ROGET'S
International
Thesaurus®

ROGET'S
International
Thesaurus®

Fifth Edition

Edited by
Robert L. Chapman

HarperPerennial
A Division of HarperCollins*Publishers*

Lithograph of Peter Mark Roget:
Edward Mansfield Burbank, *Sketches of the Lives & Work of the Honorary Medical Staff of the Manchester Infirmary, From 1752 to 1830* . . . Vol. 1, 1904. Courtesy of the New York Public Library.

HarperCollins books may be purchased for educational, business, or sales promotional use. For information, please write: Special Markets Department, HarperCollins Publishers, Inc., 10 East 53rd Street, New York, NY 10022.

FIRST HARPERPERENNIAL EDITION

Designed by C. Linda Dingler

The Library of Congress has cataloged the hardcover edition of this book as follows:

Roget's international thesaurus.—5th ed. / edited by Robert L. Chapman.
    p.   cm.
   Includes index.
   ISBN 0-06-270014-6 (thumb-indexed)—ISBN 0-06-270046-4 (plain)
   1. English language—Synonyms and antonyms.   I. Chapman, Robert L.
PE1591.R73   1992
423'.1—dc20   92-7615

ISBN 0-06-272037-6 (pbk.; world except United Kingdom and Australia)
ISBN 0-00-470470-3 (pbk.; United Kingdom and Australia)
     96 PS/RRD 10 9 8 7 6 5 4 3

Contents

P. M. Roget

Peter Mark Roget
1779–1869

The author of the "Treasury of Words" could hardly have thought that his name would become forever associated with a particular book, even though he hoped that he was suggesting a unique way of utilizing the richness and flexibility of the English language. But for almost 150 years Roget's work has been the constant companion of all those who aspire to use the language most effectively.

The career of Peter Mark Roget prior to the publication of his *Thesaurus* in 1852 when he was 73 years old, while largely devoted to science and to medicine, required of him a facility with words in the delivery of ideas and concepts. A lifetime of secretaryships for several learned societies had thoroughly familiarized him with the need for clarity and forcefulness of expression. That he was justified in his concept is made obvious by the universal acceptance of his thesaurus as an indispensable tool for all those who wish to write and speak with eloquence.

Born in London the son of a Protestant pastor who died at an early age, Roget was raised by his mother. He studied at Edinburgh University from 1793 to 1798 and received an M.D. after his successful defense of his Latin thesis dealing with the laws of chemical affinity. He was, however, too late to share in that institution's happy days as a stunning example of the Scottish Enlightenment. He was not to know William Cullen, the great nosologist, nor Alexander Monro Primus who brought Hermann Boerhaave's ethos of a medical school from Leyden; but he did learn anatomy from Monro Secundus and medicine from John Gregory. The bright stars of David Hume, denied professorship at the University for his radical thinking, and that of Adam Smith had long since blazed across the Scottish intellectual world. Moreover, Roget was too early for Sir James Young Simpson and chloroform, or for the dexterous Syme who was mentor and father-in-law to the great Lord Lister. While Roget was in Edinburgh, the soil was being prepared for the phenomenon of Paris Medicine, the next wave of medical advance, which would be built on the ruins of the French Revolution.

After his graduation, the young physician looked about for the connections he would need to launch a medical career. In this he was fortunate in having the concerned attention of his uncle, Sir Samuel Romilly, whose own promising political potential, shortened by his suicide, provided an entrée to certain segments of English scientific and intellectual life. Through his uncle, Roget was introduced to Lord Lansdowne, for whom he served briefly as personal physician, and to Jeremy Bentham. On his own initiative, Roget spent some time in Bristol in Thomas Beddoes's Pneumatic Institute, devoted to the treatment of human illness using various gases. There he may have met illustrious figures Humphry Davy, James Watt, Samuel Taylor Coleridge, William Wordsworth and Robert Southey.

In the midst of his desultory round of attendance at lectures and dispensary duties, Roget learned that his uncle had maneuvered for him an opportunity to tutor two scions of a wealthy Manchester manufacturer on a grand tour of Europe. The Peace of Amiens had been signed in 1802 and continental travel was once again open to English families anxious to provide their children with the advantages of foreign scenes.

Roget was twenty-three when he shepherded his charges across the English Channel and on to Paris, where they entered into the round of parties and dinners opened to them through letters from Sir Samuel and from the boys' family. But there was more than that. Roget hired a French tutor and supervised his charges' studies in mathematics, chemistry and geology. He also saw to it that there were the obligatory trips to museums as well as to the theatre and that the boys wrote their impressions and comments after each visit.

The little party pushed on to Geneva, not without encountering obstructions, delays and disappointments injected by the French bureaucracy. In Geneva, although the city had recently been annexed by Napoleon, the group felt secure enough to settle down to a life of studies, parties and local sightseeing. The respite was short-lived, however. The Peace of Amiens was abrogated by Napoleon in 1803 and the position of any Englishman in French territory was in doubt. Warned by Mme. de Stael that he faced internment, Roget undertook to establish for himself Genevan citizenship on the basis of his father's birth in that city. Through prodigious effort and resourcefulness remarkable in so young a man, Roget sneaked the party, dressed as peasants, into Germany. He was successful in making his way to Denmark and thence to England, delivering his charges back to their family.

Manchester now offered the best opportunity to establish a medical practice, since Roget could count on the support of the wealthy Philips family, whose sons had shared his French experience. He quickly became associated with the local infirmary and with the Manchester Literary and Philosophical Society, before which body he gave a series of lectures on physiology that historians credit as forming the basis of what became the School of Medicine in that city. As D.L. Emblen points out in his biography of Roget, "... [he] showed that his chief interest in the new science of physiology lay in the organization and order of several aspects of that subject and in the relationship of the subject to such kindred fields as anatomy." (*Peter Mark Roget: The Word and the Man*, D. L. Emblen, Thomas Crowell: New York, 1970, p. 96). It was Roget's meticulous, precise way of looking at order, at plan and at interdependence in animal economy that would eventually find expression in his unique and practical lexicographic experiment.

But the great metropolis beckoned and the young physician finally decided on a London career. Roget was never outstandingly successful as a medical practitioner. He had, however, become associated with the establishment of the Northern Dispensary, the quintessential Victorian expression of medical charity, to which he devoted a lifetime of practice. Roget's métier was teaching and institutional activities. He lectured in the Theory and Practice of Physic at the Great Windmill Street School, which served as the school of anatomy for Middlesex Hospital before that institution was eclipsed by the new University College on Gower Street. The Medical and Chirurgical Society, founded to bridge the gap between medicine and surgery, commanded much of Roget's attention during his London days. He served as the Society's secretary for twelve years and contributed to its journal *Transactions*. In 1814 he became a Fellow in the Royal Society on the basis of a paper he wrote describing a forerunner of the slide rule. He contributed many articles to the *Encyclopedia Britannica*, which were carried through several editions. In those pages he crossed swords with George Combe, the ardent promoter of phrenology, a discipline which Roget could not support. While serving as secretary of the Royal Society he wrote the Bridgewater Treatise on Physiology, which demonstrated anew Roget's ability to organize and classify the essentials of a rapidly developing science.

Although extremely occupied during these years, as a list of his extensive memberships in scientific and cultural organizations shows, Roget seems never to have captured the attention of his peers to the extent that many of his contemporaries enjoyed. There is a hint that he was always just below the top rank, never in the front. It was, after all, an age of giants, and to be even in the midst of all that ferment was remarkable enough. His active public life came to an end when he was eased out of the secretaryship of the Royal Society after a conflict over the operation of the library, and was literally forced into retirement.

An inactive retirement was not compatible with Roget's lifestyle. Since childhood, putting ideas and concepts in writing had been second nature to him. He dwelt in a world of language and his orderly, systematic mind lent itself to classification. More than a list of synonyms, more than a dictionary, the thesaurus Roget devised and constantly improved upon during this time was a unique ordering of the English language to be used by those desiring to impart an exacting and felicitous tone to written or spoken material. Grouped by ideas rather than by a mere alphabetical listing, the thesaurus enabled the user to find the exact word or phrase needed for a specific purpose. Roget had been keeping such a word list for many years. He now proposed to enlarge it and present it to the world of users of the English language.

The success of this venture was never in doubt. Roget supervised some twenty-five editions and printings of the thesaurus and was actively at work on his masterpiece when he died in 1869 at the age of ninety. *Roget's International Thesaurus®* continues to be issued. For all those who deal with words and with ideas as expressed in words it has become indispensable. It remains a monument of scholarship and a tribute to the industry and breadth of knowledge of one of the lesser-known Victorian greats.

DONALD F. KENT, M.D.

Features of
Roget's International Thesaurus®
and How to Use This Book

*R*oget's International Thesaurus® is a true thesaurus, following the principles of Dr. Peter Mark Roget's great original. It has a text of about 325,000 words and phrases, arranged in categories by their meanings, and a comprehensive index.

The search for a word that you need is a simple process that begins in the index. Suppose that you want a word to describe something that first occurred in the past:

1. In the index, look up the word first and pick the subentry closest to the meaning you want.

2. Follow its number into the text and you will find a whole paragraph of adjectives for things "previous" or "prior."

firmament 1070.2
first
  n baseball 745.1
  first ever 817.3
  adj leading 165.3
  front 216.10
  chief 249.14
  preceding 813.4
  beginning 817.15
  foremost 817.17
  previous 833.4
  novel 840.11
  adv before 216.12
  preferably 371.28
  firstly 817.18
first aid 91.14
first base 745.1
first-born
  n senior 304.5
  adj older 841.19
first-class
  superlative 249.13
  first-rate 998.17

833 PREVIOUSNESS

NOUNS 1 previousness, earliness 844, **antecedence** *or* antecedency, priority, **anteriority, precedence** *or* precedency 813, precession; *status quo ante* <L>, previous *or* prior state, earlier state; preexistence; **anticipation,** predating, antedating; antedate; **past time** 836

2 antecedent, precedent, premise; forerunner, **precursor** 815, ancestor

VERBS 3 be prior, be before *or* early *or* earlier, come on the scene *or* appear earlier, **precede, antecede, forerun,** come *or* go before, set a precedent; **herald,** usher in, proclaim, announce; **anticipate,** antedate, predate; **preexist**

ADJS 4 previous, prior, early 844.7, **earlier,** *ci-devant or ci-dessus* <Fr>, **former,** fore, prime, first, **preceding** 165.3, foregoing, above, anterior, **anticipatory,** antecedent; **preexistent;** older, elder, senior

Tracking down words in this way is the most obvious and direct use of the thesaurus. The notes that follow explain some of the other ways in which the unique features of *Roget's International Thesaurus*® will help you to solve a word problem.

The thesaurus is a device for finding specific words or phrases for general ideas. A dictionary will tell you many things about a word— spelling, pronunciation, meaning and origins. You use a thesaurus when you have an idea but do not know, or cannot remember, the word or phrase that expresses it best or when you want a more accurate or effective way of saying what you mean. A thesaurus gives you possibilities and you choose the one that you think is best. The range of possibilities includes not only meaning as we usually think of it, but the special sense and force given by nonformal words and phrases (slang and informal), of which many are included and labeled.

Roget's International Thesaurus® is a more efficient word-finder because it has a structure especially designed to stimulate thought and help you organize your ideas. The backbone of this structure is the ingenious overall arrangement of the large categories. The plan is outlined in the "Synopsis of Categories," which begins on page xix. To make good use of the thesaurus's structure all you need to remember is that it contains many sequences of closely related categories. Beginning at 448, for example, you will see HEARING, DEAFNESS, SOUND, SILENCE, FAINTNESS OF SOUND, LOUDNESS, etc., a procession of similar, contrasting and opposing concepts, all dealing with the perception and quality of sounds. So, when you are not quite satisfied with what you find in one place, glance at nearby categories too; it may be that your original intention was not the best. If you are having trouble framing a thought in a positive way, you may find that it can be more effectively expressed negatively. Seeing related terms, and antonyms, often opens up lines of thought and chains of association that had not occurred to you.

You will have already noticed that the large categories of ideas are numbered in sequence; there are 1073 of them in this edition of *Roget's International Thesaurus*®. Within each category the terms are presented in short paragraphs, and these are also numbered. References from the index to the text are made with two-part numbers such as 247.4, the first part being the number of the category, the second the number of the paragraph within that category. This system, unique to this book, makes for quick and easy pinpointing of the place where you will find the words you need.

The terms within a category are organized also by part of speech, in this order: nouns, verbs, adjectives, adverbs, prepositions, conjunctions, and interjections. This grouping by parts of speech is another aspect of the usefulness of *Roget's International Thesaurus*®. When you are casting about for a way of saying something, rather than looking for a specific word, do not limit your search to the narrow area of the category suggested by the index reference, but examine the offerings in all parts of speech.

There is a further refinement of word arrangement. The sequence of terms within a paragraph, far from being random, is determined by close, semantic relationships. The words closest in meaning are offered in clusters or "domains" that are set off with semicolons; the semicolon signals a slight change in sense or application. A close examination of the groupings will make you aware of the fine distinctions between synonyms, and you will soon recognize that few words are exactly interchangeable. As a help in focusing on the *right* word, terms with special uses—foreign terms and technical terms—are identified by labels in angle brackets.

Cross references are an important feature of the text. They suggest additional meanings of the words you are examining. Notice also that the paragraphs of text are highlighted with terms in boldface type. The bold words are those most commonly used for the idea at hand.

"Word elements" such as prefixes, suffixes, and combining forms, are listed when helpful after the final text paragraph of the category, and before any word lists.

The use of an appropriate quotation often enlivens one's prose. Here again, *Roget's International Thesaurus*® can help you, for it contains thousands of such quotes on scores of subjects. Another bonus of the thesaurus is its dozens of word lists. These contain the names of specific things— animals, poisonous plants, measurements, architectural ornaments—few of which have synonyms. The lists can save you many excursions to specialized reference books.

Thus, *Roget's International Thesaurus*® can help you in countless ways to improve your writing and speech and to enrich your active vocabulary. But you should remember the caution that very few words are true synonyms and use the thesaurus in conjunction with a good dictionary whenever a selected word or phrase is new to you.

Publisher's Preface

Like all great reference books, *Roget's International Thesaurus*® is the product of continuous improvement and long-term investment. The process began almost two centuries ago, in 1805, when Dr. Peter Mark Roget began compiling a list of useful words for his own convenience.

There have been glossaries and word lists since literature began. The revolutionary achievement of Dr. Roget, a physician with a penchant for organization, was his development of a brand new principle: *the grouping of words according to ideas*. This mechanism eliminates the need for groping through the entire alphabet posed by word books arranged in dictionary form (i.e. alphabetically), thus greatly increasing the efficiency of locating just the right word or expression for a particular circumstance. When in 1852 Roget published the first book ever to realize this concept with thoroughness and precision, he called it a "thesaurus" (from the Greek and Latin, meaning "treasury" or "storehouse"). And *thesaurus* it has remained to this day.

So successful was Roget's *Thesaurus of English Words and Phrases, Classified and Arranged so as to Facilitate the Expression of Ideas and Assist in Literary Composition* that a second edition followed one year later in 1853. By Dr. Roget's death in 1869 there had been no less than twenty-eight editions and printings.

Thomas Y. Crowell acquired the thesaurus from Roget's son, Dr. John Lewis Roget, and published the first Crowell edition in 1886. *Roget's International Thesaurus*® remained within the Crowell publishing family for the next nearly one hundred years. Each subsequent edition introduced more efficient and useful features, all of which have contributed to the quality of the present edition. Over the years, tens of thousands of new words and phrases were added, the coverage of foreign expressions increased, and the scope of the book expanded to include slang and useful quotations; a recent innovation was the numbering of the paragraphs for the user's convenience. By 1977, when the fourth edition was published by Harper & Row, *Roget's*

International Thesaurus® had become a greatly expanded and improved book, yet one which still retained Roget's brilliant organization.

It is with a very special sense of pride that we present this fifth edition of *Roget's International Thesaurus*®. Along with the addition of new words and phrases, considerable updating and refinements in format and style, the most significant changes in this fifth edition are the rearrangement of the categories and the introduction of new ones to enable fuller coverage of terms of our times. Dr. Robert L. Chapman, revising editor for this new edition, explains the details and reasoning behind these changes in his Foreword.

A work of this scope is only possible through the combined effort of many people. We wish to particularly acknowledge the superior work of Dr. Robert L. Chapman, who reorganized, rethought and rewrote this edition.

Computer technology has made working with the technical aspects of the book more efficient. We wish to thank George Alexander for his valuable contributions. Our thanks for the editorial contributions of Andrea Sargent, Mary Kay Linge, Jill Korey, Kenneth Wright, Joe Ford, Ruth Koenisberg, Pamela Marshall, Dave Prout, Ellen Zucker, Frank Gribbon and Edward Mansour.

A special thanks to John Day, supervisor of reference production, who oversaw the complexity of turning the many discs and printouts during the various stages of development into final discs for composition. Our thanks to his staff: Douglas Elam, Elaine Verriest, Celeste Bantz, Ryon Fleming, Jim Hornfischer, Dorian Yeager, and Craig Young. Our appreciation to C. Linda Dingler for the new design; to Dianne Pinkowitz, Joseph Montebello and Helen Moore. And last, we wish to acknowledge the valuable contributions of Mark Liberman and Ken Church of Bell Labs.

CAROL COHEN
Publisher, HarperReference

Peter Roget's Preface
to the First Edition
(*1852*)

It is now nearly fifty years since I first projected a system of verbal classification similar to that on which the present work is founded. Conceiving
that such a compilation might help to supply my own deficiencies, I had, in
the year 1805, completed a classed catalog of words on a small scale, but on
the same principle, and nearly in the same form, as the Thesaurus now
published. I had often during that long interval found this little collection,
scanty and imperfect as it was, of much use to me in literary composition,
and often contemplated its extension and improvement; but a sense of the
magnitude of the task, amidst a multitude of other avocations, deterred me
from the attempt. Since my retirement from the duties of Secretary of the
Royal Society, however, finding myself possessed of more leisure, and believing that a repertory of which I had myself experienced the advantage
might, when amplified, prove useful to others, I resolved to embark in an
undertaking which, for the last three or four years, has given me incessant
occupation, and has, indeed, imposed upon me an amount of labor very
much greater that I had anticipated. Notwithstanding all the pains I have
bestowed on its execution, I am fully aware of its numerous deficiencies and
imperfections, and of its falling far short of the degree of excellence that
might be attained. But, in a work of this nature, where perfection is placed
at so great a distance, I have thought it best to limit my ambition to that
moderate share of merit which it may claim in its present form; trusting to
the indulgence of those for whose benefit it is intended, and to the candor of
critics who, while they find it easy to detect faults, can at the same time duly
appreciate difficulties.

P. M. ROGET

April 29, 1852

Foreword
by Robert L. Chapman

Apart from rigorous updating and the addition of thirty new categories, the chief innovation of this fifth edition is a rearrangement of the classes and categories into which Dr. Roget organized our verbal universe. This was undertaken gingerly, since Roget's scheme had held its own for nearly a century and a half, and one hesitates to tamper with the work of a master.

Nevertheless, my own reflection and the comments of some users have convinced me that the recasting is justified. Dr. Roget wished, as he said in his original Introduction, "to obtain the greatest amount of practical utility." That should be the aim of all lexicography. Hence he adopted principles of order which seemed "the simplest and most natural, and which would not require, either for their comprehension or application, any disciplined acumen, or depth of metaphysical or antiquarian lore."

At this distance from his intellectual milieu, Roget's scheme no longer seems simple and natural. It reflects a Platonic view of the cosmos, combined with an Aristotelian marshaling of concepts. By "Platonic" I mean that he orders things as though abstract ideas exist in some supraterrestrial realm, and are made temporal and physical as they descend to Earth. By "Aristotelian" I mean that he proceeds by strict logic.

However respectable this cosmos and its deployment may be philosophically, it does not coincide with the way most people now apprehend the universe. Casting about for a more fitting arrangement, I chose what I call a "developmental–existential" scheme, which can be examined in the "Synopsis of Categories." The notion has been to make the arrangement analogous with the development of the human individual and the human race. It is more associational and durational than logical. This seems to me "the simplest and most natural" array in the mind of our own time.

I wish to acknowledge the help of Charles Courtney, a philosopher at Drew University, and of George Miller, a cognitive psychologist at

Princeton, for hearing and counseling me as I thought about the new arrangement. Dr. Donald Kent, who provides the biographical account of his fellow physician Peter Mark Roget, has also given ear to my perplexities.

This edition has benefited enormously from access to the natural-language corpora at AT&T Bell Laboratories, Murray Hill, New Jersey. In particular my thanks go to Mark Liberman and Ken Church of the Labs.

My editor Carol Cohen has been as always the mainstay of the enterprise.

And I reassert with added earnestness my debt to the library of Drew University; and to my wife Sarah, companion of my labors and the one I have most wanted to please.

Synopsis of Categories

Abbreviations Used in This Book

ADJS	adjective(s)		Hung	Hungarian
ADVS	adverb(s)		Ir	Irish
Anon	anonymous		Ital	Italian
Arab	Arabic		L	Latin
Austral	Australian		masc	masculine
Brazil Pg	Brazilian Portuguese		N	North, Northern
Brit	British		Norw	Norwegian
Can	Canadian		Pg	Portuguese
Can Fr	Canadian French		PHRS	phrase(s)
Chin	Chinese		pl	plural
CIS	Commonwealth of		Pol	Polish
	Independent States		Russ	Russian
Cz	Czechoslovakian		S	South, Southern
Dan	Danish		Scots	Scottish
E	East, Eastern		sing	singular
Eng	England, English		Skt	Sanskrit
etc	etcetera		Sp	Spanish
fem	feminine		Sp Amer	Spanish American
Fr	French		Swah	Swahili
Ger	German		Swed	Swedish
Gk	Greek		Turk	Turkish
gram	grammar		UN	United Nations
Heb	Hebrew		US	United States
Hind	Hindustani			

1 BIRTH

NOUNS **1 birth,** genesis, **nativity,** nascency, **childbirth, childbearing, having a baby, giving birth, birthing,** parturition, the stork <nonformal>; **confinement,** lying-in, being brought to bed, **childbed,** *accouchement* <Fr>; **labor,** travail, birth throes *or* pangs; **delivery,** blessed event <nonformal>; the Nativity; multiparity; **hatching;** littering, whelping, farrowing

VERBS **2 be born,** have birth, come forth, issue forth, see the light of day, come into the world; **hatch;** be illegitimate *or* born out of wedlock, have the bar sinister; be born on the wrong side of the blanket, come in through a side door <nonformal>

3 give birth, bear, bear *or* have young, **have; have a baby,** bear a child; drop, cast, throw, pup, whelp, kitten, foal, calve, fawn, lamb, yean, farrow, litter; lie in, be confined, labor, travail

ADJS **4 born,** given birth; **hatched;** cast, dropped, whelped, foaled, calved, etc; "cast naked upon the naked earth"— Pliny the Elder; née; newborn; stillborn; **bearing,** giving birth

2 THE BODY

NOUNS **1 body,** the person, carcass, anatomy, frame, bodily *or* corporal *or* corporeal entity, physical self, physical *or* bodily structure, physique, soma; organism, organic complex; the material *or* physical part

2 the skeleton, the bones, one's bones, framework, bony framework, endoskeleton; axial skeleton, appendicular skeleton, visceral skeleton; rib cage; skeletology; **bone** <see list>; cartilage

3 the muscles, myon, voluntary muscle, involuntary muscle; **musculature,** physique; **connective tissue,** connectivum; cartilage

4 the skin, skin, dermis, **epidermis,** scarfskin, ecderon; hypodermis, hypoderma; dermis, derma, corium, true skin, cutis, *cutis vera* <L>; epithelium, pavement epithelium; endothelium; mesoderm; endoderm, entoderm; blastoderm; ectoderm, epiblast, ectoblast; enderon; connective tissue

5 <castoff skin> slough, cast, desquamation, exuviae

6 membrane, membrana, pellicle, chorion; basement membrane, membrana propria; allantoic membrane; amnion, amniotic sac, arachnoid membrane; serous membrane, serosa, membrana serosa; **eardrum,** tympanic membrane, tympanum, membrana tympana; **mucous membrane; velum; peritoneum;** periosteum; pleura; pericardium; meninx, **meninges;** perineurium, neurilemma; conjunctiva; **hymen** *or* maidenhead

7 member, appendage, external organ; head, noggin *and* noodle <both nonformal>; **arm;** forearm; wrist; elbow; upper arm, biceps; **leg,** limb, shank, gam *and* pin <both nonformal>, legs, wheels <nonformal>; shin, cnemis; ankle, tarsus; calf; knee; thigh, ham; popliteal space; **hand,** paw <nonformal>; **foot,** dog *and* puppy <both nonformal>

8 teeth, dentition, ivories <nonformal>; periodontal tissue, alveolar ridge; **tooth,** fang, tusk, tush <nonformal>; snag, snaggletooth, peg; bucktooth, gagtooth *or* gang tooth <both nonformal>; pivot tooth; cuspid, bicuspid; canine tooth, canine, dogtooth, eyetooth; molar, grinder; premolar; incisor, cutter, fore-tooth; wisdom tooth; milk tooth, baby tooth, deciduous tooth; permanent tooth

9 eye, visual organ, organ of vision, oculus, optic, **orb,** peeper <nonformal>; clear eyes, bright eyes, starry orbs; saucer eyes, banjo eyes <nonformal>, popeyes, goggle eyes; naked eye, unassisted *or* unaided eye; corner of the eye; eyeball; retina; lens; cornea; sclera; optic nerve; iris; pupil; eyelid, lid, nictitating membrane

10 ear, auditory apparatus, lug <Scots>; external ear, **outer ear;** auricle, pinna; cauliflower ear; concha, conch, shell; ear lobe, lobe, lobule; auditory canal, acoustic *or* auditory meatus; **middle ear,** tympanic cavity, tympanum; eardrum, drumhead, tympanic membrane; auditory ossicles; malleus, hammer, incus, anvil; stapes, stirrup; mastoid process; eustachian *or* auditory tube; **inner ear;** round window, secondary eardrum; oval window; bony labyrinth, membraneous labyrinth; perilymph, endolymph; vestibule; semicircular canals; cochlea; basilar membrane, organ of Corti; auditory *or* acoustic nerve

11 genitals, genitalia, sex organs, reproductive organs, pudenda, private parts, privy parts, privates meat <nonformal>; **crotch,** crutch <Brit>, pubic region, perineum, pelvis; **male organs; penis, phallus,** lingam <Skt>; gonads; **testes, testicles,** balls *and* nuts *and* rocks *and* ballocks *and* family jewels <all nonformal>, cullions <old>; spermary; scrotum, bag *and* basket <both nonformal>, cod <old>; **female organs; vulva,** *yoni* <Skt>, cunt <nonformal>; **vagina;** clitoris; labia, labia majora, labia minora, lips, nymphae; cervix; ovary; uterus, womb; secondary sex characteristic, pubic hair, beard, breasts

12 **nervous system, nerves,** central nervous system, peripheral nervous system; autonomic nervous system; sympathetic *or* thoracolumbar nervous system, parasympathetic *or* craniosacral nervous system; **nerve; neuron;** nerve cell, sensory *or* afferent neuron, sensory cell; motor *or* afferent neuron; association *or* internuncial neuron; axon, dendrite, myelin *or* medullary sheath; **synapse;** effector organ; nerve trunk; **ganglion;** plexus, solar plexus; **spinal cord**

13 **brain,** encephalon

14 **viscera, vitals, internal organs, insides, innards** <nonformal>, inwards, internals, thoracic viscera, abdominal viscera; inner mechanism, works <nonformal>; peritoneum, peritoneal cavity; **guts** *and* kishkes *and* giblets <all nonformal>; **heart,** ticker *and* pump <both nonformal>, endocardium; **lung, lungs; liver;** gallbladder; spleen; pancreas; **kidney, kidneys**

15 **digestion,** ingestion, assimilation, absorption; primary digestion, secondary digestion; predigestion; salivary digestion, gastric *or* peptic digestion, pancreatic digestion, intestinal digestion; digestive system, alimentary canal, gastrointestinal tract; salivary glands, gastric glands, liver, pancreas; digestive secretions, saliva, gastric juice, pancreatic juice, intestinal juice, bile

16 <digestive system> mouth, maw, salivary glands; gullet, crop, craw, **throat,** pharynx; esophagus, gorge, weasand <old>, wizen <Brit nonformal>; fauces, isthmus of the fauces; **abdomen; stomach, belly** <nonformal>, **midriff,** diaphragm; swollen *or* distended *or* protruding *or* prominent belly, *embonpoint* <Fr>, **paunch,** ventripotence; underbelly; pylorus; **intestine, intestines, bowels;** small intestine, odenum, jejunum, ileum; blind gut, cecum; foregut, hindgut; midgut, mesogaster; **appendix,** vermiform appendix *or* process; large intestine, colon, sigmoid flexure, rectum; anus

17 <nonformal terms> goozle, guzzle; tum, tummy, tum-tum, breadbasket, **gut,** bulge, fallen chest <nonformal>, corporation, spare tire, bay window, **pot,** potbelly, potgut, beerbelly, German *or* Milwaukee goiter, pusgut, swagbelly; **guts,** tripes, stuffings

18 **metabolism,** metabolic process, tissue change; basal metabolism, acid-base metabolism, energy metabolism; **anabolism,** substance metabolism, constructive metabolism, assimilation; **catabolism,** energy metabolism, destructive metabolism, disassimilation; endogenous metabolism, exogenous metabolism; pharmacokinetic metabolism; uricotelic metabolism

19 **breathing, respiration,** aspiration, **inspiration, inhalation; expiration, exhalation;** insufflation, exsufflation; **breath,** wind, breath of air; pant, puff; wheeze, asthmatic wheeze; broken wind; gasp, gulp; snoring, snore, stertor; sniff, sniffle, snuff, snuffle; sigh, suspiration; sneeze, sternutation; cough, hack; hiccup; **artificial respiration,** kiss of life, mouth-to-mouth resuscitation

20 <respiratory system> **lungs,** bellows <nonformal>, lights <old>; **windpipe, trachea,** weasand <old>, wizen <Brit nonformal>; bronchus, bronchi <pl>, bronchial tube; epiglottis

21 **duct, vessel,** canal, passage; vasculature, vascularity, vascularization; vas, meatus; thoracic duct, lymphatic; emunctory <old>; pore; urethra, urete; vagina; oviduct, fallopian tube; salpinx; eustachian tube; ostium; fistula; **blood vessel; artery,** aorta, pulmonary artery, carotid; **vein,** jugular vein, vena cava, pulmonary vein; portal vein, varicose vein; venation; **capillary;** arteriole, veinule, venule, venule

22 <body fluids> humor, **lymph,** chyle; rheum; serous fluid, serum; **pus, matter,** purulence, peccant humor <old>; suppuration; ichor, sanies; discharge; gleet, leukorrhea, the whites; **phlegm,** snot <nonformal>; **saliva, spit <nonformal>; urine, piss** <nonformal>; **perspiration, sweat** <nonformal>; **tear,** teardrop, lachryma; **milk,** mother's milk, colostrum, lactation

23 **blood,** whole blood, lifeblood, venous blood, arterial blood, **gore;** ichor; humor; grume; **serum,** blood serum; blood substitute; **plasma,** synthetic plasma, plasma substitute, dextran, clinical dextran; **blood cell** *or* **corpuscle,** hemocyte; **red corpuscle** *or* **blood cell,** erythrocyte; **white corpuscle** *or* **blood cell,** leukocyte, blood

platelet; **hemoglobin;** blood pressure; circulation; **blood group** or **type,** type O or A or B or AB; Rh-type, Rh-positive, Rh-negative; **Rh factor** or Rhesus factor; antigen, antibody, isoantibody, globulin; opsonin; blood grouping; blood count, blood picture; hematoscope, hematoscopy, hemometer; bloodstream

ADJS **24 skeleton, skeletal; bone,** osteal; **bony,** osseous, ossiferous; ossicular; ossified; **spinal,** myelic; **muscle, muscular,** myoid; cartilage, cartilaginous

25 cutaneous, cuticular; skinlike, skinny; skin-deep; **epidermal,** epidermic, ecderonic; hypodermic, hypodermal, subcutaneous; dermal, dermic; ectodermal, ectodermic; endermic, endermatic; cortical; epicarpal; testaceous; membranous

26 eye, optic, ophthalmic; visual; **ear,** otic; aural

27 genital; phallic, penile, penial; testicular; scrotal; spermatic, seminal; vulvar, vulval; vaginal; clitoral; cervical; ovarian; uterine

28 nerve, neural; brain, cerebral, cerebellar

29 digestive; stomachal, stomachic, abdominal; ventral, celiac, **gastric,** ventricular; big-bellied 257.18; **metabolic,** basal metabolic, anabolic, catabolic; assimilative, dissimilative

30 respiratory, breathing; inspiratory, expiratory; nasal, rhinal; bronchial, tracheal; **lung,** pulmonary, pulmonic, pneumonic; puffing, huffing, snorting, wheezing, wheezy, asthmatic, stertorous, snoring, panting, heaving; sniffy, sniffly, sniffling, snuffy, snuffly, snuffling; sneezy, sternutative, sternutatory, errhine

31 circulatory, vascular, vascularized; vasiform; venous, veinal, venose; capillary; arterial, aortic; **blood,** hematal, hematic; bloody, gory, sanguinary; lymphatic, rheumy, humoral, phlegmy, ichorous, serous, sanious; chylific, chylifactive, chylifactory; **pussy,** purulent, suppurated or suppurating, suppurative; teary, tearing, tearlike, **lachrymal,** lacrimatory

32 bones

aitchbone	basilar or basioccipi-
alveolar bone	tal bone
anklebone	breastbone or ster-
anvil	num
astragalus or ankle-	calcaneus
bone	calf bone or fibula
backbone or spine or	cannon bone
spinal column or	carpal or carpus
myel	cheekbone
chin	multangular bone
clavicle	large or trapezium
coccyx	multangular bone
collarbone	small or trapezoid
costa	nasal bone
cranial bones	occipital bone
cranium	palate bone
cuboid	parietal bone
edgebone	pelvis
ethmoid bone	periotic bone or oto-
floating rib	crane
frontal bone	petrosal or petrous
funny or crazy bone	bone
hallux	phalanx or phalanges
hammer	<pl>
haunch bone	pterygoid bone
heel bone	pubis
hipbone	pyramidal bone or os
humerus	triquetrum
hyoid or lingual bone	rachidial
ilium	rachis or vertebral
incus	column
inferior maxillary	radius
innominate bone	rib
intermaxillary or pre-	sacrum or resurrec-
maxillary or	tion bone
incisive bone	scaphoid bone
interparietal or incar-	scapula
ial bone	semilunar bone
ischium	sesamoid bones
kneecap or patella or	shinbone
whirl bone	shoulder blade
lacrimal bone	skull
lenticular bone or os	sphenoid bone
orbiculare	stapes
lentiform or pisiform	stirrup
or postular bone	sutural or wormian
malar or zygomatic	bone
bone	talus
malleus	tarsal or tarsus
mandible and maxilla	temporal bone
or jawbones	thighbone or femur
mastoid	tibia
maxillary	ulna
metacarpal or meta-	vertebra
carpus	vomer
metatarsal or meta-	wishbone
tarsus	wristbone

3 HAIR

NOUNS **1 hairiness, shagginess,** hirsuteness, pilosity, fuzziness, frizziness, **furriness,** downiness, fluffiness, woolliness, fleeciness, bristliness, stubbliness, burrheadedness, mopheadedness, shockheadedness; crinosity, hispidity, villosity; hypertrichosis, pilosis, pilosism

2 hair, pile, **fur** 4.2, coat, pelt, **fleece,** wool, camel's hair, horsehair; **mane;** shag, tousled or matted hair, **mat of hair;** pubescence, pubes, pubic hair; hairlet,

villus, capillament, cilium, ciliolum
271.1; seta, setula; bristle 288.3

3 gray hair, grizzle, silver *or* silvery hair,
white hair, salt-and-pepper hair *or* beard,
graying temples, "hoary hair"—Thomas
Gray, "the silver livery of advised age"—
Shakespeare, "a crown of glory"—Bible,
"silver threads among the gold"—Eben E
Rexford

4 **head of hair,** head, crine; **crop,** crop of
hair, mat, elflock, **thatch,** mop, **shock,**
shag, fleece, **mane; locks, tresses,**
crowning glory, helmet of hair; "her
native ornament of hair"—Ovid,
"amber-dropping hair"—Milton

5 **lock, tress;** flowing locks, flowing tresses;
curl, ringlet, "wanton ringlets wav'd"—
Milton; earlock, *payess* <Yiddish>;
lovelock; frizz, frizzle; crimp; ponytail

6 **tuft, flock,** fleck; forelock, widow's peak,
quiff <Brit>, fetlock, cowlick; **bang,
bangs,** fringe

7 **braid,** plait, twist; **pigtail,** rat's-tail *or*
rat-tail, tail; **queue,** cue; coil, knot; topknot, scalplock, pigtail; bun, chignon;
widow's peak

8 **beard, whiskers;** beaver <nonformal>;
full beard, chin whiskers, side whiskers;
sideburns, burnsides, **muttonchops;
goatee,** tuft; imperial, **Vandyke,** spade
beard; adolescent beard, pappus, down,
peach fuzz, "the soft down of manhood"—Callimachus, "his phoenix
down"—Shakespeare; **stubble,**
bristles, five o'clock shadow

9 <plant beard> awn, brush, arista, pile,
pappus

10 <animal and insect whiskers> tactile
process, tactile hair, **feeler, antenna,** vibrissa; barb, barbel, barbule; cat whisker

11 **mustache,** mustachio, soup-strainer
<nonformal>, toothbrush, handle bars
or handlebar mustache, Fu Manchu mustache, Zapata mustache, walrus
mustache, tash <nonformal>

12 **eyelashes, lashes,** cilia; **eyebrows,** brows

13 false hair, switch, fall, chignon, rat
<nonformal>

14 **wig, peruke, toupee,** hairpiece, rug *and*
divot *and* doormat <all nonformal>;
periwig

15 **hairdo, hairstyle, haircut, coiffure,** coif,
headdress; wave; marcel, marcel wave;
permanent, permanent wave; home permanent; cold wave

16 **feather, plume,** pinion; **quill;** pinfeather;
contour feather, penna, down feather,
plume feather, plumule; filoplume;

hackle; scapular; **crest,** tuft, topknot;
panache

17 <parts of feathers> quill, calamus, barrel; barb, shaft, barbule, barbicel, cilium,
filament, filamentule

18 **plumage, feathers,** feather, feathering;
contour feathers; breast feathers, mail
<of a hawk>; hackle; flight feathers;
remiges, primaries, secondaries, tertia-
ries; covert, tectrices; speculum, wing
bay

19 **down, fluff,** flue, floss, **fuzz, fur,** pile; eiderdown, eider; swansdown; thistle-
down; lint

VERBS 20 grow *or* sprout hair; whisker, **be-
whisker**

21 **feather, fledge,** feather out; sprout wings

22 cut *or* dress the hair, trim, **barber, coiffure,** coif, style *or* shape the hair; pompadour, wave, marcel; process, conk; **bob,
shingle**

ADJS 23 **hairlike,** trichoid, capillary; filamentous, filamentary, filiform; bristlelike
288.10

24 **hairy, hirsute,** barbigerous, crinose,
crinite, pubescent; pilose, pilous, pileous;
furry, furred; villous; villose; ciliate, cirrose; hispid, hispidulous; **woolly, fleecy,**
lanate, lanated, flocky, flocculent, floc-
cose; woolly-headed, woolly-haired,
ulotrichous; bushy, tufty, **shaggy,**
shagged; matted, tomentose; mop-
headed, burrheaded, shockheaded,
unshorn; **bristly** 288.9; fuzzy

25 **bearded,** whiskered, whiskery, **bewhiskered,** barbate, barbigerous;
mustached *or* mustachioed; awned,
awny, pappose; goateed; unshaved, **unshaven;** stubbled, stubbly

26 **wigged,** periwigged, peruked, toupeed

27 **feathery, plumy;** hirsute; featherlike,
plumelike, pinnate, pennate; **downy,**
fluffy, nappy, velvety, peachy, fuzzy,
flossy, furry

28 **feathered, plumaged,** flighted, **pinioned,
plumed,** pennate, plumate, plumose

29 **tufted, crested,** topknotted

4 CLOTHING MATERIALS

NOUNS 1 **material, fabric, cloth, textile,** textile fabric, texture, tissue, stuff, weave,
weft, woof, web, **material, goods,** drapery, *étoffe, tissu* <both Fr>; napery, table
linen, felt; silk; lace; rag, rags

2 **fur, pelt, hide,** fell, fleece, vair <her-
aldry>; imitation fur, fake fur, synthetic
fur; furring; peltry, skins; **leather** <see
list>, rawhide; imitation leather, leather

paper, Leatheroid <trademark>, leath-
erette

3 leather

buff	patent leather
calf leather	pebble leather
capeskin	pigskin
chamois or chammy	ram leather
chamois skin	saddle leather
chrome leather	sheepskin
cordovan	shoe leather
crown leather	snakeskin
cup leather	sole leather
grain leather	stirrup leather
hat leather	suède
Hungary leather	tawed leather
kid	whitleather or white
mocha	leather
morocco	

5 CLOTHING

NOUNS **1 clothing, clothes, apparel, wear,
wearing apparel, daywear, dress,** dressing, **raiment,** garmenture, **garb, attire, array,** habit, habiliment, fashion, style
578.1, guise, **costume,** costumery, gear,
fig or full fig <both Brit>, toilette, trim,
bedizenment; **vestment,** vesture, investment, investiture; **garments,** robes,
robing, rags <nonformal>, drapery, finery, feathers; toggery or togs or **duds** or
threads <all nonformal>, sportswear;
work clothes, fatigues; linen; menswear,
men's clothing, womenswear, women's
clothing; unisex clothing, uniwear,
gender-crossing clothing; gender bender

2 wardrobe, furnishings, things, accouterments, trappings; **outfit,** livery, harness,
caparison; turnout and getup and rig and
rig-out <all nonformal>; wedding
clothes, bridal outfit, trousseau

3 garment, vestment, vesture, robe, frock,
gown, rag <nonformal>, togs and duds
<both nonformal>

4 ready-mades, ready-to-wear, store or
store-bought clothes <nonformal>

5 rags, tatters, secondhand clothes, old
clothes; worn clothes, **hand-me-downs**
and reach-me-downs <both nonformal>;
slops

6 suit <see list>, suit of clothes, **frock,**
dress, rig <nonformal>, **costume, habit,**
bib and tucker <nonformal>

7 uniform <see list>, **livery,** monkey suit
<nonformal>

8 mufti, civilian dress or clothes, **civvies**
and cits <both nonformal>, plain clothes

9 costume, costumery, character dress;
outfit and getup and rig <all nonfor-
mal>; masquerade, disguise; tights,
leotards; ballet skirt, tutu; motley, cap
and bells; buskin, sock

10 finery, frippery, fancy dress, fine or full
feather <nonformal>, full fig <Brit non-
formal>; **best clothes,** best bib and
tucker <nonformal>; **Sunday best** and
Sunday clothes and Sunday-go-to-
meeting clothes and Sunday-go-to-
meetings <all nonformal>, **glad rags**
<nonformal>, party dress

11 formal dress, formals, **evening dress, full
dress,** dress clothes, evening wear, white
tie and tails, **soup-and-fish** <nonfor-
mal>; dinner clothes; dress suit, full-
dress suit, tails <nonformal>; tuxedo,
tux <nonformal>; **regalia,** court dress;
dress uniform, full-dress uniform, special
full-dress uniform, social full-dress uniform; whites <nonformal>, dress whites;
evening gown, dinner dress or gown

12 cloak, overgarment <see list>

13 outerwear; coat, jacket <see list>; **overcoat** <see list>, great-coat, **topcoat,**
surcoat; **rainwear;** rain gear, raincoat,
slicker, rainsuit, foul weather gear

14 waistcoat, weskit <nonformal>, **vest;**
down vest

15 shirt <see list>, waist, **shirtwaist,** linen,
sark and shift <both nonformal>; **blouse,**
bodice, corsage; dickey; sweater <see
list>

16 dress <see list>, **gown, frock; skirt,** jupe
<Scots>

17 apron, tablier <Fr>; pinafore, bib,
tucker; smock

18 pants, trousers, pair of trousers or pants,
trews <Scots>, **breeches,** britches
<nonformal>, breeks <Scots>, **pan-
taloons,** jeans, **slacks**

19 waistband, belt 280.3; **sash,** cummer-
bund; **loincloth,** breechcloth or
breechclout, waistcloth, **G-string,**
loinguard, dhoti, moocha; **diaper,** dydee
<nonformal>, napkins <Brit>, nappies
<Brit nonformal>

20 dishabille, déshabillé <Fr>, **undress,**
something more comfortable; **negligee,**
négligé <Fr>; **wrap,** wrapper; sport
clothes, playwear, leisure-wear, **casual
clothes or dress,** fling-on clothes

21 nightwear, night clothes; **nightdress,
nightgown, nightie** and shortie nightie
<both nonformal>, bedgown; nightshirt;
pajamas, pyjamas <Brit>, pj's <nonfor-
mal>; sleepers

22 underclothes, underclothing, undergarments <see list>, bodywear, **underwear,
undies** <nonformal>, skivvies, body
clothes, smallclothes, unmentionables

<nonformal>, **lingerie, linen,** under-
linen; flannels, woolens

23 **corset,** stays, foundation garment, corse-
let; **girdle,** undergirdle, panty girdle;
garter belt

24 **brassiere, bra** <nonformal>, bandeau,
underbodice, *soutien-gorge* <Fr>, uplift
brassiere; falsies <nonformal>

25 **headdress,** headgear, headwear, head-
clothes, headtire; **millinery;** headpiece,
chapeau, cap, hat; lid <nonformal>;
headcloth, **kerchief,** coverchief; **handkerchief**

26 **veil,** veiling, veiler; *yashmak* <Turk>,
chador <Iranian>; mantilla

27 **footwear,** footgear, *chaussure* <Fr>;
shoes, boots; clodhoppers *and* gunboats
and waffle-stompers *and* shitkickers <all
nonformal>; wooden shoes, sabots, pat-
tens

28 **hosiery** <see list>, **hose, stockings; socks**

29 **swimwear; bathing suit,** swim suit,
swimming suit, tank suit, tank top, *maillot* or *maillot de bain* <Fr>, two-piece
suit; **trunks;** bikini, string bikini *or*
string, thong; wet suit

30 **children's wear;** rompers, jumpers;
creepers; layette, baby clothes, infant-
wear, infants' wear, baby linen; swaddling clothes, swaddle

31 garment making, **tailoring; dressmaking,
the rag trade** <nonformal>, **Seventh Avenue, the garment industry; millinery,**
hatmaking, hatting; **shoemaking,** boot-
making, **cobbling;** habilimentation

32 **clothier, haberdasher,** draper <Brit>,
outfitter; costumier, costumer; glover;
hosier; furrier; dry goods dealer, mercer
<Brit>

33 **garmentmaker, garmentworker,**
needleworker; cutter, stitcher, finisher

34 **tailor,** tailoress, *tailleur* <Fr>, sartor; fitter; busheler, bushelman; furrier,
cloakmaker

35 **dressmaker, modiste,** *couturière* or *couturier* <both Fr>; seamstress 741.2

36 **hatter,** hatmaker, **milliner**

37 **shoemaker,** bootmaker, booter, **cobbler,**
souter <Scots>

VERBS 38 **clothe,** enclothe, **dress, garb, attire,** tire, array, **apparel,** raiment, garment, habilitate, **tog** *and* tog out <both
nonformal>, dud <nonformal>, robe, en-
robe, invest, endue, **deck,** bedeck, dight,
rag out *or* up <nonformal>; drape, bedrape; wrap, enwrap, lap, envelop,
sheathe, shroud, enshroud; wrap *or* bundle *or* muffle up; swathe, swaddle

39 **cloak, mantle;** coat, jacket; gown, frock;
breech; shirt; **hat,** coif, bonnet, cap, hood;
boot, shoe; stocking, sock

40 **outfit;** equip, **accouter,** uniform, caparison, rig, rig out *or* up, fit, **fit out,** turn
out, **costume,** habit, suit; **tailor,** tailor-
make, make to order; order, bespeak

41 **dress up, get up, doll** *or* **spruce up**
<nonformal>, **primp** *and* prink *and*
prank <all nonformal>, gussy up
<nonformal>, spiff *or* fancy *or* slick up
<nonformal>, pretty up <nonformal>,
deck out *or* up, trick out *or* up, tog out *or*
up <nonformal>, rag out *or* up <nonfor-
mal>, fig out *or* up <nonformal>;
titivate, dizen, bedizen; overdress; put on
the dog *or* style <nonformal>; **dress
down,** underdress

42 **don, put on,** slip on *or* into, get on *or* into,
try on, assume, dress in; change; suit up

43 **wear, have on,** be dressed in, affect, sport
<nonformal>

ADJS 44 **clothing; dress,** vestiary, sartorial;
clothed, clad, dressed, attired, togged
<nonformal>, tired, arrayed, **garbed,**
garmented, habited, habilimented,
decked, bedecked, decked-out, turned-
out, tricked-out, rigged-out, dight <old>,
vested, vestmented, robed, gowned, rai-
mented, **appareled,** invested, endued, liveried, uniformed; **costumed,** in costume,
cloaked, mantled, disguised; breeched,
trousered, pantalooned; coifed, capped,
bonneted, hatted, hooded; **shod,** shoed,
booted, *chaussé* <Fr>

45 **dressed up, dolled** *or* **spruced up**
<nonformal>; spiffed *or* fancied *or*
slicked up <nonformal>, gussied up
<nonformal>; spruce, dressed to advan-
tage, dressed to the nines, dressed *or* fit to
kill <nonformal>; in Sunday best, *endi-
manché* <Fr>, in one's best bib and
tucker <nonformal>, in fine *or* high
feather; *en grande tenue* <Fr>, *en grande
toilette* <Fr>, in full dress, in full feather,
in white tie and tails, in tails; **well-
dressed, chic,** *soigné* <Fr>, stylish, modish, well-turned, well turned-out; **dressy;
overdressed; underdressed,** casual, casually dressed

46 **in dishabille,** *en déshabillé* <Fr>, **in negligee; casual,** nonformal, sporty

47 tailored, custom-made, bespoke <Brit>;
ready-made, store-bought *and* off-the-
rack <both nonformal>, ready-to-wear;
vestmental; sartorial

48 **suits**

bodysuit	camouflage suit *or*
boiler suit	camo
business suit	casual suit

cat suit
combination
double-breasted suit
dress suit
ensemble
foul-weather suit
jump suit
leisure suit *or* shirt-
  suit
lounge suit
mod suit
one-piece suit
pants suit
playsuit
rain suit
riding habit
romper-suit
sack suit
separates

shirt suit
shirtwaist suit
single-breasted suit
ski suit
snowsuit
sports suit
summer suit
sun suit
sweat suit
swimsuit
tailored suit
tank suit *or* top
three-piece suit
town-and-country suit
track suit
tropical suit
trouser suit
two-piece suit
zoot suit

49 uniforms

blues
continentals
dress blues
dress whites
fatigues
full dress
khaki
nauticals

olive-drab *or* OD
regimentals
sailor suit
soldier suit
stripes <prison uni-
  form>
undress
whites

50 cloaks, overgarments

academic gown
academic hood
academic robe
afghan
bachelor's gown
bleaunt
blouse
burnoose
caftan
cape
capote
cardinal
cashmere *or* cash-
  mere shawl
cassock
chlamys
doctor's gown
domino
duster
frock
gabardine
haik
houppelande
Inverness cape
judge's robe *or* gown
kaftan
kimono
kirtle
manta
manteau
mantelet
mantelletta
mantellone
mantilla

mantle
mantua
master's gown
military cloak
monk's robe
opera cloak *or*
  cape
pallium
pelerine
pelisse
peplos
peplum
plaid
poncho
robe
roquelaure
sagum
serape
shawl
shoulderette
slop
smock
soutane
stole
tabard
talma
tippet
toga
toga virilis
tunic
wrap-around
wrapover
wrapper
wrap-up

51 coats, jackets

blazer
blouse
body coat
bolero
bomber jacket
capuchin
car coat
chaqueta <Sp>
chesterfield
claw-hammer coat *or*
  claw hammer
coach coat
coatee
coolie jacket *or* coat
cutaway coat *or* cuta-
  way
denim jacket
dinner coat *or* jacket
dolman
double-breasted
  jacket
doublet
down jacket
dress coat
dressing jacket
duffel *or* duffel coat
Eisenhower jacket
Eton jacket
fingertip coat
fitted coat
flack jacket
frock coat *or* frock
happi coat
jerkin
jumper
jupe <Scots>
loden coat
lounging jacket
mackinaw *or* mack-
  inaw coat

Mao jacket
matinee jacket
maxicoat
mess jacket
midicoat
monkey jacket
morning coat
Nehru jacket
Norfolk jacket
oilskins
parka
peacoat *or* pea jacket
pilot jacket
Prince Albert *or*
  Prince Albert coat
redingote
reefer *or* reefer jacket
sack *or* sack coat
san benito
shell jacket
shirtjac *or* shirt jacket
shooting jacket
single-breasted jacket
ski jacket
sleeve waistcoat
smoking jacket
spencer
spiketail coat *or*
  spiketail
sport coat *or* jacket
sports jacket
swagger coat
swallow-tailed coat
  or swallowtail
tabard
tail coat *or* tails
tuxedo coat *or* jacket
watch coat
windbreaker
woolly

52 sweaters

bolero
bulky
cardigan *or* cardigan
  jacket
cashmere sweater
crewneck sweater
desk sweater
fisherman's sweater
hand-knit
jersey
knittie
poor boy sweater
pull-on sweater

pullover
shell
shoulderette
ski sweater
slip-on
slipover
sloppy Joe
sweatshirt
topper
turtleneck sweater
V-neck sweater
windbreaker
woolly

53 overcoats

benjamin
Burberry <trade-
  mark>
camelhair coat
capote
chesterfield
cloth coat

dreadnought
duster
fearnought
fur coat
fur-lined coat
fur-trimmed coat
greatcoat

Inverness
long coat
mackintosh or mac
Newmarket or New-
    market coat
oilskins
paletot
raglan
raincoat
slicker

slip-on
sou'wester
surtout
tarpaulin
trench coat
ulster
waterproof
wet weathers
wrap-around
wraprascal

54 shirts

basque
blouse
body shirt
body suit
button down
coat shirt
dashiki
dickey
doublet
dress shirt
evening shirt
gipon
habit shirt
hair shirt
halter
hickory shirt
jupe <Scots>
middy blouse

olive-drab or OD shirt
overblouse
polo shirt
pourpoint
pullover
sark
shell
shirt-jacket or shirt-
    jac
shirtwaist
short-sleeved shirt
sport shirt
sweatshirt
tank top
tee-shirt or T-shirt
top
tube top
workshirt

55 dresses, skirts

ballet skirt
backwrap
ball-gown
body dress
cage
cheongsam
chiton
cocktail dress
crinoline
culottes
dinner dress or gown
dirndl
divided skirt
evening dress
evening gown
farthingale
fillebeg
full skirt
granny dress
grass skirt
hobble skirt
hoop skirt
jumper
kilt or filibeg
kirtle
mantua
maxiskirt
microskirt

midiskirt
miniskirt
Mother Hubbard
muu-muu
overdress
overskirt
pannier
pantdress
pantskirt
peplum
petticoat
pinafore
sack
sari
sarong
sheath
shift
shirtdress
shirtdress or shirt-
    waist dress
slit skirt
tank dress
T-dress
tea gown
tunic dress
tutu
wrap dress

56 undergarments

all-in-one
Balmoral
bloomers
body stocking

brassiere
breechclout or loin-
    cloth
briefs

bustle
BVD's <trademark>
cami-knickers
camisole
chemise
combination
corset
crinoline
diapers
drawers
foundation garment
halter-top briefs
Jockey <trademark>
    shorts
knickers <Brit>
leotard
long underwear or
    long johns
napkins or nappies
    <Brit>
pannier
panties
pants
pantyhose

petticoat
scanties
shift
shorts
singlet <Brit>
skivvies
slip
smock
soakers
step-ins
string vest
teddy
tee-shirt or T-shirt
thermal underwear
tournure <Fr>
underdrawers
underpants
undershirt
undershorts
underskirt
undervest
union suit
unitard
vest <Brit>

57 hosiery

anklets or ankle socks
argyles
athletic socks
bobbysocks
boothose
boot socks
clock hose
crew socks
dress sheers
full-fashioned stock-
    ings
garter stockings
half hose
knee-socks
leg-warmers
lisle hose
nylons

panty-hose
rayon stockings
seamless stockings
sheer stockings or
    sheers
shin socks
silk stockings
stocking hose
stretch stockings
sweat socks
tights
trunk hose
tube socks
varsity socks
wigglers or toe
    socks
work socks

6 UNCLOTHING

NOUNS **1 unclothing,** divestment, divestiture, divesture; **removal; stripping,** de-
nudement, denudation; baring, stripping
or laying bare, uncovering, **exposure,** exposing; indecent exposure, exhibitionism, flashing <nonformal>; decortica-
tion, excoriation; desquamation, exfoliation; exuviation, ecdysis
  2 disrobing, undressing, disrobement, unclothing; uncasing, discasing; shedding,
molting, peeling; striptease
  3 nudity, nakedness, bareness; **the nude,**
the altogether and **the buff** <both nonfor-
mal>, **the raw** <nonformal>; state of
nature, **birthday suit** <nonformal>; not a
stitch, not a stitch to one's name or back;
full-frontal nudity; décolleté, décolletage,

toplessness; nudism, naturism, gymnosophy; nudist, naturist, gymnosophist;
stripper, stripteaser, ecdysiast

4 hairlessness, baldness, acomia, alopecia;
beardlessness, bald-headedness *or* -pat-
edness; baldhead, baldpate, baldy
<nonformal>; shaving, tonsure, depila-
tion; hair remover, depilatory

VERBS **5 divest, strip, strip away, remove;
uncover,** uncloak, unveil, **expose,** lay
open, bare, lay *or* strip bare, **denude,** de-
nudate; fleece, shear; pluck

6 take off, remove, doff, douse <nonfor-
mal>, off with, put off, slip *or* step out of,
slip off, slough off, cast off, throw off,
drop; unwrap, undo

7 undress, unclothe, undrape, ungarment,
unapparel, unarray, disarray; **disrobe;**
unsheathe, discase, uncase; **strip,** strip to
the buff <nonformal>, do a strip-tease

8 peel, pare, skin, strip, flay, excoriate, de-
corticate, bark; scalp

9 husk, hull, pod, **shell,** shuck

10 shed, cast, throw off, **slough, molt,** slough
off, exuviate

11 scale, flake, scale *or* flake off, desquamate, exfoliate

ADJS **12 divested, stripped, bared,** denuded,
denudated, **exposed, uncovered,** stripped
or laid bare, unveiled, showing; unsheathed, discased, uncased

**13 unclad, undressed, unclothed, unattired,
disrobed,** ungarmented, undraped, un-
garbed, unrobed, unappareled, uncased;
clothesless, garbless, garmentless, rai-
mentless; half-clothed, underclothed, *en
déshabillé* <Fr>, in dishabille, nudish;
low-necked, low-cut, décolleté, strapless,
topless; **seminude,** scantily clad

14 naked, nude; bare, peeled, raw <nonfor-
mal>, **in the raw** <nonformal>, *in puris
naturalibus* <L>, in a state of nature, in
nature's garb; in one's birthday suit, **in
the buff** *and* in native buff *and* stripped to
the buff *and* **in the altogether** <all nonfor-
mal>, with nothing on, without a stitch,
without a stitch to one's name *or* on one's
back; **stark-naked,** bare-ass <non-
formal>, bare as the back of one's hand,
naked as the day one was born, naked as a
jaybird <nonformal>, starkers <Brit
nonformal>, "naked as a worm"—
Chaucer, "naked as a needle"—William
Langland, "naked as my nail"—John
Heywood, "in naked beauty more
adorned"—Milton; nudist, naturistic,
gymnosophical

15 barefoot, barefooted, unshod; discalced,
discalceate

16 bare-ankled, bare-armed, bare-backed,
bare-breasted, topless, bare-chested,
bare-faced, bare-handed, bare-headed,
bare-kneed, bare-legged, bare-necked,
bare-throated

17 hairless, depilous; **bald,** acomous; bald as
a coot, bald as an egg; **bald-headed,** bald-
pated, tonsured; **beardless,** whiskerless,
shaven, clean-shaven, smooth-shaven,
smooth-faced; smooth, glabrous

18 exuvial, sloughy; desquamative, exfolia-
tory; denudant *or* denudatory

ADVS **19** nakedly, barely, baldly

WORD ELEMENTS **20** de—, dis—, un—

7 NUTRITION

NOUNS **1 nutrition, nourishment,** nourishing, feeding, nurture; alimentation; **food**
or **nutritive value, food intake;** food chain
or cycle

2 nutritiousness, nutritiveness, **di-
gestibility,** assimilability; healthfulness

3 nutrient, nutritive, **nutriment** 10.3, food;
nutrilite, growth factor, growth regulator; **natural food,** health food <see
list>; roughage, fiber

4 vitamin <see list>, vitamin complex;
provitamin, provitamin A *or* carotene

5 carbohydrate, carbo *or* carbs <nonfor-
mal>, simple carbohydrate, complex
carbohydrate; hydroxy aldehyde, hydroxy ketone, saccharide, monosac-
charide, disaccharide, trisaccharide,
polysaccharide *or* polysaccharose; **sugar;
starch**

6 protein *or* proteid, simple protein, conjugated protein; **amino acid,** essential
amino acid; peptide, dipeptide, polypep-
tide, etc

7 fat, glyceride, **lipid,** lipoid; fatty acid;
steroid, sterol; **cholesterol,** glycerol-
cholesterol, cephalin-cholesterol; triglyceride; **lipoprotein,** high-density
lipoprotein *or* HDL, low-density lipoprotein *or* LDL; polyunsaturated fat

8 digestion, ingestion, assimilation, absorption; primary digestion, secondary
digestion; predigestion; salivary digestion, gastric *or* peptic digestion, pancreatic digestion, intestinal digestion;
digestive system, alimentary canal, gastrointestinal tract; salivary glands,
gastric glands, liver, pancreas; digestive
secretions, saliva, gastric juice, pancreatic juice, intestinal juice, bile

9 digestant, digester, digestive; pepsin; **enzyme,** proteolytic enzyme

10 metabolism, basal metabolism, acid-base

metabolism, energy metabolism; **anabolism**, assimilation; **catabolism**, disassimilation

11 diet, dieting, dietary; dietetics; **regimen**, regime; bland diet; soft diet, pap, spoon food *or* meat, spoon victuals <nonformal>; balanced diet; diabetic diet, allergy diet, reducing diet, obesity diet; high-calorie diet, low-calorie diet, watching one's weight *or* calories, calorie-counting; liquid diet; protein-sparing diet; high-protein diet, low-carbohydrate diet; high-vitamin diet, vitamin-deficiency diet; acid-ash diet, alkaline-ash diet; low-salt diet, low-sodium diet, salt-free diet; ulcer diet; vegetarianism, macrobiotic diet; diet book, vitamin chart, calorie chart, calorie counter; fad diet

12 vitaminization, fortification, enrichment, restoration

13 nutritionist, dietitian, vitaminologist, enzymologist

14 <science of nutrition> **dietetics**, dietotherapeutics, dietotherapy; vitaminology; enzymology

VERBS **15 nourish**, feed, sustain, nutrify <old>, nurture; **sustain**, strengthen

16 digest, assimilate, absorb; metabolize; predigest

17 diet, go on a diet; watch one's weight *or* calories, count calories

18 vitaminize, **fortify, enrich**, restore

ADJS **19 nutritious**, nutritive, nutrient, **nourishing**; alimentary, alimental; digestible, assimilable

20 digestive, assimilative; peptic

21 dietary, dietetic, dietic <old>; regiminal

22 health foods

acidophilus milk	peanut flour
blackstrap molasses	powdered milk
brewer's yeast	raw vegetables
brown rice	rice polish
buckwheat flour	royal jelly
caudle	soybeans
cottonseed flour	soy flour
fiber	tiger's milk
fortified flour	unrefined flour
fortified milk	vegetables
fruits	wheat berries
liver	wheat germ
middlings	wheat grass
nonfat milk	whole wheat
nuts	whole wheat flour
oat bran	yogurt

23 vitamins

vitamin A	carotene
vitamin A$_1$ *or* anti-	cryptoxanthin
ophthalmic factor	**vitamin B**
or axerophthol	vitamin B complex
vitamin A$_2$	vitamin B$_1$ *or* thia-
mine *or* aneurin *or*	inositol
anti-beriberi factor	niacin *or* nicotinic
vitamin B$_2$ *or* vitamin	acid
G *or* riboflavin *or*	**vitamin C** *or* ascorbic
lactoflavin *or* ovo-	acid
flavin *or*	**vitamin D** *or* cal-
hepatoflavin	ciferol
vitamin M *or* vitamin	ergocalciferol
B$_c$	cholecalciferol
vitamin B$_6$ *or* py-	**vitamin E** *or*
ridoxine *or*	tocopherol
adermin	**vitamin K** *or*
biotin *or* vitamin H	naphthoquinone
choline	menadione
folic acid *or*	**vitamin P** *or* bio-
pteroylglutamic	flavinoid
acid *or* para-	
aminobenzoic acid	
or PABA	

8 EATING

NOUNS **1 eating, feeding, dining**, messing; the nosebag <nonformal>; ingestion, consumption, deglutition; **tasting**, relishing, savoring; **gourmet eating** *or* **dining**, fine dining, gourmandise; nibbling, pecking, licking, **munching**; snacking; **devouring**, gobbling, wolfing; **gorging, overeating**, gluttony, overconsumption; **chewing**, mastication, manducation, rumination; **feasting, regaling**, regalement; **appetite, hunger** 100.7; nutrition 7; **dieting** 7.11; gluttony 672; carnivorism, carnivorousness, carnivority; herbivorism, herbivority, herbivorousness, grazing, browsing, cropping, pasturing, pasture, vegetarianism, phytophagy; omnivorism, omnivorousness, pantophagy; cannibalism, anthropophagy; omophagia *or* omophagy

2 bite, morsel, taste, swallow; mouthful, gob <nonformal>; a nibble, a bite, munchies; cud, quid; bolus; **chew**, chaw <nonformal>; nip, nibble; munch; gnash; champ, chomp <nonformal>; snap

3 drinking, imbibing, imbibition, potation; lapping, slipping, tasting, nipping; quaffing, gulping, swigging <nonformal>, swilling *and* guzzling <both nonformal>, pulling <nonformal>; compotation, symposium; drunkenness 88.1,3

4 drink, potation, potion, libation; draft, dram, drench, **swig** <nonformal>, swill *and* guzzle <both nonformal>, quaff, **sip**, sup, suck, tot, bumper, snort *and* slug <both nonformal>, pull <nonformal>, lap, gulp, slurp <nonformal>; nip, peg; beverage

5 meal, repast, feed *and* sit-down <both nonformal>, mess, spread <nonformal>, table, board, meat, *repas* <Fr>; **refreshment,** refection, regalement, entertainment, treat; frozen meal, meal pack

6 <meals> breakfast, *petit déjeuner* <Fr>, continental breakfast, English breakfast; meat breakfast, *déjeuner à la fourchette* <Fr>; **brunch** <nonformal>, elevenses <Brit nonformal>; **lunch, luncheon,** tiffin, hot luncheon; **tea,** teatime, high tea, cream tea; **dinner,** *diner* <Fr>; **supper,** *souper* <Fr>; buffet supper *or* lunch; box lunch, packed lunch <Brit>; takeout; precooked frozen meal, TV dinner; **picnic, cookout,** alfresco meal, fête champêtre, **barbecue,** fish fry, clambake, wiener roast *or* wienie roast; coffee break, tea break, mash <Brit nonformal>

7 light meal, refreshments, light repast, light lunch, spot of lunch <nonformal>, collation, **snack** *and* nosh <both nonformal>, **bite** <nonformal>, *casse-croûte* <Fr>

8 hearty meal, full meal, healthy meal, large *or* substantial meal, heavy meal, **square meal,** man-sized meal, large order; three squares

9 feast, banquet, festal board; lavish *or* Lucullan feast; bean-feast *or* beano <both Brit nonformal>, blow *or* blowout <nonformal>, groaning board

10 serving, service; **portion, helping,** help; second helping; **course;** dish, plate; *plat du jour* <Fr>; antepast <old>; entree, *entrée* <Fr>, entremets; dessert; cover, place

11 <manner of service> service, table service, counter service, self-service, curb service, take-out service; table d'hôte, ordinary; à la carte; cover, *couvert* <Fr>; cover charge; American plan, European plan

12 tableware, dining utensils; **silverware,** silver, silver plate, stainless-steel ware; **flatware,** flat silver; hollow ware; **cutlery,** knives, forks, spoons; tablespoon, teaspoon; chopsticks; **dishware, china, dishes,** plates, cups, glasses, saucers, bowls, fingerbowls; **dish,** salad dish, fruit dish, dessert dish; **bowl,** cereal bowl, fruit bowl, punchbowl; **tea service, tea set,** tea things, tea strainer, tea-caddy, tea-cozy

13 table linen, napery, tablecloth, table cover, table-mat, table pad; **napkin, table napkin,** serviette <Brit>

14 menu, bill of fare, carte

15 gastronomy, gastronomics, gastrology, **epicurism,** epicureanism

16 eater, feeder, consumer, devourer; **diner,** luncher; picnicker; mouth, hungry mouth; diner-out, eater-out; boarder, board-and-roomer; **gourmet,** gastronome, epicure, gourmand, connoisseur of food *or* wine, bon vivant, high liver, Lucullus, Brillat-Savarin; **glutton,** overeater, pig <nonformal>, gourmand; omnivore, pantophagist; **flesh-eater, meat-eater, carnivore,** omophagist, predacean; **man-eater, cannibal; vegetarian,** lactovegetarian, fruitarian, plant-eater, **herbivore,** phytophagan, phytophage; grass-eater, graminivore; grain-eater, granivore; gourmand, trencherman, **glutton** 672.3

17 restaurant, eating place, eating house, dining room; eatery *and* beanery *and* hashery *and* hash house *and* greasy spoon <all nonformal>; **fast-food restaurant,** hamburger joint <nonformal>; *trattoria* <Ital>; **lunchroom,** luncheonette; **café,** *caffè* <Ital>; **tearoom,** bistro <Fr>; **coffeehouse,** coffeeroom, **coffee shop,** coffee bar, coffee-pot <nonformal>; **tea shop,** tea-room, tea-garden, teahouse; pub, tavern; chop-house; **grill,** grillroom; cookshop; buffet, smorgasbord; **lunch counter,** quick-lunch counter; hot-dog stand, hamburger stand, drive-in restaurant, drive-in; **snack bar,** *buvette* <Fr>, *cantina* <Sp>; milk bar; sushi bar; juice bar; raw bar; pizzeria; **cafeteria,** automat; mess hall, dining hall; canteen; cookhouse, cookshack, lunch wagon, chuck wagon; **diner,** dog wagon <nonformal>; **kitchen** 11.3

VERBS **18 feed, dine,** wine and dine, mess; nibble, snack, graze <nonformal>; satisfy, gratify; regale; bread, meat; board, sustain; pasture, put out to pasture, graze, grass; forage, fodder; provision 385.9

19 nourish, nurture, nutrify, aliment, foster; **nurse, suckle,** lactate, breast-feed, wet-nurse, dry-nurse; fatten, fatten up, stuff, force-feed

20 eat, feed, fare, take, partake, partake of, break bread, break one's fast; refresh *or* entertain the inner man, feed one's face *and* put on the feed bag <both nonformal>, fall to, pitch in <nonformal>; **taste,** relish, savor; hunger 100.19; **diet,** go on a diet, watch one's weight, count calories

21 dine, dinner; **sup,** breakfast; lunch; picnic, cook out; **eat out, dine out;** board; mess with, break bread with

22 devour, swallow, ingest, **consume,** take

in, tuck in or away and tuck into <all nonformal>, down, take down, get down, put away <nonformal>; **eat up;** dispatch or dispose of and get away with <all nonformal>; surround and put oneself outside of <both nonformal>

23 **gobble, gulp, bolt,** wolf, gobble or gulp or bolt or wolf down

24 **feast, banquet,** regale; eat heartily, have a good appetite, eat up, lick the platter or plate, do oneself proud <nonformal>, do one's duty, do justice to, polish the platter, put it away <nonformal>

25 **stuff, gorge** 672.4, pig out <nonformal>, engorge, glut, guttle, cram, eat one's fill, stuff or gorge oneself, gluttonize

26 **pick, peck** <nonformal>, **nibble; snack** <nonformal>, nosh <nonformal>; pick at, peck at <nonformal>, eat like a bird, show no appetite

27 **chew,** chew up, chaw <nonformal>, bite into; **masticate,** manducate; ruminate, chew the cud; **bite,** grind, champ, chomp <nonformal>; **munch;** gnash; nibble, **gnaw;** mouth, mumble; gum

28 **feed on** or **upon, feast on** or **upon,** batten upon, fatten on or upon; prey on or upon, live on or upon, pasture on, browse, graze, crop

29 **drink,** drink in, **imbibe,** wet one's whistle <nonformal>; **quaff, sip, sup,** bib, swig and swill and guzzle and pull <all nonformal>; **suck,** suckle, suck in or up; drink off or up, toss off or down, drain the cup; wash down; **toast,** drink to, pledge; tipple, **booze** 88.23

30 **lap up,** sponge or soak up, lick, lap, slurp <nonformal>

ADJS 31 **eating, feeding, gastronomical, dining,** mensal, commensal, prandial, postprandial, preprandial; **nourishing, nutritious** 7.19; **dietetic; omnivorous,** pantophagous, **gluttonous** 672.6; **flesheating, meat-eating, carnivorous,** omophagous, predacious; **man-eating, cannibal,** cannibalistic; insect-eating, insectivorous; vegetable-eating, **vegetarian,** lactovegetarian, fruitarian; plant-eating, **herbivorous,** phytivorous, phytophagous; grass-eating, graminivorous; grain-eating, granivorous

32 chewing, masticatory, manducatory; ruminant, ruminating, cud-chewing

33 **edible, eatable,** comestible, gustable, esculent; kosher; **palatable,** succulent, **delicious,** dainty, savory; **fine, fancy, gourmet**

34 **drinkable,** potable

INTERJS 35 chow down!, soup's on!, grub's

on!, come and get it!; *bon appétit!* <Fr>, eat hearty!, eat up!

WORD ELEMENTS 36 phag—, phago—, —phagia, —phagy; —phage, —vore, —vora

9 REFRESHMENT

NOUNS 1 **refreshment,** refection, refreshing, **bracing, exhilaration, stimulation,** enlivenment, vivification, **invigoration,** reinvigoration, reanimation, revival, revivification, reviviscence or revivescency, renewal, recreation; regalement, regale; **tonic,** bracer, breath of fresh air, pick-me-up and a shot in the arm and an upper <all nonformal>; cordial

VERBS 2 **refresh, freshen,** refreshen, freshen up, fresh up <nonformal>; **revive,** revivify, **reinvigorate,** reanimate; **exhilarate, stimulate, invigorate,** fortify, enliven, liven up, animate, vivify, quicken, brisk, brisken; brace, **brace up,** buck up and pick up <both nonformal>, perk up and chirk up <both nonformal>, set up, set on one's legs or feet <nonformal>; renew one's strength, put or breathe new life into, give a breath of fresh air, give a shot in the arm <nonformal>; renew, recreate, charge or recharge one's batteries <nonformal>; **regale, cheer,** refresh the inner man

ADJS 3 **refreshing,** refreshful, **fresh,** brisk, crisp, crispy, zesty, zestful, **bracing, tonic,** cordial; analeptic; **exhilarating, stimulating, stimulative, stimulatory, invigorating,** rousing, energizing; regaling, cheering

4 **refreshed, restored, invigorated, exhilarated,** stimulated, energized, recharged, animated, reanimated, **revived,** renewed, recreated

5 **unwearied, untired, unfatigued, unexhausted**

10 FOOD

NOUNS 1 **food,** foodstuff, food and drink, sustenance, kitchen stuff, victualage, **comestibles, edibles,** eatables, viands, **cuisine,** tucker <Australia>, ingesta <pl>; soul food; fast food, junk food; **fare,** cheer, creature comfort; provision, provender; meat <old>, bread, daily bread, bread and butter; health food; board, table, feast 8.9, spread <nonformal>

2 <nonformal terms> **grub,** grubbery, **eats, chow,** chuck, grits, groceries, the

nosebag, scarf *or* scoff, tuck, victuals *or* vittles

3 **nutriment, nourishment,** nurture; pabulum, pap; aliment, alimentation; **refreshment,** refection, commons <chiefly Brit>; **sustenance,** support, keep

4 **feed, fodder, provender;** forage, pasture, eatage, pasturage; grain; corn, oats, barley, wheat; meal, bran, chop; **hay,** timothy, clover, straw; ensilage, silage; chicken feed, scratch, scratch feed, mash; slops, swill; pet food, dog food, cat food; bird seed

5 **provisions, groceries,** provender, supplies, stores, larder, food supply; fresh foods, canned foods, frozen foods, dehydrated foods, precooked foods; commissariat, commissary, grocery

6 **rations,** board, meals, commons <chiefly Brit>, mess, allowance, allotment, food allotment, tucker <Australia>; short commons <chiefly Brit>; emergency rations; K ration, C ration, garrison *or* field rations

7 **dish** 11.1, culinary preparation *or* concoction; cover, **course** 8.10; casserole; grill, broil, boil, roast, fry; **main dish, entree,** *pièce de résistance* <Fr>, culinary masterpiece, dish fit for a king; side dish

8 **delicacy, dainty, goody** <nonformal>, treat, kickshaw, **tidbit,** titbit; **morsel,** choice morsel, *bonne bouche* <Fr>; savory; dessert; ambrosia, nectar, cate, manna

9 **appetizer,** whet, *apéritif* <Fr>; foretaste, antepast <old>, *antipasto* <Ital>, *Vorspeise* <Ger>; **hors d'oeuvre;** *crostato* <Ital>; smorgasbord; canapé **dip,** guacamole, salsa, clam dip, cheese dip, hummus, falafel; rumaki; zakuska; **pickle,** sour pickle, dill pickle, cornichon

10 **soup,** *potage* <Fr>, *zuppa* or *minestra* <both Ital>

11 **stew,** olla, olio, *olla podrida* <Sp>; meat stew, *étuvée* <Fr>; Irish stew, mulligan stew *or* mulligan <nonformal>; goulash, Hungarian goulash; ragout; salmi; *bouillabaisse* <Fr>, *paella* <Catalan>, oyster stew, chowder; fricassee; curry

12 **meat,** flesh, red meat, *viande* <Fr>; butcher's meat, *viande de boucherie* <Fr>; **cut of meat;** game, *menue viande* <Fr>; venison; **roast,** joint, *rôti* <Fr>; pot roast; barbecue, boiled meat, *bouilli* <Fr>; forcemeat; mincemeat, mince; hash, *hachis* <Fr>; jugged hare, *civet* <Fr>; pemmican, jerky; sausage meat, scrapple; aspic

13 **beef,** *bœuf* <Fr>; roast beef, *rosbif* <Fr>; Kobe beef; hamburger, ground beef; corned beef, bully *or* bully beef; dried beef; chipped beef; salt beef; jerky, charqui; pastrami; beef extract, beef tea, bouillon; suet

14 **veal,** *vitello* <Ital>, *veau* <Fr>; veal cutlet, *côtelette de veau* <Fr>; breast of veal, *poitrine de veau* <Fr>; fricandeau; calf's head, *tête de veau* <Fr>; calf's liver, *foie de veau* <Fr>; sweetbread, *ris de veau* <Fr>; calf's brains

15 **mutton,** *mouton* <Fr>; muttonchop; **lamb,** *agneau* <Fr>; breast of lamb, *poitrine d'agneau* <Fr>; leg of lamb, leg of mutton, *gigot* <Fr>, *jambe de mouton* <Fr>; saddle of mutton; baked sheep's head

16 **pork,** *porc* <Fr>, pig, pigmeat <nonformal>

17 **steak,** *tranche* <Fr>, **beefsteak,** *bifteck* <Fr>, *tranche de bœuf* <Fr>, *bistecca* <Ital>

18 **chop, cutlet,** *côtelette* <Fr>; pork chop, *côtelette de porc frais* <Fr>; mutton chop, *côtelette de mouton* <Fr>, Saratoga chop; veal cutlet, veal chop, *côtelette de veau* <Fr>, *Wiener Schnitzel* <Ger>

19 <variety meats> kidneys; heart; brains; liver; gizzard; tongue; sweetbread <thymus>; beef bread <pancreas>; tripe <stomach>; marrow; cockscomb; chitterlings *or* chitlins <intestines>; prairie *or* mountain oyster <testis>; haslet, giblets, *abattis* <Fr>

20 **sausage,** *saucisse* <Fr>, *saucisson* <Fr>, *salsiccia* <Ital>, *Wurst* <Ger>; **pâté**

21 **fowl,** bird, edible bird, *volaille* <Fr>

22 <parts of fowl> leg, drumstick, thigh, chicken foot, turkey foot, etc, wing, wishbone, breast; white meat, dark meat, giblets, pope's *or* parson's nose <nonformal>; oyster; neck

23 **fish,** *poisson* <Fr>; seafood; finnan haddie; kipper, kippered salmon *or* herring, gravlax; smoked salmon, lox, nova <nonformal>; smoked herring, red herring; eel, *anguille* <Fr>; fish eggs, roe, caviar; ceviche; sushi; squid, calamari; flatfish, sole, lemon sole, Dover sole, flounder, fluke, dab, sanddab

24 **shellfish,** *coquillage* <Fr>; **mollusc,** snail, *escargot* <Fr>

25 **eggs,** *œufs* <Fr>; fried eggs, *œufs sur le plat* <Fr>; boiled eggs, *œufs à la coque* <Fr>, coddled eggs; poached eggs, *œufs pochés* <Fr>; scrambled eggs, buttered eggs, *œufs brouillés* <Fr>; dropped eggs, shirred eggs, stuffed eggs, deviled eggs; omelet; soufflé Scotch egg

26 **stuffing, dressing,** forcemeat *or* farce

27 **bread,** *pain* <Fr>, *pane* <Ital>, the staff
of life; loaf of bread; crust, breadcrust,
crust of bread; breadstuff; **leaven,** leavening, ferment

28 **corn bread;** pone, ash pone, corn pone,
corn tash, ash cake, hoecake, johnnycake;
dodger, corn dodger, corn dab, hush
puppy; cracklin' bread <nonformal>;
tortilla <Sp>

29 **biscuit,** sinker <nonformal>; hardtack,
sea biscuit, ship biscuit, pilot biscuit *or*
bread; **cracker,** soda cracker *or* saltine,
graham cracker, *biscotto* <Ital>, cream
cracker, nacho, potato chip, potato crisp
<Brit>, sultana, water biscuit, butter
cracker, oyster cracker, pilot biscuit; wafer; rusk, zwieback, melba toast, Brussels
biscuit; pretzel

30 **bun, roll, muffin;** bagel, bialy *or* bi-
alystoker; brioche, croissant; English
muffin; popover; scone; hard roll, kaiser
roll, Parker House roll

31 **sandwich,** *canapé* <Fr>, *smörgåsbord*
<Swed>; club sandwich, dagwood;-
hamburger, burger; submarine *or* sub
or hero *or* grinder *or* hoagy *or* poor-
boy

32 **noodles,** *pasta* <Ital>, Italian paste,
paste; **spaghetti,** spaghettini, ziti, fed-
ellini, fettuccine, radiattore, vermicelli,
macaroni, lasagne; ravioli, *kreplach*
<Yiddish pl>, won ton; **dumpling;** spaet-
zle, dim sum, gnocchi, linguine; matzo
balls, *knaydlach* <Yiddish>

33 **cereal,** breakfast food, dry cereal, hot cereal; **flour,** meal

34 **vegetables,** produce, *légumes* <Fr>, veg
and veggies <both nonformal>; **greens;**
potherbs; **beans,** *frijoles* <Sp>, *haricots*
<Fr>; **potato,** spud <nonformal>, tater
<nonformal>, *pomme de terre* <Fr>,
Irish potato, pratie <nonformal>, white
potato; **tomato,** love apple; eggplant, *au-
bergine* <Fr>, mad apple; rhubarb,
pieplant; cabbage, *Kraut* <Ger>

35 **salad,** *salade* <Fr>; **greens,** *crudités* <Fr>

36 **fruit;** produce; stone fruit, drupe; citrus
fruit; fruit compote, fruit soup, fruit cocktail

37 **nut,** *noix* <Fr>, *noisette* <Fr>; kernel,
meat

38 **sweets,** sweet stuff, **confectionery; sweet,
sweetmeat; confection; candy;** comfit,
confiture; **jelly, jam;** preserve, conserve;
marmalade; apple butter; prune butter,
lekvar; lemon curd; gelatin, Jell-O
<trademark>; compote; mousse;
blancmange; tutti-frutti; maraschino

cherries; honey; icing, frosting, glaze;
meringue; whipped cream

39 **pastry,** *patisserie* <Fr>; French pastry,
Danish pastry; **tart;** turnover; timbale;
pie, *tarte* <Fr>, fruit pie, tart; *quiche* or
quiche Lorraine <Fr>; patty, patty cake;
patty shell, *vol-au-vent* <Fr>; rosette;
dowdy, pandowdy; filo, strudel, baklava;
puff pastry; puff, cream puff, croquem-
bouche, profiterole; cannoli, cream horn;
éclair, chocolate éclair

40 **cake,** *gâteau* <Fr>, *torte* <Ger>; *petit-
four* <Fr>

41 **cookie,** biscuit <Brit>

42 **doughnut,** friedcake, sinker <nonfor-
mal>, cymbal <old>, olykoek <non-
formal>; French doughnut, raised
doughnut; glazed doughnut; fastnacht;
cruller, twister; jelly doughnut, bis-
marck; fritter, *beignet* <Fr>; apple
fritter, *beignet aux pommes* <Fr>

43 **pancake,** griddlecake, **hot cake,** batter-
cake, flapcake, **flapjack,** flannel cake;
buckwheat cake; chapatty <India>; **waffle;** blintz, cheese blintz, *crêpe, crêpe
suzette* <both Fr>, *palacsinta* <Hung>,
Pfannkuchen <Ger>, Swedish pancake

44 **pudding,** custard, mousse, flan

45 **ice,** *glace* <Fr>, frozen dessert; **ice cream,**
ice milk, French ice-cream; **sherbet,** water
ice <Brit>, Italian ice; gelato; tortoni;
parfait; sundae, ice-cream sundae, banana split; ice-cream soda; frappé; ice-
cream cone; frozen pudding; frozen custard, soft ice cream; frozen yogurt

46 **dairy products,** milk products; **cheese;
tofu,** bean curd

47 **beverage,** drink, thirst quencher, potation, potable, drinkable <nonformal>,
liquor, liquid; **soft drink,** nonalcoholic
beverage; cold drink; carbonated water,
soda water, sparkling water, **soda,** pop,
soda pop, tonic; milk shake, frosted
shake, thick shake, shake *and* frosted
<both nonformal>; malted milk, malt
<nonformal>; hard drink, alcoholic
drink

11 COOKING

NOUNS **1 cooking, cookery, cuisine, culinary
art;** food preparation; home economics,
domestic science, culinary science; catering; nutrition 7; baking, toasting, roasting, frying, searing, blackening, sautéing,
boiling, simmering, stewing, basting,
braising, poaching, shirring, barbecuing,
steeping, brewing, grilling, broiling, pan-
broiling; broil; **dish,** manner of prepara-

tion, style of recipe; **condiment,** spice
herb; **sauce**

2 **cook, chef,** *cuisinier* or *cuisinière* <Fr>,
kitchener, culinarian, culinary artist;
chief cook, head chef, *chef de cuisine*
<Fr>; fry cook *or* grease-burner <nonfor-
mal>, short-order cook; **baker,** *boulanger*
<Fr>, pastry cook, pastry chef, *patissier*
<Fr>

3 **kitchen, cookroom,** cookery, **scullery,**
cuisine; kitchenette; **galley,** caboose *or*
camboose; cookhouse; **bakery,** bake-
house; **cookware, kitchen ware,** cooker
<see list>, pots and pans

VERBS 4 **cook,** prepare food, prepare, do,
cook up, fry up, boil up, rustle up
<nonformal>; precook; boil, heat, stew,
simmer, parboil, blanch; brew; poach,
coddle; bake, fire, ovenbake; **microwave,**
micro-cook, nuke <nonformal>; scallop;
shirr; roast; toast; fry, deep-fry *or* deep-
fat fry, griddle, pan, pan-fry; sauté, stir-
fry; frizz, frizzle; sear, blacken, braise,
brown; broil, grill, pan-broil; barbecue;
fricassee; steam; devil; curry; baste; **do to
a turn,** do to perfection

ADJS 5 **cooking, culinary,** kitchen

6 **cooked,** heated, stewed, fried, barbecued,
curried, fricasseed, deviled, sautéed,
shirred, toasted; roasted, roast; fired,
pan-fried, deep-fried *or* deep-fat fried,
stir-fried; broiled, grilled, pan-broiled;
seared, blackened, braised, browned;
boiled, simmered, parboiled; steamed;
poached, coddled; baked, fired, oven-
baked; scalloped

7 **done, well-done,** well-cooked; *bien cuit*
<Fr>, done to a turn *or* to perfection;
overcooked, **overdone;** medium, medium-
rare; doneness

8 **underdone,** undercooked, not done, **rare,**
saignant <Fr>; sodden, fallen

9 **cookers**

alcohol stove	electric roaster
baker	electric toaster
barbecue	field range
boiler	fireless cooker
broiler	fry-cooker
camp stove	galley stove
chafer	grill
chafing dish *or* pan	hibachi
coffee maker	infrared broiler
cook stove	infrared cooker
corn popper	microwave oven
Crockpot <trade-	percolator
mark>	pots, pans
double boiler	pressure cooker
Dutch oven	roaster
electric cooker	rotisserie
electric frying pan	samovar
stove	waffle iron
toaster	waterless cooker

12 EXCRETION
<bodily discharge>

NOUNS 1 **excretion,** egestion, extrusion,
elimination, discharge; emission; ec-
crisis; **exudation,** transudation;
extravasation, effusion, flux, flow; ejaculation, ejection 908; **secretion** 13

2 **defecation,** dejection, **evacuation,** voidance; movement, **bowel movement** *or*
BM, number two <nonformal>, **stool,**
shit *and* crap <both nonformal>; **diarrhea,** loose bowels, flux; trots *and* runs
and shits *and* GI's *and* GI shits <all non-
formal>; turistas *and* Montezuma's
revenge <both nonformal>; lientery;
dysentery, bloody flux; catharsis, purgation, purge

3 **excrement,** dejection, dejecta, **discharge,**
ejection; matter; **waste,** waste matter;
excreta, egesta, ejecta, ejectamenta;
exudation, exudate; transudation, trans-
udate; extravasation, extravasate;
effluent

4 **feces,** feculence; defecation, movement,
bowel movement *or* **BM; stool, shit**
<nonformal>, **ordure,** night soil, jakes
<Brit nonformal>, crap *and* ca-ca *and*
doo-doo <all nonformal>; turd <non-
formal>; dingleberry <nonformal>;
manure, dung, droppings; cow pats, cow
flops <nonformal>; cow chips, buffalo
chips; guano; coprolite, coprolith; sewage, sewerage

5 **urine,** water, **piss** <nonformal>, number
one, *pish* <Yiddish>, pee *and* pee-pee *and*
wee-wee *and* whizz <all nonformal>,
piddle, stale; **urination,** micturition, em-
iction, a piss *and* a pee *and* a whizz <all
nonformal>; urea

6 **pus; matter,** purulence, peccant humor
<old>, ichor, sanies; pussiness; **suppura-
tion, festering,** rankling, mattering,
running; gleet, leukorrhea

7 **sweat, perspiration,** water; exudation,
exudate; diaphoresis, sudor; honest
sweat, the sweat of one's brow; beads of
sweat, beaded brow; cold sweat; **lather,**
swelter, streams of sweat; sudoresis;
body odor *or* **BO,** perspiration odor

8 **hemorrhage,** hemorrhea, **bleeding;** nosebleed; ecchymosis, petechia

9 **menstruation,** menstrual discharge *or*
flow *or* flux, catamenia, catamenial
discharge, flowers <old>, **the curse**

<nonformal>, the curse of Eve; **menses, monthlies,** courses, period, that time

10 **latrine,** convenience, **toilet,** toilet room, water closet *or* WC <nonformal>; **john** *and* johnny *and* **can** *and* crapper <all nonformal>; **loo** <Brit nonformal>; **lavatory,** washroom, public convenience; **bathroom,** basement; **rest room,** comfort station *or* room; ladies' *or* women's *or* girls' *or* little girls' *or* powder room <nonformal>; men's *or* boys' *or* little boys' room <nonformal>; head; privy, outhouse, backhouse, shithouse <nonformal>, johnny house <nonformal>, earth closet <Brit>, closet *and* necessary <both nonformal>; urinal

11 **toilet,** stool, **water closet; john** *and* johnny *and* **can** *and* crapper *and* thunderbox<all nonformal>; latrine; commode, closetstool, potty-chair <nonformal>; **chamber pot,** chamber, pisspot <nonformal>, potty <nonformal>, jerry <Brit nonformal>, jordan <Brit nonformal>, thunder mug <nonformal>; throne <nonformal>; chemical toilet, chemical closet; urinal; bedpan

VERBS 12 **excrete,** egest, **eliminate, discharge,** emit, give off, pass; ease *or* relieve oneself, go to the bathroom <nonformal>; **exude,** exudate, transude; weep; effuse, extravasate; **secrete** 13.5

13 **defecate, shit** *and* crap <both nonformal>, **evacuate,** void, **stool,** dung, have a bowel movement *or* BM, take a shit *or* crap <nonformal>, ca-ca *or* number two <both nonformal>

14 **urinate, pass** *or* **make water, wet,** stale, **piss** <nonformal>, piddle, pee; pee-pee *and* wee-wee *and* whizz *and* take a whizz *and* number one <all nonformal>, spend a penny, pump bilge

15 **fester,** suppurate, matter, rankle, run, weep; ripen, come *or* draw to a head

16 **sweat, perspire,** exude; break out in a sweat, **get all in a lather** <nonformal>; sweat like a trooper *or* horse, swelter, wilt

17 **bleed, hemorrhage,** lose blood, **shed blood,** spill blood; bloody; ecchymose

18 **menstruate,** come sick, come around, have one's period

ADJS 19 **excretory,** excretive, excretionary; eliminative, egestive; exudative, transudative; **secretory** 13.7

20 **excremental,** excrementary; **fecal,** feculent, shitty *and* crappy <both nonformal>, scatologic *or* scatological, stercoral, stercorous, stercoraceous, dungy; **urinary,** urinative

21 **festering,** suppurative, rankling, mattering; pussy, purulent

22 **sweaty,** perspiry <nonformal>; sweating, perspiring; wet with sweat, beaded with sweat, **sticky** <nonformal>, **clammy;** bathed in sweat, drenched with sweat, wilted; in a sweat; sudatory, sudoric, sudorific, diaphoretic

23 **bleeding, bloody,** hemorrhaging; ecchymosed

24 **menstrual,** catamenial

13 SECRETION

NOUNS 1 **secretion,** secreta, secernment; **excretion** 12; external secretion, internal secretion; lactation; weeping, lacrimation

2 digestive secretion *or* juice, salivary secretion, gastric juice, pancreatic juice, intestinal juice; bile, gall; endocrine; prostatic fluid, semen, sperm; thyroxin; autacoid, **hormone,** chalone; mucus; tears; rheum; gland

3 **saliva, spittle, sputum, spit, expectoration;** salivation, ptyalism, sialorrhea, sialagogue, **slobber,** slabber, slaver, **drivel,** dribble, **drool;** froth, foam; mouth-watering

4 endocrinology, eccrinology, hormonology

VERBS 5 **secrete,** produce, give out; **excrete** 12.12; water; lactate; weep, tear

6 **salivate,** ptyalize; **slobber,** slabber, slaver, **drool, drivel,** dribble; **expectorate, spit,** spit up; spew; hawk, clear the throat

ADJS 7 **secretory,** secretive, secretional, secretionary; **excretory** 12.19; lymphatic, serous; seminal, spermatic; watery, watering; lactational; lacteal, lacteous; lachrymal, lacrimatory, lachrymose; rheumy; salivary, salivant, salivous, sialoid, sialagogic

8 **glandular,** glandulous; **endocrine,** humoral, exocrine, eccrine, apocrine, holocrine, merocrine; **hormonal** *or* hormonic; adrenal, pancreatic, gonadal; ovarian; luteal; prostatic; splenetic; thymic; thyroidal

14 BODILY DEVELOPMENT

NOUNS 1 **bodily** *or* **physical development,** growth, development 860.1, maturation, maturing, maturescence, coming of age, growing up, reaching one's full growth, upgrowth; growing like a weed <nonformal>; plant growth, vegetation 310.30, germination, pullulation; sexual maturity, pubescence, puberty; nubility, marriageability, marriageableness; adulthood, manhood, womanhood; reproduction, procreation 78, burgeoning, sprouting; budding, gemmation; outgrowth, excrescence; overgrowth 257.5

VERBS **2 grow, develop,** wax, **increase** 251; gather, brew; **grow up,** mature, maturate, spring up, ripen, come of age, **shoot up,** sprout up, upshoot, upspring, upsprout, upspear, overtop, tower; grow like a weed <nonformal>; burgeon, **sprout** 310.31, blossom 310.32, reproduce 78.7, procreate 78.8, grow out of, germinate, pullulate; vegetate 310.31; **flourish, thrive;** mushroom, balloon; outgrow; overgrow, hypertrophy, overdevelop, grow uncontrollably

ADJS **3 grown, full-grown, grown-up,** developed, well-developed, fully developed, **mature, adult, full-fledged; growing,** adolescent, maturescent, pubescent; nubile, marriageable; **sprouting,** crescent, budding, flowering 310.35, florescent, **flourishing,** blossoming, blooming, burgeoning, fast-growing, thriving; overgrown, hypertrophied, overdeveloped

15 STRENGTH
<inherent power>

NOUNS **1 strength, might,** mightiness, powerfulness, stamina; **force, potency, power** 18; **energy** 17; **vigor, vitality,** vigorousness, heartiness, lustiness, lustihood; **stoutness, sturdiness,** stalwartness, robustness, hardiness, ruggedness; **guts** and gutsiness <both nonformal>, fortitude, intestinal fortitude <nonformal>, **toughness** 1047, **endurance, stamina,** staying or sticking power, stick-to-it-iveness <nonformal>; **strength of will,** decisiveness, obstinacy 361

2 muscularity, brawniness; beefiness and huskiness and heftiness and hunkiness <all nonformal>, thewiness, sinewiness; **brawn,** beef <nonformal>; **muscle,** brawn, sinew, sinews, thew, thews; musculature, build, physique; tone, elasticity 1046

3 firmness, soundness, staunchness, stoutness, **sturdiness, stability,** solidity, **hardness** 1044, temper

4 impregnability, impenetrability, **invulnerability,** inexpugnability, inviolability; **unassailability,** unattackableness; resistlessness, **irresistibility; invincibility,** indomitability, insuperability, unconquerableness, unbeatableness

5 strengthening, invigoration, fortification; **hardening,** toughening, firming; case hardening, tempering; **restrengthening,** reinforcement; **reinvigoration,** refreshment, revivification

6 strong man, stalwart, tower of strength, muscle man, piledriver, bulldozer, hunk <nonformal>; **giant,** Samson, Goliath; Charles Atlas, Mr Universe; Hercules, Atlas, Antaeus, Cyclops, Briareus, colossus, Polyphemus, Titan, Brobdingnagian, Tarzan, Superman; the strong, the mighty

7 <nonformal terms> **hunk, powerhouse, muscle man,** man mountain, big bruiser, strong-arm man, bully, bullyboy, ape, tough, toughie, tough guy, bozo, bimbo, **goon** 671.10, gorilla, meat-eater

8 <comparisons> horse, ox, lion; pig-shit <nonformal>; oak, heart of oak; rock, Gibraltar; iron, steel, nails

VERBS **9 be strong,** overpower, overwhelm; have what it takes, pack a punch

10 not weaken, not flag; **bear up, hold up,** keep up, stand up; **hold out,** stay or see it out, not give up, **never say die,** not let it get one down

11 <nonformal terms> **tough it out, hang tough, hang in,** stick or take it, take it on the chin, sweat it out, stay the distance

12 exert strength, put beef or one's back into it <nonformal>; use force, get tough <nonformal>, muscle and manhandle and strong-arm <all nonformal>

13 strengthen, invigorate, fortify, beef up <nonformal>, brace, buttress, prop, shore up, support, undergird, brace up; gird, gird up one's loins; steel, harden, case harden, anneal, stiffen, **toughen,** temper, nerve; confirm, sustain; **restrengthen, reinforce; reinvigorate,** refresh, revive, recruit one's strength

14 proof, insulate, weatherproof, soundproof, muffle, quietize, fireproof, waterproof, goofproof <nonformal>, etc

ADJS **15 strong, forceful,** forcible, forcy <Scots>, **mighty, powerful,** puissant <nonformal>, **potent** 18.12; **stout, sturdy, stalwart, rugged,** hale; hunky and husky and hefty and beefy <all nonformal>, strapping, doughty <nonformal>, **hardy,** hard, hard as nails, cast-iron, iron-hard, steely; **robust,** robustious, gutty and gutsy <both nonformal>; strong-willed, obstinate 361.8; **vigorous, hearty,** nervy, **lusty,** bouncing, full- or red-blooded; bionic, sturdy as an ox, strong as a lion or an ox or a horse, strong as brandy, strong as pig-shit <nonformal>, strong as strong; full-strength, double-strength, industrial-strength <nonformal>

16 **able-bodied, well-built,** well-set, well-set-up <nonformal>, well-knit, of good or powerful physique, broad-shouldered, barrel-chested, **athletic; muscular,** well-muscled, heavily muscled, thickset, burly, **brawny;** thewy, sinewy, **wiry;** muscle-bound, all muscle

17 **herculean,** Briarean, Antaean, Cyclopean, Atlantean, gigantic, gigantesque, Brobdingnagian, huge 257.20

18 **firm, sound, stout,** sturdy, tough, hard-boiled <nonformal>, **staunch, stable,** solid; sound as a dollar, solid as a rock, firm as Gibraltar, made of iron; rigid, unbreakable, infrangible

19 **impregnable,** impenetrable, **invulnerable,** inviolable, inexpugnable; **unassailable,** unattackable, insuperable, unsurmountable; resistless, **irresistible; invincible,** indomitable, **unconquerable,** unsubduable, unyielding 361.9, incontestable, unbeatable, more than a match for; overpowering, overwhelming, avalanchine

20 **resistant, proof, tight;** impervious; foolproof; shatterproof; weatherproof; dampproof, watertight, leakproof; hermetic, airtight; soundproof, noiseproof; puncture proof, holeproof; bulletproof, ballproof, shellproof, bombproof; rustproof, corrosionproof; fireproof, flameproof, fire-resisting; burglarproof

21 **unweakened, undiminished,** unallayed, unbated, unabated, unfaded, unwithered, unshaken, unworn, unexhausted; **unweakening, unflagging, unbowed;** in full force or swing, **going strong** <nonformal>; in the plenitude of power

22 <of sounds and odors> **intense, penetrating,** piercing; **loud,** deafening, thundering 56.12; **pungent, reeking** 69.10

ADVS 23 **strongly, stoutly, sturdily,** stalwartly, robustly, ruggedly; **mightily, powerfully, forcefully,** forcibly; **vigorously, heartily,** lustily; **soundly, firmly,** staunchly; impregnably, invulnerably, **invincibly, irresistibly,** unyieldingly; resistantly, imperviously; **intensely; loudly,** at the top of one's lungs, clamorously, deafeningly; **pungently**

WORD ELEMENTS 24　muscul—, musculo—, my—, myo—; —eus

16 WEAKNESS

NOUNS 1 **weakness,** weakliness, **feebleness,** strengthlessness; **flabbiness, flaccidity,**

softness; **impotence** or impotency 19; **debility,** debilitation, prostration, invalidism, collapse; **faintness,** faintishness, dizziness, lightheadedness, shakiness, gone or blah feeling <nonformal>; **fatigue** 21, exhaustion, weariness, dullness, sluggishness, languor, lassitude, **listlessness,** tiredness, languishment, atony; anemia, bloodlessness, etiolation, asthenia, adynamia, cachexia or cachexy

2 **frailty,** slightness, **delicacy, daintiness,** lightness; **flimsiness, unsubstantiality,** wispiness, sleaziness, shoddiness; **fragility,** frangibility or frangibleness, brittleness, breakableness, destructibility; disintegration 805; **human frailty,** "amiable weakness"—Henry Fielding; gutlessness <nonformal>, cowardice 491; moral weakness, irresolution, **indecisiveness,** infirmity of will, velleity, changeableness 853; inherent vice

3 **infirmity, unsoundness,** incapacity, unfirmness, unsturdiness, **instability, unsubstantiality;** decrepitude; **unsteadiness, shakiness,** ricketiness, wobbliness, wonkiness <Brit nonformal>, caducity, senility, invalidism; wishy-washiness, insipidity, vapidity, wateriness

4 **weak point, weakness,** weak place, **weak side,** vulnerable point, chink in one's armor, Achilles' heel or heel of Achilles; feet of clay

5 **weakening, enfeeblement, debilitation,** exhaustion, inanition, attrition; languishment; **devitalization,** enervation, evisceration; fatigue; attenuation, extenuation; softening, mitigation, damping, abatement, slackening, relaxing, relaxation, blunting, deadening, dulling; **dilution,** watering, watering-down, attenuation, thinning, reduction

6 **weakling,** weak or meek soul, weak sister <nonformal>, hothouse plant, softy <nonformal>, softling, **jellyfish,** invertebrate, gutless wonder <nonformal>, **baby,** big baby, crybaby, chicken <nonformal>, Milquetoast, sop, **milksop, namby-pamby, mollycoddle,** mama's boy, mother's boy, mother's darling, teacher's pet; sissy and pansy and pantywaist <all nonformal>, pushover <nonformal>, lightweight; **wimp,** poor or weak or dull tool <nonformal>; **nonentity,** hollow man, doormat and empty suit and nebbish and sad sack <all nonformal>

7 <comparisons> a kitten, a reed, thread, matchwood, a rope of sand; a house of cards, a house built on sand, a sand cas-

tle; water, milk and water, gruel, dishwater, cambric tea

VERBS **8** <be weak> **shake,** tremble,
quiver, quaver, cringe, cower 491.9, totter, teeter, dodder; halt, limp; be on one's
last leg, have one foot in the grave

   9 <become weak> **weaken,** grow weak *or*
weaker, go soft <nonformal>; **languish,
wilt,** faint, **droop,** drop, **sink, decline,
flag, pine, fade, tail away** *or* off, fail, fall
or drop by the wayside; crumble, go to
pieces, disintegrate 805.3; go downhill,
hit the skids <nonformal>, give way,
break, collapse, cave in <nonformal>,
surrender, cry uncle <nonformal>; give
out, have no staying power, run out of gas
<nonformal>, conk *or* peter *or* poop *or*
peg *or* fizzle out <nonformal>; come
apart, come apart at the seams, come unstuck *or* unglued <both informal>; yield;
die on the vine <nonformal>; wear thin
or away

10 <make weak> **weaken, enfeeble, debilitate,** unstrengthen, unsinew, undermine,
soften up <nonformal>, unbrace, unman, unnerve, rattle, shake up <nonfor-
mal>, **devitalize, enervate,** eviscerate;
sap, sap the strength of, exhaust, gruel,
take it out of <nonformal>; shake, unstring; reduce, lay low; attenuate, extenuate, mitigate, abate; blunt, deaden,
dull, damp *or* dampen, take the edge off;
draw the teeth, defang; cramp, cripple

11 dilute, cut <nonformal>, **reduce, thin,**
thin out, attenuate, rarefy; **water,** water
down, adulterate, irrigate *and* baptize
<both nonformal>

ADJS **12 weak,** weakly, **feeble,** debilitated,
imbecile; **strengthless,** sapless, marrowless, pithless, sinewless, listless, out of
gas <nonformal>, nerveless, lustless; **impotent, powerless** 19.13; spineless, lily-
livered, whitelivered, wimpy *and* wimpish *and* chicken *and* gutless <all nonfor-
mal>, cowardly 491.10; unnerved, shook-
up <nonformal>, unstrung, faint,
faintish, lightheaded, dizzy, gone; dull,
slack; **soft, flabby,** flaccid, unhardened;
limp, limber, limp *or* limber as a dishrag,
floppy, rubbery; **languorous,** languid,
drooping, droopy, pooped <nonformal>;
asthenic, anemic, bloodless, effete, etiolated; not what one used to be

13 "weak as water"—Bible, weak as milk
and water, weak as a drink of water, weak
as a child *or* baby, weak as a chicken,
weak as a kitten, weak as a mouse, "weak
as a rained-on bee"—F R Torrence

14 frail, slight, delicate, dainty, "delicately

weak"—Pope; puny; light, lightweight;
effeminate; namby-pamby, sissified, pan-
syish; **fragile,** frangible, **breakable,**
destructible, shattery, crumbly, brittle,
fragmentable, fracturable; **unsubstantial,
flimsy,** sleazy, tacky <nonformal>,
wispy, cobwebby, gossamery, papery,
pasteboardy; gimcrack *and* gimcracky
and cheap-jack *and* ticky-tacky <all non-
formal>; jerry-built, jerry

15 unsound, infirm, unfirm, **unstable, unsubstantial,** unsturdy, unsolid, decrepit,
crumbling, fragmented, fragmentary,
disintegrating 805.5; poor, poorish; rotten, rotten at *or* rotten to the core

16 unsteady, shaky, rickety, ricketish,
wonky <Brit nonformal>, spindly, spidery, teetering, teetery, tottery, tottering,
doddering, tumbledown, ramshackle, dilapidated, rocky <nonformal>; groggy,
wobbly, staggery

17 wishy-washy, tasteless, bland, **insipid,**
vapid, neutral, watery, milky, milk-and-
water, mushy; halfhearted, infirm of will
or purpose, **indecisive,** irresolute, changeable 853.7

18 weakened, enfeebled, disabled, incapacitated; **devitalized,** drained, exhausted,
sapped, burned-out, used up, played out,
spent, *ausgespielt* <Ger>, effete, etiolated; **fatigued, enervated,** eviscerated;
wasted, rundown, worn, worn-out, worn
to a frazzle <nonformal>, worn to a
shadow, reduced to a skeleton, "weakened and wasted to skin and bone"—Du
Bartas

19 diluted, cut <nonformal>, **reduced,
thinned,** rarefied, attenuated; adulterated; watered, watered-down

**20 weakening, debilitating, enfeebling;
devitalizing,** enervating, sapping, exhausting, fatiguing, grueling, trying,
draining, unnerving

21 languishing, drooping, sinking, declining, flagging, pining, fading, failing

ADVS **22 weakly, feebly,** strengthlessly, languorously, listlessly; faintly; delicately,
effeminately, daintily; infirmly, un-
soundly, unstably, unsubstantially,
unsturdily, flimsily; shakily, unsteadily,
teeteringly, totteringly

17 ENERGY

NOUNS **1 energy, vigor, force, power, vitality,** strenuousness, **intensity, dynamism,**
demonic energy; **potency** 18; **strength** 15;
actual *or* kinetic energy; dynamic energy;
potential energy; **energy source** 1020.1,

electrical energy, hydroelectric energy, water power, nuclear energy, solar energy, wind energy

2 **vim, verve,** fire, adrenalin, **dash, drive; aggressiveness, enterprise,** initiative, proactiveness, thrust, spunk; **eagerness** 101, zeal, heartiness, keenness, gusto

3 <nonformal terms> **pep,** bang, biff, getup-and-go, ginger, gism, jazz, sizzle, kick, moxie, oomph, pepper, piss and vinegar, **pizzazz,** poop, punch, push, snap, spizzerinctum, starch, steam, zing, zip, zizz

4 **animation, vivacity,** liveliness, **ardor,** glow, warmth, enthusiasm, lustiness, robustness, mettle, **zest,** zestfulness, **gusto,** élan, impetus, impetuosity, *joie de vivre* <Fr>, *brio* <Ital>, spiritedness, **briskness,** perkiness, pertness, **life, spirit,** life force, vital force or principle, *élan vital* <Fr>; activity 330

5 <energetic disapproval or criticism> **acrimony,** acridity, acerbity, acidity, **bitterness,** tartness, **causticity,** mordancy or mordacity, **virulence; harshness,** fierceness, **rigor,** roughness, **severity, vehemence,** violence 671, stringency, astringency, stridency 58.1, **sharpness, keenness, poignancy,** trenchancy; edge, point; bite, teeth, grip, sting

6 **energizer, stimulus,** stimulator, vitalizer, arouser, needle <nonformal>, restorative; **stimulant, tonic** 86.8; **activator,** motivator, motivating force, motive power; **animator,** spark plug and human dynamo and ball of fire <all nonformal>; life, life of the party

7 <units of energy> atomerg, dinamode, dyne, erg, energid, foot-pound, horsepower-hour, horsepower-year, joule, calorie 1018.19, kilogram-meter, kilowatt-hour, photon, quantum

8 **energizing, invigoration, animation, enlivenment,** quickening, **vitalization,** revival, revitalization; **exhilaration, stimulation**

9 **activation,** reactivation; viability

VERBS 10 **energize,** dynamize; **invigorate, animate, enliven, liven, liven up,** vitalize, quicken, goose or jazz up <nonformal>; **exhilarate, stimulate,** hearten, galvanize, electrify, fire, build a fire under, inflame, warm, kindle, charge, charge up, psych or pump up <nonformal>, rouse, arouse, act like a tonic, be a shot in the arm <nonformal>, **pep** or snap or jazz or zip or perk up <nonformal>, put pep or zip into it <nonformal>

11 **have energy,** be energetic, be vigorous, **thrive,** burst or overflow with energy,

flourish, tingle, feel one's oats, be up and doing, be full of beans or pep or ginger or zip <nonformal>, be full of piss and vinegar <nonformal>, champ at the bit <nonformal>

12 **activate,** reactivate, recharge

ADJS 13 **energetic, vigorous, strenuous, forceful, forcible, strong, dynamic,** kinetic, intense, acute, keen, incisive, trenchant, vivid, vibrant; **enterprising, aggressive,** proactive, activist, can-do and gung ho and take-over and take-charge <all nonformal>; **active, lively,** living, **animated, spirited,** go-go <nonformal>, **vivacious,** brisk, bright-eyed and bushy-tailed <nonformal>, lusty, **robust,** hearty, enthusiastic, mettlesome, zesty, zestful, impetuous, spanking, smacking; pumped and pumped up and jazzed-up and charged up and switched on <all nonformal>, snappy and zingy and zippy and peppy <all nonformal>, full of pep or pizzazz or piss and vinegar <all nonformal>

14 **acrimonious, acrid,** acidulous, acid, **bitter,** tart, **caustic,** escharotic <med>, mordant or mordacious, **virulent, violent, vehement,** vitriolic; **harsh,** fierce, **rigorous,** severe, rough, stringent, astringent, strident 58.12, **sharp, keen,** sharpish, incisive, trenchant, **cutting,** biting, stinging, **scathing,** stabbing, **piercing, poignant,** penetrating, edged, double-edged

15 **energizing, vitalizing, enlivening,** quickening; tonic, bracing, rousing; **invigorating,** invigorative; **animating,** animative; **exhilarating,** exhilarative; **stimulating,** stimulative, stimulatory; activating; viable

ADVS 16 **energetically, vigorously, strenuously, forcefully,** forcibly, intensely, like a house afire and like gangbusters <both nonformal>, zestfully, lustily, heartily, keenly; **actively,** briskly; **animatedly, spiritedly,** vivaciously, with pep <nonformal>, *con brio* <Ital>

18 POWER, POTENCY
<effective force>

NOUNS 1 **power, potency** or potence, prepotency, **force, might,** mightiness, **vigor,** vitality, vim, push, drive, charge, puissance <old>; dint, virtue; moxie and oomph and pizzazz and poop and punch and bang and clout and steam <all nonformal>; powerfulness, forcefulness; virulence, vehemence; **strength** 15; **en-**

ergy 17; **virility** 76.2; cogence *or* cogency, validity, effect, impact, **effectiveness,** effectivity, effectuality, competence *or* competency; productivity, productiveness; power structure; **influence** 893, pull; **authority** 417, weight; **superiority** 249; power pack, amperage, wattage; main force, *force majeure* <Fr>, main strength, brute force *or* strength, compulsion, duress; muscle power, sinew, might and main, beef <nonformal>, strong arm; full force, full blast; power struggle; black power; flower power; mana; charisma

2 **ability, capability, capacity,** potentiality, faculty, facility, fitness, qualification, talent, flair, genius, caliber, **competence,** competency, adequacy, sufficiency, **efficiency,** efficacy; **proficiency** 413.1; the stuff *and* the goods *and* what it takes <all nonformal>; susceptibility

3 **omnipotence, almightiness, all-powerfulness;** omnicompetence

4 manpower; horsepower, brake horsepower *or* bhp, electric power, electropower, hydroelectric power; hydraulic power, water power; steam power; geothermal power; solar power; atomic power, nuclear power, thermonuclear power; rocket power, jet power; **propulsion, thrust,** impulse

5 force of inertia, *vis inertiae* <L>; dead force, *vis mortua* <L>; living force, *vis viva* <L>; force of life, *vis vitae* <L>

6 centrifugal force *or* action, centripetal force *or* action, force of gravity

7 <science of forces> dynamics, statics

8 **empowerment, enablement;** investment, endowment, enfranchisement

9 **work force,** hands, men; **fighting force,** troops, units, the big battalions, firepower; **personnel** 577.11, human resources; **forces**

VERBS 10 **empower, enable;** invest, clothe, invest *or* clothe with power, deputize; enfranchise; endue, endow, **authorize;** arm

11 **be able,** be up to, up to, **lie in one's power; can,** may, can do; make it *or* make the grade <nonformal>; hack it *and* cut it *and* cut the mustard <all nonformal>; charismatize; **wield power,** possess authority 417.13; **take charge** 417.14, get something under one's control *or* under one's thumb, hold all the aces *and* have the say-so <both nonformal>

ADJS 12 **powerful, potent,** prepotent, power-packed, **mighty,** irresistible, avalanchine, **forceful,** forcible, dynamic; **vigorous,** vital, **energetic,** puissant, ruling, in power;

cogent, striking, telling, effective, impactful, valid, operative, in force; **strong;** high-powered, high-tension, high-pressure, high-performance, high-potency, bionic; **authoritative;** armipotent, mighty in battle

13 **omnipotent, almighty, all-powerful;** plenipotentiary, absolute, unlimited, **sovereign** 417.17; **supreme** 249.13; omnicompetent

14 **able, capable, equal to,** up to, **competent,** adequate, effective, effectual, efficient, efficacious; productive; **proficient** 413.22

ADVS 15 **powerfully, potently, forcefully,** forcibly, mightily, with might and main, **vigorously, energetically,** dynamically; **cogently,** strikingly, tellingly, impactfully; **effectively,** effectually; productively; with telling effect, to good account, to good purpose, with a vengeance

16 **ably, capably, competently,** adequately, effectively, effectually, **efficiently, well; to the best of one's ability,** as lies in one's power, so far as one can, as best one can; with all one's might, with everything that is in one

17 **by force,** by main *or* brute force, by *force majeure,* with the strong arm, with a high hand, high-handedly; **forcibly,** amain, with might and main; by force of arms, at the point of the sword, by storm

PREPS 18 by dint of, by virtue of

WORD ELEMENTS 19 dynam—, dynamo—; —dynamia

19 IMPOTENCE

NOUNS 1 **impotence** *or* impotency, **powerlessness,** impuissance <old>, forcelessness, feebleness, softness, flabbiness, wimpiness *or* wimpishness <nonformal>, **weakness** 16; power vacuum

2 **inability, incapability, incapacity,** incapacitation, **incompetence** *or* incompetency, inadequacy, insufficiency, ineptitude, **inferiority** 250, inefficiency, unfitness, imbecility; disability, disablement, disqualification; legal incapacity, wardship, minority, infancy

3 **ineffectiveness, ineffectualness,** ineffectuality, inefficaciousness, **inefficacy,** counterproductiveness *or* counterproductivity, invalidity, **futility, uselessness,** bootlessness, failure 410; fatuity, inanity

4 **helplessness, defenselessness,** unprotectedness, vulnerability; **debilitation,** invalidism, effeteness, etiolation, enervation

5 **emasculation,** demasculinization, effemi-

nization, neutering, maiming, castration
255.4

6 impotent, weakling 16.6, invalid, incompetent; flash in the pan, blank cartridge,
wimp *and* dud <both nonformal>; eunuch, *castrato* <Ital>, gelding

VERBS **7** be impotent, lack force; be ineffective, avail nothing, not work *or* do not
take <nonformal>; **waste one's effort,**
bang one's head against a brick wall,
have one's hands tied, spin one's wheels,
tilt at windmills, run in circles

8 cannot, not be able, not have it *and* not
hack it *and* not cut it *and* not cut the mustard <all nonformal>, not make it *and*
not make the grade *and* not make the cut
<all nonformal>

9 disable, disenable, unfit, **incapacitate,**
drain, de-energize; enfeeble, debilitate,
weaken 16.9,10; cripple, maim, lame,
hamstring, knee-cap, defang, pull the
teeth of <nonformal>; wing, clip the
wings of; **inactivate,** disarm, unarm, put
out of action, put *hors de combat;* **put out
of order,** put out of commission <nonfor-
mal>, throw out of gear; bugger *and*
bugger up *and* queer *and* queer the works
and gum up *or* screw up <all nonfor-
mal>, throw a wrench *or* monkey wrench
in the machinery <nonformal>, sabotage, wreck; kibosh *and* put the kibosh on
<both nonformal>; spike, spike one's
guns, put a spoke in one's wheels

10 <put out of action> **paralyze,** prostrate,
shoot down in flames <nonformal>, put
hors de combat, knock out <nonformal>,
break the neck *or* back of; hamstring;
handcuff, tie the hands of, hobble, enchain, manacle, hog-tie <nonformal>, **tie
hand and foot,** truss up; throttle, strangle, get a stranglehold on; muzzle, gag,
silence; **take the wind out of one's sails,**
deflate, knock the props out from under,
cut the ground from under, not leave a leg
to stand on

11 disqualify; invalidate, knock the bottom
out of <nonformal>

12 unman, unnerve, enervate, exhaust, etiolate, **devitalize; emasculate,** cut the balls
off <nonformal>, demasculinize, effeminize; desex, desexualize; sterilize;
castrate 255.11

ADJS **13 impotent, powerless, forceless, out
of gas** <nonformal>; feeble, soft, flabby,
weak 16.12, weak as a kitten, wimpy *or*
wimpish <nonformal>

14 unable, incapable, incompetent, inefficient, ineffective; **unqualified,** inept,
unendowed, ungifted, untalented, **unfit,**

unfitted; **outmatched,** out of one's depth,
in over one's head, outgunned; **inferior**
250.6

15 ineffective, ineffectual, inefficacious,
counterproductive, feckless, not up to
scratch *or* up to snuff <nonformal>, **inadequate** 250.7; **invalid, inoperative,** of
no force; nugatory, nugacious; fatuous,
fatuitous; **vain, futile, inutile, useless,** unavailing, bootless, fruitless; all talk and
no action, all wind; **empty,** inane; **debilitated,** effete, enervated, etiolated, barren,
sterile, washed-out <nonformal>

16 disabled, incapacitated; crippled, hamstrung; disqualified, invalidated; dis-
armed; paralyzed; hog-tied <nonfor-
mal>; prostrate, **on one's back,** on one's
beam-ends

17 out of action, out of commission *and* out
of it <both nonformal>, out of gear; *hors
de combat* <Fr, out of action, literally, out
of the fight>, out of the battle, off the
field, out of the running; laid on the shelf,
obsolete, life-expired

18 helpless, defenseless, unprotected; vulnerable, like a sitting duck <nonformal>,
aidless, friendless, unfriended; fatherless,
motherless; leaderless, guideless; **untenable,** pregnable, vulnerable

19 unmanned, unnerved, enervated, debilitated, **devitalized;** nerveless, sinewless,
marrowless, pithless, lustless; **castrated,**
emasculate, emasculated, gelded, eunuchized, unsexed, deballed <non-
formal>, demasculinized, effem-
inized

ADVS **20 beyond one,** beyond one's power *or*
capacity *or* ability, beyond one's depth,
out of one's league <nonformal>, above
one's head, too much for

INTERJ **21** no can do!

20 REST, REPOSE

NOUNS **1 rest, repose, ease, relaxation,** slippered *or* unbuttoned ease, decompression
<nonformal>; **comfort** 121; restfulness,
quiet, tranquility; inactivity 331; sleep 22

2 respite, recess, rest, pause, halt, stay, lull,
break, surcease, suspension, interlude,
intermission, spell <Australia>, letup
<nonformal>, **time out** <nonformal>,
time to catch one's breath; **breathing
spell,** breathing time, breathing place,
breathing space, breath; **breather;** coffee
break, tea break, cigarette break; cocktail
hour, happy hour <nonformal>; en-
forced respite, downtime; R and R *or* rest
and recreation

3 vacation, holiday <Brit>; **time off;** day off, week off, month off, etc; paid vacation, paid holiday <Brit>; weekend; **leave, leave of absence, furlough; liberty,** shore leave; **sabbatical,** sabbatical leave *or* year; **weekend; busman's holiday;** package tour *or* holiday

4 holiday, day off; red-letter day, gala day, fete day, festival day, day of festivities; national holiday, legal holiday, bank holiday <Brit>; High Holiday, High Holy Day; holy day; feast, feast day, high day, church feast, fixed feast, movable feast; half-holiday

5 day of rest, *dies non* <L>; **Sabbath,** Sunday, Lord's day, First day

VERBS **6 rest, repose,** take rest, take one's ease, **take it easy** <nonformal>, lay down one's tools, rest from one's labors, rest on one's oars, take life easy; go to rest, settle to rest; lie down, have a lie-down, go to bed, snug down, curl up, tuck up, bed, bed down, couch, recline, lounge, drape oneself, sprawl, loll; take off one's shoes, unbuckle one's belt, get *or* take a load off one's feet, put one's feet up

7 relax, unlax <nonformal>, unbend, unwind, slack, slacken, **ease; ease up, let up,** slack up, slack off, **ease off,** let down, **slow down,** take it slow, let up, take time to catch one's breath; lay back *and* kick back *and* decompress <all nonformal>

8 take a rest, take a break, break, take time out *and* grab some R and R <both nonformal>, pause, lay off, **knock off** <nonformal>, recess, **take a recess,** take ten *and* take five <both nonformal>; stop for breath, catch one's breath, breathe; stop work, suspend operations, call it a day; go to bed with the chickens, sleep in; take a nap, catch some Zs <nonformal>

9 vacation, get away from it all, holiday, take a holiday, make holiday; **take a leave of absence,** take leave, go on leave, go on furlough, take one's sabbatical; weekend; Sunday, Christmas, etc

ADJS **10 vacational, holiday,** ferial <old>, festal; sabbatical; **comfortable** 121.11; **restful,** quiet 173.12

ADVS **11 at rest, at ease,** at one's ease; abed, in bed

12 on vacation, on leave, on furlough; off duty, on one's own time

21 FATIGUE

NOUNS **1 fatigue, tiredness, weariness,** wearifulness; **burnout,** end of one's tether, overtiredness, overstrain; faintness, goneness, weakness, enfeeblement, lack of staying power, enervation, debility, debilitation 16.1; jadedness; lassitude, languor; tension fatigue, stance fatigue, stimulation fatigue; fatigue disease, fatigue syndrome *or* post-viral fatigue syndrome; combat fatigue; mental fatigue, brain fag <nonformal>; strain, mental strain, heart strain, eyestrain; sleepiness 22.1

2 exhaustion, exhaustedness, draining; **collapse, prostration,** breakdown, crack-up <nonformal>, nervous exhaustion *or* prostration

3 breathlessness, shortness of breath, windedness, short-windedness; panting, gasping; dyspnea, labored breathing

VERBS **4 fatigue, tire, weary, exhaust,** wilt, flag, jade, harass; **wear,** wear on *or* upon, **wear down; tire out, wear out, burn out; use up; do in; wind,** put out of breath; overtire, overweary, overfatigue, overstrain; weaken, enervate, debilitate 16.10; weary *or* tire to death; prostrate

5 burn out, get tired, grow weary, tire, weary, fatigue, jade; **flag, droop,** faint, sink, feel dragged out, wilt; **play out,** run out, run down, burn out; gasp, wheeze, pant, puff, blow, puff and blow, puff like a grampus; collapse, break down, crack up <nonformal>, give out, drop, fall *or* drop by the wayside, drop in one's tracks, succumb

6 <nonformal terms> **beat, poop,** frazzle, fag, tucker; fag out, tucker out, knock out, do in, do up; **poop out,** peter out

ADJS **7 tired, weary, fatigued,** wearied, weariful, jaded, run-down, good and tired; unrefreshed, unrestored, in need of rest, ready to drop; **faint,** fainting, feeling faint, **weak,** rocky <nonformal>, enfeebled, enervated, debilitated, seedy <nonformal>, weakened 16.13,18; drooping, droopy, wilting, flagging, sagging; languid; worn, worn-down, **worn to a frazzle** *or* shadow, toilworn, wearyworn; wayworn, way-weary; foot-weary, weary-footed, footsore; tired-armed; tired-winged, weary-winged; weary-laden, "tired and weary-laden"—Bible

8 <nonformal terms> **beat, pooped, bushed,** poohed, paled, frazzled, bagged, fagged, tuckered, plumb tuckered, done, done in, all in, dead, dead beat, dead on one's feet, gone; **pooped out,** knocked out, wiped out, tuckered out, played out, fagged out; run ragged; used up, done up, beat up, washed-up

9 tired-looking, weary-looking, tired-eyed,

tired-faced, haggard, hollow-eyed, ravaged, drawn, cadaverous, worn, wan, zombiish

10 **burnt-out, exhausted,** drained, **spent,** unable to go on, gone; **tired out, worn-out,** beaten; bone-tired, bone-weary; **dog-tired,** dog-weary; **dead-tired, tired to death,** weary unto death, dead-alive *or* dead-and-alive, more dead than alive, ready to drop, on one's last legs; prostrate

11 **burnt-out, overtired, overweary,** overwearied, overstrained, overdriven, overfatigued, overspent

12 **breathless, winded;** wheezing, puffing, panting, **out of breath,** short of breath *or* wind; short-winded, short-breathed, broken-winded, touched in the wind, dyspneic

13 **fatiguing, wearying,** wearing, **tiring,** straining, stressful, trying, **exhausting,** draining, **grueling,** punishing, killing; **tiresome,** fatiguesome, **wearisome,** weariful; toilsome 725.18

ADVS 14 **out,** to the point of exhaustion

22 SLEEP

NOUNS 1 **sleepiness, drowsiness,** doziness, heaviness, lethargy, oscitation, somnolence *or* somnolency, yawning, stretching, oscitancy, pandiculation; languor 331.6; sand in the eyes, heavy eyelids; REM sleep *or* rapid-eye-movement sleep *or* dreaming sleep

2 **sleep, slumber; repose,** silken repose, *somnus* <L>, the arms of Morpheus; bye-bye *or* beddy-bye <both nonformal>; doss <Brit nonformal>, blanket drill *and* shut eye <both nonformal>; light sleep, fitful sleep, **doze, drowse,** snoozle <nonformal>; beauty sleep <nonformal>; sleepwalking, somnambulism; somniloquy; **land of Nod,** slumberland, sleepland, dreamland; hibernation, winter sleep, aestivation; bedtime, sack time <nonformal>; unconsciousness 25.2

3 **nap, snooze** <nonformal>, **catnap,** wink, **forty winks** *and* some Zs <both nonformal>, zizz <Brit nonformal>, wink of sleep, spot of sleep; **siesta,** blanket drill *and* sack *or* rack time <all nonformal>

4 sweet sleep, balmy sleep, downy sleep, soft sleep, gentle sleep, smiling sleep, golden slumbers; "folded sleep"—Tennyson, "dewy-feathered sleep"—Milton, "care-charmer Sleep, son of the sable night"—Samuel Daniel, "the honey-heavy dew of slumber"—Shakespeare; peaceful sleep, sleep of the

just; restful sleep, good night's sleep, "sleep that knits up the ravell'd sleave of care"—Shakespeare, "Brother of Death"—Sir Thomas Browne

5 **deep sleep,** profound sleep, heavy sleep, **sound sleep,** unbroken sleep, wakeless sleep, drugged sleep, dreamless sleep, the sleep of the dead, "sleep such as makes the darkness brief"—Martial; paradoxical *or* orthodox *or* dreaming *or* REM sleep, synchronized *or* S *or* NREM sleep

6 **stupor,** sopor, **coma, swoon,** lethargy <old>; **trance;** narcosis, narcohypnosis, narcoma, narcotization, narcotic stupor *or* trance; sedation; high <nonformal>; nod <nonformal>; narcolepsy; catalepsy; thanatosis, shock; sleeping sickness, encephalitis lethargica

7 **hypnosis,** mesmeric *or* **hypnotic sleep, trance,** somnipathy, hypnotic somnolence; lethargic hypnosis, somnambulistic hypnosis, cataleptic hypnosis, animal hypnosis; narcohypnosis; autohypnosis, self-hypnosis; hypnotherapy

8 **hypnotism, mesmerism;** hypnology; hypnotization, mesmerization; **animal magnetism,** od, odyl, odylic force; hypnotic suggestion, posthypnotic suggestion, autosuggestion

9 **hypnotist, mesmerist,** hypnotizer, mesmerizer; Svengali, Mesmer

10 **sleep-inducer,** sleep-producer, sleep-provoker, sleep-bringer, hypnotic, soporific, somnifacient; poppy, mandrake, mandragora, opium, opiate, morphine, morphia; nightcap; sedative 86.12; anesthetic; lullaby

11 **Morpheus,** Somnus, Hypnos; "sweet father of soft rest"—Wm Drummond; sandman, dustman <Brit>

12 **sleeper, slumberer;** sleeping beauty; **sleepyhead,** lie-abed, slugabed, sleep-walker, somnambulist; somniloquist

VERBS 13 **sleep, slumber,** rest in the arms of Morpheus; **doze, drowse; nap, catnap,** take a nap, catch a wink, sleep soundly, **sleep like a top** *or* **log,** sleep like the dead; *dormir sur les deux oreilles* <Fr>; snore, saw wood *and* saw logs <both nonformal>; have an early night, go to bed betimes; sleep in; oversleep

14 <nonformal terms> **snooze,** get some shut-eye, get some sack time, flake *or* sack out, crash, catch forty winks *or* some Zs, have a zizz <Brit>; pound the ear, kip *or* doss <both Brit>

15 **hibernate,** aestivate, lie dormant

16 **go to sleep,** settle to sleep, go off to sleep,

fall asleep, drop asleep, **drop off,** drift off, drift off to sleep, "drift gently down the tides of sleep"—Longfellow; **doze off, drowse off,** nod off, dope off <nonformal>; close one's eyes, "let fall the shadow of mine eyes"—Shakespeare

17 **go to bed, retire;** lay me down to sleep; bed, bed down; go night-night *and* go bye-bye *and* go beddy-bye <all nonformal>

18 <nonformal terms> **hit the hay, hit the sack,** crash, turn in, crawl in, flop, sack out, sack up, kip down *or* doss down <both Brit>

19 **put to bed,** bed; nestle, cradle; **tuck in**

20 **put to sleep; lull to sleep,** rock to sleep; **hypnotize, mesmerize,** magnetize; **entrance,** trance, put in a trance; narcotize, drug, dope <nonformal>; anesthetize, put under; sedate

ADJS 21 **sleepy, drowsy,** dozy, snoozy <nonformal>, **slumberous,** slumbery, dreamy; **half asleep,** asleep on one's feet; sleepful, sleep-filled; yawny, stretchy <nonformal>, oscitant, yawning, napping, **nodding,** ready for bed; heavy, **heavy-eyed, heavy with sleep,** sleep-swollen, sleep-drowned, sleep-drunk, drugged with sleep; **somnolent,** soporific; **lethargic,** comatose, narcose *or* narcous, stuporose *or* **stuporous, in a stupor,** out of it <nonformal>; narcoleptic; cataleptic; narcotized, drugged, doped <nonformal>; sedated; anesthetized; **languid**

22 **asleep, sleeping, slumbering,** in the arms *or* lap of Morpheus, in the land of Nod; **sound asleep, fast asleep,** dead asleep, deep asleep, in a sound sleep, flaked-out <nonformal>; **unconscious, oblivious, out,** out like a light, out cold; comatose; dormant; dead, **dead to the world;** unwakened, unawakened

23 **sleep-inducing,** sleep-producing, sleep-bringing, sleep-causing, sleep-compelling, sleep-inviting, sleep-provoking, sleep-tempting; **narcotic,** hypnotic, **soporific, somniferous,** somnifacient; sedative 86.45

24 **hypnotic,** hypnoid, hypnoidal, **mesmeric;** odylic; narcohypnotic

23 WAKEFULNESS

NOUNS 1 **wakefulness,** wake; **sleeplessness,** restlessness, tossing and turning; **insomnia,** insomnolence *or* insomnolency, white night, "the wakey nights"—Sir Thomas Wyatt; vigil, all-night vigil, lidless vigil, *per vigilium* <L>; insomniac;

consciousness, sentience; alertness 339.5

2 **awakening, wakening,** rousing, **arousal;** rude awakening, rousting out <nonformal>; reveille

VERBS 3 **keep awake,** keep one's eyes open; keep alert, be vigilant 339.8; stay awake, **toss and turn, not sleep a wink,** not shut one's eyes, count sheep; have a white night

4 **awake, awaken, wake, wake up, get up,** rouse, come alive <nonformal>; open one's eyes, stir <nonformal>

5 <wake someone up> **awaken, waken, rouse, arouse,** awake, wake, **wake up,** shake up, knock up <Brit>, roust out <nonformal>

6 **get up, get out of bed, arise,** rise, **rise and shine** <nonformal>, greet the day, **turn out** <nonformal>; roll out *and* pile out *and* **show a leg** *and* hit the deck <all nonformal>

ADJS 7 **wakeful, sleepless,** slumberless, **unsleeping,** insomniac, insomnious; restless; watchful, vigilant, lidless

8 **awake,** conscious, **up; wide-awake,** broad awake; alert 339.14

ADVS 9 **sleeplessly, unsleepingly; wakefully,** with one's eyes open; alertly 339.17

24 SENSATION
<physical sensibility>

NOUNS 1 **sensation, sense, feeling;** sense impression, sense-datum *or* -data, percept, perception, sense perception; experience, sensory experience; **sensuousness,** sensuosity; **consciousness,** awareness, apperception; response, response to stimuli

2 **sensibility,** sensibleness, physical sensibility, sentience *or* sentiency; openness to sensation, readiness of feeling, receptiveness, receptivity; sensation level, threshold of sensation, limen; impressionability, impressibility, affectibility; **susceptibility,** susceptivity, perceptibility

3 **sensitivity, sensitiveness;** perceptivity, perceptiveness; responsiveness; **tact, tactfulness, considerateness,** courtesy, politeness; **compassion, sympathy;** empathy, identification; **concern,** solicitousness, solicitude; capability of feeling, passibility; **delicacy, exquisiteness,** tenderness, fineness; **oversensitiveness,** oversensibility, hypersensitivity, **thin skin,** hyperesthesia, hyperpathia, supersensitivity, overtenderness; **irritability,** prickliness, soreness, **touchiness,** tetchiness; ticklishness, nervousness 128;

allergy, anaphylaxis; sensitization; photophobia

4 sore spot, sore point, soft spot, raw, exposed nerve, raw nerve, nerve ending, tender spot, the quick, where the shoe pinches, where one lives *and* in the gut <nonformal>

5 senses, five senses, sensorium; touch 74, taste 62, smell 69, sight 27, hearing 48; sixth sense; sense *or* sensory organ, sensillum, receptor; synesthesia, chromesthesia, color hearing; phonism, photism; kinesthesia, muscle sense, sense of motion

VERBS **6 sense, feel,** experience, **perceive,** apprehend, be sensible of, be conscious *or* aware of, apperceive; taste 62.7, smell 69.8, see 27.12, hear 48.11,12, touch 73.6; respond, respond to stimuli; be sensitive to, have a thing about <nonformal>

7 sensitize, make sensitive; sensibilize, sensify; **sharpen, whet, quicken,** stimulate, excite, stir, cultivate, refine

8 touch a sore spot, touch a soft spot, touch on the raw, touch a raw spot, touch to the quick, hit *or* touch a nerve *or* nerve ending, touch where it hurts, hit one where he lives <nonformal>, strike home

ADJS **9 sensory,** sensorial; **sensitive,** receptive; **sensuous;** sensorimotor, sensimotor; kinesthetic, somatosensory

10 neural, nervous, nerval; neurologic, neurological

11 sensible, sentient, sensile; **susceptible,** susceptive; **receptive,** impressionable, impressive <old>, impressible; **perceptive; conscious,** cognizant, **aware,** sensitive to, alive to

12 sensitive, responsive, sympathetic, compassionate; empathic, empathetic; passible; delicate, tactful, considerate, courteous, solicitous, tender, refined; **oversensitive, thin-skinned;** oversensible, hyperesthetic, hyperpathic, hypersensitive, supersensitive, overtender, overrefined; **irritable, touchy,** tetchy <nonformal>, quick on the draw *or* trigger *or* uptake, itchy, ticklish, prickly; goosy <nonformal>, skittish; nervous; allergic, anaphylactic

13 <keenly sensitive> **exquisite,** poignant, **acute,** sharp, **keen,** vivid, intense, extreme, excruciating

25 INSENSIBILITY
<physical unfeeling>

NOUNS **1 insensibility,** insensibleness, in-

sensitivity, insensitiveness, insentience, impassibility; **unperceptiveness,** imperceptiveness, imperception, imperceptivity, impercipience, blindness, lack of concern, obtuseness; inconsiderateness; unsolicitousness; tactlessness; discourtesy, boorishness; **unfeeling,** unfeelingness, **apathy,** affectlessness, lack of affect; thick skin *or* hide, callousness 94.3; **numbness,** dullness, hypothymia, **deadness;** pins and needles; hypesthesia; anesthesia, analgesia; narcosis, electronarcosis; narcotization

2 unconsciousness, senselessness; nothingness, oblivion, obliviousness, nirvana; nirvana principle; **faint, swoon, blackout,** syncope, athymia, lipothymy *or* lipothymia; **coma; stupor;** catalepsy, catatony *or* catatonia, sleep 22; knockout *or* KO *or* kayo <both nonformal>; semiconsciousness, grayout

3 anesthetic, general anesthetic, local anesthetic, analgesic, anodyne, balm, ointment, **pain killer,** pain-reliever, antiodontalgic, soothing syrup; tranquilizer, **sedative,** sleeping pill *or* tablet, knockout drop *and* Mickey Finn <both nonformal>; drug, dope <nonformal>, narcotic, opiate

VERBS **4 deaden, numb,** benumb, blunt, dull, obtund, **desensitize;** paralyze, palsy; **anesthetize, put to sleep,** slip one a Mickey *or* Mickey Finn <nonformal>, chloroform, etherize; narcotize, drug, dope <nonformal>; freeze, **stupefy, stun,** bedaze, besot; knock unconscious, knock senseless, **knock out,** KO *and* kayo *and* lay out *and* coldcock *and* knock stiff <all nonformal>

5 faint, swoon, drop, succumb, keel over <nonformal>, fall in a faint, fall senseless, **pass** *or* zonk out <nonformal>, **black out,** go out like a light; gray out

ADJS **6 insensible, unfeeling, insensitive,** insentient, insensate, impassible; unsympathetic, uncompassionate; unconcerned, unsolicitous, non-caring; tactless, boorish, heavy-handed; **unperceptive,** imperceptive, impercipient, blind; thick-skinned, thick-witted, **dull,** obtuse, obdurate; **numb,** numbed, benumbed, dead, **deadened,** asleep, unfelt; **unfeeling, apathetic,** affectless; callous 94.12; anesthetized, narcotized

7 stupefied, stunned, dazed, bedazed

8 unconscious, senseless, oblivious, comatose, asleep, dead, **dead to the world,** cold, out, **out cold;** nirvanic; halfconscious, semiconscious; drugged, narcotized; doped *and* stoned *and* spaced out *and* strung out *and* zonked *and* zonked out *and* out of it <all nonformal>; catatonic, cataleptic

9 **deadening,** numbing, dulling; **anesthetic,** analgesic, narcotic; stupefying, stunning, numbing, mind-boggling *or* -numbing; anesthetizing, narcotizing

26 PAIN
<physical suffering>

NOUNS 1 **pain; suffering, hurt, hurting,** misery <nonformal>, **distress,** *Schmerz* <Ger>, dolor <old>; **discomfort,** malaise; aches and pains

2 **pang,** throe, throes; seizure, spasm, paroxysm; ouch <nonformal>; **twinge,** twitch, wrench, jumping pain; crick, kink, hitch, cramp *or* cramps; **nip,** thrill, pinch, tweak, bite, prick, **stab,** stitch, sharp *or* piercing *or* stabbing pain, acute pain, **shooting pain,** darting pain, fulgurant pain, lancinating pain, shooting, shoot; boring *or* terebrant *or* terebrating pain; gnawing, gnawing *or* grinding pain; griping *and* tormen <both old>; girdle pain; stitch in the side; charley horse <nonformal>; phantom limb pain; hunger pang *or* pain; wandering pain; psychalgia, psychosomatic pain, soul pain, mind pain

3 **smart,** smarting, **sting,** stinging, urtication, **tingle,** tingling; **burn,** burning, burning pain, fire

4 **soreness, irritation,** inflammation, tenderness, sensitiveness; algesia; rankling <old>, festering; sore; sore spot 24.4

5 **ache,** aching, throbbing, throbbing ache *or* pain; **headache,** cephalalgia, misery in the head <nonformal>; splitting headache, **sick headache, migraine,** megrim, hemicrania; **backache; earache,** otalgia; **toothache,** odontalgia; **stomachache,** tummyache <nonformal>, bellyache *or* gut-ache <nonformal>; **colic,** collywobbles, gripes, gripe, gnawing, gnawing of the bowels, fret <nonformal>; **heartburn,** pyrosis; **angina**

6 **agony, anguish, torment, torture,** exquisite torment *or* torture, the rack, excruciation, crucifixion, martyrdom, martyrization, excruciating *or* agonizing *or* atrocious pain

VERBS 7 **pain,** give *or* inflict pain, **hurt, wound, afflict, distress; burn;** sting; nip, bite, tweak, pinch; pierce, prick, stab, cut, lacerate; **irritate, inflame,** harshen, exacerbate, intensify; chafe, gall, fret,

rasp, rub, grate; gnaw, grind; gripe; fester, rankle <old>; **torture, torment,** rack, put to torture, put *or* lay on the rack, **agonize, harrow,** crucify, martyr, martyrize, excruciate, wring, twist, contorse, convulse; wrench, tear, rend; prolong the agony, kill by inches

8 **suffer, feel pain,** feel the pangs, anguish 96.19; **hurt, ache,** have a misery <nonformal>, ail; **smart,** tingle; throb, pound; shoot; twinge, thrill, twitch; **wince,** blanch, shrink, make a wry face, grimace; **agonize,** writhe

ADJS 9 **pained,** in pain, **hurt,** hurting, **suffering,** afflicted, wounded, distressed, in distress; **tortured, tormented, racked, agonized, harrowed,** lacerated, crucified, martyred, martyrized, wrung, twisted, convulsed; on the rack, under the harrow

10 **painful;** hurtful, **hurting,** distressing, afflictive; **acute, sharp,** piercing, stabbing, shooting, stinging, biting, gnawing; **poignant,** pungent, **severe,** cruel, harsh, grave, hard; griping, cramping, spasmic, spasmatic, spasmodic, paroxysmal; **agonizing, excruciating,** exquisite, atrocious, torturous, tormenting, martyrizing, racking, **harrowing**

11 **sore, raw;** smarting, tingling, **burning; irritated, inflamed, tender,** sensitive, fiery, angry, red; algetic; chafed, galled; **festering,** rankling <old>

12 **aching,** achy, **throbbing;** headachy, migrainous, backachy, toothachy, stomachachy, colicky, griping

13 **irritating,** irritative, irritant; **chafing, galling,** fretting, rasping, boring, grating, grinding, stinging, scratchy

27 VISION

NOUNS 1 **vision, sight, eyesight,** seeing; **sightedness;** eye, power of sight, sense of sight, visual sense; **perception,** discernment; perspicacity, perspicuity, sharp *or* acute *or* keen sight, visual acuity, quick sight; farsight, farsightedness; clear sight, unobstructed vision; rod vision, scotopia; cone vision, photopia; color vision, twilight vision, daylight vision, day vision, night vision; eye-mindedness; **field of vision,** visual field, scope, ken, purview, horizon, sweep, range; line of vision, line of sight, sight-line; peripheral vision, peripheral field; field of view 31.3; sensitivity to light, phototonus

2 **observation,** observance; **looking, watching, viewing, seeing,** witnessing, espial;

notice, note, respect, **regard;** watch, look-out; spying, espionage

3 **look, sight,** the eye *and* a look-see *and* a gander <all nonformal>, dekko <Brit nonformal>, eye, view, regard; sidelong look; leer, leering look, lustful leer; sly look; look-in; preview; scene, prospect 33.6

4 **glance,** glance *or* flick of the eye, squiz <Australia>, slant <nonformal>, rapid glance, cast, side-glance; **glimpse,** flash, quick sight; **peek, peep;** wink, blink, flicker *or* twinkle of an eye; casual glance, **half an eye;** *coup d'œil* <Fr>

5 **gaze, stare,** gape, goggle; sharp *or* piercing *or* penetrating look; **ogle,** glad eye, come-hither look <nonformal>, bedroom eyes <nonformal>; **glare, glower,** glaring *or* glowering look; evil eye, *malocchio* <Ital>, whammy <nonformal>; withering look, hostile look, chilly look, the fisheye <nonformal>

6 **scrutiny,** overview, **survey,** contemplation; **examination, inspection** 937.3, scrutiny, the once-over <nonformal>, visual examination, a vetting <Brit nonformal>, ocular inspection, eyeball inspection <nonformal>

7 **viewpoint, standpoint, point of view,** vantage, vantage point, point *or* coign of vantage, where one stands; bird's-eye view, worm's-eye view, fly on the wall; **outlook,** angle, angle of vision, *optique* <Fr>; mental outlook 977.2

8 observation post *or* point; **observatory; lookout,** outlook, overlook, scenic overlook; **watchtower,** tower; Texas tower; beacon, lighthouse, pharos; gazebo, belvedere; bridge, conning tower, crow's nest; peephole, sighthole, loophole; **ringside,** ringside seat; **grandstand,** bleachers; **gallery,** top gallery; paradise *and* peanut gallery <both nonformal>

9 **eye,** visual organ, organ of vision, oculus, optic, **orb, peeper** <nonformal>, baby blues <nonformal>; clear eyes, bright eyes, starry orbs; saucer eyes, popeyes *and* goggle eyes *and* banjo eyes *and* googly eyes <all nonformal>; naked eye, unassisted *or* unaided eye; corner of the eye; eyeball; iris; pupil; eyelid, lid, nictitating membrane

10 **sharp eye,** keen eye, piercing *or* penetrating eye, gimlet eye, X-ray eye; **eagle eye,** hawkeye, peeled eye <nonformal>, watchful eye; **weather eye**

11 <comparisons> eagle, hawk, cat, lynx, ferret, weasel; Argus

VERBS **12 see, behold, observe, view, wit-**

ness, perceive, discern, spy, espy, **sight,** have in sight, make out, pick out, descry, spot <nonformal>, twig <Brit nonformal>, discover, notice, take notice of, have one's eye on, distinguish, recognize, ken <nonformal>, **catch sight of,** get a load of <nonformal>, take in, get an eyeful of <nonformal>, look on *or* upon, cast the eyes on *or* upon, **set** *or* **lay eyes on, clap eyes on** <nonformal>; **glimpse,** get *or* catch a glimpse of; see at a glance, see with half an eye; see with one's own eyes

13 **look, peer,** have a look, take a gander *and* take a look <both nonformal>, direct the eyes, turn *or* bend the eyes, cast one's eye, lift up the eyes; **look at,** take a look at, eye, **eyeball** <nonformal>, have a look-see <nonformal>, have a dekko <Brit nonformal>, look on *or* upon, gaze at *or* upon; **watch, observe, view, regard;** keep one's eyes peeled *or* skinned, be watchful *or* observant *or* vigilant, keep one's eyes open; keep in sight *or* view, hold in view; look after; **check** *and* **check out** <both nonformal>, scope <nonformal>, scope on *or* out <nonformal>; keep under observation, spy on, have an eye out, keep an eye out, keep an eye on, keep a weather eye on, follow, tail *and* shadow <both nonformal>, stake out; **reconnoiter,** scout, get the lay of the land; **peek, peep,** pry, take a peep *or* peek; play peekaboo

14 **scrutinize, survey, eye,** contemplate, look over, give the eye *or* the once-over <nonformal>; **ogle,** ogle at, **leer,** leer at, give one the glad eye; examine, vet <Brit nonformal>, **inspect** 937.23; **pore,** pore over, peruse; take a close *or* careful look; take a long, hard look; size up <nonformal>; take stock of

15 **gaze,** gloat <old>, fix one's gaze, fix *or* fasten *or* rivet one's eyes upon, keep one's eyes upon, feast one's eyes on; **eye, ogle; stare,** stare at, stare hard, look, goggle, **gape, gawk** *or* gawp <nonformal>, gaze open-mouthed; crane, crane the neck, stand on tiptoe; strain one's eyes; look straight in the eye, look full in the face, hold one's eye *or* gaze, stare down

16 **glare, glower,** look daggers, look black; give one the evil eye, give one a whammy <nonformal>; give one the fish eye <nonformal>

17 **glance, glimpse,** glint, cast a glance, glance at *or* upon, give a *coup d'œil* <Fr>, take a glance at, take a squint at <nonformal>

18 **look askance** *or* askant, give a sidelong look; squint, look asquint; cock the eye; **look down one's nose** <nonformal>

19 **look away,** look aside, **avert the eyes,** look another way, break one's eyes away, stop looking, turn away from, turn the back upon; drop one's eyes *or* gaze, cast one's eyes down; avoid one's gaze

ADJS 20 **visual, ocular,** eye, eyeball <nonformal>; **sighted,** seeing, having sight *or* vision; **optic, optical;** ophthalmic; retinal; visible 31.6

21 **clear-sighted,** clear-eyed; twenty-twenty; **farsighted,** farseeing, telescopic; **sharpsighted,** keen-sighted, sharp-eyed, **eagleeyed,** hawk-eyed, ferret-eyed, lynx-eyed, cat-eyed, Argus-eyed; eye-minded

ADVS 22 **at sight,** as seen, visibly, at a glance; by sight, by eyeball <nonformal>, visually; at first sight, **at the first blush,** *prima facie* <L>; out of the corner of one's eye; from where one stands, from one's viewpoint *or* standpoint

WORD ELEMENTS 23 opto—, —opsia, —opsy, —opsis; —opy, —opia; —scopy; ocul—, oculo—, ophthalm—, ophthalmo—

28 DEFECTIVE VISION

NOUNS 1 faulty eyesight, bad eyesight, defect of vision *or* sight, poor sight, impaired vision, imperfect vision, blurred vision, reduced sight, partial sightedness, partial blindness; legal blindness; **astigmatism,** astigmia; nystagmus; albinism; double vision, double sight; tunnel vision; photophobia; **blindness 30**

2 **dim-sightedness,** dull-sightedness, near-blindness, amblyopia, gravel-blindness, sand-blindness, **purblindness,** dim eyes; blurredness, blearedness, bleariness, redness, lippitude <old>

3 **nearsightedness, myopia,** shortsightedness, short sight

4 **farsightedness,** hyperopia, longsightedness, long sight; presbyopia

5 strabismus, heterotropia; cast, cast in the eye; **squint,** squinch <nonformal>; **crosseye, cross-eyedness;** convergent strabismus, esotropia; upward strabismus, anoöpsia; walleye, exotropia

6 <defective eyes> cross-eyes, cockeyes, squint eyes, lazy eye, swivel eyes <nonformal>, goggle eyes, walleyes, bug-eyes *and* popeyes <both nonformal>, saucer eyes <nonformal>

7 **winking, blinking,** fluttering the eyelids, nictitation; winker, blinkard <old>

VERBS 8 see badly *or* poorly, barely see, be half-blind; have a mote in the eye; see double

9 **squint,** squinch <nonformal>, squint the eye, look asquint, screw up the eyes, skew, goggle <old>

10 **wink, blink,** nictitate, bat the eyes <nonformal>

ADJS 11 poor-sighted; visually impaired, sight-impaired; legally blind; **blind 30.9;** **astigmatic, astigmatical;** nystagmic; **nearsighted, shortsighted, myopic,** mope-eyed <old>; **farsighted,** longsighted, presbyopic; **squinting,** squinty, asquint, squint-eyed, squinch-eyed <nonformal>, strabismal, strabismic; winking, **blinking,** blinky, blink-eyed; blinkered; photophobic

12 **cross-eyed, cockeyed,** swivel-eyed <nonformal>, goggle-eyed, bug-eyed *and* popeyed <both nonformal>, **walleyed,** saucer-eyed, glare-eyed; one-eyed, monocular, cyclopean; moon-eyed

13 **dim-sighted,** dim, dull-sighted, dim-eyed, weak-eyed, feeble-eyed, mole-eyed; **purblind,** half-blind, gravel-blind, sand-blind; bleary-eyed, blear-eyed; filmy-eyed, film-eyed; snow-blind

29 OPTICAL INSTRUMENTS

NOUNS 1 **optical instrument** <see list>, optical device, viewer; **microscope** <see list>; **spectroscope,** spectrometer <see list>

2 **lens,** glass; prism, objective prism; **camera 714.11**

3 **spectacles, specs** <nonformal>, **glasses, eyeglasses,** pair of glasses *or* spectacles, barnacles <Brit nonformal>, cheaters *and* peepers <both nonformal>; reading glasses, readers; bifocals, divided spectacles, trifocals, pince-nez, nippers <nonformal>; lorgnette, *lorgnon* <Fr>; horn-rimmed glasses; harlequin glasses; granny glasses; mini-specs <nonformal>; colored glasses, sunglasses, sunspecs <nonformal>, dark glasses, Polaroid<trademark> glasses, shades <nonformal>; goggles, blinkers; eyeglass, monocle, quizzing glass; thick glasses, thick-lensed glasses, thick lenses, Coke-bottle glasses <nonformal>; **contacts,** contact lenses, hard lenses, soft lenses

4 **telescope** <see list>, scope, **spy glass,** terrestrial telescope, glass, **field glass; binoculars,** zoom binoculars, opera glasses

5 sight; sighthole; finder, viewfinder; panoramic sight; bombsight; peep sight, open sight, leaf sight

6 mirror, glass, **looking glass,** seeing glass <Brit nonformal>, reflector, speculum; hand mirror, window mirror, rear-view mirror, cheval glass, pier glass, shaving mirror; steel mirror; convex mirror, concave mirror, distorting mirror

7 optics, optical physics; **optometry;** microscopy, microscopics; telescopy; stereoscopy; spectroscopy, spectrometry; infrared spectroscopy; spectrophotometry; electron optics; fiber optics; **photography** 714

8 oculist, ophthalmologist, **optometrist;** microscopist, telescopist; optician

ADJS **9 optic, optical,** ophthalmic, ophthalmologic, ophthalmological, optometrical; acousto-optic, acousto-optical; ocular, binocular, monocular

10 microscopic, telescopic, etc; stereoscopic, three-dimensional, 3-D

11 spectacled, bespectacled, four-eyed <nonformal>; goggled; monocled

12 optical instruments and viewers

abdominoscope	periscope
amblyoscope	pharyngoscope
bronchoscope	photometer
chromatoscope	photomultiplier
chromoscope	photoscope
cystoscope	polariscope
diaphanoscope	polemoscope
diffractometer	prism
epidiascope	pseudoscope
eriometer	radarscope
gastroscope	radioscope
goniometer	rangefinder
image orthicon	retinoscope
kaleidoscope	sniperscope
laser	snooperscope
microfilm viewer *or* reader	spectroscope
	stereopticon
ophthalmoscope	stereoscope
optometer	stroboscope
oscilloscope	thaumatrope

13 microscopes

acoustic microscope	laboratory microscope
binocular microscope	
blink microscope	light microscope
compound microscope	metallurgical microscope
dark-field microscope	optical microscope
dissecting microscope	oxyhydrogen microscope
electron microscope	phase contrast microscope *or* phase microscope
field ion microscope	
fluorescence microscope	
gravure microscope	pinion focusing microscope

polarizing microscope	stereomicroscope *or* stereoscopic microscope
power microscope	
projecting microscope	surface microscope
scanning electron microscope	transmission electron microscope
scanning microscope	ultramicroscope
simple *or* single microscope	ultraviolet microscope
	X-ray microscope

14 spectroscopes, spectrometers

analytical spectrometer	microspectroscope
diffraction spectroscope	monochromator
	ocular spectroscope
direct-reading spectrometer	prism spectroscope
	reversion spectroscope
direct-reading spectroscope	spectrograph
micro-spectrophotometer	spectrophotometer
	spectroradiometer
	star spectroscope

15 telescopes

astronomical telescope	prism telescope
	radio telescope
Cassegrainian telescope	reflecting telescope
	refracting telescope
double-image telescope	Schmidt telescope
	spotting telescope
elbow telescope	telescopic sight
finder telescope	terrestrial telescope
guiding telescope	tower telescope
inverting telescope	twin telescope
mercurial telescope	vernier telescope
Newtonian telescope	water telescope
optical telescope	zenith telescope *or* tube
panoramic telescope	

30 BLINDNESS

NOUNS **1 blindness, sightlessness,** cecity, ablepsia, unseeingness, sightless eyes, lack of vision, eyelessness; stoneblindness, total blindness; darkness, "ever-during dark," "total eclipse without all hope of day"—both Milton, "the precious treasure of his eyesight lost"—Shakespeare; legal blindness; partial blindness, reduced sight, **blind side; blind spot;** dimsightedness; snow blindness, niphablepsia; amaurosis, *gutta serena* <L>, drop serene; cataract; glaucoma; trachoma; mental *or* psychic blindness, mind-blindness, soul-blindness, benightedness, unenlightenment, spiritual blindness; **blinding,** making blind, depriving of sight, putting out the eyes, excecation <old>; blurring the eyes, blindfolding, hoodwinking, blinkering

2 day blindness, hemeralopia; **night blindness,** nyctalopia; moon blindness, moonblind

3 color blindness; dichromatism; mono-

chromatism, achromatopsia; red blindness, protanopia, green blindness,
deuteranopia, red-green blindness, Dal-
tonism; yellow blindness, xanthocyan-
opia; blue-yellow blindness, tritanopia;
violet-blindness

4 **the blind,** the sightless, the unseeing;
blind man; bat, mole; "blind leaders of
the blind"—Bible

5 blindfold; eye patch; blinkers, blinds,
blinders, rogue's badge

6 <aids for the blind> sensory aid, **braille,**
New York point, Gall's serrated type,
Boston type, Howe's American type,
Moon or Moon's type, Alston's Glasgow
type, Lucas's type, sight-saver type,
Frere's type; line letter, string alphabet,
writing stamps; noctograph, writing
frame, embosser, high-speed embosser;
visagraph; talking book; optophone,
Visotoner, Optacon; personal sonar,
Pathsounder; ultrasonic spectacles; cane;
Seeing Eye dog, guide dog

VERBS 7 **blind,** blind the eyes, deprive of
sight, **strike blind,** render or make blind,
excecate <old>; darken, dim, obscure,
eclipse; **put one's eyes out,** gouge; **blindfold,** hoodwink, bandage; throw dust in
one's eyes, benight; **dazzle,** bedazzle,
daze; glare; snow-blind

8 **be blind,** not see, walk in darkness, grope
in the dark, feel one's way; go blind, lose
one's sight or vision; be blind to, close or
shut one's eyes to, wink or blink at, look
the other way, blind oneself to, wear
blinkers or have blinders on; have a blind
spot or side

ADJS 9 **blind, sightless, unsighted,** ableptic-
al, eyeless, visionless, **unseeing,** undiscerning, unobserving, unperceiving; in
darkness, rayless, bereft of light, dark
<nonformal>, "dark, dark, dark, amid
the blaze of noon"—Milton; **stone-blind,**
stark blind, **blind as a bat,** blind as a mole
or an owl; amaurotic; dim-sighted 28.13;
hemeralopic; nyctalopic; color-blind;
mind-blind, soul-blind, mentally or psy-
chically or spiritually blind, benighted,
unenlightened

10 **blinded,** excecate <old>, darkened, obscured; **blindfolded,** blindfold, hoodwinked, blinkered; **dazzled,** bedazzled,
dazed; snow-blind, snow-blinded

11 **blinding,** obscuring; **dazzling,** bedazzling

31 VISIBILITY

NOUNS 1 **visibility,** visibleness, perceptibility, discernibleness, observability,
detectability, visuality, seeableness; exposure; manifestation; outcrop,
outcropping; the visible, the seen, what is
revealed, what can be seen; revelation,
epiphany

2 **distinctness, plainness,** evidence <old>,
evidentness, obviousness, patentness,
manifestness; **clearness, clarity,** crystal-
clearness, lucidity, limpidity; **definiteness,** definition, sharpness, microscopical
distinctness; resolution, high resolution,
low resolution; **prominence, conspicuousness,** conspicuity; **exposure,** public
exposure, high profile, low profile; high or
low visibility; atmospheric visibility, seeing, ceiling, ceiling unlimited, visibility
unlimited, CAVU or ceiling and visibility
unlimited, severe clear <nonformal>,
visibility zero

3 **field of view,** field of vision, range or
scope of vision, **sight,** limit of vision, eye-
reach, **eyesight,** eyeshot, ken; **vista, view,
horizon, prospect, perspective, outlook,**
survey; range, scan, scope; line of sight,
sightline, line of vision; naked eye; command, domination, outlook over;
viewpoint, observation point 27.8

VERBS 4 **show,** show up, show through,
shine out or through, **surface, appear**
33.8, **be visible,** be seen, be revealed, be
evident, be noticeable, meet the gaze, impinge on the eye, present to the eye, meet
or catch or hit or strike the eye; **stand out,**
stand forth, loom large, glare, **stare one in
the face,** hit one in the eye, **stick out like a
sore thumb;** dominate; emerge, come
into view, materialize

5 **be exposed,** be conspicuous, have high
visibility, stick out, hang out <nonfor-
mal>, crop out; live in a glass house;
have or keep a high profile

ADJS 6 **visible,** visual, **perceptible,** perceivable, **discernible, seeable,** viewable,
witnessable, beholdable, observable,
detectable, noticeable, recognizable, to
be seen; **in sight,** in view, in plain sight, in
full view, present to the eyes, before one's
eyes, under one's eyes, open, naked, outcropping, hanging out <nonformal>,
exposed, showing, open or exposed to
view; **evident,** in evidence, **manifest, apparent;** revealed, disclosed, unhidden,
unconcealed, unclouded, undisguised

7 **distinct, plain, clear, obvious, evident,
patent,** unmistakable, not to be mistaken,
much in evidence, plain to be seen, for all
to see, showing for all to see, plain as a
pikestaff, plain as the nose on one's face,
plain as day, clear as day, plain as plain

can be, big as life and twice as ugly; **definite, defined, well-defined**, well-marked, well-resolved, in focus; **clear-cut**, clean-cut; crystal-clear, clear as crystal; **conspicuous**, glaring, staring, **prominent**, pronounced, well-pronounced, in bold *or* strong *or* high relief, high-profile

ADVS **8 visibly, perceptibly**, perceivably, discernibly, seeably, recognizably, observably, markedly, noticeably; **manifestly, apparently**, evidently; **distinctly, clearly**, with clarity *or* crystal clarity, **plainly**, obviously, patently, definitely, unmistakably; conspicuously, undisguisedly, unconcealedly, prominently, pronouncedly, glaringly, starkly, staringly

32 INVISIBILITY

NOUNS **1 invisibility**, imperceptibility, unperceivability, undetectability, indiscernibility, unseeableness, viewlessness; nonappearance; disappearance 34; the invisible, the unseen; more than meets the eye; unsubstantiality 763, immateriality 1051, **secrecy** 345, **concealment** 346

2 inconspicuousness, half-visibility, semivisibility, low profile; **indistinctness, unclearness**, unplainness, **faintness**, paleness, feebleness, weakness, **dimness**, bedimming, bleariness, darkness, shadowiness, **vagueness**, vague appearance, indefiniteness, obscurity, uncertainty, indistinguishability; **blurriness**, blur, soft focus, defocus, **fuzziness, haziness**, mistiness, filminess, fogginess

VERBS **3** be invisible *or* unseen, escape notice; lie hid 346.8, **blush unseen**; disappear 34.2

4 blur, dim, pale, soften, film, mist, fog; defocus, lose resolution *or* sharpness *or* distinctness, go soft at the edges

ADJS **5 invisible; imperceptible**, unperceivable, **indiscernible**, undiscernible, undetectable, **unseeable**, viewless, unbeholdable, unapparent, insensible; **out of sight**, *à perte de vue* <Fr>; **secret** 345.11,15; **unseen**, sightless, unbeheld, unviewed, unwitnessed, unobserved, unnoticed, unperceived; behind the curtain *or* scenes; disguised, camouflaged, hidden, **concealed** 346.11,14; undisclosed, unrevealed, *in petto* <L>; latent, unrealized, submerged

6 inconspicuous, half-visible, semivisible, low-profile; **indistinct, unclear**, unplain, **indefinite**, undefined, ill-defined, ill-

marked, **faint**, pale, feeble, weak, **dim**, dark, **shadowy, vague, obscure**, indistinguishable, unrecognizable; half-seen, merely glimpsed; uncertain, confused, out of focus, **blurred, blurry**, bleared, bleary, blear, **fuzzy, hazy**, misty, filmy, foggy

33 APPEARANCE

NOUNS **1 appearance, appearing**, apparition, coming, forthcoming, showing-up, coming forth, coming on the scene, making the scene <nonformal>, putting in an appearance; **emergence**, issuing, issuance; **arising**, rise, rising, occurrence; **materialization, materializing**, coming into being; **manifestation**, realization, incarnation, revelation, showing-forth; epiphany, theophany, avatar, ostent <old>; **presentation, disclosure, exposure**, opening, unfolding, unfoldment, showing; rising of the curtain

2 appearance, exterior, externals, **mere externals, facade**, outside, **show, outward show, image**, display, front <nonformal>, outward *or* external appearance, surface appearance, surface show, vain show, apparent character, public image, window dressing, cosmetics; whitewash; whited sepulcher; **glitz** *and* tinsel <both nonformal>, gaudiness, speciousness, meretriciousness, **superficiality; PR** *and* flack <both nonformal>

3 aspect, look, view; feature, lineaments; **seeming, semblance, image**, imago, icon, eidolon, likeness, simulacrum; effect, impression, total effect *or* impression; **form, shape**, figure, configuration, gestalt; **manner**, fashion, wise, guise, style; **respect, regard**, reference, light; **phase; facet, side**, angle, viewpoint 27.7, slant *and* twist *and* spin <all nonformal>

4 looks, features, lineaments, traits, lines; **countenance**, face, visage, feature, favor, brow, physiognomy; cast of countenance, **cut of one's jib** <nonformal>, facial appearance *or* expression, cast, turn; **look, air, mien**, demeanor, carriage, bearing, port, posture, stance, poise, presence; guise, garb, complexion, color

5 <thing appearing> **apparition, appearance**, phenomenon; **vision, image, shape, form**, figure, presence; false image, mirage, phasm <old>, specter, **phantom** 987.1

6 view, scene, sight; prospect, **outlook, lookout, vista, perspective; scenery**, scenic view; panorama, sweep; scape,

landscape, seascape, riverscape, waterscape, airscape, skyscape, cloudscape,
cityscape, townscape; bird's-eye view,
worm's-eye view

7 **spectacle, sight;** exhibit, **exhibition,** exposition, **show, stage show** 704.4, **display,**
presentation, representation; tableau,
tableau vivant; panorama, diorama,
cosmorama, myriorama, cyclorama,
georama; *son et lumière* <Fr>, sound-
and-light show; phantasmagoria, shifting
scene, light show; psychedelic show; **pag-**
eant, pageantry; parade, pomp

VERBS 8 **appear,** become visible; **arrive,**
make one's appearance, make *or* put in
an appearance, appear on the scene,
make the scene *and* weigh in <both non-
formal>, appear to one's eyes, meet *or*
catch *or* strike the eye, **come in sight** *or*
view, show, show oneself, show one's
face, nip in <nonformal>, **show up**
<nonformal>, **turn up,** come, **material-**
ize, present oneself, present oneself to
view, **manifest oneself,** become manifest,
reveal oneself, discover oneself, uncover
oneself, declare oneself, expose *or* betray
oneself; **come to light,** see the light, see
the light of day; **emerge,** issue, issue
forth, stream forth, come forth, come to
the fore, come out, come forward, come
one's way, come to hand; enter 189.7,
come upon the stage; **rise, arise,** rear its
head; look forth, peer *or* peep out; crop
out, outcrop; loom, heave in sight, appear
on the horizon; fade in

9 **burst forth,** break forth, debouch, erupt,
irrupt, explode; **pop up, bob up** <nonfor-
mal>, start up, spring up, burst upon the
view; flare up, flash, gleam

10 appear to be, seem to be, **appear, seem,**
look, feel, sound, look to be, appear to
one's eyes, have *or* present the appearance of, give the feeling of, strike one as,
come on as <nonformal>; **appear like,**
seem like, look like, have *or* wear the look
of, **sound like; have every appearance of,**
have all the earmarks of, have all the features of, show signs of, have every sign *or*
indication of; assume the guise of, take
the shape of, exhibit the form of

ADJS 11 **apparent,** appearing, **seeming, os-**
tensible; outward, surface, superficial;
visible 31.6

ADVS 12 **apparently, seemingly, ostensibly,**
to *or* by all appearances, to *or* by all accounts, to all seeming, as it seems, to the
eye; on the face of it, *prima facie* <L>; on
the surface, outwardly, superficially; at
first sight *or* view, at the first blush

34 DISAPPEARANCE

NOUNS 1 **disappearance,** disappearing, **van-**
ishing, vanishment; **going, passing, de-**
parture, loss; dissipation, dispersion;
dissolution, dissolving, melting, evaporation, evanescence, dematerialization
1051.5; fadeout, fading, fadeaway, blackout; wipe, wipeout, wipeoff, erasure;
eclipse, occultation, blocking; vanishing
point; elimination 772.2; extinction 395.6

VERBS 2 **disappear, vanish,** vanish from
sight, do a vanishing act <nonformal>,
depart, fly, **flee** 368.10, go, be gone, **go**
away, pass, pass out *or* away, pass out of
sight, exit, pull up stakes <nonformal>,
leave the scene *or* stage, clear out, pass
out of the picture, pass *or* retire from
sight, become lost to sight, be seen no
more; **perish, die,** die off; die out *or* away,
dwindle, wane, fade, **fade out** *or* **away,** do
a fade-out <nonformal>; sink, sink away,
dissolve, melt, melt away, "melt, thaw,
and dissolve itself"—Shakespeare, dematerialize 1051.6, evaporate, evanesce,
vanish into thin air, go up in smoke; disperse, dispel, dissipate; cease, cease to
exist, **cease to be;** leave no trace, "leave
not a rack behind"—Shakespeare; waste,
waste away, erode, be consumed, wear
away; undergo *or* suffer an eclipse; **hide**
346.8

ADJS 3 **vanishing, disappearing,** passing,
fleeting, fugitive, transient, flying, fading,
dissolving, melting, evaporating, evanescent

4 **gone,** away, gone away, past and gone,
extinct, missing, no more, lost, lost to
sight *or* view, long-lost, **out of sight; un-**
accounted for; nonexistent

35 COLOR

NOUNS 1 **color, hue; tint,** tinct, tincture,
tinge, shade, tone, cast; key; **coloring, col-**
oration; color harmony, color balance,
color scheme; decorator color; **complex-**
ion, skin color *or* coloring *or* tone; chromatism, chromism; achromatism 36.1;
natural color; undercolor; pallor 36.2

2 **warmth,** warmth of color, warm color;
blush, flush, glow, healthy glow *or* hue

3 **softness,** soft color, subtle color, pale
color, **pastel,** pastel color, pastel shade

4 **colorfulness,** color, bright color, pure
color, **brightness, brilliance, vividness,**
intensity, saturation; **richness,** gorgeousness, gaiety; riot of color; Technicolor
<trademark>; Day-Glo <trademark>

5 garishness, loudness, luridness, glitz
<nonformal>, gaudiness 501.3; loud *or*
screaming color <nonformal>; shocking
pink, jaundiced yellow, arsenic green;
clashing colors, color clash

6 color quality; chroma, Munsell chroma,
brightness, purity, saturation; **hue,**
value, lightness; colorimetric quality,
chromaticity, chromaticness; tint, **tone;**
chromatic color, achromatic *or* neutral
color; warm color; cool color

7 color system, chromaticity diagram,
color triangle, Maxwell triangle; hue cycle, color circle, chromatic circle, color
cycle *or* gamut; Munsell scale; color
solid; fundamental colors; **primary color,**
primary pigment, primary; secondary
color, secondary; tertiary color, tertiary;
complementary color; chromaticity coordinate; color mixture curve *or* function;
spectral color, spectrum color, pure *or*
full color; metamer; **spectrum,** solar
spectrum, color spectrum, chromatic
spectrum, color index; monochrome;
demitint, half tint, halftone

8 <coloring matter> **color, coloring, color-
ant,** tinction, tincture, **pigment, stain;**
chromogen; **dye,** dyestuff, color filter,
color gelatin; paint, distemper, tempera;
coat, coating, **coat of paint; undercoat,**
undercoating, **primer,** priming, prime
coat, **ground, flat coat,** dead-color; interior paint, exterior paint, floor enamel;
wash, wash coat, flat wash; opaque color,
transparent color; medium, vehicle;
drier; thinner; turpentine, turps <nonfor-
mal>

9 <persons according to hair color>
brunet; blond, Goldilocks; bleached
blond, peroxide blond; ash blond, platinum blond, strawberry blond, honey
blond; **towhead; redhead,** carrottop
<nonformal>

10 <science of colors> chromatology; chromatics, chromatography,
chromatoscopy, colorimetry; spectrum
analysis, spectroscopy, spectrometry

11 <applying color> **coloring,** coloration;
staining, dyeing; tie-dyeing; tinting, ting-
ing, tinction; pigmentation; illumination,
emblazonry; color printing; lithography

12 painting, paint-work, coating, covering;
enameling, glossing, glazing; **varnishing,**
japanning, lacquering, shellacking; staining; **calcimining, whitewashing;** gilding;
stippling; frescoing, fresco; undercoating,
priming

VERBS **13 color,** hue, lay on color; **tinge, tint,**
tinct, **tincture,** tone, complexion; pig-

ment; bedizen; **stain, dye,** dip, tie-dye;
imbue; deep-dye, fast-dye, double-dye,
dye in the wool, yarn-dye; ingrain, grain;
shade, shadow; illuminate, emblazon;
paint, apply paint, paint up, **coat,** cover,
face; dab, **daub,** dedaub, smear, besmear,
brush on paint, slap *or* slop on paint;
enamel, gloss, glaze; **varnish,** japan, **lacquer, shellac; white out; calcimine,
whitewash,** parget; wash; **gild,** begild, engild; stipple; fresco; distemper;
undercoat, prime

14 <be inharmonious> **clash,** conflict, collide, fight

ADJS **15 chromatic,** colorational; **coloring,**
colorific, colorative, tinctorial, tingent;
pigmental, pigmentary; monochrome,
monochromic, monochromatic; dichromatic; many-colored, parti-colored,
medley *or* motley <both old>, rainbow,
variegated 47.9, polychromatic, kaleidoscopic; prismatic, spectral; matching,
toning, harmonious; warm, glowing;
cool, cold

16 colored, hued, in color, in Technicolor
<trademark>; **tinged, tinted,** tinctured,
tinct, toned; **painted, enameled, stained,
dyed;** tie-dyed; imbued; complexioned,
complected <nonformal>; full-colored,
full; deep, deep-colored; wash-colored;
washed

17 deep-dyed, fast-dyed, double-dyed, **dyed-
in-the-wool;** ingrained, ingrain; colorfast,
fast, fadeless, unfading, indelible, constant

18 colorful, colory; **bright, vivid,** intense,
rich, exotic, **brilliant,** burning, **gorgeous,
gay,** bright-hued, bright-colored, rich-
colored, gay-colored, high-colored, deep-
colored

19 garish, lurid, loud, screaming, shrieking,
glaring, flaring, flashy, glitzy <nonfor-
mal>, flaunting, crude, blinding, over-
bright, raw, gaudy 501.20; Day-Glo
<trademark>

20 off-color, off-tone; **inharmonious, discordant,** incongruous, **harsh,** clashing,
conflicting, colliding

21 soft-colored, soft-hued, **soft,** softened,
subdued, light, creamy, peaches-and-
cream, **pastel, pale,** palish, subtle, mellow, delicate, quiet, tender, sweet; pearly,
nacreous, mother-of-pearl, iridescent,
opalescent; patinaed; somber, simple, sober, sad; flat, eggshell, semigloss, gloss

WORD ELEMENTS **22** —choria, —
chromasia, chrom—, chromo—,
chromat—, chromato—; —phyll;
pigmento—; —chrome, —chromia,

—chromy; pallidi—; —chroic, —chroous

36 COLORLESSNESS

NOUNS **1 colorlessness,** lack *or* absence of color, huelessness, tonelessness, achromatism, achromaticity; dullness, lackluster 1026.5

2 paleness, dimness, weakness, **faintness,** fadedness; lightness, fairness; **pallor,** pallidity, pallidness, prison pallor, **wanness, sallowness,** pastiness, ashiness; wheyface; muddiness, dullness; grayness, griseousness; **anemia,** hypochromic anemia, hypochromia, chloranemia; bloodlessness, exsanguination; **ghastliness, haggardness,** lividness, sickly hue, sickliness, deadly *or* deathly pallor, deathly hue, cadaverousness

3 decoloration, decolorizing, decolorization, discoloration, achromatization, lightening; **fading, paling; dimming, bedimming; whitening,** blanching, etiolation; bleeding, bleeding white; **bleaching,** bleach; market bleach, madder bleach

4 bleach, bleacher, bleaching agent *or* substance; decolorant, decolorizer, achromatizer

VERBS **5** decolor, decolorize, discolor, achromatize, etiolate; **fade, wash out; dim, dull, tarnish,** tone down; **pale, whiten,** blanch, drain, drain of color; **bleach,** peroxide, fume

6 lose color, fade, fade out; **bleach,** bleach out; **pale, turn pale,** grow pale, **change color,** turn white, **whiten, blanch,** wan

ADJS **7 colorless, hueless,** toneless, uncolored, achromic, achromatic, achromatous; neutral; dull, flat, mat, dead, dingy, muddy, leaden, lusterless, lackluster 1026.17; **faded, washed-out,** dimmed, discolored, etiolated; **pale, dim,** weak, **faint; pallid, wan, sallow,** fallow; pale *or* blue *or* green around the gills; **white,** white as a sheet; **pasty,** mealy, waxen; **ashen,** ashy, ashen-hued, cinereous, cineritious, gray, griseous; **anemic,** hypochromic, chloranemic; bloodless, exsanguine, exsanguinated, exsanguineous, bled white; **ghastly,** livid, lurid, **haggard,** cadaverous, sickly, deadly *or* deathly pale; pale as death *or* a ghost *or* a corpse, "pale as a forpined ghost"—Chaucer, "pale as his shirt"—Shakespeare; palefaced, tallow-faced, wheyfaced

8 bleached, decolored, decolorized, achromatized, whitened, blanched, lightened, bleached out, bleached white; drained, drained of color

9 light, fair, light-colored, light-hued; pastel; whitish 37.8

WORD ELEMENTS **10** achromat—, achromato—, achro—, achroö—

37 WHITENESS

NOUNS **1 whiteness, white, whitishness;** albescence; **lightness, fairness;** paleness 36.2; silveriness; snowiness, frostiness; chalkiness; pearliness; **creaminess;** blondness; hoariness, grizzliness, canescence; milkiness, lactescence; glaucousness; glaucescence; silver; albinism, achroma, achromasia, achromatosis; albino; leukoderma, vitiligo; wheyface; white race 312.2,3

2 <comparisons> alabaster, bone, chalk, lily, lime, milk, cream, pearl, wool, sheet, swan, sheep, fleece, foam, silver, snow, driven snow, paper, phantom, flour, ivory, maggot, tallow, wax

3 whitening, albification, blanching; etiolation; **whitewashing; bleaching** 36.3; silvering, frosting, grizzling

4 whitening agent, whiting, whitening, **whitewash,** calcimine; pipe clay, Blanco <Brit, trademark>; correction fluid

VERBS **5 whiten,** white <old>, etiolate, **blanch; bleach** 36.5; silver, grizzle, frost, besnow; chalk; whitewash

6 whitewash, white <old>, calcimine; pipe-clay, Blanco <Brit>

ADJS **7 white,** pure white, white as alabaster *or* bone *or* chalk *or* snow, etc 37.2, **snow-white,** snowy, niveous, "whiter than new snow on a raven's back"—Shakespeare, frosty, frosted; **hoary,** hoar, **grizzled,** grizzly, griseous, canescent; silver, **silvery,** silvered, argent <heraldry>, argentine; platinum; chalky, cretaceous; fleece- *or* fleecy-white; swan-white; foam-white; **milk-white,** milky, lactescent; marble, marmoreal; lily-white, white as a lily, "white as the whitest lily on a stream"—Longfellow; white as a sheet, wheyfaced

8 whitish, whity, albescent; **light, fair;** pale 36.7; off-white; eggshell; glaucous, glaucescent; pearl, pearly, pearly-white, pearl-white; alabaster, alabastrine; cream, **creamy;** ivory, ivory-white; gray-white; dun-white; lint-white

9 blond; flaxen-haired, fair-haired; artificial blond, bleached-blond, peroxide-blond; ash-blond, platinum-blond, strawberry-blond, honey-blond, blond-

headed, blond-haired; **towheaded,** tow-
haired; golden-haired 43.5
10 albino, albinic, albinistic, albinal
WORD ELEMENTS **11** alb—, albo—, leuc—,
leuco—, leuk—, leuko—

38 BLACKNESS

NOUNS **1 blackness,** nigritude, nigrescence;
inkiness; **black, sable, ebony;** melanism;
black race 312.2,3; darkness 1026
2 darkness, darkishness, darksomeness,
blackishness; **swarthiness,** swartness,
swarth; **duskiness,** duskness, soberness,
sobriety, **somberness,** graveness, sadness,
funereality; hostility, sullenness, anger,
black mood, black looks, black words
3 dinginess, griminess, smokiness, sooti-
ness, fuliginousness, fuliginosity,
smudginess, smuttiness, blotchiness,
dirtiness, **muddiness,** murkiness
4 <comparisons> ebony *or* ebon <old>,
jet, ink, sloe, pitch, tar, coal, charcoal,
smoke, soot, smut, raven, crow, night,
hell, sin, one's hat <Brit>
5 blackening, darkening, nigrification,
melanization, denigration; shading;
smudging, smutching, **smirching;**
smudge, smutch, smirch, smut
6 blacking, blackening, blackening agent,
blackwash; charcoal, burnt cork, black
ink; lampblack, carbon black, stove
black, gas black, soot
VERBS **7 blacken,** black, nigrify, melanize,
denigrate; **darken,** bedarken; shade,
shadow; blackwash, ink, charcoal, cork;
smudge, smutch, **smirch,** besmirch,
murk, blotch, blot, dinge; smut, soot;
smoke, oversmoke; ebonize; **smear**
661.9/512.10, **blacken one's name** *or* **reputation,** give one a black eye, tear down
ADJS **8 black,** black as ink *or* pitch *or* tar etc
38.4; **sable** <heraldry>, nigrous; **ebony,**
"black as ebony"—Shakespeare; deep
black, of the deepest dye; **pitch-black,**
pitch-dark, pitchy, black *or* dark as pitch,
tar-black, tarry; night-black, night-dark,
black *or* dark as night; midnight, black as
midnight; **inky,** inky-black, atramentous,
ink-black, black as ink; **jet-black,** jetty;
coal-black, coaly, black as coal, coal-
black; sloe, sloe-black, sloe-colored;
raven, **raven-black,** black as a crow,
"cyprus black as e'er was crow"—
Shakespeare; **dark** 1026.13—16
9 dark, dark-colored, **darkish,** darksome,
blackish; nigrescent; **swarthy,** swart;
dusky, dusk; **somber,** sombrous, **sober,**
grave, sad, funereal; hostile, sullen, angry

10 dark-skinned, black-skinned, **dark-
complexioned; black, colored;** melan-
ian, melanic, melanotic, melanistic,
melanous
11 dingy, grimy, smoky, sooty, fuliginous,
smudgy, smutty, blotchy, dirty, **muddy,**
murky, smirched, besmirched
12 livid, black and blue
13 black-haired, raven-haired, raven-
tressed, black-locked; brunet
WORD ELEMENTS **14** atro—, mel—,
mela—, melo—, melano—, melam—

39 GRAYNESS

NOUNS **1 grayness, gray,** grayishness, canescence; glaucousness, glaucescence; silveriness; ashiness; neutral tint; smokiness; mousiness; slatiness; leadenness;
lividness, lividity; dullness, drabness, soberness, somberness; grisaille
2 gray-haired *or* **gray-headed person,** gray-
hair, graybeard, grisard
VERBS **3 gray, grizzle,** silver
ADJS **4 gray, grayish,** gray-colored, gray-
hued, gray-toned, grayed, griseous; canescent; iron-gray, steely, steel-gray,
Quaker-gray, Quaker-colored, acier, gray-
drab; dove-gray, dove-colored; pearl-
gray, pearl, pearly; silver-gray, silver, silvery, silvered; **grizzly,** grizzled, grizzle;
ash-gray, ashen, ashy, cinerous, cinereous, cineritious, cinereal; dusty, dust-
gray; smoky, smoke-gray; charcoal-gray;
slaty, slate-colored; leaden, livid, lead-
gray; glaucous, glaucescent; wolf-gray;
mousy, mouse-gray, mouse-colored;
taupe; dapple-gray, dappled-gray; gray-
spotted, gray-speckled, salt-and-pepper;
gray-white, gray-black, gray-blue, gray-
brown, gray-green, etc; **dull, dingy,** dismal, **somber, sober, sad, dreary;** winter-
gray, hoar, hoary, frost-gray, rime-gray
5 gray-haired, gray-headed, silver-headed;
hoar, hoary, hoary-haired, hoary-headed;
gray-bearded, silver-bearded

40 BROWNNESS

NOUNS **1 brownness, brownishness, brown,**
browning, infuscation; brown race 312.2
VERBS **2 brown,** embrown, infuscate; rust;
tan, bronze, suntan; sunburn; burn; fry;
sauté, scorch, braise
ADJS **3 brown, brownish;** cinnamon, hazel;
fuscous; **brunet,** brune; tawny, fulvous;
tan, tan-colored; tan-faced, tan-skinned;
tanned, sun-tanned; khaki, khaki-
colored; drab, olive-drab; **dun,** dun-

brown, dun-drab, dun-olive; beige, grege,
ecru; **chocolate,** chocolate-colored,
chocolate-brown; cocoa, cocoa-colored,
cocoa-brown; coffee, coffee-colored,
coffee-brown; toast, toast-brown; nut-
brown; walnut, walnut-brown; seal, seal-
brown; fawn, fawn-colored; grayish-
brown; brownish-gray, fuscous, taupe,
mouse-dun, mouse-brown; snuff-colored,
snuff-brown, mummy-brown; umber,
umber-colored, umber-brown; olive-
brown; **sepia;** sorrel; yellowish-brown,
brownish-yellow; lurid <old>; brown as
a berry, berry-brown

4 **reddish-brown,** rufous-brown, brownish-
red; roan; henna; terra-cotta; rufous,
foxy; livid-brown; **mahogany,** mahogany-
brown; auburn, Titian; **russet,** russety;
rust, rust-colored, rusty, ferruginous,
rubiginous; liver-colored, liver-brown;
bronze, bronze-brown, bronze-colored,
bronzed, brazen; copper, coppery,
copperish, cupreous, copper-colored;
chestnut, chestnut-brown, castaneous;
bay, bay-colored; bayard <old>; sunburned, adust <old>

5 **brunet;** brown-haired; auburn-haired;
xanthous

41 REDNESS

NOUNS 1 **redness, reddishness,** rufosity,
rubricity; **red,** *rouge* <Fr>, gules
<heraldry>; rubicundity, **ruddiness,**
color, high color, floridness, floridity;
rubor, erythema, erythroderma, "a fire-
red cherubim's face"—Chaucer; ery-
thrism; reddish brown; red race 312.3;
"any color, so long as it's red"—Eugene
Field

2 **pinkness, pinkishness; rosiness; pink,**
rose

3 **reddening,** rubefaction, rubification,
rubescence, erubescence, rufescence; **coloring,** mantling, crimsoning, **blushing,
flushing; blush,** flush, glow, bloom; hectic, hectic flush; rubefacient

VERBS 4 <make red> **redden, rouge,** rud-
dle, rubify, rubric; warm, inflame; crimson, encrimson; vermilion, madder,
miniate, henna, rust, carmine; incarnadine, pinkify; red-ink, lipstick

5 **redden,** turn *or* grow red, **color,** color up,
mantle, blush, flush, crimson; flame,
glow

ADJS 6 **red, reddish,** gules <heraldry>, red-
colored, red-hued, red-dyed, red-looking;
ruddy, ruddied, rubicund; rubric<al>,
rubricate, rubricose; rufescent, rufous,

rufulous; warm, hot, glowing; fiery, flaming, flame-colored, flame-red, fire-red, red
as fire, lurid, red as a hot *or* live coal; red-
dened, inflamed; **scarlet, vermilion,
vermeil; crimson;** rubiate; maroon; damask; puce; stammel; cerise; iron-red;
cardinal, cardinal-red; cherry, cherry-
colored, cherry-red; carmine, incar-
mined; **ruby,** ruby-colored, ruby-red;
wine, port-wine, wine-colored, wine-red,
vinaceous; carnation, carnation-red;
brick-red, brick-colored, bricky, tile-red,
lateritious; rust, rust-red, rusty, ferruginous, rubiginous; lake-colored, laky;
beet-red, red as a beet; lobster-red, red as
a lobster; red as a turkey-cock; copper-
red, carnelian; Titian, Titian-red; infrared; reddish-amber, reddish-gray, etc;
reddish-brown 40.4

7 **sanguine,** sanguineous, **blood-red,** blood-
colored, bloody-red, bloody, gory, red as
blood

8 **pink, pinkish,** pinky; **rose, rosy,** rose-
colored, rose-hued, rose-red, roseate;
primrose; flesh-color, flesh-colored, flesh-
pink, incarnadine; coral, coral-colored,
coral-red, coralline; salmon, salmon-
colored, salmon-pink

9 **red-complexioned,** ruddy-complexioned,
warm-complexioned, red-fleshed, red-
faced, ruddy-faced, apple-cheeked,
ruddy, rubicund, **florid,** sanguine, full-
blooded; blowzy, blowzed; rosy, **rosy-
cheeked;** glowing, blooming; hectic,
flushed, flush; burnt, sunburned;
erythematous

10 **redheaded,** red-haired, red-polled, red-
bearded; erythristic; red-crested, red-
crowned, red-tufted; carroty, chestnut,
auburn, Titian, xanthous

11 reddening, blushing, flushing, coloring;
rubescent, erubescent; rubificative,
rubrific; rubefacient

42 ORANGENESS

NOUNS 1 **orangeness,** oranginess; **orange**
ADJS 2 **orange, orangeish,** orangey, orange-
hued, reddish-yellow; ocherous *or* ochery,
ochreous, ochroid, ocherish; old gold;
pumpkin, pumpkin-colored; tangerine,
tangerine-colored; apricot, peach; carroty, carrot-colored; orange-red, orange-
yellow, red-orange, reddish-orange,
yellow-orange, yellowish-orange

43 YELLOWNESS

NOUNS 1 **yellowness, yellowishness;** golden-

ness, aureateness; **yellow,** gold, or
<heraldry>; gildedness; fallowness

2 yellow skin, yellow complexion, sallowness; xanthochroism; **jaundice,** yellow
jaundice, icterus, xanthoderma, xan-
thism; yellow race 312.2,3

VERBS 3 **yellow,** turn yellow; **gild,** begild,
engild; aurify; sallow; **jaundice**

ADJS 4 **yellow, yellowish,** yellowy; lutescent,
luteous, luteolous; xanthic, xanthous;
gold, golden, or <heraldry>, gold-
colored, golden-yellow; gilt, gilded, auric,
aureate; **canary,** canary-yellow; citron,
citron-yellow, citreous; **lemon,** lemon-
colored, lemon-yellow; sulfur-colored,
sulfur-yellow; pale-yellow, **sallow,**
fallow; cream, creamy, cream-colored;
straw, straw-colored, tow-colored; flaxen,
flaxen-colored, flax-colored; sandy, sand-
colored; ocherous or ochery, ochreous,
ochroid, ocherish; buff, buff-colored,
buff-yellow; beige, ecru; saffron, saffron-
colored, saffron-yellow; primrose,
primrose-colored, primrose-yellow;
topaz-yellow

5 **yellow-haired, golden-haired,** towheaded, tow-haired, auricomous, xanthous; blond 37.9

6 yellow-faced, yellow-complexioned,
sallow, yellow-cheeked; **jaundiced,** xan-
thodermatous, icteric, icterical

44 GREENNESS

NOUNS 1 **greenness,** viridity; greenishness,
virescence, viridescence; verdantness,
verdancy, **verdure,** glaucousness, glaucescence; **green,** greensickness, chlorosis,
chloremia, chloranemia; chlorophyll

2 **verdigris, patina,** aerugo; patination

VERBS 3 **green;** verdigris, patinate, patinize

ADJS 4 **green,** virid, **verdant,** verdurous, vert
<heraldry>; grassy, leafy, leaved, fo-
liaged; springlike, summerlike, summery,
vernal, vernant, aestival; **greenish,** vir-
idescent, virescent; **grass-green,** green as
grass; citrine, citrinous; **olive,** olive-
green, olivaceous; beryl-green, berylline;
leek-green, porraceous <old>; holly,
holly-green; ivy, ivy-green; emerald,
emerald-green, smaragdine; chartreuse,
yellow-green, yellowish-green, greenish-
yellow; glaucous, glaucescent, glaucous-
green; blue-green, bluish-green, green-
blue, greenish-blue; greensick, chlorotic,
chloremic, chloranemic

5 verdigrisy, verdigrised, patinous, patinaed, patinated or patinized,
aeruginous

45 BLUENESS

NOUNS 1 **blueness, bluishness;** azureness;
blue, azure; lividness, lividity; cyanosis

VERBS 2 **blue,** azure

ADJS 3 **blue, bluish,** cerulescent; cyanic, cya-
neous, cyanean; cerulean, ceruleous;
azure <heraldry>, azurine, azurean,
azureous, azured, azure-blue, azure-
colored, azure-tinted; sky-blue, sky-
colored, sky-dyed; light-blue, lightish-
blue, light-bluish, pale-blue; dark-blue,
deep-blue; peacock-blue, pavonine, pavonian; beryl-blue, berylline; turquoise,
turquoise-blue; sapphire, sapphire-blue,
sapphirine; livid; cyanotic

46 PURPLENESS

NOUNS 1 **purpleness, purplishness,** purpli-
ness; **purple; violet;** lividness, lividity

VERBS 2 **purple,** empurple, purpurate
<old>

ADJS 3 **purple,** purpure <heraldry>, pur-
pureal, purpureous, purpurean, purpurate <old>; **purplish,** purply, purples-
cent; **violet,** violaceous; plum-colored,
plum-purple; amethystine; **lavender,**
lavender-blue; lilac; magenta; mauve;
mulberry; orchid; pansy-purple, pansy-
violet; raisin-colored; livid

47 VARIEGATION
<diversity of colors>

NOUNS 1 **variegation, multicolor;** parti-
color; medley or mixture of colors, rainbow of colors, riot of color; polychrome,
polychromatism; dichromatism, trichro-
matism, etc; dichroism, trichroism, etc

2 **iridescence,** iridization, irisation, **opalescence,** nacreousness, pearliness, **play of
colors** or **light;** light show; moiré pattern,
tabby; burelé or burelage

3 **spottiness,** maculation, freckliness,
speckliness, mottledness, dappleness,
dappledness, stippledness, spottedness,
dottedness; **fleck, speck, speckle;** freckle;
spot, dot, polka dot, macula, macule,
blotch, splotch, patch, splash; **mottle,
dapple; stipple,** stippling, pointillism,
pointillage

4 **check, checker,** checks, checking, checkerboard, chessboard; **plaid,** tartan;
checker-work, variegated pattern, harlequin, colors in patches, crazy-work,
patchwork; parquet, parquetry, marque-
try, mosaic, tesserae, tessellation; crazy-
paving <Brit>

5 stripe, striping, candy-stripe, pinstripe; barber pole; **streak, streaking;** striation, striature, stria; striola, striga; crack, craze; bar, band, belt, list

6 <comparisons> spectrum, rainbow, iris, chameleon, leopard, jaguar, cheetah, ocelot, zebra, barber pole, candy cane, Dalmatian, firedog, peacock, butterfly, mother-of-pearl, nacre, tortoise shell, opal, serpentine, chrysotile, antigorite, serpentine marble, marble, ophite, mackerel, mackerel sky, confetti, crazy quilt, patchwork quilt, shot silk, moiré, watered silk, marbled paper, Joseph's coat, harlequin

VERBS **7 variegate,** motley; parti-color; polychrome, polychromize; harlequin; **mottle, dapple,** stipple, **fleck,** flake, **speck, speckle,** bespeckle, freckle, **spot,** bespot, dot, sprinkle, spangle, bespangle, pepper, stud, maculate; blotch, splotch; tattoo, stigmatize <old>; **check, checker;** tessellate; **stripe, streak,** striate, band, bar, vein; marble, marbleize; tabby

8 opalesce, opalize; iridesce

ADJS **9 variegated, many-colored,** many-hued, diverse-colored, **multicolored,** multicolor, multicolorous, **varicolored,** varicolorous, polychrome, polychromic, polychromatic; parti-colored, parti-color; of all manner of colors, of all the colors of the rainbow; versicolor, versicolored, versicolorate, versicolorous; motley, medley <old>, harlequin; colorful, colory; daedal; crazy; thunder and lightning; kaleidoscopic, kaleidoscopical; prismatic, prismatical, prismal, spectral; shot, shot through; bicolored, bicolor, dichromic, dichromatic; tricolored, tricolor, trichromic, trichromatic; two-color *or* -colored, three-color *or* -colored, two-tone *or* -toned, etc

10 iridescent, iridal, iridial, iridine, iridian; irised, irisated, **rainbowy,** rainbowlike; **opalescent,** opaline, opaloid; nacreous, nacry, *nacré* <Fr>, nacred, **pearly,** pearlish, mother-of-pearl; tortoise-shell; peacock-like, pavonine, pavonian; chatoyant; moiré, burelé

11 chameleonlike, chameleonic

12 mottled, motley; pied, piebald, skewbald, pinto; **dappled,** dapple; calico; marbled; clouded; pepper-and-salt

13 spotted, dotted, polka-dot, sprinkled, peppered, studded, pocked, pockmarked; **spotty,** dotty, patchy, pocky; **speckled, specked,** speckledy, speckly, specky; **stippled,** pointillé, pointillistic; **flecked,** fleckered; spangled, bespangled; macu-

late, maculated, macular; punctate, punctated; freckled, frecked, freckly; blotched, blotchy, splotched, splotchy; flea-bitten

14 checked, checkered, checkedy, check, **plaid,** plaided; tessellated, tessellate, mosaic

15 striped, stripy, candy-stripe, pinstripe; **streaked,** streaky; **striated,** striate, striatal, striolate, strigate *or* strigose; barred, banded, listed; veined; **brindle,** brindled, brinded; marbled, marbleized; watered, tabby

48 HEARING

NOUNS **1 hearing,** audition; sense of hearing, auditory *or* aural sense, ear; listening, heeding, attention, hushed attention, rapt attention, eager attention; auscultation, aural examination, examination by ear; audibility

2 audition, hearing, tryout, call <all nonformal>, **audience, interview,** conference; attention, favorable attention, ear; **listening,** listening in; **eavesdropping,** wiretapping, electronic surveillance, bugging <nonformal>

3 good hearing, refined *or* acute sense of hearing, sensitive ear, nice *or* quick *or* sharp *or* correct ear; **an ear for;** musical ear, ear for music; ear-mindedness; bad ear, no ear, tin ear <nonformal>

4 earshot, earreach, **hearing,** range, auditory range, reach, carrying distance, **sound of one's voice**

5 listener, hearer, auditor, audient, hearkener; **eavesdropper,** overhearer, little pitcher with big ears, snoop, listener-in <nonformal>; fly on the wall

6 audience, auditory <old>, **house, congregation;** studio audience, live audience, captive audience, theatregoers, gallery, crowd, house; orchestra, pit; groundling, boo-bird <nonformal>, spectator 917

7 ear 2.10, lug <Scots>, auditory apparatus; external ear, **outer ear;** cauliflower ear

8 listening device; hearing aid, hard-of-hearing aid; electronic hearing aid, transistor hearing aid; vacuum-tube hearing aid; ear trumpet; amplifier, speaking trumpet, megaphone; stethoscope

9 <science of hearing> otology; otoscopy, auriscopy; otoneurology, otopathy, otography, otoplasty, otolaryngology, otorhinolaryngology; acoustic phonetics, phonetics 524.14; auriscope, otoscope; audiometer

VERBS **10 listen**, hark, **hearken, heed, hear, attend**, give attention, **give ear**, give *or* lend an ear, bend an ear; **listen to**, listen at <nonformal>, attend to, give a hearing to, give audience to, sit in on; **listen in; eavesdrop**, wiretap, tap, intercept, bug <nonformal>; **keep one's ears open**, be all ears <nonformal>, listen with both ears, strain one's ears; prick up the ears, cock the ears; hang on the lips of, hang on every word; hear out; auscultate, examine by ear

11 hear, catch, get <nonformal>, take in; **overhear; hear of**, hear tell of <nonformal>; get an earful <nonformal>, get wind of; have an ear for

12 be heard, **fall on the ear**, sound in the ear, catch *or* reach the ear, come to one's ear, register, make an impression, get across <nonformal>; **have one's ear**, reach, contact, get to; make oneself heard, get through to, gain a hearing, reach the ear of; ring in the ear; caress the ear; assault *or* split *or* assail the ear

ADJS **13 auditory**, audio, audile, **hearing, aural**, auricular, otic; audio-visual; audible; otological, otoscopic, otopathic, etc; acoustic, acoustical, phonic

14 listening, attentive, open-eared, **all ears** <nonformal>

15 eared, auriculate; big-eared, cauliflower-eared, crop-eared, dog-eared, droop-eared, flap-eared, flop-eared, lop-eared, long-eared, mouse-eared, prick-eared; **sharp-eared**; tin-eared; ear-minded

INTERJS **16 hark!**, hark ye!, hear ye!, hearken!, hear!, oyez!, hear ye, hear ye!, now hear this!, list!, **listen!**, listen up!, attend!, attention!, hist!, whisht!, psst!, yo!

49 DEAFNESS

NOUNS **1 deafness, hardness of hearing**, dull hearing, deaf ears, "ears more deaf than adders"—Shakespeare; **stone-deafness;** nerve-deafness; mind deafness, word deafness; **tone deafness;** impaired hearing, hearing *or* auditory impairment; loss of hearing, **hearing loss; deaf-muteness**, deaf-mutism, surdimutism <old>

2 the deaf, the hard-of-hearing; **deaf-mute**, surdo-mute <old>, deaf-and-dumb person; lip reader

3 deaf-and-dumb alphabet, manual alphabet, finger alphabet; dactylology, sign language; lip reading, oral method

VERBS **4 be deaf;** have no ears, be earless; lose one's hearing, suffer hearing loss *or* impairment, go deaf; shut *or* stop *or* close one's ears, **turn a deaf ear;** fall on deaf ears

5 deafen, stun, split the ears *or* eardrums

ADJS **6 deaf, hard-of-hearing**, dull *or* thick of hearing, deaf-eared, dull-eared; surd <old>; deafened, stunned; **stone-deaf**, deaf as a stone, deaf as a door *or* a doorknob *or* doornail, **deaf as a post**, deaf as an adder, "like the deaf adder that stoppeth her ear"—Bible; **unhearing;** earless; word-deaf; tone-deaf; half-deaf, quasi-deaf; **deaf and dumb**, deaf-mute

50 SOUND

NOUNS **1 sound**, sonance, acoustic, acoustical *or* acoustic phenomenon; auditory phenomenon *or* stimulus, auditory effect; noise; ultrasound; sound wave, sound propagation; sound intensity, sound intensity level, amplitude, loudness 53; phone, speech sound 524.13

2 tone, pitch, frequency, audio frequency *or* AF; monotone, monotony, tonelessness; overtone, harmonic, partial, partial tone; fundamental tone, fundamental; intonation 524.7

3 timbre, tonality, **tone quality**, tone color, color, coloring, clang color *or* tint, *Klangfarbe* <Ger>

4 sounding, sonation, sonification

5 acoustics, phonics, radioacoustics; acoustical engineer, acoustician

6 sonics; subsonics; **supersonics**, ultrasonics; speed of sound 174.2; sound barrier, transonic barrier, sonic barrier *or* wall; sonic boom

7 <sound unit> **decibel**, bel, phon

8 loudspeaker, speaker, dynamic speaker; speaker unit, speaker system; crossover network; voice coil; cone, diaphragm; acoustical network; horn <nonformal>; **headphone, earphone**, stereo headset, headset

9 microphone, mike <nonformal>; radiomicrophone; concealed microphone, **bug** <nonformal>

10 audio amplifier, amplifier, amp <nonformal>; **preamplifier**, preamp <nonformal>

11 sound reproduction system, audio sound system; **high-fidelity** system *or* **hi-fi** <nonformal>; **record player, phonograph**, gramophone, Victrola; **jukebox**, nickelodeon; radio-phonograph combination; monophonic *or* monaural system, **mono** <nonformal>, stereophonic *or* binaural system, stereo <nonformal>; four-channel stereo system, discrete four-channel system, derived four-channel system, quadraphonic sound system; multitrack player *or* recorder *or* sound system; **pickup** *or* cartridge, magnetic pickup *or* cartridge, ceramic pickup *or* cartridge, crystal pickup, photoelectric pickup; stylus, needle; tone arm; turntable, transcription turntable, record changer, changer; **public-address system** *or* PA *or* PA system; sound truck; loudhailer, bullhorn; intercommunication system, **intercom** <nonformal>, squawk box *and* bitch box <both nonformal>; **tape recorder,** tape deck, cassette *or* audio-cassette player, cassette *or* audio-cassette recorder; compact disk *or* CD player; hi-fi fan *or* freak <nonformal>, audiophile

12 **record, phonograph record,** disc, wax, long-playing record *or* LP; transcription, electrical transcription, digital transcription, digital recording; **recording,** wire recording, tape recording; digital disc; tape, tape cassette, cassette; tape cartridge, cartridge; compact disk *or* CD; video-cassette recorder *or* VCR

13 **audio distortion, distortion;** scratching, shredding, hum, 60-cycle hum, rumble, hissing, howling, blurping, blooping, woomping, fluttering, flutter, wow, wow-wows, squeals, whistles, birdies, motorboating; feedback; static 1033.21

VERBS 14 **sound,** make a sound *or* noise, give forth *or* emit a sound; noise; speak 524.20; resound; **record,** tape, tape-record; prerecord; play back

ADJS 15 **sounding,** sonorous, soniferous; **sounded;** tonal; monotone, monotonic, toneless, droning

16 **audible,** hearable; **distinct, clear,** plain, definite, articulate; distinctive, contrastive; high-fidelity, hi-fi <nonformal>

17 **acoustic, acoustical,** phonic, **sonic;** subsonic, supersonic, ultrasonic, hypersonic; transonic *or* transsonic, faster than sound

ADVS 18 **audibly, aloud,** out, **out loud;** distinctly, clearly, plainly

51 SILENCE

NOUNS 1 **silence,** silentness, **soundlessness,** noiselessness, **stillness,** "lucid stillness"—T S Eliot, **quietness,** quietude, quiescence 173, **quiet, still,** peace, whisht <Scots & Ir>, **hush,** mum; lull, rest; golden silence; deathlike *or* tomblike silence, solemn *or* awful silence, the quiet *or* silence of the grave *or* the tomb;

hush *or* dead of night, dead; tacitness, taciturnity; inaudibility; tranquillity

2 **muteness,** mutism, **dumbness,** voicelessness, tonguelessness; speechlessness, wordlessness; inarticulateness; anaudia, aphasia, aphonia; hysterical mutism; deaf-muteness 49.1; standing mute, refusal to speak, stonewalling <nonformal>, the code of silence *or omertà* <Ital>, keeping one's lip buttoned <nonformal>

3 **mute,** dummy; deaf-mute 49.2

4 **silencer, muffler,** muffle, **mute,** baffle *or* baffler, quietener, cushion; **damper,** damp; dampener; **soft pedal,** sordine, sourdine, *sordino* <Ital>; hushcloth, silence cloth; **gag, muzzle;** antiknock; **soundproofing,** acoustic tile, sound-absorbing material, sound-proofing insulation

VERBS 5 **be silent,** keep silent *or* silence, **keep still** *or* **quiet; keep one's mouth shut, hold one's tongue,** keep one's tongue between one's teeth, bite one's tongue, put a bridle on one's tongue, seal one's lips, shut *or* close one's mouth, muzzle oneself, **not breathe a word,** forswear speech *or* speaking, **keep mum, hold one's peace,** not let a word escape one, not utter a word, not open one's mouth; make no sign, keep to oneself; not have a word to say, be mute, stand mute; choke up, have one's words stick in one's throat

6 <nonformal terms> **shut up,** keep one's trap *or* yap shut, button up, button one's lip, save one's breath, shut one's bazoo, dummy up, clam up, close up like a clam, not let out a peep, say nothing, not say 'boo', play dumb, stonewall

7 **fall silent, hush,** quiet, quieten, quiesce, **quiet down,** pipe down <nonformal>, check one's speech

8 **silence, put to silence, hush,** hush one up, hush-hush, **shush, quiet,** quieten, **still; soft-pedal,** put on the soft pedal; squash, squelch <nonformal>, stifle, choke, choke off, throttle, put the kibosh on <nonformal>, put the lid on *and* shut down on <both nonformal>, put the damper on <nonformal>, **gag, muzzle,** muffle, stop one's mouth, cut one short; strike dumb *or* mute, dumbfound; tonguetie

9 **muffle, mute, dull, soften, deaden,** quietize, cushion, baffle, damp, **dampen,** deafen; subdue, stop, tone down, **soft-pedal,** put on the soft pedal

ADJS 10 **silent, still,** stilly, **quiet,** quiescent 173.12, **hushed, soundless,** noiseless;

echoless; **inaudible,** subaudible, below the limen *or* threshold of hearing, unhearable; quiet as a mouse, mousy; silent as a post *or* stone, "noiseless as fear in a wide wilderness"—Keats, "silent as the shadows"—Coleridge, so quiet that one might hear a feather *or* pin drop; silent as the grave *or* tomb, still as death, "hush as death"—Shakespeare; **unsounded, unvoiced,** unvocalized, unpronounced, unuttered, unarticulated

11 **tacit, wordless, unspoken,** unuttered, unexpressed, unsaid; **implicit** 519.8

12 **mute, mum, dumb,** voiceless, tongueless, **speechless,** wordless, breathless, at a loss for words, choked up; inarticulate; **tongue-tied,** dumbstruck, dumbstricken, stricken dumb, **dumbfounded;** anaudic, aphasic, aphonic

ADVS 13 **silently,** in silence, **quietly, soundlessly,** noiselessly; inaudibly

INTERJS 14 **silence!, hush!, shush!, sh!,** sh-sh!, whist! *or* whish! <both Brit nonformal>, whisht! <Scots & Ir>, peace!, pax!, *tais toi!* <Fr>, **be quiet!,** be silent!, be still!, **keep still!,** keep quiet!, quiet!, quiet please!, soft!, belay that! *or* there!, stow it!; **hold your tongue!,** hold your jaw! *or* lip!, **shut up!** <nonformal>, **shut your mouth!** <nonformal>, save your breath!, not another word!, not another peep out of you!, mum!, mum's the word!; hush your mouth!, shut your trap!, shut your face!, button your lip!, pipe down!, clam up!, dry up!, can it!

52 FAINTNESS OF SOUND

NOUNS 1 **faintness, lowness, softness,** gentleness, subduedness, dimness, feebleness, weakness; indistinctness, unclearness, flatness; subaudibility; decrescendo

2 muffled tone, veiled voice, *voce velata* <Ital>, covered tone; **mutedness; dullness, deadness,** flatness

3 **thud,** dull thud; **thump,** flump, crump, clop, clump, clunk, plunk, tunk, plump, bump; pad, pat; **patter,** pitter-patter, pit-a-pat; **tap,** rap, **click,** tick, flick, pop; tinkle, clink, chink, tingaling

4 **murmur,** murmuring, murmuration; **mutter,** muttering; **mumble,** mumbling; soft voice, low voice, small *or* little voice, "still small voice"—Bible; **undertone,** underbreath, bated breath; susurration, susurrus; **whisper,** whispering, stage whisper, breathy voice; breath, sigh, exhalation, aspiration

5 **ripple, splash,** ripple of laughter, ripple of applause; titter, chuckle

6 **rustle,** rustling, froufrou, "a little noiseless noise among the leaves"—Keats

7 **hum, humming,** thrumming, low rumbling, booming, bombilation, bombination, **droning, buzzing,** whizzing, whirring, purring

8 **sigh, sighing, moaning,** sobbing, whining, soughing

VERBS 9 **steal** *or* **waft on the ear,** melt in the air, float in the air

10 **murmur, mutter, mumble,** mussitate <old>, maffle <Brit nonformal>; coo; susurrate; **lower one's voice, speak under one's breath; whisper,** whisper in the ear; breathe, sigh, aspirate

11 **ripple, babble, burble,** bubble, **gurgle,** guggle, **purl, trill;** lap, plash, **splash,** swish, swash, slosh, wash

12 **rustle,** crinkle; **swish,** whish

13 **hum,** thrum, bum <Brit nonformal>, boom, bombilate, bombinate, **drone, buzz,** whiz, whir, burr, birr <Scots>, purr

14 **sigh, moan, sob, whine,** sough; **whimper**

15 **thud, thump, patter,** clop, clump, clunk, plunk, flump, crump; pad, pat; **tap,** rap, **click,** tick, tick away; pop; tinkle, clink, chink

ADJS 16 **faint, low, soft, gentle, subdued, dim, feeble, weak,** faint-sounding, low-sounding, soft-sounding; soft-voiced, low-voiced, faint-voiced, weak-voiced; murmured, whispered; half-heard, scarcely heard; distant; indistinct, unclear; barely audible, subaudible, near the limit *or* threshold of hearing; piano, pianissimo; decrescendo

17 **muffled, muted, softened, dampened,** damped, **smothered,** stifled, bated, dulled, deadened, subdued; **dull, dead, flat,** *sordo* <Ital>

18 **murmuring,** murmurous, murmurish, **muttering, mumbling;** susurrous, susurrant; **whispering,** whisper, whispery; **rustling**

19 **rippling, babbling, burbling,** bubbling, **gurgling,** guggling, **purling, trilling;** lapping, splashing, plashing, sloshing, swishing

20 **humming,** thrumming, **droning,** booming, bombinating, **buzzing,** whizzing, whirring, purring, burring, birring <Scots>

ADVS 21 **faintly, softly,** gently, subduedly, hushedly, dimly, feebly, weakly, low; piano, pianissimo; *sordo* and *sordamente* <both Ital>, *à la sourdine* <Fr>

22 in an undertone, *sotto voce* <Ital>, **under one's breath,** with bated breath, in a whisper, in a stage whisper, between the teeth; aside, in an aside; out of earshot

53 LOUDNESS

NOUNS **1 loudness,** intensity, volume, amplitude, fullness; sonorousness, sonority; surge of sound, surge, crescendo, swell, swelling; loudishness

2 noisiness, noisefulness, **uproariousness,** racketiness, tumultuousness, thunderousness, clamorousness, clangorousness, boisterousness, obstreperousness; vociferousness 59.5

3 noise, loud noise, **blast** 56.3, tintamarre, **racket, din, clamor;** outcry, **uproar,** hue and cry, noise and shouting; howl; clangor, clatter, clap, jangle, rattle; roar, thunder, thunderclap 56.5; **crash, boom,** sonic boom; **bang,** percussion; brouhaha, **tumult, hubbub,** bobbery <India>; fracas, **brawl,** commotion, drunken brawl; **pandemonium,** bedlam, hell *or* bedlam let loose; charivari, shivaree <nonformal>; discord 61

4 <nonformal terms for noisy occasions> row, flap, hullabaloo, brannigan, shindy, donnybrook, free-for-all, shemozzle, rumble, rhubarb, dustup, rumpus, ruckus, ruction, rowdydow, hell broke loose, foofooraw, hoo-ha, Katy-bar-the-door, tzimmes

5 blare, blast, shriek 58.4, peal; **toot,** tootle, **honk,** beep, blat, trumpet; bay, bray; **whistle,** tweedle, squeal; trumpet call, trumpet blast *or* blare, sound *or* flourish of trumpets, Gabriel's trumpet *or* horn, **fanfare,** tarantara, tantara, tantarara; tattoo; taps

6 noisemaker; ticktack, bull-roarer, catcall, whizzer, whizgig, snapper, cricket, clapper, clack, clacker, cracker; firecracker, cherry bomb; rattle, rattlebox; horn, Klaxon <trademark>; whistle, steam whistle, siren; boiler room, boiler factory; loud-hailer, bullhorn <nonformal>

VERBS **7 din; boom,** thunder 56.9; **resound,** ring, peal, ring *or* resound in the ears, din in the ear, **blast the ear,** pierce *or* split *or* rend the ears, rend *or* split the eardrums, split one's head; **deafen,** stun; blast 56.8, **bang, crash** 56.6; **rend the air** *or* skies *or* firmament, rock the sky, fill the air, make the welkin ring; shake *or* rattle the windows; awake *or* startle the echoes, set the echoes ringing, awake the dead;

surge, swell, rise, crescendo; **shout** 59.6

8 drown out, outshout, outroar, shout down, overpower, overwhelm; jam

9 be noisy, make a noise *or* **racket,** raise a clamor *or* din *or* hue and cry, noise, racket, **clamor,** roar, clangor; brawl, row, rumpus; **make an uproar,** kick up a dust *or* racket, kick up *or* raise a hullabaloo, raise the roof, raise Cain *or* Ned, howl like all the devils of hell, raise the devil, raise hell, whoop it up, maffick <Brit>; not be able to hear oneself think

10 blare, blast; shriek 58.8; **toot,** tootle, sound, peal, wind, blow, blat; pipe, trumpet, bugle, clarion; bay, bell, bray; **whistle,** tweedle, squeal; **honk,** honk *or* sound *or* blow the horn, beep; sound taps, sound a tattoo

ADJS **11 loud,** loud-sounding, forte, fortissimo; loudish; **resounding,** ringing, plangent, pealing; full, sonorous; **deafening,** ear-deafening, **ear-splitting,** head-splitting, ear-rending, ear-piercing, piercing; **thunderous,** thundering, tonitruous, tonitruant; **crashing, booming** 56.12; window-rattling, earthshaking, enough to wake the dead *or* the seven sleepers

12 loud-voiced, loudmouthed, fullmouthed, full-throated, big-voiced, clarion-voiced, trumpet-voiced, trumpet-tongued, brazen-mouthed, **stentorian,** stentorious, stentorophonic, like Stentor, Boanergean

13 noisy, noiseful, rackety, clattery, clangorous, clanging, **clamorous,** clamoursome <Brit nonformal>, clamant, blatant, blaring, brassy, brazen, blatting; uproarious, **tumultuous,** turbulent, blustering, brawling, **boisterous,** riproaring, rowdy, mafficking <Brit>, strepitous, strepitant, obstreperous; vociferous 59.10

ADVS **14 loudly, aloud,** loud, lustily; **boomingly, thunderously, thunderingly; noisily,** uproariously; ringingly, resoundingly; with a loud voice, at the top of one's voice, at the pitch of one's breath, in full cry, with one wild yell, with a whoop and a hurrah; forte, *fortemente* <Ital>, fortissimo

54 RESONANCE

NOUNS **1 resonance, resoundingness, sonorousness,** sonority, plangency, **vibrancy;** mellowness, richness, fullness; deepness, lowness, bassness; hollowness; **snore,** snoring

2 reverberation, resounding; rumble, rum-

bling, thunder, thundering, boom, booming, growl, growling, grumble,
grumbling, reboation; rebound, resound,
echo, reecho

3 **ringing**, tintinnabulation, **pealing, chiming, tinkling**, tingling, **jingling**, dinging,
donging; **tolling**, knelling; clangor, clank-
ing, clanging; **ring, peal, chime; toll,**
knell; **tinkle**, tingle, **jingle**, dingle, ding,
dingdong, ding-a-ling, ting-a-ling; clink,
tink, ting, ping, chink; clank, clang; jangle, jingle-jangle; campanology, bell
ringing, change ringing, peal ringing; tin-
nitis, ringing of or in the ear

4 **bell** <see list>, tintinnabulum; **gong**, triangle, **chimes**, door chimes, clock chimes,
Westminster chimes; clapper, tongue;
carillon, set of bells

5 **resonator**, resounder, reverberator;
sounding board, sound box; resonant
chamber or cavity; echo chamber; loud
pedal, damper pedal, sustaining pedal

VERBS 6 **resonate, vibrate**, pulse, throb;
snore

7 **reverberate, resound**, sound, **rumble**,
roll, boom, echo, reecho, rebound, bounce
back, be reflected, be sent back, echo
back, send back, return

8 **ring**, tintinnabulate, **peal**, sound; **toll**,
knell, sound a knell; **chime**; gong; **tinkle**,
tingle, **jingle**, ding, dingdong, dong;
clink, tink, ting, chink; clank, clang, clangor; jangle, jinglejangle; ring on the air;
ring changes or peals; ring in the ear

ADJS 9 **resonant, reverberant, vibrant, sonorous**, plangent, rolling; mellow, rich,
full; resonating, reverberating, echoing,
reechoing, vibrating, pulsing, throbbing

10 **deep**, deep-toned, deep-pitched, deep-
sounding, deepmouthed, deep-echoing;
hollow, sepulchral; low, low-pitched,
low-toned, grave, heavy; **bass**; baritone;
contralto

11 **reverberating**, reverberant, reverberatory, reboant, **resounding**, rebounding,
repercussive, sounding; **rumbling**, thundering, booming, growling; echoing,
reechoing, echoic; undamped; persistent,
lingering

12 **ringing, pealing, tolling**, belling, sounding, chiming; **tinkling**, tinkly, tingling,
jingling, dinging; tintinnabular or tintin-
nabulary or tintinnabulous; campanolog-
ical

13 **bells**

alarm bell	chiming bell
Angelus bell	church bell
breakfast bell	clinkum bell
call bell	cowbell
dinner bell or gong or chimes	passing bell or death bell or end bell or mortbell
doorbell	
fire bell	Sanctus bell or sac-
fog bell	ring bell or saunce
gong bell	or sauncing bell
hand bell	school bell
harness bell	sheepbell
hour bell	shop bell
jingle bell	shriving bell
minute bell	signal bell
news bell	sleigh bell
night bell	telephone bell
pancake bell	watch bell

55 REPEATED SOUNDS

NOUNS 1 **staccato; drum, thrum, beat,
pound, roll**; drumming, tom-tom, beating, pounding, thumping; **throb**,
throbbing, pulsation 915.3; **palpitation**,
flutter; sputter, spatter, splutter; **patter,
pitter-patter**, pit-a-pat; rub-a-dub, rattat-
too, rataplan, rat-a-tat, rat-tat, rat-tat-
tat, tat-tat, tat-tat-tat; **tattoo**, devil's tattoo, ruff, ruffle, paradiddle; **drumbeat**,
drum music; drumfire, barrage

2 **clicking, ticking, tick, ticktock**, ticktack,
ticktick

3 **rattle**, rattling, brattle <Scots>, ruckle
<Brit nonformal>, rattletybang; **clatter**,
clitter, clunter <Brit nonformal>, **clit-
terclatter, chatter**, clack, clacket <non-
formal>; racket 53.3

VERBS 4 **drum, thrum, beat, pound, thump,
thump out, roll; palpitate**, flutter; sputter, splatter, splutter; patter, pitter-
patter, go pit-a-pat or pitter-patter;
throb, pulsate 915.12; beat or sound a tattoo, beat a devil's tattoo, ruffle, beat a
ruffle

5 **tick, ticktock**, ticktack, tick away

6 **rattle**, ruckle <Brit nonformal>, brattle
<Scots>; **clatter**, clitter, **chatter**, clack;
rattle around, clatter about

ADJS 7 **staccato; drumming, thrumming,
beating, pounding, thumping; throbbing**;
palpitant, fluttering; sputtering, spattering, spluttering; clicking, ticking

8 **rattly**, rattling, chattering, **clattery**, clat-
tering

56 EXPLOSIVE NOISE

NOUNS 1 **report, crash, crack, clap, bang**,
wham, slam, clash, burst; **knock, rap,
tap**, smack, whack, thwack, whop, whap,
swap <nonformal>, whomp, splat,
crump <Brit nonformal>, bump, slap,
slat <Brit nonformal>, flap, flop

2 **snap, crack;** click, clack; **crackle,** snapping, cracking, crackling, crepitation, decrepitation, sizzling, spitting; rale

3 **detonation, blast, explosion,** fulmination, **discharge, burst, bang, pop, crack,** bark; **shot,** gunshot; volley, salvo, fusillade

4 **boom,** booming, cannonade, **peal, rumble,** grumble, growl, **roll, roar**

5 **thunder,** thundering, clap or crash or peal of thunder, **thunderclap,** thunderpeal, thundercrack, thunderstroke; "heaven's artillery," "the thunder, that deep and dreadful organ-pipe," "dread rattling thunder," "deep, dread-bolted thunder"— all Shakespeare, "the crashing of the chariot of God"—William Cullen Bryant, "dry sterile thunder without rain"—T S Eliot; thunderstorm 316.3; Thor or Donar, Jupiter Tonans, Indra

VERBS 6 **crack, clap, crash,** wham, slam, **bang,** clash; **knock, rap, tap,** smack, whack, thwack, whop, whap, swap <nonformal>, whomp, splat, crump <Brit nonformal>, bump, slat <Brit nonformal>, slap, flap

7 **snap, crack;** click, clack; **crackle,** crepitate, decrepitate; spit

8 **blast, detonate, explode, discharge, burst,** go off, **bang, pop, crack,** bark, fulminate; burst on the ear

9 **boom, thunder, peal, rumble,** grumble, growl, **roll, roar**

ADJS 10 **snapping, cracking, crackling,** crackly, crepitant

11 **banging,** crashing, bursting, exploding, explosive, blasting, cracking, popping; knocking, rapping, tapping; slapping, flapping, slatting <Brit nonformal>

12 **thundering, thunderous,** thundery, fulminating, tonitruous, tonitruant, thunderlike; **booming,** pealing, rumbling, rolling, roaring; cannonading, volleying

INTERJS 13 bang!, boom!, wham!, whammo!, blam!, kerboom!, kerblam!

57 SIBILATION
<hissing sounds>

NOUNS 1 sibilation, sibilance or sibilancy; **hiss, hissing,** siss, sissing, white noise; hush, hushing, shush, shushing; sizz, sizzle, sizzling; fizz, fizzle, fizzling; effervescing, effervescence; swish, whish, whoosh; whiz, buzz, zip; siffle; wheeze, râle <Fr>, rhonchus; whistle, whistling; sneeze, sneezing, sternutation; snort; snore, stertor; **sniff,** sniffle, snuff, snuffle; spit, sputter, splutter; squash, squish, squelch; sigmatism, lisp; assibilation; frication, frictional rustling

VERBS 2 sibilate; **hiss,** siss; hush, shush; sizzle, sizz; fizzle, fizz, effervesce; whiz, buzz, zip; swish, whish, whoosh; whistle; wheeze; sneeze; snort; snore; sniff, sniffle, snuff, snuffle; spit, sputter, splutter; squash, squish, squelch; lisp; assibilate

ADJS 3 **sibilant; hissing,** hushing, sissing; sizzling, fizzling, effervescent; **sniffing,** sniffling, snuffling; snoring; wheezing, wheezy

58 STRIDENCY
<harsh and shrill sounds>

NOUNS 1 **stridency,** stridence, stridor, stridulousness, stridulation; **shrillness,** highness, sharpness, acuteness, arguteness; **screechiness, squeakiness,** creakiness, reediness, pipingness

2 **raucousness, harshness,** raucity; discord, cacophony 61.1; coarseness, rudeness, ugliness, roughness, gruffness; **raspiness,** scratchiness, scrapiness, **hoarseness,** huskiness, dryness; stertorousness; roupiness <Scots>; gutturalness, gutturalism, gutturality, thickness, throatiness; cracked voice

3 **rasp, scratch, scrape,** grind; crunch, craunch, scranch <old>, scrunch, crump; burr, chirr, buzz; snore; **jangle, clash, jar;** clank, clang, clangor, twang, twanging; blare, blat, bray; croak, caw, cackle; belch; growl, snarl; grumble, groan

4 **screech, shriek, scream, squeal,** shrill, keen, squeak, squawk, skirl, screak, skreak <nonformal>, skriech or skreigh <both Scot>; creak; **whistle,** wolf-whistle; pipe; **whine, wail, howl,** ululation, yammer; vibrato; waul, caterwaul

5 <insect sounds> **stridulation,** cricking, creaking, chirking <Scots>; crick, creak, chirk, chirp, chirping, chirrup

6 <high voices> soprano, mezzo-soprano, treble; tenor, alto; male alto, countertenor; head register, head voice, head tone, falsetto

VERBS 7 **stridulate,** crick, creak, chirk, chirp, chirrup

8 **screech, shriek,** screak, skreak <nonformal>, skriech or skreigh <both Scot>, creak, squeak, squawk, **scream, squeal,** shrill, keen; **whistle,** wolf-whistle; pipe; skirl; **whine,** wail, howl, wrawl <Brit nonformal>, yammer, ululate; waul, caterwaul

9 <sound harshly> **jangle, clash, jar;**

blare, blat, bray; croak, caw, cackle; belch; burr, chirr, buzz; snore; growl, snarl; grumble, groan; clank, clang, clangor; twang

10 **grate, rasp, scratch, scrape,** grind; crunch, craunch, scranch <old>, scrunch, crump

11 **grate on,** jar on, grate upon the ear, jar upon the ear, offend the ear, pierce or split or rend the ears, harrow or lacerate the ear, **set the teeth on edge, get on one's nerves,** jangle or wrack the nerves, make one's skin crawl

ADJS 12 **strident,** stridulant, stridulous; strident-voiced

13 **high,** high-pitched, high-toned, high-sounding; treble, soprano, mezzo-soprano, tenor, alto, falsetto, counter-tenor

14 **shrill, thin, sharp,** acute, argute, keen, keening, **piercing,** penetrating, ear-piercing; **screechy,** screeching, shrieky, shrieking, **squeaky,** squeaking, screaky, creaky, creaking; whistling, piping, skirling, reedy; whining, wailing, howling, ululating, ululant; vibrato

15 **raucous,** raucid, **harsh,** harsh-sounding; coarse, rude, rough, gruff, ragged; **hoarse, husky,** roupy <Scots>, cracked, dry; **guttural,** thick, throaty, croaky, croaking; choked, strangled; squawky, **squawking;** brassy, brazen, tinny, metallic; stertorous

16 **grating, jarring,** grinding; **jangling,** jangly; **rasping,** raspy; scratching, scratchy; scraping, scrapy

59 CRY, CALL

NOUNS 1 **cry, call, shout, yell,** hoot; halloo, hollo, yoo-hoo; **whoop, holler** <nonformal>; **cheer, hurrah; howl,** yowl, yawl <Brit nonformal>; bawl, bellow, roar; **scream, shriek,** screech, squeal, squall, caterwaul; yelp, yap, yammer, yawp, bark; war cry, battle cry, war whoop, rallying cry

2 **exclamation,** ejaculation, outburst, blurt, ecphonesis; expletive

3 hunting cry; tallyho, yoicks <old>, view halloo

4 **outcry, vociferation, clamor;** hullabaloo, hubbub, brouhaha, **uproar** 53.3; **hue and cry**

5 vociferousness, vociferance, clamorousness, clamoursomeness <Brit nonformal>, blatancy; noisiness 53.2

VERBS 6 **cry, call, shout, yell, holler** <nonformal>, hoot; hail, halloo, hollo;

whoop; **cheer** 116.6; **howl,** yowl, yammer, yawl <Brit nonformal>; squawk, yawp; **bawl, bellow,** roar, roar or bellow like a bull; cry or yell or scream bloody murder or blue murder; **scream, shriek,** screech, squeal, squall, waul, caterwaul; yelp, yap, bark

7 **exclaim,** give an exclamation, ejaculate, burst out, blurt, blurt out, jerk out, spout out; stammer out

8 **vociferate,** outcry, **cry out,** call out, bellow out, yell out, holler out <nonformal>, shout out, sing out; sound off <nonformal>, pipe up, **clamor,** make or raise a clamor; make an outcry, **raise a hue and cry,** make an uproar

9 cry aloud, raise or lift up the voice, give voice or tongue, shout or cry or thunder at the top of one's voice, split the throat or lungs, strain the voice or throat, rend the air

ADJS 10 **vociferous,** vociferant, vociferating; **clamorous,** clamoursome <Brit nonformal>; **blatant;** obstreperous, brawling; **noisy;** crying, shouting, **yelling, hollering** <nonformal>, **bawling,** screaming; yelping, yapping, yappy, yammering; loud-voiced, loudmouthed, openmouthed, stentorian, Boanergean

11 **exclamatory,** ejaculatory, blurting

60 ANIMAL SOUNDS

NOUNS 1 animal noise; **call, cry;** mating call or cry; grunt, howl, bark, howling, waul, caterwaul, ululation, barking; bird-call, note, woodnote, clang; stridulation 58.5; dawn chorus

VERBS 2 cry, call; **howl,** yowl, yawp, yawl <nonformal>, ululate; wail, whine, pule; **squeal,** squall, scream, screech, screak, squeak; troat; **roar; bellow,** blare, **bawl; moo,** low; **bleat,** blate, blat; **bray; whinny, neigh,** whicker, nicker; **bay,** bay at the moon, bell; **bark,** latrate <old>, give voice or tongue; **yelp, yap,** yip; **mew,** mewl, **meow,** miaow, waul, caterwaul

3 **grunt,** gruntle <Brit nonformal>, oink; **snort**

4 **growl, snarl,** grumble, gnarl, snap; hiss, spit

5 <birds> **warble, sing,** carol, call; pipe, whistle; **trill,** chirr, roll; **twitter,** tweet, twit, chatter, chitter; **chirp,** chirrup, chirk, **cheep,** peep, pip; **quack,** honk, cronk; **croak, caw; squawk,** scold; **crow,** cock-a-doodle-doo; **cackle,** gaggle, gabble, guggle, **cluck,** clack, chuck; **gobble; hoot,** hoo; **coo; cuckoo;** drum

ADJS **6 howling,** yowling, crying, wailing, whining, puling, bawling, ululant, blatant; lowing, mugient

61 DISCORD
<dissonant sounds>

NOUNS **1 discord,** discordance *or* discordancy, **dissonance** *or* dissonancy, diaphony, **cacophony;** stridor; **inharmoniousness,** unharmoniousness, disharmony, inharmony; **unmelodiousness,** unmusicalness, unmusicality, untunefulness, tunelessness; atonality, atonalism; flatness, sharpness, sourness <nonformal>; dissonant chord, wolf; false note, sour note *and* clinker *and* clam <all nonformal>, off note; cipher; wolf-tone

2 clash, jangle, jar; noise, mere noise, confusion *or* conflict *or* jarring *or* jostling of sounds; Babel, witches' *or* devils' chorus; harshness 58.2; clamor 53.3

VERBS **3 sound** *or* strike *or* hit a sour note <nonformal>, hit a clinker *or* a clam <nonformal>; not carry a tune; **clash, jar, jangle,** conflict, jostle; grate 58.10,11; untune, unstring

ADJS **4 dissonant, discordant, cacophonous,** absonant <old>, disconsonant, diaphonic; strident, shrill, harsh, raucous, grating 58.16; **inharmonious,** unharmonious, disharmonious, disharmonic, inharmonic; **unmelodious,** immelodious, nonmelodious; **unmusical,** musicless, untuneful, tuneless; untunable, untuned, atonal; cracked, **out of tune,** out of tone, out of pitch; **off-key, off-tone, off-pitch,** off; flat, sharp, **sour** <nonformal>; "above the pitch, out of tune, and off the hinges"—Rabelais, "like sweet bells jangled, out of tune and harsh"—Shakespeare

5 clashing, jarring, jangling, jangly, confused, conflicting, jostling, warring, ajar; **harsh, grating** 58.16

62 TASTE
<sense of taste>

NOUNS **1 taste,** gust <old>, *goût* <Fr>; **flavor,** sapor; **smack, tang; savor, relish,** sapidity; palate, tongue, tooth, stomach; taste in the mouth; sweetness, sourness, bitterness, bittersweetness, saltiness; aftertaste; savoriness 63

2 sip, sup, lick, bite, lick

3 tinge, soupçon, hint 248.4

4 sample, specimen, taste, taster, little bite, little smack; example 785.2

5 taste bud *or* bulb *or* goblet, taste *or* gustatory cell, taste hair; **tongue,** lingua; **palate**

6 tasting, savoring, gustation

VERBS **7 taste,** taste of, sample; **savor,** savor of; sip, sup <nonformal>, roll on the tongue; lick; smack

ADJS **8 gustatory,** gustative; tastable, gustable <old>

9 flavored, flavorous, flavory, sapid, saporous, saporific; savory, flavorful 63.9; sweet, sour, bitter, bittersweet, salt

10 lingual, glossal; **tonguelike,** linguiform, lingulate

63 SAVORINESS

NOUNS **1 savoriness, palatableness,** palatability, **tastiness,** toothsomeness, goodness, good taste, right taste, **deliciousness,** gustatory delightfulness, scrumptiousness *and* yumminess <both nonformal>, lusciousness, delectability, **flavorfulness,** flavorsomeness, flavorousness, flavoriness, good flavor, fine flavor, sapidity; full flavor, full-bodied flavor; gourmet quality; succulence, juiciness

2 savor, relish, zest, gusto, *goût* <Fr>

3 flavoring, flavor, flavorer; **seasoning,** seasoner, **relish, condiment, spice,** condiments

VERBS **4 taste good,** tickle *or* flatter *or* delight the palate, tempt *or* whet the appetite, make one's mouth water, melt in one's mouth

5 savor, relish, like, love, be fond of, be partial to, enjoy, delight in, have a soft spot for, appreciate; smack the lips; do justice to; taste 62.7

6 savor of, taste of, smack of, have a relish of, have the flavor of, taste like

7 flavor, savor; **season,** salt, pepper, **spice,** sauce

ADJS **8 tasty,** good, fit to eat *and* finger-lickin' good <both nonformal>, good-tasting, **savory,** savorous, **palatable, toothsome,** gusty <Scots>, gustable <old>, sapid, **good,** good to eat, nice, agreeable, likable, pleasing, to one's taste, **delicious,** delightful, delectable, exquisite; delicate, dainty; juicy, succulent, **luscious,** lush; for the gods, ambrosial, nectarous, nectareous; fit for a king, gourmet, fit for a gourmet, of gourmet quality; scrumptious *and* yummy <both nonformal>

9 flavorful, flavorsome, flavorous, flavory, well-flavored; full-flavored, full-bodied; nutty, fruity; **rich,** rich-flavored

10 appetizing, mouth-watering, tempting, tantalizing, provocative, piquant

64 UNSAVORINESS

NOUNS **1 unsavoriness, unpalatableness,** unpalatability, **distastefulness,** untastefulness; bad taste, bad taste in the mouth

2 acridness, acridity, tartness, sharpness, causticity, astringence or astringency, acerbity, **sourness 67;** pungency 68; **bitterness,** bitter taste; gall, gall and wormwood, wormwood, bitter pill

3 nastiness, foulness, vileness, loathsomeness, repulsiveness, obnoxiousness, odiousness, offensiveness, disgustingness, nauseousness; **rankness,** rancidity, rancidness, overripeness, rottenness, malodorousness, fetor, fetidness; yuckiness <nonformal>; repugnance 99.2; nauseant, emetic, sickener

VERBS **4 disgust, repel,** turn one's stomach, nauseate; make one's gorge rise; gross one out <nonformal>

ADJS **5 unsavory, unpalatable, unappetizing,** untasteful, untasty, ill-flavored, foultasting, **distasteful,** dislikable, unlikable, uninviting, unpleasant, unpleasing, displeasing, disagreeable

6 bitter, bitter as gall or wormwood, amaroidal; **acrid,** sharp, caustic, tart, astringent; hard, harsh, rough, coarse; acerb, acerbic, sour; pungent

7 nasty, offensive 98.18, fulsome, noisome, noxious, rebarbative, mawkish, cloying, brackish, **foul, vile,** bad; gross and icky and yucky <all nonformal>, **sickening, nauseating,** nauseous, nauseant, vomity and barfy <both nonformal>; poisonous, rank, rancid, maggoty, weevily, spoiled, overripe, high, rotten, stinking, putrid, malodorous, fetid

8 inedible, uneatable, not fit to eat or drink, undrinkable, impotable; unfit for human consumption

65 INSIPIDNESS

NOUNS **1 insipidness,** insipidity, **tastelessness, flavorlessness,** blandness, savorlessness, saplessness, unsavoriness; **weakness, thinness,** mildness, **wishy-washiness; flatness, staleness,** lifelessness, deadness; vapidity, inanity, jejunity, jejuneness

ADJS **2 insipid, tasteless, flavorless,** bland, spiceless, **savorless,** sapless, unsavory, unflavored; pulpy, pappy, gruelly; **weak, thin,** mild, **wishy-washy,** milktoast,

washy, watery, watered, watered-down, diluted, dilute, milk-and-water; **flat, stale,** dead, *fade* <Fr>; vapid, inane, jejune; "weary, flat, stale, and unprofitable"—Shakespeare; indifferent, neither one thing nor the other

66 SWEETNESS

NOUNS **1 sweetness,** sweet, sweetishness, saccharinity, dulcitude <old>; **sugariness,** syrupiness; oversweetness, mawkishness, cloyingness, sickly-sweetness

2 sweetening, edulcoration <old>; sweetener; sugar; sweetening agent, sugar-substitute, artificial sweetener, saccharin, aspartame, NutraSweet <trademark>, cyclamates, sodium cyclamate, calcium cyclamate; molasses, blackstrap, treacle <Brit>; syrup, maple syrup, cane syrup, corn syrup, sorghum, golden syrup or treacle <Brit>; **honey,** honeycomb, honeypot, comb honey, clover honey; honeydew; **nectar, ambrosia;** sugarcoating; sweets; sugar-making; sugaring off; saccharification

VERBS **3 sweeten,** dulcify, edulcorate or dulcorate <both old>; **sugar,** honey; sugarcoat, glaze, candy; mull; saccharify; sugar off

ADJS **4 sweet,** sweetish, sweetened; sacchariferous; **sugary,** sugared, candied, **honeyed,** syrupy; mellifluous, mellifluent <old>; melliferous, nectarous, nectareous, ambrosial; sugarsweet, honeysweet, sweet as sugar or honey, sweet as a nut; sugar-coated; bittersweet; soursweet, sweet-sour, sweet and sour, sweet and pungent

5 oversweet, saccharine, rich, **cloying,** mawkish, luscious <old>, sickly-sweet

67 SOURNESS

NOUNS **1 sourness,** sour, sourishness, **tartness,** tartishness, acerbity, verjuice; acescency; acidity, acidulousness; hyperacidity, subacidity; vinegariness; unsweetness, **dryness; pungency 68;** greenness, unripeness

2 sour; vinegar, acidulant; **pickle,** sour pickle, dill pickle, bread-and-butter pickle; verjuice; lemon, lime, crab apple, green apple, sour cherry, chokecherry; sourgrass; sour balls; sourdough; sour cream, sour milk, yogurt; **acid**

3 souring, acidification, acidulation, acetification, acescence; fermentation

VERBS **4 sour,** turn sour or acid, **acidify,** acidulate, acetify; ferment; set one's teeth on edge

ADJS **5 sour,** soured, sourish; **tart,** tartish; crab, **crabbed;** acerb, acerbic, acerbate; acescent; **vinegarish,** vinegary, sour as vinegar; pickled; lemony; **pungent** 68.6; unsweet, unsweetened, **dry,** sec; green, unripe

  6 acid, acidulous, acidulent, acidulated; acetic, acetous, acetose; hyperacid; subacid, subacidulous

68 PUNGENCY

NOUNS **1 pungency, piquancy, poignancy; sharpness, keenness,** edge, **causticity,** astringency, mordancy, severity, asperity, trenchancy, cuttingness, bitingness, penetratingness, harshness, roughness, **acridity; bitterness** 64.2; acerbity, aciduousness, acidity, **sourness** 67

  2 zest, zestfulness, zestiness, **briskness,** liveliness, raciness; **nippiness, tanginess,** snappiness; **spiciness,** pepperiness, hotness, fieriness; **tang, spice,** relish; **nip, bite;** punch, snap, zip, ginger; **kick,** guts <nonformal>

  3 strength, strongness; high flavor, highness, rankness, gaminess

  4 saltiness, salinity, brininess; brackishness; **salt; brine**

VERBS **5 bite, nip,** cut, penetrate, bite the tongue, sting, make the eyes water, go up the nose

ADJS **6 pungent, piquant, poignant; sharp, keen,** piercing, penetrating, nose-tickling, stinging, **biting, acrid,** astringent, irritating, harsh, rough, severe, asperous, cutting, trenchant; **caustic,** vitriolic, mordant, escharotic; **bitter** 64.6; acerbic, acid, **sour**

  7 zestful, zesty, **brisk,** lively, racy, zippy, **nippy,** snappy, **tangy,** with a kick; spiced, seasoned, high-seasoned; **spicy,** curried, **peppery,** hot, burning, hot as pepper; mustardy; like horseradish, like Chinese mustard

  8 strong, strong-flavored, strong-tasting; **high,** high-flavored, high-tasted; **rank, gamy**

  9 salty, salt, salted, saltish, **saline, briny; brackish;** pickled

69 ODOR

NOUNS **1 odor, smell, scent,** aroma, flavor <old>, savor; **essence,** definite odor, redolence, effluvium, emanation, exhalation, fume, breath, subtle odor, whiff, trace, detectable odor; trail, spoor; **fragrance** 70; **stink, stench** 71

  2 odorousness, smelliness, headiness, pungency 68

  3 smelling, olfaction, nosing, scenting; sniffing, snuffing, snuffling, whiffing, odorizing, odorization

  4 sense of smell, smell, smelling, scent, olfaction, olfactory sense

  5 olfactory organ; olfactory pit, olfactory cell, olfactory area, **nose; nostrils,** noseholes <nonformal>, nares; olfactory nerves; **olfactories**

VERBS **6** <have an odor> **smell,** be aromatic, smell of, be redolent of; emit or emanate or give out a smell, reach one's nostrils, yield an odor or aroma, breathe, exhale; reek, **stink** 71.4

  7 odorize; scent, perfume 70.8

  8 smell, scent, nose; **sniff,** snuff, snuffle, inhale, breathe, breathe in; get a noseful of, smell of, catch a smell of, get or take a whiff of, whiff

ADJS **9 odorous,** odoriferous, odored, odorant, **smelling, smelly,** smellful <Australia>, smellsome, **redolent, aromatic;** effluvious; **fragrant** 70.9; **stinking, malodorous** 71.5

  10 strong, strong-smelling, strong-scented; **pungent,** penetrating, nose-piercing, sharp; reeking, reeky; suffocating, stifling

  11 smellable, sniffable, whiffable

  12 olfactory, olfactive

  13 keen-scented, quick-scented, sharp- or keen-nosed, **with a nose for**

70 FRAGRANCE

NOUNS **1 fragrance,** fragrancy <old>, **perfume, aroma,** scent, redolence, balminess, **incense, bouquet,** nosegay <old>, sweet smell, sweet savor; **odor** 69; spice, spiciness; muskiness; fruitiness

  2 perfumery, *parfumerie* <Fr>; **perfume,** *parfum* <Fr>, **scent, essence,** extract; aromatic, ambrosia; attar, essential or volatile oil; aromatic water; balsam, **balm,** aromatic gum; balm of Gilead, balsam of Mecca; myrrh; bay oil, myrcia oil; champaca oil; rose oil, attar of roses, "the perfumed tincture of the roses"— Shakespeare; lavender oil, heliotrope, jasmine oil, bergamot oil; fixative, musk, civet, ambergris

  3 toilet water, Florida water; rose water, *eau de rose* <Fr>; lavender water, *eau de lavande* <Fr>; *eau de jasmin* <Fr>;

cologne, cologne water, eau de Cologne; bay rum; **lotion**, after-shave lotion

4 **incense;** joss stick; pastille; frankincense *or* olibanum; agalloch *or* aloeswood, calambac, lignaloes *or* linaloa, sandalwood

5 **perfumer,** *parfumeur* <Fr>; thurifer, censer bearer; **perfuming**, censing, thurification, odorizing

6 <articles> perfumer, *parfumoir* <Fr>, fumigator, scenter, odorator, odorizer; atomizer, purse atomizer, spray; censer, thurible, incensory, incense burner; vinaigrette, scent bottle, smelling bottle, scent box, scent ball; scent strip; scent bag, sachet; pomander, pouncet-box <old>; potpourri

VERBS 7 **be fragrant,** smell sweet, **smell good,** please the nostrils

8 **perfume, scent,** cense, incense, thurify, aromatize, odorize, fumigate, embalm

ADJS 9 **fragrant, aromatic,** odoriferous, redolent, perfumy, **perfumed, scented,** odorate *or* essenced <both old>, **sweet, sweet-smelling,** sweet-scented, savory, balmy, ambrosial, incense-breathing; thuriferous; **odorous** 69.9; sweet as a rose, fragrant as new-mown hay; flowery; fruity; musky; spicy

71 STENCH

NOUNS 1 **stench, stink,** funk, malodor, fetidness, fetidity, fetor, foul odor, offensive odor, offense to the nostrils, bad smell, niff *and* pong <both Brit nonformal>, rotten smell, noxious stench, "the rankest compound of villainous smell that ever offended nostril"—Shakespeare, smell *or* stench of decay, **reek,** reeking, nidor; fug *and* frowst <Brit nonformal>; mephitis, miasma, graveolence <old>; body odor *or* BO; halitosis, **bad breath,** foul breath

2 **fetidness,** fetidity, malodorousness, **smelliness,** stinkingness, **odorousness,** noisomeness, **rankness, foulness,** putridness, offensiveness; repulsiveness; **mustiness,** funkiness, must, frowst *or* frowstiness <Brit nonformal>, moldiness, mildew, fustiness, frowiness <nonformal>, frowziness, frowstiness <Brit nonformal>, stuffiness; **rancidness,** rancidity, reastiness <Brit nonformal>; rottenness 393.7

3 **stinker,** stinkard; skunk *or* polecat *or* rotten egg; stink ball, stinkpot, stink bomb; fart

VERBS 4 **stink,** smell, **smell bad,** niffy *and* pong <both Brit nonformal>, assail *or* offend the nostrils, stink in the nostrils,

smell to heaven *or* high heaven, **reek;** smell up, stink up; stink out

ADJS 5 **malodorous, fetid,** olid, **odorous, stinking, reeking,** reeky, nidorous, smelling, bad-smelling, **evil-smelling,** ill-smelling, heavy-smelling, **smelly,** smellful <Australia>, niffy *and* pongy <both Brit nonformal>, stenchy; **foul,** vile, putrid, bad, fulsome, noisome, fecal, feculent, excremental, offensive, repulsive, noxious, sulfurous, graveolent <old>; rotten; **rank,** strong, high, gamy; **rancid,** reasty *or* reasy <both Brit nonformal>, reechy <old>; **musty,** funky, fusty, frowy <nonformal>, frowzy, frowsty <Brit>, stuffy, moldy, mildewed, mildewy; mephitic, miasmic, miasmal

72 ODORLESSNESS

NOUNS 1 **odorlessness, inodorousness,** scentlessness, smell-lessness; inoffensiveness

2 **deodorizing,** deodorization, fumigation, ventilation

3 **deodorant,** deodorizer; antiperspirant; fumigant, fumigator

VERBS 4 **deodorize,** fumigate; ventilate, freshen the air

ADJS 5 **odorless,** inodorous, nonodorous, smell-less, **scentless,** unscented; neutral-smelling; inoffensive

6 **deodorant,** deodorizing

73 TOUCH

NOUNS 1 **touch;** sense of touch, tactile sense, cutaneous sense; taction, **contact** 223.5; **feel,** feeling; hand-mindedness; light touch, lambency, whisper, breath, **kiss, caress,** fondling, loving touch; lick, lap; **brush,** graze, grazing, glance, glancing; stroke, rub; tap, flick; fingertip caress; tentative poke

2 **touching, feeling, fingering,** palpation; **handling,** manipulation; petting, caressing, stroking, rubbing, frottage, frication, friction 1042; fondling; pressure 901.2; feeling up <nonformal>

3 touchableness, **tangibility, palpability,** tactility

4 **feeler,** tactile organ, tactor; tactile cell; tactile process, tactile corpuscle, **antenna;** tactile hair, vibrissa; cat whisker; barbel, barbule; palp, palpus

5 **finger, digit;** forefinger, index finger, index; ring finger, annulary; middle finger, medius, dactylion; little finger, pinkie <nonformal>, minimus; thumb, pollex

VERBS **6 touch, feel,** feel of, palpate; **finger,** pass or run the fingers over, feel with the fingertips, thumb; **handle,** palm, paw; **manipulate,** wield, ply; twiddle; poke at, prod; tap, flick; come in contact 223.10

7 touch lightly, touch upon; kiss, **brush,** sweep, graze, brush by, glance, scrape, skim

8 stroke, pet, caress, fondle; **nuzzle,** nose, rub noses; feel up <nonformal>; rub, rub against, massage, knead 1042.6

9 lick, lap, tongue, mouth

ADJS **10 tactile,** tactual; hand-minded

11 touchable, **palpable, tangible,** tactile

12 lightly touching, lambent, playing lightly over, barely touching

74 SENSATIONS OF TOUCH

NOUNS **1 tingle,** tingling, thrill, buzz; **prickle,** prickles, prickling, pins and needles; **sting,** stinging, urtication; paresthesia

2 tickle, tickling, **titillation,** pleasant stimulation, **ticklishness,** tickliness

3 itch, itching, itchiness, yeuk <Scots>; pruritus; prurigo

4 creeps and **cold creeps** and shivers and **cold shivers** <all nonformal>, creeping of the flesh; gooseflesh, goose bumps, goose pimples; formication

VERBS **5 tingle,** thrill; **itch;** scratch; **prickle,** prick, sting

6 tickle, titillate

7 feel creepy, feel funny, creep, crawl, **have the creeps** or **cold creeps** or the heebie-jeebies <nonformal>; have gooseflesh or goose bumps; give one the creeps or the willies <nonformal>

ADJS **8 tingly,** tingling, atingle; **prickly,** prickling

9 ticklish, tickling, tickly, **titillative**

10 itchy, itching; pruriginous

11 creepy, crawly, creepy-crawly, formicative

75 SEX

NOUNS **1 sex,** gender; maleness, masculinity 76, femaleness, femininity 77; **genitals, genitalia**

2 sexuality, sexual nature, sexualism, love-life; **love** 104, sexual activity, lovemaking 562, marriage 563; heterosexuality; homosexuality; bisexuality, ambisexuality; **carnality, sensuality** 663; sexiness, voluptuousness, flesh, fleshiness; **libido,** sex drive, sexual instinct or urge; **potency** 76.2; impotence; frigidity, coldness

3 sex appeal, sexual attraction or attractiveness or magnetism, sexiness

4 sex object; piece and meat and piece of meat and ass and piece of ass and hot number <all nonformal>; sex queen, sex goddess; stud <nonformal>

5 sexual desire, sensuous or carnal desire, bodily appetite, **biological urge,** venereal appetite or desire, sexual longing, **lust,** desire, lusts or desires of the flesh, itch, lech <nonformal>; **erection,** penile erection, hard-on <nonformal>; **passion,** carnal or sexual passion, fleshly lust, prurience or pruriency, concupiscence, hot blood, aphrodisia, the hots and hot pants and hot rocks and hot nuts <all nonformal>; lustfulness, goatishness, horniness, libidinousness; lasciviousness 665.5; **eroticism,** erotism, indecency 666; erotomania, eromania, hysteria libidinosa <L>; nymphomania, andromania, furor uterinus <L>; satyrism, satyriasis, gynecomania; infantile sexuality, polymorphous perversity; **heat,** rut; frenzy or fury of lust; estrus, estrum, estral cycle

6 aphrodisiac, love potion, philter, love philter; cantharis, blister beetle, Spanish fly

7 copulation, sex act, having sex, having intercourse, le sport <Fr>, "making the beast with two backs"—Shakespeare, coupling, mating, coition, **coitus,** pareunia, venery, copula <law>, **sex, intercourse, sexual intercourse,** cohabitation, commerce, sexual commerce, congress, sexual congress, sexual union, sexual relations, relations, marital relations, marriage act, act of love, sleeping together or with; screwing and balling and nookie and diddling and making it with <all nonformal>; meat and ass <both nonformal>, intimacy, connection, carnal knowledge, aphrodisia; foreplay; **oral sex,** oral-genital stimulation, fellatio, fellation, blow job <nonformal>, cunnilingus; **anal sex,** anal intercourse, sodomy, buggery <nonformal>; **orgasm,** climax, sexual climax; unlawful sexual intercourse, adultery, fornication 665.7; coitus interruptus, onanism; group sex, group grope <nonformal>; serial sex, gang bang <nonformal>; spouse swapping, wife swapping, husband swapping; casual sex, one-night stand or quickie; phone sex; safe sex; sex shop; **lovemaking** 562; **procreation** 78; germ cell, sperm, ovum 305.12

8 masturbation, autoeroticism, self-abuse,

onanism, manipulation, playing with oneself, jacking off *and* pulling off *and* hand job <all nonformal>; sexual fantasy; wet dream

9 **sexlessness**, asexuality, neuterness; **impotence** 19; eunuch, *castrato* <Ital>, spado, gelding; steer

10 **sexual preference; sexual orientation;** sexual normality; **heterosexuality; homosexuality,** homosexualism, homosex, homoeroticism, homophilia, *l'amour bleu* <Fr>, the love that dare not speak its name, sexual inversion; autoeroticism; **bisexuality**, bisexualism, ambisexuality, ambisextrousness, amphierotism, swinging both ways <nonformal>; **lesbianism**, sapphism, tribadism *or* tribady; **sexual prejudice**, sexism, genderism, phallicism, heterosexism, homosexism

11 **perversion**, sexual deviation, sexual deviance, sexual perversion, sexual abnormality; sexual pathology; psychosexual disorder; sexual psychopathy, *psychopathia sexualis* <L>; paraphilia; zoophilia, zooerastia, bestiality; pedophilia; algolagnia, algolagny, **sadomasochism;** active algolagnia, **sadism;** passive algolagnia, **masochism;** fetishism; narcissism; pederasty, pedophilia; exhibitionism; necrophilia; coprophilia; scotophilia, voyeurism; transvestitism, cross-dressing; **incest**, incestuousness, **sex crime; sexual abuse,** carnal abuse, molestation

12 **intersexuality**, intersexualism, epicenism, epicenity; hermaphroditism, pseudohermaphroditism; androgynism, androgyny, gynandry, gynandrism; transsexuality, transsexualism

13 **heterosexual, straight** <nonformal>, breeder <nonformal>

14 **homosexual**, gay person, homosexualist, homophile, invert; catamite, *mignon* <Fr>, Ganymede, chicken *and* punk *and* gunsel <all nonformal>; **bisexual**, bi-guy <nonformal>; **lesbian**, sapphist, tribade, fricatrice <old>

15 <nonformal terms for male homosexuals> homo, queer, faggot, fag, fruit , flit, fairy, pansy, nance, auntie, queen, drag queen, closet queen, fruitcake, poof *and* poofter *and* poove <all Brit>; <nonformal terms for female homosexuals> dyke, bull dyke, butchfemme, boondagger, diesel-dyke, lesbo, lez

16 sexual pervert; **pervert, deviant,** deviate, sex *or* sexual pervert, sex fiend, sex criminal, sexual psychopath; sodomist, sodomite, sob <Brit nonformal>, bug-

ger; pederast; paraphiliac; zoophiliac; pedophiliac; sadist; masochist; sadomasochist, algolagniac; fetishist; transvestite *or* TV, cross-dresser; narcissist; exhibitionist; necrophiliac; coprophiliac; scotophiliac, voyeur; erotomaniac, nymphomaniac, satyr; rapist 665.12

17 **intersex**, sex-intergrade, epicene; hermaphrodite, pseudohermaphrodite; androgyne, gynandroid; transsexual

18 **sexology**, sexologist; sexual counselor; sexual surrogate; sexual customs *or* mores *or* practices; sexual morality; new morality, sexual revolution; sexual freedom, free love; trial marriage

VERBS 19 sex, sexualize; genderize

20 lust, **lust after**, itch for, have a lech *and* have hot pants for <both nonformal>, **desire; be in heat** *or* **rut**, rut, come in; get physical <nonformal>; get an erection, get a hard-on <nonformal>, tumesce

21 **copulate**, couple, **mate**, unite in sexual intercourse, **have sexual relations, have sex,** make out <nonformal>, perform the act of love *or* marriage act, come together, cohabit, shack up <nonformal>, be intimate; sleep with, lie with, go to bed with; fuck *and* screw *and* lay *and* ball *and* frig *and* diddle *and* **make it with** <all nonformal>, go all the way, go to bed with, lie together; cover, mount, serve *or* service <of animals>; commit adultery, fornicate 665.19; **make love**

22 **masturbate**, play with *or* abuse oneself, jack off *and* whack off <both nonformal>; fellate, suck *and* suck off <nonformal>; sodomize, bugger *and* ream <both nonformal>

23 **climax, come**, achieve satisfaction, achieve *or* reach orgasm; **ejaculate**, get off <nonformal>

ADJS 24 **sexual**, sex, sexlike, gamic, coital, libidinal; **erotic**, sexy, amorous; nuptial; venereal; **carnal, sensual** 663.5, voluptuous, fleshly; desirable, baddable; **sexy;** erogenous, erogenic, erotogenic; sexed, oversexed, hypersexual, undersexed; procreative 78.15; potent 76.12

25 **aphrodisiac**, aphroditous, **arousing**, stimulating, eroticizing, venereal

26 **lustful, prurient, hot**, steamy, sexy, concupiscent, lickerish, libidinous, **salacious** 666.9, **passionate**, hot-blooded, itching, **horny** *and* hot to trot *and* sexed-up <all nonformal>, randy, goatish; sex-starved, unsatisfied; lascivious 665.29; **orgasmic**, orgastic, **ejaculatory**

27 **in heat, burning, hot; in rut**, rutting,

rutty, ruttish; in must, must, musty; es-
trous, estral, estrual

28 **unsexual,** unsexed; **sexless,** asexual, **neuter,** neutral; castrated, emasculated,
eunuchized; **cold, frigid; impotent;** frustrated

29 **homosexual,** homoerotic, gay, queer *and*
limp-wristed *and* faggoty <all nonfor-
mal>; **bisexual,** bisexed, ambisexual,
ambisextrous, amphierotic, AC-DC
<nonformal>, autoerotic; lesbian, sap-
phic, tribadistic; mannish 76.13, butch
and dykey <both nonformal>; effeminate 77.14; transvestite; **perverted,**
deviant

30 hermaphrodite, hermaphroditic, pseudohermaphrodite, pseudohermaphroditic,
epicene, monoclinous; androgynous, androgynal, gynandrous, gynandrian

76 MASCULINITY

NOUNS 1 **masculinity,** masculineness, maleness; **manliness,** manlihood, **manhood,**
manfulness, manlikeness; mannishness;
gentlemanliness, gentlemanlikeness

2 **male sex, male sexuality, virility,** virile-
ness, potence *or* **potency,** sexual power,
manly vigor, **machismo;** ultramascu-
linity; phallicism; male superiority, patriarchy

3 **mankind, man, men, manhood,** menfolk
or menfolks <nonformal>, the sword
side

4 **male,** male being, masculine; he, him,
his; **man,** male person, *homme* <Fr>,
hombre <Sp>; **gentleman,** gent <nonfor-
mal>

5 <nonformal terms> **guy,** fellow, feller,
lad, chap, guy, cat, bird, duck, stud, joker,
jasper, bugger, bastard, bloke *and* cove
and johnny *and* bod <all Brit nonfor-
mal>, customer, party, character, warm,
body, bean, cookie, dude, gent, Joe

6 **real man, he-man,** *and* two-fisted man
<both nonformal>, hunk *and* jockstrap
and jock <all nonformal>, man with hair
on his chest; caveman *and* bucko <both
nonformal>

7 <forms of address> **Mister, Mr,** Messrs
<pl>, Master; **sir;** *monsieur, M* <both
Fr>, *messieurs, MM* <both Fr pl>; *signor,
signore* <both Ital>, *signorino* <Ital>,
señor, Sr <both Sp>, *don* <Sp>, *senhor*
<Pg>; *Herr* <Ger>; *mein Herr* <Ger>;
mijnheer <Dutch>, *sahib* <Hind>,
bwana <Swah>

8 <male animals> cock, rooster, chanticleer; cockerel; drake; gander; peacock;

tom turkey, tom, turkey-cock, bubbly-
jock <Scots>, gobbler, turkey gobbler;
dog; boar; stag, hart, buck; stallion,
studhorse, stud, top horse <nonformal>,
entire horse, entire; tomcat, tom; he-goat,
billy goat, billy; ram, tup <Brit>;
wether; bull, bullock, top cow <non-
formal>; steer, stot <Brit nonfor-
mal>

9 <mannish female> **amazon,** virago, androgyne; lesbian, butch *and* dyke <both
nonformal>; **tomboy,** hoyden, romp
VERBS 10 masculinize, virilize
ADJS 11 **masculine, male,** bull, he—; **manly,
manlike, mannish,** manful, andric; uneffeminate; **gentlemanly,** gentlemanlike

12 **virile, potent,** viripotent; ultramasculine,
macho, he-mannish *and* hunky <both
nonformal>, two-fisted <nonformal>,
broad-shouldered, hairy-chested

13 **mannish, mannified; unwomanly, unfeminine,** uneffeminate, viraginous;
tomboyish, hoyden, rompish

77 FEMININITY

NOUNS 1 **femininity,** feminality, feminacy,
feminineness, femaleness; **womanliness,**
womanlikeness, womanishness, **womanhood,** womanity, muliebrity; girlishness,
little-girlishness; maidenhood, maidenliness; **ladylikeness,** gentlewomanliness;
matronliness, matronage, matronhood,
matronship; the eternal feminine, "*das
Ewig-Weibliche*" <Ger>—Goethe

2 **effeminacy, unmanliness,** effeminate-
ness, epicenity, epicenism,
womanishness, muliebrity, **sissiness**
<nonformal>, prissiness <nonformal>;
androgyny; feminism

3 **womankind, woman, women,** femininity,
womanhood, womenfolk *or* womenfolks
<nonformal>, the distaff side; **the female
sex;** the second sex, **the fair sex,** the gentle sex, the softer sex, **the weaker sex,** the
weaker vessel

4 **female,** female being; she, her

5 **woman,** Eve, daughter of Eve, Adam's
rib, *femme* <Fr>, distaff <old>, weaker
vessel; frow, *Frau* <Ger>, *vrouw*
<Dutch>, *donna* <Ital>, wahine
<Hawaii>; **lady,** milady, gentlewoman,
domina <L>; feme sole *and* feme covert
<both law>; married woman, wife; **ma-
tron,** dame, **dowager;** squaw; unmarried
woman, bachelor girl <nonformal>, single woman, spinster; lass, girl 302.6;
career woman, businesswoman; super-
woman

6 <nonformal terms> **gal, dame,** hen, biddy, skirt, jane, broad, doll, babe, chick, wench, bird <Brit>, tomato, bitch, minx, momma, mouse, sister, squaw, toots

7 "the female of the human species, and not a different kind of animal"—G B Shaw, "O fairest of creation! last and best of all God's works"—Milton, "a temple sacred by birth, and built by hands divine"—Dryden, "one of Nature's agreeable blunders"—Hannah Cowley

8 <forms of address> **Ms;** Mistress <old>, **Mrs; madam** or ma'am; madame, Mme <both Fr>; mesdames, Mmes <both Fr pl>; Frau <Ger>, vrouw <Dutch>, signora <Ital>, señora <Sp>, senhora <Pg>, mem-sahib <Hind>; dame <old>, donna <Ital>, doña <Sp>, dona <Pg>, lady; **Miss;** mademoiselle, Mlle <both Fr>; Fräulein <Ger>; signorina <Ital>, señorita <Sp>, senhorita <Pg>

9 <female animals> hen, Partlet, biddy; guinea hen; peahen; bitch, slut, gyp; sow; ewe, ewe lamb; she-goat, nanny goat or nanny; doe, hind, roe; jenny; mare, brood mare; filly; cow, bossy; heifer; vixen; tigress; lioness; she-bear, she-lion, etc

10 <effeminate male> **mollycoddle,** effeminate; **mother's darling, mother's boy, mama's boy,** Lord Fauntleroy, sissy, Percy, goody-goody; **pantywaist,** nancy or nance, chicken, lily; cream puff, weak sister, milksop; old woman

11 feminization, womanization, effemination, effeminization, sissification <nonformal>

VERBS 12 feminize; womanize, demasculinize, effeminize, effeminatize, effeminate, soften, sissify <nonformal>; emasculate, castrate, geld

ADJS 13 **feminine, female;** gynic, gynecic, gynecoid; muliebral, distaff, **womanly, womanish, womanlike,** petticoat; **ladylike,** gentlewomanlike, gentlewomanly; **matronly,** matronal, matronlike; **girlish,** little-girlish, kittenish; maidenly 301.11

14 **effeminate, womanish,** fem <nonformal>, old-womanish, **unmanly,** muliebrous, soft, chicken, prissy, **sissified,** sissy, **sissyish**

78 REPRODUCTION, PROCREATION

NOUNS 1 **reproduction, making, re-creation,** remaking, refashioning, reshaping, redoing, re-formation, reworking, rejiggering <nonformal>; **reconstruction,** rebuilding, redesign, restructuring, perestroika <Russ>; **revision;** reedition, reissue, reprinting, reestablishment, **reorganization,** reinstitution, reconstitution; redevelopment; **rebirth,** renascence, resurrection, revival; regeneration, regenesis, palingenesis; **duplication** 873, **imitation** 336, **copy** 784, **repetition** 848; **restoration** 396, renovation; producing or making or creating anew or over or again or once more; **birth rate,** fertility rate; baby boom or boomlet <nonformal>; baby bust <nonformal>

2 **procreation, reproduction, generation, begetting, breeding,** engenderment; **propagation, multiplication,** proliferation; linebreeding; inbreeding, endogamy; outbreeding, xenogamy; dissogeny; crossbreeding 796.4

3 **fertilization,** fecundation; **impregnation,** insemination, begetting, getting with child, knocking up <nonformal>, mating, servicing; **pollination,** pollinization; cross-fertilization, cross-pollination; self-fertilization, heterogamy, orthogamy; isogamy, artificial insemination; conjugation, zygosis

4 **conception,** conceiving, inception of pregnancy; superfetation, superimpregnation

5 **pregnancy, gestation, incubation,** parturiency, gravidness or gravidity, heaviness, greatness, bigness, the family way <nonformal>; brooding, sitting, covering

6 **birth, generation, genesis; development;** procreation; abiogenesis, archigenesis, biogenesis, blastogenesis, digenesis, dysmerogenesis, epigenesis, eumerogenesis, heterogenesis, histogenesis, homogenesis, isogenesis, merogenesis, metagenesis, monogenesis, oögenesis, orthogenesis, pangenesis, parthenogenesis, phytogenesis, sporogenesis, xenogenesis; spontaneous generation

VERBS 7 **reproduce, remake,** make or do over, **re-create,** regenerate, resurrect, revive, re-form, refashion, **reshape,** remould, recast, rework, rejigger <nonformal>, redo, **reconstruct,** rebuild, redesign, restructure, **revise;** reprint, reissue; reestablish, reinstitute, reconstitute, refound, **reorganize; redevelop;** duplicate 873.3, copy 336.5, **repeat** 848.7, **restore** 396.11, **renovate**

8 **procreate, generate, breed, beget,** get, **engender; propagate, multiply;** proliferate; mother; father, sire; reproduce in kind,

reproduce after one's kind, "multiply and replenish the earth"—Bible; breed true; inbreed, breed in and in; outbreed; cross-pollinate, crossbreed; linebreed; copulate, make love

9 **lay** <eggs>, deposit, drop, spawn

10 **fertilize,** fructify, fecundate, fecundify; **impregnate, inseminate,** spermatize, knock up <nonformal>, **get with child** or **young; pollinate** or pollinize, pollen; cross-fertilize, cross-pollinate or cross-pollinize

11 **conceive,** get in the family way <nonformal>; superfetate

12 **be pregnant,** be gravid, be great with child, **be with child** or **young;** be in the family way and have a bun in the oven and be expecting and anticipate a blessed event <all nonformal>, be infanticipating and be knocked up <both nonformal>, be blessed-eventing <nonformal>; gestate, breed, carry, carry young; **incubate, hatch; brood,** sit, set, cover

13 **give birth** 1.3

ADJS 14 **reproductive, re-creative, reconstructive,** re-formative; renascent, regenerative, resurgent, reappearing; reorganizational; revisional; **restorative** 396.22; Hydraheaded, phoenixlike

15 **reproductive, procreative,** procreant, **propagative,** life-giving; spermatic, spermatozoic, seminal, germinal, fertilizing, fecundative; multiparous

16 **genetic, generative,** genial, gametic; genital, genitive; abiogenetic, biogenetic, blastogenetic, digenetic, dysmerogenetic, epigenetic, eumerogenetic, heterogenetic, histogenetic, homogenetic, isogenetic, merogenetic, metagenetic, monogenetic, oögenetic, orthogenetic, pangenetic, parthenogenetic, phytogenetic, sporogenous, xenogenetic

17 **bred, impregnated,** inseminated; inbred, endogamic, endogamous; outbred, exogamic, exogamous; crossbred; linebred

18 **pregnant,** enceinte <Fr>, preggers and knocked-up <both nonformal>, **with child** or **young, in the family way** <nonformal>, gestating, breeding, teeming, parturient; heavy with child or young, great or big with child or young, wearing her apron high, in a delicate condition, gravid, heavy, great, big-laden; carrying, carrying a fetus or an embryo; **expecting** <nonformal>, anticipating and anticipating a blessed event <both nonformal>, infanticipating <nonformal>; superfetate, superimpregnated

79 CLEANNESS

NOUNS 1 **cleanness, cleanliness; purity,** squeaky-cleanness <nonformal>, pureness; **immaculateness,** immaculacy; **spotlessness,** unspottedness, stainlessness, whiteness; freshness; fastidiousness, daintiness, cleanly habits; asepsis, sterility, hospital cleanliness; tidiness 806.3

2 **cleansing, cleaning,** cleaning up, detersion <old>; **purge,** cleanout, cleaning out, purging, purgation, catharsis, abstersion <old>; **purification,** purifying, lustration; expurgation, bowdlerization

3 **sanitation, hygiene,** hygenics; **disinfection, decontamination, sterilization,** antisepsis; pasteurization, flash pasteurization; fumigation, disinfestation, delousing

4 **refinement, clarification, purification,** depuration; **straining,** colature; elution, elutriation; extraction 192.8; **filtering,** filtration; **percolation,** leaching, edulcoration <old>, lixiviation; **sifting,** separation, **screening,** sieving, bolting, riddling, winnowing; essentialization; sublimation; **distillation,** destructive distillation, spiritualization <old>

5 **washing, ablution;** lavation, laving, lavage; lavabo; **wash, washup;** soaping, lathering; rinse, rinsing; sponge, sponging; shampoo; washout, elution, elutriation; irrigation, flush, flushing, flushing out; douche, douching; enema; **scrub,** scrubbing, swabbing, mopping, scouring; **cleaning up** or **out,** washing up, scrubbing up or out, mopping up or down, wiping up or down

6 **laundering, laundry,** tubbing; **wash, washing;** washday

7 **bathing,** balneation

8 **bath,** bathe <Brit>, tub <nonformal>; **shower,** shower bath, needle bath, hot or cold shower; douche; sponge bath, sponge; hip bath, sitz bath; sweat bath, Turkish bath, hummum, Russian bath, Swedish bath, Finnish bath, sauna or sauna bath, Japanese bath, hot tub, whirlpool bath, Jacuzzi <trademark>, plunge bath

9 **dip, bath;** acid bath, mercury bath, fixing bath; sheepdip

10 **bathing place, bath, baths,** public baths, **bathhouse,** bagnio <old>, sauna; balneum and balneae and thermae <all L>; mikvah <Judaism>; watering place, spa; lavatory, washroom, bathroom; steam room, sweat room, sudatorium,

sudarium, caldarium, tepidarium; rest room

11 **washery, laundry;** washhouse, washshed; **coin laundry, Laundromat** <trademark>, **launderette,** coin-operated laundry, laundrette <Brit>, washateria; automatic laundry; hand laundry; car wash

12 **washbasin, washbowl,** washdish, basin; **lavatory, washstand; bathtub,** tub, bath; bidet; **shower,** showers, shower room, shower bath, shower stall, shower head, shower curtain; **sink,** kitchen sink; dishwasher, automatic dishwasher; washing machine; washer; piscina, lavabo, ewer, aquamanile; washtub, washpot, washing pot, wash boiler, dishpan; finger bowl; wash barrel

13 **refinery; refiner,** purifier, clarifier; **filter; strainer,** colander; **percolator,** lixiviator; **sifter, sieve, screen,** riddle, cribble; winnow, winnower, winnowing machine, winnowing basket or fan; cradle, rocker

14 **cleaner,** cleaner-up, cleaner-off, cleanerout; **janitor,** janitress, custodian; cleaning woman or lady or man, daily or daily woman and charwoman or char <all Brit>

15 **washer,** launderer; **laundress,** laundrywoman, **washerwoman,** washwoman, washerwife <Scots>; **laundryman,** washerman, washman; dry cleaner; **dishwasher,** pot-walloper and pearl-diver <both nonformal>, scullion, scullery maid; dishwiper

16 **sweeper; street sweeper,** crossing sweeper, whitewing, cleanser or scavenger <both Brit>; **chimney sweep** or sweeper, sweep, flue cleaner

17 **cleanser, cleaner;** cleaning agent; lotion, cream; cold cream, cleansing cream, **soap, detergent,** synthetic detergent, abstergent; shampoo; rinse; **solvent;** cleaning solvent; water softener; purifier, depurant; mouthwash, wash; dentifrice, **toothpaste, tooth powder;** pumice stone, holystone, scouring powder; purge, purgative, cathartic, enema, diuretic, emetic, nauseant; **cleaning device**

VERBS 18 **clean, cleanse, purge,** deterge, depurate; **purify,** lustrate; sweeten, **freshen;** whiten, bleach; clean up or out, clear out, sweep out, clean up after; houseclean, clean house, spring-clean; spruce, **tidy** 807.12; scavenge; **wipe,** wipe up or out, wipe off; dust, dust off; steam-clean, **dry-clean;** expurgate, bowdlerize

19 **wash, bathe,** bath <Brit>, shower, lave;

launder, tub; wash up or out or away; **rinse,** rinse out, flush, flush out, irrigate, sluice, sluice out; ritually immerse, baptize, *toivel* <Yiddish>; sponge, sponge down or off; **scrub,** scrub up or out, **swab, mop,** mop up; **scour,** holystone; hose out or down; rinse off or out; soak out or away; soap, lather; shampoo; syringe, douche; gargle

20 **groom,** dress, fettle <Brit nonformal>, **brush up; preen,** plume, titivate; manicure

21 **comb,** curry, card, hackle or hatchel, heckle <nonformal>, rake

22 **refine, clarify,** clear, purify, rectify, depurate, decrassify; try; **strain;** elute, elutriate; **extract** 192.10; **filter,** filtrate; **percolate,** leach, lixiviate, edulcorate <old>; **sift,** separate, sieve, **screen,** bolt, winnow; sublimate, sublime; **distill,** spiritualize <old>, essentialize

23 **sweep,** sweep up or out, **brush,** brush off, whisk, broom; vacuum <nonformal>, vacuum-clean

24 **sanitize,** sanitate, hygienize; **disinfect, decontaminate, sterilize,** antisepticize, radiosterilize; autoclave, boil; pasteurize, flash-pasteurize; disinfest, fumigate, delouse; chlorinate

ADJS 25 **clean, pure; immaculate, spotless,** stainless, white, fair, dirt-free, soil-free; **unsoiled, unsullied,** unmuddied, unsmirched, unbesmirched, unblotted, unsmudged, unstained, untarnished, **unspotted,** unblemished; smutless, smutfree; bleached, whitened; bright, shiny 1024.33; **unpolluted,** nonpolluted, untainted, unadulterated, **undefiled;** kosher, *tahar* <Heb>, ritually pure or clean; **sqeaky-clean** and clean as a whistle or a new penny or a hound's tooth <all nonformal>; **sweet, fresh, cleanly,** fastidious, dainty, of cleanly habits; well-washed, well-scrubbed, tubbed <nonformal>

26 **cleaned, cleansed,** cleaned up; purged, purified; expurgated, bowdlerized; refined; spruce, spick and span, **tidy** 806.8

27 **sanitary, hygienic, prophylactic; sterile,** aseptic, antiseptic, **uninfected;** disinfected, decontaminated, sterilized; autoclaved, boiled; pasteurized

28 **cleansing, cleaning;** detergent, detersive, abstergent, abstersive, depurative; **purifying,** purificatory, lustral; expurgatory; purgative, purging, cathartic, diuretic, emetic

ADVS 29 **cleanly,** clean; **purely, immaculately, spotlessly**

80 UNCLEANNESS

NOUNS **1 uncleanness,** immundity; **impurity,** unpureness; **dirtiness,** grubbiness, dinginess, griminess, messiness *and* grunginess *and* scuzziness <all nonformal>, scruffiness, slovenliness, sluttishness, untidiness 809.6; miriness, muddiness 1060.4; uncleanliness

 2 filthiness, foulness, vileness, scumminess <nonformal>, feculence, shittiness <nonformal>, muckiness, ordurousness, nastiness, grossness *and* yuckiness *and* ickiness <all nonformal>; scurfiness, scabbiness; rottenness, putridness 393.7; rankness, fetidness 71.2; odiousness, repulsiveness 98.2; nauseousness, disgustingness 64.3; hoggishness, piggishness, swinishness, beastliness

 3 squalor, squalidness, squalidity, **sordidness;** slumminess <nonformal>

 4 defilement, befoulment, dirtying, soiling, besmirchment; **pollution, contamination, infection;** abomination; ritual uncleanness *or* impurity *or* contamination

 5 soil, soilure, soilage, smut; **smirch, smudge,** smutch, smear, **spot,** blot, blotch, **stain** 1003.3

 6 dirt, grime; dust; soot, smut; **mud** 1060.8

 7 filth, muck, slime, mess, sordes, foul matter; ordure, **excrement** 12.3; mucus, snot <nonformal>; scurf, furfur, dandruff; scuzz *and* mung <both nonformal>; putrid matter, pus, corruption, gangrene, decay, carrion, **rot** 393.7; **obscenity,** smut <nonformal> 666.4

 8 slime, slop, scum, sludge, slush; glop *and* gunk <both nonformal>, **muck, mire,** ooze

 9 offal, slough, **offscourings,** scurf, scum, riffraff, scum of the earth; **carrion; garbage, swill,** slop, slops; dishwater, ditchwater, bilgewater, bilge; **sewage,** sewerage; **waste, refuse** 391.4

 10 dunghill, manure pile, midden, mixen <Brit nonformal>, colluvies; compost heap; kitchen midden, refuse heap

 11 sty, pigsty, pigpen; **stable,** Augean stables; dump *and* hole *and* shithole <all nonformal>, rathole; tenement; warren, **slum,** rookery; the inner city, the ghetto, the slums; plague spot, pesthole; hovel

 12 <receptacle of filth> **sink;** sump, **cesspool,** cesspit, septic tank; catchbasin; bilge *or* bilges; **sewer,** drain, *cloaca* and *cloaca maxima* <both L>; sewage farm, purification plant; **dump,** garbage dump, dumpsite, sanitary landfill, landfill; **swamp,** bog, mire, quagmire, marsh

 13 pig, swine, hog, slut, sloven, slattern 809.7; *Struwwelpeter* <Ger>

VERBS **14** wallow in the mire, live like a pig

 15 dirty, dirty up, dirt <old>, grime, **begrime;** muck, muck up <nonformal>; **muddy,** bemud <old>; mire, bemire; slime; dust; soot, smoke, besmoke

 16 soil, besoil; black, **blacken; smirch,** besmirch, sully, slubber <Brit nonformal>, smutch *or* smouch, besmutch, smut, **smudge, smear,** besmear, daub, bedaub; **spot, stain** 1003.6; get one's hands dirty, dirty *or* soil one's hands

 17 defile, foul, befoul; sully; foul one's own nest, shit where one eats <nonformal>, nasty *or* benasty <both nonformal>, mess *and* mess up <both nonformal>; **pollute, corrupt, contaminate, infect; taint,** tarnish

 18 spatter, splatter, splash, **bespatter,** dabble, bedabble, spot, splotch

 19 draggle, bedraggle, **drabble,** bedrabble, daggle <old>, drabble in the mud

ADJS **20 unclean, unwashed,** unbathed, unscrubbed, unscoured, unswept, unwiped; **impure,** unpure; **polluted, contaminated, infected, corrupted;** ritually unclean *or* impure *or* contaminated, *tref* <Yiddish>, *terefah* <Heb>, nonkosher; not to be handled without gloves; **uncleanly**

 21 soiled, sullied, dirtied, smirched, besmirched, smudged, spotted, **tarnished,** tainted, **stained; defiled,** fouled, **befouled;** draggled, drabbled, bedraggled

 22 dirty, grimy, grubby, grungy <nonformal>, smirchy, dingy, messy <nonformal>; scruffy, slovenly, untidy 809.15; miry, **muddy** 1060.14; **dusty;** smutty, smutchy, smudgy; sooty, smoky; snuffy

 23 filthy, foul, vile, mucky, **nasty,** icky *and* yecchy *and* yucky *and* gross *and* grungy *and* scuzzy <all nonformal>; malodorous, mephitic, rank, **fetid** 71.5; **putrid, rotten;** pollutive; nauseating, disgusting; **odious, repulsive** 98.18; **slimy,** scummy <nonformal>; barfy *and* vomity *and* puky <all nonformal>; sloppy, sludgy; gloppy *and* gunky <both nonformal>, scurfy, scabby; wormy, maggoty, flyblown; feculent, ordurous, crappy *and* shitty <both nonformal>, excremental, excrementitious, fecal 12.20

 24 hoggish, piggish, swinish, beastly

 25 squalid, sordid, wretched, shabby; slumlike, slummy

ADVS **26 uncleanly, impurely,** unpurely; **dirtily,** grimily; **filthily, foully,** nastily, vilely

81 HEALTHFULNESS

NOUNS **1 healthfulness, healthiness, sa-
lubrity,** salubriousness, salutariness,
wholesomeness, beneficialness, goodness

2 hygiene, hygienics; sanitation 79.3; public health, epidemiology; health physics;
preventive medicine, prophylaxis, preventive dentistry, prophylactodontia;
prophylactic psychology, mental hygiene; **fitness and exercise** 84

3 hygienist, hygeist, sanitarian; public
health doctor *or* physician, epidemiolo-
gist; health physicist; preventive dentist,
prophylactodontist; dental hygienist

VERBS **4 make for health,** conduce to health,
be good for, agree with

ADJS **5 healthful, healthy, salubrious, salutary, wholesome,** health-preserving,
health-enhancing, life-promoting, **beneficial,** benign, good, **good for; hygienic,
hygienical,** hygeian, sanitary; constitutional, for one's health; conditioning;
bracing, refreshing, invigorating, tonic

82 UNHEALTHFULNESS

NOUNS **1 unhealthfulness, unhealthiness,
insalubrity,** insalubriousness, unsalutari-
ness, **unwholesomeness,** badness; noxiousness, noisomeness, injuriousness,
harmfulness 999.5; pathenogenicity;
health hazard, threat *or* danger *or* menace to health; contamination, pollution,
environmental pollution, air *or* water *or*
noise pollution

2 innutritiousness, indigestibility

**3 poisonousness, toxicity, venomousness;
virulence** *or* virulency, malignancy, noxiousness, destructiveness, deadliness;
infectiousness, infectivity, contagiousness, communicability; poison, venom
1000.3

VERBS **4 disagree with,** not be good for,
sicken

ADJS **5 unhealthful, unhealthy, insalubrious,
unsalutary, unwholesome,** peccant, bad,
bad for; noxious, noisome, injurious,
baneful, harmful 999.12; **polluted,** contaminated, tainted, foul, septic; unhy-
gienic, unsanitary, insanitary; morbific,
pathogenic, pestiferous

6 innutritious, indigestible, unassimilable

7 poisonous, toxic, toxicant; **venomous,** envenomed, venenate, venenous; veneniferous, toxiferous; pollutive; **virulent, noxious, malignant,** malign, destructive,
deadly; pestiferous, pestilential; mephitic, miasmal, miasmic, miasmatic;

infectious, infective, contagious, communicable, catching

83 HEALTH

NOUNS **1 health, well-being; fitness,** health
and fitness, physical fitness 84; bloom,
flush, glow, rosiness; mental health, emotional health; physical condition; Hygeia

2 healthiness, healthfulness, soundness,
wholesomeness; healthy body, good *or*
healthy constitution; **good health,** good
state of health, "good estate of body"—
Bible, *"mens sana in corpore sano"*—
Juvenal <L, a sound mind in a sound
body>; **robust health,** rugged health,
rude health, glowing health, picture of
health, "health that snuffs the morning
air"—Grainger; **fine fettle,** fine whack
<nonformal>, fine *or* high feather
<nonformal>, **good shape,** good trim,
fine shape, top shape <nonformal>, good
condition, mint condition; eupepsia,
good digestion; clean bill of health

3 haleness, heartiness, robustness, vigorousness, ruggedness, **vitality,** lustiness,
hardiness, strength, vigor; longevity

4 immunity, resistance, nonproneness *or*
nonsusceptibility to disease; **immunization;** antibody, antigen 86.27

5 health *or* **medical care, health protection,**
health *or* **medical management, health
maintenance, medical care** 91.1; **wellness,** wellness program, disease prevention, preventive medicine; health
awareness program; health policy,
health-care policy; **health plan, health** *or*
medical insurance, health service, health-
care delivery service *or* plan, health
maintenance organization *or* HMO, Medicare, Medicaid; National Health Service
or NHS *or* National Health <all Brit>;
socialized medicine; health department,
health commissioner; health club

VERBS **6 enjoy good health,** have a clean bill
of health, be in the pink; be in the best of
health; **feel good,** feel fine, feel fit, feel like
a million dollars *or* like a million
<nonformal>, never feel better; feel
one's oats, be full of pep; burst with
health, bloom, glow, flourish; keep fit,
stay in shape; wear well, stay young

7 get well, recover 396.20, mend, be oneself
again, feel like a new person, get back on
one's feet, get over it; recuperate 396.19

ADJS **8 healthy, healthful,** enjoying health,
fine, in health, in shape, in condition, **fit,**
fit and fine; **in good health,** in the pink of
condition, in mint condition, in good

case, **in good** or **fine shape, in fine fettle**, bursting with health, full of life and vigor, feeling one's oats; eupeptic

9 <nonformal terms> **in the pink,** in fine whack, in fine or high feather, chipper, **fit as a fiddle;** alive and kicking, bright-eyed and bushy-tailed; full of beans or of piss and vinegar

10 **well, unailing, unsick, unsickly,** unfrail; all right, doing nicely, up and about, sitting up and taking nourishment, alive and well

11 **sound,** whole, wholesome; unimpaired 1001.8; sound of mind and body, sound in wind and limb, sound as a dollar <nonformal>

12 **hale, hearty,** hale and hearty, **robust,** robustious, robustuous, vital, **vigorous, strong,** strong as a horse or an ox, bionic <nonformal>, stalwart, stout, sturdy, **rugged,** rude, hardy, lusty, bouncing, well-knit, flush <old>; **fit,** in condition or shape

13 **fresh,** green, youthful, **blooming;** flush, flushed, **rosy,** rosy-cheeked, apple-cheeked, ruddy, pink, pink-cheeked; fresh-faced, fresh as a daisy or rose, fresh as April

14 **immune, resistant,** nonprone or non-susceptible to disease; health-conscious, health-protecting; immune response

84 FITNESS, EXERCISE

NOUNS 1 **fitness, physical fitness, physical conditioning, condition, shape,** trim, tone, fettle, aerobic fitness, anaerobic fitness, cardiovascular fitness, cardiorespiratory fitness; **gymnasium, gym** <nonformal>, **fitness center, health club,** health spa, work-out room, weight room, exercise track or trail, trim trail <Brit>, *parcourse* or *parcours* <both Fr>; **weight, barbell,** dumbbell, exercise machine, Atra <trademark>, Nautilus <trademark>, bench, exercise bike, rowing machine, stair-climbing machine, Indian club, wand; whirlpool bath, Jacuzzi <trademark>, hot tub, spa

2 **exercise,** motion, movement, maneuver; **program,** routine, drill, work-out; **exercise systems; warm-up, stretching,** warm-down; **calisthenics** <see list>, free exercise, setting-up exercise or set-ups, physical jerks <Brit>, daily dozen <nonformal>, constitutional; **parcourse exercise** <see list>; **gymnastic exercise, gymnastics;** slimnastics; **isometrics,** isometric or no-movement exercise; **violent** exercise, breather, wind sprint; **aerobic exercise, aerobics,** aerobic dancing or dance, dancercize or dancercizing, fitaerobics, jazz ballet or jazzercise and popmobility <all Brit>; **bodybuilding,** weightlifting, weight training, pumping iron <nonformal>, bench press, arm raise, curl, wrist curl; **running, jogging,** roadwork, distance running; obligate running; cross-training, interval training, *fartlek* <Swedish>; **walking,** fitness walking, healthwalking, aerobic walking, powerwalking, powerstriding; **swimming,** swimnastics, water exercise, aqua-robics or aquaerob or hydro-robics, aquadynamics; tub toner

3 **physical fitness test;** stress test, treadmill test; cardiovascular test

VERBS 4 **exercise, work out,** warm up, aerobicize, stretch, lift weights, pump iron <nonformal>, jog, run, bicycle, walk, fitness-walk, power-walk

5 **calisthenic exercises**

arm raise	rebounding
bench stepping	rope skipping
high jump	shuffle
hop and balance	side bend
jump and stretch	sit-up or trunk curl
jumping jack	sit-up and leg stretch
leg lift	squat thrust
place running	trunk twist
push-up	

6 **parcourse exercises**

Achilles stretch	knee lift
balance beam	leg-stretch
bench leg-raise	log hop
body-curl	push-up
chin-up	sit and reach
circle body	step-up
hand-walk	toe touch
hop-kick	vault-bar
jumping jack	

85 DISEASE

NOUNS 1 **disease** <see list>, **illness, sickness, malady, ailment, indisposition, disorder,** complaint, morbidity, *morbus* <L>, **affliction,** affection, distemper <old>, **infirmity; disability,** defect, handicap; deformity 265.3; **birth defect,** congenital defect; abnormality, condition, pathological condition; **signs, symptoms, pathology,** symptomatology, symptomology, syndrome; **sickishness,** malaise, seediness and rockiness and the pip and the crud and the creeping crud <all nonformal>; complication, secondary disease or condition; plant disease, blight 1000.2

2 fatal disease, deadly disease, terminal disease *or* illness, hopeless condition; **death** 307, clinical death, loss of vital signs; apparent death; **brain death,** local death, somatic death; sudden death, unexplained death; liver death; serum death; thymic death *or* mors thymica; cell death, molecular death; cot death *or* crib death *or* sudden infant death syndrome *or* SIDS

3 unhealthiness, healthlessness; **ill health,** poor health, delicate *or* shaky *or* frail *or* fragile health; **sickliness,** peakedness <nonformal>, **feebleness,** delicacy, weakliness, fragility, **frailty** 16.2; **infirmity, unsoundness,** debility, debilitation, enervation, exhaustion, decrepitude; wasting, languishing, languishment <old>, cachexia *or* cachexy; chronic ill health, invalidity, **invalidism;** unwholesomeness, morbidity, morbidness; hypochondria, hypochondriasis, valetudinarianism

4 infection, contagion, contamination, taint, virus; **contagiousness, infectiousness, communicability;** pestiferousness, epidemicity, inoculability; carrier, vector; **epidemiology**

5 epidemic, plague, pestilence, pest, pandemic, pandemia, scourge; white plague, tuberculosis; pesthole, plague spot

6 seizure, attack, access, visitation; arrest; blockage, stoppage, occlusion, thrombosis, thromboembolism; **stroke,** ictus, apoplexy; **spasm, throes, fit, paroxysm, convulsion,** eclampsia, frenzy; **epilepsy,** falling sickness; tonic spasm, tetany, lockjaw, trismus, tetanus; laryngospasm, laryngismus; clonic spasm, clonus; cramp; vaginismus

7 fever, feverishness, febrility, febricity, pyrexia; hyperpyrexia, hyperthermia; **heat, fire, fever heat;** flush, hectic flush; calenture; delirium 925.8

8 collapse, breakdown, crackup <nonformal>, **prostration,** exhaustion; nervous prostration *or* breakdown *or* exhaustion, neurasthenia; circulatory collapse

9 <disease symptoms> anemia; ankylosis; asphyxiation, anoxia, cyanosis; ataxia; bleeding, hemorrhage; colic; dizziness, vertigo; ague, chill, chills; hot flash, hot flush; dropsy, hydrops, edema; morning sickness; fainting; fatigue 21; fever; constipation; diarrhea, flux, dysentery; indigestion, upset stomach, dyspepsia; inflammation 85.9; necrosis; insomnia; itching, pruritus; jaundice, icterus; backache, lumbago; vomiting, nausea; paraly-

sis; skin eruption, rash; sore, abscess; hypertension, high blood pressure; hypotension, low blood pressure; tumor, growth; shock; convulsion, seizure, spasm; pain 26; fibrillation, tachycardia; shortness of breath, labored breathing, apnea, dyspnea, asthma; blennorhea; nasal discharge, rheum, coughing, sneezing; wasting, cachexia *or* cachexy, tabes, marasmus, emaciation, atrophy; sclerosis

10 inflammation, inflammatory disease, —itis; muscle *or* muscular disease *or* disorder, myopathy; collagen disease, connective-tissue disease

11 deficiency diseases <see list>, nutritional disease, vitamin-deficiency disease

12 genetic disease <see list>, gene disease, gene-transmitted disease, hereditary *or* congenital disease

13 infectious disease <see list>, infection

14 eye disease <see list>, ophthalmic disease, disease of the eye *or* of vision; cataract; conjunctivitis *or* pink eye; glaucoma; sty; eye *or* visual defect, defective vision 28

15 ear disease, otic disease *or* disorder; **deafness; earache,** otalgia; tympanitis; otosclerosis; **vertigo,** dizziness, loss of balance; Ménière's syndrome *or* disease *or* apoplectical deafness

16 respiratory disease, upper respiratory disease; lung disease

17 tuberculosis *or* **TB,** white plague, phthisis, consumption

18 venereal disease *or* VD, sexually-transmitted disease *or* STD, social disease, Cupid's itch *or* Venus's curse, dose <nonformal>; chancre, chancroid; gonorrhea *or* clap *or* the clap *or* claps <nonformal>; syphilis *or* syph *or* the syph *or* the pox <nonformal>

19 cardiovascular disease; heart disease, heart condition; vascular disease; hypertension *or* high blood pressure; angina *or* angina pectoris; cardiac *or* myocardial infarction; cardiac arrest; congenital heart disease; congestive heart failure; coronary *or* ischemic heart disease; coronary thrombosis; heart attack, coronary, heart failure; tachycardia

20 blood disease, hemic *or* hematic disease, hematopathology

21 endocrine disease, gland *or* glandular disease, endocrinism, endocrinopathy; diabetes; goiter; hyper- *or* hypoglycemia; hyper- *or* hypothyroidism

22 metabolic disease; acidosis, alkalosis; ketosis; gout, podagra; galactosemia, lactose intolerance, fructose intolerance;

phenylketonuria *or* PKU, maple syrup urine disease, congenital hypo-phosphatasia

23 liver disease, hepatic disease; gallbladder disease; jaundice *or* icterus

24 kidney disease, renal disease; nephritis

25 neural *or* **nerve disease,** neuropathy; brain disease; amyotrophic lateral sclerosis *or* Lou Gehrig's disease; palsy, cerebral palsy, Bell's palsy; chorea *or* St Vitus's dance *or* the jerks <nonformal>; Huntington's chorea; headache, migraine; multiple sclerosis *or* MS; Parkinson's disease *or* Parkinsonism; sciatica *or* sciatic neuritis; shingles *or* herpes zoster; spina fibida; emotional trauma 92.17

26 shock, trauma; traumatism

27 paralysis, paralyzation, palsy, impairment of motor function; **stroke,** apoplexy; paresis; motor paralysis, sensory paralysis; hemiplegia, paraplegia, diplegia, quadriplegia; cataplexy, catalepsy; infantile paralysis, poliomyelitis, polio <nonformal>

28 heatstroke; heat prostration *or* exhaustion; sunstroke, *coup de soleil* <Fr>, siriasis, insolation; calenture, thermic fever

29 gastrointestinal disease, disease of the digestive tract; stomach condition; colic; colitis; constipation *or* irregularity; diarrhea *or* dysentery *or* looseness of the bowels *or* flux, the trots *or* the shits <both nonformal>; gastritis; indigestion *or* dyspepsia; ulcer, peptic ulcer

30 nausea, nauseation, queasiness, squeamishness, qualmishness; qualm, pukes <nonformal>; motion sickness, travel sickness, **seasickness,** *mal de mer* <Fr>, airsickness, car sickness; vomiting 908.8

31 poisoning, intoxication, venenation; septic poisoning, blood poisoning, sepsis, septicemia, toxemia, pyemia, septicopyemia; autointoxication; food poisoning, ptomaine poisoning, milk sickness; ergotism, St Anthony's fire

32 environmental disease, occupational disease <see list>, disease of the workplace, environmental *or* occupational hazard, biohazard

33 allergy, allergic disorder; allergic rhinitis, **hay fever,** rose cold, pollinosis; **asthma,** bronchial asthma; **hives,** urticaria; eczema; conjunctivitis; cold sore; allergic gastritis; cosmetic dermatitis; Chinese restaurant syndrome *or* Kwok's disease; allergen

34 skin diseases; acne, sebaceous gland dis-

order; dermatitis; eczema; herpes; hives; itch; psoriasis

35 skin eruption, eruption, **rash,** efflorescence, breaking out; diaper rash; drug rash, vaccine rash; prickly heat, heat rash; hives, urticaria, nettle rash; papular rash; rupia

36 sore, lesion; pustule, papule, papula, fester, **pimple,** hickey *and* zit <both nonformal>; pock; ulcer, ulceration; bedsore; tubercle; blister, bleb, bulla, blain; whelk, wheal, welt, wale; **boil,** furuncle, furunculus; carbuncle; canker; canker sore; cold sore, fever blister; sty; abscess, gathering, aposteme <old>; gumboil, parulis; whitlow, felon, paronychia; bubo; chancre; soft chancre, chancroid; hemorrhoids, piles; bunion; chilblain, kibe; polyp; stigma, petechia; scab, eschar; fistula; suppuration, festering; swelling, rising 283.4

37 trauma, wound, injury hurt, lesion; **cut,** incision, scratch, gash; puncture, stab, stab wound; flesh wound; **laceration,** mutilation; abrasion, scuff, scrape, chafe, gall; frazzle, fray; run, **rip,** rent, slash, **tear; burn,** scald, scorch, first- *or* second- *or* third-degree burn; flash burn; **break, fracture,** bone-fracture, comminuted fracture, compound *or* open fracture, greenstick fracture, spiral *or* torsion fracture; rupture; crack, chip, craze, check, crackle; wrench; whiplash injury *or* whiplash; concussion; **bruise, contusion,** ecchymosis, **black-and-blue mark; black eye,** shiner *and* mouse <both nonformal>; **battering;** battered child syndrome

38 growth, neoplasm; **tumor,** intumescence; benign tumor, nonmalignant tumor, innocent tumor; malignant tumor, malignant growth, metastatic tumor, **cancer,** sarcoma, carcinoma; morbid growth; excrescence, outgrowth; proud flesh; exostosis; cyst, wen; fungus, fungosity; callus, callosity, **corn,** clavus; **wart,** verruca; **mole,** nevus

39 gangrene, mortification, necrosis, sphacelus, sphacelation; noma; moist gangrene, dry gangrene, gas gangrene, hospital gangrene; caries, cariosity, tooth decay; slough; necrotic tissue

40 <animal diseases> anthrax, splenic fever, charbon, milzbrand, malignant pustule; malignant catarrh *or* malignant catarrhal fever; bighead; blackleg, black quarter, quarter evil *or* ill; cattle plague, rinderpest; glanders; foot-and-mouth disease, hoof-and-mouth disease, aphthous fever; distemper; gapes; heaves, broken wind; hog cholera; mad cow disease; loco, loco disease, locoism; mange, scabies; pip; rot, liver rot, sheep rot; staggers, megrims, blind staggers, mad staggers; swine dysentery, bloody flux; stringhalt; Texas fever, blackwater; John's disease, paratuberculosis, pseudotuberculosis; rabies, hydrophobia; myxomatosis

41 germ, pathogen, contagium, bug <nonformal>, disease-causing agent, disease-producing microorganism; **microbe,** microorganism; **virus,** filterable virus, nonfilterable virus, adenovirus, echovirus, reovirus, rhinovirus, enterovirus, picornavirus, retrovirus; rickettsia; bacterium, **bacteria,** coccus, streptococcus, staphylococcus, bacillus, spirillum, vibrio, spirochete, gram-positive bacteria, gram-negative bacteria, aerobe, aerobic bacteria, anaerobe, anaerobic bacteria; protozoon, amoeba, trypanosome; fungus, mold, spore; **carcinogen,** cancer-causing agent

42 sick person, ill person, sufferer, victim; valetudinarian, **invalid, shut-in;** incurable, terminal case; **patient, case;** inpatient, outpatient; apoplectic, consumptive, dyspeptic, epileptic, rheumatic, arthritic, spastic; **the sick, the infirm**

43 carrier, vector, biological vector, mechanical vector; Typhoid Mary

44 cripple, defective, **handicapped person,** incapable; amputee; paraplegic, quadriplegic, paralytic; deformity 265.3; the crippled, the handicapped, "the halt, the lame, and the blind"—Bible; idiot, imbecile 923.8

VERBS **45 ail, suffer,** labor under, be affected with, complain of; **feel ill,** feel under the weather, feel awful <nonformal>, feel something terrible, not feel like anything <nonformal>, feel like the walking dead; look green about the gills <nonformal>

46 take sick or **ill, sicken; catch, contract, get,** take, sicken for <Brit>, **come down with** <nonformal>, be stricken or seized by, fall a victim to; catch cold; take one's death <nonformal>; **break out,** break out with, break out in a rash, erupt; run a temperature, fever; be laid by the heels, be struck down, be brought down, be felled; drop in one's tracks, **collapse;** overdose or **OD** <nonformal>; go into shock, be traumatized

47 fail, weaken, sink, decline, run down, lose strength, lose one's grip, dwindle, droop, flag, wilt, wither, wither away, fade, **languish,** waste, waste away, pine, peak, "dwindle, peak, and pine"—Shakespeare

48 go lame, founder

49 afflict, disorder, derange; sicken, indispose; weaken, enfeeble, enervate, reduce, debilitate, devitalize; **invalid,** incapacitate, **disable;** lay up, hospitalize

50 infect, disease, contaminate, taint

51 poison, empoison <old>, envenom

ADJS **52 disease-causing, disease-producing, pathogenic;** threatening, life-threatening; unhealthful 82.5

53 unhealthy, healthless, in poor health; **infirm, unsound,** invalid, valetudinary, valetudinarian, debilitated, cachectic, enervated, exhausted, drained; shut-in, housebound, homebound, wheelchair-bound; **sickly,** peaky or peaked <nonformal>; **weakly, feeble, frail** 16.12–21; weakened, with low resistance, **rundown,** reduced, reduced in health; **dying** 307.33, **terminal,** moribund, languishing, failing 16.21; pale 36.7

54 unwholesome, unhealthy, unsound, morbid, diseased, pathological

55 ill, ailing, sick, unwell, indisposed, taken ill, down, bad, on the sick list; **sickish, seedy** and **rocky** <both nonformal>, **under the weather, out of sorts** <nonformal>, below par <nonformal>, off-color, off one's feed <nonformal>; not quite right, not oneself; faint, faintish, feeling faint; feeling awful and feeling something terrible <both nonformal>; sick as a dog or a pig <nonformal>, laid low; in a bad way, critically ill, in danger, on the critical list, on the guarded list, in intensive care; mortally ill, sick unto death

56 nauseated, nauseous, **queasy, squeamish, qualmish,** qualmy; **sick to one's stomach;** pukish and puky and barfy <all nonformal>; seasick, carsick, airsick

57 feverish, fevered, feverous, in a fever, febrile, pyretic; **flushed,** inflamed, **hot, burning,** fiery, hectic; hyperpyretic, hyperthermic; delirious 925.31

58 laid up, invalided, hospitalized, in hospital <Brit>; **bedridden, bedfast, sick abed; down,** prostrate, flat on one's back; in childbed, confined

59 diseased, morbid, pathological, bad, **infected, contaminated,** tainted, peccant, **poisoned,** septic; cankerous, cankered, ulcerous, ulcerated, ulcerative, gangrenous, gangrened, mortified, sphacelated; **inflamed;** congested; **swollen,** edematous

60 anemic, chlorotic; bilious; dyspeptic, liverish, colicky; dropsical, edematous, hydropic; gouty, podagric; neuritic, neuralgic; palsied, paralytic; pneumonic, pleuritic, tubercular, tuberculous, phthisic, consumptive; rheumatic, arthritic; rickety, rachitic; syphilitic, pocky, luetic; tabetic, tabid <old>; allergic; allergenic; apoplectic; hypertensive; diabetic; encephalitic; epileptic; laryngitic; leprous; malarial; measly; nephritic; scabietic, scorbutic, scrofulous; variolous, variolar; tumorous; cancerous, malignant; **carcinogenic**, tumorigenic

61 **contagious, infectious**, infective, **catching**, taking, spreading, **communicable**, zymotic, inoculable; pestiferous, pestilential, **epidemic**, epidemial, pandemic; epizootic, epiphytotic; endemic; sporadic

62 kinds of disease

acute disease *or* condition	genetic disease
allergy *or* allergic disease	geriatric disease
atrophy	glandular disease
autoimmune disease	hepatic *or* liver disease
bacterial disease	hereditary disease
blood disease	hypertrophy
bone disease	iatrogenic disease
cardiovascular disease	intestinal disease
childhood *or* pediatric disease	joint disease
chronic disease *or* condition	malignant disease
chronic fatigue syndrome	muscular disease
circulatory disease	neurological disease
collagen disease	nutritional disease
congenital disease	occupational disease
connective-tissue disease	ophthalmic disease
contagious *or* infectious disease	organic disease
deficiency disease	pandemic disease
degenerative disease	parasitic disease
digestive disease	protozoan disease
endemic disease	psychogenic *or* psychosomatic disease
endocrine disease	pulmonary disease
endocrine gland disease	radiation disease
epidemic disease	renal *or* kidney disease
functional disease	respiratory disease
fungus *or* fungal disease	skin disease
gastric *or* stomach disease	urinogenital *or* urogenital disease
gastrointestinal disease	venereal *or* sexually-transmitted disease *or* STD
	virus *or* viral disease
	wasting disease
	worm disease

63 deficiency diseases and disorders

anemia	beriberi
ariboflavinosis	cachexia
chlorosis	night blindness
deficiency anemia	osteomalacia
dermatitis	osteoporosis
goiter	pellagra
greensickness	pernicious anemia
Italian *or* Lombardy leprosy	protein deficiency
keratomalacia	rickets *or* rachitis
kwashiorkor	scurvy
maidism	struma
malnutrition	vitamin deficiency
	xerophthalmia

64 genetic diseases and disorders

achromatic vision	mongolism *or* mongolianism <old>
albinism	mucoviscidosis
Christmas disease	muscular dystrophy
color blindness	neurofibromatosis
cystic fibrosis	Niemann-Pick disease
dichromatic vision	pancreatic fibrosis
Down's syndrome	sickle-cell anemia *or* disease
dysautonomia	
Hartnup's disease	Tay-Sachs disease
hemophilia	thalassemia
Huntington's chorea	Turner's syndrome
ichthyosis	Werdnig-Hoffmann disease
lipid histiocytosis	
maple syrup urine disease	
Milroy's disease	

65 infectious diseases

acquired immune deficiency syndrome *or* AIDS	cowpox
acute articular rheumatism	dandy fever
African lethargy *or* encephalitis lethargica	dengue *or* dengue fever
ague	diphtheria
AIDS-related complex *or* ARC *or* pre-AIDS	dumdum fever
alkali disease	dysentery
amebiasis	elephantiasis
amebic dysentery	enteric fever
anthrax *or* pulmonary anthrax *or* woolsorter's disease	erysipelas
	famine fever
	five-day fever
bacillary dysentery	frambesia
bastard measles	German measles
black death	glandular fever
black fever	grippe
blackwater fever	Hansen's disease *or* leprosy
breakbone fever	Haverhill fever
brucellosis	hepatitis
bubonic plague	herpes
cachectic fever	histoplasmosis
cerebral rheumatism	hookworm
Chagres fever	inflammatory rheumatism
chicken pox *or* varicella	influenza *or* flu <nonformal>
cholera *or* Asiatic cholera	jail fever
	jungle rot
	kala azar
	Kew Gardens spotted fever
	legionnaires' disease
	lepra

leprosy
leptospirosis
loaiasis or loa loa
Lyme disease
lyssa
malaria or malarial fever
marsh fever
measles or rubeola
meningitis
milzbrand
mononucleosis or infectious mononucleosis or kissing disease <nonformal>
mumps
ornithosis
osteomyelitis
paratyphoid fever
parotitis
pneumonia
poliomyelitis or infantile paralysis or polio <nonformal>
polyarthritis rheumatism
ponos
psittacosis or parrot fever
rabies or hydrophobia
rat-bite fever
relapsing fever
rheumatic fever
rickettsial pox
ringworm or tinea
Rocky Mountain spotted fever
rubella
scarlatina
scarlet fever
schistosomiasis
scrub typhus or tsutsugamushi disease

septic sore throat
shigellosis
sleeping sickness or sleepy sickness <Brit>
smallpox or variola
snail fever
splenic fever
spotted fever
St Anthony's fire
strep throat
streptococcus tonsilitis
swamp fever
tetanus or lockjaw
thrush
tick-borne typhus
tick fever
toxic shock syndrome
tracheitis
trench fever
trench mouth or Vincent's infection or Vincent's angina
trypanosomiasis
tuberculosis
tularemia or deer fly fever or rabbit fever
typhoid fever or typhoid
typhus or typhus fever
undulant fever
vaccinia
venereal disease or VD
viral dysentery
viral pneumonia
whooping cough or pertussis
yaws
yellow fever or yellow jack
zoster or shingles or zona

red-out
sunstroke
trench foot

writer's cramp or palsy or spasm

86 REMEDY

NOUNS **1 remedy, cure, corrective,** alterative, remedial measure, sovereign remedy; **relief, help, aid, assistance,** succor; balm, balsam; healing agent; restorative, analeptic; healing quality or virtue; specific, specific remedy; **prescription,** recipe, receipt

2 nostrum, patent medicine, quack remedy; snake oil

3 panacea, cure-all, universal remedy, theriac, catholicon; polychrest, broadspectrum drug or antibiotic; elixir, elixir of life, elixir vitae <L>

4 medicine, medicament, medication, medicinal, theraputant, **drug, physic,** preparation, mixture; herbs, medicinal herbs, simples, vegetable remedies, "the physic of the field"—Pope; balsam, balm; tisane, ptisan; drops; powder; inhalant; electuary, elixir, syrup, lincture, linctus; officinal; specialized drug, orphan drug; **prescription drug,** ethical drug; over-the-counter or OTC drug, counter drug, **nonprescription drug;** proprietary medicine or drug, proprietary, patent medicine; proprietary name, generic name; materia medica; **placebo,** placebo effect

5 drug, narcotic drug, controlled substance

6 dose, draft, potion, portion, **shot,** injection; broken dose; booster, booster dose, recall dose, booster shot

7 pill, bolus, **tablet, capsule,** lozenge, troche

8 tonic, bracer, cordial, restorative, analeptic, roborant, **pick-me-up** <nonformal>; **shot in the arm** <nonformal>; vitamin shot

9 stimulant; Adrenalin <trademark> or adrenaline <Brit> or epinephrine <US>, aloes; amphetamine sulphate, aromatic spirits of ammonia, caffeine, dextroamphetamine sulfate or Dexedrine <trademark>, digitalin or digitalis, methamphetamine hydrochloride or Methedrine <trademark>, smelling salts or salts

10 palliative, alleviative, alleviatory, lenitive, assuasive, assuager; soothing, abirritant

11 balm, lotion, salve, ointment, unguent, unguentum <L>, cerate, unction, balsam, oil, emollient, demulcent; **liniment,** embrocation; vulnerary; collyrium, eye-

66 environmental and occupational diseases and disorders

aeroembolism or caisson disease or decompression sickness or tunnel disease or diver's palsy or the bends <nonformal>
altitude sickness
anoxemia
anoxia
anoxic anoxia
anthrax or pulmonary anthrax or woolsorter's disease

cadmium poisoning
chilblain
frostbite
housemaid's knee
immersion foot
jet lag
lead poisoning
mercury poisoning
Minamata disease
motion sickness
pneumoconiosis or black lung <nonformal>
radiation sickness
radionecrosis

salve, eyebath, eyewater <old>, eyewash; ear-drops

12 **sedative, sedative hypnotic, depressant,**
amobarbital and secobarbital *or* Tuinal
<trademark>, amobarbital sodium *or*
Amytal <trademark>, atropine, barbital
or barbitone <Brit>, barbituric acid, bel-
ladonna, chloral hydrate *or* chloral,
laudanum, meperidine *or* Demerol
<trademark>, morphine, pentobarbital
or Nembutal <trademark>, phenobarbi-
tal *or* Luminal <trademark>, Quaalude
<trademark>, reserpine, scopolamine,
secobarbital *or* Seconal <trademark>;
sleeping pill *or* **tablet** *or* potion; **calmative, tranquilizer,** chlorpromazine,
Equanil <trademark>, Librium <trade-
mark>, meprobamate, rauwolfia, reser-
pine, Thorazine <trademark>, Triavil
<trademark>, Valium <trademark>;
abirritant, soother, soothing syrup,
quietener, pacifier; **analgesic,** aceta-
minophen *or* Datril <trademark> *or*
Tylenol <trademark>, acetanilide,
acetophenetidin, aspirin *or* acetylsali-
cylic acid *or* Bayer <trademark> *or* Em-
pirin <trademark>, buffered aspirin *or*
Bufferin <trademark>, headache *or* aspirin powder, ibuprofen *or* Advil <trade-
mark> *or* Motrin <trademark> *or* Nu-
prin <trademark>, phenacetin, propoxy-
phene *or* Darvon <trademark>, sodium
salicylate; **anodyne,** paregoric <old>;
pain killer *and* pain pill <both nonfor-
mal>; alcohol, liquor 88.13,14

13 **psychoactive drug, hallucinogen, psychedelic,** psychedelic drug

14 **antipyretic,** febrifuge, fever-reducer, fever pill <nonformal>

15 **anesthetic;** local *or* topical *or* general anesthetic; differential anesthetic; chloroform, ether, ethyl chloride, gas, laughing
gas, nitrous oxide, novocaine *or* Novocain
<trademark>, thiopental sodium *or* Pen-
tothal <trademark> *or* truth serum

16 **cough medicine,** cough syrup, cough
drops; horehound

17 **laxative, cathartic, physic, purge, purgative,** aperient, carminative, diuretic;
stool softener

18 **emetic,** vomitive *or* vomit <both ar-
chaic>, nauseant

19 **enema,** clyster, clysma, lavage, lavement
<old>

20 **prophylactic, preventive,** preventative,
protective

21 **antiseptic, disinfectant** <see list>, fumigant, fumigator, **germicide,** bactericide,
microbicide; alcohol, carbolic acid, hy-

drogen peroxide, merbromin *or* Mer-
curochrome <trademark>, tincture of
iodine

22 **dentifrice, toothpaste,** tooth powder;
mouthwash, gargle

23 **contraceptive,** birth control device, prophylactic; condom; **rubber** *and* skin *and*
bag <all nonformal>; oral contraceptive,
birth control pill, the pill <nonformal>,
Brompton *or* Brompton's mixture *or*
cocktail, morning-after pill, abortion pill;
diaphragm, pessary; spermicide, sper-
micidal jelly, contraceptive foam; intra-
uterine device *or* IUD, Dalkon shield
<trademark>, Lippes loop

24 **vermifuge,** vermicide, worm medicine,
anthelminthic

25 **antacid,** gastric antacid, alkalizer

26 **antidote,** counterpoison, alexipharmic,
theriaca *or* theriac

27 **antitoxin,** antitoxic serum; **antivenin; serum,** antiserum; interferon; **antibody,**
antigen-antibody product, anaphylactic
antibody, incomplete antibody, inhibiting antibody, sensitizing antibody;
gamma globulin, serum gamma globulin,
immune globulin, antitoxic globulin;
lysin, precipitin, agglutinin, anaphylac-
tin, bactericidin; antiantibody; antigen,
Rh antigen, Rh factor; allergen; **immu-
nosuppressive drug**

28 **vaccination, inoculation; vaccine**

29 **antibiotic,** ampicillin, bacitracin,
erythromycin, gramicidin, neomycin,
nystatin, penicillin, polymyxin, strep-
tomycin, tetracycline *or* Terramycin
<trademark>; **miracle drug, wonder
drug,** magic bullets; bacteriostat; **sulfa
drug** <see list>, sulfa, sulfanilamide, sul-
fonamide, sulfathiazole

30 diaphoretic, sudorific

31 vesicant, vesicatory, epispastic

32 **miscellaneous drugs,** anabolic steroid
or muscle pill, antihistamine, antispas-
modic, beta blocker, counterirritant, de-
congestant, expectorant, fertility drug
or pill, hormone, vasoconstrictor, vaso-
dilator

33 **dressing, application,** epithem <old>;
plaster, court plaster, mustard plaster,
sinapism; **poultice,** cataplasm; formenta-
tion; **compress,** pledget; stupe; tent;
tampon; **bandage, bandaging,** band
<old>, binder, cravat, triangular ban-
dage, roller *or* roller bandage, four-tailed
bandage; bandage compress, adhesive
compress, Band-Aid <trademark>; butterfly dressing; elastic bandage, Ace
elastic bandage *and* Ace bandage <both

trademark>; rubber bandage; plastic bandage *or* strip; **tourniquet;** sling; splint, brace; cast, plaster cast; tape, **adhesive tape;** lint, cotton, gauze, sponge

34 **pharmacology, pharmacy, pharmaceutics;** posology; materia medica

35 **pharmacist,** pharmaceutist, pharmacopolist, **druggist, chemist** <Brit>, **apothecary,** dispenser, gallipot; pharmacologist, pharmaceutical chemist, posologist

36 **drugstore, pharmacy,** chemist *and* chemist's shop <both Brit>, apothecary's shop, dispensary, dispensatory

37 **pharmacopoeia,** pharmacopedia, dispensatory

VERBS 38 remedy, cure 396.15; prescribe; treat

ADJS 39 **remedial, curative, therapeutic, healing, corrective,** disease-fighting, alterative, restorative, analeptic, sanative, sanatory; all-healing, panacean; adjuvant; **medicinal,** medicative, theriac, theriacal, iatric; anticancer

40 **palliative, lenitive, alleviative, assuasive,** soothing, balmy, balsamic, demulcent, emollient

41 **antidotal,** alexipharmic; **antitoxic; antibiotic,** synthetic antibiotic, semisynthetic antibiotic, bacteriostatic, antimicrobial; antiluetic, antisyphilitic; antiscorbutic; antiperiodic; antipyretic, febrifugal; vermifugal, anthelmintic; **antacid**

42 **prophylactic, preventive,** protective

43 **antiseptic, disinfectant, germicidal,** bactericidal

44 **tonic, stimulating, bracing, invigorating,** reviving, refreshing, restorative, analeptic, strengthening, roborant, corroborant

45 **sedative, calmative,** calmant, depressant, **soothing, tranquilizing, quietening; narcotic,** opiatic; **analgesic,** anodyne, paregoric <old>; anti-inflammatory; muscle relaxant; hypnotic, soporific, somniferous, somnifacient, sleep-inducing

46 **psychochemical,** psychoactive; ataractic; antidepressant, mood drug; hallucinogenic, **psychedelic,** mind-expanding, psychotomimetic

47 **anesthetic,** deadening, numbing

48 **cathartic,** laxative, purgative, aperient; carminative; diuretic

49 **emetic,** vomitive, vomitory <old>

87 SUBSTANCE ABUSE

NOUNS 1 **substance abuse, drug abuse,** narcotics abuse, drug use, glue-sniffing, solvent abuse; **addiction, addictedness, drug addiction,** narcotic addiction, opium addiction *or* habit, opiumism, morphine addiction *or* habit, morphinism, heroin addiction *or* habit, cocaine addiction, cocainism, coke habit <nonformal>, crack habit, barbiturate addiction, amphetamine addiction; **habit,** drug habit, drug habituation, drug dependence, physical addiction *or* dependence, psychological addiction *or* dependence, jones *and* monkey on one's back *and* Mighty Joe Young <all nonformal>; **drug experience, drug intoxication,** high *and* buzz *and* rush <all nonformal>; frightening drug experience, bad trip *and* bum trip *and* bummer *and* drag <all nonformal>; **alcoholism** 88.3, alcohol abuse, drinking habit, acute alcoholism, chronic alcoholism, dipsomania; **smoking,** smoking habit, one- *or* two- *or* three- pack-a-day habit, nicotine addiction 89.10, chain smoking; **tolerance,** acquired tolerance; **withdrawal, withdrawal sickness,** withdrawal syndrome, withdrawal symptoms, bogue *and* coming down *and* crash <both nonformal>, abrupt withdrawal *and* cold turkey <both nonformal>; **detoxification** *or* detox <nonformal>, drying out, taking the cure

2 **drug, narcotic,** dope <nonformal>, dangerous drug, controlled substance, abused substance, illegal drug, addictive drug, **hard drug;** soft drug, gateway drug; **opiate; sedative, depressant,** sedative hypnotic, **antipsychotic tranquilizer; hallucinogen,** psychedelic, psychedelic drug, psychoactive drug, psychoactive chemical *or* psychochemical, psychotropic drug, psychotomimetic drug, mind-altering drug, mind-expanding drug, mind-blowing drug; **stimulant; antidepressant; inhalant,** volatile inhalant

3 <nonformal terms for amphetamines> bennies, benz, black mollies, brain ticklers, crank, crystal, dexies, diet pills, dolls, ecstasy, footballs, hearts, ice, jelly beans, lid poppers, meth, pep pills, purple hearts, speed, uppers, ups, white crosses

4 <nonformal terms for amyl nitrate> amies, blue angels, blue devils, blue dolls, blue heavens, poppers, snappers; **barbiturates,** barbs, black beauties, candy, dolls, downers, downs, goofballs, gorilla pills, nebbies, nimbies, phennies, phenos, pink ladies, purple hearts, yellow jackets

5 <nonformal terms for chloral hydrate> joy juice, knockout drops, mickey, Mickey Finn, peter

6 <nonformal terms for cocaine> basuco, bernice, big C, blow, C, charlie, coke, crack, crack cocaine, jumps, dust, flake, girl, gold dust, her, jay, joy powder, lady, lady snow, nose candy, snow, star dust, toot, white, white girl, white lady

7 <nonformal terms for hashish> black hash, black Russian, hash

8 <nonformal terms for heroin> big H, boy, brown, caballo, crap, doojee, flea powder, garbage, H, hard stuff, henry, him, his, horse, hombre, jones, junk, mojo, P-funk, scag, schmeck, smack, white stuff

9 <nonformal terms for LSD> acid, big D, blotter, blue acid, blue cheer, blue heaven, California sunshine, cap, cubes, D, deeda, dots, electric Kool-Aid, haze, L, mellow yellows, orange cubes, pearly gates, pink owsley, strawberry fields, sugar, sunshine, tabs, yellow

10 <nonformal terms for marijuana> Acapulco gold, aunt mary, bomb, boo, bush, doobie, gage, ganja, grass, grefa, hay, hemp, herb, Indian hay, J, jane, kif, mary, maryjane, mary warner, meserole, mighty mezz, moota, muggles, pod, pot, smoke, snop, tea, Texas tea, weed, yerba

11 <nonformal terms for marijuana cigarette> joint, joy stick, kick stick, reefer, roach, stick, twist

12 <nonformal terms for mescaline> beans, big chief, buttons, cactus, mesc

13 <nonformal terms for morphine> big M, emm, hocus, M, miss emma, miss morph, morph, moocah, white stuff

14 <nonformal terms for pentobarbital> nebbies, nemmies, nimby, yellow dolls, yellows

15 <nonformal terms for opium> black pills, brown stuff, hop, O, tar

16 <nonformal terms for peyote> bad seed, big chief, buttons, cactus, P, topi

17 <nonformal terms for phencyclidine> angel dust, animal trank, DOA, dust, elephant, hog, PCP, peace, rocket fuel, supergrass, superweed

18 <nonformal terms for psilocybin> magic mushroom, mushroom, shroom

19 dose, hit *and* fix *and* toke *and* rock <all nonformal>; **shot, injection,** bang <nonformal>; **portion, packet,** bag *and* deck <both nonformal>; drug house, shooting gallery *and* needle park <both nonformal>, crack house, opium den, balloon room *and* pot party *and* dope den <all nonformal>

20 addict, drug addict, narcotics addict,

user, drug user, drug abuser, junkie *and* head *and* druggy *and* doper *and* toker *and* fiend *and* freak *and* space cadet <all nonformal>; cocaine user, cokie *and* coke head *and* crackhead *and* sniffer *and* snow drifter *and* flaky <all nonformal>; opium user, opium addict, hophead *and* hopdog *and* tar distiller <all nonformal>; heroin user *or* addict, smackhead *and* smacksack *and* schmecker <all nonformal>; methedrine user *or* methhead <nonformal>; amphetamine user, pillhead *and* pill popper *and* speed freak <all nonformal>; LSD user, acidhead *and* acid freak *and* tripper *and* cubehead <all nonformal>; marijuana smoker *and* pothead <both nonformal>; **drug seller** *or* dealer, pusher, contact, connection; **alcoholic, alcohol abuser** 88; **smoker,** heavy smoker, chain smoker, nicotine addict

VERBS **21 use, be on,** get on; use occasionally *or* irregularly, have a cotton habit *and* chip *and* chippy *and* joy pop <all nonformal>; **get a rush** *or* flush, go over the hump <nonformal>; **sniff,** snort, blow, toot, one and one <nonformal>; **smoke marijuana,** take on a number *and* blow a stick *and* toke *and* blast *and* weed out <all nonformal>; **smoke opium,** blow a fill; freebase; **inject,** mainline, shoot *and* shoot up *and* jab *and* get down *and* get off <all nonformal>, pop *and* skin pop <both nonformal>, **take pills,** pop pills <nonformal>; **withdraw,** crash *and* come down <both nonformal>, kick *or* go cold turkey *and* go a la canona *and* hang tough *and* water out <all nonformal>, detoxify, disintoxicate, detoxicate, dry out, kick *and* kick the habit <both nonformal>; **trip,** blow one's mind *and* wig out <both nonformal>; **sell drugs,** deal *and* push <both nonformal>; **buy drugs,** score *and* make *and* connect < all nonformal>; **have drugs,** be heeled *and* carry *and* hold *and* sizzle <all nonformal>; **drink** *or* booze 88.24–25; **smoke, smoke tobacco,** puff, puff away, drag, chain-smoke, smoke like a chimney

ADJS **22 intoxicated,** under the influence, nodding, narcotized, poppied

23 <nonformal terms> **high,** bent, blasted, blind, bombed out, bonged out, buzzed, coked, coked out, flying, fried, geared, geared up, geezed, gonged, gorked, hopped-up, in a zone, junked, luded out, maxed, noddy, ripped, smashed, snowed, spaced, space out, spacey, stoned, strung out, switched on, tanked, totaled, tranqued, tripping, trippy, wired, zoned, zoned out, zonked, zonked out

24 **addicted,** hooked *and* zunked *and* on the needle <all nonformal>; dependency-prone; **supplied with drugs,** holding *and* heeled *and* carrying *and* anywhere <all nonformal>; using, on, behind acid <nonformal>

88 INTOXICATION, ALCOHOLIC DRINK

NOUNS 1 **intoxication, inebriation, inebriety,** insobriety, besottedness, sottedness, **drunkenness, tipsiness,** befuddlement, fuddle, fuddlement, fuddledness, tipsification *and* tiddliness <both nonformal>; a high; Dutch courage, pot-valiance *or* pot-valiancy, pot-valor; hangover, katzenjammer, morning after <nonformal>

2 **bibulousness,** bibacity, bibaciousness, bibulosity, sottishness; serious drinking; crapulence, crapulousness; **intemperance** 669; bacchanalianism; Bacchus, Dionysus

3 **alcoholism, dipsomania,** oenomania, alcoholic psychosis *or* addiction, pathological drunkenness, problem drinking, heavy drinking, habitual drunkenness, ebriosity; delirium tremens 925.9/10; grog blossom *and* bottle nose <both nonformal>; gin drinker's liver, cirrhosis of the liver

4 **drinking, imbibing; social drinking; tippling,** guzzling, gargling, bibing; winebibbing, winebibbery; toping; hard drinking, serious drinking <nonformal>; **boozing** *and* swilling <both nonformal>, **hitting the booze** *or* **bottle** *or* **sauce** <nonformal>

5 **spree, drinking bout,** bout, **celebration,** potation, compotation, symposium, wassail, **carouse, carousal,** drunken carousal *or* revelry; bacchanal, bacchanalia, bacchanalian; **debauch, orgy**

6 <nonformal terms> **binge, drunk,** bust, tear, **bender, toot, bat,** pub-crawl <Brit>, jag, booze-up <chiefly Brit>, brannigan, guzzle, randan, rip

7 **drink,** dram, potation, potion, libation, **nip,** draft, drop, spot, finger or two, sip, sup, suck, drench, guzzle, gargle, jigger; peg, swig, swill, pull; **snort,** jolt, **shot,** snifter, wet; quickie; round, round of drinks

8 **bracer, refresher,** reviver, pickup *and* **pick-me-up** <both nonformal>, tonic,

hair of the dog *or* hair of the dog that bit one <nonformal>

9 **drink, cocktail, highball,** long drink, mixed drink; **punch; eye-opener** <nonformal>, **nightcap** <nonformal>, sundowner <Brit nonformal>; **chaser** <nonformal>, *pousse-café* <Fr>, *apéritif* <Fr>; parting cup, stirrup cup, doch-an-dorrach *or* wee doch-an-dorrach <both Scots>, one for the road; Mickey Finn *or* Mickey *and* knockout drops <all nonformal>

10 **toast, pledge**

11 **drinker,** imbiber, **social drinker,** tippler, bibber; winebibber, oenophilist; **drunkard, drunk, inebriate, sot,** toper, guzzler, swiller, soaker, lovepot, tosspot, barfly, thirsty soul, **serious drinker,** devotee of Bacchus; swigger; hard drinker, heavy drinker, **alcoholic, dipsomaniac, problem drinker,** chronic alcoholic, chronic drunk, pathological drinker; carouser, reveler, wassailer; bacchanal, bacchanalian; pot companion

12 <nonformal terms> **drunk, lush,** lusher, **soak,** sponge, hooch hound, **boozer, boozehound,** booze fighter, booze freak, dipso, juicehead, loadie, ginhound, elbow bender *or* crooker, shikker, bottle sucker, swillbelly, swillpot, swillbowl; **souse, stew,** bum, rummy, rumhound, stewbum; wino

13 **spirits, liquor,** intoxicating liquor, "the luscious liquor"—Milton, adult beverage, **hard liquor, whiskey,** firewater, spiritus frumenti, usquebaugh <Scots>, schnapps, ardent spirits, strong waters, **intoxicant,** toxicant, inebriant, **potable,** potation, **beverage, drink, strong drink,** strong liquor, alcoholic drink *or* beverage, **alcohol,** aqua vitae, water of life, brew, **grog,** social lubricant, nectar of the gods; **booze** <nonformal>; **rum,** the Demon Rum, John Barleycorn; the bottle, the cup, the cup that cheers, "the ruddy cup"—Sir Walter Scott, little brown jug; punch bowl, the flowing bowl

14 <nonformal terms> **likker, hooch, juice, sauce,** tiger milk, pig *or* tiger sweat, sheepdip, moonshine, white lightning; **medicine,** snake medicine, corpse reviver; **rotgut, poison,** rat poison, formaldehyde, embalming fluid, shellac, **panther piss**

15 **liqueur, cordial;** brandy, flavored brandy

16 **beer,** brew *and* brewskie *and* suds <all nonformal>, swipes <Brit nonformal>, "barmy beer"—Dryden; small beer

17 **wine,** *vin* <Fr>, *vino* <Sp & Ital>; vin-

tage wine, nonvintage wine; red wine, white wine, rosé wine, pink wine; dry *or* sweet wine, heavy *or* light wine, full *or* thin wine, rough *or* smooth wine, still wine, sparkling wine; extra sec *or* demi-sec *or* sec *or* brut champagne; new wine, must; imported wine, domestic wine; wine of the country, *vin du campagne* <Fr>; jug wine, plonk <Brit>

18 **bootleg liquor, moonshine** <nonformal>; hooch *and* shine *and* mountain dew <all nonformal>, white lightning *or* mule <nonformal>; bathtub gin; home brew

19 **liquor dealer,** liquor store owner; **vintner,** wine merchant; winegrower, winemaker, wine expert, oenologist; **bartender,** mixologist, barkeeper, barkeep, barman <Brit>, tapster, publican <Brit>; barmaid, tapstress; **brewer,** brewmaster; **distiller; bootlegger, moonshiner** <nonformal>

20 **bar,** barroom, *bistro* <Fr>, cocktail lounge; taproom; **tavern, pub,** pothouse, alehouse, rumshop, grogshop, dramshop, groggery, gin mill <nonformal>, **saloon,** drinking saloon, saloon bar <Brit>; lounge bar, piano bar, singles bar, gay bar; waterhole *or* watering hole <nonformal>; wine bar; public house <Brit>; public *or* local <both Brit nonformal>; beer parlor, beer garden, rathskeller; **nightclub, cabaret;** café, wine shop; barrel house *and* honky-tonk *and* dive <all nonformal>; **speakeasy** *and* blind tiger *and* blind pig *and* after-hours joint <all nonformal>

21 **distillery, still,** distiller; **brewery,** brewhouse; **winery,** wine press; bottling works

VERBS 22 **intoxicate, inebriate, addle, befuddle,** bemuse, besot, go to one's head, make one see double, make one tiddly

23 <nonformal terms> **plaster,** pickle, swack, crock, stew, souse, stone, pollute, tipsify, booze up, boozify, fuddle, overtake

24 **tipple, drink,** dram <Brit>, nip; grog, **guzzle,** gargle; **imbibe,** have a drink *or* nip *or* dram *or* guzzle *or* gargle, soak, bib, quaff, sip, sup, lap, lap up, take a drop, slake one's thirst, cheer *or* refresh the inner man, drown one's troubles *or* sorrows, commune with the spirits; **down,** toss off *or* down, toss one's drink, knock back, throw one back, drink off *or* up, drain the cup, drink bottoms-up, drink deep; **drink hard,** drink like a fish, drink seriously, **tope;** take to drink *or* drinking, "follow strong drink"—Bible

25 <nonformal terms> **booze,** swig, swill, moisten *or* wet one's whistle; **liquor, liquor up,** lush, souse, tank up, **hit the booze** *or* **bottle** *or* **sauce,** exercise *or* bend *or* crook *or* raise the elbow, dip the beak, splice the main brace; chug-a-lug, chug

26 **get drunk,** be stricken drunk, get high, put on a high, take a drop too much; **get plastered** *or* **pickled,** etc <nonformal>, tie one on *and* get a bun on <both nonformal>

27 **be drunk,** be intoxicated, have a drop too much, have more than one can hold, have a jag on <nonformal>, see double, be feeling no pain; **stagger, reel; pass out** <nonformal>

28 **go on a spree; go on a binge** *or* **drunk** *or* **toot** *or* **bat** *or* **bender** <nonformal>, **carouse, spree, revel,** wassail, debauch, "eat, drink, and be merry"—Bible, paint the town red <nonformal>, pub-crawl <Brit nonformal>

29 **drink to, toast, pledge,** drink a toast to, drink *or* pledge the health of, give you

30 **distill; brew;** bootleg, moonshine <nonformal>, moonlight <nonformal>

ADJS 31 **intoxicated, inebriated,** inebriate, inebrious, **drunk, drunken,** *shikker* <Yiddish>, **tipsy,** in liquor, **in one's cups, under the influence,** the worse for liquor; nappy, beery; **tiddly, giddy, dizzy,** muddled, addled, flustered, bemused, reeling, seeing double; **mellow, merry,** jolly, happy, gay, glorious; **full,** fou <Scots>; **besotted,** sotted, sodden, drenched, far-gone; drunk as a lord, drunk as a fiddler *or* piper, drunk as an owl; staggering drunk; crapulent, crapulous; **maudlin**

32 **dead-drunk,** blind drunk, overcome, out *and* out cold *and* passed out <all nonformal>, helpless, under the table

33 <nonformal terms> **fuddled,** muzzy, **boozy,** overtaken; **swacked, plastered,** shnockered, stewed, **pickled,** pissed, **soused,** soaked, boiled, fried, canned, tanked, potted, corned, bombed, ripped, smashed; bent, **crocked,** crocko, shellacked, sloshed, sozzled, zonked, tight, lushy, squiffy, afflicted, jug-bitten, oiled, lubricated, feeling no pain, polluted, raddled, organized, **high,** elevated, high as a kite, lit, **lit up,** lit to the gills, illuminated, **loaded, stinko,** tanked, tanked-up, stinking drunk, pie-eyed, pissy-eyed, shitfaced, cockeyed, cockeyed drunk, roaring *or* rip-roaring drunk, skunk-drunk; half-seas over, three sheets to the wind, **blotto, stiff** blind, paralyzed, **stoned**

34 full of Dutch courage, pot-valiant, pot-valorous

35 bibulous, bibacious, drunken, sottish, liquorish, given *or* addicted to drink, **liquor-loving,** liquor-drinking, drinking, hard-drinking, swilling <nonformal>, toping, tippling, winebibbing

36 intoxicating, intoxicative, **inebriating,** inebriative, inebriant, heady

37 alcoholic, spirituous, ardent, strong, hard, with a kick <nonformal>; winy, vinous

INTERJS **38** <toasts> skoal!, *skl!* <Norw>, prosit! *or* prost!, *à votre santé!* <Fr>, *¡salud!* <Sp>, *l'chaim!* <Heb>, *sláinte!* <Ir>, *salute!* <Ital>, *na zdorovye!* <Russ>, *nazdrowie!* <Pol>, to your health!, long life!, to life!, cheerio!, cheers!, down the hatch!, bottoms up!, here's how!, here's to you!, here's looking at you!, here's mud in your eye!, here's good luck!, here's to absent friends!, confusion to our enemies!

89 TOBACCO

NOUNS **1 tobacco,** *tabac* <Fr>, nicotia *or* nicotian <both old>; **the weed** <nonformal>, fragrant weed, Indian weed *or* drug, filthy weed, sot-weed <old>, "pernicious weed"—Cowper, "thou weed, who art so lovely fair and smell'st so sweet"—Shakespeare, "sublime tobacco"—Byron, "divine tobacco"—Spenser; carcinogenic substance; smoke, tobacco smoke, cigarette smoke, cigar smoke, pipe smoke; secondary smoke, secondhand smoke

2 <tobaccos> flue-cured *or* bright, fire-cured, air-cured; Broadleaf, Burley, Cuban, Havana, Havana seed, Latakia, Turkish, Russian, Maryland, Virginia; plug tobacco, bird's-eye, canaster, leaf, lugs, seconds, shag

3 smoking tobacco, smokings <nonformal>, smoke *and* smokes <both nonformal>

4 cigar, seegar <nonformal>; rope *and* stinker <both nonformal>; **cheroot, stogie,** corona, belvedere, Havana, panatella, colorado, trichinopoly; cigarillo; box of cigars, cigar box, cigar case, humidor; cigar cutter

5 cigarette; butt *and* cig *and* **fag** *and* coffin nail *and* cancer stick <all nonformal>; cigarette butt, **butt,** stub; snipe <nonformal>; pack *or* deck of cigarettes, box *or* carton of cigarettes, cigarette case

6 pipe, tobacco pipe; corncob, corncob pipe, Missouri meerschaum; briar pipe, briar; clay pipe, clay, churchwarden <Brit>; meerschaum; water pipe, hookah, nargileh, kalian, hubble-bubble; peace pipe, calumet; pipe rack, pipe cleaner, tobacco pouch

7 chewing tobacco, eating tobacco <nonformal>; navy *or* navy plug, cavendish, twist, pigtail, cut plug; **quid,** cud, fid <Brit nonformal>, **chew,** chaw <nonformal>; tobacco juice

8 snuff, snoose <nonformal>; rappee; pinch of snuff; snuff bottle, snuffbox, snuff mill <Scots>

9 nicotine, nicotia <old>

10 smoking, smoking habit, habitual smoking; chain-smoke; smoke, puff, drag <nonformal>; **chewing;** tobacco *or* nicotine addiction, tobaccoism, tabacosis, tabacism, tabagism, nicotinism; passive smoking

11 tobacco user, smoker, cigarette *or* pipe *or* cigar smoker, chewer, snuffer, snuff dipper

12 tobacconist; snuffman; tobacco store *or* shop, cigar store

13 smoking room, smoking car, **smoker**

VERBS **14** <use tobacco> **smoke;** inhale, puff, draw, drag <nonformal>, pull; smoke like a furnace *or* chimney; chain-smoke; **chew,** chaw <nonformal>; **take snuff,** dip *or* inhale snuff

ADJS **15 tobacco,** tobaccoy *or* tobaccoey, tobaccolike; **nicotinic;** smoking, chewing; snuffy

90 HEALTH CARE

NOUNS **1 medicine, medical practice, health care,** health-care industry, health-care delivery, leechcraft *and* leechdom *and* physic <all old>; **medical specialty** *or* **branch** <see list>; **treatment, therapy** 91; **health care, health insurance** 83.5; **care,** nursing care, home care, outpatient care, life care

2 surgery; operation

3 dentistry <see list>, dental medicine, dental care

4 doctor, doc <nonformal>, **physician,** Doctor of Medicine *or* **MD,** medical practitioner, **medical man, medico** <nonformal>, leech <old>, croaker *and* sawbones <both nonformal>; **general practitioner** *or* **GP;** family doctor; country doctor; **intern; resident,** house physician, resident physician; fellow; physician in ordinary; medical attendant, attending physician; **specialist**, board-certified physician *or* specialist; **medical examiner,** coroner; **osteopath, chiropractor,** podiatrist, oculist, **optometrist**

5 surgeon, sawbones <nonformal>; operator, operative surgeon

6 dentist, tooth doctor, toothdrawer; **dental surgeon,** operative dentist; Doctor of Dental Surgery *or* DDS; Doctor of Dental Science *or* DDSc; Doctor of Dental Medicine *or* DMD; **specialist,** dental specialist

7 veterinary, veterinarian, vet <nonformal>, veterinary surgeon <Brit>, horse doctor, animal doctor

8 health-care professional, health-care provider, physician, nurse, midwife, therapist, therapeutist, practitioner

9 healer, nonmedical therapist; theotherapist; Christian *or* spiritual *or* divine healer; **Christian Science practitioner,** healer; **faith healer,** witch doctor <nonformal>

10 nurse, sister *or* nursing sister <both Brit>; **probationer,** probationist, probe <nonformal>; caregiver, hospice caregiver; practical nurse; registered nurse *or* RN

11 <hospital staff> paramedic; medevac; physician's assistant *or* PA; orderly, attendant, nurse's aide; dresser; audiologist; anesthetist; dietitian; radiographer, X-ray technician; laboratory technician; radiotherapist; physical therapist, physiotherapist; dietitian; hospital administrator; ambulance driver; custodian

12 Hippocrates, Galen; Aesculapius, Asclepius

13 practice of medicine, medical practice; general practice, restricted *or* limited practice; group practice; professional association *or* PA; family practice, community medicine

VERBS **14 practice medicine,** doctor <nonformal>; treat; intern

ADJS **15 medical,** iatric, health; surgical; chiropodic, pediatric, orthopedic, obstetric, obstetrical, neurological; dental; orthodontic, periodontic, prosthodontic, exodontic; osteopathic, chiropractic, naturopathic, hydropathic, allopathic, homeopathic; clinical

16 branches of medicine

anatomy	dental surgery
anesthesiology	dentistry
audiology	dermatology
bacteriology	diagnostics
cardiography	dolorology
cardiology	embryology
chiropody	endocrinology
epidemiology	orthopedics
etiology	orthotics
family practice	otolaryngology
fetology	otology
fluoroscopy	parasitology
general medicine	pathology
geriatrics *or* gerontology	pediatrics
	physical medicine
gynecology	physiopathology
hematology	podiatry
hygiene	psychiatry
immunochemistry	psychology
immunology	psychoneuroimmunology
internal medicine	
materia medica	radiology
mental hygiene	rheumatology
midwifery	serology
mycology	surgery
neonatology	surgical anatomy
neurology	symptomatology *or* semeiology
neurosurgery	
nosology	teratology
nutrition	therapeutics
obstetrics	tocology
ophthalmology	toxicology
optometry	virology

17 kinds and specialties of dentistry

endodontics *or* endodontia	orthodontics *or* orthodontia
exodontics *or* exodontia	periodontics *or* periodontia
family dentistry	prosthetic dentistry *or* prosthodontics
general dentistry	*or* prosthodontia
operative dentistry	
oral surgery *or* surgical dentistry	radiodontics *or* radiodontia

91 THERAPY, MEDICAL TREATMENT

NOUNS **1 therapy, therapeutics,** therapeusis, **treatment, medical care** *or* **treatment,** medication; noninvasive *or* nonsurgical therapy *or* treatment; disease-fighting, healing; healing arts; psychotherapy 92; medicines 86

2 nonmedical therapy; theotherapy; **healing;** Christian *or* spiritual *or* divine healing; **faith healing**

3 hydrotherapy, hydrotherapeutics; hydropathy, water cure; cold-water cure; contrast bath, whirlpool bath

4 heat therapy, thermotherapy; heliotherapy, solar therapy; fangotherapy; hot bath, sweat bath, sunbath

5 diathermy, medical diathermy; electrotherapy, electrotherapeutics; **radiotherapy,** high-frequency treatment; shortwave diathermy, ultrashortwave diathermy, microwave diathermy; ultrasonic diathermy; surgical diatharmy, radiosurgery, electrosurgery, electrosection, electrocautery, electrocoagulation

6 **radiotherapy,** radiation therapy, radiotherapeutics; adjuvant therapy

7 **radiology,** radiography, radioscopy, fluoroscopy, etc 1036.7

8 <radiotherapeutic substances> radium; cobalt; radioisotope, tracer, labeled *or* tagged element, radioelement; radiocarbon, carbon 14, radiocalcium, radiopotassium, radiosodium, radioiodine; atomic cocktail

9 <diagnostic pictures and graphs> **X-ray,** radiograph, radiogram, roentgenogram *or* roentgenograph; photofluorograph; X-ray movie; chest X-ray; pyelogram; orthodiagram; encephalograph, encephalogram; electroencephalograph, electroencephalogram *or* EEG; electrocorticogram; electrocardiogram *or* ECG *or* EKG; electromyogram; computer-assisted tomography *or* CAT, computerized axial tomography *or* computed tomography *or* computer-assisted tomography *or* computerized tomography *or* CAT; CAT scan; magnetic resonance imaging *or* MRI; MR scan; positron emission tomography *or* PET; PET scan; ultrasound, ultrasonography; sonogram

10 case history, medical history, anamnesis; associative anamnesis; catamnesis, follow-up

11 **diagnostics,** prognostics; symptomatology, semeiology, semeiotics

12 **diagnosis; examination, physical examination;** study, test, work-up <nonformal>; blood test, blood work <nonformal>, blood count, urinalysis, uroscopy; biopsy; Pap test *or* smear; electrocardiography, electroencephalography, electromyography; mammography

13 **prognosis,** prognostication; prognostic, **symptom, sign**

14 **treatment,** medical treatment *or* attention *or* care; **cure,** curative measures; **medication,** medicamentation; **regimen,** regime, protocol; first aid; hospitalization

15 **immunization;** immunization therapy, immunotherapy; vaccine therapy, vaccinotherapy; toxin-antitoxin immunization; serum therapy, serotherapy, serotherapeutics; tuberculin test, scratch test, patch test; **immunology,** immunochemistry; immunity theory, sidechain theory; immunity; immunodeficiency

16 **inoculation, vaccination; injection,** hypodermic, hypodermic injection, shot *and* bing <both nonformal>, hypospray *or* jet injection; booster, booster shot <nonformal>; antitoxin, vaccine 86.28

17 <methods of injection> cutaneous, percutaneous, subcutaneous, intradermal, intramuscular, intravenous, intramedullary, intracardiac, intrathecal, intraspinal

18 **transfusion,** blood transfusion; serum; blood bank, blood donor center, bloodmobile; blood donor

19 **surgery,** surgical treatment, **operation,** surgical operation, surgical intervention, surgical technique *or* measure, the knife <nonformal>; **instrument,** device; respirator; unnecessary surgery, *cacoëthes operandi* <L>, tomomania

20 bloodletting, bleeding, venesection, phlebotomy; leeching; cupping

21 **hospital, clinic,** *hôpital* <Fr>, treatment center; hospice, infirmary; nursing home, rest home, sanitarium; sick bay *or* berth; trauma center; wellness center

22 **pesthouse,** lazar house, lazaretto *or* lazaret <all old>

23 **health resort, spa, watering place,** baths; mineral spring, warm *or* hot spring; pump room, pump house

VERBS 24 **treat, doctor,** minister to, care for, give care to, physic; **diagnose;** nurse; **cure, remedy, heal;** dress the wounds, bandage, poultice, plaster, strap, splint; bathe; massage, rub; operate on; physic, purge, flux <old>; **operate,** perform a procedure; transplant, replant

25 **medicate,** medicine, drug, dope <nonformal>, dose; salve, oil, anoint, embrocate

26 **irradiate,** radiumize, **X-ray,** roentgenize

27 bleed, let blood, leech, phlebotomize; cup; **transfuse,** give a transfusion; perfuse

28 **immunize, inoculate, vaccinate,** shoot <nonformal>

29 **undergo treatment,** take the cure, doctor <nonformal>, take medicine; go under the knife <nonformal>

92 PSYCHOLOGY, PSYCHOTHERAPY

NOUNS 1 **psychology** <see list>, science of the mind, science of human behavior, mental philosophy; psychologism, pop psychology *and* psychobabble <both nonformal>

2 psychological school <see list>, school *or* system of psychology, psychological theory; Adlerian psychology; behaviorism *or* behavior *or* behavioristic psychology *or*

stimulus-response psychology; Freudian psychology *or* Freudianism; Gestalt psychology *or* configurationism; Horneyan psychology; Jungian *or* analytical psychology; Pavlovian psychology; Reichian psychology *or* orgone theory; Skinnerian psychology; Sullivanian psychology

3 **psychiatry,** psychological medicine; neuropsychiatry; social psychiatry; prophylactic psychiatry

4 **psychosomatic medicine,** psychological medicine, medicopsychology; psychosocial medicine

5 **psychotherapy,** psychotherapeutics, mind cure

6 **psychoanalysis, analysis,** the couch <nonformal>; psychoanalytic therapy, psychoanalytic method; **depth psychology,** psychology of depths; group analysis; psychognosis, psychognosy; dream analysis, interpretation of dreams, dream symbolism; depth interview

7 **psychodiagnostics,** psychodiagnosis, psychological *or* psychiatric evaluation

8 **psychometrics,** psychometry, psychological measurement; **intelligence testing;** psychological screening; psychography; psychogram, psychograph, psychological profile; psychometer, IQ meter <nonformal>; lie detector, polygraph, psychogalvanometer

9 **psychological test** <see list>, mental test; standardized test; developmental test, achievement test

10 **psychologist; psychotherapist, therapist,** psychotherapeutist; clinical psychologist; licensed psychologist, psychological practitioner; **psychiatrist,** alienist, somatist; neuropsychiatrist; psychopathist, psychopathologist; psychotechnologist, industrial psychologist; psychobiologist, psychochemist, psychophysiologist, psychophysicist; psychographer; **psychoanalyst, analyst; shrink** *and* headshrinker *and* shrinker <all nonformal>; **counselor,** psychological counselor; counseling service

11 **personality tendency,** complexion <old>, humor; somatotype; **introversion,** introvertedness, ingoingness; inner-directedness; **extroversion,** extrovertedness, outgoingness; other-directedness; syntony, ambiversion; schizothymia, schizothymic *or* schizoid personality; cyclothymia, cyclothymic *or* cycloid personality; mesomorphism, mesomorphy; endomorphism, endomorphy; ectomorphism, ectomorphy

12 <personality type> **introvert, extrovert,** syntone, ambivert; schizothyme, schizoid; cyclothymic, cyclothyme, cycloid; choleric, melancholic, sanguine, phlegmatic; endomorph, mesomorph, ectomorph

13 **pathological personality,** psychopathological personality, sick personality

14 **mental disorder, emotional disorder,** psychonosema, psychopathyfunctional nervous disorder; reaction; emotional instability; **maladjustment,** social maladjustment; nervous breakdown, crack-up <nonformal>; problems in living; **insanity, mental illness** 925.1; **psychosis** 925.3; **schizophrenia** 925.4; **manic-depressive psychosis, depression,** melancholia 925.5; seasonal affective disorder *or* SAD, post-partum depression; pre-menstrual syndrome *or* PMS; **neurosis, psychoneurosis,** neuroticism, neurotic *or* psychoneurotic disorder; brain disease, nervous disorder

15 **personality disorder, character disorder,** moral insanity, sociopathy, **psychopathy; psychopathic personality;** sexual pathology, sexual psychopathy 75.18

16 **neurotic reaction,** overreaction, disproportionate reaction

17 **psychological stress, stress; frustration,** external frustration, internal frustration; conflict, ambivalence, ambivalence of impulse; **trauma,** psychological *or* emotional trauma, traumatism, mental *or* emotional shock, decompensation; rape trauma syndrome

18 **psychosomatic symptom; symptom of emotional disorder,** emotional symptom, psychological symptom; **thought disturbance,** thought disorder *or* disturbances, dissociative disorder, delirium, delusion, disorientation, hallucination; **speech abnormality** <see list>

19 **trance,** daze, stupor; catatonic stupor, catalepsy; cataplexy; dream state, reverie, daydreaming 984.2; somnambulism, sleepwalking; hypnotic trance; fugue, fugue state; **amnesia** 989.2

20 **dissociation,** mental *or* emotional dissociation, disconnection; dissociation of personality, personality disorganization *or* disintegration; **schizoid personality;** double *or* dual personality; multiple personality, split personality, alternating personality; schizoidism, schizothymia, **schizophrenia** 925.4; depersonalization; **paranoid personality; paranoia** 925.4

21 **fixation,** libido fixation *or* arrest, **arrested development;** infantile fixation, pregenital fixation, father fixation, Freudian

fixation, mother fixation, parent fixation; **regression**, retreat to immaturity

22 **complex**, inferiority complex, superiority complex, parent complex, Oedipus complex, mother complex, Electra complex, father complex, Diana complex, persecution complex; castration complex

23 **defense mechanism**, defense reaction; ego defense, psychotaxis; biological *or* psychological *or* sociological adjustive reactions; resistance; dissociation; **negativism, alienation; escapism,** escape mechanism, avoidance mechanism; escape, flight, **withdrawal; isolation,** emotional insulation; **fantasy,** fantasizing, escape into fantasy, dreamlike thinking, autistic *or* dereistic thinking, wishful thinking, autism, dereism; wish-fulfillment, wish-fulfillment fantasy; sexual fantasy; **compensation,** overcompensation, decompensation; substitution; **sublimation; projection,** blame-shifting; displacement; **rationalization**

24 **suppression, repression, inhibition,** resistance, restraint, censorship; block, psychological block, blockage, blocking; reaction formation; rigid control; **suppressed desire**

25 **catharsis,** purgation, abreaction, motor abreaction, psychocatharsis, **emotional release,** relief of tension, outlet; release therapy, acting-out, psychodrama; imaging

26 **conditioning**, classical *or* Pavlovian conditioning; instrumental conditioning; operant conditioning; psychagogy, reeducation, reorientation; conditioned reflex, conditioned stimulus, conditioned response; reinforcement, positive reinforcement, negative reinforcement; simple reflex, unconditioned reflex, **reflex** 902.1; **behavior** 321

27 **adjustment**, adjustive reaction; **readjustment, rehabilitation;** psychosynthesis, integration of personality; fulfillment, self-fulfillment; self-actualization, peak experience; integrated personality, syntonic personality

28 **psyche**, psychic apparatus, **personality, self,** personhood; **mind** 918.1,3,4; preconscious, foreconscious, coconscious; **subconscious, unconscious,** subconscious *or* unconscious mind, submerged mind, subliminal, subliminal self; **libido,** psychic *or* libidinal energy, motive force, vital impulse, ego-libido, object libido; **id,** primitive self, pleasure principle, life instinct, death instinct; **ego,** conscious self; **superego,** ethical self, conscience;

ego ideal; ego-id conflict; anima, persona; collective unconscious, racial unconscious

29 **engram,** memory trace, traumatic trace *or* memory; unconscious memory; archetype, archetypal pattern *or* image *or* symbol; imago, image, father image, etc; race *or* racial memory; cultural memory; **memory** 988

30 **symbol,** universal symbol, father symbol, mother symbol, phallic symbol, fertility symbol, etc; symbolism, symbolization

31 **surrogate,** substitute; father surrogate, father figure, father image; mother surrogate, mother figure

32 **gestalt,** pattern, figure, configuration, sensory pattern; figure-ground

33 **association, association of ideas,** chain of ideas, concatenation, mental linking; controlled association, free association, association by contiguity, association by similarity; association by sound, clang association; stream of consciousness; transference, identification, positive transference, negative transference; synesthesia 24.5

34 **cathexis,** cathection, desire concentration; charge, energy charge, cathectic energy; anticathexis, countercathexis, counterinvestment; hypercathexis, overcharge

VERBS 35 **psychologize, psychoanalyze;** abreact; fixate, obsess on <nonformal>

ADJS 36 **psychological; psychiatric,** neuropsychiatric; psychometric; **psychopathic,** psychopathological; **psychosomatic,** somatopsychic, psychophysical, psychophysiological, psychobiological; psychogenic, psychogenetic, functional; psychodynamic, psychoneurological, psychosexual, psychosocial, psychotechnical; **psychotic**

37 **psychotherapeutic;** psychiatric, psychoanalytic, psychoanalytical

38 **neurotic, psychoneurotic,** disturbed, disordered; neurasthenic, psychasthenic; hysteric<al>, hypochondriac, phobic; stressed

39 **introverted,** introvert, introversive, **subjective, ingoing,** inner-directed

40 **extroverted,** extrovert, extroversive, **outgoing,** extrospective; other-directed

41 **subconscious, unconscious;** subliminal, extramarginal; preconscious, foreconscious, coconscious

42 **kinds and branches of psychology**

abnormal psychology	analytic *or* introspective psychology
academic psychology	tive psychology
act psychology	animal psychology

applied psychology
association psychology
child psychology
clinical psychology
cognitive psychology
comparative psychology
constitutional psychology
criminal psychology
depth psychology
developmental psychology
differential psychology
dynamic or functional psychology
ecological psychology
educational psychology
empirical psychology
existential psychology
experimental psychology
faculty psychology
folk or ethnic psychology
genetic psychology
group psychology
hormic psychology
individual psychology
industrial psychology
medical psychology
morbid psychology
neuropharmacology
neuropsychology
objective psychology
ontogenetic psychology
parapsychology
phenomenological psychology
phylogenetic psychology

physiologic or physiological psychology
polygenetic psychology
popular psychology
psychoacoustics
psychoasthenics
psychobiochemistry
psychobiology
psychochemistry
psychodiagnostics
psychodynamics
psychoendocrinology
psychogenetics
psychogeriatrics
psychographics
psychohistory
psycholinguistics
psychological medicine
psychological warfare
psychomathematics
psychometrics or psychometry
psychonomy or psychonomics
psychopathology
psychopharmacology
psychophysics
psychophysiology
psychosociology
psychosomatics
psychotechnics or psychotechnology
psychotherapy or psychotherapeutics
race or racial psychology
rational psychology
reactology
reflexology
self psychology
social psychology
structural psychology
voluntaristic psychology

43 psychological and mental tests

alpha test
apperception test
aptitude test
association test
Babcock-Levy test
Bernreuter personality inventory
beta test
Binet or Binet-Simon test
Brown personality inventory
Cattell's infant intelligence scale

CAVD test
controlled association test
free association test
Gesell's development schedule
Goldstein-Scheerer test
inkblot test
intelligence quotient or IQ
intelligence test
interest inventory
IQ test
Kent mental test

Minnesota multiphasic personality inventory
Minnesota preschool scale
Oseretsky test
personality test
Rorschach test
Stanford revision

Stanford scientific aptitude test
Stanford-Binet test
Szondi test
thematic apperception test or TAT
Wechsler-Bellevue intelligence scale
word association test

93 FEELING

NOUNS **1 feeling, emotion, affect, sentiment,** affection, affections; affective faculty, affectivity; emotional charge, cathexis; **feelings, sensitiveness, sensibility,** susceptibility, thin skin; emotional life; the logic of the heart; **sense,** deep or profound sense, gut sense or sensation <nonformal>; **sensation** 24; **impression,** undercurrent; hunch, feeling in one's bones, presentiment 933.3; foreboding; **reaction, response,** gut reaction <nonformal>; **instinct** 365.1; emotional coloring or shade or nuance, **tone,** feeling tone

2 passion, passionateness, strong feeling, powerful emotion; **fervor, fervency,** fervidness, impassionedness, **ardor, ardency,** empressement <Fr>, warmth of feeling, **warmth, heat, fire,** verve, furor, **fury,** vehemence; heartiness, gusto, relish, savor; spirit, heart, soul; **liveliness** 330.2; **zeal** 101.2; **excitement** 105; **ecstasy**

3 heart, soul, spirit, esprit <Fr>, **breast, bosom,** inmost heart or soul, heart of hearts, secret or inner recesses of the heart, secret places, heart's core, heartstrings, cockles of the heart, bottom of the heart, being, innermost being, core of one's being; viscera, pit of one's stomach, **gut** or guts <nonformal>; bones

4 sensibility, sensitivity, sensitiveness, delicacy, fineness of feeling, tenderness, affectivity, susceptibility, impressionability 24.2

5 sympathy, fellow feeling, sympathetic response, responsiveness, relating, warmth, **caring,** concern; response, echo, chord, sympathetic chord, vibrations, vibes <nonformal>; **empathy,** identification; involvement, sharing; pathos

6 tenderness, tender feeling, softness, gentleness, delicacy; **tenderheartedness,** softheartedness, warmheartedness, tender or sensitive or warm heart, soft place or spot in one's heart; warmth, **fondness, weakness** 100.2

7 bad feeling, hard feelings; immediate dislike, disaffinity, personality conflict, bad vibes or chemistry <nonformal>, bad blood, **hostility**, scunner, animosity 589.4; **hard-heartedness** 94.3

8 **sentimentality, sentiment, sentimentalism,** oversentimentality, oversentimentalism, bathos; nostalgia, nostomania; romanticism; sweetness and light, hearts-and-flowers; bleeding heart; mawkishness, cloyingness, maudlinness, namby-pamby, namby-pambyness, namby-pambyism; mushiness or sloppiness <both nonformal>; **mush** and slush and slop and goo and schmaltz <all nonformal>; sob story and tearjerker <both nonformal>, soap opera

9 **emotionalism,** emotionality, lump in one's throat; emotionalizing, emotionalization; emotiveness, emotivity; visceralness; nonrationalness, unreasoningness; demonstrativeness, making scenes; **theatrics, theatricality, histrionics, dramatics,** hamminess and chewing up the scenery <both nonformal>; **sensationalism, melodrama,** melodramatics, blood and thunder; yellow journalism; emotional appeal, human interest, love interest; **overemotionalism,** hyperthymia, excess of feeling

VERBS 10 **feel,** entertain or harbor or cherish or nurture a feeling; feel deeply, feel in one's viscera or bones, feel in one's gut or guts <nonformal>; experience 830.8; have a sensation, get or receive an impression, **sense, perceive**

11 **respond, react,** be moved, be affected or touched, be inspired, echo, catch the flame or infection, be in tune; **respond to,** warm up to, take or lay to heart, open one's heart to, be turned on to <nonformal>, nourish in one's bosom, feel in one's breast, cherish at the heart's core, treasure up in the heart; enter into the spirit of, be imbued with the spirit of; care about, sympathize with, empathize with, identify with, relate to emotionally, dig and be turned on by <both nonformal>, be involved, share; color with emotion

12 **have deep feelings, be all heart, have a tender heart,** be a person of heart or sentiment; have a soft place or spot in one's heart; be a prey to one's feelings; love 104.18–20; hate 103.5

13 **emotionalize, emote** <nonformal>, give free play to the emotions, make a scene; be theatrical, theatricalize, ham it up and chew up the scenery <both nonformal>; **sentimentalize,** gush and slobber over <both nonformal>

14 **affect, touch, move, stir; melt, soften,** melt the heart, choke one up, give one a lump in the throat; **penetrate,** pierce, go through one, go deep; touch a chord, **touch a sympathetic chord, touch one's heart,** tug at the heart or heartstrings, go to one's heart, get under one's skin; come home to; **touch to the quick,** touch on the raw, flick one on the raw, smart, sting

15 **impress, affect, strike, hit,** smite, rock; **make an impression, get to one** <nonformal>; make a dent in, make an impact upon, sink in <nonformal>, strike home, come home to, hit the mark <nonformal>; tell, have a strong effect, traumatize, strike hard, impress forcibly

16 **impress upon,** bring home to, make it felt; stamp, stamp on, etch, engrave, engrave on

ADJS 17 **emotional, affective,** emotive, affectional, **feeling;** soulful, of soul, of heart, of feeling, of sentiment; visceral, gut <nonformal>; glandular; emotiometabolic, emotiomotor, emotiomuscular, emotiovascular; demonstrative, overdemonstrative

18 **fervent, fervid, passionate, impassioned,** intense, **ardent; hearty, cordial,** enthusiastic, exuberant, unrestrained, vigorous; keen, breathless, **excited** 105.18,20,22; **lively** 330.17; zealous; **warm, burning, heated, hot, volcanic,** red-hot, fiery, flaming, glowing, ablaze, afire, on fire, boiling over, steaming, steamy; delirious, fevered, feverish, febrile, flushed; intoxicated, drunk

19 **emotionalistic,** emotive, overemotional, hysteric, hysterical, sensational, sensationalistic, melodramatic, theatric, theatrical, histrionic, dramatic, overdramatic, hammy <nonformal>, nonrational, unreasoning; overemotional, hyperthymic

20 **sensitive,** sensible, emotionable, passible <old>, delicate; responsive, sympathetic, receptive; susceptible, impressionable; **tender, soft, tenderhearted, softhearted,** warmhearted

21 **sentimental,** sentimentalized, soft, **mawkish, maudlin,** cloying; sticky and gooey and schmaltzy and sappy and soppy <all nonformal>, oversentimental, oversentimentalized, bathetic; **mushy** or sloppy or gushing or teary or beery <all nonformal>, treacly <Brit nonformal>; tearjerking <nonformal>; namby-pamby, romantic; nostalgic, nostomanic

22 affecting, touching, moving, emotive, pathetic

23 affected, moved, touched, impressed; impressed with *or* by, penetrated with, seized with, imbued with, devoured by, obsessed, obsessed with *or* by; wrought up by; stricken, wracked, racked, torn, agonized, tortured; worked up, all worked up, **excited** 105.18

24 deep-felt, deepgoing, from the heart, heartfelt, homefelt <old>; **deep, profound;** indelible; pervasive, pervading, absorbing; penetrating, penetrant, piercing; **poignant,** keen, sharp, acute

ADVS **25 feelingly, emotionally,** affectively; affectingly, touchingly, movingly, **with feeling,** poignantly

26 fervently, fervidly, passionately, impassionedly, intensely, **ardently,** zealously; keenly, breathlessly, excitedly; warmly, heatedly, glowingly; heartily, cordially; enthusiastically, exuberantly, vigorously; kindly, heart and soul, with all one's heart, from the heart, from the bottom of one's heart

27 sentimentally, mawkishly, maudlinly, cloyingly; mushily *and* sloppily *and* gushingly <all nonformal>

94 LACK OF FEELING

NOUNS **1 unfeeling,** unfeelingness, affectlessness, lack of affect, lack of feeling *or* feeling tone, emotional deadness *or* numbness *or* paralysis, **anesthesia, emotionlessness,** unemotionalism, unexcitability; **dispassion,** dispassionateness, unpassionateness, **objectivity;** passionlessness, **spiritlessness, heartlessness,** soullessness; **coldness, coolness, frigidity,** chill, chilliness, frostiness, iciness; coldheartedness, cold-bloodedness; cold heart, cold blood; cold fish; **unresponsiveness,** unsympatheticness; lack of touch *or* contact, autism, self-absorption, withdrawal, catatonia; unimpressionableness, unimpressibility; insusceptibility, unsusceptibility; **impassiveness,** impassibility, impassivity; straight face *and* poker face <both nonformal>, dead pan <nonformal>; immovability, untouchability; **dullness, obtuseness; inexcitability** 106

2 insensibility, insensibleness, **unconsciousness,** unawareness, **obliviousness,** oblivion; anesthesia, narcosis

3 callousness, insensitivity, insensitiveness, philistinism; **coarseness, brutalization, hardness,** hardenedness, hardheartedness, hardness of heart, hard heart, stony-heartedness, heart of stone, stoniness, marbleheartedness, flintheartedness, flintiness; **obduracy,** obdurateness, induration, inuredness; imperviousness, **thick skin,** rhinoceros hide, thick *or* hard-shell, armor, formidable defenses

4 apathy, indifference, unconcern, lack of caring, disinterest; withdrawnness, **aloofness, detachment,** ataraxy *or* ataraxia, **dispassion; passiveness,** passivity, supineness, insouciance, nonchalance; inappetence, lack of appetite; **listlessness, spiritlessness,** burnout, blah *or* blahs <nonformal>, heartlessness, plucklessness, spunklessness; **lethargy, phlegm,** lethargicalness, phlegmaticalness, phlegmaticness, hebetude, **dullness,** sluggishness, languor, languidness; soporifousness, sopor, coma, comatoseness, torpidness, torpor, torpidity, **stupor,** stupefaction, narcosis; acedia, sloth; **resignation,** resignedness, stoicism; **numbness,** benumbedness; hopelessness 125

VERBS **5** not be affected by, remain unmoved, not turn a hair, not care less <nonformal>; have a thick skin, have a heart of stone; be cold as ice, be a cold fish, be an icicle; not affect, leave one cold *or* unmoved, unimpress, underwhelm <nonformal>

6 callous, harden, case harden, **harden one's heart,** ossify, steel, indurate, inure; brutalize

7 dull, blunt, desensitize, obtund, hebetate

8 numb, benumb, paralyze, **deaden,** anesthetize, freeze, **stun, stupefy,** drug, narcotize, anesthetize

ADJS **9 unfeeling, unemotional,** nonemotional, emotionless, affectless, emotionally dead *or* numb *or* paralyzed, anesthetized, drugged, narcotized; **unpassionate, dispassionate,** unimpassioned, **objective;** passionless, **spiritless, heartless,** soulless; lukewarm, Laodicean; **cold, cool, frigid,** frozen, chill, chilly, arctic, frosty, frosted, icy, **coldhearted, cold-blooded,** cold as charity; **unaffectionate,** unloving; **unresponsive,** unresponding, **unsympathetic;** out of touch *or* contact; in one's shell *or* armor, behind one's defenses; autistic, self-absorbed, self-centered, egocentric, catatonic; unimpressionable, unimpressible, insusceptible, unsusceptible; **impassive,** impassible; immovable, untouchable; dull, obtuse, blunt; **inexcitable** 106.10

10 **insensible, unconscious,** unaware, **oblivious,** blind to, deaf to, dead to, lost to

11 **unaffected, unmoved, untouched,** dry-eyed, unimpressed, unstruck, **unstirred,** unruffled, unanimated, uninspired

12 **callous, calloused, insensitive,** Philistine; **thick-skinned,** pachydermatous; **hard, hard-hearted, hardened,** case-hardened, coarsened, brutalized, indurated, stony, stony-hearted, marblehearted, flint-hearted, flinty, steely, impervious, inured, armored or steeled against, proof against, as hard as nails

13 **apathetic, indifferent, unconcerned,** uncaring, **disinterested, uninterested; withdrawn, aloof, detached,** Olympian, above it all; **passive,** supine; stoic, stoical; insouciant, nonchalant, blasé, **listless, spiritless,** burned-out, blah <nonformal>, heartless, pluckless, spunkless; **lethargic, phlegmatic,** hebetudinous, **dull,** desensitized, sluggish, torpid, languid, slack, soporific, comatose, **stupefied,** in a stupor, **numb,** numbed, benumbed; resigned; hopeless 125.12

ADVS 14 **unfeelingly, unemotionally,** emotionlessly; with a straight or poker face <nonformal>, deadpan <nonformal>; **dispassionately,** unpassionately; **spiritlessly, heartlessly,** coldly, coldheartedly, cold-bloodedly, **in cold blood;** with dry eyes

15 **apathetically, indifferently, unconcernedly,** disinterestedly, uninterestedly, impassively; **listlessly, spiritlessly,** heartlessly, plucklessly, spunklessly; **lethargically, phlegmatically,** dully, numbly

95 PLEASURE

NOUNS 1 **pleasure, enjoyment;** quiet pleasure, euphoria, well-being, good feeling, **contentment,** content, **ease, comfort** 121; coziness, warmth; **gratification, satisfaction,** great satisfaction, hearty enjoyment, keen pleasure or satisfaction; **self-gratification,** self-indulgence; instant gratification; luxury; **relish, zest, gusto,** joie de vivre <Fr>; sweetness of life, douceur de vivre <Fr>; kicks <nonformal>, **fun,** entertainment, amusement 743; intellectual pleasure, pleasures of the mind; **strokes** and stroking and ego massage <all nonformal>; physical pleasure, creature comforts, bodily pleasure, sense or sensuous pleasure; sexual pleasure, voluptuousness, sensual pleasure, volupté <Fr>, animal pleasure, animal comfort,

bodily comfort, fleshly or carnal delight; forepleasure, titillation, endpleasure, fruition

2 **happiness, felicity, gladness, delight,** delectation; **joy, joyfulness,** joyance <old>; **cheer,** cheerfulness, exhilaration, **exuberance, high spirits, glee,** sunshine; gaiety 109.4, overjoyfulness, overhappiness; intoxication; **rapture,** ravishment, bewitchment, **enchantment,** unalloyed happiness; elation, exaltation; **ecstasy,** ecstasies, transport; **bliss,** blissfulness; beatitude, beatification, blessedness; paradise, heaven, seventh heaven, cloud nine

3 **treat, regalement,** regale; **feast, banquet** revelment, regale, Lucullan feast; feast or banquet of the soul; round of pleasures, mad round; **festivity,** fete, fiesta, festive occasion, celebration, merrymaking, revel, revelry, jubilation, joyance; carnival, Mardi Gras

4 **pleasure-loving, pleasure principle,** hedonism, hedonics; epicureanism, Cyrenaicism, eudaemonism

VERBS 5 **please, pleasure, give pleasure,** afford one pleasure, be to one's liking, sit well with one, meet one's wishes, take or strike one's fancy, feel good or right, strike one right; do one's heart good, warm the cockles of one's heart; **suit,** suit one down to the ground

6 <nonformal terms> **hit the spot,** be just the ticket, be just what the doctor ordered, **make a hit,** go over big, go over with a bang

7 **gratify, satisfy,** sate, satiate; slake, appease, allay, assuage, quench; regale, feed, feast; do one's heart good, warm the cockles of the heart

8 **gladden,** make happy, happify; bless, beatify; cheer 109.7

9 **delight,** delectate, **tickle, titillate, thrill, enrapture, enthrall, enchant,** entrance, fascinate, captivate, bewitch, **charm,** becharm; enravish, ravish, imparadise; ecstasiate, transport, carry away

10 <nonformal terms> **give one a bang** or kick or charge or rush, knock out, knock off one's feet or dead or for a loop, knock one's socks off, thrill to death or to pieces, tickle to death, tickle pink, **wow,** slay, send, freak out; **stroke,** massage one's ego

11 **be pleased, feel happy,** feel good, sing, purr, smile, laugh, be wreathed in smiles, beam; **delight,** joy, take great satisfaction; look like the cat that swallowed the canary; brim or burst with joy, walk or tread on air, have stars in one's eyes, be in

heaven *or* seventh heaven *or* paradise, be on cloud nine; fall *or* go into raptures; die with delight *or* pleasure

12 enjoy, pleasure in, be pleased with, receive *or* derive pleasure from, take delight *or* pleasure in, get a kick *or* boot *or* bang *or* charge *or* lift *or* rush out of <nonformal>; **like, love,** adore <nonformal>; **delight in, rejoice in,** indulge in, luxuriate in, revel in, riot in, bask in, wallow in, swim in; groove on *and* get high on *and* freak out on <all nonformal>; feast on, gloat over *or* on; **relish, appreciate,** roll under the tongue, do justice to, savor, smack the lips; devour, eat up

13 enjoy oneself, have a good time, party, live it up <nonformal>, have the time of one's life

ADJS **14 pleased, delighted; glad,** gladsome; **charmed,** intrigued <nonformal>; **thrilled; tickled,** tickled to death *and* tickled pink <both nonformal>, exhilarated; **gratified, satisfied;** pleased with, taken with, favorably impressed with, sold on <nonformal>; pleased as Punch, pleased as a child with a new toy; euphoric, eupeptic; **content, contented,** easy, **comfortable** 121.11, cozy, in clover

15 happy, glad, joyful, joyous, flushed with joy, radiant, beaming, glowing, starry-eyed, sparkling, laughing, smiling, smirking, smirky, chirping, purring, singing, dancing, leaping, capering, **cheerful, gay** 109.14; **blissful,** "throned on highest bliss"—Milton; blessed; beatified, beatific; thrice happy, "thrice and four times blessed"—Virgil; happy as a lark, happy as a king, happy as the day is long, happy as a baby boy, happy as a clam at high water, happy as a pig in shit <nonformal>, happy as a sand boy <Brit>

16 overjoyed, overjoyful, overhappy, brimming *or* bursting with happiness, on top of the world; **rapturous,** raptured, **enraptured, enchanted,** entranced, enravished, ravished, rapt, possessed; sent *and* high *and* freaked-out <all nonformal>, **in raptures,** transported, in a transport of delight, **carried away,** rapt *or* ravished away, beside oneself, beside oneself with joy, all over oneself <nonformal>; **ecstatic,** in ecstasies, ecstasiating; rhapsodic, rhapsodical; imparadised, **in paradise,** in heaven, in seventh heaven, on cloud nine <nonformal>; **elated,** elate, exalted, jubilant, exultant, flushed

17 pleasure-loving, pleasure-seeking, fun-loving, hedonic, hedonistic; Lucullan; epicurean, Cyrenaic, eudaemonic

ADVS **18 happily, gladly, joyfully, joyously, delightedly,** with pleasure, to one's delight; blissfully, blessedly; **ecstatically, rapturously; elatedly,** jubilantly, exultantly

19 for fun, for the hell *or* heck *or* devil of it <nonformal>

INTERJS **20 goody!,** goody, goody!, goody gumdrops!, good-o! <Brit>; whee!, **wow!,** u-mm!, mmmm!, oooo!, oo-la-la!; oh boy!, boy oh boy!, boy!, man!, hot dog!, hot ziggety!, hot diggety!, whoopee!, wowie zowie!, out of sight! *or* outa sight!, groovy!, keen-o!, keen-o-peachy!

96 UNPLEASURE

NOUNS **1 unpleasure, unpleasantness** 98, **lack of pleasure,** joylessness, cheerlessness; unsatisfaction, nonsatisfaction, ungratification, nongratification; grimness; discontent 108; displeasure, dissatisfaction, **discomfort,** uncomfortableness, misease <old>, malaise, **painfulness; disquiet,** inquietude, **uneasiness,** unease, discomposure, vexation of spirit, **anxiety;** angst, anguish, dread, nausea, existential woe, existential vacuum; the blahs <nonformal>; **dullness,** flatness, staleness, tastelessness, savorlessness; ashes in the mouth; **boredom,** ennui, tedium, tediousness, spleen; emptiness, spiritual void, death of the heart *or* soul; unhappiness 112.2; dislike 99

2 annoyance, vexation, bothersomeness, exasperation, *tracasserie* <Fr>, **aggravation; nuisance, pest, bother,** botheration <nonformal>, public nuisance, **trouble, problem,** pain <nonformal>, difficulty, hot potato <nonformal>; **trial; bore,** crashing bore <nonformal>; **drag** *and* downer <both nonformal>; **worry,** worriment <nonformal>; downside *and* the bad news <both nonformal>; **headache** <nonformal>; **pain in the neck** *or* **in the ass** <nonformal>; **harassment,** molestation, persecution, dogging, hounding, harrying; devilment, bedevilment; vexatiousness 98.7

3 irritation, aggravation, exacerbation, worsening, salt in the wound, twisting the knife in the wound, embitterment, **provocation;** fret, gall, chafe; irritant; pea in the shoe

4 chagrin, distress; embarrassment, abashment, discomfiture, egg on one's face <nonformal>, disconcertion, disconcertment, discountenance, discomposure, disturbance, confusion; **humiliation,**

shame, shamefacedness, mortification, red face

5 **pain, distress, grief,** stress, stress of life, suffering, passion, dolor; ache, aching; pang, wrench, throes, cramp, spasm; wound, injury, hurt; **sore,** sore spot, tender spot, lesion; cut, stroke; shock, blow, hard *or* nasty blow

6 **wretchedness, despair,** bitterness, infelicity, **misery, anguish, agony, woe,** woefulness, woesomeness <old>, bale, balefulness; **melancholy,** melancholia, **depression, sadness, grief** 112.10; **heartache,** aching heart, heavy heart, bleeding heart, broken heart, agony of mind *or* spirit; suicidal despair, black night of the soul, **despondency,** despond, "Slough of Despond"—Bunyan, **desolation,** prostration, crushing; extremity, depth of misery; sloth, acedia

7 **torment, torture,** cruciation <old>, excruciation, crucifixion, passion, laceration, clawing, lancination, flaying, excoriation; the rack, the iron maiden, thumbscrews; **persecution; martyrdom; purgatory,** "frigid purgatorial fires"— T S Eliot, living death, hell, hell upon earth; holocaust; nightmare, horror

8 **affliction,** infliction; **curse, woe,** distress, grievance, **sorrow,** *tsures* <Yiddish>; **trouble,** peck *or* pack of troubles, "sea of troubles"—Shakespeare; **care,** burden of care, cankerworm of care; **burden, oppression, cross, cross to bear** *or* **be borne, load,** fardel <old>, encumbrance, weight, albatross around one's neck, millstone around one's neck; thorn, thorn in the side, crown of thorns; bitter pill, bitter draft, bitter cup, cup *or* waters of bitterness; gall, gall and wormwood; "the thousand natural shocks that flesh is heir to"—Shakespeare, "all the ills that men endure"—Abraham Cowley; Pandora's box

9 **trial, tribulation,** trials and tribulations; **ordeal,** fiery ordeal, the iron entering the soul

10 **tormentor,** torment; torturer; **nuisance, pest,** pesterer, pain *and* pain in the neck *or* ass <nonformal>, nag, nudzh <nonformal>, *nudnik* <Yiddish>, public nuisance; **tease,** teaser; annoyer, harasser, harrier, badgerer, **heckler,** plaguer, persecutor, sadist; molester, **bully**

11 **sufferer,** victim, prey; **wretch,** poor devil <nonformal>, object of compassion; martyr

VERBS 12 give no pleasure *or* joy *or* cheer *or* comfort, **disquiet,** discompose, leave unsatisfied; discontent; taste like ashes in the mouth; **bore,** be tedious, cheese off <Brit nonformal>

13 **annoy, irk, vex, nettle, provoke, pique,** miff *and* peeve <both nonformal>, distemper, **ruffle, disturb,** discompose, **roil,** rile, **aggravate,** make a nuisance of oneself, **exasperate,** exercise, try one's patience, try the patience of a saint; **put one's back up,** make one bristle; **gripe;** give one a pain <nonformal>; get, get one down, **get one's goat,** get under one's skin, get in one's hair, tread on one's toes; burn up *and* brown off <both nonformal>; **torment, molest, bother,** pother; **harass,** harry, drive up the wall <nonformal>, **hound,** dog, nag, nobble <Brit nonformal>, nudzh <nonformal>, **persecute; heckle,** pick *or* prod at, rub it in *and* rub one's nose in it <both nonformal>, badger, hector, bait, bullyrag, worry, worry at, nip at the heels of, chivy, hardly give one time to breathe, make one's life miserable, keep on at, fash <Scots>; **bug** <nonformal>, be on the back of *and* be at *and* ride <all nonformal>, **pester, tease, needle,** devil, get after *or* get on <nonformal>, **bedevil, pick on** <nonformal>, tweak the nose, pluck the beard, give a bad time to <nonformal>; **plague,** beset, beleaguer; catch in the crossfire *or* in the middle; catch one off balance, trip one up

14 **irritate, aggravate,** exacerbate, worsen, rub salt in the wound, twist the knife in the wound, step on one's corns, barb the dart; touch a soft spot *or* tender spot, touch a raw nerve, touch where it hurts; provoke, **gall, chafe, fret,** grate, grit *and* gravel <both nonformal>, rasp; **get on one's nerves, grate on,** set on edge; **set one's teeth on edge,** go against the grain; **rub one** *or* **one's fur the wrong way**

15 **chagrin, embarrass, abash, discomfit, disconcert,** discompose, confuse, throw into confusion *or* a tizzy *or* a hissy-fit, **upset,** confound, cast down, mortify, put out, put out of face *or* countenance, put to the blush

16 **distress, afflict, trouble,** burden, give one a tough row to hoe, load with care, **bother, disturb, perturb, disquiet, discomfort, agitate, upset,** put to it; **worry,** give one gray hair

17 **pain, grieve, aggrieve,** anguish; **hurt, wound,** bruise, **hurt one's feelings;** pierce, prick, stab, cut, sting; **cut up** <nonformal>, **cut to the heart,** wound *or* sting *or* cut to the quick, hit one where one

lives <nonformal>; be a thorn in one's side

18 torture, torment, agonize, harrow, savage, **rack,** scarify, crucify, impale, excruciate, lacerate, claw, rip, bloody, lancinate, macerate, convulse, wring; prolong the agony, kill by inches, make life miserable *or* not worth living; martyr, martyrize; **tyrannize,** push around <nonformal>; punish 604.10

19 suffer, hurt, ache, bleed; anguish, **suffer anguish; agonize,** writhe; go hard with, have a bad time of it, go through hell; quaff the bitter cup, drain the cup of misery to the dregs, be nailed to the cross

ADJS **20 pleasureless,** joyless, cheerless, depressed 112.22, grim; **sad, unhappy** 112.21; unsatisfied, unfulfilled, ungratified; **bored,** cheesed off <Brit nonformal>; anguished, anxious, suffering angst *or* dread *or* nausea, uneasy, unquiet, prey to malaise; **repelled,** revolted, **disgusted,** sickened, nauseated, nauseous

21 annoyed, irritated, bugged <nonformal>; galled, chafed; **bothered, troubled, disturbed, ruffled, roiled,** riled; **irked, vexed, piqued, nettled, provoked, peeved** *and* miffed <both nonformal>, **griped, aggravated, exasperated;** burnt-up *and* browned-off <both nonformal>, resentful, angry 152.28

22 distressed, afflicted, put-upon, beset, beleaguered; caught in the middle *or* in the crossfire; **troubled, bothered, disturbed, perturbed, disquieted,** discomforted, discomposed, agitated; hung up <nonformal>; **uncomfortable,** uneasy, ill at ease; **chagrined, embarrassed,** abashed, discomfited, **disconcerted, upset, confused,** mortified, **put-out,** out of countenance, cast down, chapfallen

23 pained, grieved, aggrieved; **wounded, hurt,** injured, **bruised,** mauled; **cut,** cut to the quick; **stung;** anguished, aching, bleeding

24 tormented, plagued, harassed, harried, dogged, **hounded, persecuted,** beset; nipped at, worried, chivied, **heckled,** badgered, hectored, baited, bullyragged, ragged, **pestered, teased, needled,** deviled, **bedeviled, picked on** <nonformal>, **bugged** <nonformal>

25 tortured, harrowed, savaged, **agonized,** convulsed, wrung, racked, crucified, impaled, lacerated, excoriated, clawed, ripped, bloodied, lancinated; on the rack, under the harrow

26 wretched, miserable; woeful, woebegone, woesome <old>; crushed, stricken, **cut up** <nonformal>, heartsick, heart-stricken, heart-struck; deep-troubled; desolate, disconsolate, suicidal

ADVS **27** to one's displeasure, to one's disgust

97 PLEASANTNESS

NOUNS **1 pleasantness,** pleasingness, pleasance, **pleasure** 95, pleasurefulness, **pleasurableness,** pleasurability, pleasantry <old>, felicitousness, **enjoyableness; bliss, blissfulness;** sweetness, mellifluousness, *douceur* <Fr>; mellowness; **agreeableness,** agreeability, complaisance, rapport, harmoniousness; compatibility; welcomeness; geniality, congeniality, cordiality, *Gemütlichkeit* <Ger>, affability, amicability, amiability; amenity, graciousness; goodness, goodliness, niceness; **fun** 743.2/95.1

2 delightfulness, exquisiteness, loveliness; **charm,** winsomeness, grace, **attractiveness, appeal,** appealingness, winningness; sexiness <nonformal>; **glamour;** captivation, enchantment, entrancement, bewitchment, witchery, enravishment, **fascination** 377.1; invitingness, temptingness, tantalizingness; voluptuousness, sensuousness; luxury

3 delectability, delectableness, deliciousness, lusciousness; tastiness, flavorsomeness, savoriness; juiciness; succulence

4 cheerfulness; brightness, sunniness; sunny side, bright side; fair weather

VERBS **5** make pleasant, brighten, sweeten, gild, gild the lily *or* pill; sentimentalize, saccharinize

ADJS **6 pleasant, pleasing, pleasureful, pleasurable;** fair, fair and pleasant, **enjoyable,** pleasure-giving; felicitous, felicific; **likable, desirable,** to one's liking, to one's taste, to *or* after one's fancy, after one's own heart; **agreeable,** complaisant, harmonious, *en rapport* <Fr>, compatible; **blissful;** sweet, mellifluous, honeyed, dulcet; mellow; **gratifying,** satisfying, rewarding, heartwarming, grateful; **welcome,** welcome as the roses in May; genial, congenial, cordial, *gemütlich* <Ger>, affable, amiable, amicable, gracious; good, goodly, nice, fine; cheerful 109.11

7 delightful, exquisite, lovely; thrilling, titillative; **charming, attractive, endearing, engaging, appealing,** prepossessing, heartwarming, sexy <nonformal>, **en-**

chanting, bewitching, witching, entrancing, enthralling, intriguing, fascinating; **captivating, irresistible, ravishing,** enravishing; **winning,** winsome, taking, fetching, heart-robbing; inviting, tempting, tantalizing; voluptuous, zaftig <nonformal>, sensuous; luxurious, delicious

8 <nonformal terms> **fun, kicky,** chewy, dishy, drooly, sexy, toast, yummy

9 **blissful,** beatific, saintly, divine; sublime; **heavenly,** paradisal, paradisiac, paradisiacal, paradisic, paradisical, empyreal *or* empyrean, Elysian; out of sight *or* of this world <nonformal>

10 **delectable, delicious,** luscious; tasty, flavorsome, savory; juicy, succulent

11 **bright, sunny,** fair, mild, balmy; halcyon, Saturnian

ADVS 12 **pleasantly, pleasingly, pleasurably,** fair, **enjoyably; blissfully; gratifyingly,** satisfyingly; agreeably, genially, affably, cordially, amiably, amicably, graciously, kindly; cheerfully 109.17

13 **delightfully, exquisitely; charmingly, engagingly, appealingly, enchantingly,** bewitchingly, entrancingly, intriguingly, fascinatingly; ravishingly, enravishingly; **winningly,** winsomely; invitingly, temptingly, tantalizingly, voluptuously, sensuously; luxuriously

14 **delectably,** deliciously, lusciously, tastily, succulently, savorously

98 UNPLEASANTNESS

NOUNS 1 **unpleasantness,** unpleasingness, displeasingness, displeasure; **disagreeableness,** disagreeability, *désagrément* <Fr>; **abrasiveness,** woundingess, hostility, unfriendliness; **undesirability,** unappealingness, unattractive-ness, unengagingness, uninvitingness, unprepossessingness; **distastefulness,** unsavoriness, unpalatability, **undelectability; ugliness** 1014

2 **offensiveness,** objectionability, objectionableness; repugnance, contrariety, **odiousness, repulsiveness,** repellence *or* repellency, rebarbativeness, disgustingness, nauseousness, grossness *and* yuckiness *and* grunginess *and* scuzziness <all nonformal>; **loathsomeness, hatefulness,** beastliness <nonformal>; **vileness, foulness,** putridness, putridity, rottenness, noxiousness; **nastiness,** fulsomeness, noisomeness, **obnoxiousness,** abominableness, heinousness; **contempt-** **ibleness,** contemptibility, despicability, **despicableness,** baseness, ignobleness, ignobility; unspeakableness; coarseness, grossness, crudeness, obscenity

3 **dreadfulness, horribleness,** horridness, atrociousness, atrocity, hideousness, terribleness, awfulness <nonformal>; grimness, direness, banefulness

4 **harshness, agony,** agonizingness, excruciation, excruciatingness, **torture,** torturesomeness, torturousness, **torment,** tormentingness; desolation, desolateness; heartbreak, heartsickness

5 **distressfulness, distress, grievousness, grief; painfulness,** pain 26; **harshness,** bitterness, sharpness; lamentability, lamentableness, deplorability, deplorableness, pitiableness, pitifulness, pitiability, regrettableness; **woe, sadness, sorrowfulness, mournfulness,** lamentation, woefulness, woesomeness <old>, woebegoneness, pathos, poignancy; comfortlessness, discomfort, misease <old>; dreariness, cheerlessness, joylessness, dismalness, **depression,** bleakness

6 **mortification,** humiliation, embarrassment, egg on one's face <nonformal>; disconcertedness, awkwardness

7 **vexatiousness, irksomeness, annoyance,** annoyingness, aggravation, exasperation, provocation, provokingness, tiresomeness, wearisomeness; **troublesomeness, bothersomeness,** harassment; worrisomeness, plaguesomeness, peskiness *and* pestiferousness <both nonformal>

8 **harshness, oppressiveness, burdensomeness,** onerousness, weightiness, heaviness

9 **intolerability,** intolerableness, unbearableness, insupportableness, insufferableness, **unendurability**

VERBS 10 **be unpleasant; displease;** be disagreeable *or* undesirable *or* distasteful *or* abrasive

11 **offend,** give offense, **repel,** put off, turn off <nonformal>, **revolt, disgust,** nauseate, sicken, make one sick, make one sick to *or* in the stomach, make one vomit *or* puke *or* retch, turn the stomach, gross out <nonformal>; stink in the nostrils; stick in one's throat, stick in one's crop *or* craw *or* gizzard <nonformal>; **horrify, appall,** shock; make the flesh creep *or* crawl, make one shudder

12 **agonize,** excruciate, **torture, torment,** desolate

13 **mortify,** humiliate, embarrass, disconcert, disturb

14 **distress, dismay,** grieve, mourn, lament, sorrow; pain, discomfort, misease

<old>; get in one's hair, try one's patience, give one a hard time *or* a pain *or* a pain in the neck *or* ass *or* butt <nonformal>

15 vex, irk, annoy, aggravate, exasperate, provoke; **trouble, worry,** give one gray hair, plague, harass, bother, hassle

16 oppress, burden, weigh upon, weight down, wear one down, be heavy on one, crush one; **tire, exhaust,** weary, wear out, wear upon one; prey on the mind, prey on *or* upon; **haunt,** haunt the memory, obsess

ADJS **17 unpleasant, unpleasing, unenjoyable; displeasing, disagreeable; unlikable,** dislikable; **abrasive,** wounding, hostile, unfriendly; **undesirable,** unattractive, unappealing, unengaging, uninviting, unalluring; tacky *and* low rent *and* low ride <all nonformal>; unwelcome, thankless; **distasteful,** untasteful, **unpalatable,** unsavory, unappetizing, undelicious, **undelectable; ugly** 1014.6; sour, **bitter**

18 offensive, objectionable, odious, repulsive, repellent, rebarbative, **repugnant, revolting,** forbidding; **disgusting, sickening, loathsome,** gross *and* yucky *and* grungy *and* scuzzy <all nonformal>, beastly <nonformal>, **vile, foul, nasty, nauseating** 64.7; fulsome, mephitic, miasmal, miasmic, malodorous, stinking, fetid, noisome, noxious; coarse, gross, crude, obscene; **obnoxious, abhorrent, hateful, abominable,** heinous, **contemptible, despicable,** detestable, execrable, beneath *or* below contempt, **base,** ignoble

19 horrid, horrible, horrific, **horrifying,** horrendous, unspeakable, beyond words; **dreadful, atrocious, terrible, rotten,** awful *and* beastly <both nonformal>, **hideous; tragic;** dire, grim, baneful; appalling, shocking, disgusting

20 distressing, distressful, dismaying; afflicting, afflictive; **painful,** sore, **harsh, bitter,** sharp; **grievous,** dolorous, dolorific, dolorogenic; **lamentable, deplorable,** regrettable, pitiable, piteous, rueful, woeful, woesome <old>, woebegone, **sad,** sorrowful, wretched, mournful, **depressing,** depressive; **pathetic,** affecting, touching, moving, saddening, poignant; comfortless, discomforting, uncomfortable; **desolate,** dreary, cheerless, joyless, dismal, bleak

21 mortifying, humiliating, **embarrassing,** crushing, disconcerting, awkward, disturbing

22 annoying, irritating, galling, **provoking, aggravating** <nonformal>, **exasperating; vexatious,** vexing, irking, **irksome,** tiresome, wearisome; **troublesome, bothersome, worrisome,** bothering, troubling, disturbing, plaguing, plaguesome, plaguey <nonformal>, pestilent, pestilential, **pesky** *and* pesty *and* pestiferous <all nonformal>; tormenting, harassing, worrying; pestering, teasing; importunate, importune

23 agonizing, excruciating, harrowing, racking, rending, **desolating,** consuming; **tormenting,** torturous; **heartbreaking,** heartrending, **heartsickening,** heartwounding

24 oppressive, burdensome, crushing, trying, onerous, heavy, weighty; **harsh,** wearing, wearying, exhausting; overburdensome, tyrannous, grinding

25 insufferable, intolerable, insupportable, unendurable, unbearable, past bearing, not to be borne *or* endured, for the birds <nonformal>, **too much** *or* a bit much <nonformal>, more than flesh and blood can bear, enough to drive one mad, enough to provoke a saint, enough to make a preacher swear <nonformal>, enough to try the patience of Job

ADVS **26 unpleasantly, distastefully** unpleasingly; **displeasingly, offensively, objectionably,** odiously, **repulsively,** repellently, rebarbatively, repugnantly, **revoltingly, disgustingly, sickeningly, loathsomely, vilely,** foully, nastily, fulsomely, mephitically, malodorously, fetidly, noisomely, noxiously, obnoxiously, **abhorrently, hatefully, abominably,** contemptibly, **despicably, detestably,** execrably, nauseatingly

27 horridly, horribly, dreadfully, terribly, hideously; **tragically;** grimly, direly, banefully; appallingly, shockingly

28 distressingly, distressfully; **painfully,** sorely, **grievously,** lamentably, deplorably, pitiably, ruefully, woefully, woesomely <old>, sadly, pathetically; **agonizingly, excruciatingly,** harrowingly, heartbreakingly

29 annoyingly, irritatingly, aggravatingly, provokingly, exasperatingly; vexatiously, irksomely, tiresomely, wearisomely; **troublesomely, bothersomely,** worrisomely, regrettably

30 insufferably, intolerably, unbearably, unendurably, insupportably

INTERJS **31** eeyuck! *or* yeeuck! *or* yeeuch!, phew! *or* pugh!, ugh!; *feh!* <Yiddish>; alas, alack

99 DISLIKE

NOUNS **1 dislike, distaste,** disrelish, scunner; disaffection, **disfavor,** disinclination; disaffinity; **displeasure, disapproval,** disapprobation

2 hostility, antagonism, **enmity** 589; **hatred, hate** 103; **aversion, repugnance,** repulsion, **antipathy,** allergy <nonformal>, grudge, abomination, **abhorrence, horror,** mortal horror; **disgust, loathing;** nausea; shuddering, cold sweat, creeping flesh

VERBS **3 dislike,** mislike, disfavor, not like, have no liking for, be no love lost between, **have no use for** <nonformal>, **not care for,** have no time for, have a disaffinity for, want nothing to do with, not think much of, entertain *or* conceive *or* take a dislike to, take a scunner to, not be able to bear *or* endure *or* abide, not give the time of day to <nonformal>, **disapprove of; disrelish,** have no taste for, not stomach, not have the stomach for, not be one's cup of tea; be hostile to, have it in for <nonformal>; **hate, abhor, detest, loathe** 103.5

4 feel disgust, be nauseated, **sicken at,** choke on, have a bellyful of <nonformal>; **gag, retch,** keck, heave, vomit, puke, hurl *and* upchuck *and* barf <all nonformal>

5 shudder at, have one's flesh creep *or* crawl at the thought of; shrink from, **recoil, revolt at; grimace,** make a face, make a wry face *or* mouth, turn up one's nose, look down one's nose, look askance, raise one's eyebrows, take a dim view of, show distaste for, disapprove of

6 repel, disgust 98.11, gross out <nonformal>; leave a bad taste in one's mouth

ADJS **7 unlikable, distasteful,** mislikable, dislikable, **uncongenial, displeasing,** unpleasant 98.17; **not to one's taste,** not one's sort, not one's cup of tea, counter to one's preferences, offering no delight, against the grain, uninviting; unlovable; **abhorrent, odious** 98.18; **intolerable** 98.25

8 averse, allergic <nonformal>, undelighted, out of sympathy, disaffected, disenchanted, **disinclined, displeased,** put off <nonformal>, not charmed, less than pleased; **disapproving, censorious, judgmental,** po-faced <Brit nonformal>; unamiable, **unfriendly, hostile** 589.10; death on, down on

9 disliked, uncared-for, unvalued, unprized, misprized, undervalued; **de-**spised,** lowly, spat-upon, untouchable; **unpopular, out of favor,** gone begging; **unappreciated,** misunderstood; unsung, thankless; unwept, unlamented, unmourned, undeplored, unmissed, unregretted

10 unloved, unbeloved, uncherished, loveless; **lovelorn,** forsaken, **rejected,** jilted, thrown over <nonformal>, spurned, crossed in love

11 unwanted, unwished, undesired; **unwelcome,** unasked, unbidden, uninvited, uncalled-for, unasked-for

100 DESIRE

NOUNS **1 desire, wish,** wanting, **want, need,** desideration; **hope; fancy; will, mind, pleasure,** will and pleasure; heart's desire; **urge,** drive, libido, pleasure principle; concupiscence; horme; wish fulfillment, fantasy; passion, ardor, sexual desire 75.5; **curiosity,** intellectual curiosity, thirst for knowledge, lust for learning; **eagerness** 101

2 liking, love, fondness; infatuation, crush; **affection; relish, taste,** gusto, gust <Scots>; **passion, weakness** <nonformal>

3 inclination, penchant, partiality, fancy, favor, predilection, preference, propensity, proclivity, **leaning, bent,** turn, tilt, bias, **affinity;** mutual affinity *or* attraction; **sympathy,** fascination

4 wistfulness, wishfulness, yearnfulness, **nostalgia;** wishful thinking; sheep's eyes, longing *or* wistful eye; daydream, daydreaming

5 yearning, yen <nonformal>; **longing,** desiderium, **hankering** <nonformal>, **pining,** honing <nonformal>, aching; languishment, languishing; **nostalgia, homesickness,** *Heimweh* <Ger>, *mal du pays* and *maladie du pays* <both Fr>; nostomania

6 craving, coveting, lust; hunger, thirst, appetite, "appetite, an universal wolf"— Shakespeare, appetition, appetency *or* appetence; aching void; **itch, itching,** prurience *or* pruriency; lech <nonformal>, **sexual desire** 75.5; *cacoëthes* <L>, **mania** 925.12

7 appetite, stomach, relish, taste; **hunger,** hungriness; the munchies <nonformal>, peckishness <Brit nonformal>; tapeworm <nonformal>, eyes bigger than one's stomach, wolf in one's stomach, canine appetite; empty stomach, emptiness <nonformal>, hollow hunger; **thirst,**

thirstiness, drought <nonformal>, dryness; polydipsia; torment of Tantalus; sweet tooth <nonformal>

8 greed, greediness, graspingness, **avarice, cupidity, avidity, voracity, rapacity, lust,** avariciousness, *avaritia and cupiditas* <both L>; money-grubbing; avidness, esurience, wolfishness; voraciousness, ravenousness, rapaciousness, sordidness, **covetousness,** acquisitiveness; itching palm; grasping; **piggishness, hoggishness,** swinishness; **gluttony** 672, *gula* <L>; inordinate desire, furor, craze, fury *or* frenzy of desire, overgreediness; insatiable desire, insatiability; incontinence, intemperateness 669.1

9 aspiration, reaching high, upward looking; "the desire of the moth for the star"—Shelley; high goal *or* aim *or* purpose, dream, ideals; **idealism** 985.7

10 ambition, ambitiousness, vaulting ambition; climbing, status-seeking, social climbing, careerism; opportunism; power-hunger; "the mind's immodesty"—d'Avenant, "the way in which a vulgar man aspires"—Henry Ward Beecher, "the evil shadow of aspiration"—George Macdonald, "the avarice of power"—G G Coulton, "avarice on stilts and masked"—W S Landor; noble *or* lofty ambition, magnanimity <old>; "the spur that makes man struggle with destiny"—Donald G Mitchell

11 <object of desire> **desire,** heart's desire, desideration, *desideratum* <L>; wish; **hope;** catch, quarry, prey, game, plum, prize, trophy; forbidden fruit, temptation; lodestone, magnet; golden vision, mecca, glimmering goal; land of heart's desire 985.11; something to be desired, "a consummation devoutly to be wish'd"—Shakespeare; dearest wish, ambition, the height of one's ambition; a sight for sore eyes, a welcome sight; the light at the end of the tunnel

12 desirer, wisher, wanter, hankerer <nonformal>, yearner, coveter; fancier, collector; addict, freak <nonformal>, devotee, votary; **aspirant,** aspirer, solicitant, wannabee *and* hopeful <both nonformal>, candidate; **lover,** swain, suitor

13 desirability; agreeability, acceptability, unobjectionableness; **attractiveness,** attraction, magnetism, **appeal,** seductiveness, provocativeness, pleasingness; likability, lovability 104.7

VERBS **14 desire,** desiderate, be desirous of, **wish,** lust after, bay after, kill for *and* give one's right arm for <both nonformal>,

die for <nonformal>, **want,** have a mind to, choose <nonformal>; would fain do *or* have <old>, would be glad of; **like,** have *or* acquire a taste for, fancy, take to, **take a fancy** *or* a shine to, have a fancy for; have an eye to, have one's eye on; lean toward, tilt toward, have a penchant for, have a weakness *or* soft spot in one's heart for; aim at, set one's cap for, have designs on; wish very much, wish to goodness; **love** 104.18; lust; prefer, favor 371.17

15 want to; wish to, like to, love to, dearly love to, choose to; **itch to,** burn to; ache to, long to

16 wish for, hope for, yearn for, yen for *and* have a yen for <both nonformal>, **itch for,** lust for, pant for, **long for, pine for,** hone for <nonformal>, ache for, be hurting for <nonformal>, weary for, languish for, **be dying for,** thirst for, sigh for, gape for <old>; cry for, clamor for; spoil for <nonformal>

17 want with all one's heart, want in the worst way; set one's heart on, have one's heart set on, give one's kingdom in hell for *or* one's eyeteeth for <nonformal>

18 crave, covet, hunger after, thirst after, crave after, **lust after,** have a lech for <nonformal>, pant after, run mad after, **hanker for** *or* **after** <nonformal>; crawl after; aspire after, be consumed with desire; have an itchy *or* itching palm *and* have sticky fingers <all nonformal>

19 hunger, hunger for, feel hungry, be peckish <Brit nonformal>; starve <nonformal>, be ravenous, raven; **have a good appetite,** be a good trencherman, have a tapeworm <nonformal>, have a wolf in one's stomach; eye hungrily, lick one's chops <nonformal>; **thirst,** thirst for

20 aspire, be ambitious; aspire to, try to reach; aim high, keep one's eyes on the stars, raise one's sights, set one's sights, reach for the sky, "hitch one's wagon to a star"—Emerson

ADJS **21 desirous,** desiring, desireful <old>, lickerish, **wanting, wishing,** needing, hoping; dying to <nonformal>; tempted; appetitive, desiderative, optative, libidinous, libidinal; orectic; hormic; **eager;** lascivious, **lustful**

22 desirous of *or* **to,** keen on, set on <nonformal>, bent on; fond of, with a liking for, partial to <nonformal>; fain of *or* to <old>; inclined toward, leaning toward; **itching for** *or* **to,** aching for *or* to, **dying for** *or* **to;** spoiling for <nonformal>; mad

on *or* for, wild to *or* for <nonformal>,
crazy to *or* for <nonformal> ·

23 **wistful**, wishful; **longing, yearning,**
yearnful, **hankering** <nonformal>, **languishing, pining,** honing <nonformal>;
nostalgic, homesick

24 **craving,** coveting; **hungering,** hungry,
thirsting, thirsty, athirst; **itching,** prurient; fervid; **devoured by desire,** in a
frenzy *or* fury of desire, mad with lust,
consumed with desire

25 **hungry,** hungering, peckish <Brit nonfor-
mal>; empty <nonformal>, unfilled;
ravening, **ravenous,** voracious, sharp-set,
wolfish, dog-hungry <nonformal>, hungry as a bear; **starved, famished,** starving, famishing, perishing *or* pinched with
hunger; fasting; half-starved, half-
famished

26 **thirsty,** thirsting, athirst; **dry,** parched,
droughty <nonformal>

27 **greedy, avaricious, avid, voracious, rapacious,** cupidinous, esurient, **ravening,
grasping, grabby** <nonformal>, graspy,
acquisitive, mercenary, sordid, over-
greedy; ravenous, gobbling, devouring;
miserly, money-hungry, money-grubbing, money-mad, venal; **covetous,** coveting; **piggish, hoggish,** swinish, a hog for,
greedy as a hog; **gluttonous** 672.6; omnivorous, all-devouring; insatiable, insatiate, unsatisfied, unsated, unappeased,
unappeasable, limitless, bottomless, unquenchable, quenchless, unslaked,
unslakeable, slakeless

28 **aspiring, ambitious,** sky-aspiring,
upward-looking, high-reaching; high-
flying, social-climbing, careerist, ca-
reeristic, on the make <nonformal>;
power-hungry

29 **desired, wanted,** coveted; **wished-for,**
hoped-for, longed-for; in demand, popular

30 **desirable,** sought-after, much sought-
after, to be desired, **much to be desired;
enviable,** worth having; **likable, pleasing,**
after one's own heart; **agreeable,** acceptable, unobjectionable; palatable; **attractive,** taking, winning, sexy <nonformal>,
dishy <Brit nonformal>, **seductive, provocative,** tantalizing, exciting; appetizing, tempting, toothsome, mouth-
watering; **lovable,** adorable

ADVS 31 **desirously, wistfully,** wishfully,
longingly, yearningly, piningly, lan-
guishingly; cravingly, itchingly;
hungrily, thirstily; aspiringly, ambi-
tiously

32 **greedily, avariciously,** avidly, raven-

ously, raveningly, voraciously, rapa-
ciously, **covetously,** graspingly, de-
vouringly; wolfishly, **piggishly, hoggishly,** swinishly

101 EAGERNESS

NOUNS 1 **eagerness, enthusiasm, avidity,**
avidness, keenness <chiefly Brit>, forwardness, prothymia, **readiness,** promptness, quickness, **alacrity,** cheerful readiness, *empressement* <Fr>; keen desire,
appetite 100.7; anxiousness, anxiety;
zest, zestfulness, gusto, gust <Scots>,
verve, **liveliness,** life, **vitality,** vivacity,
élan, spirit, animation; **impatience,**
breathless impatience 135.1; keen interest, fascination; **craze** 925.12

2 **zeal, ardor, ardency, fervor, fervency, fervidness, spirit, warmth, fire, heat,** heatedness, **passion,** passionateness, impassionedness, heartiness, intensity, **abandon,** vehemence; intentness, resolution
359; **devotion,** devoutness, devotedness,
dedication, commitment, committed-
ness; **earnestness, seriousness,** sincerity;
loyalty, faithfulness, faith, fidelity 644.7;
discipleship, followership

3 **overzealousness, overeagerness,** overanx-
iousness, overanxiety; unchecked enthusiasm, **overenthusiasm, infatuation;
overambitiousness; frenzy, fury; zealotry,** zealotism; mania, **fanaticism** 925.11

4 **enthusiast, zealot,** infatuate, energumen,
rhapsodist; addict; faddist; pursuer; hob-
byist, collector; **fanatic;** visionary 985.13;
devotee, votary, aficionada, aficionado,
fancier, admirer, **follower; disciple,** worshiper, idolizer, idolater; amateur, dilettante; collector

5 <nonformal terms> **fan, buff, freak,**
hound, fiend, demon, nut, bug, head,
junkie, groupie, rooter, booster, great one
for, sucker for; fan club, fanzine; eager
beaver, —aholic

VERBS 6 **jump at,** catch, grab, grab at,
snatch, snatch at, fall all over oneself, get
excited about, go at hammer and tongs *or*
tooth and nail, go hog wild <nonformal>;
go to great lengths, lean *or* bend *or* fall
over backwards; **desire** 100.14,18

7 **be enthusiastic, rave, enthuse** *and* be big
for <both nonformal>; get stars in one's
eyes, **rhapsodize, carry on over** *and* rave
on <both nonformal>, make much of,
make a fuss over, make an ado *or* much
ado about, make a to-do over *and* take on
over <both nonformal>, be *or* go on over
or about <nonformal>, rave about *and*

whoop it up about <both nonformal>; go
nuts *or* gaga *or* ape over <nonformal>;
gush, gush over; effervesce, bubble over

ADJS **8 eager, anxious,** agog, all agog; **avid,
keen,** forward, prompt, quick, ready,
ready and willing, alacritous, bursting to,
dying to, raring to; **zestful, lively,** full of
life, vital, vivacious, vivid, spirited, **animated; impatient** 135.6; breathless,
panting, champing at the bit; **desirous**
100.21

9 zealous, ardent, fervent, fervid, perfervid, **spirited, intense,** hearty, vehement,
abandoned, **passionate,** impassioned,
warm, heated, hot, hot-blooded, red-hot,
fiery, white-hot, flaming, burning, afire,
aflame, on fire, like a house afire <nonfor-
mal>; **devout, devoted;** dedicated, committed; **earnest, sincere, serious,** in earnest; loyal, faithful 644.20; intent, intent
on, resolute 359.11

10 enthusiastic, enthused *and* big <both
nonformal>, **gung ho** <nonformal>,
glowing, full of enthusiasm; enthusiastic
about, infatuated with

11 <nonformal terms> **wild about, crazy
about, mad about,** ape about *or* over,
gone on, all in a dither over, gaga over,
starry-eyed over, all hopped up about,
hepped up over, hot about *or* for *or* on,
steamed up about, **turned-on, switched-
on;** hipped on, **cracked on,** bugs on,
freaked-out, **nuts on** *or* over *or* **about,
keen on** *or* **about,** crazy *or* mad *or* nuts
about

12 overzealous, ultrazealous, **overeager,**
over-anxious; **overambitious;** over-
desirous; **overenthusiastic, infatuated;**
feverish, perfervid, febrile, at fever *or* fevered pitch; hectic, frenetic, furious,
frenzied, frantic, **wild,** hysteric, hysterical, delirious; **insane** 925.26; **fanatical**
925.32

ADVS **13 eagerly, anxiously; impatiently,**
breathlessly; **avidly,** promptly, quickly,
keenly, readily; zestfully, vivaciously, animatedly; **enthusiastically,** with enthusiasm; **with alacrity,** with zest, with gusto,
with relish, with open arms

14 zealously, ardently, fervently, fervidly,
perfervidly, heatedly, heartily, vehemently, **passionately,** impassionedly;
intently, intensely; **devoutly, devotedly;**
earnestly, sincerely, seriously

102 INDIFFERENCE

NOUNS **1 indifference,** indifferentness; indifferentism; halfheartedness, zeallessness,

perfunctoriness, fervorlessness; **coolness,**
coldness, chilliness, chill, iciness, frostiness; tepidness, **lukewarmness,** Laodiceanism; **neutrality,** neutralness, neuterness; insipidity, vapidity

**2 unconcern, disinterest, detachment; dis-
regard, dispassion,** insouciance, **carelessness,** regardlessness; easygoingness;
heedlessness, mindlessness, inattention
983; **unmindfulness, incuriosity** 981; **insensitivity;** disregardfulness, recklessness, negligence 340.1; *je-m'en-foutisme*
or je-m'en-fichisme <Fr>; unsolicitousness, unanxiousness; pococurantism;
nonchalance, inexcitability 106, ataraxy
or ataraxia, samadhi; indiscrimination,
casualness 944.1; **listlessness,** lackadaisicalness, lack of feeling *or* affect,
apathy 94.4; sloth, acedia

3 undesirousness, desirelessness; nirvana;
lovelessness, passionlessness; uneager-
ness, **unambitiousness;** lack of appetite,
inappetence

VERBS **4 not care, not mind, not give *or* care
a damn,** not give a hoot *or* shit <nonfor-
mal>, not care less *or* two hoots <non-
formal>, care nothing for *or* about, not
care a straw about; shrug off; **take no interest in,** have no desire for, have no taste
or relish for; hold no brief for; be halfhearted, temper one's zeal

5 not matter to, be all one to, take it or
leave it; make no difference, make no
never-mind <nonformal>

ADJS **6 indifferent, halfhearted,** zealless,
perfunctory, fervorless; **cool, cold** 589.9;
tepid, **lukewarm,** Laodicean; neither hot
nor cold, neither one thing nor the other,
"neither fish, nor flesh, nor good red herring"—John Heywood; **neuter, neutral**

7 unconcerned, uninterested, disinterested,
turned-off, **dispassionate,** insouciant,
careless, regardless; easygoing; incurious
981.3; mindless, **unmindful, heedless,** inattentive 983.6, disregardful; **devil-may-
care,** reckless, negligent 340.10; unsolicitous, unanxious; pococurante, **nonchalant,** inexcitable 106.10; ataractic; **blasé**
undiscriminating, casual 944.5; **listless,**
lackadaisical, sluggish; bovine; numb,
apathetic 94.13

8 undesirous, unattracted, desireless; loveless, passionless; inappetent; nirvanic;
unenthusiastic, uneager; **unambitious,**
unaspiring

ADVS **9 indifferently, with indifference,** with
utter indifference; coolly, coldly; luke-
warmly, halfheartedly; perfunctorily; for
all *or* aught one cares

10 **unconcernedly, uninterestedly, disinterestedly,** dispassionately, insouciantly, **carelessly,** regardlessly; mindlessly; **unmindfully, heedlessly,** recklessly, negligently 340.17; **nonchalantly;** listlessly, lackadaisically; numbly, **apathetically** 94.15

PHRS 11 **who cares?,** I don't care, I couldn't care less <nonformal>; it's a matter of sublime indifference; never mind!, **what does it matter?,** what's the difference?, what's the diff? <nonformal>, what are the odds?, what of it?, what boots it?, **so what?,** what the hell <nonformal>, it's all one to me, it's all the same to me, it's no skin off one's nose or ass <nonformal>; like it or lump it

12 **I should worry?,** I should fret?, that's your lookout, that's your problem, I feel for you but I can't reach you; that's your pigeon <nonformal>, that's your tough luck, tough titty and shit <both nonformal>

103 HATE

NOUNS 1 **hate, hatred; dislike** 99; **detestation, abhorrence, aversion, antipathy,** repugnance, **loathing,** execration, **abomination,** odium; **spite,** spitefulness, despite, despitefulness, **malice, malevolence,** malignity; vials of hate or wrath; misanthropy, misanthropism; misandry, misogyny; misogamy; misopedia; anti-Semitism; race hatred, racism, racialism; bigotry; Anglophobia, Russophobia, xenophobia, etc; scorn, despising, **contempt** 157

2 **enmity** 589; bitterness, **animosity** 589.4
3 <hated thing> **anathema, abomination,** detestation, aversion, abhorrence, antipathy, execration, hate; peeve, pet peeve; phobia
4 hater, man-hater, woman-hater, misanthropist, misanthrope, misogynist, anti-Semite, racist, racialist, white supremacist, bigot, redneck <nonformal>; Anglophobe, Russophobe, xenophobe, etc

VERBS 5 **hate, detest, loathe, abhor,** execrate, **abominate,** hold in abomination, take an aversion to, shudder at, utterly detest, be death on, not stand, not stand the sight of, not stomach; scorn, **despise** 157.3
6 **dislike,** have it in for <nonformal>, disrelish 99.3

ADJS 7 **hating, abhorrent,** loathing, despising, venomous, death on; averse to 99.8;

disgusted 96.20; scornful, **contemptuous** 157.8
8 **hateful, loathsome,** detestable 98.18; despiteful; unlikable 99.7; **contemptible** 661.12/98.18

WORD ELEMENTS 9 mis—, miso—; —phobia, —phobiac, —phobe

104 LOVE

NOUNS 1 **love, affection, attachment, devotion, fondness,** sentiment, warm feeling, soft spot in one's heart, weakness <nonformal>, like, **liking,** fancy, shine <nonformal>; **partiality, predilection; passion,** tender feeling or passion, **ardor,** ardency, fervor, heart, flame; physical love, Amor, Eros, bodily love, libido, sexual love, sex 75; desire, yearning 100.5; lasciviousness 665.5; charity, caritas <L>, brotherly love, Christian love, agape, loving concern, **caring;** spiritual love, platonic love; **adoration,** worship, hero worship; **regard,** admiration; idolization, idolism, idolatry; popular regard, popularity; faithful love, truelove; married love, conjugal love, uxoriousness; free love, free-lovism; **lovemaking** 562
2 "an insatiate thirst of enjoying a greedily desired object"—Montaigne, "the heart's immortal thirst to be completely known and all forgiven"—Henry Van Dyke, "Nature's second sun"—George Chapman, "tyrant sparing none"—Corneille, "the blood of life, the power of reunion of the separated"—Tillich, "the reflection of a man's own worthiness from other men"—Emerson, "a spiritual coupling of two souls"—Ben Jonson
3 **amorousness,** amativeness, lovingness, meltingness, **affection, affectionateness,** demonstrativeness; mating instinct, reproductive or procreative drive, libido; carnality, sexiness, goatishness, hot pants and horniness <both nonformal>; romantic love, romanticism, **sentimentality,** susceptibility; lovesickness, lovelornness; ecstasy, rapture; enchantment 95.2
4 **infatuation,** infatuatedness, passing fancy; **crush** and mash and pash and case <all nonformal>; **puppy love** and calf love <both nonformal>; love at first sight
5 **parental love, natural affection,** mother or maternal love, father or paternal love; filial love; parental instinct
6 **love affair, affair,** affair of the heart, **amour, romance,** romantic tie or bond, something between, thing <nonformal>,

liaison, entanglement, intrigue; **dalliance,** amorous play, the love game, flirtation, hanky-panky, lollygagging <nonformal>; triangle, eternal triangle; illicit *or* unlawful love, forbidden *or* unsanctified love, adulterous affair, adultery, unfaithfulness, infidelity, cuckoldry

7 **loveableness, likeableness,** lovability, likability, adoreableness, adorability, sweetness, loveliness, lovesomeness; cuddliness, cuddlesomeness; amiability, attractiveness 97.2, desirability, agreeability; **charm, appeal,** allurement 377; winsomeness, winning ways

8 Love, Cupid, Amor, Eros, Kama; Venus, Aphrodite, Astarte, Freya

9 <symbols> **cupid,** cupidon, amor, amourette, amoretto, *amorino* <Ital>; love-knot

10 **sweetheart, loved one, love, beloved, darling, dear, dear one,** dearly beloved, well-beloved, truelove, beloved object, **object of one's affections,** light of one's eye *or* life, light of love; sex object, prey, quarry, game

11 <nonformal terms> **sweetie, honey,** honeybunch, honey-bunny, honeypie, hon, main squeeze, sweetie-pie, sweet patootie, tootsie, tootsie-pie, tootsy-wootsy, dearie, baby, dreamboat, heartthrob, poopsy, poopsy-woopsy, sugar, sugar-bun, sweets

12 **lover, admirer,** adorer, amorist; infatuate, paramour, **suitor, wooer,** pursuer, follower; **flirt,** coquette; vampire, vamp; conquest, catch; devotee; escort, companion, date *and* steady <both nonformal>; significant other

13 **beau, inamorato, swain,** man, gallant; cavalier, squire, esquire, *caballero* <Sp>; *amoroso, cavaliere servente* <both Ital>; sugar daddy <nonformal>; gigolo; **boyfriend** *and* **fellow** *and* young man *and* flame <all nonformal>; old man <nonformal>; love-maker, lover-boy <nonformal>; **seducer, lady-killer,** ladies' man, sheik, philanderer, cocksman <nonformal>; Prince Charming, Lothario, Romeo; Casanova, Don Juan

14 **ladylove, inamorata,** *amorosa* <Ital>, lady, mistress, ladyfriend; lass, lassie, jo <Scots>, gill, jill, Dulcinea

15 <nonformal terms> **doll, angel,** baby, baby-doll, doll-baby, buttercup, ducks, ducky, pet, snookums, snooky, **girl, girlfriend,** best girl, dream girl; old lady

16 **favorite,** preference; **darling,** idol, jewel, apple of one's eye, fair-haired boy, man after one's own heart; **pet,** fondling, cosset, minion; spoiled child *or* darling, *enfant gâté* <Fr>, lap dog; teacher's pet; matinee idol; tin god, little tin god

17 **fiancé, fiancée,** bride-to-be, affianced, betrothed, future, intended <nonformal>

18 **loving couple,** soul mates, lovebirds, turtledoves, bill-and-cooers; Romeo and Juliet, Anthony and Cleopatra, Tristan and Isolde, Pelléas and Mélisande, Abélard and Héloïse, Daphnis and Chloë, Aucassin and Nicolette

VERBS 19 **love, be fond of,** be in love with, **care for, like, fancy,** have a fancy for, take an interest in, **dote on** *or* **upon,** be desperately in love, burn with love; be partial to, have a soft spot in one's heart for, have a weakness *or* fondness for

20 <nonformal terms> **go for,** have an eye *or* eyes for, only have eyes for, be sweet on, have a crush *or* mash *or* case on; have it bad, carry a torch *or* the torch for

21 **cherish, hold dear,** hold in one's heart *or* affections, think much *or* the world of, prize, treasure; **admire, regard,** esteem, revere; **adore, idolize,** worship, dearly love, think worlds *or* the world of, love to distraction

22 **fall in love, lose one's heart, become enamored,** be smitten; take to, **take a liking** *or* **fancy to,** take a shine to *and* fall for <both nonformal>, become attached to, bestow one's affections on; fall head and ears *or* head over heels in love, be swept off one's feet; cotton to <nonformal>

23 **enamor, endear;** win one's heart, win the love *or* affections of, take the fancy of, make a hit with <nonformal>; **charm,** becharm, **infatuate,** hold in thrall, command one's affection, **fascinate,** attract, allure, grow on one, strike *or* tickle one's fancy, **captivate,** bewitch, enrapture, carry away, sweep off one's feet, turn one's head, inflame with love; **seduce,** vamp <nonformal>, draw on, tempt, tantalize

ADJS 24 **beloved, loved, dear, darling, precious;** pet, favorite; **adored, admired,** esteemed, revered; **cherished,** prized, treasured, held dear; **well-liked,** popular; **well-beloved,** dearly beloved, dear to one's heart, after one's heart *or* own heart, dear as the apple of one's eye

25 **endearing, lovable, likable, adorable,** admirable, **lovely,** lovesome, sweet, winning, winsome; **charming;** angelic, seraphic; caressable, kissable; cuddlesome, cuddly

26 **amorous,** amatory, amative, erotic; **sexual** 75.28,29; loverly, loverlike; **passion-**

ate, ardent, impassioned; desirous 100.21,22; lascivious 665.29

27 loving, lovesome, fond, adoring, devoted, affectionate, demonstrative, romantic, sentimental, tender, soft <nonformal>, melting; lovelorn, lovesick, languishing; wifely, husbandly, conjugal, uxorious, faithful; parental, paternal, maternal, filial; charitable, caritative

28 enamored, charmed, becharmed, fascinated, captivated, bewitched, enraptured, enchanted; infatuated, infatuate; smitten, heartsmitten, heartstruck, lovestruck

29 in love, head over heels in love, over head and ears in love

30 fond of, enamored of, partial to, in love with, attached to, wedded to, devoted to, wrapped up in; taken with, smitten with, struck with

31 <nonformal terms> crazy about, mad or nuts or nutty or wild about, swacked on, sweet on, stuck on, gone on

ADVS 32 lovingly, fondly, affectionately, tenderly, dearly, adoringly, devotedly; amorously, ardently, passionately; with love, with affection, with all one's love

WORD ELEMENTS 33 phil—, philo—, —phily; —phile; —philic, —philous

105 EXCITEMENT

NOUNS 1 excitement, emotion, excitedness, arousal, stimulation, exhilaration; a high <nonformal>, manic state or condition

2 thrill, sensation, titillation; tingle, tingling; quiver, shiver, shudder, tremor, tremor of excitement, rush <nonformal>; flush, rush of emotion, surge of emotion

3 <nonformal terms> kick, charge, boot, bang, belt, blast, flash, hit, jolt, large charge, rush, upper, lift; jollies

4 agitation, perturbation, ferment, turbulence, turmoil, tumult, embroilment, uproar, commotion, disturbance, ado, brouhaha <Fr>, feery-fary <Scots>, to-do <nonformal>; pell-mell, flurry, ruffle, bustle, stir, swirl, swirling, whirl, vortex, eddy, hurry, hurry-scurry, hurly-burly; fermentation, yeastiness, effervescence, ebullience, ebullition; fume

5 trepidation, trepidity; disquiet, disquietude, inquietude, unrest, restlessness, fidgetiness; fidgets or shakes and shivers and dithers and antsyness <all nonformal>; quivering, quavering, quaking, shaking, trembling; quiver, quaver, shiver, shudder, didder <Brit nonformal>, twitter, tremor, tremble, flutter; palpitation, pitapatation <nonformal>, pit-a-pat, pitter-patter; throb, throbbing; panting, heaving

6 dither, tizzy <nonformal>, swivet, foofaraw, pucker <nonformal>, twitter, twitteration <nonformal>, flutter, fluster, flusteration and flustration <both nonformal>, fret, fuss, pother, bother, lather and stew and snit <all nonformal>, flap; emotional crisis, crise <Fr>

7 fever of excitement, fever pitch, fever, heat, fever heat, fire; sexual excitement, rut

8 fury, furor, furore <Brit>, fire and fury; ecstasy, transport, rapture, ravishment; intoxication, abandon; passion, rage, raging or tearing passion, towering rage or passion; frenzy, orgy, orgasm; madness, craze, delirium, hysteria

9 outburst, outbreak, burst, flare-up, blaze, explosion, eruption, irruption, upheaval, convulsion, spasm, seizure, fit, paroxysm; storm, tornado, whirlwind, cyclone, hurricane, gale, tempest, gust; steroid rage, roid rage <nonformal>

10 excitability, excitableness, perturbability, agitability; emotional instability, explosiveness, eruptiveness, inflammability, combustibility, tempestuousness, violence, latent violence; irascibility 110.2; irritability, edginess, touchiness, prickliness, sensitivity 24.3; skittishness, nervousness 128; excessive emotion, hyperthymia, emotionalism 93.9

11 excitation, excitement, arousal, arousing, stirring, stirring up, working up, working into a lather <nonformal>, lathering up, whipping up, steaming up, agitation, perturbation; stimulation, stimulus, exhilaration, animation; electrification, galvanization; provocation, irritation, aggravation, exasperation, exacerbation, fomentation, inflammation, infuriation, incitement 375.4

VERBS 12 excite, impassion, arouse, rouse, blow up <old>, stir, stir up, set astir, stir the feelings, stir the blood, cause a stir or commotion, play on the feelings; work up, work into, work up into a lather <nonformal>, lather up, whip up, key up, steam up; move 375.12; foment, incite 375.17; turn on <nonformal>; awaken, awake, wake, waken, wake up; call up, summon up, call forth; kindle, enkindle, light up, light the fuse, fire, inflame, heat, warm, set fire to, set on fire, fire or warm the blood; fan, fan the fire or flame, blow the coals, stir the embers, feed the fire, add fuel to the fire *or* flame, pour oil on the fire; raise to a fever heat *or* pitch, bring to the boiling point; overexcite; **annoy, incense; enrage, infuriate;** frenzy, madden

13 **stimulate, whet, sharpen,** pique, provoke, quicken, enliven, liven up, pick up, jazz up <nonformal>, animate, **exhilarate,** invigorate, galvanize, fillip, give a fillip to; infuse life into, give new life to, revive, renew, resuscitate

14 **agitate, perturb, disturb, trouble, disquiet, discompose,** discombobulate <nonformal>, unsettle, **stir, ruffle, shake, shake up, shock, upset,** make waves, jolt, jar, rock, stagger, electrify, bring *or* pull one up short, give one a turn <nonformal>; fuss <nonformal>, flutter, flurry, rattle, disconcert, **fluster**

15 **thrill, tickle,** thrill to death *or* to pieces, give a thrill, **give one a kick** *or* boot *or* charge *or* bang *or* lift <nonformal>; intoxicate, fascinate, titillate, take one's breath away

16 **be excitable,** excite easily; **get excited, have a fit;** catch the infection; **explode, flare up,** flash up, flame up, fire up, catch fire, take fire; **fly into a passion,** go into hysterics, have a tantrum *or* temper tantrum, come apart; ride off in all directions at once, run around like a chicken with its head cut off; **rage, rave, rant,** rant and rave, rave on, bellow, **storm,** ramp; be angry, smolder, **seethe** 152.15

17 <nonformal terms> **work oneself up,** work oneself into a sweat, lather, have a short fuse, get hot under the collar, run a temperature, race one's motor, get into a dither *or* tizzy *or* swivet *or* pucker *or* stew; blow up, **blow one's top** *or* stack *or* cool, **flip,** flip out, flip one's lid *or* wig, pop one's cork, wig out, blow a gasket, fly off the handle, **hit the ceiling,** go ape, go hog wild, go bananas, lose one's cool, go off the deep end

18 <be excited> **thrill,** tingle, **tingle with excitement,** glow; swell, swell with emotion, be full of emotion; thrill to; turn on to *and* get high on *and* freak out on <all nonformal>; heave, pant; **throb,** palpitate, go pit-a-pat; **tremble, shiver, quiver, quaver, quake,** flutter, twitter, **shake,** shake like an aspen leaf, have the shakes <nonformal>; **fidget,** have the fidgets *and* have ants in one's pants <both nonformal>; toss and turn, toss, tumble, twist and turn, wriggle, wiggle, writhe, squirm; twitch, jerk

19 **change color,** turn color, go all colors; pale, whiten, blanch, turn pale; darken, look black; turn blue in the face; **flush, blush,** crimson, glow, mantle, color, redden, turn *or* get red

ADJS 20 **excited,** impassioned; **thrilled,** agog, tingling, tingly, atingle, aquiver, atwitter; **stimulated,** exhilarated, high <nonformal>; manic; **moved, stirred,** stirred up, **aroused, roused,** switched *or* turned on <nonformal>, on one's mettle, fired, inflamed, wrought up, **worked up,** all worked up, worked up into a lather <nonformal>, lathered up, whipped up, steamed up, keyed up, hopped up <nonformal>; turned-on <nonformal>; carried away; bursting, ready to burst; effervescent, yeasty, ebullient

21 **in a dither, in a tizzy** <nonformal>, in a swivet, in a foofaraw, **in a pucker** <nonformal>, in a quiver, **in a twitter,** in a flutter, all of a twitter *or* flutter, in a fluster, in a flurry, in a pother, in a bother, in a ferment, in a turmoil, in an uproar, in a stew *and* in a sweat <both nonformal>, in a lather <nonformal>

22 **heated, passionate, warm, hot,** red-hot, flaming, **burning, fiery, glowing, fervent, fervid; feverish,** febrile, hectic, flushed; sexually excited, in rut 75.20; burning with excitement, het up <nonformal>, hot under the collar <nonformal>; seething, boiling, boiling over, steamy, steaming

23 **agitated, perturbed, disturbed, troubled, disquieted, upset,** antsy <nonformal>, unsettled, **discomposed, flustered,** ruffled, **shaken**

24 **turbulent,** tumultuous, tempestuous, boisterous, clamorous, uproarious

25 **frenzied, frantic; ecstatic,** transported, enraptured, ravished, in a transport *or* ecstasy; intoxicated, abandoned; orgiastic, orgasmic; raging, raving, roaring, bellowing, ramping, storming, howling, ranting, fulminating, frothing *or* foaming at the mouth; **wild,** hog-wild <nonformal>; **violent,** fierce, ferocious, feral, **furious; mad,** madding, **rabid,** maniac, maniacal, demonic, demoniacal, possessed; carried away, **distracted, delirious, beside oneself,** out of one's wits; uncontrollable, running mad, amok, berserk, hog-wild <nonformal>; **hysterical,** in hysterics; wild-eyed, wild-looking, haggard; blue in the face

26 **overwrought, overexcited, overstimulated, hyper** <nonformal>; **overcome,** overwhelmed, overpowered, overmastered; **upset,** *bouleversé* <Fr>

27 **restless,** restive, **uneasy,** unquiet, unsettled, unrestful, tense; **fidgety,** antsy <nonformal>, fussy, fluttery

28 **excitable, emotional,** highly emotional, overemotional, hyperthymic, perturbable, flappable <nonformal>, agitable; emotionally unstable; explosive, volcanic, eruptive, inflammable; irascible 110.19; irritable, edgy, touchy, prickly, **sensitive** 24.13; **skittish,** startlish; **highstrung,** highly strung, high-spirited, mettlesome, high-mettled; **nervous**

29 **passionate, fiery, vehement,** hotheaded, **impetuous,** violent, volcanic, furious, fierce, **wild;** tempestuous, stormy, tornadic; simmering, volcanic, ready to burst forth *or* explode

30 **exciting, thrilling,** thrilly <nonformal>, **stirring, moving, breathtaking,** eye-popping <nonformal>; agitating, agitative, perturbing, disturbing, upsetting, troubling, disquieting, unsettling, distracting, jolting, jarring; heart-stirring, heart-thrilling, heart-swelling, heart-expanding, soul-stirring, spirit-stirring, deep-thrilling, mind-blowing <nonformal>; impressive, striking, telling; **provocative** 375.27, provoking, piquant, tantalizing; **inflammatory** 375.28; **stimulating,** stimulative, stimulatory; exhilarating, heady, intoxicating, maddening, ravishing; **electric,** galvanic, charged, overcharged; **overwhelming,** overpowering, overcoming, overmastering, more than flesh and blood can bear; suspensive, **suspenseful,** cliff-hanging <nonformal>

31 **penetrating, piercing,** stabbing, cutting, stinging, biting, keen, brisk, sharp, caustic, astringent

32 **sensational, lurid,** yellow, **melodramatic,** Barnumesque; spine-chilling, eye-popping <nonformal>; blood-and-thunder, cloak-and-dagger

ADVS 33 **excitedly, agitatedly,** perturbedly; with beating *or* leaping heart, with heart beating high, with heart going pitapat *or* pitter-patter <nonformal>, thrilling all over, with heart in mouth; with glistening eyes, all agog, all aquiver *or* atwitter *or* atingle; in a sweat *or* stew *or* dither *or* tizzy <all nonformal>

34 **heatedly, passionately,** warmly, hotly, glowingly, fervently, fervidly, **feverishly**

35 **frenziedly, frantically,** wildly, furiously, violently, fiercely, madly, rabidly, distractedly, deliriously, till one is blue in the face <nonformal>

36 **excitingly, thrillingly,** stirringly, moving-ingly; **provocatively,** provokingly; stimulatingly, exhilaratingly

106 INEXCITABILITY

NOUNS 1 **inexcitability,** inexcitableness, unexcitableness, **imperturbability,** imperturbableness, unflappability <nonformal>; steadiness, evenness; inirritability, unirritableness; **dispassion,** dispassionateness, unpassionateness, ataraxy *or* ataraxia; quietism; stoicism; **even temper,** steady *or* smooth temper, good *or* easy temper; unnervousness 129; **patience** 134; **impassiveness,** impassivity, stolidity; bovinity, dullness

2 **composure,** countenance; **calm, calmness,** calm disposition, **placidity, serenity,** tranquility, soothingness, peacefulness; mental composure, peace *or* calm of mind; calm *or* quiet mind, easy mind; resignation, resignedness, acceptance, fatalism, stoic calm; philosophicalness, philosophy, philosophic composure; **quiet,** quietness of mind *or* soul, quietude; decompression, imperturbation, indisturbance, unruffledness; **coolness,** coolheadedness, cool <nonformal>, sangfroid; icy calm; Oriental calm, Buddha-like composure; shantih, the peace that passeth all understanding— Bible

3 **equanimity,** equilibrium, equability, balance; **levelheadedness,** level head, well-balanced *or* well-regulated mind; **poise,** aplomb, **self-possession, self-control,** self-command, self-restraint, restraint, possession, **presence of mind;** confidence, assurance, **self-confidence, self-assurance,** centered

4 **sedateness, staidness,** soberness, sobriety, sober-mindedness, **seriousness,** gravity, solemnity, sobersidedness; temperance, moderation; sobersides

5 **nonchalance,** casualness, offhandedness; easygoingness, lackadaisicalness; **indifference,** unconcern 102.2

VERBS 6 **be cool** *or* **composed,** not turn a hair, not have a hair out of place, keep one's cool <nonformal>, look as if butter wouldn't melt in one's mouth; **tranquilize, calm** 670.7; **set one's mind at ease** *or* **rest,** make one easy

7 **compose oneself, control oneself,** restrain oneself, collect oneself, **get hold of oneself,** get a grip on oneself <nonformal>, get organized, master one's feelings, regain one's composure; **calm down, cool off,** cool down, sober down, hold *or* keep

one's temper, simmer down *and* cool it
<both nonformal>; **relax**, decompress,
unwind, take it easy, lay *or* kick back
<nonformal>; **forget it**, get it out of one's
mind *or* head, drop it

8 <control one's feelings> **suppress, repress**, keep under, smother, stifle, choke
or hold back, fight down *or* back, inhibit;
sublimate

9 **keep cool**, keep one's cool <nonformal>,
keep calm, keep one's head, keep one's
shirt on *and* hang loose <both nonfor-
mal>, not turn a hair; take things as they
come, roll with the punches <nonfor-
mal>; keep a stiff upper lip

ADJS 10 **inexcitable, imperturbable**, undis-
turbable, unflappable <nonformal>; **un-
irritable**, inirritable; **dispassionate**, unpassionate; **steady**; stoic, stoical; **even-
tempered; impassive**, stolid; bovine, dull;
unnervous 129.2; **patient**

11 **unexcited, unperturbed**, undisturbed, untroubled, unagitated, **unruffled**, unflus-
tered, unstirred, unimpassioned

12 **calm, placid**, quiet, **tranquil, serene**,
peaceful; **cool, coolheaded**, cool as a cucumber <nonformal>; philosophical

13 **composed, collected**, recollected, **level-
headed; poised**, together <nonformal>,
in equipoise, equanimous, equilibrious,
balanced, well-balanced; **self-possessed**,
self-controlled, self-restrained; confident,
assured, **self-confident, self-assured**

14 **sedate, staid**, sober, sober-minded, **serious**, grave, solemn, sobersided; temperate, moderate

15 **nonchalant, blasé, indifferent**, unconcerned 102.7; **casual, offhand, relaxed,
laid-back** *and* throwaway <both nonfor-
mal>; **easygoing**, easy, free and easy,
devil-may-care, lackadaisical, *dégagé*
<Fr>

ADVS 16 inexcitably, **imperturbably**, inir-
ritably, **dispassionately**; steadily; stoically; **calmly, placidly**, quietly, **tranquilly, serenely; coolly, composedly**,
levelheadedly; impassively, stolidly,
stodgily, stuffily

17 **sedately, staidly, soberly, seriously**, sobersidedly

18 **nonchalantly, casually, relaxedly**, offhandedly, easygoingly, lackadaisically

107 CONTENTMENT

NOUNS 1 **contentment, content**, contented-
ness, satisfiedness; **satisfaction**, entire
satisfaction, fulfillment; ease, peace of
mind, composure 106.2; comfort 121;

quality of life; well-being, euphoria; **happiness** 95.2; **acceptance**, resignation,
reconcilement, reconciliation; clear *or*
clean conscience, dreamless sleep

2 **complacency**, complacence; **smugness,
self-complacence** *or* self-complacency,
self-approval, self-approbation, **self-
satisfaction, self-content**, self-content-
edness self-contentness; bovinity

3 **satisfactoriness, adequacy, sufficiency**
990; **acceptability**, admissibility, **tolerability**, agreeability, unobjectionability,
unexceptionability, tenability, viability

VERBS 4 **content, satisfy**; gratify; put *or* set
at ease, set one's mind at ease *or* rest,
achieve inner harmony

5 **be content, rest satisfied, rest easy**, rest
and be thankful, be of good cheer, be reconciled to, take the good the gods provide, accept one's lot, rest on one's laurels, let well enough alone, let sleeping
dogs lie, take the bitter with the sweet;
come to terms with oneself, learn to live
in one's own skin; have no kick coming
<nonformal>, not complain, not worry,
not sweat it *and* cool it *and* go with the
flow <all nonformal>; content oneself
with, settle for; settle for less, take half a
loaf, lower one's sights, cut one's losses;
be pleased 95.11

6 **be satisfactory, do, suffice** 990.4; **suit**,
suit one down to the ground

ADJS 7 **content, contented, satisfied; pleased**
95.12; **happy; easy, at ease**, at one's ease,
easygoing; composed 106.13; **comfortable** 121.11, of good comfort; euphoric,
eupeptic; carefree, without care, *sans
souci* <Fr>; accepting, resigned, reconciled; uncomplaining, unrepining

8 **untroubled, unbothered, undisturbed**,
unperturbed 106.11, unworried, unvexed,
unplagued, untormented

9 **well-content, well-pleased**, well-
contented, **well-satisfied**, highly satisfied

10 **complacent**, bovine; **smug, self-
complacent, self-satisfied**, self-content,
self-contented

11 **satisfactory, satisfying; sufficient** 990.6,
sufficing, **adequate, enough**, commensurate, proportionate, proportionable,
ample, equal to

12 **acceptable**, admissible, **agreeable**, unobjectionable, unexceptionable, tenable,
viable; **OK** *and* okay *and* all right *and* alright <all nonformal>; **passable**, good
enough

13 **tolerable, bearable, endurable, supportable, sufferable**

ADVS **14 contentedly,** to one's heart's content; **satisfiedly,** with satisfaction; **complacently, smugly,** self-complacently, self-satisfiedly, self-contentedly

15 satisfactorily, satisfyingly; **acceptably, agreeably,** admissibly; sufficiently, adequately, commensurately, amply, enough; **tolerably, passably**

16 to one's satisfaction, to one's delight, to one's great glee; to one's taste, to the king's *or* queen's taste

108 DISCONTENT

NOUNS **1 discontent,** discontentment, discontentedness; **dissatisfaction,** unsatisfaction, dissatisfiedness, unfulfillment; **resentment, envy** 154; **restlessness, restiveness, uneasiness,** unease; malaise; rebelliousness 327.3; disappointment 132; unpleasure 96; unhappiness 112.2; ill humor 110; **disgruntlement,** sulkiness, sourness, petulance, peevishness, querulousness; vexation of spirit; cold comfort; divine discontent; Faustianism

2 unsatisfactoriness, dissatisfactoriness; **inadequacy, insufficiency** 991; **unacceptability,** inadmissibility, unsuitability, undesirability, objectionability, untenability, indefensibility; **intolerability** 98.9

3 malcontent, *frondeur* <Fr>; **complainer,** complainant, **faultfinder, grumbler,** growler, smellfungus, **murmurer,** mutterer, griper, croaker, peevish *or* petulant *or* querulous person, whiner; reactionary, reactionist; rebel 327.5

4 <nonformal terms> **grouch, kvetch,** kicker, griper, moaner, moaning Minnie <Brit>, crank, crab, grouser, grump, beefer, bellyacher, bitcher, sorehead, picklepuss, sourpuss

VERBS **5 dissatisfy, discontent, disgruntle, displease,** fail to satisfy, be inadequate, not fill the bill, disappoint, leave much *or* a lot to be desired, dishearten, put out <nonformal>; **be discontented, complain**

6 <nonformal terms> **beef, bitch, kvetch,** bellyache, crab, gripe, grouch, grouse, grump, have an attitude, kick, moan, piss, make a stink, squawk

ADJS **7 discontented, dissatisfied, disgruntled,** unaccepting, unaccommodating, **displeased,** less than pleased, let down, disappointed; **unsatisfied, ungratified,** unfulfilled; resentful, dog-in-the-manger; envious 154.4; restless, restive, uneasy; rebellious 327.11; malcontent, malcontented, **complaining,** complaintful, sour,

faultfinding, grumbling, growling, murmuring, muttering, griping, croaking, **peevish, petulant,** sulky, **querulous,** querulant, whiny; unhappy 112.21; out of humor 110.17

8 <nonformal terms> **grouchy, kvetchy,** cranky, beefing, crabby, crabbing, grousing, griping, bellyaching, bitching

9 unsatisfactory, dissatisfactory; **unsatisfying, ungratifying,** unfulfilling; **displeasing** 98.17; disappointing, disheartening, not up to expectation, not good enough; **inadequate,** incommensurate, **insufficient** 991.9

10 unacceptable, inadmissible, unsuitable, undesirable, **objectionable,** exceptionable, impossible, untenable, indefensible; **intolerable** 98.25

ADVS **11 discontentedly, dissatisfiedly**

12 unsatisfactorily, dissatisfactorily; **unsatisfyingly, ungratifyingly; inadequately, insufficiently; unacceptably,** inadmissibly, unsuitably, undesirably, objectionably; intolerably 98.30

109 CHEERFULNESS

NOUNS **1 cheerfulness,** cheeriness, **good cheer, cheer,** cheery vein *or* mood; blitheness, blithesomeness; **gladness,** gladsomeness; **happiness** 95.2; **pleasantness,** winsomeness, geniality; brightness, radiance, **sunniness;** sanguineness, sanguinity, sanguine humor, euphoric *or* eupeptic mein; optimism, rosy expectation, hopefulness; **irrepressibility,** irrepressibleness

2 good humor, good spirits; high spirits, exhilaration, rare good humor

3 lightheartedness, lightsomeness, lightness, levity; **buoyancy,** buoyance, resilience, resiliency, bounce <nonformal>, springiness; springy step; **jauntiness,** perkiness, debonairness, carefreeness; **breeziness,** airiness, pertness, chirpiness, light heart

4 gaiety, gayness, *allégresse* <Fr>; **liveliness, vivacity, vitality,** life, **animation, spiritedness, spirit,** esprit, élan, **sprightliness,** high spirits, zestfulness, zest, vim, zip <nonformal>, vigor, verve, gusto, **exuberance,** heartiness; **spirits,** animal spirits; piss and vinegar <nonformal>; **friskiness,** skittishness, coltishness, rompishness, rollicksomeness, capersomeness; **sportiveness, playfulness, frolicsomeness,** gamesomeness, kittenishness

5 merriment, merriness; **hilarity,** hilariousness; **joy**, joyfulness, joyousness; **glee**, gleefulness, high glee; **jollity**, jolliness, **joviality**, jocularity, jocundity; frivolity, **levity; mirth**, mirthfulness, **amusement** 743; **fun; laughter** 116.4

VERBS **6** exude cheerfulness, radiate cheer, not have a care in the world, **beam**, burst *or* brim with cheer, glow, radiate, sparkle, sing, lilt, whistle, **chirp,** chirrup, chirp like a cricket; walk on air, dance, skip, caper, frolic, gambol, romp, caracole; **smile, laugh** 116.8

7 **cheer, gladden, brighten,** put in good humor; **encourage, hearten,** pick up <nonformal>; **inspire,** inspirit, warm the spirits, **raise the spirits,** elevate one's mood, buoy up, boost, give a lift <nonformal>, put one on top of the world *and* on cloud nine <both nonformal>; **exhilarate,** animate, invigorate, liven, enliven, vitalize; **rejoice,** rejoice the heart, do the heart good

8 **elate, exalt,** elevate, lift, uplift, flush

9 **cheer up, take heart,** drive dull care away; **brighten up,** light up, **perk up; buck up** *and* brace up *and* chirk up <all nonformal>; come out of it, snap out of it <nonformal>, revive

10 **be of good cheer,** bear up, **keep one's spirits up,** keep one's chin up <nonformal>, keep one's pecker up <Brit nonformal>, keep a stiff upper lip <nonformal>, grin and bear it

ADJS **11** **cheerful, cheery,** of good cheer, in good spirits, vogie <Scots>; in high spirits, exalted, elated, exhilarated, high <nonformal>; irrepressible; **blithe,** blithesome; **glad, gladsome; happy,** happy as a clam *or* a sand boy *or* a lark, on top of the world, sitting on top of the world, sitting pretty; **pleasant, genial,** winsome; **bright, sunny,** bright and sunny, **radiant,** riant, sparkling, beaming, glowing, flushed, rosy, smiling, laughing; sanguine, sanguineous, euphoric, eupeptic; optimistic, hopeful; **irrepressible**

12 **lighthearted,** light, lightsome; **buoyant,** corky <nonformal>, resilient; **jaunty,** perky, **debonair, carefree,** free and easy; **breezy,** airy

13 **pert,** chirk <nonformal>, chirrupy, **chirpy, chipper** <nonformal>

14 **gay,** gay as a lark; **spirited,** sprightly, **lively, animated, vivacious,** vital, zestful, zippy <nonformal>, **exuberant,** hearty; **frisky,** antic, skittish, coltish, rompish, capersome; **full of beans** *and* **feeling one's oats** <both nonformal>, full of piss and

vinegar <nonformal>; **sportive, playful,** playful as a kitten, kittenish, **frolicsome,** gamesome; rollicking, rollicky, rollicksome

15 **merry, mirthful, hilarious; joyful, joyous,** rejoicing; **gleeful,** gleesome; **jolly,** buxom; **jovial,** jocund, jocular; **frivolous;** laughter-loving, mirth-loving, risible; merry as a cricket *or* grig, "as merry as the day is long"—Shakespeare

16 **cheering, gladdening; encouraging, heartening,** heartwarming; **inspiring,** inspiriting; **exhilarating,** animating, enlivening, invigorating; cheerful, cheery, glad, joyful

ADVS **17** **cheerfully,** cheerily, with good cheer, with a cheerful heart; irrepressibly; **lightheartedly,** lightly; jauntily, perkily, airily; **pleasantly,** genially, blithely; **gladly, happily, joyfully,** smilingly; optimistically, hopefully

18 **gaily, exuberantly, heartily, spiritedly, animatedly, vivaciously,** zestfully, with zest, with vim, with élan, with zip <nonformal>, with verve, with gusto

19 **merrily, gleefully, hilariously; jovially,** jocundly, jocularly; frivolously; **mirthfully,** laughingly

PHRS **20** cheer up!, every cloud has a silver lining; don't let it get you down, illegitimati non carborundum <L, don't let the bastards grind you down>; chin up!, keep your pecker up! <Brit>; it's always darkest before the dawn

110 ILL HUMOR

NOUNS **1** **ill humor,** bad humor, **bad temper,** rotten *or* ill *or* evil temper, **ill nature,** filthy *or* rotten *or* evil humor; **sourness,** biliousness, liverishness; choler, bile, gall, spleen; **abrasiveness,** causticity, corrosiveness, asperity 144.8; **anger** 152.5; discontent 108

2 **irascibility, irritability,** excitability, short *or* quick temper, short fuse <nonformal>; **crossness,** disagreeableness, disagreeability, gruffness, shortness, peevishness, querulousness, fretfulness, crabbedness, **crankiness, testiness,** crustiness, huffiness, huffishness, churlishness, bearishness, snappishness, waspishness; **perversity,** cross-grainedness, fractiousness

3 <nonformal terms> **crabbiness, grouchiness,** cantankerousness, crustiness, grumpiness *or* grumpishness, cussedness, huffiness *or* huffishness, **meanness, orneriness,** bitchiness, cussedness, feistiness, ugliness, miffiness, saltiness, scrappiness, shirtiness <Brit>, soreheadedness

4 **hot temper, temper,** quick or short temper, irritable temper, warm temper, fiery temper, fierce temper, short fuse <nonformal>, pepperiness, feistiness and spunkiness <both nonformal>, **hotheadedness,** hot blood

5 **touchiness, tetchiness,** ticklishness, prickliness, quickness to take offense, miffiness <nonformal>, **sensitiveness,** oversensitiveness, hypersensitiveness, sensitivity, oversensitivity, hypersensitivity, thin skin; temperamentalness

6 **petulance** or petulancy, **peevishness,** pettishness, **querulousness, fretfulness,** resentfulness; shrewishness, vixenishness

7 **contentiousness, quarrelsomeness** 456.3; **disputatiousness, argumentativeness,** litigiousness; **belligerence**

8 **sullenness, sulkiness, surliness, moroseness, glumness,** grumness, grimness, mumpishness, dumpishness, bouderie <Fr>; **moodiness,** moodishness; mopishness, mopiness <nonformal>; dejection, melancholy 112.5

9 **scowl, frown,** lower, **glower, pout,** moue, mow, grimace, wry face; sullen looks, black looks, **long face**

10 **sulks,** sullens, **mopes,** mumps, dumps, grumps <nonformal>, frumps <Brit nonformal>, **blues,** blue devils, mulligrubs, dorts or dods <both Scots>, **pouts**

11 <ill-humored person> **sorehead, grouch, curmudgeon, grump, crank, crosspatch,** feist or fice <nonformal>, wasp, **bear,** grizzly bear, pit bull, junkyard dog <nonformal>; fury, Tartar, dragon, ugly customer <nonformal>; **hothead,** hotspur; fire-eater

12 **bitch** <nonformal>, **shrew, vixen,** virago, termagant, brimstone, fury, witch, beldam, cat, tigress, she-wolf, she-devil, spitfire; fishwife; **scold,** common scold; battle-ax <nonformal>

VERBS 13 have a temper, have a short fuse <nonformal>, have a devil in one, be possessed of the devil; be cross, get out on the wrong side of the bed

14 **sulk, mope,** mope around; grizzle <chiefly Brit nonformal>, grump and grouch and bitch <all nonformal>, **fret;** get oneself in a sulk

15 **look sullen,** look black, look black as thunder, gloom, pull or make a long face; frown, scowl, knit the brow, lower, glower, pout, make a moue or mow, grimace, make a wry face, make a lip, hang one's lip, thrust out one's lower lip

16 **sour,** acerbate, exacerbate; **embitter,** bitter, envenom

ADJS 17 **out of humor,** out of temper, out of sorts, **in a bad humor,** in a shocking humor, feeling evil <nonformal>; **abrasive,** caustic, corrosive, acid; angry; discontented 108.5

18 **ill-humored, bad-tempered,** ill-tempered, evil-humored, evil-tempered, **ill-natured,** ill-affected, ill-disposed

19 **irascible, irritable,** excitable, flappable <nonformal>; **cross, cranky, testy;** cankered, crabbed, spiteful, spleeny, splenetic, churlish, bearish, snappish, waspish; **gruff,** grumbly, grumbling, growling; **disagreeable; perverse,** fractious, cross-grained

20 <nonformal terms> **crabby, grouchy,** cantankerous, crusty, grumpy or grumpish, cussed, huffy or huffish, mean, mean as a junkyard dog, ornery, bitchy, cussed, feisty, ugly, miffy, salty, scrappy, shirty <Brit>, soreheaded

21 **touchy, tetchy,** miffy <nonformal>, ticklish, prickly, quick to take offense, **thin-skinned, sensitive,** oversensitive, hypersensitive, high-strung, highly strung, temperamental, prima-donnaish

22 **peevish, petulant,** pettish, **querulous, fretful,** resentful; catty; shrewish, vixenish, vixenly; nagging, naggy

23 **sour,** soured, **sour-tempered,** vinegarish; prune-faced <nonformal>; **choleric, dyspeptic, bilious,** liverish, jaundiced; **bitter,** embittered

24 **sullen, sulky, surly, morose,** dour, mumpish, dumpish, **glum,** grum, grim; **moody,** moodish; **mopish,** mopey <nonformal>, moping; **glowering,** lowering, **scowling, frowning;** dark, black; black-browed, beetle-browed; dejected, melancholy 112.23

25 **hot-tempered, hotheaded, passionate,** hot, fiery, peppery, feisty, spunky <nonformal>, **quick-tempered, short-tempered;** hasty, quick, "sudden and quick in quarrel"—Shakespeare, explosive, volcanic, combustible

26 **contentious, quarrelsome** 456.17; **disputatious,** controversial, litigious, polemic, polemical; **argumentative,** argumental; on the warpath, looking for trouble; scrappy <nonformal>; cat-and-doggish, cat-and-dog; **bellicose, belligerent**

ADVS 27 **ill-humoredly, ill-naturedly; irascibly, irritably, crossly, crankily, testily,**

huffily, cantankerously <nonformal>,
crabbedly, sourly, churlishly, crustily,
bearishly, snappily; perversely, fractiously, cross-grainedly

28 **peevishly, petulantly,** pettishly, **querulously, fretfully**

29 **grouchily** and **crabbily** and grumpily
<all nonformal>, grumblingly

30 **sullenly, sulkily, surlily, morosely,** mum-
pishly, glumly, grumly, grimly; moodily,
mopingly; gloweringly, loweringly,
scowlingly, frowningly

111 SOLEMNITY

NOUNS **1 solemnity, solemness, dignity, soberness, sobriety, gravity,** *gravitas* <L>,
weightiness, **somberness, grimness;
sedateness, staidness;** demureness,
decorousness; **seriousness, earnestness,
thoughtfulness, sober-mindedness,** sobersidedness; sobersides; long face, straight
face; **formality** 580

VERBS **2** honor the occasion, keep a straight
face, look serious, compose one's features,
wear an earnest frown; repress a smile,
not crack a smile <nonformal>, wipe the
smile off one's face, keep from laughing

ADJS **3 solemn, dignified, sober, grave,** unsmiling, weighty, **somber,** frowning,
grim; sedate, staid; demure, decorous; **serious, earnest, thoughtful; sober-minded,**
sober-sided; straight-faced, long-faced,
grim-faced, grim-visaged, stone-faced;
sober as a judge, grave as an undertaker;
formal 580.7

ADVS **4 solemnly, soberly,** gravely, somberly, grimly; **sedately, staidly,** demurely, decorously; with dignity, **seriously, earnestly,** thoughtfully, sober-
mindedly, sobersidedly; with a straight
face; formally 580.11

112 SADNESS

NOUNS **1 sadness,** sadheartedness, weight or
burden of sorrow; heaviness, **heavyheart-
edness,** heavy heart, **heaviness of heart;**
pathos, bathos

2 unhappiness, infelicity; displeasure 96.1;
discontent 108; **uncheerfulness,** cheerlessness; **joylessness,** unjoyfulness;
mirthlessness, unmirthfulness, humor-
lessness, infestivity; **grimness; wretchedness, misery**

3 dejection, depression, oppression, dejec-
tedness, **downheartedness,** downcast-
ness; **discouragement, disheartenment,**
dispiritedness; *Schmerz* and *Weltschmerz*

<both Ger>; malaise 96.1; lowness, low-
ness or depression or oppression of spirit,
downer and down trip <both nonfor-
mal>; chill, chilling effect; **low spirits,**
drooping spirits, sinking heart; despon-
dence or **despondency,** spiritlessness,
heartlessness; black or blank despondency, "Slough of Despond"—Bunyan;
demotivation, hopelessness 125, **despair**
125.2, pessimism 125.6, suicidal despair,
death wish, self-destructive urge; weariness of life, *taedium vitae* <L>; sloth,
acedia, noonday demon

4 hypochondria, hypochondriasis, morbid
anxiety

5 melancholy, melancholia, melancholi-
ness, spleen <old>; gentle melancholy,
romantic melancholy; **pensiveness, wistfulness,** tristfulness; **nostalgia,** homesickness, nostalgy <old>, *mal du pays* <Fr>

6 blues and blue devils and mulligrubs <all
nonformal>, mumps, **dumps** <nonfor-
mal>, **doldrums,** dismals, dolefuls
<nonformal>, blahs and mopes and
megrims and sulks <all nonformal>

7 gloom, gloominess, darkness, murk,
murkiness, **dismalness, bleakness, grimness, somberness, gravity, solemnity;
dreariness,** drearisomeness; wearifulness, wearisomeness

8 glumness, grumness, **moroseness, sullenness,** sulkiness, **moodiness,** mumpishness, dumpishness; mopishness, mopiness <nonformal>

9 heartache, aching heart, bleeding heart,
grieving heart; heartsickness, heartsore-
ness; **heartbreak, broken heart,** broken-
heartedness, heartbrokenness

10 sorrow, sorrowing, **grief, care,** carking
care, **woe;** heartgrief, heartfelt grief; languishment, pining; **anguish, misery,
agony;** prostrating grief, prostration; **lamentation** 115

11 sorrowfulness, mournfulness, ruefulness,
woefulness, dolefulness, woesomeness
<old>, dolorousness, **plaintiveness,** plan-
gency, grievousness, aggrievedness,
lugubriousness, funerealness; *lacrimae re-
rum* <L>, **tearfulness** 115.2

12 disconsolateness, disconsolation, **incon-
solability,** inconsolableness, unconsol-
ability, comfortlessness; **desolation,** desolateness; forlornness

13 sourpuss and picklepuss and gloomy Gus
<all nonformal>, moaning Minnie <Brit
nonformal>; mope, brooder; **melancholic,** melancholiac; depressive

14 killjoy, spoilsport, grinch and crepehanger and drag <all nonformal>;

damp, damper, **wet blanket,** party pooper; gloomster *and* doomster <both nonformal>, doomsdayer, apocalypticist, apocalyptician, awfulizer <nonformal>, crepehanger, Moaning Minnie <Brit nonformal>; skeleton at the feast; pessimist 125.7

VERBS **15** hang one's head, pull *or* make a long face, look blue, sing *or* get *or* have the blues <nonformal>; drag one down; carry the weight *or* woe of the world on one's shoulders; hang crape <nonformal>, apocalypticize, catastrophize, awfulize <nonformal>

16 lose heart, despond, give way, give oneself up *or* over to; despondency; **despair** 125.10, sink into despair, throw up one's hands in despair, be *or* become suicidal, lose the will to live; **droop,** sink, languish; reach *or* plumb the depths, touch bottom, hit rock bottom

17 grieve, sorrow; weep, mourn 115.8,10; be dumb with grief; **pine,** pine away; **brood over, mope, fret,** take on <nonformal>; **eat one's heart out,** break one's heart over; **agonize,** ache, bleed

18 sadden, darken, cast a pall *or* gloom upon, weigh *or* weigh heavy upon; **deject, depress, oppress, crush,** press down, hit one like a ton of bricks <nonformal>, **cast down,** lower, lower the spirits, get one down <nonformal>, take the wind out of one's sails, rains on one's parade, burst one's bubble, **discourage, dishearten,** take the heart out of, **dispirit;** damp, dampen, damp *or* dampen the spirits; dash, knock down, beat down; sink, sink one's soul, plunge one into despair

19 aggrieve, oppress, **grieve, sorrow,** plunge one into sorrow, embitter; draw tears, bring to tears; **anguish, tear up** *and* **cut up** <both nonformal>, wring *or* pierce *or* lacerate *or* rend the heart, pull at the heartstrings; afflict 96.16, torment 96.18; **break one's heart, make one's heart bleed;** desolate, leave an aching void; prostrate, break down, crush, bear down, inundate, overwhelm

ADJS **20 sad,** saddened; sadhearted, **sad of heart; heavyhearted,** heavy; oppressed, weighed upon, weighed *or* weighted down, bearing the woe of the world, burdened *or* laden with sorrow; sad-faced, long-faced; sad-eyed; sad-voiced

21 unhappy, uncheerful, uncheery, **cheerless, joyless, unjoyful,** unsmiling; mirthless, unmirthful, humorless, infestive; funny as a crutch <nonformal>; **grim;**

out of humor, out of sorts, in bad humor *or* spirits; **sorry,** sorryish; discontented 108.5; **wretched, miserable;** pleasureless 96.20

22 dejected, depressed, downhearted, down, downcast, cast down, bowed down, subdued; **discouraged, disheartened, dispirited,** dashed; **low, feeling low,** low-spirited, **in low spirits; down in the mouth** <nonformal>, **in the doldrums, down in the dumps** *and* **in the dumps** *and* in the doleful dumps <all nonformal>, in the depths; **despondent,** desponding; **despairing** 125.12, weary of life, suicidal, world-weary; pessimistic 125.16; spiritless, heartless, **woebegone; drooping,** droopy, languishing, pining, haggard; hypochondriac *or* hypochondriacal

23 melancholy, melancholic, splenetic <old>, **blue** <nonformal>, funky <nonformal>; atrabilious, atrabiliar; **pensive, wistful,** tristful; **nostalgic,** homesick

24 gloomy, dismal, murky, bleak, grim, somber, sombrous, **solemn, grave;** sad, *triste* <Fr>, **funereal,** funebrial, crepehanging <nonformal>, saturnine; **dark,** black, gray; **dreary,** drear, drearisome; weary, weariful, wearisome

25 glum, grum **morose, sullen,** sulky, mumpish, dumpish, long-faced, crestfallen, chapfallen; **moody,** moodish, **brooding,** broody; mopish, mopey <nonformal>, **moping**

26 sorrowful, sorrowing, sorrowed, **mournful, rueful, woeful, woesome** <old>, **doleful, plaintive,** plangent; anguished; dolorous, **grievous, lamentable,** lugubrious; **tearful; care-worn;** grieved, **grief-stricken,** griefful, aggrieved, in grief, plunged in grief, dumb with grief, prostrated by grief, cut-up *and* torn-up <both nonformal>, **inconsolable**

27 sorrow-stricken, sorrow-wounded, sorrow-struck, sorrow-torn, sorrow-worn, sorrow-wasted, sorrow-beaten, sorrow-blinded, sorrow-clouded, sorrow-shot, sorrow-burdened, sorrow-laden, sorrow-sighing, sorrow-sobbing, sorrow-sick

28 disconsolate, inconsolable, unconsolable, comfortless, prostrate *or* prostrated, **forlorn; desolate,** *désolé* <Fr>; sick, **sick at heart, heartsick,** soul-sick, heartsore

29 overcome, crushed, borne-down, overwhelmed, inundated, **stricken, cut up** <nonformal>, **desolated,** prostrate *or* prostrated, broken-down, undone; **heart-**

stricken, heart-struck; **brokenhearted,** heartbroken

30 **depressing**, depressive, depressant, **oppressive; discouraging, disheartening, dispiriting;** morale-sapping, worst-case, downbeat <nonformal>

ADVS 31 **sadly, gloomily, dismally, drearily,** heavily, bleakly, grimly, somberly, sombrously, solemnly, funereally, gravely, with a long face; **depressingly**

32 **unhappily, uncheerfully,** cheerlessly, joylessly, unjoyfully

33 **dejectedly, downheartedly; discouragedly, disheartenedly, dispiritedly; despondently,** despairingly, spiritlessly, heartlessly; **disconsolately,** inconsolably, unconsolably, forlornly

34 **melancholily, pensively,** wistfully, tristfully; nostalgically

35 **glumly,** grumly, **morosely, sullenly; moodily,** moodishly, broodingly, broodily; mopishly, mopily <nonformal>, mopingly

36 **sorrowfully, mournfully, ruefully, woefully, woesomely** <old>, **dolefully, dolorously, plaintively, grievously,** grieffully, lugubriously; with a broken voice; **heartbrokenly,** brokenheartedly; **tearfully,** with tears in one's eyes

113 REGRET

NOUNS 1 **regret, regrets,** regretting, regretfulness; **remorse,** remorsefulness, remorse of conscience, ayenbite of inwit <old>; **shame,** shamefulness, shamefacedness, shamefastness; **sorrow, grief, sorriness,** repining; **contrition,** contriteness, attrition; bitterness; apologies; wistfulness 100.4

2 **compunction, qualm, qualms,** qualmishness, scruples, scrupulosity, scrupulousness, pang, pangs, **pangs of conscience,** throes, sting or pricking or twinge or twitch of conscience, touch of conscience, **voice of conscience,** pricking of heart, better self

3 **self-reproach,** self-reproachfulness, **self-accusation, self-condemnation,** self-conviction, self-punishment, self-humiliation, self-debasement, **self-hatred,** self-flagellation; hair shirt; self-analysis, soul-searching, examination of conscience

4 **penitence, repentance, change of heart; apology,** humble or heartfelt apology, abject apology; better nature, good angel, guardian angel; reformation 857.2; deathbed repentance; mea culpa; **penance** 658.3; wearing a hairshirt or

sackcloth or sackcloth and ashes, mortification of the flesh

5 **penitent,** confessor, "a sadder and a wiser man"—Coleridge; **prodigal son,** prodigal returned; Magdalen

VERBS 6 **regret, deplore, repine, be sorry for; rue,** rue the day; **bemoan, bewail;** curse one's folly, **reproach oneself,** kick oneself <nonformal>, bite one's tongue, accuse or condemn or blame or convict or punish oneself, flagellate oneself, wear a hair shirt, make oneself miserable, humiliate or debase oneself, hate oneself for one's actions, hide one's face in shame; examine one's conscience, search one's soul, consult or heed one's better self, analyze or search one's motives; cry over spilled milk, waste time in regret

7 **repent, think better of,** change one's mind, have second thoughts; laugh out of the other side of one's mouth; **plead guilty,** own oneself in the wrong, humble oneself, **apologize** 658.5, beg pardon or forgiveness, throw oneself on the mercy of the court; **do penance** 658.6; reform

ADJS 8 **regretful, remorseful,** full of remorse, **ashamed,** shameful, shamefaced, shamefast, **sorry, rueful, repining,** unhappy about; **conscience-stricken,** conscience-smitten; **self-reproachful,** self-reproaching, self-accusing, self-condemning, self-convicting, self-punishing, self-flagellating, self-humiliating, self-debasing, self-hating; wistful 100.23

9 **penitent, repentant; penitential,** penitentiary; **contrite,** abject, humble, humbled, **sheepish, apologetic,** touched, softened, melted

10 **regrettable,** much to be regretted; **deplorable** 999.9

ADVS 11 **regretfully, remorsefully,** sorrily, ruefully, unhappily

12 **penitently,** repentantly, penitentially; **contritely,** abjectly, **humbly, sheepishly, apologetically**

114 UNREGRETFULNESS

NOUNS 1 **unregretfulness, unremorsefulness, unsorriness,** unruefulness; **remorselessness,** regretlessness, sorrowlessness; **shamelessness,** unashamedness

2 **impenitence,** impenitentness; nonrepentance, irrepentance; **uncontriteness,** unabjectness; seared conscience, heart of stone, callousness 94.3; **hardness of heart,** hardness, induration, obduracy; **defiance** 454/327.2; **insolence** 142

VERBS 3 **harden one's heart,** steel oneself;

have no regrets, not look backward, not cry over spilled milk; have no shame

ADJS **4 unregretful,** unregretting, **unremorseful, unsorry, unsorrowful,** unrueful; **remorseless,** regretless, sorrowless, griefless; unsorrowing, ungrieving, unrepining; **shameless,** unashamed

5 impenitent, unrepentant, unrepenting, unreconstructed; **uncontrite,** unabject; untouched, unsoftened, unmelted, callous 94.12; hard, hardened, obdurate; **defiant** 453.8/454.7; **insolent** 142.9

6 unregretted, unrepented

ADVS **7 unregretfully, unremorsefully,** unruefully; **remorselessly,** sorrowlessly, impenitently, shamelessly, unashamedly; **without regret,** without looking back, **without remorse,** without compunction, without any qualms *or* scruples

115 LAMENTATION

NOUNS **1 lamentation,** lamenting, **mourning, moaning, grieving, sorrowing, wailing, bewailing, bemoaning,** keening, howling, ululation, "weeping and gnashing of teeth"—Bible; **sorrow** 112.10

2 weeping, sobbing, crying, bawling, greet <Scots>; blubbering, whimpering, sniveling; **tears,** flood of tears, fit of crying; cry *and* good cry <both nonformal>; **tearfulness, weepiness** <nonformal>, lachrymosity, melting mood; tearful eyes, swimming *or* brimming *or* overflowing eyes; **tear,** teardrop, lachryma; lacrimatory, tear bottle

3 lament, plaint, *planctus* <L>; **murmur,** mutter; **moan, groan; whine, whimper; wail,** wail of woe; **sob,** *cri du coeur* <Fr>; **cry,** outcry, scream, **howl,** yowl, bawl, yawp, keen, ululation; jeremiad, tirade, dolorous tirade

4 complaint, grievance, peeve, pet peeve, **groan; dissent, protest** 333.2; hard luck story <nonformal>, tale of woe; **complaining,** scolding, groaning, **faultfinding** 510.4, sniping, destructive criticism, **grumbling, murmuring;** whining, petulance, peevishness, querulousness

5 <nonformal terms> **beef, kick, gripe,** kvetch, grouse, bellyache, howl, holler, **squawk,** bitch; **beefing, grousing, kicking, griping,** kvetching, **bellyaching,** squawking, **bitching,** yapping

6 dirge, funeral *or* **death song,** coronach, keen, elegy, epicedium, requiem, monody, threnody, threnode, knell, death knell, passing bell, funeral *or* dead

march, muffled drums; eulogy, funeral *or* graveside oration

7 <mourning garments> **mourning, weeds,** widow's weeds, crape, black; deep mourning; sackcloth, sackcloth and ashes; cypress, cypress lawn, yew; mourning band; mourning ring

8 lamenter, griever, mourner 309.7; moaner, weeper; **complainer,** faultfinder, smellfungus, malcontent 108.3

9 <nonformal terms> **grouch, kvetch,** kicker, griper, moaner, moaning Minnie <Brit>, crank, crab, grouser, beefer, bellyacher, bitcher, sorehead, picklepuss, sourpuss

VERBS **10 lament, mourn, moan, grieve, sorrow,** keen, weep over, **bewail, bemoan, deplore, repine, sigh,** give sorrow words; sing the blues <nonformal>, elegize, dirge, knell

11 wring one's hands, tear one's hair, gnash one's teeth, beat one's breast, roll on the ground

12 weep, sob, cry, greet <Scots>, **bawl,** boohoo; **blubber, whimper, snivel; shed tears,** drop a tear; **burst into tears,** burst out crying, give way to tears, melt *or* dissolve in tears, break down, break down and cry, turn on the waterworks <nonformal>; cry one's eyes out, cry oneself blind; cry before one is hurt

13 wail, ululate; **moan, groan; howl,** yowl, yawl <Brit nonformal>; **cry, squall, bawl,** yawp, **yell, scream,** shriek; cry out, make an outcry; bay at the moon; tirade

14 whine, whimper, yammer <nonformal>, pule, grizzle <chiefly Brit nonformal>

15 complain, groan; grumble, murmur, mutter, growl, clamor, croak, grunt, yelp; **fret,** fuss, make a fuss about, fret and fume; air a grievance, lodge *or* register a complaint; fault, find fault

16 <nonformal terms> **beef, bitch, kick, kvetch,** bellyache, crab, gripe, grouch, grouse, grump, have an attitude, kick, holler, howl, moan, piss, make a stink, squawk, yap; raise a howl, put up a squawk *or* howl, take on, cry *or* yell *or* scream bloody murder, give one a hard time, piss *or* kick up a storm *or* row *or* fuss, make *or* raise a stink

17 go into mourning; put on mourning, wear mourning

ADJS **18 lamenting, grieving, mourning, moaning, sorrowing;** wailing, bewailing, bemoaning; **in mourning,** in sackcloth and ashes

19 plaintive, plangent, **mournful,** moanful, wailful, lamentive, ululant; **sorrowful**

112.26; **howling,** Jeremianic; whining, whiny, whimpering, puling; **querulous, fretful,** petulant, peevish; **complaining, faultfinding** 510.24

20 <nonformal terms> **grouchy, kvetchy,** cranky, beefing, crabby, crabbing, grousing, griping, bellyaching, bitching

21 **tearful,** teary, **weepy** <nonformal>; lachrymal, lachrymose, lacrimatory; in the melting mood, on the edge of tears, ready to cry; **weeping, sobbing, crying;** blubbering, whimpering, sniveling; **in tears,** with tears in one's eyes, with tearful *or* watery eyes, with swimming *or* brimming *or* overflowing eyes, with eyes suffused *or* bathed *or* dissolved in tears, "like Niobe, all tears"—Shakespeare

22 dirgelike, knell-like, elegiac, elegiacal, epicedial, threnodic

ADVS 23 **lamentingly, plaintively, mournfully,** moanfully, wailfully; **sorrowfully** 112.36; complainingly, groaningly, querulously, fretfully, petulantly, peevishly

116 REJOICING

NOUNS 1 **rejoicing, jubilation,** jubilance, jubilant display, jubilee, show of joy, raucous happiness; **exultation,** elation, triumph; the time of one's life; whoopee *and* hoopla <both nonformal>, festivity 743.3,4, merriment 109.5; celebration 487

2 **cheer, hurrah, huzzah,** hurray, hooray, yippee, rah; **cry, shout, yell;** hosanna, hallelujah, alleluia, paean, paean *or* chorus of cheers; **applause** 509.2

3 **smile,** smiling; bright smile, gleaming *or* glowing smile, beam; silly smile *or* grin; **grin,** grinning; broad grin, ear-to-ear grin, toothful grin; stupid grin, idiotic grin; sardonic grin, **smirk, simper**

4 **laughter, laughing, hilarity** 109.5, risibility; **laugh;** boff *and* boffola *and* yuck <all nonformal>; **titter; giggle; chuckle, chortle;** cackle, crow; **snicker,** snigger, snort; ha-ha, hee-haw, hee-hee, ho-ho, tee-hee, yuk-yuk; guffaw, **horselaugh; hearty laugh, belly laugh** <nonformal>, Homeric laughter, cachinnation; **shout, shriek,** shout of laughter, burst *or* outburst of laughter, peal *or* roar of laughter, gales of laughter; fit of laughter, convulsion, "laughter holding both his sides"—Milton

VERBS 5 **rejoice,** jubilate, **exult, glory, joy, delight,** bless *or* thank one's stars *or* lucky stars, congratulate oneself, hug oneself, rub one's hands, clap hands; dance *or* skip *or* jump for joy, dance, skip, frisk,

rollick, revel, frolic, caper, gambol, caracole, romp; sing, carol, chirp, chirrup, chirp like a cricket, whistle, lilt

6 **cheer,** give a cheer, give three cheers, **cry, shout, yell,** cry for joy, yell oneself hoarse; huzzah, hurrah, hurray, hooray; shout hosanna *or* hallelujah, "make a joyful noise unto the Lord"—Bible; **applaud** 509.10

7 **smile,** crack a smile <nonformal>, break into a smile; **beam,** smile brightly; **grin,** grin like a Cheshire cat *or* chessy-cat <nonformal>; **smirk, simper**

8 **laugh,** burst out laughing, burst into laughter, burst out, laugh outright; laugh it up <nonformal>; **titter; giggle; chuckle, chortle;** cackle, crow; **snicker,** snigger, snort; ha-ha, hee-haw, hee-hee, ho-ho, tee-hee, yuk-yuk; **guffaw,** belly laugh, horselaugh; **shout, shriek,** give a shout *or* shriek of laughter; **roar,** cachinnate, roar with laughter; shake with laughter, shake like jelly; be convulsed with laughter, go into convulsions, fall about <Brit nonformal>; burst *or* split with laughter, break up *and* crack up <both nonformal>, split <nonformal>, **split one's sides,** laugh fit to burst *or* bust <nonformal>, bust a gut *and* pee in *or* wet one's pants laughing <both nonformal>, **be in stitches** <nonformal>, hold one's sides, roll in the aisles <nonformal>; laugh oneself sick *or* silly *or* limp, die *or* nearly die laughing; laugh in one's sleeve, laugh up one's sleeve, laugh in one's beard

9 **make laugh, kill** *and* **slay** <both nonformal>, "set the table on a roar"—Shakespeare, break *or* crack one up <nonformal>, get a laugh

ADJS 10 **rejoicing,** delighting, exulting; **jubilant, exultant, elated,** elate, flushed

ADVS 11 **rejoicingly,** delightingly, exultingly; **jubilantly, exultantly, elatedly**

117 DULLNESS
<being uninteresting>

NOUNS 1 **dullness, dryness,** dustiness, uninterestingness; **stuffiness, stodginess,** woodenness, stiffness; barrenness, sterility, aridity, jejunity; **insipidness,** insipidity, vapidness, vapidity, inanity, hollowness, emptiness, superficiality, **staleness, flatness,** tastelessness; characterlessness, colorlessness, pointlessness; **deadness,** lifelessness, spiritlessness, bloodlessness, paleness, pallor, etiolation, effeteness; **slowness,** pokiness, dragginess <nonformal>, unliveliness; **tediousness** 118.2; **dreariness,** drearisomeness, dismalness; **heaviness,** leadenness, ponderousness; inexcitability 106; solemnity 111; lowness of spirit 112.3

2 **prosaicness,** prosiness; prosaism, prosaicism, prose, plainness; **matter-of-factness,** unimaginativeness; matter of fact; **simplicity** 797, **plainness** 499

3 **triteness,** corniness *and* squareness <both nonformal>, **banality,** banalness, unoriginality, sameness, **hackneyedness, commonplaceness,** commonness, familiarness, platitudinousness; a familiar ring; redundancy, repetition, **staleness,** mustiness, fustiness; cliché 973.3

VERBS 4 **fall flat,** fall flat as a pancake; leave one cold *or* unmoved, go over like a lead balloon <nonformal>, lay an egg *and* bomb <both nonformal>, **wear thin**

5 prose, platitudinize, sing a familiar tune; pedestrianize; warm over; banalize

ADJS 6 **dull, dry,** dusty, dry as dust; **stuffy, stodgy,** wooden, stiff; arid, barren, blank, sterile, jejune; **insipid,** vapid, inane, hollow, empty, superficial; ho-hum *and* blah <both nonformal>, **flat,** tasteless; characterless, colorless, pointless; **dead,** lifeless, spiritless, bloodless, pale, pallid, etiolated, effete; cold; **slow,** poky, draggy <nonformal>, pedestrian, plodding, unlively; **tedious; dreary,** drearisome, dismal; **heavy,** leaden, ponderous, elephantine; dull as dish water, "weary, stale, flat and unprofitable"—Shakespeare; inexcitable 106.10; solemn 111.3; low-spirited 112.22

7 **uninteresting,** uneventful, **unexciting; uninspiring; unentertaining,** unenjoyable, **unamusing,** unfunny, unwitty

8 **prosaic,** prose, prosy, prosing, plain; **matter-of-fact,** unimaginative, unimpassioned

9 **trite;** corny *and* square *and* square-John *and* Clyde <all nonformal>, fade, **banal,** unoriginal, platitudinous, **stereotyped,** stock, set, **commonplace, common,** truistic, twice-told, **familiar,** bromidic <nonformal>, old hat <nonformal>, back-number, bewhiskered, warmed-over, **cut-and-dried; hackneyed,** hackney; well-known 927.27; **stale,** musty, fusty; **worn,** timeworn, well-worn, moth-eaten, threadbare, **worn thin**

ADVS 10 **dully, dryly,** dustily, **uninterestingly;** stuffily, stodgily; aridly, barrenly, jejunely, **insipidly, vapidly,** inanely, hollowly, emptily, superficially, tastelessly, **colorlessly,** pointlessly; lifelessly, spiritlessly, bloodlessly, pallidly, effetely; slowly, draggily <nonformal>, ploddingly; **tediously;** drearily, drearisomely, dismally; heavily, ponderously

11 **tritely,** cornily <nonformal>, **banally,** commonplacely, commonly, familiarly, hackneyedly, unoriginally, truistically, stalely

118 TEDIUM

NOUNS 1 **tedium, monotony, humdrum,** irksomeness, irk; **sameness,** sameliness, samesomeness <nonformal>, wearisome sameness, more of the same, the same old thing, the same damn thing <nonformal>; broken record, parrot; undeviation, unvariation, invariability; the round, the daily round *or* grind, the weary round, the treadmill, the squirrel cage, the rat race <nonformal>, the beaten track *or* path; time on one's hands, time hanging heavily on one's hands; **protraction, prolongation** 826.2

2 **tediousness, monotonousness, unrelievedness; humdrumness,** humdrumminess; **dullness** 117; **wearisomeness,** wearifulness; **tiresomeness, irksomeness,** drearisomeness; **boresomeness,** boringness; prolixity, **long-windedness** 538.2; redundancy, repetition, tick-tock

3 **weariness, tiredness,** wearifulness; jadedness, fed-upness, satiation, satiety; **boredom,** boredness; **ennui,** spleen <old>, melancholy, life-weariness, *taedium vitae* <L>, world-weariness; **listlessness** 94.4, **dispiritedness** 112.3

4 **bore,** crashing bore <nonformal>, frightful bore; **pest, nuisance;** dryasdust; proser, twaddler, **wet blanket;** buttonholer

5 <nonformal terms> **drag, drip, pill,** flat tire, deadass, deadfanny, dull tool; **headache,** pain in the neck *or* ass

VERBS 6 **be tedious, drag on,** go on forever; have a certain sameness, be infinitely repetitive; **weary, tire, irk,** wear, wear on *or* upon, **make one tired,** fatigue, weary *or* tire to death, jade; give one a swift pain in the ass *and* give one a bellyful *and* make one fed-up <all nonformal>, **pall, satiate,** glut

7 **bore,** leave one cold, set *or* send to sleep; **bore stiff** *or* to tears *or* to death *or* to extinction <nonformal>, bore to distraction, bore out of one's life, bore out of all patience; buttonhole

8 **harp on** *or* **upon, dwell on** *or* **upon,** harp

upon one *or* the same string, play *or* sing the same old song *or* tune, play the same broken record

ADJS **9 tedious, monotonous, humdrum,** singsong, jog-trot, treadmill, unvarying, invariable, uneventful, broken-record, parrotlike, harping, everlasting, too much with us <nonformal>; blah <nonformal>, **dreary,** drearisome, dry, dryasdust, dusty, **dull** 117.6; protracted, prolonged 826.11; prolix, **long-winded** 538.12

10 wearying, wearing, **tiring; wearisome,** weariful, fatiguing, **tiresome, irksome; boring, boresome,** stupefyingly boring, stuporific, yawny <nonformal>

11 weary, weariful; **tired,** wearied, irked; good and tired, tired to death, weary unto death; sick, **sick of, tired of, sick and tired of;** jaded, satiated, palled, fed up <nonformal>, brassed off <Brit nonformal>; **blasé;** splenetic <old>, melancholy, melancholic, life-weary, world-weary, tired of living; **listless** 94.13, **dispirited** 112.22

12 bored, uninterested; bored stiff *or* to death *or* to extinction *or* to tears <nonformal>, stupefied *or* stuporous with boredom

ADVS **13 tediously, monotonously,** harpingly, everlastingly, unvaryingly, endlessly; long-windedly; **boringly,** boresomely; **wearisomely,** fatiguingly, wearyingly, **tiresomely, irksomely,** drearisomely; dully 117.10

14 on a treadmill, in a squirrel cage, on the beaten track, on the same old round; without a change of menu *or* scenery *or* pace

PHRS **15** ho hum!, heigh ho!, what a life!, que sera sera; *plus ça change, plus c'est la même chose* <Fr, the more things change, the more they stay the same>; so what else is new?, go figure; MEGO *or* mine eyes glaze over

119 AGGRAVATION

NOUNS **1 aggravation, worsening; exacerbation,** embittering, embitterment, souring; deterioration; **intensification, heightening,** stepping-up, sharpening, deepening, **increase,** enhancement, amplification, enlargement, magnification, augmentation; **exasperation, annoyance, irritation** 96.3; deliberate aggravation, provocation; contentiousness

VERBS **2 aggravate, worsen,** make worse; **exacerbate,** embitter, sour; deteriorate; **intensify, heighten,** step up, sharpen, make acute *or* more acute, bring to a head, deepen, **increase,** enhance, amplify, enlarge, magnify, build up; augment; rub salt in the wound, twist the knife, add insult to injury, pour oil on the fire, add fuel to the fire *or* flame, heat up *and* hot up <both nonformal>; increase pressure *or* tension, tighten, tighten up, tighten the screws, put the squeeze on <nonformal>; **exasperate, annoy, irritate** 96.14; provoke, be an *agent provocateur*

3 worsen, get *or* grow worse, take a turn for the worse; go from push to shove, **go from bad to worse; jump out of the frying pan and into the fire,** avoid Scylla and fall into Charybdis, "sow the wind and reap the whirlwind"—Bible

ADJS **4 aggravated, worsened, worse,** worse and worse, exacerbated, embittered, soured, deteriorated; **intensified, heightened,** stepped-up, **increased,** enhanced, amplified, magnified, enlarged, augmented, heated *or* hotted up <nonformal>; **exasperated, irritated, annoyed** 96.21; provoked, deliberately provoked; worse-off, out of the frying pan and into the fire

5 aggravating, aggravative; **exasperating,** exasperative; **annoying, irritating** 98.22; provocative; contentious

ADVS **6** from bad to worse; aggravatingly, exasperatingly; annoyingly 98.29

120 RELIEF

NOUNS **1 relief, easement, easing,** ease; **relaxation,** relaxing, relaxation *or* easing of tension, decompression, slackening; **reduction,** diminishment, diminution, lessening, abatement, remission; **remedy** 86; **alleviation, mitigation, palliation,** softening, assuagement, allayment, defusing, appeasement, mollification, subduement; soothing, salving, anodyne; lulling; dulling, deadening, numbing, narcotizing, anesthesia, anesthetizing, analgesia; sedating, sedation; doping *or* doping up <nonformal>

2 release, deliverance, freeing, removal; suspension, intermission, respite, surcease, reprieve; discharge; catharsis, purging, purgation, purge, cleansing, cleansing away, emotional release

3 lightening, disburdening, unburdening, unweighting, unloading, disencumbrance, disembarrassment, easing of the load, a load off one's mind, something out of one's system

4 sense *or* feeling of relief, sigh of relief

VERBS **5 relieve,** give relief; **ease,** ease matters; **relax,** slacken; **reduce,** diminish, lessen, abate, remit; **alleviate, mitigate, palliate,** soften, pad, cushion, assuage, allay, defuse, lay, appease, mollify, subdue, soothe; salve, pour balm into, pour oil on; poultice, foment, stupe; slake; lull; **dull, deaden,** dull or deaden the pain, numb, benumb, anesthetize; sedate, narcotize, dope or dope up <nonformal>; temper the wind to the shorn lamb, lay the flattering unction to one's soul

6 release, free, deliver, reprieve, remove, free from; suspend, intermit, give respite or surcease; **relax,** decompress, ease, destress; act as a cathartic, **purge, purge away, cleanse,** cleanse away; give release, cut loose

7 lighten, disburden, unburden, unweight, unload, unfreight, disencumber, disembarrass, ease one's load; **set one's mind at ease** or **rest,** set at ease, **take a load off one's mind,** smooth the ruffled brow of care; relieve oneself, let one's hair down, pour one's heart out, talk it out, let it all hang out and go public <both nonformal>, get it off one's chest

8 be relieved, feel relief, feel better about, get something out of one's system, feel or be oneself again; get out from under <nonformal>; **breathe easy** or **easier,** breathe more freely, breathe again, rest easier; **heave a sigh of relief,** draw a long or deep breath

ADJS **9 relieving, easing, alleviative,** alleviating, alleviatory, **mitigative,** mitigating, **palliative,** lenitive, assuasive, softening, subduing, soothing, demulcent, emollient, balmy, balsamic; **remedial** 86.39; dulling, deadening, numbing, benumbing, anesthetic, analgesic, anodyne, pain killing; cathartic, purgative, cleansing; **relaxing**

10 relieved, breathing easy or easier or freely, able to breathe again, out from under and out of the woods <both nonformal>; **relaxed**

121 COMFORT

NOUNS **1 comfort, ease, well-being;** contentment 107; clover, velvet <nonformal>, bed of roses; life of ease 1009.1; solid comfort

2 comfortableness, easiness; restfulness, reposefulness, peace, peacefulness; softness, cushiness <nonformal>, cushioniness; **coziness, snugness;** friendliness, warmness; **homelikeness,** homeyness <nonformal>, homeliness; **commodiousness,** roominess, convenience; luxuriousness 501.5; hospitality 585

3 creature comforts, comforts, conveniences, excellent accommodations, amenities, good things of life, cakes and ale, egg in one's beer <nonformal>, all the comforts of home; all the heart can desire, luxuries, the best

4 consolation, solace, solacement, easement, heart's ease, "surcease of sorrow"—Poe; **encouragement,** aid and comfort, **assurance, reassurance,** support, **comfort,** crumb or shred of comfort, "kind words and comfortable"—William Cowper; condolence 147, sympathy; **relief** 120

5 comforter, consoler, solacer, encourager; the Holy Spirit or Ghost, the Comforter, the Paraclete

VERBS **6 comfort, console, solace,** give or bring comfort, bear up; condole with, sympathize with, extend sympathy; ease, **put** or **set at ease;** bolster, support; relieve 120.5; **assure, reassure; encourage, hearten,** pat on the back; **cheer** 109.7; wipe away the tears, "rejoice with them that do rejoice, and weep with them that weep"—Bible

7 be comforted, take comfort, take heart; take hope, lift up one's heart, pull oneself together, pluck up one's spirits; *sursum corda* <L>

8 be at ease, be or feel easy, stand easy <Brit>; **make oneself comfortable,** make oneself at home, feel at home, put one's feet up, take a load off <nonformal>; **relax,** be relaxed; live a life of ease 1009.10

9 snug, snug down or up; tuck in

10 snuggle, nestle, cuddle, cuddle up, curl up; nest; bundle; snuggle up to, snug up or together <old>

ADJS **11 comfortable,** comfy <nonformal>; contented 107.7,9,10; **easy,** easeful; **restful,** reposeful, peaceful, **relaxing;** soft, cushioned, cushy <nonformal>, cushiony; comfortable as an old shoe; **cozy, snug,** snug as a bug in a rug; friendly, warm; **homelike,** homey and down-home <both nonformal>, homely, lived-in; **commodious,** roomy, convenient; luxurious 501.21

12 at ease, at one's ease, easy, relaxed, laid-back <nonformal>; at rest, resting easy; **at home,** in one's element

13 comforting, consoling, consolatory, of good comfort; condoling, condolent, condolatory, sympathetic; **assuring, reassuring,** supportive; **encouraging,**

heartening; cheering 109.16; relieving 120.9; hospitable 585.11

ADVS **14 comfortably, easily,** with ease; **restfully,** reposefully, peacefully; **cozily, snugly; commodiously,** roomily, conveniently; luxuriously, voluptuously

15 in comfort, in ease, **in clover, on** or **in velvet** <nonformal>, on or in a bed of roses

16 comfortingly, consolingly, assuringly, reassuringly, supportively, encouragingly, hearteningly; hospitably

122 WONDER

NOUNS **1 wonder,** wonderment, sense of wonder, marveling, marvel, **astonishment, amazement,** amaze, **astoundment;** dumbfoundment, stupefaction; **surprise; awe,** breathless wonder or awe, sense of mystery, admiration; beguilement, fascination 377.1; bewilderment, puzzlement 970.3

2 marvel, wonder, prodigy, miracle, phenomenon, phenom <nonformal>; astonishment, amazement, marvelment, wonderment, wonderful thing, nine days' wonder, amazing or astonishing thing, quite a thing, really something, **sensation,** rocker and stunner <both nonformal>; one for the book and something to brag about and something to shout about and something to write home about and something else <all nonformal>; **rarity,** nonesuch, nonpareil, exception, one in a thousand, one in a way, oner <Brit nonformal>; **curiosity,** gazingstock <old>, **sight, spectacle;** wonders of the world

3 wonderfulness, wondrousness, **marvelousness,** miraculousness, phenomenalness, **prodigiousness, stupendousness, remarkableness,** extraordinariness; beguilingness, fascination, enchantingness, enticingness, seductiveness, **glamorousness; awesomeness, mysteriousness,** mystery, numinousness; **transcendence,** transcendentness, surpassingness

4 inexpressibility, ineffability, ineffableness, inenarrability, noncommunicability, noncommunicableness, incommunicability, incommunicableness, indescribability, indefinableness, **unutterability, unspeakability,** unnameableness, innominability, unmentionability

VERBS **5 wonder, marvel,** be astonished or amazed or astounded, be seized with wonder; **gaze, gape,** drop one's jaw, look or stand aghast or agog, gawk, **stare,** stare openmouthed, open one's eyes, rub one's eyes, hold one's breath; not be able to account for, not know what to make of, not believe one's eyes or ears or senses

6 astonish, amaze, astound, surprise, startle, stagger, **bewilder, perplex** 970.13, flabbergast <nonformal>, confound, overwhelm, **boggle, boggle the mind; awe,** strike with wonder or awe; **dumbfound** or dumbfounder, strike dumb, strike dead; strike all of a heap and throw on one's beam ends and knock one's socks off and bowl down or over <all nonformal>, dazzle, bedazzle, daze, bedaze; **stun, stupefy,** petrify, paralyze

7 take one's breath away, turn one's head, make one's head swim, make one's hair stand on end, make one's tongue cleave to the roof of one's mouth, make one stare, make one sit up and take notice, sweep or carry off one's feet

8 beggar or baffle description, stagger belief

ADJS **9 wondering,** wrapped or rapt in wonder, marveling, **astonished, amazed, surprised, astounded,** flabbergasted <nonformal>, **bewildered,** puzzled, confounded, **dumbfounded,** dumbstruck, staggered, overwhelmed, unable to believe one's senses or eyes; **aghast,** agape, agog, all agog, gazing, gaping, at gaze staring, gauping, wide-eyed, popeyed, open-eyed, openmouthed, **breathless; thunderstruck,** wonder-struck, wonderstricken, awestricken, awestruck, struck all of a heap <nonformal>; **awed, in awe,** in awe of; spellbound, fascinated, captivated, under a charm, beguiled, enthralled, enraptured, enravished, enchanted, entranced, bewitched, hypnotized, mesmerized, stupefied, lost in wonder or amazement

10 wonderful, wondrous, marvelous, miraculous, fantastic, fabulous, phenomenal, **prodigious, stupendous,** unheard-of, unprecedented, extraordinary, exceptional, rare, unique, singular, **remarkable,** striking, **sensational; strange,** passing strange, "wondrous strange"—Shakespeare; **beguiling, fascinating;** incredible, inconceivable, outlandish, unimaginable, incomprehensible; **bewildering, puzzling,** enigmatic

11 awesome, awful, awing, awe-inspiring; **transcendent,** transcending, surpassing; **mysterious,** numinous; weird, eerie, uncanny, bizarre

12 astonishing, amazing, surprising, startling, **astounding,** confounding, staggering, stunning <nonformal>, eye-opening, breathtaking, overwhelming, mind-boggling *or* -numbing; **spectacular**

13 **indescribable, ineffable,** inenarrable, inexpressible, unutterable, unspeakable, noncommunicable, incommunicable, indefinable, undefinable, unnameable, innominable, unwhisperable, unmentionable

ADVS 14 **wonderfully,** wondrously, **marvelously, miraculously,** fantastically, fabulously, phenomenally, prodigiously, stupendously, extraordinarily, exceptionally, remarkably, strikingly, **sensationally;** strangely, outlandishly, incredibly, inconceivably, unimaginably, incomprehensibly, **bewilderingly, puzzlingly,** enigmatically; **beguilingly,** fascinatingly

15 **awesomely,** awfully, awingly, awe-inspiringly; **mysteriously,** numinously, weirdly, eerily, uncannily, bizarrely; **transcendently,** surpassingly, surpassing, passing <old>

16 **astonishingly, amazingly, astoundingly,** staggeringly, confoundingly; **surprisingly,** startlingly, to one's surprise *or* great surprise, to one's astonishment *or* amazement; for a wonder, strange to say

17 **indescribably, ineffably,** inexpressibly, unutterably, **unspeakably,** inenarrably, indefinably, unnameably, unmentionably

18 in wonder, in astonishment, in amazement, in bewilderment, in awe, in admiration, with gaping mouth

INTERJS 19 <astonishment or surprise> my word!, I declare!, well I never!, of all things!, as I live and breathe!, what!, indeed!, really!, surely!, how now!, what on earth!, what in the world!, I'll be jiggered!, holy Christ!, holy Christmas!, holy cow!, holy mackerel!, holy Moses!, holy smoke!, holy shit! <nonformal>, hush *or* shut my mouth!, blow me down!, strike me dead!, shiver my timbers!

20 oh!, O!, ah!, la!, lo!, lo and behold!, hello!, halloo!, hey!, whew!, phew!, wow!, yipes!, yike!

21 my!, oh, my!, dear!, dear me!, goodness!, gracious!, goodness gracious!, gee!, my goodness!, my stars!, good gracious!, good heavens!, good lack!, lackadaisy!, welladay!, hoity-toity!, zounds!, 'sdeath!, gadzooks!, gad so!, bless my heart!, God bless me!, heavens and earth!, for crying out loud! <nonformal>

22 imagine!, fancy!, fancy that!, just imagine!, only think!, well!, I never!, can you feature that!, can you beat that!, it beats the Dutch!, do tell!, you don't say!, the devil *or* deuce you say!, I'll be!, what do

you know!, what do you know about that!, how about that!, who would have thought it!, did you ever!, can it be!, can such things be?, will wonders never cease!

123 UNASTONISHMENT

NOUNS 1 **unastonishment, unamazement,** unamazedness, nonastonishment, nonamazement, nonamazedness, nonwonder, nonwondering, nonmarveling, unsurprise, unsurprisedness, awelessness, wonderlessness; **calm,** calmness, coolness, **cool** <nonformal>, cool *or* calm *or* nodding acceptance, composure, composedness, sangfroid, inexcitability 106, expectation 130, unimpressibleness, refusal to be impressed *or* awed *or* amazed; poker face, straight face

VERBS 2 **accept, take for granted** *or* as a matter of course *or* in stride *or* as it comes, treat as routine, show no amazement, refuse to be impressed, not blink an eye, not turn a hair, keep one's cool <nonformal>

ADJS 3 **unastonished, unsurprised, unamazed,** unmarveling, unwondering, unastounded, undumbfounded, unbewildered; undazzled, undazed; unawed, aweless, wonderless; **unimpressed,** unmoved; calm, **cool,** cool as a cucumber, composed, inexcitable 106.10; expecting, expected 130.13,14

124 HOPE

NOUNS 1 **hope, hopefulness,** hoping, **hopes,** fond *or* fervent hope, good hope, good cheer; aspiration, **desire** 100; prospect, **expectation** 130; sanguine expectation, happy *or* cheerful expectation; **trust, confidence, faith,** assured faith, **reliance,** dependence; conviction, assurance, security, well-grounded hope; assumption, presumption; **promise, prospect,** good *or* bright *or* fair prospect, good *or* hopeful prognosis, best case; great expectations, good prospects, high hopes; hoping against hope, prayerful hope; doomed hope *or* hopes

2 "the second soul of the unhappy"— Goethe, "the dream of those that wake"— Matthew Prior, "the thing with feathers that perches in the soul"—Emily Dickinson, "the worst of all evils, because it prolongs the torments of man"— Nietzsche

3 **optimism,** optimisticalness, Pollyanna-

ism, cheerful *or* bright *or* rosy outlook, rose-colored glasses; **cheerfulness** 109; bright side, silver lining; "the noble temptation to see too much in everything"—Chesterton, "the mania of maintaining that everything is well when we are wretched"—Voltaire; philosophical optimism, Leibnizian *or* Rousseauistic optimism, utopianism, perfectionism, perfectibilism; millenarianism, chiliasm, millennialism

4 **ray of hope,** gleam *or* glimmer of hope; faint hope

5 **airy hope,** unreal hope, dream, golden dream, pipe dream <nonformal>, bubble, chimera, fool's paradise, quixotic ideal, utopia 985.11

6 **optimist,** hoper, Pollyanna <Eleanor Porter>, ray of sunshine <nonformal>, irrepressible optimist, Dr Pangloss <Voltaire>; "a proponent of the doctrine that black is white"—Ambrose Bierce, "one who makes the best of it when he gets the worst of it"—Anon, "one who makes the most of all that comes and the least of all that goes"—Sara Teasdale, Leibnizian optimist, philosophical optimist, utopian, perfectionist, perfectibilist, perfectibilitarian; millenarian, chiliast, millennialist, millennian; aspirer, aspirant, hopeful <nonformal>

VERBS 7 **hope,** be *or* live in hopes, have reason to hope, entertain *or* harbor the hope, cling to the hope, cherish *or* foster *or* nurture the hope; look for, prognosticate, **expect** 130.5; **trust,** confide, presume, feel confident, rest assured; pin one's hope upon, put one's trust in, hope in, rely on, count on, lean upon, bank on, set great store on; hope for, **aspire to, desire** 100.14; **hope against hope,** hope and pray, hope to God <nonformal>

8 **be hopeful, get one's hopes up,** keep one's spirits up, never say die, take heart, be of good hope, be of good cheer, keep hoping, keep hope alive, keep the faith <nonformal>; **hope for the best,** knock on wood, touch wood <Brit>, cross one's fingers, keep one's fingers crossed, allow oneself to hope; clutch *or* catch at straws

9 **be optimistic, look on the bright side; look through** *or* **wear rose-colored glasses,** *voir en couleur de rose* <Fr>; call the glass half full, think positively *or* affirmatively, be upbeat <nonformal>, think the best of, **make the best of it,** say that all is for the best, put a good *or* bold face upon, put the best face upon; see the light at the end of the tunnel; count one's chickens before

they are hatched, count one's bridges before they are crossed

10 **give hope, raise hope,** yield *or* afford hope, hold out hope, justify hope, inspire hope, **raise one's hopes,** raise expectations, **lead one to expect; cheer** 109.7; inspire, inspirit; **assure, reassure,** support; **promise,** hold out promise, augur well, bid fair *or* well, make fair promise, have good prospects

ADJS 11 **hopeful, hoping, in hopes,** full of hope, in good heart, of good hope, of good cheer; **aspiring** 100.28; **expectant** 130.11; **sanguine,** fond; **confident,** assured; undespairing

12 **optimistic,** upbeat <nonformal>, bright, sunny; **cheerful** 109.11; **rosy,** roseate, rose-colored, *couleur de rose* <Fr>; pollyannaish, Leibnizian, Rousseauistic, Panglossian; utopian 985.23, perfectionist, perfectibilitarian, millenarian, chiliastic, millennialistic

13 **promising,** of promise, full of promise, bright with promise, pregnant of good, best-case, **favorable,** looking up; **auspicious, propitious** 133.18; inspiring, inspiriting, **encouraging,** cheering, reassuring, supportive

ADVS 14 **hopefully,** hopingly; **expectantly** 130.15; **optimistically; cheerfully** 109.17; sanguinely, fondly; confidently

125 HOPELESSNESS

NOUNS 1 **hopelessness,** unhopefulness, no hope, not a prayer *and* not a hope in hell <both nonformal>, not the ghost of a chance; small hope, bleak outlook *or* prospect *or* prognosis, worst case, blank future, no future; inexpectation 131; futility 391.2; impossibility 966

2 **despair, desperation,** desperateness; no way <nonformal>, no way out, no exit, despondency 112.3; disconsolateness 112.12; forlornness; cave of despair, cave of Trophonius; acedia, sloth; apathy 94.4

3 **irreclaimability, irretrievability,** irredeemability, irrecoverableness, unsalvageability, unsalvability; incorrigibility, irreformability; irrevocability, **irreversibility; irreparability, incurability,** irremediableness, curelessness, remedilessness, immedicableness; unrelievability, unmitigability

4 **forlorn hope,** vain expectation, doomed *or* foredoomed hope, fond *or* foolish hope; counsel of perfection

5 dashed hopes, blighted hope, hope deferred; disappointment 132

6 pessimism, cynicism, malism, nihilism; uncheerfulness 112.2; **gloominess,** dismalness, gloomy outlook; negativism; defeatism; retreatism; "the name that men of weak nerve give to wisdom"— Bernard De Voto

7 pessimist, cynic, malist, nihilist; killjoy 112.14, gloomy Gus *and* calamity howler *and* worrywart <all nonformal>, seeksorrow, Job's comforter, prophet of doom, Cassandra, Eeyore; negativist; defeatist; retreatist; "one who is not happy except when he is miserable"—anon, "a man who feels bad when he feels good for fear he'll feel worse when he feels better"—George Burns, "one who is always building dungeons in the air"— John Galsworthy, "a man who thinks everybody as nasty as himself, and hates them for it"—G B Shaw

8 lost cause, fool's errand, wild-goose chase; hopeless case; goner *and* gone goose *or* gosling *and* dead duck <all nonformal>; terminal case

VERBS **9 be hopeless,** have not a hope *or* prayer, look bleak *or* dark; **be pessimistic, look on the dark side,** be *or* think downbeat <nonformal>, think negatively, think *or* make the worst of, put the worst face upon, call the glass half empty; "fancy clouds where no clouds be"— Thomas Hood; not hold one's breath

10 despair, despair of, **despond** 112.16, falter, lose hope, **lose heart, abandon hope,** give up hope, **give up,** give up all hope *or* expectation, give way *or* over, fall *or* sink into despair, give oneself up *or* yield to despair, throw up one's hands in despair, turn one's face to the wall; curse God and die

11 shatter one's hopes, dash *or* crush *or* blight one's hope, burst one's bubble <nonformal>, bring crashing down around one's head, dash the cup from one's lips, disappoint 132.2, drive to despair *or* desperation

ADJS **12 hopeless,** unhopeful, without hope, affording no hope, worst-case, bleak, grim, dismal, cheerless, comfortless; **desperate, despairing, in despair;** despondent 112.22; disconsolate 112.28; forlorn; apathetic 94.13

13 futile, vain 391.13; doomed, foredoomed

14 impossible, out of the question, not to be thought of, no-go *and* no-win *and* loselose <all nonformal>

15 past hope, beyond recall, past praying for; **irretrievable, irrecoverable, irreclaimable,** irredeemable, unsalvageable, unsalvable; incorrigible, irreformable; irrevocable, **irreversible; irremediable, irreparable,** inoperable, cureless, remediless, immedicable, beyond remedy, terminal; unrelievable, unmitigable; **ruined,** undone, kaput <nonformal>; lost, gone, gone to hell *and* gone to hell in a handbasket <both nonformal>

16 pessimistic, pessimist, downbeat <nonformal>, **cynical,** nihilistic; uncheerful 112.21; **gloomy,** dismal, crepehanging, funereal, lugubrious; negative, negativistic; defeatist; Cassandran *or* Cassandrian, Cassandra-like

ADVS **17 hopelessly, desperately,** forlornly; impossibly

18 irreclaimably, irretrievably, irrecoverably, irredeemably, unsalvageably, unsalvably; irrevocably, **irreversibly; irremediably, incurably, irreparably**

126 ANXIETY
<troubled thought>

NOUNS **1 anxiety, anxiousness; apprehension, apprehensiveness,** antsyness <nonformal>, misgiving, foreboding, forebodingness, suspense, strain, tension, stress, nervous strain *or* tension; **dread, fear** 127; **concern,** concernment, anxious concern, **solicitude,** zeal 101.2; **care,** cankerworm of care; **distress,** trouble, vexation, unease; **uneasiness, perturbation, disturbance,** upset, **agitation, disquiet,** disquietude, inquietude, unquietness; **nervousness** 128; malaise, angst 96.1; pucker *and* yips *and* stew *and* allovers <all nonformal>, pins and needles, tenterhooks, shpilkes <nonformal>; overanxiety; anxious seat *or* bench; anxiety neurosis, anxiety neurosis *or* hysteria

2 worry, worriment <nonformal>, worriedness; **worries,** worries and cares, troubles, concerns; worrying, fretting; harassment, torment

3 worrier, worrywart *and* nervous Nellie <both nonformal>

VERBS **4 concern,** give concern, **trouble, bother, distress, disturb, upset,** frazzle, **disquiet, agitate;** rob one of ease *or* sleep *or* rest, keep one on edge *or* on tenterhooks *or* on pins and needles *or* on shpilkes <nonformal>

5 <make anxious> **worry, upset, vex,** fret, agitate, get to <nonformal>, **harass,** harry, **torment,** dog, hound, plague, persecute, haunt, beset

6 <feel anxious> **worry,** worry oneself, worry one's head about, worry oneself sick, trouble one's head or oneself, be a prey to anxiety, lose sleep; have one's heart in one's mouth, have one's heart miss or skip a beat, have one's heart stand still, get butterflies in one's stomach; **fret, fuss, chafe,** stew and take on <both non-formal>, fret and fume; tense up, bite one's nails, walk the floor, go up the wall <nonformal>, be on tenterhooks or pins and needles or shpilkes <nonformal>

ADJS **7 anxious, concerned, apprehensive,** foreboding, misgiving, suspenseful, strained, tense, tensed up <nonformal>, nail-biting, white-knuckle <nonformal>; **fearful** 127.32; **solicitous,** zealous 101.9; **troubled, bothered; uneasy, perturbed, disturbed, disquieted, agitated; nervous** 128.11; **on pins and needles,** on tenter-hooks, on shpilkes <nonformal>, on the anxious seat or bench; anxioused up and all hot and bothered and in a pucker and in a stew <all nonformal>; over-anxious, overapprehensive

8 worried, vexed, fretted; **harassed,** har-ried, tormented, dogged, hounded, perse-cuted, haunted, beset, plagued; worried sick, worried to a frazzle, worried stiff <nonformal>

9 careworn, heavy-laden, overburdened

10 troublesome, bothersome, **distressing,** distressful, **disturbing, upsetting, dis-quieting; worrisome,** worrying; fretting, chafing; **harassing,** tormenting, plaguing; **annoying** 98.22

ADVS **11 anxiously, concernedly, apprehen-sively,** misgivingly, **uneasily;** worriedly; solicitously, zealously 101.14

127 FEAR, FRIGHTENINGNESS

NOUNS **1 fear, fright,** affright; **scare, alarm, consternation, dismay; dread,** unholy dread, **awe; terror, horror,** horrification, mortal or abject fear; **phobia** <see list>, funk or blue funk <both nonformal>; **panic,** panic fear or terror; stampede; **cowardice** 491

2 frighteningness, frightfulness, awfulness, scariness, fearfulness, fearsomeness, alarmingness, dismayingness, disquiet-ingness, startlingness, disconcertingness, terribleness, **dreadfulness, horror,** hor-ribleness, **hideousness,** appallingness, direness, **ghastliness,** grimness, grisli-ness, **gruesomeness,** ghoulishness; **creepiness, spookiness,** eeriness, weird-ness, uncanniness

3 fearfulness, afraidness; **timidity, timor-ousness, hyness;** shrinkingness, bashful-

ness, diffidence, stage fright, mike fright and flop sweat <both nonformal>; skit-tishness, startlishness, jumpiness, goosiness <nonformal>

4 apprehension, apprehensiveness, **misgiv-ing, qualm,** qualmishness, funny feeling; **anxiety** 126; doubt 954.2; foreboding

5 trepidation, trepidity, perturbation, **fear and trembling; quaking, agitation** 105.4; **uneasiness, disquiet,** disquietude, inquie-tude; nervousness 128; palpitation, heartquake; shivers or cold shivers <nonformal>, creeps or cold creeps <nonformal>, heebie-jeebies <nonfor-mal>, chills of fear or terror, icy fingers or icy clutch of dread, jimjams <nonfor-mal>; horripilation, gooseflesh, goose bumps <nonformal>; sweat, cold sweat; thrill of fear, spasm or quiver of terror; sinking stomach

6 frightening, intimidation, bullying, browbeating, cowing, bulldozing <nonformal>, hectoring; **demoraliza-tion,** psychological warfare, war of nerves

7 terrorization, terrorizing, horrification, scaremongering, panic-mongering, scare tactics; **terrorism,** terror or terroristic tactics, Schrecklichkeit <Ger>, rule by terror, reign of terror

8 alarmist, scaremonger, panic-monger; **terrorist,** bomber, assassin

9 frightener, scarer, hair-raiser; scarebabe, **bogey,** bogeyman, **bugaboo,** bugbear; hobgoblin; **scarecrow; horror, terror,** holy terror; **ogre,** ogress, **monster,** vam-pire, werewolf, ghoul, bête noire, fee-faw-fum; incubus, succubus, nightmare; witch, goblins; **ghost,** specter, phantom, revenant; Frankenstein, Dracula, Wolf-man; mythical monsters

VERBS **10 fear, be afraid; apprehend,** have qualms, misgive, eye askance; **dread,** stand in dread or awe of, be in mortal dread or terror of, stand in awe of, stand aghast; be on pins and needles, sit upon thorns; have one's heart in one's mouth, have one's heart stand still, have one's heart skip or miss a beat; **sweat,** break out in a cold sweat, sweat bullets <nonformal>

11 take fright, take alarm, push or press or hit the panic button <nonformal>; funk and go into a funk <both nonformal>, get the wind up <Brit nonformal>; lose courage 491.8; pale, grow or turn pale, change or turn color; look as if one had seen a ghost; freeze, be paralyzed with fear, throw up one's hands in horror; shit in one's pants *and* shit green <both nonformal>

12 start, startle, **jump**, jump out of one's skin, jump a mile, leap like a startled gazelle; **shy**, fight shy, start aside, boggle, jib; **panic**, stampede, skedaddle <nonformal>

13 flinch, shrink, shy, shy away from, draw back, recoil, funk <nonformal>, **quail, cringe, wince, blench, blink**, say *or* cry uncle; put one's tail between one's legs

14 tremble, shake, quake, shiver, quiver, quaver; tremble *or* **quake** *or* **shake** in one's boots *or* **shoes**, tremble like an aspen leaf, quiver like a rabbit, shake all over

15 frighten, fright, affright, funk <nonformal>, frighten *or* scare out of one's wits; **scare**, spook <nonformal>, scare one stiff *or* shitless *or* spitless <nonformal>, scare the life out of, scare the pants off of *and* scare hell out of *and* scare the shit out of <all nonformal>; scare one to death, scare the daylights *or* the living daylights *or* the wits *or* the shit out of <nonformal>; give one a fright *or* scare *or* turn; **alarm**, disquiet, raise apprehensions; shake, stagger; **startle** 131.8; **unnerve, unman**, unstring; give one goose-flesh, horripilate, give one the creeps *or* the willies <nonformal>, make one's flesh creep, chill one's spine, make one's nerves tingle, curl one's hair <nonformal>, make one's hair stand on end, make one's blood run cold, freeze *or* curdle the blood, make one's teeth chatter, make one tremble, take one's breath away, make one shit one's pants *or* shit green <nonformal>

16 put in fear, put the fear of God into, **throw a scare into** <nonformal>; **panic**, stampede, send scuttling, throw blind fear into

17 terrify, awe, strike terror into; **horrify, appall, shock**, make one's flesh creep; **frighten out of one's wits** *or* **senses**; strike dumb, **stun, stupefy, paralyze, petrify**, freeze

18 daunt, deter, shake, stop, stop in one's tracks, set back; **discourage, dishearten**; faze <nonformal>; **awe, overawe**

19 dismay, disconcert, appall, astound, confound, abash, discomfit, put out, take aback

20 intimidate, cow, browbeat, bulldoze <nonformal>, bludgeon, dragoon; **bully, hector, harass**, huff; bluster, bluster out of *or* into; **terrorize**, put in bodily fear, use

terror *or* terrorist tactics, pursue a policy of *Schrecklichkeit*, systematically terrorize; threaten 514.2; **demoralize**

21 frighten off, scare away, bluff off, put to flight

ADJS **22 afraid, scared**, scared to death <nonformal>, spooked <nonformal>; feared *or* afeared <both nonformal>; fear-stricken, fear-struck; haunted with fear, phobic

23 fearful, fearing, fearsome, **in fear; cowardly** 491.10; **timorous, timid, shy**, rabbity *and* mousy <both nonformal>, afraid of one's own shadow; **shrinking**, bashful, diffident; scary; **skittish**, skittery <nonformal>, startlish, gun-shy, jumpy, goosy <nonformal>; **tremulous**, trembling, trepidant, shaky, shivery; **nervous**

24 apprehensive, misgiving, antsy <nonformal>, **qualmish**, qualmy; anxious 126.6

25 frightened, frightened to death, affrighted, in a fright, frit <Brit nonformal>, in a funk *or* blue funk <nonformal>; **alarmed**, disquieted; consternated, **dismayed**, daunted; **startled** 131.13; more frightened than hurt

26 terrified, terror-stricken, terror-struck, terror-smitten, terror-shaken, terror-troubled, terror-riven, terror-ridden, terror-driven, terror-crazed, terror-haunted; awestricken, awestruck; **horrified**, horror-stricken, horror-struck; **appalled, astounded, aghast**; frightened out of one's wits *or* mind, **scared to death, scared stiff** *or* **shitless** *or* spitless <nonformal>; unnerved, unstrung, unmanned, undone, **cowed**, awed, **intimidated; stunned, petrified, stupefied**, paralyzed, frozen; white as a sheet, pale as death *or* a ghost, deadly pale, ashen, blanched, pallid, gray with fear

27 panicky, panic-prone, panicked, in a panic, panic-stricken, panic-struck, terror-stricken, out of one's mind with fear, prey to blind fear

28 frightening, frightful; fearful, fearsome, fear-inspiring, nightmarish, hellish; **scary**, scaring, chilling; **alarming, startling**, disquieting, dismaying, disconcerting; **unnerving, daunting**, deterring, **deterrent**, discouraging, disheartening, fazing, awing, overawing; stunning, stupefying, mind-boggling *or* -numbing

29 terrifying, terrorful, terror-striking, terror-inspiring, terror-bringing, terror-giving, terror-breeding, terror-breathing, terror-bearing, terror-fraught; **bloodcurdling, hair-raising** <nonformal>; petrifying, paralyzing, stunning, stupefying; **terrorizing, terror, terroristic;** *schrecklich* <Ger>

30 **terrible,** terrific, tremendous; **horrid, horrible, horrifying,** horrific, horrendous; **dreadful, dread,** dreaded; **awful;** awesome, awe-inspiring; **shocking, appalling,** astounding; **dire,** direful, fell; formidable, redoubtable; **hideous, ghastly,** morbid, grim, grisly, gruesome, ghoulish, macabre

31 **creepy, spooky, eerie, weird, uncanny,** unco *or* uncolike <both Scots>

ADVS 32 **fearfully, apprehensively, diffidently,** for fear of; **timorously, timidly, shyly,** mousily <nonformal>, bashfully, shrinkingly; tremulously, tremblingly, quakingly, **with** *or* **in fear and trembling;** with heart in mouth, with bated breath

33 **in fear, in terror,** in awe, in alarm, in consternation; in mortal fear, in fear of one's life

34 **frightfully, fearfully; alarmingly, startlingly,** disquietingly, dismayingly, disconcertingly; **shockingly, appallingly,** astoundingly; **terribly,** terrifically, tremendously; **dreadfully, awfully; horridly, horribly,** horrifyingly, horrifically, horrendously

35 **phobias by subject**

<albumin in the urine> albuminurophobia
<anemia> anemophobia
<animals> zoophobia
<bacteria> bacteriophobia
<beards> pogonophobia
<bears> ursaphobia
<bees> apiphobia
<being alone> autophobia *or* monophobia *or* ermitophobia
<being idle> thaasophobia
<being whipped> mastigophobia
<birds> ornithophobia
<blood> hemaphobia *or* hematophobia *or* hemophobia
<blushing> erythrophobia
<body odor> bromidrosiphobia
<bullets> ballistophobia
<bulls> taurophobia
<cancer> cancerphobia *or* cancerophobia *or* carcinophobia
<cats> ailurophobia
<certain places> topophobia
<childbirth> tocophobia
<children> pedophobia
<Chinese> Sinophobia
<cholera> cholerophobia
<church> ecclesiophobia
<clouds> nephelophobia
<coitus> coitophobia
<cold> cheimaphobia *or* cheimatophobia

<color> chromophobia
<comets> cometophobia
<constipation> coprostasophobia
<corpses> necrophobia
<crossing a bridge> gephyrophobia
<crossing a street> agyrophobia
<crowds> demophobia
<crystals> crystallophobia
<dampness> hygrophobia
<darkness> scotophobia *or* achluophobia
<dawn> eosophobia
<death> thanatophobia
<demons> demonophobia
<depth> bathophobia
<diabetes> diabetophobia
<dirt> mysophobia
<disease> pathophobia
<dogs> cynophobia
<double vision> diplopiaphobia
<draft> aerophobia
<drink> potophobia
<drugs> pharmacophobia
<duration> chronophobia
<dust> koniophobia *or* amathophobia
<electricity> electrophobia
<enclosed places> claustrophobia
<English> Anglophobia
<everything> panphobia *or* pantophobia
<eyes> ommetaphobia
<failure> kakorraphiaphobia
<fatigue> kopophobia
<fear> phobophobia
<feathers> pteronophobia

<feces> coprophobia
<fever> febriphobia
<fire> pyrophobia
<fish> ichthyophobia
<floods> antlophobia
<flowers> anthophobia
<flutes> aulophobia
<fog> homichlophobia
<food> cibophobia *or* sitophobia *or* sitiophobia
<foreigners> xenophobia
<freedom> eleutherophobia
<French> Francophobia *or* Gallophobia
<fur> doraphobia
<Germans> Germanophobia *or* Teutonophobia
<germs> spermophobia *or* spermatophobia
<ghosts> phasmophobia
<God> theophobia
<going to bed> clinophobia
<gold> aurophobia
<gravity> barophobia
<gringos> gringophobia
<hair> chaetophobia *or* trichophobia
<hair disease> trichopathophobia
<heart disease> cardiophobia
<heat> thermophobia
<heaven> uranophobia *or* ouranophobia
<hell> hadephobia *or* stygiophobia
<heredity> patroiophobia
<high places> acrophobia *or* altophobia *or* batophobia *or* hypsophobia

\<home\>
ecophobia *or*
oecophobia *or*
oikophobia
\<homosexuals\>
homophobia
\<horses\>
hippophobia
\<ice, frost\>
cryophobia
\<ideas\>
ideophobia
\<imperfection\>
atelophobia
\<infinity\>
apeirophobia
\<inoculation\>
trypanophobia *or*
vaccinophobia
\<insanity\>
lyssophobia *or*
maniaphobia
\<insects\>
entomophobia
\<insect stings\>
cnidophobia
\<itching\>
acarophobia
\<Japanese\>
Japanophobia
\<jealousy\>
zelophobia
\<Jews\>
Judeophobia
\<justice\>
dikephobia
\<lakes\>
limnophobia
\<lice\>
pediculophobia
\<light\>
photophobia
\<light flashes\>
selaphobia
\<lightning\>
astraphobia *or*
astrapophobia
\<machinery\>
mechanophobia
\<magic\>
rhabdophobia
\<marriage\>
gametophobia
\<men\> androphobia
\<meningitis\>
meningitophobia
\<metal\>
metallophobia
\<mice\>
musophobia
\<microbes\>
bacillophobia *or*
microbiophobia

\<mirrors\>
eisoptrophobia
\<mites\>
acarophobia
\<mobs\>
ochlophobia
\<money\>
chrometophobia
\<monsters\>
teratophobia
\<motion\>
dromophobia *or*
kinetophobia
\<music\>
musicophobia
\<names\>
onomatophobia
\<narrowness\>
anginophobia
\<needles\>
belonephobia
\<Negroes\>
Negrophobia
\<new things\>
neophobia
\<night\>
nyctophobia
\<nudity\>
gymnophobia *or*
nudophobia
\<old people\>
gerontophobia
\<one thing\>
monophobia
\<open places\>
agoraphobia
\<pain\> algophobia
\<parasites\>
parasitophobia
\<passing high
buildings\>
batophobia
\<pellagra\>
pellagraphobia
\<people\>
anthropophobia
\<philosophy\>
philosophobia
\<pins\> enetophobia
\<pleasure\>
hedonophobia
\<poison\>
toxiphobia *or*
toxophobia *or*
toxicophobia
\<politics\>
politicophobia
\<the Pope\>
papaphobia
\<poverty\>
peniaphobia
\<precipices\>
cremnophobia

\<priests\>
hierophobia
\<protein\>
proteinphobia
\<punishment\>
poinephobia
\<rabies\>
hydrophobobophobia
\<rectum\>
rectophobia
\<reptiles\>
batrachophobia *or*
herpetophobia
\<responsibility\>
hypegiaphobia
\<ridicule\>
katagelophobia
\<rivers\>
potamophobia
\<robbers\>
harpaxophobia
\<ruin\>
atephobia
\<Russians\>
Russophobia
\<saints\>
hagiophobia
\<Satan\>
Satanophobia
\<scabies\>
scabiophobia
\<sea\>
thalassophobia
\<sex\> erotophobia
or genophobia
\<shadows\>
sciophobia
\<sharpness\>
acrophobia
\<shock\>
hormephobia
\<sin\>
hamartophobia *or*
peccatiphobia
\<skin\>
dermatosiophobia
\<skin disease\>
dermatopatho-
phobia
\<sleep\>
hypnophobia
\<slime\>
blennophobia *or*
myxophobia
\<small things\>
microphobia
\<smell\>
olfactophobia *or*
osmophobia *or*
ophresiophobia
\<smothering\>
pnigophobia *or*
pnigerophobia

\<snakes\>
ophiciophobia *or*
ophiophobia *or*
snakephobia
\<snow\>
chionophobia
\<soiling\>
rypophobia
\<sound\>
acousticophobia
\<sourness\>
acerophobia *or*
acerbophobia
\<speech\>
lalophobia *or*
laliophobia *or*
glossophobia *or*
phonophobia
\<speed\>
tachophobia
\<spiders\>
arachnophobia
\<spirits\>
pneumatophobia
\<standing\>
stasophobia
\<stars\>
siderophobia
\<stealing\>
kleptophobia
\<string\>
linonophobia
\<sun\> heliophobia
\<swallowing\>
phagophobia
\<symmetry\>
symmetrophobia
\<syphilis\>
syphilophobia
\<taste\>
geumatophobia
\<technology\>
technophobia
\<teeth\>
odontophobia
\<telephone\>
telephonophobia
\<thinking\>
phronemophobia
\<thirteen, the
number\>
tredecaphobia *or*
triskaidekaphobia
\<thunder\>
brontophobia *or*
tonitrophobia *or*
keraunophobia
\<touch\>
haptophobia *or*
haphophobia *or*
thixophobia
\<travel\>
hodophobia

<trembling>
tremophobia
<trichinosis>
trichinophobia
<tuberculosis>
tuberculophobia *or*
phthisiophobia
<tyrants>
tyrannophobia
<urine> urophobia
<vehicles>
ochophobia
<venereal disease>
venereophobia
<void> kenophobia
<vomiting>
emetophobia
<water>
hydrophobia

<waves>
cymophobia
<weakness>
asthenophobia
<wind>
ancraophobia
<women>
gynephobia
<words> logophobia
<work> ergophobia
<worms>
vermiphobia *or*
helminthophobia
<wound, injury>
traumatophobia
<writing>
graphophobia
<young girls>
parthenophobia

36 phobias by name

acrophobia *or*
altophobia *or*
batophobia *or*
hypsophobia
<high places>
acrophobia
<sharpness>
aerophobia
<draft>
agoraphobia <open
places>
agyrophobia
<crossing a
street>
ailurophobia <cats>
albuminurophobia
<albumin in the
urine>
algophobia
<pain>
ancraophobia
<wind>
androphobia <men>
anemophobia
<anemia>
anginophobia
<narrowness>
Anglophobia
<English>
anthophobia
<flowers>
anthropophobia
<people>
antlophobia
<floods>
apeirophobia
<infinity>
apiphobia <bees>
arachnophobia
<spiders>
asthenophobia
<weakness>

astraphobia *or*
astrapophobia
<lightning>
atelophobia
<imperfection>
atephobia
<ruin>
aulophobia
<flutes>
aurophobia
<gold>
autophobia *or*
monophobia *or*
ermitophobia
<being alone>
bacillophobia *or*
microbiophobia
<microbes>
bacteriophobia
<bacteria>
ballistophobia
<bullets>
barophobia
<gravity>
bathophobia
<depth>
batophobia <passing
high buildings>
batrachophobia *or*
herpetophobia
<reptiles>
belonephobia
<needles>
blennophobia *or*
myxophobia
<slime>
bromidrosiphobia
<body odor>
brontophobia *or*
tonitrophobia *or*
keraunophobia
<thunder>

cancerphobia *or*
cancerophobia *or*
carcinophobia
<cancer>
cardiophobia <heart
disease>
chaetophobia *or*
trichophobia
<hair>
cheimaphobia *or*
cheimatophobia
<cold>
chionophobia
<snow>
cholerophobia
<cholera>
chrometophobia
<money>
chromophobia
<color>
chronophobia
cibophobia *or*
sitophobia *or*
sitiophobia
<food>
claustrophobia
<enclosed places>
clinophobia <going
to bed>
cnidophobia <insect
stings>
coitophobia
<coitus>
cometophobia
<comets>
coprophobia
<feces>
coprostasophobia
<constipation>
cremnophobia
<precipices>
cryophobia <ice>
crystallophobia
<crystals>
cymophobia
<waves>
cynophobia <dogs>
demonophobia
<demons>
demophobia
<crowds>
dermatopathophobia
<skin disease>
dermatosiophobia
<skin>
diabetophobia
<diabetes>
dikephobia
<justice>
diplopiaphobia
<double vision>
doraphobia <fur>

dromophobia *or*
kinetophobia
<motion>
ecclesiophobia
<church>
ecophobia *or*
oecophobia *or*
oikophobia
<home>
eisoptrophobia
<mirrors>
electrophobia
<electricity>
eleutherophobia
<freedom>
emetophobia
<vomiting>
enetophobia <pins>
entomophobia
<insects>
eosophobia <dawn>
ergophobia <work>
erotophobia *or*
genophobia <sex>
erythrophobia
<blushing>
febriphobia <fever>
Francophobia *or*
Gallophobia
<French>
gametophobia
<marriage>
gephyrophobia
<crossing a
bridge>
gerontophobia <old
people>
Germanophobia *or*
Teutonophobia
<Germans>
geumatophobia
<taste>
graphophobia
<writing>
gringophobia
<gringos>
gymnophobia *or*
nudophobia
<nudity>
gynephobia
<women>
hadephobia *or*
stygiophobia
<hell>
hagiophobia
<saints>
hamartophobia *or*
peccatiphobia
<sin>
haptophobia *or*
haphophobia *or*
thixophobia

harpaxophobia
<robbers>
hedonophobia
<pleasure>
heliophobia <sun>
helminthophobia
<worms>
hemaphobia *or*
hematophobia *or*
hemophobia
<blood>
hierophobia
<priests>
hippophobia
<horses>
hodophobia
<travel>
homichlophobia
<fog>
homophobia
<homosexuals>
hormephobia
<shock>
hydrophobia
<water>
hydrophobophobia
<rabies>
hygrophobia
<dampness>
hypegiaphobia
<responsibility>
hypnophobia
<sleep>
ichthyophobia
<fish>
ideophobia <ideas>
Japanophobia
<Japanese>
Judeophobia
<Jews>
kakorraphiaphobia
<failure>
katagelophobia
<ridicule>
kenophobia <void>
kleptophobia
<stealing>
koniophobia *or*
amathophobia
<dust>
kopophobia
<fatigue>
lalophobia *or*
laliophobia *or*
glossophobia *or*
phonophobia
<speech>
limnophobia
<lakes>
linonophobia
<string>
logophobia
<words>

lyssophobia *or*
maniaphobia
<insanity>
mastigophobia
<beating>
mechanophobia
<machinery>
meningitophobia
<meningitis>
metallophobia
<metal>
microphobia <small
things>
monophobia <one
thing>
musicophobia
<music>
musophobia <mice>
mysophobia <dirt>
necrophobia
<corpses>
Negrophobia
<Negroes>
neophobia <new
things>
nephophobia
<clouds>
nephophobia *or*
pathophobia
<disease>
nyctophobia
<night>
ochlophobia
<mobs>
ochophobia
<vehicles>
odontophobia
<teeth>
olfactophobia *or*
osmophobia *or*
ophresiophobia
<smell>
ommetaphobia
<eyes>
onomatophobia
<names>
ophiciophobia *or*
ophiophobia *or*
snakephobia
<snakes>
ornithophobia
<birds>
panphobia *or*
pantophobia
<everything>
papaphobia <the
Pope>
parasitophobia
<parasites>
parthenophobia
<young girls>
pathophobia
<disease>

patroiophobia
<heredity>
pediculophobia
<lice>
pedophobia
<children>
pellagraphobia
<pellagra>
peniaphobia
<poverty>
phagophobia
<swallowing>
pharmacophobia
<drugs>
phasmophobia
<ghosts>
philosophobia
<philosophy>
phobophobia <fear>
photophobia
<light>
phronemophobia
pneumatophobia
<spirits>
pnigophobia *or*
pnigerophobia
<smothering>
pogonophobia
<beards>
poinephobia
<punishment>
politicophobia
<politics>
potamophobia
<rivers>
potophobia
<drink>
proteinphobia
<protein>
pteronophobia
<feathers>
pyrophobia <fire>
rectophobia
<rectum>
rhabdophobia
<magic>
Russophobia
<Russians>
rypophobia
<soiling>
Satanophobia
<Satan>
scabiophobia
<scabies>
sciophobia
<shadows>
selaphobia <light
flashes>
siderophobia
<stars>
Sinophobia
<Chinese>

spermophobia *or*
spermatophobia
<germs>
stasophobia
<standing>
symmetrophobia
<symmetry>
syphilophobia
<syphilis>
tachophobia
<speed>
taurophobia <bulls>
technophobia
<technology>
telephonophobia
<telephone>
teratophobia
<monsters>
thaasophobia <being
idle>
thalassophobia
<sea>
thanatophobia
<death>
theophobia <God>
thermophobia
<heat>
tocophobia
<childbirth>
topophobia <certain
places>
toxiphobia *or*
toxophobia *or*
toxicophobia
<poison>
traumatophobia
<wound, injury>
tredecaphobia *or*
triskaidekaphobia
<the number
thirteen>
tremophobia
<trembling>
trichinophobia
<trichinosis>
trichopathophobia
<hair disease>
trypanophobia *or*
vaccinophobia
<inoculation>
tuberculophobia *or*
phthisiophobia
<tuberculosis>
tyrannophobia
<tyrants>
uranophobia *or*
ouranophobia
<heaven>
urophobia <urine>
ursaphobia <bears>
venereophobia
<venereal
disease>

vermiphobia or
helminthophobia
<worms>
xenophobia
<foreigners>

zelophobia
<jealousy>
zoophobia
<animals>

128 NERVOUSNESS

NOUNS **1 nervousness, nerves,** nervosity, **disquiet, uneasiness, apprehensiveness,** disquietude, qualmishness, malaise, funny or creepy feeling, **qualm, qualms, misgiving;** undue or morbid excitability, excessive irritability, state of nerves, case of nerves, spell of nerves, attack of nerves; **agitation, trepidation; fear** 127; panic; **fidgets,** fidgetiness, jitteriness, jumpiness; nail-biting; twitching, tic, vellication; stage fright, buck fever <nonformal>; nervous stomach, butterflies in one's stomach <nonformal>

2 <nonformal terms> **jitters,** willies, **heebie-jeebies,** jimjams, **jumps, shakes,** quivers, trembles, dithers, collywobbles, butterflies, shivers, cold shivers, creeps, sweat, cold sweat; antsyness, ants in one's pants, yips

3 tension, tenseness, tautness, **strain, stress,** stress and strain, mental strain, nervous tension or strain, pressure

4 frayed nerves, frazzled nerves, jangled nerves, shattered nerves, raw nerves or nerve endings, twanging or tingling nerves; neurosis; neurasthenia, nervous prostration, crackup, **nervous breakdown**

5 nervous wreck, wreck, a bundle of nerves

VERBS **6 fidget,** have the fidgets; jitter, have the jitters, etc; **tense up; tremble**

7 lose self-control, go into hysterics; lose courage 491.8; **go to pieces,** have a nervous breakdown, fall apart or to pieces, come apart, fall or come apart at the seams

8 <nonformal terms> **crack, crack up,** go haywire, **blow one's cork** or mind or stack, **flip,** flip one's lid or wig, wig out, freak out, go out of one's skull; come unglued or unstuck, go up the wall

9 get on one's nerves, jangle the nerves, **grate on, jar on,** put on edge, **set one's teeth on edge, go against the grain, send one up the wall** <nonformal>, drive one crazy; **irritate** 96.14

10 unnerve, unman, undo, unstring, unbrace, reduce to jelly, **demoralize, shake, upset,** psych out <nonformal>, dash, knock down or flat, **crush,** overcome, prostrate

ADJS **11 nervous,** nervy <Brit nonformal>; **high-strung,** overstrung, highly strung, all nerves; **uneasy, apprehensive,** qualmish, nail-biting, white-knuckle <nonformal>, frit <Brit nonformal>; nervous as a cat; **excitable; irritable,** edgy, **on edge,** nerves on edge, on the ragged edge <nonformal>, panicky, **fearful, frightened**

12 jittery <nonformal>, **jumpy,** twittery, skittish, skittery, trigger-happy <nonformal>, gun-shy; **shaky,** shivery, quivery, in a quiver; tremulous, tremulant, trembly; jumpy as a cat on a hot tin roof; **fidgety,** fidgeting, fluttery, all of a flutter or twitter; twitchy; **agitated;** shaking, trembling, quivering, shivering; shook up and all shook up <both nonformal>

13 tense, tensed-up, uptight <nonformal>, **strained,** stretched tight, taut, unrelaxed, **under a strain**

14 unnerved, unmanned, unstrung, undone, reduced to jelly, unglued <nonformal>, **demoralized, shaken, upset,** dashed, stricken, **crushed; shot,** shot to pieces; neurasthenic, prostrate, prostrated, overcome

15 unnerving, nerve-racking, nerve-rending, nerve-shaking, nerve-jangling, nerve-trying, nerve-stretching; jarring, grating

ADVS **16 nervously, shakily,** shakingly, tremulously, tremblingly, quiveringly

129 UNNERVOUSNESS

NOUNS **1 unnervousness, nervelessness; sangfroid, calmness, inexcitability** 106; unshakiness, untremulousness; **steadiness,** steady-handedness, steady nerves; no nerves, strong nerves, iron nerves, nerves of steel, icy nerves; cool head

ADJS **2 unnervous, nerveless,** without a nerve in one's body; strong-nerved, iron-nerved, steel-nerved; coolheaded, **calm, inexcitable** 106.10; calm, cool, and collected; cool as a cucumber <nonformal>; **steady,** steady as a rock, rock-steady, steady-nerved, steady-handed; unshaky, unshaken, unquivering, untremulous, without a tremor; unflinching, unfaltering, unwavering, unshrinking, unblenching, unblinking; **relaxed,** unstrained

130 EXPECTATION

NOUNS **1 expectation,** expectance or **expectancy,** state of expectancy; **predictability,** predictableness; **anticipation, prospect,** thought; contemplation; probability 967; confidence, reliance 952.1, overreliance; certainty 969; imminence 839; unastonishment 123

2 sanguine *or* cheerful expectation, optimism, eager expectation, **hope** 124; the light at the end of the tunnel

3 **suspense**, state of suspense, cliff-hanging *and* nail-biting <both nonformal>; **waiting,** expectant waiting, hushed expectancy; uncertainty 970, nervous expectation; **anxiety, dread, pessimism,** apprehension 126.1

4 **expectations,** prospects, outlook, hopes, apparent destiny *or* fate, future prospects; likelihoods, probabilities

VERBS 5 **expect,** be expectant, **anticipate, have in prospect,** face, think, **contemplate,** have in contemplation *or* mind, envision, envisage; **hope** 124.7; presume 950.10; dread; **take for granted;** not be surprised *or* a bit surprised; foresee 960.5

6 **look forward to,** reckon *or* calculate *or* count on, predict, foresee; look to, **look for, watch for,** look out for, watch out for, be on the watch *or* lookout for, keep a good *or* sharp lookout for; be ready for; forestall

7 **be expected,** be one's probable fate *or* destiny, be one's outlook *or* prospect, be in store

8 **await,** wait, wait for, wait on *or* upon, stay *or* tarry for; have *or* keep an eye out for, lie in wait for; wait around *or* about, watch, watch and wait; **bide one's time,** bide, abide, **mark time;** cool one's heels <nonformal>; be in suspense, be on tenterhooks, be on pins and needles, hold one's breath, bite one's nails, sweat *or* sweat out *or* sweat it *or* sweat it out <all nonformal>; **wait up for,** stay up for, sit up for; cross one's fingers

9 **expect to,** plan on 380.4,6,7

10 **be as expected,** be as one thought *or* looked for, turn out that way, come as no surprise; **be just like one,** be one all over <nonformal>; **expect it of,** think that way about, **not put it past** <nonformal>; **impend,** be imminent 839.2; lead one to expect 133.13

ADJS 11 **expectant,** expecting, in expectation *or* anticipation; **anticipative,** anticipant, anticipating, anticipatory; **holding one's breath; waiting,** awaiting, waiting for; forewarned, forearmed, forestalling, ready, prepared; **looking forward to,** looking for, watching for, on the watch *or* lookout for; gaping, agape, agog, all agog, atiptoe, atingle, **eager;** sanguine, optimis-

tic, hopeful 124.11; sure, confident 952.21/969.21; certain 969.13; unsurprised, not surprised

12 **in suspense, on tenterhooks,** on pins and needles, on tiptoe, **on edge, with bated breath,** tense, taut, with muscles tense, quivering, keyed-up, biting one's nails; anxious, **apprehensive; suspenseful,** cliffhanging <nonformal>

13 **expected, anticipated, awaited, predicted, foreseen;** presumed 950.14; probable 967.6; **looked-for,** hoped-for; **due, promised;** long-expected, longawaited, overdue; **in prospect, prospective; in view,** in one's eye, on the horizon; imminent 839.3

14 **to be expected,** as expected, up to *or* according to expectation, just as one thought, just as predicted, on schedule, **as one may have suspected,** as one might think *or* suppose; **expected of,** counted on, **taken for granted;** just like one, one all over <nonformal>, in character

ADVS 15 **expectantly,** expectingly; anticipatively, **anticipatingly,** anticipatorily; hopefully 124.14; **with bated breath,** in hushed expectancy, with breathless expectation; with ears pricked up, with eyes *or* ears strained

131 INEXPECTATION

NOUNS 1 **inexpectation,** nonexpectation, inexpectance *or* inexpectancy, no expectation, **unanticipation; unexpectedness;** unforeseeableness, unpredictableness, unpredictability; unreadiness, unpreparedness; the unforeseen, the unlooked-for, the last thing one expects; **improbability** 968

2 **surprise,** surprisal; **astonishment** 122.1–2; surpriser, startler, shocker, **blow,** staggerer <nonformal>, **eye-opener,** revelation; **bolt out of** *or* **from the blue,** thunderbolt, thunderclap; **bombshell,** bomb; blockbuster, earthshaker; sudden turn *or* development, *peripeteia* <Gk>, switch; surprise ending, kicker *or* joker *or* catch <all nonformal>; surprise package; surprise party

3 **start, shock, jar, jolt, turn**

VERBS 4 **not expect,** hardly expect, **not anticipate, not look for,** not bargain for, **not foresee,** not think of, have no thought of, have no expectation, think unlikely *or* improbable

5 **be startled, be taken by surprise,** be taken aback, be given a start, be given a turn *or* jar *or* jolt; **start,** startle, **jump,** jump a

mile <nonformal>, jump out of one's skin; **shy,** start aside, flinch

6 **be unexpected, come unawares,** come as a surprise *or* shock, come out of left field <nonformal>, come out of nowhere, appear unexpectedly, turn up, pop up *and* bob up <both nonformal>, drop from the clouds, appear like a bolt out of the blue, come *or* burst like a thunderclap *or* thunderbolt, burst *or* flash upon one, come *or* fall *or* pounce upon, steal *or* creep up on

7 **surprise, take by surprise,** do the unexpected, spring a surprise <nonformal>, **open one's eyes,** give one a revelation; **catch** *or* **take unawares,** catch *or* take short, take aback, pull up short, raise some eyebrows, **catch off-guard** 940.7, cross one up <nonformal>; throw a curve <nonformal>, come from behind, come from an unexpected quarter, come upon unexpectedly *or* without warning, spring *or* pounce upon; drop a bombshell, drop a brick <nonformal>; **blindside** <nonformal>, spring a mine under, ambush, bushwhack; drop in on <nonformal>; give a surprise party; **astonish** 122.6

8 **startle, shock, electrify, jar, jolt, shake,** stun, **stagger, give one a turn** <nonformal>, give the shock of one's life, make one jump out of his skin, take aback, take one's breath away, throw on one's beam ends, bowl down *or* over <nonformal>, strike all of a heap <nonformal>; frighten

ADJS 9 **inexpectant,** nonexpectant, unexpecting; **unanticipative,** unanticipating; **unsuspecting, unaware,** unguessing; uninformed, unwarned, unforewarned, unadvised, unadmonished; unready, unprepared; off one's guard 983.8

10 **unexpected, unanticipated, unlooked for,** unhoped for, unprepared for, undivined, unguessed, unpredicted, **unforeseen;** unforeseeable, unpredictable, off-the-wall <nonformal>; **improbable** 968.3; contrary to expectation, beyond *or* past expectation, out of one's reckoning, more than expected, more than one bargained for; out of the blue, dropped from the clouds, out of left field *and* from out in left field <both nonformal>; without warning, unheralded, unannounced; sudden 829.5; out-of-the-way, **extraordinary**

11 **surprising, astonishing** 122.12; eye-opening, eye-popping <nonformal>; **startling, shocking,** electrifying, staggering, stunning, jarring, jolting

12 **surprised,** struck with surprise, open-mouthed; **astonished** 122.9; **taken by surprise,** taken unawares, caught short

13 **startled, shocked, electrified,** jarred, jolted, shaken, shook <nonformal>, staggered, **given a turn** *or* **jar** *or* **jolt,** taken aback, bowled down *or* over <nonformal>, struck all of a heap <nonformal>, able to be knocked down with a feather

ADVS 14 **unexpectedly,** unanticipatedly, improbably, implausibly, unpredictably, **unforseeably,** *à l'improviste* <Fr>, **by surprise, unawares,** against *or* contrary to all expectation, when least expected, as no one would have predicted, without notice *or* warning, in an unguarded moment, like a thief in the night; **out of a clear sky, out of the blue, like a bolt from the blue;** suddenly 829.9

15 **surprisingly, startlingly, to one's surprise,** to one's great surprise; shockingly, staggeringly, stunningly, **astonishingly** 122.16

132 DISAPPOINTMENT

NOUNS 1 **disappointment,** sad *or* sore disappointment, bitter *or* cruel disappointment, failed *or* blasted expectation; **dashed hope, blighted hope,** betrayed hope, hope deferred, forlorn hope; **dash** <old>, dash to one's hopes; blow, buffet; **frustration,** discomfiture, bafflement, defeat, balk, foiling; **comedown,** setback, **letdown** <nonformal>; failure, fizzle <nonformal>, fiasco; **disillusionment** 976; tantalization, mirage, tease; dissatisfaction 108.1; fallen countenance

VERBS 2 **disappoint,** defeat expectation *or* hope; **dash,** dash *or* blight *or* blast *or* crush one's hope; **balk,** bilk, **thwart, frustrate, baffle, defeat,** foil, cross; put one's nose out of joint; **let down,** cast down; **disillusion** 976.2; tantalize, tease; dissatisfy

3 **be disappointing, let one down** <nonformal>, **not come up to expectation,** come to nothing, not live *or* measure up to expectation, go wrong, turn sour, disappoint one's expectations, come *or* fall short; peter out *or* fizzle *or* fizzle out <all nonformal>, not make it *and* not hack it <both nonformal>

4 **be disappointed,** not realize one's expectations, fail of one's hopes *or* ambitions, run into a stone wall, be let down; look blue, laugh on the wrong side of one's mouth <nonformal>; be crestfallen *or* chapfallen

ADJS 5 **disappointed,** bitterly *or* sorely disappointed; **let down**, betrayed, ill-served, ill done-by; **dashed**, blighted, blasted, crushed; **balked**, bilked, **thwarted, frustrated**, baffled, crossed, dished <Brit>, defeated, foiled; "hoist with his own petard"—Shakespeare, caught in one's own trap; disillusioned 976.5; crestfallen, chapfallen, out of countenance; soured; dissatisfied; regretful 113.8

6 **disappointing**, not up to expectation, falling short, out of the running, not up to one's hopes, second- or third-best; tantalizing, teasing; **unsatisfactory**

133 PREMONITION

NOUNS 1 **premonition, presentiment**, preapprehension, forefeeling, presage, presagement; **hunch** 933.3, **feeling in one's bones**; prediction 961

2 foreboding, boding; **apprehension, misgiving**, chill or quiver along the spine, creeping or shudder of the flesh; wind of change

3 omen, portent; **augury**, auspice, soothsay, prognostic, prognostication; **premonitory sign or symptom**, premonitory shiver or chill, **foretoken**, foretokening, tokening, betokening, betokenment, foreshowing, prefiguration, presigning <old>, presignifying, presignification, **preindication**, indicant, indication, **sign, token**, type, **promise**, sign of the times; **foreshadowing, adumbration**, foreshadow, shadow

4 **warning, forewarning**, "warnings, and portents and evils imminent, "the baby figure of the giant mass of things to come"—Shakespeare, handwriting on the wall, "*mene, mene, tekel, upharsin*"—Bible <Aramaic>

5 **harbinger, forerunner, precursor**, messenger <old>, **herald**, announcer, *buccinator novi temporis* <L>; presager, premonitor, foreshadower

6 <omens> bird of ill omen, owl, raven, stormy petrel, Mother Carey's chicken; gathering clouds, clouds on the horizon, dark or black clouds, angry clouds, storm clouds, thundercloud, thunderhead; black cat; broken mirror; rainbow; ring around the moon; shooting star; halcyon bird; woolly bear, groundhog

7 **ominousness, portentousness, portent**, bodefulness, presagefulness, suggestiveness, significance, **meaning** 518, meaningfulness; fatefulness, fatality, doomfulness, sinisterness, banefulness, balefulness, direness

8 **inauspiciousness, unpropitiousness, unfavorableness, unfortunateness, unluckiness**, ill-fatedness, ill-omenedness; fatality

9 **auspiciousness, propitiousness, favorableness; luckiness, fortunateness**, prosperousness, beneficence, benignity, benignancy, benevolence; brightness, cheerfulness, cheeriness; good omen, good auspices, *auspicium melioris aevi* <L>

VERBS 10 foreshow, presage; omen, be the omen of, auspicate <old>; **foreshadow, adumbrate**, shadow, shadow forth, cast their shadows before; **predict** 961.9; have an intimation, have a hunch <nonformal>, feel or know in one's bones, feel the wind of change

11 **forebode, bode**, portend, croak; **threaten, menace, lower**, look black, spell trouble; **warn, forewarn**, raise a warning flag, give pause; have a premonition or presentiment, apprehend, preapprehend, fear for

12 augur, hint, divine <old>; **foretoken, preindicate**, presignify, presign, presignal, pretypify, **prefigure**, betoken, token, typify, **signify, mean** 518.8, spell, **indicate**, point to, look like, **be a sign of**, show signs of

13 **promise, suggest, hint, imply**, give prospect of, make likely, give ground for expecting, raise expectation, **lead one to expect**, hold out hope, make fair promise, have a lot going for, have or show promise, **bid fair, stand fair to**

14 **herald, harbinger, forerun**, run before; speak of, announce, proclaim, preannounce; give notice, notify, talk about

ADJS 15 augured, **foreshadowed, adumbrated, foreshown; indicated, signified; preindicated**, prognosticated, **foretokened**, prefigured, pretypified, presignified, presigned <old>; presignaled; **presaged; promised, threatened; predicted** 961.14

16 **premonitory, forewarning**, augural, monitory, warning, presageful, presaging, **foretokening, preindicative**, indicative, prognostic, prognosticative, presignificant, prefigurative; **significant, meaningful** 518.10, speaking; **foreshowing, foreshadowing**; big or pregnant or heavy with meaning; forerunning, precursory, precursive; intuitive 933.5; predictive 961.11

17 **ominous, portentous**, portending; **foreboding**, boding, **bodeful; inauspicious, ill-omened**, ill-boding, of ill or fatal omen, of evil portent, loaded or laden or freighted or fraught with doom, looming,

looming over; fateful, doomful; apocalyptic; **unpropitious, unpromising, unfavorable, unfortunate, unlucky; sinister,** dark, black, gloomy, somber, dreary; **threatening, menacing, lowering;** bad, evil, ill, untoward; dire, baleful, baneful, **ill-fated,** ill-starred, evil-starred, star-crossed

18 **auspicious,** of good omen, of happy portent; **propitious, favorable,** favoring, fair, good; **promising,** of promise, full of promise; **fortunate, lucky,** prosperous; benign, benignant, bright, happy, golden

ADVS 19 **ominously, portentously, bodefully, forebodingly;** significantly, meaningly, meaningfully, speakingly, sinisterly; **threateningly, menacingly,** loweringly

20 **inauspiciously, unpropitiously, unpromisingly, unfavorably, unfortunately, unluckily**

21 **auspiciously, propitiously, promisingly, favorably; fortunately, luckily, happily;** brightly

134 PATIENCE

NOUNS 1 **patience,** patientness; **tolerance,** toleration, **acceptance; indulgence,** lenience, leniency 427; sweet reasonableness; **forbearance,** forbearing, forbearingness; **sufferance, endurance; long-suffering,** long-sufferance, longanimity; **stoicism,** fortitude, self-control; patience of Job; "the art of hoping"—Vauvenargues, "a minor form of despair, disguised as a virtue"—Ambrose Bierce; waiting game, waiting it out; **perseverance** 360

2 **resignation, meekness,** humility, humbleness; obedience; amenability; submission, **submissiveness** 433.3; acquiescence, compliance, uncomplainingness; **fatalism,** submission to fate or the inevitable or necessity; quietude, quietism, passivity, **passiveness** 329.1; *zitzflaysh* <Yiddish>; passive resistance, nonviolent resistance, nonresistance; Quakerism

3 **stoic,** Spartan, man of iron; Job, Griselda

VERBS 4 **be patient,** forbear, bear with composure, **wait,** wait it out, play a waiting game, wait around, wait one's turn, watch for one's moment, keep one's shirt or pants on <nonformal>, not hold one's breath <nonformal>; contain oneself, possess oneself, possess one's soul in patience; carry on, carry through; "have patience and endure"—Ovid

5 **endure, bear, stand,** support, sustain, **suffer, tolerate, abide,** bide, live with; perse-

vere; **bear up under, bear the brunt, bear with, put up with, stand for,** tolerate, carry or bear one's cross, take what comes, take the bitter with the sweet, abide with, brook, brave, brave out, hang in there, keep it up

6 <nonformal terms> **take it,** take it on the chin, take it like a man, not let it get one down, stand the gaff; bite the bullet; hold still or stand still for, swallow, stick, **hang in, hang in there, hang tough,** tough or stick it out; lump it

7 **accept, condone, countenance;** overlook, not make an issue of, let go by, let pass; **reconcile oneself to,** resign oneself to, yield or submit to, obey; accustom or accommodate or adjust oneself to, sit through; accept one's fate, lay in the lap of the gods, take things as they come, roll with the punches <nonformal>; **make the best of it,** make the most of it, make the best of a bad bargain, make a virtue of necessity; submit with a good grace, **grin and bear it,** grin and abide, shrug, shrug it off, slough off, not let it bother one; take in good part, take in stride; rise above

8 **take, pocket, swallow,** down, stomach, eat, digest, disregard, turn a blind eye, ignore; swallow an insult, pocket the affront, turn the other cheek, take it lying down, turn aside provocation

ADJS 9 **patient,** armed with patience, with a soul possessed in patience, patient as Job, Job-like, Griselda-like, "like patience on a monument smiling at grief"—Shakespeare; **tolerant,** tolerative, tolerating, accepting; understanding, **indulgent,** lenient; **forbearing;** philosophical; **long-suffering,** longanimous; **enduring,** endurant; stoic, stoical, Spartan; disciplined, self-controlled; **persevering**

10 **resigned,** reconciled; wait-and-see; **meek,** humble; obedient, amenable, **submissive** 433.12; acquiescent, compliant; accommodating, adjusting, adapting, adaptive; unresisting, **passive** 329.6; **uncomplaining**

ADVS 11 **patiently,** enduringly, stoically; **tolerantly, indulgently,** longanimously, leniently, forbearantly, forbearingly, philosophically, more in sorrow than in anger; perseveringly

12 **resignedly, meekly, submissively,** passively, acquiescently, compliantly, uncomplainingly

PHRS 13 Rome wasn't built in a day; all in good time; all things come to him who waits; don't hold your breath; time will tell

135 IMPATIENCE

NOUNS **1 impatience,** impatientness, unpatientness, breathless impatience; **anxiety, eagerness** 101; tense readiness, **restlessness,** restiveness, ants in one's pants <nonformal>, prothymia; **disquiet,** disquietude, unquietness, uneasiness, **nervousness** 128; sweat *and* lather *and* stew <all nonformal>, **fretfulness,** fretting, chafing; **impetuousness** 365.2; **haste** 401; excitement 105

2 intolerance, intoleration, unforbearance, nonendurance

3 the last straw, the straw that breaks the camel's back, the limit, the limit of one's patience, all one can bear *or* stand

VERBS **4 be impatient,** hardly wait; hasten 401.4,5; itch to, burn to; **champ at the bit, pull at the leash,** not be able to sit down *or* stand still; **chafe, fret, fuss,** squirm; **stew,** sweat, sweat and stew, get into a dither, get into a stew <nonformal>, work oneself into a lather *or* sweat <nonformal>, get excited; wait impatiently, sweat it out <nonformal>, pace the floor; beat the gun, jump the gun <nonformal>, go off half-cocked, shoot from the hip

5 have no patience with, be out of all patience; **lose patience,** run out of patience, call a halt, have had it <nonformal>, blow the whistle <nonformal>

ADJS **6 impatient,** unpatient; breathless; champing at the bit, rarin' to go <nonformal>; dying, **anxious, eager;** hopped-up *and* in a lather *and* in a sweat *or* stew <all nonformal>, excited 105.18; edgy, **on edge; restless,** restive, unquiet, uneasy, on *shpilkes* <Yiddish>; **fretful,** fretting, chafing, antsy-pantsy *and* antsy <both nonformal>, squirming, squirmy, about to peé *or* piss one's pants <nonformal>; **impetuous** 365.9; **hasty** 401.9

7 intolerant, unforbearing, unindulgent

ADVS **8 impatiently,** breathlessly; **anxiously;** fretfully; restlessly, restively, uneasily; intolerantly

136 PRIDE

NOUNS **1 pride,** proudness, pridefulness; **self-esteem, self-respect,** self-confidence, self-reliance, self-consequence, face, independence, self-sufficiency; pardonable pride; obstinate *or* stiff-necked pride, stiff-neckedness; **vanity, conceit** 140.4; haughtiness, **arrogance** 141; boastfulness 502.1; purse-pride

2 proud bearing, pride of bearing, military *or* erect bearing, stiff *or* straight backbone, **dignity,** dignifiedness, **stateliness,** courtliness, grandeur, **loftiness;** pride of place; **nobility,** lordliness, princeliness; **majesty,** regality, kingliness, queenliness; worthiness, augustness, venerability; **sedateness, solemnity** 111, gravity, *gravitas* <L>, sobriety

3 proudling; stiff neck; egoist 140.5; boaster 502.5; the proud

VERBS **4 be proud,** hold up one's head, hold one's head high, stand up straight, hold oneself erect, never stoop; look one in the face *or* eye; stand on one's own two feet, pay one's own way

5 take pride, pride oneself, preen oneself, plume oneself on, pique oneself, **congratulate oneself,** hug oneself; **be proud of,** glory in, exult in, **burst with pride**

6 make proud, do one's heart good, do one proud <nonformal>, **gratify, elate,** flush, turn one's head

7 save face, save one's face, preserve one's dignity, guard *or* preserve one's honor, be jealous of one's repute *or* good name

ADJS **8 proud, prideful,** proudful <nonformal>; **self-esteeming, self-respecting;** self-confident, self-reliant, **independent, self-sufficient;** proudhearted, proud-minded, proud-spirited, proud-blooded; proud-looking; proud as Punch, proud as Lucifer, proud as a peacock; erect, stiff-backed, **stiff-necked;** purse-proud, house-proud

9 vain, conceited 140.11, vogie <Scots>; haughty, **arrogant** 141.9; boastful 502.10

10 puffed up, swollen, bloated, swollen *or* bloated *or* puffed-up with pride; elated, flushed, flushed with pride

11 lofty, elevated, triumphal, high, high-flown, highfalutin *and* highfaluting <both nonformal>, high-toned <nonformal>; high-minded, lofty-minded; high-headed, high-nosed <nonformal>

12 dignified, stately, imposing, grand, courtly, magisterial, aristocratic; **noble,** lordly, princely; **majestic,** regal, royal, kingly, queenly; worthy, **august, venerable;** statuesque; **sedate, solemn** 111.3, sober, grave

ADVS **13 proudly,** pridefully, **with pride;** self-esteemingly, self-respectingly, self-confidently, self-reliantly, independently, self-sufficiently; erectly, with head erect, with head held high, with nose in air; stiff-neckedly; like a lord, *en grand seigneur* <Fr>

14 dignifiedly, with dignity; nobly, stately,

imposingly, loftily, grandly, magisterially; majestically, regally, royally; worthily, augustly, venerably; sedately, solemnly, soberly, gravely

137 HUMILITY

NOUNS **1 humility, humbleness, meekness; lowliness,** lowlihood, poorness, meanness, smallness, ingloriousness, undistinguishedness; unimportance 997; innocuousness 998.9; teachableness 570.5; submissiveness 433.3; **modesty,** unpretentiousness 139.1; plainness, simpleness, homeliness

2 humiliation, mortification <old>, egg on one's face <nonformal>, **chagrin, embarrassment** 96.4, egg on one's face <nonformal>; **abasement,** debasement, letdown, setdown, put-down *and* dump <both nonformal>; **comedown,** descent, deflation, wounded *or* humbled pride; self-diminishment, **self-abasement, self-abnegation** 652.1; **shame, disgrace;** shamefacedness, shamefastness, hangdog look

3 condescension, condescendence, deigning, lowering oneself, stooping from one's high place

VERBS **4 humiliate, humble;** mortify <old>, **embarrass** 96.15; put out, put out of face *or* countenance; **shame, disgrace,** put to shame, put to the blush, give one a red face; **deflate,** prick one's balloon; take it out of

5 abase, debase, crush, abash, **degrade, reduce,** diminish, **demean,** lower, **bring low,** bring down, trip up, take down, set down, put in one's place, put down, dump *and* dump on <both nonformal>, knock one off his perch; take down a peg *or* notch or two <nonformal>, make a fool *or* an ass *or* a monkey of one

6 <nonformal terms> beat *or* knock *or* **cut one down to size,** take the shine *or* starch out of, take the wind out of one's sails; put one's nose out of joint, put a tuck in one's tail, make one sing small

7 humble oneself, demean oneself, abase oneself, climb down *and* get down from one's high horse <both nonformal>; put one's pride in one's pocket; **eat humble pie,** eat crow *or* dirt, eat one's words, swallow one's pride, lick the dust, take *or* eat shit <nonformal>; come on bended knee, come hat in hand; go down on one's knees; pull *or* draw in one's horns *and* sing small <all nonformal>, lower one's note *or* tone, tuck one's tail; come down a

peg *or* a peg or two; **deprecate** *or* **depreciate oneself,** diminish oneself, discount oneself, belittle oneself; kiss one's ass <nonformal> 138.7

8 condescend, deign, vouchsafe; stoop, descend, lower *or* demean oneself, trouble oneself, set one's dignity aside *or* to one side; **patronize;** be so good as to, so forget oneself, dirty *or* soil one's hands; talk down to, talk *de haut en bas* <Fr, from high to low>

9 be humiliated, be put out of countenance; **be crushed, feel small, feel cheap,** look foolish *or* silly, be ready to sink through the floor; **take shame, be ashamed, feel ashamed of oneself,** be put to the blush, have a very red face; bite one's tongue; hang one's head, hide one's face, not dare to show one's face, not have a word to say for oneself; drink the cup of humiliation to the dregs

ADJS **10 humble, lowly,** low, **poor, mean,** small, inglorious, undistinguished; unimportant 997.16; innocuous; biddable, teachable 570.18; **modest, unpretentious** 139.9; **plain, simple,** homely; humble-looking, humble-visaged; humblest, lowliest, lowest, least

11 humble-hearted, humble-minded, humble-spirited, poor in spirit; **meek,** meek-hearted, meek-minded, meek-spirited, lamblike, Christlike; **abject, submissive** 433.12

12 self-abasing, self-abnegating, self-deprecating, self-depreciating 139.10, self-doubting

13 humbled, reduced, diminished, lowered, brought down *or* low, set down, bowed down, in the dust; on one's knees, on one's marrowbones <nonformal>

14 humiliated, humbled, mortified <old>, **embarrassed, chagrined, abashed, crushed,** out of countenance; blushing, ablush, **red-faced, ashamed,** shamed, ashamed of oneself, shamefaced, shamefast; crestfallen, chapfallen, hangdog

15 humiliating, humiliative, humbling, chastening, mortifying, **embarrassing,** crushing

ADVS **16 humbly, meekly;** modestly 139.14; with due deference, with bated breath, "with bated breath and whispering humbleness"—Shakespeare; submissively 433.17; **abjectly,** on bended knee, **on one's knees,** on one's marrowbones <nonformal>, on all fours, with one's tail between one's legs, hat-in-hand

138 SERVILITY

NOUNS **1 servility, slavishness,** subservience *or* subserviency, menialness, abjectness, **baseness,** meanness; **submissiveness** 433.3; slavery, helotry, helotism, serfdom, peonage

2 obsequiousness, sycophancy, fawningness, fawnery, **toadyism,** flunkyism; parasitism, sponging; **ingratiation,** insinuation; **truckling, fawning, toadying,** toadeating, groveling, cringing, **bootlicking** <nonformal>, back scratching, tufthunting <chiefly Brit old>; **apple-polishing** *and* **handshaking** <both nonformal>; ass-licking *and* ass-kissing *and* brown-nosing *and* sucking up <all nonformal>; timeserving; obeisance, prostration; mealymouthedness

3 sycophant, flatterer, toady, toad, toadeater, lickspit, lickspittle, **truckler, fawner,** courtier, led captain *and* tufthunter <both chiefly Brit old>, kowtower, groveler, cringer, spaniel; flunky, lackeyjackal; timeserver; creature, **puppet,** minion, lap dog, **tool,** cat's-paw, dupe, instrument, faithful servant, slave, helot, serf, peon; mealymouth

4 <nonformal terms> **apple-polisher, ass-kisser, brown-nose,** brown-noser, brownie, ass-licker, ass-wiper, suck-ass; **backslapper,** backscratcher, clawback, back-patter; **bootlicker,** bootlick; **handshaker; yes-man, stooge**

5 parasite, barnacle, leech; **sponger,** sponge <nonformal>, freeloader <nonformal>, smell-feast; beat *and* deadbeat <both nonformal>

6 hanger-on, adherent, dangler, appendage, **dependent, satellite, follower,** cohort, retainer, servant, man, shadow, tagtail, **henchman,** heeler <nonformal>

VERBS **7 fawn, truckle; flatter; toady,** toadeat; **bootlick** <nonformal>, lickspittle, lick one's shoes, lick the feet of; **grovel,** crawl, creep, cower, cringe, crouch, stoop, kneel, bend the knee, fall on one's knees, prostrate oneself, throw oneself at the feet of, fall at one's feet, kiss *or* lick *or* suck one's ass *and* brown-nose <all nonformal>, kiss one's feet, kiss the hem of one's garment, lick the dust, make a doormat of oneself; **kowtow,** bow, **bow and scrape**

8 toady to, truckle to, pander to, cater to, cater for <Brit>; **wait on** *or* **upon,** wait on hand and foot, dance attendance, do service, fetch and carry, do the dirty work of, do *or* jump at the bidding of

9 curry favor, court, pay court to, make court to, run after <nonformal>, dance attendance on; **shine up to,** make up to <nonformal>; **suck up to** *and* **play up to** *and* act up to <all nonformal>; be a yesman <nonformal>, agree to anything; fawn upon, fall over *or* all over <nonformal>; **handshake** *and* back-scratch *and* **polish the apple** <all nonformal>

10 ingratiate oneself, insinuate oneself, worm oneself in, creep into the good graces of, get in with *or* next to <nonformal>, **get on the good** *or* **right side of,** rub the right way <nonformal>

11 attach oneself to, pin *or* fasten oneself upon, hang about *or* around, dangle, hang on the skirts of, hang on the sleeve of, become an appendage of, **follow,** follow at heel; follow the crowd, get on the bandwagon, go with the stream, hold with the hare and run with the hounds

12 sponge *and* **sponge on** *and* **sponge off of** <all nonformal>; feed on, fatten on, batten on, live off of, use as a meal ticket

ADJS **13 servile, slavish,** subservient, **menial, base,** mean; **submissive** 433.12

14 obsequious, flattering, sycophantic, sycophantical, toadyish, fawning, flattering, truckling, ingratiating, smarmy <nonformal>, toadying, toadeating, **bootlicking** *and* back scratching *and* backslapping *and* ass-licking *and* brownnosing <all nonformal>; **groveling,** sniveling, cringing, cowering, crouching, crawling; **parasitic,** leechlike, sponging <nonformal>; timeserving; **abject,** beggarly, hangdog; obeisant, prostrate, on one's knees, on one's marrowbones <nonformal>, on bended knee; mealymouthed

ADVS **15 servilely, slavishly,** subserviently, menially, "in a bondman's key"— Shakespeare; **submissively** 433.17

16 obsequiously, sycophantically, ingratiatingly, fawningly, trucklingly; hat-in-hand, cap-in-hand; **abjectly,** obeisantly, grovelingly, on one's knees; parasitically

139 MODESTY

NOUNS **1 modesty, meekness;** humility 137; **unpretentiousness,** unassumingness, unpresumptuousness, **unostentatiousness,** unambitiousness, unobtrusiveness, unboastfulness

2 self-effacement, self-depreciation, self-deprecation, self-detraction, undervaluing of self, self-doubt, **diffidence;** hiding one's light under a bushel; low self-esteem, weak ego, lack of self-confidence *or* self-reliance, self-distrust; inferiority complex

3 reserve, restraint, constraint, backwardness, retiring disposition; low key, low visibility, low profile

4 shyness, timidity, timidness, timorousness, **bashfulness,** shamefacedness, shamefastness, pudicity, pudency, pudibundity *and* pudibundness *and* verecundity <all old>; **coyness, demureness,** demurity, skittishness, mousiness; self-consciousness, embarrassment; stammering, confusion; stagefright, mike fright *and* flop sweat <both nonformal>

5 blushing, flushing, coloring, mantling, reddening, crimsoning; **blush, flush,** suffusion, red face

6 shrinking violet, modest violet, mouse

VERBS **7 efface oneself,** depreciate *or* deprecate *or* doubt *or* distrust oneself; have low self-esteem; reserve oneself, retire, shrink, **retire into one's shell, keep in the background,** not thrust oneself forward, **keep a low profile,** keep oneself to oneself, keep one's distance, remain in the shade, take a back seat *and* play second fiddle <both nonformal>, hide one's face, hide one's light under a bushel, avoid the limelight, eschew self-advertisement; pursue the noiseless tenor of one's way, "blush unseen"—Thomas Gray, "do good by stealth and blush to find it fame"—Pope

8 blush, flush, mantle, **color,** change color, color up, redden, crimson, turn red, have a red face, get red in the face, blush up to the eyes; stammer; squirm with self-consciousness *or* embarrassment

ADJS **9 modest, meek;** humble; **unpretentious,** unpretending, **unassuming,** unpresuming, unpresumptuous, **unostentatious,** unobtrusive, unimposing, unboastful; unambitious, unaspiring

10 self-effacing, self-depreciative, self-depreciating, self-deprecating; **diffident,** deprecatory, deprecative, self-doubting, unself-confident, unsure of oneself, unself-reliant, self-distrustful, self-mistrustful; low in self-esteem

11 reserved, restrained, constrained; quiet; low-keyed, keeping low visibility *or* a low profile; **backward, retiring, shrinking**

12 shy, timid, timorous, **bashful,** shamefaced, shamefast, pudibund *and* verecund *and* verecundious <all old>; **coy, demure,** skittish, mousy; self-conscious, conscious, confused; stammering, inarticulate

13 blushing, blushful; **flushed,** red, ruddy,

red-faced, red in the face; **sheepish; embarrassed**

ADVS **14 modestly, meekly;** humbly; **unpretentiously,** unpretendingly, **unassumingly,** unpresumptuously, **unostentatiously,** unobtrusively; quietly, without ceremony, *sans façon* <Fr>

15 shyly, timidly, timorously, **bashfully, coyly, demurely,** diffidently; **shamefacedly,** shamefastly, **sheepishly,** blushingly, with downcast eyes

140 VANITY

NOUNS **1 vanity, vainness;** overproudness, overweening pride; **self-importance,** consequentiality, consequentialness, **self-esteem,** high self-esteem *or* self-valuation, positive self-image, self-respect, self-assumption; **self-admiration,** self-delight, self-worship, self-endearment, **self-love,** *amour-propre* <Fr>, self-infatuation, narcissism, narcism; autoeroticism, autoerotism, masturbation; **self-satisfaction, self-content,** ego trip <nonformal>, self-approbation, self-congratulation, self-gratulation, self-complacency, **smugness,** complacency, self-sufficiency; vainglory, vaingloriousness; "an itch for the praise of fools"—Robert Browning

2 pride 136; arrogance 141; **boastfulness** 502.1

3 egotism, egoism, egoisticalness, egotisticalness, **ego** <nonformal>, self-interest, individualism, "the tongue of vanity"—Chamfort; **egocentricity,** egocentrism, self-centeredness, self-centerment, self-obsession; selfishness 651

4 conceit, conceitedness, self-conceit, self-conceitedness, immodesty, side, self-assertiveness; **stuck-upness** <nonformal>, chestiness <nonformal>, swelledheadedness, swelled head, swollen head, big head, large hat size; **cockiness** <nonformal>, pertness, perkiness; aggressive self-confidence, obtrusiveness, bumptiousness

5 egotist, egoist, egocentric, individualist; narcissist, narcist, Narcissus; **swellhead** <nonformal>, **braggart** 502.5, know-it-all *or* know-all, smart-ass *and* wise-ass <both nonformal>, smart aleck, no modest violet, "a person of low taste, more interested in himself than in me"—Ambrose Bierce

VERBS **6 be stuck on oneself** <nonformal>, be impressed *or* overly impressed with oneself; ego-trip *and* be *or* go on an ego trip <all nonformal>; think well of one-

self, think one is it *or* one's shit doesn't
stink <nonformal>, get too big for one's
breeches, have a swelled head, know it
all, have no false modesty, have no self-
doubt, love the sound of one's own voice,
be blinded by one's own glory, lay the
flattering unction to one's soul; fish for
compliments; toot one's own horn, **boast**
502.6,7; be vain as a peacock, give oneself
airs 501.14

7 **puff up, inflate,** swell; go to one's head,
turn one's head

ADJS 8 **vain, vainglorious,** overproud, overweening; **self-important, self-esteeming,**
having high self-esteem *or* self-valuation, self-respecting, self-assuming, consequential; **self-admiring,** self-delight-
ing, self-worshiping, self-loving, self-
endeared, self-infatuated, narcissistic,
narcistic; autoerotic, masturbatory; **self-
satisfied, self-content,** self-contented,
self-approving, self-gratulating, self-
gratulatory, self-congratulating, self-
congratulatory, self-complacent, **smug,**
complacent, self-sufficient

9 **proud** 136.8; arrogant 141.9; boastful
502.10

10 **egotistic, egotistical,** egoistic, egoistical,
self-interested; **egocentric,** egocentristic,
self-centered, self-obsessed, narcissistic,
narcistic; selfish 651.5

11 **conceited, self-conceited, immodest,** self-
opinionated, vogie <Scots>; **stuck-up**
<nonformal>, **puffed up,** chesty <non-
formal>; swollen-headed, **swelled-
headed, big-headed** *and* too big for one's
shoes *or* britches *and* biggety *and* **cocky**
<all nonformal>, jumped-up <chiefly
Brit nonformal>; pert, perk, perky; peacockish, peacocky; know-all *or* know-it-
all, smart-ass *and* wise-ass <both nonfor-
mal>, smarty, smart-alecky, overwise,
wise in one's own conceit; aggressively
self-confident, obtrusive, bumptious

12 **stuck on oneself** <nonformal>, impressed with oneself, pleased with oneself, full of oneself, all wrapped up in
oneself

ADVS 13 **vainly,** self-importantly; **ego-
tistically,** egoistically; **conceitedly,** self-
conceitedly, immodestly; cockily
<nonformal>, pertly, perkily

141 ARROGANCE

NOUNS 1 **arrogance,** arrogantness; overbearingness, overbearing pride, overweening pride, stiff-necked pride, assumption of superiority, domineering,

domineeringness; **pride,** proudness; su-
perbia, sin of pride, chief of the deadly
sins; **haughtiness, hauteur; loftiness,**
Olympian loftiness *or* detachment; **toploftiness** *and* stuckupness *and* uppishness
and uppityness <all nonformal>, hoity-
toitiness, hoity-toity; haughty airs, airs of
de haut en bas; cornstarchy airs <nonfor-
mal>; high horse <nonformal>; **condescension,** condescendence, patronizing,
patronization, patronizing attitude;
purse-pride

2 **presumptuousness,** presumption, overweening, overweeningness, assumption,
total self-assurance; hubris; **insolence**
142

3 **lordliness, imperiousness,** masterfulness,
magisterialness, **high-and-mightiness,**
aristocratic presumption; elitism

4 **aloofness, standoffishness,** offishness
<nonformal>, chilliness, coolness, dis-
tantness, remoteness

5 **disdainfulness, disdain,** aristocratic disdain, **contemptuousness,**
superciliousness, contumeliousness, cav-
alierness, you-be-damnedness
<nonformal>

6 **snobbery, snobbishness,** snobbiness,
snobbism; **priggishness, priggery,** prig-
gism; snootiness *and* snottiness *and*
sniffiness *and* high-hattedness *and* high-
hattiness <all nonformal>; tufthunting

7 **snob, prig; elitist; highbrow** *and* egghead
<both nonformal>, Brahmin, mandarin;
name-dropper, tufthunter <chiefly Brit
old>; "he who meanly admires a mean
thing"—Thackeray

VERBS 8 **give oneself airs** 501.14; **hold one's
nose in the air, look down one's nose,** toss
the head, bridle; mount *or* get on one's
high horse *and* ride the high horse <all
nonformal>; **condescend, patronize,
deign,** vouchsafe, stoop, descend, lower *or*
demean oneself, trouble oneself, set one's
dignity aside *or* to one side, be so good as
to, so forget oneself, dirty *or* soil one's
hands; deal with *or* treat *de haut en bas*
<Fr, from high to low> *or* *en grand seig-
neur* <Fr, like a great lord>, talk down to,
talk *de haut en bas*

ADJS 9 **arrogant, overbearing, superior,**
domineering, **proud, haughty; lofty, toplofty** <nonformal>; high-flown, highfalutin *and* high-faluting <both nonfor-
mal>; high-headed; high-nosed *and*
stuck-up *and* uppish *and* uppity *and* **upstage** <all nonformal>; **hoity-toity,** big,
big as you please, six feet above contradiction; on one's high horse; **condescend-**

ing, patronizing, *de haut en bas* <Fr>;
purse-proud

10 **presumptuous,** presuming, assuming,
overweening, would-be, self-elect, self-
elected, self-appointed, self-proclaimed,
soi-disant <Fr>; **insolent**

11 **lordly, imperious,** aristocratic, totally
self-assured; hubristic; masterful, magisterial, **high-and-mighty;** elitist; U <Brit
nonformal>; dictatorial 417.16

12 **aloof, standoffish,** standoff, offish
<nonformal>, chilly, cool, distant, re-
mote, above all that; Olympian

13 **disdainful,** dismissive, **contemptuous, supercilious,** contumelious, cavalier, you-
be-damned <nonformal>

14 **snobbish,** snobby, toffee-nosed <Brit
nonformal>, **priggish,** snippy <nonfor-
mal>; **snooty** *and* **snotty** *and* sniffy <all
nonformal>; **high-hat** *and* high-hatted
and high-hatty <all nonformal>

ADVS 15 **arrogantly, haughtily, proudly,**
aloofly; **condescendingly, patronizingly,**
de haut en bas and *en grand seigneur*
<both Fr>; loftily, toploftily <nonfor-
mal>; imperiously, magisterially;
Olympianly; **disdainfully, contemptuously,** superciliously, contumeliously;
with nose in air, with nose turned up,
with head held high, with arms akimbo

16 **presumptuously,** overweeningly, aristo-
cratically; hubristically; **insolently**

17 **snobbishly,** snobbily, **priggishly;** snootily
and snottily <both nonformal>

142 INSOLENCE

NOUNS 1 **insolence; presumption,** presumptuousness; **audacity, effrontery,** boldness,
assurance, hardihood, bumptiousness;
hubris; overweening, overweeningness;
contempt 157, **contemptuousness,** contumely; **disdain** 141.5, *sprezzatura*
<Ital>; **arrogance** 141, uppishness *and*
uppityness <both nonformal>; obtrusiveness, pushiness <nonformal>

2 **impudence, impertinence,** flippancy, procacity *and* malapertness <both old>,
pertness, **sauciness,** sassiness <nonfor-
mal>, **cockiness,** *and* cheekiness <both
nonformal>, freshness <nonformal>,
brazenness, brazenfacedness, brassiness
<nonformal>, face of brass, **rudeness**
505.1, **brashness,** disrespect, disrespectfulness, derision, ridicule 508

3 <nonformal terms> **cheek,** face, brass,
nerve, gall, chutzpah, crust

4 **sauce** *and* sass *and* lip <nonformal>,
back talk, backchat <nonformal>

5 <impudent person> malapert <old>;
minx, hussy; whippersnapper, puppy,
pup, upstart; boldface, brazenface;
chutzpadik <Yiddish>; swaggerer
503.2

6 <nonformal terms> **smart aleck,** smarty,
smart guy, smartmouth, smart-ass, wise-
ass, smarty-pants, ho-dad, wisenheimer,
wise guy, saucebox

VERBS 7 **have the audacity, have the cheek;
have the gall** *or* a nerve *or* one's nerve
<nonformal>; **get fresh** <nonformal>,
get smart <nonformal>, forget one's
place, **dare, presume,** take liberties, make
bold *or* free; hold in contempt 157.3, ridicule, taunt, deride 508.8

8 **sauce** *and* sass <both nonformal>, **talk
back,** answer back, lip *and* give one the
lip <both nonformal>, provoke

ADJS 9 **insolent,** insulting; **presumptuous,**
presuming, overpresumptuous, overweening; **audacious, bold,** assured,
hardy, bumptious; **contemptuous** 157.8,
contumelious; **disdainful** 141.13, **arrogant** 141.9, uppish *and* uppity <both
nonformal>; hubristic; forward, pushy
<nonformal>, obtrusive, familiar; cool,
cold

10 **impudent, impertinent, pert,** malapert
and procacious <both old>, flip <nonfor-
mal>, flippant, **cocky** *and* cheeky *and*
fresh *and* facy *and* crusty *and* nervy <all
nonformal>, *chutzpadik* <Yiddish>;
uncalled-for, gratuitous, biggety <non-
formal>; **rude** 505.4,6, **disrespectful,** derisive 508.12, brash, bluff; **saucy,** sassy
<nonformal>; smart *or* smart-alecky
<nonformal>, smart-ass *or* wise-ass
<nonformal>

11 **brazen,** brazenfaced, boldfaced, bare-
faced, brassy <nonformal>, **bold,** bold as
brass <nonformal>, unblushing, unabashed, aweless, **shameless,** dead *or* lost
to shame; swaggering 503.4

ADVS 12 **insolently, audaciously,** bump-
tiously, contumeliously; **arrogantly**
141.15; **presumptuously,** obtrusively,
pushily <nonformal>; **disdainfully**
141.15

13 **impudently, impertinently,** pertly, pro-
caciously *and* malapertly <both old>,
flippantly, **cockily** *and* cheekily <both
nonformal>, saucily; **rudely** 505.8,
brashly, disrespectfully, contemptuously
157.9, derisively 508.15, in a smart-alecky
way <nonformal>, in a smart-ass fashion
<nonformal>

14 **brazenly,** brazenfacedly, **boldly,** bold-
facedly, **shamelessly,** unblushingly

143 KINDNESS, BENEVOLENCE

NOUNS **1 kindness, kindliness,** kindly disposition; **benignity,** benignancy; **goodness, decency,** niceness; **graciousness; kindheartedness,** goodheartedness, warmheartedness, softheartedness, tenderheartedness, kindness *or* goodness *or* warmth *or* softness *or* tenderness of heart, affectionateness, warmth, **loving kindness,** "milk of human kindness"—Shakespeare; soul of kindness, kind heart, heart of gold; **brotherhood,** fellow feeling, **sympathy,** fraternal feeling, feeling of kinship; **pity** 145, **mercy, compassion; humaneness,** humanity; charitableness

2 good nature, good humor, good disposition, good temper, sweetness, sweet temper *or* nature, good-naturedness, good-humoredness, good-temperedness, bonhomie; **amiability,** affability, geniality, cordiality; **gentleness,** mildness, lenity

3 considerateness, consideration, thoughtfulness, mindfulness, heedfulness, regardfulness, attentiveness, **solicitousness,** solicitude, thought, regard, concern, delicacy, **sensitivity,** tact, tactfulness; indulgence, toleration, leniency 427; complaisance, accommodatingness, **helpfulness,** obligingness, agreeableness

4 benevolence, benevolentness, benevolent disposition, well-disposedness, **beneficence, charity,** charitableness, **philanthropy; altruism,** philanthropism, **humanitarianism,** welfarism, do-goodism; utilitarianism, Benthamism, greatest good of the greatest number; **goodwill,** grace, brotherly love, charity, Christian charity *or* love, *caritas* <L>, love of mankind, good will to *or* toward man, love, *agape* <Gk>, flower power; BOMFOG *or* brotherhood of man and fatherhood of God; **bigheartedness,** largeheartedness, greatheartedness; **generosity** 485; giving 478

5 welfare; welfare work, social service, social welfare, social work; child welfare, etc; commonweal, public welfare; welfare state, welfare statism, welfarism; relief, the dole, social security <Brit>

6 benevolences, philanthropies, charities; works, **good works,** public service

7 act of kindness, kindness, favor, mercy, **benefit,** benefaction, benevolence, benignity, blessing, **service,** turn, break <nonformal>, **good turn, good** *or* **kind deed,** *mitzvah* <Heb>, office, good *or* kind offices, obligation, grace, act of grace, courtesy, kindly act, labor of love

8 philanthropist, altruist, benevolist, **humanitarian,** man of good will, **do-gooder,** goo-goo *and* bleeding heart <both nonformal>, well-doer, power for good; welfare worker, social worker, caseworker; welfare statist; almsgiver, almoner; Robin Hood, Lady Bountiful

VERBS **9 be kind,** be good *or* nice, show kindness; treat well, do right by; favor, oblige, accommodate

10 be considerate, consider, respect, regard, think of, **be thoughtful of,** have consideration *or* regard for; be at one's service, fuss over one, spoil one <nonformal>

11 be benevolent, bear good will, wish well, have one's heart in the right place; practice *or* follow the golden rule, do as you would be done by, do unto others as you would have others do unto you; make love not war

12 do a favor, do good, do a kindness, do a good turn, do a good *or* kind deed, do a *mitzvah* <Heb>, use one's good offices, render a service, confer a benefit; benefit, help 449.11

ADJS **13 kind, kindly,** kindly-disposed; **benign,** benignant; good as gold, **good, nice, decent; gracious; kindhearted, warm, warmhearted,** softhearted, tenderhearted, tender, loving, affectionate; **sympathetic,** sympathizing, **compassionate** 145.7, merciful; brotherly, fraternal; humane, human; charitable, caritative; Christian, Christly, Christlike

14 good-natured, well-natured, **good-humored, good-tempered,** bonhomous, **sweet, sweet-tempered; amiable, affable, genial, cordial; gentle,** mild, mild-mannered; easy, easy-natured, easy to get along with, able to take a joke, **agreeable**

15 benevolent, charitable, beneficent, philanthropic, altruistic, humanitarian; **bighearted,** largehearted, greathearted, freehearted; **generous** 485.4; almsgiving, eleemosynary; **welfare,** welfarist, welfaristic, welfare statist

16 considerate, thoughtful, mindful, heedful, regardful, solicitous, attentive, delicate, tactful, mindful of others; complaisant, **accommodating,** accommodative, at one's service, **helpful,** agreeable, **obliging,** indulgent, tolerant, lenient 427.7

17 well-meaning, well-meant, well-affected, well-disposed, **well-intentioned**

ADVS **18 kindly,** benignly, benignantly; **good,** nicely, well, favorably; **kindheartedly, warmly,** warmheartedly, softheartedly, tenderheartedly; humanely, humanly

19 **good-naturedly, good-humoredly,** bonhomously; **sweetly; amiably,** affably, genially, cordially; graciously, in good part

20 **benevolently, beneficently, charitably, philanthropically, altruistically,** bigheartedly, with good will

21 **considerately, thoughtfully,** mindfully, heedfully, regardfully, tactfully, **sensitively,** solicitously, attentively; well-meaningly, well-disposedly; out of consideration *or* courtesy

144 UNKINDNESS, MALEVOLENCE

NOUNS 1 **unkindness, unkindliness;** unbenignity, unbenignness; **unamiability,** uncordiality, ungraciousness, inhospitality, inhospitableness, ungeniality, unaffectionateness; unsympatheticness, uncompassionateness; disagreeableness

2 **unbenevolentness, uncharitableness,** ungenerousness

3 **inconsiderateness, inconsideration, unthoughtfulness,** unmindfulness, unheedfulness, **thoughtlessness,** heedlessness, respectlessness, disregardfulness, forgetfulness; **unhelpfulness,** unobligingness, unaccommodatingness

4 **malevolence, ill will,** bad will, bad blood, bad temper, ill nature, ill-disposedness, ill *or* evil disposition; evil eye, *malocchio* <Ital>, whammy <nonformal>, blighting glance

5 **malice, maliciousness,** maleficence; malignance *or* **malignancy,** malignity; **meanness** *and* orneriness *and* cussedness *and* bitchiness <all nonformal>, hatefulness, nastiness, invidiousness; **wickedness,** iniquitousness 654.4; deviltry, devilry, devilment; malice prepense *or* aforethought, evil intent; **harmfulness, noxiousness** 999.5

6 **spite,** despite; **spitefulness,** cattiness; gloating pleasure, unwholesome *or* unholy joy, *Schadenfreude* <Ger>

7 **rancor, virulence,** venomousness, **venom,** vitriol, gall

8 **causticity,** causticness, corrosiveness, mordancy, mordacity, bitingness; **acrimony, asperity,** acidity, acidness, acidulousness, acridity, acerbity, **bitterness,** tartness; sharpness, keenness, incisiveness, piercingness, stabbingness, trenchancy; "sharp-toothed unkindness"—Shakespeare

9 **harshness, roughness,** ungentleness; se-

verity, austerity, hardness, sternness, grimness, inclemency; stringency, astringency

10 **heartlessness, unfeeling,** unnaturalness, unresponsiveness, insensitivity, coldness, **cold-heartedness,** cold-bloodedness; **hard-heartedness,** hardness, hardness of heart, heart of stone; **callousness,** callosity; obduracy, induration; **pitilessness, unmercifulness** 146.1

11 **cruelty,** cruelness, sadistic *or* insensate cruelty, sadism, wanton cruelty; **ruthlessness** 146.1; inhumaness, **inhumanity,** atrociousness; **brutality,** mindless *or* senseless brutality, brutalness, **brutishness, bestiality, animality,** beastliness; **barbarity,** barbarousness, vandalism; **savagery, viciousness, violence,** fiendishness; **child abuse** 389.2; truculence, fierceness, ferociousness, **ferocity;** excessive force, piling on <nonformal>; bloodthirst, bloodthirstiness, bloodlust, bloodiness, bloody-mindedness, sanguineousness; cannibalism

12 **act of cruelty, atrocity,** cruelty, brutality, bestiality, barbarity, inhumanity

13 **bad deed, disservice,** ill service, **ill turn,** bad turn

14 **beast, animal, brute, monster,** monster of cruelty, **devil,** devil incarnate; **sadist,** torturer, tormenter; Attila, Torquemada, the Marquis de Sade

VERBS 15 bear malice *or* ill will; **harshen, dehumanize,** brutalize, bestialize; torture, torment; **have a cruel streak,** go for the jugular, have the killer instinct

ADJS 16 **unkind, unkindly,** ill; **unbenign,** unbenignant; **unamiable,** disagreeable, **uncordial, ungracious,** inhospitable, **ungenial,** unaffectionate, unloving; **unsympathetic,** unsympathizing, **uncompassionate,** uncompassioned

17 **unbenevolent,** unbeneficent, **uncharitable,** unphilanthropic, unaltruistic, ungenerous

18 **inconsiderate, unthoughtful,** unmindful, unheedful, disregardful, **thoughtless,** heedless, respectless, mindless, unthinking, forgetful; **tactless, insensitive;** uncomplaisant; **unhelpful, unaccommodating, unobliging,** disobliging, uncooperative

19 **malevolent, ill-disposed,** evil-disposed, **ill-natured,** ill-affected, ill-conditioned, ill-intentioned

20 **malicious,** maleficent, malefic; **malignant,** malign; **mean** *and* ornery *and* cussed *and* bitchy <all nonformal>, hateful, nasty, baleful, invidious; **wicked,**

iniquitous 654.16; **harmful, noxious** 999.12

21 **spiteful,** despiteful; **catty,** cattish, bitchy <nonformal>; **snide**

22 **rancorous, virulent,** vitriolic; **venomous,** venenate, envenomed

23 **caustic,** mordant, mordacious, corrosive, corroding; **acrimonious,** acrid, acid, acidic, acidulous, acidulent, acerb, acerbate, acerbic, **bitter,** tart; **sharp,** sharpish, keen, incisive, trenchant, **cutting,** penetrating, piercing, biting, **stinging,** stabbing, **scathing, scorching,** withering, scurrilous, abusive, thersitical, foulmouthed, harsh-tongued

24 **harsh, rough,** rugged, ungentle; **severe,** austere, **stringent,** astringent, hard, stern, dour, grim, inclement, unsparing

25 **heartless, unfeeling,** unnatural, unresponsive, insensitive, **cold,** cold of heart, coldhearted, **cold-blooded; hard, hardened,** hard of heart, **hard-hearted,** stonyhearted, marble-hearted, flint-hearted; **callous,** calloused; obdurate, indurated; **unmerciful** 146.3

26 **cruel,** cruel-hearted, sadistic; **ruthless** 146.3; **brutal,** brutish, brute, bestial, beastly, animal, animalistic; **mindless, soulless,** insensate, senseless, subhuman, dehumanized, brutalized; sharkish, wolfish, slavering; **barbarous,** barbaric, uncivilized, unchristian; **savage, ferocious,** feral, mean *and* mean as a junkyard dog <both nonformal>, **vicious,** fierce, **atrocious,** truculent, fell; **inhuman,** inhumane, unhuman; fiendish, fiendlike; demoniac *or* demoniacal, diabolic, diabolical, devilish, satanic, hellish, infernal; **bloodthirsty,** bloody-minded, bloody, sanguineous, sanguinary; cannibalistic, anthropophagous; murderous; Draconian, Tartarean

ADVS 27 **unkindly,** ill; **unbenignly,** unbenignantly; **unamiably,** disagreeably, uncordially, ungraciously, inhospitably, ungenially, unaffectionately, unlovingly; unsympathetically, uncompassionately

28 **unbenevolently,** unbeneficently, **uncharitably,** unphilanthropically, unaltruistically, ungenerously

29 **inconsiderately, unthoughtfully,** thoughtlessly, heedlessly, unthinkingly; unhelpfully, uncooperatively

30 **malevolently, maliciously,** maleficently, **malignantly; meanly** *and* ornerily *and* cussedly *and* bitchily *and* cattily <all nonformal>, hatefully, nastily, invidiously, balefully; **wickedly,** iniquitously 654.19; **harmfully, noxiously** 999.15,

spitefully, in spite; with bad intent, with malice prepense *or* aforethought

31 **rancorously, virulently,** vitriolically; venomously, venenately

32 **caustically,** mordantly, mordaciously, corrosively, corrodingly; **acrimoniously,** acridly, acidly, acerbly, acerbically, **bitterly,** tartly; **sharply,** keenly, incisively, trenchantly, **cuttingly,** penetratingly, piercingly, bitingly, **stingingly,** stabbingly, **scathingly,** scorchingly, witheringly, thersitically, scurrilously, abusively

33 **harshly, roughly; severely,** austerely, stringently, sternly, grimly, inclemently, unsparingly

34 **heartlessly, soullessly, unfeelingly, callously,** cold-heartedly; cold-bloodedly, **in cold blood**

35 **cruelly, brutally,** brutishly, bestially, animalistically, subhumanly, sharkishly, wolfishly, slaveringly; **barbarously, savagely, ferociously,** ferally, **viciously,** fiercely, **atrociously,** truculently; **ruthlessly** 146.4; **inhumanely,** inhumanly, unhumanly; fiendishly, diabolically, devilishly

145 PITY

NOUNS 1 **pity, sympathy,** feeling, fellow feeling in suffering, **commiseration,** condolence, condolences; **compassion, mercy,** ruth, rue, humanity; **sensitivity; clemency,** quarter, reprieve, mitigation, relief 120, favor, grace; **leniency,** lenity, gentleness; forbearance; **kindness, benevolence** 143; pardon, **forgiveness** 601.1; self-pity; **pathos**

2 **compassionateness, mercifulness,** ruthfulness, ruefulness, softheartedness, tenderness, lenity, gentleness; bowels of compassion *or* mercy; bleeding heart

VERBS 3 **pity, be** *or* **feel sorry for,** feel sorrow for; **commiserate,** compassionate; open one's heart; **sympathize, sympathize with,** feel for, weep for, lament for, bleed, bleed for, have one's heart bleed for *or* go out to, condole with 147.2

4 **have pity, have mercy upon, take pity on** *or* **upon;** melt, thaw; relent, forbear, relax, give quarter, spare, temper the wind to the shorn lamb, go easy on *and* let up *or* ease up on <all nonformal>, soften, unsteel; **reprieve, pardon,** remit, **forgive** 601.4; put out of one's misery; be cruel to be kind

5 <excite pity> **move, touch,** affect, reach,

soften, unsteel, melt, melt the heart, appeal to one's better feelings; sadden, grieve 112.17

6 **beg for mercy,** ask for pity, cry for quarter, beg for one's life; fall on one's knees, throw oneself at the feet of

ADJS 7 **pitying, sympathetic,** sympathizing, commiserative, condolent, understanding; **compassionate, merciful,** ruthful, rueful, **clement,** gentle, soft, melting, bleeding, tender, **tenderhearted,** softhearted, warmhearted; **humane,** human; lenient, forbearant 427.7; charitable 143.15

8 **pitiful, pitiable, pathetic, piteous, touching, moving, affecting,** heartrending, grievous, doleful 112.26

9 self-pitying, self-pitiful, sorry for oneself

ADVS 10 **pitifully,** sympathetically; **compassionately, mercifully,** ruthfully, ruefully, clemently, humanely

146 PITILESSNESS

NOUNS 1 **pitilessness, unmercifulness, uncompassionateness,** unsympatheticness, mercilessness, **ruthlessness,** unfeelingness, inclemency, relentlessness, inexorableness, unyieldingness 361.2, unforgivingness; **heartlessness,** heart of stone, hardness, steeliness, flintiness, harshness, induration, **cruelty** 144.11; remorselessness, unremorsefulness; short shrift, tender mercies

VERBS 2 **show no mercy,** give no quarter, turn a deaf ear, claim one's pound of flesh, harden or steel one's heart

ADJS 3 **pitiless,** unpitying, unpitiful; blind or deaf to pity; **unsympathetic,** unsympathizing; **uncompassionate,** uncompassioned; **merciless, unmerciful,** without mercy, unruing, **ruthless,** dog-eat-dog; unfeeling, bowelless, inclement, relentless, inexorable, unyielding 361.9, unforgiving; **heartless,** hard, hard as nails, steely, flinty, harsh, savage, **cruel;** remorseless, unremorseful

ADVS 4 **pitilessly,** unsympathetically; mercilessly, **unmercifully, ruthlessly,** uncompassionately, inclemently, relentlessly, inexorably, unyieldingly, unforgivingly; heartlessly, harshly, savagely, cruelly; remorselessly, unremorsefully

147 CONDOLENCE

NOUNS 1 **condolence, condolences,** condolement, **consolation,** comfort, balm, soothing words, **commiseration, sympathy,** sharing of grief or sorrow

VERBS 2 **condole with, commiserate, sympathize with,** feel with, empathize with, express sympathy for, send one's condolences; pity 145.3; **console,** wipe away one's tears, comfort, speak soothing words, bring balm to one's sorrow; sorrow with, share or help bear one's grief, grieve or weep with, grieve or weep for, share one's sorrow, "weep with them that weep"—Bible

ADJS 3 condoling, condolent, consolatory, comforting, commiserating, commiserative, **sympathetic,** empathic, empathetic; pitying 145.7

148 FORGIVENESS

NOUNS 1 **forgiveness,** forgivingness; unresentfulness, unrevengefulness; **condoning,** condonation, condonance, overlooking, disregard; **patience** 134; **indulgence, forbearance,** longanimity, longsuffering; **kindness, benevolence** 143; **magnanimity** 652.2; brooking, **tolerance** 978.4

2 **pardon,** excuse, sparing, **amnesty,** indemnity, exemption, immunity, reprieve, grace; **absolution,** shrift, remission, remission of sin; redemption; **exoneration, exculpation** 601.1

VERBS 3 **forgive, pardon, excuse,** give or grant forgiveness, spare; amnesty, grant amnesty to, grant immunity or exemption; hear confession, **absolve,** remit, give absolution, shrive, grant remission; **exonerate, exculpate** 601.4; blot out one's sins, wipe the slate clean

4 **condone** 134.7, **overlook, disregard, ignore,** accept, take and swallow and let go <all nonformal>, pass over, give one another chance, let one off this time and let one off easy <both nonformal>, close or shut one's eyes to, **blink or wink at,** connive at; allow for, make allowances for; bear with, endure, regard with indulgence; pocket the affront, leave unavenged, turn the other cheek, bury or hide one's head in the sand

5 **forget, forgive and forget,** dismiss from one's thoughts, think no more of, not give it another or a second thought, let it go <nonformal>, let it pass, **let bygones be bygones;** write off, charge off, charge to experience; bury the hatchet

ADJS 6 **forgiving,** sparing, placable, conciliatory; **kind, benevolent** 143.15; **magnanimous, generous** 652.6; **patient** 134.9;

forbearing, longanimous, long-suffering; unresentful, unrevengeful; **tolerant** 978.11, more in sorrow than in anger

7 **forgiven, pardoned, excused**, spared, amnestied, reprieved, remitted; overlooked, disregarded, forgotten, not held against one, wiped away, removed from the record, blotted, canceled, **condoned**, indulged; **absolved**, shriven; redeemed; exonerated, exculpated, acquitted; unresented; unavenged, unrevenged; uncondemned

149 CONGRATULATION

NOUNS 1 **congratulation, congratulations,** congrats <nonformal>, gratulation, **felicitation**, blessing, **compliment**, pat on the back; good wishes, best wishes; **applause** 509.2, **praise** 509.5, flattery 511

VERBS 2 **congratulate**, gratulate, **felicitate**, bless, **compliment**, tender or offer one's congratulations or felicitations or compliments; shake one's hand, pat one on the back; **rejoice with one**, wish one joy; **applaud** 509.10, **praise** 509.12, flatter 511.5

ADJS 3 **congratulatory**, congratulant, congratulational; gratulatory, gratulant; **complimentary** 509.16, flattering 511.8

INTERJS 4 **congratulations!**, take a bow!, nice going!, **bravo!, well done!**, good show! <Brit>

5 <nonformal terms> **congrats!, all right!, aw right!, right on!**, way to go!, attaboy!, attagirl!, good deal!, looking good!, nice going!, that's my boy!, that's my girl!

150 GRATITUDE

NOUNS 1 **gratitude, gratefulness, thankfulness, appreciation, appreciativeness;** obligation, sense of obligation or indebtedness

2 **thanks, thanksgiving**, praise, laud, hymn, paean, benediction; grace, prayer of thanks; **thank-you; acknowledgment**, cognizance, **credit**, crediting, recognition; thank offering, votary offering

VERBS 3 **be grateful, be obliged,** feel or be or lie under an obligation, be obligated or indebted, be in the debt of, give credit or due credit; **be thankful**, thank God, thank one's lucky stars, thank or bless one's stars; **appreciate**, be appreciative of; never forget; overflow with gratitude; not look a gift horse in the mouth

4 **thank, extend gratitude or thanks**, bless; give one's thanks, **express one's appreciation; offer or give thanks**, tender or

render thanks, return thanks; acknowledge, make acknowledgments of, credit, recognize, give or render credit or recognition; fall all over one with gratitude; fall on one's knees

ADJS 5 **grateful, thankful; appreciative**, appreciatory, sensible; **obliged, much obliged**, beholden, indebted to, crediting, under obligation, acknowledging, cognizant of

INTERJS 6 **thanks!, thank you!,** I thank you!, *merci!* <Fr>, *¡gracias!* <Sp>, *grazie!* <Ital>, *danke!* and *danke schön!* <both Ger>, gramercy!, *domo* and *domo arrigato* <both Japanese>, **much obliged!**, many thanks!, thank you kindly!; I thank you very much!, *merci beaucoup!* and *je vous remercie beaucoup!* <both Fr>; thanks a lot! or a bunch! or a heap! <nonformal>

151 INGRATITUDE

NOUNS 1 **ingratitude, ungratefulness, unthankfulness**, thanklessness, unappreciation, **unappreciativeness;** nonacknowledgment, nonrecognition, denial of due or proper credit; "benefits forgot"—Shakespeare; grudging or halfhearted thanks

2 **ingrate**, ungrateful wretch

VERBS 3 **be ungrateful**, feel no obligation, **not appreciate**, owe one no thanks; look a gift horse in the mouth; bite the hand that feeds one

ADJS 4 **ungrateful, unthankful**, unthanking, thankless, unappreciative, unappreciatory, unmindful, nonrecognitive, unrecognizing

5 unthanked, unacknowledged, unrecognized, nonrecognized, uncredited, denied due or proper credit, unrequited, unrewarded, forgotten, neglected, unduly or unfairly neglected, ignored; ill-requited, ill-rewarded

152 RESENTMENT, ANGER

NOUNS 1 **resentment**, resentfulness; **displeasure**, disapproval, disapprobation, dissatisfaction, **discontent; vexation**, irritation, **annoyance**, aggravation <nonformal>, exasperation

2 **offense, umbrage, pique;** glower, scowl, angry look, dirty look <nonformal>, glare, frown

3 **bitterness, bitter resentment**, bitterness of spirit, heartburning; **rancor**, virulence, **acrimony**, acerbity, asperity; causticity

144.8; **choler,** gall, bile, spleen, acid, acidity, acidulousness; hard feelings, **animosity** 589.4; soreness, rankling, slow burn <nonformal>; gnashing of teeth

4 **indignation,** indignant displeasure, righteous indignation

5 **anger, wrath, ire,** *saeva indignatio* <L>, mad <nonformal>; angriness, irateness, wrathfulness, soreness <nonformal>, "a transient madness"—Horace; infuriation, enragement; vials of wrath, grapes of wrath; **heat,** more heat than light <nonformal>

6 **temper,** dander *and* Irish <both nonformal>, monkey <Brit nonformal>; bad temper 110.1

7 **dudgeon,** high dudgeon; **huff,** pique, pet, tiff, miff *and* stew <both nonformal>, fret, **fume,** ferment

8 **fit,** fit of anger, fit of temper, rage, wax <Brit nonformal>, **tantrum,** temper tantrum; duck *or* cat fit *and* **conniption** *or* conniption fit *and* snit <all nonformal>, paroxysm, convulsion; agriothymia

9 **outburst,** outburst of anger, burst, **explosion,** eruption, blowup *and* **flare-up** <both nonformal>, access, blaze of temper; **storm, scene,** high words

10 **rage, passion; fury,** furor; livid *or* towering rage *or* passion, blind *or* burning rage, raging *or* tearing passion, furious rage; vehemence, violence; the Furies, the Eumenides, the Erinyes; Nemesis; Alecto, Tisiphone, Megaera; steroid rage, roid rage <nonformal>

11 **provocation, affront, offense,** "head and front of one's offending"—Shakespeare; *casus belli* <L>, red rag, red rag to a bull, sore point, sore spot, tender spot, raw nerve, the quick, where one lives; slap in the face

VERBS 12 **resent,** be resentful, feel *or* harbor *or* nurse resentment, feel hurt, smart, feel sore *and* have one's nose out of joint <both nonformal>; bear *or* hold *or* have a grudge

13 **take amiss,** take ill, **take in bad part,** take to heart, not take it as a joke, **mind; take offense, take umbrage,** get miffed *or* huffy <nonformal>; be cut *or* cut to the quick

14 <show resentment> redden, color, flush, mantle; **growl, snarl,** gnarl, **snap,** show one's teeth, spit; gnash *or* grind one's teeth; **glower,** lower, scowl, **glare, frown,** give a dirty look <nonformal>, look daggers; **stew,** stew in one's own juice

15 <be angry> **burn, seethe, simmer,** sizzle, smoke, smolder, steam; be pissed *or* pissed off *or* browned off <all nonformal>, be

livid, be beside oneself, **fume,** stew <nonformal>, boil, fret, chafe; foam at the mouth; breathe fire and fury; **rage, storm, rave,** rant, bluster; take on *and* go on *and* carry on <all nonformal>, rant and rave, kick up a row *or* dust *or* a shindy <nonformal>; raise Cain *or* raise hell *or* raise the devil *or* raise the roof <all nonformal>, tear up the earth; throw a fit, have a conniption *or* conniption fit *or* duck fit *or* cat fit <nonformal>, go into a tantrum; stamp one's foot

16 **vent one's anger,** vent one's rancor *or* choler *or* spleen, pour out the vials of one's wrath; **snap at, bite** *or* **snap one's nose off, bite** *or* **take one's head off, jump down one's throat;** expend one's anger on, take it out on <nonformal>

17 <become angry> **anger, lose one's temper,** become irate, forget oneself, let one's angry passions rise; **get one's gorge up,** get one's blood up, **bridle,** bridle up, **bristle,** bristle up, raise one's hackles, get one's back up; reach boiling point, boil over, climb the wall, go through the roof

18 <nonformal terms> **get mad** *or* **sore,** get one's Irish *or* dander *or* hackles up, get one's monkey up <Brit>; **see red, get hot under the collar,** flip out, work oneself into a lather *or* sweat *or* stew, get oneself in a tizzy, do a slow burn

19 **flare up, blaze up,** fire up, flame up, spunk up, ignite, kindle, take fire

20 **fly into a rage** *or* **passion** *or* **temper,** fly out, fly off at a tangent; **fly off the handle** *and* **hit the ceiling** *and* go into a tailspin *and* have a hemorrhage <all nonformal>; **explode, blow up** <nonformal>; blow one's top *or* stack <nonformal>, blow a fuse *or* gasket <nonformal>, flip one's lid *or* wig <nonformal>, wig out <nonformal>; kick *or* piss up a fuss *or* a row *or* a storm <all nonformal>

21 **offend, give offense, give umbrage,** affront, outrage; grieve, aggrieve; wound, hurt, cut, cut to the quick, hit one where one lives <nonformal>, **sting,** hurt one's feelings; step *or* tread on one's toes

22 **anger, make angry, make mad,** raise one's gorge *or* choler; make one's blood boil

23 <nonformal terms> **piss** *or* tee off, tick off, piss, **get one's goat, get one's Irish** *or* back *or* dander *or* hackles up, **make sore,** get one's mad up, make one hot under the collar, put one's nose out of joint, burn one up, burn one's ass *or* butt, steam

24 **provoke, incense,** arouse, inflame, embitter; **vex, irritate, annoy, aggravate** <non-

formal>, **exasperate, nettle**, fret, chafe; **pique, peeve** *and* miff <both nonformal>, huff; **ruffle, roil, rile** <nonformal>, ruffle one's feathers, **rankle**; bristle, put *or* get one's back up, set up, put one's hair *or* fur *or* bristles up; stick in one's craw <nonformal>; **stir up, work up**, stir one's bile, stir the blood; wave the bloody shirt

25 **enrage, infuriate, madden**, drive one mad, frenzy, lash into fury, work up into a passion, **make one's blood boil**

ADJS 26 **resentful**, resenting; **bitter**, embittered, rancorous, virulent, **acrimonious**, acerb, acerbic, acerbate; caustic; **choleric**, splenetic, acid, acidic, acidulous, acidulent; **sore** <nonformal>, rankled, burning *and* stewing <both nonformal>

27 **provoked, vexed, piqued; peeved** *and* miffed *and* huffy <all nonformal>, **nettled, irritated, annoyed**, aggravated <nonformal>, exasperated, put-out

28 **angry**, angered, **incensed, indignant, irate**, ireful; **livid**, livid with rage, beside oneself, **wroth, wrathful**, wrathy, **cross**, wrought-up, worked up, riled up <nonformal>

29 **burning, seething**, simmering, smoldering, sizzling, boiling, **steaming**; flushed with anger

30 <nonformal terms> **mad, sore**, mad as a hornet *or* as a wet hen *or* as hell, sore as a boil, pissed; **pissed-off** *or* PO'd; teed off *or* TO'd; ticked off, browned-off, waxy *and* stroppy <both Brit>, **hot**, het up, **hot under the collar**, burned up, hot and bothered, boiling, boiling *or* hopping *or* fighting *or* roaring mad, fit to be tied, good and mad, steamed, hacked, bent out of shape, in a lather *or* lava *or* pucker, red-assed

31 **in a temper, in a huff, in a pet**, in a snit *or* a stew <both nonformal>; in a wax <Brit nonformal>, **in high dudgeon**

32 **infuriated**, infuriate, in a rage *or* passion *or* fury; **furious**, fierce, wild, savage; raving mad <nonformal>, **rabid**, foaming *or* frothing at the mouth; **fuming**, in a fume; **enraged, raging, raving, ranting, storming**

ADVS 33 **angrily, indignantly, irately**, wrathfully, infuriatedly, infuriately, furiously, heatedly; **in anger**, in hot blood, in the heat of passion

153 JEALOUSY

NOUNS 1 **jealousy**, *jalousie* <Fr>, jealousness, heartburning, heartburn, **jaundice**,

jaundiced eye, green in the eye <nonformal>, "the jaundice of the soul"—Dryden; "green-eyed jealousy, "green-eyed monster, "a monster begot upon itself, born on itself"—all Shakespeare; Othello's flaw, horn-madness; **envy** 154

2 **suspiciousness**, suspicion, doubt, misdoubt, mistrust, distrust, distrustfulness

VERBS 3 suffer pangs of jealousy, have green in the eye <nonformal>, be possessive *or* overpossessive, view with a jaundiced eye; **suspect**, distrust, mistrust, doubt, misdoubt

4 make one jealous, put someone's nose out of joint

ADJS 5 **jealous, jaundiced**, jaundice-eyed, yellow-eyed, green-eyed, yellow, green, green with jealousy; horn-mad; invidious, **envious** 154.4; **suspicious**, distrustful

154 ENVY

NOUNS 1 **envy**, enviousness, **covetousness**; invidia, deadly sin of envy, **invidiousness**; grudging, grudgingness; resentment, resentfulness; **jealousy** 153; rivalry; meanness, meanspiritedness, ungenerousness

2 "the tax which all distinction must pay"—Emerson, "emulation adapted to the meanest capacity"—Ambrose Bierce, "a kind of praise"—John Gay

VERBS 3 **envy**, be envious *or* covetous of, **covet**, cast envious eyes, desire for oneself; resent; **grudge, begrudge**

ADJS 4 **envious**, envying, **invidious**, green with envy; **jealous** 153.4; **covetous**, desirous of; resentful; **grudging, begrudging**; mean, mean-spirited, ungenerous

155 RESPECT

NOUNS 1 **respect, regard**, consideration, appreciation, favor; approbation, approval; **esteem**, estimation, prestige; **reverence, veneration**, awe; **deference**, deferential *or* reverential regard; **honor, homage**, duty; great respect, high regard, **admiration**; adoration, breathless adoration, exaggerated respect, worship, hero worship, **idolization**; idolatry, deification, apotheosis; courtesy 504

2 **obeisance**, reverence, homage; **bow, nod, bob**, bend, inclination, inclination of the head, **curtsy, salaam, kowtow**, scrape, bowing and scraping, making a leg; **genuflection**, kneeling, bending the knee;

prostration; salute, salutation, namaste; presenting arms, dipping the colors *or* ensign, standing at attention; **submissiveness, submission** 433; **obsequiousness, servility** 138

3 **respects, regards,** *égards* <Fr>; duties, *devoirs* <Fr>; attentions

VERBS 4 **respect,** entertain respect for, accord respect to, **regard, esteem,** hold in esteem *or* consideration, favor, **admire,** think much of, think well of, think highly of, have *or* hold a high opinion of; **appreciate, value,** prize; **revere, reverence,** hold in reverence, **venerate, honor, look up to, defer to, bow to,** exalt, put on a pedestal, **worship,** hero-worship, deify, apotheosize, **idolize, adore,** worship the ground one walks on, stand in awe of

5 **do** *or* **pay homage to,** show *or* demonstrate respect for, pay respect to, pay tribute to, **do** *or* **render honor to,** do the **honors for;** doff one's cap to, take off one's hat to; salute, present arms, dip the colors *or* ensign, stand at *or* to attention; give the red-carpet treatment, roll out the red carpet

6 **bow, make obeisance, salaam, kowtow,** make one's bow, bow down, **nod,** incline *or* bend *or* bow the head, bend the neck, **bob,** bob down, **curtsy,** bob a curtsy, bend, make a leg, scrape, **bow and scrape; genuflect, kneel,** bend the knee, get down on one's knees, throw oneself on one's knees, fall on one's knees, fall down before, fall at the feet of, prostrate oneself, kiss the hem of one's garment

7 **command respect,** inspire respect, stand high, have prestige, rank high, be widely reputed, be up there *or* way up there <nonformal>; awe 122.6

ADJS 8 **respectful, regardful,** attentive; **deferential,** conscious of one's place, dutiful, honorific, ceremonious, cap in hand; **courteous** 504.14

9 **reverent,** reverential; admiring, **adoring, worshiping,** worshipful, hero-worshiping, **idolizing,** idolatrous, deifying, apotheosizing; **venerative,** venerational; awestruck, awestricken, awed, in awe; solemn 111.3

10 **obeisant,** prostrate, on one's knees, on bended knee; **submissive** 433.12; **obsequious**

11 **respected, esteemed, revered,** reverenced, adored, worshiped, **venerated, honored,** well-thought-of, admired, much-admired, appreciated, valued, prized, in high esteem *or* estimation, highly considered, well-considered, held in respect *or*

regard *or* favor *or* consideration, prestigious

12 **venerable, reverend, estimable, honorable,** worshipful, august, awe-inspiring, awesome, awful, dreadful; time-honored

ADVS 13 **respectfully,** regardfully, deferentially, reverentially; dutifully

ADVS, PREPS 14 **in deference to,** with due respect, with all respect, **with all due respect to** *or* **for,** saving, excusing the liberty, saving your reverence, sir-reverence; out of respect *or* consideration for, out of courtesy to

156 DISRESPECT

NOUNS 1 **disrespect, disrespectfulness,** lack of respect, low estimate *or* esteem, **disesteem,** dishonor, **irreverence;** ridicule 508; **disparagement** 512; **discourtesy** 505; **impudence,** insolence 142

2 **indignity, affront, offense, injury,** humiliation; scurrility, contempt 157, contumely, despite, flout, flouting, mockery, jeering, jeer, mock, scoff, gibe, taunt, brickbat <nonformal>; **insult, aspersion,** uncomplimentary remark, slap *or* kick in the face, left-handed *or* backhanded compliment, damning with faint praise; cut, "most unkindest cut of all"—Shakespeare; **outrage, atrocity,** enormity

3 <nonformal terms> **put-down,** dump, bringdown, brickbat, **dig,** dirty dig, ding, rank-out, rip, shot, slam

VERBS 4 **disrespect,** not respect, disesteem, hold a low opinion of, rate *or* rank low, hold in low esteem, not care much for, pay a lefthanded *or* backhanded compliment, damn with faint praise; **show disrespect for,** show a lack of respect for, **be disrespectful,** treat with disrespect, be overfamiliar with; trifle with, make bold *or* free with, take a liberty, take liberties with, play fast and loose with; **ridicule** 508.8; **disparage** 512.8

5 **offend, affront,** give offense to, disoblige, outrage, step *or* tread on one's toes; dishonor, humiliate, treat with indignity; flout, mock, jeer at, scoff at, fleer at, gibe at, taunt; **insult,** call names, kick *or* slap in the face, take *or* pluck by the beard; **add insult to injury**

6 <nonformal terms> **bad-mouth, put down, trash,** rubbish, dump on, dig at, dis, rank out, rip *or* rip on, ride, roast, slam, hurl a brickbat

ADJS 7 **disrespectful, irreverent,** aweless; **discourteous** 505.4; **insolent, impudent;**

ridiculing, **derisive** 508.12; **disparaging** 512.13

8 **insulting, insolent, abusive, offensive,** humiliating, degrading, contemptuous 157.8, contumelious, calumnious; scurrilous, scurrile; backhand, backhanded, left-handed; outrageous, atrocious, unspeakable

9 **unrespected, unregarded, unrevered,** unvenerated, unhonored, unenvied

157 CONTEMPT

NOUNS 1 **contempt, disdain, scorn,** contemptuousness, disdainfulness, superciliousness, snootiness, snottiness, sniffiness, toploftiness, scornfulness, despite, contumely, sovereign contempt; snobbishness; clannishness, cliquishness, exclusiveness, exclusivity; hauteur, airs, arrogance 141; **ridicule** 508; **insult** 156.2; **disparagement** 512

2 **snub, rebuff,** repulse; **slight,** humiliation, spurning, spurn, disregard, the go-by <nonformal>; cut, cut direct, **the cold shoulder** <nonformal>; sneer, snort, sniff; contemptuous dismissal, **dismissal** 907.2, kiss-off <nonformal>; **rejection** 372

VERBS 3 **disdain, scorn, despise,** hold in contempt, contemn, vilipend, disprize, misprize, rate *or* rank low, be contemptuous of, feel contempt for, **hold in contempt,** hold cheap, look down upon, think little *or* nothing of, feel superior to, be above, hold beneath one *or* beneath contempt, look with scorn upon, view with a scornful eye, give one the fish-eye *or* the beady eye *or* the hairy eyeball <nonformal>; **put down** *or* dump on <both nonformal>; deride, **ridicule** 508.8; **insult; disparage** 512.8; thumb one's nose at, sniff at, sneeze at, snap one's fingers at, sneer at, snort at, curl one's lip at, shrug one's shoulders at; care nothing for, couldn't care less about, think nothing of, set at naught

4 **spurn,** scout, **turn up one's nose at,** scorn to receive *or* accept, not want any part of; spit upon

5 **snub, rebuff,** cut *or* cut dead <nonformal>, drop, repulse; **high-hat** *and* upstage <both nonformal>; **look down one's nose at,** look cool *or* coldly upon; cold-shoulder *or* turn a cold shoulder upon *or* **give the cold shoulder** <nonformal>, give *or* turn the shoulder <nonformal>, give the go-by *or* the kiss-off <nonformal>; turn one's back upon, turn away from, turn on one's heel, set one's face against, slam the door in one's face, show one his place, put one in his place, wave one aside; not be at home to, not receive

6 **slight, ignore,** pooh-pooh <nonformal>, make little of, dismiss, pretend not to see, disregard, overlook, neglect, pass by, pass up *and* give the go-by <both nonformal>, leave out in the cold <nonformal>, take no note *or* notice of, look right through <nonformal>, pay no attention *or* regard to, refuse to acknowledge *or* recognize

7 **avoid** 368.6, avoid like the plague, go out of one's way to avoid, shun, dodge, steer clear of *and* have no truck with <both nonformal>; **keep one's distance,** keep at a respectful distance, **keep** *or* **stand** *or* **hold aloof;** keep at a distance, hold *or* keep at arm's length; **be stuck-up** <nonformal>, act holier than thou, give oneself airs

ADJS 8 **contemptuous, disdainful,** supercilious, snooty, snotty, sniffy, toplofty, toploftical, **scornful,** sneering, withering, contumelious; snobbish, snobby; clannish, cliquish, exclusive; stuck-up <nonformal>, **conceited** 140.11; haughty, **arrogant** 141.9

ADVS 9 **contemptuously, scornfully, disdainfully;** in *or* with contempt, in disdain, in scorn; sneeringly, with a sneer, with curling lip

INTERJS 10 **bah!,** pah!, phooey!, boo!, phoo!, pish!, ecch!, yeech!, eeyuck!, eeyuch!, yeeuck!, *feh!* <Yiddish>

158 SPACE
<indefinite space>

NOUNS 1 **space, extent,** extension, spatial extension, uninterrupted extension, space continuum, continuum; **expanse,** expansion; spread, breadth; depth, deeps; height, vertical space, air space; **measure,** volume; **dimension,** proportion; **area, expanse** tract, surface, surface *or* superficial extension; **field,** arena, sphere; acreage; **void,** empty space, emptiness, nothingness; infinite space, outer space, wastes of outer space, deep space, depths of outer space, interstellar *or* intergalactic space

2 **range, scope, compass, reach, stretch, expanse** radius, sweep, carry, fetch; **gamut, scale,** register, diapason; **spectrum**

3 **room, latitude,** swing, play, way; spare room, room to spare, room to swing a cat <nonformal>, **elbowroom, margin, lee-**

way; breathing space; sea room; head-room, clearance

4 **open space,** clear space; **clearing,** clearance, glade; open country, wide-open spaces, **terrain,** prairie, steppe, plain 236; wilderness, back country, boonies *and* boondocks <both nonformal>, outback <Austral>, desert; distant prospect *or* perspective, empty view, far horizon; **territory;** living space, *Lebensraum* <Ger>; national territory, air space

5 **spaciousness, roominess, size** commodiousness, capacity, capaciousness, amplitude, extensiveness, extent, expanse

6 **fourth dimension, space-time,** time-space, space-time continuum, four-dimensional space; four-dimensional geometry, Minkowski world *or* universe; spaceworld; other continuums; **relativity,** theory of relativity, Einstein theory, principle of relativity, principle of equivalence, general theory of relativity, special *or* restricted theory of relativity, continuum theory; time warp; cosmic constant

7 **inner space,** psychological space, the realm of the mind; personal space, room to be, individual *or* private space; semantic space

VERBS 8 **extend, reach, stretch,** sweep, spread, run, **go** *or* **go out,** cover, carry, **range,** lie; **reach** *or* stretch *or* thrust out; span, straddle, take in, hold, encompass, surround, environ

ADJS 9 **spatial,** space; **dimensional,** proportional; two-dimensional, flat, surface *or* superficial, three-dimensional *or* 3-D, spherical, cubic, volumetric; galactic, intergalactic, interstellar; stereoscopic; fourth-dimensional; space-time, spatio-temporal

10 **spacious, sizeable, roomy, commodious, capacious,** ample; **extensive,** expansive, extended, wide-ranging; far-reaching, extending, spreading, **vast,** vasty, broad, **wide,** deep, high, voluminous; widespread 863.13; **infinite** 822.3

ADVS 11 **extensively, widely,** broadly, vastly, abroad; **far and wide,** far and near; **right and left,** on all sides, on every side; infinitely

12 **everywhere,** everywheres <nonformal>, **here, there, and everywhere;** in every place, in every clime *or* region, in all places, in every quarter, in all quarters; **all over,** all round, all over hell *and* all over the map *and* all over the place *and* all over the ballpark *and* all over town

<all nonformal>, all over the world, the world over, on the face of the earth, under the sun, throughout the world, throughout the length and breadth of the land; from end to end, from pole to pole, from here to the back of beyond <Brit nonformal>, "from Dan to Beersheba"—Bible, from hell to breakfast <nonformal>; **high and low,** upstairs and downstairs, inside and out, in every nook and cranny *or* hole and corner; **universally,** in all creation

13 **from everywhere,** everywhence, "from the four corners of the earth"—Shakespeare, "at the round earth's imagined corners"—Donne, from all points of the compass, from every quarter *or* all quarters; everywhere, everywhither, to the four winds, to the uttermost parts of the earth, "unto the ends of the earth"—Bible, to hell and back <nonformal>

159 LOCATION

NOUNS 1 **location, situation, place, position,** spot, *lieu* <Fr>, placement, emplacement, stead; **whereabouts,** whereabout, ubicity; **area, district, region** 231; **locality, locale,** locus; **abode** 228; **site,** situs; **spot, point,** pinpoint, exact spot *or* point, very spot *or* point; bench mark <surveying>; *locus classicus* <L>; bearings, latitude and longitude

2 **station,** status, **stand, standing,** standpoint, pou sto; **viewpoint,** *optique* <Fr>, point of reference, reference-point, angle, perspective, distance; coign of vantage; **seat, post,** base, footing, ground, venue

3 **navigation,** guidance; dead reckoning, pilotage; coastal navigation; celestial guidance *or* astro-inertial guidance, celestial navigation *or* celo-navigation *or* astronavigation; consolan; loran; radar navigation; radio navigation; **position, orientation,** lay, lie, set, **attitude,** aspect, exposure, frontage, **bearing** *or* **bearings,** radio bearing, azimuth; position line *or* line of position; **fix**

4 **place,** stead, lieu

5 **map, chart;** hachure, contour line, isoline, layer tint; **scale,** graphic scale, representative fraction; **legend;** grid line, meridian, parallel, latitude, longitude; inset; index; **projection,** map projection, azimuthal equidistant projection *or* azimuthal projection, conic projection, Mercator projection; **cartography, mapmaking;** chorography, topography, photogrammetry, phototopography; **car-**

tographer, mapmaker, mapper; chorographer, topographer, photogrammetrist

6 <act of placing> **placement, positioning, emplacement, situation, location, siting,** localization, **locating, placing,** putting; **allocation,** collocation, **disposition,** assignment, **deployment,** posting, **stationing,** spotting; deposition, reposition, **deposit,** disposal, dumping; **stowage,** storage, warehousing; loading, lading, packing

7 **establishment, foundation,** settlement, settling, colonization, population, peopling, plantation; lodgment, fixation; anchorage, mooring; **installation,** installment, inauguration, investiture, placing in office, initiation

8 topography, geography; cartography, chorography; surveying, navigation, geodesy; geodetic satellite, orbiting geophysical observatory or OGO

VERBS 9 **have place,** be there; have its place or slot, **belong, go, fit,** fit in

10 **be located** or **situated, lie, be found,** stand, rest, repose; lie in, have its seat in

11 **locate, situate, site, place, position;** emplace, spot <nonformal>, **install,** put in place; **allocate,** collocate, **dispose, deploy,** assign; **localize,** narrow or pin down; **map, chart,** put on the map or chart; put one's finger on, **fix,** assign or consign or relegate to a place; **pinpoint,** zero in on, home in on; find or fix or calculate one's position, triangulate, find a line of position, **get a fix on** or navigational fix, navigate

12 **place, put, set, lay,** pose, posit, site, seat, stick <nonformal>, **station, post; park,** plump down <nonformal>; **dump**

13 <put violently> **clap,** slap, **thrust, fling, hurl,** throw, cast, chuck, toss; **plump;** plunk and plank and plop <all nonformal>

14 **deposit,** repose, reposit, rest, **lay,** lodge; **put down,** set down, lay down

15 **load, lade,** freight, burden; fill 793.7; **stow,** store, put in storage, warehouse; **pack,** pack away; pile, dump, heap, heap up, stack, mass; bag, sack, pocket

16 **establish, fix, plant, site,** pitch, seat, **set; found, base,** ground, lay the foundation; **build,** put up, set up; build in; **install, invest,** vest, place in office, put in

17 **settle, settle down,** sit down, locate, park <nonformal>, ensconce, ensconce oneself; take up one's abode or quarters, make one's home, **reside, inhabit** 225.7; **move,** locate, relocate, establish residence, make one's home, **take up resi-** dence, take residence at, put up or live or stay at, quarter or billet at, move in, hang up one's hat <nonformal>; take or strike root, put down roots, place oneself, plant oneself, get a footing, stand, take one's stand or position; **anchor,** drop anchor, come to anchor, moor; **squat;** camp, bivouac; perch, roost, nest, hive, burrow; domesticate, **set up housekeeping,** keep house; **colonize,** populate, people; **set up in business,** go in business for oneself, set up shop, hang up one's shingle <nonformal>

ADJS 18 **located, placed, sited, situated,** situate, **positioned,** installed, emplaced, spotted <nonformal>, **set,** seated; **stationed, posted,** deployed, assigned, positioned, prepositioned; **established,** fixed, in place, **settled,** planted, ensconced, embosomed

19 locational, positional, situational, situal; **cartographic;** topographic, geographic, chorographic, geodetic; navigational; **regional** 231.8

ADVS 20 **in place,** in position, in situ, in loco

21 **where,** whereabouts, in what place, in which place; **whither,** to what or which place

22 **wherever,** where'er, **wheresoever,** wheresoe'er, wheresomever <nonformal>, whithersoever, wherever it may be; **anywhere,** anyplace <nonformal>

23 **here,** hereat, in this place, just here, on the spot; **hereabouts,** hereabout, in this vicinity, near here; somewhere about or near; aboard, on board, with or among us; **hither,** hitherward, hitherwards, hereto, hereunto, hereinto, to this place

24 **there,** thereat, in that place, in those parts; thereabout, **thereabouts,** in that vicinity or neighborhood; **thither,** thitherward, thitherwards, to that place

25 **here and there, in places,** in various places, in spots, *passim* <L>

26 **somewhere, someplace,** in some place, someplace or other

PREPS 27 **at, in, on, by; near, next to; with, among,** in the midst of; to, toward; from

28 over, all over, here and there on or in, at about, round about; through, **all through, throughout** 793.17

PHR 29 X marks the spot

160 DISPLACEMENT

NOUNS 1 **dislocation, displacement;** disjointing 801.1, disarticulation, unjointing, unhinging, luxation; heterotopia; **shift, removal,** forcible shift or removal;

eviction; **uprooting,** ripping out, deracination; rootlessness; **disarrangement**
810; incoherence 803.1; discontinuity
812; Doppler effect, red shift, violet shift
<all physics>

2 **dislodgment;** unplacement, **unseating,**
upset, unsaddling, unhorsing; **deposal**
447

3 **misplacement, mislaying,** misputting

4 displaced person *or* DP, stateless person,
homeless person, Wandering Jew, man
without a country, exile, drifter, vagabond, deportee; displaced *or* deported
population; *déraciné* <Fr>

VERBS 5 **dislocate, displace, disjoint,** disarticulate, unjoint, luxate, unhinge, put *or*
force *or* push out of place, **put** *or* **throw
out of joint,** throw out of gear, **disarrange**
810.2

6 **dislodge,** unplace; evict; **uproot,** root up
or out, deracinate; depose 447.4, **unseat,**
unsaddle; **unhorse,** dismount; throw off,
buck off

7 **misplace, mislay,** misput

ADJS 8 dislocatory, dislocating, heterotopic

9 **dislocated, displaced; disjointed,** un-
jointed, unhinged; out, **out of joint,** out of
gear; **disarranged** 809.13

10 **unplaced,** unestablished, unsettled; **up-
rooted,** deracinated; unhoused, evicted,
unharbored, houseless, made homeless,
homeless, stateless, exiled, outcast

11 **misplaced, mislaid,** misput; **out of place,**
out of one's element, like a fish out of water, in the wrong place, in the wrong box
or pew *and* in the right church but the
wrong pew <all nonformal>

12 **eccentric, off-center,** off-balance, unbalanced, uncentered

161 DIRECTION
<compass direction or course>

NOUNS 1 **direction,** directionality; **line,** direction line, line of direction, point, quarter, **aim, way,** track, range, **bearing,**
azimuth, compass reading, **heading,
course;** current, set; tendency, trend,
inclination, bent, tenor, run, drift;
orientation, lay, lie; steering, helmsman-
ship, piloting; navigation 182.1,2; line of
march

2 <nautical & aviation terms> vector,
tack; compass direction, azimuth, compass bearing *or* heading, magnetic
bearing *or* heading, relative bearing *or*
heading, true bearing *or* heading *or*
course; lee side, weather side 218.3

3 **points of the compass,** cardinal points,

half points, quarter points, degrees, compass rose; compass card, lubber line;
rhumb, loxodrome; magnetic north, true
north, magnetic *or* compass directions,
true directions; **north,** northward, nor';
south, southward; **east,** eastward, orient,
sunrise; **west,** westward, occident, sunset; southeast, southwest, northeast,
northwest

4 **orientation, bearings;** adaptation, adjustment, accommodation, alignment,
collimation; disorientation; deviation

VERBS 5 **direct, point, aim, turn, bend, train,**
fix, set, determine; point to *or* at, hold on,
fix on, sight on; take aim, aim at, turn *or*
train upon; directionize, give a push in
the right direction

6 **direct to,** give directions to, lead *or* conduct to, point out to, show, **show** *or* **point
the way,** steer, put on the track, put on
the right track, set straight, set *or* put
right

7 <have or take a direction> **bear, head,
turn, point, aim,** take *or* hold a heading,
lead, go, steer, direct oneself, align oneself; **incline, tend, trend,** set, dispose,
verge, tend to go

8 go west, wester, go east, easter, go north,
go south

9 **head for,** bear for, **go for, make for,** hit *or*
hit out for <nonformal>, **steer for,** hold
for, put for, **set out** *or* **off for,** strike out
for, take off for <nonformal>, bend one's
steps for, lay for, bear up for, bear up to,
make up to, set in towards; set *or* direct *or*
shape one's course for, set one's compass
for, sail for 182.35; align one's march;
break for, make a break for <nonfor-
mal>, run *or* dash for, make a run *or* dash
for

10 **go directly, go straight,** follow one's nose,
go straight on, **head straight for,** vector
for, go straight to the point, steer a
straight course, follow a course, keep *or*
hold one's course, hold steady for, arrow
for, cleave to the line, keep pointed; **make
a beeline,** go as the crow flies; take the air
line, stay on the beam

11 **orient,** orientate, orient *or* orientate oneself, orient the map *or* chart, **take** *or* **get
one's bearings,** get the lay *or* lie of the
land, see which way the land lies, see
which way the wind blows; adapt, adjust,
accommodate

ADJS 12 **directional,** azimuthal; **direct,
straight,** arrow-straight, ruler-straight,
straight-ahead, straightforward, straightaway, straightway; **undeviating,** unswerving, unveering; uninterrupted, un-

broken; one-way, unidirectional, irreversible

13 **directable,** aimable, pointable, trainable; **steerable,** dirigible, guidable, leadable; **directed,** guided, aimed; well-aimed *or* -directed *or* -placed, on the mark, on the nose *or* money <nonformal>; **directional,** directive

14 **northern,** north, northernmost, northerly, northbound, **arctic,** boreal, hyperborean; **southern,** south, southernmost, southerly, southbound, meridional, **antarctic,** austral; **eastern,** east, easternmost *or* eastermost, easterly, eastbound, **oriental; western,** west, westernmost, westerly, westbound, **occidental; northeastern,** northeast, northeasterly; **southeastern,** southeast, southeasterly; **southwestern,** southwest, southwesterly; **northwestern,** northwest, northwesterly

ADVS **15 north,** N, nor', northerly, northward, north'ard, norward, northwards, northwardly; north about

16 **south,** S, southerly, southward, south'ard, southwards, southwardly; south about

17 **east,** E, easterly, eastward, eastwards, eastwardly, where the sun rises; eastabout

18 **west,** W, westerly, westernly, westward, westwards, westwardly, where the sun sets; westabout

19 **northeast** *or* NE, nor'east, northeasterly, northeastward, northeastwards, northeastwardly; north-northeast *or* NNE; northeast by east *or* NE by E; northeast by north *or* NE by N

20 **northwest** *or* NW, nor'west, northwesterly, northwestward, northwestwards, northwestwardly; north-northwest *or* NNW; northwest by west *or* NW by W; northwest by north *or* NW by N

21 **southeast** *or* SE, southeasterly, southeastward, southeastwards, southeastwardly; south-southeast *or* SSE; southeast by east *or* SE by E; southeast by south *or* SE by S

22 **southwest** *or* SW, southwesterly, southwestward, southwestwards, southwestwardly; south-southwest *or* SSW; southwest by south *or* SW by S

23 **directly, direct, straight,** straightly, **straightforward,** straightforwards, **undeviatingly,** unswervingly, unveeringly; **straight ahead,** dead ahead; due, dead, due north, etc; right, forthright; in a direct *or* straight line, in line with, in a line

for, **in a beeline, as the crow flies,** straight across; straight as an arrow

24 **clockwise,** rightward 219.7; **counterclockwise,** anticlockwise, widdershins, leftward 220.6; homeward; landward; seaward; earthward; heavenward; leeward, windward 218.9

25 **in every direction,** in all directions, in all manner of ways, every which way <nonformal>, everywhither, **everyway, everywhere,** at every turn, in all directions at once, in every quarter, on every side, all over the place *or* the ballpark *or* the map <nonformal>; around, all round, round about; forty ways *or* six ways from Sunday <nonformal>; from every quarter, everywhence; from *or* to the four corners of the earth, from *or* to the four winds

PREPS **26 toward,** towards, **in the direction of, to,** up, on, upon; against, over against, versus; headed for, bound for, on the way to, on the road *or* high road to, in transit to, en route to, on route to, in passage to

27 **through,** by, passing by *or* through, **by way of,** by the way of, **via;** over, around, round about, here and there in, all through

162 PROGRESSION
<motion forwards>

NOUNS **1 progression, progress,** going, going forward; **ongoing,** on-go, go-ahead <nonformal>, onward course, rolling, rolling on; **advance,** advancing, **advancement, promotion, furtherance,** furthering; forward motion, forwarding, forwardal; **headway,** way; **leap, jump,** forward leap *or* jump, quantum jump *or* leap, spring, forward spring; progressiveness, progressivity; **passage,** course, march, career, full career; midpassage, midcourse, midcareer; travel 177; improvement 392

VERBS **2 progress, advance, proceed, go,** go *or* move forward, step forward, go on, **go ahead,** go along, push ahead, pass on *or* along; move, travel; go fast 174.8; **make progress,** come on, **get along,** come along <nonformal>, **get ahead;** further oneself; **make headway, roll,** gather head, gather way; make strides *or* rapid strides, cover ground, get over the ground, make good time, make the best of one's way, leap *or* jump *or* spring forward, catapult oneself forward; make up for lost time, gain ground, make up leeway, make progress against, make head against, stem

3 **march on,** run on, rub on, **jog on, roll on,** flow on; drift along, go with the stream

4 **make** or **wend one's way, work** or weave one's way, worm or thread one's way, inch forward, feel one's way, muddle along or through; go slow 175.6; carve one's way; push or force one's way, fight one's way, go or swim against the current, swim upstream; come a long way, move up in the world; **forge ahead,** drive on or ahead, **push** or **press on** or **onward,** push or press forward, push, crowd

5 **advance, further, promote,** forward, hasten, contribute to, foster, aid, facilitate, expedite, abet

ADJS 6 **progressive,** progressing, advancing, proceeding, **ongoing,** oncoming, onward, forward, **forward-looking,** go-ahead <nonformal>; moving

ADVS 7 **in progress,** in mid-progress, in mid-course, in midcareer, in full career; **going on;** by leaps and bounds

8 **forward, forwards, onward, onwards, forth, on,** along, **ahead;** on the way to, on the road or high road to, en route to or for

163 REGRESSION
<motion backwards>

NOUNS 1 **regression,** regress; recession 168; **retrogression,** retrocession, retroflexion, reflux, refluence, retrogradation, retroaction, retrusion, reaction; return, reentry; **setback,** backset <nonformal>, throwback, **rollback;** back-pedalling, backward motion, backward step; sternway; **backsliding,** lapse, relapse, recidivism, recidivation

2 **retreat,** reculade <Fr>, **withdrawal,** withdrawment, strategic withdrawal, exfiltration; **retirement, fallback,** pullout, pullback; advance to the rear; rout; disengagement; **backing down** or **off** or **out** <all nonformal>; reneging, copping or weaseling out <nonformal>

3 **reverse, reversal,** reversing, reversion; **backing,** backing up, backup; **about-face,** volte-face <Fr>, about-turn, right-about, right-about-face, turn to the right-about, U-turn, turnaround, turnabout, swingaround; back track, back trail

4 **countermotion,** countermovement; countermarching, countermarch

VERBS 5 **regress,** go backwards, **recede,** return, revert; **retrogress,** retrograde, retroflex, retrocede; pull back, jerk back, reach back, cock <the arm, fist, etc>; reculer pour mieux sauter <Fr>; fall or get or go behind, fall astern, lose ground, slip back; **backslide,** lapse, relapse, recidivate

6 **retreat,** sound or beat a retreat, beat a hasty retreat, **withdraw, retire,** pull out or back, exfiltrate, advance to the rear, disengage; **fall back,** move back, go back, stand back; run back; **draw back,** draw off; **back out** or **out of** and back off and back down <all nonformal>; defer, give ground, give place, take a back seat, play second fiddle

7 **reverse,** go into reverse; **back, back up,** backpedal, back off or away; **backwater,** make sternway; **backtrack,** backtrail, take the back track; countermarch; reverse one's field; take the reciprocal course; have second thoughts, think better of it, cut one's losses

8 **turn back,** put back; double, double back, retrace one's steps; turn one's back upon; **return,** go or come back, go or come home

9 **turn round** or **around** or **about,** turn, make a U-turn, turn on a dime, turn tail, **come** or **go about,** put about, fetch about; veer, veer around; **swivel,** pivot, pivot about, swing, round, swing round; wheel, wheel about, whirl, spin; heel, turn upon one's heel

10 **about-face,** volte-face <Fr>, right-about-face, **do an about-face** or a right-about-face or an about-turn, perform a volte-face, **face about,** turn or face to the right-about, do a turn to the right-about

ADJS 11 **regressive,** recessive; **retrogressive,** retrocessive, retrograde, retral; retroactive; reactionary

12 **backward, reversed,** reflex, **turned around,** back, **backward;** wrong-way, wrong-way around, counter, ass-backwards and bassackwards <both nonformal>

ADVS 13 **backwards,** backward, retrally, **hindwards,** hindward, **rearwards,** rearward, arear, astern; **back,** away, fro, à reculons <Fr>; **in reverse,** ass-backwards <nonformal>; against the grain, à rebours <Fr>; counterclockwise, anticlockwise, widdershins

WORD ELEMENTS 14 an—, ana—, re—, retro—

164 DEVIATION
<indirect course>

NOUNS 1 **deviation,** deviance or deviancy, deviousness, **departure, digression,** diversion, **divergence,** divarication, branching off, divagation, declination, aberration, aberrancy, **variation,** indirection, exorbitation; detour, excursion, excursus, discursion; obliquity, bias, skew, slant;

circuitousness 913; **wandering**, rambling, **straying**, errantry, pererration; drift, drifting; turning, shifting, swerving, swinging; **turn, corner, bend, curve**, dog-leg, crook, hairpin, zigzag, twist, warp, swerve, **veer**, sheer, sweep; shift, double; tack, yaw; wandering *or* twisting *or* zig-zag *or* shifting course *or* path

2 **deflection, bending**, deflexure, flection, flexure; torsion, distortion, contortion, torture *or* torturing, twisting, warping; skewness; **refraction, diffraction, scatter**, diffusion, dispersion

VERBS 3 **deviate, depart from, vary, diverge**, divaricate, branch off, angle, angle off; **digress**, divagate, turn aside, go out of the way, detour, take a side road; **swerve, veer**, sheer, curve, **shift, turn**, trend, bend, heel, bear off; turn right, turn left, hang a right *or* left <nonformal>; alter one's course, make a course correction, change the bearing; tack 182.30

4 **stray**, go astray, lose one's way, err; take a wrong turn *or* turning; drift, go adrift; **wander**, wander off, ramble, rove, strag-gle, divagate, excurse, pererrate; meander, wind, twist, snake, twist and turn

5 **deflect**, deviate, **divert**, diverge, **bend**, curve, pull, crook, dogleg, hairpin, zig-zag; **warp**, bias, twist, distort, contort, torture, skew; refract, diffract, **scatter, diffuse, disperse**

6 **avoid, evade, dodge**, duck <nonformal>, turn aside *or* to the side, draw aside, **turn away**, jib, shy, shy off; gee, haw; **side-track**, shove aside, shunt, switch; **avert; head off**, turn back 907.3; **step aside**, side-step, move aside *or* to the side, sidle; **steer clear of**, make way for, get out of the way of; go off, bear off, sheer off, veer off, ease off, edge off; fly off, go *or* fly off at a tan-gent; glance, glance off

ADJS 7 **deviative**, deviatory, deviating, **devi-ant**, departing, aberrant, aberrational, aberrative, shifting, turning, swerving, veering; **digressive**, discursive, excursive, **circuitous; devious**, indirect, out-of-the-way; errant, erratic, zigzag, doglegged, **wandering**, rambling, roving, winding, twisting, meandering, snaky, serpentine, mazy, labyrinthine, vagrant, stray, desul-tory, planetary, undirected

8 **deflective**, inflective, flectional, diffrac-tive, refractive; refractile, refrangible; deflected, flexed, refracted, diffracted, scattered, diffuse, diffused, dispersed; distorted, skewed, skew

9 **avertive, evasive**, dodging, dodgy,

165 LEADING
<going ahead>

NOUNS 1 **leading, heading**, foregoing; ante-position, the lead, *le pas* <Fr>; **preced-ing**, precedence 813; priority 833.1; front, point, leading edge, cutting edge, fore-front, vanguard, van 216.2; vaunt-courier <old>, herald, precursor 815

VERBS 2 **lead, head**, spearhead, stand at the head, stand first, be way ahead <nonfor-mal>, head the line; take the lead, go in the lead, **lead the way**, break the trail, be the bellwether, lead the pack; be the point *or* point man; lead the dance; **light the way**, show the way, beacon, guide; get before, get ahead *or* in front of, come to the front, come to the fore, lap, outstrip, pace, set the pace; not look back; get *or* have the start, get a head start, steal a march upon; **precede** 813.2, **go before** 815.3

ADJS 3 **leading, heading**, precessional, prece-dent, precursory, foregoing; **first, fore-most**, headmost; **preceding**, antecedent 813.4; **prior** 833.4; **chief** 249.14

ADVS 4 **before** 813.6, in front, out in front, outfront, foremost, headmost, in the van, in the forefront, in advance 216.12

166 FOLLOWING
<going behind>

NOUNS 1 **following**, heeling, **trailing**, tailing <nonformal>, shadowing; **hounding, dogging**, chasing, **pursuit**, pursual, pur-suance; sequence 814; sequel 816; series 811.2

2 **follower**, successor; shadow *and* tail <both nonformal>; **pursuer**, pursuivant; **attendant** 768.4, **satellite, hanger-on**, dangler, adherent, appendage, depen-dent, parasite, stooge <nonformal>, flunky; **henchman**, ward heeler, partisan, supporter, votary, sectary; camp fol-lower, groupy <nonformal>; fan *and* buff <both nonformal>; courtier, *homme de cour* <Fr>, *cavaliere servente* <Ital>; trainbearer; **public; entourage, following** 768.6; disciple 572.2, discipleship

VERBS 3 **follow**, go after *or* behind, come af-ter *or* behind, move behind; **pursue, shadow** *and* **tail** <both nonformal>, **trail**, trail after, follow in the trail of, camp on the trail of, **heel**, follow *or* tread *or* step on the heels of, follow in the steps *or* foot-steps *or* footprints of, tread close upon, breathe down the neck of, follow in the wake of, hang on the skirts of, stick like the shadow of, sit on the tail of, tailgate

<nonformal>, go in the rear of, bring up the rear, eat the dust of, take or swallow one's dust; tag and **tag after** and tag along <all nonformal>; string along <nonformal>; **dog**, bedog, **hound**, chase, get after, take out or take off after, **pursue**

4 **lag, lag behind, straggle,** lag back, drag, trail, **trail behind,** hang back or behind, loiter, linger, **loiter** or **linger behind,** dawdle, get behind, fall behind or behindhand, let grass grow under one's feet

ADJS 5 **following,** trailing, on the track or trail; succeeding 814.4; back-to-back <nonformal>, consecutive 811.9

ADVS 6 **behind, after,** in the rear, in the train or wake of; in back of 217.13

167 APPROACH
<motion towards>

NOUNS 1 **approach,** approaching, coming or going toward, coming or going near, proximation, appropinquation <old>, **access,** accession, nearing; advance, oncoming; **advent, coming,** forthcoming; flowing toward, afflux, affluxion; appulse; nearness 223; imminence 839; approximation 223.1

2 **approachability, accessibility, access,** getatableness and come-at-ableness <both nonformal>, attainability, openness

VERBS 3 **approach, near, draw near** or nigh, go or come near, go or come toward, come closer or nearer, come to close quarters; **close,** close in, close in on, close with; zoom in on; **accost,** encounter, confront; proximate, appropinquate <old>; **advance,** come, **come forward,** come on, come up, bear up, step up; ease or edge or sidle up to; bear down on or upon, be on a collision course with; gain upon, narrow the gap; approximate 783.7/223.8

ADJS 4 **approaching, nearing,** advancing; attracted to, drawn to; **coming, oncoming, forthcoming,** upcoming, to come; approximate, proximate, approximative; near 223.14; imminent 839.3

5 **approachable, accessible,** getatable and come-at-able <both nonformal>, attainable, open, easy to find, meet, etc

168 RECESSION
<motion from>

NOUNS 1 **recession,** recedence, receding, retrocedence; **retreat, retirement, withdrawing, withdrawal;** retraction, retractation, retractility; fleetingness, fugitiveness, fugitivity, evanescence

VERBS 2 **recede,** retrocede; **retreat, retire, withdraw;** move off or away, stand off or away, stand out from the shore; go, **go away; die away,** fade away, drift away; erode, wash away; **diminish,** decline, sink, shrink, dwindle, **fade, ebb,** wane; shy away, tail away, tail off; go out with the tide, fade into the distance; pull away, widen the distance

3 **retract,** withdraw, **draw** or **pull back,** pull out, draw or pull in; draw in one's claws or horns; defer, take a back seat, play second fiddle; **shrink,** wince, cringe, flinch, shy, fight shy, duck

ADJS 4 **recessive,** recessional, recessionary; recedent, retrocedent

5 **receding, retreating,** retiring, withdrawing; shy; **diminishing, declining,** sinking, shrinking, eroding, dwindling, **ebbing,** waning; **fading,** dying; fleeting, fugitive, evanescent

6 **retractile,** retractable, retrahent

169 CONVERGENCE
<coming together>

NOUNS 1 **convergence,** converging, confluence, concourse, conflux; mutual approach, approach 167; **meeting,** congress, concurrence; **concentration,** concentralization, focalization 208.8, focus 208.4; meeting point, point of convergence, vanishing point; union, merger; crossing point, crossroads, crossing 170; collision course, narrowing gap; funnel, bottleneck; hub, spokes; asymptote; radius; tangent

VERBS 2 **converge, come together,** approach 167.3, run together, **meet,** unite, connect, merge; **cross, intersect** 170.6; fall in with, link up with; be on a collision course; go toward, narrow the gap, close with, close, close up, close in; funnel; taper, pinch, nip; centralize, center, **come to a center;** center on or around, concentralize, concenter, **concentrate,** come or tend to a point; **come to a focus** 208.10

ADJS 3 **converging,** convergent; **meeting,** uniting, merging; concurrent, confluent, mutually approaching, approaching; **crossing, intersecting** 170.8; connivent; **focal,** confocal, focusing, focused; centrolineal, centripetal; asymptotic, asymptotical; tangent, tangential

170 CROSSING

NOUNS 1 **crossing, intercrossing,** intersecting, **intersection;** decussation, chiasma;

traversal, transversion; cross section, transection; cruciation; **transit**, transiting

2 **crossing**, crossway, **crosswalk, crossroad**, pedestrian crosswalk, zebra *or* zebra crossing <Brit>; *carrefour* <Fr>; **intersection**, intercrossing; level crossing, grade crossing; crossover, overpass, flyover <Brit>, viaduct, undercrossing; traffic circle, rotary, roundabout <Brit>; highway interchange, **interchange**, cloverleaf, spaghetti junction <Brit>

3 **network, webwork, weaving** 740, **meshwork**, tissue, crossing over and under, interlacement, intertwinement, intertexture, texture, reticulum, reticulation; "Any thing reticulated or decussated, at equal distances, with interstices between the intersections"—Samuel Johnson; crossing-out, cancellation, scrubbing <nonformal>; **net**, netting; **mesh**, meshes; **web**, webbing; weave, weft; lace, lacery, lacing, lacework; screen, screening; sieve, riddle, raddle; wicker, wickerwork; basketwork, basketry; lattice, latticework; hachure *or* hatchure, hatching, cross-hatching; trellis, trelliswork, treillage; grate, grating; grille, grillwork; **grid**, gridiron; tracery, fretwork, fret, arabesque, filigree; plexus, plexure; reticle, reticule; wattle, wattle and daub

4 **cross**, crux, cruciform; **crucifix**, rood, tree *or* rood tree <old>; X *or* ex, exing, T, Y; **swastika**, gammadion, fylfot, *Hakenkreuz* <Ger>; crossbones; dagger

5 **crosspiece**, traverse, transverse, transversal, transept, transom, cross bitt; diagonal; **crossbar**, crossarm; swingletree, singletree, whiffletree, whippletree; doubletree

VERBS 6 **cross, crisscross**, cruciate; **intersect**, intercross, decussate; **cut across**, crosscut; **traverse**, transverse, lie across; bar, crossbar

7 net, web, mesh; lattice, trellis; grate, grid

ADJS 8 **cross, crossing, crossed; crisscross, crisscrossed; intersecting, intersected**, intersectional; crosscut, cut across; decussate, decussated; chiasmal *or* chiasmic *or* chiastic; secant

9 **transverse**, transversal, traverse; **across**, cross, crossway, **crosswise** *or* crossways, thwart, athwart, overthwart; oblique 204.13

10 **cruciform, crosslike**, cross-shaped, cruciate, X-shaped, cross, crossed; cruciferous

11 **netlike**, retiform, plexiform; **reticulated**, reticular, reticulate; cancellate, cancellated; **netted**, netty; **meshed**, meshy;

laced, lacy, lacelike; filigreed; latticed, latticelike; grated, gridded; barred, crossbarred, mullioned; streaked, striped

12 **webbed**, webby, weblike, woven, interwoven, interlaced, intertwined; webfooted, palmiped

ADVS 13 **crosswise** *or* crossways *or* crossway, decussatively; **cross, crisscross, across**, thwart, thwartly, thwartways, **athwart**, athwartwise, overthwart; **traverse**, traversely; **transverse**, transversely, transversally; obliquely 204.21; **sideways** *or* sidewise; contrariwise, contrawise; crossgrained, across the grain, against the grain; athwartship, athwartships

171 DIVERGENCE
<recession from one another>

NOUNS 1 **divergence** *or* divergency, divarication; aberration, deviation 164; **separation**, division, decentralization; centrifugence; **radial, radiating**, radiating out, raying out, beaming out; **spread**, spreading, spreading out, splaying, fanning, fanning out, deployment; ripple effect

2 **radiation**, ray, sunray, radius, spoke; radiance, diffusion, scattering, dispersion, emanation; halo, aureole, glory, corona

3 **forking**, furcation, bifurcation, biforking, trifurcation, divarication; **branching**, branching off *or* out, **ramification;** arborescence, arborization, treelikeness

4 **fork, prong**, trident; Y, V; **branch, ramification**, stem, offshoot; **crotch**, crutch; **fan, delta,** Δ; **groin**, inguen; furcula, furculum, **wishbone**

VERBS 5 **diverge**, divaricate; aberrate; **separate**, divide, separate off, split off; spread, **spread out**, outspread, splay, fan out, deploy; go off *or* away, **fly** *or* **go off at a tangent**

6 **radiate**, radiate out, ray, ray out, beam out, diffuse, emanate, spread, disperse, scatter

7 **fork**, furcate, bifurcate, trifurcate, divaricate; **branch**, stem, ramify, branch off *or* out

ADJS 8 **diverging**, divergent; divaricate, divaricating; palmate, palmated; fanlike, fan-shaped; deltoid, deltoidal, deltalike, delta-shaped; splayed; centrifugal

9 **radiating**, radial, radiate, radiated; rayed, spoked; radiative

10 **forked, forking**, furcate, biforked, bifurcate, bifurcated, forklike, trifurcate, trifurcated, tridentlike, pronged; **crotched**, Y-shaped, V-shaped; **branched**,

branching; arborescent, arboreal, arboriform, treelike, tree-shaped, dendriform,
dendritic; branchlike, ramous

172 MOTION
<motion in general>

NOUNS **1 motion; movement,** moving, **momentum; stir,** unrest, restlessness; **going,**
running, stirring; **operation,** operating,
working, ticking; **activity** 330; kinesis, kinetics, kinematics; dynamics; kinesia-
trics, kinesipathy, kinesitherapy; **actuation,** motivation; mobilization

　2 course, career, set, midcareer, **passage,**
progress, trend, **advance,** forward motion, going *or* moving on, momentum;
travel 177; **flow,** flux, flight, **trajectory;**
stream, current, run, rush, onrush, ongoing; drift, driftage; backward motion,
regression, retrogression, sternway, backing, going *or* moving backwards; back-
flowing, reflowing, refluence, reflux,
ebbing, subsiding, withdrawing; downward motion, **descent,** descending,
sinking, plunging; upward motion,
mounting, climbing, rising, **ascent,** ascending, **soaring;** oblique *or* crosswise
motion; sideward *or* sidewise *or* sideways
motion; radial motion, angular motion,
axial motion; random motion, Brownian
movement; perpetual motion

　3 mobility, motivity, motility, movable-
ness; **locomotion;** motive power

　4 velocity 174.1,2, rate, gait, pace, tread,
step, stride, clip *and* lick <both nonfor-
mal>

VERBS **5 move, budge, stir;** go, run, flow,
stream; **progress,** advance; wend, wend
one's way; **back,** back up, regress, retrogress; ebb, subside, wane; **descend,** sink,
plunge; **ascend,** mount, rise, climb, soar;
go sideways, go crabwise; go round *or*
around, circle, rotate, gyrate, spin, whirl;
travel; move over, get over; shift, change,
shift *or* change place; **speed** 174.8; **hurry**
401.5, do on the fly *or* run

　6 set in motion, move, actuate, motivate,
push, shove, nudge, **drive,** impel, propel;
mobilize

ADJS **7 moving, stirring, in motion;** transitional; **mobile,** motive, motile, motor,
motorial, motoric; motivational, impelling, propelling, propellant, driving;
traveling; **active** 330.17

　8 flowing, fluent, passing, streaming, flying, **running, going, progressive,** rushing,
onrushing; drifting; **regressive,** retrogressive, back, **backward;** back-flowing,

refluent, reflowing; descending, sinking,
plunging, **downward,** down-trending; ascending, mounting, rising, soaring,
upward, up-trending; sideward, sidewise,
sideways; **rotary,** rotatory, rotational,
round-and-round; axial, gyrational, gyratory

ADVS **9 under way,** under sail, on one's way,
on the go *or* move *or* fly *or* run *or* march,
in motion, astir; from pillar to post

WORD ELEMENTS **10** moto—; —kinesia,
kin—, kine—, kino—, kinesi—,
kinesio—, kinet—, kineto—

173 QUIESCENCE
<being at rest; absence of motion>

NOUNS **1 quiescence,** *or* quiescency, **stillness,** silence 51, quietness, **quiet,** quietude, "lucid stillness" —T S Eliot;
calmness, restfulness, **peacefulness,** imperturbability, passiveness, passivity,
"wise passiveness"—Wordsworth,
placidness, **placidity, tranquillity, serenity, peace, composure;** quietism, contemplation, satori, nirvana, samadhi,
ataraxy *or* ataraxia; **rest, repose,** silken
repose, statuelike *or* marmoreal repose;
sleep, slumber 22.2

　**2 motionlessness, immobility; inactivity,
inaction;** fixity, fixation 854.2

　3 standstill, stand, stillstand; **stop, halt,**
cessation 856; dead stop, dead stand, full
stop; deadlock, lock, dead set; running *or*
dying down, subsidence, waning, ebbing,
wane, ebb

　4 inertness, dormancy; inertia, vis inertiae;
passiveness, passivity; suspense, abeyance, latency; torpor, apathy, indifference, indolence, lotus-eating, languor;
stagnation, stagnancy, **vegetation;** stasis;
deathliness, deadliness; catalepsy, catatonia; entropy

　5 calm, lull, lull *or* calm before the storm;
dead calm, flat calm, oily calm, windless-
ness, deathlike calm; doldrums, horse
latitudes; anticyclone

　**6 stuffiness, airlessness, closeness, op-
pressiveness,** stirlessness, oppression

VERBS **7 be still, keep quiet,** lie still; **stop**
moving, cease motion, freeze *or* seize up,
come to a standstill; **rest, repose; remain,**
stay, tarry; remain motionless, freeze
<nonformal>; stand, **stand still,** be at a
standstill; stand *or* stick fast, stick, stand
firm, stay put <nonformal>; stand like a
post; **not stir,** not stir a step, not move a
muscle; not breathe, hold one's breath;
bide, bide one's time, mark time, tread

water, coast; rest on one's oars, put one's feet up, rest and be thankful

8 **quiet**, quieten, **lull, soothe**, quiesce, **calm**, calm down, tranquilize 670.7, pacify, passivize, pour oil on troubled waters; **stop** 856.7, halt, bring to a standstill; **cease** 856.6, wane, subside, ebb, run or die down, die off, dwindle, molder

9 **stagnate, vegetate**, fust <old>; sleep, slumber; smolder, hang fire; **idle**

10 **sit**, set <nonformal>, **sit down, be seated**, remain seated; perch, roost

11 **becalm**, take the wind out of one's sails

ADJS 12 **quiescent, quiet, still**, stilly <old>, stillish, hushed; quiet as a mouse; waning, subsiding, ebbing, dwindling, moldering; **at rest**, resting, reposing; restful, reposeful, relaxed; cloistered, sequestered, sequestrated, isolated, secluded, sheltered; **calm, tranquil, peaceful**, peaceable, pacific, halcyon; **placid, smooth; unruffled, untroubled**, cool, undisturbed, unperturbed, unagitated, unmoved, unstirring, laid-back <nonformal>; stolid, stoic, stoical, impassive; even-tenored; calm as a mill pond; still as death, "quiet as a street at night"—Rupert Brooke

13 **motionless, unmoving**, unmoved, moveless, **immobile**, immotive; **still, fixed, stationary, static**, at a standstill; **stock-still**, dead-still; still as a statue, statuelike; still as a mouse; at anchor, riding at anchor; **idle**, unemployed; out of commission, down

14 **inert, inactive, static, dormant**, passive, sedentary; **latent**, unaroused, suspended, abeyant, in suspense or abeyance; sleeping, slumbering, smoldering; **stagnant**, standing, foul; **torpid, languorous, languid**, apathetic, phlegmatic, **sluggish**, logy, dopey <nonformal>, groggy, heavy, leaden, **dull**, flat, slack, tame, **dead**, lifeless; catatonic, cataleptic

15 **untraveled, stay-at-home**, stick-in-the-mud <nonformal>, home-keeping

16 **stuffy, airless**, breathless, breezeless, windless; **close, oppressive, stifling, suffocating**; stirless, unstirring, not a breath of air, not a leaf stirring, "not wind enough to twirl the one red leaf"—Coleridge; ill-ventilated, unventilated, unvented

17 **becalmed**, in a dead calm

ADVS 18 quiescently, **quietly**, stilly, still; **calmly, tranquilly, peacefully; placidly**, smoothly, unperturbedly, **coolly**

19 **motionlessly**, movelessly, stationarily, fixedly

20 **inertly, inactively**, statically, dormantly, passively, latently; stagnantly; **torpidly, languorously, languidly; like a bump on a log; sluggishly**, heavily, dully, coldly, lifelessly, apathetically, phlegmatically; stoically, stolidly, impassively

174 SWIFTNESS

NOUNS 1 **velocity, speed; rapidity**, celerity, **swiftness**, fastness, **quickness**, snappiness <nonformal>, **speediness**; haste 401.1, hurry, flurry, rush, precipitation; **dispatch, expedition, promptness**, promptitude, instantaneousness; flight, flit; lightning speed; fast or swift rate, smart or rattling or spanking or lively or snappy pace, round pace; air speed, ground speed, speed over the bottom; miles per hour, knots; rpm 914.3

2 **speed of sound, sonic speed**, Mach, Mach number, Mach one, Mach two, etc; subsonic speed; supersonic or ultrasonic or hypersonic or transsonic speed; transsonic barrier, sound barrier; escape velocity; speed of light, terminal velocity; warp speed

3 **run, sprint; dash, rush**, plunge, headlong rush or plunge, **race, scurry, scamper**, scud, scuttle, **spurt**, burst, **burst of speed**; canter, **gallop**, lope; high lope, hand gallop, full gallop; dead run; **trot**, extended trot, dogtrot, jog trot; **full speed**, open throttle, flat-out speed <Brit>, wide-open speed, heavy right foot, maximum speed; **fast-forward**; fast track or lane; forced draft and flank speed <both nautical>

4 **acceleration, quickening; pickup**, getaway; step-up, speedup; thrust, drive, impetus

5 **speeder**, scorcher and hell-driver <both nonformal>, **sprinter**; flier, goer, stepper; hummer and hustler and sizzler <all nonformal>; **speed demon** or maniac or merchant <nonformal>; **racer, runner**; horse racer, turfman, jockey; Jehu

6 <comparisons> lightning, greased lightning <nonformal>, thunderbolt, flash, streak of lightning, streak, blue streak <nonformal>, bat out of hell <nonformal>, light, electricity, thought, wind, shot, bullet, cannonball, rocket, arrow, dart, quicksilver, mercury, express train, jet plane, torrent, eagle, swallow, antelope, courser, gazelle, greyhound, hare, blue darter, striped snake, scared rabbit

7 **speedometer**, accelerometer; cyclometer;

tachometer; Mach meter; knotmeter, log, log line, patent log, taffrail log, harpoon log, ground log; windsock; wind gauge, anemometer

VERBS **8 speed, go fast,** skim, **fly,** flit, fleet, wing one's way, outstrip the wind; **zoom;** make knots, foot; break the sound barrier, go at warp speed; go like the wind, go like a shot *or* flash, go like lightning *or* a streak of lightning, go like greased lightning; **rush, tear,** dash, dart, shoot, hurtle, bolt, fling, **scamper, scurry,** scour, scud, scuttle, scramble, **race,** careen; **hasten,** haste, make haste, **hurry** 401.4, hie, post; march in quick *or* double-quick time; **run, sprint, trip,** spring, **bound,** leap; gallop, lope, canter; trot; **make time,** make good time, **cover ground,** get over the ground, **make strides** *or* **rapid strides,** make the best of one's way

9 <nonformal terms> **barrel,** clip, spank *or* cut along, tear *or* tear along, bowl along, thunder along, storm along, breeze *or* breeze along, tear up the track *or* road, eat up the track *or* road, scorch, sizzle, rip, zip, whiz, whisk, sweep, brush, nip, zing, fly low, highball, ball the jack, pour it on, boom, shake *or* get the lead out, lollop <Brit>, give it the gun, skedaddle, scoot, step on it, step on the gas, hump *or* hump it, stir one's stumps, hotfoot, hightail, make tracks, step lively, step, step along, carry the mail, hop, hop along, hop it, get, git, go like a bat out of hell, run like a scared rabbit, run like mad, go at full blast, go all out, go flat out, run wide open, go at full tilt *or* steam, let her out, open her up, step on it, go hell-bent for election *or* leather, get a move on, give it the gas, go like blazes *or* blue blazes, floor it, let her rip, put the pedal to the metal, tool

10 accelerate, speed up, step up <nonformal>, **hurry up, quicken; hasten** 401.4; crack on, put on, put on steam, pour on the coal, put on more speed, open the throttle; quicken one's pace; pick up speed, gain ground; race <a motor>, rev <nonformal>

11 <naut terms> put on sail, crack *or* pack on sail, crowd sail, press her

12 spurt, make a spurt *or* dash, **dash** *or* dart *or* shoot ahead, rush ahead, put on *or* make a burst of speed; make one's move

13 overtake, outstrip, overhaul, catch up, **catch up with,** come up with *or* to, gain on *or* upon, pass, lap; outpace, outrun,

outsail; leave behind, leave standing *or* looking *or* flatfooted

14 keep up with, keep pace with, run neck and neck

ADJS **15 fast, swift, speedy, rapid; quick,** double-quick, express, **fleet, hasty, expeditious,** hustling, snappy <nonformal>, rushing, onrushing, dashing, flying, galloping, running, **agile, nimble,** lively, nimble-footed, light-footed, light-legged, light of heel; winged, eagle-winged; mercurial; quick as lightning, quick as thought, swift as an arrow, "swifter than arrow from the Tartar's bow"—Shakespeare; **breakneck,** reckless, headlong, precipitate; quick as a wink, quick on the trigger <nonformal>, hair-trigger <nonformal>; **prompt** 844.9

16 supersonic, transsonic, ultrasonic, hypersonic, faster than sound; warp; **high-speed,** high-velocity, high-geared

ADVS **17 swiftly, rapidly, quickly,** snappily <nonformal>, **speedily,** with speed, **fast, quick,** apace, amain, on eagle's wings, *ventre à terre* <Fr>; at a great rate, at a good clip <nonformal>, with rapid strides, with giant strides, *à pas de géant* <Fr>, in seven-league boots, **by leaps and bounds,** trippingly; **lickety-split** *and* lickety-cut <both nonformal>; hell-bent *and* hell-bent for election *and* hell-bent for leather <all nonformal>; **posthaste,** post, **hastily,** expeditiously, promptly, with great *or* all haste, whip and spur, **hand over hand** *or* **fist;** double-quick, in double time, in double-quick time, on the double *or* the double-quick <both nonformal>; in high gear, in high; under press of sail, all sails set, under crowded sails, under press of sail and steam, under forced draft, at flank speed <all nautical>

18 <nonformal terms> **like a shot, as if shot out of a cannon, like a flash,** like a streak, like a blue streak, like a streak of lightning, like lightning, like greased lightning, **like a bat out of hell, like a scared rabbit,** like a house afire, like sixty, like mad *and* **crazy** *and* fury, like sin, to beat the band *or* the Dutch *or* the deuce *or* the devil

19 in short order, in no time, instantaneously, immediately if not sooner, in less than no time, in nothing flat <nonformal>; in a jiff *or* jiffy <nonformal>, before you can say Jack Robinson, **in a flash,** in a twink, **in a twinkling,** "in the twinkling of an eye"—Bible, *tout de suite* <Fr>, pronto <nonformal>, PDQ *or* pretty damn quick <nonformal>

20 at full speed, with all speed, at full throttle, **at the top of one's bent, for all one is worth** <nonformal>, hit the ground running <nonformal>, as fast as one's legs will carry one, as fast as one can lay feet to the ground; **at full blast,** at full drive or pelt; under full steam, in full sail; **all out** <nonformal>, flat out <Brit>, **wide open;** full speed ahead

175 SLOWNESS

NOUNS 1 slowness, leisureliness, pokiness, slackness, creeping; **sluggishness,** sloth, laziness, idleness, indolence, sluggardy, languor, inertia, inertness, lentitude or lentor <both old>; deliberateness, deliberation, circumspection, tentativeness, cautiousness, reluctance, foot-dragging <nonformal>; drawl

2 slow motion, leisurely gait, snail's or tortoise's pace; **creep, crawl; walk,** footpace, dragging or lumbering pace, trudge, waddle, saunter, stroll; slouch, shuffle, plod, shamble; limp, claudication, hobble; dogtrot, jog trot; jog, rack; mincing steps; slow march, dead or funeral march, largo, andante

3 dawdling, lingering, loitering, tarrying, dalliance, **dallying,** dillydallying, shilly-shallying, lollygagging, dilatoriness, delaying tactic, delayed action, procrastination 845.5, lag, **lagging,** goofing off <nonformal>

4 slowing, retardation, retardment, **slackening,** flagging, slowing down; **slow-down,** slowup, **letup, letdown, slack-up, slack-off,** ease-off, ease-up; **deceleration,** negative or minus acceleration; **delay** 845.2, **detention, setback, holdup** <nonformal>, check, arrest, obstruction; lag, drag

5 slowpoke and slowcoach <both nonformal>, plodder, slow goer, slow-foot, **lingerer, loiterer, dawdler,** dawdle, **laggard,** procrastinator, foot-dragger, stick-in-the-mud <nonformal>, drone, slug, sluggard, lie-abed, sleepy-head, goof-off <nonformal>, goldbrick <nonformal>; tortoise, snail

VERBS 6 go slow or **slowly,** go at a snail's pace, take it slow, get no place fast <nonformal>; **drag,** drag out; **creep, crawl;** laze, idle; go dead slow, get nowhere fast; inch, inch along; worm, worm along; poke, **poke along;** shuffle or stagger or totter or toddle along; drag along, drag one's feet, walk, traipse and **mosey** <both nonformal>; **saunter, stroll, am-**

ble, waddle, toddle <nonformal>; jogtrot, dogtrot; limp, hobble, claudicate

7 plod, plug <nonformal>, peg, shamble, **trudge,** tramp, stump, lumber; plod along, plug along <nonformal>, schlep <nonformal>; rub on, jog on, chug on

8 dawdle, linger, loiter, tarry, delay, dally, dillydally, shilly-shally, lollygag, waste time, **take one's time,** take one's own sweet time; goof off or around <nonformal>; lag, drag, trail; flag, falter, halt

9 slow, slow down or **up, let down** or **up, ease off** or **up, slack off** or **up, slacken,** relax, moderate, taper off, lose speed or momentum; **decelerate, retard, delay** 845.8, detain, impede, obstruct, arrest, stay, **check,** curb, **hold up, hold back,** keep back, set back, hold in check; draw rein, rein in; throttle down, take one's foot off the gas; idle, barely tick over; brake, **put on the brakes,** put on the drag; reef, take in sail; backwater, backpedal; lose ground; clip the wings

ADJS 10 slow, leisurely, slack, moderate, gentle, **easy,** deliberate, go-slow, unhurried, relaxed, gradual, circumspect, tentative, cautious, reluctant, foot-dragging <nonformal>; **creeping, crawling; poking,** poky, slow-poky <nonformal>; tottering, staggering, toddling, trudging, **lumbering,** ambling, waddling, shuffling, **sauntering,** strolling; **sluggish,** languid, languorous, lazy, slothful, indolent, idle, slouchy; **slow-going, slow-moving,** slow-creeping, slow-crawling, slow-running, slow-sailing; **slow-footed,** slow-foot, slow-legged, slow-gaited, slow-paced, slow-stepped, easy-paced, slow-winged; snail-paced, snail-like, tortoiselike, turtlelike, "creeping like snail"—Shakespeare; limping, hobbling, hobbled; halting, claudicant; faltering, flagging; slow as slow, slow as molasses or molasses in January, slow as death, slower than the seven-year itch <nonformal>

11 dawdling, lingering, loitering, tarrying, dallying, dillydallying, shilly-shallying, lollygagging, procrastinatory or procrastinative, dilatory, delaying 845.17, **lagging,** dragging

12 retarded, slowed-down, eased, slackened; **delayed, detained,** checked, **arrested,** impeded, set back, backward, behind; late, **tardy** 845.16

ADVS 13 slowly, slow, **leisurely,** unhurriedly, relaxedly, easily, moderately, gently; creepingly, crawlingly; pokingly, pokily; **sluggishly,** languidly, languorously, lazily, indolently, idly, deliberately, with deliberation, circumspectly, tentatively, cautiously, reluctantly; **lingeringly,** loiteringly, tarryingly, dilatorily; limpingly, haltingly, falteringly; **in slow motion,** at a funeral pace, with faltering *or* halting steps; at a snail's *or* turtle's pace, "in haste like a snail"—John Heywood; in slow tempo, in march time; with agonizing slowness; in low gear; under easy sail

14 **gradually,** little by little 245.6

PHRS 15 **easy does it,** take it easy, go easy, slack off, slow down

176 TRANSFERAL, TRANSPORTATION

1 **transferal, transfer; transmission,** transference, transmittal, transmittance; transposition, transposal, transplacement; mutual transfer, interchange, metathesis; translocation, **transplantation,** translation; migration, transmigration; **import, importation; export, exportation;** deportation, extradition, expulsion, **transit,** transition, **passage; communication,** spread, spreading, dissemination, diffusion, contagion, ripple effect; metastasis; transmigration of souls, metempsychosis; passing over; osmosis, diapedesis; transduction, conduction, convection; transfusion, perfusion; transfer of property *or* right 629

2 **transferability, conveyability;** transmissibility, transmittability; movability, removability; **portability,** transportability; communicability, impartability; deliverability

3 **transportation, conveyance, transport, carrying,** bearing, packing, toting *and* lugging <both nonformal>; **carriage,** carry, **hauling,** haulage, portage, porterage, waft, waftage; **cartage, truckage,** drayage, wagonage; ferriage, lighterage; telpherage; **freightage,** freight, expressage, railway express; **airfreight, air express,** airlift; **package freight,** package service; **shipment, shipping,** transshipment; containerization, cargo-handling; delivery 478.1; travel 177

4 **moving, removal, movement,** relocation, shift, removement, remotion; **displacement,** delocalization

5 people mover, moving sidewalk, automated monorail; conveyor belt; elevator, lift <Brit>, escalator 911.4

6 **freight,** freightage; **shipment, consignment,** goods <Brit>; **cargo,** payload;

lading, load, pack; **baggage, luggage,** impedimenta

7 **carrier, conveyer;** transporter, hauler, carter, wagoner, drayman, shipper, trucker, common carrier, truck driver; freighter; containerizer; stevedore, cargo handler; expressman, express; **bearer, porter,** redcap, skycap; coolie; litterbearer, stretcher-bearer; caddie; shieldbearer, gun bearer; water carrier *or* bearer, water boy, bheesty <India>; the Water Bearer, Aquarius; letter carrier 353.5; cupbearer, Ganymede, Hebe

8 **beast of burden; pack** *or* **draft animal,** pack horse *or* mule, sumpter, sumpter horse *or* mule; **horse** 311.10–15, ass, mule; ox; camel, ship of the desert, dromedary, llama; reindeer; elephant; sledge dog, husky, malamute, Siberian husky

9 <geological terms> **deposit,** sediment; drift, silt, loess, moraine, scree, sinter; alluvium, alluvion, diluvium; detritus, debris

VERBS 10 **transfer, transmit, transpose,** translocate, transplace, metathesize, switch; **transplant,** translate; **pass,** pass over, **hand over,** turn over, carry over, make over, consign, assign; **deliver** 478.13; pass on, pass the buck <nonformal>, hand forward, hand on, relay; **import, export;** deport, extradite, expel; communicate, diffuse, disseminate, spread, impart; transfuse, perfuse, transfer property *or* right 629.3

11 **remove, move, relocate, shift,** send, shunt; displace, delocalize, dislodge; **take away,** cart off *or* away, carry off *or* away; manhandle; set *or* lay *or* put aside, put *or* set to one side, side

12 **transport, convey,** freight, conduct, **take; carry, bear,** pack, tote *and* lug <both nonformal>, manhandle; lift, waft, whisk, wing, fly

13 **haul, cart,** truck, bus; **ship,** barge, lighter, ferry; raft, float

14 <convey through a channel> **channel,** put through channels; **pipe,** tube, pipeline, flume, **siphon, funnel,** tap

15 **send,** send off *or* away, send forth; **dispatch,** transmit, remit, consign, forward; expedite; **ship,** ship off, freight, airfreight, embark, containerize, **transship,** pass along, send on; **express,** air-express; express-mail; package-express; **post, mail,** airmail, drop a letter; messenger; export

16 **fetch, bring, go get,** go and get, go to get, **go after,** go fetch, **go for,** call for, pick up; **get,** obtain, procure, secure; **bring back,**

retrieve; chase after, run after, shag, fetch and carry

17 **ladle, dip, scoop; bail,** bucket; **dish,** dish out *or* up; cup; **shovel,** spade, fork; spoon; **pour,** decant

ADJS 18 **transferable, conveyable; transmittable,** transmissible, transmissive, consignable, deliverable; **movable,** removable; **portable,** portative; transportable, transportative, transportive; conductive, conductional; transposable, interchangeable; **communicable,** contagious, impartable; transfusable; metastatic *or* metastatical, metathetic *or* metathetical; mailable, expressable; assignable 629.5

ADVS 19 by transfer, from hand to hand, from door to door; by freight, by express, by rail, by trolley, by bus, by steamer, by airplane, by mail, by special delivery, by package express, by messenger, by hand

20 **on the way,** along the way, on the road *or* high road, **en route, in transit,** *in transitu* <L>, on the wing, as one goes; in passing, *en passant* <Fr>; in mid-progress

177 TRAVEL

NOUNS 1 **travel,** traveling, going, journeying, touring, moving, **movement, motion, locomotion, transit, progress, passage,** course, crossing; commutation, straphanging; world travel, globetrotting <nonformal>; junketing; **tourism,** touristry

2 **travels,** journeys, **journeyings, wanderings,** voyagings, transits, peregrinations, peripatetics, migrations, transmigrations; odyssey

3 **wandering, roving, roaming, rambling, gadding,** traipsing <nonformal>, wayfaring, flitting, straying, drifting, gallivanting, peregrination, peregrinity, pilgrimage, errantry, divagation; roam, rove, ramble; **itinerancy,** itinerary; **nomadism,** nomadization, gypsydom; vagabonding, vagabondism, vagabondage; **vagrancy,** hoboism, waltzing Matilda <Australia>; bumming <nonformal>; the open road; wanderyear, *Wanderjahr* <Ger>; **wanderlust;** "afoot and lighthearted"—Whitman

4 **migration, transmigration,** passage, trek; run <of fish>, flight <of birds and insects>; swarm, swarming <of bees>; **immigration,** in-migration; **emigration,** out-migration, expatriation; remigration; intermigration

5 **journey, trip,** *jornada* <Sp>, peregrination, sally, **trek;** progress, course, run; **tour,** grand tour; tourist season, low season, high season; tourist class; travel agency *or* bureau, holiday company <chiefly Brit>; **conducted tour,** package tour *or* holiday; **excursion, jaunt, junket, outing,** pleasure trip; sight-seeing trip *or* tour, rubberneck tour <nonformal>; day-trip; round trip, circuit, turn; **cruise,** package cruise, cruise to nowhere; **expedition,** campaign; safari, hunting expedition, hunting trip, stalk, shoot, photography safari; **pilgrimage,** hajj; **voyage** 182.6

6 **riding, driving; motoring,** automobiling; busing; motorcycling, bicycling, cycling, pedaling, biking <nonformal>; **horseback riding,** horse-riding, equitation; horsemanship, manège; pony-trekking

7 **ride, drive;** spin *and* whirl <both nonformal>; joyride <nonformal>; Sunday drive; airing; lift <nonformal>, pickup <nonformal>

8 **walking,** ambulation, perambulation, pedestrianism, shank's mare *or* pony <nonformal>, going on foot *or* afoot, footing *or* hoofing, footing it *or* hoofing it; strolling, sauntering, ambling, *flânerie* <Fr>; **tramping, marching, hiking,** backpacking, trail-hiking, footslogging, trudging, treading; lumbering, waddling; toddling, staggering, tottering; **hitchhiking** *and* hitching <both nonformal>, thumbing *and* thumbing a ride <both nonformal>; jaywalking

9 **nightwalking,** noctambulation, noctambulism; night-wandering, noctivagation; **sleepwalking,** somnambulation, somnambulism; sleepwalk

10 **walk,** ramble, amble, **hike, tramp,** traipse <nonformal>; slog, trudge, schlep <nonformal>; **stroll,** saunter; **promenade;** *passeggiata* <Ital>; jaunt, airing; **constitutional** <nonformal>, stretch; turn; peripatetic journey *or* exercise, peripateticism; walking tour *or* excursion; **march,** forced march, route march; parade

11 **step, pace, stride; footstep,** footfall, tread; hoofbeat, clop; hop, jump; skip, hippety-hop <nonformal>

12 **gait, pace, walk, step, stride, tread;** saunter, stroll, strolling gait; shuffle, shamble, hobble, limp, hitch, waddle; totter, stagger, lurch; toddle, paddle; slouch, droop, drag; mince, mincing steps, scuttle, prance, flounce, stalk, strut, swagger; slink, slither, sidle; jog; swing, roll; amble, single-foot, rack, piaffer; trot, gallop

174.3; lock step; velocity 174.1,2; slowness 175

13 march; quick or quickstep march, quickstep, quick time; lockstep; double march, double-quick, double time; slow march, slow time; half step; goose step

14 leg, limb, shank; hind leg, foreleg; gamb, jamb <heraldry>; shin, cnemis; ankle, tarsus; hock, gambrel; calf; knee; thigh; popliteal space, ham, drumstick; gigot

15 <nonformal terms> gams, stems, trotters, hind legs, underpinnings, wheels, shanks, sticks, pins, stumps

16 gliding, sliding, slipping, slithering, coasting, sweeping, flowing, sailing; **skating, skiing, tobogganing, sledding;** glide, slide, slither, sweep, skim, flow

17 creeping, crawling, going on all fours; sneaking, stealing, slinking, sidling, gumshoeing and pussyfooting <both nonformal>, walking on eggs, padding, prowling, nightwalking; worming, snaking; tiptoeing, tiptoe, tippytoe; creep, crawl, scramble, scrabble; all fours

VERBS **18 travel, go, move, pass,** fare, wayfare, fare forth, fetch, flit, hie, sashay <nonformal>, cover ground; **progress** 162.2; move on or along, go along; wend, **wend one's way;** betake oneself, direct one's course, bend one's steps or course; course, run, flow, stream; roll, roll on; commute, straphang

19 <go at a given speed> **go, go at,** reach, **make, do,** hit <nonformal>, clip off <nonformal>

20 traverse, cross, travel over or through, pass through, **go** or **pass over, cover,** measure, transit, track, range, range over or through, course, do, perambulate, peregrinate, overpass, go over the ground; patrol, reconnoiter, scout; sweep, go or make one's rounds, scour, scour the country; ply, voyage 182.13

21 journey, travel, make or take or go or go on a journey, **take** or **make a trip,** fare, **wayfare, gad around** or about, get around or about, navigate, trek, jaunt, peregrinate; junket, go on a junket; **tour;** hit the trail <nonformal>, take the road, go on the road; **cruise, go on a cruise, voyage** 182.13; go abroad, go to foreign places or shores, range the world, globe-trot <nonformal>; travel light, live out of a suitcase; pilgrimage, pilgrim, go on or make a pilgrimage; campaign, go overseas, go on an expedition, go on safari; go on a sight-seeing trip, sight-see, rubberneck <nonformal>

22 migrate, transmigrate, trek; flit, take

wing; run <of fish>, swarm <of bees>; **emigrate,** out-migrate, expatriate; **immigrate,** in-migrate; remigrate; intermigrate

23 wander, roam, rove, range, nomadize, **gad,** gad around or about, follow the seasons, wayfare, flit, traipse <nonformal>, gallivant, knock around or about and bat around or about <all nonformal>, prowl, **drift, stray,** float around, straggle, **meander, ramble,** stroll, saunter, jaunt, peregrinate, pererrate, divagate, go or run about, go the rounds; **tramp,** hobo, bum or go on the bum <nonformal>, vagabond, vagabondize, take to the road, "travel the open road"—Whitman, beat one's way; **hit the road** or **trail** <nonformal>, walk the tracks and count ties <both nonformal>, pound the pavement

24 go for an outing or **airing,** take the air, get some air; go for a walk; go for a ride

25 go to, repair to, resort to, hie to, hie oneself to, arise and go to, direct one's course to, turn one's tracks to, make one's way to, set foot in, bend one's steps to, betake oneself to, **visit,** drop in or around or by, make the scene <nonformal>

26 creep, crawl, scramble, scrabble, grovel, **go on hands and knees,** go on all fours; worm, worm along, worm one's way, snake; inch, inch along; **sneak, steal,** steal along; pussyfoot and gumshoe <both nonformal>, slink, sidle, pad, prowl, nightwalk; **tiptoe,** tippytoe, go on tiptoe

27 walk, ambulate, peripateticate, pedestrianize, traipse <nonformal>; **step, tread, pace, stride,** pad; foot, foot it; leg, leg it; hoof it, ankle, go on the heel and toe, ride shank's mare or pony <nonformal>, ride the shoeleather or hobnail express, stump it <nonformal>; peg or jog or shuffle on or along; perambulate; circumambulate; jaywalk; power walk, exercise walk, speed walk, race walk

28 <ways of walking> **stroll,** saunter, flâner <Fr>; shuffle, scuff, scuffle, straggle, shamble, slouch; stride, straddle; **trudge, plod,** peg, traipse <nonformal>, clump, stump, slog, footslog, drag, **lumber, barge;** stamp, stomp <nonformal>; swing, roll, lunge; hobble, halt, limp, hitch, lurch; totter, stagger; toddle, paddle; waddle, wobble, wamble, wiggle; link, slither, sidle; stalk; **strut, swagger;** mince, sashay <nonformal>, scuttle, prance, tittup, flounce, trip, skip, foot; hop, jump, hippety-hop <nonformal>; jog, jolt; bundle, bowl along; **amble,** pace; singlefoot, rack; piaffe, piaffer

29 go for a walk, perambulate, take a walk, take one's constitutional <nonformal>, take a stretch, stretch the legs; **promenade,** *passeggiare* <Ital>, parade

30 march, mush, footslog, **tramp, hike,** backpack, trail-hike; route-march; file, defile, file off; **parade,** go on parade; goose-step, do the goose step; do the lock step

31 hitchhike *or* **hitch** <nonformal>, beat one's way, **thumb** *or* **thumb one's way** <nonformal>, **catch a ride;** hitch *or* hook *or* bum *or* cadge *or* thumb a ride <nonformal>

32 nightwalk, noctambulate; **sleepwalk,** somnambulate, walk in one's sleep

33 ride, go for a ride *or* **drive;** go for a spin <nonformal>, take *or* go for a Sunday drive; **drive, chauffeur; motor,** taxi; bus; bike *and* cycle *and* wheel *and* pedal <all nonformal>; **motorcycle, bicycle;** go by rail, entrain; joyride *or* take a joyride <nonformal>; catch *or* make a train <nonformal>

34 go on horseback, ride, horse-ride pony-trek; ride bareback; mount, take horse; hack; ride hard, clap spurs to one's horse; trot, amble, pace, canter, gallop, tittup, lope; prance, frisk, curvet, piaffe, caracole

35 glide, coast, skim, sweep, flow; **sail, fly,** flit; **slide,** slip, skid, skitter, sideslip, slither, glissade; skate, ice-skate, roller-skate, skateboard; ski; toboggan, sled, sleigh; bellywhop <nonformal>

ADJS **36 traveling, going, moving,** trekking, passing; **progressing; itinerant,** itinerary, circuit-riding; **journeying, wayfaring,** strolling; **peripatetic;** ambulant, ambulatory; ambulative; perambulating, perambulatory; peregrine, peregrinative, pilgrimlike; locomotive; **walking, pedestrian, touring,** on tour, globe-trotting <nonformal>, globe-girdling, mundivagant <old>; touristic, touristical, touristy <nonformal>; expeditionary

37 wandering, roving, roaming, ranging, **rambling, meandering,** strolling, **straying,** straggling, shifting, flitting, landloping, errant, divagatory, discursive, circumforaneous; **gadding,** traipsing <nonformal>, gallivanting; **nomad,** nomadic, floating, drifting, gypsyish *or* gypsylike; **transient,** transitory, fugitive; **vagrant,** vagabond, vagabondish; **footloose,** footloose and fancy-free; **migratory,** migrational, transmigrant, transmigratory

38 nightwalking, noctambulant, noctambulous; night-wandering, noctivagant;

sleepwalking, somnambulant, somnambular

39 creeping, crawling, on hands and knees, on all fours; reptant, repent, reptile, reptatorial; **on tiptoe,** on tippytoe, atiptoe, tiptoeing, tiptoe, tippytoe

40 traveled, well-traveled, cosmopolitan

41 wayworn, way-weary, road-weary, leg-weary, **travel-worn,** travel-weary, travel-tired; travel-sated, travel-jaded; travel-soiled, travel-stained, dusty

ADVS **42 on the move** *or* **go,** en route, in transit, on the wing *or* fly; on the run, on the jump <nonformal>, on the road, on the tramp *or* march; on the gad <nonformal>, on the bum <nonformal>

43 on foot, afoot, by foot, footback *or* on footback <nonformal>; on the heel and toe, on *or* by shank's mare *or* pony <nonformal>

44 on horseback, horseback, by horse, mounted

178 TRAVELER

NOUNS **1 traveler, goer,** viator, comer and goer; **wayfarer, journeyer,** trekker; **tourist,** tourer; **tripper** <Brit>, day-tripper; cicerone, travel *or* tourist guide; **visitor,** visiting fireman <nonformal>; **excursionist, sightseer,** rubberneck *or* rubbernecker <nonformal>; **voyager,** cruise-goer, cruiser, sailor, mariner 183; **globetrotter** <nonformal>, globe-girdler, world-traveler, cosmopolite; jet set, jet-setter; **pilgrim,** palmer, hajji; **passenger,** fare; **commuter,** straphanger <nonformal>; transient; passerby; adventurer, alpinist, climber, mountaineer; explorer, forty-niner, pioneer, pathfinder, voortrekker, trailblazer, trailbreaker; camper; astronaut 1073.8

2 wanderer, rover, roamer, rambler, stroller, straggler, mover; **gad, gadabout** <nonformal>, runabout, go-about <nonformal>; **itinerant,** peripatetic, rolling stone, peregrine, peregrinator, bird of passage, visitant; **drifter** *and* **floater** <both nonformal>; Wandering Jew, Ahasuerus, Ancient Mariner <Samuel Taylor Coleridge>, Argonaut, Flying Dutchman, Oisin, Ossian, Gulliver <Jonathan Swift>, Ulysses, Odysseus <Homer>; wandering scholar, Goliard, *vaganti* <L>; strolling player, wandering minstrel, troubadour

3 vagabond, vagrant, vag <nonformal>; **bum** *or* bummer <nonformal>, loafer, wastrel, losel <old>, *lazzarone* <Ital>;

tramp, turnpiker, piker, knight of the road, easy rider, **hobo** or bo <nonformal>, rounder <nonformal>, stiff or bindlestiff <nonformal>; landloper, sundowner or swagman or swagsman <all Australian nonformal>; beggar 440.8; **waif,** homeless waif, dogie, stray, waifs and strays; ragamuffin, tatterdemalion; **gamin,** gamine, urchin, street urchin, dead-end kid <nonformal>, mudlark, guttersnipe <nonformal>; beachcomber, loafer, idler; ski bum, beach bum, surf · bum, tennis bum; ragman, ragpicker

4 **nomad,** Bedouin, Arab; gypsy, Bohemian, Romany, zingaro <Ital>, Zigeuner <Ger>, tzigane <Fr>

5 **migrant,** migrator, trekker; **immigrant,** in-migrant; migrant or migratory worker, wetback <nonformal>; **emigrant,** out-migrant, émigré <Fr>; expatriate; **evacuee,** évacué <Fr>; displaced person or DP, stateless person, exile

6 **pedestrian, walker,** walkist; foot traveler, foot passenger, hoofer <nonformal>, footbacker <nonformal>, ambulator, peripatetic; **hiker,** backpacker, trailsman, tramper; marcher, footslogger, foot soldier, infantryman, paddlefoot <nonformal>; **hitchhiker** <nonformal>; jaywalker; power walker, exercise walker, speed walker, race walker

7 **nightwalker,** noctambulist, noctambule, **sleepwalker,** somnambulist, somnambulator, somnambule

8 **rider, equestrian, horseman,** horserider, horseback rider, horsebacker, caballero <Sp>, cavalier, knight, chevalier; horse soldier, cavalryman, mounted policeman; horsewoman, equestrienne; cowboy, cowgirl, puncher or cowpuncher or cowpoke <all nonformal>, vaquero, gaucho <both Sp>; broncobuster <nonformal>, buckaroo; postilion, postboy; roughrider; **jockey;** steeplechaser; circus rider, trick rider

9 **driver,** reinsman, whip, Jehu, skinner <nonformal>; **coachman,** coachy <nonformal>, cocher <Fr>, cochero <Sp>, voiturier <Fr>, vetturino <Ital>, gharry-wallah <India>; stage coachman; charioteer; harness racer; **cabdriver,** cabman, cabby <nonformal>, hackman, hack or hacky <nonformal>, jarvey <Brit nonformal>; wagoner, wagonman, drayman, truckman; **carter,** cartman, carman; **teamster;** muleteer, mule skinner <nonformal>; bullwhacker; elephant driver, mahout; cameleer

10 **driver, motorist,** automobilist; **chauffeur; taxidriver,** cabdriver, cabby <nonformal>, hackman, **hack** or hacky <nonformal>, hackdriver; jitney driver; **truck driver, teamster,** truckman, **trucker; bus driver,** busman, bus jockey <nonformal>; speeder 174.5, road hog <nonformal>, Sunday driver, joyrider <nonformal>; hit-and-run driver; backseat driver

11 cyclist, cycler; **bicyclist,** bicycler; **motorcyclist,** motorcycler, biker <nonformal>

12 **engineer,** engineman, engine driver <Brit>; hogger or hoghead <nonformal>; Casey Jones; **motorman;** gripman

13 **trainman,** railroad man, **railroader;** conductor, guard <Brit>; brakeman, brakie <nonformal>; fireman, footplate man <Brit>, stoker; smoke agent and bakehead <both nonformal>; switchman; yardman; yardmaster; trainmaster; dispatcher; stationmaster; lineman; baggage man, baggagesmasher <nonformal>; porter, redcap; trainboy; butcher <nonformal>

179 VEHICLE
<means of conveyance>

NOUNS 1 **vehicle, conveyance,** carrier, means of carrying or transporting, means of transport, medium of transportation, carriage; watercraft 180.1, aircraft 181

2 **wagon,** waggon <Brit>, wain; haywagon, milkwagon; dray, van, caravan; covered wagon, prairie schooner, Conestoga wagon

3 **cart,** two-wheeler; oxcart, horsecart, ponycart, dogcart; dumpcart, coup-cart <Scots>; **handcart,** barrow, wheelbarrow; jinrikisha, ricksha

4 **carriage,** four-wheeler, voiture <Fr>, gharry <India>; **chaise,** shay <nonformal>, "one hoss shay"—Oliver Wendell Holmes

5 **rig, equipage,** turnout <nonformal>, coach-and-four; team, pair, span; tandem, random; spike, spike team, unicorn; three-in-hand, four-in-hand, etc; three-up, four-up, etc

6 **baby carriage,** baby buggy <nonformal>, perambulator, pram <Brit>; go-cart; **stroller,** walker

7 **wheel chair,** Bath chair, push chair

8 **cycle,** wheel <nonformal>; **bicycle,** bike <nonformal>, velocipede; **tricycle,** three-wheeler, trike <nonformal>; **motorcycle,** motocycle, bike and iron <both nonformal>, pig <nonformal>, chopper <nonformal>; pedicab

9 **automobile** <see list>, **car, auto,** motor-car, motocar, autocar, **machine,** motor, motor vehicle, motorized vehicle, *voiture* <Fr>

10 <nonformal terms> **jalopy,** banger, bus, buggy, wheels, tub, tuna wagon, heap, boat, short, crate, wreck, clunker, junker, junkheap, junkpile

11 **police car, patrol car; prowl car,** squad car, cruiser; **police van,** patrol wagon; wagon *and* paddy wagon *and* Black Maria <all nonformal>

12 **truck** <see list>, lorry <Brit>, *camion* <Fr>; trailer truck, truck trailer, tractor trailer, semitrailer, rig *and* semi <both nonformal>; eighteen-wheeler <nonformal>

13 <public vehicles> **commercial vehicle; bus,** omnibus, chartered bus, autobus, motorbus, motor coach, articulated bus, jitney <nonformal>; express bus, local bus; schoolbus; **cab, taxicab, taxi,** hack <nonformal>, gypsy cab <nonformal>; rental car; hired car, limousine, limo *and* stretch limo <both nonformal>

14 **train,** railroad train; choo-choo *and* choo-choo train <both nonformal>; passenger train, Amtrak; aerotrain, bullet train, *train de haute vitesse* <Fr>; local, way train, milk train, accommodation train; shuttle train, shuttle; express train, express; lightning express, flier, cannonball express <nonformal>; local express; special, limited; parliamentary train *or* parliamentary <Brit>; freight train, goods train <Brit>, freight, freighter, rattler <nonformal>; baggage train, luggage train; electric train; cable railroad; funicular; cog railroad *or* railway, rack-and-pinion railroad; subway, *métro* <Fr>, tube, underground <Brit>; elevated, el <nonformal>; monorail; streamliner; rolling stock

15 **railway car,** car, waggon <Brit>; baggage car, boxcar, caboose, coach; diner, dining car *or* compartment; drawing room; freight car; parlor car; Pullman *or* Pullman car; refrigerator car *or* reefer <nonformal>; roomette, sleeper *or* sleeping car or *wagon-lit* <Fr>; smoker *or* smoking car *or* compartment

16 **handcar,** go-devil; push car, trolley, truck car, rubble car

17 **streetcar, trolley** *or* trolley car, **tram** *or* tramcar <both Brit>; electric car, electric <nonformal>; trolley bus, trackless trolley; horsecar, horse box <Brit>; cable car, grip car

18 **tractor,** traction engine; Caterpillar trac-tor <trademark>, Caterpillar <trademark>, Cat <nonformal>, tracked vehicle; bulldozer, dozer <nonformal>, calfdozer

19 **trailer,** trail car; house trailer, mobile home; recreation vehicle *or* RV; truck trailer, **semitrailer,** highway trailer; camp *or* camping trailer, caravan <Brit>; **camper,** camping bus

20 **sled, sleigh,** *traîneau* <Fr>; snowmobile, Sno-Cat, weasel, Skimobile; runner, blade; toboggan

21 **skates,** ice skates, hockey skates, figure skates; roller skates, skateboard, bob skates; **skis, snowshoes**

22 **Hovercraft** <trademark>, hovercar, air-cushion vehicle *or* ACV, cushioncraft, ground-effect machine *or* GEM, captured-air vehicle *or* CAV, captured-air bubble *or* CAB, surface-effect ship

ADJS 23 **vehicular,** transportational; automotive, locomotive

24 **automobiles**

brougham	rocket car
cabriolet	runabout
compact car	saloon <Brit>
convertible	sedan
coupe	sedan limousine
hardtop	sports car
hatchback	station wagon
jeep	stock car
limousine *or* limo	stretch limousine *or*
mini-bus	limo
minicar	tourer <Brit>
phaeton	touring car
race car *or* racer *or*	two-door
racing car	two-seater <Brit>
roadster	

25 **trucks**

duck *or* DUKW	recreation vehicle *or*
fork *or* forklift	recvee *or* rec-v *or*
truck	RV
four-by-four *or* 4x4	six-by-six
minivan	tractor *or* tractor
panel truck	truck *or* truck
pick-up truck *or*	tractor
pickup	van

180 SHIP, BOAT

NOUNS 1 **ship,** argosy, cargo ship, container ship, cruise ship, dredge, freighter, liner, merchant ship *or* merchantman, motorship, oceanographic research ship, paddle boat *or* steamer, refrigeration ship, roll-on roll-off ship *or* ro-ro, side-wheeler, supertanker, tanker, trawler, ULCC *or* ultra-large crude carrier, VLCC *or* very large crude carrier, whaler; **boat,** ark, canoe, gondola, kayak, lifeboat, motorboat, shell, skiff, whaleboat, workboat; vessel, craft, bottom, bark, hull, hulk, keel, watercraft; tub *and* bucket *and* rustbucket *and* hooker <all nonformal>, packet; leviathan; "that packet of assorted miseries which we call a ship"—Kipling, "the ship, a fragment detached from the earth"—Joseph Conrad

2 steamer, steamboat, steamship; motor ship

3 sailboat, sailing vessel, sailing boat, wind boat, ragboat <nonformal>, sailing yacht, sailing cruiser, sailing ship, tall *or* taunt ship, sail, sailer, **windjammer** <nonformal>, windship, windboat; **galley; yacht,** pleasure boat, a hole in the water into which one pours money <nonformal>

4 motorboat, powerboat, speedboat, stinkpot <nonformal>; **launch,** motor launch, steam launch, naphtha launch; **cruiser,** power cruiser, **cabin cruiser,** sedan cruiser, outboard cruiser

5 liner, ocean liner, ocean greyhound <nonformal>, passenger steamer, floating hotel *or* palace, luxury liner; **cruise ship**

6 warship, war vessel, naval vessel; warship; **man-of-war,** man-o'-war, ship of war, armored vessel; USS *or* United States Ship; HMS *or* His *or* Her Majesty's Ship; line-of-battle ship, ship of the line; aircraft carrier *or* flattop <nonformal>, assault transport, battle cruiser, battleship, coast guard cutter, communications ship, cruiser, destroyer, destroyer escort, guided missile cruiser, heavy cruiser, hospital ship, mine layer, mine ship, mine sweeper

7 battleship, battlewagon <nonformal>, capital ship; **cruiser,** battle-cruiser; **destroyer,** can *or* tin can <nonformal>

8 carrier, aircraft carrier, seaplane carrier, **flattop** <nonformal>

9 submarine, sub, submersible, underwater craft; **U-boat,** U-boot *or* Unterseeboot <both Ger>, pigboat <nonformal>; nuclear *or* nuclear-powered submarine; Polaris submarine; Trident submarine; hunter-killer submarine

10 ships, shipping, merchant *or* mercantile marine, merchant navy *or* fleet, bottoms, tonnage; **fleet,** flotilla, argosy; line; fishing fleet, whaling fleet, etc; **navy** 461.26

11 float, raft; balsa, balsa raft, Kon Tiki; life raft, Carling float; boom; pontoon; buoy, life buoy; **life preserver** 397.5; surfboard; cork; bob

12 rigging, rig, **tackle,** tackling, **gear; ropework,** roping; service, serving, whipping; standing rigging, running rigging; boatswain's stores; ship chandlery

13 spar, timber; **mast,** pole, stick *and* tree <both nonformal>; bare pole

14 sail, canvas, muslin, cloth, rag <nonformal>; **full** *or* **plain sail,** press *or* crowd of sail; reduced sail, reefed sail; square sail; fore-and-aft sail; luff, leech, foot, earing, reef point, boltrope, clew, cringle, head

15 oar, remi—; **paddle,** scull, sweep, pole; steering oar

16 anchor, mooring, hook *and* mudhook <both nonformal>; **anchorage,** moorings; **berth,** slip; mooring buoy

ADJS **17 rigged,** decked, trimmed; square-rigged, fore-and-aft rigged, Marconi-rigged, gaff-rigged, lateen-rigged

18 seaworthy, sea-kindly, fit for sea, **snug, bold; watertight,** waterproof; **A1,** A1 at Lloyd's; stiff, tender; weatherly; yare

19 trim, in trim; apoise, on an even keel

20 shipshape, Bristol fashion, shipshape and Bristol fashion, trim, trig, neat, tight, taut, ataunt, all ataunto, bungup and bilge-free

181 AIRCRAFT

NOUNS **1 aircraft, airplane,** aeroplane <Brit>, **plane, ship,** fixed-wing aircraft, flying machine <old>, *avion* <Fr>; aerodyne, heavier-than-air craft; kite <Brit nonformal>; **shuttle, space shuttle,** lifting body; **airplane part; flight instrument,** aircraft instrument; **aircraft engine; piston engine,** radial engine, rotary engine, pancake engine; **jet engine,** fanjet engine, rocket motor, turbofan, turbojet, turboprop, pulse jet, ramjet, reaction engine *or* motor

2 propeller plane, single-prop, double-prop *or* twin-prop, multi-prop; tractor, tractor plane; pusher, pusher plane; piston plane; turbo-propeller plane, turbo-prop, prop-jet

3 jet plane, jet; turbojet, ramjet, pulsejet, blowtorch <nonformal>; single-jet, twin-jet, multi-jet; Jet Liner, business jet; deltaplanform jet, tailless jet, twin-tailboom jet; jumbo jet; subsonic jet; supersonic jet, supersonic transport *or* SST, Concorde

4 rocket plane, repulsor; rocket ship, spaceship 1073.2; rocket 1072.2

5 rotor plane, rotary-wing aircraft, rotocraft, rotodyne; gyroplane, gyro, **autogiro,** windmill <nonformal>; **helicopter,**

copter *and* whirlybird *and* chopper *and*
eggbeater <all nonformal>

6 **ornithopter,** orthopter, wind flapper, mechanical bird

7 **flying platform,** flying ring, Hiller-
CNR machine, flying bedstead *or* bed-
spring; **Hovercraft** <trademark>, air
car, ground-effect machine, air-cushion
vehicle, hovercar, cushioncraft; flying
crow's nest, flying motorcycle, flying
bathtub

8 **seaplane,** waterplane, **hydroplane,**
aerohydroplane, aeroboat, **floatplane,**
float seaplane; **flying boat,** clipper, boat
seaplane; **amphibian,** triphibian

9 **military aircraft, warplane,** battleplane,
combat plane; carrier fighter, carrier-
based plane, dive bomber, fighter, helicopter gunship, jet bomber, jet fighter,
jet tanker, night fighter, photo-
reconnaissance plane, Stealth Bomber,
Stealth Fighter, tactical support bomber,
torpedo bomber, troop carrier *or* transport; suicide plane, kamikaze; bogey,
bandit, enemy aircraft; air fleet, air armada; air force 461.29

10 **trainer;** Link trainer; **flight simulator;**
dual-control trainer; basic *or* primary
trainer, intermediate trainer, advanced
trainer; crew trainer, flying classroom;
navigator-bombardier trainer, radio-
navigational trainer, etc

11 **aerostat,** lighter-than-air craft; **airship,**
ship, dirigible balloon, **blimp** <nonfor-
mal>; rigid airship, semirigid airship;
dirigible, zeppelin, Graf Zeppelin; gasbag, ballonet; **balloon,** *ballon* <Fr>

12 **glider,** gliding machine; **sailplane,** soaring plane; rocket glider; student glider;
air train, glider train

13 **parachute, chute** <nonformal>, umbrella <nonformal>, brolly <Brit non-
formal>; pilot chute, drogue chute;
rip cord, safety loop, shroud lines, harness, pack, vent; parachute jump, brollyhop <Brit nonformal>; sky dive; brake *or*
braking *or* deceleration parachute; para-
wing *or* paraglider *or* parafoil

14 **kite,** box kite, Eddy kite, Hargrave *or* cellular kite, tetrahedral kite

182 WATER TRAVEL

NOUNS 1 water travel, travel by water, marine *or* ocean *or* sea travel, **navigation,**
navigating, **seafaring, sailing,** steaming,
passage-making, voyaging, **cruising,**
coasting, gunkholing <nonformal>;
boating, yachting, motorboating, canoe-

ing, rowing, sculling; circumnavigation,
periplus; navigability

2 <methods> celestial navigation, astronavigation; radio navigation, radio beacon; loran; consolan, shoran; coastal
or coastwise navigation; dead reckoning;
point-to-point navigation; pilotage; sonar, radar, sofar; plane *or* traverse *or*
spherical *or* parallel *or* middle *or* latitude
or Mercator *or* great-circle *or* rhumbline
or composite sailing; fix, line of position;
sextant, chronometer, tables

3 **seamanship,** shipmanship; seamanliness,
seamanlikeness; weather eye; sea legs

4 **pilotship,** pilotry, pilotage, **helmsman-
ship;** steerage; proper piloting

5 embarkation 188.3; disembarkation
186.2

6 **voyage,** ocean *or* sea trip, **cruise,** sail;
course, **run, passage; crossing;** shakedown cruise; leg

7 **wake,** track; wash, backwash

8 <submarines> **surfacing,** breaking water; **submergence, dive;** stationary dive,
running dive, crash dive

9 **way, progress; headway,** steerageway,
sternway, leeway, driftway

10 **seaway, waterway,** fairway, road, channel, ocean *or* sea lane, ship route, steamer
track *or* lane; approaches

11 aquatics, **swimming, bathing,** natation,
balneation, **swim, bathe;** crawl, freestyle,
trudgen, Australian crawl, breaststroke,
butterfly, sidestroke, dog *or* doggie paddle, backstroke; treading water; floating;
diving 367.3; wading; fin; flipper, flapper;
fishtail; waterskiing, aquaplaning, surf-
boarding; surfing; windsurfing, board-
sailing

12 **swimmer, bather,** natator, merman;
bathing girl, mermaid; bathing beauty;
frogman; diver 367.4

VERBS 13 **navigate, sail, cruise,** steam, run,
seafare, voyage, ply, go on shipboard, go
by ship, go on *or* take a voyage, "go down
to the sea in ships"—Bible; go to sea, sail
the sea, sail the ocean blue; **boat, yacht,**
motorboat, canoe, row, scull; surf, wind-
surf, boardsail; steamboat; bear *or* carry
sail; cross, traverse, make a passage *or*
run; sail round, circumnavigate; coast

14 **pilot,** helm, coxswain, **steer,** guide, be at
the helm *or* tiller, direct, manage, handle,
run, operate, **conn** *or* cond, be at *or* have
the conn; **navigate,** shape *or* chart a
course

15 **anchor,** come to anchor, lay anchor, **cast
anchor,** let go the anchor, drop the hook;
carry out the anchor; kedge, kedge off;

dock, tie up; **moor,** pick up the mooring;
run out a warp *or* rope; lash, lash and tie;
foul the anchor; disembark 186.8

16 **ride at anchor,** ride, lie, rest; ride easy;
ride hawse full; lie athwart; set an anchor
watch

17 **lay** *or* **lie to,** lay *or* lie by; lie near *or* close
to the wind, head to wind *or* windward,
be under the sea; lie ahull; lie off, lie off
the land; lay *or* lie up

18 **weigh anchor,** up-anchor, bring the anchor home, break out the anchor, cat the
anchor, break ground, loose for sea; **un-
moor,** drop the mooring, cast off *or* loose
or away

19 **get under way,** put *or* have way upon, **put**
or **push** *or* **shove off;** hoist the blue Peter;
put to sea, put out to sea, go to sea, head
for blue water, go off soundings; **sail,** sail
away; embark

20 **set sail,** hoist sail, unfurl *or* spread sail,
heave out a sail, **make sail,** trim sail;
square away, square the yards; **crowd** *or*
clap *or* **crack** *or* **pack on sail,** put on
<more> sail; clap on, crack on, pack on;
give her beans <nonformal>

21 **make way,** gather way, **make headway,**
make sternway; make knots, foot; **go full
speed ahead,** go full speed astern; go *or*
run *or* steam at flank speed

22 run, **run** *or* **sail before the wind,** run *or*
sail with the wind, run *or* sail down the
wind, make a spinnaker run, sail off the
wind, sail free, sail with the wind aft, sail
with the wind abaft the beam; tack down
wind; run *or* sail with the wind quartering

23 **bring off the wind, pay off,** bear off *or*
away, put the helm to leeward, bear *or*
head to leeward, pay off the head

24 **sail against the wind,** sail on *or* by the
wind, sail to windward, bear *or* head to
windward; **bring in** *or* **into the wind,**
bring by *or* on the wind, haul the wind *or*
one's wind; uphelm, put the helm up;
haul, haul off, haul up; **haul to, bring to,
heave to;** sail in *or* into the wind's eye *or*
the teeth of the wind; sail to the windward of, weather

25 **sail near the wind,** sail close to the wind,
lie near *or* close to the wind, sail full and
by, hold a close wind, **sail close-hauled,**
close-haul; work *or* go *or* beat *or* eat to
windward, **beat, ply; luff,** luff up, sail
closer to the wind; sail too close to the
wind, sail fine, touch the wind, pinch

26 **gain to windward of,** eat *or* claw to windward of, eat the wind out of, have the
wind of, be to windward of

27 **chart** *or* **plot** *or* **lay out a course;** shape a
course, lay *or* lie a course

28 take *or* follow a course, **keep** *or* **hold the
course** *or* **a course,** hold on the course *or* a
course, stand on *or* upon a course, stand
on a straight course, maintain *or* keep the
heading, keep her steady, keep pointed

29 **drift off course, yaw,** yaw off, pay off,
bear off, drift, sag; sag *or* bear *or* ride *or*
drive to leeward, make leeway, drive,
fetch away; be set by the current, drift
with the current, fall down

30 **change course,** change the heading, bear
off *or* away, bear to starboard *or* port;
sheer, swerve; **tack,** cast, break, yaw,
slew, shift, turn; **cant,** cant round *or*
across; **beat, ply; veer, wear, wear ship;
jibe** *or* gybe <both Brit>, jibe all standing, make a North River jibe; **put about,**
come *or* go *or* bring *or* fetch about, beat
about, cast *or* throw about; bring *or*
swing *or* heave *or* haul round; **about ship,**
turn *or* put back, turn on her heel, wind;
swing the stern; box off; back and fill;
stand off and on; double *or* round a point;
miss stays

31 put the rudder hard left *or* right, put the
rudder *or* helm hard over, put the rudder
amidships, ease the rudder *or* helm, give
her more *or* less rudder

32 **veer** *or* **wear short,** bring by the lee,
broach to, lie beam on to the seas

33 <come to a stop> **fetch up, heave to,**
haul up, fetch up all standing

34 **backwater,** back, reverse, go astern; **go
full speed astern;** make sternway

35 **sail for, put away for, make for** *or* toward, make at, **run for,** stand for, head *or*
steer toward, lay for, **lay a** *or* **one's course
for,** bear up for; bear up to, **bear down on**
or **upon,** run *or* bear in with, **close with;**
make, reach, fetch; heave *or* go alongside;
lay *or* go aboard; lay *or* lie in; **put in** *or*
into, put into port, approach anchorage

36 **sail away from,** head *or* steer away from,
run from, **stand from,** lay away *or* off
from; **stand off,** bear off, put off, shove
off, haul off; stand off and on

37 **clear the land,** bear off the land, lay *or*
settle the land, make *or* get sea room

38 **make land,** reach land; close with the
land, stand in for the land; sight land;
smell land; make a landfall

39 **coast,** sail coast-wise, stay in soundings,
range the coast, skirt the shore, lie along
the shore, **hug the shore** *or* **land** *or* **coast**

40 **weather the storm,** weather, ride, **ride
out,** outride, ride *or* ride out a storm;
make heavy *or* bad weather

41 sail into, run down, run in *or* into, **ram; come** *or* **run foul** *or* **afoul of, collide,** fall aboard; nose *or* head into, run prow *or* end *or* head on, run head and head; run broadside on

42 shipwreck, wreck, pile up <nonformal>, cast away; **go** *or* **run aground,** ground, take the ground, beach, strand, run on the rocks; ground hard and fast

43 careen, list, heel, tip, cant, heave *or* lay down, lie along; be on beam ends

44 capsize, upset, overset, **overturn,** turn over, turn turtle, upset the boat, keel, keel over *or* up; pitchpole, somersault; **sink, founder,** be lost, go down, go to the bottom, go to Davy Jones's locker; scuttle

45 go overboard, go by the board, go over the board *or* side

46 maneuver, execute a maneuver; heave in together, keep in formation, maintain position, **keep station,** keep pointed, steam in line, steam in line of bearing; convoy

47 <submarines> **surface,** break water; **submerge, dive,** crash-dive, go below; rig for diving; flood the tanks, flood negative

48 <activities aboard ship> lay, lay aloft, lay forward, etc; traverse a yard, brace a yard fore and aft; heave, haul; kedge; warp; boom; heave round, heave short, heave apeak; log, heave *or* stream the log; haul down, board; spar down; ratline down, clap on ratlines; batten down the hatches; unlash, cut *or* cast loose; clear hawse

49 trim ship, trim, trim up; trim by the head *or* stern, put in proper fore-and-aft trim, give greater draft fore and aft, **put on an even keel; ballast,** shift ballast, wing out ballast; break out ballast, break bulk, shoot ballast; **clear the decks,** clear for action, take action stations

50 reduce sail, shorten *or* take in sail, hand a sail, **reef,** reef one's sails; double-reef; lower sail, dowse sail; run under bare poles; snug down; **furl,** put on a harbor furl

51 take bearings, cast a traverse; correct distance and maintain the bearings; run down the latitude, **take a sight,** shoot the sun, bring down the sun; **box the compass; take soundings** 275.9

52 signal, make a signal, speak, hail and speak; dress ship; unfurl *or* hoist a banner, unfurl an ensign, **break out a flag;** hoist the blue Peter; show one's colors, **exchange colors;** salute, dip the ensign

53 row, paddle, ply the oar, **pull, scull, punt;** give way, row away; catch *or* cut a crab *or* lobster <nonformal>; feather, feather an oar; sky an oar <nonformal>; row dry <Brit nonformal>; pace, shoot; ship oars

54 float, ride, drift; **sail, scud, run,** shoot; skim, foot; ghost, glide, slip; ride the sea, plow the deep, walk the waters

55 pitch, toss, tumble, toss and tumble, pitch and toss, **plunge,** hobbyhorse, pound, **rear, rock, roll, reel, swing, sway, lurch, yaw, heave,** scend, **flounder, welter, wallow;** make heavy weather

56 swim, bathe, go in swimming *or* bathing; tread water; **float,** float on one's back, do the deadman's float; **wade,** go in wading; skinny-dip; dive 367.6

ADJS **57 nautical, marine, maritime, naval, navigational; seafaring, seagoing, oceangoing,** seaborne, water-borne; seamanly, seamanlike, **salty** <nonformal>; pelagic, oceanic 240.8

58 aquatic, water-dwelling, water-living, water-growing, water-loving; **swimming,** balneal, natant, natatory, natatorial; shore, seashore; tidal, estuarine, littoral, grallatorial; riverine; deep-sea 275.14

59 navigable, boatable

60 floating, afloat, awash; water-borne

61 adrift, afloat, unmoored, untied, loose, unanchored, aweigh; cast-off, started

ADVS **62 on board,** on shipboard, on board ship, **aboard,** all aboard, afloat; **on deck,** topside; aloft; in sail; before the mast; athwart the hawse, athwarthawse

63 under way, making way, with steerageway, with way on; **at sea,** on the high seas, off soundings, in blue water; **under sail** *or* **canvas,** with sails spread; under press of sail *or* canvas *or* steam; under steam *or* power; under bare poles; on *or* off the heading *or* course; in soundings, homeward bound

64 before the wind, with the wind, down the wind, running free; off the wind, with the wind aft, with the wind abaft the beam, wing and wing, under the wind, under the lee; on a reach, on a beam *or* broad reach, with wind abeam

65 against the wind, on the wind, in *or* into the wind, up the wind, by the wind, head to wind; in *or* into the wind's eye, in the teeth of the wind

66 near the wind, close to the wind, **closehauled,** on a beat, full and by

67 coastward, landward, to landward; **coastwise,** coastways

68 leeward, to leeward, alee, downwind; **windward,** to windward, weatherward, aweather, upwind

69 aft, abaft, baft, **astern;** fore and aft

70 alongside, board and board, yardarm to yardarm
71 at anchor, riding at anchor; lying to, hove to; lying ahull
72 afoul, foul, in collision; head and head, head *or* end *or* prow on; broadside on
73 aground, on the rocks; hard and fast
74 overboard, over the board *or* side, by the board; aft the fantail

183 MARINER

NOUNS **1 mariner, seaman, sailor,** sailor-man, **navigator, seafarer,** seafaring man, bluejacket, sea *or* water dog <nonformal>, crewman, shipman, jack, jacky, jack afloat, jack-tar, **tar, salt** <nonformal>, hearty, lobscouser <nonformal>, *matelot* <Fr>, windsailor, windjammer; limey *or* limejuicer <nonformal>, lascar <India>; common *or* ordinary seaman, OD; able *or* able-bodied seaman, AB; deep-sea man, saltwater *or* bluewater *or* deepwater sailor; fresh-water sailor; fair-weather sailor; whaler, fisherman, lobsterman; viking, sea rover, buccaneer, privateer, pirate; Jason, Argonaut, Ancient Mariner, Flying Dutchman; Neptune, Poseidon, Varuna, Dylan; **yachtsman, yachtswoman,** sailor, cruising sailor, racing sailor
2 <novice> **lubber, landlubber;** polliwog
3 <veteran> **old salt** *and* old sea dog *and* shell-back *and* barnacle-back <all nonformal>; **master mariner**
4 navy man, man-of-war's man, **bluejacket; gob** *and* swabbie *and* swabber <all nonformal>; **marine, leatherneck** *and* gyrene *and* devil dog <all nonformal>, Royal Marine, jolly <Brit nonformal>; horse marine; boot <nonformal>; **midshipman,** midshipmate, middy <nonformal>; cadet, naval cadet; coastguardsman, Naval Reservist, Seabee, frogman
5 boatman, boatsman, boat-handler, **boater,** waterman; **oarsman,** oar, rower, sculler, punter; galley slave; **ferryman,** ferrier; **bargeman,** barger, bargee <Brit>, bargemaster; lighterman, wherryman; **gondolier,** *gondoliere* <Ital>
6 hand, **deckhand,** deckie <Brit>, roustabout <nonformal>; stoker, fireman, bakehead <nonformal>; black gang; wiper, oiler, boilerman; cabin boy; yeoman, ship's writer; purser; ship's carpenter, chips <nonformal>; ship's cooper, bungs *or* Jimmy Bungs <nonformal>; ship's tailor, snip *or* snips <non-

formal>; steward, stewardess, commissary steward, mess steward, hospital steward; commissary clerk; mail orderly; navigator; radio operator, sparks <nonformal>; landing signalman; gunner, gun loader, torpedoman; afterguard; complement; watch
7 <ship's officers> **captain,** shipmaster, **master, skipper** <nonformal>, **commander,** the Old Man <nonformal>, *patron* <Fr>; navigator, navigating officer, sailing master; deck officer, officer of the deck *or* OD; watch officer, officer of the watch; **mate,** first *or* chief mate, second mate, third mate, boatswain's mate; **boatswain,** bos'n, pipes <nonformal>; quartermaster; sergeant-at-arms; chief engineer, engine-room officer; naval officer 575.20
8 steersman, helmsman, wheelman, wheelsman, boatsteerer; quartermaster; **coxswain,** cox <nonformal>; **pilot,** conner, sailing master; harbor pilot, docking pilot
9 longshoreman, wharf hand, dockhand, docker, dockworker, dock-walloper <nonformal>; **stevedore,** loader; **roustabout** <nonformal>, lumper

184 AVIATION

NOUNS **1 aviation, aeronautics;** airplaning, skyriding, **flying, flight,** winging; volation, volitation; aeronautism, aerodromics; powered flight, jet flight, subsonic *or* supersonic flight; cruising, cross-country flying; bush flying; **gliding,** sail-planing, soaring, sailing; volplaning; ballooning, balloonery, lighter-than-air aviation; barnstorming <nonformal>; high-altitude flying; blind *or* instrument flight *or* flying, instrument flight rules *or* IFR; contact flying, visual flight *or* flying, visual flight rules *or* VFR, pilotage; skywriting; cloud-seeding; in-flight training, ground school; **air traffic,** airline traffic, air-traffic control, air-traffic controller; commercial aviation, general aviation, private aviation, private flying; astronautics 1073.1; air show, flying circus
2 air sciences <see list>, aeronautical sciences
3 airmanship, pilotship; **flight plan;** briefing, brief, rundown <nonformal>, debriefing; flight *or* pilot training, flying lessons; washout <nonformal>
4 air-mindedness, aerophilia; air legs
5 airsickness; aerophobia, aeropathy

6 **navigation,** avigation, aerial *or* air navigation; celestial navigation, astronavigation; electronic navigation, automatic electronic navigation, radio navigation, navar, radar, consolan, tacan, teleran, loran, shoran; omnidirectional range, omni-range, visual-aural range *or* VAR

7 <aeronautical organizations> Civil Aeronautics Administration *or* CAA; Federal Aviation Agency *or* FAA; Bureau of Aeronautics, BuAer; National Advisory Committee for Aeronautics *or* NACA; Office of Naval Research *or* ONR; Civil Air Patrol *or* CAP; Caterpillar Club; Airline Pilots Association; Aircraft Recognition Society *or* ARS; Air Force 461.29

8 **takeoff,** hopoff <nonformal>; taxiing, takeoff run, takeoff power, rotation; daisy-clipping *and* grass-cutting <both nonformal>; ground loop; level-off; jet-assisted takeoff *or* JATO, booster rocket, takeoff rocket; catapult, electropult

9 **flight, trip, run; hop** *and* **jump** <both nonformal>; powered flight; solo flight, **solo;** inverted flight; supersonic flight; test flight, **test hop** <nonformal>; **airlift;** airdrop

10 **air travel,** air transport, air transportation; **airfreight, air cargo; airline travel, airline,** airline service, air service, feeder airline, commuter airline, scheduled airline, charter airline, nonscheduled airline *or* nonsked <nonformal>, short-hop airline; **shuttle,** air shuttle, shuttle service, shuttle trip; air taxi

11 <Air Force> **mission,** flight operation; training mission; gunnery mission; combat rehearsal, **dry run** <nonformal>; transition mission; reconnaissance mission, reconnaissance, observation flight, search mission; **milk run** <nonformal>; box-top mission <nonformal>; combat flight; **sortie,** scramble <nonformal>; **air raid;** shuttle raid; bombing mission; bombing, strafing 459.7; **air support** <for ground troops>, **air cover,** cover, umbrella, air umbrella

12 flight formation, formation flying, formation; close formation, loose formation, wing formation; V formation, echelon

13 <maneuvers> acrobatic *or* tactical evolutions *or* maneuvers, acrobatics, **aerobatics;** stunting *and* **stunt flying** <both nonformal>, rolling, crabbing, banking, porpoising, fishtailing, diving; **dive, nose dive, power dive; zoom,** chandelle; stall, whip stall; **glide,** volplane; spiral, split 'S', lazy eight, sideslip, pushdown, pull-up, pull-out

14 **roll, barrel roll,** aileron roll, outside roll, **snap roll**

15 **spin,** autorotation, **tailspin,** flat spin, inverted spin, normal spin, power spin, uncontrolled spin, falling leaf; whipstall

16 **loop,** spiral loop, ground loop, normal loop, outside loop, inverted normal *or* outside loop, dead-stick loop, wingover, looping the loop; Immelmann turn, reverse turn, reversement; flipper turns

17 **buzzing,** flathatting *and* **hedgehopping** <both nonformal>

18 **landing,** coming in <nonformal>, touching down, touchdown; arrival; landing run, landing pattern; approach, downwind leg, approach leg; holding pattern, stack up <nonformal>; ballooning in, parachute approach; blind *or* instrument landing, dead-stick landing, glide landing, stall landing, fishtail landing, sideslip landing, level *or* two-point landing, normal *or* three-point landing, Chinese landing <nonformal>, tail-high landing, tail-low landing, thumped-in landing <nonformal>, pancake landing, belly landing, crash landing, noseover, nose-up; practice landing, bounce drill

19 flying and landing guides marker, pylon; beacon; radio beacon, radio range station, radio marker; fan marker; radar beacon, racon; beam, radio beam; beacon lights; runway lights, high-intensity runway approach lights, sequence flashers, flare path; wind indicator, wind cone *or* sock, air sleeve; instrument landing system *or* ILS; touchdown rate of descent indicator *or* TRODI; ground-controlled approach *or* GCA; talking-down system, talking down

20 **crash, crack-up,** prang <Brit nonformal>; crash landing; collision, mid-air collision; near-miss, near collision

21 **blackout;** grayout; anoxia; useful consciousness; pressure suit, antiblackout suit

22 **airport, airfield, airdrome,** aerodrome <Brit>, drome, port, air harbor <Can>, aviation field, **landing field,** landing, field, airship station; **air terminal, jetport; air base,** air station, naval air station; airpark; **heliport,** helidrome; control tower, island; Air Route Traffic Control Center; baggage pickup, baggage carousel

23 **runway, taxiway,** strip, landing strip, **airstrip, flight strip,** take-off strip; fairway, launching way; stopway; clearway; transition strip; apron; **flight deck,** landing deck; helipad

24 **hangar,** housing, dock, airdock, shed, airship shed; mooring mast
25 <propulsion> rocket propulsion, rocket
power; **jet propulsion,** jet power; turbojet
propulsion, pulse-jet propulsion, ram-jet
propulsion, resojet propulsion; constant
or ram pressure, air ram; reaction propulsion, reaction, action and reaction;
aeromotor, aircraft engine, power plant
26 **lift,** lift ratio, lift force or component, lift
direction; aerostatic lift, dynamic lift,
gross lift, useful lift, margin of lift
27 **drag,** resistance; drag ratio, drag force or
component, induced drag, wing drag,
parasite or parasitic or structural drag,
profile drag, head resistance, drag direction, cross-wind force
28 **drift,** drift angle; lateral drift, leeway
29 flow, air flow, laminar flow; **turbulence,**
turbulent flow, burble, burble point, ed-
dies
30 wash, wake, stream; downwash; backwash, **slipstream,** propeller race,
propwash; **exhaust,** jet exhaust, blow
wash; **vapor trail,** condensation trail,
contrail, vortex
31 <speed> **air speed,** true air speed, operating or flying speed, cruising speed,
knots, minimum flying speed, hump
speed, peripheral speed, pitch speed, terminal speed, sinking speed, get-away or
take-off speed, landing speed, ground
speed, speed over the ground; **speed of
sound** 174.2; zone of no signal, Mach
cone; **sound barrier,** sonic barrier or wall;
sonic boom, shock wave, Mach wave
32 <air, atmosphere> **airspace,** navigable
airspace; aerosphere; **aerospace;** space,
empty space; **weather, weather conditions; ceiling,** ballonet ceiling, service
ceiling, static ceiling, absolute ceiling;
ceiling and visibility unlimited or CAVU;
severe clear <nonformal>; cloud layer or
cover, ceiling zero; visibility, visibility
zero; **overcast,** undercast; fog, soup
<nonformal>; high-pressure area, low-
pressure area; trough, trough line; front;
air pocket or **hole,** air bump, pocket, hole,
bump; **turbulence;** clear-air turbulence
or CAT; roughness; head wind, unfavorable wind; tail wind, favorable or favoring wind; cross wind; atmospheric tides;
jetstream
33 **airway, air lane, air line,** air route, sky-
way, corridor, flight path, lane, path
34 **course, heading,** vector; compass heading
or course, compass direction, magnetic
heading, true heading or course
35 <altitude> altitude of flight, absolute altitude, critical altitude, density altitude,
pressure altitude, sextant altitude; clearance; ground elevation
VERBS **36 fly,** be airborne, wing, take wing,
wing one's way, take or make a flight,
take to the air, take the air, volitate, be
wafted; **jet;** aviate, airplane, aeroplane;
travel by air, go or travel by airline, go by
plane or air, take to the airways, ride the
skies; hop <nonformal>; **soar,** drift,
hover; **cruise; glide,** sailplane, sail, volplane; hydroplane, seaplane; balloon;
ferry; airlift; break the sound barrier;
navigate, avigate
37 **pilot,** control, be at the controls, **fly,** manipulate, drive <nonformal>, fly left
seat; **copilot,** fly right seat; solo; **barnstorm** <nonformal>; fly blind, fly by the
seat of one's pants <nonformal>; follow
the beam, ride the beam, fly on instruments; fly in formation, take position;
peel off
38 **take off,** hop or jump off <nonformal>,
become airborne, get off or leave the
ground, take to the air, go or fly aloft,
clear; rotate, power off; **taxi**
39 **ascend,** climb, gain altitude, mount;
zoom, hoick <nonformal>, chandelle
40 <maneuver> **stunt** <nonformal>, perform aerobatics; crab, fishtail; **spin,** go
into a tailspin; **loop,** loop the loop; **roll,**
wingover, spiral, undulate, porpoise,
feather, yaw, sideslip, skid, bank, dip,
nose down, nose up, pull up, push down,
pull out, plow, mush through
41 **dive,** nose-dive, power-dive, go for the
deck; lose altitude, settle, dump altitude
<nonformal>
42 **buzz,** flathat and **hedgehop** <both non-
formal>
43 **land,** set her down <nonformal>, **alight,
light,** touch down; **descend,** come down,
dump altitude <nonformal>, fly down;
come in, come in for a landing; **level off,**
flatten out; upwind, downwind; overshoot, undershoot; make a dead-stick
landing; pancake, thump in <nonfor-
mal>; bellyland, settle down, balloon in;
fishtail down; **crash-land;** ditch <nonfor-
mal>; nose up, nose over; talk down
44 **crash, crack up,** prang <Brit nonfor-
mal>, spin in, fail to pull out
45 **stall,** lose power, conk out <nonformal>;
flame out
46 **black out,** gray out
47 **parachute, bail out, jump,** make a parachute jump, hit the silk, make a brollyhop
<Brit nonformal>, sky-dive
48 **brief,** give a briefing; debrief

ADJS **49 aviation, aeronautic, aeronautical,**
aerial; **aviatorial,** aviational; aerodontic,
aerospace, aerotechnical, aerostatic,
aerostatical, aeromechanic, aeromechanical, aerodynamic, aerodynamical, avi-
onic, aeronomic, aerophysical; aeroma-
rine; aerobatic; airworthy, air-minded,
air-conscious, aeromedical; air-wise; airsick
50 flying, airborne, winging, soaring; volant,
volitant, volitational, hovering, fluttering; gliding; jet-propelled, rocket-
propelled
ADVS **51 in flight, on the wing** or fly, while
airborne
52 air sciences

aeroballistics	aerostation
acronomy	aerotechnics
aerial photography	aircraft hydraulics
aerocartography	aviation medicine or
aerodontia	aeromedicine
aerodynamics	aviation technology
aerogeography	avionics
aerogeology	climatology
aerography	hydrostatics
aerology	jet engineering
aeromechanics	kinematics
aerometry	kinetics
aeronautical engi-	meteorology
neering	micrometry
aeronautical mete-	photometry
orology	pneumatics
aerophotography	rocket engineering
aerophysics	rocketry
aeroscopy	supersonic aerody-
aerospace research	namics
aerostatics	supersonics

185 AVIATOR

NOUNS **1 aviator, airman, flier, pilot,** air pilot, licensed pilot, private pilot, airline
pilot, commercial pilot, aeronaut, flyboy
and airplane driver *and* birdman <all
nonformal>; aircrew member; captain,
chief pilot; copilot, second officer; flight
engineer, third officer; jet pilot, jet jockey
<nonformal>; instructor; test pilot; bush
pilot; astronaut 1073.8; cloud seeder,
rainmaker; cropduster; barnstormer
<nonformal>; stunt man, stunt flier
2 aviatrix, aviatress, **airwoman,** bird-
woman <nonformal>; stuntwoman
3 military pilot, naval pilot, combat pilot;
fighter pilot; bomber pilot; observer; **aviation cadet,** air *or* flying cadet, pilot
trainee; flyboy <nonformal>; ace; air
force 461.29
4 crew, aircrew, flight crew; crewman,
crewmate, crewmember, aircrewman;

navigator, avigator; **bombardier;** gunner,
machine gunner, belly gunner, tail gunner; crew chief; aerial photographer;
meteorologist; **flight attendant, steward,
stewardess,** hostess, stew <nonformal>
5 ground crew, landing crew, plane han-
dlers; crew chief
6 aircraftsman, aeromechanic, aircraft mechanic, mechanic, grease monkey <non-
formal>; rigger; aeronautical engineer,
jet engineer, rocket engineer 1072.11;
ground tester, flight tester
7 balloonist, ballooner, aeronaut
8 parachutist, chutist *or* chuter <nonfor-
mal>, parachute jumper, sports parachutist; sky diver; smoke jumper; **paratrooper;** paradoctor, paramedic; jump-
master
9 <mythological fliers> Daedalus, Icarus

186 ARRIVAL

NOUNS **1 arrival, coming, advent,** approach,
appearance, **reaching; attainment, accomplishment, achievement**
2 landing, landfall; docking, mooring,
tying up, dropping anchor; **getting off,
disembarkation,** disembarkment, debarkation, coming *or* going ashore;
deplaning
3 return, homecoming, recursion; reentrance, **reentry;** remigration
4 welcome, greetings 585.3
5 destination, goal, bourn <old>; port, haven, harbor, anchorage, **journey's end;**
end of the line, terminus, **terminal,** terminal point; stop, stopping place, last stop;
airport, air terminal 184.22
VERBS **6 arrive,** arrive at, arrive in, come,
come *or* **get to,** approach, access, **reach,
hit** <nonformal>; find, **gain,** attain, attain to, accomplish, achieve, make, **make
it** <nonformal>, fetch, fetch up at, get
there, reach one's destination, come to
one's journey's end, end up; **come to rest,**
settle, settle in; **make** *or* **put in an appearance, show up** <nonformal>, turn up,
surface, pop *or* bob up *and* make the
scene <all nonformal>; **get in, come in,**
blow in <nonformal>, pull in, roll in;
check in; clock *or* punch *or* ring *or* time in
<all nonformal>, sign in; hit town <non-
formal>; come to hand, be received
7 arrive at, come at, get at, **reach,** arrive
upon, **come upon, hit upon,** strike upon,
fall upon, light upon, pitch upon, stumble
on *or* upon
8 land, come to land, make a landfall, set
foot on dry land; reach *or* make land,

make port; put in *or* into, put into port;
dock, moor, tie up, anchor, drop anchor;
go ashore, **disembark,** debark, unboat;
detrain, debus, **deplane, disemplane;**
alight

ADJS **9 arriving,** approaching, entering, **coming,** incoming; inbound, inwardbound;
homeward, homeward-bound

ADVS **10 arriving,** on arrival *or* arriving

187 RECEPTION

NOUNS **1 reception, taking in,** receipt, receiving; **welcome,** welcoming, cordial
welcome, open *or* welcoming arms; refuge 1008

 2 admission, admittance, acceptance; im-
mission <old>, intromission 191.1;
installation, installment, instatement, inauguration, initiation; baptism, investiture, ordination; enlistment, enrollment,
induction

 3 entree, entrée, in <nonformal>, entry,
entrance 189, **access,** opening, **open door,**
open arms; a foot in the door, opening
wedge

 4 ingestion; eating 8; **drinking** 8.3, imbibing, imbibition; engorgement, ingurgita-
tion, engulfment; **swallowing,** gulping;
swallow, gulp, slurp

 5 <drawing in> **suction,** suck, sucking; **inhalation,** inhalement, inspiration,
aspiration; snuff, snuffle, sniff, sniffle

 6 sorption, **absorption,** adsorption, chem-
isorption *or* chemosorption, engrossment, digestion, **assimilation,** infiltration; **sponging, blotting; seepage,**
percolation; **osmosis,** endosmosis, exos-
mosis, electroosmosis; absorbency;
absorbent, adsorbent, **sponge, blotter,**
blotting paper

 7 <bringing in> **introduction; importing,**
import, **importation**

 8 readmission; reabsorption, resorbence

 9 receptivity, receptiveness, welcoming,
welcome, invitingness, openness, hospitality, cordiality, recipience *or*
recipiency; receptibility, admissibility

VERBS **10 receive, take in; admit, let in,** im-
mit <old>, intromit, give entrance *or* admittance to; **welcome,** bid welcome, give
a royal welcome, roll out the red carpet;
give an entree, open the door to, give refuge *or* shelter *or* sanctuary to, throw open
to

 11 ingest, eat 8.18, tuck away, put away; imbibe, **drink; swallow, devour,** ingurgi-
tate; **engulf,** engorge; **gulp,** gulp down,
swill, swill down, wolf down, gobble

 12 draw in, suck, suckle, suck in *or* up, aspirate; **inhale,** inspire, breathe in; snuff,
snuffle, sniff, sniffle, snuff in *or* up, slurp

 13 absorb, adsorb, chemisorb *or* chemosorb,
assimilate, engross, digest, **drink,** imbibe,
take up *or* in, drink up *or* in, slurp up,
swill up; blot, **blot up, soak up,** sponge;
osmose; infiltrate, filter in; **soak in, seep
in,** percolate in

 14 bring in, introduce, import

 15 readmit; reabsorb, resorb

ADJS **16 receptive,** recipient; welcoming,
open, hospitable, cordial, inviting, invitatory; introceptive; **admissive,** admissory;
receivable, receptible, admissible; intro-
missive, intromittent; ingestive, imbibitory

 17 sorbent, **absorbent,** adsorbent, chem-
isorptive *or* chemosorptive, **assimilative,**
digestive; bibulous, imbibitory, thirsty,
soaking, blotting; spongy, spongeous; os-
motic, endosmotic, exosmotic; resorbent

 18 introductory, introductive; **initiatory,**
initiative, baptismal

188 DEPARTURE

NOUNS **1 departure, leaving, going,** passing,
parting; exit, walkout <nonformal>;
egress 190.2; **withdrawal,** removal, retreat 163.2, retirement; evacuation,
abandonment, desertion; decampment;
escape, flight, getaway <nonformal>; exodus, hegira; migration, mass migration;
defection, voting with one's feet

 2 start, starting, start-off, setoff, setout,
takeoff *and* getaway <both nonformal>;
the starting gun *or* pistol; break; the
green light

 3 embarkation, embarkment, boarding;
entrainment; enplanement *or* emplane-
ment, **takeoff,** hopoff <nonformal>

 4 leave-taking, leave, parting, departure,
congé; **send-off,** Godspeed; **adieu,** one's
adieus, **farewell,** aloha, **good-bye;** valedictory address, valedictory, valediction,
parting words; parting *or* Parthian shot;
swan song; viaticum; stirrup cup, one for
the road, *doch-an-dorrach* or *doch-an-
dorris* <Gaelic>

 5 point of departure, starting place *or*
point, takeoff, **start,** base, baseline, basis;
line of departure; starting line *or* post *or*
gate, starting blocks; stakeboat; port of
embarkation

VERBS **6 depart,** make off, begone, be off,
take oneself off *or* away, take one's departure, take leave *or* take one's leave, **leave,
go, go away, go off, get off** *or* **away,** get

under way, come away, go one's way, go *or* get along, be getting along, gang along <Scots>, go on, get on; move off *or* away, move out, march off *or* away; **pull out;** decamp; exit; take *or* break *or* tear oneself away, take oneself off, take wing *or* flight

7 <nonformal terms> **beat it, split,** scram, up and go, trot, toddle, stagger along, mosey *or* sashay along, buzz off, buzz along, bug out, bugger off <Brit>, fuck off *or* f off, get rolling, hightail it, pull up stakes, check out, clear out, cut out, haul ass, hit the road *or* trail, piss off <chiefly Brit>, get lost, flake off, get going, shove off, push along, push off, get out, get *or* git, clear out, get the hell out, make oneself scarce, vamoose, take off, skip, skip out, lam, take it on the lam, powder, take a powder, take a runout powder, skedaddle, absquatulate <old>

8 **set out, set forth,** put forth, go forth, **sally forth,** sally, issue, issue forth, launch forth, set forward, **set off,** be off, be on one's way, outset, **start, start out** *or* **off, strike out,** get off, get away, get off the dime <nonformal>; get the green light, break; set sail

9 **quit, vacate,** evacuate, abandon, desert, turn one's back on, walk away from, leave to one's fate, leave flat *or* high and dry; leave *or* desert a sinking ship; **withdraw,** retreat, **beat a retreat,** retire, remove; walk away, abscond, disappear, vanish; **bow out** <nonformal>, make one's exit; jump ship

10 **hasten off, hurry away; scamper off, dash off,** whiz off, whip off *or* away, nip *and* nip off <both nonformal>, tear off *or* out, **light out** <nonformal>, dig *or* skin out *and* burn rubber <all nonformal>

11 **fling out** *or* **off,** flounce out *or* off

12 **run off** *or* **away,** run along, flee, take to flight, fly, take to one's heels, cut and run *and* hightail *and* make tracks *and* absquatulate <old> <all nonformal>, scarper <Brit nonformal>; run for one's life; beat a retreat *or* a hasty retreat; run away from 368.10

13 **check out;** clock *and* ring *and* punch out <all nonformal>, sign out

14 **decamp, break camp,** strike camp *or* tent, **pull up stakes**

15 **embark, go aboard,** board, go on board; go on shipboard, take ship; hoist the blue Peter; **entrain,** enplane *or* emplane, embus; weigh anchor, up-anchor, put to sea 182.19

16 say *or* bid good-bye *or* farewell, take leave, make one's adieus; bid Godspeed, give one a send-off *or* a big send-off, see off *or* out, "speed the parting guest"— Pope; drink a stirrup cup, have one for the road

17 **leave home,** go from home; leave the country, emigrate, out-migrate, expatriate, defect; vote with one's feet; burn one's bridges

ADJS 18 **departing, leaving; parting,** last, final, farewell; valedictory; outward-bound

19 **departed, left, gone,** gone off *or* away

ADVS 20 **hence,** thence, whence; off, **away,** forth, out; therefrom, thereof

PREPS 21 **from, away from;** out, out of

INTERJS 22 **farewell!, good-bye!, adieu!, so long!, I'm outa here** <both nonformal>, cheerio! <Brit>, *au revoir!* <Fr>, *¡adios!* <Sp>, *¡hasta la vista!* <Sp>, *¡hasta luego!* <Sp>, *¡vaya con Dios!* <Sp>, *auf Wiedersehen!* <Ger>, *addio!* <Ital>, *arrivederci!, arrivederla!* <both Ital>, *ciao!* <Ital nonformal>, *do svidanye!* <Russ>, *shalom!* <Heb>, *sayonara!* <Japanese>, *vale!, vive valeque!* <both L>, aloha!, **until we meet again!,** until tomorrow!, *à demain!* <Fr>, **see you later!,** see you!, tata, toodleoo, I'll be seeing you!, see you around!, we'll see you!, *à bientôt!* <Fr>, *à toute a l'heure!* <Fr>, *a domani* <Ital>; be good!, keep in touch!, come again!; *bon voyage!* <Fr>, pleasant journey!, have a nice trip!, *tsetchem leshalom!* <Heb>, *glückliche Reise!* <Ger>, happy landing!; Godspeed!, peace be with you!, *pax vobiscum!* <L>; all good go with you!, God bless you!

23 **good night!,** nighty-night! <nonformal>, *bonne nuit!* <Fr>, *gute Nacht!* <Ger>, *¡buenas noches!* <Sp>, *buona notte!* <Ital>

189 ENTRANCE

NOUNS 1 **entrance, entry,** access, entree, entrée; **ingress,** ingression; **admission, reception** 187; **ingoing, incoming,** income; **importation,** import, importing; **input, intake; penetration,** interpenetration, injection; infiltration, percolation, seepage, leakage; insinuation; intrusion 214; introduction, **insertion** 191

2 **influx, inflow,** inflooding, incursion, indraft, indrawing, inpour, inrun, inrush; afflux

3 **immigration,** in-migration, incoming population, foreign influx; border-crossing

4 **incomer, entrant,** comer, arrival; **visitor,** visitant; **immigrant,** in-migrant; newcomer 773.4; settler 227.9; **trespasser, intruder** 214.3

5 **entrance,** entry, gate, door, portal, **entranceway,** entryway; **inlet,** ingress, intake, adit, approach, **access,** means of access, in <nonformal>, way in; a foot in the door, an opening wedge, the camel's nose under the wall of the tent; **opening** 292; **passageway,** corridor, companionway, hall, hallway, passage, way; jetway, jet bridge; gangway, gangplank; **vestibule** 197.19; air lock

6 **porch,** propylaeum; **portal, threshold,** doorjamb, gatepost, doorpost, lintel; **door, doorway,** French door; **gate, gateway; hatch,** hatchway, scuttle

VERBS 7 **enter, go in** or **into,** access, cross the threshold, **come in,** find one's way into, put in or into; be admitted, gain admission or admittance, have an entree, have an in <nonformal>; **set foot in,** step in, walk in; **get in,** jump in, leap in, hop in; **drop in,** look in, visit, drop by or in, pop in <nonformal>; **breeze in,** come breezing in; break or burst in, bust or come busting in <nonformal>; **barge in** or come barging in *and* wade in <all nonformal>; thrust in, push or press in, crowd in, jam in, wedge in, pack in, squeeze in; slip or creep in, wriggle or worm oneself into, get one's foot in the door, edge in, work in, insinuate oneself, weigh in <nonformal>; irrupt, intrude 214.5; take in, admit 187.10; insert 191.3

8 **penetrate,** interpenetrate, **pierce,** pass or go through, get through, get into, make way into, make an entrance, gain entree; crash <nonformal>

9 **flow in,** inpour, **pour in**

10 **filter in, infiltrate, seep in,** percolate into, leak in, soak in, perfuse

11 **immigrate,** in-migrate; cross the border

ADJS 12 **entering,** ingressive, **incoming, ingoing;** in, inward; **inbound,** inward-bound; inflowing, influent, inflooding, inpouring, inrushing; invasive, intrusive, irruptive; ingrowing

ADVS 13 **in,** inward, inwards, inwardly; thereinto

PREPS 14 **into, in,** to

190 EMERGENCE

NOUNS 1 **emergence,** coming out, coming forth, coming into view, rising to the surface, surfacing; **issuing,** issuance, issue; extrusion; **emission,** emitting, giving forth, giving out; emanation; **vent,** venting, discharge

2 **egress,** egression; **exit,** exodus; outgoing, outgo, going out; emersion or egress <astronomy>; **departure** 188; extraction 192

3 **outburst** 671.6, ejection 908

4 **outflow,** outflowing; discharge; **outpouring,** outpour; effluence, effusion, exhalation; **efflux,** effluxion, defluxion; **exhaust; runoff, flowoff;** outfall; drainage, drain; gush 238.4

5 **leakage,** leaking, weeping <nonformal>; **leak; dripping,** drippings, **drip,** dribble, drop, trickle; distillation

6 **exuding,** exudation, transudation; **filtration,** exfiltration, filtering; straining; **percolation,** percolating; leaching, lixiviation; effusion, extravasation; **seepage,** seep; perfusion; **oozing,** ooze; weeping, weep; **excretion** 12

7 **emigration,** out-migration, remigration; exile, expatriation, defection, deportation

8 **export,** exporting, exportation

9 **outlet,** egress, **exit,** outgo, outcome, out <nonformal>, way out; loophole, escape; **opening** 292; outfall, estuary; chute, flume, sluice, weir, floodgate; **vent,** ventage, venthole, port; safety valve; avenue, channel; spout, tap; debouch; **exhaust;** door 189.6; outgate, sally port; vomitory; emunctory; pore; blowhole, spiracle

10 **goer,** outgoer, leaver, departer; **emigrant, émigré,** out-migrant; defector, refugee

VERBS 11 **emerge, come out, issue,** issue forth, come into view, extrude, **come forth; surface,** rise to the surface; sally, sally forth, come to the fore; emanate, effuse, arise, come; debouch, disembogue; jump out, leap out, hop out; bail out; **burst forth, break forth, erupt;** break cover, **come out in the open;** protrude

12 **exit,** make an exit, **make one's exit;** egress, **go out,** get out, walk out, march out, run out, pass out, bow out *and* include oneself out <both nonformal>; walk out on, leave cold <nonformal>; **depart** 188.6

13 **run out,** empty, find vent; **exhaust, drain,** drain out; **flow out,** outflow, outpour, **pour out,** sluice out, well out, gush or spout out, spew, flow, pour, well, surge, gush, jet, spout, spurt, vomit forth, blow out, spew out

14 **leak, leak out, drip,** dribble, drop, trickle, trill, distill

15 **exude,** exudate, transude, transpire, reek; **emit, discharge,** give off; **filter,** filtrate, exfiltrate; strain; **percolate;** leach, lixivi-

ate; effuse, extravasate; **seep, ooze;** bleed; weep; excrete 12.12

16 emigrate, out-migrate, remigrate; exile, expatriate, defect; deport

17 export, send abroad

ADJS **18 emerging,** emergent; **issuing,** arising, surfacing, coming, forthcoming; emanating, emanent, emanative, transeunt, transient

19 outgoing, outbound, outward-bound; **outflowing,** outpouring, effusive, effluent; effused, extravasated

20 exudative, exuding, transudative; percolative; porous, permeable, pervious, oozy, runny, weepy, leaky; excretory 12.19

ADVS **21 forth; out,** outward, outwards, outwardly

PREPS **22 out of,** ex; **from; out, forth**

191 INSERTION
<*putting in*>

NOUNS **1 insertion, introduction,** insinuation, injection, infusion, perfusion, inoculation, intromission; **entrance** 189; **penetration** 292.3; interjection, interpolation 213.2; graft, grafting, engrafting, transplant, transplantation; infixing, implantation, embedment, tessellation, impactment, impaction

2 insert, insertion; **inset, inlay;** gore, godet, gusset; **graft,** scion *or* cion; tessera

VERBS **3 insert, introduce,** insinuate, inject, infuse, perfuse, inoculate, intromit; **enter** 189.7; **penetrate; put in, stick in,** set in, throw in, pop in, tuck in, whip in; slip in, ease in; interject

4 install, instate, inaugurate, initiate, invest, ordain; enlist, enroll, induct, sign up, sign on

5 inset, inlay; embed *or* bed, bed in

6 graft, engraft, **implant,** imp <old>; bud; inarch

7 thrust in, drive in, run in, plunge in, force in, push in, **ram in,** press in, stuff in, crowd in, squeeze in, cram in, jam in, tamp in, pound in, pack in, poke in, knock in, wedge in, impact

8 implant, transplant; infix 854.9; fit in, **inlay;** tessellate

192 EXTRACTION
<*taking or drawing out*>

NOUNS **1 extraction, withdrawal,** removal; **drawing, pulling,** drawing out; ripping *or* tearing *or* wresting out; eradication, **uprooting,** unrooting, deracination; squeezing out, pressing out, expressing, expression; avulsion, evulsion, cutting out, exsection, extirpation, excision, enucleation; extrication, evolvement, disentanglement, unravelment; excavation, mining, quarrying, drilling; dredging

2 disinterment, exhumation, disentombment, **unearthing,** uncovering, digging out

3 drawing, drafting, sucking, **suction,** aspiration, pipetting; pumping, siphoning, tapping, broaching; milking; drainage, draining, emptying; cupping; bloodletting, bleeding, phlebotomy, venesection

4 evisceration, gutting, **disembowelment**

5 elicitation, eduction, drawing out *or* forth, bringing out *or* forth; **evocation,** calling forth; arousal

6 extortion, exaction, claim, demand; **wresting, wrenching, wringing, rending,** tearing, ripping; wrest, wrench, wring

7 <obtaining an extract> **squeezing, pressing,** expression; **distillation;** decoction; **rendering,** rendition; **steeping,** soaking, infusion; concentration

8 extract, extraction; **essence, quintessence, spirit, elixir;** decoction; **distillate,** distillation; **concentrate,** concentration; infusion; refinement, purification

9 extractor, separator; siphon; aspirator, pipette; pump, vacuum pump; press, wringer; corkscrew; forceps, pliers, pincers, tweezers; crowbar; smelter

VERBS **10 extract, take out,** get out, **withdraw, remove;** pull, draw; **pull out, draw out,** tear out, rip out, wrest out, pluck out, pick out, weed out, rake out; **pry out,** prize out, winkle out <Brit>; **pull up,** pluck up; **root up** *or* **out, uproot,** unroot, eradicate, deracinate, pull *or* pluck out by the roots, pull *or* pluck up by the roots; cut out, excise, exsect; enucleate; gouge out, avulse, evulse; extricate, evolve, disentangle, unravel; **dig up** *or* **out,** grub up *or* out, excavate, **unearth,** mine, quarry; dredge, dredge up *or* out; smelt

11 disinter, exhume, disentomb, unbury, unsepulcher, dig up, uncover

12 draw off, draft off, draft, draw, draw from; **suck,** suck out *or* up, **siphon off;** pipette; pump, pump out; tap, broach; let, let out; bleed; let blood, venesect, phlebotomize; milk; **drain,** decant; exhaust, empty

13 eviscerate, disembowel, gut

14 elicit, educe, deduce, induce, derive, obtain, procure, secure; **get from,** get out of; **evoke, call up, summon up,** call *or*

summon forth, call out; rouse, arouse, stimulate; **draw out** *or* **forth,** bring out *or* forth, pry *or* prize out, winkle out <Brit>, drag out, worm out, bring to light; wangle, wangle out of, worm out of

15 extort, exact, squeeze, claim, demand; **wrest, wring from, wrench from, rend from,** wrest *or* tear from

16 <obtain an extract> **squeeze** *or* **press out,** express, wring, wring out; **distill,** distill out, elixirate <old>; **filter,** filter out; decoct; **render,** melt down; refine; **steep,** soak, infuse; **concentrate,** essentialize

ADJS **17** extractive, eductive; educible; eradicative, uprooting; elicitory, **evocative,** arousing; **exacting,** exactive; **extortionate,** extortionary, extortive

18 essential, quintessential, pure 797.6

193 ASCENT
<motion upwards>

NOUNS **1 ascent,** ascension, levitation, **rise, rising,** uprising, **uprise,** uprisal; **upgoing,** upgo, uphill, upslope, upping, upgang <Scots>; upcoming; **taking off,** leaving the ground, takeoff; **soaring,** zooming, gaining altitude, leaving the earth behind; spiraling *or* gyring up; shooting *or* rocketing up; **jump,** vault, spring, saltation, **leap** 366; mount, **mounting; climb, climbing,** upclimb, anabasis, clamber, escalade; surge, upsurge, upsurgence, upleap, upshoot, uprush; **gush, jet,** spurt, spout, fountain; updraft; upswing, upsweep; upgrowth; upgrade 204.6; **uplift,** elevation 911; **uptick** <nonformal>, **increase** 251

2 upturn, uptrend, upcast, upsweep, upbend, upcurve

3 stairs, stairway, staircase, *escalier* <Fr>, flight of stairs, pair of stairs; **steps,** treads and risers; stepping-stones; spiral staircase, winding staircase, cockle stairs <nonformal>; companionway, companion; stile; back stairs; perron; fire escape; landing, landing stage; ramp, incline

4 ladder, scale; stepladder, folding ladder, rope ladder, fire ladder; hook ladder, extension ladder; Jacob's ladder, companion ladder, accommodation ladder, boarding ladder, side ladder, gangway ladder, quarter ladder, stern ladder

5 step, stair, footstep, rest, footrest, stepping-stone; **rung, round,** rundle, spoke, stave, scale; doorstep; tread; riser; bridgeboard, string; step stool

6 climber, ascender, upclimber; mountain climber, **mountaineer,** alpinist, rock climber, rock-jock <nonformal>, cragsman

7 <comparisons> rocket, skyrocket; lark, skylark, eagle

VERBS **8 ascend, rise, mount,** arise, up, uprise, levitate, upgo, **go up,** rise up, come up; go onwards and upwards, go up and up; upsurge, **surge,** upstream, upheave; swarm up, upswarm, sweep up; upwind, upspin, spiral, spire, curl upwards; stand up, **rear,** rear up, **tower,** loom; upgrow, grow up

9 shoot up, spring up, jump up, **leap up,** vault up, start up, fly up, pop up, bob up; float up, surface, break water; **gush, jet,** spurt, fountain; upshoot, upstart, upspring, upleap, upspear, rocket, **skyrocket**

10 take off, leave the ground, leave the earth behind, gain altitude, claw skyward; become airborne; **soar,** zoom, fly, plane, kite, fly aloft; aspire; spire, spiral *or* gyre upward; **hover,** hang, poise, float, float in the air

11 climb, climb up, upclimb, **mount,** clamber, **clamber up,** scramble *or* scrabble up, claw one's way up, struggle up, inch up, shin, shinny *or* shin up <nonformal>, ramp <nonformal>, work *or* inch one's way up, climb the ladder; **scale,** escalade, scale the heights; climb over, surmount

12 mount, get on, climb on, back; **bestride,** bestraddle; **board,** go aboard, go on board; **get in,** jump in, hop in, pile in <nonformal>

13 upturn, turn up, cock up; trend upwards, slope up; upcast, upsweep, upbend, upcurve

ADJS **14 ascending,** in the ascendant, **mounting, rising,** uprising, upgoing, upcoming; ascendant, ascensional, ascensive, anabatic; **leaping,** springing, saltatory; spiraling, skyrocketing; **upward,** upwith <Scots>; uphill, uphillward, upgrade, upsloping; uparching, rearing, rampant; climbing, scandent, scansorial

15 upturned, upcast, uplifted, **turned-up,** retroussé

ADVS **16 up, upward, upwards,** upwith <Scots>; skyward, heavenward; uplong, upalong; upstream, upstreamward; uphill; uphillward; upstairs; up attic *and* up steps <both nonformal>; uptown; up north

INTERJS **17 alley-oop!, upsy-daisy!;** excelsior!, onward and upward!

194 DESCENT
<motion downward>

NOUNS **1 descent, descending,** descension *or* downcome <both old>, **comedown,** down; **dropping, falling,** plummeting, **drop, fall, free-fall,** *chute* <Fr>, **downfall,** debacle, **collapse,** crash; **swoop,** stoop, pounce, downrush, downflow, cascade, waterfall, cataract, **downpour,** defluxion; downturn, downcurve, downbend, downward trend, downtrend; declension, declination, inclination; gravitation; downgrade 204.5; **down tick; decrease** 252

2 sinkage, lowering, **decline, slump,** subsidence, submergence, lapse, decurrence; cadence; **droop, sag,** swag; catenary

3 tumble, fall, *culbute* <Fr>, cropper *and* **spill** <both nonformal>, **flop** <nonformal>; **header** <nonformal>; **sprawl; pratfall** <nonformal>; **stumble,** trip; **dive, plunge** 367; forced landing

4 slide; slip, slippage; **glide,** coast, glissade; glissando; slither; **skid,** sideslip; **landslide,** mudslide, landslip, subsidence; **snowslide,** snowslip <Brit>; **avalanche**

VERBS **5 descend, go** *or* **come down,** down, dip down, lose altitude, dump altitude <nonformal>; gravitate; **fall, drop,** precipitate, rain, rain *or* pour down, fall *or* drop down; **collapse,** crash; **swoop,** stoop, pounce; **pitch, plunge** 367.6, **plummet;** cascade, cataract, parachute; come down a peg <nonformal>; **fall off,** drop off; trend downward, down-tick, go downhill

6 sink, go down, sink down, submerge; **set, settle,** settle down; **decline,** lower, **subside,** give way, lapse, cave, cave in; **droop,** slouch, **sag,** swag; **slump,** slump down; flump, flump down; flop *and* flop down <both nonformal>; plump, plop *or* plop down, plunk *or* plunk down <nonformal>; founder 367.8

7 get down, alight, touch down, **light; land,** settle, perch, come to rest; **dismount, get off,** uphorse; climb down

8 tumble, fall, fall down, come *or* fall *or* get a cropper <nonformal>, take a fall *or* tumble, take a flop *or* spill <nonformal>, precipitate oneself; fall over, tumble over, trip over; **sprawl,** sprawl out, take a pratfall <nonformal>, spread-eagle <nonformal>, measure one's length; fall headlong, **take a header** <nonformal>; fall prostrate, fall flat, fall on one's face, fall flat on one's ass <nonformal>; **fall over,** topple down *or* over; capsize, turn

turtle; **topple,** lurch, pitch, **stumble,** stagger, totter, careen, list, tilt, trip, flounder

9 slide, slip, slidder <nonformal>, slip *or* slide down; **glide,** skim, coast, glissade; **slither; skid,** sideslip; avalanche

10 light upon, alight upon, settle on; **descend upon, come down on, fall on,** drop on, hit *or* strike upon

ADJS **11 descending,** descendant, on the descendant; **down,** downward, declivitous; decurrent, deciduous; **downgoing,** downcoming; down-reaching; **dropping, falling, plunging, plummeting,** downfalling; **sinking,** downsinking, foundering, submerging, setting; declining, **subsiding;** collapsing, tumbledown, tottering; drooping, sagging; on the downgrade, downhill 204.16

12 downcast, downturned; hanging, downhanging

ADVS **13 down,** downward, **downwards,** from the top down, *de haut en bas* <Fr>; downwith <Scots>, adown, below; downright; downhill, downgrade; downstreet; downline; downstream; downstairs; downtown; south, down south

195 CONTAINER

NOUNS **1 container, receptacle;** receiver 479.3, holder, vessel, utensil; basin, pot, pan, cup, glass, ladle, bottle; cask; box, case; basket; luggage, baggage; cabinet, cupboard

2 bag, sack, sac, poke <nonformal>; **pocket,** fob; **balloon, bladder**

196 CONTENTS

NOUNS **1 contents, content,** what is contained *or* included *or* comprised; **insides** 207.4, innards <nonformal>, guts; **components, constituents, ingredients,** elements, **items, parts, divisions,** subdivisions; **inventory,** index, census, list 870; part 792; whole 791; composition 795

2 load, lading, cargo, freight, charge, burden; payload; boatload, busload, carload, cartload, container-load, shipload, trailerload, trainload, truckload, vanload, wagonload

3 lining, liner; **interlining,** interlineation; inlayer, inside layer; **inlay,** inlaying; **filling,** filler; **packing,** padding, wadding, **stuffing;** facing; doubling, doublure; bushing, bush; wainscot; insole

4 <contents of a container> cup, cupful, etc

5 <essential content> **substance, sum and**

substance, stuff, material, matter, medium, building blocks, fabric; gist, heart, soul, meat, nub; the nitty-gritty *and* the bottom line *and* the name of the game <all nonformal>, core, kernel, marrow, pith, sap, spirit, essence, quintessence, elixir, distillate, distillation, distilled essence; sine qua non, irreducible *or* indispensable content

6 enclosure, the enclosed

VERBS 7 fill, pack 793.7, load; line, interline, interlineate; inlay; face; wainscot, ceil; pad, wad, stuff; feather, fur

197 ROOM
<compartment>

NOUNS 1 room, chamber, *chambre* <Fr>, *salle* <Fr>, four walls

2 compartment, chamber, space, enclosed space; cavity, hollow, hole, concavity; cell, cellule; booth, stall, crib, manger; box, pew; crypt, vault

3 nook, corner, cranny, niche, recess, cove, bay, oriel, alcove; cubicle, roomlet, carrel, hole-in-the-wall <nonformal>, cubby, cubbyhole, snuggery, hidey-hole <nonformal>

4 hall; assembly hall, exhibition hall, convention hall; gallery; meetinghouse, meeting room; auditorium; concert hall; theater, music hall; stadium, dome, sports dome, arena 463; lecture hall, lyceum, amphitheater; operating theater; dance hall; ballroom, grand ballroom; chapel 703.3

5 parlor, living room, sitting room, morning room, drawing *or* withdrawing room, front room, best room <nonformal>, foreroom <nonformal>, salon, saloon <old>; sun parlor *or* sunroom, sun lounge, sunporch, solarium

6 library, stacks; study, studio, *atelier* <Fr>, workroom; office, workplace; loft, sail loft

7 bedroom, boudoir, chamber, sleeping chamber, bedchamber, master bedroom, guest room, sleeping room, cubicle, cubiculum; nursery; dormitory

8 <private chamber> sanctum, sanctum sanctorum, holy of holies, adytum; den, retreat, closet, cabinet

9 <ships> cabin, stateroom; saloon; house, deckhouse, trunk cabin, cuddy, shelter cabin

10 <trains> drawing room, stateroom, parlor car, Pullman car, roomette

11 dining room, *salle à manger* <Fr>, dinette, dining hall, refectory, mess *or*

messroom *or* mess hall, commons; dining car *or* diner; restaurant, cafeteria

12 playroom, recreation room, rec room <nonformal>, family room, game room, rumpus room <nonformal>; gymnasium

13 utility room, laundry room, sewing room

14 kitchen 11.3, storeroom 386.6, smoking room 89.13

15 closet, clothes closet, wardrobe, cloakroom; checkroom; linen closet; dressing room, fitting room, pantry

16 attic, attic room, garret, loft, sky parlor; cockloft, hayloft; storeroom, junk room, lumber room <Brit>

17 cellar, cellarage, basement; subbasement; wine cellar, potato cellar, storm cellar, cyclone cellar; coal bin *or* hole, hold, hole, bunker

18 corridor, hall, hallway; passage, passageway; gallery, loggia; arcade, colonnade, pergola, cloister, peristyle; areaway; breezeway

19 vestibule, portal, portico, entry, entryway, entrance, entrance hall, entranceway, threshold; lobby, foyer; propylaeum, stoa; narthex, galilee

20 anteroom, antechamber; side room, byroom; waiting room, *salle d'attente* <Fr>; reception room, presence chamber *or* room, audience chamber; throne room; lounge, greenroom, wardroom

21 porch, stoop, veranda, piazza <nonformal>, patio, lanai, gallery; sleeping porch

22 balcony, gallery, terrace

23 floor, story, level, flat; first floor *or* story, ground *or* street floor, *rez-de-chaussée* <Fr>; mezzanine, mezzanine floor, *entresol* <Fr>; clerestory

24 showroom, display room, exhibition room, gallery

25 hospital room; ward, maternity ward, fever ward, charity ward, prison ward, etc; private room, semi-private room; examining *or* examination room, consulting *or* consultation room, treatment room; operating room *or* OR, operating theater, surgery; labor room, delivery room; recovery room; emergency, emergency room; intensive care unit *or* ICU; pharmacy, dispensary; clinic, nursery; laboratory *or* blood bank; nurses' station

26 bathroom, lavatory, washroom 79.10, water closet *or* WC, closet, rest room, comfort station, toilet 12.10

27 <for vehicles> garage, carport; coach *or* carriage house; carbarn; roundhouse; hangar; boathouse

198 TOP

NOUNS **1 top,** top side, upper side, upside; surface 206.2; topside *or* topsides; upper story, top floor; clerestory; **roof,** ridgepole *or* roofpole; rooftop

2 summit, top; **tip-top, peak** 3.6, pinnacle; **crest, brow;** ridge, edge; **crown,** cap, **tip,** point, spire, pitch; highest pitch, no place higher, **apex,** vertex, **acme,** *ne plus ultra* <Fr>, **zenith, climax,** apogee, pole; **culmination; extremity, maximum, limit,** upper extremity, highest point, very top, top of the world, extreme limit, utmost *or* upmost *or* uppermost height, "the very acme and pitch" —Pope; **sky,** heaven *or* heavens, seventh heaven, cloud nine <nonformal>; meridian, noon, high noon; mountaintop

3 topping, icing, frosting

4 <top part>**head,** heading, **headpiece,** cap, *caput* <L>, capsheaf, **crown, crest;** topknot; pinhead, nailhead

5 architectural topping, capital <see list>, head, crown, cap; bracket capital; cornice

6 head, headpiece, **pate,** poll <nonformal>, crown, **sconce** *and* **noodle** *and* **noddle** *and* **noggin** *and* **bean** *and* **dome** <all nonformal>; brow, ridge; "the dome of Thought, the palace of the Soul"—Byron

7 skull, cranium, pericranium, epicranium; brainpan, brain box *or* case

8 phrenology, craniology, metoposcopy, physiognomy; phrenologist, craniologist, metoposcopist, physiognomist

VERBS **9 top,** top off, **crown, cap,** crest, **head,** tip, peak, surmount; overtop *or* outtop, have the top place *or* spot, over-arch; **culminate,** consummate, climax; ice, frost <a cake>; fill, top up

ADJS **10 top,** topmost, **uppermost,** upmost, overmost, **highest;** tip-top, tip-crowning, **maximum,** maximal, ultimate; summital, apical, vertical, zenithal, climactic, climactical, **consummate;** acmic, acmatic; meridian, meridional; **head,** headmost, capital, chief, paramount, supreme, preeminent; **top-level,** highest level, top-echelon, top-flight, top-ranking, top-drawer <nonformal>

11 topping, crowning, capping, heading, surmounting, overtopping *or* outtopping, overarching; **culminating,** consummating, perfecting, climaxing

12 topped, headed, **crowned, capped,** crested, plumed, tipped, peaked

13 topless, headless, crownless

14 cranial; cephalic, encephalic

ADVS **15 atop, on top,** at *or* on the top, topside <nonformal>; at the top of the tree *or* ladder, on top of the roost *or* heap; on the crest *or* crest of the wave; at the head, at the peak *or* pinnacle *or* summit

PREPS **16 atop, on, upon,** on top of, surmounting, topping

17 capital styles

Byzantine	Ionic
Corinthian	Moorish
Doric	Roman Corinthian
Gothic	Roman Doric
Greek	Romanesque
Greek Corinthian	Roman Ionic
Greek Ionic	Tuscan

199 BOTTOM

NOUNS **1 bottom,** bottom side, **underside,** nether side, lower side, downside, **underneath,** fundament; belly, underbelly; buttocks 217.4, breech; **rock bottom, bedrock,** bed, hardpan; **grass roots;** substratum, underlayer, lowest level *or* layer *or* stratum, nethermost level *or* layer *or* stratum; **nadir,** the pits <nonformal>

2 base, basement, **foot,** footing, sole, toe; **foundation** 900.6; baseboard, mopboard, shoemold; wainscot, dado; skeleton, bare bones, chassis, frame; keel, keelson

3 ground covering, **ground,** earth, *terra firma* <L>; **floor,** flooring; parquet; **deck; pavement,** *pavé* <Fr>, paving, surfacing, asphalt, blacktop, macadam, concrete; **cover,** carpet, floor covering; artificial turf, Astroturf <trademark>

4 bed, bottom, floor, ground, **basin, channel,** coulee; seabed, ocean bottom 275.4

5 foot, extremity, pes, pedes, *pied* <Fr>, trotter, pedal extremity, dog, tootsy <nonformal>; **hoof,** ungula; **paw,** pad, pug, *patte* <Fr>; forefoot, forepaw; harefoot, splay-foot, clubfoot; **toe,** digit; **heel; sole,** pedi *or* pedio; instep, arch; pastern; fetlock

VERBS **6 base on, found on, ground on, build on,** bottom on, bed on, set on; root in; **underlie,** undergird; bottom, bottom out; hit bottom

ADJS **7 bottom,** bottommost, **undermost,** nethermost, lowermost, deepest, **lowest; rock-bottom,** bedrock; ground

8 basic; basal, basilar; **underlying, fundamental,** essential, elementary, elemental, primary, primal, primitive, rudimentary, original, grass-roots; radical; nadiral

9 pedal; plantar; footed, hoofed, ungulate, clawed, taloned; toed

200 VERTICALNESS

NOUNS **1 verticalness,** verticality, verticalism; **erectness, uprightness;** stiffness *or* erectness of posture, position of attention, brace; straight up-and-downness, up-and-downness; steepness, sheerness, precipitousness, plungingness, **perpendicularity,** plumbness, aplomb; right-angledness *or* -angularity, squareness, orthogonality

2 vertical, upright, perpendicular, plumb, normal; right angle, orthodiagonal; vertical circle, azimuth circle

3 precipice, cliff, sheer *or* yawning cliff *or* precipice *or* drop, steep, bluff, wall, face, scar; crag, craig <Scots>; scarp, **escarpment; palisade,** palisades

4 erection, erecting, **elevation; rearing,** raising; **uprearing,** upraising, lofting, uplifting, heaving up *or* aloft; standing on end *or* upright *or* on its feet *or* on its base *or* on its legs *or* on its bottom

5 rising, uprising, ascension, ascending, ascent; vertical height *or* dimension; **gradient,** rise, uprise

6 <instruments> square, T square, try square, set square, carpenter's square; plumb, plumb line, plumb rule, plummet, bob, plumb bob, lead

VERBS **7 stand, stand erect, stand up, stand upright, stand up straight,** be erect, be on one's feet; hold oneself straight *or* stiff, stand ramrod-straight, have an upright carriage; stand at attention, brace, stand at parade rest <all military>

8 rise, arise, ascend, mount, uprise, **rise up, get up,** get to one's feet; **stand up, stand on end; stick up,** cock up; bristle; **rear,** ramp, uprear, rear up, rise on the hind legs; upheave; sit up, sit bolt upright; jump up, spring to one's feet

9 erect, elevate, rear, raise, pitch, **set up,** raise *or* lift *or* cast up; raise *or* heave *or* rear aloft; uprear, upraise, uplift, upheave; upright; **upend,** stand upright *or* on end; set on its feet *or* legs *or* base *or* bottom

10 plumb, plumb-line, set *à plomb;* **square,** square up

ADJS **11 vertical, upright,** bolt upright, ramrod straight, **erect,** upstanding, standing up, stand-up; rearing, rampant; **upended,** upraised, upreared; downright

12 perpendicular, plumb, straight-up-and-down, straight-up, **up-and-down;** sheer, steep, precipitous, plunging; **right-angled,** right-angle, right-angular, orthogonal, orthodiagonal

ADVS **13 vertically, erectly,** upstandingly, uprightly, **upright,** up, stark *or* bolt upright; **on end,** up on end, right on end, endwise, endways; on one's feet *or* legs, on one's hind legs <nonformal>; at attention, braced, at parade rest <all military>

14 perpendicularly, sheer, sheerly; up and down, **straight up and down; plumb,** *à plomb* <Fr>; **at right angles,** square

201 HORIZONTALNESS

NOUNS **1 horizontalness,** horizontality; **levelness, flatness,** planeness, evenness, smoothness, flushness; unbrokenness, unrelievedness

2 recumbency, recumbence, decumbency *or* decumbence, accumbency; accubation; **prostration,** proneness; supineness, reclining, reclination; lying, lounging, **repose** 20; sprawl, loll

3 horizontal, plane, level, flat, dead level *or* flat, homaloid; **horizontal** *or* level plane; horizontal *or* level line; horizontal projection; horizontal surface, fascia; horizontal parallax; horizontal axis; horizontal fault; water level, sea level, mean sea level; ground, earth, steppe, **plain, flatland,** prairie, savanna, sea of grass, bowling green, table, billiard table; floor, platform, ledge, terrace

4 horizon, skyline, rim of the horizon; sea line; apparent *or* local *or* visible horizon, sensible horizon, celestial *or* rational *or* geometrical *or* true horizon, artificial *or* false horizon; azimuth

VERBS **5 lie, lie down,** lay <nonformal>, **recline, repose,** lounge, sprawl, loll, drape *or* spread oneself, splay, lie limply; **lie flat** *or* prostrate *or* prone *or* supine, lie on one's face *or* back, lie on a level, hug the ground *or* deck; **grovel, crawl,** kowtow

6 level, flatten, even, equalize, align, smooth *or* smoothen, level out, smooth out, flush; grade, roll, roll flat, steamroller *or* steamroll; **lay,** lay down *or* out; **raze,** rase, lay level, lay level with the ground; lay low *or* flat; **fell** 912.5

ADJS **7 horizontal, level, flat,** flattened; **even,** smooth, smoothened, smoothed out; table-like, tabular; **flush;** homaloidal; **plane,** plain; rolled, trodden, squashed, rolled *or* trodden *or* squashed flat; flat as a pancake, "flat as a cake"—Erasmus, flat as a table *or* billiard table *or* bowling green *or* tennis court, flat as a board, "flat as a flounder"—John Fletcher, level as a plain.

8 **recumbent,** accumbent, procumbent, decumbent; **prostrate, prone,** flat; **supine,** resupine; couchant, *couché* <Fr>; **lying, reclining, reposing,** flat on one's back; sprawling, lolling, lounging; sprawled, spread, splay, splayed, draped; groveling, crawling, flat on one's belly *or* nose

ADVS 9 **horizontally, flat,** flatly, flatways, flatwise; **evenly,** flush; **level, on a level;** lengthwise, lengthways, at full length, on one's back *or* belly *or* nose

202 PENDENCY

NOUNS 1 **pendency,** pendulousness *or* pendulosity, pensileness *or* pensility; **hanging, suspension,** dangling *or* danglement, suspense, dependence *or* dependency

2 **hang, droop,** dangle, swing, fall; **sag,** swag, bag

3 **overhang, overhanging,** impendence *or* impendency, **projection,** beetling, jutting; cantilever

4 **pendant,** hanger; **hanging,** drape; **lobe,** ear lobe, lobule, lobus, lobation, lappet, wattle; **uvula**

5 **suspender, hanger,** supporter; **suspenders,** pair of suspenders, braces <Brit>, galluses <nonformal>

VERBS 6 **hang,** hang down, fall; **depend,** pend; **dangle,** swing, flap, flop <nonformal>; flow, drape, cascade; **droop,** lop; nod, weep; **sag,** swag, bag; **trail, drag, draggle,** drabble, daggle

7 **overhang,** hang over, hang out, **impend,** impend over, **project,** project over, beetle, **jut,** beetle *or* jut *or* thrust over, stick out over

8 **suspend, hang, hang up,** put up, fasten up; sling

ADJS 9 **pendent,** pendulous, pendulant, pendular, penduline, pensile; **suspended,** hung; **hanging,** pending, depending, dependent; **falling; dangling,** swinging, falling loosely; weeping; flowing, cascading

10 **drooping, droopy,** limp, loose, nodding, floppy <nonformal>, loppy, lop; **sagging,** saggy, swag, sagging in folds; **bagging,** baggy, ballooning; lop-eared

11 **overhanging,** overhung, overhung, lowering, **impending,** impendent, **pending;** incumbent, superincumbent; **projecting, jutting; beetling,** beetle; beetle-browed

12 lobular, lobar, lobed, lobate, lobated

203 PARALLELISM

<*physically parallel direction or state*>

NOUNS 1 **parallelism,** coextension, nonconvergence, nondivergence, collaterality, concurrence, equidistance; collineation, collimation; alignment; parallelization; parallelotropism; **analogy** 942.1

2 **parallel,** paralleler; parallel line, parallel dash, parallel bar, parallel file, parallel series, parallel column, parallel trench, parallel vector; parallelogram, parallelepiped *or* parallelepipedon

3 <instruments> parallel rule *or* rules *or* ruler, parallelograph, parallelometer

VERBS 4 **parallel,** be parallel, coextend; run parallel, go alongside, go beside, run abreast; match, equal

5 **parallelize,** place parallel to, equidistance; line up, align, realign; collineate, collimate; match; correspond, follow, equate

ADJS 6 **parallel,** paralleling; coextending, coextensive, nonconvergent, nondivergent, **equidistant,** equispaced, collateral, concurrent; lined up, aligned; equal, even; parallelogrammical, parallelogrammatical; parallelepipedal; parallelotropic; parallelodrome, parallelinervate; analogous 942.8

ADVS 7 **in parallel,** parallelwise, parallelly; side-by-side, alongside, abreast; equidistantly, nonconvergently, nondivergently; collaterally, coextensively

204 OBLIQUITY

NOUNS 1 **obliquity,** obliqueness; **deviation** 164, deviance, divergence, digression, divagation, vagary, excursion, skewness, aberration, squint, declination; deflection, deflexure; nonconformity 867; diagonality, crosswiseness, transverseness; indirection, indirectness, deviousness, circuitousness 913

2 **inclination, leaning,** lean, angularity; **slant,** slaunch <nonformal>, rake, **slope; tilt, tip,** pitch, **list, cant,** swag, sway; leaning tower, tower of Pisa

3 **bias, bend,** bent, **crook, warp, twist, turn, skew,** slue, **veer,** sheer, **swerve,** lurch

4 **incline,** inclination, **slope, grade,** gradient, pitch, **ramp,** launching ramp, bank, talus, gentle *or* easy slope, glacis; rapid *or* steep slope, stiff climb, scarp, chute; helicline, inclined plane <phys>; **bevel,** bezel, fleam; hillside, side; hanging gardens; shelving beach

5 **declivity, descent,** dip, drop, fall, falling-off *or* -away, **decline;** hang, hanging; **downgrade,** downgate <Scots>, **downhill**

6 **acclivity, ascent,** climb, **rise,** rising, uprise, uprising, rising ground; **upgrade, uphill,** upgo, upclimb, uplift, steepness, precipitousness, abruptness, verticalness 200

7 **diagonal,** oblique, transverse, bias, bend <heraldry>, oblique line, slash, **slant,** virgule, scratch comma, separatrix, solidus; oblique angle *or* figure, rhomboid

8 **zigzag,** zig, zag; zigzaggery, flexuosity, **crookedness,** crankiness; switchback, hairpin, dogleg; chevron

VERBS 9 **oblique, deviate, diverge,** deflect, divagate, **bear off;** angle, **angle off, swerve,** shoot off at an angle, **veer,** sheer, sway, slue, **skew, twist, turn,** bend, bias; crook

10 **incline, lean; slope, slant,** slaunch <nonformal>, rake, pitch, grade, bank, shelve; **tilt, tip, list, cant,** careen, keel, sidle, swag, sway; **ascend, rise,** uprise, climb, **go uphill; descend, decline,** dip, drop, fall, fall off *or* away, **go downhill;** retreat

11 cut, cut *or* slant across, cut crosswise *or* transversely *or* diagonally, catercorner, diagonalize, slash, slash across

12 **zigzag,** zig, zag, **stagger,** crank *or* crankle <old>, wind in and out

ADJS 13 **oblique; devious,** deviant, deviative, divergent, digressive, divagational, deflectional, excursive; **indirect,** side, sidelong; left-handed, sinister, sinistral; backhand, backhanded; circuitous 913.7

14 **askew, skew,** skewed; skew-jawed *and* skewgee *and* skew-whiff *and* askewgee *and* agee *and* agee-jawed <all nonformal>; **awry,** wry; askance, askant, asquint, squinting, **cockeyed** <nonformal>; **crooked** 265.10; slaunchwise *or* slaunchways <nonformal>; wamper-jawed *and* catawampous *and* yaw-ways <all nonformal>, wonky <Brit nonformal>

15 **inclining,** inclined, inclinatory, inclinational; **leaning,** recumbent; **sloping,** sloped, aslope; raking, pitched; **slanting,** slanted, slant, aslant, slantways, slantwise; bias, biased; shelving, shelvy; **tilting,** tilted, atilt, tipped, **tipping,** tipsy, listing, **canting,** careening; sideling, sidelong; out of the perpendicular *or* square *or* plumb, bevel, beveled

16 <sloping downward> **downhill, downgrade; descending,** falling, dropping,

dipping; **declining,** declined; declivous, declivitous, declivate

17 <sloping upward> **uphill, upgrade; rising,** uprising, **ascending,** climbing; acclivous, acclivitous, acclinate

18 **steep, precipitous, bluff,** plunging, abrupt, bold, **sheer,** sharp, rapid; headlong, breakneck; vertical 200.11

19 **transverse,** crosswise *or* crossways, thwart, athwart, across 170.9; **diagonal,** bendwise; catercorner *or* **catercornered** *or* cattycorner *or* cattycornered *or* kittycorner *or* kittycornered; slant, bias, biased, biaswise *or* biasways

20 **crooked, zigzag,** zigzagged, zigzaggy, zigzagwise *or* zigzagways, dogleg *or* doglegged; flexuous, twisty, hairpin, bendy, curvy; staggered, crankled <old>; chevrony, chevronwise *or* chevronways <all architecture>

ADVS 21 **obliquely, deviously,** deviately, **indirectly,** circuitously 913.9; divergently, digressively, excursively, divagationally; **sideways** *or* sidewise, sidelong, sideling, on *or* to one side; at an angle

22 **askew, awry; askance,** askant, asquint

23 **slantingly, slopingly,** aslant, aslope, atilt, rakingly, tipsily, slopewise, slopeways, slantwise, slantways, aslantwise, on *or* at a slant; slaunchwise *and* slaunchways <both nonformal>; off plumb *or* the vertical; **downhill, downgrade; uphill, upgrade**

24 transversely, crosswise *or* crossways, athwart, across 170.13

25 **diagonally,** diagonalwise; **on the bias,** bias, biaswise; **cornerwise,** cornerways; catercornerways *or* **catercorner** *or* cattycorner *or* kittycorner

205 INVERSION

NOUNS 1 **inversion,** turning over *or* around *or* upside down, the other way round; eversion, turning inside out, invagination, intussusception; introversion, turning inward; **reversing, reversal** 858.1, turning front to back *or* side to side; **reversion,** turning back *or* backwards, retroversion, retroflexion, revulsion; devolution, atavism; recidivism; **transposition,** transposal; topsy-turvydom *or* topsy-turviness; the world turned upside-down, the tail wagging the dog; pronation, supination, resupination

2 **overturn, upset,** overset, **overthrow,** upturn, **turnover,** spill <nonformal>; subversion; **revolution** 859; **capsizing,** capsize, capsizal, turning turtle; **somer-**

sault, somerset, *culbute* <Fr>; turning head over heels

3 <grammatical and rhetorical terms> metastasis, metathesis; anastrophe, chiasmus, hypallage, hyperbaton, hysteron proteron, palindrome, parenthesis, synchysis, tmesis

4 **inverse, reverse, converse, opposite** 215.5, other side of the coin *or* picture, the flip side *and* B side <both nonformal>

VERBS 5 **invert,** inverse, turn over *or* around *or* upside down; introvert, turn in *or* inward; **turn down; turn inside out,** turn out, evert, invaginate, intussuscept; **revert,** recidivate, relapse, lapse, backslide; **reverse** 858.4, **transpose,** convert; put the cart before the horse; turn into the opposite, turn about, turn the tables, turn the scale *or* balance; rotate, revolve, pronate, supinate, resupinate

6 **overturn, turn over, turn upside down,** turn bottom side up, upturn, **upset,** overset, **overthrow,** subvert, *culbuter* <Fr>; go *or* turn ass over elbows *or* ass over tincups <all nonformal>, turn a somersault, go *or* turn head over heels; **turn turtle, turn topsy-turvy,** topsy-turvy, topsy-turvify; **tip over,** keel over, topple over; **capsize;** careen, set on its beam ends, set on its ears

ADJS 7 **inverted,** inversed, back-to-front, **backwards,** retroverted, **reversed, transposed, back side forward, tail first; inside out,** outside in, everted, invaginated, wrong side out; reverted, lapsed, recidivist *or* recidivistic; atavistic; devolutional; **upside-down, topsy-turvy,** ass over elbows *and* ass over tincups *and* arsy-varsy <all nonformal>; **capsized,** head-over-heels; hyperbatic, chiastic, palindromic; resupinate; introverted

ADVS 8 **inversely, conversely,** contrarily, contrariwise, **vice versa,** the other way around, **backwards,** turned around; **upside down,** over, **topsy-turvy; bottom up,** bottom side up; head over heels, heels over head

206 EXTERIORITY

NOUNS 1 **exteriority,** externalness, externality, **outwardness,** outerness; appearance, outward appearance, seeming, mien, **front,** manner; window-dressing, cosmetics; openness; extrinsicality 767; **superficiality, shallowness** 276; extraterritoriality, foreignness

2 **exterior,** external, **outside; surface,** superficies, covering 295, skin 2.4, outer

skin *or* layer, epidermis, integument, envelope, crust, cortex, rind, shell 295.16; cladding, plating; top, superstratum; **periphery, fringe,** circumference, outline, lineaments, border; **face,** outer face *or* side, facade, **front;** facet; extrados, back; store-front, shop-front, shop-window, street-front

3 **outdoors,** outside, **the out-of-doors,** the great out-of-doors, the open, **the open air;** outland

4 **externalization,** exteriorization, bringing into the open, show, showing, display, displaying; **objectification,** actualization, realization

VERBS 5 **externalize,** exteriorize, bring into the open, bring out, show, display, exhibit; **objectify,** actualize, project, realize

6 **scratch the surface;** give a lick and a promise, do a cosmetic job, give a once-over-lightly, whitewash, give a nod

ADJS 7 **exterior, external;** extrinsic 767; **outer, outside, out, outward,** outward-facing, outlying, outstanding; **outermost,** outmost; surface, superficial 276.5, epidermic, cortical; cosmetic, merely cosmetic; peripheral, **fringe,** roundabout; apparent, seeming; open 348.10, public 352.17; exomorphic

8 **outdoor, out-of-door,** out-of-doors, **outside, without-doors; open-air,** alfresco; out and about

9 extraterritorial, exterritorial; extraterrestrial, exterrestrial, extramundane; extragalactic, extralateral, extraliminal, extramural, extrapolar, extrasolar, extraprovincial, extratribal; foreign, outlandish, **alien**

ADVS 10 **externally, outwardly,** on the outside, exteriorly; **without, outside, outwards, out;** apparently, to all appearances; openly, publicly, to judge by appearances; superficially, on the surface

11 **outdoors, out of doors, outside,** abroad; in the open, **in the open air,** alfresco, *en plein air* <Fr>

WORD ELEMENTS 12 e—, ec—, ect—, ecto—, ex—, ef—, epi—, eph—, extra—, hyper—, peripher—, periphero—

207 INTERIORITY

NOUNS 1 interiority, internalness, internality, **inwardness, innerness,** inness; introversion, internalization; **intrinsicality** 766; depth 275

2 **interior, inside,** inner, inward, internal, intern; inner recess, recesses, **innermost** *or* **deepest recesses,** penetralia, intimate

places, secret place *or* places; bosom, secret heart, heart, heart of hearts, soul, vitals, vital center; inner self, inner life, inner landscape, inner *or* interior man, inner nature; intrados; core, center 208.2

3 inland, inlands, **interior,** up-country; **midland,** midlands; heartland; hinterland 233.2; Middle America

4 insides, innards <nonformal>, inwards, internals; inner mechanism, what makes it tick *and* work <both nonformal>; **guts** <nonformal>, **vitals, viscera,** *kishkes* <Yiddish>, giblets; entrails, bowels, guts; tripes *and* stuffings <both nonformal>

VERBS **5** internalize, put in, keep within; enclose, embed, surround, contain, comprise, include, enfold, take to heart, assimilate

ADJS **6 interior, internal, inner, inside, inward;** intestine; **innermost,** inmost, **intimate,** private; visceral, gut <nonformal>; **intrinsic** 766.7; deep 275.10; central 208.11; indoor; live-in

7 inland, interior, up-country, up-river; hinterland; **midland,** mediterranean; Middle American

8 intramarginal, intramural, intramundane, intramontane, intraterritorial, intracoastal, intragroupal

ADVS **9 internally, inwardly,** interiorly, inly, **intimately,** deeply, profoundly, under the surface; **intrinsically** 766; centrally

10 in, inside, within; herein, therein, wherein

11 inward, inwards, inwardly, withinward, withinwards; inland, inshore

12 indoors, indoor, withindoors

PREPS **13 in, into; within,** at, inside, **inside of,** in the limits of; to the heart *or* core of

WORD ELEMENTS **14** en—, em—, end—, endo—, ent—, ento—, eso—, infra—, in—, im—, il—, ir—, inter—, intra—, ob—

208 CENTRALITY

NOUNS **1 centrality,** centralness, middleness, central *or* middle *or* mid position; equidistance; centricity, centricality; concentricity; centripetalism

2 center, centrum; **middle** 818, **heart, core, nucleus; core of one's being, where one lives; kernel; pith,** marrow, medulla; **nub, hub,** nave, axis, pivot; **navel,** umbilicus, omphalos, belly button <nonformal>; bull's-eye; dead center; "the still point of the turning world"—T S Eliot; storm center, eye of the storm

3 <biological terms> central body, centriole, centrosome, centrosphere

4 focus, focal point, prime focus, point of convergence; **center of interest** *or* attention, focus of attention; center of consciousness; **center of attraction, centerpiece,** clou, mecca, cynosure, cynosure of all eyes; polestar, lodestar; magnet

5 nerve center, ganglion, center of activity, vital center; control center, guidance center

6 headquarters *or* **HQ,** central station, central office, main office, central administration, seat, base, **base of operations,** center of authority; general headquarters *or* **GHQ,** command post *or* **CP,** company headquarters

7 metropolis, capital; urban center, art center, cultural center, medical center, shopping center, shipping center, railroad center, garment center, manufacturing center, tourist center, trade center, etc

8 centralization, centering; nucleation; **focalization,** focus, focusing; convergence 169; **concentration,** concentralization, pooling; centralism

VERBS **9 centralize, center,** middle; center round, center on *or* in

10 focus, focalize, come to a point *or* focus, bring to *or* into focus; bring *or* come to a head, get to the heart of the matter, home in on; zero in on; draw a bead on *and* get a handle on <nonformal>; **concentrate,** concenter, get it together <nonformal>; **channel,** direct, canalize, channelize; converge 169.2

ADJS **11 central,** centric, **middle** 818; centermost, middlemost, **midmost; equidistant;** centralized, concentrated; umbilical, omphalic; axial, **pivotal,** key; centroidal; centrosymmetric; geocentric

12 nuclear, nucleate

13 focal, confocal; converging; centrolineal; centripetal

14 concentric; homocentric; **coaxial,** coaxal

ADVS **15 centrally,** in the center *or* middle of, at the heart of

209 ENVIRONMENT

NOUNS **1 environment, surroundings, environs,** surround, ambience, entourage, circle, circumjacencies, circumambiencies, **circumstances,** environing circumstances, *alentours* <Fr>; **precincts,** ambit, purlieus, **milieu; neighborhood,**

vicinity, vicinage; **suburbs;** outskirts, outposts, borderlands; borders, boundaries, limits, periphery, perimeter, compass, circuit; **context, situation;** habitat 228; total environment, configuration, gestalt

2 **setting, background,** backdrop, ground, surround, field, scene, arena, theater, locale; back, rear, hinterland, distance; stage, stage setting, stage set, *mise-en-scène* <Fr>

3 <surrounding influence or condition> **milieu, ambience, atmosphere, climate, air,** aura, spirit, feeling, feel, quality, color, local color, sense, sense of place, note, tone, overtone, undertone

4 <natural or suitable environment> **element,** medium; **the environment**

5 **surrounding, encompassment,** environment, circumambience *or* circumambiency, circumjacence *or* circumjacency; containment, **enclosure** 212; **encirclement,** cincture, encincture, circumcincture, circling, girdling, girding; **envelopment,** enfoldment, encompassment, encompassing, compassing, embracement; circumposition; circumflexion; inclusion 771, involvement 897

VERBS 6 **surround, environ,** compass, **encompass,** enclose, close; go round *or* around, compass about; **envelop,** enfold, lap, wrap, enwrap, embrace, enclasp, embosom, embay, involve, invest

7 **encircle, circle,** ensphere, belt, belt in, zone, cincture, encincture; **girdle,** gird, begird, engird; ring, band; loop; wreathe, wreathe *or* twine around

ADJS 8 **environing, surrounding,** encompassing, enclosing; **enveloping,** wrapping, enwrapping, enfolding, embracing; **encircling,** circling; bordering, peripheral; circumjacent, circumferential, circumambient, ambient; circumfluent, circumfluous; circumflex; **roundabout,** suburban, neighboring

9 **environmental,** environal; **ecological**

10 **surrounded,** environed, compassed, **encompassed,** enclosed; **enveloped,** wrapped, enfolded, lapped, wreathed

11 **encircled, circled,** ringed, cinctured, encinctured, belted, girdled, girt, begirt, zoned

ADVS 12 **around,** round, **about,** round about, in the neighborhood *or* vicinity *or* vicinage; close, close about

13 **all round, all about,** on every side, on all sides, on all hands, right and left

WORD ELEMENTS 14 amph—, amphi—, circum—, peri—

210 CIRCUMSCRIPTION

NOUNS 1 **circumscription, limiting,** circumscribing, **bounding, demarcation,** delimitation, definition, determination, specification; limit-setting, inclusion-exclusion, circling-in *or* -out, encincture, boundary-marking

2 **limitation, limiting, restriction,** restricting, confinement 212.1, prescription, proscription, restraint, discipline, moderation, continence; qualification, **hedging;** bounds 211, boundary, limit 211.3; time-limit, time constraint; small space 258.3

3 **patent, copyright,** certificate of invention, *brevet d'invention* <Fr>; **trademark, logo** *or* logotype, registered trademark, trade name, service mark

VERBS 4 **circumscribe, bound; mark off** *or* mark out, stake out, lay off, rope off; **demarcate,** delimit, delimitate, draw *or* mark *or* set *or* lay out boundaries, circle in *or* out, hedge in, set the limit, mark the periphery; **define,** determine, fix, specify; surround 209.6; enclose 212.5

5 **limit, restrict, restrain, bound, confine,** ground <nonformal>; straiten, narrow, tighten; specialize; stint, scant; **condition,** qualify, hedge, hedge about; draw the line, set an end point *or* a stopping place; discipline, moderate, contain; restrain oneself, pull one's punches <nonformal>; **patent, copyright,** register

ADJS 6 **circumscribed,** circumscript; ringed *or* circled *or* hedged about; **demarcated, delimited, defined,** definite, determined, determinate, specific, stated, set, fixed; surrounded 209.10, encircled 209.11

7 **limited, restricted,** bound, **bounded, finite; confined** 212.10, prescribed, proscribed, cramped, strait, straitened, narrow; conditioned, qualified, hedged; disciplined, moderated; **deprived,** in straitened circumstances, pinched, on short commons, on short rations, strapped; patented, registered, protected, copyrighted

8 **restricted,** out of bounds, off-limits

9 **limiting, restricting,** defining, determining, determinative, confining; limitative, limitary, restrictive, definitive, exclusive

10 **terminal,** limital; limitable, terminable

211 BOUNDS

NOUNS 1 **bounds, limits,** boundaries, limitations, **confines, pale,** marches, bourns,

verges, edges, outlines, outer markings,
skirts, outskirts, **fringes,** metes, metes
and bounds; periphery, **perimeter;** coordinates, parameters; **compass, circumference,** circumscription 210

2 **outline, contour,** delineation, lines, lineaments, shapes, figure, figuration, **configuration,** gestalt; **features,** main features;
profile, silhouette; relief; skeleton, framework, armature

3 **boundary, bound, limit,** limitation, extremity 793.5; **barrier,** block, claustrum;
delimitation, hedge, break or breakoff
point, cutoff, cutoff point, terminus; time
limit, time frame, term, deadline, target
date, terminal date, time allotment; finish, **end** 819, tail end; **start,** starting line
or point, mark; **limiting factor,** determinant, limit or boundary condition;
bracket, brackets, **bookends** <nonfor-
mal>; threshold, limen; upper limit, ceiling, apogee, high-water mark; lower
limit, floor, low-water mark, nadir; **confine,** march, mark, bourn, mete, compass,
circumscription; **boundary line, line, border line,** frontier, division line, interface,
break, boundary, line of demarcation or
circumvallation

4 **border,** limbus, bordure <heraldry>,
edge, limb, **verge, brink,** brow, **brim, rim,
margin,** marge, **skirt, fringe, hem,** list,
selvage or selvedge, side; **forefront, cutting edge,** front line, vanguard 216.2;
sideline; shore, bank, coast; **lip,** labium,
labrum, labellum; flange; ledge; frame,
enframement, mat; featheredge; ragged
edge

5 **frontier, border, borderland,** border
ground, marchland, march, marches;
outskirts, outpost; frontier post; iron curtain, bamboo curtain, Berlin wall; Pillars
of Hercules; three-mile or twelve-mile
limit

6 **curb,** kerb <Brit>, curbing; border
stone, curbstone, kerbstone <Brit>,
edgestone

7 **edging, bordering,** bordure <heraldry>,
trimming, binding, skirting; fringe,
fimbriation, fimbria; **hem,** selvage, list,
welt; frill, frilling; beading, flounce, fur-
below, galloon, motif, ruffle, valance

VERBS 8 **bound,** circumscribe 210.4, surround 209.6, limit 210.5, enclose 212.5,
divide, separate

9 **outline,** contour; **delineate;** silhouette,
profile, limn

10 **border, edge, bound, rim, skirt, hem, hem
in, ringe,** befringe, lap, list, margin,
marge, marginate, march, verge, line,

side; **adjoin** 223.9; **frame,** enframe, set
off; trim, bind; purl; purfle

ADJS 11 **bordering, fringing,** rimming, skirting; **bounding,** boundary, **limiting,** limit,
determining or determinant or determinative; threshold, liminal, limbic;
extreme, terminal; **marginal, borderline,**
frontier; coastal, littoral

12 **bordered,** edged; margined, marged,
marginate; marginated; **fringed,** befringed, trimmed, skirted, fimbriate,
fimbriated

13 lipped, labial, labiate

14 outlining, delineatory; peripheral, peri-
metric, perimetrical, circumferential;
outlined, **in outline**

ADVS 15 **on the verge, on the brink,** on the
borderline, on the point, on the edge, on
the ragged edge, at the threshold, at the
limit or bound; **peripherally,** marginally,
at the periphery

16 **thus far,** so far, thus far and no farther

212 ENCLOSURE

NOUNS 1 **enclosure; confinement,** containing, containment, circumscription 210,
immurement, walling- or hedging- or
hemming- or boxing- or fencing- or
walling-in; **imprisonment,** incarceration,
jailing, locking-up, lockdown; **siege,** be-
sieging, beleaguerment, blockade,
blockading, cordoning, quarantine, besetment; inclusion 771; **envelopment**
209.5

2 **packaging, packing,** package; boxing,
crating, encasement; canning, tinning
<Brit>; bottling; **wrapping,** enwrap-
ment, bundling; shrink-wrapping

3 <enclosed place> enclosure, close, **confine,** precinct, enclave, pale, paling, list,
cincture; **cloister; pen, coop,** fold; **yard,**
park, court, courtyard, curtilage, toft;
square, quadrangle, quad <nonformal>;
field, delimited field, **arena,** theater,
ground; **container** 195

4 **fence, wall,** boundary 211.3, **barrier;**
stone wall; paling, palisade; rail, railing;
balustrade, balustrading; arcade

VERBS 5 **enclose,** close in, bound, include,
contain; compass, encompass; **surround,**
encircle 209.7; **shut** or **pen in,** coop in;
fence in, wall in, wall up, rail in, rail off,
screen off, curtain off; **hem** or **hedge in,**
box in, pocket; shut or coop or mew up;
pen, coop, corral, cage, impound, mew;
imprison, incarcerate, jail, lock up, lock
down; **besiege,** beset, beleaguer, leaguer,
cordon, cordon off, quarantine, blockade;

yard, yard up; house in; chamber; stable, kennel, shrine, enshrine; **wrap** 295.20

6 **confine, immure;** cramp, straiten, encase; cloister, closet, cabin, crib; entomb, coffin, casket; bottle up *or* in, box up *or* in

7 **fence, wall,** fence in, fence up; pale, rail, bar; hem, hem in, hedge, hedge in, hedge out; picket, palisade; bulkhead in

8 parenthesize, bracket, precede and follow, bookend

9 **package, pack, parcel;** box, box up, case, encase, crate, carton; can, tin <Brit>; bottle, jar, pot; barrel, cask, tank; sack, bag; basket, hamper; capsule, encyst; **wrap,** enwrap, bundle; shrink-wrap

ADJS 10 **enclosed,** closed-in; **confined,** bound, immured, cloistered, "cabined, cribbed, confined"—Shakespeare; **imprisoned,** incarcerated, jailed; caged, cramped, restrained, corralled; besieged, beleaguered, leaguered, beset, cordoned, cordoned off, quarantined, blockaded; **shut-in,** pent-up, penned, cooped, mewed, walled- *or* hedged- *or* hemmed- *or* boxed- *or* fenced-in, fenced, walled, paled, railed, barred; hemmed, hedged

11 enclosing, confining, **cloistered,** cloisterlike, claustral, parietal, surrounding 209.8; limiting 210.9

12 **packed, packaged,** boxed, crated, canned, tinned <Brit>, parceled, cased, encased; bottled; capsuled, encapsuled; **wrapped,** enwrapped, bundled; shrink-wrapped; prepacked; vacuum-packed

213 INTERPOSITION
<a putting or lying between>

NOUNS 1 **interposition, interposing,** interposal, interlocation, intermediacy, interjacence; **intervention,** intervenience, intercurrence, slipping-in, sandwiching; leafing-in, interleaving, interfoliation, tipping-in; **intrusion** 214

2 **interjection, interpolation,** introduction, throwing- *or* tossing-in, **injection,** insinuation; intercalation, interlineation; **insertion** 191; interlocution, remark, parenthetical *or* side *or* incidental *or* casual remark, *obiter dictum* <L>, aside, parenthesis; episode; infix, insert

3 **interspersion, interfusion,** interlardment, interpenetration

4 **intermediary,** intermedium, mediary, medium; link, **connecting link,** tie, connection, **go-between,** liaison; middleman, broker, agent, wholesaler, jobber, distributor; **mediator** 466.3

5 **partition, dividing wall,** division, separa-

tion, *cloison* <Fr>; **wall, barrier;** panel; paries, parietes; brattice <mining>; bulkhead; diaphragm, midriff, midsection; septum, interseptum, septulum, dissepiment; **border** 211.4, **dividing line,** property line, party wall; **buffer, bumper,** mat, fender, cushion, pad, shock pad, collision mat; buffer state

VERBS 6 **interpose, interject, interpolate,** intercalate, interjaculate; **mediate, go between,** liaise <Brit nonformal>; **intervene;** put between, sandwich; **insert in,** stick in, introduce in, insinuate in, sandwich in, slip in, inject in, implant in; leaf in, interleaf, tip in, interfoliate; **foist in,** fudge in, work in, drag in, lug in, drag *or* lug in by the heels, worm in, squeeze in, smuggle in, throw in, run in, thrust in, edge in, wedge in; **intrude** 214.5

7 **intersperse, interfuse,** interlard, interpenetrate; intersow, intersprinkle

8 **partition,** set apart, separate, divide; **wall off,** fence off, screen off, curtain off

ADJS 9 interjectional, interpolative, intercalary; parenthetical, episodic

10 intervening, intervenient, **interjacent,** intercurrent; **intermediate,** intermediary, medial, mean, medium, mesne, median, **middle**

11 partitioned, walled; mural; septal, parietal

PREPS 12 **between, betwixt,** 'twixt, betwixt and between <nonformal>; **among, amongst,** 'mongst; **amid, amidst,** mid, 'mid, midst, 'midst; in the midst of, in the thick of

WORD ELEMENTS 13 medi—, medio—, mes—, meso—; inter—, intra—

214 INTRUSION

NOUNS 1 **intrusion,** obtrusion, **interloping;** interposition 213, interposal, imposition, insinuation, **interference,** intervention, interventionism, interruption, injection, interjection 213.2; **encroachment,** entrenchment, trespass, trespassing, unlawful entry; impingement, **infringement,** invasion, incursion, inroad, influx, irruption, infiltration; entrance 189

2 **meddling,** intermeddling; butting-in *and* kibitzing *and* sticking one's nose in<all nonformal>; **meddlesomeness, intrusiveness, forwardness,** obtrusiveness; **officiousness,** impertinence, presumption, presumptuousness; inquisitiveness 980.1

3 **intruder, interloper, trespasser;** crasher

and gate-crasher <both nonformal>, unwelcome *or* uninvited guest; invader, encroacher, infiltrator

4 meddler, intermeddler; **busybody, pry,** Paul Pry, prier, Nosey Parker *or* nosey Parker *or* Nosy Parker <all nonformal>, snoop *or* snooper, *yenta* <Yiddish>, **kibitzer** *and* backseat driver <both nonformal>

VERBS **5 intrude,** obtrude, **interlope;** come between, **interpose** 213.6, insert oneself, **intervene, interfere,** insinuate, impose; **encroach, infringe,** impinge, **trespass,** trespass on *or* upon, trench, entrench, invade, infiltrate; **break in upon,** break in, burst in, charge in, crash in, smash in, storm in; **barge in** <nonformal>, irrupt, **cut in,** thrust in 191.7, push in, press in, rush in, throng in, crowd in, squeeze in, elbow in, muscle in <nonformal>; **butt in** *and* **horn in** *and* chisel in <all nonformal>; appoint oneself; crash *and* crash the gates <both nonformal>; **get in,** get in on, creep in, steal in, sneak in, slink in, slip in; foist in, worm *or* work in, edge in, put in *or* shove in one's oar; **foist oneself upon,** thrust oneself upon; put on *or* upon, impose on *or* upon, put one's two cents in <nonformal>

6 interrupt, put in, cut in, break in; jump in, chime in *and* chip in *and* put in one's two-cents worth <all nonformal>

7 meddle, intermeddle, busybody, not mind one's business; **meddle with, tamper with,** mix oneself up with, inject oneself into, monkey with, fool with *or* around with <nonformal>, mess with *or* around with <nonformal>; **pry,** Paul-Pry, snoop, nose, **stick** *or* **poke one's nose in,** stick one's long nose into; have a finger in, have a finger in the pie; kibitz <nonformal>

ADJS **8 intrusive,** obtrusive, **interfering,** intervenient, invasive, interruptive

9 meddlesome, meddling; **officious,** over-officious, self-appointed, impertinent, presumptuous; **busybody,** busy; pushing, pushy, forward; **prying,** nosy *or* nosey *and* snoopy <both nonformal>; inquisitive 980.5

PHRS **10** <nonformal terms> **none of your business;** what's it to you?, **mind your own business,** keep your nose out of this, **butt out,** go soak your head, go sit on a tack, go roll your hoop, go peddle your fish, go fly a kite, go chase yourself, go jump in the lake; too many cooks spoil the broth

215 CONTRAPOSITION
<a placing over against>

NOUNS **1** contraposition, anteposition, posing against *or* over against; **opposition,** opposing, opposure; **antithesis,** contrast, ironic *or* contrastive juxtaposition; confrontment, **confrontation;** polarity, polar opposition, **polarization; contrariety** 778; contention 457; hostility 451.2

2 opposites, antipodes, polar opposites, contraries; **poles,** opposite poles, antipoles, counterpoles, North Pole, South Pole; antipodal points, antipoints; contrapositives <logic>; night and day, black and white

3 opposite side, other side, the other side of the picture *or* coin, other face; **reverse, inverse, obverse, converse;** heads, tails <of a coin>; flip side *and* B-side <both nonformal>

VERBS **4** contrapose, **oppose,** contrast, match, **set over against,** pose against *or* over against, put in opposition, set *or* pit against one another; **confront,** face, front, stand *or* lie opposite, stand opposed *or* vis-à-vis; be at loggerheads, be eyeball to eyeball, bump heads, meet head-on; counteract 451.3; contend; subtend; **polarize;** contraposit <logic>

ADJS **5** contrapositive, **opposite,** opposing, **facing,** confronting, confrontational, confrontive, eyeball-to-eyeball, one-on-one; **opposed,** on opposite sides, adversarial, at loggerheads, at daggers drawn, antithetic, antithetical; **reverse, inverse, obverse, converse; antipodal; polar,** polarized one-on-one, up against

ADVS **6 opposite, poles apart,** at opposite extremes; contrary, contrariwise, counter; just opposite, **face-to-face,** vis-à-vis, *front à front* <Fr>, nose to nose, one on one, eyeball-to-eyeball, back to back

PREPS **7 opposite to,** in opposition to, against, over against; versus, v *or* vs; **facing, across, fronting,** confronting, **in front of;** toward

WORD ELEMENTS **8** ant—, anti—, anth—, cat—, cata—, cath—, kat—, kata—, co—, contra—, counter—, enantio—, ob—

216 FRONT

NOUNS **1 front, fore,** forepart, forequarter, foreside, forefront, forehand; **priority,** anteriority; front office; **frontier** 211.5; foreland; **foreground;** proscenium; frontage; front page; frontispiece; **preface,** front matter, foreword; prefix; front view, front elevation; **head**, heading; **face**, facade, frontal; fascia; **false front**, window dressing, display; front man; bold *or* brave front, brave face; facet; obverse <of a coin or medal>, head <of a coin>; lap

2 **vanguard**, van, point, point man; **spearhead**, advance guard, **forefront, cutting edge**, avant-garde, outguard; scout; **pioneer; precursor** 815; **front-runner**, leader, first in line; **front**, battlefront, line, front line, battle line, line of departure; front rank, first line, first line of battle; **outpost**, farthest outpost; **bridgehead**, beachhead, airhead, railhead; advanced base

3 **prow, bow, stem**, rostrum, figurehead, nose, beak; bowsprit, jib boom; forecastle, forepeak; foredeck

4 **face**, facies, **visage**; physiognomy, phiz *and* dial <both nonformal>; **countenance**, features, lineaments, favor; mug *and* mush *and* pan *and* kisser *and* map *and* puss <all nonformal>

5 **forehead, brow**, lofty brow

6 **chin**, point of the chin, button <nonformal>

VERBS 7 be *or* stand in front, **lead, head**, head up; **get ahead of**, steal a march on, take the lead, come to the front *or* fore, forge ahead; be the front-runner, lead, lead the pack *or* field, be first; **pioneer**; front, front for, represent, speak for

8 **confront, front**, affront <old>, **face, meet, encounter**, breast, stem, brave, meet squarely, square up to, come to grips with, head *or* wade into, meet face to face *or* eyeball to eyeball *or* one-on-one, come face to face with, look in the face *or* eye, stare in the face, stand up to, stand fast, hold one's ground, hang tough *and* tough it out *and* gut it out <all nonformal>; call someone's bluff, call *or* bring someone to account; **confront with, face with**, bring face to face with, tell one to one's face, cast *or* throw in one's teeth, present to, **put** *or* **bring before**, set *or* place before, lay before, put *or* lay it on the line; bring up, bring forward; put it to, put it up to; **challenge**, dare, defy, fly in the teeth of, throw down the gauntlet, ask for trouble, start something, do something about it

9 **front on, face upon, give upon**, face *or* look toward, look out upon, look over, **overlook**

ADJS 10 **front, frontal, anterior; full-face, full-frontal; fore, forward**, forehand; foremost, headmost; first, earliest, **pi-**oneering, **trail-blazing, advanced; leading**, up-front <nonformal>, first, chief, head, prime, primary; **confronting**, confrontational, head-on, one-on-one *and* eyeball-to-eyeball <both nonformal>; **ahead, in front**, one-up, one jump *or* move ahead

11 **fronting, facing**, looking on *or* out on, opposite

ADVS 12 **before, ahead**, out *or* up ahead, **in front**, in the front, in the lead, in the van, in advance, **in the forefront**, in the foreground; **to the fore**, to the front; foremost, headmost, first; before one's face *or* eyes, under one's nose

13 **frontward**, frontwards, **forward**, forwards, vanward, **headward**, headwards, **onward**, onwards; **facing** 215.7

217 REAR

NOUNS 1 **rear, rear end, hind end**, hind part, hinder part, afterpart, rearward, **posterior, behind**, breech, stern, tail, tail end; **afterpiece**, tailpiece, heelpiece, heel; **back**, back side, reverse <of a coin or medal>, tail <of a coin>; back door, postern, postern door; back seat, rumble seat; hindhead, occiput

2 rear guard, rear, rear area

3 **back**, dorsum, ridge; dorsal region, lumbar region; hindquarter; loin

4 **buttocks, rump**, bottom, posterior, derrière; croup, crupper; podex; haunches; gluteal region; nates

5 <nonformal terms> **ass**, arse *and* bum <both chiefly Brit>, behind, backside, **butt, can**, cheeks, hind end, nether cheeks, stern, tail, rusty-dusty, **fanny**, prat, keister, popo, rear, rear end, tuchis *or* tushy *or* tush

6 **tail**, cauda, caudation, caudal appendage; tailpiece, scut <of a hare, rabbit, or deer>, brush <of a fox>, fantail <of fowls>; rattail, rat's-tail; dock, stub; caudal fin; **queue**, cue, **pigtail**

7 **stern**, heel; poop, transom, counter, fantail; sternpost, rudderpost

VERBS 8 <be behind> **bring up the rear**, come last, **follow**, come after; trail, trail behind, lag behind, draggle, **straggle**; fall behind, fall back, fall astern; **back up, back**, go back, go backwards, regress 163.5, retrogress, get behind; revert 858.4

ADJS 9 **rear**, rearward, **back**, backward, retrograde, **posterior**, postern, tail; after *or* aft; **hind, hinder; hindmost**, hindermost, hindhand, posteriormost, **aftermost**, aftmost, rearmost

10 <anatomy> posterial, dorsal, retral, tergal, lumbar, gluteal, sciatic, occipital

11 tail, caudal, caudate, caudated, tailed; taillike, caudiform

12 backswept, swept-back

ADVS **13 behind, in the rear, in back of;** in the background; behind the scenes; behind one's back; back to back; tandem

14 after; aft, abaft, baft, astern; aback

15 rearward, rearwards, to the rear, **hindward,** hindwards, **backward,** backwards, posteriorly, retrad, tailward, tailwards

218 SIDE

NOUNS **1 side, flank, hand;** laterality, sidedness, handedness; unilaterality, unilateralism, bilaterality, bilateralism, etc, multilaterality, many-sidedness; border 211.4; parallelism 203; bank, shore, coast; siding, planking; beam; broadside; quarter; hip, haunch; cheek, jowl, chop; temple; **profile,** side-view, half-face view

2 lee side, lee, leeward; lee shore; lee tide; lee wheel, lee helm, lee anchor, lee sheet, lee tack

3 windward side, windward, windwards, weather side, weather, weatherboard; weather wheel, weather helm, weather anchor, weather sheet, weather tack, weather rail, weather bow, weather deck; weather roll; windward tide, weathergoing tide, windward ebb, windward flood

VERBS **4 side, flank;** edge, skirt, border 211.10

5 go sideways, sidle, lateral, lateralize, **edge, veer, angle, slant, skew,** sidestep; go crabwise; **sideslip, skid;** make leeway

ADJS **6 side, lateral;** flanking, skirting; **beside,** to the side, off to one side; **alongside, parallel** 203.6; next-beside; **sidelong,** sideling, **sidewise,** sideway, **sideways,** sideward, **sidewards,** glancing; leeward, lee; windward, weather

7 sided, flanked, handed; lateral; **onesided,** unilateral, unilateralist, **two-sided, bilateral,** bilateralist, etc; dihedral, bifacial; **three-sided, trilateral,** trihedral, triquetrous; **four-sided, quadrilateral,** tetrahedral, etc; **many-sided, multilateral,** multifaceted, polyhedral

ADVS **8 laterally,** laterad; **sideways,** sideway, **sidewise, sidewards,** sideward, sideling, sidling, sidelong, aside, crabwise; side-to-side; **edgeways,** edgeway, **edgewise; widthwise, widthways, thwartwise; askance,** askant, asquint, glancingly; broadside, **broadside on,** on the beam; on

its side, on its beam ends; on the other hand; right and left

9 leeward, to leeward, alee, downwind; **windward,** to windward, weatherward, aweather, upwind

10 aside, on one side, **to one side,** to the side, sidelong, on the side, on the one hand, on one hand, on the other hand; **alongside,** in parallel 203.7, side-by-side; nearby, in juxtaposition 223.21; away

PREPS **11 beside, alongside, abreast,** abeam, by, on the flank of, along by, **by the side of,** along the side of

PHRS **12 side by side,** cheek to cheek, cheek by cheek, cheek by jowl, shoulder to shoulder, yardarm to yardarm

219 RIGHT SIDE

NOUNS **1 right side, right,** off side <of a horse or vehicle>, starboard; Epistle side, decanal side; recto <of a book>; right field; starboard tack; right wing; right-winger, conservative, reactionary

2 rightness, dextrality; dexterity, **right-handedness;** dextroversion, dextrocularity, dextroduction; dextrorotation, dextrogyration

3 right-hander; righty <nonformal>

ADJS **4 right, right-hand,** dextral, dexter; off, **starboard;** rightmost; dextrorse; dextropedal; dextrocardial; dextrocerebral; dextrocular; **clockwise,** dextrorotary, dextrogyrate, dextrogyratory; rightwing, right-wingish, right-of-center, conservative, reactionary, dry <Brit nonformal>

5 right-handed, dextromanual, dexterous

6 ambidextrous, ambidextral, ambidexter; dextrosinistral, sinistrodextral

ADVS **7 rightward,** rightwards, rightwardly, **right, to the right,** dextrally, dextrad; on the right, dexter; starboard, astarboard

220 LEFT SIDE

NOUNS **1 left side, left, left hand,** left-hand side, wrong side <nonformal>, near *or* nigh side <of a horse or vehicle>, portside, port, larboard; Gospel side, cantorial side, verso <of a book>; left field; port tack; left wing, left-winger, radical, liberal, progressive

2 leftness, sinistrality, **left-handedness;** sinistration; levoversion, levoduction; levorotation, sinistrogyration

3 left-hander, southpaw *and* lefty *and* portsider <all nonformal>

ADJS **4 left, left-hand,** sinister, sinistral;

near, nigh; **larboard, port;** sinistrorse; sinistrocerebral; sinistrocular; counterclockwise, levorotatory, sinistrogyrate; left-wing, left-wingish, left-of-center, radical, liberal, progressive, wet <Brit nonformal>

5 **left-handed,** sinistromanual, sinistral, lefty *and* southpaw <both nonformal>

ADVS 6 **leftward,** leftwards, leftwardly, **left, to the left,** sinistrally, sinister, sinistrad; on the left; larboard, port, aport

221 PRESENCE

NOUNS 1 **presence,** being here *or* there, hereness, thereness, physical *or* actual presence, spiritual presence; **immanence,** indwellingness, **inherence;** whereness, **immediacy;** ubiety; availability, accessibility; nearness 223; **occurrence** 830.2, existence 760

2 **omnipresence,** all-presence, **ubiquity;** continuum, plenum; infinity

3 **permeation, pervasion,** penetration; **suffusion,** transfusion, perfusion, diffusion, imbuement; absorption; **overrunning,** overspreading, ripple effect, overswarming, whelming, overwhelming

4 **attendance,** frequenting, frequence; number present; turnout *and* box office *and* draw <all nonformal>

5 **attender, visitor,** churchgoer, moviegoer, etc; **patron; fan** *and* buff <both nonformal>, aficionado, supporter; **frequenter,** habitué, haunter; spectator 917; theatergoer; audience 48.6

VERBS 6 **be present,** be located *or* situated 159.10, be there, be found, be met with; **occur** 830.5, exist 760.8; lie, stand, remain; fall in the way of; dwell in, indwell, inhere

7 **pervade, permeate,** penetrate; **suffuse,** inform, transfuse, perfuse, diffuse, leaven, imbue; **fill,** extend throughout, leave no void, occupy; **overrun,** overswarm, overspread, bespread, run through, meet one at every turn, whelm, overwhelm; creep *or* crawl *or* swarm with, be lousy with <nonformal>, teem with; honeycomb

8 **attend, be at,** be present at, find oneself at, **go** *or* **come to; appear** 33.8, turn up, set foot in, show up <nonformal>, show one's face, make *or* put in an appearance, give the pleasure of one's company, make a personal appearance, **visit, take in** *and* do *and* catch <all nonformal>; sit in *or* at; be on hand, be on deck <nonformal>;

watch, see; witness, look on, *assister* <Fr>

9 **revisit,** return to, go back to, come again

10 **frequent, haunt,** resort to, hang *and* hang around *and* hang about *and* hang out <all nonformal>

11 **present oneself, report;** report for duty

ADJS 12 **present,** attendant; **on hand,** on deck <nonformal>, on board; **immediate,** immanent, indwelling, inherent, **available, accessible, at hand,** in view, within reach *or* sight *or* call, in place

13 **omnipresent, all-present,** ubiquitous, everywhere; continuous, uninterrupted, infinite

14 **pervasive,** pervading, suffusive, perfusive, suffusing

15 **permeated,** saturated, shot through, filled with, perfused, suffused; honeycombed; crawling, creeping, swarming, teeming, lousy with <nonformal>

ADVS 16 **here, there**

17 **in person,** personally, bodily, **in the flesh** <nonformal>, in one's own person, *in propria persona* <L>

PREPS 18 **in the presence of,** in the face of, under the eyes *or* nose of, **before**

PHRS 19 all present and accounted for; standing room only *or* SRO

222 ABSENCE

NOUNS 1 **absence,** nonpresence, awayness; nowhereness, **nonexistence** 761; want, **lack,** total lack, blank, deprivation; nonoccurrence, neverness; **subtraction** 255

2 **vacancy,** vacuity, voidness, **emptiness,** blankness, hollowness, inanition; **bareness,** barrenness, desolateness, bleakness, desertedness; **nonoccupancy,** nonoccupation, vacancy, noninhabitance, nonresidence; vacancy, job vacancy, opening, open place *or* post, vacant post

3 **void, vacuum,** blank, emptiness, empty space, inanity; **nothingness;** *tabula rasa* <L>, clean slate; **nothing** 761.2

4 **absence,** nonattendance, **absenting, leaving,** taking leave, **departure** 188; "to leave is to die a little"—French saying, "Say, is not absence death to those who love?"—Pope; running away, fleeing, decamping, bolting, skedaddling *and* absquatulating <old informal>, abscondence, scarpering <Brit nonformal>; **disappearance** 34, escape 369; **absentation,** nonappearance, default, unauthorized *or* unexcused absence; **truancy, hooky** <nonformal>, French leave, **cut** <nonformal>; **absence without leave** *or* AWOL; **absenteeism,**

truantism; **leave, leave of absence,** furlough; **vacation,** holiday, paid vacation, paid holiday, day off, comp *or* compensation time; authorized *or* excused absence, sick leave; sabbatical leave

5 **absentee, truant,** no-show

6 **nobody, no one,** no man, not one, not a single one *or* person, **not a soul** *or* **blessed soul** *or* **living soul,** never a one, ne'er a one, nary one <nonformal>, nobody on earth *or* under the sun, nobody present; nonperson, unperson

VERBS 7 **be absent, stay away,** keep away, keep out of the way, not come, not show up <nonformal>, turn up missing <nonformal>, stay away in droves <nonformal>, fail to appear, default, sit out, include oneself out <nonformal>

8 **absent oneself, take leave** *or* **leave of absence,** go on leave *or* furlough; **vacation,** go on vacation *or* holiday, take time off, take off from work; slip off *or* away, duck *or* sneak out <nonformal>, slip out, make oneself scarce <nonformal>, leave the scene, bow out, exit, **depart** 188.6, **disappear** 34.2, escape 369.6

9 **play truant, go AWOL,** take French leave; play hooky, cut classes; jump ship

10 <nonformal terms> **split,** bugger off, fuck off, f off, make tracks, pull up stakes, push along, scarper <Brit>, push off, skedaddle *or* absquatulate <old>, **haul ass,** bag ass, **beat it, blow,** boogie, bug out, cut, **cut out,** cut and run, make tracks, peel out, piss off *and* scarper <Brit nonformal>, scram, shove off

ADJS 11 **absent,** not present, nonattendant, **away, gone,** departed, disappeared, vanished, absconded, out of sight; **missing,** among the missing, wanting, **lacking,** not found, nowhere to be found, omitted, taken away, subtracted, deleted; no longer present *or* with us *or* among us; long-lost; **nonexistent;** conspicuous by its absence

12 **nonresident,** not in residence, from home, **away from home,** on leave *or* vacation *or* holiday, on sabbatical leave; on tour, on the road; abroad, overseas

13 **truant,** absent without leave *or* **AWOL**

14 **vacant, empty,** hollow, inane, **bare, vacuous, void,** without content, with nothing inside, devoid, null, null and void; **blank,** clear, white, bleached; featureless, unrelieved, characterless, bland, insipid; **barren** 890.4

15 **available, open,** free, **unoccupied,** unfilled, **uninhabited,** unpopulated, unpeopled, untaken, untenanted, tenant-less, untended, unmanned, unstaffed; **deserted,** abandoned, forsaken, godforsaken <nonformal>

ADVS 16 **absently; vacantly, emptily,** hollowly, vacuously, blankly

17 **nowhere,** in no place, neither here nor there; nowhither

18 **away** 188.21, **elsewhere,** somewhere else, not here; elsewhither

PREPS 19 absent, lacking, sans; void of, empty of, free of, **without** 991.17

223 NEARNESS

NOUNS 1 **nearness, closeness,** nighness, **proximity,** propinquity, intimacy, immediacy; approximation, approach, convergence; a rough idea <nonformal>; **vicinity,** vicinage, **neighborhood,** environs, surroundings, surround, setting, grounds, purlieus, confines, precinct; **foreground,** immediate foreground

2 **short distance, short way,** little ways, **step,** short step, span, brief span, short piece <nonformal>, a little, intimate distance; short range; close quarters *or* range *or* grips; middle distance; **stone's throw,** spitting distance <nonformal>, bowshot, gunshot, pistol shot; earshot, earreach, a whoop *and* a whoop and a holler *and* two whoops and a holler <all nonformal>, ace, bit <nonformal>, **hair, hairbreadth** *or* **hairsbreadth,** cunt-hair <nonformal>, finger's breadth *or* width, an inch; hair space

3 **juxtaposition, apposition,** adjacency; **contiguity,** contiguousness, conterminousness *or* coterminousness; butting, abuttal, abutment; adjunction, junction 799.1, connection, union; **conjunction,** conjugation; appulse, syzygy; perigee, perihelion

4 **meeting,** meeting up, joining, joining up, **encounter;** confrontation; rencontre; near-miss, collision course, near thing, narrow squeak *or* brush

5 **contact, touch,** touching, *attouchement* <Fr>, taction, tangency, contingence; gentle *or* tentative contact, caress, brush, glance, nudge, kiss, rub, graze; impingement, impingence; osculation

6 **neighbor,** neighborer, next-door *or* immediate neighbor; borderer; abutter; adjoiner; bystander, onlooker, looker-on; tangent

VERBS 7 **near, come near,** nigh, draw near *or* nigh, **approach** 167.3, come within shouting distance; **converge,** shake hands

<nonformal>; come within an ace *or* an inch

8 **be near** *or* **around,** be in the vicinity *or* neighborhood, **approximate, approach,** get warm <nonformal>, come near, have something at hand *or* at one's fingertips; give *or* get a rough idea <nonformal>

9 **adjoin,** join, conjoin, **connect,** butt, **abut,** abut on *or* upon, be contiguous, be in contact; **neighbor,** border, **border on** *or* **upon,** verge on *or* upon; lie by, stand by

10 **contact, come in contact, touch, feel, impinge,** bump up against, hit; osculate; **graze,** caress, kiss, nudge, rub, brush, glance, scrape, sideswipe, skim, skirt, shave; grope *and* feel up *and* cop a feel <all nonformal>; have a near miss, brush *or* graze *or* squeak by

11 **meet, encounter; come across, run across,** meet up, fall across, cross the path of; **come upon,** run upon, fall upon, light *or* alight upon; come among, fall among; **meet with,** meet up with <nonformal>, come face to face with, **confront,** meet head-on *or* eyeball to eyeball; **run into, bump into** *and* run smack into <both nonformal>, join up with, come *or* run up against <nonformal>, run *and* fall foul of; burst *or* pitch *or* pop *or* bounce *or* plump upon <all nonformal>; be on a collision course

12 **stay near, keep close to;** stand by, lie by; go with, march with, follow close upon, breathe down one's neck, tread *or* stay on one's heels, stay on one's tail, tailgate <nonformal>; hang about *or* around, hang upon the skirts of, hover over; **cling to,** clasp, hug, huddle; hug the shore *or* land, keep hold of the land, stay inshore

13 **juxtapose,** appose, join 799, **adjoin, abut,** butt against, neighbor; bring near, put with, place *or* set side by side

ADJS 14 **near, close, nigh,** close-in, nearish, nighish, intimate, cheek-by-jowl, side-by-side, hand-in-hand, arm-in-arm, *bras-dessus-bras-dessous* <Fr>; **approaching,** nearing, approximate *or* approximating, proximate, proximal, propinque <old>; **short-range;** near the mark; warm *or* hot *or* burning <all nonformal>

15 **nearby, handy, convenient,** neighboring, vicinal, propinquant *or* propinquous, ready at hand, easily reached *or* attained

16 **adjacent, next,** immediate, contiguous, **adjoining, abutting; neighboring,** neighbor; **juxtaposed,** juxtapositional; **bordering,** conterminous *or* coterminous, connecting; **face-to-face** 215.6; end-to-end, endways, endwise; **joined**

17 **in contact,** contacting, **touching, meeting,** contingent; impinging, impingent; tangent, tangential; osculatory; grazing, kissing, glancing, brushing, rubbing, nudging

18 **nearer,** nigher, **closer**

19 **nearest,** nighest, **closest,** nearmost, next, immediate

ADVS 20 **near, nigh, close;** hard, at close quarters; **nearby, close by,** hard by, fast by, not far *or* far off, in the vicinity *or* **neighborhood of,** at hand, at close range, **near** *or* **close at hand;** thereabout *or* thereabouts, hereabout *or* hereabouts; nearabout *or* nearabouts *or* nigh about <all dial>; **about, around** <nonformal>, close about, along toward <nonformal>; at no great distance, only a step; as near as no matter *or* makes no difference <nonformal>; **within reach** *or* **range,** within call *or* hearing, within earshot *or* earreach, within a whoop *or* two whoops and a holler <nonformal>, within a stone's throw, a stone's throw away, in spitting distance <nonformal>, at one's elbow, at one's feet, at one's fingertips, under one's nose, at one's side, within one's grasp; just around the corner, just across the street, next-door, right next door, just next door

21 **in juxtaposition, in conjunction,** in apposition; beside 218.11

22 **nearly, near,** pretty near <nonformal>, close, **closely; almost,** all but, not quite, as good as, as near as makes no difference; **well-nigh, just about;** nigh, nigh hand

23 **approximately,** approximatively, practically <nonformal>, for practical purposes *or* all practical purposes, at a first approximation, give or take a little, **more or less; roughly,** roundly, in round numbers; **generally,** generally speaking, roughly speaking, say; in the ballpark <nonformal>

PREPS 24 **near, nigh,** near to, **close to,** near upon, close upon, hard on *or* upon, bordering on *or* upon, **verging on** *or* upon, on the confines of, at the threshold of, **on the brink** *or* **verge of,** on the edge of, at next hand, at *or* on the point of, on the skirts of; **not far from;** next door to, at one's door; nigh about *or* nearabout *or* nigh on *or* nigh onto <all dial>

25 **against,** up against, on, upon, over against, opposite, nose to nose with, vis-à -vis, in contact with

26 **about, around,** just about, circa, c, somewhere about *or* near, near *or* close upon,

give or take, near enough to, upwards of <nonformal>, —ish, —something; **in the neighborhood** *or* **vicinity of**

224 INTERVAL
<space between>

NOUNS **1 interval, gap, space** 158, intervening *or* intermediate space, **interspace**, distance *or* space between, interstice; **clearance**, margin, leeway, **room** 158.3; discontinuity 812, jump, leap, interruption; hiatus, caesura, lacuna; half space, single space, double space, em space, en space, hair space; time interval, interim 825

2 crack, cleft, cranny, chink, check, craze, chap, **crevice**, fissure, scissure, incision, notch, score, cut, gash, slit, split, **rift**, rent; **opening**, excavation, cavity, concavity, hole; **gap**, gape, **abyss**, abysm, **gulf, chasm**, void 222.3; **breach, break**, fracture, rupture; fault, flaw; slot, groove, furrow, moat, ditch, trench, dike; joint, seam; **valley**

VERBS **3 interspace, space**, make a space, set at intervals, dot, scatter 770.4, **space out, separate**, split off, part, dispart, set *or* keep apart

4 cleave, crack, check, incise, craze, **cut, cut apart**, gash, slit, **split**, rive, rent, rip open; **open; gap**, breach, break, fracture, rupture; slot, groove, furrow, ditch, trench

ADJS **5** intervallic, intervallary, interspatial, interstitial

6 interspaced, spaced, intervaled, **spaced out**, set at intervals, with intervals *or* an interval, dotted, scattered 770.9, **separated, parted**, disparted, split-off

7 cleft, cut, cloven, **cracked**, sundered, rift, rent, chinky, chapped, crazed; **slit, split**; gaping, gappy; hiatal, caesural, lacunar; fissured, fissural

225 HABITATION
<an inhabiting>

NOUNS **1 habitation**, inhabiting, inhabitation, habitancy, inhabitancy, **tenancy, occupancy**, occupation, **residence** *or* **residency**, residing, abiding, **living**, nesting, **dwelling**, commorancy <law>, lodging, staying, stopping, sojourning, staying over; squatting; cohabitation, living together, sharing quarters; living in sin; **abode, habitat** 228

2 peopling, peoplement, empeoplement, **population**, inhabiting; **colonization, settlement**, plantation

3 housing, domiciliation; lodgment, **lodging**, transient lodging, doss <Brit>, **quartering**, billeting, hospitality; living quarters; **housing development**, subdivision, tract; housing problem, housing bill

4 camping, tenting, **encampment**, bivouacking; camp 228.29

5 sojourn, sojourning, sojournment, temporary stay; **stay**, stop; **stopover**, stopoff, stayover, layover

6 habitability, inhabitability, **livability**

VERBS **7 inhabit, occupy**, tenant, move in *or* into, take up one's abode, make one's home; rent, lease; **reside, live, live in, dwell, lodge, stay**, remain, abide, hang *or* hang out <nonformal>, domicile, domiciliate; **room**, bunk, crash <nonformal>, berth, doss down <Brit>; perch *and* roost *and* squat <all nonformal>; nest; room together; cohabit, live together; live in sin

8 sojourn, stop, stay, **stop over**, stay over, lay over

9 people, empeople, **populate, inhabit**, denizen; colonize, **settle**, settle in, plant

10 house, domicile, domiciliate; provide with a roof, have as a guest *or* lodger, shelter, harbor; **lodge, quarter, put up**, billet, room, bed, berth, bunk; stable

11 camp, encamp, tent; pitch, **pitch camp**, pitch one's tent, drive stakes <nonformal>; bivouac; go camping, camp out, sleep out, rough it

ADJS **12 inhabited, occupied**, tenanted; **peopled**, empeopled, populated, colonized, settled; populous

13 resident, residentiary, **in residence; residing, living, dwelling**, commorant, lodging, **staying**, remaining, abiding, living in; cohabiting, live-in

14 housed, domiciled, domiciliated, **lodged**, quartered, billeted; stabled

15 habitable, inhabitable, occupiable, lodgeable, tenantable, **livable, fit to live in, fit for occupation**; homelike 228.33

ADVS **16 at home**, in the bosom of one's family, *chez soi* <Fr>; in one's element; back home *and* down home <both nonformal>

226 NATIVENESS

NOUNS **1 nativeness**, nativity, nativebornness, indigenousness *or* indigenity, aboriginality, autochthonousness, **nationality;** nativism

2 citizenship, native-born citizenship, citizenship by birth, citizenhood, subjecthood; civism

3 **naturalization**, naturalized citizenship,
citizenship by naturalization *or* adoption,
nationalization, adoption, admission, affiliation, **assimilation;** indigenization;
Americanization, Anglicization, etc; acculturation, enculturation; papers, citizenship papers; culture shock

VERBS 4 **naturalize**, grant *or* confer citizenship, adopt, admit, affiliate, **assimilate;**
Americanize, Anglicize, etc; acculturate,
acculturize; indigenize, go native
<nonformal>

ADJS 5 **native**, natal, **indigenous**, endemic,
autochthonous; mother, maternal, original, aboriginal, primitive; native-born,
home-grown, homebred, native to the soil
or place *or* heath

6 **naturalized**, adopted, **assimilated;** indoctrinated, Americanized, Anglicized, etc;
acculturated, acculturized; indigenized

227 INHABITANT, NATIVE

NOUNS 1 **population, inhabitants,**
habitancy, dwellers, **populace, people,**
whole people, people at large, citizenry,
folk, souls, living souls, body, whole
body, warm bodies <nonformal>; **public,** general public; community, society,
nation, commonwealth, constituency,
body politic, electorate; speech *or* linguistic community, ethnic *or* cultural
community; **census,** head count; population statistics, demography, demographics

2 **inhabitant**, inhabiter, habitant; **occupant,** occupier, **dweller, tenant, denizen,**
inmate; **resident,** residencer, residentiary, resider; inpatient; resident *or* live-
in maid; writer- *or* poet- *or* artist- *or*
composer-in-residence; house detective; incumbent, *locum tenens* <L>; sojourner; addressee

3 **native**, indigene, autochthon, earliest inhabitant, first comer, primitive settler;
primitive; **aborigine,** aboriginal; local
and local yokel <both nonformal>

4 **citizen, national**, subject; **naturalized citizen,** nonnative citizen, citizen by adoption, immigrant, metic; hyphenated
American, hyphenate; **cosmopolitan,** cosmopolite, citizen of the world

5 **fellow citizen,** fellow countryman,
compatriot, congener, **countryman,**
countrywoman, *landsman* <Yiddish>,
paesano <Ital>, *paisano* <Sp>; fellow
townsman, home boy *and* home girl *and*
hometowner <all nonformal>

6 **townsman, townswoman,** towny *and*
towner <both nonformal>, **villager,** oppidan, city dweller, city person; big-city
person, **city slicker** <nonformal>; urban-
ite; suburbanite; exurbanite; burgher,
burgess, *bourgeois* <Fr>; townspeople,
townfolks, townfolk

7 **householder,** homeowner, house-owner,
proprietor, freeholder; cottager, cotter,
cottier, crofter; head of household

8 **lodger, roomer,** paying guest; **boarder,**
board-and-roomer, **transient,** transient
guest *or* boarder; **renter, tenant,** leaser *or*
lessee, subleaser *or* sublessee

9 **settler,** *habitant* <Canadian & Louisiana
Fr>; **colonist,** colonizer, colonial, immigrant, planter; **homesteader; squatter,**
nester; **pioneer;** sooner; precursor 815

10 wilderness settler *or* hinterlander;
frontiersman, mountain man; **back-
woodsman,** woodlander, woodsman,
woodman, woodhick <nonformal>;
mountaineer, hillbilly *and* ridge runner
<both nonformal>, brush ape *and* briar-
hopper <both nonformal>; cracker *and*
redneck <both nonformal>, desert rat
<nonformal>, clam digger <nonfor-
mal>, piny <nonformal>

11 <regional inhabitants> **Easterner,** east-
lander; **Midwesterner; Westerner,**
westlander; **Southerner,** southlander;
Northerner, northlander, Yankee; North-
man; New Englander, Down-Easter
Yankee; Maritimer <Canada>

228 ABODE, HABITAT
<place of habitation or resort>

NOUNS 1 **abode, habitation, place, dwelling,**
dwelling place, abiding place, place to
live, where one lives *or* resides, where one
is at home, roof, roof over one's head, **residence,** place of residence, **domicile,**
domus <L>; **lodging,** lodgment, lodging
place; seat, nest, living space, houseroom,
sleeping place, place to rest one's head,
crash pad <nonformal>; native heath,
turf, home turf; **address,** permanent residence; **housing; affordable housing,** low-
cost housing, low-and-middle-income
housing, public housing, public-sector
housing, scattersite housing; council
house <Brit>; private housing, private-
sector housing, market-rate housing

2 **home,** home sweet home, "the place
where, when you go there, They have to
take you in"—Robert Frost, "the place
to do things you want to do"—Zelda
Fitzgerald; **fireside, hearth,** hearth and
home, hearthstone, fireplace, *foyer* <Fr>,

chimney corner, ingle, ingleside *or* inglenook; **household,** ménage; **homestead,**
home place, home roof, roof, rooftree, toft
<Brit old>; paternal roof *or* domicile,
family homestead, ancestral halls; **homi-
ness** *or* homeyness

3 **domesticity;** housewifery, **housekeeping,
homemaking;** householding, householdry

4 **quarters, living quarters; lodgings,** lodging, lodgment; diggings *and* digs <both
Brit nonformal>, pad *and* crib <both
nonformal>, room; **rooms,** berth, roost,
accommodations; **housing** 225.3, shelter,
gîte <Fr>

5 **house,** dwelling, dwelling house, *casa*
<Sp & Ital>; house and grounds, house
and lot, homesite; **building, structure, edifice,** fabric, erection, **hall** 197.4; roof;
lodge; manor house, hall; town house, *rus
in urbe* <L>; country house, *dacha*
<Russ>, country seat; ranch house,
farmhouse, farm; prefabricated house,
modular house; sod house, adobe house;
lake dwelling 241.3; houseboat; cave *or*
cliff dwelling; penthouse; split-level; parsonage 703.7, **rectory,** vicarage, deanery,
manse; official residence, White House,
10 Downing Street, governor's mansion;
presidential palace; embassy, consulate

6 **farmstead; ranch,** *rancho, hacienda*
<both Sp>, toft *or* steading <both Brit
old>, grange

7 **estate; mansion,** palatial residence,
stately home <Brit>; **villa, château,** *hôtel*
<Fr>, **castle,** tower; **palace,** *palais* <Fr>,
palazzo <Ital>, court

8 **cottage,** cot *or* cote, **bungalow,** box;
cabin, log cabin; **second home, vacation
home;** chalet, lodge, snuggery; home
away from home, *pied-à-terre* <Fr>

9 **hut,** hutch, **shack, shanty,** crib, hole-in-
the-wall <nonformal>, **shed; lean-to;
booth,** bothy *or* boothy <both Scots>,
stall; tollbooth *or* tollhouse, sentry box,
gatehouse, porter's lodge; **outhouse,** outbuilding; privy; **pavilion,** kiosk; Quonset
hut *or* Nissen hut; hutment

10 <American Indian houses> wigwam, tepee, hogan, wickiup, jacal, longhouse;
tupik, igloo <both Eskimo>; ajouba

11 **hovel, dump** <nonformal>, rathole, hole,
sty, pigsty, pigpen, tumbledown shack

12 **summerhouse,** arbor, bower, **gazebo,** pergola, kiosk, alcove, retreat; **conservatory,
greenhouse,** glasshouse <Brit>, lathhouse

13 **apartment, flat,** tenement, chambers
<Brit>, rooms; studio apartment *or* flat;
bed-sitter <Brit>, granny flat, flatlet;

suite, suite *or* set of rooms; walkup, cold-
water flat; **penthouse;** garden apartment;
duplex apartment; railroad *or* shotgun
flat

14 **apartment house, flats, tenement;** duplex, duplex house; apartment complex;
cooperative apartment house *or* co-op
<nonformal>, condominium *or* condo
<nonformal>; high-rise apartment
building *or* high rise

15 **inn, hotel,** hostel, hostelry, **tavern,** *posada*
<Sp>; tourist hotel, *parador* <Sp>;
roadhouse, caravansary *or* caravanserai,
guest house, bed and breakfast; youth
hostel, hospice, elder hostel; **lodging
house,** rooming house; **boardinghouse,**
pension <Fr>, *pensione* <Ital>; **dormitory,** dorm <nonformal>, fraternity *or*
sorority house; bunkhouse; **flophouse** *and*
fleabag <both nonformal>, dosshouse
<Brit nonformal>

16 **motel,** motor court, motor inn, motor hotel, auto court; boatel

17 **trailer,** house *or* camp trailer, **mobile
home,** camper, caravan <Brit>; trailer
court *or* camp *or* park, campground

18 **habitat,** home, **range,** stamping grounds,
locality, native environment

19 **zoo, menagerie,** *Tiergarten* <Ger>, zoological garden *or* park

20 **barn, stable,** stall; **cowbarn,** cowhouse,
cowshed, cowbyre, byre; mews

21 **kennel, doghouse;** pound, dog pound;
cattery

22 **coop, chicken house** *or* **coop,** henhouse,
hencote, hennery; brooder

23 **birdhouse, aviary,** bird cage; dovecote,
pigeon house *or* loft, columbary; roost,
perch, roosting place; rookery, heronry;
eyrie

24 vivarium, terrarium, aquarium; fishpond

25 **nest,** nidus; **beehive, apiary,** hive, bee
tree, hornet's nest, wasp's nest, vespiary

26 **lair, den,** cave, **hole,** covert, mew, form;
burrow, tunnel, earth, run, couch, lodge

27 **resort, haunt,** purlieu, **hangout** <nonfor-
mal>, **stamping ground** <nonformal>;
gathering place, rallying point, meeting
place, clubhouse, club; casino, gambling
house; health resort; **spa,** baths, springs,
watering place

28 <disapproved place> **dive** <nonfor-
mal>, **den, lair,** den of thieves; hole *and*
dump *and* **joint** <all nonformal>; gyp *or*
clip joint <nonformal>; **whorehouse,**
cathouse <nonformal>, sporting house,
brothel, bordello, stews, fleshpots

29 **camp, encampment,** *Lager* <Ger>; bivouac; barrack *or* **barracks,** casern, *caserne*

<Fr>, cantonment, lines <Brit>; hobo jungle *or* camp; detention camp, concentration camp, *Konzentrationslager* <Ger>; campground *or* campsite
30 <deities of the household> lares and penates, Vesta, Hestia
VERBS **31 keep house,** housekeep <nonformal>, practice domesticity, maintain *or* run a household
ADJS **32 residential,** residentiary; domestic, domiciliary, domal; **home, household;** mansional, manorial, palatial
33 homelike, homish, **homey** <nonformal>, homely; comfortable, friendly, cheerful, peaceful, cozy, snug, intimate; simple, plain, unpretending
34 domesticated, tame, tamed, broken; housebroken

229 FURNITURE

NOUNS **1 furniture,** furnishings, movables, home furnishings, house furnishings, household effects, household goods, office furniture, school furniture, church furniture, library furniture, furnishments <old>; **cabinetmaking,** cabinetwork, cabinetry; **furniture design, furniture style,** <see list>; period furniture; **piece of furniture, furniture piece,** chair, sofa, bed, table, desk, cabinet, mirror, clock, screen; **suite, set of furniture,** ensemble, decor

2 furniture styles and periods

Adam	Chippendale
Adapted Colonial	Colonial *or* Campaign
Adirondack	Contemporary
American Chippen-	Cotswold School
dale *or* Pilgrim	Country Chippendale
American Empire	Cromwellian *or* Com-
American Jacobean	monwealth
American Moderne	De Stijl
American Queen	Desornamentado
Anne	Directoire
American Regency *or*	Duncan Phyfe
Directory	Early Georgian
American Restora-	Eastlake
tion *or* Pillar and	Egyptian
Scroll	Empire
Anglo-Dutch	French Provincial
Art Deco	French Renaissance
Art Nouveau	Georgian
Arts and Crafts	Gothic
Baroque	Gothic-Renaissance
Bauhaus	Hepplewhite
Biedermeier	International
Block-front	Italian Renaissance
Boston Chippendale	Jacobean
Byzantine	Japonisme
Chinese Chippendale	Late Regency
Chinoiserie	Later Victorian
Louis XIII	Queen Anne
Louis XIV	Renaissance Revival
Louis XV	Restoration *or* Car-
Louis XVI	olean
Mannerist	Rococo
Mission	Rococo Revival *or*
Modern	Louis Philippe *or*
Moderne	Louis XV Revival
National Romanti-	Romano-Byzantine *or*
cism	Italo-Byzantine *or*
Naturalistic	Romanesque
Neoclassical *or le style*	Scandinavian Mod-
antique <Fr>	ern
Neo-Gothic *or* Cathé-	Shaker
drale	Sheraton
Neo-Grec	Spanish Renaissance
New York Chippen-	Stuart
dale	Tudor
Newport Chippen-	Turkish
dale	Venetian
Palladian	Victorian
Pennsylvania Dutch	Viking Revival *or*
Philadelphia Chip-	Dragonesque
pendale	William and Mary
Pop Art	

230 TOWN, CITY

NOUNS **1 town,** township; **city, metropolis,** metro, metropolitan area, greater city, megalopolis, supercity, conurbation, urban complex, spread city, urban sprawl, urban corridor, strip city, **municipality,** *urbs* <L>, *polis* <Gk>, city *or* municipal government, metro; *ville* <Fr>, *Stadt* <Ger>; **borough, burg** <nonformal>, bourg, burgh <Scots>; **suburb,** suburbia, burbs <nonformal>, slurb, stockbroker belt <Brit nonformal>, outskirts, *faubourg* <Fr>, *banlieue* <Fr>; exurb, exurbia; market town <Brit>; small town; twin town; boom town, ghost town
2 village, hamlet; ham *and* thorp *and* wick <all old>; country town, crossroads, wide place in the road; "a little one-eyed, blinking sort o' place"—Thomas Hardy, "a hive of glass, where nothing unobserved can pass"—C H Spurgeon
3 <nonformal terms> one-horse town, jerkwater town, one-gas-station town, **tank town** *or* station, **whistle-stop,** jumping-off place; **hick town,** rube town, podunk; hoosier town; wide place in the road
4 capital, capital city, **seat,** seat of government; **county seat** *or* county site, county town *or* shiretown <Brit>
5 town hall, city hall, municipal building; courthouse; police headquarters *or* station, station house, precinct house; firehouse, fire station, station house;

county building, county courthouse; community center

6 <city districts> East Side *or* End, West Side *or* End; **downtown,** uptown, midtown; city center, city centre <Brit>, urban center, central *or* center city, core, core city, inner city, suburbs, suburbia, burbs <nonformal>, outskirts, greenbelt, residential district, business district *or* section, shopping center; Chinatown, Little Italy, Little Hungary, etc; **asphalt** *or* **concrete jungle,** mean streets; **slum** *or* **slums,** the other side *or* the wrong side of the tracks, blighted area *or* neighborhood *or* section, run-down neighborhood, tenement district, shanty-town, hell's kitchen *or* half-acre; tenderloin, red-light district, Bowery, **skid row** *or* skid road <both nonformal>; **ghetto, inner city,** urban ghetto, barrio

7 block, city block, square

8 square, plaza, *place* <Fr>, *piazza* <Ital>, *campo* <Ital>, **marketplace,** market, mart, rialto, forum, agora

9 circle, circus <Brit>; crescent

10 city planning, urban planning; urban studies, urbanology

ADJS **11 urban, metropolitan, municipal,** metro, burghal, **civic,** oppidan; citywide; city, town, village; citified; suburban; interurban; downtown, uptown, midtown; **inner-city,** core, core-city, ghetto; small-town; boom-town

231 REGION

NOUNS **1 region, area, zone,** belt, **territory,** terrain; **place** 159.1; **space** 158; **country** 232, **land** 234, ground, soil; territoriality; territorial waters, twelve- *or* three-mile limit, continental shelf, offshore rights; air space; heartland; hinterland; **district, quarter, section,** department, division; salient, corridor; part, parts; **neighborhood,** vicinity, vicinage, neck of the woods <nonformal>, purlieus; premises, confines, precincts, environs, milieu

2 sphere, hemisphere, orb, **orbit,** ambit, circle; **circuit,** judicial circuit, **beat, round,** walk; **realm,** demesne, **domain,** dominion, jurisdiction, bailiwick; border, borderland, march; **province,** precinct, department; **field,** pale, arena

3 zone; climate *or* clime <both old>; **longitude,** longitude in arc, longitude in time; meridian, prime meridian; **latitude,** parallel; equator, the line; tropic, Tropic of Cancer, Tropic of Capricorn; tropics, subtropics, Torrid Zone; Temperate *or* Variable Zones; Frigid Zones, Arctic Zone *or* Circle, Antarctic Zone *or* Circle; horse latitudes, roaring forties

4 plot, plot of ground *or* land, parcel of land, plat, **patch, tract, field;** lot; air space; block, square; section <square mile>, forty <sixteenth of a section>; close, quadrangle, quad, enclave, pale, *clos* <Fr>, croft <Brit>, kraal <Africa>; real estate

5 <territorial divisions> **state, territory, province,** region, duchy, electorate, government, principality; **county,** shire, canton, *oblast, okrug* <both Russ>, *département* <Fr>, *Kreis* <Ger>; **borough, ward,** riding, *arrondissement* <Fr>; **township,** hundred, commune, wapentake; metropolis, metropolitan area, **city, town** 230; **village,** hamlet; **district,** congressional district, electoral district, precinct; magistracy, soke, bailiwick; shrievalty, sheriffalty, sheriffwick, constablewick <all England>; archdiocese, archbishopric, stake; **diocese,** bishopric, parish

6 <regions of the world> continent, landmass; **Old World,** the old country; **New World,** America; **Northern Hemisphere,** North America; Central America; **Southern Hemisphere,** South America; Latin America; **Western Hemisphere, Occident,** West; **Eastern Hemisphere, Orient,** Levant, East, eastland; Far East, Mideast *or* Middle East, Near East; Asia, Europe, Eurasia, Asia Major, Asia Minor, Africa; Antipodes, down under, Australasia, Oceania

7 <regions of the US> the West, westland, the wild West, the West Coast, the Coast, the left Coast <nonformal>; the Northwest, the Pacific Northwest; the Rockies; the Southwest, the Middle West, Middle America; the Great Plains, the heartlands; the North Central region; the Rust Belt; the East, eastland, the East Coast, the Middle Atlantic; the Northeast, the Southeast; the North, the northland, the Snow Belt, the Frost Belt; Appalachia; the South, the southland, Dixie, Dixieland; the Deep South, the Old South; the Delta, the bayous; the Bible Belt; the Sunbelt; the Gulf Coast; New England, Down East, Yankeeland <nonformal>

ADJS **8 regional, territorial, geographical,** areal, sectional, zonal, topographic *or* topographical

9 local, localized, of a place, geographically limited, topical, vernacular, parochial, provincial, insular, limited, confined

10 state mottoes and nicknames

Alabama "We dare defend our rights"; Heart of Dixie *or* Camellia State

Alaska "North to the future"; The Last Frontier

Arizona "Diat Deus"; Grand Canyon State

Arkansas "Regnat populus"; Land of Opportunity

California "Eureka"; Golden State

Colorado "Nil sine numine"; Centennial State

Connecticut "Qui transtulit sustinet"; Constitution State; Nutmeg State

Delaware "Liberty and independence"; First State *or* Diamond State

District of Columbia "Justitia Omnibus"; Capital City

Florida "In God we trust"; Sunshine State

Georgia "Wisdom, justice, and moderation"; Empire State of the South; Peach State

Hawaii "The life of the land is perpetuated in righteousness"; Aloha State

Idaho "Esto perpetua"; Gem State

Illinois "State sovereignty—national union"; Prairie State

Indiana "Crossroads of America"; Hoosier State

Iowa "Our liberties we prize and our rights we will maintain"; Hawkeye State

Kansas "Ad astra per aspera"; Sunflower State

Kentucky "United we stand, divided we fall"; Bluegrass State

Louisiana "Union, justice and confidence"; Pelican State

Maine "Dirigo"; Pine Tree State

Maryland "Fatti maschii, parole femine"; Old Line State *or* Free State

Massachusetts "Ense petit placidam sub libertate"; Bay State; Colony State

Michigan "Si quaeris peninsulam amoenam"; Great Lake State *or* Wolverine State

Minnesota "L'Etoile du nord"; North Star State *or* Gopher State

Mississippi "Virtute et armis"; Magnolia State

Missouri "Salus populi suprema lex esto"; Show-Me State

Montana "Oro y plato"; Treasure State

Nebraska "Equality before the law"; Cornhusker State

Nevada "All for our country"; Sagebrush State *or* Battle-Born State

New Hampshire "Live free or die"; Granite State

New Jersey "Liberty and prosperity"; Garden State

New Mexico "Crescit eundo"; Land of Enchantment

New York "Excelsior"; Empire State

North Carolina "Esse quam videri"; Tar Heel State *or* Old North State

North Dakota "Liberty and union, now and forever, one and inseparable"; Peace Garden State

Ohio "With God, all things are possible"; Buckeye State

Oklahoma "Labor omnia vincit"; Sooner State

Oregon "The union"; Beaver State

Pennsylvania "Virtue, liberty and independence"; Keystone State

Rhode Island "Hope"; Little Rhody; Ocean State

South Carolina "Dum spiro spero"; Palmetto State

South Dakota "Under God, the people rule"; Coyote State *or* Sunshine State

Tennessee "Agriculture and commerce"; Volunteer State

Texas "Friendship"; Lone Star State

Utah "Industry"; Beehive State

Vermont "Freedom and unity"; Green Mountain State

Virginia "Sic semper tyrannis"; Old Dominion

Washington "Alki"; Evergreen State

West Virginia "Montani semper liberi"; Mountain State

Wisconsin "Forward"; Badger State

Wyoming "Equal rights"; Equality State

10 United State Territories and Commonwealths; mottoes

American Samoa "Samoa Muamua le Atua"

Guam "Where America's day begins"

Puerto Rico "Joannes est nomen eius"

Virgin Islands none

232 COUNTRY

NOUNS **1 country,** land; **nation,** nationality, **state,** nation-state, sovereign nation *or* state, polity, **body politic; power,** superpower, world power; microstate; **republic,** people's republic, **commonwealth,** commonweal; **kingdom,** sultanate; **empire,** empery; **realm,** dominion, domain; **principality,** principate; duchy, dukedom; grand duchy, archduchy, archdukedom, earldom, county, palatinate, seneschalty; chieftaincy, chieftainry; toparchy, *toparchia* <L>; city-state, *polis* <Gk>, free city; **province,** territory, possession; colony, settlement; protectorate, mandate, mandated territory, mandant, mandatee, mandatory; buffer state; **ally,** military ally, cobelligerent, treaty partner; satellite, puppet regime *or* government; free nation, captive nation, iron-curtain country; nonaligned *or* unaligned *or* neutralist nation; developed nation, in-

dustrial *or* industrialized nation; underdeveloped nation, third-world nation

2 fatherland, *Vaterland* <Ger>, *patria*
<L>, *la patrie* <Fr>, **motherland,** mother
country, **native land,** native soil, one's native heath *or* ground *or* soil *or* place, the
old country, country of origin, **birthplace,**
cradle; **home, homeland,** homeground,
"home is where one starts"—T S Eliot,
God's country; the home front

3 United States, United States of America,
US, USA, US of A <nonformal>, **America,** Columbia, the States, Uncle Sugar
and Yankeeland <both nonformal>,
Land of Liberty, the melting pot; stateside

**4 Britain, Great Britain, United Kingdom,
the UK,** Britannia, Albion, Blighty <Brit
nonformal>, Limeyland <US nonfor-
mal>, Tight Little Island, Land of the
Rose, "This royal throne of kings, this
scepter'd isle, This earth of majesty, this
seat of Mars, This other Eden, demi-
paradise"—Shakespeare, Sovereign of
the Seas; British Empire, Commonwealth of Nations, British Commonwealth of Nations, the Commonwealth;
perfidious Albion

5 <national personifications> Uncle Sam
or Brother Jonathan <US>; John Bull
<England>

6 nationhood, peoplehood, **nationality;
statehood, nation-statehood, sovereignty,**
sovereign nationhood *or* statehood,
independence, self-government, self-
determination; internationality, internationalism; **nationalism**

7 <derog terms> dago, Guinea, greaseball,
wop <Italian>; frog <Frenchman>;
Kraut, Krauthead, Jerry, Boche
<German>; Mick, Mickey, Paddy
<Irishman>; squarehead <Scandana-
vian>; polack <Pole>; Hunk, Hunkie,
Bohunk <Eastern European>; Canuck,
Pepsi <Canadian Fr>; greaser, wetback
<Mexican>; spic <Latin American>;
Chink <Chinese>; Jap <Japanese>;
limey <Briton>; Aussie <Australian>

233 THE COUNTRY

NOUNS **1 the country,** agricultural region,
farm country, farmland, arable land,
grazing region *or* country, rural district,
rustic region, province *or* **provinces,**
countryside, woodland 310.11, grassland
310.8, woods and fields, meadows and
pastures, the soil, grass roots; **the sticks**

and the tall corn *and* yokeldom *and* hick-
dom <all nonformal>; cotton belt,
tobacco belt, black belt, farm belt, corn
belt, fruit belt, wheat belt, citrus belt;
dust bowl; highlands, moors, uplands,
foothills; lowlands, veld *or* veldt, savanna
or savannah, plains, prairies, steppes,
wide-open spaces

2 hinterland, back country, outback
<Australia>, up-country, boonies *and*
boondocks <both nonformal>; **the bush,**
bush country, bushveld, **woods,** wood-
lands, **backwoods,** forests, timbers, the
big sticks <nonformal>, brush; wilderness, wilds, uninhabited region, virgin
land *or* territory; **wasteland** 890.2; **frontier,** borderland, outpost; wild West, cow
country

3 rusticity, ruralism, inurbanity, agrarianism, bucolicism, **provincialism,**
provinciality, simplicity, pastoral simplicity, unspoiledness; yokelism, hick-
ishness, backwoodsiness; **boorishness,**
churlishness, unrefinement, uncultivation

4 ruralization, countrification, rustication,
pastoralization

VERBS **5 ruralize, countrify, rusticate,** pas-
toralize; farm 1067.16; return to the soil

ADJS **6 rustic, rural, country, provincial,
farm, pastoral, bucolic,** Arcadian, **agrarian,** agrestic; **agricultural** 1067.20;
lowland, low-lying, upland, highland,
prairie, plains

7 countrified, inurbane; country-born,
country-bred, up-country; farmerish,
hobnailed, clodhopping, clodhopperish;
boorish, clownish, loutish, lumpish,
lumpen, cloddish, churlish, **uncouth,** unpolished, uncultivated, uncultured,
unrefined; country-style, country-fashion

8 <nonformal terms> **hick,** hicky, hick-
ified, from the sticks, rube, hayseed,
yokel, yokelish, down-home, shit-kicking,
hillbilly, redneck

9 hinterland, back, **back-country,** up-
country, backroad, outback <Australia>,
wild, wilderness, virgin; wild-West, cow-
country; **waste** 890.4; backwood *or* **backwoods,** back of beyond, backwoodsy;
woodland, sylvan

234 LAND

NOUNS **1 land, ground,** landmass, earth,
glebe <old>, **sod,** clod, **soil, dirt,** dust,
clay, marl, mold <Brit nonformal>; *terra*
<L>, **terra firma;** terrain; **dry land;** ar-

able land; marginal land; grassland
310.8, woodland 310.11; crust, earth's
crust, lithosphere; regolith; topsoil, sub-
soil; alluvium, alluvion; eolian *or*
subaerial deposit; **real estate,** real property, landholdings, acres, territory,
freehold; region 231; the country 233;
earth science 1069

2 **shore, coast,** *côte* <Fr>; **strand,** *playa*
<Sp>, **beach,** beachfront, beachside
shingle, plage, lido, riviera, sands, berm;
waterside, **waterfront;** shoreline, coast-
line; foreshore; bank, embankment;
riverside; lakefront, lakeshore; **seashore,
coast, seacoast, seaside, seaboard,** sea-
beach, seacliff, seabank, sea margin,
oceanfront, oceanside, seafront, seaside,
shorefront, tidewater, tideland, coast-
land, littoral; wetland, wetlands; **bay,**
bayfront, bayside; drowned *or* submerged coast; rockbound coast, ironbound coast; loom of the land

3 **landsman,** landman, **landlubber**

ADJS 4 **terrestrial,** terrene <old>, **earth,
earthly,** telluric, tellurian; earthbound;
sublunar, subastral; geophilous; terra-
queous; fluvioterrestrial

5 earthy, earthen, soily, loamy, marly,
gumbo; clayey, clayish; adobe

6 **alluvial,** estuarine, fluviomarine

7 **coastal, littoral, seaside, shore,** shoreside;
shoreward; riparian *or* riparial *or* ripar-
ious; riverain, riverine; riverside; lakefront, lakeshore; oceanfront, oceanside;
seaside, seafront, shorefront, shoreline;
beachfront, beachside; bayfront, bayside;
tideland, tidal, wetland

ADVS 8 **on land,** on dry land, on terra firma;
onshore, ashore; alongshore; shoreward;
by land, overland

9 **on earth,** on the face of the earth *or* globe,
in the world, in the wide world, in the
whole wide world; **under the sun,** under
the stars, beneath the sky, under heaven,
below, **here below**

235 BODY OF LAND

NOUNS 1 **continent, mainland,** main <old>,
landform, continental landform, landmass; North America, South America,
Africa, Europe, Asia, Eurasia, Eurasian
landmass, Australia, Antarctica; subcon-
tinent, India, Greenland; peninsula;
plate, crustal plate, crustal segment, Pacific plate, American plate, African plate,
Eurasian plate, Antarctic plate, Indian
plate; continental divide, continental
drift

2 **island, isle; islet,** holm, ait <Brit nonfor-
mal>; continental island; oceanic island;
key, cay; sandbank, sandbar, bar; **reef,**
coral reef, coral head; coral island, atoll;
archipelago, island group *or* chain; insularity; islandology

3 **continental,** mainlander; continentalist

4 **islander,** islandman, island-dweller,
islesman, insular; islandologist

VERBS 5 insulate, isolate, island, enisle;
island-hop

ADJS 6 **continental,** mainland

7 **insular,** insulated, isolated; island, is-
landy *or* islandish, islandlike; islanded,
isleted, island-dotted; seagirt; archi-
pelagic *or* archipelagian

236 PLAIN

  <open country>

NOUNS 1 **plain, plains,** flat country, flatland,
flats, flat, level; champaign, champaign
country, open country, **wide-open spaces;
prairie,** grassland 310.8, sea of grass,
steppe, pampas, *pampa* <Sp>, savanna,
tundra, vega, campo, llano, sebkha; **veld,**
grass veld, bushveld, tree veld; wold,
weald; **moor,** moorland, down, **downs,**
lande, **heath,** fell <Brit>; lowland, lowlands, bottomland; basin, playa; sand
plain, sand flat, strand flat; tidal flat, salt
marsh; salt pan; salt flat, alkali flat; **desert** 890.2; **plateau,** upland, tableland,
table, **mesa,** mesilla; peneplain; coastal
plain, tidal plain, alluvial plain, delta,
delta plain; mare, lunar mare

ADJS 2 champaign, **plain, flat,** open; cam-
pestral *or* campestrian

237 HIGHLANDS

NOUNS 1 **highlands, uplands,** highland, upland, high country, elevated land, dome,
plateau, tableland, upland area, piedmont, moor, moorland, **hills, heights,** hill
or hilly country, downs, wold, foothills,
rolling country, **mountains,** mountain *or*
mountainous country, high terrain,
peaks, range, *massif* <Fr>

2 **slope, declivity,** steep, versant, incline,
rise, talus, brae <Scots>, mountainside,
hillside, bank, gentle *or* easy slope, glacis,
angle of repose, steep *or* rapid slope, fall
line, bluff, cliff, precipice, steep, wall,
palisade, scar <Brit>, escarpment,
scarp, fault scarp, rim, face; upper
slopes, upper reaches, timberline *or*
tree line

3 **plateau, tableland,** high plateau, table,

mesa, table mountain, butte, moor, fell
<Brit>, hammada

4 **hill,** down <chiefly Brit>, "the earth's
gesture of despair for the unreachable"—
Rabindranath Tagore; brae *and* fell
<both Scots>; **hillock, knob,** butte,
kopje, kame, monticle, monticule, mo-
nadnock, **knoll,** hummock, hammock,
eminence, rise, mound, swell, barrow, tumulus, kop, tel, jebel; **dune,** sand dune;
moraine, drumlin; anthill, molehill;
dune, sand dune, sandhill

5 **ridge,** ridgeline, *arête* <Fr>, chine, spine,
horst, kame, comb <Brit>, esker, cuesta,
serpent kame, Indian ridge, moraine, terminal moraine; **saddle, hogback,** hog's-
back, saddleback, horseback, col; **pass,**
gap, notch, wind gap, water gap

6 **mountain** <see list>, mount, alp, hump,
tor, height, dizzying height, nunatak,
"the beginning and the end of all natural
scenery"—Ruskin, dome; **peak, pinnacle,
summit** 198.2, mountaintop, point, topmost point *or* pinnacle, **crest,** tor, *pic*
<Fr>, *pico* <Sp>; crag, spur, cloud-
capped *or* cloud-topped *or* snow-clad
peak, the roof of the world; needle,
aiguille, pyramidal peak, horn; **volcano,**
volcanic mountain, volcanic spine, volcanic neck; seamount, submarine mountain, guyot; **mountain range,** range, massif; **mountain system, chain,** mountain
chain, cordillera, sierra, cordilleran
belt, fold belt; "alps on alps"—Pope, hill
heaped upon hill; mountain-building,
orogeny, folding, faulting, block-faulting,
volcanism

7 **valley,** vale, glen, dale, dell, hollow,
holler <nonformal>, flume, cleuch
<Scots>, cwm <Welsh>; **ravine, gorge,
canyon,** box canyon, *arroyo* <Sp>, bar-
ranca, bolson, coulee, gully, gulch, combe
<Brit>, dingle, rift, rift valley, kloof,
donga, graben, gully, draw, wadi, basin,
cirque, corrie, hanging valley; **crevasse;**
chimney, **defile,** pass, passage, col; **crater,**
volcanic crater, caldera, meteorite *or* meteoritic crater

ADJS 8 **hilly, rolling,** undulating; **mountainous,** montane, alpine

9 **famous and high mountains**

Aconcagua <Argentina 22,835 feet>	Ben Nevis <Scotland 4,406 feet>
Annapurna <Nepal 26,504 feet>	Carstensz <New Guinea 16,503 feet>
Ararat <Turkey 17,011 feet>	Cho Oyo <Nepal and Tibet 26,750 feet>
Communism Peak <Commonwealth of Independent States 24,590 feet>	Manaslu <Nepal 26,760 feet>
Cook <New Zealand 12,349 feet>	Matterhorn <Switzerland 14,690 feet>
Cotopaxi <Ecuador 19,700 feet>	McKinley <Alaska 20,320 feet>
Dhaulagiri <Nepal 26,810 feet>	Mitchell <North Carolina 6,684 feet>
Elbert <Colorado 14,331 feet>	Mont Blanc <France 15,771 feet>
Elbrus <Commonwealth of Independent States 18,481 feet>	Mount Saint Helens <Washington 8,364 feet>
Erebus <Antarctica 13,202 feet>	Mulhacen <Spain 11,420 feet>
Etna <Sicily 10,900 feet>	Olympus <Greece 9,570 feet>
Everest <Nepal and Tibet 29,028 feet>	Orizaba <Mexico 18,700 feet>
Fuji <Japan 12,388 feet>	Pikes Peak <Colorado 14,110 feet>
Grand Teton <Wyoming 13,766 feet>	Popocatépetl <Mexico 17,887 feet>
Jungfrau <Switzerland 13,668 feet>	Rainier <Washington 14,410 feet>
K2 <India 28,741 feet>	Rushmore <South Dakota 6,050 feet>
Kanchenjunga <Nepal and Sikkim 28,208 feet>	Snowdon <Wales 3,560 feet>
Kilimanjaro <Tanzania 19,340 feet>	Teide <Canary Islands 12,198 feet>
Kosciusko <Australia 7,314 feet>	Toubaki <Morocco 13,881 feet>
Lhotse <Nepal and Tibet 27,923 feet>	Vesuvius <Italy 3,891 feet>
Logan <Yukon 19,850 feet>	Vinson Massif <Antarctica 16,864 feet>
Makalu <China and Nepal 27,824 feet>	Washington <New Hampshire 6,288 feet>
	Whitney <California 14,494 feet>

238 STREAM
<*running water*>

NOUNS 1 **stream, waterway, watercourse**
239.2, **channel** 239; meandering stream,
flowing stream, lazy stream, racing
stream, braided stream; spill stream; adolescent stream; **river;** navigable river,
underground *or* subterranean river,
"moving road"—Pascal, "a strong brown
god"—T S Eliot; dry stream, stream bed,
winterbourne, wadi, *arroyo* <Sp>, *donga*
<Africa>, nullah <India>; **brook,**
branch; kill, bourn, run <Brit nonfor-
mal>, **creek,** crick <nonformal>; **rivulet,**

rill, **streamlet**, brooklet, runlet, runnel, rundle <nonformal>, rindle <Brit nonformal>, beck <Brit>, gill <Brit>, burn <Scots>, sike <Brit nonformal>; **freshet**, fresh; millstream, race; midstream, midchannel; stream action, fluviation

2 **headwaters, headstream**, headwater, head, riverhead; **source**, fountainhead 885.6

3 **tributary**, feeder, **branch, fork**, prong <nonformal>, confluent, confluent stream, affluent; effluent, anabranch; bayou; billabong <Australia>; dendritic drainage pattern

4 **flow**, flowing, **flux**, fluency, profluence, fluid motion *or* movement; hydrodynamics; **stream, current**, set, trend, tide, water flow; drift, driftage; **course**, onward course, **surge, gush, rush**, onrush, spate, run, race; millrace, mill run; undercurrent, undertow; crosscurrent, crossflow; affluence, afflux, affluxion, confluence, concourse, conflux; **downflow**, downpour; defluxion; inflow 189.2; outflow 190.4

5 **torrent, river, flood**, flash flood, wall of water, waterflood, **deluge**; spate, **pour**, freshet, fresh

6 **overflow**, spillage, spill, spillover, overflowing, overrunning, alluvion, alluvium, **inundation, flood, deluge**, whelming, overwhelming, engulfment, submersion 367.2, cataclysm; the Flood, the Deluge; washout

7 **trickle**, tricklet, **dribble, drip**, dripping, stillicide <old>, drop, spurtle; percolation, leaching, lixiviation; distillation, condensation, sweating; seeping, seepage

8 **lap, swash, wash, slosh, plash, splash**; lapping, washing, etc

9 **jet, spout, spurt**, spurtle, squirt, spit, spew, spray, spritz <nonformal>; rush, **gush, flush; fountain**, fount, font, *jet d'eau* <Fr>; geyser, spouter <nonformal>

10 **rapids, rapid**, white water, wild water; ripple, **riffle**, riff <nonformal>; chute, shoot, sault

11 **waterfall, cataract**, fall, **falls, Niagara, cascade**, force <Brit>, linn <Scots>, sault; nappe; watershoot

12 **eddy**, back stream, gurge, **swirl**, twirl, whirl; **whirlpool**, vortex, gulf, **maelstrom**; Maelstrom, Charybdis; countercurrent, counterflow, counterflux, backflow, reflux, refluence, regurgitation, backwash, backwater, snye <Can>

13 **tide**, tidal current *or* stream, tidal flow *or* flood, **tide race; tidewater**; tideway, tide gate; **riptide**, rip, tiderip, overfalls; direct tide, opposite tide; **spring tide; high tide**, high water, full tide; **low tide**, low water; **neap tide**, neap; lunar tide, solar tide; **flood tide, ebb tide**; rise of the tide, flux, flow, flood; ebb, reflux, refluence; ebb and flow, flux and reflux; tidal amplitude, tidal range; tide chart *or* table, tidal current chart; tide gauge, thalassometer

14 **wave, billow**, surge, **swell**, heave, undulation, lift, rise, send, scend; trough, peak; **sea**, heavy swell, ocean swell, ground swell; **roller**, roll; **comber**, comb; **surf, breakers**; wavelet, **ripple**, riffle; **tidal wave**, tsunami; gravity wave, water wave; tide wave; bore, tidal bore, eagre, traveling wave; **whitecap**, white horse; rough *or* heavy sea, rough water, dirty water *or* sea, choppy *or* chopping sea, popple, lop, chop, choppiness; standing wave

15 water gauge, fluviograph, fluviometer; marigraph; Nilometer

VERBS 16 **flow, stream, issue, pour, surge, run, course, rush, gush, flush, flood**; empty into, flow into, join, join with, mingle waters; set, make, trend; flow in 189.9; flow out 190.13; flow back, surge back, ebb, regurgitate

17 **overflow**, flow over, wash over, **run over, well over, brim over**, lap, lap at, lap over, overbrim, overrun, pour out *or* over, **spill, slop, slosh**, spill out *or* over; **cataract, cascade**; **inundate**, engulf, swamp, sweep, whelm, overwhelm, **flood**, deluge, submerge 367.7

18 **trickle, dribble**, dripple, **drip**, drop, spurtle; **filter**, percolate, leach, lixiviate; distill, condense, sweat; seep, weep; **gurgle** 52.11

19 **lap, plash, splash, wash, swash, slosh**

20 **jet, spout, spurt**, spurtle, **squirt**, spit, spew, spray, spritz <nonformal>, play, **gush**, well, surge; vomit, vomit out *or* forth

21 **eddy**, gurge, **swirl**, whirl, purl, reel, spin

22 **billow, surge, swell**, heave, lift, rise, send, scend, toss, popple, **roll**, wave, **undulate; peak**, draw to a peak, be poised; comb, **break**, dash, crash, smash; rise and fall, ebb and flow

ADJS 23 **streamy**, rivery, brooky, creeky; streamlike, riverine; fluvial, fluviatile *or* fluviatic

24 **flowing, streaming, running, pouring**, fluxive, fluxional, coursing, racing, gushing, rushing, onrushing, surging, surgy, torrential, rough, whitewater; **fluent**, profluent, affluent, defluent, decurrent,

confluent, diffluent; tidal; gulfy, vortical;
meandering, mazy, sluggish, serpentine

25 **flooded,** deluged, inundated, engulfed,
swamped, swept, whelmed, drowned,
overwhelmed, afloat, awash; washed,
water-washed; in flood, at flood, in spate

239 CHANNEL

NOUNS 1 **channel, conduit, duct,** canal,
course; **way, passage, passageway;**
trough, troughway, troughing; tunnel;
ditch, trench 290.2; adit; ingress, entrance 189; egress, exit; **stream** 238

2 **watercourse, waterway, aqueduct,** water
channel, water gate, water carrier, culvert, **canal;** side-channel, intrariverine
channel, snye <Can>; streamway, river-
way; **bed,** stream bed, river bed, creek
bed, runnel; water gap; dry bed, *arroyo*
<Sp>, wadi, winterbourne, *donga*
<Africa>, *nullah* <India>, **gully,** gully-
hole, gulch; swash, swash channel; race,
headrace, tailrace; flume; sluice; spillway; spillbox; irrigation ditch, water
furrow; waterworks

3 **gutter, trough,** eave *or* eaves trough;
flume, chute, shoot; pentrough, penstock;
guide

4 <metal founding> gate, ingate, runner,
sprue, tedge

5 **drain,** sough <Brit nonformal>, sluice,
scupper; **sink,** sump; piscina; **gutter,** kennel; **sewer,** cloaca, headchute; cloaca
maxima

6 **tube; pipe; tubing, piping,** tubulation; tu-
bulure; nipple, pipette, tubulet, tubule;
reed, stem, straw; **hose,** hosepipe <Brit>,
garden hose, fire hose; pipeline; catheter;
siphon; tap; efflux tube, adjutage; funnel;
snorkel; siamese, siamese connection *or*
joint

7 **main,** water main, gas main, fire main

8 **spout,** beak, waterspout, downspout; gargoyle

9 **nozzle,** bib nozzle, pressure nozzle, spray
nozzle, nose, snout; rose, rosehead;
shower head, sprinkler head

10 **valve,** gate; **faucet, spigot, tap;** cock, **pet-
cock,** draw cock, stopcock, sea cock, drain
cock, ball cock; bunghole; needle valve;
valvule, valvula

11 **floodgate,** flood-hatch, gate, **head gate,**
penstock, water gate, **sluice,** sluice gate;
tide gate, aboiteau <Can>; weir; **lock,**
lock gate, dock gate; air lock

12 **hydrant,** fire hydrant, **plug,** water plug,
fireplug

13 air passage, air duct, airway, air shaft,
shaft, **air hole,** air tube; speaking tube *or*
pipe; **blowhole,** breathing hole, spiracle;
nostril; touchhole; spilehole, **vent, venthole,** ventage, ventiduct; **ventilator,**
ventilating shaft; transom, louver, lou-
verwork; wind tunnel

14 **chimney, flue,** flue pipe, funnel,
stovepipe, stack, smokestack, smoke
pipe, smokeshaft; Charley Noble;
fumarole

VERBS 15 **channel,** channelize, canalize,
conduct, convey, put through; pipe, funnel, siphon; trench 290.3; direct 573.8

ADJS 16 **tubular,** tubate, tubiform, tubelike;
pipelike; cylindrical; tubed, piped; can-
nular; tubal

17 **valvular,** valval, valvelike; valved

240 SEA, OCEAN

NOUNS 1 **ocean, sea,** ocean sea, great *or*
main sea, *thalassa* <Gk>, **main** *or* ocean
main, the bounding main, tide, salt sea,
salt water, blue water, deep water, open
sea, **the brine,** the briny *and* the big pond
<both nonformal>, the briny deep, "the
vasty deep"—Shakespeare, **the deep,** the
deep sea, the deep blue sea, drink *and* big
drink <both nonformal>, **high sea, high
seas;** the seven seas; hydrosphere; **ocean
depths,** ocean deeps and trenches
275.4,17

2 "great Neptune's ocean, "unpath'd waters, "the always wind-obeying deep"—
all Shakespeare, "thou deep and dark
blue ocean"—Byron, "Uterine Sea of our
dreams and Sea haunted by the true
dream, "Sea of a thousand creases, like
the infinitely pleated tunic of the god in
the hands of women of the sanctuary"—
both S-J Perse, "the great naked sea
shouldering a load of salt"—Sandburg,
"the wine-dark sea"—Homer, "the wavy
waste"—Thomas Hood, "old ocean's
gray and melancholy waste"—William
Cullen Bryant, "the world of waters
wild"—James Thomson, "the rising
world of waters dark and deep"—Milton,
"the glad, indomitable sea"—Bliss Carman, "the clear hyaline, the glassy sea"—
Milton

3 **ocean** <see list>; **sea,** tributary sea <see
list>, gulf, bay

4 spirit of the sea, "the old man of the
sea"—Homer, sea devil, Davy, **Davy
Jones;** sea god, **Neptune,** Poseidon,
Oceanus, Triton, Nereus, Oceanid,
Nereid, Thetis; Varuna, Dylan; **mermaid,**
siren; merman, seaman

5 <ocean zones> pelagic zone, benthic zone, estuarine area, sublittoral, littoral, intertidal zone, splash zone, supralittoral

6 oceanography, thalassography, hydrography, bathymetry; marine biology; aquaculture

7 oceanographer, thalassographer, hydrographer

ADJS 8 **oceanic, marine, maritime**, pelagic, thalassic; nautical 182.57; oceanographic, oceanographical, hydrographic, hydrographical, bathymetric, bathymetrical, bathyorographical, thalassographic, thalassographical; terriginous; deep-sea 275.14

ADVS 9 **at sea**, on the high seas; afloat 182.62; by water, by sea

10 **oversea, overseas**, beyond seas, over the water, transmarine, across the sea

11 **oceanward**, oceanwards, **seaward**, seawards, off; offshore, off soundings, out of soundings, in blue water

WORD ELEMENTS 12 mari—, thalass—, thalasso—; oceano—; bathy—

13 **oceans**

Antarctic	South Atlantic
Arctic	North Pacific
Indian	Pacific
North Atlantic	South Pacific

14 **tributary seas**

Andaman Sea	Gulf of California
Arabian Sea	Gulf of Guinea
Arafura Sea	Gulf of Mexico
Baffin Bay	Gulf of Saint
Bali Sea	Lawrence
Baltic Sea	Hudson Bay
Banda Sea	Kara Sea
Barents Sea	Laptev Sea
Bay of Bengal	Macassar Strait
Bequfort Sea	Mediterranean
Bering Sea	Sea
Black Sea	Molukka Sea
Caribbean Sea	North Sea
Celebes Sea	Norwegian Sea
Ceram Sea	Persian Gulf
Chukchi Sea	Red Sea
Coral Sea	Savu Sea
East China Sea	Sea of Japan
East Siberian Sea	Sea of Okhotsk
Flores Sea	South China Sea
Great Australian	Sulu Sea
Bight	Timor Sea
Greenland Sea	White Sea
Gulf of Alaska	Yellow Sea

241 LAKE, POOL

NOUNS 1 **lake**, landlocked water, loch <Scots>, lough <Ir>, nyanza <Africa>, mere, freshwater lake; oxbow lake, bayou lake, glacial lake; volcanic lake; tarn; inland sea; **pool**, lakelet, **pond**, pondlet, dew pond, linn <Scots>, dike <Brit nonformal>, *étang* <Fr>; standing water, still water, stagnant water, dead water; **water** or watering hole, water pocket; **oasis**; farm pond; fishpond; millpond, millpool; salt pond, salina, tidal pond or pool; **puddle**, plash, sump <nonformal>; **lagoon**, *laguna* <Sp>; **reservoir**, artificial lake; dam; **well, cistern**, tank, artesian well, flowing well, **spring**

2 **lake dweller,** lacustrian, lacustrine dweller or inhabitant, **pile dweller** or builder; laker

3 **lake dwelling,** lacustrine dwelling, **pile house** or **dwelling**, palafitte; crannog

4 limnology, limnologist; limnimeter, limnograph

ADJS 5 **lakish**, laky, lakelike; lacustrine, lacustral, lacustrian; pondy, pondlike, lacuscular; limnologic, limnological

WORD ELEMENTS 6 limn—, limno—, limni—, —limnion

242 INLET, GULF

NOUNS 1 **inlet, cove,** creek <Brit>, arm of the sea, arm, armlet, canal, reach, loch <Scots>, **bay, fjord**, bight; cove; **gulf; estuary,** firth or frith, bayou, mouth, *boca* <Sp>; **harbor**, natural harbor; road or roads, roadstead; **strait** or straits, kyle <Scots>, **narrow** or **narrows**, euripus, belt, gut, narrow seas; **sound**

ADJS 2 gulfy, gulflike; gulfed, bayed, embayed; estuarine, fluviomarine, tidewater; drowned

243 MARSH

NOUNS 1 **marsh**, marshland, **swamp**, swampland, fen, fenland, **morass**, mere or marish <both old>, *marais* <Fr>, *maremma* <Ital>, **bog, mire, quagmire,** sump <nonformal>, wash, baygall; glade, everglade; slough, swale, wallow, hog wallow, buffalo wallow, sough <Brit>; bottom, **bottoms**, bottomland, slob land, holm <Brit>, water meadow, meadow; **moor**, moorland, moss <Scots>, peat bog; salt marsh; quicksand; taiga; mud flat, **mud** 1060.8,9

VERBS 2 **mire**, bemire, sink in, **bog**, mire or bog down, stick in the mud; stodge

ADJS 3 **marshy, swampy**, swampish, **moory**, moorish, fenny, marish <old>, paludal or paludous; **boggy**, boggish, **miry**, mirish, quaggy, quagmiry, spouty, poachy;

muddy 1060.14; swamp-growing, ulig-
inous

| teaspoon *or* teaspoon-ful | thimble *or* thimbleful |
| tub *or* tubful |

244 QUANTITY

NOUNS **1 quantity,** quantum, amount,
whole 791; mass, **bulk,** substance, matter, magnitude, amplitude, **extent, sum;
measure,** measurement; strength, force,
numbers
2 amount, quantity, large amount, small
amount, **sum, number,** count, group, total, reckoning, **measure,** parcel, passel
<nonformal>, **part** 792, **portion,** clutch,
ration, share, issue, allotment, lot, deal;
batch, bunch, heap <nonformal>, pack,
mess <nonformal>, gob *and* chunk *and*
hunk <all nonformal>, budget <old>,
dose
3 some, somewhat, something; **aught; any,**
anything
VERBS **4 quantify,** quantize, **count, number
off, enumerate, number** 1016.10, rate, fix;
parcel, apportion, mete out, issue, allot,
divide 801.18; **increase** 251.4,6, **decrease**
252.6, reduce 252.7; quantitate, **measure**
300.11
ADJS **5 quantitative,** quantitive, quantified,
quantized, measured; **some,** certain, one;
a, an; **any**
ADVS **6 approximately,** nearly, some, about,
circa; more or less, *plus ou moins* <Fr>,
by and large, upwards of
PREPS **7 to the amount of,** to the tune of
<nonformal>; as much as, all of
<nonformal>, no less than, upwards
of

8 indefinite quantities

armful *or* armload	kettle *or* kettleful
bag *or* bagful	lapful
bargeload	mouthful
barrel *or* barrelful	mug *or* mugful
basin *or* basinful	pail *or* pailful
basket *or* basketful	pitcher *or* pitcherful
bin *or* binful	planeful *or* planeload
bottle *or* bottleful	plate *or* plateful
bowl *or* bowlful	pocketful
box *or* boxful	pot *or* potful
bucket *or* bucketful	roomful
can *or* canful	sack *or* sackful *or*
cap *or* capful	sackload
carton *or* cartonful	scoop *or* scoopful
case *or* caseful	shovel *or* shovelful
crate *or* crateful	skepful
cup *or* cupful	spoon *or* spoonful
flask *or* flaskful	tablespoon *or* table-
glass *or* glassful	spoonful
handful	tank *or* tankful
jar *or* jarful	tankerload
keg *or* kegful	teacup *or* teacupful

245 DEGREE

NOUNS **1 degree, grade, step,** *pas* <Fr>,
leap; round, rung, tread, stair; **point,**
mark, peg, tick; **notch,** cut; **plane,** level,
plateau; **period,** space, interval; **extent,
measure,** amount, ratio, proportion,
stint, standard, height, pitch, reach, remove, compass, range, scale, scope,
caliber; **shade,** shadow, nuance
2 rank, standing, level, footing, **status,**
station; **position,** place, sphere, orbit,
echelon; **order,** estate, precedence, condition; rate, rating; **class,** caste; **hierarchy,**
power structure
3 gradation, graduation, grading, staging,
phasing, tapering, shading
VERBS **4 graduate, grade,** calibrate; phase
in, phase out, taper off, shade off; **increase** 251, **decrease** 252.6,7
ADJS **5 gradual,** gradational, calibrated,
graduated, phased, staged, tapered, sca-
lar; regular, progressive; hierarchic,
hierarchical
ADVS **6 by degrees,** degreewise; **gradually,**
gradatim; **step by step,** grade by grade, *di
grado in grado* <Ital>, **bit by bit, little by
little,** inch by inch, inchmeal, step by
step, drop by drop; a little, fractionally;
a little at a time, by slow degrees, by
inches, by little and little, a little at a
time; slowly 175.13
7 to a degree, to some extent, in a way, in a
measure, in some measure; somewhat,
kind of <nonformal>, sort of <nonfor-
mal>, rather, pretty, quite, fairly; a little,
a bit; slightly, scarcely, to a small degree
248.9,10; very, extremely, to a great degree 247.19–22

246 MEAN

NOUNS **1 mean, median, middle** 818; **golden
mean,** *juste milieu* <Fr>; **medium,** happy
medium; middle of the road, middle
course, *via media* <L>; middle state *or*
ground *or* position *or* echelon *or* level *or*
point, midpoint; **average,** balance, par,
normal, norm, rule, run, generality; **mediocrity,** averageness, passableness,
adequacy; averaging, mediocritization;
center 208.2
VERBS **2 average,** average out, **split the difference,** take the average, strike a balance, pair off; strike *or* hit a happy

medium; keep to the middle, avoid extremes; **do**, just do, pass, barely pass; mediocritize

ADJS **3 medium**, mean, **intermediate**, intermediary, median, medial, mid-level, middle-echelon; **average**, normal, standard, par for the course; middle-of-the-road, moderate; **middling, ordinary**, usual, routine, common, mediocre, merely adequate, passing, banal, so-so; **central** 208.11

ADVS **4 mediumly**, medianly; medially, midway 818.5, intermediately, in the mean; **centrally** 208.15

5 on the average, in the long run, over the long haul; taking one thing with another, taking all things together, **all in all, on the whole**, all things considered, on balance; **generally** 863.17

WORD ELEMENTS **6** medi—, mes—, mezzo—, semi—

247 GREATNESS

NOUNS **1 greatness, magnitude,** muchness; **amplitude**, ampleness, fullness, plenitude, great scope or compass or reach; **grandeur**, grandness; **immensity**, enormousness or enormity, **vastness**, vastitude, tremendousness, expanse, boundlessness, infinity 822; stupendousness, formidableness, prodigiousness, humongousness <nonformal>; **might**, mightiness, strength, power, intensity; **largeness** 257.6, **hugeness**, gigantism, bulk; **superiority** 249

2 glory, eminence, preeminence, majesty, loftiness, prominence, distinction, outstandingness, consequence, notability; **magnanimity**, nobility, sublimity ; **fame,** renown, celebrity; heroism

3 quantity 244, **numerousness** 883; **quantities, much, abundance,** copiousness, superabundance, superfluity, profusion, plenty, plenitude; **volume, mass,** mountain, load; peck, bushel; bag, barrel, ton; world, acre, ocean, sea; flood, spate; **multitude** 883.3, countlessness 822.1

4 lot, lots, deal, no end of, **good** or **great deal, considerable,** sight, **heap, pile, stack,** loads, **raft, slew,** whole slew, spate, wad, **batch,** mess, mint, peck, pack, pot, **tidy sum,** quite a little; **oodles, gobs, scads,** bags and masses and lashings <all Brit>

VERBS **5 loom, bulk,** loom large, bulk large, stand out; **tower,** rear, soar, outsoar; **tower above,** rise above, overtop; **exceed, transcend,** outstrip

ADJS **6 great, grand, considerable,** consequential; **mighty,** powerful, strong, irresistible, intense; main, maximum, **total, full,** plenary, comprehensive, exhaustive; grave, **serious,** heavy, deep

7 large 257.16, **immense, enormous, huge** 257.20; **gigantic,** mountainous, titanic, colossal, mammoth, Gargantuan, gigantesque, monster, monstrous, outsize, sizable, larger-than-life, overgrown, king-size, monumental; **massive,** massy, weighty, bulky, voluminous, **vast,** vasty, boundless, **infinite** 822.3, immeasurable, cosmic, astronomical, galactic; **spacious,** amplitudinous, extensive; **tremendous,** stupendous, awesome, prodigious

8 much, many, beaucoup <nonformal>, ample, **abundant,** copious, generous, overflowing, superabundant, multitudinous, plentiful, **numerous** 883.6, countless 822.3

9 eminent, prominent, outstanding, standout, high, elevated, towering, soaring, overtopping, exalted, **lofty,** sublime; august, majestic, noble, distinguished; **magnificent,** magnanimous, heroic, godlike, superb; famous, renowned, lauded, glorious

10 remarkable, outstanding, extraordinary, **superior** 249.12, **marked,** of mark, signal, conspicuous, **striking; notable,** much in evidence, noticeable, noteworthy; **marvelous,** wonderful, formidable, exceptional, uncommon, astonishing, appalling, humongous <nonformal>, fabulous, fantastic, incredible, egregious

11 <nonformal terms> **terrific,** terrible, horrible, **dreadful, awful,** fearful, frightful, deadly; **whacking, thumping, rousing,** howling

12 downright, outright, out-and-out; absolute, utter, perfect, consummate, superlative, surpassing, the veriest, positive, definitive, classical, pronounced, decided, regular <nonformal>, proper <Brit nonformal>, precious, profound, stark; **thorough,** thoroughgoing, **complete,** total; **unmitigated,** unqualified, unrelieved, unspoiled, undeniable, unquestionable, unequivocal; **flagrant,** arrant, shocking, shattering, egregious, intolerable, unbearable, unconscionable, glaring, stark-staring, **rank,** crass, gross

13 extreme, radical, out of this world, way or far out <nonformal>, too much <nonformal>; **greatest,** furthest, **most, utmost,** uttermost, the max <nonformal>; **ultra,** ultra-ultra; at the height or peak or limit or summit or zenith

14 undiminished, unabated, unreduced, unrestricted, unretarded, unmitigated

ADVS **15 greatly, largely,** to a large *or* great extent, in great measure, on a large scale; **much,** muchly <nonformal>, pretty much, very much, so, so very much, ever so much, ever so, never so; **considerably,** considerable <nonformal>; abundantly, plenty <nonformal>, no end of, no end, not a little, galore <nonformal>, **a lot,** a deal <nonformal>, **a great deal,** *beaucoup* <Fr>; **highly,** to the skies; like *or* as all creation <nonformal>, like *or* as all get-out <nonformal>, in spades *and* with bells on *and* with bells on one's toes <all nonformal>; **undiminishedly,** unabatedly, unreducedly, unrestrictedly, unretardedly, unmitigatedly

16 vastly, immensely, enormously, hugely, tremendously, gigantically, colossally, titanically, prodigiously, stupendously, humongously <nonformal>

17 by far, far and away, far, far and wide, by a long way, by a great deal, by a long shot *or* long chalk <nonformal>, out and away, by all odds

18 very, exceedingly, awfully *and* terribly *and* terrifically <all nonformal>, **quite,** just, so, **really,** real *and* right <both nonformal>, **pretty,** only too, mightily, **mighty** *and* almighty *and* powerfully *and* powerful <all nonformal>

19 <in a positive degree> **positively, decidedly, clearly,** manifestly, unambiguously, patently, **obviously,** visibly, unmistakably, unquestionably, observably, **noticeably,** demonstrably, sensibly, quite; **certainly,** actually, **really, truly,** verily, **undeniably,** indubitably, without doubt, assuredly, **indeed,** for a certainty, for real <nonformal>, seriously, in all conscience

20 <in a marked degree> **intensely, acutely,** exquisitely, **exceptionally,** surpassingly, superlatively, eminently, preeminently; **remarkably, markedly, notably, strikingly,** signally, emphatically, pointedly, prominently, conspicuously, pronouncedly, impressively, famously, glaringly; **particularly, singularly,** peculiarly; uncommonly, extraordinarily, **unusually; wonderfully,** wondrous, amazingly, magically, surprisingly, astonishingly, marvelously, exuberantly, incredibly, awesomely; **abundantly,** richly, profusely, amply, **generously,** copiously; **magnificently,** splendidly, nobly, worthily, magnanimously

21 <in a distressing degree> **distressingly,**

sadly, sorely, bitterly, piteously, grievously, miserably, **cruelly,** woefully, lamentably, balefully, dolorously, shockingly; **terribly, awfully, dreadfully, frightfully, horribly,** abominably, **painfully,** excruciatingly, torturously, **agonizingly,** deathly, deadly, something awful *or* fierce *or* terrible *and* in the worst way <all nonformal>, within an inch of one's life; shatteringly, staggeringly; **excessively,** exorbitantly, extravagantly, **inordinately,** preposterously; **unduly, improperly,** intolerably, unbearably; **inexcusably,** unpardonably, unconscionably; **flagrantly,** blatantly, egregiously; **unashamedly,** unabashedly, baldly, nakedly, brashly, openly; **cursedly,** confoundedly, **damnably,** deucedly <nonformal>, infernally, hellishly

22 <in an extreme degree> **extremely, utterly, totally** in the extreme, **most,** *à outrance* <Fr, to the utmost>; **immeasurably,** incalculably, indefinitely, **infinitely;** beyond compare *or* comparison, **beyond measure,** beyond all bounds, all out <nonformal>, flat out <Brit nonformal>; **perfectly, absolutely,** essentially, fundamentally, radically; **purely, totally,** completely; unconditionally, with no strings attached, unequivocally, downright, dead; with a vengeance

23 <in a violent degree> **violently,** furiously, hotly, fiercely, severely, **desperately,** madly, **like mad** <nonformal>; **wildly,** demonically, like one possessed, **frantically,** frenetically, fanatically, uncontrollably

WORD ELEMENTS **24** meg—, mega—, multi—, super—

248 INSIGNIFICANCE

NOUNS **1 insignificance,** inconsiderableness, unimportance 997, inconsequentialness, inconsequentiality, lowness, pettiness, meanness, triviality, nugacity, nugaciousness; **smallness,** tininess, diminutiveness, minuteness, exiguity *or* exiguousness; **slightness,** moderateness, scantiness, puniness, picayunishness, meanness, meagerness; daintiness, delicacy; **littleness** 258; **fewness** 884; insufficiency 991

2 modicum, minim; **minimum; little, bit,** little *or* wee *or* tiny bit <nonformal>, bite, **particle,** fragment, spot, **speck,** flyspeck, fleck, point, dot, jot, tittle, **iota,** ounce, **dab** <nonformal>, mote, **mite** <nonformal> 258.7; whit, ace, **hair,** scruple, groat, farthing, pittance, dole, trifling amount, **smidgen** *and* skosh *and* smitch <all nonformal>, pinch, gobbet, dribble, driblet, dram, drop, drop in a bucket *or* in the ocean, tip of the iceberg; grain, granule, pebble; molecule, **atom;** thimbleful, spoonful, handful, nutshell; trivia, minutiae; dwarf

3 **scrap,** tatter, smithereen <nonformal>, patch, **stitch, shred,** tag; snip, **snippet,** snick, chip, nip; splinter, sliver, shiver; **morsel,** *morceau* <Fr>, **crumb**

4 **hint,** *soupçon* <Fr>, **suspicion, suggestion,** intimation; tip of the iceberg; **trace, touch, dash,** cast, **smattering,** sprinkling; tinge, tincture; **taste, lick, smack,** sip, sup, **smell;** look, **thought,** idea; **shade,** shadow; gleam, spark, scintilla

5 **hardly anything, mere nothing,** next to nothing, less than nothing, **trifle,** bagatelle, **a drop in the bucket** *or* **in the ocean;** the shadow of a shade, the suspicion of a suspicion

ADJS **6** **insignificant, small, inconsiderable, inconsequential, negligible,** no great shakes, footling, one-horse *and* pint-size *and* vest-pocket <all nonformal>; unimportant, no skin off one's nose *or* ass, **trivial,** trifling, nugacious, nugatory, petty, mean, niggling, picayune *or* picayunish, nickel-and-dime *and* penny-ante *and* Mickey-Mouse *and* chickenshit <all nonformal>; shallow, depthless, cursory, superficial, skin-deep; **little** 258.10, **tiny** 258.11, **weeny, miniature** 258.12, **meager** 991.10, **few** 884.4; **short** 268.8; **low** 274.7

7 **dainty, delicate, gossamer, diaphanous; subtle,** subtile, tenuous, thin 270.16, rarefied 299.4

8 **mere, sheer,** stark, bare, bare-bones, plain, simple, unadorned, unenhanced

ADVS **9** <in a small degree> **scarcely, hardly,** not hardly <nonformal>, **barely,** only just, by a hair, by an ace *or* a jot *or* a whit *or* an iota, **slightly,** lightly, exiguously, fractionally, scantily, inconsequentially, **insignificantly, negligibly,** imperfectly, minimally, inappreciably, **little; minutely,** meagerly, triflingly, faintly, weakly, feebly; **a little, a bit,** just a bit, to a small extent, on a small scale; ever so little, *tant soit peu* <Fr>, as little as may be

10 <in a certain or limited degree> **to a degree, to a certain extent, to some degree,** in some measure, to such an extent, *pro tanto* <L>; **moderately,** mildly, **somewhat,** detectably, just visibly, modestly,

appreciably, visibly, **fairly,** tolerably, **partially,** partly, part, in part, incompletely, not exhaustively, not comprehensively; **comparatively, relatively; merely,** simply, purely, only; **at least,** at the least, leastwise, at worst, at any rate; **at most,** at the most, at best, at the outside <nonformal>; in a manner, in a manner of speaking, **in a way,** after a fashion; so far, thus far

11 <in no degree> **noway,** noways, **nowise,** in no wise, in no case, in no respect, **by no means,** by no manner of means, **on no account, not on any account, not for anything in the world, under no circumstances,** at no hand, nohow <nonformal>, **not in the least,** not much, **not at all,** never, not by a damn sight <nonformal>, not by a long shot <nonformal>; not nearly, **nowhere near; not a bit,** not a bit of it, not a whit, not a speck, not a jot, not an iota

249 SUPERIORITY

NOUNS **1** **superiority, preeminence, greatness** 247, **lead,** transcendence *or* transcendency, ascendancy *or* ascendance, prestige, favor, prepotence *or* prepotency, preponderance; predominance *or* predominancy, hegemony; precedence 813, **priority,** prerogative, privilege, right-of-way; **excellence** 998.1, virtuosity, inimitability, incomparability; **seniority,** precedence, deanship; **success** 409, accomplishment 407, **skill** 413

2 **advantage,** vantage, odds, leg up *and* inside track *and* pole position <all nonformal>; **upper hand,** whip hand; start, head *or* flying *or* running start; **edge,** bulge *and* jump *and* drop <all nonformal>; **card up one's sleeve** <nonformal>, ace in the hole <nonformal>, something extra *or* in reserve; vantage ground *or* point, coign of vantage

3 **supremacy, primacy,** paramountcy, **first place,** height, acme, zenith, be-all and end-all, summit, top spot <nonformal>; **sovereignty, rule, hegemony, control** 417.5; kingship, **dominion** 417.6, lordship, imperium, world power; **command,** sway; **mastery,** mastership 417.7; **leadership,** headship, presidency; **authority** 417, directorship, management, jurisdiction, power, say *and* last word <both nonformal>; **influence** 893; effectiveness; **maximum,** highest, most, *ne plus ultra* <L, no more beyond>, the max <nonformal>; **championship,** crown, laurels, palms, first prize, blue ribbon, new high, record

4 superior, chief, head, boss 575.1, honcho <nonformal>, commander, **ruler, leader,** dean, *primus inter pares* <L, first among equals>, **master** 575; higher-up <nonformal>, senior, principal, big shot <nonformal>; superman, **genius** 413.12; prodigy, nonpareil, paragon, virtuoso, ace, **star, superstar,** champion, winner, top dog *and* top banana <both nonformal>, one in a thousand, one in a million, etc, laureate, fugleman, Cadillac *and* Rolls-Royce <both trademark>, A per se, A 1, A number 1, standout, money-maker, record-breaker, the greatest *and* the most whiz *and* whizbang *and* world-beater *and* a tough act to follow <all nonformal>

5 the best 998.8, the top of the line <nonformal>; the best people, nobility 608; **aristocracy,** barons, top people <nonformal>, **elite,** cream, top of the milk, upper crust, upper class, one's betters; **the brass** <nonformal>, the VIP's <nonformal>, higher-ups, movers and shakers, lords of creation, ruling circles, **establishment,** power elite, power structure, **ruling class,** bigwigs <nonformal>

VERBS **6 excel, surpass, exceed, transcend,** get *or* have the ascendancy, get *or* have the edge, have it all over <nonformal>, overcome, overpass, best, **better,** improve on, perfect, go one better <nonformal>; **cap,** trump; top, tower above *or* over, overtop; **predominate,** prevail, preponderate; **outweigh,** overbalance, overbear

7 best, beat, beat out, defeat 412.6; beat all hollow <nonformal>, trounce, clobber *and* take to the cleaners *and* smoke *and* skin *and* skin alive <all nonformal>, worst, whip *and* lick *and* have it all over *and* cut down to size <all nonformal>; bear the palm, take the cake <nonformal>, bring home the bacon <nonformal>; **triumph; win** 411.4

8 overshadow, eclipse, throw into the shade, top, extinguish, take the shine out of <nonformal>; put to shame, show up <nonformal>, put one's nose out of joint, put down <nonformal>, fake out <nonformal>

9 outdo, outrival, outvie, outachieve, edge out, **outclass, outshine,** overmatch, outgun <nonformal>; **outstrip,** outgo, outrange, outreach, outpoint, **outperform;** outplay, overplay, outmaneuver, outwit; outrun, outstep, outpace, outmarch, run rings *or* circles around

<nonformal>; outride, override; outjump, overjump; outleap, overleap

10 outdistance, distance; pass, surpass, overpass; **get ahead,** pull ahead, shoot ahead, walk away *or* off <nonformal>; **leave behind,** leave at the post, leave in the dust, leave in the lurch; **come to the front,** have a healthy lead <nonformal>, hold the field; steal a march

11 rule, command, lead, possess authority 417.13, have the authority, have the say *or* the last word, have the whip hand *and* hold all the aces <both nonformal>; **take precedence, precede** 813.2; **come** *or* **rank first, outrank,** rank, rank out <nonformal>; **come to the fore,** come to the front, **lead** 165.2; play first fiddle, **star**

ADJS **12 superior, greater,** better, finer; **higher,** upper, over, super, above; ascendant, in the ascendant, in ascendancy, coming <nonformal>; **eminent,** outstanding, rare, distinguished, marked, of choice, chosen; **surpassing, exceeding, excellent** 998.12, **excelling, rivaling, eclipsing,** capping, topping, **transcending,** transcendent *or* transcendental; **ahead,** a cut *or* stroke above, one up on <nonformal>; more than a match for

13 superlative, supreme, greatest, best, highest, veriest, maximal, maximum, most, utmost, outstanding, stickout <nonformal>; top, topmost, **uppermost,** tip-top, top-level, top-echelon, top-notch *and* top-of-the-line <both nonformal>, **first-rate,** first-class, of the first water, top of the line, highest-quality, best-quality, far and away the best, the best by a long shot *or* long chalk, head and shoulders above, of the highest type, A1, A number 1, drop-dead <nonformal>

14 chief, main, principal, paramount, **foremost,** headmost, **leading, dominant,** crowning, capital, **cardinal;** great, arch, banner, master, magisterial; central, focal, prime, **primary,** primal, first; **preeminent,** supereminent; **predominant,** preponderant, prevailing, hegemonic *or* hegemonical; ruling, overruling; **sovereign** 417.17; topflight, highest-ranking, ranking; **star,** superstar, stellar, world-class;

15 peerless, matchless, champion; unmatched, unmatchable, makeless <old>, unrivaled, unparagoned, unparalleled, immortal, **unequaled,** never-to-be-equaled, unpeered, unexampled, unapproached, unapproachable, **unsurpassed, unexcelled;** unsurpassable; inimitable, **incomparable,** beyond compare *or* comparison, **unique;** without equal *or* par-

allel, *sans pareil* <Fr>; in a class by itself, *sui generis* <L>, easily first, *facile
princeps* <L>; second to none, *nulli secundus* <L>; **unbeatable**, invincible
ADVS **16 superlatively, exceedingly, surpassingly;** eminently, egregiously, prominently; supremely, paramountly,
preeminently, **the most,** transcendently,
to crown all, *par excellence* <Fr>; inim-
itably, incomparably; to or in the highest
degree, far and away
17 chiefly, mainly, in the main, in chief;
dominantly, **predominantly; mostly, for
the most part; principally, especially,
particularly,** peculiarly; **primarily, in the
first place,** first of all, **above all; indeed,**
even, yea, still more, more than ever, all
the more, *a fortiori* <L>; ever so, never
so, no end
18 peerlessly, matchlessly, unmatchably;
unsurpassedly, unsurpassably; inimita-
bly, **incomparably; uniquely,** second to
none, *nulli secundus* <L>; **unbeatably,**
invincibly
19 advantageously, to or with advantage, favorably; melioratively, amelioratively,
improvingly
WORD ELEMENTS **20** preter—, super—,
supra—, sur—, trans—, ultra—, arch—,
prot—

250 INFERIORITY

NOUNS **1 inferiority, subordinacy,** subordination, secondariness; **juniority,** minority; **subservience, subjection,** servility, lowliness, humbleness, humility;
back seat *and* second fiddle <both non-
formal>, second or third string <non-
formal>
2 inferior, underling, understrapper
<Brit>, **subordinate,** subaltern, **junior;**
secondary, second fiddle *and* second
stringer *and* third stringer *and* benchwarmer *and* low man on the totem pole
<all nonformal>, loser *and* nonstarter
<both nonformal>; lightweight, fol-
lower, pawn, cog, flunky, yes-man,
creature; lower class or orders or ranks,
commonalty; infrastructure or commonality, *hoi polloi* <Gk>, masses
3 inadequacy, mediocrity 1004, deficiency,
imperfection, insufficiency 991; **incompetence,** or incompetency, maladroitness,
unskillfulness 414; **failure** 410; smallness
248.1; littleness 258; meanness, lowness,
baseness, pettiness, triviality, shabbiness, vulgarity 497; **fewness** 884;
subnormality

VERBS **4 be inferior, not come up to, not
measure up, fall** or **come short, fail** 410.8,
not make or hack it *and* not cut the mustard *and* not make the cut <all nonfor-
mal>; want, leave much to be desired, be
found wanting; **not compare,** have nothing on <nonformal>, **not hold a candle to**
<nonformal>, not approach, not come
near; serve, subserve, rank under or beneath, follow, play second fiddle *and* take
a back seat *and* sit on the bench <all non-
formal>
5 bow to, hand it to <nonformal>, tip the
hat to <nonformal>, yield the palm; retire into the shade; give in <nonformal>,
lose face
ADJS **6 inferior, subordinate,** subaltern, sub,
small-scale, **secondary; junior, minor;**
second or third string *and* one-horse *and*
penny-ante *and* dinky <all nonformal>,
second or third rank, low in the pecking
order, low-rent *and* downscale <both
nonformal>; **subservient,** subject, servile, low, **lowly,** humble, modest; **lesser,**
less, lower; in the shade, thrown into the
shade; **common,** vulgar, **ordinary;** underprivileged, disadvantaged; **beneath one's
dignity** or station, infra dig, demeaning
7 inadequate, mediocre, deficient, imperfect, **insufficient; incompetent,** unskillful,
maladroit; small, little, mean, base,
petty, trivial, shabby; **not to be compared, not comparable, not a patch on**
<nonformal>; **outclassed,** not in it *and*
not in the same street or league with <all
nonformal>, out of it *and* out of the picture *and* **out of the running** *and* left a mile
behind <all nonformal>
8 least, smallest, littlest, slightest, **lowest,**
shortest; minimum, minimal, minim;
few 884.4
ADVS **9 poorly, incompetently, inadequately,**
badly, maladroitly; least of all, at the bottom of the scale, at the nadir, at the bottom of the heap *and* in the gutter <both
nonformal>; at a disadvantage
WORD ELEMENTS **10** sub—, hyp—, hypo—

251 INCREASE

NOUNS **1 increase, gain,** augmentation,
greatening, **enlargement, amplification,
growth,** development, widening, spread,
broadening, elevation, **extension,** aggrandizement, access, accession, **increment,**
accretion; **addition** 253; **expansion** 259;
inflation, swelling, ballooning, edema,
fattening, tumescence, bloating; **multi-
duplication, proliferation,** productive-

ness 889; accruement, accrual, accumulation; **advance,** appreciation, ascent, mounting, crescendo, waxing, snowballing, **rise** or raise, fattening and boost and hike <all nonformal>, **up** and upping <both nonformal>, buildup; **upturn,** uptick <nonformal>, uptrend, upsurge, upswing; **leap,** jump; **flood,** surge, gush

2 **intensification, heightening, deepening,** tightening, turn of the screw; **strengthening,** beefing-up <nonformal>, enhancement, **magnification,** blowup, blowing up, exaggeration; aggravation, exacerbation, heating-up; **concentration,** condensation, consolidation; **reinforcement,** redoubling; pickup and step-up <both nonformal>, **acceleration,** speedup, accelerando; **boom, explosion,** baby boom, population explosion, information explosion

3 **gains,** winnings, cut and take <both nonformal>, increase <old>, **profits** 472.3

VERBS 4 **increase, enlarge,** aggrandize, **amplify, augment, extend,** maximize, **add to; expand** 259.4, **inflate;** lengthen, broaden, fatten, fill out, thicken; **raise,** exalt, boost <nonformal>, hike and hike up and jack up and jump up <all nonformal>, mark up, put up, **up** <nonformal>; **build, build up;** pyramid, parlay

5 **intensify, heighten, deepen,** enhance, **strengthen,** beef up <nonformal>, aggravate, exacerbate; **exaggerate,** blow up and puff up <both nonformal>, **magnify;** whet, sharpen; **reinforce,** double, redouble, triple; **concentrate,** condense, consolidate; **complicate,** ramify, make complex; give a boost to, **step up** <nonformal>, accelerate; key up, hop up and soup up and jazz up <all nonformal>; add fuel to the flame or the fire, heat or hot up <nonformal>

6 **grow, increase, advance,** appreciate; **spread, widen,** broaden; **gain,** get ahead; wax, swell, balloon, bloat, mount, **rise,** go up, crescendo, snowball; **intensify, develop,** gain strength, strengthen; accrue, accumulate; **multiply, proliferate,** breed, teem; run or shoot up, **boom, explode**

ADJS 7 **increased, heightened,** raised, elevated, stepped-up <nonformal>; **intensified,** deepened, reinforced, strengthened, fortified, beefed-up <nonformal>, tightened, stiffened; **enlarged, extended,** augmented, aggrandized, amplified, **enhanced,** boosted, hiked <nonformal>; broadened, widened, spread; **magnified, inflated, expanded,** swollen, bloated; **multiplied,** proliferated; **accelerated,**

hopped-up and jazzed-up <both nonformal>

8 **increasing, rising,** fast-rising, skyrocketing, meteoric; on the upswing, on the increase, on the rise; crescent, **growing,** fast-growing, flourishing, burgeoning, blossoming, waxing, swelling, lengthening, **multiplying,** proliferating; spreading, spreading like a cancer or like wildfire, expanding; tightening, intensifying; incremental; **on the increase,** crescendoing, snowballing, mushrooming, growing like a mushroom

ADVS 9 **increasingly,** growingly, more, **more and more,** on and on, greater and greater, ever more; in a crescendo

252 DECREASE

NOUNS 1 **decrease,** decrescence, decrement, **diminishment,** diminution, **reduction, lessening, lowering,** waning, shrinking or shrinkage, withering, withering away, scaling down, scaledown, downsizing, build-down; miniaturization; depression, damping, dampening; **letup** <nonformal>, abatement, easing, easing off; de-escalation; **alleviation,** relaxation, mitigation; attenuation, extenuation, weakening, sagging, dying, dying off or away, trailing off, tailing off, tapering off, fade-out, languishment; depreciation, **deflation; deduction** 255.1; subtraction, **abridgment** 268.3; **contraction** 260; simplicity 797

2 **decline,** declension, **subsidence,** slump <nonformal>, lapse, **drop,** downtick <nonformal>; **collapse,** crash; dwindling, wane, ebb; downturn, downtrend, retreat, remission; **fall, plunge,** dive, decline and fall; decrescendo, diminuendo; catabasis, deceleration, slowdown

3 **decrement, waste, loss,** dissipation, wear and tear, erosion, ablation, wearing away, depletion, corrosion, attrition, consumption, shrinkage, exhaustion; deliquescence, dissolution

4 **curtailment, retrenchment,** cut, cutback, drawdown, rollback, scaleback, pullback

5 **minimization,** minification, making light of, devaluing, undervaluing, **belittling,** belittlement, detraction; qualification 958

VERBS 6 **decrease, diminish, lessen; let up,** bate, abate; **decline, subside,** shrink, wane, wither, ebb, ebb away, dwindle, languish, sink, sag, die down or away, wind down, taper off and trail off or away and tail off or away <all nonformal>;

drop, drop off, dive, take a nose dive, plummet, plunge, fall, fall off, fall away, fall to a low ebb, run low; **waste,** wear, waste *or* wear away, crumble, erode, ablate, corrode, consume, consume away, be eaten away; melt away, deliquesce

7 **reduce, decrease, diminish, lessen,** take from; **lower, depress,** de-escalate, damp, dampen, **step down** *and* tune down *and* phase down *or* out *and* scale back *or* down *and* roll back *or* down <all nonformal>; **downgrade;** depreciate, **deflate; curtail,** retrench; **cut,** cut down *or* back, trim away, chip away at, whittle away *or* down, pare, roll back <nonformal>; deduct 255.9; **shorten** 268.6, abridge; **compress** 260.7, shrink, downsize; **simplify** 797.4

8 **abate,** bate, ease; **weaken,** dilute, water, water down, attenuate, extenuate; alleviate, mitigate, slacken, remit

9 **minimize,** minify, **belittle,** detract from; dwarf, bedwarf; play down, underplay, downplay, de-emphasize

ADJS 10 **reduced, decreased, diminished, lowered,** dropped, fallen; bated, **abated; deflated,** contracted, shrunk, shrunken; **simplified** 797.9; back-to-basics, no-frills; dissipated, **eroded,** consumed, ablated, **worn;** curtailed, shorn, retrenched, cutback; weakened, attenuated, watereddown; scaled-down, miniaturized; minimized, belittled; **lower,** less, lesser, smaller, shorter; off-peak

11 **decreasing, diminishing, lessening, subsiding, declining,** languishing, dwindling, waning, on the wane, wasting; decrescent, reductive, deliquescent, **contractive;** diminuendo, decrescendo

ADVS 12 **decreasingly, diminishingly,** less, **less and less,** ever less; decrescendo, diminuendo; on a declining scale, at a declining rate

253 ADDITION

NOUNS 1 **addition,** accession, annexation, affixation, suffixation, prefixation, agglutination, attachment, junction, **joining** 799, adjunction, uniting; **increase** 251; **augmentation, supplementation, complementation,** reinforcement; superaddition, superposition, superjunction, superfetation, suppletion; juxtaposition 223.3; adjunct 254, add-on

2 <math terms> plus sign, plus; addend; sum, summation, total; subtotal

3 **adding,** totalizing *or* totalization, computation; **adding machine,** calculator

VERBS 4 **add,** plus <nonformal>, put with, **join** *or* **unite with, bring together, affix, attach,** annex, adjoin, append, conjoin, subjoin, prefix, suffix, infix, postfix, tag, tag on, **tack on** <nonformal>, slap on <nonformal>, hitch on <nonformal>; glue on, paste on, agglutinate; superpose, superadd; burden, encumber, saddle with; **complicate,** ornament, decorate

5 **add to, augment, supplement; increase** 251.4; **reinforce,** strengthen, fortify, beef up <nonformal>; recruit, swell the ranks of

6 **compute,** add up; sum, total, totalize, total up, tot *and* tot up *and* tote *and* tote up <all nonformal>, tally

7 **be added,** advene, supervene

ADJS 8 **additive,** additional, additory; **cumulative,** accumulative; summative *or* summational

9 **added,** affixed, add-on, **attached,** annexed, appended, appendant; adjoined, adjunct, conjoined, subjoined; superadded, superposed, superjoined

10 **additional, supplementary, supplemental; extra,** plus, further, farther, fresh, **more,** new, **other,** another, ulterior; **auxiliary,** ancillary, supernumerary, contributory, **accessory,** collateral; **surplus,** spare

ADVS 11 **additionally, in addition, also,** and then some, even more, more so, and also, and all <nonformal>, and so, **as well, too,** else, beside, **besides, to boot, not to mention, let alone, into the bargain;** on top of, over, above; **beyond, plus; extra,** on the side <nonformal>, for lagniappe; **more, moreover,** *au reste* <Fr>, *en plus* <Fr>, thereto, farther, further, **furthermore,** at the same time, then, again, yet; similarly, likewise, by the same token, by the same sign; item; therewith, withal <old>; all included, altogether; among other things, *inter alia* <L>

PREPS 12 **with, plus, including,** inclusive of, **along** *or* **together with,** coupled with, **in conjunction with; as well as,** to say nothing of, not to mention, let alone; over and above, **in addition to,** added to, linked to; with the addition of, attended by

CONJS 13 **and, also,** and also

PHRS 14 **et cetera, etc, and so forth, and so on,** *und so weiter* <Ger>; **et al,** *et alii* <L>, **and all** <nonformal>, and others, and other things, *cum multis aliis* <L, with many others>; and everything else, **and more of the same, and the rest, and the like;** blah blah blah blah *and* dah-dah dah-dah dah-dah *and* and suchlike *or* and all that sort of thing *and* and all that *and*

and all like that *and* and stuff like that
and and all that jazz <all nonformal>;
and what not *and* and what have you *and*
and I don't know what *and* and God
knows what *and* and then some *and* you
name it<all nonformal>; and the following, *et sequens* <L>, et seq

WORD ELEMENTS **15** super—, pleo—,
pleio—

254 ADJUNCT
<thing added>

NOUNS **1 adjunct, addition,** increase, **increment,** augmentation, supplementation,
complementation, *additum* <L>, addita-
ment, additory, addendum, addenda
<pl>, accession, fixture; **annex,** annexa-
tion; **appendage,** appendant, pendant,
appanage, tailpiece, coda; undergirding,
reinforcement; appurtenance, appurte-
nant; **accessory,** attachment; **supplement,** complement, continuation, extrapolation, extension; offshoot, side issue,
corollary, sidebar <nonformal>, side effect, spin-off <nonformal>, **concomitant, accompaniment** 768, **additive,** adjuvant

2 <written text> **postscript, appendix;**
rider, allonge, codicil; **epilogue,** envoi,
coda, tail; back matter, front matter;
note, marginalia, scholia, commentary;
interpolation, interlineation; affix, prefix,
suffix, infix; enclitic, proclitic

3 <building> wing, **addition, annex,** extension, ell *or* L

4 extra, bonus, premium, something extra,
extra dash, extra added attraction, lagniappe, something into the bargain,
something for good measure, baker's
dozen; **padding,** stuffing, filling; trimming, **frill,** flourish, filigree, decoration,
ornament; bells and whistles <nonfor-
mal>; superaddition; fillip, wrinkle,
twist

255 SUBTRACTION

NOUNS **1 subtraction, deduction,** subduc-
tion, **removal,** taking away; abstraction,
ablation, sublation; erosion, abrasion,
wearing, wearing away; refinement, purification

2 reduction, diminution, decrease 252,
build-down, phasedown, drawdown, decrement, impairment, **cut** *or* **cutting,**
curtailment, shortening, truncation;
shrinkage, depletion, **attrition,** remission; **depreciation,** detraction, disparage-

ment, derogation; retraction, retrenchment; **extraction**

3 excision, abscission, rescission, extirpation; **elimination,** exclusion, extinction,
eradication, destruction 395, annihilation; cancellation, write-off, erasure;
amputation, mutilation

4 castration, gelding, emasculation, deball-
ing <nonformal>, altering *and* fixing
<both nonformal>, spaying

5 <written text> **deletion,** erasure, cancellation, omission; editing, blue-
penciling, striking *or* striking out; expurgation, bowdlerization, censoring
or censorship; abridgment, abbreviation

6 <math terms> subtrahend, minuend;
negative; minus sign, minus

7 <thing subtracted> **deduction,** decre-
ment, minus

8 <result> **difference, remainder** 256,
epact <astronomy>, discrepancy, net,
balance, surplus 992.5, deficit, credit

VERBS **9 subtract, deduct,** subduct, take
away, take from, **remove,** withdraw, ab-
stract; **reduce,** shorten, curtail, retrench,
lessen, **diminish, decrease,** phase down,
impair, bate, abate; **depreciate,** dispar-
age, detract, derogate; **erode,** abrade, eat
or wear *or* rub *or* shave *or* file away; **ex-
tract,** leach, drain, wash away; thin, thin
out, weed; **refine,** purify

10 excise, cut out, cut, extirpate, enucleate;
cancel, write off; **eradicate,** root out, wipe
or stamp out, **eliminate,** kill, kill off, liq-
uidate, annihilate, destroy 395.10,
extinguish; **exclude,** except, take out, can-
cel, cancel out, censor out, bleep out
<nonformal>, rule out, bar, ban; set
aside *or* apart, isolate, pick out, cull; **cut
off** *or* **away,** shear *or* take *or* strike *or*
knock *or* lop off, truncate; **amputate,** mu-
tilate, abscind; **prune,** pare, peel, clip,
crop, bob, dock, lop, nip, shear, shave,
strip, strip off *or* away

11 castrate, geld, emasculate, eunuchize,
neuter, spay, fix *or* alter <both nonfor-
mal>, unsex, deball <nonformal>

12 <written text> **delete,** erase, expunge,
cancel, omit; **edit,** edit out, blue-pencil;
strike, strike out *or* off, rub *or* blot out,
cross out *or* off, kill, cut; void, rescind;
censor, bowdlerize, expurgate; abridge,
abbreviate

ADJS **13 subtractive, reductive,** deductive;
ablative, erosive; censorial

PREPS **14 off, from; minus,** less, without, ex-
cluding, except *or* excepting, with the ex-
ception of, save, leaving out *or* aside,

barring, exclusive of, not counting, exception taken of, discounting

256 REMAINDER

NOUNS **1 remainder, remains, remnant, residue,** residuum, **rest, balance;** holdover; **leavings, leftovers, oddments; refuse,** odds and ends, scraps, rags, **rubbish, waste,** orts, candle ends; scourings, offscourings; parings, sweepings, filings, shavings, sawdust; chaff, straw, stubble, husks; **debris,** detritus, ruins; end, fag end; stump, butt or butt end, roach <nonformal>, rump; survival, vestige, trace, hint, shadow, afterimage, afterglow; **fossil,** relics

2 dregs, grounds, lees, dross, slag, draff, scoria, feces; **sediment, settlings, deposits,** deposition; precipitate, precipitation, sublimate <chem>; alluvium, alluvion, diluvium; silt, loess, moraine; scum, off-scum, froth; ash, ember, cinder, sinter, clinker; soot, smut

3 survivor, heir, successor; **widow,** widower, relict, war widow, **orphan**

4 excess 992, **surplus,** surplusage, overplus, overage; superfluity, redundancy

VERBS **5 remain, be left** or **left over, survive,** subsist, rest

6 leave, leave over, leave behind

ADJS **7 remaining, surviving, extant,** vestigial, over, left, **leftover, still around, remnant,** remanent, odd; **spare,** to spare; unused, unconsumed; **surplus,** superfluous; **outstanding,** unmet, unresolved; net

8 residual, residuary; sedimental, sedimentary

257 SIZE, LARGENESS

NOUNS **1 size, largeness, bigness, greatness** 247, vastness, vastitude, **magnitude,** order of magnitude, amplitude; mass, bulk, **volume,** body; **dimensions, proportions,** dimension, caliber, scantling, proportion; **measure,** measurement 300, gauge, **scale; extent,** extension, expansion, expanse, square footage or yardage etc, **scope,** reach, range, ballpark <nonformal>, spread, coverage, area, circumference, ambit, girth, diameter, radius, boundary, border, periphery; linear measure or dimension, length, height, procerity <depth>; depth, breadth, width; wheelbase, wingspan

2 capacity, volume, content, holding capacity, cubic footage or yardage etc,

accommodation, room, space, measure, limit, burden; gallonage, tankage; poundage, tonnage, cordage; stowage; **quantity** 244

3 full size, full growth; life size

4 large size, economy size, family size, **king size,** queen size, giant size

5 oversize, outsize; overlargeness, overbigness; **overgrowth,** wild or uncontrolled growth, overdevelopment, sprawl; **overweight,** overheaviness; overstoutness, overfatness, overplumpness, bloat, bloatedness, obesity; gigantism, giantism, titanism; hypertrophy, acromegalic gigantism, pituitary gigantism, normal gigantism

6 <large size> **sizableness, largeness, bigness,** greatness, grandness, grandeur, grandiosity; largishness, biggishness; voluminousness, capaciousness, generousness, copiousness, ampleness; tallness, toweringness; broadness, wideness; profundity; extensiveness, expansiveness, comprehensiveness; spaciousness 158.5

7 <very large size> **hugeness, vastness,** vastitude; humongousness <nonformal>; **enormousness, immenseness, enormity, immensity,** tremendousness, **prodigiousness,** stupendousness, mountainousness; **gigantism,** giganticness, giantism, giantlikeness; monumentalism; **monstrousness, monstrosity**

8 corpulence, obesity, stoutness, largeness, bigness, embonpoint <Fr>; **fatness,** fattishness, adiposis or adiposity, fleshiness, beefiness, meatiness, heftiness, grossness; **plumpness,** buxomness, rotundity, fubsiness <Brit>, tubbiness <nonformal>, roly-poliness; pudginess, podginess; chubbiness, chunkiness <nonformal>, stockiness, squattiness, dumpiness, portliness; paunchiness, bloatedness, puffiness, pursiness, blowziness; middle-age spread; hippiness <nonformal>; steatopygia or steatopygy; bosominess, bustiness <nonformal>

9 bulkiness, bulk, hulkingness or hulkiness, **massiveness,** lumpishness, clumpishness; **ponderousness,** cumbrousness, cumbersomeness; clumsiness, awkwardness, unwieldiness, clunkiness <nonformal>

10 lump, clump, **hunk** and **chunk** <both nonformal>, wodge <Brit nonformal>; **mass,** piece, **gob** and glob <both nonformal>, gobbet; batch, **wad,** block, loaf; pat <of butter>; clod; nugget; **quantity** 244

11 <something large> **whopper** and

thumper *and* lunker *and* whale *and* jumbo <all nonformal>; monster, hulk

12 <corpulent person> **heavyweight, pig,** porker, heavy <nonformal>, human *or* man mountain <nonformal>; big *or* large person; **fat person, fatty** *and* **fatso** <both nonformal>, roly-poly, **tub, tub of lard,** tun, tun of flesh, whale, blimp <nonformal>, hippo <nonformal>, **potbelly,** gorbelly <old or dial>, swagbelly

13 giant <see list> giantess, **amazon, colossus, titan,** *nephilim* <Heb pl>

14 behemoth, leviathan, monster; mammoth, mastodon; elephant, jumbo <nonformal>; whale; hippopotamus, hippo <nonformal>; **dinosaur**

VERBS **15 size, adjust, grade,** group, range, rank, graduate, sort, match; gauge, **measure** 300.11, proportion; **bulk** 247.5; **enlarge** 259.4,5; fatten

ADJS **16 large, sizable, big, great** 247.6, **grand,** tall <nonformal>, **considerable, goodly,** healthy, tidy <nonformal>, **substantial,** bumper; as big as all outdoors; numerous 883.6; largish, biggish; large-scale, larger than life; man-sized <nonformal>; large-size *or* -sized, man-sized, king-size, queen-size; good-sized, life-size *or* -sized

17 voluminous, capacious, generous, ample, copious, broad, wide, extensive, expansive, comprehensive; **spacious**

18 corpulent, stout, fat, overweight, fattish, **obese,** adipose, gross, fleshy, beefy, meaty, hefty, porky, porcine; paunchy, paunched, bloated, puffy, blowzy, distended, swollen, pursy; abdominous, big-bellied, full-bellied, potbellied, gorbellied <old or dial>, swag-bellied, pot-gutted *and* pussle-gutted <both nonformal>, **plump, buxom,** *zaftig* <Yiddish>, pleasantly plump, full, huggy <nonformal>, rotund, fubsy <Brit>, **tubby** <nonformal>, roly-poly; **pudgy,** podgy; thick-bodied, thick-girthed, **heavyset, thickset, chubby,** chunky <nonformal>, fubsy <Brit nonformal>, **stocky,** squat, squatty, dumpy, square; pyknic, endomorphic; **stalwart, brawny, burly;** lusty, strapping <nonformal>; **portly,** imposing; well-fed, corn-fed, grain-fed; chubby-faced, round-faced, moonfaced; hippy <nonformal>, full-buttocked, steatopygic *or* steatopygous, fat-assed *and* lard-assed <both nonformal>, broad in the beam <nonformal>; bosomy, full-bosomed, chesty, busty <nonformal>, top-heavy; plump as a dumpling *or* partridge, fat as a quail, fat as a pig *or* hog,

"fat as a pork hog"—Malory, "fat as a porpoise"—Swift, "fat as a fool"—John Lyly, "fat as butter"—Shakespeare, fat as brawn *or* bacon

19 bulky, hulky, hulking, lumpish, lumpy, lumping <nonformal>, clumpish, lumbering, lubberly; **massive,** massy; elephantine, hippopotamic; **ponderous,** cumbrous, cumbersome; **clumsy,** awkward, **unwieldy;** clunky <nonformal>

20 huge, immense, vast, enormous, astronomic, astronomical, humongous *and* jumbo <both nonformal>, king-size, queen-size, tremendous, prodigious, stupendous, macro, mega, giga; great big, larger than life, Homeric, mighty, **titanic, colossal, monumental,** heroic, heroical, epic, epical, towering, mountainous; profound, abysmal, deep as the ocean *or* as China; **monster,** monstrous; **mammoth,** mastodonic; **gigantic, giant,** giantlike, gigantesque, gigantean; Cyclopean, Brobdingnagian, Gargantuan, Herculean, Atlantean; elephantine, jumbo <nonformal>; dinosaurian, dinotherian; **infinite** 822.3

21 <nonformal terms> **whopping, walloping, whaling, whacking,** spanking, slapping, lolloping, thumping, thundering, bumping, banging

22 full-sized, full-size, full-scale; **full-grown, full-fledged,** full-blown; full-formed, **life-sized,** large as life, larger than life

23 oversize, oversized; **outsize,** outsized, giant-size, **king-size, queen-size,** record-size, **overlarge,** overbig, too big; **overgrown,** overdeveloped; **overweight,** overheavy; overfleshed, overstout, overfat, overplump, overfed, obese

24 this big, so big, yay big <nonformal>, this size, about this size

ADVS **25** largely, on a large scale, in a big way; in the large; as can be

WORD ELEMENTS **26** hyper—, macr—, macro—, maxi—, meg—, mega—, megal—, megalo—, super—

27 giants

Abominable Snowman *or* yeti	Blunderbore
	Briareüs
Aegaeon	Brobdingnagian
Aegir	Cormoran
Alifanfaron	Cottus
Amarant	Cyclops
Antaeus	Enceladus
Ascapart	Ephialtes
Atlas	Fafner
Balan	Fenrir
Bellerus	Ferragus
Big Foot *or* Sasquatch *or* Omah	Fierabras
	Firbauti

Galapas   Magog
Galligantus   Mimir
Gargantua   Morgante
Geryoneo   Og
Godzilla   Orgoglio
Gog   Orion
Goliath   Pantagruel
Grantorto   Paul Bunyan
Gyes   Polyphemus
Hercules *or* Heracles   Titan
Hlér   Tityus
Hymir   Typhon
Jötunn   Urdar
King Kong   Ymir

258 LITTLENESS

NOUNS **1 littleness, smallness,** smallishness, **diminutiveness,** miniatureness, slightness, exiguity; puniness, pokiness, dinkiness <nonformal>; tininess, **minuteness;** undersize; petiteness; dwarfishness, stuntedness, runtiness, shrimpiness; **shortness** 268; **scantiness** 884.1

2 infinitesimalness; undetectability, inappreciability, evanescence; intangibility, impalpability, tenuousness, imponderability; imperceptibility, invisibility

3 <small space> **tight spot** *and* corner *and* squeeze *and* **pinch** <all nonformal>, not enough room to swing a cat <nonformal>; hole, pigeonhole; hole-in-the-wall; cubby, cubbyhole; cubbyhouse, dollhouse, playhouse, doghouse; cuddy, cuddy cabin

4 <small person or creature> **runt, shrimp** <nonformal>, wart <nonformal>, diminutive, wisp, chit, slip, snip, snippet, minikin <old>, **peanut** *and* **peewee** <both nonformal>, pip-squeak, shorty, fingerling, small fry <nonformal>, dandiprat *and* tiddler <Brit old>; lightweight, featherweight; bantam, banty <nonformal>; pony; minnow, mini *and* minny <both nonformal>; mouse, tit, titmouse, tomtit <nonformal>; nubbin, button

5 <creature small by species or birth> **dwarf,** dwarfling, **midget,** midge, **pygmy,** manikin, homunculus, atomy, micromorph, hop-o'-my-thumb; elf, gnome, brownie; Lilliputian, Pigwiggen, Tom Thumb, Thumbelina, Alberich, Alviss, Andvari, Nibelung, Regin

6 miniature, mini; scaled-down *or* miniaturized version; microcosm, microcosmos; baby; doll, puppet; microvolume; Elzevir, Elzevir edition; duodecimo, twelvemo

7 <minute thing> minutia, **minutiae**

<pl>, minim, **drop,** droplet, **mite** <nonformal>, **point,** vanishing point, mathematical point, point of a pin, pinpoint, pinhead, **dot;** mote, fleck, **speck,** flyspeck, jot, tittle, jot nor tittle, iota, **trace,** trace amount, suspicion, *soupçon* <Fr>; **particle,** crumb, scrap, bite, snip, snippet; grain, grain of sand; barleycorn, millet seed, mustard seed; midge, gnat; microbe, **microorganism,** amoeba, bacillus, bacteria, diatom, germ, microbe, paramecium, protozoon, virus

8 atom, atomy, monad; **molecule,** ion; **electron,** proton, meson, neutrino, quark, parton, subatomic *or* nuclear particle

9 make small, contract 260.7; **shorten** 268.6; **miniaturize,** minify, scale down; **reduce** 252.7, scale back

ADJS **10 little, small** 248.6, smallish; **slight,** exiguous; **puny, trifling,** poky, piffling *and* pindling *and* piddling *and* piddly <all nonformal>, **dinky** <nonformal>; cramped, limited; one-horse, two-by-four <nonformal>; pintsized <nonformal>, half-pint; knee-high, knee-high to a grasshopper; petite; short 268.8

11 tiny; teeny *and* teeny-weeny *and* eentsy-weentsy <all nonformal>, wee *and* peewee <both nonformal>, bitty *and* bitsy *and* little-bitty *and* little-bitsy *and* itsy-bitsy *and* itsy-witsy <all nonformal>; **minute,** fine

12 miniature, diminutive, minuscule, minuscular, mini, micro, miniaturized, subminiature, minikin <old>, **smallscale,** minimal; pony, bantam, banty <nonformal>; **baby,** baby-sized; pocket, pocketsized, **vest-pocket; toy;** handy, compact; duodecimo, twelvemo

13 dwarf, dwarfed, dwarfish, **pygmy, midget,** nanoid, elfin; Lilliputian, Tom Thumb; **undersized,** undersize, squat, dumpy; **stunted,** undergrown, runty, pint-size *or* -sized *and* sawed-off <all nonformal>; shrunk, shrunken, wizened, shriveled; meager, scrubby, scraggy; rudimentary, rudimental

14 infinitesimal, microscopic, ultramicroscopic; evanescent, thin, tenuous; inappreciable; impalpable, imponderable, intangible; imperceptible, indiscernible, invisible, unseeable; atomic, subatomic; molecular; granular, corpuscular, microcosmic<al>; embryonic, germinal

15 microbic, microbial, **microorganic;** animalcular, bacterial; microzoic; protozoan, microzoan, amoebic *or* amoeboid

ADVS **16 small,** little, **slightly** 248.9, fractionally; **on a small scale,** in a small compass, in a small way, on a minuscule *or* infinitesimal scale; **in miniature,** in the small; in a nutshell

WORD ELEMENTS 17 micr—, micro—, ultramicr—, ultramicro—; granul—, granulo—, granuli—, chondr—, chondro—; —cle, —ee, —een, —el, —ella, —illa, —et, —ette, —idium, —idion, —ie, —y, —ey, —ium, —kin, —let, —ling, —ock, —sy, —ula, —ule, —ulum, —ulus

259 EXPANSION, GROWTH
<increase in size>

NOUNS **1 expansion, extension, enlargement, increase** 251, uptick, crescendo, upping, raising, hiking, magnification, aggrandizement, amplification, ampliation <old>, broadening, widening; **spread,** spreading, creeping, fanning out, dispersion, ripple effect; **flare,** splay; deployment; augmentation, **addition** 253; adjunct 254

2 distension, stretching; **inflation,** sufflation, blowing up; **dilation,** dilatation, dilating; diastole; **swelling,** swell 283.4; puffing, puff, puffiness, **bloating,** bloat, **flatulence** *or* flatulency, flatus, gassiness, windiness; **turgidity,** turgidness, turgescence; tumidness *or* tumidity, tumefaction; tumescence, intumescence; **swollenness,** bloatedness; dropsy, edema; tympanites, tympany, tympanism

3 growth, development 860.1; **bodily development** 14, **maturation,** maturing, coming of age, growing up, upgrowth; vegetation 310.30; reproduction, procreation 78, germination, pullulation; burgeoning, sprouting; budding, gemmation; outgrowth, excrescence; overgrowth 257.5

VERBS **4** <make larger> **enlarge, expand, extend, widen, broaden,** build, build up, aggrandize, **amplify,** crescendo, **magnify, increase** 251.4, augment, add to 253.5, raise, up, scale up, hike *or* hike up; develop, bulk *or* bulk up; **stretch, distend, dilate, swell, inflate,** sufflate, **blow up,** puff up, huff, puff, bloat; pump, pump up; rarefy

5 <become larger> **enlarge, expand, extend, increase,** greaten, crescendo, **develop, widen, broaden,** bulk; **stretch, distend, dilate, swell, swell up, swell out, puff up, puff out, pump up, bloat,** tumefy, balloon, fill out; snowball

6 spread, spread out, outspread, out-

stretch; **expand, extend,** widen; open, **open up,** unfold; **flare,** flare out, broaden out, splay; spraddle, sprangle, sprawl; branch, branch out, ramify; fan, fan out, disperse, deploy; spread like wildfire; overrun, overgrow

7 grow, develop, wax, **increase** 251; gather, brew; **grow up,** mature, spring up, ripen, come of age, **shoot up,** sprout up, upshoot, upspring, upsprout, upspear, overtop, tower; burgeon, **sprout** 310.31, blossom 310.32, reproduce 78.7, procreate 78.8, grow out of, germinate, pullulate; vegetate 310.31; **flourish, thrive,** grow like a weed; mushroom; outgrow; overgrow, hypertrophy, overdevelop, grow uncontrollably

8 fatten, fat, plump, pinguefy *and* engross <both old>; **gain weight,** gather flesh, take *or* put on weight, become overweight

ADJS **9 expansive, extensive;** expansional, extensional; expansile, extensile, elastic; expansible, inflatable; distensive, dilatant; inflationary

10 expanded, extended, enlarged, increased 251.7, upped, raised, hiked, **amplified,** ampliate <old>, crescendoed, widened, broadened, built-up, beefed-up <nonformal>

11 spread, spreading; sprawling, sprawly; **outspread, outstretched,** spreadout, stretched-out; open, unfolded, gaping, patulous; widespread, wide-open; flared, spraddled, sprangled, splayed; flaring, flared, flared-out, spraddling, sprangling, splaying; splay; fanned, fanning; fanlike, fan-shaped, fan-shape, flabelliform, deltoid

12 grown, full-grown, grown-up, mature, developed, well-developed, fully developed, full-fledged; growing, sprouting, crescent, budding, flowering 310.35, florescent, **flourishing,** blossoming, blooming, burgeoning, fast-growing, thriving; overgrown, hypertrophied, overdeveloped

13 distended, dilated, inflated, sufflated, **blown up, puffed up, swollen,** swelled, **bloated,** turgid, tumid, plethoric, incrassate; **puffy,** pursy; flatulent, gassy, windy, ventose; tumefacient; dropsical, edematous; enchymatous; fat; puffed out, bouffant, bouffed up *and* bouffy <both nonformal>

260 CONTRACTION
<decrease in size>

NOUNS **1 contraction,** contracture; systole;

compression, compressure, pressurizing, pressurization; **compacting,** compaction, compactedness; **condensation, concentration,** consolidation, solidification; **circumscription, narrowing;** reduction, diminuendo, **decrease** 252; abbreviation, curtailment, shortening 268.3; **constriction,** stricture or striction, astriction, strangulation, **choking,** choking off, coarctation; bottleneck, chokepoint, hourglass, hourglass figure, nipped or wasp waist; neck, cervix, isthmus, narrow place; astringency, constringency; puckering, pursing; knitting, wrinkling

2 **squeezing,** compression, clamping or clamping down, tightening; **pressure,** press, crush; **pinch, squeeze, tweak, nip**

3 **shrinking,** shrinkage, atrophy; **shriveling, withering;** searing, parching, drying or drying up; attenuation, thinning; wasting, consumption, emaciation, emaceration <old>; skin and bones; preshrinking, preshrinkage, Sanforizing <trademark>

4 **collapse,** prostration, cave-in; implosion; **deflation**

5 contractibility, contractility, compactability, **compressibility,** condensability, reducibility; collapsibility

6 contractor, constrictor, clamp, compressor, vise, pincer, squeezer; thumbscrew; **astringent,** styptic; alum, astringent bitters, styptic pencil

VERBS 7 **contract, compress,** cramp, compact, condense, concentrate, consolidate, solidify; **reduce, decrease** 252; abbreviate, curtail, **shorten** 268.6; **constrict,** constringe, circumscribe, coarct, **narrow,** draw, draw in or together; strangle, strangulate, choke, choke off; **pucker,** pucker up, **purse; knit, wrinkle**

8 **squeeze,** compress, clamp, cramp, cramp up, tighten; roll or wad up, roll up into a ball, ensphere; **press,** pressurize, crush; **pinch, tweak, nip**

9 **shrink, shrivel, wither,** sear, parch, dry up; **wizen,** weazen; consume, waste, waste away, attenuate, thin, emaciate, macerate or emacerate <old>; preshrink, Sanforize <trademark>

10 **collapse, cave, cave in,** fall in; fold, fold up; implode; **deflate,** let the air out of, take the wind out of; puncture

ADJS 11 **contractive,** contractional, contractible, contractile, compactable; **astringent,** constringent, styptic; **compressible,** condensable, reducible; **collapsible,** foldable; deflationary; consumptive

12 **contracted, compressed,** cramped, compact or compacted, concentrated, condensed, consolidated, solidified; **constricted,** strangled, strangulated, choked, choked off, coarcted, **squeezed,** clamped, nipped, pinched or pinched-in, waspwaisted; puckered, pursed; knitted, wrinkled

13 **shrunk,** shrunken; **shriveled,** shriveled up; **withered,** sear, parched, corky, dried-up; **wasted,** wasted away, consumed, emaciated, emacerated, thin, attenuated; **wizened,** wizen, weazened; wizen-faced; preshrunk, Sanforized <trademark>

14 **deflated, punctured, flat,** holed

261 DISTANCE, REMOTENESS

NOUNS 1 **distance, remoteness,** farness, far-offness, longinquity; **separation,** separatedness, divergence, clearance, margin, leeway; **extent, length,** space 158, **reach,** stretch, range, compass, span, stride, haul, a way, ways and piece <both nonformal>; perspective, aesthetic distance, distancing; astronomical or interstellar or galactic or intergalactic distance, deep space, depths of space, **infinity** 822; **mileage,** light-years, parsecs

2 **long way,** good ways <nonformal>, **great distance, far cry,** far piece <nonformal>; long step, tidy step, giant step or stride; long run or haul, long road or trail; long range; apogee, aphelion

3 **the distance, remote distance, offing;** horizon, the far horizon, where the earth meets the sky, vanishing point, background

4 <remote region> jumping-off place and godforsaken place and God knows where and the middle of nowhere <all nonformal>, the back of beyond, the end of the rainbow, Thule or Ultima Thule, Timbuktu, Siberia, Darkest Africa, the South Seas, Pago Pago, the Great Divide, China, Outer Mongolia, pole, antipodes, end of the earth, North Pole, South Pole, Tierra del Fuego, Greenland, Yukon, Pillars of Hercules, remotest corner of the world; outpost, outskirts; the sticks and the boondocks and the boonies <all nonformal>; **nowhere;** frontier, outback <Australia>; the moon; outer space

VERBS 5 **reach out, stretch out,** extend, extend out, go or go out, range out, carry out; outstretch, outlie, outdistance, outrange

6 **extend to,** stretch to, stretch away to, **reach to,** lead to, go to, get to, come to, run to, carry to

7 keep one's distance, distance oneself, remain at a distance, maintain distance *or* clearance, keep at a respectful distance, separate oneself, **keep away,** stand off *or* away; keep away from, keep *or* stand clear of, **steer clear of** <nonformal>, hold away from, give a wide berth to, keep a good leeway *or* margin *or* offing, keep out of the way of, keep at arm's length, not touch with a ten-foot pole <nonformal>, keep *or* stay *or* stand aloof; maintain one's perspective, keep one's esthetic distance

ADJS **8 distant,** distal, **remote, removed, far, far-off,** away, **faraway,** way-off, at a distance, exotic, separated, apart, asunder; long-distance, long-range

9 out-of-the-way, godforsaken, back of beyond, upcountry; **out of reach, inaccessible,** ungetatable, unapproachable, untouchable, hyperborean, antipodean

10 thither, ulterior; **yonder,** yon; **farther, further,** remoter, more distant

11 transoceanic, transmarine, ultramarine, oversea, overseas; transatlantic, transpacific; tramontane, transmontane, ultramontane, transalpine; transarctic, transcontinental, transequatorial, transpolar, transpontine, ultramundane

12 farthest, furthest, farthermost, farthest off, furthermost, ultimate, extreme, remotest, most distant

ADVS **13 yonder,** yon; **in the distance,** in the remote distance; **in the offing,** on the horizon, in the background

14 at a distance, away, off, aloof, at arm's length; distantly, remotely

15 far, far off, far away, **afar,** afar off, a long way off, a good ways off <nonformal>, a long cry to, "over the hills and far away"—John Gay, as far as the eye can see, out of sight; clear to hell and gone <nonformal>

16 far and wide, far and near, distantly and broadly, wide, widely, broadly, abroad

17 apart, away, aside, wide apart, wide away, "as wide asunder as pole and pole"—J A Froude, "as far as the east is from the west"—Bible

18 out of reach, beyond reach, **out of range,** beyond the bounds, out-of-the-way, out of the sphere of; out of sight, *à perte de vue* <Fr>; out of hearing, out of earshot *or* earreach

19 wide, clear; wide of the mark, abroad, all abroad, astray, afield, far afield

PREPS **20 as far as, to, all the way to,** the whole way to

21 beyond, past, over, across, the other *or* far side of

262 FORM

NOUNS **1 form, shape, figure;** figuration, **configuration;** formation, **conformation; structure** 266; **build,** make, frame; **arrangement** 807; makeup, format, layout; **composition** 795; cut, set, stamp, type, turn, cast, mold, impression, pattern, matrix, model, mode, modality; archetype, prototype 785.1, Platonic form *or* idea; style, fashion; aesthetic form, inner form, significant form; art form, genre

2 contour, *tournure* <Fr>, *galbe* <Fr>; broad lines, silhouette, profile, **outline** 211.2; organization 806.1

3 appearance 33, lineaments, features, physiognomy

4 <human form> **figure, form,** shape, frame, anatomy, **physique,** build, body-build, person; body 1050.3

5 forming, shaping, molding, modeling, fashioning, making, making up; **formation,** conformation, figuration, configuration; sculpture; morphogeny, morphogenesis; creation

6 <grammatical terms> form, morph, allomorph, morpheme; morphology, morphemics

VERBS **7 form,** formalize, **shape, fashion,** tailor, frame, figure, **lick into shape;** <nonformal> work, knead; set, fix; **forge,** drop-forge; **mold,** model, sculpt *or* sculpture; cast, found; thermoform; stamp, mint; carve, whittle, cut, chisel, hew, hew out; roughhew, roughcast, rough out, block out, lay out, sketch out; hammer *or* knock out; whomp out *or* up <nonformal>, cobble up; create; organize 806.4

8 <be formed> **form,** take form, shape, **shape up, take shape;** materialize

ADJS **9 formative,** formal, formational, plastic, morphotic; **formed, shaped,** patterned, fashioned, tailored, framed; **forged,** molded, modeled, sculpted; cast, founded; stamped, minted; carved, cut, whittled, chiseled, hewn; roughhewn, roughcast, roughed-out, blocked-out, laid-out, sketched-out; hammered-out, knocked-out, cobbled-up; **made, produced**

10 <biological terms> plasmatic, plasmic, protoplasmic, plastic, metabolic

11 <grammatical terms> morphologic, morphological, morphemic

WORD ELEMENTS **12** morph—, morpho—, —morph, —morphism, —morphy,

—form, —iform, —morphic,
—morphous

263 FORMLESSNESS

NOUNS **1 formlessness, shapelessness;** un-
formedness, amorphousness, amorphism; misshapenness; **chaos** 809.2,
confusion, messiness, mess, muddle
809.2, orderlessness, untidiness; **disorder**
809; entropy; anarchy 418.2; **indeterminateness, indefiniteness,** indecisiveness, vagueness, mistiness, haziness,
fuzziness, blurriness, unclearness, obscurity; lumpiness, lumpishness

2 unlicked cub, diamond in the rough, raw
material

VERBS **3 deform, distort** 265.5; misshape;
unform, unshape; disorder, jumble, mess
up, muddle, confuse; obfuscate, obscure,
fog up, blur

ADJS **4 formless, shapeless,** featureless, characterless, nondescript, inchoate, lumpy,
lumpish, blobby *and* baggy <both non-
formal>, inform; amorphous, **chaotic,
orderless,** disorderly 809.13, unordered,
unorganized, confused, anarchic 418.6;
kaleidoscopic; **indeterminate, indefinite,**
undefined, indecisive, vague, misty, hazy,
fuzzy, blurred *or* blurry, unclear, obscure; obfuscatory

5 unformed, unshaped, unshapen, unfashioned, unlicked; unstructured; uncut,
unhewn

264 SYMMETRY

NOUNS **1 symmetry,** symmetricalness, **proportion,** proportionality, **balance** 789.1,
equilibrium; **regularity,** uniformity 780,
evenness; equality 789; finish; harmony,
congruity, consistency, conformity 866,
correspondence, keeping; eurythmy, eurythmics; dynamic symmetry; bilateral
symmetry, trilateral symmetry, etc, multilateral symmetry; parallelism 203,
polarity; shapeliness

2 symmetrization, regularization, balancing, harmonization; evening, equaliza-
tion; coordination, integration; **compensation,** playing off, playing off against,
posing against *or* over against

VERBS **3** symmetrize, regularize, **balance,**
balance off, compensate; harmonize; **proportion,** proportionate; even, even up,
equalize; coordinate, integrate; play off,
play off against

ADJS **4 symmetric, symmetrical, balanced,**
balanced off, proportioned, eurythmic,

harmonious; **regular,** uniform 780.5,
even, equal 789.7, equal on both sides,
fifty-fifty <nonformal>, square, squared-
off; coequal, coordinate, equilateral;
well-balanced, well-set, well-set-up
<nonformal>; finished

5 shapely, well-shaped, well-proportioned,
well-made, **well-formed,** well-favored;
comely; trim, trig <old>, neat, spruce,
clean, clean-cut, clean-limbed

265 DISTORTION

NOUNS **1 distortion,** torsion, twist, twistedness, **contortion, crookedness,** tortuosity;
asymmetry, unsymmetry, disproportion,
lopsidedness, imbalance, irregularity, **deviation; twist,** quirk, turn, screw, wring,
wrench, wrest; **warp,** buckle; knot, gnarl;
anamorphosis; anamorphism

2 perversion, corruption, misdirection,
misrepresentation 350, misinterpretation, misconstruction; **falsification** 354.9;
twisting, false coloring, bending the
truth, **spin,** spin control, slanting, straining, torturing; misuse 389

3 deformity, deformation, **malformation,**
malconformation, monstrosity 869.6, teratology, freakishness, misproportion,
misshapenness, misshape; **disfigurement,
defacement;** mutilation, truncation;
humpback, hunchback, crookback, camelback, kyphosis; swayback, lordosis;
wryneck, torticollis; clubfoot, talipes,
flatfoot, splayfoot; knock-knee; bowlegs;
valgus; harelip; cleft palate

4 grimace, wry face, wry mouth, rictus,
snarl; moue, mow, pout

VERBS **5 distort, contort,** turn awry; **twist,**
turn, screw, wring, wrench, wrest;
writhe; **warp,** buckle, crumple; knot,
gnarl; **crook,** bend, spring

**6 pervert, falsify, twist, garble, put a false
construction upon, give a spin, give a
false coloring,** color, varnish, slant,
strain, torture; put words in someone's
mouth; **bias;** misrepresent 350.3, misconstrue, misinterpret, misrender, misdirect; misuse 389.4; send *or* deliver the
wrong signal *or* message

7 deform, misshape, twist, torture, disproportion; **disfigure, deface;** mutilate,
truncate; blemish, mar

8 grimace, make a face, make a wry face *or*
mouth, pull a face, **screw up one's face,**
mug <nonformal>, mouth, make a
mouth, mop, mow, mop and mow; pout

ADJS **9** distortive, contortive, contortional,
torsional

10 distorted, contorted, warped, twisted, crooked; tortuous, labyrinthine, buckled, sprung, bent, bowed; cockeyed <nonformal>, crazy; crunched, crumpled; unsymmetric, unsymmetrical, asymmetric, asymmetrical, nonsymmetric, nonsymmetrical; irregular, deviative, anamorphous; one-sided, lopsided; askew 204.14, off-center, left *or* right of center

11 falsified, perverted, twisted, garbled, slanted, doctored, biased, crooked; strained, tortured; misrepresented, misquoted

12 deformed, malformed, misshapen, misbegotten, misproportioned, ill-proportioned, ill-made, ill-shaped, **out of shape;** dwarfed, stumpy; bloated; **disfigured,** defaced, blemished, marred; mutilated, truncated; grotesque, **monstrous 869.13;** sway-backed, round-shouldered; bowlegged, bandy-legged, bandy; knock-kneed; rickety, rachitic; club-footed, talipedic; flatfooted, splay-footed, pigeon-toed; pug-nosed, snub-nosed, simous

13 humpbacked, hunchbacked, bunchbacked, crookbacked, crooked-backed, camelback, humped, gibbous, kyphotic

266 STRUCTURE

NOUNS **1 structure, construction,** architecture, tectonics, architectonics, **frame,** make, **build,** fabric, tissue, warp and woof *or* weft, web, weave, texture, contexture, mold, **shape, pattern, plan,** fashion, arrangement, **organization 806.1;** organism, organic structure, **constitution, composition; makeup,** getup <nonformal>, setup; **formation,** conformation, **format; arrangement 807,** configuration; **composition 795;** making, building, creation, production, forging, fashioning, molding, fabrication, manufacture, shaping, structuring, patterning; anatomy, physique; form 262; **morphology,** science of structure

2 structure, building, edifice, construction, construct, erection, establishment, fabric; house; tower, pile, pyramid, skyscraper, ziggurat; prefabrication, prefab, packaged house; air structure, bubble <nonformal>, air hall <Brit>; superstructure; flat-slab construction, post-and-beam construction, steel-cage construction, steel construction

3 understructure, understruction, under-

building, undercroft, crypt; **substructure,** substruction; infrastructure

4 frame, framing; braced framing; **framework, skeleton,** fabric, cadre, chassis, shell, armature; lattice, latticework; sash, casement, case, casing; window case *or* frame, doorframe; picture frame

VERBS **5 construct, build; structure; organize 806.4; form** 262.7

ADJS **6 structural,** formal, morphological, edificial, tectonic, textural; **anatomic,** anatomical, **organic,** organismal, organismic; **structured, patterned,** shaped, formed; **architectural,** architectonic; constructional; superstructural, substructural

267 LENGTH

NOUNS **1 length,** longness, lengthiness, overall length; wheelbase; **extent,** extension, **measure, span, reach, stretch; distance 261;** footage, yardage, mileage; infinity 822; perpetuity 828; long time 826.4; linear measures; oblongness; longitude

2 a length, **piece, portion,** part; coil, **strip,** bolt, roll; run

3 line, strip, bar; stripe 517.6; string

4 lengthening, prolongation, elongation, production, protraction; prolixity, prolixness; **extension,** stretching, stretching *or* spinning *or* stringing out

VERBS **5 be long, be lengthy, extend,** be prolonged, **stretch; stretch out,** extend out, reach out; stretch oneself, crane, crane one's neck, rubberneck; stand on tiptoes; outstretch, outreach; sprawl, straggle

6 lengthen, prolong, prolongate, **elongate, extend,** produce, **protract,** continue; make prolix; lengthen out, let out, **draw** *or* drag *or* stretch *or* string *or* spin out; **stretch,** draw, pull

ADJS **7 long, lengthy;** longish, longsome; tall; **extensive, far-reaching,** fargoing, far-flung; sesquipedalian, sesquipedal; as long as one's arm, a mile long; **time-consuming,** interminable, without end, no end of *or* to

8 lengthened, prolonged, prolongated, **elongated, extended, protracted; prolix; long-winded; drawn-out,** dragged out, long-drawn-out, stretched *or* spun *or* strung out, straggling; **stretched,** drawn, pulled

9 oblong, oblongated, oblongitudinal, **elongated;** rectangular; elliptical

ADVS **10** lengthily, extensively, at length, *in extenso* <L>, *ad infinitum* <L>, ad nauseam

11 lengthwise or lengthways, **longwise** or longways, longitudinally, along, in length, at length; **endwise** or endways, endlong

268 SHORTNESS

NOUNS **1 shortness, briefness, brevity; succinctness,** curtness, terseness, summariness, compendiousness, compactness; **conciseness** 537; **littleness** 258; transience 827, short time 827.3, instantaneousness 829

2 stubbiness, stumpiness <nonformal>, **stockiness, fatness** 257.8, chubbiness, chunkiness <nonformal>, blockiness, squatness, squattiness, dumpiness; pudginess, podginess; snubbiness; **lowness** 274

3 shortening, abbreviation; reduction; abridgment, condensation, compression, conspectus, epitome, epitomization, summary, summation, précis, abstract, recapitulation, recap <nonformal>, wrapup, synopsis, encapsulation; **curtailment,** truncation, retrenchment; telescoping; elision, ellipsis, syncope, apocope; foreshortening

4 shortener, cutter, abridger; abstracter, epitomizer or epitomist

5 shortcut, cut, cutoff; shortest way; **beeline,** air line

VERBS **6 shorten, abbreviate, cut; reduce** 260.7; **abridge, condense,** compress, contract, **boil down,** abstract, sum up, summarize, recapitulate, recap <nonformal>, synopsize, epitomize, encapsulate, capsulize; **curtail,** truncate, retrench; bowdlerize; elide, **cut short,** cut down, cut off short, cut back, take in; **dock,** bob, shear, shave, trim, clip, snub, nip; mow, reap, **crop; prune,** poll, pollard; stunt, check the growth of; telescope; foreshorten

7 take a short cut, short-cut; **cut across,** cut through; **cut a corner,** cut corners; **make a beeline,** take the air line, go as the crow flies

ADJS **8 short, brief, abbreviated,** abbreviatory, "short and sweet"—Thomas Lodge; **concise** 537.6; **curt,** curtal <old>, curtate, decurtate; **succinct, summary,** synoptic, synoptical, compendious, compact; **little** 258.10; **low** 274.7; transient 827.7, instantaneous 829.4

9 shortened, abbreviated; abridged, compressed, condensed, epitomized, digested, abstracted, capsule, capsulized, encapsulated; bowdlerized; nutshell,

vest-pocket; **curtailed,** cut short, shortcut, **docked,** bobbed, sheared, shaved, trimmed, clipped, snub, snubbed, nipped; mowed, mown, reaped, **cropped; pruned,** polled, pollarded; elided, elliptic, elliptical

10 stubby, stubbed, stumpy <nonformal>, undergrown, **thickset, stocky,** blocky, **chunky** <nonformal>, **fat** 257.18, **chubby,** tubby <nonformal>, dumpy; **squat,** squatty, squattish; **pudgy,** podgy; pug, **pugged;** snub-nosed; turned-up, retroussé <Fr>

11 short-legged, breviped; **short-winged,** brevipennate

ADVS **12 shortly, briefly,** summarily, tout court <Fr>, in brief compass, economically, sparely, curtly, succinctly, in a nutshell, in two or a few words; abbreviatedly, for short; **concisely** 537.7, compendiously, synoptically

13 short, abruptly, suddenly 829.9, all of a sudden

269 BREADTH, THICKNESS

NOUNS **1 breadth, width,** broadness, wideness, fullness, amplitude, latitude, distance across or crosswise or crossways, extent, **span, expanse, spread;** beam

2 thickness, the third dimension, distance through, depth; **mass, bulk, body;** corpulence, fatness 257.8, bodily size; **coarseness,** grossness 294.2

3 diameter, bore, caliber; radius, semidiameter

VERBS **4 broaden, widen,** deepen; **expand,** extend, extend to the side or sides; **spread** 259.6, spread out or sidewise or sideways, outspread, outstretch

5 thicken, grow thick, thick; incrassate, inspissate; fatten 259.8

ADJS **6 broad, wide,** deep; broad-scale, widescale, wide-ranging, exhaustive, comprehensive, in-depth, extensive; spread-out, **expansive;** spacious, **roomy;** ample, full; widespread 863.13; "broad as the world"—James Russell Lowell, "wide as a church door"—Shakespeare

7 broad of beam, broad-beamed, broadsterned, beamy; broad-ribbed, wideribbed, laticostate; broad-toothed, widetoothed, latidentate

8 thick, three-dimensional; **thickset, heavyset,** thick-bodied, broad-bodied, thick-girthed; **massive, bulky** 257.19, corpulent 257.18; coarse, heavy, gross, crass, fat; full-bodied, full, viscous; **dense** 1043.12; thicknecked, bullnecked

ADVS **9** breadthwise *or* breadthways, in breadth; widthwise *or* widthways; broadwise *or* broadways; broadside, broad side foremost; side-wise *or* -ways; through, depth-wise *or* -ways, in depth

270 NARROWNESS, THINNESS

NOUNS **1 narrowness, slenderness; closeness,** nearness; **straitness,** restriction, restrictedness, limitation, strictness, confinement; crowdedness, incapaciousness, incommodiousness; **tightness,** tight squeeze; hair, hairbreadth *or* hairsbreadth; finger's breadth *or* width; narrow gauge

2 narrowing, tapering, taper; **contraction** 260; stricture, constriction, strangulation, coarctation

3 <narrow place> narrow, **narrows, strait; bottleneck,** chokepoint; isthmus; channel 239; canal; pass, defile; neck, throat, craw

4 thinness, slenderness, slimness, frailty, slightness, gracility, lightness, airiness, delicacy, flimsiness, wispiness, laciness, paperiness, gauziness, gossameriness, diaphanousness, insubstantiality, ethereality, mistiness, vagueness; light *or* airy texture; **fineness** 294.3; **tenuity, rarity,** subtility, exility, exiguity; **attenuation;** dilution, dilutedness, wateriness 1059.1, weakness

5 leanness, skinniness, fleshlessness, slightness, frailness, twigginess, spareness, meagerness, **scrawniness, gauntness,** lankness, **lankiness,** gawkiness, **boniness,** skin and bones; haggardness, poorness, paperiness, peakedness <nonformal>, puniness, "lean and hungry look"— Shakespeare; undernourishment, undernutrition, underweight; hatchet face, lantern jaws

6 emaciation, emaceration <old>, attenuation, atrophy, tabes, marasmus

7 <comparisons> paper, wafer, lath, slat, **rail,** rake, splinter, slip, shaving, streak, vein; gruel, soup; shadow, mere shadow; **skeleton**

8 <thin person> **slim, lanky;** twiggy, **shadow, skeleton,** stick, walking skeleton, corpse, barebones, bag *or* stack of bones; rattlebones *or* **spindleshanks** *or* spindlelegs <all nonformal>, gangleshanks *and* gammerstang <both nonformal>, lathlegs *and* sticklegs <both nonformal>, **beanpole,** beanstalk, broomstick, clothes pole, stilt

9 reducing, slenderizing, slimming down; weight-watching, calorie-counting

10 thinner, solvent 1062.4

VERBS **11 narrow,** constrict, diminish, draw in, go in; restrict, limit, straiten, confine; **taper; contract** 260.7

12 thin, thin down, thin away *or* off *or* out, down; **rarefy,** subtilize, **attenuate;** dilute, water, water down, weaken; undernourish; **emaciate,** emacerate <old>

13 slenderize, reduce, reduce *or* lose *or* take off weight, watch one's weight, lose flesh, weight-watch, count calories, diet; slim, **slim down,** thin down

ADJS **14 narrow, slender;** narrowish, narrowy; **close,** near; **tight, strait,** isthmic, isthmian; close-fitting; **restricted,** limited, circumscribed, **confined,** constricted; **cramped,** cramp; incapacious, incommodious, crowded; **meager,** scant, scanty; narrow-gauge *or* narrow-gauged; angustifoliate, angustirostrate, angustiseptal, angustisellate

15 tapered, taper, tapering, cone- *or* wedge-shaped

16 thin, slender, slim, gracile, "imperially slim"—E A Robinson; thin-bodied, thin-set, narrow- *or* wasp-waisted; **svelte,** slinky, sylphlike, willowy; girlish, boyish; thinnish, slenderish, slimmish; **slight,** slight-made; **frail,** delicate, light, airy, wispy, lacy, gauzy, papery, gossamer, diaphanous, insubstantial, ethereal, misty, vague, flimsy, wafer-thin, **fine; finespun,** thin-spun, fine-drawn, wiredrawn; threadlike, slender as a thread; **tenuous,** subtle, rare, **rarefied;** attenuated, attenuate, **watery, weak,** diluted, watered *or* watered-down, small

17 lean, lean-looking, **skinny** <nonformal>, fleshless, lean-fleshed, thin-fleshed, **spare,** meager, **scrawny,** scraggy, thin-bellied, **gaunt, lank, lanky; gangling** *and* gangly <both nonformal>, gawky, **spindling,** spindly; flat-chested, flat <nonformal>; **bony, rawboned,** bare-boned, rattleboned <nonformal>, skeletal, **mere skin and bones, all skin and bones, nothing but skin and bones;** twiggy; **underweight,** undersized, undernourished, spidery, thin *or* skinny as a lath *or* rail, "lean as a rake"—Chaucer

18 lean-limbed, thin-legged, lath- *or* stick-legged <nonformal>, spindle-legged *or* -shanked <nonformal>, gangle-shanked <nonformal>, stilt-legged

19 lean- *or* horse- *or* thin-faced, thin-featured, **hatchet-faced;** wizen- *or* weazen-faced; lean- *or* thin-cheeked; lean- *or* lantern-jawed

20 haggard, poor, puny, **peaked** *and* peaky

<both nonformal>, **pinched;** shriveled, withered; **wizened,** weazeny; **emaciated,** emaciate, emacerated, **wasted,** attenuated, corpselike, skeletal, hollow-eyed, wraithlike, cadaverous; tabetic, tabid, marantic, marasmic; **starved,** starveling, starved-looking; **undernourished,** underfed, jejune; worn to a shadow, "worn to the bones"—Shakespeare, "weakened and wasted to skin and bone"—Du Bartas

21 **slenderizing,** reducing, slimming

ADVS 22 **narrowly,** closely, nearly, **barely,** hardly, only just, **by the skin of one's teeth**

23 thinly, thin; meagerly, sparsely, sparingly, scantily

271 FILAMENT

NOUNS 1 **filament; fiber; thread; strand,** suture; filature; **hair** 3; artificial fiber, natural fiber, animal fiber; fibril, fibrilla; cilium, ciliolum; **tendril,** cirrus; flagellum; **web,** cobweb, gossamer, spider *or* spider's web; denier

2 **cord, line, rope, wire,** braided rope, twisted rope, flattened-strand rope, wire rope, locked-wire rope, **cable,** wire cable; **yarn,** spun yarn, skein, hank; **string, twine;** braid; **ligament,** ligature, ligation; **tendon**

3 **cordage,** cording, **ropework,** roping; tackle, tack, gear, rigging; ship's ropes

4 **strip, strap,** strop; **lace,** thong; **band,** bandage, fillet, fascia, taenia; **belt,** girdle; **ribbon,** ribband; **tape,** tapeline, tape measure; slat, lath, batten, spline, strake, plank; ligule, ligula

5 **spinner,** spinster; silkworm, spider; spinning wheel, spinning jenny, jenny, mule, mule-jenny; spinning frame, bobbin and fly frame; spinneret; rope walk

VERBS 6 <make threads> **spin; braid,** twist

ADJS 7 **threadlike,** thready; **stringy,** ropy, wiry; **hairlike** 3.23, hairy 3.24; filamentary, filamentous, filiform; fibrous, fibered, fibroid, fibrilliform; ligamental; capillary, capilliform; cirrose, cirrous; funicular, funiculate; flagelliform; taeniate, taeniform; ligulate, ligular; gossamer, gossamery, flossy, silky

272 HEIGHT

NOUNS 1 **height,** heighth <nonformal>, vertical *or* perpendicular distance; **highness, tallness,** procerity; **altitude, elevation,** ceiling; **loftiness,** sublimity, exaltation;

hauteur, toploftiness 141.1; eminence, prominence; **stature**

2 **height, elevation,** eminence, **rise,** raise, **uprise,** lift, rising ground, vantage point *or* ground; **heights,** soaring *or* towering *or* Olympian heights, aerial heights, dizzy *or* dizzying heights; upmost *or* uppermost *or* utmost *or* extreme height; sky, stratosphere, ether, heaven *or* heavens; **zenith, apex, acme**

3 **highlands** 237.1, highland, upland, uplands, moorland, moors, downs, wold, rolling country

4 **plateau,** tableland, table, mesa, table mountain, bench; **hill; ridge; mountain; peak; mountain range**

5 **watershed,** water parting, **divide;** Great Divide, Continental Divide

6 **tower; turret,** *tour* <Fr>; campanile, bell tower, belfry, "topless towers"—Marlowe; **spire,** church spire; **lighthouse,** light tower; cupola, lantern; dome; martello, martello tower; barbican; **derrick,** pole; windmill tower, observation tower, fire tower; **mast,** radio *or* television mast, antenna tower; water tower, standpipe; **spire,** pinnacle; **steeple,** *flèche* <Fr>; minaret; stupa, tope, pagoda; pyramid; pylon; **shaft,** pillar, column; pilaster; obelisk; monument; colossus; skyscraper

7 <tall person> **longlegs** *and* longshanks *and* highpockets *and* long drink of water <all nonformal>; beanpole 270.8; **giant** 257.13; six-footer, seven-footer, grenadier <Brit>

8 **high tide,** high water, mean high water, flood tide, spring tide, flood; storm surge

9 <measurement of height> altimetry, hypsometry, hypsography; altimeter, hypsometer

VERBS 10 **tower, soar,** spire, "buss the clouds"—Shakespeare; **rise, uprise, ascend, mount, rear;** stand on tiptoe

11 **rise above, tower above** *or* **over,** clear, overtop, o'er top, outtop, **top, surmount; overlook,** look down upon *or* over; **command,** dominate, overarch, overshadow, command a view of; bestride, bestraddle

12 <become higher> **grow,** grow up, upgrow; uprise, **rise** *or* **shoot up,** mount

13 **heighten, elevate** 911.5

ADJS 14 **high,** high-reaching, high-up, **lofty, elevated,** altitudinous, uplifted *or* upreared, uprearing, **eminent, exalted, prominent,** supernal, **superlative,** sublime; **towering,** towery, **soaring,** spiring, aspiring, mounting, ascending; towered, turreted, steepled; **topping,** outtopping *or* overtopping; overarching, **overlooking,** dominating; airy, aerial, ethereal; Olympian; monumental, colossal; high as a steeple; topless; high-set, high-pitched; high-rise, multistory; **haughty** 141.9/157.8, toplofty

15 skyscraping, **sky-high**, heaven-reaching *or* -aspiring, heaven-high, heaven-kissing, "as high as Heaven and as deep as Hell"—Beaumont and Fletcher; cloud-touching *or* -topped *or* -capped; **mid-air**

16 **giant** 257.20, gigantic, colossal, statuesque; **tall, lengthy**, long 267.8; **rangy, lanky**, lank, tall as a maypole; **gangling** *and* gangly <both nonformal>; **long-legged**, long-limbed, leggy

17 **highland**, upland; hill-dwelling, mountain-dwelling

18 **hilly**, knobby, rolling; **mountainous**, mountained, **alpine**, alpen, alpestrine, alpigene; subalpine; monticuline, monticulous

19 **higher**, superior, greater; **over, above**; upper, upmost *or* uppermost, outtopping, overtopping; highest 198.10

20 altimetric, altimetrical, hypsometrical, hypsographic

ADVS 21 **on high**, high up, high; **aloft**, aloof; **up**, upward, upwards, straight up, to the zenith; **above, over**, o'er, **overhead**; above one's head, over head and ears; skyward, airward, in the air, in the clouds; on the peak *or* summit *or* crest *or* pinnacle; upstairs, abovestairs; tiptoe, on tiptoe; on stilts; on the shoulders of; supra, *ubi supra* <L>, hereinabove, hereinbefore

273 SHAFT

NOUNS 1 **shaft, pole, bar, rod, stick**, scape, scapi—; **stalk, stem;** thill; tongue, wagon tongue; flagstaff; totem pole; Maypole; utility *or* telephone *or* telegraph pole; tent pole

2 **staff**, stave; **cane, stick, walking stick**, handstaff, shillelagh; Malacca cane; baton, marshal's baton, drum-major's baton, conductor's baton; swagger stick, swanking stick; pilgrim's staff, pastoral staff, shepherd's staff, crook; crosier, cross-staff, cross, paterissa; pikestaff, alpenstock; quarterstaff; lituus, thyrsus; **crutch**, crutch-stick

3 **beam, timber**, pole, spar

4 **post, standard, upright;** king post, queen post, crown post; newel; banister, baluster; balustrade, balustrading; gatepost, swinging *or* hinging post, shutting post; doorpost, jamb, doorjamb; signpost,

milepost; stile, mullion; stanchion; hitching post, snubbing post, Samson post

5 **pillar, column,** post, pier, pilaster; colonnette, columella; caryatid; atlas, atlantes <pl>; telamon, telamones; **colonnade, arcade,** pilastrade, portico, peristyle

6 **leg,** shank; **stake,** peg; pile, spile, stud; picket, pale, palisade

274 LOWNESS

NOUNS 1 **lowness, shortness,** squatness, squattiness, stumpiness; **prostration,** supineness, proneness, recumbency, **lying, lying down, reclining;** depression, debasement; subjacency

2 **low tide,** low water, mean low water, dead low water *or* tide, ebb tide, neap tide, neap

3 lowland, **lowlands,** bottomland, swale; water meadow

4 **base, bottom** 199, lowest point, nadir; the lowest of the low; lowest *or* underlying level, lower strata, bedrock

VERBS 5 **lie low, squat, crouch,** lay low <nonformal>, couch; crawl, grovel, lie prone *or* supine *or* prostrate, hug the earth; lie under, underlie

6 lower, debase, depress 912.4

ADJS 7 **low, unelevated, flat, low-lying; short, squat,** squatty, stumpy, runty 258.13; **lowered,** debased, depressed 912.12; demoted; **reduced** 252.10; prone, supine, prostrate *or* prostrated, couchant, crouched, stooped, recumbent; laid low, knocked flat, decked <nonformal>; low-set, low-hung; **low-built,** low-sized, low-statured, low-bodied; low-level, low-leveled; neap; knee-high, knee-high to a grasshopper <nonformal>

8 **lower,** inferior, **under, nether,** subjacent; down; less advanced; earlier; lowest 199.7

ADVS 9 **low,** near the ground; at a low ebb

10 **below,** down below, **under;** infra, hereunder, hereinafter, hereinbelow; thereunder; belowstairs, downstairs, below deck; underfoot; below par, below the mark

PREPS 11 **below, under, underneath, beneath,** neath, at the foot of, at the base of

275 DEPTH

NOUNS 1 **depth, deepness,** profoundness, profundity; deep-downness, extreme innerness, deep-seatedness, deep-rootedness; bottomlessness, plumblessness, fathomlessness; subterraneity, undergroundness; interiority 207

2 pit, deep, depth, hole, hollow, **cavity,** shaft, well, **gulf, chasm, abyss,** abysm, yawning abyss; crater; crevasse; valley

3 depths, deeps, bowels, bowels of the earth; bottomless pit; infernal pit, hell, nether world, underworld; dark *or* unknown *or* yawning *or* gaping depths, unfathomed deeps; outer *or* deep space

4 ocean depths, the deep sea, the deep, trench, deep-sea trench <see list>, hadal zone, **the deeps, the depths,** bottomless depths, inner space, abyss; bottom waters; abyssal zone, Bassalia *or* Bassalian realm, bathyal zone, pelagic zone; **seabed, bottom of the sea,** ocean bottom *or* floor *or* bed, ground, benthos, benthonic division, benthonic zone; Davy Jones's locker <nonformal>

5 sounding *or* **soundings,** fathoming, depth sounding; **echo sounding,** echolocation; **depth indicator;** oceanography, bathometry, bathymetry; fathomage, water <depth of water>

6 draft, submergence, submersion, sinkage, **displacement**

7 deepening, lowering, depression; sinking, sinkage; excavation, digging, mining, tunneling; drilling, probing

VERBS **8 deepen, lower, depress, sink;** countersink; **dig,** excavate, tunnel, mine, **drill;** pierce to the depths; **dive** 367.6

9 sound, take soundings, make a sounding, heave *or* cast *or* sling the lead, **fathom, plumb,** plumb-line, plumb the depths

ADJS **10 deep, profound,** deep-down; deepish, deepsome; **deep-going,** deep-lying, deep-reaching; **deep-set,** deep-laid; deepsunk, deep-sunken, deep-sinking; **deepseated, deep-rooted,** deep-fixed, deepsettled; deep-cut, deep-engraven; kneedeep, ankle-deep

11 abysmal, abyssal, yawning, cavernous, gaping, plunging; **bottomless,** without bottom, soundless, unsounded, plumbless, **fathomless,** unfathomed, unfathomable; deep as a well, deep as the sea *or* ocean, deep as hell

12 underground, subterranean, subterraneous, buried, deep-buried

13 underwater, subaqueous; **submarine, undersea;** submerged, submersed, immersed, buried, engulfed, inundated, flooded, drowned, sunken

14 deep-sea, deep-water, blue-water; oceanographic, bathyal; benthic, benthal, benthonic; abyssal, Bassalian; bathyorographic, bathyorographical, bath-

ymetric, bathymetrical; benthopelagic, bathypelagic

15 deepest, deepmost, profoundest; bedrock, rock-bottom

ADVS **16 deep; beyond one's depth,** out of one's depth; over one's head, over head and ears; at bottom, at the core, at rock bottom

17 deep-sea trenches and deeps

Aleutian Trench 29,194 feet	Peru-Chile *or* Atacama Trench,
Cayman Trench 24,576 feet	Bartholomew Deep 26,160 feet
Diamantina Fracture, Ob Trench 22,553 feet	Philippine Trench, Galathea Deep 34,578 feet
Guatemala Trench 21,228 feet	Puerto Rico Trench, Milwaukee Deep
Japan Trench, Ramapo Deep 34,038 feet	27,498 feet Romanche Trench 25,050 feet
Java *or* Sunda Trench, Planet Deep 25,344 feet	Solomon Trench 29,988 feet South Sandwich
Kuril-Kamchatka Trench 34,062 feet	Trench, Meteor Deep 27,112 feet Tonga-Kermadec
Mariana Trench, Challenger Deep 35,760 feet	Trench, Vityaz II *or* Tonga Deep 35,589 feet
Nansei Shoto *or* Ryukyu Trench 24,630 feet	Vityaz Trench 20,142 feet Yap Trench 26,280 feet

276 SHALLOWNESS

NOUNS **1 shallowness, depthlessness;** shoalness, shoaliness, no water, no depth; **superficiality,** exteriority, triviality, **cursoriness,** slightness; insufficiency 991; a lick and a promise *and* once-overlightly <both nonformal>; **surface,** superficies, skin, rind, epidermis; veneer, gloss; pinprick, scratch, mere scratch

2 shoal, shallow, shallows, shallow *or* shoal water, flat, shelf; **bank, bar,** sandbank, sandbar, tombolo; **reef,** coral reef; ford; wetlands, tidal flats

VERBS **3 shoal,** shallow; fill in *or* up, silt up

4 scratch the surface, touch upon, hardly touch, skim, skim over, skim *or* graze the surface, hit the high spots *and* give a lick and a promise *and* give it once over lightly <all nonformal>, apply a Band-Aid <trademark> <nonformal>

ADJS **5 shallow,** shoal, **depthless,** not deep, unprofound; **surface,** on *or* near the surface, merely surface; **superficial, cursory,** slight, light, cosmetic, merely cosmetic, thin, jejune, trivial; **skin-deep,** epidermal; ankle-deep, knee-deep; shallow-rooted, shallow-rooting; shallow-draft *or* -bottomed *or* -hulled; shallow-sea

6 shoaly, shelfy; reefy; unnavigable

277 STRAIGHTNESS

NOUNS **1 straightness,** directness, unswervingness, lineality, **linearity,** rectilinearity; verticalness 200; flatness, horizontalness 201

2 straight line, straight, right line, direct line; straight course *or* stretch, straightaway; **beeline,** air line; **shortcut** 268.5; great-circle course; streamline; edge, side, diagonal, secant, transversal, chord, tangent, perpendicular, normal, segment, directrix, diameter, axis, radius, vector, radius vector <all mathematics>

3 straightedge, rule, ruler; square, T square, triangle

VERBS **4** be straight, have no turning *or* turns; arrow; go straight, make a beeline

5 straighten, set *or* **put straight,** rectify, make right *or* good, square away; **unbend,** unkink, uncurl, unsnarl, disentangle 797.5; straighten up, square up; straighten out, extend; flatten, smooth 201.6

ADJS **6 straight;** straight-lined, dead straight, straight as an edge *or* a ruler, ruler-straight, even, right, true, straight as an arrow, arrowlike; **rectilinear,** rectilineal; **linear,** lineal, in a line; **direct, undeviating, unswerving,** unbending, undeflected; **unbent, unbowed,** unturned, uncurved, undistorted; **uninterrupted, unbroken;** straight-side, straight-front, straight-cut; upright, vertical 200.11; flat, level, smooth, horizontal 201.7

ADVS **7 straight,** straightly, on the straight, unswervingly, undeviatingly, **directly;** straight to the mark; down the alley *and* down the pipe *and* in the groove *and* on the beam *and* on the money <all nonformal>

278 ANGULARITY

NOUNS **1 angularity,** angularness, crookedness, hookedness; squareness, orthogonality, right-angledness, rectangularity; flection, flexure

2 angle, point, bight; vertex, apex 198.2; **corner,** quoin, coin; nook; **crook, hook,** crotchet; **bend,** curve, swerve, veer, inflection, deflection; ell, L; cant; furcation, bifurcation, fork 171.4; zigzag, zig, zag;

chevron; elbow, knee, dogleg <nonformal>; crank

3 <angular measurement> goniometry; trigonometry

4 <instruments> goniometer, radiogoniometer; pantometer, clinometer, graphometer, astrolabe; azimuth compass, azimuth circle; theodolite, transit theodolite, transit, transit instrument, transit circle; sextant, quadrant; bevel, bevel square; protractor, bevel protractor

VERBS **5 angle, crook, hook, bend,** elbow; crank; angle off *or* away, curve, swerve, veer, veer off, slant off, go off on a tangent; furcate, bifurcate, branch, fork 171.7; zigzag, zig, zag

ADJS **6 angular;** cornered, **crooked, hooked, bent,** flexed, flexural; akimbo; knee-shaped, geniculate, geniculated, dog-legged <nonformal>; crotched, Y-shaped, V-shaped; furcate, furcal, forked 171.10; sharp-cornered, **sharp, pointed;** zigzag, jagged, serrate, sawtooth *or* saw-toothed

7 right-angled, rectangular, right-angular, right-angle; **orthogonal,** orthodiagonal, orthometric; **perpendicular,** normal

8 triangular, trilateral, trigonal, oxygonal, deltoid; wedgeshaped, cuneiform, cuneate, cuneated

9 quadrangular, quadrilateral, quadrate, quadriform; **rectangular, square;** foursquare, orthogonal; tetragonal, tetrahedral; **oblong;** trapezoid *or* trapezoidal, rhombic *or* rhombal, rhomboid *or* rhomboidal; **cubic** *or* **cubical,** cubiform, cuboid, cube-shaped, cubed, diced; rhombohedral, trapezohedral

10 pentagonal, hexagonal, heptagonal, octagonal, decagonal, dodecagonal, etc; pentahedral, hexahedral, octahedral, dodecahedral, icosahedral, etc

11 multilateral, multiangular, polygonal; polyhedral, pyramidal, pyramidic *or* pyramidal; prismatic, prismoid

279 CURVATURE

NOUNS **1 curvature,** curving, curvation, arcing; incurvature, incurvation; excurvature, excurvation; decurvature, decurvation; recurvature, recurvity, recurvation; rondure; **arching, vaulting,** arcuation, concameration; aduncity, aquilinity, crookedness, hookedness; sinuosity, sinuousness, tortuosity, tortuousness; circularity 280; convolution 281; rotundity 282; convexity 283; concavity 284; curvaceousness

2 **curve,** sinus; **bow, arc; crook, hook;** parabola, hyperbola, witch of Agnesi; ellipse; caustic, catacaustic, diacaustic; catenary, festoon, swag; conchoid; lituus; tracery; circle 280.2; curl 281.2

3 **bend,** bending; **bow,** bowing, oxbow; Cupid's bow; **turn,** turning, sweep, meander, hairpin turn *or* bend, S-curve, U-turn; **flexure,** flex, **flection,** conflexure, inflection, deflection; reflection; geanticline, geosyncline

4 **arch, span, vault,** vaulting, concameration, camber; ogive; apse; **dome,** cupola, geodesic dome, igloo, concha; cove; arched roof, ceilinged roof; **arcade, archway,** arcature; voussoir, keystone, skewback

5 **crescent, semicircle,** scythe, sickle, meniscus; crescent moon, half-moon; lunula, lunule; horseshoe

VERBS 6 **curve, turn,** arc, sweep; **crook, hook,** loop; incurve, incurvate; recurve, decurve, bend back, retroflex; sag, swag <nonformal>; **bend,** flex; deflect, inflect; reflect, reflex; **bow,** embow; **arch,** vault; dome; **hump,** hunch; wind, curl 281.5; round 282.6

ADJS 7 **curved,** curve, curvate, curvated, **curving,** curvy, curvaceous <nonformal>, curvesome, curviform; curvilinear, curvilineal; wavy, undulant, billowy, billowing; sinuous, tortuous, serpentine, mazy, labyrinthine, meandering; **bent,** flexed, flexural; incurved, incurving, incurvate, incurvated; recurved, recurving, recurvate, recurvated; geosynclinal, geanticlinal

8 **hooked, crooked, aquiline,** aduncous; **hook-shaped,** hooklike, uncinate, unciform; hamulate, hamate, hamiform; claw-like, unguiform, down-curving; **hook-nosed,** beak-nosed, parrot-nosed, aquiline-nosed, Roman-nosed, crooknosed, crookbilled; **beaked,** billed; **beak-shaped,** beak-like; bill-shaped, bill-like; rostrate, rostriform, rhamphoid

9 turned-up, upcurving, upsweeping, *retroussé* <Fr>

10 **bowed,** embowed, bandy; bowlike, bow-shaped, oxbow, Cupid's-bow; **convex, concave** 284.16, convexoconcave; arcuate, arcuated, arcual, arciform, arclike; **arched,** vaulted; **humped,** hunched, humpy, hunchy; gibbous, gibbose; humpbacked 265.13

11 **crescent-shaped,** crescentlike, crescent, crescentic, crescentiform; meniscoid <al>, menisciform; S-shaped, ess, S, sigmoid; **semicircular,** semilunar; horn-shaped, hornlike, horned, corniform; bicorn, two-horned; sickle-shaped, sicklelike, falcate, falciform; moon-shaped, moonlike, lunar, lunate, lunular, luniform

12 lens-shaped, lenticular, lentiform

13 parabolic, parabolical, paraboloid, saucer-shaped; elliptic, elliptical, ellipsoid; bell-shaped, bell-like, campanular, campanulate, campaniform

14 pear-shaped, pearlike, pyriform

15 heart-shaped, heartlike; cordate, cardioid, cordiform

16 kidney-shaped, kidneylike, reniform

17 turnip-shaped, turniplike, napiform

18 shell-shaped, shell-like; conchate, conchiform

19 shield-shaped, shieldlike, peltate; scutate, scutiform; clypeate, clypeiform

20 helmet-shaped, helmetlike, galeiform, cassideous

280 CIRCULARITY

NOUNS 1 **circularity, roundness,** ring-shape, ringliness, annularity; annulation

2 **circle,** circus, rondure, **ring,** annulus, O; **circumference,** radius; **round,** roundel, rondelle; **cycle, circuit;** orbit 1070.16; closed circle *or* arc; vicious circle, eternal return; magic circle, charmed circle, fairy ring; logical circle, circular reasoning, petitio principii; **wheel** 914.4; **disk,** discus, saucer; **loop,** looplet; noose, lasso; crown, diadem, coronet, corona; garland, chaplet, wreath; halo, glory, areola, aureole; annular muscle, sphincter

3 <thing encircling> **band, belt, cincture,** cingulum, **girdle, girth,** girt, zone, fascia, fillet; collar, collarband, neckband; necktie; necklace, bracelet, armlet, torque, wristlet, wristband, anklet; ring, earring, nose ring, finger ring; hoop; quoit; zodiac, ecliptic, equator, great circle

4 **rim,** felly; **tire**

5 circlet, **ringlet,** roundlet, annulet, eye, **eyelet,** grommet

6 **oval,** ovule, ovoid; ellipse

7 cycloid; epicycloid, epicycle; hypocycloid; lemniscate; cardioid; Lissajous figure

8 **semicircle,** half circle, hemicycle; crescent 279.5; quadrant, sextant, sector

9 <music and poetry> **round,** canon; rondo, rondino, rondeau, rondelet

VERBS 10 **circle, round;** orbit; **encircle** 209.7, surround, encompass, girdle

ADJS 11 **circular, round,** rounded, circinate, annular, annulate, ring-shaped, ringlike;

annulose; disklike, discoid; cyclic, cyclical, cycloid, cycloidal; epicyclic; planetary; coronal, crownlike

12 **oval,** ovate, ovoid, oviform, egg-shaped, obovate

281 CONVOLUTION
<complex curvature>

NOUNS 1 **convolution,** involution, circumvolution, **winding, twisting, turning; meander, meandering;** crinkle, crinkling; circuitousness, circumlocution, circumbendibus, circumambages, ambagiousness, ambages; Byzantinism; tortuousness, tortuosity; torsion, intorsion; sinuousness, **sinuosity,** sinuation, slinkiness; anfractuosity; snakiness; flexuousness, flexuosity; undulation, wave, waving; rivulation; **complexity** 798

2 **coil, whorl,** roll, **curl,** curlicue, ringlet, pigtail, **spiral,** helix, volute, volution, involute, evolute, gyre, scroll; **kink, twist, twirl;** screw, corkscrew; tendril, cirrus; whirl, swirl, vortex

3 curler, curling iron; curlpaper, papillote

VERBS 4 convolve, **wind, twine,** twirl, **twist, turn, twist and turn, meander,** crinkle; serpentine, snake, slink, worm; screw, corkscrew; whirl, swirl; whorl; scallop; wring; intort; contort

5 **curl, coil;** crisp, kink, crimp

ADJS 6 **convolutional, winding, twisting,** twisty, **turning; meandering,** meandrous, mazy, labyrinthine; **serpentine,** snaky, anfractuous; roundabout, circuitous, ambagious, circumlocutory; labyrinthine; Byzantine; **sinuous,** sinuose, sinuate; **tortuous,** torsional, tortile; flexular, flexuous, flexuose; involutional, involute, involuted; rivose, rivulose; sigmoidal; wreathy, wreathlike; ruffled, whorled

7 **coiled,** tortile, **snakelike, snaky,** snake-shaped, **serpentine,** serpentlike, serpentiform; anguine <old>, anguiform; eellike, eelshaped, anguilliform; wormlike, vermiform, lumbricoid, lumbricine, lumbriciform

8 **spiral,** spiroid, volute, voluted; **helical,** helicoid, helicoidal; anfractuous; screw-shaped, corkscrew, corkscrewy; verticillate, whorled, scrolled, cochlear, cochleate; turbinal, turbinate

9 **curly, curled; kinky,** kinked; **frizzly,** frizzy, frizzled, frizzed; crisp, crispy, crisped

10 **wavy, undulant,** undulatory, undulative,

undulating, undulate, undulated; **billowy,** billowing, surgy, rolling

ADVS 11 **windingly, twistingly,** sinuously, tortuously, serpentinely, meanderingly, meandrously; in waves; wavily; **in and out,** round and round

282 SPHERICITY, ROTUNDITY

NOUNS 1 **sphericity, rotundity, roundness,** ball-likeness, rotundness, orbicularness, orbicularity, orbiculation, orblikeness, **sphericalness,** sphericality, globularity, globularness, globosity, globoseness; spheroidity, spheroidicity; belly; cylindricality; convexity 283

2 **sphere; ball,** orb, orbit, **globe,** rondure; geoid; spheroid, globoid, ellipsoid, oblate spheroid, prolate spheroid; spherule, globule, globelet, orblet; glomerulus; **pellet;** boll; **bulb,** bulbil *or* bulbel, bulblet; knob, knot; **gob,** glob <nonformal>, blob, gobbet; pill, bolus; **balloon,** bladder, bubble

3 **drop,** droplet; dewdrop, raindrop, teardrop; bead, pearl

4 **cylinder,** cylindroid, pillar, column; barrel, drum, cask; pipe, tube; roll, rouleau, roller, rolling pin; bole, trunk

5 **cone,** conoid, conelet; complex cone, cone of a complex; funnel; ice-cream cone, cornet <Brit>; pine cone; cop

VERBS 6 **round; round out, fill out;** cone

7 **ball, snowball;** sphere, spherify, globe, conglobulate; roll; bead; balloon, mushroom

ADJS 8 **rotund, round,** rounded, rounded out, round as a ball; bellied, bellylike; convex, bulging

9 **spherical,** sphereic, spheriform, spherelike, sphere-shaped; **globular, global,** globed, globose, globate, globelike, globe-shaped; orbicular, orbiculate, orbiculated, orbed, orb, orby <old>, orblike; spheroid, spheroidal, globoid, ellipsoid, ellipsoidal; hemispheric, hemispherical; **bulbous,** bulblike, bulging; ovoid, obovoid

10 **beady,** beaded, bead-shaped, beadlike

11 **cylindric, cylindrical,** cylindroid, cylindroidal; **columnar,** columnal, columned, columelliform; **tubular,** tubeshaped; barrel-shaped, drum-shaped

12 **conical,** conic, coned, cone-shaped, conelike; conoid, conoidal; spheroconic; funnel-shaped, funnellike, funnelled, funnelform, infundibuliform, infundibular

283 CONVEXITY, PROTUBERANCE

NOUNS **1 convexity,** convexness, convexedness; excurvature, excurvation; camber; gibbousness, gibbosity; tuberousness, tuberosity; **bulging,** bellying, puffing, puffing out

2 protuberance or protuberancy, **projection, protrusion, extrusion;** prominence, eminence, salience, boldness, **bulging,** bellying; gibbousness, gibbosity; excrescence or excrescency; tuberousness, tuberosity, puffiness; salient; relief, high relief, *alto-rilievo* <Ital>, low relief, basrelief, *basso-rilievo* <Ital>, embossment

3 bulge, bilge, bow, convex; **bump;** thankyou-ma'am *and* whoopdedoo <both nonformal>, cahot <Can>; speed bump, sleeping policeman <Brit>; hill, mountain; **hump,** hunch; **lump,** clump, bunch, blob; nubbin, nubble, nub; **mole,** nevus; **wart,** papilloma, verruca; **knob,** boss, bulla, button, bulb; stud, jog, joggle, peg, dowel; flange, lip; tab, ear, flap, loop, ring, handle; **knot,** knur, knurl, gnarl, burl, gall; **ridge,** rib, cost<o>— or costi—, chine, spine, shoulder; welt, wale; blister, bleb, vesicle <anat>, blain; bubble; condyle; bubo; tubercle or tubercule

4 swelling, swollenness, edema; **rising, lump, bump,** pimple; pock, furuncle, boil, carbuncle; corn; pustule; dilation, dilatation; turgidity, turgescence or turgescency, tumescence, intumescence; tumor, tumidity, tumefaction; wen, cyst, sebaceous cyst; bunion; distension 259.2

5 node, nodule, nodulus, nodulation, nodosity

6 breast, bosom, bust, chest, crop, brisket; thorax; pigeon breast; **breasts,** dugs, teats; **nipple,** papilla, pap, mammilla, *mamelon* and *téton* <both Fr>; mammillation, mamelonation; mammary gland, udder, bag

7 <nonformal terms> **tits,** titties, **boobs,** boobies, bubbies, jugs, headlights, **knockers,** knobs, *nénés* <Fr>, bazooms, bags, bazongas, coconuts, hooters

8 nose, olfactory organ; **snout, snoot** <nonformal>, nozzle <nonformal>, **muzzle; proboscis,** antlia, **trunk; beak,** rostrum; **bill** *and* pecker <both nonformal>; nib, neb; smeller *and* beezer *and* bugle *and* schnozzle *and* schnoz *and* schnozzola *and* conk <all nonformal>; muffle, rhinarium; nostrils, noseholes <Brit nonformal>, nares

9 <point of land> **point,** hook, spur, **cape,** tongue, bill; **promontory,** foreland, head-

land, head, mull <Scots>; naze, ness; **peninsula,** chersonese; **delta; spit,** sandspit; **reef,** coral reef; breakwater 900.4

VERBS **10 protrude, protuberate, project, extrude; stick out,** jut out, poke out, stand out, shoot out; **stick up,** bristle up, start up, cock up, shoot up

11 bulge, bilge, bouge <nonformal>, **belly,** bag, balloon, **pouch,** pooch <nonformal>; pout; **goggle,** bug <nonformal>, pop; **swell, swell up, dilate, distend,** billow; swell out, **belly out,** round out

12 emboss, boss, chase, raise; ridge

ADJS **13 convex,** convexed; excurved, excurvate, excurvated; **bowed,** bowed-out, outbowed, arched 279.10; gibbous, gibbose; humped 279.10; rotund 282.8

14 protruding, protrusive, protrudent; protrusile, protrusible; **protuberant,** protuberating; **projecting, extruding,** jutting, outstanding; prominent, eminent, salient, bold; prognathous; excrescent, excrescential; protrusile, emissile

15 bulging, swelling, distended, bloated, potbellied, bellying, pouching, bagging, baggy; rounded, hillocky, hummocky, moutonnée; billowing, billowy, bosomy, ballooning, pneumatic; **bumpy,** bumped; bunchy, bunched; **bulbous,** bulbose; warty, verrucose, verrucated

16 bulged, bulgy, bugged-out <nonformal>; swollen 259.13, turgid, tumid, turgescent, tumescent, tumorous; bellied, ventricose; pouched, pooched <nonformal>; goggled, goggle; exophthalmic, bug-eyed <nonformal>, popeyed <nonformal>

17 studded, knobbed, knobby, knoblike, nubbled, nubby, nubbly, torose; **knotty, knotted; gnarled,** knurled, knurly, burled, gnarly; noded, nodal, nodiform; noduled, nodular; nodulated; bubonic; tuberculous, tubercular; tuberous, tuberose

18 in relief, in bold or high relief, bold, raised, *repoussé* <Fr>; chased, bossed, embossed, bossy

19 pectoral, chest, thoracic; pigeonbreasted; mammary, mammillary, mammiform; mammalian, mammate; papillary, papillose, papulous; breasted, bosomed, chested; teated, titted <nonformal>, nippled; busty, bosomy, chesty

20 peninsular; deltaic, deltal

284 CONCAVITY

NOUNS **1 concavity, hollowness;** incurvature, incurvation; depression, impression; emptiness 222.2

2 cavity, concavity, concave; **hollow,** hollow shell, shell; **hole, pit, depression, dip,** sink, fold <Brit>; scoop, pocket; **basin,** trough, **bowl,** punch bowl, cup, container 195; **crater;** antrum; lacuna; alveola, alveolus, alveolation; vug *or* vugg *or* vugh; crypt; armpit; socket; funnel chest *or* breast

3 pothole, sinkhole, pitchhole, chuckhole, **mudhole, rut** 290.1

4 pit, well, shaft, sump; **chasm, gulf, abyss,** abysm; **excavation,** dig, diggings, workings; mine, quarry

5 cave, cavern, cove <Scots>, **hole, grotto,** grot, antre, subterrane; lair 228.26; **tunnel, burrow,** warren; subway; bunker, foxhole, dugout, *abri* <Fr>; sewer

6 indentation, indent, indention, indenture, **dent,** dint; gouge, **furrow** 290; sunken part *or* place, **dimple; pit,** pock, pockmark; impression, impress; imprint, print; alveolus, alveolation; honeycomb, Swiss cheese; **notch** 289

7 recess, recession, **niche, nook,** inglenook, corner; cove, alcove; bay; pitchhole

8 <hollow in the side of a mountain> combe, cwm, cirque, corrie

9 valley, vale, dale, dell, dingle; **glen,** bottom, bottoms, bottom glade, intervale, strath <Scots>, gill <Brit>, wadi, grove; trench, trough, lunar rill; gap, pass, ravine

10 excavator, digger; sapper; **miner;** tunneler, sandhog *and* groundhog <both nonformal>; driller; steam shovel, navvy <Brit>; dredge, dredger

11 excavation, digging; mining; indentation, **engraving**

VERBS **12** <be concave> **sink, dish,** cup, bowl, hollow; retreat, retire; incurve

13 hollow, hollow out, concave, **dish,** cup, bowl; cave, cave in

14 indent, dent, dint, **depress,** press in, stamp, tamp, punch, punch in, impress, imprint; **pit;** pock, pockmark; dimple; **recess,** set back; set in; **notch** 289.4; engrave

15 excavate, dig, dig out, **scoop,** scoop out, **gouge,** gouge out, grub, shovel, spade, dike, delve, scrape, scratch, scrabble; dredge; **trench,** trough, furrow, groove; **tunnel, burrow;** drive <min>, sink, lower; **mine,** sap; quarry; drill, bore

ADJS **16 concave,** concaved, **incurved,** incurving, incurvate; **sunk,** sunken; retreating, recessed, retiring; **hollow,** hollowed, empty; palm-shaped; dish-shaped, dished, dishing, dishlike, bowl-shaped; bowllike, crater-shaped, craterlike, saucer-shaped; spoon-like; **cupped,** cup-

shaped, scyphate; funnel-shaped, infundibular, infundibuliform; funnel-chested, funnel-breasted; boat-shaped, boatlike, navicular, naviform, cymbiform, scaphoid; **cavernous,** cavelike

17 indented, dented, depressed; **dimpled; pitted;** cratered; pocked, pockmarked; honeycombed, alveolar, alveolate, faveolate; **notched** 289.5; **engraved**

285 SHARPNESS

NOUNS **1 sharpness, keenness, edge;** acuteness, acuity; **pointedness,** acumination; thorniness, prickliness, spinosity; mucronation; cornification; acridity 68.1

2 <sharp edge> **edge, cutting edge, honed edge, knife-edge, razor-edge;** featheredge, fine edge; edge tool; weapon 462.21–26

3 point, tip, cusp; acumination, mucro; **nib,** neb; needle; hypodermic needle, hypodermic syringe; **drill,** borer, auger, bit; **prick, prickle;** sting, acus *or* aculeus; **tooth** 2.8

4 <pointed projection> **projection,** spur, jag, **snag,** snaggle; **horn,** antler; cornicle; crag, peak, arête; spire, steeple, flèche; **cog, sprocket,** ratchet; sawtooth; harrow, rake; comb, pecten

5 thorn, bramble, brier, nettle, burr, prickle, sticker <nonformal>; **spike,** spikelet, spicule, spiculum; **spine;** bristle; quill; **needle,** pine needle; **thistle,** catchweed, cleavers, goose grass, cactus; yucca, Adam's-needle

VERBS **6** come *or* taper to a point, acuminate; prick, sting, stick, bite; be keen, have an edge, cut; bristle with

7 sharpen, edge, acuminate, aculeate, spiculate, taper; **whet, hone,** oilstone, file, grind; strop, strap; set, reset; **point;** barb, spur, file to a point

ADJS **8 sharp, keen, edged, acute,** fine, **cutting,** knifelike; sharp-edged, keen-edged, razor-edged, knife-edged, sharp as broken glass; featheredged, fine-edged; acrid 68.6; two-edged, double-edged; sharp as a razor *or* needle *or* tack, "sharp as a two-edged sword"—Bible, "sharper than a serpent's tooth"—Shakespeare; sharpened, set

9 pointed, pointy, acuminate, acuate, aculeate, aculeated, acute, unbated; tapered, tapering; cusped, cuspate, cuspated, cuspidal, cuspidate, cuspidated; **sharp-pointed; needlelike,** needle-sharp, needle-pointed, needly, acicular, aculeiform; mucronate, mucronated; toothed; **spiked,**

spiky, spiculate; **barbed, tined, pronged;
horned,** horny, cornuted, corniculate,
cornified, ceratoid; **spined, spiny,**
spinous, hispid, acanthoid, acanthous;
"like quills upon the fretful porpen-
tine"—Shakespeare

10 **prickly,** pricky <nonformal>, muricate,
echinate, acanaceous, aculeolate; pricking, stinging; **thorny,** brambly, briery,
thistly, nettly, burry; bristly

11 **arrowlike,** arrowy, arrowheaded; sagit-
tal, sagittate, sagittiform

12 **spearlike,** hastate; lancelike, lanciform,
lanceolate, lanceolar; **spindle-shaped,** fu-
siform

13 **swordlike,** gladiate, ensate, ensiform

14 **toothlike,** dentiform, dentoid, odontoid;
toothed, toothy, **fanged, tusked;** snaggle-
toothed, snaggled

15 **star-shaped, starlike,** star-pointed

286 BLUNTNESS

NOUNS 1 **bluntness, dullness,** unsharpness,
obtuseness, obtundity; bluffness; abruptness; flatness; toothlessness, lack of bite
or incisiveness

VERBS 2 **blunt, dull,** disedge, retund, obtund, **take the edge off;** turn, turn the
edge or point of; weaken, repress; draw
the teeth or fangs; bate

ADJS 3 **blunt, dull,** obtuse, obtundent; blunt-
ish, dullish; **unsharp,** unsharpened; **un-
edged,** edgeless; rounded, faired,
smoothed, streamlined; **unpointed,**
pointless; blunted, dulled; blunt-edged,
dull-edged; blunt-pointed, dull-pointed,
blunt-ended; bluff, abrupt

4 **toothless,** teethless, edentate, edental,
biteless

287 SMOOTHNESS

NOUNS 1 **smoothness, flatness, levelness,**
evenness, uniformity, regularity; **sleekness,** glossiness; **slickness,** slipperiness,
lubricity, oiliness, greasiness, frictionlessness; silkiness, satininess, velvetiness; glabrousness, glabriety; downiness; suavity 504.5

2 **polish, gloss, glaze,** burnish, **shine, luster,**
finish; **patina**

3 <smooth surface> smooth, **plane, level,
flat;** tennis court, bowling alley or green,
billiard table or ball; slide; glass, ice;
marble, alabaster, ivory; silk, satin,
velvet, a baby's ass <nonformal>;
mahogany

4 **smoother;** roller, lawn-roller; sleeker,

slicker; **polish,** burnish; **abrasive,**
abrader, abradant; lubricant

VERBS 5 **smooth, flatten, plane,** planish,
level, even, equalize; **dress,** dub, dab;
smooth down or out, lay; plaster, plaster
down; roll, roll smooth; harrow, drag;
grade; mow, shave; lubricate, oil, grease

6 **press,** hot-press, **iron, mangle,** calender;
roll

7 **polish, shine, burnish, furbish,** sleek,
slick, slick down, gloss, glaze, glance, luster; **rub,** scour, **buff;** wax, varnish; finish

8 **grind, file, sand, scrape,** sandpaper, emery, pumice; abrade; sandblast

ADJS 9 **smooth;** smooth-textured or -sur-
faced, **even, level, plane, flat,** regular, uniform, **unbroken;** unrough, unroughened,
unruffled, unwrinkled; glabrous, gla-
brate, glabrescent; downy; silky, satiny,
velvety, smooth as silk or satin or velvet, smooth as a billiard ball or baby's
ass <nonformal>; leiotrichous, lisso-
trichous; smooth-shaven 6.17; suave
504.18

10 **sleek, slick, glossy,** shiny, gleaming;
silky, silken, satiny, velvety; **polished,**
burnished, furbished; buffed, rubbed, finished; varnished, lacquered, shellacked,
glazed, glacé <Fr>; **glassy,** smooth as
glass

11 **slippery,** slippy, **slick,** slithery and slid-
dery <both nonformal>, slippery as an
eel; lubricious, lubric, oily, oleaginous,
greasy, buttery, soaped; lubricated, oiled,
greased

ADVS 12 **smoothly, evenly,** regularly, uniformly; **like clockwork,** on wheels

288 ROUGHNESS

NOUNS 1 **roughness, unsmoothness, unevenness,** irregularity, ununiformity, nonuniformity 781, inequality; **bumpiness,**
pockedness, pockiness, holeyness; **abrasiveness, abrasion,** harshness, asperity;
ruggedness, rugosity; **jaggedness,** raggedness, cragginess, scraggliness; joltiness,
bumpiness; rough air, turbulence; choppiness; tooth; granulation; hispidity,
bristliness, spininess, thorniness; nubbi-
ness, nubbliness

2 <rough surface> **rough,** broken ground;
broken water, chop, lop; **corrugation,** ripple, washboard; washboard or corduroy
road, corduroy; gooseflesh, goose bumps,
goose pimples, horripilation; sandpaper

3 **bristle,** barb, barbel, striga, setule, setula, seta; **stubble;** whisker

VERBS 4 **roughen,** rough, rough up, harshen;

coarsen; granulate; gnarl, knob, stud, boss; pimple, horripilate

5 **ruffle,** wrinkle, corrugate, crinkle, crumple, **rumple; bristle; rub the wrong way, go against the grain,** set on edge

ADJS 6 **rough, unsmooth; uneven,** ununiform, unlevel, inequal, **broken,** irregular, textured; jolty, **bumpy,** rutty, rutted, pitted, pocky, potholed; horripilant, pimply; **corrugated,** ripply, wimpled; **choppy;** ruffled, unkempt; **shaggy,** shagged; **coarse,** rank, unrefined; unpolished; rough-grained, coarse-grained, cross-grained; grainy, granulated; roughhewn, rough-cast; homespun, linseywoolsey

7 **rugged,** ragged, harsh; rugose, rugous, wrinkled, crinkled, crumpled, corrugated; **scratchy, abrasive,** rough as a cob <nonformal>; **jagged,** jaggy; **snaggy,** snagged, snaggled; scraggy, scragged, scraggly; sawtooth, sawtoothed, serrate, serrated; **craggy,** cragged; **rocky,** gravelly, stony; rockbound, ironbound

8 **gnarled,** gnarly; **knurled,** knurly; **knotted,** knotty, knobbly, nodose, nodular, studded, lumpy

9 **bristly, bristling,** bristled, hispid, hirsute, whiskery; barbellate, whiskered, glochidiate, setaceous, setous, setose; strigal, strigose, strigate, studded; **stubbled,** stubbly; hairy 3.24

10 bristlelike, setiform, aristate, setarious

ADVS 11 **roughly,** rough, in the rough; **unsmoothly,** brokenly, **unevenly,** irregularly, raggedly, choppily, jaggedly; **abrasively**

12 cross-grained, **against the grain,** the wrong way

289 NOTCH

NOUNS 1 **notch, nick,** nock, **cut,** cleft, **incision, gash,** hack, blaze, scotch, **score,** kerf, crena, depression, jag; jog, joggle; **indentation** 284.6

2 **notching, serration,** serrulation, saw, saw tooth *or* teeth; denticulation, dentil, dentil band, dogtooth; crenation, crenelation, crenature, crenulation; **scallop;** rickrack; picot edge, Vandyke edge; deckle edge; cockscomb, crest

3 battlement, crenel, merlon, embrasure, castellation, machicolation

VERBS 4 **notch, nick, cut, incise, gash,** slash, chop, crimp, scotch, **score,** blaze, jag, scarify; **indent** 284.14; **scallop,** crenellate, crenulate, machicolate; serrate, pink, mill, knurl, tooth, picot, Vandyke

ADJS 5 **notched, nicked,** incised, gashed, scotched, scored, chopped, blazed; **indented** 284.17; serrate, serrated, serrulated, **saw-toothed,** saw-edged, sawlike; crenate, crenated, crenulate, crenellated, battlemented, embrasured; scalloped; dentate, dentated, **toothed,** toothlike, tooth-shaped; lacerate, lacerated; **jagged,** jaggy; erose

290 FURROW

NOUNS 1 **furrow, groove,** scratch, crack, cranny, chase, chink, score, **cut,** gash, striation, streak, stria, **gouge,** slit, incision; sulcus, sulcation; **rut,** ruck <nonformal>, wheeltrack, well-worn groove; wrinkle 291.3; **corrugation;** flute, fluting; rifling; chamfer, bezel, rabbet, dado; microgroove; **engraving** 713.2

2 **trench, trough, channel, ditch,** dike <old>, fosse, **canal,** cut, gutter, kennel <Brit>; moat; sunk fence, ha-ha; aqueduct 239.2; entrenchment 460.5; canalization; pleat, crimp, goffer

VERBS 3 **furrow, groove,** score, scratch, incise, cut, carve, chisel, gash, striate, streak, gouge, slit, crack; plow; rifle; **channel, trough, flute,** chamfer, rabbet, dado; **trench,** canal, canalize, **ditch,** dike <old>, gully, **rut; corrugate;** wrinkle 291.6; pleat, crimp, goffer; **engrave** 713.10

ADJS 4 **furrowed, grooved,** scratched, scored, incised, cut, gashed, gouged, slit, striated; **channeled, troughed,** trenched, ditched; fluted, chamfered, rabbeted, dadoed; rifled; sulcate, sulcated; canaliculate, canaliculated; **corrugated,** corrugate; corduroy, corduroyed, **rutted,** rutty; wrinkled 291.8, pleated, crimped, goffered; **engraved;** ribbed, costate

291 FOLD

NOUNS 1 **fold, double,** fold on itself, doubling, duplicature; ply; plication, plica, plicature; flection, flexure; **crease,** creasing; crimp; **tuck, gather;** ruffle, frill, ruche, ruching; flounce; lappet; lapel; dog-ear

2 **pleat,** pleating, plait *or* plat; accordion pleat, box pleat, knife pleat

3 **wrinkle, corrugation,** ridge, **furrow** 290, **crease, crimp,** ruck, **pucker,** cockle; **crinkle,** crankle, rimple, ripple, wimple; crumple, rumple; crow's-feet

4 **folding, creasing,** infolding, infoldment

or enfoldment; plication, plicature; paper-folding, origami

VERBS **5 fold**, fold on itself, fold up; **double, ply**, plicate; fold over, double over, lap over, turn over *or* under; **crease, crimp;** crisp; **pleat**, plait, plat <nonformal>; **tuck, gather**, tuck up, ruck, ruck up; ruffle, ruff, frill; flounce; twill, quill, flute; dog-ear; **fold in**, enfold *or* infold, wrap, lap; interfold

6 wrinkle, corrugate, shirr, ridge, **furrow, crease**, crimp, crimple, cockle, cocker, **pucker, purse; knit;** ruck, ruckle; **crumple**, rumple; **crinkle**, rimple, ripple, wimple

ADJS **7 folded, doubled;** plicate, plicated; **pleated**, plaited; **creased**, crimped; tucked, gathered; flounced, ruffled; twilled, quilled, fluted; dog-eared; **foldable**, folding, flexural, flexible, pliable, pliant, willowy

8 wrinkled, wrinkly; corrugated, corrugate; **creased**, rucked, **furrowed** 290.4, ridged; cockled, cockly; puckered, puckery; pursed, pursy; knitted, knotted; rugged, rugose, rugous; **crinkled**, crinkly, cranklety <nonformal>, rimpled, rippled; crimped, crimpy; **crumpled**, rumpled

292 OPENING

NOUNS **1 opening, aperture, hole**, hollow, **cavity** 284.2, **orifice; slot**, split, crack, check, leak; opening up, unstopping, uncorking, clearing, throwing open, laying open, broaching, cutting through; passageway; inlet 189.5; outlet 190.9; **gap**, gape, yawn, hiatus, lacuna, gat, space, interval; **chasm, gulf;** cleft 224.2; fontanel; foramen, fenestra; stoma; pore, porosity; fistula; **disclosure** 351

2 gaping, yawning, oscitation, oscitancy, dehiscence, pandiculation; **gape, yawn;** the gapes

3 hole, perforation, penetration, piercing, empiercement, **puncture**, goring, boring, puncturing, punching, pricking, lancing, broach, transforation, terebration; acupuncture, acupunctuation; trephining, trepanning; **impalement**, skewering, fixing, transfixion, transfixation; bore, borehole, drill hole

4 mouth; maw, oral cavity, gob <nonformal>, gab <Scots>; **muzzle**, jaw, lips, embouchure; bazoo *or* kisser *or* mug *or* mush *or* trap *or* yap <all nonformal>; **jaws**, mandibles, chops, chaps, jowls; premaxilla

5 anus; asshole *and* bumhole *and* bunghole <all nonformal>; bung

6 door, doorway 189.6; **entrance, entry** 189.5

7 window, casement; **windowpane**, window glass, pane, light; window frame, window ledge, window-sill, window bay

8 porousness, porosity; sievelikeness, cribriformity, cribrosity; screen, sieve, strainer, colander, riddle, cribble, net; honeycomb; sponge

9 permeability, perviousness

10 opener; can opener, tin opener <Brit>; corkscrew, bottle screw, bottle opener, church key <nonformal>; latchstring; **key**, clavis; latchkey; passkey, *passepartout* <Fr>; master key, skeleton key; open sesame; plastic key

VERBS **11 open**, ope <old>, **open up;** lay open, throw open; fly open, spring open, swing open; **tap, broach;** cut open, cut, cleave, split, slit, crack, chink, fissure, crevasse, incise; rift, rive; tear open, rent, tear, rip, rip open, part, dispart, separate, divide, divaricate; spread, spread out, open out, splay, splay out

12 unclose, unshut; **unfold**, unwrap, unroll; **unstop, unclog, unblock**, clear, unfoul, free, deobstruct; **unplug**, uncork, uncap; crack; **unlock**, unlatch, undo; unseal, unclench, unclutch; **uncover**, uncase, unsheathe, unveil, undrape, uncurtain; **disclose** 351.4, expose, reveal, bare, take the lid off, manifest

13 make an opening, find an opening, make place *or* space, **make way, make room**

14 breach, rupture; **break open**, force *or* pry *or* prize open, crack *or* split open, rip *or* tear open; break into, break through; break in, burst in, bust in <nonformal>, stave *or* stove in, cave in

15 perforate, pierce, empierce, **penetrate, puncture, punch, hole**, prick; **tap, broach; stab, stick**, pink, run through; **transfix**, transpierce, fix, **impale**, spit, skewer; gore, spear, lance, spike, needle; **bore, drill**, auger; **ream**, ream out, countersink, gouge, gouge out; trepan, trephine; punch full of holes, make look like Swiss cheese *or* a sieve, **riddle, honeycomb**

16 gape, gap <nonformal>, **yawn**, oscitate, dehisce, hang open

ADJS **17 open, unclosed**, uncovered; **unobstructed, unstopped, unclogged;** clear, cleared, free; wide-open, unrestricted; **disclosed** 348.10; bare, exposed, unhidden 348.11, naked, bald

18 gaping, yawning, agape, oscitant, slack-jawed, openmouthed; dehiscent, ringent; ajar, half-open, cracked

19 apertured, slotted, **holey;** pierced, **perforated,** perforate, holed; honeycombed, like Swiss cheese, riddled, *criblé* <Fr>, shot through, peppered; windowed, fenestrated; leaky

20 porous, porose; poriferous; like a sieve, sievelike, cribose, cribriform; spongy, spongelike; percolating, leachy

21 permeable, pervious, penetrable, openable, accessible

22 mouthlike, oral, orificial; mandibular, maxillary

INTERJS **23 open up!,** open sesame!, **gangway!,** passageway!, **make way!**

293 CLOSURE

NOUNS **1 closure, closing, shutting,** shutting up, occlusion; **shutdown,** shutting down; **exclusion** 772, shutting out, **ruling out;** blockade, embargo

2 imperviousness, impermeability, impenetrability, impassability; imperforation

3 obstruction, clog, block, blockade, sealing off, **blockage,** strangulation, choking, choking off, **stoppage,** stop, **bar, barrier, obstacle,** impediment; **bottleneck,** chokepoint; **congestion,** jam, traffic jam, gridlock, rush hour; gorge; constipation, obstipation, costiveness; infarct, infarction; embolism, embolus; bottleneck; **blind alley,** blank wall, **dead end,** cul-de-sac, dead-end street, impasse; cecum, blind gut

4 stopper, stop, **stopple,** stopgap; **plug, cork,** bung, spike, spill, spile, tap, faucet, spigot, valve, check valve, cock, sea cock, peg, pin; lid 295.5

5 stopping, **wadding, stuffing,** padding, **packing,** pack, tampon; gland; gasket

VERBS **6 close, shut,** occlude; close up, shut up, contract, constrict, strangle, strangulate, choke, choke off, squeeze, squeeze shut; **exclude** 772.4, shut out, squeeze out; **rule out** 444.3; **fasten,** secure; **lock,** lock up, lock out, key, padlock, latch, bolt, bar, barricade; **seal,** seal up, seal in, seal off; button, button up; snap; zipper, zip up; batten, batten down; put *or* slap the lid on, **cover;** contain; **shut the door,** slam, clap, bang

7 stop, stop up; obstruct, bar, stay; **block,** block up; **clog,** clog up, foul; **choke,** choke up *or* off; **fill,** fill up; **stuff,** pack, jam; **congest,** stuff up; **plug,** plug up; **stopper,** stopple, **cork,** bung, spile; cover; **dam,** dam up; stanch, stench <Scots>; chink;

caulk; blockade, embargo; constipate, obstipate, bind

8 close shop, **close up** *or* **down,** shut up, **shut up shop, shut down,** go out of business, fold *or* fold up *and* pull an el foldo <all nonformal> shutter, put up the shutters; cease 856.6

ADJS **9 closed, shut, unopen,** unopened; unvented, unventilated; **excluded** 772.7, shut-out; **ruled out, barred** 444.7; contracted, constricted, choked, choked off, choked up, squeezed shut, strangulated; blank; blind, cecal, dead; dead-end, blind-alley, closed-end, closed-ended; **exclusive,** exclusionary, closed-door, in-camera, private, closed to the public

10 unpierced, pierceless, **unperforated,** imperforate, intact; **untrodden,** pathless, wayless, trackless

11 stopped, stopped up; obstructed, infarcted, **blocked; plugged,** plugged up; **clogged,** clogged up; foul, fouled; **choked,** choked up, strangulated, strangled; **full, stuffed,** packed, jammed, bumper-to-bumper <nonformal>, jam-packed, like sardines; **congested,** stuffed up; constipated, obstipated, costive, bound

12 close, tight, compact, fast, shut fast, **snug,** staunch, firm; **sealed;** hermetic, hermetical, hermetically sealed; airtight, dusttight *or* dustproof, gastight *or* gasproof, lighttight *or* lightproof, oil-tight *or* oil-proof, raintight *or* rainproof, smoketight *or* smokeproof, stormtight *or* stormproof, watertight *or* waterproof, windtight *or* windproof; water-repellant *or* -resistant

13 impervious, impenetrable, impermeable; impassable, unpassable; unpierceable, unperforable; **punctureproof,** nonpuncturable, holeproof

294 TEXTURE
<surface quality>

NOUNS **1 texture,** surface texture; **surface; finish,** feel; **grain,** granular texture, fineness *or* coarseness of grain; **weave,** woof 740.3, wale; **nap,** pile, shag, nub, knub, protuberance 283; **pit,** pock, indentation 284.6; structure 266

2 roughness 288; irregularity; bumpiness, lumpiness; **coarseness, grossness, unrefinement,** coarse-grainedness; cross-grainedness; **graininess,** granularity, granulation, grittiness; pockiness; hardness 1044

3 smoothness 287, **fineness, refinement,** fine-grainedness; **delicacy, daintiness;**

filminess, gossameriness 1028.1; down, **downiness,** fluff, fluffiness, velvet, velvetiness, fuzz, fuzziness, peach fuzz, pubescence; satin, satininess; silk, silkiness; softness 1045

VERBS **4 coarsen; grain,** granulate; tooth, **roughen** 288.4; smooth 287.5

ADJS **5 textural, textured,** —surfaced

6 rough 288.6, **coarse, gross, unrefined, coarse-grained;** cross-grained; grained, **grainy,** granular, granulated, gritty, gravelly, gravelish

7 nappy, pily, **shaggy,** hairy, hirsute; nubby or nubbly; bumpy, lumpy; studded, knobbed; pocked, pitted 284.17

8 smooth 287.9; **fine, refined,** attenuate, attenuated, **fine-grained; delicate, dainty; finespun,** thin-spun, fine-drawn, wiredrawn; gauzy, filmy, gossamer, gossamery 1028.4, **downy,** fluffy, velvety, velutinous, fuzzy, pubescent; satin, satiny, silky

295 COVERING

NOUNS **1** <act of covering> **covering,** coverage, obduction; **coating,** cloaking; **screening,** shielding, hiding, curtaining, **veiling,** clouding, obscuring, befogging, fogging, fuzzing, masking, mantling, shrouding, blanketing; blocking, blotting out, eclipse, eclipsing, occultation; **wrapping,** enwrapping, enwrapment, sheathing, envelopment; **overlaying,** overspreading, laying on or over, superimposition, superposition; superincumbence; upholstering, upholstery; plasterwork, stuccowork, brickwork, cementwork, pargeting; incrustation

2 cover, covering, coverage, covert, coverture, housing, hood, cowl, cowling, **shelter; screen,** shroud, shield, veil, pall, mantle, curtain, hanging, drape, drapery; **coat,** cloak, mask, guise; vestment 5.1

3 skin, dermis; **cuticle; rind; flesh;** bare skin or flesh, the buff; integument, tegument 206.2, tegmen, tegmentum; **pelt, hide coat, jacket, fell, fleece, fur, hair,** vair <heraldry>; **peel, peeling, rind; skin,** epicarp; **bark;** cork, phellum; cortex, cortical tissue; periderm, phelloderm; peridium; dermatogen

4 overlayer, overlay; appliqué, **lap, overlap,** overlapping, imbrication; **flap,** fly, tentfly

5 cover, lid, top, cap, screw-top; operculum; stopper 293.4

6 roof, roofing, roofage, top, **housetop,** rooftop; roof-deck, roof garden, penthouse;

roofpole, ridgepole, rooftree; shingles, slates, tiles; eaves; **ceiling,** plafond <Fr>, overhead; skylight, lantern, cupola; widow's walk or captain's walk

7 umbrella, gamp or brolly <both Brit nonformal>, bumbershoot <nonformal>; **sunshade, parasol,** beach umbrella

8 tent, canvas; top, whitetop, round top, big top; tentage

9 rug, carpet, floor cover or covering; carpeting, wall-to-wall carpet or carpeting; **mat;** drop cloth, ground cloth, groundsheet; **flooring,** floorboards, duckboards; **tiling; pavement,** pavé

10 blanket, coverlet, coverlid <nonformal>, space blanket, cover, covers, **spread,** robe, buffalo robe, **afghan,** rug <Brit>; lap robe; **bedspread; bedcover;** counterpane, counterpin <nonformal>; comfort, **comforter, down comforter, duvet, continental quilt** <Brit>, **quilt,** feather bed, eiderdown; patchwork quilt; **bedding, bedclothes,** clothes; **linen,** bed linen; **sheet,** sheeting, bedsheet, fitted sheet, contour sheet; **pillowcase,** pillow slip, case, slip; duvet cover

11 horsecloth, **horse blanket;** caparison, housing; **saddle blanket,** saddlecloth

12 blanket, coating, coat; **veneer, facing,** veneering, revetment; pellicle, **film, scum,** skin, scale; slick, oil slick; varnish, enamel, lacquer, paint 35.8

13 plating, plate, cladding; nickel plate, silver plate, gold plate, copperplate, chromium plate, anodized aluminum; electroplating, electrocoating

14 crust, incrustation, shell; piecrust, pastry shell; stalactite, stalagmite; scale, scab, eschar

15 shell, seashell, lorication, lorica, conch; test, testa, episperm, pericarp, elytron, scute, scutum; **armor,** mail, **shield; carapace,** plate, chitin; **protective covering,** cortex, thick skin or hide, elephant skin

16 hull, shell, pod, capsule, case, **husk, shuck;** cornhusk, corn shuck; bark, jacket; chaff, bran, palea

17 case, casing, encasement; **sheath,** sheathing

18 wrapper, wrapping, gift wrapping, wrap; wrapping paper, waxed paper, aluminum foil, tin foil, plastic wrap, clingfilm <Brit>; **binder,** binding; **bandage,** bandaging; **envelope,** envelopment; **jacket,** jacketing; dust jacket

VERBS **19 cover,** cover up; apply to, **put on,** lay on; **superimpose,** superpose; **lay over,** overlay; **spread over,** overspread; **clothe, cloak,** mantle, muffle, blanket, canopy, cope, cowl, hood, **veil,** curtain, **screen, shield,** screen off, mask, cloud, obscure, fog, befog, fuzz; block, eclipse, occult; film, film over, scum

20 **wrap,** enwrap, wrap up, wrap about *or* around; **envelop, sheathe;** surround, encompass, lap, smother, enfold, embrace, invest; shroud, enshroud; swathe, swaddle; **box, case,** encase, **crate,** pack, embox; **containerize; package,** encapsulate

21 **top, cap,** tip, crown; put the lid on, cork, stopper, plug; hood, hat, coif, bonnet; roof, roof in *or* over; ceil; dome, endome

22 **floor; carpet; pave,** causeway, cobblestone, flag, pebble; cement, concrete; **pave, surface,** pave over, repave, resurface; blacktop, tar, asphalt, metal <old>, macadamize

23 **face, veneer,** revet; **sheathe;** board, plank, weatherboard, clapboard, lath; shingle, shake; tile, stone, brick, slate; thatch; glass, glaze, fiberglass; paper, wallpaper; wall in *or* up

24 **coat,** spread on, **spread with;** smear, **smear on,** besmear, slap on, dab, daub, bedaub, plaster, beplaster; flow on, pour on; lay on, lay it on thick, slather; undercoat, prime; enamel, gild, gloss, lacquer; butter; tar

25 **plaster,** parget, stucco, cement, concrete, mastic, grout, mortar; face, line; roughcast, pebble-dash, spatter-dash

26 **plate,** chromium-plate, copperplate, gold-plate, nickel-plate, silver-plate; **electroplate, galvanize,** anodize

27 **crust, incrust,** encrust; loricate; effloresce; scab, scab over

28 **upholster,** overstuff

29 **re-cover,** reupholster, recap

30 **overlie,** lie over; **overlap,** lap, **lap over,** override, imbricate, jut, shingle; **extend over,** span, bridge, bestride, bestraddle, arch over, overarch, hang over, overhang

ADJS 31 **covered,** covert, under cover; **cloaked,** mantled, blanketed, muffled, canopied, coped, cowled, hooded, **shrouded, veiled,** clouded, obscured, fogged, fogged in; eclipsed, occulted, curtained, **screened,** screened-in, screened-off; shielded, masked; **housed;** tented, under canvas; roofed, roofed-in *or* -over, domed; walled, walled-in; **wrapped,** enwrapped, jacketed, **enveloped,** sheathed, swathed; **boxed, cased,** encased, encapsuled *or* encapsulated, **packaged, coated,** filmed, filmed-over, scummed; shelled, loricate, loricated; armored; ceiled; **floored; paved, surfaced;** plastered, stuccoed

32 **cutaneous,** cuticular; skinlike, skinny; skin-deep; **epidermal,** epidermic, dermal, dermic; ectodermal, ectodermic; endermic, endermatic; cortical; epicarpal; testaceous; hairy, furry 3.24; integumental, integumentary, tegumentary, tegumental, tegmental; vaginal; thecal

33 **plated,** chromium-plated, copperplated, gold-plated, nickel-plated, silver-plated; electroplated, galvanized, anodized

34 upholstered, overstuffed

35 **covering, coating;** cloaking, blanketing, shrouding, obscuring, **veiling, screening,** shielding, sheltering; wrapping, **enveloping,** sheathing

36 **overlying,** incumbent, superincumbent, superimposed; **overlapping,** lapping, shingled, equitant; imbricate, imbricated; spanning, bridging; overarched, overarching

PREPS 37 **on, upon, over,** o'er, **above, on top of**

296 LAYER

NOUNS 1 **layer,** thickness; **level, tier,** stage, story, floor, gallery, step, ledge, deck; **stratum,** seam, *couche* <Fr>, belt, band, **bed, course,** measures; zone; shelf; **overlayer, superstratum,** overstory, topsoil; **underlayer, substratum,** understratum, understory; floor, bedding

2 lamina, lamella; **sheet,** leaf, *feuille* <Fr>, foil; wafer, disk; **plate,** plating, cladding; covering 295; **coat,** coating, veneer, film, patina, scum, membrane, pellicle, peel, skin, rind, hide; slick, oil slick; **slice,** cut, rasher, collop; **slab,** plank, deal <Brit>, slat, tablet, table; panel, pane; **fold,** lap, flap, **ply,** plait; laminated glass, safety glass; laminated wood, plywood, layered fiberglass

3 **flake,** flock, floccule, flocculus; **scale, scurf,** dandruff; chip; shaving, paring, swarf

4 **stratification, lamination,** lamellation; foliation; delamination, exfoliation; desquamation, furfuration; flakiness, scaliness

VERBS 5 **layer,** lay down, lay up, **stratify,** arrange in layers *or* levels *or* strata *or* tiers, **laminate;** flake, scale; delaminate, desquamate, exfoliate

ADJS 6 **layered,** in layers; **laminated,** laminate, laminous; lamellated, lamellate, lamellar, lamelliform; plated, coated; veneered, faced; two-ply, three-ply, etc; two-level, bilevel, three-level, trilevel, etc; one-story, single story, two-story,

double-story, etc; **stratified,** stratiform;
foliated, foliaceous, leaflike

7 **flaky,** flocculent; **scaly,** scurfy, squamous,
lentiginous, furfuraceous, lepidote;
scabby, scabious, scabrous

WORD ELEMENTS 8 strati—, lamin—,
lamino—, lamini—, lamell—, lamelli—

297 WEIGHT

NOUNS 1 **weight, heaviness, weightiness,
ponderousness,** ponderosity, ponderability, leadenness, heftiness *and* heft
<both nonformal>; body weight, avoir-
dupois <nonformal>, fatness 257.8, beef
and beefiness <both nonformal>;
poundage, tonnage; deadweight, live
weight; gross weight, gr wt; **net weight,**
neat weight, nt wt, net, nett <Brit>;
short-weight; underweight; overweight;
overbalance, overweightage; **solemnity,
gravity** 111.1, 580.1

2 onerousness, **burdensomeness, oppressiveness, deadweight, overburden,
cumbersomeness,** cumbrousness; massiveness, massiness <old>, bulkiness
257.9, lumpishness, unwieldiness

3 <sports> bantamweight, featherweight,
flyweight, heavyweight, light heavyweight, lightweight, middleweight,
cruiser weight, welterweight; catch-
weight; fighting weight; jockey weight

4 **counterbalance** 899.4; makeweight; **ballast,** ballasting

5 <physics terms> **gravity, gravitation,** G,
supergravity; specific gravity; gravitational field, gravisphere; graviton;
geotropism, positive geotropism, apo-
geotropism, negative geotropism; G suit,
anti-G suit; **mass;** atomic weight, molecular weight, molar weight

6 **weight,** paperweight, letterweight;
sinker, lead, plumb, plummet, bob; sash
weight; sandbag

7 **burden,** burthen <old>, pressure, **oppression, deadweight;** burdening,
saddling, charging, taxing; overburden,
overburdening, overtaxing, overweight-
ing, weighing *or* weighting down; charge,
load, loading, lading, freight, cargo, bale;
cumber, cumbrance, **encumbrance;** incubus; incumbency *or* superincumbency
<old>; handicap, drag, millstone; sur-
charge, overload

8 <systems of weight> avoirdupois
weight, troy weight, apothecaries'
weight; atomic weight, molecular
weight; **pound, ounce, gram** etc, **unit of
weight** <see list>

9 **weighing,** hefting <nonformal>, balancing; weighing-in, weigh-in, weighing-out,
weigh-out; **scale,** weighing instrument

VERBS 10 **weigh,** weight; **heft** <nonformal>,
balance, weigh in the balance, strike a
balance, hold the scales, put on the
scales, lay in the scales; **counterbalance;
weigh in,** weigh out; be heavy, weigh
heavy, lie heavy, have weight, carry
weight; **tip the scales,** turn *or* depress *or*
tilt the scales

11 **weigh on** *or* **upon,** rest on *or* upon, bear
on *or* upon, lie on, press, press down,
press to the ground

12 **weight, weigh** *or* **weight down;** hang like
a millstone; **ballast;** lead, sandbag

13 **burden,** burthen <old>, **load,** load down
or up, lade, cumber, **encumber, charge,
freight,** tax, handicap, hamper, saddle;
oppress, weigh one down, weigh on *or*
upon, weigh heavy on, bear *or* rest hard
upon, lie hard *or* heavy upon, press hard
upon, be an incubus to; **overburden,** overweight, overtax, **overload** 992.15

14 **outweigh,** overweigh, overweight, overbalance, **outbalance,** outpoise, over-
poise

15 **gravitate, descend** 194.5, drop, plunge
367.6, precipitate, sink, settle, subside;
tend, tend to go, **incline,** point, head,
lead, lean

ADJS 16 **heavy, ponderous, massive,** massy,
weighty, hefty <nonformal>, fat 257.18;
leaden, heavy as lead; deadweight;
heavyweight; overweight; **solemn, grave**
111.3/580.8

17 **onerous, oppressive, burdensome,** incumbent *or* superincumbent, **cumbersome,**
cumbrous; massive; lumpish, **unwieldy**

18 **weighted, weighed** *or* **weighted down;
burdened, oppressed, laden,** cumbered,
encumbered, charged, loaded, fraught,
freighted, taxed, saddled, hampered;
overburdened, overloaded, overladen,
overcharged, overfreighted, overfraught,
overweighted, overtaxed; borne-down,
sinking, foundering

19 **weighable,** ponderable; **appreciable,** palpable, sensible

20 **gravitational,** mass

ADVS 21 **heavily,** heavy, weightily, leadenly;
burdensomely, onerously, oppressively;
ponderously, cumbersomely, cumbrously

22 **units of weight** *or* **force** *or* **mass**

assay ton	decagram *or* dkg *or*
carat *or* c	decigram *or* dg
carat grain	displacement ton
centigram *or* cg	dram *or* dram avoir-
dead-weight ton	dupois *or* dr

dram apothecaries' *or*
  dr ap
dyne
grain *or* gr
gram *or* g
gram equivalent *or*
  gram equivalent
  weight
gram molecule *or*
  gram-molecular
  weight
gross ton
hectogram *or* hg
hundredweight *or*
  cwt
international carat
kilogram *or* kilo *or* kg
kiloton
long hundredweight
long ton *or* lt
measurement ton
megaton
metric carat
metric ton *or* MT *or* t
microgram *or* mcg
milligram *or* mg
mole *or* mol
myriagram *or* myg

net ton
newton
ounce *or* ounce avoir-
  dupois *or* oz *or* oz
  av
ounce apothecaries'
  or oz ap
ounce troy *or* oz t
pearl grain
pennyweight *or* dwt
  or pwt
pound *or* pound
  avoirdupois *or* lb *or*
  lb av
poundal
pound apothecaries'
  or lb ap
pound troy *or* lb t
quintal *or* q
scruple *or* s ap
shipping ton
short hundredweight
short ton *or* st
slug
sthene
stone *or* st
ton *or* tn

298 LIGHTNESS

NOUNS **1 lightness, levity,** unheaviness, lack of weight; **weightlessness; buoyancy,** buoyance, floatability; levitation, ascent 193; **volatility; airiness,** ethereality, foaminess, frothiness, bubbliness, yeastiness; downiness, fluffiness, gossameriness 1028.1; softness, gentleness, delicacy, daintiness, tenderness; light touch, gentle touch; frivolity 922.1/109.5

2 <comparisons> air, ether, feather, down, thistledown, flue, fluff, fuzz, sponge, gossamer, cobweb, fairy, straw, chaff, dust, mote, cork, chip, bubble, froth, foam, spume

3 lightening, easing, **easement, alleviation, relief;** disburdening, **disencumberment,** unburdening, **unloading,** unlading, unsaddling, untaxing, unfreighting; unballasting

4 leavening, fermentation; leaven, ferment

5 <indeterminacy of weight> **imponderableness** *or* imponderability, unweighableness *or* unweighability; imponderables, imponderabilia

VERBS **6 lighten,** make light *or* lighter, reduce weight; unballast; **ease, alleviate, relieve; disburden, disencumber,** unburden, unload, unlade, off-load; **be light,** weigh lightly, have little weight, kick the beam

7 leaven, raise, **ferment**

8 buoy, buoy up; float, float high, ride high, waft; **sustain, hold up,** bear up, uphold, upbear, uplift, upraise; refloat

9 levitate, rise, ascend 193.8; hover, **float**

ADJS **10 light,** unheavy, imponderous; **weightless; airy, ethereal; volatile;** frothy, foamy, spumy, spumous, spumescent, bubbly, yeasty; downy, feathery, fluffy, gossamery 1028.4; *soufflé, moussé, léger* <all Fr>; "lighter than vanity"—Bible, "light as any wind that blows"—Tennyson; light as air *or* a feather *or* gossamer, etc 298.2; **frivolous** 921.20/109.15

11 lightened, eased, unburdened, disburdened, disencumbered, unencumbered, relieved, alleviated, out from under, breathing easier; mitigated

12 light, gentle, soft, delicate, dainty, tender, **easy**

13 lightweight, bantamweight, featherweight; underweight

14 buoyant, floaty, floatable; floating, supernatant

15 levitative, levitational

16 lightening, easing, alleviating, alleviative, alleviatory, relieving, disburdening, unburdening, disencumbering

17 leavening, raising, **fermenting,** fermentative, working; yeasty, barmy; enzymic, diastatic

18 imponderable, unweighable

299 RARITY
   <lack of density>

NOUNS **1 rarity,** rareness; **thinness, tenuousness,** tenuity; **subtlety,** subtility; **fineness,** slightness, flimsiness, **unsubstantiality** *or* **insubstantiality** 763; **ethereality,** airiness, immateriality, incorporeality, bodilessness, insolidity; **diffuseness,** dispersedness, scatter, scatteredness; "airy nothing,"— *and* "such stuff as dreams are made on"—both Shakespeare

2 rarefaction, attenuation, subtilization, etherealization; **diffusion,** dispersion, scattering; **thinning,** thinning-out, dilution, adulteration, watering, watering-down; decompression

VERBS **3 rarefy, attenuate,** thin, thin out; dilute, adulterate, water, water down, cut; subtilize, **etherealize; diffuse,** disperse, scatter; expand 259.4; decompress

ADJS **4 rare,** rarefied; **subtle; thin,** thinned, dilute, attenuated, attenuate; thinned-out, diluted, adulterated, watered, watered-down, cut; **tenuous, fine,** flimsy,

slight, **unsubstantial** *or* **insubstantial**
763; **airy, ethereal,** vaporous, gaseous,
windy; **diffused,** diffuse, dispersed, scattered; uncompact, uncompressed,
decompressed

5 rarefactive, rarefactional

300 MEASUREMENT

NOUNS 1 **measurement, measure;** mensuration, measuring, **gauging;** admeasure-
ment; metage; **estimation,** estimate,
rough measure, approximation, ballpark
figure <nonformal>; **quantification,**
quantitation, quantization; **appraisal,**
appraisement, **stocktaking, assay,** assaying; **assessment,** determination, rating,
valuation, evaluation; assizement, assize,
sizing up <nonformal>; **survey,** surveying; triangulation; **instrumentation;**
telemetry, telemetering; metric system;
metrication; English system of measurement; calibration, correction, computation, calculation

2 **measure,** measuring instrument, **meter,
instrument, gauge,** barometer, **rule, yardstick,** measuring rod *or* stick, **standard,**
norm, canon, **criterion,** test, touchstone,
check; **pattern,** model, type; **scale,** graduated *or* calibrated scale; meter-reading,
reading, readout, value, degree, quantity;
parameter

3 **extent,** quantity 244, degree 245, size 257,
distance 261, length 267, breadth 269;
weight 297

4 <measures> US liquid measure, British
imperial liquid measure, US dry measure, British imperial dry measure,
apothecaries' measure, linear measure
<see list>, square measure, circular
measure, cubic measure, volume measure <see list>, area measure <see list>,
surface measure, surveyor's measure,
land measure, board measure

5 coordinates, Cartesian coordinates, rectangular coordinates, polar coordinates,
cylindrical coordinates, spherical coordinates, equator coordinates; latitude,
longitude; altitude, azimuth; declination,
right ascension; ordinate, abscissa

6 **waterline;** watermark, tidemark, flood-
mark, **high-water mark;** load waterline,
load line mark, Plimsoll mark *or* line

7 **measurability,** mensurability, comput-
ability, determinability, quantifiability

8 science of measurement, **mensuration,**
metrology

9 **measurer,** meter, gauger; **geodesist,** geodetic engineer; **surveyor,** land surveyor,
quantity surveyor; topographer, cartog-
rapher, mapmaker, oceanographer,
chorographer; **appraiser, assessor;** assayer; valuer, valuator, evaluator;
estimator

VERBS 10 **measure, gauge, quantify,** quantitate, quantize, mete <old>, take the measure of, mensurate, triangulate, apply the
yardstick to; **estimate,** make an approximation; **assess, rate, appraise, valuate,
value,** evaluate, appreciate, prize; **assay;**
size *or* size up <nonformal>, take the dimensions of; **weigh,** weigh up 297.10;
survey; plumb, probe, sound, fathom;
span, pace, step; calibrate, graduate; divide; caliper; meter; read the meter, take
a reading, check a parameter; compute,
calculate

11 **measure off, mark off, lay off,** set off, rule
off; **step off,** pace off *or* out; **measure out,**
mark out, lay out; put at

ADJS 12 **measuring, metric, metrical,**
mensural, mensurative, mensurational;
valuative, valuational; **quantitative,** numerative; approximative, estimative;
geodetic, geodetical, geodesic, geodesical,
hypsographic, hypsographical, hypso-
metric, hypsometrical; topographic, topographical, chorographic, chorographi-
cal, cartographic, cartographical,
oceanographic, oceanographical

13 **measured, gauged,** metered, **quantified,**
quantitated, quantized; **appraised, assessed, valuated,** valued, rated, ranked;
assayed; surveyed, plotted, mapped, ad-
measured, triangulated; known by
measurement

14 **measurable,** mensurable, **quantifiable,**
numerable, meterable, gaugeable, fathomable, **determinable,** computable,
calculable; quantifiable, quantitatable,
quantizable; estimable; assessable, ap-
praisable, ratable; appreciable, perceptible, noticeable

ADVS 15 **measurably, appreciably, perceptibly, noticeably**

16 **linear measures**

absolute angstrom	cubit
Admiralty mile	decameter *or* dkm
angstrom *or* ang-	decimeter *or* dm
strom unit *or* a *or* å	ell
or A *or* Å	em
arpent	en
astronomical unit	fathom *or* fthm
block	fingerbreadth *or* fin-
board foot *or* bd ft	ger
cable length	foot *or* ft
centimeter *or* cm	footstep
chain *or* Gunter's	furlong *or* fur
chain *or* chn	hand

handbreadth *or* hands- breadth	millimicron *or* micro- millimeter
hectometer *or* hm	myriameter *or* mym nail
inch *or* in	nautical mile *or* naut
international ang- strom	mi
kilometer *or* km	pace
land mile	palm
league	parsec
light-year	perch
line	pica
link *or* li	point *or* pt
meter *or* m	pole *or* p
micron *or* μ	rod *or* r
mil	statute mile *or* stat mi
mile *or* mi	step
millimeter *or* mm	stride wavelength yard *or* yd

17 volume measures

barrel	gill *or* gi
bushel *or* bu	hectoliter *or* hl
centiliter *or* cl	hogshead *or* hhd
cord *or* cd	jeroboam
cubic foot *or* yard *or* etc	jigger kiloliter *or* kl
cubic meter	liquid pint *or* quart *or* etc
cup	liter *or* l
decaliter *or* dkl	magnum
decastere *or* dks	milliliter *or* ml
deciliter *or* dl	minim *or* min
drop	peck *or* pk
dry pint *or* quart *or* etc	pint *or* pt pony
fifth	quart *or* qt
finger	stere *or* s
fluidounce *or* fl oz	tablespoon *or* tbs
fluidram *or* fl dr	teaspoon *or* tsp
gallon *or* gal	

18 area measures

acre *or* a *or* ac	rood
are *or* a	section *or* sec
arpent	square inch *or* foot *or*
centare *or* ca	mile *or* etc
hectare *or* ha	square meter *or* kilo-
perch	meter *or* etc
pole *or* p	

301 YOUTH

NOUNS 1 youth, youthhead <Scots>, **youthfulness,** youthiness <Scots>, **juvenility,** juvenescence, tenderness, tender age, early years, school age, *jeunesse* <Fr>, prime of life, flower of life, salad days, springtime *or* springtide of life, seedtime of life, flowering time, bloom, florescence, budtime, "the very May-morn of his youth"—Shakespeare, "the summer of your youth"—Edward Moore, "the red sweet wine of youth"—Rupert Brooke, golden season of life, "the glad season of life"—Carlyle, heyday of youth *or* of the blood, young blood, "my burning youth"—Yeats, "my green age"—Dylan Thomas

2 childhood, "childhood's careless days"—William Cullen Bryant; **boyhood; girlhood,** maidenhood *or* maidenhead; puppyhood, calfhood; subteens, pre-teens

3 immaturity, undevelopment, inexperience, **callowness, unripeness,** greenness, rawness, sappiness, freshness, juiciness, dewiness, **minority,** juniority, infancy, nonage

4 childishness, childlikeness, **puerility; boyishness,** boylikeness; **girlishness,** girl-likeness, maidenliness

5 infancy, babyhood, the cradle, the crib, the nursery, "my Angel-infancy"—Henry Vaughan

6 adolescence, maturation, maturement, pubescence, **puberty;** nubility

7 teens, teen years *or* age, **awkward age,** age of growing pains <nonformal>

VERBS 8 make young, youthen, **rejuvenate,** reinvigorate; turn back the clock

ADJS 9 young, youngling, youngish, **juvenile,** juvenal, juvenescent, **youthful,** youthy <Scots>, youthlike, in the flower *or* bloom of youth, blooming, florescent, flowering, dewy, fresh-faced; "towering in confidence of twenty-one"—Samuel Johnson; young-looking, well-preserved

10 immature, unadult; **inexperienced,** unseasoned, unfledged, new-fledged, **callow, unripe,** ripening, unmellowed, **raw, green,** vernal, primaveral, dewy, juicy, sappy, budding, tender, virginal, intact, innocent, naive, ingenuous, **undeveloped,** growing, unformed, unlicked, wet *or* not dry behind the ears; **minor,** underage

11 childish, childlike, kiddish <nonformal>, **puerile; boyish,** boylike, beardless; **girlish,** girl-like, maiden, maidenly; puppyish, puppylike, puplike, calflike, coltish, coltlike

12 infant, infantile, infantine, **babyish,** baby; dollish, doll-like; kittenish, kittenlike; **newborn,** neonatal; in the cradle *or* crib *or* nursery, in swaddling clothes, in diapers, in nappies <Brit>, in arms, at the breast, tied to mother's apron strings

13 adolescent, pubescent, nubile, marriageable

14 teen-age, teen-aged, teenish, **in one's teens;** sweet sixteen <nonformal>

15 junior, Jr; **younger,** puisne

PHRS 16 "Young men are fitter to invent than to judge"—Francis Bacon; "To be young is to be one of the Immortals"—

W C Hazlitt, "To be young was very Heaven!"—Wordsworth

302 YOUNGSTER

NOUNS **1 youngster**, young person, **youth, juvenile**, youngling, young'un <nonformal>, juvenal <old>; **stripling**, slip, sprig, sapling; fledgling; hopeful, young hopeful; **minor**, infant; **adolescent**, pubescent; **teenager**, teener, teenybopper <nonformal>; junior, younger, youngest, baby

2 young people, youth, young, **younger generation**, rising or new generation, young blood, young fry <nonformal>, *ragazze* <Ital>; **children**, tots, childkind; small fry and **kids** and **little kids** and little guys <all nonformal>; boyhood, girlhood; babyhood

3 child, one <Scots>; nipper, **kid** and kiddy and kiddo <all nonformal>, **little one**, little fellow or guy, little bugger <nonformal>, shaver and little shaver <both nonformal>, little squirt <nonformal>, **tot, little tot**, wee tot, pee-wee, tad or little tad, tyke, mite, chit <nonformal>, innocent, little innocent, moppet, poppet; darling, cherub, lamb, lambkin, kitten, **offspring** 561.3

4 brat, urchin; minx, imp, puck, elf, gamin, little monkey, **whippersnapper**, young whippersnapper, *enfant terrible* <Fr>, little terror, holy terror; spoiled brat; snotnose kid <nonformal>; juvenile delinquent, JD <nonformal>; punk and punk kid <both nonformal>

5 boy, lad, laddie, **youth**, manchild, manling, young man, *garçon* <Fr>, *muchacho* <Sp>, schoolboy, schoolkid <nonformal>, fledgling, hobbledehoy; fellow 76.5; pup, puppy, whelp, cub, colt; master; sonny, sonny boy; bud and buddy <both nonformal>; bub and bubba <both nonformal>; buck, young buck; schoolboy

6 girl, girlie <nonformal>, **maid, maiden, lass**, girlchild, **lassie**, young thing, young creature, young lady, damsel in distress, **damsel**, damoiselle, demoiselle, *jeune fille* <Fr>, *mademoiselle* <Fr>, *muchacha* <Sp>, miss, missy, little missy, slip, wench <dial or nonformal>, colleen <Irish>

7 <nonformal terms> **gal**, dame, **chick**, tomato, **babe** or baby, **broad**, frail, **doll**, skirt, jill, chit, cutie, filly, heifer; teenybopper and weenybopper <both nonformal>

8 schoolgirl, schoolmaid, schoolmiss, junior miss, subteen, subteener; subdebutante, subdeb <nonformal>; bobbysoxer <nonformal>, **tomboy**, hoyden, romp; piece <nonformal>, nymphet; virgin, *virgo intacta* <L>

9 infant, baby, babe, babe in arms, little darling or angel or doll or cherub, bouncing baby, puling infant, mewling infant, babykins <nonformal>, baby bunting; papoose, *bimbo* <Ital> or *bambino* <Ital>; **toddler; suckling**, nursling, fosterling, weanling; neonate; yearling, yearold; premature baby, preemie <nonformal>, incubator baby; preschooler; crumbcrusher and -cruncher and -grinder and -snatcher; carpet rat and rug ape and carpet ape and curtain-climber <all nonformal>

10 <animals> **fledgling**, birdling, nestling; **chick**, chicky, chickling; **pullet**, fryer; **duckling**; gosling; **kitten**, kit, catling; **pup**, puppy, whelp; **cub; calf**, dogie, weaner; **colt**, foal; piglet, pigling, shoat; **lamb**, lambkin; kid, yeanling; fawn; **tadpole**, polliwog; litter, nest

11 <plants> **sprout, seedling**, set; sucker, shoot, slip; **twig**, sprig, scion, sapling

12 <insects> **larva, chrysalis**, aurelia, **cocoon**, pupa; nymph, nympha; wriggler, wiggler; caterpillar, maggot, grub

303 AGE
<time of life>

NOUNS **1 age**, years, "the days of our years" "the measure of my days"—both Bible; time or stage of life; lifespan, life expectancy

2 maturity, adulthood, majority, grownupness, full growth, mature age, legal age, voting age, driving age, drinking age, *legalis homo* <L>; age of consent; ripe age, riper years, full age or growth or bloom, flower of age, **prime, prime of life**, age of responsibility, age or years of discretion, age of matured powers; **manhood**, man's estate, virility, *toga virilis* <L>, masculinity, maleness, manliness; **womanhood**, womanness, femininity, femaleness, womanliness

3 seniority, eldership, deanship, primogeniture

4 middle age, middle life, meridian of life, the middle years, the wrong side of forty, the dangerous age

5 old age, oldness, eld <old>, **elderliness**, senectitude, advanced age or years; superannuation, pensionable age, age of retirement; **ripe old age,** the golden years, senior citizenship, hoary age, gray *or* white hairs; **decline of life,** declining years, youth deficiency, the vale of years, "an incurable disease," "the downward slope"—both Seneca, "slow-consuming age"—Thomas Gray, "a tyrant, which forbids the pleasures of youth on pain of death"—La Rochefoucauld, "old age is fifteen years older than I"—Bernard Baruch, "crabbed age"—The Passionate Pilgrim, "the arctic regions of our lives"—Longfellow, the shady side <nonformal>; "the sere, the yellow leaf, "the silver livery of advised age"—both Shakespeare, "a crown of glory"—Bible; sunset *or* twilight *or* evening *or* autumn *or* winter of one's days; **decrepitude,** ricketiness, infirm old age, infirmity of age, infirmity, debility, caducity, feebleness; **dotage,** second childhood; senility 921.10, anility; **longevity,** long life, length of years, green *or* hale old age

6 **maturation, development,** growth, ripening, blooming, blossoming, flourishing; **mellowing,** seasoning, tempering; **aging,** senescence

7 **change of life, menopause,** climacteric, grand climacteric

8 **geriatrics,** gerontology

VERBS 9 **mature, grow up,** grow, **develop, ripen,** flower, flourish, bloom, blossom; fledge, leave the nest, put up one's hair, not be in pigtails, put on long pants; **come of age,** come to maturity, attain majority, **reach one's majority,** reach twenty-one, reach voting age, reach the age of consent, reach manhood *or* womanhood, write oneself a man, come to *or* into man's estate, put on long trousers *or* pants, assume the toga virilis, come into years of discretion, be in the prime of life, cut one's wisdom teeth *or* eyeteeth <nonformal>, have sown one's wild oats, settle down; **mellow,** season, temper

10 **age, grow old,** senesce, get on *or* along, **get on** *or* **along in years,** grow *or* have whiskers, be over the hill <nonformal>, turn gray *or* white; **decline,** wane, fade, fail, sink, waste away; **dodder,** totter, shake; wither, wrinkle, shrivel, wizen; **live to a ripe old age,** cheat the undertaker <nonformal>; be in one's dotage *or* second childhood

11 **have had one's day,** have seen one's day *or* best days, **have seen better days; show one's age,** show marks of age, have one foot in the grave

ADJS **12 adult, mature, of age,** out of one's teens, big, grown, **grown-up;** old enough to know better; **marriageable,** of marriageable age, marriable, nubile

13 **mature, ripe,** ripened, of full *or* ripe age, **developed,** fully developed, well-developed, **full-grown,** full-fledged, fully fledged, full-blown, in full bloom, in one's prime; **mellow** *or* mellowed, seasoned, tempered, aged

14 **middle-aged,** mid-life, *entre deux âges* <Fr>, fortyish, matronly

15 **past one's prime,** senescent, on the shady side <nonformal>, overblown, overripe, of a certain age, over the hill <nonformal>; "fall'n into the sere, the yellow leaf"—Shakespeare

16 **aged, elderly, old,** grown old in years, along *or* up *or* advanced *or* on in years, years old, advanced, advanced in life, **at an advanced age, ancient,** geriatric, gerontic; **venerable,** old as Methuselah *or* as God *or* as the hills; patriarchal, hoary, hoar, **gray,** white, gray- *or* white-headed, gray- *or* white-haired, gray- *or* white-crowned, gray- *or* white-bearded, gray *or* white with age; wrinkled, prune-faced <nonformal>; wrinkly, with crow's feet, marked with the crow's foot

17 **aging,** growing old, senescent, **getting on** *or* **along,** getting on *or* along *or* up in years, not as young as one used to be, long in the tooth; **declining,** sinking, waning, fading, wasting, doting

18 **stricken in years, decrepit, infirm,** weak, debilitated, feeble, geriatric, timeworn, the worse for wear, rusty, moth-eaten *or* mossbacked <nonformal>, fossilized, wracked *or* ravaged with age, run to seed; **doddering,** doddery, doddered, tottering, tottery, rickety, shaky, palsied; on one's last legs, with one foot in the grave; **wizened,** crabbed, **withered,** shriveled, like a prune, mummylike, papery-skinned; **senile** 921.23, anile

304 ADULT OR OLD PERSON

NOUNS 1 **adult, grownup,** mature man *or* woman, grown man *or* woman, big boy *and* big girl <both nonformal>; **man, woman;** major, *legalis homo* <L>; no chicken *and* no spring chicken <both nonformal>

2 **old man, elder, oldster** <nonformal>; golden-ager, senior citizen, geriatric; old chap, old party, **old gentleman,** old gent <nonformal>, old codger <nonformal>, geezer *and* old geezer <both nonformal>,

gramps <nonformal>, gaffer, old duffer <nonformal>, old dog *and* old-timer <both nonformal>, dotard, veteran, pantaloon; **patriarch,** graybeard *or* greybeard, reverend *or* venerable sir; grandfather, grandsire; Father Time, Methuselah, Nestor, Old Parr; sexagenarian, septuagenarian, octogenarian, nonagenarian, centenarian; "the quiet-voiced elders"—T S Eliot, "a paltry thing, a tattered coat upon a stick"—Yeats

3 **old woman, old lady,** dowager, granny, old granny, dame, **grandam,** trot *and* old trot <both nonformal>; old dame *and* hen *and* bag *and* girl <all nonformal>; old bag *and* old bat *and* old battleax <all nonformal>; **crone,** hag, witch, beldam, frump <nonformal>, old wife; grandmother

4 <elderly couples> Darby and Joan, Baucis and Philemon

5 **senior,** Sr, *senex* <L>, **elder,** older; dean, *doyen* <Fr>, *doyenne* <Fr>; father, sire; firstling, first-born, **eldest,** oldest

VERBS 6 **mature** 303.9; grow old 303.10
ADJS 7 **mature** 303.12; middle-aged 303.14; aged 303.16, older 841.19

305 ORGANIC MATTER

NOUNS 1 **organic matter,** animate *or* living matter, all that lives, living nature, organic nature, organized matter; **biology** 1066; **flesh, tissue,** fiber, brawn, plasm; **flora and fauna,** plant and animal life, animal and vegetable kingdom, biosphere, biota, ecosphere, noosphere

2 **organism,** organization, organic being, life-form, form of life, **living being** *or* **thing,** being, creature, created being, **individual,** genetic individual, physiological individual, morphological individual; zoon, zooid; virus; aerobic organism, anaerobic organism; heterotrophic organism, autotrophic organism; microbe, microorganism

3 **biological classification,** taxonomy, kingdom, phylum, etc

4 **cell,** bioplast, cellule; procaryotic cell, eucaryotic cell; plant cell, animal cell; germ cell, somatic cell; corpuscle; unicellularity, multicellularity; germ layer, ectoderm, endoderm, mesoderm; **protoplasm,** energid; trophoplasm; chromatoplasm; germ plasm; cytoplasm; ectoplasm, endoplasm; cellular tissue, reticulum; plasmodium, coenocyte, syncytium

5 **organelle;** plastid; chromoplast, plastosome, chloroplast; mitochondrion; Golgi apparatus; ribosome; spherosome, microbody; vacuole; central apparatus, cytocentrum; centroplasm; centra body, microcentrum; centrosome; centrosphere; centriole, basal body; pili, cilia, flagella, spindle fibers; aster; kinoplasm; plasmodesmata; cell membrane

6 **metaplasm;** cell wall, cell plate; structural polysaccharide; bast, phloem, xylem, xyl— *or* xylo—, cellulose, chitin

7 **nucleus,** cell nucleus; macronucleus, meganucleus; micronucleus; nucleolus; plasmosome; karyosome, chromatin strands; nuclear envelope; chromatin, karyotin; basichromatin, heterochromatin, oxychromatin

8 **chromosome;** allosome; heterochromosome, sex chromosome, idiochromosome; W chromosome; X chromosome, accessory chromosome, monosome; Y chromosome; Z chromosome; euchromosome, autosome; homologous chromosomes; univalent chromosome, chromatid; centromere; gene-string, chromonema; genome; chromosome complement; chromosome number, diploid number, haploid number; polyploidy

9 **genetic material, gene;** allele; operon; cistron, structural gene, regulator gene, operator gene; altered gene; deoxyribonucleic acid *or* **DNA;** DNA double helix, superhelix *or* supercoil; nucleotide, codon; ribonucleic acid *or* **RNA;** messenger RNA, mRNA; transfer RNA, tRNA; ribosomal RNA; anticodon; gene pool, gene complex, gene flow, genetic drift; genotype, biotype; **hereditary character,** heredity 560.6; genetic counseling; genetic screening; **recombinant DNA technology,** gene mapping, gene splicing; gene transplantation, gene transfer, germline insertion; intronizing, intron *or* intervening sequence; exonizing, exon; **genetic engineering;** designer gene

10 **gamete, germ cell,** reproductive cell; macrogamete, megagamete; microgamete; planogamete; genetoid; gamone; gametangium, gametophore; gametophyte; germ plasm, idioplasm

11 **sperm, spermatozoa, seed, semen,** jism *or* gism *and* come *or* cum *and* scum *and* spunk <all nonformal>; seminal *or* spermatic fluid, milt; **sperm cell,** male gamete; spermatozoon, spermatozoid, antherozoid; antheridium; spermatium, spermatiophore *or* spermatophore, sper-

magonium; pollen; spermatogonium; androcyte, spermatid, spermatocyte

12 **ovum, egg, egg cell,** female gamete, oösphere; oöcyte; oögonium; ovicell, oöecium; ovule; stirp; ovulation; donor egg

13 **spore;** microspore; macrospore, megaspore; swarm spore, zoospore, planospore; spore mother cell, sporocyte; zygospore; sporocarp, cystocarp; basidium; sporangium, megasporangium, microsporangium; sporocyst; gonidangium; sporogonium, sporophyte; sporophore; sorus

14 **embryo,** zygote, oösperm, oöspore, blastula; *Anlage* <Ger>; **fetus,** germ, germen <old>, rudiment; **larva,** nymph

15 **egg;** ovule; bird's egg; **roe,** fish eggs, caviar, spawn; **yolk,** yellow, vitellus; white, **egg white,** albumen, glair; eggshell

16 **cell division; mitosis;** amitosis; metamitosis, eumitosis; endomitosis, promitosis; haplomitosis, mesomitosis; karyomitosis; karyokinesis; interphase, prophase, metaphase, anaphase, telophase, diaster, cytokinesis; **meiosis**

ADJS 17 **organic,** organismic; organized; **animate, living,** vital, zoetic; **biological,** biotic; physiological

18 **protoplasmic,** plasmic, plasmatic; **genetic,** genic, hereditary

19 **cellular,** cellulous; unicellular, multicellular; corpuscular

20 gametic, gamic, sexual; **spermatic,** spermic, **seminal,** spermatozoal, spermatozoan, spermatozoic; sporal, sporous, sporoid; sporogenous

21 **nuclear,** nucleal, nucleary, nucleate; multinucleate; nucleolar, nucleolate, nucleolated; **chromosomal;** chromatinic; haploid, diploid, polyploid

22 **embryonic, germinal,** germinant, germinative, germinational; larval; fetal; in the bud; germiparous

23 **egglike,** ovicular, eggy; ovular; albuminous, albuminoid; yolked, yolky; oviparous

306 LIFE

NOUNS 1 **life, living, vitality,** being alive, having life, animation, animate existence; breath; liveliness, animal spirits, vivacity, spriteliness; long life, longevity; life expectancy, life-span; viability; lifetime 826.5; immortality 828.3; birth 1; existence 760

2 "one dem'd horrid grind"—Dickens, "a beauty chased by tragic laughter"—John Masefield, "a little gleam of Time between two eternities"—Carlyle, "a tale told by an idiot, full of sound and fury, signifying nothing"—Shakespeare, "a perpetual instruction in cause and effect"—Emerson, "a flame that is always burning itself out"—G B Shaw, "a dome of many-colored glass"—Shelley, "a long lesson in humility"—J M Barrie, "a fiction made up of contradiction"—William Blake, "a fatal complaint, and an eminently contagious one"—O W Holmes, Sr., "a play of passion"—Sir W Raleigh, "a comedy to those who think, a tragedy to those who feel"—H Walpole

3 **life force, soul,** spirit, indwelling spirit, force of life, living force, *vis vitae* or *vis vitalis* <both L>, **vital force** or energy, animating force or power or principle, inspiriting force or power or principle, archeus, élan vital, impulse of life, vital principle, **vital spark** or **flame,** spark of life, divine spark, life principle, vital spirit, vital fluid, anima; **breath,** life breath, **breath of life,** breath of one's nostrils, divine breath, life essence, essence of life, pneuma; prana, atman, jivatma, jiva; blood, **lifeblood,** heartblood, heart's blood; **heart,** heartbeat, beating heart; seat of life; growth force, bathmism; **life process;** biorhythm, biological clock, life cycle

4 **the living,** the living and breathing, all animate nature, the quick; the quick and the dead

5 vivification, vitalization, animation, quickening

6 biosphere, ecosphere, noosphere; biochore, biotype, biocycle

VERBS 7 **live,** be alive or animate or vital, have life, exist 760.8, breathe, respire, live and breathe, fetch or draw breath, draw the breath of life, walk the earth, subsist

8 **come to life,** come into existence or being, come into the world, see the light, be incarnated, **be born** or begotten or conceived; quicken; **revive, come to,** come alive, show signs of life; **awake, awaken;** rise again, live again, rise from the grave, resurge, resuscitate, reanimate, return to life

9 **vivify, vitalize, energize, animate, quicken,** inspirit, imbue or endow with life, give life to, put life or new life into, breathe life into, bring to life, bring or call into existence or being; conceive; give birth

10 **keep alive,** keep body and soul together,

endure, survive, persist, last, last out, hang on, hang in <nonformal>, be spared, have nine lives like a cat; support life; cheat death

ADJS **11 living, alive,** having life, live, very much alive, alive and well, alive and kicking <nonformal>, conscious, breathing, quick <old>, **animate,** animated, **vital,** zoetic, instinct with life, imbued or endowed with life, vivified, enlivened, inspirited; in the flesh, among the living, in the land of the living, on this side of the grave, above-ground; existent 760.13; long-lived, tenacious of life; capable of life or survival, viable

12 life-giving, animating, animative, quickening, vivifying, energizing

307 DEATH

NOUNS **1 death, dying,** somatic death, clinical death, biological death, abiosis, **decease, demise;** brain death; perishing, release, **passing away,** passing, passing over, "crossing the bar"—Tennyson, leaving life, making an end, departure, parting, going, going off or away, exit, ending, **end** 819, end of life, cessation of life, end of the road or line <nonformal>; **loss of life,** ebb of life, expiration, **dissolution, extinction,** bane, annihilation, extinguishment, quietus; doom, summons of death, final summons, sentence of death, death knell, knell; **sleep, rest,** eternal rest or sleep, last sleep, last rest; **grave** 309.16; reward, debt of nature, last debt; last muster, last roundup, curtains <nonformal>; jaws of death, hand or finger of death, shadow or shades of death; rigor mortis; near-death experience or NDE

2 "the journey's end, "the undiscovered country from whose bourn no traveler returns, "dusty death"—all Shakespeare, "that dreamless sleep"—Byron, "a debt we all must pay"—Euripides, "the tribute due unto nature"—Laurence Sterne, "the sleeping partner of life"—Horace Smith, "a knell that summons thee to heaven or to hell, "that fell arrest without all bail"—both Shakespeare, "kind Nature's signal of retreat"—Samuel Johnson, "the latter end, "a little sleep, a little slumber, a little folding of the hands to sleep"—both Bible, "the seamouth of mortality"—Robinson Jeffers, "that good night"—Dylan Thomas, "the downward path"—Horace, "the gate of life"—St Bernard, "the crown of life"—Edward

Young, "an awfully big adventure"—J M Barrie; "the big sleep"—Raymond Chandler

3 <personifications and symbols> **Death,** "Black Death"—Ovid, "Pale Death"—Horace, "the pale priest of the mute people"—R Browning, "that grim ferryman, "that fell sergeant"—both Shakespeare, "Hell's grim Tyrant"—Pope, "the king of terrors"—Bible, **Grim Reaper,** Reaper; pale horse, pale rider; angel of death, death's bright angel, Azrael; scythe or sickle of Death; **skull,** death's-head, grinning skull, crossbones, skull and crossbones; *memento mori* <L>; white cross

4 river of death, Styx, Stygian shore, Acheron; Jordan, Jordan's bank; "valley of the shadow of death"—Bible; Heaven 681; Hell 682

5 early death, early grave, **untimely end,** premature death; sudden death; stroke of death, death stroke; deathblow

6 violent death; killing 308; suffocation, smothering, smotheration <nonformal>; asphyxiation; choking, choke, strangulation, strangling; drowning, watery grave; starvation; liver death, serum death; megadeath

7 natural death; easy or quiet or peaceful death or end, euthanasia, blessed or welcome release

8 dying day, deathday, "the supreme day and the inevitable hour"—Vergil; final or fatal hour, dying hour, running-out of the sands, deathtime

9 moribundity, extremity, last or final extremity; **deathbed;** deathwatch; death struggle, agony, last agony, death agony, death throes, throes of death; last breath or gasp, dying breath; **death rattle,** death groan

10 swan song, *chant du cygne* <Fr>, death song

11 bereavement 473.1

12 deathliness, deathlikeness, deadliness; **weirdness, eeriness, uncanniness,** unearthliness; ghostliness, ghostlikeness; **ghastliness, grisliness, gruesomeness,** macabreness; paleness, haggardness, wanness, luridness, pallor; cadaverousness, corpselikeness; *facies Hippocratica* <L>, Hippocratic face or countenance, mask of death

13 death rate, death toll; **mortality,** mortalness; transience 827; mutability 853.1

14 obituary, obit <nonformal>, necrology, necrologue; register of deaths, roll of the dead, death roll, mortuary roll, bill of mortality; casualty list; martyrology; death toll, body count

15 terminal case; **dying**

16 **corpse,** dead body, dead man *or* woman, dead person, **cadaver, carcass, body; corpus delicti** <L>; **stiff** <nonformal>; **the dead,** the defunct, **the deceased,** the departed, the loved one; **decedent,** late lamented; **remains,** mortal *or* organic remains, bones, skeleton, dry bones, relics, reliquiae; dust, ashes, earth, clay, tenement of clay; **carrion,** crowbait, food for worms; **mummy,** mummification; embalmed corpse

17 **dead,** the majority, the great majority; one's fathers, one's ancestors; the choir invisible

18 **autopsy, postmortem, inquest,** postmortem examination, ex post facto examination, necropsy, necroscopy, medical examiner, coroner, mortality committee

VERBS 19 **die, decease, succumb, expire, perish,** be taken by death, up and die <nonformal>, cease to be *or* live, part, depart, quit this world, make one's exit, go, go the way of all flesh, go out, pass, pass on *or* over, **pass away, meet one's death** *or* **end** *or* **fate,** end one's life *or* days, depart this life, "shuffle off this mortal coil"—Shakespeare, put off mortality, **lose one's life,** fall, be lost, relinquish *or* surrender one's life, resign one's life *or* being, **give up the ghost,** yield the ghost *or* spirit, yield one's breath, take one's last breath, breathe one's last, stop breathing, fall asleep, close one's eyes, take one's last sleep, pay the debt of *or* to nature, go out with the ebb, "go the way of all earth"—Bible, return to dust *or* the earth

20 <nonformal terms> **croak,** go west, kick the bucket, kick in, pop off, conk off, conk out, cop it, drop off, step off, go to the wall, go home feet first, knock off, pipe off, kick off, shove off, bow out, pass out, peg out, push up daisies, go for a burton <Brit>, belly up, go belly up, bite the dust, take the last count; check out, check in, cash in, hand *or* pass *or* cash in one's checks *or* chips; turn up one's toes; slip one's cable; buy the farm *or* the ranch, farm, have one's time *and* have it *and* buy it <all Brit>

21 **meet one's Maker,** go to glory, go to kingdom come <nonformal>, go to the happy hunting grounds, go to *or* reach a better place *or* land *or* life *or* world, go to one's rest *or* reward, go home, go home feet first <nonformal>, go to one's last home, go to one's long account, go over to *or* join the majority *or* great majority, **be gathered to one's fathers,** join one's ancestors, join the angels, join the choir invisible, die in the Lord, go to Abraham's bosom, pass over Jordan, "walk through the valley of the shadow of death"—Bible, cross the Stygian ferry, give an obolus to Charon; awake to life immortal, "put on immortality"—Bible

22 **drop dead, fall dead,** fall down dead; come to an untimely end; predecease

23 die in harness, die with one's boots on, make a good end, die fighting, die in the last ditch, die like a man

24 die a natural death; die a violent death, be killed; **starve,** famish; smother, **suffocate;** asphyxiate; choke, strangle; **drown,** go to a watery grave, go to Davy Jones's locker <nonformal>; catch one's death, catch one's death of cold

25 **lay down** *or* **give one's life for one's country, die for one's country,** "*pro patria mori*"—Horace, make the supreme sacrifice, do one's bit

26 be dying, be moribund, be terminal; die out, become extinct

27 be dead, be no more, sleep *or* be asleep with the Lord, sleep with one's fathers *or* ancestors; lie in the grave, lie in Abraham's bosom <nonformal>

28 **bereave;** leave, leave behind; orphan, widow

ADJS 29 **deathly, deathlike,** deadly; **weird, eerie, uncanny,** unearthly; ghostly, ghostlike; **ghastly, grisly, gruesome, macabre;** pale, deathly pale, wan, lurid, blue, livid, haggard; **cadaverous,** corpselike; mortuary

30 **dead, lifeless,** breathless, without life, inanimate 1053.5, exanimate, without vital functions; **deceased, demised, defunct,** croaked <nonformal>, departed, departed this life, destitute of life, **gone, passed on,** gone the way of all flesh, gone west <nonformal>, dead and gone, done for <nonformal>, dead and done for <nonformal>, no more, finished <nonformal>, taken off *or* away, released, fallen, bereft of life, gone for a burton <Brit nonformal>; **at rest,** resting easy <nonformal>, still, out of one's misery; **asleep,** sleeping, reposing; asleep in Jesus, with the Lord, asleep *or* dead in the Lord; **called home,** out of the world, gone to a better world *or* place *or* land, launched into eternity, gone to glory, joined the choir invisible, gone to king-

dom come <nonformal>, "gathered to his fathers"—Bible, with the saints, sainted, numbered with the dead; in the grave, six feet under *and* pushing up daisies <both nonformal>; carrion, food for worms; martyred; death-struck, death-stricken, smitten with death; stillborn; late, late lamented

31 stone-dead; dead as a doornail *and* dead as a dodo *and* dead as a herring *and* dead as mutton <all nonformal>; cold, stone-cold, "as cold as any stone"—Shakespeare, stiff <nonformal>

32 drowned, in a watery grave *or* bier, in Davy Jones's locker

33 dying, terminal, expiring, going, slipping, slipping away, sinking, sinking fast, low, despaired of, given up, given up for dead, not long for this world, hopeless, bad, **moribund,** near death, near one's end, at the end of one's rope <nonformal>, done for <nonformal>, at the point of death, **at death's door,** at the portals of death, *in articulo mortis* <L>, *in extremis* <L>, in the jaws of death, facing *or* in the face of death; **on one's last legs** <nonformal>, with one foot in the grave, tottering on the brink of the grave; on one's deathbed; at the last gasp; terminal; nonviable, unviable, incapable of life

34 mortal, perishable, subject to death, ephemeral, transient 827.7, mutable 853.6

35 bereaved, bereft, deprived; widowed; orphan, **orphaned,** parentless, fatherless, motherless

36 postmortem, postmortal, postmortuary, postmundane, post-obit, postobituary, **posthumous**

ADVS **37 deathly, deadly;** to the death, *à la mort* <Fr>

PHRS **38** one's hour is come, one's days are numbered, one's race is run, one's doom is sealed, life hangs by a thread, one's number is up, Death knocks at the door, Death stares one in the face, the sands of life are running out

308 KILLING

NOUNS **1 killing** <see list>, **slaying, slaughter, dispatch, extermination, destruction,** destruction of life, taking of life, death-dealing, dealing of death, bane; kill; **bloodshed,** bloodletting, blood, gore, flow of blood; mercy killing, euthanasia, negative *or* passive euthanasia; ritual murder *or* killing, immolation, sacrifice; *auto-da-fé* <Sp, literally, act of faith>, martyr-

dom, martyrization; lynching; stoning, lapidation; defenestration; braining; shooting; poisoning; execution 604.7; mass killing, biocide, ecocide, genocide; Holocaust; mass murder

2 homicide, manslaughter; negligent homicide; murder, bloody murder <nonformal>; serial killing; hit *and* bump-off *and* bumping-off <all nonformal>, gangland-style execution; kiss of death; foul play; **assassination;** removal, elimination; liquidation, purge, purging; thuggery, thuggism, thuggee; justifiable homicide

3 butchery, butchering, **slaughter,** shambles, occision, slaughtering, hecatomb, holocaust

4 carnage, massacre, bloodbath, decimation, saturnalia of blood; **mass murder, mass destruction,** mass extermination, wholesale murder, pogrom, race-murder, genocide, race extermination, **the Holocaust,** the final solution

5 suicide, autocide, self-murder, self-homicide, self-destruction, death by one's own hand, *felo-de-se* <L>, self-immolation, self-sacrifice; **disembowelment,** ritual suicide, *hara-kiri, seppuku* <both Jap>, suttee, sutteeism; car of Jagannath *or* Juggernaut; mass suicide, race suicide

6 suffocation, smothering, smotheration <nonformal>, **asphyxiation,** asphyxia; **strangulation,** strangling, burking, throttling, stifling, garrote, garroting; **choking,** choke; **drowning**

7 fatality, fatal accident, violent death, **casualty,** disaster, calamity; DOA *or* dead-on-arrival

8 deadliness, lethality, mortality, fatality; **malignance** *or* malignancy, malignity, **virulence, perniciousness,** banefulness

9 deathblow, death stroke, final stroke, fatal *or* mortal *or* lethal blow, *coup de grâce* <Fr>

10 killer, slayer, slaughterer, butcher, bloodshedder; massacrer; **manslayer, homicide, murderer,** man-killer, blood-letter, Cain; **assassin,** assassinator; **cutthroat,** thug, desperado, bravo, gorilla <nonformal>, apache, gunman; professional killer, hired killer, hit man *or* button man *or* gun *or* trigger man *or* torpedo *or* gunsel <all nonformal>; **hatchet man;** poisoner; strangler, garroter, burker; cannibal, maneater, anthropophagus; headhunter; mercy killer; thrill killer, homicidal maniac; serial killer; executioner 604.8; matador; exterminator, eradicator; death squad; poison, pesticide 1000.3

11 <place of slaughter> aceldama, field of blood *or* bloodshed; **slaughterhouse,** butchery <Brit>, shambles, abattoir; stockyard; gas chamber, concentration camp, death camp, killing fields; Auschwitz, Belsen, etc

VERBS **12 kill, slay, put to death,** deprive of life, bereave of life, **take life,** take the life of, take one's life away, **do away with,** make away with, **put out of the way,** put to sleep, end, **put an end to,** end the life of, **dispatch, do to death,** do for, finish, finish off, kill off, take off, **dispose of, exterminate, destroy,** annihilate; **liquidate,** purge; carry off *or* away, remove from life; put down, put away, put one out of one's misery; launch into eternity, send to glory, send to kingdom come <nonformal>, send to one's last account; **martyr,** martyrize; immolate, sacrifice; lynch; cut off, cut down, nip in the bud; poison; chloroform; starve; euthanatize; **execute**

13 <nonformal terms> **waste, zap,** nuke, rub out, croak, snuff, bump off, knock off, bushwhack, lay out, polish off, blow away, blot out, erase, wipe out, blast, do in, off, hit, ice, gun down, pick off, put to bed with a shovel, scrag, take care of, take out, take for a ride, give the business *or* works, get, fix, settle

14 shed blood, spill blood, let blood, bloody one's hands with, dye one's hands in blood, have blood on one's hands, pour out blood like water, wade knee-deep in blood

15 murder, commit murder; **assassinate;** remove, **purge, liquidate,** eliminate, get rid of

16 slaughter, butcher, massacre, decimate, commit carnage, depopulate, murder *or* kill *or* slay en masse; commit mass murder *or* destruction, murder wholesale, commit genocide

17 strike dead, fell, bring down, lay low; drop, drop *or* stop in one's tracks; **shoot,** shoot down, pistol, shotgun, machinegun, gun down, riddle, shoot to death; cut down, cut to pieces *or* ribbons, **put to the sword,** stab to death, jugulate, cut *or* slash the throat; **deal a deathblow,** give the quietus *or coup de grâce* <Fr>, silence; knock in *or* on the head; **brain,** blow *or* knock *or* dash one's brains out, poleax; **stone,** lapidate, stone to death; defenestrate; blow up, blow to bits *or* pieces *or* kingdom come, frag; disinte-

grate, vaporize; burn to death, incinerate, burn at the stake

18 strangle, garrote, **throttle, choke,** burke; **suffocate, stifle, smother, asphyxiate,** stop the breath; **drown**

19 condemn to death, sign one's death warrant, strike the death knell of, finger <nonformal>, give the kiss of death to

20 be killed, get killed, die a violent death, **come to a violent end,** meet with foul play; welter in one's own blood

21 commit suicide, take one's own life, kill oneself, die by one's own hand, do away with oneself, put an end to oneself; blow one's brains out, take an overdose <of a drug>, overdose *or* OD <nonformal>; commit hara-kiri *or* seppuku; sign one's own death warrant, doom oneself

ADJS **22 deadly, deathly,** deathful, **killing, destructive,** death-dealing, deathbringing, feral <old>; savage, brutal; internecine; **fatal, mortal, lethal, malignant,** malign, **virulent, pernicious,** baneful; **life-threatening, terminal**

23 murderous, slaughterous; cutthroat; redhanded; **homicidal,** man-killing, deathdealing; biocidal, genocidal; suicidal, self-destructive; soul-destroying; cruel; **bloodthirsty,** bloody-minded; **bloody, gory,** sanguinary

24 types of killing and killers

aborticide *or* feticide <fetus>	ovicide <sheep>
amicicide <friend>	parenticide <parent>
ceticide <whales>	parricide <kinsman>
deicide <god>	patricide <father>
elephanticide <elephants>	pesticide <pest>
formicicide <ants>	regicide <king>
fratricide <brother>	rodenticide <rodent>
fungicide <fungi>	sororicide <sister>
genocide <race>	spermicide *or* spermatozoicide <spermatozoa>
giganticide <giant>	
gynecide *or* femicide <woman>	suicide *or* autocide <self>
herbicide <plants>	
homicide <person>	tauricide <bulls>
infanticide <infant>	tickicide <ticks>
insecticide <insects>	tyrannicide <tyrant>
mariticide <spouse, especially husband>	uxoricide <wife>
	vaticide <prophet>
matricide <mother>	vermicide *or* filaricide <worms>
microbicide *or* germicide <germs>	vespacide <wasps>
	viricide <viruses>

309 INTERMENT

NOUNS **1 interment, burial,** burying, inhumation, sepulture, **entombment;** encoffinment, inurning, inurnment, urn burial; primary burial; secondary burial, reburial; disposal of the dead; burial *or* funeral *or* funerary customs

2 **cremation, incineration, burning,** reduction to ashes

3 **embalmment,** embalming; mummification

4 **last offices,** last honors, **last rites,** funeral rites, last duty *or* service, funeral service, burial service, exequies, **obsequies;** Office of the Dead, Memento of the Dead, requiem, requiem mass, dirge <old>; **extreme unction;** viaticum; funeral oration *or* sermon, eulogy; **wake,** deathwatch

5 **funeral, burial,** burying; funeral procession, cortege; dead march, muffled drum, last post <Brit>, taps; dirge; burial at sea, deep six <nonformal>

6 **knell,** passing bell, death bell, funeral ring, tolling, tolling of the knell

7 **mourner, griever, lamenter,** keener; mute, professional mourner; **pallbearer,** bearer

8 **undertaker, mortician,** funeral director; embalmer; gravedigger; sexton

9 **mortuary, morgue,** deadhouse <old>, charnel house, lichhouse <Brit nonformal>; ossuary *or* ossuarium; **funeral home** *or* **parlor,** undertaker's establishment; **crematorium,** crematory, cinerarium; pyre, funeral pile; burning ghat

10 **hearse,** funeral car *or* coach; catafalque

11 **coffin, casket,** burial case, box, kist <Scots>; wooden kimono *or* overcoat <nonformal>; **sarcophagus;** mummy case

12 **urn,** cinerary urn, funerary *or* funeral urn *or* vessel, bone pot, ossuary *or* ossuarium

13 **bier,** litter

14 **graveclothes, shroud,** winding sheet, cerecloth, cerements; pall

15 **graveyard, cemetery, burial ground** *or* **place,** burying place *or* ground, *campo santo* <Ital>, boneyard *and* bone orchard <both nonformal>, burial yard, necropolis, polyandrium, **memorial park,** city *or* village of the dead; **churchyard,** God's acre; **potter's field;** Golgotha, Calvary; urnfield; lych-gate

16 **tomb, sepulcher; grave,** gravesite, burial, pit, deep six <nonformal>; resting place, "the lone couch of his everlasting sleep"—Shelley; last home, long home, narrow house, house of death, low house, low green tent; **crypt, vault,** burial chamber; ossuary *or* ossuarium; charnel house, bone house; **mausoleum; catacombs;** mastaba; cist grave, box grave, passage grave, shaft grave, beehive tomb; **shrine,** reliquary, monstrance, tope, stupa; cenotaph; dokhma, tower of silence; pyramid, mummy chamber; burial mound, tumulus, barrow, cist, cromlech, dolmen

17 monument, gravestone 549.12

18 **epitaph,** inscription, *hic jacet* <L>, tombstone marking

VERBS 19 **inter,** inhume, **bury,** sepulture, in-earth <old>, **lay to rest, consign to the grave,** lay in the grave *or* earth, lay under the sod, put six feet under <nonformal>; **tomb, entomb,** ensepulcher, hearse; enshrine; inurn; encoffin, coffin; hold *or* conduct a funeral

20 **cremate, incinerate, burn,** reduce to ashes

21 **lay out; embalm; mummify;** lie in state

ADJS 22 **funereal,** funeral, funerary, funebrial, funebrous *or* funebrious, *funèbre* <Fr>, feral <old>; mortuary, exequial, obsequial; graveside; sepulchral, tomblike; cinerary; necrological, obituary, epitaphic; **dismal** 112.24; **mournful** 112.26; dirgelike

ADVS 23 beneath the sod, underground, six feet under <nonformal>, "in the dark union of insensate dust"—Byron; at rest, resting in peace

PHRS 24 **RIP,** *requiescat in pace* <L singular>, *requiescant in pace* <L plural>, rest in peace; *hic jacet* <L>, *ci-gît* <Fr>, here lies; ashes to ashes and dust to dust—Book of Common Prayer

310 PLANTS

NOUNS 1 **plants, vegetation; flora, plant life,** vegetable life; **vegetable kingdom,** plant kingdom; herbage, flowerage, verdure, greenery, greens; botany 1,5,6,7; vegetation spirit 1067.4

2 **growth,** stand, crop; plantation, planting; **clump,** tuft, tussock, hassock

3 **plant; vegetable; weed;** seedling; cutting; vascular plant; seed plant, spermatophyte; gymnosperm; angiosperm, flowering plant; monocotyledon *or* monocot *or* monocotyl; dicotyledon *or* dicot *or* dicotyl; polycotyledon *or* polycot *or* polycotyl; thallophyte, fungus; gametophyte, sporophyte; exotic, hothouse plant; ephemeral, annual, biennial, triennial, perennial; evergreen, deciduous plant; cosmopolite; aquatic plant, hydrophyte, amphibian

4 <varieties> **legume,** pulse, vetch, bean, pea, lentil; **herb** <see list>, pot-herb; succulent; **vine** <see list>, grapevine, creeper, ivy, climber, liana; **fern** <see list>, bracken; **moss; wort,** liverwort; **algae; seaweed,** kelp, sea moss, rockweed, gulfweed, sargasso *or* sargassum, sea lentil, wrack, sea wrack; **fungus,** mold, rust, smut, puffball, mushroom, toad-stool; lichen; parasitic plant, parasite, saprophyte, perthophyte, heterophyte, autophyte; plant families 1066.3; fruits and vegetables

5 **grass,** gramineous *or* graminaceous plant, pasture *or* forage grass, lawn grass, ornamental grass; aftergrass, fog <nonformal>; **cereal,** cereal plant, farinaceous plant, **grain,** corn <Brit>; sedge; rush, reed, cane, bamboo

6 **turf, sod, sward,** greensward; divot

7 **green, lawn;** artificial turf, Astroturf <trademark>; grassplot, greenyard; grounds; **common, park, village green;** golf course *or* links, fairway; bowling green, putting green; grass court

8 **grassland,** grass; parkland; **meadow,** meadow land, mead <old>, swale, lea, haugh *or* haughland <Scots>, vega; bottomland, water meadow; **pasture,** pastureland, pasturage, pasture land, park <Brit nonformal>; **range,** grazing, grazing land; **prairie, savanna, steppe,** steppeland, **pampas,** pampa, campo, llano, **veld,** grass veld

9 **shrubbery; shrub, bush;** scrub, bramble, brier, brier bush; topiary

10 **tree** <see list>, timber; shade tree, fruit tree, timber tree; softwood tree, hardwood tree; sapling, seedling; conifer, evergreen; pollard, pollarded tree

11 **woodland, wood, woods, timberland; timber,** stand of timber, **forest,** forest land, forest cover, forest preserve, state *or* national forest; forestry, dendrology, silviculture; afforestation, reforestation; boondocks <nonformal>; wildwood, **bush,** scrub; bushveld, tree veld; shrubland, scrubland; pine barrens, palmetto barrens; hanger; **park,** parkland, chase <Brit>; park forest; arboretum

12 **grove, woodlet; holt** <nonformal>, hurst, spinney <Brit>, tope <India>, shaw <nonformal>, bosk <old>; **orchard;** wood lot; coppice, copse; *bocage* <Fr>

13 **thicket,** thickset, **copse, coppice,** copsewood, frith <Brit nonformal>; bosket <old>, boscage; covert; motte; **brake,** canebrake; chaparral; chamisal; ceja

14 **brush, scrub,** bush, **brushwood,** shrubwood, scrubwood

15 **undergrowth, underwood, underbrush,** copsewood, undershrubs, boscage, frith <Brit nonformal>; ground cover

16 **foliage, leafage,** leafiness, umbrage, foliation; frondage, frondescence; vernation

17 **leaf, frond;** leaflet, foliole; ligule; lamina, **blade,** spear, spire, pile, flag; **needle,** pine needle; floral leaf, **petal,** sepal; bract, bractlet, bracteole, spathe, involucre, involucrum, glume, lemma; cotyledon, seed leaf; stipule, stipula

18 **branch,** fork, **limb, bough;** deadwood; **twig, sprig,** switch; spray; **shoot,** offshoot, spear, frond; scion; **sprout,** sprit, slip, burgeon, thallus; sucker; **runner,** stolon, flagellum, sarmentum, sarment; bine; **tendril;** ramage; branchiness, branchedness, ramification

19 **stem, stalk, stock,** axis, *caulis* <L>; **trunk,** bole; spear, spire; straw; reed; cane; culm, haulm <Brit>; caudex; footstalk, pedicel, peduncle; leafstalk, petiole, petiolus, petiolule; seedstalk; caulicle; tigella; funicule, funiculus; stipe, anthrophore, carpophore, gynophore

20 **root,** radix, radicle; rootlet; **taproot,** tap; **rhizome,** rootstock; **tuber,** tubercle; **bulb,** bulbil, corm, earthnut

21 **bud,** burgeon, gemma; gemmule, gemmula; plumule, acrospire; leaf bud, flower bud

22 **flower** <see list>, **posy, blossom, bloom,** blow <old>; floweret, floret, floscule; **wildflower; gardening,** horticulture, floriculture; hortorium

23 **bouquet, nosegay, posy,** boughpot, flower arrangement; **boutonniere,** buttonhole <Brit>; **corsage; spray; wreath;** festoon; **garland,** chaplet, lei

24 **flowering,** florescence, efflorescence, flowerage, **blossoming, blooming;** inflorescence; **blossom, bloom,** blowing, blow; unfolding, unfoldment; anthesis, full bloom

25 <types of inflorescence> raceme, corymb, umbel, panicle, cyme, thyrse, spadix, verticillaster; head, capitulum; spike, spikelet; ament, catkin; strobile, cone, pine cone

26 <flower parts> petal, perianth; calyx, epicalyx; corolla, corolla tube, corona; androecium, anther, stamen, microsporophyll; pistil, gynoecium; style; stigma, carpel, megasporophyll; receptacle, torus

27 **ear,** spike; auricle; ear of corn, mealie; **cob,** corncob

28 **seed vessel, seedcase,** seedbox, pericarp; hull, husk; **capsule, pod,** cod <nonformal>, seed pod; pease cod, legume, legumen, boll, burr, follicle, silique

29 **seed; stone, pit, nut;** pip; fruit; **grain, kernel, berry;** flaxseed, linseed; hayseed; bird seed

30 **vegetation, growth;** germination, pullulation; burgeoning, sprouting; budding, luxuriation

VERBS 31 **vegetate, grow;** germinate, pullulate; root, take root, strike root; sprout up, shoot up, upsprout, upspear; **burgeon,** put forth, burst forth; **sprout,** shoot; **bud,** gemmate, put forth or put out buds; **leaf,** leave, leaf out, put out or put forth leaves; flourish, luxuriate, riot, grow rank or lush; overgrow, overrun

32 **flower,** be in flower, **blossom, bloom,** be in bloom, blow, effloresce, floreate, burst into bloom

ADJS 33 **vegetable,** vegetal, vegetative, vegetational, vegetarian; **plantlike; herbaceous,** herbal, herbous, herbose, herby; leguminous, leguminose, leguminiform; cereal, farinaceous; weedy; fruity, fruitlike; tuberous, bulbous; rootlike, rhizoid, radicular, radicated, radiciform; botanic, botanical

34 algal, fucoid, confervoid; phytoplanktonic, diatomaceous; fungous, fungoid, fungiform

35 **floral; flowery, florid** <old>; **flowered,** floreate, floriate, floriated; **flowering, blossoming, blooming,** abloom, bloomy, florescent, inflorescent, efflorescent, in flower, in bloom, in blossom; uniflorous, multiflorous; radiciflorous, rhizanthous; **garden,** horticultural, hortulan, floricultural

36 **arboreal,** arborical, arboresque, arboreous, arborary; **treelike,** arboriform, arborescent, dendroid, dendriform, dendritic; deciduous, nondeciduous; evergreen; softwood, hardwood; piny; coniferous; citrous; **bosky,** bushy, shrubby, scrubby, scrubbly; bushlike, shrublike, scrublike

37 **sylvan, woodland, forest,** forestal; dendrologic, dendrological, silvicultural, afforestational, reforestational; **wooded,** timbered, forested, arboreous; **woody,** woodsy, bosky, bushy, shrubby, scrubby; copsy, braky

38 **leafy,** leavy <old>, bowery; foliated, foliate, foliose, foliaged, leaved; **branched,** branchy, branching, ramified, ramate, ramous or ramose; twiggy

39 **verdant, verdurous,** verdured; **mossy,** moss-covered, moss-grown; **grassy,** grasslike, gramineous, graminaceous; turfy, swardy, turflike, caespitose, tufted; meadowy

40 **luxuriant,** flourishing, **rank, lush,** riotous, exuberant; dense, impenetrable, thick, heavy, gross; jungly, jungled; overgrown, overrun; **weedy,** unweeded, weed-choked, weed-ridden; gone to seed

41 **perennial,** ephemeral; hardy, half-hardy; **deciduous,** evergreen

42 **herbs**

angelica	horehound
anise	hyssop
balm	licorice
basil	liverwort
belladonna	mandrake
boneset	marijuana
borage	marjoram
burning bush	mayapple
calendula	mint
camomile	monkshood
caraway	mullein
cardamom	mustard
castor-oil plant	oregano or origanum
catnip or catmint	parsley
chervil	peppermint
chicory	rosemary
clover	rue
coriander	sage
Cretan dittany	savory
deadly nightshade	sorrel
death camas	spearmint
dill	sweet cicely
dittany	sweet woodruff
fennel	tansy
feverroot	tarragon
figwort	thyme
fraxinella or gas plant	tobacco
ginseng	wall rue
hemp	wild marjoram
henbane	wintergreen

43 **vines**

bittersweet	morning glory
clematis	poison ivy
dewberry	travellers joy
English ivy	trumpet creeper
grape	trumpet flower
greenbrier	trumpet honeysuckle
honeysuckle	Virginia creeper
hop	virgins-bower
ivy	wisteria
jasmine	woodbine
liana	

44 **ferns**

adder's fern	bladder fern
basket fern	boulder fern
beech fern	bracken

chain fern
cliff brake
climbing fern
curly grass
grape fern
hart's tongue
holly fern
lady fern
lip fern
maidenhair
marsh fern
moonwort

oak fern
osmunda
ostrich fern
rattlesnake fern
rock brake
shield fern
snuffbox fern
tree fern
walking fern
wall fern
wood fern
woodsia

45 trees

acacia
abele
ailanthus *or* tree of
 heaven
alder
allspice
almond
apple
apricot
ash
aspen
avocado *or* alligator
 pear
bald cypress
balsa
balsam
banyan
basswood
bay
bayberry
beech
betel palm
birch
boxwood
Brazil-nut
breadfruit
buckeye
butternut
buttonwood
cacao
camphor tree
candleberry
cashew
cassia
catalpa
cedar
cherry
chestnut
chinaberry tree *or*
 China tree
chinquapin
cinnamon
citron
clove
coconut *or* coco
cork oak
cottonwood
cypress
date palm

dogwood
ebony
elder
elm
eucalyptus
ficus
fig
fir
frankincense
ginkgo
grapefruit
guava
gum
hawthorn
hazel *or* hazelnut
hemlock
henna
hickory
holly
hop tree
hornbeam
horse chestnut
ironwood
juniper
kumquat
laburnum
lancewood
larch
laurel
lemon
lignum vitae
lime
linden
litchi *or* litchi nut
locust
logwood
madroña
magnolia
mahogany
mango
mangrove
maple
medlar
mimosa
monkey puzzle
mountain ash
mulberry
nutmeg
nux vomica

oak
olive
orange
osier
palm
papaw
papaya
peach
pear
pecan
persimmon
pine
pistachio
pitch pine
plane
plum
pomegranate
poplar
quince
raffia palm
rain tree
redwood
rosewood
rubber plant
sandalwood
sassafras
satinwood
senna
sequoia
serviceberry
silk oak
silver birch
spruce
sycamore
tamarack
tamarind
tamarugo
tangerine

46 flowers

acacia
African violet
amaryllis
anemone *or* wind-
 flower
arbutus
arrowhead
asphodel
aster
azalea
baby's breath
baby-blue-eyes
bachelor button
begonia
bitterroot
black-eyed Susan
bleeding heart
bloodroot
bluebell
bluet
bridal wreath
broom
buttercup

teak
thorn tree
thuja
torchwood
trembling poplar
tulip oak
tulip tree
turpentine tree
umbrella tree
upas
varnish tree
walnut
wandoo
wax palm
wax tree
wayfaring tree
weeping willow
western hemlock
white birch
white cedar
white gum
white oak
white pine
white poplar
white spruce
whitebeam
whitethorn
wicopy
willow
witch hazel
woollybutt
wychelm
yellow poplar
yellowwood *or* go-
 pher wood
yew
ylang-ylang
zebrawood

cactus
calendula
camas
camellia
camomile
campanula
candytuft
carnation
cat's-paw
cattail
century plant
Chinese lantern
Christmas rose
chrysanthemum
cineraria
clematis
clethra
cockscomb
columbine
cornel
cornflower
cosmos
cowslip

crocus
cyclamen
daffodil
dahlia
daisy
damask rose
dandelion
delphinium
dogwood
duckweed
Dutchman's-breeches
edelweiss
eglantine
elderflower
fireweed
flax
fleur-de-lis <Fr>
forget-me-not
forsythia
foxglove
foxtail
freesia
fuchsia
gardenia
gentian
geranium
gladiolus
goldenrod
groundsel
guelder rose
harebell
hawthorn
heather
hepatica
hibiscus
hollyhock
honeysuckle
horehound
hyacinth
hydrangea
impatience
Indian paintbrush
indigo
iris
jack-in-the-pulpit
japonica
jasmine
jonquil
kingcup
knotweed
lady's-slipper
larkspur
lavender
lilac
lily
lily of the valley
lobelia
lotus
love-lies-bleeding
lupine
magnolia
mallow
marguerite

marigold
marsh marigold
marshmallow
mayflower
Michaelmas daisy
mignonette
mimosa
moccasin flower
mock orange
monkshood
morning-glory
moss rose
motherwort
myrtle
narcissus
nasturtium
oleander
opium poppy
orchid
oxalis
oxeye daisy
pansy
passion flower
peony
periwinkle
petunia
phlox
pink
poinsettia
polyanthus
poppy
portulaca
primrose
primula
Queen Anne's lace
ragged robin
ragwort
rambler rose
ranunculus
resurrection plant
rhododendron
rose
shooting star
smilax
snapdragon
snowball
snowberry
snowdrop
spiraea
stock
strawflower
sunflower
sweet alyssum
sweet pea
sweet william
tick trefoil
tiger lily
trailing arbutus
trillium
trumpet vine
tulip
twayblade
twinflower

umbrella plant
valerian
Venus's flytrap
verbena
vetch
viburnum
viola
violet
wake-robin
wallflower
water hyacinth
water lily
water milfoil

water pimpernel
wax flower
waxplant
white clover
wisteria
wolfbane
wood anemone
wood hyacinth
woody nightshade
yarrow
yellow water lily
yucca
zinnia

311 ANIMALS, INSECTS

NOUNS **1 animal life, animal kingdom,**
brute creation, **fauna,** Animalia <zo-
ology>, animality; animal behavior, biology ; birds, beasts, and fish; the beasts of
the field, the fowl of the air, and the fish of
the sea; domestic animals, livestock,
stock <nonformal>, cattle; wild animals
or beasts, beasts of field, wildlife, denizens of the forest or jungle or wild, furry
creatures; predators, beasts of prey;
game, big game, small game

2 animal, creature, critter <nonformal>,
living being or thing, creeping thing;
brute, beast, varmint <nonformal>,
dumb animal or creature, dumb friend

3 <varieties> **vertebrate; invertebrate; biped, quadruped; mammal,** mammalian
primate <see list>; **marsupial,** marsu-
pialian; canine; **feline; rodent,** gnawer;
ungulate; ruminant; insectivore, herbivore, carnivore, omnivore; cannibal;
scavenger; reptile; amphibian; aquatic;
cosmopolite; vermin, varmint <nonfor-
mal>

4 pachyderm; elephant, Jumbo, hathi
<India>, "heffalump"—A A Milne;
mammoth, woolly mammoth; mastodon;
rhinoceros, rhino; **hippopotamus,** hippo,
river horse

5 <hoofed animals> **deer, buck, doe, fawn;**
red deer, **stag,** hart, hind; roe deer, roe,
roebuck; musk deer; fallow deer; hog-
deer; white-tailed or Virginia deer; mule
deer; **elk,** wapiti; **moose; reindeer,** car-
ibou; deerlet; **antelope;** gazelle, kaama,
wildebeest or gnu, hartebeest, springbok,
reebok, dik-dik, eland or Cape elk, koo-
doo; **camel,** dromedary, ship of the
desert; **giraffe,** camelopard, okapi

6 cattle <see list>, kine <old pl>, neat;
beef cattle, beef, beeves <pl>; dairy cattle or cows; bovine animal, **bovine,** critter
<nonformal>; **cow,** moo-cow and bossy

<both nonformal>; milk or milch cow,
milker, milcher, dairy cow; **bull,** bullock,
top cow <nonformal>; **steer,** stot <Brit
nonformal>, **ox,** oxen <pl>; **calf, heifer,**
yearling, fatling, stirk <Brit>; **dogie,**
leppy <both W US>; maverick <W US>;
hornless cow, butthead and muley head
<both nonformal>, muley cow; zebu,
Brahman; yak; musk-ox, **buffalo,** water
buffalo, Indian buffalo, carabao; bison,
aurochs, wisent
7 **sheep** <see list>, jumbuck <Australia>;
lamb, lambkin, yeanling; teg <Brit>;
ewe, yow <nonformal>; ewe lamb; **ram,**
tup <Brit>, wether; bellwether; mutton
8 **goat;** he-goat, buck, **billy goat** and billy
<both nonformal>; she-goat, doe, **nanny
goat** and nanny <both nonformal>; **kid,**
doeling; mountain goat
9 **swine** <see list>, **pig, hog,** porker; **shoat,**
piggy, piglet, pigling; sucking or suckling
pig; gilt; **boar, sow;** barrow; wild boar,
tusker, razorback; warthog, babirusa
10 **horse;** horseflesh, hoss <nonformal>,
critter <nonformal>; **equine,** mount, **nag**
<nonformal>; **steed,** prancer, dobbin;
charger, courser, war-horse, destrier
<old>; Houyhnhnm <Jonathan Swift>;
colt, foal, filly; **mare,** brood mare; **stallion, studhorse, stud,** top horse <nonfor-
mal>, entire horse, entire; gelding, purebred horse, blood horse; wild horse,
Przewalsky's horse, tarpan; **pony,** Shetland pony, Shetland, shelty, Iceland
pony, Galloway; **bronco,** bronc, range
horse, Indian pony, cayuse, mustang;
bucking bronco, buckjumper, sunfisher,
broomtail; cowcutting horse, stock horse,
roping horse, cow pony
11 <colored horses> appaloosa, bay, bayard, chestnut, gray, dapple-gray, grizzle,
roan, sorrel, dun, buckskin <W US>,
pinto, paint, piebald, skewbald, calico
pony, painted pony
12 <inferior horse> **nag, plug,** hack, jade,
crock, garron <Scots & Ir>, crowbait
<nonformal>, scalawag, rosinante; goat
and stiff and dog <all nonformal>;
roarer, whistler; balky horse, balker, jughead; rogue; rackabones, scrag, stack of
bones
13 **hunter;** stalking-horse; **saddle horse,** sad-
dler, rouncy <old>, **riding horse,** rider,
palfrey, **mount;** remount; polo pony;
post-horse; cavalry horse; **driving horse,**
road horse, roadster, carriage horse,
coach horse, gigster; hack, hackney; **draft
horse,** dray horse, cart horse, **workhorse,**

plow horse; shaft horse, pole horse, thill
horse, thiller, fill horse or filler <nonfor-
mal>; wheelhorse, wheeler, lead, leader;
pack horse, jument <old>, sumpter,
sumpter horse, bidet; pit-pony
14 **race horse; show-horse, gaited horse,**
galloper, trotter, pacer, sidewheeler
<nonformal>; stepper, high-stepper,
cob, prancer; ambler, padnag, pad;
racker; single-footer
15 <distinguished horses> Al Borak
<Mohammed's winged horse of ascen-
sion>, Baiardo <Rinaldo's bay horse>,
Black Beauty, Black Bess <Dick Turpin's
horse>, Black Saladin <Warwick's
horse>, Bucephalus <Alexander the
Great's horse>, Buttermilk <Dale Evans'
horse>, Champion <Gene Autry's
horse>, Copenhagen <Wellington's horse
at Waterloo>, Grani <Sigurd's magic
horse>, Incitatus <Caligula's horse>,
Marengo <Napoleon's white horse>,
Pegasus <winged horse of the Muses>,
Roan Barbary <favorite horse of Richard
II>, Rosinante <Don Quixote's bony
horse>, Silver <the Lone Ranger's
horse>, Sleipnir <Odin's eight-legged
horse>, Trigger <Roy Rogers' horse>,
Topper <Hopalong Cassidy's horse>,
Traveller <Robert E Lee's horse>, Veg-
liantino or Veillantif <Orlando's horse>,
White Surrey <favorite horse of Richard
III>; <race horses> Affirmed, Alydar, Assault, Citation, Dr Fager, Forego, John
Henry, Kelso, Man O'War, Nashua, Native Dancer, Ruffian, Seabiscuit, Seattle
Slew, Secretariat, Spectacular Bid,
Swaps, Whirlaway
16 **ass, donkey, burro,** neddy or cuddy
<both Brit nonformal>, moke <Brit non-
formal>, Rocky Mountain canary <W
US>; **jackass,** jack, dickey <Brit nonfor-
mal>; jenny, jenny ass, jennet; **mule,**
sumpter mule, sumpter; hinny, jennet
17 **dog** <see list>, **canine, pooch** and bowwow <both nonformal>; **pup, puppy,**
puppy-dog and perp <both nonformal>,
whelp; bitch, gyp <S US>, slut; toy dog,
lap dog; working dog; ratter; watchdog,
bandog; sheep dog, shepherd or shepherd's dog; Seeing Eye dog, guide dog;
sled dog; gazehound, sighthound; show
dog, fancy dog; kennel, pack of dogs
18 sporting dog, **hunting dog,** hunter, field
dog, bird dog, gundog, water dog
19 **cur, mongrel,** lurcher <Brit>, **mutt**
<nonformal>; pariah dog
20 **fox,** reynard; **wolf,** timber wolf, lobo <W

US>, **coyote,** brush wolf, prairie wolf, medicine wolf <W US>; dingo, jackal, **hyena;** Cape hunting dog, African hunting dog

21 **cat** <see list>, **feline,** pussy *and* **puss** *and* **pussycat** <all nonformal>, tabby, grimalkin; house cat; **kitten, kitty** *and* kittycat <both nonformal>; kit, kitling <Brit nonformal>; **tomcat,** tom; gib *or* gib-cat <both Brit nonformal>; mouser; ratter; Cheshire cat, Chessycat <nonformal>; silver cat, Chinchilla cat; blue cat, Maltese cat; tiger cat, tabby cat; tortoiseshell cat, calico cat; alley cat

22 <wild cats> **big cat, jungle cat; lion,** Leo <nonformal>, *simba* <Swah>; **tiger,** Siberian tiger; **leopard,** panther, jaguar, cheetah; cougar, painter <S US>, puma, mountain lion, catamount *or* cat-a-mountain; lynx, ocelot; wildcat, bobcat, steppe cat, Pallas's cat

23 <wild animals> **bear,** bar <nonformal>; guinea pig, cavy; hedgehog, **porcupine,** quill pig <nonformal>; woodchuck, **groundhog, whistle-pig** <nonformal>; prairie dog, prairie squirrel; **raccoon,** coon; **opossum, possum; weasel,** mousehound <Brit>; **wolverine,** glutton; ferret, monk <nonformal>; **skunk,** polecat <nonformal>; zoril, stink cat <South Africa>, Cape polecat; foumart; **primate, simian; ape; monkey,** monk <nonformal>, chimpanzee, chimp

24 **hare,** leveret, jackrabbit; **rabbit, bunny** *and* bunny rabbit <both nonformal>, lapin; cottontail; Belgian hare, leporide; buck, doe

25 **reptile,** reptilian; **lizard;** saurian, dinosaur; crocodile, crocodilian, alligator, gator <nonformal>; tortoise, turtle, terrapin

26 **serpent, snake,** ophidian; **viper,** pit viper; sea snake

27 **amphibian,** batrachian, croaker, paddock <nonformal>; **frog,** rani—, tree toad *or* frog, bullfrog; **toad,** hoptoad *or* hoppytoad; newt, salamander; **tadpole, polliwog**

28 **bird, fowl;** dicky-bird *and* birdy *and* birdie <all nonformal>; fowls of the air, birdlife, avifauna, feathered friends; baby bird, chick, nestling, fledgling; wildfowl, game bird; waterfowl, water bird, wading bird, diving bird; sea bird; shore bird; migratory bird, migrant, bird of passage; **songbird,** oscine bird, warbler, passerine bird, perching bird; cage bird; flightless bird, ratite; seed-eating bird, insect-

eating bird, fruit-eating bird, fish-eating bird; **raptor,** bird of prey; **eagle,** bird of Jove, eaglet; **hawk, falcon; owl,** bird of Minerva, bird of night; peafowl, peahen, **peacock,** bird of Juno; **swan,** cygnet; **pigeon, dove,** squab; stormy *or* storm petrel, Mother Carey's chicken; fulmar, Mother Carey's goose

29 **poultry, fowl,** domestic fowl, barnyard fowl, barn-door fowl, dunghill fowl; **chicken** <see list>, chick, chicky *and* chickabiddy <both nonformal>; **cock, rooster,** chanticleer; **hen,** biddy <nonformal>, partlet; cockerel, pullet; setting hen, brooder, broody hen; capon, poulard; broiler, fryer, spring chicken, roaster, stewing chicken; Bantam, banty <nonformal>; game fowl; guinea fowl, guinea cock, guinea hen; **goose,** gander, gosling; **duck,** drake, duckling; **turkey,** gobbler, turkey gobbler; turkey-cock, tom, tom turkey; hen turkey; poult

30 marine animal <see list>, denizen of the deep; **whale,** cetacean; **porpoise, dolphin,** sea pig; **sea serpent,** sea snake, Loch Ness monster, sea monster, Leviathan <Bible>; **fish,** game fish, tropical fish, panfish; **shark,** man-eating shark, maneater; **salmon,** kipper, grilse, smolt, parr, alevin; **minnow** *or* minny <nonformal>, fry, fingerling; **sponge; plankton,** zooplankton, nekton, benthon, benthos, zoobenthos; **crustacean,** lobster, spiny lobster, **crab,** blueclaw, Dungeness crab, king crab, spider crab, land crab, stone crab, soft-shell crab; crayfish *or* crawfish *or* crawdaddy; **mollusc,** wentletrap, whelk, snail, cockle, mussel, **clam, oyster,** razor clam, quahog, steamer, toheroa, tridachna *or* giant clam

31 **insect, bug; beetle;** arthropod; hexapod, myriapod; centipede, chilopod; millipede, diplopod; **mite; arachnid, spider,** tarantula, black widow spider, daddy longlegs *or* harvestman; **scorpion; tick;** larva, maggot, nymph, **caterpillar; insect; fly**

32 **ant,** emmet <nonformal>, pismire, pissant *and* antymire <both nonformal>; red ant, black ant, fire ant, house ant, agricultural ant, carpenter ant, army ant; slave ant, slave-making ant; **termite,** white ant; queen, worker, soldier

33 **bee,** honeybee, bumblebee, carpenter bee; queen, queen bee, worker, drone, Africanized bee; **wasp; hornet,** yellow jacket

34 **locust,** acridian; **grasshopper,** hopper,

hoppergrass <nonformal>; **cricket;** cicada, cicala, dog-day cicada, seventeen-year locust

35 vermin; parasite; **louse,** head louse, body louse, grayback, cootie <nonformal>; crab, crab louse; weevil; nit; **flea,** sand flea, dog flea, cat flea, chigoe, chigger, jigger, red bug, mite, harvest mite; **roach, cockroach,** *cucaracha* <Sp>

36 bloodsucker, parasite; **leech; tick,** wood tick, deer tick; **mosquito,** skeeter <nonformal>, culex; bedbug, housebug <Brit>

37 worm; earthworm, angleworm, fishworm, night crawler, nightwalker <N US>; measuring worm, inchworm; tapeworm, helminth

ADJS **38 animal,** animalian, animalic, animalistic, animal-like, theriomorphic, zoic, zooidal; zoologic, zoological; **brutish, brutal,** brute, brutelike; **bestial, beastly,** beastlike; **wild,** feral; subhuman, soulless; dumb, "that wants discourse of reason"—Shakespeare; instinctual *or* instinctive, mindless, nonrational; half-animal, half-human, anthropomorphic, therianthropic

39 vertebrate, chordate, mammalian; viviparous; marsupial, cetacean

40 canine, doggish, doggy, doglike; vulpine, foxy, foxlike; lupine, wolfish, wolflike

41 feline, felid, cattish, catty, catlike; kittenish; leonine, lionlike; tigerish, tigerlike

42 ursine, bearish, bearlike

43 rodent, rodential; verminous; mousy, mouselike; ratty, ratlike

44 ungulate, hoofed, hooved; **equine,** hippic, horsy, horselike; **equestrian;** asinine, mulish; bovid, ruminant, "that chew the cud"—Bible; **bovine,** cowlike, cowish; bull-like, bullish, taurine; cervine, deerlike; caprine, caprid, hircine, goatish, goatlike; ovine, sheepish, sheeplike; porcine, swinish, piggish, hoggish

45 elephantlike, elephantine, pachydermous

46 reptile, reptilian, **reptilelike,** reptiloid, reptiliform; reptant, repent, creeping, crawling, slithering; **lizardlike,** saurian; crocodilian; **serpentine,** serpentile, serpentoid, serpentiform, **serpentlike;** snakish, **snaky, snakelike,** colubrine, ophidian, anguine <old>; viperish, viperous, vipery, viperine, viperoid, viperiform, viperlike; amphibian, batrachian, froggy, toadish, salamandrian

47 birdlike, birdy; avian, avicular; gallinaceous, rasorial; oscine, passerine, perching; columbine, columbaceous, dovelike; psittacine; aquiline, hawklike; anserine, anserous, goosy; nidificant, nesting, nest-building; nidicolous, altricial; nidifugous, precocial

48 fishlike, fishy; piscine, pisciform; piscatorial, piscatory; eellike; selachian, sharklike, sharkish

49 invertebrate, invertebral; protozoan, protozoal, protozoic; crustaceous, crustacean; molluscan, molluscoid

50 insectile, insectlike, buggy; verminous; lepidopterous, lepidopteran; weevily

51 wormlike, vermicular, vermiform; wormy

52 planktonic, nektonic, benthonic, zooplanktonic, zoobenthoic

53 primates

angwantibo	howling monkey
anthropoid ape	king monkey
ape	langur
aye-aye	lemur
baboon	lion-tailed monkey *or*
Barbary ape	macaque
Bengal monkey	macaque
bonnet monkey *or*	man
macaque	mandrill
capuchin	marmoset
chacma	mountain gorilla
chimpanzee	orangutan *or* orang
colobus	owl monkey
drill	proboscis monkey
entellus	rhesus
gibbon	saki
gorilla	siamang
grivet	sloth monkey
guenon	spider monkey
guereza	squirrel monkey
hanuman	vervet

54 breeds of cattle

Aberdeen Angus *or*	Holstein *or* Holstein-
Angus *or* black	Friesian
Angus	Jersey
Africander	Kobe cattle
Alderney	Lincoln Red *or*
Ayrshire	Lincoln Red
Belted Galloway	Shorthorn
Brahman *or*	Longhorn
Brahmany	Polled Durham *or*
Brown Swiss	Shorthorn
Charbray	Polled Hereford
Charolais	Red Poll *or* Red
Devon	Polled
Dexter	Red Sindhi
Durham	Santa Gertrudis
Dutch Belted	Shorthorn
French Canadian	Sussex
Galloway	Welsh *or* Welsh
Guernsey	Black
Hereford	West Highland

55 breeds of sheep

black face Highland
blackhead Persian
broadtail
Cheviot
Columbia
Corriedale
Cotswold
Dorset Down
Hampshire *or* Hampshire Down
Karaku
Kerry Hill
Leicester
Lincoln
Merino
Oxford *or* Oxfordshire Down
Panama
Rambouillet
Romanov
Romeldale
Romney *or* Romney Marsh
Ryeland
Scottish blackface
Shropshire
Southdown
Suffolk
Targhee
Welsh Mountain
Wensleydale

56 breeds of swine

Berkshire
Cheshire
Chester White
Duroc *or* Duroc-Jersey
Hampshire
Hereford
Landrace
large black
large white
Mangalitza
middle white
miniature pig
Poland China
Spotted Poland China
Tamworth
Vietnamese pot-bellied pig
Wessex saddleback
Yorkshire

57 breeds of dogs

affenpinscher
Afghan hound
Airedale *or* Airedale terrier
Alaskan malamute
Alsatian
American foxhound
American water spaniel
Australian terrier
badger dog
barbet
Basenji
basset *or* basset hound
beagle
Bedlington terrier
Belgian sheep dog *or* shepherd
Bernese mountain dog
Blenheim spaniel
bloodhound *or* sleuth *or* sleuthhound
boarhound
Border terrier
borzoi
Boston bull *or* terrier
Bouvier des Flandres
boxer
Briard
Brittany spaniel
Brussels griffon
bulldog *or* bull
bull mastiff
bull terrier
Cairn terrier
Chesapeake Bay retriever
Chihuahua
chow *or* chow chow
clumber spaniel
Clydesdale terrier
cocker spaniel
collie
coonhound
dachshund *or* sausage dog *or* sausage hound
Dalmatian *or* coach dog
Dandie Dinmont terrier
deerhound
Doberman pinscher
elkhound
English bulldog
English cocker spaniel
English foxhound
English setter
English springer spaniel
English toy spaniel
Eskimo dog
field spaniel
flat-coated retriever
foxhound
fox terrier
French bulldog
gazelle hound
German shepherd *or* police dog
German short-haired pointer
German wire-haired pointer
giant schnauzer
golden retriever
Gordon setter
Great Dane
Great Pyrenees
greyhound
griffon
Groenendael
harrier
hound *or* hound-dog <S US>
husky
Irish setter
Irish terrier
Irish water spaniel
Irish wolfhound
Italian greyhound
Jack Russell terrier
Japanese spaniel
keeshond
Kerry blue terrier
King Charles spaniel
komondor
kuvasz
Labrador retriever
lakeland terrier
Lhasa apso
malamute
Malinois
Maltese
Manchester terrier
mastiff
Mexican hairless
miniature pinscher
miniature poodle
miniature schnauzer
Newfoundland
Nizinny
Norfolk spaniel
Norwegian elkhound
Norwich terrier
Old English sheep dog
otterhound
papillon
Pekingese
pointer
Pomeranian
poodle
pug *or* pug dog *or* mops
puli
rat terrier
retriever
Rhodesian ridgeback
Rottweiler
Russian owtchar
Russian wolfhound
St Bernard
Saluki
Samoyed
schipperke
schnauzer
Scottish deerhound
Scottish terrier
Sealyham terrier
setter
shepherd dog
Shetland sheep dog
Shih Tzu
Siberian husky
silky terrier
Skye terrier
spaniel
spitz
springer spaniel
staghound
Sussex spaniel
terrier
toy poodle
toy spaniel
toy terrier
turnspit
Vizsla
water spaniel
Weimaraner
Welsh collie
Welsh corgi
Welsh springer spaniel
Welsh terrier
West Highland white terrier
whippet
wire-haired terrier
wolfhound
Yorkshire terrier

58 breeds and varieties of domestic cats

Abyssinian cat
Angora cat
Archangel cat
blue-point Siamese cat
Burmese cat
chartreuse cat
Chinese cat
chocolate-point Siamese cat
domestic shorthair cat
Egyptian cat
Havana brown cat

Himalayan cat
Madagascar cat
Maine coon cat
Malayan cat
Maltese *or* blue cat
Manx cat
marmalade cat
Oriental Shorthair
Persian cat
Rex cat

Russian blue cat
seal-point Siamese
  cat
Siamese cat
Spanish cat
tabby *or* tabby-cat
Tobolsk cat
tortoise-shell cat
Turkish cat

59 breeds of chickens

Ancona
Andalusian
Araucanian
Australorp
Bantam
Barred Plymouth
  Rock
black Minorca
black Orpington
black Spanish
black Sumatra
blue Andalusian
blue Orpington
Brahma
buff Orpington
Campine
Cochin
Cornish
dark Cornish
Dorking
Faverolle
Hamburg

Houdan
Jersey white giant
Langshan
Leghorn
Minorca
New Hampshire *or*
  New Hampshire
  red
Orpington
Plymouth Rock
Rhode Island red
Rhode Island white
Rock Cornish
speckled Sussex
Sumatra
Sussex
white Leghorn
white Orpington
white Plymouth Rock
white Wyandotte
Wyandotte

60 marine animals

crustacean
dugong
elephant seal
fur seal
harbor seal
manatee
octopus *or* octopod
sea calf
sea cow

sea dog
sea elephant
seal
sea lion
sea urchin
shellfish
squid
walrus

312 HUMANKIND

NOUNS **1 humankind, mankind, man,** human species, **human race,** race of man, human family, the family of man, **humanity,** human beings, mortals, mortality, flesh, mortal flesh, clay; generation of man <old>, *le genre humain* <Fr>, "the plumeless genus of bipeds"—Plato, homo, genus Homo, **Homo sapiens,** Hominidae, hominids; archaic Homo; **race,** strain, stock, subrace, infrarace, subspecies; **culture** 373.3; ethnic group; ethnicity, ethnicism; **society,** speech community, **ethnic group;** community, **the people, the populace; nationality, nation**

2 <races of humankind> **Caucasoid** *or*

Caucasian *or* **white race;** Nordic subrace, Alpine subrace, Mediterranean subrace; dolichocephalic people, brachycephalic people; xanthochroi, melanochroi; Archaic Caucasoid *or* archaic white *or* Australoid race; Polynesian race; **Negroid** *or* **black race;** Nilotic race, Melanesian race, Papuan race; Pygmoid race; Bushman race; **Mongoloid** *or* **Mongolian** *or* **yellow race;** Malayan *or* Malaysian *or* brown race; prehistoric races; majority, racial *or* ethnic majority; minority, racial *or* ethnic minority; persons of color

3 Caucasian, white man *or* **woman, white person,** paleface *and* ofay *and* the Man *and* Mister Charley *and* whitey *and* honky <all nonformal>; Australian aborigine, blackfellow <Australia>; **Negro, black man** *or* **woman, black,** colored person, person of color, darky *and* spade *and* nigger <all nonformal>; African-American; negritude, Afroism, blackness; pygmy, Negrito, Negrillo; Bushman; **Indian,** American Indian, Amerind, Red Indian <Brit>, red man *or* woman; injun *and* redskin <both nonformal>; Mongolian, yellow man *or* woman, **Oriental;** gook *and* slant-eye <both nonformal>; Malayan, brown man

4 the people 606, the populace, the population, the public

5 person, human, human being, man, woman, child, member of the human race *or* family, Adamite, daughter of Eve; ethnic; **mortal,** life, **soul,** living soul; **being,** creature, clay, ordinary clay; **individual,** "single, separate person"—Whitman; personage, **personality, personhood,** individuality; **body;** somebody, one, someone; earthling, groundling, terran, worldling, tellurian; **ordinary person;** head, hand, nose; fellow <nonformal> 76.5; gal <nonformal> 77.6

6 human nature, humanity; frail *or* fallen humanity, Adam, the generation of Adam, Adam's seed *or* offspring

7 God's image, lord of creation; homo faber, symbol-using animal; "a god in ruins"—Emerson, "the aristocrat amongst the animals"—Heine, "the measure of all things"—Protagoras, "a reasoning animal"—Seneca, "the most intelligent of animals—and the most silly"—Diogenes, "a thinking reed"—Pascal, "a tool-using animal"—Carlyle, "a tool-making animal"—Benjamin Franklin, "the only animal that blushes Or needs to"—Mark Twain, "an intel-

ligence served by organs"—Emerson, rational animal, animal capable of reason,
"an ingenious assembly of portable
plumbing"—Christopher Morley, "Nature's sole mistake"—W S Gilbert, "that
unfeather'd two-legged thing"—Dryden, "but breath and shadow, nothing
more"—Sophocles, "this quintessence
of dust"—Shakespeare, "political animal"—Aristotle; "the naked ape"—
Desmond Morris

8 **humanness, humanity,** mortality; **human
nature,** the way you are; **frailty,** human
frailty, weakness, **human weakness,**
weakness of the flesh, "thy nature's
weakness"—Whittier, "one touch of
nature"—Shakespeare, the weaknesses
human flesh is heir to; human equation

9 **humanization,** humanizing; **anthropomorphism,** pathetic fallacy, anthropo-
pathism, anthropomorphology

10 **anthropology,** science of man; anthro-
pogeny, anthropography, anthropoge-
ography, human geography, demography, human ecology, anthropometry,
craniometry, craniology, ethnology, eth-
nography; behavioral science, sociology,
social anthropology, social psychology,
psychology 92; anatomy; **anthropologist,**
ethnologist, ethnographer; sociologist;
demographics, population study, population statistics; demographer

11 **humanism;** naturalistic humanism, scientific humanism, secular humanism;
religious humanism; Christian humanism, integral humanism; new humanism;
anthroposophy

VERBS 12 **humanize,** anthropomorphize,
make human, civilize

ADJS 13 **human;** hominal; creaturely, creatural; Adamite or Adamitic; **frail, weak,**
fleshly, finite, **mortal; only human;** earthborn, of the earth, earthy, tellurian,
unangelic; humanistic; man-centered,
homocentric, anthropocentric; anthropological, ethnographic, ethnological;
demographic

14 **manlike, anthropoid,** humanoid, hominid; anthropomorphic, anthropopathic,
therioanthropic

15 **personal, individual,** private, peculiar,
idiosyncratic; person-to-person, one-to-
one, one-on-one

16 **public, general, common; communal, societal, social;** civic, civil; **national,** state;
international, cosmopolitan, superna-
tional, supranational

ADVS 17 **humanly,** mortally, after the manner of men

WORD ELEMENTS 18 anthrop—,
anthropo—, homin—, homini—

313 SEASON
<time of year>

NOUNS 1 **season,** time of year, season of the
year, "the measure of the year"—Keats,
period, annual period; dry or rainy or
cold season, monsoon; theatrical or opera
or concert season; **social season,** the season; dead or off-season; baseball season,
football season, basketball season, etc;
seasonality, periodicity 849.2; **seasonableness** 842.1

2 **spring,** springtide, **springtime,** seedtime
or budtime, Maytime, Eastertide; *pri-
mavera* <Ital>, prime, prime of the year,
"the boyhood of the year"—Tennyson,
"Sweet Spring, full of sweet days and
roses"—George Herbert, "Daughter of
heaven and earth, coy Spring"—
Emerson, "the time of the singing of
birds"—Bible, "when the hounds of
spring are on winter's traces"—
Swinburne

3 **summer,** summertide, **summertime,**
good old summertime; growing season;
midsummer; **dog days,** canicular days;
the silly season

4 **autumn, fall,** fall of the year, fall of the
leaf, harvest, harvest time, harvest home;
"Season of mists and mellow
fruitfulness!"—Keats

5 **Indian summer,** St Martin's summer, St
Luke's summer, little summer of St Luke,
St Austin's or St Augustine's summer,
"the dead Summer's soul"—Mary Clem-
mer

6 **winter,** wintertide, **wintertime,** "ruler of
th'inverted year"—William Cowper;
midwinter; Christmastime or Christmas-
tide, Yule or Yuletide

7 **equinox,** vernal equinox, autumnal equinox; **solstice,** summer solstice, winter
solstice

VERBS 8 **summer, winter, overwinter,**
spend or pass the spring, summer,
etc

ADJS 9 **seasonal,** in or out of season, in sea-
son and out of season, off-season; early-
season, mid-season, late-season; **spring,**
springlike, vernal; **summer,** summery,
summerly, summerlike, canicular, aestival; midsummer; **autumn,** autumnal;
winter, wintry, wintery, hibernal, hiemal, brumal, boreal, arctic 1022.14,
winterlike, snowy, icy; midwinter; equinoctial, solstitial

314 MORNING, NOON

NOUNS **1 morning,** morn, morningtide, morning time, morntime, matins, morrow <old>, waking time, reveille, get-up time <nonformal>, **forenoon;** *ante meridiem* <L> or **AM,** Ack Emma <Brit old>; "dewy morn"—Byron, "incense-breathing morn"—Thomas Gray, "grey-eyed morn, "the morn, in russet mantle clad"—both Shakespeare, "rosy-finger'd morn"—Homer; this morning, this AM <nonformal>

2 Morning, Aurora, Eos; "daughter of the dawn" —Homer, "meek-eyed Morn, mother of dews" —James Thomson, "mild blushing goddess" —L P Smith

3 dawn, the dawn of day, dawning, **daybreak,** dayspring, day-peep, **sunrise, sunup** <nonformal>, cockcrowing or cocklight <Brit nonformal>, light 1024, first light, daylight, aurora; **break of day,** peep of day, **crack of dawn,** prime, prime of the morning, first blush or flush of the morning, brightening or first brightening; "the opening eyelids of the morn"—Milton, "vestibule of Day"—Bayard Taylor, "golden exhalations of the dawn"—Schiller; chanticleer or chantecler

4 foredawn, twilight, morning twilight, half-light, glow, dawnlight, first light, "the dawn's early light"—Francis Scott Key, crepuscule, aurora; **the small hours;** alpenglow

5 noon, noonday, noontide, nooning <nonformal>, noontime, **high noon, midday,** meridian, *meridiem* <L>, twelve o'clock, 1200 hours, eight bells; noonlight, "the blaze of noon"—Milton; meridian devil or *daemonium meridianum* <L>, "the destruction that wasteth at noonday"—Bible

ADJS **6 morning,** matin, matinal, matutinal, **antemeridian;** auroral, dawn, dawning

7 noon, noonday, noonish, **midday,** meridian, twelve-o'clock; noonlit

ADVS **8 in the morning,** before noon, mornings <nonformal>; at sunrise, at dawn, at dawn of day, at cockcrow, at first light, **at the crack** or **break of dawn;** with the sun, with the lark

9 at noon, at midday, at twelve-o'clock sharp

315 EVENING, NIGHT

NOUNS **1 afternoon,** *post meridiem* <L> or **PM;** this afternoon, this aft <nonformal>, this PM <nonformal>

2 evening, eve, even, evensong time or hour, **eventide,** vesper; **close of day,** decline or fall of day, shut of day, gray of the evening, grayness 39, evening's close, when day is done; **nightfall, sunset, sundown,** setting sun, going down of the sun, cockshut and cockshut time and cockshut light <all nonformal>, retreat; shank of the afternoon or evening <nonformal>, the cool of the evening; "the expiring day"—Dante, "evening's calm and holy hour"—S G Bulfinch, "the gray-hooded Ev'n"—Milton, "the pale child, Eve, leading her mother, Night"—Alexander Smith, "the evening is spread out against the sky, Like a patient etherized upon a table"—T S Eliot

3 dusk, dusking time or -tide, dusk-dark and dust-dark and dusty-dark <all nonformal>, **twilight,** evening twilight, crepuscule, crepuscular light, gloam, **gloaming,** glooming; duskiness, duskishness, brown of dusk, brownness 40, candlelight, candlelighting, owllight or owl's light, cocklight <Brit nonformal>, "the pale dusk of the impending night"—Longfellow

4 night, nighttime, nighttide, lights-out, taps, bedtime, sleepy time <nonformal>, **darkness** 1026, blackness 38, "sable-vested Night, eldest of things"—Milton, "sable night, "darkeyed night"—both Shakespeare, "cowlèd night"—Francis Thompson, "empress of silence, and the queen of sleep"—Christopher Marlowe; dark of night, "the suit of night"—Shakespeare, "the mystic wine of Night"—Louis Untermeyer

5 eleventh hour, curfew

6 midnight, dead of night, hush of night, the witching hour; "the very witching time of night"—Shakespeare, "noonday night, "outpost of advancing day"—both Longfellow

ADJS **7 afternoon,** postmeridian

8 evening, evensong, vesper, vespertine or vespertinal; **twilight,** twilighty, crepuscular; **dusk,** dusky, duskish

9 nocturnal, night, **nightly,** nighttime; nightlong, all-night; night-fallen; midnight

10 benighted, night-overtaken

ADVS **11 nightly,** nights <nonformal>, at or by night; **overnight,** through the night, all through the night, nightlong, the whole night, all night

WORD ELEMENTS **12** noc—, nocto—, nocti—, nyct—, nycto—, nycti—

316 RAIN

NOUNS **1 rain, rainfall,** fall, **precipitation,** moisture, wet, rainwater; **shower, sprinkle,** flurry, patter, pitter-patter, splatter; streams of rain, sheet of rain, splash *or* spurt of rain; **drizzle,** mizzle; **mist,** misty rain, Scotch mist; evening mist; fog drip; blood rain; raindrop, unfrozen hydrometeor

2 rainstorm, brash *and* scud <both Scots>; **cloudburst,** rainburst, burst of rain, torrent of rain, torrential rain *or* downpour; waterspout, spout, rainspout, **downpour,** downflow, downfall, pour, pouring *or* pelting *or* teeming *or* drowning rain, spate <Scots>, plash <nonformal>, **deluge, flood,** heavy rain, driving *or* gushing rain, drenching *or* soaking rain, drencher, soaker, goosedrownder <nonformal>, "smoky rain"—Chaucer, lovely weather for ducks

3 thunderstorm, thundersquall, thundergust, thundershower

4 wet weather, raininess, rainy weather, stormy *or* dirty weather, cat-and-dog weather <nonformal>, spell of rain, wet; rainy day; **rains,** rainy *or* wet season, spring rains, **monsoon;** predominance of Aquarius, reign of St Swithin

5 rainmaking, seeding, cloud seeding, nucleation, artificial nucleation; **rainmaker,** rain doctor, cloud seeder; dry ice, silver iodide

6 Jupiter Pluvius, Zeus; Thor

7 rain gauge, pluviometer, pluvioscope, pluviograph; ombrometer, ombrograph; udometer, udomograph; hyetometer, hyetometrograph, hyetograph

8 <science of precipitation> hydrometeorology, hyetology, hyetography; pluviography, pluviometry, ombrology

VERBS **9 rain, precipitate,** rain down, fall; weep; **shower,** shower down; **sprinkle,** spit *and* spritz <both nonformal>, spatter, patter, pitter-patter; **drizzle,** mizzle; **pour,** stream, stream down, pour with rain, **pelt,** pelt down, drum, tattoo, come down in torrents *or* sheets *or* buckets *or* curtains, **rain cats and dogs** <nonformal>, "rain dogs and pole-cats"— Richard Brome, rain tadpoles *or* bullfrogs *or* pitchforks <nonformal>, "rain daggers with their points downward"— Robert Burton; rainmake, seed clouds

ADJS **10 rainy, showery;** pluvious *or* pluviose *or* pluvial; **drizzly,** drizzling, mizzly, drippy; **misty,** misty-moisty; torrential, pouring, streaming, pelting, drumming, driving, blinding, cat-and-doggish <nonformal>

11 pluviometric *or* pluvioscopic *or* pluviographic, ombrometric *or* ombrographic, udometric *or* udographic, hyetometric, hyetographic, hyetometrographic; hydrometeorological, hyetological

317 AIR, WEATHER

NOUNS **1 air;** ether; ozone <nonformal>; thin air

2 atmosphere; aerosphere, gaseous envelope *or* environment *or* medium *or* blanket, welkin, lift <nonformal>; biosphere, ecosphere, noosphere; air mass; atmospheric component, atmospheric gas; atmospheric layer *or* stratum *or* belt <see list>

3 weather, climate, clime; **the elements,** forces of nature; microclimate, macroclimate; fair weather, calm weather, halcyon days, good weather; stormy weather 671.4; rainy weather 316.4; windiness 318.15; heat wave, hot weather 1018.7; cold wave, cold weather 1022.3

4 weather map; isobar, isobaric *or* isopiestic line; isotherm, isothermal line; isometric, isometric line; high, high-pressure area; low, low-pressure area; front, wind-shift line, squall line; cold front, polar front, cold sector; warm front; occluded front, stationary front; air mass; cyclone, anticyclone

5 meteorology, weather science, aerology, aerography, air-mass analysis, weatherology, climatology, climatography, microclimatology, forecasting, long-range forecasting; barometry; pneumatics 1038.5; anemology 318.16; nephology 319.4

6 meteorologist, weather scientist, aerologist, aerographer, weatherologist; climatologist, microclimatologist; **weatherman, weather forecaster,** weather prophet; **weather report,** weather forecast; weather bureau; weather ship; weather station; weather-reporting network

7 weather instrument, meteorological *or* aerological instrument; **barometer,** aneroid barometer, glass, weatherglass; barograph, barometrograph, recording barometer; aneroidograph; vacuometer; hygrometer; weather balloon, radiosonde; weather satellite; hurricane-hunter aircraft; weather vane 318.17

8 ventilation, cross-ventilation, **airing,** aerage, perflation, refreshment; **aeration; air conditioning,** air cooling; oxygenation, oxygenization

9 **ventilator; aerator; air conditioner,** air filter, air cooler, ventilating *or* cooling system; blower; heat pump; air passage; fan

VERBS 10 **air,** air out, **ventilate,** cross-ventilate, wind, refresh, freshen; **air-condition,** air-cool; **fan,** winnow; **aerate,** airify; oxygenate, oxygenize

ADJS 11 **airy,** aery, **aerial,** aeriform, airlike, **pneumatic,** ethereal; exposed, roomy, light; airish, breezy; open-air, alfresco; **atmospheric,** tropospheric, stratospheric

12 **climatal,** climatic, climatical, climato-graphical, **elemental;** meteorological, aerologic, aerological, aerographic, aerographical, climatologic, climato-logical; macroclimatic, microclimatic, microclimatologic; barometric, baromet-rical, baric, barographic; isobaric, iso-piestic, isometric; high-pressure, low-pressure; cyclonic, anti-cyclonic

13 **atmospheric layers**

boundary layer	mesosphere
chemosphere	outer atmosphere
exosphere	ozone layer *or*
F₁ layer	ozonosphere
F₂ *or* Appleton layer	stratosphere
Heaviside *or*	substratosphere
Heaviside-Kennelly	thermosphere
layer *or* region	tropopause
ionosphere	troposphere
isothermal region	upper atmosphere
lower atmosphere	Van Allen belt *or* radi-
magnetosphere	ation belt

318 WIND
<air flow>

NOUNS 1 **wind,** current, **air current,** current of air, **draft,** movement of air, stream, stream of air, flow of air; updraft, uprush; downdraft, downrush, microburst; in-draft, inflow; inrush; crosscurrent, undercurrent; fall wind, gravity wind, katabatic wind, head wind, tail wind, following wind; wind aloft; jet stream, upper-atmosphere *or* upper-atmospheric wind

2 "scolding winds"—Shakespeare, "the felon winds"—Milton, "the wings of the wind"—Bible, "O wild West Wind, thou breath of Autumn's being"—Shelley, "the wind that sang of trees uptorn and vessels tost"—Wordsworth

3 <wind god; the wind personified> Ae-olus, Vayu; Boreas <north wind>; Eurus <east wind>; Zephyr *or* Zephyrus, Fa-vonius <west wind>; Notus <south wind>; Caurus <northwest wind>; After <southwest wind>

4 **puff,** puff of air *or* wind, breath, breath of air, flatus, waft, capful of wind, whiff, whiffet, stir of air

5 **breeze,** light *or* gentle wind *or* breeze, softblowing wind, **zephyr,** gale <old>, air, light air, moderate breeze; fresh *or* stiff breeze; cool *or* cooling breeze; sea breeze, onshore breeze, ocean breeze, cat's-paw

6 **gust,** wind gust, **blast,** blow, flaw, **flurry,** scud <Scots>

7 **hot wind;** snow eater, thawer; chinook, **chinook wind;** simoom, samiel; foehn *or* föhn; khamsin; harmattan; sirocco *or* yugo; solano; Santa Ana; volcanic wind

8 **wintry wind,** winter wind, raw wind, chilling *or* freezing wind, bone-chilling wind, sharp *or* piercing wind, cold *or* icy wind, biting wind, the hawk <nonfor-mal>, nipping *or* nippy wind, "a nipping and an eager air"—Shakespeare, icy blasts; Arctic *or* boreal *or* hyperboreal *or* hyperborean blast; wind chill *or* wind chill factor

9 **north wind, norther,** mistral, bise, tra-montane, Etesian winds, meltemi, vardarac, Papagayo wind; northeaster, **nor'easter,** Euroclydon *or* gregale *or* gre-gal *or* gregau, bura, Tehuantepec wind, Tehuantepecer; northwester, **nor'wester;** southeaster, **sou'easter;** southwester, **sou'wester,** kite-wind, libeccio; **east wind,** easter, easterly, levanter, sharav; **west wind,** wester, westerly; **south wind,** souther, southerly buster <Australia>

10 prevailing wind; polar easterlies; prevail-ing westerlies, antitrades; trade wind, trades; doldrums, wind-equator; horse latitudes; roaring forties

11 <naut terms> **head wind, beam wind, tail wind,** following wind, fair *or* favor-able wind, apparent *or* relative wind, backing wind, veering wind, slant of wind; onshore wind, offshore wind

12 **windstorm,** big *or* great *or* fresh *or* strong *or* stiff *or* high *or* howling *or* spanking wind, ill *or* dirty *or* ugly wind; storm, storm wind, stormy winds, **tempest,** tem-pestuous wind; **blow,** violent *or* heavy blow; **squall,** thick squall, black squall, white squall; squall line, wind-shift line, line squall; line storm; equinoc-tial; **gale,** half a gale, whole gale; tropical cyclone, **hurricane,** typhoon, tropical storm, **blizzard** 1022.8; **thundersquall,** thundergust; wind shear

13 dust storm, sandstorm, shaitan, peesash, devil, khamsin, sirocco, simoom, samiel, harmattan

14 whirlwind, whirlblast, tourbillion, wind eddy; **cyclone, tornado, twister,** rotary storm, typhoon, *baguio* <Sp>; sandspout, sand column, dust devil; waterspout, rainspout

15 windiness, gustiness; airiness, **breeziness;** draftiness

16 anemology, anemometry; **wind direction; wind force, Beaufort scale,** half-Beaufort scale, International scale; wind rose, barometric wind rose, humidity wind rose, hyetal *or* rain wind rose, temperature wind rose, dynamic wind rose; wind arrow, wind marker

17 weather vane, weathercock, vane, cock, wind vane, wind indicator, wind cone *or* sleeve *or* sock, anemoscope; anemometer, wind-speed indicator, anemograph, anemometrograph

18 blower, bellows; blowpipe, blowtube, blowgun

19 fan, flabellum; punkah, thermantidote, electric fan, blower, window fan, attic fan, exhaust fan; ventilator; windsail, windscoop, windcatcher

VERBS **20 blow, waft; puff,** huff, whiff; whiffle; **breeze;** breeze up, freshen; **gather, brew,** set in, blow up, pipe up, come up, **blow up a storm;** bluster, squall; **storm,** rage, "blow, winds, and crack your cheeks, rage, blow"—Shakespeare, blast, blow great guns, blow a hurricane; blow over

21 sigh, sough, whisper, mutter, murmur, **sob, moan,** groan, growl, snarl, **wail, howl,** scream, screech, shriek, **roar,** whistle, pipe, sing, sing in the shrouds

ADJS **22 windy, blowy; breezy, drafty,** airy, airish; brisk, fresh; **gusty,** blasty, puffy, flawy; **squally;** blustery, blustering, blusterous; aeolian, favonian, boreal; ventose

23 stormy, tempestuous, raging, storming, angry; turbulent; dirty, foul; cyclonic, tornadic, typhonic, typhoonish; rainy 316.10; cloudy 319.7

24 windblown, blown; **windswept,** bleak, raw, exposed

25 anemological, anemographic, anemometric, anemometrical

319 CLOUD

NOUNS **1 cloud,** high fog; "the clouds—the only birds that never sleep"—Victor Hugo, "the argosies of cloudland"—

J T Trowbridge, "islands on a dark-blue sea"—Shelley, "fair, frail, palaces"—T B Aldrich, "the low'ring element"—Milton; fleecy cloud, cottony cloud, billowy cloud; **cloud bank,** cloud mass, cloud cover, cloud drift; cloudling, cloudlet; cloudscape, cloud band; cloudland, Cloudcuckooland *or* Nephelococcygia <Aristophanes>

2 fog, pea soup *and* peasouper *and* peasoup fog <all nonformal>; London fog, London special <Brit nonformal>; fog-bank; **smog** <smoke-fog>, smaze <smoke-haze>; frost smoke; mist, drizzling mist, drisk <nonformal>; haze, gauze, film; vapor 1065

3 cloudiness, haziness, mistiness, fogginess, nebulosity, nubilation, nimbosity, **overcast,** heavy sky, dirty sky, lowering *or* louring sky

4 nephology, nephelognosy; nephologist

5 nephelometer, nepheloscope

VERBS **6 cloud,** becloud, encloud, cloud over, overcloud, cloud up, clabber up <nonformal>, **overcast,** overshadow, shadow, shade, **darken** 1026.9, darken over, nubilate, obnubilate, obscure; **smoke,** oversmoke; **fog,** befog, fog in; smog; **mist,** mist over, mist up, bemist, enmist; **haze**

ADJS **7 cloudy,** nebulous, nubilous, nimbose, nebulosus; **clouded,** overclouded, **overcast;** dirty, heavy, lowering *or* louring; dark 1026.13; **gloomy** 1026.14; cloud-flecked; cirrous, cirrose; cumulous, cumuliform, stratous, stratiform; lenticularis, mammatus, castellatus; thunderheaded, stormy, squally

8 cloud-covered, cloud-laden, cloud-curtained, cloud-crammed, cloud-crossed, cloud-decked, cloud-hidden, cloud-wrapped, cloud-enveloped, cloud-surrounded, cloud-girt, cloud-flecked, cloud-eclipsed, **cloud-capped,** cloud-topped

9 foggy, soupy *or* pea-soupy <nonformal>, nubilous; fog-bound, fogged-in; smoggy; hazy, misty; so foggy the seagulls are walking, so thick you can cut it with a knife

10 nephological

320 BUBBLE

NOUNS **1 bubble,** bleb, **globule;** vesicle, bulla, **blister,** blood blister, fever blister; balloon, bladder 195.2; air bubble, soap bubble

2 foam, froth; spume, sea foam, scud;

spray, surf, breakers, white water, spoondrift or spindrift, "stinging, ringing spindrift"—Kipling; suds, lather, soapsuds; beer-suds, head; scum, off-scum; head, collar; puff, mousse, soufflé, meringue

3 bubbling, bubbliness, effervescence or effervescency, sparkle, spumescence, frothiness, frothing, foaming; fizz, fizzle, carbonation; ebullience or ebulliency; ebullition, boiling; fermentation, ferment

VERBS 4 bubble, bubble up, burble; effervesce, fizz, fizzle; hiss, sparkle; ferment, work; foam, froth, froth up; have a head, foam over; boil, seethe, simmer; plop, blubber; guggle, gurgle; bubble over, boil over

5 foam, froth, spume, cream; lather, suds, sud; scum, mantle; aerate, whip, beat, whisk

ADJS 6 bubbly, burbly, bubbling, burbling; effervescent, spumescent, fizzy, sparkling, mousseux <Fr>, spumante <Ital>; carbonated; ebullient; puffed, soufflé or souffléed, beaten, whipped, chiffon; blistered, blistery, blebby, vesicated, vesicular; blistering, vesicant, vesicatory

7 foamy, foam-flecked, frothy, spumy, spumous or spumose; yeasty, barmy; sudsy, suddy, lathery, soapy, soapsudsy, soapsuddy; heady, with a head or collar on

321 BEHAVIOR

NOUNS 1 behavior, conduct, deportment, comportment, manner, manners, demeanor, mien, maintien <Fr>, carriage, bearing, port, poise, posture, guise, air, address, presence; tone, style, lifestyle; way of life, habit of life, modus vivendi; way, way of acting, ways; trait behavior, behavior trait; methods, method, methodology; practice, praxis; procedure, proceeding; actions, acts, goings-on, doings, what one is up to, movements, moves, tactics; action, doing 328.1; activity 330; objective or observable behavior; motions, gestures; pose, affectation 500; pattern, behavior pattern; Type A behavior, Type B behavior; culture pattern, behavioral norm, folkway, custom 373; behavioral science, social science

2 good behavior, sanctioned behavior; good citizenship; good manners, correct deportment, etiquette 580.3; courtesy 504; social behavior, sociability 582; bad or poor behavior, misbehavior 322; discourtesy 505

3 behaviorism, behavioral science, behavior or behavioristic psychology, Watsonian psychology, Skinnerian psychology; behavior modification, behavior therapy ethology, animal behavior, human behavior, social behavior

VERBS 4 behave, act, do, go on; behave oneself, conduct oneself, manage oneself, handle oneself, guide oneself, comport oneself, deport oneself, demean oneself, bear oneself, carry oneself; acquit oneself, quit oneself <old>; proceed, move, swing into action; misbehave 322.4

5 behave oneself, behave, act well, clean up one's act <nonformal>, act one's age, be good, be nice, do right, do what is right, do the right or proper thing, keep out of mischief, play the game and mind one's P's and Q's <both nonformal>, be on one's good or best behavior, play one's cards right

6 treat, use, do by, deal by, act or behave toward, conduct oneself toward, act with regard to, conduct oneself vis-à-vis or in the face of; deal with, cope with, handle; respond to

ADJS 7 behavioral; behaviorist, behavioristic; ethological; behaved, behaviored, mannered, demeanored

322 MISBEHAVIOR

NOUNS 1 misbehavior, misconduct, misdemeanor <old>; unsanctioned or non-sanctioned behavior; frowned-upon behavior; naughtiness, badness; impropriety; venial sin; disorderly conduct, disorder, disorderliness, disruptiveness, disruption, rowdiness, rowdyism, riotousness, ruffianism, hooliganism, hoodlumism, aggro <Brit nonformal>; vandalism, trashing, roughhouse, horseplay; discourtesy 505; vice 654; misfeasance, malfeasance, misdoing, delinquency, wrongdoing 655

2 mischief, mischievousness; devilment, deviltry, devilry; roguishness, roguery, scampishness; waggery, waggishness; impishness, devilishness, puckishness, elfishness; prankishness, pranksomeness; sportiveness, playfulness, espièglerie <Fr>; high spirits, youthful spirits; foolishness 922

3 mischief-maker, mischief, rogue, devil, knave, rascal, rapscallion, scapegrace, scamp; wag 489.12; buffoon 707.10; funmaker, joker, jokester, practical joker, prankster, life of the party, cutup

<nonformal>; **rowdy**, ruffian, hoodlum, hood <nonformal>, hooligan; **imp, elf, puck**, pixie, **minx**, bad boy, bugger *and* booger <both nonformal>, little devil, little rascal, little monkey, *enfant terrible* <Fr>

VERBS **4 misbehave**, misdemean <old>, **misbehave oneself, misconduct oneself**, misdemean oneself <old>, behave ill; get into mischief; **act up** *and* make waves *and* **carry on** *and* carry on something scandalous <all nonformal>, sow one's wild oats; **cut up** <nonformal>, horse around <nonformal>, roughhouse *and* cut up rough <both nonformal>; play the fool 922.6

ADJS **5 misbehaving, unbehaving; naughty, bad**; improper, not respectable; out-of-order *and* off-base *and* out-of-line <all nonformal>; **disorderly**, disruptive, **rowdy**, rowdyish, **ruffianly**

 6 mischievous, mischief-loving, full of mischief, full of the devil *or* old nick; **roguish**, scampish, scapegrace, arch, knavish; **devilish; impish, puckish, elfish**, elvish; **waggish, prankish**, pranky, pranksome, trickish, tricksy; **playful**, sportive, high-spirited, *espiègle* <Fr>; foolish 922.8,9

ADVS **7 mischievously, roguishly**, knavishly, scampishly, devilishly; impishly, puckishly, elfishly; waggishly; prankishly, playfully, sportively, in fun

323 WILL

NOUNS **1 will, volition; choice**, determination, **decision** 371.1; **wish, mind, fancy**, discretion, pleasure, **inclination, disposition**, liking, appetence, appetency, **desire** 100; half a mind *or* notion, idle wish, velleity; **appetite, passion, lust, sexual desire** 75.5; animus, **objective, intention** 380; **command** 420; **free choice**, one's own will *or* choice *or* discretion *or* initiative, **free will** 430.6; conation, conatus; will power, **resolution** 359

VERBS **2 will, wish** see *or* think fit, think good, think proper, **choose to, have a mind to**; have half a mind *or* notion to; **choose**, determine, **decide** 371.14,16; **resolve** 359.7; command, decree; **desire** 100.14,18

 3 have one's will, **have *or* get one's way, get one's wish, have one's druthers** <nonformal>, **write one's own ticket**, have it all one's way, do *or* go as one pleases, please oneself; take the bit in one's teeth, take charge of one's destiny; stand on one's

rights; take the law into one's own hands; have the last word, impose one's will

ADJS **4 volitional, volitive; willing, voluntary;** conative; *ex gratia* <L>

ADVS **5 at will**, at choice, at pleasure, *al piacere* <Ital>, **at one's pleasure**, *a beneplacito* <Ital>, at one's will and pleasure, at one's own sweet will, **at one's discretion**, *à discrétion* <Fr>; *ad arbitrium* <L>; *ad libitum* <L>, ad lib; as one wishes, as it pleases *or* suits oneself, **in one's own way**, in one's own sweet way *or* time <nonformal>, **as one thinks best**, as it seems good *or* best, as far as one desires; of one's own free will, of one's own accord, on one's own; without coercion, unforced

324 WILLINGNESS

NOUNS **1 willingness, gameness** <nonformal>, readiness; **unreluctance**, unloathness, ungrudgingness; agreeableness, **agreeability**, favorableness; **acquiescence, consent** 441; **compliance**, cooperativeness; receptivity, receptiveness, responsiveness; amenability, tractableness, tractability, docility, biddability, biddableness, pliancy, pliability, malleability; **eagerness**, keenness, promptness, forwardness, alacrity, zeal, zealousness, ardor, enthusiasm; goodwill, cheerful consent; **willing heart** *or* mind *or* humor, **favorable disposition**, positive *or* right *or* receptive mood, willing ear

 2 voluntariness, volunteering; **gratuitousness; spontaneity**, spontaneousness, unforcedness; **self-determination**, self-activity, self-action, autonomy, autonomousness, independence, free will 430.5–7; **volunteerism**, voluntaryism, voluntarism; volunteer

VERBS **3 be willing, be game** <nonformal>, be ready; be of favorable disposition, take the trouble, find it in one's heart, find one's heart <old>, have a willing heart; **incline, lean;** look kindly upon; be open to, bring oneself, **agree**, be agreeable to; **acquiesce, consent** 441.2; not hesitate to, would as lief, would as leave <nonformal>, would as lief as not, not care *or* mind if one does <nonformal>; **play** *or* **go along** <nonformal>, do one's part *or* bit; be eager, be keen, be dying to, fall all over oneself, be spoiling for, be champing at the bit; be Johnny on the spot, step into the breach; **enter with a will**, lean *or* bend over backward, go into heart and soul, go the extra mile, plunge into; **cooperate,** collaborate 450.3; lend *or* give *or* turn a willing ear

4 **volunteer,** do voluntarily, do ex gratia, **do of one's own accord,** do of one's own volition, **do of one's own free will *or* choice;** do independently

ADJS 5 **willing, willinghearted, ready, game** <nonformal>; **disposed, inclined, minded, willed,** fain *and* prone <both old>; **well-disposed,** well-inclined, favorably inclined *or* disposed; predisposed; **favorable, agreeable, cooperative; compliant,** content <old>, **acquiescent** 332.13, **consenting** 441.4; **eager;** keen, prompt, quick, alacritous, forward, ready and willing, zealous, ardent, enthusiastic; in the mood *or* vein *or* humor *or* mind, in a good mood; receptive, responsive; amenable, tractable, docile, pliant

6 **ungrudging,** ungrumbling, **unreluctant,** unloath, **nothing loath,** unaverse, unshrinking

7 **voluntary, volunteer; ex gratia** <L>, gratuitous; spontaneous, free, freewill; offered, proffered; **discretionary,** discretional, nonmandatory, **optional,** elective; arbitrary; **self-determined,** self-determining, autonomous, independent, selfactive, self-acting; **unsought,** unbesought, **unasked,** unrequested, **unsolicited, uninvited,** unbidden, uncalled-for; **unforced,** uncoerced, unpressured, unrequired, uncompelled; unprompted, uninfluenced

ADVS 8 **willingly, with a will,** with good will, with right good will, *de bonne volonté* <Fr>; **eagerly,** with zest, with relish, with open arms, without question, zealously, ardently, enthusiastically; **readily,** promptly, at the drop of a hat <nonformal>

9 **agreeably, favorably, compliantly;** lief, lieve <nonformal>, fain, as lief, as lief as not; **ungrudgingly,** ungrumblingly, **unreluctantly, nothing loath,** without reluctance *or* demur *or* hesitation, unstintingly, unreservedly

10 **voluntarily, freely, gratuitously, spontaneously;** optionally, electively, by choice; **of one's own accord,** of one's own free will, of one's own volition, without reservation, of one's own choice, at one's own discretion; without coercion *or* pressure *or* compulsion *or* intimidation; independently

325 UNWILLINGNESS

NOUNS 1 refusal 442, **unwillingness, disinclination,** nolition, **indisposition,** indisposedness, **reluctance,** renitency, renitence, grudgingness, grudging consent; unenthusiasm, lack of enthusiasm *or* zeal *or* eagerness, slowness, backwardness, dragging of the feet *and* foot-dragging <both nonformal>; sullenness, sulk, sulks, sulkiness; cursoriness, perfunctoriness; recalcitrance *or* recalcitrancy, disobedience, refractoriness, fractiousness, intractableness, indocility, mutinousness; averseness, aversion, repugnance, antipathy, distaste, disrelish; **obstinacy, stubbornness** 361.1; opposition 451; **resistance** 453; **disagreement,** dissent 456.3

2 **demur,** demurral, **scruple, qualm,** qualm of conscience, reservation, compunction; **hesitation,** hesitancy *or* hesitance, pause, boggle, **falter;** qualmishness, scrupulousness, scrupulosity; **stickling,** boggling; **faltering;** shrinking; shyness, **diffidence,** modesty, bashfulness; recoil; **protest, objection** 333.2

VERBS 3 refuse 442.3, **be unwilling, would** *or* **had rather not, not care to,** not feel like <nonformal>, not find it in one's heart to, not have the heart *or* stomach to; **mind,** object to, draw the line at, be dead set against, **balk at;** grudge, begrudge

4 **demur, scruple,** have qualms *or* scruples; **stickle, stick at,** boggle, strain; falter, waver; **hesitate,** pause, be half-hearted, **hang back,** hang off, hold off; **fight shy of,** shy at, shy, crane, shrink, recoil, blench, flinch, wince, quail, pull back; make bones about *or* of

ADJS 5 **unwilling, disinclined, indisposed,** not in the mood, averse; **unconsenting** 442.6; dead set against, opposed 451.8; **resistant** 453.5; **disagreeing,** differing, at odds 456.16; disobedient, recalcitrant, refractory, fractious, sullen, sulky, indocile, mutinous; cursory, perfunctory; **involuntary, forced**

6 **reluctant,** renitent, **grudging, loath;** backward, laggard, dilatory, slow, slow to; unenthusiastic, unzealous, indifferent, apathetic, perfunctory; balky, balking, restive

7 **demurring, qualmish,** boggling, stickling, hedging, squeamish, **scrupulous; diffident,** shy, modest, bashful; **hesitant,** hesitating, faltering; shrinking

ADVS 8 **unwillingly, involuntarily, against one's will,** *à contre coeur* <Fr>; under compulsion *or* coercion *or* pressure; in spite of oneself, *malgré soi* <Fr>

9 **reluctantly, grudgingly,** sullenly, sulkily; unenthusiastically, perfunctorily; with

dragging feet, with a bad *or* an ill grace, **under protest**; with a heavy heart, with no heart *or* stomach; over one's dead body, not on one's life

326 OBEDIENCE

NOUNS **1 obedience** *or* **obediency**, compliance; acquiescence, consent 441; **deference** 155.1, self-abnegation, submission, submissiveness 433.3; servility 138; eagerness *or* readiness *or* willingness to serve, **dutifulness**, duteousness; **service**, servitium, homage, fealty, **allegiance**, **loyalty**, faithfulness, faith, suit and service *or* suit service, observance <old>; doglike devotion *or* obedience; **conformity** 866, lockstep; law-abidingness

VERBS **2 obey, mind, heed, keep, observe**, listen *or* hearken to; **comply, conform** 866.3, walk in lockstep; stay in line *and* not get out of line *and* not get off base <all nonformal>, **toe the line** *or* mark, fall in, fall in line, obey the rules, follow the book, **do what one is told;** do as one says, do the will of, defer to 155.4, do one's bidding, come at one's call, lie down and roll over for <nonformal>; take orders, attend to orders, do suit and service, follow the lead of; **submit** 433.6,9

ADJS **3 obedient, compliant**, complying, allegiant; **acquiescent**, consenting 441.4, **submissive** 433.12, deferential 155.8, self-abnegating; willing, **dutiful**, duteous; loyal, faithful, devoted; uncritical, unshakeable, doglike; conforming, in conformity; law-abiding

4 at one's command, at one's whim *or* pleasure, at one's disposal, at one's nod, at one's call, **at one's beck and call**

5 henpecked, tied to one's apron strings, on a string, on a leash, in leading strings; wimpish <nonformal>; milk-toast *or* milquetoast, Caspar Milquetoast

ADVS **6 obediently, compliantly; acquiescently, submissively** 433.17; willingly, **dutifully**, duteously; loyally, faithfully, devotedly; in obedience to, in compliance *or* conformity with

7 at your service *or* command *or* orders, as you please, as you will, as thou wilt <old>

327 DISOBEDIENCE

NOUNS **1 disobedience**, nonobedience, **noncompliance; undutifulness**, unduteousness; willful disobedience; **insubordination**, indiscipline; **unsubmissiveness, in-** tractability, indocility 361.4, recusancy; **nonconformity** 867; **disrespect** 156; **lawlessness**, waywardness, frowardness, naughtiness; violation, transgression, infraction, infringement, lawbreaking; civil disobedience, passive resistance; uncooperativeness, noncooperation; **dereliction**, deliberate negligence, default, delinquency, nonfeasance

2 defiance, refractoriness, recalcitrance *or* recalcitrancy, recalcitration, defiance of authority, contumacy, **contumaciousness, obstreperousness, unruliness**, restiveness, fractiousness, orneriness *and* feistiness <both nonformal>; wildness 430.3; **obstinacy, stubbornness** 361.1

3 rebelliousness, mutinousness; riotousness; insurrectionism, insurgentism; factiousness, **sedition**, seditiousness; treasonableness, traitorousness, subversiveness; extremism 611.4

4 revolt, rebellion, revolution, mutiny, insurrection, insurgence *or* insurgency, *émeute* <Fr>, **uprising**, rising, outbreak, general uprising, *levée en masse* <Fr>, **riot**, civil disorder; peasant revolt, *jacquerie* <Fr>; putsch, coup d'état; **strike, general strike**; intifada

5 rebel, revolter; **insurgent**, insurrectionary, insurrecto, **insurrectionist;** malcontent, *frondeur* <Fr>; **insubordinate; mutineer**, rioter, brawler; maverick <nonformal>, noncooperator, troublemaker, refusenik <nonformal>; nonconformist 867.3; agitator 375.11; extremist 611.12; revolutionary, revolutionist 859.3; traitor, subversive 357.11; freedom fighter

VERBS **6 disobey**, not mind, not heed, not keep *or* observe, not listen *or* hearken, pay no attention to, **ignore, disregard, defy**, set at defiance, fly in the face of, snap one's fingers at, scoff at, flout, go counter to, set at naught, set naught by, care naught for; be a law unto oneself, step out of line, get off-base <nonformal>, refuse to cooperate; not conform 867.4, hear a different drummer; **violate**, transgress 435.4; break the law 674.5

7 revolt, rebel, kick over the traces, reluct, reluctate; **rise up**, rise, arise, rise up in arms, mount the barricades; mount *or* make a coup d'état; **mutiny**, mutineer <old>; insurge *and* insurrect <both old>, **riot**, run riot; revolutionize, revolution, revolute, subvert, overthrow 859.4; call a general strike, strike 727.8; secede, break away

ADJS **8 disobedient, transgressive**, uncom-

plying, violative, lawless, wayward,
froward, naughty; recusant, nonconforming 867.5; **undutiful,** unduteous; self-
willed, willful, obstinate 361.8; **defiant**
454.7; **undisciplined,** ill-disciplined, in-
disciplined

9 **insubordinate, unsubmissive,** indocile,
uncompliant, uncooperative, noncooperative, noncooperating, **intractable**
361.12

10 **defiant, refractory, recalcitrant, contumacious, obstreperous, unruly,** restive,
impatient of control *or* discipline; fractious, ornery *and* feisty <both nonfor-
mal>; wild, untamed 430.29

11 **rebellious,** rebel, breakaway; **mutinous,**
mutineering; **insurgent, insurrectionary,**
riotous, turbulent; factious, **seditious,** seditionary; revolutionary, revolutional;
traitorous, treasonable, subversive; extreme, extremistic 611.20

ADVS 12 **disobediently,** uncompliantly,
against *or* contrary to order and discipline; **insubordinately, unsubmissively,**
indocilely, **uncooperatively;** unresign-
edly; disregardfully, floutingly, **defiantly;**
intractably 361.17; obstreperously, contumaciously, restively, fractiously; **re-
belliously,** mutinously; riotously

328 ACTION
<voluntary action>

NOUNS 1 **action, activity** 330, act, willed action *or* activity; **acting, doing,** activism,
direct action, not words but action; **practice,** actual practice, praxis; **exercise,**
drill; **operation,** working, function, functioning; play; **operations,** affairs, workings; **business,** employment, work, occupation; **behavior** 321

2 **performance, execution,** carrying out,
enactment; **transaction; discharge,
dispatch;** conduct, **handling,** management, administration; **achievement,
accomplishment, effectuation, implementation; commission, perpetration;**
completion 407.2

3 **act, action, deed, doing,** thing, thing
done; **turn; feat, stunt** *and* **trick** <both
nonformal>; **master stroke,** *tour de force*
<Fr>, **exploit,** adventure, gest, **enter-
prise, initiative,** achievement,
accomplishment, **performance,** production, track record <nonformal>; effort,
endeavor, job, undertaking; **transaction;**
dealing, deal <nonformal>; passage; **operation, proceeding, step, measure,
maneuver, move, movement;** *démarche*

<Fr>, coup, stroke; blow, go <nonfor-
mal>; accomplished fact, *fait accompli*
<Fr>, done deal <nonformal>; overt act
<law>; acta, *res gestae* <L>, **doings,
dealings; works;** work, handiwork, hand
VERBS 4 **act, serve, function; operate, work,
move,** practice, do one's stuff *or* one's
thing <all nonformal>; **move,** proceed;
make, play, **behave** 321.4

5 **take action, take steps** *or* **measures; proceed,** proceed with, go ahead with, go
with, go through with; do something, go
or swing into action, **do something about,
act on** *or* **upon,** take it on, run with it
<nonformal>, get off the dime *or* one's
ass *or* one's dead ass <nonformal>, get
with it *or* the picture <nonformal>; fish
or cut bait, shit or get off the pot *and* put
up or shut up *and* put one's money where
one's mouth is <all nonformal>; **go,** have
a go <chiefly Brit nonformal>, take a
whack *or* a cut <nonformal>, lift a finger,
take *or* **bear a hand;** play a role *or* part in;
stretch forth one's hand, strike a blow;
maneuver, make moves <nonformal>

6 **do, effect,** effectuate, **make; bring about,**
bring to pass, **bring off, produce, deliver**
<nonformal>, **do the trick,** put across *or*
through; swing *or* swing it *and* hack it
and cut it *and* cut the mustard <all non-
formal>; **do one's part,** carry one's
weight, carry the ball <nonformal>, hold
up one's end *or* one's end of the bargain;
tear off <nonformal>, **achieve, accomplish,** realize 407.4; **render, pay; inflict,
wreak,** do to; **commit, perpetrate;** pull off
<nonformal>; go and do, up and do *or*
take and do <both nonformal>

7 **carry out,** carry through, go through, fulfill, work out; **bring off,** carry off; **put
through,** get through; **implement; put
into effect, put in** *or* **into practice,** carry
into effect, carry into execution, **translate
into action;** suit the action to the word;
rise to the occasion, come through
<nonformal>

8 **practice,** put into practice, exercise, **employ, use; carry on,** conduct, prosecute,
wage; follow, pursue; **engage in,** work at,
devote oneself to, **do,** turn to, apply oneself to, employ oneself in; play at; **take
up,** take to, **undertake, tackle,** take on,
address oneself to, have a go at, turn one's
hand to, **go in** *or* **out for** <nonformal>,
make it one's business, follow as an occupation, set up shop; specialize in 865.4

9 **perform, execute, enact; transact; discharge, dispatch;** conduct, **manage,
handle;** dispose of, take care of, **deal with,**

cope with; **make, accomplish,** complete 407.6

ADJS **10 acting,** performing, practicing, serving, functioning, functional, operating, operative, operational, working; in action 888.11; behavioral 321.7

329 INACTION
<voluntary inaction>

NOUNS **1 inaction,** passiveness, "a wise passiveness"—Wordsworth, **passivity,** passivism; passive resistance, nonviolent resistance; nonresistance, nonviolence; pacifism; neutrality, neutralness, neutralism, **nonparticipation, noninvolvement;** standpattism <nonformal>; **do-nothingism,** do-nothingness, do-nothing policy, **laissez-faireism;** *laissez-faire, laissez-aller* <both Fr>; watching and waiting, watchful waiting, waiting game, a wait-and-see attitude; **inertia,** inertness, **immobility,** dormancy, stagnation, stagnancy, vegetation, stasis, paralysis; **procrastination; idleness,** indolence, torpor, torpidity, torpidity, sloth; **immobility** 852.1; equilibrium, dead center; **inactivity** 331; **quietude, serenity, quiescence** 173; **quietism,** contemplation, meditation, passive self-annihilation; contemplative life, *vita contemplativa* <L>

VERBS **2 do nothing,** not stir, not budge, **not lift a finger** *or* **hand,** not move a foot, **sit back, sit on one's hands** <nonformal>, sit on one's ass *or* dead ass *or* butt *or* duff <nonformal>, sit on the sidelines, be a sideliner, sit it out, take a raincheck <nonformal>, fold one's arms, twiddle one's thumbs; **cool one's heels** *or* jets <nonformal>; **bide one's time, delay,** watch and wait, wait and see, play a waiting game, lie low; hang fire, not go off half-cocked; lie *or* sit back, lie *or* rest upon one's oars, rest, put one's feet up *and* kick back <both nonformal>, be still 173.7; repose on one's laurels; drift, coast; **stagnate,** vegetate, veg out <nonformal>, lie dormant, hibernate; lay down on the job <nonformal>, idle 331.11

3 refrain, abstain, hold, **spare, forbear, forgo,** keep from; hold *or* stay one's hand, sit by *or* idly by, sit on one's hands

4 let alone, leave alone, **leave** *or* **let well enough alone;** look the other way, not make waves, not look for trouble, not rock the boat; **let be,** leave be <nonformal>, let things take their course, let it

have its way; leave things as they are; *laisser faire, laisser passer, laisser aller* <all Fr>, live and let live; **take no part in,** not get involved in, **have nothing to do with,** have no hand in, stand *or* hold *or* remain aloof

5 let go, let pass, **let slip, let slide** *and* let ride <both nonformal>; procrastinate

ADJS **6 passive; neutral,** neuter; standpat <nonformal>, **do-nothing;** *laissez-faire, laissez-aller* <both Fr>; **inert,** like a bump on a log <nonformal>, immobile, dormant, stagnant, stagnating, vegetative, vegetable, static, stationary, motionless, immobile, unmoving, paralyzed, paralytic; procrastinating; **inactive, idle** 331.16; quiescent 173.12; quietist, quietistic, contemplative, meditative

ADVS **7 at a stand** *or* **standstill,** at a halt; as a last resort

PHRS **8** if it ain't broke don't fix it, let sleeping dogs lie; *dolce far niente* <Ital>

330 ACTIVITY

NOUNS **1 activity, action,** activeness; **movement,** motion, **stir; proceedings, doings, goings-on; activism,** political activism, judicial activism, etc; **militancy;** business 724

2 liveliness, animation, vivacity, vivaciousness, **sprightliness, spiritedness,** bubbliness, ebullience, effervescence, **briskness, breeziness, peppiness** <nonformal>; **life, spirit, verve,** energy, adrenalin; pep *and* moxie *and* oomph *and* pizzazz *and* piss and vinegar <all nonformal>, **vim** 17.2

3 quickness, swiftness, speediness, alacrity, celerity, readiness, smartness, sharpness, briskness; **promptness,** promptitude; dispatch, expeditiousness, expedition; **agility, nimbleness, spryness,** springiness

4 bustle, fuss, flurry, flutter, fluster, scramble, ferment, stew, sweat, whirl, swirl, vortex, maelstrom, **stir,** hubbub, hullabaloo, hoo-ha *and* foofaraw *and* flap <all nonformal>, schemozzle <Brit nonformal>, feery-fary <Scots>, ado, to-do <nonformal>, bother, botheration <nonformal>, pother; fussiness, flutteriness; tumult, commotion, **agitation; restlessness,** unquiet, fidgetiness; **spurt, burst,** fit, spasm

5 busyness, press of business; plenty to do, many irons in the fire, much on one's plate; the battle of life, the rat race <nonformal>

6 industry, industriousness, assiduousness,

assiduity, diligence, application, concentration, laboriousness, sedulity, **sedulousness,** unsparingness, relentlessness, zealousness, ardor, fervor, vehemence; **energy,** energeticalness, strenuousness, strenuosity, tirelessness, indefatigability

7 **enterprise,** enterprisingness, dynamism, **initiative,** aggression, **aggressiveness,** killer instinct, force, forcefulness, push-fulness, pushingness, **pushiness, push, drive, hustle, go,** getup, get-up-and-get *or* **get-up-and-go** <both nonformal>, go-ahead, go-getting, go-to-itiveness <nonformal>, **up-and-comingness; adventurousness,** venturousness, venturesomeness, adventuresomeness; spirit, gumption *and* spunk <both nonformal>; **ambitiousness** 100.10; "the strenuous life"—Theodore Roosevelt

8 **man** *or* **woman of action, doer,** man of deeds; **hustler** *and* self-starter <both nonformal>, bustler; go-getter *and* ball of fire *and* live wire *and* powerhouse *and* human dynamo *and* spitfire <all nonformal>; **workaholic,** overachiever; beaver, busy bee, **eager beaver** <nonformal>; operator *and* big-time operator *and* wheeler-dealer <all nonformal>; winner <nonformal>; **activist,** political activist, **militant;** enthusiast 101.4; new broom, take-charge guy <nonformal>

9 **overactivity,** hyperactivity; hyperkinesia *or* hyperkinesis; franticness, frenziedness; overexertion, overextension; officiousness 214.2

VERBS 10 **be busy, have one's hands full,** have many irons in the fire, have a lot on one's plate; not have a moment to spare, not have a moment to call one's own, not be able to call one's time one's own; do it on the run; have other things to do, have other fish to fry; **work, labor, drudge** 725.14; **busy oneself** 724.10,11

11 **stir,** stir about, **bestir oneself,** stir one's stumps <nonformal>, get down to business, sink one's teeth into it, take hold, be up and doing

12 **bustle, fuss,** make a fuss, stir, stir about, rush around *or* about, tear around, hurry about, buzz *or* whiz about, dart to and fro, run *or* go around like a chicken with its head cut off

13 **hustle** <nonformal>, **drive,** drive oneself, **push, scramble,** go all out <nonformal>, **make things hum,** step lively <nonformal>, make the sparks *or* chips fly <nonformal>; make up for lost time; press on, drive on; go ahead, forge ahead, shoot ahead, go full steam ahead

14 <nonformal terms> **hump,** get cutting, break one's neck, bear down on it, put one's back into it, get off the dime, get off one's ass *or* duff *or* dead ass, **hit the ball,** pour it on, lean on it, shake a leg, go to town, get the lead out, floor it

15 **keep going, keep on,** keep on the go, keep on keeping on, keep on trucking <nonformal>, **carry on,** peg *or* plug away <nonformal>, **keep at it,** keep moving, keep driving, **keep the pot boiling,** keep the ball rolling; keep busy, **keep one's nose to the grindstone,** stay on the treadmill

16 make the most of one's time, improve the shining hour, make hay while the sun shines, not let the grass grow under one's feet; get up early

ADJS 17 **active, lively, animated, spirited,** bubbly, ebullient, effervescent, **vivacious, sprightly,** chipper *and* perky <both nonformal>, pert; **spry, breezy, brisk, energetic,** eager, keen, can-do <nonformal>; smacking, spanking; alive, live, full of life, full of pep *or* go *and* pizzazz *or* moxie <nonformal>; **peppy** *and* snappy *and* zingy <all nonformal>; frisky, bouncing, bouncy, mercurial, quick-silver; **activist,** activistic, **militant**

18 **quick, swift, speedy, expeditious, snappy** <nonformal>, celeritous, alacritous, dis-patchful <old>, **prompt,** ready, smart, sharp, quick on the draw *or* trigger *or* up-swing <nonformal>; **agile, nimble, spry, springy**

19 **astir, stirring,** afoot, **on foot;** in full swing

20 **bustling,** fussing, fussy; **fidgety,** restless, fretful, jumpy, unquiet, unsettled 105.23; **agitated, turbulent**

21 **busy,** full of business; **occupied, engaged, employed, working;** at it; **at work,** on duty, on the job, in harness; hard at work, **hard at it; on the move, on the go,** on the run, **on the hop** *or* **jump** <nonformal>; busy as a bee *or* beaver, busier than a one-armed paper hanger <nonformal>; up to one's ears *or* elbows *or* asshole *or* neck *or* eyeballs in <nonformal>; tied up

22 **industrious, assiduous, diligent, sedulous,** laborious, **hardworking;** hard, unremitting, unsparing, relentless, zealous, ardent, fervent, vehement; **energetic,** strenuous; never idle; sleepless, unsleeping; tireless, unwearied, unflagging, indefatigable

23 **enterprising, aggressive, dynamic,** activist, proactive, driving, forceful, **pushing,** pushful, **pushy, up-and-coming, go-ahead** *and* **hustling** <both nonformal>; adven-

turous, venturous, venturesome, adventuresome; **ambitious** 100.28

24 **overactive,** hyperactive, hyper <nonformal>; hectic, frenzied, frantic, frenetic; hyperkinetic; intrusive, officious 214.9

ADVS **25 actively, busily; lively,** sprightly, **briskly, breezily, energetically, animatedly, vivaciously, spiritedly,** with life and spirit, with gusto; allegro, allegretto; full tilt, in full swing, all out <nonformal>; like a house afire

26 **quickly, swiftly, expeditiously,** with dispatch, readily, **promptly; agilely, nimbly, spryly**

27 **industriously, assiduously, diligently, sedulously,** laboriously; unsparingly, relentlessly, zealously, ardently, fervently, vehemently; **energetically,** strenuously, tirelessly, indefatigably

331 INACTIVITY

NOUNS **1 inactivity, inaction** 329, inactiveness; lull, suspension; suspended animation; dormancy, hibernation; immobility, motionlessness, quiescence 173; **inertia** 329.1; underactivity

2 **idleness,** unemployment, nothing to do, otiosity, inoccupation; **leisure,** leisureliness, unhurried ease; idle hands, idle hours, time on one's hands; "a life of dignified otiosity"—Thackeray; **relaxation,** letting down, unwinding, putting one's feet up, slippered ease

3 **unemployment,** lack of work, joblessness, inoccupation; layoff, furlough; normal unemployment, seasonal unemployment, technological unemployment, cyclical unemployment; unemployment insurance

4 **idling, loafing,** lazing, *flânerie* <Fr>, goofing off <nonformal>, goldbricking <nonformal>; *dolce far niente* <Ital>; trifling; dallying, dillydallying, mopery, dawdling; loitering, tarrying, lingering; lounging, **lolling**

5 **indolence, laziness, sloth,** slothfulness, bone-laziness; laggardness, slowness, dilatoriness, remissness, do-nothingness, faineancy, *fainéantise* <Fr>; inexertion, inertia; **shiftlessness,** do-lessness <nonformal>; hoboism, vagrancy; spring fever; ergophobia

6 **languor,** languidness, languorousness, languishment <old>, lackadaisicalness, lotus-eating; **listlessness,** lifelessness, inanimation, enervation, slowness, lenitude *or* lentor <both old>, **dullness,**

sluggishness, heaviness, dopiness <nonformal>, hebetude, supineness, **lassitude, lethargy,** loginess; kef, nodding; phlegm, **apathy, indifference, passivity;** torpidness, **torpor,** torpidity; stupor, stuporousness, stupefaction; **sloth,** slothfulness, acedia; **sleepiness, somnolence, oscitancy, yawning, drowsiness** 22.1; **weariness, fatigue** 21; jadedness, satedness 993.2; world-weariness, ennui, boredom 118.3

7 **lazybones,** lazyboots, lazylegs, indolent, lie-abed, slugabed

8 **idler, loafer, lounger,** loller, layabout <Brit nonformal>, couch potato <nonformal>, lotus-eater, *flâneur, flâneuse* <both Fr>, **do-nothing,** dolittle, *fainéant* <Fr>, goof-off *and* fuck-off *and* goldbrick *and* goldbricker <all nonformal>, clock watcher; **sluggard,** slug, slouch, sloucher, lubber, stick-in-the-mud <nonformal>, gentleman of leisure; **time waster,** time killer; **dallier, dillydallier,** mope, moper, doodler, diddler <nonformal>, **dawdler,** dawdle, laggard, **loiterer,** lingerer; waiter on Providence; trifler, **putterer,** potterer

9 **bum,** stiff <nonformal>, derelict, skidrow bum, Bowery bum, *lazzarone* <Ital>; beachcomber; **good-for-nothing,** good-for-naught, **ne'er-do-well,** wastrel; drifter, vagrant, hobo, tramp 178.3; beggar 440.8

10 homeless person; street person; shopping-bag lady *or* woman

11 **nonworker, drone;** cadger, bummer *and* moocher <both nonformal>, **sponger,** freeloader, lounge lizard <nonformal>, social parasite, parasite, spiv <Brit>; beggar, mendicant, panhandler <nonformal>; **the unemployed;** the unemployable; the chronically unemployed, discouraged workers, lumpen proletariat; leisure class, rentiers, coupon-clippers, idle rich

VERBS **12 idle,** do nothing, **laze,** lazy <nonformal>, take one's ease *or* leisure, take one's time, **loaf, lounge;** "I loafe and invite my soul, I lean and loafe at my ease"—Walt Whitman; **lie around,** lounge around, loll around, lollop about <Brit nonformal>, moon, moon around, sit around, sit on one's ass *or* butt *or* duff <nonformal>, stand *or* hang around, **loiter about** *or* **around,** slouch, slouch around, **bum around** *and* mooch around <both nonformal>; **shirk,** avoid work, **goof off** *and* fuck off *and* **lie down on the job** <all nonformal>; sleep at one's post;

let the grass grow under one's feet; twiddle one's thumbs, fold one's arms

13 **waste time,** consume time, **kill time,** idle *or* trifle *or* fritter *or* fool away time, loiter away *or* loiter out the time, beguile the time, **while away the time,** pass the time, lose time, waste the precious hours, burn daylight <old>; **trifle,** dabble, fribble, footle, putter, potter, piddle, diddle, doodle

14 **dally, dillydally,** piddle, diddle, diddle-daddle, doodle, **dawdle, loiter,** lollygag <nonformal>, linger, lag, poke, take one's time

15 **take it easy,** take things as they come, **drift,** drift with the current, go with the flow, swim with the stream, coast, lead an easy life, **live a life of ease,** eat the bread of idleness, lie *or* rest on one's oars; rest *or* repose on one's laurels, lie back on one's record

16 **lie idle, lie fallow;** aestivate, hibernate, lie dormant; lie *or* lay off, charge *or* recharge one's batteries <nonformal>; lie up, lie on the shelf; ride at anchor, lay *or* lie by, lay *or* lie to; have nothing to do, have nothing on <nonformal>

ADJS 17 **inactive,** unactive; stationary, static, at a standstill; sedentary; **quiescent,** motionless 173.13

18 **idle,** fallow, otiose; **unemployed, unoccupied,** disengaged, *désœuvré* <Fr>, **jobless, out of work,** out of employ, out of a job, out of harness; free, available, at liberty, at leisure; at loose ends; unemployable, lumpen; leisure, leisured; off duty, off work, off

19 **indolent, lazy,** bone-lazy, **slothful,** workshy, ergophobic; **do-nothing,** *fainéant* <Fr>, **laggard,** slow, **dilatory,** procrastinative, remiss, slack, lax; easy; **shiftless,** do-less <nonformal>; **unenterprising,** nonaggressive; good-for-nothing, ne'er-do-well; drony, dronish, spivvish <Brit>, parasitic, cadging, sponging, scrounging

20 **languid, languorous, listless,** lifeless, inanimate, enervated, debilitated, **pepless** <nonformal>, lackadaisical, slow, wan, **lethargic,** logy, hebetudinous, supine, lymphatic, apathetic, **sluggish,** dopey <nonformal>, drugged, nodding, droopy, **dull,** heavy, leaden, lumpish, **torpid,** stultified, stuporous, **inert,** stagnant, stagnating, vegetative, vegetable, dormant; phlegmatic, numb, benumbed; moribund, dead, exanimate; sleepy, somnolent 22.21; **pooped** <nonformal>, weary; jaded, sated 993.6; **blasé,** world-weary, bored

332 ASSENT

NOUNS 1 **assent, acquiescence, concurrence, concurring, concurrency, compliance, agreement, acceptance,** accession; eager *or* hearty *or* warm assent, welcome; assentation; agreement in principle, general agreement; support; **consent** 441

2 **affirmative; yes,** yea, aye, amen; nod, nod of assent; thumbs-up; **affirmativeness,** affirmative attitude, yea-saying; **me-too-ism;** toadying, automatic agreement, knee-jerk assent, subservience, asslicking <nonformal>

3 **acknowledgment, recognition, acceptance;** appreciation; **admission,** confession, concession, allowance; avowal, profession, declaration

4 **ratification, endorsement, acceptance, approval, approbation** 509.1, subscription, subscribership, signing-off, imprimatur, **sanction, permission, the OK** *and* the okay *and* **the green light** *and* **the go-ahead** *and* the nod <all nonformal>, **certification, confirmation, validation, authentication,** authorization, warrant; **affirmation,** affirmance; stamp, rubber stamp, **stamp of approval;** seal, signet, sigil; **subscription, signature,** John Hancock <nonformal>; countersignature; visa, *visé* <Fr>; notarization

5 **unanimity,** unanimousness, universal *or* univocal *or* unambiguous assent; **likemindedness, meeting of minds,** one *or* same mind; total agreement; **understanding,** mutual understanding; **concurrence, consent,** general consent, common assent *or* consent, consentaneity, **accord,** accordance, **concord,** concordance, **agreement,** general agreement; **consensus,** consensus of opinion <nonformal>; *consensus omnium* <L>, universal agreement *or* accord, *consensus gentium* <L>, agreement of all, shared sense, sense of the meeting; **acclamation,** general acclamation; unison, harmony, **chorus, concert,** one *or* single voice, one accord; general voice, vox pop, *vox populi* <L>

6 **assenter, consenter, accepter,** covenanter, covenantor; assentator, yea-sayer; **yes-man,** toady, creature, ass-licker *and* ass-kisser *and* brown-nose *and* boot-licker <all nonformal>

7 **endorser, subscriber, ratifier,** approver, upholder, certifier, confirmer; **signer,** signatory, the undersigned; cosigner, cosignatory, party; underwriter, guarantor, insurer; notary, notary public

VERBS 8 **assent,** give *or* yield assent, **acqui-**

esce, consent 441.2, **comply, accede, agree,** agree to *or* with, have no problem with; find it in one's heart; take kindly to *and* hold with <both nonformal>; **accept,** receive, buy <nonformal>, take one up on <nonformal>; **subscribe to,** acquiesce in, abide by; yes, **say 'yes' to; nod,** nod assent, vote for, cast one's vote for, give one's voice for; welcome, hail, cheer, acclaim, applaud, accept in toto

9 **concur, accord,** coincide, **agree, agree with,** agree in opinion; enter into one's view, enter into the ideas *or* feelings of, **see eye to eye, be at one with,** be of one mind with, go with, **go along with,** fall *or* chime *or* strike in with, close with, meet, conform to, side with, join *or* identify oneself with; cast in one's lot, fall in *or* into line, lend oneself to, play *or* go along, take kindly to; **echo,** ditto <nonformal>, say 'ditto' to, say 'amen' to; join in the chorus, go along with the crowd <nonformal>, run with the pack, go *or* float *or* swim with the stream *or* current; get on the bandwagon <nonformal>

10 **come to an agreement, agree, concur on, settle on,** agree with, **agree on** *or* **upon, arrive at an agreement, come to an understanding, come to terms, reach an understanding** *or* **agreement** *or* **accord,** strike *or* hammer out a bargain, covenant, get together <nonformal>; **shake hands on,** shake on it <nonformal>; come around to

11 **acknowledge, admit, own, confess, allow,** avow, **grant,** warrant, **concede,** yield <old>; **accept, recognize;** agree in principle, express general agreement, go along with, not oppose *or* deny, agree provisionally *or* for the sake of argument; bring oneself to agree, assent grudgingly *or* under protest

12 **ratify, endorse,** sign off on, second, support, **certify, confirm, validate, authenticate, accept,** give the nod *or* the green light *or* the go-ahead *or* the OK <all nonformal>, give a nod of assent, give one's imprimatur, permit, give permission, **approve** 509.9; sanction, **authorize,** warrant, accredit; **pass,** pass on *or* upon, give thumbs up <nonformal>; amen, say amen to; visa, *visé* <Fr>; underwrite, subscribe to; **sign,** undersign, sign on the dotted line, put one's John Hancock on <nonformal>, initial, put one's mark *or* X *or* cross on; autograph; cosign, countersign; seal, sign and seal, set one's seal, **set one's hand and seal;** affirm, swear and affirm, take one's oath, swear to; rubber stamp <nonformal>; notarize

ADJS 13 **assenting, agreeing,** acquiescing, **acquiescent, compliant,** consenting, consentient, consensual, submissive, unmurmuring, conceding, concessive, assentatious, **agreed, content**

14 **accepted, approved,** received; acknowledged, admitted, allowed, granted, conceded, recognized, professed, confessed, avowed, warranted; self-confessed; **ratified, endorsed, certified,** confirmed, validated, authenticated; certificatory, confirmatory, validating, warranting; **signed,** sealed, signed and sealed, countersigned, underwritten; stamped; sworn to, notarized, affirmed, sworn and affirmed

15 **unanimous, solid,** consentaneous, **with one consent** *or* **voice;** uncontradicted, unchallenged, uncontroverted, uncontested, unopposed; **concurrent,** concordant, **of one accord; agreeing, in agreement, likeminded, of one mind,** of the same mind; of a piece, **at one,** at one with, agreed on all hands, carried by acclamation

ADVS 16 **affirmatively,** assentingly, in the affirmative

17 **unanimously,** concurrently, consentaneously, **by common** *or* **general consent,** with one consent, **with one accord,** with one voice, without contradiction, *nemine contradicente* <L>, nem con, without a dissenting voice, *nemine dissentiente* <L>, in chorus, in concert, in unison, in one voice, univocally, unambiguously, to a man, **together,** all together, all agreeing, **as one,** as one man, one and all, on all hands; by acclamation

INTERJS 18 **yes, yea,** aye, *oui* <Fr>, *sí* <Sp>, *da* <Russ>, *ja* <Ger>; yes sir, yes ma'am; why yes, *mais oui* <Fr>; **indeed,** yes indeed; **surely, certainly,** assuredly, most assuredly, **right, right you are, exactly, precisely,** just so, absolutely, positively, really, truly, rather <Brit>, quite, to be sure; **all right, right, good,** well and good, good enough, **very well,** *très bien* <Fr>; naturally, *naturellement* <Fr>; **of course,** as you say, **by all means,** by all manner of means; **amen;** hear hear <Brit>

19 <nonformal terms> **yeah,** yep, yup, uh-huh; yes sirree, same here, likewise, indeedy, yes indeedy, sure, sure thing, sure enough, surest thing you know; right on!, righto!; OK, okay, Roger, Roger-dodger; fine; you bet!, bet your ass!, you can bet

on it!, you can say that again!, you said
it!, you better believe it

20 PHRS **so be it,** be it so, so mote it be
<old>, so shall it be, *amen* <Heb>; so it
is, so is it; agreed, done, that's about the
size of it; *c'est bien* <Fr>; that takes care
of that, that's that, that's right; that
makes two of us

333 DISSENT

NOUNS **1 dissent, dissidence,** dissentience;
nonassent, nonconsent, nonconcurrence,
nonagreement, agreement to disagree;
minority opinion *or* report *or* position;
disagreement, difference, variance, diversity, disparity; **dissatisfaction,**
disapproval, disapprobation; repudiation, **rejection; refusal, opposition** 451;
dissension, disaccord 456; **alienation,**
withdrawal, dropping out, secession; recusance *or* recusancy, **nonconformity**
867; apostasy 363.2; counterculture, underground

2 objection, protest; kick and **beef** and
bitch and squawk and howl <all nonfor-
mal>, protestation; **remonstrance,**
remonstration, expostulation; **challenge;**
demur, demurrer; **reservation, scruple,**
compunction, qualm, twinge *or* qualm of
conscience; **complaint, grievance; excep-**
tion; peaceful *or* nonviolent protest;
demonstration, demo <nonformal>, protest demonstration, counterdemonstra-
tion, **rally,** march, sit-in, teach-in, boycott, strike, picketing, indignation
meeting; grievance committee; **rebellion**
327.4

3 dissenter, dissident, dissentient, recusant; **objector,** demurrer; minority *or*
opposition voice; **protester,** protestant;
separatist, schismatic; sectary, sectarian,
opinionist; nonconformist 867.3; apostate 363.5

VERBS **4 dissent,** dissent from, be in dissent,
say nay, **disagree,** discord with, **differ,**
not agree, disagree with, agree to disagree *or* differ; divide on, be at variance;
take exception, withhold assent, **take is-**
sue, beg to differ, raise an objection, rise
to a point of order; be in opposition to,
oppose; refuse to conform, kick against
the pricks, march to *or* hear a different
drummer, swim against the tide *or*
against the current *or* upstream; **split off,**
withdraw, drop out, secede, separate *or*
disjoin oneself

5 object, protest, kick and **beef** <both non-
formal>, put up a struggle *or* fight; **bitch**

and **beef** and **squawk** and howl and holler
and put up a squawk and raise a howl
<all nonformal>; exclaim *or* cry out
against, make *or* create *or* raise a stink
about <all nonformal>; yell bloody
murder <nonformal>; **remonstrate,**
expostulate; raise *or* press objections,
raise one's voice against, enter a protest;
complain, exclaim at, state a grievance,
air one's grievances; **dispute, challenge,**
call in question; **demur, scruple,** boggle,
dig in one's heels; **demonstrate, demon-**
strate against, rally, march, sit-in, teach-
in, boycott, strike, picket; **rebel** 327.7

ADJS **6 dissenting, dissident,** dissentient, recusant; **disagreeing, differing; opposing**
451.8, in opposition; alienated; counterculture, antiestablishment, underground;
breakaway <Brit>; at variance with, at
odds with; schismatic, schismatical, sectarian, sectary; nonconforming 867.5;
rebellious 327.11; resistant 453.5

7 protesting, protestant; **objecting,** expostulative, expostulatory, remonstrative,
remonstrant; under protest

334 AFFIRMATION

NOUNS **1 affirmation,** affirmance, **assertion,**
asseveration, averment, **declaration,**
vouch <old>, allegation; **avouchment,**
avowal; position, stand, stance; profession, **statement, word,** say, saying, say-so
<nonformal>, positive declaration *or*
statement; manifesto, position paper;
statement of principles, **creed** 952.3;
pronouncement, proclamation, announcement, annunciation, enunciation;
proposition, conclusion; predication,
predicate; protest, protestation; utterance, dictum, *ipse dixit* <L>

2 affirmativeness; assertiveness, positiveness, absoluteness, speaking out, table-
thumping <nonformal>

3 deposition, sworn statement, affidavit,
statement under oath, notarized statement, sworn testimony, affirmation;
vouching, swearing; attestation; certification; **testimony**

4 oath, vow, avow <old>, **word, assurance,**
guarantee, warrant, solemn oath *or* affirmation *or* word *or* declaration; **pledge**
436.1; Bible oath, ironclad oath; judicial
oath, extrajudicial oath; oath of office, official oath; oath of allegiance, loyalty
oath, test oath

VERBS **5 affirm, assert,** assever <old>, asseverate, **aver,** protest, lay down, avouch,
avow, **declare,** say, say loud and clear,

say out loud, sound off <nonformal>, have one's say, speak, speak one's piece *or* one's mind, speak up *or* out, **state**, set down, express, put, put it, put in one's two-cents worth <nonformal>; **allege**, profess; stand on *or* for; predicate; issue a manifesto *or* position paper, manifesto; announce, **pronounce**, annunciate, enunciate, **proclaim; maintain**, have, **contend**, argue, **insist**, **hold**, submit, maintain with one's last breath

6 **depose**, depone; **testify**, take the stand, witness; **warrant**, **attest**, certify, **guarantee**, **assure**; **vouch**, **vouch for**, **swear to**, swear the truth, **assert under oath**; make *or* take one's oath, **vow**; swear by bell, book, and candle; call heaven to witness, declare *or* swear to God, swear on the Bible, kiss the book, swear to goodness, hope to die, cross one's heart *or* cross one's heart and hope to die; swear till one is black *or* blue in the face <nonformal>

7 administer an oath, **place** *or* **put under oath**, put to one's oath, put upon oath; **swear, swear in**, adjure <old>

ADJS 8 **affirmative**, affirming, affirmatory, certifying, certificatory; **assertive**, assertative, assertional; **declarative**, declaratory; predicative, predicational; **positive**, absolute, emphatic, decided, table-thumping <nonformal>, unambiguously, unmistakably, loud and clear

9 **affirmed**, **asserted**, asseverated, avouched, avowed, averred, **declared**; **alleged**, professed; **stated**, pronounced, announced, enunciated; predicated; manifestoed; **deposed**, warranted, **attested**, **certified**, vouched, **vouched for**, vowed, pledged, **sworn**, **sworn to**

ADVS 10 **affirmatively**, assertively, declaratively, predicatively; **positively**, absolutely, decidedly, loudly, loud and clear, at the top of one's voice *or* one's lungs; emphatically, with emphasis; without fear of contradiction; under oath, on one's honor *or* one's word

335 NEGATION, DENIAL

NOUNS 1 **negation**, negating, abnegation; negativeness, negativity, **negativism**, negative attitude, naysaying; **obtuseness**, perversity, orneriness <nonformal>, cross-grainedness; **negative, no**, nay, nix <nonformal>

2 **denial, disavowal, disaffirmation, disownment**, disallowance; disclamation; disclaimer; **renunciation, retraction**, retractation, **repudiation,** recantation; revocation, nullification, annulment, abrogation; abjuration, abjurement, forswearing; **contradiction,** flat *or* absolute contradiction, contravention, contrary assertion, controversion, countering, crossing, gainsaying, impugnment; **refutation, disproof** 957; **apostasy, defection** 363.2; **about-face, reversal** 363.1

VERBS 3 **negate**, abnegate, negative; **say 'no'**; shake the head, wag *or* waggle the beard

4 **deny, not admit, not accept,** refuse to admit *or* accept; **disclaim, disown, disaffirm, disavow, disallow,** abjure, forswear, **renounce, retract,** take back, recant; revoke, nullify, **repudiate; contradict,** fly in the face of, cross, assert the contrary, contravene, controvert, impugn, **dispute,** gainsay, **oppose, counter,** go counter to, go contra, contest, take issue with, join issue upon, run counter to; belie, give the lie to, give one the lie direct *or* in his throat; **refute** 957.5, **disprove** 957.4; **reverse oneself** 363.6; **defect, apostatize** 363.7

ADJS 5 **negative**, negatory, abnegative; **denying, disclaiming,** disowning, disaffirming, disallowing, disavowing, renunciative, renunciatory, repudiative, recanting, abjuratory, revocative *or* revocatory; **contradictory,** contradicting, **opposing, contrary,** contra, nay-saying, adversative, repugnant; **obtuse,** perverse, ornery <nonformal>, crossgrained, contrarious <nonformal>

ADVS 6 **negatively, in the negative;** in denial, in contradiction

CONJS 7 **neither,** not either, **nor,** nor yet, or not, and not, also not

INTERJS 8 **no, nay,** negative, *non* <Fr>, *nein* <Ger>, *nyet* <Russ>; certainly not, absolutely no; no sir, no ma'am; **not,** not a bit *or* whit *or* jot, I think not, not really; to the contrary, *au contraire* <Fr>, quite the contrary, far from it; no such thing, nothing of the kind *or* sort, not so

9 **by no means, by no manner of means; on no account,** in no respect, **in no case, under no circumstances, on no condition,** no matter what; **not at all,** not in the least, **never;** in no wise, noways, noway, nohow <nonformal>; out of the question; **not for the world,** not for anything in the world, not if one can help it, not if I know it, not at any price, not for love or money, not for the life of me, over one's dead body; to the contrary, *au contraire* <Fr>,

quite the contrary, far from it; God forbid
510.27
10 <nonformal or nonformal terms> nope,
nix, no dice, unhunh, no sirree; no way,
no way José, not on your life, not by a
long chalk, not by a long shot or sight, not
by a darn or damn sight, not a bit of it,
not much, not a chance, fat chance, nothing doing, forget it, that'll be the day

336 IMITATION

NOUNS 1 imitation, copying, counterfeiting,
repetition; me-tooism <nonformal>, emulation, the sincerest form of flattery,
following, mirroring; copycat crime
<nonformal>; simulation 354.3, model-
ing; fakery, forgery, plagiarism, plagiarizing, plagiary; imposture, impersonation, takeoff and hit-off <both nonfor-
mal>, impression, burlesque, pastiche,
pasticcio <Ital>; mimesis; parody,
onomatopoeia
 2 mimicry, mockery, apery, parrotry,
mimetism; protective coloration or mimicry, aggressive mimicry, aposematic or
synaposematic mimicry and cryptic
mimicry <both biology>, playing possum
 3 reproduction, duplication, imitation
784.1, copy 784.1, dummy, mock-up,
replica, facsimile, representation, paraphrase, approximation, model, version,
knockoff <nonformal>; computer model
or simulation; parody, burlesque, pastiche, pasticcio <Ital>, travesty 508.6
 4 imitator, simulator, me-tooer <nonfor-
mal>, impersonator, impostor 357.6,
mimic, mimicker, mimer, mime, mocker;
mockingbird, cuckoo; parrot, polly, poll-
parrot or polly-parrot, ape, aper, monkey;
echo, echoer, echoist; copier, copyist,
copycat <nonformal>; faker, imposter,
counterfeiter, forger, plagiarist; dissimulator, dissembler, deceiver, gay deceiver,
hypocrite, phony <nonformal>, poseur;
conformist, sheep
VERBS 5 imitate, copy, repeat, ditto
<nonformal>; do like <nonformal>, do
<nonformal>, act or go or make like
<nonformal>; mirror, reflect; echo,
reecho, chorus; borrow, steal one's stuff
<nonformal>, take a leaf out of one's
book; assume; affect; simulate; counterfeit, fake <nonformal>, hoke and hoke up
<both nonformal>, forge, plagiarize,
crib, lift <nonformal>; parody, pastiche;
paraphrase, approximate
 6 mimic, impersonate, mime, ape, parrot,

copycat <nonformal>; do an impression;
take off, hit off, hit off on, take off on
 7 emulate, follow, follow in the steps or
footsteps of, walk in the shoes of, put oneself in another's shoes, follow in the wake
of, follow the example of, follow suit, follow like sheep, jump on the bandwagon;
copy after, model after, model on, pattern
after, pattern on, shape after, take after,
take a leaf out of one's book, take as a
model
ADJS 8 imitation, mock, sham, copied, fake
and phony <both nonformal>, counterfeit, forged, plagiarized, unoriginal,
ungenuine; pseudo, synthetic, synthetical, ersatz, hokey and hoked-up <both
nonformal>, quasi
 9 imitative, simulative, me-too <nonfor-
mal>; mimic, mimetic, apish, parrotlike;
emulative; echoic, onomatopoetic, onomatopoeic
10 imitable, copiable, duplicable, replicable
ADVS 11 imitatively, apishly, apewise, par-
rotwise; onomatopoetically; synthetically; quasi
PREPS 12 like, in imitation of, after, in the
semblance of, on the model of, à la <Fr>
WORD ELEMENTS 13 quasi—, mim—,
ne—, near—, semi—; —ish, —like

337 NONIMITATION

NOUNS 1 nonimitation, originality, novelty,
newness, innovation, freshness, uniqueness; authenticity; inventiveness,
creativity, creativeness 985.3
 2 original, model 785, archetype, prototype
785.1, pattern, mold, pilot model; innovation, new departure
 3 autograph, holograph, first edition
VERBS 4 originate, invent; innovate; create;
revolutionize
ADJS 5 original, novel, unprecedented;
unique, sui generis <L>; new, fresh
840.7; underived, firsthand; authentic,
imaginative, creative 985.18; avant-
garde, revolutionary; pioneer, bellwether, trail-blazing
 6 unimitated, uncopied, unduplicated, un-
reproduced, unprecedented, unexampled; archetypal, archetypical, archetypic, prototypal 785.9; prime, primary,
primal, primitive, pristine

338 COMPENSATION

NOUNS 1 compensation, recompense, repayment, payback, indemnity, indemnification, measure for measure, rectification,

restitution, **reparation; amends,** expiation, atonement; **redress,** satisfaction; commutation, substitution; **offsetting,** balancing, **counterbalancing,** counteraction; **retaliation** 506, revenge, *lex talionis* <L>

2 **offset,** setoff; **counterbalance,** counterpoise, equipoise, counterweight, makeweight; **balance,** ballast; **trade-off,** equivalent, consideration, something of value, *quid pro quo* <L, something for something>, tit for tat, give-and-take 862.1

3 **counterclaim,** counterdemand

VERBS 4 **compensate,** make compensation, make good, set right, restitute, pay back, rectify, **make up for; make amends,** expiate, do penance, atone; **recompense,** pay back, repay, indemnify, cover; **trade off,** give and take; **retaliate** 506

5 **offset** 778.4, set off, **counteract,** countervail, **counterbalance,** counterweigh, counterpoise, **balance,** play off against, set against, set over against, equiponderate; **square,** square up

ADJS 6 **compensating, compensatory;** recompensive, amendatory, indemnificatory, reparative, rectifying; **offsetting,** counteracting *or* counteractive, countervailing, balancing, **counterbalancing,** zero-sum; **expiatory,** penitential; **retaliatory** 506

ADVS 7 **in compensation,** in return, back; in consideration, for a consideration

ADVS, CONJS 8 **notwithstanding,** but, all the same <nonformal>, still, yet, even; **however, nevertheless,** nonetheless; **although,** when, though; howbeit, albeit; **at all events,** in any event, **in any case,** at any rate; **be that as it may,** for all that, even so, **on the other hand,** rather, again, at the same time, all the same, just the same, **however, that may be;** after all, after all is said and done

ADVS, PREPS 9 **in spite of,** spite of <nonformal>, **despite,** in despite of, with, even with; **regardless of,** regardless, irregardless <nonformal>, irrespective of, without respect *or* regard to; cost what it may, regardless of cost, at any cost, at all costs, whatever the cost

339 CAREFULNESS
<*close or watchful attention*>

NOUNS 1 **carefulness, care, heed, concern, regard; attention** 982; **heedfulness,** regardfulness, mindfulness, **thoughtfulness; consideration,** solicitude, caring, loving care, tender loving care, TLC

<nonformal>, caregiving; circumspectness, circumspection; forethought, anticipation, preparedness; **caution** 494

2 **painstakingness,** painstaking, **pains; diligence,** assiduousness, assiduity, sedulousness, industriousness, industry; **thoroughness,** thoroughgoingness

3 **meticulousness,** exactingness, **scrupulousness,** scrupulosity, **conscientiousness,** punctiliousness, attention to detail, finetuning; **particularness,** particularity, circumstantiality; **fussiness, criticalness,** criticality; **finicalness,** finickingness, finickiness, finicality; **exactness, exactitude, accuracy, preciseness, precision,** precisionism, precisianism, punctuality, correctness, prissiness; **strictness, rigor,** rigorousness, spit and polish; nicety, niceness, delicacy, detail, subtlety, refinement, minuteness, exquisiteness

4 **vigilance, wariness,** prudence, **watchfulness,** watching, observance, **surveillance; watch, vigil, lookout;** *qui vive* <Fr>; invigilation, proctoring, monitoring; watch and ward; custody, custodianship, guardianship, stewardship; **guard,** guardedness; **sharp eye, weather eye,** peeled eye, watchful eye, eagle eye, lidless *or* sleepless *or* unblinking *or* unwinking eye

5 **alertness, attentiveness; attention** 982; **wakefulness,** sleeplessness; **readiness,** promptness, promptitude, punctuality; **quickness,** agility, nimbleness; **smartness,** brightness, keenness, sharpness, acuteness, acuity

VERBS 6 **care, mind, heed,** reck, think, consider, regard, pay heed to, take heed *or* thought of; **take an interest,** be concerned; **pay attention** 982.8

7 **be careful, take care** *or* good care, take heed, have a care, exercise care; **be cautious** 494.5; **take pains,** take trouble, **be painstaking,** go to great pains, go to great lengths, go out of one's way, go the extra mile <nonformal>, bend over backwards <nonformal>, use every trick in the book, not miss a trick; mind what one is doing *or* about, mind one's business, **mind one's P's and Q's** <nonformal>; **watch one's step** <nonformal>, pick one's steps, tread on eggs, place one's feet carefully, feel one's way; treat gently, **handle with gloves** *or* **kid gloves**

8 **be vigilant,** be watchful, never nod *or* sleep, **be on the watch** *or* **lookout,** be on the *qui vive* <Fr>, keep a good *or* sharp lookout, keep in sight *or* view; **keep watch,** keep watch and ward, keep vigil; **watch, look sharp,** look about one, look

with one's own eyes, **be on one's guard,** keep an eye out, sleep with one eye open, have all one's eyes *or* wits about one, keep one's eye on the ball <nonformal>, keep one's eyes open, keep a weather eye open *and* **keep one's eyes peeled** <both nonformal>, keep the ear to the ground, keep a nose to the wind; keep alert, **be on the alert; look out, watch out;** look lively *or* alive; stop, look, and listen

9 look after, nurture, foster, **tend, take care of** 1007.19

ADJS **10 careful, heedful, regardful, mindful, thoughtful, considerate, caring,** solicitous, loving, tender, curious <old>; circumspect; **attentive** 982.15; **cautious** 494.8

11 painstaking, diligent, assiduous, sedulous, **thorough, thoroughgoing,** operose, industrious, elaborate

12 meticulous, exacting, scrupulous, conscientious, religious, punctilious, punctual, **particular, fussy, critical, attentive,** scrutinizing; **thorough,** thoroughgoing, thoroughpaced; **finical,** finicking, finicky; **exact, precise,** precisionistic, precisionistic, prissy, **accurate, correct;** close, narrow; **strict,** rigid, **rigorous,** spit-and-polish, exigent, demanding; nice, delicate, subtle, fine, refined, minute, detailed, exquisite

13 vigilant, wary, prudent, **watchful,** lidless, sleepless, observant; **on the watch, on the lookout,** *aux aguets* <Fr>; **on guard,** on one's guard, guarded; with open eyes, with one's eyes open, with one's eyes peeled *or* with a weather eye open <both nonformal>; open-eyed, sharp-eyed, keen-eyed, Argus-eyed, eagle-eyed, hawk-eyed; all eyes, all ears, **all eyes and ears;** custodial

14 alert, on the alert, on the *qui vive* <Fr>, **on one's toes, on top** *and* **on the job** *and* on the ball <all nonformal>, **attentive; awake,** wakeful, **wide-awake,** sleepless, unsleeping, unblinking, unwinking, unnodding, alive, ready, prompt, quick, agile, nimble, quick on the trigger *or* draw *or* uptake <all nonformal>; **smart, bright, keen, sharp**

ADVS **15 carefully, heedfully,** regardfully, **mindfully,** thoughtfully, **considerately,** solicitously, tenderly, lovingly; circumspectly; **cautiously** 494.12; **with care,** with great care; **painstakingly, diligently,** assiduously, industriously, sedulously, thoroughly, thoroughgoingly, nine ways to Sunday *and* to a t *or* a turn *and* to a fare-thee-well <all nonformal>

16 **meticulously, exactingly, scrupulously, conscientiously,** religiously, punctiliously, punctually, fussily; strictly, rigorously; exactly, **accurately, precisely, with exactitude, with precision;** nicely, with great nicety, refinedly, minutely, in detail, exquisitely

17 **vigilantly, warily,** prudently, **watchfully,** observantly; **alertly,** attentively; sleeplessly, unsleepingly, unwinkingly, unblinkingly, lidlessly, unnoddingly

340 NEGLECT

NOUNS **1 neglect,** neglectfulness, **negligence,** inadvertence *or* inadvertency, malperformance, dereliction, *culpa* <L>, culpable negligence, criminal negligence; **remissness,** laxity, laxness, slackness, looseness, laches; unrigorousness, permissiveness; noninterference, *laissez-faire* <Fr>, nonrestriction; **disregard,** airy disregard, slighting; **inattention** 983; **oversight,** overlooking; **omission,** nonfeasance, nonperformance, lapse, failure, **default;** poor stewardship *or* guardianship *or* custody; procrastination 845.5

2 **carelessness, heedlessness, unheedfulness,** disregardfulness, regardlessness; unperceptiveness, impercipience, blindness, deliberate blindess; uncaring, unsolicitude, unsolicitousness, **thoughtlessness,** tactlessness, inconsiderateness, **inconsideration;** unthinkingness, unmindfulness, oblivion, forgetfulness; **unpreparedness,** unreadiness, lack of foresight *or* forethought; **recklessness** 493.2; **indifference** 102, *je-m'en-fichisme* and *je-m'en-foutisme* <both Fr>; **laziness** 331.5; perfunctoriness; cursoriness, hastiness, offhandedness, casualness; easiness; nonconcern, insouciance; abandon, careless abandon, *sprezzatura* <Ital>

3 **slipshodness,** slipshoddiness, **slovenliness,** slovenry, sluttishness, untidiness, **sloppiness** *and* **messiness** <both nonformal>; haphazardness; slapdash, slapdashness, a lick and a promise <all nonformal>, loose ends; bad job, sad work, botch, slovenly performance; bungling 414.4

4 **unmeticulousness,** unexactingness, **unscrupulousness,** unrigorousness, **unconscientiousness,** unpunctiliousness, unpunctuality, unparticularness, unfussiness, unfinicalness, **uncriticalness;** inexactness, **inexactitude,** inaccuracy, imprecision, unpreciseness

5 **neglecter,** negligent <old>, ignorer, dis-

regarder; *je-m'en-fichiste* and *je-m'en-foutiste* <both Fr>; **procrastinator,** waiter on Providence, Micawber <Dickens>; slacker, shirker, malingerer, dodger, goof-off *and* goldbrick <both nonformal>, idler; skimper <nonformal>; trifler; sloven, slut; bungler 414.8

VERBS **6 neglect, overlook, disregard,** not heed, not attend to, take for granted, **ignore;** not care for, not take care of; **pass over,** gloss over; **let slip, let slide** <nonformal>, let the chance slip by, **let go,** let ride <nonformal>, let take its course; let the grass grow under one's feet; not think *or* consider, not give a thought to, take no thought *or* account of, blind oneself to, turn a blind eye to, leave out of one's calculation; lose sight of, lose track of; **be neglectful *or* negligent,** fail in one's duty, **fail,** lapse, **default,** let go by default; not get involved; nod, nod *or* sleep through, sleep <old>, be caught napping, be asleep at the switch <nonformal>

7 **leave undone,** leave, **let go,** leave half-done, pretermit, **skip,** jump, **miss, omit,** cut *and* blow off <both nonformal>, let be *or* alone, pass over, pass up <nonformal>, abandon; leave a loose thread, leave loose ends, let dangle; **slack, shirk,** malinger, goof off *and* goldbrick <both nonformal>; trifle; **procrastinate** 845.11

8 **slight;** turn one's back on, turn a cold shoulder to, get *or* give the cold shoulder *and* get *or* give the go-by *and* cold-shoulder <all nonformal>, leave out in the cold; not lift a finger, leave undone; scamp, skimp <nonformal>; slur, **slur over,** pass over, skate over <Brit>, slubber over, slip *or* **skip over,** dodge, waffle <Brit nonformal>, fudge, blink, carefully ignore; skim, **skim over,** skim the surface, **touch upon,** touch upon lightly *or* in passing, pass over lightly, go once over lightly, **hit the high spots** *and* **give a lick and a promise** <both nonformal>; **cut corners,** cut a corner

9 **do carelessly,** do by halves, do in a half-assed way <nonformal>, do in a slipshod fashion, do anyhow, do in any old way <nonformal>; botch, **bungle** 414.11; **trifle with,** play *or* play at fast and loose with, mess around *or* about with *and* muck around *or* about with *and* piss around *or* about with <all nonformal>; **do offhand,** dash off, knock off *and* throw off <both nonformal>, **toss off** *or* **out** <nonformal>; **roughhew,** roughcast, rough out; **knock out** <nonformal>, hammer *or* pound out, bat out <nonfor-

mal>; toss *or* **throw together,** knock together, throw *or* slap together, cobble up, patch together, patch, patch up, fudge up, fake up, whomp up <nonformal>, lash up <Brit nonformal>, slap up <nonformal>; jury-rig

ADJS **10 negligent, neglectful,** neglecting, derelict, culpably negligent; inadvertent, uncircumspect; **inattentive** 983.6; unwary, unwatchful, asleep at the switch, off-guard, unguarded; **remiss,** slack, lax, relaxed, laid-back <nonformal>, loose, loosey-goosey <nonformal>, unrigorous, permissive, overly permissive; noninterfering, *laissez-faire* <Fr>, nonrestrictive; slighting; slurring, scamping, skimping <nonformal>; procrastinating 845.17

11 **careless, heedless, unheeding, unheedful, disregardful,** disregardant, regardless, **unsolicitous, uncaring;** tactless, respectless, **thoughtless, unthinking, inconsiderate,** untactful, undiplomatic, mindless of, **unmindful,** forgetful, oblivious; **unprepared,** unready; **reckless** 493.8; **indifferent** 102.6; lazy; perfunctory, cursory, casual, offhand; easygoing, *dégagé* <Fr>, airy, flippant, insouciant, free and easy, free as a bird

12 **slipshod,** slipshoddy, **slovenly,** sloppy *and* **messy** *and* half-assed <all nonformal>, sluttish, untidy; **clumsy, bungling** 414.20; **haphazard, promiscuous, hit-or-miss,** hit-and-miss; deficient, half-assed <nonformal>, botched

13 **unmeticulous, unexacting, unpainstaking, unscrupulous,** unrigorous, **unconscientious,** unpunctilious, unpunctual, **unparticular, unfussy, unfinical, uncritical;** inexact, inaccurate, unprecise

14 **neglected,** unattended to, untended, unwatched, unchaperoned, uncared-for; **disregarded,** unconsidered, unregarded, **overlooked, missed,** omitted, passed by, passed over, passed up <nonformal>, gathering dust, **ignored, slighted;** unasked, unsolicited; half-done, undone, left undone; deserted, abandoned; in the cold *and* out in the cold <both nonformal>; on the shelf, shelved, pigeonholed, on hold *and* on the back burner <both nonformal>, **put** *or* **laid aside,** sidetracked *and* sidelined <both nonformal>, shunted

15 **unheeded, unobserved, unnoticed, unnoted, unperceived, unseen,** undiscerned, undescried, unmarked, unremarked, unregarded, unminded, unconsidered, unthought-of, unmissed

16 **unexamined, unstudied,** unconsidered,

unsearched, unscanned, unweighed, un-
sifted, unexplored, uninvestigated,
unindagated, unconned

ADVS **17 negligently, neglectfully,** inadvertently; **remissly,** laxly, slackly, loosely;
unrigorously, permissively; nonrestric-
tively; **slightingly,** lightly, slurringly;
scampingly, skimpingly <nonformal>

18 carelessly, heedlessly, unheedingly, un-
heedfully, disregardfully, regardlessly,
**thoughtlessly, unthinkingly, unsolici-
tously,** tactlessly, **inconsiderately,** unmindfully, forgetfully; **inattentively,
unwarily,** unvigilantly, unguardedly, un-
watchfully; **recklessly** 493.11; perfunctorily; once over lightly, cursorily; casually, offhand, offhandedly, airily;
clumsily, bunglingly 414.24; **sloppily** and
messily <both nonformal>, sluttishly,
shoddily, shabbily; haphazardly, promiscuously, hit or miss and hit and miss and
helter-skelter and slapdash and anyhow
and any old way and any which way <all
nonformal>

**19 unmeticulously, unscrupulously, uncons-
cientiously,** unfussily, **uncritically;**
inexactly, inaccurately, unprecisely, im-
precisely, unrigorously, unpunctually

341 INTERPRETATION

NOUNS **1 interpretation, construction, reading,** way of seeing or understanding or
putting; constructionism, strict constructionism, loose constructionism; **diagnosis; definition,** description; **meaning** 518;
overinterpretation, laboring

2 rendering, rendition; text, edited text,
diplomatic text, normalized text; **version;** reading, lection, variant, variant
reading; **edition,** critical or scholarly edition; variorum edition or variorum;
conflation, composite reading or text

3 translation, transcription, transliteration; Englishing; **paraphrase,** loose or
free translation; decipherment, decoding;
amplification, restatement, rewording;
metaphrase, literal or verbal or faithful or
word-for-word translation; **pony** and trot
and crib <all nonformal>; interlinear,
interlinear translation, bilingual text
or edition; **gloss, glossary;** key, clavis
<L>

4 explanation, explication, unfolding, **elu-
cidation,** illumination, enlightenment,
light, **clarification,** éclaircissement <Fr>,
simplification; take <nonformal>; **exposition,** expounding, exegesis; **illustration,
demonstration,** exemplification; **reason,**

rationale; euhemerism, demythologiza-
tion, allegorization; decipherment, decoding, cracking, unlocking, **solution** 939;
editing, emendation; critical revision, re-
scension, diaskeuasis

5 <explanatory remark> **comment, word
of explanation; annotation,** notation,
note, note of explanation, footnote, gloss,
scholium; exegesis; apparatus criticus
<L>; commentary, commentation
<old>

6 interpretability, interpretableness, con-
struability; **definability, describability;**
translatability; **explicability,** explain-
ableness, accountableness

7 interpreter, exegete, exegetist, exegesist,
hermeneut; constructionist, strict constructionist, loose constructionist;
commentator, annotator, scholiast;
critic, textual critic, **editor,** diaskeuast,
emender, emendator; cryptographer,
cryptologist, decoder, decipherer, crypt-
analyst; **explainer,** lexicographer, de-
finer, **explicator,** exponent, expositor, expounder, clarifier; demonstrator,
euhemerist, demythologizer, allegorist;
go-between 576.4; **translator,** meta-
phrast, paraphrast; oneirocritic; guide,
cicerone <Ital>, dragoman

8 <science of interpretation> exegetics,
hermeneutics; tropology; criticism, literary criticism, textual criticism; paleography, epigraphy; cryptology, cryptography, cryptanalysis; lexicography; diagnostics, symptomatology, semeiology, semeiotics; pathognomy; physiognomics,
physiognomy; metoposcopy; oneirology,
oneirocriticism

VERBS **9 interpret, diagnose; construe,** put a
construction on, **take;** understand, **understand by, take to mean,** take it that; **read;
read into,** read between the lines; see in a
special light, read in view of, take an approach to, **define, describe**

10 explain, explicate, expound, make of, exposit; **give the meaning,** tell the meaning
of; **spell out,** unfold; **account for,** give reason for; **clarify, elucidate,** clear up, clear
the air, **cover** and cover the waterfront or
the territory <all nonformal>, **make
clear,** make plain; **simplify,** popularize;
illuminate, enlighten, **shed** or **throw
light upon;** rationalize, euhemerize, demythologize, allegorize; tell or show how,
show the way; **demonstrate, show, illustrate,** exemplify; get to the bottom of or to
the heart of, make sense of, make head or
tails of; decipher, crack, unlock, find the
key to, unravel, read between the lines,

read into, **solve** 939.2; explain oneself; explain away; overinterpret

11 **comment upon,** commentate, remark upon; **annotate,** gloss; **edit,** make an edition

12 **translate, render,** transcribe, transliterate, put *or* turn into, transfuse the sense of; construe; English

13 **paraphrase, rephrase, reword, restate,** rehash; give a free *or* loose translation

ADJS 14 **interpretative,** interpretive, interpretational, exegetic, exegetical, hermeneutic, hermeneutical; constructive, constructional; **diagnostic;** symptomatological, semeiological; tropological; **definitional, descriptive**

15 **explanatory,** explaining, exegetic, exegetical, **explicative,** explicatory; **expository,** expositive; **clarifying, elucidative, elucidatory; illuminating,** illuminative, enlightening; **demonstrative, illustrative,** exemplificative; glossarial, annotative, critical, editorial, scholiastic; rationalizing, rationalistic, euhemeristic, demythologizing, allegorizing

16 **translational,** translative; paraphrastic, metaphrastic

17 **interpretable, construable; definable,** describable; translatable, renderable; Englishable <old>; explainable, explicable, accountable; diagnosable

ADVS 18 **by interpretation,** as here interpreted, as here defined, according to this reading; **in explanation, to explain; that is,** that is to say, as it were, *id est* <L>, i.e.; **to wit, namely,** *videlicet* <L>, viz, *scilicet* <L>, sc; **in other words,** in words to that effect

342 MISINTERPRETATION

NOUNS 1 **misinterpretation, misunderstanding,** *malentente* <Fr>, misintelligence, **misapprehension, misreading, misconstruction,** mistaking, malobservation, **misconception; misrendering,** mistranslation, eisegesis; misexplanation, misexplication, misexposition; misapplication; gloss; **perversion, distortion,** wrenching, twisting, contorting, torturing, squeezing, garbling; reversal; abuse of terms, misuse of words, catachresis; misquotation, miscitation; "blunders round about a meaning"—Pope; misjudgment 947; **error** 974

VERBS 2 **misinterpret, misunderstand,** misconceive, **mistake, misapprehend; mis-**

read, **misconstrue,** put a false construction on, miss the point, **take wrong, get wrong,** get one wrong, take amiss, take the wrong way; **get backwards,** reverse, have the wrong way round, put the cart before the horse; misapply; misexplain, misexplicate, misexpound; **misrender,** mistranslate; quote out of context; misquote, miscite, give a false coloring, give a false impression *or* idea, gloss; **garble, pervert, distort,** wrench, contort, torture, squeeze, twist the words *or* meaning, stretch *or* strain the sense *or* meaning, misdeem, **misjudge** 947.2; bark up the wrong tree

ADJS 3 **misinterpreted, misunderstood, mistaken, misapprehended, misread,** eisegetical, misconceived, **misconstrued; garbled, perverted, distorted,** catachrestic, catechrestical; backwards, reversed, arsy-varsy <Brit>, ass-backwards <nonformal>

4 **misinterpretable, misunderstandable,** mistakable

343 COMMUNICATION

NOUNS 1 **communication,** communion, congress, **commerce, intercourse; speaking, speech** 524, utterance, speech act, talking, linguistic intercourse, speech situation, speech circuit, converse, **conversation** 541; **contact, touch, connection; interpersonal communication, intercommunication,** intercommunion, grokking <nonformal>, **interplay,** interaction; **exchange,** interchange; answer, response, reply; one-way communication, two-way communication; **dealings,** dealing, **traffic, truck** <nonformal>; information 551; message 552.4; ESP, telepathy 689.9; correspondence 553; social intercourse 582.4; miscommunication

2 **informing, telling,** imparting, impartation, impartment, **conveyance, telling, transmission,** transmittal, transfer, transference, sharing, giving, sending, signaling; notification, alerting, **announcement** 352.2, publication 352, **disclosure** 351

3 **communicativeness, talkativeness** 540, **sociability** 582; **unreserve,** unreservedness, **unreticence, unrestraint, unconstraint,** unrestriction; **unrepression,** unsuppression; **unsecretiveness,** untaciturnity; candor, **frankness** 644.4; **openness,** plainness, freeness, outspokenness, plainspokenness; **accessibility,** approachability, conversableness; **extro-**

version, outgoingness; **uncommunicativeness** 344, reserve, taciturnity

4 **communicability, impartability, conveyability, transmittability,** transmissibility, transferability; contagiousness

5 **communications,** electronic communications, communications industry, media, communications medium *or* media, communications network; telecommunication 347.1; radio communication, wire communication; communication *or* information theory 551.7

VERBS 6 **communicate, be in touch** *or* **contact,** be in connection *or* intercourse, have intercourse, hold communication; **intercommunicate,** interchange, commune with; grok <nonformal>; commerce with, **deal with, traffic with, have dealings with, have truck with** <nonformal>; **speak, talk,** be in a speech situation, **converse** 541.9, pass the time of day

7 **communicate, impart, tell,** lay on one <nonformal>, **convey, transmit,** transfer, send, send word, deliver *or* send a signal *or* message, **disseminate,** broadcast, pass, **pass on** *or* **along, hand on; report, render, make known,** get across *or* over; give *or* send *or* leave word; **signal;** share, share with; **leak,** let slip out, **give** 478.12; tell 551.8

8 **communicate with, get in touch** *or* **contact with, contact** <nonformal>, **make contact with,** raise, reach, get to, get through to, get hold of, make *or* establish connection, get in connection with; **make advances,** make overtures, **approach,** make up to <nonformal>; relate to; keep in touch *or* contact with, maintain connection; **answer,** respond *or* reply to, get back to; **question,** interrogate; **correspond,** drop a line

ADJS 9 **communicational, communicating,** communional; transmissional; speech, **verbal,** linguistic, oral; **conversational** 541.13; **intercommunicational,** intercommunicative, intercommunional, interactional, interactive, interacting, interresponsive, responsive, answering; questioning, interrogative, interrogatory; telepathic

10 **communicative, talkative** 540.9, gossipy, newsy; **sociable; unreserved, unreticent,** unshrinking, **unrestrained, unconstrained,** unhampered, unrestricted; demonstrative, expansive, effusive; **unrepressed, unsuppressed; unsecretive,** unsilent, untaciturn; candid, **frank** 644.17; self-revealing, self-revelatory; **open,** free, outspoken, free-speaking, free-spoken, free-tongued; **accessible, approachable,** conversable, easy to speak to; **extroverted,** outgoing; **uncommunicative** 344.8

11 **communicable, impartable, conveyable, transmittable,** transmissible, transferable; contagious

12 communicatively; verbally, talkatively, by word of mouth, orally, viva voce

344 UNCOMMUNICATIVENESS

NOUNS 1 **uncommunicativeness,** closeness, indisposition to speak, disinclination to communicate; unconversableness, **unsociability** 583; nondisclosure, **secretiveness** 345.1; lack of message *or* meaning, meaninglessness 520

2 **taciturnity, untalkativeness,** unloquaciousness; **silence** 51; **speechlessness,** wordlessness, dumbness, **muteness** 51.2; quietness, quietude; laconicalness, laconism, curtness, shortness, terseness; brusqueness, briefness, brevity, conciseness, economy *or* sparingness of words, pauciloquy <old>

3 **reticence** *or* reticency; **reserve,** reservedness, restraint, low key, **constraint;** guardedness, discreetness, discretion; suppression, repression; subduedness; backwardness, retirement, low profile; **aloofness, standoffishness,** distance, remoteness, **detachment,** withdrawal, withdrawnness, reclusiveness, solitariness; impersonality; **coolness,** coldness, frigidity, iciness, frostiness, chilliness; **inaccessibility, unapproachability; undemonstrativeness,** unexpansiveness, unaffability, uncongeniality; **introversion;** modesty, bashfulness 139.4, pudency; expressionlessness, blankness, impassiveness, impassivity; straight *or* poker face, mask

4 **prevarication, equivocation,** tergiversation, **evasion,** shuffle, fencing, dodging, parrying, waffling *and* tap-dancing <both nonformal>; *suppressio veri* <L>; weasel words

5 **man of few words,** clam <nonformal>, strong silent type, laconic <old>; Spartan, Laconian; evader, weasel

VERBS 6 **keep to oneself,** keep one's own counsel; not open one's mouth, not say a word, not breathe a word, stand mute, **hold one's tongue** 51.5, clam up <nonformal>; bite one's tongue; have little to say, refuse comment, say neither yes nor no, waste no words, save one's breath; retire; **keep one's distance,** keep at a distance, keep oneself to oneself, **stand aloof,** hold oneself aloof; keep secret 345.7

7 **prevaricate, equivocate,** waffle <nonformal>, tergiversate, evade, dodge, side-step, say in a roundabout way, parry, duck, weasel *and* weasel out <both nonformal>, palter; hum and haw, **hem and haw,** back and fill; **mince words,** mince the truth, euphemize

ADJS 8 **uncommunicative,** indisposed *or* disinclined to communicate; unconversational, unconversable <old>; **unsociable** 583.5; **secretive** 345.15; meaningless 520.6

9 **taciturn, untalkative,** unloquacious, indisposed to talk; **silent, speechless,** wordless, **mum; mute** 51.12, dumb, quiet; close, **closemouthed,** close-tongued, snug <nonformal>, **tight-lipped;** close-lipped, tongue-tied, word-bound; **laconic,** curt, brief, terse, brusque, short, concise, **sparing of words,** economical of words, of few words

10 **reticent, reserved,** restrained, nonassertive, low-key, low-keyed, constrained; **suppressed,** repressed; subdued; guarded, discreet; backward, **retiring,** shrinking; **aloof, standoffish,** offish <nonformal>, standoff, **distant,** remote, removed, **detached,** Olympian, withdrawn; impersonal; **cool,** cold, frigid, icy, frosty, chilled, chilly; **inaccessible, unapproachable,** forbidding; **undemonstrative,** unexpansive, unaffable, uncongenial, ungenial; **introverted;** modest, verecund, verecundious, *pudique* <Fr>, bashful 139.12; expressionless, blank, impassive

11 **prevaricating, equivocal,** tergiversating, tergiversant, waffling <nonformal>, **evasive,** weaselly, weasel-worded

345 SECRECY

NOUNS 1 **secrecy,** secretness, airtight secrecy, close secrecy; **crypticness;** the dark; hiddenness, **concealment** 346; **secretiveness,** closeness; discreetness, discretion, **uncommunicativeness** 344; **evasiveness,** evasion, subterfuge; huggermugger, hugger-muggery

2 **privacy,** retirement, isolation, sequestration, seclusion; incognito, anonymity; **confidentialness,** confidentiality; closed meeting, executive session, private conference

3 **veil of secrecy,** veil, curtain, pall, wraps; iron curtain, "curtains of fog and iron"—

Churchill, bamboo curtain; wall *or* barrier of secrecy; **suppression,** repression, stifling, smothering; **censorship,** blackout <nonformal>, **hush-up, cover-up; seal of secrecy,** official secrecy, classification, official classification; security, ironbound security; pledge *or* oath of secrecy

4 **stealth,** stealthiness, **furtiveness, clandestineness,** clandestinity, clandestine behavior; **surreptitiousness, covertness,** slyness, shiftiness, sneakiness, slinkiness, underhand dealing, undercover *or* underground activity, **covert activity** *or* **operation;** prowl, prowling; stalking

5 **secret, confidence;** private *or* personal matter, privity <old>; trade secret; confidential *or* **privileged information** *or* **communication;** doctor-patient *or* lawyer-client confidentiality; secret of the confessional; more than meets the eye; deep, dark secret; solemn secret; guarded secret, hush-hush matter, classified information, eyes-only *or* top-secret information, restricted information; inside information, inside skinny <nonformal>; **mystery, enigma** 522.8; the arcane, arcanum, *arcanum arcanorum* <L>; esoterica, cabala, the occult, hermetism, hermeticism, hermetics; deep *or* profound secret, sealed book, mystery of mysteries; skeleton in the closet *or* cupboard

6 **cryptography,** cryptoanalysis, cryptoanalytics; **code, cipher;** secret language; code book, code word, code name; **secret writing,** coded message, cryptogram, cryptograph; secret *or* invisible *or* sympathetic ink; cryptographer

VERBS 7 **keep secret, keep mum, veil,** keep dark; keep it a deep, dark secret; secrete, **conceal;** keep to oneself 344.6, keep *in petto* <Ital>, bosom, keep close, keep snug <nonformal>, keep back, keep from, **withhold,** hold out on <nonformal>; not let it go further, keep within these walls, keep within the bosom of the lodge, keep between us; **not tell,** hold one's tongue 51.5, never let on <nonformal>, make no sign, not breathe *or* whisper a word, clam up <nonformal>, be the soul of discretion; **not give away** <nonformal>, "tell it not in Gath"— Bible, **keep it under one's hat** <nonformal>, keep under wraps <nonformal>, keep buttoned up <nonformal>, keep one's own counsel; play one's cards close to the chest *or* to one's vest; play dumb; not let the right hand know what the left is doing; keep in ignorance, keep *or* leave in the dark; classify; file and forget; **have secret** or **confidential information,** be in on the secret *and* know where the bodies are buried <both nonformal>

8 **cover up,** muffle up; **hush up, hush,** hush-hush, shush, hugger-mugger; **suppress,** repress, **stifle,** muffle, **smother,** squash, quash, squelch, kill, sit on *or* upon, put the lid on <nonformal>; **censor,** black out <nonformal>

9 **tell confidentially,** tell for one's ears only, mention privately, **whisper, breathe, whisper in the ear;** tell one a secret; take aside, see one alone, talk to in private, speak in privacy; say under one's breath

10 code, encode, encipher, cipher

ADJS 11 **secret,** close, closed, closet; cryptic, dark; unuttered, unrevealed, undivulged, undisclosed, unspoken, untold; **hush-hush, top secret,** supersecret, eyes-only, classified, restricted, under wraps <nonformal>, under security *or* security restrictions; **censored,** suppressed, stifled, smothered, hushed-up, under the seal *or* ban of secrecy; **unrevealable, undivulgable, undisclosable, untellable,** unwhisperable, unbreatheable, unutterable; latent, ulterior, concealed, hidden 346.11; arcane, esoteric, occult, cabalistic, hermetic; enigmatic, mysterious 522.18

12 **covert, clandestine,** quiet, unobtrusive, hugger-mugger, hidlings <Scots>; **surreptitious, undercover,** underground, under-the-counter, under-the-table, **cloak-and-dagger,** backdoor, hole-and-corner <nonformal>, underhand, **underhanded; furtive, stealthy,** privy, backstairs, **sly, shifty, sneaky,** sneaking, skulking, slinking, slinky, feline

13 **private, privy, closed-door; intimate, inmost,** innermost, interior, inward, **personal; privileged,** protected; **secluded, sequestered,** isolated, withdrawn, retired; incognito, anonymous

14 **confidential,** auricular, **inside** <nonformal>, esoteric; *in petto* <Ital>, close to one's chest *or* vest <nonformal>, under one's hat <nonformal>; **off the record,** not for the record, not to be minuted, within these four walls, in the bosom of the lodge, for no other ears, eyes-only, between us; not to be quoted, not for publication *or* release; not for attribution; unquotable, unpublishable, sealed; sensitive, privileged, under privilege

15 **secretive,** close-lipped, secret, close, dark; discreet; evasive, shifty; **uncommunicative, close-mouthed**

16 coded, encoded; ciphered, enciphered; cryptographic, cryptographical

ADVS 17 **secretly, in secret,** in *or* up one's sleeve; in the closet; nobody the wiser; **covertly,** stownlins *and* in hidlings <both Scots>, **undercover,** *à couvert* <Fr>, under the cloak of; **behind the scenes,** in the background, in a corner, in the dark, in darkness, behind the veil *or* curtain, behind the veil of secrecy; *sub rosa* <L>, under the rose; underground; *sotto voce* <Ital>, under the breath, with bated breath, in a whisper

18 **surreptitiously, clandestinely, secretively, furtively, stealthily, slyly,** shiftily, sneakily, sneakingly, skulkingly, slinkingly, slinkily; by stealth, **on the sly** *and* **on the quiet** *and* on the qt <all nonformal>, *à la dérobée* <Fr>, *en tapinois* <Fr>, behind one's back, by a side door, **like a thief in the night,** underhand, underhandedly, under the table, in holes and corners *and* in a hole-and-corner way <both nonformal>

19 **privately,** privily, **in private,** in privacy, in privy; apart, aside; **behind closed doors,** *januis clausis* <L>, *à huis clos* <Fr>, *in camera* <L>, in chambers, in secret *or* closed meeting, in executive session, in private conference

20 **confidentially, in confidence,** in strict confidence, under the seal of secrecy, **off the record; between ourselves,** strictly between us, *entre nous* <Fr>, *inter nos* <L>, for your ears *or* eyes only, between you and me, from me to you, between you and me and the bedpost *or* lamppost <nonformal>

346 CONCEALMENT

NOUNS 1 **concealment, hiding, secretion;** burial, burying, interment, putting away; **cover, covering,** covering up, masking, screening 295.1; mystification, obscuration; darkening, obscurement, clouding 1026.6; hiddenness, concealedness, **covertness,** occultation; **secrecy** 345; uncommunicativeness 344; invisibility 32; **subterfuge, deception** 356

2 **veil,** curtain, **cover, screen** 295.2; fig leaf; **wraps** <nonformal>; **cover, disguise**

3 **ambush,** ambushment, **ambuscade,** *guet-apens* <Fr>; surveillance, shadowing 937.9; lurking hole *or* place; blind, stalking-horse; booby trap, trap

4 **hiding place, hideaway, hideout,** hidey-hole <nonformal>, hiding, concealment, **cover,** secret place; safe house; drop, ac-

commodation address <Brit>; **recess, corner,** dark corner, nook, cranny, niche; **hole,** bolt-hole, foxhole, funk hole, dug-out, lair, den; **asylum, sanctuary, retreat, refuge** 1008; covert, coverture, under-covert; **cache,** stash <nonformal>; cubbyhole, cubby, pigeonhole

5 **secret passage,** covert way, secret exit; **back way, back door, side door;** bolt-hole, escape route, escape hatch, escapeway; secret staircase, *escalier dérobé* <Fr>, **back stairs; underground,** underground route, underground railroad

VERBS 6 **conceal, hide,** ensconce; **cover, cover up,** blind, **screen, cloak, veil,** screen off, curtain, blanket, shroud, enshroud, envelop; **disguise, camouflage, mask,** dis-semble; plain-wrap, wrap in plain brown paper; whitewash <nonformal>; **paper over,** gloss over, varnish, slur over; dis-tract attention from; **obscure,** obfuscate, cloud, becloud, befog, throw out a smoke screen, shade, throw into the shade; **eclipse,** occult; put out of sight, sweep un-der the rug, keep under cover; cover up one's tracks, lay a false scent, hide one's trail; hide one's light under a bushel

7 **secrete, hide away,** keep hidden, put away, store away, stow away, file and for-get, bottle up, lock up, seal up, put out of sight; **keep secret** 345.7; **cache,** stash <nonformal>, deposit, plant <nonfor-mal>; **bury;** bosom, embosom <old>

8 <hide oneself> **hide, conceal oneself, take cover, hide out** <nonformal>, hide away, **go into hiding,** go to ground; stay in hiding, **lie hid** *or* **hidden,** lie *or* lay low <nonformal>, lie *perdue,* lie snug *or* close <nonformal>, lie doggo *and* sit tight <both nonformal>, burrow <old>, **hole up** <nonformal>, **go underground;** play peekaboo *or* bopeep *or* hide and seek; keep out of sight, retire from sight, drop from sight, disappear 34.2, crawl *or* re-treat into one's shell, keep in the back-ground, keep a low profile, stay in the shade; **disguise oneself,** masquerade, take an assumed name, assume a cover, change one's identity, go under an alias, remain anonymous, be incognito, go *or* sail under false colors, wear a mask

9 **lurk,** couch; **lie in wait,** lay wait; **sneak, skulk, slink, prowl,** nightwalk, **steal, creep,** pussyfoot <nonformal>, gumshoe <nonformal>, tiptoe; stalk, shadow 937.34

10 **ambush,** ambuscade, **waylay; lie in am-bush,** lay wait for, **lie in wait for,** lay for <nonformal>; stalk; set a trap for

ADJS 11 **concealed, hidden, hid,** occult, re-condite <old>, blind; **covered** 295.31; **covert, under cover,** under wraps <non-formal>; code-named; **obscured,** obfus-cated, clouded, clouded over, wrapped in clouds, in a cloud *or* fog *or* mist *or* haze, beclouded, befogged; eclipsed, in eclipse, under an eclipse; in the wings; buried; underground; close, secluded, secluse, se-questered; in purdah, under house arrest, incommunicado; **obscure,** abstruse, mys-terious 522.18; **secret** 345.11; unknown 929.17, latent 519.5

12 **unrevealed, undisclosed,** undivulged, **unexposed;** unapparent, **invisible, un-seen,** unperceived, unspied, undetected; undiscovered, unexplored, untraced, untracked; unaccounted for, unex-plained, unsolved

13 **disguised, camouflaged, in disguise;** masked, masquerading; **incognito,** incog <nonformal>; in plain wrapping *or* plain brown paper <nonformal>

14 **in hiding,** hidden out, **under cover,** in a dark corner, lying hid, doggo <nonfor-mal>; in ambush *or* ambuscade; waiting concealed, lying in wait; in the wings; lurking, skulking, prowling, sneaking, stealing; pussyfooted, pussyfoot, on tip-toe; stealthy, furtive, surreptitious 345.12

15 **concealing, hiding,** obscuring, obfusca-tory; covering; unrevealing, nonreveal-ing, undisclosing

347 COMMUNICATIONS

NOUNS 1 **communications,** signaling, tele-communication, comms <Brit nonfor-mal>; electronic communication, elec-trical communication; satellite commu-nication; wire communication, wireless communication; communication engi-neering, communication technology; communications engineer; media, com-munications medium *or* media; commu-nication *or* information theory 551.7; communication *or* information explosion

2 **telegraph, telegraph recorder,** ticker; **telegraphy,** telegraphics; **teleprinter,** Telex <trademark>, teletypewriter; tele-printer exchange *or* telex; wire service; code 345.6; electricity 1031; **key,** inter-rupter, transmitter, sender; receiver, **sounder**

3 **radio** 1033, **radiotelephony, radiotelegra-phy,** wireless <Brit>, wireless telephony, wireless telegraphy; line radio, wire *or* wired radio, wired wireless <Brit>, wire wave communication; radiophotogra-

phy; **television** 1034; electronics 1032

4 telephone, phone *and* horn <both nonformal>, dog <Brit nonformal>, telephone set; telephony, telephonics, telephone mechanics, telephone engineering; high-frequency telephony; receiver, telephone receiver; mouthpiece, transmitter; telephone extension, extension; wall telephone, desk telephone; dial telephone, touch-tone telephone, push-button telephone; beeper; scrambler; telephone booth, telephone box, call box <Brit>, public telephone, coin telephone, pay station, pay phone; mobile telephone *or* phone <nonformal>, cellular telephone *or* phone <nonformal>; caller ID service

5 radiophone, radiotelephone, wireless telephone, wireless; headset, headphone 50.8

6 intercom <nonformal>, Interphone, intercommunication system

7 telephone exchange, telephone office, central office, **central;** automatic exchange, machine-switching office; step-by-step switching, panel switching, crossbar switching, electronic switching

8 switchboard; PBX *or* private branch *or* business exchange; in *or* A board, out *or* B board

9 telephone operator, operator, switchboard operator, telephonist, **central;** long distance; PBX operator

10 telephone man; telephone mechanic; telephonic engineer; lineman

11 telephoner, phoner <nonformal>, caller, **party,** calling party

12 telephone number, **phone number** <nonformal>, unlisted number; telephone directory, phone book <nonformal>; telephone directory, phone book <nonformal>; telephone exchange, exchange; telephone area, area code; calling zone

13 telephone call, **phone call** <nonformal>, **call, ring** *and* buzz <both nonformal>; local call, toll call, long-distance call; long distance, direct distance nondialing, DDD; trunk call; station-to-station call; person-to-person call; collect call; mobile call; dial tone, busy signal; conference call, video teleconference, teleconference; hot line; chat *or* talk *or* gab line, messagerie; voicemail, phonemail; telemarketing

14 telegram, telegraph, wire <nonformal>, telex; **cablegram, cable; radiogram,** radiotelegram; **day letter, night letter;** fast telegram

15 Telephoto <trademark>, Wirephoto

<trademark>, Telecopier <trademark>, **facsimile, fax** <nonformal>; telephotograph, radiophotograph, Photoradiogram <trademark>

16 telegrapher, telegraphist, telegraph operator; **sparks** *and* brass pounder *and* ditda artist <all nonformal>; radiotelegrapher; wireman, wire chief

17 line, wire line, telegraph line, telephone line; private line, direct line; party line; hot line; trunk, trunk line; WATS *or* wide area telecommunications service, WATS line; cable, telegraph cable; concentric cable, coaxial cable, co-ax <nonformal>

VERBS **18 telephone, phone** <nonformal>, **call,** call on the phone <nonformal>, put in *or* make a call, **call up, ring,** ring up, give a ring *or* buzz <nonformal>, buzz <nonformal>; listen in; hold the phone *or* wire; hang up, ring off <Brit>

19 telegraph, telegram, flash, **wire** *and* send a wire <both nonformal>, telex; **cable;** Teletype; radio; sign on, sign off

ADJS **20 communicational,** telecommunicational, **communications,** communication, signal; **telephonic,** magnetotelephonic, microtelephonic, monotelephonic, thermotelephonic; **telegraphic; Teletype;** Wirephoto, facsimile; phototelegraphic, telephotographic; **radio,** wireless <Brit>; radiotelegraphic

348 MANIFESTATION

NOUNS **1 manifestation, appearance; expression,** evincement; **indication, evidence,** proof 956; embodiment, incarnation, bodying forth, materialization; epiphany, theophany, angelophany, Satanophany, Christophany, pneumatophany, avatar; **revelation, disclosure** 351, showing forth; dissemination, **publication** 352

2 display, demonstration, show, showing; presentation, showing forth, presentment, ostentation <old>, **exhibition, exhibit, exposition,** retrospective; production, performance, representation, enactment, projection; opening, unfolding, unfoldment; **showcase,** showcasing, unveiling, exposure, varnishing day, *vernissage* <Fr>

3 manifestness, apparentness, obviousness, plainness, clearness, crystal-clearness, perspicuity, distinctness, microscopical distinctness, patency, patentness, palpability, tangibility; evidentness, evidence <old>, **self-evidence; openness,** openness

to sight, overtness; visibility 31; unmistakableness, unquestionability
969.3

4 **conspicuousness, prominence, salience**
or saliency, bold *or* high *or* strong relief,
boldness, **noticeability**, pronouncedness,
strikingness, outstandingness; highlighting, spotlighting, featuring; obtrusiveness; **flagrance** *or* flagrancy, arrantness,
blatancy, notoriousness, notoriety; ostentation 501

VERBS 5 **manifest, show, exhibit, demonstrate, display,** breathe, unfold, develop;
present, represent <old>, **evince, evidence; indicate,** give sign *or* token, token,
betoken, mean 518.8; **express,** show forth,
set forth; show off, showcase; **make plain,
make clear;** produce, bring out, roll out,
trot out <nonformal>, bring forth, bring
forward *or* to the front, bring to notice,
expose to view, bring to *or* into view; **reveal, divulge, disclose** 351.4; **illuminate,
highlight, spotlight, feature,** bring to the
fore, place in the foreground, bring out in
bold *or* strong *or* high relief; **flaunt,** dangle, wave, **flourish,** brandish, parade;
affect, make a show *or* a great show of;
perform, enact, dramatize; **embody,** incarnate, body forth, **materialize**

6 <manifest oneself> **come out, come into
the open,** come out of the closet <nonfor-
mal>, come forth, **surface; show one's
colors** *or* true colors, wear one's heart
upon one's sleeve; **speak up, speak out,**
raise one's voice, **assert oneself,** let one's
voice be heard, speak one's piece *or* one's
mind, **stand up and be counted,** take a
stand; open up, show one's mind, have no
secrets; **appear, materialize**

7 **be manifest,** be there for all to see, make
an appearance, be no secret *or* revelation,
surface, lie on the surface, be seen with
half an eye; need no explanation, **speak
for itself,** tell its own story *or* tale; **go
without saying,** *aller sans dire* <Fr>; **leap
to the eye,** *sauter aux yeux* <Fr>, **stare
one in the face,** hit one in the eye, strike
the eye, glare, shout; come across, project; stand out, stick out, stick out a mile,
stick out like a sore thumb, hang out
<nonformal>

ADJS 8 **manifest, apparent, evident, self-
evident,** axiomatic, indisputable, **obvious, plain, clear,** perspicuous, distinct,
palpable, patent, tangible; **visible, perceptible, perceivable, discernible,** seeable, observable, **noticeable, much in evidence; to be seen,** easy to be seen, plain to
be seen; plain as day, plain as the nose on

one's face, plain as a pikestaff, big as life,
big as life and twice as ugly; **crystal-clear,**
clear as crystal; **express, explicit, unmistakable,** not to be mistaken, open-and-
shut <nonformal>; self-explanatory,
self-explaining; **indubitable** 969.15

9 **manifesting, manifestative,** showing, displaying, showcasing, demonstrating,
demonstrative, presentational, expository, expositional, exhibitive, exhibi-
tional, **expressive;** evincive, evidential;
indicative, indicatory; appearing, incarnating, incarnational, materializing;
epiphanic, theophanic, angelophanic, Sa-
tanophanic, Christophanic, pneumatoph-
anic; **revelational,** revelatory, **disclosive**
351.10; promulgatory 352.18

10 **open,** overt, open to all, open as day, out
of the closet <nonformal>; unclassified;
revealed, disclosed, exposed; bare, bald,
naked

11 **unhidden, unconcealed,** unscreened, un-
curtained, unshaded, veilless; **unobscure,**
unobscured, undarkened, unclouded; **undisguised,** uncamouflaged

12 **conspicuous, noticeable, notable,** ostensible, **prominent, bold, pronounced, salient,** in relief, in bold *or* high *or* strong
relief, **striking, outstanding,** in the foreground, sticking *or* hanging out <nonfor-
mal>; highlighted, spotlighted, featured;
obtrusive; **flagrant,** arrant, blatant,
notorious; **glaring,** staring, stark-
staring

13 **manifested,** demonstrated, exhibited,
shown, displayed, showcased; **manifest-
able,** demonstrable, exhibitable, dis-
playable

ADVS 14 **manifestly, apparently, evidently,
obviously, patently, plainly, clearly,**
distinctly, **unmistakably,** expressly,
explicitly, palpably, tangibly; **visibly,
perceptibly,** perceivably, discernibly, observably, **noticeably**

15 **openly, overtly,** before one, **before one's
eyes** *or* very eyes, under one's nose
<nonformal>; to one's face, face-to-face;
publicly, in public; **in the open,** out in the
open, in open court, **in plain sight,** in
broad daylight, in the face of day *or*
heaven, for all to see, in public view, in
plain view, in the marketplace; aboveboard, on the table

16 **conspicuously, prominently, noticeably,**
ostensibly, **notably, markedly, pronouncedly, saliently, strikingly, boldly, outstandingly;** obtrusively; arrantly, flagrantly, blatantly, notoriously; glaringly,
staringly

349 REPRESENTATION, DESCRIPTION

NOUNS **1 representation, delineation,** presentment, drawing, **portrayal, portraiture, depiction,** depictment, rendering, rendition, characterization, charactering <old>, picturization, figuration, limning, imaging; prefigurement; **illustration,** exemplification, demonstration; projection, **realization;** imagery, iconography; **art** 712; **drama** 704.1,4–6; conventional representation, plan, diagram, schema, schematization, **blueprint, chart, map; notation,** mathematical notation, musical notation, score, tablature; dance notation, Laban dance notation system *or* labanotation, choreography; **writing,** script, written word, text; **writing system; alphabet,** syllabary; alphabetic symbol, syllabic symbol, letter, ideogram, pictogram, logogram, logograph, hieroglyphic; **printing** 548; **symbol**

2 description, portrayal, portraiture, **depiction,** rendering, rendition, **delineation,** limning, **representation** 349; imagery; **word painting** *or* **picture, picture, portrait, image,** photograph; evocation, impression; **sketch,** vignette, cameo; **characterization,** character, character sketch, profile; vivid description, exact description, realistic *or* naturalistic description, slice of life, *tranche de vie* <Fr>, graphic account; specification, particularization, details, itemization, catalog, cataloging; **narration**

3 account, recounting, statement, report, word; play-by-play description, blow-by-blow account *or* description; case study

4 impersonation, personation; mimicry, mimicking, mime, miming, pantomime, pantomiming, aping, dumb show; mimesis, **imitation** 336; personification, embodiment, incarnation; **characterization,** portrayal; **acting,** playing, dramatization, enacting, enactment, performing, performance; **posing,** masquerade

5 image, likeness; resemblance, semblance, similitude, simulacrum; **effigy,** icon, idol; **copy** 784, fair copy; **picture; portrait,** likeness; **photograph** 714.3,6; **perfect** *or* **exact likeness, duplicate, double;** match, fellow, mate, companion, **twin;** living image, very image, very picture, living picture, dead ringer <nonformal>, spitting image *or* spit and image <nonformal>; miniature, model; **reflection,** shadow, mirroring; trace, tracing; rubbing

6 figure, figurine; doll, dolly <nonformal>; teddy bear; **puppet, marionette,** *fantoche* <Fr>, *fantoccino* and *fantoccio* <both Ital>, hand puppet, glove puppet; **mannequin** *or* manikin, model, dummy, lay figure; wax figure, waxwork; scarecrow, corn dolly <Brit>, woman *or* man of straw, snowman, snowwoman, gingerbread woman *or* man; **sculpture, bust, statue, statuette,** statuary, monument <old>; portrait bust *or* statue; death mask, life mask; carving, wood carving; figurehead

7 representative, representation, **type, specimen,** typification, embodiment, type specimen; **cross section;** exponent; **example** 785.2, exemplar; exemplification, typicality, typicalness, representativeness

VERBS **8 represent, delineate, depict,** render, characterize, hit off, character <old>, **portray, picture,** picturize, limn, draw, paint 712.20; **register,** convey an impression of; take *or* catch a likeness; **notate, write,** print, map, chart, diagram, schematize; trace, trace out, trace over; rub, take a rubbing; **symbolize** 517.18

9 describe, portray, picture, render, **depict, represent, delineate,** limn, **paint,** draw; evoke, bring to life, make one see; outline, sketch; **characterize,** character; **express,** set forth, give words to; **write** 547.21

10 go for *or* **as, pass for** *or* **as, count for** *or* **as,** answer for *or* as, stand in the place of, be taken as, be regarded as, be the equivalent of; **serve as,** be accepted for

11 image, mirror, hold the mirror up to nature, reflect, figure; **embody,** body forth, incarnate, **personify,** personate, impersonate; **illustrate,** demonstrate, exemplify; project, realize; shadow, shadow forth; **prefigure, pretypify,** foreshadow, adumbrate

12 impersonate, personate; **mimic,** mime, pantomime, take off, do *or* give an impression of, mock; ape, copy; **pose as, masquerade as,** affect the manner *or* guise of, pass for, pretend to be, represent oneself to be; **act,** enact, perform, do; **play, act as,** act *or* play a part, act the part of, act out

ADJS **13 representational, representative, depictive, delineatory, resemblant; illustrative,** illustrational; pictorial, graphic, vivid; ideographic, pictographic, figurative; **representing, portraying,** limning, illustrating; **typifying, symbolizing,** personifying, incarnating, embodying; imitative, mimetic, simulative, apish, mimish; echoic, onomatopoeic

14 descriptive, depictive, expositive, **representative, delineative; expressive, vivid,
graphic,** well-drawn; realistic, naturalistic, true to life, lifelike, faithful

15 typical, typic, typal; exemplary, sample;
characteristic, distinctive, distinguishing, quintessential; **realistic, naturalistic;
natural, normal,** usual, regular, par for
the course <nonformal>; **true to type,
true to form,** the nature of the beast
<nonformal>

ADVS **16 descriptively,** representatively; **expressively, vividly, graphically;** faithfully, realistically, naturalistically

350 MISREPRESENTATION

NOUNS **1 misrepresentation, perversion, distortion,** deformation, garbling, twisting,
slanting; inaccuracy; **coloring,** miscoloring, **false coloring; falsification** 354.9,
spin, spin control, disinformation; misteaching 569; injustice, unjust representation; misdrawing, mispainting; misstatement, misreport, misquotation;
nonrepresentationalism, nonrealism, ab-
stractionism, expressionism, calculated
distortion; overstatement, exaggeration,
hyperbole, overdrawing; understatement, litotes

2 bad likeness, **daub,** botch; scribble,
scratch, hen tracks or scratches <nonfor-
mal>; distortion, distorted image,
anamorphosis, astigmatism; **travesty,**
parody, **caricature, burlesque,** gross exaggeration

VERBS **3 misrepresent, belie,** give a wrong
idea, pass or pawn or foist or fob off as,
send or deliver the wrong signal or message; put in a false light, **pervert, distort,
garble, twist,** warp, wrench, slant, put a
spin on, twist the meaning of; **color,** miscolor, **give a false coloring,** put a false
construction or appearance upon, falsify
354.18; misteach 569.3; **disguise,** camouflage; misstate, misreport, misquote, put
words into one's mouth, quote out of context; overstate, exaggerate, overdraw,
blow up, blow out of all proportion; understate; **travesty,** parody, **caricature,
burlesque**

4 misdraw, mispaint; daub, botch,
butcher, scribble, scratch

351 DISCLOSURE

NOUNS **1 disclosure,** disclosing; **revelation,**
revealment, revealing, making public,
publicizing, broadcasting; apocalypse;

discovery, discovering; manifestation
348; unfolding, unfoldment, **uncovering,**
unwrapping, uncloaking, taking the
wraps off, taking from under wraps, re-
moving the veil, **unveiling, unmasking;
exposure,** exposition, **exposé; baring,**
stripping, stripping or laying bare; outing
<nonformal>; **showing up,** showup

2 divulgence, divulging, divulgement, di-
vulgation, evulgation <old>, letting out;
betrayal, unwitting disclosure, indiscretion; leak, communication leak; **giveaway** and dead giveaway <both nonfor-
mal>; telltale, telltale sign, obvious clue;
blabbing and blabbering <both nonfor-
mal>, babbling; **tattling**

3 confession, confessing, shrift, **acknowledgment, admission,** concession, avowal,
self-admission, self-concession, self-
avowal, owning, owning up and coming
clean <both nonformal>, unbosoming,
unburdening oneself, getting a load off
one's mind <nonformal>, fessing up
<nonformal>, making a clean breast,
baring one's breast; rite of confession

VERBS **4 disclose, reveal, let out, show,** impart, discover, develop <old>, **leak,** let
slip out, let the cat out of the bag and spill
the beans <both nonformal>; manifest
348.5; unfold, unroll; **open,** open up, lay
open, break the seal, bring into the open,
get out in the open, bring out of the
closet; **expose, show up; bare,** strip or lay
bare, blow the lid off and blow wide open
and rip open and crack wide open <all
nonformal>; take the lid off, **bring to
light,** bring into the open, hold up to
view; hold up the mirror to; **unmask,** dis-
mask, tear off the mask, **uncover,** unveil,
take the lid off <nonformal>, ventilate,
take out from under wraps, take the
wraps off, lift or draw the veil, raise the
curtain, let daylight in, unscreen, uncloak, undrape, unshroud, unfurl, unsheathe, unwrap, unpack, unkennel;
put one wise and clue one in and bring
one up to speed <all nonformal>, put one
in the picture <chiefly Brit nonformal>,
open one's eyes

5 divulge, divulgate, evulgate <old>; **reveal, make known, tell,** breathe, utter,
vent, ventilate, air, give vent to, **give out,
let out** <Brit>, let get around, out with
<nonformal>, come out with; break it to,
break the news; let in on or to, **confide,**
confide to, let one's hair down <nonfor-
mal>, unbosom oneself, let into the
secret; **publish** 352.10

6 betray, inform, **inform on** 551.12, talk

and peach <both nonformal>; rat *and* stool *and* sing *and* squeal <all nonformal>, turn state's evidence; leak <nonformal>, spill <nonformal>, **spill the beans** <nonformal>; **let the cat out of the bag** <nonformal>, speak before one thinks, be unguarded *or* indiscreet, kiss and tell, **give away** *and* give the show away *and* give the game away <all nonformal>, betray a confidence, tell secrets, reveal a secret; have a big mouth *or* bazoo <nonformal>, **blab** *or* blabber <nonformal>; babble, **tattle,** tell *or* tattle on, tell tales, **tell tales out of school;** talk out of turn, let slip, let fall *or* drop; **blurt, blurt out**

7 **confess,** break down and confess, **admit, acknowledge,** tell all, avow, concede, grant, **own, own up** <nonformal>, let on, implicate *or* incriminate oneself, come clean <nonformal>; spill *and* spill it *and* spill one's guts <all nonformal>; **tell the truth,** tell all, admit everything, let it all hang out <nonformal>, throw off all disguise; **plead guilty,** own oneself in the wrong, cop a plea <nonformal>; **unbosom oneself, make a clean breast, get it off one's chest** <nonformal>, **get it out of one's system** <nonformal>, disburden *or* unburden one's mind *or* conscience *or* heart, **get a load off one's mind** <nonformal>, fess up <nonformal>; out with it *and* spit it out *and* open up <all nonformal>; throw oneself on the mercy of the court; **reveal oneself,** show one's colors *or* true colors, come out of the closet <nonformal>, show one's hand *or* cards, put *or* lay one's cards on the table

8 **be revealed, become known, surface, come to light,** appear, manifest itself, come to one's ears, transpire, **leak out, get out, come out,** out, come home to roost, come out in the wash, break forth, show its face; show its colors, be seen in its true colors, stand revealed; blow one's cover <nonformal>

ADJS 9 **revealed, disclosed** 348.10

10 **disclosive, revealing,** revelatory, revelational; **disclosing,** showing, exposing, betraying; kiss-and-tell; eye-opening; **talkative** 343.10/540.9; admitted, confessed, self-confessed

11 confessional, admissive

352 PUBLICATION

NOUNS 1 **publication, publishing, promulgation,** evulgation, **propagation, dissemination, diffusion, broadcast,** broadcasting, **spread, spreading,** spreading abroad, **circulation,** ventilation, airing, noising, bandying, bruiting, bruiting about; **display;** issue, issuance; telecasting, videocasting; printing 548; book, periodical 555

2 **announcement,** annunciation, enunciation; **proclamation,** pronouncement, pronunciamento; **report,** communiqué, **declaration, statement;** public declaration *or* statement, program, programma, **notice, notification,** public notice; circular, encyclical, encyclical letter; manifesto, position paper; broadside; rationale; white paper, white book; ukase, edict 420.4; bulletin board, notice board

3 **press release,** release, handout, bulletin, official bulletin, notice

4 **publicity,** publicness, **notoriety, fame,** famousness, notoriousness, notice, public notice, **celebrity,** *réclame, éclat* <both Fr>; **limelight** *and* **spotlight** <both nonformal>, daylight, bright light, glare, public eye *or* consciousness, **exposure, currency,** common *or* public knowledge, widest *or* maximum dissemination; **ballyhoo** *and* hoopla <both nonformal>; report, public report; cry, hue and cry; **public relations** *or* PR, flackery <nonformal>; **publicity story,** press notice; **writeup, puff** <nonformal>, **plug** <nonformal>, **blurb** <nonformal>

5 **promotion, buildup** *and* promo <both nonformal>, flack <nonformal>, publicization, publicizing, promoting, advocating, advocacy, bruiting, drumbeating, tub-thumping, press-agentry; **advertising,** salesmanship 734.2, Madison Avenue, hucksterism <nonformal>; advertising campaign; advertising agency; advertising medium *or* media; advocacy, advocacy group

6 **advertisement, ad** <nonformal>, advert <Brit nonformal>, notice; **commercial,** message, important message, message *or* words from the sponsor; spot commercial *or* spot, network commercial; reader, reading notice; display ad; want ad <nonformal>, classified ad; spread, two-page spread, testimonial

7 **poster, bill, placard, sign,** show card, banner, *affiche* <Fr>; **signboard, billboard,** highway sign, hoarding <Brit>; sandwich board; marquee

8 **advertising matter,** promotional material, public relations handout *or* release, literature <nonformal>; **leaflet,** leaf, **folder, handbill, bill, flier, throwaway, handout, circular,** broadside, broadsheet

9 publicist, publicizer, public relations
man, public relations officer, PR man,
flack *and* pitchman *or* pitchperson <all
nonformal>, public relations specialist,
publicity man *or* agent, **press agent,** flack
<nonformal>; **advertiser; adman** *and*
huckster *and* pitchman <all nonformal>;
ad writer <nonformal>, copywriter; **promoter, booster** <nonformal>, plugger
<nonformal>; **ballyhooer** *or* **ballyhoo
man** <nonformal>; **barker,** spieler
<nonformal>, skywriter; billposter;
sign-painter; sandwich boy *or* man

VERBS **10 publish, promulgate, propagate,
circulate,** circularize, **diffuse, disseminate,** distribute, **broadcast,** televise,
telecast, videocast, air, **spread,** spread
around *or* about, spread far and wide,
publish abroad, **pass the word around,**
bruit, **bruit about, advertise,** repeat, retail, put about, **bandy about, noise about,**
cry about *or* abroad, noise *or* sound
abroad, bruit abroad, set news afloat,
spread a report; rumor, launch a rumor,
voice <old>, whisper, buzz, **rumor
about,** whisper *or* buzz about

11 make public, go public with <nonfor-
mal>; bring *or* lay *or* drag before the public, **display,** take one's case to the public,
give *or* **put out,** give to the world, **make
known; divulge** 351.5; **ventilate,** air, give
air to, bring into the open, get out in the
open, open up, broach, give vent to, ventilate

12 announce, annunciate, enunciate; **declare, state,** declare roundly, affirm,
pronounce, give notice; **say,** make a statement, send a message *or* signal; **report,**
make an announcement *or* a report, issue
a statement, publish *or* issue a manifesto,
present a position paper, issue a white
paper, hold a press conference

13 proclaim, cry, cry out, **promulgate,** give
voice to; **herald,** herald abroad; **blazon,**
blaze, blaze *or* blazon about *or* abroad,
blare, blare forth *or* abroad, thunder,
declaim, shout, trumpet, trumpet *or*
thunder forth, announce with flourish of
trumpets *or* beat of drum; shout from the
housetops, proclaim at the crossroads *or*
market cross, proclaim at Charing Cross
<Brit>

14 issue, bring out, put out, get out, launch
get off, emit, put *or* give *or* send forth, offer to the public, pass out

15 publicize, give publicity; go public with
<nonformal>; bring *or* drag into the
limelight, throw the spotlight on <non-
formal>; **advertise, promote,** build up,

cry up, sell, puff <nonformal>, **boost**
<nonformal>, **plug** <nonformal>, **bally-
hoo** <nonformal>; put on the map,
make a household word of, establish;
bark *and* spiel <both nonformal>; make
a pitch for *and* beat the drum for *and*
thump the tub for <all nonformal>;
write up, give a write-up, press-agent
<nonformal>; circularize; bulletin; bill;
post bills, post, post up, placard; sky-
write

16 <be published> **come out, appear,**
break, hit the streets <nonformal>, **issue,** go *or* come forth, find vent, **see the
light,** see the light of day, become public;
circulate, spread, spread about, have currency, **get around** *or* about, get abroad,
get afloat, get exposure, go *or* fly *or* buzz
or blow about, **go the rounds,** pass from
mouth to mouth, be on everyone's lips, go
through the length and breadth of the
land; spread like wildfire

ADJS **17 published, public,** made public, **cir-
culated,** in circulation, promulgated,
propagated, **disseminated,** issued,
spread, diffused, distributed; in print;
broadcast, telecast, televised; **announced,**
proclaimed, declared, **stated,** affirmed;
reported, brought to notice; common
knowledge, common property, current; **open,** accessible, open to the
public

18 publicational, promulgatory, propaga-
tory; proclamatory, annunciatory,
enunciative; declarative, declaratory;
heraldic; promotional

ADVS **19 publicly, in public; openly** 348.15;
in the public eye, in the glare of publicity,
in the limelight *or* spotlight <nonfor-
mal>, reportedly

353 MESSENGER

NOUNS **1 messenger,** message-bearer,
dispatch-bearer, commissionaire
<Brit>, nuncio <old>, **courier,** diplo-
matic courier, carrier, **runner,** express
<Brit>, dispatch-rider, pony-express
rider, post <old>, postboy, postrider,
estafette <Fr>; bicycle *or* motorcycle
messenger; **go-between** 576.4; **emissary**
576.6; Mercury, Hermes, Iris, Pheidip-
pides, Paul Revere; post office, courier
service, package service, message service
or center; answering service

2 herald, harbinger, forerunner, vaunt-
courier; evangel, evangelist, bearer of
glad tidings; herald angel, Gabriel, *buccinator* <L>

3 **announcer,** annunciator, enunciator; nunciate <old>; **proclaimer; crier, town crier,** bellman

4 errand boy, office boy, messenger-boy, copyboy; bellhop <nonformal>, bellboy, bellman, callboy, caller

5 **postman, mailman,** mail carrier, letter carrier; postmaster, postmistress; postal clerk

6 <mail carriers> carrier pigeon, carrier, homing pigeon, homer <nonformal>; pigeon post; post-horse, poster; post coach, mail coach; post boat, packet boat *or* ship, mail boat, mail packet, mailer <old>; mail train, mail car, post car, post-office car, railway mail car; mail truck; mailplane

354 FALSENESS

NOUNS 1 **falseness, falsehood,** falsity, inveracity, untruth, **truthlessness, untrueness; fallaciousness,** fallacy, **erroneousness** 974.1

2 **spuriousness, phoniness** <nonformal>, bogusness, **ungenuineness, unauthenticity,** unrealness, artificiality, factitiousness, syntheticness

3 **sham, fakery,** faking, falsity, feigning, pretending; feint, pretext, **pretense,** hollow pretense, **pretension, false pretense** *or* **pretension;** humbug, humbuggery; **bluff,** bluffing, four-flushing <nonformal>; speciousness, meretriciousness; cheating, fraud; imposture; deception, delusion 356.1; acting, playacting; representation, **simulation,** simulacrum; dissembling, **dissemblance, dissimulation;** seeming, semblance, appearance, face, ostentation, **show, false show,** outward show, false air; window dressing, front, **false front, façade,** gloss, varnish; gilt; color, coloring, false color; masquerade, facade, disguise; posture, pose, posing, attitudinizing; mannerism, affectation 500

4 **falseheartedness, falseness,** doubleheartedness, doubleness of heart, doubleness, **duplicity, two-facedness,** double-facedness, **double-dealing,** ambidexterity; double standard; **dishonesty,** improbity, lack of integrity, Machiavellianism, bad faith; low cunning, **cunning,** artifice, wile 415.1,3; **deceitfulness** 356.3; faithlessness, treachery 645.6

5 **insincerity, uncandidness,** uncandor, **unfrankness,** disingenuousness; emptiness, hollowness; mockery, hollow mockery; crossed fingers, tongue in cheek, un-

seriousness; halfheartedness; sophistry, jesuitry, casuistry 935.1

6 **hypocrisy,** hypocriticalness; Tartuffery, Tartuffism, Pecksniffery, pharisaism, **sanctimony** 693, sanctimoniousness, religiosity, false piety, ostentatious devotion, pietism, Bible-thumping <nonformal>; **mealymouthedness, unctuousness,** oiliness, smarminess *or* smarm <nonformal>; **cant,** mummery, snuffling <old>, **mouthing; lip service;** tokenism; token gesture, empty gesture; smooth tongue, smooth talk, sweet talk *and* soft soap <both nonformal>; crocodile tears

7 **quackery, chicanery,** quackishness, quackism, **mountebankery, charlatanry,** charlatanism; **imposture; humbug,** humbuggery

8 **untruthfulness, dishonesty,** falsehood, **unveracity,** unveraciousness, truthlessness, **mendaciousness, mendacity;** credibility gap; **lying, fibbing,** fibbery, pseudology; pathological lying, mythomania, *pseudologia phantastica* <L>

9 **deliberate falsehood, disinformation, falsification,** disinforming, falsifying; confabulation; **perversion, distortion,** straining, **bending; misrepresentation,** misconstruction, misstatement, coloring, false coloring, miscoloring, slanting, imparting a spin <nonformal>; tampering, cooking *and* fiddling <both nonformal>; stretching, fictionalization, **exaggeration** 355; **prevarication,** equivocation 344.4; **perjury,** false swearing, oath breaking

10 **fabrication, invention, concoction, disinformation;** canard, base canard; **forgery; fiction,** figment, **myth,** fable, romance, extravaganza

11 **lie, falsehood,** falsity, **untruth,** untruism, mendacity, **prevarication, fib,** taradiddle <nonformal>, flimflam *or* flam, a crock *and* a crock of shit <both nonformal>, *blague* <Fr>; **fiction,** pious fiction, legal fiction; **story** <nonformal>, **trumped-up story,** farrago; **yarn** <nonformal>, **tale,** fairy tale <nonformal>, ghost story; farfetched story, tall tale *and* **tall story** <both nonformal>, **cock-and-bull story,** fish story <nonformal>; exaggeration 355; half-truth, stretching of the truth, slight stretching, white lie, little white lie; *suggestio falsi* <L>; a pack of lies

12 monstrous lie, consummate lie, deep-dyed falsehood, out-and-out lie, **whopper** <nonformal>, gross *or* flagrant *or* shameless falsehood, **barefaced lie, dirty lie** <nonformal>; **slander, libel** 512.3; the big lie

13 fake, fakement *and* put-up job <both nonformal>, **phony** <nonformal>, **rip-off** <nonformal>, **sham, mock, imitation,** simulacrum, dummy; paste, tinsel, *clinquant* <Fr>, pinchbeck, shoddy, junk; **counterfeit, forgery;** put-up job *and* frame-up <both nonformal>, put-on <nonformal>; **hoax, cheat, fraud, swindle** 356.8; whited sepulcher, whitewash job <nonformal>; impostor 357.6

14 humbug, humbuggery; **bunk** <nonformal>, **bunkum;** hooey *and* hoke *and* **hokum** <all nonformal>, **bosh** <nonformal>, bull *and* **bullshit** *and* crap <all nonformal>, baloney <nonformal>, flimflam, flam, smoke and mirrors <nonformal>, claptrap, moonshine, eyewash, hogwash, gammon <Brit nonformal>, *blague* <Fr>, jiggery-pokery <Brit>

VERBS **15** ring false, **not ring true**

16 falsify, belie, misrepresent, miscolor; misstate, misquote, misreport, miscite; overstate, understate; **pervert, distort,** strain, warp, **slant, twist,** impart spin <nonformal>; garble; put a false appearance upon, give a false coloring, give a color to, **color, gild,** gloss, gloss over, whitewash, varnish, paper over <nonformal>; fudge <nonformal>, dress up, titivate, embellish, embroider, trick *or* prink out; deodorize, make smell like roses; **disguise, camouflage, mask**

17 tamper with, manipulate, fake, juggle, sophisticate, **doctor** *and* **cook** <both nonformal>, rig, cook *or* juggle the books *or* the accounts <nonformal>; pack, stack; **adulterate;** retouch; **load; salt,** plant <nonformal>, salt a mine

18 fabricate, invent, manufacture, trump up, make up, hatch, concoct, cook up *and* make out of whole cloth <both nonformal>, fudge <nonformal>, fake, hoke up <nonformal>; **counterfeit, forge;** fantasize, fantasize about

19 lie, tell a lie, falsify, speak falsely, speak with forked tongue <nonformal>, be untruthful, trifle with the truth, deviate from the truth, **fib, story** <nonformal>; **stretch the truth,** strain *or* bend the truth; draw the longbow; **exaggerate** 355.3; lie flatly, lie in one's throat, lie through one's teeth, lie like a trooper, **prevaricate,** equivocate 344.7; **deceive, mislead**

20 swear falsely, forswear oneself <old>, **perjure oneself, bear false witness**

21 sham, fake <nonformal>, **feign, counterfeit, simulate,** put up <nonformal>; gammon <Brit nonformal>; **pretend,**

make a pretense, **make believe, make a show of,** make like <nonformal>, make as if *or* as though; go through the motions <nonformal>; let on, let on like <nonformal>; **affect,** profess, **assume,** put on; **dissimulate, dissemble,** cover up; **act, play,** play-act, **put on an act** *or* a charade <nonformal>, act *or* play a part; **put up a front** <nonformal>, put on a front *or* false front <nonformal>; four-flush <nonformal>, **bluff,** pull *or* put up a bluff <nonformal>; **play possum** <nonformal>, roll over and play dead

22 pose as, masquerade as, impersonate, pass for, assume the guise *or* identity of, set up for, act the part of, represent oneself to be, claim *or* pretend to be, **make false pretenses,** go under false pretenses, **sail under false colors**

23 be hypocritical, act *or* play the hypocrite; cant, be holier than the Pope *or* thou, reek of piety; shed crocodile tears, snuffle <old>, snivel, mouth; give mouth honor, render *or* give lip service; sweet-talk, soft-soap, blandish 511.5

24 play a double game *or* **role, play both ends against the middle,** work both sides of the street, have it both ways at once, have one's cake and eat it too, run with the hare and hunt with the hounds <Brit>; two-time <nonformal>

ADJS **25 false, untrue, truthless, not true,** void *or* devoid of truth, contrary to fact, in error, **fallacious, erroneous** 974.16; unfounded 935.13; disinformative

26 spurious, ungenuine, unauthentic, supposititious, bastard, **pseudo, quasi,** apocryphal, **fake** <nonformal>, **phony** <nonformal>, **sham, mock, counterfeit,** colorable, **bogus,** queer <nonformal>, dummy, **make-believe,** so-called, **imitation** 336.8; not what it's cracked up to be <nonformal>; **falsified;** dressed up, titivated, embellished, embroidered; garbled; twisted, distorted, warped, perverted, slanted; **simulated, faked, feigned,** colored, fictitious, fictive, **counterfeited, pretended, affected, assumed, put-on; artificial, synthetic,** ersatz; unreal; factitious, unnatural, man-made; illegitimate; *soi-disant* <Fr>, self-styled; pinchbeck, brummagem <Brit>, tinsel, shoddy, tin, junky

27 specious, meretricious, gilded, tinsel, **seeming,** apparent, colored, colorable, plausible, **ostensible**

28 quack, quackish; charlatan, charlatanish, charlatanic

29 fabricated, invented, manufactured, **con-**

cocted, hatched, trumped-up, made-up, put-up, cooked-up <nonformal>; forged; fictitious, fictional, figmental, mythical, fabulous, legendary; fantastic, fantasied, fancied

30 tampered with, manipulated, cooked and doctored <both nonformal>, juggled, rigged, engineered; packed

31 falsehearted, false, false-principled, false-dealing; double, duplicitous, ambidextrous, double-dealing, doublehearted, double-minded, double-tongued, doublefaced, two-faced, Janus-faced; Machiavellian, dishonest; crooked, deceitful; creative, artful, cunning, crafty 415.12; faithless, perfidious, treacherous 645.21

32 insincere, uncandid, unfrank, mealy-mouthed, unctuous, oily, disingenuous, smarmy <nonformal>; dishonest; empty, hollow; tongue in cheek, unserious; sophistic or sophistical, jesuitic or jesuitical, casuistic 935.10

33 hypocritic or hypocritical, canting, Pecksniffian, pharisaic, pharisaical, pharisean, sanctimonious, goody-goody <nonformal>, holier-than-the-Pope, holier-than-thou, simon-pure

34 untruthful, dishonest, unveracious, unveridical, truthless, lying, mendacious; perjured, forsworn; prevaricating, equivocal 344.11

ADVS 35 falsely, untruly, truthlessly; erroneously 974.20; untruthfully, unveraciously; spuriously, ungenuinely; artificially, synthetically; unnaturally, factitiously; speciously, seemingly, apparently, plausibly, ostensibly; nominally, in name only

36 insincerely, uncandidly; emptily, hollowly; unseriously; hypocritically, mealy-mouthedly, unctuously

355 EXAGGERATION

NOUNS 1 exaggeration, exaggerating; overstatement, big or tall talk <nonformal>, hyperbole, hyperbolism; superlative; extravagance, profuseness, prodigality 486; magnification, enlargement, amplification <old>, dilation, dilatation, inflation, expansion, blowing up, puffing up, aggrandizement; stretching, heightening, enhancement; overemphasis, overstressing; overestimation 948; exaggerated lengths, extreme, exorbitance, inordinacy, overkill, excess 992; burlesque, travesty, caricature; sensationalism, puffery and ballyhoo <both nonformal>, touting, huckstering; grandiloquence 545

2 overreaction, much ado about nothing, storm or tempest in a teapot, making a mountain out of a molehill

VERBS 3 exaggerate, hyperbolize; overstate, overspeak <old>, overreach, overdraw, overcharge; overstress; overdo, carry too far, go to extremes; push to the extreme, indulge in overkill, overestimate 948.2; overpraise, oversell, tout, puff and ballyhoo <both nonformal>; stretch, stretch the truth, stretch the point, draw the longbow; magnify, inflate, amplify <old>; aggrandize, build up; pile or lay it on and pour or spread or lay it on thick and lay it on with a trowel <all nonformal>; pile Pelion on Ossa; talk big <nonformal>, talk in superlatives, deal in the marvelous, make much of; overreact, make a Federal case out of it <nonformal>, something out of nothing, make a mountain out of a molehill, cry over spilt milk; caricature, travesty, burlesque

ADJS 4 exaggerated, hyperbolical, magnified, amplified <old>, inflated, aggrandized; stretched, disproportionate, blown up out of all proportion; overpraised, oversold, touted, puffed and ballyhooed <both nonformal>; overemphasized, overemphatic, overstressed; overemphatic, overstressed; overstated, overdrawn; overdone, overwrought; overestimated 948.3; overlarge, overgreat; extreme, pushed to the extreme, exorbitant, inordinate, excessive 992.16; superlative, extravagant, profuse, prodigal 486.8; high-flown, grandiloquent 545.8

5 exaggerating, exaggerative, hyperbolical

356 DECEPTION

NOUNS 1 deception, calculated deception, deceptiveness, subterfuge, gimmickry or gimmickery, trickiness; falseness 354; fallaciousness, fallacy; self-deception, fond illusion, wishful thinking, willful misconception; vision, hallucination, phantasm, mirage, will-o'-the-wisp, delusion, delusiveness, illusion 975; deceiving, victimization, dupery; bamboozlement <nonformal>, hoodwinking; swindling, defrauding, conning, flimflam or flimflammery <nonformal>; fooling, befooling, tricking, kidding and putting on <both nonformal>; spoofing and spoofery <both nonformal>; bluffing; circumvention, overreaching, outwitting; ensnarement, entrapment, enmeshment, entanglement

2 misleading, misguidance, misdirection;

bum steer <nonformal>; misinformation 569.1

3 deceit, deceitfulness, guile, falseness, insidiousness, **underhandedness; shiftiness, furtiveness,** surreptitiousness, indirection; **hypocrisy** 354.6; **falseheartedness, duplicity** 354.4; **treacherousness** 645.6; **artfulness,** craft, **cunning** 415; sneakiness 345.4; sneak attack

4 chicanery, chicane, **skulduggery** <nonformal>, **trickery,** dodgery, pettifogging, pettifoggery, *supercherie* <Fr>, **artifice,** sleight, machination; **sharp practice, underhand dealing, foul play;** connivery, connivance, collusion, conspiracy, covin <law>

5 juggling, jugglery, **trickery,** dirty pool <nonformal>, *escamotage* <Fr>, prestidigitation, conjuration, **legerdemain, sleight of hand,** smoke and mirrors <nonformal>; mumbo jumbo, **hocuspocus,** hanky-panky *and* monkey business *and* hokey-pokey <all nonformal>, nobbling *and* jiggery-pokery <both Brit nonformal>

6 trick, artifice, device, ploy, gambit, stratagem, **scheme,** design, *ficelle* <Fr>, **subterfuge,** blind, **ruse, wile,** chouse <nonformal>, shift, **dodge,** artful dodge, sleight, pass, feint, fetch, chicanery; **bluff;** gimmick, joker, catch; curve, curve-ball, googly *or* bosey *or* wrong'un <all Brit nonformal>; **dirty trick,** dirty deal, fast deal, scurvy trick; sleight of hand, sleight-of-hand trick, hocus-pocus <old>; juggle, juggler's trick; **bag of tricks,** tricks of the trade

7 hoax, deception, spoof <nonformal>, **humbug,** flam, **fake** *and* fakement, **rip-off** <nonformal>, **sham;** mare's nest

8 fraud, fraudulence *or* fraudulency, **dishonesty; imposture; imposition, cheat, cheating,** cozenage, **swindle,** dodge, fishy transaction, piece of sharp practice; customer-gouging, insider-trading, short weight, chiseling; **gyp joint** <nonformal>; **racket** <nonformal>, illicit business 732; **graft** <nonformal>, grift <nonformal>; bunco; cardsharping; ballot-box stuffing, gerrymandering

9 <nonformal terms> **gyp,** diddle, diddling, scam, flimflam flam, ramp <Brit>, scam, snow job, song and dance, number, bill of goods, burn, the business, dipsy-doodle, double cross, fiddle, hosing, the old army game, reaming, suckering, sting

10 confidence game, con game <nonformal>, **skin game** <nonformal>, **bunco game; shell game,** thimblerig, thimble-rigging; bucket shop, boiler room <nonformal>; goldbrick; bait-andswitch, the wire, the pay-off, the rag, pastposting

11 cover, disguise, camouflage, protective coloration; **false colors, false front** 354.3; **incognito;** smoke screen; **masquerade,** masque, mummery; **mask,** visor, vizard, vizard mask <old>, false face, domino, domino mask

12 trap, gin; pitfall, trapfall, deadfall; flytrap, mousetrap, mole trap, rattrap, bear trap; deathtrap, firetrap; Venus's flytrap, Dionaea; spring gun, set gun; baited trap; **booby trap, mine; decoy** 357.5

13 snare, springe; noose, lasso, lariat; bola; **net,** trawl, dragnet, seine, purse seine, pound net, gill net; cobweb; **meshes, toils; fishhook, hook,** sniggle; **bait,** ground bait; **lure,** fly, jig, squid, plug, wobbler, spinner; lime, birdlime

VERBS **14 deceive, beguile, trick, hoax, dupe,** gammon, **gull,** pigeon, play one for a fool *or* sucker, **bamboozle** *and* snow *and* **hornswoggle** *and* diddle *and* scam <all nonformal>, nobble <Brit nonformal>, **humbug, take in,** put on *and* hocus-pocus <both nonformal>, string along, **put something over** *or* **across,** slip one over on <nonformal>, pull a fast one on; **play games** <nonformal>; **delude,** mock; **betray,** let down, leave in the lurch, leave holding the bag, play one false, **doublecross** <nonformal>, cheat on; two-time <nonformal>; juggle, conjure; **bluff;** cajole, **circumvent,** get around, forestall; **overreach,** outreach, outwit, outmaneuver, outsmart

15 fool, befool, make a fool of, practice on one's credulity, **pull one's leg,** make an ass of; **trick; spoof** *and* kid *and* put one on <all nonformal>; **play a trick on,** play a practical joke upon, send on a fool's errand; fake one out <nonformal>; sell one a bill of goods, give one a snow job

16 mislead, misguide, misdirect, lead astray, lead up the garden path, **give a bum steer** <nonformal>; feed one a line <nonformal>, throw off the scent, throw off the track *or* trail, put on a false scent, drag *or* draw a red herring across the trail; throw one a curve *or* curve ball <nonformal>, bowl a googly *or* bosey *or* wrong 'un <Brit nonformal>; misinform 569.3

17 hoodwink, blindfold, blind, blind one's eyes, blear the eyes of <old>, throw dust in one's eyes, **pull the wool over one's eyes**

18 cheat, victimize, gull, pigeon, fudge, swindle, defraud, practice fraud upon, euchre, con, finagle, fleece, mulct, fob <old>, bilk, cozen, cog <old>, chouse, cheat out of, do out of, chouse out of, beguile of or out of; obtain under false pretenses; live by one's wits; bunco, play a bunco game; sell gold bricks <nonformal>; shortchange, shortweight, skim off the top; stack the cards or deck, pack the deal <nonformal>, deal off the bottom of the deck, play with marked cards; cog the dice, load the dice; thimblerig; crib <nonformal>; throw a fight or game <nonformal>, take a dive <nonformal>

19 <nonformal terms> gyp, clip, scam, rope in, hose, shave, beat, rook, flam, flimflam, diddle, dipsy-doodle, do a number on, hustle, fuck, screw, have, pull something, pull a trick or stunt, give the business, ramp <Brit>, stick, sting, burn, gouge, chisel, hocus, hocus-pocus, play or take for a sucker, make a patsy of, do, run a game on, slicker, take for a ride

20 trap, entrap, gin, catch, catch out, catch in a trap; ensnare, snare, hook, hook in, sniggle, noose; inveigle; net, mesh, enmesh, snarl <old>, ensnarl, wind, tangle, entangle, entoil, enweb; trip, trip up; set or lay a trap for, bait the hook, spread the toils; lime, birdlime; lure, allure, decoy 377.3

ADJS 21 deceptive, deceiving, misleading, beguiling, false, fallacious, delusive, delusory; hallucinatory, illusive, illusory; tricky, trickish, tricksy <old>, catchy; fishy <nonformal>, questionable, dubious

22 deceitful, false; fraudulent, sharp, guileful, insidious, slippery, slippery as an eel, shifty, tricky, trickish, cute, finagling, chiseling <nonformal>; underhand, underhanded, furtive, surreptitious, indirect; collusive, covinous; falsehearted, two-faced; treacherous 645.21; sneaky 345.12; cunning, artful, gimmicky <nonformal>, wily, crafty 415.12; calculating, scheming

ADVS 23 deceptively, beguilingly, falsely, fallaciously, delusively, trickily, misleadingly, with intent to deceive; under false colors, under cover of, under the garb of, in disguise

24 deceitfully, fraudulently, guilefully, insidiously, shiftily, trickily; underhandedly, furtively, surreptitiously, indirectly, like a thief in the night; treacherously 645.25

357 DECEIVER

NOUNS 1 deceiver, deluder, duper, misleader, beguiler, bamboozler <nonformal>; actor, playactor <nonformal>, role-player; dissembler, dissimulator; confidence man; double-dealer, Machiavelli, Machiavel, Machiavellian; dodger, Artful Dodger <Charles Dickens>, counterfeiter, forger, faker; plagiarizer, plagiarist; entrancer, enchanter, charmer, befuddler, hypnotizer, mesmerizer; seducer, Don Juan, Casanova; tease, teaser; jilt, jilter; gay deceiver; fooler, joker, jokester, hoaxer, practical joker; spoofer and kidder and ragger and leg-puller <all nonformal>

2 trickster, tricker; juggler, sleight-of-hand performer, magician, illusionist, conjurer, prestidigitator, escamoteur <Fr>

3 cheat, cheater; two-timer <nonformal>; swindler, defrauder, cozener, juggler; sharper, sharp, spieler, pitchman, pitchperson; confidence man, confidence trickster, horse trader, horse coper <Brit>; cardsharp, cardsharper; thimblerigger; shortchanger; shyster and pettifogger <both nonformal>; land shark, land pirate, land grabber, mortgage shark; carpetbagger; crimp

4 <nonformal terms> gyp, gypper, gyp artist, flimflammer, flimflam man, blackleg, chiseler, bilker, fleecer, diddler, crook, sharpie, shark, jackleg, slicker, con man, con artist, bunco, bunco artist, bunco steerer, scammer, clip artist, smoothie, dipsy-doodle, hustler, hoser

5 shill, decoy, come-on man <nonformal>, plant, capper, stool pigeon, stoolie <nonformal>; agent provocateur <Fr>

6 impostor, ringer; impersonator; pretender; sham, shammer, humbug, blagueur <Fr>, fraud <nonformal>, fake and faker and phony <all nonformal>, fourflusher <nonformal>, bluff, bluffer; charlatan, quack, quacksalver, quackster, mountebank, saltimbanco; wolf in sheep's clothing, ass in lion's skin, jackdaw in peacock's feathers; poser, poseur; malingerer

7 masquerader, masker; impersonator, personator; mummer, guiser <Scots>, guisard; incognito, incognita

8 hypocrite, phony <nonformal>, sanctimonious fraud, pharisee, whited sepulcher, canter, snuffler, mealy-mouth, "a saint abroad and a devil at home"—Bunyan; Tartuffe <Molière>, Pecksniff and Uriah Heep <both Charles Dickens>,

Joseph Surface <Richard B Sheridan>;
false friend, fair-weather friend; summer
soldier

9 **liar, fibber,** fibster, fabricator, fabulist,
pseudologist; falsifier; **prevaricator,**
equivocator, mudger <Brit nonformal>,
waffler <nonformal>, palterer; **storyteller;** yarner *and* yarn spinner *and* spinner of yarns <all nonformal>; Ananias;
Satan, Father of Lies; Baron Münchau-
sen; Sir John Mandeville; consummate
liar, "liar of the first magnitude"—
Congreve; *menteur à triple étage* <Fr>,
dirty liar; pathological liar, mytho-
maniac, pseudologue, confirmed *or*
habitual liar; **perjurer,** false witness

10 **traitor,** treasonist, **betrayer, quisling, rat**
<nonformal>, serpent, snake, cockatrice,
snake in the grass, double-crosser
<nonformal>, double-dealer; double
agent; trimmer, time-server; turncoat
363.5; informer 551.6; archtraitor; Judas,
Judas Iscariot, Benedict Arnold, Quisling,
Brutus; **schemer, plotter,** intriguer, *intrigant* <Fr>, conspirer, **conspirator,** conniver, machinator

11 **subversive; saboteur, fifth columnist,**
crypto; security risk; **collaborationist,**
collaborator, fraternizer; fifth column,
underground; Trojan horse

358 DUPE

NOUNS 1 **dupe, gull,** gudgeon, *gobe-mouches*
<Fr>; **victim;** gullible *or* dupable *or*
credulous person, trusting *or* simple soul,
innocent, *naïf* <Fr>, babe, babe in the
woods; greenhorn; toy, plaything; monkey; **fool** 923; stooge, **cat's-paw**

2 <nonformal terms> **sucker, patsy,** pigeon, chicken, fall guy, doormat, mug
<Brit>, fish, jay <chiefly Brit>, easy
mark, sitting duck, juggin <chiefly Brit>,
pushover, cinch, mark, vic, easy pickings,
greeny, greener, chump, boob, schlemiel,
sap, saphead, prize sap, easy touch, soft
touch

359 RESOLUTION

NOUNS 1 **resolution,** resolve, resolvedness,
determination, decision, fixed *or* firm
resolve, **will,** purpose; **resoluteness,**
determinedness, determinateness, decisiveness, decidedness, **purposefulness;**
definiteness; **earnestness, seriousness,**
sincerity, devotion, dedication, commitment, total commitment; "the dauntless
spirit of resolution, "the native hue of

resolution"—both Shakespeare; single-
mindedness, relentlessness, persistence,
tenacity, perseverance 360; self-will, obstinacy 361

2 **firmness,** firmness of mind *or* spirit,
staunchness, settledness, steadiness, constancy, steadfastness, fixedness, unshakableness; **stability** 854; concentration;
flintiness, steeliness; inflexibility, rigidity, unyieldingness 361.2; trueness,
loyalty 644.7

3 **pluck, spunk** <nonformal>, **mettle,**
backbone <nonformal>, **grit,** true grit,
spirit, **stamina, guts** *and* moxie <both
nonformal>, pith <old>, bottom, **toughness** <nonformal>; pluckiness, spunkiness <nonformal>, **gameness,** feistiness
<nonformal>, mettlesomeness; courage
492

4 **will power, will,** power, **strong-
mindedness,** strength of mind, strength
or fixity of purpose, strength, fortitude,
moral fiber; iron will, will of iron *or* steel;
a will *or* mind of one's own, law unto oneself; the courage of one's convictions,
moral courage

5 **self-control, self-command, self-
possession,** self-mastery, self-government, self-domination, **self-restraint,** self-
conquest, self-discipline, **self-denial;** control, restraint, constraint, discipline;
composure, possession, aplomb; **independence** 430.5

6 **self-assertion,** self-assertiveness, forwardness, **nerve** *and* pushiness <both
nonformal>, importunateness, importunacy; self-expression, self-expressive-
ness

VERBS 7 **resolve, determine, decide, will,**
purpose, make up one's mind, make *or*
take a resolution, make a point of; **settle,**
settle on, fix, seal; conclude, come to a determination *or* conclusion *or* decision,
determine once for all

8 **be determined,** be resolved; **have a mind**
or **will of one's own,** know one's own
mind; **be in earnest, mean business**
<nonformal>, mean what one says; have
blood in one's eyes *and* be out for blood
<both nonformal>, **set one's mind** *or*
heart upon; put one's heart into, devote
or commit *or* dedicate oneself to, give
oneself up to; buckle oneself, buckle
down, buckle to; steel oneself, brace oneself, grit one's teeth, set one's teeth *or*
jaw; put *or* lay *or* set one's shoulder to the
wheel; take the bull by the horns, take the
plunge, cross the Rubicon; nail one's colors to the mast, burn one's bridges *or*

boats, go for broke *and* shoot the works <both nonformal>, kick down the ladder, throw away the scabbard; never say die, die hard, die fighting, die with one's boots on

9 remain firm, stand fast *or* **firm, hold out,** hold fast, get tough <nonformal>, **take one's stand,** set one's back against the wall, **stand** *or* **hold one's ground,** keep one's footing, hold one's own, hang in *and* hang in there *and* hang tough <all nonformal>, dig in, dig one's heels in; **stick to one's guns,** stick, stick with it, stick fast, stick to one's colors, adhere to one's principles; not listen to the voice of the siren; take what comes, stand the gaff; **put one's foot down** <nonformal>, stand no nonsense

10 not hesitate, think nothing of, think little of, **make no bones about** <nonformal>, have *or* make no scruple of <old>, **stick at nothing,** stop at nothing; not look back; go the whole hog <nonformal>, carry through, face out; go the whole nine yards <nonformal>

ADJS **11 resolute, resolved, determined,** bound *and* bound and determined <both nonformal>, **decided,** decisive, **purposeful;** definite; **earnest, serious,** sincere; devoted, dedicated, committed; wholehearted; single-minded, relentless, persistent, tenacious, persevering; **obstinate** 361.8

12 firm, staunch, standup <nonformal>, fixed, settled, steady, steadfast, constant, set *or* sot <both nonformal>, flinty, steely; unshaken, not to be shaken, unflappable <nonformal>; undeflectable, **unswerving,** not to be deflected; immovable, unbending, inflexible, **unyielding** 361.9; true, loyal 644.20

13 unhesitating, unhesitant, **unfaltering,** unflinching, unshrinking; stick-at-nothing <nonformal>

14 plucky, spunky *and* feisty *and* gutty *or* gutsy <all nonformal>, gritty, **mettlesome,** dauntless, **game,** game to the last *or* end; **courageous** 492.17

15 strong-willed, strong-minded, firm-minded; **self-controlled,** controlled, self-disciplined, self-restrained; **self-possessed; self-assertive,** self-asserting, forward, pushy <nonformal>, importunate; self-expressive; **independent**

16 determined upon, resolved upon, decided upon, intent upon, fixed upon, settled upon, **set on,** dead set on <nonformal>, sot on <nonformal>, **bent on,** hell-bent on <nonformal>

ADVS **17 resolutely, determinedly, decidedly,** decisively, resolvedly, **purposefully, with a will;** firmly, steadfastly, steadily, fixedly, with constancy, staunchly; **seriously,** in all seriousness, **earnestly,** in earnest, in good earnest, sincerely; devotedly, with total dedication, committedly; hammer and tongs, tooth and nail, *bec et ongles* <Fr>; heart and soul, with all one's heart *or* might, wholeheartedly; **unswervingly;** singlemindedly, relentlessly, persistently, tenaciously, like a bulldog, like a leech, perseveringly; **obstinately, unyieldingly, inflexibly** 361.15

18 pluckily, spunkily *and* feistily *and* gutsily <all nonformal>, mettlesomely, **gamely,** dauntlessly, manfully, like a man; on one's mettle; **courageously, heroically** 492.23

19 unhesitatingly, unhesitantly, **unfalteringly,** unflinchingly, unshrinkingly

PHRS **20 come what may,** *venga lo que venga* <Sp>, *vogue la galère* <Fr>, **cost what it may,** *coûte que coûte* <Fr>, whatever the cost, at any price *or* cost *or* sacrifice, at all risks *or* hazards, **whatever may happen,** *ruat caelum* <L>, though the heavens may fall, at all events, live or die, survive or perish, sink or swim, rain or shine, come hell or high water; in some way or other

360 PERSEVERANCE

NOUNS **1 perseverance, persistence** *or* persistency, insistence *or* insistency, singleness of purpose; **resolution** 359; **steadfastness, steadiness,** stability 854; **constancy, permanence** 852.1; loyalty, fidelity 644.7; **single-mindedness,** concentration, undivided *or* unswerving attention, engrossment, preoccupation 982.3; **endurance, stick-to-itiveness** <nonformal>, staying power, bitterendism, **pertinacity,** pertinaciousness, **tenacity,** tenaciousness, **doggedness,** unremittingness, relentlessness, dogged perseverance, bulldog tenacity, unfailing *or* leechlike grip; plodding, plugging, slogging; **obstinacy, stubbornness** 361.1; **diligence,** application, sedulousness, sedulity, industry, industriousness, assiduousness, assiduity; **tirelessness, indefatigability, stamina; patience,** patience of Job 134.1

VERBS **2 persevere, persist, carry on,** go on, **keep on,** keep up, keep at, **keep at it,** keep going, keep driving, keep trying, try and try again, **keep the ball rolling,** keep the pot boiling, keep up the good work; not take 'no' for an answer; not accept compromise *or* defeat; **endure, last, continue** 826.6

3 keep doggedly at, **plod,** drudge, slog *or* slog away, soldier on, put one foot in front of the other, peg away *or* at *or* on; **plug,** plug at, plug away *or* along; pound *or* hammer away; **keep one's nose to the grindstone**

4 **stay with it, hold on,** hold fast, **hang on,** hang on like a bulldog *or* leech, **stick to one's guns;** not give up, **never say die,** not give up the ship, not strike one's colors; come up fighting, come up for more; **stay it out, stick out, hold out;** hold up, last out, **bear up,** stand up; **live with it,** live through it; stay the distance *or* the course; sit tight, be unmoved *or* unmoveable; "wear this world out to the ending doom," "bears it out even to the edge of doom"—both Shakespeare; brazen it out

5 prosecute to a conclusion, **go through with it, carry through, follow through, see it through,** see it out, follow out *or* up; go through with it, go to the bitter end, go the distance, go all the way, go to any length, go the whole length; **leave no stone unturned,** leave no avenue unexplored, overlook nothing, exhaust every move; move heaven and earth, go through fire and water

6 **die trying,** die in the last ditch, die in harness, **die with one's boots on** *or* die in one's boots, die at one's post, die in the attempt, die game, die hard, **go down with flying colors**

7 <nonformal terms> **stick,** stick to it, stick with it, stick it, stick it out, hang on for dear life, hang in hang in there, hang tough, tough it out, keep on trucking, keep on keeping on; **go the limit,** go the whole hog, go the whole nine yards, go all out, shoot the works, go for broke, go through hell and high water

ADJS 8 **persevering,** perseverant, **persistent,** persisting, insistent; **enduring,** permanent, **constant, lasting;** continuing 852.7; **stable, steady, steadfast** 854.12; immutable, inalterable; **resolute** 359.11; **diligent, assiduous, sedulous,** industrious; dogged, plodding, slogging, plugging; **pertinacious, tenacious, stick-to-itive** <nonformal>; loyal, faithful 644.20; **unswerving,** unremitting, unabating, unintermitting, uninterrupted; single-minded, utterly attentive; rapt, preoccupied 982.17; **unfaltering, unwavering,** unflinching; relentless, **unrelenting; ob-**

stinate, **stubborn** 361.8; **unrelaxing,** unfailing, **untiring,** unwearying, unflagging, never-tiring, **tireless,** weariless, **indefatigable,** unwearied, unsleeping, undrooping, unnodding, unwinking, sleepless; undiscouraged, undaunted, indomitable, unconquerable, invincible, game to the last *or* to the end; **patient,** patient as Job 134.9

ADVS 9 **perseveringly, persistently,** persistingly, insistently; resolutely 359.17; loyally, faithfully, devotedly 644.25; **diligently,** industriously, assiduously, sedulously; **doggedly,** sloggingly, ploddingly; pertinaciously, tenaciously; unremittingly, unabatingly, unintermittingly, uninterruptedly; unswervingly, unwaveringly, unfalteringly, unflinchingly; relentlessly, unrelentingly; **indefatigably, tirelessly,** wearilessly, untiringly, unwearyingly, unflaggingly, unrestingly, unsleepingly; **patiently**

10 **through thick and thin,** through fire and water, come hell or high water, through evil report and good report, rain or shine, fair or foul, in sickness and in health; **come what may** 359.20, **all the way, down to the wire,** to the bitter end

361 OBSTINACY

NOUNS 1 **obstinacy,** obstinateness, pertinacity, restiveness, **stubbornness, willfulness,** self-will, hardheadedness, **headstrongness,** strongheadedness; mind *or* will of one's own, set *or* fixed mind, inflexible will; **perseverance** 360, **doggedness, determination,** tenaciousness, tenacity, "tough tenacity of purpose"—J A Symonds, bitterendism; **bullheadedness, pigheadedness, mulishness; obduracy,** unregenerateness; stiff neck, stiff-neckedness; sullenness, sulkiness; balkiness; uncooperativeness; dogmatism, opinionatedness 969.6; overzealousness, fanaticism 925.11; intolerance, bigotry 979.1

2 **unyieldingness,** unbendingness, stiff temper, **inflexibility,** inelasticity, impliability, ungivingness, **obduracy,** toughness, **firmness,** stiffness, adamantness, rigorism, **rigidity,** strait-lacedness *or* straight-lacedness, stuffiness; **hard line,** hardbittenness, hard-nosedness <nonformal>; unalterability, unchangeability, immutability, immovability; irreconcilability, uncompromisingness, **intransigence** *or* intransigency, *intransigeance* <Fr>, intransigentism; **implacability,** inexorability, **relentlessness,** unrelenting-

ness; sternness, grimness, dourness, flintiness, **steeliness**

3 **perversity,** perverseness, **contrariness, wrongheadedness, waywardness,** forwardness, difficultness, crossgrainedness, cantankerousness, feistiness *and* orneriness *and* cussedness <all nonformal>; sullenness, sulkiness, dourness, stuffiness; irascibility 110.2

4 **ungovernability, unmanageability,** uncontrollability; indomitability, untameableness, **intractability,** refractoriness, shrewishness; incorrigibility; **unsubmissiveness,** unbiddability <Brit>, **indocility;** irrepressibility, insuppressibility; unmalleability, unmoldableness; recidivism; **recalcitrance** *or* recalcitrancy, contumacy, contumaciousness; **unruliness,** obstreperousness, restiveness, fractiousness, wildness; defiance 454; resistance 453

5 **unpersuadableness,** deafness, blindness; closed-mindedness; positiveness, dogmatism 969.6

6 <obstinate person> **mule** *and* donkey <both nonformal>, ass, perverse fool; bullethead, pighead; hardnose <nonformal>, hardhead, hammerhead <nonformal>, hard-liner; standpat *and* **standpatter, stickler; intransigent,** maverick; dogmatist, positivist, bigot, fanatic, purist; **diehard, bitter-ender,** last-ditcher

VERBS 7 **balk, stickle;** hold one's ground, not budge, **stand pat** <nonformal>, **not yield an inch,** stick to one's guns; hold out, stand out; take no denial, not take 'no' for an answer; take the bit in one's teeth; die hard; cut off one's nose to spite one's face; **persevere** 360.2,7

ADJS 8 **obstinate, stubborn, pertinacious, restive; willful, self-willed,** strong-willed, hardheaded, **headstrong,** strongheaded, *entêté* <Fr>; **dogged,** bulldogged, **tenacious, perserving; bullheaded,** bulletheaded, **pigheaded, mulish** <nonformal>, stubborn as a mule; set, **set in one's ways,** case-hardened, stiff-necked; sullen, sulky; balky, balking; unregenerate, uncooperative; bigoted, intolerant 979.11, overzealous, fanatic, fanatical 925.32; dogmatic, opinionated 969.22

9 **unyielding, unbending, inflexible, hard, hard-line,** inelastic, impliable, ungiving, **firm, stiff, rigid,** rigorous, stuffy; rock-ribbed, rock-hard, rock-like; **adamant,** adamantine; unmoved, unaffected; **immovable,** not to be moved; **unalterable,** unchangeable, immutable; **uncompromising,** intransigent, irreconcilable,

hard-shell *and* hard-core <both nonformal>; implacable, inexorable, **relentless,** unrelenting; stern, grim, dour; iron, cast-iron, flinty, steely

10 **obdurate,** tough, **hard,** hard-set, hard-mouthed, hard-bitten, hard-nosed *and* hard-boiled <both nonformal>

11 **perverse, contrary, wrongheaded, wayward, froward, difficult,** cross-grained, cantankerous, feisty, ornery <nonformal>; sullen, sulky, stuffy; irascible 110.19

12 **ungovernable, unmanageable, uncontrollable, indomitable,** untamable, **intractable, refractory;** shrewish; **incorrigible, unreconstructed; unsubmissive,** unbiddable <Brit>, **indocile;** irrepressible, insuppressible; unmalleable, unmoldable; recidivist, recidivistic; **recalcitrant,** contumacious; obstreperous, **unruly, restive,** wild, fractious, breachy <nonformal>; beyond control, out of hand; **resistant, resisting** 453.5; **defiant** 454.7

13 **unpersuadable,** deaf, blind; closed-minded; positive; dogmatic 969.22

ADVS 14 **obstinately, stubbornly,** pertinaciously; willfully, headstrongly; **doggedly,** tenaciously; **bullheadedly,** pigheadedly, mulishly; unregenerately; uncooperatively; with set jaw, with sullen mouth, with a stiff neck

15 **unyieldingly, unbendingly, inflexibly, adamantly,** obdurately, **firmly,** stiffly, rigidly, rigorously; unalterably, unchangeably, immutably, immovably, unregenerately; uncompromisingly, intransigently, irreconcilably; implacably, inexorably, relentlessly, unrelentingly; sternly, grimly, dourly

16 **perversely, contrarily,** contrariwise, waywardly, wrongheadedly, frowardly, crossgrainedly, cantankerously, feistily, sullenly, sulkily

17 **ungovernably, unmanageably, uncontrollably,** indomitably, untamably, intractably; shrewishly; incorrigibly; unsubmissively; irrepressibly, insuppressibly; contumaciously; unrulily, obstreperously, restively, fractiously

362 IRRESOLUTION

NOUNS 1 **irresolution, indecision,** unsettlement, unsettledness, irresoluteness, undeterminedness, **indecisiveness,** undecidedness, infirmity of purpose; mugwumpery, mugwumpism, fence-sitting, fence-straddling; double-mindedness, **ambivalence,** ambitendency; dubiety, dubiousness, **uncertainty** 970; **instability, inconstancy,** changeableness 853; capriciousness, mercuriality, fickleness 364.3; change of mind, second thoughts, tergiversation 363.1

2 **vacillation, fluctuation,** oscillation, pendulation, mood swing, **wavering,** wobbling, waffling <nonformal>, shilly-shally, **shilly-shallying,** blowing hot and cold; equivocation 344.4

3 **hesitation,** hesitance, **hesitancy,** hesitating, holding back, dragging one's feet; falter, faltering, shilly-shally, shilly-shallying; diffidence, tentativeness, caution, cautiousness

4 **weak will, weak-mindedness;** feeble-mindedness <old>, **weakness,** feebleness, faintness, faintheartedness, **frailty, infirmity; wimpiness** or wimpishness <nonformal>, spinelessness, invertebracy; abulia; fear 127; cowardice 491; **pliability** 1045.2

5 **vacillator, shillyshallyer,** shilly-shally, **waverer,** wobbler; mugwump, fence-sitter, fence-straddler; ass between two bundles of hay; **wimp** <nonformal>, weakling, jellyfish, Milquetoast; quitter

VERBS 6 **not know one's own mind,** not know where one stands, **be of two minds,** have two minds, have mixed feelings, be in conflict, be conflicted <nonformal>; stagger, stumble, boggle

7 **hesitate, pause, falter, hang back,** hover; shilly-shally, hum and haw, **hem and haw;** wait to see how the cat jumps or the wind blows, scruple, jib, demur <old>, stick at, stickle, strain at; think twice about, stop to consider, ponder, wrinkle one's brow; debate, deliberate, see both sides of the question, balance, weigh one thing against another, consider both sides of the question; be divided, come down squarely in the middle, sit on or straddle the fence, fall between two stools; yield, back down 433.7; retreat, withdraw 163.6, wimp or chicken or cop out <all nonformal>; pull back, drag one's feet; **flinch, shy away from, shy** 902.7, back off <nonformal>; fear; not face up to, hide one's head in the sand

8 **vacillate, waver, waffle** <nonformal>, **fluctuate,** pendulate, oscillate, wobble, wobble about, teeter, totter <old>, dither, swing from one thing to another, **shilly-shally,** back and fill, keep off and on, will and will not, keep or leave hanging in midair; blow hot and cold 364.4; **equivocate** 344.7, fudge and mudge <Brit nonformal>; change one's mind, ter-

giversate; vary, **alternate** 853.5; shift, change horses in midstream, **change** 851.5

ADJS 9 **irresolute,** irresolved, **unresolved; undecided, indecisive, undetermined,** unsettled, infirm of purpose; dubious, **uncertain** 970.15; at loose ends, at a loose end; **of two minds,** in conflict, double-minded, ambivalent, ambitendent; changeable, mutable 853.6; capricious, mercurial, fickle 364.6; mugwumpian, mugwumpish, fence-sitting, fence-straddling

10 **vacillating,** vacillatory, waffling <nonformal>, oscillatory, wobbly, **wavering, fluctuating,** pendulating, oscillating, **shilly-shallying,** shilly-shally, "at war 'twixt will and will not"—Shakespeare

11 **hesitant,** hesitating, pikerish; faltering; shilly-shallying; diffident, tentative, timid, cautious; scrupling, jibbing, demurring <old>, sticking, straining, stickling

12 **weak-willed, weak-minded,** feeble-minded <old>, weak-kneed, **weak,** wimpy or wimpish <nonformal>, feeble, fainthearted, **frail, faint, infirm; spineless,** invertebrate; without a will of one's own, unable to say 'no'; abulic; afraid, **chicken** and chicken-hearted and chicken-livered <all nonformal>, cowardly 491.10; like putty, **pliable** 1045.9

ADVS 13 **irresolutely,** irresolvedly, **undecidedly, indecisively, undeterminedly; uncertainly;** hesitantly, hesitatingly, falteringly; waveringly, vacillatingly, shilly-shally, shilly-shallyingly

363 CHANGING OF MIND

NOUNS 1 **reverse, reversal,** flip and flip-flop and U-turn <all nonformal>, turnabout, turnaround, **about-face,** about turn <Brit>, volte-face <Fr>, right-about-face, right-about turn <Brit>, right-about, a turn to the right-about; tergiversation, tergiversating; **change of mind;** second thoughts, better thoughts, afterthoughts, mature judgment

2 **apostasy,** recreancy; **treason,** misprision of treason, betrayal, turning traitor, turning one's coat, changing one's stripes, ratting <nonformal>, going over, joining or going over to the opposition, siding with the enemy; **defection;** bolt, bolting, secession, breakaway; **desertion** 370.2; **recidivism,** recidivation, relapse, backsliding 394.2; faithlessness, **disloyalty** 645.5

3 recantation, withdrawal, disavowal, denial, reneging, **unsaying, repudiation,** palinode, palinody, **retraction,** retractation; **disclaimer,** disclamation, **disownment,** disowning, abjurement, abjuration, **renunciation,** renouncement, forswearing; expatriation, self-exile

4 timeserver, timepleaser <old>, temporizer, opportunist, trimmer, weathercock; mugwump; chameleon, Vicar of Bray

5 apostate, turncoat, turnabout, **recreant, renegade,** renegado, renegate *or* runagate <old>, **defector,** tergiversator, tergiversant; **deserter,** turntail, quisling, fifth columnist, collaborationist, collaborator, **traitor** 357.10; strikebreaker; **bolter, seceder,** secessionist, **separatist,** schismatic; **backslider,** recidivist; reversionist; convert, proselyte

VERBS **6 change one's mind** *or* **song** *or* **tune** *or* **note,** sing a different tune, dance to another tune; come round, wheel, do an about-face, reverse oneself, do a flip-flop *or* U-turn <nonformal>; swing from one thing to another; think better of it, have second thoughts, be of another mind; bite one's tongue

7 apostatize *or* apostacize, go over, change sides, switch, switch over, change one's allegiance, **defect; turn one's coat,** turn cloak; desert *or* leave a sinking ship; secede, break away, bolt, fall off *or* away; desert

8 recant, retract, repudiate, withdraw, take back, unswear, renege, welsh <nonformal>, **abjure, disavow, disown; deny,** disclaim, unsay, unspeak; **renounce, forswear, eat one's words,** eat one's hat, swallow, eat crow, eat humble pie; **back down** *or* **out,** climb down, crawfish out <nonformal>, backwater, weasel

9 be a timeserver, trim, temporize, change with the times; sit on *or* straddle the fence

ADJS **10 timeserving, trimming, temporizing;** supple, neither fish nor fowl

11 apostate, recreant, renegade, tergiversating, tergiversant; **treasonous, treasonable, traitorous,** forsworn; collaborating; faithless, **disloyal** 645.20

12 repudiative, repudiatory; abjuratory, renunciative, renunciatory; schismatic; **separatist,** secessionist, breakaway <nonformal>; **opportunistic,** mugwumpian, mugwumpish, fence-straddling, fence-sitting

364 CAPRICE

NOUNS **1 caprice, whim,** *capriccio* <Ital>, *boutade* <Fr>, humor, **whimsy,** freak, whim-wham; **fancy,** fantasy, **conceit, notion,** flimflam, toy, freakish inspiration, crazy idea, fantastic notion, fool notion <nonformal>, harebrained idea, brainstorm, **vagary,** megrim; **fad, craze, passing fancy; quirk, crotchet,** crank, kink; maggot, maggot in the brain, bee in one's bonnet <nonformal>, flea in one's nose <nonformal>

2 capriciousness, caprice, **whimsicalness,** whimsy, whimsicality; humorsomeness, **fancifulness,** fantasticality, **freakishness;** crankiness, crotchetiness, quirkiness; **moodiness,** temperamentalness, primadonnaism; petulance 110.6; **arbitrariness,** motivelessness

3 fickleness, flightiness, skittishness, inconstancy, **lightness, levity,** *légèreté* <Fr>; volatility, mercurialness, mercuriality; **mood swing;** faddishness, faddism; **changeableness** 853; unpredictability 970.1; unreliability, undependability 645.4; coquettishness; frivolousness 921.7

VERBS **4 blow hot and cold,** keep off and on, have as many phases as the moon, chop and change, **fluctuate** 853.5, vacillate 362.8; act on impulse

ADJS **5 capricious, whimsical,** freakish, humorsome, vagarious; **fanciful, notional,** fantasied <old>, fantastic *or* fantastical, maggoty, **crotchety,** kinky, harebrained, cranky, flaky <nonformal>, quirky; wanton, wayward, vagrant; **arbitrary, unreasonable,** motiveless; **moody, temperamental,** prima-donnaish; petulant 110.22; unrestrained

6 fickle, flighty, skittish, **light;** coquettish, flirtatious, toying; versatile, **inconstant, changeable** 853.7; vacillating 362.10; volatile, mercurial, quicksilver; faddish; **scatterbrained** 984.16, unpredictable; **impulsive;** unreliable, undependable 645.19

ADVS **7 capriciously, whimsically,** fancifully, at one's own sweet will <nonformal>; **flightily, lightly;** arbitrarily, unreasonably, without rhyme or reason

365 IMPULSE

NOUNS **1 impulse;** natural impulse, blind impulse, **instinct,** urge, drive; vagrant *or* fleeting impulse; involuntary impulse, reflex, knee jerk, automatic response; gut response *or* reaction <nonformal>; **notion, fancy; sudden thought,** flash, inspiration, brainstorm, brain wave, quick hunch

2 impulsiveness, impetuousness, impulsivity, impetuosity; **hastiness,** over-hastiness, haste, quickness, suddenness; **precipitateness,** precipitance, precipitancy, precipitation; hair-trigger; **recklessness, rashness** 493; impatience 135

3 thoughtlessness, unthoughtfulness, **heedlessness** 983.1, **carelessness,** inconsideration, inconsiderateness; **negligence** 102.2, caprice 364

4 unpremeditation, indeliberation, **undeliberateness,** uncalculatedness, undesignedness, **spontaneity, spontaneousness,** unstudiedness; involuntariness 962.5; snap judgment *or* decision; snap shot, offhand shot

5 improvisation, extemporization, improvision, improvising, extempore <old>, **impromptu, ad-lib,** ad-libbing *and* playing by ear <both nonformal>, **ad hoc measure** *or* solution, adhocracy <nonformal>, ad hockery *or* hocery *or* hocism <nonformal>; extemporaneousness, extemporariness; temporary measure *or* arrangement, *pro tempore* measure *or* arrangement, **stopgap, makeshift,** jury-rig <naut>; cannibalization; bricolage

6 improviser, improvisator, *improvvisatore* and *improvvisatrice* <both Ital>, **extemporizer,** ad-libber <nonformal>; cannibalizer; bricoleur

VERBS **7 act on the spur of the moment,** obey one's impulse, let oneself go; shoot from the hip <nonformal>, be too quick on the trigger *or* the uptake *or* the draw; **blurt out,** come out with, let slip out, say what comes uppermost, say the first thing that comes into one's head *or* to one's mind; be unable to help oneself

8 improvise, extemporize, improvisate, improv *and* tapdance *and* talk off the top of one's head <all nonformal>, speak off the cuff, think on one's feet, make it up as one goes along, play it by ear <nonformal>, throw away *or* depart from the prepared text, throw away the speech, scrap the plan, **ad-lib** <nonformal>, **do offhand,** wing it <nonformal>, vamp, fake <nonformal>, play by ear <nonformal>; **dash off, strike off,** knock off, throw off, toss off *or* out; make up, whip up, **cook up,** run up, rustle up *or* whomp up <nonformal>, slap up *or* together *and* throw *or* slap together <all nonformal>, lash up <Brit>, cobble up; jury-rig; cannibalize

ADJS **9 impulsive, impetuous, hasty,** over-

hasty, quick, sudden; quick on the draw *or* trigger *or* uptake, hair-trigger; **precipitate,** headlong; **reckless, rash** 493.7; impatient 135.6

10 unthinking, unreasoning, unreflecting, uncalculating, unthoughtful, **thoughtless, inadvertent,** reasonless, **heedless, careless,** inconsiderate; unguarded; arbitrary, capricious 364.5

11 unpremeditated, unmeditated, **uncalculated,** undeliberated, **spontaneous, undesigned, unstudied;** unintentional, unintended, inadvertent, unwilled, **indeliberate,** undeliberate; **involuntary,** reflex, reflexive, knee-jerk <nonformal>, automatic, goose-step, lockstep; gut <nonformal>, unconscious; **unconsidered,** unadvised, snap, casual, offhand, throwaway <nonformal>; **ill-considered,** ill-advised, ill-devised; act-first-and-think-later

12 extemporaneous, extemporary, extempore, **impromptu,** unrehearsed, **improvised,** improvisatory, improvisatorial, improviso, *improvisé* <Fr>; **ad-lib,** *ad libitum* <L>; **ad-hoc,** stopgap, makeshift, jury-rigged; **offhand,** off the top of one's head *and* off-the-cuff <both nonformal>, **spur-of-the-moment, quick and dirty** <nonformal>

ADVS **13 impulsively, impetuously, hastily,** suddenly, quickly, **precipitately,** headlong; **recklessly, rashly** 493.10

14 on impulse, on a sudden impulse, **on the spur of the moment; without premeditation,** unpremeditatedly, uncalculatedly, undesignedly; unthinkingly, unreflectingly, unreasoningly, unthoughtfully, thoughtlessly, heedlessly, carelessly, inconsiderately, unadvisedly; unintentionally, inadvertently, without willing, indeliberately, involuntarily

15 extemporaneously, extemporarily, extempore, *à l'improviste* <Fr>, **impromptu, ad lib, offhand,** out of hand; at *or* on sight; by ear, off the hip *and* off the top of one's head *and* off the cuff <all nonformal>; at short notice

366 LEAP

NOUNS **1 leap, jump, hop, spring, skip, bound,** bounce; **pounce;** upleap, upspring, jump-off; **hurdle; vault,** pole vault; demivolt, curvet, capriole; jeté, grand jeté, tour jeté, saut de basque; jig, galliard, lavolta, Highland fling, morris; standing *or* running *or* flying jump; long jump, broad jump, standing *or* running broad jump; high jump, standing *or* running high jump; leapfrog; jump shot; handspring; buck, buckjump; ski jump, jump turn, geländesprung, gelände jump; steeplechase; hippety-hop <nonformal>; jump-hop; hop, skip, and jump

2 caper, dido <nonformal>, **gambol, frisk,** curvet, cavort, capriole; **prance,** caracole; *gambade* <Fr>, gambado; falcade

3 leaping, jumping, bouncing, bounding, hopping, capering, cavorting, prancing, skipping, **springing,** saltation; **vaulting,** pole vaulting; **hurdling,** the hurdles, hurdle race, timber topping <nonformal>, steeplechase; leapfrogging

4 jumper, leaper, hopper; broad jumper, high jumper; **vaulter,** pole vaulter; **hurdler,** hurdle racer, timber topper <nonformal>; jumping jack; bucking bronco, buckjumper, sunfisher <nonformal>; jumping bean; kangaroo, gazelle, stag, jackrabbit, goat, frog, grasshopper, flea; salmon

VERBS **5 leap, jump, vault, spring, skip, hop, bound,** bounce; upleap, upspring, updive; leap over, jump over, etc; overleap, overjump, overskip, leapfrog; **hurdle,** clear, negotiate; curvet, capriole; buck, buckjump; ski jump; steeplechase; start, start up, start aside; **pounce,** pounce on *or* upon; hippety-hop <nonformal>

6 caper, cut capers, cut a dido <nonformal>, curvet, cavort, capriole; **gambol,** gambado, **frisk,** flounce, **trip, skip,** bob, bounce, jump about; **romp,** ramp <nonformal>; **prance;** caracole

ADJS **7 leaping, jumping,** springing, hopping, skipping, prancing, bouncing, bounding; saltant, saltatory, saltatorial

367 PLUNGE

NOUNS **1 plunge, dive, pitch, drop, fall;** free-fall; header <nonformal>; **swoop, pounce,** stoop; swan dive, gainer, jackknife, cannonball; belly flop *and* belly buster *and* belly whopper <all nonformal>; nose dive, power dive; parachute jump, sky dive; bungee jump; crash dive, stationary dive, running dive

2 submergence, submersion, immersion, immergence, engulfment, **inundation,** ‧ burial; **dipping, ducking,** dousing, sousing, dunking <nonformal>, sinking; **dip, duck, souse;** baptism

3 diving, plunging; skydiving; bungee jumping; fancy diving, high diving; scuba diving, snorkeling, skin diving, pearl diving, deep-sea diving

4 diver, plunger; high diver; bungee jumper; parachute jumper, jumper, sky diver, sport jumper, paratrooper, smoke jumper, paramedic; skin diver, snorkel diver, scuba diver, free diver, pearl diver, deep-sea diver, frogman

5 <diving equipment> diving bell, diving chamber, bathysphere, bathyscaphe, benthoscope, aquascope; submarine 180.9; diving boat; scuba *or* self-contained underwater breathing apparatus, Aqua-Lung <trademark>; Scuba; diving goggles, diving mask, swim fins; wet suit; air cylinder; diving suit; diving helmet, diving hood; snorkel, periscope

VERBS **6 plunge, dive, pitch, plummet, drop, fall;** skydive; bungee jump; free-fall; plump, plunk, plop; swoop, swoop down, stoop, **pounce,** pounce on *or* upon; nosedive, make *or* take a nose dive; parachute, sky-dive; skin-dive; sound; take a header <nonformal>

7 submerge, submerse, **immerse,** immerge, merge, **sink,** bury, engulf, **inundate,** deluge, drown, overwhelm, whelm; **dip, duck, dunk** <nonformal>, douse, souse, plunge in water; baptize

8 sink, scuttle, send to the bottom, send to Davy Jones's locker; **founder, go down,** go to the bottom, sink like lead, go down like a stone; get out of one's depth

ADJS **9 submersible,** submergible, immersible, sinkable

368 AVOIDANCE

NOUNS **1 avoidance, shunning; forbearance,** refraining; hands-off policy, **nonintervention,** noninvolvement, neutrality; **evasion,** elusion; side-stepping, getting around <nonformal>, **circumvention;** prevention, forestalling, forestallment; **escape** 369; evasive action, the runaround <nonformal>; zigzag, jink *and* juke <both nonformal>, slip, dodge, duck, side step, shy; shunting off, sidetracking; evasiveness, elusiveness; **equivocation** 344.4, fudging, fudge and mudge <Brit nonformal>; avoiding reaction, defense mechanism *or* reaction

2 shirking, slacking, goldbricking <nonformal>, soldiering, goofing *and* goofing off *and* fucking off <all nonformal>; clockwatching; **malingering,** skulking <Brit>; **dodging,** ducking; welshing <nonformal>; truancy; tax evasion, tax dodging

3 shirker, shirk, **slacker,** eye-servant *or* eye-server <both old>, soldier *or* old soldier, **goldbricker,** goldbrick <nonformal>;

clock watcher; **welsher** <nonformal>; **malingerer,** skulker *or* skulk <both Brit>; truant; tax dodger

4 **flight,** fugitation, exit, quick exit, making oneself scarce *and* getting the hell out <both nonformal>, bolt, scarpering <Brit nonformal>, disappearing act <nonformal>, hasty retreat; **running away, decampment;** skedaddle *and* skedaddling *and* scramming *and* absquatulation <old> <all nonformal>; **elopement;** disappearance 34; French leave, absence without leave *or* AWOL; **desertion** 370.2; hegira

5 **fugitive,** fleer, person on the run, **runaway,** runagate, **bolter,** skedaddler <nonformal>; **absconder, eloper; refugee, evacuee,** boat person, *émigré* <Fr>; **displaced person** *or* DP, stateless person; **escapee** 369.5; illegal immigrant, wetback <nonformal>, day-crosser

VERBS 6 **avoid, shun, fight shy of, shy away from,** keep from, **keep away from, circumvent,** keep clear of, avoid like the plague, **steer clear of** <nonformal>, give a miss to <nonformal>, skate around <Brit informal>, keep *or* get out of the way of, **give a wide berth,** keep remote from, stay detached from; make way for, give place to; **keep one's distance,** keep at a respectful distance, keep *or* stand *or* hold aloof; give the cold shoulder to <nonformal>, have nothing to do with, **have no truck with** <nonformal>; not meddle with, let alone, let well enough alone, keep hands off, not touch, not touch with a ten-foot pole; turn away from, turn one's back upon, slam the door in one's face

7 **evade, elude,** beg, **get out of,** shuffle out of, skirt, **get around** <nonformal>, circumvent; give one the run-around; ditch *and* shake *and* shake off <all nonformal>, get away from, give the runaround *or* the slip <nonformal>; throw off the scent; play at hide and seek; lead one a chase *or* merry chase, lead one a dance *or* pretty dance; escape 369.6–8

8 **dodge, duck; take evasive action,** juke *and* jink <both nonformal>, zig-zag; throw off the track *or* trail; shy, shy off *or* away; swerve, sheer off; pull away *or* clear; pull back, shrink, recoil 902.6,7; **sidestep,** step aside; parry, fence, ward off; have an out *or* escape hatch; shift, shift *or* put off; **hedge,** pussyfoot <nonformal>, be *or* sit on the fence, beat around *or* about the bush, hem and haw, beg the question, tapdance <nonformal>, dance

around, equivocate 344.7, fudge and mudge <Brit nonformal>

9 **shirk, slack, lie** *or* **rest upon one's oars,** not pull fair, not pull one's weight; **lie down on the job** <nonformal>; soldier, duck duty, **goof off** *and* dog it <both nonformal>, **goldbrick** <nonformal>; **malinger,** skulk <Brit>; **get out of,** sneak *or* slip out of, slide out of, dodge, duck; welsh <nonformal>

10 **flee, fly, take flight,** take to flight, take wing, fugitate, **run, cut and run** <nonformal>, make a precipitate departure, **run off** *or* **away,** run away from, bug out <nonformal>, **decamp,** pull up stakes, **take to one's heels,** make off, **depart** 188.6, do the disappearing act, make a quick exit, **beat a retreat** *or* **a hasty retreat, turn tail,** show the heels, show a clean *or* light pair of heels; **run for it,** "show it a fair pair of heels and run for it"—Shakespeare, **bolt, run for one's life;** make a run for it; advance to the rear, make a strategic withdrawal; **take French leave,** go AWOL, slip the cable; **desert; abscond,** levant <Brit>, **elope,** run away with; skip *or* jump bail

11 <nonformal terms> **beat it, blow, scram,** lam, book, air out, shemozzle *and* bugger off <both Brit>, **take it on the lam,** take a powder *or* runout powder, make tracks, cut ass, cut and run, peel out, **split,** skin out, **skip,** skip out, duck out, duck and run, dog it, vamoose, absquatulate <old> *and* skedaddle <both old>, **clear out,** make oneself scarce, get the hell out, make a break for it, warp out

12 **slip away, steal away, sneak off,** shuffle off, slink off, slide off, slither off, skulk away, mooch off *and* duck out <both nonformal>, slip out of

13 **not face up to,** hide one's head in the sand, not come to grips with, put off, procrastinate, temporize

ADJS 14 **avoidable, escapable,** eludible; evadable; preventable

15 **evasive, elusive,** elusory; **shifty,** slippery, slippery as an eel; cagey <nonformal>; shirking, malingering

16 **fugitive, runaway,** in flight, on the lam <nonformal>, hot <nonformal>; disappearing 34.3

369 ESCAPE

NOUNS 1 **escape; getaway** *and* break *and* breakout <all nonformal>; **deliverance; delivery,** riddance, **release,** setting-free, freeing, **liberation, extrication, rescue;**

emergence, issuance, issue, outlet, vent;
leakage, leak; jailbreak, prisonbreak,
break, breakout; evasion 368.1; **flight**
368.4; escapology; escapism

2 **narrow escape**, hairbreadth escape, **close
call** *or* **shave** <nonformal>, **near miss**,
near go *or* thing <Brit nonformal>, near
or narrow squeak <Brit nonformal>,
close *or* tight squeeze <nonformal>,
squeaker <nonformal>

3 bolt-hole, escape hatch, fire escape, life
net, lifeboat, life raft, life buoy, lifeline,
sally port, slide, inflatable slide, ejection
or ejector seat, emergency exit, escapeway

4 **loophole, way out,** way of escape, hole to
creep out of, escape hatch, escape clause,
saving clause; pretext 376; **alternative,**
choice 371

5 **escapee**, escaper, evader; escape artist;
escapologist; **fugitive** 368.5; escapist

VERBS 6 **escape**, make *or* effect one's escape,
make good one's escape; **get away, make
a getaway** <nonformal>; **free oneself**, deliver oneself, gain one's liberty, **get free,
get clear of**, bail out, **get out, get out of,**
get well out of; **break loose**, cut loose,
break away, break one's bonds *or* chains,
slip the collar, shake off the yoke; **jump**
and **skip** <both nonformal>; **break jail**
or **prison**, escape prison, fly the coop
<nonformal>; leap over the wall; evade
368.7; flee 368.10

7 **get off, go free**, win freedom, go at liberty, **go scot free**, escape with a whole
skin, escape without penalty, walk *and*
beat the rap <both nonformal>; **get
away with** <nonformal>, get by, get by
with, get off easy *or* lightly, get away with
murder <nonformal>, **get off cheap**; cop
a plea *and* cop out <nonformal>

8 scrape *or* squeak through, squeak by, escape with *or* by the skin of one's teeth,
have a close call *or* close shave <nonfor-
mal>

9 **slip away, give one the slip**, slip through
one's hands *or* fingers; slip *or* sneak
through; **slip out of,** slide out of, crawl
or creep out of, sneak out of, wiggle *or*
squirm *or* shuffle *or* wriggle *or* worm out
of, find a loophole

10 **find vent**, issue forth, come forth, exit,
emerge, issue, debouch, erupt, break out,
break through, come out, run out, **leak
out**, ooze out

ADJS 11 **escaped, loose,** on the loose, disengaged, out of, well out of; fled, flown; fugitive, runaway; free as a bird, scot-free, at
large, **free**

370 ABANDONMENT

NOUNS 1 **abandonment, forsaking, leaving;**
jettison, jettisoning, throwing overboard
or away *or* aside, casting away *or* aside;
withdrawal, evacuation, pulling out, absentation; cessation 856; disuse,
desuetude

2 **desertion, defection,** ratting <nonfor-
mal>; dereliction; **secession**, bolt, breakaway, walkout; betrayal 645.8; schism,
apostasy 363.2; deserter 363.5

3 <giving up> **relinquishment, surrender,
resignation, renouncement**, renunciation,
abdication, waiver, abjurement, abjuration, ceding, cession, handing over,
standing *or* stepping down, **yielding, forswearing; withdrawing, dropping out**
<nonformal>

4 **derelict**, castoff; jetsam, flotsam, lagan,
flotsam and jetsam; waifs and strays;
rubbish, junk, trash, refuse, waste, waste
product, solid waste; liquid waste, wastewater; **dump**, dumpsite, garbage dump,
landfill, sanitary landfill, junkheap, junkpile, scrap heap, midden; abandonee,
waif, throwaway, orphan, dogie <nonfor-
mal>; **castaway;** foundling; wastrel,
reject, **discard** 390.3

VERBS 5 **abandon, desert, forsake; quit,
leave**, leave behind, take leave of, depart
from, absent oneself from, turn one's
back upon, turn one's tail upon, say good-
bye to, bid a long farewell to, walk away,
walk *or* **run out on** <nonformal>, **leave
flat** *and* leave high and dry *or* holding the
bag *or* in the lurch <all nonformal>,
leave one to one's fate, throw to the
wolves <nonformal>; **withdraw, back
out, drop out** <nonformal>, pull out,
stand down <nonformal>; **go back on, go
back on one's word;** cry off <Brit>, beg
off, renege; **vacate**, evacuate; quit cold
and leave flat <both nonformal>, toss
aside; jilt, throw over <nonformal>; maroon; **jettison; junk**, deep-six <nonfor-
mal>, **discard** 390.7; let fall into disuse *or*
desuetude

6 **defect, secede, bolt**, break away; pull out
<nonformal>, withdraw one's support;
sell out *and* sell down the river <both
nonformal>, **betray** 645.14; turn one's
back on; apostatize

7 **give up, relinquish, surrender, yield,**
yield up, waive, **forgo, resign, renounce,**
throw up, abdicate, **abjure, forswear,
give up on, have done with**, give up as a
bad job, cede, hand over, lay down, wash
one's hands of, **write off**, drop, drop all

idea of, drop like a hot potato; **cease** 856.6, **desist from,** leave off, give over; hold *or* stay one's hand, cry quits, acknowledge defeat, **throw in the towel** *or* **sponge** 433.8

ADJS **8 abandoned, forsaken, deserted,** left; disused; **derelict,** castaway, jettisoned; marooned; junk, junked, discarded 390.11

371 CHOICE

NOUNS **1 choice, selection, election,** preference, decision, **pick, choosing,** free choice; alternativity; co-option, co-optation; **will,** volition, free will 430.6,7; preoption, first choice; the pick 998.7

2 option, discretion, pleasure, will and pleasure; optionality; possible choice, alternative, alternate choice

3 dilemma, Scylla and Charybdis, the devil and the deep blue sea; *embarras de choix* <Fr>; choice of Hercules; Hobson's choice, **no choice,** only choice, zero option; limited choice, positive discrimination <Brit>, affirmative action

4 adoption, embracement, acceptance, espousal; affiliation

5 preference, predilection, proclivity, bent, affinity, prepossession, predisposition, partiality, inclination, leaning, tilt, penchant, bias, tendency, taste; favor, fancy; prejudice; personal choice, particular choice <old>, druthers <nonformal>; chosen kind *or* sort, style, one's cup of tea <nonformal>, type, bag *and* thing <both nonformal>; way of life, lifestyle

6 vote, voting, **suffrage,** franchise, enfranchisement, voting right, right to vote; **voice, say;** representation; **poll,** polling, canvass, canvassing, division <Brit>, counting heads *or* noses, exit poll; **ballot,** balloting, secret ballot, Australian ballot; ballot-box, voting machine; **plebiscite,** plebiscitum, **referendum;** yeas and nays, yea, aye, yes, nay, no; voice vote, *viva voce* vote; rising vote; hand vote, show of hands; absentee vote, proxy; casting vote, deciding vote; write-in vote, write-in; faggot vote <Brit old>; graveyard vote; single vote, plural vote; transferable vote, nontransferable vote; Hare system, list system, cumulative voting, preferential voting, proportional representation; **straw vote** *or* **poll;** record vote, snap vote

7 selector, chooser, optant, elector, **voter; electorate**

8 nomination, designation, naming, proposal

9 election, appointment; political election

10 selectivity, selectiveness, picking and choosing; **choosiness** 495.1; eclecticism; **discrimination** 943

11 eligibility, qualification, fitness, fittedness, **suitability,** acceptability, worthiness, desirability; eligible

12 elect, elite, the chosen

VERBS **13 choose, elect,** pick, go with <nonformal>, opt, opt for, co-opt, make *or* take one's choice, make choice of, have one's druthers <nonformal>, use *or* take up *or* exercise one's option; **shop around** <nonformal>, pick and choose

14 select, make a selection; **pick,** handpick, **pick out, single out,** choose out, smile on, give the nod <nonformal>, jump at, seize on; extract, excerpt; **decide between, choose up sides** <nonformal>, cull, glean, winnow, sift; separate the wheat from the chaff *or* tares, separate the sheep from the goats

15 adopt; approve, ratify, pass, carry, endorse, sign off on <nonformal>; **take up, go in for** <nonformal>; accept, take one up on <nonformal>, **embrace,** espouse; affiliate

16 decide upon, determine upon, settle upon, fix upon, resolve upon; make *or* take a decision, **make up one's mind**

17 prefer, have preference, **favor, like better** *or* **best,** prefer to, set before *or* above, regard *or* honor before; rather <nonformal>, **had** *or* **have rather,** choose rather, had rather *or* sooner, had *or* would as soon; think proper, see *or* think fit, think best, think please; tilt *or* incline *or* lean *or* tend toward, have a bias *or* partiality *or* penchant

18 vote, cast one's vote, ballot, cast a ballot; have a say *or* a voice; hold up one's hand, exercise one's suffrage *or* franchise, stand up and be counted; plump *or* plump for <Brit>; divide <Brit>; **poll,** canvass

19 nominate, name, designate; put up, propose, submit, name for office; run, run for office

20 elect, vote in, place in office; **appoint**

21 put to choice, offer, present, set before; put to vote, have a show of hands

ADJS **22 elective;** volitional, voluntary, volitive; **optional,** discretional; **alternative,** disjunctive

23 selective, selecting, choosing; eclectic *or* eclectical; elective, electoral; appointing, appointive, constituent; adoptive; exclusive, discriminating 943.7; **choosy** <nonformal>, particular 495.9

24 eligible, qualified, fit, fitted, **suitable,** ac-

ceptable, admissible, worthy, desirable;
with voice, with vote, with voice and
vote, enfranchised

25 **preferable,** of choice or preference, **better,** preferred, **to be preferred,** more
desirable, favored; preferential, prefer-
ring, favoring

26 **chosen, selected, picked;** select, elect;
handpicked, singled-out; **adopted,** accepted, embraced, espoused, approved,
ratified, passed, carried; **elected,** unanimously elected, elected by acclamation;
appointed; **nominated,** designated,
named

ADVS 27 **at choice, at will,** at one's will and
pleasure, at one's pleasure, electively, at
one's discretion, at the option of, if one
wishes; on approval; **optionally;** alter-
natively

28 **preferably, by choice** or **preference,** in
preference; by vote, by election or suffrage; **rather than,** sooner than, first,
sooner, rather, before

CONJS 29 or, either . . . or; and/or

PHRS 30 one man's meat is another man's
poison, there's no accounting for taste

372 REJECTION

NOUNS 1 **rejection, repudiation;** abjurement, abjuration, **renouncement** 370.3;
disownment, disavowal, disclamation,
recantation 363.3; **exclusion,** exception
772.1; **disapproval, nonacceptance,** non-
approval, declining, declination, **refusal**
442; contradiction, **denial** 335.2; passing
by or up <nonformal>, ignoring, noncon-
sideration, discounting, dismissal, disregard 983.1; throwing out or away, putting
out or away, chucking and chucking out
<both nonformal>; discard 390.3; turn-
ing out or away, repulse, a flea in one's
ear, rebuff 907.2; **spurning,** kiss-off and
brush-off <both nonformal>, scouting,
despising, despisal, contempt 157; scorn,
disdain

VERBS 2 **reject, repudiate,** abjure, forswear,
renounce 370.7, **disown, disclaim, recant;**
vote out; except, **exclude** 772.4, deselect,
include out <nonformal>, close out,
close the door on, leave out in the cold,
cut out, blackball, blacklist; **disapprove,
decline, refuse** 442.3; contradict, **deny**
335.4; pass by or up <nonformal>,
waive, ignore, not hear of, wave aside,
brush away or aside, refuse to consider,
discount, **dismiss; disregard** 983.2; throw
out or away, chuck and chuck out <both
nonformal>, **discard** 390.7; turn out or

away, shove away, push aside, repulse,
repel, slap or smack down <nonformal>,
rebuff 907.2, send away with a flea in
one's ear, send about one's business, send
packing; turn one's back on; **spurn,** scout,
disdain, scorn, contemn, make a face at,
turn up one's nose at, look down one's
nose at, raise one's eyebrows at, **despise**
157.3

ADJS 3 **rejected, repudiated; renounced,** forsworn, **disowned; denied,** refused; excluded, excepted; **disapproved, declined;**
ignored, discounted, not considered, **dismissed,** dismissed out of hand; **discarded;**
repulsed, rebuffed; **spurned,** scouted, **dis-
dained, scorned,** contemned, **despised;**
out of the question, not to be thought of,
declined with thanks

4 rejective; renunciative, abjuratory; declinatory; dismissive; contemptuous,
despising, **scornful,** disdainful

373 CUSTOM, HABIT

NOUNS 1 custom, **convention,** use, **usage,**
standard usage, standard behavior, **wont,**
wonting, **way,** established way, time-
honored practice, **tradition,** standing custom, **folkway,** manner, **practice,** praxis,
prescription, **observance,** ritual, consue-
tude, **mores;** proper thing, what is done,
social convention 579; bon ton, **fashion**
578; manners, etiquette 580.3; way of life,
lifestyle; conformity 866; **generalization**
863.1, labeling, stereotyping

2 "a second nature, and no less powerful"—Montaigne, "the universal sovereign"—Pindar, "that unwritten law, by
which the people keep even kings in
awe"—D'Avenant, "often only the antiquity of error"—Cyprian

3 **culture, society, civilization;** trait, culture trait; key trait; complex, culture
complex, trait-complex; culture area;
culture center; shame culture, memory
culture; **folkways, mores,** system of
values, **ethos, culture pattern;** cultural
change; cultural lag; culture conflict; acculturation, enculturation; culture contact <Brit>, cultural drift

4 **habit,** habitude, **custom, second nature;**
use, **usage,** trick, wont, **way,** practice,
praxis; bad habit; stereotype; "the petrifaction of feelings"—L E Landon;
pattern, **habit pattern;** stereotyped behavior; force of habit; creature of habit;
knee-jerk <nonformal>, automatism
962.5; peculiarity, characteristic 864.4

5 **rule, norm,** procedure, **common practice,**

the way things are done, form, prescribed *or* set form; common *or* ordinary run of things, matter of course, par for the course <nonformal>; standard operating procedure *or* SOP, drill <Brit>; standing orders

6 **routine**, run, **round**, beat, track, beaten path *or* track; jog trot, **rut, groove**, well-worn groove; **treadmill**, squirrel cage; the working day, nine-to-five, the grind *or* the daily grind <nonformal>; **red tape**, red-tapeism, **bureaucracy**, bureaucratism, *chinoiseries* <Fr>

7 **customariness**, accustomedness, wonted-ness, **habitualness; inveteracy**, inverater-ateness, confirmedness, settledness, fix-edness; commonness, prevalence 863.2

8 **habituation, accustoming; conditioning**, seasoning, training; **familiarization**, nat-uralization <old>, breaking-in <nonfor-mal>, orientation; **domestication, tam-ing**, breaking, housebreaking; acclima-tion, acclimatization; **inurement**, harden-ing, case hardening; adaption, adjust-ment, accommodation 866.1

9 **addiction** 87.1; **addict** 87.2

VERBS 10 **accustom, habituate**, wont; **condi-tion**, season, **train**; familiarize, naturalize <old>, break in <nonformal>, orient, orientate; **domesticate**, domesticize, **tame**, break, gentle, housebreak; put through the mill; acclimatize, acclimate; inure, harden, case harden; adapt, adjust, accommodate 787.7; confirm, fix, estab-lish 854.9; acculturate, enculturate

11 **become a habit**, take root, become fixed, **grow on one**, take hold of one, take one over

12 **be used to, be wont**, wont, **make a prac-tice of**; get used to, get into the way of, **take to**, accustom oneself to, make a prac-tice of; contract *or* fall into a habit, addict oneself to

13 **get in a rut, be in a rut**, move *or* travel in a groove *or* rut, run on in a groove, follow the beaten path *or* track, go round like a horse in a mill, go on in the old jog-trot way

ADJS 14 **customary, wonted**, consuetudi-nary; traditional, time-honored; familiar, everyday, ordinary, **usual; established**, received, accepted; set, prescribed, pre-scriptive; **normative, normal; standard**, regular, stock, regulation; prevalent, pre-vailing, widespread, obtaining, generally accepted, popular, **current** 863.12; **con-ventional** 579.5; conformist, conformable 866.5

15 **habitual, regular**, frequent, constant, per-

sistent; repetitive, recurring, recurrent; stereotyped; knee-jerk <nonformal>, goose-step, lockstep, automatic 962.14; **routine**, nine-to-five, workaday, well-trodden, well-worn, beaten; trite, hack-neyed 117.9

16 **accustomed, wont, wonted, used to; con-ditioned**, trained, seasoned; experienced, **familiarized**, naturalized <old>, broken-in, run-in <nonformal>, oriented, orien-tated; acclimated, acclimatized; inured, hardened, case-hardened; adapted, ad-justed, accommodated; housebroken, potty-trained

17 **used to, familiar with**, conversant with, **at home in** *or* **with**, no stranger to, an old hand at

18 **habituated**, *habitué* <Fr>; **in the habit of**, used to; never free from; **in a rut**

19 **confirmed, inveterate, chronic, estab-lished**, long-established, **fixed, settled, rooted**, thorough; incorrigible, irrevers-ible; **deep-rooted**, deep-set, deep-settled, **deep-seated**, deep-fixed, deep-dyed; **in-fixed, ingrained**, fast, dyed-in-the-wool; implanted, inculcated, instilled; set, **set in one's ways**, settled in habit

ADVS 20 **customarily**, conventionally, accus-tomedly, wontedly; normatively, nor-mally, **usually; as is the custom**; as is usual, *comme d'habitude* <Fr>; as things go, as the world goes

21 **habitually, regularly**, routinely, fre-quently, persistently, repetitively, recur-ringly; **inveterately, chronically**; from habit, **by** *or* **from force of habit**, as is one's wont

374 UNACCUSTOMEDNESS

NOUNS 1 **unaccustomedness, newness**, un-wontedness, disaccustomedness, unused-ness, unhabituatedness; shakiness <non-formal>; **unfamiliarity**, unacquaintance, unconversance, unpracticedness, new-ness to; inexperience 414.2; ignorance 929

VERBS 2 **disaccustom, cure, break off**, stop, **wean**

3 **break the habit, cure oneself of**, disac-custom oneself, wean oneself from, break the pattern, break one's chains *or* fetters; **give up**, leave off, **abandon**, drop, stop, discontinue, kick *and* shake <both non-formal>, throw off, rid oneself of; get on the wagon, swear off 668.8

ADJS 4 **unaccustomed, new**, disaccustomed, **unused, unwonted**; uninured, unsea-soned, untrained, unhardened; shaky

<nonformal>, tyronic; unhabituated,
not in the habit of; out of the habit of,
rusty; unweaned; **unused to, unfamiliar
with,** unacquainted with, unconversant
with, unpracticed, new to, a stranger to;
cub, greenhorn; inexperienced 414.17; ignorant 929.12

375 MOTIVATION, INDUCEMENT

NOUNS **1 motive, reason, cause,** source,
spring, mainspring; matter, score, consideration; **ground, basis** 885.1; sake;
aim, goal 380.2, end, end in view, telos,
final cause; **ideal,** principle, **ambition,**
aspiration, inspiration, guiding light *or*
star, lodestar; calling, vocation; intention
380; ulterior motive

2 motivation, moving, **actuation, prompting, stimulation,** animation, triggering,
setting-off, setting in motion, getting
under way; direction, inner-direction,
other-direction; **influence** 893

3 inducement, enlistment, engagement, solicitation, **persuasion,** suasion; exhortation, hortation, preaching, preachment;
selling, sales talk, salesmanship, hard
sell, high pressure, hawking, huckstering,
flogging <Brit>; jawboning *and* arm-
twisting <both nonformal>; **lobbying;**
coaxing, wheedling, working on <nonfor-
mal>, cajolery, cajolement, conning,
snow job *and* smoke and mirrors <both
nonformal>, nobbling <Brit nonfor-
mal>, blandishment, sweet talk *and* soft
soap <both nonformal>, soft sell
<nonformal>; **allurement** 377

4 incitement, incitation, **instigation, stimulation, arousal, excitement, agitation,
inflammation,** excitation, fomentation,
firing, stirring, stirring-up, impassioning,
whipping-up, rabble-rousing; waving the
bloody shirt; **provocation,** irritation, exasperation; pep talk, pep rally

5 urging, pressure, pressing, pushing; **encouragement,** abetment; **insistence,**
instance; **goading, prodding,** goosing
<nonformal>, spurring, pricking, nee-
dling

6 urge, urgency; impulse, impulsion, compulsion; press, **pressure, drive,** push;
sudden *or* rash impulse; constraint, exigency, stress, pinch

7 incentive, inducement, encouragement,
persuasive, **invitation, provocation, incitement; stimulus, stimulation,** stimulative, fillip, whet; carrot; reward, payment
624; **profit** 472.3; bait, **lure** 377.2; palm
oil <nonformal>, bribe 378.2; sweeten-

ing *and* sweetener <both nonformal>, interest, percentage, what's in it for one
<nonformal>

8 goad, spur, prod, prick <old>, sting, **gadfly;** oxgoad; rowel; whip, lash, whiplash,
gad <nonformal>

9 inspiration, infusion, infection; fire,
firing, spark, sparking; **animation,
exhilaration,** enlivenment; afflatus,
divine afflatus; genius, animus, moving *or* animating spirit; muse; the
Muses

10 prompter, mover, prime mover, motivator, impeller, energizer, galvanizer,
inducer, **actuator, animator,** moving
spirit; **encourager,** abettor, **inspirer,** firer,
spark, sparker, spark plug <nonformal>;
persuader; **stimulator, gadfly; tempter**
377.3; coaxer, coax <nonformal>,
wheedler, cajoler, pleader

11 instigator, inciter, exciter, urger; **pro-
voker,** *provocateur* <Fr>, *agent provocateur* <Fr>, catalyst; **agitator, fomenter,**
inflamer; agitprop; **rabble-rouser,** rouser,
**demagogue; firebrand, incendiary; sedi-
tionist,** seditionary; **troublemaker,**
makebate <old>, mischief-maker, ringleader

VERBS **12 motivate, move,** set in motion, **actuate,** move to action, **impel,** propel;
stimulate, energize, galvanize, **animate,
spark;** promote, foster; force, compel
424.4; ego-involve

13 prompt, provoke, evoke, elicit, call up,
summon up, muster up, call forth, **inspire;** bring about, **cause**

14 urge, press, push, work on <nonformal>,
twist one's arm <nonformal>; **sell,** flog
<Brit>; **insist,** push for, not take no for
an answer, **importune, nag, pressure,
high-pressure,** bring pressure to bear
upon, throw one's weight around, throw
one's weight into the scale, jawbone *and*
build a fire under <both nonformal>,
talk round *or* around; grind in; **lobby;
coax,** wheedle, cajole, blandish, plead
with, sweet-talk *and* soft-soap <both non-
formal>, **exhort,** call on *or* upon, advocate, recommend, put in a good word,
buck for *and* hype <both nonformal>; insist, insist upon

15 goad, prod, poke, nudge, prod at, goose
<nonformal>, **spur,** prick, sting, needle;
whip, lash; pick at *or* on, nibble at, nibble
away at

16 urge on *or* **along, egg on** <nonformal>,
hound on, hie on, hasten on, hurry on,
speed on; **goad on, spur on,** drive on,
whip on *or* along; cheer on, root on

<nonformal>, root from the sidelines <nonformal>

17 **incite, instigate, put up to** <nonformal>; set on, sic on; **foment,** ferment, **agitate, arouse, excite, stir up,** work up, whip up; rally; **inflame,** incense, **fire,** heat, heat up, impassion; **provoke,** pique, whet, tickle; nettle; lash into a fury *or* frenzy; wave the bloody shirt; pour oil on the fire, feed the fire, add fuel to the flame, fan, fan the flame, blow the coals, stir the embers

18 **kindle,** enkindle, **fire, spark, spark off, trigger, trigger off, touch off,** set off, light the fuse, **enflame,** set afire *or* on fire

19 **rouse, arouse,** raise, raise up, **waken, awaken,** wake up, turn on <nonformal>, charge *or* psych *or* pump up <nonformal>, stir, **stir up,** set astir, **pique**

20 **inspire,** inspirit, spirit, spirit up; fire, **fire one's imagination; animate, exhilarate,** enliven; **infuse, infect,** inject, inoculate, imbue, inform

21 **encourage, hearten, embolden,** give encouragement, pat *or* clap on the back, stroke <nonformal>; **invite,** ask for; **abet,** aid and abet, countenance, keep in countenance; **foster, nurture,** nourish, feed

22 **induce, prompt, move one to, influence, sway,** incline, **dispose,** carry, bring, lead, **lead one to; lure; tempt;** determine, decide; enlist, procure, engage <old>, interest in, get to do

23 **persuade, prevail on** *or* **upon,** prevail with, **sway,** convince, lead to believe, **bring round,** bring to reason, bring to one's senses; **win, win over,** win around, bring over, draw over, gain, gain over; **talk over, talk into,** argue into, out-talk <nonformal>; wangle, wangle into; hook *and* hook in <both nonformal>, con *and* do a snow job on <both nonformal>, nobble <Brit nonformal>, sell *and* sell one on <both nonformal>, **charm, captivate;** wear down, overcome one's resistance, arm-twist *and* twist one's arm <both nonformal>; **bribe** 378.3, grease *or* oil *or* cross one's palm <nonformal>

24 **persuade oneself, make oneself easy about,** make sure of, make up one's mind; be persuaded, rest easy

ADJS 25 **motivating, motivational, motive, moving, animating, actuating, impelling, driving,** impulsive, inducive, directive; **urgent, pressing, driving;** compelling; causal, causative

26 **inspiring, inspirational,** inspiriting; infusive; animating, exhilarating, enlivening

27 **provocative, provoking,** piquant, **excit-**ing, challenging, prompting, **rousing, stirring, stimulating,** stimulant, stimulative, stimulatory, energizing, electric, galvanizing, galvanic; **encouraging,** inviting, **alluring**

28 **incitive,** inciting, incentive; **instigative,** instigating; **agitative,** agitational; **inflammatory, incendiary,** fomenting, rabble-rousing

29 **persuasive,** suasive, persuading; wheedling, cajoling; hortative, hortatory; exhortative, exhortatory

30 **moved, motivated, prompted, impelled, actuated;** stimulated, animated; minded, inclined, of a mind to, with half a mind to; inner-directed, other-directed

31 **inspired, fired,** afire, on fire

376 PRETEXT

NOUNS 1 **pretext, pretense, pretension,** lying pretension, **show,** ostensible *or* announced *or* public *or* professed motive; **front,** facade, **sham** 354.3; **excuse,** apology, protestation, poor excuse, lame excuse; **occasion,** mere occasion; put-off <nonformal>; handle, peg to hang on, leg to stand on, *locus standi* <L>; **subterfuge,** refuge, device, stratagem, feint, dipsy-doodle <nonformal>, **trick** 356.6; dust thrown in the eye, smoke screen, **screen, cover,** stalking-horse, **blind;** guise, semblance; mask, cloak, veil; **cosmetics,** mere cosmetics, gloss, varnish, color, coat of paint, whitewash <nonformal>; spit and polish; **cover,** cover-up, cover story, alibi; band-aid

2 **claim,** profession, allegation

VERBS 3 **pretext,** make a pretext of, take as an excuse *or* reason *or* occasion, urge as a motive, **pretend,** make a pretense of; put up a front *or* false front; **allege, claim,** profess, purport, avow; protest too much

4 **hide under,** cover oneself with, shelter under, take cover under, wrap oneself in, cloak *or* mantle oneself with, take refuge in; conceal one's motive with; **cover,** cover up, gloss *or* varnish over, apply a coat of paint *or* whitewash, stick on a band-aid

ADJS 5 **pretexted, pretended, alleged, claimed, professed, purported,** avowed; **ostensible,** hypocritical, **specious;** so-called, in name only

ADVS 6 **ostensibly, allegedly,** purportedly, professedly, avowedly; for the record, for public consumption; under the pretext of, **as a pretext,** as an excuse, as a cover *or* a cover-up *or* an alibi

377 ALLUREMENT

NOUNS **1 allurement, allure, enticement, inveiglement,** invitation, come-hither <nonformal>, blandishment, cajolery; inducement 375.7; **temptation,** tantalization; **seduction,** seducement; **beguilement,** beguiling; **fascination, captivation,** enthrallment, entrapment, snaring; **enchantment,** witchery, bewitchery, bewitchment; **attraction, interest, charm, glamour, appeal,** magnetism; charisma; star quality; wooing; flirtation

2 **attractiveness, allure,** charmingness, bewitchingness, impressiveness, **seductiveness,** winsomeness, winning ways, winningness; **sexiness,** sex appeal or SA <nonformal>

3 **lure,** charm, **come-on** <nonformal>, attention-getter or -grabber, **attraction, draw** or drawer or crowd-drawer, crowd-pleaser, headliner; clou, hook and gimmick <both nonformal>, drawing card, drawcard; **decoy,** decoy duck; **bait,** ground bait, baited trap, baited hook; **snare,** trap; **endearment** 562; the song of the Sirens, the voice of the tempter, honeyed words; forbidden fruit

4 **tempter, seducer, enticer,** inveigler, **charmer,** enchanter, fascinator, tantalizer, teaser; coquette, flirt; Don Juan; Pied Piper of Hamelin; **temptress,** enchantress, seductress, **siren;** Siren, Circe, Lorelei, Parthenope; **vampire,** vamp <nonformal>, *femme fatale* <Fr>

VERBS **5 lure,** allure, **entice, seduce, inveigle, decoy,** draw, **draw on, lead on;** come on to and give the come-on and give a come-hither look and bat the eyes at and make goo-goo eyes at <all nonformal>, flirt with, flirt; **woo;** coax, cajole, blandish; **ensnare;** draw in, suck in and rope in <both nonformal>; bait, offer bait to, bait the hook, angle with a silver hook

6 **attract, interest, appeal, engage,** impress, charismatize, fetch <nonformal>, catch or get one's eye, command one's attention, rivet one, attract one's interest, be attractive, take or tickle one's fancy; **invite,** summon, beckon; **tempt, tantalize, titillate,** tickle, **tease,** whet the appetite, make one's mouth water, dangle before one

7 **fascinate, captivate, charm,** becharm, spell, spellbind, cast a spell, put under a spell, **beguile, intrigue, enthrall,** infatuate, **enrapture, transport, enravish, entrance, enchant,** witch, **bewitch;** carry away, sweep off one's feet, turn one's

head, knock one's socks off <nonformal>; hypnotize, mesmerize; vamp <nonformal>; charismatize

ADJS **8 alluring, fascinating, captivating, riveting, charming, glamorous,** exotic, **enchanting,** spellful, spellbinding, **entrancing,** ravishing, **enravishing, intriguing, enthralling,** witching, **bewitching; attractive, interesting, appealing,** dishy <Brit nonformal>, sexy <nonformal>, engaging, taking, eye-catching, catching, fetching, winning, winsome, prepossessing; exciting; charismatic; **seductive,** seducing, **beguiling, enticing, inviting,** come-hither <nonformal>; flirtatious, coquettish; coaxing, cajoling, blandishing; **tempting, tantalizing,** teasing, titillating, titillative, tickling; **provocative,** *provoquant* <Fr>; appetizing, mouth-watering, piquant; **irresistible;** siren, sirenic; hypnotic, mesmeric

ADVS **9 alluringly, fascinatingly,** captivatingly, charmingly, enchantingly, entrancingly, enravishingly, intriguingly, beguilingly, glamorously, bewitchingly; attractively, appealingly, engagingly, winsomely; **enticingly, seductively,** with bedroom eyes <nonformal>; **temptingly,** provocatively; **tantalizingly,** teasingly; piquantly, appetizingly; irresistibly; hypnotically, mesmerically

378 BRIBERY

NOUNS **1 bribery,** bribing, subornation, **corruption, graft,** bribery and corruption

2 **bribe,** bribe money, sop, sop to Cerberus, gratuity, gratification <old>, payoff <nonformal>, boodle <nonformal>; hush money <nonformal>; payola <nonformal>; protection

VERBS **3 bribe,** throw a sop to; grease and **grease the palm** or hand and oil the palm and tickle the palm <all nonformal>; **purchase;** buy and **buy off** and pay off <all nonformal>; suborn, **corrupt,** tamper with; reach and get at and get to <all nonformal>; approach, try to bribe; **fix, take care of**

ADJS **4 bribable,** corruptible, purchasable, buyable; approachable; fixable; on the take and on the pad <both nonformal>; **venal, corrupt,** bought and paid for, in one's pocket

379 DISSUASION

NOUNS **1 dissuasion,** talking out of <nonformal>, remonstrance, expostulation, admonition, monition, **warning,** caveat, **caution,** cautioning; intimidation, **determent,** deterrence, scaring *or* frightening off, turning around

2 **deterrent,** determent; **discouragement,** disincentive, chilling effect, demotivation; damp, damper, **wet blanket,** cold water, chill

VERBS 3 **dissuade,** convince to the contrary, convince otherwise, **talk out of** <nonformal>, kid out of <nonformal>; unconvince, unpersuade; remonstrate, expostulate, admonish, cry out against; **warn, warn off** *or* **away, caution;** enter a caveat; **intimidate,** scare *or* frighten off, daunt; turn around

4 **disincline, indispose,** disaffect, disinterest; **deter,** repel, turn from, turn away *or* aside; divert, deflect; distract, put off *and* turn off <both nonformal>; wean from; **discourage; pour** *or* **dash** *or* **throw cold water on,** throw *or* lay a wet blanket on, damp, dampen, demotivate, **cool, chill,** quench, blunt; take the starch out of, take the wind out of one's sails

ADJS 5 **dissuasive,** dissuading, disinclining, **discouraging; deterrent,** off-putting; expostulatory, admonitory, monitory, cautionary; intimidating

380 INTENTION

NOUNS 1 **intention, intent,** intendment, mindset, **aim,** effect, meaning, view, study, animus, **point, purpose,** function, set *or* settled *or* fixed purpose; sake; **design, plan, project,** idea, notion; **quest,** pursuit; **proposal,** prospectus; **resolve,** resolution, mind, will; **motive** 375.1; determination 359.1; desideratum, desideration, **ambition,** aspiration, **desire** 100; striving, nisus

2 **objective, object, aim, end, goal,** destination, mark, object in mind, **end in view,** telos, final cause, ultimate aim; end in itself; **target,** butt, bull's-eye, quintain; quarry, prey, game; reason for being, *raison d'être* <Fr>; by-purpose, by-end; "the be-all and the end-all" Shakespeare; teleology

3 **intentionality, deliberation, deliberateness,** directedness; express intention, expressness, **premeditation, predeliberation,** preconsideration, **calculation, calculatedness, predetermination,** preresolution, forethought, aforethought

VERBS 4 **intend, purpose, plan,** purport, **mean,** think, **propose; resolve,** determine 359.7; project, **design,** destine; **aim,** aim

at, take aim at, draw a bead on, set one's sights on, have designs on, go for, drive at, aspire to *or* after, be after, set before oneself, purpose to oneself; harbor a design; **desire** 100.14,18

5 **contemplate, meditate; envisage,** envision, **have in mind, have in view;** have an eye to, have every intention, have a mind *or* notion, have half a mind *or* notion, have a good *or* great mind *or* notion

6 **plan, plan on, figure on,** plan for *or* out, count on, figure out, calculate, calculate on, reckon, reckon *or* bargain on, bargain for, bank on *or* upon, make book on <nonformal>

7 **premeditate, calculate, preresolve, predetermine,** predeliberate, preconsider, direct oneself, forethink, work out beforehand; plan; plot, scheme

ADJS 8 **intentional, intended,** proposed, purposed, telic, **projected, designed,** of design, aimed, aimed at, **meant, purposeful,** purposive, **willful, voluntary, deliberate;** deliberated; considered, studied, advised, **calculated, contemplated, envisaged,** envisioned, meditated, **conscious,** knowing, witting; planned; teleological

9 **premeditated, predeliberated,** preconsidered, predetermined, preresolved, prepense, **aforethought**

ADVS 10 **intentionally, purposely,** purposefully, purposively, pointedly, **on purpose,** with purpose, with a view *or* an eye to, **deliberately, designedly, willfully, voluntarily,** of one's own accord *or* one's own free will; **wittingly, consciously, knowingly; advisedly, calculatedly,** contemplatedly, meditatedly, premeditatedly, **with premeditation, with intent,** with full intent, **by design,** with one's eyes open; with malice aforethought, in cold blood

PREPS, CONJS 11 **for, to; in order to** *or* **that,** so, **so that, so as to; for the purpose of,** to the end that, with the intent that, with the view of, with a view to, with an eye to; in contemplation of, in consideration of; **for the sake of**

381 PLAN

NOUNS 1 **plan, scheme, design,** method, **program,** device, contrivance, game, envisagement, conception, enterprise, **idea, notion;** organization, rationalization, systematization, schematization; charting, mapping, graphing, blueprinting; **planning,** calculation, figuring; planning function; long-range planning, long-range plan; **master plan,** the picture *and* the big picture <both nonformal>; approach, attack, plan of attack; way, procedure; **arrangement,** prearrangement, system, disposition, layout, setup, lineup; **schedule,** timetable, timescheme, time frame; deadline; plan of work; **schema,** schematism, scheme of arrangement; blueprint, **guideline, guidelines,** program of action; methodology; working plan, ground plan, tactical plan, strategic plan; tactics, **strategy,** game plan <nonformal>; contingency plan; operations research; **intention** 380; forethought, foresight 960

2 project, projection, scheme; proposal, prospectus, proposition; **scenario, game plan** <nonformal>

3 diagram, plot, chart, blueprint, graph, bar graph, pie *or* circle graph *or* chart, area graph; flow diagram, flow chart; **table; design, pattern,** copy <old>, cartoon; **sketch, draft, drawing,** working drawing, rough; *brouillon, ébauche, esquisse* <all Fr>; **outline, delineation,** skeleton, figure, profile; house plan, ground plan, ichnography; elevation, projection; **map, chart** 159.5

4 policy, polity, principles, guiding principles; **procedure,** course, line, plan of action; creed 952.3; **platform;** position paper

5 intrigue, web of intrigue, **plot, scheme,** deep-laid plot *or* scheme, underplot, game *or* little game <both nonformal>, trick, stratagem, finesse; counterplot; **conspiracy,** confederacy, covin, complot <old>, cabal; **complicity, collusion, connivance; artifice** 415.3; **contrivance,** contriving; **scheming,** schemery, plotting; finagling <nonformal>, **machination,** manipulation, **maneuvering,** engineering, rigging; frame-up <nonformal>; wire-pulling <nonformal>

6 planner, designer, deviser, contriver, framer, projector; enterpriser, entrepreneuer; organizer, promoter, developer, engineer; expediter, facilitator, animator; **policymaker, decision-maker; architect, tactician, strategist, strategian**

7 schemer, plotter, counterplotter, finagler <nonformal>, Machiavellian; **intriguer,** *intrigant, intrigante* <both Fr>, cabalist; **conspirer, conspirator,** coconspirator, **conniver;** maneuverer, machinator, operator <nonformal>, opportunist, pothunter, exploiter; wire-puller <nonformal>

VERBS **8 plan, devise, contrive, design,** frame, shape, cast, concert, lay plans; organize, rationalize, systematize, schematize, methodize, configure, pull together, sort out; **arrange,** prearrange, make arrangements, set up, work up, work out; **schedule;** lay down a plan, shape *or* mark out a course; program; **calculate,** figure; **project,** cut out, make a projection, forecast <old>, plan ahead; intend 380.4

9 plot, scheme, intrigue, be up to something; **conspire, connive,** collude, complot <old>, cabal; **hatch, hatch up,** cook up <nonformal>, brew, concoct, hatch *or* lay a plot; **maneuver,** machinate, finesse, operate <nonformal>, engineer, rig, wangle <nonformal>, angle, finagle <nonformal>; frame *or* frame up <both nonformal>; counterplot, countermine

10 plot; map, chart 159.11, **blueprint; diagram,** graph; **sketch,** sketch in *or* out, draw up a plan; map out, plot out, **lay out,** set out, mark out; lay off, mark off

11 outline, line, **delineate,** chalk out, brief; **sketch, draft,** trace; block in *or* out; rough in, rough out

ADJS **12 planned, devised, designed,** shaped, set, **blueprinted,** charted, **contrived; plotted;** arranged; organized, rationalized, systematized, schematized, methodized; worked out, calculated, figured; **projected; scheduled,** on the agenda, in the works, in the pipeline <nonformal>, on the calendar, on the docket, on the anvil, on the carpet, on the tapis <old>, *sur le tapis* <Fr>; tactical, **strategic**

13 scheming, calculating, designing, contriving, plotting, intriguing; manipulatory, **manipulative;** opportunist, **opportunistic;** Machiavellian, Byzantine; **conniving,** connivent <old>, conspiring, collusive; stratagemical

14 schematic, diagrammatic

382 PURSUIT

NOUNS **1 pursuit,** pursuing, pursuance, prosecution <old>; **quest,** seeking, hunting, searching; **following,** follow, follow-up; **tracking,** trailing, tracking down, dogging, shadowing, stalking; **chase,** hot pursuit; hue and cry

2 hunting, gunning, shooting, venery, cynegetics, sport, sporting; **hunt, chase,** chevy *or* chivy <both Brit>, shikar <India>, coursing; blood-sport; fox hunt, fox hunting; hawking, falconry; stalking, still hunt

3 **fishing,** fishery; **angling,** piscatology
<old>, halieutics

4 **pursuer,** pursuant, **chaser,** follower;
hunter, quester, **seeker**

5 **hunter, huntsman,** sportsman, **Nimrod;**
huntress, sportswoman; stalker; courser;
trapper; big game hunter, shikari <In-
dia>, white hunter; jacklighter, jacker;
gamekeeper; beater, whipper-in; fal-
coner; gundog

6 **fisher, fisherman, angler,** *piscator* <L>,
piscatorian, piscatorialist; Waltonian,
"The Compleat Angler"—Izaak Wal-
ton; dibber, dibbler, troller, trawler,
trawlerman, dragger, jacker, jigger, bob-
ber, guddler, tickler, drifter, drift net-
ter, whaler, clam digger, lobsterman,
etc

7 **quarry, game, prey,** venery, beasts of
venery, victim, the hunted; kill; big
game

VERBS 8 **pursue,** prosecute <old>, **follow,**
follow up, **go after,** take out *or* off after
<nonformal>, bay after, run after, run in
pursuit of, make after, go in pursuit of;
raise the hunt, raise the hue and cry,
hollo after; **chase, give chase,** chivy;
hound, dog; **quest,** quest after, **seek,** seek
out, hunt, **search** 937.29,30

9 **hunt,** go hunting, hunt down, chase, run,
shikar <India>, sport; engage in a blood
sport; shoot, gun; course; ride to hounds,
follow the hounds; **track,** trail; **stalk,**
prowl after, still-hunt; hound, dog; hawk,
falcon; fowl; flush, start; drive, beat; jack,
jacklight

10 **fish,** go fishing, **angle;** cast one's hook *or*
net; bait the hook; shrimp, whale, clam,
grig, still-fish, fly-fish, troll, bob, dap, dib
or dibble, gig, jig, etc; reel in

ADJS 11 **pursuing,** pursuant, following;
questing, seeking, searching 937.37; **in
pursuit,** in hot pursuit, in full cry; hunting, cynegetic, fishing, piscatory, piscatorial, halieutic, halieutical

PREPS 12 **after, in pursuit** *or* **pursuance of,** in
search of, on the lookout for, in the mar-
ket for, out for; on the track *or* trail of, on
the scent of

INTERJS 13 <hunting cries> view halloo!,
yoicks! <old>; so-ho!, tallyho!, tallyho
over!, tallyho back!

383 ROUTE, PATH

NOUNS 1 **route, path, way,** itinerary, **course,**
track, run, line, road; trajectory, traject,
trajet <Fr>; circuit, tour, orbit; walk,
beat, round; trade route, **sea lane, air
lane,** flight path; path of least resistance,
primrose path, garden path; shortcut

2 **path, track, trail, pathway,** footpath,
footway, *piste* <Fr>; walkway, catwalk,
skybridge *or* skywalk *or* flying bridge *or*
walkway; **sidewalk, walk,** fastwalk, *trot-
toir* <Fr>, foot pavement <Brit>;
boardwalk; hiking trail; public walk,
promenade, esplanade, alameda, parade,
prado <Sp>, mall; towpath *or* towing
path; bridle path *or* road *or* trail *or* way;
bicycle path; berm; run, runway; beaten
track *or* path, rut, groove; garden path

3 **passageway, pass, passage, defile; avenue, artery; corridor, aisle, alley, lane;
channel, conduit** 239.1; ford, ferry, traject, *trajet* <Fr>; opening, aperture;
access, inlet 189.5; exit, outlet 190.9; connection, communication; covered way,
gallery, arcade, portico, colonnade, cloister, ambulatory; underpass, overpass,
flyover <Brit>; tunnel, railroad tunnel,
vehicular tunnel; junction, interchange,
intersection 170.2

4 **byway, bypath,** byroad, by-lane, bystreet,
side road, side street; **bypass, detour,**
roundabout way; bypaths and crooked
ways; back way, back stairs, back door,
side door; back road, back street

5 **road** <see list>, highway, roadway, car-
riageway <Brit>, right-of-way; **street**
<see list>

6 **pavement,** paving; macadam, blacktop,
bitumen, asphalt, tarmacadam, tarmac,
tarvia, bituminous macadam; cement,
concrete; tile, brick, paving brick; stone,
paving stone, pavestone, flag, flagstone,
flagging; cobblestone, cobble; road metal
<Brit>; gravel; washboard; curbstone,
kerbstone <Brit>, edgestone; curb, kerb
<Brit>, curbing; gutter, kennel <Brit>

7 **railway** <see list>, **railroad,** rail, line,
track, trackage, railway *or* railroad *or* rail
line; junction; terminus, terminal, the
end of the line; roadway, roadbed, embankment; bridge, trestle

8 **cableway,** ropeway, wireway, wire ropeway, cable *or* rope railway, funicular *or*
funicular railway; *téléphérique* <Fr>, telpher, telpherway, telpher ropeway, telpher line *or* railway; ski lift

9 **bridge, span, viaduct;** cantilever bridge,
clapper bridge, drawbridge, footbridge,
pontoon bridge, rope bridge, skybridge *or*
skywalk *or* flying bridge *or* walkway *or*
skywalk, suspension bridge, toll bridge;
overpass, overcrossing, overbridge *or*
flyover <both Brit>; stepping-stone,
stepstone; Bifrost

10 roads, highways

access road
arterial high-
 way
artery
Autobahn <Ger>
autoroute <Fr>
autostrada <Ital>
beltway *or* circum-
 ferential *or* ring
 road *or* belt high-
 way
causeway
expressway
freeway
highroad <Brit>

main road *or* main
 drag <nonformal>
motorway <Brit>
parkway
pavé <Fr>
pike
post road
private road
shunpike
speedway
superhighway
throughway *or* thru-
 way
toll road
turnpike

11 streets, alleys

alley *or* alleyway
avenue
blind alley
boulevard
close <Brit>
court
crescent
cul-de-sac
dead-end street

drive
lane
mews
one-way street
place
row
vennel <Scots>
wynd <Scots>

12 railways

cable railway
cog railway
electric railway
elevated railway *or*
 elevated *or* el *or* L
 <nonformal>
gravity-operated rail-
 way *or* gravity
 railroad
mainline
métro <Fr>
monorail

rack *or* rack-and-
 pinion railway
subway
tram *or* tramline *or*
 tramway *or* tram-
 road <Brit>
trolley *or* streetcar
 line
trunk *or* trunk line
underground *or* tube
 <Brit>

384 MANNER, MEANS

NOUNS **1 manner, way,** wise, **means, mode,**
modality, form <old>, **fashion, style,**
tone, guise <old>; **method,** method-
ology, **system;** algorithm <math>; **ap-
proach,** attack, tack; **technique, pro-
cedure, process,** proceeding, course, prac-
tice; order; lines, line, line of action;
modus operandi <L>, mode of operation
or MO, manner of working, mode of pro-
cedure; **routine;** the way of, the how, the
how-to, the drill <Brit>

2 means, ways, **ways and means,** means to
an end; **wherewithal,** wherewith; funds
728.14; **resources,** disposable resources,
capital 728.15; bankroll <nonformal>;
stock in trade, stock, supply 386; power,
capacity, ability 18.2; power base, con-
stituency, backing, support; recourses,
resorts, devices; method

3 instrumentality, agency; machinery,
mechanism, modality; gadgetry <nonfor-
mal>; mediation, going between, inter-
mediation, service; **expedient,** recourse,
resort, device 994.2

4 instrument, tool, implement, appliance,
device; contrivance, lever, mechanism;
vehicle, organ; agent 576; medium, medi-
ator, intermedium, intermediary, inter-
mediate, interagent, liaison, go-between
576.4; expediter, facilitator, animator;
midwife, servant, slave, handmaid, hand-
maiden, *ancilla* <L>; **cat's-paw, puppet,
dummy, pawn,** creature, minion, stooge
<nonformal>; stalking horse; toy, play-
thing; dupe 358

VERBS **5 use, utilize,** adopt, effect; **approach,
attack;** proceed, practice, go about; rou-
tinize

6 find means, find a way, provide *or* have
the wherewithal; get by hook or by crook,
obtain by fair means or foul; beg, borrow,
or steal

7 be instrumental, **serve, subserve,** serve
one's purpose, come in handy, stand in
good stead, fill the bill; minister to, act
for, act in the interests of, **promote, ad-
vance, forward, assist,** facilitate; medi-
ate, go between; liaise

ADJS **8** modal; **instrumental, implemental;**
agential, agentive, agentival; **useful,**
utile, handy, employable, **serviceable;
helpful,** conducive, forwarding, favoring,
promoting, assisting, facilitating; subser-
vient, ministering, ministerial; mediat-
ing, mediatorial, intermediary

ADVS **9 how, in what way** *or* **manner,** by
what mode *or* means; to what extent; in
what condition; by what name; at what
price; after this fashion, in this way, in
such wise, along these lines; **thus, so,** just
so, thus and so; as, like, on the lines of

10 anyhow, anyway, anywise, anyroad
<Brit nonformal>, in any way, **by any
means, by any manner of means;** in any
event, at any rate, leastways <nonfor-
mal>, in any case; **nevertheless, none-
theless, however, regardless,** irregard-
less <nonformal>; at all, nohow <non-
formal>

11 somehow, in some way, in some way or
other, someway <nonformal>, by some
means, **somehow or other,** somehow or
another, in one way or another, in some
such way, after a fashion; no matter how,
by hook or by crook, by fair means or foul

12 herewith, therewith, wherewith, where-
withal; whereby, thereby, hereby

PREPS **13 by means of, by** *or* **through the**

agency of, by *or* through the good offices of, through the instrumentality of, by the aid of, thanks to, by use of, **by way of,** by dint of, by the act of, through the medium of, by *or* in virtue of, at the hand of, at the hands of; **with, through, by,** per

PHRS **14** it isn't what you do, it's how you do it; there's more than one way to skin a cat

385 PROVISION, EQUIPMENT

NOUNS **1 provision,** providing; **equipment, accouterment,** fitting out, outfitting; **supply,** supplying, finding; **furnishing,** furnishment; chandlery, **retailing, selling** 734.2; **logistics;** procurement 472.1; investment, endowment, subvention, subsidy, subsidization; provisioning, victualing, purveyance, catering; armament; resupply, replenishment, reinforcement; supply line, line of supply; **preparation** 405

2 provisions, supplies 386.1; provender 10.5; **merchandise** 735

3 accommodations, accommodation, facilities; **lodgings;** bed, board, full board; **room and board,** bed and board; **subsistence,** keep, fostering

4 equipment, matériel, equipage, munitions; **furniture, furnishings,** furnishments <old>; **fixtures, fittings, appointments, accouterments, appurtenances,** installations, plumbing; **appliances, utensils, conveniences; outfit, apparatus, rig,** machinery; stock-in-trade; **plant,** facility, facilities; paraphernalia, things, **gear, stuff** <nonformal>, impedimenta <pl>, **tackle;** rigging; armament, munition; **kit,** duffel, effects, personal effects

5 harness, caparison, trappings, **tack,** tackle

6 provider, supplier, furnisher; donor 478.11; patron; **purveyor,** provisioner, **caterer,** victualer, sutler; *vivandier or vivandière* <both Fr>; chandler, retailer, merchant 730.2; commissary, commissariat, quartermaster, storekeeper, stock clerk, steward, manciple

VERBS **7 provide, supply,** find, dish up *and* rustle up <both nonformal>, **furnish;** accommodate; invest, endow, fund, subsidize; donate, give, afford, contribute, kick in <nonformal>, yield, present 478.12; make available; stock, store; provide for, make provision *or* due provision for; prepare 405.6; support, maintain, keep; fill, fill up; replenish, restock, recruit

8 equip, furnish, outfit, gear, **prepare, fit,** fit up *or* out, fix up <nonformal>, **rig,** rig up

or out, **turn out,** appoint, accouter, clothe, dress, arm, heel <nonformal>, munition; man, staff

9 provision, provender, cater, victual, plenish <old>; provide a grubstake <nonformal>; **board,** feed; forage; fuel, gas, gas up, fill up, top off, coal, oil, bunker; **purvey,** sell 734.8

10 accommodate, furnish accommodations; house, lodge 225.10; **put up,** board

11 make a living, earn a living *or* livelihood, **make** *or* **earn one's keep**

12 support oneself, make one's way; **make ends meet, keep body and soul together, keep the wolf from the door,** keep *or* hold one's head above water, keep afloat; **survive, subsist, cope, eke out,** make out, scrape along, manage, get by

ADJS **13 provided, supplied, furnished,** provisioned, purveyed, catered; invested, endowed; **equipped, fitted,** fitted out, outfitted, rigged, accoutered; armed, heeled <nonformal>; staffed, manned; readied, in place, **prepared** 405.16

14 well-provided, well-supplied, well-furnished, well-stocked, well-found; **well-equipped, well-fitted,** well-appointed; well-armed

386 STORE, SUPPLY

NOUNS **1 store, hoard, treasure,** treasury; plenty, plenitude, abundance, cornucopia; heap, mass, stack, pile, dump, rick; **collection, accumulation,** cumulation, **amassment,** budget, **stockpile; backlog;** repertory, repertoire; stock-in-trade; **inventory, stock,** supply on hand; lock, stock, and barrel; **stores, supplies, provisions,** provisionment, rations; larder, commissariat, commissary; munitions; matériel; material, materials 1052

2 supply, fund, resource, resources; means, assets, liquid assets, balance, pluses <nonformal>, black-ink items, **capital,** capital goods, capitalization, available means *or* resources *or* funds, cash flow, stock in trade; venture capital; grist, grist for the mill; holdings, property 471

3 reserve, reserves, reservoir, resource; proved *or* proven reserve; **stockpile, cache,** backup, reserve supply, something in reserve *or* in hand, something to fall back on, reserve fund, **nest egg, savings,** sinking fund; proved reserves; backlog, unexpended balance; ace in the hole <nonformal>, a card up one's sleeve; spare *or* replacement part

4 source of supply, source, staple, resource;

well, fountain, fount, font <old>, spring, wellspring; mine, **gold mine, bonanza,** luau <nonformal>; quarry, lode, vein; oilfield, oil well, oil rig; cornucopia

5 **storage, stowage;** preservation, conservation, safekeeping, warehousing; cold storage, cold store, dry storage, dead storage; storage space, shelf-room; custody, guardianship 1007.2; sequestration, escrow

6 **storehouse, storeroom,** stock room, lumber room, store, storage, **depository, repository,** conservatory <old>, reservoir, repertory, depot, supply depot, supply base, magazine, *magasin* <Fr>, warehouse, godown; bonded warehouse, entrepôt; dock; hold, cargo dock; attic, cellar, basement; closet, cupboard; wine cellar, buttery; **treasury,** treasure house, treasure room, exchequer; bank, vault 729.12, strongroom, strongbox; **archives, library,** stack room; armory, arsenal, dump; lumberyard; drawer, shelf; bin, bunker, bay, crib; rack, rick; vat, tank; crate, box; chest, **locker,** hutch; bookcase, stack; sail locker, chain locker, lazaret, lazaretto, glory hole

7 **garner, granary,** grain bin, elevator, grain elevator, **silo;** mow, haymow, hayloft, hayrick; crib, corncrib

8 **larder, pantry,** buttery <nonformal>; spence <Brit nonformal>, stillroom <Brit>; root cellar; dairy, dairy house *or* room

9 **museum; gallery,** art gallery, picture gallery, pinacotheca; salon; Metropolitan Museum, National Gallery, Museum of Modern Art, Guggenheim Museum, Tate Gallery, British Museum, Louvre, Hermitage, Prado, Uffizi, Rijksmuseum; museology, curatorship

VERBS 10 **store, stow,** lay in store; **lay in,** lay in a supply *or* stock *or* store, store away, stow away, **put away, lay away,** put *or* lay by, pack away, bundle away, lay down, stow down, salt down *or* away *and* sock away *and* squirrel away <all nonformal>; **deposit,** reposit, lodge; **cache,** stash <nonformal>, bury away; **bank,** coffer, hutch <old>; warehouse, reservoir; file, file away

11 **store up, stock up, lay up,** put up, **save up,** hoard up, treasure up, garner up, **heap up,** pile up, build up a stock *or* an inventory; **accumulate,** cumulate, **collect, amass, stockpile;** backlog; garner, gather into barns; **hoard,** treasure, save, keep, hold, squirrel, squirrel away; hide, secrete 346.7

12 **reserve, save, conserve, keep,** retain, husband, husband one's resources, keep *or* hold back, withhold; **keep in reserve,** keep in store, keep on hand, keep by one; sequester, put in escrow; **preserve** 397.7; **set** *or* **put aside,** set *or* put apart, put *or* lay *or* set by; save up, save to fall back upon, keep as a nest egg, **save for a rainy day,** provide for *or* against a rainy day

13 **have in store** *or* **reserve,** have to fall back upon, have something to draw on, have something laid by, have something laid by for a rainy day, have something up one's sleeve

ADJS 14 **stored, accumulated,** amassed, laid up; gathered, garnered, collected; **stockpiled;** backlogged; **hoarded,** treasured

15 **reserved, preserved, saved,** conserved, put by, kept, retained, held, withheld, held back, kept *or* held in reserve; spare

ADVS 16 **in store,** in stock, in supply, **on hand**

17 **in reserve,** back, aside, by

387 USE

NOUNS 1 **use, employment,** utilization, employ <old>, **usage; exercise, exertion,** active use; good use; ill use, wrong use, misuse 389; hard use, hard *or* rough usage; hard wear, heavy duty; **application,** appliance; expenditure, expending, using up, exhausting, dissipation, dissipating, **consumption** 388

2 **usage, treatment, handling,** management; way *or* means of dealing; stewardship, custodianship, guardianship, care

3 **utility, usefulness, usability, use,** utilizability, avail, good, **serviceability, helpfulness,** functionality, profitability, applicability, availability, **practicability,** practicality, practical utility, operability, **effectiveness,** efficacy, efficiency

4 **benefit, use, service, avail, profit, advantage,** point, percentage *and* mileage <all nonformal>, what's in it for one <nonformal>, convenience; interest, behalf, behoof; **value, worth**

5 **function, use, purpose, role,** part, end use, immediate purpose, ultimate purpose, operational purpose, operation; work, duty, office

6 **functionalism, utilitarianism;** pragmatism, pragmaticism; functional design, functional furniture *or* housing, etc

7 <law terms> usufruct, imperfect usufruct, perfect usufruct, right of use, user, enjoyment of property; *jus primae noctis* <L>, *droit du seigneur* <Fr>

8 **utilization,** using, making use of, making

instrumental, using as a means *or* tool; **employment,** employing; **management,** manipulation, handling, working, operation, **exploitation,** recruiting, recruitment, calling upon, calling into service; mobilization, mobilizing

9 **user,** employer; **consumer,** enjoyer

VERBS 10 **use, utilize, make use of,** do with; **employ,** practice, ply, work, manage, handle, manipulate, operate, **wield,** play; **have** *or* **enjoy the use of;** exercise, **exert**

11 **apply, put to use** *or* **good use,** carry out, put into execution, **put into practice** *or* **operation,** put in force, enforce; bring to bear upon

12 **treat, handle,** manage, use, **deal with, cope with,** come to grips with, take on, tackle <nonformal>, contend with, do with; steward, care for

13 **spend,** consume, expend, **pass,** employ, **put in;** devote, bestow, give to *or* give over to, devote *or* consecrate *or* dedicate to; while, while away, wile; dissipate, **exhaust, use up**

14 **avail oneself of, make use of, resort to, put to use** *or* **good use,** have recourse to, **turn to,** look to, recur to, refer to, take to <nonformal>, betake oneself to; revert to, fall back on *or* upon; convert *or* turn to use, put in *or* into requisition, press *or* enlist into service, lay under contribution, impress, **call upon,** call *or* bring into play, draw on *or* upon, recruit, muster

15 **take advantage of, avail oneself of, make the most of,** use to the full, make good use of, improve, **turn to use** *or* **profit** *or* **account** *or* **good account,** turn to advantage *or* good advantage, use to advantage, put to advantage, find one's account *or* advantage in; improve the occasion 842.8; **profit by, benefit from,** reap the benefit of; **exploit, capitalize on, make capital of,** make a good thing of <nonformal>, make hay <nonformal>, **trade on,** cash in on <nonformal>; make the best of, make a virtue of necessity, "make necessity a virtue"—Quintilian

16 <take unfair advantage of> **exploit, take advantage of, use,** make use of, **use for one's own ends;** make a paw *or* cat's-paw of, sucker *and* play for a sucker <both nonformal>; **manipulate,** work on, work upon, stroke, play on *or* upon; play both ends against the middle; **impose upon,** presume upon; use ill, ill-use, abuse, misuse 389.4; batten on; milk, bleed, bleed white <nonformal>; drain, suck the blood of *or* from, suck dry; exploit one's

position, feather one's nest <nonformal>, **profiteer**

17 **avail,** be of use, be of service, serve, **suffice, do,** answer, **answer** *or* **serve one's purpose,** serve one's need, fill the bill *and* do the trick <both nonformal>; bestead <old>, **stand one in stead** *or* **good stead,** be handy, stand one in hand <nonformal>; advantage, be of advantage *or* service to; **profit, benefit,** pay *and* pay off <both nonformal>, give good returns, yield a profit

ADJS 18 **useful,** employable, of use, of service, **serviceable,** commodious <old>; good for; **helpful,** of help 449.21; **advantageous, to one's advantage** *or* **profit, profitable,** remuneratory, beneficial 998.12; **practical,** banausic, pragmatical, **functional, utilitarian,** of general utility *or* application; fitting, proper, appropriate, expedient 994.5; well-used, well-thumbed

19 **using, exploitive,** exploitative, manipulative, manipulatory

20 **handy, convenient; available,** accessible, **ready, at hand,** to hand, **on hand,** on tap, on deck <nonformal>, on call, at one's call *or* beck and call, at one's elbow, at one's fingertips, just around the corner, at one's disposal; versatile, adaptable, all-around <nonformal>, of all work; crude but effective, quick and dirty <nonformal>

21 **effectual, effective,** active, efficient, efficacious, operative

22 **valuable,** of value, all for the best, all to the good, **profitable,** yielding a return, well-spent, **worthwhile,** rewarding; gainful, remunerative

23 **usable, utilizable; applicable,** appliable; practical, operable; **reusable; exploitable;** manipulable, pliable, compliant 433.12

24 **used, employed,** exercised, exerted, **applied;** previously owned *or* pre-owned, secondhand 841.18

25 **in use, in practice,** in force, in effect, in service, in operation, in commission

ADVS 26 **usefully,** to good use; **profitably, advantageously, to advantage,** to profit, to good effect; effectually, effectively, efficiently; serviceably, functionally, **practically;** handily, conveniently; by use of, by dint of

388 CONSUMPTION

NOUNS 1 **consumption, consuming, using** *or* **eating up;** burning up; absorption, assimilation, digestion, ingestion, **expenditure,** expending, spending; squandering, wastefulness 486.1; finishing; **depletion,** drain, exhausting, **exhaustion,** impoverishment; **waste,** wastage, wasting away, erosion, ablation, wearing down, wearing away, attrition; throwing away

2 consumable, consumable item *or* **goods;** nonrenewable *or* nonreusable *or* nonrecyclable item *or* resource; **throwaway,** throwaway item, disposable goods *or* item; throwaway culture *or* psychology, instant obsolescence

VERBS **3 consume, spend, expend, use up;** absorb, assimilate, digest, ingest, eat, **eat up,** swallow, swallow up, gobble, gobble up; burn up; **finish,** finish off; **exhaust, deplete,** impoverish, drain, drain of resources; suck dry, bleed white <nonformal>, suck one's blood; wear away, erode, erode away, ablate; waste away; **throw away, squander** 486.3

4 be consumed, be used up, waste; **run out, give out,** peter out <nonformal>; run dry, dry up

ADJS **5 used up, consumed,** eaten up, burnt up; finished; gone; unreclaimable, irreplaceable; nonrenewable, nonrecyclable, nonreusable; **spent,** exhausted, effete, dissipated, depleted, impoverished, drained, worn-out; worn away, eroded, ablated; **wasted** 486.9

6 consumable, expendable, spendable; exhaustible; replaceable; disposable, throwaway, no-deposit, no-deposit-no-return

389 MISUSE

NOUNS **1 misuse, misusage, abuse; misemployment, misapplication; mishandling,** mismanagement, poor stewardship; corrupt administration, malversation, breach of public trust, maladministration; diversion, defalcation, misappropriation, conversion, **embezzlement,** peculation, pilfering; perversion, prostitution; profanation, violation, pollution, fouling, befoulment, desecration, defilement, debasement; malpractice, abuse of office, misconduct, malfeasance, misfeasance

2 mistreatment, ill-treatment, maltreatment, ill-use, ill-usage, **abuse; molesting, molestation,** child abuse *or* molestation; **violation,** outrage, violence, injury, atrocity; cruel and unusual punishment

3 persecution, oppression, harrying, hounding, tormenting, bashing <nonfor-

mal>, harassment, nobbling <Brit nonformal>, victimization; **witch-hunting,** witch-hunt, red-baiting <nonformal>, McCarthyism; open season, piling on <nonformal>

VERBS **4 misuse, misemploy, abuse, misapply; mishandle,** mismanage, maladminister; divert, misappropriate, convert, defalcate <old>, embezzle, pilfer, peculate, feather one's nest <nonformal>; pervert, prostitute; profane, violate, pollute, foul, foul one's own nest, befoul, desecrate, defile, debase

5 mistreat, maltreat, ill-treat, ill-use, abuse, injure, **molest;** do wrong to, do wrong by; outrage, do violence to, do one's worst to; mishandle, manhandle; buffet, batter, bruise, **savage,** manhandle, maul, knock about, rough, rough up

6 <nonformal terms> **screw,** screw over, shaft, stiff, give the short *or* the shitty end of the stick, fuck, fuck over

7 persecute, oppress, **torment,** victimize, play cat and mouse with, **harass,** get *or* keep after, get *or* keep at, harry, hound, beset, nobble <Brit nonformal>; pursue, hunt

ADVS **8** on one's back *and* on one's case *and* in one's face <all nonformal>

390 DISUSE

NOUNS **1 disuse,** disusage, desuetude; **nonuse, nonemployment; abstinence, abstention;** nonprevalence, unprevalence; **obsolescence,** obsoleteness, obsoletism, obsoletion, planned obsolescence; superannuation, retirement, pensioning off

2 discontinuance, cessation, desisting, desistance; **abdication,** relinquishment, forbearance, resignation, renunciation, renouncement, abjurement, abjuration; waiver, nonexercise; abeyance, suspension, back burner *and* cold storage <all nonformal>; **phaseout, abandonment** 370

3 discard, discarding, jettison, deep six <nonformal>, disposal, dumping, **waste disposal,** solid waste disposal, burning, incineration, ocean burning *or* incineration; compacting; **scrapping, junking** <nonformal>; removal, elimination 772.2; **rejection** 372; **reject,** throwaway, castaway, castoff, rejectamenta <pl>; **refuse** 391.4

VERBS **4 cease to use; abdicate, relinquish; discontinue, disuse,** quit, stop, drop <nonformal>, give up, give over, lay off <nonformal>, **phase out,** phase down, put behind one, let go, leave off, come off <nonformal>, cut out, desist from, have done with; waive <old>, resign, renounce, abjure; nol-pros, not pursue *or* proceed with

5 **not use, do without,** dispense with, **let alone,** not touch, hold off; **abstain, refrain,** forgo, forbear, spare, waive; keep *or* hold back, reserve, save, save up, sock *or* squirrel away, tuck away, put under the mattress, hoard; keep in hand, have up one's sleeve; see the last of

6 **put away,** lay away, **put aside,** lay *or* set *or* wave *or* cast *or* push aside, sideline <nonformal>, put *or* lay *or* set by; stow, store 386.10; **pigeonhole, shelve,** put on the shelf, put in mothballs; **table,** lay on the table; table the motion, pass to the order of the day; put on hold *or* on the back burner <nonformal>, postpone, delay 845.8

7 **discard, reject, throw away, throw out,** chuck *or* chuck away *and* shit-can *and* eighty-six <all nonformal>, cast, cast off *or* away *or* aside; **get rid of,** get quit of, get shut *or* shet of <nonformal>, rid oneself of, shrug off, **dispose of,** slough, **dump, ditch** <nonformal>, **jettison, throw** *or* **heave** *or* **toss overboard,** deep-six <nonformal>, throw out the window, throw *or* cast to the dogs, cast to the winds; sell off *or* out; throw over, jilt; part with, give away; throw to the wolves, write off, walk away from, **abandon** 370.5; remove, **eliminate** 772.5

8 **scrap, junk** <nonformal>, consign to the scrap heap, throw on the junk heap <nonformal>; superannuate, retire, pension off, put out to pasture *or* grass

9 **obsolesce,** fall into disuse, go out, pass away; be superseded; superannuate

ADJS 10 **disused, abandoned,** deserted, **discontinued,** done with; out, **out of use;** old; relinquished, resigned, renounced, abjured; **outworn,** worn-out, past use, not worth saving; **obsolete,** obsolescent, life-expired, superannuated, superannuate; superseded, outdated, out-of-date, outmoded, desuete; retired, pensioned off; on the shelf; antique, antiquated, old-fashioned, old

11 **discarded,** rejected, **castoff,** castaway

12 **unused,** unutilized, **unemployed,** unapplied, unexercised; in abeyance, suspended; waived; **unspent,** unexpended, unconsumed; held back, held out, put by, put aside, saved, held in reserve, in hand, spare, to spare, extra,

reserve; stored 386.14; untouched, unhandled, untapped; untrodden, unbeaten; **new,** original, pristine, fresh, fresh off the assembly line, mint, in mint condition, factory-fresh

391 USELESSNESS

NOUNS 1 **uselessness,** inutility; **needlessness,** unnecessity; unserviceability, **unusability,** unemployability, inoperativeness, inoperability, disrepair; unhelpfulness; inapplicability, unsuitability, unfitness; functionlessness; otioseness, otiosity; **superfluousness** 992.4

2 **futility,** vanity, emptiness, hollowness; **fruitlessness,** bootlessness, unprofitableness, profitlessness, unprofitability, otiosity, worthlessness, valuelessness; triviality, nugacity, nugaciousness; unproductiveness 890; **ineffectuality,** ineffectiveness, inefficacy 19.3; **impotence** 19.1; **pointlessness,** meaninglessness, purposelessness, aimlessness, fecklessness; the absurd, absurdity; inanity, fatuity; vicious circle *or* cycle; **rat race** <nonformal>

3 **labor in vain,** labor lost, labor for naught; labor of Sisyphus, work of Penelope, Penelope's web; **wild-goose chase,** snipe hunt, bootless errand; waste of labor, waste of breath, waste of time, wasted effort, wasted breath, wasted labor

4 **refuse, waste,** wastage, waste matter, waste stream, waste product, solid waste, liquid waste, wastewater, effluent, sewage, sludge; incinerator ash; industrial waste, hazardous waste, toxic waste, atomic waste; medical waste; **offal; leavings,** sweepings, dust <Brit>, **scraps,** orts; **garbage,** gash <nonformal>, swill, pig-swill, slop, slops, hogwash <nonformal>; bilgewater; draff, lees, **dregs** 256.2; **offscourings,** scourings, rinsings, dishwater; parings, raspings, filings, shavings; **scum;** chaff, stubble, husks; weeds, tares; deadwood; rags, bones, wastepaper, shard, potsherd; scrap iron; slag, culm, slack

5 **rubbish, rubble, trash, junk** <nonformal>, shoddy, riffraff, raff <Brit nonformal>, **scrap,** dust <Brit>, **debris, litter,** lumber, clamjamfry <Scots>, truck <nonformal>

6 **trash pile,** rubbish heap, junkheap *and* junkpile <both nonformal>, scrap heap, dustheap, midden, kitchenmidden; wasteyard, **junkyard** <nonformal>, scrapyard, **dump,** dumpsite, garbage

dump, landfill, sanitary landfill, toxic waste dump

7 wastepaper basket, wastebasket, shitcan <nonformal>; litter basket, litter bin; garbage bag, garbage can, wastebin, dustbin <Brit>, trash can; Dumpster <trademark>, skip <Brit>; waste disposal unit, compactor, garbage grinder <nonformal>

VERBS 8 **be useless, be futile, make no difference, cut no ice; die aborning; labor in vain, go on a wild-goose chase,** run in circles, go around in circles, spin one's wheels *and* bang one's head against a brick wall <both nonformal>, beat the air, lash the waves, tilt at windmills, sow the sand, bay at the moon, waste one's effort *or* breath, preach *or* speak to the winds, beat *or* flog a dead horse, roll the stone of Sisyphus, carry coals to Newcastle, milk the ram, milk a he-goat into a sieve, pour water into a sieve, hold a farthing candle to the sun, look for a needle in a haystack, lock the barn door after the horse is stolen

ADJS 9 **useless,** of no use, no go <nonformal>; **aimless,** meaningless, **purposeless,** of no purpose, **pointless,** feckless; **unavailing,** of no avail, failed; ineffective, **ineffectual** 19.15; impotent 19.13; **superfluous** 992.17

10 **needless, unnecessary, unessential,** nonessential, **unneeded, uncalled-for,** unrequired; unrecognized, neglected, "born to blush unseen"—Thomas Gray

11 **worthless, valueless, good-for-nothing,** good-for-naught, no-good *or* NG <nonformal>, no-account <nonformal>, dear at any price, worthless as tits on a boar <nonformal>, not worth a dime *or* a red cent *or* a hill of beans *or* shit *or* bubkes <nonformal>, not worthwhile, not worth having, not worth mentioning *or* speaking of, not worth a thought, not worth a rap *or* a continental *or* a damn, not worth the powder to blow it to hell, not worth the powder and shot, not worth the pains *or* the trouble, of no earthly use, fit for the junk yard <nonformal>; trivial, pennyante <nonformal>, nugatory, nugacious; **junk** *and* **junky** <both nonformal>; **cheap,** shoddy, trashy, **shabby**

12 **fruitless,** gainless, profitless, bootless, otiose, **unprofitable,** unremunerative, nonremunerative; uncommercial; **unrewarding,** rewardless; abortive; barren, sterile, unproductive 890.4

13 **vain, futile,** hollow, empty, "weary, stale, flat, and unprofitable"—Shakespeare, idle; absurd; inane, fatuous, fatuitous

14 **unserviceable, unusable,** unemployable, inoperative, inoperable, unworkable; out of order, out of whack *and* on the blink *and* on the fritz <all nonformal>, in disrepair; **unhelpful,** unconducive; inapplicable; unsuitable, unfit; functionless, nonfunctional, otiose, nonutilitarian

ADVS 15 **uselessly; needlessly,** unnecessarily; bootlessly, fruitlessly; **futilely, vainly;** purposelessly, to little purpose, to no purpose, **aimlessly, pointlessly,** fecklessly

392 IMPROVEMENT

NOUNS 1 **improvement, betterment,** bettering, change for the better; melioration, **amelioration; mend,** mending, **amendment; progress,** progression, headway; breakthrough, quantum jump *or* leap; **advance,** advancement; upward mobility; **promotion, furtherance,** preferment; **rise,** ascent, **lift, uplift,** uptick <nonformal>, upswing, uptrend, upbeat; **increase** 251, upgrade, upping *and* boost *and* pickup <all nonformal>; gentrification; **enhancement, enrichment;** euthenics, eugenics; **restoration,** revival, retro, recovery

2 **development, refinement,** elaboration, **perfection;** beautification, embellishment; maturation, coming-of-age, ripening, evolution, seasoning

3 **cultivation, culture, refinement, polish,** civility; cultivation of the mind; **civilization;** acculturation; enculturation, socialization; enlightenment, education 927.4

4 **revision,** revise, revisal; revised edition; **emendation, amendment, correction, corrigenda, rectification;** editing, redaction, recension, revampment; **rewrite,** rewriting, rescript, rescription <old>; **polishing,** touching up, putting on the finishing touches, putting the gloss on, finishing, perfecting, tuning, fine-tuning; retrofitting

5 **reform, reformation;** regeneration 857.2; **transformation; conversion** 857; reformism, meliorism; gradualism, Fabianism, revisionism; utopianism; progressiveness, progressivism, progressism; radical reform, extremism, radicalism 611.4; revolution 859

6 **reformer,** reformist, meliorist; gradualist, Fabian, revisionist; utopian, utopist; progressive, progressivist, progressionist,

progressist; radical, extremist 611.12; revolutionary 859.3

VERBS **7** <get better> **improve, grow better,** look better, show improvement, **mend,** amend <old>, meliorate, ameliorate; **look up** or **pick up** or **perk up** <all nonformal>; **develop,** shape up; **advance, progress, make progress, make headway, gain,** gain ground, go forward, get or go ahead, come on, come along and come along nicely <both nonformal>, get along; make strides or rapid strides, take off and skyrocket <both nonformal>, make up for lost time; graduate

8 rally, come about or round, **take a favorable turn,** get over <nonformal>, take a turn for the better, gain strength; come a long way <nonformal>; **recuperate, recover** 396.20

9 improve, better, change for the better, make an improvement; transform, transfigure; improve upon, refine upon, **mend, amend,** emend; meliorate, **ameliorate; advance, promote,** foster, favor, nurture, forward, bring forward; **lift,** elevate, **uplift,** raise, boost <nonformal>; upgrade; gentrify; **enhance, enrich,** fatten, lard <old>; make one's way, better oneself; be the making of; **reform,** put or set straight; reform oneself, turn over a new leaf, mend one's ways, straighten out, straighten oneself out, go straight <nonformal>; get it together and get one's ducks in a row <both nonformal>; **civilize,** acculturate, socialize; enlighten, edify; **educate**

10 develop, elaborate; beautify, embellish; **cultivate;** come of age, come into its own, mature, ripen, evolve, season

11 perfect, touch up, finish, put on the finishing touches, polish, fine down, fine-tune <nonformal>, tone up, **brush up, furbish,** furbish up, spruce, **spruce up,** freshen, vamp, vamp up, rub up, brighten up, polish, polish up, shine <nonformal>; retouch; **revive, renovate** 396.17, 17; **repair, fix** 396.14; retrofit

12 revise, redact, recense, **revamp, rewrite,** redraft, **rework,** work over; **emend, amend,** emendate, **rectify,** correct; **edit,** blue-pencil

ADJS **13 improved, bettered;** changed for the better, advanced, ameliorated, enhanced, enriched; developed, perfected; beautified, embellished; upgraded; gentrified; **reformed; transformed,** transfigured, converted; **cultivated,** cultured, **refined,** polished, civilized; **educated** 927.18

14 better, better off, better for, all the better for; before-and-after

15 improving, bettering; meliorative, ameliorative, amelioratory; progressive, progressing, advancing, ongoing; mending, **on the mend;** on the lift or rise or upswing or upbeat or upgrade <nonformal>, looking up <nonformal>

16 emendatory, corrective; revisory, revisional; reformatory, reformative, reformational; **reformist,** reformistic, progressive, progressivist, melioristic; gradualistic, Fabian, revisionist; utopian; radical 611.20; revolutionary 859.5

17 improvable, ameliorable, corrigible, revisable, perfectible; **emendable** 396.25

393 IMPAIRMENT

NOUNS **1 impairment, damage, injury, harm,** mischief, scathe, **hurt, detriment,** loss, weakening, sickening; **worsening,** disimprovement; disablement, incapacitation; encroachment, inroad, infringement 214.1; **disrepair, dilapidation,** ruinousness; breakage; **breakdown, collapse,** crash and crack-up <both nonformal>; **malfunction,** glitch <nonformal>; bankruptcy; hurting, spoiling, ruination; sabotage, monkey-wrenching <nonformal>; mayhem, mutilation, crippling, hobbling, hamstringing, laming, maiming; destruction 395

2 corruption, pollution, contamination, vitiation, **defilement,** fouling, befouling; **poisoning,** envenoming; infection, festering, suppuration; **perversion,** prostitution, misuse 389; denaturing, adulteration

3 deterioration, decadence or decadency, **degradation, debasement,** derogation, deformation; **degeneration,** degeneracy, degenerateness, effeteness; etiolation, loss of tone, failure of nerve; depravation, depravedness; **retrogression,** retrogradation, retrocession, **regression;** devolution, involution; demotion 447; downward mobility; **decline,** declination, declension, comedown, **descent,** downtick <nonformal>, downtrend, downward trend, downturn, depreciation, **decrease** 252, **drop, fall, plunge,** free-fall, falling-off, lessening, slippage, slump, lapse, fading, dying, failing, failure, wane, ebb

4 waste, wastage, **consumption;** withering, wasting, wasting away, atrophy, wilting, marcescence; emaciation 270.6

5 wear, use, hard wear; **wear and tear;** erosion, **weathering,** ablation, ravages of time

6 **decay, decomposition, disintegration, dissolution,** resolution, degradation, bio-degradation, breakup, disorganization, **corruption, spoilage, dilapidation; corrosion,** oxidation, oxidization, rust; mildew, mold 1000.2; degradability, biodegradability

7 **rot, rottenness, foulness, putridness,** putridity, rancidness, rancidity, rankness, **putrefaction,** putrescence, spoilage, decay, decomposition; carrion; dry rot, wet rot

8 **wreck, ruins, ruin, total loss;** hulk, carcass, skeleton; mere wreck, wreck of one's former self; nervous wreck; rattletrap

VERBS 9 **impair, damage,** endamage, **injure, harm, hurt,** irritate; **worsen,** make worse, disimprove, deteriorate, put or set back, aggravate, exacerbate, embitter; **weaken; dilapidate;** add insult to injury, rub salt in the wound

10 **spoil, mar,** botch, **ruin,** wreck, blight, **play havoc with; destroy** 395.10

11 <nonformal terms> **screw up, foul up,** fuck up, bitch up, **blow,** louse up, queer, snafu, snarl up, balls up <Brit>, bugger, bugger up, gum up, ball up, bollix, bollix up, **mess up,** hash up, muck up; play hob with, play hell with, play merry hell with, play the devil with, rain on one's picnic or parade; upset the apple cart, cook, sink, shoot down in flames; **total**

12 **corrupt, debase, degrade,** degenerate, **deprave, debauch, defile,** violate, desecrate, deflower, ravish, ravage, despoil; **contaminate,** confound, **pollute, vitiate, poison, infect, taint;** canker, ulcerate; **pervert,** warp, twist, distort; prostitute, misuse 389.4; denature; **cheapen,** devalue; coarsen, vulgarize, drag in the mud; adulterate, alloy, water, water down

13 <inflict an injury> **injure, hurt;** draw blood, wound, scotch <old>; **traumatize;** stab, stick, pierce, puncture; cut, incise, slit, slash, gash, scratch; abrade, eat away at, scuff, scrape, chafe, fret, gall, bark, skin; break, fracture, rupture; crack, chip, craze, check; lacerate, claw, tear, rip, rend; run; frazzle, fray; burn, scorch, scald; mutilate, maim, rough up <nonformal>, make mincemeat of, maul, batter, savage; sprain, strain, wrench; bloody; **blemish** 1003.4; **bruise, contuse,** bung and bung up <both nonformal>; **buffet,** batter, bash <nonformal>,

maul, pound, beat, beat black and blue; give a black eye

14 **cripple, lame,** maim; **hamstring,** hobble; wing; emasculate, castrate; incapacitate, **disable** 19.9

15 **undermine,** sap, mine, sap the foundations of, honeycomb; sabotage, monkeywrench and throw or toss a monkeywrench in the works <all nonformal>, subvert

16 **deteriorate, sicken, worsen, get** or **grow worse,** get no better fast <nonformal>, disimprove, **degenerate;** slip back, **retrogress,** retrograde, regress, relapse, fall back; jump the track; go to the bad 395.24; let oneself go, let down, slacken; be the worse for, be the worse for wear and have seen better days <both nonformal>

17 **decline, sink, fail, fall,** slip, fade, die, wane, ebb, subside, lapse, **run down,** go down, **go downhill, fall away, fall off,** go off <nonformal>, slide, slump, hit a slump, take a nose dive <nonformal>, go into a tailspin, take a turn for the worse; hit the skids <nonformal>; reach the depths, hit or touch bottom, hit rock bottom, have no lower to go

18 **languish, pine, droop, flag, wilt; fade,** fade away; **wither, shrivel,** shrink, diminish, wither or die on the vine, **dry up,** desiccate, wizen, wrinkle, sear; "fall'n into the sere, the yellow leaf"—Shakespeare

19 **waste, waste away, wither away,** atrophy, consume, consume away, erode away, emaciate, pine away; trickle or dribble away; run to waste, run to seed

20 **wear, wear away, wear down, wear off;** abrade, fret, whittle away, rub off; fray, frazzle, tatter, wear ragged; **wear out;** weather, erode, ablate

21 **corrode, erode,** eat, gnaw, eat into, eat away, nibble away, gnaw at the root of; canker; **oxidize, rust**

22 **decay, decompose, disintegrate;** go or fall into decay, go or fall to pieces, break up, crumble, crumble into dust; **spoil,** corrupt, canker, **go bad; rot, putrefy,** putresce; fester, suppurate, rankle <nonformal>; **mortify,** necrose, gangrene, sphacelate; mold, molder, molder away, rot away, rust away, mildew

23 **break, break up,** fracture, **come apart,** come unstuck, **come** or **fall to pieces, fall apart, disintegrate;** burst, rupture; crack, split, fissure; snap; break open, give way or away, start, spring a leak, come apart

at the seams, come unstuck <nonformal>

24 break down, founder, collapse; crash <nonformal>, cave *or* fall in, come crashing *or* tumbling down, topple, topple down *or* over, tremble *or* nod *or* totter to one's fall; totter, sway

25 get out of order, malfunction, get out of gear; get out of joint; go wrong

26 <nonformal terms> **get out of whack,** get out of kilter, get out of commission, go kaput, **go on the blink** *or* **fritz, go haywire,** fritz out, go blooey *or* kerflooey, give out, **break down,** pack up <Brit>, conk out

ADJS **27 impaired, damaged, hurt, injured, harmed; deteriorated, worsened,** cut to the quick, aggravated, exacerbated, irritated, embittered; weakened; **worse,** worse off, the worse for, all the worse for; imperfect; lacerated, mangled, cut, split, rent, torn, slit, slashed, mutilated, chewed-up; **broken** 801.24, **shattered, smashed,** in bits, in pieces, in shards, burst, busted <nonformal>, ruptured, sprung; cracked, chipped, crazed, checked; burned, scorched, scalded; **damaging, injurious,** traumatic, degenerative

28 spoiled *or* spoilt, **marred,** botched, blighted, **ruined,** wrecked; **destroyed** 395.28

29 <nonformal terms> **queered, screwed up, fouled up,** loused up, snafued, buggered, buggered up, gummed up, snarled up, balled up, bollixed up, **messed up,** hashed up, mucked up, botched up; beat up, clapped-out <Brit>; **totaled,** kaput, finished, packed-up <Brit>, done for, cooked, sunk, shot

30 crippled, game <nonformal>, bad, handicapped, maimed; **lame, halt,** halting, hobbling, limping; knee-sprung; hamstrung; spavined; **disabled, incapacitated;** emasculated, castrated

31 worn, well-worn, deep-worn, worn-down, the worse for wear, dog-eared; timeworn; shopworn, shopsoiled <Brit>, shelfworn; worn to the stump, worn to the bone; **worn ragged,** worn to rags, worn to threads; **threadbare,** bare, sere <old>

32 shabby, shoddy, seedy, scruffy, **tacky** <nonformal>, dowdy, tatty, ratty; holey, full of holes; raggedy, raggedy-ass <nonformal>, **ragged, tattered, torn;** patchy; **frayed, frazzled;** in rags, in tatters, in shreds; **out at the elbows,** out at the heels, **down-at-heel** *or* **-heels, down-at-the-heel** *or* **-heels**

33 dilapidated, ramshackle, decrepit,

shacky, tottery, slummy <nonformal>, **tumbledown, broken-down, run-down,** in ruins, ruinous, ruined, derelict, gone to wrack and ruin, the worse for wear; **battered,** beaten up, **beat-up** <nonformal>

34 weatherworn, weather-beaten, weathered, weather-battered, weather-wasted, weather-eaten, weather-bitten, weather-scarred; eroded; **faded,** washed-out, bleached, blanched, etiolated

35 wasted, atrophied, shrunken; **withered,** sere, shriveled, wilted, wizened, dried-up, desiccated; wrinkled, wrinkled like a prune; brittle, papery, parchment; **emaciated** 270.20; starved, worn to a shadow, reduced to a skeleton, skin and bones, "worn to the bones"—Shakespeare

36 worn-out, used up <nonformal>, worn to a frazzle, frazzled, fit for the dust hole *or* wastepaper basket; **exhausted, tired,** fatigued, pooped <nonformal>, **spent,** effete, etiolated, played out, *ausgespielt* <Ger>, shotten <nonformal>, jaded, emptied, done *and* done up <both nonformal>; **run-down,** dragged-out <nonformal>, laid low, at a low ebb, in a bad way, far-gone, on one's last legs

37 in disrepair, out of order, malfunctioning, out of working order, out of condition, out of repair, inoperative; out of tune, out of gear; out of joint; **broken** 801.24

38 <nonformal terms> **out of whack** *or* **kilter** *or* kelter *or* sync *or* commission, on the fritz, fritzed, on the blink, blooey, kerflooey, haywire, wonky <Brit>

39 putrefactive, putrefacient, rotting; **septic;** saprogenic, saprogenous; saprophilous, saprophytic, saprobic

40 decayed, decomposed; spoiled, corrupt, peccant, bad, **gone bad; rotten, rotting, putrid, putrefied, foul;** putrescent, **mortified,** necrosed, necrotic, sphacelated, gangrened, gangrenous; carious; cankered, ulcerated, festering, suppurating, suppurative; rotten at *or* to the core

41 tainted, off, blown, frowy <nonformal>; **stale; sour,** soured, turned; **rank,** reechy <old>, **rancid,** strong <nonformal>, **high,** gamy

42 blighted, blasted, ravaged, despoiled; blown, **flyblown,** wormy, weevily, maggoty; **moth-eaten, worm-eaten; moldy,** moldering, **mildewed,** smutty, smutted; **musty, fusty,** frowzy *or* frowsy, frowsty <Brit>

43 corroded, eroded, eaten; **rusty,** rust-eaten, rust-worn, rust-cankered

44 corrupting, corruptive; corrosive, corroding; erosive, eroding, **damaging, injurious** 999.12; pollutive

45 **deteriorating, worsening,** disintegrating, coming apart *or* unstuck, crumbling, cracking, fragmenting, going to pieces; **decadent, degenerate,** effete; **retrogressive,** retrograde, regressive, from better to worse; **declining, sinking, failing,** failing, waning, subsiding, **slipping,** sliding, slumping; **languishing, pining,** drooping, flagging, wilting; ebbing, draining, dwindling; **wasting,** fading, fading fast, **withering,** shriveling; tabetic, marcescent

46 **on the wane, on the decline,** on the downgrade, on the downward track, on the skids <nonformal>; tottering, nodding to its fall, on the way out

47 degradable, biodegradable, decomposable, putrefiable, putrescible

ADVS 48 out of the frying pan into the fire, from better to worse; for the worse

394 RELAPSE

NOUNS 1 **relapse, lapse,** falling back; **reversion, regression** 858.1; **reverse, reversal,** backward deviation, devolution, **setback,** backset; **return,** recurrence, renewal, recrudescence; throwback, atavism

2 **backsliding,** backslide; **fall, fall from grace;** recidivism, recidivation; apostasy 363.2

3 **backslider,** recidivist, reversionist; apostate 363.5

VERBS 4 **relapse, lapse, backslide,** slide back, lapse back, **slip back,** sink back, **fall back,** have a relapse, devolve; **return to, revert to,** recur to, yield again to, fall again into, recidivate; revert, **regress** 858.4; **fall, fall from grace**

ADJS 5 **relapsing, lapsing, lapsarian, backsliding,** recidivous; recrudescent; **regressive** 858.7; apostate 363.11

395 DESTRUCTION

NOUNS 1 **destruction, ruin, ruination,** rack, **rack and ruin,** blue ruin <nonformal>; perdition, damnation, eternal damnation; universal ruin; **wreck;** devastation, ravage, havoc, holocaust, firestorm, hecatomb, carnage, shambles, slaughter, bloodbath, **desolation; waste, consumption;** decimation; **dissolution, disintegration,** breakup, disruption, disorganization, undoing, lysis; vandalism, depredation, spoliation, despoliation, despoilment; the road to ruin *or* wrack and ruin

2 **end, fate, doom,** death, death knell, bane, deathblow, death warrant, *coup de grâce* <Fr>, final blow, quietus, cutoff

3 **fall, downfall,** prostration; **overthrow, overturn, upset, upheaval,** *bouleversement* <Fr>; convulsion, **subversion,** sabotage, monkey-wrenching <nonformal>

4 **debacle, disaster, cataclysm, catastrophe; breakup,** breaking up; **breakdown, collapse; crash,** smash, **smashup,** crackup <nonformal>; **wreck,** wrack, shipwreck; cave-in, cave; washout; total loss

5 **demolition,** demolishment; wrecking, wreckage, leveling, razing, flattening, smashing, tearing down, bringing to the ground; **dismantlement,** disassembly, unmaking

6 **extinction, extermination, elimination, eradication,** extirpation; rooting out, deracination, uprooting, tearing up root and branch; **annihilation,** extinguishment, **snuffing out; abolition,** abolishment; annulment, **nullification,** voiding, **negation; liquidation, purge; suppression;** choking, choking off, suffocation, stifling, strangulation; silencing

7 **obliteration, erasure, effacement,** expunction, blot <old>, blotting, **blotting out, wiping out;** washing out *and* scrubbing <both nonformal>, cancellation, cancel; deletion

8 **destroyer, ruiner, wrecker, bane,** wiperout, demolisher; **vandal,** hun; exterminator, annihilator; **iconoclast,** idoloclast, idol breaker; biblioclast; nihilist; terrorist, syndicalist; **bomber,** dynamiter, dynamitard; burner, arsonist

9 **eradicator,** expunger; **eraser,** rubber, India rubber, sponge

VERBS 10 **destroy,** deal *or* unleash destruction, unleash the hurricane, nuke <nonformal>; **ruin,** ruinate <nonformal>, bring to ruin, lay in ruins, play *or* raise hob with; throw into disorder, upheave; **wreck,** wrack, shipwreck; damn, seal the doom of, **condemn,** confound; **devastate, desolate,** waste, **lay waste, ravage,** havoc, wreak havoc, despoil, depredate; vandalize; **decimate;** devour, consume, engorge, gobble, gobble up, swallow up; gut, gut with fire, incinerate, vaporize, ravage with fire and sword; dissolve, lyse

11 **do for, fix** <nonformal>, settle, sink, cook *and* cook one's goose *and* cut one down to size *and* cut one off at the knees *and* pull the plug on *and* pull the rug out from under <all nonformal>, dish, scuttle, put the kibosh on *and* put the skids under <both nonformal>, do in, **undo,**

knock in or on the head, poleax, torpedo, knock out, KO and banjax <both nonformal>, deal a knockout blow to, zap and shoot down and shoot down in flames <all nonformal>; break the back of; make short work of; **defeat** 412.6

12 **put an end to,** make an end of, **end, finish,** finish off <nonformal>, put paid to <Brit>, give the *coup de grâce* <Fr> to, give the quietus to, deal a deathblow to, dispose of, get rid of, do in, do away with; cut off, take off, be the death of, sound the death knell of; put out of the way, put out of existence, **slaughter,** make away with, off and waste and blow away <all nonformal>, kill off, strike down, **kill** 308.13; nip, nip in the bud or head; cut short

13 **abolish, nullify,** void, abrogate, annihilate, annul, tear up, repeal, revoke, negate, negative, invalidate, **undo, cancel,** cancel out, bring to naught, put or lay to rest

14 **exterminate, eliminate, eradicate,** deracinate, **extirpate, annihilate; wipe out** <nonformal>; cut out, root up or out, uproot, pull or pluck up by the roots, cut up root and branch, strike at the root of, lay the ax to the root of; **liquidate, purge;** remove, sweep away, wash away

15 **extinguish, quench, snuff out,** put out, stamp or trample out, trample underfoot; **smother,** choke, stifle, strangle, suffocate; silence; **suppress, quash,** squash and squelch <both nonformal>, **quell,** put down

16 **obliterate, expunge, efface, erase,** raze <old>, blot, sponge, **wipe out,** wipe off the map, rub out, **blot out,** sponge out, wash away; cancel, strike out, cross out, scratch, scratch out, rule out; bluepencil; **delete** or dele, kill

17 **demolish, wreck,** total and rack up <both nonformal>, undo, unbuild, unmake, **dismantle, disassemble; take apart, tear apart, tear asunder, rend, take** or **pull** or **pick** or **tear to pieces,** pull in pieces, tear to shreds or rags or tatters; sunder, cleave, **split; disintegrate, fragment,** break to pieces, make mincemeat of, reduce to rubble, atomize, pulverize, **smash,** shatter 801.13

18 **blow up,** blast, spring, explode, blow to pieces or bits or smithereens or kingdom come, bomb, bombard, blitz; mine; selfdestruct

19 **raze,** rase, **fell, level,** flatten, smash, prostrate, raze to the ground or dust; steamroller, bulldoze; **pull down, tear down, take down,** bring down, bring

down about one's ears, bring tumbling or crashing down, break down, throw down, cast down, beat down, knock down or over; cut down, chop down, mow down; blow down; burn down

20 **overthrow, overturn; upset,** overset, upend, **subvert,** throw down or over; undermine, honeycomb, **sap,** sap the foundations, **weaken**

21 **overwhelm,** whelm, swamp, engulf; inundate

22 <be destroyed> **fall,** fall to the ground, tumble, come tumbling or crashing down, topple, tremble or nod to its fall, bite the dust <nonformal>; **break up,** crumble, crumble to dust, disintegrate, go or fall to pieces; go by the board, go out the window or up the spout <nonformal>, go down the tube or tubes <nonformal>; self-destruct

23 **perish, expire, succumb, die, cease, end,** come to an end, go, pass, **pass away, vanish, disappear,** fade away, run out, peg or conk out <nonformal>, come to nothing or naught, be no more, be done for; be all over with, be all up with <nonformal>

24 **go to ruin, go to rack and ruin,** go to rack and manger <old>, **go to the bad,** go wrong, **go to the dogs** or **pot** <nonformal>, go or run to seed, go to hell in a handbasket <nonformal>, go to the deuce or devil <nonformal>, go to hell <nonformal>, go to the wall, go to perdition or glory <nonformal>; go up <nonformal>, go under; **go to smash,** go to shivers, go to smithereens <nonformal>

25 **drive to ruin,** drive to the bad, **force to the wall,** drive to the dogs <nonformal>, hound or harry to destruction

ADJS 26 **destructive,** destroying; **ruinous,** ruining; demolishing, demolitionary; **disastrous, calamitous, cataclysmic,** cataclysmal, **catastrophic;** fatal, fateful, doomful, baneful; bad news <nonformal>; **deadly;** consumptive, consuming, withering; **devastating, desolating,** ravaging, wasting, wasteful, spoliative, depredatory; vandalic, vandalish, vandalistic; subversive, subversionary; nihilist, nihilistic; suicidal, selfdestructive; fratricidal, internecine, internecive

27 **exterminative,** exterminatory, **annihilative, eradicative,** extirpative, extirpatory; all-destroying, all-devouring, allconsuming

28 **ruined, destroyed, wrecked, blasted, undone,** down-and-out, broken, bankrupt; spoiled; irremediable 125.15; fallen, over-

thrown; **devastated, desolated, ravaged,** blighted, wasted; ruinous, in ruins; gone to wrack and ruin

29 <nonformal terms> **shot, done for,** done in, finished, *ausgespielt* <Ger>, kaput; gone to pot, gone to the dogs, gone to hell in a handbasket, phut, belly up, blooey, kerflooey, dead in the water, washed up, all washed up, history, **dead meat, down the tube** *or* **tubes,** zapped, nuked, tapped out, wiped out

396 RESTORATION

NOUNS 1 **restoration, restitution, reestablishment, redintegration, reinstatement,** reinstation, reformation <old>, reinvestment, reinvestiture, instauration, reversion, reinstitution, reconstitution, recomposition; replacement; **rehabilitation,** redevelopment, reconversion, reactivation, reenactment; improvement 392

2 **reclamation, recovery, retrieval,** salvage, salving; redemption, salvation

3 **revival,** revivification, revivescence *or* revivescency, **renewal,** resurrection, resuscitation, restimulation, reanimation, resurgence, recrudescence; retro; **refreshment** 9; second wind; renaissance, renascence, **rebirth,** new birth; **rejuvenation,** rejuvenescence, second youth, new lease on life; **regeneration,** regeneracy, regenerateness; regenesis, palingenesis

4 **renovation, renewal;** refreshment; **redecorating; reconditioning,** furbishment, refurbishment, refurbishing; retread *and* retreading <both nonformal>; facelifting *or* face-lift; slum clearance, urban renewal

5 **reconstruction, re-creation, remaking,** recomposition, remodeling, **rebuilding,** refabrication, refashioning; reassembling, reassembly; reformation; restructuring, perestroika

6 **reparation, repair,** repairing, **fixing, mending,** making *or* setting right, repairwork; servicing, maintenance; **overhaul,** overhauling; troubleshooting <nonformal>; **rectification, correction, remedy; redress,** making *or* setting right, amends, satisfaction, compensation, **recompense**

7 **cure, curing, healing, remedy** 86; **therapy** 91

8 **recovery, rally, comeback** <nonformal>, return; **recuperation, convalescence**

9 **restorability, reparability,** curability, recoverability, reversibility, remediability,

retrievability, redeemability, salvageability, corrigibility

10 **mender, fixer,** doctor <nonformal>, restorer, renovator, repairer, **repairman, repairwoman,** maintenance man *or* woman, **serviceman, servicewoman;** trouble man *and* **troubleshooter** <both nonformal>; Mr Fixit *and* little Miss Fixit <both nonformal>; **mechanic** *or* mechanician; tinker, tinkerer; cobbler; salvor, salvager

VERBS 11 **restore, put back, replace, return,** place in *status quo ante;* **reestablish,** redintegrate, reform <old>, reenact, **reinstate,** restitute; **reinstall,** reinvest, revest, reinstitute, reconstitute, recompose, recruit, **rehabilitate,** redevelop; reintegrate, reconvert, reactivate; refill, replenish; give back 481.4

12 **redeem, reclaim, recover, retrieve;** ransom; rescue; salvage, salve; recycle; win back, **recoup**

13 **remedy, rectify, correct, right,** patch up, emend, amend, **redress,** make good *or* right, **put right,** set right, put *or* set to rights, put *or* set straight, set up, heal up, knit up, make all square; pay reparations, give satisfaction, requite, restitute, recompense, compensate, remunerate

14 **repair, mend, fix,** fix up <nonformal>, do up, doctor <nonformal>, put in repair, put in shape, set to rights, put in order *or* condition; **condition, recondition,** commission, put in commission, ready; **service, overhaul;** patch, **patch up;** tinker, tinker up, fiddle, fiddle around; cobble; sew up, darn; recap, retread

15 **cure,** work a cure, recure <old>, **remedy, heal, restore to health,** heal up, knit up, bring round *or* around, pull round *or* around, give a new *or* fresh lease on life, make better, make well, fix up, pull through, set on one's feet *or* legs; snatch from the jaws of death

16 **revive,** revivify, **renew,** recruit; **reanimate,** reinspire, **regenerate, rejuvenate, revitalize,** put *or* breathe new life into, restimulate; **refresh** 9.2; **resuscitate,** bring to, bring round *or* around; recharge; **resurrect,** bring back, call back, recall to life, raise from the dead; rewarm, warm up *or* over; **rekindle,** relight, reheat the ashes, stir the embers

17 **renovate, renew; recondition,** refit, revamp, furbish, refurbish; refresh, face-lift

18 **remake,** reconstruct, remodel, recompose, reconstitute, re-create, **rebuild,** refabricate, re-form, refashion, reassemble

19 recuperate, recruit, **gain strength**, recruit *or* renew one's strength, catch one's breath, **get better; improve** 392.7; **rally, pick up,** perk up *and* brace up <both nonformal>, take a new *or* fresh lease on life; **take a favorable turn,** turn the corner, be out of the woods, take a turn for the better; **convalesce;** sleep it off

20 recover, rally, revive, get well, get over, pull through, pull round *or* around, come round *or* around <nonformal>, come back <nonformal>, make a comeback <nonformal>; get about, get back in shape <nonformal>, be oneself again, feel like a new person; **survive,** weather the storm; **come to,** come to oneself, show signs of life; come up smiling *and* bounce back <both nonformal>, get one's second wind; come *or* pull *or* snap out of it <nonformal>

21 heal, heal over, close up, scab over, cicatrize, granulate; heal *or* right itself; **knit, set**

ADJS **22 tonic, restorative, restitutive,** restitutory, restimulative; analeptic; reparative, reparatory; remedial, **curative** 86.39

23 recuperative, recuperatory; reviviscent; **convalescent;** buoyant, resilient, elastic

24 renascent, redivivus, redux, resurrected, renewed, revived, reborn, resurgent, recrudescent, reappearing, phoenix-like

25 remediable, curable; medicable, treatable; emendable, amendable, **correctable,** rectifiable, corrigible; **improvable,** ameliorable; **reparable,** repairable, **mendable, fixable;** restorable, recoverable, salvageable, retrievable, reversible, reclaimable, recyclable, redeemable; renewable

397 PRESERVATION

NOUNS **1 preservation,** preserval, **conservation, saving, salvation,** salvage, **keeping, safekeeping,** maintenance, upkeep, support; custody, custodianship, guardianship, curatorship; protectiveness, protection 1007; conservationism, environmental conservation; nature conservation *or* conservancy, soil conservation, forest conservation, forest management, wildlife conservation, stream conservation, water conservation, wetlands conservation

2 food preservation; curing, seasoning, salting, brining, pickling, marinating, corning; **drying,** dry-curing, jerking; dehydration, anhydration, evaporation, desiccation; **smoking,** fuming, smoke-curing, kippering; **refrigeration,** freezing, quick-freezing, blast-freezing; freeze-drying, lyophilization; irradiation; **canning,** tinning <Brit>; bottling, potting

3 embalming, mummification; taxidermy, stuffing; tanning

4 preservative, preservative medium; salt, brine, vinegar, formaldehyde, formalin *or* formol, embalming fluid

5 preserver, saver, conservator, keeper, safekeeper; taxidermist; lifesaver, rescuer, deliverer, savior; **conservationist,** preservationist; National Wildlife Service, Audubon Society, Sierra Club; **ranger, forest ranger,** Smoky the Bear, fire warden, game warden

6 life preserver, life jacket, life vest, life belt, cork jacket, Mae West <nonformal>; life buoy, life ring, buoy, floating cushion; man-overboard buoy; water wings; breeches buoy; lifeboat, life raft, rubber dinghy <Brit>; life net; lifeline; safety belt; **parachute;** ejection seat *or* ejector seat, ejection capsule

7 preserve, reserve, reservation; park, paradise; national park, state park; national seashore; forest preserve *or* reserve; national *or* state forest; wilderness preserve; Indian reservation; **refuge, sanctuary** 1008.1, game preserve *or* reserve, bird sanctuary, wildlife sanctuary *or* preserve; museum, library 558, archives 549.2, bank, store 386

VERBS **8 preserve, conserve, save,** spare; **keep,** keep safe, keep inviolate *or* intact; patent, copyright, register; not endanger, not destroy; not use up, not waste, not expend; **guard, protect** 1007.18; **maintain, sustain,** uphold, support, **keep up,** keep alive

9 preserve, cure, season, salt, brine, marinate *or* marinade, pickle, corn, **dry, drycure,** jerk, dry-salt; dehydrate, anhydrate, evaporate, desiccate; vacuumpack; **smoke,** fume, **smoke-cure,** smokedry, kipper; **refrigerate,** freeze, quickfreeze, blast-freeze; freeze-dry, lyophilize; irradiate

10 embalm, mummify; stuff; tan

11 put up, do up; **can,** tin <Brit>; bottle, jar, pot

ADJS **12 preservative,** preservatory, conservative, conservatory; custodial, curatorial; **conservational,** conservationist; preserving, conserving, saving, keeping; **protective** 1007.23

13 preserved, conserved, **kept,** saved, spared; protected 1007.21; **untainted, unspoiled;** intact, all in one piece, undamaged 1001.8; **well-preserved,** well-conserved, **well-kept,** in a good state of preservation, none the worse for wear

398 RESCUE

NOUNS **1 rescue, deliverance,** delivery, **saving;** lifesaving; **extrication, release, freeing, liberation** 431; **bailout; salvation,** salvage, **redemption,** ransom; **recovery, retrieval**

  2 rescuer, lifesaver, lifeguard; coast guard, lifesaving service, air-sea rescue; savior 592.2; lifeboat; salvager, salvor

VERBS **3 rescue,** come to the rescue, **deliver, save,** be the saving of, **redeem,** ransom, **salvage; recover, retrieve** 481.6; **free,** set free, **release, extricate,** extract, **liberate** 431.4; snatch from the jaws of death; save one's bacon *and* save one's neck *or* ass *and* bail one out <all nonformal>

ADJS **4 rescuable, savable;** redeemable; deliverable, extricable; salvageable

399 WARNING

NOUNS **1 warning, caution,** caveat, **admonition,** monition, admonishment; **notice,** notification; **word to the wise,** *verbum sapienti* <L>, verb sap, enough said; **hint,** broad hint, measured words, flea in one's ear <nonformal>, little birdy <nonformal>; tip-off <nonformal>; **lesson,** object lesson, **example,** deterrent example, warning piece; moral, moral of the story; **alarm** 400; final warning *or* notice, ultimatum; **threat** 514

  2 forewarning, prewarning, **premonition,** precautioning; advance warning *or* notice, plenty of notice, prenotification; presentiment, hunch *and* funny feeling <both nonformal>, **foreboding; portent,** "warnings, and portents and evils imminent"—Shakespeare

  3 warning sign, premonitory sign, danger sign; preliminary sign *or* signal *or* token; **symptom,** early symptom, premonitory symptom, prodrome, prodroma, prodromata <pl>; **precursor** 815; **omen** 133.3,6; **handwriting on the wall,** "*mene, mene, tekel, upharsin*"—Bible <Aramaic>; straw in the wind; gathering clouds, clouds on the horizon; thundercloud, thunderhead; falling barometer *or* glass; storm *or* stormy petrel, **red light,** red flag; quarantine flag, yellow flag, yellow jack; death's-head, skull and crossbones; **high sign** <nonformal>, **warning**

signal, alert, red alert; siren, klaxon, tocsin, alarm bell

  4 warner, cautioner, admonisher, monitor; prophet *or* messenger of doom, Cassandra, Jeremiah; **lookout, lookout man; sentinel, sentry; signalman,** signaler, flagman; lighthouse keeper

VERBS **5 warn, caution, advise, admonish; give warning,** give fair warning, utter a caveat, address a warning to, put a flea in one's ear <nonformal>, have a word with one, say a word to the wise; tip *and* tip off <both nonformal>; notify, put on notice, give notice *or* advance notice *or* advance word; tell once and for all; issue an ultimatum; **threaten** 514.2; **alert,** warn against, put on one's guard, warn away *or* off; **give the high sign** <nonformal>; **put on alert,** cry havoc, sound the alarm 400.3

  6 forewarn, prewarn, precaution, premonish; prenotify, tell in advance, give advance notice; **portend, forebode**

ADJS **7 warning,** cautioning, **cautionary; monitory,** monitorial, admonitory, admonishing; notifying, notificational; exemplary, deterrent

  8 forewarning, premonitory; portentous, foreboding 133.17; **precautionary,** precautional; precursive, precursory, forerunning, prodromal, prodromic

400 ALARM

NOUNS **1 alarm,** alarum, alarm signal *or* bell, **alert;** hue and cry; **red light,** danger signal, amber light, caution signal; **alarm button,** panic button <nonformal>, nurse's signal; **beeper,** buzzer; note of alarm; air-raid alarm; all clear; tocsin, alarm bell; signal of distress, SOS, Mayday, upside-down flag, flare; *sécurité* <Fr>, notice to mariners; storm warning, storm flag *or* pennant *or* cone, hurricane watch *or* warning *or* advisory, gale warning, small-craft warning *or* advisory, tornado watch *or* warning, winterstorm watch *or* advisory, severe thunderstorm watch *or* warning; fog signal *or* alarm, foghorn, fog bell; burglar alarm; fire alarm, fire bell, fire flag, still alarm; siren, whistle, horn, klaxon, hooter <Brit>; police whistle, watchman's rattle; alarm clock; five-minute gun, two-minute gun; lighthouse, beacon; blinking light, flashing light, occulting light

  2 false alarm, cry of wolf; bugbear, bugaboo; bogy; flash in the pan *and* dud <both nonformal>

VERBS **3 alarm, alert, arouse,** put on the alert; **warn** 399.5; fly storm warnings; **sound the alarm,** give *or* raise *or* beat *or* turn in an alarm, ring *or* sound the tocsin, cry havoc, raise a hue and cry; give a false alarm, cry before one is hurt, **cry wolf;** frighten *or* scare out of one's wits *or* to death, **frighten,** startle 131.8

ADJS **4 alarmed, aroused;** alerted; frit <Brit nonformal>, frightened to death *or* out of one's wits, **frightened; startled** 131.13

401 HASTE
<rapidity of action>

NOUNS **1 haste, hurry, scurry, rush, race,** dash, drive, scuttle, scamper, **scramble,** hustle <nonformal>, **bustle,** flutter, **flurry,** hurry-scurry, helter-skelter; no time to be lost

2 hastiness, hurriedness, quickness, swiftness, expeditiousness, alacrity, promptness 330.3; **speed** 174.1,2; furiousness, feverishness; **precipitousness,** precipitance *or* precipitancy, precipitation; suddenness, abruptness; **impetuousness** 365.2, impetuosity, **impulsiveness, rashness** 493, impulsivity; eagerness, zealousness, **overeagerness, overzealousness**

3 hastening, hurrying, festination, speeding, forwarding, quickening, **acceleration;** forced march, double time, double-quick time, double-quick; fast-forward

VERBS **4 hasten,** haste, **hurry, accelerate, speed,** speed up, **hurry up,** hustle up <nonformal>, **rush,** quicken, hustle <nonformal>, bustle, bundle, precipitate, forward; **dispatch, expedite; whip,** whip along, spur, **urge** 375.14,16; push, press; crowd, stampede; **hurry on,** hasten on, drive on, hie on, push on, press on; **hurry along,** lollop <chiefly Brit>, rush along, speed along, **speed on its way; push through,** railroad through <nonformal>, steamroll

5 make haste, hasten, festinate, **hurry, hurry up, race, run,** post, **rush, chase, tear, dash,** spurt, leap, plunge, **scurry,** hurry-scurry, **scamper, scramble, scuttle, hustle** <nonformal>, bundle, **bustle;** bestir oneself, move quickly 174.9; hurry on, dash on, press *or* push on, crowd; double-time, go at the double; break one's neck *or* fall all over oneself <both nonformal>; lose no time, not lose a moment; rush through, romp through, hurry through; dash off; make short *or* fast work of, make the best of one's time *or*

way, make up for lost time; do on the run *or* on the fly

6 <nonformal terms> **step on it, snap to it,** hop to it, hotfoot, bear down on it, shake it up, **get moving** *or* **going,** get a move on, get cracking <chiefly Brit>, get *or* shake the lead out, get the lead out of one's ass, get one's ass in gear, give it the gun, hump, hump it, hump oneself, shag ass, tear ass, **get a hustle** *or* **move** *or* **wiggle on,** stir one's stumps, not spare the horses

7 rush into, plunge into, dive into, plunge, plunge ahead *or* headlong; **not stop to think,** go off half-cocked *or* at half cock <nonformal>, leap before one looks, cross a bridge before one comes to it

8 be in a hurry, be under the gun <nonformal>, have no time to lose *or* spare, not have a moment to spare, hardly have time to breathe, work against time *or* the clock, work under pressure, have a deadline

ADJS **9 hasty, hurried,** festinate, **quick,** flying, **expeditious,** prompt 330.18; quick-and-dirty <nonformal>, **immediate,** instant, on the spot; onrushing, **swift, speedy; urgent;** furious, feverish; slapbang, slapdash, **cursory,** passing, cosmetic, snap <nonformal>, **superficial;** spur-of-the-moment, last-minute

10 precipitate, precipitant, precipitous; **sudden,** abrupt; **impetuous, impulsive, rash;** headlong, breakneck; breathless, panting

11 hurried, rushed, pushed, pressed, crowded, **pressed for time,** hard-pushed *or* -pressed, hard-run; double-time, double-quick, on *or* at the double

ADVS **12 hastily, hurriedly, quickly; expeditiously,** promptly, with dispatch; all in one breath, in one word, in two words; apace, amain, hand over fist, **immediately,** instantly, in a second *or* split second *or* jiffy, at once, as soon as possible *or* ASAP; **swiftly, speedily,** on *or* at fast-forward; with haste, with great *or* all haste, in *or* with a rush, in a mad rush, at fever pitch; furiously, feverishly, in a sweat *or* lather of haste, hotfoot; by forced marches; **helter-skelter, hurry-scurry,** pellmell; slapdash, cursorily, superficially, on the run *or* fly, in passing, on the spur of the moment

13 posthaste, in posthaste; post, express; by express, by airmail, by return mail; by cable, by telegraph, by fax

14 in a hurry, in haste, in hot haste, in all haste; in short order; against time, against the clock

15 precipitately, precipitantly, precipitously, slap-bang; **suddenly,** abruptly; **impetuously, impulsively, rashly; headlong,** headfirst, headforemost, head over heels, heels over head <old>, *à corps perdu* <Fr>

INTERJS **16 make haste!,** make it quick!, **hurry up!; now!; at once!,** rush!, immediate!, **urgent!,** instanter!; **step lively!,** look alive!, on the double!

17 <nonformal terms> **step on it!,** snap to it!, **make it snappy!, get a move on!,** get a wiggle on!, **chop-chop!, shake a leg!,** stir your stumps!, get the lead out!, **get moving!, get going!,** get cracking!, get with it!, hop to it!, move your tail!, move your fanny!, get on the ball!, don't spare the horses!

402 LEISURE

NOUNS **1 leisure, ease, convenience,** freedom; retirement, semiretirement; rest, repose 20; **free time, spare time,** goof-off time <nonformal>, odd moments, idle hours; time to spare *or* burn *or* kill, time on one's hands, time at one's disposal *or* command; time, one's own sweet time <nonformal>; downtime

2 leisureliness, unhurriedness, unhastiness, hastelessness, relaxedness; *dolce far niente* <Ital>; **inactivity** 331; **slowness** 175; deliberateness, deliberation

VERBS **3 have time,** have time enough, have time to spare, have plenty of time, have nothing but time, be in no hurry

4 take one's leisure, take one's ease, **take one's time, take one's own sweet time** <nonformal>, do at one's leisure *or* convenience *or* pleasure; go slow 175.6; ride the gravy train *and* lead the life of Riley <both nonformal>

ADJS **5 leisure, leisured;** idle, unoccupied, free, open, spare; retired, semiretired

6 leisurely, unhurried, laid-back <nonformal>, unhasty, hasteless, easy, relaxed; deliberate; inactive 331.17; **slow** 175.10

ADVS **7 at leisure, at one's leisure, at one's convenience,** at one's own sweet time <nonformal>, when one gets around to it, when it is handy, when one has the time, when one has a minute to spare, when one has a moment to call one's own

INTERJS **8** easy does it!, take it easy!

403 ENDEAVOR

NOUNS **1 endeavor,** effort, striving, struggle, strain; **all-out effort,** best effort, college try *or* old college try <nonformal>; **exer-**

tion 725; determination, resolution 359; **enterprise** 330.7

2 attempt, trial, effort, essay, assay <old>, first attempt, *coup d'essai* <Fr>; **endeavor, undertaking;** approach, move; coup, stroke 328.3, step; gambit, offer, **bid,** strong bid; experiment, tentative; tentation, trial and error

3 <nonformal terms> **try, whack, fling, shot, crack,** bash, belt, go, stab, lick, rip, ripple, cut, hack, smack

4 one's best, one's level best, one's utmost, one's damndest *or* darndest <nonformal>, one's best effort *or* endeavor, the best one can, the best one knows how, all one can do, all one's got, all one's got in one, one's all <nonformal>, the top of one's bent, as much as in one lies

VERBS **5 endeavor, strive, struggle,** strain, sweat, sweat blood, labor, get one's teeth into, come to grips with, take it on, make an all-out effort, move heaven and earth, **exert oneself,** apply oneself, use some elbow grease <nonformal>; spend oneself; seek, study, aim; resolve, be determined 359.8

6 attempt, try, essay, assay, offer; try one's hand *or* wings, try it on <chiefly Brit>; **undertake** 404.3, **approach,** come to grips with, engage, take the bull by the horns; venture, venture on *or* upon, chance; **make an attempt** *or* **effort,** lift a finger *or* hand

7 <nonformal terms> **tackle, take on, make a try, give a try,** have a go <chiefly Brit>, take a shot *or* stab *or* crack *or* try *or* whack at; try on for size, **go for it,** go for the brass ring, **have a fling** *or* **go at,** give a fling *or* a go *or* a whirl, **make a stab at,** have a shot *or* stab *or* crack *or* try *or* whack at

8 try to, try and <nonformal>, **attempt to, endeavor to,** strive to, seek to, study to, aim to, venture to, dare to, pretend to

9 try for, strive for, strain for, struggle for, contend for, pull for <nonformal>, bid for, make a bid *or* strong bid for, make a play for <nonformal>

10 see what one can do, see what can be done, see if one can do, do what one can, use one's endeavor; try anything once; **try one's hand,** try one's luck; make a cautious *or* tentative move, experiment, feel one's way, test the waters

11 make a special effort, go out of the way, go out of one's way, take special pains, **put oneself out,** put oneself out of the way, lay oneself out *and* fall *or* bend *or* lean over backward <all nonformal>, fall all over oneself, trouble oneself, **go to the trouble,** take trouble, **take pains,** redouble one's efforts

12 **try hard, push** <nonformal>, make a bold push, **put one's back to** or **into,** put one's heart into, try until one is blue in the face, die trying, **try and try;** try, try again; exert oneself 725.9

13 **do one's best** or **level best, do one's utmost,** try one's best or utmost, **do all** or **everything one can,** do the best one can, **do the best one knows how,** do all in one's power, do as much as in one lies, do what lies in one's power; put all one's strength into, put one's whole soul in, **strain every nerve; give it one's all;** be on one's mettle, **die trying**

14 <nonformal terms> **knock oneself out, break one's neck,** break or bust one's balls, bust a gut, bust one's ass or hump, rupture oneself, do it or know why not, do it or break a leg, do it or bust a gut, do or try one's damndest or darndest, go all out, go the limit, go for broke, shoot the works, give it all one's got, give it one's best shot, go for it

15 **make every effort, spare no effort** or **pains, go all lengths, go to great lengths,** go the whole length, go through fire and water, not rest, not relax, not slacken, move heaven and earth, leave no stone unturned, leave no avenue unexplored

ADJS 16 trial, tentative, experimental; venturesome, willing; determined, resolute 359.11; utmost, damndest

ADVS 17 **out for,** out to, trying for, **on the make** <nonformal>

18 **at the top of one's bent,** to one's utmost, as far as possible

404 UNDERTAKING

NOUNS 1 **undertaking, enterprise, operation,** work, **venture, project,** proposition and deal <both nonformal>; **program, plan** 381; **affair, business, matter, task** 724.2, concern, interest; **initiative,** effort, attempt 403.2; **action** 328.3; **engagement, contract, obligation, commitment** 436.2; démarche <Fr>

2 **adventure,** emprise, **mission;** quest, pilgrimage; expedition, exploration

VERBS 3 **undertake, assume,** accept, **take on, take upon oneself,** take in hand, take upon one's shoulders, take up, go with, **tackle,** attack; engage or contract or obligate or commit oneself; **put** or **set** or **turn one's hand to, engage in, devote oneself to, apply oneself to,** betake oneself to

<old>, address oneself to, give oneself up to; join oneself to, associate oneself with, **come aboard** <nonformal>; busy oneself with 724.11; **take up,** move into, go into, **go in** or **out for** <nonformal>, **enter on** or **upon,** proceed to, embark in or upon, **venture upon,** go upon, launch forth, set forward, get going, get under way; set about, go about, lay about, go to do; **go** or **swing into action, set to, turn to, buckle to, fall to; pitch into** <nonformal>, plunge into, fall into, **launch into** or **upon;** go at, set at, have at <nonformal>, knuckle or buckle down to; put one's hand to the plow, put or lay one's shoulder to the wheel; take the bull by the horns; **endeavor, attempt**

4 **have in hand, have one's hands in,** have on one's hands or shoulders

5 **be in progress** or **process,** be on the anvil, be in the fire, be in the works or hopper or pipeline <nonformal>, **be under way**

6 **bite off more than one can chew** <nonformal>, overextend or overreach oneself, have too many irons in the fire, have too much on one's plate

ADJS 7 **undertaken, assumed,** accepted, **taken on** <nonformal>; **ventured,** attempted, chanced; **in hand,** on the anvil, in the fire, **in progress** or **process,** on one's plate, in the works or hopper or pipeline <nonformal>, on the agenda, **under way**

8 **enterprising,** venturesome, adventurous, plucky, keen, eager

405 PREPARATION

NOUNS 1 **preparation,** preparing, prep and prepping <both nonformal>, **readying,** getting or making ready, makeready; warm-up, getting in shape or condition; mobilization; walk-up, **run-up; prearrangement** 964, lead time, advance notice, warning, advance warning, alerting; **planning** 381.1; trial, dry run, **tryout** 941.3; **provision, arrangement;** preparatory or preliminary act or measure or step; **preliminary, preliminaries;** clearing the decks <nonformal>; **grounding,** propaedeutic, preparatory study or instruction; basic training, familiarization, briefing; prerequisite; processing, treatment, pretreatment; equipment 385; training 568.3; manufacture; **spadework,** groundwork, foundation 900.6

2 **fitting,** checking the fit, fit; **conditioning; adaptation, adjustment,** tuning; **qualification,** capacitation, enablement; **equipment, furnishing** 385.1

3 <a preparation> **concoction,** decoction, *decoctum* <L>, brew, **confection; composition, mixture** 796.5, combination 804

4 preparedness, readiness; fitness, fittedness, suitedness, suitableness, **suitability;** condition, trim; **qualification,** qualifiedness, credentials, record, track record <nonformal>; **competence** or competency, **ability, capability, proficiency,** mastery; ripeness, maturity, seasoning, tempering

5 preparer, preparator, preparationist; trainer, coach, instructor, mentor, teacher; **trailblazer, pathfinder; forerunner** 815.1; **paver of the way**

VERBS **6 prepare, make** or **get ready,** prep <nonformal>, trim <old>, **ready, fix** <nonformal>; provide <old>, **arrange; make preparations** or **arrangements,** sound the note of preparation, clear the decks <nonformal>, clear for action, settle preliminaries, tee up <nonformal>; mobilize, marshal, deploy, marshal or deploy one's forces or resources; **prearrange; plan; try out** 941.8; fix or ready up <both nonformal>, put in or into shape; dress; treat, pretreat, process; cure, tan, taw

7 make up, get up, fix up and rustle up <both nonformal>; **concoct,** decoct, brew; **compound, compose, put together, mix;** make

8 fit, condition, adapt, adjust, suit, tune, attune, put in tune or trim or working order; **qualify,** enable, capacitate; **equip, furnish** 385.7,8

9 prime, load, charge, cock, set; wind, wind up; steam up, get up steam, warm up

10 prepare to, get ready to, get set for <nonformal>, fix to <nonformal>; be about to, be on the point of; ready oneself to, hold oneself in readiness

11 prepare for, provide for, arrange for, make arrangements or dispositions for, look to, look out for, see to, **make provision** or **due provision for;** provide against, make sure against, forearm, **provide for** or **against a rainy day,** prepare for the evil day; lay in provisions, lay up a store, keep as a nest egg, save to fall back upon, lay by, husband one's resources, salt or squirrel something away; set one's house in order

12 prepare the way, pave the way, smooth the path or road, **clear the way,** open the way, open the door to; **break the ice;** go in advance, be the point, **blaze the trail; prepare the ground,** cultivate the soil, sow

the seed; do the spadework, lay the groundwork or foundation, lay the first stone; lead up to

13 prepare oneself, brace oneself, **get ready, get set** <nonformal>, put one's house in order, strip for action, get into shape or condition, roll up one's sleeves, spit on one's hands, limber up, warm up, flex one's muscles, gird up one's loins, buckle on one's armor, get into harness, shoulder arms; sharpen one's tools, whet the knife or sword; **run up to,** build up to, gear up, tool up

14 be prepared, be ready, stand by, stand ready, hold oneself in readiness, keep one's powder dry, "put your trust in God, my boys, and keep your powder dry"—Cromwell

15 <be fitted> **qualify, measure up,** meet the requirements, check out <nonformal>, have the credentials or qualifications or prerequisites; be up to *and* be just the ticket *and* fill the bill <all nonformal>

ADJS **16 prepared, ready,** well-prepared, prepped <nonformal>, in readiness or ready state, all ready, good and ready, prepared and ready; psyched or pumped up <nonformal>, eager, keen, champing at the bit; alert, vigilant 339.13; **ripe, mature; set** *and* **all set** <both nonformal>, on the mark *and* teed up <nonformal>; about to, fixing to <nonformal>; **prearranged; planned; primed,** loaded, cocked, **loaded for bear** <nonformal>; familiarized, briefed, informed, put into the picture <Brit nonformal>; groomed, coached; ready for anything, "prepared for either course"—Vergil; in the saddle, booted and spurred; armed and ready, in arms, up in arms, **armed** 460.14; in battle array, mobilized; **provided, equipped** 385.13; dressed; treated, pretreated, processed; cured, tanned, tawed; **readied,** available 221.12

17 fitted, adapted, adjusted, suited; qualified, fit, competent, able, capable, proficient; checked out <nonformal>; well-qualified, well-fitted, well-suited

18 prepared for, ready for, alert for, set or all set for <nonformal>; loaded for, primed for; up for <nonformal>; equal to, up to

19 ready-made, ready-formed, ready-mixed, ready-furnished, ready-dressed, ready-cooked; ready-built, prefabricated, prefab <nonformal>, preformed; ready-to-wear, ready-for-wear, off-the-rack; ready-cut, cut-and-dried or cut-and-dry

20 preparatory, preparative; propaedeutic; prerequisite; provident, provisional

ADJS, ADVS **21 in readiness, in store, in reserve;** in anticipation

22 in preparation, in course of preparation, **in progress** *or* **process,** under way, **going on,** in embryo, **in production,** on stream, under construction, **in the works** *or* hopper *or* pipeline <nonformal>, on the way, **in the making, in hand,** on the anvil, on the fire, in the oven; under revision; brewing, forthcoming

23 afoot, on foot, afloat, astir

PREPS **24 in preparation for,** against, for; in order to; ready for, set for *and* fixing to <both nonformal>

406 UNPREPAREDNESS

NOUNS **1 unpreparedness, unreadiness,** unprovidedness, nonpreparedness, nonpreparation, lack of preparation; vulnerability 1005.4; extemporaneousness, improvisation, ad lib <nonformal>, planlessness; **unfitness,** unfittedness, unsuitedness, unsuitableness, **unsuitability, unqualifiedness,** unqualification, lack of credentials, poor track record <nonformal>, **disqualification,** incompetence *or* incompetency, incapability

2 improvidence, thriftlessness, unthriftiness, poor husbandry, lax stewardship; **shiftlessness,** fecklessness, thoughtlessness, heedlessness; happy-go-luckiness; hastiness 401.2; negligence 340.1

3 <raw or original condition> **naturalness,** inartificiality; **natural state,** nature, **state of nature,** nature in the raw; pristineness, intactness, virginity; natural man, "unaccommodated man"—Shakespeare; artlessness 416

4 undevelopment, nondevelopment; **immaturity,** immatureness, callowness, unfledgedness, cubbishness, **rawness, unripeness, greenness; unfinish,** unfinishedness, unpolishedness, **unrefinement, uncultivation; crudity,** crudeness, **rudeness, coarseness,** roughness, the rough; **oversimplification,** oversimplicity, simplism, reductionism

5 raw material; crude, crude stuff <nonformal>; ore, rich ore, rich vein; unsorted *or* unanalyzed mass; rough diamond, **diamond in the rough;** unlicked cub; **virgin soil**

VERBS **6 be unprepared** *or* **unready,** not be ready; go off half-cocked *or* at half cock <nonformal>; be taken unawares *or* aback, be blindsided <nonformal>, be caught napping, be caught with one's pants down <nonformal>, be surprised; **extemporize,** improvise, ad-lib *and* play by ear <both nonformal>; have no plan, be innocent of forethought

7 make no provision, take no thought of tomorrow *or* the morrow, seize the day, *carpe diem* <L, Horace>, let tomorrow take care of itself, live for the day, live like the grasshopper, live from hand to mouth; "eat, drink, and be merry"—Bible

ADJS **8 unprepared, unready,** unprimed; surprised, caught short, caught napping, caught with one's pants down <nonformal>, taken by surprise, taken aback, taken unawares, blindsided <nonformal>, caught off balance, caught off base <nonformal>, tripped up; **unarranged,** unorganized, haphazard; makeshift, rough-and-ready, **extemporaneous,** extemporized, improvised, ad-lib *and* off the top of one's head <both nonformal>; impromptu, snap <nonformal>; **unmade,** unmanufactured, unconcocted, unhatched, uncontrived, undevised, unplanned, unpremeditated, undeliberated, unstudied; hasty, precipitate 401.10; unbegun

9 unfitted, unfit, ill-fitted, **unsuited, unadapted, unqualified,** disqualified, incompetent, incapable; **unequipped, unfurnished,** unarmed, ill-equipped, ill-furnished, **unprovided,** ill-provided 991.12

10 raw, crude; uncooked, unbaked, unboiled; underdone, undercooked, rare, red

11 immature, unripe, underripe, unripened, impubic, **raw, green,** callow, wet behind the ears, cub, cubbish, unfledged, fledgling, unseasoned, unmellowed; ungrown, half-grown, adolescent, juvenile, puerile, boyish, girlish; undigested, ill-digested; half-baked <nonformal>; half-cocked *and* at half cock <both nonformal>

12 undeveloped, unfinished, unlicked, unformed; unfashioned, unwrought, unlabored, unworked, unprocessed, untreated; unblown; uncut, unhewn; **underdeveloped;** backward, arrested, stunted; **crude, rude, coarse, unpolished, unrefined; uncultivated, uncultured; rough,** roughcast, roughhewn, **in the rough; rudimentary,** rudimental; embryonic, in embryo, fetal, *in ovo* <L>; **oversimple, simplistic,** reductive, reductionistic

13 <in the raw or original state> **natural,**

native, in a state of nature, in the raw; in-artificial, artless 416.5; virgin, virginal, pristine, untouched, unsullied

14 **fallow,** untilled, uncultivated, unsown

15 **improvident, prodigal,** unproviding; **thriftless, unthrifty,** uneconomical; grasshopper; hand-to-mouth; **shiftless, feckless, thoughtless, heedless;** happy-go-lucky; negligent 340.10

407 ACCOMPLISHMENT
<act of accomplishing; entire performance>

NOUNS 1 **accomplishment, achievement, fulfillment, performance, execution, effectuation,** implementation, carrying out *or* through, **discharge, dispatch, consummation, realization, attainment,** production, fruition; **success** 409; track record *or* track <nonformal>; *fait accompli* <Fr>, accomplished fact, done deal <nonformal>; mission accomplished

2 **completion,** completing, **finish,** finishing, **conclusion, end,** ending, **termination,** terminus, **close, windup** <nonformal>, rounding off *or* out, topping off, wrapping up, wrap-up, finalization; **perfection,** culmination 1001.3; ripeness, maturity, maturation, full development

3 **finishing touch,** final touch, last touch, last stroke, final *or* finishing stroke, finisher <nonformal>, icing the cake, the icing on the cake; copestone, capstone, crown, crowning of the edifice; capper <nonformal>, climax 198.2

VERBS 4 **accomplish, achieve, effect, effectuate, compass, consummate, do, execute, produce, deliver, make,** enact, **perform, discharge, fulfill, realize, attain,** run with *and* hack *and* swing <all nonformal>; **work,** work out; **dispatch, dispose of,** knock off <nonformal>, polish off <nonformal>, take care of <nonformal>, **deal with,** put away, make short work of; succeed, manage 409.12; come through *and* do the job <both nonformal>, **do** *or* **turn the trick** <nonformal>

5 **bring about, bring to pass,** bring to effect, bring to a happy issue; **implement, carry out, carry through,** carry into execution; **bring off, carry off, pull off** <nonformal>; **put through,** get through, **put over** *or* **across** <nonformal>; come through with <nonformal>

6 **complete, perfect, finish, finish off, conclude, terminate, end,** bring to a close, carry to completion, prosecute to a conclusion; **get through, get done;** come off

of, get through with, get it over, get it over with, **finish up;** clean up *and* wind up *and* button up *and* sew up *and* wrap up *and* mop up <all nonformal>, close up *or* out; put the lid on *and* call it a day <both nonformal>; **round off** *or* **out, wind up** <nonformal>, **top off;** top out, crown, cap 198.9; climax, culminate; **give the finishing touches** *or* **strokes,** put the finishing touches *or* strokes on, lick *or* whip into shape, finalize, put the icing on the cake

7 **do to perfection, do up brown** <nonformal>, **do to a turn,** do to a T *or* to a frazzle *or* down to the ground <nonformal>, not do by halves, do oneself proud <nonformal>, use every trick in the book, leave no loose ends, leave nothing hanging; go all lengths, go to all lengths, go the whole length *or* way, go the limit *and* go whole hog *and* go all out *and* shoot the works *and* go for broke <all nonformal>

8 **ripen,** ripe <nonformal>, **mature,** maturate; bloom, blow, blossom, flourish; come to fruition, bear fruit; **mellow;** grow up, reach maturity, reach its season; come *or* draw to a head; bring to maturity, bring to a head

ADJS 9 **completing,** completive, completory, **finishing,** consummative, culminating, terminative, conclusive, **concluding,** fulfilling, finalizing, crowning; ultimate, **last, final,** terminal

10 **accomplished, achieved, effected,** effectuated, implemented, **consummated, executed, discharged, fulfilled, realized,** compassed, **attained; dispatched, disposed of,** set at rest; wrought, wrought out

11 **completed, done, finished, concluded, terminated, ended,** finished up; signed, sealed, and delivered; cleaned up *and* wound up *and* sewed *or* sewn up *and* wrapped up *and* mopped up <all nonformal>; washed up <nonformal>, **through,** done with; all over with, all said and done, all over but the shouting; perfective

12 **complete, perfect, consummate,** polished; exhaustive, thorough 793.10; fully realized

13 **ripe, mature,** matured, maturated, seasoned; blooming, abloom; **mellow,** full-grown, fully developed

ADVS 14 **to completion,** to the end, to the full, to the limit; to a turn, to a T <nonformal>, to a finish, to a frazzle <nonformal>

408 NONACCOMPLISHMENT

NOUNS **1 nonaccomplishment, nonachievement, nonperformance,** inexecution, non-
execution, nondischarging, **noncompletion,** nonconsummation, nonfulfillment,
unfulfillment; nonfeasance, omission; **neglect** 340; loose ends, rough edges; endless task, work of Penelope, Sisyphean
labor *or* toil *or* task; **disappointment**
132; **failure** 410

VERBS **2** neglect, leave undone 340.7, fail
410.8–10,13; be disappointed 132.4

ADJS **3 unaccomplished, unachieved, unperformed,** unexecuted, undischarged, unfulfilled, unconsummated, unrealized,
unattained; **unfinished, uncompleted, undone;** open-ended; **neglected** 340.14;
disappointed 132.5

409 SUCCESS

NOUNS **1 success, successfulness,** fortunate
outcome, prosperous issue, favorable termination; **prosperity** 1009; accomplishment 407; **victory** 411

2 sure success, foregone conclusion, surefire proposition <nonformal>; **winner**
and **natural** <both nonformal>; shoo-in
and **sure thing** *and* sure bet *and* **cinch** *and*
lead-pipe cinch <all nonformal>

3 great success, triumph, resounding triumph, brilliant success, striking success,
meteoric success; **stardom; success story;**
brief *or* momentary success, nine days'
wonder, flash in the pan, fad; best seller

4 <nonformal terms> **smash, hit,** smash
hit, gas, gasser, blast, boffo, showstopper,
barn-burner, howling *or* roaring success,
one for the book, wow, wowser, sensation, overnight sensation, sensaysh,
phenom, sockeroo

5 score, hit, bull's-eye; goal, touchdown;
slam, grand slam; strike; hole, hole in
one; home run, homer <nonformal>

6 <successful person> **winner,** star, star in
the firmament, success, superstar *and*
megastar <both nonformal>; phenom
and comer <both nonformal>; **victor**
411.2

VERBS **7 succeed, prevail,** be successful, be
crowned with success, meet with success,
do very well, do famously, deliver, come
through *and* make a go of it <both non-
formal>; **go, come off,** go off; **prosper**
1009.7; fare well, work well, do *or* work

wonders, go to town *or* go great guns
<both nonformal>; **make a hit** <nonfor-
mal>, click *and* connect <both nonfor-
mal>, **catch on** *and* take <both nonfor-
mal>, catch fire, have legs <nonformal>;
go over *and* go over big *or* with a bang
<all nonformal>; pass, graduate, qual-
ify, win one's spurs *or* wings, get one's
credentials, be blooded; pass with flying
colors

8 achieve one's purpose, gain one's end *or*
ends, secure one's object, attain one's objective, do what one set out to do, reach
one's goal, bring it off, pull it off *and* hack
it *and* swing it <all nonformal>; make
one's point; play it *or* handle it just right
<nonformal>, not put a foot wrong, play
it like a master

9 score a success, score, notch one up
<nonformal>, hit it, hit the mark, ring
the bell <nonformal>, turn up trumps,
break the bank *or* make a killing <both
nonformal>, hit the jackpot <nonfor-
mal>

**10 make good, come through, achieve suc-
cess,** make a success, have a good thing
going <nonformal>, **make it** <nonfor-
mal>, get into the zone *or* bubble
<nonformal>, wing *and* cruise, <both
nonformal>, hit one's stride, **make one's
mark, give a good account of oneself,**
bear oneself with credit, do all right by
oneself *and* **do oneself proud,** make out
like a bandit <all nonformal>; **advance,
progress,** make one's way, make headway, **get on,** come on <nonformal>, **get
ahead** <nonformal>; go places, **go far;**
rise, **rise in the world,** work one's way up,
step up, come *or* move up in the world,
claw *or* scrabble one's way up, mount the
ladder of success, pull oneself up by one's
bootstraps; **arrive,** get there <nonfor-
mal>, make the scene <nonformal>;
come out on top, come out on top of the
heap <nonformal>; **be a success,** have it
made *or* hacked *or* wrapped up <nonfor-
mal>, have the world at one's feet, eat *or*
live high on the hog <nonformal>; **make
a noise in the world** <nonformal>, cut a
swath, set the world *or* river *or* Thames
on fire; break through, score *or* make a
breakthrough

11 succeed with, crown with success; **make
a go of it; accomplish,** compass, **achieve**
407.4; **bring off, carry off, pull off** <non-
formal>, turn *or* do the trick <nonfor-
mal>, **put through,** bring through; **put
over** *or* **across** <nonformal>; get away
with it *and* get by <both nonformal>

12 manage, contrive, succeed in; make out, get on *or* **along** <nonformal>, come on *or* along <nonformal>, go on; **scrape along,** worry along, **muddle through** <Brit>, get by, **manage somehow; make it** <nonformal>, **make the grade,** cut the mustard *and* hack it <both nonformal>; **clear,** clear the hurdle; **negotiate** <nonformal>, **engineer; swing** <nonformal>, put over <nonformal>, put through

13 win through, win out <nonformal>, come through <nonformal>, rise to the occasion, beat the game *and* beat the system <both nonformal>; **triumph** 411.3; weather out, **weather the storm,** live through, keep one's head above water; come up fighting *or* smiling, not know when one is beaten, persevere 360.2

ADJS **14 successful,** succeeding, crowned with success; **prosperous,** fortunate 1009.14; **triumphant;** ahead of the game, out in front, on top, sitting on top of the world *and* sitting pretty <both nonformal>, on top of the heap <nonformal>; assured of success, surefire, made; coming *and* on the up-and-up <both nonformal>

ADVS **15 successfully,** swimmingly <nonformal>, well, to some purpose, to good purpose; beyond all expectation, beyond one's fondest dreams, from rags to riches, with flying colors

410 FAILURE

NOUNS **1 failure, unsuccessfulness,** unsuccess, successlessness, nonsuccess; no go <nonformal>; ill success; futility, uselessness 391; **defeat** 412; losing game, **no-win situation;** "lame and impotent conclusion"—Shakespeare; nonaccomplishment 408; **bankruptcy** 625.3

2 <nonformal terms> **flop,** flopperoo, megaflop, gigaflop, **bust,** frost, **fizzle,** lemon, clinker, dud, non-starter, **loser, washout,** turkey, bomb, flat failure, dull thud, total loss

3 collapse, crash, smash, comedown, breakdown, derailment, **fall,** pratfall <nonformal>, stumble, tumble, **downfall,** cropper <chiefly Brit nonformal>; nose dive *and* tailspin <both nonformal>; deflation, bursting of the bubble, letdown, **disappointment** 132

4 miss, near-miss; **slip, slipup** <nonformal>, slip 'twixt cup and lip; **error, mistake** 974.3

5 abortion, miscarriage, miscarrying, abortive attempt, vain attempt; wild-goose chase, merry chase; **misfire, flash in the pan,** wet squib, malfunction, glitch <nonformal>; **dud** <nonformal>; **flunk** <nonformal>, **washout** <nonformal>

6 fiasco, botch, botch-up, cock-up *and* balls-up <both Brit nonformal>, bungle, hash, mess, muddle, foozle *and* bollix *and* bitch-up *and* screw-up *and* fuck-up <all nonformal>

7 <unsuccessful person> **failure,** flash in the pan; bankrupt 625.4

8 <nonformal terms> **loser, non-starter,** born loser, **flop,** washout, false alarm, **dud,** also-ran, bum, dull tool, bust, schlemiel, turkey

VERBS **9 fail,** be unsuccessful, fail of success, not work *and* not come off <both nonformal>, come to grief, **lose,** not make the grade, be found wanting, not come up to the mark; not pass, **flunk** *and* **flunk out** <both nonformal>; go to the wall, **go on the rocks;** labor in vain 391.8; come away empty-handed; tap out <nonformal>, go bankrupt 625.7

10 <nonformal terms> **lose out,** get left, **not make it,** not hack it, not get to first base, drop the ball, go for a Burton *and* come a cropper <both Brit>, **flop,** flummox, fall flat on one's ass, lay an egg, go over like a lead balloon, draw a blank, bomb, drop a bomb; fold, fold up; take it on the chin, take the count; crap out; strike out, fan, whiff

11 sink, founder, go down, go under <nonformal>; **slip,** go downhill, be on the skids <nonformal>

12 fall, fall down <nonformal>, fall *or* drop by the wayside, fall flat, fall flat on one's face; fall down on the job <nonformal>; **fall short, fall through,** fall to the ground; fall between two stools; **fall dead; collapse,** fall in; **crash,** go to smash <nonformal>

13 come to nothing, hang up *and* get nowhere <both nonformal>; **poop out** *and* go phut <both nonformal>; be all over *or* up with; fail miserably *or* ignominiously; fizz out *and* fizzle *and* fizzle out *and* peter out *and* poop out <all nonformal>; **misfire,** flash in the pan, hang fire; **blow up, blow up in one's face, explode, end** *or* **go up in smoke,** go up like a rocket and come down like a stick

14 miss, miss the mark, miss one's aim; slip, slip up <nonformal>; goof <nonformal>, blunder, foozle <nonformal>, **err** 974.9; **botch, bungle** 414.11,12; waste one's effort, run around in circles, spin one's wheels

15 miscarry, abort, be stillborn, die aborning; **go amiss,** go astray, **go wrong,** go on a wrong tack, take a wrong turn, derail, go off the rails

16 stall, stick, die, go dead, **conk out** <nonformal>, sputter and stop, run out of gas *or* steam, come to a shuddering halt, come to a dead stop

17 flunk *or* **flunk out** <both nonformal>; **fail,** pluck *and* plough <both Brit nonformal>, bust *and* wash out <both nonformal>

ADJS **18 unsuccessful,** successless, failing; failed, *manqué* <Fr>, stickit <Scots>; **unfortunate** 1010.14; **abortive,** miscarrying, miscarried, stillborn, died aborning; fruitless, bootless, no-win <nonformal>, futile, useless 391.9; lame, **ineffectual,** ineffective, inefficacious, of no effect; malfunctioning, glitchy <nonformal>

ADVS **19 unsuccessfully,** successlessly, **without success;** fruitlessly, bootlessly, ineffectually, ineffectively, inefficaciously, lamely; to little *or* no purpose, **in vain**

411 VICTORY

NOUNS **1 victory, triumph, conquest,** subduing, subdual; a feather in one's cap <nonformal>; total victory, grand slam; **championship,** crown, laurels, cup, trophy, belt, blue ribbon, first prize; V-for-victory sign *or* V-sign, raised arms; victory lap; **winning,** win <nonformal>; knockout *or* KO <nonformal>; easy victory, walkover *and* walkaway <both nonformal>, pushover *and* picnic <both nonformal>; runaway victory, laugher *and* romp *and* shellacking <all nonformal>; landslide victory, landslide; Pyrrhic victory, Cadmean victory; moral victory; winning streak <nonformal>; winning ways, triumphalism; **success** 409; ascendancy 417.6; mastery 612.2

2 victor, winner, victress, victrix, triumpher; **conqueror,** defeater, **vanquisher,** subduer, subjugator, *conquistador* <Sp>; top dog <nonformal>; master, master of the situation; hero, conquering hero; champion, champ *and* number one <both nonformal>; easy winner, sure winner, shoo-in <nonformal>; pancratiast; runner-up

VERBS **3 triumph, prevail, be victorious,** come out ahead, come out on top <nonformal>, clean up, chain victory to one's car; **win, gain, capture, carry;** win out <nonformal>, **win through,** carry it,

carry off *or* away; **win** *or* **carry** *or* **gain the day,** win the battle, come out first, finish in front, make a killing <nonformal>, remain in possession of the field; get *or* have the last laugh; **win the prize,** win the palm *or* bays *or* laurels, bear the palm, take the cake <nonformal>, win one's spurs *or* wings; fluke *and* win by a fluke <both nonformal>; **win by a nose** *and* nose out *and* edge out <all nonformal>; **succeed;** break the record, set a new mark <nonformal>

4 win hands down *and* win going away <both nonformal>, win in a canter *and* walk *and* waltz <all nonformal>, romp *or* breeze *or* waltz home <all nonformal>, **walk off** *or* **away with,** waltz off with <nonformal>, walk off with the game, **walk over** <nonformal>; have the game in one's own hands, have it all one's way; **take** *or* **carry by storm,** sweep aside all obstacles, carry all before one, make short work of

5 defeat 412.6, **triumph over, prevail over,** best, get the best of <nonformal>, **beat** <nonformal>, **get the better** *or* **best of;** surmount, overcome, outmatch, rise above

6 gain the ascendancy, come out on top <nonformal>, **get the advantage, gain the upper** *or* **whip hand,** dominate the field, get the edge on *or* jump on *or* drop on <nonformal>, get a leg up on <nonformal>, get a stranglehold on

ADJS **7 victorious, triumphant,** triumphal, **winning, prevailing;** conquering, vanquishing, defeating, overcoming; ahead of the game, ascendant, in the ascendant, in ascendancy, sitting on top of the world *and* sitting pretty <both nonformal>, dominant 612.18; successful; flushed with success *or* victory

8 undefeated, unbeaten, unvanquished, unconquered, unsubdued, unquelled, unbowed

ADVS **9 triumphantly,** victoriously, **in triumph;** by a mile

412 DEFEAT

NOUNS **1 defeat; beating,** drubbing, thrashing; clobbering *and* hiding *and* lathering *and* whipping *and* lambasting *and* trimming *and* licking <all nonformal>, trouncing; **vanquishment, conquest, conquering,** mastery, subjugation, subduing, subdual; **overthrow,** overturn, overcoming; **fall, downfall,** collapse, smash, crash, **undoing, ruin,** debacle, derailing, derailment; **destruction** 395; deathblow, quietus; Waterloo; failure 410

2 **discomfiture, rout, repulse,** rebuff; **frustration,** bafflement, confusion; **checkmate,** check, balk, foil <old>; **reverse,** reversal, **setback**

3 **utter defeat,** total defeat, overwhelming defeat, crushing defeat, smashing defeat, decisive defeat; no contest; **smearing** *and* **pasting** *and* creaming *and* **clobbering** *and* **shellacking** *and* whopping *and* whomping <all nonformal>; whitewash *or* **whitewashing** <nonformal>, **shutout**

4 **ignominious defeat,** abject defeat, inglorious defeat, disastrous defeat, utter rout, bitter defeat, stinging defeat, embarrassing defeat

5 **loser,** defeatee <nonformal>; the vanquished; good loser, game loser, sport *or* **good sport** <nonformal>; poor sport, poor loser; **underdog, also-ran;** booby *and* duck <both nonformal>; stooge *and* fall guy <both nonformal>; victim 96.11

VERBS 6 **defeat, worst, best, get the better** *or* **best of,** be too good for, be too much for, be more than a match for; **outdo,** outgeneral, outmaneuver, outclass, outshine, outpoint, outsail, outrun, outfight, etc; **triumph over; knock on the head,** deal a deathblow to, put *hors de combat;* undo, ruin, destroy 395.10; beat by a nose *and* nose out *and* edge out <all nonformal>

7 **overcome,** surmount; **overpower, overmaster,** overmatch; **overthrow, overturn,** overset; put the skids to <nonformal>; **upset,** trip, trip up, lay by the heels, send flying *or* sprawling; silence, floor, deck, make bite the dust; overcome oneself, master oneself; kick the habit <nonformal>

8 **overwhelm,** whelm, snow under <nonformal>, overbear, defeat utterly, deal a crushing *or* smashing defeat; **discomfit, rout, put to rout,** put to flight, scatter, stampede, panic; confound; put out of court

9 <nonformal terms> **clobber, trim, skin alive, beat,** skunk, drub, massacre, marmelize <Brit nonformal>, lick, whip, thrash, knock off, trim, hide, cut to pieces, run rings *or* circles around, throw for a loss, lather, trounce, **lambaste,** skin alive; fix, settle, settle one's hash, make one say 'uncle,' do in, lick to a frazzle, beat all hollow, beat one's brains out, cook one's goose, make hamburger *or* mincemeat out of, mop up the floor with, sandbag, banjax, bulldoze, steamroller,

smear, paste, cream, **shellac,** whup, whop, whomp, shut out

10 **conquer, vanquish,** quell, **suppress, put down, subdue, subjugate,** put under the yoke, master; **reduce,** prostrate, fell, **flatten, break, smash, crush, humble,** bend, **bring one to his knees;** roll *or* trample in the dust, tread *or* trample underfoot, trample down, ride down, ride *or* run roughshod over, override; have one's way with

11 **thwart, frustrate,** dash, check, deal a check to, checkmate 1011.15

12 **lose,** lose out <nonformal>, lose the day, come off second best, **get** *or* **have the worst of it, meet one's Waterloo; fall,** succumb, tumble, bow, go down, go under, **bite** *or* **lick the dust,** take the count <nonformal>; snatch defeat from the jaws of victory; throw in the towel, say 'uncle'; have enough

ADJS 13 **lost,** unwon

14 **defeated, worsted, bested, outdone; beaten, discomfited,** put to rout, **routed,** scattered, stampeded, panicked; confounded; **overcome, overthrown,** upset, overturned, overmatched, **overpowered, overwhelmed,** whelmed, **overmastered,** overborne, overridden; **fallen,** down; floored, silenced; **undone, done for** <nonformal>, **ruined,** kaput *and* on the skids <both nonformal>, *hors de combat* <Fr>; all up with <nonformal>

15 <nonformal terms> **beat, clobbered, licked, whipped,** trimmed, sandbagged, banjaxed, done in, lathered, creamed, shellacked, trounced, lambasted, settled, fixed; skinned alive; thrown for a loss

16 **shut out,** skunked *and* blanked *and* whitewashed <all nonformal>, scoreless, not on the scoreboard

17 **conquered, vanquished,** quelled, suppressed, put down, **subdued, subjugated,** mastered; **reduced,** prostrate *or* prostrated, felled, **flattened,** smashed, **crushed,** broken; **humbled,** brought to one's knees

18 **irresistible, overpowering, overcoming, overwhelming, overmastering,** overmatching, avalanching

413 SKILL

NOUNS 1 **skill,** skillfulness, **expertness, expertise, proficiency,** callidity <old>, craft, moxie <nonformal>, **cleverness; dexterity,** dexterousness *or* dextrousness; **adroitness,** address, **adeptness, deftness,** handiness, hand, practical ability; coordination, timing; quickness, readiness; **competence,** capability, capacity, ability; efficiency; **facility, prowess;** grace, style, finesse; **tact, tactfulness, diplomacy;** *savoir-faire* <Fr>; **artistry;** artfulness; **craftsmanship,** workmanship, artisanship; **know-how** *and* savvy *and* bag of tricks <all nonformal>; technical skill, **technique, touch,** technical brilliance, technical mastery, **virtuosity,** bravura, wizardry; brilliance 919.2; cunning 415; **ingenuity,** ingeniousness, resource, resourcefulness, wit; **mastery,** mastership, **command,** control, grip; steady hand; marksmanship, seamanship, airmanship, horsemanship, etc

2 **agility, nimbleness, spryness,** lightness, featliness

3 **versatility, ambidexterity,** many-sidedness, all-roundedness <nonformal>, Renaissance versatility; **adaptability,** adjustability, flexibility; broad-gauge, many hats; Renaissance man *or* woman

4 **talent, flair,** strong flair, **gift, endowment,** dowry, dower, natural gift *or* endowment, **genius,** instinct, **faculty,** bump <nonformal>; **power, ability, capability, capacity,** potential; caliber; **forte,** speciality, métier, long suit, strong point; **equipment, qualification;** talents, powers, naturals <old>, parts; the goods *and* the stuff *and* the right stuff *and* what it takes *and* the makings <all nonformal>

5 **aptitude,** inborn *or* innate aptitude, aptness, felicity, flair; **bent, turn,** propensity, **leaning,** inclination, tendency; turn for, capacity for, gift for, genius for; an eye for, an ear for, a hand for, a way with

6 **knack, art, hang, trick,** way; **touch,** feel

7 **art, science, craft; skill; technique,** technic, **technics,** technology, technical knowledge *or* skill, technical know-how <nonformal>; **mechanics,** mechanism; method

8 **accomplishment, acquirement, attainment;** finish

9 **experience, practice,** practical knowledge *or* skill, hands-on experience <nonformal>, field-work; background, past experience, seasoning, tempering; **worldly wisdom,** knowledge of the world, blaséness, **sophistication;** sagacity 919.4

10 **masterpiece, masterwork,** *chef d'œuvre* <Fr>; **master stroke,** *coup de maître* <Fr>; **feat,** *tour de force* <Fr>

11 **expert, adept,** proficient; **artist, craftsman,** artisan, skilled workman, journeyman; technician; seasoned *or* experienced hand; shark *or* sharp *or* sharpy *and* no slouch *and* tough act to follow <all nonformal>; graduate; **professional, pro** <nonformal>; **jack-of-all-trades,** handyman, Admirable Crichton <J M Barrie>; **authority,** maven <nonformal>; professor; **consultant,** expert consultant, attaché, technical adviser; boffin <Brit nonformal>, pundit, savant 928.3; diplomatist, diplomat; politician, statesman, elder statesman; connoisseur, *connaisseur* <Fr>; *cordon bleu* <Fr>; marksman, crack shot, dead shot

12 **talented person, talent,** man *or* woman of parts, gifted person, prodigy, natural <nonformal>, **genius,** mental genius, intellectual genius, intellectual prodigy, mental giant; rocket scientist *and* brain surgeon <both nonformal>; phenom <nonformal>; gifted child, **child prodigy,** wunderkind, whiz kid *and* boy wonder <both nonformal>

13 **master, past master;** master hand, world-class performer, **good hand,** dab hand <Brit nonformal>, skilled *or* practiced hand; **prodigy; wizard,** magician; **virtuoso; genius,** man *or* woman of genius; mastermind; master spirit, mahatma, sage 920.1

14 <nonformal terms> **ace, star, superstar, crackerjack,** great, all-time great, topnotcher, first-rater, whiz, flash, hot stuff, pisser, piss-cutter, pistol, no slouch, world-beater, hot rock, the one who wrote the book

15 **champion,** champ <nonformal>, titleholder, world champion; **record holder,** world-record holder; laureate; medal winner, Olympic medal winner, medalist, award winner, prizeman, prizetaker, **prizewinner;** hall of famer

16 **veteran,** vet <nonformal>, seasoned *or* grizzled veteran, **old pro** <nonformal>; **old hand, old-timer** <nonformal> one of the old guard, old stager <Brit>; old campaigner, war-horse *or* old war-horse <nonformal>; salt *and* old salt *and* old sea dog <all nonformal>, shellback <nonformal>

17 **sophisticate,** man of experience, **man of the world;** slicker *and* city slicker <both nonformal>; man-about-town; **cosmopolitan,** cosmopolite, citizen of the world

VERBS 18 **excel in** *or* **at, shine in** *or* **at** <nonformal>, be master of; write the book <nonformal>, have a good command of, feel comfortable with, be at home in; **have a gift** *or* **flair** *or* **talent** *or* **bent** *or* **faculty** *or* **turn for,** have a bump for <nonformal>, be a natural *and* be cut out *or* born to be <both nonformal>, **have a good head for,** have an ear for, have an eye for, be born for, show aptitude *or* talent for, have something to spare; have the knack *or* touch, have a way with, have the hang of it, have a lot going for one <nonformal>, be able to do it blindfolded *or* standing on one's head <nonformal>; have something *or* plenty on the ball <nonformal>

19 **know backwards and forwards, know one's stuff** *or* **know one's onions** <both nonformal>, **know the ropes** *and* **know all the ins and outs** <both nonformal>, know from A to Z *or* alpha to omega, know like the back of one's hand *or* a book, know from the ground up, know all the tricks *or* moves, know all the tricks of the trade, know all the moves of the game; **know what's what, know a thing or two, know what it's all about, know the score** *and* know all the answers <both nonformal>, "know a hawk from a handsaw"—Shakespeare; have savvy <nonformal>; **know one's way about,** know the ways of the world, have been around <nonformal>, have been around the block <nonformal>, have been through the mill <nonformal>, have cut one's wisdom teeth *or* eyeteeth <nonformal>, be long in the tooth, **not be born yesterday;** get around <nonformal>

20 **exercise skill,** handle oneself well, demonstrate one's ability, **strut one's stuff** *and* hotdog *and* grandstand *and* showboat <all nonformal>, show expertise; cut one's coat according to one's cloth, play one's cards well

21 **be versatile,** double in brass *and* wear more than one hat <both nonformal>

ADJS 22 **skillful, good,** goodish, excellent, **expert, proficient; dexterous,** callid <old>, **adroit, deft, adept, coordinated,** well-coordinated, **apt,** no mean, **handy;** quick, ready; **clever,** cute *and* slick *and* slick as a whistle <all nonformal>, neat, clean; fancy, graceful, stylish; some *or* quite some *or* quite a *or* every bit a <all nonformal>; **masterly, masterful;** magisterial; authoritative, professional; the compleat *or* the complete; crack *or* crackerjack <both nonformal>; whiz-kid <nonformal>; **virtuoso,** bravura, technically superb; **brilliant** 919.14; cunning 415.12; tactful, diplomatic, politic, statesmanlike; **ingenious,** resourceful, daedal, Daedalian; **artistic; workmanlike, well-done**

23 **agile, nimble, spry,** sprightly, fleet, featly,

peart <nonformal>, light, graceful, nimble-footed, light-footed, sure-footed; nimble-fingered, neat-fingered, neat-handed

24 **competent, capable, able, efficient, qualified, fit, fitted, suited, worthy;** journeyman; fit *or* fitted for; **equal to, up to;** up to snuff <nonformal>, up to the mark <nonformal>, *au fait* <Fr>; well-qualified, well-fitted, well-suited

25 **versatile, ambidextrous,** two-handed, **all around** <nonformal>, broad-gauge, **well-rounded, many-sided,** generally capable; **adaptable,** adjustable, flexible, resourceful, supple; amphibious

26 **skilled, accomplished; practiced; professional,** career; trained, coached, prepared, primed, finished; at one's best, at concert pitch; initiated, initiate; technical; conversant

27 **skilled in,** proficient in, adept in, versed in, **good at,** expert at, **handy at, a hand** *or* **good hand at,** master of, strong in, at home in; **up on,** well up on, well-versed 927.20

28 **experienced, practiced,** mature, matured, ripe, ripened, **seasoned,** tried, well-tried, tried and true, **veteran,** old, an old dog at <nonformal>; sagacious 919.16; **worldly, worldly-wise,** world-wise, wise in the ways of the world, knowing, **sophisticated,** cosmopolitan, cosmopolite, blasé, dry behind the ears, not born yesterday, long in the tooth

29 **talented, gifted, endowed,** with a flair; born for, made for, cut out for <nonformal>, with an eye for, with an ear for, with a bump for <nonformal>

30 **well-laid, well-devised,** well-contrived, well-designed, well-planned, well-worked-out; well-invented, *ben trovato* <Ital>; **well-weighed, well-reasoned,** well-considered, well-thought-out; **cunning, clever**

ADVS 31 **skillfully, expertly, proficiently,** excellently, well; **cleverly,** neatly, ingeniously, resourcefully; cunningly 415.13; **dexterously, adroitly, deftly, adeptly,** aptly, handily; agilely, nimbly, featly, spryly; **competently, capably, ably,** efficiently; **masterfully;** brilliantly, superbly, with genius, with a touch of genius; **artistically,** artfully; with skill, with consummate skill, with finesse

414 UNSKILLFULNESS

NOUNS 1 **unskillfulness,** skill-lessness, **inexpertness, unproficiency, uncleverness;**

unintelligence 921; inadeptness, **undex-terousness,** indexterity, **undeftness;** inefficiency; **incompetence** *or* incompetency, **inability, incapability, incapacity,** inadequacy; ineffectiveness, **ineffectuality; mediocrity,** pedestrianism; **inaptitude,** inaptness, unaptness, ineptness, maladroitness; unfitness, unfittedness; untrainedness, unschooledness; thoughtlessness, inattentiveness; maladjustment; rustiness <nonformal>

2 **inexperience,** unexperience, unexperiencedness, unpracticedness; **rawness, greenness,** unripeness, callowness, unfledgedness, unreadiness, immaturity; ignorance 929; **unfamiliarity,** unacquaintance, unacquaintedness, unaccustomedness; **amateurishness,** amateurism, unprofessionalness, unprofessionalism

3 **clumsiness, awkwardness,** bumblingness, **maladroitness, unhandiness,** lefthandedness, heavy-handedness, fumblitis *and* ham-handedness <both nonformal>, ham-fistedness <Brit nonformal>; handful of thumbs; **ungainliness,** uncouthness, **ungracefulness,** gracelessness, inelegance; **gawkiness,** gawkishness; **lubberliness, oafishness,** loutishness, boorishness, clownishness, lumpishness; **cumbersomeness,** hulkiness, **ponderousness; unwieldiness, unmanageability**

4 **bungling, blundering,** boggling, **fumbling,** malperformance, muffing, **botching,** botchery, blunderheadedness; **sloppiness, carelessness** 340.2; too many cooks

5 **bungle, blunder, botch,** flub, boner *and* bonehead play <both nonformal>, boggle, bobble *and* boo-boo *and* screw-up *and* fuck-up <all nonformal>, foozle <nonformal>, bevue; **fumble, muff,** fluff, miscue <nonformal>; **slip,** trip, stumble; *gaucherie, étourderie, balourdise* <all Fr>; hash *and* mess <both nonformal>; bad job, sad work, clumsy performance; off day; **error, mistake** 974.3

6 **mismanagement, mishandling,** misdirection, misguidance, misconduct, **misgovernment,** misrule; misadministration, maladministration; malfeasance, malpractice, misfeasance, wrongdoing 655; nonfeasance, omission, **negligence,** neglect 340.6; bad policy, impolicy, inexpedience *or* inexpediency 995

7 **incompetent,** incapable; dull tool, mediocrity, duffer *and* hacker <both nonformal>, no great shakes, no prize, no prize package, no brain surgeon, no rocket scientist; no conjurer; one who will not set the Thames on fire <Brit>; greenhorn 929.8

8 **bungler, blunderer,** blunderhead, boggler, slubberer, bumbler, **fumbler, botcher;** bull in a china shop, ox; lubber, lobby, **lout, oaf,** gawk, boor, **clown,** slouch; clodhopper, clodknocker, yokel; **clod,** clot <Brit>, **dolt,** blockhead 923.4; awkward squad; blind leading the blind

9 <nonformal terms> **goof,** goofer, goofball, goofus, foul-up, fuck-up, screw-up, bobbler, bonehead, dub, foozler, clumsy, fumble-fist, klutz, **butterfingers,** muff, muffer, stumblebum, stumblebunny, duffer, lummox, **slob,** lump, dub; gowk <Brit>, rube, hick

VERBS 10 not know how, not have the knack, not have it in one <nonformal>; not be up to <nonformal>; not be versed; muddle along, pedestrianize

11 **bungle, blunder,** bumble, boggle, **muff,** muff one's cue *or* lines, **fumble,** be all thumbs, have a handful of thumbs; **flounder,** muddle, lumber; stumble, **slip,** trip, trip over one's own feet, get in one's own way, miss one's footing, miscue; commit a *faux pas*, commit a gaffe; blunder on *or* upon *or* into; blunder away, be not one's day; **botch,** mar, **spoil, butcher, murder,** make sad work of; play havoc with, play mischief with

12 <nonformal terms> **goof, pull a boner,** bobble, lay an egg, put *or* stick one's foot in it, stub one's toe, step on one's schvantz *or* pecker, drop the ball, drop a brick, bonehead into it; **blow,** blow it, bitch, bitch up, hash up, **mess up,** flub, flub the dub, **make a mess** *or* **hash of,** foul up, fuck up, goof up, bollix up, **screw up, louse up, gum up,** gum up the works, bugger, bugger up, play the deuce *or* devil *or* hell *or* merry hell with; go at it assbackwards; put one's foot in one's mouth

13 **mismanage, mishandle, misconduct,** misdirect, misguide, **misgovern, misrule;** misadminister, maladminister; be negligent 340.6

14 not know what one is about, not know one's interest, lose one's touch, make an ass of oneself, **make a fool of oneself,** stultify oneself, put oneself out of court, stand in one's own light, not know on which side one's bread is buttered, not know one's ass from one's elbow *or* a hole in the ground, kill the goose that lays the golden egg, cut one's own throat, dig one's own grave, behave self-destructively, **play with fire,** burn one's fingers, jump out of the frying pan into the

fire, "sow the wind and reap the whirl-wind"—Bible, lock the barn door after the horse is stolen, **count one's chickens before they are hatched,** buy a pig in a poke, aim at a pigeon and kill a crow, **put the cart before the horse,** put a square peg into a round hole, run before one can walk

ADJS **15 unskillful,** skill-less, artless, **inexpert, unproficient, unclever;** inefficient; **undexterous, undeft, inadept, unfacile; unapt, inapt, inept,** hopeless, half-assed *and* clunky <both nonformal>, **poor;** mediocre, pedestrian; thoughtless, inattentive; unintelligent 921.13

16 unskilled, unaccomplished, untrained, untaught, unschooled, untutored, uncoached, unimproved, uninitiated, **unprepared,** unprimed, unfinished, unpolished; **untalented, ungifted, unendowed; amateurish,** unprofessional, unbusinesslike, semiskilled

17 inexperienced, unexperienced, unversed, unconversant, **unpracticed;** undeveloped, unseasoned; **raw, green,** green as grass, unripe, callow, unfledged, immature, unmatured, fresh, wet behind the ears, not dry behind the ears, **untried;** unskilled in, unpracticed in, unversed in, unconversant with, unaccustomed to, unused to, unfamiliar *or* unacquainted with, new to, uninitiated in, a stranger to, a novice *or* tyro at; ignorant 929.12

18 out of practice, out of training *or* form, soft <nonformal>, out of shape *or* condition, stiff, **rusty;** gone *or* run to seed *and* over the hill *and* not what one used to be <all nonformal>, losing one's touch, slipping, on the downgrade

19 incompetent, incapable, unable, inadequate, unequipped, unqualified, ill-qualified, out of one's depth, outmatched, **unfit, unfitted,** unadapted, not equal *or* up to, not cut out for <nonformal>; ineffective, **ineffectual;** unadjusted, maladjusted

20 bungling, blundering, blunderheaded, bumbling, fumbling, mistake-prone, accident-prone; **clumsy, awkward, uncoordinated,** maladroit, unhandy, left-hand, left-handed, heavy-handed, ham-handed <nonformal>, ham-fisted *and* cack-handed <both Brit nonformal>, clumsy-fisted, butterfingered <nonformal>, **all thumbs,** fingers all thumbs, with a handful of thumbs; stiff; **ungainly,** uncouth, **ungraceful,** graceless, inelegant, *gauche* <Fr>; **gawky,** gawkish; **lubberly, loutish, oafish,** boorish, clownish, lump-

ish, slobbish <nonformal>; **sloppy, careless** 340.11; **ponderous, cumbersome,** lumbering, hulking, hulky; **unwieldy**

21 botched, bungled, fumbled, muffed, spoiled, **butchered,** murdered; **ill-managed,** ill-done, ill-conducted, ill-devised, ill-contrived, ill-executed; mismanaged, misconducted, **misdirected, misguided;** impolitic, ill-considered, ill-advised; negligent 340.10

22 <nonformal terms> **goofed-up, bobbled,** bitched, bitched-up, hashed-up, **messed-up, fouled-up, fucked-up, screwed-up, bollixed-up, loused-up,** gummed-up, buggered, buggered-up, snafued; clunky, half-assed; ass-backwards

ADVS **23 unskillfully, inexpertly, unproficiently, uncleverly;** inefficiently; **incompetently, incapably,** inadequately, unfitly; **undexterously, undeftly, inadeptly,** unfacilely; **unaptly, inaptly, ineptly,** poorly

24 clumsily, awkwardly; bunglingly, blunderingly; maladroitly, unhandily; **ungracefully,** gracelessly, inelegantly, uncouthly; **ponderously, cumbersomely,** lumberingly, hulkingly, hulkily; ass-backwards <nonformal>

415 CUNNING

NOUNS **1 cunning,** cunningness, **craft, craftiness,** callidity <old>, **artfulness, art, artifice, wiliness,** wiles, guile, **slyness,** insidiousness, suppleness <Scots>, **foxiness,** slipperiness, shiftiness, trickiness; low cunning, animal cunning; gamesmanship *and* one-upmanship <both nonformal>; **canniness, shrewdness,** sharpness, acuteness, astuteness, **cleverness** 413.1; **resourcefulness, ingeniousness, wit,** inventiveness, readiness; subtlety, subtleness, Italian hand, fine Italian hand, finesse; acuteness, cuteness *and* cutification <both nonformal>; Jesuitism, Jesuitry, **sophistry** 935; "the ape of wisdom"—Locke; satanic cunning, the cunning of the serpent; sneakiness, **stealthiness, stealth** 345.4; cageyness <nonformal>, wariness 494.2

2 Machiavellianism, Machiavellism; **politics, diplomacy,** diplomatics; jobbery, jobbing

3 stratagem, artifice, art <old>, **craft, wile,** strategy, **device,** wily device, **contrivance, expedient, design, scheme, trick,** cute trick, fetch, fakement <nonformal>, gimmick <nonformal>, **ruse, red herring, shift,** tactic, **maneuver, stroke,**

stroke of policy, master stroke, **move,** coup, gambit, **ploy, dodge,** artful dodge; **game,** little game, racket *and* grift <both nonformal>; **plot,** conspiracy, **intrigue;** sleight, feint, jugglery; method in one's madness; **subterfuge,** blind, dust in the eyes; chicanery, knavery, deceit, trickery 356.4

4 **machination, manipulation, wire-pulling** <nonformal>; influence, political influence, behind-the-scenes influence *or* pressure; **maneuvering,** maneuvers, tactical maneuvers; **tactics,** devices, expedients, gimmickry <nonformal>

5 **circumvention,** getting round *or* around; **evasion,** elusion, the slip <nonformal>; the runaround *and* buck-passing *and* passing the buck <all nonformal>; **frustration, foiling, thwarting** 1011.3; **outwitting,** outsmarting, outguessing, **outmaneuvering**

6 **slyboots,** sly dog <nonformal>, **fox,** reynard, dodger, Artful Dodger <Charles Dickens>, crafty rascal, smooth *or* slick citizen <nonformal>, smooth *or* cool customer <nonformal>, glib tongue, smooth *or* sweet talker, smoothie <nonformal>, charmer; **trickster,** shyster <nonformal>, shady character, Philadelphia lawyer <nonformal>; horse trader, Yankee horse trader; **swindler** 357.3

7 **strategist, tactician; maneuverer, machinator, manipulator, wire-puller** <nonformal>; calculator, schemer, **intriguer**

8 **Machiavellian,** Machiavel, Machiavellianist; **diplomat,** diplomatist, **politician** 610; political realist; influence peddler; powerbroker, kingmaker; power behind the throne, gray eminence, *éminence grise* <Fr>

VERBS 9 **live by one's wits,** play a deep game; use one's fine Italian hand, finesse; shift, dodge, twist and turn, zig and zag; have something up one's sleeve, hide one's hand, cover one's path, have an out *or* a way out *or* an escape hatch; **trick, deceive** 356.14

10 **maneuver, manipulate,** pull strings *or* wires; **machinate, contrive,** angle <nonformal>, **jockey, engineer;** play games <nonformal>; **plot, scheme, intrigue; finagle, wangle;** gerrymander

11 **outwit, outfox, outsmart,** outguess, outfigure, **outmaneuver,** outgeneral, outflank, outplay; get the better *or* best of, go one better, know a trick worth two of that; play one's trump card; **overreach,** outreach; **circumvent,** get round *or* around, **evade,** stonewall <nonformal>,

elude, frustrate, foil, give the slip *or* runaround <nonformal>; pass the buck <nonformal>; pull a fast one <nonformal>, steal a march on; make a fool of, make a sucker *or* patsy of <nonformal>; be too much for, be too deep for; throw a curve <nonformal>, **deceive, victimize** 356.18

ADJS 12 **cunning, crafty, artful, wily,** callid <old>, guileful, **sly,** insidious, supple <Scots>, **shifty,** pawky <Brit>, arch, **smooth, slick** *and* slick as a whistle <both nonformal>, **slippery,** snaky, serpentine, **foxy,** vulpine, feline; **canny, shrewd,** knowing, sharp, razor-sharp, cute *or* cutesy *or* cutesy-poo <nonformal>, acute, astute, **clever;** resourceful, ingenious, inventive, ready; subtle; Jesuitical, **sophistical** 935.10; **tricky,** trickish, tricksy <old>, gimmicky <nonformal>; **Machiavellian,** Machiavellic, politic, diplomatic; strategic, tactical; deep, deep-laid; cunning as a fox *or* serpent, crazy like a fox <nonformal>, slippery as an eel, too clever by half; sneaky, **stealthy** 345.12; cagey <nonformal>, wary 494.9; **scheming, designing; manipulative,** manipulatory; **deceitful**

ADVS 13 **cunningly, craftily, artfully,** wilily, guilefully, insidiously, shiftily, foxily, trickily, smoothly, slick <nonformal>; **slyly,** on the sly; **cannily, shrewdly,** knowingly, astutely, **cleverly;** subtly; cagily <nonformal>, warily 494.13; diplomatically

416 ARTLESSNESS

NOUNS 1 **artlessness, ingenuousness, guilelessness; simplicity,** simpleness, plainness; simpleheartedness, simplemindedness; **unsophistication,** unsophisticatedness; *naïveté* <Fr>, naivety, naiveness, childlikeness; **innocence;** trustfulness, trustingness, unguardedness, unwariness, unsuspiciousness; **openness,** openheartedness, sincerity, **candor** 644.4; **integrity,** single-heartedness, single-mindedness, singleness of heart; directness, bluffness, bluntness, outspokenness

2 **naturalness,** naturalism, nature; state of nature; unspoiledness; **unaffectedness,** unaffectation, **unassumingness,** unpretendingness, unpretentiousness, undisguise; **inartificiality,** unartificialness, genuineness

3 **simple soul,** unsophisticate, naïf, **ingenue, innocent, child,** mere child, infant,

babe, baby, newborn babe, babe in the woods, lamb, dove; child of nature, noble savage; primitive; yokel, rube *and* hick <both nonformal>; oaf, lout 923.5; dupe 358

VERBS **4** wear one's heart on one's sleeve, look one in the face

ADJS **5 artless, simple,** plain, **guideless;** simplehearted, simpleminded; **ingenuous,** *ingénu* <Fr>; **unsophisticated, naive;** childlike, born yesterday; **innocent;** trustful, trusting, unguarded, unwary, unreserved, confiding, unsuspicious; **open,** openhearted, sincere, candid, **frank** 644.17; single-hearted, single-minded; direct, bluff, blunt, outspoken

6 natural, naturelike, native; in the state of nature; primitive, primal, pristine, unspoiled, untainted, uncontaminated; **unaffected, unassuming, unpretending,** unpretentious, unfeigning, undisguising, undissimulating, undissembling, undesigning; **genuine, inartificial,** unartificial, unadorned, unvarnished, unembellished; homespun; **pastoral, rural,** arcadian, bucolic

ADVS **7 artlessly, ingenuously, guilelessly;** simply, plainly; naturally, genuinely; naïvely; openly, openheartedly

417 AUTHORITY

NOUNS **1 authority, prerogative, right, power,** faculty, competence *or* competency; **mandate,** popular authority *or* mandate, people's mandate, electoral mandate; regality, royal prerogative; constituted authority, vested authority; inherent authority; legal *or* lawful *or* rightful authority, legitimacy; derived *or* delegated authority, vicarious authority, indirect authority; **the say** *and* **the say-so** <both nonformal>; divine right, *jus divinum* <L>; absolute power, absolutism 612.9

2 authoritativeness, authority, power, powerfulness, magisterialness, **potency** *or* potence, puissance, **strength,** might, mightiness, clout <nonformal>

3 authoritativeness, masterfulness, lordliness, magistrality, magisterialness; **arbitrariness,** peremptoriness, imperativeness, **imperiousness,** autocraticalness, high-handedness, dictatorialness, overbearingness, overbearance, overbearing, domineering, domineeringness, tyrannicalness, authoritarianism, bossism <nonformal>

4 prestige, authority, influence, influen-

tialness; pressure, **weight,** weightiness, moment, **consequence;** eminence, **stature,** rank, seniority, preeminence, priority, precedence; **greatness** 247; **importance, prominence** 996.2

5 governance, authority, jurisdiction, control, command, power, rule, reign, regnancy, **dominion, sovereignty,** empire, empery, raj <India>, imperium, **sway; government** 612; administration, disposition 573.3; **control, grip,** claws, **clutches,** hand, hands, iron hand, talons

6 dominance *or* dominancy, **dominion, domination; preeminence, supremacy, superiority** 249; **ascendance** *or* ascendancy; **upper** *or* **whip hand, sway; sovereignty,** suzerainty, suzerainship, **overlordship;** primacy, principality, **predominance** *or* predominancy, predomination, prepotence *or* prepotency, hegemony; preponderance; balance of power; eminent domain

7 mastership, masterhood, masterdom, **mastery; leadership, headship, lordship;** hegemony; supervisorship, directorship 573.4; hierarchy, nobility, aristocracy, **ruling class** 575.15; chair, chairmanship; chieftainship, chieftaincy, chieftainry, chiefery; presidentship, presidency; premiership, prime-ministership, primeministry; governorship; princeship, princedom, principality; rectorship, rectorate; suzerainty, suzerainship; regency, regentship; prefectship, prefecture; proconsulship, proconsulate; provostship, provostry; protectorship, protectorate; seneschalship, seneschalsy; pashadom, pashalic; sheikhdom; emirate, viziership, vizierate; magistrateship, magistrature, magistracy; mayorship, mayoralty; sheriffdom, sheriffcy, sheriffalty, shrievalty; consulship, consulate; chancellorship, chancellery, chancellorate; seigniory; tribunate, aedileship; deanship, decanal authority, deanery; patriarchate, patriarchy <old>; bishopric, episcopacy; archbishopric, archiepiscopacy, archiepiscopate; metropolitanship, metropolitanate; popedom, popeship, popehood, papacy, pontificate, pontificality; dictatorship, dictature

8 sovereignty, royalty, regnancy, **majesty,** empire, empery, imperialism, **emperorship; kingship,** kinghood; queenship, queenhood; kaisership, kaiserdom; czardom; rajaship; sultanship, sultanate; caliphate; the throne, the Crown, the purple; royal insignia 647.3

9 scepter, rod, staff, wand, staff *or* rod *or*

wand of office, baton, mace, truncheon, fasces; crosier, crook, cross-staff; caduceus; gavel; mantle; chain of office; portfolio

10 <seat of authority> **saddle** <nonformal>, **helm, driver's seat** <nonformal>; seat, **chair,** bench; woolsack <England>; seat of state, seat of power; curule chair; dais

11 **throne,** royal seat; musnud *or* gaddi <both India>; Peacock throne

12 <acquisition of authority> **accession; succession,** rightful *or* legitimate succession; **usurpation,** arrogation, assumption, taking over, seizure; anointment, anointing, consecration, coronation; **delegation,** deputation, assignment, **appointment; election; authorization,** empowerment

VERBS 13 **possess** *or* **wield authority, have power,** have the power, have in one's hands, have the right, have the say *or* say-so <nonformal>, have the whip hand, wear the crown, hold the prerogative, have the mandate; exercise sovereignty; be vested *or* invested, carry authority, have clout <nonformal>, have what one says go, have one's own way; show one's authority, crack the whip, throw one's weight around *and* ride herd <both nonformal>; **rule** 612.14, **control;** supervise 573.10

14 **take command, take charge, take over,** take the helm, take the reins of government, take the reins into one's hand, get the power into one's hands, gain *or* get the upper hand, take the lead; ascend *or* mount *or* succeed *or* accede to the throne; **assume command,** assume, **usurp,** arrogate, seize; usurp *or* seize the throne *or* crown *or* mantle, usurp the prerogatives of the crown; seize power, execute a *coup d'état*

ADJS 15 **authoritative,** clothed *or* vested *or* invested with authority, **commanding, imperative; governing, controlling, ruling** 612.18; **preeminent, supreme,** leading, **superior** 249.12; **powerful, potent,** puissant, mighty; dominant, ascendant, hegemonic, hegemonistic; **influential, prestigious, weighty,** momentous, consequential, eminent, substantial, considerable; great 247.6; important, prominent; ranking, senior; authorized, empowered, duly constituted, competent; **official,** *ex officio* <L>; authoritarian; absolute, autocratic, monocratic; **totalitarian**

16 **imperious,** imperial, **masterful,** authoritative, feudal, aristocratic, **lordly,** magistral, **magisterial;** arrogant 141.9; **arbi-**

trary, peremptory, imperative; absolute, absolutist, absolutistic; **dictatorial, authoritarian; bossy** <nonformal>, **domineering, high-handed, overbearing,** overruling; autocratic, monocratic, **despotic, tyrannical;** tyrannous, grinding, oppressive 98.24; repressive, suppressive 428.11; strict, severe 425.6

17 **sovereign; regal, royal, majestic,** purple; **kinglike, kingly,** "every inch a king"— Shakespeare; **imperial,** imperious *or* imperatorious <both old>; **imperatorial;** monarchic *or* monarchical, monarchal, monarchial; tetrarchic; princely, princelike; **queenly,** queenlike; dynastic

ADVS 18 **authoritatively,** with authority, by virtue of office; **commandingly, imperatively; powerfully, potently,** puissantly, mightily; **influentially, weightily,** momentously, consequentially; **officially,** *ex cathedra* <L>

19 **imperiously, masterfully,** magisterially; **arbitrarily, peremptorily; autocratically, dictatorially, high-handedly, domineeringly, overbearingly, despotically, tyrannically**

20 **by authority of,** in the name of, in *or* by virtue of

21 **in authority,** in power, in charge, in control, in command, at the reins, at the head, **at the helm,** at the wheel, **in the saddle** *or* driver's seat <nonformal>, on the throne; "drest in a little brief authority"—Shakespeare

418 LAWLESSNESS
<absence of authority>

NOUNS 1 **lawlessness; licentiousness,** license, uncontrol, anything goes, unrestraint 430.3; indiscipline, insubordination, mutiny, disobedience 327; permissiveness; **irresponsibility,** unaccountability; willfulness, unchecked *or* rampant will; interregnum, power vacuum

2 **anarchy,** anarchism; **disorderliness, unruliness,** misrule, **disorder,** disruption, disorganization, confusion, **turmoil, chaos,** primal chaos, tohubohu; antinomianism; **nihilism;** syndicalism *and* anarcho-syndicalism *and* criminal syndicalism <all old>, lynch law, mob rule *or* law, mobocracy, ochlocracy; **law of the jungle;** revolution 859; rebellion 327.4

3 **anarchist,** anarch; antinomian; **nihilist,** syndicalist *and* anarcho-syndicalist <both old>; revolutionist 859.3; mutineer, rebel 327.5

VERBS 4 **reject** *or* **defy authority,** enthrone

one's own will; **take the law in one's own hands,** act on one's own responsibility; do *or* go as one pleases, indulge oneself; be a law unto oneself, answer to no man, "swear allegiance to the words of no master"—Horace

ADJS **5 lawless; licentious, ungoverned,** undisciplined, unrestrained; permissive; insubordinate, mutinous, disobedient 327.8; **uncontrolled,** uncurbed, unbridled, unchecked, rampant, untrammeled, unreined, reinless, anything goes; **irresponsible,** wildcat, unaccountable; selfwilled, willful, headstrong, heady

6 anarchic, anarchical, anarchial, anarchistic; **unruly, disorderly,** disorganized, **chaotic;** antinomian; **nihilistic**

ADVS **7 lawlessly,** licentiously; anarchically, chaotically

419 PRECEPT

NOUNS **1 precept,** prescript, **prescription, teaching; instruction, direction, charge,** commission, **injunction,** dictate; **order,** command 420

2 rule, law, canon, maxim, dictum, moral, moralism; **norm, standard;** formula, form; rule of action *or* conduct, moral precept; commandment, *mitzvah* <Heb>; **tradition;** ordinance, imperative, **regulation,** reg <nonformal>, *règlement* <Fr>; **principle,** principium, settled principle, general principle *or* truth, tenet, convention; **guideline,** ground rule, rubric, protocol, working rule, working principle, standard procedure; guiding principle, golden rule; **code**

3 formula, form <old>, **recipe,** receipt; **prescription;** formulary

ADJS **4 preceptive,** didactic, instructive, moralistic, **prescriptive;** prescript, prescribed, mandatory, hard-and-fast, binding, dictated; formulary, standard, regulation, official, authoritative, canonical, statutory, rubric, rubrical, protocolary, protocolic; **normative; conventional;** traditional

420 COMMAND

NOUNS **1 command, commandment, order,** direct order, command decision, **bidding,** behest, hest <old>, imperative, **dictate,** dictation, **will, pleasure,** say-so <nonformal>, word, word of command, *mot d'ordre* <Fr>; special order; **authority** 417

2 injunction, charge, commission, **mandate**

3 direction, directive, instruction, rule, regulation; prescript, prescription, **precept** 419; general order

4 decree, decreement <old>, decretum, decretal, rescript, fiat, **edict,** *edictum* <L>; **law** 673.3; **rule, ruling,** dictum, ipse dixit; **ordinance,** *ordonnance* <Fr>, appointment <old>; **proclamation,** pronouncement, pronunciamento, **declaration,** ukase; bull, brevet <old>; decree-law, *décret-loi* <Fr>; *senatus consultum* <L>, senatus consult; diktat

5 summons, bidding, beck, call, calling, nod, **beck and call,** preconization; **convocation,** convoking; evocation, calling forth, invocation; requisition, indent <chiefly Brit>

6 court order, injunction, legal order

7 process server, summoner

VERBS **8 command, order, dictate, direct, instruct,** mandate, **bid, enjoin, charge,** commission, call on *or* upon; issue a writ *or* an injunction; **decree, rule, ordain,** promulgate; give an order *or* a direct order, issue a command, say the word, give the word *or* word of command; call the shots *or* tune *or* signals *or* play <nonformal>; order about *or* around; **speak, proclaim, declare,** pronounce 352.12

9 prescribe, require, demand, dictate, impose, lay down, set, fix, appoint, make obligatory *or* mandatory; decide once and for all, carve in stone, set in concrete <nonformal>; authorize 443.11

10 lay down the law, put one's foot down <nonformal>, read the riot act, lower the boom <nonformal>, set the record straight

11 summon, call, demand, preconize; call for, send for *or* after, bid come; **cite, summons** <nonformal>, **subpoena,** serve; page; convoke, convene, call together; call away; muster, invoke, conjure; order up, summon up, muster up, call up, conjure up, magic *or* magic up <Brit>; evoke, call forth, summon forth, call out; recall, call back, call in; requisition, indent <chiefly Brit>

ADJS **12 mandatory,** mandated, **imperative, compulsory,** prescript, prescriptive, **obligatory,** must <nonformal>; dictated, imposed, required, entailed, decretory; decisive, final, peremptory, absolute, eternal, written, hard-and-fast, carved in stone, set in concrete <nonformal>, ultimate, conclusive, binding, irrevocable, without appeal

13 commanding, imperious, imperative, jussive, peremptory, abrupt; **directive, instructive; mandating,** dictating, compelling, obligating, **prescriptive,** preceptive; decretory, decretive, decretal; **authoritative** 417.15

ADVS **14 commandingly, imperatively,** peremptorily

15 by order or **command,** at the word of command, as ordered or required, to order; mandatorily, compulsorily, obligatorily

421 DEMAND

NOUNS **1 demand, claim, call; requisition,** requirement, stated requirement, order, rush order, indent <chiefly Brit>; seller's market, land-office business; strong or heavy demand, draft, drain, levy, tax, taxing; imposition, impost, tribute, duty, contribution; insistent demand, rush; exorbitant or extortionate demand, exaction, extortion, blackmail; **ultimatum,** nonnegotiable demand; notice, warning 399

2 stipulation, provision, proviso, condition; **terms;** exception, reservation; **qualification** 958

3 <nonformal terms> catch, Catch-22, kicker, zinger, snag, joker; strings, strings attached; ifs, ands, and buts; whereases, howevers, howsomevers

4 insistence, exigence, importunity, importunateness, importunacy, **demandingness,** pertinaciousness, pertinacity; pressure, pressingness, **urgency, exigency** 996.4; **persistence** 360.1

VERBS **5 demand, ask, ask for,** make a demand; **call for,** call on or upon one for, appeal to one for; call out for, cry or cry out for, clamor for; **claim,** challenge, **require;** levy, **impose,** impose on one for; **exact, extort,** squeeze, screw; blackmail; **requisition,** make or put in requisition, indent <chiefly Brit>, **confiscate; order,** put in or place an order, order up; deliver or issue an ultimatum; warn 399.5

6 claim, pretend to, lay claim to, stake a claim <nonformal>, put or have dibs on <nonformal>, assert or vindicate a claim or right or title to; have going for it or one <nonformal>; **challenge**

7 stipulate, stipulate for, specifically provide, set conditions or terms, make reservations; **qualify** 958.3

8 insist, insist on or **upon,** stick to <nonformal>, set one's heart or mind upon; **take one's stand upon,** stand on or upon, put or

lay it on the line <nonformal>, make no bones about it; stand upon one's rights, **put one's foot down** <nonformal>; brook or take no denial, not take no for an answer; **maintain, contend,** assert; urge, press 375.14; **persist** 360.2

ADJS **9 demanding, exacting,** exigent; draining, taxing, exorbitant, extortionate, grasping; **insistent,** instant, **importunate,** urgent, pertinacious, pressing, loud, clamant, crying, clamorous; persistent

10 claimed, spoken for; requisitioned; requisitorial, requisitory

ADVS **11 demandingly, exactingly,** exigently; exorbitantly, extortionately; **insistently, importunately, urgently,** pressingly, clamorously, loudly, clamantly

12 on demand, at demand, **on call,** upon presentation

422 ADVICE

NOUNS **1 advice, counsel, recommendation, suggestion;** proposal; advising, advocacy; **direction, instruction,** guidance, briefing; **exhortation,** hortation <old>, enjoinder, expostulation, remonstrance; **sermons,** sermonizing, preaching, preachiness; **admonition,** monition, monitory or monitory letter, caution, caveat, **warning** 399; **idea,** thought, opinion 952.6; **consultancy,** consultantship, **consultation,** parley 541.6; council 423; **counseling;** guidance counseling, educational counseling, vocational guidance

2 piece of advice, **word of advice, word to the wise,** verbum sapienti <L>, verb or verbum sap <nonformal>, word in the ear, **hint, broad hint, flea in the ear** <nonformal>, **tip** <nonformal>, a few words of wisdom, one's two cents' worth <nonformal>, intimation, insinuation

3 adviser, counsel, counselor, consultant, professional consultant, expert, maven <nonformal>, boffin <Brit nonformal>; instructor, guide, **mentor,** nestor, orienter; confidant, personal adviser; admonisher, monitor, Dutch uncle; Polonius <Shakespeare>, preceptist; **teacher** 571; meddler, buttinsky and yenta and kibitzer and backseat driver <all nonformal>

4 advisee, counselee; client

VERBS **5 advise, counsel, recommend, suggest, advocate,** propose, submit; **instruct,** coach, guide, direct, brief; prescribe; weigh in with advice <nonformal>, give a piece of advice, give a hint or broad hint, hint at, intimate, insinuate, put a flea in one's ear <nonformal>, have a word with one, speak words of wisdom; meddle, kibitz <nonformal>; confer, consult with 541.11

6 **admonish, exhort,** expostulate, remonstrate, preach; **enjoin, charge,** call upon one to; caution, issue a caveat, wag one's finger <nonformal>; warn away, warn off, **warn** 399.5,6; move, prompt, **urge, incite, encourage, induce, persuade** 375.23; **implore** 440.11

7 **take** or **accept advice, follow advice,** follow, follow implicitly, go along with <nonformal>, buy or buy into <nonformal>; solicit advice, desire guidance, implore counsel; **be advised by;** have at one's elbow, take one's cue from

ADJS 8 **advisory,** recommendatory; **consultative,** consultatory; directive, instructive; **admonitory,** monitory, monitorial, cautionary, **warning** 399.7; **expostulative,** expostulatory, **remonstrative,** remonstratory, remonstrant; **exhortative,** exhortatory, hortative, hortatory, preachy <nonformal>, **didactic,** moralistic, sententious

PHRS 9 too many cooks spoil the broth, another country heard from

423 COUNCIL

NOUNS 1 **council,** conclave, *concilium* <L>, deliberative or advisory body, **assembly;** deliberative assembly, consultative assembly; chamber, house; **board,** court, bench; **full assembly,** plenum, plenary session; **congress,** diet, synod, senate, soviet; **legislature** 613; **cabinet,** divan, council of ministers, council of state, US Cabinet, British Cabinet; kitchen cabinet, camarilla; staff; junta, directory; Sanhedrin; privy council; common council, county council, parish council, borough or town council, city or municipal council, village council; brain trust <nonformal>, brains trust <Brit nonformal>, group or corps or body of advisers, inner circle; council of war; council fire; syndicate, **association** 617; **conference** 541.6; **assembly** 769.2; **tribunal** 595

2 **committee,** subcommittee, standing committee; select committee, special committee, ad hoc committee; committee of one

3 **forum, conference,** discussion group, buzz session <nonformal>, **round table, panel;** open forum, colloquium, symposium; town meeting; **powwow** <nonformal>

4 ecclesiastical council, chapter, classis, conclave, conference, congregation, consistory, convention, convocation, presbytery, session, synod, vestry; parochial council, parochial church council; diocesan conference, diocesan court; provincial court, plenary council; ecumenical council; Council of Nicaea, Council of Trent, Lateran Council, Vatican Council, Vatican Two; conciliarism

ADJS 5 **conciliar,** council, councilmanic, aldermanic; **consultative, deliberative, advisory;** synodal, synodic, synodical

ADVS 6 **in council, in conference, in consultation, in a huddle** <nonformal>, in conclave; **in session,** sitting

424 COMPULSION

NOUNS 1 **compulsion, obligation,** obligement; **command** 420; **necessity** 962; **inevitability** 962.7; **irresistibility, compulsiveness; forcing,** enforcement; command performance; **constraint,** coaction; **restraint** 428

2 **force,** *ultima ratio* <L>; **brute force,** naked force, rule of might, big battalions, **main force,** physical force; the right of the strong, the law of the jungle; **tyranny** 612.10; steamroller <nonformal>

3 **coercion,** intimidation, scare tactics, headbanging and arm-twisting <both nonformal>, **duress; the strong arm** and strong-arm tactics <both nonformal>, a pistol or gun to one's head, the sword, the mailed fist, the bludgeon, the boot in the face, the jackboot, the big stick, the club, *argumentum baculinum* <L>; **pressure, high pressure,** high-pressure methods; **violence** 671

VERBS 4 **compel, force, make;** have, cause, cause to; **constrain, bind,** tie, tie one's hands; **restrain** 428.7; enforce, **drive,** impel; dragoon, use force upon, force one's hand, hold a pistol or gun to one's head

5 **oblige, necessitate, require,** exact, demand, **dictate,** impose, call for; take or brook no denial; leave no option or escape, admit of no option

6 **press; bring pressure to bear upon, put pressure on,** bear down on, bear against, bear hard upon

7 **coerce,** use violence, ride roughshod, intimidate, bully, bludgeon, blackjack; hijack, shanghai, dragoon

8 <nonformal terms> **twist one's arm, arm-twist, twist arms, knock** or **bang heads,** knock or bang heads together, **strong-arm, steamroller, bulldoze, pres-**

sure, high-pressure, lean on, squeeze; put the screws on *or* to, get one over a barrel *or* under one's thumb, hold one's feet to the fire, put the heat on; pull rank; ram *or* cram down one's throat

9 **be compelled, be coerced,** have to 962.10; be stuck with <nonformal>, can't help but

ADJS 10 **compulsory, compulsive,** compulsatory, **compelling; pressing, driving,** imperative, imperious; constraining, coactive; **restraining** 428.11; **irresistible**

11 **obligatory, compulsory,** imperative, mandatory, required, dictated, **binding;** involuntary; **necessary** 962.12; **inevitable** 962.15

12 **coercive, forcible;** steamroller *and* bulldozer *and* sledgehammer *and* strong-arm <all nonformal>; violent

ADVS 13 **compulsively,** compulsorily, **compellingly,** imperatively, imperiously

14 **forcibly, by force,** by main force, by *force majeure,* by a strong arm; by force of arms, *vi et armis* <L>, at gunpoint, with a pistol *or* gun to one's head, at the point of a gun, at the point of the sword *or* bayonet, at bayonet point

15 **obligatorily,** compulsorily, mandatorily, by stress of, under press of; under the lash *or* gun; of necessity

425 STRICTNESS

NOUNS 1 **strictness, severity, harshness, stringency,** astringency, **hard line; discipline,** strict *or* tight *or* rigid discipline, regimentation, spit and polish; **austerity, sternness,** grimness, ruggedness, **toughness** <nonformal>; **belt-tightening;** Spartanism; authoritarianism; demandingness, exactingness; **meticulousness** 339.3

2 **firmness, rigor, rigorousness,** rigidness, rigidity, stiffness, **hardness,** obduracy, obdurateness, **inflexibility,** inexorability, unyieldingness, unbendingness, impliability, unrelentingness, **relentlessness; uncompromisingness;** stubbornness, obstinacy 361; purism; precisianism, puritanism, fundamentalism, orthodoxy

3 **firm hand, iron hand,** heavy hand, strong hand, tight hand, tight rein; tight *or* taut ship

VERBS 4 **hold** *or* **keep a tight hand upon,** keep a firm hand on, keep a tight rein on, rule with an iron hand, rule with a rod of iron, knock *or* bang heads together <nonformal>; regiment, discipline; run a tight *or* taut ship, ride herd, keep one in line; maintain the highest standards, not spare

oneself nor anyone else, go out of one's way, go the extra mile <nonformal>

5 **deal hardly** *or* **harshly with,** deal hard measure to, lay a heavy hand on, bear hard upon, **take a hard line,** not pull one's punches <nonformal>

ADJS 6 **strict, exacting,** exigent, demanding, not to be trifled with, **stringent,** astringent; disciplined, spit-and-polish; **severe, harsh,** dour, unsparing; **stern, grim, austere,** rugged, **tough** <nonformal>; Spartan, Spartanic; **hard-line,** authoritarian 417.16; **meticulous** 339.12

7 **firm, rigid, rigorous,** rigorist, rigoristic, stiff, **hard,** iron, steel, steely, hard-shell, obdurate, **inflexible,** ironhanded, inexorable, dour, **unyielding,** unbending, impliable, **relentless,** unrelenting, procrustean; **uncompromising;** stubborn, obstinate 361.8; purist, puristic; puritan, puritanic, puritanical, fundamentalist, orthodox; ironbound, rockbound, musclebound, ironclad <nonformal>; straitlaced, hidebound

ADVS 8 **strictly, severely, stringently, harshly; sternly,** grimly, **austerely,** ruggedly, toughly <nonformal>

9 **firmly, rigidly, rigorously,** stiffly, stiff, hardly, obdurately, **inflexibly,** impliably, inexorably, unyieldingly, unbendingly; **uncompromisingly, relentlessly,** unrelentingly; ironhandedly, with a firm *or* a strong *or* a heavy *or* a tight *or* an iron hand

426 LAXNESS

NOUNS 1 **laxness, laxity, slackness, looseness,** relaxedness; loosening, relaxation; imprecision, sloppiness <nonformal>, carelessness, remissness, negligence 340.1; indifference 102; weakness 16; impotence 19; unrestraint 430.3

2 **unstrictness,** nonstrictness, undemandingness, unsevereness, unharshness; leniency 427; **permissiveness,** overpermissiveness, overindulgence, **softness;** unsternness, unauster/eness; easygoingness, easiness; **flexibility,** pliancy

VERBS 3 **hold a loose rein, give free rein to,** give the reins to, **give one his head,** give a free course to, give rope enough to; permit all *or* anything

ADJS 4 **lax, slack, loose,** relaxed; imprecise, sloppy <nonformal>, careless, slipshod; remiss, negligent 340.10; indifferent 102.6; weak 16.12; impotent 19.13; untrammeled, unrestrained

5 **unstrict,** undemanding, **unexacting; un-**

severe, unharsh; unstern, unaustere; lenient 427.7; permissive, overpermissive,
overindulgent, soft; easy, easygoing, laid-
back <nonformal>; flexible, pliant,
yielding

427 LENIENCY

NOUNS **1 leniency** or lenience, lenientness,
lenity; **clemency**, clementness, **mercifulness,** mercy, **humaneness,** humanity,
pity, **compassion** 145.1; **mildness, gentleness,** tenderness, softness, moderateness;
easiness, easygoingness; laxness 426;
forbearance, forbearing, patience 134;
acceptance, **tolerance** 978.4

 2 compliance, complaisance, obligingness,
accommodatingness, **agreeableness;** affability, graciosity, graciousness, generousness, decency, amiability; kindness,
kindliness, benignity, **benevolence** 143

 3 indulgence, humoring, obliging; favoring, gratification, pleasing; **pampering,**
cosseting, **coddling,** mollycoddling, petting, **spoiling; permissiveness,** overpermissiveness, overindulgence; sparing the
rod

 4 spoiled child or **brat,** enfant gâté <Fr>,
pampered darling, mama's boy, mollycoddle, sissy; enfant terrible <Fr>,
naughty child

VERBS **5 be easy on,** ease up on, handle with
kid or velvet gloves, use a light hand or
rein, slap one's wrist, spare the rod; **tolerate,** bear with 134.5

 6 indulge, humor, oblige; favor, please,
gratify, satisfy, **cater to; give way to,** yield
to, let one have his own way; **pamper,**
cosset, **coddle,** mollycoddle, pet, make a
lap dog of, **spoil;** spare the rod

ADJS **7 lenient, mild, gentle,** mild-mannered,
tender, humane, compassionate, **clement,**
merciful 145.7; soft, moderate, **easy,** easygoing; lax 426.4; forgiving 148.6; **fore-
bearing, forbearant,** patient 134.9; accepting, **tolerant** 978.11

 8 indulgent, compliant, complaisant, **obliging, accommodating, agreeable,** amiable,
gracious, generous, benignant, affable,
decent, kind, kindly, benign, benevolent
143.15; **hands-off** <nonformal>, permissive, overpermissive, overindulgent

 9 indulged, pampered, coddled, spoiled,
spoiled rotten <nonformal>

428 RESTRAINT

NOUNS **1 restraint, constraint; inhibition;**
legal restraint, injunction, enjoining, en-

joinder, interdict; **control, curb, check,**
rein, arrest, arrestation; **retardation,** deceleration, slowing down; cooling and
cooling off and cooling down <all nonfor-
mal>; retrenchment, curtailment; self-
control 359.5; **hindrance** 1011; rationing;
thought control; restraint of trade, monopoly, protection, protectionism, protective tariff, tariff wall; clampdown and
crackdown <both nonformal>, proscription, **prohibition** 444

 2 suppression, repression, subdual, quelling, putting down, shutting or closing
down, smashing, crushing; quashing,
squashing and squelching <both nonfor-
mal>; smothering, stifling, suffocating,
strangling, throttling; extinguishment,
quenching; **censorship** censoring, bleeping or bleeping out <nonformal>

 3 restriction, limitation, confinement;
Hobson's choice, no choice, zero option;
circumscription 210; stint, cramping,
cramp; qualification 958

 4 shackle, restraint, **restraints, fetter, hamper,** trammel, trammels, **manacle,** gyves,
bond, **bonds,** irons, chains, Oregon boat;
stranglehold; **handcuffs,** cuffs; stocks,
bilbo, pillory; **tether,** spancel, leash, lead
<chiefly Brit>, leading string; **rein;** hob-
ble, hopple; straitjacket, strait-waistcoat
<Brit>, camisole; yoke, collar; bridle,
halter; **muzzle, gag;** electronic ankle
bracelet and offender's tag and monitor

 5 lock, bolt, bar, padlock, catch, safety
catch; barrier 1011.5

 6 restrictionist, protectionist, monopolist;
censor

VERBS **7 restrain, constrain, control, govern,**
guard, contain, keep under control, put or
lay under restraint; **inhibit,** straiten
<old>; enjoin, clamp or crack down on
<nonformal>, proscribe, prohibit 444.3;
curb, check, arrest, bridle, get under control, rein, snub, snub in; **retard,** slow
down, decelerate; **cool** and **cool off** and
cool down <all nonformal>; retrench,
curtail; hold, **hold in,** keep, withhold,
hold up <nonformal>, **keep from;** hinder
1011.10; **hold back, keep back,** pull, set
back; **hold in, keep in,** pull in, rein in;
hold or **keep in check, hold at bay,** hold in
leash, tie one down, tie one's hands; hold
fast, keep a tight hand on; restrain oneself, not go too far, not go off the deep end
<nonformal>

 8 suppress, repress, stultify; **keep down,**
hold down, keep under; **close** or shut
down; **subdue, quell, put down,** smash,
crush; quash, squash and **squelch** <both

nonformal>; **extinguish,** quench, stanch, damp down, pour water on, dash *or* pour cold water on, drown, kill; **smother, stifle,** suffocate, asphyxiate, strangle, throttle, choke off, **muzzle, gag;** censor, bleep *or* bleep out <nonformal>, silence; sit on *and* sit down on *and* slap *or* smack down <all nonformal>; jump on *and* crack down on *and* clamp down on <all nonformal>, put *or* keep the lid on <nonformal>; bottle up, cork, cork up

9 **restrict, limit, narrow, confine,** tighten; ground, restrict to home, barracks, bedroom, quarters, etc; circumscribe 210.4; keep in *or* within bounds, keep from spreading, localize; **cage in,** hem, hem in, box, box in *or* up; **cramp,** stint; qualify 958.3

10 **bind, restrain, tie,** tie up, put the clamps on, **strap,** lash, leash, pinion, fasten, secure, make fast; **hamper, trammel,** entrammel; rope; **chain,** enchain; **shackle, fetter, manacle,** gyve, **put in irons; handcuff, tie one's hands; tie hand and foot,** hog-tie <nonformal>; straitjacket; hobble, hopple, fetter, leash, put on a lead <chiefly Brit>, spancel; tether, picket, moor, anchor; tie down, pin down, peg down; get a stranglehold on, put a half nelson on <nonformal>; **bridle**

ADJS 11 **restraining, constraining; inhibiting,** inhibitive; **suppressive, repressive,** stultifying; controlling, on top of <nonformal>

12 **restrictive,** limitative, restricting, **narrowing, limiting, confining,** cramping; censorial

13 **restrained, constrained, inhibited,** pent up; guarded; controlled, curbed, bridled; **under restraint,** under control, in check, under discipline; grounded, out of circulation; slowed down, retarded, arrested, in remission; in *or* on leash, in leading strings

14 **suppressed, repressed; subdued,** quelled, put down, smashed, crushed; quashed, squashed *and* squelched <both nonformal>; smothered, stifled, suffocated; censored

15 **restricted, limited, confined;** circumscribed 210.6, "cabined, cribbed, confined"— Shakespeare, hemmed in, hedged in *or* about, boxed in; landlocked; **shut-in,** stormbound, weatherbound, windbound, icebound, snowbound; cramped, stinted; qualified 958.10

16 **bound, tied,** bound hand and foot, tied up, tied down, strapped, hampered, trammeled, shackled, handcuffed, fet-

tered, manacled, tethered; **in bonds,** in irons *or* chains, ironbound

429 CONFINEMENT

NOUNS 1 **confinement,** locking-up, lockup, lockdown, caging, penning, putting behind barriers, impoundment, **restraint,** restriction; check, **restraint, constraint** 428.1

2 **quarantine, isolation,** cordoning off, segregation, separation, sequestration, seclusion; walling in *or* up *or* off; sanitary cordon, *cordon sanitaire* <Fr>, cordon; quarantine flag, yellow flag, yellow jack

3 **imprisonment, jailing,** incarceration, **internment,** immurement, immuration; **detention, captivity,** duress, durance, durance vile; close arrest, house arrest; term of imprisonment; preventive detention; minimum- *or* maximum-security imprisonment *or* detention; lockdown

4 **commitment,** committal, consignment; recommitment, remand; mittimus <law>; institutionalization

5 **custody,** custodianship, keep <old>, **keeping, care, change, ward,** guarding, hold, protective *or* preventive custody; protection, safekeeping 1007.1

6 **arrest,** arrestment, arrestation, pinch *and* bust *and* collar <all nonformal>; **capture, apprehension, seizure,** netting <nonformal>

7 **place of confinement,** close quarters, not enough room to swing a cat; limbo, hell, purgatory; pound, pinfold *or* penfold; **cage; enclosure,** pen, coop 212.3

8 **prison,** prisonhouse, correctional *or* correction facility, minimum- *or* maximum-security facility, **penitentiary,** pen <nonformal>, keep, penal institution, bastille, state prison, federal prison; house of detention, detention center, detention home; **jail, gaol** <Brit>, jailhouse, lockup, toolbooth <Scots>, bridewell <Brit>; maximum- *or* minimum-security prison; **military prison, guardhouse, stockade, brig; dungeon,** oubliette, black hole; **reformatory,** house of correction, reform school, training school, industrial school, borstal *or* borstal institution <both Brit>; debtor's prison *and* sponging house <both old>; **prison camp,** internment camp, detention camp, labor camp, forced-labor camp, gulag, **concentration camp;** prisoner-of-war camp *or* stockade, POW camp; cell; bullpen; solitary confinement, the hole

<nonformal>; **cell,** prison *or* jail cell; **detention cell,** holding cell, lockup; tank *and* drunk tank <both nonformal>; cellblock, cellhouse; condemned cell, death cell, death house *or* row; penal settlement *or* colony, Devil's Island

9 <nonformal terms> **slammer, slam, jug,** can, coop, cooler, hoosegow, stir, clink, pokey, nick *and* quod *and* chokey <all Brit>; **joint,** big house, big school, big cage, big joint, brig, tank

10 **jailer, gaoler** <Brit>, correctional *or* correction *or* corrections officer; **keeper, warder,** prison guard, **turnkey,** bull *and* screw <both nonformal>; **warden,** governor <Brit>, commandant, principal keeper; custodian, guardian 1007.6; **guard** 1007.9

11 **prisoner, captive,** *détenu* <Fr>, cageling; arrestee; **convict,** con <nonformal>; **jailbird** <nonformal>, gaolbird <Brit nonformal>, stir bird <nonformal>; **detainee; internee; prisoner of war** *or* POW; enemy prisoner of war *or* EPWS; political prisoner, prisoner of conscience; lifer <nonformal>; trusty; parolee, ticket-of-leave man *or* ticket-of-leaver <both Brit>; ex-convict; chain gang

VERBS 12 **confine, shut in,** shut away, coop in, hem in, fence in *or* up, wall in *or* up, rail in; **shut up, coop up, pen up,** box up, mew up, bottle up, cork up, seal up, **impound;** pen, coop, pound <old>, crib, mew, cloister, immure, cage, cage in, encage; **enclose** 212.5; **hold, keep in,** hold *or* keep in custody, **detain,** keep in detention, constrain, ground, **restrain,** hold in restraint; check, inhibit 428.7; restrict 428.9; shackle 428.10

13 **quarantine, isolate,** segregate, separate, seclude; **cordon, cordon off,** seal off, rope off; wall off, set up barriers, put behind barriers

14 **imprison, incarcerate, intern,** immure; **jail,** gaol <Brit>, jug <nonformal>, throw into jail, throw under the jailhouse <nonformal>; throw *or* cast in prison, clap up, clap in jail *or* prison, send up the river <nonformal>; **lock up,** lock in, bolt in, put *or* keep under lock and key; hold captive, hold prisoner, hold in captivity; hold under close *or* house arrest

15 **arrest,** make an arrest, put under arrest, pick up; catch flat-footed; catch with one's pants down *or* hand in the till <nonformal>, catch one in the act *or* redhanded *or* in flagrante delicto, catch *or* have one dead to rights; run down, run to earth, **take captive, take prisoner, appre-**hend, **capture,** seize, net <nonformal>, lay by the heels, **take into custody**

16 <nonformal terms> **bust, pinch,** make a pinch, nab, pull in, **run in,** collar

17 **commit,** consign, commit to prison, send to jail, send up *and* send up the river <both nonformal>; commit to an institution, institutionalize; recommit, remit, remand

18 **be imprisoned, do** *or* **serve time** <nonformal>; pay one's debt to society

ADJS 19 **confined,** in confinement, **shut-in,** pent, **pent-up,** kept in, under restraint; "cabined, cribbed, confined"—Shakespeare; impounded; grounded, out of circulation; **detained;** restricted 428.15; cloistered, enclosed 212.10

20 **quarantined,** isolated, segregated, separated; cordoned, cordoned *or* sealed *or* roped off

21 **jailed,** jugged <nonformal>, **imprisoned, incarcerated, interned,** immured; **in prison,** in stir <nonformal>, in captivity, **behind bars,** locked up, under lock and key, in durance vile

22 **under arrest, in custody,** in hold, in charge <Brit>, under *or* in detention; under close arrest, under house arrest

430 FREEDOM

NOUNS 1 **freedom, liberty; license,** loose <old>; run *and* the run of <both nonformal>, "the right to live as we wish"—Epictetus, "the will to be responsible to ourselves"—Nietzsche, "political power divided into small fragments"—Thomas Hobbes, "the choice of working or starving"—Samuel Johnson, "the recognition of necessity"—Friedrich Engels; **civil liberty,** the Four Freedoms <F D Roosevelt>: freedom of speech and expression, freedom of worship, freedom from want, freedom from fear; constitutional freedom; academic freedom

2 **right, rights, civil rights,** civil liberties, constitutional rights, legal rights; Bill of Rights, Petition of Right, Declaration of Right, Declaration of the Rights of Man, Magna Charta *or* Carta; **unalienable rights, human rights,** natural rights, "life, liberty, and the pursuit of happiness"—Thomas Jefferson

3 **unrestraint, unconstraint,** noncoercion, nonintimidation; **unreserve,** irrepressibleness, irrepressibility, uninhibitedness, exuberance 109.4; **immoderacy, intemperance,** incontinence, uncontrol, unruliness, indiscipline; **aban-**

don, abandonment, **licentiousness,** wantonness, riotousness, wildness; permissiveness, unstrictness, **laxness** 426

4 **latitude, scope, room,** range, way, field, maneuvering space *or* room, room to swing a cat <nonformal>; **margin,** clearance, **space,** open space *or* field, elbowroom, breathing space, **leeway** <nonformal>, sea room, wide berth; **tolerance; free scope,** full *or* ample scope, **free hand,** free play, free course; **carte blanche,** blank check; no holds barred; swing, play, full swing; rope, long rope *or* tether, rope enough to hang oneself

5 **independence, self-determination, self government,** self-direction, **autonomy,** home rule; autarky, autarchy, self-containment, self-sufficiency; **individualism,** rugged individualism, individual freedom; **self-reliance,** self-dependence; inner-direction; Declaration of Independence

6 **free will,** free choice, **discretion,** option, choice, say, say-so *and* druthers <both nonformal>, free decision; **full consent;** absolute *or* unconditioned *or* noncontingent free will

7 **own free will, own account, own accord, own hook** *and* own say-so <both nonformal>, own discretion, own choice, **own initiative,** personal initiative, own responsibility, personal *or* individual responsibility, own volition, own authority, own power; own way, own sweet way <nonformal>; law unto oneself

8 **exemption,** exception, **immunity; release,** discharge; **franchise, license,** charter, patent, liberty; diplomatic immunity, congressional *or* legislative immunity; special case *or* privilege; grandfather clause, grandfathering; privilege; permission 443

9 **noninterference, nonintervention; isolationism; laissez-faireism,** let-alone principle *or* doctrine *or* policy, deregulation; *laissez-faire, laissez-aller* <both Fr>; liberalism, free enterprise, free competition, self-regulating market; capitalism 611.8; free trade

10 **liberalism,** libertarianism, latitudinarianism; broad-mindedness, open-mindedness, toleration, tolerance; unbigotedness 978.1; libertinism, **freethinking,** free thought; liberalization, **liberation** 431

11 **freeman,** freewoman; citizen, free citizen, burgess; franklin; emancipated *or* manumitted slave, freedman, freedwoman; dedititian

12 **free agent, independent, free lance;** indi-

vidualist, rugged individualist; free spirit; **liberal,** libertarian, latitudinarian; libertine, freethinker; free trader; **nonpartisan,** neutral, mugwump; isolationist; nonaligned nation; third world, third force

VERBS 13 **liberalize,** ease; **free, liberate** 431.4

14 **exempt, free, release,** discharge, **let go** *and* **let off** <both nonformal>, set at liberty, spring <nonformal>; **excuse,** spare, except, grant immunity, make a special case of; grandfather; **dispense,** dispense from, give dispensation from; dispense with, save the necessity; remit, remise; absolve 601.4

15 **give a free hand,** let one have his head, **give one his head; give the run of** <nonformal>, give the freedom of; give one leeway <nonformal>, give full play; give one scope *or* space *or* room; **give rein** *or* **free rein to,** give the reins to, give bridle to, give one line, give one rope; **give one carte blanche, give one a blank check;** let go one's own way, let one go at will

16 **not interfere, leave** *or* **let alone, let be,** leave *or* let well enough alone, let sleeping dogs lie; **keep hands off,** not tamper, not meddle, not involve oneself, not get involved, let it ride <nonformal>, let nature take its course; live and let live, leave one to oneself, leave one in peace; mind one's own business; **decontrol, deregulate**

17 <nonformal terms> **get off one's back** *or* **one's case** *or* **one's tail,** get out of one's face *or* hair, **butt out, back off,** leave be, call off the dogs, keep one's nose out, get lost, take a walk

18 **be free,** feel free, feel free as a bird, feel at liberty; **go at large,** breathe free, breathe the air of freedom; **have free scope,** have one's druthers <nonformal>, have a free hand, have the run of <nonformal>; be at home, feel at home; be freed, be released; be exonerated, go *or* get off scotfree, walk

19 **let oneself go,** let go, let loose *and* cut loose *and* let one's hair down <all nonformal>, **give way to,** open up, let it all hang out <nonformal>; go all out, go flat out <Brit>, pull out all the stops; go unrestrained, run wild, have one's fling, sow one's wild oats

20 **stand on one's own two feet, shift for oneself, fend for oneself,** stand on one's own, strike out for oneself, trust one's good right arm, look out for number one <nonformal>; **go it alone, be one's own man,**

pull a lone oar, play a lone hand <nonformal>, **paddle one's own canoe** <nonformal>; suffice to oneself, do for oneself, make *or* pay one's own way; ask no favors, ask no quarter; **be one's own boss** <nonformal>, answer only to oneself, ask leave of no man; **go one's own way,** take one's own course; do on one's own, do on one's own initiative, do on one's own hook *or* say-so <nonformal>, do in one's own sweet way <nonformal>; **have a will of one's own,** have one's own way, do what one likes *or* wishes *or* chooses, **do as one pleases,** go as one pleases, please oneself <nonformal>, **suit oneself;** have a free mind; free-lance, be a free agent

ADJS **21 free; at liberty, at large,** on the loose, **loose,** unengaged, disengaged, detached, unattached, uncommitted, uninvolved, clear, in the clear, go-as-you-please, easygoing, footloose, footloose and fancy-free, "afoot and light-hearted"—Whitman, free and easy; free as air, free as a bird, free as the wind; scot-free; **freeborn; freed, liberated, emancipated,** manumitted, released, uncaged, sprung <nonformal>

22 independent, self-dependent; free-spirited, freewheeling, free-floating, free-standing; **self-determined,** self-directing, one's own man; inner-directed, **individualistic;** self-governed, **self-governing, autonomous,** sovereign; stand-alone, self-reliant, self-sufficient, self-subsistent, self-supporting, self-contained, autarkic, autarchic; nonpartisan, neutral, **nonaligned;** third-world, third-force

23 free-acting, free-going, free-moving, free-working; freehand, freehanded; **free-spoken,** outspoken, **plain-spoken, open, frank,** direct, candid, blunt 644.17

24 unrestrained, unconstrained, unforced, uncompelled, uncoerced; unmeasured, **uninhibited, unsuppressed, unrepressed, unreserved,** go-go <nonformal>, exuberant 109.14; **uncurbed, unchecked, unbridled,** unmuzzled; **unreined,** reinless; **uncontrolled,** unmastered, unsubdued, ungoverned, **unruly;** out of control, out of hand, out of one's power; **abandoned,** intemperate, immoderate, **incontinent, licentious,** loose, wanton, rampant, riotous, wild; irrepressible; lax 426.4

25 nonrestrictive, unrestrictive; **permissive,** hands-off <nonformal>; indulgent 427.8; lax 426.4; **liberal,** libertarian, latitudinarian; broad-minded, open-minded, tolerant; unbigoted 978.8; libertine; free-thinking

26 unhampered, untrammeled, unhandicapped, unimpeded, unhindered, unprevented, unclogged, unobstructed; clear, unencumbered, unburdened, unladen, unembarrassed, disembarrassed

27 unrestricted, unconfined, uncircumscribed, unbound <old>, unbounded, unmeasured; **unlimited,** limitless, illimitable; unqualified, unconditioned, **unconditional,** without strings, no strings, no strings attached; **absolute,** perfect, unequivocal, full, plenary; open-ended, open, **wide-open** <nonformal>; decontrolled, deregulated

28 unbound, untied, **unfettered,** unshackled, unchained; unmuzzled, ungagged; uncensored; declassified

29 unsubject, ungoverned, unenslaved, **unenthralled;** unvanquished, unconquered, unsubdued, unquelled, **untamed,** unbroken, undomesticated, unreconstructed

30 exempt, immune; exempted, **released, excused,** excepted, let off <nonformal>, spared; grandfathered; **privileged, licensed,** favored, chartered; permitted; dispensed; **unliable,** unsubject, irresponsible, unaccountable, unanswerable

31 quit, clear, free, rid; free of, clear of, quit of, rid of, shut of, shed of <nonformal>

ADVS **32 freely,** free; **without restraint,** without stint, **unreservedly,** with abandon; outright

33 independently, alone, by oneself, all by one's lonesome <nonformal>, under one's own power *or* steam, **on one's own** *and* **on one's own hook** <both nonformal>, on one's own initiative, on one's own bottom <old>; **on one's own account** *or* **responsibility,** on one's own say-so <nonformal>; **of one's own free will, of one's own accord,** of one's own volition, at one's own discretion

431 LIBERATION

NOUNS **1 liberation, freeing,** setting free, setting at liberty; **deliverance, delivery; rescue** 398; **emancipation,** disenthrallment, manumission; enfranchisement, affranchisement; Emancipation Proclamation; women's liberation; gay liberation; women's *or* gay *or* men's lib <nonformal>

2 release, freeing, unhanding, loosing, unloosing; unbinding, untying, unbuckling, unshackling, unfettering, unlashing, unstrapping, untrussing *and* unpinioning <both old>, unmanacling, **unleashing,** unchaining, untethering, unhobbling, unharnessing, unyoking, unbridling; unmuzzling, ungagging; unlocking, unlatching, unbolting, unbarring; unpenning, uncaging; **discharge, dismissal;** parole; convict release, springing <nonformal>; demobilization, separation from the service

3 **extrication,** freeing, releasing, clearing; **disengagement, disentanglement,** untangling, unsnarling, unraveling, disentwining, disinvolvement, unknotting, disembarrassment, disembroilment; dislodgment, breaking out or loose, busting out or loose <nonformal>

VERBS 4 **liberate, free, deliver, set free,** set at liberty, set at large; **emancipate,** manumit, disenthrall; enfranchise, affranchise; **rescue** 398.3

5 **release, unhand, let go, let loose, turn loose,** cast loose, let out, let off, let go free; **discharge, dismiss;** let out on bail, grant bail to, go bail for <nonformal>; parole, put on parole; release from prison, spring <nonformal>; demobilize, separate from the service

6 **loose,** loosen, let loose, cut loose or free, unloose, unloosen; **unbind, untie,** unstrap, unbuckle, unlash, untruss and unpinion <both old>; **unfetter, unshackle,** unmanacle, unchain, unhandcuff, untie one's hands; **unleash,** untether, unhobble; unharness, unyoke, unbridle; unmuzzle, ungag; unlock, unlatch, unbolt, unbar; unpen, uncage

7 **extricate, free, release, clear,** get out; **disengage,** disentangle, untangle, unsnarl, unravel, disentwine, disinvolve, unknot, disembarrass, disembroil; dislodge, break out or loose, cut loose, tear loose

8 **free oneself from,** deliver oneself from, **get free of,** get quit of, **get rid of,** get clear of, **get out of,** get well out of, get around, extricate oneself, get out of a jam <nonformal>; **throw off, shake off;** break out, bust out <nonformal>, **escape** 369.6; wriggle out of

9 **go free,** go scot free, go at liberty, **get off,** get off scot-free, get out of, beat the rap and walk <both nonformal>

ADJS 10 **liberated, freed, emancipated, released;** delivered, rescued, ransomed, redeemed; extricated, unbound, untied, unshackled, etc; free 430.20; on parole

432 SUBJECTION

NOUNS 1 **subjection, subjugation; domination** 612.2; **restraint, control** 428.1; **bondage, captivity; thrall, thralldom,** enthrallment; **slavery,** enslavement, master-slave relationship; **servitude,** compulsory or involuntary servitude, servility, bond service, indentureship; **serfdom,** serfhood, villenage, **vassalage;** helotry, helotism; debt slavery, **peonage;** feudalism, feudality; absolutism, tyranny 612.9,10; deprivation of freedom, disenfranchisement, disfranchisement

2 **subservience** or subserviency, subjecthood, subordinacy, **subordination,** juniority, **inferiority;** lower status, subordinate role, satellite status; back seat and second fiddle and hind tit <all nonformal>; **service,** servitorship 577.12

3 **dependence** or dependency, tutelage, chargeship, wardship; clientship, clientage

4 **subdual, quelling,** crushing, trampling or treading down, reduction, **humbling, humiliation; breaking, taming,** domestication, gentling; conquering 412.1; **suppression** 428.2

5 **subordinate,** junior, secondary, second-in-command, lieutenant, **inferior; underling,** understrapper, low man on the totem pole <nonformal>, errand boy, flunky, gofer <nonformal>; assistant, personal assistant, helper 616.6; strong right arm, **right-hand man** 616.7; **servant, employee** 577

6 **dependent, charge, ward,** client, protégé, encumbrance; pensioner, pensionary; public charge, ward of the state; foster child; dependency or dependent state, client state, satellite or satellite state, puppet government, creature

7 **subject, vassal,** liege, liege man, liege subject, homager; **captive; slave,** servant, chattel, chattel slave, **bondsman,** bondman, **bondslave,** theow, thrall; indentured servant; laborer, esne; bondwoman, bondswoman, bondmaid; odalisque, concubine; galley slave; **serf,** helot, villein; churl; debt slave, **peon**

VERBS 8 **subjugate, subject, subordinate; dominate** 612.15; disfranchise, disenfranchise, divest or deprive of freedom; **enslave,** enthrall, hold in thrall, make a chattel of; take captive, lead captive or into captivity; **hold in subjection,** hold in bondage, **hold captive,** hold in captivity; **hold down,** keep down, keep under; **keep** or **have under one's thumb,** have tied to one's apron strings, hold in leash, hold in leading strings, hold in swaddling clothes, hold or keep at one's beck and call; vassalize, make dependent or tributary; peonize

9 subdue, master, overmaster, **quell, crush, reduce,** beat down, **break,** break down, overwhelm; tread underfoot, trample on *or* down, trample underfoot, roll in the dust, trample in the dust, drag at one's chariot wheel; **suppress** 428.8; make one give in *or* say 'uncle' <nonformal>, **conquer** 412.10; kick around <nonformal>, tyrannize 612.16; unman 19.12; bring low, **bring to terms, humble,** humiliate, take down a notch *or* peg, bend, **bring one to his knees, bend to one's will**

10 have subject, twist *or* turn *or* wind around one's little finger, make lie down and roll over, have eating out of one's hand, **lead by the nose,** make a puppet of, make putty of, make a sport *or* plaything of; use as a doormat, treat like dirt under one's feet

11 domesticate, tame, break, bust *and* gentle <both nonformal>, break in, break to harness; housebreak

12 depend on, be at the mercy of, be the sport *or* plaything *or* puppet of, be putty in the hands of; not dare to say one's soul is one's own; eat out of one's hands; play second fiddle, suck hind tit <nonformal>, take a back seat

ADJS **13 subject, dependent,** tributary, client; **subservient, subordinate, inferior;** servile; liege, **vassal,** feudal, feudatory

14 subjugated, subjected, **enslaved, enthralled, in thrall, captive,** bond, unfree; disenfranchised, disfranchised, **oppressed, suppressed** 428.14; **in subjection, in bondage, in captivity,** in slavery, in bonds, in chains; under the lash, under the heel; **in one's power,** in one's control, in one's hands *or* clutches, in one's pocket, **under one's thumb,** at one's mercy, under one's command *or* orders, at one's beck and call, at one's feet, at one's pleasure; **subordinated,** playing second fiddle; at the bottom of the ladder, sucking hind tit <nonformal>

15 subdued, quelled, crushed, broken, reduced, mastered, overmastered, humbled, humiliated, brought to one's knees, brought low, made to grovel; **tamed, domesticated,** broken to harness, gentled; housebroken *or* housebroke

16 downtrodden, downtrod <old>, kept down *or* under, ground down, overborne, trampled, **oppressed, abused,** misused; **henpecked, browbeaten,** led by the nose, in leading strings, tied to one's apron strings, ordered *or* kicked around <nonformal>, regimented, tyrannized; slavish, servile, submissive 433.12; un-

manned 19.19; treated like dirt under one's feet

PREPS **17 under, below, beneath,** underneath, subordinate to; at the feet of; under the heel of; at the beck and call of, at the whim *or* pleasure of

433 SUBMISSION

NOUNS **1 submission,** submittal, **yielding; compliance,** complaisance, **acquiescence, acceptance;** going along with <nonformal>, **assent** 332; **consent** 441; **obedience** 326; subjection 432; **resignation,** resignedness, stoicism, philosophical attitude; **deference,** homage, kneeling, obeisance; **passivity, unassertiveness,** passiveness, supineness, longanimity, long-suffering, long-sufferance <old>, nonresistance, nonopposition, nonopposal, quietness, nondissent, quietude, quietism; **cowardice** 491

2 surrender, capitulation; renunciation, giving over, abandonment, relinquishment, **cession;** giving up *or* in, backing off *or* down <nonformal>, retreat, recession, recedence

3 submissiveness, docility, tractability, biddability, yieldingness, compliableness <old>, pliancy, pliability, flexibility, malleability, moldability, ductility, plasticity, facility; agreeableness, agreeability; subservience, **servility** 138

4 manageability, governability, controllability, manipulability, manipulatability, corrigibility, untroublesomeness; **tameness,** housebrokenness; tamableness, domesticability; milk-toast, milquetoast, Caspar Milquetoast

5 meekness, gentleness, tameness, mildness, mild-manneredness, peaceableness, lamblikeness, dovelikeness; **self-abnegation, humility** 137

VERBS **6 submit, comply, take, accept,** go along with <nonformal>, suffer, bear, brook, **acquiesce,** be agreeable, accede, **assent** 332.8; **consent** 441.2; relent, **succumb,** resign, resign oneself, give oneself up, not resist; take one's medicine, swallow the pill, face the music; **bite the bullet; knuckle down** *or* **under,** knock under <old>, take it, swallow it; jump through a hoop, dance to another's tune; take it lying down; put up with it, grin and bear it, make the best of it, take the bitter with the sweet, shrug, shrug off, **live with it;** obey 326.2

7 yield, cede, give way, give ground, back down, give up, give in, cave in <nonfor-

mal>, withdraw from or quit the field, break off combat, cease resistance, have no fight left

8 **surrender, give up, capitulate,** acknowledge defeat, **cry quits,** cry pax <Brit>, **say 'uncle'** <nonformal>, beg a truce, pray for quarter, implore mercy, **throw in the towel** or **sponge** <nonformal>, show or wave the white flag, lower or haul down or strike one's flag or colors, throw down or lay down or deliver up one's arms, hand over one's sword, yield the palm, pull in one's horns <nonformal>, come to terms; renounce, abandon, relinquish, **cede,** give over, hand over

9 **submit to, yield to, defer to,** bow to, give way to, knuckle under to, succumb to

10 **bow down,** bow, bend, stoop, crouch, **bow one's head,** bend the neck, bow submission; genuflect, curtsy; **bow to,** bend to, knuckle to <nonformal>, bend or bow to one's will, bend to one's yoke; kneel to, **bend the knee to, fall on one's knees before,** crouch before, **fall at one's feet,** throw oneself at the feet of, prostrate oneself before, **truckle to,** cringe to; **kowtow,** bow and scrape, grovel, do obeisance or homage; kiss ass <nonformal>

11 **eat dirt, eat crow, eat humble pie,** lick the dust, kiss the rod

ADJS 12 **submissive, compliant,** compliable <old>, complaisant, complying, **acquiescent,** consenting 441.4; **assenting,** accepting, agreeable; subservient, abject, **obedient** 326.3; servile; **resigned,** uncomplaining; unassertive; **passive,** supine, **unresisting,** nonresisting, unresistant, nonresistant, nonresistive, long-suffering, longanimous, nonopposing, nondissenting

13 **docile, tractable,** biddable, unmurmuring, **yielding,** pliant, pliable, flexible, malleable, moldable, ductile, plastic, facile <old>, like putty in one's hands

14 **manageable, governable, controllable,** manipulable, manipulatable, handleable, corrigible, restrainable, untroublesome; domitable, tamable, domesticable; milktoast or milquetoast

15 **meek, gentle, mild,** mild-mannered, peaceable, pacific, quiet; **subdued, chastened, tame,** tamed, broken, housebroken, domesticated; lamblike, gentle as a lamb, dovelike; humble

16 **deferential, obeisant; subservient, obsequious,** servile 138.13; crouching, prostrate, prone, on one's belly, on one's knees, on one's marrowbones <nonformal>, on bended knee

ADVS 17 **submissively, compliantly,** complaisantly, acquiescently, agreeably; **obediently** 326.6; **resignedly,** uncomplainingly, with resignation; **passively,** supinely, unresistingly, unresistantly, nonresistively

18 **docilely, tractably,** biddably, **yieldingly,** pliantly, pliably, malleably, flexibly, plastically, facilely <old>

19 **meekly, gently, tamely, mildly,** peaceably, pacifically, quietly, like a lamb

434 OBSERVANCE

NOUNS 1 **observance,** observation; **keeping,** adherence, heeding; compliance, conformance, conformity, accordance; **faith,** faithfulness, fidelity; **respect, deference** 155.1; **performance, practice,** execution, discharge, carrying out or through; dutifulness 641.2, acquittal, acquittance <both old>, fulfillment, satisfaction; heed, care 339.1

VERBS 2 **observe, keep, heed, follow,** keep the faith; regard, defer to, **respect** 155.4, attend to, **comply with,** conform to; hold by, **abide by,** adhere to; **live up to,** act up to, practice what one preaches, **be faithful to,** keep faith with, do justice to, do the right thing by; **fulfill,** fill, meet, satisfy; **make good,** keep or make good one's word or promise, be as good as one's word, redeem one's pledge, stand to one's engagement

3 **perform, practice,** do, execute, discharge, carry out or through, carry into execution, do one's duty 641.10, do one's office, fulfill one's role, discharge one's function

ADJS 4 **observant,** respectful 155.8, regardful, mindful; **faithful,** devout, devoted, true, loyal, constant; dutiful 641.13, duteous; as good as one's word; **practicing,** active; compliant, conforming; punctual, punctilious, scrupulous, meticulous, conscientious 339.12

435 NONOBSERVANCE

NOUNS 1 **nonobservance,** inobservance, unobservance, nonadherence; nonconformity, disconformity, **nonconformance, noncompliance;** apostasy; inattention, indifference, **disregard** 983.1; laxity 426.1; **nonfulfillment, nonperformance,** nonfeasance, failure, **dereliction, delinquency,** omission, default, slight, oversight; **negligence; neglect** 340; abandonment 370

2 violation, infraction, breach, breaking; **infringement, transgression, trespass,** contravention; offense 674.4; breach of promise, breach of contract, breach of trust *or* faith, bad faith, breach of privilege; breach of the peace

VERBS **3 disregard,** lose sight of, pay no regard to; **neglect** 340.6; renege, abandon 370.5; defect 857.13

4 violate, break, breach; infringe, transgress, trespass, contravene, trample on *or* upon, trample underfoot, do violence to, make a mockery of, outrage; **defy,** set at defiance, flout, set at naught, set naught by; take the law into one's own hands; break one's promise, break one's word

ADJS **5 nonobservant,** inobservant, unobservant, nonadherent; nonconforming, unconforming, noncompliant, uncompliant; inattentive, **disregardful** 983.6; **negligent** 340.10; unfaithful, untrue, unloyal, inconstant, lapsed, renegade 857.20/363.11

436 PROMISE

NOUNS **1 promise, pledge,** solemn promise, troth, plight, faith, parole, **word, word of honor,** solemn declaration *or* word; **oath, vow;** avouch, avouchment; **assurance, guarantee,** warranty; entitlement

2 obligation, commitment, agreement, engagement, undertaking, recognizance; **understanding,** gentlemen's agreement; verbal agreement, nonformal agreement, pactum <law>; tacit *or* unspoken agreement; **contract** 437.1; designation, committal, earmarking

3 betrothal, betrothment, espousal, **engagement,** handfasting *and* affiance <both old>, troth, marriage contract *or* vow, plighted troth *or* faith *or* love; banns, banns of matrimony; prenuptial agreement *or* contract

VERBS **4 promise,** give *or* make a promise, hold out an expectation; **pledge,** plight, troth, **vow; give one's word,** pledge *or* pass one's word, give one's parole, **give one's word of honor,** plight one's troth *or* faith, pledge *or* plight one's honor; cross one's heart *and* cross one's heart and hope to die <both nonformal>, **swear;** vouch, avouch, **warrant, guarantee, assure;** underwrite, countersign

5 commit, engage, undertake, obligate, bind, **agree to,** answer for, be answerable for, take on oneself, be responsible for, be security for, go bail for, accept obligation *or* responsibility, bind oneself to, put oneself down for; have an understanding; enter into a gentlemen's agreement; take the vows *or* marriage vows; shake hands on; contract; designate, commit, earmark

6 be engaged, affiance, betroth, troth, plight one's troth, **contract,** contract an engagement, pledge *or* promise in marriage; publish the banns

ADJS **7 promissory,** votive; under *or* upon oath, on one's word, on one's word of honor, on the Book, under hand and seal

8 promised, pledged, bound, committed, compromised, **obligated; sworn,** warranted, **guaranteed,** assured, underwritten; contracted 437.12; **engaged, plighted, affianced, betrothed,** intended

ADVS **9** on one's honor *or* word *or* word of honor *or* parole; solemnly

437 COMPACT

NOUNS **1 compact, pact, contract,** legal contract, valid contract, **covenant,** convention, transaction, paction <Scots>, accord, **agreement,** mutual agreement, agreement between *or* among parties, signed *or* written agreement, formal agreement, legal agreement, undertaking, stipulation; adjustment, accommodation; **understanding, arrangement, bargain,** dicker *and* **deal** <both nonformal>; **settlement,** negotiated settlement; **labor contract, union contract** 727.3, wage contract, employment contract, collective agreement; cartel, consortium; protocol; bond, binding agreement, ironclad agreement, covenant of salt; gentleman's *or* gentlemen's agreement; promise 436

2 treaty, international agreement, *entente, entente cordiale* <both Fr>, concord, concordat, cartel, convention, paction, capitulation; **alliance, league;** nonaggression pact, mutual-defense treaty; NATO *or* North Atlantic Treaty Organization; SEATO *or* Southeast Asia Treaty Organization; Warsaw Pact

3 signing, signature, sealing, closing, conclusion, solemnization; handshake

4 execution, completion; transaction; carrying out, discharge, fulfillment, prosecution, effectuation; enforcement; observance 434

VERBS **5 contract,** compact, **covenant, bargain, agree, engage,** undertake, commit, mutually commit, make a deal <nonformal>, do a deal <Brit nonformal>, stipulate, agree to, bargain for, contract for; preset, prearrange, **promise** 436.4; subcontract, outsource

6 **treat with, negotiate, bargain,** make terms, sit down with, sit down at the bargaining table

7 **sign, shake hands** or shake <nonformal>, affix one's John Hancock <nonformal>, seal, formalize, make legal and binding, solemnize; agree on terms, come to an agreement 332.10; strike a bargain 731.18; plea-bargain

8 **arrange, settle; adjust,** fine-tune, accommodate, reshuffle, rejigger <nonformal>, **compose,** fix, make up, straighten out, put or set straight, work out, sort out and square away <both nonformal>; **conclude,** close, **close with,** settle with

9 **execute, complete, transact,** promulgate, **make;** make out, fill out; **discharge, fulfill,** render, administer; **carry out,** carry through, put through, prosecute; effect, effectuate, set in motion, implement; enforce, put in force; **abide by, honor, live up to,** adhere to, live by, **observe** 434.2

ADJS 10 contractual, covenantal, conventional

11 **contracted,** compacted, **covenanted, agreed upon, bargained for,** agreed <Brit>, stipulated; engaged, undertaken; **promised** 436.8; arranged, settled; under hand and seal, **signed,** sealed; signed sealed and delivered

ADVS 12 **contractually, as agreed upon, as promised,** as contracted for, by the terms of the contract, according to the contract or bargain or agreement

438 SECURITY
<thing given as a pledge>

NOUNS 1 **security, surety,** indemnity, **guaranty, guarantee, warranty, insurance,** warrant, assurance; **obligation** 436.2, full faith and credit; **bond,** tie; stocks and bonds 738.1

2 **pledge, gage,** pignus, vadium <both L>; undertaking; **earnest,** earnest money, god's penny, handsel; escrow; token payment; pawn, hock <nonformal>; **bail,** bond, vadimonium; replevin, replevy, recognizance; mainprise; **hostage,** surety

3 **collateral,** collateral security or warranty; deposit, stake, forfeit; caution money, caution; margin; cosigned promissory note

4 **mortgage,** mortgage deed, deed of trust, lien, security agreement; vadium mortuum or mortuum vadium; dead pledge; vadium vivum, living pledge, antichresis; hypothec, hypothecation, bottomry, bottomry bond; adjustment mortgage,

blanket mortgage, chattel mortgage, closed mortgage, participating mortgage, installment mortgage, leasehold mortgage, trust mortgage; first mortgage, second mortgage, third mortgage; adjustable-rate mortgage or ARM, variable-rate mortgage or VRM, fixed-rate mortgage; equity loan; reverse equity

5 **lien,** general lien, particular lien; pignus legale, common-law lien, statutory lien, judgment lien, pignus judiciale, tax lien, mechanic's lien; mortgage bond

6 **guarantor,** warrantor, guaranty, guarantee; mortgagor; insurer, underwriter; sponsor, surety; godparent, godfather, godmother; bondsman, bailsman, mainpernor

7 **warrantee,** mortgagee; insuree, policyholder; godchild, godson, goddaughter

8 guarantorship, **sponsorship,** sponsion

VERBS 9 **secure, guarantee, guaranty, warrant, assure, insure,** ensure, bond, **certify;** countersecure; **sponsor,** be sponsor for, sign for, sign one's note, **back,** stand behind or back of, stand up for; **endorse;** sign, cosign, **underwrite,** undersign, subscribe to; confirm, attest

10 **pledge,** impignorate and handsel <both old>, **deposit, stake,** post, put in escrow, **put up,** put up as collateral, lay out or down; **pawn,** put in pawn, spout or put up the spout <both old>, **hock** and **put in hock** <both nonformal>; mortgage, hypothecate, bottomry, bond; **put up** or **go bail,** bail out

ADJS 11 **secured,** covered, **guaranteed, warranted,** certified, **insured,** ensured, **assured;** certain, sure 969.13

12 **pledged,** staked, posted, deposited, in escrow, **put up,** put up as collateral; on deposit, at stake; as earnest; **pawned,** in pawn, **in hock** <nonformal>, up the spout <old>

13 **in trust,** held in trust, held in pledge, fiduciary; in escrow

439 OFFER

NOUNS 1 **offer,** offering, proffer, presentation, **bid,** submission; **advance, overture,** approach, invitation; hesitant or tentative or preliminary approach, feeling-out, **feeler** <nonformal>; asking price; **counteroffer, counterproposal**

2 **proposal, proposition, suggestion,** instance; **motion,** resolution; sexual advance or approach or invitation or overture, indecent proposal, pass <nonfor-

mal>, improper suggestion; request 440

3 **ultimatum,** last or final word or offer, firm bid or price, sticking point

VERBS **4 offer, proffer, present,** tender, offer up, **put up, submit, extend,** prefer <old>, **hold out,** hold forth, place in one's way, lay at one's feet, put or place at one's disposal, put one in the way of

5 **propose, submit,** prefer; **suggest,** recommend, **advance,** commend to attention, **propound, pose, put forward,** bring forward, put or set forth, put it to, put or set or lay or bring before, dish up and come out or up with <both nonformal>; put a bee in one's bonnet, put ideas into one's head; **bring up, broach, moot,** introduce, open up, launch, start, kick off <nonformal>; **move, make a motion,** offer a resolution; postulate 950.12

6 **bid,** bid for, make a bid

7 **make advances,** approach, overture, **make an overture,** throw or fling oneself at one <nonformal>; **solicit, importune**

8 <nonformal terms> **proposition, come on to,** hit on, put or make a move on, jump one's bones, make or throw a pass, george, **make a play for,** play footsie with, pitch, mash <old>

9 **urge upon, press upon,** ply upon, push upon, force upon, thrust upon; **press, ply;** insist

10 **volunteer, come** or **step forward, offer** or **proffer** or **present oneself,** be at one's service, not wait to be asked, not wait for an invitation, need no prodding, step into the breach, be Johnny-on-the-spot <nonformal>

440 REQUEST

NOUNS **1 request,** asking; the touch <nonformal>; desire, wish, expressed desire; **petition,** petitioning, impetration, address; **application; requisition,** indent <Brit>; demand 421

2 **entreaty, appeal, plea, bid,** suit, call, cry, clamor, cri de cœur <Fr>, beseeching, impetration, obtestation; **supplication, prayer,** rogation, **beseechment,** imploring, imploration, obsecration, obtestation, adjuration, imprecation; **invocation,** invocatory plea or prayer

3 **importunity,** importunateness, urgency, pressure, high pressure and hard sell <both nonformal>; **urging, pressing, plying;** buttonholing; dunning; **teasing,** pestering, plaguing, nagging, nudging

<nonformal>; **coaxing,** wheedling, cajolery, cajolement, blandishment

4 **invitation, invite** and **bid** <both nonformal>, engraved invitation, bidding, biddance, **call,** calling, **summons**

5 **solicitation, canvass, canvassing; suit,** addresses; **courting, wooing**

6 **beggary,** mendicancy, mendicity; **begging,** cadging, scrounging; mooching and bumming and panhandling <all nonformal>

7 **petitioner, supplicant,** suppliant, suitor; **solicitor** 730.7; **applicant,** solicitant, claimant; **aspirant,** seeker, wannabee <nonformal>; **candidate,** postulant; bidder

8 **beggar, mendicant,** scrounger, **cadger; bum** and bummer and **moocher** and **panhandler** <all nonformal>; schnorrer <Yiddish>; hobo, tramp 178.3; loafer 331.8; mendicant friar; mendicant order

VERBS **9 request, ask,** make a request, **beg leave,** make bold to ask; **desire,** wish, wish for, express a wish for, crave; **ask for,** order, put in an order for, bespeak, call for, trouble one for; whistle for <nonformal>; **requisition,** make or put in a requisition, indent <Brit>; make application, **apply for,** file for, **put in for;** demand 421.4

10 **petition,** present or prefer a petition, sign a petition, circulate a petition; **pray,** sue; **apply to, call on** or **upon;** memorialize

11 **entreat, implore, beseech, beg,** crave, **plead, appeal, pray, supplicate,** impetrate, obtest; adjure, conjure; invoke, imprecate <old>, **call on** or **upon,** cry on or upon, **appeal to,** cry to, run to; go cap or hat in hand to; kneel to, go down on one's knees to, fall on one's knees to, go on bended knee to, throw oneself at the feet of, get or come down on one's marrowbones <nonformal>; **plead for,** clamor for, cry for, cry out for; call for help

12 **importune, urge, press,** pressure <nonformal>, prod, prod at, apply or exert pressure, push, **ply;** dun; **beset, buttonhole,** besiege, take or grasp by the lapels; work on <nonformal>, **tease,** pester, plague, nag, nag at, make a pest or nuisance of oneself, try one's patience, bug <nonformal>, nudge; **coax,** wheedle, cajole, blandish, flatter, soft-soap <nonformal>

13 **invite, ask, call, summon, call in, bid come,** extend or issue an invitation, request the presence of, request the pleasure of one's company, send an engraved invitation

14 solicit, canvass; court, woo, address, sue, sue for, pop the question <nonformal>; seek, bid for, look for; fish for, angle for

15 beg, scrounge, cadge; mooch *and* bum *and* panhandle <all nonformal>; hit *and* hit up *and* touch *and* put the touch on *and* make a touch <all nonformal>; pass the hat <nonformal>

ADJS **16** supplicatory, suppliant, supplicant, supplicating, prayerful, precative; petitionary; begging, mendicant, cadging, scrounging, mooching <nonformal>; on one's knees *or* bended knees, on one's marrow-bones <nonformal>; with joined *or* folded hands

17 imploring, entreating, beseeching, begging, pleading, appealing, precatory, precative, adjuratory

18 importunate; teasing, pesty, pesky <nonformal>, pestering, plaguing, nagging, dunning; coaxing, wheedling, cajoling, flattering, soft-soaping <nonformal>; insistent, demanding, urgent

19 invitational, inviting, invitatory

INTERJS **20** please, prithee <old>, pray, do, pray do; be so good as to, be good enough, have the goodness; will you, may it please you; if you please, *s'il vous plaît* <Fr>; I beg you, *je vous en prie* <Fr>; for God's *or* goodness *or* heaven's *or* mercy's sake; be my guest, feel free; gimme a break!, cut me some slack!

441 CONSENT

NOUNS **1** consent, assent, agreement, accord <old>, acceptance, approval, blessing, approbation, sanction, endorsement, ratification, backing; affirmation, affirmative, affirmative voice *or* vote, yea, aye, nod *and* okay *and* OK <all nonformal>; leave, permission 443; willingness, readiness, promptness, promptitude, eagerness, unreluctance, unloathness, ungrudgingness, tacit *or* unspoken *or* silent *or* implicit consent, connivance; acquiescence, compliance; submission 433

VERBS **2** consent, assent, give consent, yield assent, be willing, be amenable, be persuaded, accede to, accord to *and* grant <both old>, say yes *or* aye *or* yea, vote affirmatively, vote aye, nod, nod assent; accept, play *or* go along <nonformal>, agree to, sign off on <nonformal>, go along with <nonformal>; be in accord with, be in favor of, take kindly to, approve of, hold with; approve, give one's blessing to, okay *or* OK <nonformal>; sanction, endorse, ratify; consent to si-

lently *or* by implication *or in petto* <Ital>; wink at, connive at; be willing, turn a willing ear; deign, condescend; have no objection, not refuse; permit 443.9

3 acquiesce, comply, comply with, fall in with, take one up on <nonformal>, be persuaded, come round *or* around, come over, come to <nonformal>, see one's way clear to; submit 433.6,9

ADJS **4** consenting, assenting, affirmative, amenable, persuaded, approving, agreeing, favorable, accordant, consentient, consentual; sanctioning, endorsing, ratifying; acquiescent, compliant, compliable <old>; submissive 433.12; willing, agreeable, content; ready, prompt, eager, unreluctant, unloath, nothing loath, unmurmuring, ungrudging, unrefusing; permissive 443.14

ADVS **5** consentingly, assentingly, affirmatively, approvingly, favorably, positively, agreeably, accordantly; acquiescently, compliantly; willingly 324.8; yes 332.18

442 REFUSAL

NOUNS **1** refusal, rejection, turndown, turning down; thumbs-down <nonformal>, *pollice verso* <L>; nonconsent, nonacceptance; declining, declination, declension, declinature; denial, disclamation, disclaimer, disallowance; decertification, disaccreditation; repudiation 372.1; disagreement, dissent 333; recantation 363.3; contradiction 335.2; negation, abnegation, negative, negative answer, nay, no, nix <nonformal>; unwillingness 325; disobedience 327; noncompliance, nonobservance 435; withholding, holding back, retention, deprivation

2 repulse, rebuff, peremptory *or* flat *or* point-blank refusal, summary negative; a flea in one's ear; kiss-off *and* slap in the face *and* kick in the teeth <all nonformal>; short shrift

VERBS **3** refuse, decline, not consent, refuse consent, reject, turn down <nonformal>, decline to accept, not have, not buy <nonformal>; not hold with, not think *or* hear of; say no, say nay, vote nay, vote negatively *or* in the negative, side against, disagree, beg to disagree, dissent 333.4; shake one's head, negative, negate; vote down, turn thumbs down on; be unwilling 325.3; turn one's back on, turn a deaf ear to, set oneself against, set one's face against, be unmoved, harden one's heart, resist entreaty *or* persuasion; stand aloof, not lift a finger, have nothing to do with, wash one's hands of; hold out against; put *or* set one's foot down, refuse point-blank *or* summarily; decline politely *or* with thanks, beg off; **repudiate,** disallow, disclaim 372.2; decertify, disaccredit

4 **deny, withhold,** hold back; grudge, begrudge; close the hand *or* purse; deprive one of

5 **repulse, rebuff, repel,** kiss one off *and* slap one in the face *and* kick one in the teeth <all nonformal>, send one away with a flea in one's ear, give one short shrift, shut *or* slam the door in one's face, turn one away; slap *or* smack one down <nonformal>; deny oneself to, refuse to receive, not be at home to, cut, **snub** 157.5

ADJS 6 **unconsenting,** nonconsenting, **negative; unwilling** 325.5; **uncompliant,** uncomplying, uncomplaisant, inacquiescent, uncooperative; disobedient; rejective, declinatory; deaf to, not willing to hear of

PHRS 7 **I refuse, I won't,** I will not, I will do no such thing; over my dead body, far be it from me, not if I can help it, not likely, not on your life, count me out, include me out, I'm not taking any, I won't buy it, it's no go, like hell I will, I'll be hanged if I will, try and make me, you have another guess coming, you should live so long, I'll see you in hell first, nothing doing <all nonformal>; out of the question, not to be thought of, impossible; **no,** by no means, **no way, no way José, there's no way;** in a pig's eye *or* ear *or* ass, my eye *or* ass

443 PERMISSION

NOUNS 1 **permission, leave, allowance,** vouchsafement; **consent** 441; permission to enter, admission, ticket, ticket of admission; **license,** liberty 430.1; **okay** *and* **OK** *and* **nod** *and* **go-ahead** *and* **green light** *and* **go sign** *and* **thumbs-up** <all nonformal>; special permission, charter, patent, dispensation, release, waiver; zoning variance, variance

2 **sufferance, tolerance,** toleration, **indulgence;** winking, overlooking, connivance; permissiveness

3 **authorization, authority, sanction, licensing,** countenance, **warrant,** warranty, fiat; empowerment, enabling, entitlement, enfranchisement, certification; clearance, security clearance; ratification

332.4; legalization, legitimation, decriminalization

4 **carte blanche,** blank check <nonformal>, **full authority,** full power, free hand, open mandate

5 **grant, concession;** charter, franchise, liberty, diploma, patent, letters patent, brevet; royal grant

6 **permit, license, warrant;** building permit, learner's permit; driver's license, marriage license, hunting license, fishing license, etc; nihil obstat, imprimatur

7 **pass, passport, safe-conduct,** safeguard, protection; visa, entry visa, exit visa; **clearance,** clearance papers; bill of health, clean bill of health, pratique, full pratique

8 **permissibility,** permissibleness, **allowableness; admissibility,** admissibleness; justifiableness, warrantableness, sanctionableness; **validity,** legitimacy, lawfulness, licitness, legality

VERBS 9 **permit, allow, admit, let,** leave <nonformal>, give permission, give leave, make possible; **allow** *or* **permit of;** give *or* leave room for, open the door to; consent 441.2; **grant,** accord, vouchsafe; **okay** *and* **OK** *and* **give the nod** *or* **go-ahead** *or* **green light** *or* **go sign** <all nonformal>, say *or* give the word <nonformal>; dispense, release, waive

10 **suffer, countenance,** have, **tolerate, condone,** brook, endure, stomach, bear, bear with, put up with, stand for, hear of *and* go along with <both nonformal>; indulge 427.6; shut one's eyes to, **wink at,** blink at, overlook, connive at; leave the door *or* way open to

11 **authorize, sanction, warrant;** give official sanction *or* warrant, legitimize, validate, legalize; empower, give power, enable, entitle; **license; privilege;** charter, patent, enfranchise, franchise; accredit, certificate, certify; ratify 332.12; **legalize,** legitimate, legitimize, decriminalize

12 **give carte blanche,** issue *or* accord *or* give a blank check <nonformal>, give full power *or* authority, give an open mandate *or* invitation, give free rein, give a free hand, leave alone, leave it to one; permit all *or* anything, open the floodgates, remove all restrictions

13 **may,** can, have permission, **be permitted** *or* **allowed**

ADJS 14 **permissive,** admissive, permitting, allowing; consenting 441.4; **unprohibitive,** nonprohibitive; tolerating, obliging, **tolerant;** suffering, **indulgent, lenient** 427.7; hands-off <nonformal>; lax 426.4

15 permissible, allowable, admissible; justifiable, warrantable, sanctionable; licit, **lawful, legitimate, legal,** legitimized, legalized, legitimated, decriminalized

16 permitted, allowed, admitted; tolerated, on sufferance; unprohibited, unforbidden, unregulated, unchecked

17 authorized, empowered, entitled; **warranted, sanctioned; licensed, privileged;** chartered, patented; franchised, enfranchised; accredited, certificated

ADVS **18 permissively,** admissively; **tolerantly, indulgently**

19 permissibly, allowably, admissibly; with permission, by one's leave; licitly, lawfully, legitimately, legally

PHRS **20 by your leave,** with your permission, if you please, with respect, may I?

444 PROHIBITION

NOUNS **1 prohibition, forbidding,** forbiddance; **ruling out, disallowance,** denial, rejection 372; refusal 442; **repression, suppression** 428.2; **ban, embargo, enjoinder, injunction,** prohibitory injunction, **proscription,** inhibition, **interdict,** *interdictum* <L>, interdiction; **index,** *Index Expurgatorius, Index Librorum Prohibitorum* <both L>; **taboo;** thou-shalt-not *and* don't *and* no-no <all nonformal>; law, statute 673.3; preclusion, exclusion, **prevention** 1011.2; forbidden fruit, contraband; sumptuary law *or* ordinance; zoning, zoning law, restrictive convenant; **forbidden ground** *or* **territory,** no-man's land <nonformal>

2 veto, negative <old>; absolute veto, qualified *or* limited *or* negative veto, suspensive *or* suspensory veto, item veto, pocket veto; **thumbs-down** <nonformal>, *pollice verso* <L>

VERBS **3 prohibit, forbid; disallow, rule out** *or* **against;** deny, **reject** 372.2; say no to, **refuse** 442.3; **bar,** debar, preclude, exclude, exclude from, shut out, shut *or* close the door on, **prevent** 1011.14; **ban,** put under the ban, **outlaw; repress, suppress** 428.8; **enjoin,** put under an injunction, issue an injunction against, issue a prohibitory injunction; **proscribe,** inhibit, **interdict,** put *or* lay under an interdict *or* interdiction; put on the index; embargo, **lay** *or* **put an embargo on; taboo**

4 not permit *or* **allow, not have, not suffer** *or* **tolerate,** not endure, not stomach, not bear, not bear with, **not countenance,** not brook, brook no, not condone, not accept, not put up with, not go along with <nonformal>; not stand for *and* not hear of <both nonformal>, put *or* set one's foot down on <nonformal>

5 veto, put one's veto upon, decide *or* rule against, **turn thumbs down on** <nonformal>, **negative,** kill

ADJS **6 prohibitive,** prohibitory, prohibiting, **forbidding;** inhibitive, inhibitory, **repressive, suppressive** 428.11; proscriptive, interdictive, interdictory; preclusive, exclusive, **preventive** 1011.19

7 prohibited, forbidden, forbade, forbid, *verboten* <Ger>, **barred; vetoed; unpermissible,** nonpermissible, not permitted *or* allowed, unchartered, **unallowed;** disallowed, ruled out, contraindicated; beyond the pale, off limits, out of bounds; unauthorized, **unsanctioned,** unlicensed; banned, under the ban, **outlawed,** contraband; taboo, tabooed, untouchable; **illegal,** unlawful, illicit

445 REPEAL

NOUNS **1 repeal, revocation,** revoke, revokement; reneging, renigging *and* going back on *and* welshing <all nonformal>, **rescinding,** rescindment, rescission, **reversal, striking down, abrogation,** cessation, reversal; suspension; waiving, **waiver, setting aside; countermand,** counterorder; **annulment,** nullification, withdrawal, **invalidation,** voiding, voidance, vacation, vacatur, defeasance; **cancellation,** canceling, cancel, write-off; **abolition,** abolishment, **recall,** retraction, recantation 363.3

VERBS **2 repeal, revoke, rescind, reverse, strike down, abrogate;** renege, renig *and* go back on *and* welsh <all nonformal>; suspend; **waive, set aside; countermand,** counterorder; **abolish,** do away with; **cancel,** write off; **annul,** nullify, disannul, withdraw, **invalidate,** void, vacate, make void, declare null and void; **overrule,** override; **recall,** retract, recant; unwish

ADJS **3 repealed, revoked, rescinded,** struck down, set aside; **invalid,** void, **null and void**

446 PROMOTION

NOUNS **1 promotion, preferment, advancement, advance,** step-up *and* upping <both nonformal>, rise, elevation, upgrading, jump, step up, step up the ladder; **raise, boost** <nonformal>; kicking *or* bumping upstairs <nonformal>; exaltation, aggrandizement; ennoblement, knighting; graduation, passing; pay raise

VERBS **2 promote, advance,** prefer <old>, up *and* boost <both nonformal>, elevate, upgrade, jump; kick *or* bump upstairs <nonformal>; **raise;** exalt, aggrandize; **ennoble,** knight; pass, graduate; raise one's pay, up *or* boost one's pay <nonformal>

447 DEMOTION, DEPOSAL

NOUNS **1 demotion,** degrading, degradation, disgrading, downgrading, debasement; abasement, humbling, humiliation, casting down; **reduction,** bump *and* bust <both nonformal>; stripping of rank, depluming, displuming

2 deposal, deposition, removal, displacement, outplacement, supplanting, supplantation, replacement, deprivation, **ousting,** unseating; **cashiering, firing** <nonformal>, **dismissal** 908.5; reduction in forces *or* RIF; forced resignation; kicking upstairs <nonformal>; **superannuation,** pensioning off, putting out to pasture, **retirement,** the golden handshake *or* parachute <nonformal>; **suspension;** impeachment; purge, **liquidation; overthrow,** overthrowal; **dethronement,** disenthronement, discrownment; **disbarment,** disbarring; unfrocking, defrocking, unchurching; deconsecration, expulsion, excommunication 908.4

VERBS **3 demote, degrade,** disgrade, downgrade, debase, abase, humble, humiliate, **lower, reduce,** bump *and* bust <both nonformal>; strip of rank, cut off one's spurs, deplume, displume

4 depose, remove from office, send to the showers *and* give the gate <both nonformal>, divest *or* deprive *or* strip of office, **remove,** displace, outplace, supplant, replace; **oust; suspend; cashier,** drum out, strip of rank, **break,** bust <nonformal>; **dismiss** 908.19; **purge, liquidate; overthrow; retire,** superannuate, pension, pension off, put out to pasture, give the golden handshake *or* parachute <nonformal>; kick upstairs <nonformal>; **unseat,** unsaddle; **dethrone,** disenthrone, unthrone, uncrown, discrown; **disbar; unfrock,** defrock, unchurch; strike off the roll, read out of; **expel,** excommunicate 908.17; deconsecrate

448 RESIGNATION, RETIREMENT

NOUNS **1 resignation,** demission, **withdrawal, retirement,** pensioning, pensioning off, golden handshake *or* parachute <nonformal>, retiral <Scots>, superannuation, emeritus status; **abdication;** voluntary resignation; forced resignation, deposal 447; relinquishment 370.3

VERBS **2 resign,** demit, **quit,** leave, **vacate,** withdraw from; **retire,** superannuate, be superannuated, be pensioned *or* pensioned off, be put out to pasture, get the golden handshake *or* parachute <nonformal>; relinquish, give up 370.7; retire from office, stand down, stand *or* step aside, give up one's post, hang up one's spurs <nonformal>; **tender** *or* **hand in one's resignation,** send in one's papers, turn in one's badge *or* uniform; **abdicate,** renounce the throne, give up the crown; pension off 447.4; be invalided out

ADJS **3 retired,** in retirement, superannuated, on pension, pensioned, pensioned off, emeritus, emerita <fem>

449 AID

NOUNS **1 aid, help, assistance, support, succor, relief, comfort,** ease, remedy; mutual help *or* assistance; **service, benefit** 387.4; ministry, ministration, office, offices, good offices; yeoman's service; therapy 91; protection 1007; **bailout** <nonformal>, **rescue** 398

2 assist, helping hand, hand, lift; boost *and* leg up <both nonformal>; help in time of need; **support group,** self-help group, Alcoholics Anonymous *or* AA, Gamblers Anonymous, etc, 12-step group

3 support, maintenance, sustainment, sustentation, **sustenance, subsistence,** provision, total support, meal ticket <nonformal>; **keep, upkeep; livelihood, living,** meat, bread, daily bread; **nurture, fostering,** nurturance, nourishment, nutriture <old>, mothering, parenting, rearing, fosterage, foster-care, **care, caring,** care-giving, tender loving care *or* TLC <nonformal>; manna, manna in the wilderness; economic support, price support, subsidy, subsidization, subvention, endowment; **support services, social services**

4 patronage, fosterage, tutelage, sponsorship, backing, auspices, aegis, coattails <nonformal>, care, guidance, **championing, championship,** seconding; interest, advocacy, encouragement, **backing, abet-**

ment; countenance, **favor, goodwill,** charity, **sympathy**

5 **furtherance, helping along, advancement,** advance, **promotion, forwarding,** facilitation, speeding, easing *or* smoothing of the way, clearing of the track, greasing of the wheels, expedition, expediting, rushing; special *or* preferential treatment

6 **self-help,** self-helpfulness, **self-support,** self-sustainment, self-improvement; independence 430.5

7 helper, assistant 616.6; benefactor 592; facilitator, animator

8 **reinforcements, support, relief,** auxiliaries, reserves, reserve forces

9 **facility, accommodation, appliance, convenience,** amenity, appurtenance; advantage

10 **helpfulness,** aidfulness <old>; serviceability, utility, **usefulness** 387.3; **advantageousness,** profitability, favorableness, beneficialness 998.1

VERBS 11 **aid, help, assist,** comfort, abet <old>, **succor,** relieve, **ease,** doctor, remedy; be of some help, put one's oar in <nonformal>; do good, do a world of good, **benefit, avail** 998.10; **favor, befriend; give help,** render assistance, offer *or* proffer aid, come to the aid of, rush *or* fly to the assistance of, lend aid, **give** *or* **lend** *or* **bear a hand** *or* **helping hand,** stretch forth *or* hold out a helping hand, cater for <chiefly Brit>; take by the hand, take in tow; **give an assist, give a leg up** *or* lift *or* boost <nonformal>, help a lame dog over a stile; **save,** redeem, bail out <nonformal>, **rescue** 398.3; protect 1007.18; set up, put on one's feet; give new life to, resuscitate, rally, reclaim, revive, **restore** 396.11,15; be the making of, set one up in business; see one through

12 **support, lend support,** give *or* furnish *or* afford support; **maintain, sustain, keep,** upkeep <Brit>; **uphold,** hold up, bear, upbear, **bear up,** bear out; reinforce, undergird, bolster, **bolster up,** buttress, shore, shore up, prop, prop up, crutch; **finance,** fund, subsidize, subvention, subventionize; comp *and* pick up the tab *or* check <all nonformal>

13 **back, back up, stand behind, stand back of** *or* in back of, get behind, get in behind, get in back of; **stand by,** stick by *and* **stick up for** <both nonformal>, **champion; second, take the part of,** take up *or* adopt *or* espouse the cause of, take under one's wing, **go to bat for** <nonformal>, take up the cudgels for, run interference for

<nonformal>, **side with,** take sides with, associate oneself with, join oneself to, align oneself with, come down *or* range oneself on the side of, find time for

14 **abet, aid and abet, encourage,** hearten, embolden, comfort <old>; advocate, hold a brief for <nonformal>, countenance, keep in countenance, **endorse, lend oneself to,** lend one's countenance to, lend one's favor *or* support to, lend one's offices, put one's weight in the scale, plump for *and* thump the tub for <both nonformal>, lend one's name to, give one's support *or* countenance to, give moral support to, hold one's hand, make one's cause one's own, weigh in for <nonformal>; subscribe <Brit>, **favor, go for** <nonformal>, smile upon, shine upon

15 **patronize, sponsor,** take up

16 **foster, nurture,** nourish, mother, care for, lavish care on, feed, parent, rear, sustain, cultivate, **cherish;** pamper, coddle, cosset, fondle <old>; **nurse,** suckle, cradle; dry-nurse, wet-nurse; spoon-feed

17 **be useful, further, forward, advance, promote,** stand in good stead, encourage, **boost** <nonformal>, favor, advantage, **facilitate,** set *or* put *or* push forward, give an impulse to; speed, expedite, quicken, hasten, lend wings to; conduce to, make for, contribute to

18 **serve, lend** *or* **give oneself,** render service to, do service for, **work for, labor in behalf of; minister to,** cater to; attend 577.13; pander to

19 **oblige, accommodate, favor,** do a favor, do a service

ADJS 20 **helping,** assisting, serving; **assistant, auxiliary,** adjuvant, subservient, subsidiary, ancillary, accessory; ministerial, ministering, ministrant; fostering, nurtural; care, caring, care-giving; instrumental

21 **helpful, useful,** utile, aidful <old>; **profitable, salutary,** good for, **beneficial** 998.12; remedial, therapeutic; **serviceable, useful** 387.18; **contributory,** contributing, conducive, **constructive, positive,** promotional, furthersome <old>; at one's service, at one's command, at one's beck and call

22 **favorable, propitious;** kind, kindly, kindly-disposed, all for <nonformal>, **well-disposed,** well-affected, well-intentioned, well-meant, **well-meaning;** benevolent, beneficent, benign, benignant; friendly, amicable, neighborly; cooperative

23 self-helpful, self-helping, self-improving; **self-supporting, self-sustaining;** self-supported, self-sustained; independent

ADVS **24 helpfully,** helpingly; **beneficially,** favorably, profitably, advantageously, to advantage, to the good; serviceably, **usefully**

PREPS **25** helped by, with the help *or* assistance of, by the aid of; **by means of**

26 for, on *or* **in behalf of,** in aid of <chiefly Brit>, in the name of, on account of, **for the sake of,** in the service of, in furtherance of, in favor of; remedial of

27 behind, back of <nonformal>, supporting, **in support of**

450 COOPERATION

NOUNS **1 cooperation, collaboration, coaction,** concurrence, synergy, synergism; **consensus, commonality; community,** harmony, concordance, concord, fellowship, fellow feeling, solidarity, concert, **teamwork;** pulling *or* working together, communal *or* community activity, joining of forces, pooling, pooling of resources, joining of hands; bipartisanship, **mutualism,** mutuality, mutual assistance, coadjuvancy; **reciprocity;** joint effort, common effort, combined *or* joint operation, common enterprise *or* endeavor, collective *or* united action, mass action; job-sharing; coagency; coadministration, cochairmanship, codirectorship; duet, duumvirate; trio, triumvirate, troika; quartet, quintet, sextet, septet, octet; government by committee; symbiosis, commensalism; **cooperativeness,** collaborativeness, team spirit, morale, esprit, *esprit de corps* <Fr>; communism, communalism, communitarianism, collectivism; ecumenism, ecumenicism, ecumenicalism; **collusion,** complicity

2 affiliation, alliance, allying, alignment, association, consociation, combination, **union,** unification, **coalition,** fusion, merger, coalescence, coadunation, amalgamation, **league, federation, confederation,** confederacy, consolidation, incorporation, inclusion, integration; hookup *and* tie-up *and* tie-in <all nonformal>; **partnership,** copartnership, copartnery <old>, cahoots <nonformal>; colleagueship, **collegialism, collegiality; fraternity,** confraternity, fraternization, fraternalism; sorority; **fellowship,** sodality; comradeship, camaraderie, freemasonry

VERBS **3 cooperate, collaborate,** do business *and* **play ball** <both nonformal>, coact, concur; concert, harmonize, concord; **join,** band, league, **associate, affiliate,** ally, **combine, unite,** fuse, merge, coalesce, amalgamate, federate, confederate, consolidate; hook up *and* tie up *and* tie in <all nonformal>; partner, be in league, **go into partnership with,** go partners <nonformal>, go *or* be in cahoots with; **join together,** club together, league together, band together; **work together,** get together *and* team up *and* buddy up <all nonformal>, work as a team, act together, act in concert, **pull together; hold together, hang together,** keep together, **stand together,** stand shoulder to shoulder; lay *or* put *or* get heads together; **close ranks,** make common cause, throw in together <nonformal>, unite efforts, join in; reciprocate; **conspire,** collude

4 side with, take sides with, **unite with; join, join with,** join up with *and* get together with *and* team up with <all nonformal>, strike in with <old>; **throw in with** *and* string along with *and* swing in with <all nonformal>, **go along with; line up with** <nonformal>, align with, align oneself with, range with, range oneself with, stand up with, stand in with; **join hands with,** be hand in glove with, go hand in hand with; act with, take part with, **go in with;** cast in one's lot with, join one's fortunes with, stand shoulder to shoulder with, be cheek by jowl with, sink or swim with, stand or fall with; **close ranks with,** fall in with, make common cause with, pool one's interests with; enlist under the banner of, rally round, flock to

ADJS **5 cooperative, cooperating,** cooperant, **hand in glove; collaborative,** coactive, coacting, coefficient, synergetic, synergic, synergical, synergistic *or* synergistical; **fellow;** concurrent, concurring, concerted, **in concert; consensus,** consensual, agreeing, in agreement, of like mind; harmonious, harmonized, concordant, **common, communal,** collective; **mutual,** reciprocal; **joint, combined** 804.5; coadjuvant, coadjutant; symbiotic, commensal; uncompetitive, noncompetitive, communalist, communalistic, communist, communistic, communitarian, collectivist, collectivistic, ecumenic *or* ecumenical; **conniving, collusive**

ADVS **6 cooperatively,** cooperatingly, coactively, coefficiently, concurrently; in consensus, consensually; **jointly,** combinedly, **conjointly,** concertedly, in concert with; harmoniously, concordantly; communally, collectively, **together;** as one, with one voice, unanimously, in chorus, in unison, as one man, en masse; **side by side, hand in hand, hand in glove, shoulder to shoulder, back to back,** "all for one, one for all"—Dumas père

7 **in cooperation, in collaboration, in partnership, in cahoots** <nonformal>, **in collusion,** in league

PREPS 8 **with, in cooperation with,** etc

451 OPPOSITION

NOUNS 1 **opposition,** opposing, opposure, crossing, oppugnancy, bucking <nonformal>, standing against; contraposition 778.1; **resistance 453; noncooperation; contention 457;** negation 335; **rejection** 372, refusal; **counteraction,** counterworking 899.1; refusal 442; **contradiction,** challenge, contravention, contraversion, rebutment, rebuttal, denial, impugnation, impugnment; countercurrent, head wind; crosscurrent, undercurrent, undertow

2 **hostility, antagonism,** oppugnancy, oppugnance *and* oppugnation <both old>, **antipathy,** enmity, bad blood, inimicalness; **contrariness, contrariety,** orneriness <nonformal>, repugnance *or* repugnancy, perverseness, **obstinacy** 361; fractiousness, refractoriness, recalcitrance 327.2; uncooperativeness, noncooperation, negativeness, **obstructionism,** traversal, bloody-mindedness <Brit>; **friction, conflict,** clashing, **collision,** cross-purposes, dissension, disaccord 456; rivalry, vying, competition 457.2

VERBS 3 **oppose, counter, cross,** go *or* act in opposition to, **go against,** run against, **run counter to,** fly in the face of, fly in the teeth of; kick out against, make waves <nonformal>, **protest** 333.5; set oneself against, set one's face *or* heart against; be *or* play at cross-purposes, **obstruct,** traverse, sabotage; **take issue with, take one's stand against,** lift *or* raise a hand against, declare oneself against, stand and be counted against, side against, vote against, vote nay, veto; make a stand against, make a dead set against; join the opposition; not put up with, not abide, not be content with; counteract, counterwork, countervail 899.6; **resist,** withstand 453.3

4 **contend against,** militate against, **contest, combat, battle, clash with, clash** "each thing meets in mere oppug-

nancy"—Shakespeare, **fight against, strive against,** struggle against, labor against, **take on** <nonformal>, grapple with, join battle with, close with, come to close quarters with, go the the mat with <nonformal>, antagonize <old>, **fight, buck** <nonformal>, **counter;** buffet, beat against, beat up against, breast, stem, breast *or* stem the tide *or* current *or* flood, breast the wave, buffet the waves; rival, compete with *or* against, vie with *or* against; fight back, **resist, offer resistance** 453.3

5 **confront, affront,** front, go eyeball-to-eyeball *or* one-on-one with <nonformal>, **meet, face, meet head-on; encounter**

6 **contradict,** cross, traverse, contravene, controvert, rebut, deny, **gainsay;** challenge, contest; oppugn, call into question; **belie,** be contrary to, come in conflict with, negate 335.3; **reject** 372.2

7 **be against,** be agin <nonformal>; discountenance 510.11; not hold with, not have anything to do with; have a crow to pluck *or* pick, have a bone to pick

ADJS 8 **oppositional, opponent, opposing, opposed; anti** <nonformal>, contra, confrontational, confrontive; at odds, at loggerheads; **adverse, adversary,** adversarial, adversative, oppugnant, antithetic, antithetical, repugnant, con <nonformal>, **set** *or* **dead set against; contrary, counter; negative; opposite,** oppositive, death on; overthwart <old>, cross; **contradictory;** unfavorable, unpropitious 133.17; **hostile, antagonistic,** unfriendly, enemy, inimical, alien, antipathetic, antipathetical; fractious, refractory, recalcitrant 327.10; uncooperative, noncooperative, **obstructive,** bloody-minded <Brit>; ornery <nonformal>, perverse, obstinate 361.8; **conflicting, clashing,** dissentient, disaccordant 456.15; rival, competitive

ADVS 9 **in opposition, in confrontation,** eyeball-to-eyeball *and* one-on-one <both nonformal>, head-on, **at variance, at cross-purposes, at odds,** at issue, at war with, up in arms, with crossed bayonets, at daggers drawn, at daggers, in hostile array, poised against one another; contra, contrariwise, counter, cross, athwart; against the tide *or* wind *or* grain

PREPS 10 **opposed to, adverse to,** counter to, **in opposition to,** in conflict with, at cross-purposes with; **against,** agin <nonformal>, dead against, athwart; **versus,** vs; **con,** contra, face to face with, *vis-à-vis* <Fr>

452 OPPONENT

NOUNS **1 opponent, adversary, antagonist, assailant, foe,** foeman, **enemy,** archenemy; adverse *or* opposing party, opposite camp, opposite *or* opposing side, **the opposition,** the loyal opposition; **combatant** 461

2 competitor, contestant, contender, corrival, vier, player, entrant; **rival,** archrival; emulator; the field; finalist, semifinalist, etc

3 oppositionist, opposer; obstructionist, obstructive, negativist, naysayer; contra; **objector, protester,** dissident, dissentient; **resister;** noncooperator; **disputant,** litigant, plaintiff, defendant; quarreler, irritable man, scrapper <nonformal>, wrangler, brawler; die-hard, bitterender, last-ditcher, intransigent, irreconcilable

453 RESISTANCE

NOUNS **1 resistance,** withstanding, countering, renitence *or* renitency, repellence *or* repellency; **defiance** 454; **opposing, opposition** 451; **stand; repulsion,** repulse, rebuff; **objection, protest,** remonstrance, **dispute,** challenge, **demur; complaint;** dissentience, **dissent** 333; reaction, hostile *or* combative reaction, **counteraction** 899; revolt 327.4; recalcitrance *or* recalcitrancy, recalcitration, fractiousness, refractoriness 327.2; **reluctance** 325.1; **obstinacy** 361; passive resistance, noncooperation; uncooperativeness, negativism

VERBS **2 resist, withstand; stand; endure** 134.5; **stand up, bear up, hold up, hold out; defy** 454.3, tell one where to get off <nonformal>, throw down the gauntlet; be proof against, bear up against; **repel, repulse,** rebuff

3 offer resistance, fight back, bite back, not turn the other cheek, show fight, lift *or* raise a hand, stand *or* hold one's ground, **withstand,** stand, **take one's stand,** make a stand, make a stand against, take one's stand against, square off *and* put up one's dukes <both nonformal>, **stand up to,** stand up against, stand at bay; front, **confront,** meet head-on, fly in the teeth *or* face of, **face up to,** face down, face out; **object, protest,** remonstrate, **dispute,** challenge, **complain,** complain loudly, exclaim at; **dissent** 333.4; make waves <nonformal>; make a determined resistance; kick against, kick out against,

recalcitrate, "kick against the pricks"—Bible; put up a fight *or* struggle <nonformal>, not take lying down, hang tough *and* tough it out <both nonformal>; **revolt** 327.7; **oppose** 451.3; **contend with** 457.18; **strive against** 451.4

4 stand fast, stand *or* **hold one's ground,** make a resolute stand, **hold one's own,** remain firm, stick *and* stuck fast <both nonformal>, **stick to one's guns, stay it out, stick it out** <nonformal>, **hold out,** not back down, not give up, not submit, **never say die; fight to the last ditch,** die hard, sell one's life dearly, go down with flying colors

ADJS **5 resistant, resistive,** resisting, renitent, up against, **withstanding,** repellent; obstructive, retardant, retardative; **unyielding,** unsubmissive 361.12; rebellious 327.11; **proof against; objecting, protesting,** disputing, disputatious, complaining, dissentient, dissenting 333.6; recalcitrant, fractious, refractory 327.10; **reluctant** 325.6; noncooperative, uncooperative; up in arms, on the barricades, not lying down

454 DEFIANCE

NOUNS **1 defiance,** defying, defial <old>; **daring,** daringness, **audacity,** boldness, bold front, brash bearing, brashness, brassiness <nonformal>, brazenness, bravado, insolence; bearding, beardtweaking, nose-tweaking; **arrogance** 141; **sauciness, cheekiness** <nonformal>, pertness, impudence, impertinence; bumptiousness, cockiness; **contempt,** contemptuousness, derision, **disdain,** disregard, despite; **risk-taking,** tightrope walking, funambulism

2 challenge, dare, double dare; fighting words; **defy** *or* defi; gage, gage of battle, gauntlet, glove, chip on one's shoulder, slap of the glove, invitation *or* bid to combat, call to arms; war cry, war whoop, battle cry, rebel yell

VERBS **3 defy,** bid defiance, hurl defiance, snarl *or* shout *or* scream defiance; **dare,** double-dare, outdare; **challenge,** call out, throw *or* fling down the gauntlet *or* glove *or* gage, knock the chip off one's shoulder, cross swords; beard, beard the lion in his den, face, face out, look in the eye, stare down, stare out <Brit>, **confront, affront,** front, say right to one's face, square up to, go eyeball-to-eyeball *or* one-on-one with <nonformal>; tweak the nose, pluck by the beard, slap one's face, double *or* shake one's fist at; give one the finger; **ask for it** <nonformal>, ask *or* look for trouble, make something of it <nonformal>, show fight, show one's teeth, bare one's fangs; dance the war dance; **brave** 492.11

4 **flout**, disregard, **slight**, slight over, treat with contempt, set at defiance, fly in the teeth *or* face of, **snap one's fingers at; thumb one's nose at**, cock a snook at, bite the thumb at; **disdain, despise, scorn** 157.3; laugh at, laugh to scorn, laugh out of court, laugh in one's face; hold in derision, scout, scoff at, **deride** 508.8

5 **show** *or* **put up a bold front**, bluster, throw out one's chest, strut, crow, look big, stand with arms akimbo

6 **take a dare**, accept a challenge, **take one up on** *and* **call one's bluff** <both nonformal>; **start something**, take up the gauntlet

ADJS 7 **defiant**, defying, challenging; **daring, bold**, brash, brassy <nonformal>; brazen, **audacious**, insolent; arrogant 141.9; saucy, cheeky <nonformal>, pert, impudent, impertinent; bumptious, cocky; **contemptuous**, disdainful, derisive, disregardful, greatly daring, regardless of consequences

ADVS 8 **in defiance of**, in the teeth of, in the face of, under one's very nose

455 ACCORD
<harmonious relationship>

NOUNS 1 **accord**, accordance, **concord**, concordance, **harmony**, symphony; **rapport**; good vibrations <nonformal>, good vibes <nonformal>, good karma; amity 587.1; frictionlessness; *rapprochement* <Fr>; **sympathy**, empathy, identity, feeling of identity, fellow feeling, **fellowship**, kinship, togetherness, **affinity; agreement, understanding, like-mindedness, congruence**; congeniality, **compatibility; oneness**, unity, unison, union; **community**, communion, community of interests; solidarity, team spirit, esprit, *esprit de corps* <Fr>; mutuality, sharing, reciprocity, mutual supportiveness; bonds of harmony, ties of affection, cement of friendship; happy family; peace 464; **love**, *agape* <Gk>, charity, *caritas* <L>, brotherly love; correspondence 787.1

VERBS 2 **get along**, harmonize, **agree with, agree, get along with**, get on with, cotton to *or* hit it off with <both nonformal>, harmonize with, **be in harmony with**, be in tune with, fall *or* chime in with, blend

in with, go hand in hand with, **be at one with**; sing in chorus, be on the same wavelength <nonformal>; **sympathize**, empathize, identify with, respond to, understand one another, enter into one's views, enter into the ideas *or* feelings of; **accord**, correspond 787.6; reciprocate, interchange 862.4

ADJS 3 **in accord**, accordant <old>, **harmonious, in harmony**, congruous, congruent, in tune, attuned, agreeing, in concert, **in rapport**, *en rapport* <Fr>, amicable 587.15,18; frictionless; **sympathetic**, simpatico <nonformal>, empathic, empathetic, **understanding; like-minded**, akin, of the same mind, of one mind, at one, united, together; concordant, corresponding 787.9; agreeable, congenial, **compatible; peaceful** 464.9

456 DISACCORD
<unharmonious relationship>

NOUNS 1 **disaccord, discord**, discordance *or* discordancy, asynchrony, **unharmoniousness**, inharmoniousness, disharmony, inharmony, incongruence, disaffinity, incompatibility, incompatibleness; culture gap, generation gap, gender gap; noncooperation; **conflict**, open conflict *or* war, **friction**, rub; jar, **jarring**, jangle, clash, clashing; touchiness, strained relations, **tension**; bad blood; **unpleasantness**; mischief; contention 457; **enmity** 589; Eris, Discordia; the Apple of Discord

2 **disagreement, difficulty, misunderstanding, difference**, difference of opinion, agreement to disagree, **variance**, division, dividedness; cross-purposes; polarity of opinion, polarization; **disparity** 788.1

3 **dissension, dissent**, dissidence, flak <nonformal>; bickering, infighting, faction, factiousness, partisanship, partisan spirit; **divisiveness; quarrelsomeness;** litigiousness; pugnacity, bellicosity, combativeness, **aggressiveness**, contentiousness, belligerence; feistiness <nonformal>, **touchiness, irritability**, shrewishness, irascibility 110.2

4 **falling-out, breach of friendship**, parting of the ways, bust-up <nonformal>; **alienation, estrangement, disaffection**, disfavor; **breach, break, rupture, schism, split, rift**, cleft, **disunity, disunion, disruption**, separation, cleavage, divergence, division, dividedness; division in the camp, house divided against itself; open rupture, breaking off of negotiations, recall of ambassadors

5 quarrel, open quarrel, dustup, **dispute, argument,** polemic, argy-bargy *and* slanging match <both Brit>, fliting <old>, lovers' quarrel, **controversy,** altercation, **fight, squabble, contention,** strife, **tussle,** bicker, wrangle, snarl, **tiff, spat,** fuss; **breach of the peace; fracas,** donnybrook *or* donnybrook fair; broil, embroilment, imbroglio; words, sharp words, war of words, logomachy; **feud,** blood feud, vendetta; brawl 457.5

6 <nonformal terms> **row, rumpus,** row-de-dow, ruckus, ruction, brannigan, shindy, foofooraw, hoo-ha, barney *and* shemozzle <both Brit>, set-to, run-in, **scrap, hassle,** rhubarb; knock-down-and-drag-out, knock-down-and-drag-out quarrel *or* fight; the dozens

7 bone of contention, apple of discord, sore point, tender spot, delicate *or* ticklish issue, rub, beef <nonformal>; **bone to pick,** crow to pluck *or* pick *or* pull; *casus belli* <L>, grounds for war

VERBS **8 disagree, differ,** differ in opinion, hold opposite views, discaccord, **be at variance,** not get along, pull different ways, be at cross-purposes, have no measures with, misunderstand one another; **conflict, clash,** collide, jostle, jangle, jar; live like cat and dog, live a cat-and-dog life

9 have a bone to pick with, have a crow to pluck with *or* pick with *or* pull with, have a beef with <nonformal>

10 fall out, have a falling-out, **break with, split,** separate, **diverge,** divide, agree to disagree, **part company,** come to *or* reach a parting of the ways

11 quarrel, dispute, oppugn, flite <old>, altercate, **fight, squabble,** tiff, spat, **bicker, wrangle,** spar, broil, have words, set to, join issue, make the fur fly; cross swords, **feud, battle; brawl;** be quarrelsome *or* contentious, be thin-skinned, be touchy *or* sensitive, get up on the wrong side of the bed

12 <nonformal terms> **row, scrap, hassle,** make *or* kick up a row; mix it up, lock horns, bump heads

13 pick a quarrel, fasten a quarrel on, look for trouble, pick a bone with, pluck a crow with; have a chip on one's shoulder; add insult to injury

14 sow dissension, stir up trouble, make *or* borrow trouble; **alienate, estrange,** separate, **divide, disunite,** disaffect, **come between; irritate, provoke,** aggravate; **set at odds,** set at variance; **set against,** pit against, **sic on** *or* **at, set on,** set by the

ears, set at one's throat; add fuel to the fire *or* flame, fan the flame, pour oil on the blaze, light the fuse, stir the pot <nonformal>

ADJS **15 disaccordant, unharmonious,** inharmonious, disharmonious, out of tune, asynchronous, unsynchronized, out of sync <nonformal>, **discordant,** out of accord, dissident, dissentient, **disagreeing, differing; conflicting,** clashing, colliding; like cats and dogs; **divided,** faction-ridden, fragmented

16 at odds, at variance, at loggerheads, at square <old>, at cross-purposes; at war, at strife, at feud, at swords' points, at daggers *or* at daggers drawn, up in arms

17 partisan, polarizing, **divisive,** factional, factious; **quarrelsome,** bickering, disputatious, wrangling, eristic, eristical, polemical; litigious, pugnacious, combative, **aggressive,** bellicose, belligerent; feisty <nonformal>, touchy, irritable, shrewish, **irascible** 110.19

457 CONTENTION

NOUNS **1 contention, contest,** contestation, combat, **fighting, conflict, strife, war, struggle,** blood on the floor, cut and thrust; fighting at close quarters, infighting; **warfare** 458; **hostility,** enmity 589; **quarrel, altercation, controversy,** dustup, polemic, debate, forensics, **argument, dispute, disputation;** litigation; words, war of words, paper war, logomachy; **fighting,** scrapping *and* hassling <both nonformal>; **quarreling, bickering, wrangling, squabbling;** oppugnancy, contentiousness, disputatiousness, litigiousness, **quarrelsomeness** 456.3; cat-and-dog life; Kilkenny cats; **competitiveness,** vying, rivalrousness, competitorship

2 competition, rivalry, trying conclusions *or* the issue, vying, emulation, jockeying <nonformal>; cutthroat competition; run for one's money; **sportsmanship, gamesmanship,** lifemanship, one-upmanship, **competitive advantage**

3 contest, engagement, encounter, match, matching, meet, meeting, derby, pissing match <nonformal>, **trial, test,** *concours and rencontre* <both Fr>; **close contest, hard contest,** closely fought contest, close *or* tight one, horse race *and* crapshoot <all nonformal>; fight, bout, go <nonformal>; joust, tilt; tournament, tourney; rally; **game** 743.9; **games,** Olympic games, Olympics, gymkhana; cookoff, Bake-Off <trademark>

4 **fight, battle, fray,** affray, combat, action, conflict, embroilment; gun battle; **clash; brush, skirmish,** scrimmage; tussle, **scuffle, struggle,** scramble, shoving match; exchange of blows, *passage d'armes* <Fr>, passage at or of arms, clash of arms; **quarrel** 456.5; pitched battle; battle royal; unarmed combat; **fistfight,** punch-out *and* duke-out <both nonformal>, punch-up <Brit nonformal>; **hand-to-hand fight,** stand-up fight <nonformal>, running fight *or* engagement; tug-of-war; bull-fight, tauromachy; dogfight, cockfight; street fight, rumble <nonformal>; air *or* aerial combat, sea *or* naval combat, ground combat, armored combat, infantry combat, fire fight, hand-to-hand combat, house-to-house combat; **internal struggle,** intestine *or* internecine struggle *or* combat

5 **free-for-all, knock-down-and-drag-out** <nonformal>, **brawl,** broil, melee, scrimmage, **fracas,** riot

6 **death struggle, life-and-death** *or* **life-or-death struggle, struggle** *or* **fight** *or* **duel to the death,** *guerre à mort* and *guerre à outrance* <both Fr>, all-out war, total war, last-ditch fight, fight to the last ditch, fight with no quarter given

7 **duel,** single combat, monomachy, satisfaction, **affair of honor,** *affaire d'honneur* <Fr>

8 **fencing, swordplay;** swordsmanship

9 **boxing** 754, **fighting,** noble *or* manly art of self-defense, **fisticuffs, pugilism, prizefighting,** the fights <nonformal>, the ring; **boxing match, prizefight,** spar, bout; shadowboxing; close fighting, infighting, the clinches <nonformal>; Chinese boxing; savate

10 **wrestling,** rassling <nonformal>, grappling, *sumo* <Japanese>; **martial arts;** catch-as-catch-can; wrestling match, wrestling meet; Greco-Roman wrestling, Cornish wrestling, Westmorland wrestling, Cumberland wrestling

11 **racing, track,** track sports; **horse racing** 757, the turf, the sport of kings; dog racing, automobile racing 756

12 **race,** contest of speed *or* fleetness; derby; **horse race; automobile race; heat, lap,** bell lap, victory lap; footrace, run, running event; torch race; match race, obstacle race, three-legged race, sack race, potato race; walk; ride and tie; endurance race, motorcycle race, bicycle race; boat race, yacht race, regatta; air race; dog race

VERBS 13 **contend, contest,** jostle; **fight, bat-** tle, **combat, war, declare** *or* **go to war,** take *or* take up arms, put up a fight <nonformal>; wage war; **strive, struggle,** scramble, go for the brass ring; make the fur *or* feathers fly, **tussle, scuffle; quarrel** 456.11,12; clash, collide; **wrestle,** rassle <nonformal>, grapple, grapple with, go to the mat with; **come to blows,** close, try conclusions, **mix it up** *and* go toe-to-toe <both nonformal>, exchange blows *or* fisticuffs, **box,** spar, give and take; cut and thrust; **cross swords, fence,** thrust and parry; **joust, tilt, tourney,** run a tilt *or* a tilt at, break a lance with; **duel,** fight a duel, give satisfaction; feud; skirmish; fight one's way; fight the good fight; **brawl,** broil; **riot**

14 **lift** *or* **raise one's hand against;** make war on; draw the sword against, take up the cudgels, couch one's lance; square up *or* off <nonformal>, come to the scratch; have at, jump; lay on, lay about one; **pitch into** *and* **sail into** *and* light into *and* lay into *and* rip into <all nonformal>, strike the first blow, draw first blood; **attack** 459.15

15 **encounter, come** *or* **go up against,** fall *or* run foul *or* afoul of; close with, come to close quarters, bring to bay, meet *or* fight hand-to-hand

16 **engage, take on** <nonformal>, go against *or* up against, close with, try conclusions with, enter the ring *or* arena with, put on the gloves with, match oneself against; **join issue** *or* **battle, do** *or* **give battle,** engage in battle *or* combat

17 **contend with, engage with,** cope with, **fight with, strive with, struggle with,** wrestle with, grapple with, bandy with <old>, try conclusions with, measure swords with, tilt with, **cross swords with;** exchange shots, shoot it out with <nonformal>; **lock horns** *and* **bump heads** <both nonformal>, fall *or* go to loggerheads <old>; **tangle with** *and* **mix it up with** <both nonformal>, have a brush with; have it out, fight *or* battle it out, settle it; **fight** *or* **go at it hammer and tongs** *or* tooth and nail, fight it out, duke it out <nonformal>, fight like devils, ask and give no quarter, make blood flow freely, battle *à outrance*, fight to the death

18 **compete, contend, vie,** try conclusions *or* the issue, jockey <nonformal>; **compete with** *or* **against, vie with, challenge,** cope <old>, enter into competition with, give a run for one's money, **meet;** try *or* test one another; **rival,** emulate, outvie; keep up with the Joneses

19 race, race with, run a race; horse-race, boat-race

20 contend for, strive for, struggle for, fight for, vie for; stickle for, stipulate for, hold out for, make a point of

21 dispute, contest, oppugn, take issue with; **fight over, quarrel over, wrangle over, squabble over,** bicker over, strive *or* contend about

ADJS **22 contending,** contesting; **contestant,** disputant; striving, struggling; fighting, battling, warring; **warlike; quarrelsome** 456.17

23 competitive, competitory, competing, **vying,** rivaling, **rival,** rivalrous, emulous, in competition, in rivalry; **cutthroat**

458 WARFARE

NOUNS **1 war, warfare, warring, warmaking, combat, fighting,** *la guerre* <Fr>; armed conflict, armed combat, military operations, the sword, arbitrament of the sword, appeal to arms *or* the sword, resort to arms, force *or* might of arms, bloodshed; **state of war, hostilities,** belligerence *or* belligerency, open war *or* warfare *or* hostilities; **hot war, shooting war;** total war, **all-out war; wartime;** battle 457.4; **attack** 459; **war zone, theater of operations;** trouble spot

2 "an epidemic insanity"—Emerson, "a brain-spattering, windpipe-slitting art, "the feast of vultures, and the waste of life"—both Byron, "the business of barbarians"—Napoleon, "the trade of kings"—Dryden, "a by-product of the arts of peace"—Ambrose Bierce, "a conflict which does not determine who is right—but who is left"—anon, "the continuation of politics by other means"— von Clausewitz, "an emblem, a hieroglyphic, of all misery"—Donne, "politics with bloodshed"—Mao Tse-tung

3 battle array, order of battle, **disposition, deployment, marshaling;** open order; close formation; echelon

4 campaign, war, **drive, expedition,** hostile expedition; **crusade,** holy war, jihad

5 operation, action; **movement; mission; operations,** military operations, naval operations; combined operations, joint operations, coordinated operations; active operations, amphibious operations, airborne operations, fluid operations, major operations, minor operations, night operations, overseas operations; war plans, staff work; logistic; war game, dry run, kriegspiel, maneuver, maneuvers; **strategy, tactics; battle**

6 military science, art *or* rules *or* science of war; siegecraft; warcraft, war, **arms,** profession of arms; **generalship,** soldiership; chivalry, knighthood, knightly skill

7 declaration of war, challenge; defiance 454

8 call to arms, call-up, call to the colors, **rally; mobilization; muster,** levy; conscription, recruitment; **rallying cry,** slogan, watchword, catchword, exhortation; **battle cry,** war cry, war whoop, rebel yell; banzai, gung ho, St George, Montjoie, Geronimo, go for broke; **bugle call,** trumpet call, clarion, clarion call; remember the Maine *or* the Alamo *or* Pearl Harbor

9 service, military service; active service *or* duty; military obligation; selective service, national service <Brit>; reserve status

10 militarization, activation, **mobilization;** war *or* wartime footing, national emergency; **war effort, war economy;** martial law, suspension of civil rights; garrison state, military dictatorship; remilitarization, reactivation; arms race; war clouds, war scare

11 warlikeness, unpeacefulness, war *or* warlike spirit, ferocity, fierceness; **hard line; combativeness, contentiousness; hostility, antagonism;** unfriendliness 589.1; aggression, **aggressiveness;** aggro <Brit nonformal>; belligerence *or* belligerency, **pugnacity,** pugnaciousness, **bellicosity, bellicoseness, truculence,** fight <nonformal>; chip on one's shoulder <nonformal>; militancy, **militarism,** martialism, militaryism; saber rattling; **chauvinism, jingoism,** hawkishness <nonformal>, **warmongering;** waving of the bloody shirt; warpath; oppugnancy, **quarrelsomeness** 456.3

12 <rallying devices and themes> battle flag, banner, colors, gonfalon, bloody shirt, bluidy sark <Scots>, fiery cross *or* crostarie, atrocity story, enemy atrocities; martial music, war song, battle hymn, national anthem; national honor, face; foreign threat, totalitarian threat, Communist threat, colonialist *or* neocolonialist *or* imperialist threat, Western imperialism, yellow peril; expansionism, manifest destiny; independence, self-determination

13 war-god, Mars, Ares, Odin *or* Woden *or* Wotan, Tyr *or* Tiu *or* Tiw; war-goddess, Athena, Minerva, Bellona, Enyo, Valkyrie

VERBS **14 war, wage war, make war, carry on war** or **hostilities,** engage in hostilities, wield the sword; battle, **fight;** spill or shed blood

15 make war on, levy war on, "let slip the dogs of war"—Shakespeare; **attack** 459.15,17; **declare war, challenge,** throw or fling down the gauntlet; defy 454.3; open hostilities, plunge the world into war; launch a holy war on, go on a crusade against

16 go to war, break or breach the peace, take up the gauntlet, **go on the warpath, rise up in arms, take** or **resort to arms,** take arms, take up arms, take up the cudgels or sword, fly or appeal to the sword, unsheathe one's weapon, come to cold steel; take the field

17 campaign, undertake operations, pursue a strategy, make an expedition, go on a crusade

18 serve, do duty; fulfill one's military obligation, wear the uniform; **soldier,** see or do active duty; **bear arms,** carry arms, shoulder arms, shoulder a gun; see action or combat, hear shots fired in anger

19 call to arms, call up, call to the colors, **rally; mobilize; muster,** levy; **conscript, recruit;** sound the call to arms, give the battle cry, wave the bloody shirt, beat the drums, blow the bugle or clarion

20 militarize, activate, mobilize, go on a wartime footing, gird or gird up one's loins, muster one's resources; reactivate, remilitarize, take out of mothballs and retread <both nonformal>

ADJS **21 warlike, militant,** fighting, warring, battling; **martial, military,** soldierly, soldierlike; **combative, contentious,** gladiatorial; trigger-happy <nonformal>; **belligerent, pugnacious, truculent, bellicose,** scrappy <nonformal>, full of fight; **aggressive,** offensive; fierce, ferocious, savage, bloody, bloody-minded, bloodthirsty, sanguinary, sanguineous; **unpeaceful,** unpeaceable, unpacific; **hostile, antagonistic, enemy,** inimical; unfriendly 589.9; **quarrelsome** 456.17

22 militaristic, warmongering, saberrattling; **chauvinistic,** chauvinist, **jingoistic,** jingoist, jingoish, jingo; **hardline, hawkish** <nonformal>, of the war party

23 embattled, battled, **engaged,** at grips, in combat; **arrayed, deployed,** ranged, in battle array, in the field; **militarized; armed** 460.14; war-ravaged, war-torn

ADVS **24 at war, up in arms;** in the midst of battle, in the thick of the fray or combat; in the cannon's mouth, at the point of the gun; at swords' points, at the point of the bayonet or sword

25 wars

Algerian War	Persian Gulf Conflict
American Revolution	or Operation Desert
Arab-Israeli War	Storm
Balkan Wars	Persian Wars
Boer War	Punic Wars
Civil War <US>	Russian Revolution
Civil War	Russo-Japanese War
<England>	Samnite Wars
Civil War <Spain>	Seven Weeks' War
Civil Wars <China>	Seven Years' War
Civil Wars	Sino-Japanese War
<Roman>	Six Day War
Crimean War	Southeast Asian War
Crusades	Spanish-American
Franco-Prussian War	War
French and Indian	Thirty Years' War
War	Vietnam War
French Revolution	War Between the
Gallic Wars	States
Greco-Persian Wars	War of the Austrian
Hundred Years' War	Succession
Indian Wars	War of the Polish Suc-
Indochina War	cession
Italian Wars of Inde-	War of the Spanish
pendence	Succession
Korean War	Wars of the French
Macedonian-Persian	Revolution
War	Wars of the Roses
Manchurian War	World War I or Great
Mexican War	War or War of the
Napoleonic Wars	Nations
Norman Conquest	World War II
Peloponnesian Wars	Yom Kippur War

459 ATTACK

NOUNS **1 attack, assault,** assailing, assailment; **offense, offensive; aggression; onset, onslaught; strike;** surgical strike, first strike, preventive war; descent on or upon; **charge,** rush, dead set at, run at or against; **drive, push** <nonformal>; **sally, sortie;** infiltration; coup de main <Fr>; frontal attack or assault, head-on attack, flank attack; mass attack, kamikaze attack; banzai attack or charge, suicide attack or charge; hit-and-run attack; breakthrough; **counterattack, counteroffensive;** amphibious attack; gas attack; diversionary attack, diversion; assault and battery, simple assault, mugging <nonformal>, aggravated assault, armed assault, unprovoked assault; **preemptive strike; blitzkrieg, blitz,** lightning attack, lightning war, panzer warfare, sudden or devastating or crippling attack, deep strike, shock tactics; atomic or thermonuclear attack, first-strike capacity, megadeath, overkill

2 surprise attack, surprise, surprisal, unforeseen attack, **sneak attack** <nonformal>; Pearl Harbor; stab in the back

3 thrust, pass, lunge, swing, cut, stab, jab; feint; home thrust

4 raid, foray, razzia; **invasion, incursion,** inroad, irruption; **air raid, air strike,** air attack, shuttle raid, fire raid, saturation raid; escalade, scaling, boarding, **tank** or **armored attack,** panzer attack

5 siege, besiegement, beleaguerment; encompassment, investment, encirclement, envelopment; blockading, blockade; cutting of supply lines; vertical envelopment; pincer movement

6 storm, storming, taking by storm, overrunning

7 bombardment, bombing, air bombing; strafing

8 gunfire, fire, firing, musketry, **shooting,** fireworks or gunplay <both nonformal>; gunfight, shoot-out; **firepower,** offensive capacity, bang <nonformal>

9 volley, salvo, burst, spray, **fusillade,** drumfire, **cannonade,** cannonry, **broadside,** enfilade; **barrage, artillery barrage**

10 stabbing, piercing, sticking <nonformal>; **knifing,** bayonetting; the sword; **impalement, transfixion**

11 stoning, lapidation

12 assailant, assailer, **attacker;** assaulter, mugger <nonformal>; **aggressor;** invader, raider

13 zero hour, H hour; D-day, target day

VERBS **14 attack, assault, assail,** harry, assume or take the offensive; commit an assault upon; **strike, hit, pound; go at, come at,** have at, **launch out against,** make a set or dead set at; **fall on** or **upon, set on** or **upon, descend on** or upon, come down on, swoop down on; pounce upon; **lift** or **raise** or **lift a hand against,** draw the sword against, take up arms or the cudgels against; **lay hands on,** lay a hand on, bloody one's hands with; gang up on, attack in force; surprise, **ambush; blitz,** attack or hit like lightning

15 <nonformal terms> **pitch into, light into, lambaste,** pile into, sail into, wade into, lay into, plow into, tie into, rip into; **let one have it,** let one have it with both barrels; **land on,** land on like a ton of bricks, climb all over, crack down on, lower the boom on, tee off on; **mug,** jump, bushwhack, sandbag, scrag; swipe at, lay

at, **go for, go at;** blindside, blind-pop, sucker-punch; **take a swing** or **crack** or **swipe** or **poke** or punch or **shot at**

16 lash out at, strike out at, hit out at, let drive at, let fly at, strike out at; **strike at,** hit at, poke at, thrust at, **swing at,** swing on, make a thrust or pass at, lunge at, aim or deal a blow at, flail at, flail away at, take a fling or shy at; cut and thrust; feint

17 launch an attack, kick off an attack, mount an attack, **push, thrust,** mount or open an offensive, **drive; advance against** or **upon, march upon** or **against,** bear down upon; **infiltrate; strike;** flank; press the attack, follow up the attack; **counterattack**

18 charge, rush, **rush at, fly at,** run at, dash at, make a dash or rush at; tilt at, go full tilt at, make or run a tilt at, ride full tilt against; **jump off,** go over the top <nonformal>

19 besiege, lay siege to, encompass, surround, **encircle,** envelope, invest, set upon on all sides, get in a pincers, close the jaws of the pincers or trap; **blockade; beset, beleaguer, harry, harass,** drive or press one hard; soften up

20 raid, foray, make a raid; **invade,** inroad, make an inroad, make an irruption into; escalade, scale, scale the walls, board; storm, take by storm, overwhelm, inundate

21 pull a gun on, draw a gun on; **get the drop on** and **beat to the draw** <both nonformal>

22 pull the trigger, fire upon, fire at, **shoot at,** pop at and take a pop at <both nonformal>, take or fire or let off a shot at, blaze away at <nonformal>; **open fire,** commence firing, open up on <nonformal>; aim at, take aim at, level at <old>, zero in on, take dead aim at, draw a bead on; **snipe,** snipe at; **bombard, blast, strafe, shell,** cannonade, mortar, barrage, blitz; pepper, fusillade, fire a volley; rake, enfilade; pour a broadside into; cannon; **torpedo; shoot**

23 bomb, drop a bomb, lay an egg <nonformal>; dive-bomb, glide-bomb, skip-bomb, pattern-bomb, etc; atom-bomb, hydrogen-bomb

24 mine, plant a mine, trigger a mine

25 stab, stick <nonformal>, **pierce,** plunge in; **run through, impale,** spit, **transfix,** transpierce; **spear,** lance, poniard, bayonet, saber, sword, put to the sword; **knife,** dirk, dagger, stiletto; spike

26 gore, horn, tusk

27 pelt, stone, lapidate <old>, pellet; brickbat *or* egg <both nonformal>
28 hurl at, throw at, cast at, heave at, chuck
at <nonformal>, fling at, sling at, toss at,
shy at, fire at, let fly at; hurl against, hurl
at the head of
ADJS **29 attacking,** assailing, assaulting,
charging, driving, thrusting, advancing;
invading, invasive, invasionary, incur-
sive, incursionary, irruptive
30 offensive, combative, on the offensive *or*
attack; **aggressive**
ADVS **31 under attack, under fire;** under
siege
INTERJS **32 attack!,** advance!, **charge!,** over
the top!, up and at 'em!, have at them!,
give 'em hell!, let 'em have it!, fire!, open
fire!; banzai!, Geronimo!

460 DEFENSE

NOUNS **1 defense,** defence <Brit>, **guard,**
ward; **protection** 1007; resistance 453;
self-defense, self-protection, self-
preservation; deterrent capacity; defense
in depth; the defensive; covering one's ass
or rear-end <nonformal>; defenses, psychological defenses, ego defenses, defense
mechanism, escape mechanism, avoidance reaction, negative taxis *or* tropism;
bunker atmosphere *or* mentality
2 military defense, national defense, defense capability; Air Defense Command;
civil defense; CONELRAD *or* control of
electromagnetic radiation for civil defense, Emergency Broadcast System *or*
EBS, Civil Defense Warning System;
radar defenses, distant early warning
or DEW Line; antimissile missile, anti-
ballistic-missile system *or* ABM; strategic defense initiative *or* Star Wars
3 armor, armature; armor plate; body armor, suit of armor, plate armor; panoply,
harness; **mail,** chain mail, chain armor;
bulletproof vest; **battlegear; protective
covering,** cortex, **thick skin,** carapace,
shell 295.15; spines, needles
4 fortification, work, defense work, **bulwark, rampart, fence, barrier** 1011.5;
enclosure 212.3
5 entrenchment, trench, ditch, fosse; **moat;
dugout,** abri <Fr>; **bunker; foxhole,** slit
trench; approach trench, communication
trench, fire trench, gallery, parallel, cou-
pure; tunnel, fortified tunnel; undermining, sap, single *or* double sap, flying sap;
mine, countermine
6 stronghold, hold, safehold, fasthold,
strong point, **fastness,** keep, ward, **bas-**
tion, donjon, **citadel, castle,** tower, tower
of strength, strong point; mote *or* motte;
fort, fortress, post; **bunker, pillbox,**
blockhouse, garrison *or* trenches *or* barricades; garrison house; acropolis; peel,
peel tower; rath; martello tower, martello; **bridgehead, beachhead**
**7 defender, champion, advocate; upholder;
guardian angel, supporter** 616.9; vindicator, apologist; **protector** 1007.5; **guard**
1007.9; paladin; guard dog, attack dog,
junkyard dog
VERBS **8 defend, guard, shield,** screen, secure, guard against; defend tooth and
nail *or* to the death *or* to the last breath;
safeguard, protect 1007.18; stand by the
side of, flank; **advocate, champion** 600.10;
defend oneself, cover one's ass *or* rear-
end <nonformal>, CYA *or* cover your ass
<nonformal>
9 fortify, embattle *or* battle <old>; **arm;
armor,** armor-plate; **man;** garrison, man
the garrison *or* trenches *or* barricades;
barricade, blockade; bulwark, wall, palisade, fence; castellate, crenellate; bank;
entrench, **dig in;** mine
**10 fend off, ward off, stave off, hold off,
fight off,** keep off, beat off, parry, fend,
counter, turn aside; **hold** *or* **keep at bay,**
keep at arm's length; **hold the fort, hold
the line,** stop, check, block, hinder, obstruct; **repel, repulse, rebuff, drive back,**
put back, push back; go on the defensive,
fight a holding *or* delaying action, fall
back to prepared positions
ADJS **11 defensive,** defending, **guarding,**
shielding, screening; **protective** 1007.23;
self-defensive, self-protective, self-
preservative
12 fortified, battlemented, embattled *or* battled <old>; castellated, crenellated,
casemated, machicolated
13 armored, armor-plated; in armor, pan-
oplied, armed cap-a-pie, armed at all
points, in harness, "in complete steel"—
Shakespeare; mailed, mailclad, ironclad;
loricate, loricated
14 armed, heeled *and* carrying *and* gun-
toting <all nonformal>; accoutered, **in
arms,** bearing *or* wearing *or* carrying
arms, under arms, sword in hand; **well-
armed,** heavy-armed, full-armed, bristling with arms, **armed to the teeth;** light-
armed; **garrisoned,** manned
15 defensible, defendable, tenable
ADVS **16 defensively, in defense,** in self-
defense; **on the defensive,** on guard; **at
bay,** aux abois <Fr>, with one's back to
the wall

461 COMBATANT

NOUNS **1 combatant, fighter, battler,** scrapper <nonformal>; **contestant, contender, competitor, rival;** disputant, wrangler, squabbler, bickerer, quarreler; struggler, tussler, scuffler; brawler, rioter; feuder; **belligerent,** militant; gladiator; jouster, tilter; **knight,** belted knight; swordsman, blade, sword, *sabreur, beau sabreur* <both Fr>; fencer, foilsman, swordplayer <old>; duelist; gamecock, fighting cock; **tough,** rough, rowdy, **ruffian,** thug, **hoodlum, hood** <nonformal>, hooligan, streetfighter, bully, bullyboy, bravo; gorilla *and* goon *and* plug-ugly <all nonformal>; hatchet man *and* enforcer <both nonformal>, strong-arm man, strong arm, strong-armer; swashbuckler

2 boxer, pugilist, pug *or* palooka <both nonformal>; **street fighter,** scrapper, pit bull

3 wrestler, rassler *and* grunt-and-groaner <both nonformal>, grappler, scuffler, matman

4 bullfighter, toreador, *torero* <Sp>; banderillero, picador, matador

5 militarist, warmonger, war dog *or* hound, war hawk, **hawk** <nonformal>; **chauvinist, jingo,** jingoist

6 military man *or* **woman, serviceman, servicewoman,** navy man *or* woman; air service-man *or* -woman; **soldier, warrior,** brave, fighting man, legionary, hoplite, **man-at-arms,** rifleman, rifle; **cannon fodder,** food for powder; warrioress, Amazon; spearman, pikeman, halberdier

7 <common soldiers> **GI,** GI Joe, dough *and* doughfoot *and* Joe Tentpeg *and* John Dogface <all nonformal>, **doughboy, Yank;** Tommy Atkins *or* **Tommy** *or* Johnny *or* swaddy <all Brit>; redcoat; *poilu* <Fr>; Aussie, Anzac, digger <all Australian>; jock <Scots>; Fritz, Jerry, Heinie, Hun, Boche, Kraut, krauthead <German soldier>; Janissary <Turkish soldier>; sepoy <India>; askari <Africa>

8 enlisted man, noncommissioned officer 575.19; **common soldier, private, private soldier,** buck private <nonformal>; private first class *or* pfc

9 infantryman, foot soldier; light infantryman, chasseur, *Jäger* <Ger>, Zouave; **rifleman,** rifle, musketeer; fusileer, carabineer; **sharpshooter,** marksman, expert rifleman, *bersagliere* <Ital>; **sniper;** grenadier

10 <nonformal terms> **grunt, dogface,** footslogger, paddlefoot, doughfoot, blisterfoot, crunchie, line doggie, ground-pounder

11 artilleryman, artillerist, **gunner,** guns <nonformal>, cannoneer, machine gunner; **bomber,** bomb thrower, bombardier

12 cavalryman, mounted infantryman, **trooper;** dragoon, light *or* heavy dragoon; lancer, lance, uhlan, hussar; cuirassier; spahi; cossack

13 tanker, tank corpsman, tank crewman

14 engineer, combat engineer, pioneer, Seabee; sapper, sapper and miner

15 elite troops, special troops, **shock troops,** storm troops, elite corps; rapid deployment force *or* RDF; commandos, rangers, Special Forces, Green Berets, marines, paratroops; guardsmen, guards, household troops; Life Guards, Horse Guards, Foot Guards, Grenadier Guards, Coldstream Guards, Scots Guards, Irish Guards; Swiss Guards

16 irregular, casual; **guerrilla,** partisan, franctireur; **bushfighter,** bushwhacker <nonformal>; underground, resistance, maquis; Vietcong *or* VC, Charley <nonformal>; SWAPO *or* South West African People's Organization guerrilla; Shining Path Guerrilla; Contra; *maquisard* <Fr>, underground *or* resistance fighter

17 mercenary, hireling, *condottiere* <Ital>, free lance, free companion, **soldier of fortune,** adventurer; gunman, gun, hired gun, hired killer, professional killer

18 recruit, rookie <nonformal>, **conscript,** drafted man, **draftee, inductee, selectee, enlistee,** enrollee, trainee, boot <nonformal>; **raw recruit,** tenderfoot; awkward squad <nonformal>; draft, levy

19 veteran, vet <nonformal>, campaigner, old campaigner, old soldier, war-horse <nonformal>

20 defense forces, services, the service, armed forces, armed services, fighting machine; **the military,** the military establishment

21 branch, branch of the service, corps <see list>; **service, arm of the service,** Air Force, Army, Navy, Marine Corps, Coast Guard, Merchant Marine

22 <military units> **unit, organization,** tactical unit, **outfit** <nonformal>; **army,** field army, army group, corps, **division,** infantry division, armored division, airborne division, triangular division, pentomic division, Reorganization Objective Army Division *or* ROAD; **regiment, battle group,** battalion, garrison, **company,** troop, brigade, legion, pha-

lanx, cohort, **platoon,** section, **battery,**
maniple; **combat team,** combat command; **task force; squad,** squadron; detachment, detail, posse; kitchen police
or KP; column, flying column; rank, file;
train, field train; cadre

23 **army,** this man's army <nonformal>,
soldiery, forces, troops, host, array, le-
gions; ranks, rank and file; **standing
army, regular army,** regulars, professional *or* career soldiers; the line, troops
of the line; line of defense, first *or* second
line of defense; ground forces, ground
troops; storm troops; **airborne troops,**
paratroops; ski troops, mountain troops;
occupation force

24 **militia,** organized militia, national militia, mobile militia, territorial militia,
reserve militia; home reserve; **National
Guard,** Air National Guard, state guard;
home guard <chiefly Brit>; minutemen,
trainband, yeomanry

25 **reserves,** auxiliaries, **second line of defense,** landwehr, army reserves, home
reserves, territorial reserves, territorial
or home defense army <Brit>, supplementary reserves, organized reserves; US
Army Reserve, US Naval Reserve, US
Marine Corps Reserve, US Air Force Reserve, US Coast Guard Reserve

26 **volunteers, enlistees,** volunteer army,
volunteer militia, volunteer navy

27 **navy,** naval forces, **first line of defense;
fleet,** flotilla, argosy, armada, squadron,
escadrille, division, task force, task
group; mosquito fleet; United States
Navy *or* USN; Royal Navy *or* RN; marine,
mercantile *or* merchant marine, merchant navy, merchant fleet; naval militia;
naval reserve; coast guard; Seabees, Naval Construction Battalion

28 **marines,** sea soldiers, Marine Corps,
Royal Marines; **leathernecks** *and* devil
dogs *and* gyrenes <all nonformal>, jollies <Brit nonformal>

29 **air force,** air corps, air service, air arm;
US Air Force *or* USAF; strategic air force,
tactical air force; squadron, escadrille,
flight, wing

30 **war-horse, charger,** courser, trooper

31 **US Army branches and corps**

Adjutant General	Corps of Cadets
Corps	<West Point>
Armored Corps	Corps of Engineers
Army Air Corps	Dental Corps
Army Nurse Corps	General Staff Corps
Army Service Corps	Judge Advocate Gen-
Chemical Warfare	eral Corps
Service	Medical Corps

Military Police Corps	Signal Corps
Ordnance Corps	Transportation Corps
Quartermaster Corps	

462 ARMS

NOUNS **1 arms, weapons,** deadly weapons,
instruments of destruction, offensive
weapons, **military hardware,** matériel,
**weaponry, armament, munitions, ord-
nance,** munitions of war, *apparatus belli*
<L>; musketry; missilery; small arms;
side arms; stand of arms; conventional
weapons, nonnuclear weapons; **nuclear
weapons,** atomic weapons, thermonuclear weapons, A-weapons; biological
weapons; weapons of mass destruction;
arms industry, arms maker, military-
industrial complex

2 **armory, arsenal,** magazine, dump; ammunition depot, ammo dump <nonfor-
mal>; park, gun park, artillery park,
park of artillery; atomic arsenal, thermonuclear arsenal

3 **ballistics, gunnery,** musketry, artillery;
rocketry, missilery; archery

4 **fist, clenched fist; brass knuckles;** knucks
and brass knucks <both nonformal>,
knuckles, knuckle-dusters; **club,** blunt instrument

5 **sword, blade,** good *or* trusty sword; steel,
cold steel; Excalibur; **knife; dagger; axe**

6 **arrow, shaft, dart,** reed, **bolt;** quarrel;
chested arrow, footed arrow, bobtailed
arrow, cloth yard shaft; arrowhead, barb;
flight, volley

7 **bow,** longbow, carriage bow; **bow and arrow;** crossbow, arbalest

8 **spear,** throwing spear, javelin

9 **sling, slingshot;** throwing-stick, throw
stick, spear-thrower, atlatl, wommera;
catapult, arbalest, ballista, trebuchet

10 **gun, firearm;** shooting iron *and* gat *and*
rod *and* heater *and* piece <all nonfor-
mal>; shoulder weapon *or* gun *or* arm;
gun make; gun part; stun gun; automatic,
BB gun, blunderbuss <old>, Bren,
Browning automatic rifle, burp gun
<nonformal>, carbine, derringer,
flintlock, forty-five *or* .45, forty-four *or*
.44, Gatling gun, handgun, machine gun,
musket, pistol, repeater, revolver, rifle,
Saturday night special, sawed-off shotgun, shotgun, six-gun *or* six-shooter
<nonformal>, submachine gun, thirty-
eight *or* .38, thirty-thirty *or* .30-30, thirty-
two *or* .32, Thompson submachine gun *or*
tommy gun <nonformal>, twenty-two *or*
.22, Uzi submachine gun, zip gun

11 **artillery, cannon,** cannonry, ordnance,
engines of war, Big Bertha, howitzer;
field artillery; heavy artillery, heavy field
artillery; siege artillery, bombardment
weapons; breakthrough weapons; siege
engine; mountain artillery, coast artillery, trench artillery, anti-aircraft artillery, flak <nonformal>; battery

12 **antiaircraft gun** or AA gun, ack-ack
<nonformal>, pom-pom <nonformal>,
Fliegerabwehrkanone <Ger>, skysweeper,
Bofors, Oerlikon

13 **ammunition, ammo** <nonformal>, **powder and shot,** iron rations <nonformal>

14 **explosive,** high explosive; cellulose nitrate, cordite, dynamite, gelignite,
guncotton, gunpowder, nitroglycerin,
plastic explosive or plastique, powder,
trinitrotoluene or trinitrotoluol or TNT

15 **fuse, detonator,** exploder; **cap,** blasting
cap, percussion cap, mercury fulminate,
fulminating mercury; electric detonator
or exploder; detonating powder; **primer,**
priming; primacord

16 **charge, load;** blast; warhead, payload

17 **cartridge,** cartouche, **shell;** ball cartridge; blank cartridge, dry ammunition

18 **missile, projectile,** bolt; brickbat, stone,
rock, alley apple and Irish confetti <both
nonformal>; boomerang; bola; throwing-
stick, throw stick, waddy <Austral>;
ballistic missile, cruise missile, Exocet
missile, surface-to-air missile or SAM,
surface-to-surface missile, Tomahawk
missile; **rocket** 1072.2–6,14; **torpedo**

19 **shot; ball,** cannonball, rifle ball, minié
ball; **bullet,** slug, pellet; dumdum bullet,
expanding bullet, explosive bullet, man-
stopping bullet, manstopper, copkiller or
Teflon bullet <trademark>; tracer bullet, tracer; **shell,** high-explosive shell,
shrapnel

20 **bomb,** bombshell; antipersonnel bomb,
atomic bomb or atom bomb or A-bomb,
atomic warhead, blockbuster, depth
charge or depth bomb or ash can
<nonformal>, fire bomb or incendiary
bomb or incendiary, grenade, hand grenade, hydrogen bomb or H-bomb, letter
bomb, Molotov cocktail, napalm bomb,
neutron bomb, nuclear warhead, pipe
bomb, plastic or plastique bomb, plutonium bomb, smart bomb, stench or
stink bomb, time bomb; clean bomb,
dirty bomb; **mine**

21 **launcher,** projector, bazooka; rocket
launcher, grenade launcher, hedgehog,
mine thrower, *Minenwerfer* <Ger>, **mortar**

463 ARENA

NOUNS 1 **arena, scene of action, site,** scene,
setting, background, **field, ground,** terrain, sphere, place, locale, milieu,
precinct, purlieu; course, range, walk
<old>; campus; **theater,** stage, stage set
or setting, scenery; **platform; forum,**
agora, marketplace, open forum, public
square; **amphitheater,** circus, **hippo-
drome, coliseum,** colosseum, **stadium,
bowl; hall, auditorium;** gymnasium, gym
<nonformal>, palaestra; **lists,** tiltyard,
tilting ground; floor, **pit,** cockpit; bear
garden; **ring,** prize ring, boxing ring,
canvas, squared circle <nonformal>,
wrestling ring, mat, bull ring; parade
ground; athletic field, field, playing field;
stamping ground, turf, bailiwick 893.4

2 **battlefield, battleground,** battle site,
field, combat area, **field of battle;** field of
slaughter, field of blood or bloodshed,
aceldama, killing ground or field, shambles; **battlefront, the front,** front line,
line, enemy line or lines, firing line, battle
line, line of battle; combat zone; **theater,
theater of operations,** theater or seat of
war; communications zone, zone of communications; no-man's-land; demilitarized zone or DMZ; jump area or zone,
landing beach

3 campground, camp, encampment, bivouac, tented field

464 PEACE

NOUNS 1 **peace,** *pax* <L>; **peacetime,** "piping time of peace"—Shakespeare, the
storm blown over; freedom from war,
cessation of combat, exemption from hostilities, public tranquillity, "liberty in
tranquillity"—Cicero; **harmony,** accord
455

2 **peacefulness, tranquillity, serenity,
calmness, quiet,** peace and quiet, quietude, quietness, quiet life, restfulness;
order, orderliness, law and order

3 **peace of mind,** peace of heart, peace of
soul or spirit, peace of God, "peace which
passeth all understanding"—Bible; ataraxia, shanti

4 **peaceableness, unpugnaciousness,** un-
contentiousness, nonaggression; ireni-
cism, dovelikeness, dovishness <nonfor-
mal>, **pacifism,** pacificism; peaceful
coexistence; **nonviolence;** meekness,
lamblikeness 433.5

5 **noncombatant,** nonbelligerent, nonresistant, nonresister; **civilian,** citizen

6 **pacifist,** pacificist, peacenik <nonformal>, **peace lover, dove** *and* dove of peace <both nonformal>; pacificator, peacemaker, bridgebuilder; peacemonger; **conscientious objector,** conchie <nonformal>

VERBS 7 **keep the peace,** remain at peace, wage peace; refuse to shed blood, keep one's sword in its sheath; forswear violence, beat one's swords into plowshares; pursue the arts of peace, pour oil on troubled waters; defuse

8 "be at peace among yourselves," "follow after the things which make for peace, "follow peace with all men, "as much as lieth in you, live peaceably with all men, "seek peace, and pursue it, "have peace one with another, "be of one mind, live in peace"—all Bible

ADJS 9 **pacific, peaceful, peaceable; tranquil, serene;** idyllic, pastoral; halcyon, soft, piping, **calm, quiet,** restful, **untroubled,** orderly, **at peace;** concordant 455.3; bloodless; peacetime

10 **unbelligerent, unhostile,** unbellicose, **unpugnacious, uncontentious,** unmilitant, unmilitary, **nonaggressive,** noncombative, nonmilitant; noncombatant, civilian; **antiwar, pacific, peaceable,** peaceloving, dovish <nonformal>; meek, lamblike 433.15; **pacifistic,** pacifist, irenic; **nonviolent;** conciliatory 465.12

INTERJS 11 **peace!, peace be with you!,** peace be to you!, *pax vobiscum!, pax tecum!* <both L>; *shalom!, shalom aleichem!* <both Hebrew>, *salaam aleikum!* <Arabic>; "peace be to this house!, "peace be within thy walls, and prosperity within thy palaces, "let the peace of God rule in your hearts"—all Bible; go in peace!, *vade in pace!* <L>

465 PACIFICATION

NOUNS 1 **pacification, peacemaking,** peacemongering, **conciliation, propitiation, placation, appeasement, mollification,** dulcification; **calming, soothing,** tranquilization; détente, relaxation of tension, easing of relations; mediation 466; placability; peace-keeping force, United Nations troops

2 **peace offer,** offer of parley, parley; peace feelers; **peace offering,** propitiatory gift; **olive branch; white flag,** truce flag, flag of truce; calumet, peace pipe, **pipe of peace;** downing of arms, hand of friendship, empty hands, outstretched hand; **cooling off, cooling-off period**

3 **reconciliation,** reconcilement, *rapprochement* <Fr>, **reunion,** shaking of hands, making up *and* kissing and making up <both nonformal>

4 **adjustment,** accommodation, resolution, composition of differences, compromise, arrangement, settlement, terms; consensus building, consensus seeking

5 **truce, armistice, peace; pacification,** treaty of peace, suspension of hostilities, **cease-fire,** stand-down, breathing spell, cooling-off period; Truce *or* Peace of God, Pax Dei, Pax Romana; temporary arrangement, *modus vivendi* <L>; hollow truce, *pax in bello* <L>; demilitarized zone, buffer zone, neutral territory

6 **disarmament,** reduction of armaments; unilateral disarmament; **demilitarization,** deactivation, disbanding, disbandment, **demobilization,** mustering out, reconversion, decommissioning; civilian life, mufti *and* civvy street <both Brit>

VERBS 7 **pacify, conciliate, placate, propitiate, appease, mollify,** dulcify; **calm, settle, soothe,** tranquilize 670.7; smooth, smooth over *or* out, smooth down, smooth one's feathers; allay, lay, lay the dust; pour oil on troubled waters, pour balm on, take the edge off of, take the sting out of; cool <nonformal>, defuse; clear the air

8 **reconcile, bring to terms, bring together,** reunite, heal the breach; bring about a détente; **harmonize,** restore harmony, put in tune; **iron** *or* **sort out,** adjust, settle, compose, accommodate, arrange matters, settle differences, resolve, compromise; **patch things up,** fix up <nonformal>, patch up a friendship *or* quarrel, smooth it over; weave peace between, mediate 466.6

9 **make peace,** cease hostilities, cease fire, stand down, raise a siege; **cool it** *and* **chill out** <both nonformal>, **bury the hatchet, smoke the pipe of peace;** negotiate a peace, dictate peace; make a peace offering, hold out the olive branch, hoist *or* show *or* wave the white flag

10 **make up** *and* **kiss and make up** *and* make it up *and* make matters up <all nonformal>, **shake hands,** come round, come together, come to an understanding, **come to terms,** let the wound heal, let bygones be bygones, forgive and forget, put it all behind one, settle *or* compose one's differences, meet halfway

11 **disarm, lay down one's arms,** unarm, turn in one's weapons, down *or* ground one's arms, sheathe the sword, turn

swords into plowshares; **demilitarize,** deactivate, **demobilize, disband,** reconvert, decommission

ADJS **12 pacificatory, pacific,** irenic, **conciliatory,** reconciliatory, **propitiatory,** propitiative, **placative,** placatory, **mollifying, appeasing; pacifying, soothing** 670.15, appeasable

13 pacifiable, placable, appeasable, propitiable

ADVS **14 pacifically, peaceably; with no hard feelings**

466 MEDIATION

NOUNS **1 mediation,** mediating, intermediation, **intercession; intervention,** interposition, putting oneself between, stepping in, declaring oneself in, involvement, interagency; interventionism

2 arbitration, arbitrament, compulsory arbitration, binding arbitration; nonbinding arbitration; umpirage, refereeship, mediatorship

3 mediator, intermediator, intermediate agent, intermediate, intermedium, **intermediary,** interagent, internuncio; **medium; intercessor,** interceder; ombudsman; **intervener,** intervenor; interventionist; **go-between, middleman** 576.4; connection <nonformal>; front *and* front man <both nonformal>; deputy, agent 576; **spokesman, spokeswoman,** spokesperson, spokespeople; **mouthpiece; negotiator,** negotiant, negotiatress *or* negotiatrix; Little Miss Fixit

4 arbitrator, arbiter, impartial arbitrator, third party, unbiased observer; **moderator; umpire, referee, judge;** magistrate 596.1

5 peacemaker, make-peace, reconciler, smoother-over; **pacifier,** pacificator; **conciliator,** propitiator, **appeaser;** marriage counselor, family counselor; patcher-up

VERBS **6 mediate,** intermediate, **intercede,** go between; **intervene,** interpose, step in, step into the breach, declare oneself a party, involve oneself, put oneself between disputants, use one's good offices, act between; butt in *and* put one's nose in <both nonformal>; represent 576.14; **negotiate,** bargain, **treat with,** make terms, meet halfway; **arbitrate,** moderate; **umpire, referee,** judge

7 settle, arrange, compose, patch up, adjust, straighten out, bring to terms *or* an understanding; make peace 465.9

ADJS **8 mediatory,** mediatorial, mediative, mediating, going *or* coming between; intermediatory, intermediary, intermedial, intermediate, **middle,** intervening, mesne, interlocutory; interventional, arbitrational, arbitrative; **intercessory,** intercessional; pacificatory 465.12

467 NEUTRALITY

NOUNS **1 neutrality, neutralism,** strict neutrality; noncommitment, noninvolvement; **independence, nonpartisanism, unalignment, nonalignment;** anythingarianism *or* nothingarianism <both nonformal>; mugwumpery, mugwumpism, fence-sitting *or* -straddling, trimming; **evasion, cop-out** <nonformal>, abstention; **impartiality** 649.4

2 indifference, indifferentness, Laodiceanism; passiveness 329.1; apathy 94.4

3 middle course *or* **way,** *via media* <L>; **middle ground,** neutral ground *or* territory, center; meeting ground, interface; gray area, penumbra; **middle of the road,** sitting on *or* straddling the fence <nonformal>; medium, **happy medium;** mean, **golden mean;** moderation, moderateness 670.1; compromise 468; halfway measures, half measures, half-and-half measures

4 neutral, neuter; **independent, nonpartisan;** mugwump, fence-sitter *or* -straddler, trimmer; anythingarian *and* nothingarian <both nonformal>; unaligned *or* nonaligned nation, third force, third world

VERBS **5 remain neutral,** stand neuter, hold no brief, **keep in the middle of the road, straddle** *or* **sit on the fence** *and* sit out *and* sit on the sidelines <all nonformal>, trim; **evade,** evade the issue, duck the issue *and* waffle *and* **cop out** <all nonformal>, abstain

6 steer a middle course, hold *or* keep *or* preserve a middle course, walk a middle path, follow the *via media,* strike *or* preserve a balance, **strike** *or* **keep a happy medium,** keep the golden mean, steer between *or* avoid Scylla and Charybdis; be moderate 670.5

ADJS **7 neutral,** neuter; noncommitted, uncommitted, noninvolved, uninvolved; anythingarian *and* nothingarian <both nonformal>; **indifferent,** Laodicean; passive 329.6; apathetic 94.13; neither one thing nor the other, neither hot nor cold; even, half-and-half, fifty-fifty <nonformal>; **on the fence** *or* **sidelines** <nonformal>, **in the middle of the road,** centrist, moderate, midway; **independent,**

nonpartisan; **unaligned, nonaligned,**
third-force, third-world; **impartial** 649.10

468 COMPROMISE

NOUNS **1 compromise,** composition, adjustment, accommodation, settlement, mutual concession, give-and-take; abatement of differences; bargain, deal <non-
formal>, arrangement, understanding;
concession, giving way, yielding; surrender, desertion of principle, evasion of
responsibility, cop-out <nonformal>

VERBS **2 compromise,** make or reach a compromise, compound, compose, accommodate, adjust, settle, make an adjustment
or arrangement, **make a deal** <nonfor-
mal>, do a deal <Brit nonformal>, come
to an understanding, strike a bargain, do
something mutually beneficial; plea-
bargain; strike a balance, take the mean,
meet halfway, split the difference, go
fifty-fifty <nonformal>, give and take;
play politics; steer a middle course 467.6;
make concessions, give way, yield, wimp
or chicken out <nonformal>; **surrender**
433.8, desert one's principles, evade responsibility, sidestep, duck responsibility and cop out and punt <all nonfor-
mal>

PHRS **3** half a loaf is better than none; you
can't win them all

469 POSSESSION

NOUNS **1 possession,** possessing, outright
possession, free-and-clear possession;
owning, having title to; seisin, nine
points of the law, de facto possession, de
jure possession, lawful or legal possession; property rights, proprietary rights;
title, absolute title, free-and-clear title,
original title; derivative title; adverse
possession, squatting, squatterism,
squatter's right; claim, legal claim, lien;
usucapion, usucaption <old>, prescription; **occupancy,** occupation; **hold,**
holding, tenure; tenancy, tenantry, **lease,**
leasehold, sublease, underlease, under-
tenancy; gavelkind; villenage, villein
socage, villeinhold; socage, free socage;
burgage; frankalmoign, lay fee; tenure in
chivalry, knight service; fee fief, fiefdom,
feud, feodum; freehold, alodium; fee
simple, fee tail, fee simple absolute, fee
simple conditional, fee simple defeasible
or fee simple determinable; fee position;
dependency, colony, mandate; prepossess-
sion <old>, preoccupation, preoccu-

pancy; chose in possession, bird in hand;
property 471

2 ownership, title, possessorship, domi-
nium <L>, **proprietorship,** proprietary,
property right or rights; lordship, **overlordship,** seigniory; **dominion, sovereignty** 417.5; landownership, landowning, landholding, land tenure

3 monopoly, monopolization; **corner** and
cornering and a corner on <all nonfor-
mal>; exclusive possession; engrossment, forestallment

VERBS **4 possess, have, hold,** have and hold,
possess outright or free and clear, **occupy,
fill, enjoy,** boast; be possessed of, have
tenure of, have in hand, be seized of, have
in one's grip or grasp, have in one's possession, be enfeoffed of; **command,** have
at one's command or pleasure or disposition or disposal, have going for one <non-
formal>; claim, usucapt; **squat,** squat on,
claim squatter's right

5 own, have title to, have for one's own or
very own, have to one's name, call one's
own, have the deed for, hold in fee simple,
etc

6 monopolize, hog and grab all of and gobble up <all nonformal>, take it all, have
all to oneself, have exclusive possession of
or exclusive rights to; engross, forestall,
tie up; **corner** and get a corner on and corner the market <all nonformal>

7 belong to, pertain to, appertain to; vest in

ADJS **8 possessed, owned,** held; in seisin, in
fee, in fee simple, **free and clear; own,** of
one's own; **in one's possession, in hand,** in
one's grip or grasp, at one's command or
disposal; on hand, by one, in stock, in
store

9 possessing, having, holding, having and
holding, **occupying, owning; in possession of, possessed of,** seized of, master
of; tenured; enfeoffed; endowed with,
blessed with; worth; propertied, prop-
erty-owning, landed, landowning, landholding

10 possessive, possessory, **proprietary**

11 monopolistic, monopolist, monopolizing,
hogging or hoggish <both nonformal>

ADVS **12 free and clear, outright;** bag and
baggage; by fee simple, etc

470 POSSESSOR

NOUNS **1 possessor, holder,** keeper, haver,
enjoyer; a have <nonformal>

2 proprietor, proprietary, **owner;** rentier
<Fr>; titleholder, deedholder; propri-
etress, proprietrix; **master, mistress, lord,**

laird <Scots>; **landlord, landlady;** lord of the manor, mesne lord, mesne, feudatory, feoffee; squire, country gentleman; householder; beneficiary, cestui, cestui que trust, cestui que use

3 **landowner,** landholder, property owner, propertied *or* landed person, man of property, freeholder; landed interests, landed gentry, slumlord, rent gouger; absentee landlord

4 **tenant, occupant,** occupier, incumbent, **resident; lodger,** roomer, paying guest; **renter,** hirer <Brit>, **lessee,** leaseholder; subtenant, sublessee, underlessee, undertenant; tenant at sufferance, tenant at will; tenant from year to year, tenant for years, tenant for life; squatter; homesteader

5 **trustee,** fiduciary, holder of the legal estate; depository, depositary

471 PROPERTY

NOUNS 1 **property, properties, possessions, holdings,** havings, goods, chattels, goods and chattels, **effects,** estate and effects, what one can call one's own, what one has to one's name, all one owns *or* has, all one can lay claim to, one's all; household possessions *or* effects, lares and penates; hereditament, corporeal hereditament, incorporeal hereditament; acquest; acquisitions, receipts 627; **inheritance** 479.2

2 **belongings, appurtenances,** trappings, paraphernalia, appointments, accessories, perquisites, appendages, appanages, choses local; **things,** material things, mere things; consumer goods; choses, choses in possession, choses in action; **personal effects,** chattels personal, movables, choses transitory

3 **impedimenta, luggage, dunnage, baggage,** bag and baggage, traps, tackle, apparatus, truck, gear, kit, outfit, duffel

4 **estate, interest, equity, stake,** part, percentage; **right, title** 469.1, **claim,** holding; use, trust, benefit; absolute interest, vested interest, contingent interest, beneficial interest, equitable interest; easement, right of common, common, right of entry; limitation; settlement, strict settlement

5 **freehold,** estate of freehold; alodium, alod; frankalmoign, lay fee, tenure in *or* by free alms; mortmain, dead hand

6 **real estate, realty,** real property, land, land and buildings, chattels real, tenements; immovables; *praedium* <L>, landed property *or* estate, **land, lands,**

property, grounds, acres; lot, lots, parcel, plot, plat, quadrat; demesne, domain <old>; messuage, manor, honor, toft <Brit>

7 **assets, means, resources,** total assets *or* resources; stock, stock-in-trade; **worth,** net worth, what one is worth; circumstances, funds 728.14; wealth 618; **material assets,** tangible assets, tangibles; intangible assets, intangibles; current assets, deferred assets, fixed assets, frozen assets, liquid assets, quick assets, assets and liabilities, net assets; assessed valuation

ADJS 8 **propertied,** proprietary; **landed**

9 real, praedial; manorial, seignioral, seigneurial; feudal, feudatory, feodal

10 freehold, leasehold, copyhold; alodial

472 ACQUISITION

NOUNS 1 **acquisition,** gaining, getting, getting hold of <nonformal>, coming by, **acquirement, obtainment,** obtention, **attainment,** securement, winning; trover; accession; addition 253; **procurement,** procural, procurance, procuration; **earnings,** making, pulling *or* dragging *or* knocking down <nonformal>, moneymaking, moneygetting, moneygrubbing

2 **collection, gathering,** gleaning, bringing together, assembling, putting *or* piecing together, **accumulation,** cumulation, **amassment,** heaping up, grubbing

3 **gain, profit,** percentage <nonformal>, get <Brit nonformal>, **take** *or* take-in *and* piece *and* slice *and* end *and* rakeoff *and* skimmings <all nonformal>; **gains, profits, earnings, winnings, return, returns, proceeds, bottom line** <nonformal>, ettings, makings; **income** 624.4; **receipts** 627; **fruits,** pickings, gleanings; **booty, spoils** 482.11; pelf, lucre, filthy lucre; perquisite, perk *or* perks; **pile** *and* bundle *and* cleanup *and* killing *and* mint <all nonformal>; net *or* neat profit, clean *or* clear profit, net; gross profit, gross; paper profits; capital gains; interest, dividends; hoard, store 386; wealth 618

4 **profitableness, profitability,** gainfulness, remunerativeness, rewardingness, bang for the buck <nonformal>

5 **yield, output,** make, production; **proceeds, produce,** product; **crop, harvest,** fruit, vintage, bearing; second crop, aftermath; bumper crop

6 **find,** finding, **discovery; trove,** *trouvaille* <Fr>; treasure trove, buried treasure; **windfall,** windfall money, windfall profit,

found money, money in the bank, **bonus, gravy** <nonformal>, bunce <Brit nonformal>

7 **godsend, boon, blessing;** manna, manna from heaven, loaves and fishes, gift from on high

VERBS 8 **acquire, get, gain, obtain, secure, procure; win,** score; **earn,** make; **reap, harvest;** contract; take, catch, capture; **net;** come or enter into possession of, **come into, come by,** come in for, be seized of; draw, derive

9 <nonformal terms> **grab, latch** or glom on to, corral, bag, get or lay hold of, rake in or up or off, skim or skim off, catch, collar, cop, dig up, grub up, round up, drum up, get hold of, get or lay one's hands or mitts on, get one's fingers or hands on, get one's hooks into, snag, snaffle, grub up, scratch together, hook, land, throw together, nab, pick up, nail, scare or scrape up; take home, pull or drag or knock down

10 **take possession, appropriate, take up,** take over, make one's own, move in or move in on <nonformal>, annex

11 **collect, gather, glean, pick, pluck,** cull, **take up,** pick up, get or gather in, gather to oneself, bring or get together, scrape together; heap up, amass, assemble, accumulate 386.11

12 **profit, make** or **draw** or **realize** or **reap profit, come out ahead, make money;** rake it in and coin money and make a bundle or pile or killing or mint and clean up <all nonformal>; gain by, **capitalize on,** commercialize, make capital out of, **cash in on** and make a good thing of <both nonformal>, turn to profit or account, **realize on,** make money by, obtain a return, turn a penny or an honest penny; **gross, net; realize, clear;** kill two birds with one stone, turn to one's advantage; make a fast or quick buck <nonformal>

13 **be profitable,** pay, repay, pay off <nonformal>, yield a profit, show a percentage, be gainful, be worthwhile or worth one's while, be a good investment

ADJS 14 **obtainable, attainable, available,** accessible, to be had

15 **acquisitive,** acquiring; grasping, graspy, hoggy and grabby <both nonformal>; **greedy** 100.27

16 **gainful,** productive, **profitable, remunerative, remuneratory, lucrative,** fat, **paying,** well-paying, high-yield, high-yielding; advantageous, worthwhile; banausic, moneymaking, breadwinning

ADVS 17 **profitably, gainfully,** remuneratively, lucratively, **at a profit,** in the black; for money; advantageously, to advantage, to profit, to the good

473 LOSS

NOUNS 1 **loss, losing, privation,** getting away, losing hold of; **deprivation, bereavement,** taking away, stripping, dispossession, despoilment, despoliation, spoliation, robbery; divestment, denudation; **sacrifice, forfeit, forfeiture,** giving up or over, denial; nonrestoration; **expense, cost, debit;** detriment, injury, damage; **destruction, ruin,** perdition, total loss, dead loss; losing streak <nonformal>; **loser** 412.5

2 **waste,** wastage, **exhaustion, depletion,** sapping, depreciation, dissipation, diffusion, **wearing, wearing away, erosion,** ablation, leaching away; molting, shedding, casting or sloughing off; **using, using up, consumption, expenditure, drain;** stripping, clear-cutting; impoverishment, shrinkage, leakage, evaporation; decrement, decrease 252

3 **losses,** losings; red ink; net loss, bottom line <nonformal>

VERBS 4 **lose,** incur loss, **suffer loss,** undergo privation or deprivation, be bereaved or bereft of, have no more, meet with a loss; drop and kiss good-bye <both nonformal>; let slip, let slip through one's fingers; **forfeit,** default; **sacrifice; miss,** wander from, go astray from; **mislay,** misplace; lose out; **lose everything,** go broke and lose one's shirt and take a bath or to the cleaners and tap out and go to Tap City <all nonformal>

5 **waste, deplete, depreciate,** dissipate, wear, wear away, erode, ablate, consume, drain, **shrink,** dribble away; **molt, shed,** cast or slough off; decrease 252.6; squander 486.3

6 **go to waste,** come to nothing, come to naught, go up in smoke and go down the drain <both nonformal>; run to waste, go to pot <nonformal>, run or go to seed; dissipate, leak, leak away, scatter to the winds, "waste its sweetness on the desert air"—Thomas Gray

ADJS 7 **lost, gone;** forfeited, forfeit; by the board, out the window and down the drain or tube <all nonformal>; **nonrenewable;** long-lost; lost to; wasted, consumed, depleted, dissipated, diffused, **expended; worn away, eroded,** ablated, used, used up, shrunken; stripped, clear-cut; squandered 486.9; irretrievable 125.15

8 bereft, bereaved, divested, denuded, **deprived of,** shorn of, parted from, bereaved of, stripped of, dispossessed of, despoiled of, robbed of; **out of,** minus <nonformal>, wanting, lacking; cut off, cut off without a cent; out-of-pocket; **penniless, destitute, broke** and cleaned out and tapped out and wiped out <all nonformal>

ADVS **9 at a loss, unprofitably,** to the bad <nonformal>; in the red <nonformal>; out, out-of-pocket

474 RETENTION

NOUNS **1 retention,** retainment, **keeping, holding, maintenance, preservation;** prehension; keeping or holding in, **bottling** or corking up <nonformal>, locking in, suppression, repression, inhibition, retentiveness, retentivity; **tenacity** 802.3

2 hold, purchase, grasp, grip, clutch, clamp, clinch, clench; seizure 480.2; bite, nip, tooth-hold; **cling,** clinging; toehold, foothold, footing; **clasp, hug, embrace,** bear hug; grapple; firm hold, tight grip, iron grip, grip of iron or steel, death grip

3 <wrestling holds> half nelson, full nelson, quarter nelson, three-quarter nelson, stranglehold, toehold, lock, hammerlock, headlock, scissors, bear hug

4 clutches, claws, talons, pounces, unguals; **nails,** fingernails; **pincers,** nippers, chelae; **tentacles; fingers,** digits, hooks <nonformal>; **hands,** paws and meathooks and mitts <all nonformal>; palm; prehensile tail; **jaws,** mandibles, maxillae; **teeth,** fangs

VERBS **5 retain, keep, save,** save up, pocket and hip-pocket <both nonformal>; **maintain, preserve;** keep or hold in, **bottle** or cork up <both nonformal>, lock in, suppress, repress, inhibit, keep to oneself; persist in; hold one's own, hold one's ground

6 hold, grip, grasp, clutch, clip, **clinch, clench;** bite, nip; grapple; **clasp, hug, embrace; cling, cling to,** cleave to, stick to, adhere to, freeze to; **hold on to,** hold fast or tight, hang on to, keep a firm hold upon; **hold on, hang on** <nonformal>, hold on like a bulldog, stick like a leech, cling like a winkle, hang on for dear life; keep hold of, never let go; **seize** 480.14

7 hold, keep, harbor, bear, have, have and hold, hold on to; **cherish,** fondle, entertain, treasure, treasure up; **foster, nur-**

ture, nurse; embrace, hug, clip <Brit nonformal>, cling to; bosom or embosom <both old>, take to the bosom

ADJS **8 retentive,** keeping, holding, gripping, grasping; **tenacious,** clinging; viselike; anal

9 prehensile, raptorial; fingered, digitate or digitated, digital; clawed, taloned, jawed, toothed, dentate, fanged

ADVS **10 for keeps** <nonformal>, to keep, **for good,** for good and all, for always; forever 828.12

475 RELINQUISHMENT

NOUNS **1 relinquishment, release,** giving up, letting go, dispensation; **disposal,** disposition, riddance, getting rid of, dumping 390.3; **renunciation,** forgoing, forswearing, swearing off, resignation, abjuration, **abandonment** 370; recantation, retraction 363.3; **surrender,** cession, handover, turning over, **yielding;** sacrifice

2 waiver, quitclaim, deed of release

VERBS **3 relinquish, give up,** render up, **surrender, yield,** cede, hand or turn over; take one's hands off, loose one's grip on; spare; resign, vacate; drop, **waive,** dispense with; **forgo,** do without, get along without, forswear, abjure, **renounce,** swear off; walk away from, **abandon** 370.5; recant, retract; disgorge, throw up; have done with, wash one's hands of; **part with,** give away, dispose of, rid oneself of, get rid of, see the last of, dump 390.7; kiss goodbye or off <nonformal>; **sacrifice,** make a sacrifice; quitclaim; sell off

4 release, let go, leave go <nonformal>, **let loose of,** unhand, unclutch, unclasp, relax one's grip or hold

ADJS **5 relinquished,** released, disposed of; waived, dispensed with; forgone, forsworn, renounced, abjured, **abandoned** 370.8; recanted, retracted; **surrendered,** ceded, yielded; sacrificed

476 PARTICIPATION

NOUNS **1 participation, partaking, sharing,** having a part or share or voice, contribution, association; **involvement,** engagement; complicity; **voting** 609.18, **suffrage** 609.17; **power-sharing;** partnership, copartnership, copartnery, joint control, cochairmanship, joint chairmanship; joint tenancy, cotenancy; joint ownership, condominium or condo, cooperative or coop; communal ownership, commune

2 communion, community, communal effort *or* enterprise, **cooperation,** cooperative society; social life, socializing; **collectivity,** collectivism, collective enterprise, collective farm, kibbutz, kolkhoz; **democracy,** participatory democracy, town meeting, self-rule; collegiality; common ownership, public ownership, state ownership, communism, socialism 611.5,6; profit sharing; sharecropping

3 communization, communalization, **socialization, nationalization, collectivization**

4 participator, participant, partaker, player, sharer; party, **a party to,** accomplice, accessory; partner, copartner; cotenant; shareholder

VERBS **5 participate, take part, partake, contribute,** chip in, involve *or* engage oneself, get involved; **have** *or* **take a hand in,** get in on, have a finger in, have a finger in the pie, have to do with, have a part in, be an accessory to, be implicated in, be a party to, be a player in; **participate in,** partake of *or* in, **take part in,** take an active part in, **join, join in,** figure in, make oneself part of, join oneself to, associate oneself with, play *or* perform a part in, play a role in, get in the act <nonformal>; **join up,** sign on, enlist; climb on the bandwagon; **have a voice in,** help decide, be in on the decisions, **vote,** have suffrage, be enfranchised; **enter into,** go into; make the scene <nonformal>; sit in, sit on; bear a hand, pull an oar; come out of one's shell

6 share, share in, come in for a share, **go shares,** be partners in, have a stake in, have a percentage *or* piece of <nonformal>, **divide with, divvy up with** <nonformal>, halve, go halves; go halvers *and* **go fifty-fifty** *and* go even stephen <all nonformal>, split the difference, **share and share alike;** do one's share *or* part, pull one's weight; cooperate 450.3; apportion 477.6

7 communize, communalize, **socialize, collectivize, nationalize**

ADJS **8 participating, participative,** participant, participatory; involved, engaged, **in** *or* **in on** <nonformal>; implicated, accessory; **partaking, sharing**

9 communal, common, general, public, collective, popular, social, societal; **mutual,** commutual <old>, reciprocal, associated, **joint,** conjoint, **in common,** share and share alike; **cooperative** 450.5; power-sharing, profit-sharing; collectivistic, **communistic,** socialistic 611.22

477 APPORTIONMENT

NOUNS **1 apportionment, apportioning, portioning, division,** divvy <nonformal>, **partition,** repartition, partitionment, partitioning, parceling, budgeting, rationing, **dividing, sharing,** share-out, sharing out, splitting, cutting, slicing, cutting the pie *and* divvying up <both nonformal>; reapportionment

2 distribution, dispersion, **disposal,** disposition; dole, doling, doling out, giving out, passing around; **dispensation,** administration, issuance; disbursal, disbursement, paying out; redistribution; maldistribution

3 allotment, assignment, appointment, setting aside, **earmarking,** tagging; underallotment, overallotment; appropriation; **allocation;** misallocation; reallocation

4 dedication, commitment, devoting, devotion, consecration

5 portion, share, interest, part, stake, stock, **piece,** bit, segment; **bite** *and* **cut** *and* **slice** *and* **chunk** *and* slice of the pie *or* melon *and* piece of the action <all nonformal>, **lot, allotment, end** <nonformal>, **proportion, percentage,** measure, quantum, **quota,** deal *or* dole <both nonformal>, meed, moiety, mess, helping; contingent; dividend; **commission,** rake-off <nonformal>; equal share, half; **lion's share,** bigger half, big end <nonformal>; small share, modicum; **allowance, ration, budget; load,** work load; fate, destiny 963.2

VERBS **6 apportion, portion, parcel, partition, part, divide,** share; share with, cut *or* deal one in <nonformal>, share and share alike, divide with, go halvers *or* fifty-fifty *or* even stephen with <nonformal>; divide into shares, **share out** *or* **around,** divide up, divvy *or* divvy up *or* out <nonformal>, **split,** split up, carve, cut, slice, carve up, slice up, cut up, cut *or* slice the pie *or* melon <nonformal>; divide *or* split fifty-fifty

7 proportion, proportionate, **prorate,** divide *pro rata*

8 parcel out, portion out, measure out, serve out, spoon *or* ladle *or* dish out, **deal out, dole out, hand out, mete out,** ration out, give out, hand around, pass around; mete, dole, deal; **distribute,** disperse; **dispense,** dispose <old>, issue, administer; disburse, pay out

9 allot, lot, **assign, appoint, set,** detail; **allocate,** make assignments *or* allocations, schedule; **set apart** *or* **aside, earmark,** tag, mark out for; set off, mark off, portion off;

assign to, appropriate to *or* for; reserve, restrict to, restrict 210.5; **ordain, destine, fate**

10 **budget, ration;** allowance, put on an allowance

11 **dedicate, commit, devote, consecrate,** set apart

ADJS 12 **apportioned,** portioned out, parceled, allocated, etc; **apportionable,** allocable, divisible, distributable, committable, appropriable, dispensable, donable, severable

13 **proportionate,** proportional; prorated, *pro rata* <L>; half; halvers *or* fifty-fifty *or* even stephen <all nonformal>, half-and-half, equal; **distributive,** distributional; **respective,** particular, per head, per capita, several

ADVS 14 **proportionately, in proportion,** *pro rata* <L>; **distributively; respectively,** severally, each to each; share and share alike, in equal shares, half-and-half; fifty-fifty *and* even stephen <both nonformal>

478 GIVING

NOUNS 1 **giving, donation,** bestowal, bestowment; **endowment,** gifting <nonformal>, **presentation,** presentment; **award,** awarding; grant, granting; accordance, vouchsafement <old>; conferment, conferral; investiture; **delivery,** deliverance, surrender; **concession,** communication, impartation, impartment; **contribution,** subscription; tithing; accommodation, supplying, furnishment, provision 385; **offer** 439; **liberality** 485

2 **commitment, consignment,** assignment, **delegation,** relegation, commendation, remanding, **entrustment;** enfeoffment, infeudation *or* infeodation

3 **charity,** almsgiving; **philanthropy** 143.4

4 **gift, present,** presentation, *cadeau* <Fr>, **offering,** fairing <Brit>; tribute, **award;** free gift, freebie *and* gimme <both nonformal>; oblation 696.7; handsel; box <Brit>; Christmas present *or* gift, birthday present *or* gift; peace offering

5 **gratuity, largess, bounty,** liberality, donative, sportula; perquisite, perks <Brit nonformal>; consideration, fee <old>, **tip,** *pourboire* <Fr>, *Trinkgeld* <Ger>, sweetener, inducement; grease *and* salve *and* palm oil <all nonformal>; **premium, bonus,** something extra, **gravy** <nonformal>, bunce <Brit nonformal>, lagniappe; baker's dozen; honorarium; incentive pay, time and a half, double time; bribe 378.2

6 **donation,** donative; **contribution, subscription; alms,** pittance, **charity, dole, handout** <nonformal>, alms fee, widow's mite; Peter's pence; **offering,** offertory, votive offering, collection; tithe

7 **benefit,** benefaction, benevolence, **blessing, favor, boon,** grace; manna, manna from heaven

8 **subsidy,** subvention, subsidization, support, price support, depletion allowance, tax benefit *or* write-off; **grant,** grant-in-aid, bounty; **allowance, stipend,** allotment; **aid,** assistance, financial assistance; **help,** pecuniary aid; scholarship, fellowship; honorarium; **welfare,** public welfare, public assistance, relief, relief *or* welfare payments, welfare aid, dole, aid to dependent children; guaranteed annual income; alimony; annuity; pension, old-age insurance, retirement benefits, social security, remittance; unemployment insurance

9 **endowment,** investment, **settlement,** foundation; **dowry,** *dot* <Fr>, portion, marriage portion; **dower,** widow's dower; jointure, legal jointure, thirds; appanage

10 **bequest,** bequeathal, **legacy,** devise; inheritance 479.2; **will, testament,** last will and testament; probate, attested copy; codicil

11 **giver, donor,** donator, gifter <nonformal>, presenter, bestower, conferrer, grantor, awarder, imparter, vouchsafer; fairy godmother, Lady Bountiful, Santa Claus, sugar daddy <nonformal>; cheerful giver; **contributor, subscriber,** supporter, backer, financer, funder, angel <nonformal>; subsidizer; patron, patroness, Maecenas; tither; almsgiver, almoner; **philanthropist** 143.8; assignor, consignor; settler; testate, testator, testatrix; feoffor

VERBS 12 **give, present, donate,** slip <nonformal>, let have; **bestow, confer, award, allot, render,** bestow on; impart, let one know, communicate; **grant,** accord, **allow,** vouchsafe, yield, afford, make available; **tender,** proffer, offer, extend, come up with <nonformal>; **issue, dispense,** administer; serve, help to; **distribute;** deal, dole, mete; **give out, deal out, dole out, mete out, hand** *or* dish out <nonformal>, fork *or* shell out <nonformal>; make a present of, gift *or* gift with <nonformal>, give as a gift; **give generously,** give the shirt off one's back; be generous *or* liberal with, give freely;

pour, shower, rain, snow, heap, lavish
486.3; give in addition *or* as lagniappe,
give into the bargain

13 **deliver, hand, pass,** reach, forward, render, put into the hands of; transfer; **hand
over,** give over, deliver over, fork over
<nonformal>, **pass over, turn over,** come
across with <nonformal>; hand out, give
out, pass out, distribute, circulate; hand
in, give in; **surrender,** resign

14 **contribute, subscribe, chip in** *and* kick in
and pony up *and* pay up <all nonfor-
mal>, give one's share *or* fair share; put
oneself down for, pledge; contribute to,
give to, **donate to,** gift *and* gift with
<both nonformal>; put something in the
pot, sweeten the kitty

15 **furnish, supply, provide, afford,** provide
for; **make available to,** put one in the way
of; **accommodate with,** favor with, indulge with; **heap upon,** pour on, shower
down upon, **lavish upon**

16 **commit, consign, assign, delegate,** relegate, confide, commend, remit, remand,
give in charge; **entrust,** trust, give in
trust; enfeoff, infeudate

17 **endow,** invest, vest; endow with, favor
with, bless with, grace with, vest with;
settle on *or* **upon; dower**

18 **bequeath, will,** will and bequeath, **leave,
devise, will to,** hand down, hand on, pass
on, transmit; **make a will,** draw up a will,
execute a will, make a bequest, write
one's last will and testament, write into
one's will; add a codicil; entail

19 **subsidize, finance,** bankroll *and* green-
back <both nonformal>, fund; angel
<nonformal>; **aid, assist, support, help,**
pay the bills, pick up the check *or* tab *and*
spring for *and* pop for <all nonformal>;
pension, pension off

20 **thrust upon, force upon, press upon,** push
upon, obtrude on, ram *or* cram down
one's throat

21 **give away,** dispose of, part with, sacrifice,
spare

ADJS 22 philanthropic, eleemosynary, **charitable** 143.15; giving, generous to a fault,
liberal, **generous** 485.4

23 **giveable,** presentable, bestowable; impartable, communicable; bequeathable,
devisable; allowable; committable; fund-
able

24 **given,** allowed, accorded, granted, vouch-
safed, bestowed, etc; gratuitous 634.5;
God-given, providential

25 donative, contributory; concessive; testate, testamentary; intestate

26 **endowed,** dowered, invested; dower,

dowry, dotal; subsidiary, stipendiary,
pensionary

ADVS 27 as a gift, gratis, on one, on the
house, free; to his heirs, to the heirs of his
body, to his heirs and assigns, to his exec-
utors *or* administrators and assigns

479 RECEIVING

NOUNS 1 **receiving, reception,** receival, **receipt, getting, taking; acquisition** 472;
derivation; **assumption, acceptance;** admission, admittance; **reception** 187

2 **inheritance,** heritance <old>, **heritage,
patrimony, birthright, legacy, bequest,**
bequeathal; reversion; entail; heirship;
succession, line of succession, mode of
succession, law of succession; primogeniture, ultimogeniture, postremogeniture,
borough-English, coheirship, coparcen-
ary, gavelkind; hereditament, corporeal
or incorporeal hereditament; **heritable;
heirloom**

3 **recipient, receiver,** accepter, getter,
taker, acquirer, obtainer, procurer;
payee, endorsee; addressee, consignee;
holder, trustee; **hearer,** viewer, beholder,
audience, auditor, listener, looker, spectator; the receiving end

4 **beneficiary,** allottee, **donee, grantee,** pat-
entee; **assignee, assign; devisee, legatee,**
legatary <old>; feoffee; almsman, almswoman; stipendiary; pensioner, pensionary; annuitant

5 **heir,** heritor, inheritor, *heres* <L>;
heiress, inheritress, inheritrix; coheir,
joint heir, fellow heir, coparcener; heir
portioner <Scots>; heir expectant; **heir
apparent,** apparent heir; **heir presumptive,** presumptive heir; statutory next of
kin; legal heir, heir at law, heir general,
heir of line *or* heir whatsoever <both
Scots>; heir of inventory *or* beneficiary
heir <both Scots>; heir of provision
<Scots>, heir by destination; heir of
the body; heir in tail, heir of entail;
fideicommissary heir, fiduciary heir; reversioner; remainderman; **successor,**
next in line

VERBS 6 **receive, get, gain, secure,** have,
come by, be in receipt of, be on the receiving end; **obtain, acquire** 472.8,9; **admit,
accept, take,** take off one's hands; **take in**
187.10; assume, take on, take over; **derive, draw,** draw *or* derive from; have an
income of, drag down *and* pull down *and*
rake in <all nonformal>, have coming in,
take home

7 **inherit,** be heir to, **come into,** come in for,

come by, fall *or* step into; step into the shoes of, succeed to

8 **be received, come in,** come to hand, pass *or* fall into one's hands, go into one's pocket, come *or* fall to one, fall to one's share *or* lot; **accrue,** accrue to

ADJS 9 **receiving,** on the receiving end; **receptive,** recipient 187.16

10 **received, accepted, admitted, recognized, approved**

480 TAKING

NOUNS 1 **taking,** possession, taking possession, taking away; **claiming,** staking one's claim; **acquisition** 472; **reception** 479.1; **theft** 482

2 **seizure, seizing, grab,** grabbing, snatching, snatch; **kidnapping, abduction,** forcible seizure; **power grab** <nonformal>, coup, coup d'état, seizure of power; **hold** 474.2; **catch,** catching; **capture,** collaring <nonformal>, nabbing <nonformal>; **apprehension,** prehension; **arrest,** arrestation, taking into custody; picking up *and* taking in *and* running in <all nonformal>; dragnet

3 **sexual possession,** taking; sexual assault, ravishment, **rape,** violation, indecent assault, date rape *or* acquaintance rape, serial rape *or* gang bang <nonformal>; statutory rape; defloration, deflowerment, devirgination

4 **appropriation, taking over, takeover** <nonformal>, **adoption, assumption, usurpation,** arrogation; requisition, indent <Brit>; preoccupation, prepossession, preemption; **conquest,** occupation, subjugation, enslavement, colonization

5 **attachment, annexation,** annexure <Brit>; **confiscation,** sequestration; impoundment; **commandeering, impressment;** expropriation, nationalization, socialization, communalization, communization, collectivization; levy; distraint, distress; garnishment; execution; eminent domain, angary, right of eminent domain, right of angary

6 **deprivation, deprival,** privation, divestment, bereavement; relieving, disburdening, disburdenment; curtailment, abridgment <old>; disentitlement

7 **dispossession,** disseisin, expropriation; reclaiming, repossessing, **repossession,** foreclosure; **eviction** 908.2; disendowment; **disinheritance,** disherison, disownment

8 **extortion, shakedown** <nonformal>,

blackmail, bloodsucking, vampirism; protection racket; badger game

9 **rapacity,** rapaciousness, ravenousness, sharkishness, wolfishness, **predaciousness,** predacity; pillaging, looting

10 **take, catch, bag,** capture, seizure, **haul;** booty 482.11

11 **taker;** partaker; **catcher, captor,** capturer

12 **extortionist,** extortioner, **blackmailer,** racketeer, shakedown artist <nonformal>, **bloodsucker,** leech, **vampire; predator,** raptor, bird of prey, beast of prey; harpy; **vulture,** shark; profiteer; rackrenter

VERBS 13 **take,** possess, take possession; **get,** get into one's hold *or* possession; pocket, palm; draw off, drain off; skim *and* skim off *and* take up front <all nonformal>; **claim,** stake one's claim, enforce one's claim; partake; **acquire** 472.8,9; **receive** 479.6; **steal** 482.13

14 **seize,** take *or* get hold of, **lay hold of,** catch *or* grab hold of, glom *or* latch on to <nonformal>, **get** *or* **lay hands on,** clap hands on <nonformal>, put one's hands on, get into one's grasp *or* clutches; get one's fingers *or* hands on, get between one's finger and thumb; **grab, grasp, grip,** gripe <old>, **grapple, snatch,** snatch up, nip, nail <nonformal>, **clutch,** claw, clinch, clench; **clasp, hug, embrace;** snap up, nip up, whip up, catch up; pillage, loot; take by assault *or* storm; **kidnap, abduct,** snatch <nonformal>, carry off; shanghai; take by the throat, throttle

15 **possess sexually,** take; **rape,** commit rape, commit date *or* acquaintance rape, ravish, violate, assault sexually, lay violent hands on, have one's will of; deflower, deflorate, devirginate

16 **seize on** *or* **upon,** fasten upon; spring *or* pounce upon, jump <nonformal>, swoop down upon; **catch at, snatch at,** snap at, jump at, make a grab for, scramble for

17 **catch, take,** catch flatfooted, land *and* nail <both nonformal>, hook, **snag, snare,** sniggle, spear, harpoon; ensnare, enmesh, entangle, tangle, foul, tangle up with; **net,** mesh; **bag,** sack; **trap,** entrap; lasso, rope, noose

18 **capture, apprehend, collar** <nonformal>, run down, run to earth, **nab** <nonformal>, grab <nonformal>, lay by the heels, take prisoner; **arrest,** place *or* put under arrest, take into custody; pick up *or* take in *or* run in <all nonformal>

19 **appropriate, adopt, assume, usurp,** arrogate, accroach; requisition, indent <Brit>; **take possession of,** possess one-

self of, take for oneself, arrogate to oneself, take up, **take over, help oneself to,**
make use of, make one's own, make free
with, dip one's hands into; take it all, take
all of, hog <nonformal>, monopolize, sit
on; preoccupy, prepossess, preempt;
jump a claim; **conquer,** overrun, occupy,
subjugate, enslave, colonize; squat on

20 **attach, annex; confiscate,** sequester, sequestrate, impound; **commandeer,** press,
impress; expropriate, nationalize, socialize, communalize, communize, collectivize; exercise the right of eminent domain,
exercise the right of angary; levy, distrain, replevy, replevin; garnishee, garnish

21 **take from,** take away from, **deprive of,** do
out of <nonformal>, relieve of, dis-
burden of, lighten of, ease of; **deprive,
bereave, divest;** tap, milk, mine, drain,
bleed, curtail, abridge <old>; cut off;
disentitle

22 **wrest,** wring, wrench, **rend,** rip; **extort,
exact,** squeeze, screw, **shake down**
<nonformal>, **blackmail,** levy black-
mail, badger *and* play the badger game
<both nonformal>; **force from, wrest
from, wrench from, wring from, tear
from, rip from, rend from,** snatch from,
pry loose from

23 **dispossess,** disseise, expropriate, foreclose; **evict** 908.15; disendow; **disinherit,**
disherison, **disown,** cut out of one's will,
cut off, cut off with a shilling, cut off
without a cent

24 **strip,** strip bare *or* clean, **fleece** <nonfor-
mal>, **shear,** denude, skin *and* pluck
<both nonformal>, flay, **despoil, divest,**
pick clean, pick the bones of; deplume,
displume; **milk; bleed, bleed white;** exhaust, drain, dry, suck dry; **impoverish,**
beggar; clean out *and* take to the cleaners
<both nonformal>; eat out of house and
home

ADJS 25 **taking, catching;** private, depriva-
tive; confiscatory, annexational, expro-
priatory; **thievish** 482.21

26 **rapacious, ravenous,** ravening, vulturous,
vulturine, sharkish, **wolfish,** lupine, predacious, **predatory,** raptorial; vampirish,
bloodsucking, parasitic; **extortionate;
grasping,** graspy, grabby <nonformal>,
insatiable 100.27; all-devouring, all-
engulfing

481 RESTITUTION

NOUNS 1 **restitution, restoration,** restoring,
giving back, sending back, remitting,

remission, **return;** reddition <old>;
extradition, rendition; repatriation; recommitment, remandment, remand

2 **reparation, recompense,** paying back,
squaring <nonformal>, repayment, reimbursement, refund, remuneration,
compensation, indemnification; retribution, **atonement,** redress, satisfaction,
amends, making good, **requital**

3 **recovery,** regaining; **retrieval,** retrieve;
recuperation, recoup, recoupment; **retake,** retaking, recapture; **repossession,**
resumption, reoccupation; **reclamation,**
reclaiming; **redemption,** ransom, salvage, trover; replevin, replevy; **revival,
restoration** 396, retro

VERBS 4 **restore, return, give back,** restitute,
hand back, put back; take back, bring
back; put the genie back into the bottle,
put the toothpaste back into the tube; **remit,** send back; repatriate; extradite;
recommit, remand

5 **make restitution,** make reparation, **make
amends,** make good, make up for, atone,
give satisfaction, redress, **recompense,**
pay back, square <nonformal>, repay,
reimburse, refund, remunerate, **compensate, requite,** indemnify, make up for,
make it up; pay damages, pay reparations; pay conscience money; overcompensate

6 **recover, regain, retrieve,** recuperate, **recoup, get back,** come by one's own;
redeem, ransom; **reclaim; repossess,** resume, reoccupy; **retake,** recapture, take
back; replevin, replevy; revive, renovate,
restore 396.11,15

ADJS 7 **restitutive,** restitutory, **restorative;**
compensatory, indemnificatory, retribu-
tive, reparative; reversionary, reversional, revertible; redeeming, redemptive, redemptional; reimbursable

ADVS 8 **in restitution,** in reparation, in recompense, in compensation, to make up
for, in return for, in retribution, in requital, in amends, in atonement, to atone
for

482 THEFT

NOUNS 1 **theft, thievery,** stealage, **stealing,**
thieving, **purloining;** swiping *and* lifting
and snatching *and* snitching *and* pinching
<all nonformal>; conveyance <old>, **ap-
propriation,** conversion, liberation *and*
annexation <both nonformal>; **pilfering,**
pilferage, **filching,** scrounging <nonfor-
mal>; abstraction; sneak thievery; shop-
lifting, boosting <nonformal>; poach-

ing; **graft**; **embezzlement** 389.1; **fraud, swindle** 356.8

2 **larceny**, petit or petty larceny, petty theft, grand larceny, grand theft, simple larceny, mixed or aggravated larceny; automobile theft

3 **theft, robbery**, robbing; bank robbery; banditry, highway robbery; **armed robbery, holdup**, assault and robbery, **mugging**, push-in job or crime; purse snatching; **pocket picking**, jostling; **hijacking**, asportation <old>; cattle stealing, **cattle rustling** and cattle lifting <both nonformal>; **extortion** 480.8

4 <nonformal terms> **heist, stickup**, job, stickup job, bag job, boost, burn, knockover, **ripoff**

5 **burglary**, burglarizing, housebreaking, **breaking and entering**, break and entry, break-in, unlawful entry; second-story work <nonformal>; safebreaking, **safecracking, safeblowing**

6 **plundering, pillaging, looting, sacking**, freebooting, ransacking, rifling, spoiling, **despoliation**, despoilment, despoiling; rapine, spoliation, depredation, direption <old>, **raiding**, reiving <Scots>, ravage, ravaging, ravagement, rape, ravishment; **pillage, plunder**, sack; brigandage, brigandism, banditry; **marauding**, foraging; raid, foray, razzia

7 **piracy, buccaneering, privateering, freebooting**; letters of marque, letters of marque and reprisal; **air piracy**, airplane hijacking, skyjacking

8 **plagiarism**, plagiarizing, plagiary, **piracy**, literary piracy, appropriation, borrowing, cribbing; infringement of copyright; autoplagiarism

9 **abduction, kidnapping, snatching** <nonformal>; **shanghaiing**, impressment, crimping

10 **grave-robbing**, body-snatching <nonformal>, resurrectionism

11 **booty**, spoil, **spoils, loot, swag** <nonformal>, ill-gotten gains, **plunder**, prize, haul, take, pickings, stealings, stolen goods, hot goods or items <nonformal>; **boodle** and squeeze and **graft** <all nonformal>; perquisite, perks <Brit nonformal>, pork barrel, spoils of office, public trough; till, public till; blackmail

12 **thievishness**, larcenousness, taking ways <nonformal>, light fingers, sticky fingers; kleptomania, bibliokleptomania, etc

VERBS 13 **steal, thieve, purloin, appropriate, take**, snatch, palm, **make off with**, walk off with, run off or away with, abstract,

disregard the distinction between *meum* and *tuum;* have one's hand in the till; **pilfer, filch**; shoplift; poach; rustle; **embezzle** 389.4; defraud, swindle; **extort** 480.22

14 **rob**, commit robbery; pick pockets, jostle; hold up

15 **burglarize**, burgle <nonformal>, commit burglary; crack or blow a safe

16 <nonformal terms> **swipe, pinch**, bag, **lift**, hook, crib, **cop**, nip, snitch, snare, boost, annex, borrow, burn, clip, **rip off**, nick and nobble <both Brit>; **heist, knock off** or **over**, tip over; **stick up; mug**; roll, jackroll; hijack

17 **plunder, pillage, loot, sack**, ransack, rifle, freeboot, spoil, spoliate, despoil, depredate, prey on or upon, **raid**, reive <Scots>, ravage, ravish, raven, sweep, gut; **fleece** 480.24; maraud, foray, forage

18 **pirate**, buccaneer, privateer, freeboot

19 **plagiarize, pirate**, borrow and crib <both nonformal>, appropriate; **pick one's brains;** infringe a copyright

20 **abduct**, abduce, spirit away, **carry off** or **away**, magic away <Brit>, run off or away with; **kidnap**, snatch <nonformal>, hold for ransom; skyjack; **shanghai**, crimp, impress

ADJS 21 **thievish, thieving, larcenous, light-fingered, sticky-fingered**; kleptomaniacal, burglarious; brigandish, piratical, piratelike; fraudulent

22 **plunderous, plundering, looting**, pillaging, ravaging, marauding, spoliatory; predatory, predacious

23 **stolen**, pilfered, purloined; pirated, plagiarized; hot <nonformal>

483 THIEF

NOUNS 1 **thief, robber**, stealer, purloiner, lifter <nonformal>, *ganef* <Yiddish>, **crook** <nonformal>; larcenist, larcener; **pilferer, filcher**, petty thief, chicken thief; sneak thief, prowler; shoplifter, booster <nonformal>; poacher; **grafter**, petty grafter; jewel thief; **swindler**, con man 357.3,4; land pirate, land shark, land-grabber; grave robber, body snatcher, resurrectionist, ghoul; embezzler, peculator, white-collar thief; den of thieves

2 **pickpocket**, cutpurse, fingersmith and dip <both nonformal>; **purse snatcher;** light-fingered gentry

3 **burglar**, yegg and cracksman <both nonformal>; housebreaker, cat burglar, cat man, second-story thief or worker; **safecracker**, safebreaker, safeblower; pete

blower *or* pete man *or* peterman <all nonformal>

4 bandit, brigand, dacoit; **gangster** *and* mobster <both nonformal>; racketeer; **thug, hoodlum** 593.4

5 robber, holdup man *and* stickup man <both nonformal>; highwayman, highway robber, footpad, road agent, bushranger <Austral>; **mugger** <nonformal>, sandbagger; train robber; bank robber, **hijacker** <nonformal>

6 plunderer, pillager, looter, marauder, rifler, sacker, spoiler, despoiler, spoliator, depredator, **raider,** moss-trooper, freebooter, rapparee, reiver <Scots>, forayer, forager, ravisher, ravager; wrecker

7 pirate, corsair, buccaneer, privateer, sea rover, rover, picaroon; viking, sea king; Blackbeard, Captain Kidd, Jean Lafitte, Henry Morgan; Captain Hook <J M Barrie>, Long John Silver <Stevenson>; air pirate, airplane hijacker, skyjacker

8 cattle thief, abactor, rustler *and* **cattle rustler** <both nonformal>

9 plagiarist, plagiarizer, cribber <nonformal>, **pirate,** literary pirate, copyright infringer

10 abductor, kidnapper; shanghaier, snatcher *and* baby-snatcher <both nonformal>; crimp, crimper

11 <famous thieves> Barabbas, Robin Hood, Jesse James, Clyde Barrow, John Dillinger, Claude Duval, Jack Sheppard, Willie Sutton, Dick Turpin, Jonathan Wild; Autolycus, Macheath <John Gay>, Thief of Baghdad, Jean Valjean <Hugo>, Jimmy Valentine <O Henry>, Raffles <E W Hornung>, Bill Sikes <Dickens>

484 PARSIMONY

NOUNS **1 parsimony,** parsimoniousness; frugality 635.1; **stinting, pinching, scrimping,** skimping, cheeseparing; economy, economy of means, economy of assumption, law of parsimony, Ockham's razor, elegance

2 niggardliness, penuriousness, **meanness,** minginess, shabbiness, sordidness

3 stinginess, ungenerosity, illiberality, cheapness, chintziness *and* tightness *and* narrowness <all nonformal>, tight purse strings, nearness, closeness, closefistedness, closehandedness <old>, tightfistedness, hardfistedness, **miserliness,** pennypinching, hoarding; **avarice** 100.8

4 niggard, tightwad *and* **cheapskate** <both nonformal>, **miser,** hard man with a buck <nonformal>, **skinflint,** scrooge,

penny pincher, pinchfist, pinchgut <old>, churl, curmudgeon <old>, muckworm, save-all <nonformal>, Harpagon <Molière>, Silas Marner <George Eliot>

VERBS **5 stint, scrimp, skimp, scamp,** scant, screw, **pinch,** starve, famish; **pinch pennies,** rub the print off a dollar bill, rub the picture off a nickel; live upon nothing; grudge, begrudge

6 withhold, hold back, hold out on <nonformal>

ADJS **7 parsimonious, sparing,** cheeseparing, **stinting, scamping, scrimping,** skimping; frugal 635.6; too frugal, overfrugal, frugal to excess; penny-wise, penny-wise and pound-foolish

8 niggardly, niggard, pinchpenny, penurious, **grudging, mean,** mingy, shabby, sordid

9 stingy, illiberal, ungenerous, chintzy, miserly, save-all, **cheap** *and* **tight** *and* narrow <all nonformal>, **near, close, closefisted,** closehanded <old>, tightfisted, pinchfisted, hardfisted; near as the bark on a tree, "as close as a vise" — Hawthorne; pinching, **penny-pinching; avaricious** 100.27

ADVS **10 parsimoniously,** stintingly, scrimpingly, skimpingly

11 niggardly, stingily, illiberally, ungenerously, closefistedly, tightfistedly; meanly, shabbily, sordidly

485 LIBERALITY

NOUNS **1 liberality,** liberalness, freeness, freedom; **generosity,** generousness, largeness, **unselfishness, munificence,** largess; bountifulness, bounteousness, **bounty;** hospitality, welcome, graciousness; **openhandedness,** freehandedness, open *or* free hand, easy purse strings; **givingness;** open-heartedness, bigheartedness, largeheartedness, greatheartedness, freeheartedness; open heart, big *or* large *or* great heart, heart of gold; **magnanimity** 652.2

2 cheerful giver, free giver; Lady Bountiful; Santa Claus

VERBS **3 give freely,** give cheerfully, give with an open hand, give with both hands, put one's hands in one's pockets, open the purse, loosen *or* untie the purse strings; **spare no expense,** spare nothing, not count the cost, let money be no object; **heap upon,** lavish upon, shower down upon; give the coat *or* shirt off one's back, give more than one's share, **give until it hurts;** give of oneself, give of one's substance, not hold back, offer oneself; keep the change!

ADJS **4 liberal, free,** free with one's money, free-spending; **generous, munificent,** large, princely, handsome; **unselfish,** ungrudging; **unsparing, unstinting,** stintless, unstinted; **bountiful,** bounteous, **lavish,** profuse; hospitable, gracious; **openhanded,** freehanded, open; **giving;** openhearted, **bighearted,** largehearted, greathearted; **magnanimous** 652.6

ADVS **5 liberally, freely; generously, munificently,** handsomely; **unselfishly,** ungrudgingly; **unsparingly, unstintingly; bountifully,** bounteously, **lavishly,** profusely; hospitably, graciously; **openhandedly,** freehandedly; openheartedly, bigheartedly, largeheartedly, greatheartedly, freeheartedly; with open hands, with both hands, with an unsparing hand, without stint

486 PRODIGALITY

NOUNS **1 prodigality, overliberality,** overgenerousness, overgenerosity; profligacy, **extravagance,** pound-foolishness, recklessness, reckless spending *or* expenditure; incontinence, intemperance 669; lavishness, profuseness, profusion; **wastefulness, waste; dissipation, squandering,** squandermania; *carpe diem* <L>; slack *or* loose purse strings, leaking purse; conspicuous consumption *or* waste

2 prodigal, wastrel, waster, **squanderer; spendthrift,** wastethrift, spender, spendall, big-time spender <nonformal>; Diamond Jim Brady; prodigal son

VERBS **3 squander, lavish,** slather, blow <nonformal>, play ducks and drakes with; **dissipate,** scatter <old>, sow broadcast, scatter to the winds; **run through,** go through; **throw away,** throw one's money away, throw money around, **spend money like water,** hang the expense, let slip *or* flow through one's fingers, spend as if money grew on trees, spend money as if it were going out of style, throw money around, spend like a drunken sailor; gamble away; burn the candle at both ends; seize the day, live for the day, let tomorrow take care of itself

4 waste, consume, spend, expend, use up, exhaust; lose; spill, pour down the drain *or* rathole; pour water into a sieve, cast pearls before swine, kill the goose that lays the golden egg, *manger son blé en herbe* <Fr>, throw out the baby with the bath water

5 fritter away, fool away, fribble away, dribble away, drivel away, **trifle away,** dally away, potter away, piss away <nonformal>, muddle away, diddle away <nonformal>, squander in dribs and drabs; idle away, while away

6 misspend, throw good money after bad, throw the helve after the hatchet, throw out the baby with the bathwater

7 overspend, spend more than one has, spend what one hasn't got; overdraw, overdraw one's account, live beyond one's means, have champagne tastes on a beer budget

ADJS **8 prodigal, extravagant, lavish,** profuse, **overliberal,** overgenerous, overlavish, **spendthrift, wasteful,** profligate, dissipative; incontinent, intemperate 669.7; pound-foolish, penny-wise and pound-foolish; easy come, easy go

9 wasted, squandered, dissipated, consumed, spent, used, lost; **gone to waste,** run *or* gone to seed; down the drain *or* spout *or* rathole <nonformal>; misspent

487 CELEBRATION

NOUNS **1 celebration,** celebrating; **observance,** formal *or* solemn *or* ritual observance, **solemnization;** marking *or* honoring the occasion; **commemoration,** memorialization, remembrance, memory; jubilee; red-letter day, **holiday** 20.4; anniversaries; **festivity** 743.3,4; **revel** 743.6; rejoicing 116; **ceremony,** rite 580.4; religious rites 701; ovation, triumph; **tribute;** testimonial, testimonial banquet *or* dinner; toast; roast; **salute;** salvo; flourish of trumpets, fanfare, fanfaronade; dressing ship

VERBS **2 celebrate, observe, keep, mark,** solemnly mark, **honor; commemorate,** memorialize; **solemnize,** signalize, hallow, mark with a red letter; hold jubilee, jubilize, jubilate, maffick <Brit nonformal>; **make merry;** kill the fatted calf; sound a fanfare, blow the trumpet, beat the drum, fire a salute; dress ship

ADJS **3 celebrative,** celebratory, celebrating; **commemorative,** commemorating; memorial; solemn

ADVS **4 in honor of, in commemoration of,** in memory *or* remembrance of, to the memory of

488 HUMOROUSNESS

NOUNS **1 humorousness, funniness,** amusingness, laughableness, laughability, hilarity, hilariousness; wittiness 489.2; **drollness,** drollery; **whimsicalness,** quizzicalness; **ludicrousness, ridiculousness, absurdity,** absurdness, quaintness, eccentricity, incongruity, bizarreness, bizarrerie; richness, pricelessness <nonformal>; the funny side

2 comicalness, comicality, funiosity; farcicalness, **farcicality,** slapstick quality, broadness

3 bathos; anticlimax, comedown

ADJS **4 humorous, funny, amusing; witty** 489.15; **droll, whimsical,** quizzical; **laughable,** risible, good for a laugh; **ludicrous, ridiculous, hilarious, absurd,** quaint, eccentric, incongruous, bizarre

5 <nonformal terms> **funny ha-ha,** priceless, too funny or too killing for words, hardy-har or hardy-har-har or har-har-har, rich, hysterical

6 comic or **comical; farcical,** slapstick, broad; **burlesque** 508.14; tragicomic, serio-comic, mock-heroic

ADVS **7 humorously, amusingly,** funnily, **laughably;** wittily 489.18; drolly, whimsically, quizzically; **comically,** farcically, broadly; **ludicrously, ridiculously, absurdly,** quaintly, eccentrically, incongruously, bizarrely

489 WIT, HUMOR

NOUNS **1 wit, humor,** pleasantry, *esprit* <Fr>, salt, spice or savor of wit; Attic wit or salt, Atticism; ready wit, quick wit, nimble wit, agile wit, pretty wit; dry wit, subtle wit; **comedy** 704.6; black humor, sick humor, gallows humor; **satire,** sarcasm, irony; Varonnian satire, Menippean satire; **parody, lampoon,** lampoonery, travesty, **caricature, burlesque,** squib; **farce,** mere farce; **slapstick,** slapstick humor, broad humor; visual humor

2 wittiness, humorousness 488, **funniness; facetiousness,** pleasantry, **jocularity,** jocoseness, jocosity; **joking,** japery, joshing <nonformal>; smartness, cleverness, brilliance; pungency, saltiness; keenness, sharpness; keen-wittedness, quick-wittedness, nimble-wittedness

3 drollery, drollness; **whimsicality,** whimsicalness, humorsomeness, antic wit

4 waggishness, waggery; roguishness 322.2; **playfulness,** sportiveness, **levity, frivolity,** flippancy, merriment 109.5; **prankishness,** pranksomeness; trickery, trickiness, tricksiness, trickishness

5 buffoonery, buffoonism, clownery, clowning, clowning around, harle-

quinade; **clownishness,** buffoonishness; **foolery,** fooling, **tomfoolery;** horseplay; shenanigans and monkey tricks and monkeyshines <all nonformal>; **banter** 490

6 joke, jest, gag and one-liner <both nonformal>, **wheeze,** jape; **fun, sport, play;** story, yarn, **funny story,** good story; dirty story or joke, blue story or joke, *double entendre* <Fr>; shaggy-dog story; sick joke <nonformal>; ethnic joke; capital joke, good one, laugh, belly laugh, rib tickler, sidesplitter, thigh-slapper, howler, wow, scream, riot, panic; visual joke, sight gag <nonformal>; **point,** punch line, gag line, tag line; cream of the jest; jest-book; sight gag

7 witticism, pleasantry, *plaisanterie, boutade* <both Fr>; **play of wit,** *jeu d'esprit* <Fr>; **crack** and smart crack and **wisecrack** <all nonformal>; **quip,** conceit, bright or happy thought, bright or brilliant idea; **mot, bon mot,** smart saying, stroke of wit, one-liner and zinger <both nonformal>; epigram, turn of thought, aphorism, apothegm; flash of wit, scintillation; **sally,** flight of wit; **repartee,** backchat, retort, riposte, snappy comeback <nonformal>; facetiae <pl>, quips and cranks; **gibe, dirty** or **nasty crack** <nonformal>; persiflage 490.1

8 wordplay, play on words, *jeu de mots* <Fr>, missaying, corruption, paronomasia, *calembour* <Fr>, abuse of terms; **pun,** punning; equivoque, equivocality; anagram, logogram, logogriph, metagram; acrostic, double acrostic; amphiboly, amphibologism; palindrome; spoonerism; malapropism

9 old joke, old wheeze or turkey, **trite joke,** hoary-headed joke, joke with whiskers; **chestnut** and corn and **corny joke** and oldie <all nonformal>; Joe Miller, Joe Millerism; twice-told tale, retold story, warmed-over cabbage <nonformal>

10 prank, trick, practical joke, waggish trick, *espièglerie* <Fr>, antic, caper, frolic; **monkeyshines** and **shenanigans** <both nonformal>

11 sense of humor, risibility, funny bone

12 humorist, wit, funnyman, comic, *bel-esprit* <Fr>, life of the party; **joker,** jokester, gagman <nonformal>, **jester, quipster, wisecracker** and gagster <both nonformal>; wag, wagwit; zany, madcap, cutup <nonformal>; **prankster; comedian,** stand-up comic or comedian, banana <nonformal>; **clown** 707.10; punster, punner; epigrammatist; satirist, ironist; burlesquer, caricaturist, parodist, lampooner; reparteeist; witling; gag writer <nonformal>, jokesmith

VERBS **13 joke, jest, wisecrack** and crack wise <both nonformal>, utter a mot, **quip,** jape, josh <nonformal>, fun <nonformal>, make fun, **kid** or **kid around** <both nonformal>; **make a funny** <nonformal>; **crack a joke,** get off a joke, tell a good story; pun, play on words; scintillate, sparkle; **make fun of,** gibe at, fleer at, mock, scoff at, poke fun at, make the butt of one's humor, be merry with; ridicule 508.8

14 trick, play a practical joke, play tricks or pranks, **play a joke** or **trick on,** make merry with; **clown around,** pull a stunt or trick; pull one's leg and put one on <both nonformal>

ADJS **15 witty, amusing,** spirituel <Fr>; **humorous** 488.4,5, **comic, comical, farcical** 488.6; **funny; jocular,** joky <nonformal>, **joking, jesting, jocose, tongue-in-cheek; facetious,** joshing <nonformal>, **whimsical, droll,** humorsome; smart, clever, brilliant, scintillating, sparkling, sprightly; keen, sharp, rapier-like, pungent, pointed, biting, mordant; satiric, **satirical, sarcastic, ironic,** ironical; salty, salt, Attic; **keen-witted, quick-witted, nimble-witted**

16 clownish, buffoonish

17 waggish; roguish 322.6; **playful, sportive; prankish,** pranky, pranksome; tricky, trickish, tricksy

ADVS **18 wittily, humorously; jocularly, jocosely; facetiously; whimsically, drolly**

19 in fun, in sport, in play, in jest, in joke, as a joke, jokingly, jestingly, with tongue in cheek; for fun, for sport

490 BANTER

NOUNS **1 banter, badinage, persiflage, pleasantry, fooling, fooling around, kidding** and **kidding around** <both nonformal>, **raillery,** rallying, **sport,** good-natured banter, harmless teasing; ridicule 508; exchange, give-and-take; side-talk, **byplay,** asides; flyting, slanging, the dozens <nonformal>

2 bantering, twitting, chaffing, joking, jesting, japing, **fooling, teasing,** hazing; playing the dozens <nonformal>

3 <nonformal terms> **kidding,** joshing, jollying, jiving, fooling around; **ribbing,** ragging, razzing, **roasting**

4 banterer, persifleur <Fr>, **chaffer, twitter; kidder** and josher <both nonformal>

VERBS **5 banter, twit, chaff,** rally, **joke, jest,**

jape, **tease,** haze; have a slanging match, play the dozens <nonformal>

6 <nonformal terms> **kid,** jolly, josh, fool around, jive, rub, put on; **razz, roast,** ride, needle

ADJS **7 bantering, chaffing, twitting; jollying** and **kidding** and joshing etc <all nonformal>, **fooling, teasing,** quizzical

491 COWARDICE

NOUNS **1 cowardice, cowardliness; fear** 127; **faintheartedness,** faintheart, weakheartedness, chickenheartedness, henheartedness, pigeonheartedness; **yellowness,** white-liveredness and lily-liveredness and chicken-liveredness <all nonformal>, weak-kneedness; weakness, softness; unmanliness, unmanfulness; timidness, **timidity,** timorousness, milksoppiness, milksoppishness, milksopism

2 uncourageousness, unvaliantness, unvalorousness, unheroicness, ungallantness, unintrepidness; **plucklessness, spunklessness** and gritlessness and gutlessness <all nonformal>, spiritlessness, heartlessness

3 dastardliness, pusillanimousness, **pusillanimity, poltroonery,** poltroonishness, poltroonism, baseness, **cravenness;** desertion under fire, bugout and skedaddling <both nonformal>

4 cold feet <nonformal>, weak knees, **faintheart,** chicken heart, **yellow streak** <nonformal>, white feather

5 coward, jellyfish, invertebrate, **weakling,** weak sister <nonformal>, milksop, milquetoast, mouse, **sissy, wimp** <nonformal>, baby, **big baby, chicken** <nonformal>; **yellow-belly,** and white-liver and lily-liver and chicken-liver <all nonformal>, white feather; fraid-cat and fraidy-cat and scaredy-cat <all nonformal>; funk and funker <both nonformal>; "one who in a perilous emergency thinks with his legs"—Ambrose Bierce

6 dastard, craven, poltroon, recreant, caitiff, arrant coward; **sneak**

VERBS **7 dare not; have a yellow streak** <nonformal>, **have cold feet** <nonformal>, be unable to say 'boo' to a goose

8 lose one's nerve, lose courage, **get cold feet** <nonformal>, **show the white feather;** falter, boggle, funk <nonformal>, **chicken** <nonformal>; put one's tail between one's legs, back out, funk out <nonformal>, **wimp** or **chicken out** <both nonformal>; desert under fire, turn tail, bug out *and* skedaddle <both nonformal>, **run scared** <nonformal>, scuttle

9 **cower, quail, cringe, crouch, skulk, sneak, slink**

ADJS 10 **cowardly,** coward; **afraid, fearful** 127.32,34; timid, timorous, overtimorous, overtimid, rabbity *and* mousy <both nonformal>; **fainthearted,** weakhearted, chicken-hearted, henhearted, pigeonhearted; white-livered *and* lilylivered *and* chicken-livered *and* milklivered <all nonformal>; **yellow** *and* yellow-bellied *and* with a yellow streak <all nonformal>; **weak-kneed, chicken** <nonformal>, afraid of one's shadow; weak, soft; **wimpy** *or* wimpish <nonformal>, unmanly, unmanful, sissy, sissified; milksoppy, milksoppish; panicky, panic-prone, funking *and* funky <both nonformal>; daunted, dismayed, unmanned, cowed, intimidated

11 **uncourageous, unvaliant, unvalorous, unheroic,** ungallant, **unintrepid, undaring,** unable to say 'boo' to a goose; unsoldierlike, unsoldierly; **pluckless, spunkless** *and* gritless <both nonformal>, **gutless** <nonformal>, spiritless, heartless

12 **dastardly,** dastard; hit-and-run; **poltroonish,** poltroon; **pusillanimous,** base, craven, recreant, caitiff; dunghill, dunghilly

13 **cowering, quailing, cringing; skulking, sneaking, slinking,** sneaky, slinky

ADVS 14 **cravenly,** poltroonishly, like a coward, **cowardly, uncourageously,** unvaliantly, unvalorously, unheroically, ungallantly, unintrepidly, undaringly; plucklessly, spunklessly *and* gritlessly <both nonformal>, spiritlessly, heartlessly; faintheartedly, weakheartedly, chickenheartedly; wimpishly

492 COURAGE

NOUNS 1 **courage,** courageousness, **nerve,** pluck, **bravery,** braveness, ballsiness *and* gutsiness *or* guttiness <all nonformal>, **boldness, valor,** valorousness, valiance, valiancy, **gallantry,** conspicuous gallantry, gallantry under fire *or* beyond the call of duty, gallantness, **intrepidity,** intrepidness, **prowess,** virtue; doughtiness, stalwartness, stoutness, stouthearted-ness, lionheartedness, greatheartedness; **heroism,** heroicalness; chivalry, chivalrousness, knightliness; military *or* martial spirit, soldierly quality *or* vir-

tues; **manliness,** manfulness, **manhood,** virility, machismo; Dutch courage <nonformal>, pot-valor

2 "fear that has said its prayers"—Dorothy Bernard, "fear holding on a minute longer"—George Patton, "taking hard knocks like a man when occasion calls"—Plautus, "doing without witnesses that which we would be capable of doing before everyone"—La Rochefoucauld

3 **fearlessness,** dauntlessness, **undauntedness, unfearfulness,** unfearingness, unafraidness, **unapprehensiveness; confidence** 969.5; untimidness, untimorousness, unshrinkingness, unshyness, unbashfulness

4 <nonformal terms> **balls, guts,** intestinal fortitude, spunk, brass balls, cojones, moxie, spizzerinctum, **backbone,** chutzpah

5 **daring,** derring-do, deeds of derring-do; **bravado,** bravura; **audacity,** audaciousness, overboldness; **venturousness,** venturesomeness, risk-taking, tightrope walking, funambulism; **adventurousness,** adventuresomeness, enterprise; foolhardiness 493.3

6 **fortitude, hardihood,** hardiness; **pluckiness; spunkiness** *and* grittiness *and* nerviness <all nonformal>, mettlesomeness; **gameness,** gaminess; grit, **stamina,** toughness, pith <old>, **mettle,** bottom; **heart,** spirit, stout heart, heart of oak; **resolution** 359, resoluteness, tenaciousness, tenacity, pertinaciousness, pertinacity, bulldog courage

7 **exploit, feat, deed, enterprise, achievement, adventure,** gest, **bold stroke,** heroic act *or* deed; aristeia

8 <brave person> **hero, heroine;** brave, stalwart, gallant, valiant, man *or* woman of courage *or* mettle, a man, valiant knight, good soldier; demigod, paladin; demigoddess; the brave; decorated hero; Hector, Achilles, Roland, David; lion, **tiger,** bulldog, fighting cock, gamecock

9 **encouragement, heartening, inspiration,** inspiriting, inspiritment, emboldening, assurance, reassurance, pat *or* clap on the back

VERBS 10 **dare, venture, make bold to,** make so bold as to, take risks, walk the tightrope, **have the nerve, have the guts** *or* the balls <nonformal>, have the courage of one's convictions, be a man, "dare do all that may become a man"—Shakespeare, "be strong, and quit yourselves like men"—Bible; defy 454.3

11 **brave, face, confront,** affront, front, look

one in the eye, say to one's face, **face up to**, meet, **meet head-on** or boldly, square up to, stand up to or against, go eyeball-to-eyeball or one-on-one with <nonformal>; set at defiance 454.4; speak up, speak out, stand up and be counted; not flinch or shrink from, bite the bullet <nonformal>, look full in the face, put a bold face upon, show or present a bold front; head into, face up, come to grips with, grapple with; face the music <nonformal>; **brazen,** brazen out or through; beard, "beard the lion in his den"—Sir Walter Scott; put one's head in the lion's mouth, fly into the face of danger, take the bull by the horns, march up to the cannon's mouth, bell the cat, go through fire and water, go in harm's way, throw caution to the wind, run the gauntlet, take one's life in one's hands, put one's ass or life on the line <nonformal>

12 **outbrave, outdare; outface,** face down, face out; **outbrazen,** brazen out; **outlook, outstare,** stare down, stare out <Brit>, stare out of countenance

13 **steel oneself, get up nerve,** nerve oneself, muster or summon up or gather courage, pluck up heart, screw up one's nerve or courage, "screw your courage to the sticking place"—Shakespeare, stiffen one's backbone <nonformal>

14 **take courage, take heart,** pluck up courage, take heart of grace; **brace** or **buck up** <nonformal>

15 keep up one's courage, bear up, **keep one's chin up** <nonformal>, keep one's pecker up <Brit nonformal>, **keep a stiff upper lip** <nonformal>, hold up one's head, take what comes; hang in or hang in there or hang tough or stick it out <all nonformal>, stick to one's guns

16 **encourage, hearten, embolden, nerve,** pat or clap on the back, **assure, reassure,** bolster, support, cheer on, root for; **inspire,** inspirit; buck or brace up <nonformal>; put upon one's mettle, make a man of; cheer 109.7

ADJS 17 **courageous, plucky, brave, bold, valiant, valorous, gallant, intrepid,** doughty, **hardy,** stalwart, stout, stouthearted, ironhearted, lionhearted, greathearted, bold-spirited, bold as a lion; **heroic,** herolike; **chivalrous,** chivalric, knightly, knightlike, soldierly, soldierlike; **manly,** manful, virile, macho

18 **resolute, tough, game; spirited,** spiritful, red-blooded, **mettlesome;** bulldoggish, tenacious, pertinacious

19 <nonformal terms> **ballsy,** gutsy, gutty,

stand-up, dead game, gritty, spunky, nervy

20 **unafraid, unfearing, unfearful; unapprehensive,** undiffident; **confident** 969.21; **fearless, dauntless,** aweless, dreadless; **unfrightened,** unscared, unalarmed, unterrified; **untimid,** untimorous, unshy, unbashful

21 **undaunted, undismayed,** uncowed, unintimidated, unappalled, unabashed, unawed; **unflinching, unshrinking,** unquailing, uncringing, unwincing, unblenching, unblinking

22 **daring, audacious,** overbold; **adventurous, venturous, venturesome,** adventuresome, enterprising; foolhardy 493.9

ADVS 23 **courageously, bravely, boldly, heroically, valiantly,** valorously, **gallantly, intrepidly,** doughtily, stoutly, hardily, stalwartly; **pluckily, spunkily** <nonformal>, gutsily <nonformal>, **resolutely, gamely,** tenaciously, pertinaciously, bulldoggishly, **fearlessly,** unfearingly, unfearfully; **daringly,** audaciously; chivalrously, knightly, yeomanly; like a man, like a soldier

493 RASHNESS

NOUNS 1 **rashness, brashness,** brazen boldness, **incautiousness,** overboldness, **imprudence, indiscretion,** injudiciousness, improvidence; **unwariness,** unchariness; overcarelessness; overconfidence, oversureness, overweeningness; **impudence,** insolence 142; **gall** and brass and cheek and chutzpah <all nonformal>; hubris; **temerity,** temerariousness; heroics

2 **recklessness,** devil-may-careness; heedlessness, **carelessness** 340.2; **impetuousness** 365.2, impetuosity, hotheadedness; **haste** 401, **hastiness,** hurriedness, overeagerness, overzealousness, overenthusiasm; **furiousness,** desperateness, wantonness, wildness, wild oats; **precipitateness,** precipitousness, precipitance, precipitancy, precipitation

3 **foolhardiness,** harebrainedness; **audacity,** audaciousness; more guts than brains <nonformal>, courage fou <Fr>; forwardness, boldness, **presumption,** presumptuousness; **daring,** daredeviltry, daredevilry, fire-eating; playing with fire, flirting with death, courting disaster, stretching one's luck, going for broke <nonformal>, brinkmanship, tightrope walking, funambulism; adventurousness

4 **daredevil,** devil, **madcap,** madbrain, wild man, hotspur, hellcat, rantipole, harum-

scarum *and* fire-eater <both nonformal>; **adventurer,** adventuress, adventurist; brazen-face

VERBS **5** be rash, be reckless, carry too much sail, sail too near the wind, go out of one's depth, go too far, go to sea in a sieve, take a leap in the dark, buy a pig in a poke, count one's chickens before they are hatched, catch at straws, lean on a broken reed, put all one's eggs in one basket, live in a glass house; go out on a limb <nonformal>, leave oneself wide open <nonformal>, drop one's guard, stick one's neck out *and* ask for it <both nonformal>

6 court danger, mock *or* defy danger, go in harm's way, thumb one's nose at the consequences, **tempt fate** *or* **the gods** *or* **Providence,** tweak the devil's nose, bell the cat, play a desperate game, ride for a fall; play with fire, flirt with death, stretch one's luck, march up to the cannon's mouth, put one's head in a lion's mouth, beard the lion in his den, sit on a barrel of gunpowder, sleep on a volcano, play Russian roulette, playing with a loaded pistol *or* gun, working without a net; **risk all,** go for broke *and* shoot the works <both nonformal>

ADJS **7 rash, brash, incautious,** overbold, **imprudent, indiscreet,** injudicious, improvident; **unwary, unchary;** overcareless; overconfident, oversure, overweening, **impudent,** insolent, brazenfaced, brazen; hubristic; temerarious

8 reckless, devil-may-care; careless 340.11; **impetuous,** hotheaded; **hasty** 401.9, hurried, overeager, overzealous, overenthusiastic; **furious,** desperate, mad, wild, wanton, harum-scarum <nonformal>; precipitate, **precipitous, precipitant; headlong, breakneck;** slapdash, slap-bang; accident-prone

9 foolhardy, harebrained, madcap, **wild,** wild-ass <nonformal>, madbrain, mad-brained; **audacious;** forward, bold, **presumptuous; daring,** daredevil, fire-eating, death-defying; adventurous

ADVS **10 rashly, brashly, incautiously, imprudently, indiscreetly,** injudiciously, improvidently; **unwarily,** uncharily; overconfidently, overweeningly, **impudently,** insolently, **brazenly,** hubristically, temerariously

11 recklessly, happen what may; heedlessly, **carelessly** 340.18; **impetuously,** hotheadedly; **hastily,** hurriedly, overeagerly, overzealously, overenthusiastically; **furiously,** desperately, wildly, wantonly,

madly, like mad *or* crazy *and* like there was no tomorrow <all nonformal>; **precipitately,** precipitously, precipitantly; **headlong,** headfirst, headforemost, **head over heels,** heels over head, *à corps perdu* <Fr>; slapdash, slap-bang *or* slam-bang <both nonformal>; helter-skelter, ramble-scramble <nonformal>, hurry-scurry, holus-bolus

12 foolhardily, daringly, audaciously, presumptuously, harebrainedly

494 CAUTION

NOUNS **1 caution, cautiousness;** slowness to act *or* commit oneself *or* make one's move; **care, heed, solicitude; carefulness, heedfulness,** mindfulness, regardfulness, thoroughness; paying mind *or* attention; **guardedness;** uncommunicativeness 344; **gingerliness, tentativeness,** hesitation, hesitancy, unprecipitateness; slow and careful steps, deliberate stages, wait-and-see attitude *or* policy; **prudence,** prudentialness, **circumspection, discretion,** canniness <Scots>; **coolness, judiciousness** 919.7; calculation, **deliberateness,** deliberation, careful consideration, prior consultation; **safeness,** safety first, no room for error; **hedge, hedging,** hedging one's bets, cutting one's losses

2 wariness, chariness, cageyness *and* **leeriness** <both nonformal>; **suspicion,** suspiciousness; **distrust,** distrustfulness, mistrust, mistrustfulness

3 precaution, precautiousness; **forethought, foresight,** foresightedness, forehandedness, forethoughtfulness; **providence,** provision, forearming; precautions, steps, measures, steps and measures; **safeguard,** protection 1007, preventive measure, safety net, safety valve, sheet anchor; **insurance**

4 overcaution, overcautiousness, overcarefulness, overwariness

VERBS **5 be cautious, be careful;** think twice, give it a second thought; make haste slowly, take it easy *or* slow <nonformal>; put the right foot forward, take one step at a time, pick one's steps, go step by step, feel one's ground *or* way; pussyfoot, tiptoe, go *or* walk on tiptoe, walk on eggs *or* eggshells *or* thin ice; pull *or* draw in one's horns

6 take precautions, take steps *or* **measures,** take steps and measures; **prepare** *or* **provide for** *or* **against,** forearm; **guard against, make sure against,** make sure, "make assurance double sure"—

Shakespeare; **play safe** <nonformal>, keep on the safe side; leave no stone unturned, forget *or* leave out nothing, overlook no possibility, leave no room *or* margin for error, leave nothing to chance, consider every angle; **look before one leaps;** see how the land lies *or* the wind blows, see how the cat jumps <nonformal>; clear the decks, batten down the hatches, shorten sail, reef down, tie in *or* tuck in *or* take in a reef, get out a sheet-anchor, have an anchor to windward; **hedge,** provide a hedge, hedge one's bets, cut one's losses; take out insurance; keep something for a rainy day

7 **beware, take care, have a care,** take heed, take heed at one's peril; keep at a respectful distance, keep out of harm's way; mind, mind one's business; **be on one's guard,** be on the watch *or* lookout, be on the *qui vive;* **look out, watch out** <nonformal>; **look sharp,** keep one's eyes open, keep a weather eye out *or* open <nonformal>, keep one's eye peeled <nonformal>, **watch one's step** <nonformal>, look about one, look over one's shoulder; stop, look, and listen; not stick one's neck out <nonformal>, not go out on a limb <nonformal>, not expose oneself, not be too visible, **keep a low profile,** lie low, stay in the background, blend with the scenery; not blow one's cover <nonformal>; hold one's tongue 51.5

ADJS 8 **cautious, careful,** heedful, mindful, regardful, **thorough; prudent, circumspect,** slow to act *or* commit oneself *or* make one's move, noncommittal, uncommitted; canny <Scots>; sly, crafty, scheming; **discreet, politic, judicious** 919.19, Polonian, Macchiavelian; unadventurous, unenterprising, undaring; **gingerly; guarded,** on guard, on one's guard; uncommunicative 344.8; **tentative,** hesistant, unprecipitate, cool; **deliberate;** safe, on the safe side, leaving no stone unturned, forgetting *or* leaving out nothing, overlooking no possibility, leaving no room *or* margin for error

9 **wary, chary, cagey** <nonformal>, **leery** <nonformal>, **suspicious,** suspecting, **distrustful,** mistrustful, shy

10 **precautionary,** precautious, precautional; **preventive,** preemptive, prophylactic; **forethoughtful,** forethoughted, **foresighted,** foreseeing, forehanded; **provident,** provisional

11 **overcautious, overcareful,** overwary

ADVS 12 **cautiously, carefully,** heedfully,

mindfully, regardfully; **prudently, circumspectly,** cannily <Scots>, pawkily <Brit>, **discreetly,** judiciously; **gingerly,** guardedly, easy <nonformal>, with caution, with care

13 **warily, charily,** cagily <nonformal>; **askance,** askant, suspiciously, leerily <nonformal>, distrustfully

INTERJS 14 careful!, be careful!, **take care!,** have a care!, **look out!, watch out!, watch your step!,** watch it!, take heed!, steady!, look sharp!, easy!, take it easy!, easy does it!, go easy!

495 FASTIDIOUSNESS

NOUNS 1 **fastidiousness, particularity,** particularness; **scrupulousness,** scrupulosity; punctiliousness, punctilio, spit and polish; preciseness, precision; **meticulousness, conscientiousness,** criticalness; **taste** 496; **sensitivity, discrimination** 943, discriminatingness, discriminativeness; **selectiveness,** selectivity, pickiness <nonformal>, choosiness; **strictness** 339.3, **perfectionism,** precisianism, **purism; puritanism, priggishness, prudishness, prissiness** <nonformal>, propriety, strait-lacedness, censoriousness, judgmentalness

2 **finicalness,** finickiness, finickingness, finicality; **fussiness,** pernicketiness *or* persnicketiness <both nonformal>; squeamishness, queasiness

3 **nicety,** niceness, **delicacy,** delicateness, daintiness, exquisiteness, fineness, refinement, **subtlety**

4 overfastidiousness, **overscrupulousness, overparticularity, overconscientiousness,** overmeticulousness, overniceness, **overnicety; overcriticalness,** hypercriticism, hairsplitting; overrefinement, oversubtlety, supersubtlety; oversqueamishness, oversensitivity, hypersensitivity, morbid sensibility

5 **exclusiveness,** exclusivity, selectness, selectiveness, selectivity; **cliquishness,** clannishness; **snobbishness,** snobbery, snobbism

6 **perfectionist,** precisian, precisianist, stickler, nitpicker <nonformal>, captious critic 945.7

7 **fussbudget, fusspot** <nonformal>, fuss, fusser, **fuddy-duddy** <nonformal>, granny, old woman, old maid; Mrs Grundy

VERBS 8 **be hard to please,** want everything just so, **fuss,** fuss over; pick and choose; **turn up one's nose,** look down one's nose, disdain, scorn, spurn; not dirty *or* soil one's hands

ADJS **9 fastidious, particular, scrupulous, meticulous, conscientious,** exacting, precise, punctilious, spit-and-polish; **sensitive, discriminating** 943.7, discriminative; **selective,** picky <nonformal>, choosy, choicy <nonformal>; critical, "nothing if not critical"—Shakespeare; **strict** 339.12, perfectionistic, precisianistic, puristic; puritanic, puritanical, priggish, prudish, prissy, proper, strait-laced, censorious, judgmental

10 finical, finicky, finicking, finikin; **fussy,** fuss-budgety <nonformal>; **squeamish,** pernickety *and* persnickety <both nonformal>, difficult, hard to please

11 nice, dainty, delicate, *délicat* <Fr>, fine, refined, exquisite, **subtle**

12 overfastidious, queasy, **overparticular, overscrupulous, overconscientious,** overmeticulous, **overnice,** overprecise; **overcritical,** hypercritical, ultracritical, hairsplitting; overrefined, oversubtle, supersubtle; oversqueamish, oversensitive, hypersensitive, morbidly sensitive; **compulsive,** anal, anal-compulsive

13 exclusive, selective, **select,** elect, elite; **cliquish,** clannish; **snobbish,** snobby

ADVS **14 fastidiously, particularly, scrupulously, meticulously, conscientiously,** critically, punctiliously; discriminatingly, discriminatively, selectively; **finically,** finickily, finickingly; **fussily; squeamishly,** queasily; refinedly, subtly

496 TASTE, TASTEFULNESS

NOUNS **1 taste, good taste,** sound critical judgment, discernment *or* appreciation of excellence, preference for the best, *goût raffiné* <Fr>; **tastefulness,** quality, excellence, choiceness, **elegance,** grace, gracefulness, gracility, graciousness, graciosity; **refinement,** finesse, **polish, culture, cultivation,** civilizedness, refined *or* cultivated *or* civilized taste; niceness, nicety, delicacy, daintiness, **subtlety, sophistication; discrimination** 943, fastidiousness 495; acquired taste, "caviare to the general"—Shakespeare

2 "good sense delicately put in force"—Chévier, "the microscope of the judgment"—Rousseau, "a fine judgment in discerning art"—Horace, "the literary conscience of the soul"—Joseph Joubert, "the fundamental quality which sums up all other qualities"—Lautréamont, "the enemy of creativeness"—Picasso

3 decorousness, decorum, decency, properness, propriety, rightness, right thinking, **seemliness,** becomingness, fittingness, fitness, appropriateness, suitability, meetness, happiness, felicity; gentility, genteelness; civility, urbanity 504.1

4 restraint, restrainedness, **understatement,** unobtrusiveness, quietness, subduedness, quiet taste; simplicity 499.1

5 aesthetic *or* **artistic taste,** virtuosity, virtu, **expertise,** expertism, connoisseurship; dilettantism; fine art of living; epicurism, epicureanism; gastronomy, *friandise* <Fr>; aesthetics

6 aesthete, person of taste, lover of beauty

7 connoisseur, *connaisseur* <Fr>, *cognoscente* <Ital>; **judge,** good judge, **critic, expert,** authority, maven <nonformal>, arbiter, arbiter of taste, *arbiter elegantiarum* <L>, tastemaker, trend-setter; **epicure,** epicurean; **gourmet, gourmand,** *bon vivant* <Fr>, good *or* refined palate; virtuoso; dilettante, amateur; culture vulture <nonformal>; collector

ADJS **8 tasteful, in good taste,** in the best taste; excellent, of quality, of the best, of the first water; **aesthetic,** artistic, pleasing, well-chosen, choice, of choice; pure, chaste; classic *or* classical, Attic, restrained, understated, unobtrusive, quiet, subdued, simple, unaffected 499.7

9 elegant, graceful, gracile, gracious; **refined, polished, cultivated,** civilized, **cultured;** nice, fine, delicate, dainty, **subtle, sophisticated, discriminating** 943.7, fastidious 495.9

10 decorous, decent, proper, right, right-thinking, **seemly, becoming,** fitting, appropriate, suitable, meet, happy, felicitous; genteel; civil, urbane 504.14

ADVS **11 tastefully, with taste,** in good taste, in the best taste; aesthetically, artistically; elegantly, gracefully; decorously, genteelly, decently, properly, seemly, becomingly; quietly, unobtrusively; simply 499.10

497 VULGARITY

NOUNS **1 vulgarity,** vulgarness, vulgarism, commonness, meanness; **inelegance** *or* inelegancy, **indelicacy, impropriety, indecency, indecorum,** indecorousness, unseemliness, unbecomingness, unfittingness, inappropriateness, unsuitableness, unsuitability; ungentility; **untastefulness,** tastelessness, unaestheticness, unaestheticism, tackiness <nonformal>;

low *or* bad *or* poor taste, *mauvais goût* <Fr>; vulgar taste, bourgeois taste, Babbittry, philistinism; popular taste, pop culture *and* pop <both nonformal>; campiness, camp, high *or* low camp; kitsch

2 **coarseness, grossness,** *grossièreté* <Fr>, **rudeness, crudeness,** crudity, **crassness,** rawness, roughness, **earthiness;** ribaldness, ribaldry; raunchiness <nonformal>, **obscenity** 666.4; meretriciousness, **loudness** <nonformal>, **gaudiness** 501.3

3 **unrefinement, uncouthness, uncultivation,** uncultivatedness, unculturedness; uncivilizedness, wildness; impoliteness, incivility, ill breeding 505.1; **barbarism,** barbarousness, barbarity, philistinism, Gothicism; **savagery,** savagism; **brutality,** brutishness, bestiality, animality, **mindlessness;** Neanderthalism, troglodytism

4 **boorishness, churlishness,** carlishness, **loutishness,** lubberliness, lumpishness, cloddishness, clownishness, yokelism; ruffianism, rowdyism, hooliganism; parvenuism, arrivism, upstartness

5 **commonness, commonplaceness,** ordinariness, homeliness; **lowness, baseness, meanness; ignobility,** plebeianism

6 **vulgarian,** low *or* vulgar *or* ill-bred fellow, mucker <nonformal>, guttersnipe <nonformal>, *épicier* <Fr>; Babbitt, Philistine, bourgeois; *parvenu, arriviste, nouveau riche* <all Fr>, upstart; bounder <nonformal>, cad, **boor,** churl, clown, **lout,** yahoo, redneck <nonformal>, looby, peasant, groundling, yokel; rough, **ruffian,** roughneck <nonformal>, **rowdy,** hooligan; vulgarist, ribald

7 **barbarian, savage,** Goth, animal, brute; Neanderthal, troglodyte

8 **vulgarization,** coarsening; popularization; *haute vulgarisation* <Fr>; dumbing down <nonformal>

VERBS 9 vulgarize, coarsen; popularize; dumb down <nonformal>; **pander**

ADJS 10 **vulgar, inelegant, indelicate, indecorous, indecent, improper, unseemly,** unbeseeming, unbecoming, unfitting, inappropriate, unsuitable, **ungenteel,** undignified; **untasteful,** tasteless, in bad *or* poor taste, tacky *and* chintzy *and* Mickey Mouse <all nonformal>; **offensive,** offensive to gentle ears

11 **coarse, gross, rude, crude, crass,** raw, rough, **earthy;** ribald; raunchy <nonformal>, **obscene** 666.9; meretricious, **loud** <nonformal>, **gaudy** 501.20

12 **unrefined, unpolished, uncouth,** un-

kempt, uncombed, unlicked; **uncultivated, uncultured; uncivilized,** noncivilized; impolite, uncivil, ill-bred 505.6; **wild,** untamed; **barbarous,** barbaric, barbarian; outlandish, Gothic; primitive; **savage, brutal,** brutish, bestial, animal, **mindless;** Neanderthal, troglodytic; wild-and-woolly, rough-and-ready

13 **boorish, churlish,** carlish, **loutish,** redneck <nonformal>, lubberly, lumpish, cloddish, clownish, loobyish, yokelish; rowdy, **rowdyish, ruffianly,** roughneck <nonformal>, hooliganish, raffish, raised in a barn

14 **common, commonplace, ordinary;** plebeian; homely, homespun; **general, public, popular,** pop <nonformal>; vernacular; Babbittish, Philistine, bourgeois; campy, high-camp, low-camp, kitschy

15 **low, base, mean, ignoble,** vile, scurvy, sorry, scrubby, beggarly; low-minded, base-minded

ADVS 16 **vulgarly, uncouthly, inelegantly,** indelicately, indecorously, indecently, improperly, unseemly, untastefully, offensively; **coarsely, grossly, rudely, crudely,** crassly, roughly; ribaldly

498 ORNAMENTATION

NOUNS 1 **ornamentation, ornament; decoration,** decor; **adornment, embellishment,** embroidery, elaboration; nonfunctional addition *or* adjunct; garnish, garnishment, garniture; trimming, trim; flourish; emblazonment, emblazonry; illumination; **color,** color scheme, color pattern, color compatibility, color design, color arrangement; **arrangement,** flower arrangement, floral decoration, furniture arrangement; table setting *or* decoration; window dressing; **interior decoration** *or* decorating, room decoration, interior design; **redecoration, refurbishment** 396.4, redoing

2 **ornateness, elegance, fanciness,** fineness, **elaborateness; ostentation** 501; richness, luxuriousness, luxuriance; **floweriness,** floridness, floridity; dizenment <old>, **bedizenment; gaudiness, flashiness** 501.3; flamboyance *or* flamboyancy, chi-chi; **overelegance,** overelaborateness, overornamentation, busyness; clutteredness; baroqueness, baroque, rococo, arabesque, moresque, chinoiserie

3 **finery,** frippery, gaudery, gaiety, bravery, trumpery, folderol, trickery, chiffon, trappings, festoons, superfluity; **frills,** frills and furbelows, bells and whistles

and gimmickry *and* Mickey Mouse *and* glitz <all nonformal>, **frillery,** frilling, frilliness; foofaraw <nonformal>, fuss <nonformal>, froufrou; gingerbread; **tinsel,** clinquant, pinchbeck, paste; gilt, gilding

4 trinket, gewgaw, **knickknack** *or* nicknack, knack <old>, **gimcrack,** kickshaw, whim-wham, **bauble,** fribble, bibelot, toy, gaud; bric-a-brac

5 jewelry, bijouterie, ice <nonformal>; costume jewelry, glass, paste, junk jewelry <nonformal>

6 jewel, bijou, **gem,** stone, precious stone; rhinestone; pin, brooch, stickpin, breastpin, scatter pin, chatelaine; cuff-link, tie clasp *or* clip, tie bar, tiepin *or* scarfpin, tie tack *or* tie tac; **ring,** band, wedding band, engagement ring, mood ring, signet ring, school *or* class ring, circle, earring, nose ring; bracelet, wristlet, wristband, armlet, anklet; chain, necklace, torque; locket; beads, chaplet, wampum; bangle; charm; fob; crown, coronet, diadem, tiara

7 motif, ornamental motif, **figure, detail,** form, touch, repeated figure; **pattern, theme,** design, ornamental theme, ornamental *or* decorative composition; foreground detail, background detail; **background,** setting, foil, **style,** ornamental *or* decorative style, national style, **period style**

VERBS 8 ornament, decorate, adorn, dress, trim, garnish, array, **deck,** bedeck, dizen <old>, bedizen; prettify; **beautify; redecorate,** refurbish, redo; gimmick *or* glitz *or* sex up <nonformal>; **embellish, furbish,** embroider, enrich, grace, set off *or* out, paint, color, blazon, emblazon, paint in glowing colors; **dress up; spruce up** *and* gussy up *and* doll up *and* fix up <all nonformal>, **primp up,** prink up, prank up, trick up *or* out, deck out, bedight <old>, fig out; primp, prink, prank, preen; smarten, smarten up, dandify, titivate

9 figure, filigree; **spangle, bespangle;** bead; tinsel; jewel, bejewel, gem, diamond; ribbon, beribbon; flounce; flower, garland, wreathe; feather, plume; flag; illuminate; paint 35.13; engrave

ADJS 10 ornamental, decorative, adorning, embellishing

11 ornamented, adorned, decorated, embellished, bedecked, decked out, tricked out, garnished, trimmed, dizened <old>, bedizened; figured; flowered; festooned, befrilled, wreathed; spangled, be-

spangled, spangly; jeweled, bejeweled; beaded; studded; plumed, feathered; beribboned

12 ornate, elegant, fancy, fine, chichi, pretty-pretty; picturesque; **elaborate,** overornamented, overornate, overelegant, etc, labored, high-wrought; **ostentatious** 501.18; **rich, luxurious,** luxuriant; **flowery,** florid; flamboyant, fussy, frilly, frilled, flouncy, gingerbread *or* gingerbready; **overelegant,** overelaborate, overlabored, overworked, overwrought, overornamented, busy; cluttered; **baroque,** rococo, arabesque, moresque; gimmicked- *or* glitzed- *or* sexed-up <nonformal>

499 PLAINNESS
<unaffectedness>

NOUNS 1 plainness, simplicity 797, **simpleness, ordinariness, commonness, commonplaceness,** homeliness, prosaicness, prosiness, matter-of-factness; **purity,** chasteness, classic *or* classical purity, Attic simplicity

2 naturalness, inartificiality; **unaffectedness,** unassumingness, **unpretentiousness;** directness, straightforwardness; innocence, naïveté

3 unadornment, unembellishment, unadornedness, unornamentation; **no frills,** no nonsense, back-to-basics; **uncomplexity,** uncomplication, uncomplicatedness, **unsophistication,** unadulteration; bareness, baldness, nakedness, nudity, undress, beauty unadorned

4 inornateness, unelaborateness, unfanciness, unfussiness; **austerity,** severity, starkness, Spartan simplicity

VERBS 5 simplify 797.4; chasten, restrain, purify; put in words of one syllable, spell out

ADJS 6 simple 797.6, **plain, ordinary, nondescript, common, commonplace, prosaic,** prosy, **matter-of-fact, homely, homespun,** everyday, workday, workaday, household, garden, common- *or* garden-variety; pure, **pure and simple,** chaste, classic *or* classical, Attic

7 natural, native; **inartificial,** unartificial; **unaffected, unpretentious,** unpretending, unassuming, unfeigning, direct, straightforward, honest, candid; innocent, naive

8 unadorned, undecorated, unornamented, unembellished, ungarnished, unfurbished, unvarnished, untrimmed; olde *and* olde-worlde <both nonformal>; back-to-basics, no-frills, no-nonsense, vanilla or plain-vanilla and white-bread or white-bready <all nonformal>; back-to-nature; **uncomplex,** uncomplicated, **unsophisticated,** unadulterated; **undressed,** undecked, unarrayed; bare, bald, blank, naked, nude

9 **inornate,** unornate, **unelaborate,** unfancy, unfussy; austere, monkish, cloistral, severe, stark, Spartan

ADVS **10 plainly, simply,** ordinarily, commonly, commonplacely, prosaically, matter-of-factly

11 **unaffectedly, naturally,** unpretentiously, unassumingly, directly, straightforwardly

500 AFFECTATION

NOUNS 1 **affectation, affectedness; pretension, pretense, airs,** putting on airs, put-on <nonformal>; **show, false show,** mere show; front, false front <nonformal>, **facade,** mere facade, **image,** public image; feigned belief, **hypocrisy** 354.6; phoniness <nonformal>, sham 354.3; artificiality, unnaturalness, insincerity; prunes and prisms, airs and graces; stylishness, mannerism

2 **mannerism,** minauderie <Fr>, **trick of behavior,** trick, **quirk,** habit, peculiarity, peculiar trait, idiosyncrasy, trademark

3 **posing, pose, posturing,** attitudinizing, attitudinarianism; peacockery, peacockishness

4 **foppery, foppishness, dandyism,** coxcombry, puppyism, conceit

5 **overniceness,** overpreciseness, **overrefinement, elegance,** exquisiteness, preciousness, preciosity; goody-goodyism and goody-goodness <both nonformal>; purism, formalism, formality, pedantry, precisionism, precisianism; euphuism; euphemism

6 **prudery, prudishness, prissiness, priggishness, primness, smugness, stuffiness** <nonformal>, old-maidishness, **straitlacedness,** stiff-neckedness, hidebound, narrowness, censoriousness, sanctimony, sanctimoniousness, **puritanism,** puritanicalness; **false modesty,** overmodesty, demureness, mauvaise honte <Fr>

7 **phony** and **fake** and **fraud** <all nonformal> 354.13; affecter; mannerist; **pretender,** actor, playactor <nonformal>, performer; paper tiger, hollow man, straw man, man of straw, empty suit <nonformal>

8 **poser, poseur,** striker of poses, **posturer,** posturist, posture maker, attitudinarian, attitudinizer

9 **dandy, fop,** coxcomb, macaroni, gallant, dude and swell and sport <all nonformal>, ponce and toff <both Brit nonformal>, exquisite, blood, fine gentleman, puppy, jackanapes, jack-a-dandy, fribble, clotheshorse, fashion plate; beau, Beau Brummel, spark, blade, ladies' man, lady-killer <nonformal>, masher, cocksman <nonformal>; man-about-town, boulevardier

10 **fine lady,** grande dame, précieuse <both Fr>; belle, toast

11 **prude, prig,** priss, puritan, bluenose, goody-goody <nonformal>, wowser <Brit nonformal>, old maid; Victorian, mid-Victorian

VERBS 12 **affect, assume, put on,** assume or put on airs, wear, **pretend, simulate, counterfeit, sham, fake** <nonformal>, **feign,** make out like <nonformal>, make a show of, play, playact <nonformal>, act or play a part, play a scene, do a bit <nonformal>, put up a front <nonformal>, dramatize, histrionize, lay it on thick <nonformal>, overact, ham and ham it up and chew up the scenery and emote <all nonformal>, tug at the heartstrings

13 **pose, posture, attitudinize,** peacock, strike a pose, strike an attitude, pose for effect

14 **mince,** mince it, prink <Brit nonformal>; **simper,** smirk, bridle

ADJS **15 affected, pretentious,** la-di-da, posy <Brit nonformal>; **mannered,** maniéré <Fr>; **artificial, unnatural,** insincere; theatrical, stagy, histrionic; overdone, overacted, hammed up <nonformal>

16 **assumed, put-on, pretended,** simulated, **phony** and **fake** and **faked** <all nonformal>, feigned, counterfeited; spurious, sham; hypocritical

17 **foppish, dandified,** dandy, coxcombical, conceited

18 <affectedly nice> **overnice,** overprecise, precious, précieuse <Fr>, exquisite, **overrefined, elegant,** mincing, simpering, namby-pamby; **goody-goody** and goody good-good <both nonformal>; puristic, formalistic, pedantic, precisionistic, precisian, precisianistic, euphuistic, euphemistic

19 **prudish, priggish, prim, prissy, smug, stuffy** <nonformal>, old-maidish, **overmodest,** demure, **straitlaced,** stiff-necked, hide-bound, narrow, censorious, po-faced

<Brit>, sanctimonious, **puritanical**, Victorian, mid-Victorian

ADVS **20 affectedly, pretentiously;** elegantly, mincingly; for effect, for show

21 prudishly, priggishly, primly, smugly, stuffily <nonformal>, straitlacedly, stiffneckedly, puritanically

501 OSTENTATION

NOUNS **1 ostentation,** ostentatiousness, ostent; **pretentiousness, pretension, pretense;** loftiness, lofty affectations, **triumphalism**

2 pretensions, vain pretensions; **airs,** lofty airs, airs and graces, vaporing, highfalutin or highfaluting ways <nonformal>, side, swank <nonformal>

3 showiness, flashiness, flamboyance, panache, dash, jazziness <nonformal>, jauntiness, sportiness <nonformal>, gaiety, glitter, glare, dazzle, dazzlingness; extravaganza; **gaudiness,** gaudery, glitz and gimmickry and razzmatazz and razzledazzle <all nonformal>, **tawdriness,** meretriciousness; gorgeousness, colorfulness; **garishness,** loudness <nonformal>, **blatancy,** flagrancy, shamelessness, brazenness, luridness, extravagance, sensationalism, obtrusiveness, vulgarness, crudeness, extravagation

4 display, show, demonstration, manifestation, **exhibition, parade,** *étalage* <Fr>; **pageantry,** pageant, **spectacle;** vaunt, fanfaronade, blazon, flourish, flaunt, flaunting; daring, brilliancy, éclat, bravura, flair; dash and splash and splurge <all nonformal>; figure; **exhibitionism,** showing-off; theatrics, histrionics, dramatics, staginess; false front, **sham** 354.3

5 grandeur, grandness, grandiosity, **magnificence,** gorgeousness, **splendor,** splendidness, splendiferousness, resplendence, brilliance, glory; nobility, proudness, **state, stateliness, majesty;** impressiveness, imposingness; **sumptuousness, elegance, elaborateness, lavishness, luxuriousness;** ritziness or poshness or plushness or swankness or swankiness <all nonformal>; **luxury,** barbaric or Babylonian splendor

6 pomp, circumstance, pride, **state,** solemnity, formality; **pomp and circumstance,** "pride, pomp, and circumstance"—Shakespeare; heraldry, "trump and solemn heraldry"—Coleridge

7 pompousness, pomposity, pontification, pontificality, **stuffiness** <nonformal>, self-importance, inflation; grandiloquence, turgidity, orotundity

8 swagger, strut, swank <nonformal>, bounce, brave show; swaggering, strutting; swash, **swashbucklery,** swashbuckling, swashbucklering; peacockishness, peacockery

9 stuffed shirt <nonformal>, blimp <nonformal>, Colonel Blimp; bloated aristocrat

10 strutter, swaggerer, swanker <Brit>, swash, swasher, **swashbuckler,** peacock, miles gloriosus

11 show-off <nonformal>, **exhibitionist,** flaunter; **grandstander** or grandstand player or hot dog or **hotshot** or showboat <all nonformal>

VERBS **12 put** or **thrust oneself forward,** come forward, step to the front or fore, step into the limelight, take center stage, attract attention, make oneself conspicuous

13 cut a dash, make a show, put on a show, make one's mark, cut a swath, **cut** or **make a figure;** make a splash or a splurge <nonformal>; **splurge** and splash <both nonformal>; shine, glitter, glare, dazzle

14 give oneself airs, put on airs, put on, put on side, put on the dog <nonformal>, put up a front <nonformal>, ritz it <nonformal>, look big, **swank** <nonformal>, swell, swell it, act the grand seigneur; pontificate, play the pontiff

15 strut, swagger, swank <Brit>, prance, stalk, peacock, swash, swashbuckle

16 show off <nonformal>, **grandstand** and hotdog and showboat <all nonformal>, play to the gallery or galleries <nonformal>, please the crowd; exhibit or parade one's wares <nonformal>, strut one's stuff <nonformal>, go through one's paces, show what one has

17 flaunt, vaunt, **parade, display, demonstrate,** manifest, make a great show of, **exhibit,** air, put forward, put forth, hold up, flash and sport <both nonformal>; advertise; **flourish,** brandish, wave; dangle, dangle before the eyes; emblazon, blazon forth; trumpet, trumpet forth

ADJS **18 ostentatious, pretentious,** posy <Brit nonformal>; **ambitious,** vaunting, **lofty, highfalutin** and highfaluting <both nonformal>, **high-flown,** high-flying; **high-toned,** tony <both nonformal>, **fancy,** classy <nonformal>, flossy <nonformal>

19 showy, flaunting, flashy, snazzy, flashing,

glittering, **jazzy** *and* **glitzy** *and* gimmicky *and* splashy *and* splurgy <all nonformal>; exhibitionistic, showoffy <nonformal>, bravura; **gay,** jaunty, rakish, **dashing;** gallant, brave, braw <Scots>, daring; **sporty** *or* dressy <both nonformal>; **frilly, flouncy,** frothy, chichi

20 **gaudy, tawdry;** gorgeous, colorful; **garish, loud** <nonformal>, **blatant, flagrant,** shameless, **brazen,** brazenfaced, lurid, extravagant, sensational, **spectacular,** glaring, flaring, flaunting, screaming <nonformal>, obtrusive, vulgar, crude; meretricious, low-rent *and* low-ride *and* tacky <all nonformal>

21 **grandiose, grand, magnificent, splendid,** splendiferous, splendacious <nonformal>, **glorious,** superb, fine, superfine, fancy, superfancy, swell <nonformal>; **imposing, impressive,** larger-than-life, awful, awe-inspiring, awesome; **noble, proud, stately, majestic,** princely; **sumptuous, elegant, elaborate, luxurious,** extravagant, deluxe; executive *and* plush *and* posh *and* ritzy *and* swank *and* swanky <all nonformal>, Corinthian; palatial, Babylonian; barbaric

22 **pompous, stuffy** <nonformal>, **self-important,** impressed with oneself, pontific, pontifical; **inflated, swollen,** bloated, tumid, turgid, flatulent, gassy <nonformal>, stilted; grandiloquent, **bombastic** 545.9; solemn 111.3, formal

23 **strutting, swaggering;** swashing, **swashbuckling,** swashbucklering; peacockish, peacocky; too big for one's britches

24 **theatrical, theatric, stagy, dramatic, histrionic;** spectacular

ADVS 25 **ostentatiously, pretentiously, loftily;** with flourish of trumpet, with beat of drum, with flying colors

26 **showily, flauntingly,** flashily, with a flair, glitteringly; gaily, jauntily, **dashingly;** gallantly, bravely, daringly

27 **gaudily, tawdrily;** gorgeously, colorfully; **garishly, blatantly, flagrantly,** shamelessly, **brazenly,** brazenfacedly, luridly, sensationally, **spectacularly,** glaringly, flaringly, obtrusively

28 **grandiosely, grandly, magnificently, splendidly,** splendiferously, splendaciously <nonformal>, gloriously, superbly; nobly, proudly, majestically; imposingly, impressively; **sumptuously, elegantly,** elaborately, luxuriously, **extravagantly;** palatially

29 **pompously, pontifically,** stuffily <nonformal>, **self-importantly;** stiltedly; **bombastically** 545.12

502 BOASTING

NOUNS 1 **boasting, bragging,** vaunting; **boastfulness, braggadocio, braggartism; boast, brag,** vaunt; side, bombast, bravado, vauntery, fanfaronade, blowing-off *or* blowing *or* tooting one's own horn <all nonformal>, gasconade, gasconism, rodomontade; bluster, swagger 503.1; vanity, conceit 140.4; jactation, jactitation; heroics

2 <nonformal terms> **big talk,** fine talk, fancy talk, tall talk, highfalutin *or* highfaluting, **hot air,** gas, bunk, bunkum, **bullshit;** tall story, fish story

3 **self-approbation,** self-praise, self-laudation, self-gratulation, self-applause, self-boosting, self-puffery, self-vaunting, self-advertising, self-advertisement, self-adulation, self-glorification, self-dramatizing, self-dramatization, self-promoting, self-promotion; **vainglory,** vaingloriousness

4 **crowing,** exultation, elation, triumph, jubilation; **gloating**

5 **braggart, boaster,** brag, braggadocio, hector, fanfaron, Gascon, gasconader, miles gloriosus; **blowhard** *and* blower *and* big mouth *and* bullshit artist *and* hot-air artist *and* gasbag *and* windbag *and* big bag of wind *and* windjammer *and* windy <all nonformal>; blusterer 503.2; Texan, Fourth-of-July orator; Braggadocchio <Spenser>, Captain Bobadil <Ben Jonson>, Thraso <Terence>, Parolles <Shakespeare>

VERBS 6 **boast, brag,** make a boast of, vaunt, flourish, gasconade, vapor, puff, draw the longbow, advertise oneself, **blow one's own trumpet, toot one's own horn,** sing one's own praises, exaggerate one's own merits; bluster, swagger 503.3; speak for Buncombe

7 <nonformal terms> **blow,** blow off, mouth off, **blow hard, talk big,** sound off, blow off *and* toot *or* blow one's own horn, **bullshit,** shoot the shit, spread oneself, lay it on thick, brag oneself up

8 **flatter oneself,** conceit oneself, **congratulate oneself,** hug oneself, shake hands with oneself, form a mutual admiration society with oneself, **pat oneself on the back,** take merit to oneself; think one's shit doesn't stink <nonformal>

9 **exult,** triumph, glory, delight, joy, jubilate; **crow** *or* crow over, crow like a rooster *or* cock; **gloat,** gloat over

ADJS 10 **boastful, boasting, braggart, bragging,** thrasonical, thrasonic, big-mouthed

<nonformal>, vaunting, vaporing, gas-conading, Gascon, fanfaronading, fan-faron; vain, conceited 140.11; **vainglorious**

11 **self-approving**, self-approbatory, self-praising, self-gratulating, self-boosting, self-puffing, self-adulating, self-adulatory, self-glorifying, self-glorying, self-glorious, self-lauding, self-laudatory, self-congratulatory, self-applauding, self-praising, self-flattering, self-vaunting, self-advertising, self-dramatizing, self-promoting

12 **inflated, swollen, windy** *and* gassy <both nonformal>, **bombastic**, high-swelling, **high-flown, highfalutin** *and* highfaluting <both nonformal>, **pretentious**, extravagant, big, tall <nonformal>

13 **crowing**, exultant, exulting, elated, elate, jubilant, **triumphant, flushed**, cock-a-hoop, in high feather; **gloating**

ADVS 14 **boastfully**, boastingly, braggingly, vauntingly, vaingloriously; **self-approvingly**, self-praisingly, etc

15 **exultantly**, exultingly, elatedly, jubilantly, triumphantly, triumphally, in triumph; **gloatingly**

503 BLUSTER

NOUNS 1 **bluster**, blustering, hectoring, bullying, **swagger**, swashbucklery, side; **bravado**, rant, rodomontade, fanfaronade; sputter, splutter; fuss, bustle, fluster, flurry; bluff, bluster and bluff; intimidation 127.6; **boastfulness** 502.1

2 **blusterer, swaggerer**, swasher, swashbuckler, fanfaron, bravo, **bully**, bullyboy, bucko, roisterer, cock of the walk, vaporer, blatherskite <nonformal>; ranter, raver, hectorer, hector, Herod; slanger <Brit>; bluff, bluffer; **braggart** 502.5

VERBS 3 **bluster**, hector; **swagger**, swashbuckle; bully; bounce, vapor, roister, rollick, gasconade, kick up a dust <nonformal>; sputter, splutter; rant, rage, rave, rave on, storm, "out-herod Herod"—Shakespeare; slang <Brit>; bluff, bluster and bluff, put up a bluff <nonformal>; intimidate; shoot off one's mouth, sound off, **brag** 502.6

ADJS 4 **blustering**, blustery, blusterous, hectoring, **bullying, swaggering**, swashing, swashbuckling, boisterous, roisterous, roistering, rollicking; ranting, raging, raving, storming; tumultuous; noisy, "full of sound and fury"—Shakespeare

504 COURTESY

NOUNS 1 **courtesy**, courteousness, common courtesy, **politeness, civility**, *politesse* <Fr>, amenity, agreeableness, urbanity, comity, affability; **graciousness**, gracefulness; complaisance; **thoughtfulness, considerateness** 143.3, **tactfulness**, tact, consideration, **solicitousness, solicitude; respect**, respectfulness, deference; civilization, quality of life

2 **gallantry**, gallantness, **chivalry**, chivalrousness, knightliness; courtliness, courtly behavior *or* politeness; *noblesse oblige* <Fr>

3 **mannerliness, manners, good manners**, excellent *or* exquisite manners, good *or* polite deportment, good *or* polite behavior, *bienséance* <Fr>; *savoir-faire, savoir-vivre* <both Fr>; correctness, correctitude, **etiquette** 580.3

4 **good breeding, breeding; refinement, finish, polish, culture, cultivation; gentility**, gentleness, genteelness, elegance; gentlemanliness, gentlemanlikeness, ladylikeness

5 **suavity, suaveness, smoothness, smugness**, blandness; **unctuousness**, oiliness, oleaginousness, smarm *or* smarminess <nonformal>; **glibness**, slickness <nonformal>, fulsomeness; sweet talk, fair words, soft words *or* tongue, sweet *or* honeyed words *or* tongue, incense; soft soap *and* butter <both nonformal>

6 **courtesy, civility**, amenity, urbanity, attention, polite act, act of courtesy *or* politeness, graceful gesture; old-fashioned courtesy *or* civility, courtliness

7 **amenities, courtesies, civilities**, gentilities, graces, elegancies; dignities; formalities, ceremonies, rites, rituals, observances

8 **regards, compliments, respects,** *égards, devoirs* <both Fr>; **best wishes**, one's best, good wishes, best regards, kind *or* kindest regards, love, best love; greetings 585.3; remembrances, kind remembrances; compliments of the season

9 **gallant, cavalier**, chevalier, **knight**, "a verray parfit gentil knight"—Chaucer

10 "the very pink of courtesy"—Shakespeare, "the very pineapple of politeness"—R B Sheridan, "the mirror of all courtesy"—Shakespeare

VERBS 11 **mind one's manners**, mind one's P's and Q's <nonformal>; keep a civil tongue in one's head; mend one's manners; observe etiquette, observe *or* follow protocol

12 **extend courtesy, do the honors, pay one's respects, make one's compliments,** present oneself, pay attentions to, do service, wait on *or* upon

13 **give one's regards** *or* **compliments** *or* love, give one's best regards, give one's best, send one's regards *or* compliments *or* love; wish one joy, wish one luck, bid Godspeed

ADJS 14 **courteous, polite, civil, urbane, gracious,** graceful, agreeable, affable, fair; complaisant; obliging, accommodating; **thoughtful, considerate,** tactful, solicitous; respectful, deferential, attentive

15 **gallant, chivalrous,** chivalric, knightly; **courtly; formal,** ceremonious; old-fashioned, old-world

16 **mannerly, well-mannered,** good-mannered, **well-behaved,** well- *or* fair-spoken; **correct,** correct in one's manners *or* behavior; housebroken <nonformal>

17 **well-bred,** highbred, **well-brought-up; cultivated, cultured, polished, refined, genteel,** gentle; gentlemanly, gentleman-like, ladylike

18 **suave, smooth, smug,** bland, **glib, unctuous,** oily, oleaginous, smarmy <nonformal>, soapy *and* buttery <both nonformal>, fulsome, ingratiating, disarming; suave-spoken, fine-spoken, fair-spoken, soft-spoken, smooth-spoken, smooth-tongued, oily-tongued, honey-tongued, honey-mouthed

ADVS 19 **courteously, politely, civilly,** urbanely, mannerly; **gallantly, chivalrously,** courtly, knightly; **graciously,** gracefully, with a good grace; complaisantly, complacently; out of consideration *or* courtesy; obligingly, accommodatingly; respectfully, attentively, deferentially

505 DISCOURTESY

NOUNS 1 **discourtesy,** discourteousness; **impoliteness,** unpoliteness; **rudeness, incivility,** inurbanity, **ungraciousness, ungallantness,** uncourtesy, uncourtliness, ungentlemanliness, **unmannerliness,** mannerlessness, bad *or* ill manners, **ill breeding,** conduct unbecoming a gentleman, caddishness; inconsiderateness, inconsideration, unsolicitousness, unsolicitude, tactlessness, **insensitivity; grossness, crassness,** gross *or* crass behavior, **boorishness, vulgarity, coarseness,**

crudeness, offensiveness, loutishness, nastiness

2 disrespect, disrespectfulness 156.1; **insolence** 142

3 **gruffness, brusqueness,** *brusquerie* <Fr>, **curtness,** shortness, sharpness, abruptness, bluntness, brashness; **harshness,** roughness, severity; truculence, aggressiveness; **surliness,** crustiness, bearishness, beastliness, churlishness

ADJS 4 **discourteous,** uncourteous; **impolite,** unpolite; **rude, uncivil, ungracious, ungallant,** uncourtly, inaffable, uncomplaisant, unaccommodating; disrespectful; **insolent**

5 **unmannerly,** unmannered, mannerless, **ill-mannered, ill-behaved,** ill-conditioned

6 **ill-bred, ungenteel,** ungentle, caddish; **ungentlemanly,** ungentlemanlike; **unladylike,** unfeminine; **vulgar, boorish, unrefined** 497.12, **inconsiderate, unsolicitous, tactless, insensitive; gross,** offensive, crass, **coarse, crude,** loutish, nasty

7 **gruff, brusque, curt,** short, sharp, snippy <nonformal>, abrupt, **blunt,** bluff, brash, cavalier; **harsh,** rough, severe; truculent, aggressive; **surly,** crusty, bearish, beastly, churlish

ADVS 8 **discourteously, impolitely, rudely,** uncivilly, ungraciously, ungallantly, ungenteelly, caddishly; inconsiderately, unsolicitously, tactlessly, insensitively

9 **gruffly, brusquely, curtly,** shortly, sharply, snippily <nonformal>, abruptly, bluntly, bluffly, brashly, cavalierly; harshly, crustily, bearishly, churlishly, **boorishly,** nastily

506 RETALIATION

NOUNS 1 **retaliation, reciprocation,** exchange, interchange, give-and-take; **retort, reply,** return, comeback <nonformal>; counter, counterblow, counterstroke, counterblast, recoil, boomerang, backlash

2 **reprisal, requital, retribution; recompense, compensation** 338, **reward,** comeuppance <nonformal>, desert, deserts, **just deserts,** what is merited, what is due *or* condign, what's coming to one *and* a dose of one's own medicine <both nonformal>; quittance, return of evil for evil; **revenge** 507; **punishment** 604

3 **tit for tat, measure for measure,** like for like, quid pro quo, something in return, blow for blow, a Roland for an Oliver, a game two can play, **an eye for an eye,** a

tooth for a tooth, "eye for eye, tooth for tooth, hand for hand, foot for foot"— Bible, law of retaliation *or* equivalent retaliation, *lex talionis* <L>, talion

VERBS **4 retaliate, retort,** counter, **strike back,** hit back at <nonformal>, give in return; **reciprocate,** give in exchange, give and take; **get** *or* **come back at** <nonformal>, turn the tables upon

5 requite, quit, make requital *or* reprisal *or* retribution, get satisfaction, recompense, compensate, make restitution, indemnify, reward, redress, make amends, **repay,** pay, **pay back,** pay off; **give one his comeuppance** <nonformal>, give one his desserts *or* just desserts, serve one right, give one what is coming to him <nonformal>

6 give in kind, cap, match, give as good as one gets *or* as was sent; repay in kind, **pay one in one's own coin** *or* **currency, give one a dose of one's own medicine** <nonformal>; return the like, return the compliment; return like for like, **return evil for evil;** return blow for blow, **give one tit for tat,** give a quid pro quo, give as good as one gets, give measure for measure, give *or* get an eye for an eye and a tooth for a tooth, follow *or* observe the *lex talionis*

7 get even with <nonformal>, even the score, **settle** *or* **settle up with, settle** *or* **square accounts** *and* settle the score *and* fix <all nonformal>, pay off old scores, pay back in full measure, be *or* make quits; fix one's wagon <nonformal>, **take revenge** 507.4; **punish** 604.10,11

ADJS **8 retaliatory,** retaliative; **retributive,** retributory; reparative, compensatory, restitutive, recompensing, recompensive, reciprocal; punitive

ADVS **9 in retaliation, in exchange,** in reciprocation; **in return,** in reply; **in requital, in reprisal,** in retribution, in reparation, in amends; **in revenge,** *en revanche* <Fr>

PHRS **10** what goes around comes around, one's chickens come home to roost; the shoe is on the other foot

507 REVENGE

NOUNS **1 revenge, vengeance, avengement,** sweet revenge, getting even, evening of the score; **wrath;** revanche, revanchism; **retaliation, reprisal** 506.2; vendetta, feud, blood feud; the wrath of God

2 revengefulness, vengefulness, vindictiveness, rancor, grudgefulness, irreconcil-

ableness, unappeasableness, implacableness, implacability

3 avenger, vindicator; revanchist; Nemesis, the Furies, the Erinyes, the Eumenides

VERBS **4 revenge, avenge, take** *or* **exact revenge,** have one's revenge, wreak one's vengeance; **retaliate, even the score, get even with** 506.4–7; launch a vendetta

5 harbor revenge, breathe vengeance; have accounts to settle, have a crow to pick *or* pluck *or* pull with; nurse one's revenge, brood over, dwell on *or* upon, keep the wound open, wave the bloody shirt

6 reap *or* **suffer** *or* **incur vengeance** *or* revenge; sow the wind and reap the whirlwind; live by the sword and die by the sword

ADJS **7 revengeful, vengeful,** avenging; **vindictive,** vindicatory; revanchist; **punitive,** punitory; **wrathful,** rancorous, grudgeful, irreconcilable, unappeasable, implacable, unwilling to forgive and forget, unwilling to let bygones be bygones; **retaliatory** 506.8

508 RIDICULE

NOUNS **1 ridicule, derision, mockery, raillery,** rallying, chaffing; panning *and* razzing *and* roasting *and* ragging <all nonformal>, **scoffing, jeering, sneering,** snickering, sniggering, smirking, grinning, leering, fleering, snorting, levity, flippancy, smartness, smart-aleckiness *and* joshing <both nonformal>, fooling, japery, twitting, taunting, booing, hooting, catcalling, hissing; **banter** 490

2 gibe, scoff, jeer, fleer, flout, mock, barracking <Brit>, **taunt, twit,** quip, jest, jape, put-on *and* leg-pull <both nonformal>, foolery; **insult** 156.2; scurrility, caustic remark; **cut,** cutting remark, verbal thrust; gibing retort, rude reproach, short answer, back answer, comeback <nonformal>, parting shot, Parthian shot

3 boo, booing, **hoot, catcall;** Bronx cheer *and* **raspberry** *and* razz <all nonformal>; **hiss, hissing,** the bird <nonformal>

4 scornful laugh *or* smile, snicker, snigger, **smirk,** sardonic grin, leer, fleer, **sneer,** snort

5 sarcasm, irony, cynicism, satire, satiric wit *or* humor, invective, innuendo; causticity 144.8

6 burlesque, lampoon, squib, **parody, satire, farce,** mockery, imitation, wicked imitation *or* pastiche, takeoff <nonformal>, **travesty, caricature**

7 **laughingstock,** jestingstock, gazingstock, derision, mockery, **figure of fun,** byword, byword of reproach, jest, joke, **butt,** target, stock, **goat** <nonformal>, toy, game, **fair game,** victim, dupe, fool, everybody's fool, monkey, mug <Brit nonformal>

VERBS 8 **ridicule, deride,** ride <nonformal>, make a laughingstock *or* a mockery of; roast <nonformal>, **insult** 156.5; **make fun** *or* **game of, poke fun at,** make merry with, put one on *and* pull one's leg <both nonformal>; **laugh at,** laugh in one's face, grin at, smile at, snicker *or* snigger at; **laugh to scorn,** hold in derision, laugh out of court, hoot down; point at, point the finger of scorn; pillory

9 **scoff, jeer,** gibe, barrack <Brit>, **mock, revile, rail at, rally,** chaff, **twit, taunt,** jape, flout, scout, have a fling at, cast in one's teeth; cut at; jab, jab at, dig at, take a dig at; pooh, **pooh-pooh;** sneer, **sneer at,** fleer, curl one's lip

10 **boo, hiss, hoot,** catcall, give the raspberry *or* Bronx cheer <nonformal>, give the bird <nonformal>, whistle at

11 **burlesque, lampoon, satirize, parody, caricature,** travesty, hit *or* take off on

ADJS 12 **ridiculing, derisive,** derisory; **mocking,** railing, rallying, chaffing; panning *and* razzing *and* roasting *and* ragging <all nonformal>, **scoffing,** jeering, sneering, snickering, sniggering, smirky, smirking, grinning, leering, fleering, snorting, flippant, smart, smart-alecky *and* smart-ass *and* wise-ass <all nonformal>; joshing *and* jiving <both nonformal>, fooling, japing, twitting, taunting, booing, hooting, catcalling, hissing, bantering, kidding, teasing, quizzical

13 **satiric, satirical; sarcastic, ironic, ironical, sardonic, cynical,** Rabelaisian, dry; caustic

14 **burlesque, farcical, broad,** slapstick; parodic, caricatural, macaronic, doggerel

ADVS 15 **derisively, mockingly, scoffingly,** jeeringly, sneeringly, "with scoffs and scorns and contumelious taunts"— Shakespeare

509 APPROVAL

NOUNS 1 **approval, approbation;** "Our polite recognition of another's resemblance to ourselves"—Ambrose Bierce, "the daughter of ignorance"—Franklin; **sanction,** acceptance, countenance, **favor; admiration, esteem, respect** 155; endorse-

ment, vote, favorable vote, yea vote, yea, voice, adherence, blessing, seal of approval, nod, stamp of approval, **OK** 332.4

2 **applause,** plaudit, éclat, **acclaim, acclamation; popularity;** clap, handclap, **clapping,** handclapping, clapping of hands; **cheer** 116.2; burst of applause, peal *or* thunder of applause; **round of applause, hand, big hand; ovation,** standing ovation

3 **commendation,** good word, acknowledgment, recognition, appreciation; boost *and* buildup <both nonformal>; **puff,** promotion; **blurb** *and* **plug** *and* promo *and* hype <all nonformal>; honorable mention

4 **recommendation,** recommend <Brit nonformal>, letter of recommendation; **advocacy,** advocating, advocation, patronage; **reference, credential,** letter of reference, voucher, **testimonial;** character reference, character, certificate of character, good character; letter of introduction

5 **praise,** bepraisement; **laudation,** laud; **glorification,** glory, exaltation, magnification, **honor; eulogy,** *éloge* and *hommage* <both Fr>, eulogium; **encomium,** accolade, kudos, panegyric, paean; **tribute,** homage, meed of praise; congratulation 149.1; flattery 511; overpraise, excessive praise, idolizing, idolatry, deification, apotheosis, adulation, lionizing, hero worship

6 **compliment,** polite commendation, complimentary *or* flattering remark, stroke <nonformal>; **bouquet** *and* posy <both nonformal>, trade-last *or* TL <both old nonformal>

7 **praiseworthiness, laudability,** laudableness, commendableness, estimableness, meritoriousness, exemplariness, admirability

8 commender, eulogist, eulogizer; **praiser,** lauder, extoller, encomiast, panegyrist, **booster** <nonformal>, puffer, promoter; plugger *and* tout *and* touter <all nonformal>; **applauder,** *claqueur* <Fr>; claque; rooter *and* fan *and* buff <all nonformal>, adherent; appreciator; **flatterer** 138.3, 511.4

VERBS 9 **approve, approve of,** think well of, take kindly to; **sanction, accept; admire, esteem, respect** 155.4; endorse, bless, sign off on <nonformal>, OK 332.12; **countenance,** keep in countenance; hold with, uphold; **favor,** be in favor of, view with favor, take kindly to

10 **applaud, acclaim, hail; clap,** clap one's

hands, give a hand *or* big hand, have *or* hear a hand *or* big hand for, hear it for <nonformal>; **cheer** 116.6; root for <nonformal>, cheer on; encore; cheer *or* applaud to the very echo

11 **commend, speak well** *or* **highly of,** speak in high terms of, speak warmly of, have *or* say a good word for; boost *and* give a boost to <both nonformal>, puff, promote, cry up; plug *and* tout *and* hype; pour *or* spread *or* lay it on thick <all nonformal>; **recommend, advocate,** put in a word *or* good word for, support, back, lend one's name *or* support *or* backing to, make a pitch for <nonformal>

12 **praise,** bepraise, talk one up <nonformal>; **laud,** belaud; **eulogize,** panegyrize, pay tribute, salute, hand it to one <nonformal>; **extol, glorify,** magnify, exalt, bless; cry up, blow up, puff, puff up; boast of, brag about <nonformal>, make much of; celebrate, emblazon, sound *or* resound the praises of, ring one's praises, sing the praises of, trumpet; praise to the skies, *porter aux nues* <Fr>; flatter 511.5; overpraise, praise to excess, idolize, deify, apotheosize, adulate, lionize, heroworship; put on a pedestal

13 **espouse,** join *or* associate oneself with, take up, take for one's own; **campaign for, crusade for,** put on a drive for, take up the cudgels for, push for <nonformal>; carry the banner of, march under the banner of; beat the drum for, thump the tub for; lavish oneself on, fight the good fight for; devote *or* dedicate oneself to, spend *or* give *or* sacrifice oneself for

14 **compliment, pay a compliment,** make one a compliment, give a bouquet *or* posy <nonformal>, say something nice about; hand it to *and* have to hand it to <both nonformal>, pat on the back, take off one's hat to, doff one's cap to, congratulate 149.2

15 **meet with approval,** find favor with, **pass muster,** recommend itself, do credit to; redound to the honor of; ring with the praises of

ADJS 16 **approbatory, approbative, commendatory, complimentary, laudatory,** acclamatory, eulogistic, panegyric, panegyrical, encomiastic, **appreciative, appreciatory; admiring, regardful, respectful** 155.8; flattering 511.8

17 **approving, favorable,** favoring, in favor of, **pro,** well-disposed, well-inclined, supporting, backing, **advocating;** promoting, promotional; touting *and* puffing *and* hyping <all nonformal>

18 **uncritical,** uncriticizing, **uncensorious,** unreproachful; overpraising, overappreciative, unmeasured *or* excessive in one's praise, idolatrous, adulatory, lionizing, hero-worshiping, fulsome; knee-jerk <nonformal>

19 **approved,** favored, backed, advocated, supported; favorite; **accepted,** received, admitted; **recommended,** bearing the seal of approval, highly touted <nonformal>, **admired** 155.11, **applauded,** wellthought-of, in good odor, **acclaimed,** cried up; **popular**

20 **praiseworthy,** worthy, **commendable,** estimable, **laudable,** admirable, meritorious, creditable; exemplary, model, unexceptionable; deserving, well-deserving; beyond all praise, *sans peur et sans reproche* <Fr>; **good** 998.12,13

PREPS 21 **in favor of, for, pro,** all for

INTERJS 22 **bravo!,** bravissimo!, **well done!,** ¡ole! <Sp>, *bene!* <Ital>, hear, hear!, aha!; hurrah!; **good!,** fine!, excellent!, whizzo! <Brit>, great!, beautiful!, swell!, good for you!, good enough!, not bad!, now you're talking!; way to go, attaboy!, attababy!, attagirl!, attagal!, good boy!, good girl!; that's the idea!, that's the ticket!; encore!, bis!, take a bow!, three cheers!, one cheer more!, **congratulations!** 149.4

23 **hail!,** all hail!, *ave!* <L>, *vive!* <Fr>, *viva!, evviva!* <both Ital>, live live!, long life to!, glory be to!, honor be to!

510 DISAPPROVAL

NOUNS 1 **disapproval, disapprobation,** disfavor, disesteem, disrespect 156; dim view, poor *or* low opinion, low estimation, adverse judgment; **displeasure,** distaste, **dissatisfaction,** discontent, discontentment, discontentedness, disgruntlement, indignation, **unhappiness;** disillusion, disillusionment, disenchantment, disappointment; disagreement, **opposition** 451, opposure; rejection, thumbs-down, exclusion, ostracism, blackballing, blackball, ban; **complaint, protest,** objection, **dissent** 333

2 **deprecation,** discommendation, dispraise, denigration, disvaluation; **ridicule** 508; depreciation, disparagement 512; **contempt** 157

3 **censure, reprehension,** stricture, reprobation, **blame, denunciation,** denouncement, decrying, decrial, bashing *and* trashing <both nonformal>, impeachment, arraignment, indictment, **con-**

demnation, damnation, fulmination, anathema; castigation, flaying, skinning alive <nonformal>, fustigation, excoriation; pillorying

4 **criticism,** adverse criticism, harsh *or* hostile criticism, flak <nonformal>, bad notices, bad press, animadversion, imputation, reflection, **aspersion,** stricture, obloquy; **knock** *and* **swipe** *and* **slam** *and* **rap** *and* hit <all nonformal>, home thrust; minor *or* petty criticism, niggle, cavil, quibble, exception, nit <nonformal>; **censoriousness,** reproachfulness, priggishness; **faultfinding,** taking exception, carping, caviling, pettifogging, quibbling, captiousness, niggling, nitpicking, pestering, nagging; hypercriticism, hypercriticalness, overcriticalness, hairsplitting, trichoschistism

5 **reproof,** reproval, reprobation, a flea in one's ear; **rebuke, reprimand, reproach,** reprehension, **scolding, chiding,** rating, **upbraiding,** objurgation; **admonishment, admonition; correction,** castigation, chastisement, spanking, rap on the knuckles; lecture, lesson, sermon; **disrecommendation,** low rating, adverse report, wolf ticket

6 <nonformal terms> piece *or* bit of one's mind, **talking-to,** speaking-to, roasting, raking-down, **raking-over,** raking over the coals, dressing, dressing-down, setdown; **bawling-out,** cussing-out, **calling-down,** jacking-up, going-over, chewing-out, chewing, reaming-out, reaming, ass-chewing, ass-reaming, what-for, ticking-off

7 **berating,** rating, tongue-lashing; **revilement, vilification,** blackening, **execration, abuse, vituperation,** invective, contumely, hard *or* cutting *or* bitter words; **tirade, diatribe,** jeremiad, screed, philippic; **attack, assault,** onslaught, assailing; **abusiveness; acrimony**

8 **reproving look,** dirty *or* nasty look <nonformal>, black look, frown, scowl

9 **faultfinder,** *frondeur* <Fr>, momus, basher *and* tracher *and* boo-bird <all nonformal>; **critic** 945.7, captious critic, criticizer, **nitpicker** <nonformal>, smellfungus, belittler, censor, censurer, carper, caviler, quibbler, pettifogger; **scold,** common scold; kvetch, **complainer** 108.3

VERBS 10 **disapprove, disapprove of,** not approve, raise an objection, go *or* side against, go contra; **disfavor, view with disfavor, raise one's eyebrows, frown at** *or* **on,** look black upon, look askance at,

make a wry face at, grimace at, **turn up one's nose at,** shrug one's shoulders at; **take a dim view of** <nonformal>, not think much of, think ill of, think little of, not take kindly to, not hold with, hold no brief for *and* not sign off on <both nonformal>; not hear of, not go for *and* not get all choked up over *and* be turned off by <all nonformal>; not want *or* have any part of, wash one's hands of, dissociate oneself from; **object to,** take exception to; **oppose** 451.3, set oneself against, set one's face *or* heart against; **reject,** categorically reject, disallow, not hear of; **turn thumbs down on** *and* thumb down <both nonformal>, vote down, veto, frown down, exclude, ostracize, blackball, ban; say no to, shake one's head at; **dissent from, protest, object** 333.4,5; turn over in one's grave

11 **discountenance,** not countenance, **not tolerate,** not brook, not condone, not suffer, not abide, not endure, not bear with, not put up with, **not stand for** <nonformal>

12 **deprecate,** discommend, dispraise, disvalue, not be able to say much for, denigrate, **fault,** faultfind, find fault with, put down <nonformal>, pick at *or* on, pick holes in, pick to pieces; **ridicule** 508.8; **depreciate, disparage** 512.8; **hold in contempt,** disdain, **despise** 157.3

13 **censure,** reprehend; **blame,** lay *or* cast blame upon; **bash** *and* trash *and* rubbish <all nonformal>; **reproach,** impugn; **condemn,** damn, take out after; damn with faint praise; fulminate against, anathematize, anathemize, put on the Index; **denounce,** denunciate, **accuse** 599.7,9, **decry,** cry down, impeach, arraign, indict, call to account, exclaim *or* declaim *or* inveigh against, peg away at, cry out against, cry out on *or* upon, cry shame upon, raise one's voice against, raise a hue and cry against, shake up <old>; reprobate, hold up to reprobation; animadvert on *or* upon, reflect upon, cast reflection upon, cast a reproach *or* slur upon, complain against; throw a stone at, cast *or* throw the first stone

14 **criticize; pan** *and* **knock** *and* **slam** *and* **hit** *and* rap *and* take a rap *or* swipe at <all nonformal>, snipe at, strike out at, tie into *and* tee off on *and* rip into *and* open up on *and* plow into <all nonformal>

15 **find fault,** take exception, fault-find, pick holes, cut up, pick *or* pull apart, pick *or* pull *or* tear to pieces; tear down, carp, cavil, quibble, **nitpick,** pick nits, pettifog, catch at straws

16 **nag,** niggle, **carp at, fuss at, fret at,** yap *or* **pick at** <nonformal>, peck at, nibble at, **pester, henpeck, pick on** *and* pick at <all nonformal>, bug *and* hassle <nonformal>

17 **reprove, rebuke, reprimand,** reprehend, put a flea in one's ear, **scold, chide,** rate, **admonish, upbraid,** objurgate, have words with, take a hard line with; **lecture,** read a lesson *or* lecture to; **correct,** rap on the knuckles, **chastise,** spank, turn over one's knees; **take to task,** call to account, bring to book, call on the carpet, read the riot act, give one a tongue-lashing, tonguelash; take down, set down, set straight, straighten out

18 <nonformal terms> **call down** *or* **dress down, speak** *or* **talk to, tell off,** tell a thing or two, pin one's ears back, **give a piece** *or* **bit of one's mind, rake** *or* **haul over the coals,** rake up one side and down the other, give it to, let one have it, let one have it with both barrels, trim, come down on *or* down hard on, jump on *or* all over *or* down one's throat; give one a hard time *or* what for; **bawl out,** give a bawling out, chew, **chew out,** chew ass, ream, ream out, ream ass, cuss out, jack up, sit on *or* upon, lambaste, give a going-over, tell where to get off; give the deuce *or* devil, give hell, give hail Columbia

19 **berate,** rate, betongue, jaw <nonformal>, clapper-claw <nonformal>, **tongue-lash, rail at,** rag, thunder *or* fulminate against, rave against, yell at, bark *or* yelp at; **revile, vilify,** blacken, **execrate, abuse,** vituperate, load with reproaches

20 <criticize or reprove severely> **attack, assail; castigate, flay,** skin alive <nonformal>, lash, slash, **excoriate,** fustigate, scarify, scathe, **roast** <nonformal>, scorch, blister, trounce

ADJS 21 **disapproving, disapprobatory,** unapproving, turned-off, **displeased, dissatisfied,** less than pleased, discontented, disgruntled, indignant, **unhappy;** disillusioned, disenchanted, disappointed; **unfavorable,** low, poor, **opposed** 451.8, **opposing, con,** against, agin <nonformal>, dead set against, death on, down on, **dissenting** 333.6; **uncomplimentary;** unappreciative

22 **condemnatory, censorious,** censorial, damnatory, **denunciatory, reproachful,** blameful, reprobative, objurgatory, po-faced <Brit>, priggish, judgmental; deprecative, deprecatory; **derisive, ridiculing, scoffing** 508.12; **depreciative, disparaging** 512.13; **contemptuous** 157.8;

invective, inveighing; reviling, vilifying, blackening, execrating, execrative, execratory, abusive, vituperative

23 **critical, faultfinding,** carping, picky *and* nitpicky <both nonformal>, caviling, quibbling, pettifogging, captious, cynical; nagging, niggling; hypercritical, ultracritical, overcritical, hairsplitting, trichoschistic

24 **unpraiseworthy, illaudable; uncommendable,** discommendable; **objectionable,** exceptionable, unacceptable, not to be thought of, beyond the pale

25 **blameworthy,** blamable, to blame, at fault, much at fault; **reprehensible,** censurable, reproachable, reprovable, open to criticism *or* reproach; **culpable,** chargeable, impeachable, accusable, indictable, arraignable, imputable

ADVS 26 **disapprovingly, askance,** askant, **unfavorably;** censoriously, critically, reproachfully, rebukingly; captiously

INTERJS 27 **God forbid!,** Heaven forbid!, Heaven forfend!, forbid it Heaven!; by no means!, not for the world!, not on your life!, over my dead body!, not if I know it!, nothing doing!, no way! *and* no way José! <both nonformal>, perish the thought!, I'll be hanged *or* damned if!, **shame!,** for shame!, tuttut!

511 FLATTERY

NOUNS 1 **flattery, adulation; praise** 509.5; **blandishment,** palaver, **cajolery,** cajolement, wheedling; **blarney** *and* bunkum *and* **soft soap** *and* soap *or* butter salve <all nonformal>, oil, grease, eyewash <nonformal>; strokes *and* stroking *and* ego massage <all nonformal>, sweet talk, fair *or* sweet *or* honeyed words, soft *or* honeyed phrases, incense, pretty lies, sweet nothings; trade-last <old nonformal>, **compliment** 509.6; ass-kissing <nonformal>, **fawning, sycophancy** 138.2

2 **unction,** "that flattering unction"— Shakespeare; **unctuousness,** oiliness; slobber, gush, smarm *and* smarminess <both nonformal>; flattering tongue; insincerity 354.5

3 **overpraise,** overprizing, excessive praise, overcommendation, overlaudation, overestimation; idolatry 509.5

4 **flatterer,** *flatteur* <Fr>, adulator, courtier; **cajoler, wheedler; backslapper,** backscratcher; blarneyer *and* soft-soaper <both nonformal>; ass-kisser <nonformal>, brown-noser, **sycophant** 138.3

VERBS **5 flatter,** adulate, conceit; **cajole, wheedle, blandish,** palaver; slaver *or* slobber over, beslobber, beslubber; oil the tongue, lay the flattering unction to one's soul, make fair weather; **praise, compliment** 509.14, praise to the skies; scratch one's back, kiss ass <nonformal>, fawn upon 138.9

6 <nonformal terms> **soft-soap,** butter, honey, **butter up,** soften up; stroke <nonformal>, massage the ego <nonformal>; **blarney,** jolly, pull one's leg; lay it on <nonformal>, pour *or* spread *or* lay it on thick *or* with a trowel <nonformal>, overdo it, soap, oil; string along, kid along; play up to, get around

7 overpraise, overprize, overcommend, overlaud; overesteem, overestimate, overdo it, protest too much; idolize 509.12, put on a pedestal

ADJS **8 flattering,** adulatory; **complimentary** 509.16; **blandishing, cajoling, wheedling,** blarneying *and* soft-soaping <both nonformal>; fair-spoken, fine-spoken, smooth-spoken, smooth-tongued, **mealy-mouthed,** honey-mouthed, honey-tongued, honeyed, oily-tongued; fulsome, slimy, slobbery, gushing, protesting too much, smarmy <nonformal>, insinuating, oily, buttery <nonformal>, soapy <nonformal>, **unctuous,** smooth, bland; insincere; courtly, courtierly; **fawning, sycophantic, obsequious**

512 DISPARAGEMENT

NOUNS **1 disparagement, faultfinding, depreciation, detraction,** deprecation, derogation, bad-mouthing *and* running down *and* knocking *and* putting down <all nonformal>, **belittling;** sour grapes; slighting, minimizing, faint praise, lukewarm support, discrediting, decrying, decrial; **disapproval** 510; **contempt** 157; indignity, disgrace, comedown <nonformal>

2 defamation, malicious defamation, defamation of character, injury of *or* to one's reputation; **vilification,** revilement, defilement, blackening, denigration; **smear,** character assassination, *ad hominem* <L> *or* personal attack, name-calling, smear word, smear campaign; **muckraking, mudslinging**

3 slander, scandal, libel, traducement; calumny, calumniation; backbiting, cattiness *and* bitchiness <both nonformal>

4 aspersion, slur, **remark, reflection,** imputation, **insinuation,** suggestion, sly suggestion, innuendo, whispering campaign; disparaging *or* uncomplimentary remark; personality, personal

5 lampoon, send-up <nonformal>, pasquinade, pasquin, pasquil, squib, lampoonery, **satire,** malicious parody, **burlesque** 508.6; poison pen, hatchet job

6 disparager, depreciator, decrier, detractor, basher *and* trasher *and* boo-bird <all nonformal>, belittler, debunker, deflater, slighter, derogator, **knocker** <nonformal>, caustic critic, hatchet man; **slanderer,** libeler, defamer, backbiter; calumniator, traducer; **muckraker, mudslinger,** social critic; **cynic,** railer, Thersites, "A man who knows the price of everything, and the value of nothing"— Oscar Wilde

7 lampooner, lampoonist, **satirist,** pasquinader; poison-pen writer

VERBS **8 disparage, depreciate, belittle,** slight, minimize, make little of, degrade, debase, **run** *or* **knock down** <nonformal>, **put down** <nonformal>; **discredit,** bring into discredit, reflect discredit upon, disgrace; detract from, derogate from, cut down to size <nonformal>; **decry,** cry down; speak ill of; speak slightingly of, not speak well of; disapprove of 510.10; hold in contempt 157.3; submit to indignity *or* disgrace, bring down, bring low

9 defame, malign, bad-mouth *and* poormouth <both nonformal>; **asperse, cast aspersions on,** cast reflections on, injure one's reputation, damage one's good name, give one a black eye <nonformal>; **slur,** cast a slur on, do a number *or* a job on <nonformal>, tear down

10 vilify, revile, defile, sully, soil, smear, smirch, besmirch, bespatter, tarnish, **blacken,** denigrate, blacken one's good name, give a black eye <nonformal>; **call names,** give a bad name, give a dog a bad name, stigmatize 661.9; **muckrake, throw mud at,** mudsling, heap dirt upon, drag through the mud; engage in personalities

11 slander, libel; calumniate, traduce; stab in the back, backbite, speak ill of behind one's back

12 lampoon, satirize, pasquinade; parody, send up <nonformal>; dip the pen in gall, **burlesque** 508.11

ADJS **13 disparaging, derogatory,** derogative, **depreciatory,** depreciative, deprecatory, slighting, belittling, minimizing, detractory, pejorative, back-biting, catty *and* bitchy <both nonformal>, contumelious, contemptuous, derisive, derisory, ridiculing 508.12; **snide,** insinuating; censorious; **defamatory,** vilifying, **slanderous, scandalous, libelous;** calumnious, calumniatory; **abusive,** scurrilous, scurrile <old>

513 CURSE

NOUNS **1 curse, malediction,** malison, damnation, denunciation, commination, imprecation, execration; blasphemy; anathema, fulmination, thundering, excommunication; ban, proscription; hex, evil eye, *malocchio* <Ital>, whammy <nonformal>

2 vilification, abuse, revilement, **vituperation, invective,** opprobrium, obloquy, contumely, calumny, scurrility, blackguardism; **disparagement** 512

3 cursing, cussing <nonformal>, **swearing, profanity,** profane swearing, foul *or* profane *or* obscene *or* blue *or* bad *or* strong *or* unparliamentary *or* indelicate language, vulgar language, vile language, colorful language, unrepeatable expressions, dysphemism, billingsgate, ribaldry, evil speaking, **dirty language** *or* **talk** <nonformal>, **obscenity,** scatology, coprology, **filthy language, filth**

4 oath, profane oath, curse; cuss *or* cuss word *and* dirty word *and* four-letter word *and* **swearword** <all nonformal>, naughty word, no-no <nonformal>, foul invective, **expletive, epithet,** dirty name <nonformal>, dysphemism, obscenity

VERBS **5 curse,** accurse, **damn,** darn, **confound,** blast, anathematize, fulminate *or* thunder against, execrate, imprecate; excommunicate; call down evil upon, call down curses on the head of; put a curse on; curse up hill and down dale; curse with bell, book, and candle; blaspheme; hex, give the evil eye, throw a whammy <nonformal>

6 curse, swear, cuss <nonformal>, curse and swear, execrate, rap out *or* rip out an oath, take the Lord's name in vain; swear like a trooper, cuss like a sailor, make the air blue, swear till one is blue in the face; **talk dirty** <nonformal>, scatologize, coprologize, dysphemize, use strong language

7 vilify, abuse, revile, vituperate, blackguard, call names, epithet, epithetize; **swear at,** damn, cuss out <nonformal>

ADJS **8 cursing, maledictory,** imprecatory, **damnatory,** denunciatory, epithetic, epithetical; **abusive,** vituperative, contumelious; calumnious, calumniatory;

execratory, comminatory, fulminatory, excommunicative, excommunicatory; **scurrilous,** scurrile <old>; blasphemous, **profane, foul, foulmouthed, vile,** thersitical, **dirty** <nonformal>, **obscene,** dysphemistic, scatologic, scatological, coprological, toilet, sewer, cloacal; ribald, Rabelaisian, raw, risqué

9 cursed, accursed, bloody <Brit nonformal>, **damned, damn, damnable,** goddamned, goddamn, **execrable**

10 <euphemisms> **darned,** danged, **confounded,** deuced, blessed, **blasted,** dashed, blamed, goshdarn, doggone *or* doggoned, goldarned, goldanged, dadburned; blankety-blank; ruddy <Brit>

INTERJS **11** damn!, damn it!, God damn it! *or* goddam it!, confound it!, hang it!, devil take!, a plague upon!, a pox upon!, *parbleu!* <Fr>, *verdammt!* <Ger>

12 <euphemistic oaths> darn!, dern!, dang!, dash!, drat!, blast!, doggone!, goldarn!, goldang!, golding!, gosh-darn!, cripes!, crikey! <Brit>, drat!, golly!, gosh!, heck!

514 THREAT

NOUNS **1 threat, menace,** threateningness, threatfulness, promise of harm, knife poised at one's throat, arrow aimed at one's heart, sword of Damocles; imminent threat, powder keg, timebomb, imminence 839; **foreboding; warning** 399; saber-rattling, muscle-flexing, woofing <nonformal>, bulldozing, scare tactics, **intimidation** 127.6, arm-twisting <nonformal>; denunciation, commination; veiled *or* implied threat, idle *or* hollow *or* empty threat

VERBS **2 threaten, menace,** bludgeon, bulldoze, put the heat *or* screws *or* squeeze on <nonformal>, lean on <nonformal>; hold a pistol to one's head, terrorize, **intimidate,** twist one's arm *and* arm-twist <both nonformal>; utter threats against, shake *or* double *or* clench one's fist at; hold over one's head; denounce, comminate; **lower,** spell *or* mean trouble, look threatening, loom, loom up; **be imminent** 839.2; **forebode** 133.11; **warn** 399.5

ADJS **3 threatening, menacing,** threatful, minatory, minacious; **lowering; imminent** 839.3; **ominous,** foreboding 133.17; denunciatory, comminatory, abusive; fear-inspiring, **intimidating,** bludgeoning, muscle-flexing, saber-rattling, bulldozing, browbeating, bullying, hectoring, blustering, terrorizing, terroristic

ADVS **4** under duress or threat, under the gun, at gunpoint or knifepoint

515 FASTING

NOUNS **1 fasting,** abstinence from food; starvation; punishment of Tantalus; hunger strike

2 fast, lack of food; spare or meager diet, Lenten diet, Lenten fare, "Lenten entertainment"—Shakespeare; short commons or rations, starvation diet, water diet, bread and water, bare subsistence; xerophagy, xerophagia; Barmecide or Barmecidal feast

3 fast day, jour maigre <Fr>; **Lent,** Quadragesima; Yom Kippur, Tishah B'Av or Ninth of Av; Ramadan

VERBS **4 fast,** not eat, go hungry, dine with Duke Humphrey; eat sparingly

ADJS **5 fasting,** uneating, unfed; **Lenten,** quadragesimal

516 SOBRIETY

NOUNS **1 sobriety, soberness;** unintoxicatedness, uninebriatedness, undrunkenness; temperance 668

VERBS **2 sober up,** sober off; sleep it off; bring one down, take off a high <nonformal>; dry out

ADJS **3 sober,** in one's sober senses, in one's right mind, in possession of one's faculties; clearheaded; **unintoxicated, uninebriated,** uninebriate, uninebrious, undrunk, undrunken, untipsy, unbefuddled; cold or stone sober <nonformal>, **sober as a judge;** able to walk the chalk, able to walk the chalk mark or line <nonformal>; dry, straight, temperate 668.9

4 unintoxicating, nonintoxicating, uninebriating; **nonalcoholic, soft**

517 SIGNS, INDICATORS

NOUNS **1 sign,** telltale sign, sure sign, tip-off <nonformal>, **index,** indicant, **indicator,** signal <old>, measure; tip of the iceberg; **symptom;** note, keynote, **mark, earmark,** hallmark, **badge,** device, banner, stamp, signature, sigil, seal, trait, **characteristic,** character, peculiarity, idiosyncrasy, **property,** differentia; image, picture, **representation,** representative; **insignia** 647

2 symbol, emblem, icon, token, cipher <old>, type; **allegory; symbolism, symbology,** iconology, charactery; conventional symbol; symbolic system; **symbolization; ideogram,** logogram, pictogram;

logo <nonformal>, logotype; **totem,** totem pole; love knot

3 indication, signification, identification, differentiation, denotation, **designation,** denomination; characterization, highlighting; **specification,** naming, pointing, pointing out or to, fingering <nonformal>, picking out, selection; symptomaticness, indicativeness; **meaning** 518; hint, suggestion 551.4; **expression, manifestation** 348; show, showing, disclosure 351

4 pointer, index, **lead; direction, guide;** fist, index finger or mark; **arrow;** hand, hour hand, minute hand, **needle,** compass needle, lubber line; **signpost,** guidepost, finger post, direction post; milepost; blaze; guideboard, signboard 352.7

5 mark, marking; watermark; **scratch,** scratching, engraving, graving, **score,** scotch, cut, hack, gash, blaze; bar code; nick, notch 289; **scar,** cicatrix, scarification, cicatrization; **brand, earmark; stigma; stain, discoloration** 1003.2; blemish, macula, **spot,** blotch, splotch, flick, patch, splash; mottle, dapple; **dot,** point; polka dot; tittle, jot; **speck, speckle,** fleck; tick, **freckle,** lentigo, mole; **birthmark,** strawberry mark, port-wine stain, vascular nevus, nevus, hemangioma; beauty mark or spot; caste mark; **check,** checkmark; prick, puncture; tattoo, tattoo mark

6 line, score, **stroke,** slash, virgule, diagonal, **dash, stripe, strip, streak, striation,** striping, streaking, bar, band; squiggle; hairline; dotted line; lineation, delineation; sublineation, **underline,** underlining, underscore, underscoring; hatching, cross-hatching, hachure

7 print, imprint, impress, impression; dint, dent, indent, indentation, indention, concavity; sitzmark; **stamp,** seal, sigil, signet; colophon; **fingerprint,** finger mark, thumbprint, thumbmark, dactylogram, dactylograph; **footprint,** footmark, footstep, step, vestige; hoofprint, hoofmark; pad, paw print, pawmark, pug, pugmark; claw mark; fossil print or footprint, ichnite, ichnolite; **bump,** boss, stud, pimple, lump, excrescence, convexity, embossment

8 track, trail, path, course, piste <Fr>, **line, wake;** vapor trail, contrail, condensation trail; **spoor,** signs, traces, scent

9 clue, cue, key, tip-off <nonformal>, telltale, smoking gun <nonformal>, straw in the wind; **trace, vestige, spoor,** scent, whiff; **lead** and hot lead <both nonfor-

mal>; catchword, cue word, key word; **evidence** 956; **hint, intimation, suggestion** 551.4

10 **marker, mark;** bookmark; **landmark,** seamark; bench mark; **milestone,** milepost; cairn, menhir, catstone; **lighthouse,** lightship, tower, Texas tower; platform, watchtower, pharos; **buoy,** aid to navigation, bell, gong, lighted buoy, nun, can, spar buoy, wreck buoy, junction buoy, special-purpose buoy; **monument** 549.12

11 **identification,** identification mark; **badge,** identification badge, identification tag, dog tag <military>, personal identification number *or* PIN number *or* PIN, **identity card** *or* **ID card** *or* **ID; card,** business card, calling card, visiting card, *carte de visite* <Fr>, press card; letter of introduction; signature, initials, monogram, calligram; credentials; serial number; countersign, countermark; theme, theme tune *or* song; **criminal identification,** forensic tool, DNA print, genetic fingerprint, voiceprint; fingerprint 517.7

12 **password, watchword, countersign;** token; open sesame; secret grip; shibboleth

13 **label, tag;** ticket, docket <Brit>, tally; **stamp, sticker; seal,** sigil, signet; cachet; stub, counterfoil; **token,** check; **brand, brand name, trade name,** trademark name; **trademark,** registered trademark; government mark, government stamp, broad arrow <Brit>; **hallmark,** countermark; price tag; plate, bookplate, book stamp, colophon, *ex libris* <L>, logotype *or* logo; International Standard Book Number *or* ISBN; masthead, imprint, title page; letterhead, billhead; running head *or* title

14 **gesture, gesticulation; motion,** movement; carriage, bearing, posture, poise, pose, stance, way of holding oneself; body language, kinesics; beck, beckon; shrug; charade, dumb show, **pantomime;** sign language, gesture language; dactylology, deaf-and-dumb alphabet; hand signal; chironomy

15 **signal, sign; high sign** *and* the wink *and* the nod <all nonformal>; wink, flick of the eyelash, glance, leer; look in one's eyes, tone of one's voice; nod; nudge, elbow in the ribs, poke, kick, touch; **alarm** 400; **beacon,** signal beacon, marker beacon, radio beacon; signal light, signal lamp *or* lantern; blinker; signal fire, beacon fire, watch fire, balefire; **flare,** parachute flare; rocket, signal rocket, Roman candle; signal gun, signal shot;

signal siren *or* whistle, signal bell, bell, signal gong, **police whistle,** watchman's rattle; fog signal *or* alarm, fog bell, **foghorn,** diaphone, fog whistle, fog bell; **traffic signal,** traffic light, red *or* stop light, amber *or* caution light, green *or* go light; heliograph; signal flag; **semaphore,** semaphore telegraph, semaphore flag; **wigwag,** wigwag flag; international alphabet flag, international numeral pennant; red flag; white flag; yellow flag, quarantine flag; blue peter; pilot flag *or* jack; signal post, signal mast, signal tower; telecommunications

16 call, summons; whistle; moose call, bird call, duck call, hog call, goose call, crow call, hawk call, dog whistle; **bugle call,** trumpet call; **reveille, taps,** last post <Brit>; alarm, alarum; **battle cry,** war cry, war whoop, rebel yell, rallying cry; Angelus, Angelus bell

VERBS 17 **signify, betoken,** stand for, identify, differentiate, note <old>, speak of, talk, **indicate,** be indicative of, be an indication of, be significant of, connote, denominate, argue, bespeak, be symptomatic *or* diagnostic of, symptomize, **characterize, mark,** highlight, be the mark *or* sign of, give token, **denote, mean** 518.8; testify, give evidence; **show, express, display, manifest** 348.5, **hint,** suggest 551.10, reveal, **disclose** 351.4; entail, involve 771.4

18 **designate, specify;** denominate, name, denote; stigmatize; **symbolize, stand for,** typify, be taken as, symbol, emblematize, figure <old>; **point to,** refer to, advert to, allude to, make an allusion to; pick out, select; **point out,** point at, put *or* lay one's finger on, finger <nonformal>

19 **mark,** make a mark, put a mark on; pencil, chalk; mark out, demarcate, delimit, define; **mark off, check, check off,** tick, tick off, chalk up; punctuate, point; **dot, spot,** blotch, splotch, dash, **speck, speckle,** fleck, freckle; mottle, dapple; blemish; **brand,** stigmatize; **stain, discolor** 1003.6; stamp, seal, punch, impress, imprint, **print, engrave; score, scratch,** gash, scotch, scar, scarify, cicatrize; nick, notch 289.4; **blaze,** blaze a trail; **line, seam,** trace, **stripe, streak, striate;** hatch; **underline, underscore;** prick, puncture, tattoo, riddle, pepper

20 **label, tag,** tab, ticket; stamp, seal; **brand, earmark;** hallmark; bar-code

21 **gesture, gesticulate; motion,** motion to; beckon, wiggle the finger at; wave the arms, wig-wag, saw the air; shrug, shrug

the shoulders; pantomime, mime, ape, take off

22 **signal,** signalize, sign, give a signal, make a sign; speak; flash; **give the high sign** or **the nod** or a high five <all nonformal>; nod; nudge, poke, kick, dig one in the ribs, touch; wink, glance, raise one's eyebrows, leer; hold up the hand; **wave,** wave the hand, wave a flag, **flag,** flag down; **unfurl a flag,** hoist a banner, break out a flag; **show one's colors,** exchange colors; **salute,** dip; dip a flag, hail, hail and speak; half-mast; give or sound an alarm, raise a cry; beat the drum, sound the trumpet

ADJS 23 **indicative,** indicatory; connotative, indicating, signifying, signalizing; **significant,** significative, meaningful; symptomatic, symptomatologic, symptomatological, diagnostic, pathognomonic, pathognomonical; evidential, **designative,** denotative, denominative, naming; **suggestive,** implicative; **expressive,** demonstrative, exhibitive; representative; identifying, identificational; individual, peculiar, idiosyncratic; **emblematic, symbolic,** emblematical, symbolical; symbolistic, symbological, typical; figurative, figural, metaphorical; ideographic; semiotic, semantic

24 **marked, designated,** flagged; signed, signposted; monogrammed, individualized, personal; own-brand, own-label

25 **gestural,** gesticulative, gesticulatory; kinesic; pantomimic, **in pantomime,** in dumb show

518 MEANING

NOUNS 1 **meaning, significance, signification,** significatum <L>, signifié <Fr>, point, **sense,** idea, **purport, import,** where one is coming from <nonformal>; **reference, referent;** intension, extension; **denotation;** dictionary meaning, lexical meaning; emotive or affective meaning, undertone, overtone, coloring; relevance, bearing, **relation,** pertinence or pertinency; **substance, gist,** pith, spirit, essence, gravamen, last word, name of the game and meat and potatoes and bottom line <all nonformal>; **drift,** tenor; sum, sum and substance; **literal meaning, true** or **real meaning, unadorned meaning; secondary meaning, connotation** 519.2; more than meets the eye, what is read between the lines; effect, force, impact, consequence, practical consequence, response; shifted or displaced

meaning, implied meaning, **implication** 519.2; Aesopian or Aesopic meaning, Aesopian or Aesopic language; totality of associations or references or relations, value; syntactic or structural meaning, grammatical meaning; symbolic meaning; metaphorical or transferred meaning; semantic field, semantic domain, semantic cluster; range or span of meaning, scope

2 **intent, intention, purpose, aim, object, design,** plan

3 **explanation, definition,** construction, sense-distinction, **interpretation** 341

4 **acceptation,** acception, accepted or received meaning; **usage,** acceptance

5 **meaningfulness,** suggestiveness, expressiveness, pregnancy; **significance,** significancy, significantness; intelligibility, interpretability, readability; pithiness, meatiness, sententiousness

6 <units> sign, symbol, significant, significant, type, token, icon, verbal icon, lexeme, sememe, morpheme, glosseme, **word,** term, phrase, utterance, lexical form or item, linguistic form, semantic or semiotic or semasiological unit; text

7 **semantics,** semiotic, semiotics, significs, semasiology; lexicology

VERBS 8 **mean, signify, denote, connote,** import, spell, have the sense of, be construed as, have the force of; be talking and be talking about <both nonformal>; **stand for, symbolize; imply,** suggest, argue, breathe, bespeak, betoken, **indicate; refer to; mean something,** mean a lot, have impact, come home, hit one where one lives and hit one close to home <both nonformal>

9 **intend,** have in mind, seek to communicate

ADJS 10 **meaningful,** meaning, **significant,** significative; **denotative, connotative,** denotational, connotational, intensional, extensional, associational; **referential; symbolic, metaphorical,** figurative, allegorical; transferred, extended; intelligible, interpretable, definable, readable; **suggestive,** indicative, **expressive; pregnant,** full of meaning, loaded or laden or fraught or freighted or heavy with significance; **pithy, meaty,** sententious, substantial, full of substance; pointed, full of point

11 **meant,** implied 519.7, **intended**

12 **semantic,** semantological, semiotic, semasiological; lexological; **symbolic,** signific, iconic, lexemic, sememic, glos-

sematic, morphemic, **verbal**, phrasal, lexical; structural

ADVS **13 meaningfully,** meaningly, **significantly;** suggestively, indicatively; **expressively**

519 LATENT MEANINGFULNESS

NOUNS **1 latent meaningfulness, latency,** latentness, delitescence, latent content; **potentiality,** virtuality, possibility; dormancy 173.4

2 implication, connotation, import, latent *or* underlying *or* implied meaning, ironic suggestion *or* implication, more than meets the eye, what is read between the lines; meaning 518; **suggestion,** allusion; coloration, tinge, undertone, overtone, undercurrent, more than meets the eye *or* ear, something between the lines, intimation, touch, nuance, innuendo; **code word,** weasel word; **hint** 551.4; **inference, supposition,** presupposition, assumption, presumption; secondary *or* transferred *or* metaphorical sense; undermeaning, undermention, subsidiary sense, subsense, **subtext;** Aesopian *or* Aesopic meaning, cryptic *or* hidden *or* esoteric *or* arcane meaning, occult meaning; **symbolism, allegory**

VERBS **3 be latent, underlie, lie under the surface, lurk,** lie hid *or* low, lie beneath, hibernate, lie dormant, smolder; be read between the lines; make no sign, escape notice

4 imply, implicate, involve, import, connote, entail 771.4; **mean** 518.8; **suggest,** lead one to believe, bring to mind; **hint, insinuate, infer, intimate** 551.10; **allude to,** point to from afar, point indirectly to; write between the lines; allegorize; **suppose, presuppose,** assume, presume, take for granted; mean to say *or* imply *or* suggest

ADJS **5 latent, lurking,** lying low, delitescent, **hidden** 346.11, obscured, obfuscated, veiled, muffled, covert, occult, mystic <old>, cryptic; esoteric; **underlying, under the surface,** submerged; **between the lines;** hibernating, sleeping, dormant 173.14; **potential,** unmanifested, virtual, possible

6 suggestive, allusive, allusory, **indicative, inferential; insinuating,** insinuative, insinuatory; ironic; **implicative,** implicatory, implicational; referential

7 implied, implicated, involved; **meant,** indicated; **suggested, intimated, insinuated, hinted;** inferred, supposed, as-

sumed, presumed, presupposed; hidden, arcane, esoteric, **cryptic,** Aesopian *or* Aesopic

8 tacit, implicit, implied, understood, taken for granted

9 unexpressed, unpronounced, **unsaid, unspoken, unuttered,** undeclared, unbreathed, unvoiced, wordless, silent; **unmentioned,** untalked-of, **untold,** unsung, unproclaimed, unpublished; unwritten, unrecorded

10 symbolic, symbolical, allegoric, allegorical, figural, figurative, tropological, **metaphoric,** metaphorical, anagogic, anagogical

ADVS **11 latently,** underlyingly; **potentially,** virtually

12 suggestively, allusively, inferentially, insinuatingly; impliedly; by suggestion, by allusion, etc

13 tacitly, implicitly, unspokenly, wordlessly, silently

520 MEANINGLESSNESS

NOUNS **1 meaninglessness, unmeaningness, senselessness,** nonsensicality; **insignificance,** unsignificancy; **noise,** mere noise, static, empty sound, talking to hear oneself talk, phatic communion; inanity, emptiness, nullity; "sounding brass and a tinkling cymbal"—Bible, "a tale told by an idiot, full of sound and fury, signifying nothing"—Shakespeare; purposelessness, aimlessness, futility; dead letter

2 nonsense, stuff and nonsense, pack of nonsense, **folderol, balderdash,** *niaiserie* <Fr>, flummery, trumpery, **rubbish,** trash, *narrishkeit* <Yiddish>, vaporing, fudge; **humbug,** gammon, hocus-pocus; rant, claptrap, fustian, rodomontade, bombast, absurdity 922.3; stultiloquence, **twaddle,** twiddle-twaddle, fiddle-faddle, fiddledeedee, fiddlesticks, **blather, babble,** babblement, bibble-babble, **gabble,** gibble-gabble, **blabber, gibber, jabber,** prate, **prattle,** palaver, rigmarole *or* rigamarole, galimatias, skimble-skamble, drivel, drool; **gibberish,** jargon, mumbo jumbo, **double-talk,** amphigory, gobbledygook <nonformal>; glossolalia, speaking in tongues

3 <nonformal terms> **bullshit,** shit, crap, horseshit, horsefeathers, bull, poppycock, bosh, tosh <Brit>, applesauce, bunkum, bunk, garbage, guff, jive, bilge, piffle, moonshine, flapdoodle, moonshine, a crock *or* a crock of shit, claptrap, tommyrot, rot, hogwash, malarkey, double

Dutch, hokum, hooey, bushwa, blah,
balls <Brit>, blah, baloney, blarney,
tripe, hot air, gas, wind, waffle <Brit>

VERBS **4 be meaningless, mean nothing,** signify nothing, not mean a thing, not convey anything; not make sense, not figure
<nonformal>, not compute; **not register,**
not ring any bells

5 talk nonsense, twaddle, piffle, waffle
<Brit>, **blather, blabber, babble, gabble,**
gibble-gabble, **jabber, gibber,** prate, **prattle,** rattle; talk through one's hat; gas *and*
bull *and* **bullshit** *and* throw the bull *and*
shoot off one's mouth *and* shoot the bull
<all nonformal>; **drivel,** vapor, drool,
run off at the mouth <nonformal>; speak
in tongues

ADJS **6 meaningless,** unmeaning, **senseless,**
purportless, importless, nondenotative,
nonconnotative; **insignificant,** unsignifi-
cant; empty, inane, null; phatic, garbled,
scrambled; **purposeless, aimless,** designless, **without rhyme or reason**

7 nonsensical, silly, poppycockish
<nonformal>; **foolish, absurd;** twad-
dling, twaddly; rubbishy, trashy;
skimble-skamble; Pickwickian

ADVS **8 meaninglessly,** unmeaningly, non-
denotatively, nonconnotatively, **senselessly, nonsensically;** insignificantly,
unsignificantly; **purposelessly,** aimlessly

521 INTELLIGIBILITY

NOUNS **1 intelligibility, comprehensibility,
apprehensibility,** prehensibility, grasp-
ability, **understandability,** knowability,
cognizability, scrutability, penetrability,
fathomableness, decipherability; recog-
nizability, readability, interpretability;
articulateness

2 clearness, clarity; plainness, distinctness,
microscopical distinctness, explicitness,
clear-cutness, definition; **lucidity,** limpidity, pellucidity, crystal *or* crystalline
clarity, crystallinity, perspicuity, trans-
picuity, transparency; **simplicity,**
straightforwardness, directness, literalness; unmistakableness, unequivocalness, unambiguousness; **coherence,** connectedness, consistency, structure; plain
language, plain style, plain English, plain
speech, unadorned style; clear, plaintext,
unencoded text

3 legibility, decipherability, **readability**

VERBS **4 be understandable, make sense;** be
plain *or* clear, be obvious, be self-evident,
be self-explanatory; **speak for itself,** tell
its own tale, speak volumes, have no se-

crets, put up no barriers; read easily

5 <be understood> **get over** *or* **across**
<nonformal>, come through, **register**
<nonformal>, **penetrate, sink in,** soak in;
dawn on, be glimpsed

6 make clear, make it clear, **let it be understood,** make oneself understood, get *or*
put over *or* across <nonformal>; **simplify,** put in plain words *or* plain English,
put in words of one syllable, spell out
<nonformal>; elucidate, **explain,** expli-
cate, **clarify** 341.10; put one in the picture
<Brit>; demystify, descramble; **decode,
decipher;** make available to all, popularize, vulgarize

7 understand, comprehend, apprehend,
have, **know, conceive, realize,** appreciate,
have no problem with, ken <Scots>,
savvy <nonformal>, sense, make sense
out of, make something of; **fathom, follow; grasp, seize,** get hold of, grasp *or*
seize the meaning, be seized of, take, **take
in,** catch, **catch on,** get the meaning of,
get the hang of; **master, learn** 570.6–15;
assimilate, absorb, digest

8 <nonformal terms> **read one loud and
clear,** read, read one, dig, get the idea, be
with one, be with it, get the message, get
the word, get the picture, get up to speed,
get into *or* through one's head *or* thick
head, get, get it, catch *or* get the drift,
have it taped, have it down pat, see where
one is coming from, hear loud and clear,
hear what one is saying, grok, have hold
of, have a fix on, know like the back *or*
palm of one's hand, know inside out

9 perceive, see, discern, make out, descry;
see the light, see daylight <nonformal>,
wake up, wake up to, tumble to <nonfor-
mal>, come alive; **see through,** see to the
bottom of, penetrate, see into, pierce,
plumb; see at a glance, see with half an
eye; get *or* have someone's number *and*
read someone like a book <both nonfor-
mal>

ADJS **10 intelligible, comprehensible, apprehensible,** prehensible, graspable, **knowable,** cognizable, scrutable, **fathomable,**
decipherable, plumbable, penetrable, interpretable; **understandable,** easily
understood, easy to understand, exoteric;
readable; articulate

11 clear, crystal-clear, clear as crystal, clear
as day, clear as the nose on one's face;
plain, distinct, microscopically distinct,
plain as pikestaffs; **definite,** defined, well-
defined, **clear-cut,** clean-cut, crisp; **direct,
literal;** simple, **straightforward; explicit,
express; unmistakable, unequivocal,** uni-

vocal, unambiguous, unconfused; **loud and clear** <nonformal>; **lucid,** pellucid, limpid, crystal-clear, crystalline, perspicuous, transpicuous, **transparent,** translucent, luminous; **coherent,** connected, consistent

12 **legible, decipherable, readable,** fair; uncoded, unenciphered, in the clear, clear, plaintext

ADVS 13 **intelligibly, understandably, comprehensibly,** apprehensibly; articulately; **clearly, lucidly,** limpidly, pellucidly, perspicuously, **simply, plainly, distinctly,** definitely; **coherently; explicitly, expressly; unmistakably, unequivocally,** unambiguously; in plain terms or words, in plain English, in no uncertain terms, in words of one syllable

14 **legibly,** decipherably, readably, fairly

522 UNINTELLIGIBILITY

NOUNS 1 **unintelligibility, incomprehensibility,** inapprehensibility, ungraspability, unseizability, **ununderstandability,** unknowability, incognizability, inscrutability, impenetrability, unfathomableness, unsearchableness, numinousness; **incoherence,** unconnectedness, ramblingness; inarticulateness; **ambiguity** 539

2 **abstruseness,** reconditeness; crabbedness, crampedness, knottiness; **complexity,** intricacy, **complication** 798.1; **hardness, difficulty; profundity,** profoundness, deepness; esotericism, esotery

3 **obscurity,** obscuration, obscurantism, obfuscation, mumbo jumbo <nonformal>, mystification; perplexity; **unclearness,** unclarity, unplainness, opacity; **vagueness,** indistinctness, indeterminateness, fuzziness, shapelessness, amorphousness; murkiness, murk, mistiness, mist, fogginess, fog, darkness, dark

4 **illegibility,** unreadability; undecipherability, indecipherability; scribble, scrawl, hen track <nonformal>

5 **unexpressiveness,** inexpressiveness, **expressionlessness,** impassivity; uncommunicativeness; straight face, dead pan <nonformal>, poker face <nonformal>

6 **inexplicability,** unexplainableness, uninterpretability, indefinability, undefinability, unaccountableness; insolvability, inextricability; **enigmaticalness,** mysteriousness, mystery, strangeness, weirdness

7 <something unintelligible> Greek, Choctaw, double Dutch; gibberish, babble, jargon, garbage, rubbish, gobbledygook, noise, Babel; scramble, jumble, garble; argot, cant, slang, secret language, Aesopian or Aesopic language, code, cipher, cryptogram; glossolalia, gift of tongues

8 **enigma, mystery, puzzle,** puzzlement; Chinese puzzle, crossword puzzle, jigsaw puzzle; **problem,** puzzling or baffling problem, why; question, question mark, vexed or perplexed question, enigmatic question, sixty-four dollar question <nonformal>; **perplexity;** knot, knotty point, crux, point to be solved; **puzzler,** poser, brain twister or teaser <nonformal>, sticker <nonformal>; mindboggler, **floorer** or **stumper** <all nonformal>; nut to crack, **hard** or **tough nut to crack;** tough proposition <nonformal>, "a perfect nonplus and baffle to all human understanding"—Southey, "a riddle wrapped in a mystery inside an enigma" —Winston Churchill

9 **riddle, conundrum,** charade, rebus; logogriph, anagram; riddle of the Sphinx

VERBS 10 **be incomprehensible, not make sense,** be too deep, go over one's head, be beyond one, beat one <nonformal>, elude or escape one, lose one, need explanation or clarification or translation, be Greek to, pass comprehension or understanding, not penetrate; **baffle, perplex** 970.13, riddle, be sphinxlike, speak in riddles; speak in tongues; talk double Dutch, babble, gibber, ramble, drivel

11 **not understand, be unable to comprehend,** not have the first idea, not get <nonformal>, be unable to get into or through one's head or thick skull; be out of one's depth, be at sea, be lost; **not know what to make of,** make nothing of, not be able to account for, not make head or tail of; be unable to see, not see the wood for the trees; go over one's head, escape one; give up, pass <nonformal>

12 **make unintelligible, scramble,** jumble, garble; **obscure,** obfuscate, mystify, shadow; **complicate** 798.3

ADJS 13 **unintelligible, incomprehensible,** inapprehensible, ungraspable, unseizable, **ununderstandable,** unknowable, incognizable; **unfathomable, inscrutable,** impenetrable, unsearchable, numinous; **ambiguous; incoherent,** unconnected, rambling; **inarticulate; past comprehension,** beyond one's comprehension, beyond understanding; Greek to one

14 **hard to understand, difficult, hard,** tough <nonformal>, beyond one, **over one's head,** beyond or out of one's depth;

knotty, cramp, crabbed; intricate, **complex,** overtechnical, perplexed, **complicated** 798.4; **scrambled,** jumbled, **garbled; obscure,** obscured, obfuscated

15 **obscure, vague, indistinct,** indeterminate, fuzzy, shapeless, amorphous; unclear, unplain, opaque, muddy, **clear as mud** and clear as ditch water <both nonformal>; **dark,** dim, blind <old>, shadowy; **murky,** cloudy, foggy, fogbound, hazy, misty, nebulous

16 **recondite, abstruse,** abstract, transcendental; **profound, deep; hidden** 346.11; arcane, **esoteric,** occult; **secret** 345.11

17 **enigmatic,** enigmatical, cryptic, cryptical; sphinxlike; **perplexing, puzzling;** riddling; logogriphic, anagrammatic

18 **inexplicable, unexplainable,** uninterpretable, undefinable, indefinable, funny, funny peculiar <nonformal>, **unaccountable; insolvable,** unsolvable, insoluble, inextricable; mysterious, mystic, mystical, shrouded or wrapped or enwrapped in mystery

19 **illegible, unreadable, unclear; undecipherable,** indecipherable

20 **inexpressive,** unexpressive, impassive, po-faced <Brit>; uncommunicative; **expressionless; vacant, empty, blank;** glassy, glazed, glazed-over, fishy, wooden; deadpan, poker-faced <nonformal>

ADVS 21 **unintelligibly, incomprehensibly,** inapprehensibly, ununderstandably

22 **obscurely, vaguely, indistinctly,** indeterminately; **unclearly,** unplainly; illegibly

23 **reconditely, abstrusely;** esoterically, occultly

24 **inexplicably, unexplainably,** undefinably, bafflingly, **unaccountably, enigmatically; mysteriously,** mystically

25 **expressionlessly, vacantly, blankly, emptily,** woodenly, glassily, fishily

PREPS 26 **beyond,** past, above; **too deep for**

PHRS 27 **I don't understand, I can't see,** I don't see how or why, **it beats me** <nonformal>, you've got me <nonformal>, **it's beyond me,** it's too deep for me, it has me guessing, I don't have the first or foggiest idea, it's Greek to me, I'm clueless <Brit>; **I give up,** I pass <nonformal>

523 LANGUAGE

NOUNS 1 **language** <see list>, speech, tongue, *lingua* <L>, spoken language, natural language; **talk, parlance, locu-**tion, phraseology, **idiom, lingo** <nonformal>; dialect; idiolect, personal usage, individual speech habits or performance, parole; code or system of oral communication, individual speech, competence, langue; **usage; language type; language family, subfamily, language group;** area language, regional language; world language, universal language

2 **dead language,** ancient language, lost language; parent language; classical language; living language, vernacular; sacred language or tongue

3 **mother tongue,** native language or tongue, natal tongue, native speech, vernacular, first language

4 **standard language,** standard or prestige dialect, acrolect; national language, official language; educated speech or language; literary language, written language, formal written language; classical language; correct or good English, **Standard English, the King's** or **Queen's English,** Received Standard, Received Pronunciation

5 **nonformal language** or **speech,** nonformal standard speech, **spoken language, colloquial language** or **speech,** vernacular language or speech, vernacular; **slang;** colloquialism, colloquial usage, conversationalism, vernacularism; ordinary language or speech; nonformal English, conversational English, colloquial English, English as it is spoken

6 **substandard** or nonstandard language or **speech,** nonformal language or speech; vernacular language or speech, **vernacular,** demotic language or speech, vulgate, vulgar tongue, common speech; uneducated speech, illiterate speech; substandard usage; basilect; **nonformal**

7 **dialect,** idiom; class dialect; regional or local dialect; subdialect; folk speech or dialect, patois; **provincialism, localism, regionalism,** regional accent 524.9; Canadian French, French Canadian; Pennsylvania Dutch, Pennsylvania German; Yankee, New England dialect; Brooklynese; Southern dialect or twang; Black English, Afro-Americanese; Cockney; Yorkshire; Midland, Midland dialect; Anglo-Indian; Australian English; Gullah; Acadian, Cajun; dialect atlas, linguistic atlas; isogloss, bundle of isoglosses; speech community; linguistic community; linguistic ambience; speech or linguistic island, relic area

8 <idioms> Anglicism, Briticism, Englishism; Americanism, Yankeeism; Western-

ism, Southernism; Gallicism, Frenchism; Irishism, Hibernicism; Canadianism, Scotticism, Germanism, Russianism, Latinism, etc

9 **jargon, lingo** <nonformal>, **slang, cant, argot, patois, patter, vernacular;** vocabulary, phraseology; gobbledygook, mumbo jumbo, gibberish; **nonformal;** taboo language, vulgar language; obscene language, scatology; doublespeak, bizspeak, mediaspeak, policyspeak, spookspeak, technospeak, winespeak

10 <jargons> Academese, cinemese, collegese, constablese, economese, sociologese, legalese, pedagese, societyese, stagese, telegraphese, Varietyese, Wall Streetese, journalese, newspaperese, officialese, federalese, Pentagonese, Washingtonese, medical Greek, medicalese, businessese *or* businessspeak, computerese, technobabble, psychobabble; Yinglish, Franglais, Spanglish; Euro-jargon; man-talk, bloke-talk <Brit nonformal>, woman-talk, hen-talk <nonformal>; shoptalk

11 **lingua franca,** jargon, **pidgin,** trade language; auxiliary language, interlanguage; creolized language, creole language, creole; koine; pidgin English, talkee-talkee, Bêche-de-Mer, Beach-la-mar; Kitchen Kaffir; Chinook *or* Oregon Jargon; Sabir; Esperanto

12 **linguistics,** linguistic science, science of language; glottology, glossology <old>; linguistic analysis; linguistic terminology, metalanguage; **philology;** paleography; speech origins, language origins, bowwow theory, dingdong theory, pooh-pooh theory; language study, foreign-language study

13 **linguist,** linguistic scientist, linguistician, linguistic scholar; philologist, philologer, philologian; philologaster; **grammarian,** grammatist; grammaticaster; **etymologist,** etymologer; **lexicologist; lexicographer,** glossographer, glossarist; phoneticist, phonetician, phonemicist, phonologist, orthoepist; dialectician, dialectologist; semanticist, semasiologist; paleographer

14 **polyglot,** linguist, **bilingual** *or* diglot, trilingual, multilingual

15 **colloquializer;** jargonist, jargoneer, jargonizer; slangster

VERBS 16 **speak, talk,** use language, communicate orally *or* verbally; use nonformal speech *or* style, colloquialize, vernacularize; jargon, jargonize, cant; patter

ADJS 17 **linguistic,** lingual, glottological; de-

scriptive, structural, glottochronological, lexicostatistical, psycholinguistic, sociolinguistic, metalinguistic; **philological;** lexicological, lexicographic, lexicographical; syntactic, syntactical, **grammatical;** grammatic, semantic 518.12; phonetic 524.31, phonemic, phonological; morphological; morphophonemic, graphemic, paleographic, paleographical

18 **vernacular, colloquial, conversational, unliterary, nonformal,** demotic, spoken, vulgar, vulgate; unstudied, familiar, common, everyday; **substandard,** nonformal, uneducated

19 **jargonish,** jargonal; **slang,** slangy; taboo; scatological; rhyming slang

20 **idiomatic; dialect,** dialectal, dialectological; provincial, regional, local

WORD ELEMENTS 21 lingu—, linguo—, lingui—, gloss—, glosso—, glott—, glotto—

22 **types of language**

affixing	monosyllabic
agglutinative	polysyllabic
analytic	polysynthetic
fusional	polytonic
incorporative	symbolic
inflectional	synthetic
isolating	tone

524 SPEECH
<utterance>

NOUNS 1 **speech, talk,** the power *or* faculty of speech, the verbal *or* oral faculty, talking, speaking, **discourse,** oral communication, vocal *or* voice *or* viva-voce communication, communication; **palaver, prattle, gab** *and* jaw-jaw <both nonformal>; rapping *and* yakking *and* yakkety-yak <all nonformal>; **words, accents;** chatter 540.3; conversation 541; elocution 543.1; **language** 523

2 "the mirror of the soul"—Publilius Syrus, "the image of life"—Democritus, "a faculty given to man to conceal his thoughts"—Talleyrand, "but broken light upon the depth of the unspoken"—George Eliot

3 **utterance, speaking,** *parole* <Fr>, locution <old>, phonation; **speech act,** linguistic act *or* behavior; string, utterance string, sequence of phonemes; **voice, tongue;** word of mouth, parol, the spoken word; vocable, **word** 526

4 **remark, statement,** earful *and* crack *and* one's two cents' worth <all nonformal>, **word,** say, **saying, utterance, observation, reflection, expression; note,** thought,

mention; **assertion,** averment, allegation, affirmation, pronouncement, position, dictum; **declaration;** interjection, exclamation; question 937.10; answer 938; address, greeting, apostrophe; sentence, phrase; subjoinder, Parthian shot

5 **articulateness,** articulacy, oracy, readiness *or* facility of speech; **eloquence** 544

6 **articulation,** uttering, phonation, voicing, giving voice, **vocalization; pronunciation, enunciation,** utterance; **delivery, attack**

7 **intonation, inflection, modulation;** intonation pattern *or* contour, intonation *or* inflection of voice, speech tune *or* melody; suprasegmental, suprasegmental phoneme; **tone, pitch;** pitch accent, tonic accent

8 manner of speaking, way of saying, mode of expression; **tone of voice, voice,** *voce* <Ital>, **tone;** voice quality, vocal style, **timbre;** voice qualifier; paralinguistic communication

9 **accent,** regional accent, brogue, twang, burr, drawl, broad accent; **foreign accent;** broken English

10 pause, juncture, open juncture, close juncture; terminal, clause terminal, rising terminal, falling terminal; sandhi; word boundary, clause boundary; pause

11 **accent,** accentuation, stress accent; **emphasis, stress, word stress;** ictus, beat, rhythmical stress; rhythm, rhythmic pattern, **cadence;** prosody, prosodics, metrics; stress pattern; level of stress; primary stress, secondary stress, tertiary stress, weak stress

12 vowel quantity, **quantity,** mora; long vowel, short vowel, full vowel, reduced vowel

13 **speech sound,** phone, vocable, phonetic unit *or* entity; puff of air, aspiration; stream of air, airstream, glottalic airstream; articulation, manner of articulation; **stop,** plosive, explosive, mute, check, occlusive, **affricate,** continuant, **liquid,** lateral, **nasal;** point *or* place of articulation; voice, voicing; sonority; aspiration, palatalization, labialization, pharyngealization, glottalization; surd, voiceless sound; sonant, voiced sound; **consonant; semivowel,** glide, transition sound; vocalic, syllabic nucleus, syllabic peak, peak; vocoid; **vowel;** monophthong, **diphthong,** triphthong; **syllable; phoneme,** segmental phoneme, morphophoneme; modification, assimilation, dissimilation; **allophone;** parasitic vowel, epenthetic vowel, svarabhakti vowel,

prothetic vowel; vowel gradation, vowel mutation; doubletalk

14 **phonetics,** articulatory phonetics, acoustic phonetics; phonology; morphophonemics; orthoepy; sound *or* phonetic law; sound shift, *Lautverschiebung* <Ger>; umlaut, mutation, ablaut, gradation; rhotacism, betacism; Grimm's law, Verner's law, Grassmann's law

15 **phonetician,** phonetist, phoneticist; orthoepist

16 **ventriloquism,** ventriloquy; **ventriloquist**

17 talking machine, sonovox, voder, vocoder

18 **talker, speaker,** sayer, utterer, patterer; chatterbox 540.4; conversationalist 541.8

19 **vocal** *or* **speech organ,** articulator; tongue, apex, tip, blade, dorsum, back; vocal cords *or* bands, vocal processes, vocal folds; voice box, larynx, Adam's apple; syrinx; arytenoid cartilages; glottis, vocal chink; lips, teeth, palate, hard palate, soft palate, velum, alveolus, teeth ridge, alveolar ridge; nasal cavity, oral cavity; pharynx, throat *or* pharyngeal cavity

VERBS 20 **speak, talk;** patter *or* gab *or* wag the tongue <all nonformal>; mouth; chatter 540.5; converse 541.9; declaim 543.10

21 <nonformal terms> **yak,** yap, yakkety-yak, gab, spiel, chin, jaw, shoot off one's face *or* mouth, shoot *or* bat the breeze, beat *or* bat one's gums, bend one's ear, make chin music, rattle away, talk a blue streak, talk someone's ear *or* head off, flap one's jaw, natter <Brit>, spout off, sound off

22 **speak up, speak out, speak one's piece** *or* **one's mind, pipe up, open one's mouth,** open one's lips, say out, say loud and clear, say out loud, sound off, lift *or* raise one's voice, break silence, find one's tongue; take the floor; put in a word, get in a word edgewise *or* edgeway; **have one's say,** put in one's two cents worth <nonformal>, relieve oneself, get a load off one's mind <nonformal>, give vent *or* voice to, pour one's heart out

23 **say, utter, breathe,** sound, **voice,** vocalize, phonate, **articulate, enunciate, pronounce,** lip, give voice, give tongue, give utterance; whisper; **express,** give expression, verbalize, put in words, find words to express; **word,** formulate, put into words, couch, phrase 532.4; **present,** deliver; **emit,** give, raise, **let out,** out with, come *or* give out with, put *or* set forth, pour forth; throw off, fling off; chorus,

chime; **tell, communicate** 343.6,7; **convey, impart, disclose** 351.4

24 **state, declare, assert,** aver, affirm, asseverate, allege; **say,** make a statement, send a message; **announce,** tell the world; **relate, recite;** quote; proclaim, nuncupate

25 **remark, comment, observe, note; mention,** speak <old>, let drop *or* fall, say by the way, make mention of; refer to, allude to, touch on, make reference to, call attention to; muse, reflect; opine <nonformal>; interject; blurt, blurt out, exclaim

26 <utter in a certain way> murmur, mutter, mumble, whisper, breathe, buzz, sigh; gasp, pant; exclaim, yell 59.6,8; sing, lilt, warble, chant, coo, chirp; pipe, flute; squeak; cackle, crow; bark, yelp, yap; growl, snap, snarl; hiss, sibilate; grunt, snort; roar, bellow, blare, trumpet, bray, blat, bawl, thunder, rumble, boom; scream, shriek, screech, squeal, squawk, yawp, squall; whine, wail, keen, blubber, sob; drawl, twang

27 **address, speak to, talk to,** bespeak, beg the ear of; **appeal to,** invoke; apostrophize; **approach; buttonhole,** take by the button *or* lapel; take aside, talk to in private, closet oneself with; **accost, call to, hail,** halloo, greet, salute, speak, speak fair

28 **pass one's lips, escape one's lips,** fall from the lips *or* mouth

29 inflect, modulate, intonate

ADJS 30 **speech; language, linguistic,** lingual; **spoken, uttered, said,** vocalized, **voiced, verbalized, pronounced, sounded, articulated, enunciated;** vocal, voiceful; **oral, verbal, unwritten,** *viva voce* <L>, nuncupative, parol

31 **phonetic,** phonic; articulatory, acoustic; intonated; pitched, pitch, **tonal,** tonic, oxytone, oxytonic, paroxytonic, barytone; **accented, stressed,** strong, heavy; unaccented, unstressed, weak, light, pretonic, atonic, posttonic; articulated; stopped, muted, checked, occlusive, nasal, nasalized, twangy, continuant, liquid, lateral, affricated; alveolabial, alveolar, alveolingual, etc; low, high, mid, open, broad, close; front, back, central; wide, lax, tense, narrow; voiced, sonant, voiceless, surd; rounded, unrounded, flat; aspirated; labialized; palatalized, soft, *mouillé* <Fr>; unpalatalized, hard; pharyngealized, glottalized; **consonant,** consonantal, semivowel, glide, **vowel;** vowellike, vocoid, vocalic, syllabic; monophthongal, diphthongal, triphthon-

gal; **phonemic,** allophonic; assimilated, dissimilated

32 **speaking, talking;** articulate, talkative 540.9; **eloquent** 544.8, well-spoken; true-speaking, clean-speaking, plain-speaking, plain-spoken, **outspoken,** free-speaking, free-spoken, loud-speaking, loud-spoken, soft-speaking, soft-spoken; English-speaking, etc

33 ventriloquial, ventriloquistic

ADVS 34 **orally, vocally, verbally, by word of mouth,** *viva voce* <L>; from the lips of, from his own mouth

525 IMPERFECT SPEECH

NOUNS 1 **speech defect,** speech impediment, impairment of speech; dysarthria, dysphasia, dysphrasia; dyslalia, dyslogia; idioglossia, idiolalia; **broken speech,** cracked *or* broken voice, broken tones *or* accents; indistinct *or* blurred *or* muzzy speech; loss of voice, aphonia; **nasalization,** nasal tone *or* accent, **twang,** nasal twang, talking through one's nose; **falsetto,** childish treble, artificial voice; **shake, quaver,** tremor; **lisp,** lisping; hiss, sibilation; **croak,** choked voice, hawking voice; crow; harshness, dysphonia, hoarseness 58.2

2 **inarticulateness,** inarticulacy; thickness of speech

3 **stammering, stuttering,** hesitation, faltering, traulism, dysphemia, *balbuties* <L>; palilalia; stammer, stutter

4 **mumbling, muttering,** maundering; droning, drone; mumble, mutter; jabber, jibber, gibber, gibbering, gabble; whispering, whisper, susurration; mouthing; murmuring

5 **mispronunciation,** misspeaking, cacology, cacoepy; lallation, lambdacism, paralambdacism; rhotacism, pararhotacism; gammacism; mytacism; **corruption,** language pollution

6 **aphasia, agraphia;** aphrasia, aphrasia paranoica; **aphonia,** loss of speech, aphonia clericorum, hysterical aphonia, stage fright, aphonia paralytica, aphonia paranoica, spastic aphonia, mutism, muteness 51.2

VERBS 7 **speak poorly,** talk incoherently, be unable to put two words together; have an impediment in one's speech, have a bone in one's neck *or* throat; speak thickly; **croak; lisp; shake, quaver; drawl;** mince, clip one's words; lose one's voice, get stage fright, clank *or* clank up *and* freeze <all nonformal>

8 **stammer, stutter,** stammer out; hesitate, falter, halt, mammer <Brit nonformal>, stumble; hem, haw, hum, **hum and haw, hem and haw**

9 **mumble, mutter,** maunder; drone, drone on; swallow one's words, speak drunkenly or incoherently; jabber, gibber, gabble; splutter, sputter; blubber, sob; whisper, susurrate; murmur; mouth

10 nasalize, whine, **speak through one's nose,** twang, snuffle

11 **mispronounce,** misspeak, missay, **murder the King's or Queen's English**

ADJS 12 <imperfectly spoken> inarticulate, indistinct, blurred, muzzy; **mispronounced; shaky,** shaking, **quavering,** tremulous, titubant; **drawling,** drawly; **lisping; throaty, guttural,** thick, velar; stifled, choked, choking, strangled; **nasal, twangy,** breathy, adenoidal, snuffling; croaking, hawking; harsh, dysphonic, hoarse 58.15

13 **stammering, stuttering,** halting, hesitating, faltering, stumbling, balbutient; **aphasic;** aphrasic; aphonic, dumb, **mute** 51.12

526 WORD

NOUNS 1 **word,** free form, minimum free form, **term,** expression, locution, linguistic form, lexeme; content word, function word; *logos* <Gk>, *verbum* <L>; verbalism, vocable, utterance, articulation; **usage;** syllable, polysyllable; homonym, homophone, homograph; monosyllable; synonym; metonym; antonym

2 **root,** etymon, primitive; eponym; derivative, derivation; cognate; doublet

3 **morphology,** morphemics; morphophonemics; **morpheme;** morph, allomorph; bound morpheme or form, free morpheme or form; difference of form, formal contrast; accidence; **inflection,** conjugation, declension; paradigm; derivation, word-formation; formative; root, radical; theme, stem; word element, combining form; **affix, suffix, prefix,** infix; proclitic, enclitic; affixation, infixation, suffixation, prefixation; morphemic analysis, immediate constituent or IC analysis, cutting; morphophonemic analysis

4 **word form,** formation, construction; back formation; clipped word; spoonerism; **compound;** *tatpurusha, dvandva, karmadharaya, dvigu, avyayibhava, bahuvrihi* <all Skt>; endocentric compound, exocentric compound; acronym, acrostic; paronym, conjugate

5 **technical term,** technicality; jargon word; jargon 523.9,10

6 **barbarism, corruption, vulgarism, impropriety,** taboo word, dirty word *and* four-letter word <both nonformal>; **colloquialism, slang, localism** 526.6

7 **loan word,** borrowing, borrowed word, paronym; loan translation, calque; foreignism

8 **neologism,** neology, neoterism, new word or term, newfangled expression; **coinage;** new sense or meaning; **nonce word;** ghost word or name

9 **catchword,** catch phrase, shibboleth, slogan, cry; **pet expression,** byword, cliché; **buzzword,** vogue word, fad word, in-word; euphemism, **code word**

10 long word, hard word, jawbreaker or jaw-twister *and* two-dollar or five-dollar word <all nonformal>, polysyllable; sesquipedalian, sesquipedalia <pl>; lexiphanicism, grandiloquence 545

11 hybrid word, **hybrid;** macaronicism, macaronic; hybridism, contamination; blendword, blend, portmanteau word, portmanteau, portmantologism, telescope word, **counterword**

12 **archaism,** archaicism, antiquated word or expression; obsoletism, obsolete

13 **vocabulary, lexis, words, word stock,** wordhoard, stock of words; phraseology; **thesaurus,** Roget's; lexicon

14 **lexicology; lexicography,** lexigraphy, glossography; onomastics 527.1, toponymics; **meaning** 518, semantics, semasiology

15 **etymology, derivation, origin,** word origin, word history, semantic history; historical linguistics, comparative linguistics; eponymy; folk etymology

16 echoic word, onomatopoeic word, onomatope; onomatopoeia; bowwow theory

17 **neologist, word-coiner,** neoterist; phraser, phrasemaker, phrasemonger

ADJS 18 **verbal,** vocabular, vocabulary

19 lexical, lexicologic, lexicological; lexigraphic, lexigraphical, **lexicographical,** lexicographic; glossographic, glossographical; etymological, etymologic, derivational; onomastic, onomatologic; onomasiological; echoic, onomatopoeic; conjugate, paronymous, paronymic

20 neological, neoterical

21 **morphological,** morphemic; morphophonemic; inflective, inflectional, paradigmatic, derivational; affixal, prefixal, infixal, suffixal

WORD ELEMENTS 22 log—, logo—, onomato—, —onym, —onymy

527 NOMENCLATURE

NOUNS **1 nomenclature, terminology,** orismology, glossology <old>; onomatology, onomastics; toponymics, toponymy, place-names, place-naming; antonomasia; polyonymy; **taxonomy,** classification, systematics, biosystematics, cytotaxonomy, binomial nomenclature, binomialism, Linnaean method, trinomialism; kingdom, phylum, class, order, family, genus, species

2 naming, calling, denomination, appellation, designation, designating, styling, terming, definition, identification; **christening,** baptism; dubbing; nicknaming

3 name, appellation, appellative, **denomination, designation, style,** nomen <L>, **cognomen,** cognomination, full name; proper name or noun; moniker and handle <both nonformal>; **title,** honorific; empty title or name; **label, tag; epithet,** byword; **scientific name,** trinomen, trinomial name, binomen, binomial name; nomen nudum <L>, hyponym; tautonym; typonym; middle name; eponym; namesake; secret name, cryptonym, euonym

4 first name, forename, **Christian name, given name,** baptismal name; **middle name**

5 surname, last name, family name, cognomen, byname; **maiden name;** married name; patronymic, matronymic

6 <Latin terms> praenomen, nomen, agnomen, cognomen

7 nickname, sobriquet, byname, cognomen; epithet, agnomen; **pet name,** diminutive, hypocoristic, affectionate name

8 alias, pseudonym, anonym, **assumed name,** false or fictitious name, nom de guerre <Fr>; **pen name, nom de plume;** stage name, nom de théâtre <Fr>, professional name; John Doe, Jane Doe, Richard Roe

9 misnomer, wrong name

10 signature, sign manual, **autograph, hand, John Hancock** <nonformal>; mark, mark of signature, cross, christcross, X; initials; subscription; countersignature, countersign, countermark, counterstamp; endorsement; visa, visé <Fr>; monogram, cipher, device; seal, sigil, signet

VERBS **11 name, denominate,** nominate, **designate, call, term, style, dub,** color <nonformal>; specify; define, identify; **title,** entitle; **label, tag; nickname; christen,** baptize

12 misname, misnomer, **miscall,** misterm, misdesignate

13 be called, be known by or as, go by, go as, **go by the name of,** go or pass under the name of, bear the name of, rejoice in the name of; go under an assumed or a false name, have an alias

ADJS **14 named, called,** yclept <old>, **styled, titled,** denominated, denominate <old>, **known as,** known by the name of, designated, termed, dubbed, identified as; christened, baptized; what one may well or fairly or properly or fitly call

15 nominal, cognominal; **titular, in name only,** nominative, formal; **so-called,** quasi; would-be, soi-disant <Fr>; **selfcalled, self-styled,** self-christened; honorific; agnominal, epithetic, epithetical; hypocoristic, diminutive; by name, by whatever name, under any other name; **alias,** a k a <also known as>

16 denominative, nominative, appellative; eponymous, eponymic

17 terminological, nomenclatural, orismological; onomastic; toponymic, toponymous; taxonomic, classificatory, binomial, Linnaean, trinomial

WORD ELEMENTS **18** onomato—, —onym, —onymy

528 ANONYMITY

NOUNS **1 anonymity, anonymousness, namelessness; incognito;** cover, cover name; code name; anonym

2 what's-its-name and **what's-his-name** and what's-his-face and what's-her-name and **what-you-may-call-it** and what-you-may-call-'em and what-d'ye-call-'em and what-d'ye-call-it and whatzit <all nonformal>; je ne sais quoi <Fr>, I don't know what; such-and-such; **so-and-so,** certain person, Mr X; you-know-who

ADJS **3 anonymous, anon; nameless, unnamed,** unidentified, undesignated, unspecified, innominate, without a name, **unknown;** undefined; unacknowledged; **incognito;** cryptonymous, cryptonymic

529 PHRASE

NOUNS **1 phrase, expression, locution, utterance,** usage, term, verbalism; **wordgroup,** construction, endocentric construction, headed group, syntagm; syntactic structure; noun phrase, verb phrase, verb complex, adverbial phrase, adjectival phrase, prepositional phrase; **clause; sentence,** period, periodic sentence; **paragraph; idiom,** idiotism, phrasal idiom; turn of phrase *or* expression, peculiar expression, manner *or* way of speaking; set phrase *or* term; conventional *or* common *or* standard phrase; phraseogram, phraseograph

2 diction, phrasing

3 phraser, phrasemaker, phrasemonger, phraseman

ADJS **4 phrasal,** phrase; phrasey

5 in set phrases *or* terms, in good set terms, in round terms

530 GRAMMAR

NOUNS **1 grammar,** rules of language, linguistic structure, syntactic structure; "the rule and pattern of speech"— Horace; grammaticalness, well-formedness, grammaticality, grammatical theory; **traditional grammar, school grammar;** descriptive grammar, **structural grammar;** case grammar; phrase-structure grammar; generative grammar, **transformational grammar, transformational generative grammar;** tagmemic analysis; glossematics; stratificational grammar; **parsing,** grammatical analysis; **morphology** 526.3; **phonology** 524.14

2 syntax, structure, syntactic structure, word order, word arrangement; syntactics, syntactic analysis; immediate constituent analysis *or* IC analysis, cutting; phrase structure; surface structure, shallow structure, deep structure, underlying structure; levels, ranks, strata; tagmeme, form-function unit, slot, filler, slot and filler; **function, subject, predicate, complement, object,** direct object, indirect object, **modifier,** qualifier, sentence *or* construction modifier, appositive, attribute, attributive

3 part of speech, form class, major form class, function class; function *or* empty *or* form word; **adjective,** adjectival, attributive; **adverb,** adverbial; **preposition;** verbal adjective, gerundive; **participle,** present participle, past participle, perfect participle; **conjunction,** subordinating conjunction, coordinating conjunction, conjunctive adverb, adversative conjunction, copulative, copulative conjunction, correlative conjunction, disjunctive, disjunctive conjunction; **interjection,** exclamatory noun *or* adjective; **particle**

4 verb, transitive, transitive verb, intransitive, intransitive verb, impersonal verb, neuter verb, deponent verb, defective verb; finite verb; linking verb, copula; verbal, verbid, nonfinite verb form; **infinitive; auxiliary verb,** auxiliary, modal auxiliary; phrasal verb; verb phrase

5 noun, pronoun, substantive, substantival, common noun, proper noun, concrete noun, abstract noun, collective noun, quotation noun, hypostasis, adherent noun, adverbial noun; verbal noun, gerund; nominal; noun phrase; mass noun, count noun

6 article, definite article, indefinite article; determiner, noun determiner, determinative, post-determiner

7 person; first person; second person, proximate; third person; fourth person, obviative

8 number; singular, dual, trial, plural

9 case; common case, subject case, nominative; object *or* objective case, accusative, dative, possessive case, genitive; local case, locative, essive, superessive, inessive, adessive, abessive, lative, allative, illative, sublative, elative, ablative, delative, terminative, approximative, prolative, perlative, translative; comitative, instrumental, prepositional, vocative; oblique case

10 gender, masculine, feminine, neuter, common gender; grammatical gender, natural gender; animate, inanimate

11 mood, mode; indicative, subjunctive, imperative, conditional, potential, obligative, permissive, optative, jussive

12 tense; present; historical present; **past,** preterit *or* preterite; aorist; imperfect; future; **perfect,** present perfect, future perfect; past perfect, **pluperfect;** progressive tense, durative; point tense

13 aspect; perfective, imperfective, inchoative, iterative, frequentative, desiderative

14 voice; active voice, active, passive voice, passive; middle voice, middle; mediopassive; reflexive

15 punctuation, punctuation marks <see list>; diacritical mark *or* sign <see list>; reference mark <see list>, reference; point, tittle; stop, end stop

VERBS **16** grammaticize; **parse,** analyze; inflect, **conjugate, decline; punctuate,** mark, point; parenthesize, hyphenate, bracket; diagram, notate

ADJS **17 grammatical, syntactical,** formal, structural; correct, well-formed; tagmemic, glossematic; **functional;** substantive, nominal, pronominal; verbal, transitive, intransitive; linking, copulative; attributive, adjectival, adverbal,

participial; prepositional, postpositional; conjunctive

18 punctuation marks

ampersand <&>	period, full stop
angle brackets	<Brit>, point,
<<>>	decimal point, dot
apostrophe <'>	<.>
braces <{}>	question mark *or*
brackets <[]>	interrogation mark
colon <:>	*or* point <?>
comma <,>	quotation marks,
dash <—, –>	quotes <"">
ellipsis, suspension	semicolon <;>
periods < ... > *or*	single quotation
<***>	marks, single
exclamation mark *or*	quotes <''>
point <!>	virgule, diagonal,
hyphen <->	solidus, slash mark
interrobang <‽>	</>
parentheses *or* parens	
<nonformal>	
<()>	

19 diacritical marks

acute accent <'>	grave accent <`>
breve <˘>	*hač* <Cz>, wedge
cedilla <,>	<ˇ>
circumflex accent	macron <¯>
<^, *or* ˜>	tilde <˜>
diaeresis, umlaut	
<¨>	

20 reference marks

asterisk, star <*>	double prime <″>
asterism <***>	index *or* fist <☞>
bullet, centered dot	leaders <.......>
<•>	paragraph <¶>
caret <ˆ>	parallels <‖>
dagger *or* obelisk	prime <′>
<†>	section <§>
ditto mark <">	
double dagger, diesis	
<‡>	

531 UNGRAMMATICALNESS

NOUNS **1 ungrammaticalness, bad** *or* faulty grammar, faulty syntax; lack of concord *or* agreement, faulty reference, misplaced *or* dangling modifier, shift of tense, shift of structure, anacoluthon, faulty subordination, faulty comparison, faulty coordination, faulty punctuation, lack of parallelism, sentence fragment, comma fault, comma splice; abuse of terms, corruption of speech, broken speech

2 solecism, ungrammaticism, **misusage, missaying, misconstruction,** barbarism, infelicity; corruption; antiphrasis, malapropism 974.7

VERBS **3** solecize, commit a solecism, use faulty *or* inadmissible *or* inappropriate grammar, ignore *or* disdain *or* violate

grammar, murder the King's *or* Queen's English, break Priscian's head <old>

ADJS **4 ungrammatic, ungrammatical,** solecistic, solecistical, **incorrect,** barbarous; faulty, erroneous 974.16; infelicitous, improper 788.7; careless, slovenly, slipshod 809.15; loose, imprecise 974.17

532 DICTION

NOUNS **1 diction,** words, wordage, verbiage, word-usage, **usage,** *usus loquendi* <L>, use *or* choice of words, formulation, way of putting *or* couching, word garment, word dressing; **rhetoric,** speech, talk <nonformal>; **language,** dialect, parlance, locution, expression, **grammar** 530; **idiom;** composition

2 style; mode, manner, strain, vein; fashion, way; **rhetoric; manner of speaking,** mode of expression, literary style, style of writing, command of language *or* idiom, form of speech, expression of ideas; feeling for words *or* language, way with words, sense of language, *Sprachgefühl* <Ger>; gift of gab *or* of the gab <nonformal>, blarney *or* the blarney <nonformal>; the power *or* grace of expression; linguistic tact *or* finesse; personal style; mannerism, trick, pecularity; affectation; "the dress of thought"—Charles Dickens, "a certain absolute and unique manner of expressing a thing"—Walter Pater; inflation, exaggeration, grandiloquence 545; the grand style, the sublime style, the sublime; the plain style; **stylistics,** stylistic analysis

3 stylist, master of style; rhetorician, rhetor, rhetorizer <old>; mannerist

VERBS **4 phrase, express,** find a phrase for, give expression *or* words to, **word,** state, **frame,** conceive, style, couch, **put in** *or* **into words,** clothe *or* embody in words, couch in terms, express by *or* in words, find words to express; put, present, set out; **formulate,** formularize; paragraph; rhetorize <old>

ADJS **5 phrased,** expressed, worded, formulated, styled, put, presented, couched; stylistic

533 ELEGANCE
<of *language*>

NOUNS **1 elegance,** elegancy; **grace,** gracefulness, gracility; **taste,** tastefulness, good taste; **correctness,** seemliness, comeliness, **propriety,** aptness, fittingness; **refinement,** precision, exactitude, lapidary quality, finish; **discrimination,** choice; **restraint; polish, finish,** terseness, neatness; smoothness, flow, **fluency; felicity,** felicitousness, **ease;** clarity, clearness, lucidity, limpidity, pellucidity, perspicuity; distinction, dignity; **purity,** chastity, chasteness; **plainness,** straightforwardness, directness, **simplicity,** naturalness, unaffectedness, Atticism, unadorned simplicity, gracility, Attic quality; classicism, classicalism; well-rounded or well-turned periods, flowing periods; the right word in the right place, fittingness, appropriateness

2 **harmony, proportion,** symmetry, **balance,** equilibrium, order, orderedness, measure, measuredness, concinnity; rhythm; **euphony,** sweetness, beauty

3 <affected elegance> **affectation,** affectedness, studiedness, **pretentiousness, mannerism,** posiness <Brit>, manneredness, artifice, artfulness, **artificiality,** unnaturalness; **euphuism,** Gongorism, Marinism; **preciousness,** preciosity; euphemism; purism; overelegance, overelaboration, overniceness, overrefinement, hyperelegance, etc

4 purist, classicist, Atticist, plain stylist

5 euphuist, Gongorist, Marinist, précieux <Fr>, précieuse <Fr fem>; phrasemaker, phrasemonger

ADJS 6 **elegant, tasteful, graceful, polished,** finished, round, terse; neat, trim, **refined, exact,** lapidary or lapidarian; **restrained; clear,** lucid, limpid, pellucid, perspicuous; **simple, unaffected, natural,** unlabored, fluent, flowing, **easy; pure,** chaste; **plain,** straightforward, direct, unadorned, gracile, no-frills and vanilla and plain vanilla <all nonformal>; classic, classical; Attic, Ciceronian

7 **appropriate, fit, fitting,** just <old>, **proper, correct, seemly,** comely; **felicitous,** happy, **apt, well-chosen; well-put,** well-expressed, inspired

8 **harmonious, balanced,** symmetrical, orderly, ordered, measured, concinnate, concinnous; **euphonious,** euphonic, euphonical <old>, sweet; **smooth,** tripping, smooth-sounding, fluent, flowing

9 <affectedly elegant> **affected,** euphuistic, euphuistical; elaborate, elaborated; **pretentious, mannered, artificial, unnatural,** posy <Brit>, studied; precious, précieux, précieuse <both Fr>, overnice, overrefined, overelegant, overelaborate, hyperelegant, etc; Gongoristic, Gongoresque, Marinistic

534 INELEGANCE
<of language>

NOUNS 1 **inelegance,** inelegancy; inconcinnity <old>, infelicity; **clumsiness,** cumbrousness, clunkiness and klutziness <both nonformal>, leadenness, heavy-handedness, ham-handedness, hamfistedness <chiefly Brit>, heavy-footedness, heaviness, stiltedness, **ponderousness,** unwieldiness; sesquipedalianism, sesquipedality; turgidity, bombasticness, pompousness 545.1; **gracelessness,** ungracefulness; **tastelessness,** bad taste, **impropriety,** indecorousness, unseemliness; incorrectness, impurity; **vulgarity,** vulgarism, Gothicism <old>, barbarism, barbarousness, **coarseness, unrefinement,** roughness, grossness, rudeness, crudeness, uncouthness; dysphemism; cacology, poor diction; cacophony, uneuphoniousness, harshness; loose or slipshod construction, ill-balanced sentences; lack of finish or polish

ADJS 2 **inelegant, clumsy, clunky** and **klutzy** <both nonformal>, heavy-handed, heavy-footed, ham-handed, ham-fisted <chiefly Brit>, graceless, ungraceful, inconcinnate and inconcinnous <both old>, infelicitous, unfelicitous; **tasteless,** in bad taste, offensive to ears polite; **incorrect, improper; indecorous, unseemly,** uncourtly, undignified; **unpolished, unrefined;** impure, unclassical; **vulgar,** barbarous, barbaric, rude, **crude, uncouth,** Doric, outlandish; low, gross, **coarse,** dysphemistic, doggerel; cacologic, cacological, cacophonous, uneuphonious, harsh, ill-sounding

3 **stiff, stilted, formal,** Latinate, guindé <Fr>, **labored,** ponderous, elephantine, lumbering, cumbrous, leaden, heavy, unwieldy, sesquipedalian, inkhorn, turgid, bombastic, pompous 545.8; **forced,** awkward, cramped, halting; crabbed

535 PLAIN SPEECH

NOUNS 1 **plain speech,** plain speaking, plain-spokenness, plain style, unadorned style, gracility, **plain English,** plain words, common speech, vernacular, household words, words of one syllable; **plainness,** simpleness, simplicity; "more matter with less art"—Shakespeare; soberness, restrainedness; severity, austerity; spareness, leanness, baldness, bareness, starkness, unadornedness, naturalness, unaffectedness; **directness, straightforwardness,** calling a spade a spade, mincing no words, making no bones about it <nonformal>; unimaginativeness, prosaicness, matter-of-factness, prosiness, unpoeticalness; homespun, rustic style; **candor,** frankness, openness

VERBS **2 speak plainly,** waste no words, **call a spade a spade,** come to the point, lay it on the line, not beat about the bush, mince no words, make no bones about it *and* talk turkey <both nonformal>

ADJS **3 plain-speaking,** simple-speaking; **plain,** common; **simple,** unadorned, unvarnished, pure, neat; sober, severe, austere, ascetic, spare, lean, bald, bare, stark, Spartan; **natural, unaffected;** direct, straightforward, woman-to-woman, man-to-man, one-on-one; commonplace, homely, homespun, rustic; **candid,** upfront <nonformal>, plain-spoken, frank, straight-out <nonformal>, open; **prosaic,** prosing, prosy; unpoetical, unimaginative, dull, dry, **matter-of-fact**

ADVS **4 plainly, simply,** naturally, unaffectedly, matter-of-factly; in plain words, plain-spokenly, **in plain English,** in words of one syllable; **directly,** point-blank, to the point; candidly, frankly

PHRS **5** read my lips, I'll spell it out

536 FIGURE OF SPEECH

NOUNS **1 figure of speech** <see list>, **figure, image,** trope, turn of expression, manner *or* way of speaking, ornament, device, flourish, flower; purple passage; imagery, nonliterality, nonliteralness, figurativeness, figurative language; figured *or* florid *or* flowery style, Gongorism, floridity, euphuism

VERBS **2** metaphorize, figure <old>; similize; personify, personalize; symbolize

ADJS **3 figurative,** tropologic, tropological; **metaphorical,** trolatitious; allusive, referential; mannered, figured, ornamented, **flowery** 545.11

ADVS **4 figuratively,** tropologically; **metaphorically;** symbolically; **figuratively speaking,** so to say *or* speak, in a manner of speaking, **as it were**

5 figures of speech

agnomination	anaphora
alliteration	anastrophe
allusion	antiphrasis
anacoluthon	antithesis
anadiplosis	antonomasia
analogy	apophasis
aporia	metalepsis
aposiopesis	metaphor
apostrophe	metonymy
catachresis	mixed metaphor
chiasmus	onomatopoeia,
circumlocution	onomatopy
climax	oxymoron
conversion	paradiastole
ecphonesis	paralepsis
emphasis	paregmenon
enallage	parenthesis
epanaphora	periphrasis
epanodos	personification
epanorthosis	pleonasm
epidiplosis	ploce
epiphora	polyptoton
eroteme	polysyndeton
exclamation	preterition
gemination	prolepsis
hendiadys	prosopopoeia
hypallage	regression
hyperbaton	repetition
hyperbole	rhetorical question
hypozeugma	sarcasm
hypozeuxis	simile, similitude
hysteron-proteron	spoonerism
inversion	syllepsis
irony	symploce
kenning	synecdoche
litotes	Wellerism
malapropism	zeugma
meiosis	

537 CONCISENESS

NOUNS **1 conciseness,** concision, briefness, brachylogy, **brevity,** "the soul of wit"—Shakespeare; shortness, compactness; **curtness,** brusqueness, **crispness, terseness,** summariness; taciturnity 344.2, reserve 344.3; **pithiness,** succinctness, pointedness, sententiousness; compendiousness

2 laconicness, laconism, laconicism, economy of language; laconics

3 aphorism, epigram 973.1; **abridgment** 557

4 abbreviation, shortening, clipping, cutting, pruning, truncation; ellipsis, aposiopesis, contraction, syncope, apocope, elision, crasis, syneresis <all rhetoric>

VERBS **5 be brief, come to the point,** get to the bottom line *or* the nitty-gritty <nonformal>, **make a long story short,** cut the matter short, cut the shit <nonformal>, be telegraphic, waste no words, put it in few words, give more matter and less art; shorten, condense, **abbreviate** 268.6

ADJS **6 concise, brief, short,** "short and

sweet"—Thomas Lodge; **condensed, compressed,** tight, close, compact; compendious 268.8; **curt,** brusque, **crisp, terse,** summary; taciturn 344.9; reserved 344.10; **pithy, succinct; laconic,** Spartan; **abridged, abbreviated,** vest-pocket, synopsized, shortened, clipped, cut, pruned, contracted, truncated, docked; elliptic, aposiopestic; sententious, epigrammatic, epigrammatical, gnomic, aphoristic<al>, **pointed,** to the point

ADVS **7 concisely, briefly,** shortly, standing on one leg; laconically; **curtly,** brusquely, **crisply, tersely,** summarily; **pithily, succinctly,** pointedly; sententiously, aphoristically, epigrammatically

8 in brief, in short, for short, *tout court* <Fr>; in substance, in epitome, in outline; **in a nutshell,** in a capsule; **in a word,** in two words, in a few words, without wasting *or* mincing words; **to be brief,** to come to the point, to cut the matter short, **to make a long story short**

538 DIFFUSENESS

NOUNS **1 diffuseness,** diffusiveness, diffusion; shapelessness, **formlessness** 263, amorphousness, blobbiness <nonformal>, unstructuredness; obscurity 522.3

2 wordiness, verbosity, verbiage, verbalism, verbality; **prolixity, long-windedness,** longiloquence; flow *or* flux of words, cloud of words; **profuseness,** profuseness, profusion; **effusiveness,** effusion, gush, gushing; outpour, tirade; logorrhea, verbal diarrhea, diarrhea of the mouth; **talkativeness 540; copiousness, exuberance,** rampancy, amplitude, extravagance, prodigality, fertility, fecundity, rankness, teemingness, prolificity, prolificacy, productivity, abundance, overflow, fluency <old>; superfluity, superflux, superabundance, overflow, inundation; **redundancy,** pleonasm, repetitiveness, reiterativeness, reiteration, iteration, tautology, macrology; repetition for effect *or* emphasis, palilogy

3 discursiveness, desultoriness, digressiveness, aimlessness; rambling, maundering, meandering, wandering, roving

4 digression, departure, deviation, **discursion,** excursion, excursus, sidetrack, side path, side road, byway, bypath; episode

5 circumlocution, roundaboutness, circuitousness, ambages <old>; deviousness, obliqueness, **indirection;** periphrase, periphrasis

6 amplification, expatiation, enlargement,

expansion, dilation, dilatation, dilating; **elaboration, laboring; development,** explication, unfolding, working-out, fleshing-out, detailing, filling in the empty places

VERBS **7 amplify, expatiate, dilate, expand,** enlarge, **enlarge on,** expand on, **elaborate;** relate *or* rehearse in extenso; detail, particularize; **develop,** open out, fill in, flesh out, evolve, unfold; work out, explicate; descant, relate at large

8 protract, extend, spin out, string out, draw out, stretch out, go on *or* be on about, **drag out,** run out, drive into the ground <nonformal>; pad, fill out; perorate; **speak at length,** spin a long yarn, never finish; verbify, chatter, talk one to death 540.5,6

9 digress, wander, **get off the subject, wander from the subject,** get sidetracked, excurse, ramble, maunder, stray, go astray; depart, **deviate,** turn aside, jump the track; **go off on a tangent,** go up blind alleys

10 circumlocute <nonformal>, say in a roundabout way, talk in circles, **go round about,** go around and around, **beat around** *or* **about the bush,** go round Robin Hood's barn; periphrase

ADJS **11 diffuse,** diffusive; **formless** 263.4, unstructured; **profuse,** profusive; **effusive,** gushing, gushy; copious, exuberant, extravagant, prodigal, fecund, teeming, prolific, productive, abundant, superabundant, overflowing; **redundant,** pleonastic, repetitive, reiterative, iterative, tautologous, parrotlike

12 wordy, verbose; talkative 540.9; **prolix,** windy <nonformal>, **long-winded,** longiloquent; **protracted,** extended, *de longue haleine* <Fr>, lengthy, long, **long-drawn-out,** long-spun, spun-out, endless, unrelenting; padded, filled out

13 discursive, aimless, loose; **rambling, maundering, wandering,** peripatetic, roving; excursive, **digressive,** deviative, **desultory,** episodic; by the way

14 circumlocutory, circumlocutional, **roundabout, circuitous,** ambagious <old>, oblique, indirect; periphrastic

15 expatiating, dilative, dilatative, enlarging, amplifying, expanding; **developmental**

ADVS **16 at length,** *ad nauseam* <L>, at large, in full, *in extenso* <L>, in detail

539 AMBIGUITY

NOUNS **1 ambiguity,** ambiguousness; **equivocalness,** equivocacy, equivocality; **dou-**

ble meaning, amphibology, multivocality, polysemy, polysemousness; punning, paronomasia; double reference, double entendre; twilight zone, gray area; six of one and half dozen of the other; inexplicitness, uncertainty 970; irony, contradiction, oxymoron, enantiosis; levels of meaning, richness of meaning, complexity of meaning

2 <ambiguous word or expression> **ambiguity,** equivoque, equivocal, equivocality; equivocation, amphibology, double entendre; counterword, portmanteau word; polysemant; weasel word; squinting construction; pun 489.8

VERBS 3 equivocate, weasel; ironize; have mixed feelings, be uncertain 970.9

ADJS 4 **ambiguous, equivocal,** equivocatory; multivocal, polysemous, polysemantic, amphibolous, amphibological; two-edged, two-sided, either-or, betwixt and between; bittersweet, mixed; inexplicit, uncertain 970.15; ironic; obscure, mysterious, funny, funny peculiar <nonformal>; enigmatic 522.17

540 TALKATIVENESS

NOUNS 1 **talkativeness, loquacity,** loquaciousness; overtalkativeness, loose tongue, big mouth <nonformal>; gabbiness *and* windiness *and* gassiness <all nonformal>; **garrulousness,** garrulity; **long-windedness, prolixity, verbosity** 538.2; multiloquence, multiloquy; **volubility, fluency, glibness;** fluent tongue, flowing tongue, **gift of gab** <nonformal>; openness, candor, frankness 644.4; effusion, gush, slush; gushiness, **effusiveness;** flow *or* flux *or* spate of words; *flux de bouche, flux de mots,* and *flux de paroles* <all Fr>; **communicativeness** 343.3; gregariousness, sociability, conversableness 582

2 **logomania, logorrhea, diarrhea of the mouth, verbal diarrhea,** *cacoëthes loquendi, furor loquendi* <both L>

3 **chatter, jabber,** gibber, **babble,** babblement, prate, **prating, prattle, palaver,** chat, natter <Brit>, **gabble, gab** *and* jaw-jaw <both nonformal>, blab, **blabber, blather,** blether, blethers <Scots>, clatter, clack, cackle, talkee-talkee; *caquet, caqueterie, bavardage* <all Fr>, twaddle, twattle, **gibble-gabble, bibble-babble, chitter-chatter, prittle-prattle, tittle-tattle,** mere talk, idle talk *or* chatter, "the hare-brained chatter of irresponsible frivolity"—Disraeli; **guff** *and* **gas** *and* **hot air** *and* blah-blah *and* yak *and* yakkety-yak <all nonformal>; **gossip;** nonsense talk 520.2

4 **chatterer, chatterbox, babbler, jabberer, prater, prattler, gabbler,** gibble-gabbler, **gabber** <nonformal>, **blabberer, blabber,** blatherer, patterer, word-slinger, *moulin à paroles* <Fr>, blab, rattle, "agreeable rattle"—Goldsmith; magpie, jay; **windbag** *and* gasbag *and* windjammer *and* hot-air artist *and* motor-mouth *and* ratchet-jaw <all nonformal>; idle chatterer, talkative person, **big** *or* **great talker** <nonformal>, spendthrift of one's tongue

VERBS 5 **chatter, chat, prate, prattle, patter,** palaver, **babble, gab** <nonformal>, natter <Brit>, **gabble, gibble-gabble,** tittle-tattle, **jabber,** gibber, **blab, blabber, blather,** blether, clatter, twaddle, twattle, rattle, clack, natter *and* haver <both Brit>, dither, spout *or* **spout off** <nonformal>, pour forth, **gush,** have a big mouth <nonformal>, love the sound of one's own voice, talk to hear one's head rattle <nonformal>; **jaw** *and* **gas** *and* yak *and* yakkety-yak *and* run off at the mouth *and* beat one's gums <all nonformal>, **shoot off one's mouth** *or* **face** <nonformal>; reel off; **talk on,** talk away, **go on** <nonformal>, run on, rattle on, run on like a mill race; ramble on; talk oneself hoarse, talk till one is blue in the face, talk oneself out of breath; "varnish nonsense with the charms of sound"—Charles Churchill; **talk too much; gossip;** talk nonsense 520.5

6 <nonformal terms> **talk one to death, talk one's head** *or* **ear off,** talk one deaf and dumb, talk one into a fever, talk the hind leg off a mule

7 **outtalk,** outspeak, **talk down,** outlast; filibuster

8 be loquacious *or* garrulous, be a windbag *or* gasbag <nonformal>; have a big mouth *or* bazoo <nonformal>

ADJS 9 **talkative, loquacious, talky,** big-mouthed <nonformal>, overtalkative, garrulous, chatty; gossipy, newsy; gabby *and* windy *and* gassy <all nonformal>, all jaw <nonformal>; multiloquent, multiloquious; **longwinded, prolix, verbose** 538.12; **voluble, fluent; glib,** flip <nonformal>, smooth; candid, frank 644.17; **effusive,** gushy; expansive, **communicative;** conversational; gregarious, sociable

10 **chattering, prattling, prating,** gabbling, jabbering, gibbering, babbling, blabbing, blabbering, blathering

ADVS **11 talkatively, loquaciously,** garru-
lously; **volubly, fluently,** glibly; effu-
sively, gushingly

541 CONVERSATION

NOUNS **1 conversation, converse,** convers-
ing, rapping <nonformal>; interlocution, colloquy; **exchange;** verbal intercourse, conversational interchange, interchange of speech, give-and-take, cross-
talk, rapping <nonformal>, **repartee,**
backchat; **discourse,** colloquial discourse; **communion, intercourse,
communication** 343

2 the art of conversation, "a game of circles, "our account of ourselves"—both
Emerson; "the sweeter banquet of the
mind, "the feast of reason and the flow of
soul"—both Pope

3 talk, palaver, speech, words; confabulation, **confab** <nonformal>; **chinfest** and
chinwag and **talkfest** and **bull session**
<all nonformal>; **dialogue,** duologue,
trialogue; **interview,** question-and-
answer session

4 chat, cozy chat, friendly chat or talk, **little talk,** coze, causerie, **visit** <nonfor-
mal>, gam, tête-à-tête <Fr>, **heart-to-
heart talk** or heart-to-heart; pillow-talk,
intimate discourse

5 chitchat, chitter-chatter, tittle-tattle,
small talk, by-talk, cocktail-party chitchat, beauty-parlor chitchat, tea-table
talk, table talk, idle chat, gossip, backchat

**6 conference, congress, convention, parley,
palaver, confab** <nonformal>, confabulation, **conclave, powwow, huddle**
<nonformal>, **consultation,** pourparler
<Fr>, **meeting;** session, sitting, sit-down
<nonformal>, séance; exchange or inter-
change of views; **council,** council of war;
**discussion; interview, audience; news
conference,** press conference; photo opportunity, photo op <nonformal>; high-
level talk, conference at the summit, summit, summit conference; summitry;
negotiations, bargaining, bargaining session; confrontation, eyeball-to-eyeball
encounter <nonformal>; teleconference;
council fire; conference table, negotiating
table

7 discussion, debate, debating, **deliberation, nonformalogue,** exchange of views,
canvassing, ventilation, airing, review,
treatment, consideration, investigation,
examination, study, analysis, logical
analysis; logical discussion, dialectic;

buzz session <nonformal>, rap or rap
session <nonformal>; **panel,** panel discussion, open discussion, joint discussion, symposium, colloquium, conference, seminar; **forum,** open forum, town
meeting

8 conversationalist, converser, conversa-
tionist; talker, discourser, verbalist,
confabulator; colloquist, colloquialist,
collocutor; conversational partner; interlocutor, interlocutress or interlocutrice or
interlocutrix; parleyer, palaverer; dialog-
ist; Dr Johnson

VERBS **9 converse, talk together, talk** or
speak with, converse with, strike up a
conversation, visit with <nonformal>,
discourse with, **commune with,** communicate with, take counsel with, commerce
with, **have a talk with,** have a word with,
chin <nonformal>, **chew the rag** or **fat**
<nonformal>, **shoot the breeze** <non-
formal>, hold or carry on or join in or engage in a conversation; confabulate, confab <nonformal>; colloque, colloquize;
"inject a few raisins of conversation
into the tasteless dough of existence"—
O Henry; **bandy words; communicate**
343.6,7

10 chat, visit <nonformal>, gam, coze, pass
the time of day, touch base with, have a
friendly or cozy chat; **have a little talk,**
have a heart-to-heart talk, let one's hair
down; talk with one in private, talk with
one tête-à-tête, be closeted with, make
conversation or talk, engage in small talk;
prattle, prittle-prattle, tittle-tattle; **gossip**

11 confer, hold a conference, parley, palaver, powwow, sit down together, meet
around the conference table, **go into a
huddle** <nonformal>, deliberate, take
counsel, counsel, **lay** or **put heads together;** collogue; **confer with,** sit down
with, **consult with, advise with, discuss
with, take up with,** reason with; **discuss,**
talk over; **consult,** refer to, call in; **compare notes,** exchange observations or
views; have conversations; negotiate,
bargain

12 discuss, debate, reason, deliberate, deliberate upon, exchange views or opinions,
talk, **talk over, hash over** <nonformal>,
talk of or about, rap <nonformal>, comment upon, reason about, discourse
about, **consider, treat,** dissertate on, handle, deal with, take up, **go into, examine,**
investigate, talk out, **analyze,** sift, **study,**
canvass, review, pass under review, controvert, ventilate, air, thresh out, reason

the point, consider pro and con; **kick** or **knock around** <nonformal>

ADJS **13** conversational, colloquial, confabulatory, interlocutory; communicative; chatty, chitchatty, cozy

ADVS **14** conversationally, colloquially; *tête-à-tête* <Fr>

542 SOLILOQUY

NOUNS **1 soliloquy**, monology, self-address; **monologue;** aside; solo; monodrama; apostrophe

2 soliloquist, soliloquizer, Hamlet; **monologist**

VERBS **3 soliloquize**, monologize; **talk to oneself,** say to oneself, tell oneself, think out loud or aloud; address the four walls; say aside; do all the talking, monopolize the conversation, hold forth without interruption

ADJS **4** soliloquizing, monologic, monological, self-addressing; apostrophic; soloistic; monodramatic

543 PUBLIC SPEAKING

NOUNS **1 public speaking, declamation, speechmaking, speaking,** speechification <nonformal>, lecturing, speeching; after-dinner speaking; **oratory**, platform oratory or speaking; campaign oratory, stump speaking, the stump, the hustings <Brit>; the soap box; **elocution; rhetoric,** art of public speaking; **eloquence** 544; forensics, **debating;** speechcraft, wordcraft; **preaching**, pulpit oratory, Bible-thumping <nonformal>, the pulpit, homiletics; demagogism, demagogy <chiefly Brit>, demagoguery, rabble-rousing; **pyrotechnics**

2 speech, speeching, speechification <nonformal>, **talk, oration, address,** declamation, harangue; public speech or address, formal speech, set speech, prepared speech or text; campaign speech, stump speech; say; **tirade,** screed, **diatribe,** jeremiad, philippic, invective; after-dinner speech; funeral oration, eulogy; allocution, exhortation, hortatory address, forensic, forensic address; **recitation,** recital, reading; salutatory, salutatory address; valediction, valedictory, valedictory address; inaugural address, inaugural; chalk talk <nonformal>; pep talk <nonformal>; pitch, sales talk 734.5; talkathon, filibuster; peroration; debate

3 lecture, prelection, **discourse; sermon,** sermonette, homily, religious or pulpit discourse; preachment, preaching, preachification <nonformal>; **evangelism,** televison or TV evangelism; travel talk, travelogue

4 speaker, talker, public speaker, speechmaker, speecher, speechifier <nonformal>, spieler and jawsmith <both nonformal>; after-dinner speaker; **spokesman,** spokeswoman; **demagogue,** rabble-rouser; declaimer, ranter, tub-thumper <nonformal>, haranguer, spouter <nonformal>; valedictorian, salutatorian; panelist, debater

5 lecturer, praelector, discourser, reader; **preacher;** sermonizer, sermonist, sermoner, homilist <old>, pulpitarian, pulpiteer <nonformal>, Boanerges, hellfire preacher; **evangelist,** television or TV evangelist; **expositor,** expounder; chalk talker <nonformal>

6 orator, public speaker, platform orator or speaker; rhetorician, rhetor; silver-tongued orator, **spellbinder;** Demosthenes, Cicero, Franklin D Roosevelt, Winston Churchill, William Jennings Bryan, Martin Luther King; **soapbox orator,** soapboxer, stump orator

7 elocutionist, elocutioner; **recitationist,** reciter, diseur, diseuse; reader; improvisator, *improvvisatore* <Ital>

8 rhetorician, teacher of rhetoric, rhetor, elocutionist; speech-writer

VERBS **9 make a speech, give a talk, deliver an address,** speechify <nonformal>, **speak, talk, discourse; address;** stump <nonformal>, go on or take the stump; platform, soapbox; take the floor

10 declaim, hold forth, **orate,** elocute <nonformal>, spout <nonformal>, spiel <nonformal>, mouth; **harangue, rant,** "out-herod Herod"—Shakespeare, tub-thump, perorate, rodomontade; **recite,** read; debate; demagogue, rabble-rouse

11 lecture, prelect, read or deliver a lecture; **preach,** Bible-thump and preachify <both nonformal>, **sermonize,** read a sermon

ADJS **12 declamatory, elocutionary, oratorical, rhetorical,** forensic; eloquent 544.8; demagogic, demagogical

544 ELOQUENCE

NOUNS **1 eloquence, rhetoric, silver tongue,** eloquent tongue, fecundity; **articulateness;** gift of gab <nonformal>, **glibness,** smoothness, slickness; **felicitousness,** felicity; **oratory** 543.1; expression,

expressiveness, command of words *or* language, gift of gab *or* of the gab <nonformal>, gift of expression, vividness, graphicness; pleasing or effective style; **meaningfulness** 518.5

2 **fluency, flow; smoothness, facility, ease; grace,** gracefulness, poetry; **elegance** 533

3 **vigor, force,** power, strength, vitality, drive, sinew, sinewiness, nervousness, nervosity, vigorousness, forcefulness, effectiveness, impressiveness, pizzazz *and* punch *and* clout <all nonformal>; incisiveness, trenchancy, cuttingness, poignancy, bitingness, bite, mordancy; strong language, "thoughts that breathe and words that burn"—Thomas Gray

4 **spirit,** pep <nonformal>, liveliness, raciness, sparkle, vivacity, dash, verve, vividness; piquancy, poignancy, pungency

5 **vehemence, passion,** impassionedness, enthusiasm, **ardor,** ardency, **fervor,** fervency, fire, fieriness, glow, warmth

6 **loftiness,** elevation, sublimity; grandeur, **nobility,** stateliness, majesty, gravity, *gravitas* <L>, solemnity, **dignity**

VERBS 7 **have the gift of gab** *or* **of the gab** <nonformal>, have a tongue in one's head; **spellbind;** shine, "pour the full tide of eloquence along"—Pope

ADJS 8 **eloquent, silver-tongued,** silver; well-speaking, well-spoken, **articulate,** fecund; **glib, smooth,** smooth-spoken, smooth-tongued, **slick; felicitous;** facile, slick as a whistle <nonformal>, spellbinding; Demosthenic, Demosthenian; Ciceronian, Tullian

9 **fluent, flowing,** tripping; **smooth,** pleasing, facile, **easy, graceful, elegant** 533.6

10 **expressive, graphic, vivid,** suggestive, imaginative; well-turned; **meaningful** 518.10

11 **vigorous,** strong, **powerful,** imperative, **forceful,** forcible, vital, driving, sinewy, sinewed, punchy *and* full of piss and vinegar *and* zappy <all nonformal>, **striking, telling, effective,** impressive; incisive, trenchant, cutting, biting, piercing, poignant, penetrating, slashing, mordant, acid, corrosive; sensational

12 **spirited, lively,** peppy *and* gingery <both nonformal>, racy, sparkling, vivacious; piquant, poignant, pungent

13 **vehement,** emphatic, **passionate, impassioned,** enthusiastic, **ardent,** fiery, **fervent,** burning, glowing, warm; urgent, stirring, exciting, stimulating, provoking

14 **lofty, elevated, sublime, grand, majestic,** noble, stately, grave, solemn, dignified; serious, weighty; moving, inspiring

ADVS 15 **eloquently; fluently,** smoothly, glibly, trippingly on the tongue; **expressively,** vividly, graphically; **meaningfully** 518.13; **vigorously,** powerfully, forcefully, spiritedly; tellingly, strikingly, effectively, impressively; **vehemently, passionately,** ardently, fervently, warmly, glowingly, in glowing terms

545 GRANDILOQUENCE

NOUNS 1 **grandiloquence,** magniloquence, lexiphanicism, **pompousness,** pomposity, orotundity; **rhetoric,** mere rhetoric, rhetoricalness; high-flown diction, big *or* tall talk <nonformal>; grandioseness, grandiosity; loftiness, stiltedness; fulsomeness; **pretentiousness,** pretension, **affectation** 533.3; ostentation; **flamboyancy,** showiness, flashiness, gaudiness, meretriciousness, bedizenment, **glitz** <nonformal>, garishness; sensationalism, luridness, Barnumism; **inflation, inflatedness,** swollenness, turgidity, turgescence, flatulence *or* flatulency, tumidness, tumidity, sententiousness, pontification; swollen phrase *or* diction, swelling utterance; platitudinous ponderosity, polysyllabic profundity, pompous prolixity; Johnsonese; prose run mad; convolution, tortuosity, tortuousness, ostentatious complexity *or* profundity

2 **bombast,** bombastry, **fustian,** highfalutin <nonformal>, **rant,** rodomontade; **hot air** <nonformal>; balderdash, gobbledygook <nonformal>

3 high-sounding words, lexiphanicism, hard words; **sesquipedalian word,** big *or* long word, twodollar *or* five-dollar word <nonformal>, **jawbreaker,** jawtwister, mouthful; antidisestablishmentarianism, honorificabilitudinitatibus <Shakespeare>, pneumonoultramicroscopicsilicovolcanoconiosis; polysyllabism, sesquipedalianism, sesquipedality; Latinate diction; academic Choctaw, technical jargon

4 **ornateness, floweriness,** floridness, floridity, lushness, luxuriance; flourish, flourish of rhetoric, flowers of speech *or* rhetoric, **purple patches** *or* **passages,** beauties, fine writing; **ornament,** ornamentation, **adornment, embellishment,** elegant variation, **embroidery, frill,** colors *or* colors of rhetoric <both old>, figure, **figure of speech** 536

5 **phrasemonger,** rhetorician; phraseman, phrasemaker, fine writer, wordspinner; euphuist, Gongorist, Marinist; pedant

VERBS 6 **talk big** <nonformal>, talk highfalutin <nonformal>, phrasemake, **pontificate, blow** <nonformal>, **vapor,** Barnumize; inflate, bombast, lay *or* pile it on <nonformal>, lay it on thick *and* lay it on with a trowel <both nonformal>; smell of the lamp

7 **ornament, decorate, adorn, embellish, embroider,** enrich; overcharge, overlay, overload, load with ornament, festoon, weight down with ornament, flourish <old>; **gild,** gild the lily, trick out, varnish; paint in glowing colors, tell in glowing terms; "to gild refined gold, to paint the lily, to throw a perfume on the violet"—Shakespeare; elaborate, convolute, involve

ADJS 8 **grandiloquent,** magniloquent, **pompous, orotund; grandiose;** fulsome; lofty, elevated, tall <nonformal>, **stilted; pretentious, affected** 533.9; overdone, overwrought; **showy, flashy, ostentatious,** gaudy, glitzy <nonformal>, meretricious, flamboyant, flaming, bedizened, flaunting, garish; lurid, sensational, sensationalistic; **high-flown, high-falutin** <nonformal>, high-flying; high-flowing, **high-sounding, big-sounding,** greatsounding, grandisonant <old>, sonorous; **rhetorical,** declamatory; **pedantic,** inkhorn, lexiphanic <old>; sententious, Johnsonian; convoluted, tortuous, labyrinthine, overelaborate, overinvolved; euphuistic, Gongoresque

9 **bombastic,** fustian, mouthy, **inflated, swollen,** swelling, turgid, turgescent, tumid, tumescent, flatulent, windy *and* gassy <both nonformal>; overadorned, fulsome

10 sesquipedalian, sesquipedal, polysyllabic, jawbreaking *and* jawtwisting <both nonformal>

11 **ornate,** purple <nonformal>, colored, **fancy;** adorned, **embellished, embroidered,** lavish, decorated, festooned, overcharged, overloaded, befrilled; **flowery, florid,** lush, luxuriant; figured, **figurative** 536.3

ADVS 12 **grandiloquently,** magniloquently, **pompously,** grandiosely, fulsomely, loftily, stiltedly, pretentiously; **ostentatiously,** showily; **bombastically,** turgidly, tumidly, flatulently, windily <nonformal>

13 **ornately,** fancily; **flowerily,** floridly

546 LETTER

NOUNS 1 **letter, written character, character, sign, symbol,** graph, digraph, grapheme, allograph, alphabetic character *or* symbol, phonetic character *or* symbol; diacritic, diacritical mark, vowel point; logographic *or* lexigraphic character *or* symbol; ideographic *or* ideogrammic *or* ideogrammatic character *or* symbol; syllabic character *or* symbol, syllabic, syllabogram; pictographic character *or* symbol; cipher, device; monogram; graphy, *mater lectionis* <L>; **writing** 547

2 <phonetic and ideographic symbols> **phonogram;** phonetic symbol; **logogram,** logograph, grammalogue; word letter; **ideogram,** ideograph, phonetic, radical, determinative; **pictograph,** pictogram; **hieroglyphic,** hieroglyph, hieratic symbol, demotic character; **rune,** runic character *or* symbol; **cuneiform, character;** wedge, arrowhead, ogham; kana, hiragana, katakana; **shorthand** 547.8; hieroglyphics

3 **writing system, script, letters; alphabet,** letters of the alphabet, **ABC's;** christcross-row; **phonetic alphabet,** International Phonetic Alphabet *or* IPA; Initial Teaching Alphabet *or* ITA; phonemic alphabet; runic alphabet, futhark; alphabetism; **syllabary;** alphabetics, alphabetology, graphemics; paleography; speech sound 524.13

4 **spelling,** orthography; phonetic spelling *or* respelling, phonetics, phonography; normalization; spelling reform; spelling match *or* bee, spelldown; bad spelling, cacography; spelling pronunciation

5 **lettering,** initialing; **inscription,** epigraph, graffito; alphabetization; transliteration, romanization, pin-yin, Wade-Giles system; transcription

VERBS 6 **letter, initial, inscribe,** character, sign, mark; **capitalize; alphabetize,** alphabet; transliterate, transcribe

7 **spell,** orthographize; spell *or* respell phonetically; spell out, write out, trace out; spell backward; outspell, spell down; syllabify, syllabize, syllable, syllabicate

ADJS 8 **literal, lettered; alphabetic, alphabetical;** abecedarian; graphemic, allographic; large-lettered, majuscule, majuscular, uncial; **capital,** capitalized, upper-case; small-lettered, minuscule, minuscular, lower-case; logographic, logogrammatic, lexigraphic, ideographic, ideogrammic, ideogrammatic, pictographic; transliterated, transcribed

547 WRITING

NOUNS 1 writing, scrivening *or* scrivenery <both old>, inscription, lettering; engrossment; pen, **pen-and-ink;** inkslinging *and* ink spilling <both nonformal>, pen *or* pencil driving *or* pushing <nonformal>; **typing, typewriting;** macrography, micrography; stroke *or* dash of the pen, *coup de plume* <Fr>; secret writing, cryptography 345.6; **alphabet, writing system** 546.3

2 authorship, writing, authorcraft, pencraft, wordsmanship, **composition,** the art of composition, inditing, inditement; one's pen; **creative writing,** literary art, verbal art, literary composition, literary production, verse-writing, short-story writing, novel-writing, playwriting, drama-writing; essay-writing; **expository writing;** technical writing; journalism, newspaper writing, editorial-writing, feature-writing, rewriting; magazine writing; songwriting, lyric-writing, libretto-writing; artistry, literary power, literary artistry, literary talent *or* flair, skill with words *or* language, facility in writing, ready pen; **writer's itch,** graphomania, scribblemania, graphorrhea, *cacoëthes scribendi* <L>; automatic writing; writer's cramp, graphospasm

3 handwriting, hand, script, fist <nonformal>, chirography, **calligraphy,** autography; **manuscript,** scrive <Scots>; **autograph,** holograph; **penmanship,** penscript, pencraft; stylography; graphology, graphanalysis, graphometry; paleography

4 handwriting style; **printing,** handprinting, block letter, **lettering; stationery; writing materials,** paper, foolscap, note paper, pad, papyrus, parchment, tracing paper, typing paper, vellum

5 <good writing> **calligraphy,** fine writing, elegant penmanship, **good hand,** fine hand, good fist <nonformal>, fair hand, copybook hand

6 <bad writing> **cacography, bad hand,** poor fist <nonformal>, cramped *or* crabbed hand, botched writing, childish scrawl, illegible handwriting, *griffonage* <Fr>

7 scribbling, scribblement; **scribble,** scrabble, **scrawl, scratch,** *barbouillage* <Fr>; *pattes de mouche* <Fr>, hen tracks *and* hen scratches <both nonformal>, pothookery, pothooks, pothooks and hangers

8 stenography, shorthand, brachygraphy, tachygraphy; speedwriting; phonography, stenotype; contraction

9 letter, written character 546.1; **alphabet, writing system** 546.3; punctuation 530.15, 18–20

10 <written matter> **writing, the written word; piece;** piece of writing, text, screed; **copy, matter;** printed matter, literature, reading matter; the written word, *literae scriptae* <L>; nonfiction; fiction 722; **composition, work,** opus, production, literary production, literary artefact *or* artifact, lucubration, brainchild; essay, article 556.1; poem; play 704.4; letter 553.2; **document** 549.5,8; **paper,** parchment, scroll; **script,** scrip, scrive <Scots>; **penscript, typescript; manuscript** *or* MS *or* Ms *or* ms, holograph, autograph; **draft,** first draft, second draft, etc, recension, **version;** edited version, finished version, final draft; transcription, transcript, fair copy, engrossment; flimsy; original, author's copy; camera-ready copy; printout, computer printout, hard copy

11 <ancient manuscript> **codex;** scroll; palimpsest, *codex rescriptus* <L>; papyrus, parchment

12 literature, letters, belles lettres, polite literature, humane letters, *litterae humaniores* <L>, republic of letters; **work, literary work, text, literary text; works, complete works, oeuvre, canon, literary canon, author's canon;** serious literature; **classics,** ancient literature; medieval literature, Renaissance literature, etc; national literature, English literature, French literature, etc; contemporary literature; underground literature; pseudonymous literature; folk literature; travel literature; wisdom literature; erotic literature, erotica; pornographic literature, pornography, porn *and* hard porn *and* soft porn <all nonformal>, obscene literature, scatological literature; popular literature, pop literature <nonformal>; kitsch

13 writer, scribbler <nonformal>, **penman,** pen, penner; pen *or* pencil driver *or* pusher <nonformal>, word-slinger, **ink-slinger** *and* ink spiller <both nonformal>, knight of the plume *or* pen *or* quill <nonformal>; **scribe, scrivener, amanuensis, secretary,** recording secretary, **clerk;** letterer; **copyist,** copier, transcriber; chirographer, calligrapher

14 writing expert, graphologist, handwriting expert, graphometrist; paleographer

15 author, writer, scribe <nonformal>,

composer, inditer; authoress, penwoman; **creative writer,** *littérateur* <Fr>, literary artist, literary craftsman *or* artisan *or* journeyman, belletrist, man of letters, literary man; wordsmith, word painter; free lance, free-lance writer; ghostwriter, ghost <nonformal>; collaborator, coauthor; prose writer, logographer; fiction writer, fictioneer <nonformal>; story writer, **short story writer;** storyteller; **novelist;** novelettist; diarist; **newspaperman; annalist; poet** 720.13; **dramatist,** humorist 489.12; scriptwriter, scenario writer, scenarist; nonfiction writer; article writer, magazine writer; **essayist;** monographer; reviewer, critic, literary critic, music critic, art critic, drama critic, dance critic; columnist; pamphleteer; technical writer; copywriter, advertising writer; compiler, encyclopedist, bibliographer

16 **hack writer,** hack, literary hack, Grub Street writer <Brit>, **penny-a-liner, scribbler** <nonformal>, **potboiler** <nonformal>

17 **stenographer,** brachygrapher, tachygrapher; phonographer, stenotypist

18 **typist;** printer

VERBS 19 **write, pen, pencil,** drive *or* push the pen *or* pencil <nonformal>; stain *or* spoil paper <nonformal>, shed *or* spill ink <nonformal>, **scribe,** scrive <Scots>; inscribe, scroll; superscribe; enface; take pen in hand; **put in writing,** put in black and white; **draw up, draft, write out,** make out; **write down, record** 549.16; take down in shorthand; **type; transcribe,** copy out, engross, make a fair copy, copy; trace; **rewrite, revise, edit,** recense, make a recension, make a critical revision

20 **scribble,** scrabble, **scratch, scrawl,** make hen tracks *or* hen *or* chicken scratches <nonformal>, doodle

21 **write,** author, **compose, indite,** formulate, produce, prepare; dash off, knock off *or* out <nonformal>, throw on paper, pound *or* crank *or* grind *or* churn out; free-lance; collaborate, coauthor; ghostwrite, ghost <nonformal>; novelize; scenarize; pamphleteer; editorialize

ADJS 22 **written,** penned, penciled; **inscribed;** engrossed; **in writing, in black and white,** on paper; scriptural, scriptorial, graphic; calligraphic, chirographic, chirographical; stylographic, stylographical; manuscript, autograph, autographic, holograph, holographic, holographical, in one's own hand, under

one's hand; **longhand,** in longhand, in script; **shorthand,** in shorthand; italic, italicized; cursive, running, flowing; graphologic, graphological, graphometric, graphometrical; graphoanalytic, graphoanalytical; typewritten; printed

23 **scribbled,** scrabbled, **scratched, scrawled; scribbly, scratchy, scrawly**

24 **literary,** belletristic; classical

25 auctorial, authorial; polygraphic; graphomaniac, graphomaniacal, scribblemaniac, scribblemaniacal, scripturient <old>

26 **alphabetic,** ideographic, etc 546.8

27 stenographic, stenographical; **shorthand,** in shorthand

28 **clerical, secretarial**

WORD ELEMENTS 29 grapho—, —graphy, —graphia; —graph, —gram; —grapher

548 PRINTING

NOUNS 1 **printing,** publishing, publication, photographic reproduction, photochemical process, phototypography, phototypy; **photoengraving; letterpress,** relief printing, **typography,** letterpress photoengraving; zincography, photozincography; line engraving, halftone engraving; stereotypy; wood-block printing, xylotypography, chromoxylography; intaglio printing, **gravure;** rotogravure, rotary photogravure; planographic printing, planography, **lithography,** typolithography, photolithography, lithogravure, lithophotogravure; offset lithography, offset, dry offset, photo-offset; photogelatin process, albertype, collotype; electronography, electrostatic printing, onset, xerography, xeroprinting; stencil, mimeograph, silk-screen printing; color printing, chromotypography, chromotypy, two-color printing, three-color printing; book printing, job printing, sheetwork; history of printing, palaeotypography; photography 714; **graphic arts, printmaking** 713.1

2 **composition, typesetting, setting,** composing; hand composition, machine composition; hot-metal typesetting, cold-type typesetting, photosetting, photocomposition; imposition; justification; composing stick, galley chase, furniture, quoin; typesetting machine, phototypesetter, phototypesetting machine; computer composition, computerized typesetting; composition tape; line of type, slug; layout, dummy

3 **print, imprint, stamp, impression, im-**

press, letterpress; reprint, reissue; off-print; offcut; offset, setoff, mackle

4 **copy,** printer's copy, manuscript, type-script; **camera-ready copy; matter;** composed matter, live matter, dead matter, standing matter

5 **proof,** proof sheet, pull <Brit>, trial impression; galley, **galley proof,** slip; page proof, foundry proof, plate proof, stone proof, press proof, cold-type proof, color proof, computer proof, engraver's proof, reproduction *or* repro proof, blueprint, blue <nonformal>, vandyke, progressive proof; author's proof; revise

6 **type, print, stamp, letter; type size;** type body *or* shank *or* stem, body, shank, stem, shoulder, belly, back, bevel, beard, feet, groove, nick, face, counter; ascender, descender, serif; lower case, minuscule; upper case, majuscule; capital, cap <nonformal>, small capital, small cap <nonformal>; ligature, logotype; bastard type, bottle-assed type, fat-faced type; **pi;** type lice; **font; face,** typeface; type class, roman, sans serif, script, italic, black letter; case, typecase; point, pica; en, em; typefounders, typefoundry

7 **space,** spacing, patent space, justifying space, justification space; spaceband, slug; quadrat, quad; em quad, en quad; em, en; three-em space, thick space; four-em space, five-em space, thin space; hair space

8 **printing surface, plate,** printing plate; typeform, locked-up page; duplicate plate, electrotype, stereotype, plastic plate, rubber plate; zincograph, zincotype; **printing equipment**

9 **presswork,** makeready; **press, printing press,** printing machine <Brit>; platen press, flatbed cylinder press, cylinder press, rotary press, web press, rotogravure press; bed, platen, web

10 **printed matter; reading matter, text,** letterpress <Brit>; advertising matter; advance sheets

11 **press,** printing office, print shop, printery, printers; publishers, **publishing house; pressroom,** composing room, proofroom

12 **printer,** printworker; **compositor, typesetter,** typographer, Linotyper; keyboarder; stoneman, makeup man; proofer; stereotyper, stereotypist, electrotyper; apprentice printer, devil, printer's devil; **pressman**

13 **proofreader,** reader, printer's reader <Brit>, copyholder; **copyreader,** copy editor

VERBS 14 **print; imprint, impress, stamp,** enstamp <old>; engrave; run, run off, strike; **publish, issue, put in print, bring out, put out, get out;** put to press, put to bed, see through the press; prove, proof, prove up, make *or* pull a proof, pull; overprint; reprint, reissue; mimeograph, hectograph; multigraph

15 autotype, electrotype, Linotype <trademark>, monotype, palaeotype, stereotype; keyboard

16 **compose,** set, set in print; **make up,** impose; justify, overrun; pi, pi a form

17 **copy-edit; proofread,** read, read *or* correct copy

18 <be printed> go to press, come off press, come out, appear in print

ADJS 19 **printed, in print;** typeset

20 **typographic, typographical;** phototypic, phototypographic; chromotypic, chromotypographic; stereotypic, palaeotypographical; **boldface,** bold-faced, blackface, black-faced, full-faced; **lightface,** light-faced; **upper-case, lower-case**

549 RECORD

NOUNS 1 **record, recording,** documentation, written word; **chronicle, annals,** history, story; roll, **rolls,** pipe roll <Brit>; **account; register, registry,** rota, roster, scroll, catalog, inventory, table, list 870; letters, correspondence; **vestige, trace,** memorial, token, relic, remains

2 **archives,** public records, government archives, government papers, presidential papers, historical documents, historical records, memorabilia; cartulary; biographical records, life records, biographical material, papers, ana; parish rolls *or* register *or* records

3 registry, registry office; archives, files; chancery; National Archives, Library of Congress; Somerset House <Brit>

4 **memorandum, memo** <nonformal>, memoir, *aide-mémoire* <Fr>, memorial; **reminder** 988.6; **note, notation,** annotation, jotting, docket, marginal note, marginalia, scholium, scholia, adversaria, footnote; **entry,** register, **registry,** item; **minutes**

5 **document,** official document, legal document, legal paper, legal instrument, **instrument,** writ, **paper,** parchment, scroll, roll, **writing,** script, scrip; holograph, chirograph; **papers,** ship's papers; docket, **file,** personal file, **dossier;** blank, form

6 **certificate,** certification, **ticket; author-**

ity, authorization; **credential, voucher, warrant,** warranty, testimonial; note; **affidavit,** sworn statement, notarized statement, deposition, witness, attestation, *procès-verbal* <Fr>; **visa,** *visé* <Fr>; **bill of health,** clean bill of health; navicert <Brit>; **diploma,** sheepskin <nonformal>; certificate of proficiency, testamur <Brit>; birth certificate, death certificate

7 **report, bulletin, brief, statement, account,** accounting; account rendered, *compte rendu* <Fr>; **minutes,** the record, proceedings, transactions, acta; **yearbook,** annual; **returns,** census report *or* returns, election returns, tally

8 <official documents> state paper, white paper; blue book, green book, Red Book <Brit>, white book, yellow book, *livre jaune* <Fr>; gazette, official journal, Congressional Record, Hansard

9 <registers> genealogy, pedigree, studbook; Social Register, blue book; directory; Who's Who; Almanach de Gotha; Burke's Peerage Baronetage and Knightage; Debrett's Peerage Baronetage Knightage and Companionage; Red Book, Royal Kalendar; Lloyd's Register

10 <recording media> bulletin board, notice board; scoresheet, scorecard, scoreboard; **tape,** magnetic tape, videotape, ticker tape; **computer disk,** diskette, floppy disk *or* floppy, hard disk, disk cartridge; memory; compact disk *or* CD; phonograph record, disc *or* disk, platter <nonformal>; film, motion-picture film; slip, card, index card, filing card; library catalog, catalog card; microcard, microfiche, microdot, microfilm; **file** 870.3

11 <record books> **notebook, pocketbook,** pocket notebook, blankbook; loose-leaf notebook, spiral notebook; **memorandum book,** memo book <nonformal>, commonplace book, adversaria; address book; workbook; **blotter,** police blotter; docket, court calendar; **calendar,** desk calendar, appointment calendar, appointment schedule, engagement book, agenda; **tablet,** table <old>, writing tablet; diptych, triptych; pad, **scratch pad; scrapbook,** memory book, **album; diary, journal; log,** ship's log, **logbook; account book, ledger,** daybook; **cashbook,** petty cashbook; Domesday Book; catalog, classified catalog; yearbook, annual; guestbook, guest register, register

12 **monument,** monumental *or* memorial record, **memorial;** necrology, obituary, **memento,** remembrance, testimonial;

cup, trophy, prize, ribbon, plaque; **marker;** inscription; **tablet,** stone, hoarstone <Brit>, boundary stone, memorial stone; **pillar,** stele *or* stela, shaft, column, memorial column, rostral column, manubial column; cross; war memorial; arch, memorial arch, triumphal arch; memorial statue, bust; monolith, obelisk, **pyramid; tomb,** grave 309.16; **gravestone, tombstone;** memorial tablet, brass; headstone, footstone; mausoleum; cenotaph; cairn, mound, barrow, cromlech, dolmen, megalith, menhir, cyclolith; **shrine,** reliquary, tope, stupa

13 recorder, registrar 550.1

14 **registration, register, registry; recording,** record keeping, recordation; archiving; minuting, **enrollment,** matriculation, enlistment; impanelment; **listing, tabulation, cataloging,** inventorying, indexing; chronicling; **entry,** insertion, entering, posting; docketing, inscribing, **inscription; booking, logging;** recording instruments

VERBS 15 **record,** put *or* place upon record; **inscribe,** enscroll; **register, enroll,** matriculate, check in; impanel; poll; **file,** index, **catalog,** calendar, **tabulate, list,** docket; **chronicle;** minute, put in the minutes *or* on the record, spread on the record; commit to *or* preserve in an archive, archive; **write,** commit *or* reduce to writing, put in writing, put in black and white, put on paper; **write out; make out,** fill out; **write up,** chalk, chalk up; **write down, mark down, jot down, put down, set down, take down; note,** note down, make a note, make a memorandum; **post,** post up; **enter,** make an entry, insert, write in; **book, log;** cut, carve, grave, engrave, incise; put on tape, tape, taperecord, cut; videotape

ADJS 16 **recording,** recordative <old>, registrational; certificatory

17 **recorded,** registered; inscribed, written down, down; **filed,** indexed, enrolled, **entered,** logged, booked, posted; documented; minuted; **on record,** on file, on the books; official, legal, of record

18 **documentary,** documentational, documental, archival; epigraphic, inscriptional; necrological, obituary; testimonial

550 RECORDER

NOUNS 1 **recorder,** recordist; **registrar,** register, prothonotary; archivist, documentalist; master of the rolls <Brit>, *custos*

rotulorum <L>; librarian; **clerk,** record
clerk, penpusher <nonformal>, filing
clerk; town *or* municipal clerk, county
clerk; bookkeeper, accountant; **scribe,**
scrivener; **secretary,** amanuensis; **stenographer** 547.17; notary, notary public;
marker; scorekeeper, scorer, official
scorer, timekeeper; engraver, stonecutter

2 **annalist,** genealogist, chronicler;
cliometrician; historian

551 INFORMATION

NOUNS 1 **information,** info <nonformal>,
gen <Brit nonformal>, **facts, data,
knowledge** 927; public knowledge, open
secret, common knowledge; general information; factual information, hard
information; **evidence, proof** 956; **enlightenment,** light; incidental information, sidelight; **acquaintance,** familiarization, briefing; **instruction** 568.1; **intelligence; the dope** *and* the goods *and* **the
scoop** *and* the skinny *and* the straight
skinny *and* the inside skinny <all nonfor-
mal>; transmission, **communication**
343; **report, word,** message, presentation,
account, **statement,** mention; white paper, white book, blue book, command
paper <Brit>; dispatch, bulletin, communiqué, handout <nonformal>, fact
sheet, release; publicity, promotional
material, broadside; **notice,** notification;
notice board, bulletin board; announcement, publication 352; directory,
guidebook 574.10

2 **inside information,** private *or* confidential information; **the lowdown** *and* **inside
dope** *and* inside wire *and* **hot tip** <all
nonformal>; insider; pipeline <nonfor-
mal>; privileged information, classified
information

3 **tip** *and* tip-off *and* **pointer** <all nonfor-
mal>, clue, cue; steer <nonformal>;
advice; whisper, passing word, **word to
the wise,** word in the ear, bug in the ear
<nonformal>, bee in the bonnet <non-
formal>; warning, caution, monition,
alerting, sound bite

4 **hint,** gentle hint, **intimation, indication,
suggestion,** mere *or* **faint suggestion, suspicion, inkling,** whisper, **glimmer, glimmering; cue, clue,** index, **symptom, sign,**
spoor, track, scent, sniff, whiff, telltale,
tip-off <nonformal>; **implication, insinuation, innuendo;** broad hint, gesture,
signal, nod, wink, look, nudge, kick,
prompt

5 **informant, informer, source,** teller, inter-

viewee, enlightener; **adviser,** monitor; **reporter,** notifier, **announcer,** annunciator;
spokesperson, spokespeople, spokeswoman, spokesman, press secretary, press
officer, information officer, mouthpiece;
communicator, communicant, publisher;
authority, witness, expert witness; **tipster**
<nonformal>, **tout** <nonformal>; news-
monger, gossipmonger; **information
medium** *or* **media, mass media,** print media, electronic media, the press, radio,
television; channel, the grapevine; information network, network; information
center; public relations officer

6 **informer, betrayer,** double-crosser
<nonformal>, delator <old>; **snitch** *and*
snitcher <both nonformal>; whistle-
blower <nonformal>; **tattler, tattletale,
telltale, talebearer; blab** *or* blabber *or*
blabberer *or* blabbermouth <all nonfor-
mal>; **squealer** *and* preacher *and* **stool
pigeon** *and* stoolie *and* **fink** *and* rat <all
nonformal>, nark <Brit nonformal>;
spy 576.9

7 information *or* communication theory;
data storage *or* retrieval, EDP *or* electronic data processing; signal, noise;
encoding, decoding; bit; redundancy,
entropy; channel; information *or* communication explosion

VERBS 8 **inform, tell, speak on** *or* **for,** apprise, **advise, advertise,** advertise of, **give
word,** mention to, **acquaint, enlighten,** familiarize, brief, verse, give the facts, give
an account of, give by way of information; **instruct;** possess *or* seize one of the
facts; **let know, have one to know, give** *or*
lead one to believe *or* **understand;** tell
once and for all; notify, give notice *or* notification, serve notice; **communicate**
343.6,7; bring *or* send *or* leave word; **report** 552.11; **disclose** 351.4; put in a
new light, shed new *or* fresh light upon

9 **post** *and* **keep one posted** <both nonfor-
mal>; wise up *and* clue *or* fill in *and* bring
up to speed *or* date *and* put in the picture
<all nonformal>

10 **hint, intimate, suggest, insinuate, imply,
indicate,** adumbrate, lead *or* leave one to
gather, justify one in supposing, give *or*
drop *or* throw out a hint, give an inkling
of, **hint at; leak,** let slip out; allude to,
make an allusion to, glance at <old>;
prompt, give the cue, put onto; put in *or*
into one's head, put a bee in one's bonnet

11 **tip** *and* tip off *and* **give one a tip** <all non-
formal>, alert; **give a pointer to** <nonfor-
mal>; put hep *or* hip <nonformal>, **let in
on,** let in on the know <nonformal>; let

next to *and* put next to *and* **put on to** *and* put on to something hot <all nonformal>; **confide**, confide to, entrust with information, give confidential information, mention privately *or* confidentially, whisper, buzz, breathe, whisper in the ear, **put a bug in one's ear** <nonformal>

12 **inform on** *or* **against, betray; tattle;** turn informer; testify against, **bear witness against;** turn state's evidence, turn king's *or* queen's evidence <Brit>

13 <nonformal terms> **sell one out** *or* **down the river,** tell on, blab, snitch, squeal, peach <old>, sell out, sing, rat, stool, fink, nark, finger, put the finger on, blow the whistle, shop <Brit>, dime, drop a dime, spill one's guts, spill the beans, squawk, weasel

14 **learn, come to know, be informed** *or* **apprised of,** have it reported, get the facts, **get wise to** <nonformal>, **get hep to** *and* **next to** *and* **on to** <all nonformal>; become conscious *or* aware of, become alive *or* awake to, awaken to, tumble to <nonformal>, open one's eyes to

15 **know** 927.12, be informed *or* apprised, have the facts, be in the know <nonformal>, **come to one's knowledge,** come to *or* reach one's ears; be told, **hear, overhear,** hear tell of *and* hear say <both nonformal>; get scent *or* wind of; **know well** 927.13; have inside information, know where the bodies are buried <nonformal>

16 **keep informed,** keep posted <nonformal>, stay briefed, **keep up on,** keep up to date *or* au courant, keep abreast of the times; **keep track of,** keep count *or* account of, keep watch on, keep tab *or* tabs on <nonformal>, keep a check on, keep an eye on

ADJS 17 **informed** 927.18–20; informed of, in the know 927.16, clued-in *or* clued-up <nonformal>

18 **informative,** informing, informational; **instructive, enlightening;** educative, educational; advisory, monitory; **communicative**

19 telltale, tattletale, kiss-and-tell

ADVS 20 from information received, according to reports *or* rumor, from notice given, as a matter of general information, by common report, from what one can gather, as far as anyone knows

552 NEWS

NOUNS 1 **news, tidings, intelligence, information, word,** advice; newsiness

<nonformal>; newsworthiness; a nose for news; **journalism,** reportage, coverage, news coverage; **the press,** the fourth estate, the press corps, print journalism, electronic journalism, broadcast journalism, broadcast news, radio journalism, television journalism; **news medium** *or* **media,** newspaper, newsletter, newsmagazine, radio, television, press association, news service, news agency, press agency, wire service, telegraph agency; press box, press gallery; yellow press, tabloid press; pack journalism

2 **good news,** good word, **glad tidings;** gospel, evangel; bad news

3 **news item,** piece *or* budget of news; **article, story,** piece; copy; scoop *and* beat <both nonformal>, exclusive; breaking story, newsbreak; follow-up, sidebar; spot news; outtake; sound bite

4 **message, dispatch, word, communication, communiqué,** advice, press release, release; express <Brit>; embassy, embassage <old>; **letter** 553.2; **telegram** 347.14; pneumatogram, *petit bleu* <Fr>

5 **bulletin,** news report, **flash**

6 **report, rumor,** flying rumor, unverified *or* unconfirmed report, **hearsay,** *on-dit* <Fr>, **scuttlebutt** *and* latrine rumor <both nonformal>; **talk, whisper, buzz, rumble,** bruit, cry; idea afloat, news stirring; **common talk,** town talk, **talk of the town,** topic of the day, *cause célèbre* <Fr>; **grapevine; canard,** roorback

7 **gossip,** gossiping, gossipry, gossip-mongering, mongering, back-fence gossip <nonformal>, newsmongering; **talebearing,** taletelling; **tattle,** tittle-tattle, chit-chat, **talk,** idle talk, small talk, by-talk; "putting two and two together, and making it five"—Pascal; piece of gossip, groundless rumor, tale, story

8 **scandal, dirt** <nonformal>, **malicious gossip,** "gossip made tedious by morality"—Oscar Wilde; juicy morsel, tidbit, choice bit of dirt <nonformal>; **scandalmongering;** gossip column; character assassination, **slander** 512.3; whispering campaign

9 **newsmonger, rumormonger, scandalmonger, gossip,** gossipmonger, gossiper, *yenta* <Yiddish>, quidnunc, **busybody,** tabby <nonformal>; **talebearer,** taleteller, telltale, **tattletale** <nonformal>, tattler, tittle-tattler, "a tale-bearing animal"—J Harrington; gossip columnist; reporter, newspaperman

10 <secret news channel> **grapevine, grape-**

vine telegraph, bush telegraph <Australia>; **pipeline;** a litle bird *or* birdie

VERBS **11 report,** give a report, give an account of, tell, relate, rehearse <old>; write up, make out *or* write up a report; gather the news, newsgather; dig *or* dig up dirt <nonformal>; bring word, tell the news, break the news, give tidings of; bring glad tidings, give the good word; announce 352.12; put around, spread, **rumor** 352.10; clue in *or* clue up <nonformal>, **inform** 551.8

12 gossip, talk over the back fence <nonformal>; **tattle,** tittle-tattle; clatter <Scots>, **talk;** retail gossip, **dish the dirt** <nonformal>, tell idle tales

ADJS **13 newsworthy,** front-page, with news value, newsy; reportorial

14 gossipy, gossiping, newsy; **talebearing,** taletelling

15 reported, rumored, whispered; rumored about, talked about, whispered about, bruited about, bandied about; **in the news, in circulation, in the air, going around,** going about, **current, rife,** afloat, in every one's mouth, on all tongues, on the street, all over the town; made public 352.17

ADVS **16** reportedly, allegedly, as they say, as it is said, **as the story goes** *or* runs, as the fellow says <nonformal>, it is said

553 CORRESPONDENCE

NOUNS **1 correspondence, letter writing,** written communication, exchange of letters, epistolary intercourse *or* communication; personal correspondence, business correspondence; mailing, mass mailing

2 letter <see list>, **epistle, message, communication, dispatch, missive,** favor <old>; personal letter, business letter; **note, line,** chit, billet <old>; **reply, answer, acknowledgment,** rescript

3 card, postcard, postal card, lettercard <Brit>; picture postcard

4 mail, post <chiefly Brit>, **postal services,** letter bag; post day <Brit>; mailing list; junk mail <nonformal>; direct mail, direct-mail advertising *or* selling, mail-order selling; mail solicitation; fan mail

5 postage; stamp, postage stamp; frank; postmark, cancellation; postage meter

6 mailbox, postbox *and* letter box <both chiefly Brit>, pillar box <Brit>; letter drop, mail drop; mailing machine *or* mailer; mailbag, postbag <Brit>

7 postal service, postal system; post office

or PO, general post office *or* GPO, sub post office, sea post office, mailboat; **mailman, postman;** mail clerk, post-office *or* postal clerk; postal union, Universal Postal Union

8 correspondent, letter writer, writer, communicator; pen pal <nonformal>; addressee

9 address, name and address, direction <old>, **destination,** superscription; zone, postal zone, zip code *or* zip, postal code <Canada>, postcode <Brit>; letterhead, billhead; drop, accommodation address <Brit>

VERBS **10 correspond,** correspond with, **communicate with, write, write to,** write a letter, send a letter to, send a note, **drop a line** <nonformal>; use the mails; keep up a correspondence, exchange letters

11 reply, answer, acknowledge; reply by return mail

12 mail, post, dispatch, send; airmail

13 address, direct, superscribe

ADJS **14** epistolary; **postal,** post; letter; mail-order, direct-mail; mail-in; mailable; send-in, sendable

PHRS **15** please reply, RSVP *or répondez s'il vous plaît* <Fr>

16 kinds of letters

aerogram	letter of delegation
air letter	letter of introduction
airgraph <Brit>	letter of marque
apostolic *or* papal brief	letter of request
	letter of resignation
bull	letter overt
chain letter	letter patent
circular letter	letter rogatory
cover *or* covering letter	letter testamentary
	love letter *or billet*
dead letter	*doux* <Fr>
dimissory letter *or* dimissorial	market letter
	monitory *or* monitory letter
drop letter	newsletter
encyclical	open letter
encyclical letter	paschal letter
fan letter	pastoral letter
form letter	poison-pen letter
letter credential	round robin
letter of credence	
letter of credit	

554 BOOK

NOUNS **1 book, volume, tome;** publication, writing, **work, opus, production;** title; opusculum, opuscule; **trade book; textbook,** schoolbook; **reference book,** playbook; songbook 708.28; notebook 549.11; storybook, **novel; best seller;** coffee-table book; nonbook; **children's**

book, juvenile book, juvenile; picture book; coloring book, sketchbook; prayer book, psalter, psalmbook; **classic,** the book, the bible, magnum opus, great work, standard work, definitive work

2 **publisher,** book publisher; publishing house, press, small press, vanity press; **editor,** trade editor, reference editor, juvenile editor, textbook editor, dictionary editor, college editor, line editor; acquisitions editor, executive editor, managing editor, editor-in-chief; picture editor; packager; copy editor, production editor, permissions editor; **printer,** book printer; **bookbinder,** bibliopegist; **bookdealer, bookseller,** book agent, book salesman; book manufacturer, press

3 **book, printed book, bound book,** bound volume, cased book, casebound book, cloth-bound book, clothback, leather-bound book; manufactured book, finished book; packaged book; **hardcover,** hardcover book, hardbound, hardbound book, hard book; **paperback,** paper-bound book; pocket book, soft-cover, soft-bound book, limp-cover book

4 **volume, tome;** folio; quarto *or* 4to; octavo *or* 8vo; twelvemo *or* 12mo; sextodecimo *or* sixteenmo *or* 16mo; octodecimo *or* eighteenmo *or* 18mo; imperial, super, royal, medium, crown; trim size

5 **edition,** issue; volume, number; **printing,** impression, press order, print order, print run; copy; series, set, boxed set, collection, library; library edition; back number; **trade edition,** subscription edition, subscription book; school edition, text edition

6 **rare book,** early edition; first edition; Elzevir, Elzevir book *or* edition; Aldine, Aldine book *or* edition; manuscript, scroll, codex; incunabulum, cradle book

7 **compilation,** omnibus; symposium; collection, collectanea, miscellany; collected works, selected works, complete works, *œuvres* <Fr>, canon; **miscellanea,** analects; ana; chrestomathy, delectus; **anthology,** garland, florilegium; flowers, beauties; garden; *Festschrift* <Ger>; quotation book; album, photograph album; scrapbook

8 **handbook, manual,** enchiridion, vade mecum, gradus, how-to book <nonformal>; **cookbook,** cookery book <Brit>; nature book, field guide; travel book, **guidebook** 574.10

9 **reference book,** work of reference; **encyclopedia,** cyclopedia; **concordance;** catalog; calendar; index; classified catalog, *catalogue raisonné* <Fr>, dictionary catalog; **directory,** city directory; telephone directory, telephone book, phone book <nonformal>; **atlas, gazetteer;** studbook; source book, casebook; record book 549.11; **language reference book** <see list>; **dictionary,** lexicon, wordbook, Webster's; glossary, gloss, **vocabulary,** onomasticon, nomenclator; **thesaurus, Roget's,** storehouse *or* treasury of words

10 **textbook, text, schoolbook, manual,** manual of instruction; **primer,** alphabet book, abecedary, abecedarium; hornbook, battledore; gradus, exercise book, workbook; **grammar, reader;** spelling book, speller, casebook

11 **booklet, pamphlet, brochure, chapbook, leaflet, folder, tract;** circular 352.8; comic book

12 **makeup, design;** front matter, preliminaries, text, back matter; head, fore edge, back, tail; page, leaf, folio; type page; trim size; flyleaf, endpaper, endleaf, endsheet, signature; recto, verso *or* reverso; title page, half-title page; title, bastard title, binder's title, subtitle, running title; copyright page, imprint, printer's imprint, colophon; catchword, catch line; dedication, inscription; acknowledgments, preface, foreword, introduction; contents, contents page, table of contents; errata; bibliography; index

13 **part, section,** book, volume; article; serial, installment, *livraison* <Fr>; fascicle; **passage,** phrase, clause, verse, paragraph, chapter, column

14 **bookbinding,** bibliopegy; **binding, cover, book cover,** case, bookcase, hard binding, soft binding, mechanical binding, spiral binding, comb binding, plastic binding; library binding; headband, footband, tailband; **jacket, book jacket, dust jacket,** dust cover, wrapper; slipcase, slipcover; book cloth, binder's cloth, binder's board, binder board; folding, tipping, gathering, collating, sewing; **signature;** collating mark, niggerhead; Smyth sewing, side sewing, saddle stitching, wire stitching, stapling, perfect binding; smashing, gluing-off, trimming, rounding, backing, lining, lining-up; casemaking, stamping, casing-in

15 <bookbinding styles> Aldine, Arabesque, Byzantine, Canevari, cottage, dentelle, Etruscan, fanfare, Grolier, Harleian, Jansenist, Maioli, pointillé, Roxburgh

16 **bookstore, bookshop,** *librairie* <Fr>,

bookseller's; **bookstall**, bookstand; **book club**

17 **bookholder, bookrest**, book support, **book end; bookcase**, revolving bookcase *or* bookstand, bookrack, bookstand, **bookshelf**; stack, bookstack; book table, book tray, book truck; folder, folio; **portfolio**

18 **booklover**, philobiblist, bibliophile, bibliolater, book collector, bibliomane, bibliomaniac, bibliotaph; **bookworm**, bibliophage; book-stealer, biblioklept

19 **bibliology**, bibliography; bookcraft, bookmaking, book printing, book production, book manufacturing, bibliogenesis, bibliogony; bookselling, bibliopolism

ADJS 20 **bibliological**, bibliographical; bibliothecal, bibliothecary; bibliopolic; bibliopegic

21 **language reference books**

bilingual dictionary	foreign-language dictionary
biographical dictionary	geographical dictionary *or* gazetteer
children's dictionary	
college dictionary	
desk dictionary	glossary
dialect dictionary	idiom dictionary
dictionary of quotations	rhyming dictionary
	Roget's Thesaurus
dictionary of science, electronic, psychology, philosophy, etc	school dictionary
	synonym dictionary
	thesaurus
etymological dictionary *or* etymologicon	unabridged dictionary
	usage dictionary

555 PERIODICAL

1 **periodical, serial, journal**, gazette; ephemeris; **magazine**, book *and* zine <both nonformal>; pictorial; review; organ, **house organ; trade journal**, trade magazine; daily, weekly, biweekly, bimonthly, fortnightly, monthly, quarterly; annual, yearbook; daybook, diary 549.11

2 **newspaper**, news, **paper**, sheet *or* rag <both nonformal>, **gazette**, daily newspaper, daily, weekly newspaper, weekly, neighborhood newspaper, national newspaper; newspaper of record; **tabloid**, extra, special, extra edition, special edition

3 **the press**, journalism, the public press, **the fourth estate;** print medium, the print media, print journalism, the print press, the public print; Fleet Street <Brit>; **wire service**, newswire, Associated Press, AP; United Press International, UPI; Reuters; **publishing, newspaper publishing, magazine publishing; the publishing industry, communications**, mass media,

the communications industry, public communication; satellite publishing

4 **journalist, newspaperman, newspaperwoman, newsman, newswoman**, journo <Brit nonformal>, newspeople, ink-stained wretch, pressman <Brit>, newswriter, gazetteer <old>, gentleman *or* representative of the press; **reporter**, newshawk *and* newshound <both nonformal>; leg man <nonformal>; interviewer; investigative reporter; **cub reporter; correspondent, foreign correspondent**, war correspondent, special correspondent, own correspondent, stringer; publicist; rewriter, **rewrite man;** reviser, diaskeuast; **editor**, subeditor, managing editor, city editor, news editor, sports editor, woman's editor, feature editor, **copy editor**, copyman, copy chief, slotman; reader, **copyreader;** editorial writer, leader writer <Brit>; **columnist**, paragrapher, paragraphist; **photographer, news photographer**, photojournalist; paparazzo

ADJS 5 **journalistic**, journalese <nonformal>; **periodical**, serial; magazinish, magaziny; newspaperish, newspapery; **editorial; reportorial**

556 TREATISE

NOUNS 1 **treatise**, piece, treatment, handling, tractate, tract; contribution; examination, survey, **discourse, discussion**, disquisition, descant, exposition, screed; homily; memoir; dissertation, **thesis; essay**, theme; pandect; excursus; **study**, lucubration, étude; **paper**, research paper, term paper; **sketch**, outline, aperçu; causerie; **monograph**, research monograph; *morceau* <Fr>, paragraph, **note;** preliminary study, introductory study, first approach, prolegomenon; **article**, feature, special article

2 **commentary**, commentation <old>; **comment, remark; criticism**, critique, *compte-rendu critique* <Fr>, analysis; **review**, critical review, **report**, notice, **write-up** <nonformal>; **editorial**, leading article *or* leader <both Brit>; gloss, running commentary

3 **discourser**, discusser, disquisitor, expositor, descanter; symposiast, discussant; **essayist;** monographer, monographist; tractation, tractator <old>; **writer, author** 547.15

4 **commentator**, commenter; expositor, expounder; annotator, scholiast; glossarist, glossographer; **critic; reviewer**, book re-

viewer; **editor;** editorial writer, editorialist, leader writer <Brit>; news analyst; publicist

VERBS **5 write upon,** touch upon, **discuss, treat, treat of, deal with,** take up, handle, go into, inquire into, survey; discourse, dissert, dissertate, descant; **comment upon,** remark upon; **criticize, review, write up**

ADJS **6** dissertational, disquisitional, discoursive; expository, expositorial, expositive; essayistic; monographic, commentative, commentatorial; critical

557 ABRIDGMENT

NOUNS **1 abridgment,** compendium, compend, *abrégé* <Fr>, **condensation,** short *or* shortened version, condensed version, abbreviation, abbreviature, brief, digest, **abstract,** epitome, **précis, capsule,** nutshell *or* capsule version, capsulization, encapsulation, sketch, thumbnail sketch, **synopsis,** conspectus, syllabus, *aperçu* <Fr>, **survey, review,** overview, pandect, bird's-eye view; **outline,** skeleton, draft; topical outline; head, rubric

2 summary, résumé, recapitulation, recap <nonformal>, rundown, run-through; **summation;** sum, substance, sum and substance, **wrapup** <nonformal>; pith, meat, gist, core, essence, main point 996.6

3 excerpt, extract, selection, extraction, excerption, snippet; passage, selected passage; **clip** <nonformal>, film clip, outtake, sound bite <nonformal>

4 excerpts, *excerpta* <L>, **extracts, gleanings,** cuttings, clippings, snippets; flowers, florilegium, **anthology;** fragments; analects; **miscellany,** miscellanea; **collection,** collectanea; ana

VERBS **5 abridge, shorten** 268.6, **condense, cut, clip; summarize,** synopsize, wrap up <nonformal>; **outline, sketch,** sketch out, hit the high spots; capsule, capsulize, encapsulate; **put in a nutshell**

ADJS **6 abridged,** condensed; shortened, clipped; nutshell, compendious, **brief** 268.8

ADVS **7** in brief, in summary, in sum, in a nutshell 537.8

558 LIBRARY

1 library, book depository; learning center; media center, media resource center, information center; **public library,** town *or* city *or* municipal library, county library, state library; school library, community college library, college library, university library; **special library,** medical library, law library, art library, etc; **circulating library, lending library** <Brit>; rental library; **book wagon, bookmobile;** bookroom, bookery <old>, *bibliothèque* <Fr>, *bibliotheca* <L>, athenaeum; reading room; **national library,** Bibliothèque Nationale, Bodleian Library, British Library, Deutsche Bücherei, Library of Congress, Vatican Library, Faculty of Advocates Library; American Library Association *or* ALA, Association of College and Research Libraries, Special Libraries Association, International Federation of Library Associations, American Society for Information Science, Medical Library Association, Association of Library and Information Service Educators, Art Library Society of North America, etc

2 librarianship, professional librarianship; **library science,** information science, library services, library and information services, library and information studies

3 librarian, professional librarian, library professional; **director, head librarian, chief librarian;** head of service; library services director

4 bibliography <see list>, Modern Language Association Bibliography; **index** <see list>; Books in Print, Paperbound Books in Print; **publisher's catalog,** publisher's list, backlist; National Union Catalog, Library of Congress Catalog, General Catalogue of Printed Books <Brit>, Union List of Serials; **library catalog,** computerized catalog, on-line catalog, integrated online system; CD-ROM workstation

5 bibliographies

annotated bibliography	cumulative bibliography
annual bibliography	national bibliography
bibliography of bibliographies	period bibliography
critical bibliography	subject bibliography
	trade bibliography

6 indexes to periodicals

Art Index	Humanities Index
Bibliography Index	Index Medicus
Business Periodicals Index	New York Times Index
Cumulative Book Index	PsycLIT
Dissertation Abstracts Ondisc	Public Affairs Information Service Bulletin *or* PAIS
Education Index	Reader's Guide to Periodical Literature
General Science Index	

Religion Index
Social Sciences Index
Sociofile

The Philosopher's
Index

559 RELATIONSHIP BY BLOOD

NOUNS **1 blood relationship,** blood, ties of
blood, consanguinity, common descent
or ancestry, biological *or* genetic relationship, **kinship,** kindred, **relation,
relationship,** sibship; propinquity; cognation; agnation, enation; filiation,
affiliation; alliance, connection, **family
connection** *or* tie; motherhood, maternity; fatherhood, paternity; patrocliny,
matrocliny; patrilineage, matrilineage;
patriliny, matriliny; patrisib, matrisib;
brotherhood, brothership, fraternity; sisterhood, sistership; cousinhood, cousin-
ship; **ancestry** 560
2 kinfolk *and* **kinfolks** <both nonformal>,
kinsmen, kinsfolk, kindred, kinnery
<nonformal>, **kin,** kith and kin, **fam-
ily, relatives, relations, people,** folks
<nonformal>, connections; **blood re-
lation** *or* **relative,** flesh, blood, flesh
and blood, uterine kin, consanguinean;
cognate; agnate, enate; kinsman, kins-
woman, sib, sibling; german; near relation, distant relation; next of kin;
collateral relative, collateral; distaff *or*
spindle side, distaff *or* spindle kin; sword
or spear side, sword *or* spear kin; **tribes-
man,** tribespeople, clansman *or* -woman;
ancestry 560, **posterity** 561
3 brother, bub *and* bubba *and* bro *and* bud
and buddy <all nonformal>, frater;
brethren 700.1; **sister,** sis *and* sissy <both
nonformal>; sistern <nonformal>; kid
brother *or* sister; blood brother *or* sister,
uterine brother *or* sister, brother- *or*
sister-german; half brother *or* sister, foster brother *or* sister, stepbrother *or*
stepsister; **aunt,** auntie <nonformal>;
uncle, unc *and* uncs *and* nunks *and* nunky
and nuncle <all nonformal>, **nephew,
niece; cousin,** cousin-german; first
cousin, second cousin, etc; cousin once
removed, cousin twice removed, etc;
country cousin; great-uncle, granduncle;
great-granduncle; great-aunt, grandaunt;
great-grandaunt; grandnephew, grand-
niece; **father, mother; son, daughter**
561.2
**4 race, people, folk, family, house, clan,
tribe, nation;** patriclan, matriclan, deme,
sept, gens, phyle, phratry, totem; **lineage,**
line, blood, strain, stock, stem, species,
stirps, **breed,** brood, kind; plant *or* ani-

mal kingdom, class, order, etc 808.5; **ethnicity,** tribalism, clannishness
5 family, brood, nuclear family, binuclear
family, extended family, one-parent *or*
single-parent family; **house, household,**
hearth, hearthside, ménage, people, **folk,**
homefolk, folks *and* homefolks <both
nonformal>; **children,** issue, descendants, progeny, **offspring,** get, kids
<nonformal>
ADJS **6 related, kindred, akin;** consanguineous *or* consanguinean *or* consan-
guineal, consanguine, by *or* of the blood;
biological, genetic; **natural, birth,** by
birth; cognate, uterine, agnate, enate; sib,
sibling; allied, affiliated, congeneric;
german, germane; collateral; foster,
novercal; patrilineal, matrilineal; patroclinous, matroclinous; patrilateral,
matrilateral; avuncular; intimately *or*
closely related, remotely *or* distantly related
7 racial, ethnic, tribal, national, family,
clannish, totemic, **lineal; ethnic;** phyletic,
phylogenetic, genetic; gentile, gentilic
WORD ELEMENTS **8** adelpho—, phyl—

560 ANCESTRY

NOUNS **1 ancestry,** progenitorship; parentage, parenthood; grandparentage,
grandfatherhood, grandmotherhood
2 paternity, fatherhood, fathership; natural *or* birth *or* biological fatherhood;
fatherliness, paternalness; adoptive fatherhood
3 maternity, motherhood, mothership; natural *or* birth *or* biological motherhood;
motherliness, maternalness; adoptive
motherhood; surrogate motherhood
4 lineage, line, bloodline, descent, descen-
dancy, line of descent, ancestral line,
succession, **extraction,** derivation, birth,
blood, breed, **family,** house, **strain,** sept,
stock, race, stirps, seed; direct line, phylum; **branch,** stem; filiation, affiliation,
apparentation; side, father's side,
mother's side; enate, agnate, cognate;
male line, spear *or* sword side; female
line, distaff *or* spindle side; consanguinity, common ancestry 559.1
5 genealogy, pedigree, stemma, *Stamm-
baum* <Ger>, genealogical tree, **family
tree,** tree; genogram
6 heredity, heritage, inheritance, birth; patrocliny, matrocliny; endowment, inborn
capacity *or* tendency *or* susceptibility *or*
predisposition; diathesis; inheritability,
heritability, hereditability; Mendel's law,

Mendelism or Mendelianism; Weismann theory, Weismannism; Altmann theory, De Vries theory, Galtonian theory, Verworn theory, Wiesner theory; **genetics,** pharmacogenetics, genesiology, eugenics; **gene,** factor, inheritance factor, determiner, determinant; **character,** dominant or recessive character, allele or allelomorph; germ cell, germ plasm; **chromosome;** sex chromosome, X chromosome, Y chromosome; chromatin, chromatid; genetic code; DNA, RNA, replication

7 **ancestors, antecedents, predecessors,** ascendants, **fathers, forefathers, forebears,** progenitors, primogenitors; **grandparents,** grandfathers; patriarchs, elders

8 **parent, progenitor, ancestor,** procreator, begetter; natural or birth or biological parent; grandparent; ancestress, progenitress, progenitrix; stepparent; adoptive parent; surrogate parent

9 **father, sire,** genitor, paternal ancestor, pater <nonformal>, the old man <nonformal>, governor <nonformal>, *abba* <Heb>; patriarch, paterfamilias; stepfather; foster father, adoptive father; birth father

10 <nonformal terms> **papa,** pa, pap, pappy, **pop,** pops, **dad, daddy,** daddums, daddyo, big daddy, the old man, the governor, pater

11 **mother,** genetrix, dam, maternal ancestor, matriarch, materfamilias; stepmother; foster mother, adoptive mother; birth mother

12 <nonformal terms> **mama,** mater, the old woman, mammy, mam, **ma, mom, mommy,** mummy, mumsy, mimsy, motherkin, motherkins

13 **grandfather,** grandsire; old man 304.2; great-grandfather

14 <nonformal terms> **grandpa,** grampa, gramper, gramp, gramps, grandpapa, grandpap, grandpappy, **granddad,** granddaddy, granddada, granfer, gramfer, granther, pop, grandpop

15 **grandmother,** grandam; great-grandmother

16 <nonformal terms> **grandma,** granma, old woman 304.3; grandmamma, grandmammy, **granny,** grammy, gammy, grannam, gammer

ADJS 17 **ancestral,** ancestorial, patriarchal; **parental,** parent; **paternal,** fatherly, fatherlike; **maternal,** motherly, motherlike; grandparental; grandmotherly, grandmaternal; grandfatherly, grandpaternal

18 **lineal,** family, genealogical; enate or enatic, agnate or agnatic, cognate or cognatic; direct, in a direct line; phyletic, phylogenetic; diphyletic

19 **hereditary,** patrimonial, **inherited, innate;** genetic, genic; patroclinous, matroclinous

20 **inheritable,** heritable, hereditable

561 POSTERITY

NOUNS 1 **posterity, progeny, issue, offspring,** fruit, seed, brood, breed, family; **descent,** succession; lineage 560.4, blood, bloodline; **descendants,** heirs, inheritors, sons, **children, kids** <nonformal>, little ones, little people <nonformal>, treasures, hostages to fortune, youngsters, younglings; grandchildren, great-grandchildren; new or young or rising generation

2 <of animals> **young, brood,** get, **spawn,** spat, fry; **litter,** farrow <of pigs>; clutch, hatch

3 **descendant; offspring, child, scion; son,** son and heir, a chip of or off the old block, sonny; **daughter,** heiress; grandchild, grandson, granddaughter; stepchild, stepson, stepdaughter; foster child

4 <derived or collateral descendant> **offshoot,** offset, **branch,** sprout, shoot, filiation

5 **bastard,** illegitimate, illegitimate or bastard child, whoreson, by-blow, child born out of wedlock or without benefit of clergy or on the wrong side of the blanket, natural or love child, *nullius filius* <L>; illegitimacy, bastardy, bar or bend sinister; hellspawn

6 sonship, sonhood; daughtership, daughterhood

ADJS 7 **filial,** sonly, sonlike; **daughterly,** daughterlike

562 LOVEMAKING, ENDEARMENT

NOUNS 1 **lovemaking,** dalliance, amorous dalliance, billing and cooing; **fondling, caressing,** hugging, kissing; cuddling, snuggling, nestling, nuzzling; bundling; sexual intercourse 75.7

2 <nonformal terms> **making out, necking, petting,** spooning, smooching, lollygagging, canoodling, playing kissy-face or kissy-kissy or kissy-poo or kissy-huggy or lickey-face or smacky-lips, pitching or flinging woo, sucking face, swapping spit

3 **embrace, hug, squeeze,** fond embrace,

embracement, clasp, enfoldment, bear hug <nonformal>

4 kiss, buss, smack, smooch <nonformal>, **osculation;** French kiss, soul kiss

5 endearment; caress, pat; sweet talk, soft words, honeyed words, sweet nothings; line <nonformal>, blandishments, artful endearments; love call, mating call, wolf whistle

6 <terms of endearment> **darling, dear,** deary, **sweetheart, sweetie, sweet,** sweets, sweetkins, **honey,** hon, honeybun, honey-bunny, honeybunch, honey child, sugar, love, lover, precious, precious heart, pet, petkins, babe, **baby, doll,** baby-doll, cherub, angel, chick, chickabiddy, butter-cup, duck, duckling, ducks, lamb, lambkin, snookums, poppet <Brit>

7 courtship, courting, wooing; court, suit, suing, amorous pursuit, addresses; gal-lantry; serenade

8 proposal, marriage proposal, offer of marriage, popping of the question; en-gagement 436.3

9 flirtation, flirtiness, coquetry, dalliance; flirtatiousness, coquettishness, coyness; sheep's eyes, goo-goo eyes <nonformal>, amorous looks, coquettish glances, come-hither look; ogle, side-glance; bedroom eyes <nonformal>

10 philandering, philander, lady-killing <nonformal>; lechery, licentiousness, unchastity 665

11 flirt, coquette, gold digger *and* vamp <both nonformal>; strumpet, whore 665.14,16

12 philanderer, philander, woman chaser, **ladies' man,** heartbreaker; masher, lady-killer, wolf, skirt chaser, man on the make *and* make-out artist <both nonfor-mal>; libertine, lecher, cocksman <non-formal>, seducer 665.12, Casanova, Don Juan

13 love letter, billet-doux, mash note <nonformal>; valentine

VERBS **14 make love,** bill and coo; dally, toy, trifle, wanton, make time; sweet-talk <nonformal>, whisper sweet nothings; go steady, keep company; copulate

15 <nonformal terms> **make out, neck,** pet, spoon, smooch, lollygag, canoodle, pitch *or* fling woo, play kissy-face *or* kissy-kissy *or* kissy-huggy *or* kissy-poo *or* lickey-face *or* smacky-lips, suck face, swap spit

16 caress, pet, pat; feel *or* feel up <nonfor-mal>, **fondle,** dandle, coddle, cocker, cosset; pat on the head *or* cheek, chuck under the chin

17 cuddle, snuggle, nestle, nuzzle; lap; bundle

18 embrace, hug, clasp, press, squeeze <nonformal>, fold, **enfold,** bosom, em-bosom, put *or* throw one's arms around, take to *or* in one's arms, fold to the heart, press to the bosom

19 kiss, osculate, buss, smack, smooch <nonformal>; blow a kiss

20 flirt, coquet; philander, gallivant, play the field <nonformal>, run *or* play around, sow one's oats; **make eyes at, ogle,** eye, cast coquettish glances, cast sheep's eyes at, make goo-goo eyes at <nonformal>, *faire les yeux doux* <Fr>, look sweet upon <nonformal>; play hard to get

21 court, woo, sue, press one's suit, **pay court** *or* **suit to,** make suit to, cozy up to <nonformal>, eye up *and* chat up <Brit nonformal>, pay one's court to, address, pay one's addresses to, pay attention to, lay siege to, fling oneself at, throw oneself at the head of; **pursue,** follow; chase <nonformal>; set one's cap at *or* for <nonformal>; serenade; spark <nonfor-mal>, squire, esquire, beau, sweetheart <nonformal>, swain

22 propose, pop the question <nonformal>, ask for one's hand; become engaged

ADJS **23** amatory, amative; sexual 75.28,29; caressive; **flirtatious,** flirty; **coquettish,** coy, come-hither

563 MARRIAGE

NOUNS **1 marriage, matrimony, wedlock, married status,** holy matrimony, holy wedlock, match, matching, match-up, splicing <nonformal>, union, matrimo-nial union, alliance, "a world-without-end bargain"—Shakespeare, "a dignified and commodious sacrament"—T S Eliot, marriage sacrament, sacrament of matri-mony, bond of matrimony, wedding knot, conjugal bond *or* tie *or* knot, nuptial bond *or* tie *or* knot; married state *or* status, wedded state *or* status, wedded bliss, weddedness, wifehood, husbandhood, spousehood; coverture, cohabitation; bed, marriage bed, bridebed; intermar-riage, mixed marriage, interfaith marriage, interracial marriage; mis-cegenation; misalliance, *mésalliance* <Fr>, ill-assorted marriage

2 marriageability, nubility, ripeness

3 wedding, marriage, marriage ceremony, nuptial mass; church wedding, civil wed-ding, civil ceremony; espousement, bridal; banns; **nuptials,** spousals, es-pousals, hymeneal rites; *chuppah*

<Heb>, wedding canopy; white wedding; wedding song, marriage song, nuptial song, prothalamium, epithalamium, epithalamy, hymen, hymeneal; wedding veil, saffron veil or robe; bridechamber, bridal suite, nuptial apartment; **honeymoon;** forced marriage, shotgun wedding; Gretna Green wedding, elopement

4 **wedding party;** wedding attendant, usher; **best man,** bridesman, groomsman; paranymph; **bridesmaid,** bridemaiden, maid or matron of honor

5 **newlywed; bridegroom, groom; bride,** plighted bride, blushing bride; war bride, GI bride <nonformal>; honeymooner

6 **spouse, mate,** yokemate, partner, consort, **better half** <nonformal>, "bone of my bones, and flesh of my flesh"—Bible

7 **husband, married man,** man, benedict, goodman <old>, old man <nonformal>

8 **wife, married woman,** wedded wife, goodwife or goody <both old>, squaw, woman, lady, matron, old lady and old woman and little woman and ball and chain <all nonformal>, feme, feme covert, **better half** <nonformal>, **helpmate,** helpmeet, rib, wife of one's bosom; wife in name only; wife in all but name, concubine, common-law wife

9 **married couple,** wedded pair, happy couple, **man and wife,** husband and wife, man and woman, vir et uxor <L>, one flesh; newlyweds, **bride and groom**

10 **harem, seraglio,** serai, gynaeceum; zenana, purdah

11 **monogamist,** monogynist; **bigamist;** digamist, deuterogamist; trigamist; **polygamist,** polygynist, polyandrist; Bluebeard

12 **matchmaker, marriage broker,** matrimonial agent, shadchen <Yiddish>; matrimonial agency or bureau

13 <god> Hymen; <goddesses> Hera, Teleia; Juno, Pronuba; Frigg

VERBS 14 <join in marriage> **marry,** wed, nuptial, **join, unite, hitch** and **splice** <both nonformal>, couple, match, match up, make or arrange a match, join together, **unite in marriage,** join or unite in holy wedlock, tie the knot, tie the nuptial or wedding knot, make one; give away, give in marriage; marry off, find a mate for, find a husband or wife for

15 <get married> **marry, wed,** contract matrimony, mate, couple, espouse, wive, **take to wife,** take to oneself a wife, **get hitched** or spliced <both nonformal>, tie the knot, become one, be made one, pair

off, give one's hand to, bestow one's hand upon, lead to the altar, take for better or for worse; remarry, rewed; intermarry, interwed, miscegenate

16 **honeymoon,** go on a honeymoon

17 **cohabit,** live together, live as man and wife, share one's bed and board

ADJS 18 **matrimonial, marital, conjugal, connubial, nuptial,** wedded, married, hymeneal; epithalamic; **spousal;** husbandly, uxorious; bridal, wifely, uxorial

19 **monogamous,** monogynous, monandrous; **bigamous,** digamous; **polygamous,** polygynous, polyandrous; morganatic; miscegenetic

20 **marriageable,** nubile, ripe, of age, of marriageable age

21 **married, wedded,** one, one bone and one flesh, mated, matched, coupled, partnered, paired, hitched and spliced <both nonformal>

WORD ELEMENTS 22 —gamy; —gamous

564 RELATIONSHIP BY MARRIAGE

NOUNS 1 **marriage relationship,** affinity, marital affinity; connection, family connection, marriage connection, matrimonial connection

2 **in-laws** <nonformal>, **relatives-in-law;** brother-in-law, sister-in-law, father-in-law, mother-in-law, son-in-law, daughter-in-law

3 stepfather, stepmother; stepbrother, stepsister; stepchild, stepson, stepdaughter

ADJS 4 **affinal,** affined, by marriage

565 CELIBACY

NOUNS 1 **celibacy, singleness,** singlehood, single blessedness, single or unmarried or unwed state or condition; **bachelorhood,** bachelordom, bachelorism, bachelorship; **spinsterhood,** maidenhood, maidenhead, **virginity,** maiden or virgin state; **monasticism,** monachism; misogamy, misogyny; sexual abstinence or abstention, continence 664.3

2 **celibate,** célibataire <Fr>; monk, monastic, priest, nun; misogamist, misogynist; unmarried, single <nonformal>

3 **bachelor,** bach and old bach <both nonformal>, confirmed bachelor, **single man**

4 **single** or unmarried woman, spinster, spinstress, **old maid,** maid, maiden, bachelor girl, single girl, single woman, lone woman, maiden lady, feme sole; **virgin,**

virgo intacta, cherry <nonformal>; vestal, vestal virgin
VERBS **5 be unmarried, be single, live alone,**
enjoy single blessedness, **bach** *and* **bach it**
<both nonformal>, keep bachelor quar-
ters, keep one's freedom
ADJS **6 celibate; monastic,** monachal, **monkish;** misogamic, misogynous; sexually abstinent *or* continent, abstinent, abstaining
  7 unmarried, unwedded, unwed, single,
sole, spouseless, wifeless, husbandless;
bachelorly, bachelorlike; **spinsterly,** spin-
sterish, spinsterlike; **old-maidish,** old-
maidenish; maiden, maidenly; virgin,
virginal

566 DIVORCE, WIDOWHOOD

NOUNS **1 divorce,** divorcement, grass-
widowhood, civil divorce, **separation,**
legal *or* judicial separation, separate
maintenance; interlocutory decree; dissolution of marriage; annulment, decree of
nullity; broken marriage, broken home
  2 divorcé, divorced person, divorced man,
divorced woman, *divorcée* <Fr>; di-
vorcer; grass widow, grass widower
  3 widowhood, viduity <old>; **widower-
hood,** widowership; weeds, widow's
weeds
  4 widow, widow woman <nonformal>,
relict; dowager, queen dowager, etc; **widower,** widowman <nonformal>
VERBS **5 divorce, separate,** part, split up *and*
split the sheets <both nonformal>, un-
marry, put away, obtain a divorce, come
to a parting of the ways, untie the knot,
sue for divorce, file suit for divorce; grant
a divorce, grant a final decree; grant an
annulment, grant a decree of nullity, annul a marriage, put asunder
  6 widow, bereave
ADJS **7** widowly, widowish, widowlike; **widowed,** widowered; **divorced;** separated,
legally separated

567 SCHOOL

NOUNS **1 school** <see list>, **educational institution,** teaching institution, academic
or scholastic institution, teaching and research institution, **institute, academy,**
seminary, *Schule* <Ger>, *école* <Fr>, *es-
cuela* <Sp>; alternative school; magnet
school
  2 preschool, infant school <Brit>, nursery,
nursery school; day nursery, **day-care
center,** crèche; playschool; **kindergarten**

  3 elementary school, grade school *or*
graded school, the grades; **primary
school;** junior school <Brit>; **grammar
school;** folk school, *Volksschule* <Ger>
  4 secondary school, middle school, **academy,** *Gymnasium* <Ger>; *lycée* <Fr>,
lyceum; **high school,** high <nonformal>;
junior high school, junior high <nonfor-
mal>, intermediate school; **senior high
school,** senior high <nonformal>; **preparatory school,** prep school <nonfor-
mal>, public school <Brit>, seminary;
grammar school <Brit>, Latin school,
Progymnasium <Ger>; *Realschule*
<Ger>; *Realgymnasium* <Ger>
  5 college, university, institution of higher
education *or* learning, degree-granting
institution; graduate school, postgraduate school, coeducational school; academe, academia, the groves of Academe,
the campus, the halls of learning *or* ivy,
ivied halls; alma mater
  6 service school, service academy <see
list>, military academy, naval academy
  7 art school, performing arts school, music
school, conservatory, arts conservatory,
school of the arts, dance school
  8 religious school <see list>, parochial
school, church-related school, church
school; Sunday school
  9 reform school, reformatory, correctional
institution, industrial school, training
school; borstal *or* borstal school *or* remand school <all Brit>
  10 schoolhouse, school building; little red
schoolhouse; classroom building; hall;
campus
  11 schoolroom, classroom; recitation room;
lecture room *or* hall; auditorium; theater,
amphitheater
  12 governing board, board; board of education, school board; college board, board
of regents, board of trustees, board of vis-
itors
ADJS **13 scholastic, academic,** institutional,
school, classroom; **collegiate; university;**
preschool; interscholastic, intercollegiate, extramural; intramural

  14 schools

adult-education school	day school
alternate *or* alterna- tive school	elementary *or* grade school
boarding school	extension school *or* program
business college *or* school	finishing school
correspondence school	junior high school *or* junior school *or* intermediate school
country day school	

military school *or*
academy
night school
open-classroom
school
playschool
polytechnic school *or*
polytechnic
<chiefly Brit>
preparatory school *or*
prep school
<nonformal>
primary school
private school

public school
school of continuing
education *or* con-
tinuation school
secondary school *or*
high school *or*
senior high school
summer school
technical school *or*
tech <nonformal>
university extension
vocational *or* trade
school

15 service schools or academies

air university
command and
general staff school
École de l'Air <Salon-
de-Provence>
École Navale
<Brest>
École Spéciale
Militaire Interarmes
<St Cyr>
naval college
officer candidate
school *or* OCS
Royal Air Force Col-
lege <Cranwell>
Royal Military
Academy
<Woolwich>
Royal Military Col-
lege <Sandhurst>

Royal Military Col-
lege of Canada
<Kingston>
Royal Naval College
<Dartmouth>
staff college
US Air Force Acad-
emy <Colorado
Springs>
US Coast Guard
Academy <New
London>
US Merchant Marine
Academy <Kings
Point>
US Military Academy
<West Point>
US Naval Academy
<Annapolis> war
college

16 religious schools

Bible institute
Bible school
church school
convent school
denominational
school
divinity school
Hebrew school *or*
heder <Yiddish>
mesivta
parish school

religious *or* parochial
school
Sabbath school
seminary
Sunday school
Talmud Torah
theological seminary
or school
vacation church
school
yeshiva

568 TEACHING

NOUNS **1 teaching, instruction, education,
schooling, tuition; edification, enlightenment,** illumination; tutelage, tutorage,
tutorship; tutoring, coaching, private
teaching, teacher 571; spoon-feeding; direction, guidance; **pedagogy,** pedagogics,
didactics, didacticism; catechization;
computer-aided instruction, programmed instruction; self-teaching, self-
instruction; information 551; reeducation 857.4; **school** 567; **formal education,**
coursework, school-work

2 inculcation, indoctrination, catechization, inoculation, **implantation,** infixation, infixion, **impression, instillment,**
instillation, impregnation, **infusion,** imbuement; absorption and regurgitation;
dictation; conditioning, brainwashing;
reindoctrination 857.5

3 training, preparation, readying <nonfor-
mal>, **conditioning, grooming,** cultivation, development, improvement;
discipline; breaking, housebreaking;
upbringing, bringing-up, fetching-up
<nonformal>, **rearing, raising, breeding,
nurture,** nurturing, fostering; **practice,**
rehearsal, **exercise, drill,** drilling; **apprenticeship,** in-service training, on-the-
job training; work-study; military training, basic training; manual training,
sloyd; vocational training *or* education

4 preinstruction, pre-education; **priming,**
cramming <nonformal>

**5 elementary education; initiation, intro-
duction,** propaedeutic; **rudiments,**
grounding, first steps, elements, **ABC's,
basics;** reading, writing, and arithmetic,
three R's; primer, hornbook, abecedarium, abecedary

6 instructions, directions, orders; briefing,
final instructions

7 lesson, teaching, instruction, lecture,
lecture-demonstration, harangue, **discourse,** disquisition, exposition, **talk,**
homily, **sermon,** preachment; chalk talk
<nonformal>; skull session <nonfor-
mal>; **recitation,** recital; **assignment,
exercise,** task, set task, homework; **moral,**
morality, moralization, moral lesson; object lesson

8 study, branch of learning; **discipline,** subdiscipline; **field, specialty,** academic
specialty, area; **course,** course of study,
curriculum; subject; major, minor; requirement *or* required course, elective
course, core curriculum; refresher
course; summer *or* summer-session
course, intersession course; gut course
<nonformal>; **seminar,** proseminar

9 physical education, physical culture,
gymnastics, calisthenics, eurythmics

VERBS **10 teach, instruct,** give instruction,
give lessons in, **educate, school; edify, enlighten,** civilize, illumine; **direct, guide;**
get across, **inform** 551.8; **show,** show
how, show the ropes, demonstrate; give
an idea of; put in the right, set right; improve one's mind, enlarge *or* broaden the
mind; sharpen the wits, open the eyes *or*
mind; teach a lesson, give a lesson to;
ground, teach the rudiments *or* elements

or basics; catechize; teach an old dog new tricks; reeducate 857.14

11 tutor, coach; prime, cram <nonformal>, cram with facts, stuff with knowledge

12 inculcate, indoctrinate, catechize, inoculate, **instill, infuse,** imbue, impregnate, **implant,** infix, impress; **impress upon the mind** *or* **memory,** urge on the mind, beat into, beat *or* knock into one's head, grind in, drill into, drum into one's head *or* skull; **condition, brainwash, program**

13 train; drill, exercise; practice, rehearse; keep in practice, keep one's hand in; **prepare,** ready, **condition, groom,** fit, put in tune, form, **lick into shape** <nonformal>; **rear, raise, bring up,** fetch up <nonformal>, bring up by hand, **breed; cultivate,** develop, improve; **nurture, foster,** nurse; **discipline,** take in hand; put through the mill *or* grind <nonformal>; break, break in, housebreak, house-train <Brit>; put to school, send to school, apprentice

14 preinstruct, pre-educate; **initiate,** introduce

15 give instructions, give directions; **brief,** give a briefing

16 expound, exposit; explain 341.10; **lecture, discourse,** harangue, hold forth, give *or* read a lesson; **preach,** sermonize; **moralize,** point a moral

17 assign, give *or* make an assignment, give homework, set a task, set hurdles; lay out a course, make a syllabus

ADJS **18 educational,** educative, educating, teaching, **instructive,** instructional, **tuitional,** tuitionary; **cultural, edifying, enlightening,** illuminating; informative; didactic, preceptive; self instructional, self-teaching, autodidactic; lecturing, preaching, hortatory, exhortatory, homiletic, homiletical; initiatory, introductory, propaedeutic; **disciplinary;** coeducational

19 scholastic, academic, schoolish, pedantic, donnish <Brit>; **scholarly; pedagogical;** graduate, professional, graduate-professional, postgraduate; interdisciplinary, cross-disciplinary; curricular

20 extracurricular, extraclassroom; nonscholastic, noncollegiate

569 MISTEACHING

NOUNS **1 misteaching,** misinstruction; **misguidance,** misdirection, misleading; sophistry 935; perversion, corruption; mystification, obscuration, obfuscation, obscurantism; **misinformation,** mis-

knowledge; the blind leading the blind; college of Laputa

2 propaganda; propagandism, indoctrination; brainwashing; **propagandist,** agitprop; **disinformation**

VERBS **3 misteach,** misinstruct, miseducate; **misinform;** misadvise, **misguide,** misdirect, **mislead;** pervert, corrupt; mystify, obscure, obfuscate

4 propagandize, carry on a propaganda; indoctrinate; **disinform,** brainwash

ADJS **5 mistaught,** misinstructed; **misinformed;** misadvised, **misguided,** misdirected, **misled**

6 misteaching, misinstructive, miseducative, **misinforming; misleading,** misguiding, misdirecting, obscuring, mystifying, obfuscatory; propagandistic, indoctrinational; disinformational

570 LEARNING

NOUNS **1 learning,** intellectual acquirement *or* acquisition *or* attainment, stocking *or* storing the mind, mental cultivation, mental culture, improving *or* broadening the mind; **mastery,** mastery of skills; **self-education,** self-instruction; **knowledge, erudition** 927.5; education 568.1; memorization 988.4

2 absorption, ingestion, imbibing, assimilation, taking-in, getting, getting hold of, getting the hang of <nonformal>, soaking-up, digestion

3 study, studying, application, conning; **reading, perusal;** restudy, restudying, brushing up, boning up <nonformal>, **review; contemplation** 930.2; **inspection** 937.3; **engrossment; brainwork, headwork,** lucubration, mental labor; exercise, **practice, drill;** grind *and* grinding *and* boning <all nonformal>, **cramming** *and* cram <both nonformal>, swotting <Brit nonformal>; extensive study, wide reading; subject 568.8

4 studiousness, scholarliness, scholarship; bookishness, diligence 330.6

5 teachableness, teachability, educability, trainableness; **aptness, aptitude,** quickness, **readiness; receptivity,** mind like a blotter, ready grasp, quick mind, quick study; **willingness, motivation,** hunger *or* thirst for learning; docility, **malleability,** moldability, pliability, facility, plasticity, **impressionability,** susceptibility, formability; brightness, cleverness, **intelligence** 919

VERBS **6 learn,** get, get hold of <nonformal>, get into one's head, get through one's thick skull <nonformal>; **gain knowledge,** pick up information, gather or collect or glean knowledge or learning; stock or store the mind, improve or broaden the mind; stuff or cram the mind; burden or load the mind; **find out, ascertain, discover,** find, determine; **become informed,** gain knowledge or understanding of, acquire information or intelligence about, **learn about, find out about;** acquaint oneself with, make oneself acquainted with, become acquainted with; be informed 551.14

7 **absorb, acquire, take in,** ingest, imbibe, get by osmosis, **assimilate, digest, soak up,** drink in; **soak in, seep in,** percolate in

8 **memorize** 988.17, get by rote; fix in the mind 988.18

9 **master,** attain mastery of, make oneself master of, **gain command of, become adept in,** become familiar or conversant with, become versed or well-versed in, **get up in** or **on,** gain a good or thorough knowledge of, **learn all about, get down pat** <nonformal>, get down cold <nonformal>, get taped <Brit nonformal>, get to the bottom or heart of; **get the hang** or **knack of; learn the ropes,** learn the ins and outs; know well 927.13

10 **learn by experience,** learn by doing, **live and learn,** go through the school of hard knocks, learn the hard way <nonformal>; teach or school oneself; **learn a lesson,** be taught a lesson

11 **be taught, receive instruction,** be tutored, undergo schooling, pursue one's education, attend classes, go to or attend school, take lessons, matriculate, enroll, register; **train,** prepare oneself, ready oneself, go into training; serve an apprenticeship; apprentice oneself to; **study with,** read with, sit at the feet of, learn from, have as one's master; monitor, audit

12 **study,** regard studiously, apply oneself to, con, crack a book and hit the books <both nonformal>; **read, peruse,** go over, read up or read up on, have one's nose in a book <nonformal>; restudy, **review; contemplate** 930.12; **examine** 937.23; give the mind to 982.5; **pore over,** vet <Brit nonformal>; be highly motivated, hunger or thirst for knowledge; bury oneself in, wade through, plunge into; **dig** and **grind** and **bone** and bone up on <all nonformal>, swot <Brit nonformal>; lucubrate, elucubrate, **burn the midnight oil;** make a study of; **practice, drill**

13 **browse, scan, skim, dip into,** thumb over or through, run over or through, glance or run the eye over or through, turn over the leaves, have a look at, hit the high spots

14 **study up, get up,** study up on, read up on, get up on; **review, brush up,** polish up <nonformal>, rub up, **cram** or cram up <nonformal>, **bone up** <nonformal>

15 **study to be, study for, read for,** read law, etc; **specialize in, go in for,** make one's field; major in, minor in

ADJS 16 educated, **learned** 927.21,22; self-taught, self-instructed, autodidactic

17 **studious,** devoted to studies, **scholarly,** scholastic, academic, professorial, tweedy, donnish <Brit>; owlish; rabbinic, mandarin; pedantic, dryasdust; bookish 927.22; diligent 330.22

18 **teachable, instructable, educable,** schoolable, trainable; **apt,** quick, **ready,** ripe for instruction; **receptive, willing,** motivated; hungry or thirsty for knowledge; docile, **malleable, moldable,** pliable, facile, plastic, **impressionable,** susceptible, formable; bright, clever, **intelligent** 919.12

571 TEACHER

NOUNS 1 **teacher, instructor, educator,** preceptor, **mentor; master,** maestro; **pedagogue,** pedagogist, educationist; schoolman; **schoolteacher, schoolmaster,** schoolkeeper; dominie <Scots>, abecedarian <old>, certified or licensed teacher; **professor, academic,** member of academy; don <Brit>, fellow; guide 574.7, docent; rabbi, melamed <Heb>, pandit, pundit, guru, mullah <Persian>, starets <Russ>

2 <woman teachers> instructress, educatress, preceptress, **mistress; schoolmistress; schoolma'am** or **schoolmarm,** dame, schooldame; **governess,** duenna

3 <academic ranks> professor, associate professor, assistant professor, instructor, tutor, associate, assistant, lecturer, reader <Brit>; visiting professor; emeritus, professor emeritus, retired professor

4 teaching fellow, teaching assistant; teaching intern, intern; practice teacher, apprentice teacher, student or pupil teacher; teacher's aide, paraprofessional; monitor, proctor, prefect, praepostor <Brit>; student assistant, graduate assistant

5 **tutor,** tutorer; **coach,** coacher; **private instructor,** Privatdocent, Privatdozent <both Ger>; crammer <Brit nonformal>

6 trainer, handler, groomer; driller, drill-master; **coach,** athletic coach

7 lecturer, lector, **reader** <Brit>, praelec-tor, **preacher,** homilist

8 principal, headmaster, headmistress; president, chancellor, vice-chancellor, rector, provost, master; **dean,** academic dean, dean of the faculty, dean of women, dean of men; administrator, educational administrator; administration

9 faculty, staff <Brit>, faculty members, professorate, professoriate, professors, professordom, teaching staff

10 instructorship, teachership, precep-torship, schoolmastery; **tutorship,** tutorhood, tutorage, tutelage; **profes-sorship,** professorhood, professorate, professoriate; **chair,** endowed chair; lectureship, readership <Brit>; fellowship

ADJS **11 pedagogic, pedagogical,** precep-torial, tutorial; **teacherish,** teachery, teacherlike, teachy, **schoolteacherish,** schoolteachery, **schoolmasterish,** school-masterly, schoolmastering, schoolmas-terlike; schoolmistressy, schoolmarmish <nonformal>; **professorial,** professor-like, academic, tweedy, donnish <Brit>; pedantic 927.22

572 STUDENT

NOUNS **1 student, pupil, scholar,** learner, studier, educatee, **trainee,** *élève* <Fr>; tutee; inquirer; mature student, adult-education *or* continuing education stu-dent; self-taught person, autodidact; auditor; **reader,** reading enthusiast, great reader, printhead <nonformal>

2 disciple, follower, apostle, convert, pros-elyte 857.7; **discipleship,** disciplehood, pupilage, tutelage, studentship, follower-ship

3 schoolchild, school kid <nonformal>; **schoolboy,** school lad; **schoolgirl;** day-pupil, day boy, day girl; preschool child, preschooler, nursery school child, infant <Brit>; kindergartner, grade schooler, primary schooler, intermediate schooler; secondary schooler, prep schooler, prep-pie <nonformal>, high schooler; school-mate, schoolfellow, fellow student, class-mate

4 special *or* exceptional student, gifted stu-dent; special education *or* special ed <nonformal> student; learning disabled *or* LD student; learning impaired stu-dent; slow learner, underachiever; handicapped *or* retarded student; emo-

tionally disturbed student; culturally dis-advantaged student

5 college student, collegian, collegiate, uni-versity student, **varsity student** <Brit nonformal>, college boy *or* girl; co-ed <nonformal>; seminarian, seminarist; *bahur* <Heb>, *yeshiva bocher* <Yiddish>

6 undergraduate, undergrad <nonfor-mal>, cadet, midshipman; underclass-man, **freshman,** freshie <nonformal>, plebe, **sophomore,** soph <nonformal>; **upperclassman, junior, senior**

7 <Brit terms> commoner, pensioner, sizar, servitor <old>, exhibitioner, fel-low commoner; sophister, questionist <both old>; wrangler, optime; passman

8 graduate, grad <nonformal>; **alumnus,** alumni, alumna, alumnae; old boy <Brit>; **graduate student,** grad student <nonformal>, master's degree candi-date, doctoral candidate; **postgraduate,** postgrad <nonformal>; degrees; college graduate, college man *or* woman, edu-cated man *or* woman, educated class; meritocracy

9 novice, novitiate *or* noviciate, **tyro,** abe-cedarian, alphabetarian, **beginner** 817.2, entrant, **neophyte, tenderfoot** *and* **green-horn** <both nonformal>, freshman, **fledgling;** catechumen, initiate, debutant; new boy <Brit>, newcomer 773.4; igno-ramus 929.8; **recruit, raw recruit,** inductee, **rookie** *and* yardbird<both non-formal>, boot; **probationer,** probationist, postulant; **apprentice,** articled clerk

10 nerd *and* grind *or* greasy grind <all non-formal>, swotter *or* mugger <both Brit nonformal>; bookworm 928.4

11 class, form <Brit>, **grade;** track; year

ADJS **12 studentlike,** schoolboyish, school-girlish; undergraduate, graduate, post-graduate; **collegiate,** college-bred; sophomoric; sophomorical; autodidactic; **studious** 570.17; **learned, bookish** 927.22; exceptional, gifted, special

13 probationary, probational, on probation; in detention

573 DIRECTION, MANAGEMENT

NOUNS **1 direction, management, manag-ing,** managery <old>, handling, **running** <nonformal>, **conduct;** governance, **command, control, chiefdom, govern-ment** 612, controllership; **authority** 417; **regulation,** ordering, husbandry; manip-ulation; **guidance, lead, leading; steering, navigation,** pilotage, conning, the conn, the helm, the wheel

2 **supervision, superintendence,** intendance *or* intendancy, heading, heading up *and* **bossing** *and* running <all nonformal>; **surveillance,** oversight, eye; **charge, care, auspices, jurisdiction; responsibility,** accountability 641.2

3 **administration,** executive function *or* role, command function, say-so *and* last word <both nonformal>; **decision-making; disposition,** disposal, **dispensation;** officiation

4 **directorship, leadership, managership,** directorate, headship, governorship, chairmanship, convenership <Brit>, presidency, generalship, captainship; mastership 417.7; dictatorship, sovereignty 417.8; superintendence *or* **superintendency,** intendancy, foremanship, overseership, supervisorship; stewardship, custody, guardianship, shepherding, proctorship; collective leadership

5 **helm,** conn, rudder, tiller, wheel, steering wheel; **reins,** reins of government

6 **domestic management, housekeeping,** homemaking, housewifery, ménage, husbandry <old>; domestic economy, home economics

7 **efficiency engineering,** scientific management, bean-counting <nonformal>, industrial engineering, management engineering, management consulting; management theory; efficiency expert, management consultant; time and motion study, time-motion study, time study; therblig

VERBS 8 **direct, manage, regulate, conduct, carry on, handle, run** <nonformal>; **control, command, head, govern** 612.12, **boss** *and* head up *and* pull the strings *and* **mastermind** *and* quarterback *and* call the signals <all nonformal>; **order, prescribe;** lay down the law, make the rules, call the shots *or* tune <nonformal>; **head,** head up, office, captain, skipper <nonformal>; **lead,** take the lead, lead on; manipulate, maneuver, engineer; take command 417.14; be responsible for

9 **guide, steer, drive, run** <nonformal>; herd, shepherd; channel; **pilot,** take the helm, be at the helm *or* wheel *or* tiller *or* rudder, hold the reins, **be in the driver's seat** <nonformal>

10 **supervise, superintend, boss, oversee,** overlook, ride herd on <nonformal>, stand over, keep an eye on *or* upon, keep in order; cut work out for; straw-boss <nonformal>; take care of 1007.19

11 **administer,** administrate; **officiate; pre**-side, preside over, preside at the board; chair, chairman, occupy the chair

ADJS 12 **directing, directive,** directory, directorial; **managing, managerial; commanding, controlling, governing** 612.18; regulating, regulative, regulatory; **head, chief;** leading, guiding

13 **supervising, supervisory,** overseeing, **superintendent, boss; in charge** 417.21

14 **administrative, administrating;** ministerial, **executive; officiating, presiding**

ADVS 15 in the charge of, in the hands of, in the care of; **under the auspices of,** under the aegis of; in one's charge, on one's hands, under one's care, under one's jurisdiction

574 DIRECTOR

NOUNS 1 **director,** *directeur* <Fr>, director general, **governor,** rector, **manager, administrator,** intendant, **conductor;** person in charge, responsible person; ship's husband, supercargo; impresario; producer; deputy, agent 576

2 **superintendent; supervisor, foreman,** monitor, **head,** headman, overman, **boss,** chief, gaffer *and* ganger <both Brit nonformal>, taskmaster; sirdar <India>, **overseer,** overlooker; inspector, surveyor, visitor; proctor; subforeman, **straw boss** <nonformal>; slave driver; boatswain; floorman, floorwalker, floor manager; noncommissioned officer 575.19; controller, comptroller, auditor

3 **executive,** officer, official, pinstriper <nonformal>; **president,** prexy <nonformal>, chief executive officer, chief executive, managing director <Brit>; provost, prefect, warden, archon; policymaker, agenda-setter; magistrate; **chairman of the board; chancellor,** vice-chancellor; vice-president *or* VP *or* veep <nonformal>; secretary; treasurer; dean; executive officer, executive director, executive secretary; **management,** the administration 574.11

4 **steward,** bailiff <Brit>, reeve <old>, factor <Scots>, seneschal; majordomo, butler, housekeeper, *maître d'hôtel* <Fr>; master of ceremonies *or* MC *and* emcee <both nonformal>, master of the revels; proctor, procurator, attorney; guardian, custodian 1007.6; curator, librarian; croupier

5 **chairman,** chairwoman, **chair,** convener <Brit>, speaker, presiding officer; co-chairman, etc

6 **leader,** conductor <old>; file leader, fu-

gleman; pacemaker, pacesetter; bell-wether, bell mare, bell cow, Judas goat; standard-bearer, torchbearer; **leader of men**, born leader, charismatic leader *or* figure, inspired leader; messiah, Mahdi; führer, duce; forerunner 815.1; ringleader 375.11; precentor, coryphaeus, choragus, symphonic conductor, choirmaster 710.18

7 **guide**, guider; **shepherd**, herd, herdsman, drover, cowherd, goatherd, etc; tour guide, tour director *or* conductor, ci-cerone, mercury <old>, courier, dragoman; **pilot**, river pilot, navigator, **helmsman**, timoneer, steersman, steerer, coxswain, boatsteerer, boatheader; auto-matic pilot, Gyropilot; pointer, fingerpost <Brit>, guidepost 517.4

8 **guiding star**, cynosure <old>, **polestar**, polar star, lodestar, Polaris, **North Star**

9 **compass**, magnetic compass, gyrocom-pass, gyroscopic compass, gyrostatic compass, Gyrosin compass, surveyor's compass, mariner's compass; needle, magnetic needle; direction finder, radio compass, radio direction finder *or* RDF

10 **directory, guidebook**, handbook, Baedeker; city directory, business direc-tory; telephone directory, telephone book, phone book <nonformal>, clas-sified directory, Yellow Pages; **bibliog-raphy;** catalog, index, handlist, check-list, finding list; itinerary, road map, roadbook; gazetteer, reference book

11 **directorate**, directory, **management, the administration**, the brass *and* top brass <both nonformal>, the people upstairs *and* the people in the front office <both nonformal>, executive hierarchy; the ex-ecutive, executive arm *or* branch; middle management; **cabinet; board**, governing board *or* body, board of directors, board of trustees, board of regents; steering committee, executive committee, inter-locking directorate; cadre, executive council; infrastructure; council 423

575 MASTER

NOUNS **1 master, lord, lord and master**, overlord, seigneur, paramount, lord para-mount, liege, liege lord, *padrone* <Ital>, *patron* and *chef* <both Fr>, patroon; **chief, boss**, sahib <India>, *bwana* <Swah>; employer; husband, man of the house, master of the house, goodman <old or nonformal>, paterfamilias; pa-triarch, elder; teacher, rabbi, guru, starets; church dignitary, ecclesiarch

2 **mistress**, governess, dame <old>, madam; **matron, housewife,** homemaker, goodwife <Scots>, lady of the house, chatelaine; housemistress, housemother; rectoress, abbess, mother superior; great lady, first lady; matriarch, dowager

3 **chief**, principal; **master**, dean, doyen, doyenne; high priest <nonformal>, supe-rior, senior; **leader** 574.6; important person, personage 996.8

4 <nonformal terms> **top dog**, boss man, big boy, Big Daddy, big cheese, kingpin, kingfish, el supremo, honcho *or* head hon-cho, top banana, big enchilada, himself, herself, man *or* woman upstairs; queen bee, heavy momma, Big Momma

5 **figurehead**, nominal head, dummy, lay figure, front man *and* front <both nonfor-mal>, stooge *and* Charlie McCarthy <both nonformal>, puppet, creature

6 **governor, ruler; captain, master, com-mander,** commandant, commanding officer, intendant, castellan, chatelain, chatelaine; **director, manager, executive** 574.3

7 **head of state, chief of state; premier, prime minister, chancellor,** grand vizier, dewan <India>; doge; **president**, chief executive, the man in the White House

8 **potentate, sovereign, monarch, ruler, prince,** dynast, **crowned head, emperor,** *imperator* <L>, king-emperor, **king**, anointed king, majesty, royalty, royal, royal personage; petty king, tetrarch, kinglet; grand duke; paramount, lord paramount, suzerain, overlord, overking, high king; **chief, chieftain,** high chief; prince consort 608.7

9 <rulers> **caesar,** kaiser, **czar;** Holy Ro-man Emperor; Dalai Lama; **pharaoh;** pendragon, rig, ardri; **mikado,** tenno; shogun, tycoon; khan *or* cham; shah, padishah; negus; bey; **sheikh;** sachem, sagamore; Inca; cacique; kaid

10 <Muslim rulers> **sultan,** Grand Turk, grand seignior; caliph, imam; hakim; khan *or* cham; nizam, nabab; emir; Great Mogul, Mogul

11 **sovereign queen, sovereign princess, princess, queen,** queen regent, queen reg-nant, **empress,** czarina, *Kaiserin* <Ger>; rani, maharani <both India>; grand duchess; queen consort

12 **regent,** protector, prince regent, queen regent

13 <regional governors> **governor,** governor-general, lieutenant governor; **viceroy,** vice-king, exarch, proconsul, khedive, stadtholder, vizier; nabob *and*

nabab *and* subahdar <all India>; gau-
leiter; eparch; palatine; tetrarch; bur-
grave; collector; hospodar, vaivode; dey,
bey *or* beg, beglerbeg, wali *or* vali, satrap;
provincial

14 **tyrant, despot,** warlord; **autocrat,** au-
tarch; oligarch; absolute ruler *or* master
or monarch, omnipotent *or* all-powerful
ruler; **dictator,** duce, führer, commissar,
pharaoh, caesar, czar; usurper, arrogator; **oppressor, hard master,** driver,
slave driver, Simon Legree <Harriet B
Stowe>; **martinet, disciplinarian,** stickler

15 **the authorities, the powers that be,** ruling
class *or* classes, the lords of creation, **the
Establishment,** the interests, the power
elite, **the power structure; they,** them; the
inner circle; the ins *and* the in-group *and*
those on the inside <all nonformal>;
management, the administration; higher
echelons, **top brass** <nonformal>;
higher-ups *and* the people upstairs *or* in
the front office <all nonformal>; **the top**
<nonformal>, the corridors of power;
prelacy, hierarchy; ministry; **bureaucracy, officialdom;** directorate 574.11

16 **official, officer,** officiary, functionary,
fonctionnaire <Fr>, apparatchik; **public
official,** public servant; officeholder,
office-bearer *and* placeman <both Brit>;
government *or* public employee; **civil servant; bureaucrat,** mandarin, red-tapist,
rond-de-cuir <Fr>; petty tyrant, jack-in-
office

17 <public officials> **minister,** secretary,
secretary of state <Brit>, undersecretary, cabinet minister, cabinet member,
minister of state <Brit>; chancellor;
warden; archon; magistrate; syndic;
commissioner; commissar; county commissioners; city manager, mayor, *maire*
<Fr>, lord mayor, burgomaster; head-
man, induna <Africa>; **councilman,**
councilwoman, councillor, city councilman, elder, city father, alderman, bailie
<Scots>, selectman; supervisor, county
supervisor; reeve, portreeve; legislator
610.3

18 **commissioned officer, officer;** top brass
and the brass <both nonformal>; **commander in chief,** generalissimo, captain
general; hetman, sirdar; general of the
army, general of the air force, five-star
general <nonformal>, **marshal,** *maréchal*
<Fr>, field marshal; general officer, **gen-
eral,** four-star general <nonformal>;
lieutenant general, three-star general
<nonformal>; major general, two-star

general <nonformal>, brigadier general,
one-star general <nonformal>, brigadier
<Brit>; field officer; **colonel,** chicken col-
onel <nonformal>; lieutenant colonel;
major; company officer; **captain; lieutenant,** first lieutenant; second lieutenant,
shavetail <nonformal>, subaltern *and*
sublieutenant <both Brit>; warrant officer, chief warrant officer; **commander,**
commandant, the Old Man <nonfor-
mal>; **commanding officer** *or* CO, old
man <nonformal>; executive officer,
exec <nonformal>; chief of staff; aide,
aide-de-camp *or* ADC; officer of the day *or*
OD, orderly officer <Brit>; staff officer;
senior officer, junior officer

19 **Army noncommissioned officer,** noncom
or NCO <nonformal>; centurion; sergeant, sarge <nonformal>, havildar
<India>; sergeant major of the Army,
command sergeant major, sergeant major, first sergeant, top sergeant *and*
topkick *and* first man <all nonformal>,
master sergeant, sergeant first class, technical sergeant, staff sergeant, sergeant,
specialist seven, platoon sergeant, mess
sergeant, color sergeant, acting sergeant,
lance sergeant <Brit>; **corporal,** acting
corporal, lance corporal <Brit>, lance-
jack <Brit nonformal>; **Air Force noncommissioned officer,** chief master
sergeant of the Air Force, chief master
sergeant, senior master sergeant, master
sergeant, technical sergeant, staff sergeant, sergeant, airman first class

20 **Navy** *or* **naval officer; fleet admiral,** na-
varch, **admiral,** vice admiral, rear
admiral, **commodore, captain, commander,** lieutenant commander,
lieutenant, lieutenant junior grade, ensign; warrant officer; Navy *or* naval
noncommissioned officer, master chief
petty officer of the Navy, master chief
petty officer, senior chief petty officer,
chief petty officer, petty officer first class,
petty officer second class, petty officer
third class; **Marine Corps noncommissioned officer,** sergeant major of the
Marine Corps, sergeant major, master
gunnery sergeant, first sergeant, master
sergeant, gunnery sergeant, staff sergeant, sergeant, corporal, lance corporal

21 <heraldic officials> herald, king of arms,
king at arms, earl marshal; Garter, Garter King of Arms, Clarenceux, Clarenceux
King of Arms, Norroy and Ulster, Norroy
and Ulster King of Arms, Norroy, Norroy
King of Arms, Lyon, Lyon King of Arms;
College of Arms

576 DEPUTY, AGENT

NOUNS **1 deputy, proxy, representative, substitute,** vice, vicegerent, **alternate,** backup *and* stand-in <both nonformal>, alter ego, **surrogate,** procurator, secondary, understudy, pinch hitter <nonformal>, utility man *or* woman, the bench <nonformal>; second in command, executive officer; exponent, advocate, pleader, paranymph, attorney, champion; **lieutenant;** vicar, vicar general; locum tenens *or* locum <chiefly Brit>; amicus curiae; **puppet,** dummy, creature, cat's-paw, figurehead

2 delegate, legate; **commissioner,** commissary, *commissionaire* <Fr>, commissar; **messenger,** herald, **emissary, envoy; minister,** secretary

3 agent, instrument, implement, implementer; expediter, facilitator; **tool; steward** 574.4; **functionary; official** 575.16; clerk, **secretary;** amanuensis; factor, consignee; puppet, cat's-paw; dupe 358

4 go-between, middleman, intermediary, medium, intermedium, intermediate, interagent, **internuncio,** broker; connection <nonformal>, **contact; negotiator,** negotiant; interpleader; arbitrator, mediator 466.3

5 spokesman, spokeswoman, spokesperson, spokespeople, official spokesman *or* -woman *or* -person, press officer, speaker, **voice,** mouthpiece <nonformal>; herald; prolocutor, prolocutress *or* prolocutrix; reporter, rapporteur

6 diplomat, diplomatist, diplomatic agent, diplomatic <old>; **emissary, envoy, legate, minister,** foreign service officer; **ambassador,** ambassadress, ambassador-at-large; envoy extraordinary, plenipotentiary, **minister plenipotentiary;** nuncio, internuncio, apostolic delegate; vice-legate; resident, minister resident; chargé d'affaires, chargé, chargé d'affaires ad interim; secretary of legation, chancellor <Brit>; **attaché,** commercial attaché, military attaché, **consul,** consul general, vice-consul, consular agent; career diplomat

7 foreign office, foreign service, diplomatic service; diplomatic mission, diplomatic staff *or* corps, *corps diplomatique* <Fr>; **embassy, legation;** consular service

8 vice-president, vice-chairman, vice-governor, vice-director, vice-master, vice-chancellor, vice-premier, vice-warden, vice-consul, vice-legate; vice-regent, vice-roy, vicegerent, vice-king, vice-queen, vice-reine, etc

9 secret agent, operative, cloak-and-dagger operative, **undercover man,** inside man <nonformal>; **spy,** espionage agent; counterspy, double agent; **spotter; scout,** reconnoiterer; **intelligence agent** *or* **officer;** CIA man, military-intelligence man, naval-intelligence man; spymaster; spy-catcher <nonformal>, counterintelligence agent

10 detective, operative, investigator, sleuth, Sherlock Holmes <A Conan Doyle>; police detective, Bow Street runner *or* officer <Brit old>, **plainclothesman;** private detective *or* dick, private investigator *or* PI, inquiry agent <Brit>; hotel detective, house detective, house dick <nonformal>, store detective; arson investigator; narcotics agent, narc <nonformal>; FBI agent *or* G-man <nonformal>; treasury agent *or* T-man <nonformal>; Federal *or* fed <nonformal>; Federal Bureau of Investigation *or* FBI; Secret Service

11 <nonformal terms> **dick,** gumshoe, gumshoe man, hawkshaw, sleuthhound, beagle, flatfoot, tec; eye, private eye; skip tracer, spotter

12 secret service, intelligence service, intelligence bureau *or* department; intelligence, military intelligence, naval intelligence; **counterintelligence**

13 <group of delegates> **delegation, deputation, commission, mission;** committee, subcommittee

VERBS **14 represent, act for,** act on behalf of, substitute for, appear for, answer for, speak for, be the voice of, give voice to, be the mouthpiece of <nonformal>, hold the proxy of, hold a brief for, act in the place of, stand in the stead of, serve in one's stead, pinch-hit for <nonformal>; understudy, double for *and* stand in for *and* back up <all nonformal>; front for <nonformal>; deputize, commission

ADJS **15 deputy,** deputative; **acting,** representative

16 diplomatic, ambassadorial, consular, ministerial, plenipotentiary

ADVS **17** by proxy, indirectly; in behalf of 861.12

577 SERVANT, EMPLOYEE

NOUNS **1 retainer,** dependent, follower; myrmidon, yeoman; vassal, liege, liege man, feudatory, homager; inferior, **underling, subordinate,** understrapper;

minion, creature, hanger-on, lackey, flunky, stooge <nonformal>; peon, serf, slave 432.7

2 **servant**, servitor, help; **domestic**, domestic help, domestic servant, house servant; live-in help, day help; **menial**, drudge, slavey <nonformal>; scullion, turnspit

3 **employee**; pensioner, **hireling, mercenary**, myrmidon; hired man, hired hand, man *or* girl Friday, right-hand man, assistant 616.6; worker 726

4 **man**, manservant, serving man, gillie <Scots>, **boy**, *garçon* <Fr>, houseboy, houseman; butler; valet, *valet de chambre* <Fr>, gentleman, gentleman's gentleman; driver, chauffeur, coachman; gardener; lord-in-waiting, lord of the bedchamber, equerry

5 **attendant**, tender, usher, squire, yeoman; errand boy *or* girl, gofer <nonformal>, office boy *or* girl, copyboy; page, footboy; bellboy, bellman, bellhop; cabin boy, purser; printer's devil; chore boy; caddie; bootblack, boots <Brit>; trainbearer; cupbearer, Ganymede, Hebe; orderly, batman <Brit>; **cabin** *or* **flight attendant, steward, stewardess, hostess,** airline stewardess *or* hostess, stew <nonformal>

6 **lackey, flunky,** livery *or* liveried servant; **footman,** *valet de pied* <Fr>

7 **waiter, waitress;** carhop; counterman, soda jerk <nonformal>; busboy; headwaiter, *maître d'hôtel* <Fr>, maître d' <nonformal>; hostess; wine steward, sommelier; bartender, barkeeper *or* barkeep, barman, barmaid <Brit>

8 **maid, maidservant,** servitress, **girl,** servant girl, *bonne* <Fr>, serving girl, wench, biddy <nonformal>, hired girl; lady-help <Brit>, au pair girl, ayah <India>, amah <China>; live-in maid, live-out maid; **handmaid,** handmaiden; **lady's maid,** waiting maid *or* woman, gentlewoman, abigail, soubrette; lady-in-waiting, maid-in-waiting, lady of the bedchamber; companion; chaperon; betweenmaid, tweeny <both Brit>; duenna; parlormaid; kitchenmaid, scullery maid; cook; housemaid, chambermaid, *femme de chambre, fille de chambre* <both Fr>, upstairs maid; nursemaid 1007.8

9 **factotum, do-all** <old>, general servant <Brit>, man of all work; maid of all work, domestic drudge, slavey <nonformal>

10 **major-domo, steward,** house steward, **butler,** chamberlain, *maître d'hôtel* <Fr>, seneschal; **housekeeper**

11 **staff, personnel, employees,** help, hired help, the help, **crew, gang,** men, force, servantry, retinue 768.6

12 **service,** servanthood, servitude <old>, servitorship, *servitium* <L>; **employment, employ; ministry, ministration, attendance,** tendance; serfdom, peonage, slavery 432.1

VERBS 13 **serve, work for,** be in service with, serve one's every need; minister *or* administer to, pander to, do service to; **help** 449.11; **care for,** do for <nonformal>, **look after,** wait on hand and foot, take care of; **wait, wait on** *or* **upon, attend,** tend, attend on *or* upon, dance attendance upon; lackey, valet, maid, chore; drudge 725.14

ADJS 14 **serving,** servitorial, servitial, **ministering,** waiting, **attending,** attendant; in the train of, in one's pay *or* employ; helping 449.20; **menial, servile**

578 FASHION

NOUNS 1 **fashion, style, mode, vogue,** trend, prevailing taste; proper thing, ton, bon ton; custom 373; convention 579.1,2; the swim <nonformal>, current *or* stream of fashion; height of fashion; the new look, the season's look; high fashion, *haute couture* <Fr>

2 **fashionableness,** ton, bon ton, fashionability, **stylishness, modishness,** voguishness; with-itness <nonformal>; **popularity,** prevalence, currency 863.2

3 **smartness, chic,** elegance; style-consciousness, clothes-consciousness; **spruceness, nattiness,** neatness, trimness, sleekness, **dapperness,** jauntiness; sharpness *and* spiffiness *and* classiness *and* niftiness <all nonformal>; swankness *and* swankiness <both nonformal>; foppery, foppishness, coxcombry, dandyism; hipness <nonformal>

4 **the rage,** the thing, **the last word** <nonformal>, *le dernier cri* <Fr>, **the latest thing,** the in thing *and* the latest wrinkle <both nonformal>

5 **fad, craze, rage;** wrinkle <nonformal>; new take <nonformal>; novelty 840.2; faddishness, faddiness <nonformal>, faddism; **faddist;** the bandwagon, metooism

6 **society,** *société* <Fr>, fashionable society, **polite society, high society,** high life, *beau monde, haut monde* <both Fr>, good society; best people, people of fashion, right people; *monde* <Fr>, world of fashion, Vanity Fair; **smart set** <nonformal>;

the Four Hundred, **upper crust** *and* upper cut <both nonformal>; **cream of society,** *crème de la crème* <Fr>, elite, carriage trade; café society, jet set, beautiful people, in-crowd, the glitterati <nonformal>; *jeunesse dorée* <Fr>; drawing room, salon; social register

7 person of fashion, fashionable, man-about-town, man *or* woman of the world, nob, *mondain, mondaine* <both Fr>; leader *or* arbiter of fashion, tastemaker, trendsetter, tonesetter, *arbiter elegantiae* <L>; ten best-dressed, fashion plate, clotheshorse, sharpy <nonformal>, "the glass of fashion and the mold of form"— Shakespeare, Beau Brummel; fop, dandy 500.9; **socialite; clubwoman,** clubman; salonist, salonnard; jet setter; swinger <nonformal>; **debutante,** subdebutante, deb *and* subdeb <both nonformal>

VERBS 8 **catch on,** become popular, **become the rage,** catch *or* take fire

9 **be fashionable, be the style, be the rage,** be the thing; have a run; cut a figure in society <nonformal>, give a tone to society, set the fashion *or* style *or* tone; dress to kill

10 **follow the fashion, get in the swim** <nonformal>, get *or* climb *or* jump on the bandwagon <nonformal>, join the parade, follow the crowd, go with the stream *or* tide *or* current *or* flow; keep in step, do as others do; keep up, **keep up appearances,** keep up with the Joneses

ADJS 11 **fashionable, in fashion, smart, in style, in vogue; all the rage,** all the thing; **popular,** prevalent, current 863.12; **up-to-date,** up-to-datish, up-to-the-minute, switched-on *and* hip *and* with-it <all nonformal>, trendy <nonformal>, new-fashioned, modern, new 840.9,10,12−14; **in the swim;** sought-after, much sought-after

12 **stylish, modish,** voguish, vogue; dressy <nonformal>; *soigné or soignée* <both Fr>; *à la mode* <Fr>, in the mode

13 **chic, smart,** elegant; style-conscious, clothes-conscious; **well-dressed,** well-groomed, *soignée or soignée* <both Fr>, dressed to advantage, all dressed up, dressed to kill, dressed to the teeth, dressed to the nines, well-turned-out; **spruce, natty,** neat, trim, sleek, smug, trig, tricksy <old>; **dapper,** dashing, jaunty, braw <Scots>; sharp *and* spiffy *and* classy *and* nifty *and* snazzy <all nonformal>; **swank** *or* **swanky** <nonformal>, posh <nonformal>, ritzy <nonformal>, swell *and* nobby <both non-

formal>; genteel; exquisite, *recherché* <Fr>; cosmopolitan, sophisticated

14 **ultrafashionable,** ultrastylish, ultra-smart; chichi; foppish, dandified, dandyish, dandiacal

15 **trendy** <nonformal>, **faddish,** faddy <nonformal>

16 **socially prominent, in society,** high-society, elite; café-society, jet-set; lace-curtain, silk-stocking

ADVS 17 **fashionably, stylishly, modishly,** *à la mode* <Fr>, in the latest style *or* mode

18 **smartly,** dressily, chicly, elegantly, exquisitely; **sprucely, nattily,** neatly, trimly, sleekly; **dapperly,** jauntily, dashingly, swankly *or* swankily <nonformal>; foppishly, dandyishly

579 SOCIAL CONVENTION

NOUNS 1 **social convention, convention,** conventional usage, what is done, what one does, **social usage, form, formality; custom** 373; **conformism, conformity** 866; **propriety, decorum,** decorousness, correctness, *convenance, bienséance* <both Fr>, decency, seemliness, civility <old>, good form, etiquette 580.3; **conventionalism, conventionality, Grundyism; Mrs Grundy**

2 **the conventions, the proprieties, the mores,** the right things, accepted *or* sanctioned conduct, what is done, civilized behavior; **dictates of society,** dictates of Mrs Grundy

3 conventionalist, Grundy, Mrs Grundy; conformist 866.2

VERBS 4 **conform,** observe the proprieties, play the game, follow the rules 866.4, fall in *or* into line

ADJS 5 **conventional, decorous,** orthodox, **correct,** right, **right-thinking, proper,** decent, seemly, meet; **accepted, recognized,** acknowledged, received, admitted, approved, being done; *comme il faut, de rigueur* <both Fr>; **traditional, customary;** formal 580.7; conformable 866.5

ADVS 6 **conventionally,** decorously, orthodoxly; **customarily, traditionally;** correctly, properly, as is proper, as it should be, *comme il faut* <Fr>; according to use *or* custom, according to the dictates of society *or* Mrs Grundy

580 FORMALITY

NOUNS 1 **formality, form, formalness; ceremony,** ceremonial, **ceremoniousness; the red carpet; ritual,** rituality; extrinsicality, impersonality 767.1; formalization, stylization, conventionalization; **stiffness, stiltedness,** primness, prissiness, rigidness, starchiness, buckram <old>, **dignity,** gravity, weight, *gravitas* <L>, weighty dignity, staidness, reverend seriousness, **solemnity** 111; **pomp** 501.6; pomposity 501.7

2 **formalism, ceremonialism, ritualism;** legalism; pedantry, pedantism, pedanticism; precisianism, preciseness, preciousness, preciosity, purism; punctiliousness, punctilio, scrupulousness

3 **etiquette,** social code, rules *or* code of conduct; **formalities,** social procedures, social conduct, what is done, what one does; **manners,** good manners, exquisite manners, quiet good manners, **politeness,** *politesse* <Fr>; natural politeness, comity, civility 504.1; **amenities,** decencies, civilities, elegancies, **social graces, mores, proprieties;** decorum, good form; **courtliness,** elegance 533; **protocol,** diplomatic code; punctilio, point of etiquette; convention, social usage; table manners

4 <ceremonial function> **ceremony,** ceremonial; **rite, ritual, formality; solemnity, service, function,** office, **observance,** performance; **exercise,** exercises; **celebration,** solemnization; **liturgy,** religious ceremony; **rite of passage,** *rite de passage* <Fr>; convocation; commencement, commencement exercises; graduation, graduation exercises; baccalaureate service; inaugural, inauguration; initiation; formal; empty formality *or* ceremony, mummery

VERBS 5 **formalize,** ritualize, solemnize, **celebrate,** dignify; **observe;** conventionalize, stylize

6 **stand on ceremony,** observe the formalities, follow protocol

ADJS 7 **formal,** formulary; formalist, formalistic; legalistic; pedantic, pedantical; stylized, conventionalized; extrinsic, outward, impersonal 767.3; surface, **superficial, nominal** 527.15

8 **ceremonious, ceremonial; red-carpet; ritualistic, ritual;** hieratic, hieratical, sacerdotal, liturgic; **grave, solemn** 111.3; **pompous** 501.22; **stately** 501.21; well-mannered 504.16; **conventional,** decorous 579.5

9 **stiff, stilted,** prim, prissy, rigid, starch, starchy, starched; buckram *and* in buckram <both old>

10 **punctilious, scrupulous, precise,** precisian, precisionist, precious, puristic; by-the-book; exact, **meticulous** 339.12; **orderly, methodical** 806.6

ADVS 11 **formally,** in due form, in set form; **ceremoniously, ritually,** ritualistically; **solemnly** 111.4; for form's sake, *pro forma* <L>, **as a matter of form;** by the book

12 **stiffly, stiltedly,** starchly, primly, rigidly

581 INFORMALITY

NOUNS 1 **informality, informalness, unceremoniousness; casualness,** offhandedness, **ease, easiness,** easygoingness; **relaxedness;** affability, graciousness, cordiality, sociability 582; Bohemianism, unconventionality 867.2; **familiarity; naturalness,** simplicity, plainness, homeliness, homeyness, folksiness <nonformal>, common touch, **unaffectedness,** unpretentiousness 499.2; unconstraint, unconstrainedness, looseness; irregularity

VERBS 2 **not stand on ceremony,** let one's hair down <nonformal>, be oneself, be at ease, come as you are; relax

ADJS 3 **informal, unceremonious; casual, offhand,** offhanded, throwaway <nonformal>, unstudied, easy, easygoing, free and easy; *dégagé* <Fr>; **relaxed;** affable, gracious, cordial, sociable; Bohemian, unconventional 867.6; **familiar; natural,** simple, plain, homely, homey, down-home *and* folksy <both nonformal>, *haymish* <Yiddish>; **unaffected, unassuming** 499.7; unconstrained, loose; irregular; unofficial

ADVS 4 **informally, unceremoniously,** without ceremony, *sans cérémonie, sans façon* <both Fr>; **casually,** offhand, offhandedly; relaxedly; familiarly; **naturally,** simply, plainly; **unaffectedly, unassumingly** 499.11; unconstrainedly, unofficially; *en famille* <Fr>

582 SOCIABILITY

NOUNS 1 **sociability,** sociality, sociableness, fitness *or* fondness for society, social-mindedness, **gregariousness, affability,** companionability, compatibility, geniality, *Gemütlichkeit* <Ger>, **congeniality;** hospitality 585; clubbability <nonformal>, clubbishness, clubbiness, clubbism; intimacy, familiarity; amiability, **friendliness** 587.1; **communicativeness** 343.3; social grace, civility, urbanity, courtesy 504

2 **camaraderie,** comradery, comradeship, **fellowship, good-fellowship;** male bond-

ing; consorting, hobnobbing, hanging *and* hanging out <both nonformal>

3 **conviviality, joviality, jollity,** gaiety, heartiness, cheer, good cheer, festivity, partying, merrymaking, merriment, revelry

4 **social life, social intercourse,** social activity, **intercourse, communication, communion,** intercommunion, **fellowship,** intercommunication, **community,** collegiality, commerce, congress, converse, conversation, social relations

5 **social circle** *or* **set,** social class, one's crowd *or* set, clique, coterie, crowd <nonformal>; **association** 617

6 **association,** consociation, affiliation, bonding, social bonding, **fellowship, companionship, company, society;** fraternity, **fraternization;** membership, participation, partaking, sharing, cooperation 450

7 **visit, social call,** call; formal visit, duty visit, required visit; exchange visit; flying visit, look-in; visiting, visitation; round of visits; social round, social whirl, mad round

8 **appointment, engagement, date** <nonformal>, double date *and* blind date <both nonformal>; arrangement, interview; engagement book

9 **rendezvous, tryst, assignation, meeting;** trysting place, meeting place, place of assignation; assignation house; love nest <nonformal>

10 **social gathering, social,** sociable, social affair, social hour, hospitality hour, affair, gathering, get-together <nonformal>; **reception,** at home, salon, levee, soiree; matinee; reunion, family reunion; wake

11 **party,** <see list> **entertainment,** party time, **festivity** 743.3,4

12 <nonformal terms> **brawl, bash,** blast, clambake, wingding, hoodang, blowout, shindig, shindy, do *and* bean-feast *and* knees-up *and* rave *and* rave-up <all Brit>

13 **tea,** afternoon tea, five-o'clock tea, high tea, cream tea

14 bee, quilting bee, raising bee, husking bee, cornhusking, corn shucking, husking

15 **debut, coming out** <nonformal>, presentation

16 <sociable person> joiner, mixer *and* **good mixer** <both nonformal>, good *or* pleasant company, excellent companion, life of the party, bon vivant; man-about-town, playboy, social lion, nightclub habitué; clubman, clubwoman; salonnard, salonist

VERBS 17 **associate with,** assort with, sort with, consort with, hobnob with, fall in with, go around with, **mingle with, mix with, touch** *or* **rub elbows** *or* **shoulders with,** eat off the same trencher; **fraternize,** fellowship, join in fellowship; **keep company with,** bear one's company, walk hand in hand with; **join; flock together,** herd together, club together

18 <nonformal terms> **hang with,** hang out *or* around with, clique, clique with, gang up with, run with, chum, chum together, pal, pal with, pal up *or* around with, run around with, run with; take *or* tie up with

19 **visit,** make *or* pay a visit, **call on** *or* **upon, drop in,** run *or* stop in, look in, look one up, see, stop off *or* over <nonformal>, drop *or* run *or* stop by, drop around *or* round; leave one's card; exchange visits

20 have *or* give a party, entertain

21 <nonformal terms> **throw a party; party,** have fun, live it up, have a ball, ball, boogie, jam, kick up one's heels, make whoopee, whoop it up

ADJS 22 **sociable, social,** social-minded, fit for society, fond of society, **gregarious, affable; companionable,** companionate, compatible, genial, *gemütlich* <Ger>, **congenial;** hospitable 585.11; clubby, clubbable <both nonformal>, clubbish; **communicative** 343.10; amiable, **friendly;** civil, urbane, courteous 504.14

23 **convivial,** boon, free and easy, hail-fellow-well-met; **jovial, jolly,** hearty, festive, gay

24 **intimate, familiar,** cozy, chatty, *tête-à-tête* <Fr>; man-to-man, woman-to-woman

ADVS 25 **sociably,** socially, gregariously, affably; friendlily, companionably, arm in arm, hand in hand, hand in glove

26 **types of parties**

ball	masquerade party *or*
birthday party	mask *or* masque *or*
cocktail party	masquerade
coffee party *or* kaffee	open house
klatsch *or* coffee	pajama party
klatsch	shower
dinner party	smoker <nonfor-
fête champêtre	mal>
<Fr>	stag *or* stag party
garden party	<nonformal>
house-warming	surprise party
masked ball *or* bal	tea party
masqué <Fr>	*thé dansante* <Fr>

583 UNSOCIABILITY

NOUNS 1 **unsociability,** insociability, unsociableness, dissociability, dissociableness; **ungregariousness,** uncompanionability; unclubbableness *or* unclubbability <both nonformal>, ungeniality, **uncon-geniality**; incompatibility, social incompatibility; **unfriendliness** 589.1; **uncommunicativeness** 344; sullenness, mopishness, moroseness; self-sufficiency, self-containment; autism, catatonia; bashfulness 139.4

2 **aloofness, standoffishness**, offishness, withdrawnness, **remoteness**, distance, detachment; **coolness**, coldness, frigidity, chill, chilliness, iciness, frostiness; cold shoulder; inaccessibility, unapproachability

3 seclusiveness, **seclusion** 584; exclusiveness, exclusivity

VERBS 4 **keep to oneself**, keep oneself to oneself, not mix *or* mingle, enjoy *or* prefer one's own company, stay at home, shun companionship, be a poor mixer, **stand aloof**, hold oneself aloof *or* apart, keep one's distance, keep at a distance, keep in the background, retire, retire into the shade, creep into a corner, seclude oneself; have nothing to do with 586.5, be unfriendly, not give one the time of day

ADJS 5 **unsociable**, insociable, dissociable, unsocial; **ungregarious**, nongregarious; **uncompanionable**, ungenial, uncongenial; incompatible, socially incompatible; unclubbable <nonformal>; **unfriendly** 589.9; **uncommunicative** 344.8; sullen, mopish, mopey, morose; close, snug; self-sufficient, self-contained; autistic, catatonic; bashful 139.12

6 **aloof, standoffish**, offish, standoff, **distant, remote**, withdrawn, removed, detached, Olympian; **cool**, cold, cold-fish, frigid, chilly, icy, frosty; seclusive; exclusive; inaccessible, unapproachable; tight-assed <nonformal>

584 SECLUSION

NOUNS 1 **seclusion**, reclusion, **retirement, withdrawal, retreat**, recess; renunciation *or* forsaking of the world; cocooning; **sequestration**, quarantine, separation, detachment, apartness; segregation, apartheid, Jim Crow; **isolation**, "splendid isolation"—Sir William Goschen; ivory tower, ivory-towerism, ivory-towerishness; **privacy**, privatism, **secrecy**; rustication; privatization; isolationism

2 **hermitism**, hermitry, eremitism, anchoritism, anchoretism, cloistered monasticism

3 **solitude**, solitariness, **aloneness**, loneness, singleness; **loneliness, lonesomeness**

4 **forlornness, desolation**; friendlessness, kithlessness, fatherlessness, motherlessness, homelessness, rootlessness; helplessness, defenselessness; abandonment, desertion

5 **recluse, loner**, solitaire, solitary, solitudinarian; **shut-in**, invalid, bedridden invalid; cloistered monk *or* nun; **hermit**, eremite, anchorite, anchoret; marabout; hermitess, anchoress; **ascetic**; closet cynic; stylite, pillarist, pillar saint; Hieronymite, Hieronymian; Diogenes, Timon of Athens, St Simeon Stylites, St Anthony, desert saints, desert fathers; outcast, pariah 586.4; **stay-at-home, homebody; isolationist**, seclusionist; ivory-towerist, ivory-towerite

6 **retreat** 1008.5, **hideaway, cell, ivory tower**, hidey-hole <nonformal>, lair, sanctum, sanctum sanctorum, inner sanctum

VERBS 7 **seclude oneself, go into seclusion, retire, go into retirement**, retire from the world, abandon *or* forsake the world, live in retirement, lead a retired life, lead a cloistered life, sequester *or* sequestrate oneself, be *or* remain incommunicado, shut oneself up, live alone, live apart, retreat to one's ivory tower; stay at home; rusticate; take the veil; cop out <nonformal>, opt out *or* drop out of society

ADJS 8 **secluded, seclusive, retired, withdrawn; isolated**, shut off, insular, **separate**, separated, **apart**, detached, removed; segregated, quarantined; **remote, out-of-the-way**, up-country, in a backwater, out-of-the-world, out-back *and* back of beyond <both Austral>; **unfrequented**, unvisited, off the beaten track; untraveled

9 **private**, privatistic, reclusive; ivory-towered, ivory-towerish

10 **recluse, reclusive, sequestered, cloistered**, sequestrated, shut up *or* in; hermitlike, hermitic, hermitical, eremitic, eremitical, hermitish; anchoritic, anchoritical; stay-at-home, domestic; homebound

11 **solitary, alone; in solitude**, by oneself, all alone; **lonely, lonesome, lone**; lonely-hearts

12 **forlorn**, lorn; **abandoned, forsaken, deserted, desolate**, godforsaken <nonformal>, friendless, unfriended, kithless, fatherless, motherless, homeless; helpless, defenseless; outcast 586.10

ADVS 13 **in seclusion, in retirement**, in retreat, in solitude; in privacy, in secrecy; "far from the madding crowd's ignoble strife"—Thomas Gray, "the world forgetting by the world forgot"—Pope

585 HOSPITALITY, WELCOME

NOUNS **1 hospitality,** hospitableness, receptiveness; honors *or* freedom of the house; **cordiality,** amiability, graciousness, **friendliness,** neighborliness, geniality, heartiness, bonhomie, **generosity,** liberality, openheartedness, warmth, warmness, warmheartedness; open door

2 **welcome,** welcoming, **reception,** *accueil* <Fr>; cordial *or* warm *or* hearty welcome, pleasant *or* smiling reception, the glad hand <nonformal>, **open arms; embrace, hug;** welcome mat

3 **greetings, salutations,** salaams; **regards,** best wishes 504.8

4 **greeting, salutation,** salute; **hail, hello,** how-do-you-do; accost, address; nod, bow, bob; curtsy 155.2; wave; handshake, handclasp; namaste; open arms, embrace, hug, kiss; smile, smile *or* nod of recognition, nod

5 **host,** mine host; hostess, receptionist, greeter; landlord 470.2

6 **guest, visitor,** visitant; **caller,** company; invited guest, invitee; frequenter, habitué, haunter; uninvited guest, gatecrasher <nonformal>; moocher *and* freeloader <both nonformal>

VERBS **7 receive, admit,** accept, take in, let in, open the door to; **be at home to,** have the latchstring out, keep a light in the window, put out the welcome mat, keep the door open, keep an open house, keep the home fires burning

8 **entertain,** entertain guests, guest; host, preside, do the honors <nonformal>; give a party, throw a party <nonformal>; spread oneself <nonformal>

9 **welcome,** make welcome, bid one welcome, bid one feel at home, make one feel welcome *or* at home *or* like one of the family, do the honors of the house, give one the freedom of the house, hold out the hand, extend the right hand of friendship; glad hand *and* give the glad hand *and* glad eye <all nonformal>; **embrace, hug, receive** *or* **welcome with open arms;** give a warm reception to, "kill the fatted calf"—Bible, roll out the red carpet, give the red-carpet treatment, receive royally, make feel like a king *or* queen

10 **greet, hail, accost,** address; **salute,** make one's salutations; **bid** *or* **say hello,** bid

good day *or* good morning, etc; exchange greetings, **pass the time of day; give one's regards** 504.13; shake hands, shake *and* give one some skin *and* give a high *or* a low five <all nonformal>, press the flesh <nonformal>, press *or* squeeze one's hand; nod to, bow to; curtsy 155.6; tip the hat to, lift the hat, touch the hat *or* cap; take one's hat off to, uncover; pull *or* tug at the forelock; kiss, greet with a kiss, kiss hands *or* cheeks

ADJS **11 hospitable, receptive,** welcoming; **cordial,** amiable, gracious, **friendly,** neighborly, genial, hearty, open, openhearted, warm, warmhearted; **generous,** liberal

12 **welcome,** welcome as the roses in May, wanted, desired, wished-for; **agreeable,** desirable, acceptable; **grateful,** gratifying, pleasing

ADVS **13 hospitably, with open arms;** friendlily

INTERJS **14 welcome!,** *soyez le bienvenu!* <Fr>, *¡bien venido!* <Sp>, *benvenuto!* <Ital>, *Willkommen!* <Ger>; glad to see you!

15 **greetings!,** salutations!, **hello!,** hullo!, hail!, hey! *or* heigh!, **hi!,** aloha!, *¡hola!* <Sp>; **how do you do?, how are you?,** *comment allez-vous?, comment ça va?* <both Fr>, *¿cómo está Usted?* <Sp>, *come sta?* <Ital>, *wie geht's?* <Ger>; **good morning!,** *guten Morgen!* <Ger>; good day!, *bon jour!* <Fr>, *¡buenos días!* <Sp>, *buon giorno!* <Ital>, *guten Tag!* <Ger>; **good afternoon!,** *¡buenas tardes!* <Sp>; **good evening!,** *bon soir!* <Fr>, *buona sera!* <Ital>, *guten Abend!* <Ger>

16 <nonformal terms> **howdy!,** howdy-do!, how-de-do!, how-do-ye-do!, how-d'ye-do!, how you doin'?, hi ya!; how's things?, how's tricks?, how goes it?, how's every little thing?, how's the world treating you?, **yo!,** ahoy!, hey!; long time no see!

586 INHOSPITALITY

NOUNS **1 inhospitality,** inhospitableness, unhospitableness, unreceptiveness; **uncordialness,** ungraciousness, **unfriendliness,** unneighborliness; nonwelcome, nonwelcoming

2 unhabitability, uninhabitability, unlivability

3 **ostracism,** ostracization, thumbs down; **banishment** 908.4; **proscription, ban; boycott,** boycottage; **blackball,** blackballing, blacklist; **rejection** 442.1

4 **outcast,** social outcast, outcast of society,

castaway, **derelict,** Ishmael; **pariah, untouchable,** leper; outcaste; *déclassé*
<Fr>; **outlaw; expellee, evictee; dis-
placed person** *or* **DP; exile, expatriate,**
man without a country; undesirable; *persona non grata* <L>, unacceptable person
VERBS **5 have nothing to do with,** have no
truck with <nonformal>, refuse to associate with, steer clear of <nonformal>,
spurn, turn one's back upon, not give one
the time of day <nonformal>; deny oneself to, refuse to receive, not be at home
to; shut the door upon
6 **ostracize,** turn thumbs down, disfellowship; **reject** 442.3, **exile, banish** 908.17;
proscribe, ban, outlaw 444.3, put under
the ban; **boycott, blackball,** blacklist
ADJS **7 inhospitable,** unhospitable; **unreceptive,** closed; **uncordial,** ungracious, **unfriendly,** unneighborly
8 **unhabitable, uninhabitable,** nonhabita-
ble, unoccupiable, untenantable, **unlivable, unfit to live in,** not fit for man
or beast
9 **unwelcome, unwanted; unagreeable,** undesirable, unacceptable; **uninvited,** unasked, unbidden
10 **outcast, cast-off, castaway, derelict;** outlawed 444.7, outside the pale, outside the
gates; **rejected, disowned; abandoned,
forsaken**

587 FRIENDSHIP

NOUNS **1 friendship, friendliness; amicability,** amicableness, amity, peaceableness, unhostility; **amiability,** amiable-
ness, **congeniality,** well-affectedness;
neighborliness, neighborlikeness; sociability 582; **affection, love** 104; **loving
kindness, kindness** 143
2 **fellowship, companionship, comradeship,** colleagueship, chumship <non-
formal>, palship <nonformal>, freemasonry, consortship, boon companionship; comradery, camaraderie, male
bonding; **brotherhood, fraternity,** fraternalism, sodality, confraternity; **sisterhood, sorority;** brotherliness, sisterliness;
community of interest, *esprit de corps*
<Fr>
3 **good terms, good understanding,** good
footing, friendly relations; **harmony,**
sympathy, fellow feeling, **rapport** 455.1;
favor, goodwill, good graces, regard, respect, mutual regard, favorable regard,
the good *or* right side of <nonformal>;
an in <nonformal>
4 **acquaintance,** acquaintedness, close ac-

quaintance; **introduction,** presentation,
knockdown <nonformal>
5 **familiarity, intimacy,** intimate acquaintance, closeness, nearness, inseparable-
ness, inseparability; **affinity,** special affinity, mutual affinity; **chumminess**
<nonformal>, palliness *or* palsiness *or*
palsy-walsiness <nonformal>, matey-
ness <Brit nonformal>
6 **cordiality, geniality,** heartiness, bonhomie, ardency, warmth, warmness,
affability, warmheartedness; hospitality
585
7 **devotion, devotedness;** dedication, commitment; fastness, steadfastness,
firmness, constancy, staunchness; tried-
ness, trueness, true-blueness, tried-and-
trueness
8 cordial friendship, warm *or* ardent
friendship, devoted friendship, bosom
friendship, intimate *or* familiar friendship, sincere friendship, beautiful
friendship, fast *or* firm friendship,
staunch friendship, loyal friendship, lasting friendship, undying friendship
VERBS **9 be friends,** have the friendship of,
have the ear of; be old friends *or* friends of
long standing, be long acquainted, go
way back; **know, be acquainted with;** associate with; cotton to *and* hit it off
<both nonformal>, get on well with,
hobnob with, fraternize with; be close
friends with, be best friends, be inseparable; **be on good terms,** enjoy good *or*
friendly relations with; keep on good
terms, have an in with <nonformal>
10 **befriend, make friends with,** gain the
friendship of, **strike up a friendship,** get
to know one another, take up with
<nonformal>, shake hands with, **get ac-
quainted,** make *or* scrape acquaintance
with, pick up an acquaintance with; win
friends, win friends and influence people
11 <nonformal terms> **be buddy-buddy** *or*
palsy-walsy with, click, have good *or*
great chemistry, team up; **get next to, get
palsy** *or* **palsy-walsy with,** get cozy with,
cozy *or* snuggle up to, get close to, get
chummy with, buddy *or* pal up with, play
footsie with
12 **cultivate,** cultivate the friendship of,
court, pay court to, pay addresses to, seek
the company of, **run after** <nonformal>,
shine up to, make up to <nonformal>,
play up to *and* suck up to <both nonfor-
mal>, hold out *or* extend the right of
friendship *or* fellowship; **make advances,**
approach, break the ice
13 **get on good terms with,** get into favor,

win the regard of, **get in the good graces
of, get in good with,** get in with *or* on the
in with *and* get next to <all nonformal>,
get on the good *or* **right side of** <nonformal>; stay friends with, keep in with
<nonformal>

14 **introduce, present, acquaint,** make acquainted, give an introduction, give a
knockdown <nonformal>, do the honors
<nonformal>

ADJS 15 **friendly,** friendlike; **amicable,
peaceable,** unhostile; **harmonious** 455.3;
amiable, congenial, *simpático* <Sp>,
simpatico <Ital>, *sympathique* <Fr>,
pleasant, agreeable, favorable, well-affected, well-disposed, well-intentioned,
well-meaning, well-meant; brotherly, fraternal; sisterly; neighborly, neighborlike;
sociable; kind 143.13

16 **cordial, genial,** hearty, ardent, warm,
warmhearted, affable; hospitable 585.11

17 **friends with,** friendly with, at home with;
acquainted

18 **on good terms,** on a good footing, on
friendly *or* amicable terms, **on speaking
terms,** on a first-name basis, on visiting
terms; **in good with,** in with *and* on the in
with *and* in <all nonformal>, **in favor, in
one's good graces,** in one's good books, on
the good *or* right side of <nonformal>

19 **familiar, intimate, close,** near, inseparable, on familiar *or* intimate terms; just
between the two, one-on-one, man-to-man, woman-to-woman; hand-in-hand,
hand and glove *or* hand in glove; **thick,
thick as thieves** <nonformal>

20 **chummy** <nonformal>, matey <Brit
nonformal>; pally *and* palsy *and* palsy-walsy *and* buddy-buddy <all nonformal>

21 **devoted,** dedicated, committed, **fast,**
steadfast, constant, faithful, staunch;
tried, true, **tried and true,** true-blue,
tested

ADVS 22 **amicably,** friendly, friendlily,
friendliwise; **amiably, congenially,** pleasantly, agreeably, favorably; **cordially,
genially,** heartily, ardently, warmly, with
open arms; familiarly, intimately; arm in
arm, hand in hand, hand in glove

588 FRIEND

NOUNS 1 **friend, acquaintance,** close acquaintance; confidant, confidante, repository; **intimate,** familiar, **close friend,**
intimate *or* familiar friend; **bosom friend,**
friend of one's bosom, inseparable friend,
best friend; alter ego, other self; brother,

fellow, fellowman, fellow creature, neighbor; **sympathizer,** well-wisher, partisan,
advocate, favorer, backer, **supporter**
616.9; casual acquaintance; pickup
<nonformal>; lover 104.12; live-in lover,
POSSLQ *or* person of opposite sex sharing living quarters, significant other

2 **good friend, best friend,** great friend, **devoted friend,** warm *or* ardent friend,
faithful friend, trusted *or* trusty friend,
fidus Achates <L>, constant friend,
staunch friend, fast friend, "a friend that
sticketh closer than a brother"—Bible;
friend in need, friend indeed

3 **companion, fellow,** fellow companion,
comrade, *camarade* <Fr>, amigo <nonformal>, mate <Brit>, comate, company, **associate** 616, consociate, compeer,
confrere, consort, **colleague, partner,** copartner, side partner, **crony,** old crony,
gossip; girlfriend <nonformal>; **roommate,** chamberfellow; flatmate; bunkmate, bunkie <nonformal>; bedfellow,
bedmate; **schoolmate,** schoolfellow,
classmate, classfellow, school companion, school chum, fellow student *or* pupil;
playmate, playfellow; **teammate,** yokefellow, yokemate; workmate, workfellow
616.5; shipmate; messmate; comrade in
arms

4 <nonformal terms> **pal, buddy,** bud,
buddy-boy, bosom buddy, asshole buddy,
main man, home boy, goombah, landsman, paesan, paesano, pally, palsy-walsy,
road dog, walkboy, cobber <Austral>,
pardner, pard, sidekick, tillicum, **chum,**
ace, mate *and* butty <both Brit>

5 **boon companion,** boonfellow; **good fellow,** jolly fellow, hearty, *bon vivant*
<Fr>; pot companion

6 <famous friendships> Achilles and Patroclus, Castor and Pollux, Damon and
Pythias, David and Jonathan, Diomedes
and Sthenelus, Epaminondas and Pelopidas, Hercules and Iolaus, Nisus and
Euryalus, Pylades and Orestes, Theseus
and Pirithoüs, Christ and the beloved disciple; the Three Musketeers

589 ENMITY

NOUNS 1 **enmity, unfriendliness,** inimicality; **uncordiality,** unamiability, ungeniality, disaffinity, incompatibility,
incompatibleness; personal conflict,
strain, **tension;** coolness, coldness, chilliness, chill, frost, iciness, the freeze;
inhospitality 586, unsociability 583

2 **disaccord** 456; ruffled feelings, strained

relations, alienation, **disaffection, estrangement** 456.4

3 **hostility, antagonism, repugnance, antipathy,** spitefulness, spite, despitefulness, malice, malevolence, malignity, **hatred, hate** 103; **conflict, contention** 457, collision, clash, clashing, **friction;** quarrelsomeness 456.3; belligerence

4 **animosity,** animus; **ill will,** ill feeling, bitter feeling, **hard feelings,** no love lost; **bad blood,** ill blood, feud, blood feud, vendetta; **bitterness,** sourness, soreness, **rancor,** acrimony, virulence, venom, vitriol

5 **grudge, spite,** crow to pick *or* pluck *or* pull, bone to pick; peeve *and* pet peeve <both nonformal>

6 **enemy, foe,** foeman **adversary, antagonist;** bitter enemy; sworn enemy; open enemy; public enemy; archenemy, devil; "my nearest and dearest enemy"— Thomas Middleton; the other side, the opposition; **bane** 395.8, bête noire

VERBS 7 **antagonize,** set against, set at odds, set at each other's throat, sick on each other <nonformal>; aggravate, exacerbate, heat up, **provoke,** envenom, **embitter,** infuriate, madden; **alienate,** estrange 456.14; be alienated *or* estranged, draw *or* grow apart

8 **bear ill will,** bear malice, have it in for <nonformal>, hold it against, be down on <nonformal>; **bear** *or* **harbor** *or* **nurse a grudge,** owe a grudge, have a bone to pick with; no love is lost between; have a crow to pick *or* pluck *or* pull with; pick a quarrel; **hate** 103.5

ADJS 9 **unfriendly, inimical, unamicable; uncordial,** unamiable, ungenial, incompatible; strained, tense; disaccordant, unharmonious; cool, cold, chill, chilly, frosty, icy; inhospitable 586.7; unsociable 583.5

10 **hostile, antagonistic,** repugnant, antipathetic, set against, snide, spiteful, despiteful, malicious, malevolent, malignant, hateful, full of hate *or* hatred; virulent, **bitter,** sore, rancorous, acrid, caustic, venomous, vitriolic; conflicting, clashing, colliding; quarrelsome 456.17; **provocative,** off-putting; belligerent

11 **alienated, estranged,** pffft <nonformal>, disaffected, separated, divided, disunited, torn; irreconcilable

12 **at outs, on the outs** <nonformal>, at enmity, at variance, **at odds,** at loggerheads, at cross-purposes, at sixes and sevens, at each other's throat, at swords points, at daggers drawn

13 **on bad terms,** not on speaking terms; in bad with <nonformal>, in bad odor with, in one's bad *or* black books, on one's shitlist *or* drop-dead list <nonformal>

ADVS 14 **unamicably,** inimically; **uncordially,** unamiably, ungenially; coolly, coldly, chillily, frostily; **hostilely, antagonistically**

590 MISANTHROPY

NOUNS 1 **misanthropy,** misanthropism, people-hating, Timonism, cynicism, antisociality, antisocial sentiments *or* attitudes; unsociability 583; **man-hating,** misandry; **woman-hating,** misogyny; **sexism,** sex discrimination, sexual stereotyping, male *or* female chauvinism

2 **misanthrope,** misanthropist, people-hater, cynic, Timon, Timonist; **man-hater,** misandrist; **woman-hater,** misogynist; **sexist,** male *or* female chauvinist, chauvinist

ADJS 3 **misanthropic,** people-hating, Timonist, Timonistic, cynical, **antisocial;** unsociable 583.5; **man-hating,** misandrist; **woman-hating,** misogynic, misogynistic, misogynous; **sexist,** male- *or* female-chauvinistic, chauvinistic

591 PUBLIC SPIRIT

NOUNS 1 **public spirit,** social consciousness *or* responsibility; **citizenship, good citizenship,** citizenism, civism; altruism

2 **patriotism,** love of country; "the last refuge of a scoundrel"—Samuel Johnson; **nationalism,** nationality, ultranationalism; Americanism, Anglicism, Briticism, etc; **chauvinism, jingoism,** overpatriotism; patriotics, flag-waving; saber-rattling

3 **patriot;** nationalist; ultranationalist; **chauvinist,** chauvin, **jingo,** jingoist; patrioteer <nonformal>, flag waver, superpatriot, hard hat <nonformal>, hundred-percenter, hundred-percent American; hawk

ADJS 4 **public-spirited, civic; patriotic; nationalistic;** ultranationalist, ultranationalistic; overpatriotic, superpatriotic, flagwaving, **chauvinist, chauvinistic,** jingoist, jingoistic; hawkish

592 BENEFACTOR

NOUNS 1 **benefactor,** benefactress, **benefiter,** succorer, befriender; ministrant, ministering angel; Samaritan, **good**

Samaritan; **helper,** aider, assister, help, aid, helping hand, "a very present help in time of trouble"—Bible; Johnny-on-the-spot <nonformal>, jack-at-a-pinch <old Brit nonformal>; angel <nonformal>, **patron, backer** 616.9, angel *and* cash cow <both nonformal>; **good person** 659

2 **savior, redeemer,** deliverer, **liberator,** rescuer, freer, **emancipator,** manumitter

VERBS 3 **benefit, aid,** assist, succor; befriend, take under one's wing; back, support; save the day, save one's neck *or* skin *or* bacon

ADJS 4 benefitting, aiding, befriending, assisting; backing, supporting; saving, salving, salvational, redemptive, redeeming; liberating, freeing, emancipative, emancipating, manumitting

ADVS 5 by one's aid *or* good offices, with one's support, on one's shoulders *or* coattails

PREPS 6 with *or* by benefit of, with *or* by the aid of

593 EVILDOER

NOUNS 1 **evildoer, wrongdoer,** worker of ill *or* evil, **malefactor,** malfeasant, malfeasor, misfeasor, malevolent, public enemy, **sinner, villain,** villainess, transgressor, delinquent; bad *or* bad guy *and* baddy *and* meany *and* wrongo *and* black hat <all nonformal>, wrong'un <Brit nonformal>; **criminal,** outlaw, felon, **crook** <nonformal>, lawbreaker, perpetrator, perp <nonformal>, gangster *and* mobster <both nonformal>, racketeer, thief; **bad person** 660; deceiver 357

2 **troublemaker, mischief-maker;** agitator 375.11

3 **ruffian,** rough, bravo, **rowdy, thug,** desperado, cutthroat, kill-crazy animal, mad dog; gunman; bully, bullyboy, bucko; devil, hellcat, hell-raiser; killer

4 <nonformal terms> **roughneck, tough,** bruiser, mug, mugger, bimbo, bozo, ugly customer, **hoodlum, hood, hooligan,** gorilla, ape, plug-ugly, strong-arm man, muscle man, **goon;** gun, gunsel, trigger man, rodman, torpedo, hatchet man; hellion, terror, holy terror, shtarker, ugly customer

5 **savage, barbarian, brute, beast, animal,** tiger, shark, hyena; wild man; cannibal, man-eater, anthropophagite; **wrecker, vandal,** nihilist, destroyer

6 **monster, fiend,** fiend from hell, **demon, devil,** devil incarnate, hellhound, hellkite; **vampire,** lamia, **harpy, ghoul;**

werewolf, ape-man; ogre, ogress; Frankenstein's monster

7 **witch, hag, vixen,** hellhag, hellcat, she-devil, virago, brimstone, termagant, grimalkin, Jezebel, beldam, she-wolf, tigress, wildcat, bitch-kitty <nonformal>, siren, fury

594 JURISDICTION
<administration of justice>

NOUNS 1 **jurisdiction,** legal authority *or* power *or* right *or* sway, the confines of the law; original *or* appellate jurisdiction, exclusive *or* concurrent jurisdiction, civil *or* criminal jurisdiction, common-law *or* equitable jurisdiction, *in rem* jurisdiction, *in personam* jurisdiction; voluntary jurisdiction

2 **judiciary,** judicial *or* legal *or* court system, judicature, judicatory, court, the courts; criminal-justice system; **justice,** the wheels of justice, judicial process; judgment 945

3 **magistracy,** magistrature, magistrateship; **judgeship,** justiceship; mayoralty, mayorship

4 **bureau, office, department;** secretariat, ministry, commissariat; municipality, bailiwick; constabulary, constablery, sheriffry, sheriffalty, shrievalty; constablewick, sheriffwick

VERBS 5 **administer justice,** administer, administrate; preside, preside at the board; **sit in judgment** 598.17; **judge** 945.8

ADJS 6 **jurisdictional,** jurisdictive; **judicatory,** judicatorial, judicative, **juridic** *or* **juridical; judicial, judiciary;** magisterial

595 TRIBUNAL

NOUNS 1 **tribunal, forum, board,** curia, Areopagus; judicature, judicatory, judiciary 594.2; council 423; inquisition, the Inquisition

2 **court, law court, court of law** *or* **justice,** court of arbitration, legal tribunal, judicature; **United States court** <see list>, federal court; **British court** <see list>, Crown court

3 <ecclesiastical courts> Papal Court, Curia, Rota, Sacra Romana Rota, Court of Arches *and* Court of Peculiars <both Brit>

4 **military court, court-martial,** general *or* special *or* summary court-martial, drumhead court-martial; naval court, captain's mast

5 **seat of justice, judgment seat,** mercy

seat, siege of justice <old>; **bench;** woolsack <Brit>

6 **courthouse, court;** county *or* town hall, town house; **courtroom;** jury box; witness stand *or* box, dock

ADJS 7 **tribunal, judicial,** judiciary, court, curial; appellate

8 **United States courts**

Court of Private Land Claims	Territorial court
Federal Court of Claims	United States Circuit Court of Appeals
Supreme Court *or* United States Supreme Court	United States District Court

9 **British courts**

Board of Green Cloth Council	Court of the Duchy of Lancaster
court of admiralty	Green Cloth
Court of Appeal	High Court
court of attachments	High Court of Appeal
Court of Common	High *or* Supreme
Court of Common Bank	Court of Judicature
Court of Common Pleas	High Court of Justice
Court of Criminal Appeal	Judicial Committee of the Privy
Court of Divorce and Matrimonial Causes	Council
	Lords Justices' Court
	Palatine Court
Court of Exchequer	Rolls Court
Court of Exchequer Chamber	Stannary Court
	superior courts of Westminster
court of piepoudre *or* dustyfoot	Teind Court <Scots>
Court of Queen's *or* King's Bench	Vice Chancellor's Court
Court of Session <Scots>	Wardmote *or* Wardmote Court
	Woodmote

596 JUDGE, JURY

NOUNS 1 **judge, magistrate, justice,** adjudicator, bencher, man *or* woman on the bench, beak <Brit nonformal>; **justice of the peace** *or* JP; arbiter, arbitrator, moderator; umpire, referee; his honor, his worship, his lordship; Mr Justice; critic 945.7; **special judge** <see list>

2 <historical> tribune, praetor, ephor, archon, syndic, podesta; Areopagite; justiciar, justiciary; dempster, deemster, doomster, doomsman

3 <Muslim> mullah, ulema, hakim, mufti, cadi

4 Chief Justice, Associate Justice, Justice of the Supreme Court; Lord Chief Justice, Lord Justice, Lord Chancellor, Master of the Rolls, Baron of the Exchequer; Judge Advocate General

5 Pontius Pilate, Solomon, Minos, Rhadamanthus, Aeacus

6 **jury** <see list>, **panel,** jury of one's peers, sessions <Scots>, country, twelve men in a box; inquest; jury panel, jury list, venire facias; hung *or* deadlocked jury

7 **juror, juryman, jurywoman,** venire-man *or* -woman, talesman; foreman of the jury, foreman, jury chancellor <Scots>; grand-juror, grand-juryman; petit-juror, petit-juryman; recognitor

8 **special judges**

amicus curiae	master
assessor *or* legal assessor	military judge
	ombudsman
bankruptcy judge	ordinary *or* judge ordinary
barmaster <Brit>	
chancellor	police judge *or* justice
circuit judge	*or* magistrate *or* PJ
district judge	presiding judge
judge advocate *or* JA	probate judge
judge *or* justice of assize	puisne judge *or* justice
jurat	recorder
justice in eyre	tax judge
lay judge	vice-chancellor

9 **kinds of jury**

blue-ribbon jury *or* panel	jury of the vicinage
	petit jury *or* petty
common jury	jury *or* traverse
coroner's jury	jury
elisor jury	police jury
grand jury	pyx jury
Jedburgh jury <Scots>	special jury
	struck jury
jury of inquest	trial jury
jury of matrons *or* women	

597 LAWYER

NOUNS 1 **lawyer, attorney, attorney-at-law,** barrister, barrister-at-law, **counselor,** counselor-at-law, **counsel,** legal counsel *or* counselor, legal adviser, legal expert, **solicitor, advocate, pleader;** member of the bar, legal practitioner, officer of the court; smart lawyer, pettifogger, Philadelphia lawyer; proctor, procurator; friend at *or* in court, amicus curiae; deputy, agent 576; intercessor 466.3; sea lawyer, latrine *or* guardhouse lawyer <nonformal>, self-styled lawyer, legalist

2 legist, jurist, jurisprudent, jurisconsult; law member of a court-martial

3 <nonformal terms> **shyster, mouthpiece, ambulance chaser,** lip, fixer, legal eagle

4 **bar,** legal profession, members of the bar; representation, counsel, pleading, attorneyship; **practice,** legal practice, criminal

practice, corporate practice, etc; legal-aid *or* pro bono practice; **law firm,** legal firm, partnership

VERBS **5 practice law,** practice at the bar; be admitted to the bar; take silk <Brit>

ADJS **6 lawyerly,** lawyerlike, barristerial; representing, of counsel

598 LEGAL ACTION

NOUNS **1 lawsuit, suit,** suit in *or* at law; countersuit; **litigation, prosecution, action, legal action,** proceedings, legal proceedings, legal process; legal remedy; **case, court case,** cause, cause in court, legal case; **judicial process**

2 **summons, subpoena,** writ of summons; **writ, warrant**

3 **arraignment, indictment, impeachment; complaint, charge** 599.1; presentment; information; bill of indictment, true bill; **bail** 438.2

4 **jury selection, impanelment,** venire, venire facias, venire facias de novo

5 **trial, jury trial,** trial by jury, trial at the bar, **hearing, inquiry, inquisition,** inquest, assize; court-martial; **examination,** cross-examination; retrial; mistrial; change of venue

6 **pleadings,** arguments at the bar; **plea,** pleading, argument; **defense,** statement of defense; demurrer, general *or* special demurrer; refutation 957.2; rebuttal 938.2

7 **declaration, statement,** allegation, allegation *or* statement of facts, procès-verbal; **deposition,** affidavit; claim; complaint; bill, bill of complaint; libel, narratio; nolle prosequi, nol pros; nonsuit

8 **testimony; evidence** 956; **argument,** presentation of the case; resting of the case; **summing up,** summation, charge to the jury, charging of the jury

9 **judgment, decision,** landmark decision; **verdict, sentence** 945.5; acquittal 601; condemnation 602, penalty 603

10 **appeal,** appeal motion, application for retrial, appeal to a higher court; writ of error; certiorari, writ of certiorari

11 **litigant, litigator,** litigationist; suitor, **party,** party to a suit; injured *or* aggrieved party, **plaintiff** 599.5; **defendant** 599.6; witness; accessory, accessory before *or* after the fact; panel, parties litigant

VERBS **12 sue, litigate, prosecute,** go into litigation, **bring suit,** put in suit, sue *or* prosecute at law, **go to law,** seek in law, appeal to the law, seek justice *or* legal re-

dress, implead, **bring action against,** prosecute a suit against, take *or* institute legal proceedings against; law *or* have the law in <both nonformal>; take to court, bring into court, hale *or* haul *or* drag into court, bring a case before the court *or* bar, bring before a jury, bring to justice, bring to trial, **put on trial,** bring to the bar, take before the judge; set down for hearing

13 **summons, issue a summons,** subpoena

14 **arraign, indict, impeach,** find an indictment against, present a true bill, prefer *or* file a claim, have *or* pull up <nonformal>, bring up for investigation; **prefer charges** 599.7

15 **select** *or* **impanel a jury,** impanel, panel

16 **call to witness,** bring forward, put on the stand; swear in 334.7; take oath; take the stand, testify

17 **try,** try a case, conduct a trial, **hear,** give a hearing to, sit on; charge the jury, deliver one's charge to the jury; **judge, sit in judgment**

18 **plead, enter a plea** *or* **pleading,** implead, conduct pleadings, argue at the bar; **plead** *or* **argue one's case,** present one's case, make a plea, tell it to the judge <nonformal>; hang the jury <nonformal>; rest, rest one's case; sum up one's case; throw oneself on the mercy of the court

19 **bring in a verdict, pass** *or* **pronounce sentence** 945.13; acquit 601.4; convict 602.3; penalize 603.4

ADJS **20** litigious, litigant, litigatory; causidical, lawyerly; litigable, actionable, prosecutable; prosecutorial; **moot,** sub judice; unactionable, unprosecutable, unlitigable, frivolous, without merit

PHRS **21 in litigation,** in court, in chancery, in jeopardy, **at law,** at bar, at the bar, **on trial,** up for investigation *or* hearing, before the court *or* bar *or* judge

599 ACCUSATION

NOUNS **1 accusation,** accusal, finger-pointing <nonformal>, **charge, complaint,** plaint, count, **blame, imputation,** delation, reproach, taxing; **accusing, bringing of charges,** laying of charges, bringing to book; **denunciation,** denouncement; **impeachment, arraignment, indictment,** bill of indictment, true bill; **allegation,** allegement; **imputation,** ascription; **insinuation, implication, innuendo,** veiled accusation, unspoken accusation; information, information against, bill of particulars; charge sheet;

specification; gravamen of a charge; prosecution, suit, lawsuit 598.1

2 incrimination, crimination, **inculpation**, implication, **citation**, involvement, impugnment; attack, assault; **censure** 510.3

3 recrimination, retort, countercharge

4 trumped-up charge, false witness; **put-up job** *and* **frame-up** *and* **frame** <all nonformal>

5 accuser, accusant, accusatrix; incriminator, delator, allegator, impugner; informer 551.6; impeacher, indictor; **plaintiff, complainant**, claimant, appellant, petitioner, libelant, suitor, **party**, party to a suit; **prosecutor**, the prosecution

6 accused, defendant, respondent, codefendant, corespondent, libelee, suspect, prisoner

VERBS **7 accuse**, bring accusation; **charge, press charges, prefer** *or* **bring charges**, lay charges; complain, **lodge a complaint**, lodge a plaint; **impeach, arraign, indict**, bring in *or* hand up an indictment, return a true bill, article, **cite**, cite on several counts; book; **denounce**, denunciate; **finger** *and* point the finger at *and* put *or* lay the finger on <all nonformal>, **inform on** *or* **against** 551.12,13; **impute**, ascribe; allege, insinuate, imply; bring to book; tax, task, take to task *or* account; **reproach**, twit, taunt with; report, put on report

8 blame, blame on *or* upon <nonformal>, lay on, hold against, **put** *or* **place** *or* **lay the blame on**, lay *or* cast blame upon, place *or* fix the blame *or* responsibility for; fasten on *or* upon, pin *or* hang on <nonformal>

9 accuse of, charge with, tax *or* task with, saddle with, lay to one's charge, place to one's account, lay at one's door, bring home to, cast *or* throw in one's teeth, throw up to one, throw *or* thrust in the face of

10 incriminate, criminate, **inculpate**, implicate, involve; cry out against, cry out on *or* upon, cry shame upon, raise one's voice against; attack, assail, impugn; **censure** 510.13; throw a stone at, cast *or* throw the first stone

11 recriminate, countercharge, retort an accusation

12 trump up a charge, bear false witness; frame *and* **frame up** *and* **set up** *and* **put up a job on** <all nonformal>

ADJS **13 accusing, accusatory**, accusatorial, accusative; imputative, denunciatory; recriminatory; prosecutorial; **condemnatory**

14 incriminating, incriminatory, criminatory; delatorian; inculpative, inculpatory

15 accused, charged, blamed, tasked, taxed, reproached, **denounced, impeached, indicted, arraigned; under a cloud** *or* a cloud of suspicion; incriminated, inculpated, implicated, involved, in complicity; **cited**, impugned; under attack, under fire

600 JUSTIFICATION

NOUNS **1 justification, vindication; clearing**, clearing of one's name *or* one's good name, clearance, purging, purgation, destigmatizing, destigmatization, **exculpation** 601.1; no bill, failure to indict; explanation, rationalization; reinstatement, restoration, **rehabilitation**

2 defense, plea, pleading; argument, statement of defense; answer, reply, counterstatement, response, riposte; **refutation** 957.2, **rebuttal** 938.2; demurrer, general *or* special demurrer; denial, objection, exception; **special pleading**; self-defense, plea of self-defense, Nuremberg defense, the devil-made-me-do-it defense, blame-the-victim defense

3 apology, apologia, apologetic

4 excuse, cop-out *and* **alibi** *and* **out** <all nonformal>; lame excuse, poor excuse, likely story; escape hatch, way out

5 extenuation, mitigation, palliation, softening; extenuative, palliative, saving grace; **whitewash, whitewashing**, decontamination; gilding, gloss, varnish, color, putting the best color on; qualification, allowance; extenuating circumstances, diminished responsibility

6 warrant, reason, good reason, **cause**, call, **right, basis**, substantive *or* material basis, **ground, grounds**, foundation, substance

7 justifiability, vindicability, defensibility; explainability, explicability; **excusability**, pardonableness, forgivableness, remissibility, veniality; warrantableness, allowableness, admissibility, reasonableness, reasonability, legitimacy

8 justifier, vindicator; defender, pleader; **advocate**, successful advocate *or* defender, proponent, **champion; apologist**, apologizer, apologetic; whitewasher

VERBS **9 justify, vindicate**, do justice to, make justice *or* right prevail; fail to indict, no-bill; **warrant**, account for, show sufficient grounds for, give good reasons for; **rationalize**, explain; cry sour grapes, "make a virtue of necessity"—Shakespeare; get off the hook <nonformal>, **exculpate** 601.4; **clear,** clear one's name or one's good name, purge, destigmatize, reinstate, restore, rehabilitate

10 **defend,** offer or say in defense, allege in support or vindication, **support, uphold, sustain, maintain,** assert; **answer,** reply, respond, riposte, counter; refute 957.5, **rebut** 938.5; **plead for,** make a plea, offer as a plea, plead one's case or cause, put up a front or a brave front; **advocate,** champion, go to bat for <nonformal>, espouse, join or associate oneself with, stand or stick up for, speak up for, contend for, speak for, argue for, urge reasons for, put in a good word for

11 **excuse,** alibi <nonformal>, offer excuse for, give as an excuse, cover with excuses, **explain,** offer an explanation; plead ignorance or insanity or diminished responsibility; **apologize for,** make apology for; alibi out of <nonformal>, crawl or worm or squirm out of, lie out of, have an out or alibi or story <all nonformal>

12 **extenuate, mitigate, palliate,** soften, lessen, diminish, **ease,** mince; **soft-pedal;** slur over, ignore, pass by in silence, give the benefit of the doubt, not hold it against one, **explain away, gloss** or **smooth over,** put a gloss upon, put a good face upon, varnish, **white-wash,** color, lend a color to, put the best color or face on, show in the best colors, show to best advantage; **allow for,** make allowance for; give the Devil his due

ADJS 13 **justifying,** justificatory; **vindicative,** vindicatory, rehabilitating; refuting 957.6; **excusing,** excusatory; **apologetic, apologetical; extenuating,** extenuative, **palliative**

14 **justifiable, vindicable, defensible; excusable, pardonable, forgivable,** expiable, remissible, exemptible, venial; **condonable,** dispensable; **warrantable,** allowable, admissible, reasonable, colorable, legitimate; innocuous, unobjectionable, inoffensive

601 ACQUITTAL

NOUNS 1 **acquittal,** acquittance; **exculpation,** disculpation, verdict of acquittal or not guilty; **exoneration, absolution, vindication, remission,** compurgation, purgation, purging; **clearing,** clearance, destigmatizing, destigmatization, quietus; **pardon, excuse, forgiveness, free pardon; discharge, release, dismissal,**

setting free; quashing of the charge or indictment

2 **exemption, immunity,** impunity; **amnesty,** indemnity, nonprosecution, non prosequitur, nolle prosequi; stay

3 **reprieve,** respite, grace

VERBS 4 **acquit, clear, exculpate, exonerate, absolve,** give absolution, bring in or return a verdict of not guilty; **vindicate,** justify; **pardon, excuse, forgive;** remit, grant remission, remit the penalty of; amnesty, grant or extend amnesty; **discharge, release, dismiss, free, set free,** let off <nonformal>, let go; quash the charge or indictment, withdraw the charge; **exempt,** grant immunity, exempt from, dispense from; clear the skirts of, shrive, purge; blot out one's sins, wipe the slate clean; **whitewash,** decontaminate; destigmatize; non-pros

5 **reprieve,** respite, give or grant a reprieve

602 CONDEMNATION

NOUNS 1 **condemnation, damnation, doom,** guilty verdict, verdict of guilty; proscription, excommunication, anathematizing; **denunciation,** denouncement; **censure** 510.3; **conviction; sentence, judgment,** rap <nonformal>; capital punishment, death penalty, death sentence, death warrant

2 **attainder,** attainture, attaintment; bill of attainder

VERBS 3 **condemn, damn, doom; denounce,** denunciate; **censure** 510.13; **convict,** find guilty, bring home to; proscribe, excommunicate, anathematize; blacklist, put on the Index; pronounce judgment 945.13; **sentence,** pronounce sentence, pass sentence on; penalize 603.4; attaint; sign one's death warrant

4 **stand condemned,** be convicted, be found guilty

ADJS 5 **condemnatory, damnatory,** denunciatory, proscriptive; **censorious**

603 PENALTY

NOUNS 1 **penalty,** penalization, penance, penal retribution; **sanctions,** penal or punitive measures; **punishment** 604; **reprisal** 506.2, retaliation 506, compensation, price; the devil to pay

2 **handicap,** disability, **disadvantage** 1011.6

3 **fine,** monetary or financial penalty, mulct, amercement, sconce, **damages,** punitive damages, compensatory dam-

ages; distress, distraint; forfeit, forfeiture; escheat, escheatment

VERBS **4 penalize,** put *or* impose *or* inflict a penalty *or* sanctions on; **punish** 604.10; **handicap,** put at a disadvantage

5 fine, mulct, amerce, sconce, estreat; distrain, levy a distress; award damages

ADVS **6 on pain of,** under *or* upon pain of, **on** *or* **under penalty of**

604 PUNISHMENT

NOUNS **1 punishment,** punition, **chastisement, chastening, correction, discipline,** disciplinary measure *or* action, **castigation,** infliction, scourge, ferule, what-for <nonformal>; pains, pains and punishments; pay, payment; **retribution,** retributive justice, nemesis; judicial punishment; punishment that fits the crime, condign punishment, well-deserved punishment; **penalty,** penal retribution; penology; cruel and unusual punishment; judgment; what's coming to one, **just desserts, desserts**

2 <forms of punishment> penal servitude, jailing, imprisonment, incarceration, confinement; hard labor, rock pile; galleys; torture, torment, martyrdom; the gantlet, keelhauling, tar-and-feathering, railriding, picketing, the rack, impalement, dismemberment; strappado, estrapade

3 slap, smack, whack, whomp, **cuff, box,** buffet, belt; blow 901.4; **rap on the knuckles,** box on the ear, slap in the face; slap on the wrist, token punishment

4 corporal punishment, whipping, beating, thrashing, spanking, flogging, flagellation, scourging, flailing, trouncing, basting, drubbing, buffeting, belaboring; **lashing, lacing,** stripes; horse-whipping, strapping, belting, rawhiding, cowhiding; **switching; clubbing,** cudgeling, caning, truncheoning, fustigation, bastinado; pistol-whipping; battery

5 <nonformal terms> licking, larruping, walloping, whaling, lathering, leathering, **hiding, tanning, dressing-down; paddling,** swingeing

6 <old nonformal terms> strap oil, hazel oil, hickory oil, birch oil; dose of strap oil, etc

7 capital punishment, execution; legal *or* judicial murder; **hanging,** the gallows, the rope *or* noose; summary execution; **lynching,** necktie party *or* sociable <nonformal>, vigilantism, vigilante justice; the necklace; **crucifixion; electro-**

cution, the chair <nonformal>, the hot seat <nonformal>; gassing, the gas chamber; lethal injection; **decapitation,** decollation, beheading, the guillotine, the ax, the block; **strangling,** strangulation, garrote; **shooting,** fusillade, firing squad; **burning,** burning at the stake; **poisoning,** hemlock; stoning, lapidation; defenestration

8 punisher, discipliner, chastiser, chastener; **executioner,** executionist, deathsman <old>, Jack Ketch <Brit>; **hangman; lyncher;** electrocutioner; headsman, **beheader,** decapitator; strangler, garroter; sadist, torturer

9 penologist; jailer 429.10

VERBS **10 punish, chastise, chasten, discipline, correct, castigate, penalize; take to task,** bring to book, bring *or* call to account; deal with, settle with, settle *or* square accounts, **give one his desserts** *or* **just desserts,** serve one right; inflict upon, visit upon; teach *or* give one a lesson, make an example of; pillory; masthead

11 <nonformal terms> **attend to,** do for, take care of, serve one out, **give it to,** take *or* have it out of; pay, pay out, **fix, settle,** fix one's wagon, settle one's hash, settle the score, give one his gruel, make it hot for one, **give one his comeuppance;** lower the boom, put one through the wringer, come down on *or* down hard on, throw the book at, throw to the wolves; **give what-for,** give a going-over, climb one's frame, let one have it, light into, lay into, land on, mop *or* wipe up the floor with, skin live, have one's hide

12 slap, smack, whack, whomp, **cuff, box,** buffet; strike 901.13; slap the face, box the ears, give a rap on the knuckles

13 whip, give a whipping *or* beating *or* thrashing, **beat, thrash, spank, flog,** scourge, flagellate, flail, whale; **smite,** thump, trounce, baste, **pummel,** pommel, **drub, buffet, belabor,** lay on; **lash, lace,** cut, stripe; horsewhip; knout; **strap,** belt, rawhide, cowhide; **switch,** birch, give the stick; **club, cudgel,** cane, truncheon, fustigate, bastinado; pistol-whip

14 thrash soundly, batter, bruise

15 <nonformal terms> **beat up,** rough up, clobber, marmelize <Brit>, work over, lick, larrup, wallop, whop, swinge, beat one's brains out, whale, whale the tar out of, beat *or* kick the shit out of, beat to a jelly, **beat black and blue, knock one's lights out, nail,** welt, trim, flax, lather, leather, **hide,** tan, **tan one's hide,** dress down, **kick ass,** give a dressing-down, knock head, knock heads together; **paddle; lambaste, clobber,** dust one's jacket, give a dose of birch oil or strap oil or hickory oil or hazel oil, take it out of one's hide or skin

16 torture, put to the question; rack, put on or to the rack; dismember, tear limb from limb; draw and quarter, break on the wheel, tar and feather, ride on a rail, picket, keelhaul, impale, grill

17 execute, put to death, inflict capital punishment; **electrocute,** burn and fry <nonformal>; send to the gas chamber; **behead, decapitate,** decollate, guillotine, bring to the block; **crucify; shoot,** execute by firing squad; burn, **burn at the stake; strangle,** garrote, bowstring; stone, lapidate; defenestrate

18 hang, hang by the neck; **string up** and scrag and stretch <all nonformal>; gibbet, noose, neck, bring to the gallows; **lynch;** hang, draw, and quarter

19 be hanged, suffer hanging, **swing,** dance upon nothing, kick the air or wind or clouds

20 be punished, suffer, suffer for, **suffer the consequences** or **penalty,** get it and **catch it** <both nonformal>, get or catch it in the neck <nonformal>, catch hell or the devil <nonformal>, get or take a licking or shellacking <nonformal>; **get one's desserts** or **just desserts** 639.6; get it coming and going <nonformal>, be doubly punished, sow the wind and reap the whirlwind; get hurt, get one's fingers burned, have or get one's knuckles rapped

21 take one's punishment, bow one's neck, take the consequences, **take one's medicine** or what is coming to one, swallow the bitter pill or one's medicine, pay the piper, face the music <nonformal>, stand up to it, make one's bed and lie on it; take the rap <nonformal>

22 deserve punishment, have it coming <nonformal>, be for it or in for it, be heading for a fall, be cruising for a bruising <nonformal>

ADJS **23 punishing, chastising,** chastening, corrective, disciplinary; retributive; grueling <nonformal>; **penal, punitive,** punitory, inflictive; castigatory; baculine; penological

605 INSTRUMENTS OF PUNISHMENT

NOUNS **1 whip, lash, scourge,** flagellum, strap, thong, rawhide, cowhide, blacksnake, kurbash, sjambok, belt, razor strap; knout; bullwhip, bullwhack; horsewhip; crop; quirt; rope's end; cat, cat-o'-nine-tails; whiplash

2 rod, stick, switch; paddle, ruler, ferule, pandybat; birch, rattan; cane; club

3 <devices> **pillory, stocks,** finger pillory; cucking stool, ducking stool, trebuchet; whipping post, branks, triangle or triangles, wooden horse, treadmill, crank

4 <instruments of torture> **rack,** wheel, Iron Maiden of Nuremberg; screw, thumbscrew; boot, iron heel, scarpines; Procrustean bed or bed of Procrustes

5 <instruments of execution> **scaffold; block, guillotine,** ax, maiden; **stake; cross; gallows,** gallows-tree, gibbet, tree, drop; **hangman's rope, noose,** rope, halter, hemp, hempen collar or necktie or bridle <nonformal>; **electric chair,** death chair, the chair <nonformal>, hot seat <nonformal>; **gas chamber,** lethal chamber, death chamber; the necklace

606 THE PEOPLE
<the population>

NOUNS **1 the people, the populace, the public,** the general public, people in general, everyone, everybody; **the population,** the citizenry, the whole people, the polity, the body politic; **the community, the commonwealth, society,** the society, the social order or fabric, the nation; the commonalty or commonality, commonage, commoners, commons, demos <Gk>; **common people, ordinary people** or **folk, persons, folk, folks,** gentry; the common sort, plain people or folks, the common run <nonformal>, the rank and file, "the unknown ranks"—Woodrow Wilson, Brown Jones and Robinson, John Q. Public, Middle America; Tom, Dick, and Harry; the salt of the earth, Everyman, Everywoman, the man or woman in the street, the common man, you and me, John Doe, Joe Sixpack <nonformal>, vulgus <L>, the third estate; **the upper class; the middle class; the lower class;** demography, demographics; social anthropology

2 the masses, the hoi polloi, hoi polloi <Gk>, the many, **the multitude,** the crowd, **the mob,** "the hateful, hostile mob"—Petrarch, the horde, the million, "the booboisie"—H L Mencken, **the majority,** the mass of the people, the herd, the great unnumbered, the great unwashed, **the vulgar** or **common herd;** profanum vulgus, ignobile vulgus, mobile *vulgus* <all L>; "the multitude of the gross people"—Erasmus, "many-headed multitude" —Sir Philip Sidney, "the beast with many heads, "the blunt monster with uncounted heads, the still-discordant wavering multitude"—both Shakespeare

3 **rabble,** rabblement, rout, ruck, common ruck, canaille, *racaille* <Fr>, ragtag <informal>, "the tagrag people"—Shakespeare, **ragtag and bobtail;** rag, tag, and bobtail; **riffraff, trash,** raff, chaff, **rubbish,** dregs, sordes, offscourings, off-scum, **scum, scum of the earth, dregs** *or* **scum** *or* **off-scum** *or* **offscourings of society,** swinish multitude, vermin, cattle.

4 **the underprivileged,** the disadvantaged, the poor, ghetto-dwellers, slum-dwellers, welfare cases, chronic poor, underclass, depressed class, poverty subculture, the wretched of the earth, outcasts, the homeless, the dispossessed, the powerless, the unemployable, lumpen, the lumpenproletariat *or* lumpenprole <nonformal>

5 **common man, commoner,** little man, **little fellow, average man,** ordinary man, typical man, **man in the street,** one of the people, man of the people, Everyman; **plebeian,** pleb <slang>; **proletarian,** prole <Brit nonformal>, *roturier* <Fr>; ordinary *or* average Joe *and* Joe Doakes *and* Joe Sixpack <all nonformal>, John Doe, Jane Doe, John Smith, Mr *or* Mrs Brown *or* Smith

6 **peasant, countryman,** countrywoman, **provincial,** son of the soil, tiller of the soil; **peon,** hind, fellah, muzhik; "hewers of wood and drawers of water"—Bible; **farmer 1067.5, hick** *and* yokel *and* rube *and* hayseed *and* shit-kicker <all nonformal>, **bumpkin,** country bumpkin, clod, **clodhopper** <nonformal>, hillbilly *and* woodhick <both nonformal>, **boor,** clown, lout, looby

7 **upstart, parvenu,** adventurer, sprout <nonformal>, "an upstart crow beautified in our feathers"—Robert Greene; *bourgeois gentilhomme* <Fr>, would-be gentleman; *nouveau riche, nouveau roturier* <both Fr>, *arriviste* <Fr>, **newly-rich,** pig in clover <nonformal>; **social climber,** climber, name-dropper, tufthunter, status seeker

ADJS 8 **populational,** population; **demographic,** demographical; national, societal; **popular,** public, mass, grass-roots, **common,** common as dirt, commonplace,

plain, ordinary, lowly, low, mean, base; **humble,** homely; **lowborn,** lowbred, baseborn, earthborn, earthy, "of the earth earthy"—Bible, plebeian; third-estate; ungenteel, shabby-genteel; **vulgar, rude,** coarse, below the salt; **parvenu, upstart,** risen from the ranks, jumped-up <nonformal>; **newly-rich,** *nouveau-riche* <Fr>

607 SOCIAL CLASS AND STATUS

NOUNS 1 **class, social class, economic class,** social group *or* grouping, status group, accorded status, social category, order, grade, caste, estate, rank; **status, social status, economic status,** socioeconomic status *or* background, standing, footing, prestige, rank, ranking, place, station, position, level, degree, stratum; **social structure, hierarchy,** social system, social gamut, social differentiation, class structure, class distinction, status system, power structure, ranking, stratification, ordering, social scale, gradation, division, social inequality, inequality, haves and have-nots, "the classes and the masses"—William Ewart Gladstone, "the Privileged and the People"—Benjamin Disraeli; **social bias, class conflict,** class identity, class difference, class prejudice, class struggle, class politics; **mobility, social mobility,** upward mobility, downward mobility, vertical mobility, horizontal mobility

2 **upper class, upper classes, aristocracy,** patriciate, second estate, ruling class, ruling circles, elite, elect, the privileged, the classes, the quality, the better sort, upper circles, upper cut *and* upper crust *and* crust *and* cream <all nonformal>, upper-income group *or* higher-income group, gentry, gentlefolk, lords of creation; **high society,** high life, the Four Hundred, bon ton, *haut monde* <Fr>, First Families of Virginia *or* FFV; Social Register, Bluebook; nobility, gentry 608

3 **aristocracy, aristocratic status,** aristocraticalness, aristocraticness, high status, high rank, quality, high estate, gentility, social distinction, social prestige; **birth,** high birth, distinguished ancestry *or* descent *or* heritage *or* blood, **blue blood**

4 **aristocrat, patrician,** Brahmin, blue-blood, thoroughbred, member of the upper class, socialite, swell *and* upper-cruster <both nonformal>, grandee, grand dame, dowager, magnifico, lord of

creation; **gentleman, lady,** person of
breeding

5 **middle class,** middle order or orders,
lower middle class, upper middle class,
bourgeoisie, educated class, professional
class, middle-income group, white-collar
workers, salaried workers; suburbia;
Middle America, silent majority

6 **bourgeois,** member of the middle class,
white-collar worker 726.2, salaried
worker; pillar of society, solid citizen

7 **lower class, lower classes,** lower orders,
plebs, workers, working class, working
people, proletariat, proles <Brit nonfor-
mal>, laboring class or classes, toilers,
toiling class or classes, the other half,
low-income group, wage-earners, hourly
worker, blue-collar workers

8 **the underclass, the underprivileged**

9 **worker 726.2, workman, working man,
working woman,** working girl, proletarian, laborer, laboring man, toiler, stiff
and working stiff <both nonformal>, artisan, mechanic, industrial worker,
factory worker

ADJS 10 **upper-class, aristocratic, patrician,
upscale;** gentle, genteel, of gentle blood;
gentlemanly, gentlemanlike; ladylike,
quite the lady; **wellborn, well-bred, blue-
blooded,** of good breed; **thoroughbred,**
purebred, pure-blooded, pur sang <Fr>,
full-blooded; **highborn,** highbred; born to
the purple, "to the manner born"—
Shakespeare, born with a silver spoon in
one's mouth; **high-society,** socialite,
hoity-toity <nonformal>, posh; **middle-
class, bourgeois,** petit-bourgeois <Fr>,
petty-bourgeois, suburban; **working
class, blue collar,** proletarian, lower-
class, born on the wrong side of the
tracks; **class-conscious; mobile, socially
mobile,** upwardly mobile, downwardly
mobile, vertically mobile, horizontally
mobile, déclassé

608 ARISTOCRACY, NOBILITY, GENTRY
<noble rank or birth>

NOUNS 1 **aristocracy, nobility,** titled aristocracy, hereditary nobility, noblesse, **aristocracy; elite,** upper class, elect, the
classes, **upper classes** or circles, upper cut
and **upper crust** <both nonformal>, upper ten <Brit nonformal>, **upper ten
thousand,** the Four Hundred, high society, high life, haut monde <Fr>; old
nobility, ancienne noblesse <Fr>, noblesse de robe, noblesse d'épée <both Fr>;

First Families of Virginia or FFV; **peerage,** baronage, lords temporal and
spiritual; baronetage; knightage, chivalry; royalty

2 **nobility, nobleness, aristocracy,** aristocraticalness; **gentility,** genteelness;
quality, rank, distinction; birth, high or
noble birth, ancestry, high or honorable
descent; blood, **blue blood;** royalty 417.8

3 **gentry,** gentlefolk, gentlefolks, gentlepeo-
ple, better sort; lesser nobility, petite
noblesse <Fr>; samurai <Japanese>;
landed gentry, squirearchy

4 **nobleman, noble, gentleman; peer; aristocrat, patrician,** Brahman, **blue blood,**
thoroughbred, silk-stocking, lace-curtain,
swell and upper-cruster <both nonfor-
mal>; **grandee,** magnifico, magnate,
optimate; **lord,** laird <Scots>, lordling;
seignior, seigneur, hidalgo <Sp>; **duke,**
grand duke, archduke, marquis, **earl,
count,** viscount, **baron,** daimio, **baronet;**
squire; esquire, armiger; palsgrave,
waldgrave, margrave, landgrave

5 **knight, cavalier,** chevalier, caballero
<Sp>, Ritter <Ger>, "a verray parfit
gentil knight"—Chaucer; **knight-errant,**
knight-adventurer; companion; bachelor,
knight bachelor; baronet, knight baronet;
banneret, knight banneret; Bayard, Ga-
wain, Lancelot, Sidney, Sir Galahad, Don
Quixote

6 **noblewoman, peeress, gentlewoman;
lady,** dame, doña <Sp>, khanum;
duchess, grand duchess, archduchess,
marchioness, viscountess, **countess, bar-
oness,** margravine

7 **prince,** Prinz, Fürst <both Ger>, knez,
atheling, sheikh, sherif, mirza, khan,
emir, shahzada <India>; princeling,
princelet; crown prince, heir apparent;
heir presumptive; prince consort; prince
regent; **king;** princes of India; Muslim
rulers 575.10

8 **princess,** princesse <Fr>, infanta <Sp>,
rani and maharani and begum and shah-
zadi and kumari or kunwari and raj-
kumari and malikzadi <all India>;
crown princess; **queen** 575.11

9 <rank or office> lordship, ladyship;
dukedom, marquisate, earldom, barony,
baronetcy; viscountship, viscountcy, vis-
county; knighthood, knight-errantship;
seigniory, seigneury, seignioralty; pasha-
ship, pashadom; princeship, princedom;
kingship, queenship 417.8

ADJS 10 **noble,** of rank, high, exalted; **aristocratic, patrician; gentle,** genteel, of gentle
blood; gentlemanly, gentlemanlike; lady-

like, quite the lady; knightly, chivalrous; ducal, archducal; princely, princelike; **regal** 417.17, kingly, kinglike, "every inch a king"—Shakespeare; queenly, queenlike; titled

11 **wellborn, well-bred, blue-blooded,** wellconnected, of good breed; **thoroughbred,** purebred, pure-blooded, *pur sang* <Fr>, full-blooded; **highborn,** highbred; born to the purple

609 POLITICS

NOUNS 1 **politics,** polity, the art of the possible, "economics in action"—Robert La Follette, "the people's business, the most important business there is"—Adlai Stevenson; practical politics, *Realpolitik* <Ger>; empirical politics; **party** *or* **partisan politics, partisanism; politicization;** reform politics; multiparty politics; power politics, *Machtpolitik* <Ger>; machine politics, bossism <nonformal>, Tammany Hall, Tammanism <nonformal>; confrontation *or* confrontational *or* confro politics; **interest politics,** singleissue politics, interest-group politics, pressure-group politics, PAC *or* political action committee politics; consensus politics; fusion politics; career politics; petty politics, peanut politics <nonformal>; pork-barrel politics; kid-glove politics <nonformal>; silk-stocking politics <nonformal>; ward politics; electronic *or* technological politics

2 **political science,** poli-sci <nonformal>, **politics, government, civics;** political philosophy, political theory; political behavior; political economy, comparative government, international relations, public administration; political geography, geopolitics, *Geopolitik* <Ger>

3 **statesmanship, statecraft,** political *or* governmental leadership, national leadership; transpartisan *or* suprapartisan leadership; "the wise employment of individual meanness for the public good"—Lincoln; kingcraft, queencraft; senatorship

4 **policy, polity,** public policy; line, **party line,** party principle *or* doctrine *or* philosophy, **position,** bipartisan policy; noninterference, nonintervention, *laissez-faire* <Fr>, laissez-faireism; free enterprise; go-slow policy; government control, governmentalism; planned economy, managed currency, price supports, pump-priming <nonformal>; autarky, economic self-sufficiency; free trade; protection, protectionism; bimetallism; strict constructionism; localism, sectionalism, states' rights, nullification

5 **foreign policy, foreign affairs;** world politics; **diplomacy,** diplomatic *or* diplomatics <both old>; "the police in grand costume"—Napoleon; shirt-sleeve diplomacy; shuttle diplomacy; dollar diplomacy, dollar imperialism; gunboat diplomacy; brinkmanship; **nationalism, internationalism;** expansionism, imperialism, manifest destiny, colonialism, neocolonialism; spheres of influence; balance of power; containment; deterrence; militarism, preparedness; tough policy, the big stick <nonformal>, twisting the lion's tail; nonresistance, isolationism, neutralism, coexistence, peaceful coexistence; détente; compromise, appeasement; peace offensive; good-neighbor policy; open-door policy, open door; Monroe Doctrine; Truman Doctrine; Eisenhower Doctrine; Nixon Doctrine

6 **program;** Square Deal <Theodore Roosevelt>, New Deal <Franklin D Roosevelt>, Fair Deal <Harry S Truman>, New Frontier <John F Kennedy>, Great Society <Lyndon B Johnson>; austerity program; Beveridge Plan <Brit>; Thatcherism <Brit>

7 **platform,** party platform, **program,** declaration of policy; **plank; issue;** keynote address, keynote speech; position paper

8 **political convention, convention;** conclave, powwow <nonformal>; national convention, quadrennial circus <nonformal>; state convention, county convention, preliminary convention, nominating convention; constitutional convention

9 **caucus,** legislative *or* congressional caucus, packed caucus; secret caucus

10 **candidacy,** candidature <chiefly Brit>, **running, running for office,** throwing *or* tossing one's hat in the ring <nonformal>, standing *or* standing for office <both Brit>

11 **nomination,** caucus nomination, direct nomination, petition nomination; acceptance speech

12 **electioneering,** campaigning, politicking <nonformal>, **stumping** *and* **whistlestopping** <both nonformal>; **rally,** clambake <nonformal>; campaign dinner, fund-raising dinner

13 **campaign,** all-out campaign, hardhitting campaign, hoopla *or* hurrah campaign <nonformal>; **canvass,**

solicitation; front-porch campaign; grass-roots campaign; stump excursion *and* stumping tour *and* **whistle-stop campaign** <all nonformal>; TV *or* media campaign; campaign commitments *or* promises; campaign fund, campaign contribution; campaign button

14 **smear campaign,** mudslinging campaign, negative campaign; **whispering campaign;** muckraking, **mudslinging** *and* **dirty politics** *and* **dirty tricks** *and* dirty pool <all nonformal>, character assassination; political canard, roorback; last-minute lie

15 **election,** general election, by-election; congressional election, presidential election; partisan election, nonpartisan election; **primary,** primary election; direct primary, open primary, closed primary, nonpartisan primary, mandatory primary, optional primary, preference primary, presidential primary, presidential preference primary, runoff primary; caucus 609.9; runoff, runoff election; disputed *or* contested election; referendum; close election, horse race *and* toss-up <both nonformal>

16 **election district, precinct, ward, borough;** congressional district; safe district; swing district <nonformal>; close borough *and* pocket borough *and* rotten borough <all Brit>; gerrymander, gerrymandered district, shoestring district; silk-stocking district *or* ward; single-member district *or* constituency

17 **suffrage, franchise, the vote,** right to vote; universal suffrage, manhood suffrage, woman *or* female suffrage; suffragism, suffragettism; suffragist, woman-suffragist, suffragette; household franchise; one man one vote

18 **voting,** going to the polls, casting one's ballot; preferential voting, preferential system, alternative vote; proportional representation *or* PR, cumulative system *or* voting, Hare system, list system; single system *or* voting, single transferrable vote; plural system *or* voting; single-member district 609.16; absentee voting; proxy voting, card voting; voting machine; election fraud, colonization, floating, repeating, ballot-box stuffing; **vote** 371.6

19 **ballot, slate, ticket,** proxy <nonformal>; straight ticket, split ticket; Australian ballot; Massachusetts ballot, office-block ballot; Indiana ballot, party-column ballot; absentee ballot; long ballot, blanket ballot, jungle ballot <nonformal>; short ballot; nonpartisan ballot; sample ballot; party emblem

20 **polls,** poll, polling place, polling station <Brit>, balloting place; voting booth, polling booth; ballot box; voting machine; pollbook

21 **returns,** election returns, **poll,** count, official count; **recount;** landslide, tidal wave

22 **electorate,** electors; **constituency,** constituents; electoral college

23 **voter, elector, balloter;** registered voter; fraudulent voter, floater, repeater, ballot-box stuffer; proxy

24 **political party** <see list>, **party,** major party, minor party, third party, splinter party; "the madness of many for the gain of a few"—Pope; party in power, opposition party, loyal opposition; **fraction, camp; machine,** political *or* party machine, Tammany Hall; city hall; one-party system, two-party system, multiple party system, multiparty system

25 **partisanism,** partisanship, partisanry; Republicanism; Conservatism, Toryism; Liberalism; Whiggism, Whiggery

26 **nonpartisanism, independence,** neutralism; mugwumpery, mugwumpism

27 **partisan, party member,** party man *or* woman; regular, stalwart, loyalist; wheelhorse, party wheelhorse; heeler, ward heeler, **party hack;** party faithful

28 **nonpartisan, independent, neutral, mugwump,** undecided *or* uncommitted voter, centrist; swing vote

29 **political influence, wire-pulling** <nonformal>; **social pressure, public opinion, special-interest pressure,** group pressure; **influence peddling; lobbying,** lobbyism; **logrolling,** back scratching

30 **wire-puller** <nonformal>; **influence peddler,** four-percenter, power broker, fixer <nonformal>, five-percenter <nonformal>; logroller

31 **pressure group,** interest group, special-interest group, political action committee *or* PAC, single-issue group; **special interest;** vested interest; financial interests, farm interests, labor interests, etc; minority interests, ethnic vote, black vote, Jewish vote, Italian vote, etc; **Black Power,** White Power, Polish Power, etc

32 **lobby,** legislative lobby, special-interest lobby; **lobbyist,** registered lobbyist, lobbyer, parliamentary agent <England>

33 **front, movement,** coalition, political front; popular front, people's front, communist front, etc; grass-roots movement, ground swell, the silent majority

34 <political corruption> **graft,** boodling
<nonformal>, jobbery; pork-barrel legis-
lation *or* pork-barreling; political
intrigue

35 **spoils of office; graft,** boodle <nonfor-
mal>; slush fund <nonformal>; cam-
paign fund, campaign contribution;
public tit *and* public trough <both non-
formal>; spoils system; cronyism,
nepotism

36 **political patronage, patronage, favors of
office, pork** *and* **pork barrel** <both non-
formal>, plum, melon <nonformal>

37 **political** *or* **official jargon; officialese** *and*
federalese *and* Washingtonese *and* gob-
bledygook <all nonformal>; bafflegab
<nonformal>; political doubletalk, dou-
blespeak, bunkum <nonformal>;
pussyfooting; pointing with pride and
viewing with alarm

VERBS **38** **politick** <nonformal>, politicize;
look after one's fences *and* mend one's
fences <both nonformal>; caucus; gerrymander

39 **run for office,** run; **throw** *or* **toss one's hat
in the ring** <nonformal>, announce for,
enter the lists *or* arena, stand *and* stand
for office <both Brit>; contest a seat
<Brit>

40 **electioneer, campaign; stump** *and* take
the stump *and* take to the stump *and*
stump the country *and* take to the hustings *and* hit the campaign trail *and*
whistle-stop <all nonformal>; **canvass,**
go to the voters *or* electorate, solicit
votes, ring doorbells; shake hands and
kiss babies

41 **support, back** *and* **back up** <both nonfor-
mal>, come out for, **endorse;** go with the
party, follow the party line; **get on the
bandwagon** <nonformal>; **nominate,
elect, vote** 371.18,20

42 **hold office,** hold *or* occupy a post, fill an
office, be the incumbent, be in office

ADJS **43** **political,** politic; governmental,
civic; geopolitical; statesmanlike; diplomatic; suffragist; politico-commer-
cial, politico-diplomatic, politico-
ecclesiastical, politico-economic,
politico-ethical, politico-geographical,
politico-judicial, politico-military,
politico-moral, politico-religious,
politico-scientific, politico-social,
politico-theological

44 **partisan, party;** bipartisan, biparty, two-
party

45 **nonpartisan, independent,** neutral, mugwumpian *and* mugwumpish <both
nonformal>, **on the fence**

WORD ELEMENT **46** politico—

47 **political parties**

American Labor Party	Liberal Republican Party
American Party *or* Know-Nothing Party	Liberty Party
	Militant Tendency <Brit>
Anti-Masonic Party	National Republican Party
Anti-Monopoly Party	
Bull Moose Party	People's *or* Populist Party
Communist Party	
Conservative Party	Progressive Party
Conservative Party <Brit>	Prohibition Party
	Republican Party *or* GOP <Grand Old Party>
Constitutional Union Party	
Democratic Party	Social Democratic Party *or* SDP <Brit>
Democratic-Republican Party	
Farmer-Labor Party	Socialist Labor Party
Federalist Party	Socialist Party
Free Soil Party	Socialist Workers Party
Greenback Party	
Labour Party <Brit>	States' Rights Demo-cratic Party *or* Dixiecrats <nonformal>
Liberal Party	
Liberal Party <Brit>	Whig Party

610 POLITICIAN

NOUNS **1 politician,** politico, political
leader, professional politician; party
leader, party boss *and* party chieftain
<both nonformal>; machine *or* club-
house politician, **political hack,**
Tammany man <old>; **pol** <nonfor-
mal>; old campaigner, war-horse;
wheelhorse; reform politician, reformer

2 **statesman,** stateswoman, solon, public
man *or* woman, national leader; "a politician who is held upright by equal
pressure from all directions"—Eric John-
ston, "a successful politician who is
dead"—Thomas B Reed; elder statesman

3 **legislator, lawmaker,** solon, lawgiver;
congressman, congresswoman, Member
of Congress; **senator; representative;**
Speaker of the House; majority leader,
minority leader; floor leader; whip, party
whip; Member of Parliament *or* MP; state
senator, assemblyman, assemblywoman,
chosen, freeholder, councilman, alderman, city father

4 <petty politician> **two-bit** *or* **peanut politician** <nonformal>, politicaster,
statemonger <old>, political dabbler;
hack, party hack

5 <corrupt politician> **dirty** *or* **crooked
politician** *and* jackleg politician <both
nonformal>; **grafter,** boodler <nonfor-

mal>; spoilsman, spoilsmonger; influence peddler 609.30

6 <political intriguer> strategist, machinator, gamesman, wheeler-dealer <nonformal>; operator *and* finagler *and* **wire-puller** <all nonformal>; **logroller,** pork-barrel politician; Machiavellian; behind-the-scenes operator, gray eminence, *éminence grise* <Fr>, power behind the throne, kingmaker <nonformal>, **powerbroker** 893.6

7 <political leader> **boss** <nonformal>, higher-up *or* man higher up <nonformal>, cacique *and* sachem <both old>; keynoter <nonformal>, policy maker; standard-bearer; ringleader 375.11; **big shot** <nonformal> 996.9

8 **henchman,** cohort, hanger-on, buddy *and* sidekick <both nonformal>; heeler *and* **ward heeler** <both nonformal>; hatchet man

9 **candidate, aspirant,** hopeful *and* political hopeful *and* wannabee <all nonformal>, office seeker *or* hunter, baby kisser <nonformal>; running mate; leading candidate, head of the ticket *or* slate; **dark horse;** stalking-horse; favorite son; presidential timber; defeated candidate, also-ran *and* dud <both nonformal>

10 **campaigner,** electioneer, **stumper** <nonformal>, whistle-stopper <nonformal>, stump speaker *or* orator <nonformal>

11 **officeholder,** office-bearer <Brit>, jack-in-office, public servant, public official, **incumbent;** holdover, lame duck; new broom <nonformal>; president-elect; ins, the powers that be

12 **political worker, committeeman,** committeewoman, precinct captain, precinct leader, district leader; party chairman, state chairman, national chairman, chairman of the national committee

VERBS **13** go into politics; **run,** get on the ticket; **campaign,** stump

ADJS **14 statesmanlike,** statesmanly

611 POLITICO-ECONOMIC PRINCIPLES

NOUNS **1 conservatism, conservativeness, rightism;** standpattism <nonformal>, unprogressiveness, backwardness; **ultraconservatism, reaction,** archconservative, reactionism, reactionarism, reactionaryism, reactionariness, diehardism <nonformal>

2 moderatism, moderateness, moderatism, middle-of-the-roadism; middle of the road, moderate position, via media, **center,** centrism; third force, nonalignment

3 liberalism, progressivism, leftism; left, left wing, progressiveness

4 radicalism, extremism, ultraism; radicalization; revolutionism; ultraconservatism 611.1; extreme left, extreme left wing, left-wing extremism, loony left <Brit nonformal>; New Left, Old Left; Jacobinism, sans-culottism, *sans-culotterie* <Fr>; **anarchism, nihilism,** syndicalism *and* anarcho-syndicalism *and* criminal syndicalism <all old>; extreme rightism, radical rightism, know-nothingism; extreme right, extreme right wing; social Darwinism; laissez-faireism 329.1; **royalism, monarchism;** Toryism, Bourbonism

5 communism, Bolshevism, Marxism, Marxism-Leninism, Leninism, Trotskyism, Stalinism, Maoism, Titoism, Castroism, revisionism; Marxian socialism; dialectical materialism; democratic centralism; dictatorship of the proletariat; **Communist Party;** Communist International, Comintern; Communist Information Bureau, Cominform; iron curtain 1011.5

6 socialism, collective ownership, collectivization, public ownership; **collectivism;** creeping socialism; state socialism, *Staatsozialismus* <Ger>; guild socialism; Fabian socialism, Fabianism; utopian socialism; Marxian socialism, Marxism 611.5; phalansterism; Owenism; Saint-Simonianism, Saint-Simonism; **nationalization**

7 welfarism, welfare statism; womb-to-tomb security, cradle-to-grave security; social welfare; social security, social insurance; old-age and survivors insurance; unemployment compensation, unemployment insurance; workmen's compensation, workmen's compensation insurance; health insurance, Medicare, Medicaid, state medicine, **socialized medicine;** sickness insurance; public assistance, **welfare, relief,** welfare payments, aid to dependent children *or* ADC, old-age assistance, aid to the blind, aid to the permanently and totally disabled; guaranteed income, guaranteed annual income; welfare state; welfare capitalism

8 capitalism, capitalistic system, **free enterprise,** private enterprise, free-enterprise economy, free-enterprise system, free economy; finance capitalism; *laissez-faire* <Fr>, laissez-faireism; private sector; private ownership; state capitalism; **individualism**, rugged individualism

.9 **conservative,** conservatist, **rightist, right-winger;** dry <Brit nonformal>, "a person who has something to conserve"—Edward Young, "the leftover progressive of an earlier generation" —Edmund Fuller; standpat *and* standpatter <both nonformal>; hard hat; social Darwinist; ultraconservative, arch-conservative, extreme right-winger, **reactionary,** reactionarist, reactionist, diehard; **royalist, monarchist,** Bourbon, Tory, imperialist; **right, right wing; radical right**

10 **moderate,** moderatist, moderationist, **centrist,** middle-of-the-roader <nonformal>; independent; center

11 **liberal,** liberalist, wet <Brit nonformal>, **progressive,** progressivist, **leftist, left-winger;** welfare stater; Lib-Lab <Brit nonformal>; **left**

12 **radical, extremist,** ultra, ultraist; **revolutionary,** revolutionist; subversive; extreme left-winger, left-wing extremist, **red** <nonformal>, Bolshevik; yippie; Jacobin, sansculotte; **anarchist,** nihilist; mild radical, parlor Bolshevik <nonformal>, pink *and* parlor pink *and* pinko <all nonformal>; lunatic fringe

13 **Communist,** Bolshevist; Bolshevik, **Red** *and* commie *and* bolshie <all nonformal>; Marxist, Leninist, Marxist-Leninist, Trotskyite *or* Trotskyist, Stalinist, Maoist, Titoist, Castroite, revisionist; card-carrying Communist, avowed Communist; fellow traveler, Communist sympathizer, comsymp <nonformal>

14 **socialist,** collectivist; social democrat; state socialist; Fabian, Fabian socialist; Marxist 611.13; utopian socialist; Fourierist, phalansterian; Saint-Simonian; Owenite

15 **capitalist;** coupon-clipper <nonformal>; rich man 618.7

VERBS 16 **politicize;** democratize, republicanize, socialize, communize; nationalize 476.7; deregulate, privatize, denationalize; radicalize

ADJS 17 **conservative, right-wing,** right of center, dry <Brit nonformal>; old-line, die-hard, unreconstructed, standpat <nonformal>, unprogressive; ultraconservative, **reactionary,** reactionist

18 **moderate,** centrist, middle-of-the-road <nonformal>, independent

19 **liberal, liberalistic,** liberalist, wet <Brit nonformal>, bleeding-heart <nonformal>; **progressive,** progressivistic; **leftist, left-wing,** on the left, left of center

20 **radical, extreme, extremist,** extremistic, ultraist, ultraistic; revolutionary, revolutionist; subversive; ultraconservative 611.17; extreme left-wing, **red** <nonformal>; anarchistic, nihilistic, syndicalist *and* anarcho-syndicalist <both old>; mildly radical, pink <nonformal>

21 **Communist, communistic,** Bolshevik, Bolshevist, commie *and* bolshie *and* Red <all nonformal>; **Marxist,** Leninist, Marxist-Leninist, Trotskyite *or* Trotskyist, Stalinist, Maoist, Titoist, Castroite; revisionist

22 **socialist, socialistic,** collectivistic; social-democratic; Fabian; Fourieristic, phalansterian; Saint-Simonian

23 **capitalist, capitalistic,** bourgeois, individualistic, nonsocialistic, free-enterprise, private-enterprise

612 GOVERNMENT

NOUNS 1 **government,** governance, **discipline, regulation; direction, management, administration,** dispensation, disposition, oversight, **supervision** 573.2; **regime,** regimen; **rule, sway, sovereignty, reign,** regnancy; empire, empery; social order, civil government, political government; form *or* system of government, political organization, polity

2 **control, mastery, mastership, command, power, jurisdiction, dominion, domination; hold, grasp,** grip, gripe; hand, hands, iron hand, clutches; talons, claws; helm, reins of government

3 **the government, the authorities; the powers that be,** national government, central government, the Establishment; the corridors of power, government circles; Uncle Sam, Washington; John Bull, the Crown, His *or* Her Majesty's Government, Whitehall

4 <kinds of government> **federal government,** federation; **constitutional government; republic,** commonwealth; **democracy,** representative government, representative democracy, direct *or* pure democracy, town-meeting democracy; "government of the people, by the people, for the people"—Lincoln, "the worst form of government except all those other forms that have been tried from time to time"—Winston Churchill, "the recurrent suspicion that more than half of the people are right more than half of the

time" —E B White; **parliamentary government;** social democracy, welfare state; mob rule, tyranny of the majority, mobocracy <nonformal>, ochlocracy; minority government; pantisocracy; aristocracy, hierarchy, oligarchy; feudal system; monarchy, absolute monarchy, constitutional monarchy, limited monarchy; dictatorship, tyranny, autocracy, autarchy; dyarchy, duarchy, duumvirate; triarchy, triumvirate; **totalitarian government** *or* regime, police state; **fascism, communism;** stratocracy, **military government,** militarism, garrison state; martial law, rule of the sword; regency; hierocracy, theocracy, thearchy; patriarchy, patriarchate; gerontocracy; technocracy, meritocracy; **autonomy, self-government,** self-rule, self-determination, home rule; heteronomy, dominion rule, colonial government, colonialism, neocolonialism; provisional government; coalition government

5 matriarchy, matriarchate, gynarchy, gynocracy, gynecocracy; petticoat government

6 <nonformal terms> foolocracy, gunocracy, mediocracy, moneyocracy, landocracy, cottonocracy, beerocracy, oiligarchy, parsonarchy, pedantocracy, pornocracy, snobocracy, squirearchy

7 **supranational government,** supergovernment, **world government,** World Federalism; League of Nations, United Nations 614

8 <principles of government> democratism, power-sharing, republicanism; constitutionalism, rule of law, parliamentarism, parliamentarianism; monarchism, royalism; feudalism, feudality; imperialism; fascism, neofascism, Nazism, national socialism; statism, governmentalism; collectivism, communism 611.5, socialism 611.6; federalism; centralism; pluralism; political principles 611

9 **absolutism, dictatorship, despotism,** tyranny, autocracy, autarchy, monarchy, absolute monarchy; **authoritarianism;** totalitarianism; one-man rule, one-party rule; Caesarism, Stalinism, kaiserism, czarism; benevolent despotism, paternalism

10 **despotism, tyranny, fascism,** domineering, domination, oppression; heavy hand, high hand, iron hand, iron heel *or* boot; big stick, *argumentum baculinum* <L>; **terrorism,** reign of terror; thought control

11 **officialism, bureaucracy;** beadledom,

bumbledom; **red-tapeism** *and* red-tapery *and* **red tape** <all nonformal>; federalese, official jargon 609.37

VERBS 12 **govern, regulate; wield authority** 417.13; **command,** officer, captain, **head, lead,** be master, be at the head of, **preside over,** chair; **direct, manage, supervise, administer,** administrate 573.11; discipline; stand over

13 **control, hold in hand,** have in one's power, gain a hold upon; hold the reins, hold the helm, call the shots *or* tune *and* be in the driver's seat *or* saddle <all nonformal>; have control of, **have under control, have in hand** *or* **well in hand;** be master of the situation, have it all one's own way, have the game in one's own hands, hold all the aces <nonformal>; pull the strings *or* wires

14 **rule, sway, reign,** bear reign, have the sway, wield the scepter, wear the crown, sit on the throne; rule over, overrule

15 **dominate, predominate,** preponderate, prevail; **have the ascendancy, have the upper** *or* **whip hand,** get under control, have on the hip <old>; **master,** have the mastery of; bestride; dictate, lay down the law; **rule the roost** *and* wear the pants *and* crack the whip *and* ride herd <all nonformal>; take the lead, play first fiddle; **lead by the nose, twist** *or* **turn around one's little finger; keep under one's thumb,** bend to one's will

16 **domineer,** dominate over, **lord it over;** browbeat, order around, henpeck <nonformal>, intimidate, bully, cow, bulldoze <nonformal>, walk over, walk all over; castrate, unman; daunt, terrorize; **tyrannize,** tyrannize over, push *or* kick around <nonformal>, despotize; **grind,** grind down, break, **oppress,** suppress, repress, weigh *or* press heavy on; keep under, keep down, beat down, clamp down on <nonformal>; overbear, overmaster, overawe; override, ride over, trample *or* stamp *or* tread upon, trample *or* tread down, **trample** *or* **tread underfoot,** keep down, crush under an iron heel, **ride roughshod over;** hold *or* keep a tight hand upon, rule with a rod of iron, rule with an iron hand *or* fist; enslave, subjugate 432.8; compel, coerce 424.7

ADJS 17 **governmental,** gubernatorial; **political, civil,** civic; **official,** bureaucratic; democratic, republican, fascist, fascistic, oligarchal, oligarchic, oligarchical, aristocratic, aristocratical, theocratic, **federal,** federalist, federalistic, **constitutional,** parliamentary, parliamentarian;

monarchic *or* monarchical, monarchial, monarchal <old>; autocratic, monocratic, absolute; **authoritarian;** despotic, **dictatorial; totalitarian;** pluralistic; paternalistic, patriarchal, patriarchic, patriarchical; matriarchal, matriarchic, matriarchical; heteronomous; autonomous, self-governing

18 **governing, controlling, regulating,** regulative, regulatory, **commanding; ruling, reigning, sovereign,** regnant; **master, chief,** general, **boss, head; dominant, predominant,** predominate, preponderant, preponderate, prepotent, prepollent, prevalent, **leading, paramount, supreme,** number one <nonformal>, hegemonic, hegemonistic; ascendant, in the ascendant, in ascendancy; at the head, in chief; in charge 417.21

19 **executive, administrative,** ministerial; official, bureaucratic; **supervisory, directing, managing** 573.12

ADVS 20 **under control, in hand,** well in hand; **in one's power,** under one's control

WORD ELEMENTS 21 —archy, —cracy, —ocracy

613 LEGISLATURE, GOVERNMENT ORGANIZATION

NOUNS 1 **legislature** <see list>, legislative body; **parliament, congress, assembly,** general assembly, house of assembly, legislative assembly, **national assembly, chamber of deputies,** federal assembly, diet, soviet, court; unicameral legislature, bicameral legislature; legislative chamber, **upper chamber *or* house** <see list>, **lower chamber *or* house** <see list>; state legislature, state assembly; provincial legislature, provincial parliament; city council, city board, board of aldermen, common council, commission; representative town meeting, town meeting

2 United States Government, Federal Government; Cabinet <see list>; Executive Department <see list>; government agency; House of Representatives committee; Senate committee

3 **cabinet,** ministry, British cabinet <see list>, **council,** advisory council, council of state, privy council, divan; shadow cabinet; kitchen cabinet, camarilla

4 **capitol, statehouse; courthouse;** city hall

5 **legislation, lawmaking,** legislature <old>; **enactment,** enaction, constitution, passage, passing; **resolution,** con-

current resolution, joint resolution; act 673.3

6 <legislative procedure> introduction, first reading, committee consideration, tabling, filing, second reading, deliberation, **debate,** third reading, **vote,** division, roll call; **filibustering,** filibuster, talkathon <nonformal>; cloture 856.5; **logrolling;** steamroller methods; guillotine <Brit>

7 **veto,** executive veto, absolute veto, qualified *or* limited veto, suspensive *or* suspensory veto, item veto, pocket veto; veto power; veto message; senatorial courtesy

8 **referendum,** constitutional referendum, statutory referendum, optional *or* facultative referendum, compulsory *or* mandatory referendum; **mandate; plebiscite,** plebiscitum; initiative, direct initiative, indirect initiative; recall

9 **bill,** omnibus bill, hold-up bill, companion bills amendment; **clause, proviso;** enacting clause, dragnet clause, escalator clause, saving clause; **rider;** joker <nonformal>; **calendar, motion;** question, previous question, privileged question

VERBS 10 **legislate,** make *or* enact laws, **enact, pass,** constitute, ordain, put in force; **put through, jam *or* steamroller *or* railroad through** <nonformal>, lobby through; table, pigeonhole; take the floor, get the floor, have the floor; yield the floor; **filibuster; logroll,** roll logs; **veto, pocket, kill; decree** 420.8

ADJS 11 **legislative,** legislatorial, lawmaking; deliberative; **parliamentary, congressional;** senatorial; bicameral, unicameral

12 **legislatures**

Althing <Iceland>	Federal Assembly
Chamber of Deputies	<Czechoslovakia,
<Lebanon, Luxem-	Switzerland,
bourg>	Yugoslavia>
Chamber of Repre-	Federal National As-
sentatives	sembly
<Morocco>	<Cameroon>
Congress <Chile,	Federal Parliament
Colombia,	<Australia>
Honduras,	Folketing <Den-
Liberia,	mark>
Mexico, US,	Grand National As-
Venezuela>	sembly <Turkey>
Cortes <Spain>	Great and General
Council of the Valleys	Council <San
<Andorra>	Marino>
Diet <Japan>	Great People's
Eduskunta <Fin-	Khural <Mon-
land>	golia>

House of Representa-
tives <Cyprus,
Gambia, Malta,
New Zealand,
Sierra Leone>
Knesset <Israel>
Legislative Assembly
<Costa Rica,
Mauritius,
Nauru,
Western Samoa,
Tonga>
Legislative Chamber
<Haiti>
National Assembly
<Bhutan,
Botswana,
Bulgaria,
Republic of China,
El Salvador,
Gabon, Guinea,
Equatorial Guinea,
Guyana, Hungary,
Ivory Coast, Jor-
dan, Kenya, South
Korea, Kuwait,
Malawi,
Mauritania,
Pakistan, Rwanda,
Senegal, Tanzania,
Thailand, Tunisia,
Uganda, Upper
Volta, North Viet-
nam, Zaïre,
Zambia>
National Congress
<Brazil, Domini-
can Republic,
Ecuador, Guate-
mala>
National Council
<Monaco>

National People's
Congress <People's
Republic of
China>
Oireachtas <Ire-
land>
Parliament <Afghan-
istan, Austria,
Barbados, Belgium,
Canada, Ethiopia,
Fiji, France, Ger-
many, India, Iran,
Italy, Jamaica,
Laos, Liechten-
stein, Malagasy
Republic, Ma-
laysia, Rhodesia,
Rumania,
Singapore, South
Africa, Swaziland,
Trinidad and To-
bago, United
Kingdom>
People's Assembly
<Albania, Egypt>
People's Consultative
Congress <Indo-
nesia>
People's Council
<Maldive Islands,
Syria>
Riksdag <Sweden>
Sejm <Poland>
States General
<Netherlands>
Storting <Norway>
Supreme People's As-
sembly <North
Korea>
Supreme Soviet
<Russian Federa-
tion>

Malagasy Republic,
Malaysia, Mexico,
Nicaragua, Para-
guay, Philip-
pines, Rhodesia,

14 lower houses
Bundestag
<Germany>
Chamber of Deputies
<Brazil, Chile, Do-
minican Republic,
Ecuador, Ethiopia,
Italy, Jordan, Mex-
ico, Nicaragua,
Paraguay, Ven-
ezuela>
Chamber of Repre-
sentatives
<Belgium, Colom-
bia>
Chamber of the
People
<Czechoslovakia>
Council of the Federa-
tion <Russian
Federation>
Dáil <Ireland>
House of Assembly
<Barbados,
Rhodesia, South
Africa, Swaziland>

South Africa,
Swaziland,
Trinidad and
Tobago, US,
Venezuela>

House of Commons
<Canada, United
Kingdom>
House of
Representatives
<Australia,
Fiji, Jamaica,
Japan, Liberia,
Malaysia, Philip-
pines, US>
House of the People
<Afghanistan>
Lok Sabha
<India>
Majlis <Iran>
National Assembly
<France, Laos,
Malagasy Republic,
Portugal, Turkey>
National Council
<Switzerland>
Odelsting <Nor-
way>
Second Chamber
<Netherlands>

15 US Cabinet
Attorney General
Secretary of Agricul-
ture
Secretary of Com-
merce
Secretary of Defense
Secretary of Health,
Education, and
Welfare
Secretary of Housing
and Urban
Development

Secretary of Labor
Secretary of State
Secretary of the Inte-
rior
Secretary of the Trea-
sury
Secretary of Trans-
portation
Secretary of Veterans
Affairs

13 upper houses
Bundesrat <Austria,
Germany>
Chamber of Nations
<Czechoslovakia>
Chamber of Notables
<Jordan>
Corporative Chamber
<Portugal>
Council of
Nationalities
<Russian
Federation>
Council of States
<Switzerland>
First Chamber
<Netherlands>
House of Councillors
<Japan>
House of Elders
<Afghanistan>

House of Lords
<United King-
dom>
King's Council
<Laos>
Lagting <Norway>
Rajya Sabha
<India>
Republican Senate
<Turkey>
Senate <Australia,
Barbados, Belgium,
Brazil, Canada,
Chile, Colombia,
Dominican Repub-
lic, Ecuador,
Ethiopia, Fiji,
France, Iran, Ire-
land, Italy,
Jamaica, Liberia,

16 US executive departments
Department of Agri-
culture
Department of Com-
merce
Department of De-
fense
Department of
Health, Education,
and Welfare
Department of Hous-
ing and Urban
Development

Department of Jus-
tice
Department of Labor
Department of State
Department of the In-
terior
Department of the
Treasury
Department of Trans-
portation
Department of Vet-
erans Affairs

17 British Cabinet
Chancellor of the Ex-
chequer
Chief Secretary, Trea-
sury

First Lord of the Ad-
miralty
First Lord of the Trea-
sury

First Secretary of
State
Lord Chancellor
Lord President of the
Council
Lord Privy Seal
Minister of Agricul-
ture, Fisheries and
Food
Minister of Housing
and Local Govern-
ment
Minister of Power
Minister of Technol-
ogy
Minister of Transport
Paymaster-General
President of the
Board of Education
President of the
Board of Trade
Prime Minister

Secretary of State for
Defence
Secretary of State for
Economic Affairs
Secretary of State for
Education and Sci-
ence
Secretary of State for
Employment and
Productivity
Secretary of State for
Foreign and Com-
monwealth Affairs
Secretary of State for
Northern Ireland
Secretary of State for
Scotland
Secretary of State for
the Home Depart-
ment
Secretary of State for
Wales

614 UNITED NATIONS, INTERNATIONAL ORGANIZATIONS

NOUNS **1 United Nations** or **UN;** League of
Nations
  2 <United Nations organs> Secretariat;
General Assembly; Security Council;
Trusteeship Council; International Court
of Justice; **United Nations agency** <see
list>, Economic and Social Council or
ECOSOC, ECOSOC commission
  3 international organization, non-UN international organization
  4 United Nations agencies

Food and Agri-
cultural
Organization or
FAO
General Agreement
on Tariffs and
Trade or GATT
Intergovernmental
Maritime Consulta-
tive Organization
or IMCO
International Atomic
Energy Agency or
IAEA
International Bank
for Reconstruction
and Development
or World Bank
International Civil
Aviation Organiza-
tion or ICAO
International Devel-
opment Association
or IDA

International Finance
Corporation or IFO
International Labor
Organization ILO
International Mone-
tary Fund or the
Fund
International Tele-
communication
Union or ITU
United Nations Chil-
dren's Fund or
UNICEF
United Nations
Educational,
Scientific and
Cultural
Organization or
UNESCO
United Nations Relief
and Works Agency
or UNRWA
Universal Postal
Union or UPU

World Health
Organization or
WHO

World Meteorological
Organization or
WMO

615 COMMISSION

NOUNS **1 commission,** commissioning, **delegation,** devolution, devolvement, vesting,
investing, investment, investiture; **deputation;** commitment, entrusting, entrustment, **assignment,** consignment;
errand, task, office; care, cure, **responsibility,** purview, jurisdiction; **mission,**
legation, embassy; **authority** 417; **authorization,** empowerment, power to act, full
power, plenipotentiary power, vicarious
or delegated authority; **warrant,** license,
mandate, charge, trust, brevet, exe-
quatur; **agency,** agentship, factorship;
regency, regentship; lieutenancy; trusteeship, executorship; **proxy,** procuration,
power of attorney
  2 appointment, assignment, designation,
nomination, naming, selection, tabbing
<nonformal>; **ordainment,** ordination;
posting, transferral
  3 installation, installment, **instatement,**
induction, placement, **inauguration,**
investiture, taking office; **accession,** ac-
cedence; coronation, enthronement
  **4 engagement, employment, hiring, ap-
pointment,** taking on <nonformal>,
recruitment, recruiting; executive recruiting, executive search; retaining,
retainment, briefing <Brit>; preengage-
ment, bespeaking; reservation, booking
  5 executive search agency or firm; executive recruiter, executive recruitment
consultant, executive development specialist; **headhunter** and body snatcher
and flesh peddler and talent scout <all
nonformal>
  6 rental, rent; lease, let <Brit>; hire, hiring; sublease, subrent; **charter,** bareboat
charter; lend-lease
  **7 enlistment, enrollment; conscription,
draft, drafting, induction,** impressment,
press; call, draft call, call-up, summons,
call to the colors, letter from Uncle Sam
<nonformal>; **recruitment,** recruiting;
muster, mustering, mustering in, levy,
levying; mobilization; selective service,
compulsory military service
  8 indenture, binding over; **apprenticeship**
  9 assignee, appointee, selectee, nominee,
candidate; licensee, licentiate; deputy,
agent 576
VERBS **10 commission, authorize,** empower,
accredit; **delegate,** devolute, devolve, de-

volve upon, vest, invest; depute, **deputize; assign,** consign, **commit, charge,
entrust,** give in charge; license, charter,
warrant; detail, detach, post, transfer,
send out, mission, send on a mission

11 **appoint, assign,** designate, **nominate,**
name, select, tab <nonformal>; **ordain,**
ordinate <old>

12 **install,** instate, induct, **inaugurate,** invest, put in, place, **place in office;** chair;
crown, throne, enthrone, anoint

13 **be instated, take office,** accede; take *or*
mount the throne; attain to

14 **employ, hire,** give a job to, take into employment, take into one's service, take
on <nonformal>, recruit, headhunt
<nonformal>, **engage,** sign up *or* on
<nonformal>; retain, brief <Brit>; be-
speak, preengage; sign up for <nonfor-
mal>, **reserve,** book

15 **rent, lease, let** <Brit>, hire, job, **charter;
sublease, sublet,** underlet

16 **rent out, rent; lease,** lease out; let *and* let
off *and* let out <all Brit>; **hire out,** hire;
charter; **sublease, sublet,** underlet; lend-
lease, lease-lend; lease-back; farm, farm
out; job

17 **enlist,** list <old>, **enroll, sign up** *or* on
<nonformal>; **conscript, draft, induct,**
press, impress, commandeer; detach, detach for service; summon, call up, call to
the colors; **mobilize,** call to active duty;
recruit, muster, levy, raise, muster in;
join 617.14

18 indenture, article, bind, bind over; **apprentice**

ADJS 19 **commissioned, authorized, accredited;** delegated, deputized, appointed

20 **employed, hired, hireling, paid,** mercenary; rented, leased, let <Brit>; sublet,
underlet, subleased; chartered

21 **indentured,** articled, bound over; **appren-
ticed, apprentice,** prentice *or* 'prentice

ADVS 22 **for hire,** for rent, to let, to lease

616 ASSOCIATE

NOUNS 1 **associate, confederate,** consociate,
colleague, fellow member, **companion,
fellow,** bedfellow, **crony,** consort, cohort,
compeer, compatriot, confrere, brother,
brother-in-arms, **ally,** adjunct, coadjutor;
comrade in arms, **comrade** 588.3

2 **partner,** pardner *or* pard <nonformal>,
copartner, side partner, buddy <nonfor-
mal>, **sidekick** *and* sidekicker <both
nonformal>; **mate; business partner,**
nominal *or* holding-out *or* ostensible *or*
quasi partner, general partner, special

partner, silent partner, secret partner,
dormant *or* sleeping partner

3 **accomplice,** cohort, confederate, fellow
conspirator, coconspirator, partner *or* accomplice in crime; *particeps criminis,
socius criminis* <both L>; **accessory,** accessory before the fact, accessory after
the fact; **abettor**

4 **collaborator,** cooperator; coauthor; **collaborationist**

5 **co-worker, workfellow, workmate, fellow worker, buddy** <nonformal>, butty
<Brit nonformal>; **teammate, yokefel-
low,** yokemate; benchfellow, shopmate

6 **assistant, helper,** auxiliary, aider, **aid,**
aide, paraprofessional; **help, helpmate,
helpmeet;** deputy, **agent** 576; **attendant,
second,** acolyte; best man, groomsman,
paranymph; **servant, employee** 577; adjutant, aide-de-camp; lieutenant, executive
officer; coadjutant, coadjutor; coad-
jutress, coadjutrix; sidesman <Brit>;
supporting actor *or* player; supporting instrumentalist, sideman

7 **right-hand man** *or* **woman, right hand,**
strong right hand *or* arm, **man** *or* **gal Friday,** fidus Achates, second self, alter ego,
confidant

8 **follower, disciple,** adherent, votary; **man,
henchman,** camp follower, hanger-on,
satellite, creature, lackey, flunky, stooge
<nonformal>, jackal, minion, myr-
midon; yes-man <nonformal>, sycophant 138.3; goon <nonformal>, thug
593.3; puppet, cat's-paw; dummy, figurehead

9 **supporter, upholder,** maintainer, sustainer; support, **mainstay, standby**
<nonformal>, stalwart, reliance, de-
pendence; **abettor, seconder,** second;
endorser, sponsor; **backer, promoter,** angel <nonformal>, rabbi <nonformal>;
patron, Maecenas; friend at *or* in court;
champion, defender, apologist, **advocate,**
exponent, **protagonist; well-wisher,** favorer, encourager, sympathizer; **partisan,**
sider <old>, sectary, votary; **fan** *and* buff
<both nonformal>, aficionado, **admirer,**
lover

617 ASSOCIATION

NOUNS 1 **association, society,** body; **alliance, coalition, league, union;** council;
bloc, axis; **partnership; federation, confederation,** confederacy, grouping,
assemblage 769; **combination,** combine;
Bund, Verein <both Ger>; **unholy alliance, gang** *and* **ring** *and* **mob** <all non-

formal>; machine, **political machine;** economic community, common market, free trade area, customs union; credit union; cooperative, cooperative society, consumer cooperative, Rochdale cooperative; college, **group,** corps, band 769.3; labor union 727

2 **community, society, commonwealth;** body; **kinship group, clan,** sept <Scots>, moiety, totemic *or* totemistic group, phyle, phratry *or* phratria, gens, caste, subcaste, endogamous group; **family,** extended family, nuclear family, binuclear family; order, **class, social class** 607, economic class; colony, settlement; **commune,** ashram

3 **fellowship,** sodality; **society,** guild, order; **brotherhood, fraternity,** confraternity, confrerie, fraternal order *or* society; **sisterhood, sorority; club,** country club; secret society, **cabal**

4 **party, interest, camp, side;** interest group, pressure group, ethnic group; minority group, vocal minority; silent majority; **faction,** division, **sect,** wing, **caucus,** splinter, splinter group, breakaway group, offshoot; **political party** 609.24

5 **school, sect,** class, order; **denomination, communion,** confession, faith, church; **persuasion, ism; disciples, followers,** adherents

6 **clique, coterie, set, circle,** ring, junto, junta, cabal, camarilla, **clan,** group; **crew** *and* mob *and* **crowd** *and* **bunch** *and* outfit <all nonformal>; cell; cadre, inner circle; closed *or* charmed circle; ingroup, we-group; elite, elite group; leadership group; **old-boy network**

7 **team, outfit,** squad, string; eleven, nine, eight, five, etc; **crew,** rowing crew; varsity, first team, first string; bench, reserves, second team, second string, third string; platoon; complement; **cast,** company

8 **organization,** establishment, **foundation, institution, institute**

9 **company, firm, business firm, concern, house,** *compagnie* <Fr>, *compañía* <Sp>, *Aktiengesellschaft* <Ger>, *aktiebolag* <Swed>; **business, industry, enterprise,** business establishment, commercial enterprise; **trust, syndicate, cartel,** combine, pool, consortium, plunderbund <nonformal>; combination in restraint of trade; chamber of commerce; junior chamber of commerce; trade association

10 **branch, organ, division,** wing, arm, off-

shoot, **affiliate; chapter,** lodge, post; chapel; **local;** branch office

11 **member,** affiliate, belonger, insider, initiate, one of us, cardholder, card-carrier, card-carrying member; **enrollee,** enlistee; **associate,** socius, **fellow;** brother, sister; comrade; honorary member; life member; member in good standing, dues-paying member; charter member; clubman, clubwoman, clubber <nonformal>; fraternity man, fraternity *or* frat brother, Greek <nonformal>, sorority woman; sorority sister, guildsman; committeeman; conventionist, conventioner, conventioneer; joiner <nonformal>; pledge

12 **membership,** members, associates, affiliates, body of affiliates, constituency

13 **partisanism,** partisanship, **partiality; factionalism, sectionalism,** faction; sectarianism, denominationalism; **cliquism,** cliquishness, cliqueyness; **clannishness,** clanship; exclusiveness, exclusivity; ethnocentricity; party spirit, *esprit de corps* <Fr>; the old college spirit

VERBS 14 **join,** join up <nonformal>, **enter, go into,** come into, get into, make oneself part of, swell the ranks of; **enlist, enroll, affiliate, sign up** *or* **on** <nonformal>, take up membership, take out membership; inscribe oneself, put oneself down; associate oneself with, affiliate with, league with, team *or* team up with; sneak in, creep in, insinuate oneself into; **combine, associate** 804.4

15 **belong,** hold membership, be a member, be on the rolls, be inscribed, subscribe, hold *or* carry a card, be in <nonformal>

ADJS 16 **associated, corporate,** incorporated; **combined** 804.5; non-profit-making, nonprofit, not-for-profit

17 **associational, social, society, communal;** organizational; coalitional; sociable

18 **cliquish,** cliquey, **clannish;** ethnocentric; exclusive

19 **partisan,** party; **partial,** interested; **factional, sectional,** sectarian, sectary, denominational

ADVS 20 **in association, conjointly** 450.6

618 WEALTH

NOUNS 1 **wealth, riches, opulence** *or* opulency 990.2, **luxuriousness** 501.5; richness, wealthiness; **prosperity,** prosperousness, **affluence,** comfortable *or* easy circumstances, independence; **money,** lucre, pelf, gold, mammon; **substance, property, possessions,** material wealth; **assets** 728.14; **fortune, treasure,** handsome fortune; full *or* heavy *or* well-lined *or* bottomless *or* fat *or* bulging purse, deep pockets <nonformal>; *embarras de richesses* <Fr>, money to burn <nonformal>; high income, six-figure income; high tax bracket, upper bracket

2 **large sum,** good sum, tidy sum *and* **pretty penny, king's ransom;** heaps of gold; thousands, millions, cool million, billion, etc

3 <nonformal terms> **bundle, big bucks,** megabucks, gigabucks, big money, serious money, gobs, heaps, heavy lettuce, heavy jack, heavy money, important money, pot, potful, power, mint, barrel, raft, load, **loads,** pile, wad, wads, nice hunk of change, packet <Brit>

4 <rich source> **mine,** mine of wealth, **gold mine,** bonanza, luau <nonformal>, lode, rich lode, mother lode, Eldorado, Golconda, Seven Cities of Cibola; gravy train <nonformal>; rich uncle; cash cow <nonformal>

5 **the golden touch,** Midas touch; philosophers' stone; Pactolus

6 **the rich, the wealthy,** the well-to-do, the haves <nonformal>; **plutocracy,** timocracy

7 **rich man** *or* **woman,** wealthy man *or* woman, warm man *or* woman <Brit nonformal>, **moneyed man** *or* **woman,** man *or* woman of wealth, **man** *or* **woman of means** *or* **substance,** fat cat <nonformal>, richling, deep pocket *and* moneybags *and* Mr Moneybags <all nonformal>, Daddy Warbucks <Harold Gray>, coupon-clipper, **nabob; capitalist, plutocrat,** bloated plutocrat; **millionaire,** multimillionaire, megamillionaire, millionairess, multibillionaire, multimillionairess, billionaire; parvenu

8 Croesus, Midas, Plutus, Dives, Timon of Athens, Danaë; Rockefeller, Vanderbilt, Whitney, DuPont, Ford, Getty, Rothschild, Onassis, Hughes, Hunt, Trump

VERBS 9 **enrich, richen**

10 **grow rich, get rich,** fill *or* line one's pockets, feather one's nest, **make** *or* **coin money,** have a gold mine, have the golden touch, **make a fortune,** make one's pile <nonformal>; **strike it rich;** come into money; make good, get on in the world, do all right by oneself *and* rake it in <both nonformal>

11 **have money,** command money, **be loaded** *and* have deep pockets <both nonformal>, have the wherewithal, have means, have independent means; **afford,** well afford

12 **live well,** live high, live high on the hog <nonformal>, **live in clover,** roll *or* wallow in wealth, roll *or* live in the lap of luxury; have all the money in the world, have a mint, have money to burn <nonformal>

13 worship mammon, worship the golden calf

ADJS 14 **wealthy, rich, affluent, moneyed** *or* **monied,** in funds *or* cash, **well-to-do,** well-to-do in the world, **well-off, well-situated, prosperous,** comfortable, provided for, well provided for, fat, **flush,** flush with *or* of money, abounding in riches, worth a great deal, frightfully rich, rich as Croesus; independent, independently rich, independently wealthy; **luxurious** 501.21; **opulent** 990.7; privileged, born with a silver spoon in one's mouth; higher-income, upper-income, well-paid

15 <nonformal terms> **loaded, well-heeled, filthy rich,** warm <Brit>, in the money *or* dough, well-fixed, made of money, **rolling in money,** rolling *or* wallowing in it, disgustingly rich, big-rich, rich-rich, oofy, lousy rich, upscale

619 POVERTY

NOUNS 1 **poverty,** poorness, impecuniousness, impecuniosity; **straits,** difficulties, **hardship** 1010.1; financial distress *or* embarrassment, **embarrassed** *or* **reduced** *or* **straitened circumstances,** tight squeeze, hard pinch, crunch <nonformal>, cash *or* credit crunch <nonformal>; cash-flow shortage, cash-flow blowout <nonformal>; slender *or* narrow means, insolvency, light purse; unprosperousness; broken fortune; genteel poverty; vows of poverty, voluntary poverty

2 **indigence, penury, pennilessness,** penuriousness, moneylessness; **pauperism,** pauperization, **impoverishment,** grinding *or* crushing poverty, chronic pauperism; **beggary,** beggarliness, mendicancy; homelessness; **destitution, privation, deprivation; neediness, want,** need, lack, pinch, gripe, necessity, disadvantagedness, necessitousness, **homelessness; hand-to-mouth existence,** bare subsistence, wolf at the door, bare cupboard, empty purse *or* pocket

3 **the poor, the needy,** the have-nots <nonformal>, the down-and-out, the disadvantaged, the underprivileged, the distressed, the underclass; the urban poor, ghetto-dwellers, barrio-dwellers; welfare rolls, welfare clients, welfare

families; the homeless, the ranks of the homeless; "wretched of the earth" —E Pottier, "houseless heads and unfed sides"—Shakespeare; the other America; the forgotten man, "the forgotten man at the bottom of the economic pyramid" —F D Roosevelt; depressed population, depressed area, chronic poverty area; underdeveloped nation, third world

4 **poor man,** poorling, poor devil, down-and-out *or* down-and-outer, **pauper,** indigent, penniless man, hard case, starveling; homeless person, bag woman *or* lady, shopping-bag lady, shopping-cart woman *or* lady, homeless *or* street person, skell <nonformal>; **beggar** 440.8; welfare client; almsman, almswoman, charity case, casual; bankrupt 625.4

VERBS 5 **be poor,** be hard up <nonformal>, find it hard going, have seen better days, be on one's uppers, be pinched *or* strapped, **be in want,** want, need, lack; **starve,** not know where one's next meal is coming from, **live from hand to mouth,** eke out *or* squeeze out a living; **not have a penny** *or* **sou,** not have a penny to bless oneself with, not have one dollar to rub against another; go on welfare

6 **impoverish,** reduce, **pauperize, beggar;** eat out of house and home; **bankrupt** 625.8

ADJS 7 **poor, ill off,** badly *or* poorly off, hard up <nonformal>, downscale, impecunious, **unmoneyed; unprosperous;** reduced, in reduced circumstances; **straitened, in straitened circumstances,** narrow, in narrow circumstances, feeling the pinch, strapped, **financially embarrassed** *or* distressed, **pinched,** feeling the pinch, squeezed, put to one's shifts *or* last shifts, at the end of one's rope, on the edge *or* ragged edge <nonformal>, down to bedrock, in Queer Street; short, **short of money** *or* **funds** *or* **cash,** out-of-pocket; unable to make ends meet, unable to keep the wolf from the door; poor as a church mouse, "poor as Job"—John Gower; land-poor

8 **indigent, poverty-stricken; needy,** necessitous, **in need, in want,** disadvantaged, deprived, underprivileged; **beggared,** beggarly, mendicant; **impoverished, pauperized,** starveling; ghettoized; bereft, bereaved; stripped, fleeced; **down at heels,** down at the heel, on *or* down on one's uppers, out at the heels, out at elbows, in rags; on welfare, on relief, on the dole <Brit>

9 **destitute, down-and-out,** in the gutter;

penniless, moneyless, fortuneless, out of funds, **without a sou,** without a penny to bless oneself with, without one dollar to rub against another; insolvent, in the red, **bankrupt** 625.11; homeless; propertyless, landless

10 <nonformal terms> **broke, dead broke,** busted, **flat, flat broke,** flat on one's ass, flat-ass, down for the count, stone *or* stony broke, stony, **strapped,** skint <Brit>, beat, down to one's last penny *or* cent, cleaned out, tapped out, Tap City, oofless, wasted, wiped out, without a pot to piss in

620 LENDING

NOUNS 1 **lending, loaning;** moneylending, lending at interest; advance, advancing, advancement; **usury,** loan-sharking *and* shylocking <both nonformal>; lend-lease; **interest,** interest rate, lending rate, the price of money; points, mortgage points

2 **loan,** the lend <nonformal>, **advance,** accommodation

3 **lender, loaner;** loan officer; commercial banker; **moneylender,** moneymonger; money broker; banker 729.10; **usurer,** shylock *and* loan shark <both nonformal>; **pawnbroker;** mortgagee, mortgage holder

4 **lending institution,** savings and loan association *or* thrift *or* thrift institution *or* savings institution; savings and loan *or* thrift industry; building society <Brit>; finance company *or* corporation, loan office, mortgage company; commercial bank, **bank** 729.13; **credit union; pawnshop, pawnbroker,** pawnbrokery, **hock shop** <nonformal>, *mont-de-piété* <Fr>, sign of the three balls

VERBS 5 **lend, loan, advance,** accommodate with; loan-shark <nonformal>; float *or* negotiate a loan; lend-lease, lease-lend

ADJS 6 **loaned, lent**

ADVS 7 **on loan,** on security; in advance

621 BORROWING

NOUNS 1 **borrowing,** money-raising; touching *or* hitting *or* hitting-up <all nonformal>; financing, mortgaging; installment buying, installment plan, hire purchase <Brit>; debt, debtor 623.4

2 **adoption, appropriation, taking,** deriving, **derivation, assumption; imitation,** simulation, copying, mocking; borrowed plumes; a leaf from someone else's book;

plagiarism, plagiary, pastiche, pasticcio; infringement, pirating

VERBS **3 borrow,** borrow the loan of, get on credit *or* trust, get on tick *and* get on the cuff <both nonformal>; get a loan, float *or* negotiate a loan, go into the money market, **raise money; touch** *and* **hit up** *and* hit one for *and* put the arm *or* bite *or* touch on <all nonformal>; run into debt 623.6; pawn 438.10

4 adopt, appropriate, take, take on, take over, assume, make use of, take a leaf from someone's book, derive from; **imitate,** simulate, copy, mock, steal one's stuff <nonformal>; plagiarize, steal; pirate, infringe

622 FINANCIAL CREDIT

NOUNS **1 credit, trust,** tick <nonformal>; borrowing power *or* capacity; commercial credit, cash credit, bank credit, book credit, tax credit, investment credit; credit line, line of credit; installment plan, installment credit, consumer credit, store credit, hire purchase plan <Brit>, never-never <Brit nonformal>; **credit standing,** standing, **credit rating,** rating, Dun and Bradstreet rating, solvency 729.6; credit squeeze, insolvency; credit bureau *or* agency; credit insurance, credit life insurance; credit union, cooperative credit union

2 account, credit account, charge account; bank account, savings account, checking account; share account; bank balance; expense account; current *or* open account

3 credit instrument; paper credit; **letter of credit,** *lettre de créance* <Fr>, circular note; credit slip, credit memorandum, deposit slip, certificate of deposit; share certificate; negotiable instruments 728.11; **credit card,** plastic, plastic money *or* credit, affinity card *or* affinity credit card *or* affinity-group card *or* affinity-group credit card, custom credit card *or* customized credit card *or* custom card, gold card, charge card, charge plate; smart card, supersmart card

4 creditor, creditress; debtee; mortgagee, mortgage-holder; note-holder; credit man; bill collector, collection agent; dunner, dun

VERBS **5 credit, credit with; credit to one's account,** place to one's credit *or* account

6 give *or* **extend credit** *or* a line of credit; sell on credit, trust, entrust; give tick <nonformal>; carry, carry on one's books

7 receive credit, take credit, **charge,** charge to one's account, keep an account with, go on tick <nonformal>, buy on credit, buy on the cuff <nonformal>, buy on the installment plan, buy on time, put on the lay-away plan; go in hock for <nonformal>; have one's credit good for

ADJS **8 credited,** of good credit, **well-rated**

ADVS **9 to one's credit** *or* **account,** to the credit *or* account of, to the good

10 on credit, on account, on trust, on tick *and* **on the cuff** <both nonformal>; on terms, on good terms, on easy terms, on budget terms, in installments, on time

623 DEBT

NOUNS **1 debt, indebtedness,** indebtment, **obligation, liability,** financial commitment, due, **dues,** score, pledge, unfulfilled pledge, amount due, outstanding debt; **bill, bills,** chits <nonformal>, **charges;** floating debt; funded debt, unfunded debt; accounts receivable; accounts payable; borrowing 621; maturity; bad debts, uncollectibles; **national debt,** public debt; deficit, national deficit; megadebt <nonformal>; debt explosion

2 arrears, arrear, arrearage, back debts, back payments; **deficit,** default, deferred payments; cash *or* credit crunch <nonformal>; overdraft, bounced *or* bouncing check, rubber check <nonformal>; dollar gap, unfavorable trade balance *or* balance of payments; deficit financing

3 interest, premium, price, rate; interest rate, rate of interest, prime interest rate *or* **prime rate,** bank rate, lending rate, borrowing rate, the price of money; discount rate; **usury** 620.1, excessive *or* exorbitant interest; points, mortgage points; simple interest, compound interest; net interest, gross interest; compensatory interest; lucrative interest; penal interest

4 debtor, borrower; mortgagor

VERBS **5 owe, be indebted,** be obliged *or* obligated for, be financially committed, lie under an obligation, be bound to pay

6 go in debt, get into debt, run into debt, plunge into debt, incur *or* contract a debt, go in hock <nonformal>, be overextended, **run up a bill** *or* a score *or* an account *or* a tab; run *or* show a deficit, operate at a loss; borrow

7 mature, accrue, fall due

ADJS **8 indebted, in debt,** plunged in debt, in difficulties, embarrassed, in embarrassed circumstances, in the hole *and* in hock

<both nonformal>, in the red, encumbered, mortgaged, mortgaged to the hilt, tied up, involved; deep in debt, involved *or* deeply involved in debt, burdened with debt, head over heels *or* up to one's ears in debt <nonformal>; cash poor

9 chargeable, obligated, liable, pledged, responsible, answerable for

10 due, owed, owing, payable, receivable, redeemable, mature, **outstanding, unpaid,** in arrear *or* arrears, back

624 PAYMENT

NOUNS **1 payment, paying,** paying off, paying up <nonformal>, payoff; **defrayment,** defrayal; paying out, doling out, **disbursal** 626.1; **discharge, settlement, clearance, liquidation, amortization,** amortizement, retirement, satisfaction; quittance; acquittance *or* acquitment *or* acquittal <all old>; **debt service, interest payment,** sinking-fund payment; **remittance;** installment, installment plan, layaway plan; hire purchase *or* hire purchase plan *or* never-never <all Brit>; regular payments, monthly payments, weekly payments, quarterly payments, etc; down payment, deposit, earnest, earnest money, binder; god's penny; the King's shilling <Brit>; **cash,** hard cash, spot cash, cash payment, cash on the nail *and* cash on the barrelhead <both nonformal>; pay-as-you-go; prepayment; **postponed** *or* **deferred payment,** contango *or* carryover *and* continuation *and* backwardation <all Brit>; payment in kind

2 reimbursement, recoupment, recoup, return, restitution; **refund,** refundment; kickback <nonformal>; payback, chargeback, **repayment** 481.2

3 recompense, remuneration, compensation; requital, requitement, quittance, **retribution, reparation, redress,** satisfaction, **atonement, amends,** return, restitution 481; blood money, wergild <old>; **indemnity,** indemnification; price, consideration; **reward,** meed, guerdon; honorarium; workmen's compensation *or* comp <nonformal>, solatium, damages, smart money; salvage

4 pay, payment, remuneration, compensation, total compensation, wages plus fringe benefits, financial package, pay and allowances, financial remuneration; rate of pay; **salary, wage, wages, income, earnings,** hire; real wages, purchasing power; payday, pay check, pay envelope,

pay packet <Brit>; take-home pay *or* income, wages after taxes, pay *or* income *or* wages after deductions, net income *or* wages *or* pay *or* earnings, taxable income; gross income; living wage; minimum wage, base pay; portal-to-portal pay; severance pay, discontinuance *or* dismissal wage; wage scale; escalator plan, escalator clause, sliding scale; guaranteed income, guaranteed annual income, negative income tax; fixed income; wage freeze, wage rollback, wage reduction, wage control; guaranteed annual wage, guaranteed income plan; overtime pay; danger money, combat pay, flight pay; back pay; strike pay; **payroll**

5 fee, stipend, allowance, emolument, tribute; **reckoning,** account, bill; assessment, scot; initiation fee, footing <old>; retainer, retaining fee; hush money, blackmail; blood money; mileage

6 <extra pay or allowance> **bonus, premium, fringe benefit** *or* **benefits,** bounty, perquisite, perquisites, perks <nonformal>, gravy <nonformal>, lagniappe, solatium; **tip** 478.5; overtime pay; bonus system

7 dividend; royalty; commission, rake-off *and* cut <both nonformal>

8 <the bearing of another's expense> **treat,** standing treat, picking up the check *or* tab <nonformal>; paying the bills, maintenance, support 449.3; subsidy 478.8

9 payer, remunerator, compensator, recompenser; paymaster, purser, bursar, cashier, treasurer 729.11; defrayer; liquidator; **taxpayer, ratepayer** <Brit>

VERBS **10 pay,** render, tender; **recompense, remunerate, compensate, reward,** guerdon, indemnify, satisfy; salary, fee; remit; prepay; pay by *or* in installments, pay on, pay in; make payments to *or* towards *or* on

11 repay, pay back, restitute, **reimburse,** recoup; **requite,** quit, **atone,** redress <old>, **make amends,** make good, make up for, make up to, make restitution, make reparation 481.5; pay in kind, pay one in his own coin, give tit for tat; **refund,** kick back <nonformal>

12 settle with, reckon with, account with <old>, pay out, **settle** *or* **square accounts with,** square oneself with, get square with, **get even with,** get quits with; even the score <nonformal>, wipe *or* clear off old scores, pay old debts, clear the board

13 pay in full, pay off, pay up <nonformal>, **discharge, settle,** square, **clear, liquidate,**

amortize, retire, take up, lift, take up and pay off, honor, acquit oneself of <old>; satisfy; meet one's obligations *or* commitments, redeem, redeem one's pledge *or* pledges, tear up *or* burn one's mortgage, have a mortgage-burning party, settle *or* square accounts, make accounts square, strike a balance; pay the bill, pay the shot

14 pay out, fork out *or* **over** <nonformal>, **shell out** <nonformal>; **expend** 626.5

15 pay over, hand over; ante, **ante up,** put up; put down, lay down, lay one's money down, show the color of one's money

16 <nonformal terms> **kick in, fork over,** pony up, pay up, cough up, stump up <Brit>, come across, come through with, come across with, come down with, come down with the needful, plank down, plunk down, post, tickle *or* grease the palm, cross one's palm with, lay on one; pay to the tune of

17 pay cash, make a cash payment, cash, **pay spot cash, pay cash down,** pay cash on the barrelhead <nonformal>, plunk down the money *and* put one's money on the line <both nonformal>, pay at sight; pay in advance; pay as you go; pay cash on delivery *or* pay COD

18 pay for, pay *or* stand the costs, **bear the expense** *or* **cost,** pay the piper <nonformal>; **finance, fund** 729.15; **defray,** defray expenses; pay the bill, **foot the bill** *and* pick up the check *or* tab *and* spring *or* pop for <all nonformal>; honor a bill, acknowledge, redeem; pay one's way; pay one's share, chip in <nonformal>, go Dutch <nonformal>

19 treat, treat to, **stand treat,** go treat, stand to <nonformal>, pick up the check *or* tab <nonformal>, pay the bill, set up, blow to <nonformal>; stand drinks; maintain, support 449.12; subsidize 478.19

20 be paid, draw wages, be salaried, work for wages, be remunerated, collect for one's services, **earn,** get an income, pull down *and* drag down <both nonformal>

ADJS **21 paying, remunerative, remuneratory; compensating,** compensative, compensatory; retributive, retributory; **rewarding,** rewardful; lucrative, moneymaking, profitable; repaying, satisfying, reparative

22 paid, paid-up, discharged, settled, liquidated, acquitted <old>, paid in full, receipted, remitted; **spent, expended;** salaried, waged, hired; prepaid, postpaid

23 unindebted, unowing, **out of debt,** above water, out of the hole *or* the red <nonformal>, **clear,** all clear, free and clear, all straight; solvent 729.17

ADVS **24 in compensation,** as compensation, in recompense, for services rendered, for professional services, **in reward,** in requital, in reparation, in retribution, in restitution, in exchange for, **in amends,** in atonement, to atone for

25 cash, cash on the barrelhead <nonformal>, strictly cash; **cash down, money down,** down; cash on delivery *or* **COD;** on demand, on call; pay-as-you-go

625 NONPAYMENT

NOUNS **1 nonpayment, default, delinquency,** delinquence <old>, nondischarge of debts, nonremittal, failure to pay; defection; protest, repudiation; dishonor, dishonoring; bad debt, uncollectible, dishonored *or* protested bill

2 moratorium, grace period; **write-off,** cancellation, obliteration 395.7

3 insolvency, bankruptcy, receivership, Chapter 11, **failure; crash,** collapse, bust <nonformal>; run on a bank; insufficient funds, overdraft, overdrawn account, not enough to cover, bounced *or* bouncing check, kited check

4 insolvent, insolvent debtor; **bankrupt,** failure; **loser,** heavy loser, lame duck <nonformal>

5 defaulter, delinquent, nonpayer; **welsher** <nonformal>, levanter; tax evader, tax dodger *or* cheat <nonformal>

VERBS **6 not pay;** dishonor, repudiate, disallow, protest, stop payment, refuse to pay; **default, welsh** <nonformal>, levant; button up one's pockets, draw the purse strings; **underpay;** bounce *or* kite a check <nonformal>

7 go bankrupt, go broke <nonformal>, go into receivership, become insolvent *or* bankrupt, **fail,** break, bust <nonformal>, crash, collapse, **fold, fold up,** belly up *and* go up *and* go belly up *and* **go under** <all nonformal>, shut down, shut one's doors, go out of business, **be ruined,** go to ruin, go on the rocks, go to the wall, go to pot <nonformal>, go to the dogs; take a bath *and* be taken to the cleaners *and* be cleaned out *and* lose one's shirt *and* tap out <all nonformal>

8 bankrupt, ruin, break, bust *and* wipe out <both nonformal>; put out of business, drive to the wall, scuttle, sink; impoverish 619.6

9 declare a moratorium; write off, forgive,

absolve, **cancel**, nullify, wipe the slate clean; wipe out, obliterate 395.16

ADJS **10 defaulting**, nonpaying, **delinquent**; behindhand, in arrear *or* arrears

11 insolvent, bankrupt, in receivership, in the hands of receivers, belly-up <nonformal>, broken, **broke** *and* busted <both nonformal>, **ruined,** failed, out of business, unable to pay one's creditors, unable to meet one's obligations, on the rocks; destitute 619.9

12 unpaid, unremunerated, uncompensated, unrecompensed, **unrewarded,** unrequited; underpaid

13 unpayable, irredeemable, inconvertible

626 EXPENDITURE

NOUNS **1 expenditure, spending,** expense, disbursal, **disbursement;** debit, debiting; budgeting, scheduling; costing, costing-out; **payment** 624; deficit spending; **use** 387; **consumption** 388

2 spendings, disbursements, payments, outgoings, outgo, outflow, **outlay,** money going out

3 expenses, costs, charges, disbursals, **liabilities; expense, cost,** burden of expenditure; budget, budget item, budget line, line item; **overhead,** operating expense *or* expenses *or* costs *or* budget, general expenses; expense account, swindle sheet <nonformal>; business expenses, overhead; nonremunerated business expenses, out-of-pocket expenses; direct costs, indirect costs; distributed costs, undistributed costs; material costs; labor costs; carrying charge; unit cost; replacement cost; prime cost; cost of living, cost-of-living index, cost-of-living allowance *or* COLA

4 spender, expender, expenditor, disburser

VERBS **5 spend, expend, disburse, pay out,** fork out *or* over <nonformal>, shell out <nonformal>, **lay out,** outlay; go to the expense of; **pay** 624.10; put one's hands in one's pockets, open the purse, loosen *or* untie the purse strings *and* throw money around <both nonformal>, go on a spending spree, splurge, spend money like a drunken sailor *and* spend money as if it were going out of style <both nonformal>, go *or* run through, **squander** 486.3; **invest,** sink money in <nonformal>, put out; throw money at the problem; **incur costs** *or* **expenses;** budget, schedule, cost, cost out; **use** 387.13; **consume**

6 be spent, burn in one's pocket, burn a hole in one's pocket

7 afford, well afford, spare, spare the price, bear, stand, support, endure, undergo, meet the expense of, swing

627 RECEIPTS

NOUNS **1 receipts,** receipt, **income, revenue, profits, earnings, returns, proceeds,** avails <old>, **take,** takings, intake, take *or* take-in <nonformal>, get <Brit nonformal>; credit, credits; gains 472.3; gate receipts, gate, box office; net receipts, net; gross receipts, gross; national income; net income, gross income; earned income, unearned income; **dividend** 738.7, dividends, payout, payback; royalties, commissions; receivables; disposable income; make, produce, **yield, output** 892.2, bang for the buck <nonformal>, fruits, first fruits

2 <written acknowledgment> **receipt, acknowledgment, voucher,** warrant <Brit>; canceled check; **receipt in full,** receipt in full of all demands, release, acquittance, quittance, discharge

VERBS **3 receive** 479.6, **pocket, acquire** 472.8,9; acknowledge receipt of, receipt, mark paid

4 yield, bring in, afford, pay, pay off <nonformal>, **return; gross, net**

628 ACCOUNTS

NOUNS **1 accounts; outstanding accounts,** uncollected *or* unpaid accounts; **accounts receivable,** receipts, assets; **accounts payable,** expenditures, liabilities; **budget,** budgeting; costing out

2 account, reckoning, tally, rendering-up, score; account current; account rendered, *compte rendu* <Fr>, account stated; balance, trial balance

3 statement, bill, itemized bill, bill of account, **account, reckoning, check,** *l'addition* <Fr>, score *or* tab <both nonformal>; **dun; invoice,** manifest, bill of lading

4 account book, ledger, journal, daybook; **register,** registry, **record book,** books; inventory, catalog; **log,** logbook; **cashbook; bankbook,** passbook; balance sheet; cost sheet, cost card

5 entry, item, line item, minute, note, notation; single entry, double entry; **credit, debit**

6 accounting, accountancy, bookkeeping, double-entry bookkeeping *or* accounting, single-entry bookkeeping *or* accounting; comptrollership *or* controllership; business *or* commercial *or* monetary arithmetic; cost accounting, costing <Brit>, cost system, cost-accounting system; **audit, auditing;** stocktaking

7 **accountant, bookkeeper; clerk,** actuary <old>, registrar, recorder, journalizer; calculator, reckoner; cost accountant, cost keeper; certified public accountant *or* CPA; chartered accountant *or* CA <Brit>; **auditor,** bank examiner; bank accountant; accountant general; comptroller *or* controller

VERBS 8 **keep accounts, keep books,** make up *or* cast up *or* render accounts; make an entry, enter, post, post up, journalize, book, docket, log, note, minute; **credit, debit;** charge off, write off; capitalize; carry, carry on one's books; carry over; **balance,** balance accounts, balance the books, strike a balance; close the books, close out

9 **take account of, take stock,** overhaul; **inventory; audit,** examine *or* inspect the books

10 **falsify accounts,** garble accounts, cook *or* doctor accounts <nonformal>, salt; surcharge

11 **bill,** send a statement; **invoice;** call, call in, demand payment, **dun**

ADJS 12 accounting, bookkeeping; budget, budgetary

629 TRANSFER OF PROPERTY OR RIGHT

NOUNS 1 **transfer,** transference; **conveyance,** conveyancing; **giving** 478; **delivery,** deliverance; **assignment,** assignation; **consignment,** consignation; conferment, conferral, settling, settlement; vesting; bequeathal 478.10; **sale** 734; surrender, cession; transmission, transmittal; disposal, disposition, deaccession, deaccessioning; demise; alienation, abalienation; amortization, amortizement; enfeoffment; deeding; bargain and sale; lease and release; **exchange,** barter, trading; entailment

2 devolution, succession, reversion; shifting use, shifting trust

VERBS 3 **transfer, convey, deliver,** hand, pass, negotiate; **give** 478.12–14,16,21; **hand over, turn over, pass over; assign, consign,** confer, settle, settle on; cede, surrender; bequeath 478.18; entail; **sell** 734.8,11,12, sell off, deaccession; **make over, sign over,** sign away; transmit, **hand down, hand on, pass on,** devolve upon; demise; alienate, alien, abalienate,

amortize; enfeoff; **deed,** deed over, give title to; **exchange,** barter, trade, trade away

4 **change hands,** change ownership; devolve, pass on, descend, succeed <old>

ADJS 5 **transferable, conveyable,** negotiable, alienable; **assignable,** consignable; devisable, bequeathable; heritable, inheritable

630 PRICE, FEE

NOUNS 1 **price, cost, expense,** expenditure, **charge,** damage *and* score *and* tab <all nonformal>; rate, figure, amount; **quotation,** quoted price, price tag *and* **ticket** *and* **sticker** <all nonformal>; **price list,** prices current; stock market quotations

2 **worth, value,** account, rate; face value, face; par value; market value; street value; net worth; conversion factor *or* value; money's worth, pennyworth, value received; bang for the buck <nonformal>

3 **valuation, evaluation,** value-setting, value-fixing, pricing, price determination, **assessment, appraisal,** appraisement, estimation, rating; unit pricing, dual pricing

4 **price index,** business index; wholesale price index; consumer price *or* retail price index; cost-of-living index; price level; price ceiling, ceiling price, ceiling, top price; floor price, floor, bottom price; demand curve; rising prices, **inflation,** inflationary spiral

5 **price controls,** price-fixing, valorization; managed prices, fair-trading, fair trade, fair-trade agreement; **price supports,** rigid supports, flexible supports; price freeze; rent control

6 **fee, dues, toll, charge, charges, demand, exaction,** exactment, scot, shot, scot and lot; hire; **fare,** carfare; user fee; airport fee *or* charge; license fee; entrance *or* entry *or* admission fee, admission; cover charge; portage, towage; wharfage, anchorage, dockage; pilotage; storage, cellarage; brokerage; salvage

7 freightage, freight, haulage, carriage, cartage, drayage, expressage, lighterage; poundage, tonnage

8 **rent, rental;** rent-roll; rent charge; rack rent, quitrent; ground rent, wayleave rent

9 **tax, taxation, duty, tribute,** taxes, rates <Brit>, contribution, **assessment, revenue enhancement,** cess <Brit>, **levy, toll, impost,** imposition; tax code, tax law; **tithe;** indirect taxation, direct taxation; **tax burden,** overtaxation, undertaxation;

bracket *or* tax-bracket creep; progressive taxation, graduated taxation; regressive taxation; tax withholding; tax return, separate returns, joint return; tax evasion *or* avoidance; tax haven *or* shelter; **tax deduction, deduction; tax write-off,** write-off, tax relief; tax exemption, tax-exempt status; tax structure, tax base; taxable income *or* goods *or* land *or* property, ratables

10 **tax collector,** taxer, taxman, publican; collector of internal revenue, internal revenue agent; tax farmer, farmer; assessor, **tax assessor;** exciseman <Brit>, revenuer; Internal Revenue Service *or* IRS; Inland Revenue *or* IR <Brit>; **customs agent; customs,** US Customs Service, Bureau of Customs and Excise <Brit>; customhouse

VERBS 11 **price,** set *or* name a price, fix the price of; place a value on, **value, evaluate,** valuate, **appraise, assess, rate,** prize, apprize; quote a price; set an arbitrary price on, control *or* manage the price of, valorize; mark up, mark down, **discount;** fairtrade; reassess

12 **charge, demand, ask,** require; overcharge, undercharge; **exact, assess, levy, impose; tax,** assess a tax upon, slap a tax on <nonformal>, lay *or* put a duty on, make dutiable, subject to a tax *or* fee *or* duty, collect a tax *or* duty on; tithe; prorate, assess *pro rata;* charge for, stick for <nonformal>

13 **cost, sell for, fetch, bring,** bring in, stand one *and* set *or* move one back <all nonformal>, knock one back <Brit nonformal>; **come to,** run to *or* into, **amount to,** mount up to, come up to, total up to

ADJS 14 **priced, valued,** evaluated, assessed, appraised, rated, prized; **worth,** valued at; good for; ad valorem, pro rata

15 **chargeable, taxable,** ratable <Brit>, assessable, dutiable, leviable, declarable; tithable

16 tax-free, nontaxable, nondutiable, taxexempt; deductible, tax-deductible; dutyfree

ADVS 17 **at a price,** for a consideration; to the amount of, to the tune of *and* in the neighborhood of <both nonformal>

631 DISCOUNT

NOUNS 1 **discount, cut, deduction,** slash, abatement, reduction, price reduction, price-cutting, price-cut, rollback <nonformal>; underselling; **rebate,** rebatement; bank discount, cash discount,

chain discount, time discount, trade discount; write-off, charge-off; **depreciation; allowance,** concession; setoff; drawback, **refund,** kickback <nonformal>; **premium,** percentage, agio; trading stamp

VERBS 2 **discount, cut, deduct,** bate, abate; **take off,** write off, charge off; **depreciate,** reduce; sell at a loss; **allow,** make allowance; rebate, **refund,** kick back <nonformal>; take a premium *or* percentage

ADVS 3 **at a discount,** at a reduction, at a reduced rate, below par, below *or* under cost

632 EXPENSIVENESS

NOUNS 1 **expensiveness, costliness, dearness,** high *or* great cost, highness, stiffness *or* **steepness** <both nonformal>, priceyness; **richness, sumptuousness, luxuriousness**

2 **preciousness, dearness, value,** high *or* great value, **worth,** extraordinary worth, price *or* great price <both old>, **valuableness; pricelessness, invaluableness**

3 **high price,** high *or* big price tag *and* big ticket *and* big sticker price <all nonformal>, **fancy price,** good price, steep *or* stiff price <nonformal>, luxury price, a pretty penny *or* an arm and a leg <both nonformal>, exorbitant *or* unconscionable *or* extortionate price; famine price, scarcity price; rack rent; inflationary prices, rising *or* soaring *or* spiraling prices, soaring costs; sellers' market; **inflation,** cost *or* cost-push inflation *or* costpush, inflationary trend *or* pressure, hot economy, inflationary spiral, inflationary gap; reflation; stagflation, slumpflation

4 **exorbitance,** exorbitancy <old>, **extravagance,** excess, **excessiveness,** inordinateness, immoderateness, immoderation, undueness, unreasonableness, outrageousness, preposterousness; unconscionableness, extortionateness

5 **overcharge,** surcharge, overassessment; gouging *or* price-gouging; **extortion,** extortionate price; **holdup** *and* armed robbery *and* highway robbery <all nonformal>; profiteering

VERBS 6 **cost much,** cost money *and* cost you <both nonformal>, cost a pretty penny *or* an arm and a leg *or* a packet <nonformal>, **run into money;** be overpriced, price out of the market

7 **overprice,** set the price tag too high; **overcharge,** surcharge, overtax; **hold up** *and* **soak** *and* **stick** *and* **sting** *and* **clip** <all

nonformal>, **make pay through the nose, gouge;** victimize, swindle 356.18; exploit, skin <nonformal>, **fleece,** screw *and* put the screws to <both nonformal>, bleed, bleed white; profiteer; rack *or* rack up the rents, rack rent

8 **overpay,** overspend, pay too much, pay more than it's worth, **pay dearly,** pay exorbitantly, pay, **pay through the nose,** be had *or* taken <both nonformal>

9 **inflate,** heat *or* heat up the economy; reflate

ADJS 10 **precious, dear, valuable,** worthy, rich, golden, of great price <old>, worth a pretty penny <nonformal>, worth a king's ransom, worth its weight in gold, good as gold, precious as the apple of one's eye; **priceless, invaluable,** inestimable, without *or* **beyond price,** not to be had for love or money, not for all the tea in China

11 **expensive, dear, costly,** of great cost, dear-bought, **high, high-priced,** premium, at a premium, top; big ticket <nonformal>, **fancy** *and* stiff *and* steep <all nonformal>, pricey; beyond one's means, not affordable, more than one can afford; unpayable; upmarket, upscale <nonformal> rich, sumptuous, executive *and* posh <both nonformal>, **luxurious** 501.21, gold-plated

12 **overpriced,** grossly overpriced, **exorbitant, excessive, extravagant, inordinate, immoderate,** undue, unwarranted, unreasonable, fancy, unconscionable, outrageous, preposterous, out of bounds, out of sight <nonformal>, **prohibitive; extortionate,** cutthroat, **gouging, usurious,** exacting; **inflationary,** spiraling, skyrocketing; stagflationary, slumpflationary; reflationary

ADVS 13 **dear, dearly;** at a high price, at great cost, at a premium, at a great rate, at heavy cost, at great expense

14 **preciously, valuably,** worthily; pricelessly, invaluably, inestimably

15 **expensively,** richly, sumptuously, luxuriously

16 **exorbitantly, excessively,** grossly, **extravagantly, inordinately,** immoderately, unduly, unreasonably, unconscionably, outrageously, preposterously; **extortionately,** usuriously, gougingly

633 CHEAPNESS

NOUNS 1 **cheapness, inexpensiveness,** affordableness, affordability, reasonableness, modestness, moderateness, nominalness; drug *or* glut on the market; shabbiness, shoddiness 997.2

2 **low price, nominal price,** reasonable price, modest *or* manageable price, sensible price, moderate price; low *or* nominal *or* reasonable charge; bargain prices, budget prices, economy prices, easy prices, popular prices, rock-bottom prices; buyers' market; low *or* small price tag *and* low sticker price *and* low tariff <all nonformal>; **reduced price,** cut price, sale price; cheap *or* reduced rates

3 **bargain,** advantageous purchase, **buy** <nonformal>, **good buy, steal** <nonformal>; money's worth, pennyworth, good pennyworth

4 **cheapening, depreciation, devaluation,** reduction, lowering; deflation, deflationary spiral, cooling *or* cooling off of the economy; **buyers' market; decline,** plummet, plummeting, plunge, dive, nosedive *and* slump *and* sag <all nonformal>, free fall; price fall; break; **price cut** *or* **reduction,** cut, slash, **markdown**

VERBS 5 **be cheap,** cost little, not cost anything *and* cost nothing *and* next to nothing <all nonformal>; **buy dirt cheap** *or* for a song *or* for nickels and dimes *or* for peanuts <all nonformal>, buy at a bargain, buy for a mere nothing; get one's money's worth, get a good pennyworth; buy at wholesale prices *or* at cost

6 **cheapen, depreciate, devaluate,** lower, reduce, **mark down, cut prices, cut,** slash, shave, trim, pare, underprice, knock the bottom out of <nonformal>; deflate, cool *or* cool off the economy; beat down; come down *or* fall in price; **fall,** decline, plummet, dive, nose-dive <nonformal>, drop, crash, head for the bottom, plunge, sag, slump; break, give way; reach a new low

ADJS 7 **cheap, inexpensive,** unexpensive, **low, low-priced,** frugal, reasonable, sensible, manageable, modest, moderate, affordable, to fit the pocketbook, budget, easy, economy, economic, economical; within means, within reach *or* easy reach; nominal, token; worth the money, well worth the money; cheap *or* good at the price, cheap at half the price; shabby, shoddy; deflationary

8 **dirt cheap,** cheap as dirt, dog-cheap <nonformal>, **a dime a dozen,** bargain-basement, five-and-ten, dime-store

9 **reduced,** cut, cut-price, slashed, **marked down;** cut-rate; half-price; giveaway <nonformal>, sacrificial; **lowest,** rock-bottom, bottom, best

ADVS 10 **cheaply, cheap,** on the cheap <Brit

nonformal>; **inexpensively,** reasonably, moderately, nominally; **at a bargain,** *à bon marché* <Fr>, for a song *or* mere song <nonformal>, for pennies *or* nickels and dimes *or* peanuts <all nonformal>, at small cost, at a low price, at budget prices, at piggy-bank prices, at a sacrifice; at cost *or* cost price, at prime cost, wholesale, at wholesale; at reduced rates

634 COSTLESSNESS
<absence of charge>

NOUNS **1 costlessness,** gratuitousness, gratuity, **freeness,** expenselessness, complimentariness, no charge; free ride <nonformal>; freebie *and* gimme <both nonformal>; labor of love; **gift** 478.4

2 complimentary ticket, pass, comp <nonformal>, free pass *or* ticket, paper <nonformal>, free admission, guest pass *or* ticket, Annie Oakley <nonformal>; discount ticket, twofer <nonformal>

3 freeloader, free rider, pass holder, deadhead <nonformal>

VERBS **4 give, present** 478.12, comp <nonformal>; freeload, sponge

ADJS **5 gratuitous, gratis, free, free of charge,** for free, **for nothing,** free for nothing, free for the asking, free gratis *and* free gratis for nothing <both nonformal>, for love, free as air; freebie *and* freebee *and* freeby <all nonformal>; costless, expenseless, untaxed, without charge, free of cost *or* expense; no charge; unbought, unpaid-for; **complimentary, on the house, comp** <nonformal>, given 478.24; giftlike; eleemosynary, charitable 143.15

ADVS **6 gratuitously, gratis, free, free of charge,** for nothing, for the asking, at no charge, without charge, with the compliments of the management, as our guest, on the house

635 THRIFT

NOUNS **1 thrift, economy, thriftiness,** economicalness, savingness, sparingness, unwastefulness, **frugality,** frugalness; tight purse strings; parsimony, **parsimoniousness** 484.1; false economy; carefulness, care, chariness, canniness; **prudence,** providence, forehandedness; **husbandry,** management, good management *or* stewardship, custodianship, prudent *or* prudential administration; **austerity,** austerity program, belt-tightening; economic planning; economy of means 484.1

2 economizing, economization, reduction of spending *or* government spending; **cost-effectiveness; saving,** scrimping, skimping <nonformal>, scraping, sparing, cheeseparing; **retrenchment, curtailment,** reduction of expenses, cutback, rollback, slowdown, cooling, cooling off *or* down, low growth rate; reduction in forces *or* RIF

3 economizer, economist <old>, **saver,** string-saver

VERBS **4 economize, save,** make *or* enforce economies; **scrimp, skimp** <nonformal>, **scrape,** scrape and save; **manage, husband,** husband one's resources; live frugally, get along on a shoestring, get by on little; keep within compass <old>, keep *or* stay within one's means *or* budget, balance income with outgo, live within one's income, make ends meet, cut one's coat according to one's cloth, keep *or* stay ahead of the game; put something aside, **save up,** save for a rainy day, have a nest egg; supplement *or* eke out one's income

5 retrench, cut down, cut *or* pare down expenses, **curtail expenses; cut corners, tighten one's belt,** cut back, roll back, take a reef, slow down

ADJS **6 economical, thrifty, frugal,** economic, unwasteful, conserving, **saving,** economizing, spare, **sparing;** Scotch; **prudent,** prudential, provident, forehanded; careful, chary, canny; scrimping, skimping <nonformal>, cheeseparing; pennywise; **parsimonious** 484.7; **cost-effective, cost-efficient; efficient,** labor-saving, time-saving, money-saving

ADVS **7 economically, thriftily, frugally,** husbandly <old>; **cost-effectively, cost-efficiently;** prudently, providently; carefully, charily, cannily; sparingly, with a sparing hand

636 ETHICS

NOUNS **1 ethics, principles,** standards, norms, principles of conduct *or* behavior, principles of professional practice; **morals,** moral principles; code, ethical *or* moral code, **ethic,** code of morals *or* ethics, ethical system, value system, axiology; **norm,** behavioral norm, normative system; moral climate, **ethos,** *Zeitgeist* <Ger>; Ten Commandments, decalogue; social ethics, professional ethics, bioethics, medical ethics, legal ethics, business ethics, etc

2 ethical *or* moral philosophy, ethonomics,

aretaics, eudaemonics, casuistry, deontology, empiricism, evolutionism, hedonism, ethical formalism, intuitionism, perfectionism, Stoicism, utilitarianism, categorical imperative, golden rule; egoistic ethics, altruistic ethics; Christian ethics; situation ethics; comparative ethics

3 morality, morals, morale; virtue 653; ethicality, ethicalness

4 amorality, unmorality; amoralism

5 conscience, grace, **sense of right and wrong;** inward monitor, inner arbiter, moral censor, censor, ethical self, superego; **voice of conscience,** still small voice within, guardian *or* good angel; tender conscience; clear *or* clean conscience; social conscience; conscientiousness 644.2; twinge of conscience 113.2

ADJS **6 ethical, moral,** moralistic; ethological; axiological

637 RIGHT

NOUNS **1 right,** rightfulness, rightness; what is right *or* proper, what should be, what ought to be, the seemly, the thing, the right *or* proper thing, the right *or* proper thing to do, what is done

2 propriety, decorum, decency, good behavior *or* conduct, correctness, correctitude, rightness, properness, decorousness, goodness, goodliness, niceness, seemliness, cricket <Brit nonformal>; fitness, fittingness, appropriateness, suitability 994.1; normativeness, normality; proprieties, decencies; rightmindedness, **righteousness** 653.1

ADJS **3 right,** rightful; fit, suitable 994.5; **proper, correct, decorous,** good, nice, decent, seemly, **due, appropriate,** fitting, condign, **right and proper,** as it should be, as it ought to be, *comme il faut* <Fr>; kosher *and* according to Hoyle <both nonformal>; in the right; normative, normal; rightminded, right-thinking, **righteous**

ADVS **4 rightly, rightfully,** right; **by rights,** by right, with good right, **as is right** *or* **only right; properly,** correctly, as is proper *or* fitting, **duly, appropriately,** fittingly, condignly, **in justice,** in equity; in reason, in all conscience

638 WRONG

NOUNS **1 wrong,** wrongfulness, wrongness; **impropriety, indecorum;** incorrectness, improperness, indecorousness, unseemliness; unfitness, unfittingness, inappropriateness, unsuitability 995.1; infraction, violation, delinquency, criminality, illegality, unlawfulness; abnormality, deviance *or* deviancy, aberrance *or* aberrancy; sinfulness, wickedness, unrighteousness; **dysfunction,** malfunction; maladaptation, maladjustment; malfeasance, malversation, malpractice; malformation

2 abomination, horror, terrible thing; **scandal, disgrace, shame, pity,** atrocity, profanation, desecration, violation, sacrilege, infamy, ignominy

ADJS **3 wrong, wrongful; improper, incorrect, indecorous,** undue, unseemly; unfit, unfitting, inappropriate, unsuitable 995.5; delinquent, criminal, illegal, unlawful; fraudulent, creative <nonformal>; abnormal, deviant, aberrant; **dysfunctional; evil, sinful, wicked, unrighteous;** not the thing, hardly the thing, not done, not cricket <Brit>; **off-base** *and* **out-of-line** *and* **off-color** <all nonformal>; abominable, terrible, scandalous, disgraceful, shameful, shameless, atrocious, sacrilegious, infamous, ignominious; maladapted, maladjusted

ADVS **4 wrongly, wrongfully,** wrong; **improperly,** incorrectly, indecorously

WORD ELEMENTS **5** mis—, dis—; dys—, caco—

639 DUENESS

NOUNS **1 dueness, entitlement,** entitledness, deservingness, deservedness, meritedness, expectation, just *or* justifiable expectation, expectations, outlook, prospect, prospects; **justice** 649

2 due, one's due, what one merits *or* is entitled to, what one has earned, what is owing, what one has coming, what is coming to one, acknowledgment, cognizance, recognition, credit, crediting; **right**

3 desserts, just desserts, deservings, merits, dues, due reward *or* punishment, **comeuppance** <nonformal>, all that is coming to one; the wrath of God; retaliation 506, vengeance 507.1

VERBS **4 be due,** be one's due, **be entitled to,** have a right or title to, have a rightful claim to *or* upon, claim as one's right, **have coming,** come by honestly

5 deserve, merit, earn, rate *and* be in line for <both nonformal>, **be worthy of,** be deserving, richly deserve

6 get one's deserts, get one's dues, **get one's**

comeuppance *and* get his *or* hers <all nonformal>, get what is coming to one; get justice; serve one right, be rightly served; get for one's pains, reap the fruits *or* benefit of, reap where one has sown, come into one's own

ADJS **7 due, owed, owing,** payable, redeemable, coming, **coming to**

8 rightful, condign, appropriate, proper; fit, becoming 994.5; **fair, just** 649.8

9 warranted, justified, entitled, qualified, worthy; **deserved, merited,** richly deserved, earned, well-earned

10 due, entitled to, with a right to; **deserving, meriting, meritorious, worthy of;** attributable, ascribable

ADVS **11 duly,** rightfully, condignly, as is one's due *or* right

PHRS **12** what's sauce for the goose is sauce for the gander; give the devil his due; give credit where credit is due; he's made his bed let him lie in it; let the punishment fit the crime

640 UNDUENESS

NOUNS **1 undueness, undeservedness,** undeservingness, unentitledness, unentitlement, unmeritedness; disentitlement; lack of claim *or* title, false claim *or* title, invalid claim *or* title, no claim *or* title, empty claim *or* title; unearned increment; **inappropriateness** 995.1; **impropriety** 638.1; **excess** 992

2 presumption, assumption, **imposition; license,** licentiousness, **undue liberty,** liberties, familiarity, **presumptuousness,** freedom *or* liberty abused, hubris; lawlessness 418; injustice 650

3 usurpation, arrogation, seizure, unlawful seizure, **appropriation,** assumption, adoption, infringement, encroachment, invasion, trespass, trespassing; playing God

4 usurper, arrogator, pretender

VERBS **5 not be entitled to,** have no right *or* title to, have no claim upon, not have a leg to stand on

6 presume, assume, venture, hazard, dare, pretend, attempt, **make bold** *or* so bold, make free, **take the liberty,** take upon oneself, go so far as to

7 presume on *or* **upon, impose on** *or* **upon,** encroach upon, obtrude upon; **take liberties,** take a liberty, overstep, overstep one's rights *or* bounds *or* prerogatives, make free with *or* of, abuse one's rights, abuse a privilege, give an inch and take an ell; **inconvenience,** bother, trouble, cause to go out of one's way

8 <take to oneself unduly> **usurp, arrogate,** seize, grab *and* latch on to <both nonformal>, **appropriate,** assume, adopt, take over, arrogate *or* accroach to oneself, pretend to, infringe, encroach, invade, trespass; play God

ADJS **9 undue, unowed, unowing,** not coming, not outstanding; **undeserved, unmerited,** unearned; **unwarranted, unjustified,** unprovoked; unentitled, undeserving, unmeriting, nonmeritorious, unworthy; preposterous, outrageous

10 inappropriate 995.5; **improper** 638.3; **excessive** 992.16

11 presumptuous, presuming, licentious; hubristic 493.7

PHRS **12** give him an inch he'll take a mile; let a camel get his nose under the tent and he'll come in

641 DUTY
<moral obligation>

NOUNS **1 duty, obligation,** charge, **onus, burden,** mission, devoir, must, ought, imperative, bounden duty, proper *or* assigned task, what ought to be done, what one is responsible for, where the buck stops <nonformal>, "stern daughter of the voice of God"—Wordsworth, deference, respect 155, fealty, allegiance, loyalty, homage; devotion, dedication, **commitment;** self-commitment, self-imposed duty; **business** 724, function, province, place 724.3; ethics 636; line of duty; call of duty; duties and responsibilities, assignment, work load

2 responsibility, incumbency; **liability, accountability,** accountableness, answerability, answerableness, amenability; product liability; **responsibleness, dutifulness,** duteousness, devotion *or* dedication to duty, sense of duty *or* obligation

VERBS **3 should, ought to,** had best, had better, be expedient

4 behoove, become, befit, beseem, be bound, be obliged *or* obligated, be under an obligation; **owe it to,** owe it to oneself

5 be the duty of, be incumbent on *or* **upon,** be his *or* hers to, stand on *or* upon, be a must *or* an imperative for, duty calls one to

6 be responsible for, answer for, stand responsible for, **be liable for,** be answerable *or* accountable for; be on the hook for *and* take the heat *or* rap for <all nonformal>

7 be one's responsibility, be one's office, be one's charge *or* mission, **rest with,** lie upon, devolve on, rest on the shoulders of, lie on one's head or one's door or one's doorstep, fall to one or to one's lot

8 **incur a responsibility,** become bound to, become sponsor for

9 **take** or **accept the responsibility, take upon oneself,** take upon one's shoulders, commit oneself; be where the buck stops <nonformal>; **answer for,** respect or defer to one's duty; sponsor, be or stand sponsor for; do at one's own risk or peril; **take the blame,** be in the hot seat or on the spot and take the heat or rap for <all nonformal>

10 **do one's duty,** perform or fulfill or discharge one's duty, do what one has to do, pay one's dues <nonformal>, **do what is expected,** do the needful, do the right thing, do justice to, **do** or **act one's part,** play one's proper role; answer the call of duty, do one's bit or part

11 **meet an obligation,** satisfy one's obligations, stand to one's engagement, stand up to, **acquit oneself, make good,** redeem one's pledge

12 **obligate, oblige, require,** make incumbent or imperative, tie, **bind,** pledge, commit, saddle with, put under an obligation; call to account, hold responsible or accountable or answerable

ADJS 13 **dutiful, duteous;** moral, ethical; conscientious, scrupulous, observant; obedient 326.3; deferential, respectful 155.8

14 **incumbent on** or **upon,** chargeable to, behooving

15 **obligatory, binding, imperative,** imperious, peremptory, mandatory, must, de rigueur <Fr>; **necessary,** required 962.13

16 **obliged, obligated,** obligate, **under obligation; bound, duty-bound,** in duty bound, tied, pledged, committed, saddled, beholden, bounden; **obliged to,** beholden to, bound or bounden to, **indebted to**

17 **responsible, answerable; liable, accountable,** amenable, unexempt from, chargeable, on one's head, at one's doorstep, on the hook <nonformal>; responsible for, at the bottom of; to blame

ADVS 18 **dutifully, duteously, in the line of duty,** as in duty bound; beyond the call of duty

642 PREROGATIVE

NOUNS 1 **prerogative, right, due,** droit; power, authority, prerogative of office; faculty, appurtenance; **claim,** proper claim, demand, **interest, title,** pretension, pretense, prescription; birthright; natu-

ral right, presumptive right, inalienable right; divine right; vested right or interest; property right; conjugal right

2 **privilege, license, liberty, freedom, immunity;** franchise, patent, copyright, grant, warrant, blank check, carte blanche; favor, indulgence, **special favor,** dispensation

3 **human rights,** rights of man; constitutional rights, rights of citizenship, **civil rights** 430.2, civil liberties; rights of minorities, minority rights; gay rights, gay liberation

4 **women's rights,** rights of women; **feminism, women's liberation,** women's lib <nonformal>, womanism, women's movement or liberation movement, sisterhood

5 **women's rightist, feminist, women's liberationist,** women's liberation advocate or adherent or activist, womanist, women's libber and libber <both nonformal>; **suffragette,** suffragist

VERBS 6 have or claim or assert a right, exercise a right; defend a right

643 IMPOSITION

<a putting or inflicting upon>

NOUNS 1 **imposition, infliction,** laying on or upon, charging, taxing, tasking; burdening, weighting or weighting down, freighting, loading or loading down, heaping on or upon, imposing an onus; **exaction, demand** 421; unwarranted demand, obtrusiveness, presumptuousness 142.1; inconvenience, trouble, bother; inconsiderateness 144.3

2 administration, giving, bestowal; applying, application, dosing, dosage, meting out, prescribing; **forcing,** forcing on or upon, enforcing

3 **charge, duty, tax,** task; **burden,** weight, freight, cargo, load, onus

VERBS 4 **impose, impose on** or **upon, inflict on** or **upon, put on** or **upon, lay on** or **upon,** enjoin; **put, place, set, lay,** put down; **levy, exact, demand** 421.4; **tax,** task, **charge,** burden with, weight or freight with, weight down with, yoke with, **fasten upon,** saddle with, stick with <nonformal>; subject to

5 **inflict, wreak, do to,** bring, bring upon, bring down upon, bring on or down on one's head, visit upon

6 **administer, give, bestow; apply, put on** or **upon,** lay on or upon, dose, dose with, dish out <nonformal>, mete out, prescribe; **force, force upon,** impose by force

or main force, strongarm <nonformal>, force down one's throat, enforce upon

7 **impose on** *or* **upon, take advantage of** 387.16; **presume upon** 640.7; **deceive,** play *or* work on, out on *or* upon, put over *or* across <nonformal>; palm *or* pass *or* fob off on, fob *or* foist on; shift the blame *or* responsibility, **pass the buck** <nonformal>

ADJS 8 **imposed, inflicted,** piled *or* heaped on; burdened with, stuck with <nonformal>; self-inflicted; exacted, demanded

644 PROBITY

NOUNS 1 **probity,** assured probity, **honesty, integrity, rectitude, uprightness,** up-standingness, erectness, **virtue,** virtuousness, **righteousness, goodness;** cleanness, **decency; honor,** honorableness, worthiness, estimableness, reputability, nobility; unimpeachableness, unimpeachability, irreproachableness, irreproachability, blamelessness; immaculacy, unspottedness, stainlessness, pureness, purity; respectability; principles, high principles, high ideals, high-mindedness; **character,** good *or* sterling character, moral strength, moral excellence; **fairness,** justness, justice 649

2 **conscientiousness, scrupulousness,** scrupulosity, **scruples,** punctiliousness, meticulousness; scruple, point of honor, punctilio; qualm 325.2; twinge of conscience 113.2; overconscientiousness, overscrupulousness; fastidiousness 495

3 **honesty, veracity,** veraciousness, verity, **truthfulness,** truth, veridicality, truth-telling, truth-speaking; truth-loving; credibility, absolute credibility

4 **candor, candidness, frankness,** plain dealing; sincerity, genuineness, authenticity; ingenuousness; artlessness 416; **openness,** openheartedness; freedom, freeness; **unreserve,** unrestraint, unconstraint; **forthrightness, directness, straightforwardness; outspokenness,** plainness, plainspokenness, plain speaking, roundness, broadness; **bluntness,** bluffness, brusqueness

5 **undeceptiveness, undeceitfulness, guilelessness**

6 **trustworthiness,** faithworthiness, trustiness, trustability, **reliability, dependability,** dependableness, sureness; answerableness, responsibility 641.2; unfalseness, unperfidiousness, untreacherousness; incorruptibility, inviolability

7 **fidelity, faithfulness, loyalty,** faith; con-stancy, **steadfastness,** staunchness, firmness; trueness, troth, true blue; good faith, *bona fides* <L>, *bonne foi* <Fr>; **allegiance, fealty, homage;** bond, tie; attachment, adherence, adhesion; devotion, devotedness

8 **person** *or* **man** *or* **woman of honor,** man of his word, woman of her word; gentleman, *gentilhomme* <Fr>, *galantuomo* <Ital>; **honest man,** good man; **lady, real lady; honest woman, good woman;** salt of the earth; square *or* straight shooter *and* straight arrow <all nonformal>; true blue, truepenny; trusty, faithful

VERBS 9 **keep faith,** not fail, **keep one's word** *or* **promise,** keep troth, show good faith, be as good as one's word, one's word is one's bond, redeem one's pledge, play by the rules, acquit oneself, make good; practice what one preaches

10 shoot straight <nonformal>, draw a straight furrow, **put one's cards on the table,** level with one <nonformal>

11 **speak** *or* **tell the truth,** speak *or* tell true, paint in its true colors, tell the truth and shame the devil; tell the truth, the whole truth, and nothing but the truth

12 **be frank, speak plainly,** speak out, speak one's mind, say what one thinks, **call a spade a spade,** tell it like it is

ADJS 13 **honest, upright,** uprighteous, **upstanding,** erect, right, **righteous, virtuous, good,** clean, squeaky-clean <nonformal>, **decent; honorable,** full of integrity, **reputable,** estimable, creditable, worthy, noble, sterling, manly, yeomanly; Christian <nonformal>; unimpeachable, irreproachable, blameless, immaculate, spotless, stainless, unstained, unspotted, unblemished, untarnished, unsullied, undefiled, pure; **respectable,** highly respectable; **ethical, moral; principled, high-principled,** high-minded, right-minded; uncorrupt, uncorrupted, inviolate; truehearted, true-souled, true-spirited; true-dealing, true-disposing, true-devoted; **law-abiding,** law-loving, law-revering; **fair, just** 649.8

14 **straight, square,** foursquare, straight-arrow <nonformal>, honest and above-board, right as rain; **fair and square; square-dealing,** square-shooting, straight-shooting, up-and-up, **on the up-and-up** *and* **on the level** *and* on the square <all nonformal>; **aboveboard, open and aboveboard;** bona fide, good-faith; authentic, all wool and a yard wide, veritable, genuine; single-hearted; honest as the day is long

15 **conscientious**, tender-conscienced; **scrupulous**, careful 339.10; punctilious, punctual, meticulous, religious, strict, nice; fastidious 495.9; overconscientious, overscrupulous

16 **honest, veracious, truthful**, true, true to one's word, veridical; truth-telling, truth-speaking, truth-declaring, truth-passing, truth-bearing, truth-loving, truth-seeking, truth-desiring, truth-guarding, truth-filled; true-speaking, true-meaning, true-tongued

17 **candid, frank, sincere**, genuine, ingenuous, frankhearted; **open**, openhearted, transparent, open-faced; artless 416.5; **straightforward, direct**, up-front *and* straight <both nonformal>, **forthright**, downright, straight-out <nonformal>; plain, broad, round; **unreserved**, unrestrained, unconstrained, unchecked; unguarded, uncalculating; free; **outspoken, plain-spoken**, free-spoken, free-speaking, free-tongued; explicit, unequivocal; **blunt**, bluff, brusque; heart-to-heart

18 **undeceptive, undeceitful, undissembling,** undissimulating, undeceiving, undesigning, uncalculating; **guileless**, unbeguiling, unbeguileful; unassuming, unpretending, unfeigning, undisguising, unflattering; undissimulated, undissembled; unassumed, unaffected, unpretended, unfeigned, undisguised, unvarnished, untrimmed

19 **trustworthy, trusty**, trustable, faithworthy, **reliable, dependable, responsible,** straight <nonformal>, sure, to be trusted, **to be depended** *or* **relied upon,** to be counted *or* reckoned on, as good as one's word; tried, true, **tried and true,** tested, proven; unfalse, unperfidious, untreacherous; incorruptible, inviolable

20 **faithful, loyal**, devoted, allegiant; **true, true-blue**, true to one's colors; **constant, steadfast**, unswerving, steady, consistent, stable, unfailing, staunch, firm, solid, "marble-constant"—Shakespeare

ADVS 21 **honestly, uprightly, honorably**, upstandingly, erectly, **virtuously, righteously, decently**, worthily, reputably, nobly; unimpeachably, irreproachably, blamelessly, immaculately, unspottedly, stainlessly, purely; high-mindedly, morally; **conscientiously, scrupulously,** punctiliously, meticulously, fastidiously 495.14

22 **truthfully, truly**, veraciously; to tell the truth, to speak truthfully; in truth, in sooth <old>, of a truth, with truth, in good *or* very truth

23 **candidly, frankly, sincerely,** genuinely, in all seriousness *or* soberness, from the heart, in all conscience; in plain words *or* English, straight from the shoulder, not to mince the matter, not to mince words, without equivocation, with no nonsense, all joking aside *or* apart; **openly,** openheartedly, **unreservedly,** unrestrainedly, unconstrainedly, **forthrightly, directly, straightforwardly, outspokenly, plainly,** plain-spokenly, broadly, roundly, **bluntly,** bluffly, brusquely

24 **trustworthily**, trustily, **reliably, dependably, responsibly;** undeceptively, undeceitfully, guilelessly; incorruptibly, inviolably

25 **faithfully, loyally,** devotedly; **constantly, steadfastly**, steadily, responsibly, consistently, unfailingly, unswervingly, staunchly, firmly; in *or* with good faith, *bona fide* <L>

645 IMPROBITY

NOUNS 1 **improbity, dishonesty**, dishonor; **unscrupulousness**, unconscientiousness; **corruption**, corruptness, corruptedness; **crookedness**, criminality, feloniousness, **fraudulence** *or* fraudulency, underhandedness, unsavoriness, fishiness *and* shadiness <both nonformal>, indirection, shiftiness, slipperiness, deviousness, evasiveness, unstraightforwardness, trickiness

2 **knavery, roguery, rascality,** rascalry, **villainy**, reprobacy, scoundrelism; chicanery 356.4; knavishness, roguishness, scampishness, villainousness; **baseness, vileness**, degradation, turpitude, moral turpitude

3 **deceitfulness; falseness** 354; perjury, forswearing, untruthfulness 354.8, credibility gap; **insincerity**, unsincereness, uncandidness, uncandor, unfrankness, disingenuousness; sharp practice 356.4; fraud 356.8; artfulness, craftiness 415.1; intrigue

4 **untrustworthiness**, unfaithworthiness, untrustiness, **unreliability, undependability**, irresponsibility

5 **infidelity, unfaithfulness**, unfaith, faithlessness, trothlessness; **inconstancy, unsteadfastness**, fickleness; **disloyalty,** unloyalty; **falsity**, falseness, untrueness; disaffection, recreancy, dereliction; bad faith, *mala fides* <L>, Punic faith; breach of promise, breach of trust *or* faith, barratry; breach of confidence

6 **treachery**, treacherousness; **perfidy**, per-

fidiousness, falseheartedness 354.4, two-facedness, doubleness; **duplicity, double-dealing,** foul play, dirty work *and* dirty pool *and* dirty trick *and* dirty game <all nonformal>

7 **treason,** petty treason, misprision of treason, high treason; lese majesty, sedition; quislingism, fifth-column activity; collaboration, fraternization

8 **betrayal,** betrayment, letting down <nonformal>, **double cross** *and* sellout <both nonformal>, Judas kiss, kiss of death, stab in the back

9 **corruptibility, venality,** bribability, purchasability

10 criminal 660.10, perpetrator, perp <nonformal>, scoundrel 660.3, traitor 357.10, deceiver 357

VERBS 11 <be dishonest> live by one's wits; shift, shift about, evade; deceive; cheat; falsify; lie; sail under false colors

12 **be unfaithful,** not keep faith *or* troth, **go back on** <nonformal>, **fail,** break one's word *or* promise, renege, go back on one's word <nonformal>, break faith, perjure *or* forswear oneself; forsake, desert 370.5; pass the buck <nonformal>; shift the responsibility *or* blame

13 **play one false,** prove false; **stab one in the back,** knife one <nonformal>; bite the hand that feeds one; play dirty pool <nonformal>; shift *or* move the goalposts *and* change the rules <both nonformal>

14 **betray, double-cross** *and* two-time <both nonformal>, sell out *and* sell down the river <both nonformal>, turn in; **mislead,** lead one down the garden path; let down *and* let down one's side <both nonformal>; inform on 551.12

15 **act the traitor,** turn against, go over to the enemy, turn one's coat, sell oneself, sell out <nonformal>; collaborate, fraternize

ADJS 16 **dishonest, dishonorable; unconscientious,** unconscienced, conscienceless, unconscionable, shameless, without shame *or* remorse, **unscrupulous, unprincipled,** unethical, immoral, amoral; **corrupt,** corrupted, rotten; **crooked, criminal,** felonious, **fraudulent,** creative <nonformal>, underhand, underhanded; shady <nonformal>, up to no good, not kosher <nonformal>, unsavory, dark, sinister, insidious, indirect, slippery, devious, tricky, shifty, evasive, unstraightforward; fishy <nonformal>, questionable, suspicious, doubtful, dubious; ill-gotten, ill-got

17 **knavish, roguish, scampish, rascally, scoundrelly,** blackguardly, villainous, reprobate, recreant, **base, vile,** degraded; **infamous, notorious**

18 **deceitful;** falsehearted; perjured, forsworn, untruthful 354.34; **insincere,** unsincere, uncandid, unfrank, disingenuous; artful, crafty 415.12; calculating, scheming; **tricky,** cute *and* dodgy <both nonformal>, slippery as an eel

19 **untrustworthy,** unfaithworthy, untrusty, trustless, **unreliable, undependable,** fly-by-night, irresponsible, unsure, not to be trusted, not to be depended *or* relied upon

20 **unfaithful,** faithless, of bad faith, trothless; **inconstant, unsteadfast,** fickle; **disloyal,** unloyal; false, **untrue,** not true to; disaffected, recreant, derelict, barratrous

21 **treacherous, perfidious,** falsehearted; **shifty,** slippery, tricky; **double-dealing,** double, ambidextrous; **two-faced**

22 **traitorous,** turncoat, double-crossing *and* two-timing <both nonformal>, betraying; Judas-like, Iscariotic; **treasonable,** treasonous; quisling, quislingistic, fifth-column, Trojan-horse

23 **corruptible, venal,** bribable, purchasable, on the pad <nonformal>, mercenary, hireling

ADVS 24 **dishonestly, dishonorably; unscrupulously,** unconscientiously; **crookedly,** criminally, feloniously, **fraudulently,** underhandedly, like a thief in the night, insidiously, deviously, shiftily, evasively, fishily <nonformal>, suspiciously, dubiously, by fair means or foul; **deceitfully;** knavishly, roguishly, villainously; basely, vilely; infamously, notoriously

25 **perfidiously,** falseheartedly; **unfaithfully,** faithlessly; **treacherously;** traitorously, treasonably

646 HONOR

NOUNS 1 **honor,** great honor, distinction, glory, credit, ornament; "blushing honors"—Shakespeare

2 **award, reward, prize;** first prize, second prize, etc; blue ribbon; consolation prize; booby prize; Nobel Prize, Pulitzer Prize; sweepstakes; jackpot; Oscar, Academy Award

3 **trophy,** laurel, **laurels,** bays, palm, palms, crown, chaplet, wreath, garland, **feather in one's cap** <nonformal>; civic crown *or* garland *or* wreath; **cup,** loving cup, pot <nonformal>; America's Cup,

Old Mug; **belt,** championship belt, black belt, brown belt, etc; banner, flag

4 **citation,** eulogy, mention, honorable mention, kudos, **accolade, tribute, praise** 511.1

5 **decoration,** decoration of honor, order, ornament; ribbon, riband; blue ribbon, *cordon bleu* <Fr>; red ribbon, red ribbon of the Legion of Honor; cordon, grand cordon; garter; star, gold star

6 **medal, military honor** <see list>, order, medallion; military medal, service medal, war medal, soldier's medal; lifesaving medal, Carnegie hero's medal; police citation, departmental citation

7 scholarship, fellowship

VERBS **8 honor, do honor,** pay regard to, give *or* pay *or* render honor to, **recognize; cite; decorate,** pin a medal on; crown, crown with laurel; hand it to *or* take off one's hat to one <nonformal>, pay tribute, praise 511.5; give credit where credit is due; give one the red carpet treatment, roll out the red carpet

ADJS **9 honored, distinguished;** laureate, crowned with laurel

10 honorary, honorific, honorable

ADVS **11 with honor,** with distinction; *cum laude, magna cum laude, summa cum laude, insigne cum laude, honoris causa* <all L>

12 military honors

Air Medal	Distinguished Unit
Bronze Star Medal	Citation
Congressional Medal	Médaille Militaire
of Honor	<France>
Croix de Guerre	Medal of Honor
<France>	Military Cross
Distinguished	Navy Cross
Conduct Medal	Order of the Purple
Distinguished Flying	Heart
Cross	Silver Star Medal
Distinguished Service	Unit Citation
Cross	Victoria Cross
Distinguished Service	<Britain>
Medal	
Distinguished Service	
Order	

647 INSIGNIA

NOUNS **1 insignia, regalia,** ensign, **emblem, badge, symbol,** logo <nonformal>, marking, attribute; badge of office, mark of office, chain, chain of office, collar; wand, verge, *fasces* <L>, **mace, staff, baton;** livery, uniform, mantle, dress; tartan, tie, old school tie, regimental tie; ring, school ring, class ring; pin, button, lapel pin *or* button; cap and gown, mortarboard;

cockade; brassard; figurehead, eagle; cross 170.4, skull and crossbones, swastika, hammer and sickle, rose, thistle, shamrock, fleur-de-lis; medal, **decoration** 646.5; **heraldry,** armory, blazonry, sigillography, sphragistics

2 <heraldry terms> heraldic device, achievement, bearings, coat of arms, arms, armorial bearings, armory, blazonry, blazon; hatchment; shield, escutcheon, scutcheon, lozenge; charge, field; crest, torse, wreath, garland, bandeau, chaplet, mantling, helmet; crown, coronet; device, motto; pheon, broad arrow; animal charge, lion, unicorn, griffin, yale, cockatrice, falcon, alerion, eagle, spread eagle; marshaling, quartering, impaling, impalement, dimidiating, differencing, difference; ordinary, bar, bend, bar sinister, bend sinister, baton, chevron, chief, cross, fess, pale, paly, saltire; subordinary, billet, bordure, canton, flanch, fret, fusil, gyron, inescutcheon, mascle, orle, quarter, rustre, tressure; fess point, nombril point, honor point; cadency mark, file, label, crescent, mullet, martlet, annulet, fleur-de-lis, rose, cross moline, octofoil; tincture, gules, azure, vert, sable, purpure, tenne; metal, or, argent; fur, ermine, ermines, erminites, erminois, pean, vair; heraldic officials 575.21

3 <royal insignia> regalia; scepter, rod, rod of empire; orb; armilla; purple, ermine, robe of state *or* royalty; purple pall; crown, royal crown, coronet, tiara, diadem; cap of maintenance *or* dignity *or* estate, triple plume, Prince of Wales's feathers; uraeus; seal, signet, great seal, privy seal

4 <ecclesiastical insignia> tiara, triple crown; ring, keys; miter, crosier, crook, pastoral staff; pallium; cardinal's hat, red hat

5 <military insignia> insignia of rank, grade insignia, chevron, stripe; star, bar, eagle, spread eagle, chicken <nonformal>, pip <Brit>, oak leaf; branch of service insignia, insignia of branch *or* arm; unit insignia, organization insignia, shoulder patch, patch; shoulder sleeve insignia, badge, aviation badge *or* wings; parachute badge, submarine badge; service stripe, hash mark <nonformal>, overseas bar, Hershey bar <nonformal>; epaulet

6 **flag, banner,** oriflamme, **standard,** gonfalon *or* gonfanon, guidon, *vexillum* <L>, *labarum* <L>; **pennant,** pennon, pennoncel, banneret, banderole, swallowtail, burgee, **streamer; bunting;** coachwhip, long pennant; **national flag, colors;** royal standard; **ensign,** merchant flag, jack, Jolly Roger, black flag; house flag; <US> Old Glory, Stars and Stripes, Star-Spangled Banner, red, white, and blue; <Confederacy> Stars and Bars; <France> tricolor, *le drapeau tricolore* <Fr>; <Britain> Union Jack, Union Flag, white *or* red *or* blue ensign; <Denmark> Dannebrog; vexillology; signal flag 517.15

648 TITLE

NOUNS **1 title, honorific, honor,** title of honor; **handle** *and* handle to one's name <both nonformal>; courtesy title

2 <honorifics> Excellency, Eminence, Reverence, Grace, Honor, Worship, Your *or* His *or* Her Excellency; Lord, My Lord, milord, Lordship, Your *or* His Lordship; Lady, My Lady, milady, Ladyship, Your *or* Her Ladyship; Highness, Royal Highness, Imperial Highness, Serene Highness, Your *or* His *or* Her Highness; Majesty, Royal Majesty, Imperial Majesty, Serene Majesty, Your *or* His *or* Her Majesty

3 Sir, sire, sirrah; Esquire; Master, Mister 76.7; mirza, effendi, sirdar, emir, khan, sahib

4 Mistress, madame 77.8

5 <ecclesiastical titles> Reverend, His Reverence, His Grace; Monsignor; Holiness, His Holiness; Dom, Brother, Sister, Father, Mother; Rabbi

6 degree, academic degree <see list>; **bachelor,** baccalaureate, *baccalaureus* <L>, bachelor's degree; **master,** master's degree; **doctor,** doctorate, doctor's degree

ADJS **7 titular,** titulary; honorific; honorary

8 the Noble, the Most Noble, the Most Excellent, the Most Worthy, the Most Worshipful; the Honorable, the Most Honorable, the Right Honorable; the Reverend, the Very Reverend, the Right Reverend, the Most Reverend

9 academic degrees

AA *or* Associate of Arts	ABLS *or* Bachelor of Arts in Library Science
AAS *or* Associate in Applied Science	AdjA *or* Adjunct in Arts
AB *or* Bachelor of Arts <*Artium Baccalaureus*>	AM *or* Master of Arts <*Artium Magister*>

AMusD *or* Doctor of Musical Arts	LLD *or* Doctor of Laws
AN *or* Associate in Nursing	LLM *or* Master of Laws
ArtsD *or* Doctor of Arts	MA *or* Master of Arts
BA *or* Bachelor of Arts	MALS *or* Master of Arts in Library Science
BAN *or* Bachelor of Arts in Nursing	MArch *or* Master of Architecture
BCL *or* Bachelor of Civil Law	MAT *or* Master of Arts in Teaching
BD *or* Bachelor of Divinity	MB *or* Bachelor of Medicine <Brit>
BLitt *or* Bachelor of Literature	MBA *or* Master in Business Administration
BMus *or* Bachelor of Music	MD *or* Doctor of Medicine
BNS *or* Bachelor of Naval Science	MDiv *or* Master of Divinity
BS *or* Bachelor of Science	MEd *or* Master of Education
BSArch *or* Bachelor of Science in Architecture	MFA *or* Master of Fine Arts
DD *or* Doctor of Divinity	MLitt *or* Master of Literature
DDS *or* Doctor of Dental Surgery	MLS *or* Master of Library Science
DEd *or* Doctor of Education	MPhil *or* Master of Philosophy
DMD *or* Doctor of Dental Medicine	MRE *or* Master of Religious Education
DMin *or* Doctor of Ministry	MS *or* Master of Science
DMus *or* Doctor of Music	MusD *or* Doctor of Music
DO *or* Doctor of Osteopathy	OD *or* Doctor of Optometry
DPH *or* Doctor of Public Health	PhD *or* Doctor of Philosophy
DPhil *or* Doctor of Philosophy <Brit>	SB *or* Bachelor of Science
DS *or* Doctor of Science	ScD *or* Doctor of Science
DSC *or* Doctor of Surgical Chiropody	SM *or* Master of Science
EdD *or* Doctor of Education	STD *or* Doctor of Sacred Theology
JCD *or* Doctor of Canon Law	ThB *or* Bachelor of Theology
JD *or* Doctor of Jurisprudence	ThD *or* Doctor of Theology
LittD *or* Doctor of Letters	ThM *or* Master of Theology
LLB *or* Bachelor of Laws	

649 JUSTICE

NOUNS **1 justice, justness; equity,** equitableness, level playing field <nonformal>; **evenhandedness,** measure for measure, give-and-take; balance, equality 789;

right, rightness, rightfulness, meetness, properness, propriety, what is right; dueness 639; justification, **justifiableness,** justifiability, warrantedness, warrantability, defensibility; poetic justice; retributive justice, nemesis; summary justice, drumhead justice, rude justice; scales of justice; lawfulness, legality 673

2 "truth in action"—Disraeli, "right reason applied to command and prohibition"—Cicero, "the firm and continuous desire to render to everyone that which is his due"—Justinian, "the ligament which holds civilized beings and civilized nations together"—Daniel Webster

3 fairness, fair-mindedness, candor; the fair thing, the right *or* proper thing, the handsome thing <nonformal>; level playing field, **square deal** *and* **fair shake** <both nonformal>; **fair play,** cricket <nonformal>; sportsmanship, good sportsmanship, sportsmanliness, sportsmanlikeness

4 impartiality, detachment, **dispassion,** loftiness, Olympian detachment, **dispassionateness, disinterestedness,** disinterest, unbias, unbiasedness, a fair field and no favor; **neutrality** 467; selflessness, unselfishness 652

5 <personifications> Justice, Justitia, blind *or* blindfolded Justice; Rhadamanthus, Minos; <deities> Jupiter Fidius, Deus Fidius; Fides, Fides publica Romani, Fides populi Romani; Nemesis, Dike, Themis; Astraea

VERBS **6 be just, be fair,** do the fair thing, do the handsome thing <nonformal>, do right, be righteous, do it fair and square, do the right thing by; **do justice to,** see justice done, see one righted *or* redressed, redress a wrong *or* an injustice, remedy an injustice, serve one right, shoot straight with *and* **give a square deal** *or* **fair shake** <all nonformal>; give the Devil his due; give and take; bend *or* lean over backwards, go out of one's way, go the extra mile <nonformal>

7 play fair, play the game <nonformal>, be a good sport, show a proper spirit; judge on its own merits, hold no brief

ADJS **8 just, fair,** square, **fair and square; equitable,** balanced, level <nonformal>, **even,** evenhanded; **right, rightful;** justifiable, justified, warranted, warrantable, defensible; **due** 639.7,10, deserved, merited; meet, meet and right, right and proper, fit, **proper, good,** as it should *or* ought to be; lawful, legal 673.10

9 fair-minded; **sporting,** sportsmanly, sportsmanlike; square-dealing *and* square-shooting <both nonformal>

10 impartial, impersonal, evenhanded, equitable, **dispassionate, disinterested,** detached, objective, lofty, Olympian; **unbiased,** uninfluenced, unswayed; **neutral** 467.7; selfless, unselfish 652.5

ADVS **11 justly, fairly,** fair, in a fair manner; rightfully, rightly, duly, deservedly, meetly, properly; **equitably, equally, evenly,** upon even terms; justifiedly, justifiably, warrantably, warrantedly; **impartially, impersonally, dispassionately, disinterestedly,** without distinction, without regard *or* respect to persons, without fear or favor

12 in justice, in equity, in reason, in all conscience, in all fairness, **to be fair,** as is only fair *or* right, as is right *or* just *or* fitting *or* proper

650 INJUSTICE

NOUNS **1 injustice, unjustness; inequity,** iniquity, inequitableness, iniquitousness; inequality 790, inequality of treatment *or* dealing; **wrong, wrongness,** wrongfulness, unmeetness, improperness, **impropriety;** undueness 640; what should not be, what ought not *or* must not be; unlawfulness, illegality 674

2 unfairness; unsportsmanliness, **unsportsmanlikeness;** foul play, foul, a hit below the belt, dirty pool <nonformal>

3 partiality, onesidedness; bias, leaning, inclination, tendentiousness; undispassionateness, undetachment, interest, involvement, **partisanism,** partisanship, *parti pris* <Fr>, *Tendenz* <Ger>; unneutrality; **slant,** angle, spin <nonformal>; **favoritism,** preference, nepotism; unequal *or* preferential treatment, discrimination, unjust legal disability, inequality

4 injustice, wrong, injury, grievance, disservice; raw *or* rotten deal *and* bad rap <all nonformal>; imposition; mockery *or* miscarriage of justice; great wrong, grave *or* gross injustice; atrocity, outrage

5 unjustifiability, unwarrantability, indefensibility; **inexcusability,** unconscionableness, **unpardonability,** unforgivableness, inexpiableness, irremissibility

VERBS **6** not play fair, hit below the belt, give a raw deal *or* rotten deal *or* bad rap <nonformal>

7 do one an injustice, wrong, do wrong, do wrong by, **do one a wrong,** do a disservice; do a great wrong, do a grave *or* gross injustice, commit an atrocity *or* outrage

8 **favor**, prefer, show preference, **play favorites**, treat unequally, discriminate; **slant**, angle, put on spin <nonformal>

ADJS 9 **unjust, inequitable**, unequitable, iniquitous, **unbalanced, discriminatory, uneven, unequal** 790.4; **wrong, wrongful**, unrightful; **undue** 640.9, unmeet, undeserved, unmerited; unlawful, illegal 674.6

10 **unfair**, not fair; **unsporting**, unsportsmanly, **unsportsmanlike**, not done, not kosher <nonformal>, not cricket <Brit nonformal>; **dirty** <nonformal>, foul, below the belt

11 **partial, interested**, involved, **partisan**, unneutral, **one-sided**, all on *or* way over to one side, undetached, interested, unobjective, **undispassionate, biased**, tendentious, tendential, warped, influenced, swayed, slanted

12 **unjustifiable, unwarrantable**, unallowable, unreasonable, indefensible; **inexcusable**, unconscionable, **unpardonable, unforgivable**, inexpiable, irremissible

ADVS 13 **unjustly, unfairly**; wrongfully, wrongly, undeservedly; inequitably, iniquitously, unequally, unevenly; partially, interestedly, one-sidedly, undispassionately; **unjustifiably, unwarrantably**, unallowably, unreasonably, indefensibly; inexcusably, unconscionably, unpardonably, unforgivably, inexpiably, irremissibly

651 SELFISHNESS

NOUNS 1 **selfishness**, selfism, **self-seeking**, self-serving, self-pleasing, **self-indulgence**, hedonism; self-advancement, self-promotion, self-advertisement; **careerism**, personal ambition; **narcissism, self-love**, self-devotion, self-jealousy, **self-consideration**, self-solicitude, self-sufficiency, self-absorption, ego trip, self-occupation; self-containment, self-isolation; autism, catatonia, remoteness 583.2; **self-interest**, self-interestedness, interest; self-esteem, self-admiration 140.1; **self-centeredness, self-obsession, narcissism, egotism** 140.3; **avarice, greed**, graspingness, grabbiness <nonformal>, acquisitiveness, possessiveness; **individualism** 430.5, personalism, privatism, private *or* personal desires, private *or* personal aims

2 **ungenerousness, unmagnanimousness, illiberality**, meanness, smallness, little-ness, paltriness, minginess, pettiness; **niggardliness, stinginess** 484.3

3 **self-seeker**, self-pleaser, self-advancer; member of the me generation; **narcissist, egotist** 140.5; timepleaser, timeserver, temporizer; fortune hunter, tufthunter, name-dropper; self-server, careerist; monopolist, hog, road hog; dog in the manger; **individualist**, loner *and* lone wolf <both nonformal>

VERBS 4 **please oneself**, gratify oneself; ego-trip *and* be *or* go on an ego trip <all nonformal>, be full of oneself; indulge *or* pamper *or* coddle oneself, consult one's own wishes, look after one's own interests, know which side one's bread is buttered on, take care of *or* look out for number one *or* numero uno <nonformal>; want everything, have one's cake and eat it

ADJS 5 **selfish, self-seeking, self-serving**, self-advancing, self-promoting, self-advertising, careerist, ambitious for self, **self-indulgent**, self-pleasing, hedonistic, self-jealous, self-sufficient, **self-interested**, self-considerative, self-besot, self-devoted, self-occupied, self-absorbed, wrapped up in oneself, self-contained, autistic, remote 583.6; self-esteeming, self-admiring 140.8; **self-centered, self-obsessed, narcissistic, egotistical** 140.10; possessive; **avaricious, greedy**, grasping, graspy *and* grabby <both nonformal>, acquisitive; **individualistic**, personalistic, privatistic

6 **ungenerous, illiberal**, unchivalrous, mean, small, little, paltry, mingy, petty; **niggardly, stingy** 484.9

ADVS 7 **selfishly, for oneself**, in one's own interest, from selfish *or* interested motives, to gain some private ends

652 UNSELFISHNESS

NOUNS 1 **unselfishness, selflessness**; self-subjection, self-subordination, self-suppression, self-abasement, self-effacement; **humility** 137; modesty 139; self-neglect, self-neglectfulness, self-forgetfulness, **self-renunciation**, self-renouncement; **self-denial**, self-abnegation; **self-sacrifice**, sacrifice, self-immolation, self-devotion, devotion, dedication, commitment, consecration; disinterest, disinterestedness; unpossessiveness, unacquisitiveness; **altruism** 143.4

2 **magnanimity**, magnanimousness, greatness of spirit *or* soul, **generosity**, generousness, openhandedness, **liberality**, lib-

eralness; **bigness, bigheartedness,** great-heartedness, largeheartedness, big *or* large *or* great heart, greatness of heart; noble-mindedness, **high-mindedness, idealism; benevolence** 143.4; **nobleness,** nobility, princeliness, greatness, **loftiness,** elevation, exaltation, sublimity; chivalry, chivalrousness, knightliness, errantry, knight-errantry; heroism

VERBS **3** not have a selfish bone in one's body, think only of others; be generous to a fault; put oneself out, go out of the way, lean over backwards; sacrifice, make a sacrifice; subject oneself, subordinate oneself, abase oneself

4 observe the golden rule, do as one would be done by, do unto others as you would have others do unto you

ADJS **5 unselfish, selfless;** self-unconscious, self-forgetful, self-abasing, self-effacing; **altruistic** 143.15, **humble; unpretentious, modest** 139.9; self-neglectful, self-neglecting; **self-denying,** self-renouncing, self-abnegating, self-abnegatory; **self-sacrificing,** self-immolating, sacrificing, self-devotional, self-devoted, devoted, dedicated, committed, consecrated, unsparing of self, disinterested; unpossessive, unacquisitive

6 magnanimous, great-souled *or* -spirited; **generous,** generous to a fault, open-handed, **liberal; big, bighearted,** great-hearted, largehearted, great of heart *or* soul; noble-minded, **high-minded, idealistic; benevolent** 143.15, **noble,** princely, handsome, great, high, elevated, **lofty,** exalted, sublime; chivalrous, knightly; heroic

ADVS **7 unselfishly, altruistically,** forgetful of self; for others

8 magnanimously, generously, open-handedly, **liberally; biheartedly,** greatheartedly, largeheartedly; **nobly,** handsomely; chivalrously, knightly

653 VIRTUE

NOUNS **1 virtue, virtuousness, goodness, righteousness,** rectitude, right conduct *or* behavior, the straight and narrow, the straight and narrow way, the right thing; **probity** 644; **morality,** moral fiber *or* rectitude *or* virtue, morale; **saintliness,** saintlikeness, angelicalness; **godliness** 692.2

2 "the health of the soul"—Joseph Joubert, "the fount whence honour springs"—Marlowe, "the beauty of the soul, "the

adherence in action to the nature of things"—both Emerson, "victorious resistance to one's vital desire to do this, that or the other"—James Branch Cabell, "to do unwitnessed what we should be capable of doing before all the world"—La Rochefoucauld

3 purity, immaculacy, immaculateness, spotlessness, unspottedness; **uncorruptness,** uncorruptedness, incorruptness; **unsinfulness, sinlessness,** unwickedness, uniniquitousness; undegenerateness, undepravedness, undissoluteness, undebauchedness; **chastity** 664; guiltlessness, innocence 657

4 cardinal virtues, natural virtues; prudence, justice, temperance, fortitude; theological virtues *or* supernatural virtues; faith, hope, charity *or* love

VERBS **5 be good,** do no evil, do the right thing; keep in the right path, walk the straight path, follow the straight and narrow, keep on the straight and narrow way *or* path; fight the good fight

ADJS **6 virtuous, good, moral;** upright, honest 644.13,14,16; **righteous,** just, straight, rightminded, right-thinking; **angelic,** seraphic; **saintly,** saintlike; **godly** 692.9

7 chaste, immaculate, spotless, pure 664.4; **clean,** squeaky-clean <nonformal>; guiltless, **innocent** 657.6

8 uncorrupt, uncorrupted, incorrupt, incorrupted; **unsinful,** sinless; **unwicked,** uniniquitous, unerring, unfallen; undegenerate, undepraved, undemoralized, undissolute, undebauched

654 VICE

NOUNS **1 vice,** viciousness; criminality, **wrongdoing** 655; **immorality,** unmorality, evil; **amorality** 636.4; **unvirtuousness,** ungoodness; **unrighteousness, ungodliness,** unsaintliness, unangelicalness; **uncleanness, impurity, unchastity** 665, fallenness, fallen state, lapsedness; waywardness, wantonness, prodigality; delinquency, moral delinquency; peccability; backsliding, recidivism; **evil nature, carnality** 663.2

2 vice, weakness, weakness of the flesh, **flaw,** moral flaw *or* blemish, **frailty, infirmity; failing,** failure; weak point, weak side, foible; bad habit, besetting sin; **fault, imperfection** 1002

3 iniquity, evil, bad, wrong, error, obliquity, villainy, knavery, reprobacy, peccancy, **abomination, atrocity, infamy,**

shame, disgrace, scandal, unforgivable
or cardinal *or* mortal sin, **sin** 655.2

4 **wickedness, badness,** naughtiness, **evilness, viciousness, sinfulness, iniquitousness; baseness,** rankness, **vileness,** foulness, arrantness, nefariousness, **heinousness,** infamousness, villainousness, flagitiousness; fiendishness, hellishness; devilishness, devilry, deviltry

5 **turpitude, moral turpitude; corruption,** corruptedness, corruptness, rottenness, moral pollution *or* pollutedness, lack *or* absence of moral fiber; **decadence** *or* decadency, debasement, **degradation,** demoralization, abjection; **degeneracy,** degenerateness, degeneration, reprobacy, **depravity,** depravedness, depravation; **dissoluteness, profligacy;** abandonment, abandon

6 **obduracy, hardheartedness, hardness, callousness,** heartlessness, hardness of heart, heart of stone

7 **sewer, gutter, pit, sink, sink of corruption; den of iniquity,** den, **fleshpots,** hellhole; hole *and* joint *and* the pits <all nonformal>; Sodom, Gomorrah, Babylon; **brothel** 665.9

VERBS 8 **do wrong, sin** 655.5; misbehave, misdemean *and* misdo <both old>

9 **go wrong,** stray, go astray, **err,** deviate, deviate from the path of virtue, leave the straight and narrow, step out of line, get *or* go off base <nonformal>; **fall, lapse,** slip, trip; **degenerate; go to the bad** 395.24; **relapse,** recidivate, backslide 394.4

10 **corrupt; sully, soil, defile;** demoralize, vitiate, drive to the dogs

ADJS 11 vice-prone, vice-laden, vicious, **steeped in vice; immoral,** unmoral; **amoral,** nonmoral; unethical

12 **unvirtuous,** virtueless, ungood; **unrighteous, ungodly,** unsaintly, unangelic; **unclean, impure,** spotted, flawed, blemished, maculate <old>, **unchaste** 665.23; fleshly, carnal 663.6, wayward, wanton, prodigal; erring, **fallen, lapsed,** postlapsarian; frail, weak, infirm; Adamic; peccable; **relapsing, backsliding,** recidivist, recidivistic; of easy virtue 665.26

13 **diabolic, diabolical, devilish,** demonic, demoniac, demoniacal, **satanic,** Mephistophelian; **fiendish,** fiendlike; **hellish,** hellborn; **infernal**

14 **corrupt,** corrupted, vice-corrupted, polluted, morally polluted, rotten, tainted, contaminated, vitiated; warped, perverted; **decadent,** debased, degraded, reprobate, **depraved, debauched, disso-**

lute, degenerate, profligate, abandoned, gone to the bad *or* dogs, sunk *or* steeped in iniquity, rotten at *or* to the core, in the sewer *or* gutter

15 **evil-minded,** evilhearted, **blackhearted; base-minded,** low-minded; low-thoughted, dirty *or* dirty-minded <nonformal>

16 **wicked, evil, vicious, bad, naughty, wrong, sinful, iniquitous,** peccant, reprobate; dark, black; **base, low, vile,** foul, rank, flagrant, arrant, nefarious, **heinous,** villainous, criminal, up to no good, knavish, flagitious; abominable, atrocious, monstrous, unspeakable, execrable, damnable; shameful, disgraceful, scandalous, **infamous, unpardonable,** unforgivable; **improper,** reprehensible, blamable, blameworthy, unworthy

17 **hardened, hard, case-hardened, obdurate,** inured, indurated; **callous,** calloused, **seared; hardhearted,** heartless; **shameless,** lost to shame, blind to virtue, lost to all sense of honor, conscienceless, unblushing, **brazen**

18 **irreclaimable,** irredeemable, unredeemable, unregenerate, **irreformable,** incorrigible, past praying for; shriftless, graceless; **lost**

ADVS 19 **wickedly, evilly, sinfully, iniquitously,** peccantly, **viciously;** basely, vilely, foully, rankly, arrantly, flagrantly, flagitiously

655 WRONGDOING

NOUNS 1 **wrongdoing, evildoing, wickedness,** misdoing <old>, wrong conduct, **misbehavior** 322, **misconduct,** misdemeaning, misfeasance, malfeasance, malversation, **malpractice,** evil courses, machinations of the devil; **sin,** "thou scarlet sin"—Shakespeare, "the transgression of the law"—Bible; **crime, criminality,** lawbreaking, feloniousness; criminal tendency; habitual criminality, criminosis; viciousness, **vice** 654; misprision, negative *or* positive misprision, misprision of treason *or* felony

2 **misdeed, misdemeanor,** misfeasance, malfeasance, malefaction, criminal *or* guilty *or* sinful act, **offense,** injustice, injury, **wrong, iniquity, evil,** peccancy, *malum* <L>; tort; **error, fault,** breach; **impropriety,** slight *or* minor wrong, venial sin, **indiscretion,** peccadillo, misstep, trip, slip, lapse; **transgression,** trespass; **sin,** "deed without a name"—Shakespeare; **cardinal** *or* **deadly** *or* **mortal**

sin, grave *or* heavy sin, unutterable sin, unpardonable *or* unforgivable *or* inexpiable sin; sin against the Holy Ghost; sin of commission; sin of omission, nonfeasance, omission, failure, dereliction, delinquency; **crime, felony;** capital crime; white-collar crime, execu-crime; computer crime; copycat crime <nonformal>; war crime, crime against humanity, genocide; **outrage, atrocity,** enormity

3 **original sin,** fall from grace, fall, fall of man, fall of Adam *or* Adam's fall, sin of Adam

VERBS 4 **do wrong,** do amiss, misdo <old>, misdemean oneself, **misbehave** 322.4, **err,** offend; **sin,** commit sin; **transgress,** trespass

ADJS 5 **wrongdoing, evildoing,** malefactory, malfeasant; **wrong,** iniquitous, **sinful, wicked** 654.16; **criminal,** felonious, criminous <old>; crime-infested, crime-ridden

656 GUILT

NOUNS 1 **guilt, guiltiness; criminality,** peccancy; guilty *or* wrongful *or* criminal involvement; **culpability,** reprehensibility, blamability, blameworthiness; chargeability, answerability, much to answer for; censurability, censurableness, reproachability, reproachableness, reprovability, reprovableness, inculpation, implication, involvement, complicity, impeachability, impeachableness, indictability, indictableness, arraignability, arraignableness; bloodguilt *or* -guiltiness, red-handedness, dirty hands, red *or* bloody hands, "hangman's hands"— Shakespeare; much to answer for; **ruth,** ruefulness, remorse, guilty conscience, guilt feelings; onus, burden

VERBS 2 **be guilty,** look guilty, look like the cat that swallowed the canary, blush, stammer; have on one's hands *or* to one's discredit, have much to answer for; have a red face; be caught in the act *or* flatfooted *or* redhanded, be caught with one's pants down *or* with one's hand in the till *or* with one's hand in the cookie jar <nonformal>

ADJS 3 **guilty,** guilty as hell, peccant, **criminal, to blame, at fault,** faulty, on one's head; **culpable,** reprehensible, censurable, reproachable, reprovable, inculpated, implicated, involved, impeachable, indictable, arraignable; redhanded, bloodguilty; caught in the act *or*

flatfooted *or* red-handed, caught with one's pants down *or* with one's hand in the till *or* with one's hand in the cookie jar <nonformal>

ADVS 4 **red-handed,** red-hand, **in the act,** in the very act, *in flagrante delicto* <L>

5 **guilty,** shamefacedly, sheepishly, with a guilty conscience

657 INNOCENCE

NOUNS 1 **innocence,** innocency, innocentness; unfallen *or* unlapsed *or* prelapsarian state; unguiltiness, **guiltlessness,** faultlessness, blamelessness, reproachlessness, **sinlessness,** offenselessness; **spotlessness,** stainlessness, taintlessness, unblemishedness; **purity,** cleanness, cleanliness, whiteness, immaculateness, immaculacy, impeccability; clean hands, clean slate, clear conscience, nothing to hide

2 childlikeness 416.1; lamblikeness, dovelikeness, angelicness; unacquaintance with evil, uncorruptedness, incorruptness, pristineness, undefiledness

3 **inculpability,** unblamability, unblamableness, **unblameworthiness,** irreproachability, irreproachableness, impeccability, impeccableness, unexceptionability, unexceptionableness, **irreprehensibility,** irreprehensibleness, uncensurability, uncensurableness, unimpeachability, unimpeachableness, unindictableness, unarraignableness

4 **innocent,** baby, babe, babe in arms, newborn babe, infant, babe in the woods, child, mere child, lamb, dove, angel

VERBS 5 know no wrong, have clean hands, have a clear conscience, look as if butter would not melt in one's mouth

ADJS 6 **innocent;** unfallen, unlapsed, prelapsarian; **unguilty,** not guilty, **guiltless, faultless, blameless,** reproachless, **sinless,** offenseless, with clean hands, "blameless in life and pure of crime"— Horace; clear, in the clear; without reproach, *sans reproche* <Fr>; innocent as a lamb, lamblike, dovelike, angelic, childlike 416.5; unacquainted with *or* untouched by evil, uncorrupted, incorrupt, pristine, undefiled

7 **spotless,** stainless, taintless, unblemished, unspotted, **untainted, unsoiled, unsullied, undefiled; pure, clean, immaculate,** impeccable, white, pure *or* white as driven snow, squeakyclean <nonformal>, "without unspotted, innocent within"—Dryden

8 inculpable, unblamable, unblameworthy, **irreproachable**, irreprovable, **irreprehensible**, uncensurable, unimpeachable, unindictable, unarraignable, unobjectionable, unexceptionable, above suspicion

ADVS **9 innocently, guiltlessly, unguiltily**, with a clear conscience; **unknowingly**, unconsciously, unawares

658 ATONEMENT

NOUNS **1 atonement, reparation, amends**, making amends, **restitution, propitiation, expiation, redress, recompense**, compensation, setting right, making right *or* good, making up, squaring, redemption, reclamation, satisfaction, quittance; making it quits; indemnity, indemnification; compromise, composition; expiatory offering *or* sacrifice, piaculum, peace offering

2 apology, excuse, regrets; acknowledgment, penitence, contrition, breast-beating, *mea culpa* <L>, confession 351.3; abject apology

3 penance, penitence, repentance; penitential act *or* exercise, **mortification**, maceration, flagellation, lustration; **asceticism** 667, **fasting** 515; **purgation**, purgatory, "cold purgatorial fires"— T S Eliot; **sackcloth and ashes**; hair shirt; **Lent**; Day of Atonement, Yom Kippur

VERBS **4 atone, atone for, propitiate, expiate**, compensate, restitute, recompense, redress, redeem, repair, satisfy, give satisfaction, **make amends, make reparation** *or* **compensation** *or* **expiation** *or* **restitution**, make good *or* right, set right, **make up for**, make matters up, square it, square things, make it quits, pay the forfeit *or* penalty, pay one's dues <nonformal>, wipe off old scores; wipe the slate clean; set one's house in order; live down, unlive

5 apologize, beg pardon, ask forgiveness, beg indulgence, express regret; take back; get *or* fall down on one's knees, get down on one's marrowbones <nonformal>

6 do penance, flagellate oneself, mortify oneself, mortify one's flesh, make oneself miserable, shrive oneself, purge oneself, cleanse oneself of guilt, stand in a white sheet, repent in sackcloth and ashes, wear a hair shirt, wear sackcloth *or* sackcloth and ashes; receive absolution

ADJS **7 atoning, propitiatory, expiatory**, piacular, reparative, reparatory, restitutive, restitutory, restitutional, redressing, recompensing, compensatory, compensational, righting, squaring; redemptive, redeeming, reclamatory, satisfactional; **apologetic, apologetical;** repentant, repenting; **penitential**, purgative, purgatorial; lustral, lustrative, lustrational, cleansing, purifying; ascetic

659 GOOD PERSON

NOUNS **1** good person, fine person, good *or* fine man *or* woman *or* child, worthy, prince, nature's nobleman *or* -woman, man *or* woman after one's own heart; *persona grata* <L>, acceptable person; **good fellow**, capital fellow, **good sort**, right sort, a decent sort of fellow, good lot <Brit nonformal>, no end of a fellow; real person, real man *or* woman, mensch <nonformal>; **gentleman**, perfect gentleman, a gentleman and a scholar; **lady**, perfect lady; **gem**, jewel, pearl, diamond; rough diamond, diamond in the rough; honest man 644.8

2 <nonformal terms> **good guy**, crackerjack, brick, trump, good egg, stout fellow, nice guy, Mr Nice Guy, good Joe, likely lad, no slouch, doll, living doll, pussycat, **sweetheart, sweetie**

3 **good** *or* **respectable citizen**, excellent *or* exemplary citizen, good neighbor, burgher, taxpayer, **pillar of society**, pillar of the church, salt of the earth; Christian *and* true Christian <both nonformal>

4 **paragon, ideal**, beau ideal, nonpareil, person to look up to, *chevalier sans peur et sans reproche* <Fr>, **good example, role model**, shining example; exemplar, epitome; **model, pattern, standard**, norm, mirror, "the observed of all observers"— Shakespeare; *Übermensch* <Ger; Nietzsche>; **standout**, one in a thousand *or* ten thousand, man of men, a man among men, woman of women, a woman among women

5 hero, god, demigod, phoenix; **heroine, goddess**, demigoddess; **idol**

6 holy man; great soul, mahatma; guru, *rishi* <Skt>; *starets* <Russ>; saint, angel 679

660 BAD PERSON

NOUNS **1** bad person, bad man *or* woman *or* child, unworthy *or* disreputable person, unworthy, disreputable, **undesirable**, *persona non grata* <L>, unacceptable *or* unwanted *or* objectionable person, baddy *and* wrongo *and* bad news <all nonformal>; bad example

2 **wretch**, mean *or* miserable wretch, **beggarly fellow, beggar, blighter** <Brit nonformal>; **bum** *and* bummer *and* lowlifer *and* lowlife *and* **mucker** <all nonformal>, caitiff, budmash <India>, pilgarlic; devil, **poor devil**, *pauvre diable* <Fr>, poor creature, *mauvais sujet* <Fr>; **sad case**, sad sack *and* sad sack of shit <both nonformal>; **good-for-nothing, good-for-naught, no-good** <nonformal>, **ne'er-do-well**, wastrel, *vaurien* <Fr>, worthless fellow; **derelict**, skid-row bum, Bowery bum, tramp, hobo, beachcomber, **drifter**, drunkard, vagrant, vag <nonformal>, vagabond, truant, stiff *and* bindlestiff <both nonformal>, swagman *or* sundowner <both Austral>; human wreck

3 **rascal**, precious rascal, rogue, knave, **scoundrel**, villain, blackguard, **scamp, scalawag** <nonformal>, spalpeen <Ir>, rapscallion, **devil**; shyster; sneak

4 "a rascally yeaforsooth knave, "a foul-mouthed and calumnious knave, "poor cuckoldy knave, "a poor, decayed, ingenious, foolish, rascally knave, "an arrant, rascally, beggarly, lousy knave, "a slipper and subtle knave, a finder of occasions, "a whoreson, beetle-headed, flap-ear'd knave, "filthy, worsted-stocking knave, "a lily-livered, action-taking knave, "a knave; a rascal; an eater of broken meats; a base, proud, shallow, beggarly, three-suited, hundred-pound, filthy, worsted-stocking knave"—all Shakespeare

5 **reprobate**, recreant, **miscreant**, bad *or* sorry lot <Brit nonformal>, bad egg *and* wrongo *and* wrong number <all nonformal>, bad'un *or* wrong'un <both Brit nonformal>; scapegrace, black sheep; lost soul, lost sheep, *âme damnée* <Fr>, backslider, recidivist, fallen angel; degenerate, pervert; profligate, **lecher** 665.11; trollop, **whore** 665.14,16; **pimp** 665.18

6 <nonformal terms> **asshole, prick, bastard, son of a bitch** *or* **SOB, jerk, horse's ass**, creep, motherfucker, mother, dork, **shit**, turd, birdturd, shithead, shitface, cuntface, dickhead, fart, **louse, meanie, heel, shitheel, rat, stinker**, stinkard, pill, bugger, dirtbag, dork, geek, dweeb, twerp, sleaze, sleazoid, sleazebag, bad lot <Brit>; **hood, hooligan** 593.4

7 beast, **animal; cur**, dog, hound, whelp, mongrel; **reptile**, viper, serpent, snake; vermin, varmint <nonformal>, hyena; **swine**, pig; **skunk**, polecat; insect, worm

8 cad, bounder *and* rotter <nonformal>

9 **wrongdoer, malefactor, sinner**, transgressor, delinquent; malfeasor, misfeasor, nonfeasor; misdemeanant, misdemeanist; **culprit, offender; evil person, evil man** *or* **woman** *or* **child, evildoer** 593

10 **criminal, felon, perpetrator, crook** *and* perp <both nonformal>, public enemy, **lawbreaker**, scofflaw; **gangster** *and* mobster *and* wiseguy <all nonformal>, **racketeer; swindler** 357.3; thief 483; **thug** 593.3; **desperado**, desperate criminal; **outlaw**, fugitive, **convict**, jailbird, gaolbird <Brit>; gallows bird <nonformal>; **traitor**, betrayer, quisling, Judas, doubledealer, two-timer <nonformal>, **deceiver** 357

11 **the underworld**, gangland, gangdom, **organized crime**, organized crime family, the rackets, the mob, the syndicate, the Mafia, Cosa Nostra, Black Hand; **gangsterism; gangster**, ganglord, gangleader, caporegime *or* capo, button man, soldier

12 **the wicked**, the bad, the evil, the unrighteous, the reprobate; sons of men, sons of Belial, sons *or* children of the devil, limbs *or* get *or* imps of Satan, children of darkness; **scum of the earth**, dregs of society

661 DISREPUTE

NOUNS 1 **disrepute, ill repute**, bad repute, bad *or* poor reputation, evil repute *or* reputation, ill fame, shady *or* unsavory reputation, **bad name**, bad odor, bad report, bad character; **disesteem, dishonor**, public dishonor, **discredit; disfavor**, illfavor; disapprobation 510.1

2 **disreputability**, disreputableness, **notoriety**; discreditableness, dishonorableness, unsavoriness, **unrespectability**; disgracefulness, **shamefulness**

3 **baseness, lowness, meanness, crumminess** <nonformal>, poorness, pettiness, paltriness, smallness, littleness, pokiness, cheesiness <nonformal>, beggarliness, **shabbiness, shoddiness, squalor**, scrubbiness, scumminess, scabbiness, scurviness, scruffiness, shittiness <nonformal>; **abjectness, wretchedness**, miserableness, despicableness, contemptibleness, contemptibility, abominableness, execrableness, obnoxiousness; **vulgarity**, tastelessness, crudity, crudeness, tackiness *and* chintziness <both nonformal>; **vileness** 98.2, foulness, rankness, fulsomeness, grossness, nefariousness, heinousness, **atrociousness**, monstrousness, enor-

mity; degradation, debasement, depravity

4 **infamy**, infamousness; **ignominy**, ignominiousness; ingloriousness, **ignobility**, odium, obloquy, opprobrium, "a long farewell to all my greatness"—Shakespeare; depluming, displuming, loss of honor *or* name *or* repute *or* face; degradation, comedown <nonformal>, **demotion** 447

5 **disgrace, scandal, humiliation; shame,** dirty shame *and* low-down dirty shame <both nonformal>, crying *or* burning shame; **reproach,** byword, byword of reproach, a disgrace to one's name

6 **stigma,** stigmatism, onus; **brand,** badge of infamy; **slur,** reproach, censure, reprimand, imputation, aspersion, reflection, stigmatization; pillorying; **black eye** <nonformal>, black mark; **disparagement** 512; **stain, taint,** attaint, **tarnish,** blur, **smirch,** smutch *or* smooch, smudge, **smear,** spot, blot, blot on *or* in one's escutcheon *or* scutcheon; bend *or* bar sinister <heraldry>; baton, champain, point champain <all heraldry>; mark of Cain; broad arrow <Brit>

VERBS 7 **incur disgrace,** incur disesteem *or* dishonor *or* discredit, get a black eye <nonformal>, be shamed, earn a bad name *or* reproach *or* reproof, forfeit one's good opinion, fall into disrepute, seal one's infamy; lose one's good name, **lose face,** lose countenance, lose credit, **lose caste; disgrace oneself,** lower oneself, demean oneself, drag one's banner in the dust, degrade *or* debase oneself, act beneath oneself, dirty *or* soil one's hands, get one's hands dirty, sully *or* lower oneself, derogate, stoop, descend, ride to a fall, fall from one's high estate, foul one's own nest; **scandalize,** make oneself notorious, put one's good name in jeopardy; compromise oneself; raise eyebrows, cause eyebrows to raise, cause tongues to wag

8 **disgrace, dishonor, discredit,** reflect discredit upon, bring into discredit, reproach, cast reproach upon, be a reproach to; **shame, put to shame,** impute shame to, hold up to shame; hold up to public shame *or* public scorn *or* public ridicule, pillory, bring shame upon, **humiliate** 137.4; **degrade, debase** 447.3, deplume, displume, defrock, unfrock, bring low

9 **stigmatize, brand; stain, besmirch,** smirch, tarnish, taint, attaint, blot, **blacken, smear,** bespatter, **sully,** soil, de-

file, vilify, **slur,** cast a slur upon, blow upon; disapprove 510.10; **disparage, defame** 512.9; censure, reprimand, **give a black eye** <nonformal>, give a black mark, put in one's bad *or* black books; give a bad name, give a dog a bad name; expose, expose to infamy; pillory, gibbet; burn *or* hang in effigy; **skewer,** impale, crucify

ADJS 10 **disreputable, discreditable, dishonorable,** unsavory, shady, **seamy, sordid; unrespectable, ignoble, ignominious, infamous,** inglorious; notorious; unpraiseworthy; derogatory 512.13

11 **disgraceful, shameful,** pitiful, deplorable, opprobrious, sad, sorry, too bad; degrading, debasing, demeaning, beneath one, beneath one's dignity, *infra dignitatem* <L>, infra dig <nonformal>, unbecoming, unworthy of one; cheap, gutter; **humiliating,** humiliative; **scandalous,** shocking, outrageous

12 **base, low,** low rent *and* low ride *and* low-down *and* cotton-picking <all nonformal>, **mean,** crummy <nonformal>, poor, petty, paltry, small, little, **shabby, shoddy, squalid,** lumpen, scrubby, scummy, scabby, **scurvy,** scruffy, mangy <nonformal>, measly *and* cheesy <both nonformal>, poky, beggarly, **wretched, miserable,** abject, **despicable, contemptible,** abominable, execrable, obnoxious, **vulgar,** tasteless, crude, **tacky** *and* chintzy <both nonformal>; **disgusting, odious** 98.18, vile, foul, **dirty,** rank, fulsome, gross, flagrant, grave, arrant, nefarious, heinous, reptilian, **atrocious,** monstrous, unspeakable, unmentionable; degraded, debased, depraved

13 **in disrepute,** in bad repute, in bad odor; **in disfavor,** in discredit, **in bad** <nonformal>, in one's bad *or* black books, out of favor, out of countenance, at a discount; **in disgrace,** in Dutch *and* **in the doghouse** <both nonformal>, under a cloud; scandal-plagued *or* -ridden; stripped of reputation, disgraced, discredited, dishonored, shamed, loaded with shame, unable to show one's face; **in trouble**

14 **unrenowned,** renownless, nameless, inglorious, **unnotable, unnoted,** unnoticed, unremarked, **undistinguished, unfamed,** uncelebrated, unsung, unhonored, unglorified, unpopular; no credit to; **unknown,** little known, obscure, unheard-of, *ignotus* <L>

ADVS 15 **disreputably, discreditably, dishonorably, unrespectably, ignobly, ignominiously, infamously,** ingloriously

16 disgracefully, scandalously, shockingly, deplorably, outrageously; **shamefully,** to one's shame, to one's shame be it spoken

17 basely, meanly, poorly, pettily, **shabbily, shoddily,** scurvily, **wretchedly, miserably,** abjectly, **despicably, contemptibly,** abominably, execrably, obnoxiously, **odiously** 98.26, **vilely,** foully, grossly, flagrantly, arrantly, nefariously, heinously, **atrociously,** monstrously

662 REPUTE

NOUNS **1 repute, reputation,** "the bubble reputation"—Shakespeare; **name,** character, figure; **fame,** famousness, **renown,** "that last infirmity of noble mind"—Milton, **kudos,** report, **glory,** éclat, **celebrity, popularity,** recognition, a place in the sun; popular acceptance *or* favor, vogue; **acclaim, public acclaim,** réclame, **publicity; notoriety,** notoriousness, talk of the town; **exposure;** play *and* air-play <both nonformal>

2 reputability, reputableness; good reputation, good name, **good** *or* **high repute,** good report, good track record <nonformal>, good odor, face, fair name, name to conjure with

3 esteem, estimation, **honor, regard, respect,** approval, approbation, account, favor, consideration, **credit,** points *and* Brownie points <both nonformal>

4 prestige, honor; dignity; rank, standing, stature, high place, position, station, face, **status**

5 distinction, mark, note; importance, consequence, significance; **notability, prominence, eminence, preeminence, greatness,** conspicuousness, outstandingness; **stardom;** elevation, exaltation, exaltedness, loftiness, high and mightiness <nonformal>; nobility, grandeur, sublimity; excellence 998.1, supereminence 998.2

6 illustriousness, luster, brilliance *or* brilliancy, radiance, splendor, resplendence *or* resplendency, refulgence *or* refulgency, refulgentness, **glory,** blaze of glory, nimbus, halo, aura, envelope; charisma, mystique, glamour, numinousness, magic; cult of personality, personality cult

7 <posthumous fame> **memory, remembrance,** blessed *or* sacred memory, legend, heroic legend *or* myth; **immortality,** lasting *or* undying fame, niche in the hall of fame, secure place in history;

immortal name, "ghost of a great name"—Lucan

8 glorification, ennoblement, dignification, **exaltation,** elevation, enskying, enskyment, magnification, aggrandizement; enthronement; immortalization, enshrinement; beatification, canonization, sainting, sanctification; **deification, apotheosis;** lionization

9 celebrity, man *or* woman of mark *or* note, person of note *or* consequence, **notable, notability, luminary, great man** *or* **woman,** master spirit, worthy, name, **big name,** figure, public figure, **somebody; important person, VIP** *and* **standout** <both nonformal>, personage 996.8, one in a hundred *or* thousand *or* million etc; cynosure, model, very model, ideal type, "the observed of all observers"—Shakespeare, **idol,** popular idol, tin god *or* little tin god <nonformal>; lion, social lion; hero, heroine, popular hero, pop hero <nonformal>, folk hero, superhero; **star, superstar,** megastar, hot stuff <nonformal>; cult figure; **immortal;** luminaries, galaxy, pleiad, constellation; semicelebrity

VERBS **10 be somebody,** be something, **impress,** charismatize; **figure,** make *or* cut a figure, cut a dash *and* make a splash <both nonformal>, **make a noise in the world,** make *or* leave one's mark; live, **flourish; shine,** glitter, gleam, glow

11 gain recognition, be recognized, get a reputation, **make a name** *or* make a name for oneself, make oneself known, come into one's own, come to the front *or* fore, come into vogue; **burst onto the scene,** become an overnight celebrity, come onto the scene <nonformal>, come out of the woods *or* out of nowhere *or* out of left field <all nonformal>; make points *or* Brownie points <nonformal>

12 honor, confer *or* bestow honor upon; **dignify,** adorn, grace; **distinguish,** signalize, confer distinction on, give credit where credit is due

13 glorify, glamorize; **exalt,** elevate, ensky, raise, uplift, set up, **ennoble,** aggrandize, magnify, exalt to the skies; crown; throne, enthrone; immortalize, enshrine, hand one's name down to posterity, make legendary; beatify, canonize, saint, sanctify; **deify,** apotheosize, apotheose; **lionize**

14 reflect honor, lend credit *or* distinction, shed a luster, redound to one's honor, give one a reputation

ADJS **15 reputable,** highly reputed, **esti-**

mable, **esteemed**, much *or* highly esteemed, **honorable**, honored; **meritorious**, worth one's salt, noble, worthy, creditable; respected, respectable, highly respectable; revered, reverend, venerable, venerated, worshipful; **well-thought-of**, highly regarded, held in esteem, in good odor, in favor, in high favor; in one's good books; prestigious

16 **distinguished**, distingué; **noted, notable**, marked, of note, of mark; **famous**, famed, honored, **renowned, celebrated, popular**, acclaimed, much acclaimed, sought-after, hot *and* world-class <both nonformal>, **notorious, well-known**, best-known, in everyone's mouth, on everyone's tongue *or* lips, talked-of, talked-about; far-famed, far-heard; fabled, legendary, mythical

17 **prominent, conspicuous, outstanding**, stickout <nonformal>, much in evidence, to the front, in the limelight <nonformal>; **important**, consequential, significant

18 **eminent, high, exalted**, elevated, enskyed, lofty, sublime, held in awe, awesome; immortal; **great**, big <nonformal>, **grand**; excellent 998.12,13,15, supereminent, mighty, high and mighty <nonformal>; glorified, ennobled, magnified, aggrandized; enthroned, throned; immortalized, shrined, enshrined; beatified, canonized, sainted, sanctified; **idolized, godlike, deified**, apotheosized

19 **illustrious**, lustrous, glorious, brilliant, radiant, splendid, splendorous, splendrous, splendent, resplendent, bright, shining; charismatic, glamorous, numinous, magic, magical

ADVS 20 **reputably, estimably, honorably**, nobly, respectably, worthily, creditably

21 **famously, notably, notedly, notoriously**, popularly, celebratedly; **prominently, eminently**, conspicuously, outstandingly; **illustriously**, gloriously

663 SENSUALITY

NOUNS 1 **sensuality**, sensualness, sensualism; appetitiveness, appetite; **voluptuousness**, luxuriousness, luxury; **unchastity** 665; **pleasure-seeking**; sybaritism; **self-indulgence, hedonism**, Cyrenaic hedonism, Cyrenaicism, ethical hedonism, psychological hedonism, hedonics, hedonic calculus; epicurism, epicureanism; pleasure principle, *Lustprinzip* <Ger>; **instant gratification**; sensuousness 24.1

2 **carnality**, carnal-mindedness; **fleshliness**,

flesh; animal *or* carnal nature, the flesh, the beast, Adam, the Old Adam, the offending Adam, fallen state *or* nature, lapsed state *or* nature, postlapsarian state *or* nature; **animality, animalism, bestiality**, beastliness, brutishness, **brutality**; coarseness, grossness; swishness; **earthiness**, unspirituality, nonspirituality, materialism

3 **sensualist, voluptuary, pleasure-seeker**, sybarite, Cyrenaic, Sardanapalus, Heliogabalus, **hedonist**, *bon vivant* <Fr>, carpet knight; epicure, epicurean; gourmet, gourmand; swine

VERBS 4 sensualize, carnalize, coarsen, brutify; *carpe diem* <L, seize the day>, live for the moment

ADJS 5 **sensual**, sensualist, sensualistic; appetitive; **voluptuous**, luxurious; **unchaste** 665.23, **hedonistic, pleasure-seeking**, pleasure-bent, bent on pleasure, luxury-loving, hedonic, epicurean, sybaritic; Cyrenaic; sensory, sensuous

6 **carnal**, carnal-minded, **fleshly**, bodily, physical; Adamic, fallen, lapsed, postlapsarian; animal, animalistic; **brutish, brutal**, brute; **bestial**, beastly, beastlike; Circean; coarse, gross; swinish; orgiastic; **earthy**, unspiritual, nonspiritual, material, materialistic

664 CHASTITY

NOUNS 1 **chastity, virtue**, virtuousness, honor; **purity**, cleanness, cleanliness; whiteness, snowiness; **immaculacy**, immaculateness, spotlessness, stainlessness, taintlessness, blotlessness, unspottedness, unstainedness, unblottedness, untaintedness, unblemishedness, unsoiledness, unsulliedness, undefiledness, untarnishedness; uncorruptness; sexual innocence, innocence 657

2 **decency, seemliness, propriety, decorum**, decorousness, elegance, delicacy; **modesty**, shame, pudicity, pudency

3 **continence** *or* continency; abstemiousness, abstaining, abstinence 668.2; celibacy; **virginity**, intactness, maidenhood, maidenhead; Platonic love; marital fidelity *or* faithfulness

ADJS 4 **chaste, virtuous; pure**, purehearted, pure in heart; **clean**, cleanly; **immaculate, spotless**, blotless, stainless, taintless, white, snowy, pure *or* white as driven snow; **unsoiled, unsullied, undefiled**, untarnished, unstained, unspotted, untainted, unblemished, unblotted, uncorrupt; "as chaste as Diana, "as chaste

as unsunn'd snow"—both Shakespeare,
"chaste as morning dew"—Edward
Young; sexually innocent, innocent
657.6,7

5 **decent, modest, decorous,** delicate, elegant, proper, becoming, seemly

6 **continent;** abstemious, abstinent 668.10;
celibate; virginal, **virgin,** maidenly, vestal, intact; Platonic

7 **undebauched, undissipated, undissolute,**
unwanton, unlicentious

665 UNCHASTITY

NOUNS 1 **unchastity,** unchasteness; unvirtuousness; **impurity,** uncleanness, uncleanliness, taintedness, soiledness,
sulliedness; **indecency** 666

2 **incontinence,** uncontinence; intemperance 669; unrestraint 430.3

3 **profligacy, dissoluteness, licentiousness,**
license, unbridledness, wildness, fastness, rakishness, gallantry, **libertinism,**
libertinage; **dissipation, debauchery,** debauchment; venery, wenching, whoring,
womanizing

4 **wantonness, waywardness; looseness,**
laxity, lightness, loose morals, easy
virtue, whorishness, chambering,
promiscuity, sleeping around *and*
swinging <both nonformal>

5 **lasciviousness, lechery, lecherousness,
lewdness,** bawdiness, **dirtiness,** salacity,
salaciousness, **carnality,** animality, fleshliness, **sexuality, sexiness, lust, lustfulness,** "an expense of spirit in a waste of
shame is lust in action"—Shakespeare;
obscenity 666.4; **prurience** *or* pruriency,
sexual itch, concupiscence, lickerish-
ness, libidinousness, randiness, horniness <nonformal>, lubricity, lubricious-
ness, **sensuality,** eroticism, goatishness;
satyrism, satyriasis, gynecomania; nymphomania, *furor uterinus* <L>, hysteromania, uteromania, clitoromania; erotomania, eroticomania, aphrodisiomania

6 **seduction,** seducement, **betrayal; violation,** abuse; **debauchment, defilement,**
ravishment, ravage, despoilment, fate
worse than death; priapism; defloration,
deflowering; **rape,** sexual *or* criminal assault; date *or* acquaintance rape

7 <illicit sexual intercourse> **adultery,**
criminal conversation *or* congress *or* cohabitation, extramarital *or* premarital
sex, extramarital *or* premarital relations,
extracurricular sex *or* relations <nonfor-
mal>, **fornication;** free love, free-lovism;
incest; concubinage; cuckoldry

8 **prostitution, harlotry,** whoredom, **streetwalking;** soliciting, solicitation; Mrs
Warren's profession; whoremongering,
whoremastery, pimping, pandering

9 **brothel, house of prostitution,** house of
assignation, house of joy *or* ill repute *or* ill
fame, **whorehouse,** bawdyhouse, massage
parlor, sporting house, disorderly house,
cathouse, bordello, bagnio, stew, dive,
den of vice, den *or* sink of iniquity, crib,
joint; panel house *or* den; red-light district, tenderloin, stews, street of fallen
women

10 **libertine, swinger** <nonformal>, **profligate, rake,** rakehell, rip <nonformal>,
roué, wanton, womanizer, cocksman
<nonformal>, walking phallus, de-
bauchee, rounder <old>, **wolf**
<nonformal>, woman chaser, skirt
chaser <nonformal>, gay dog, gay deceiver, gallant, philanderer, lover-boy
<nonformal>, lady-killer, Lothario, Don
Juan, Casanova

11 **lecher, satyr, goat,** old goat, **dirty old
man;** whorer *or* whoremonger <both
old>, whoremaster, whorehound
<nonformal>; Priapus; gynecomaniac;
erotomaniac, eroticomaniac, aphro-
disiomaniac

12 **seducer, betrayer,** deceiver; **debaucher,
ravisher,** ravager, violator, despoiler, de-
filer; raper, **rapist**

13 **adulterer, cheater, fornicator; adulteress,**
fornicatress, fornicatrix

14 **strumpet, trollop, wench, hussy, slut,
jade, baggage,** *cocotte* <Fr>, grisette;
tart *and* **chippy** *and* **floozy** *and* broad <all
nonformal>, bitch, drab, trull, quean,
harridan, Jezebel, wanton, whore <non-
formal>, bad woman, **loose woman,** easy
woman <nonformal>, easy lay <nonfor-
mal>, woman of easy virtue, frail sister;
pickup; nymphomaniac, nympho <non-
formal>, hysteromaniac, uteromaniac,
clitoromaniac; nymphet

15 **demimonde,** demimondaine, demirep;
courtesan, adventuress, **seductress,**
femme fatale, vampire, vamp, temptress;
hetaera, houri, harem girl, odalisque;
Jezebel, Messalina, Delilah, Thais,
Phryne, Aspasia, Lais

16 **prostitute, harlot, whore,** *fille de joie*
<Fr>, daughter of joy, call girl *and* B-girl
<both nonformal>, **scarlet woman,** un-
fortunate woman, painted woman, fallen
woman, erring sister, **streetwalker,** hustler *and* **hooker** <both nonformal>,
woman of the town, *poule* <Fr>, stew,
meretrix, Cyprian, Paphian; white slave

17 **mistress,** woman, **kept woman,** kept mistress, **paramour,** concubine, doxy, playmate, spiritual *or* unofficial wife; live-in lover <nonformal>

18 **procurer, pimp,** pander *or* panderer, *maquereau* <Fr>, mack *or* mackman, ponce <Brit nonformal>; **bawd; gigolo,** fancy man; procuress, **madam** <nonformal>; white slaver

VERBS 19 **be promiscuous,** sleep around *and* swing <both nonformal>; **debauch, wanton,** rake, chase women, womanize, whore, sow one's wild oats; **philander; dissipate** 669.6; fornicate, **cheat, commit adultery,** get a little on the side <nonformal>; grovel, wallow, wallow in the mire

20 **seduce, betray, deceive,** mislead, lead astray, lead down the garden *or* the primrose path; **debauch, ravish,** ravage, despoil, ruin; deflower, pop one's cherry <nonformal>; **defile,** soil, sully; **violate,** abuse; **rape,** force

21 **prostitute oneself,** sell *or* peddle one's ass <nonformal>, streetwalk; pimp, procure, pander

22 **cuckold;** wear horns, wear the horn

ADJS 23 **unchaste, unvirtuous,** unvirginal; **impure, unclean; indecent** 666.5; soiled, sullied, smirched, besmirched, defiled, tainted, maculate

24 **incontinent,** uncontinent; **orgiastic;** intemperate 669.7; unrestrained

25 **profligate, licentious,** unbridled, untrammeled, uninhibited, free; **dissolute, dissipated, debauched,** abandoned; **wild, fast,** gallant, gay, rakish; rakehell, rakehellish, rakehelly

26 **wanton, wayward,** Paphian; **loose,** lax, slack, loose-moraled, of loose morals, of easy virtue, easy <nonformal>, **light,** no better than she should be, whorish, chambering, **promiscuous**

27 freeloving; **adulterous,** illicit, extramarital, premarital; incestuous

28 **prostitute, prostituted, whorish, harlot,** scarlet, fallen, meretricious, streetwalking, hustling <nonformal>, on the town *or* streets, on the *pavé,* in the life

29 **lascivious, lecherous, sexy, salacious, carnal,** animal, **sexual, lustful,** ithyphallic, **hot,** horny *and* sexed-up *and* hot to trot <all nonformal>; prurient, itching, itchy <nonformal>; concupiscent, lickerish, libidinous, randy, horny <nonformal>, lubricious; **lewd, bawdy,** adult, X-rated, hard, pornographic, porno <nonformal>, **dirty, obscene** 666.9; erotic, **sensual,** fleshly; goatish, satyric, priapic, gynecomaniacal; nymphomaniacal, hys-

teromaniacal, uteromaniacal, clitoromaniacal; erotomaniacal, eroticomaniacal, aphrodisiomaniacal

666 INDECENCY

NOUNS 1 **indecency, indelicacy,** inelegance *or* inelegancy, **indecorousness,** indecorum, **impropriety** 638.1, inappropriateness, unseemliness, indiscretion, indiscreetness; **unchastity** 665

2 **immodesty,** unmodestness, impudicity; exhibitionism; **shamelessness,** unembarrassedness; **brazenness** 142.2, brassiness, pertness, forwardness, boldness, procacity, bumptiousness; **flagrancy,** notoriousness, scandal, scandalousness

3 **vulgarity** 497, **uncouthness, coarseness, crudeness, grossness,** rankness, rawness, raunchiness <nonformal>; **earthiness,** frankness; **spiciness, raciness,** saltiness

4 **obscenity, dirtiness,** bawdry, raunch <nonformal>, **ribaldry, pornography,** porno *and* porn <both nonformal>, hard *or* hard-core pornography, soft *or* soft-core pornography, salacity, **smut, dirt, filth; lewdness, bawdiness,** salaciousness, **smuttiness, foulness, filthiness,** nastiness, vileness, offensiveness; scurrility, fescenninity; Rabelaisianism; erotic art *or* literature, pornographic art *or* literature; sexploitation; blue movie *and* dirty movie *and* porno film *and* skin flick <all nonformal>, adult movie, stag film <nonformal>, X-rated movie; pornographomania, erotographomania, iconolagny, erotology; **dirty talk, scatology** 523.9

ADJS 5 **indecent, indelicate, inelegant, indecorous, improper,** inappropriate, **unseemly, unbecoming,** indiscreet

6 **immodest,** unmodest; exhibitionistic; **shameless,** unashamed, unembarrassed, unabashed, unblushing, **brazen,** brazenfaced, brassy; **forward,** bold, pert, procacious <old>, bumptious; **flagrant,** notorious, scandalous

7 **risqué,** risky, **racy,** salty, spicy, **off-color,** suggestive, scabrous

8 **vulgar, uncouth, coarse, gross,** rank, raw, broad, low, foul, gutter; **earthy,** frank, pulling no punches

9 **obscene, lewd, adult, bawdy,** ithyphallic, **ribald, pornographic, salacious,** sultry <nonformal>, lurid, **dirty, smutty,** raunchy <nonformal>, blue, smoking-room, impure, unchaste, unclean, **foul, filthy, nasty,** vile, fulsome, offensive, unprintable, unrepeatable, not fit for mixed company; scurrilous, scurrile, Fescen-

nine; **foulmouthed,** foul-tongued, foul-
spoken; Rabelaisian

667 ASCETICISM

NOUNS **1 asceticism, austerity, self-denial,**
self-abnegation, **rigor; puritanism,** eremitism, anchoritism, anchorite *or* anchoritic monasticism, monasticism, monachism; Sabbatarianism; Albigensia-
nism, Waldensianism, Catharism; Yoga;
mortification, self-mortification, maceration, flagellation; **abstinence** 668.2; belt-
tightening, fasting 515; voluntary poverty, mendicantism, Franciscanism;
Trappism

2 ascetic, puritan, Sabbatarian; Albigensian, Waldensian, Catharist; **abstainer**
668.4; anchorite, **hermit** 584.5; yogi, yogin; sannyasi, bhikshu, dervish, fakir,
flagellant, Penitente; mendicant, Franciscan, Discalced *or* barefooted Carmelite;
Trappist

VERBS **3** deny oneself; abstain, tighten one's
belt; flagellate oneself, wear a hair shirt,
make oneself miserable

ADJS **4 ascetic, austere,** self-denying, self-
abnegating, **rigorous, rigoristic; puritanical,** eremitic, anchoritic, Sabbatarian; **penitential;** Albigensian, Waldensian, Catharist; **abstinent** 668.10;
mendicant, discalced, barefoot, wedded
to poverty, Franciscan; Trappist; flagellant

668 TEMPERANCE

NOUNS **1 temperance,** temperateness, **moderation,** moderateness, sophrosyne;
golden mean, via media, *juste milieu*
<Fr>; nothing in excess, sobriety, sober-
ness, frugality, forbearance, abnegation;
renunciation, renouncement, forgoing;
denial, **self-denial;** restraint, constraint,
self-restraint; self-control, self-reining,
self-mastery, **discipline,** self-discipline

2 abstinence, abstention, abstainment, **abstemiousness,** refraining, refrainment,
avoidance, eschewal, denying *or* refusing
oneself, saying no to, passing up <nonfor-
mal>; **total abstinence, teetotalism,**
nephalism, Rechabitism; the pledge; En-
cratism, Shakerism; Pythagorism,
Pythagoreanism; sexual abstinence, celibacy 565; chastity 664; gymnosophy;
Stoicism; vegetarianism, veganism,
fruitarianism; plain living, spare diet,
simple diet; Spartan fare, Lenten fare;
fish day, Friday, banyan day; fast 515.2,3;

continence 664.3; **asceticism** 667; smoke-
out

3 prohibition, prohibitionism; Eighteenth
Amendment, Volstead Act

4 abstainer, abstinent; **teetotaler,** teeto-
talist; nephalist, Rechabite, hydropot,
water-drinker; vegetarian, vegan, fruitarian; banian, banya; gymnosophist;
Pythagorean, Pythagorist; Encratite,
Apostolici, Shaker; **ascetic** 667.2; nonsmoker, nondrinker, etc

5 prohibitionist, dry <nonformal>; Anti-
Saloon League; Women's Christian Temperance Union *or* WCTU

VERBS **6 restrain oneself,** constrain oneself,
curb oneself, hold back, **avoid excess;
limit oneself, restrict oneself; control
oneself,** control one's appetites, repress *or*
inhibit one's desires, contain oneself, discipline oneself, master oneself, exercise
self-control *or* self-restraint, keep oneself
under control, keep in *or* within bounds,
keep within compass *or* limits, know
when one has had enough, **deny** *or* refuse
oneself, **say no** *or* just say no; live plainly
or simply *or* frugally; mortify oneself,
mortify the flesh, control the fleshy lusts,
control the carnal man *or* the old Adam,
"let the passions be amenable to reason"—Cicero; eat to live, not live to eat;
eat sparingly

7 abstain, abstain from, refrain, **refrain
from, forbear, forgo,** spare, withhold,
hold back, **avoid, shun,** eschew, **pass up**
<nonformal>, **keep from,** keep *or* stand
or hold aloof from, have nothing to do
with, take no part in, have no hand in, **let
alone,** let well enough alone, let go by,
deny oneself, do without, go without,
make do without, not *or* never touch,
keep hands off

8 swear off, renounce, forswear, **give up,**
abandon, stop, discontinue; take the
pledge, get on the wagon *or* water wagon
<nonformal>; **kick** *and* kick the habit
<both nonformal>, dry out

ADJS **9 temperate, moderate,** sober, frugal, restrained, **sparing,** stinting, measured

10 abstinent, abstentious, **abstemious;** tee-
total, sworn off, on the wagon *or* water
wagon <nonformal>; nephalistic, Rechabite; Encratic, Apostolic, Shaker;
Pythagorean; sexually abstinent, celibate, chaste; Stoic; vegetarian, veganis-
tic, fruitarian; Spartan, Lenten; maigre,
meatless; **continent** 664.6; **ascetic**

11 prohibitionist, antisaloon, dry <nonfor-
mal>

ADVS **12 temperately, moderately, sparingly,** stintingly, frugally, in moderation, within compass *or* bounds

669 INTEMPERANCE

NOUNS **1 intemperance,** intemperateness, **indulgence, self-indulgence; overindulgence,** overdoing; **unrestraint,** unconstraint, indiscipline, uncontrol; **immoderation,** immoderacy, immoderateness; inordinacy, inordinateness; **excess, excessiveness,** too much, too-muchness <nonformal>; prodigality, extravagance; crapulence *or* crapulency, crapulousness; **incontinence** 665.2; **swinishness, gluttony** 672; **drunkenness** 88.1

2 dissipation, licentiousness; riotous living, free living, high living <nonformal>, fast *or* killing pace, burning the candle at both ends; **debauchery,** debauchment; **carousal** 88.5, carousing, carouse; **debauch, orgy,** saturnalia

3 dissipater, rounder <old>, free liver, high liver <nonformal>; nighthawk *and* nightowl <both nonformal>; **playboy,** partyer, partygoer, party girl

VERBS **4 indulge,** indulge oneself, indulge one's appetites, "indulge in easy vices"—Samuel Johnson, deny oneself nothing *or* not at all; **give oneself up to,** give free course to, give free rein to; live well *or* high, live high on the hog <nonformal>, live off the fat of the land; indulge in, luxuriate in, wallow in; roll in

5 overindulge, overdo, carry to excess, carry too far, go the limit, go whole hog <nonformal>, know no limits, not know when to stop, bite off more than one can chew, spread oneself too thin; dine not wisely but too well; live above *or* beyond one's means

6 dissipate, plunge into dissipation, **debauch, wanton, carouse,** run riot, live hard *or* fast, squander one's money in riotous living, burn the candle at both ends, keep up a fast *or* killing pace, sow one's wild oats, have one's fling, **party** <nonformal>, "eat, drink, and be merry"—Bible

ADJS **7 intemperate, indulgent, self-indulgent; overindulgent,** overindulging, unthrifty, unfrugal, **immoderate,** inordinate, **excessive,** too much, prodigal, extravagant, extreme, unmeasured, unlimited; crapulous, crapulent; undisciplined, uncontrolled, unbridled, unconstrained, uninhibited, **unrestrained; in-**

continent 665.24; **swinish, gluttonous** 672.6; **bibulous**

8 licentious, dissipated, riotous, dissolute, debauched; free-living, high-living <nonformal>

9 orgiastic, saturnalian, corybantic

ADVS **10 intemperately,** prodigally, **immoderately,** inordinately, excessively, **in** *or* **to excess,** to extremes, beyond all bounds *or* limits, without restraint; high, high on the hog <nonformal>

670 MODERATION

NOUNS **1 moderation,** moderateness; **restraint,** constraint, control; **judiciousness,** prudence; steadiness, evenness, balance, equilibrium, **stability** 854; **temperateness,** temperance, sobriety; self-abnegation, self-restraint, self-control, self-denial; abstinence, continence, abnegation; **mildness,** lenity, gentleness; calmness, serenity, tranquillity, repose, calm, cool <nonformal>; unexcessiveness, unextremeness, unextravagance, nothing in excess, *meden agan* <Gk>; **happy medium, golden mean,** *juste-milieu* <Fr>, middle way *or* path, *via media* <L>, balancing act <nonformal>; moderationism, **conservatism** 852.3; **nonviolence,** pacifism; impartiality, neutrality, dispassion; irenics, ecumenism

2 modulation, **abatement,** remission, **mitigation,** diminution, defusing, de-escalation, **reduction,** lessening, falling-off; **relaxation,** relaxing, slackening, **easing,** loosening, letup *and* letdown <both nonformal>; **alleviation,** assuagement, allayment, palliation, leniency, relenting, lightening, **tempering, softening,** subdual; **deadening, dulling,** damping, blunting; drugging, narcotizing, sedating, sedation; **pacification, tranquilization,** tranquilizing, mollification, demulsion, dulcification, **quieting,** quietening, lulling, **soothing, calming,** hushing

3 moderator, mitigator, modulator, stabilizer, temperer, assuager; **mediator, bridge-builder,** calming *or* restraining hand, wiser head; **alleviator,** alleviative, palliative, lenitive; **pacifier, soother,** comforter, peacemaker, pacificator, dove of peace, mollifier; **drug,** anodyne, dolorifuge, soothing syrup, **tranquilizer,** calmative; **sedative** 86.12; balm, salve; cushion, shock absorber

4 moderate, moderatist, moderationist, middle-of-the-roader, **centrist,** neutral, compromiser; **conservative** 852.4

VERBS **5 be moderate, keep within bounds,**
keep within compass; practice self-
control or self-denial, live within one's
means, live temperately, do nothing in
excess, strike a balance, strike or keep a
happy medium, seek the golden mean,
steer or preserve an even course, keep to
the middle path or way, steer or be between Scylla and Charybdis; keep the
peace, not resist, espouse or practice nonviolence, be pacifistic; not rock the boat
and not make waves or static <all nonfor-
mal>; cool it and keep one's cool <both
nonformal>, keep one's head or temper;
sober down, settle down; remit, relent;
take in sail; go out like a lamb; be conservative 852.6

6 moderate, restrain, constrain, control,
keep within bounds; modulate, mitigate,
defuse, abate, weaken, **diminish, reduce,**
de-escalate, slacken, lessen, slow down;
alleviate, assuage, allay, lay, lighten, palliate, extenuate, **temper,** attemper, lenify;
soften, subdue, tame, hold in check, keep
a tight rein, chasten, underplay, play
down, downplay, de-emphasize, tone or
tune down; turn down the volume, lower
the voice; **drug,** narcotize, sedate, tranquilize, deaden, dull, blunt, obtund, take
the edge off, take the sting or bite out;
smother, suppress, stifle; **damp, dampen,**
bank the fire, reduce the temperature,
throw cold water on, throw a wet blanket
on; sober, sober down or up; clear the air

7 calm, calm down, **stabilize, tranquilize,**
pacify, mollify, appease, dulcify; **quiet,**
hush, still, rest, compose, **lull, soothe,**
gentle, rock, cradle, rock to sleep; cool,
subdue, quell; ease, steady, smooth,
smoothen, smooth over, smooth down,
even out; keep the peace, be the dove of
peace, pour oil on troubled waters, pour
balm into

8 cushion, absorb the shock, **soften the**
blow, break the fall, deaden, damp or
dampen, soften, suppress, neutralize, offset; show pity or mercy or consideration
or sensitivity, temper the wind to the
shorn lamb

9 relax, unbend; ease, **ease up,** ease off, **let**
up, let down; abate, bate, remit, mitigate;
slacken, slack, slake, slack off, slack up;
loose, **loosen;** unbrace, unstrain, unstring

ADJS **10 moderate, temperate,** sober; **mild,**
soft, bland, **gentle,** tame; mild as milk or
mother's milk, mild as milk and water,
gentle as a lamb; nonviolent, peaceable,
peaceful, pacifistic; **judicious, prudent**

11 restrained, constrained, limited, con-

trolled, **stable,** in control, in hand; tempered, **softened,** hushed, **subdued,**
quelled, chastened

12 unexcessive, unextreme, unextravagant,
conservative; reasonable

13 equable, even, low-key or low-keyed,
cool, even-tempered, level-headed, dispassionate; tranquil, reposeful, serene,
calm 173.12

14 mitigating, assuaging, abating, **diminish-**
ing, reducing, lessening, allaying, **allevi-**
ating, relaxing, easing; tempering, **soft-**
ening, chastening, **subduing;** deadening,
dulling, blunting, damping, dampening,
cushioning

15 tranquilizing, pacifying, mollifying, appeasing; cooling-off; **calming,** lulling,
gentling, rocking, cradling, hushing, quietening, stilling; **soothing,** soothful, restful; dreamy, drowsy

16 palliative, alleviative, alleviatory, assuasive, lenitive, **calmative,** calmant, **nar-**
cotic, sedative, demulcent, anodyne; anti-
orgastic, anaphrodisiac

ADVS **17 moderately, in moderation,** re-
strainedly, subduedly, in or within reason, within bounds or compass, in balance; **temperately,** soberly, prudently, judiciously, dispassionately; composedly,
calmly, coolly, evenly, steadily, equably,
tranquilly, serenely; soothingly, conser-
vatively

671 VIOLENCE
<vehement action>

NOUNS **1 violence, vehemence, virulence,**
venom, furiousness, force, rigor, roughness, harshness, ungentleness, extremity,
impetuosity, inclemency, **severity, inten-**
sity, acuteness, **sharpness; acrimony**
17.5; fierceness, ferociousness, furiousness, viciousness, insensateness,
savagery, destructiveness, **destruction,**
vandalism; terrorism, barbarity, brutal-
ity, atrocity, inhumanity, bloodlust,
killer instinct, murderousness, malignity,
mercilessness, pitilessness, mindlessness,
animality, brutishness; **rage,** raging, **an-**
ger 152

2 turbulence, turmoil, chaos, upset, **fury,**
furor, furore <Ital>, **rage, frenzy, pas-**
sion, fanaticism, zealousness, zeal,
tempestuousness, storminess, wildness,
tumultuousness, **tumult, uproar,** racket,
cacophony, pandemonium, hubbub, **com-**
motion, disturbance, agitation, bluster,
broil, brawl, embroilment, brouhaha,
fuss, flap <Brit nonformal>, **row,**

rumpus, ruckus <nonformal>, foofaraw <nonformal>, **ferment,** fume, boil, boiling, seething, ebullition, fomentation

3 **unruliness, disorderliness,** obstreperousness, Katy-bar-the-door <nonformal>; **riot, rioting;** looting, pillaging, plundering, rapine; wilding <nonformal>; laying waste, sowing with salt, sacking; scorched earth; **attack** 459, **assault,** onslaught, battering; **rape, violation,** forcible seizure; **killing** 308, butchery, massacre, slaughter

4 **storm, tempest,** squall, line squall, **tornado, cyclone, hurricane,** tropical cyclone, typhoon, storm-center, tropical storm, eye of the storm *or* hurricane, war of the elements, "Nature's elemental din"—Thomas Campbell, "tempestuous rage, "groans of roaring wind and rain"—both Shakespeare; stormy weather, rough weather, foul weather, dirty weather; rainstorm 316.2; thunderstorm 316.3; windstorm 318.12; **snowstorm** 1022.8; **firestorm**

5 **upheaval, convulsion,** cataclysm, catastrophe, disaster; **fit,** spasm, **paroxysm,** apoplexy, stroke; climax; **earthquake,** quake, temblor, diastrophism, epicenter, shock-wave; tidal wave, *tsunami* <Japanese>

6 **outburst, outbreak, eruption,** debouchment, eructation, belch, spew; **burst,** dissilience *or* dissiliency; meltdown, atomic meltdown; **torrent,** rush, gush, spate, cascade, spurt, jet, rapids, **volcano,** volcan, burning mountain

7 **explosion, discharge, blowout,** blowup, detonation, fulmination, **blast, burst, report** 56.1; flash, flash *or* flashing point, flare, flare-up, fulguration; bang, boom 56.4; backfire

8 **concussion, shock, impact,** crunch, smash; percussion, repercussion

9 <violent person> berserk *or* berserker; **hothead,** hotspur; **devil, demon, fiend, brute,** hellhound, hellcat, hellion, hellraiser; **beast,** wild beast, tiger, dragon, mad dog, wolf, monster, mutant, savage; **rapist, mugger, killer;** Mafioso, hit man <nonformal>, contract killer, hired killer, hired gun; **fury,** virago, vixen, termagant, beldam, she-wolf, tigress, witch; firebrand, revolutionary 859.3, **terrorist,** incendiary, bomber, guerrilla

10 <nonformal terms> **goon, gorilla,** ape, knuckle dragger, muscle man, plug-ugly, shtarker, cowboy, bimbo, bozo, bruiser, hardnose, tough guy, tough, hoodlum, hood, meat-eater, gunsel, terror, holy ter-

ror, fire-eater, spitfire, tough *or* ugly customer

VERBS 11 **rage, storm, rant, rave,** roar; **rampage,** ramp, **tear,** tear around; go *or* carry on <nonformal>; come in like a lion; **destroy, wreck,** wreak havoc, ruin; sow chaos *or* disorder; **terrorize,** sow terror, vandalize, barbarize, brutalize; **riot,** loot, burn, pillage, sack, lay waste; **slaughter, butcher; rape,** violate; **attack, assault,** batter, savage, mug, maul, hammer; go for the jugular

12 **seethe, boil, fume,** foam, simmer, stew, ferment, stir, churn

13 **erupt, burst forth** *or* **out, break out, blow out** *or* **open,** eruct, belch, **vomit,** spout, spew, disgorge, **discharge,** eject, throw *or* hurl forth

14 **explode, blow up, burst,** go off, go up, blow out, blast, bust <nonformal>; **detonate,** fulminate; **touch off,** trigger, trip, set off, let off; **discharge,** fire, shoot; backfire; melt down

15 **run amok, go berserk, go on a rampage,** cut loose, run riot, run wild

ADJS 16 **violent, vehement, virulent, venomous, severe, rigorous, furious, fierce, intense,** sharp, acute, keen, cutting, splitting, piercing; **destructive;** rough, bruising, tough <nonformal>; **drastic,** extreme, outrageous, excessive, exorbitant, unconscionable, intemperate, immoderate, extravagant; acrimonious 17.14

17 **unmitigated, unsoftened, untempered,** unallayed, unsubdued, unquelled; unquenched, unextinguished, unabated; unmixed, unalloyed; **total**

18 **turbulent, tumultuous, raging, chaotic,** hellish, anarchic, **storming,** stormy, **tempestuous,** troublous, **frenzied, wild, wildeyed, frantic, furious,** infuriate, insensate, **mad,** demented, insane, raging, enraged, ravening, raving, slavering; **angry; blustering,** blustery, blusterous; **uproarious,** rip-roaring <nonformal>; pandemoniac; orgastic, orgasmic

19 **unruly, disorderly,** obstreperous; **unbridled; riotous,** wild, rampant; **terroristic,** anarchic, nihilistic, revolutionary 859.5

20 **boisterous, rampageous, rambunctious** <nonformal>, rumbustious, roisterous, wild, rollicking, **rowdy,** rough, hoody <nonformal>, harum-scarum <nonformal>; knockabout, rough-and-tumble, knock-down-and-drag-out <nonformal>

21 **savage, fierce, ferocious, vicious, murderous, cruel, atrocious, mindless, brutal,**

brutish, **bestial,** mindless, insensate, monstrous, mutant, inhuman, pitiless, ruthless, merciless, bloody, sanguinary, kill-crazy <nonformal>; malign, malignant; feral, ferine; **wild,** untamed, tameless, undomesticated, ungentle; **barbarous,** barbaric; **uncivilized,** noncivilized

22 **fiery, heated, inflamed,** flaming, scorching, hot, red-hot, white-hot; **fanatic, zealous,** totally committed, hard-core, hard-line, ardent, passionate; **hot-headed**

23 **convulsive,** cataclysmic, disastrous, upheaving; seismic; **spasmodic,** paroxysmal, spastic, jerky, herky-jerky <nonformal>; orgasmic

24 **explosive,** bursting, detonating, explosible, explodable, fulminating, fulminant, fulminatory; dissilient; **volcanic,** eruptive

ADVS 25 **violently, vehemently, virulently, venomously, rigorously, severely, fiercely, drastically; furiously,** wildly, madly, **like mad,** like fury <nonformal>, like blazes; all to pieces, with a vengeance

26 **turbulently, tumultuously,** riotously, uproariously, stormily, tempestuously, troublously, **frenziedly, frantically, furiously, ragingly, enragedly, madly;** angrily 152.33

27 **savagely, fiercely, ferociously, atrociously, viciously, murderously,** brutally *or* brutishly, mindlessly, bestially, barbarously, inhumanly, insensately, ruthlessly, pitilessly, mercilessly; **tooth and nail,** tooth and claw, *bec et ongles* <Fr>

672 GLUTTONY

NOUNS 1 **gluttony,** gluttonousness, **greed,** greediness, voraciousness, voracity, ravenousness, edacity, crapulence *or* crapulency, gulosity, rapacity, insatiability; omnivorousness; **piggishness, hoggishness,** swinishness, "swinish gluttony" — Milton; **overindulgence, overeating;** eating disorder, polyphagia, hyperphagia, bulimia, bulimia nervosa, binge-purge syndrome; **intemperance** 669

2 **epicurism, epicureanism, gourmandise;** gastronomy

3 **glutton,** greedy eater, big *or* hefty *or* husky eater <nonformal>, trencherman, trencherwoman, belly-god, gobbler, greedygut *or* greedyguts <nonformal>, gorger, **gourmand,** gourmandizer, gormand, gormandizer, guttler, cormorant;

animal, **hog** *and* **pig** *and* chow hound *and* khazer <all nonformal>

VERBS 4 **gluttonize,** gormandize, **indulge one's appetite,** live to eat; **gorge,** engorge, glut, cram, **stuff,** batten, guttle, guzzle, **devour,** raven, bolt, gobble, gulp, **wolf,** gobble *or* gulp *or* bolt *or* wolf down, eat like a horse, stuff oneself *and* hog it down *and* eat one's head off *and* fork *or* shovel it in <all nonformal>, eat one out of house and home

5 **overeat,** overgorge, **overindulge, make a pig** *or* **hog of oneself,** pig out *or* pork out *or* scarf out <nonformal>; stuff oneself

ADJS 6 **gluttonous, greedy,** voracious, ravenous, edacious, rapacious, insatiable, polyphagic, bulimic, hyperphagic, Apician; **piggish, hoggish,** swinish; crapulous, crapulent; intemperate 669.7; omnivorous, all-devouring; **gorging,** cramming, glutting, guttling, stuffing, guzzling, wolfing, bolting, **gobbling, gulping,** gluttonizing

7 overfed, overgorged, overindulged

ADVS 8 **gluttonously, greedily,** voraciously, ravenously, edaciously; **piggishly, hoggishly, swinishly**

673 LEGALITY

NOUNS 1 **legality, legitimacy, lawfulness, legitimateness, licitness,** rightfulness, validity, scope, applicability; **jurisdiction** 594; actionability, justiciability, **constitutionality,** constitutional validity; legal process, legal form, **due process;** legalism, constitutionalism; **justice** 649

2 **legalization, legitimation, legitimatization, decriminalization;** money-washing *or* -laundering; validation; authorization, sanction; legislation, enactment

3 **law,** *lex, jus* <both L>, **statute,** rubric, **canon,** institution; **ordinance; act, enactment, measure,** legislation; **rule, ruling; prescript,** prescription; **regulation,** *règlement* <Fr>, reg <nonformal>; **dictate,** dictation; form, formula, formulary, formality; standing order; bylaw; **edict, decree** 420.4; **bill**

4 **law,** legal system, system of laws, legal branch *or* specialty

5 **code, digest,** pandect, capitulary, **body of law,** corpus juris, legal code, code of laws, digest of law; **codification; civil code, penal code;** Justinian Code; Napoleonic code, *Code Napoléon* <Fr>; lawbook, statute book, compilation; Blackstone; Uniform Code of Military Justice

6 **constitution,** written constitution, unwritten constitution; constitutional amendment; Bill of Rights, constitutional guarantees; constitutional interpretation

7 **jurisprudence, law,** legal science; nomology, nomography; **forensic science,** forensic *or* legal medicine, medical jurisprudence, medico-legal medicine; forensic psychiatry; forensic *or* legal chemistry; criminology

VERBS 8 **legalize, legitimize,** legitimatize, legitimate, make legal, declare lawful, **decriminalize;** wash *or* launder money; validate; **authorize, sanction;** constitute, ordain, establish, put in force; prescribe, formulate; regulate, make a regulation; **decree; legislate, enact; enforce; litigate** 598.12, take legal action

9 **codify,** digest; compile, publish

ADJS 10 **legal, legitimate,** legit *and* kosher <both nonformal>, competent, **licit, lawful,** rightful, according to law, within the law; **actionable,** litigable, justiciable, within the scope of the law; **enforceable,** legally binding; **judicial,** juridical; **authorized, sanctioned,** valid, applicable; **constitutional;** statutory, statutable; **legislative, lawmaking;** lawlike; **just** 649.8

11 jurisprudent, jurisprudential; **legalistic; forensic;** nomistic, nomothetic; criminological

ADVS 12 **legally, legitimately, licitly, lawfully,** by law, *de jure* <L>, in the eyes of the law

674 ILLEGALITY

NOUNS 1 **illegality, unlawfulness, illicitness, lawlessness,** wrongfulness; unauthorization, impermissibility, **unconstitutionality;** legal *or* technical flaw, legal irregularity; **outlawry; anarchy,** collapse *or* breakdown *or* paralysis of authority, anomie; illicit business 732

2 **illegitimacy, illegitimateness,** illegitimation; **bastardy,** bastardism; bend *or* bar sinister, baton

3 **lawbreaking, violation,** breach *or* violation of law, infringement, contravention, infraction, **transgression,** trespass, trespassing; **criminality,** criminalism, habitual criminality, delinquency; flouting *or* making a mockery of the law

4 **offense, wrong,** illegality; **violation** 435.2; **wrongdoing** 655; much to answer for; **crime, felony; misdemeanor;** tort; delict, delictum

VERBS 5 **break** *or* **violate the law,** breach the law, infringe, contravene, infract, violate 435.4, **transgress, trespass,** disobey the law, offend against the law, flout the law, make a mockery of the law, fly in the face of the law, set the law at defiance, snap one's fingers at the law, set the law at naught, circumvent the law, disregard the law, **take the law into one's own hands,** twist *or* torture the law to one's own ends *or* purposes; commit a crime; have much to answer for; live outside the law

ADJS 6 **illegal, unlawful, illegitimate, illicit,** nonlicit, nonlegal, lawless, wrongful, fraudulent, creative <nonformal>, **against the law; unauthorized,** unallowed, impermissible, unwarranted, unwarrantable, unofficial; unstatutory; **unconstitutional,** nonconstitutional; flawed, irregular, contrary to law; actionable, chargeable, justiciable, litigable; triable, punishable; **criminal, felonious; outlaw, outlawed; contraband,** bootleg, black-market; under-the-table, under-the-counter; unregulated, unchartered; anarchic, anarchistic, anomic

7 **illegitimate, spurious,** false; **bastard,** misbegot, **misbegotten,** miscreated, gotten on the wrong side of the blanket, baseborn, born out of wedlock, without benefit of clergy

ADVS 8 **illegally, unlawfully, illegitimately, illicitly;** impermissibly; criminally, feloniously; contrary to law, in violation of law

675 RELIGIONS, CULTS, SECTS

NOUNS 1 **religion,** religious belief *or* faith, **belief, faith,** teaching, doctrine, creed, credo, theology 676, orthodoxy 687; system of beliefs; tradition

2 **cult, ism;** cultism; **mystique**

3 **sect** <see list>, sectarism, religious order, **denomination, persuasion,** faction, **church,** communion, community, group, fellowship, affiliation, order, school, party, society, body, organization; branch, variety, version, segment; offshoot; **schism,** division

4 **sectarianism,** sectarism, **denominationalism,** partisanism, the clash of creeds; schismatism; syncretism, eclecticism

5 **theism; monotheism; polytheism,** multitheism, myriotheism; **ditheism,** dyotheism, dualism; **tritheism;** tetratheism; **pantheism,** cosmotheism, theopantism, acosmism; physitheism, psychotheism,

animotheism; physicomorphism; hylotheism; anthropotheism, anthropomorphism; anthropolatry; allotheism; monolatry, henotheism; autotheism; zootheism, theriotheism; **deism**

6 **animism, animistic religion** or cult; voodooism, voodoo, hoodoo, wanga, juju, jujuism, obeah, obeahism; shamanism; fetishism, totemism; nature worship, naturism; primitive religion

7 **Christianity** <see list>, Christianism, Christendom; Latin or Roman or Western Christianity; Eastern or Orthodox Christianity; Protestant Christianity; Judeo-Christian religion or tradition or belief; fundamentalism, Christian fundamentalism

8 **Catholicism,** Catholicity; **Roman Catholicism,** Romanism, Rome; papalism; popery and popeism and papism and papistry <all nonformal>; ultramontanism; Catholic Church, **Roman Catholic Church,** Church of Rome; Eastern Rites, Uniate Rites, Uniatism, Alexandrian or Antiochian or Byzantine Rite

9 Orthodoxy; **Eastern Orthodox Church, Holy Orthodox Catholic Apostolic Church,** Greek Orthodox Church, Russian Orthodox Church; patriarchate of Constantinople, patriarchate of Antioch, patriarchate of Alexandria, patriarchate of Jerusalem

10 **Protestantism,** Reform, Reformationism; Evangelicalism; Zwinglianism; dissent 333; apostasy 363.2; new theology

11 **Anglicanism;** High-Churchism, Low-Churchism; Anglo-Catholicism; Church of England, Established Church; High Church, Low Church; Broad Church, Free Church

12 **Judaism;** Hebraism, Hebrewism; Israelitism; Orthodox Judaism, Conservative Judaism, Reform Judaism, Reconstructionism; Hasidism; rabbinism, Talmudism; Pharisaism; Sadduceeism; Karaism or Karaitism

13 **Islam, Muslimism,** Islamism, Moslemism, Muhammadanism, Mohammedanism; Sufism, Wahabiism, Sunnism, Shiism; Black Muslimism; Muslim fundamentalism, militant Muslimism

14 **Christian Science;** New Thought, Higher Thought, Practical Christianity, Mental Science, Divine Science Church

15 **religionist,** religioner; **believer** 692.4; cultist, ist

16 **theist; monotheist; polytheist,** multitheist, myriotheist; ditheist, dualist; tritheist; tetratheist; **pantheist,** cos-

motheist; psychotheist; physitheist; hylotheist; anthropotheist; anthropolater; allotheist; henotheist; autotheist; zootheist, theriotheist; **deist**

17 **Christian,** Nazarene, Nazarite; Christian sectarian

18 **sectarian,** sectary, **denominationalist,** factionist, schismatic

19 **Catholic,** Roman Catholic or RC <nonformal>, Romanist, papist <nonformal>; ultramontane; Eastern-Rite Christian, Uniate

20 **Protestant,** non-Catholic, Reformed believer, Reformationist, Evangelical; Zwinglian; dissenter 333.3; apostate 363.5

21 **Jew, Hebrew,** Judaist, Israelite; Orthodox or Conservative or Reform Jew, Reconstructionist; Hasid; Rabbinist, Talmudist; Pharisee; Sadducee; Karaite

22 **Mormon,** Latter-day Saint, Josephite <nonformal>

23 **Muslim,** Muhammadan and Mohammedan <both nonformal>, Mussulman, Moslem, Islamite; Shiite, Shia, Sectary; Motazilite, Sunni, Sunnite, Wahabi, Sufi; dervish; abdal; Black Muslim; Muslim fundamentalist or militant

24 **Christian Scientist,** Christian Science Practitioner

ADJS 25 **religious, theistic; monotheistic; polytheistic,** ditheistic, tritheistic; **pantheistic,** cosmotheistic; physicomorphic; anthropomorphic, anthropotheistic; **deistic**

26 **sectarian,** sectary, **denominational,** schismatic, schismatical

27 **nonsectarian, undenominational, nondenominational;** interdenominational

28 **Protestant,** non-Catholic, Reformed, Reformationist, Evangelical; Lutheran, Calvinist, Calvinistic, Zwinglian; dissentient 333.6; apostate 363.11

29 **Catholic; Roman Catholic** or RC <nonformal>, Roman; Romish and popish and papish and papist and papistical <all nonformal>; ultramontane

30 **Jewish, Hebrew,** Judaic, Judaical, Israelite, Israelitic, Israelitish; Orthodox, Conservative, Reform, Reconstructionist; Hasidic

31 **Muslim, Islamic,** Moslem, Islamitic, Islamistic, Muhammadan, Mohammedan; Shiite, Sunni, Sunnite

32 <Oriental> Buddhist, Buddhistic; Brahmanic, Brahmanistic; Vedic, Vedantic; Confucian, Confucianist; Taoist, Taoistic, Shintoist, Shintoistic; Zoroastrian, Zarathustrian, Parsee

33 religions and sects

anthroposophy
Babism or Babi
Bahhá'í or Bahaism
Brahmanism
Brahmoism
Buddhism
Ch'an Buddhism
Chen Yen Buddhism
Ching-t'u Buddhism
Christianity
Confucianism
Conservative Judaism
Dakshincharin Hinduism
Eleusinianism
Ethical Culture
Gnosticism
gymnosophy
Hinduism
Islam
Jainism
Jodo Buddhism
Judaism
Lamaism
Lingayat Hinduism
Magianism
Mahayana Buddhism
Mandaeism
Mithraism
Nichiren Buddhism
Orphism
Orthodox Judaism
Parsiism or Parsism
Reconstructionism

Reform Judaism
reincarnationism
Rosicrucianism
Sabaeanism
Saivism
Shaivite Hinduism
Shiite Muslimism
Shin Buddhism
Shingon Buddhism
Shinto or Shintoism
Sikhism
Soka Gakkai Buddhism
Sufism
Sunni Muslimism
Taoism
Tendai Buddhism
Theosophy
Theravada or Hinayana Buddhism
T'ien-t'ai Buddhism
Unitarianism
Vaishnavite Hinduism
Vajrayana Buddhism
Vamacharin Hinduism
Vedanta or Vedantism
Wahabiism
Yoga or Yogism
Zen or Zen Buddhism
Zoroastrianism or Zoroastrism

34 Christian denominations

Adventism or Second Adventism
Amish
Anabaptism
Anglicanism
Anglo-Catholicism
antinomianism
Arianism
Athanasianism
Boehmenism
Calvinism
Catholicism
Christian Science
Congregationalism
Eastern Orthodox Christianity
Episcopalianism
Erastianism
homoiousianism
homoousianism
Jansenism
latitudinarianism
Laudism or Laudianism
Liberal Catholicism
Lutheranism

Mennonitism
Methodism
Moral Rearmament
Mormonism
New Thought
Origenism
Orthodox Christianity
Oxford Movement
Practical Christianity
Presbyterianism
Puritanism
Puseyism
Quakerism
quietism
Roman Catholicism
Rosicrucianism
Sabellianism
Salvation Army
Socinianism
Stundism
Swedenborgianism
Tractarianism
Trinitarianism
Ubiquitarianism
Uniatism

Unitarianism
Universalism

Wesleyanism or Wesleyism

676 THEOLOGY

NOUNS **1 theology** <see list>, **religion, divinity;** theologism; doctrinism, doctrinalism

2 doctrine, dogma 952.2; **creed,** credo; credenda, articles of religion or faith; Apostles' Creed, Nicene Creed, Athanasian Creed; Catechism

3 theologian, theologist, theologizer, theologer, theologician; **divine;** scholastic, schoolman; theological or divinity student, theological, theologue; canonist

ADJS **4 theological, religious; divine;** doctrinal, doctrinary; canonic or canonical; physicotheological

5 kinds and branches of theology

apologetics
canonics
Christology
crisis theology
doctrinal theology
dogmatics or dogmatic theology
eschatology
existential theology
feminist theology
hagiology
hierography or hagiography
hierology
liberation theology
Mercersburg theology
natural or rational theology
neoorthodoxy or neoorthodox theology

nonformalogical theology
patristics or patristic theology
phenomenological theology
philosophical theology
physicotheology
rationalism
school theology or scholastic theology
secularism
soteriology or Christology or logos theology or logos Christology
systematics or systematic theology
theological hermeneutics

677 DEITY

NOUNS **1 deity, divinity,** divineness; **godliness,** godlikeness; **godhood,** godhead, godship, Fatherhood; heavenliness; **transcendence**

2 God; Jehovah; *Yahweh, Adonai, Elohim* <all Heb>; **Allah;** the Great Spirit, Manitou

3 <Hinduism> **Brahma,** the Supreme Soul, the Essence of the Universe; **Atman,** the Universal Ego or Self; **Vishnu,** the Preserver; **Siva,** the Destroyer, the Regenerator

4 <Buddhism> **Buddha,** the Blessed One, the Teacher, **the Lord Buddha,** bodhisattva

5 <Zoroastrianism> **Ahura Mazda,** Ormazd, Mazda, the Lord of Wisdom, the

Wise Lord, the Wise One, the King of Light, the Guardian of Mankind

6 <Christian Science> **Mind, Divine Mind,** Spirit, Soul Principle, Life, Truth, Love

7 **world spirit** or **soul,** *anima mundi* <L>, universal life force, world principle, **world-self,** universal ego or self, infinite spirit, supreme soul or principle, **oversoul, nous, Logos,** World Reason

8 **Nature, Mother Nature,** Dame Nature, Natura, "Beldame Nature"—Milton

9 **Godhead, Trinity;** Trimurti, Hindu trinity or triad

10 **Christ**

11 **the Word, Logos,** the Word Made Flesh, **the Incarnation,** the Hypostatic Union

12 God the Holy Ghost, **the Holy Ghost, the Holy Spirit,** the Spirit of God, the Spirit of Truth, the Paraclete, the Comforter, the Consoler, the Intercessor, the Dove

13 <divine functions> creation, preservation, dispensation; **providence, divine providence,** dealings or dispensations or visitations of providence

14 <functions of Christ> salvation, redemption; atonement, propitiation; mediation, intercession; judgment

15 <functions of the Holy Ghost> inspiration, unction, regeneration, sanctification, comfort, consolation, grace, witness

ADJS **16 divine,** heavenly, celestial, empyrean; **godly, godlike** 692.9; **transcendent,** superhuman, supernatural; self-existent; Christly, Christlike, redemptive, salvational, propitiative, propitiatory, mediative, mediatory, intercessive, intercessional; incarnate, incarnated, made flesh; messianic

17 **almighty, omnipotent,** all-powerful; creating, creative, making, shaping; **omniscient,** all-wise, all-knowing, allseeing; **infinite,** boundless, limitless, unbounded, unlimited, undefined, omnipresent, ubiquitous; eternal, everlasting, timeless, perpetual, immortal, permanent; one; immutable, unchanging, changeless, eternally the same; supreme, sovereign, highest; holy, hallowed, sacred, numinous; glorious, radiant, luminous; majestic; good, just, loving, merciful; triune, tripersonal, three-personed, three-in-one

678 MYTHICAL AND POLYTHEISTIC GODS AND SPIRITS

NOUNS **1 the gods,** the immortals; the major deities, the greater gods, *di majores* <L>; the minor deities, the lesser gods, *di minores* <L>; pantheon; theogony; **spirits,** animistic spirit or powers, manitou, huaca, nagual, mana, pokunt, tamanoas, wakan, zemi

2 **god,** *deus* <L>; **deity, divinity,** immortal, heathen god, pagan deity or divinity; **goddess,** *dea* <L>; deva, devi, the shining ones; **idol,** false god, devil-god

3 godling, godlet, godkin; **demigod,** halfgod, hero; cult figure; demigoddess, heroine

4 **god; goddesses; Greek and Roman deities** <see list>; **Norse and Germanic deities** <see list>; **Celtic deities** <see list>; **Hindu deities** <see list>; **avatars of Vishnu; Egyptian deities** <see list>; **Semitic deities; Chinese deities; Japanese deities; specialized** or **tutelary deities** <see list>

5 **spirit,** intelligence, supernatural being; **genius,** daemon, demon, atua; **specter** 987; **evil spirits** 680

6 **elemental,** elemental spirit; sylph, spirit of the air; gnome, spirit of the earth, earth-spirit; salamander, fire-spirit; undine, water spirit, water-sprite

7 **fairyfolk,** elfenfolk, shee or sidhe <Ir>, **the little people** or **men,** the good folk or people, denizens of the air; **fairyland,** faerie

8 **fairy, sprite, fay,** fairy man or woman; **elf, brownie, pixie, gremlin,** ouphe, hob, cluricaune, puca or pooka or pwca, kobold, nisse, peri; **imp, goblin** 680.8; **gnome,** dwarf; **sylph,** sylphid; **banshee; leprechaun;** fairy queen; Ariel, Mab, Oberon, Puck, Titania, Béfind, Corrigan, Finnbeara

9 **nymph;** nymphet, nymphlin; **dryad,** hamadryad, wood nymph; vila or willi; tree nymph; oread, mountain nymph; limoniad, meadow or flower nymph; Napaea, glen nymph; Hyades; Pleiades, Atlantides

10 **water god, water spirit** or **sprite** or **nymph;** undine, nix, nixie, kelpie; **naiad,** limniad, fresh-water nymph; Oceanid, Nereid, sea nymph, ocean nymph, **mermaid,** sea-maid, sea-maiden, siren; Thetis; **merman,** man fish; **Neptune,** "the old man of the sea"—Homer; Oceanus, Poseidon, Triton; Davy Jones, Davy

11 **forest god, sylvan deity,** vegetation spirit or daemon, field spirit, fertility god, corn spirit, **faun, satyr,** silenus, panisc, paniscus, panisca; **Pan,** Faunus; Cailleac; Priapus; Vitharr or Vidar, the goat god; Jack-in-the-green, Green Man

12 **familiar spirit**, familiar; **genius, good genius**, daemon, demon, *numen* <L>, totem; **guardian, guardian spirit, guardian angel**, angel, good angel, ministering angel, **fairy godmother**; guide, control, attendant godling *or* spirit, invisible helper, special providence; **tutelary** *or* **tutelar god** *or* **genius** *or* **spirit**; *genius tutelae, genius loci, genius domus, genius familiae* <all L>; **household gods**; *lares familiaris, lares praestites, lares compitales, lares viales, lares permarini* <all L>; penates, lares and penates; ancestral spirits; manes, pitris

13 **Santa Claus**, Santa, Saint Nicholas, Saint Nick, Kriss Kringle, Father Christmas

14 **mythology**, mythicism; **legend, lore, folklore**, mythical lore; fairy lore, fairyism; mythologist

ADJS 15 **mythic, mythical, mythological; fabulous, legendary;** folkloric

16 **divine, godlike**

17 **fairy**, faery, **fairylike**, fairyish, fay; sylphine, sylphish, sylphy, sylphidine, sylphlike; **elfin**, elfish, elflike; gnomish, gnomelike; pixieish

18 nymphic, nymphal, nymphean, nymphlike

19 **Greek and Roman deities**

Apollo *or* Apollon *or* Phoebus *or* Phoebus Apollo	Mars *or* Ares Mercury *or* Hermes Mithras
Ate	Momus
Athena *or* Minerva *or* Pallas Athena	Neptune *or* Poseidon Nike
Bacchus *or* Dionysus	Olympic gods *or* Olympians
Cronus	
Cupid *or* Amor *or* Eros	Persephone *or* Proserpina *or* Proserpine
Cybele *or* Agdistis *or* Great Mother *or* Magna Mater *or* Mater Turrita	Pluto *or* Hades *or* Dis *or* Orcus Rhea *or* Ops
Demeter *or* Ceres	Saturn Venus *or* Aphrodite
Despoina	Vesta
Diana *or* Artemis	Vulcan *or* Hephaestus
Ge *or* Gaea *or* Gaia *or* Tellus	Zeus *or* Jupiter *or* Jove *or* Jupiter Fulgur *or* Fulminator *or* Jupiter Tonans *or* Jupiter Pluvius *or* Jupiter Optimus Maximus *or* Jupiter Fidius
Helios *or* Hyperion *or* Phaëthon	
Hestia	
Hymen	
Juno *or* Hera *or* Here	
Kore *or* Cora	

20 **Norse and Germanic deities**

Aesir	Forseti
Balder	Frey *or* Freyr
Bor	Freya *or* Freyja
Bori	Frigg *or* Frigga
Bragi	Heimdall
Hel	Sigyn
Höder *or* Hödr	Thor *or* Donar
Hoenir	Tyr *or* Tiu
Ing	Ull *or* Ullr
Ithunn *or* Idun	Vali
Loki	Vanir
Nanna	Vitharr *or* Vidar
Nerthus *or* Hertha	Völund
Njorth *or* Njord	Wayland
Odin *or* Woden *or* Wotan	Weland Wyrd
Reimthursen	Ymir
Sif	

21 **Celtic deities**

Aine	Dôn
Amaethon	Dylan
Angus Og	Epona
Arawn	Goibniu
Arianrhod	Lir
Blodenwedd	Llew Llaw Gyffes
Bóann	Lug
Bodb	Macha
Brigit	Morrigan
Dagda	Neman
Danu	

22 **Hindu deities**

Aditi	Ka
Agni	Kala
Aryaman	Kali
Asapurna	Kama
Asvins	Kamsa
Avalokita *or* Avalokitesvara	Karttikeya Lakshmi
Bhaga	Marut
Bhairava	Mitra
Bhairavi	Parjanya
Bhudevi	Parvati
Brahma	Pushan
Brihaspati	Rahu
Chandi	Rhibhus
Chitragupta	Rudra
Daksha	Sarasvati
Devaki	Savitar
Devi	Sita
Dharma	Siva
Dharti Mai	Soma
Durga	Surya
Dyaus	Uma
Ganesa *or* Ganesh *or* Ganesha *or* Ganapati	Ushas Vaja
Garuda	Varuna
Gauri	Varuni
Hanuman	Vayu
Himavat	Vibhu
Indra	Vishnu
Jaganmati	Yama

23 **Egyptian deities**

Anubis	Min
Bast	Neph
Horus	Nephthys
Isis	Nut
Khem	Osiris

Ptah	Set
Ra *or* Amen-Ra	Thoth

24 specialized deities, tutelary deities

agricultural deities 1067.4	gods of lightning 1024.17
deities of fertility 889.5	gods of marriage 563.13
deities of justice 649.5	love deities 104.8
deities of the house- hold 228.30	moon goddesses 1070.12
deities of the nether world 682.5	Muses 985.2
earth goddesses 1070.10	music Muses 710.22 poetry Muses 720.10
Fates 963.3	rain gods 316.6
forest gods 678.11	sea gods 240.4
goddesses of discord 456.1	sun gods 1070.14 thunder gods 56.5
gods of commerce 731.10	war gods 458.13 water gods 678.10
gods of evil 680.5	wind gods 318.3

679 ANGEL, SAINT

NOUNS **1 angel,** celestial, celestial *or* heavenly being; messenger of God; **seraph,** seraphim <pl>, angel of love; **cherub, cherubim** <pl>, angel of light; principality, archangel; recording angel; **saint,** beatified soul, canonized mortal; patron saint; martyr; redeemed *or* saved soul, soul in glory

2 heavenly host, host of heaven, choir invisible, angelic host, heavenly hierarchy, Sons of God, ministering spirits; Amesha Spentas

3 <celestial hierarchy of Pseudo-Dionysius> seraphim, cherubim, thrones; dominations *or* dominions, virtues, powers; principalities, archangels, angels; angelology

4 Azrael, angel of death, death's bright angel; Abdiel, Chamuel, Gabriel, Jophiel, Michael, Raphael, Uriel, Zadkiel

5 the Madonna; the Immaculate Conception; Mariology; Mariolatry

ADJS **6 angelic, seraphic, cherubic; heavenly, celestial;** archangelic; **saintly, sainted,** beatified, canonized; martyred; saved, redeemed, glorified, in glory

680 EVIL SPIRITS

NOUNS **1 evil spirits, demons, demonkind,** powers of darkness, spirits of the air, host of hell, hellish host, hellspawn, denizens of hell, inhabitants of Pandemonium, souls in hell, damned spirits, lost souls, the lost, the damned

2 devil, *diable* <Fr>, *diablo* <Sp>, *diabolus* <L>, deil <Scots>, *Teufel* <Ger>

3 Satan <see list>, Satanas

4 Beelzebub, Belial, Eblis, Azazel, Ahriman *or* Angra Mainyu; Mephistopheles, Mephisto; Shaitan, Sammael, Asmodeus; Abaddon, Apollyon; Lilith; Aeshma, Pisacha, Putana, Ravana

5 <gods of evil> Set, Typhon, Loki; Nemesis; gods of the nether world

6 demon, fiend, fiend from hell, **devil,** Satan, daeva, rakshasa, dybbuk, shedu, gyre <Scots>, bad *or* evil *or* unclean spirit; **hellion** <nonformal>, hellhound, hellkite <old>, she-devil; cacodemon, incubus, succubus; **jinni,** genie, genius, jinniyeh, afreet; evil genius; barghest; **ghoul,** lamia, Lilith, yogini, Baba Yaga, **vampire,** the undead

7 imp, pixie, sprite, elf, puck, kobold, *diablotin* <Fr>, tokoloshe, poltergeist, **gremlin,** Dingbelle, Fifinella, **bad fairy,** bad peri; little *or* young devil, devilkin, deviling; erlking; Puck, Robin Goodfellow, Hob, Hobgoblin

8 goblin, hobgoblin, hob, ouphe

9 bugbear, bugaboo, bogey, bogle, boggart; **booger, bugger,** bug <old>, **booger-man, bogeyman, boogeyman;** bête noire, fee-faw-fum, Mumbo Jumbo

10 Fury, avenging spirit; the Furies, the Erinyes, the Eumenides, the Dirae; Alecto, Megaera, Tisiphone

11 changeling, elf child; shape-shifter

12 werefolk, were-animals; werewolf, lycanthrope, *loup-garou* <Fr>; werejaguar, jaguar-man, uturuncu; wereass, werebear, werecalf, werefox, werehyena, wereleopard, weretiger, werelion, wereboar, werecrocodile, werecat, werehare

13 devilishness, demonishness, **fiendishness;** devilship, devildom; horns, the cloven hoof, the Devil's pitchfork

14 Satanism, diabolism, devil-worship, **demonism, devilry, diablerie, demonry;** demonomy, demonianism; black magic; Black Mass; sorcery 690; demonolatry, demon *or* devil *or* chthonian worship; demonomancy; demonology, diabololology *or* diabology, demonography, devil lore

15 Satanist, Satan-worshiper, diabolist, devil-worshiper, **demonist; demonomist,** demoniast; demonologist, demonologer; demonolater, chthonian, demon worshiper; sorcerer 690.5

VERBS **16 demonize, devilize,** diabolize; possess, **obsess; bewitch,** bedevil

ADJS **17 demoniac** *or* **demoniacal,** demonic *or* demonical, demonish, demonlike; **devilish,** devil-like; **satanic, diabolic, diabol-**

ical; **hellish** 682.8; **fiendish**, fiendlike;
ghoulish, ogreish; foul, unclean, damned;
inhuman

18 **impish, puckish, elfish**, elvish; mischievous 322.6

19 **designations of Satan**

His Satanic Majesty	the Author or Father
Lucifer	of Evil
Old or Auld Clootie	the Common Enemy
<Scots nonfor-	the Demon
mal>	the Deuce <nonfor-
Old Bendy <nonfor-	mal>
mal>	the Devil Incarnate
Old Gooseberry	the Dickens <nonfor-
<nonformal>	mal>
Old Harry <nonfor-	the Evil One
mal>	the Evil Spirit
Old Horny <nonfor-	the Father of Lies
mal>	the Fiend
Old Ned <nonfor-	the Foul Fiend
mal>	the Old Enemy
Old Nick <nonfor-	the Old Gentleman
mal>	<nonformal>
Old Poker <nonfor-	the Old Serpent
mal>	the Prince of the
Old Scratch <nonfor-	Devils
mal>	the Prince of the
the Adversary	power of the air
the Angel or Prince of	the Prince of this
darkness	world
the Angel of the bot-	the serpent
tomless pit	the Tempter
the Arch-fiend	the Wicked One
the archenemy	

681 HEAVEN
<abode of the deity and blessed dead>

NOUNS 1 **Heaven** <see list>; "my Father's house"—Bible, "God's residence"—Emily Dickinson, "mansions in the sky"—Isaac Watts, "the bosom of our rest"—Cardinal Newman, "the treasury of everlasting joy"—Shakespeare, "the great world of light, that lies behind all human destinies"—Longfellow

2 **the hereafter**, the afterworld, the afterlife 838.2, life after death

3 Holy City, **Zion**, New Jerusalem, Heavenly or Celestial City, City Celestial, Heavenly City of God, City of God, *Civitas Dei* <L>, "heaven's high city"—Francis Quarles

4 **heaven of heavens, seventh heaven**, the empyrean, throne of God, God's throne, celestial throne, the great white throne

5 <Christian Science> bliss, harmony, spirituality, the reign of Spirit, the atmosphere of Soul

6 <Mormon> celestial kingdom, terrestrial kingdom, telestial kingdom

7 <Muslim> Alfardaws, Assama; Falak al aflak

8 <Hindu, Buddhist, and Theosophical> nirvana; Buddha-field; devaloka, land of the gods; kamavachara, kamaloka; devachan; samadhi

9 <mythological> Olympus, Mount Olympus; Elysium, Elysian fields; fields of Aalu; Islands or Isles of the Blessed, Happy Isles, Fortunate Isles or Islands; Avalon; garden of the Gods, garden of the Hesperides, Bower of Bliss; Tir-na-n'Og, Annwfn

10 <Norse> Valhalla, Asgard, Fensalir, Glathsheim, Vingolf, Valaskjalf, Hlithskjalf, Thruthvang or Thruthheim, Bilskirnir, Ydalir, Sökkvabekk, Breithablik, Folkvang, Sessrymnir, Noatun, Thrymheim, Glitnir, Himinbjorg, Vithi

11 <removal to heaven> **apotheosis, resurrection, translation,** gathering, **ascension,** the Ascension; **assumption**, the Assumption; removal to Abraham's bosom

ADJS 12 **heavenly,** heavenish; **paradisal, paradisaic, paradisaical,** paradisiac, paradisiacal, paradisic, paradisical; **celestial,** supernal, ethereal; **unearthly,** unworldly; **otherworldly,** extraterrestrial, extramundane, transmundane, transcendental; Elysian, Olympian; blessed, beatified, beatific or beatifical, glorified, in glory; from on high

ADVS 13 **celestially,** paradisally, supernally, ethereally; in heaven, in Abraham's bosom, *in sinu Abraham* <L>, on high, among the blest, in glory

14 **designations of Heaven**

a better place	Land of the Leal
abode of the	<Scots>
blessed	my Father's house
Abraham's bosom	Paradise
better world	the happy land
Beulah	the heavenly king-
Beulah Land	dom
eternal home	the kingdom of
eternity	glory
glory	the kingdom of
God's kingdom	God
God's presence	the kingdom of
happy hunting	heaven
ground	the otherworld
heaven above	the place up there
high heaven	the presence of
inheritance of	God
the saints in	the Promised
light	Land
kingdom come	the realm of light
<nonformal>	the world above

682 HELL

NOUNS **1 hell, Hades,** Sheol, Gehenna, Tophet, Abaddon, Naraka, jahannan, avichi, **perdition,** Pandemonium, **inferno,** the pit, **the bottomless pit,** the abyss, "a vast, unbottom'd, boundless pit"—Robert Burns, **nether world,** lower world, underworld, infernal regions, abode *or* world of the dead, abode of the damned, place of torment, the grave, shades below; **purgatory; limbo**

2 hellfire, fire and brimstone, lake of fire and brimstone, everlasting fire *or* torment, "the fire that never shall be quenched"—Bible

3 <mythological> **Hades,** Orcus, Tartarus, Avernus, Acheron, pit of Acheron; Amenti, Aralu; Hel, Niflhel, Niflheim, Naströnd

4 <rivers of Hades> Styx, Stygian creek; Acheron, River of Woe; Cocytus, River of Wailing; Phlegethon, Pyriphlegethon, River of Fire; Lethe, River of Forgetfulness

5 <deities of the nether world> Pluto, Orcus, Hades *or* Aides *or* Aidoneus, Dis *or* Dis pater, Rhadamanthus, Erebus, Charon, Cerberus, Minos; Osiris; Persephone, Proserpine, Proserpina, Persephassa, Despoina, Kore *or* Cora; Hel, Loki; Satan 680.3

VERBS **6 damn,** doom, send *or* consign to hell, cast into hell, doom to perdition, condemn to hell *or* eternal punishment

7 go to hell *or* to the devil, be damned, go the other way *or* to the other place <nonformal>

ADJS **8 hellish, infernal,** sulfurous, brimstone, fire-and-brimstone; chthonic, chthonian; pandemonic, pandemoniac; devilish; Plutonic, Plutonian; Tartarean; Stygian; Lethean; Acherontic; purgatorial, hellborn

ADVS **9 hellishly, infernally,** in hell, in hellfire, below, in torment

683 SCRIPTURE

NOUNS **1 scripture, scriptures, sacred writings** *or* **texts, bible;** canonical writings *or* books, sacred canon

2 Bible, Holy Bible, Scripture, the Scriptures, Holy Scripture, Holy Writ, the Book, the Good Book, the Book of Books, the Word, the Word of God; Vulgate, Septuagint, Douay Bible, Authorized *or* King James Version, Revised Version, American Revised Version; Revised Standard Version; Jerusalem Bible; Testament; canon

3 Old Testament, Tenach; Hexateuch, Octateuch; Pentateuch, Chumash, Five Books of Moses, **Torah,** the Law, the Jewish *or* Mosaic Law, Law of Moses; the Prophets, Nebiim, Major *or* Minor Prophets; the Writings, Hagiographa, Ketubim; Apocrypha, noncanonical writings

4 New Testament; Gospels, Evangels, the Gospel, Good News, Good *or* Glad Tidings; Synoptic Gospels, Epistles, Pauline Epistles, Catholic Epistles, Johannine Epistles; Acts, Acts of the Apostles; Apocalypse, Revelation

5 Talmud, Mishnah, Gemara; Masorah

6 Koran, Alkoran *or* Alcoran; Avesta, **Zend-Avesta;** Granth, Adigranth; Tripitaka, agama; Tao Tê Ching; Analects of Confucius; the Eddas; Arcana Caelestia; **Book of Mormon;** Science and Health with Key to the Scriptures

7 <Hindu> **the Vedas, Veda,** Rig-Veda, Yajur-Veda, Sama-Veda, Atharva-Veda, sruti; Brahmana, Upanishad, Aranyaka; Samhita; shastra, Smriti, Purana, Tantra, Agama; Bhagavad-Gita

8 <Buddhist> Vinaya Pitaka, Sutta Pitaka, Abhidamma Pitaka; Dhammapada, Jataka; The Diamond-Cutter, The Lotus of the True Law, Prajna-Paramita Sutra, Pure Land Sutras

9 revelation, divine revelation; inspiration, afflatus, divine inspiration; theopneusty, theopneustia; theophany, theophania, epiphany; **mysticism,** direct *or* immediate intuition *or* communication, mystical experience, mystical intuition, contemplation, ecstasy; **prophecy,** prophetic revelation, apocalypse

ADJS **10 scriptural, Biblical,** Old-Testament, New-Testament, Gospel, Mosaic, Yahwist, Yahwistic, Elohist; **revealed, revelational;** prophetic, apocalyptic, apocalyptical; **inspired,** theopneustic; evangelic, evangelical, evangelistic, gospel; apostolic, apostolical; textual, textuary; canonical

11 Talmudic, Mishnaic, Gemaric, Masoretic; rabbinic

12 epiphanic, mystic, mystical

13 Koranic; Avestan; Eddic; Mormon

14 Vedic; tantrist

684 PROPHETS, RELIGIOUS FOUNDERS

NOUNS **1 prophet** 961.4, *vates sacer* <L>; Old Testament prophets <see list>

2 <Christian founders> **evangelist, apostle, disciple,** saint; Matthew, Mark, Luke, John; Paul; Peter; **the Fathers, fathers of the church**

3 Martin Luther, John Calvin, John Wycliffe, Jan Hus, John Wesley, John Knox, George Fox <Protestant reformers>; Emanuel Swedenborg <Church of the New Jerusalem>; Mary Baker Eddy <Christian Science>; Joseph Smith <Church of Jesus Christ of Latter-day Saints>

4 Buddha, Gautama Buddha <Buddhism>; Mahavira *or* Vardhamana *or* Jina <Jainism>; Mirza Ali Muhammad of Shiraz *or* the Bab <Babism>; Muhammad *or* Mohammed <Islam>; Confucius <Confucianism>; Lao-tzu <Taoism>; Zoroaster *or* Zarathustra <Zoroastrianism>; Nanak <Sikhism>; Ram Mohan Roy <Brahmo-Samaj>

5 Old Testament prophets

Abraham	Jonah
Amos	Joseph
Daniel	Joshua
Ezekiel	Malachi
Habakkuk	Micah
Haggai	Moses
Hosea	Nahum
Isaac	Obadiah
Isaiah	Samuel
Jacob	Zechariah
Jeremiah	Zephaniah
Joel	

685 SANCTITY
<sacred quality>

NOUNS **1 sanctity,** sanctitude; **sacredness, holiness,** hallowedness, numinousness; sacrosanctness, sacrosanctity; heavenliness, transcendence, divinity, divineness 677.1; venerableness, **venerability, blessedness;** awesomeness, awfulness; inviolableness, **inviolability;** ineffability, unutterability, unspeakability, inexpressibility, inenarrableness; godliness 692.2; odor of sanctity

2 the sacred, the holy, the holy of holies, the numinous, the ineffable, the unutterable, the unspeakable, the inexpressible, the inenarrable, the transcendent

3 sanctification, hallowing; purification; beatitude, blessing; **glorification,** exaltation, enskying; **consecration,** dedication, devotion, setting apart; sainting, canonization, enshrinement; **sainthood, beatification; blessedness; grace,** state of grace; justification, justification by faith, justification by works

4 redemption, redeemedness, **salvation,** conversion, regeneration, new life, reformation, adoption; **rebirth, new birth, second birth;** circumcision, spiritual purification *or* cleansing

VERBS **5 sanctify, hallow; purify,** cleanse, wash one's sins away; **bless,** beatify; **glorify,** exalt, ensky; **consecrate,** dedicate, devote, set apart; **beatify, saint, canonize;** enshrine

6 redeem, regenerate, reform, convert, save, give salvation

ADJS **7 sacred, holy,** numinous, **sacrosanct, religious, spiritual,** heavenly, divine; **venerable,** awesome, awful; inviolable, **inviolate,** untouchable; **ineffable,** unutterable, unspeakable, inexpressible, inenarrable

8 sanctified, hallowed; blessed, consecrated, devoted, dedicated, set apart; **glorified, exalted,** enskied; **saintly,** sainted, beatified, canonized

9 redeemed, saved, converted, regenerated, regenerate, justified, reborn, born-again, renewed; circumcised, spiritually purified *or* cleansed

WORD ELEMENTS **10** sacr—, sacro—, hier—, hiero—, hagi—, hagio—

686 UNSANCTITY

NOUNS **1 unsanctity,** unsanctitude; **unsacredness, unholiness,** unhallowedness, unblessedness; profanity, profaneness; unregenerateness, reprobation; **worldliness,** secularity, secularism; secular humanism

2 the profane, the unholy; the temporal, the secular, **the worldly,** the fleshly, the mundane; the world, the flesh, and the devil

ADJS **3 unsacred,** nonsacred, **unholy,** unhallowed, unsanctified, unblessed; profane, **secular, temporal, worldly,** fleshly, mundane; unsaved, unredeemed, unregenerate, reprobate

687 ORTHODOXY

NOUNS **1 orthodoxy,** orthodoxness, orthodoxism; **soundness,** soundness of doctrine, rightness, right belief *or* doctrine; **authoritativeness,** authenticity, canonicalness, canonicity; traditionalism; the truth, religious truth, gospel truth

2 the faith, true faith, apostolic faith, primitive faith, "the faith once delivered unto the saints"—Bible; old-time religion, faith of our fathers

3 the Church, the true church, Holy

Church, Church of Christ, the Bride of the
Lamb, body of Christ, temple of the Holy
Ghost, body of Christians, members in
Christ, disciples *or* followers of Christ;
apostolic church; universal church, the
church universal; church visible, church
invisible; church militant, church triumphant

4 **true believer,** orthodox Christian; Sunni
Muslim; Orthodox Jew; orthodox, ortho-
doxian, orthodoxist; textualist, textuary;
canonist; fundamentalist; the orthodox

5 **strictness,** strict interpretation, scrip-
turalism, evangelicalism; hyperortho-
doxy, puritanism, puritanicalness, purism; staunchness; straitlacedness, stiff-
neckedness, hideboundness; hard line
<nonformal>; **bigotry** 979.1; **dogmatism**
969.6; **fundamentalism,** literalism, precisianism; bibliolatry; Sabbatarianism;
sabbatism

6 **bigot** 979.5; **dogmatist** 969.7

ADJS 7 **orthodox,** orthodoxical; of the faith,
of the true faith; **sound,** firm, faithful,
true, true-blue, right-thinking; Christian;
evangelical; scriptural, canonical; traditional, traditionalistic; literal, textual;
standard, customary, conventional; **authoritative,** authentic, accepted, received,
approved; correct, right, proper

8 **strict,** scripturalistic, evangelical; hyper-
orthodox, puritanical, purist *or* puristic,
straitlaced; staunch; hidebound, hardline
<nonformal>, creedbound; **bigoted**
979.10; **dogmatic** 969.22; **fundamentalist,**
precisianist *or* precisianistic, literalist *or*
literalistic; Sabbatarian

688 UNORTHODOXY

NOUNS 1 **unorthodoxy, heterodoxy;** unor-
thodoxness, **unsoundness,** un-Scriptural-
ity; **unauthoritativeness,** unauthenticity,
uncanonicalness, uncanonicity; **nonconformity** 867

2 **heresy,** false doctrine, **misbelief; fallacy,
error** 974

3 **infidelity,** infidelism; unchristianity; gen-
tilism; **atheism, unbelief** 695.5

4 **paganism, heathenism;** paganry, hea-
thenry; pagandom, heathendom; pagano-
Christianism; allotheism; animism, animatism; idolatry 697

5 **heretic, misbeliever;** heresiarch; nonconformist 867.3; antinomian, Albigensian,
Arian, Donatist, etc

6 **gentile;** non-Christian; **non-Jew,** goy,
goyim, non-Jewish man *or shegets*
<Yiddish>, non-Jewish woman *or shiksa*

<Yiddish>; non-Muslim, non-Moslem,
non-Muhammadan, non-Mohammedan,
giaour <Turk>, kaffir; zendik, zendician,
zendikite; non-Mormon; infidel; unbeliever 695.11

7 **pagan, heathen;** allotheist; animist; idolater 697.4

VERBS 8 **misbelieve, err,** stray, deviate, wander, go astray, stray from the path, step
out of line <nonformal>, go wrong, fall
into error; be wrong, be mistaken, be in
error; serve Mammon

ADJS 9 **unorthodox,** nonorthodox, **heterodox,
heretical; unsound; unscriptural,** un-
canonical, apocryphal; **unauthoritative,**
unauthentic, unaccepted, unreceived, un-
approved; **fallacious,** erroneous 974.16;
antinomian, Albigensian, Arian, Donatist, etc

10 **infidel,** infidelic, misbelieving; **atheistic,**
unbelieving 695.19; **unchristian,** non-
Christian; gentile, non-Jewish, goyish,
uncircumcised; non-Muslim, non-
Muhammadan, non-Mohammedan, non-
Moslem, non-Islamic; non-Mormon

11 **pagan, paganish,** paganistic; **heathen,
heathenish;** pagano-Christian; allotheis-
tic; animist, animistic; idolatrous 697.7

689 OCCULTISM

NOUNS 1 **occultism, esoterics,** esotericism,
esoterism, esotery; cabalism, cabala *or*
kabala *or* kabbala; yoga, yogism, yo-
geeism; **theosophy,** anthroposophy;
symbolics, symbolism; anagogics; ana-
goge; mystery; mystification, hocus-
pocus, mumbo jumbo; mysticism 683.9

2 **supernaturalism,** supranaturalism, preternaturalism, **transcendentalism; the
supernatural,** the supersensible, the paranormal

3 **metaphysics,** hyperphysics, transphysi-
cal science, the first philosophy *or*
theology

4 **psychics,** psychism, psychicism; **parapsychology, psychical research;** meta-
psychics, metapsychism; psychosophy;
panpsychism; psychic monism

5 **spiritualism,** spiritism; mediumism; necromancy; séance, sitting; spirit 987.1

6 psychic *or* psychical phenomena, spirit
manifestation; materialization; spirit
rapping, table tipping *or* turning; polter-
geistism, poltergeist; telekinesis, psychokinesis, power of mind over matter, teles-
thesia, teleportation; levitation; trance
speaking; psychorrhagy; automatism,
psychography, automatic *or* trance *or*

spirit writing; Ouija board, Ouija; planchette

7 **ectoplasm,** exteriorized protoplasm; aura, emanation, effluvium; ectoplasy

8 **extrasensory perception** or ESP; **clairvoyance,** lucidity, second sight, insight, sixth sense; intuition 933; foresight 960; premonition 133.1; clairsentience, clairaudience, crystal vision, psychometry, metapsychosis

9 **telepathy, mental telepathy, mind reading,** thought transference, telepathic transmission; telepathic dream, telepathic hallucination

10 **divination** 961.2; **sorcery** 690

11 **occultist,** esoteric, mystic, mystagogue, cabalist, supernaturalist, transcendentalist; adept, mahatma; yogi, yogin, yogist; theosophist, anthroposophist

12 **parapsychologist;** psychist, psychicist; **metapsychist;** panpsychist; **metaphysician,** metaphysicist

13 **psychic; spiritualist,** spiritist, **medium,** ecstatic, spirit rapper, automatist, psychographist; necromancer

14 **clairvoyant;** clairaudient; psychometer, psychometrist

15 **telepathist, mental telepathist, mind reader,** thought reader

16 **diviner** 961.4; **sorcerer** 690.5

17 **astral body,** astral, linga sharira, design body, subtle body, vital body, etheric body, bliss body, Buddhic body, spiritual body, soul body; kamarupa, desire or kamic body; causal body; mental or mind body

18 <seven principles of man, theosophy> spirit, atman; mind, manas; soul, buddhi; life principle, vital force, prana; astral body, linga sharira; physical or dense or gross body, sthula sharira; principle of desire, kama

19 **spiritualization,** etherealization, idealization; **dematerialization,** immaterialization, unsubstantialization; **disembodiment,** disincarnation

VERBS 20 **spiritualize,** spiritize; etherealize; idealize; **dematerialize,** immaterialize, unsubstantialize; **disembody,** disincarnate

21 practice spiritualism, hold a séance or sitting; call up spirits 690.11

22 **telepathize, read one's mind**

ADJS 23 **occult, esoteric, esoterical, mysterious,** mystic, mystical, anagogic, anagogical; metaphysic, metaphysical; cabalic, cabalistic; **paranormal, supernatural** 869.15; theosophical, theosophist, anthroposophical

24 **psychic, psychical, spiritual; spiritualistic,** spiritistic; mediumistic; **clairvoyant,** second-sighted, clairaudient, clairsentient, **telepathic; extrasensory,** psychosensory; supersensible, supersensual, pretersensual; telekinetic, psychokinetic; automatist

690 SORCERY

NOUNS 1 **sorcery, necromancy, magic,** sortilege, **wizardry,** theurgy, gramarye <old>, rune, glamour; **witchcraft,** spellcraft, spellbinding, spellcasting; **witchery,** witchwork, bewitchery, enchantment; **voodooism, voodoo,** hoodoo, wanga, juju, jujuism, obeah, obeahism; shamanism; magism, magianism; fetishism; vampirism; thaumaturgy, thaumaturgia, thaumaturgics, thaumaturgism; alchemy; white or natural magic; sympathetic magic; **divination** 961.2; spell, charm 691

2 **black magic,** the black art; **diabolism, demonism,** Satanism

3 <practices> magic circle; ghost dance; Sabbath, witches' meeting or Sabbath; ordeal, ordeal by battle or fire or water or lots

4 **conjuration,** conjurement, evocation, invocation; **exorcism,** exorcisation; exsufflation; **incantation** 691.4

5 **sorcerer, necromancer, wizard, wonderworker,** warlock, theurgist; warlock, male witch; thaumaturge, thaumaturgist, miracle- or wonder-worker; alchemist; **conjurer; diviner** 961.4; dowser, water witch or diviner; diabolist; Faust, Comus

6 **magician,** mage, magus, magian; Merlin; prestidigitator, illusionist 357.2

7 **shaman,** shamanist; **voodoo,** voodooist, wangateur, **witch doctor,** obeah doctor, **medicine man,** mundunugu, isangoma; witch-hunter, witch-finder; exorcist, exorciser; unspeller

8 **sorceress,** shamaness; **witch,** witchwoman <nonformal>, witchwife <Scots>, **hex, hag,** lamia; witch of Endor; coven, witches' coven, Weird Sisters <Shakespeare>

9 **bewitcher, enchanter, charmer, spellbinder; enchantress, siren,** vampire; Circe; Medusa, Medea, Gorgon, Stheno, Euryale

VERBS 10 **sorcerize, shamanize;** make or work magic, wave a wand, rub the ring or lamp; ride a broomstick; alchemize

11 **conjure, conjure up,** evoke, invoke, raise,

summon, call up; **call up spirits,** conjure
or conjure up spirits, summon spirits,
raise ghosts, evoke from the dead, "call
spirits from the vasty deep"—Shakespeare

12 **exorcise,** lay; lay ghosts, **cast out devils;**
unspell

13 cast a spell, bewitch 691.9

ADJS 14 sorcerous, necromantic, **magic,
magical,** magian, numinous,
thaumaturgic, thaumaturgical, miraculous, cantrip *or* weird <both Scots>,
wizardlike, wizardly; alchemical, alche-
mistic, alchemistical; shaman, shamanic,
shamanist *or* shamanistic; witchlike,
witchy, witch; voodoo, hoodoo <nonfor-
mal>, voodooistic; incantatory,
incantational; talismanic

691 SPELL, CHARM

NOUNS 1 **spell,** magic spell, **charm,** glamour, weird *or* cantrip <both Scots>,
wanga; hand of glory; evil eye, *malocchio*
<Ital>, whammy <nonformal>; **hex,
jinx, curse; exorcism**

2 **bewitchment, witchery, bewitchery; enchantment, entrancement,** fascination,
captivation; illusion, maya; bedevilment;
possession, obsession

3 **trance, ecstasy,** ecstasis, transport, mystic transport; meditation, contemplation;
rapture; yoga trance, dharana, dhyana,
samadhi; hypnosis 22.7

4 **incantation, conjuration,** magic words
or formula; hocus-pocus, abracadabra,
mumbo jumbo; open sesame

5 **charm, amulet, talisman, fetish,** periapt,
phylactery; **voodoo, hoodoo,** juju, obeah,
mumbo jumbo; **good-luck charm,** good-
luck piece, **lucky piece,** rabbit's-foot,
lucky bean, four-leaf clover, whammy
<nonformal>; mascot; madstone; love
charm, philter; scarab, scarabaeus, scar-
abee; veronica, sudarium; swastika,
fylfot, gammadion

6 **wish-bringer,** wish-giver; **wand, magic
wand,** Aaron's rod; Aladdin's lamp,
magic ring, magic belt, magic spectacles,
magic carpet, seven-league boots; wishing well, wishing stone, wishing cap,
Fortunatus's cap; cap of darkness, Tarn-
kappe, Tarnhelm; fern seed; **wishbone,**
wishing bone, merrythought <Brit>

VERBS 7 cast a spell, spell, **spellbind; entrance,** trance, put in a trance; **hypnotize,
mesmerize**

8 **charm,** becharm, **enchant, fascinate,** captivate, glamour

9 **bewitch,** witch, **hex, jinx;** voodoo,
hoodoo; **possess, obsess;** bedevil, diabolize, demonize; hagride; overlook, look
on with the evil eye, cast the evil eye

10 **put a curse on,** put a hex on, put a juju on,
put obeah on, give the evil eye, give the
malocchio, give a whammy <nonfor-
mal>

ADJS 11 **bewitching, witching;** illusory, illusive, illusionary; **charming, enchanting,
entrancing, spellbinding, fascinating,**
glamorous, Circean

12 **enchanted, charmed,** becharmed, charm-
struck, charm-bound; **spellbound,** spell-
struck, spell-caught; **fascinated,** captivated; **hypnotized, mesmerized;** under a
spell, in a trance

13 **bewitched,** witched, witch-charmed,
witch-held, witch-struck; hag-ridden;
possessed, taken over, obsessed

692 PIETY

NOUNS 1 **piety, piousness,** pietism; **religion,
faith; religiousness, religiosity,** religionism, religious-mindedness; theism; love
of God, adoration; **devoutness,** devotion,
devotedness, worship 696, worshipful-
ness, prayerfulness, cultism; faithfulness,
dutifulness, observance, churchgoing,
conformity 866; **reverence,** veneration;
discipleship, followership; daily communion

2 **godliness,** godlikeness; fear of God; **sanctity,** sanctitude; odor of sanctity, beauty
of holiness; **righteousness, holiness,** goodness; **spirituality,** spiritual-mindedness,
holy-mindedness, heavenly-mindedness,
godly-mindedness; **purity,** pureness,
pure-heartedness, pureness of heart;
saintliness, saintlikeness; saintship,
sainthood; angelicalness, seraphicalness;
heavenliness, **unworldliness,** unearthliness, other-worldliness

3 **zeal,** zealousness, zealotry, zealotism;
evangelism, revival, evangelicalism, re-
vivalism; pentecostalism, charismatic
movement; charismatic renewal, baptism in the spirit; charismatic gift, gift of
tongues, glossolalia; **overreligiousness,
religiosity,** overpiousness, overrighteous-
ness, **overzealousness,** overdevoutness;
bibliolatry; fundamentalism, militance,
fanaticism 925.11; **sanctimony** 693

4 **believer,** truster, accepter, receiver; God-
fearing man, pietist, religionist, saint,
theist; **devotee,** devotionalist, votary;
zealot, zealotist, fundamentalist, militant; **churchgoer,** churchman, churchite;

pillar of the church; communicant, daily communicant; **convert**, proselyte, neophyte, catechumen; **disciple**, follower, servant, faithful servant; **fanatic**

5 **the believing, the faithful**, the righteous, the good; the elect, the chosen, the saved; the children of God, the children of light; Christendom, the Church 687.3

VERBS 6 **be pious, be religious; have faith**, trust in God, love God, fear God; witness, bear witness, affirm, **believe** 952.10; keep the faith, fight the good fight, let one's light shine, praise and glorify God, walk humbly with one's God; be observant, follow righteousness

7 **be converted, get religion** <nonformal>, receive *or* accept Christ, stand up for Jesus, be washed in the blood of the Lamb; be born again, see the light

ADJS 8 **pious**, pietistic; **religious**, religious-minded; theistic; **devout**, devoted, worshipful, prayerful, cultish, cultist, cultistic; **reverent**, reverential, venerative, venerational, adoring, solemn; faithful, dutiful; affirming, witnessing, believing 952.21; **observant, practicing**

9 **godly, godlike; God-fearing; righteous, holy**, good; **spiritual**, spiritual-minded, holy-minded, godly-minded, heavenly-minded; **pure**, purehearted, pure in heart; **saintly**, saintlike; **angelic, angelical**, seraphic, seraphical; heavenly; **unworldly**, unearthly, otherworldly, not of the earth, not of this world

10 **regenerate**, regenerated, **converted, redeemed, saved**, reborn, **born-again**; sanctified 685.8

11 **zealous**, zealotical; **overreligious**, ultra-religious, overpious, overrighteous, **overzealous**, overdevout; **fanatical** 925.32; sanctimonious 693.5

693 SANCTIMONY

NOUNS 1 **sanctimony, sanctimoniousness; pietism**, piety, **piousness**, pietisticalness, false piety; religionism, religiosity; **self-righteousness**; goodiness *and* goody-goodiness <both nonformal>; pharisaism, pharisaicalness; Tartuffery, Tartuffism; **falseness, insincerity, hypocrisy** 354.6; affectation 500; **cant**, mummery, snivel, snuffle; unction, unctuousness, oiliness, smarm *and* smarminesss <both nonformal>, mealymouthedness

2 **lip service, mouth honor**, mouthing, lip homage *or* worship *or* devotion *or* praise *or* reverence; formalism, solemn mock-ery; BOMFOG *or* brotherhood of man and fatherhood of God

3 **pietist**, religionist, **hypocrite**, religious hypocrite, canting hypocrite, pious fraud, religious *or* spiritual humbug, whited sepulcher, **pharisee**, Holy Willie <Robert Burns>, "a saint abroad and a devil at home"—Bunyan; bleeding heart <nonformal>; **canter**, ranter, snuffler, sniveler; dissembler, dissimulator; affecter, poser 500.8; **lip server**, lip worshiper, formalist; Pharisee, scribes and Pharisees; Tartuffe, Pecksniff, Mawworm, Joseph Surface

VERBS 4 **be sanctimonious**, be hypocritical; cant, snuffle, snivel; give mouth honor, render *or* pay lip service

ADJS 5 **sanctimonious**, sanctified, **pious, pietistic, pietistical**, self-righteous, pharisaic, pharisaical, **holier-than-thou**, holier-than-the-pope <nonformal>; goody *and* goody-goody *and* goo-goo <all nonformal>; **false, insincere, hypocritical** 354.32; affected 500.15; Tartuffish, Tartuffian; canting, sniveling, unctuous, mealymouthed, smarmy <nonformal>

694 IMPIETY

NOUNS 1 **impiety, impiousness; irreverence**, undutifulness; desertion, renegadism, apostasy, recreancy; backsliding, recidivism, lapse, fall *or* lapse from grace; **atheism, irreligion; unsanctity** 686

2 **sacrilege, blasphemy**, blaspheming, impiety; **profanity**, profaneness; sacrilegiousness, blasphemousness; **desecration, profanation**; tainting, pollution, contamination

3 sacrilegist, **blasphemer**, Sabbath-breaker; deserter, renegade, apostate, recreant; backslider, recidivist; **atheist**, unbeliever 695.11

VERBS 4 **desecrate, profane**, dishonor, unhallow, commit sacrilege

5 **blaspheme**; vilify, abuse 513.7; curse, swear 513.6; take in vain; taint, pollute, contaminate

ADJS 6 **impious, irreverent**, undutiful; **profane**, profanatory; **sacrilegious, blasphemous**; renegade, apostate, recreant, backsliding, recidivist *or* recidivistic, lapsed, fallen, lapsed *or* fallen from grace; atheistic, **irreligious** 695.17; **unsacred** 686.3

695 NONRELIGIOUSNESS

NOUNS 1 **nonreligiousness, unreligiousness; undevoutness**; indevoutness, indevotion,

undutifulness, nonobservance; adiaphor-
ism, indifferentism, Laodiceanism,
lukewarm piety; indifference 102; **lai-
cism,** unconsecration; **deconsecration,
secularization,** laicization, desacraliza-
tion

2 **secularism, worldliness,** earthliness,
earthiness, mundaneness; **unspirituality,**
carnality; worldly-mindedness, earthly-
mindedness, carnal-mindedness; materialism, Philistinism

3 **ungodliness,** godlessness, **unrighteousness, irreligion, unholiness,** unsaintliness, unangelicalness; unchristianliness,
un-Christliness; impiety 694; **wickedness,
sinfulness** 654.4

4 **unregeneracy,** unredeemedness, **reprobacy,** gracelessness, shriftlessness

5 **unbelief, disbelief** 954.1; infidelity, infidelism, faithlessness; **atheism;** nullifidianism, minimifidianism

6 **agnosticism; skepticism, doubt, incredulity,** Pyrrhonism, Humism; scoffing 508.1

7 **freethinking,** free thought, **latitudinarianism; humanism,** secular humanism

8 **antireligion;** antichristianism, antichris-
tianity; antiscripturism

9 **iconoclasm,** iconoclasticism, image
breaking

10 **irreligionist; worldling,** earthling; **materialist;** iconoclast, idoloclast; anti-
Christian, antichrist

11 **unbeliever, disbeliever,** nonbeliever;
atheist, infidel, pagan, heathen; nullifidian, minimifidian; secularist; **gentile**
688.6

12 **agnostic; skeptic, doubter,** dubitante,
doubting Thomas, scoffer, Pyrrhonist,
Humist

13 **freethinker, latitudinarian,** *esprit fort*
<Fr>; humanist, secular humanist

VERBS 14 **disbelieve,** doubt 954.6; scoff
508.9; **laicize,** deconsecrate, **secularize,**
desacralize

ADJS 15 **nonreligious, unreligious,** having no
religious preference; **undevout,** indevout,
indevotional, undutiful, nonobservant,
nonpracticing; adiamorphic, indifferen-
tist *or* indifferentistic, Laodicean,
lukewarm, indifferent 102.6; unconse-
crated, **deconsecrated, secularized,**
laicized, desacralized

16 **secularist, secularistic, worldly, earthly,**
earthy, terrestrial, **mundane,** temporal;
unspiritual, profane, carnal, **secular;** humanistic, secular-humanistic; worldly
minded, earthly minded, carnal-minded;
materialistic, material, Philistine

17 **ungodly,** godless, **irreligious, un-**

righteous, unholy, unsaintly, unangelic,
unangelical; impious 694.6; **wicked, sinful** 654.16

18 **unregenerate,** unredeemed **unconverted,**
godless, reprobate, graceless, shriftless,
lost, damned; lapsed, fallen, recidivist,
recidivistic

19 **unbelieving, disbelieving, faithless;** infi-
del, infidelic; **pagan, heathen; atheistic,**
atheist; nullifidian, minimifidian

20 **agnostic; skeptic, skeptical, doubtful, dubious, incredulous,** Humean, Pyrrhonic;
Cartesian

21 **freethinking, latitudinarian**

22 **antireligious;** antichristian; antiscrip-
tural; **iconoclastic**

696 WORSHIP

NOUNS 1 **worship,** worshiping, **adoration,
devotion, homage, veneration, reverence,**
"transcendent wonder"—Carlyle; cult,
cultus, cultism; latria, dulia, hyperdulia;
falling down and worshiping, prostration; co-worship; idolatry 697

2 **glorification,** glory, **praise,** laudation,
laud, exaltation, magnification

3 **paean,** laud; hosanna, hallelujah, alleluia; **hymn,** hymn of praise, **doxology,
psalm, anthem,** motet, canticle, chorale;
chant, versicle; mantra, Vedic hymn *or*
chant; Introit, Miserere; Gloria, Gloria in
Excelsis, Gloria Patri; Te Deum, Agnus
Dei, Benedicite, Magnificat, Nunc Di-
mittis; response, responsory, report,
answer; Trisagion; antiphon, antiphony;
offertory, offertory sentence *or* hymn;
hymnody, hymnology, hymnography,
psalmody

4 **prayer, supplication, invocation,** imploration, impetration, entreaty, beseechment, appeal, petition, suit, aid
prayer, bid *or* bidding prayer, orison, obsecration, obtestation, rogation, **devotions;** silent prayer, meditation, contemplation, communion; intercession; **grace,
thanks, thanksgiving;** litany; breviary,
canonical prayers; collect, collect of the
Mass, collect of the Communion; Angelus; Paternoster, the Lord's Prayer;
Hail Mary, Ave, Ave Maria; Kyrie Elei-
son; chaplet; rosary, beads, beadroll;
Kaddish, Mourner's Kaddish; prayer
wheel *or* machine

5 **benediction, blessing,** benison, invocation, benedicite; sign of the cross; laying
on of hands

6 **propitiation,** appeasement 465.1; atonement 658

7 **oblation, offering, sacrifice, immolation,** incense; libation, drink offering; burnt offering, holocaust; thank offering, votive *or* ex voto offering; heave offering, peace offering, sacramental offering, sin *or* piacular offering, whole offering; human sacrifice, mactation, infanticide, hecatomb; self-sacrifice, self-immolation; sutteeism; scapegoat, suttee; offertory, collection

8 divine service, **service,** public worship, **liturgy** 701.3, office, duty, exercises, **devotions;** meeting; church service, church; **revival,** revival meeting, camp meeting, tent meeting, praise meeting; watch meeting, watch-night service, watch night; **prayer meeting,** prayers, prayer; morning devotions *or* services *or* prayers, matins, lauds; prime, prime song; tierce, undersong; sext; none, nones; novena; evening devotions *or* services *or* prayers, vesper, vespers, vigils, evensong; compline, night song *or* prayer; bedtime prayer; Mass

9 **worshiper,** adorer, venerator, votary, communicant, daily communicant, celebrant, churchgoer, chapelgoer; prayer, suppliant, supplicant, supplicator, petitioner; orans, orant; beadsman; revivalist, evangelist; congregation; **idolater** 697.4

VERBS 10 **worship, adore, reverence, venerate, revere, honor,** do *or* pay homage to, pay divine honors to, do service, lift up the heart, bow down and worship, humble oneself before; **idolize** 697.5

11 **glorify, praise, laud, exalt, extol,** magnify, bless, celebrate; praise God, praise *or* glorify the Lord, bless the Lord, praise God from whom all blessings flow; praise Father, Son, and Holy Ghost; sing praises, sing the praises of, sound *or* resound the praises of; doxologize, hymn

12 **pray, supplicate,** invoke, petition, make supplication, *daven* <Yiddish>; **implore, beseech** 440.11, obtest; offer a prayer, send up a prayer, commune with God; **say one's prayers;** tell one's beads, recite the rosary; **say grace, give *or* return thanks;** pray over

13 **bless, give one's blessing,** give benediction, confer a blessing upon, invoke benefits upon; cross, make the sign of the cross over *or* upon; lay hands on

14 **propitiate,** make propitiation; appease 465.7; **offer sacrifice,** sacrifice, make sacrifice to, immolate before, offer up an oblation

ADJS 15 **worshipful,** worshiping; **adoring,** adorant; **devout,** devotional; **reverent,** reverential; **venerative,** venerational; solemn; at the feet of; **prayerful, supplicatory,** supplicant, suppliant, precatory, precative, imploring, on one's knees, on bended knee; prone *or* prostrate before, in the dust; blessing, benedictory, benedictional; propitiatory

INTERJS 16 **hallelujah!,** alleluia!, **hosanna!, praise God!,** praise the Lord!, praise ye the Lord!, "praise Him·all His hosts!"— Bible, Heaven be praised!, glory to God!, glory be to God!, glory be to God in the highest!, bless the Lord!, "bless the Lord, O my soul, and all that is within me, bless His holy name!, "hallowed be Thy Name!"—both Bible; thanks be to God!, *Deo gratias!* <L>; sursum corda! <Hinduism>; om!, om mani padme hum!

17 O Lord!, our Father which art in heaven!; God grant!, pray God that!; God bless!, God save!, God forbid!

697 IDOLATRY

NOUNS 1 **idolatry,** idolatrousness, idolism, idolodulia, **idol worship;** heathenism, paganism; image worship, iconolatry, iconoduly; **fetishism; demonism,** demonolatry, demon *or* devil worship, Satanism; animal worship, snake worship, fire worship, pyrolatry, Parsiism, Zoroastrianism; sun worship, star worship, Sabaism; tree worship, plant worship, Druidism, nature worship; phallic worship, phallicism; hero worship; idolomancy

2 **idolization,** fetishization; **deification,** apotheosis

3 **idol; fetish,** totem, joss; **graven image, golden calf;** devil-god, "the god of my idolatry"—Shakespeare; Baal, Jaganatha *or* Juggernaut; sacred cow

4 **idolater,** idolatress, idolizer, idolatrizer, idolist, idol worshiper, image-worshiper; fetishist, totemist; demon *or* devil worshiper, demonolater, chthonian; animal worshiper, zoolater, theriolater, therolater, snake worshiper, ophiolater; fire worshiper, pyrolater, Parsi, Zoroastrian; sun worshiper, heliolater; star worshiper, Sabaist; tree worshiper, arborolater, dendrolater, plant worshiper, Druid, nature worshiper; phallic worshiper; anthropolater, archaeolater, etc

VERBS 5 **idolatrize,** idolize, idolify, idol; fetishize, fetish; **make an idol of, deify,** apotheosize

6 **worship idols,** worship the golden calf, *adorer le veau d'or* <Fr>

ADJS **7 idolatrous,** idolatric or idolatrical, **idol worshiping;** idolistic, fetishistic, totemistic; heathen, pagan; demonolatrous, chthonian; heliolatrous; bibliolatrous; zoolatrous

698 THE MINISTRY

NOUNS **1 the ministry, pastorate,** pastorage, pastoral care, cure or care of souls, **the Church,** the cloth, the pulpit, the desk; **priesthood,** priestship; apostleship; call, vocation, sacred calling; holy orders; rabbinate

2 ecclesiasticalism, ecclesiology, priestcraft

3 clericalism, sacerdotalism; priesthood; priestism; episcopalianism; ultramontanism

4 monasticism, monachism, monkery, **monkhood,** friarhood; celibacy 565

5 ecclesiastical office <see list>, church office, dignity

6 papacy, papality, **pontificate,** popedom, the Vatican, Apostolic See, See of Rome, the Church

7 hierarchy, hierocracy; theocracy

8 diocese, see, archdiocese, bishopric, archbishopric; province; synod, conference; **parish**

9 benefice, living, **incumbency,** glebe, advowson; curacy, cure, charge, cure or care of souls; prelacy, rectory, vicarage

10 holy orders, orders 699.4, major orders, apostolic orders, minor orders; calling, election, nomination, appointment, preferment, induction, institution, installation, investiture; conferment, presentation; **ordination,** ordainment, consecration, canonization, reading in <Brit>

VERBS **11 be ordained, take holy orders,** take orders, take vows, read oneself in <Brit>; **take the veil,** wear the cloth

12 ordain, frock, **canonize, consecrate;** saint

ADJS **13 ecclesiastic, ecclesiastical, churchly; ministerial, clerical,** sacerdotal, **pastoral; priestly,** priestish; prelatic, prelatical, prelatial; episcopal, episcopalian; archiepiscopal; primatal, primatial, primatical; canonical; capitular, capitulary; abbatical, abbatial; ultramontane; **evangelistic;** rabbinic, rabbinical; priest-ridden

14 monastic, monachal, **monasterial, monkish;** conventual

15 papal, pontific, pontifical, apostolic, apostolical; **popish** or papist or papistic or papistical or papish <all nonformal>

16 hierarchical, hierarchal; theocratic, theocratist

17 ordained; in orders, in holy orders, of the cloth

18 ecclesiastical offices

abbacy	episcopate or episcopacy
archbishopric or archiepiscopate or archiepiscopacy	pastorate or pastorship
archdeaconry	prebend or prebendaryship or prebendal stall
bishopric or bishopdom	prelacy or prelature or prelateship or prelatehood
canonry or canonicate	
cardinalate or cardinalship	presbytery or presbyterate
chaplaincy or chaplainship	primacy or primateship
curacy	
deaconry or deaconship	rectorate or rectorship
deanery or deanship	vicariate or vicarship

699 THE CLERGY

NOUNS **1 clergy, ministry,** the cloth; clerical order, clericals; **priesthood;** priestery; presbytery; prelacy; Sacred College; rabbinate

2 clergyman, clergywoman, man or woman of the cloth, **divine, ecclesiastic, churchman, cleric,** clerical; clerk, clerk in holy orders, tonsured cleric; **minister, minister of the Gospel, parson, pastor,** abbé, curé <both Fr>, **rector,** curate, man or woman of God, servant of God, shepherd, sky pilot and Holy Joe <both nonformal>, reverend <nonformal>; supply minister or preacher, supply clergy; **chaplain;** military chaplain, padre <nonformal>; the Reverend, the Very or Right Reverend; Doctor of Divinity or DD

3 preacher, sermoner, sermonizer, sermonist, homilist; pulpiter, pulpiteer; predicant, predikant; preaching friar; circuit rider; television or TV preacher, telepreacher <nonformal>

4 holy orders, major orders, priest or presbyter, deacon or diaconus, subdeacon or subdiaconus; minor orders, acolyte or acolytus, exorcist or exorcista, reader or lector, doorkeeper or ostiarius; ordinand, candidate for holy orders

5 priest, gallach <Heb>, **father,** father in Christ, **padre,** cassock, presbyter; curé, parish priest; confessor, father confessor, spiritual father or director or leader, holy father; penitentiary

6 evangelist, revivalist, evangel, evangelicalist; **missionary,** missioner; missionary apostolic, missionary rector, colporteur; television *or* TV evangelist, televangelist <nonformal>

7 **benefice-holder, beneficiary, incumbent;** resident, residentiary

8 church dignitary, ecclesiarch, ecclesiast, hierarch; minor *or* lay officer

9 <Mormon> deacon, teacher, priest, elder, Seventy, high priest, bishop, patriarch, apostle; Aaronic priesthood, Melchizedek priesthood

10 <Jewish> **rabbi**, rabbin; chief rabbi; *baal kore* <Yiddish>; cantor; priest, *kohen* <Heb>, high priest; Levite; scribe

11 <Muslim> imam, qadi, sheikh, mullah, murshid, mufti, hajji, muezzin, dervish, abdal, fakir, santon

12 <Hindu> Brahman, pujari, purohit, pundit, guru, bashara, vairagi *or* bairagi, Ramwat, Ramanandi; sannyasi; yogi, yogin; bhikshu, bhikhari

13 <Buddhist> bonze, bhikku, poonghie, talapoin; lama; Grand Lama, Dalai Lama, Panchen Lama

14 <pagan> Druid, Druidess; flamen; hierophant, hierodule, hieros, daduchus, mystes, epopt

15 **religious**, *religieux* <Fr>; **monk**, monastic; brother, lay brother; cenobite, conventual; caloyer, hieromonach; **mendicant, friar;** pilgrim, palmer; stylite, pillarist, pillar saint; beadsman; prior, claustral *or* conventual prior, grand prior, general prior; abbot; lay abbot, abbacomes; hermit 584.5; ascetic 667.2; celibate 565.2

16 religious orders <see list>

17 **nun**, sister, *religieuse* <Fr>, clergywoman, conventual; abbess, prioress; **mother superior,** lady superior, superioress, the reverend mother, holy mother; canoness, regular *or* secular canoness; novice, postulant

18 **religious orders**

Augustinian *or*	Crutched Friars *or*
Austin Friars	Crossed Friars
Augustinian	Discalced Carmelite
Hermit	Dominican *or* Black
Benedictine *or*	Friars
Black Monks	Franciscan *or* Gray
Bernardine	Friars
Bonhomme	Friars Minor
Brigittine	Friars Preacher
Capuchin	Gilbertine
Carmelite *or* White	Hospitaler
Friars	Jesuit *or* Loyolite
Carthusian	Lorettine
Cistercian	Marist
Cluniac	Maryknoll
Conventual	Maturine
Minorite	Premonstratensian
Observant	Recollect *or* Recollet
Oratorian	Redemptorist
preaching Friars *or*	Templar
brothers	Trappist

700 THE LAITY

NOUNS 1 **the laity, lay persons,** laymen, laywomen, nonclerics, nonordained persons, seculars; brothers, sisters, brethren, sistren <nonformal>, people; flock, fold, sheep; **congregation,** parishioners, churchgoers, assembly; *minyan* <Heb>; **parish,** society; class

2 **layman,** laic, secular, churchman, **parishioner,** church member; brother, sister, lay brother, lay sister; laywoman, churchwoman; catehumen; communicant

ADJS 3 **lay,** laic *or* laical; **nonecclesiastical,** nonclerical, nonministerial, nonpastoral, nonordained; nonreligious; **secular,** secularist; secularistic; temporal, popular, civil; congregational

701 RELIGIOUS RITES

NOUNS 1 **ritualism,** rituality, **ceremonialism, formalism,** liturgism; symbolism, symbolics; **cult,** cultus, cultism; sacramentalism, sacramentarianism; sabbatism, Sabbatarianism; ritualization, **solemnization,** solemn observance, **celebration;** liturgics, liturgiology

2 **ritualist, ceremonialist,** liturgist, **formalist,** formulist, formularist; sacramentalist, sacramentarian; sabbatist, Sabbatarian; High-Churchman, High-Churchist

3 **rite** <see list>, **ritual,** rituality, **liturgy,** holy rite; order of worship; **ceremony, ceremonial; observance,** ritual observance; **formality,** solemnity; **form,** formula, formulary, form of worship *or* service, mode of worship; prescribed form; service, function, duty, office, practice; **sacrament,** sacramental, mystery; ordinance; institution

4 **seven sacraments,** mysteries: baptism, confirmation, the Eucharist, penance, extreme unction, holy orders, matrimony

5 **unction,** sacred unction, sacramental anointment, chrism *or* chrisom, chrismation, chrismatory; **extreme unction, last rites,** viaticum; ointment; chrismal

6 **baptism,** baptizement; **christening; immersion,** total immersion; **sprinkling,** aspersion, aspergation; affusion, infusion; baptism for the dead; baptismal

regeneration; baptismal gown *or* dress *or* robe, chrismal; baptistery, **font; confirmation,** bar *or* bas mitzvah <both Jewish>

7 **Eucharist, Lord's Supper, Last Supper, Communion,** Holy Communion, **the Sacrament,** the Holy Sacrament; intinction; consubstantiation, impanation, subpanation, transubstantiation; real presence; elements, consecrated elements, bread and wine, body and blood of Christ; Host, wafer, loaf, bread, altar bread, consecrated bread; Sacrament Sunday

8 **Mass,** *Missa* <L>, Eucharistic rites; **the Liturgy,** the Divine Liturgy; **parts of the Mass**

9 **sacred object** *or* **article; ritualistic manual,** Book of Common Prayer, breviary, canon, haggadah <Jewish>, missal *or* Mass book, prayer book, siddur *and* machazor <Jewish>

10 **psalter, psalmbook;** Psalm Book, Book of Common Order; the Psalms, Book of Psalms, the Psalter, the Psaltery

11 **holy day,** hallowday <nonformal>, holytide; feast, fast; Sabbath; Sunday, Lord's day; saint's day; church calendar, ecclesiastical calendar

12 Christian holy days <see list>; Jewish holy days <see list>

13 <Muslim holy days> Ramadan <month>, Bairam, Muharram

VERBS **14 celebrate, observe, keep, solemnize;** celebrate Mass; communicate, administer Communion; attend Communion, receive the Sacrament, partake of the Lord's Supper; attend Mass

15 **minister, officiate,** do duty, **perform a rite,** perform service *or* divine service; administer a sacrament, administer the Eucharist, etc; anoint, chrism; confirm, impose, lay hands on; make the sign of the cross

16 **baptize, christen;** dip, immerse; sprinkle, asperge; circumcise

17 **confess,** make confession, receive absolution; **shrive,** hear confession; **absolve,** administer absolution; administer extreme unction

ADJS **18 ritualistic, ritual; ceremonial, ceremonious; formal,** formular, formulary; **liturgic, liturgical,** liturgistic, liturgistical; High-Church; **sacramental,** sacramentarian; eucharistic, eucharistical, baptismal; paschal; Passover

19 **rites**

aspersion *or* asperges	circumcision *and* bar
celebration	mitzvah *and* bas

mitzvah <all Jewish>.

confession *or* auricular confession *or* the confessional *or* the confessionary

confirmation

greater *or* lesser litany

high celebration

imposition *or* laying on of hands

invocation

invocation of saints

litany

love feast *or* agape

lustration

pax *or* kiss of peace

processional

reciting the rosary *or* telling one's beads

sign of the cross *or* *signum crucis* <L> *or* signing *or* crossing oneself

thurification *or* censing

20 **Christian holy days**

Advent	Lammas *or* Lammas
Annunciation *or* Annunciation Day *or* Lady Day	Day *or* Lammastide *or* Feast of St Peter's Chains
Ascension Day *or* Holy Thursday	Lent *or* Lententide Martinmas
Ash Wednesday	Michaelmas *or* Michaelmas Day *or*
Candlemas *or* Candlemas Day	chaelmas Day *or* Michaelmastide
Christmas	Palm Sunday
Corpus Christi	Pentecost *or* Whitsuntide *or* Whitsun *or*
Easter *or* Eastertide	tide *or* Whitsun *or*
Easter Saturday *or* Easter Sunday	Whitsunday
Ember days	Quadragesima *or* Quadragesima
Epiphany *or* Three Kings' Day	Sunday
Good Friday	Septuagesima
Hallowmas *or* Allhallowmas *or*	Shrove Tuesday *or* Mardi Gras *or* Carnival *or* Pancake
Allhallowtide *or*	Day
Halloween *or* Allhallows *or* All Saints' Day *or* All	Trinity Sunday Twelfth-tide *or* Twelfth-night *or*
Souls' Day	Twelfth-day
Holy Thursday *or* Maundy Thursday	Whitweek *and* Whitmonday *and*
Holy Week *or* Passion Week	Whit-Tuesday, etc

21 **Jewish holy days**

Fast of Av *or* Ninth of Av *or* Tishah b'Av	Shabuoth *or* Pentecost *or* Feast of
Hanukkah *or* Feast of the Dedication	Weeks
High Holy Days	Simhath Torah *or* Rejoicing over the
Lag b'Omer	Law
Passover *or* Pesach	Sukkoth *or* Feast of
Purim	Tabernacles
Rosh Hashanah *or* New Year	Yom Kippur *or* Day of Atonement

702 ECCLESIASTICAL ATTIRE

NOUNS **1 canonicals,** clericals <nonformal>, robes, cloth; **vestments,** vesture; liturgical garments, ceremonial attire; pontificals, pontificalia, episcopal vestments

2 robe, frock, mantle, gown, cloak
3 staff, pastoral staff, **crosier, cross,** cross-staff, crook, paterissa
ADJS **4 vestmental,** vestmentary

703 RELIGIOUS BUILDINGS

NOUNS **1 church,** kirk <Scots>, bethel, **meetinghouse,** church house, **house of God,** place of worship, house of worship *or* prayer; conventicle; **mission;** basilica, major *or* patriarchal basilica, minor basilica; **cathedral,** cathedral church, *duomo* <Ital>; collegiate church
2 temple, fane; **tabernacle; synagogue,** *shul* <Yiddish>; **mosque,** masjid; dewal, girja; pagoda; kiack; pantheon
3 chapel, chapel of ease, chapel royal, side chapel, school chapel, sacrament chapel, Lady chapel, oratory, oratorium; chantry; sacellum, sacrarium
4 shrine, holy place, dagoba, naos; sacrarium, delubrum; tope, stupa; reliquary, *reliquaire* <Fr>
5 sanctuary, holy of holies, sanctum, sanctum sanctorum, adytum, sacrarium
6 cloister, monastery, house, abbey, friary; priory, priorate; lamasery; **convent, nunnery**
7 parsonage, pastorage, pastorate, manse, **church house,** clergy house; presbytery, **rectory,** vicarage, deanery; glebe; chapter house
8 bishop's palace; Vatican; Lambeth, Lambeth Palace
9 <church interior> vestry, sacristy, sacrarium, diaconicon *or* diaconicum; baptistery; ambry, apse, blindstory, chancel, choir, choir screen, cloisters, confessional, confessionary <old>, crypt, Easter sepulcher, nave, porch, presbytery, rood loft, rood stair, rood tower *or* spire *or* steeple, transept, triforium; organ loft
10 <church furnishings> piscina; stoup, holy-water stoup *or* basin; baptismal font; patent; reredos; jube, rood screen, rood arch, chancel screen; altar cloth, cerecloth, chrismal; communion *or* sacrament cloth, corporal, fanon, oblation cloth; rood cloth; baldachin, *baldacchino* <Ital>; kneeling stool, *prie-dieu* <Fr>; prayer rug *or* carpet *or* mat
11 <vessels> cruet; chalice; ciborium, pyx; chrismal, chrismatory; monstrance, ostensorium; reliquary; font, holy-water font
12 altar, scrobis; bomos, eschara, hestia;

Lord's table, holy table, **Communion table,** chancel table, table of the Lord, God's board; rood altar; altar desk, missal stand; credence, prothesis, table *or* altar of prothesis, predella; superaltar, retable, retablo, ancona, gradin; altarpiece, altar side, altar rail, altar carpet, altar stair; altar facing *or* front, frontal; altar slab, altar stone, mensal
13 pulpit, rostrum, ambo; **lectern,** desk, reading desk
14 <seats> **pew; stall;** mourners' bench, anxious bench *or* seat, penitent form; amen corner; sedilia
ADJS **15 churchly,** churchish, **ecclesiastical;** churchlike, templelike; cathedral-like, cathedralesque; tabernacular; synagogical, synagogal; pantheonic
16 claustral, cloistered; monastic, monachal, **monasterial; coventual,** conventicular

704 SHOW BUSINESS, THEATER

NOUNS **1 show business,** show biz <nonformal>, the entertainment industry; **the theater, the footlights, the stage, the boards,** the bright lights, Broadway, the Great White Way, the scenes <old>, traffic of the stage; avant-garde theater, contemporary theater, experimental theater, total theater, epic theater, theater of the absurd, theater of cruelty, guerrilla theater, street theater; stagedom, theater world, stage world, stageland, playland; **drama,** legitimate stage *or* theater, legit <nonformal>, off Broadway, off-off-Broadway; music *or* musical theater; café theater, dinner theater; regional theater; repertory drama *or* theater, stock; summer stock, straw hat *or* straw hat circuit <nonformal>; **vaudeville,** variety; **burlesque; circus,** carnival; theatromania, theatrophobia
2 dramatics; dramatization, dramaticism, dramatism; **theatrics,** theatricism, **theatricalism,** theatricality, staginess; theatricals, amateur theatricals; **histrionics,** histrionism; dramatic *or* histrionic *or* Thespian art; dramatic stroke, *coup de théâtre* <Fr>; **melodramatics,** sensationalism; **dramaturgy,** dramatic structure, play construction, dramatic form; dramatic irony, tragic irony
3 theatercraft, stagecraft, stagery, scenecraft; **showmanship**
4 stage show, show; play, stage play, piece, vehicle, work; **hit** *or* hit show <nonformal>, gasser <nonformal>, success,

critical success, audience success, word-of-mouth success; failure, **flop** *and* bomb *and* turkey <all nonformal>

5 **tragedy,** tragic drama; tragic flaw; buskin, cothurnus; tragic muse, Melpomene

6 **comedy;** comic relief, comedy relief; comic muse, Thalia; sock, coxcomb, cap and bells, motley, bladder, slapstick

7 **act, scene, number, turn,** bit *and* shtick <both nonformal>, routine <nonformal>; curtain raiser *or* lifter; introduction; expository scene; **prologue,** epilogue; **entr'acte,** intermezzo, intermission, interlude, *divertissement* <Fr>, *divertimento* <Ital>; **finale,** afterpiece; exodus, exode; chaser <nonformal>; curtain call, curtain; hokum *or* hoke act <nonformal>; song and dance; burlesque act, striptease; stand-up comedy act; sketch, skit

8 **acting, playing,** playacting, performing, **performance,** taking a role *or* part; **representation, portrayal, characterization,** projection; **impersonation,** personation, miming, mimicking, mimicry, mimesis; pantomiming, mummery; ham *and* hammy acting *and* hamming *or* hamming up <all nonformal>, overacting; stage presence; stage directions, **business,** stage business, *jeu de théâtre* <Fr>, acting device; stunt *and* gag <both nonformal>; hokum *or* hoke <nonformal>; buffoonery, slapstick; patter; stand-up comedy

9 **repertoire, repertory;** stock

10 **role, part,** piece <nonformal>; cue, **lines,** side; cast; **character,** person, personage; lead, starring *or* lead *or* leading role, fat part, leading man, leading woman *or* lady, hero, heroine; antihero; title role, protagonist, principal character; supporting role, supporting character; ingenue, *jeune première* or *jeune premier* <Fr>, romantic lead; soubrette; villain, heavy <nonformal>; antagonist; bit, bit part, minor role; feeder, straight part; walking part, walk-on; top banana, second banana; **actor** 707.2

11 **engagement,** playing engagement, booking; **run; stand,** one-night stand *or* one-nighter; **circuit,** vaudeville circuit, borscht circuit; **tour, bus-and-truck, production tour;** date

12 theatrical performance, **performance, show, presentation,** presentment, **production,** entertainment, stage presentation *or* performance; bill; **exhibit, exhibition;** benefit performance, benefit; personal appearance, flesh show <nonfor-

mal>; showcase, tryout; premiere, premier performance, debut; farewell performance, swan song <nonformal>

13 **production,** mounting, staging, putting on; stage management; **direction,** *mise-en-scène* <Fr>; blocking; **rehearsal,** dress rehearsal, walk-through, run-through, technical *or* tech rehearsal *or* run, final dress, gypsy rehearsal *or* run-through *or* run

14 **theater, playhouse, house,** theatron, odeum; **auditorium; opera house,** opera; **hall,** music hall, concert hall; **amphitheater;** circle theater, arena theater, theater-in-the-round; vaudeville theater; burlesque theater; **little theater,** community theater; open-air theater, outdoor theater; Greek theater; children's theater; Elizabethan theater, Globe Theatre; showboat; dinner theater; cabaret, nightclub, club, night spot, *boîte de nuit* <Fr>

15 **auditorium;** parquet, orchestra, **pit** <Brit>; **orchestra circle,** parquet circle, parterre; **dress circle;** fauteuil *or* theatre stall *or* **stall** <all Brit>; **box,** box seat, **loge,** *baignoire* <Fr>; stage box; proscenium boxes, parterre boxes; balcony, gallery; **peanut gallery** *and* paradise <both nonformal>; standing room

16 **stage,** the boards; acting area, playing *or* performing area; thrust stage, three-quarter-round stage, theater-in-the-round; apron, passerelle, apron stage, forestage; proscenium stage, proscenium arch, proscenium; bridge; revolving stage; orchestra, pit, orchestra pit; **bandstand,** shell, band shell; stage right, **R;** stage left, **L;** upstage, downstage, backstage; **wings,** coulisse; dressing room, greenroom; flies, fly gallery, fly floor; gridiron, grid <nonformal>; board, lightboard, switchboard; dock; prompter's box; curtain, grand drape, safety curtain, asbestos curtain, fire curtain; stage door

17 <stage requisites> **property, prop;** practical piece *or* prop <nonformal>; costume 5.9; theatrical makeup, makeup, greasepaint, blackface, clown white; spirit gum

18 lights, instruments; **footlights,** foots <nonformal>, floats; floodlight, flood; bunch light; **limelight,** follow spot, spotlight *or* spot <nonformal>, arc light, arc, klieg *or* klieg light; color filter, medium, gelatin *or* gel; dimmer; marquee; light plot

19 **setting, stage setting,** stage set, **set,** *mise-en-scène* <Fr>; location, locale

20 scenery, decor; **scene;** screen, **flat;** cyclorama or cyc; batten; side scene, **wing,** coulisse; border; tormentor, **teaser;** wingcut, woodcut; transformation, transformation scene; flipper; counterweight; **curtain,** rag <nonformal>, hanging; **drop,** drop scene, drop curtain, scrim, cloth; **backdrop,** back cloth <Brit>; act drop or curtain; tab, tableau curtain

21 playbook, script, text, **libretto;** promptbook; book; **score; scenario,** continuity, shooting script; scene plot; lines, actor's lines, cue, sides; stage direction; prompt book

22 dramatist; playwright, playwriter, dramaturge; doctor and play doctor and play fixer <all nonformal>; dramatizer; **scriptwriter, scenario writer,** scenarist, **scenarioist, screenwriter; gagman,** joke writer, jokesmith; **librettist;** tragedian, comedian; farcist, farceur, farceuse <both Fr>, farcer; melodramatist; monodramatist; mimographer; **choreographer**

23 theater man, theatrician; **showman,** exhibitor, **producer, impresario; director,** auteur; stage director, **stage manager;** set designer, scenewright; costume designer, costumer, costumier, costumière <both Fr>; wardrobe master or mistress; dresser; hair or wigmaker or designer; makeup man or artist, visagiste; propsmaster or propsmistress; prompter; callboy; playreader; master of ceremonies, MC or emcee <nonformal>; ticket collector; usher, usherer, usherette; ringmaster, equestrian director; barker, ballyhoo man and spieler <both nonformal>

24 stage technician, stagehand, machinist <old>, sceneman, **sceneshifter;** flyman; carpenter; **electrician;** scene painter, scenic artist, scenewright

25 agent, actor's agent, playbroker, tenpercenter <nonformal>; **booking agent;** advance agent, advance man; publicity man or agent

26 patron, patroness; **backer, angel** <nonformal>; Dionysus

27 playgoer, theatergoer; attender 221.5, spectator 917, audience 48.6; moviegoer, **motion-picture fan** <nonformal>; firstnighter; standee, groundling <old>; claqueur <Fr>, hired applauder; pass holder, deadhead <nonformal>

VERBS **28 dramatize,** theatricalize; melodramatize; scenarize; **present, stage, produce, mount, put on,** put on the stage; **put on a show;** try out, preview; give a performance; premiere; **open,** open a show, open a show cold <nonformal>; set the stage; ring up the curtain, ring down the curtain; **star, feature** <nonformal>, bill, **headline,** give top billing to; succeed, make or be a hit and have legs <all nonformal>, be a gas or gasser and run out of gas <all nonformal>; fail, flop and bomb and bomb out <all nonformal>

29 act, perform, play, playact, tread the boards, strut one's stuff <nonformal>; appear, **appear on the stage;** act like a trouper; register; emotionalize, emote <nonformal>; pantomime, mime; patter; sketch; troupe, barnstorm <nonformal>; steal the show, upstage, steal the spotlight; **debut,** make one's debut or bow, come out; act as foil or feeder, stooge <nonformal>, be straight man for; **star,** play the lead, get top billing, have one's name in lights

30 enact, act out; represent, depict, portray; act or play or perform a part or role, take a part, sustain a part, act or play the part of; create a role or character; **impersonate,** personate; play opposite, support

31 overact, overdramatize, chew up the scenery <nonformal>, act all over the stage; **ham** and ham it up <both nonformal>; **mug** <nonformal>, grimace; spout, rant, roar, declaim, "out-herod Herod"—Shakespeare; milk a scene; **underact,** throw away <nonformal>

32 rehearse, practice, go through, walk or run through, go over; go through one's part, read one's lines; con or study one's part; be a fast or slow study

ADJS **33 dramatic,** dramatical <old>, **dramaturgic, dramaturgical; theatric, theatrical, histrionic, thespian;** scenic; **stagy;** theaterlike, stagelike; **spectacular; melodramatic;** ham or hammy <nonformal>; overacted, overplayed, milked <nonformal>; underacted, underplayed, thrown away; **operatic;** ballet, balletic; legitimate; stellar, all-star; stagestruck, starstruck; stageworthy, actor-proof

34 tragic, heavy; buskined, cothurned

35 comic, light; tragicomical, **farcical, slapstick;** camp or campy <nonformal>

ADVS **36 on the stage** or boards, before an audience, before the footlights; **in the limelight** or spotlight; onstage; downstage, upstage; backstage, off stage, behind the scenes; down left or DL; down right or DR; up left or UL; up right or UR

705 DANCE

NOUNS **1 dancing** <see list>, terpsichore, **dance;** the light fantastic; **choreography;**

dance drama, choreodrama; **hoofing** <nonformal>

2 **dance, hop** <nonformal>, dancing party, **shindig** and shindy <both nonformal>; **ball,** *bal* <Fr>; masked ball, masque, mask, masquerade ball, masquerade, *bal masqué* <Fr>, *bal costumé* <Fr>, fancy-dress ball, cotillion; promenade, **prom** <nonformal>, formal <nonformal>; country dance, square dance, barn dance; mixer, stag dance; record hop; dinner-dance, tea dance, *thé dansant* <Fr>

3 **dancer,** danseur, terpsichorean, **hoofer** <nonformal>, step dancer, tap dancer, clog dancer, etc; **ballet dancer; ballerina,** danseuse, coryphée; *première danseuse, danseur noble* <both Fr>; **modern dancer;** *corps de ballet* <Fr>; figurant, figurante; **chorus girl, chorine,** chorus boy or man; chorus line; geisha or geisha girl; nautch girl, bayadere; hula girl; taxi dancer; topless dancer; burlesque dancer, strip-teaser, stripper and bump-and-grinder <both nonformal>; choreographer

4 **ballroom, dance hall,** dancery; dance palace; casino

VERBS 5 **dance, trip the light fantastic,** "trip it as we go, on the light fantastic toe"— Milton, trip, skip, hop, foot, prance <nonformal>, **hoof** <nonformal>, clog, tap-dance, fold-dance, etc; shake, shimmy, shuffle; waltz, one-step, two-step, foxtrot, etc; choreograph

ADJS 6 **dancing, dance, terpsichorean;** balletic; choreographic

7 **kinds of dancing**

ballet	folk dancing
ballroom dancing	interpretive dancing
belly dancing	jazz dancing
break dancing	jazz tap
character dancing	modern ballet
choral dancing	modern dance
classical ballet	morris dancing
clog dancing	round dancing
comedy ballet	slam dancing
country dancing	social dancing
couple dancing	soft-shoe dancing
dirty or touch danc-	solo dancing
ing	square dancing
disco dancing	step dancing
flamenco	tap dancing
folklorico	taxi dancing

706 MOTION PICTURES

NOUNS 1 **motion pictures, movies, the movies, the pictures,** moving pictures, films, the film, the cinema, the screen, the big screen, the silver screen, the flicks and the flickers <both nonformal>; **motion picture, movie, picture, film,** flick and flicker <both nonformal>, picture show, motion-picture show, moving-picture show, photoplay, photodrama; **sound film,** silent film or silent; cinéma vérité or direct cinema; vérité; magic realism; **documentary film** or **movie,** docudrama, docutainment; **feature,** feature film, feature-length film, main attraction; theatrical film, big-screen film; **motion-picture genre** or **type;** TV film or movie, made-for-television movie or film; **short,** short movie, short subject; preview, sneak preview; **B-movie,** B-picture, Grade B movie, low-budget picture; **educational film** or **movie,** training film, promotional film, trigger film; **underground film** or **movie,** experimental film or movie, avant-garde film or movie, representational film or movie, art film or movie, surrealistic film or movie; **cartoon,** animated cartoon, animation, cel animation, claymation, computer graphics; animatron, audioanimatron; **rated movie** or **film,** rating system, rating, G or general audience, PG or parental guidance suggested, PG-13 or parents strongly cautioned, R or Restricted, NC-17 or no children under 17 admitted, X or no one under 17 admitted

2 **script, screenplay,** motion-picture play or script, shooting script, storyboard, scenario, treatment, original screenplay; **dialogue,** book; **role,** lead, romantic lead, stock character, ingenue, soubrette, cameo, bit, silent bit

3 **motion-picture studio, movie studio,** film studio, dream factory <nonformal>, animation studio, lot, back lot, sound stage, location; **set, motion-picture set, film set,** *mise-en-scène* <Fr>, properties or props, set dressing; **motion-picture company, film company,** production company; **producer,** filmmaker, moviemaker, **director,** auteur, screenwriter or scriptwriter or scenarist, editor or film editor, **actor, actress, film actor, film actress,** player, cinemactor, cinemactress, star, starlet, character actor, featured player, supporting actor or actress, supporting player, bit player, extra; **crew,** film crew

4 **motion-picture photography, photography,** cinematography, camera work, cinematics, camera angle, camera position, **shot, take,** footage, retake; screen test; **special effects,** rear-screen projection, mechanical effects, optical effects, process photography, FX; **color photogra-**

phy, black-and-white, color, colorization; **cameraman** *or* **camerawoman, motion-picture cameraman** *or* **camerawoman,** cinematographer, director of photography *or* DP, first cameraman, lighting cameraman

5 **motion-picture editing, film editing, editing,** cutting; **transition,** fade, fade-out/fade-in, dissolve, lap *or* overlap dissolve, out-focus-dissolve, match dissolve, cross dissolve, mix

6 **motion-picture theater, movie theater,** picture theater, film theater, cinema <Brit>, movie palace, dream palace <nonformal>, circuit theater, drive-in theater *or* movie, grind house <nonformal>; **screen,** movie screen, motion-picture screen, silver screen, aspect ratio *or* format, screen proportion, widescreen, Cinerama *and* Cinemascope *and* VistaVision *and* Todd-AO *and* Ultra-Panavision <all trade names>

VERBS 7 **film, shoot,** cinematize, filmmake; colorize

ADJS 8 **motion-picture, movie, film,** cinema, cinematic, filmistic, filmic; colorized; animated; animatronic, audioanimatronic

707 ENTERTAINER

NOUNS 1 **entertainer,** public entertainer, performer; artist, artiste; impersonator, female impersonator; **vaudevillian,** vaudevillist; dancer 705.3, hoofer <nonformal>; song and dance man; chorus girl, show girl, chorine <nonformal>; coryphée; chorus boy *or* man; burlesque queen <nonformal>, **stripteaser,** exotic dancer, ecdysiast; stripper *and* peeler *and* stripteuse *and* bump-and-grinder <all nonformal>; dancing girl, nautch girl, belly dancer; go-go dancer; geisha, geisha girl; mountebank; **magician,** conjurer, prestidigitator, sleight-of-hand artist; mummer, guiser <Scots>, guisard; singer, musician 710; performance artist

2 **actor, actress, player,** stage player *or* performer, playactor, histrion, histrio, thespian, Roscius, theatrical <nonformal>, trouper; child actor; mummer, pantomime, pantomimist; monologist, diseur, diseuse, reciter; dramatizer; mime, mimer, mimic; strolling player, stroller; barnstormer <nonformal>; character actor *or* actress, character man *or* woman, character; **villain,** antagonist, **bad guy** *or* **heavy** *or* black hat <all nonformal>, villainess; juvenile, ingenue;

jeune premier and *jeune première* <both Fr>; soubrette; foil, feeder *and* stooge <both nonformal>, straight man *or* person; utility man *or* person; protean actor; matinee idol <nonformal>; romantic lead

3 circus artist *or* performer; trapeze artist, aerialist, flier <nonformal>; high-wire artist, tightrope walker, slack-roper artist, equilibrist; acrobat, tumbler; bareback rider; juggler; lion tamer, sword swallower; snake charmer; clown; ringmaster, equestrian director

4 **motion-picture actor,** movie actor; **movie star,** film star; starlet; day player, under-five player, contract player

5 **ham** *or* ham actor <both nonformal>; grimacer

6 **lead,** leading man *or* lady, leading actor *or* actress, principal, **star,** superstar, megastar, headliner, headline *or* feature attraction; costar; **hero, heroine,** protagonist; juvenile lead, *jeune premier, jeune première* <both Fr>; first tragedian, heavy lead <nonformal>; **prima donna,** diva, singer 710.13; première danseuse, prima ballerina, *danseur noble* <Fr>

7 **supporting actor** *or* **actress; support,** supporting cast; **supernumerary,** super *or* supe <nonformal>, spear-carrier <nonformal>, **extra;** bit player; walking gentleman *or* lady <nonformal>, walk-on, mute; figurant, figurante; **understudy, stand-in,** standby, substitute, swing

8 **tragedian,** tragedienne

9 **comedian,** comedienne, **comic, funnyman;** farcist, farcer, *farceur, farceuse* <both Fr>; stand-up comic *or* comedian <nonformal>, light comedian, genteel comedian, low comedian, slapstick comedian, hokum *or* hoke comic <nonformal>

10 **buffoon,** *buffo* <Ital>, **clown, fool, jester, zany, merry-andrew,** jack-pudding, pickle-herring, **motley fool,** motley, wearer of the cap and bells; harlequin; Pierrot; Pantaloon, Pantalone; Punch, Punchinello, Pulcinella, Polichinelle; Punch and Judy; Hanswurst; Columbine; Harlequin; Scaramouch

11 **cast,** cast of characters, characters, persons of the drama, *dramatis personae* <L>; supporting cast; **company,** acting company, **troupe;** repertory company, stock company; ensemble, chorus, *corps de ballet* <Fr>; circus troupe

708 MUSIC

NOUNS 1 **music** <see list>, harmonious sound, "the speech of angels"—Carlyle, "the mosaic of the Air"—Andrew Marvell, "the harmonious voice of creation; an echo of the invisible world" — Giuseppe Mazzini, "the only universal tongue"—Samuel Rogers, "the universal language of mankind"—Longfellow, "the poor man's Parnassus"—Emerson, "the brandy of the damned"—G B Shaw, "nothing else but wild sounds civilized into time and tune"—Thomas Fuller

2 **melody,** melodiousness, **tunefulness,** musicalness, musicality; **tune, tone,** musical sound, musical quality, tonality; sweetness, dulcetness, mellifluence, mellifluousness

3 **harmony, concord,** concordance, concert, consonance *or* consonancy, consort, accordance, **accord,** monochord, concentus, symphony, diapason; synchronism, synchronization; **attunement,** tune, attune; chime, chiming; unison, unisonance, homophony, monody; **euphony;** light *or* heavy harmony; two-part *or* three-part harmony, etc; harmony *or* music of the spheres; harmonics 709

4 **air,** aria, **tune, melody,** line, melodic line, refrain, note, **song,** solo, solo part, soprano part, treble, lay, descant, lilt, **strain,** measure; canto, cantus

5 **piece,** opus, **composition,** production, work; **score; arrangement,** adaptation, orchestration, harmonization, setting; **form**

6 **classical music,** classic; concert music, serious music, longhair music <nonformal>, symphonic music; semiclassic, semiclassical music

7 **popular music,** pop music, light music, popular song *or* air *or* tune, **ballad;** hit, song hit, hit tune; Tin Pan Alley

8 **dance music,** ballroom music, **dances;** syncopated music, **syncopation; ragtime** *or* rag

9 **jazz;** hot jazz, Dixieland, Basin Street, traditional jazz *or* trad <Brit nonformal>; **swing,** jive <nonformal>; bebop, bop <nonformal>; mainstream jazz; avant-garde jazz, the new music <nonformal>; boogie *or* boogie-woogie; walking bass, stride *or* stride piano

10 **rock-and-roll, rock music,** rock'n'roll, rock, hard rock, acid rock, folk rock, country rock, full-tilt boogie

11 **folk music,** folk songs, ethnic music, ethnomusicology; folk ballads, balladry; border ballads; country music, hillbilly music; country-and-western music, western swing; old-time country music *or* old-timey music; bluegrass; field holler; the

blues, talking blues, country blues, city blues

12 **march,** martial *or* military music; military march, quick *or* quickstep march; processional march, recessional march; funeral *or* dead march; wedding march

13 **vocal music, song; singing,** caroling, warbling, lyricism, vocalism, **vocalization;** operatic singing, bel canto, coloratura, bravura; choral singing; folk singing; croon, crooning; yodel, yodeling; scat, scat singing; intonation; hum, humming; solmization, tonic sol-fa, solfeggio, solfège, sol-fa, sol-fa exercise

14 **song,** lay, *Lied* <Ger>, *chanson* <Fr>, carol, **ditty,** canticle, lilt; **ballad,** ballade, *ballata* <Ital>; *canzone* <Ital>; canzonet, *canzonetta* <Ital>

15 **solo; aria;** operatic aria

16 <Italian terms for arias> arietta, arioso; aria buffa, aria da capo, aria d'agilità, aria da chiesa, aria d'imitazione, aria fugata, aria parlante; bravura, aria di bravura; coloratura, aria di coloratura; cantabile, aria cantabile; recitativo

17 **sacred music, church music,** liturgical music; **hymn,** hymn-tune, hymnody, hymnology; **psalm,** psalmody; **chorale,** choral fantasy, anthem; motet; **oratorio;** passion; **mass;** requiem mass, requiem, missa brevis, missa solemnis; offertory, offertory sentence *or* hymn; **cantata;** doxology, introit, canticle, paean, prosodion; recessional

18 **part music,** polyphonic music, part song, part singing, ensemble music, ensemble singing; **duet,** duo, *duettino* <Ital>; **trio,** terzet, *terzetto* <Ital>; **quartet; quintet; sextet,** sestet; **septet,** septuor; **octet;** cantata, lyric cantata; madrigal, *madrigaletto* <Ital>; **chorus** 710.16, chorale, glee club, choir; choral singing; four-part, soprano-alto-tenor-base *or* SATB

19 **round, rondo,** rondeau, **roundelay,** catch, troll; rondino, rondoletto; **fugue,** canon, fugato

20 **polyphony,** polyphonism; **counterpoint,** contrapunto; **plainsong,** Gregorian chant, Ambrosian chant; *faux-bourdon* <Fr>; musica ficta, false music

21 monody, monophony, homophony

22 **part,** melody *or* voice part, **voice** 709.5, **line;** descant, canto, cantus, cantus planus *or* firmus, plain song, plain chant; prick song, cantus figuratus; soprano, tenor, treble, alto, contralto, baritone, bass, bassus; undersong; drone; **accompaniment;** continuo, basso continuo, figured bass, thorough bass; ground bass,

basso ostinato; drone, drone bass, bourdon, burden

23 response, responsory report, answer; echo; antiphon, antiphony, antiphonal chanting *or* singing

24 passage, phrase, musical phrase, strain, part, motive, motif, theme, subject, figure; leitmotiv; **movement;** introductory phrase, anacrusis; statement, exposition, development, variation; division; period, musical sentence; section; **measure;** figure; **verse, stanza;** burden, bourdon; **chorus, refrain,** response; folderol, **ornament** 709.18, cadence 709.23, harmonic close, resolution; **coda,** tailpiece; ritornello; intermezzo, interlude; bass passage; tutti, tutti passage; bridge, bridge passage

25 <fast, slow, etc passages> presto, prestissimo; allegro, allegretto; scherzo, scherzando; adagio, adagietto; andante, andantino; largo, larghetto, larghissimo; crescendo; diminuendo, decrescendo; rallentando, ritardando, ritenuto; piano, pianissimo; forte, fortissimo; staccato, marcato, marcando; pizzicato; spiccato; legato; stretto

26 overture, prelude, *Vorspiel* <Ger>, **introduction,** operatic overture, dramatic overture, concert overture, voluntary, descant, vamp; curtain raiser

27 impromptu, extempore, improvisation, interpolation; cadenza; **ornament** 709.18, flourish, ruffles and flourishes, grace note, appoggiatura, mordent, upper mordent, inverted mordent; **run,** melisma; vamp; lick, hot lick, riff

28 score, musical score *or* copy, **music,** notation, musical notation, written music, copy, draft, transcript, transcription, version, edition, text, arrangement; part; full *or* orchestral score, compressed *or* short score, piano score, vocal score, instrumental score; tablature, lute tablature; opera score, opera; **libretto;** sheet music; **songbook,** songster; hymnbook, hymnal; music paper; music roll

29 staff, stave <Brit>; line, ledger line; bar, bar line; space, degree; brace

30 execution, performance; rendering, rendition, music-making, **touch, expression;** fingering; pianism; intonation; repercussion; pizzicato, staccato, spiccato, parlando, legato, cantando, rubato, demilegato, mezzo staccato, slur; glissando

31 musicianship; musical talent *or* flair, musicality; virtuosity; pianism; musical ear, ear for music; musical sense, sense of rhythm; absolute *or* perfect pitch; relative pitch

32 musical occasion; choral service, service of lessons and carols, service of song, sing <nonformal>, singing, community singing *or* sing, singfest, songfest, sing-in; folk-sing *and* hootenanny <both nonformal>; **festival,** music festival; opera festival; folk-music festival, jazz festival, rock festival; *Sängerfest* <Ger>, *eisteddfod* <Welsh>; jam session <nonformal>

33 performance, musical performance, **program,** musical program, program of music; **concert,** symphony concert, chamber concert; philharmonic concert, philharmonic; popular concert, pops *and* pop concert <both nonformal>; promenade concert, prom <nonformal>; band concert; **recital;** service of music; concert performance <of an opera>; **medley,** potpourri; swan song, farewell performance

34 musical theater, music theater, lyric theater, musical stage, lyric stage; **music drama,** lyric drama; song-play, *Singspiel* <Ger>; **opera,** grand opera, light opera, ballad opera; comic opera, *opéra bouffe* <Fr>, *opera buffa* <Ital>; **operetta; musical comedy; musical;** Broadway musical; **ballet,** *opéra ballet* <Fr>, comedy ballet, *ballet d'action* <Fr>, *ballet divertissement* <Fr>; dance drama; chorus show; **song-and-dance act;** minstrel, minstrel show

VERBS **35 harmonize,** be harmonious, be in tune *or* concert, chord, **accord,** symphonize, synchronize, **chime, blend,** blend in; tune, attune, atone, sound together, sound in tune; assonate; melodize, musicalize

36 tune, tune up, attune, atone, chord, **put in tune;** voice, string; tone up, tone down

37 strike up, strike up a tune, **strike up the band,** break into music, pipe up, pipe up a song, yerk out <nonformal>, **burst into song**

38 sing, vocalize, carol, descant, lilt, troll, line out *and* belt out *and* tear off <all nonformal>; **warble,** trill, tremolo, quaver, shake; **chirp,** chirrup, twit <Brit nonformal>, **twitter;** pipe, whistle, tweedle, tweedledee; **chant; intone,** intonate; **croon; hum; yodel;** roulade; chorus, choir, sing in chorus; **hymn,** anthem, psalm, "make a joyful noise unto the Lord"—Bible; sing the praises of; minstrel; ballad; **serenade;** sol-fa, do-re-mi, solmizate

39 play, perform, execute, render, do; interpret; make music; concertize; symphonize; chord; accompany; play by ear; play at, pound out *and* saw away at <both nonformal>

40 strum, thrum, pluck, plunk, **pick,** twang, sweep the strings

41 fiddle <nonformal>, play violin *or* the violin; scrape *and* saw <both nonformal>

42 blow a horn, sound *or* wind the horn, sound, blow, wind, **toot,** tootle, pipe, tweedle; bugle, carillon, clarion, fife, flute, trumpet, whistle; bagpipe, doodle <Brit nonformal>; lip, tongue, double-tongue, triple-tongue

43 syncopate, play jazz, swing, jive <nonformal>, rag <nonformal>

44 beat time, keep time, tap, tap out the rhythm; count, count the beats; beat the drum, **drum** 55.4, play drum *or* the drums, thrum, beat, thump, pound; tom-tom; ruffle; beat *or* sound a tattoo

45 conduct, direct, lead, wield the baton

46 compose, write, arrange, score, set, set to music, put to music; musicalize, melodize, **harmonize; orchestrate;** instrument, instrumentate, **adapt,** make an adaptation; transcribe, transpose

ADJS **47 musical, musically inclined,** musicianly, with an ear for music; virtuoso, virtuose, virtuosic; **music-loving,** music-mad, musicophile, philharmonic; absolute, aleatory

48 melodious, melodic; **musical,** music-like; **tuneful,** tunable; fine-toned, **pleasant-sounding,** agreeable-sounding, pleasant, appealing, agreeable, catchy, singable; **euphonious** *or* euphonic, **lyric, lyrical,** melic; **lilting,** songful, songlike; **sweet, dulcet,** sweet-sounding, achingly sweet, sweet-flowing; honeyed, mellifluent, mellifluous, mellisonant, music-flowing; rich, mellow; sonorous, canorous; golden, golden-toned; silvery, silver-toned; sweet-voiced, golden-voiced, silver-voiced, silver-tongued, golden-tongued, music-tongued; ariose, arioso, cantabile

49 harmonious, harmonic, symphonious; harmonizing, **chiming,** blending, well-blended, blended; **concordant,** consonant, accordant, according, **in accord,** in concord, in concert; synchronous, synchronized, in sync <nonformal>, **in tune,** tuned, attuned; in unison, in chorus; unisonous, unisonant; homophonic, monophonic, monodic; assonant, assonantal

50 vocal, singing; **choral,** choric; four-part; operatic; hymnal; psalmic, psalmodic, psalmodial; sacred, liturgical; treble, soprano, tenor, alto, falsetto; coloratura, lyric, bravura, dramatic, heroic; baritone; bass

51 instrumental, orchestral, symphonic, concert; dramatico-musical; jazz, syncopated, jazzy, rock, swing

52 polyphonic, contrapuntal

ADJS, ADVS **53** <directions, style> legato; staccato; spiccato; pizzicato; forte, fortissimo; piano, pianissimo; sordo; crescendo, accrescendo; decrescendo, diminuendo, morendo; dolce; amabile; affettuoso, con affetto; amoroso, con amore; lamentabile; agitato, con agitazione; leggiero; agilmente, con agilità; capriccioso, a capriccio; scherzando, scherzoso; appassionato, appassionatamente; abbandono; brillante; parlando; a cappella; trillando, tremolando, tremoloso; sotto voce; stretto

54 <slowly> largo, larghetto, allargando; adagio, adagietto; andante, andantino, andante moderato; calando; a poco; lento; ritardando, rallentando

55 <fast> presto, prestissimo; veloce; accelerando; vivace, vivacissimo; desto, con anima, con brio; allegro, allegretto; affrettando, moderato

56 varieties of music

absolute music	ensemble music
Afro-beat	field music
aleatory music	folk music
art music	folk rock
art rock	funk
atonal music *or* atonalism	fusion
ballet music	gospel music
baroque music	hard rock
beach music	heavy metal
big band	heavy rock
bluegrass	hillbilly music
cathedral music	house music *or* House
chamber music	inspirational music
church music	instrumental music
circus music	jazz music *or* jazz
classical music	jazz rock
country music	Latin rock
country-and-western music	loft jazz
dance hall	martial *or* military music
dance music	new age
deca-rock *or* glitter rock	part music
Delta blues	piped music
ear candy <nonformal>	political rock
easy listening music	pomp rock
electronic *or* synthesized music	polyphonic music
elevator music *or* Muzak <trademark>	pop-rock
	popular *or* pop music
	pop funk
	program music
	progressive rock
	progressive soul
	psychobilly

punkabilly
raga-rock
ragtime music *or* rag-
time
rap music
reggae
rhythm and blues *or*
R and B *or* the
blues
rock music *or*
rock'n'roll
rockabilly
rococo music
romantic music
sacred music

salon music
semiclassical music
ska
swing music *or* swing
technopop
thirdstream music
through-composed
music
twelve-tone music *or*
serialism
vocal music
wind music
Zopf music
zydeco

709 HARMONICS, MUSICAL ELEMENTS

NOUNS **1 harmonics,** harmony; melodics;
rhythmics; musicality; music, **music theory,** theory; musicology; musicography

**2 harmonization; orchestration, instru-
mentation;** arrangement, setting, adaptation, transcription; chordal progression; phrasing, modulation, intonation,
preparation, suspension, solution, resolution; tone painting

3 tone, tonality 50.3

4 pitch, tuning, tune, **tone, key, note,** register, tonality; height, depth; pitch range,
tessitura; classical pitch, high pitch, diapason *or* normal *or* French pitch, international *or* concert *or* new philharmonic
pitch, standard pitch, low pitch, Stutt-
gart *or* Scheibler's pitch, philharmonic
pitch, philosophical pitch; temperament

5 voice, *voce* <Ital>; *voce di petto* <Ital>,
chest voice; *voce di testa* <Ital>, head
voice; **soprano,** mezzo-soprano, dramatic
soprano, soprano spinto, lyric soprano,
coloratura soprano; boy soprano; male
soprano, castrato; alto, contralto; tenor,
lyric tenor, operatic tenor, heldentenor *or*
heroic tenor *or* Wagnerian tenor; counter-
tenor *or* male alto; baritone, light *or* lyric
baritone; **bass,** basso, basso profundo,
basso cantante *or* lyric bass, basso buffo
or comic bass; treble, falsetto

6 scale, gamut, register, compass, range,
diapason; diatonic scale, chromatic scale,
enharmonic scale, major scale, minor
scale, natural *or* harmonic *or* melodic
minor, whole-tone scale; great scale; octave scale, dodecuple scale, pentatonic
scale; tetrachordal scale; twelve-tone *or*
dodecuple scale, tone block, tone row,
tone cluster

7 sol-fa, tonic sol-fa, do-re-mi; Guidonian
syllables, ut, re, mi, fa, sol, la; sol-fa syllables, do, re, mi, fa, sol, la, ti *or* si, do;
fixed-do system, movable-do system; solmization; bobization

8 <diatonic series> tetrachord, chromatic
tetrachord, enharmonic tetrachord, Dorian tetrachord; hexachord, hard hexachord, natural hexachord, soft hexachord; pentachord

9 octave, *ottava* <Ital>, eighth; *ottava alta*
<Ital>, *ottava bassa* <Ital>; small oc-
tave, great octave; contraoctave, subcon-
traoctave, double contraoctave; one-line
octave, two-line octave, four-line octave,
two-foot octave, four-foot octave; tenor
octave

10 mode, octave species; major mode, minor
mode; Greek modes, Ionian mode, Dorian
mode, Phrygian mode, Lydian mode,
mixolydian mode, Aeolian mode, Locrian
mode; hypoionian mode, hypodorian
mode, hypophrygian mode, hypolydian
mode, hypoaeolian mode, hypomixoly-
dian mode, hypolocrian mode; Gregorian
or ecclesiastical *or* church *or* medieval
mode; plagal mode, authentic mode; Indian *or* Hindu mode, raga

11 form, arrangement, pattern, model, design; song *or* lied form, primary form;
sonata form, sonata allegro, ternary
form, symphonic form, canon form, toc-
cata form, fugue form, rondo form

12 notation, character, mark, symbol, signature, sign, *segno* <Ital>; dot; custos,
direct; cancel; bar, measure; measure *or*
time signature, key signature; tempo
mark, metronome *or* metronomic mark;
fermata, hold, pause; *presa* <Ital>, lead;
slur, tie, ligature, vinculum, enharmonic
tie; swell; accent, accent mark, expression mark

13 clef; C clef, soprano clef, alto *or* viola clef,
tenor clef; F *or* **bass clef,** G *or* **treble clef**

14 note, musical note, notes of a scale; **tone**
50.2; **sharp, flat, natural; accidental;** double whole note, breve; whole note,
semibreve; half note, minim; quarter
note, crotchet; eighth note, quaver; sixteenth note, semiquaver; thirty-second
note, demisemiquaver; sixty-fourth note,
hemidemisemiquaver; tercet, triplet; sustained note, dominant, dominant note;
enharmonic, enharmonic note; separation, hammering, staccato, spiccato;
connected, smooth, legato; responding
note, report; shaped note, patent note

15 key, key signature, tonality, sharps and
flats; **keynote,** tonic; tonic key; major,
minor, major *or* minor key, tonic major *or*
minor; supertonic, mediant, submediant,

dominant, subdominant, subtonic; pedal point, organ point

16 **harmonic,** harmonic tone, overtone, upper partial tone; flageolet tone

17 **chord,** *concento* <Ital>, combination of tones *or* notes; major *or* minor chord, tonic chord, dominant chord

18 **ornament,** grace, arabesque, embellishment, *fioritura* <Ital>; **flourish,** roulade, flight, run; passage, division 708.24; florid phrase *or* passage; coloratura; incidental, incidental note; grace note, appoggiatura; rubato; mordent, single mordent, double *or* long mordent; inverted mordent, pralltriller; turn, back *or* inverted turn; cadence, cadenza

19 **trill,** trillo; trillet, *trilleto* <Ital>; **tremolo,** tremolant, tremolando; quaver, quiver, tremble, tremor, flutter, falter, shake; **vibrato,** *Bebung* <Ger>

20 **interval,** degree, **step,** note, tone; second, third, fourth, fifth, sixth, seventh, octave; prime *or* unison interval, major *or* minor interval, harmonic *or* melodic interval, enharmonic interval, diatonic interval; parallel *or* consecutive intervals, parallel fifths, parallel octaves; whole step, major second; half step, halftone, semitone, minor second; augmented interval; diminished interval; diatonic semitone, chromatic semitone, less semitone, quarter semitone, tempered *or* mean semitone; quarter step, enharmonic diesis; diatessaron, diapason; *tierce de Picardie* <Fr> *or* Picardy third; augmented fourth *or* tritone

21 **rest,** pause; whole rest, breve rest, semibreve rest, half rest, minim, quarter rest, eighth rest, sixteenth rest, thirty-second rest, sixty-fourth rest

22 **rhythm, beat, meter, measure,** number *or* numbers, movement, **lilt, swing;** prosody, metrics; rhythmic pattern *or* phrase

23 cadence *or* cadency, authentic cadence, plagal cadence, mixed cadence, perfect *or* imperfect cadence, half cadence, deceptive *or* false cadence, interrupted *or* suspended cadence

24 **tempo, time, beat,** time pattern, timing; time signature; simple time *or* measure, compound time *or* measure; two-part *or* duple time, three-part *or* triple time, triplet, four-part *or* quadruple time, five-part *or* quintuple time, six-part *or* sextuple time, seven-part *or* septuple time, nine-part *or* nonuple time; two-four time, six-eight time, etc; tempo rubato, rubato; mixed times; **syncopation,** syncope; **ragtime,** rag <nonformal>; waltz time,

three-four *or* three-quarter time, andante tempo, march tempo, etc; largo, etc; presto, etc

25 **accent,** accentuation, rhythmical accent *or* accentuation, ictus, emphasis, stress arsis, thesis

26 **beat,** throb, pulse, pulsation; downbeat, upbeat, offbeat; bar beat

ADJS 27 **tonal,** tonic; chromatic, enharmonic; semitonic

28 **rhythmic, rhythmical,** cadent, cadenced, **measured, metric, metrical;** in rhythm, in numbers; beating, throbbing, pulsing, pulsating, pulsative, pulsatory

29 **syncopated; ragtime,** ragtimey <nonformal>; **jazz;** jazzy *and* jazzed *and* jazzed up <all nonformal>, hot, swingy <nonformal>

ADVS 30 **in time,** in tempo 709.24, *a tempo* <Ital>

710 MUSICIAN

NOUNS 1 **musician,** musico, **music maker,** professional musician; performer, executant, interpreter, tunester, artiste, artist, concert artist, **virtuoso,** virtuosa; maestro; recitalist; **soloist,** duettist; street musician, busker <chiefly Brit>

2 **popular** *or* pop musician; ragtime musician; **jazz musician, jazzman;** swing musician; big-band musician; **rock** *or* **rock'n'roll musician**

3 **player, instrumentalist,** instrumental musician; bandman, bandsman; orchestral musician; symphonist; concertist; accompanist, accompanyist

4 **wind player,** wind-instrumentalist, horn player, French-horn player *or* hornist, horner, piper, tooter; bassoonist, bugler, clarinetist, cornettist, fifer, oboist, piccoloist, saxophonist, trombonist; trumpeter, trumpet major; fluegelhornist; flutist *or* flautist

5 **string musician,** strummer, picker <nonformal>, thrummer, twanger; banjoist, banjo-picker <nonformal>, citharist, guitarist, guitar-picker <nonformal>, classical guitarist, folk guitarist, lute player, lutenist, lutist, lyrist, mandolinist, theorbist; violinist, fiddler <nonformal>; bass violinist, bassist, bass player, contrabassist; violoncellist, cellist, celloist; violist; harpist, harper; zitherist, psalterer

6 xylophonist, marimbaist, vibist *or* vibraphonist

7 **pianist,** pianiste, pianofortist, piano player, ivory tickler *or* thumper <nonfor-

mal>; keyboard player *or* keyboardist;
harpsichordist, clavichordist, mono-
chordist; accordionist, concertinist

8 **organist,** organ player

9 organ-grinder, hurdy-gurdist, hurdy-
gurdyist, hurdy-gurdy man

10 **drummer, percussionist,** tympanist,
kettle-drummer; taborer

11 **cymbalist,** cymbaler; bell-ringer, **car-
illoneur,** campanologist, campanist

12 **orchestra, band, ensemble,** combo
<nonformal>, group; strings, woodwind
or woodwinds, brass *or* brasses, string *or*
woodwind *or* brass section, string *or*
woodwind *or* brass choir; desks

13 **singer, vocalist,** vocalizer, voice, songster, songbird, warbler; lead singer,
caroler, melodist, minstrel, cantor; song-
stress, singstress, cantatrice, chanteuse,
song stylist, canary <nonformal>;
chanter, chantress; aria singer, lieder
singer, opera singer, diva, prima donna;
improvisator; rap singer; blues singer,
torch singer <nonformal>; crooner, rock
or rock-and-roll singer; yodeler; country
singer, folk singer *or* folkie <nonformal>;
psalm singer, hymner; Meistersinger;
singing voice, voice 709.5

14 **minstrel, ballad singer,** balladeer, **bard,**
rhapsode, rhapsodist; wandering *or*
strolling minstrel, **troubadour,** trovatore,
trouvère, minnesinger; scop, gleeman,
fili, jongleur; street singer, wait; ser-
enader; **folk singer,** folk-rock singer;
country-and-western singer

15 **choral singer,** choir member, chorister,
chorus singer, choralist; choirman, **choirboy; chorus girl,** chorine <nonformal>

16 **chorus, chorale, choir,** choral group, choral society, oratorio society, chamber
chorus *or* Kammerchor <Ger>, chorale,
men's *or* women's chorus, male chorus *or*
Männerchor <Ger>, mixed chorus, ensemble, voices; **glee club,** *Liedertafel* and
Liederkranz <both Ger>, singing club *or*
society; *a cappella* choir; choral symphony

17 **conductor,** leader, symphonic conductor,
music director, director, *Kapellmeister*
<Ger>; **orchestra leader, band leader,**
bandmaster, band major, drum major

18 **choirmaster,** choral director *or* conductor, song leader, *Kapellmeister* <Ger> *or*
maestro di cappella <Ital>; choir chaplain, minister of music, precentor, cantor,
chorister

19 **concertmaster,** concertmeister, *Konzert-
meister* <Ger>, first violinist; first chair

20 **composer, scorer, arranger,** musicogra-
pher; melodist, melodizer; harmonist,
harmonizer; **orchestrator;** symphonist;
tone poet; ballad maker *or* writer, balladeer, balladist, balladmonger; madri-
galist; lyrist; hymnist, hymnographer,
hymnologist; contrapuntist; song writer,
songsmith, tunesmith; lyricist, librettist;
musicologist, ethnomusicologist

21 **music lover,** philharmonic person, **music
fan** *and* music buff <both nonformal>,
musicophile; musicmonger; concertgoer,
operagoer; tonalist

22 <patrons> the Muses, the Nine, sacred
Nine, tuneful Nine, Pierides; Apollo, Apol-
lo Musagetes; Orpheus; Erato, Euterpe,
Polymnia *or* Polyhymnia, Terpsichore, St
Cecilia

23 **songbird,** singing bird, **songster,** feathered songster, warbler; nightingale,
Philomel; bulbul, canary, cuckoo, lark,
mavis, mockingbird, oriole, ringdove,
song sparrow, thrush

711 MUSICAL INSTRUMENTS

1 **musical instrument,** instrument of music; electronic instrument, synthesizer,
Mellotron <trademark>, Moog synthesizer <trademark>

2 **string** *or* **stringed instrument,**
chordophone; strings, string choir

3 **harp, lyre**

4 **plucked stringed instrument** <see list>

5 **viol** *or* violin family <see list>, chest of
viols; Stradivarius, Stradivari, Strad
<nonformal>; Amati, Cremona, Guar-
nerius; bow, fiddlestick, fiddlebow;
bridge, sound hole, soundboard, fingerboard, tuning peg, scroll; string, G string,
D string, A string, E string

6 **wind instrument,** wind; aerophone; **horn,**
pipe, tooter; mouthpiece, embouchure,
lip, chops <nonformal>; valve, bell,
reed, double reed, key, slide

7 **brass wind** <see list> brass *or* brass-
wind instrument; brasses, brass choir

8 **woodwind** <see list>, wood *or* woodwind
instrument; woods, woodwind choir;
reed instrument, **reed;** double-reed instrument, **double reed; single-reed
instrument,** single reed

9 **bagpipe** *or* bagpipes, pipes, union pipes,
war pipes, Irish pipes, doodlesack, *Dud-
elsack* <Ger>; cornemuse, musette;
sordellina; chanter, drone; pipe bag

10 **mouth organ,** mouth harp, harp, French
harp <nonformal>, **harmonica,** harmon-
icon; jaws *or* Jew's harp, mouth bow;
kazoo

11 accordion, piano accordion; **concertina;** squeeze box <nonformal>; mellophone; bandonion

12 keyboard instrument <see list>, **piano, harpsichord, clavichord, player piano;** music roll, piano player roll

13 organ, keyboard wind instrument

14 hurdy-gurdy, vielle, **barrel organ,** hand organ, grind organ, street organ

15 music box, musical box; orchestrion, orchestrina

16 percussion instrument <see list>, percussion, **drum;** drumstick, jazz stick, tymp stick

17 keyboard, fingerboard; console, **keys,** manual, claviature; piano keys, ivories <nonformal>, eighty-eight <nonformal>, organ manual, great, swell, choir, solo, echo; pedals

18 carillon, chimes 711.18, chime of bells; electronic carillon

19 organ stop, stop rank, register

20 string, chord, steel string, wound string, nylon string; fiddlestring, catgut; horsehair; music wire, piano wire

21 plectrum, plectron, pick

22 <aids> metronome, rhythmometer; tone measurer, monochord, sonometer; tuning fork, tuning bar, diapason; pitch pipe, tuning pipe; mute; music stand, music lyre; baton, conductor's baton, stick <nonformal>

23 plucked stringed instruments

archlute	Hawaiian guitar
balalaika	mando-bass
bandore	mando-cello
bandurria <Sp>	mandolin *or* mandola
banjo	mandolute
banjo-ukulele *or* ban-	mandore
juke *or* banjulele *or*	oud
banjo-uke	pandora
banjo-zither	samisen
banjorine	sitar
bass guitar	Spanish guitar
bouzouki	steel guitar
centerhole guitar	tamboura
classical guitar	theorbo
concert guitar	troubadour fiddle
Dobro guitar	ukulele *or* uke
<trademark>	<nonformal>
electric guitar	vina
F-hole guitar	

24 viol or violin family

alto *or* tenor viol	contrabass
baritone viol *or* viola	crowd <old>
d'amore	descant viol
baryton	double bass *or* vio-
basso da camera	lone *or* bass viol *or*
<Ital>	bass *or* doghouse *or*
bass viol *or* viola da	bull fiddle <both
gamba	nonformal>

kit	viol *or* viola di fagotto
kit violin	viola *or* tenor
pocket *or* kit fiddle	viola alta
rebec	viola bastarda
treble viol	viola pomposa
trumpet marine *or*	violette
tromba marina	violin *or* fiddle
vielle	<nonformal>
viol *or* viola da brac-	violinette
cio	violino piccolo
viol *or* viola da spalla	violoncello *or* cello
viol *or* viola di bor-	violoncello piccolo
done	violotta

25 brass wind instruments, brasses

alpenhorn *or* alphorn	lur
althorn *or* alto horn	mellophone
ballad horn	nyas taranga
baritone horn	ophicleide
bass horn	orchestral horn
bombardon	pocket trumpet
bugle *or* bugle horn	post horn
clarion	sackbut
cornet *or* cornet-	saxcornet
à-pistons	saxhorn
cornopean	saxtuba
double-bell eupho-	serpent
nium	slide trombone *or*
E-flat horn	sliphorn <nonfor-
euphonium	mal>
F horn	sousaphone
flugelhorn	tenor tuba
French horn	tromba
helicon	trombone
horn	trumpet
hunting horn *or* corno	tuba
di caccia <Ital>	valve trombone
key trumpet	valve trumpet
lituus	

26 woodwinds

bass *or* basset oboe	oaten reed
basset horn	oboe *or* hautboy *or*
bassoon	hautbois
bombard	*oboe d'amore* <Ital>
bombardon	*oboe da caccia*
clarinet *or* licorice	<Ital>
stick <nonfor-	ocarina *or* sweet
mal>	potato <nonfor-
contrabassoon *or*	mal>
contrafagotto	Pandean pipe
double bassoon	panpipe
English horn *or* cor	pibgorn
anglais <Fr>	piccolo
fife	pipe
fipple flute *or* pipe	pommer
flageolet	recorder
flute	saxophone *or* sax
heckelphone	<nonformal>
hornpipe	shawm
krummhorn *or*	sonorophone
cromorne *or*	syrinx *or* shepherd's
cromorna	pipe
musette	tabor pipe
nose-flute	tenoroon

tin-whistle *or* penny-whistle

transverse flute whistle

27 keyboard stringed instruments

baby grand	melodion
cembalo	melopiano
clarichord	monochord
clavichord	pair of virginals
clavicittern	parlor grand
clavicymbal *or* clavi-cembalo	pianette
	pianino
clavicytherium	piano *or* pianoforte
clavier	piano-violin
concert grand	Pianola <trademark>
console piano	
cottage piano	player *or* mechanical piano
couched harp	
digital piano	sostinente pianoforte
dulcimer harpsichord	spinet
grand piano	square piano
hammer dulcimer	street piano
harmonichord	upright *or* upright piano
harpsichord	
lyrichord	violin piano
manichord	virginal

28 percussion instruments, drums

bass drum	nagara <India>
bells	naker
bones	orchestral bells
bongo drum	rattle
carillon	rattlebones
castanets	ride cymbal
celesta	side drum
chime	sizzler
chimes	snappers
clappers	snare drum
conga	tabor
crash cymbal	tam-tam
cymbals *or* potlids <nonformal>	tambourine
	tenor drum
drumhead	timbrel
drumskin	timpani *or* kettledrums
finger cymbals	
gamelan	tintinnabula
glockenspiel	thumb piano
gong	tom-tom
handbells	tonitruone
highhat cymbal <nonformal>	triangle
	troll-drum
kettledrum *or* timbal	tubular bells
lyra	vibraphone *or* vibraharp *or* vibes <nonformal>
maraca	
marimba	
mbira *or* kalimba	war drum
membranophone	xylophone
metallophone	

712 VISUAL ARTS

NOUNS **1 visual arts; art, artwork,** the arts; **fine arts,** *beaux arts* <Fr>; arts of design, **design,** designing; art form; abstract art, representative art; **graphic arts 713;** plastic art; **arts and crafts;** primitive art, cave art; folk art; calligraphy; commercial art, applied art; sculpture 715; ceramics 742; photography 714; etching, engraving 713.2; decoration 498.1; artist 716

2 "a treating of the commonplace with the feeling of the sublime"—J F Millet, "the conveyance of spirit by means of matter"—Salvador de Madariaga, "the expression of one soul talking to another"—Ruskin, "an instant arrested in eternity"—James Huneker, "a handicraft in flower"—George Iles, "science in the flesh"—Jean Cocteau, "life upon the larger scale"—E B Browning, "the perfection of nature"—Sir Thomas Browne, "the conscious utterance of thought, by speech or action, to any end"—Emerson, "the wine of life"—Jean Paul Richter, "a shadow of the divine perfection"—Michelangelo, "life seen through a temperament"—Zola, "a form of catharsis"—Dorothy Parker

3 craft, manual art, industrial art, **handicraft,** artisan work, craftwork, artisanship; industrial design; woodcraft, woodwork, metalcraft, stonecraft

4 <act or art of painting> **painting,** coloring, "a noble and expressive language"—Ruskin; the brush

5 <art of drawing> **drawing, draftsmanship, sketching, delineation; black and white,** charcoal; mechanical drawing, drafting; freehand drawing

6 scenography, ichnography, orthographic *or* orthogonal projection

7 artistry, art, talent, artistic skill, flair, artistic flair, artistic invention; artiness *and* arty-craftiness *and* artsy-craftsiness <all nonformal>; artistic temperament; virtu, artistic quality

8 style; lines; genre; **school,** movement <see list>; the grand style

9 treatment; technique, draftsmanship, brushwork, painterliness; **composition, design,** arrangement; grouping, balance; **color,** values; atmosphere, tone; shadow, shading; **line;** perspective

10 work of art, object of art, objet d'art, art object, art work, artistic production, piece, **work, study, design, composition;** creation, brainchild; virtu, article *or* piece of virtu; **masterpiece,** *chef d'œuvre* <Fr>, masterwork, master <old>, old master, classic; museum piece; grotesque; statue; mobile, stabile; nude, still life; pastiche, *pasticcio* <Ital>; artware, artwork; bric-a-brac; kitsch

11 picture; image, likeness, representation, tableau; "a poem without words"—

Horace; photograph 714.3; **illustration, illumination;** miniature; copy, reproduction; print, color print; engraving 713.2; stencil, block print; daub; abstraction, abstract; mural, fresco, wall painting; cyclorama, panorama; montage, collage, assemblage; still life, study in still life; tapestry, mosaic, stained glass, stained glass window, **icon,** altarpiece, diptych, triptych

12 **scene, view, scape; landscape;** waterscape, riverscape, seascape, seapiece; airscape, skyscape, cloudscape; snowscape; cityscape, townscape; farmscape; pastoral; treescape; diorama; exterior, interior

13 **drawing; delineation;** line drawing; **sketch, draft; black and white,** chiaroscuro; **charcoal, crayon, pen-and-ink,** pencil drawing, charcoal drawing, pastel, pastel painting; silhouette; vignette; doodle; rough draft *or* copy, rough outline, cartoon, sinopia, **study,** design; *brouillon, ébauche, esquisse* <all Fr>; diagram, graph; silver-print drawing, tracing

14 **painting, canvas,** easel-picture, "a pretty mocking of the life"—Shakespeare, "silent poetry"—Simonides, "the intermediate somewhat between a thought and a thing"—Coleridge; **oil painting,** oil; **watercolor,** water, aquarelle, wash, wash drawing; finger painting; tempera, egg tempera; *gouache* <Fr>

15 **portrait, portraiture, portrayal;** head; profile; silhouette, shadow figure; miniature

16 **cartoon, caricature; comic strip;** comic section, comics, funny paper *and* funnies <both nonformal>; comic book; animated cartoon

17 **studio,** *atelier* <Fr>; **gallery** 386.9

18 <art equipment> palette; easel; paintbox; art paper, drawing paper; sketchbook, sketchpad; canvas, artists' canvas; canvas board; scratchboard; lay figure; camera obscura, camera lucida; maulstick; palette knife, spatula; brush, paintbrush; air brush, spray gun; pencil, drawing pencil; crayon, charcoal, chalk, pastel; stump; painter's cream; ground; pigments, medium; siccative, drier; fixative, varnish; **paint** 35.8

VERBS 19 **portray, picture,** picturize, **depict, limn,** draw *or* paint a picture; **paint** 35.13; brush, brush in; color, tint; spread *or* lay on a color; **daub** <nonformal>; scumble; **draw, sketch, delineate; draft;** pencil, chalk, crayon, charcoal; draw in, pencil in; dash off, scratch <nonformal>;

doodle; design; diagram; cartoon; copy, trace; stencil; hatch, crosshatch, shade

ADJS 20 **artistic,** painterly; **arty** *or* artycrafty *or* artsy-craftsy *or* artsy-fartsy <nonformal>; **art-minded,** art-conscious; **aesthetic; tasteful; beautiful; decorative, ornamental** 498.10; **wellcomposed,** well-grouped, well-arranged, well-varied; of consummate art; in the grand style

21 **pictorial,** pictural, **graphic, picturesque;** picturable; photographic 714.17; scenographic; painty, pastose; scumbled; monochrome, polychrome; freehand

22 **art schools, groups, movements**

American	Mannerist
Art Nouveau	Milanese
Ashcan school *or* the	Modenese
Eight	Momentum
Barbizon	'N'
Bauhaus	Neapolitan
Bolognese	Neonism
British	New Objectivity
classical abstraction	New York
Cobra	Origine
Dada	Paduan
De Stijl	Parisian
Der Blaue Reiter	Phases
Die Brücke	plein-air
Dutch	Pre-Raphaelite
eclectic	Raphaelite
Flemish	Reflex
Florentine	Restany
Fontainebleau	Roman
French	Scottish
Honfleur	Sienese
Hudson River	Spur
Italian	Suprematism
L'Age d'or	The Ten
letrist	Tuscan
Lombard	Umbrian
Madinensor	Venetian
Madrid	Washington

713 GRAPHIC ARTS

NOUNS 1 **graphic arts, graphics; printmaking; painting; drawing; relief-carving; photography** 714; **printing** 548; graphic artist 716.8

2 **engraving** <see list>, engravement, graving, enchasing, **tooling,** chiseling, incising, incision, lining, scratching, slashing, scoring; **inscription,** inscript; type-cutting; **marking,** line, scratch, slash, score; hatching, cross-hatching; etch, etching; stipple, stippling; tint, demitint, half tint; burr; photoengraving 548.1

3 **lithography,** planography, autolithography, artist lithography; chromolithog-

raphy; photolithography, offset lithography 548.1

4 stencil printing, stencil; silk-screen printing, serigraphy; monotype; glass printing, decal, decalcomania; cameography

5 **print**, numbered print, imprint, impression, first impression, impress; negative; color print; **etching; lithograph;** autolithograph; chromolithograph; lithotype; crayon engraving, graphotype; **block, block print,** linoleum-block print, rubber-block print, wood engraving, **woodprint,** xylograph, **cut, woodcut,** woodblock; vignette

6 **plate,** steel plate, copperplate, chalcograph; zincograph; stone, lithographic stone; printing plate 548.8

7 **proof,** artist's proof, proof before letter, open-letter proof, remarque proof

8 **engraving tool, graver,** burin, tint tool, style, point, etching point, needle, etching needle; etching ball; etching ground *or* varnish; scorper; rocker; **die,** punch, stamp, intaglio, seal

VERBS **9 engrave, grave, tool, enchase, incise, sculpture, inscribe,** character, **mark,** line, crease, score, scratch, scrape, cut, carve, chisel; groove, furrow 290.3; stipple, cribble; hatch, crosshatch; lithograph, autolithograph; **be a printmaker** *or* graphic artist; make prints *or* graphics; print 548.14

10 etch, eat, eat out, corrode, bite, bite in

ADJS **11 engraved, graven,** graved, glypt— *or* glypto—; tooled, enchased, inscribed, incised, marked, lined, creased, cut, carved, glyphic, **sculptured,** insculptured, "insculp'd upon"—Shakespeare; grooved, furrowed 290.4; **printed, imprinted, impressed, stamped,** numbered

12 glyptic, glyptical, glyptographic, lapidary, lapidarian; xylographic, woodblock; lithographic, autolithographic, chromolithographic; aquatint, aquatinta, mezzotint

13 kinds of engraving

acid-blast	electric engraving
aquatint	etching
black-line engraving	gem-engraving
cerography	glass-cutting
chalcography	glyptics *or* glyptography
chalk engraving	
copperplate engraving	intaglio
	line engraving
crayon engraving	linocut
cribbling *or manière criblée* <Fr>	metal cut
	mezzotint
drypoint *or* drawpoint engraving	photochemical engraving *or* photoetching
eccentric engraving	

photoengraving
plate engraving
pyrography *or* pyrogravure *or* pokerwork
relief etching
relief method
soft-ground etching
steel engraving

stipple engraving
woodburning *or* xylopyrography
woodcut *or* wood engraving
xylography
zinc etching
zincography *or* zinc engraving

714 PHOTOGRAPHY

NOUNS **1 photography** <see list>, picture-taking; **cinematography,** motion-picture photography; color photography; photochromy, heliochromy; **3-D,** three-dimensional photography; photofinishing; photogravure; radiography, X-ray photography; photogrammetry, phototopography

2 photographer 716.5, shutter-bug <nonformal>, press photographer, lensman

3 **photograph, photo** <nonformal>, heliograph, **picture,** shot <nonformal>; **snapshot,** snap <nonformal>; black-and-white photograph; color photograph, color print, heliochrome; slide, diapositive, transparency; candid photograph; still, still photograph; photomural; montage, photomontage; aerial photograph, photomap; facsimile *or* fax transmission; telephotograph, Telephoto <trademark>, Wirephoto <trademark>; photomicrograph, microphotograph; metallograph; microradiograph; electron micrograph; photochronograph, chronophotograph; **portrait;** pinup <nonformal>, cheesecake *and* beefcake <both nonformal>; police photograph, **mug** *or* mug shot <nonformal>; rogues' gallery; photobiography

4 **tintype** *or* ferrotype, ambrotype, **daguerreotype,** calotype *or* talbotype, collotype, photocollotype, autotype, vitrotype

5 **print,** photoprint, positive; glossy, matte, semi-matte; **enlargement, blowup;** photocopy, Photostat <trademark>, photostatic copy, Xerox <trademark>, Xerox copy; microprint, microcopy; blueprint, cyanotype; **slide,** transparency, lantern slide; contact printing, projection printing; photogravure; hologram

6 shadowgraph, shadowgram, skiagraph, skiagram; radiograph, radiogram, scotograph; **X ray,** X-ray photograph, roentgenograph, roentgenogram; photofluorogram; photogram

7 spectrograph, spectrogram; spectrohelio-gram

8 <motion pictures> **shot; take, retake;** close-up, long shot, medium shot, full shot, group shot, deuce shot, matte shot, process shot, boom shot, travel shot, trucking shot, follow-focus shot, pan shot *or* panoramic shot, rap shot, reverse *or* reverse-angle shot, wild shot, zoom shot; motion picture; kinescope

9 **exposure,** time exposure; shutter speed; f-stop, lens opening; film rating, **film speed,** film gauge, ASA exposure index, **DIN** *or Deutsche Industrie Normen* number; exposure meter, light meter

10 **film; negative;** printing paper, photographic paper; **plate;** dry plate; vehicle; motion-picture film, panchromatic film, monochromatic film, orthochromatic film, black-and-white film, color film, color negative film, color reversal film; microfilm, bibliofilm; sound-on-film, sound film; sound track, soundstripe; roll, cartridge; pack, bipack, tripack; frame; emulsion, dope, backing

11 **camera,** Kodak <trademark>; motion-picture camera, cinematograph *or* kinematograph <both Brit>

12 **projector;** motion-picture projector, cineprojector, cinematograph *or* kinematograph <both Brit>, vitascope; **slide projector,** magic lantern, stereopticon; slide viewer

13 **processing solution;** developer, soup <nonformal>; fixer, fixing bath, sodium thiosulfate *or* sodium hyposulfite *or* hypo; stop bath, short-stop, short-stop bath

VERBS **14** **photograph, shoot** <nonformal>, take a photograph, **take a picture,** take one's picture; **snap,** snapshot, snapshoot; **film,** get *or* capture on film; **mug** <nonformal>; daguerreotype, talbotype, calotype; Photostat <trademark>; xerox; microfilm; photomap; pan; **X-ray,** radiograph, roentgenograph

15 **process; develop; print;** blueprint; **blow up, enlarge**

16 **project, show, screen**

ADJS **17** **photographic,** photo; **photogenic,** picturesome; photosensitive, photoactive; panchromatic; telephotographic, telephoto; tintype; three-dimensional, 3-D

18 **types of photography**

acoustical holography	animation photography
aerophotography *or* aerial photography *or* air photography	astrophotography available-light photography
candid photography	photomicrography
chronophotography	pyrophotography
cinematography	radiation-field *or* Kirlian photography
cinephotomicrography	
color photography	radiography
electrophotography	schlieren photography
flash photography	
heliophotography	skiagraphy
holography	spectroheliography
infrared photography	spectrophotography
integral photography	stereophotography
laser photography	stroboscopic photography
macrophotography	
microphotography	telephotography
miniature photography	time-lapse photography
phonophotography	uranophotography
photoheliography	xerography
photomacrography	X-ray photography

715 SCULPTURE

NOUNS **1** **sculpture, sculpturing;** plastic art, **modeling; statuary; stonecutting;** gem-cutting, masonry; **carving,** bone-carving, cameo carving, scrimshaw, *taille directe* <Fr>, whittling, woodcarving *or* xyloglyphy; embossing, **engraving** 713.2, **chasing,** toreutics, founding, casting, molding, plaster casting, lost-wax process, *cire perdue* <Fr>; sculptor 716.6

2 <sculptured piece> **sculpture; glyph; statue;** marble, bronze, terra cotta; mobile, stabile; cast 784.6; found object, *objet trouvé* <Fr>

3 **relief,** relievo; **embossment,** boss; half relief, *mezzo-rilievo* <Ital>; high relief, *alto-rilievo* <Ital>; low relief, bas-relief, *basso-rilievo* <Ital>, *rilievo stiacciato* <Ital>; sunk relief, *cavo-rilievo* <Ital>, coelanaglyphic sculpture, **intaglio,** *intaglio rilievo, intaglio rilevato* <both Ital>; *repoussé* <Fr>; glyph, anaglyph; glyptograph; **mask;** plaquette; **medallion; medal; cameo,** cameo glass, sculptured glass; cut glass

4 <tools, materials> chisel, point, mallet, modeling tool, spatula; cutting torch, welding torch, soldering iron; solder; modeling clay, Plasticine <trademark>, sculptor's wax; plaster

VERBS **5** **sculpture,** sculp *or* sculpt <nonformal>, insculpture <old>; **carve,** chisel, cut, grave, engrave, chase; weld, solder; assemble; **model, mold;** cast, found

ADJS **6** **sculptural,** sculpturesque, sculptitory; **statuary; statuesque,** statuelike; **monumental,** marmoreal

7 **sculptured,** sculpted; sculptile; **molded,**

modeled, ceroplastic; **carved,** chiseled; **graven,** engraven; in relief, in high *or* low relief; glyphic, glyptic, anaglyphic, anaglyptic; anastatic; embossed, chased, hammered, toreutic; *repoussé* <Fr>

716 ARTIST

NOUNS **1 artist,** *artiste* <Fr>, "a dreamer consenting to dream of the actual world"—Santayana, creator, maker; master, **old master;** dauber, daubster; copyist; **craftsman, artisan** 726.6

2 limner, delineator, depicter, picturer, portrayer, imager; **illustrator;** illuminator; calligrapher; commercial artist

3 draftsman, sketcher, delineator; drawer, architectural draftsman; crayonist, charcoalist, pastelist; **cartoonist, caricaturist**

4 painter, *artiste-peintre* <Fr>; **colorist;** luminist, luminarist; **oil painter,** oilcolorist; **watercolorist;** aquarellist; finger painter; monochromist, polychromist; genre painter, historical painter, landscapist, miniaturist, portrait painter, portraitist, marine painter, still-life painter; pavement artist; scene painter, scenewright, scenographer

5 photographer, photographist, lensman, **cameraman; cinematographer;** snapshotter, snap shooter, shutterbug <nonformal>; daguerreotypist, calotypist, talbotypist; skiagrapher, shadowgraphist, radiographer, X-ray technician

6 sculptor, sculptress, sculpturer; earth artist, environmental artist; statuary; figurer, *figuriste* <Fr>, **modeler,** molder, wax modeler, clay modeler; graver, chaser, carver; stonecutter, mason, monumental mason, wood carver, xyloglyphic artist, whittler; ivory carver, bone carver, shell carver; gem carver, glyptic *or* glyptographic artist

7 ceramist, ceramicist, potter; china decorator *or* painter, tile painter, majolica painter; glassblower, glazer, glass decorator, pyroglazer, glass cutter; enamelist, enameler

8 printmaker, graphic artist; **engraver,** graver, burinist; inscriber, carver; **etcher;** line engraver; **lithographer,** autolithographer, chromolithographer; serigrapher, silk-screen artist; cerographer, cerographist; chalcographer; gem engraver, glyptographer, lapidary; wood engraver, xylographer; pyrographer, xylopyrographer; zincographer

9 designer, stylist, styler; costume designer, dress designer, *couturier* <Fr>, *couturière* <Fr fem>; furniture designer, rug designer, textile designer

10 architect, civil architect; landscape architect, landscape gardener; city *or* urban planner, urbanist; functionalist

11 decorator, expert in decor, ornamentist, ornamentalist; **interior decorator** *or* designer, house decorator, room decorator, floral decorator, table decorator; window decorator *or* dresser; confectionery decorator

717 ARCHITECTURE, DESIGN

NOUNS **1 architecture,** architectural design, building design, the art and technique of building, "inhabited sculpture"—Brancusi, "frozen music"—Goethe, "music in space"—Schelling, "the art of significant forms in space"—Claude Bragdon; **architectural science,** architectural engineering, structural engineering, architectural technology, building science, building technology; **architectural style** <see list>; **architectural specialty** <see list>; landscape architecture, landscape gardening 1067.2

2 architectural element; ornamentation, architectural ornamentation; column order, Doric, Ionic, Corinthian, Composite; **type of construction** <see list>, building type

3 architect; landscape architect, landscape gardener 1067.6; city *or* urban planner, urbanist, urbanologist

4 design, styling, patterning, planning, shaping, "the conscious effort to impose meaningful order"—Victor Papanek; **design specialty** <see list>

5 designer, stylist, styler

ADJS **6 architectural, design, designer**

7 architectural styles and types

absolute	churrigueresque *or*
academic	churrigueresco
action	Cistercian
additive	classical
American colonial	conceptual *or* invisi-
American Georgian	ble *or* imaginary *or*
Art Deco *or* Art Mod-	nowhere
erne	de Stijl
Art Nouveau	directed *or* pro-
arts and crafts	grammed
baroque	duck
Bauhaus	early English
Beaux Arts	early Gothic
brutalist	early Renaissance
Byzantine	earthwork
Chicago School	eclectic
Chinese	ecological

Egyptian
Elizabethan
endless
English decorated
  Gothic
English Georgian
English Renaissance
flamboyant Gothic
formalist
French Renaissance
functionalist
funk
German Renaissance
Gothic
Great West Road
Greco-Roman
Greek
Greek Revival
hard
high Gothic
high Renaissance
hi-tech
indeterminate
international
Islamic
Italian Gothic
Italian Mannerism
Jacobean
Japanese
Jesuit
kinetic
mechanist

Mesopotamian
Mestizo
moderne
neo-Gothic
neoclassical
new brutalist
Norman
organicist
Palladian
perpendicular
Persian
pneumatic
postmodern
Prairie
Queen Anne
rayonnant Gothic
Renaissance
rococo
rococo Gothic
Roman
Romanesque
Romanesque Revival
Romantic
Spanish
tensile
Tudor
Utopian *or* fantastic
  or visionary
vernacular
Victorian
Victorian Gothic

8 architectural specialties
church *or* religious *or*
  ecclesiastical archi-
  tecture
college architecture
commercial architec-
  ture
domestic architecture
governmental archi-
  tecture

industrial architec-
  ture
institutional architec-
  ture
library architecture
museum architecture
recreational architec-
  ture

9 elements of architecture
aesthetic quality *or*
  venustas <L>
aesthetic unity
applied ornament
circulation
columniation
commodity *or utilitas*
  <L>
decoration *or* orna-
  ment *or* detail

facilitation
fenestration
materials
mimetic ornament
organic ornament
proportions
repetitions
scale
strength *or firmitas*
  <L>

10 design specialties
accessory design
appearance design
architectural
  design
automotive design
book design
carpet design
clothing design
costume design

ergonomics *or* ergon-
  omy *or* human
  engineering
  or human factors
  engineering
fashion design
furniture design
graphics design
high-tech

industrial *or* product
  design
interior design
jewelry design
landscape architec-
  ture
lighting design

package design
pottery design
special effects design
stage design
textile design
typographic design

718 LITERATURE

NOUNS **1 literature, letters, belles lettres,**
polite literature, humane letters, *litterae
humaniores* <L>, republic of letters;
**work, literary work, text, literary text;
works, complete works, oeuvre, canon,
literary canon, author's canon;** serious
literature; **classics,** ancient literature;
medieval literature, Renaissance literature, etc; national literature, English
literature, French literature, etc; ethnic
literature, black *or* Afro-American literature, Latino literature, etc; contemporary
literature; underground literature;
pseudonymous literature; folk literature;
travel literature; wisdom literature;
erotic literature, erotica; pornographic
literature, pornography, porn *and* hard
porn *and* soft porn <all nonformal>, obscene literature, scatological literature;
popular literature, pop literature
<nonformal>; kitsch

2 authorship, writing, authorcraft, pencraft, wordsmanship, **composition,** the
art of composition, inditing, inditement;
one's pen; **creative writing,** literary art,
verbal art, literary composition, literary
production, verse-writing, short-story
writing, novel-writing, playwriting,
drama-writing; essay-writing; **expository
writing;** technical writing; journalism,
newspaper writing, editorial-writing,
feature-writing, rewriting; magazine
writing; songwriting, lyric-writing, libretto-writing; artistry, literary power,
literary artistry, literary talent *or* flair,
skill with words *or* language, facility in
writing, ready pen; **writer's itch,** graphomania, scribblemania, graphorrhea,
cacoëthes scribendi <L>

3 writer, scribbler <nonformal>, **penman,**
pen, penner; pen *or* pencil driver *or*
pusher <nonformal>, word-slinger, **ink-
slinger** *and* ink spiller *and* inkstained
wretch <all nonformal>, knight of the
plume *or* pen *or* quill <nonformal>

4 author, writer, scribe <nonformal>,
composer, inditer; authoress, penwoman;
creative writer, *littérateur* <Fr>, literary
artist, literary craftsman *or* artisan *or*

journeyman, belletrist, man of letters, literary man; wordsmith, word painter; free lance, free-lance writer; ghostwriter, ghost <nonformal>; collaborator, co-author; prose writer, logographer; fiction writer, fictioneer <nonformal>; story writer, **short story writer**; story-teller; **novelist**; novelettist; diarist; **news-paperman; annalist; poet** 720.13; **drama-tist**, humorist 489.12; scriptwriter, sce-nario writer, scenarist; nonfiction writer; article writer, magazine writer; **essayist**; monographer; reviewer, critic, literary critic, music critic, art critic, drama critic, dance critic; columnist; pam-phleteer; technical writer; copywriter, advertising writer; compiler, encyclo-pedist, bibliographer

5 **hack writer**, hack, literary hack, Grub Street writer <Brit>, **penny-a-liner, scribbler** <nonformal>, **potboiler** <nonformal>

VERBS 6 **write**, author, pen, **compose, indite**, formulate, produce, prepare; dash off, knock off or out <nonformal>, throw on paper, pound or crank or grind or churn out; free-lance; collaborate, coauthor; ghostwrite, ghost <nonformal>; novel-ize; scenarize; pamphleteer; editorialize

ADJS 7 **literary**, belletristic; classical

8 auctorial, authorial

719 HISTORY

NOUNS 1 **history**, the historical discipline, the investigation of the past, the record of the past, the story of mankind; historical research; **annals, chronicles**, memora-bilia, chronology; chronicle, record 549; historical method, historical approach, philosophy of history, **historiography**; cliometrics; narrative history, **oral his-tory**, oral record, survivors' or witnesses' accounts; **biography, memoir**, memorial, **life**, story, **life story**, adventures, for-tunes, experiences; résumé, vita, curric-ulum vitae or CV; life and letters; legend, saint's legend, hagiology, hagiography; **autobiography, memoirs**, memorials; **journal, diary**, confessions; **profile, bio-graphical sketch**; obituary, necrology, martyrology; photobiography; case his-tory; historiography, theory of history; Clio, Muse of history; **the past** 836; **re-cord, recording** 549

2 <history> "a set of lies agreed upon"— Napoleon, "a voice forever sounding across the centuries the laws of right and wrong"—J A Froude, "a cyclic poem

written by Time upon the memories of man"—Shelley, "the essence of innumer-able biographies"—Carlyle, "philosophy learned from examples"—Dionysius of Halicarnassus, "a shallow village tale"—Emerson, "History is more or less bunk"—Henry Ford, "history is merely gossip"—Oscar Wilde, "a realm in which human freedom and natural necessity are curiously mingled"—Reinhold Niebuhr

3 **story, tale, yarn, account, narrative**, nar-ration, chronicle; **anecdote**, anecdotage; **epic**, epos, **saga**

4 **historian**, cliometrician, historiographer; **chronicler**, annalist; **biographer**, memo-rialist, Boswell; autobiographer, auto-biographist; diarist, Pepys

VERBS 5 **chronicle**, write history, historify; historicize; biograph, biography, biogra-phize; immortalize; **record** 549.16

6 **narrate, tell, relate, recount**, report, **re-cite**, rehearse, give an account of

ADJS 7 **historical, historic**, historied, histori-cally accurate; fact-based; historicized; historiographical; cliometric; **chronicled**; chronologic, chronological; **traditional, legendary**; biographical, autobiographic, autobiographical; hagiographic, hagio-graphical, martyrologic, martyrological; necrologic, necrological

8 **narrative**, narrational; **fictional**

ADVS 9 **historically**, historically speaking; as chronicled, as history tells us, according to or by all accounts; as the record shows

720 POETRY

NOUNS 1 **poetry**, poesy, **verse, song, rhyme**; "musical thought, "the harmonious uni-son of man with nature"—both Carlyle, "the supreme fiction"—Wallace Stevens, "the spontaneous overflow of powerful feelings recollected in tranquility"— Wordsworth, "the rhythmical creation of beauty"—Poe, "painting with the gift of speech"—Simonides, "the poet's inner-most feeling issuing in rhythmic lan-guage"—John Keble, "the record of the best and happiest moments of the happi-est and best minds"—Shelley, "the journal of a sea animal living on land, wanting to fly in the air, "the achieve-ment of the synthesis of hyacinths and biscuits"—both Sandburg, "the best words in the best order"—Coleridge, "the rhythmic, inevitably narrative, move-ment from an overclothed blindness to a naked vision"—Dylan Thomas, "not the thing said but a way of saying it"—A E

Housman, "the art of uniting pleasure
with truth, by calling imagination to the
help of reason"—Samuel Johnson, "the
emotion of life rhythmically remembering beauty"—Fiona MacLeod, "the music
of the soul, and above all of great and of
feeling souls"—Voltaire, "adolescence
fermented and thus preserved"—J Or-
tega Y Gasset

2 poetics, poetcraft, versecraft, versification, versemaking, *ars poetica* <L>; "my
craft and sullen art"—Dylan Thomas; **poetic language,** poeticism; **poetic license,
poetic justice**

3 bad poetry, doggerel, versemongering,
poetastering, poetastery; poesy; crambo,
crambo clink *or* jingle <Scots>, Hudibrastic verse; nonsense verse, amphigory;
macaronics, macaronic verse; lame
verses, limping meters, halting meters

4 poem, verse, rhyme, "imaginary gardens
with real toads in them"—Marianne
Moore; verselet, versicle

5 book of verse, garland, **collection, anthology;** poetic works, poesy

6 metrics, prosody, versification; scansion,
scanning; metrical pattern *or* form, prosodic pattern *or* form, meter, numbers,
measure; quantitative meter, syllabic
meter, accentual meter; free verse, *vers li-
bre* <Fr>; alliterative meter, *Stabreim*
<Ger>

7 meter, measure, numbers; **rhythm, cadence,** movement, lilt, jingle, swing;
sprung rhythm; **accent,** accentuation,
metrical accent, stress, emphasis, ictus,
beat; arsis, thesis; quantity, mora; metrical unit; **foot, metrical foot** <see list>;
triseme, tetraseme; metrical group,
metron, colon, period; dipody, syzygy,
tripody, tetrapody, pentapody, hexapody,
heptapody; dimeter, trimeter, tetrame-
ter, pentameter, hexameter, heptameter;
iambic pentameter, dactylic hexameter;
Alexandrine; Saturnian meter; elegiac,
elegiac couplet *or* distich, elegiac pentameter; heroic couplet; counterpoint;
caesura, diaeresis, masculine caesura,
feminine caesura; catalexis; anacrusis

8 rhyme; clink, crambo; **consonance, assonance; alliteration;** eye rhyme; male *or*
masculine *or* single rhyme, female *or* feminine *or* double rhyme; initial rhyme, end
rhyme; tail rhyme, rhyme royal; near
rhyme, slant rhyme; rhyme scheme;
rhyming dictionary; unrhymed poetry,
blank verse

9 <poetic divisions> **measure, strain; syllable; line;** verse; stanza, stave; strophe,

antistrophe, epode; **canto,** book; **refrain,
chorus,** burden; envoi; monostich, distich, tristich, tetrastich, pentastich, hexastich, heptastich, octastich; **couplet;** triplet, tercet, *terza rima* <Ital>; **quatrain;**
sextet, sestet; septet; octave, octet, *ottava
rima* <Ital>; rhyme royal; Spenserian
stanza

10 Muse; the Muses, Pierides, *Camenae*
<L>; Apollo, Apollo Musagetes; Calliope,
Polyhymnia, Erato, Euterpe; Helicon,
Parnassus; Castilian Spring, Pierian
Spring, Hippocrene; Bragi; **poetic genius,**
poesy, afflatus, fire of genius, **creative
imagination** 985.2, **inspiration** 919.8

11 poet, poetess, poetress <old>, maker
<old>; "the painter of the soul"—Dis-
raeli, "a nightingale who sits in darkness
and sings to cheer its own solitude with
sweet sounds," "the unacknowledged leg-
islators of the world"—both Shelley, "all
who love, who feel great truths, and tell
them"—Philip James Bailey, "literalists
of the imagination"—Marianne Moore;
ballad maker, balladmonger; **bard, minstrel,** scop, fili, baird, skald, **jongleur,
troubadour,** *trovatore* <Ital>, trouveur,
trouvère <Fr>, *Meistersinger* <Ger>, minnesinger; minor poet, major poet, arch-
poet; laureate, **poet laureate;** occasional
poet; **lyric poet;** epic poet; pastoral poet,
pastoralist, idyllist, bucoliast <old>;
rhapsodist, rhapsode; vers-librist, *vers li-
briste* <Fr>; elegist, librettist; lyricist,
lyrist; odist; satirist; sonneteer; modernist, imagist, symbolist; Parnassian; beat
poet

12 bad poet, rhymester, rhymer; metrist;
versemaker, versesmith, versifier, verse-
man, versemonger; poetling, **poetaster,**
poeticule; balladmonger

VERBS **13 poetize, versify,** verse, write *or*
compose poetry, build the stately rime,
sing deathless songs, make immortal
verse; tune one's lyre, climb Parnassus, mount Pegasus; **sing,** "lisp in numbers"—Pope; elegize; poeticize

14 rhyme, assonate, alliterate; **scan;** jingle;
cap verses *or* rhymes

ADJS **15 poetic, poetical,** poetlike; **lyrical,
narrative,** dramatic, lyrico-dramatic;
bardic; runic, skaldic; epic, heroic; mock-
heroic, Hudibrastic; pastoral, bucolic,
eclogic, idyllic, Theocritean; didactic; elegiac, elegiacal; dithyrambic, rhapsodic,
rhapsodical, Alcaic, Anacreontic, Homeric, Pindaric, sapphic; Castalian,
Pierian; poetico-mythological; poetico-
mystical, poetico-philosophic

16 **metric, metrical, prosodic, prosodical;
rhythmic, rhythmical, measured,** cadenced, scanning; iambic, dactylic,
spondaic, pyrrhic, trochaic, anapestic,
antispastic, etc

17 **rhyming; assonant,** assonantal; **alliterative;** jingling; musical, lilting

ADVS 18 **poetically, lyrically; metrically,
rhythmically,** in measure; musically

19 **metrical feet**

amphibrach	iamb *or* iambus *or*
anapest	iambic
antispast	ionic
bacchius	molossus
chloriambus *or* chlo-	paeon
riamb	proceleusmatic
cretic *or* amphimacer	pyrrhic
dactyl	spondee
dochmiac	tribrach
epitrite	trochee

721 PROSE

NOUNS 1 **prose,** "words in their best
order"—Coleridge; prose fiction, nonfiction prose, expository prose; prose
rhythm; prose style; poetic prose, polyphonic prose, prose poetry

2 **prosaism, prosaicism, prosaicness,** prosiness, pedestrianism, **unpoeticalness;
matter-of-factness,** unromanticism, unidealism; **unimaginativeness** 986; **plainness,** commonness, commonplaceness,
unembellishedness; insipidness, flatness,
vapidity; **dullness** 117

VERBS 3 **prose,** write prose *or* in prose; pedestrianize

ADJS 4 **prose,** in prose; unversified, nonpoetic, nonmetrical

5 **prosaic, prosy, prosing;** unpoetical, poet-
ryless; **plain, common, commonplace,
ordinary,** unembellished, mundane;
matter-of-fact, unromantic, unidealistic,
unimpassioned; pedestrian, **unimaginative** 986.5; insipid, vapid, flat; humdrum,
tiresome, **dull** 117.6

722 FICTION

NOUNS 1 **fiction,** narrative, narrative literature, imaginative narrative, prose fiction;
narration, relation, relating, recital, rehearsal, telling, retelling, recounting, recountal, review, portrayal, graphic narration, description, delineation, presentation; **storytelling,** tale-telling, yarn-spin-
ning *and* yarning <both nonformal>;
narrative poetry; operatic libretto; computer *or* interactive fiction

2 **narration, narrative, relation, recital,** rehearsal, telling, retelling, recounting,
recountal, review; **storytelling,** tale-telling, yarn spinning *or* yarning <both non-
formal>

3 **story** <see list>, **short story,** tale, narrative, yarn, account, narration, chronicle,
relation, version; **novel** <see list>, *roman*
<Fr>

4 <story elements> **plot,** fable, argument,
story, line, story line, subplot, secondary
plot, mythos; **structure,** plan, architecture, architectonics, scheme, design; **subject, topic, theme,** motif; thematic development, development, continuity; **action,**
movement; incident, episode; **complication;** rising action, climax, falling action,
peripeteia <Gk>, switch <nonformal>;
anagnorisis <Gk>, recognition; denouement, catastrophe; *deus ex machina* <L>;
device, contrivance, **gimmick** <nonfor-
mal>; angle *and* slant *and* twist <all non-
formal>; **character,** characterization;
speech, dialogue; **tone, atmosphere,**
mood; **setting,** locale, world, milieu,
background, region, local color

5 **narrator,** relator, reciter, recounter, *ra-
conteur* <Fr>; **anecdotist; storyteller,**
storier, taleteller, teller of tales, spinner
of yarns *and* yarn spinner <both nonfor-
mal>; word painter; **persona,** central
consciousness, the I of the story; point-of-
view <see list>; **author, writer,** short-
story writer, **novelist,** novelettist, fiction-
ist; fabulist, fableist, fabler, mythmaker,
mythopoet; romancer, romancist; saga-
man

VERBS 6 **narrate, tell, relate, recount,** report,
recite, rehearse, give an account of; tell a
story, unfold a tale, a tale unfold, fable,
fabulize; storify, fictionalize; romance;
novelize; mythicize, mythify, mythologize, allegorize; retell

ADJS 7 **fictional,** fictionalized; **novelistic,**
novelized, novelettish; mythical, mythological, **legendary, fabulous;** myth-
opoeic, mythopoetic *or* mythopoetical;
allegorical *or* allegoric, parabolic *or* parabolical; **romantic,** romanticized; historical, historicized, fact-based

8 **narrative, narrational;** storied, storified;
anecdotal, anecdotic; epic *or* epical

9 **types of stories**

adventure story	classical detective story
allegory	*conte* <Fr>
apologue	detective story *or* de-
beast fable	tective yarn *or*
bedtime story	whodunit <nonfor-
chivalric romance	mal>

dime novel *or* penny
dreadful <nonfor-
mal>
epic *or* epos
exemplum *or* didactic
tale *or* moral tale
fable
fabliau
fairy tale *or* Märchen
<Ger>
fantasy
folktale *or* folk story
gest
ghost story
hard-boiled detective
story *or* tough-tec
story <nonfor-
mal>
hero tale
horror story *or* chiller
and chiller-diller
<both nonformal>
lai
legend
love story

Milesian tale
mystery *or* mystery
story
myth *or* mythos
nursery tale
parable
romance
romantic adventure
saga
saint's legend
science fiction story
or sci-fi story
<nonformal>
short short story *or*
short-short
short story
sketch
suspense story
thriller *or* thriller-
diller <nonfor-
mal>
vignette
Western *or* Western
story *or* cowboy
story

10 types of novels

adventure novel
antinovel *or* anti-
roman *or* nouveau
roman
Bildungsroman
<Ger>
collage novel
comic novel
detective novel
dystopia *or* cacotopia
entertainment
epistolary novel
erotic novel
experimental novel
fictional *or* fiction-
alized biography
Gothic novel
historical novel
historical romance *or*
bodice-ripper
<nonformal>
Kunstlerroman
<Ger>
lyrical novel
naturalistic novel
nouveau roman
novel of character
novel of ideas
novel of incident
novel of manners

novel of sensibility
novel of the soil
novelette
novella *or* nouvelle
<Fr>
picaresque novel
political novel
pornographic novel
problem novel
proletarian novel
propaganda novel
psychological novel
realistic novel
regional novel
roman à clef <Fr>
roman-fleuve <Fr> *or*
river novel
satirical novel
science-fiction novel
sentimental novel
social melodrama
sociological novel
stream-of-
consciousness
novel
surrealistic novel
techno-thriller
thesis novel
utopia *or* utopian
novel

11 narrative points of view

documentary *or*
camera-eye ob-
server
fallible observer
first-person past nar-
rator

first-person present
narrator
omniscient observer
stream of conscious-
ness *or* interior
monologue

third-person past nar-
rator

third-person present
narrator

723 CRITICISM OF THE ARTS

NOUNS **1 criticism,** criticism of the arts, esthetic *or* artistic criticism, aesthetic *or*
artistic evaluation, aesthetic *or* artistic
analysis, aesthetic *or* artistic interpretation, critical commentary, critique, critical analysis, critical interpretation, critical evaluation, metacriticism, exegetics,
hermeneutics; **art criticism,** formalist
criticism, expressionist criticism, neofor-
malist criticism; music criticism; dramatic criticism; dance criticism; aesthetics

2 review, critical notice, commentary,
compte rendu critique <Fr>, critical
treatment *or* treatise

3 literary criticism, Lit-Crit <nonformal>,
literary analysis *or* evaluation *or* interpretation *or* exegetics *or* hermeneutics,
poetics; **critical approach *or* school** <see
list>; **literary theory,** theory of literature,
critical theory, theory of criticism

4 critic, interpreter, exegete, analyst, explicator, theoretician, aesthetician; reviewer

VERBS **5 criticize,** critique, evaluate, interpret, explicate, analyze, judge; theorize

ADJS **6 critical,** evaluative, interpretive, exegetical, analytical, explicative

7 literary critical approaches

archetypal criticism
contextualist criti-
cism
deconstruction *or* de-
constructionism
epistemological ap-
proach
ethical criticism
feminist criticism
formalist criticism
Freudian criticism
genre *or* generic criti-
cism
impressionistic criti-
cism
Jungian criticism
literary history
Marxist criticism
myth criticism

New Criticism
ontological approach
post-structuralist
criticism *or* post-
structuralism
practical criticism
psychological *or* psy-
choanalytic
criticism
reader-response criti-
cism
revisionist criticism
rhetorical criticism
sociological criticism
speech-act criticism
structuralist criti-
cism *or*
structuralism
textual criticism

724 OCCUPATION

NOUNS **1 occupation, work, job, employment,** business, employ, **activity, function,** enterprise, undertaking, **work,
affairs,** labor; thing *and* bag <both non-

formal>; **affair, matter, concern**, concernment, **interest**, lookout <nonformal>; what one is doing or about; **commerce** 731

2 **task, work, stint, job**, labor, piece of work, **chore**, chare, odd job; **assignment, charge**, project, errand, **mission**, commission, **duty**, service, exercise; things to do, matters in hand, irons in the fire, fish to fry; homework; busywork, makework

3 **function, office, duty, job**, province, place, **role**, *rôle* <Fr>, part; **capacity**, character, **position**

4 <sphere of work or activity> **field, sphere**, profession, province, bailiwick, turf <nonformal>, department, area, discipline, subdiscipline, orb, orbit, realm, arena, domain, walk; **specialty**, speciality <Brit>, line of country <Brit nonformal>; beat, round; shop

5 **position, job**, employment, gainful employment, situation, **office, post, place**, station, berth, billet, **appointment**, engagement, gig <nonformal>; incumbency, tenure; opening, vacancy; second job, moonlighting <nonformal>

6 **vocation, occupation, business, work, line, line of work**, line of business or endeavor, number <nonformal>, walk, **walk of life, calling**, mission, **profession, practice, pursuit, specialty**, specialization, *métier* <Fr>, mystery <old>, **trade**, racket and game <both nonformal>; **career**, lifework, life's work; career track, Mommy track <nonformal>; **craft**, art, handicraft; careerism, career building

7 **avocation, hobby**, hobbyhorse <old>, sideline, by-line, side interest, pastime, spare-time activity; amateur pursuit, amateurism; unpaid work, volunteer work

8 **professionalism**, professional standing or status

9 **nonprofessionalism, amateurism**, amateur standing or status

VERBS 10 **occupy, engage, busy**, devote, spend, **employ**, occupy oneself, busy oneself, go about one's business, devote oneself; pass or employ or spend the time; occupy one's time, take up one's time; attend to business, attend to one's work; mind one's business, mind the store <nonformal>, stick to one's last or knitting <nonformal>

11 **busy oneself with, do**, occupy or engage oneself with, employ oneself in or upon, pass or employ or spend one's time in; **engage in, take up**, devote oneself to, apply oneself to, address oneself to, have one's hands in, turn one's hand to; concern oneself with, make it one's business; **be about, be doing**, be occupied with, be engaged or employed in, be at work on; practice, follow as an occupation

12 **work**, work at, work for, have a job, be employed, **ply one's trade**, labor in one's vocation, do one's number <nonformal>, follow a trade, practice a profession, carry on a business or trade, keep up; **do or transact business**, carry on or conduct business; set up shop, set up in business, hang out one's shingle <nonformal>; stay employed, hold down a job <nonformal>; moonlight <nonformal>; labor, toil 725.13,14

13 **officiate, function, serve; perform as, act as**, act or play one's part, **do duty**, discharge or perform or exercise the office or duties or functions of, serve in the office or capacity of

14 **hold office**, fill an office, occupy a post

ADJS 15 **occupied, busy**, working; practical, realistic 986.6; banausic, moneymaking, breadwinning, utilitarian 387.18; materialistic 695.16; workaday, workday, prosaic 117.8; **commercial** 731.21

16 **occupational, vocational**, functional; **professional**, pro <nonformal>; official; technical, industrial; all in the day's work

17 **avocational**, hobby, amateur, nonprofessional

ADVS 18 **professionally**, vocationally; as a profession or vocation; in the course of business

725 EXERTION

NOUNS 1 **exertion, effort, energy**, elbow grease; **endeavor** 403; **trouble, pains**; great or mighty effort, might and main, muscle, one's back, nerve, and sinew, hard or strong or long pull, "a long pull, a strong pull, and a pull all together"— Dickens

2 **strain**, straining, **stress**, stressfulness, **stress and strain**, taxing, **tension**, stretch, rack; tug, pull, haul, heave; overexertion, overstrain, overtaxing, overextension, overstress

3 **struggle, fight, battle, tussle, scuffle, wrestle**, hassle <nonformal>

4 **work, labor, employment, industry, toil**, moil, travail, toil and trouble, sweat of one's brow; **drudgery, sweat**, slavery, spadework, rat race <nonformal>; treadmill; unskilled labor, hewing of wood and drawing of water; dirty work, grunt work and donkey work and shit-work and scut work <all nonformal>; **makework**, te-

dious *or* stupid *or* idiot *or* tiresome work, humdrum toil, grind <nonformal>, fag <chiefly Brit>; rubber room work *or* job *or* assignment, no-work job; **manual labor,** handwork, handiwork; hand's turn, stroke of work, stroke; lick *and* lick of work *and* stitch of work <all nonformal>; man-hour; **workload,** work schedule; task 724.2; fatigue 21

5 **hard work** *or* **labor, backbreaking work,** warm work, uphill work, hard *or* tough grind <nonformal>; **hard job** 1012.2; labor of Hercules; **laboriousness, toilsomeness,** effortfulness, **strenuousness, arduousness,** operosity, operoseness; onerousness, oppressiveness, burdensomeness; troublesomeness

6 **exercise** 84, exercising; **practice, drill, workout;** yoga; constitutional <nonformal>, stretch; violent exercise; physical education

7 exerciser; horizontal bar, parallel bars, horse, side horse, long horse, rings; trapeze; trampoline; Indian club; medicine ball; punching bag; rowing machine; weight, dumbbell, barbell

VERBS 8 **exert, exercise, ply, employ, use, put forth,** put out *and* make with <both nonformal>; practice

9 **exert oneself,** use some elbow grease <nonformal>, spread oneself, put forth one's strength, bend every effort, bend might and main, spare no effort, put on a full-court press <nonformal>, tax one's energies, break a sweat <nonformal>; put *or* lay oneself out <nonformal>, go all out <nonformal>; endeavor 403.4; **do one's best; apply oneself,** come to grips with; hump *and* hump it *and* hump oneself <all nonformal>, **buckle** *or* **knuckle** *or* bear <nonformal>, lay to; lay to the oars, ply the oar

10 **strain, tense, stress, stretch, tax,** press, rack; **pull, tug,** haul, **heave;** strain the muscles, strain every nerve *or* every nerve and sinew; put one's back into it <nonformal>; sweat blood; take on too much, spread oneself too thin, overexert, overstrain, overtax, overextend; drive *or* whip *or* flog oneself

11 **struggle, strive, contend, fight, battle,** buffet, scuffle, tussle, wrestle, hassle <nonformal>, work *or* fight one's way, agonize, huff and puff, grunt and sweat, sweat it <nonformal>, make heavy weather of it

12 **work, labor;** busy oneself 724.10,11; turn a hand, do a hand's turn, do a lick of work, earn one's keep; chore, do the chores, char *or* do chars, chare <Brit>

13 **work hard; scratch** *and* **hustle** *and* **sweat** <all nonformal>, **slave, sweat and slave** <nonformal>, slave away, toil away; **hit the ball** *and* bear down *and* pour it on <all nonformal>; work one's head off <nonformal>, work one's fingers to the bone, break one's back, bust one's hump *or* ass <nonformal>; beaver *or* beaver away <Brit nonformal>, work like a beaver, work like a horse *or* cart horse *or* dog, work like a slave *or* galley slave, work like a coal heaver, work like a Trojan; work overtime, be a workaholic <nonformal>, do double duty, work double hours *or* tides, **work day and night,** work late, **burn the midnight oil;** lucubrate, elucubrate; overwork 992.10

14 **drudge, grind** *and* **dig** <both nonformal>, fag <Brit>, **grub, toil,** moil, toil and moil, travail, **plod, slog, peg, plug** <nonformal>, hammer, peg away *or* along, plug away *or* along <nonformal>, hammer away, pound away, struggle along, struggle on, work away; **get** *or* **keep one's nose to the grindstone;** wade through

15 **set to work, get rolling, get busy, get down to business** *or* **work,** roll up one's sleeves, spit on one's hands, gird up one's loins; fall to work, **fall to, buckle** *or* **knuckle down to** <nonformal>, **turn to, set to** *or* **about,** put *or* set one's hand to, start in, set up shop, enter on *or* upon, launch into *or* upon; **get on the job** *and* get going <both nonformal>; **go to it** *and* **get with it** *and* get cracking *and* have at it *and* get one's teeth into it <all nonformal>; hop *or* jump to it <nonformal>; **attack,** set at, **tackle** <nonformal>; **plunge into,** dive into; **pitch in** *or* **into** <nonformal>; light into *and* wade into *and* tear into *and* sail into <all nonformal>, put *or* lay one's shoulder to the wheel, put one's hand to the plow; take on, undertake 404.3

16 **task, work, busy,** keep busy, fag <Brit>, sweat <nonformal>, **drive, tax;** overtask, overtax, **overwork,** overdrive; burden, oppress 297.13

ADJS 17 **laboring, working; struggling, striving,** straining; **drudging, toiling,** slaving, sweating *and* grinding <both nonformal>, grubbing, **plodding,** slogging, pegging, plugging <nonformal>; hardworking

18 **laborious, toilsome, arduous, strenuous,** painful, effortful, operose, troublesome,

onerous, oppressive, burdensome; wearisome; **heavy,** hefty <nonformal>, tough
<nonformal>, uphill, **backbreaking,** gru-
eling, punishing, crushing, killing, Herculean; **labored,** forced, strained; straining, tensive, **intensive;** hard-fought, hard-
earned

ADVS **19 laboriously, arduously, toilsomely,
strenuously,** operosely; effortfully, with
effort, **hard,** by the sweat of one's brow;
the hard way; with all one's might, for all
one is worth, with a will, **with might and
main,** with a strong hand, manfully;
hammer and tongs, tooth and nail, *bec et
ongles* <Fr>, heart and soul; **industriously** 330.27

726 WORKER, DOER

NOUNS **1 doer, agent,** actor, **performer,
worker, practitioner,** perpetrator; **producer, maker,** creator, fabricator, **author,**
mover, prime mover; architect; **agent,**
medium; **executor,** executant, executrix;
operator, operative, operant; subject *and*
agent <both grammar>

2 worker, laborer, toiler, moiler; member
of the working class, proletarian, prole
<Brit nonformal>, blue-collar *or* lunch-
bucket worker, laboring man, stiff *and*
working stiff <both nonformal>; **workman, workingman; workwoman, work-
ingwoman,** workfolk, workpeople; working girl, workgirl; **factory worker,** industrial worker; autoworker, steelworker;
construction worker; **commuter;** home
worker, telecommuter; **office worker,
white-collar worker;** career woman, career girl; **jobholder,** wageworker, **wage
earner,** salaried worker; **breadwinner;**
wage slave; employee, servant 577; **hand,
workhand; laborer,** common laborer, **unskilled laborer,** navvy <Brit>, day laborer, roust-about; casual, casual laborer;
agricultural worker 1067.5; migrant
worker, migrant; menial, flunky; piece-
worker, jobber; full-time worker, part-
time worker; temporary employee, temporary, office temporary, temp <nonfor-
mal>; free-lance worker, free lance, free-
lancer; self-employed person; **labor force,
work force,** shop floor <Brit>; labor
market

3 drudge, grub, hack, fag, plodder, slave,
galley slave, **workhorse,** beast of burden,
slogger; "hewers of wood and drawers of
water"—Bible; grind *and* greasy grind
<both nonformal>, swot <Brit nonfor-
mal>; slave labor, sweatshop labor

4 professional, member of a learned profession, professional practitioner; pro *and*
old pro <both nonformal>, seasoned professional; gownsman; doctor, lawyer,
member of the clergy, teacher, accountant; social worker; health-care professional, military professional; law-
enforcement professional, etc

5 amateur, nonprofessional, layman, member of the laity, laic

6 skilled worker, skilled laborer, **journeyman,** mechanic; **craftsman, handicrafts-
man;** craftswoman; craftsperson; crafts-
people; **artisan,** artificer, artist <old>;
maker, *fabbro* <Ital>; **wright; technician;** apprentice, prentice <nonformal>;
master, master craftsman, master workman, master carpenter, etc

7 engineer, professional engineer; **technician,** technical worker, techie <nonfor-
mal>; engineering, technology

8 smith; farrier <Brit>, forger, forgeman,
metalworker; Vulcan, Hephaestus, Way-
land *or* Völund

727 UNIONISM, LABOR UNION

NOUNS **1 unionism,** trade unionism, trades
unionism <Brit>, labor unionism;
**unionization; collective bargaining; arbi-
tration,** nonbinding arbitration; industrial relations, labor relations

2 labor union, trade union, trades union
<Brit>; organized labor; collective bar-
gaining; **craft union,** horizontal union;
industrial union, vertical union; **local,**
union local, local union; company union

3 union shop, preferential shop, **closed
shop;** open shop; nonunion shop; **labor
contract, union contract,** sweetheart contract, yellow-dog contract; maintenance
of membership

**4 unionist, labor unionist, trade unionist,
union member,** trades unionist <Brit>,
organized *or* unionized worker, cardholder; shop steward, bargainer,
negotiator; business agent; union officer;
union *or* labor organizer, organizer;
union contractor

5 strike, walkout *or* tie-up <both nonfor-
mal>, industrial action <Brit>, **job
action;** slowdown, rulebook slowdown,
sick-in *and* sickout *and* blue flu <all non-
formal>; work stoppage, sit-down strike,
sit-down, wildcat strike, outlaw strike;
sympathy strike; **slowdown,** work-to-
rule, rule-book slowdown; general strike;
boycott, boy-cottage; buyer's *or* consumer's strike; **lock-out;** revolt 327.4

6 **striker;** sitdown striker; holdout <nonformal>

7 <strike enforcer> **picket; goon** <nonformal>, strong-arm man; flying squadron *or* squad, goon squad <nonformal>

8 **strikebreaker, scab** *and* **rat** *and* **fink** *and* scissorbill <all nonformal>, **blackleg** <Brit>

VERBS **9 organize, unionize;** bargain, bargain collectively; arbitrate; submit to arbitration

10 **strike, go on strike, go out, walk, walk out;** hit the bricks <nonformal>, shut it down; slow down; sit down; **boycott;** picket; hold out <nonformal>; **lock out;** revolt 327.7

11 **break a strike; scab** *and* **rat** *and* **fink** <all nonformal>, **blackleg** <Brit>

728 MONEY

NOUNS **1 money, currency, legal tender, medium of exchange,** circulating medium, sterling <Brit>, **cash,** hard cash, cold cash; specie, coinage, mintage, coin of the realm, gold; **silver;** dollars; pounds, shillings, and pence; **the wherewithal,** the wherewith; lucre, **filthy lucre** <nonformal>, the almighty dollar, pelf, root of all evil, mammon; "the sinews of war"—Libanius, "the sinews of affairs"—Laertius, "the ruling spirit of all things"—Publilius Syrus, "coined liberty"—Dostoyevsky; **hard currency,** soft currency; fractional currency, postage currency, postal currency; managed currency; necessity money, scrip, emergency money

2 <nonformal terms> **dough, bread, jack, kale,** scratch, sugar, change, mazuma, mopus, gelt, gilt, coin, spondulics, oof, ooftish, wampum, possibles, moolah, boodle, blunt, dinero, do-re-mi, **sugar,** brass, tin, rocks, simoleons, shekels, berries, chips, **bucks,** green, green stuff, the needful, grease, ointment, oil of palms, cabbage, whip-out, the necessary, loot

3 wampum, wampumpeag, peag, sewan, roanoke; cowrie

4 specie, hard money; coin, piece, piece of money, piece of silver *or* gold; roll of coins, rouleau; **gold piece;** ten-dollar gold piece, eagle; five-dollar gold piece, half eagle; twenty-dollar gold piece, double eagle; guinea, sovereign, pound sovereign, crown, half crown; doubloon; ducat; napoleon, louis d'or; moidore

5 paper money; bill, dollar bill, etc; **note,** negotiable note, legal-tender note; **bank note,** Federal Reserve note; national bank note; government note, treasury note; silver certificate; gold certificate; scrip; fractional note, shinplaster <nonformal>; fiat money, assignat

6 <nonformal terms> **folding money, green stuff,** the long green, folding green, lean green, mint leaves, lettuce, greenbacks, frogskins, skins

7 <US denominations> mill; cent, penny, copper, red cent <nonformal>; five cents, nickel; ten cents, dime; twenty-five cents, quarter, two bits <nonformal>; fifty cents, half-dollar, four bits <nonformal>; dollar, dollar bill; buck *and* smacker *and* frogskin *and* fish *and* skin <all nonformal>; silver dollar, beau dollar <old>, cartwheel *and* iron man <both nonformal>; two-dollar bill, two-spot <nonformal>; five-dollar bill; fiver *and* five-spot *and* fin <all nonformal>; ten-dollar bill; tenner *and* ten-spot *and* sawbuck <all nonformal>; twenty-dollar bill, double sawbuck <nonformal>; fifty-dollar bill, half a C <nonformal>; hundred-dollar bill; C *and* C-note *and* century *and* bill <all nonformal>; five hundred dollars, half grand <nonformal>, five-hundred-dollar bill, half G <nonformal>; thousand dollars, G *and* grand <both nonformal>, thousand-dollar bill, G-note *and* yard *and* big one <all nonformal>

8 <British denominations> mite; farthing; halfpenny *or* ha'penny, bawbee <Brit nonformal>, mag *or* meg <both Brit nonformal>; penny; pence, p; new pence, np; two-pence *or* tuppence; threepence *or* thrippence, threepenny bit *or* piece; fourpence, fourpenny, groat; sixpence, tanner <Brit nonformal>, teston; shilling, bob <Brit nonformal>; florin; half crown, half-dollar <Brit nonformal>; crown, dollar <Brit nonformal>; pound, quid <nonformal>; guinea; fiver <£5>, tenner <£10>, pony <£25>, monkey <£500>, plum <£100,000>, marigold <£1,000,000> <all Brit nonformal>

9 foreign money, foreign denominations; **convertibility, foreign exchange;** rate of exchange *or* exchange rate; parity of exchange; agio

10 counterfeit, counterfeit money, funny *or* phony *or* bogus money <nonformal>, false *or* bad money, queer <nonformal>, base coin, green goods <nonformal>; **forgery,** bad check, rubber check *and* bounced check *and* kite <all nonformal>

11 negotiable instrument *or* **paper,** commercial paper, paper, bill; **bill of exchange,**

bill of draft; certificate, certificate of deposit or CD; **check**, cheque <Brit>; blank check; bank check, teller's check; treasury check; cashier's check, certified check; traveler's check or banker's check; letter of credit, commercial letter of credit; **money order** or MO; postal order or postoffice order <both Brit>; draft, warrant, voucher, debenture; **promissory note, note, IOU**; note of hand; credit note; acceptance, acceptance bill, bank acceptance, trade acceptance; due bill; demand bill, sight bill, demand draft, sight draft; time bill, time draft; exchequer bill or treasury bill <both Brit>; checkbook

12 **token, counter**, slug; **scrip, coupon; check, ticket**, tag; hat check, baggage check

13 **sum**, amount of money; round sum, lump sum

14 **funds, finances, moneys**, exchequer, purse, budget, pocket; treasury, treasure, substance, **assets**, resources, total assets, worth, net worth, **pecuniary resources, means**, available means or resources or funds, cash flow, wherewithal, command of money; balance; pool, **fund, kitty** <nonformal>; war chest; checking account, bank account; Swiss bank account, unnumbered or unregistered bank account; reserves, cash reserves; savings, savings account, nest egg <nonformal>; life savings; bottom dollar <nonformal>

15 **capital, fund**; moneyed capital; principal, corpus; circulating capital, floating capital; fixed capital, working capital, equity capital, **risk** or **venture capital**; capital structure; capital gains distribution; capitalization

16 **money market**, supply of short-term funds; tight money, cheap money; **borrowing** 621; **lending** 620; discounting, note discounting, note shaving, dealing in commercial paper

17 **bankroll**; roll or wad <both nonformal>

18 **cash, ready money** or **cash**, the ready <nonformal>, available funds, money in hand, cash in hand, balance in hand, immediate resources, **liquid assets**, cash supply, **cash flow**; treasury

19 **petty cash, pocket money, pin money**, spending money, mad money, **change**, small change; nickels and dimes and chicken feed and peanuts <all nonformal>

20 precious metals; **gold**, yellow stuff <nonformal>; nugget, gold nugget; **silver, copper, nickel**, coin gold or silver; bullion, ingot, bar

21 standard of value, gold standard, silver standard; monometallism, bimetallism; money of account

22 <science of coins> **numismatics**, numismatology; numismatist, numismatologist

23 monetization; issuance, circulation; remonetization; demonetization; revaluation, devaluation

24 **coining**, coinage, mintage, striking, stamping; **counterfeiting, forgery**; coin-clipping

25 **coiner**, minter, mintmaster, moneyer; **counterfeiter, forger**; coin-clipper

VERBS 26 monetize; **issue**, utter, **circulate**; remonetize, reissue; demonetize; revalue, devalue, devaluate

27 discount, discount notes, deal in commercial paper, shave; borrow, lend 620.5

28 **coin, mint; counterfeit, forge**; utter, pass or shove the queer <nonformal>

29 **cash**, cash in <nonformal>, liquidate, convert into cash

ADJS 30 **monetary, pecuniary**, nummary, **financial**; capital; fiscal; sumptuary; numismatic; sterling

31 convertible, liquid, negotiable

729 FINANCE, INVESTMENT

NOUNS 1 **finance, finances, money matters**; world of finance, financial world, financial industry, **high finance**, investment banking, international banking, Wall Street banking, Lombard Street; the gnomes of Zurich; economics 731

2 **financing, funding, backing**, financial backing, **sponsorship, patronization**, support, financial support; **stake** and **grubstake** <both nonformal>; subsidy 478.8; **capitalizing**, capitalization, provision of capital; deficit financing

3 **investment, venture, risk**, plunge <nonformal>, speculation; prime investment; ethical or conscience investment; **divestment**, disinvestment

4 **banking**, money dealing, money changing; investment banking; banking industry

5 **financial condition**, state of the exchequer; **credit rating**, Dun & Bradstreet rating

6 **solvency**, soundness, solidity; credit standing, creditworthiness; unindebtedness

7 **crisis**, financial crisis; dollar crisis, dollar gap

8 **financier**, moneyman, **capitalist**, finance capitalist; Wall Streeter; investor; finan-

cial expert, economist, authority on money and banking; international banker

9 **financer, backer,** funder, **sponsor, patron, supporter,** angel <nonformal>, Maecenas; cash cow *and* staker *and* grubstaker <all nonformal>, meal ticket <nonformal>; **fundraiser**

10 **banker, money dealer,** moneymonger; money broker; discounter, note broker, bill broker <Brit>; moneylender 620.3; money changer, cambist; investment banker; bank president, bank manager, bank officer, loan officer, trust officer, banking executive; bank clerk, cashier, teller

11 **treasurer,** financial officer, bursar, purser, purse bearer, **cashier,** cashkeeper; accountant, auditor, controller *or* comptroller, bookkeeper; chamberlain, curator, steward, trustee; depositary, depository; receiver, liquidator; **paymaster;** Secretary of the Treasury, Chancellor of the Exchequer

12 **treasury, treasure-house;** subtreasury; **depository,** repository; storehouse 386.6; gold depository, Fort Knox; **strongbox, safe,** money chest, **coffer, locker, chest;** piggy bank, penny bank, bank; **vault,** strong room; safe-deposit *or* safety-deposit box *or* vault; cashbox, coin box, cash register, **till;** bursary; exchequer, fisc; **public treasury,** public funds, taxpayer funds *or* money, pork barrel, public crib *or* trough *or* till <nonformal>

13 **bank,** banking house, lending institution, savings institution; automated teller machine *or* ATM, cash machine; **central bank,** Bank of England *or* the Old Lady of Threadneedle Street, Bank of France; Federal Reserve Bank *or* System; World Bank, International Monetary Fund; clearing house

14 **purse, wallet, pocketbook, bag, handbag,** porte-monnaie, **billfold,** money belt, money clip, poke <nonformal>, **pocket;** moneybag; purse strings

VERBS 15 **finance, back, fund, sponsor, patronize, support,** provide for, capitalize, provide capital *or* money for, pay for, bankroll <nonformal>, angel <nonformal>, put up the money; **stake** *or* **grubstake** <both nonformal>; subsidize 478.19; set up, set up in business; refinance

16 **invest,** place, put, sink; **risk, venture;** make an investment, lay out money, place out *or* put out at interest; reinvest, roll over, plow back into <nonformal>;

invest in, put money in, sink money in, pour money into, tie up one's money in; buy in *or* into, buy a piece *or* share of; financier; plunge <nonformal>, speculate 737.23

ADJS 17 **solvent, sound,** substantial, solid, good, sound as a dollar, creditworthy; **able to pay,** good for, unindebted 624.23, out of the hole *or* the red

18 **insolvent,** unsound, indebted 623.8

730 BUSINESSMAN, MERCHANT

NOUNS 1 **businessman,** businesswoman, businessperson, businesspeople; enterpriser, entrepreneur, man of commerce; small *or* little businessman; big businessman, magnate, tycoon <nonformal>, baron, king, top executive, business leader; director, manager 574.1; big boss; **industrialist,** captain of industry; banker, financier; robber baron

2 **merchant,** merchandiser, marketer, **trader,** trafficker, **dealer,** monger, chandler; **tradesman,** tradeswoman; **storekeeper, shopkeeper;** regrater; **wholesaler,** jobber, middleman; importer, exporter; **distributor; retailer,** retail merchant, retail dealer *or* seller; **dealership, distributorship;** franchise; concession

3 **salesman,** seller, salesperson, salesclerk; **saleswoman,** saleslady, salesgirl; **clerk,** shop clerk, store clerk, shop assistant; floorwalker; **agent, sales agent,** selling agent; sales engineer; sales manager; salespeople, sales force, sales personnel; scalper *and* ticket scalper <both nonformal>

4 **traveling salesman, traveler, commercial traveler,** traveling agent, traveling man *or* woman, knight of the road, bagman <Brit>, drummer <old>; detail man; door-to-door salesman, canvasser

5 **vendor, peddler, huckster, hawker,** butcher <old>, higgler, cadger <Scots>, colporteur, chapman <Brit>; cheap-jack *and* cheap-john <both nonformal>; coster *or* costermonger <both Brit>; sidewalk salesman

6 **solicitor,** canvasser

7 <nonformal terms> tout, touter, **pitchman** *or* **-woman** *or* person, barker, spieler, ballyhooer, **ballyhoo man**

8 **auctioneer,** auction agent

9 **broker,** note broker, bill broker <Brit>, discount broker, cotton broker, hotel broker, insurance broker, mortgage broker, diamond broker, furniture

broker, ship broker, grain broker; stockbroker 737.10; pawnbroker 620.3; money
broker, money changer, cambist; land
broker, real estate broker, realtor, real estate agent, estate agent <Brit>

10 **ragman**, old-clothesman, rag-and-bone
man <Brit>; **junkman**, junk dealer

11 **tradesmen**, **tradespeople**, tradesfolk,
merchantry

ADJS 12 **business**, **commercial**, mercantile;
entrepreneurial

731 COMMERCE, ECONOMICS

NOUNS 1 **commerce**, **trade**, **traffic**, truck, intercourse, **dealing**, **dealings**; **business**,
business dealings or affairs or relations,
commercial affairs or relations; the business world, the world of trade or commerce, the marketplace; merchantry,
mercantile business; **market**, marketing,
state of the market, buyers' market,
sellers' market; **industry** 725.4; big business, small business; fair trade, free
trade, reciprocal trade, unilateral trade,
multilateral trade; most favored nation;
balance of trade; restraint of trade

2 **trade**, **trading**, **doing business**, **traffick-
ing**; barter, bartering, **exchange**,
interchange, swapping <nonformal>;
give-and-take, horse trading <nonfor-
mal>, **dealing**, **deal-making**, wheeling
and dealing <nonformal>; **buying and
selling**; **wholesaling**, jobbing; brokerage, agency; **retailing**, merchandising
734.2

3 **negotiation**, **bargaining**, **haggling**, hig-
gling, **dickering**, **chaffering**, chaffer,
haggle; hacking out or working out or
hammering out a deal, coming to terms;
collective bargaining, package bargaining, pattern bargaining

4 **transaction**, business or commercial
transaction, **deal**, business deal, negotiation <old>, operation, turn; package
deal

5 **bargain**, **deal** <nonformal>, dicker;
trade, **swap** <nonformal>; horse trade
<nonformal>; trade-in; blind bargain,
pig in a poke; hard bargain

6 **custom**, patronage, trade; **goodwill**, repute, good name

7 **economy**, **economic system**, capitalist or
capitalistic economy, free-enterprise or
private-enterprise economy, market
economy, socialist or socialistic economy,
collectivized economy; hot or overheated
economy; healthy or sound economy;
gross national product or **GNP**; economic

sector, public sector, private sector; economic self-sufficiency, autarky

8 **standard of living**, standard of life, standard of comfort; real wages, take-home
pay or take-home; **cost of living**; cost-of-
living index, consumer price index

9 **business cycle**, **economic cycle**, business
fluctuations; peak, peaking; low, bottom-
ing out <nonformal>; prosperity, boom
<nonformal>; boomlet or miniboom;
crisis, **recession**, **depression**, slow-down,
cooling off, slump and bust <both nonfor-
mal>, downturn, downtick <nonfor-
mal>; upturn, uptick <nonformal>, expanding economy, recovery; **growth**,
economic growth, business growth, high
growth rate, expansion, market expansion, **economic expansion**; **trade cycle**;
trade deficit, trade gap, balance of payments; **monetary cycle**; **inflation**, deflation, stagflation

10 **economics**, eco or econ <nonformal>,
economic science, the dismal science; political economy; dynamic economics;
theoretical economics, plutology; classical economics; Keynesian economics,
Keynesianism; supply side economics;
econometrics; economism, economic determinism; economic man

11 **economist**, economic expert or authority;
political economist

12 **commercialism**, mercantilism; indus-
trialism; mass marketing

13 **commercialization**; industrialization

VERBS 14 **trade**, **deal**, **traffic**, **truck**, **buy and
sell**, **do business**; **barter**; **exchange**,
change, interchange, give in exchange,
take in exchange, **swap** <nonformal>,
switch; swap horses and horse-trade
<both nonformal>; trade off; trade in;
trade sight unseen, make a blind bargain,
sell a pig in a poke; **ply one's trade** 724.12

15 **deal in**, **trade in**, **traffic in**, **handle**, carry,
be in; market, merchandise, **sell**, retail,
wholesale, job

16 **trade with**, **deal with**, **traffic with**, **do
business with**, have dealings with, have
truck with, transact business with; frequent as a customer, shop at, trade at,
patronize, take one's business or trade to;
open an account with, have an account
with

17 **bargain**, **drive a bargain**, **negotiate**, **haggle**, higgle, chaffer, huckster, **deal**, **dicker**,
make a deal, do a deal <Brit>, hack out
or work out or hammer out a deal; **bid**,
bid for, cheapen, beat down; underbid,
outbid; drive a hard bargain

18 **strike a bargain**, make a bargain, make a

dicker, **make a deal,** get oneself a deal, put through a deal, shake hands, shake on it <nonformal>; bargain for, agree to; **come to terms** 332.10; be a bargain, be a go *and* be a deal <both nonformal>, be on <nonformal>

19 put on a business basis *or* footing, make businesslike; commercialize; industrialize

20 <adjust the economy> cool *or* cool off the economy; heat *or* heat up the economy

ADJS 21 **commercial, business, trade,** trading, **mercantile,** merchant; commercialistic, mercantilistic; industrial; wholesale, retail

22 **economic;** socio-economic, politico-economic *or* -economical

732 ILLICIT BUSINESS

NOUNS 1 illicit business, illegitimate business, illegal operations, illegal commerce *or* traffic, shady dealings, **racket** <nonformal>; **the rackets** <nonformal>, the syndicate, **organized crime, Mafia,** Cosa Nostra; **black market,** gray market; **drug** *or* **narcotics traffic;** narcoterrorism; **prostitution,** streetwalking; **pimping,** traffic in women, white slavery; usury 623.3, loan-sharking *and* shylocking <both nonformal>; protection racket; bootlegging, moonshining <nonformal>; gambling 759.7

2 **smuggling,** contrabandage, contraband; narcotics smuggling, dope smuggling <nonformal>, jewel smuggling, cigarette smuggling; gunrunning, rumrunning

3 **contraband,** smuggled goods; narcotics, drugs, dope <nonformal>, jewels, cigarettes; bootleg liquor; stolen goods *or* property, hot goods *or* items <nonformal>

4 **racketeer;** Mafioso, **black marketeer,** gray marketeer; bootlegger, moonshiner <nonformal>; pusher *and* dealer <both nonformal>, narcotics *or* dope *or* drug pusher <nonformal>; **drug lord;** Medellin cartel

5 **smuggler,** contrabandist, runner; drug smuggler, mule <nonformal>; gunrunner, rumrunner

6 **fence,** receiver, **receiver of stolen goods,** swagman *and* swagsman <both nonformal>, bagman, bagwoman

VERBS 7 <deal in illicit goods> push *and* shove <both nonformal>; **sell under the counter; black-market,** black-marketeer; bootleg, moonshine <nonformal>; fence <nonformal>

8 **smuggle,** run, sneak

733 PURCHASE

NOUNS 1 purchase, buying, purchasing; **shopping, marketing;** shopping around, comparison shopping; window-shopping; impulse buying; shopping spree; repurchase, rebuying; mail-order buying, catalog buying; installment buying, hire purchase <Brit>; layaway purchase; **buying up,** cornering, coemption <old>; **buying** *or* **purchasing power; consumerism;** consumer society, consumer sovereignty, consumer power, acquisitive society; retail *or* consumer price index; wholesale price index

2 **option,** first option, **first refusal,** refusal, preemption, right of preemption, prior right of purchase

3 **market,** public, purchasing public; urban market, rural market, youth market, suburban market, etc; **clientele, customers,** clientage, **patronage, custom,** trade; carriage trade

4 **customer, client; patron,** patronizer <nonformal>, regular customer *or* buyer, regular; **prospect;** mark *or* sucker <both nonformal>

5 **buyer,** purchaser, emptor, **consumer,** vendee; **shopper,** marketer; windowshopper, browser; purchasing agent, customer agent

6 by-bidder, decoy, come-on man *and* shill <both nonformal>

VERBS 7 **purchase, buy,** procure, make *or* complete a purchase, make a buy, make a deal for, blow oneself to <nonformal>; **buy up,** regrate, **corner,** monopolize, engross; buy out; buy in, buy into, buy a piece of; repurchase, rebuy, buy back; buy on credit, buy on the installment plan; buy sight unseen *or* blind; trade up

8 **shop, market, go shopping,** go marketing; **shop around;** window-shop, comparison-shop, **browse;** impulse-buy

9 **bid,** make a bid, offer, offer to buy, make an offer; give the asking price; by-bid, shill <nonformal>; bid up; bid in

ADJS 10 **purchasing, buying,** in the market; cliental

11 **bought,** store-bought, boughten *or* store-boughten <both nonformal>, purchased

734 SALE

NOUNS 1 sale; wholesale, retail; market, demand, outlet; buyers' market, sellers' market; mass market; conditional sale; tie-in sale, tie-in; turnover; bill of sale; cash sale, cash-and-carry

**2 selling, merchandising, marketing;
wholesaling,** jobbing; **retailing;** direct
selling; mail-order selling, direct-mail
selling, catalog selling; television *or* video
selling; **vending, peddling, hawking,
huckstering;** hucksterism; market *or*
marketing research, consumer research,
consumer preference study, consumer
survey; sales campaign, promotion, sales
promotion; **salesmanship,** high-pressure
salesmanship, hard sell <nonformal>,
low-pressure salesmanship, soft sell
<nonformal>; sellout

3 sale, closing-out sale, going-out-of-
business sale, inventory-clearance sale,
distress sale, fire sale; bazaar; rummage
sale, white elephant sale, garage sale, flea
market; tax sale

4 auction, auction sale, vendue, outcry,
sale at *or* by auction, sale to the highest
bidder; Dutch auction; **auction block,
block**

5 sales talk, sales pitch, patter; **pitch** *or*
spiel *or* ballyhoo <all nonformal>

6 sales resistance, consumer *or* buyer resistance

7 salability, salableness, commerciality,
merchandisability, **marketability,** ven-
dibility

VERBS **8 sell, merchandise, market,** move,
turn over, sell off, make *or* effect a sale;
convert into cash, turn into money; **sell
out,** close out; sell up <Brit>; **retail,** sell
retail, sell over the counter; **wholesale,**
sell wholesale, job, be jobber *or* wholesaler for; dump, unload, flood the market
with; sacrifice, sell at a sacrifice *or* loss;
resell, sell over; undersell, undercut, cut
under; sell short; sell on consignment

9 vend, dispense, **peddle, hawk, huckster**

10 put up for sale, put up, ask bids *or* offers
for, offer for sale, offer at a bargain

11 auction, auction off, auctioneer, sell at
auction, sell by auction, put up for auction, **put on the block,** bring under the
hammer; knock down, sell to the highest
bidder

12 be sold, sell, bring, realize, sell for; sell
like hotcakes

ADJS **13 sales,** selling, market, **marketing,
merchandising, retail,** retailing, wholesale, wholesaling

14 salable, marketable, retailable, merchan-
disable, merchantable, commercial,
vendible; in demand

15 unsalable, nonsalable, **unmarketable;** on
one's hands, on the shelves, not moving,
not turning over, unbought, unsold

ADVS **16 for sale,** to sell, up for sale, in *or* on

the market, in the marts of trade; at a
bargain, marked down

17 at auction, at outcry, at public auction *or*
outcry, by auction, **on the block,** under
the hammer

735 MERCHANDISE

NOUNS **1 merchandise, commodities, wares,
goods,** effects, vendibles; **items,** oddments; **consumer goods,** consumer items,
retail goods, goods for sale; **stock, stock-
in-trade;** staples; **inventory; line,** line of
goods; sideline; job lot; mail-order goods,
catalog goods; **luxury goods,** high-ticket
or big-ticket *or* upscale items

2 commodity, ware, vendible, **product,
article, item,** article of commerce *or*
merchandise; staple, staple item, standard article; special, feature, leader, lead
item, loss leader; seconds; drug, drug on
the market

3 dry goods, soft goods; textiles; yard
goods, white goods, linens, napery; men's
wear, ladies' wear, children's wear, infants' wear; sportswear, sporting goods;
leatherware, leather goods

4 hard goods, durables, durable goods; fixtures, white goods, **appliances** 385.4;
tools and machinery 1039; **hardware,**
ironmongery <Brit>; sporting goods,
housewares, home furnishings, kitchen-
ware; tableware, dinnerware; flatware,
hollow ware; metalware, brassware, cop-
perware, silverware, ironware, tinware;
woodenware; glassware; chinaware,
earthenware, clayware, stoneware, gran-
iteware; enamelware; ovenware

5 furniture 229, furnishings, home furnishings

6 notions, sundries, novelties, knickknacks,
odds and ends; toilet goods, toiletries;
cosmetics; giftware

7 groceries, grocery <Brit>, food items,
edibles, victuals, baked goods, packaged
goods, canned goods, tinned goods
<Brit>; green goods, **produce,** truck

736 MARKET
<place of trade>

NOUNS **1 market, mart, store, shop,** salon,
boutique, wareroom, emporium, house,
establishment, *magasin* <Fr>; **retail
store; wholesale house, discount store,
discount house, outlet store;** warehouse;
mail-order house; **general store,** country
store; **department store; co-op** <nonfor-
mal>, cooperative; **variety store,** variety

shop, **dime store; ten-cent store** or five-and-ten or five-and-dime <all nonformal>; chain store; concession; **trading post,** post; **supermarket**

2 **marketplace, mart, market, open market,** market overt; **shopping center, shopping plaza** or **mall,** plaza, mall, shopping or shop or commercial complex; emporium, rialto; staple; **bazaar, fair,** trade fair, show, auto show, boat show, etc, exposition; flea market, flea fair, street market, *marché aux puces* <Fr>

3 **booth, stall, stand;** newsstand, kiosk, news kiosk

4 **vending machine,** vendor, coin machine, coin-operated machine, slot machine, **automat;** redeemer or reverse vending machine

5 **salesroom,** wareroom; showroom; auction room

6 **counter,** shopboard <old>; notions counter; showcase; peddler's cart, pushcart

737 STOCK MARKET

NOUNS 1 **stock market, the market, Wall Street;** ticker market; open market, competitive market; steady market, strong market, hard or stiff market; unsteady market, spotty market; weak market; long market; top-heavy market; market index, stock price index, Dow-Jones Industrial Average

2 **active market,** brisk market, lively market

3 **inactive market,** slow market, stagnant market, flat market, tired market, sick market; investors on the sidelines

4 **rising market,** booming market, buoyant market; **bull market,** bullish market, bullishness

5 **declining market,** sagging market, retreating market, off market, soft market; **bear market,** bearish market, bearishness; **slump,** sag; break, break in the market; profit-taking, selloff; **crash,** smash

6 **rigged market,** manipulated market, pegged market, put-up market; **insider trading**

7 **stock exchange, exchange,** Wall Street, change <Brit>, **stock market,** bourse, **board;** the Exchange, New York Stock Exchange, the Big Board; American Stock Exchange, Amex, curb, curb market, curb exchange; over-the-counter market, telephone market, outside market; third market; exchange floor; commodity exchange, pit, corn pit, wheat

pit, etc; quotation board; **ticker,** stock ticker; ticker tape

8 **financial district,** Wall Street, the Street; Lombard Street

9 **stockbrokerage,** brokerage, brokerage house, brokerage office; wire house; bucket shop and boiler room <both nonformal>

10 **stockbroker,** sharebroker <Brit>, **broker,** jobber, stockjobber, dealer, stock dealer; Wall Streeter; stock-exchange broker, *agent de bourse* <Fr>; floor broker, floor trader, floorman, specialist, market maker; pit man; curb broker; odd-lot dealer; two-dollar broker; broker's agent, customer's broker or customer's man, registered representative; bond crowd

11 **speculator,** adventurer, operator; big operator, smart operator; **plunger,** gunslinger; scalper; stag <Brit>; lame duck; margin purchaser; **arbitrager** or arbitrageur or arb <nonformal>; inside trader

12 **bear,** short, short seller; shorts, short interest, short side; short account, bear account

13 **bull,** long, longs, long interest, long side; long account, bull account

14 **stockholder,** stockowner, **shareholder, shareowner;** bondholder, coupon-clipper <nonformal>; stockholder of record

15 **stock company,** joint-stock company; issuing company; stock insurance company

16 **trust,** investment company; investment trust, holding company; closed-end investment company, closed-end fund; open-end fund, mutual fund, money-market fund; unit trust <Brit>; load fund, no-load fund, low-load fund, back-end fund; growth fund, income fund, dual purpose fund; trust fund; blind trust

17 **pool,** bear pool, bull pool, blind pool

18 **stockbroking,** brokerage, stockbrokerage, jobbing, stockjobbing, stockjobbery, stock dealing; bucketing, legal bucketing

19 **trading,** stock-market trading, market-trading; computer or programmed selling; playing the market <nonformal>; **speculation,** stockjobbing, stockjobbery; **venture,** flutter; flier, plunge; scalping; liquidation, profit taking; **arbitrage,** arbitraging; buying in, covering shorts; short sale; spot sale; round trade or transaction, turn; risk or venture capital, equity capital; money-market trading, foreign-exchange trading, agiotage; **buyout, take-**

over, hostile takeover, takeover bid; leveraged buyout; greenmail; **leverage**

20 **manipulation, rigging; raid,** bear raid, bull raid; **corner,** corner in, corner on the market, monopoly; washing, washed *or* wash sale

21 **option,** stock option, right, **put, call,** put and call, right of put and call; straddle, spread; strip; strap

22 **panic,** bear panic, rich man's panic

VERBS 23 **trade, speculate,** venture, operate, **play the market,** buy *or* sell *or* deal in futures; **arbitrage; plunge,** take a flier <nonformal>; scalp; bucket, bucketshop; stag *or* stag the market <both Brit>; trade on margin; pyramid; be long, go long, be long of the market, be on the long side of the market; be short, be short of the market, be on the short side of the market; margin up, apply *or* deposit margin; wait out the market, hold on; be caught short, miss the market, overstay the market; scoop the market, make a scoop *or* killing *or* bundle *or* pile <all nonformal>

24 **sell,** convert, liquidate; throw on the market, dump, unload; **sell short,** go short, make a short sale; cover one's short, fulfill a short sale; make delivery, clear the trade; close out, sell out, terminate the account

25 manipulate the market, **rig the market;** bear, **bear the market;** bull, **bull the market;** raid the market; hold *or* peg the market; whipsaw; wash sales

26 corner, get a corner on, **corner the market;** monopolize, engross; buy up, absorb

738 SECURITIES

NOUNS 1 **securities** <see list>, **stocks and bonds,** investment securities

2 **stock** <see list>, shares <Brit>, equity, equity security, corporate stock; stock split, split; reverse split; stock list; stock ledger, share ledger <Brit>; **holdings, portfolio,** investment portfolio

3 **share, lot;** preference share; dummy share; holding, holdings, stockholding, stockholdings; block; round lot, full lot, even lot, board lot; odd lot, fractional lot

4 **stock certificate,** certificate of stock; street certificate; interim certificate; **coupon**

5 **bond** <see list>; nominal rate, coupon rate, current yield, yield to maturity

6 **issue,** issuance; **flotation;** stock issue, secondary issue; bond issue; poison pill <nonformal>

7 **dividend;** regular dividend; extra dividend, special dividend, plum *and* melon <both nonformal>; payout ratio; cumulative dividend, accumulated dividends, accrued dividends; interim dividend; cash dividend; stock dividend; optional dividend; scrip dividend; liquidating dividend; phony dividend; **interest** 623.3; **return, yield,** return on investment, payout, payback

8 **assessment,** Irish dividend

9 **price, quotation;** bid-and-asked prices, bid price, asked *or* asking *or* offering price; actual *or* delivery *or* settling price, put price, call price; opening price, closing price; high, low; market price, quoted price, flash price; issue price; fixed price; parity; **par,** issue par; par value, nominal value, face value; stated value; book value; market value; bearish prices, bullish prices; swings, fluctuations; flurry, flutter; rally, decline

10 **margin;** thin margin, shoestring margin; exhaust price

11 <commodities> spots, spot grain, etc; futures, future grain, etc

VERBS 12 **issue, float,** put on the market; issue stock, go public <nonformal>; float a bond issue

13 **declare a dividend,** cut a melon <nonformal>

ADVS 14 dividend off, ex dividend; dividend on, cum dividend; coupon off, ex coupon; coupon on, cum coupon; warrants off, ex warrants; warrants on, cum warrants; when issued

15 **kinds of securities**

active securities	governments
American Depository Receipts *or* ADRs	international securities
banker's acceptance	junior securities
callable securities	legal securities
certificate of accrual *or* treasury securities *or* CATS	liquid yield option notes *or* LYONs
certificate of deposit *or* CD	listed securities
	margined securities
convertible securities *or* convertibles *or* CVs	marketable securities
	money-market certificate
corporation securities	municipal securities
debenture *or* certificate of indebtedness	negotiable securities *or* negotiables
	noncallable securities
digested securities	note
foreign securities	obsolete securities
futures contract	outside securities
gilt-edged securities	outstanding securities
government securities	over-the-counter securities

registered securities
senior securities
separate trading of
   registered interest
   and principal secu-
   rities or STRIPS
short-term note
speculative securities
   or cats and dogs
   <nonformal>
stamped securities
treasury bill

treasury bond
treasury certificate
treasury investment
   growth receipts or
   TIGRs
treasury note
undigested securities
unlisted securities
unregistered securi-
   ties
warrant

16 kinds of stock

active stock
assessable stock
authorized capital
   stock
blue chip stock or
   blue chip
borrowed stock
capital stock
common stock or or-
   dinary shares
   <Brit>
convertible preferred
   stock
cumulative convert-
   ible preferred stock
cumulative preferred
   stock
cyclical stock
debenture stock
defensive stock
deferred stock
eighth stock
floating stock
growth stock
guaranteed stock
high-grade stock
hypothecated stock
inactive stock
income stock
industrials or rails or
   utilities, etc
issued capital stock
letter stock

loaned stock
long stock
new issue
no-par stock
nonassessable stock
nonvoting stock
pale blue chip
participating pre-
   ferred stock
penny stock
preferred stock or
   preference stock
   <Brit>
protective stock
quality stock
quarter stock
seasoned stock
short stock
small cap stock
special situation
   stock
specialty stock
speculative stock
standard stock
ten-share unit stock
treasury stock
unissued capital
   stock
voting stock
voting-right certifi-
   cate
watered stock

17 kinds of bond

adjustment bond
annuity bond
appreciation bond
assented bond
assumed bond
baby bond
bearer bond
bearer certificate
bond anticipation
   note
callable bond
collateral trust bond
consolidated annu-
   ities or consols or
   bank annuities
   <Brit>

consolidated stock
convertible bond
convertible deben-
   ture
corporate bond
corporation stock
   <Brit>
coupon bond
current income bond
deep-discount bond
defense bond
deferred bond
definitive bond
discount bond
equipment bond
equipment note

equipment trust
equipment trust bond
equipment trust cer-
   tificate
extended bond
Fannie Mae bond
Federal Agency bond
FICO bonds
first mortgage bond
   or first
Freddie Mac bond
general mortgage
   bond
general obligation
   bond
Ginnie Mae bond
government bond
guaranteed bond
high-grade bond
high-yield bond or
   junk bond
   <nonformal>
income bond
indenture
installment bond
interchangeable bond
interim bond
joint bond
Liberty bond
long-term bond
mortgage bond
municipal bond
negotiable bond
noncallable bond
nonnegotiable bond

optional bond
par bond
participating bond
perpetual bond
premium bond
purchase money bond
redeemable bond
refunding bond
registered bond
registered certificate
revenue bond
savings bond
second mortgage
   bond or second
secured bond
serial bond
Series EE bond
Series HH bond
short-term bond
sinking-fund bond
small bond
state bond
tax anticipation note
tax-exempt bond
tax-free bond
treasury bond
trust indenture
trustee mortgage
   bond
turnpike bond
unsecured bond
voting bond
war bond
zero coupon bond

739 WORKPLACE

NOUNS **1 workplace,** worksite, **workshop, shop;** shop floor, workspace, working space, loft; **bench,** workbench, worktable; counter, worktop; **work station; desk,** desktop; **workroom; studio,** atelier <Fr>; parlor, beauty parlor, funeral parlor, etc; **establishment, facility,** installation; **company,** institution, house, firm, concern, agency, organization, **corporation; financial institution, stock exchange** 737, **bank** 729; **market, store** 736, mall, shopping mall; **restaurant, eating place** 8.17

2 hive, hive of industry, beehive; factory or mill or manufacturing town; hub of industry, center of manufacture

3 **plant, factory, works,** manufactory <old>, manufacturing plant, usine <Fr>; main plant, assembly plant, subassembly plant, feeder plant; foreign-owned plant, transplant; push-button plant, automated or cybernated or automatic or robot factory; assembly or production line; defense plant, munitions

plant, armory, arsenal; **power plant**
1031.18; atomic energy plant; **machine
shop; mill,** sawmill, flour mill, etc; **yard,**
yards, railroad yard, brickyard, shipyard,
dockyard, boatyard; rope-walk; mint; refinery, oil refinery, sugar refinery, etc;
distillery, brewery, winery; boilery; bind-
ery, bookbindery; packinghouse; can-
nery; dairy, creamery; pottery; tannery;
factory district, industrial zone, industrial park, industrial estate <Brit>;
factory belt, manufacturing quarter; enterprise zone

4 **foundry,** metalworks; steelworks, steel
mill; forge, furnace, bloomery; smelter;
smithy, smithery, stithy, blacksmith shop
or blacksmith's shop

5 **repair shop,** fix-it shop <nonformal>;
garage; roundhouse; hangar

6 **laboratory, lab** <nonformal>; research
laboratory, research installation *or* facility *or* center

7 **office,** shop <nonformal>; home *or* head
or main office, headquarters, executive
office, corporate headquarters; office
suite, executive suite; chambers <chiefly
Brit>; closet, cabinet <old>, **study,** den,
carrel; **embassy,** consulate, legation,
chancery, chancellery; box office, booking office, ticket office; branch, branch
office, local office; office *or* executive park

740 WEAVING

NOUNS 1 **weaving,** weave, warpage,
weftage, warp and woof *or* weft, texture,
tissue; **fabric, web; interweaving,** inter-
weavement, intertexture; **interlacing,**
interlacement, interlacery; **intertwining,**
intertwinement; intertieing, interknit-
ting, interthreading, intertwisting;
lacing, enlacement; **twining,** entwining,
entwinemént; wreathing, knitting, twisting; **braiding,** plaiting

2 **braid,** plait, **wreath,** wreathwork

3 **warp; woof, weft,** filling; shoot, pick

4 **weaver,** interlacer, webster <old>;
weaverbird, weaver finch, whirligig
beetle

5 **loom,** weaver; hand loom; Navajo loom;
knitting machine; shuttle

VERBS 6 **weave,** loom, tissue; **interweave,
interlace, intertwine,** interknit, inter-
thread, intertissue, intertie, intertwist;
inweave, intort; web, net; **lace,** enlace;
twine, entwine; **braid,** plait, pleach,
wreathe, raddle, **knit,** twist, mat, wattle;
twill, loop, noose; splice

ADJS 7 **woven,** loomed, textile; **interwoven,**

interlaced, interthreaded, **intertwined,**
interknit, intertissued, intertied, inter-
twisted; handwoven; **laced,** enlaced;
wreathed, fretted, raddled, knit; **twined,**
entwined; **braided,** plaited, platted,
pleached

8 **weaving, twining,** entwining; **intertwining, interlacing,** interweaving

741 SEWING

NOUNS 1 **sewing, needlework,** stitchery,
stitching; suture; **fancywork;** tailoring,
garment making 5.31

2 **sewer, needleworker, seamstress,** semp-
stress, needlewoman; seamster, semp-
ster, **tailor,** needleman <old>, needler
<Brit>; embroiderer, embroideress;
knitter; garmentmaker 5.33

3 **sewing machine,** sewer, Singer
<trademark>

VERBS 4 **sew, stitch,** needle; stitch up, sew
up; **tailor**

742 CERAMICS

NOUNS 1 **ceramics** <see list>, **pottery;** potting

2 **ceramic ware, ceramics; pottery, crock-
ery; china, porcelain;** enamelware;
refractory, cement; bisque, biscuit; pot,
crock, vase, urn, jug, bowl; tile, tiling;
brick, firebrick, refractory brick, adobe;
glass 1028.2

3 <materials> clay; potter's clay *or* earth,
fireclay, refractory clay; porcelain clay,
kaolin, china clay; china stone, feldspar,
petuntse; flux; slip; glaze

4 **potter's wheel,** wheel; kick wheel, pedal
wheel, power wheel

5 **kiln, oven, stove, furnace;** acid kiln, brick
kiln, cement kiln, enamel kiln, muffle
kiln, limekiln, reverberatory, reverberatory kiln; pyrometer, pyrometric cone,
Seger cone

VERBS 6 pot, shape, **throw,** throw *or* turn a
pot; mold; **fire,** bake; glaze

ADJS 7 **ceramic,** earthen, clay, enamel,
china, porcelain; fired, baked, glazed;
refractory

8 **ceramics**

Albion ware	bone china
Allervale pottery	Castleford ware
Aretine ware	Castor ware
basalt *or* basaltes	champlevé *or*
Belleek ware	champlevé
Berlin ware	enamel
biscuit ware	china *or* chinaware
blackware	clayware

cloisonné *or* cloisonné
  enamel
cottage china
crackle *or* crackle-
  ware
crouch ware
Crown Derby ware
delft *or* delftware
Dresden china
earthenware
eggshell porcelain
enamel *or* enamel-
  ware
faience
glassware
glazed ware
gombroon
hard-paste porcelain
Hirado ware
Hizen porcelain
Imari ware
ironstone *or* ironstone
  china
Jackfield ware
jasper *or* jasper ware
Kinkozan ware
Leeds pottery
Limoges *or* Limoges
  ware
Lowestoft ware
lusterware *or* luster
  pottery
majolica

Meissen ware
Nabeshima ware
Old Worcester ware
Palissy ware
Parian ware
porcelain
queensware
refractory ware
Rockingham ware
salt-glazed ware
Samian ware
sanda ware
Satsuma ware
Sèvres *or* Sèvres ware
Seto ware
soft-paste porcelain
Spode
spongeware
Staffordshire *or*
  Staffordshire ware
stoneware
terra cotta
terra sigillata
ting ware *or* ting yao
Toft ware
Wedgwood *or* Wedg-
  wood ware
whiteware *or* white
  pottery
Worcester ware
yi-hsing ware *or* yi-
  hsing yao

743 AMUSEMENT

NOUNS **1 amusement, entertainment, diversion,** solace, divertisement, *divertissement*
<Fr>, **recreation, relaxation,** regale-
ment; **pastime,** *passe-temps* <Fr>; **mirth**
109.5; **pleasure, enjoyment** 95

2 fun, action <nonformal>; funmaking,
fun and games, **play, sport,** game; **good
time,** lovely time, pleasant time; big time
and **high time** *and* high old time <all non-
formal>, picnic *and* laughs *and* lots of
laughs *and* ball <all nonformal>, great
fun, time of one's life; a short life and a
merry one; wild oats

**3 festivity, merrymaking, merriment, gai-
ety, jollity,** jollification <nonformal>,
joviality, conviviality, whoopee *and*
hoopla <both nonformal>; larking
<nonformal>, cavorting, skylarking,
racketing, mafficking <Brit nonformal>,
holiday-making; **revelry,** revelment, re-
veling, revels; nightlife

4 festival, festivity, festive occasion, *fiesta*
<Sp>, **fete,** gala, **gala affair, blowout**
<nonformal>, **jamboree** <nonformal>;
high jinks, do, great doings <all non-

formal>; *fête champêtre* <Fr>; **feast,
banquet** 8.9; picnic 8.6; party 582.11;
waygoose <Brit nonformal>, wayz-
goose; **fair,** carnival; kermis; *Oktoberfest*
<Ger>; Mardi Gras; Saturnalia; harvest
festival, harvest home <Brit>; **field day;**
gala day, feria

5 frolic, play, romp, rollick, frisk, gambol,
caper, dido <nonformal>

6 revel, lark, escapade, ploy; **celebration**
487; **party** 582.11; **spree, bout, fling,**
wingding *and* randan <both nonfor-
mal>, randy <Scots>; **carouse, drinking
bout** 88.5

7 round of pleasure, mad round, **whirl,**
merry-go-round, the rounds, the dizzy
rounds

8 sports 744; **athletics,** agonistics; athleti-
cism

9 game; card game; board game; parlor
game; **play; contest** 457.3; race 457.12;
event, meet; bout, match, go <nonfor-
mal>; gambling 759

10 tournament, tourney, gymkhana, **field
day;** rally; **regatta**

11 playground; field, athletic field, playing
field; football field, gridiron; baseball
field, diamond; infield, outfield; soccer
field; archery ground, cricket ground,
polo ground, croquet ground *or* lawn,
bowling green; bowling alley; links, golf
links, golf course; fairway, putting green;
gymnasium, gym <nonformal>; **court,**
badminton court, basketball court, tennis
court, racket court, squash court; billiard
parlor, poolroom, pool hall; racecourse,
track, course turf, oval; stretch; rink, gla-
ciarium, ice rink, skating rink; **playroom**
197.12

12 swimming pool, pool, swimming bath
<Brit>, plunge, plunge bath, natator-
ium; swimming hole; wading pool

**13 entertainment; entertainment industry,
show business,** show biz <nonformal>;
theater; dinner theatre; **cabaret, tavern,
roadhouse;** café dansant, chantant; **nightclub,** night spot *or* nitery *and* hot spot
<all nonformal>, *boîte, boîte de nuit*
<both Fr>; juke joint <nonformal>, dis-
cothèque *or* disco <nonformal>; dance
hall, dancing pavilion, ballroom, dance
floor; casino; **resort** 228.27

14 park, public park, pleasure garden *or*
ground, pleasance, paradise, common,
commons; **amusement park,** Tivoli, fun
fair, carnival; fairground; **theme park,** safari park

15 merry-go-round, carousel, roundabout,
ride, whirligig, whip, flying horses; Ferris

wheel; seesaw, teeter-totter; slide; swing; roller coaster; chutes, chute-the-chutes; —drome

16 **toy, plaything,** sport; bauble, knickknack, gimcrack, gewgaw, kickshaw, whimwham, trinket; **doll,** paper doll, golliwog, rag doll, teddy bear, puppet, glove puppet, marionette, toy soldier, tin soldier; **dollhouse,** doll carriage; **hobbyhorse,** cockhorse, rocking horse; **hoop,** hula hoop; **top,** spinning top, teetotum; pinwheel; **jack-in-the-box;** jacks, jackstones; **jackstraws,** pick-up sticks; **blocks; checkerboard,** chessboard; **marble,** mig, agate, steelie, taw; pop-gun, BB gun, air gun; slingshot, catapult <Brit>

17 **chessman,** man, piece; **bishop, knight, king, queen, pawn, rook** or castle

18 **player, frolicker,** frisker, **funmaker,** funster, gamboler; **pleasure-seeker,** pleasurer, pleasurist, **playboy** <nonformal>; **reveler, celebrant, merrymaker,** rollicker, skylarker, **carouser,** cutup <nonformal>; contestant 452.2

19 **athlete,** jock <nonformal>, **player,** amateur athlete, professional athlete, competitor, sportsman; letter man

20 **master of ceremonies, MC** or **emcee** <both nonformal>, compère <Brit>, marshal; **toastmaster;** host, master of the revels, revel master; Lord of Misrule, Abbot of Unreason <Scots>; social director

VERBS 21 **amuse, entertain, divert,** regale, beguile, solace, recreate, refresh, enliven, exhilarate, put in good humor; **relax,** loosen up; **delight, tickle, titillate,** tickle pink or to death <nonformal>, tickle the fancy; **make one laugh, strike one as funny,** raise a smile or laugh, convulse, set the table on a roar, be the death of; wow and slay and knock dead and kill and break one up and crack one up and fracture one <all nonformal>; have them rolling in the aisles; keep them in stitches

22 **amuse oneself,** pleasure oneself, take one's pleasure, give oneself over to pleasure; get one's kicks or jollies <both nonformal>; **relax,** let oneself go, loosen up; **have fun, have a good time,** have a ball and have lots of laughs <both nonformal>, live it up and laugh it up <both nonformal>; drown care, drive dull care away; beguile the time, kill time, while away the time; get away from it all

23 **play, sport, disport; frolic, rollick, gambol, frisk, romp, caper,** cut capers <nonformal>, lark about <Brit nonformal>, antic, curvet, cavort, caracole, flounce, trip, skip, dance; **cut up** <nonfor-

mal>, cut a dido <nonformal>, horse around <nonformal>, fool around, carry on <nonformal>

24 **make merry, revel, roister,** jolly, lark <nonformal>, skylark, **make whoopee** <nonformal>, let oneself go, **blow** or **let off steam;** cut loose, let loose, let go, let one's hair down <nonformal>, whoop it up, **kick up one's heels;** hell around and raise hell and blow off the lid <all nonformal>; step out <nonformal>, go places and do things, go on the town, see life, **paint the town red** <nonformal>; go the dizzy rounds, go on the merry-go-round <nonformal>; **celebrate** 487.2; spree, **go on a spree,** go on a bust or toot or bender or binge or rip or tear <all nonformal>; **carouse,** jollify <nonformal>, wanton, debauch, pub-crawl <chiefly Brit>; **sow one's wild oats, have one's fling**

25 "eat, drink, and be merry"—Bible, feast, banquet

ADJS 26 **amused,** entertained; diverted, **delighted,** tickled, tickled pink or to death <nonformal>, titillated; "pleased with a rattle, tickled with a straw"—Pope

27 **amusing, entertaining, diverting,** beguiling; **fun,** funsome and more fun than a barrel of monkeys <both nonformal>; recreative, recreational; **delightful,** titillative, titillating; humorous 488.4

28 **festive, festal; merry, gay, jolly, jovial, joyous, joyful,** gladsome, convivial, gala, hilarious; merrymaking, on the loose <nonformal>; on the town, out on the town

29 **playful, sportive,** sportful; **frolicsome,** gamesome, rompish, larkish, capersome; waggish 322.6

30 **sporting,** sports; **athletic,** agonistic; **gymnastic,** palaestral; **acrobatic**

ADVS 31 **in fun,** for amusement, **for fun,** for the fun of it; for kicks and for laughs <both nonformal>, for the devil or heck or hell of it <all nonformal>; just to be doing

744 SPORTS

NOUNS 1 **sport, sports, athletics,** athletic competition, game, sports activity, play, contest; aeronautical or air sport <see list>; animal sport <see list>; water or aquatic sport <see list>; **ball game; track and field** 755; **gymnastics** <see list>; **outdoor sport** <see list>; **winter sport** <see list>; **combat sport,** martial art <see list>; **decathlon; triathlon,** biathlon; **bicycling,** bicycle touring, cross-country cycling, cyclo-cross, bicycle moto-cross, road racing, track racing; **motor sport,** automobile racing 756, go-carting, jet skiing, water skiing, motor-cycling, moto-cross, dirt-biking, snow-mobiling, soapbox racing; **in-line skating** or blading or Roller-blading <trade-mark>, roller skating, roller hockey, skateboarding; **target sport,** archery, field archery, darts, marksmanship, target shooting, skeet shooting, trap shooting; **throwing sport** <see list>; **weightlifting, bodybuilding,** iron-pumping <nonfor-mal>, Olympic lifting, powerlifting, weight training

VERBS **2 play, compete;** practice, train, work out; try out, go out for; follow

3 aeronautical or air sports

aerotow	hydroplane racing
ballooning	parachuting
flying	parasailing
gliding	sky-diving
hang gliding	soaring

4 animal sports

barrel racing	horseback riding
bronc riding and bronco busting	horsemanship
	pack riding
bull riding	pole bending
bullfighting	polo
calf roping	pony trekking
camel racing	rodeo
chuckwagon racing	show jumping
cockfighting	steeplechase
cross-country riding	steer roping
dog racing	steer wrestling
dressage	team penning
driving	team roping
endurance riding	three-day event
equestrian sport	trail riding
harness racing 463	vaulting
horse racing	Western riding

5 aquatic or water sports

birling	snorkeling
boating	sprint swimming
body surfing	surfing
canoeing	swimming
canoe slalom	synchronized swim-ming
distance swimming	
diving	underwater diving
dragon boat racing	underwater hockey
fin swimming	underwaterball
fishing	water polo
inner tube water polo	water skiing
kayaking	windsurfing or boardsailing or sailboarding
lifesaving	
rafting	
rowing	yachting
scuba diving	

6 gymnastics

balance beam	mini-trampolining
floor exercises	parallel bars
horizontal bar	uneven parallel bars
pommel horse	vaulting
rings	modern rhythmic gymnastics
trampolining	
tumbling	Swedish gymnastics

7 outdoor sports

backpacking	rock climbing
camping	speleology or spelunking
hiking	
mountaineering or al-pinism	<nonformal>
	superalpinism
orienteering	wilderness survival

8 winter sports

Alpine skiing	ringette
bandy	skating
biathlon	ski jumping
bobsledding	skibobbing
broomball	skiing
cross-country skiing	skijoring
curling	slalom
downhill skiing	skiing
figure skating	sledding
freestyle skiing or hotdogging <nonformal>	snowboarding
	snowshoeing
	snow tubing
hockey	speed skating
ice boating or sailing	tobogganing
luge	

9 combat sports, martial arts

aikido or aiki-jutsu	judo
arm and wrist wrestling	jujutsu
	jukendo
arnis	kalari payat
bando	karate
bersilat	kenjutsu
bojutsu	kiaijutsu
boxing	kobu-jutsu
capoeira	kung-fu
Cornish wrestling	kyujutsu
dumog	lua
escrima	main tindju
fencing	naginata-jutsu
glimae	ninjutsu
go-ti	pankation
Greco-Roman wrestling	pentjak-silat
	pukulan
Greek boxing	sambo wrestling
hapkido	savate
hwarang-do	stick fighting
Iaido	sumo wrestling
Iaijutsu	tae kwon do
Icelandic wrestling	tegumi
jeet kune do	Thai kick boxing
jobajutsu	wrestling
jojutsu	wu shu
jousting	

10 throwing sports

boomeranging	shot put
caber tossing	ultimate Frisbee <trademark> or ultimate or air-borne soccer
discus throw	
Frisbee <trademark>	
hammer throw	
horseshoe pitching	ultimate skate Fris-bee <trademark>
javelin throw	

745 BASEBALL

NOUNS **1 baseball, ball,** the national pastime; **organized baseball, league,** loop, circuit, **major league,** big league, the majors *and* the big time *and* the bigs <all nonformal>, the National League *or* Senior Circuit, the American League *or* Junior Circuit; **minor league,** triple-A, the minors *and* bush leagues *and* the bushes <all nonformal>; division championship, playoff, League Championship Series, league championship *or* pennant, World Series, All-Star Game; **farm team,** farm club, farm, farm system; **ball park, ball field,** field, park; **stands, grandstand,** boxes, lower deck, upper deck, outfield stands, bleachers; **diamond;** dugout; **home plate, the plate,** platter *and* dish <both nonformal>; **base line, line,** base path; **base, bag,** sack, **first,** first base, **second,** second base, keystone *and* keystone sack <both nonformal>, **third,** third base, hot corner <nonformal>; **infield,** infield grass *or* turf; **outfield,** warning track, fences; foul line, foul pole; **mound,** pitcher's mound, hill; **equipment** <see list>, gear

2 baseball team, team, nine, roster, squad, the boys of summer, **club,** ball club, personnel, crew; **starting lineup, lineup batting order; starter, regular;** substitute, sub, utility player, benchwarmer *and* bench jockey <both nonformal>, the bench; **pitcher,** hurler <nonformal>, motion, pitching motion, herky-jerky motion <nonformal>, **right-hander,** right-hand pitcher, righty <nonformal>, **left-hander, left-hand pitcher, lefty** *and* **southpaw** *and* portsider <all nonformal>; **starting pitcher, starter,** fifth starter, spot starter; starting rotation, rotation, pitching rotation; **relief pitcher, reliever,** fireman *and* closer *and* stopper <both nonformal>, long reliever, middle *or* inner reliever, short reliever, the bull pen; **battery; catcher,** backstop *and* receiver <both informal>; **fielder,** glove man, outfielder, infielder, cover man, cutoff man, relay man; **first baseman,** first bagger *and* first sacker <both informal>; **second baseman,** second bagger *and* second sacker *and* keystone bagger *and* keystone sacker <all nonformal>; **third baseman,** third bagger *and* third sacker *and* hot-corner man <all nonformal>; shortstop; **outfielder,** left fielder, center fielder, right fielder; designated hitter *or* DH *or* desi; **batter, hitter,** man at the plate, man in the box *or* batter's box, **stance,** batting stance, pull hitter, power hitter, long-ball hitter, slugger <nonformal>, spray hitter, contact hitter, banjo hitter <nonformal>, switch hitter, leadoff hitter, cleanup hitter; **manager, pilot, coach,** batting coach, pitching coach, bench coach, bullpen coach, first-base coach, third-base coach; scout, talent scout

3 game, ball game, play, strategy; **umpire,** home-plate umpire, plate umpire, umpire in chief, umpire crew, first-base umpire, second-base umpire, third-base umpire; **pitch** <see list>, set, windup, kick, delivery, stuff, offering; **strike zone,** wheelhouse *and* kitchen <both nonformal>; **throwing arm,** arm, cannon *and* soupbone <nonformal>; **balk; count,** balls and strikes, full count; **hit, base hit,** tater *and* bingle *and* dinger <all nonformal>, opposite-field hit; hard-hit ball, shot *and* bullet *and* scorcher <all nonformal>; **single,** seeing-eye hit *and* excuse-me hit *and* banjo hit <all nonformal>; **double,** two-base hit, two-base shot, two-bagger; **triple,** three-base hit or three-base shot, three-bagger; **home run, homer,** four-bagger, tater *and* round trip *and* round tripper *and* circuit clout *and* big salami *and* dinger <all nonformal>, grand-slam home run, grand-slammer, cheap homer *and* Chinese homer <both nonformal>; **fly,** pop fly, pop-up, can of corn *and* looper *and* blooper *and* bloop *and* Texas Leaguer <all nonformal>, sacrifice fly *or* sac fly <nonformal>; **line drive, liner,** line shot, rope *and* clothesline <both nonformal>; **ground ball,** grounder, wormburner <nonformal>, slow roller, roller, bunt, drag bunt, bleeder *and* squibbler *and* nubber *and* dying quail <all nonformal>, comebacker, chopper; **foul ball, foul; base on balls, walk,** intentional pass, free ticket *and* free ride <nonformal>; error, passed ball, unearned run, earned run; **out,** strikeout *or* K *or* punchout, put-out, foul-out, force-out, double play, DP, double killing *and* twin killing <both nonformal>, triple play, triple killing <nonformal>; **assist; catch,** shoestring catch, basket catch, circus catch; squeeze play, hit-and-run play, pickoff play, pickoff, pitch-out; **base runner,** baseburner <nonformal>, pinch-runner; **run; inning,** frame, top of the inning, bottom of the inning, extra innings

4 statistics, averages, stats and numbers

<nonformal>, percentages; batting average, earned-run average, slugging average or slugging percentage, fielding average, run batted in or RBI, ribby <nonformal>; **the record book,** the book
VERBS **5 play,** play ball; **umpire,** call balls and strikes, officiate; **pitch, throw,** deliver, fire, offer, offer up, bring it and burn it and throw smoke and blow it by and throw seeds <all nonformal>; throw a bean ball, dust the batter off, back the batter off; **relieve,** put out the fire <nonformal>; **bat, be up,** step up to the plate, be in the batter's box; **hit,** belt and clout and connect <all nonformal>, golf, chop, tomahawk; **fly,** hit a fly, sky it and pop and pop up <all nonformal>; **ground,** bounce, lay it down, lay down a bunt; sacrifice, hit a sacrifice fly; **hit,** get a base hit, put on one's hitting shoes <nonformal>; **connect,** blast it and cream it and tear the cover off and hit it right on the screws and hit it right on the button and hit with the good wood and get good wood on it <all nonformal>; **hit a home run, homer,** hit it out; **single, double, triple;** get aboard, be a base runner; **walk, get a free ride** or free pass <both nonformal>; **strike out,** go down or out on strikes, go down swinging, fan and whiff <both nonformal>, be called out on strikes, be caught looking <nonformal>; ground out, fly out, pop out; catch, haul in, grab and glove and flag down <all nonformal>; misplay, make an error, bobble and boot <both nonformal>

6 baseball equipment

bar mask	batting glove
base	batting helmet
baseball or ball or pill and apple <both nonformal>	birdcage mask
	catcher's mask
	pine-tar rag
bat or lumber <nonformal>	rosin bag
	shinpads
batting cage	

7 baseball pitches

back door	eefus ball
beanball or beaner	fast ball or smoke or bullet or heater or hummer
bender	
breaking ball	
Captain Hook	floater
change-of-pace ball or change-up	forkball
	gopher ball
curve ball or curve or breaking ball or bender or Captain Hook or slurve	knuckleball or knuckler
	knucklecurve
	Linda Ronstadt fastball
cut fastball	
dime	off-speed pitch
duster	palmball

roundhouse curve	slow ball
sailing fastball	spitball or spitter
screwball	split-finger fastball
screwgy <nonformal>	splitter
sinker	Uncle Charlie
slider	wild pitch

746 FOOTBALL

NOUNS **1 football, ball,** American football; **organized football, college football,** conference, league, Big Eight, Big Ten, Ivy League, Pacific Ten; conference championship, post-season game, bowl invitation, Cotton Bowl, Gator Bowl, Orange Bowl, Rose Bowl, Sugar Bowl, national championship or mythical national championship; **professional football,** pro football <nonformal>, National Football League or NFL; division championship, playoff, Super Bowl, Super Bowl championship; **stadium,** bowl, domed stadium, dome; **field, gridiron; line,** sideline, end line, end zone, goal line, goalpost, crossbar, yard line, midfield stripe, inbounds marker or hash mark; **equipment** <see list>, gear, armament

2 football team, eleven, team, squad, roster, personnel; first team, regulars, starting lineup, offensive team or platoon, defensive team or platoon, kicking team; substitute or sub, benchwarmer; **ball,** football, pigskin and prolate spheroid <both nonformal>; **line, linemen, forward wall,** front four, **end, tackle, nose tackle, guard, noseguard, center, tight end; backfield,** back, **quarterback, halfback, fullback,** kicker, tailback, plunging back, slotback, flanker back, running back, blocking back, linebacker, cornerback, safety, free safety, strong safety, weak safety; **pass receiver, receiver,** wide receiver or wide out, primary receiver

3 game, strategy, game plan, ball control; **official** <see list>, zebra <nonformal>; **kickoff,** kick, coin-toss or -flip, place kick, squib kick, free kick, onside kick, runback, kickoff return; **play** <see list>, down, first down, second down, third down, fourth down; **line,** line of scrimmage or scrimmage line, flat; **lineup, formation** <see list>; **pass from center, snap,** hand-to-hand snap; live ball, ball in play, ball out of play, dead ball, play stopped, ball whistled dead; **running play, passing play, kick; ball-carrier,** ball-handling, tuck, feint, hand-off, pocket, straightarm; **block,** blocking, body block, brush block, chop block, screen block, shoulder block; **tackle,** neck tackle, shirt tackle, face-mask tackle, sack; **yardage,** gain, loss, long yardage, short yardage; **forward pass, pass,** pass pattern <see list>, pitchout, screen pass, quick release, bomb <nonformal>, incomplete pass, completed pass, pass completion; **pass rush,** blitz; **possession,** loss of possession, turnover, fumble, pass interception, interception; in bounds, out of bounds; **penalty** <see list>, infraction, foul, flag on the play; **punt, kick,** quick kick, squib kick or knuckler; punt return, fair catch; **touchdown,** conversion, field goal, safety; **period, quarter, half,** halftime, intermission, two-minute warning, thirty-second clock, sudden-death overtime; **gun,** final gun

4 **statistics, averages,** stats and numbers <both nonformal>, average running yardage, average passing yardage, average punting yardage, average punt-return yardage

VERBS 5 **play,** kick, kick off, run, scramble, pass, punt; complete a pass, catch a pass; **block, tackle,** double-team, blindside, sack, blitz, red-dog; **lose possession,** fumble, bobble <nonformal>, give up the ball; **score,** get on the scoreboard; **officiate,** blow the whistle, whistle the ball dead, drop a flag, call a penalty

6 **football equipment**

cleats	numbers
face mask	pads
football	pants
helmet	shirt or jersey
hip pads	shoes
kicking tee	shoulder pads
kneepads	thigh pads
mouth guard	

7 **football officials**

back judge	referee
field judge	side judge
head linesman	umpire
line judge	

8 **football plays and calls**

automatic or audible	naked bootleg
blitz or red dog	naked reverse
bootleg	off-tackle slant
buck lateral	option
conversion	plunge
counter	power sweep
draw	quick kick
end run	reverse
fair catch	rollout
flea-flicker	scramble
keeper	slant
lateral pass or lateral	Statue of Liberty
man in motion	trap
mousetrap	two-point conversion

9 **football formations**

3-4 defense	short punt formation
4 3 2 2	single wing or wing-
4-3 defense	back
6 2 2 1	slot
7 diamond	split end
double wing or wing-	split T
back	straight T
flexbone	strong side
huddle	T formation
I	tight end
Notre Dame box	veer
option	weak side
overshift	wedge or flying wedge
power I	wing T
pro set	wishbone T
run-and-shoot offense	zone blocking
shotgun offense	zone defense

10 **football pass patterns**

buttonhook	screen pass
circle	sideline pass
crossing pattern	slant-in pattern
curl	square-in
down and out	square-out
flag pattern	streak pattern
flare or swing pass	up the middle or the
flood	gut
fly	zig in
hook pattern	zig out
look-in pass	

11 **football penalties**

clipping	more than 11 players
delay of game	on the field
encroachment	offside
excessive time-	out-of-bounds kickoff
outs	pass interference
grabbing the face	personal foul
mask	piling on
holding	roughing the kicker
illegal blocking below	roughing the passer
the waist	running into the
illegal formation	kicker
illegal position	tackling by the face-
illegal procedure	mask
illegal shift	tripping
ineligible receiver	unnecessary rough-
downfield	ness
kick-catching inter-	unsportsmanlike con-
ference	duct

747 BASKETBALL

NOUNS 1 **basketball,** hoop, hoop sport, ball; **organized basketball, college basketball,** NCAA or National Collegiate Athletic Association; **professional basketball,** pro basketball <nonformal>, National Basketball Association or NBA; **tournament,** competition, championship, Olympic Games, NCAA or National Collegiate Athletic Association Tournament, NIT or National Invitational Tournament, Final

Four, NAIA *or* National Association of Intercollegiate Athletics Tournament, Dixie Classic, Rose City Classic; **basketball court, court,** hardwood *and* pine <both nonformal>, forecourt, midcourt, backcourt, end line *or* base line, sideline, basket *or* hoop, iron <nonformal>, backboard, glass <nonformal>, defensive board, offensive board, free throw line, charity line <nonformal>, free throw lane *or* foul lane, key *and* keyhole <both nonformal>, foul line

2 **basketball team, five,** team, roster, squad, personnel; **basketball player,** hoopster, center, right forward, left forward, corner man, right guard, left guard, point guard, point player *or* playmaker, swingman, trailer, backcourt man, disher-upper, gunner

3 **basketball game,** game, play, strategy, defense <see list>, offense <see list>; **official, referee,** umpire, official scorekeeper, timer; **foul,** violation <see list>, infraction; **play, strategy,** running game, fast break, passing game, draw and kick game; **jump,** center jump, jump ball, live ball; **pass,** passing, pass ball, assist, bounce pass, dish *and* feed <both nonformal>; **tactics, action,** dribble, fake, handoff, ball control, ball-handling, sky shot *or* air ball, clear-out *or* outlet pass, basket hanging, freelancing, pivot *or* post, high post, low post, one-on-one, screening, pick, pick and roll, trap, turnover, steal *or* burn, out-of-bounds, dead ball, throw-in, corner throw, buzzer play; **restrictions,** three-second rule, five-second rule, ten-second rule, twenty-four-second rule, thirty-second rule; **shot** <see list>, **score, basket** *or* **field goal,** bucket <nonformal>, three-point play *or* three-pointer, free throw *or* foul shot; **quarter,** half, overtime period *or* overtime

VERBS 4 **play,** play basketball, play ball, ride the pine <nonformal>, **dribble,** fake, pass, dish <nonformal>, work the ball around, take it coast to coast, give and go, sky it, clear the ball, hand off, **guard,** play tight, play loose, double-team, handcheck, block, screen, pick, set a pick, steal, burn, freelance, **shoot, score,** sink one *and* can *and* swish <all nonformal>, finger-roll, tip it in, shoot a brick <nonformal>, rebound, clear the board, freeze the ball, kill the clock; **foul,** commit a foul *or* violation, foul out

5 **basketball defensive strategies**

box-and-one defense	man-to-man defense
combination defense	matchup defense
multiple defense	set pattern
pressure defense	slough
sagging *or* collapsing defense	stack defense
	zone defense *or* zone

6 **basketball offensive strategies**

clear out one side	motion offense
delay offense	press
flip-flop offense	pressure offense
full-court press	rotation offense
full-court zone press	run and gun offense
gap offense	shuffle offense
give and go offense	stack offense
half-court press	stall offense

7 **basketball fouls**

blocking	offensive foul
charging	palming
disqualifying foul	personal foul *or* personal
double dribble	
double foul	pushing off
force-out	technical foul *or* technical
goaltending	
hacking	three-second violation
held ball	
intentional foul	traveling
multiple foul	

8 **basketball shots**

bank shot	hook shot *or* hook
brick <nonformal>	jump shot *or* jumper
bunny <nonformal>	lay-up
charity toss *and* charity throw *and* charity shot <all nonformal>	one-and-one
	pivot shot
	penalty free throw
	scoop shot
cripple <nonformal>	set shot
dunk <nonformal>	slam dunk <nonformal>
finger-roll	swish <nonformal>
free throw	tip-in

748 TENNIS

NOUNS 1 **tennis,** lawn tennis, indoor tennis, outdoor tennis, singles, doubles, mixed doubles, Canadian doubles, team tennis; court *or* real *or* royal tennis; **organized tennis,** International Tennis Federation *or* ITF, United States Tennis Association *or* USTA; **tournament,** tennis competition <see list>, championship, crown, match, trophy; **tennis ball, ball, tennis racket, racket** <see list>, bat <nonformal>, sweet spot; **tennis court, court,** sideline, alley, doubles sideline, baseline, center mark, service line, half court line, backcourt, forecourt, midcourt, net, band; **surface,** slow surface, fast surface, grass surface *or* grass, concrete surface, wood *or* wooden surface, synthetic fiber surface, competition court, all-weather court, clay court

2 **game,** strategy, serve-and-volley, power

game; **official, umpire,** baseline umpires *or* linesmen, line umpires *or* linesmen, service-line umpire *or* linesman, net-court judge; **play,** coin-toss, racket-flip, grip, Eastern grip, Continental grip, Western grip, two-handed grip, **stroke** <see list>, **shot,** service *or* serve, return, spin, top-spin, let ball *or* let, net-cord ball, rally, fault, double fault, foot fault; error, unforced error; **score, point,** service ace *or* ace, love, deuce, advantage *or* ad, game point, service break, break point, set point, match point, tiebreaker, lingering death <nonformal>, Van Alen Streamlined Scoring System *or* VASSS

VERBS **3 play tennis, play,** serve, return, drive, volley, smash, lob, place the ball, serve and volley, play serve-and-volley tennis, fault, foot-fault, double-fault, make an unforced error; **score** *or* **make a point,** score, ace one's opponent, break service, break back

4 tennis competitions

Australian Open	Italian Open
Big Four	King's Cup
British Open *or* Wimbledon	Masters Tournament
	Olympic Games
Federation Cup	South African Open
French Open	US Open
Grand Prix	Virginia Slims Circuit
International Lawn Tennis Challenge Trophy *or* Davis Cup	West German Open
	Wightman Cup

5 tennis rackets

aluminum racket	graphite racket
Fiberglas <trademark> racket	steel racket
	wooden *or* wood racket
Prince <trademark> racket	

6 tennis strokes

backhand	lob volley
backhand drive	overhead
chop	passing shot
drive	slice
drop shot	service *or* serve
forehand	smash
forehand drive	two-handed backhand
ground stroke	
half-volley	volley
lob	

749 HOCKEY

NOUNS **1 hockey,** ice hockey, Canadian national sport; **professional hockey,** National Hockey League *or* NHL, Clarence Campbell Conference, Smythe Division, Norris Division, Prince of Wales Conference, Patrick Division, Adams Division; **amateur hockey,** bantam hockey, midget hockey, pee-wee hockey, junior hockey, Canadian Amateur Hockey Association, Amateur Hockey Association of the United States, International Ice Hockey Federation; **competition,** series, championship, cup, Olympic Games, Stanley Cup, All-Star Game; **rink,** hockey rink, boards, end zone, defending *or* defensive zone, attacking *or* offensive zone, neutral zone *or* center ice, blue line, red line, goal line, crease, goal *and* net *and* cage, face-off spot, face-off circle, penalty box, penalty bench, players' bench; **equipment,** gear <see list>

2 hockey team, team, skaters, squad, bench; line, forward line, center, right wingman, left wingman; **defense,** right defenseman, left defenseman, goaltender *or* goalie; specialized player, playmaker, penalty killer, point *or* point man, enforcer <nonformal>

3 game, match; **referee,** linesman, goal judge, timekeepers, scorer; **foul,** penalty <see list>, infraction, offside, icing *or* icing the puck; **play,** skating, stick *or* puck handling, ragging, deking, checking, backchecking, forechecking, passing, shooting; **pass,** blind pass, drop pass, through-pass; **check** <see list>; **offense,** breakout, Montreal offense, headmanning, Toronto offense, play-off hockey, give-and-go, breakaway; **shot,** slap shot, wrist shot, backhand shot, flip, sweep shot; power play; **score,** point, finish off a play, feed, assist, hat trick; **period,** overtime *or* overtime period, sudden death overtime, shoot-out

4 field hockey, banty *or* bandy, hurley *or* hurling, shinty *or* shinny; International Hockey Board, *Fédération Internationale de Hockey* <Can Fr>, International Federation of Women's Hockey Associations, United States Field Hockey Association, Field Hockey Association of America; **hockey field,** field, pitch, goal line, center line, center mark, bully circle, sideline, 7-yard line, alley, 25-yard line, striking *or* shooting circle, goalpost, goal, goal mouth; **equipment,** gear, stick, ball, shin pads

5 team, attack, outside left, inside left, center forward, inside right, outside right, defense, left halfback, center halfback, right halfback, left fullback, right fullback, goalkeeper

6 game, match; **umpire,** timekeeper; **foul,** infraction, advancing, obstructing, sticks, undercutting, **penalty,** free hit, corner hit, defense hit, penalty bully, penalty shot;

play, bully, bully-off, pass-back, stroke <see list>, marking, pass, tackle, circular tackle, out-of-bounds, roll-in or push-in, hit-in; **goal**, point, score; **period**, half

VERBS **7 play, skate**, pass, check, block, stick-handle or puck-handle, rag, deke, give-and-go, headman, break out, shoot, score, clear, dig, freeze the puck, center, ice or ice the puck; tackle, mark

8 hockey equipment

chest protector	leg pads
elbow pads	neutral stick
face mask	puck
gloves	right-handed stick
goaltender's stick	shin guards
helmet	shoulder pads
hip pads	skates
knee guards	stick
left-handed stick	

9 hockey fouls and penalties

bench minor penalty	interference
board-checking	kneeing
butt-ending	match penalty
charging	major or five-minute
clipping	penalty
cross checking	minor or two-minute
ejection	penalty
elbowing	misconduct penalty
falling on the puck	penalty shot
fighting	poke checking
handling the puck	slashing
high-sticking	spearing
holding	tripping
hooking	

10 hockey checks

board check or board-ing	hip check
body check	poke check
cross check	stick check
	sweep check

11 field hockey strokes

clearing	left-hand lunge
dribble	push
drive	right cut
flick	right drive
job	right-hand lunge
left drive	scoop

750 BOWLING

NOUNS **1 bowling**, kegling or kegeling <nonformal>, tenpin bowling or tenpins, candlepin bowling, duckpin bowling, fivepin bowling, rubberband duckpin bowling; **bowling organization**, league, American Bowling Congress or ABC, Regular Division, Classic Division, Women's International Bowling Congress or WIBC, American Junior Bowling Congress; amateur bowling, league bowling; **professional bowling**, pro bowling <nonformal>, tour, Professional Bowlers Association or PBA, Professional Women's Bowling Association, Fédération Internationale des Quilleurs <Fr>; **tournament**, competition, match-play tournament, round-robin tournament, ABC tournament, All-Star Tournament, Bowling Proprietors Association Open, Firestone Tournament of Champions, ABC Masters, WIBC Queens; **alley, lane**, gutter, foul line, bed, spot, pin spot; **equipment, pin**, candlepin, duckpin, fivepin, rubberband duckpin, tenpin, **ball**, two-hole ball, three-hole ball, shoe, leather- or vinyl- or rubber-soled shoe

2 game or string, frame; **delivery**, grip, two-finger grip, three-finger grip, conventional grip, semi-fingertip grip, full-fingertip grip, **approach**, three-step approach, four-step approach, five-step approach, push-away, downswing, backswing, timing step, release, follow-through, straight ball, curve ball, backup, hook ball, gutter ball; **pocket**, Brooklyn side, Brooklyn hit or Jersey hit or crossover, **strike** or ten-strike, mark, double, turkey, foundation; **spare**, mark, leave, spare leave, split <see list>, railroad, open frame; **score**, pinfall, miss, perfect game or 300 game, Dutch

3 lawn bowling, lawn bowls, bowling on the green, bowls; American Lawn Bowling Association; **bowling green**, green, crown green, rink, ditch; **ball**, bowl, jack or kitty, mat or footer; **team**, side, rink, lead or leader, second player, third player, skip

4 spare leaves and splits

baby split	fence
bed posts or fence-posts or goal posts	fit-in split
	Golden Gate
bucket	left fence
Christmas tree	mother-in-law
Cincinnati	right fence
converted split	washout
double pinochle	Woolworth
double wood or tandem	

751 GOLF

NOUNS **1 golf**, the royal and ancient; **professional golf**, pro golf <nonformal>, tour, Professional Golfers Association of America or PGA, Ladies' Professional Golfers' Association or LPGA; **amateur golf**, club, Royal and Ancient Golf Club, United States Golf Association or USGA; **tournament** <see list>, championship, title, cup; **golf course**, course, links, penal course, strategic course, green, tee, teeing ground, back or championship marker, middle or men's marker, front or womens' marker, hole, par-3 hole, par-4 hole, par-5 hole, front nine or side, back nine or side, water hole, fairway, dogleg, obstruction, rub of the green, casual water, rough, hazard, water hazard, bunker, sand hazard, sand trap, beach <nonformal>, collar, apron, fringe, putting green, grass green, sand green, pin, flagstick, flag, lip, cup; **equipment,** gear, club, club parts <see list>

2 **golfer,** player, scratch golfer or player, handicapped golfer, dub and duffer and hacker <all nonformal>, **team,** twosome, threesome, foursome

3 **round,** 9 holes, 18 holes, 72 holes, match, stroke play, match play, medal play, fourball match, three-ball match, best ball, Scotch foursome; **official,** referee, official observer, marker; **play,** golfing grip, overlapping or Vardon grip, reverse overlap, interlocking grip, full-finger grip, address, stance, closed stance, square stance, open stance, waggle, swing, backswing, downswing, followthrough, pivot, body pivot, tee-off; **stroke, shot** <see list>, backspin, bite, distance, carry, run, lie, plugged lie, blind, stymie; **score,** scoring, strokes, eagle, double eagle, birdie, par, bogey, double bogey, penalty, hole-in-one and ace, halved hole, gross, handicap, net

VERBS **4** **play, shoot,** tee up, tee off, drive, hit, sclaff, draw, fade, pull, push, hook, slice, top, sky, loft, dunk, putt, can <nonformal>, borrow, hole out, sink, eagle, double eagle, birdie, par, bogey, double bogey; play through; concede, default

INTERJ **5 fore!**

6 golf tournaments

Australian Masters	PGA Championship
Bing Crosby National	Ryder Cup
Pro-AM	US Open
British Open	US Womens' Open
Colgate-Dinah Shore	USGA National Amateur
Winners Circle	teur
Curtis Cup	USGA Womens' Amateur
Grand Slam	teur
Halford Hewitt	Walker Cup
LPGA Championship	World Amateur Team
Masters Golf Tourna-	Championship
ment	World Cup

7 golf equipment

1 iron or driving iron	5 iron or mashie
2 iron or midiron	6 iron or spade
3 iron or mid mashie	mashie
4 iron or mashie	7 iron or mashie
iron	niblick

8 iron or pitching	number 3 wood or
niblick	spoon
9 iron or niblick	number 4 wood or
ball or pill <nonfor-	cleek or short
mal>	spoon
chipping iron club	number 5 wood or
driver	baffy
golf cart	pitching wedge
golf glove	putter
iron	sand wedge
lofter or lofting iron	short iron
long iron	tee
middle iron	Texas wedge
number 1 wood or	utility iron
driver	wedge
number 2 wood or	wood
brassie	

8 golf shots

approach shot or ap-	lag
proach	lob
blast	long iron shot
chip shot or chip	Mulligan or Shapiro
chip-and-run	pitch
cut shot	pitch-and-run
draw	punch
drive	putt
duck hook	run-up
fade	sand shot
fairway wood shot	slice
full shot	snake
gimme <nonfor-	tee shot
mal>	water shot
hook	

752 SOCCER

NOUNS **1 soccer,** football, association football, assoc fooball, soccer football; **league,** college soccer, Intercollegiate Soccer Football Association of America, National Collegiate Athletic Association or NCAA, Federation of International Football Associations or FIFA; **tournament,** competition <see list>, championship, cup; **professional soccer,** pro soccer, North American Soccer League or NASL; **soccer field,** field, soccer pitch, pitch, goal line, touch line, halfway line, penalty area, penalty spot or penalty-kick mark, goal area, goal, goalpost, crossbar, corner area, corner flag, center mark, center circle; **equipment,** gear, ball, suit, uniform, shirt, shorts, knee socks, shin guards, soccer shoes

2 **team,** squad, side, forward, striker, outside right, inside right, center forward, lineman, midfielder, inside left, outside left, right half, center half, left half, defender, back, right back, left back, back four, goalkeeper or goaltender or goalie

3 **game, match; official,** referee, linesman;

play, coin-toss or -flip, 3-3-4 offense, 5-2 offense, man-to-man offense, kickoff, kick <see list>, throw-in, goal kick, corner kick, offside, ball-control, pass, back-heel pass, outside-of-the-foot pass, push pass, tackle, sliding tackle, sliding block tackle, trap, chest trap, thigh trap, breakaway, header, shot, save; **rule,** law; **foul** <see list>; **penalty,** caution, red card, direct free kick, indirect free kick, caution; **goal,** score, point, tie-breaker, series of penalty kicks, shootout, bonus point; **period,** quarter, overtime period

VERBS **4 play,** kick, kick off, trap, pass, dribble, screen, head, center, clear, mark, tackle, save

5 soccer competitions

Coupe de France	National Challenge or
Cup Winners Cup	Dewar Cup
European Cup	National Junior Cup
Libertadores Cup	NCAA Championship
NAIA Champion-	Norway Cup
ship	Olympic Games
National Amateur	Women's World Cup
Cup	World Cup

6 soccer kicks

bicycle kick	lofted kick
chip	low drive
flick kick	overhead volley
half-volley	punt
instep or inside-of-	scissors kick
the-foot kick	volley or volley kick

7 soccer fouls

charging dangerously	holding an opponent
charging from behind	jumping at an oppo-
charging the goal-	nent
keeper	kicking an opponent
continual breaking of	offside
rules	pushing an opponent
dangerous play	spitting at an oppo-
dissenting from ref-	nent
eree's decision	striking an opponent
foul or abusive lan-	tripping an opponent
guage	ungentlemanly con-
handling the ball	duct

753 SKIING

NOUNS **1 skiing,** snow-skiing, Alpine skiing, downhill skiing, **Nordic skiing,** cross-country skiing or langlauf, ski-jumping, jumping, freestyle skiing or hotdog skiing or hotdogging, skijoring, pulk skiing, helicopter skiing or heli-skiing, grass skiing, dry skiing; **organized skiing,** competition skiing, _Fédération Internationale de Ski_ <Fr> or FIS, International Freestyle Skiers Association, World Hot Dog Ski Association; **competition** <see list>, **championship,** cup, race; **slope,** ski slope, ski run, nursery or beginner's slope, ex-

pert's slope, intermediate slope, expert's trail, course, trail, mogul; **ski lift, lift,** rope tow, J-bar, chair lift, T-bar; **race course,** downhill course, slalom course, giant slalom course, super giant slalom course, parallel or dual slalom course; starting gate, fall line, drop or vertical drop, control gate, obligatory gate, flag-stick, open gate, closed or blind gate, hairpin, flush, H, men's course, women's course, **ski-jump,** ramp, inrun, outrun, hill rating, 60-point hill, normal hill, big hill, cross-country course; **equipment,** gear <see list>

2 skier, snow-skier, cross-country skier, ski-jumper, racer, downhill racer, fore-runner, forejumper, skimeister

3 race, downhill race, slalom, giant slalom, super giant slalom or super G, parallel or dual slalom, cross-country race, biathlon; **technique,** style, Arlberg technique, Lil-ienfeld technique, wedeln, **position,** tuck _and_ egg, Vorlage, sitting position, inrun position, fish position, flight position; **maneuver, turn** <see list>

VERBS **4 ski,** run, schuss, traverse, turn, check

5 skiing competitions

Alpine Combined	FIS World Champion-
Arlberg-Kandahar or	ship
A-K Championship	Holmenkollen
Benson & Hedges	Nordic Combined
Professional Tour	Olympic Games
Dalarna Cross-	Silver Belt
Country Race	

6 skiing equipment

aluminum alloy pole	jumping ski
Alpine boot	laminated wood ski
Arlberg or safety	metal ski
strap	molded boot
basket or snow basket	plastic ski
bent pole	pole or stick
cross-country binding	release binding
cross-country pole	ski-boot
cross-country ski	slalom ski
double boot	steel pole
downhill pole	step-in binding
downhill ski	toe clamp
fiberglass pole	

7 skiing maneuvers and turns

check	sideslip
Christiania or	sidestep
christie	snap
diagonal stride	snowplow or double
double-pole stride	stem
double-poling	stem turn
edging	stem christie
Geländesprung	step acceleration
herringbone	step turn
jump turn	Telemark
kick turn	tempo
parallel turn	unweighting

754 BOXING

NOUNS **1 boxing, prizefighting,** fighting, pugilism, noble *or* manly art of self-defense, the noble *or* sweet science, fisticuffs, the fistic sport, the fights *and* the fight game <both nonformal>, the ring; **amateur boxing,** Olympic Games, International Amateur Boxing Association *or* AIBA, Amateur Athletic Union *or* AAU, Golden Gloves; **professional boxing,** World Boxing Council *or* WBC, World Boxing Association *or* WBA, European Boxing Union, club boxing *or* fighting; Queensbury rules, Marquess of Queensbury rules; **boxing ring, ring,** prize ring, square circle *or* ring, canvas, corner; **equipment, gloves,** mitts *and* mittens <both nonformal>, tape, bandages, mouthpiece

2 boxer, fighter, pugilist, prize-fighter, pug *and* palooka <both nonformal>, slugger, mauler; **weight** <see list>; division; **manager; trainer; handler,** second, sparring partner

3 fight, match, bout, battle, duel, slugfest <nonformal>; **official, referee,** ref <nonformal>, judge, timekeeper; **strategy, fight-plan, style,** stance, footwork, **offense, punch** <see list>, blow, belt *and* biff *and* sock <all nonformal>; **defense,** blocking, ducking, parrying, slipping, feint, clinching; **foul** <see list>; **win, knockout** *or* **KO,** technical knockout *or* TKO, decision, unanimous decision, split decision, win on points; **round,** canto *and* stanza <both nonformal>

VERBS **4 fight, box,** punch, spar, mix it up <nonformal>, clinch, break, block, catch, slip a punch, duck, feint, parry, heel, thumb, knock down, knock out, slug, maul, go down, go down for the count, hit the canvas <nonformal>, shadow-box

5 weight divisions

light flyweight	welterweight
flyweight	light middleweight
bantamweight	middleweight
super bantamweight	light heavyweight
featherweight	cruiserweight
junior lightweight	heavyweight
lightweight	super-heavyweight
light welterweight	

6 boxing punches

backhand *or* back-hander	chop
backstroke	combination
body blow *or* body slam	corkscrew punch
bolo punch	counter-punch
	cross
	flanker

follow-up	short-arm blow
haymaker	sideswipe
hook	sidewinder
jab	sneak punch *or* sucker punch
left *or* left-hander *or* portsider	solar-plexus punch
Long Melford	straight punch
mishit *or* mislick	swing
rabbit punch	swipe
right *or* right-hander	the one-two *or* the old one-two
round-arm blow	uppercut
roundhouse	

7 boxing fouls

backhanding	hitting with open glove
butting	holding
elbowing	kidney punch
heeling	kneeing
hitting below the belt	pivot blow
hitting downed opponent	rabbit punch
hitting while breaking	thumbing

755 TRACK AND FIELD

NOUNS **1 track, track and field,** athletics <Brit>, light athletics <Germany and Commonwealth of Independent States>; governing organization, International Athletic Federation *or* IAAF, Amateur Athletic Union of the US *or* AAU, Amateur Athletic Federation of Canada, Amateur Athletic Union of Canada, National Federation of State High School Athletic Associations; **games,** competition <see list>, cup; **stadium, arena,** oval, armory, field house; **track,** oval, lane, start line, starting block, finish line, **infield** <see list>; lap, lap of honor, victory lap

2 track meet, meet, games, program; **running event; field event** <see list>; **all-around event,** decathlon <see list>, heptathlon <see list>, pentathlon <see list>; triathlon <see list>; **walking, race walking,** the walk, heel-and-toe racing

3 track and field competitions

Americas versus Europe Games	Maccabiah Games
Asian Games	Mediterranean Games
Central American and Caribbean Games	Melrose Games
Colgate Games	Olympic Games
Commonwealth Games	Pacific Games
Empire State Games	Pan-American Games
European Cup	South Pacific Games
European Veteran Games	Special Olympics
International Paraplegic Games	World Cup
	World University Games

4 infield sites

cinder surface
crossbar
dirt surface
discus-throw circuit
hammer-throw circle
hammer-throw
  sector
high-jump runway *or*
  run-up
javelin-throw runway
  or run-up
javelin-throw sector
landing area
landing pit

long-jump runway *or*
  run-up
pole-vault runway *or*
  run-up
shot-put circle
shot-put sector
shot-put stopboard
take-off board
take-off box
triple-jump runway
  or run-up
weight-throw circle
weight-throw sector
wood surface

5 field events

discus throw
hammer throw
high jump
javelin throw

long jump
pole vault
shot put
triple jump

6 heptathlon

100-meter hurdles
200-meter run
800-meter run
high jump

javelin
long jump
shot put

7 decathlon

100-meter run
110-meter hurdles
400-meter run
1500-meter run
discus

high jump
javelin
long jump
pole vault
shot put

8 pentathlon

100-meter hurdles
200-meter run
high jump

javelin
long jump

9 triathlon

100-meter dash
high jump

shot put

756 AUTOMOBILE RACING

NOUNS **1 automobile racing, auto racing, car racing,** motor sport; **racing association; race,** competition, championship; **track,** speedway, Indianapolis Motor Speedway *or* the Brickyard <nonformal>, closed course, road course *or* circuit, dirt track, super speedway; **car, racing car** <see list>, racer; **racing engine** <see list>; **supercharger,** turbocharger, blower *and* windmill <both nonformal>; **tires, racing tires,** shoes <nonformal>, slicks; **body,** body work, spoiler, sidepod, roll bar, roll cage; **wheel,** wire wheel *or* wire, magnesium wheel *or* mag; **fuel, racing fuel,** methanol, nitromethane *or* nitro, blend, pop *and* juice <both nonformal>

2 race driving, racing driver, driver, fast driver *or* leadfoot <nonformal>, slow

driver *or* balloon foot, novice driver *or* yellowtail

3 race, driving, start, Le Mans start, flying start, paced start, grid start; **position,** qualifying, qualifying heat, starting grid, inside position, pole *or* pole position, bubble; **track,** turn, curve, hairpin, switchback, banked turn, corner, chicane, groove, shut-off, drift, straightaway *or* chute, pit, pit area; **signal,** black flag, white flag, checkered flag; **lap,** pace lap, victory lap *or* lane

VERBS **4 drive, race,** start, jump, rev, accelerate, put the hammer down <nonformal>, slow down, back off, stroke it, draft, fishtail, nerf, shut the gate

ADVS **5 at top speed,** flat-out, full-bore, tentenths ride the rail, spin, spin out, crash, t-bone

6 racing cars

championship car
compact sprint car
dirt car
dragster
experimental car *or*
  X-car
Formula A
formula car
Formula F
Formula One
Formula Super Vee
Formula Vee
fuel dragster *or* sling-
  shot *or* rail job
fueler
funny car
gas dragster

grand touring car *or*
  GT
hobby car
Indy car
late-model sportsman
midget car
modified stock car
production car
prototype
quarter-midget car
sedanFormula SCCA
sportsman
sports-racing car
sprint car or big car
stock car
turbine car

7 racing engines

big banger <nonfor-
  mal>
non-supercharged en-
  gine with overhead
  cams
normally aspirated
  engine
Offenhauser engine *or*
  Offy
production engine

stock-block engine
supercharged engine
  or blown engine
supercharged engine
  with overhead
  cams
supercharged stock-
  block engine
turbine engine

757 HORSE RACING

NOUNS **1 horse racing, the turf,** the sport of kings, the turf sport, the racing world *or* establishment; **flat racing; harness racing,** trotting, pacing; **Jockey Club,** Trotting Horse Club, Thoroughbred Racing Association *or* TRA, Thoroughbred Racing Protective Bureau *or* TRPB, state racing commission; **General Stud Book, American Stud Book,** Wallace's Trotting Register; **Triple Crown,** Kentucky Derby,

Preakness Stakes, Belmont Stakes; Grand National, Derby, 2000 Guineas, Sty Leger, Gold Cup Race, Oaks; **racetrack, track,** racecourse, turf, oval, course, strip; rail, inside rail, infield, paddock; turf track, steeplejack course; gate *and* barrier; **track locations** <see list> *and* **calls; track conditions** <see list>, footing; racing equipment, tack

2 **jockey,** jock, rider, race rider, pilot, bug boy <nonformal>, money rider; apprentice jockey, bug <nonformal>; breeder, owner; trainer; steward, racing secretary; **railbird** *and* race bird <both nonformal>, turf-man; **racehorse, pony,** thoroughbred, standardbred, mount, flyer, running horse, trotter, pacer, quarter horse, bangtail *and* daisy-cutter *and* filly *and* gee-gee <all nonformal>; **sire, dam,** stallion, stud, stud horse, racing stud, mare, brood mare, gelding, ridgeling *or* rigling; **horse,** aged horse, three-year-old, sophomore, two-year-old, juvenile, colt, racing colt, filly, baby, foal, tenderfoot, bug, maiden *or* maiden horse, yearling, weanling; **favorite,** chalk, choice, odds-on favorite, public choice, top horse; runner, front-runner, pacesetter; strong horse, router, stayer; winner *or* win horse, place horse, show horse, also-ran; **nag** *and* race-nag *and* beagle *and* beetle *and* hayburner *and* nine of hearts *and* palooka *and* pelter *and* pig *and* plater *and* selling plater <all nonformal>; **rogue,** bad actor, cooler

3 **horse race, race;** race meeting, race card, scratch sheet; **starters,** field, weigh-in *or* weighing-in, post parade, post time, post position *or* PP; **start, break,** off; easy race, romp, shoo-in, armchair ride, hand ride; **finish,** dead heat, blanket finish, photo finish, Garrison finish; **dishonest race,** boat race *and* fixed race <both nonformal>

4 **statistics, records,** condition book, chart, form, **racing form,** daily racing form, past performance, **track record,** dope *or* tip *or* tout sheet <nonformal>, par time, parallel-time chart; **betting;** pari-mutuel 759.4; horse-racing bets

VERBS 5 **race, run; start, break, be off;** air *and* breeze; make a move, drive, extend, straighten out; fade, come back; screw in *or* through; ride out, run wide; **win,** romp *or* breeze in; **place, show,** be in the money; be out of the money

ADJS 6 **winning, in the money;** losing, out of the money; on the chinstrap; out in front, on the Bill Daley

7 **track locations** *or* **calls**

backstretch	mile pole *or* post
clubhouse turn	post
eighth pole *or* post	quarter pole *or* post
far turn	sixteenth pole *or* post
five-eighths pole *or* post	straightaway *or* home stretch *or* home straight
half-mile pole *or* post	

8 **track conditions**

fast	pasteboard
good	sloppy
muddy	slow
off	

758 CARDPLAYING

NOUNS 1 **cardplaying,** shuffling, dealing; **card game,** game; gambling 759, gambling games

2 **card, playing card,** board, pasteboard; **deck, pack; suit,** hearts, diamonds, spades, clubs, puppy-feet <nonformal>; **face card,** blaze, coat card, coat, count card, court card, paint, paint-skin, picture card, redskin; **king,** figure, cowboy *and* sergeant from K Company <both nonformal>, one-eyed king, king of hearts *or* suicide king; **queen,** bitch *and* hen *and* lady *and* mop-squeezer *and* whore <all nonformal>, queen of spades, Black Maria *and* Maria *and* slippery Anne <all nonformal>; **jack,** knave, boy *and* fishhook *and* j-bird *and* j-boy *and* john <all nonformal>, one-eyed jack, jack of trumps *or* right bower, left bower; **joker,** bower, best bower; spot card, rank card, plain card; **ace,** bull *and* bullet *and* seed *and* spike <all nonformal>, ace of diamonds *or* pig's eye <nonformal>, ace of clubs *or* puppyfoot <nonformal>; **two, deuce,** two-spot, duck <nonformal>, two of spades *or* curse of Mexico <nonformal>; **three, trey,** three-spot; **four,** four-spot, four of clubs *or* devil's bedposts <nonformal>; **five,** fivespot, fever <nonformal>; **six,** six-spot; **seven,** seven-spot, fishhook <nonformal>; **eight,** eight-spot; **nine,** nine-spot, nine of diamonds *or* curse of Scotland <nonformal>; **ten,** ten-spot

3 **bridge,** auction bridge, contract bridge, rubber bridge, duplicate *or* tournament bridge; **bridge player,** partner, dummy, North and South, East and West, left hand opponent *or* LHO, bidder, responder, declarer, senior; **suit,** major suit, minor suit, trump suit, trump *or* trumps, lay suit *or* plain suit *or* side suit; **call, bid** <see list>; pass; **hand** <see list>; **play,** lead, opening lead, **trick,**

quick trick *or* honor trick, high-card trick, overtrick, odd trick; **score,** adjusted score, grand slam, little slam *or* small slam, game, rubber, premium, honors, set *or* setback

VERBS **4 shuffle,** make up, make up the pack, fan *and* wash <both nonformal>; cut; **deal,** serve, pitch <nonformal>

5 bridge bids

asking bid	overbid *or* overcall
borderline bid	rebid
business double	redouble
demand bid	response
forcing bid	sacrifice bid
forcing pass	score bid
free bid	shut-out bid
insufficient bid	sign-off
jump bid	skip bid
no-trump bid	suit bid
opening bid	takeout double
original bid	

6 bridge hands

balanced hand	piano hand
doubleton	pianola hand
exposed hand	side strength
long trump	singleton
long suit	short suit
major tenace	tenace
minor tenace	unbalanced hand
offensive strength	void
perfect tenace	yarborough

759 GAMBLING

NOUNS **1 gambling, playing, betting, action,** wagering, punting, hazarding, risking, staking, gaming, laying, taking *or* giving *or* laying odds, sporting <old>; **speculation, play;** drawing *or* casting lots, tossing *or* flipping a coin, sortition

2 gamble, chance, risk, risky thing, hazard; gambling *or* **gambler's chance,** betting proposition, bet, matter of chance, sporting chance, **luck of the draw,** hazard of the die, roll *or* cast *or* throw of the dice, turn *or* roll of the wheel, turn of the table, turn of the cards, fall of the cards, flip *or* toss of a coin, toss-up, toss; heads or tails, touch and go; blind bargain, pig in a poke; leap in the dark, shot in the dark; potshot, random shot, potluck; **speculation, venture,** flier *and* plunge <both nonformal>; calculated risk; uncertainty 970; fortune, luck 971.1

3 bet, wager, stake, hazard, lay, play *and* chunk *and* shot <all nonformal>; cinch bet *or* sure thing, mortal cinch *and* mortal lock *and* nuts <all nonformal>; long shot; **ante;** parlay, double or nothing;

dice bet, craps bet, golf bet, **horse-racing bet, poker bet,** roulette bet, telebet

4 betting system; pari-mutuel, off-track betting *or* OTB

5 pot, jackpot, pool, stakes, kitty; bank; office pool

6 gambling odds, odds, price; **even** *or* **square odds,** even break; **short odds, long odds,** long shot; even chance, good chance, small chance, no chance 971.10; **handicapper,** odds maker, pricemaker

7 gambling game <see list>, game of chance, game, friendly game; card games

8 dice, bones *and* rolling bones *and* ivories *and* babies *and* cubes *and* devil's bones *or* teeth *and* galloping dominoes *and* golf balls *and* marbles *and* Memphis dominoes *and* Mississippi marbles *and* Missouri marbles <all nonformal>, **craps,** crap shooting, crap game, bank craps *or* casino craps, muscle craps, African dominoes *and* African golf *and* alley craps *and* army craps *and* blanket craps *and* army marbles *and* Harlem tennis *and* poor man's roulette <all nonformal> floating crap game, floating game, sawdust game; poker dice; **false** *or* crooked *or* loaded dice

9 <throw of dice> **throw, cast, rattle, roll, shot,** hazard of the die; dice points and rolls <see list>

10 poker, draw poker *or* draw *or* five-card draw *or* open poker, stud poker *or* stud *or* closed poker, five-card stud *or* seven-card stud, up card *or* open card, down card *or* closed card; common *or* community *or* communal card; highball, high-low, lowball; **straight** *or* **natural poker,** wild-card poker; **poker hand,** duke *and* mitt <both nonformal>, good hand *or* cards, lock *or* cinch *or* cinch hand *or* ironclad hand *or* iron duke *or* mortal cinch *or* nut hand *or* nuts *or* immortals; bad hand *or* cards, trash *and* rags <both nonformal>; **openers,** progressive openers, bet, raise *or* kick *or* bump *or* pump *or* push, showdown

11 blackjack *or* **twenty-one** *or* vingt-et-un; deal, card count, stiff, hard seventeen, hard eighteen, soft count, soft hand, soft eighteen, hit, blackjack *or* natural *or* snap *or* snapper, California blackjack; cut card *or* indicator card *or* sweat card; card-counting *or* ace-count *or* number count

12 roulette, American roulette, European roulette; **wheel,** American wheel, European wheel, wheel well, canoe, fret; **layout,** column, damnation alley, outside; zero, double zero, knotholes *or* house numbers

13 **cheating**, cheating scheme, cheating method, angle, con *and* grift *and* move *and* racket *and* scam *and* sting <all nonformal>; deception 356

14 **lottery**, drawing, sweepstakes *or* sweepstake *or* sweep; draft lottery; **raffle; state lottery**, Lotto, Pick Six, Pick Four; tombola <Brit>; number lottery, numbers pool, **numbers game** *or* **policy**, Chinese lottery <nonformal>; interest lottery, Dutch *or* class lottery; tontine; grab bag *or* barrel *or* box

15 **bingo**, slow death <nonformal>, beano, keno, lotto; bingo card, banker, counter

16 <gambling device> gambling wheel, wheel of fortune, big six wheel, Fortune's wheel, raffle wheel *or* paddle wheel; roulette wheel, American wheel, European wheel; raffle wheel; cage, birdcage; goose *or* shaker, gooseneck; pinball machine; slot machine, slot, the slots, one-armed bandit <nonformal>; **layout** *or* green cloth, gambling table, craps table, Philadelphia layout, roulette table; **cheating device**, gaff *and* gimmick *and* tool <all nonformal>

17 pari-mutuel, pari-mutuel machine; totalizator, totalizer, tote *and* tote board <both nonformal>, odds board

18 **chip, check, counter** bean *and* fish <both nonformal>

19 **casino, gambling house, house**, store *and* shop <both nonformal>, gaming house, betting house, betting parlor, gambling den, gambling hall, sporting house <old>, gambling hell <nonformal>; luxurious casino, carpet joint *and* rug joint <both nonformal>; honest gambling house, right joint <nonformal>; disreputable gambling house, crib *and* dive *and* joint *and* sawdust joint *and* store *and* toilet <all nonformal>; illegal gambling house, cheating gambling house, brace house *and* bust-out joint *and* clip joint *and* deadfall *and* flat joint *and* flat store *and* hell *and* juice joint *and* low den *and* nick joint *and* peek store *and* skinning house *and* snap house *and* sneak joint *and* steer joint *and* wire joint *and* wolf trap <all nonformal>; **handbook, book, sports book, bookie joint** <nonformal>, racebook, horse parlor, horse room, off-track betting parlor, OTB

20 **bookmaker, bookie** <nonformal>, turf accountant; **tout,** turf consultant; numbers runner; bagman

21 **gambler, player,** gamester, sportsman *or* sporting man <both archaic>, sport, hazarder <old>; **speculator,** venturer, adventurer; **bettor,** wagerer, punter; high-stakes gambler, money player, high roller, plunger; petty gambler, low roller, piker *and* tinhorn *and* tinhorn gambler <all nonformal>; **professional gambler,** pro *and* nutman <both nonformal>; **skillful gambler, sharp, shark,** sharper, dean *and* professor *and* river gambler *and* dice gospeller *and* sharpie <all nonformal>; **cardsharp** *or* cardshark, cardsharper; **card counter,** counter, caser, matrix player; crap shooter *and* boneshaker <both nonformal>; compulsive gambler; **spectator, kibitzer,** lumber *and* sweater *and* wood <all nonformal>

22 **cheater,** cheat, air bandit *and* bilk *and* bunco artist *and* dildock *and* grec *and* greek *and* grifter *and* hustler *and* mechanic *and* mover *and* rook *and* worker <all nonformal>; deceiver 357; **dupe, victim,** coll *and* flat *and* john *and* lamb *and* lobster *and* mark *and* monkey *and* patsy *and* **sucker** <all nonformal>

VERBS 23 **gamble,** game, sport <old>, play, **try one's luck** *or* **fortune; speculate; run** *or* **bank a game;** draw lots, draw straws, lot, cut lots, **cast lots;** cut the cards *or* deck; match coins, toss, flip a coin, call, call heads or tails; shoot craps, play at dice, roll the bones <nonformal>; play the ponies <nonformal>; raffle off

24 **chance, risk, hazard,** set at hazard, **venture,** wager, take a flier <nonformal>; **gamble on,** take a gamble on; **take a chance,** take one's chance, take the chances of, try the chance, **chance it,** "stand the hazard of the die"— Shakespeare; **take** *or* **run the risk,** run a chance; **take chances,** tempt fortune; **leave** *or* **trust to chance** *or* **luck,** rely on fortune, take a leap in the dark; buy a pig in a poke; take potluck

25 **bet, wager, gamble, hazard, stake,** punt, lay, lay down, put up, **make a bet, lay a wager,** give *or* take *or* lay odds, make book, get a piece of the action <nonformal>; plunge <nonformal>; **bet on** *or* **upon, back;** bet *or* play against; play *or* follow the ponies <nonformal>; parlay; **ante, ante up; cover, call,** match *or* meet a bet, see, fade; **check, sandbag** <nonformal>, **pass,** stand pat *or* stand stiff

26 **cheat, pluck** *and* skin *and* rook <all nonformal>; load the dice, mark the cards

ADJS 27 speculative, **uncertain** 970.15; **hazardous, risky** 1005.10, dicey <nonformal>; **lucky,** winning, hot *and* red hot *and* on a roll <all nonformal>; **unlucky,** losing, cold <nonformal>

28 gambling games

all fours	loo
auction bridge	lottery
baccarat	lotto
banker	lowball poker
bezique	monte
bingo	numbers *or* policy
blind poker	ombre
bridge	paddle wheel *or* raffle
canasta	wheel
casino	penny ante
chemin de fer	picquet
chuck-a-luck *or* bird-	pinball
cage	pinochle
chuck-farthing	pitch and toss
contract bridge *or*	poker
contract	poker dice
crack-loo	quinze
craps	romesteq
cribbage	rouge et noir
draw poker	roulette
écarté	rum
euchre	rummy
fan tan	seven-up
faro	skat
gin	straight poker
gin rummy	stud poker
hazard	three-card monte
hearts	trente-et-quarante
high, low, jack and	twenty-one *or* black-
the game	jack *or* vingt-et-un
keno	wheel of fortune *or*
liar dice	big six wheel
liar's poker	whist

29 dice points and rolls

blanket roll *or*	Chicago *or* little joe
soft-pad roll	from Kokomo
boxes *or* hard	greek shot
eight	little natural *or* slow
craps	crap
doublet	nine *or* carolina *or*
drop shot	carolina nina *or*
dump over shot	nina from caroliner
eight *or* eighter from	*or* nina from caro-
Decatur *or* Ada	lina
from Decatur *or*	number *or* point
Ada Ross *or* Ada	puppy feet
Ross the stable hoss	seven *or* natural *or* lit-
English *or* ass English	tle natural *or* pass
or body English *or*	*or* craps *or* skinny
Jonah	Dugan
even roll	six *or* captain hicks *or*
fimps *or* hard ten	sister hicks *or*
five *or* fee-bee *or* fever	Jimmy Hicks *or*
or phoebe *or* little	sixie from dixie
Phoebe	*or* sixty days *or*
four *or* little Dick	sice
Fisher *or* little Dick	ten *or* big dick *or* big
or little joe *or* little	Joe from Boston *or*
joe from Baltimore	slow crap
or little joe from	three *or* cock-eyes

twelve *or* boxcars *or* high noon *or* Gary Cooper

two *or* snake eyes *or* Dolly Parton

760 EXISTENCE

NOUNS **1 existence, being;** subsistence, entity, essence, isness, absolute *or* transcendental essence, *l'être* <Fr>, pure being, *Ding-an-sich* <Ger, thing-in-itself>, noumenon; **occurrence,** presence; **materiality** 1050, **substantiality** 762; **life** 306

2 reality, actuality, factuality, empirical *or* demonstrable *or* objective existence, the here and now; historicity; **truth** 972; **authenticity;** sober *or* grim reality, hardball *and* the nitty-gritty <both nonformal>, not a dream, more truth than poetry

3 fact, the case, the truth of the matter, not opinion, not guesswork, what's what *and* where it's at <both nonformal>; **matter of fact,** "plain, plump fact"—R Browning; **bare fact,** naked fact, bald fact, **simple fact,** sober fact, simple *or* sober truth; **cold fact,** hard fact, **stubborn fact, brutal fact,** painful fact, the nitty-gritty *and* the bottom line <both nonformal>; **actual fact,** positive fact, absolute fact; **self-evident fact,** axiom, postulate, premise, accomplished fact, *fait accompli* <Fr>; **accepted fact,** conceded fact, admitted fact, fact of experience, well-known fact, established fact, inescapable fact, irreducible fact, indisputable fact, undeniable fact; **demonstrable fact,** provable fact; empirical fact; protocol, protocol statement *or* sentence *or* proposition; given fact, given, donné datum, **circumstance** 765; **salient fact,** significant fact

4 the facts, the information 551, the particulars, the details, the specifics, **the data;** the dope *and* the scoop *and* the score *and* the skinny *and* the inside skinny <all nonformal>; the picture <nonformal>, the gen <Brit nonformal>; the fact *or* facts *or* truth of the matter, the facts of the case, the whole story <nonformal>; "irreducible and stubborn facts"—W James; essentials, basic *or* essential facts, brass tacks <nonformal>

5 self-existence, uncreated being, noncontingent existence, aseity, innascibility

6 mere existence, simple existence, **vegetable existence, vegetation,** mere tropism

7 (philosophy of being) ontology, metaphysics, existentialism

VERBS **8 exist, be,** be in existence, be extant, have being; breathe, **live** 306.7; subsist, stand, obtain, hold, prevail, be the case; **occur,** be present, be there, be found, be met with, happen to be

9 **live on,** continue to exist, persist, last, stand the test of time, endure 826.6

10 **vegetate,** merely exist, just be, pass the time

11 **exist in, consist in,** subsist in, lie in, rest in, repose in, reside in, abide in, inhabit, dwell in, **inhere in,** be present in, be a quality of, be comprised in, be contained in, be constituted by, be coextensive with

12 **become,** come to be, go, get, get to be, turn out to be; be converted into, turn into 857.17; grow 860.5; be changed

ADJS 13 **existent, existing,** in existence, de facto; **subsistent,** subsisting; **being,** in being; **living** 306.11; **present, extant, prevalent, current,** in force *or* effect, afoot, on foot, under the sun, on the face of the earth

14 **self-existent,** self-existing, innascible; uncreated, increate

15 **real, actual,** factual, veritable, for real <nonformal>, de facto, simple, sober, **hard; absolute, positive; self-evident,** axiomatic; accepted, conceded, stipulated, given; admitted, well-known, **established, inescapable, indisputable, undeniable; demonstrable,** provable; empirical, **objective,** historical; **true** 972.12; honest-to-God <nonformal>, genuine, card-carrying <nonformal>, **authentic; substantial** 762.6

ADVS 16 **really, actually; factually; genuinely,** veritably, **truly; in reality,** in actuality, in effect, in fact, de facto, in point of fact, as a matter of fact; positively, absolutely; no buts about it <nonformal>; no ifs, ands, or buts <nonformal>; obviously, manifestly 348.14

WORD ELEMENTS 17 onto—

761 NONEXISTENCE

NOUNS 1 **nonexistence,** nonsubsistence; **nonbeing,** unbeing, not-being, nonentity; **nothingness,** nullity, nihility; vacancy, deprivation, emptiness, inanity, vacuity 222.2; vacuum, void 222.3; "the intense inane"—Shelley; negativeness, negation, negativity; nonoccurrence; **unreality,** nonreality, unactuality; nonpresence, absence 222

2 **nothing,** nil, *nihil* <L>, *nichts* <Ger>, *nada* <Sp>, **naught, aught;** zero, cipher; nothing whatever, nothing at all, nothing on earth *or* under the sun, no such thing; thing of naught 763.2

3 <nonformal terms> **zilch, zip,** zippo, nix, goose egg, Billy be damn, diddly, shit, diddly shit, squat, diddly squat, Sweet Fanny Adams <Brit>, bubkes, beans, a hill of beans, a hoot, **a fart,** a fuck, fuck all *and* bugger all <both Brit>, jack-shit, a rat's ass

4 **none,** not any, none at all, not a one, not a blessed one <nonformal>, never a one, ne'er a one, nary one <nonformal>; **not a bit,** not a whit, not a hint, not a smitch *or* smidgen <nonformal>, not a speck, not a mite, not a particle, not an iota, not a jot, not a scrap, not a trace, not a lick *or* a whiff <nonformal>, not a shadow, not a suspicion, not a shadow of a suspicion, neither hide nor hair

VERBS 5 **not exist,** not be in existence, not be met with, not occur, not be found, found nowhere, be absent *or* lacking *or* wanting

6 **cease to exist** *or* **be, be annihilated,** be destroyed, **be wiped out,** be extirpated, be eradicated; **go, vanish,** be no more, leave no trace, "leave not a rack behind"—Shakespeare; **vanish, disappear** 34.2, evaporate, fade, fade away *or* out, fly, flee, dissolve, melt away, die out *or* away, pass, pass away, pass out of the picture <nonformal>, turn to nothing *or* naught, peter out <nonformal>, come to an end, wind down, tail off *and* trail off <both nonformal>; **perish, expire,** pass away, **die** 307.19

7 **annihilate** 395.13, **exterminate** 395.14, eradicate, extirpate, **eliminate,** liquidate, **wipe out, stamp out,** waste *and* take out *and* nuke *and* zap <all nonformal>, put an end to 395.12

ADJS 8 **nonexistent,** unexistent, inexistent, nonsubsistent, unexisting, without being, nowhere to be found; **minus, missing,** lacking, wanting; **null, void,** devoid, empty, inane, vacuous; **negative,** less than nothing

9 **unreal,** unrealistic, unactual, not real; merely nominal; **immaterial** 1051.7; **unsubstantial** 763.5; **imaginary, imagined, fantastic, fanciful, fancied** 985.19–22; illusory

10 **uncreated, unmade,** unborn, unbegotten, unconceived, unproduced

11 **no more, extinct, defunct, dead** 307.30, expired, passed away; vanished, gone glimmering; perished, annihilated; gone, all gone; all over with, had it <nonformal>, finished *and* phut *and* pffft *and* kaput <all nonformal>, down the tube *and* down the drain *and* up the spout <all

nonformal>, done for *and* dead and done
for <both nonformal>

ADVS **12 none, no,** not at all, in no way, to no
extent

WORD ELEMENTS **13** nulli—

762 SUBSTANTIALITY

NOUNS **1 substantiality,** substantialness;
materiality 1050; **substance, body,** mass;
solidity, density, concreteness, **tangibility,** palpability, ponderability; **sturdiness, stability,** soundness, firmness,
steadiness, stoutness, toughness,
strength, durability

2 substance, stuff, fabric, material, matter
1050.2, medium, the tangible; **elements,**
constituent elements, constituents, ingredients, components, atoms, building
blocks, parts

3 something, thing, an existence; **being, entity,** unit, individual, entelechy, monad;
person, persona, personality, body, soul;
creature, created being, contingent being; **organism,** life form, living thing, life;
object 1050.4

4 embodiment, incarnation, materialization, substantiation, concretization,
hypostasis, reification

VERBS **5 embody,** incarnate, **materialize,**
concretize, body forth, lend substance to,
reify, entify, hypostatize

ADJS **6 substantial,** substantive; **solid, concrete; tangible,** sensible, appreciable, palpable, ponderable; **material** 1050.9; **real**
760.15; **created,** creatural, organismic *or*
organismal, contingent

7 sturdy, stable, **solid,** sound, firm, steady,
tough, stout, **strong,** "strong as flesh and
blood"—Wordsworth, rugged; **durable,**
lasting, enduring; **hard, dense,** unyielding, steely, adamantine; **well-made,**
well-constructed, well-built, well-knit;
well-founded, well-established, well-
grounded; **massive,** bulky, heavy, chunky

ADVS **8 substantially,** essentially, materially

WORD ELEMENTS **9** stere—, ont—

763 UNSUBSTANTIALITY

NOUNS **1 unsubstantiality,** insubstantiality,
unsubstantialness; **immateriality** 1051;
bodilessness, incorporeality, unsolidity,
unconcreteness; **intangibility,** impalpability, imponderability; **thinness, tenuousness,** attenuation, tenuity, evanescence, subtlety, subtility, fineness, airiness, mistiness, vagueness, ethereality;
fragility, frailness; flimsiness 16.2; **tran-**

sience 827, **ephemerality,** ephemeralness,
fleetingness, fugitiveness

2 thing of naught, nullity, zero; **nonentity,
nobody** *and* nonstarter *and* nebbish <all
nonformal>, nonperson, unperson, cipher, man of straw, jackstraw <old>, lay
figure, puppet, dummy, hollow man;
flash in the pan, dud <nonformal>; **trifle**
997.5; *nugae* <L>; nothing 761.2

3 spirit, air, **thin air,** "airy nothing"—
Shakespeare, breath, mere breath,
smoke, vapor, mist, ether, **bubble,**
"such stuff as dreams are made on"—
Shakespeare, **shadow,** mere shadow; "a
spume that plays upon a ghostly paradigm of things"—Yeats; illusion 975;
phantom 987.1

VERBS **4 spiritualize, disembody,** dematerialize; etherealize, **attenuate,**
subtilize, rarefy, fine, refine; **weaken,**
enervate, sap

ADJS **5 unsubstantial,** insubstantial, nonsub-
stantial, unsubstanced; intangible, impalpable, imponderable; **immaterial**
1051.7; **bodiless,** incorporeal, unsolid, un-
concrete; weightless 298.10; **transient**
827.7, ephemeral, fleeting, fugitive

6 thin, tenuous, subtile, subtle, evanescent,
fine, overfine, refined, rarefied; **ethereal,**
airy, windy, spirituous, vaporous, gaseous; air-built, cloud-built; **chimerical,**
gossamer, gossamery, gauzy, shadowy,
phantomlike 987.7; dreamlike, **illusory,
unreal;** fatuous, fatuitous, inane; **imaginary,** fanciful 985.20

7 fragile, frail 1048.4; **flimsy,** shaky, weak,
papery, paper-thin, **unsound,** infirm
16.15

8 baseless, groundless, ungrounded, **without foundation,** unfounded, not well-
founded, built on sand, "writ on water"—
Keats

WORD ELEMENTS **9** pseudo—

764 STATE

NOUNS **1 state,** mode, modality; **status, situation,** status quo *or* status in quo, position, standing, footing, location, bearings, spot; **rank,** estate, station, place,
place on the ladder, **standing; condition,**
circumstance 765; **case, lot; predicament,
plight,** pass, pickle *and* picklement *and*
fix *and* jam *and* spot *and* bind <all non-
formal>

2 the state of affairs, the nature *or* shape of
things, the way it shapes up <nonfor-
mal>, the way of the world, how things
stack up <nonformal>, **how things**

stand, how things are, the way of things, the way it is, like it is, where it's at <nonformal>, **the way things are,** the way of it, the way things go, how it goes, the way the cookie crumbles, **how it is,** the status quo or status in quo, the size of it <nonformal>; how the land lies, the lay of the land

3 **good condition, bad condition;** adjustment, fettle, form, order, repair, **shape** <nonformal>, trim

4 **mode, manner, way,** tenor, vein, fashion, style, lifestyle, way of life, preference, thing and bag <both nonformal>; **form,** shape, guise, complexion, make-up; **role,** capacity, character, part

VERBS 5 **be in** or **have** a certain state, be such or so or thus, **fare,** go on or along; **enjoy** or **occupy** a certain position; **get on** or **along,** come on or along <nonformal>; **manage** <nonformal>, **contrive, make out** <nonformal>, come through, get by; **turn out,** come out, stack up <nonformal>, shape up <nonformal>

ADJS 6 conditional, modal, formal, situational, statal

7 **in condition** or **order** or repair or shape; **out of order,** out of commission and **out of kilter** or kelter and out of whack <all nonformal>

765 CIRCUMSTANCE

NOUNS 1 **circumstance, occurrence, occasion, event** 830, **incident;** juncture, conjuncture, contingency, eventuality; **condition** 764.1

2 **circumstances,** total situation, existing conditions or situation, set of conditions, terms of reference, **environment** 209, environing circumstances, context, frame, setting, surround, surrounding conditions, parameters, status quo or status in quo; **the picture,** the whole picture, full particulars, ins and outs, play-by-play description, blow-by-blow account

3 **particular, instance, item, detail,** point, count, case, fact, matter, article, datum, element, part, ingredient, factor, facet, aspect, thing; **respect, regard,** angle; minutia, minutiae <pl>, trifle, petty or trivial matter; incidental, minor detail

4 **circumstantiality,** particularity, specificity, thoroughness, minuteness of detail; accuracy

5 **circumstantiation,** itemization, particularization, specification, spelling-out, detailing, anatomization, atomization, analysis 800

VERBS 6 **itemize, specify,** circumstantiate, particularize, **spell out, detail,** go or enter into detail, descend to particulars, give full particulars, atomize, anatomize; **analyze** 800.6; **cite,** instance, adduce, document, give or quote chapter and verse; **substantiate**

ADJS 7 **circumstantial,** conditional, provisional; **incidental,** occasional, contingent, adventitious, **accidental, chance,** fortuitous, casual, aleatory, unessential or inessential or nonessential

8 environmental, environing, surrounding, conjunctive, conjoined, contextual, attending, attendant, limiting, determining, parametric

9 **detailed, minute, full, particular,** meticulous, fussy, finicky or finicking or finical, picayune, picky <nonformal>, nice <old>, precise, exact, specific, special

ADVS 10 **thus, thusly** <nonformal>, in such wise, thuswise, this way, this-a-way <nonformal>, thus and thus, thus and so, **so,** just so, like so and yea <both nonformal>, like this, like that, just like that; similarly 783.18, precisely

11 **accordingly, in that case, in that event, at that rate,** that being the case, such being the case, that being so, **under the circumstances,** the condition being such, as it is, as matters stand, as the matter stands, **therefore** 887.7, **consequently; as the case may be,** as it may be, according to circumstances; as it may happen or turn out, as things may fall; **by the same token,** equally

12 **circumstantially,** conditionally, provisionally; provided 958.12

13 **fully, in full, in detail,** minutely, specifically, particularly, in particular, wholly 791.13, in toto <L>, completely 793.14, **at length,** in extenso <L>, ad nauseam <L>

766 INTRINSICALITY

NOUNS 1 **intrinsicality,** internality, innerness, **inwardness; inbeing,** indwelling, immanence; **innateness, inherence,** indigenousness; essentiality, fundamentality; **subjectivity,** internal reality, nonobjectivity

2 **essence, substance,** stuff, very stuff, inner essence, essential nature, quiddity; **quintessence, epitome,** embodiment, incarnation, model, pattern, purest type, typification, perfect example or exemplar, elixir, flower; **essential,** principle, essential principle, fundamental, hypostasis,

postulate, axiom; **gist,** gravamen, **nub**
<nonformal>, nucleus, center, focus, ker-
nel, **core, pith,** meat; **heart,** soul, heart
and soul, spirit, sap, marrow

3 <nonformal terms> **meat and potatoes,**
nuts and bolts, the nitty-gritty, the guts,
the name of the game, the bottom line,
where it's at, what it's all about, the ball
game, the payoff, the score, where the
rubber meets the road

4 **nature, character, quality,** suchness; **constitution,** crasis <old>, composition,
characteristics, makeup, constituents;
physique 262.4, physio; **build,** body-
build, somatotype, frame, constitution,
genetic make-up, system; complexion
<old>, humor *and* humors <both old>;
temperament, temper, fiber, **disposition,**
spirit, ethos, genius, dharma; **way, habit,**
tenor, cast, hue, tone, grain, vein, streak,
stripe, mold, brand, stamp; **kind** 808.3,
sort, type, ilk; **property, characteristic**
864.4; **tendency** 895; the way of it, the nature of the beast <nonformal>

5 **inner nature,** inside, insides <nonfor-
mal>, internal *or* inner *or* esoteric *or* intrinsic reality, iniety, true being, essential nature, what makes one tick <nonfor-
mal>, center of life, vital principle, nerve
center; **spirit, indwelling spirit, soul,
heart, heart and soul, breast, bosom, inner person,** heart of hearts, secret heart,
inmost heart *or* soul, secret *or* innermost
recesses of the heart, heart's core, bottom
or cockles of the heart; vitals, the quick,
depths of one's being, guts *and* kishkes
<both nonformal>, where one lives
<nonformal>; **vital principle,** archeus,
life force, *élan vital* <Fr> <Henri Berg-
son>

VERBS 6 **inhere,** indwell, belong to *or* permeate by nature, makes one tick <nonfor-
mal>; run in the blood, run in the family,
inherit, be born so, have it in the genes,
be made that way, be built that way
<nonformal>

ADJS 7 **intrinsic,** internal, **inner,** inward; **inherent,** resident, implicit, immanent, indwelling; inalienable, unalienable,
uninfringeable, unquestionable, un-
challengeable, irreducible, qualitative;
ingrained, in the very grain; infixed, implanted, inwrought, deep-seated; **subjective,** esoteric, private, secret

8 **innate, inborn,** born, congenital; **native,
natural,** natural to, connatural, native to,
indigenous; **constitutional,** bodily, physical, temperamental, organic; **inbred,
genetic, hereditary,** inherited, bred in the

bone, in the blood, running in the blood
or race *or* strain, radical, rooted; connate,
connatal, coeval; **instinctive,** instinctual,
atavistic, primal

9 **essential,** of the essence, **fundamental;
primary,** primitive, primal, elementary,
elemental, simple, bare-bones *and* no-
frills *and* bread-and-butter <all nonfor-
mal>, original, *ab ovo* <L>, **basic, gut**
<nonformal>, basal, underlying; **sub-
stantive,** substantial, material; constitutive, constituent

ADVS 10 **intrinsically, inherently,** innately;
internally, **inwardly,** immanently; originally, primally, primitively; **naturally,
congenitally,** genetically, **by birth, by nature**

11 **essentially, fundamentally, primarily,
basically;** at bottom, *au fond* <Fr>, at
heart; in essence, at the core, in substance, in the main; substantially, materially, most of all; per se, of *or* in itself, as
such, qua

WORD ELEMENTS 12 physi—, physic—

767 EXTRINSICALITY

NOUNS 1 **extrinsicality,** externality, outwardness, **extraneousness,** otherness, discreteness; foreignness; **objectivity,** non-
subjectivity, impersonality

2 **nonessential,** inessential *or* unessential,
nonvitalness, carrying coals to Newcastle, gilding the lily; **accessory, extra,**
collateral; the other, not-self; **appendage,**
appurtenance, auxiliary, supernumerary,
supplement, addition, addendum, superaddition, adjunct 254; **subsidiary,** subordinate, secondary; **contingency,** contingent, incidental, accidental, accident,
happenstance, mere chance; **superfluity,**
superfluousness; fifth wheel *and* tits on a
boar <both nonformal>

ADJS 3 **extrinsic, external,** outward, outside,
outlying; **extraneous,** foreign; **objective,**
nonsubjective, impersonal, extraorgan-
ismic *or* extraorganismal

4 **unessential,** inessential *or* nonessential,
unnecessary, nonvital, superfluous; **accessory, extra,** collateral, auxiliary,
supernumerary; adventitious, appurte-
nant, adscititious; **additional, supplementary,** supplemental, superadded,
supervenient, make-weight; **secondary,**
subsidiary, subordinate; **incidental,** circumstantial, contingent; **accidental,
chance,** fortuitous, casual, aleatory;
indeterminate, unpredictable, capricious

768 ACCOMPANIMENT

NOUNS **1 accompaniment,** concomitance *or* concomitancy, withness *and* togetherness <both nonformal>; synchronism, **simultaneity** 835, simultaneousness; coincidence, co-occurrence, **concurrence,** concurrency; parallelism

2 company, association, consociation, **society,** community; **companionship, fellowship,** consortship, partnership

3 attendant, concomitant, corollary, **accessory,** appendage; **adjunct** 254

4 accompanier, accompanist; attendant, companion, fellow, mate, comate, consort, **partner;** companion piece

5 escort, conductor, usher, shepherd; **guide,** tourist guide, cicerone; **squire,** esquire, swain, cavalier; **chaperon,** duenna; **bodyguard,** guard, **convoy;** companion, sidekick <nonformal>, fellow traveler, travel companion, satellite, outrider

6 attendance, following, cortege, retinue, entourage, suite, followers, followership, rout, train, body of retainers; **court,** cohort; parasite 138.5

VERBS **7 accompany,** bear *or* keep one company, **keep company with,** companion, go *or* travel *or* run with, go along for the ride <nonformal>, **go along with, attend,** wait on *or* upon; **associate with,** assort with, sort with, **consort with,** couple with, hang around with *and* hang out with *and* hang with <all nonformal>, go hand in hand with; **combine** 804.3, **associate,** consociate, confederate, flock *or*
. band *or* herd together

8 escort, conduct, have in tow <nonformal>, marshal, **usher,** shepherd, **guide, lead; convoy,** guard; **squire,** esquire, **attend,** wait on *or* upon, **take out** <nonformal>; **chaperon**

ADJS **9 accompanying, attending, attendant, concomitant,** accessory, collateral; **combined** 804.5, **associated,** coupled, paired; **fellow, twin, joint, joined** 799.13, conjoint, hand-in-hand, hand-in-glove, mutual; **simultaneous, concurrent,** coincident, synchronic, synchronized; correlative; parallel

ADVS **10 hand in hand** *or* glove, arm in arm, side by side, cheek by jowl, shoulder to shoulder; therewith, therewithal, herewith

11 together, collectively, mutually, jointly, unitedly, in conjunction, conjointly, *en masse* <Fr>, communally, corporately, **in a body,** all at once, *ensemble* <Fr>, in association, in company; simultaneously, coincidentally, concurrently, at once

PREPS **12 with, in company with, along with, together with,** in association with, coupled *or* paired *or* partnered with, in conjunction with

WORD ELEMENTS **13** co—, con—, col—, com—, cor—, meta—, syn—, sym—

769 ASSEMBLAGE

NOUNS **1 assemblage, assembly, collection, gathering,** ingathering, **congregation;** concourse, concurrence, conflux, confluence, convergence; collocation, juxtaposition, junction 799.1; combination 804; mobilization, call-up, muster, *attroupement* <Fr>; roundup, rodeo, corralling; **comparison** 942; canvass, census, data-gathering, survey, inventory

2 assembly <of persons>, *assemblée* <Fr>, **gathering, forgathering, congregation,** congress, conference, convocation, concourse, **meeting,** meet, **get-together** *and* turnout <both nonformal>; convention, conventicle, synod, council, diet, **conclave,** levee; caucus; mass meeting, **rally,** sit-in, demonstration, demo <nonformal>; **session,** séance, sitting, sit-down <nonformal>; **panel,** forum, symposium, colloquium; committee, commission; *eisteddfod* <Welsh>; plenum, quorum; **party, festivity** 743.4, fete, at home, housewarming, soiree, reception, **dance,** ball, prom, do <chiefly Brit>, shindig *and* brawl <both nonformal>; rendezvous, date, assignation

3 company, group, grouping, groupment, network, **party, band, knot, gang, crew,** complement, cast, outfit, pack, cohort, troop, troupe, tribe, **body,** corps, stable, bunch *and* mob *and* crowd <all nonformal>; squad, platoon, battalion, regiment, brigade, division, fleet; **team,** squad, string; covey, bevy; posse, detachment, contingent, detail, *posse comitatus* <L>; phalanx; **party, faction,** movement, wing, persuasion; in-group, old-boy network, out-group, peer group, age group; coterie, salon, clique, **set;** junta, cabal

4 throng, multitude, horde, host, heap <nonformal>, army, panoply, legion; flock, cluster, galaxy; **crowd,** press, crush, flood, spate, deluge, mass; **mob,** rabble, rout, ruck, jam, *cohue* <Fr>, everybody and his uncle *or* his brother <nonformal>

5 <animals> **flock, bunch, pack,** colony, host, troop, army, **herd, drove,** drive, drift, trip; pride <of lions>, sloth <of bears>, skulk <of foxes>, gang <of elk>, kennel <of dogs>, clowder <of cats>, pod <of seals>, gam <of whales>, **school** *or* shoal <of fish>; <animal young> **litter**

6 <birds, insects> **flock,** flight, **swarm,** cloud; covey <of partridges>, bevy <of quail>, skein <of geese in flight>, gaggle <of geese on water>, watch <of nightingales>, charm <of finches>, murmuration <of starlings>, spring <of teal>; hive <of bees>, plague <of locusts>

7 **bunch, group,** grouping, groupment, crop, **cluster, clump,** knot; grove, copse, thicket; **batch, lot,** slew <nonformal>, **mess** <nonformal>; tuft, wisp; tussock, hassock; shock, stook

8 **bundle,** bindle <nonformal>, **pack, package,** packet, deck, budget, **parcel,** fardel <nonformal>, sack, bag, poke <nonformal>, rag-bag <nonformal>, bale, truss, **roll,** rouleau, bolt; fagot, fascine, fasces; quiver, sheaf; bouquet, nosegay, posy

9 **accumulation,** cumulation, gathering, **amassment,** congeries, acervation; agglomeration, conglomeration, glomeration, conglomerate, agglomerate; **aggregation,** aggregate; conglobation; **mass, lump,** gob <nonformal>, chunk *and* hunk <both nonformal>, wad; snowball; stockpile, stockpiling

10 **pile, heap, stack; mound, hill;** molehill, anthill; bank, embankment, dune; haystack, hayrick, haymow, haycock, cock, mow, rick; drift, snowdrift; pyramid

11 **collection,** collector's items, collectibles; **holdings,** fund, treasure; corpus, corpora, **body,** data, raw data; compilation, collectanea; ana; anthology, florilegium, treasury; *Festschrift* <Ger>; chrestomathy; **museum, library,** zoo, menagerie, aquarium

12 **set, suit, suite, series,** outfit *and* kit <both nonformal>

13 **miscellany,** miscellanea, collectanea; **assortment, medley, variety, mixture** 796; hodgepodge, conglomerate, **conglomeration,** omnium-gatherum <nonformal>; **sundries,** oddments, **odds and ends**

14 <a putting together> **assembly,** assemblage; assembly line, production line; assembly-line production

15 **collector,** gatherer, accumulator, connoisseur, fancier, enthusiast, pack rat *and* magpie <both nonformal>; collection agent, bill collector, dunner; tax collec-

tor, tax man, exciseman <Brit>, customs agent, *douanier* <Fr>; **miser** 484.4

VERBS **16 come together, assemble, congregate, collect,** come from far and wide, come *or* arrive in a body; league 804.4, ally; **unite** 799.5; muster, **meet, gather, forgather,** gang up <nonformal>, mass; **merge,** converge, flow together, fuse; flock together; herd together; **throng, crowd,** swarm, teem, hive, surge, seethe, mill, stream, horde; **be crowded,** be mobbed, burst at the seams, be full to overflowing; **cluster,** bunch, bunch up, clot; gather around, gang around <nonformal>; rally, rally around; **huddle,** go into a huddle, close ranks; rendezvous, date; **couple,** copulate, link, link up

17 **convene, meet,** hold a meeting *or* session, sit; **convoke,** summon, call together

18 <bring or gather together> **assemble, gather;** drum up, muster, rally, **mobilize; collect,** collect up, fund-raise, take up a collection, raise, take up; **accumulate,** cumulate, **amass,** mass, bulk, batch; agglomerate, conglomerate, aggregate; **combine** 804.3, **network, join** 799.5, **bring together,** get together, **gather together,** draw *or* lump *or* batch *or* bunch together, pack, pack in, cram, cram in; **bunch,** bunch up; **cluster,** clump; **group,** aggroup; **gather in,** get *or* whip in; scrape *or* scratch together, scrape up, together, rake *or* dredge *or* dig up; round up, corral, drive together; **put together,** make up, compile, colligate; collocate, **juxtapose,** pair, match, partner; hold up together, **compare** 942.4

19 **pile, pile on, heap, stack,** heap *or* pile *or* stack up; mound, hill, bank, bank up; rick; pyramid; drift

20 **bundle,** bundle up, **package,** parcel, parcel up, **pack,** bag, sack, truss, truss up; bale; wrap, **wrap up,** do *or* tie *or* bind up; roll up

ADJS **21 assembled, collected, gathered;** congregate, congregated; meeting, in session; **combined** 804.5; **joined** 799.13; joint, leagued 804.6; **accumulated,** cumulate, massed, **amassed;** heaped, stacked, piled; glomerate, agglomerate, conglomerate, aggregate; **clustered,** bunched, lumped, clumped, knotted; bundled, packaged, wrapped up; fascicled, fasciculated

22 **crowded, packed, crammed;** bumper-to-bumper <nonformal>, jam-packed, packed *or* crammed like sardines <nonformal>; **compact,** firm, solid, dense,

close, serried; **teeming, swarming, crawling**, bristling, populous, **full** 793.11

23 **cumulative,** accumulative, total, overall

770 DISPERSION

NOUNS 1 **dispersion** or **dispersal, scattering,** scatter, scatteration, diffraction; ripple effect; **distribution, spreading,** strewing, sowing, broadcasting, **broadcast, spread,** narrowcast, publication 352, **dissemination,** propagation, dispensation; **radiation,** divergence 171; expansion, splay; **diffusion,** circumfusion; **dilution,** attenuation, thinning, thinning-out, watering, watering-down, weakening; **evaporation,** volatilization, dissipation; fragmentation, shattering, pulverization; sprinkling, spattering; peppering, buckshot or shotgun pattern

2 **decentralization,** deconcentration

3 **disbandment,** dispersion or dispersal, diaspora, separation, parting; breakup, split-up <nonformal>; **demobilization,** deactivation, **release,** detachment; dismissal 908.5; dissolution, disorganization, disintegration 805

VERBS 4 **disperse, scatter,** diffract; **distribute, broadcast, sow,** narrowcast, disseminate, propagate, pass around or out, publish 352.10; **diffuse, spread,** dispread, circumfuse, strew, bestrew, dot; **radiate,** diverge 171.5; expand, splay, branch or fan or spread out; **issue, deal out,** retail, utter, dispense; sow broadcast, scatter to the winds; overscatter, overspread, oversow

5 **dissipate, dispel,** dissolve, attenuate, dilute, thin, thin out, water, water down, weaken; **evaporate,** volatilize; drive away, clear away, cast forth, blow off

6 **sprinkle,** besprinkle, asperge, **spatter,** splatter, splash; **dot,** spot, speck, speckle, stud; **pepper,** powder, dust; flour, crumb, bread, dredge

7 **decentralize,** deconcentrate

8 **disband, disperse, scatter, separate, part,** break up, split up; part company, go separate ways; **demobilize,** demob <nonformal>, deactivate, muster out, debrief, **release,** detach, discharge, let go; dismiss 908.18; **dissolve,** disorganize, disintegrate 805.3

ADJS 9 **dispersed, scattered, distributed,** dissipated, disseminated, strown, strewn, broadcast, **spread,** dispread; **widespread,** diffuse, discrete, sparse; **diluted,** thinned, thinned-out, watered, watered-down, weakened; **sporadic;** straggling, straggly;

all over the lot or place <nonformal>, from hell to breakfast <nonformal>

10 **sprinkled,** spattered, splattered, asperged, splashed, **peppered,** spotted, dotted, powdered, dusted, specked, speckled, **studded**

11 dispersive, **scattering, spreading,** diffractive or diffractional, **distributive,** disseminative, diffusive, dissipative, attenuative

ADVS 12 **scatteringly, dispersedly,** diffusely, sparsely, **sporadically,** passim <L>, **here and there;** in places, **in spots** <nonformal>; at large, everywhere, throughout, wherever you look or turn <nonformal>, in all quarters

771 INCLUSION

NOUNS 1 **inclusion, comprisal, comprehension,** coverage, envisagement, embracement, encompassment, incorporation, embodiment, assimilation, reception; **membership,** participation, admission, admissibility, eligibility, legitimation, legitimization; **power-sharing,** enablement, enfranchisement; **completeness** 793, **inclusiveness, comprehensiveness,** exhaustiveness; **whole** 791; openness, toleration or tolerance

2 **entailment, involvement, implication;** assumption, presumption, presupposition, subsumption

VERBS 3 **include, comprise, contain, comprehend,** hold, **take in; cover,** cover a lot of ground <nonformal>, occupy, take up, fill; fill in or out, build into, **complete** 793.6; **embrace,** encompass, enclose, encircle, incorporate, assimilate, embody, admit, receive, envisage; **legitimize,** legitimatize; **share power,** enable, enfranchise, cut in and deal in and give a piece of the action <all nonformal>; among, count in, work in; **number among,** take into account or consideration

4 <include as a necessary circumstance or consequence> **entail, involve, implicate,** imply, assume, presume, presuppose, subsume, affect, take in, contain, comprise, **call for, require,** take, bring, lead to

ADJS 5 **included, comprised,** comprehended, envisaged, embraced, encompassed, added-in, covered, subsumed; bound up with, forming or making a part of, built-in, tucked-in; **involved** 897.3

6 **inclusive, including, containing, comprising, covering, embracing,** encompassing, enclosing, encircling, assimilating, incorporating, envisaging;

counting, numbering; broad-brush *and* ballpark <both nonformal>

7 comprehensive, sweeping, complete 793.9; **whole** 791.9; **all-comprehensive,** all-inclusive 863.14; without omission *or* exception, **overall,** universal, global, wall-to-wall <nonformal>, around-the-world, **total,** blanket, omnibus, across-the-board; encyclopedic, compendious; synoptic; bird's-eye, panoramic

772 EXCLUSION

NOUNS **1 exclusion, barring,** debarring, debarment, preclusion, exception, omission, nonadmission, cutting-out, leaving-out; **restriction, circumscription,** narrowing, demarcation; **rejection,** repudiation; **ban,** bar, taboo, injunction; relegation; prohibition, embargo, blockade; boycott, lockout; inadmissibility, excludability, exclusivity

2 elimination, riddance, culling, culling out, winnowing-out, shakeout, eviction, chasing, bum's rush <nonformal>; **severance** 801.2; withdrawal, **removal,** detachment, disjunction 801.1; discard, eradication, clearance, **ejection,** expulsion, suspension; **deportation, exile,** expatriation, ostracism, outlawing *or* outlawry; disposal, disposition; **liquidation, purge**

3 exclusiveness, narrowness, tightness; **insularity,** snobbishness, parochialism, ethnocentrism, ethnicity, xenophobia, know-nothingism; **segregation, separation, separationism,** division; **isolation,** insulation, seclusion; quarantine; racial segregation, apartheid, color bar, Jim Crow, race hatred; **out-group; outsider,** non-member, stranger, the other, they; **foreigner, alien** 773.3, outcast 586.4, outlaw; *persona non grata* <L>

VERBS **4 exclude, bar,** debar, bar out, lock out, **shut out, keep out,** count out <nonformal>, close the door on, close out, cut out, cut off, preclude; **reject, repudiate,** blackball *and* turn thumbs down on <both nonformal>, read *or* drum out, ease *or* freeze out *and* leave *or* keep out in the cold <all nonformal>, send to Coventry <Brit>, ostracize, wave off *or* aside; **ignore,** turn a blind eye, turn a deaf ear, filter out, tune out; **ban,** prohibit, proscribe, taboo, **leave out,** omit, pass over, ignore; relegate; **blockade,** embargo; **tariff,** trade barrier

5 eliminate, get rid of, rid oneself of, **get quit of,** get shut of <nonformal>, **dispose**

of, **remove,** abstract, eject, expel, give the bum's rush <nonformal>, kick downstairs, cast off *or* out, chuck <nonformal>, throw over *or* overboard <nonformal>; **deport, exile,** outlaw, expatriate; clear, clear out, clear away, clear the decks; **weed out,** pick out; **cut out,** strike off *or* out, elide; eradicate, root up *or* out; **purge, liquidate**

6 segregate, separate, separate out *or* off, divide, cordon, cordon off; **isolate,** insulate, seclude; **set apart,** keep apart; **quarantine,** put in isolation; put beyond the pale, ghettoize; **set aside,** lay aside, put aside, keep aside; **sort** *or* **pick out,** cull out, sift, screen, sieve, bolt, riddle, winnow, winnow out; thresh, thrash, gin

ADJS **7 excluded, barred,** debarred, precluded, kept-out, **shut-out, left-out,** left out in the cold <nonformal>, passed-over; not included, not in it, not in the picture <nonformal>; **ignored;** relegated; **banned,** prohibited, proscribed, tabooed; **expelled,** ejected, **purged,** liquidated; deported, exiled; **blockaded,** embargoed

8 segregated, separated, cordoned-off, divided; isolated, insulated, secluded; **set apart,** sequestered; **quarantined; ghettoized,** beyond the pale

9 exclusive, excluding, exclusory; seclusive, preclusive, exceptional, inadmissible, prohibitive, preventive, prescriptive, restrictive; separative, segregative, closed-door; select, selective; narrow, insular, parochial, ethnocentric, xenophobic, snobbish

PREP **10 excluding, barring,** bar, exclusive of, precluding, omitting, without, absent, **leaving out; excepting, except, except for,** with the exception of, outside of <nonformal>, **save,** saving, save and except, let alone; **besides,** beside, **aside from**

773 EXTRANEOUSNESS

NOUNS **1 extraneousness, foreignness;** otherness, alienism, alienage, alienation; **extrinsicality** 767; **exteriority** 206; nonassimilation, nonconformity; intrusion

2 intruder, foreign body *or* element, foreign intruder *or* intrusion, interloper, encroacher; **impurity,** blemish 1003; speck 258.7, spot, macula, blot; mote, splinter *or* sliver, **weed,** misfit 788.4; oddball 869.4; black sheep

3 alien, stranger, foreigner, outsider, nonmember, not one of us, not our sort, not the right sort, the other, outlander,

Uitlander <Afrikaans>, tramontane, ultramontane, barbarian, foreign devil <China>, *gringo* <Sp Amer>; **exile**, outcast, outlaw, wanderer, refugee, émigré, displaced person *or* DP, *déraciné* <Fr>; the Wandering Jew

4 **newcomer, new arrival**, *novus homo* <L>; *arriviste* <Fr>, Johnny-come-lately <nonformal>, new boy <Brit>; **tenderfoot**, greenhorn; settler, emigrant, immigrant; recruit, rookie <nonformal>; **intruder, squatter**, gate-crasher, stowaway

ADJS 5 **extraneous, foreign, alien**, strange, exotic, foreign-looking; unearthly, extraterrestrial 1070.26; exterior, **external**; extrinsic 767.3; ulterior, outside, outland, outlandish; barbarian, barbarous, barbaric; foreign-born; intrusive

ADVS 6 **abroad**, in foreign parts; oversea, **overseas**, beyond seas; on one's travels

WORD ELEMENTS 7 ep—, epi—, eph—, ex—, exo—, ef—, xen—, xeno—

774 RELATION

NOUNS 1 **relation, relationship, connection;** relatedness, connectedness, **association** 617, **affiliation**, filiation, bond, union, alliance, **tie**, tie-in <nonformal>, link, linkage, linking, linkup, liaison, **addition** 253, adjunct 254, junction 799.1, **combination** 804, assemblage 769; deduction 255.1, disjunction 801.1, **contrariety** 778, **disagreement** 788, negative *or* bad relation; **positive** *or* **good relation, affinity, rapport**, mutual attraction, sympathy, accord 455; **closeness**, propinquity, **proximity**, approximation, contiguity, nearness 223, intimacy; **relations, dealings**, affairs, business, transactions, doings *and* truck <both nonformal>, intercourse; **similarity** 783, homology

2 **relativity**, dependence, contingency; **relativism**, indeterminacy, uncertainty, variability, variance; **interrelation, correlation** 776

3 **kinship**, common source *or* stock *or* descent *or* ancestry, consanguinity, agnation, cognation, enation, blood relationship 559; family relationship, affinity 564.1

4 **relevance, pertinence**, pertinency, cogency, relatedness, materiality, **appositeness**, germaneness; application, applicability, effect, appropriateness; **connection**, reference, **bearing**, concern, concernment, interest, respect, regard

VERBS 5 **relate to**, refer to, **apply to, bear on** *or* **upon**, respect, regard, **concern, involve**, touch, affect, interest; **pertain, pertain to**, appertain, appertain to, belong to, fit; **agree, agree with**, answer to, correspond to, chime with; **have to do with**, have connection with, link with *or* link up with, connect, tie in with <nonformal>, liaise with <nonformal>, deal with, treat of, touch upon

6 **relate, associate, connect**, interconnect, ally, link, link up, wed, marry, marry up, weld, bind, tie, couple, bracket, equate, identify; bring into relation with, bring to bear upon, apply; **parallel**, parallelize, draw a parallel; **interrelate**, relativize, **correlate** 776.4

ADJS 7 **relative, comparative**, relational; **relativistic**, indeterminate, uncertain, variable; **connective, linking**, associative; **relating**, pertaining, appertaining, pertinent, referring, referable

8 **approximate**, approximating, approximative, proximate; **near, close** 223.14; **comparable**, relatable, commensurable; **proportional**, proportionate, proportionable; correlative; **like**, homologous, similar 783.10

9 **related, connected; linked**, tied, coupled, knotted, twinned, wedded, wed, married *or* married up, welded, conjugate, bracketed, bound, yoked, spliced, conjoined, conjoint, conjunct, joined 799.13; **associated, affiliated**, filiated, **allied**, associate, affiliate; interlocked, **interrelated**, interlinked, involved, implicated, overlapping, interpenetrating, **correlated;** in the same category, of that kind *or* sort *or* ilk; parallel, collateral; **congenial**, *en rapport* <Fr>, sympathetic, compatible, affinitive

10 **kindred, akin, related**, of common source *or* stock *or* descent *or* ancestry, agnate, cognate, enate, connate, connatural, congeneric *or* congenerous, consanguine *or* consanguineous, genetically related, related by blood 559.6, affinal 564.4

11 **relevant, pertinent**, appertaining, **germane, apposite**, cogent, material, admissible, applicable, applying, pertaining, belonging, involving, appropriate, **apropos**, *à propos* <Fr>, to the purpose, **to the point**, in point, *ad rem* <L>

ADVS 12 **relatively**, comparatively, proportionately, not absolutely, to a degree, to an extent, to some extent; **relevantly**, pertinently, appositely, germanely

PREPS 13 **with** *or* **in relation to**, with *or* in reference to, **with** *or* **in regard to**, with respect to, in respect to *or* of, in what concerns, relative to, **relating** *or* **pertaining to,** pertinent to, appertaining to, referring to, in relation with, **in connection with,** apropos of, speaking of; **as to,** as for, as respects, as regards; in the matter of, on the subject of, in point of, on the score of; re, *in re* <L>; **about,** anent, of, on, upon, **concerning,** touching, respecting, **regarding**

775 UNRELATEDNESS

NOUNS **1 unrelatedness,** irrelativeness, irrelation; **irrelevance,** irrelevancy, impertinence, inappositeness, uncogency, ungermaneness, immateriality, inapplicability; inconnection *or* disconnection, inconsequence, independence; **unconnectedness,** separateness, delinkage, discreteness, dissociation, disassociation, disjuncture, disjunction 801.1

2 misconnection, misrelation, wrong *or* invalid linking, **mismatch,** mismatching, misalliance, *mésalliance* <Fr>; misapplication, misapplicability, misreference

3 an irrelevance, *or* irrelevancy, quite another thing, something else again *and* a whole nother thing *and* a whole different story *and* a whole different ball game <all nonformal>

VERBS **4 not concern,** not involve, not imply, not implicate, not entail, not relate to, not connect with, have nothing to do with, have no business with, cut no ice *and* make no never mind <both nonformal>

5 foist, drag in 213.6; impose on 643.7

ADJS **6 unrelated,** irrelative, unrelatable, unrelational, **unconnected,** unallied, unlinked, **unassociated,** unaffiliated *or* disaffiliated; disrelated, disconnected, dissociated, detached, discrete, disjunct, removed, **separated,** segregated, apart, other, independent, marked off, bracketed; **isolated,** insular; **foreign, alien,** strange, exotic, outlandish; incommensurable, incomparable; extraneous 767.3

7 irrelevant, irrelative; **impertinent, inapposite,** ungermane, uncogent, inconsequent, inapplicable, immaterial, inappropriate, inadmissible; wide of *or* away from the point, *nihil ad rem* <L>, **beside the point,** beside the mark, wide of the mark, **beside the question,** off the subject, not to the purpose, **nothing to do with the case,** not at issue, out-of-the-way; **unessential,** nonessential, extraneous, extrinsic 767.3; incidental, parenthetical

8 farfetched, remote, distant, out-of-the-way, strained, forced, dragged in, neither here nor there, brought in from nowhere; **imaginary** 985.19; improbable 968.3

ADVS **9 irrelevantly,** irrelatively, impertinently, inappositely, ungermanely, uncogently, amiss; without connection, without reference *or* regard

776 CORRELATION

NOUNS **1 correlation,** corelation; correlativity, correlativism; **reciprocation,** reciprocity, reciprocality, two-edged sword, relativity 774.2; **mutuality,** communion, community, commutuality; **common denominator,** common factor; proportionality, direct *or* inverse relationship, direct *or* inverse ratio, direct *or* inverse proportion, covariation; **equilibrium, balance,** symmetry 264; **correspondence, equivalence,** equipollence, coequality

2 interrelation, interrelationship; **interconnection,** interlocking, interdigitation, intercoupling, interlinking, interlinkage, interalliance, interassociation, interaffiliation, interdependence, interdependency

3 interaction, interworking, intercourse, intercommunication, **interplay;** alternation, seesaw; **meshing,** intermeshing, mesh, engagement; **complementation,** complementary relation, complementary distribution; **interweaving,** interlacing, intertwining 740.1; **interchange** 862, tit for tat, trade-off, *quid pro quo* <L>; **concurrence** 898, coaction, **cooperation** 450; codependency

4 correlate, correlative; **correspondent,** analogue, counterpart; reciprocator, reciprocatist; each other, one another

VERBS **5 correlate,** corelate; **interrelate, interconnect,** interassociate, interlink, intercouple, interlock, interdigitate, interally, intertie, interjoin, interdepend

6 interact, interwork, **interplay;** mesh, intermesh, engage, fit, fit like a glove, dovetail, mortise; **interweave,** interlace, intertwine; **interchange;** coact, **cooperate;** codepend

7 reciprocate, correspond, correspond to, respond to, answer, answer to, go tit-for-tat; **complement,** coequal; **cut both ways,** cut two ways

ADJS **8 correlative,** corelative, correlational, corelational; **correlated,** corelated; **interrelated, interconnected,** interassociated, interallied, interaffiliated, interlinked, in-

terlocked, intercoupled, intertied, interdependent

9 **interacting,** interactive, interworking, in-
terplaying; in gear, in mesh; dovetailed,
mortised; **cooperative,** cooperating 450.5

10 **reciprocal,** reciprocative, tit-for-tat, seesaw, seesawing; **corresponding,** correspondent, answering, analogous, homologous, equipollent, tantamount, equivalent, coequal; **complementary,** complemental

11 **mutual,** commutual, **common, joint,
communal,** shared, sharing, conjoint; respective, two-way

ADVS 12 **reciprocally,** back and forth, backward and forward, backwards and forwards, alternately, seesaw, to and fro;
vice versa

13 **mutually, commonly,** communally,
jointly; respectively, each to each; *entre
nous* <Fr>, *inter se* <L>

WORD ELEMENTS 14 equi—

777 SAMENESS

NOUNS 1 **sameness, identity,** identicalness,
selfsameness, indistinguishability, un-
differentiation, nondifferentiation, two
peas in a pod; **coincidence,** correspondence, agreement, congruence; **equivalence, equality** 789, coequality; **syn-
onymousness,** synonymity, synonymy;
oneness, unity, homogeneity, consubstantiality

2 **identification,** likening, unification, coalescence, combination, union, fusion,
merger, blending, melding, synthesis

3 **the same, selfsame,** very same, one and
the same, identical same, no other, none
other, very *or* actual thing, a distinction
without a difference, the same difference
<nonformal>; **equivalent** 783.3; **syn-
onym;** homonym, homograph, homophone; ditto <nonformal>, *idem* <L>,
ipsissima verba <L, the very words>; **duplicate,** double, clone *and* cookie-cutter
copy <both nonformal>, *Doppelgänger*
<Ger>, twin, very image, look-alike,
dead ringer <nonformal>, the image of,
the picture of, spitting image *and* spit and
image <both nonformal>, **exact counterpart, copy** 784.1,3–5, replica, facsimile,
carbon copy

VERBS 4 **coincide, correspond,** agree, chime
with, match, tally, go hand in glove with,
twin

5 **identify,** make one, **unify,** unite, join,
combine, coalesce, synthesize, merge,
blend, meld, fuse 804.3

6 **reproduce,** copy, reduplicate, **duplicate,**
ditto <nonformal>, clone

ADJS 7 **identical,** identic; **same, selfsame,**
one, **one and the same,** all the same, all
one, of the same kidney; **indistinguishable,** without distinction, without difference, undifferent, undifferentiated; **alike,
all alike, like** 783.10, just alike, exactly
alike, like two peas in a pod; **duplicate,**
reduplicated, twin; **homogeneous,** consubstantial

8 **coinciding,** coincident, coincidental; **corresponding,** correspondent, congruent;
synonymous, equivalent, six of one and
half a dozen of the other <nonformal>;
equal 789.7, coequal, coextensive, coterminous; in *or* at parity

ADVS 9 **identically,** synonymously, **alike;**
coincidentally, correspondently, correspondingly, congruently; **equally** 789.11,
coequally, coextensively, coterminously;
on the same footing, on all fours with;
likewise, the same way, just the same, as
is, ditto, same here <nonformal>; *ibid
and ibidem* <both L>

778 CONTRARIETY

NOUNS 1 **contrariety, oppositeness, opposition** 451; **antithesis, contrast,** contraposition 215, counterposition, contradiction,
contraindication, contradistinction; **antagonism,** repugnance, oppugnance,
oppugnancy, **hostility,** perversity, nay-
saying, negativeness, orneriness <nonfor-
mal>, inimicalness, **antipathy,** scunner
<nonformal>; **confrontation,** showdown,
standoff, Mexican standoff <nonfor-
mal>, clashing, collision, cross-purposes
456.2, conflict; polarity; discrepancy, inconsistency, **disagreement** 788

2 **the opposite, the contrary, the antithesis,
the reverse,** the other way round *or*
around, the inverse, the converse, the obverse, the counter; **the other side,** the
mirror *or* reverse image, the other side of
the coin, the flip *or* B side <nonformal>;
the direct *or* polar opposite, the other *or*
opposite extreme; antipode, antipodes;
countercheck *or* counterbalance *or* counterpoise, offset, setoff; **opposite pole,**
antipole, counterpole, counterpoint; opposite number <nonformal>, vis-à-vis;
antonym, opposite, opposite term, coun-
terterm

3 (contrarieties when joined or coexisting)
self-contradiction, **paradox** 788.2, antinomy, oxymoron, ambivalence, **irony,**
enantiosis, equivocation, **ambiguity**

VERBS **4 go contrary to, run counter to,** counter, **contradict,** contravene, controvert, fly in the face of, be *or* play at cross-purposes, go against; **oppose,** be opposed to, go *or* run in opposition to, side against; **conflict with,** come in conflict with, oppugn, conflict, clash; contrast with, **offset,** set off, countercheck *or* counterbalance, countervail; **counteract,** counterwork; counterpose *or* contrapose, counterpoise, juxtapose in opposition

5 reverse, transpose 205.5, flip <nonformal>

ADJS **6 contrary;** contrarious, perverse, **opposite,** antithetic, antithetical, **contradictory,** counter, contrapositive, contrasted; **converse, reverse,** obverse, inverse; **adverse,** adversative *or* adversive, adversarial, **opposing, opposed,** oppositive, oppositional; anti <nonformal>, dead against; **antagonistic,** repugnant, oppugnant, perverse, contrarious, ornery <nonformal>, nay-saying, negative, hostile, combative, bellicose, belligerent, inimical, antipathetic, antipathetical, discordant; inconsistent, discrepant, conflicting, clashing, at cross-purposes, confronting, **confrontational,** confrontive, squared off <nonformal>, eyeball to eyeball *and* toe-to-toe <both nonformal>, at loggerheads; contradistinct; antonymous; countervailing, counterpoised, balancing, counterbalancing, compensating

7 diametric, diametrical, diametrically opposite, at opposite poles, in polar opposition, antipodal *or* antipodean; opposite as black and white *or* light and darkness *or* day and night *or* fire and water *or* the poles, etc, "Hyperion to a satyr"—Shakespeare

8 self-contradictory, **paradoxical,** antinomic, oxymoronic, ambivalent, **ironic;** equivocal, **ambiguous**

ADVS **9** contrarily, contrariwise, counter, conversely, inversely, **vice versa,** topsy-turvy, upside down, arsy-varsy <nonformal>, **on the other hand,** *per contra* <L>, **on** *or* **to the contrary,** *tout au contraire* <Fr>, at loggerheads, in flat opposition; rather, nay rather, quite the contrary, otherwise 779.11, just the other way, just the other way around, **oppositely,** just the opposite *or* reverse; by contraries, by way of opposition; against the grain, *à rebours* <Fr>; contrariously, perversely, ornerily <nonformal>

PREPS **10 opposite,** over against, contra, in contrast with, contrary to, vis-à-vis

WORD ELEMENTS **11** con—, contra—, counter—

779 DIFFERENCE

NOUNS **1 difference,** otherness, separateness, discreteness, distinctness, **distinction;** unlikeness, **dissimilarity** 786; **variation,** variance, variegation, variety, **mixture** 796, **heterogeneity, diversity; deviation,** divergence *or* divergency, departure; **disparity,** gap, inequality 790, odds; **discrepancy,** inconsistency, inconsonance, incongruity, discongruity, unconformity *or* nonconformity, disconformity, **strangeness** 869, unorthodoxy 688, incompatibility, irreconcilability; culture gap; **disagreement, dissent** 333, disaccord *or* disaccordance, inaccordance, discordance, dissonance, inharmoniousness, inharmony; **contrast,** opposition, **contrariety** 778; a far cry, a whale of a difference <nonformal>

2 margin, wide *or* narrow margin, **differential;** differentia, distinction, point of difference; **nicety, subtlety,** refinement, delicacy, nice *or* fine *or* delicate *or* **subtle distinction,** fine point; shade *or* particle of difference, **nuance,** hairline; **seeming difference,** distinction without a difference

3 a different thing, a different story <nonformal>, **something else,** something else again <nonformal>, *tertium quid* <L, a third something>, *autre chose* <Fr>, another kettle of fish <nonformal>, another tune, different breed of cat <nonformal>, another can of worms, horse of a different color, bird of another feather; **nothing of the kind,** no such thing, **quite another thing; other, another,** tother *and* whole nother thing *and* different ball game *and* whole different ball game <all nonformal>

4 differentiation, differencing, **discrimination,** distinguishing, **distinction;** demarcation, limiting, drawing the line; **separation, separateness,** discreteness 801.1, division, atomization, anatomization, analysis, disjunction, segregation, severance, severalization; **modification, alteration, change** 851, variation, diversification, disequalization; **particularization,** specification, individualization, individuation, personalization, specialization

VERBS **5 differ, vary,** diverge, stand apart, be distinguished *or* distinct; **deviate from,** diverge from, divaricate from, depart from; **disagree with,** disaccord with, conflict with, contrast with, stand over against, clash with, jar with; not be like, bear no resemblance to 786.2, not square with, not accord with, not go on all fours with

6 **differentiate,** difference; **distinguish, make a distinction, discriminate, secern; separate,** sever, severalize, segregate, divide; **demarcate,** mark, mark out *or* off, set off, set apart, draw a line, set limits; **modify,** vary, diversify, disequalize, **change** 851.5,6; **particularize,** individualize, individuate, personalize, specify, specialize; atomize, analyze, anatomize, disjoin; split hairs, sharpen *or* refine a distinction, chop logic

ADJS 7 **different,** differing; unlike, not like, **dissimilar** 786.4; **distinct,** distinguished, differentiated, discriminated, discrete, separated, separate, disjoined 801.21, widely apart; **various,** variant, varying, varied, heterogeneous, multifarious, motley, assorted, variegated, diverse, divers, **diversified** 782.4; **several,** many; **divergent,** deviative, diverging, deviating, departing; **disparate,** unequal 790.4; **discrepant,** inconsistent, inconsonant, incongruous, incongruent, unconformable, incompatible, irreconcilable; **disagreeing,** in disagreement; **at odds,** at variance, clashing, inaccordant, disaccordant, discordant, dissonant, inharmonious, out of tune; **contrasting,** contrasted, poles apart, poles asunder, worlds apart; **contrary** 778.6; **discriminable,** separable, severable

8 **other, another,** whole nother <nonformal>, else, otherwise, other than *or* from; not the same, not the type <nonformal>, not that sort, of another sort, of a sort *and* of sorts <both nonformal>; **unique,** one of a kind, rare, **special,** peculiar, *sui generis* <L, of its own kind>, in a class by itself

9 **differentiative,** differentiating, diacritic, diacritical, differential; **distinguishing,** discriminating, discriminative, discriminatory, characterizing, individualizing, individuating, personalizing, differencing, separative; diagnostic; **distinctive,** contrastive, characteristic, peculiar, idiosyncratic

ADVS 10 **differently,** diversely, variously; in a different manner, in another way, with a difference; differentiatingly, distinguishingly

11 **otherwise,** in other ways, **in other respects;** elsewise, else, or else; than; other

than; **on the other hand;** contrarily 778.9; alias

WORD ELEMENTS **12** all—, de—, dis—, heter—, xen—

780 UNIFORMITY

NOUNS 1 **uniformity, evenness,** equability; **steadiness,** stability 854, steadfastness, firmness, unbrokenness, seamlessness, constancy, unwaveringness, undeviatingness, persistence, perseverance, continuity, **consistency;** consonance, correspondence, accordance; unity, **homogeneity,** consubstantiality, monolithism; **equanimity,** equilibrium, unruffledness, serenity, tranquility, calm, calmness, cool <nonformal>

2 **regularity, constancy,** invariability, unvariation, undeviation, even tenor *or* pace, smoothness, clockwork regularity; **sameness** 777, **monotony,** monotonousness, undifferentiation, the same old thing <nonformal>, the daily round *or* routine, the treadmill; monotone, drone, dingdong, singsong, monologue

VERBS 3 **persist, prevail,** persevere, run true to form *or* type, continue the same; drag on *or* along; hum, drone

4 **make uniform,** uniformize; **regulate,** regularize, normalize, stabilize, damp; **even, equalize,** symmetrize, harmonize, balance, balance up, equilibrize; **level,** level out *or* off, smooth, smooth out, even, even out, flatten; **homogenize, assimilate,** standardize, stereotype; clone <nonformal>

ADJS 5 **uniform, equable,** equal, **even; level,** flat, smooth; **regular, constant,** steadfast, persistent, continuous; **unvaried,** unruffled, unbroken, seamless, undiversified, undifferentiated, unchanged; invariable, unchangeable, immutable; **unvarying,** undeviating, unchanging, steady, stable; cloned *or* clonish *and* cookie-cutter <all nonformal>; **ordered,** balanced, measured; **orderly,** methodical, systematic, mechanical, faceless, robotlike, automatic; **consistent,** consonant, correspondent, accordant, homogeneous, **alike,** all alike, all of a piece, of a piece, consubstantial, monolithic

6 **same,** wall-to-wall, back-to-back; **monotonous, humdrum,** unrelieved, repetitive, drab, gray, ho-hum <nonformal>, samey <Brit nonformal>, usual, as usual; tedious, boring

ADVS 7 **uniformly,** equably, **evenly;** monot-

onously, in a rut or groove, dully, tediously, routinely, unrelievedly

8 **regularly; constantly, steadily,** continually; **invariably,** without exception, at
every turn, every time one turns around,
all the time, all year round, week in week
out, year in year out, day in day out,
never otherwise; methodically, orderly,
systematically; **always** 828.11; like clockwork

WORD ELEMENTS 9 equi—, hol—, hom—,
is—, mon—

781 NONUNIFORMITY

NOUNS 1 **nonuniformity, unevenness, irregularity,** raggedness, crazy-quilt, choppiness, jerkiness, **disorder** 809; **difference**
779; inequality; **inconstancy, inconsistency,** variability, changeability, changeableness, mutability, capriciousness,
mercuriality, wavering, **instability, unsteadiness; variation, deviation,** deviance, divergence, differentiation, divarication, ramification; versatility,
diversity, diversification, nonformaliza-
tion; **nonconformity,** nonconformism,
unconformity, unconformism, **unorthodoxy; pluralism,** variegation, variety,
variousness, motleyness, dappleness;
multiculturalism, multiculturism

VERBS 2 **diversify, vary,** variegate 47.7, chop
and change, waver, mutate; **differentiate,**
divaricate, diverge, ramify; **differ** 779.5;
dissent 333.4; **disunify,** break up, break
down, fragment, partition, **analyze** 800.6

ADJS 3 **nonuniform,** ununiform, **uneven, irregular,** ragged, erose, choppy, jerky, jagged, rough, disorderly, unsystematic;
different 779.7, unequal, unequable; **inconstant, inconsistent, variable,** varying,
changeable, changing, mutable, capricious, impulsive, mercurial, erratic,
spasmodic, sporadic, wavery, wavering,
unstable, unsteady; deviating, deviative,
deviatory, divergent, divaricate, ramified; **diversified,** variform, diversiform,
nonformal; **nonconformist,** unorthodox;
pluralistic, variegated, various, motley
47.9,12; multicultural, multiracial

ADVS 4 **nonuniformly,** ununiformly, unequally, **unevenly, irregularly,** inconstantly, **inconsistently,** unsteadily,
erratically, spasmodically, by fits and
starts, capriciously, impulsively, sporadically; unsystematically, chaotically,
helter-skelter, higgledy-piggledy; in all
manner of ways, every which way <non-
formal>, all over the shop and all over

the ball park <both nonformal>; here
there and everywhere

WORD ELEMENTS 5 diversi—, vari—,
heter—

782 MULTIFORMITY

NOUNS 1 **multiformity,** multifariousness,
variety, nonuniformity 781, **diversity,** diversification, variation, variegation 47,
variability, versatility, proteanism,
manifoldness, multiplicity, heterogeneity; omniformity, omnifariousness, everything but the kitchen sink <nonformal>,
polymorphism, heteromorphism; al-
lotropy or allotropism <chemistry>;
Proteus, shapeshifting, shapeshifter;
"God's plenty"—Dryden, "her infinite
variety"—Shakespeare

VERBS 2 **diversify, vary,** change form,
change shape, shift shape, ring changes,
cover the spectrum, **variegate** 47.7

ADJS 3 **multiform,** diversiform, variable,
versatile, "of every shape that was not
uniform"—James Russell Lowell; **protean,** proteiform; **manifold,** multifold,
multiplex, multiple, multifarious, multi-
phase; polymorphous, polymorphic,
heteromorphous, heteromorphic, metamorphic; omniform, omniformal, omnifarious, omnigenous; allotropic or al-
lotropical <chemistry>

4 **diversified, varied, assorted,** heterogeneous; **various,** many and various,
divers <old>, diverse, sundry, **several,
many;** of all sorts or conditions or kinds
or shapes or descriptions or types

ADVS 5 **variously, severally,** sundrily, multi-
fariously, diversely, manifoldly

WORD ELEMENTS 6 allo—, diversi—,
heter—, multi—, omni—, parti—,
party—, poecil— or poikil—, poly—,
vari—

783 SIMILARITY

NOUNS 1 **similarity, likeness,** alikeness,
sameness, similitude; **resemblance,** semblance; **analogy, correspondence,** conformity, accordance, agreement, comparability, comparison, **parallelism, parity,**
community, alliance, consimilarity; **approximation,** approach, closeness, nearness; assimilation, likening, **simile, metaphor; simulation, imitation,** copying,
aping, mimicking, taking-off, takeoff,
burlesque, pastiche, pasticcio <Ital>;
identity 777.1

2 **kinship,** affinity, family resemblance or

likeness, family favor, generic or genetic resemblance; connaturality or connaturalness, connature, connateness, congeneracy

3 **likeness,** like, the like of or **the likes of** <nonformal>; suchlike, such; **analogue, parallel;** cognate, congener; **counterpart, complement, correspondent,** pendant, similitude, tally; **approximation,** rough idea, sketch; coordinate, reciprocal, obverse, equivalent; correlate, correlative; **close imitation** or reproduction or copy or facsimile or replica, near duplicate, simulacrum; **close match, match-up, fellow, mate;** soul mate, kindred spirit or soul, **companion, twin,** brother, sister; *mon semblable* <Fr>, second self, alter ego; a chip off the old block; **look-alike,** the image of, the picture of

4 **close** or **striking resemblance,** startling or marked or decided resemblance; close or near likeness; **faint** or **remote resemblance,** mere hint or shadow

5 **set,** group, matching pair or set, his and hers <nonformal>, couple, pair, twins, look-alikes, two of a kind, birds of a feather, peas in a pod

6 (of words or sounds) assonance, alliteration, rhyme, slant rhyme, near rhyme, jingle, clink; pun, paronamasia

VERBS 7 **resemble,** be like, bear resemblance; put one in mind of <nonformal>, remind one of, bring to mind, be reminiscent of, suggest, evoke, call up, call to mind; **look like,** favor <nonformal>, mirror; **take after,** partake of, follow, appear or seem like, sound like; savor or smack of, be redolent of; **have all the earmarks of,** have every appearance of, have all the features of, have all the signs of, have every sign or indication of; **approximate,** approach, near, come near, come close; **compare with,** stack up with <nonformal>; **correspond, match, parallel;** not tell apart, not tell one from the other; **imitate** 336.5, **simulate,** copy, ape, mimic, take off, counterfeit; nearly reproduce or duplicate or reduplicate

8 **similarize,** approximate, assimilate, bring near; connaturalize

9 **assonate,** alliterate, rhyme, chime; pun

ADJS 10 **similar,** like, alike, something like, not unlike; **resembling,** resemblant, following, favoring <nonformal>, savoring or smacking of, suggestive of, **on the order of;** consimilar; **simulated, imitated,** imitation, copied, aped, mimicked, taken off, fake or phony <both nonformal>, counterfeit, **mock,** synthetic, ersatz; nearly

reproduced or duplicated or reduplicated; uniform with, homogeneous, identical 777.7

11 **analogous,** comparable; **corresponding,** correspondent, equivalent; **parallel,** paralleling; **matching,** cast in the same mold, of a kind, of a size, of a piece; duplicate, twin, of the same hue or stripe

12 **such as,** suchlike, so

13 **akin,** affinitive; connatural, connate, cognate, agnate, enate, conspecific, correlative; congenerous, congeneric, congenerical; brothers or sisters under the skin

14 **approximating,** approximative, approximate, approximable; **near, close;** much of a muchness <Brit nonformal>, much the same, much at one, nearly the same, same but different, "like—but oh! how different"—Wordsworth; quasi

15 **very like, mighty like,** powerful like <nonformal>, uncommonly like, remarkably like, extraordinarily like, strikingly like, **ridiculously like, for all the world like,** as like as can be; a lot alike, pretty much the same, the same difference *and* damned little difference <both nonformal>; as like as two peas in a pod, "as lyke as one pease is to another"—John Lyly, "as like as eggs"—Shakespeare, *comme deux gouttes d'eau* <Fr, like two drops of water>; faintly or remotely like

16 **lifelike,** speaking, faithful, living, breathing, to the life, **true to life** or nature; **realistic, natural**

17 (of words or sounds) assonant, assonantal, alliterative, alliteral; **rhyming,** jingling, chiming, punning

ADVS 18 **similarly,** correspondingly, **like, likewise,** either; in the same manner, **in like manner,** in kind; in that way, like that, like this; **thus** 765.10; so; by the same token, by the same sign; identically 777.9

19 **so to speak,** in a manner of speaking, **as it were,** in a manner, in a way; kind of *and* sort of <both nonformal>

784 COPY

NOUNS 1 **copy, representation, facsimile, image,** likeness 783.3, **resemblance,** semblance, similitude, picture, portrait, life mask, death mask, icon, simulacrum; ectype; pastiche, *pasticcio* <Ital>; fair copy, faithful copy; certified copy; **imitation** 336.3, **counterfeit** 354.13, forgery, fake *and* phony <both nonformal>

2 reproduction, duplication, reduplication;

reprography; transcription; tracing, rubbing; mimeography, xerography, hectography

3 duplicate, duplication, dupe *and* ditto <both nonformal>; **double,** cookie-cutter copy, clone; representation, **reproduction, replica,** repro <nonformal>, reduplication, facsimile, model, **counterpart;** a chip off the old block; triplicate, quadruplicate, etc; repetition 848

4 transcript, transcription, apograph, tenor <law>; **transfer,** tracing, rubbing, **carbon copy,** carbon; manifold <old>; microcopy, microform; microfiche, fiche; recording

5 print, offprint; **impression,** impress; **reprint,** proof, reproduction proof, repro proof *and* repro <both nonformal>, second edition; photostatic copy, Photostat <trademark>, stat <nonformal>; mimeograph copy, Ditto copy <trademark>, hectograph copy, xerographic copy, Xerox copy <trademark> *or* Xerox <trademark>; **facsimile,** fax <nonformal>; **photograph,** positive, negative, print, enlargement, contact print, photocopy

6 cast, casting; mold, **molding,** die, stamp, seal

7 reflection, reflex; **shadow,** silhouette, outline 211.2; **echo**

VERBS **8 copy, reproduce,** replicate, **duplicate,** dupe <nonformal>; clone; reduplicate; **transcribe;** trace; double; triplicate, quadruplicate, etc; manifold <old>, multigraph, mimeograph, mimeo, Photostat <trademark>, stat <nonformal>, facsimile, fax <nonformal>, hectograph, ditto, Xerox <trademark>; microcopy, microfilm

ADVS **9** in duplicate, in triplicate, etc

785 MODEL
<thing copied>

NOUNS **1 model, pattern, standard, criterion,** classic example, rule, mirror, paradigm; showpiece, showplace; **original,** urtext, *locus classicus* <L>; **type, prototype,** antetype, **archetype,** genotype, biotype, type specimen, type species; **precedent**

2 example, exemplar; **representative,** type, symbol, emblem, exponent; **exemplification,** illustration, demonstration, explanation; **instance,** relevant instance, **case,** typical example *or* case, case in point, object lesson

3 sample, specimen; piece, taste, swatch; instance, for-instance <nonformal>

4 ideal, beau ideal, ego ideal, ideal type, acme, highest *or* perfect *or* best type; cynosure, apotheosis, idol; **shining example,** role-model, **hero, superhero; model,** the very model, role model, mirror, paragon, epitome, "The glass of fashion and the mould of form, The observ'd of all observers"—Shakespeare; cult figure

5 artist's model, dressmaker's model, photographer's model, mannequin; dummy, lay figure; clay model, wood model, pilot model, mock-up

6 mold, form 262, cast, template, matrix, negative; **die,** punch, stamp, intaglio, seal, mint; last, shoe last

VERBS **7 set an example,** set the pace, lead the way; **exemplify,** epitomize, fit the pattern; **emulate,** follow, hold up as a model, model oneself on

ADJS **8 model, exemplary,** precedential, typical, paradigmatic, representative, standard, normative, classic; ideal

9 prototypal, prototypic, prototypical, archetypal, archetypic, archetypical, antitypic, antitypical

786 DISSIMILARITY

NOUNS **1 dissimilarity,** unsimilarity; **dissimilitude,** dissemblance, **unresemblance; unlikeness,** unsameness; **disparity,** diversity, divergence, gap, **contrast, difference** 779; nonuniformity 781; uncomparability, uncomparableness, incomparability, incomparableness, uncommensurableness, uncommensurability, incommensurableness, incommensurability; culture gap; **disguise,** dissimilation, camouflage, masking; cosmetics; poor imitation, bad likeness *or* copy, botched copy, mere caricature *or* counterfeit

VERBS **2 not resemble, bear no resemblance,** not look like, **not compare with; differ** 779.5; have little *or* nothing in common

3 disguise, dissimilate, camouflage; do a cosmetic job on; vary 851.6

ADJS **4 dissimilar,** unsimilar, unresembling, unresemblant; **unlike, unalike,** unidentical; **disparate,** diverse, divergent, **contrasting, different** 779.7; nonuniform 781.3; scarcely like, hardly like, a bit *or* mite different; **off,** a bit on the off side, offbeat <nonformal>; unmatched, odd, counter, out

5 nothing like, not a bit alike, not a bit of it, **nothing of the sort,** nothing of the kind, something else, something else again

<nonformal>, different as night from day, quite another thing, cast in a different mold, not the same thing at all; not so you could tell it *and* not that you would know it *and* **far from it** *and* far other <all nonformal>; way off, away off, a mile off, way out, no such thing, no such a thing <nonformal>; "no more like than an apple to an oyster"—Sir Thomas More

6 uncomparable, not comparable, not to be compared, incomparable; incommensurable, uncommensurable, uncommensurate, incommensurate

ADVS **7 dissimilarly, differently** 779.10, with a difference, disparately, contrastingly

787 AGREEMENT

NOUNS **1 agreement, accord** 455, accordance; **concord,** concordance; **harmony, cooperation** 450, peace 464, *rapport* <Fr>, concert, consort, **consonance,** unisonance, **unison,** union, chorus, oneness; **correspondence,** coincidence, intersection, overlap, parallelism, symmetry, tally, equivalence 777.1; congeniality, compatibility, affinity; **conformity,** conformance, conformation, uniformity 780; congruity, congruence, congruency; **consistency,** self-consistency, coherence; synchronism, sync <nonformal>, timing; **assent** 332

2 understanding, entente; mutual *or* cordial understanding, consortium, *entente cordiale* <Fr>; **compact** 437

3 <general agreement> consensus, consentaneity, consentaneousness, *consensus omnium* <L, consent of all> *and consensus gentium* <L, consent of the people>, sense, **unanimity** 332.5; **likemindedness,** meeting *or* intersection *or* confluence of minds, sense of the meeting

4 adjustment, adaptation, mutual adjustment, **compromise,** coaptation, arbitration, arbitrament; **regulation,** attunement, harmonization, **coordination,** accommodation, squaring, integration, assimilation; reconciliation, reconcilement, synchronization; consensus-building *or* -seeking

5 fitness *or* fittedness, **suitability, appropriateness,** propriety, admissibility; **aptness,** aptitude, qualification; **relevance** 774.4, felicity, appositeness, applicability

VERBS **6 agree, accord** 455.2, **harmonize, concur** 332.9, have no problem with, go along with <nonformal>, **cooperate**

450.3, **correspond, conform,** coincide, parallel, intersect, overlap, **match,** tally, hit, register, lock, interlock, check <nonformal>, square, dovetail, jibe <nonformal>; **be consistent,** cohere, stand *or* hold *or* hang together, fall in together, fit together, chime, chime with, chime in with; **assent** 332.8, come to an agreement 332.10, be of one *or* the same *or* like mind, see eye to eye, sing in chorus, have a meeting of the minds, climb on the bandwagon; **go together,** go with, conform with, be uniform with, square with, sort *or* assort with, go on all fours with, consist with, register with, answer *or* respond to

7 <make agree> **harmonize,** coordinate, bring into line, accord, make uniform 780.4, equalize 789.6, similarize, assimilate, homologize; **adjust, set,** regulate, **accommodate, reconcile,** synchronize, sync <nonformal>; adapt, fit, tailor, measure, proportion, adjust to, trim to, cut to, gear to, key to; fix, **rectify,** true, true up, right, set right, make plumb; **tune,** attune, put in tune

8 suit, fit, suit *or* fit to a tee, fit like a glove, **qualify, do,** serve, answer, be OK <nonformal>, do the job *and* do the trick *and* fill the bill *and* cut the mustard <all nonformal>

ADJS **9 agreeing, in agreement; in accord, concurring,** positive, affirmative, in rapport, *en rapport* <Fr>, **in harmony,** in accordance, in sync <nonformal>, **at one,** on all fours, of one *or* the same *or* like mind, **like-minded,** consentient, consentaneous, **unanimous** 332.15, unisonous *or* unisonant; **harmonious,** accordant, **concordant,** consonant; **consistent,** self-consistent; uniform, coherent, conformable, of a piece, equivalent, **coinciding** 777.8, coincident, corresponding *or* correspondent; answerable, reconcilable; commensurate, proportionate; **congruous,** congruent; **agreeable,** congenial, compatible, cooperating *or* cooperative 450.5, coexisting *or* coexistent, symbiotic; **synchronized,** synchronous, synchronic

10 apt, apposite, appropriate, suitable; applicable, relevant, likely, sortable, seasonable, opportune; **fitting,** befitting, **suiting,** becoming; **fit,** fitted, qualified, **suited,** adapted, geared, tailored, dovetailing, meshing; **right,** just right, well-chosen, **pat,** happy, felicitous, just what the doctor ordered <nonformal>; to the point, to the purpose, *ad rem* <L>, *à propos* <Fr>, **apropos,** on the button *and* on the money <both nonformal>, spot-on <Brit nonformal>

ADVS 11 in step, in concert, **in unison,** in chorus, **in line, in conformity, in keeping,** hand in glove, just right; with it <nonformal>; **unanimously, as one, with one voice, harmoniously,** concordantly, consonantly, in synchronization, in sync <nonformal>, **by consensus;** agreeably, congenially, compatibly; fittingly

PREPS 12 in agreement with, together with, with, right with, in there with, right along there with; in line with, in keeping with; together on

PHRS 13 that's it, that's the thing, that's just the thing, that's the very thing, that's the idea *and* that's the ticket <both nonformal>; right on <nonformal>; touché

788 DISAGREEMENT

NOUNS 1 disagreement, discord, discordance *or* discordancy; **disaccord** 456, disaccordance, inaccordance; disunity, disunion; **disharmony,** unharmoniousness; dissonance, dissidence; **jarring,** clashing; **difference** 779, **variance,** divergence, diversity; **disparity,** discrepancy, inequality; antagonism, **opposition** 451, **conflict,** controversy, faction, oppugnancy, repugnance, dissension 456.3, argumentation 934.4; **dissent** 333, negation 335, contradiction

2 inconsistency, incongruity, asymmetry, inconsonance, incoherence; **incompatibility,** irreconcilability, incommensurability; disproportion, disproportionateness, nonconformity *or* unconformity, nonconformability *or* unconformability, heterogeneity, heterodoxy, unorthodoxy, heresy; self-contradiction, paradox, antinomy, oxymoron, **ambiguity 539.2,** ambivalence, equivocality, equivocalness, mixed message *or* signal

3 unfitness, inappropriateness, unsuitability, impropriety; **inaptness,** inaptitude, **inappositeness, irrelevance** *or* irrelevancy, infelicity, uncongeniality, inapplicability, inadmissibility; abnormality, anomaly; **maladjustment,** misjoining, misjoinder; mismatch, mismatchment; misalliance, *mésalliance* <Fr>

4 misfit, nonconformist, individualist, inner-directed person, oddball <nonformal>; **freak,** sport, anomaly; naysayer, crosspatch; a fish out of water, a square peg in a round hole <nonformal>

VERBS 5 disagree, differ 779.5, vary, not see eye-to-eye, be at cross-purposes, tangle assholes <nonformal>, **disaccord** 456.8, **conflict,** clash, **jar,** jangle, jostle, collide, square off, cross swords, break, break off; **mismatch,** mismate, mismarry, misally; **dissent** 333.4, agree to disagree, object, **negate** 335.3, **contradict,** counter; be *or* march out of step, "hear a different drummer"—Thoreau

ADJS 6 disagreeing, differing 779.7, **discordant** 456.15, disaccordant; dissonant, dissident; **inharmonious,** unharmonious, disharmonious; discrepant, disproportionate; divergent, variant; at variance, **at odds,** at war, at daggers drawn, at opposite poles, at loggerheads, at cross-purposes; **hostile,** antipathetic, antagonistic, repugnant; inaccordant, out of accord, out of whack <nonformal>; **jarring,** clashing, grating, jangling; **contradictory, contrary; disagreeable,** cross, cranky, ornery <nonformal>, negative, uncongenial, incompatible; immiscible <chem>

7 inappropriate, inapt, unapt, inapposite, misplaced, **irrelevant,** malapropos, *mal à propos* <Fr>; **unsuited,** ill-suited; **unfitted,** ill-fitted; **maladjusted,** unadapted, ill-adapted; ill-sorted, ill-assorted, ill-chosen; ill-matched, ill-mated, mismatched, mismated, mismarried, misallied; **unfit,** inept, unqualified; unfitting, unbefitting; **unsuitable,** improper, **unbecoming,** unseemly; infelicitous, inapplicable, inadmissible; **unseasonable, untimely,** ill-timed; **out of place,** out of line, out of keeping, out of character, out of proportion, out of joint, out of tune, out of time, out of season, out of its element

8 inconsistent, incongruous, inconsonant, inconsequent, incoherent, **incompatible,** irreconcilable; incommensurable, incommensurate; disproportionate, out of proportion, self-contradictory, paradoxical, oxymoronic, **absurd; abnormal,** anomalous

9 nonconformist, individualistic, inner-directed, perverse; **unorthodox,** heterodox, heretical

PREPS 10 in disagreement with, against, agin <nonformal>, counter to, clean counter to, **contrary to,** in defiance of, in contempt of, in opposition to; out of line with, not in keeping with

WORD ELEMENTS 11 contra—, counter—, dis—, ill—, mal—, mis—

789 EQUALITY

NOUNS **1 equality, parity,** par, equation, **identity** 777.1; equivalence *or* equivalency, convertibility, **correspondence,** parallelism , equipollence, coequality; **likeness,** levelness, evenness, coextension; **balance,** poise, equipoise, **equilibrium,** equiponderance; symmetry, proportion; level playing field; **justice** 649, equity

2 equating, equation; equalizing, equilibration, evening, evening up; coordination, integration, accommodation, adjustment; **even break** *and* fair shake <both nonformal>, affirmative action, equal opportunity

3 the same 777.3; **tie, draw, standoff** *and* Mexican standoff *and* wash *and* dead heat <all nonformal>, stalemate, deadlock, impasse, neck-and-neck race, photo finish, even money; tied *or* knotted score; a distinction without a difference, six of one and half a dozen of the other, Tweedledum and Tweedledee

4 equal, match, mate, twin, fellow, **like, equivalent,** opposite number, counterpart, answer <nonformal>, vis à vis, equipollent, coequal, parallel, ditto <nonformal>; **peer,** compeer, colleague, peer group

VERBS **5 equal, match, rival, correspond, be even-steven,** be tantamount to, be equal to; **keep pace with, keep step with, run abreast; amount to,** come to, come down to, run to, reach, touch; **measure up to,** come up to, stack up with <nonformal>, match up with; lie on a level with, **balance, parallel,** ditto <nonformal>; break even <nonformal>; **tie, draw,** knot

6 equalize; equate; even, equal out, even up, even off, square, level, level out, level off, make both ends meet; **balance,** strike a balance, poise, balance out, balance the accounts, balance the books; **compensate,** make up for, counterpoise; countervail, counterbalance, cancel; coordinate, integrate, proportion; fit, accommodate, adjust

ADJS **7 equal, equalized,** like, **alike, even,** level, par, **on a par,** at par, at parity, au pair, commensurate, proportionate; on the same level, on the same plane, on the same *or* equal footing; on terms of equality, **on even** *or* **equal terms,** on even ground; on a level, on a level playing field, on a footing, in the same boat; **square,** quits, zero-sum, even steven <nonformal>; half-and-half, **fifty-fifty;**

nip and tuck, **drawn, tied,** neck-and-neck <nonformal>, too close to call, deadlocked, stalemated, knotted

8 equivalent, tantamount, equiparant, equipollent, coequal, coordinate; **identical** 777.7; corresponding *or* correspondent; convertible, much the same, as broad as long, neither more nor less, **all one,** all the same, neither here nor there

9 balanced, poised, apoise, **on an even keel;** equibalanced, equiponderant *or* equiponderous

10 equisized, equidimensional, equiproportional, equispaced; equiangular, isogonic, isometric; equilateral, equisided

ADVS **11 equally, correspondingly, proportionately,** equivalently, **evenly; identically** 777.9; without distinction, indifferently; to the same degree, *ad eundem* <L>; as, **so;** as well; to all intents and purposes, other things being equal, *ceteris paribus* <L>; as much as to say

12 to a standoff <nonformal>, to a tie *or* draw

WORD ELEMENTS **13** co—, equi—, aequi—, homal—, is—, pari—

790 INEQUALITY

NOUNS **1 inequality, disparity, unevenness,** contrariety 778, **difference** 779; **irregularity,** nonuniformity 781, heterogeneity; **disproportion,** asymmetry; **unbalance,** imbalance, disequilibrium, overbalance, inclination of the balance, overcompensation, tippiness; **inadequacy,** insufficiency, shortcoming; **odds,** handicap; **injustice,** inequity, unfair discrimination, second-class citizenship, untouchability

VERBS **2 unequalize,** disproportion

3 unbalance, disbalance, disequilibrate, overbalance, overcompensate, **throw off balance,** upset, skew

ADJS **4 unequal,** disparate, **uneven; irregular** 781.3; disproportionate, **out of proportion,** skew, skewed, asymmetric *or* asymmetrical; mismatched *or* ill-matched, ill-sorted; **inadequate,** insufficient

5 unbalanced, ill-balanced, overbalanced, off-balance, tippy, listing, heeling, leaning, canted, top-heavy; **lopsided,** slaunchways *and* cockeyed *and* skewgee *and* skygodlin <all nonformal>, skew-whiff <Brit nonformal>; **unstable,** unsteady, tender <nautical>

ADVS **6 unequally,** disparately, disproportionately, variously, **unevenly;** nonuniformly 781.4

791 WHOLE

NOUNS **1 whole, totality, entirety,** collectivity; complex; integration, embodiment; **unity, integrity, wholeness;** organic unity, oneness; integer

2 total, sum, sum total, sum and substance, **the amount,** whole *or* gross amount, grand total

3 all, the whole, the entirety, everything, all the above *or* all of the above <both nonformal>, the aggregate, the assemblage, one and all, all and sundry, each and every <nonformal>; **package,** set, complement, package deal; **the lot,** the corpus, all she wrote <nonformal>, **the ensemble; be-all,** be-all and end-all, beginning and end, "alpha and omega"— Bible, A to Z, A to izzard, the whole range *or* spectrum, length and breadth; everything from soup to nuts *and* everything but the kitchen sink <both nonformal>

4 <nonformal terms> **whole bunch, whole mess, whole caboodle, the kit and caboodle, whole kit and caboodle,** whole kit and boodle, whole bit *or* shtick, whole megillah, **whole shooting match,** whole hog, whole animal <old>, **whole deal,** whole schmear, **whole shebang,** whole works, the works, whole ball of wax, whole show, whole nine yards

5 wholeness, totality, **completeness** 793, **unity, fullness,** inclusiveness, exhaustiveness, comprehensiveness; holism, holistic *or* total approach; universality

6 major part, best part, better part, **most; majority,** generality, plurality; **bulk, mass,** body, main body; **lion's share; substance,** gist, meat, essence, thrust, gravamen

VERBS **7 form** *or* **make a whole,** constitute a whole; **integrate,** unite, form a unity

8 total, amount to, come to, run to *or* **into,** mount up to, add up to, tot *or* tot up to <nonformal>, tote *or* tote up to <nonformal>, reckon up to <nonformal>, aggregate to; aggregate, unitize; **number, comprise,** contain, encompass

ADJS **9** <not partial> **whole, total, entire,** aggregate, gross, all; integral, integrated; **one,** one and indivisible; **inclusive,** all-inclusive, **exhaustive,** comprehensive, omnibus, all-embracing; holistic; universal

10 intact, untouched, undamaged 1001.8, all in one piece <nonformal>, unimpaired, virgin, pristine, unspoiled

11 undivided, uncut, unsevered, unclipped, uncropped, unshorn; **undiminished,** unreduced, complete

12 unabridged, uncondensed, unexpurgated

ADVS **13** <not partially> **wholly, entirely,** all; **totally,** *in toto* <L>, from start to finish, from soup to nuts <nonformal>, from A to Z, from A to izzard, across the board; **altogether, all put together,** in its entirety, *tout ensemble* <Fr>; **in all,** on all counts, in all respects, at large; **as a whole, in the aggregate,** in the lump, in the gross, in bulk, in the mass, *en masse* <Fr>, *en bloc* <Fr>; **collectively, corporately,** bodily, in a body, as a body; lock, stock, and barrel; hook, line, and sinker

14 on the whole, in the long run, over the long haul, all in all, to all intents and purposes, on balance, **by and large, in the main, mainly, mostly, chiefly,** substantially, essentially, effectually, **for the most part,** almost entirely, for all practical purposes, **virtually;** approximately, nearly, all but

WORD ELEMENTS **15** pan—, pant—, panta—, coen—

792 PART

NOUNS **1 part, portion, fraction;** percentage; **division** 801.1; **share,** parcel, dole, quota, piece *or* piece of the action <nonformal>; cut *and* slice *and* vigorish <all nonformal>; **section,** sector, **segment;** quarter, quadrant; **item,** detail, particular; installment; **subdivision,** subset, subgroup, subspecies; detachment, contingent; **cross section,** sample, random sample, sampling; **component** 795.2, module, constituent, ingredient; **adjunct** 254; **remainder** 256

2 <part of writing> section, front *or* back matter, prologue, epilogue, foreword, preface, introduction, afterword, text, chapter, verse, article; sentence, clause, phrase, segment, string, constituent, paragraph, passage; number, book, fascicle; sheet, folio, page, signature, gathering

3 piece, particle, bit, scrap 248.3, bite, **fragment, morsel, crumb,** shard, potsherd, snatch, snack; **cut,** cutting, clip, clipping, paring, shaving, rasher, snip, snippet, chip, slice, collop, dollop, scoop; **tatter, shred,** stitch; **splinter,** sliver; **shiver, smithereen** <nonformal>; **lump,** gob <nonformal>, gobbet, **hunk, chunk; stump,** butt, end, butt-end, fag-end, tail-end; modicum 248.2, moiety; sound bite, outtake

4 member, organ; appendage; **limb**; **branch**, imp, bough, twig, sprig, spray, switch; runner, tendril; **off-shoot**, ramification, scion, spur; **arm** 905.5, **leg**, tail; hand 474.4; **wing**, pinion; lobe, lobule, hemisphere

5 dose, portion; slug *and* shot *and* nip *and* snort *and* dram <all nonformal>

VERBS **6 separate**, apportion, share, share out, distribute, cut, cut up, slice, slice up, divide 801.18; **analyze** 800.6

ADJS **7 partial**, part; **fractional**, sectional, componential; segmentary, segmental, modular; **fragmentary**; incomplete 794.4, open-ended

ADVS **8 partly, partially**, part, **in part**

9 piece by piece, bit by bit, part by part, **little by little**, inch by inch, foot by foot, drop by drop; **piecemeal**, piecewise, bitwise, inchmeal, by inchmeal; **by degrees**, by inches; **by** *or* **in snatches**, by *or* in installments, in lots, in small doses, in driblets, in dribs and drabs; in detail

WORD ELEMENTS **10** organo—; chir—; ali—, pter—, pterus—, pteryg—

793 COMPLETENESS

NOUNS **1 completeness, totality; wholeness** 791.5, entireness, **entirety; unity, integrity,** integrality, undividedness, intactness, untouchedness, unbrokenness; solidity, solidarity; **thoroughness,** exhaustiveness, unstintedness, inclusiveness, comprehensiveness, universality; pervasiveness, ubiquity, omnipresence; **universe,** cosmos, plenum

2 fullness, full; **amplitude, plenitude;** impletion, **repletion,** plethora; saturation, saturation point, satiety, congestion

3 full measure, fill, full house, "good measure, pressed down, and shaken together, and running over"—Bible; **load, capacity, complement,** lading, **charge;** the whole bit <nonformal>; bumper, brimmer; bellyful *and* snootful <both nonformal>, skinful *or* mouthful <both nonformal>; **crush,** cram <nonformal>, jam-up <nonformal>

4 completion, fulfillment, consummation, culmination, perfection, realization, actualization, **accomplishment** 407, topping-off, closure

5 limit, end 819, **extremity,** extreme, **acme,** apogee, climax, **maximum,** max <nonformal>, ceiling, **peak,** summit, **pinnacle,** crown, top; **utmost,** uttermost, utmost extent, highest degree, nth degree *or* power, *ne plus ultra* <L>; **all, the whole** 791.3, 4

VERBS **6** <make whole> **complete,** bring to completion *or* fruition, mature; **fill in, fill out,** piece out, top off, eke *or* eke out, round out; **make up,** make good, replenish, refill; **accomplish** 407.4, fulfill

7 fill, charge, load, lade, freight, weight; **stuff, wad,** pad, **pack,** crowd, **cram,** jam, jam-pack, ram in, chock; **fill up,** fill to the brim, brim, top up *or* top off, fill to overflowing, fill the measure of; supercharge, saturate, satiate, congest; overfill 992.15, make burst at the seams, surfeit

8 <be thorough> **go to all lengths, go all out, go the limit** <nonformal>, go the whole way, **go the whole hog** <nonformal>, cover a lot of ground, make a federal case of *and* make a big deal of *and* do up brown *and* do with a vengeance <all nonformal>, **see it through** <nonformal>, follow out *or* up, follow *or* prosecute to a conclusion; leave nothing undone, not overlook a bet *and* use every trick in the book <both nonformal>; **move heaven and earth, leave no stone unturned**

ADJS **9 complete, whole, total,** global, **entire,** intact, solid; **full, full-fledged,** full-dress, **full-scale;** full-grown, mature, matured, ripe, developed; **uncut,** unabbreviated, undiminished, unexpurgated

10 thorough, thoroughgoing, thorough-paced, exhaustive, intensive, broad-based, wall-to-wall <nonformal>, house-to-house *and* door-to-door <both nonformal>, A-to-Z, comprehensive, all-embracing, all-encompassing, omnibus, radical, sweeping; **pervasive,** all-pervading, ubiquitous, omnipresent, **universal; unmitigated, unqualified, unconditional,** unrestricted, unreserved, **all-out,** wholesale, whole-hog <nonformal>; **out-and-out, through-and-through,** outright, downright, straight; congenital, born, **consummate,** unmitigated, unalloyed, perfect, veritable, egregious, deep-dyed, dyed-in-the-wool; **utter, absolute, total; sheer,** clear, clean, **pure,** plumb <nonformal>, **plain,** regular <nonformal>

11 full, filled, **replete,** plenary, capacity, flush, round; **brimful,** brimming; **chock-full,** chock-a-block, chuck-full, **cram-full,** topful; **jam-full, jam-packed, overcrowded;** stuffed, overstuffed, **packed,** crammed, *farci* <Fr>; **swollen** 259.13, bulging, bursting, bursting at the seams, ready to burst, full to bursting, fit to bust <nonformal>; as full as a tick, packed like sardines *or* herrings; standing room only *or* SRO; **saturated,** satiated, soaked; congested; overfull 992.20, surfeited

12 **fraught,** freighted, **laden, loaded, charged,** burdened; heavy-laden; full-laden, full-fraught, full-charged, super-charged

13 **completing, fulfilling,** filling; completive *or* completory, consummative *or* consummatory, culminative, perfective; **complementary,** complemental

ADVS 14 **completely, totally,** globally, **entirely, wholly, fully,** integrally, roundly, **altogether,** hundred percent, **exhaustively,** inclusively, comprehensively, bag and baggage *and* lock, stock, and barrel <both nonformal>; **unconditionally,** unrestrictedly, unreservedly, with no strings attached, no ifs, ands, or buts; **one and all;** outright, *tout à fait* <Fr>; **thoroughly,** inside out <nonformal>; in full, in full measure; to the hilt

15 **absolutely, perfectly, quite,** right, stark, clean, sheer, plumb <nonformal>, plain; irretrievably, unrelievedly, irrevocably

16 **utterly, to the utmost,** all the way, **all out,** flat out <Brit>, *à outrance* <Fr>, *à toute outrance* <Fr>, hammer and tongs *and* tooth and nail <both nonformal>; **to the full, to the limit,** to the max <nonformal>, to the backbone, to the marrow, to the nth degree *or* power, to the sky *or* skies, to the top of one's bent, **to a fare-thee-well,** to a fare-you-well *or* fare-ye-well, to beat the band *or* the Dutch *and* nine ways to Sunday <both nonformal>, with a vengeance, all hollow <nonformal>

17 **throughout, all over,** overall, **inside and out, through and through;** through thick and thin, down to the ground <nonformal>, **from the ground up,** from the word 'go' *and* from the git-go <both nonformal>; **to the end** *or* **bitter end,** to the death; **at full length,** *in extenso* <L>, *ad infinitum* <L>; every inch, every whit, every bit; root and branch, head and shoulders, heart and soul; to the brim, to the hilt, neck deep, up to the ears, up to the eyes; **in every respect,** in all respects, you name it <nonformal>; **on all counts,** at all points, for good and all

18 **from beginning to end, from start to finish,** from end to end, **from first to last, from A to Z,** from A to izzard, from soup to nuts *and* from hell to breakfast <both nonformal>, from cover to cover; **from top to bottom,** *de fond en comble* <Fr>; from top to toe, **from head to foot,** *a cap-*

ite ad calcem <L>, cap-a-pie; **from stem to stern,** from clew to earing, fore and aft; from soup to nuts <nonformal>, *ab ovo usque ad mala*—<L, from eggs to apples>—Horace

WORD ELEMENTS 19 hol—, integri—, pan—, per—, tel—, teleut—

794 INCOMPLETENESS

NOUNS 1 **incompleteness,** incompletion; **deficiency,** defectiveness, imperfection, **inadequacy;** underdevelopment, hypoplasia, **immaturity,** callowness, arrestment; **sketchiness,** scrappiness, patchiness; short measure *or* weight

2 <part lacking> **deficiency,** want, **lack, need, deficit,** defect, **shortage,** shortfall, underage; wantage, outage, ullage; defalcation, arrearage; **omission,** gap, hiatus, hole, vacuum, break, lacuna, discontinuity, interval

VERBS 3 **lack** 991.7, want, want for; fall short 910.2; be arrested, underdevelop, undergrow

ADJS 4 **incomplete, uncompleted, deficient,** defective, unfinished, imperfect, unperfected, **inadequate; undeveloped,** underdeveloped, undergrown, stunted, hypoplastic, **immature,** callow, infant, arrested, embryonic, **wanting, lacking,** needing, missing, **partial,** part, failing; in default, in arrear *or* arrears; **in short supply,** scanty; **short,** scant, shy <nonformal>; **sketchy,** patchy, scrappy

5 **mutilated,** garbled, hashed, **mangled, butchered,** docked, hacked, lopped, truncated, castrated, cut short

ADVS 6 **incompletely, partially,** by halves, by *or* in half measures, in installments, in *or* by bits and pieces; **deficiently,** imperfectly, inadequately

WORD ELEMENTS 7 semi—, parti—

795 COMPOSITION
<manner of being composed>

NOUNS 1 **composition, constitution, construction, formation,** fabrication, fashioning, shaping, organization; **embodiment,** incorporation, incarnation; **make, makeup,** getup *or* setup <both informal>; **building,** buildup, structure, structuring, shaping-up; **assembly,** assemblage, putting *or* piecing together; synthesis, syneresis; **combination** 804; **compound** 796.5; **junction** 799.1; **mixture** 796

2 **component, constituent, ingredient,**

integrant, makings *and* fixings <both nonformal>, **element, factor, part** 792, player, module, part and parcel; appurtenance, adjunct 254; **feature,** aspect, specialty, circumstance, detail, item

VERBS **3 compose, constitute,** construct, fabricate; **incorporate,** embody, incarnate; **form, organize,** structure, shape, shape up; **enter into,** go into, go to make up; **make, make up, build,** build up, assemble, put *or* piece together; **consist of,** be a feature of, form a part of, combine *or* unite in, merge in; **consist,** be made up of, be constituted of, contain; **synthesize; combine** 804.3; join 799.5; **mix**

ADJS **4 composed of,** formed of, **made of,** made up of, made out of, compact of, consisting of; composing, comprising, constituting, including, inclusive of, containing, incarnating, embodying, subsuming; contained in, embodied in

5 component, constituent, modular, integrant, integral; **formative,** elementary

796 MIXTURE

NOUNS **1 mixture,** mixing, blending; **admixture,** composition, commixture, immixture, intermixture, **mingling,** minglement, commingling *or* comminglement, intermingling *or* interminglement, interlarding *or* interlardment; **eclecticism,** syncretism; **pluralism,** melting pot, multiculturism *or* multiculturalism, ethnic *or* racial *or* cultural diversity; **fusion,** interfusion, conflation; amalgamation, **integration,** alloyage, coalescence; **merger, combination** 804

2 imbuement, impregnation, infusion, suffusion, decoction, infiltration, instillment, instillation, permeation, pervasion, interpenetration, penetration; saturation, steeping, soaking, marination

3 adulteration, corruption, contamination, denaturalization, **pollution, doctoring** <nonformal>; fortifying, lacing, spiking <nonformal>; **dilution,** cutting <nonformal>, watering, watering down; debasement, bastardizing

4 crossbreeding, crossing, **interbreeding,** miscegenation; **hybridism,** hybridization, mongrelism, mongrelization

5 compound, mixture, admixture, intermixture, immixture, commixture, **composite, blend,** meld, composition, confection, concoction, **combination,** combo <nonformal>, ensemble, marriage; amalgam, alloy; paste, magma

6 hodgepodge, hotchpotch, hotchpot; **med-**

ley, **miscellany,** mélange, pastiche, *pasticcio* <Ital>, **conglomeration, assortment,** assemblage, mixed bag, ragbag, grab bag, olio, *olla podrida* <Sp>, **scramble, jumble,** mingle-mangle, **mix,** mishmash, **mess,** can of worms <nonformal>, dog's breakfast <Can nonformal>, mare's nest, rat's nest, hurrah's nest <nautical nonformal>, hash, patchwork, salad, gallimaufry, salmagundi, **potpourri,** stew, sauce, slurry, omnium-gatherum, Noah's ark, **odds and ends,** oddments, all sorts, everything but the kitchen sink <nonformal>, "God's plenty"—Dryden, broad spectrum, what you will

7 <slight admixture> **tinge, tincture, touch, dash, smack,** taint, tinct, tint, **trace,** vestige, hint, inkling, intimation, soupçon, suspicion, suggestion, whiff, thought, shade, tempering; sprinkling, seasoning, sauce, spice, infusion

8 hybrid, crossbreed, cross, mixed-blood, mixblood, **half-breed,** half-bred, half blood, half-caste; **mongrel;** *ladino* <Sp>; mustee *or* mestee, *mestizo* <Sp>, *mestiza* <Sp fem>, *métis* <Fr>, *métisse* <Fr fem>; Eurasian; *mulatto,* high yellow <nonformal>, quadroon, quintroon, octoroon; sambo, zambo, *cafuso* <Brazil Pg>, Cape Colored <S Africa>, griqua <S Africa>; griffe; zebrule, zebrass, cattalo, mule, hinny, liger, tigon; tangelo, citrange, plumcot

9 mixer, blender, beater, agitator, food processor; cement mixer, eggbeater, churn; homogenizer, colloid mill, emulsifier; crucible, melting pot

VERBS **10 mix,** admix, commix, immix, **intermix, mingle,** bemingle, commingle, immingle, **intermingle,** interlace, interweave, intertwine, interlard; syncretize; **blend,** interblend, stir in; **amalgamate, integrate,** alloy, coalesce, **fuse, merge,** meld, compound, compose, conflate, concoct; **combine** 804.3; mix up, hash, stir up, **scramble,** conglomerate, shuffle, **jumble,** jumble up, mingle-mangle, throw *or* toss together; knead, work; homogenize, emulsify

11 imbue, imbrue, **infuse,** suffuse, transfuse, breathe, **instill,** infiltrate, **impregnate, permeate,** pervade, penetrate, leaven; **tinge, tincture,** entincture, temper, color, dye, flavor, season, dredge, besprinkle; **saturate,** steep, decoct, brew

12 adulterate, corrupt, contaminate, **debase,** denaturalize, pollute, denature, bastardize, **tamper with, doctor** *and* doctor up

<both nonformal>; **fortify,** spike
<nonformal>, lace; **dilute,** cut <nonformal>, water, water down <nonformal>
13 **hybridize, crossbreed, cross, interbreed,**
miscegenate, mongrelize
ADJS 14 **mixed, mingled,** blended, compounded, amalgamated; **combined** 804.5;
composite, compound, **complex,** many-sided, multifaceted, intricate; **conglomerate,** pluralistic, multiracial, multicultural, multiethnic, multinational, heterogeneous, varied, **miscellaneous,** medley,
motley, dappled, patchy; promiscuous,
indiscriminate, **scrambled, jumbled,**
thrown together; half-and-half, fifty-fifty
<nonformal>; amphibious; equivocal,
ambiguous, ambivalent, ironic; syncretic, eclectic
15 **hybrid, mongrel,** interbred, **crossbred,**
crossed, cross; **half-breed,** half-bred, half-blooded, half-caste
16 miscible, mixable, assimilable, integrable
PREPS 17 **among,** amongst, 'mongst; **amid,**
mid, amidst, midst, **in the midst of, in the
thick of; with,** together with

797 SIMPLICITY
<freedom from mixture or
complexity>

NOUNS 1 **simplicity, purity,** simpleness,
plainness, no frills, starkness, severity;
unmixedness, monism; **unadulteration,**
unsophistication, unspoiledness, intactness, fundamentality, elementarity,
primitiveness *or* primitivity, primariness; **singleness,** oneness, unity; integrity,
homogeneity, uniformity 780
2 **simplification,** streamlining, refinement,
purification, distillation; **disentanglement,** disinvolvement; uncluttering,
unscrambling, unsnarling, unknotting;
stripping, stripping away *or* down, narrowing, confining, bracketing; **analysis**
800
3 **oversimplification, oversimplicity,** oversimplifying; **simplism,** reductivism;
intellectual childishness *or* immaturity,
conceptual crudity
VERBS 4 **simplify,** streamline, **reduce,** reduce to elements *or* essentials, factorize;
purify, refine, distill; strip, strip down;
narrow, confine, bracket, zero in <nonformal>; oversimplify; **analyze** 800.6
5 **disinvolve,** disintricate, unmix, disembroil, **disentangle,** untangle, **unscramble,
unsnarl,** unknot, untwist, unbraid, unweave, untwine, unwind, uncoil, un-

thread, **unravel,** ravel; **unclutter,** clarify,
clear up, disambiguate, sort out, get to
the core *or* nub *or* essence
ADJS 6 **simple, plain,** bare, bare-bones *and*
no-frills <both nonformal>, mere; **single,**
uniform, homogeneous, of a piece; **pure,**
simon-pure, pure and simple; **essential,**
elementary, indivisible, **primary,** primal,
primitive, prime, pristine, **irreducible,
fundamental,** basic; undifferentiable *or*
undifferentiated, undifferenced, monolithic; **austere,** chaste, unadorned, uncluttered, spare, stark, severe; homely,
homespun, grass-roots, bread-and-butter,
down-home *and* vanilla *or* plain-vanilla
and white-bread <all nonformal>; beginning, entry-level
7 **unmixed, unmingled,** unblended, **uncombined,** uncompounded; unleavened;
unadulterated, unspoiled, untouched, intact, virgin, uncorrupted, unsophisticated, unalloyed, untinged, undiluted,
unfortified; **clear,** clarified, purified, refined, **distilled,** rectified; **neat, straight,**
absolute, sheer, naked, bare
8 **uncomplicated, uninvolved,** incomplex,
straightforward
9 **simplified,** streamlined, stripped down
10 **oversimplified,** oversimple; **simplistic,**
reductive; intellectually childish *or* immature, conceptually crude
ADVS 11 **simply, plainly, purely;** merely,
barely; **singly, solely,** only, **alone,** exclusively, just, simply and solely
WORD ELEMENTS 12 hapl—

798 COMPLEXITY

NOUNS 1 **complexity, complication, involvement,** complexness, involution, convolution, tortuousness, Byzantinism,
chinoiserie <Fr>, tanglement, **entanglement,** perplexity, **intricacy,** intricateness,
ramification, crabbedness, technicality,
subtlety
2 **complex,** perplex <nonformal>, **tangle,**
tangled skein, **mess** *and* snafu *and* fuck-up <all nonformal>, ravel, snarl, snarl-up; knot, Gordian knot; **maze,** meander,
Chinese puzzle, **labyrinth;** webwork,
mesh; **wilderness, jungle,** morass, quagmire; Rube Goldberg contraption, Heath
Robinson device <Brit>, wheels within
wheels; mare's nest, rat's nest, hurrah's
nest <nautical nonformal>, can of
worms <nonformal>, snake pit
VERBS 3 **complicate, involve, perplex,** ramify; **confound, confuse,** muddle, **mix up,**
mess up *and* ball up *and* bollix up *and*

screw up *and* foul up *and* fuck up *and* snafu *and* muck up *and* louse up <all non-formal>, implicate; **tangle**, entangle, embrangle, **snarl, snarl up**, ravel, knot, tie in knots

ADJS **4 complex, complicated,** many-faceted, multifarious, ramified, perplexed, **confused,** confounded, **involved,** implicated, crabbed, **intricate,** elaborate, involuted, convoluted, multilayered, multilevel; **mixed up,** balled up *and* bollixed up *and* screwed up *and* loused up *and* fouled up *and* fucked up *and* snafued *and* mucked up *and* messed up <all nonformal>; **tangled,** entangled, tangly, embrangled, **snarled,** knotted, matted, twisted, raveled; mazy, daedal, **labyrinthine,** labyrinthian, meandering; **devious,** roundabout, deep-laid, Byzantine, subtle

5 inextricable, irreducible, unknottable, unsolvable

799 JOINING

NOUNS **1 joining, junction,** joinder, jointure, **connection, union,** unification, bond, bonding, connectedness *or* connectivity, conjunction, conjoining, conjugation, liaison, marriage, hookup <nonformal>, splice, tie, tie-up *and* tie-in <both informal>, knotting; merger, merging; symbiosis; **combination 804;** conglomeration, **aggregation,** agglomeration, congeries; **coupling,** copulation, accouplement, coupledness, **bracketing,** yoking, pairing, splicing, wedding; **linking,** linkup, linkage, bridging, **concatenation,** chaining, articulation, agglutination; **meeting,** meeting place *or* point, confluence, convergence, concurrence, concourse, gathering, massing, clustering; communication, intercommunication, intercourse

2 interconnection, interjoinder, **interlinking,** interlocking, interdigitation; **interassociation,** interaffiliation

3 fastening, attachment, affixation, annexation; ligature, ligation, ligating; **binding,** bonding, gluing, sticking, tying, lashing, splicing, knotting, linking, trussing, girding, hooking, clasping, zipping, buckling, buttoning; knot <see list>; adhesive 802.4; splice, bond, fastener

4 joint, join, joining, **juncture, union, connection,** link, connecting link, **coupling, accouplement;** clinch, embrace; articulation <anatomy and botany>, symphysis <anatomy>; **pivot, hinge; knee; elbow; wrist; ankle; knuckle; hip; shoulder;**

neck, cervix; ball-and-socket joint, pivot joint, hinged joint, gliding joint; toggle joint; connecting rod, tie rod; seam, suture, stitch, closure, mortise and tenon, miter, butt, scarf, dovetail, rabbet, weld; boundary, interface

VERBS **5 put together, join,** conjoin, **unite,** unify, bond, **connect,** associate, league, band, merge, **assemble,** accumulate; **join up,** become a part of, associate oneself, enter into, come aboard <nonformal>; **gather,** mobilize, marshal, mass, amass, **collect,** conglobulate; **combine 804.3; couple,** pair, accouple, copulate, conjugate, marry, wed, tie the knot <nonformal>, **link,** link up, build bridges, yoke, knot, splice, tie, chain, bracket; **concatenate,** articulate, agglutinate; glue, tape, cement, solder, weld; **put together,** fix together, lay together, piece together, clap together, tack together, stick together, lump together, roll into one; bridge over *or* between, span; **include,** encompass, take in, cover, embrace, comprise

6 interconnect, interjoin, intertie, interassociate, interaffiliate, **interlink,** interlock, interdigitate

7 fasten, fix, attach, affix, annex, put to, set to; graft, engraft; **secure,** anchor, moor; cement, knit, set, grapple, belay, **make fast;** clinch, clamp, cramp; tighten, trim, trice up, screw up; cinch *or* cinch up

8 hook, hitch; **clasp,** hasp, clip, snap; **button,** buckle, zipper; lock, latch; **pin,** skewer, peg, nail, nail up, tack, staple, toggle, screw, bolt, rivet; **sew,** stitch; **wedge,** jam, stick; rabbet, butt, scarf, mortise, miter, dovetail; batten, batten down; cleat; **hinge,** joint, articulate

9 bind, tie, brace, truss, **lash,** leash, rope, strap, lace, wire, chain; **splice,** bend; **gird,** girt, belt, girth, girdle, band, cinch; **tie up,** bind up, do up; **wrap,** wrap up, bundle; shrink-wrap; **bandage,** bandage up, swathe, swaddle

10 yoke, hitch up, hook up; harness, harness up; halter, bridle; saddle; tether, fetter

11 <be joined> join, connect, unite, meet, meet up, link up, merge, converge, **come together;** communicate, intercommunicate; knit, grow together; cohere, adhere, hang *or* hold together, clinch, embrace

ADJS **12 joint, combined,** joined, **conjoint,** conjunct, conjugate, corporate, compact, cooperative, cooperating; concurrent, coincident; inclusive, comprehensive

13 joined, united, connected, copulate, **coupled,** linked, knit, bridged, tight-knit, knitted, bracketed, associated, conjoined, incorporated, integrated, **merged,** gathered, assembled, accumulated, **collected; associated,** joined up, on board; **allied,** leagued, banded together; hand-in-hand, hand-in-glove, intimate; unseparated, undivided; **wedded,** matched, married, paired, yoked, mated; **tied, bound,** knotted, spliced, lashed

14 **fast, fastened, fixed,** secure, firm, close, tight, set; **bonded,** glued, cemented, taped; **jammed,** wedged, stuck, frozen, seized, seized up

15 **inseparable,** impartible, **indivisible,** undividable, indissoluble, inalienable, inseverable, bound up in *or* with

16 **joining, connecting,** meeting; **communicating,** intercommunicating; **connective,** connectional; conjunctive, combinative, combinatorial, copulative, linking, bridging, binding

17 jointed, articulate

ADVS 18 **jointly,** conjointly, corporately, **together; in common,** in partnership, mutually, in concord; **all together,** as one, in unison, in agreement, in harmony; concurrently, at once, at *or* in one fell swoop

19 **securely, firmly, fast,** tight; **inseparably,** indissolubly

20 **knots**

anchor knot	loop knot
becket knot	magnus hitch
Blackwall hitch	manrope knot
bow	marlinespike hitch
bowknot	marling hitch
bowline	Matthew Walker knot
bowline knot	mesh knot
builder's knot	midshipman's hitch
carrick bend	netting knot
cat's-paw	open hand knot
clinch	outside clinch
clove hitch	prolonge knot
cuckold's neck	reef knot
diamond knot	reeving-line bend
double hitch	rolling hitches
Englishman's tie	rope-yarn knot
figure-of-eight knot	round seizing
fisherman's bend	round turn and half
flat knot	hitch
Flemish knot	running bowline
French shroud knot	running knot
German knot	sheepshank
granny knot	Shelby knot
half crown	shroud knot
half hitch	single knot
half-Windsor knot	slide knot
harness hitch	slipknot
hawser bend	square knot
hawser fastening	stevedore's knot
heaving-line bend	stopper's knot
inside clinch	studding-sail halyard
lanyard knot	bend

stunner hitch	truelove knot
surgeon's knot	wall knot
tack bend	weaver's knot *or* hitch
timber knot *or* hitch	Windsor knot
truckman's knot	

800 ANALYSIS

NOUNS 1 **analysis,** analyzation, **breakdown,** breaking down, breakup, breaking up; anatomy, anatomizing, dissection; separation, **division, subdivision,** segmentation, reduction to elements *or* parts; chemical analysis, **assay** *or* assaying, resolution, titration, docimasy <old>, qualitative analysis, quantitative analysis, volumetric analysis, gravimetric analysis; ultimate analysis, proximate analysis; microanalysis, semimicroanalysis

2 **itemization,** enumeration, detailing, breakout, isolation; outlining, schematization, blocking, blocking out; resolution; scansion, parsing

3 **classification, categorization, sorting,** taxonomy, sorting out, sifting, sifting out, grouping, factoring, winnowing, shakeout; **weighing, evaluation,** gauging, assessment, appraisal, position statement *or* paper, **judgment** 945; impact statement

4 **outline,** structural outline, **plan,** scheme, schema, chart, flow chart, graph; table, table of contents, index; **diagram,** block diagram, exploded view, **blueprint; catalog,** catalogue raisonné <Fr>

5 **analyst, analyzer, examiner** 937.16; taxonomist

VERBS 6 **analyze, break down,** break up, anatomize, dissect, atomize, unitize; **divide, subdivide,** segment; assay, titrate; separate, make discrete, isolate, reduce, reduce to elements, resolve

7 **itemize,** enumerate, factorize, number, detail, break out; **outline,** schematize, block out, diagram, graph, chart; resolve; scan, parse

8 **classify,** class, **categorize,** catalog, sort, sort out, sift, group, factor, winnow, thrash out; weigh, weigh up, **evaluate, judge,** gauge 945.9, assess, appraise 945.9

ADJS 9 **analytical,** analytic; segmental; classificatory, enumerative; schematic

ADVS 10 **analytically,** by parts *or* divisions *or* sections; by categories *or* types

801 SEPARATION

NOUNS 1 **separation, disjunction,** severalty, disjointure, disjointing, split-up, splitting-up, demerger, delinkage, disarticulation, **disconnection,** disconnectedness, discontinuity, incoherence, disengagement, disunion, nonunion, disassociation, segregation; **parting,** alienation, estrangement, **removal,** withdrawal, isolation, detachment, sequestration, abstraction; **subtraction** 255; divorce, divorcement; **division,** subdivision, partition, compartmentalization, segmentation, marking off; districting, zoning; **dislocation,** luxation; separability, partibility, dividableness, divisibility; separatism; **separateness,** discreteness, singleness, monism, unitariness

2 **severance,** disseverment *or* disseverance, **sunderance,** scission, fission, cleavage, dichotomy; **cutting, slitting,** slashing, **splitting,** slicing; **rending, tearing,** ripping, laceration, hacking, chopping, butchering, mutilation; section, resection; **surgery**

3 **disruption, dissolution,** abruption, cataclasm; revolution 859; **disintegration** 805, breakup, crack-up, shattering, splintering, fragmentizing, fragmentation; **bursting,** dissilience *or* dissiliency; **scattering,** dispersal, diffusion; **stripping,** scaling, exfoliation

4 **break,** breakage, **breach,** burst, **rupture, fracture; crack,** cleft, **fissure, cut, split,** slit; slash, slice; **gap, rift,** rent, rip, tear; chip, splinter, scale

5 **dissection, analysis** 800, vivisection, resolution, breakdown, diaeresis; anatomy

6 **disassembly, dismantlement,** taking down *or* apart, dismemberment, dismounting; undoing, unbuilding; **stripping,** stripping away *or* down, divestiture, divestment, defoliation, deprivation; disrobing, unclothing, doffing

7 **separator,** sieve, centrifuge, ultracentrifuge; creamer, cream separator; breaker, stripper, mincer; slicer, cutter, microtome; analyzer

VERBS 8 **separate, divide, disjoin, disunite,** draw apart, dissociate, disassociate, grow apart, **disjoint,** disengage, disarticulate, **disconnect;** uncouple, unyoke; **part,** cut the knot, **divorce,** estrange; **alienate, segregate,** separate off, factor out, sequester, isolate, curtain off, shut off, set apart *or* aside, split off, cut off *or* out *or* loose *or* adrift; **withdraw, leave, depart,** take one's leave, cut out *and* split <both nonformal>; pull out *or* away *or* back, stand apart *or* aside *or* aloof, step aside; subtract 255.9; delete 255.12; **expel,** eject, throw off *or* out, cast off *or* out

9 **come apart,** spring apart, fly apart, come unstuck, come unglued, come undone, come apart at the seams, **come** *or* **drop** *or* fall to pieces, **disintegrate, come to pieces,** go to pieces, fall apart, fall apart at the seams, fall to pieces, atomize, unitize, fragmentize, pulverize, break up, bust up <nonformal>, unravel; come *or* fall off, peel off, carry away; get loose, give way, start

10 **detach, remove,** disengage, take *or* lift off, doff; **unfasten, undo,** unattach, unfix; **free, release,** liberate, loose, unloose, unleash, unfetter; **unloosen,** loosen; cast off, weigh anchor; **unhook,** unhitch, unclasp, unclinch, unbuckle, unbutton, unsnap, unscrew, unpin, unbolt; **untie,** unbind, unknit, unbandage, unlace, unzip, unstrap, unchain; unstick, unglue

11 **sever, dissever,** cut off *or* away *or* loose, shear off, hack through, hack off, ax, amputate; **cleave, split,** fissure; sunder, cut in two, dichotomize, halve, bisect; **cut,** incise, carve, **slice,** pare, prune, trim, trim away, resect, excise 255.10; slit, snip, lance, scissor; **chop, hew,** hack, **slash;** gash, whittle, butcher; saw, jigsaw; **tear, rend,** rive, rend asunder

12 **break, burst,** bust <nonformal>, breach; **fracture, rupture; crack,** split, check, craze, fissure; snap; chip, scale, exfoliate

13 **shatter, splinter,** shiver, break to *or* into pieces, fragmentize, break to *or* into smithereens <nonformal>; **smash,** crush, crunch, squash, squish <nonformal>; **disrupt,** demolish, break up, smash up; **scatter,** disperse, diffuse; **fragment,** fission, atomize; **pulverize** 1049.9, grind, cut to pieces, mince, make mincemeat of, make hamburger of <nonformal>

14 **tear** *or* **rip apart,** take *or* pull apart, **pick** *or* **rip** *or* **tear to pieces,** tear to rags *or* tatters, **shred,** rip to shreds; **dismember,** tear limb from limb, draw and quarter; **mangle,** lacerate, mutilate, maim; skin, flay, strip, peel, denude; defoliate

15 **disassemble,** take apart *or* down, tear down; **dismantle, demolish,** dismount, unrig <nautical>

16 **disjoint,** unjoint, **unhinge,** disarticulate, **dislocate,** luxate, throw out of joint, unseat

17 **dissect, analyze** 800.6, vivisect, anatomize, break down

18 **apportion, portion,** section, partition, compartmentalize, segment; **divide,** divide up, divvy *and* divvy up <both nonformal>, **parcel,** parcel up *or* out,

split, split up, cut up, subdivide; district, zone

19 **part company, part, separate,** split up, dispel, disband, scatter, **disperse,** break up, break it up <nonformal>, **go separate ways,** diverge

ADJS 20 **separate, distinct, discrete; unjoined, unconnected, unattached,** unaccompanied, unattended, unassociated; **apart,** asunder, **in two;** discontinuous, noncontiguous, divergent; **isolated,** insular, detached, detachable, free-standing, free-floating, autonomous; **independent,** self-contained, stand-alone <nonformal>; noncohesive, noncohering, incoherent 803.4; bipartite, dichotomous, multipartite, multisegmental; **subdivided,** partitioned, curtained-off, marked-off, compartmentalized

21 **separated,** disjoined, disjoint, disjointed, disjunct, **disconnected,** disengaged, detached, **disunited, divided,** removed, divorced, **alienated,** estranged, distanced, **segregated,** sequestered, isolated, cloistered, shut off; **scattered,** dispersed, helter-skelter; disarticulated, dislocated, luxated, out of joint

22 **unfastened, unbound,** uncaught, unfixed, **undone, loose, free,** loosened, unloosened, clear; **untied, unbound,** unknit, unleashed, unfettered, unchained, unlaced, unbandaged, unhitched; unstuck, unglued; unclasped, unclinched, unbuckled, unbuttoned, unzipped, unsnapped; unscrewed, unpinned, unbolted; **unanchored,** adrift, afloat, floating, free, free-floating

23 **severed, cut,** cleaved, cleft, cloven, riven, hewn, sheared; **splintered,** shivered, cracked, **split,** slit, reft, **rent, torn;** tattered, shredded, in shreds; quartered, **dismembered,** in pieces

24 **broken,** busted <nonformal>, **burst, ruptured,** dissilient; sprung; **shattered,** broken up, broken to pieces *or* bits, fragmentized, fragmentary, fragmented, in shards, in smithereens <nonformal>

25 **separating, dividing,** parting, distancing; separative, disjunctive

26 **separable,** severable, **divisible,** alienable, cleavable, partible; **fissionable,** fissile, scissile; dissoluble, dissolvable

ADVS 27 **separately,** severally, piecemeal, one by one; **apart,** adrift, asunder, **in two,** in twain; apart from, away from, aside from; abstractly, in the abstract, objectively, impersonally

28 **disjointedly,** unconnectedly, sporadically, spasmodically, discontinuously, by bits and pieces, by fits and starts

29 **to pieces,** all to pieces, **to bits, to smithereens** <nonformal>, to splinters, to shards, to tatters, to shreds

802 COHESION

NOUNS 1 **cohesion,** cohesiveness, **coherence, adherence, adhesion, sticking,** sticking together, cling, clinging, binding, colligation, inseparability; cementation, conglutination, agglutination; concretion, condensation, accretion, solidification, set, congelation, congealment, clotting, coagulation; **conglomeration,** conglobation, compaction, agglomeration, consolidation; **clustering,** massing, bunching, nodality

2 **consistency** 787.1, connection, **connectedness; junction** 799.1; continuity, **seriality,** sequence 814, sequentialness, **consecutiveness** 811.1, orderliness

3 **tenacity,** tenaciousness, **adhesiveness,** cohesiveness, retention; **tightness,** snugness; stickiness, **tackiness,** gluiness, gumminess, **viscidity,** consistency, viscosity, glutinosity; persistence *or* persistency, **stick-to-itiveness** <nonformal>, toughness, **stubbornness, obstinacy** 361, bulldoggedness *or* bulldoggishness, bullheadedness

4 <something adhesive or tenacious> **adhesive,** adherent, adherer; **bulldog,** barnacle, leech, limpet, remora; burr, cocklebur, clotbur, bramble, brier, prickle, thorn; sticker, bumper sticker, decalcomania, decal<nonformal>; **glue, cement,** mucilage, epoxy resin, paste, stickum *and* gunk <both nonformal>; **plaster,** adhesive plaster, court plaster; syrup, molasses, honey

5 **conglomeration, conglomerate,** breccia <geology>, agglomerate, agglomeration, cluster, bunch, mass, clot; concrete, concretion

VERBS 6 **cohere, adhere, stick, cling,** cleave, hold; **persist,** stay, stay put <nonformal>; cling to, freeze to <nonformal>; hang on, hold on; take hold of, clasp, grasp, hug, embrace, clinch; **stick together, hang** *or* **hold together;** grow to, grow together; **solidify, set,** conglomerate, agglomerate, conglobate; **congeal,** coagulate, clabber <nonformal>, **clot; cluster,** mass, bunch

7 **be consistent** 787.6, **connect,** connect with, follow; **join** 799.11, link up

8 **hold fast, stick close,** stick like glue, stick

like a wet shirt *or* wet T-shirt *or* second skin, stick closer than a brother, stick like a barnacle *or* limpet *or* leech, cling like ivy *or* a burr, hold on like a bulldog

9 **stick together, cement, bind, colligate, paste, glue,** agglutinate, conglutinate, gum; **weld,** fuse, **solder,** braze

ADJS 10 **cohesive,** cohering, coherent; adhering, **sticking, clinging,** inseparable, cleaving, holding together; **cemented,** stuck, agglutinative, agglutinated, agglutinate, conglutinate, conglutinated; **concrete, condensed, solidified, set, congealed,** clotted, coagulated; conglomerated, conglobate, **compacted, consolidated,** agglomerated; **clustered,** massed, bunched, nodal

11 **consistent** 787.9, **connected;** continuous 811.8, **serial,** uninterrupted, contiguous, sequential, sequent, **consecutive** 811.9; orderly, tight; **joined** 799.13

12 **adhesive, adherent,** stickable, self-adhesive, retentive; **tenacious,** clingy; **sticky, tacky,** gluey, gummy, **viscid,** glutinous; **persistent,** tough, **stubborn, obstinate** 361.8, bulldoggish *or* bulldogged *or* bulldoggy, bullheaded

803 NONCOHESION

NOUNS 1 **noncohesion,** uncohesiveness, incoherence, inconsistency, discontinuity 812, nonadhesion, unadhesiveness, unadherence, untenacity; **separateness,** discreteness, aloofness, standoffishness <nonformal>; **disjunction** 801.1, unknitting, unraveling, dismemberment; **dislocation; dissolution, chaos** 809.2, anarchy, **disorder** 809, confusion, entropy; **scattering,** dispersion *or* dispersal; diffusion

2 **looseness, slackness,** bagginess, **laxness,** laxity, relaxation; sloppiness, shakiness, ricketiness

VERBS 3 **loosen, slacken, relax;** slack, slack off; ease, ease off, let up; **loose, free,** let go, unleash; **disjoin,** unknit, unravel, dismember; **sow confusion,** open Pandora's box; unstick, unglue; **scatter,** disperse, diffuse

ADJS 4 **incoherent,** uncoherent, noncoherent, **inconsistent, uncohesive, unadhesive,** nonadhesive, noncohesive, nonadherent, like grains of sand, **untenacious, unconsolidated,** tenuous; unjoined 801.20, disconnected, unconnected, unraveled, dismembered, gapped, open; **disordered** 809.12, **chaotic, anarchic,** anomic, confused; **discontinuous** 812.4, broken, detached, discrete, aloof, standoffish <nonformal>

5 **loose, slack, lax, relaxed,** easy, sloppy; shaky, rickety; flapping, streaming; hanging, drooping, dangling; bagging, baggy

804 COMBINATION

NOUNS 1 **combination,** combine, combo <nonformal>, composition; **union, unification,** marriage, wedding, coupling, accouplement, linking, linkage, yoking; **incorporation,** aggregation, agglomeration, conglomeration, congeries; **amalgamation, consolidation,** assimilation, **integration,** solidification, **encompassment,** inclusion, ecumenism; **junction** 799.1; conjunction, conjugation; **alliance,** affiliation, reaffiliation, **association** 617, merger, league, hookup <nonformal>, tie-up <nonformal>; **taking** 480, buyout, takeover, leveraged buyout; **federation, confederation,** confederacy; federalization, centralization, cartel; **fusion,** blend, blending, meld, melding; coalescence, coalition; **synthesis,** syncretism, syneresis; syndication; **conspiracy,** cabal, junta; *enosis* <Gk>, *Anschluss* <Ger>; package, package deal; **agreement** 787; **addition** 253

2 **mixture** 796, **compound** 796.5

VERBS 3 **combine, unite, unify,** marry, wed, couple, link, yoke, yoke together; **incorporate, amalgamate, consolidate,** assimilate, **integrate,** solidify, coalesce, compound, put *or* lump together, roll into one, come together, make one, unitize; **connect, join** 799.5; **mix; add** 253.4; **merge,** meld, **blend,** stir in, merge *or* blend *or* meld *or* shade into, **fuse,** flux, melt into one, conflate; interfuse, interblend; **encompass,** include, comprise; **take,** take over, buy out; **synthesize,** syncretize; syndicate; reembody

4 **league, ally, affiliate, associate,** consociate; unionize, organize, cement a union; **federate, confederate,** federalize, centralize; **join forces,** join *or* unite with, join *or* come together, join up with <nonformal>, hook up with <nonformal>, tie up *or* in with <nonformal>, **throw in with** <nonformal>, stand up with, go *or* be in cahoots <nonformal>, **pool one's interests, join fortunes with,** stand together, close ranks, make common cause with; **marry, wed, couple, yoke,** yoke together, link; **band together,** club together, bunch, bunch up <nonformal>, gang up <nonformal>, gang, club; team with, **team up with** <nonformal>, couple, pair, double up, buddy up <nonformal>, pair

off, partner; go in partnership, go in partners <nonformal>; **conspire,** cabal

ADJS **5 combined, united, amalgamated, incorporated, consolidated, integrated,** assimilated, one, unitary, unitive, unitized,
joined 799.13, joint 799.12, conjoint; conjunctive, combinative *or* combinatory,
connective, conjugate; **merged,** blended,
fused; **mixed; synthesized,** syncretized,
syncretistic, eclectic

6 leagued, enleagued, **allied, affiliated,** affiliate, **associated,** associate, corporate;
federated, confederated, federate, confederate; **in league,** in cahoots <nonfor-
mal>, in with; **conspiratorial,** cabalistic;
partners with, in partnership; teamed,
coupled, paired, married, wed, wedded,
coupled, yoked, yoked together, linked,
linked up

7 combining, uniting, unitive, unitizing, incorporating; merging, blending, fusing;
combinative, combinatory; associative;
federative, federal; corporative, incor-
porative, corporational

805 DISINTEGRATION

NOUNS **1 disintegration, decomposition, dissolution, decay,** coming-apart, resolution, disorganization, degradation,
breakup, breakdown, fragmentation, atomization; **ruination, destruction** 395;
erosion, corrosion, crumbling, dilapidation, wear, wear and tear, waste, wasting,
wasting away, ablation, ravagement, ravages of time; **disjunction** 801.1; **incoherence** 803.1; **impairment** 393

2 dissociation; catalysis, dialysis, hydroly-
sis, proteolysis, thermolysis, photolysis
<all chemistry>; catalyst, hydrolyst
<chemistry>; hydrolyte <chemistry>;
decay, fission <physics>, splitting

VERBS **3 disintegrate, decompose, decay,**
dissolve, come apart, disorganize, **break
up** 395.22, go to rack and ruin 395.24,
crack up, disjoin, unknit, split, fission, atomize, **come** *or* **fall to pieces; erode,**
corrode, ablate, consume, wear *or* waste
away, molder, molder away, crumble,
crumble into dust

4 <chemical terms> dissociate; catalyze,
dialyze, hydrolyze, electrolyze, photolyze

ADJS **5 disintegrative,** decomposing, disintegrating, disruptive, disjunctive; **destructive, ruinous** 395.26; **erosive,** corrosive, ablative; resolvent, solvent, separative; **dilapidated,** disintegrated, ruinous, shacky, worn-out, worn, clapped-out
<Brit nonformal>, moldering, ravaged,

wrecked, totaled <nonformal>; disin-
tegrable, decomposable, degradable,
biodegradable

6 <chemical terms> dissociative; catalytic, dialytic, hydrolytic, proteolytic,
thermolytic, electrolytic, photolytic

WORD ELEMENTS **7** —lysis, lyso—, lysi—,
—lyte

806 ORDER

NOUNS **1 order, arrangement** 807; **organization** 807.2; **disposition,** disposal, deployment, marshaling; **formation, structure,
configuration,** array, makeup, lineup,
setup, layout; system; routine, even
tenor, standard operating procedure;
peace, quiet, quietude, **tranquillity;
regularity,** uniformity 780; symmetry,
proportion, concord, **harmony,** order, the
music of the spheres, Tao *or* Dào; "the
eternal fitness of things"—Samuel
Clarke, "Heav'n's first law"—Pope

2 continuity, logical order, serial order;
degree 245; **hierarchy, gradation,**
subordination, superordination, rank,
place; **sequence** 814

3 orderliness, trimness, tidiness, neatness;
good shape <nonformal>, good condi-
tion, fine fettle, good trim, apple-pie
order <nonformal>, a place for everything and everything in its place;
discipline, method, methodology, methodicalness, system, systematicness;
anality, compulsiveness, compulsive
neatness <all psychoanalysis>

VERBS **4 order, arrange** 807.8, get it together
<nonformal>, **organize, regulate;** dis-
pose, deploy, marshal; **form,** form up,
configure, structure, array, pull it together, get *or* put one's ducks in a row
<nonformal>, straighten it out, get *or*
put one's house in order, line up, set up,
lay out; **pacify,** quiet, cool off *or* down
<nonformal>, **tranquilize; regularize,**
harmonize; **systematize,** methodize, normalize, standardize, routinize; hierar-
chize, grade, rank

5 form, take form, take order, **take shape,**
crystallize, **shape up;** arrange *or* range itself, place itself, take its place, fall in, **fall**
or **drop into place,** fall into line *or* order
or series, fall into rank, take rank; come
together, draw up, gather around, rally
round

ADJS **6 orderly,** ordered, **regular, well-
regulated, well-ordered, methodical, formal,** regular as clockwork, uniform 780.5,
systematic, symmetrical, **harmonious;**

businesslike, routine, steady, normal, habitual, usual, en règle, in hand; **arranged** 807.14

7 **in order, in trim**, to rights *and* in apple-pie order <both nonformal>; **in condition,** in good condition, in kilter *or* kelter <nonformal>, **in shape**, in good shape <nonformal>, **in good form**, in fine fettle, in good trim, in the pink <nonformal>, in the pink of condition; **in repair**, in commission, in adjustment, in working order, fixed; up to scratch *or* snuff <nonformal>

8 **tidy, trim, natty, neat,** spruce, sleek, slick *and* slick as a whistle <nonformal>, smart, trig, dinky <Brit nonformal>, snug, tight, **shipshape**, shipshape and Bristol fashion; **well-kept,** well-kempt, well-cared-for, well-groomed; neat as a button *or* pin <nonformal>

ADVS 9 **methodically, systematically, regularly,** through channels, uniformly, harmoniously, like clockwork

10 **in order, in turn, in sequence, in succession,** hierarchically, in series, *seriatim* <L>; step by step, by stages

807 ARRANGEMENT
<putting in order>

NOUNS 1 **arrangement, ordering,** structuring, shaping, forming, configurating, configuration, constitution; **disposition, disposal, deployment,** placement, marshaling, **arraying; distribution,** collation, collocation, allocation, allotment, apportionment; **formation,** formulation, **configuration,** form, array; regimentation; syntax; **order** 806

2 **organization, methodization,** ordering, planning, charting, codification, regulation, regularization, routinization, normalization, rationalization; **adjustment,** harmonization, tuning, fine-tuning, tune-up, tinkering; **systematization,** ordination, coordination

3 **grouping, classification** 808, categorization, taxonomy; **gradation,** subordination, superordination, **ranking,** placement; **sorting,** sorting out, assortment, sifting, screening, triage, culling, selection, shakeout

4 **table,** code, digest, **index, inventory,** census; table of organization

5 **arranger, organizer,** coordinator, spreadsheet; **sorter,** sifter, **sieve,** riddle, **screen,** bolter, colander, grate, grating

6 <act of making neat> **cleanup,** red-up <nonformal>; tidy-up, trim-up, police-up <nonformal>

7 **rearrangement, reorganization,** reconstitution, **reordering, restructuring,** *perestroika* <Russ>, shake-up <nonformal>; **redeployment,** redisposition, realignment

VERBS 8 **arrange,** order 806.4, reduce to order, **put** *or* **get** *or* **set in order,** right, prioritize, put first things first, get one's ducks in a row <nonformal>; **put** *or* **set to rights, get it together** <nonformal>, **pull it together,** put in *or* into shape, whip into shape <nonformal>, sort out <chiefly Brit>, unsnarl, make sense out of <nonformal>

9 **dispose, distribute, fix, place,** set out, collocate, allocate, **compose,** space, **marshal,** rally, array; align, line, **line up,** form up, range; regiment; **allot, apportion,** parcel out, deal, **deal out**

10 **organize,** methodize, **systematize,** rationalize, regularize, get *or* put one's house in order; **harmonize,** synchronize, **tune,** tune up; **regularize,** routinize, normalize, standardize; **regulate,** adjust, coordinate, fix, settle; **plan,** chart, codify

11 **classify** 808.6, **group,** categorize; **grade,** gradate, rank, subordinate; **sort,** sort out <chiefly Brit>, assort; **separate,** divide; collate; **sift,** size, sieve, **screen,** bolt, riddle

12 tidy, **tidy up,** neaten, trim, **put in trim,** trim up, trig up <chiefly Brit>, **straighten up,** fix up <nonformal>, **clean up,** police *and* police up <both nonformal>, groom, spruce *and* spruce up <both nonformal>, **clear up,** clear the decks

13 **rearrange, reorganize,** reconstitute, **reorder, restructure,** reshuffle, rejigger <nonformal>, tinker *or* tinker with, tune, tune up, fine-tune; **shake up,** shake out; redispose, redistribute, reallocate, realign

ADJS 14 **arranged, ordered, disposed,** configured, composed, constituted, fixed, placed, aligned, ranged, arrayed, marshaled, grouped, ranked, **graded;** organized, methodized, **regularized,** routinized, normalized, standardized, **systematized;** regulated, harmonized, synchronized; **classified** 808.8, categorized, **sorted,** assorted; **orderly** 806.6

15 **organizational,** formational, structural

WORD ELEMENTS 16 tax—, taxi—, —taxia, —taxis

808 CLASSIFICATION

NOUNS 1 **classification, categorization,** classing, placement, ranging, **pigeon-**

holing, **sorting**, **grouping**; **grading**, stratification, ranking, rating, classing; division, subdivision; **cataloging**, codification, tabulation, rationalization, indexing, filing; **taxonomy**, typology; analysis 800, **arrangement** 807

2 **class**, **category**, **head**, **order**, **division**, branch, set, **group**, grouping, bracket, pigeonhole; **section**, heading, rubric, **label**, title; **grade**, rank, rating, status, estate, stratum, level, station, position; **caste**, clan, race, strain, blood, kin, sept; **subdivision**, subgroup, suborder

3 **kind**, **sort**, **ilk**, **type**, breed of cat <nonformal>, lot <nonformal>, **variety**, **species**, **genus**, *genre* <Fr>, phylum, denomination, designation, description, style, manner, **nature**, **character**, persuasion, the like *or* likes of <nonformal>; **stamp**, **brand**, feather, color, stripe, line, grain, kidney; **make**, mark, label, shape, cast, form, mold; tribe, clan, race, strain, blood, kin, breed

4 **hierarchy**, class structure, power structure, pyramid, establishment, pecking order; natural hierarchy, order *or* chain of being, domain, realm, **kingdom**, animal kingdom, vegetable kingdom, mineral kingdom

5 <botanical and zoological classifications, in descending order> **kingdom**; subkingdom, **phylum** <zoology>, branch <botany>; superclass, **class**, subclass, superorder, **order**, suborder, superfamily, **family**, subfamily, tribe, subtribe, **genus**, subgenus, series, section, superspecies, **species**; subspecies, **variety**; biotype, genotype

VERBS 6 **classify**, class, assign, designate; **categorize**, type, put down as, **pigeonhole**, place, **group**, **arrange** 807.8, range; **order** 806.4, put in order, rank, rate, **grade**; **sort**, assort; **divide**, **analyze** 800.6, subdivide, break down; **catalog**, list, file, tabulate, rationalize, **index**, alphabetize, digest, codify

ADJS 7 **classificational**, classificatory; **categorical**, **taxonomic** *or* **taxonomical**, typologic *or* typological; ordinal; divisional, divisionary, subdivisional; **typical**, typal; **special**, specific, characteristic, particular, peculiar, denominative, differential, distinctive, defining, varietal

8 **classified**, **cataloged**, **pigeonholed**, indexed, sorted, assorted, **graded**, **grouped**, ranked, rated, stratified, hierarchic, pyramidal; placed; filed, on file; tabular

ADVS 9 **any kind** *or* sort, **of any description**, **at all**, whatever, soever, whatsoever

WORD ELEMENTS 10 speci—, specie—, gen—

809 DISORDER

NOUNS 1 **disorder**, **disorderliness**, **disarrangement**, derangement, disarticulation, disjunction 801.1, **disorganization**; discomposure, **dishevelment**, **disarray**, upset, disturbance, discomfiture, disconcertedness; **irregularity**, randomness, turbulence, perturbation, ununiformity *or* nonuniformity, unsymmetry *or* nonsymmetry, **disproportion**, **disharmony**; indiscriminateness, promiscuity, promiscuousness, haphazardness; **randomness**, randomicity, vagueness, trendlessness; entropy; **disruption** 801.3, destabilization; **incoherence** 803.1; untogetherness <nonformal>; disintegration 805; "most admired disorder"—Shakespeare, "inharmonious harmony"—Horace

2 **confusion**, **chaos**, anarchy, misrule, license; **Babel**, cognitive dissonance; **muddle**, morass, **mix-up** *and* foul-up *and* fuck-up *and* snafu *and* screw-up <all nonformal>, ball-up <nonformal>, balls-up <Brit nonformal>, hoo-ha *and* fine howde-do <all nonformal>, pretty kettle of fish, pretty piece of business, nice piece of work; "Chaos and old Night"—Milton, "the seed of Chaos, and of Night"—Pope, "mere anarchy is loosed upon the world," "fabulous formless darkness"—both Yeats

3 **jumble**, **scramble**, **tumble**, **snarl-up**, **mess**, bloody *or* holy *or* unholy *or* godawful mess <nonformal>, shemozzle <Brit>, **turmoil**, welter, mishmash, hash, helter-skelter, farrago, crazy-quilt, higgledy-piggledy; **clutter**, **litter**, **hodgepodge** 796.6, rat's nest, mare's nest, hurrah's nest <nautical>; topsyturviness *or* topsy-turvydom, arsyvarsiness, hysteron proteron

4 **commotion**, **hubbub**, **Babel**, **tumult**, turmoil, **uproar**, **racket**, riot, **disturbance**, **rumpus** <nonformal>, ruckus *and* ruction <both nonformal>, **fracas**, **hassle**, shemozzle <Brit nonformal>, shindy <nonformal>, rampage; **ado**, to-do <nonformal>, trouble, bother, pother, dustup <Brit nonformal>, stir <nonformal>, **fuss**, brouhaha, foofaraw <nonformal>; **row** *and* hassle <both nonformal>, **brawl**, free-for-all <nonformal>, donnybrook *or* donnybrook fair, broil, embroil-

ment, melee, scramble; helter-skelter, pell-mell, **roughhouse, rough-and-tumble**

5 **pandemonium**, "confusion worse confounded"—Milton, **hell, bedlam,** witches' Sabbath, Babel, confusion of tongues; **cacophony**, din, noise, static, racket

6 slovenliness, **slipshodness,** carelessness, negligence; **untidiness,** unneatness, looseness, **messiness** <nonformal>, **sloppiness,** dowdiness, seediness, **shabbiness,** tawdriness, chintziness <nonformal>, shoddiness, tackiness <nonformal>, grubbiness <nonformal>, frowziness, blowziness; **slatternliness,** frumpishness <nonformal>, sluttishness; **squalor,** squalidness, sordidness

7 **slob** <nonformal>, **slattern, sloven,** frump <nonformal>, sloppy Joe, schlep, schlump, *Strüwelpeter* <Ger>; drab, **slut, trollop; pig,** swine; **litterbug**

VERBS 8 lapse into disorder, come apart, come apart at the seams, dissolve into chaos, slacken 803.3, come unstuck *or* unglued <nonformal>, disintegrate 805.3, degenerate, detune, untune

9 **disorder, disarrange** 810.2, **disorganize,** dishevel; **confuse** 810.3, sow confusion, open Pandora's box, **muddle,** jumble, jumble up; **discompose** 810.4, **upset,** destabilize, unsettle, **disturb,** perturb

10 **riot, roister,** roil, carouse; **create a disturbance, make a commotion,** make trouble, cause a stir *or* commotion, **make an ado** *or* **to-do,** create a riot, **cut loose, run wild, run riot,** run amok, go on a rampage, go berserk

11 <nonformal terms> **kick up a row,** kick up a shindy *or* a fuss *or* a storm, piss up a storm, **raise the devil,** raise the deuce *or* dickens, raise a rumpus *or* a storm, raise a ruckus, raise Cain, **raise hell,** raise sand, raise the roof, whoop it up, hell around, horse around *or* about; **carry on,** go on, maffick <Brit>; **cut up,** cut up rough, **roughhouse**

ADJS 12 **unordered, orderless, disordered, unorganized, random, entropic, unarranged,** ungraded, unsorted, unclassified; untogether <nonformal>; **unmethodical,** immethodical; **unsystematic,** systemless, nonsystematic; disjunct, unjoined 801.20; disarticulated, **incoherent** 803.4; discontinuous; **formless,** amorphous, inchoate, shapeless; ununiform *or* nonuniform, unsymmetrical *or* nonsymmetrical, disproportionate, misshapen; **irregular, haphazard,** desultory, **erratic,** sporadic,

spasmodic, fitful, promiscuous, indiscriminate, casual, frivolous, capricious, random, hit-or-miss, vague, dispersed, wandering, planless, undirected, **aimless,** straggling, straggly; senseless, meaningless, gratuitous

13 **disorderly, in disorder,** disordered, **disorganized, disarranged, discomposed,** dislocated, deranged, convulsed; **upset, disturbed,** perturbed, unsettled, discomfited, disconcerted; **turbulent,** turbid, roily; **out of order,** out of place, misplaced, shuffled; **out of kilter** *or* **kelter** <nonformal>, **out of whack** <nonformal>, out of gear, out of joint, out of tune, on the fritz <nonformal>; **cockeyed** *and* skewgee *and* slaunchways *and* skygodlin <all nonformal>, skew-whiff <Brit <nonformal>, awry, amiss, askew, on the blink *and* haywire <both nonformal>

14 **disheveled, mussed up** <nonformal>, messed up <nonformal>, slobby <nonformal>, **rumpled,** tumbled, ruffled, snarled, snaggy; **tousled,** tously; uncombed, shaggy, matted

15 **slovenly, slipshod, careless, loose, slack,** nonformal, negligent; **untidy, unsightly,** unneat, slobby *and* scuzzy <both nonformal>, **unkempt; messy** <nonformal>, mussy <nonformal>, **sloppy** <nonformal>, scraggly, poky, seedy <nonformal>, **shabby,** shoddy, schlocky <nonformal>, lumpen, chintzy, grubby <nonformal>, **frowzy, blowzy,** tacky <nonformal>; **slatternly, sluttish, frumpish,** frumpy, draggletailed, drabbletailed, draggled, bedraggled; down at the heel, out at the heels, out at the elbows, in rags, ragged, raggedy-ass *or* ragged-ass <nonformal>, raggedy, tattered; **squalid,** sordid; dilapidated, ruinous, **beat-up** *and* shacky <both nonformal>

16 **confused, chaotic,** anarchic, **muddled, jumbled,** scattered, helter-skelter <nonformal>, higgledy-piggledy, hugger-mugger, skimble-skamble, in a mess; **topsy-turvy,** arsy-varsy, upside-down, ass-backwards <nonformal>; **mixed up, balled** *or* **bollixed up** <nonformal>, **screwed up** <nonformal>, mucked up <nonformal>, **fouled up** *and* fucked up *and* snafu <all nonformal>

ADVS 17 **in disorder, in disarray, in confusion,** Katy bar the door <nonformal>, in a jumble, in a tumble, in a muddle, in a mess; higgledy-piggledy, helter-skelter <nonformal>, hugger-mugger, skimble-skamble, harum-scarum <nonformal>, willy-nilly <nonformal>, all over, all over hell <nonformal>, **all over the place, all over the shop** <nonformal>

18 **haphazardly, unsystematically,** unmethodically, irregularly, desultorily, **erratically,** capriciously, promiscuously, indiscriminately, **sloppily** <nonformal>, **carelessly,** randomly, **fitfully;** by *or* at intervals, sporadically, spasmodically, by fits, **by fits and starts,** by *or* in snatches, in spots <nonformal>; every now and then *and* every once in a while <both nonformal>; **at random,** at haphazard, **by chance, hit or miss**

19 **chaotically, anarchically,** turbulently, **riotously; confusedly,** dispersedly, vaguely, wanderingly, **aimlessly,** planlessly, senselessly

810 DISARRANGEMENT
<bringing into disorder>

NOUNS 1 **disarrangement, derangement,** misarrangement, convulsion, dislocation; **disorganization,** shuffling; **discomposure,** disturbance, perturbation; **disorder** 809; insanity 925

VERBS 2 **disarrange, derange,** misarrange; **disorder, disorganize,** throw out of order, put out of gear, dislocate, upset the applecart, **disarray; dishevel,** rumple, ruffle; tousle <nonformal>, muss *and* **muss up** <both nonformal>, mess *and* **mess up** <both nonformal>; **litter, clutter,** scatter

3 **confuse, muddle, jumble,** confound, garble, tumble, scramble, snarl, tie in knots, fumble, pi; **shuffle,** riffle; **mix up,** snarl up, **ball** *or* **bollix up** <nonformal>, **foul up** *and* fuck up *and* **screw up** *and* muck up *and* snafu <all nonformal>; make a hash *or* mess of <nonformal>, play hob with <nonformal>

4 **discompose,** throw into confusion, **upset, unsettle, disturb,** trip up, perturb, trouble, distract, throw <nonformal>, throw into a tizzy *or* snit *or* stew <nonformal>, agitate, convulse, embroil; **psych** *and* spook *and* bug <all nonformal>

ADJS 5 **disarranged** 809.13, **confused** 809.16, **disordered** 809.12

811 CONTINUITY
<uninterrupted sequence>

NOUNS 1 **continuity, uninterruption, uninterruptedness,** featurelessness, unrelievedness, monotony, unintermittedness, unbrokenness, **uniformity** 780, un-differentiation; fullness, plenitude; seamlessness, jointlessness, gaplessness, smoothness; **consecutiveness,** successiveness; continuousness, **endlessness, ceaselessness, incessancy; constancy** 846.2, continualness, constant flow; steadiness, steady state, equilibrium, stability 854

2 **series, succession,** run, **sequence,** consecution, progression, course, gradation; **continuum,** plenum; lineage, descent, filiation; **connection, concatenation,** catenation, catena, **chain,** chaining, linkup, articulation, reticulation, nexus; chain reaction, powder train; **train,** range, rank, **file, line, string,** thread, queue, **row,** bank, tier; windrow, swath; single file, Indian file; array; **round, cycle,** rotation, routine, the daily grind <nonformal>, recurrence, periodicity, flywheel effect, pendulum; endless belt *or* chain, Möbius band *or* strip, *la ronde* <Fr>, endless round; gamut, spectrum, scale; drone, monotone, hum, buzz

3 **procession, train, column, line, string, cortege;** stream, steady stream; cavalcade, caravan, motorcade; **parade,** pomp; dress parade; promenade, review, march-past, flyover, flypast <Brit>, funeral; skimmington <Brit>; chain gang, coffel; mule train, pack train

VERBS 4 **continue,** be continuous, **connect, connect up, concatenate,** continuate, catenate, **join** 799.5, link *or* link up, **string together,** string, thread, chain *or* chain up, link *or* link up, follow in *or* form a series, run on, maintain continuity

5 **align, line, line up,** string out, rank, array, range, get *or* put in a row

6 **line up, get in** *or* **get on line,** queue *or* queue up <Brit>, make *or* form a line, get in formation, **fall in,** fall in *or* into line, fall into rank, take rank, take one's place

7 **file,** defile, file off; **parade,** go on parade, promenade, march past, fly over, fly past <Brit>

ADJS 8 **continuous,** continued, **continual,** continuing; **uninterrupted, unintermittent,** unintermitted, featureless, unrelieved, monotonous; **connected, joined** 799.13, linked, chained, concatenated, catenated, articulated; **unbroken,** serried, **uniform** 780.5, homogeneous, homogenized, cloned *or* clonish *and* cookie-cutter <all nonformal>, undifferentiated, wall-to-wall *and* back-to-back <both nonformal>, seamless, jointless, gapless, smooth, unstopped; unintermitting, unremitting; **incessant, constant, steady, stable, ceaseless,** unceasing, **endless,** unending, never-ending, **interminable,** perennial; **cyclical,** repetitive, **recurrent,** periodic; straight, running, **nonstop; round-the-clock,** twenty-four-hour, all-hours; immediate, direct

9 **consecutive, successive,** successional, back-to-back <nonformal>; progressive; **serial,** ordinal, seriate, catenary; sequent, **sequential;** linear, lineal, in-line

ADVS 10 **continuously, continually; uninterruptedly, unintermittently; without cease,** without stopping, with every other breath, without a break, back-to-back *and* wall-to-wall <both nonformal>, unbrokenly, gaplessly, seamlessly, jointlessly, **connectedly,** together, cumulatively, on end; unceasingly, **endlessly,** *ad infinitum* <L>, perennially, **interminably,** again and again, repeatedly, time after time, time and again, time and time again, repetitively, cyclically, monotonously, unrelievedly, week in week out, year in year out, year-round, on and on, at *or* on a stretch; round the clock, all day long, all the livelong day

11 **consecutively, progressively,** sequentially, successively, **in succession,** one after the other, back-to-back <nonformal>, **in turn,** turn about, turn and turn about; step by step; running, hand running <nonformal>; **serially,** in a series, *seriatim* <L>; **in a line,** in a row, in column, in file, in a chain, in single file, in Indian file

812 DISCONTINUITY
<interrupted sequence>

NOUNS 1 **discontinuity,** discontinuousness, discontinuation, discontinuance, noncontinuance; **incoherence** 803.1, **disconnectedness,** disconnection, delinkage, decoupling, discreteness, **disjunction** 801.1; **nonuniformity** 781; irregularity, **intermittence,** fitfulness 850.1; brokenness; nonseriality, nonlinearity, non sequitur; incompleteness 794; episode, parenthesis; broken thread

2 **interruption, suspension, break,** fissure, breach, gap, hiatus, lacuna, caesura; **interval, pause,** interim 825, lull, cessation, letup <nonformal>, **intermission**

VERBS 3 **discontinue, interrupt** 856.10, **break,** break off, **disjoin; disarrange** 810.2; intermit 850.2

ADJS 4 **discontinuous,** noncontinuous, unsuccessive, **incoherent** 803.4, nonserial, nonlinear, nonsequential, discontinued, **disconnected,** unconnected, unjoined 801.20, delinked, decoupled, *décousu* <Fr>, **broken;** nonuniform 781.3, irregular; broken, broken off, fragmentary, **interrupted,** suspended; disjunctive, discrete, discretive; **intermittent, fitful** 850.3; scrappy, snatchy, spotty, patchy, jagged; choppy, chopped-off, herky-jerky <nonformal>, jerky, spasmodic; episodic, parenthetic

ADVS 5 **discontinuously, disconnectedly,** brokenly, fragmentarily; at intervals; **haphazardly** 809.18, randomly, occasionally, infrequently, now and then, now and again, intermittently, fitfully, **by fits and starts,** by fits, by snatches, by catches, by jerks, spasmodically, episodically, by skips, skippingly, *per saltum* <L>; willy-nilly, **here and there,** in spots, sporadically, patchily

813 PRECEDENCE
<in order>

NOUNS 1 **precedence** *or* precedency, antecedence *or* antecedency, anteposition, anteriority, precession; the lead, front position, front seat, pole position, first chair; **priority,** preference, urgency; top priority; prefixation, prothesis; **superiority** 249; **dominion** 417.6; **precursor** 815; prelude 815.2; preliminaries, run-up *and* walk-up <both nonformal>; preceding 165.1

VERBS 2 **precede,** antecede, **come first,** come *or* go before, **go ahead of, go in advance,** stand first, stand at the head, **head,** head up <nonformal>, front, **lead** 165.2, take precedence, have priority; lead off, kick off, usher in; head the table *or* board, sit on the dais; rank, outrank, rate

3 <place before> **prefix, preface,** premise, prelude, prologize, preamble, introduce

ADJS 4 **preceding,** precedent, **prior,** antecedent, anterior, precessional, **leading** 165.3; **preliminary,** precursory, prevenient, prefatory, exordial, prelusive, preludial, proemial, preparatory, initiatory, propaedeutic, inaugural; **first, foremost,** headmost, **chief** 249.14

5 **former,** foregoing; aforesaid, aforementioned, beforementioned, abovementioned, aforenamed, forenamed, forementioned, said, named, same

ADVS 6 **before** 216.12; above, hereinbefore, hereinabove, *supra* <L>, *ante* <L>

814 SEQUENCE

NOUNS **1 sequence,** logical sequence, **succession,** successiveness, consecution, **consecutiveness,** following, coming after; descent, lineage, line; **series** 811.2; **order,** order of succession; **priority; progression,** procession, rotation; **continuity** 811; **continuation,** prolongation, extension, posteriority; suffixation, subjunction, postposition

VERBS **2 succeed, follow, ensue,** come or go after, **come next; inherit,** take the mantle of, step into the shoes or place of, take over

3 <place after> suffix, append, subjoin

ADJS **4 succeeding, successive, following, ensuing,** sequent, sequential, sequacious, posterior, **subsequent,** consequent; proximate, **next;** appendant, suffixed, postpositive, postpositional

815 PRECURSOR

NOUNS **1 precursor, forerunner,** foregoer, *voorlooper* <Dutch>, vaunt-courier, avant-courier, front- or lead-runner; pioneer, *voortrekker* <Dutch>, frontiersman, bushwhacker; scout, pathfinder, explorer, point, point man, trailblazer or trailbreaker, guide; **leader** 574.6, leadoff man or woman, bellwether, fugleman; **herald,** announcer, *buccinator* <L>, messenger, harbinger, stormy petrel; **predecessor,** forebear, precedent, antecedent, **ancestor; vanguard, avant-garde,** avant-gardist, innovator, groundbreaker

2 curtain raiser, countdown, run-up and walk-up <both nonformal>, lead-in, warm-up, kickoff, opening gun or shot; **opening episode,** first episode, prequel; **prelude, preamble, preface,** prologue, foreword, introduction, *avant-propos* <Fr>, protasis, proem, proemium, prolegomenon or prolegomena, exordium; **prefix,** prefixture; frontispiece; **preliminary,** front matter; overture, voluntary, verse; premise, presupposition, postulate, prolepsis; **innovation, breakthrough** <nonformal>, leap

VERBS **3 go before, pioneer,** blaze or break the trail, break new ground, be in the van or vanguard; guide; **lead** 165.2, lead or show the way; **precede** 813.2; herald, count down, run up, lead in, forerun, usher in, introduce

ADJS **4 preceding** 813.4; preliminary, exploratory, pioneering, trailblazing, door-

opening, kickoff, inaugural; **advanced,** avant-garde, original 337.5

816 SEQUEL

NOUNS **1 sequel,** sequela or sequelae, sequelant, sequent, sequitur, **consequence** 886.1; **continuation,** continuance, **follow-up** or **follow-through** <nonformal>; caboose; **supplement,** addendum, appendix, back matter; postfix, suffix; postscript or PS, subscript, postface; postlude, **epilogue,** conclusion, peroration, codicil; refrain, chorus, coda; envoi, colophon, tag; afterthought, second thought, double take <nonformal>, *arrière-pensée* <Fr>, *espirit d'escalier* <Fr>; parting or Parthian shot; last words, swan song, dying words, famous last words

2 afterpart, afterpiece; **wake,** trail, train, queue; **tail,** tailpiece, rear, rear end; tab, tag, trailer

3 aftermath, afterclap, afterglow, afterimage, aftereffect, side effect, by-product, spin-off, aftertaste; **aftergrowth,** aftercrop; **afterbirth,** placenta, secundines; afterpain

4 successor, replacement, backup, backup man or woman, substitute, stand-in; **descendant,** posterity, **heir,** inheritor

VERBS **5 succeed,** follow, come next, come after, come on the heels of; **follow through,** carry through, take the next step, drop the other shoe

817 BEGINNING

NOUNS **1 beginning, commencement, start,** running or flying start, starting point, square one <nonformal>, **outset,** outbreak, **onset,** oncoming; dawn; **creation, foundation, establishment, establishing, institution, origin,** origination, establishment, setting-up, setting in motion; **launching,** launch, launch or launching pad; alpha, A; **opening,** rising of the curtain; first crack out of the box <nonformal>, leadoff, kickoff and jump-off and send-off and start-off and take-off and blast-off and git-go and square one <all nonformal>, the word 'go' <nonformal>; fresh start, new departure; **opening wedge,** leading edge, cutting edge, thin end of the wedge; entry level, bottom rung, bottom of the ladder, low place on the totem pole

2 beginner, neophyte, tyro; newcomer 773.4, new arrival, Johnny-come-lately

<nonformal>; entry-level employee, low man on the totem pole; entrant, **novice,** novitiate, probationer, catechumen; **recruit,** raw recruit, rookie <nonformal>; **apprentice,** trainee, learner; baby, infant; nestling, fledging; freshman 572.6; tenderfoot, greenhorn, greeny <nonformal>; debutant, deb <nonformal>

3 **first,** first ever, prime, primal, primary, **initial,** alpha; **initiation,** initialization, first move, opening move, gambit, **first step,** baby step, *le premier pas* <Fr>, openers, starters, first lap, first round, first inning, first stage; breaking-in, warming-up; first blush, first glance, first sight, first impression

4 **origin,** origination, **genesis, inception,** incipience *or* incipiency, inchoation; **divine creation,** creationism, creation science; **birth,** birthing, bearing, parturition, pregnancy, nascency *or* nascence, nativity; **infancy,** babyhood, childhood, youth; freshman year; incunabula, beginnings, cradle

5 **inauguration,** installation *or* installment, induction, **introduction,** initiation; embarkation *or* embarkment, **launching,** floating, flotation, unveiling; debut, first appearance, coming out <nonformal>; opener <nonformal>, preliminary, curtain raiser *or* lifter; maiden speech, inaugural address

6 **basics, essentials, rudiments, elements, nuts and bolts** <nonformal>; **principles,** principia, first principles, first steps, **outlines, primer,** hornbook, grammar, alphabet, **ABC's,** abecedarium; introduction, induction

VERBS 7 **begin, commence, start; start up, kick** *or* **click in** <nonformal>; **start in, start off, start out, set out,** set sail, set in, set to *or* about, go *or* swing into action, get to *or* down to, **turn to,** fall to, pitch in <nonformal>, dive in <nonformal>, plunge into, head into <nonformal>, **go ahead,** let her rip <nonformal>, fire *or* blast away <nonformal>, take *or* jump *or* kick *or* tee *or* blast *or* send off <all nonformal>, get the show on the road <nonformal>, get *or* set *or* start the ball rolling <nonformal>, roll it *and* let it roll <both nonformal>

8 **make a beginning,** make a move <nonformal>, **start up,** get going <nonformal>, get off, set forth, set out, launch forth, get off the ground <nonformal>, **get under way,** set up shop, get in there <nonformal>; set a course, get

squared away <nonformal>; make an auspicious beginning, **get off to a good start,** make a dent; get in on the ground floor <nonformal>; **break in, warm up,** get one's feet wet <nonformal>, cut one's teeth

9 enter, **enter on** *or* **upon** *or* **into, embark in** *or* **on** *or* **upon,** take up, go into, have a go at <chiefly Brit>, take a crack *or* whack *or* shot at <nonformal>; **debut,** make one's debut

10 **initiate, originate, create,** invent; **precede** 813.2, **take the initiative, take the first step,** take the lead, pioneer 815.3; **lead,** lead off, lead the way; **ahead,** head up <nonformal>, stand at the head, stand first; **break the ice,** take the plunge, break ground, cut the first turf, lay the first stone

11 **inaugurate,** institute, **found, establish,** set up <nonformal>; **install,** initiate, induct; **introduce,** broach, bring up, lift up, raise; **launch,** float; christen <nonformal>; **usher in,** ring in <nonformal>; **set on foot,** set abroach, set agoing, turn on, kick-start *and* jump-start <both nonformal>, start up, start going, start the ball rolling <nonformal>

12 **open,** open up, breach, open the door to; open fire

13 **originate, take** *or* **have origin,** be born, take birth, come into the world, **become,** come to be, get to be <nonformal>, see the light of day, rise, **arise,** take rise, take its rise, **come forth, issue,** issue forth, come out, spring *or* crop up; burst forth, break out, erupt, irrupt

14 **engender, beget, procreate** 78.8; **give birth to, bear,** birth, bring to birth; father, mother, sire

ADJS 15 **beginning, initial,** initiatory *or* initiative; **incipient,** inceptive, **introductory,** inchoative, inchoate; inaugural *or* inauguratory; **prime,** primal, **primary,** primitive, primeval; **original, first,** first ever, first of all; aboriginal, autochthonous; **elementary,** elemental, **fundamental,** foundational; **rudimentary,** rudimental, abecedarian; **ancestral,** primogenital *or* primogenitary; **formative, creative,** procreative, inventive; embryonic, in embryo, in the bud, budding, fetal, gestatory, parturient, pregnant, in its infancy; infant, infantile, incunabular; **natal,** nascent, prenatal, antenatal, neonatal

16 **preliminary, prefatory,** preludial, proemial; entry-level, door-opening; prepositive, prefixed

17 **first, foremost,** front, up-front <nonfor-

mal>, **head, chief, principal**, premier, **leading, main**, flagship; maiden

ADVS **18 first**, firstly, **at first**, first off, first thing, for openers *or* starters <nonformal>, as a gambit, up front <nonformal>, **in the first place**, first and foremost, before everything, *primo* <L>; **principally**, mainly, chiefly, most of all; **primarily**, initially; **originally, in the beginning**, *in limine* <L>, **at the start**, at first glance *or* first blush, at the outset, at the first go-off <nonformal>; from the ground up, from the foundations, from the beginning, **from scratch** <nonformal>, from the first, **from the word 'go'** *and* from the git-go <both nonformal>, *ab origine* <L>, *ab initio* <L>; *ab ovo* <L>

WORD ELEMENTS **19** acro—, arche—, eo—, ne—, neo—, proto—; *Ur—* <Ger>

818 MIDDLE

NOUNS **1 middle**, median, midmost, **midst**; thick, thick of things; **center** 208.2; **heart, core**, nucleus, kernel; **mean** 246; interior 207.2; midriff, diaphragm; **waist**, waistline, zone, girth, tummy *and* belly girt <both nonformal>; equator; diameter

2 mid-distance, middle distance; **equidistance; half**, moiety; **middle ground**, middle of the road, centrism; halfway point *or* place, midway, midcourse, halfway house; bisection

VERBS **3** seek the middle, bisect; average 246.2; double, fold, middle <nautical>

ADJS **4 middle, medial**, median, mesial, middling, mediocre, average, **medium** 246.3, mezzo <music>, **mean, mid; midmost**, middlemost; **central** 208.11, core, nuclear; interior; **intermediate**, intermediary; equidistant, halfway, midway, equatorial; midland, mediterranean; midships, amidships; centrist, moderate, middle-of-the-road; center-seeking, centripetal

ADVS **5 midway, halfway, in the middle**, betwixt and between <nonformal>, halfway in the middle <nonformal>; plump *or* smack *or* slap-'*or* smack-dab in the middle <nonformal>; half-and-half, neither here nor there, *mezzo-mezzo* <Ital>; medially, mediumly; in the mean; *in medias res* <L>; **in the midst of**, in the thick of; midships, amidships

WORD ELEMENTS **6** mid—, medi—, medio—, mes—, meso—, mesio—; intermedi—, intermedio—

819 END

NOUNS **1 end**, end point, ending, perfection, be-all and end-all, **termination, terminus, terminal**, terminating, term, period, **expiration**, expiry, phaseout, phasedown, discontinuation, closeout, **cessation** 856, ceasing, consummation, culmination, **conclusion, finish, finis, finale**, the end, finishing, finalizing *or* finalization, a wrap <nonformal>, quietus, stoppage, windup *and* payoff <both nonformal>, curtain, curtains <nonformal>, all she wrote <nonformal>, fall of the curtain, end of the road *or* line <nonformal>; decease, taps, **death** 307; **last**, "latter end"—Bible, last gasp *or* breath, final twitch, last throe, last legs, last hurrah <nonformal>; omega, Ω, izzard, Z; **goal**, destination, stopping place, resting place, finish line, tape *and* wire <both nonformal>; denouement, catastrophe, final solution, resolution; last *or* final words, peroration, swan song, dying words, envoi, coda, epilogue; **fate, destiny**, last things, eschatology, last trumpet, Gabriel's trumpet, crack of doom, doom; **effect** 886; **happy ending**, Hollywood ending, walking into the sunset

2 extremity, extreme; limit 793.5, ultimacy, definitiveness, **boundary**, farthest bound, jumping-off place, Thule, *Ultima Thule* <L>, **pole; tip**, point, nib; tail, **tail end**, butt end, tag, tag end, fag end; bitter end; stub, stump, butt; bottom dollar <nonformal>, bottom of the barrel <nonformal>

3 close, closing, cessation; decline, lapse; **homestretch, last lap** *or* **round** *or* **inning** <nonformal>, last stage; beginning of the end

4 finishing stroke, ender, **end-all**, quietus, stopper, **deathblow**, death stroke, *coup de grâce* <Fr>, kiss of death; **finisher**, clincher, equalizer, crusher, **settler**; knockout *and* knockout blow <both nonformal>; sockdolager, KO *or* kayo *and* kayo punch <all nonformal>; final stroke, finishing *or* perfecting *or* crowning touch, last dab *or* lick <nonformal>

VERBS **5 end, terminate**, determine, close, close out, close the books on, phase out *or* down, **finish, conclude**, finish with, resolve, finish *or* wind up <nonformal>; **put an end to**, put a period to, put paid to <Brit>, put *or* lay to rest, **make an end of**, bring to an end, bring to a close *or* halt, end up; **get it over**, get over with *or* through with <nonformal>; bring down *or* drop the curtain; put the lid on <nonformal>, fold up <nonformal>, wrap *and* wrap up <both nonformal>, sew up <nonformal>; call off <nonformal>, call all bets off <nonformal>; **dispose of**, polish off <nonformal>; kibosh *and* put the kibosh on <both nonformal>, put the skids under <nonformal>; **stop, cease** 856.6; perorate; abort; scrap *and* scratch <both nonformal>; **kill** 308.13, extinguish, scrag *and* waste *and* take out *and* zap <all nonformal>, **give the quietus,** put the finisher *or* settler on <nonformal>, knock on *or* in the head, knock out <nonformal>, kayo *or* KO <both nonformal>, shoot down *and* shoot down in flames <both nonformal>, stop dead in one's tracks, wipe out <nonformal>; **cancel, delete,** expunge, censor, censor out, blank out, erase

6 **come to an end, draw to a close, expire, die** 307.19, come to rest, end up, land up; lapse, become void *or* extinct *or* defunct, run out, run its course, have its time *and* have it <both nonformal>, pass, **pass away,** die away, wear off *or* away, go out, blow over, be all over, be no more

7 **complete** 793.6, perfect, finish, finish off, finish up, put the last *or* final *or* finishing touches on, finalize <nonformal>

ADJS 8 **ended, at an end, terminated, concluded, finished, complete** 793.9, perfected, settled, decided, set at rest; **over, all over,** all up <nonformal>; all off <nonformal>, all bets off <nonformal>; **done,** done with, over with, over and done with, through *and* through with <both nonformal>; wound up <nonformal>, washed up <nonformal>; all over but the shouting <nonformal>; **dead** 307.30, **defunct,** extinct; **finished,** defeated, out of action, disabled, *hors de combat* <Fr>; **canceled, deleted,** expunged, censored *or* censored out, blanked *or* blanked out, bleeped *or* bleeped out

9 <nonformal terms> **belly-up, dead meat,** kaput, shot, done for, SOL *or* shit out of luck, scragged, shot down, shot down in flames, down in flames, wasted, zapped, pffft *or* phut, wiped out, washed up, down and out, down the tubes, totaled

10 **ending, closing, concluding, finishing,** culminating *or* culminative, consummative *or* consummatory, **ultimate,** definitive, perfecting *or* perfective, terminating, crowning, capping

11 **final, terminal,** terminating *or* terminative, determinative, definitive, **conclusive; last,** last-ditch <nonformal>, last

but not least, eventual, farthest, extreme, boundary, border, limbic, limiting, polar, **endmost, ultimate;** caudal, tail, tail-end

ADVS 12 **finally,** in fine; **ultimately, eventually, as a matter of course; lastly,** last, **at last,** at the last *or* end *or* conclusion, at length, at long last; **in conclusion, in sum;** conclusively, once and for all

13 **to the end, to the bitter end, all the way,** to the last gasp, the last extremity, **to a finish,** *à outrance* <Fr>, till hell freezes over <nonformal>, "to the edge of doom, "to the last syllable of recorded time"— both Shakespeare

PHRS 14 **that's all for, that's final, that's that,** that's all she wrote *and* that buttons it up <both nonformal>, that's the end of the matter, so much for that, nuf said *and* enough said <both nonformal>; the subject is closed, the matter is ended, the deal is off <nonformal>; "the rest is silence"—Shakespeare

WORD ELEMENTS 15 acr—, acro—, tel—, telo—, tele—

820 TIME

NOUNS 1 **time, duration,** *durée* <Fr>, lastingness, continuity 811, term, while, tide, space; real time; psychological time; tense 530.12; **period** 823, time frame; time warp; cosmic time; kairotic time; space-time 158.6; the past 836, the present 837, the future 838; timebinding; **chronology** 831.1

2 Time, **Father Time,** Cronus, Kronos; "Old Time, that greatest and longest established spinner of all"—Dickens, "that old bald cheater, Time"—Ben Jonson; "Old Time, the clocksetter, that bald sexton Time, "that old common arbitrator, Time, "the nurse and breeder of all good"—all Shakespeare, "the soul of the world"—Pythagoras, "the author of authors"—, "the greatest innovator"— both Francis Bacon, "the devourer of things"—Ovid, "the illimitable, silent, never-resting thing called Time"— Carlyle, "a short parenthesis in a long period"—Donne, "a sandpile we run our fingers in"—Sandburg

3 tract of time, corridors of time, whirligig of time, glass *or* hourglass of time, sands of time, ravages of time, noiseless foot of Time, scythe of Time, "the dark backward and abysm of time, "the tooth of time"—both Shakespeare

4 **passage of time, course of time, lapse of time,** progress of time, process of time,

succession of time, time-flow, flow *or* flowing *or* flux of time, sweep of time, stream *or* current *or* tide of time, march *or* step of time, flight of time, time's caravan, "Time's revolving wheels"—Petrarch, "Time's wingèd chariot"—Andrew Marvell

VERBS **5 elapse,** lapse, **pass, expire,** run its course, run out, go *or* pass by; **flow,** tick away *or* by *or* on, run, proceed, advance, roll *or* press on, flit, fly, slip, slide, glide; **continue** 811.4, last, **endure,** go *or* run *or* flow on

6 spend time, pass time, put in time, employ *or* use time, fill *or* occupy time, kill time <nonformal>, consume time, take time, take up time, while away the time; find *or* look for time; race with *or* against time, buy time, work against time, run out of time, make time stand still; weekend, winter, summer; keep time, measure time

ADJS **7 temporal, chronological;** durational, durative; lasting, continuous 811.8

ADVS **8 when, at which time,** what time *and* whenas <both old>, at which moment *or* instant, on which occasion, **upon which, whereupon,** at which, in which time, at what time, in what period, on what occasion, whenever

9 at that time, on that occasion, at the same time as, at the same time *or* moment that, then, concurrently, simultaneously, contemporaneously

10 in the meantime, meanwhile 825.5; during the time; for the duration; at a stretch

11 then, thereat, thereupon, **at that time,** at that moment *or* instant, in that case *or* instance, on that occasion; **again,** at another time, at some other time, anon

12 whenever, whene'er, whensoever, whensoe'er, **at whatever time,** at any time, anytime, no matter when; if ever, once

13 in the year of our Lord, *anno Domini* <L>, AD, in the Common *or* Christian Era, CE; *ante Christum* <L>, AC, before Christ, BC, before the Common *or* Christian era, BCE; *anno urbis conditae* <L>, AUC; *anno regni* <L>, AR

PREPS **14 during,** pending, *durante* <law>; **in the course of,** in the process of, in the middle of; **in the time of,** at the time of, in the age *or* era of; over, through, **throughout,** throughout the course of, **for the period of;** until the conclusion of

15 until, till, to, unto, **up to,** up to the time of

16 CONJS **when, while,** whilst <chiefly Brit>, the while; **during the time that,** at the time that, at the same time that, at *or* during which time; **whereas, as long as,** as far as

17 PHRS **time flies,** *tempus fugit* <L>, time runs out, time marches on, "Time rolls his ceaseless course"—Sir Walter Scott, "Time and tide stayeth for no man"—Richard Braithwaite

WORD ELEMENTS **18** chron—, chrono—, —chronous

821 TIMELESSNESS

NOUNS **1 timelessness,** neverness, datelessness, eternity 828.1,2; no time, no time at all, running out of time; time out of time, stopping time; everlasting moment

2 <a time that will never come> Greek calends *or* kalends, when hell freezes over, the thirtieth of February, "till Birnam Wood do come to Dunsinane"—Shakespeare

ADJS **3 timeless, dateless**

ADVS **4 never,** ne'er, **not ever,** at no time, on no occasion, not at all; **nevermore;** never in the world, never on earth; not in donkey's years <Brit>, never in all one's born days <nonformal>, never in my life, *jamais de la vie* <Fr>

5 without date, *sine die* <L>, open, open-ended

822 INFINITY

NOUNS **1 infinity,** infiniteness, infinitude, the all, the be-all and end-all; **boundlessness, limitlessness, endlessness;** illimitability, interminability, termlessness; **immeasurability,** unmeasurability, immensity, incalculability, innumerability, incomprehensibility; measurelessness, countlessness, unreckonability, numberlessness; exhaustlessness, inexhaustibility; universality, "world without end"—Bible; **all-inclusiveness,** all-comprehensiveness; **eternity** 828.1,2, **perpetuity** 828, forever; "a dark illimitable ocean, without bound"—Milton

VERBS **2 have no limit** *or* **bounds,** have *or* know no end, be without end, **go on and on,** go on forever, never cease *or* end

ADJS **3 infinite, boundless, endless, limitless,** termless, shoreless; unbounded, uncircumscribed, **unlimited,** illimited, infinitely continuous *or* extended, stretching *or* extending everywhere, without bound, without limit *or* end, no end of *or* to; illimitable, **interminable,** interminate; **immeasurable,** incalculable, unreckonable, innumerable, incomprehensible, unfathomable; measureless, countless, sumless; **unmeasured,** unmeasurable, immense, unplumbed, untold, unnumbered, without measure or number or term; exhaustless, inexhaustible; **all-inclusive,** all-comprehensive 863.14, **universal** 863.14; **perpetual, eternal** 828.7; "as boundless as the sea"—Shakespeare

ADVS **4 infinitely, illimitably,** boundlessly, limitlessly, **interminably; immeasurably,** measurelessly, immensely, incalculably, innumerably, incomprehensibly; **endlessly,** without end or limit; ad infinitum <L>, to infinity; **forever, eternally** 828.10, in perpetuity, "to the last syllable of recorded time"—Shakespeare

823 PERIOD
<portion or point of time>

NOUNS **1 period, point, juncture,** stage; **interval,** lapse of time, time frame, space, span, timespan, stretch, time-lag, timegap; **time,** while, **moment,** minute, instant, hour, day, **season;** psychological moment; pregnant or fateful moment, fated moment, kairos, moment of truth; **spell** 824; "this bank and shoal of time"—Shakespeare

2 <periods> **moment, second,** millisecond, microsecond, nanosecond; **minute,** New York minute <nonformal>; hour, manhour; **day,** sun; weekday; **week;** fortnight; **month,** moon, lunation; calendar month, lunar month; **quarter; semester,** trimester, term, session, academic year; **year,** annum, sun, twelvemonth; common year, regular year, intercalary year, leap year, bissextile year, defective year, perfect or abundant year; solar year, lunar year, sidereal year; fiscal year; calendar year; quinquennium, lustrum, luster; **decade,** decennium, decennary; **century; millennium**

3 term, time, duration, **tenure;** spell 824

4 age, generation, time, day, date, cycle; **eon** or aeon; Platonic year, great year, annus magnus <L>

5 era, epoch, age; Golden Age, Silver Age; Ice Age, glacial epoch; stone Age, Bronze Age, Iron Age, steel Age; Middle Ages, Dark Ages; Era of Good Feeling; Jacksonian Age; Reconstruction Era and Gilded Age <1870s and '80s>; Gay Nineties and Naughty Nineties and Mauve Decade and Golden Age and Gilded Age <1890s>; Roaring Twenties and Golden Twenties and Mad Decade and Age of the Red-Hot

Mamas and Jazz Age and Flapper Era <1920s>; Depression Era; New Deal Era; Prohibition Era

6 <modern age> Technological Age, Automobile Age, Air Age, Jet Age, Supersonic Age, Atomic Age, Electronic Age, Computer Age, Space Age, Age of Anxiety, Age of Aquarius

7 geological time periods

Algonkian	Oligocene
Archean	Ordovician
Archeozoic	Paleocene
Cambrian	Paleozoic
Carboniferous	Pennsylvanian
Cenozoic	Permian
Comanchean	Pleistocene
Cretaceous	Pliocene
Devonian	Precambrian
Eocene	Proterozoic
Glacial	Quaternary
Holocene	Recent
Jurassic	Silurian
Lower Cretaceous	Tertiary
Lower Tertiary	Triassic
Mesozoic	Upper Cretaceous
Miocene	Upper Tertiary
Mississippian	

824 SPELL
<period of duty, etc>

NOUNS **1 spell,** fit, stretch, go <nonformal>

2 turn, bout, round, inning, innings <Brit>, **time,** time at bat, place, say, whack and go <both nonformal>; opportunity, chance; **relief, spell;** one's turn, one's move <nonformal>, one's say

3 shift, work shift, **tour,** tour of duty, stint, bit, **watch, trick,** time, **turn,** relay, spell or turn of work; day shift, night shift, swing shift, graveyard shift <nonformal>, dogwatch, anchor watch; lobster trick or tour, sunrise watch; split shift, split schedule; flextime or flexitime; halftime, part-time, full-time; **overtime**

4 term, time; **tenure,** continuous tenure, tenure in or of office; **enlistment, hitch** <nonformal>, tour; prison term, stretch <nonformal>

VERBS **5 take one's turn,** have a go <nonformal>; **take turns,** alternate, turn and turn about; **time off, spell** and **spell off** <both nonformal>, **relieve,** cover, **fill in for,** take over for; put in one's time, work one's shift; **stand one's watch** or **trick,** keep a watch; have one's innings <Brit>; do a stint; hold office, have tenure or tenure of appointment; **enlist,** sign up; reenlist, re-up <nonformal>; do a hitch

<nonformal>, do a tour *or* tour of duty; serve *or* do time

825 INTERIM

<intermediate period>

NOUNS **1 interim, interval, interlude, intermission,** pause, break, **time-out,** recess, coffee break, halftime *or* halftime intermission, interruption; **lull,** quiet spell, resting point, point of repose, plateau, letup, relief, vacation, holiday, time off, off-time; downtime; **respite** 20.2; **intermission,** interval <Brit>, entr'acte; *intermezzo* <Ital>; interregnum
2 meantime, meanwhile, while, the while
VERBS **3 intervene,** interlude, interval; **pause,** break, **recess,** declare a recess; call a halt *or* break *or* intermission; **call time** *or* time-out; take five *and* ten, etc *and* take a break <all nonformal>
ADJS **4 interim, temporary,** tentative, provisional, provisory
ADVS **5 meanwhile, meantime, in the meanwhile** *or* **meantime,** in the interim, *ad interim* <L>; between acts *or* halves *or* periods, betweenwhiles, betweentimes, between now and then; till *or* until then; *en attendant* <Fr>, in the intervening time, during the interval, at the same time, for the nonce, for a time *or* season; *pendente lite* <L>

826 DURATION

NOUNS **1 durability, endurance,** duration, durableness, **lastingness,** *longueur* <Fr>, perenniality, abidingness, long-lastingness, perdurability; **continuance,** maintenance, **steadfastness,** constancy, **stability** 854, **persistence, permanence** 852, standing, long standing; **longevity,** long-livedness; **antiquity, age; survival,** survivability, viability, defiance *or* defeat of time; **service life,** serviceable life, useful life, shelf life, mean life; **perpetuity** 828
2 protraction, prolongation, continuation, extension, lengthening, drawing- *or* stretching- *or* dragging- *or* spinning-out, lingering; procrastination 845.5
3 length of time, distance of time, vista *or* stretch *or* desert of time, "deserts of vast eternity"—Andrew Marvell, "the dark backward and abysm of time"—Shakespeare; corridor *or* tunnel of time
4 long time, long while, long; **age** *and* **ages** <both nonformal>, aeon, **century, eternity,** years, **years on end,** coon's age

<nonformal>, donkey's years <Brit nonformal>, month of Sundays <nonformal>, right smart spell <nonformal>
5 lifetime, life, life's duration, life expectancy, lifespan, expectation of life, "threescore years and ten"—Bible, period of existence, all the days of one's life; **generation, age;** all one's born days *or* natural life <nonformal>
VERBS **6 endure, last** *or* **last out,** bide, **abide,** dwell, perdure, **continue,** run, extend, **go on,** carry on, hold on, keep on, stay on, run on, stay the course, go the distance, go through with, grind *or* slog on, grind *or* plug away; live, **live on,** continue to be, subsist, exist, tarry; get *or* keep one's head above water; **persist;** hang in *and* hang in there *and* hang tough <all nonformal>; maintain, sustain, **remain, stay,** keep, hold, stand, prevail, last long, hold out; **survive,** defy *or* defeat time; live to fight another day; perennate; **survive,** live on, live through; wear, wear well
7 linger on, linger, tarry, go on, **go on and on, wear on,** crawl, creep, drag, **drag on,** drag along, drag its slow length along, drag a lengthening chain
8 outlast, outstay, last out, outwear, **outlive, survive**
9 protract, prolong, continue, **extend, lengthen,** lengthen out, **draw out, spin out,** drag *or* stretch out; linger on, dwell on; dawdle, procrastinate, temporize, drag one's feet
ADJS **10 durable,** perdurable, **lasting, enduring,** perduring, **abiding, continuing,** remaining, staying, **stable** 854.12, persisting, **persistent,** perennial; inveterate, agelong; **steadfast, constant,** intransient, immutable, unfading, evergreen, sempervirent, **permanent** 852.7, perennial, **long-lasting,** long-standing, of long duration *or* standing, diuturnal; long-term; **long-lived,** tough, hardy, vital, longevous *or* longeval; **ancient,** aged, antique; macrobiotic; chronic; **perpetual** 828.7
11 protracted, prolonged, extended, lengthened; **long,** overlong, time-consuming, interminable, marathon, lasting, **lingering,** languishing; long-continued, long-continuing, long-pending; drawn- *or* stretched- *or* dragged- *or* spun-out, long-drawn, **long-drawn-out;** long-winded, prolix, verbose 538.12
12 daylong, nightlong, weeklong, monthlong, yearlong
13 lifelong, livelong, lifetime, for life
ADVS **14 for a long time, long, for long,** inter-

minably, unendingly, undyingly, persistently, protractedly, enduringly; for ever so long <nonformal>, for many a long day, for life *or* a lifetime, for an age *or* ages, for a coon's *or* dog's age <nonformal>, for a month of Sundays <nonformal>, for donkey's years <Brit nonformal>, **forever and a day, forever and ever, for years on end, for days on end, etc;** all the year round, all the day long, the livelong day, as the day is long; morning, noon, and night; hour after hour, day after day, month after month, year after year; day in day out, month in month out, year in year out; till hell freezes over <nonformal>, till you're blue in the face <nonformal>, till the cows come home <nonformal>, till shrimps learn to whistle <nonformal>, till doomsday, from now till doomsday, from here to eternity, till the end of time; since time began, from way back, long ago, long since, time out of mind, time immemorial

827 TRANSIENCE
<short duration>

NOUNS **1 transience** *or* **transiency,** transientness, **impermanence** *or* **impermanency,** transitoriness, changeableness 853, rootlessness, **mutability, instability, temporariness,** fleetingness, **momentariness;** finitude; **ephemerality,** ephemeralness, short duration; evanescence, volatility, fugacity, **short-livedness; mortality,** death, perishability, corruptibility, caducity; **expedience** 994, ad hoc, ad hockery *or* ad hocism, adhocracy

2 brevity, briefness, shortness; swiftness 174, fleetness

3 short time, little while, little, **instant, moment** 829.3, mo <nonformal>, small space, span, spurt, **short spell;** no time, less than no time; bit *or* **little bit,** a breath, the wink of an eye, pair of winks <nonformal>; **two shakes** *and* two shakes of a lamb's tail <both nonformal>

4 transient, transient guest *or* boarder, temporary lodger; **sojourner;** passer, passerby; **wanderer; vagabond,** drifter, derelict, homeless person, tramp, hobo, bum <nonformal>

5 ephemeron, ephemera, ephemeral; ephemerid, ephemeris, ephemerides <pl>; mayfly; bubble, smoke; nine days' wonder, flash in the pan; snows of yesteryear, *neiges d'antan* <Fr>

VERBS **6** <be transient> **flit, fly,** fleet; pass, **pass away, vanish, evaporate,** dissolve, evanesce, disappear, fade, melt, sink; fade like a shadow *or* dream, vanish like a dream, burst like a bubble, **go up in smoke,** melt like snow; "leave not a rack behind"—Shakespeare

ADJS **7 transient, transitory,** transitive; **temporary,** temporal; **impermanent,** unenduring, undurable, nondurable, nonpermanent; frail, brittle, fragile, insubstantial; changeable 853.6, **mutable, unstable,** inconstant 853.7; capricious, fickle, impulsive, impetuous; **short-lived, ephemeral,** fly-by-night, evanescent, volatile, **momentary;** deciduous; **passing,** fleeting, flitting, flying, fading, dying; fugitive, fugacious; perishable, mortal, corruptible; "as transient as the clouds"—Robert Green Ingersoll, here today and gone tomorrow; **expedient** 994.5, ad-hoc

8 brief, short, short-time, quick, brisk, swift, fleet, speedy, "short and sweet"—Thomas Lodge; meteoric, cometary, flashing, flickering; short-term, short-termed

ADVS **9 temporarily,** for the moment, for the time, *pro tempore* <L>, pro tem, for the nonce, **for the time being,** for a time, awhile

10 transiently, impermanently, evanescently, transitorily, changeably, mutably, ephemerally, fleetingly, flittingly, flickeringly, **briefly, shortly,** swiftly, quickly, **for a little while,** for a short time; **momentarily,** for a moment; **in an instant** 829.7

11 PHRS "all flesh is grass"—Bible

828 PERPETUITY
<endless duration>

NOUNS **1 perpetuity,** perpetualness; **eternity,** eternalness, sempiternity, infinite duration; everness, foreverness, **everlastingness, permanence** 852, everduringness, duration 826, perdurability, indestructibility; **constancy,** stability, immutability, continuance, continualness, perennialness *or* perenniality, **ceaselessness,** unceasingness, incessancy; timelessness 821; **endlessness,** neverendingness, **interminability; infinity** 822; coeternity

2 forever, an eternity, endless time, **time without end;** "a moment standing still for ever"—James Montgomery, "a short parenthesis in a long period"—Donne, "deserts of vast eternity"—Andrew Marvell

3 **immortality**, eternal life, **deathlessness**, imperishability, undyingness, incorruptibility *or* incorruption, athanasy *or* athanasia; eternal youth, fountain of youth

4 **perpetuation**, preservation, eternalization, immortalization; eternal recreation, eternal return *or* recurrence; steady-state universe

VERBS 5 **perpetuate, preserve,** preserve from oblivion, keep fresh *or* alive, perennialize, **eternalize,** eternize, **immortalize;** monumentalize; freeze, embalm

6 last *or* endure forever, **go on forever,** go on and on, live forever, **have no end,** have no limits *or* bounds *or* term, never cease *or* end *or* die *or* pass

ADJS 7 **perpetual, everlasting,** everliving, ever-being, ever-abiding, ever-during, ever-durable, permanent 852.7, perdurable, indestructible; **eternal,** sempiternal, eterne <old>, **infinite** 822.3, aeonian *or* eonian; dateless, ageless, timeless, immemorial; **endless,** unending, never-ending, without end, **interminable,** nonterminous, nonterminating; **continual,** continuous, steady, **constant, ceaseless,** nonstop, unceasing, never-ceasing, **incessant,** unremitting, unintermitting, uninterrupted, "continuous as the stars that shine"—Wordsworth; coeternal

8 **perennial,** indeciduous, **evergreen,** sempervirent, ever-new, ever-young; ever-blooming, ever-bearing

9 **immortal,** everlasting, **deathless,** undying, never-dying, **imperishable,** incorruptible, amaranthine; fadeless, **unfading,** never-fading, ever-fresh; frozen, embalmed

ADVS 10 **perpetually,** in perpetuity, **everlastingly, eternally, permanently** 852.9, perennially, perdurably, indestructibly, **constantly,** continually, steadily, **ceaselessly,** unceasingly, never-ceasingly, **incessantly,** never-endingly, **endlessly,** unendingly, **interminably,** without end, world without end, time without end, "from everlasting to everlasting"—Bible; **infinitely,** *ad infinitum* <L> 822.4

11 **always, all along, all the time,** all the while, at all times, *semper et ubique* <L, always and everywhere>; ever and always, **invariably,** without exception, never otherwise, *semper eadem* <L, ever the same; Elizabeth I>

12 **forever, forevermore, for ever and ever,** forever and aye; forever and a day

<nonformal>, now and forever, *ora e sempre* <Ital>, "yesterday and today and forever"—Bible; **ever, evermore,** ever and anon, ever and again; aye, for aye; **for good,** for keeps <nonformal>, for good and all, for all time; throughout the ages, from age to age, in all ages, "for ages of ages"—Douay Bible; **to the end of time,** till time stops *or* runs out, "to the last syllable of recorded time"—Shakespeare, to the crack of doom, to the last trumpet, till doomsday; till you're blue in the face <nonformal>, till hell freezes over <nonformal>, till the cows come home <nonformal>

13 **for life,** for all one's natural life, for the term of one's days, while life endures, while one draws breath, in all one's born days <nonformal>; from the cradle to the grave, from the womb to the tomb; **till death,** till death do us part

829 INSTANTANEOUSNESS
<imperceptible duration>

NOUNS 1 **instantaneousness** *or* **instantaneity,** momentariness, **momentaneousness** <old>, **immediateness** *or* immediacy, near-simultaneity *or* -simultaneousness; simultaneity 835

2 **suddenness, abruptness, precipitateness,** precipitance *or* precipitancy; **unexpectedness,** unanticipation, inexpectation 131

3 **instant, moment, second,** sec <nonformal>, split second, millisecond, microsecond, nanosecond, half a second, half a mo <Brit nonformal>, minute, **trice,** twinkle, **twinkling, twinkling** *or* **twinkle of an eye,** twink, **wink,** bat of an eye <nonformal>, **flash,** crack, tick, stroke, coup, breath, twitch; two shakes of a lamb's tail *and* two shakes *and* shake *and* half a shake *and* **jiffy** *and* jiff *and* half a jiffy <all nonformal>

ADJS 4 **instantaneous,** instant, momentary, momentaneous <old>, **immediate,** presto, quick as thought *or* lightning; lightning-like, lightning-swift; nearly simultaneous; simultaneous

5 **sudden, abrupt,** precipitant, **precipitate, precipitous; hasty,** headlong, impulsive, impetuous; speedy, swift, quick; **unexpected** 131.10, unanticipated, unpredicted, unforeseen, unlooked-for; **surprising** 131.11, startling, electrifying, shocking, nerve-shattering

ADVS 6 **instantly,** instanter, momentaneously <old>, momentarily, momently, instantaneously, immediately, **right off the bat** <nonformal>; on the instant, on the dot <nonformal>, on the nail

7 **quickly, in an instant, in a trice, in a second,** in a moment, in a mo *or* half a mo <Brit nonformal>, in a bit *or* little bit, in a jiff *or* jiffy *or* half a jiffy <nonformal>, in a flash, in a wink <nonformal>, in a twink, **in a twinkling, in the twinkling of an eye, as quick as a wink,** as quick as greased lightning <nonformal>, in two shakes *or* a shake *or* half a shake <nonformal>, in two shakes of a lamb's tail <nonformal>, before you can say 'Jack Robinson' <nonformal>; **in no time,** in less than no time, in nothing flat <nonformal>, in short order; at the drop of a hat *or* handkerchief, like a shot, like a shot out of hell <nonformal>; with the speed of light

8 **at once,** at once and on the spot, **then and there, now, right now, right away, right off,** straightway, straightaway, forthwith, this minute, this very minute, **without delay,** without the least delay, in a hurry <nonformal>, *pronto* <Sp>, *subito* <Ital>; **simultaneously,** at the same instant, in the same breath; **all at once,** all together, at one time, at a stroke, at one stroke, at a blow, at one blow, at one swoop, "at one fell swoop"— Shakespeare; at one jump, *per saltum* <L>, *uno saltu* <L>

9 **suddenly,** sudden, of a sudden, on a sudden, **all of a sudden, all at once: abruptly,** sharp; **precipitously** *or* precipitately, precipitantly, impulsively, impetuously, hastily; dash; smack, bang, slap, plop, plunk, plump, pop; **unexpectedly** 131.14, out of a clear blue sky, when least expected, before you know it; on short notice, without notice *or* warning, without further ado, unawares, **surprisingly** 131.15, startlingly, like a thunderbolt *or* thunderclap, like a flash, like a bolt from the blue

10 **PHRS** no sooner said than done

830 EVENT

NOUNS 1 event, eventuality, eventuation, effect 886, issue, outcome, result, aftermath, consequence; **realization,** materialization, coming to be *or* pass, incidence; contingency, contingent; accident 971.6

2 **event, occurrence, incident, episode, experience, adventure,** hap, **happening,** happenstance, **phenomenon,** fact, matter of fact, reality, particular, circumstance, **occasion,** turn of events; **nonevent,** pseudo-event, media event *or* happening, photo opportunity; what's happening

3 **affair, concern, matter,** thing, concernment, interest, **business,** job <nonformal>, **transaction,** proceeding, doing; current affairs *or* events; cause célèbre, matter of moment

4 **affairs, concerns, matters,** circumstances, relations, **dealings, proceedings,** doings, goings-on <nonformal>; course *or* run of events, run of things, the way of things, the way things go, what happens, current of events, march of events; the world, life, the times; order of the day; **conditions, state of affairs,** environing *or* ambient phenomena, state *or* condition of things

VERBS 5 occur, happen 971.11, hap, eventuate, **take place,** come *or* go down <nonformal>, go on, **transpire,** be realized, come, **come off** <nonformal>, **come about,** come true, **come to pass,** pass, pass off, go off, fall, **befall,** betide; **be found,** be met with

6 **turn up, show up** <nonformal>, **come along,** come one's way, cross one's path, come into being *or* existence, chance, **crop up,** spring up, pop up <nonformal>, arise, come forth, come *or* draw on, appear, approach, materialize, present itself, be destined for one

7 **turn out, result** 886.5

8 **experience, have, know, feel,** taste; **encounter, meet,** meet with, meet up with <nonformal>; run up against <nonformal>; **undergo, go through,** pass through, be subjected to, be exposed to, stand under, labor under, **endure, suffer,** sustain, pay, spend

ADJS 9 happening, occurring, current, actual, passing, taking place, on, **going on,** ongoing <nonformal>, **prevalent, prevailing,** that is, that applies, in the wind, afloat, afoot, under way, in hand, **on foot,** ado, doing; incidental, circumstantial, accompanying; accidental; occasional; resultant; eventuating

10 **eventful, momentous, stirring,** bustling, full of incident; phenomenal

11 **eventual, coming, final,** last, **ultimate; contingent,** collateral, secondary, indirect

ADVS 12 eventually, ultimately, finally, in the end, after all is said and done, in the long run, over the long haul; in the course of things, in the natural way of things, as things go, as times go, as the world goes, as the tree falls, the way the cookie crumbles <nonformal>, as things turn out, as it may be *or* happen *or* turn out, as luck *or* fate *or* destiny wills

CONJS **13 in the event that, if, in case,** if it should happen that, just in case, in any case, in either case, in the contingency that, in case that; provided 958.12

831 MEASUREMENT OF TIME

NOUNS **1 chronology,** timekeeping, timing, clocking, horology, **chronometry,** horometry, chronoscopy; watch- *or* clock-making; calendar-making; **dating,** carbon-14 dating, dendrochronology

2 time of day, time 820, **the time; hour,** minute; stroke of the hour, time signal, bell

3 standard time, civil time, zone time, slow time <nonformal>; mean time, solar time, mean solar time, sidereal time, apparent time, local time; universal time *or* Greenwich time *or* Greenwich mean time *or* GMT, Eastern time, Central time, Mountain time, Pacific time; Atlantic time; Alaska time, Yukon time; daylight-saving time, fast time <nonformal>, summer time <Brit>; **time zone**

4 date, point of time, time, day; postdate, antedate; datemark; date line, International Date Line

5 epact, annual epact, monthly *or* menstrual epact

6 timepiece, timekeeper, **timer, chronometer,** ship's watch; horologe, horologium; **clock,** Big Ben, ticker <nonformal>, **watch,** turnip <nonformal>; hourglass, sundial; watch *or* clock movement, clockworks, watchworks

7 almanac, The Old Farmer's Almanac, Ephemeris and Nautical Almanac, Information Please Almanac, Nautical Almanac, Poor Richard's Almanac, Reader's Digest Almanac, Whitaker's Almanack, World Almanac

8 calendar, calends; calendar stone, chronogram; almanac *or* astronomical calendar, ephemeris; perpetual calendar; Chinese calendar, church *or* ecclesiastical calendar, Cotsworth calendar, Gregorian calendar, Hebrew *or* Jewish calendar, Hindu calendar, international fixed calendar, Julian calendar, Muslim calendar, Republican *or* Revolutionary calendar, Roman calendar

9 chronicle, chronology, register, registry, record; **annals,** journal, diary; time sheet, time book, **log,** daybook; timecard, time

ticket, clock card, check sheet; datebook; date slip; **timetable,** schedule, timeline, time schedule, time chart; time scale; time study, motion study, time and motion study

10 chronologist, chronologer, chronographer, horologist, horologer; watchmaker *or* clockmaker; timekeeper, timer; **chronicler,** annalist, diarist; calendar maker, calendarist

VERBS **11 time, fix** *or* **set the time,** mark the time; **keep time,** mark time, measure time, beat time; **clock** <nonformal>

12 punch the clock *and* punch in *and* punch out *and* **time in** *and* **time out** <all nonformal>; ring in, ring out; clock in, clock out; check in, check out; check off

13 date, be dated, date at *or* from, date back, bear a date of, bear the date of; fix *or* set the date, make a date; **predate,** backdate, antedate; **postdate; update,** bring up to date; datemark; date-stamp; dateline

14 chronologize, chronicle, calendar, intercalate

ADJS **15 chronologic<al>,** temporal, timekeeping; **chronometric<al>,** chronoscopic, chronographic *or* chronographical, chronogrammatic *or* chronogrammatical, horologic *or* horological, horometric *or* horometrical, metronomic *or* metronomical, calendric *or* calendrical, intercalary *or* intercalated; dated; annalistic, diaristic; calendarial

ADVS **16 o'clock,** of the clock, by the clock; half past, half *or* half after <Brit>; a quarter of *or* to, a quarter past *or* after

832 ANACHRONISM

<false estimation or knowledge of time>

NOUNS **1 anachronism,** chronological *or* historical error, **mistiming, misdating,** misdate, postdating, antedating; parachronism, metachronism, prochronism; prolepsis, anticipation; earliness, lateness, tardiness, unpunctuality

VERBS **2 mistime, misdate;** antedate, foredate, postdate; lag

ADJS **3 anachronous** *or* anachronistical *or* **anachronistic,** parachronistic, metachronistic, prochronistic, unhistorical, unchronological; **mistimed, misdated;** antedated, foredated, postdated; ahead of time, **beforehand, early;** behind time, **behindhand, late,** unpunctual, tardy; **overdue,** past due; unseasonable, out of season; **dated,** out-of-date

833 PREVIOUSNESS

NOUNS **1 previousness, earliness** 844, **ante-cedence** or antecedency, priority, **anteriority, precedence** or precedency 813, precession; *status quo ante* <L>, previous or prior state, earlier state; preexistence; **anticipation,** predating, antedating; antedate; **past time** 836

2 antecedent, precedent, premise; forerunner, **precursor** 815, ancestor

VERBS **3 be prior,** be before or early or earlier, come on the scene or appear earlier, **precede, antecede, forerun,** come or go before, set a precedent; **herald,** usher in, proclaim, announce; **anticipate,** antedate, predate; **preexist**

ADJS **4 previous, prior, early** 844.7, **earlier,** *ci-devant* or *ci-dessus* <Fr>, **former,** fore, prime, first, **preceding** 165.3, foregoing, above, anterior, **anticipatory,** antecedent; **preexistent;** older, elder, senior

5 prewar, ante-bellum, before the war; prerevolutionary; premundane or antemundane; prelapsarian, before the Fall; antediluvian, before the Flood; protohistoric, prehistoric 836.10; precultural; pre-Aryan; pre-Christian; premillenarian, premillennial; ante-classical, preclassical, pre-Roman, pre-Renaissance, pre-Romantic, pre-Victorian, etc

ADVS **6 previously,** priorly, **hitherto, heretofore,** thitherto, theretofore; **before, early** 844.11, **earlier,** ere, erenow, ere then, or ever; already, yet; before all; **formerly** 836.13

PREPS **7 prior to, previous to, before,** in advance of, in anticipation of, in preparation for

WORD ELEMENTS **8** ante—, anti—, fore—, pre—, pro—, prot—, proto—, proter—, protero—, supra—

834 SUBSEQUENCE
   <later time>

NOUNS **1 subsequence,** posteriority, **succession, ensuing, following** 166, sequence, coming after, supervenience, supervention; lateness 845; afterlife, next life; remainder 256, hangover <nonformal>; postdating; postdate; future time 838

2 sequel 816, **follow-up,** sequelae, **aftermath; consequence, effect** 886; **posterity,** offspring, descendant, heir, inheritor; **successor;** replacement, line, **lineage,** dynasty, family

VERBS **3 come** or **follow** or **go after, follow,**
follow on or upon, succeed, replace, take the place of, displace, overtake, supervene; **ensue,** issue, emanate, attend, **result;** follow up, trail, track, come close on or tread on the heels of, "follow hard upon"—Shakespeare, dog the footsteps of; **step into** or **fill the shoes of,** don the mantle of, assume the robe of

ADJS **4 subsequent, after, later,** after-the-fact, *post factum* and *ex post facto* <both L>, posterior, **following, succeeding,** successive, sequent, lineal, consecutive, ensuing, attendant; **junior,** cadet, puisne <law>, younger

5 posthumous, afterdeath; **postprandial,** postcibal, postcenal, after-dinner; **postwar,** *postbellum* <L>, after the war; **postdiluvian,** postdiluvial, after the flood; postlapsarian, after the Fall, post-industrial, post-modern, post-millenial, etc

ADVS **6 subsequently, after, afterwards,** after that, after all, **later, next,** since; **thereafter,** thereon, thereupon, therewith, **then;** in the process or course of time, as things worked out, in the sequel; at a subsequent or later time, in the aftermath; *ex post facto* <L>; hard on the heels or on the heels

7 after which, on or upon which, **whereupon,** whereon, whereat, whereto, whereunto, wherewith, wherefore, on, upon; hereinafter

PREPS **8 after, following, subsequent to,** later than, past, beyond, behind; below, farther down or along

WORD ELEMENTS **9** ante—, anti—, fore—, pre—, pro—, prot—, proto—, proter—, protero—, supra—; epi—, eph—, infra—, meta—, post—

835 SIMULTANEITY

NOUNS **1 simultaneity** or **simultaneousness,** coincidence, co-occurrence, concurrence or concurrency, concomitance or concomitancy; **coexistence; contemporaneousness** or contemporaneity, coetaneousness or coetaneity, coevalness or coevalneity; unison; **synchronism,** synchronization; isochronism; accompaniment 768, agreement 787

2 contemporary, coeval, concomitant

3 tie, dead heat, draw, wash <nonformal>

VERBS **4 coincide,** co-occur, concur; **coexist;** coextend; **synchronize,** isochronize, put or be in phase, be in time, keep time, time; contemporize; **accompany** 768.7, **agree** 787.6, match, go along with, go hand in hand, keep pace with, keep in step

ADJS 5 simultaneous, concurrent, co-occurring, coinstantaneous, concomitant; **tied,** neck-and-neck; coexistent, coexisting; **contemporaneous,** contemporary, coetaneous, coeval; coterminous, conterminous; unison, unisonous; isochronous, isochronal; coeternal; accompanying 768.9, collateral; agreeing 787.9

6 synchronous, synchronized, synchronic *or* synchronal, in sync <nonformal>; **in time,** in step, in tempo, in phase, with *or* on the beat

ADVS 7 simultaneously, concurrently, coinstantaneously; **together,** all together, **at the same time,** at one and the same time, as one, as one man, in concert with, in chorus, with one voice, in unison, in a chorus, in the same breath; at one time, at a clip <nonformal>; **synchronously,** synchronically, isochronously, in phase, **in sync** <nonformal>, with *or* on the beat, on the downbeat

836 THE PAST

NOUNS 1 the past, past, foretime, former times, past times, times past, water under the bridge, **days** *or* **times gone by, bygone times** *or* **days, yesterday, yesteryear;** recent past, just *or* only yesterday; **history,** past history; dead past, dead hand of the past, "the dead cold hand of the Past"—Oliver Wendell Holmes; the years that are past, "the days that are no more"—Tennyson, "the irrevocable Past"—Longfellow, "a bucket of ashes"—Carl Sandburg

2 old *or* **olden times,** early times, **old** *or* **olden days,** the olden time, times of old, **days of old, days** *or* **times of yore,** yore, yoretime, eld <old>, good old times *or* days, the way it was, lang syne *or* auld lang syne <both Scots>, **the long ago,** time out of mind, days beyond recall; the old story, the same old story

3 antiquity, ancient times, time immemorial, ancient history, remote age *or* time, remote *or* far *or* dim *or* **distant past,** distance of time, "the dark backward and abysm of time"—Shakespeare; ancientness 841

4 memory 988, **remembrance, recollection, reminiscence, fond remembrance, retrospection,** musing on the past, looking back; "the remembrance of things past"—Shakespeare, *"la recherche du*

temps perdu"—Proust; **reliving,** reexperiencing; revival 396.3; youth 301

5 <grammatical terms> past tense, preterit, perfect tense, past perfect tense, pluperfect, historical present tense, past progressive tense; aorist; perfective aspect; preterition

VERBS 6 pass, be past, **be a thing of the past,** elapse, lapse, slip by *or* away, be gone, fade, fade away, be dead and gone, be all over, have run its course, have run out, have had its day; **disappear** 34.2; **die** 307.19

ADJS 7 past, gone, by, **gone-by, bygone,** gone glimmering, bypast, ago, **over,** departed, passed, passed away, elapsed, lapsed, vanished, faded, no more, irrecoverable, never to return, not coming back; **dead** 307.30, dead as a dodo, expired, extinct, dead and buried, defunct, deceased; run out, blown over, finished, forgotten, wound up; **passé, obsolete,** has-been, dated, antique, **antiquated**

8 reminiscent 988.22, **retrospective, remembered** 988.23, **recollected; relived, reexperienced; restored, revived**

9 <grammatical terms> past, preterit *or* preteritive, pluperfect, past perfect; aorist, aoristic; perfective

10 former, past, fore, **previous,** late, recent, **once, onetime,** sometime, **erstwhile,** then, quondam; **prior** 833.4; **ancient, immemorial,** early, primitive, primeval, prehistoric; **old,** olden

11 foregoing, aforegoing, **preceding** 813.4; last, latter

12 back, backward, into the past; early; retrospective, retroactive, *ex post facto* <L>, *a priori* <L>

ADVS 13 formerly, previously, priorly 833.6; **earlier, before,** before now, erenow, erst, whilom, erewhile, **hitherto, heretofore,** thitherto, aforetime, beforetime, **in the past,** in times past; then; **yesterday,** only yesterday, recently; **historically,** prehistorically, in historic *or* prehistoric times

14 once, once upon a time, one day, one fine morning, time was

15 ago, since, gone by; back, back when; backward, to *or* into the past; **retrospectively,** reminiscently, retroactively

16 long ago, long since, **a long while** *or* **time ago,** some time ago *or* since, some time back, a way *or* away back <nonformal>, ages ago, **years ago,** donkey's years ago <Brit nonformal>; **in times past,** in times gone by, in the old days, in the good old days; **anciently, of old, of yore,** in ancient times, in olden times, in the olden times, **in days of yore,** early, in the memory of man, time out of mind

17 since, ever since, until now; **since long ago, long since,** from away back <nonformal>, since days of yore, ages ago, **from time immemorial,** from time out of mind, aeons ago, since the world was made, since the world was young, since time began, since the year one, since Hector was a pup *and* since God knows when <both nonformal>

WORD ELEMENTS **18** archae—, archaeo—, archeo—; pale—, paleo—, praeter—, preter—, retro—; —ed, y— <old>

837 THE PRESENT

NOUNS **1 the present,** presentness, present time, the here and now; **now,** the present juncture *or* occasion, the present hour *or* moment, this instant *or* second *or* moment, **the present day** *or* **time** *or* hour *or* minute, etc; **the present age,** "the living sum-total of the whole Past"—Carlyle; **today,** this day, **this day and age; this point,** this stage, this hour, **now,** nowadays, the now, the way things are, the nonce, **the time being; the times,** our times, these days; **contemporaneousness** *or* contemporaneity, nowness, actuality, topicality; **newness** 840, modernity; the Now Generation, the me generation; historical present, present tense <both grammatical>

ADJS **2 present, immediate,** latest, current, running, extant, existent, **existing,** actual, topical, being, that is, as is, that be; **present-day,** present-time, present-age, **modern** 840.13, modern-day; **contemporary,** contemporaneous; up-to-date, up-to-the-minute, fresh, **new** 840.7

ADVS **3 now, at present, at this point,** at this juncture, at this stage *or* at this stage of the game, on the present occasion, **at this time,** at this moment *or* instant, at the present time, "upon this bank and shoal of time"—Shakespeare; **today,** this day, in these days, **in this day and age,** in our time, **nowadays;** this night, **tonight;** here, hereat, **here and now,** *hic et nunc* <L>, even now, but now, **just now,** as of now, as things are; on the spot; for the nonce, for the time being; for this occasion

4 until now, hitherto, till now, thitherto, **hereunto,** heretofore, until this time, by this time, **up to now,** up to the present, up to this time, to this day, to the present moment, to this very instant, **so far,** thus

far, **as yet, to date,** yet, already, still, now *or* then as previously

WORD ELEMENTS **5** ne—, neo—, nov—, novo—; cen—, ceno—, caen—, caeno—, —cene

838 THE FUTURE

NOUNS **1 the future,** future, futurity, what is to come, imminence 839, subsequence 834, eventuality 830.1, **hereafter,** aftertime, afteryears, **time to come,** years to come, etc; **futurism,** futuristics; **tomorrow,** the morrow, the morning after, *mañana* <Sp>; **immediate** *or* **near future,** time just ahead, immediate prospect, offing, next period; **distant future,** remote *or* deep *or* far future; **by-and-by,** the sweet by-and-by <nonformal>; time ahead, course ahead, **prospect,** outlook, anticipation, expectation, project, probability, prediction, extrapolation, forward look, foresight, prevision, prevenience, envisionment, envisagement, prophecy, divination, clairvoyance, crystal ball; what is to be *or* come; determinism; future tense; futurism; the womb of time, "the past again, entered through another gate"—Pinero, "an opaque mirror"—Jim Bishop

2 destiny 963.2, **fate,** doom, karma, kismet, what bodes *or* looms, what is fated *or* destined *or* doomed, what is written, what is in the books, "whatever limits us"—Emerson; the Fates, the Parcae *or* Parcae Fates, Lachesis, Clotho, Atropos, Moira, Moirai, **the hereafter,** the great hereafter, "the good hereafter"—Whittier, a better place, Paradise, Heaven, Elysian Fields, Happy Isles, the Land of Youth *or* Tir na n'Og, Valhalla; Hades, the Underworld, Hell, Gehenna; **the afterworld,** the otherworld, **the next world,** the world to come, life *or* world beyond the grave, **the beyond,** the great beyond, the unknown, the great unknown, **the grave,** home *or* abode *or* world of the dead, eternal home; "the world of light"—Henry Vaughan, "the great world of light, that lies behind all human destinies"—Longfellow; **afterlife, postexistence,** future state, **life to come,** life after death

3 doomsday, doom, day of doom, day of reckoning, crack of doom, trumpet *or* trump of doom; **Judgment Day,** Day of Judgment, the Judgment; eschatology, last things, **last days**

4 futurity; ultimateness, eventuality, finality

5 advent, coming, approach of time, time drawing on

VERBS **6 come,** come on, **approach,** near, **draw on** or **near;** be to be or come; be fated or destined or doomed, be in the books, be in the cards; **loom,** threaten, await, stare one in the face, be imminent 839.2; lie ahead or in one's course; **predict,** foresee, envision, envisage, see ahead, previse, foretell, prophesy; **anticipate, expect,** hope, hope for, look for, look forward to, **project,** plot, plan, scheme, think ahead, extrapolate

7 live on, postexist, survive, get by or through, make it <nonformal>

ADJS **8 future, later,** hereafter; **coming, forthcoming, imminent** 839.3, approaching, nearing, **prospective; eventual** 830.11, ultimate, to-be, **to come; projected,** plotted, planned, looked- or hoped-for, desired, emergent, **predicted,** prophesied, foreseen, anticipated, anticipatory, previsional, prevenient, envisioned, envisaged, probable, extrapolated; determined, fatal, fatidic, fated, destinal, destined, doomed; eschatological; futuristic

ADVS **9 in the future,** in aftertime, **afterward** or afterwards, **later,** at a later time, after a time or while, anon; **by and by,** in the sweet by-and-by <nonformal>; **tomorrow,** mañana <Sp>, the day after tomorrow; proximo <L>, prox, **in the near** or **immediate future,** just around the corner, **imminently** 839.4, **soon, before long;** probably, predictably, hopefully; fatally, by destiny or necessity

10 in future, **hereafter,** hereinafter, thereafter, **henceforth, henceforward** or henceforwards, thence, **thenceforth,** thenceforward or thenceforwards, over the long haul or short haul <nonformal>, from this time forward, from this day on or forward, from this point, from this or that time, from then on, **from here** or **now on, from now on in** <nonformal>, from here in or out <nonformal>, from this moment on

11 in time, in due time, in due season or course, all in good time, **in the fullness of time,** in God's good time, in the course or process of time, **eventually** 830.12, **ultimately,** in the long run

12 sometime, someday, some of these days, one of these days, some fine day or morning, one fine day or morning, some sweet day, sometime or other, somewhen, **sooner or later,** when all is said and done

PREPS **13 about to,** at or **on the point of,** on

the eve of, on the brink or edge or verge of, near to, close upon, in the act of

839 IMMINENCE
    <future event>

NOUNS **1 imminence** or **imminency,** impendence or impendency, forthcomingness; **forthcoming,** coming, **approach, loom;** immediate or near future; futurity 838.1

VERBS **2 be imminent, impend, overhang,** hang or lie over, **loom,** hang over one's head, hover, **threaten, menace,** lower; brew, gather; **come** or **draw on,** draw near or nigh, rush up on one, forthcome, **approach, loom up, near,** be on the horizon, be in the offing, be just around the corner, await, face, **confront, loom,** stare one in the face, be in store, breathe down one's neck, be about to be borning

ADJS **3 imminent, impending,** impendent, **overhanging,** hanging over one's head, waiting, lurking, **threatening, looming,** lowering, **menacing,** lying in ambush, "in danger imminent"—Spenser; **brewing,** gathering, preparing; **coming, forthcoming, upcoming, to come,** about to be, about or going to happen, **approaching, nearing,** looming, looming up, looming in the distance or future; **near, close,** immediate, instant, soon to be, **at hand,** near at hand, close at hand; **in the offing,** on the horizon, **in prospect,** already in sight, just around the corner, in view, in one's eye, in store, in reserve, **in the wind,** in the womb of time; on the knees or lap of the gods, in the cards <nonformal>; that will be, that is to be; future 838.8

ADVS **4 imminently,** impendingly; **any time,** any time now, any moment, any second, any minute, any hour, any day; **to be expected,** as may be expected, as may be

CONJS **5 on the point of, on the verge of,** on the eve of

840 NEWNESS

NOUNS **1 newness,** freshness, maidenhood, dewiness, pristineness, mint condition, new-mintedness, newbornness, virginity, intactness, greenness, immaturity, rawness, callowness, brand-newness; presentness, nowness, **recentness,** recency, lateness; **novelty,** gloss of novelty, newfangledness or newfangleness; originality 337.1; **uncommonness,** unusualness, strangeness, unfamiliarity

2 novelty, innovation, newfangled device or contraption <nonformal>, neoism, neonism, **new** *or* **latest wrinkle** <nonformal>, **the last word** *or* **the latest thing** <both nonformal>, *dernier cri* <Fr>; what's happening *and* what's in *and* the in thing *and* where it's at <all nonformal>; new ball game; new look, latest fashion *or* fad; advance guard, vanguard, **avant-garde;** neophilia, neophiliac

3 modernity, modernness; modernism; modernization, updating, *aggiornamento* <Ital>; postmodernism, space age

4 modern, modern man; modernist; modernizer; neologist, neoterist, neology, neologism, neoterism, neoteric; modern *or* rising *or* new generation; neonate, fledgling, stripling, *novus homo* <L>, new man, upstart, *arriviste* <Fr>, *nouveau riche* <Fr>, parvenu; Young Turk, bright young man, comer <nonformal>

VERBS **5 innovate, invent,** make from scratch *or* from the ground up, coin, newmint, mint, inaugurate, neologize, neoterize; **renew,** renovate 396.17

6 modernize, streamline; update, **bring up to date,** keep *or* stay current, move with the times

ADJS **7 new,** young, **fresh,** fresh as a daisy, fresh as the morning dew; **unused, firsthand, original;** untried, untouched, unhandled, unhandseled, untrodden, unbeaten; virgin, virginal, intact, maiden, maidenly; green, vernal; dewy, pristine, ever-new, sempervirent, evergreen; **immature,** undeveloped, raw, callow, fledgling, unfledged, nestling

8 fresh, additional, further, other, another; **renewed**

9 new-made, new-built, new-wrought, new-shaped, new-mown, new-minted, new-coined, uncirculated, in mint condition, mint, new-begotten, new-grown, new-laid; **newfound;** newborn, neonatal, new-fledged; **new-model,** late-model, like new, factory-new, factory-fresh, in its original carton

10 <nonformal terms> **brand-new,** firenew, **brand-spanking new,** spanking, **spanking new; just out; hot,** hottest, hot off the fire *or* griddle *or* spit, hot off the press; newfangled *or* newfangle

11 novel, original, unique, different; strange, unusual, uncommon; unfamiliar, unheard-of; **first, first ever** 817.15

12 recent, late, newly come, of yesterday; latter, later

13 modern, contemporary, present-day, present-time, twentieth-century, latterday, space-age, neoteric, now <nonformal>, **newfashioned,** fashionable,

modish, mod, *à la mode* <Fr>, **up-to-date,** up-to-datish, **up-to-the-minute, in,** abreast of the times; **advanced,** progressive, forward-looking, modernizing, **avant-garde;** ultramodern, ultra-ultra, ahead of its time, far out, way out, modernistic, modernized, streamlined; postmodern

14 state-of-the-art, newest, latest, the very latest, up-to-the-minute, last, most recent, newest of the new, farthest out

ADVS **15 newly,** freshly, new, **anew,** once more, from the ground up, from scratch <nonformal>, *ab ovo* <L>, *de novo* <L>, **afresh, again;** as new

16 now, recently, lately, latterly, **of late,** not long ago, a short time ago, the other day, only yesterday; just now, right now <nonformal>; neoterically

841 OLDNESS

NOUNS **1 oldness, age,** eld <old>, hoary eld; elderliness, seniority, senior citizenship, senility, **old age** 303.5; **ancientness, antiquity,** dust of ages, rust *or* cobwebs of antiquity; venerableness, eldership, primogeniture, great *or* hoary age, "the ancient and honourable"—Bible; old order, old style, *ancien régime* <Fr>; **primitiveness,** primordialism *or* primordiality, aboriginality; atavism

2 tradition, custom, immemorial usage; Sunna <Muslim>; Talmud, Mishnah <both Jewish>, ancient wisdom, ways of the fathers; traditionalism *or* traditionality; myth, mythology, legend, lore, folklore, folktale, folk motif; racial memory, archetypal myth *or* image *or* pattern, "Spiritus Mundi"—Yeats

3 antiquation, superannuation, staleness, disuse; **old-fashionedness,** unfashionableness, out-of-dateness; **old-fogyishness,** fogyishness, stuffiness, stodginess, fuddyduddiness

4 antiquarianism; classicism, medievalism, Pre-Raphaelitism, longing *or* yearning *or* nostalgia for the past; **archaeology;** Greek archaeology, Roman archaeology, etc, Assyriology, Egyptology, Sumerology; crisis archeology, industrial archeology, underwater *or* marine archeology, paleology, epigraphy, paleontology, human paleontology, paleethnology, paleonanthropology, paleoethnography; paleozoology, paleornithology

5 antiquarian, antiquary, *laudator temporis acti* <L>; dryasdust, the Rev Dr Dryasdust, Jonathan Oldbuck <both Sir Walter Scott>, Herr Teufelsdröckh <Carlyle>; **archaeologist;** classicist, medievalist, Miniver Cheevy <E A Robinson>, Pre-Raphaelite; antique dealer, antique collector, antique-car collector; archaist

6 antiquity, antique, archaism; **relic,** relic of the past; **remains,** survival, vestige, ruin *or* ruins; old thing, oldie *and* golden oldie <nonformal>; **fossil;** petrification, petrified wood, petrified forest; **artifact,** eolith, mezzolith, microlith, neolith, paleolith, plateaulith; cave painting, petroglyph; ancient manuscript 547.11

7 ancient, man *or* woman *or* person of old, old Homo, **prehistoric mankind** <see list>; preadamite, antediluvian; anthropoid, humanoid, primate, fossil man, protohuman, prehuman, missing link, apeman, hominid; **primitive, aboriginal,** aborigine, bushman, autochthon; **caveman,** cave dweller, troglodyte; bog man, bog body, Lindow man; Stone Age man, Bronze Age man, Iron Age man

8 <antiquated person> back number <nonformal>; pop *and* pops *and* dad <all nonformal>, dodo *and* old dodo <both nonformal>; fossil *and* antique *and* relic <all nonformal>; **mossback** <nonformal>, longhair *and* square <both nonformal>, **mid-Victorian,** antediluvian; old liner, old believer, conservative, hard-shell, traditionalist, reactionary; has-been; **fogy, old fogy,** regular old fogy, old poop *or* crock <nonformal>, **fud** *and* **fuddy-duddy** <both nonformal>; granny <nonformal>, **old woman,** matriarch; **old man,** patriarch, elder, *starets* <Russ>, old-timer <nonformal>, Methuselah

VERBS **9 age,** grow old 303.10, grow *or* have whiskers; **antiquate,** fossilize, date, **superannuate,** outdate; obsolesce, go out of use *or* style, molder, fust, rust, fade, perish; lose currency *or* novelty; become obsolete *or* extinct; belong to the past, be a thing of the past

ADJS **10 old, age-old,** auld <Scots>, olden <old>, old-time, old-timey <nonformal>; **ancient, antique,** venerable, hoary; of old, of yore; dateless, timeless, ageless; **immemorial,** old as Methuselah *or* Adam, old as God, old as history, old as time, old as the hills; **elderly** 303.16

11 primitive, prime, **primeval,** primogenital, primordial, pristine; atavistic; **aboriginal,** autochthonous; ancestral, patriarchal; **prehistoric,** protohistoric, pregla-

cial, preadamite, antepatriarchal; prehuman, protohuman, humanoid

12 traditional; mythological, heroic; **legendary,** unwritten, oral, handed down; true-blue, tried and true; **prescriptive, customary,** conventional, understood, admitted, recognized, acknowledged, received; **hallowed, time-honored,** immemorial; **venerable,** hoary, worshipful; **long-standing, of long standing,** long-established, established, fixed, inveterate, rooted; **folk, of the folk,** folkloric

13 antiquated, grown old, **superannuated, antique, old,** age-encrusted, of other times, old-world; Victorian, mid-Victorian; classical, medieval, Gothic; antediluvian; **fossil,** fossilized, petrified

14 stale, fusty, musty, rusty, dusty, moldy, mildewed; **worn, timeworn,** time-scarred; **moth-eaten,** moss-grown, crumbling, moldering, gone to seed, dilapidated, ruined, ruinous

15 obsolete, passé, extinct, gone out, gone-by, dead, past, run out, **outworn**

16 old-fashioned, old-fangled, old-timey <nonformal>, **dated, out, out-of-date, outdated, outmoded,** out of style *or* fashion, out of use, disused, out of season, **unfashionable,** styleless, **behind the times,** of the old school, old hat *and* back-number *and* has-been <all nonformal>

17 old-fogyish, fogyish, old-fogy; fuddy-duddy, square *and* corny *and* cornball <all nonformal>; **stuffy, stodgy; aged** 303.16, senile, bent *or* wracked *or* ravaged with age

18 secondhand, used, worn, previously owned, **unnew,** not new, pawed-over; hand-me-down *and* reach-me-down <both nonformal>

19 older, senior, Sr, major, elder, dean; **oldest,** eldest; first-born, firstling, primogenitary; former 836.10

20 archaeological, paleological; antiquarian; paleolithic, eolithic, neolithic, mezzolithic

ADVS **21** anciently 836.16

22 Stone Age cultures

Acheulean	Magdalenian
Aurignacian	Mousterian
Azilian	Neolithic
Chellean	Paleolithic
Combe-Capelle	Pre-Chellean
Cro-Magnon	Solutrean
Eolithic	

23 prehistoric men and manlike primates

Aurignacian man	Australopithecus
	Australopithecus afarensis
Australanthropus	

Australopithecus afri-
  canus
Australopithecus
  boisei
Australopithecus
  robustus
Brünn race
caveman
Cro-Magnon man
Dawn man <the Pilt-
  down hoax>
eolithic man
Florisbad man
Furfooz or Grenelle
  man
Galley Hill man
Gigantopithecus
Grimaldi man
Heidelberg man

Java man
Lucy
Meganthropus
Neanderthal man
neolithic man
Oreopithecus
paleolithic man
Paranthropus
Peking man
Piltdown man
  <hoax>
Pithecanthropus
Plesianthropus
Rhodesian man
Sinanthropus
Stone Age man
Swanscombe man
Zinjanthropus

24 prehistoric animals
allosaurus
ammonite
anatosaurus
ankylosaurus
apatosaurus
archaeohippus
archaeopteryx
archaeornis
archaeotherium
archelon
arthrodiran
atlantosaurus
aurochs
baryonyx Walker
bothriolepis
brachiosaurus
brontops
brontosaurus
brontothere
camarasaurus
cantius trigonodus
ceratopsid
ceratosaurus
cetiosaurus
coccostean
coelodont
compsognathus
coryphodon
cotylosaur
creodont
crossopterygian
cynodictis
deinonychus
denversaurus
diacodexis
diatryma
dimetrodon
dinichthyid
dinothere
diplodocus
dipnoan
diprotodon
duck-billed dinosaur

edaphosaurid
elasmosaurus
eohippus
eryopsid
eurypterid
eurypterus remipes
giant sloth
glyptodont
gorgosaurus
hadrosaurus
hesperornis
hoplophoneus
hyaenodon
hyracodont
hyracothere
ichthyornis
ichthyosaurus
iguanodon
imperial mammoth
  or elephant
labyrinthodont
machairodont
mamenchisaurus
mammoth
mastodon
megalosaurus
megathere
merodus
merychippus
merycoidodon
merycopotamus
mesohippus
miacis
mosasaurus
nummulite
ornithomimid
ornithopod
ostracoderm
palaeodictyopteron
palaeomastodon
palaeoniscid
palaeophis
palaeosaur

palaeospondylus
pelycosaur
phytosaur
pinchosaurus
plesiosaurus
protoceratops
protohippus
protylopus
pteranodon
pteraspid
pterichthys
pterodactyl
pterosaur
quetzalcoatlus north-
  ropii
rhamphorhynchus
saber-toothed cat,
  formerly saber-
  tooth tiger
sauropod
scelidosaurus

smilodon
stegocephalian
stegodon
stegosaurus
struthiomimus
teleoceras
therapsid
theriodont
theropod
thrinaxodon lio-
  rhinus
titanosaurus
titanothere
trachodon
triceratops
trilobite
tyrannosaurus
uintathere
urus
woolly or northern
  mammoth

842 TIMELINESS

NOUNS **1 timeliness, seasonableness, opportuneness,** convenience; **expedience** or **expediency,** meetness, fittingness, fitness,
appropriateness, rightness, propriety,
suitability; **favorableness, propitiousness,** auspiciousness, felicitousness;
ripeness, pregnancy, cruciality, criticality, criticalness, expectancy,
loadedness, chargedness

**2 opportunity, chance, time, occasion;
opening,** room, scope, space, place, liberty, "world enough and time"—Andrew
Marvell; clear stage, fair field, level playing field, fair game, fair shake and even
break <both nonformal>; **opportunism;**
equal opportunity, nondiscrimination,
affirmative action, positive discrimination <Brit>; trump card; a leg up,
stepping-stone, rung of the ladder; time's
forelock

3 good opportunity, good chance, favorable
opportunity, golden opportunity, well-
timed opportunity, the chance of a lifetime, a once-in-a-lifetime chance, "a tide
in the affairs of men"—Shakespeare;
suitable occasion, proper occasion, suitable or proper time, **good time,** high time,
due season; propitious or well-chosen
moment

4 crisis, critical point, crunch, crucial period, climax, climacteric; **turning point,**
hinge, turn, turn of the tide, cusp; **emergency, exigency,** juncture or conjuncture
or convergence of events, critical juncture, crossroads; **pinch,** clutch <nonfor-
mal>, rub, push, pass, strait, extremity,

spot <nonformal>; **emergency,** state of
emergency, red alert, race against time

5 **crucial moment,** critical moment, loaded
or charged moment, decisive moment,
kairotic moment, kairos, pregnant moment, defining moment, turning point,
climax, **moment of truth,** crunch *and*
when push comes to shove <both nonfor-
mal>, when the balloon goes up <Brit
nonformal>; **psychological moment,**
right moment; nick of time, eleventh
hour; **zero hour,** H-hour, D-day, A-day,
target date, deadline

VERBS 6 **be timely,** suit *or* befit the time *or*
season *or* occasion, come *or* fall just right

7 **take** *or* **seize the opportunity,** use the occasion, take the chance; take the bit in the
teeth, leap into the breach, take the bull
by the horns, bite the bullet, **make one's
move,** cross the Rubicon, *prendre la balle
au bond* <Fr, take the ball on the re-
bound>; **commit oneself,** make an
opening, drive an entering wedge

8 **improve the occasion,** "improve each
shining hour"—Isaac Watts, turn to account *or* good account, avail oneself of,
take advantage of, put to advantage,
profit by, **cash in** *or* **capitalize on;** take
time by the forelock, seize the opportunity, seize the present hour, *carpe diem*
<L, seize the day>, make hay while the
sun shines; strike while the iron is hot;
not be caught flatfooted, not be behindhand, not be caught looking <nonfor-
mal>, don't let the chance slip by, get
going *and* get off the dime <both nonfor-
mal>

ADJS 9 **timely, well-timed, seasonable, opportune,** convenient; **expedient,** meet, fit,
fitting, befitting, suitable, sortable, appropriate; **favorable, propitious,** ripe,
auspicious, lucky, providential, heaven-
sent, fortunate, happy, felicitous

10 **critical, crucial,** pivotal, climactic, climacteric *or* climacterical, decisive;
pregnant, kairotic, loaded, charged; exigent, emergent

11 **incidental, occasional, casual,** accidental; parenthetical, by-the-way

ADVS 12 **opportunely, seasonably, propitiously,** auspiciously, in proper time *or*
season, in due time *or* course *or* season, in
the fullness of time, **in good time,** all in
good time; in the nick of time, just in
time, at the eleventh hour; now or never

13 **incidentally, by the way, by the by;** while
on the subject, speaking of, *à propos*
<Fr>, apropos *or* apropos of; **in passing,**
en passant <Fr>; parenthetically, by way

of parenthesis, *par parenthése* <Fr>; for
example, *par exemple* <Fr>

14 a bird in the hand is worth two in the
bush, better late than never, every minute *or* moment counts; live for the
moment, you can't take it with you

843 UNTIMELINESS

NOUNS 1 **untimeliness, unseasonableness,**
inopportuneness, inopportunity, unripeness, inconvenience; **inexpedience,** irrelevance *or* irrelevancy; **awkwardness,**
inappropriateness, impropriety, unfitness, unfittingness, wrongness, unsuitability; **unfavorableness,** unfortunateness, inauspiciousness, unpropitiousness,
infelicity; **intrusion,** interruption; **prematurity** 844.2; **lateness** 845, afterthought, thinking too late, *l'esprit de
l'escalier* <Fr>

2 **wrong time, bad time,** wrong *or* bad *or*
poor timing, unsuitable time, unfortunate time; evil hour, unlucky day *or* hour,
off-year, *contretemps* <Fr>

VERBS 3 **ill-time, mistime,** miss the time;
lack the time, not have time, have other
or better things to do, be otherwise occupied, be engaged, be preoccupied, have
other fish to fry <nonformal>

4 **talk out of turn,** speak inopportunely, interrupt, **put one's foot in one's mouth**
<nonformal>, intrude, butt in *and* stick
one's nose in <both nonformal>, **go off
half-cocked** <nonformal>, open one's big
mouth *or* big fat mouth <nonformal>;
blow it <nonformal>, speak too late *or*
too soon

5 **miss an opportunity, miss the chance,
miss out, miss the boat,** miss one's turn,
lose the opportunity, ignore opportunity's knock, lose the chance, blow the
chance <nonformal>, throw away *or*
waste *or* neglect the opportunity, allow
the occasion to go by, let slip through
one's fingers, be left at the starting gate *or*
post, be caught looking <nonformal>,
oversleep, lock the barn door after the
horse is stolen

ADJS 6 **untimely, unseasonable, inopportune, ill-timed,** ill-seasoned, mistimed,
unripe, unready, ill-considered, too late
or soon, out of phase *or* time *or* sync; **inconvenient,** unhandy; **inappropriate,**
irrelevant, improper, unfit, wrong, out of
line, off-base, unsuitable, **inexpedient,**
unfitting, unbefitting, untoward, malapropos, *mal à propos* <Fr>, intrusive;
unfavorable, unfortunate, infelicitous, in-

auspicious, **unpropitious,** unhappy, unlucky, misfortuned; **premature** 844.8; **late** 845.16

ADVS **7 inopportunely, unseasonably,** inconveniently, inexpediently; **unpropitiously,** inauspiciously, unfortunately, in an evil hour, at just the wrong time

844 EARLINESS

NOUNS **1 earliness,** early hour, time to spare; **head start,** running start, ground floor, first crack, beginnings, first *or* early stage, very beginning, preliminaries; **anticipation, foresight,** prevision, prevenience; advance notice, lead time, a stitch in time, readiness, preparedness, preparation

2 prematurity, prematureness; **untimeliness** 843; precocity, **precociousness,** forwardness; precipitation, haste, hastiness, **overhastiness,** rush, impulse, impulsivity, impulsiveness

3 promptness, promptitude, punctuality, punctualness, readiness; instantaneousness 829, immediateness *or* immediacy, summariness, decisiveness, **alacrity, quickness** 174.1, speediness, swiftness, rapidity, expeditiousness, expedition, dispatch

4 early bird <nonformal>, early riser, early comer, first arrival, first on the scene; **precursor** 815

VERBS **5 be early,** be ahead of time, take time by the forelock, be up and stirring, be beforehand *or* betimes, be ready and waiting, be off and running; gain time, draw on futurity *or* on the future

6 anticipate, foresee, foreglimpse, previse, see the handwriting on the wall, foretaste, pave the way for, prevent <old>; **forestall,** forerun, go before, **get ahead of,** win the start, break out ahead, get a head start, steal a march on, beat someone to the punch *or* the draw <nonformal>; **jump the gun,** beat the gun, go off half-cocked <nonformal>; take the words out of one's mouth

ADJS **7 early,** bright and early *and* with the birds <both nonformal>, **beforetime,** in good time *or* season; **forehand,** forehanded; foresighted, **anticipative** *or* **anticipatory,** prevenient, previsional

8 premature, too early, too soon, oversoon; previous *and* a bit previous <both nonformal>; **untimely; precipitate,** hasty 829.5, **overhasty,** too soon off the mark, too quick on the draw *or* trigger *or* uptake <nonformal>; **unprepared,** unripe, im-

pulsive, rushed, unmatured; unpremeditated, unmeditated, ill-considered, **half-cocked** *and* **half-baked** <both nonformal>, unjelled, uncrystallized, not firm; **precocious, forward, advanced,** far ahead, born before one's time

9 prompt, punctual, immediate, instant, instantaneous 829.4, **quick** 174.19, speedy, swift, expeditious, summary, decisive, apt, alert, **ready,** Johnny-on-the-spot <nonformal>

10 earlier, previous 833.4

ADVS **11 early, bright and early, beforehand, beforetime,** early on, betimes, precociously, **ahead of time,** foresightedly, in advance, in anticipation, ahead, before, **with time to spare**

12 in time, in good time, soon enough, time enough, early enough; just in time, **in the nick of time,** with no time to spare, just under the wire, without a minute to spare

13 prematurely, too soon, oversoon, untimely, too early, before its *or* one's time; **precipitately,** impulsively, in a rush, hastily, **overhastily;** at half cock <nonformal>

14 punctually, precisely, exactly, sharp; **on time,** on the minute *or* instant, to the minute *or* second, **on the dot** <nonformal>, spot on *and* bang on <Brit nonformal>, at the gun

15 promptly, without delay, without further delay *or* ado, directly, **immediately,** immediately if not sooner <nonformal>, **instantly** 829.6, instanter, on the instant, on the spot, **at once,** right off, **right away, straightway,** straightaway, **forthwith,** *pronto* <Sp>, *subito* <Ital>, PDQ *or* pretty damned quick <both nonformal>, **quickly,** swiftly, speedily, with all speed, **summarily,** decisively, smartly, expeditiously, apace, in no time, in less than no time; no sooner said than done

16 soon, presently, directly, shortly, in a short time *or* while, **before long,** ere long, in no long time, in a while, **in a little while, after a while, by and by,** anon, betimes, *bientôt* <Fr>, in due time, in due course, at the first opportunity; in a moment *or* minute, *tout à l'heure* <Fr>

PHRS **17** the early bird gets the worm

845 LATENESS

NOUNS **1 lateness, tardiness, belatedness, unpunctuality;** late hour, small hours; eleventh hour, last minute, high time; unreadiness, unpreparedness; untimeliness 843

2 delay, stoppage, jam *and* logjam <both nonformal>, obstruction, tie-up *and* bind <both nonformal>, **block,** blockage, **hang-up** <nonformal>; delayed reaction, double take, afterthought; **retardation** *or* retardance, slowdown *and* slow-up <both nonformal>, slowness, lag, time lag, lagging, dragging, dragging one's feet *and* foot-dragging <both nonformal>; **detention,** suspension, holdup <nonformal>, **obstruction, hindrance;** delaying action; **wait, halt, stay, stop,** down-time, break, pause, interim 825, respite; reprieve, stay of execution; moratorium; **red tape,** red-tapery, red-tapeism, bureaucratic delay, *paperasserie* <Fr>

3 waiting, cooling one's heels <nonformal>, **tarrying,** tarriance <old>; **lingering, dawdling,** dalliance, dallying, dilly-dallying

4 postponement, deferment *or* **deferral,** prorogation, putting-off, tabling, holding up, holding in suspension, carrying over; **prolongation,** protraction, continuation, extension of time; **adjournment** *or* adjournal, adjournment sine die

5 procrastination, "the thief of time"— Edward Young, hesitation 362.3; **temporization, a play for time, stall** *and* tap-dancing <both nonformal>; Micawberism, Fabian policy; **dilatoriness,** slowness, backwardness, remissness, slackness, laxness

6 latecomer, late arrival, Johnny-come-lately; slow starter, dawdler, dallier, dillydallier; late bloomer *or* developer; retardee; late riser, slug-abed

VERBS **7 be late, not be on time,** be overdue, be behindhand, show up late, miss the boat; keep everyone waiting; **stay late,** stay up late *or* into the small hours, burn the midnight oil, keep late hours; get up late, keep banker's hours; oversleep

8 delay, retard, detain, make late, slacken, lag, drag, drag one's feet *and* stonewall <both nonformal>, slow down, **hold up** <nonformal>, hold *or* keep back, check, **stay, stop,** arrest, impede, **block,** hinder, obstruct, throw a monkey wrench in the works <nonformal>, confine; tie up with red tape

9 postpone, delay, defer, put off, give one a rain check <nonformal>, shift off, hold off *or* up <nonformal>, prorogue, put on hold *or* ice *or* the back burner <all nonformal>, reserve, waive, **suspend,** hang up, stay, hang fire; protract, drag *or* stretch out <nonformal>, **prolong, extend,** spin *or* string out, continue, adjourn,

recess, take a recess, prorogue; **hold over,** lay over, stand over, let the matter stand, **put aside,** lay *or* set *or* push aside, lay *or* set by, **table,** lay on the table, pigeonhole, **shelve,** put on the shelf, put on ice <nonformal>; consult one's pillow about, sleep on

10 be left behind, be outrun *or* outdistanced, make a slow start, be slow *or* late *or* last off the mark, be left at the post *or* starting gate; bloom *or* develop late

11 procrastinate, be dilatory, hesitate, let something slide, hang, hang back, hang fire; **temporize,** gain *or* make time, **play for time,** drag one's feet <nonformal>, hold off <nonformal>; **stall,** stall off, **stall for time,** stall *or* stooge around *and* tap-dance <all nonformal>; talk against time, filibuster

12 wait, delay, stay, bide, abide, **bide** *or* **abide one's time; take one's time,** take time, mark time; **tarry, linger, loiter,** dawdle, dally, dillydally; hang around *or* about *or* out <nonformal>, stick around <nonformal>; **hold on** <nonformal>, sit tight <nonformal>, hold one's breath; wait a minute *or* second, wait up; hold everything *and* hold your horses *and* hold your water *and* keep your shirt on <all nonformal>; wait *or* stay up, sit up; **wait and see,** bide the issue, see which way the cat jumps, see how the cookie crumbles *or* the ball bounces <nonformal>; wait for something to turn up; **await** 130.8

13 wait impatiently, tear one's hair *and* sweat it out *and* champ *or* chomp at the bit <all nonformal>

14 be kept waiting, be stood up <nonformal>, be left; **cool one's heels** <nonformal>

15 overstay, overtarry

ADJS **16 late, belated, tardy,** slow, slow on the draw *or* uptake *or* trigger <all nonformal>, **behindhand,** never on time, backward, back, **overdue, long-awaited, untimely; unpunctual,** unready; latish; **delayed,** detained, **held up** <nonformal>, **retarded, arrested,** blocked, **hung up** *and* in a bind <both nonformal>, obstructed, stopped, jammed, congested; weather-bound; **postponed, in abeyance,** held up, put off, **on hold** *or* put on hold <nonformal>, on the back burner *or* put on the back burner <nonformal>; delayed-action; moratory

17 dilatory, delaying, Micawberish; slow *or* late *or* last off the mark; **procrastinating,** procrastinative *or* procrastinatory, go-slow; **obstructive,** obstructionist *or* ob-

structionistic, bloody-minded <Brit non-
formal>; **lingering,** loitering, lagging,
dallying, dillydallying, **slow,** sluggish,
laggard, foot-dragging, shuffling, backward; easygoing, **lazy, lackadaisical;
remiss,** slack, work-shy, lax

18 later 834.4; last-minute, eleventh-hour,
deathbed

ADVS **19 late, behind, behindhand, belat-
edly,** backward, slow, **behind time,** after
time; far on, deep into; late in the day, at
the last minute, at the eleventh hour,
none too soon, in the nick of time, under
the wire

20 **tardily, slow, slowly,** deliberately, dilatorily, sluggishly, lackadaisically,
leisurely, at one's leisure, lingeringly;
until all hours, into the night

846 FREQUENCY

NOUNS **1 frequency,** frequence, **oftenness;
commonness,** usualness, prevalence,
common occurrence, routineness, habitualness; **incidence,** relative incidence

2 **constancy, continualness,** steadiness, sustainment, **regularity,** noninterruption or
uninterruption, nonintermission or unin-
termission, incessancy, ceaselessness,
constant flow, continuity 811; perpetuity
828; repetition 848; **rapidity** 174.1; rapid
recurrence or succession, rapid or quick
fire, tattoo, **staccato,** chattering, stuttering; **vibration,** shuddering, juddering
<Brit>, pulsation, **oscillation** 915

VERBS **3** be frequent, occur often, have a
high incidence, continue 811.4, recur
849.5; shudder, judder <Brit>, vibrate,
oscillate 915.10

ADJS **4 frequent,** oftentime, many, many
times, **recurrent, oft-repeated,** thick-
coming; **common,** of common occurrence, not rare, thick on the ground
<Brit>, **prevalent,** usual, routine, habit-
ual, ordinary, everyday; frequentative
<grammar>

5 **constant, continual** 811.8, **perennial;**
steady, sustained, **regular; incessant,
ceaseless, unceasing,** unintermitting,
unintermittent or unintermitted,
unremitting, relentless, unrelenting, unchanging, unvarying, uninterrupted,
unstopped, unbroken; **perpetual** 828.7;
repeated 848.12; **rapid, staccato,** stuttering, chattering, machine gun; pulsating,
juddering <Brit>, vibrating, **oscillating**
915.15

ADVS **6 frequently, commonly,** usually, ordinarily, routinely, habitually; **often,** oft,

oftentimes, oft times; **repeatedly** 848.16,
**again and again, time after time; most
often** or frequently, in many instances,
many times, many a time, full many a
time, many a time and oft, as often as can
be, as often as not, more often than not; **in
quick** or **rapid succession;** often enough,
not infrequently, not seldom, unseldom;
as often as you wish or like, whenever you
wish or like

7 **constantly, continually** 811.10, **steadily,**
sustainedly, **regularly,** as regular as
clockwork, with every other breath, every
time one turns around, right along <non-
formal>, unvaryingly, uninterruptedly,
unintermittently, **incessantly,** unceasingly, **ceaselessly,** without cease or ceasing, perennially, all the time, at all times,
ever, ever and anon, on and on, without
letup or break or intermission, without
stopping; **perpetually, always** 828.11;
rapidly; all year round, every day, every
hour, every moment; daily, hourly, daily
and hourly; **night and day,** day and night;
morning, noon, and night; hour after
hour, day after day, month after month,
year after year; **day in day out,** month in
month out, year in year out

847 INFREQUENCY

NOUNS **1 infrequency,** infrequence, unfre-
quentness, seldomness; occasionalness;
rarity, scarcity, scarceness, rareness, **uncommonness,** uniqueness, unusualness;
sparsity 884.1; **slowness** 175

ADJS **2 infrequent,** unfrequent, **rare,** scarce,
scarce as hens' teeth, scarcer than hens'
teeth, **uncommon,** unique, unusual,
almost unheard-of, seldom met with,
seldom seen, few and far between, **sparse**
884.5; one-time, one-shot, once in a lifetime; **slow** 175.10

3 **occasional, casual, incidental; odd,** sometime, extra, side, off, off-and-on, out-of-
the-way, spare, sparetime, **part-time**

ADVS **4 infrequently,** unfrequently, **seldom,
rarely, uncommonly,** scarcely, hardly,
scarcely or **hardly ever,** very seldom, not
often, only now and then, at infrequent
intervals, unoften, off-and-on; **sparsely**
884.8

5 **occasionally,** on occasion, **sometimes,
at times,** at odd times, every so often
<nonformal>, at various times, on divers
occasions, **now and then,** every now and
then <nonformal>, now and again, **once
in a while,** every once in a while <nonfor-
mal>, every now and then, every now

and again, once and again, once or twice, betweentimes, betweenwhiles, at intervals, **from time to time;** only occasionally, only when the spirit moves, only when necessary, only now and then, at infrequent intervals, once in a blue moon *and* once in a coon's age <both nonformal>; irregularly, sporadically

6 **once, one-time,** on one occasion, just *or* only once, just this once, once and no more, once for all, once and for all *or* always

848 REPETITION

NOUNS 1 **repetition, reproduction,** duplication 873, reduplication, doubling, redoubling; **recurrence,** reoccurrence, cyclicality, return, reincarnation, rebirth, reappearance, renewal, resumption; resurfacing, reentry; echo, reecho, parroting; regurgitation, rehearsal, rote recitation; **quotation; imitation** 336; plagiarism 621.2; **reexamination,** second *or* another look

2 **iteration, reiteration, recapitulation,** recap *and* wrapup <both nonformal>, retelling, recounting, recountal, **recital, rehearsal, restatement,** rehash <nonformal>; reissue, reprint; review, summary, précis, résumé, summing up; going over *or* through, practicing; reassertion, reaffirmation; elaboration, dwelling upon; copy 784

3 **redundancy, tautology,** tautologism, pleonasm, macrology, battology; stammering, stuttering; padding, filling, expletive

4 **repetitiousness,** repetitiveness, stale *or* unnecessary repetition; harping; **monotony,** monotone, drone; **tedium** 118, the daily round *or* grind; **humdrum,** dingdong, singsong, chime, jingle, jinglejangle, trot, pitter-patter; **rhyme, alliteration,** assonance, slant *or* near rhyme; **repeated sounds** 55

5 **repeat,** repetend, bis, ditto <nonformal>, echo; **refrain,** burden, chant, undersong, chorus, bob; bob wheel, bob and wheel; ritornel, *ritornello* <Ital>

6 **encore,** repeat performance, repeat, **reprise;** replay, replaying, return match

VERBS 7 **repeat, redo,** do again, do over, do a repeat, **reproduce, duplicate** 873.3, reduplicate, double, redouble, ditto <nonformal>, **echo, parrot,** reecho; **rattle off,** reel off, regurgitate; renew, reincarnate, revive; come again *and* run it by again <both nonformal>, say again,

repeat oneself, **quote,** repeat word for word *or* verbatim, repeat like a broken record; **copy, imitate** 336.5; plagiarize 621.4,336.5; **reexamine,** take *or* have a second look, take *or* have another look

8 **iterate, reiterate, rehearse, recapitulate, recount,** rehash <nonformal>, **recite, retell,** retail, **restate,** reword, review, run over, sum up, summarize, précis, resume, encapsulate; reissue, reprint; do *or* say over again, **go over** *or* **through,** practice, say over, go over the same ground, give an encore, quote oneself, go the same round, fight one's battles over again; **tautologize,** battologize, pad, fill; **reaffirm,** reassert

9 **dwell on** *or* **upon,** insist upon, **harp on,** beat a dead horse, have on the brain, constantly recur *or* revert to, labor, belabor, hammer away at, always trot out, sing the same old song *or* tune, play the same old record, plug the same theme, never hear the last of; **thrash** *or* **thresh over,** cover the same ground, go over again and again, go over and over

10 **din, ding;** drum 55.4, beat, hammer, pound; **din in the ear,** din into, drum into, say over and over

11 <be repeated> **repeat, recur,** reoccur, **come again,** come round again, go round again, come up again, resurface, reenter, **return, reappear, resume;** resound, reverberate, echo; revert, turn *or* go back; keep coming, come again and again, happen over and over, run through like King Charles's head

ADJS 12 **repeated,** reproduced, doubled, redoubled; **duplicated,** reduplicated; regurgitated, recited by rote; **echoed,** reechoed, parroted; **quoted,** plagiarized; **iterated, reiterated,** reiterate; retold, **twice-told;** warmed up *or* over, *réchauffé* <Fr>

13 **recurrent,** recurring, **returning,** reappearing, revenant, ubiquitous, everrecurring, cyclical, periodic, yearly, monthly, weekly, daily, circadian, thickcoming, frequent, incessant, continuous 811.8, year-to-year, month-to-month, week-to-week, etc; haunting, thematic

14 **repetitious,** repetitive, repetitional *or* repetitionary, repeating; **duplicative,** reduplicative; **imitative** 336.9, parrotlike; echoing, reechoing, echoic; **iterative, reiterative,** reiterant; recapitulative, recapitulatory; battological, **tautological** *or* **tautologous, redundant**

15 **monotonous,** monotone; **tedious;** harping, labored, belabored, cliché-ridden; **humdrum,** singsong, chiming, chanting,

dingdong <nonformal>, jog-trot, jingle-jangle; **rhymed, rhyming, alliterative,** alliterating, assonant

ADVS **16 repeatedly, often, frequently, recurrently, every time one turns around,** with every other breath, like a tolling bell, **again and again, over and over,** over and over again, many times over, time and again, **time after time,** times without number, **ad nauseam;** year in year out, week in week out, etc, year after year, day after day, day by day, "tomorrow and tomorrow and tomorrow"—Shakespeare; **many times,** several times, a number of times, many a time, many a time and oft, full many a time and oft; every now and then, every once in a while

17 again, over, over again, **once more,** *encore, bis* <both Fr>, two times, twice over, ditto; **anew,** *de novo* <L>, afresh; from the beginning, *da capo* <Ital>

INTERJS **18 encore!,** *bis!* <Fr>, once more!, again!

849 REGULARITY OF RECURRENCE

NOUNS **1 regularity,** regularness, clockwork regularity, predictability, punctuality, smoothness, **steadiness, evenness, unvariableness, methodicalness,** systematicalness; **repetition** 848; **uniformity** 780; **constancy** 846.2

2 periodicity, periodicalness; cyclical motion, piston motion, pendulum motion, regular wave motion, undulation, **pulsation; intermittence** *or* intermittency, alternation; rhythm 709.22, meter, beat; **oscillation** 915; **recurrence,** go-round, reoccurrence, reappearance, return, the eternal return, **cyclicalness,** cyclicality, seasonality; resurfacing, reentry

3 round, revolution, rotation, cycle, circle, wheel, **circuit; beat,** upbeat, downbeat, thesis, arsis, **pulse;** systole, diastole; course, series, **bout, turn,** spell 824

4 anniversary, commemoration; immovable feast, annual holiday; biennial, triennial, quadrennial, quinquennial, sextennial, septennial, octennial, nonennial, decennial, tricennial, jubilee, silver jubilee, golden jubilee, diamond jubilee; centennial, centenary; quasquicentennial; sesquicentennial; bicentennial, bicentenary; tercentennial, tercentenary; tricentenary; quincentennial, quincentenary; **wedding anniversary,** silver wedding anniversary, golden wedding anniversary; **birthday,** birthdate, natal day; saint's day, name day; leap year, bissextile day; **religious holiday,** holy day

VERBS **5** <occur periodically> **recur, reoccur, return, repeat** 848.7, reappear, **come again,** come up again, be here again, resurface, reenter, **come round** *or* **around,** come round again, come in its turn; **rotate, revolve,** turn, circle, wheel, cycle, **roll around,** roll about, wheel around, go around, go round; **intermit,** alternate, **come and go;** undulate 915.11; **oscillate** 915.10, **pulse, pulsate** 915.12

ADJS **6 regular, systematic** *or* systematical, methodical, ordered, orderly, regular as clockwork; **uniform** 780.5; **constant** 846.5

7 periodic *or* periodical, seasonal, epochal, **cyclic** *or* cyclical, serial, isochronal, metronomic; measured, steady, even, **rhythmic** *or* rhythmical 709.28; **recurrent,** recurring, reoccurring; **intermittent,** reciprocal, alternate, every other; circling, wheeling, rotary, wavelike, undulant, undulatory, oscillatory 915.15, pulsing, beating 915.18

8 momentary, momently, **hourly; daily,** diurnal, quotidian, circadian; **weekly,** tertian, hebdomadal, hebdomadary; biweekly, semiweekly; fortnightly; **monthly,** menstrual, catamenial; bimonthly, semimonthly; quarterly; biannual, semiannual, semiyearly, half-yearly, semestral; **yearly, annual;** biennial, triennial, decennial, etc; centennial, centenary, secular

ADVS **9 regularly, systematically, methodically,** like clockwork, at regular intervals, punctually, steadily; at stated times, at fixed *or* established periods; intermittently, every so often, every now and then; **uniformly** 780.7; **constantly** 846.7

10 periodically, recurrently, seasonally, cyclically, epochally; rhythmically, on the beat, in time, synchronously, **hourly, daily,** etc; every hour, every day, etc; hour by hour, day by day, etc; from hour to hour, from day to day, *de die in diem* <L>

11 alternately, by turns, in turns, in rotation, turn about, **turn and turn about,** reciprocally, every other, one after the other; to and fro, up and down, from side to side; off and on, make and break, round and round

PHRS **12 what goes around comes around,** *plus ça change plus c'est la même chose* <Fr>

850 IRREGULARITY OF RECURRENCE

NOUNS **1 irregularity,** unmethodicalness, unsystematicness; **inconstancy, unevenness, unsteadiness,** uncertainty, desultoriness; **variability,** capriciousness, unpredictability, whimsicality, eccentricity; stagger, wobble, weaving, erraticness; roughness; **fitfulness, sporadicity** *or* sporadicalness, spasticity, jerkiness, fits and starts, patchiness, spottiness, choppiness, brokenness, disconnectedness, discontinuity 812; **intermittence, fluctuation; nonuniformity** 781; arrhythmia, fibrillation <both medical>

VERBS **2 intermit, fluctuate,** vary, lack regularity, go by fits and starts

ADJS **3 irregular,** unregular, unsystematic, unmethodical *or* immethodical; **inconstant, unsteady, uneven, unrhythmical,** unmetrical, rough, unequal, uncertain, unsettled; **variable,** deviative, heteroclite; **capricious, erratic,** off-again-on-again, eccentric; wobbly, wobbling, weaving, staggering, lurching, careening; **fitful, spasmodic** *or* spasmodical, spastic, spasmic, **jerky,** herky-jerky <nonformal>, halting; **sporadic,** patchy, spotty, scrappy, snatchy, catchy, choppy, **broken, disconnected, discontinuous** 812.4; **nonuniform** 781.3; **intermittent,** intermitting, **desultory, fluctuating, wavering,** wandering, rambling, veering; flickering, guttering

ADVS **4 irregularly,** unsystematically, unmethodically; **inconstantly, unsteadily, unevenly,** unrhythmically, roughly, uncertainly; **variably,** capriciously, unpredictably, whimsically, eccentrically, wobblingly, lurchingly, erratically; **intermittently, disconnectedly, discontinuously** 812.5; **nonuniformly** 781.4; **brokenly, desultorily,** patchily, spottily, in spots, in snatches; **by fits and starts,** by fits, by jerks, by snatches, by catches; **fitfully, sporadically, jerkily, spasmodically,** haltingly; **off and on,** at irregular intervals, sometimes and sometimes not; when the mood strikes, when the spirit moves, at random

851 CHANGE

NOUNS **1 change, alteration, modification; variation,** variety, difference, diversity, diversification; **deviation,** diversion, aberrance *or* aberrancy, **divergence; switch, switchover, changeover, turn,** turnabout, about-face, **reversal,** flip-flop <nonformal>; apostasy, defection, change of heart; **shift,** transition, **modulation,** qualification; **conversion, renewal,** revival, revivification, retro; remaking, reshaping, re-creation, redesign, restructuring, *perestroika* <Russ>; realignment, **adaptation, adjustment,** accommodation, fitting; **reform,** reformation, **improvement,** amelioration, melioration, mitigation, constructive change, **betterment,** change for the better; **take** *and* **new take** <both nonformal>; **social mobility,** vertical mobility, horizontal mobility, upward *or* downward mobility; gradual change, progressive change, **continuity** 811; **degeneration, deterioration,** worsening, degenerative change, change for the worse, disorder 809, entropy; changeableness 853; "the ever whirling wheels of Change"—Spenser, "Nature's mighty law"—Robert Burns, "a sea-change, Into something rich and strange"—Shakespeare, "the changes and chances of this mortal life"—Book of Common Prayer

2 revolution, break, break with the past, sudden change, radical *or* revolutionary *or* violent *or* total change, catastrophic change, **upheaval,** overthrow, **quantum jump** *or* **leap,** sea change; **discontinuity** 812

3 transformation, transmogrification; **translation; metamorphosis,** metamorphism; **mutation,** transmutation, permutation; **mutant,** mutated form, sport; **transfiguration** *or* transfigurement; metathesis, transposition, translocation, **displacement,** metastasis, heterotopia; **transubstantiation,** consubstantiation; transanimation, transmigration, reincarnation, metempsychosis avatar; metasomatism, metasomatosis; catalysis; metabolism, anabolism, catabolism; metagenesis; transformism

4 innovation, introduction, discovery, invention, launching; neologism, neoterism, coinage; **breakthrough,** leap, quantum jump *or* leap, new phase; **novelty** 840.2

5 transformer, transmogrifier, **innovator,** innovationist, introducer; precursor 815; **alterant,** alterer, alterative, **agent,** catalytic agent, catalyst; the wind *or* winds of change; **leaven,** yeast, ferment; **modifier,** modificator

VERBS **6 be changed, change, undergo a change,** go through a change, sing *or* dance to a different tune <nonformal>, be converted into, turn into 857.17; **alter,** mutate, modulate; **vary,** checker, diversify; **deviate, diverge,** turn, take a turn, take a new turn, turn aside, turn the corner, **shift,** veer, jibe, tack, come about, come round *or* around, haul around, chop, chop and change, swerve, warp; change sides, change horses in midstream; **revive,** be renewed, feel like a new person; **improve,** ameliorate, meliorate, mitigate; **degenerate, deteriorate, worsen;** hit bottom, bottom out <nonformal>, reach the nadir, flop <nonformal>

7 **change, work** *or* **make a change, alter,** change someone's tune; **mutate; modify;** adapt; modulate, accommodate, adjust, fine-tune, fit, **qualify; vary, diversify; convert, renew, recast, revamp** <nonformal>, change over, exchange, **revive;** remake, reshape, re-create, redesign, **rebuild,** reconstruct, restructure; realign; refit; **reform, improve,** better, ameliorate, meliorate, mitigate; **revolutionize,** turn upside down, subvert, overthrow, break up; worsen, deform, denature; ring the changes; give a turn to, give a twist to, turn the tide, turn the tables, turn the scale *or* balance; shift the scene; shuffle the cards; turn over a new leaf; **about-face,** do an about-face, do a 180 <nonformal>, reverse oneself, turn one's coat, sing *or* dance to a different tune, flip-flop <nonformal>

8 **transform, transfigure, transmute,** transmogrify; **translate;** transubstantiate, metamorphose; metabolize

9 **innovate,** make innovations, invent, discover, make a breakthrough, make a quantum jump *or* leap, **pioneer** 815.3, **revolutionize, introduce,** introduce new blood; neologize, neoterize, coin

ADJS 10 **changed, altered, modified,** qualified, **transformed,** transmuted, **metamorphosed;** translated, metastasized; deviant, aberrant, mutant; divergent; **converted, renewed,** revived, **rebuilt; reformed,** improved, **better,** ameliorative, ameliatory; before-and-after; **degenerate, worse,** unmitigated; subversive, **revolutionary;** changeable 853.6,7

11 **innovational,** innovative

12 **metamorphic, metabolic,** anabolic, catabolic; metastatic, **catalytic**

13 presto, presto chango, hey presto <Brit>

PHRS 14 the shoe is on the other foot

852 PERMANENCE

NOUNS 1 **permanence** *or* permanency, **immutability, changelessness,** unchanging-ness, invariableness *or* invariability; **unchangeableness,** unchangeability, unchangingness, inalterability *or* inalterableness, inconvertibility *or* inconvertibleness; **fixedness, constancy,** steadfastness, firmness, solidity, immovableness *or* immovability, persistence *or* persistency, faithfulness, **lastingness, abidingness, endurance,** duration, standing, long standing, inveteracy; durableness, durability 826; **perpetualness** 828.1; **stability** 854; **unchangeability** 854.4; **immobility,** stasis, frozenness, hardening, **rigidity; quiescence,** torpor, coma

2 **maintenance, preservation** 397, **conservation**

3 **conservatism, conservativeness,** opposition *or* resistance to change, unprogressiveness, fogyism, fuddy-duddyism, backwardness, old-fashionedness, standpattism <nonformal>; ultraconservatism, arch-conservatism; misocainea, misoneism; political conservatism, rightism 611.1; laissez-faireism 329.1; old school tie <Brit>; "adherence to the old and tried, against the new and untried"— Lincoln, "be not the first by whom the new is tried"—Pope

4 **conservative,** conservatist; conservationist; ultraconservative, arch-conservative, knee-jerk conservative <nonformal>, **diehard,** standpat *and* standpatter <both nonformal>, **old fogy,** fogy, stick-in-the-mud <nonformal>, mossback <nonformal>, *laudator temporis acti* <L>, **rightist, right-winger** 611.9, "the leftover progressive of an earlier generation"—Edmund Fuller; old school

VERBS 5 **remain, endure** 826.6, last, stay, persist, bide, abide, stand, hold, subsist; be ever the same

6 **be conservative,** save, preserve, oppose change, stand on ancient ways; stand pat *and* stand still <both nonformal>; **let things take their course,** leave things as they are, let be, let *or* leave alone, stick with it *and* let it ride <both nonformal>, follow a hands-off policy, let well enough alone, do nothing; stop *or* turn back the clock

ADJS 7 **permanent, changeless, unchanging, immutable,** unvarying, unshifting; **unchanged,** unchangeable, unvaried, **unaltered,** inalterable, inviolate, undestroyed, intact; **constant, persistent,** sustained, fixed, firm, solid, steadfast, like the Rock of Gibraltar, faithful; unchecked, unfailing, unfading; **lasting,**

enduring, abiding, remaining, staying, continuing; **durable** 826.10; **perpetual** 828.7; stable 854.12; **unchangeable** 854.17; **immobile, static,** stationary, frozen, **rigid; quiescent,** torpid, comatose, vegetable

8 **conservative, preservative,** old-line, **diehard,** standpat <nonformal>, opposed to change; backward, backward-looking, old-fashioned, **unprogressive,** nonprogressive, unreconstructed, status-quo, stuck-in-the-mud; ultraconservative, misoneistic, fogyish, **old-fogyish; right-wing** 611.17; *laissez-faire* <Fr>, hands-off; noninvasive, noninterventionist

ADVS 9 **permanently,** abidingly, lastingly, steadfastly, unwaveringly, changelessly, unchangingly; enduringly, **perpetually,** invariably, **forever, always** 828.11; statically, rigidly, inflexibly

10 *in status quo* <L>, as things are, **as is, as usual,** as per usual <nonformal>; at a stand *or* standstill, without a shadow of turning

PHRS 11 *plus ça change, plus c'est la même chose* <Fr, the more it changes, the more it's the same thing>; if it isn't broken don't fix it, let sleeping dogs lie

853 CHANGEABLENESS

NOUNS 1 **changeableness,** changefulness, **changeability, alterability,** convertibility, modifiability; **mutability,** permutability, impermanence, **transience,** transitoriness; mobility, motility, movability; plasticity, malleability, workability, rubberiness, fluidity; **resilience, adaptability,** adjustability, **flexibility,** suppleness; **nonuniformity** 781

2 **inconstancy, instability,** changefulness, unstableness, **unsteadiness,** unsteadfastness, unfixedness, unsettledness, rootlessness; **uncertainty,** undependability, inconsistency, shiftiness, unreliability; **variability,** variation, variety, restlessness, deviability; unpredictability, irregularity 850.1; **desultoriness,** waywardness, wantonness; **erraticism, eccentricity;** freakishness, freakery; flightiness, impulsiveness *or* impulsivity, mercuriality, moodiness, whimsicality, **capriciousness, fickleness** 364.3

3 **changing, fluctuation,** vicissitude, **variation, shiftingness;** alternation, oscillation, **vacillation,** pendulation; **mood swings; wavering,** shifting, shuffling, teetering, tottering, seesawing, teeter-

tottering; **exchange,** trading, musical chairs

4 <comparisons> Proteus, kaleidoscope, chameleon, shifting sands, rolling stone, April showers, cloud shapes, feather in the wind; water; wheel of fortune; whirligig; mercury, quicksilver; the weather, weathercock, weather vane; moon, phases of the moon

VERBS 5 **change, fluctuate, vary; shift; alternate, vacillate,** oscillate, pendulate, waffle <Brit nonformal>, blow hot and cold <nonformal>; ebb and flow, wax and wane; go through phases, waver, shuffle, swing, sway, wobble, wobble about, flounder, stagger, teeter, totter, **seesaw, teeter-totter;** back and fill, turn, blow hot and cold, ring the changes, have as many phases as the moon; **exchange,** trade, play musical chairs

ADJS 6 **changeable, alterable,** alterative, modifiable; mutable, permutable, impermanent, transient, **transitory; variable,** checkered, ever-changing, many-sided, kaleidoscopic; **movable,** mobile, motile; plastic, malleable, rubbery, fluid; **resilient, adaptable,** adjustable, **flexible,** supple, able to adapt, able to roll with the punches *or* bend without breaking; protean, proteiform; metamorphic; **nonuniform** 781.3

7 **inconstant, changeable, changeful, changing, shifting,** uncertain, inconsistent; **shifty,** unreliable, undependable; **unstable, unfixed,** infirm, restless, **unsettled,** unstaid, **unsteady,** wishy-washy, spineless, shapeless, amorphous, indecisive, irresolute, waffling <Brit nonformal>, blowing hot and cold <nonformal>, like a feather in the wind, unsteadfast, unstable as water; **variable,** deviable, dodgy <nonformal>; unaccountable, unpredictable; vicissitudinous *or* vicissitudinary; whimsical, **capricious, fickle** 364.6, off-again-on-again; **erratic, eccentric,** freakish; volatile, giddy, dizzy, ditzy <nonformal>, scatterbrained, mercurial, moody, flighty, impulsive, impetuous; **fluctuating,** alternating, **vacillating, wavering,** wavery, wavy, mazy, flitting, flickering, guttering, fitful, shifting, shuffling; irregular, spasmodic 850.3; **desultory,** rambling, roving, vagrant, wanton, wayward, wandering, afloat, adrift; **unrestrained, undisciplined,** irresponsible, uncontrolled, fast and loose

ADVS 8 **changeably, variably, inconstantly,** shiftingly, shiftily, uncertainly, **unsteadily,** unsteadfastly, whimsically, capriciously, desultorily, erratically, waveringly; **impulsively, impetuously,** precipitately; back and forth, to and fro, in and out, off and on, on and off, round and round

854 STABILITY

NOUNS **1 stability, firmness, soundness, substantiality, solidity; security,** secureness, securement; **rootedness,** fastness; reliability 969.4; **steadiness,** steadfastness; constancy 846.2, invariability, undeflectability; **imperturbability,** unflappability <nonformal>, nerve, steady or unshakable nerves, unshakableness, unsusceptibility, unimpressionability, stolidness or stolidity, stoicism, **cool** <nonformal>, *sang-froid* <Fr>; **equilibrium, balance,** stable state, stable equilibrium, homeostasis; steady state; emotional stability, balanced personality; aplomb; **uniformity** 780

2 fixity, fixedness, fixture, fixation; infixion, implantation, embedment; **establishment, stabilization,** confirmation, entrenchment; inveteracy, deep-rootedness, **deep-seatedness**

3 immobility, immovability, unmovability, immovableness, irremovability, immotility; inextricability; **firmness,** solidity, unyieldingness, rigidity, **inflexibility** 1044.3; inertia, *vis inertiae* <L>, inertness; immobilization

4 unchangeableness, unchangeability, unalterability, inalterability, unmodifiability, **immutability,** incommutability, inconvertibility; nontransferability; lastingness, **permanence** 852; irrevocability, indefeasibility, **irreversibility;** irretrievability, unreturnableness, unrestorableness; intransmutability

5 indestructibility, imperishability, incorruptibility, inextinguishability, immortality, **deathlessness;** invulnerability, invincibility, inexpugnability, impregnability; ineradicability, indelibility, ineffaceability, inerasableness

6 <comparisons> rock, Rock of Gibraltar, bedrock, pillar or tower of strength, foundation; leopard's spots

VERBS **7 stabilize,** stabilitate or stabilify <old>; **firm, firm up** <nonformal>; **steady, balance,** counterbalance, ballast; **immobilize,** freeze, keep, retain; **transfix,** stick, hold, pin or nail down <nonformal>

8 secure, make sure or secure, tie, tie off or up, chain, tether; cleat, belay; **wedge,**

jam, seize; **make fast, fasten,** fasten down; **anchor,** moor; batten *and* batten down; "build one's house upon a rock"— Bible; **confirm,** ratify

9 fix, define, set, **settle; establish,** found, ground, lodge, seat, **entrench; root;** infix, ingrain, set in, plant, implant, engraft, bed, embed; **print,** imprint, **stamp,** inscribe, **etch,** engrave, impress; deep-dye, **dye in the wool;** stereotype

10 <become firmly fixed> **root, take root,** strike root; **stick,** stick fast; seize, seize up, freeze; **catch, jam,** lodge, foul

11 stand fast, stand or remain firm, **stand pat** <nonformal>, stay put <nonformal>, hold fast, not budge, not budge an inch, **stand or hold one's ground,** hold one's own, dig in one's heels, take one's stand, **stick to one's guns,** put one's foot down <nonformal>; **hold out,** stick or gut or tough it out *and* hang tough <all nonformal>, stay the course; **hold up; weather,** weather the storm, ride it out, get home free <nonformal>; be imperturbable, be unflappable *and* not bat an eye or eyelash *and* keep one's cool <all nonformal>

ADJS **12 stable, substantial, firm, solid, sound,** stabile; firm as Gibraltar, solid as a rock, rock-like, built on bedrock; **fast, secure; steady,** unwavering, steadfast; **balanced,** in equilibrium, in a stable state; **well-balanced; imperturbable,** unflappable <nonformal>, unshakable, **cool** <nonformal>, unimpressionable, unsusceptible, impassive, stolid, stoic; without nerves, without a nerve in one's body, unflinching; **reliable** 969.17, predictable; fiducial

13 established, stabilized, **entrenched,** vested, firmly established; **well-established, well-founded, well-grounded,** on a rock, in or on bedrock; old-line, long-established; **confirmed, inveterate; settled, set;** well-settled, well-set, in place; **rooted,** well-rooted; **deep-rooted, deep-seated,** deep-set, deep-settled, deep-fixed, deep-dyed, deep-engraven, deep-grounded, deep-laid; **infixed, ingrained,** implanted, engrafted, embedded, ingrown, inwrought; impressed, indelibly impressed, imprinted; engraved, etched, graven, embossed; **dyed-in-the-wool**

14 fixed, fastened, anchored, riveted; **set, settled, stated;** staple

15 immovable, unmovable, **immobile,** immotile, unmoving, **irremovable, stationary,** frozen, not to be moved, at a standstill, on dead center; **firm, unyielding,**

adamant, adamantine, rigid, **inflexible**
1044.12; pat, standpat <nonformal>

16 **stuck, fast,** stuck fast, **fixed, transfixed,
caught,** fastened, tied, chained, tethered,
anchored, moored, held, inextricable;
jammed, impacted, congested, packed,
wedged; seized, seized up, frozen;
aground, grounded, stranded, high
and dry

17 **unchangeable,** not to be changed, changeless, unchanged, unchanging, unvarying,
unvariable, **unalterable,** unaltered, un-
alterative, **immutable,** incommutable,
inconvertible, unmodifiable; insusceptible of change; **constant, invariable,**
undeviating, undeflectable; lasting, unremitting, **permanent** 852.7; irrevocable,
indefeasible, **irreversible,** nonreversible,
reverseless; irretrievable, unrestorable,
unreturnable, nonreturnable; intransmutable, inert, noble <chemistry>

18 **indestructible,** undestroyable, **imperishable,** nonperishable, incorruptible;
deathless, immortal, undying; **invulnerable, invincible,** inexpugnable,
impregnable, indivisible; **ineradicable,**
indelible, ineffaceable, inerasable; **inextinguishable,** unquenchable, quenchless,
undampable

PHRS 19 **stet, let it stand; what's done is
done**

855 CONTINUANCE
<continuance in action>

NOUNS 1 **continuance, continuation,
ceaselessness,** unceasingness, uninterruptedness, unremittingness, **continualness**
811.1; **prolongation, extension, protraction, perpetuation,** lengthening, spinning
or stringing out; **survival** 826.1, holding
out, hanging on *or* in; **maintenance,** sustenance, sustained action *or* activity;
pursuance; run, way, straight *or* uninterrupted course; **progress,** progression;
persistence, perseverance 360; **endurance**
826.1, **stamina,** staying power; **continuity**
811; **repetition** 848

2 **resumption, recommencement,** rebegin-
ning, recommencement, reestablishment,
revival, recrudescence, resuscitation, **renewal,** reopening, reentrance, reappearance; **fresh start,** new beginning; another
try, another shot *or* crack *or* go <nonfor-
mal>

VERBS 3 **continue** 811.4, keep *or* stay with it,
keep *or* stay at it, carry on; **remain,** bide,
abide, stay, tarry, linger; **go on,** go along,
keep on, keep on keeping on, keep going,

carry on, see it through, stay on, hold on,
hold one's way *or* course *or* path, hold
steady, run on, jog on, drag on, bash
ahead *or* on <nonformal>, slog on, soldier on, plug away <nonformal>, grind
away *or* on, stagger on, put one foot in
front of the other; never cease, cease not;
endure 826.6

4 **sustain, protract, prolong, extend,** perpetuate, lengthen, spin *or* string out;
maintain, keep, hold, retain, preserve;
keep up, keep going, keep alive, **survive**
826.6

5 **persist, persevere,** keep at it 360.2, stick it
out, stick to it, stick with it, never say die,
see it through, hang in *and* hang tough
and not know when one is licked <all
nonformal>; survive, make out, manage,
get along, get on, eke out an existence,
keep the even tenor of one's way; go on,
go on with, go on with the show <nonfor-
mal>, press on; perseverate, iterate,
reiterate, **harp,** go on about, chew one's
ear off *and* run off at the mouth <both
nonformal>, beat a dead horse

6 **resume, recommence,** rebegin, **renew,**
reestablish; **revive,** resuscitate, re-
crudesce; reenter, reopen, **return to,** go
back to, begin again, take up again, make
a new beginning, make a fresh start, start
all over, have another try, have another
shot *or* crack *or* go <nonformal>

ADJS 7 **continuing, abiding** 826.10; staying,
remaining, sticking; **continuous** 811.8,
ceaseless, unceasing, unending, endless,
incessant, unremitting, steady, sustained,
protracted, undying, indefatigable, **persistent; repetitious, repetitive** 848.14;
resumed, recommenced, rebegun, renewed, reopened

856 CESSATION

NOUNS 1 **cessation, discontinuance,** discontinuation, phaseout, phasedown, scratching *and* scrubbing *and* breakoff <all
nonformal>; **desistance,** desinence,
cease, surcease, **ceasing,** ending, halting,
stopping, termination; **close,** closing,
shutdown; sign-off; log-off; **relinquishment,** renunciation, abandonment

2 **stop,** stoppage, **halt, stay, arrest,** check,
cutoff <nonformal>; stand, **standstill;**
full stop, dead stop, screaming *or* grinding *or* shuddering *or* squealing halt;
strike 727.7, walkout, work stoppage, sit-
down strike, lockout; sick-out *and* blue flu
<both nonformal>; **end,** ending, end-
game, final whistle, gun, bell, checkmate;

tie, stalemate, deadlock, wash *and* toss-up <both nonformal>, standoff *and* Mexican standoff <both nonformal>; **terminal,** end of the line, rest stop, stopping place, terminus

3 **pause, rest, break,** caesura, **recess, intermission,** interim 825, intermittence, interval, interlude, *intermezzo* <Ital>; **respite,** letup <nonformal>; **interruption, suspension,** time-out, break in the action, breathing spell, cooling-off period; **postponement** 845.4, rain-out; **remission;** abeyance, stay, drop, lull, lapse; truce, cease-fire, stand-down; **vacation, holiday,** time off, day off, recess, playtime, leisure

4 <grammatical terms> pause, juncture, boundary, caesura; <punctuation> stop *or* point *or* period, comma, colon, semicolon

5 <legislatures> **cloture,** *clôture* <Fr>; cloture by compartment, kangaroo cloture; guillotine <Brit>

VERBS 6 **cease, discontinue, end, stop, halt,** end-stop, terminate, close the books on, close the books, put paid to <Brit>, abort, cancel, scratch *and* scrub <both nonformal>, hold, **quit,** stay, belay <nonformal>; **desist, refrain,** leave off, lay off <nonformal>, give over, **have done with;** cut it out *and* drop it *and* knock it off <all nonformal>, relinquish, renounce, abandon; **come to an end** 819.6, draw to a close

7 **stop, come to a stop** *or* halt, **halt,** stop in one's tracks, skid to a stop, stop dead, **stall; bring up, pull up,** pull in, head in, draw up, **fetch up; stop short,** come up short, bring up short, come to a screaming *or* squealing *or* grinding *or* shuddering halt, stop on a dime <nonformal>, come to a full stop, come to a stand *or* standstill, grind to a halt, fetch up all standing; **stick,** jam, hang fire, seize, seize up, freeze; **cease fire,** stand down; run into a brick wall

8 <stop work> **lay off, knock off** <nonformal>, call it a day <nonformal>, call it quits <nonformal>; lay down one's tools, **shut up shop,** close shop, shut down, close down, secure <nautical nonformal>; **strike,** walk out, call a strike, go *or* go out on strike, stand down; work to rule

9 **pause, rest,** let up *and* take it easy <both nonformal>, **relax,** rest on one's oars; **recess,** take *or* call a recess; **take a break,** break, take ten

10 **interrupt, suspend,** intermit, **break, break off,** take a break <nonformal>, cut off, break *or* snap the thread

11 **put a stop to, call a halt to,** get it over with, blow the whistle on <nonformal>, **put an end to** 819.5, put paid to <Brit nonformal>, call off the dogs <nonformal>; **stop, stay, halt, arrest, check,** flag down, wave down; block, brake, dam, stem, stem the tide *or* current; pull up, draw rein, put on the brakes, hit the brake pedal; **bring to a stand** *or* **standstill,** bring to a close *or* halt, freeze, bring to, bring up short, **stop dead** *or* dead in one's tracks, set one back on his heels, stop cold, stop short, cut short, check in full career; checkmate, stalemate, deadlock

12 **turn off, shut off,** shut, shut down, close; **phase out,** phase down, taper off, wind up *or* down; **kill, cut,** cut off short, switch off

INTERJS 13 **cease!, stop!, halt!,** *halte!* <Fr>, hold!, freeze!, stay!, desist!, quit it!; **let up!,** easy!, take it easy!, relax!, get off it!, **leave off!,** *arrêtez!* <Fr>, stop it!, forget it!, no more!, have done!, *tenez!* <Fr>, **hold everything!, hold it!,** hold to!, hold on!, whoa!, that's it!, that's enough!, that will do!, enough!, enough is enough!, genug!, all right already!, *basta!* <Ital>

14 <nonformal terms> **cut it out!,** cool it!, bag it!, chill out!, call it quits!, can it!, turn it off!, chuck it!, stow it!, drop it!, lay off!, all right already!, come off it!, **knock it off!,** break it off!, break it up!

857 CONVERSION
<change to something different>

NOUNS 1 **conversion,** reconversion, **changeover,** turning into, becoming; convertibility; **change** 851, sea change, **transformation,** transubstantiation, transmutation; **transition,** transit, **switch** *and* **switchover** <both nonformal>, passage, **shift; reversal,** about-face *and* flip-flop <both nonformal>, *volte-face* <Fr>; **relapse,** lapse, descent; **breakthrough; growth,** progress, development; transcendence; **resolution** 939.1; reduction, simplification; **assimilation,** naturalization, adoption, assumption; alchemy

2 **new start, new beginning,** fresh start, clean slate, square one <nonformal>; **reformation, reform, regeneration, revival, reclamation,** redemption, amendment, improvement 392, renewal, recrudescence, **rebirth,** renascence, new birth, **change of heart;** change of mind *or* commitment *or* allegiance *or* loyalty *or* conviction

3 apostasy, renunciation, **defection, deser-**

tion, treason, crossing-over, abandonment; degeneration 393.3

4 **rehabilitation,** reconditioning, recovery, readjustment, reclamation, restoration; **reeducation,** reinstruction; **repatriation**

5 **indoctrination,** reindoctrination, counterindoctrination; **brainwashing,** menticide; subversion, alienation, corruption

6 **conversion,** proselytization, proselytism, evangelization, persuasion 375.3

7 **convert, proselyte,** neophyte, catechumen, disciple

8 **apostate, defector,** turncoat, traitor, deserter, **renegade**

9 **converter, proselyter,** proselytizer, **missionary, apostle, evangelist**

10 <instruments> philosopher's stone, melting pot, crucible, alembic, test tube, caldron, retort, mortar; potter's wheel, anvil, lathe; converter, transformer, transducer, engine, motor, machine 1039.4

VERBS 11 **convert,** reconvert; **change over,** switch *and* switch over <both nonformal>, **shift; do over,** re-do, make over, rejigger <nonformal>; **change, transform** 851.5,8, transmute; **change into, turn into, become,** resolve into, assimilate to, bring to, reduce to, naturalize; **make,** render; **reverse,** do an about-face; change one's tune, sing a different tune, dance to another tune; turn back 858.5

12 **re-form,** remodel, reshape, refashion, recast; regroup, redeploy, rearrange 807.13; **renew,** new-model; be reborn, be born again, be a new person, feel like a new person; get it together *and* get one's act *or* shit together *and* get one's ducks in a row <all nonformal>; **regenerate, reclaim,** redeem, amend, set straight; **reform, rehabilitate,** set on the straight and narrow, make a new man of, restore self-respect; mend *or* change one's ways, **turn over a new leaf,** put on the new man

13 **defect,** renege, wimp *or* chicken *or* cop out <nonformal>, turn one's coat, desert, apostatize, change one's colors, turn against, turn traitor; leave *or* desert a sinking ship; lapse, relapse; degenerate

14 **rehabilitate,** recondition, reclaim, recover, restore, readjust; **reeducate,** reinstruct; **repatriate**

15 **indoctrinate, brainwash,** reindoctrinate, counterindoctrinate; subvert, alienate, win away, corrupt

16 **convince, persuade,** wean, bring over, sweep off one's feet <nonformal>, **win over;** proselyte, **proselytize,** evangelize

17 be converted into, **turn into** *or* **to, become** 760.12, **change into,** alter into, run *or* fall *or* pass into, slide *or* glide into, **grow into,** ripen into, **develop** *or* **evolve into,** merge *or* blend *or* melt into, shift into, lapse into, open into, resolve itself *or* settle into, come round to

ADJS 18 **convertible,** changeable, resolvable, transmutable, **transformable, transitional, modifiable;** reformable, reclaimable, renewable

19 **converted, changed, transformed;** naturalized, assimilated; **reformed,** regenerated, renewed, redeemed, reborn, born-again

20 **apostate, treasonable, traitorous,** degenerate, **renegade**

858 REVERSION
<change to a former state>

NOUNS 1 **reversion,** reverting, retroversion, retrogradation, **retrogression,** retrocession, regress, **relapse** 394, **regression, backsliding,** lapse, slipping back, backing, recidivism, recidivation; reconversion; **reverse, reversal,** turnabout, about-face, right about-face, 180-degree shift, flip-flop <nonformal>, **turn; return,** returning; disenchantment; **reclamation, rehabilitation,** redemption, return to the fold; **reinstatement,** restitution, restoration

2 **throwback,** atavism

3 **returnee, repeater;** prodigal son, lost lamb; reversioner, reversionist; recidivist, habitual criminal *or* offender, two-time loser <nonformal>; backslider

VERBS 4 **revert,** retrovert, **regress, retrogress,** retrograde, retrocede, **reverse, return,** return to the fold; backslide, slip back, recidivate, lapse, lapse back, relapse 394.4

5 **turn back, change back, go back, hark back,** cry back, break back, **turn,** turn around *or* about; do an about-face *and* flip-flop *and* do a flip-flop *and* hang a 180 <all nonformal>; put the genie back into the bottle, put the toothpaste back into the tube; go back to go *or* to square one *or* to the drawing board <nonformal>

6 **revert to, return to,** recur to, go back to; hark *or* cry back to

ADJS 7 **reversionary,** reversional, **regressive,** recessive, **retrogressive, retrograde;** reactionary; recidivist *or* recidivistic, recidivous, lapsarian; retroverse, retrorse; atavistic; revertible, returnable, reversible, recoverable

WORD ELEMENTS 8 retro—

859 REVOLUTION
<sudden or radical change>

NOUNS **1 revolution, radical** *or* **total change, violent change,** striking alteration, sweeping change, clean sweep, clean slate, square one <nonformal>, tabula rasa; transilience, quantum leap *or* jump; **overthrow,** overturn, upset, *bouleversement* <Fr>, convulsion, spasm, subversion, coup d'état; breakup, breakdown; **cataclysm, catastrophe,** debacle, *débâcle* <Fr>; **revolution,** revolutionary war, war of national liberation; bloodless revolution, palace revolution; technological revolution, electronic *or* communications *or* computer *or* information revolution; green revolution; counterrevolution; **revolt** 327.4

2 revolutionism, revolutionariness, anarchism, syndicalism, terrorism; Bolshevism *or* Bolshevikism <both Russia>, Carbonarism <Italy>, Sinn Feinism <Ireland>, Jacobinism <France>; sansculottism <France>, *sans-culotterie* <Fr>, Castroism <Cuba>, Maoism <China>, Shining Path <Peru>, Sandinistism <Nicaragua>

3 revolutionist, revolutionary, revolutionizer; **rebel** 327.5; anarchist, anarch, syndicalist, criminal syndicalist, terrorist 671.9; subversive; red; Red Republican <France>, *bonnet rouge* <Fr>; Jacobin <France>, sans-culotte, sans-culottist; Yankee *or* Yankee Doodle *or* Continental <all US>; Puritan *or* Roundhead <both England>; Bolshevik *or* Bolshevist *or* Bolshie <all Russia>, Marxist, Leninist, Communist, Commie <nonformal>, Red, Trotskyite *or* Trotskyist, Castroist *or* Castroite <Cuba>, Guevarist, Maoist; Vietcong *or* VC, Cong, Charley <all Vietnam>; *Carbonaro* <Italy>, Carbonarist <Italy>; Sinn Feiner, Fenian <both Ireland>; revolutionary junta

VERBS **4 revolutionize, make a radical change,** make a clean sweep, break with the past; **overthrow, overturn,** throw the rascals out *and* let heads roll <both nonformal> *boulverse* <Fr>, upset; revolt 327.7

ADJS **5 revolutionary;** revulsive, revulsionary; transilient; cataclysmic, catastrophic; **radical,** sweeping 793.10; **insurrectionary** 327.11

6 revolutionist, revolutionary, anarchic *or* anarchical, syndicalist, terrorist *or* terroristic, agin the government <nonformal>; Bolshevistic, Bolshevik; sansculottic, sans-culottish; Jacobinic *or* Jacobinical, Carbonarist, Fenian, Marxist, Leninist, Communist, Trotskyist *or* Trotskyite, Guevarist, Castroist *or* Castroite, Maoist, Vietcong, Mau-Mau

860 EVOLUTION

NOUNS **1 evolution, evolving,** evolvement; evolutionary change, gradual change, step-by-step change, peaceful *or* nonviolent change; **development, growth,** rise, incremental change, developmental change, natural growth *or* development; flowering, blossoming; ripening, coming of age, maturation 303.6; accomplishment 407; **advance,** advancement, furtherance; **progress,** progression; **elaboration,** enlargement, amplification, **expansion;** devolution, degeneration 393.3

2 unfolding, unfoldment, unrolling, unfurling, unwinding; revelation, gradual revelation

3 <biological terms> **genesis;** phylogeny, phylogenesis; ontogeny, ontogenesis; physiogeny, physiogenesis; **biological evolution;** natural selection, adaptation; horotely, bradytely, tachytely

4 evolutionism, theory of evolution; **Darwinism,** Darwinianism, punctuated equilibrium, Neo-Darwinism, organic evolution, survival of the fittest; Haeckelism, Lamarckism *or* Lamarckianism, Neo-Lamarckism, Lysenkoism, Weismannism, Spencerianism; social Darwinism, social evolution

VERBS **5 evolve; develop, grow,** wax, change gradually *or* step-by-step; **progress, advance,** come a long way; accomplish 407.4; ripen, mellow, mature 303.9, maturate; flower, bloom, blossom, bear fruit; degenerate

6 elaborate, develop, work out, enlarge, enlarge on *or* upon, amplify, **expand,** expand on *or* upon, detail, go *or* enter into detail, go into, flesh out, **pursue,** spell out <nonformal>; complete 407.6

7 unfold, unroll, unfurl, unwind, unreel, uncoil, reveal, reveal *or* expose gradually

ADJS **8 evolutionary,** evolutional, evolutionist *or* evolutionistic; **evolving, developing, unfolding; maturing,** maturational, maturative; **progressing, advancing;** devolutionary, degenerative; genetic, phylogenetic, ontogenetic, physiogenetic; horotelic, bradytelic, tachytelic

861 SUBSTITUTION
<change of one thing for another>

NOUNS **1 substitution, exchange, change,** switch, switcheroo <nonformal>, commutation, subrogation; **surrogacy;** vicariousness, **representation,** deputation, **delegation;** deputyship, **agency, power of attorney; supplanting,** supplantation, succession; **replacement,** displacement; provision, provisionalness *or* provisionality, adhocracy, ad hockery *or* ad hocery, ad hocism; superseding, supersession *or* supersedure; tit for tat, *quid pro quo* <L>

2 substitute, sub <nonformal>, **substitution, replacement,** backup, second *or* third string <nonformal>, secondary, utility player, succedaneum; **change, exchange; ersatz,** phony *and* fake <both nonformal>, counterfeit, imitation 336, copy 784; surrogate; reserves, bench <nonformal>, backup, backup personnel, spares; **alternate,** alternative, next best thing; **successor,** supplanter, superseder, capper <nonformal>; **proxy,** dummy, ghost; vicar, agent, representative; **deputy** 576; locum tenens, vice, vice-president, vice-regent, etc; **relief,** fill-in, **stand-in, understudy, pinch hitter** *or* runner <nonformal>; double; **equivalent,** equal; ringer <nonformal>; ghostwriter; **analogy,** comparison; **metaphor,** metonymy, synecdoche <all grammatical>; **symbol, sign,** token, icon; makeshift 994.2

3 scapegoat, goat <nonformal>, fall guy *and* can-carrier *and* patsy *and* catch dog <all nonformal>, **whipping boy**

VERBS **4 substitute, exchange, change,** take *or* ask *or* offer in exchange, switch, ring in <nonformal>, **put in the place of,** change for, make way for, give place to; commute, redeem, compound for; **pass off,** pawn *or* foist *or* fob off; rob Peter to pay Paul; dub in; make do with, shift with, put up with

5 substitute for, sub for <nonformal>, subrogate; **act for,** double for *or* as, stand *or* sit in for, understudy for, fill in for, don the mantle of, change places with, swap places with <nonformal>, stand in the stead of, step into *or* fill the shoes of, pinch-hit *and* pinch-run <both nonformal>; **relieve,** spell *and* spell off <both nonformal>, cover for; ghost, ghostwrite; **represent** 576.14; **supplant, supersede,**

succeed, **replace,** displace, **take the place of,** crowd out, cut out <nonformal>

6 <nonformal terms> **cover up for,** front for; **take the rap for,** *and* take the fall for <both nonformal>, carry the can *and* be the goat *or* patsy *or* fall guy <all nonformal>

7 delegate, deputize, commission, give the nod to <nonformal>, designate an agent *or* a proxy

ADJS **8 substitute, alternate, alternative,** other, tother <nonformal>, equivalent, token, dummy, pinch, utility, backup, secondary; ad hoc, provisional; **vicarious,** ersatz, mock, phony *and* fake *and* bogus <all nonformal>, counterfeit, imitation 336.8; **proxy;** makeshift, reserve, **spare,** stopgap, temporary, provisional, tentative

9 substitutional, substitutionary, substitutive, supersessive; **substituted,** substituent

10 replaceable, substitutable, supersedable, expendable

ADVS **11 instead, rather,** *faute de mieux* <Fr>; in its stead *or* place; in one's stead, in one's behalf, in one's place, in one's shoes; by proxy; as an alternative; *in loco parentis* <L>

PREPS **12 instead of,** in the stead of, rather than, sooner than, **in place of,** in the place of, **in** *or* **on behalf of, in lieu of; for,** as proxy for, as a substitute for, as representing, in preference to, as an alternative to; **replacing,** as a replacement for, vice

WORD ELEMENTS **13** pro—, vice—, quasi—, pseudo—

862 INTERCHANGE
<double or mutual change>

NOUNS **1 interchange, exchange,** counterchange; **transposition,** transposal; mutual transfer *or* replacement; mutual admiration, mutual support; **cooperation** 450; commutation, permutation, intermutation; alternation; **interplay, tradeoff, compromise, reciprocation** 776.1, reciprocality, reciprocity, mutuality; **give-and-take,** something for something, *quid pro quo* <L>, measure for measure, **tit for tat,** an eye for an eye, "an eye for an eye and a tooth for a tooth"—Bible; **retaliation,** *lex talionis* <L>; cross fire; battledore and shuttlecock

2 trading, swapping <nonformal>; trade, swap <nonformal>, even trade, even-steven trade, **switch;** barter 731.2; log-rolling, back scratching, pork barrel

3 **interchangeability,** exchangeability, changeability, standardization; convertibility, commutability, permutability

VERBS 4 **interchange, exchange,** change, counterchange; alternate; **transpose;** convert, commute, permute; **trade, swap** <nonformal>, **switch;** bandy, bandy about, play at battledore and shuttlecock; **reciprocate, trade off,** compromise, settle, settle for, respond, keep a balance; **give and take,** give tit for tat, give a Roland for an Oliver, give as much as one takes, give as good as one gets, return the compliment or favor, pay back, compensate, **requite,** return; **retaliate,** get back at, get even with, be quits with; logroll, scratch each other's back, **cooperate** 450.3

ADJS 5 **interchangeable, exchangeable,** changeable, standard; equivalent; **even,** equal; returnable, **convertible,** commutable, permutable; commutative; retaliatory, equalizing; **reciprocative or reciprocating, reciprocatory, reciprocal, traded-off; mutual,** give-and-take; **exchanged, transposed,** switched, **swapped** <nonformal>, traded, **interchanged**

ADVS 6 **interchangeably, exchangeably; in exchange, in return; even, evenly** au pair <Fr>; **reciprocally,** mutually; **in turn,** each in its turn, every one in his turn, by turns, turn about, turn and turn about

PHRS 7 one good turn deserves another; you scratch my back I scratch yours

863 GENERALITY

NOUNS 1 **generality, universality,** cosmicality, inclusiveness 771.1; worldwideness, globality or globalism, globaloney <nonformal>, ecumenicity or ecumenicalism; catholicity; **internationalism,** cosmopolitanism; **generalization,** universalization, globalization, ecumenization, internationalization; **labeling,** stereotyping

2 **prevalence, commonness,** commonality, usualness, **currency,** occurrence; **extensiveness,** widespreadness, sweepingness, rifeness, rampantness; **normality,** normalness, averageness, ordinariness, routineness, habitualness, standardness

3 **average,** ruck, **run,** general or common or average or ordinary run, **run of the mill;** any Tom, Dick, or Harry; Everyman; common or average man, the man in the street, John Q Public, John or Jane Doe,

ordinary Joe, Joe Six-pack; girl next door; everyman, everywoman; homme moyen sensuel <Fr>

4 **all, everyone, everybody, each and every-one, one and all,** all comers and all hands and every man Jack and every mother's son <all nonformal>, every living soul, **all the world,** tout le monde <Fr>, the devil and all <nonformal>, **whole, totality** 791.1; **everything,** all kinds or all manner of things; you name it and what have you and all the above <all nonformal>

5 **any, anything,** any one, aught, either; **anybody, anyone**

6 **whatever,** whate'er, **whatsoever,** whatsoe'er, **what, whichever,** anything soever which, no matter what or which

7 **whoever,** whoso, **whosoever, whomever,** whomso, **whomsoever,** anyone, no matter who

8 <idea or expression> **generalization,** general idea, **abstraction,** generalized proposition; glittering generality, sweeping statement; **truism, platitude, conventional wisdom,** commonplace, lieu commun <Fr>, locus communis <L>; **cliché,** tired cliché, bromide, trite or hackneyed expression

VERBS 9 **generalize, universalize,** catholicize, ecumenicize, globalize, internationalize; **broaden, widen, expand,** extend, spread; make a generalization, deal in generalities or abstractions; **label,** stereotype

10 **prevail, predominate, obtain,** dominate, reign, rule; be in force or effect; be the rule or fashion, be the rage or thing <nonformal>, be in <nonformal>

ADJS 11 **general, generalized, nonspecific,** generic, **indefinite,** indeterminate, vague, abstract, nebulous, unspecified, undifferentiated, featureless, uncharacterized, bland, neutral

12 **prevalent, prevailing, common,** popular, **current,** running; regnant, reigning, **ruling, predominant,** predominating, **dominant; rife, rampant,** pandemic, epidemic, besetting; **ordinary, normal, average, usual,** routine, standard, par for the course <nonformal>, stereotyped

13 **extensive, broad, wide,** liberal, diffuse, large-scale, broad-scale, broad-scope, broadly-based, wide-scale, **sweeping; cross-disciplinary,** interdisciplinary; widespread, far-spread, far-stretched, **far-reaching,** far-going, far-embracing, far-extending, far-spreading, far-flying, far-ranging, **far-flung,** wide-flung, wide-

reaching, wide-extending, wide-extended, wide-ranging, wide-stretching; **wholesale, indiscriminate**

14 **universal,** cosmic *or* cosmical, heaven-wide, galactic, planetary, world-wide, transnational, planet-wide, **global; total,** allover, holistic; catholic, **all-inclusive,** all-including, **all-embracing,** all-encompassing, all-comprehensive, all-comprehending, all-filling, all-pervading, all-covering; nonsectarian, nondenominational, ecumenic *or* ecumenical; **cosmopolitan,** international; **national,** nation-wide, country-wide, state-wide

15 **every, all,** any, whichever, whichsoever; **each,** each one; every one, each and every, each and all, **one and all, all and sundry,** all and some

16 **trite, commonplace,** hackneyed, platitudinous, truistic, overworked, stereotyped

ADVS 17 **generally, in general; generally speaking,** speaking generally, **broadly,** broadly speaking, **roughly,** roughly speaking, as an approximation; **usually, as a rule, ordinarily, commonly, normally,** routinely, as a matter of course, in the usual course; **by and large,** at large, altogether, overall, over the long haul <nonformal>, **all things considered,** taking one thing with another, taking all things together, on balance, **all in all,** taking all in all, taking it for all in all, **on the whole,** as a whole, **in the long run,** for the most part, for better or for worse; **prevailingly, predominantly, mostly,** chiefly, mainly

18 **universally,** galactically, cosmically; **everywhere, all over,** the world over, all over the world, internationally; in every instance, without exception, **invariably, always,** never otherwise

WORD ELEMENTS 19 glob—, globo—, omn—, omni—, pan—, pano—, pant—, panto—, panta—

864 PARTICULARITY

NOUNS 1 **particularity, individuality, singularity, differentiation,** differentness, distinctiveness, uniqueness; identity, individual *or* separate *or* concrete identity; **personality,** personship, personal identity; soul; **selfness,** selfhood, **egohood,** self-identity, "a single separate person"—Whitman; oneness 871.1, wholeness, integrity; personal equation, human factor; **nonconformity** 867; **individualism,** particularism; nominalism

2 **speciality, specialness,** specialty, specificality, **specificness,** definiteness; special case

3 **the specific,** the special, **the particular,** the concrete, the individual, the unique; "all things counter, original, spare, strange"—G M Hopkins

4 **characteristic, peculiarity, singularity,** particularity, specialty, individualism, **character,** nature, **trait,** quirk, point of character, bad point, good point, saving grace, redeeming feature, mannerism, keynote, trick, **feature,** distinctive feature, lineament; **mark,** marking, **earmark,** hallmark, index; badge, token; **brand,** cast, stamp, cachet, seal, mold, cut, figure, shape, configuration; impress, impression; differential, differentia; **idiosyncrasy,** idiocrasy; **quality, property, attribute;** savor, flavor, taste, gust, aroma, odor, smack, tang, taint

5 **self, ego; oneself, I,** myself, me, myself, my humble self, number one <nonformal>, yours truly <nonformal>; yourself, himself, herself, itself; ourselves, yourselves; themselves; you; he, she; him, her; they, them; it; inner self, inner man; subliminal *or* subconscious self; superego, better self, ethical self; other self, alter ego, alter, *alterum* <L>

6 **specification, designation, stipulation,** specifying, designating, stipulating, singling-out, featuring, highlighting, focusing on, denomination; **allocation,** attribution, fixing, selection, assignment, pinning down

7 **particularization, specialization;** individualization, peculiarization, personalization; localization; itemization 765.5

8 **characterization,** distinction, **differentiation;** definition, description

VERBS 9 **particularize, specialize; individualize,** peculiarize, personalize; **descend to particulars,** get precise, get down to brass tacks *or* to cases <nonformal>, get down to the nitty-gritty <nonformal>, come to the point, lay it on the line <nonformal>; **itemize** 765.6, detail, spell out

10 **characterize, distinguish, differentiate, define, describe; mark, earmark,** mark off, mark out, demarcate, **set apart,** make special *or* unique; keynote <nonformal>, sound the keynote, set the tone *or* mood, set the pace; be characteristic, **be a feature *or* trait of**

11 **specify, specialize, designate, stipulate,** determine, single out, feature, highlight, focus on, mention, select, pick out, **fix,** set, assign, pin down; **name,** denominate,

state, mark, check, check off, **indicate,
signify,** point out, put *or* lay one's finger
on

ADJS **12 particular, special, especial, specific, express,** precise, **concrete; singular,
individual,** individualist *or* individualistic; **personal,** private, intimate, inner,
solipsistic, esoteric; respective, several;
fixed, definite, defined, distinct, different,
different as night and day, determinate,
certain, absolute; **distinguished,** noteworthy, **exceptional, extraordinary;**
minute, detailed

13 characteristic, peculiar, singular, single,
quintessential, intrinsic, unique, qualitative, **distinctive,** marked, distinguished,
notable, nameable; appropriate, proper;
idiosyncratic, idiocratic, **in character,
true to form**

14 this, this and no other, this one, this single; **these; that,** that one; those

ADVS **15 particularly, specially, especially,
specifically, expressly,** concretely, exactly, precisely, **in particular,** to be
specific; **definitely, distinctly; minutely,**
in detail, item by item, singly, separately

16 personally, privately, idiosyncratically,
individually; in person, in the flesh, *in
propria persona* <L>; as for me, for all of
me, **for my part, as far as I am concerned**

17 characteristically, peculiarly, singularly,
intrinsically, **uniquely,** markedly, **dis-
tinctively,** in its own way, like no other

18 namely, nominally, **that is to say,** *videlicet* <L>, viz, *scilicet* <L>, scil, sc, **to
wit**

19 each, apiece; severally, respectively, one
by one, each to each; *per annum, per diem,
per capita* <all L>

PREPS **20 per, for each**

WORD ELEMENTS **21** —ness, —hood, —
dom; aut—, auto—, idio—, self—; —
acean, —aceous, —ey, —y, —ious, —ous,
—ish, —ist, —istic, —istical, —itious, —
itic, —ose, —some

865 SPECIALTY

*<object of special attention or
preference>*

NOUNS **1 specialty,** speciality, **line, pursuit,
pet subject, business, line of business,
line of country** <Brit>, **field,** area, main
interest; **vocation** 724.6; **forte, métier,
strong point,** long suit; specialism, specialization; technicality; **way,** manner,
style, type; **lifestyle,** way of life, preferences; cup of tea *and* bag *and* thing *and*
thang *and* weakness <all nonformal>

2 special, feature, main feature; **leader,**
lead item, leading card

3 specialist, specializer, **expert, authority,**
savant, scholar, connoisseur, maven
<nonformal>; technical expert, tech-
nician, techie <nonformal>, nerd
<nonformal>; pundit, critic; amateur,
dilettante; fan, buff, freak *and* nut <both
nonformal>, aficionado

VERBS **4 specialize, feature; narrow, restrict,** limit, confine; specialize in, **go in
for,** be into <nonformal>, have a weakness *or* taste for, be strong in, follow,
pursue, **make one's business;** major
in, minor in; do one's thing <nonfor-
mal>

ADJS **5 specialized,** specialist, specialistic;
down one's alley <nonformal>, cut out
for one, fits one like a glove; technical; **restricted, limited,** confined; **featured,**
feature; **expert, authoritative,** knowledgeable

866 CONFORMITY

NOUNS **1 conformity; conformance,** conformation, other-directedness; **compliance,**
acquiescence, goose step, lockstep, obedience, observance, traditionalism,
orthodoxy; strictness; **accordance,** accord, **correspondence,** harmony, agreement, **uniformity** 780; **consistency,** congruity; **accommodation,** adaptation,
adaption, pliancy, malleability, flexibility, adjustment; reconciliation,
reconcilement; **conventionality** 579.1

2 conformist, conformer, sheep, trimmer,
parrot, yes-man, organization man; **conventionalist,** Mrs Grundy, Babbitt,
Philistine, middle-class type, button-
down *or* white-bread type <nonformal>,
bourgeois, burgher, Middle American,
plastic person *and* clone *and* square <all
nonformal>, three-piecer *and* yuppie
<both nonformal>, Barbie Doll
<trademark> <nonformal>; model
child; teenybopper <nonformal>; **formalist,** methodologist, perfectionist,
precisianist *or* precisian; anal character,
compulsive character; pedant

VERBS **3 conform, comply, correspond,** accord, harmonize; **adapt,** adjust, **accommodate,** bend, meet, suit, fit, shape;
comply with, agree with, tally with,
chime *or* fall in with, go by, be guided
or regulated by, observe, follow, bend,
yield, take the shape of; **adapt to,** adjust
to, gear to, assimilate to, **accommodate
to *or* with; reconcile,** settle, compose;

rub off corners; **make conform,** shape, lick into shape, mold, force into a mold; straighten, rectify, correct, **discipline**

4 **follow the rule, toe the mark,** do it according to Hoyle *or* by the book <nonformal>, play the game <nonformal>; go through channels; **fit in, follow the crowd,** follow the fashion, swim *or* go with the stream *or* tide *or* current, get on the bandwagon, trim one's sails to the breeze, follow the beaten path, **do as others do, get** *or* **stay in line,** fall in *or* into line, fall in with; **keep in step,** goose-step, walk in lockstep; keep up to standard, pass muster, come up to scratch <nonformal>

ADJS 5 **conformable, adaptable,** adaptive, adjustable; **compliant,** pliant, complaisant, malleable, flexible, plastic, acquiescent, unmurmuring, other-directed, submissive, tractable, obedient

6 **conformist, conventional** 579.5, bourgeois, plastic *and* square *and* straight *and* white-bread *and* white-bready *and* button-down *and* buttoned-down <all nonformal>, cloned *and* clonish *and* cookie-cutter <all nonformal>; **orthodox,** traditionalist *or* traditionalistic; kosher; **formalistic,** legalistic, precisianistic, anal, compulsive; pedantic, stuffy *and* hidebound <both nonformal>, uptight <nonformal>; in accord, in keeping, in line, in step, in lockstep; **corresponding,** accordant, concordant, harmonious

ADVS 7 conformably, conformingly, in conformity, **obediently, pliantly,** flexibly, malleably, complaisantly, yieldingly, **compliantly,** submissively; **conventionally,** traditionally, anally, **compulsively;** pedantically

8 **according to rule,** *en règle* <Fr>, according to regulations; **according to Hoyle** *and* **by the book** *and* by the numbers <all nonformal>

PREPS 9 **conformable to, in conformity with,** in compliance with; **according to, in accordance with, consistent with, in harmony with,** in agreement with, in correspondence to; adapted to, adjusted to, accommodated to; proper to, suitable for, agreeable to, agreeably to; answerable to, in obedience to; congruent with, uniform with, in uniformity with; **in line with,** in step with; in lock-step with, **in keeping with; after, by, per, as per**

PHRS 10 **don't rock the boat, don't make waves,** get in line, shape up, shape up or ship out <all nonformal>; when in Rome do as the Romans do

867 NONCONFORMITY

NOUNS 1 **nonconformity,** unconformity, nonconformism, **inconsistency,** incongruity; **inaccordance,** disaccord, disaccordance; originality 337.1; **nonconformance,** disconformity; **nonobservance, noncompliance,** nonconcurrence, **dissent** 333, **protest** 333.2, disagreement, contrariety, recalcitrance, refractoriness, recusance *or* recusancy; **deviation** 869.1, deviationism

2 **unconventionality, unorthodoxy** 688, revisionism, heterodoxy, heresy, originality, Bohemianism, beatnikism, hippiedom, counterculture; alternative lifestyle *or* society

3 **nonconformist,** unconformist, **original,** eccentric, gonzo <nonformal>, deviant, deviationist, maverick <nonformal>, dropout, Bohemian, beatnik, hippie, hipster, freak <nonformal>, flower child, street people, yippie; **misfit,** square peg in a round hole, ugly duckling, fish out of water; **dissenter** 333.3; **heretic** 688.5; sectary, sectarian; nonjuror

VERBS 4 **not conform,** nonconform, not comply; **get out of line** *and* **rock the boat** *and* make waves <all nonformal>, **leave the beaten path, go out of bounds,** upset the apple cart, break step, break bounds; drop out, opt out; **dissent** 333.4, swim against the current *or* against the tide *or* upstream, **protest** 333.5; *"épater le bourgeois"*—Baudelaire, "hear a different drummer"—Thoreau

ADJS 5 **nonconforming,** unconforming, nonconformable, unadaptable, unadjustable; **uncompliant,** unsubmissive; **nonobservant;** contrary, recalcitrant, refractory, recusant; **deviant,** deviationist, atypic *or* atypical, unusual; **dissenting** 333.6, **dissident**

6 **unconventional, unorthodox, eccentric,** gonzo <nonformal>, heterodox, heretical; unfashionable, not done, not kosher, not cricket <Brit nonformal>; offbeat <nonformal>, way out *and* far out *and* kinky *and* out in left field <all nonformal>, fringy, breakaway, **out-of-the-way; original,** maverick, Bohemian, beat, hippie, counterculture; **nonformal,** free and easy <nonformal>, "at ease and light-hearted"—Whitman

7 **out of line, out of keeping,** out of order *or* place, misplaced, **out of step,** out of turn <nonformal>, out of tune

868 NORMALITY

NOUNS **1 normality**, normalness, typicality, normalcy, **naturalness**; health,
wholesomeness, propriety, **regularity**;
naturalism, naturism, realism; **order**
806

2 **usualness, ordinariness, commonness,**
commonplaceness, averageness, mediocrity; **generality** 863, **prevalence,**
currency

3 **the normal, the usual, the ordinary, the
common,** the commonplace, the day-to-
day, the way things are, the normal order
of things; common *or* garden variety, the
run of the mine *or* the mill

4 **rule, law, principle, standard,** criterion,
canon, code, code of practice, maxim,
prescription, guideline, rulebook, the
book <nonformal>, regulation, reg *or*
regs <nonformal>; **norm, model,** rule of
behavior, ideal, ideal type, specimen
type, exemplar; **rule** *or* **law** *or* **order of nature,** natural *or* universal law; **form,
formula,** formulary, formality, prescribed *or* set form; standing order,
standard operating procedure; **hard-
and-fast rule,** Procrustean law

5 **normalization, standardization, regularization; codification,** formalization

VERBS **6 normalize, standardize, regularize;
codify,** formalize

7 **do the usual thing, make a practice of,**
carry on, carry on as usual, do business as
usual

ADJS **8 normal, natural; general** 863.11; typical, unexceptional; **normative,** prescribed, model, ideal, desired, white-
bread *or* white-bready <nonformal>;
naturalistic, naturistic, realistic; **orderly**
806.6

9 **usual, regular; customary,** habitual,
accustomed, wonted, **normative,** prescriptive, standard, regulation, conventional; **common, commonplace, ordinary,
average, everyday,** mediocre, familiar,
household, vernacular, stock; **prevailing,
predominating,** current, popular; **universal** 863.14

ADVS **10 normally, naturally; normatively,**
prescriptively, **regularly; typically,** usually, commonly, ordinarily, customarily,
habitually, generally; mostly, chiefly,
mainly, for the most part, most often *or*
frequently; **as a rule,** as a matter of
course; **as usual,** as per usual <nonfor-
mal>; **as may be expected,** to be
expected, as things go

WORD ELEMENTS **11** norm—, normo—

869 ABNORMALITY

NOUNS **1 abnormality,** abnormity; **unnaturalness,** unnaturalism, strangeness;
anomaly, anomalousness, anomalism;
aberration, aberrance *or* aberrancy; **atyp-
icality,** atypicalness; **irregularity, deviation,** divergence, **difference** 779; **eccentricity,** erraticism, unpredictability, unpredictableness, randomness; **monstrosity,** teratism <see list>, amorphism, heteromorphism; **subnormality; inferiority**
250; **superiority** 249; **derangement** 810.1

2 **unusualness, uncommonness,** unordina-
riness, unwontedness, exceptionalness,
exceptionality, extraordinariness; **rarity,**
rareness, **uniqueness; prodigiousness,**
marvelousness, wondrousness, fabulousness, mythicalness, remarkableness, stupendousness; **incredibility** 954.3, incred-
itability, inconceivability, **impossibility**
966

3 **oddity, queerness,** curiousness, quaintness, **peculiarity, absurdity** 966.1,
singularity; **strangeness,** outlandishness,
bizarreness, *bizarrerie* <Fr>; fantasticality, anticness; **freakishness, grotesque-
ness,** grotesquerie, strangeness, weirdness, gonzo <nonformal>, monstrousness, monstrosity, malformation, deformity, teratism

4 <odd person> oddity, **character** <non-
formal>, type, **case** <nonformal>,
natural, original, odd fellow, queer
specimen; **oddball** *and* **weirdo** <both
nonformal>, odd *or* queer fish, queer
duck, rum one <Brit nonformal>; **rare
bird,** *rara avis* <L>; eccentric 926.3;
meshuggenah <Yiddish>; **freak** *and*
screwball *and* **crackpot** *and* **kook** *and* **nut**
and bird *and* gonzo <all nonformal>; **fanatic, crank,** zealot; **outsider, alien,**
foreigner; **alien,** extraterrestrial, Martian, little green man, visitor from
another planet; pariah, loner, lone wolf,
solitary, hermit; hobo, tramp; maverick;
outcast, outlaw, scapegoat; **nonconformist** 867.3

5 <odd thing> **oddity, curiosity, wonder**
funny *or* peculiar *or* strange thing; **abnormality, anomaly; rarity,** improbability,
exception, one in a thousand *or* million;
prodigy, prodigiosity; curio, conversation
piece; museum piece

6 **monstrosity, monster** <see list>, mis-
creation, abortion, teratism, abnormal *or*
defective birth, abnormal *or* defective
fetus; **freak,** freak of nature, *lusus naturae*
<L>

7 supernaturalism, supernaturalness, supernaturality, supranaturalism, supernormalness, **preternaturalism**, supersensibleness, superphysicalness, superhumanity; **the paranormal**; numinousness; **unearthliness**, unworldliness, **otherworldliness**, eeriness; transcendentalism; New Age; the supernatural, **the occult**, the supersensible; **paranormality**; supernature, supranature; **mystery**, mysteriousness, miraculousness, strangeness; faerie, witchery, elfdom

8 miracle, sign, signs and portents, prodigy, wonder, wonderwork, ferlie <Scots>; thaumatology, thaumaturgy; fantasy, enchantment

ADJS **9 abnormal, unnatural; anomalous**, anomalistic; **irregular**, eccentric, erratic, deviative, divergent, **different** 779.7; **aberrant**, stray, straying, wandering; heteroclite, heteromorphic; formless, shapeless, amorphous; **subnormal**

10 unusual, unordinary, **uncustomary**, unwonted, **uncommon, unfamiliar**, atypic *or* atypical, unheard-of, *recherché* <Fr>; **rare, unique**, *sui generis* <L, of its own kind>; **out of the ordinary**, out of this world, out-of-the-way, out of the common, out of the pale, **off the beaten track**, offbeat, breakaway; unexpected, not to be expected, unthought-of, undreamed-of

11 odd, queer, peculiar, absurd 966.7, **singular, curious, oddball** <nonformal>, weird *and* kooky *and* freaky *and* freaked-out <all nonformal>, quaint, **eccentric**, gonzo <nonformal>, funny, rum <Brit nonformal>; **strange, outlandish**, off-the-wall <informal>, surreal, not for real <nonformal>, passing strange, "wondrous strange"—Shakespeare; **weird**, unearthly; off, out

12 fantastic, fantastical, fanciful, antic, **unbelievable** 954.10, **impossible, incredible**, logic-defying, incomprehensible, unimaginable, unexpected, unaccountable, inconceivable

13 freakish, freak *or* freaky <nonformal>; **monstrous, deformed**, malformed, misshapen, **misbegotten**, teratogenic, teratoid; **grotesque, bizarre**, baroque, rococo

14 extraordinary, exceptional, remarkable, noteworthy, **wonderful, marvelous**, fabulous, mythical, legendary; **stupendous**, stupefying, prodigious, portentous, phenomenal; unprecedented, unexampled, unparalleled, not within the memory of man; indescribable, unspeakable, ineffable

15 supernatural, supranatural, **preter-**natural; **supernormal**, hypernormal, preternormal, **paranormal; superphysical**, hyperphysical; numinous; **supersensible**, supersensual, pretersensual; **superhuman**, preterhuman, unhuman, nonhuman; **supramundane**, extramundane, transmundane, extraterrestrial; **unearthly, unworldly, otherworldly, eerie**; fey; psychical, **spiritual, occult**; **transcendental; mysterious**, arcane, esoteric

16 miraculous, wondrous, wonder-working, thaumaturgic *or* thaumaturgical, necromantic, **prodigious; magical**, enchanted, bewitched

ADVS **17 unusually, uncommonly, incredibly, unnaturally**, abnormally, unordinarily, **uncustomarily**, unexpectedly; **rarely, seldom**, seldom if ever, once in a thousand years, hardly, hardly ever

18 extraordinarily, exceptionally, remarkably, wonderfully, marvelously, prodigiously, fabulously, unspeakably, ineffably, phenomenally, stupendously

19 oddly, queerly, peculiarly, singularly, curiously, quaintly, **strangely**, outlandishly, **fantastically**, fancifully; **grotesquely, monstrously; eerily, mysteriously**, supernaturally

WORD ELEMENTS **20** terat—, terato—; medus—, medusi—, —pagus, anom—, anomo—, anomal—, anomalo—, anomali—, dys—, dis—, mal—, ne—, neo—, par—, para—, poly—, pseud—, pseudo—

21 mythical and imaginary monsters

abominable snowman *or* yeti	hippocampus
	hippocentaur
Argus	hippocerf
basilisk	hippogriff
Bigfoot *or* Sasquatch	hircocervus
Briareus	Hydra
bucentur	Kraken
Cacus	Ladon
Caliban	Loch Ness monster
centaur	manticore
Cerberus	Medusa
Ceto	mermaid
Charybdis	merman
chimera	Midgard serpent
cockatrice	Minotaur
Cyclops	nixie
dipsas	ogre
dragon	ogress
drake <old>	opinicus
Echidna	Orthos *or* Orthros
Geryon	Pegasus
Gigantes	Python
Gorgon	roc
Grendel	Sagittary
griffin	salamander
Harpy	satyr

Scylla	Typhon
sea horse	unicorn
sea serpent	vampire
simurgh	werewolf
siren	windigo
Sphinx	wivern
Talos	xiphopagus
troll	zombie
Typhoeus	

870 LIST

NOUNS **1 list, enumeration, itemization,** listing, shopping list *and* laundry list *and* want list *and* wish list *and* hit list *and* shit list *and* drop-dead list <all nonformal>, items, **schedule, register,** registry; **inventory,** repertory, tally; **spreadsheet,** electronic spreadsheet; **checklist;** tally sheet; active list, civil list <Brit>, retired list, sick list; waiting list; blacklist; short list

2 table, contents, table of contents

3 catalog; classified catalog, *catalogue raisonné* <Fr>; **card catalog, bibliography,** finding list, handlist; publisher's catalog *or* list; **file,** filing system, letter file, pigeonholes

4 dictionary, word list, **lexicon, glossary, thesaurus, Roget's, vocabulary,** terminology, nomenclator; promptorium, gradus; **gazetteer**

5 bill, statement, account, ledger, books; **bill of fare, menu,** carte; **bill of lading,** manifest, waybill, invoice

6 roll, roster, scroll, rota; **roll call,** muster, **census,** nose *or* head count <nonformal>, **poll,** questionnaire, returns, census report *or* returns; property roll, tax roll, cadastre; muster roll; checkroll, checklist; jury list *or* panel; **calendar,** docket, **agenda,** order of business; **program,** dramatis personae, lineup, beadroll; honor roll, dean's list

7 index, listing, tabulation; **cataloging, itemization,** filing, card file, card index, Rolodex <trademark>, thumb index, indexing; **registration,** registry, enrollment

VERBS **8 list, enumerate, itemize, tabulate, catalog,** tally; **register,** post, enter, **enroll, book;** impanel; **file,** pigeonhole; **index;** inventory; calendar; score, keep score; **schedule,** program

ADJS **9 listed, enumerated, entered, itemized, cataloged,** tallied, inventoried; filed, **indexed, tabulated; scheduled,** programmed; put on the agenda; inventorial, cadastral

871 ONENESS

<state of being one>

NOUNS **1 oneness, unity, singleness,** singularity, **individuality,** identity, selfsameness; **particularity** 864; **uniqueness;** intactness, inviolability, purity, simplicity 797, irreducibility, **integrity,** integrality; **unification,** uniting, integration, fusion, combination 804; **solidification,** solidity, solidarity, **indivisibility,** undividedness, **wholeness** 791.5; univocity, organic unity; uniformity 780; "the sacredness of private integrity"—Emerson

2 aloneness, loneness, **loneliness, lonesomeness,** soleness, singleness; **privacy,** solitariness, **solitude;** separateness, aloofness, detachment, seclusion, sequestration, **withdrawal, alienation,** standing *or* moving *or* keeping apart, **isolation,** "splendid isolation"—Sir William Goschen; celibacy, single blessedness

3 one, I, unit, ace, atom; monad; one and only, none else, no other, nothing else, nought beside

4 individual, single, unit, **integer, entity,** singleton, **item,** article, point, module; person, wight <old>, persona, soul, body, warm body <nonformal>; **individuality,** personhood

VERBS **5 unify,** reduce to unity, unitize, make one; **integrate, unite** 804.3

6 stand alone, stand *or* move *or* keep apart, keep oneself to oneself, withdraw, alienate *or* seclude *or* sequester *or* isolate oneself, feel out of place; individuate, become an individual

ADJS **7 one, single, singular, individual, sole, unique,** a certain, **solitary, lone;** exclusive; **integral,** indivisible, irreducible, monadic, monistic, unanalyzable, noncompound, atomic, unitary, unitive, unary, undivided, solid, whole-cloth, seamless, uniform 780.5, simple 797.6, whole 791.9; an, any, any one, either

8 alone, solitary, solo, *solus* <L>; **isolated,** insular, apart, separate, separated, alienated, withdrawn, aloof, standoffish, detached, removed; **lone, lonely, lonesome,** lonely-hearts; **private,** reserved, reticent, reclusive, shy, nonpublic, ungregarious; **friendless,** kithless, homeless, rootless, companionless, **unaccompanied,** unescorted, unattended; **unaided,** unassisted, unabetted, unsupported, unseconded; **single-handed,** solo, oneman, one-woman, one-person

9 sole, unique, singular, absolute, unre-

peated, **alone,** lone, **only,** only-begotten,
one and only, first and last; odd, impair,
unpaired, azygous; celibate

10 **unitary, integrated,** integral, integrant;
unified, united, rolled into one, composite

11 **unipartite,** unipart, **one-piece;** monadic
or monadal; **unilateral, one-sided;** unilateralist, uniangulate, unibivalent,
unibranchiate, unicameral, unicellular,
unicuspid, unidentate, unidigitate; **uni-
dimensional, unidirectional;** uniflorous,
unifoliate, unifoliolate, unigenital, uni-
globular, unilinear, uniliteral, unilobed,
unilobular, unilocular, unimodular, un-
imolecular, uninuclear, uniocular;
unipolar, **univalent, univocal**

12 **unifying, uniting,** unific; **combining,**
combinative 804.5,7, combinatory; connective, connecting, connectional; conjunctive 799.16, conjunctival; coalescing,
coalescent

ADVS 13 **singly, individually,** particularly,
severally, one by one, one at a time; **singularly,** in the singular; **alone,** by itself,
per se <L>; **by oneself,** by one's lonesome
<nonformal>, on one's own, under one's
own steam, **single-handedly, solo, unaided;** separately, apart; **once** 847.6

14 **solely, exclusively, only,** merely, **purely,**
simply; **entirely,** wholly, totally; **integrally, indivisibly,** irreducibly,
unanalyzably, undividedly

872 DOUBLENESS

NOUNS 1 **doubleness, duality,** dualism, du-
plexity, **twoness;** twofoldness, biformity;
polarity; conjugation, pairing, coupling,
yoking; **doubling,** duplication 873, twinning, bifurcation; **dichotomy,** bisection
874, halving, splitting down the middle
or fifty-fifty; **duplicity,** two-facedness,
double-think, hypocrisy; **irony,** enantiosis, ambiguity, equivocation, equivocality, **ambivalence;** Janus

2 **two,** twain <old>; **couple, pair, matching pair, twosome,** set of two, duo, duet,
brace, team, span, yoke, double harness;
match, matchup, mates; **couplet,** distich,
doublet; duad, dyad; the two, **both**

3 **deuce;** pair, doubleton; **craps** *and* **snake
eyes** <both crapshooting>

4 **twins,** pair of twins <nonformal>, identical twins, fraternal twins, exact mates,
look-alikes, dead ringers <nonformal>;
Tweedledum and Tweedledee, Siamese
twins; Twin stars, Castor and Pollux,
Gemini

VERBS 5 **double,** duplicate, replicate, dual-

ize, twin; **halve,** split down the middle *or*
fifty fifty <nonformal>, bifurcate, dichotomize, bisect; team, **yoke,** yoke together,
span, double-team, double-harness;
mate, match, couple, conjugate; **pair,**
pair off, pair up, couple up, team up,
match up, buddy up <nonformal>; talk
out of both sides of one's mouth at once

ADJS 6 **two,** twain <old>; **dual, double,** duplex, doubled, twinned, duplicated, replicated, dualized; **dualistic;** dyadic;
duadic; biform; bipartite, bipartisan, bilateral, either-or, two-sided, double-
sided; dichotomous; bifurcated, bisected,
dichotomized, split down the middle *or*
fifty fifty <nonformal>; twin, identical,
matched, twinned, duplicated; **two-
faced,** duplicitous, hypocritical, doublefaced, Janus-like

7 **both,** the two, the pair; for two, tête-
à-tête, *à deux* <Fr>

8 **coupled, paired,** yoked, yoked together,
matched, matched up, mated, paired off,
paired up, teamed up, buddied up
<nonformal>; **bracketed;** conjugate,
conjugated; biconjugate, bigeminate; bi-
jugate

PHRS 9 it takes two to tango *and* it's not a
one-way street <both nonformal>

WORD ELEMENTS 10 ambi—, amph—,
amphi—, bi—, bin—, bis—, deut—,
deuto—, deuter—, deutero—, di—,
dis—, didym—, didymo—, duo—,
dyo—, gem—, twi—, zyg—, zygo—

873 DUPLICATION

NOUNS 1 **duplication, reduplication,** replication, conduplication; **reproduction, repro** <nonformal>, **doubling;** twinning,
gemination, ingemination; **repetition**
848, iteration, reiteration, echoing; **imitation** 336, parroting; **copying** 336.1;
duplicate 784.3

2 repeat, encore, repeat performance; echo

VERBS 3 **duplicate,** dupe <nonformal>,
ditto <nonformal>; **double,** double up;
multiply by two; twin, geminate, ingemi-
nate; **reduplicate, reproduce,** replicate,
redouble; **repeat** 848.7; **copy**

ADJS 4 **double, doubled, duplicate,** duplicated, reproduced, replicated, cloned,
twinned, geminate, geminated, dualized

ADVS 5 **doubly; twofold,** as much again,
twice as much; twice, two times

6 **secondly,** second, secondarily, **in the second place** *or* instance

7 **again,** another time, **once more,** once
again, over again, yet again, *encore, bis*

<both Fr>; **anew,** afresh, new, freshly, newly

WORD ELEMENTS 8 bi—, bis—, deuter—, deutero—, di—, dis—, diphy—, diphyo—, dipl—, diplo—, diss—, disso—, twi—

874 BISECTION

NOUNS 1 **bisection,** halving, bipartition, bifidity; **dichotomy, halving, division, in half** *or* **by two,** splitting *or* dividing *or* cutting in two, splitting *or* dividing fifty-fifty <nonformal>; subdivision; bifurcation, forking, ramification, branching

2 **half,** moiety; hemisphere, semisphere, semicircle, **fifty percent;** half-and-half *and* fifty-fifty <both nonformal>

3 bisector, diameter, equator, halfway mark, divider, partition 213.5, line of demarcation, boundary 211.3

VERBS 4 **bisect, halve, divide, in half** *or* **by two,** transect, subdivide; cleave, fission, **divide** *or* split *or* **cut in two,** share and share alike, go halfers *or* go Dutch <both nonformal>, **dichotomize;** bifurcate, fork, ramify, branch

ADJS 5 **half, part, partly, partial,** halfway

6 **halved, bisected, divided;** dichotomous; bifurcated, forked *or* forking, ramified, branched, branching; riven, **split,** cloven, cleft

7 **bipartite,** bifid, biform, bicuspid, biaxial, bicameral, binocular, binomial, binominal, biped, bipetalous, bipinnate, bisexual, bivalent, unibivalent

ADVS 8 **in half,** in halves, **in two,** in twain, by two, down the middle; half-and-half *and* fifty-fifty <both nonformal>; apart, asunder

WORD ELEMENTS 9 bi—, demi—, dich—, dicho—, hemi—, semi—, sesqui—

875 THREE

NOUNS 1 **three, trio, threesome,** trialogue, set of three, tierce <cards>, leash, troika; **triad,** trilogy, trine, **trinity,** triunity, ternary, ternion; **triplet,** tercet, terzetto; trefoil, shamrock, clover; tripod, trivet; **triangle,** tricorn, trihedron, trident, trisul, triennium, trimester, trinomial, trionym, triphthong, triptych, triplopy, trireme, triseme, triskelion, triumvirate; triple crown, triple threat; trey *and* three-spot <both cards>, deuce-ace <dice>

2 **threeness,** triplicity, triality, tripleness; triunity, trinity

ADJS 3 **three, triple,** triplex, trinal, trine, trial; triadic<al>; triune, three-in-one,

tria juncta in uno <L>; triform; **triangular,** deltoid, fan-shaped

WORD ELEMENTS 4 tri—, ter—, ternati—

876 TRIPLICATION

NOUNS 1 **triplication,** triplicity, trebleness, **threefoldness;** triplicate, second carbon

VERBS 2 **triplicate, triple, treble, multiply by three,** threefold; cube

ADJS 3 **triple,** triplicate, **treble, threefold,** triplex, trinal, trine, tern, ternary, ternal, ternate; three-ply; trilogic *or* trilocial

4 **third, tertiary**

ADVS 5 **triply, trebly,** trinely; **threefold; thrice,** three times, again and yet again

6 **thirdly,** in the third place

WORD ELEMENTS 7 cub—, cubo—, cubi—; ter—; tert—, trit—, trito—

877 TRISECTION

NOUNS 1 **trisection,** tripartition, trichotomy

2 **third,** tierce, third part, one-third; *tertium quid* <L, a third something>

VERBS 3 **trisect, divide in thirds** *or* **three,** third, trichotomize; trifurcate

ADJS 4 **tripartite,** trisected, triparted, **three-parted,** trichotomous; three-sided, trihedral, trilateral; **three-dimensional;** three-forked, three-pronged, trifurcate; trident, tridental, tridentate, trifid; tricuspid; three-footed, tripodic, tripedal; trifoliate, trifloral, triflorate, triflorous, tripetalous, triadelphous, triarch; trimerous, 3-merous; three-cornered, tricornered, tricorn; trigonal, trigonoid; triquetrous, triquetral; trigrammatic, triliteral; **triangular,** triangulate, deltoid

878 FOUR

NOUNS 1 **four,** tetrad, quatern, quaternion, quaternary, quaternity, **quartet, quadruplet, foursome;** Little Joe *and* Little Joe from Kokomo *and* Little Dick Fisher <all crapshooting>; quadrennium; tetralogy; tetrapody; tetraphony, four-part diaphony; quadrille, square dance; quatrefoil *or* quadrifoil, four-leaf clover; tetragram, tetragrammaton; quadrangle, quad <nonformal>, rectangle; tetrahedron; tetragon, square; biquadrate; quadrinomial; quadrature, squaring; quadrilateral

2 **fourness,** quaternity, quadruplicity

VERBS 3 **square, quadrate,** form *or* make four; form fours *or* squares; **cube, dice**

ADJS 4 **four;** foursquare; quaternary, quartile, quartic, quadric, quadratic; tetrad, tetradic; quadrinomial, biquadratic; tetractinal, four-rayed, **quadruped,** four-legged; quadrivalent, tetravalent; quadrilateral 278.9

WORD ELEMENTS 5 quadr—, quadri—, quadru—, tetr—, tetra—, tessar—, tessara—, tri—, trip—, tripl—, triplo—, tris—

879 QUADRUPLICATION

NOUNS 1 **quadruplication,** quadruplicature

VERBS 2 **quadruple, quadruplicate,** fourfold, form or make four, multiply by four; biquadrate, quadruplex

ADJS 3 **quadruplicate, quadruple,** quadraple, **quadruplex, fourfold,** four-ply, four-part, tetraploid, quadrigeminal, biquadratic

WORD ELEMENTS 4 quadr—, quadri, quadru—, quater—, tetr—, tetra—, tetrakis—

880 QUADRISECTION

NOUNS 1 **quadrisection,** quadripartition, **quartering**

  2 **fourth,** one-fourth, **quarter,** one-quarter, fourth part, twenty-five percent, twenty-five cents, two bits <old or nonformal>; quartern; quart; farthing; quarto or 4to or 4°

VERBS 3 **divide by four** or **into four; quadrisect, quarter**

ADJS 4 **quadrisected, quartered,** quarter-cut; quadripartite, quadrifid, quadriform; quadrifoliate, quadrigeminal, quadripinnate, quadriplanar, quadriserial, quadrivial, quadrifurcate, quadrumanal or quadrumanous

  5 **fourth, quarter**

ADVS 6 **fourthly,** in the fourth place; quarterly, by quarters

881 FIVE AND OVER

NOUNS 1 **five,** V, cinque <cards and dice>, Phoebe and Little Phoebe and fever <all crapshooting>; **quintet, fivesome,** quintuplets, quints <nonformal>, cinquain, quincunx, pentad; **five dollars,** fiver and fin and finniff and five bucks <all nonformal>; pentagon, pentahedron, pentagram; pentapody, pentameter, pentastich; pentarchy; Pentateuch; pentachord; pentathlon; five-pointed star, pentacle, pentalpha, mullet <heraldry>

  2 **six,** sixie from Dixie and sister Hicks and

Jimmy Hicks and Captain Hicks <all crapshooting>, **half a dozen, sextet,** sestet, sextuplets, hexad; hexagon, hexahedron, hexagram, six-pointed star, estoile <heraldry>, Jewish star, star of David, *Magen David* <Heb>; hexameter, hexapody, hexastich; hexapod; hexarchy; Hexateuch; hexastyle; hexachord

  3 **seven,** heptad, little natural <crapshooting>; septet, heptad; heptagon, heptahedron; heptameter, heptastich; septemvir, heptarchy; Septuagint, Heptateuch; heptachord; **week**

  4 **eight,** ogdoad, eighter or Ada from Decatur <crapshooting>, Ada Ross and Ada Ross the stable hoss <both crapshooting>; octad, octonary; octagon, octahedron; octastylos or oktostylos; octave, octavo or 8vo; octachord; octet or octal, octameter; Octateuch

  5 **nine,** niner <radio communication>, Nina from Carolina and Nina Ross the stable hoss and Nina Nina ocean liner <all crapshooting>; ennead; nonagon or enneagon, enneahedron; novena; enneastylos

  6 **ten,** X, Big Dick and Big Dick from Battle Creek <both crapshooting>; **decade;** decagon, decahedron; decagram, decigram, decaliter, deciliter, decare, decameter, decimeter, decastere; decapod; decastylos; decasyllable; decemvir, decemvirate, decurion; decennium, decennary; Ten Commandments or Decalogue

  7 <eleven to ninety> **eleven; twelve, dozen,** boxcar and boxcars <both crapshooting>, duodecimo or twelvemo or 12mo; **teens; thirteen,** long dozen, baker's dozen; **fourteen,** two weeks, fortnight; **fifteen,** quindecima, quindene, quindecim, quindecennial; **sixteen,** sixteenmo or 16mo; **twenty, score; twenty-four,** four and twenty, two dozen, twenty-fourmo or 24mo; **twenty-five,** five and twenty, quarter of a hundred or century; **thirty-two,** thirty-twomo or 32mo; **forty,** twoscore; **fifty,** L, half a hundred; **sixty,** sexagenary; Sexagesima; sexagenarian, threescore; **sixty-four,** sixty-fourmo or 64mo or sexagesimo-quarto; **seventy,** septuagenarian, threescore and ten; **eighty,** octogenarian, fourscore; **ninety,** nonagenarian, fourscore and ten

  8 **hundred, century,** C, one C <nonformal>; centennium, centennial, centenary; centenarian; cental, centigram, centiliter, centimeter, centare, centistere; hundredweight or cwt;

hecatomb; centipede; centumvir, cen-
tumvirate, centurion; <120> great *or*
long hundred; <144> gross; <150> sesquicentennial, sesquicentenary; <200>
bicentenary, bicentennial; <300> tercentenary, tercentennial, etc

9 five hundred, D, five centuries; five C's
<nonformal>

10 thousand, M, chiliad; **millennium;** G *and*
grand *and* thou *and* yard <all nonfor-
mal>; chiliagon, chiliahedron *or* chiliaë-
dron; chiliarchia *or* chiliarch; millepede;
milligram, milliliter, millimeter, kilogram *or* kilo, kiloliter, kilometer;
kilocycle, kilohertz; **ten thousand,** myriad; **one hundred thousand,** lakh
<India>

11 million; ten million, crore <India>

12 billion, thousand million, milliard

13 trillion, quadrillion, quintillion, sex-
tillion, septillion, octillion, nonillion,
decillion, undecillion, duodecillion, tre-
decillion, quattuordecillion, quindecil-
lion, sexdecillion, septendecillion, octo-
decillion, novemdecillion, vigintillion;
googol, googolplex; zillion *and* jillion
<both nonformal>

14 <division into five or more parts> quin-
quesection, quinquepartition, sextipar-
tition, etc; decimation, decimalization;
fifth, sixth, etc; **tenth, tithe,** decima

VERBS **15** <divide by five, etc> quin-
quesect; decimalize

16 <multiply by five, etc> fivefold, sixfold,
etc; quintuple, quintuplicate; sextuple,
sextuplicate; centuple, centuplicate

ADJS **17 fifth,** quinary; **fivefold, quintuple,**
quintuplicate; quinquennial; quinque-
partite, pentadic, quinquefid; quincun-
cial, pentastyle; pentad, pentavalent,
quinquevalent

18 sixth, senary; **sixfold, sextuple;** sexpar-
tite, hexadic, sextipartite, hexapartite;
hexagonal, hexahedral, hexangular;
hexad, hexavalent; sextuplex, hexastyle;
sexennial

19 seventh, septimal; **sevenfold, septuple,**
septenary; septempartite, heptadic, sep-
temfid; heptagonal, heptahedral, hep-
tangular; heptamerous

20 eighth, octonary; **eightfold, octuple;** oc-
tadic; octal, octofid, octaploid; octagonal,
octahedral, octan; octangular; octo-
syllabic; octastyle

21 ninth, novenary, nonary; **ninefold, nonuple,** enneadic; enneahedral, enneastyle

22 tenth, denary, **decimal,** tithe; **tenfold,
decuple;** decagonal, decahedral; decasyl-
labic

23 eleventh, undecennial, undecennary

24 twelfth, duodenary, duodenal; duodecimal

25 thirteenth, fourteenth, etc; eleventeenth,
umpteenth <nonformal>; in one's
teens

26 twentieth, vicenary, vicennial, vigesimal,
vicesimal

27 sixtieth, sexagesimal, sexagenary

28 seventieth, septuagesimal, septuagenary

29 hundredth, centesimal, **centennial,** centenary, centurial; **hundredfold, centuple,**
centuplicate; secular; centigrado

30 thousandth, millenary, **millennial; thou-
sandfold**

31 millionth; billionth, quadrillionth, quin-
tillionth, etc

WORD ELEMENTS **32** pent—, penta—,
pen—, quinqu—, quinque—,
quintquinti—; hex—, hexa—, sex—,
sexi—, sexti—; hept—, hepta—, sept—,
septi—; oct—, octa—, octo—; non—
nona—, ennea—; deca—, deka—, deci—;
undec—, hendec—, hendeca—; dodec—,
dodeca—; icos—, icosa—, icosi—,
eicos—, eicosa—, cent—, centi—, hect—,
hecto—, hecato—, hecaton; kilo—,
milli—; meg—, mega—, micro—;
giga—, nano—; pico—

882 PLURALITY
<more than one>

NOUNS **1 plurality,** pluralness; a greater
number, a certain number; **several,** some,
a few 884.2, more; plural number, the
plural; compositeness, nonsingleness,
nonuniqueness; **pluralism** 781.1, variety;
numerousness 883

2 majority, plurality, more than half, the
greater number, the greatest number,
most, preponderance *or* preponderancy,
bulk, mass; lion's share

3 pluralization, plurification <old>

4 multiplication, multiplying, proliferation, **increase** 251; duplication 873;
multiple, multiplier, multiplicand;
multiplication table

VERBS **5 pluralize,** plurify <old>; raise to *or*
make more than one

6 multiply, proliferate, **increase** 251.4,6,
duplicate 873.3

ADJS **7 plural,** pluralized, more than one,
more, several, severalfold; **some,** certain;
not singular, composite, nonsingle, non-
unique; plurative <logic>; **pluralistic**
781.3, various; many, beaucoup <nonfor-
mal>, numerous 883.6

8 multiple, multiplied, multifold, **manifold**

883.6; **increased** 251.7; multinomial, polynomial <both mathematics>
9 **majority, most,** the greatest number
ADVS **10 in the majority;** and others, et al, et cetera 253.14; plurally
WORD ELEMENTS 11 multi—; —fold

883 NUMEROUSNESS

NOUNS **1 numerousness, multiplicity, manyness,** manifoldness, multifoldness, multitudinousness, multifariousness, teemingness, swarmingness, rifeness, profuseness, profusion; **plenty, abundance** 990.2; **countlessness,** innumerability, infinitude
2 <indefinite number> **a number,** a certain number, one or two, two or three, **a few, several,** parcel, passel <nonformal>; eleventeen *and* umpteen <both nonformal>
3 <large number> **multitude, throng** 769.4; a many, numbers, quantities, lots 247.4, flocks, **scores;** an abundance of, all kinds *or* sorts of, no end of, quite a few, tidy sum; muchness, any number of, **large amount; host, army,** more than one can shake a stick at, fistful *and* slew *and* shitload *and* shithouse full <all nonformal>, legion, rout, ruck, mob, jam, clutter; **swarm, flock** 769.5, flight, cloud, hail, bevy, covey, shoal, hive, nest, pack, litter, bunch 769.7; a world of, a mass of, worlds of, masses of
4 <immense number> **a myriad,** a thousand, **a thousand and one,** a lakh <India>, a crore <India>, a million, a billion, a quadrillion, a nonillion, etc 881.13; a zillion *or* jillion <nonformal>; googol, googolplex
VERBS **5 teem with,** overflow with, **abound with,** burst with, bristle with, pullulate with, **swarm with,** throng with, creep with, **crawl with, be alive with, have coming out of one's ears** *and* **have up the gazoo** *and* **kazoo** <both nonformal>; clutter, crowd, jam, pack, overwhelm, overflow; multiply 882.6; outnumber
ADJS **6 numerous, many, manifold,** not a few, no few; **very many,** full many, **ever so many,** considerable *and* quite some <both nonformal>; **multitudinous,** multitudinal, multifarious, multifold, multiple, **myriad,** thousand, million, billion; zillion *and* jillion <both nonformal>; heaped-up; numerous as the stars, numerous as the sands, numerous as the hairs on the head, "numerous as glitter-

ing gems of morning dew"—Edward Young
7 **several,** divers, **sundry,** various; fivish, sixish, etc; some five or six, etc; upwards of
8 **abundant,** copious, ample, plenteous, **plentiful** 990.7, thick on the ground <Brit>
9 **teeming, swarming, crowding,** thronging, overflowing, overcrowded, overwhelming, bursting, **crawling, alive with,** lousy with <nonformal>, populous, prolific, proliferating, crowded, packed, jammed, bumper-to-bumper <nonformal>, jam-packed, like sardines in a can <nonformal>, thronged, studded, bristling, rife, lavish, prodigal, superabundant, **profuse,** in profusion, thick, **thick with,** thick-coming, thick as hail *or* flies; "thick as autumnal leaves that strow the brooks in Vallombrose"—Milton
10 **innumerable, numberless,** unnumbered, **countless,** uncounted, uncountable, unreckonable, untold, incalculable, immeasurable, unmeasured, measureless, inexhaustible, endless, infinite, without end *or* limit, more than one can tell, more than you can shake a stick at <nonformal>, no end of *or* to; countless as the stars *or* sands; **astronomical,** galactic; millionfold, trillionfold, etc
11 **and many more,** *cum multis aliis* <L>, and what not, and heaven knows what
ADVS **12 numerously,** multitudinously, **profusely,** swarmingly, teemingly, thickly, copiously, **abundantly, prodigally; innumerably,** countlessly, infinitely, incalculably, inexhaustibly, immeasurably; in throngs, in crowds, in swarms, in heaps, *acervatim* <L>; **no end** <nonformal>
WORD ELEMENTS 13 multi—, myri—, myrio—, pluri—, poly—

884 FEWNESS

NOUNS **1 fewness,** infrequency, **sparsity,** sparseness, **scarcity, paucity, scantiness, meagerness,** miserliness, niggardliness, tightness, thinness, stringency, restrictedness; chintziness *and* chinchiness *and* stinginess <all nonformal>, scrimpiness *and* skimpiness <both nonformal>; **rarity,** exiguity; smallness 258.1
2 **a few,** too few, mere *or* piddling *or* piddly few, only a few, **small number,** limited *or* piddling *or* piddly number, not enough to count *or* matter, not enough to shake a

stick at, **handful, scattering**, corporal's guard, sprinkling, trickle

3 minority, least; the minority, the few; minority group; "we happy few"—Shakespeare

ADJS **4 few, not many**; hardly *or* scarcely any, precious little *or* few, of small number, to be counted on one's fingers

5 sparse, scant, **scanty**, exiguous, **infrequent**, scarce, scarce as hen's teeth <nonformal>, poor, piddling, piddly, thin, slim, **meager**; miserly, niggardly, cheeseparing, tight; chintzy *and* chinchy *and* stingy <all nonformal>, scrimpy *and* skimpy <both nonformal>, skimping *and* scrimping <both nonformal>; **scattered**, sprinkled, spotty, **few and far between**; **rare**, seldom met with, seldom seen, not thick on the ground <Brit>

6 fewer, less, smaller, not so much *or* many

7 minority, least

ADVS **8 sparsely**, *sparsim* <L>, **scantily, meagerly**, exiguously, piddlingly; stingily *and* scrimpily *and* skimpily <all nonformal>, thinly; **scarcely**, rarely, infrequently; **scatteringly**, scatterdly, spottily, in dribs and drabs *and* in bits and pieces <both nonformal>, **here and there**, in places, in spots

885 CAUSE

NOUNS **1 cause, occasion**, antecedents, **grounds**, ground, background, stimulus, base, **basis**, element, principle, factor; **determinant**, determinative; causation, causality, cause and effect; etiology

2 reason, reason why, rationale, reason for *or* behind, underlying reason, rational ground, **explanation, the why**, the wherefore, the whatfor *or* whyfor <nonformal>, **the why and wherefore**, the idea <nonformal>, the big idea <nonformal>; stated cause, pretext, pretense, excuse

3 immediate cause, proximate cause, trigger, spark; **domino effect**, causal sequence, chain *or* nexus of cause and effect, ripple effect, slippery slope, contagion effect, knock-on *or* knock-on effect <chiefly Brit>; transient cause, occasional cause; formal cause; efficient cause; ultimate cause, immanent cause, remote cause, causing cause, *causa causans* <L>, first cause; **final cause**, *causa finalis* <L>, **end**, end in view, teleology; provocation, **last straw**, straw that broke the camel's back, match in the powder barrel; butterfly effect *or* strange

attraction *or* sensitive dependence on initial conditions

4 author, agent, **originator**, generator, begetter, engenderer, producer, maker, beginner, **creator**, mover; **parent, mother, father**, sire; **prime mover**, *primum mobile* <L>; causer, effector; inspirer, instigator, catalyst

5 source, origin, genesis, original, origination, **derivation, rise, beginning**, conception, inception, commencement, **head**; provenance, provenience, background; **root**, radix, radical, taproot, grass roots; stem, stock

6 fountainhead, headwater, headstream, riverhead, springhead, headspring, **mainspring**, wellspring, wellhead, well, **spring, fountain**, fount, font, *fons et origo* <L>; mine, quarry

7 vital force *or* **principle**, *élan vital* <Fr>, reproductive urge, a gleam in one's father's eye <nonformal>; **egg**, ovum 305.12, **germ**, germen <old>, spermatozoon 305.11, nucleus 305.7, **seed**; **embryo** 305.14; bud 310.21; loins; **womb**, matrix, uterus

8 birthplace, breeding place, breeding ground, birthsite, rookery, hatchery; **hotbed**, forcing bed; incubator, brooder; **nest**, nidus; **cradle**, nursery

9 <a principle or movement> **cause, principle**, interest, issue, burning issue, commitment, faith, great cause, lifework; reason for being, *raison d'être* <Fr>; **movement**, mass movement, activity; **drive, campaign, crusade**; zeal, passion, fanaticism

VERBS **10 cause**, be the cause of, lie at the root of; **bring about, bring to pass**, effectuate, **effect**, bring to effect, realize; **impact**, impact on, influence; **occasion, make, create, engender**, generate, **produce**, breed, work, do; **originate**, give origin to, give occasion to, **give rise to**, spark, spark off, set off, trigger, trigger off; **give birth to, beget**, bear, bring forth, labor *or* travail and bring forth, author, **father**, sire, sow the seeds of; gestate, **conceive**, have the idea, have a bright idea <nonformal>; set up, set afloat, **set on foot**; found, establish, inaugurate, institute

11 induce, lead, procure, get, obtain, contrive, **effect**, bring, **bring on**, draw on, **call forth, elicit, evoke, provoke**, inspire, influence, instigate, egg on, **motivate**; draw down, open the door to; suborn; superinduce

12 determine, decide, turn the scale, have

the last word; **necessitate,** entail, require;
contribute to, lead to, conduce to; **advance, forward,** influence, subserve; **spin
off,** hive off <Brit>

ADJS **13 causal,** causative; chicken-and-egg
<nonformal>; occasional; originative,
institutive, constitutive; **at the bottom
of,** behind the scenes; **formative,** determinative, effectual, decisive, pivotal;
etiological

14 original, primary, primal, primitive,
pristine, primo <nonformal>, primeval,
aboriginal, **elementary,** elemental, **basic,**
basal, **rudimentary,** crucial, central, radical, **fundamental;** embryonic, in embryo,
in ovo <L>, germinal, seminal, pregnant;
generative, genetic, protogenic

WORD ELEMENTS **15** uter—, utero—,
metr—, metro—, —metrium, venter;
etio—, aetio—, prot—, proto—;
—facient, —factive, —fic, —ic, —ical,
—etic

886 EFFECT

NOUNS **1 effect, result,** resultant, **consequence,** consequent, sequent, sequence,
sequel, sequela, sequelae; event, eventuality, eventuation, **upshot, outcome,**
logical outcome, possible outcome, scenario; **outgrowth,** spin-off, offshoot,
offspring, issue, aftermath, legacy; **product** 892, precipitate, distillate, **fruit,** first
fruits, crop, harvest; development, corollary; derivative, derivation, by-product

2 **impact,** force, **repercussion,** reaction;
backwash, backlash, reflex, recoil, response; mark, print, imprint, impress,
impression

3 aftereffect, aftermath, aftergrowth, aftercrop, **afterclap,** aftershock, afterimage,
afterglow, aftertaste; wake, trail, track;
domino effect

VERBS **4 result, ensue, issue, follow,** attend,
accompany; **turn out, come out,** fall out,
redound, **work out,** pan out <nonfor-
mal>, fare; have a happy result, turn out
well, come up roses <nonformal>; turn
out to be, prove, prove to be; **become of,**
come of, come about; **develop,** unfold;
eventuate, terminate, end; **end up,** land
up <Brit>, come out, wind up

5 result from, be the effect of, be due to,
originate in *or* from, **come from,** come out
of, grow from, **grow out of,** follow from *or*
on, proceed from, descend from, emerge
from, issue from, ensue from, emanate
from, flow from, **derive from,** accrue
from, rise *or* arise from, take its rise from,

spring from, stem from, sprout from, bud
from, germinate from; **spin off; depend
on,** hinge *or* pivot *or* turn on, hang on, be
contingent on

ADJS **6 resultant, resulting, following, ensuing; consequent,** consequential, following, sequent, sequential, sequacious;
necessitated, entailed, required; **final;** derivative, derivational

ADVS **7 consequently, as a result,** as a consequence, in consequence, in the event, naturally, *naturellement* <Fr>, necessarily,
of necessity, inevitably, of course, as a
matter of course, and so, it follows that;
therefore; accordingly 765.11; **finally**

CONJS **8 resulting from,** coming from, arising from, deriving *or* derivable from, consequent to, in consequence of; **owing to,
due to;** attributed *or* attributable to, dependent *or* contingent on; **caused by,**
occasioned by, **at the bottom of;** required
by, entailed by, following from, following
strictly from

PHRS **9** one thing leads to another, *post hoc,
ergo propter hoc* <L>, what goes up must
come down <nonformal>, what goes
around comes around <nonformal>

887 ATTRIBUTION
<assignment of cause>

NOUNS **1 attribution, assignment,** assignation, **ascription, imputation,** arrogation,
placement, application, attachment, saddling, **charge, blame; indictment;
responsibility,** answerability; **credit,**
honor; accounting for, reference to, derivation from, connection with; etiology

2 acknowledgment, citation, tribute; confession; **reference;** trademark, signature;
by-line, credit line

VERBS **3 attribute, assign, ascribe, impute,**
give, place, put, apply, attach, refer

4 attribute to, ascribe to, impute to, assign to, **lay to,** put *or* set down to, apply
to, refer to, point to; **pin on,** pinpoint
<nonformal>, fix on *or* upon, attach to,
acrete to, connect with, fasten upon, hang
on <nonformal>, **saddle on *or* upon,**
place upon, **father upon,** settle upon, saddle with; blame, **blame for,** blame on *or*
upon, charge on *or* upon, place *or* put the
blame on, place the blame *or* responsibility for, indict, **fix the responsibility
for,** point to one, put the finger on *and* finger <both nonformal>, fix the burden of,
charge to, lay to one's charge, place to
one's account, set to the account of, account for, lay at the door of, bring home

to; acknowledge, confess; **credit** or **accredit with;** put words in one's mouth

5 **trace to,** follow the trail to; **derive from,** trace the origin or derivation of; affiliate to, filiate to, father, fix the paternity of

ADJS 6 **attributable, assignable, ascribable, imputable,** traceable, referable, accountable, explicable; owing, **due,** assigned or referred to, derivable from, derivative, derivational; **charged,** alleged, imputed, putative; **credited, attributed**

ADVS 7 **hence, therefore,** therefor, **wherefore,** wherefrom, whence, then, thence, ergo <L>, for which reason; **consequently** 886.7; **accordingly** 765.11; **because of that,** for that, by reason of that, for that reason, for the reason that, in consideration of something, from or for that cause, **on that account,** on that ground, thereat; **because of this, on this account,** for this cause, on account of this, propter hoc <L>, for this reason, hereat; thus, thusly <nonformal>, thuswise; on someone's head, on or at someone's doorstep

8 **why,** whyever, whyfor and for why <both nonformal>, how come <nonformal>, how is it that, **wherefore, what for,** for which, **on what account,** on account of what or which, for what or whatever reason, from what cause, pourquoi <Fr>

PREPS 9 **because of,** by reason of, **as a result of,** by or in virtue of, **on account of,** on the score of, for the sake of, **owing to, due to,** thanks to; **considering,** in consideration of, **in view of;** after

CONJS 10 **because,** parce que <Fr>, **since,** as, for, **whereas, inasmuch as, forasmuch as, insofar as, insomuch as,** as things go; in that, for the cause that, for the reason that, in view of the fact that, taking into account that, **seeing that,** seeing as how <nonformal>, being as how <nonformal>; **resulting from** 886.8

888 OPERATION

NOUNS 1 **operation, functioning, action, performance,** performing, **working, work,** workings, exercise, practice; agency; operations; **management** 573, **direction, conduct, running, carrying-on** or **-out,** execution, seeing to, overseeing, oversight; **handling,** manipulation; responsibility 641.2; **occupation** 724

2 **process, procedure,** proceeding, course; what makes it tick; **act,** step, measure, initiative, démarche <Fr>, move, maneuver, motion

3 **workability, operability,** operativeness, performability, negotiability <nonformal>, manageability, compassability, manipulatability, maneuverability; **practicability, feasibility,** viability

4 **operator,** operative, operant; **handler,** manipulator; **manager** 574.1, **executive** 574.3; functionary, agent; driver

VERBS 5 **operate, function, run, work; manage, direct** 573.8, **conduct; carry on** or **out** or **through,** make go or work, carry the ball <nonformal>, perform; **handle,** manipulate, maneuver; deal with, see to, take care of; occupy oneself with 724.10; be responsible for 641.6

6 **operate on, act on** or **upon, work on, affect, influence,** bear on, impact, impact on; have to do with, treat, focus or concentrate on; bring to bear on

7 <be operative> **operate, function, work, act, perform, go, run,** be in action or operation or commission; percolate and perk and tick <all nonformal>; be effective, go into effect, have effect, take effect, militate; have play, have free play

8 **function as,** work as, **act as,** act or play the part of, have the function or role or job or mission of

ADJS 9 **operative, operational,** go <nonformal>, **functional, practical; effective,** effectual, efficient, efficacious

10 **workable, operable,** operatable, **performable,** actable, **doable,** manageable, compassable, negotiable, manipulatable, maneuverable; **practicable, feasible,** practical, viable

11 **operating, operational, working, functioning,** operant, functional, acting, active, running, **going,** going on, ongoing; **in operation,** in action, **in practice, in force,** in play, in exercise, at work, on foot; **in process,** in the works, on the fire, in the pipe or pipeline <nonformal>, in hand

12 operational, functional; **managerial** 573.12; agential, agentive or agentival; manipulational

WORD ELEMENTS 13 —age, —al, —ance, —ence, —ation, —ing, —ion, —ism, —ization, —isation, —ment, —osis, —sis, —th, —ure

889 PRODUCTIVENESS

NOUNS 1 **productiveness, productivity,** productive capacity; **fruitfulness,** fructification, procreativeness, progenitiveness, **fertility,** fecundity, prolificness, prolificity, prolificacy; **pregnancy; luxuriance, exuberance,** generousness, bountifulness, plentifulness, plenteousness, richness, lushness, **abundance** 990.2, superabundance, copiousness, teemingness, swarmingness; teeming womb *or* loins

2 proliferation, multiplication, fructification, pullulation, teeming; **reproduction 78, production 891**

3 **fertilization, enrichment,** fecundation; insemination, impregnation 78.4

4 **fertilizer,** dressing, top dressing, enricher, richener; organic fertilizer, manure, muck, night soil, dung, guano, compost, leaf litter, leaf mould, humus, peat moss, castor-bean meal, bone meal; commercial fertilizer, inorganic fertilizer, chemical fertilizer, phosphate, superphosphate, ammonia, nitrogen, nitrate, potash

5 <goddesses of fertility> Demeter, Ceres, Isis, Astarte *or* Ashtoreth, Venus of Willenburg; <gods> Frey, Priapus, Dionysus, Pan, Baal

6 <comparisons> rabbit, Hydra, warren, seed plot, hotbed, rich soil, land flowing with milk and honey

VERBS 7 **produce, be productive, proliferate,** pullulate, fructify, be fruitful, **multiply,** spin off, hive off <Brit>, engender, beget, teem; **reproduce** 78.7,8

8 **fertilize, enrich,** richen, fatten, feed; fructify, fecundate, fecundify, prolificate; inseminate, impregnate 78.10; crossfertilize, cross-pollinate; dress, top-dress, manure

ADJS 9 **productive, fruitful,** fructiferous, fecund; **fertile, pregnant,** seminal, **rich,** flourishing, thriving, blooming; **prolific,** proliferous, uberous, **teeming,** swarming, bursting, bursting out, plenteous, **plentiful,** copious, generous, bountiful, **abundant** 990.7, **luxuriant, exuberant, lush,** superabundant; creative

10 **bearing, yielding, producing;** fruitbearing, fructiferous

11 **fertilizing, enriching,** richening, fattening, fecundatory, fructificative, **seminal,** germinal

890 UNPRODUCTIVENESS

NOUNS 1 **unproductiveness,** unproductivity, ineffectualness 19.3; **unfruitfulness, barrenness,** nonfruition, dryness, aridity, dearth, famine, sterileness, **sterility,** unfertileness, **infertility,** infecundity; wasted *or* withered loins, dry womb; **birth control, contraception,** family planning, planned parenthood; abortion; impotence 19, incapacity

2 **wasteland, waste,** desolation, barren *or* **barrens,** barren land, "weary waste"— Southey, "Rock and no water and the sandy road," "An old man in a dry season"—both T S Eliot; heath; **desert,** Sahara, "a barren waste, a wild of sand"—Addison, karroo <Africa>, badlands, dust bowl, salt flat, Death Valley, Arabia Deserta, lunar waste *or* landscape; desert island; **wilderness,** howling wilderness, wild, wilds; treeless plain; bush, brush, outback <Australia>

VERBS 3 be unproductive, **come to nothing,** come to naught, hang fire, flash in the pan, fizzle *or* peter out <nonformal>; **lie fallow**

ADJS 4 **unproductive,** nonproductive *or* nonproducing; **infertile, sterile,** unfertile *or* nonfertile, **unfruitful,** unfructuous, acarpous <botany>, infecund, unprolific *or* nonprolific; **impotent,** gelded 19.19; **ineffectual** 19.15; **barren, desert, arid,** dry, dried-up, sere, exhausted, drained, leached, sucked dry, wasted, gaunt, **waste, desolate,** jejune; **childless,** issueless, without issue, *sine prole* <L>; fallow, unplowed, unsown, untilled, uncultivated, unfecundated; celibate; virgin; menopausal

5 **uncreative,** noncreative, nonseminal, nongerminal, unfructified, unpregnant; uninventive, unoriginal, derivative

891 PRODUCTION

NOUNS 1 **production, creation, making, origination, invention, conception,** originating, engenderment, engendering, genesis, beginning; **devising,** hatching, fabrication, **concoction,** coinage, mintage, **contriving,** contrivance; **authorship;** creative effort, **generation** 78.6; improvisation, making do; **gross national product** *or* **GNP,** net natonal product *or* NNP, national production of goods and services

2 **production, manufacture** *or* **manufacturing, making, producing,** devising, design, fashioning, framing, forming, formation, formulation; engineering, tooling-up; processing, conversion; casting, **shaping,** molding; machining, milling, finishing; **assembly,** composition, elaboration; **workmanship, craftsmanship, skill** 413; **construction, building,** erection, architecture; **fabrication,** prefabrication; handiwork, handwork, handicraft, crafting; **mining,** extraction, smelting, **refining; growing,** cultivation, **raising,** harvesting

3 **industrial production, industry, mass**

production, volume production, **assembly-line production;** production line, assembly line; modular production *or* assembly, standardization; division of labor, industrialization; **cottage industry;** piecework, farmed-out work

4 **establishment, foundation,** constitution, institution, installation, formation, **organization,** inauguration, **inception, setting-up,** realization, materialization, effectuation; spinning-off, hiving-off <Brit>

5 **performance, execution, doing, accomplishment, achievement,** productive effort *or* effect, realization, bringing to fruition, fructification, effectuation, operation 888; overproduction, glut; underproduction, scarcity; **productiveness** 889, fructuousness

6 **bearing, yielding, birthing; fruition,** fruiting, fructification

7 **producer, maker,** craftsman, wright, smith; **manufacturer,** industrialist; **creator,** begetter, engenderer, **author,** mother, **father,** sire; **ancestors** 560.7; **precursor** 815; **originator,** initiator, establisher, inaugurator, introducer, institutor, beginner, mover, prime mover, motive force, instigator; **founder,** organizer, founding father, founding *or* founder member, founding partner, cofounder; **inventor,** discoverer, deviser; developer; engineer; **builder,** constructor, artificer, **architect,** planner, **conceiver,** designer, **shaper,** master *or* leading spirit; executor, executrix; facilitator, animator; **grower,** raiser; effector, realizer; **apprentice, journeyman, master,** master craftsman *or* workman, artist, past master; *"il miglior fabbro"*—T S Eliot, <Ital, the better craftsman, literally, the better smith>

VERBS 8 **produce, create, make, manufacture, form,** formulate, evolve, mature, elaborate, fashion, **fabricate,** prefabricate, cast, shape, configure, carve out, mold, extrude, frame; **construct, build,** erect, put up, set up, run up, raise, rear; make up, get up, prepare, compose, write, indite, devise, design, concoct, compound, churn out *and* crank out *and* pound out *and* hammer out *and* grind out *and* rustle up *and* gin up <all nonformal>; **put together, assemble,** piece together, patch together, whomp up *and* fudge together *and* slap up *or* together <all nonformal>, improvise 365.8; **make to order,** custom-make, custom-build, purpose-build <Brit>

9 **process,** convert 857.11; mill, machine; carve, chisel; **mine,** extract, pump, smelt, **refine; raise,** rear, **grow,** cultivate, harvest

10 **establish, found,** constitute, institute, install, form, **set up, organize,** equip, endow, inaugurate, realize, materialize, effect, effectuate

11 **perform, do,** work, act, execute, **accomplish, achieve** 407.4, **deliver,** come through with, realize, engineer, effectuate, **bring about,** bring to fruition *or* into being, cause; mass-produce, volume-produce, industrialize; overproduce; underproduce; **be productive** 889.7

12 **originate, invent, conceive,** discover, **make up, devise, contrive,** concoct, fabricate, coin, mint, frame, hatch, hatch *or* cook up, strike out; improvise, make do with; think up, think out, dream up, **design,** plan, set one's wits to work; **generate, develop,** mature, **evolve;** breed, engender, beget, spawn, hatch; bring forth, give rise to, give being to, bring *or* call into being; procreate 78.8

13 **bear, yield, produce,** furnish; **bring forth,** usher into the world; fruit, **bear fruit,** fructify

ADJS 14 **productional, creational,** formational; executional; **manufacturing,** manufactural, fabricational, **industrial,** smokestack

15 **constructional, structural,** building, housing, edificial; **architectural,** architectonic

16 **creative, originative,** causative, **productive** 889.9, **constructive,** formative, fabricative, demiurgic; inventive; generative 78.16

17 **produced, made, caused, brought about;** effectuated, executed, performed, done; grown, raised

18 **made,** man-made; **manufactured,** created, crafted, formed, shaped, molded, cast, forged, machined, milled, fashioned, **built, constructed,** fabricated; **mass-produced,** volume-produced, assembly-line; **well-made,** well-built, well-constructed; **homemade,** homespun, **handmade,** handcrafted, handicrafted, self-made, DIY *or* do it yourself; machine-made; **processed; assembled,** put together; **custom-made,** custom-built, purpose-built <Brit>, custom, made to order, bespoke; **ready-made,** ready-formed, ready-prepared, ready-to-wear, ready-for-wear, off-the-shelf, off-the-rack; prefabricated, prefab <nonformal>;

mined, extracted, smelted, refined; grown, raised, harvested, gathered

19 invented, originated, conceived, discovered, newfound; fabricated, coined, minted, new-minted; made-up, made out of whole cloth

20 manufacturable, producible, productible

ADVS 21 in production; in the works, in hand, on foot; under construction; in the pipeline; on-line

892 PRODUCT

NOUNS 1 product, end product, production, manufacture; work, œuvre <Fr>, handiwork, artifact; creation; creature; offspring, child, fruit, fruit of one's loins; result, effect 886, issue, outgrowth, outcome; invention, origination, coinage, mintage or new mintage, brainchild; concoction, composition; opus, opuscule; apprentice work; journeyman work; masterwork, masterpiece, chef d'œuvre <Fr>, Meisterstück <Ger>, work of an artist or a master or a past master, crowning achievement; gross national product 891.1

2 production, produce, proceeds, net, yield, output, throughput; crop, harvest, take <nonformal>, return, bang <nonformal>

3 extract, distillation, essence; by-product, secondary or incidental product, spin-off, outgrowth, offshoot; residue, leavings, waste, waste product, industrial waste, solid waste, lees, dregs, ash

4 <amount made> make, making; batch, lot, run, boiling

893 INFLUENCE

NOUNS 1 influence, influentiality; power 18, force, clout <nonformal>, potency, pressure, effect, indirect or incidental power, say, the final say, the last word, say-so and a lot to do with or to say about <all nonformal>, veto power; prestige, favor, good feeling, credit, esteem, repute, personality, leadership, charisma, magnetism, charm, enchantment; weight, moment, consequence, importance, eminence; authority 417, control, domination, hold; sway 612.1, reign, rule; mastery, ascendancy, supremacy, dominance, predominance, preponderance; upper hand, whip hand, trump card; leverage, purchase; persuasion 375.3, suasion, suggestion, subtle influence, insinuation

2 favor, special favor, interest; pull and drag and suction <all nonformal>; connections, the right people, inside track <nonformal>

3 backstairs influence, intrigues, deals, schemes, games, Machiavellian or Byzantine intrigues, ploys; wires and strings and ropes <all nonformal>; wire-pulling <nonformal>; influence peddling; lobbying, lobbyism

4 sphere of influence, orbit, ambit; bailiwick, vantage, stamping ground, footing, territory, turf, home turf, constituency, power base

5 influenceability, swayableness, movability; persuadability, persuadableness, persuasibility, suasibility, openness, open-mindedness, get-at-ableness <Brit nonformal>, perviousness, accessibility, receptiveness, responsiveness, amenableness; suggestibility, susceptibility, impressionability, malleability; weakness 16; putty in one's hands

6 <influential person or thing> influence, good influence; bad influence, sinister influence; person or woman or man of influence, an influential, an affluential, a presence, a palpable presence, a mover and shaker <nonformal>, a person to be reckoned with, a player or player on the scene; heavyweight, big wheel and biggie and heavy or long-ball hitter and piledriver <all nonformal>, very important person or VIP <nonformal>; wheeler-dealer <nonformal>, influencer, wire-puller <nonformal>; powerbroker; power behind the throne, gray eminence, éminence grise <Fr>, hidden hand, manipulator, friend at or in court, kingmaker; influence peddler, five-percenter, lobbyist; Svengali, Rasputin; pressure group, special-interest group, special interests, single-issue group, PAC or political action committee; lobby; the Establishment, ingroup, court, powers that be 575.15, lords of creation; key, key to the city, access, open sesame

VERBS 7 influence, make oneself felt, affect, weigh with, sway, bias, bend, incline, dispose, predispose, move, prompt, lead; color, tinge, tone, slant, impart spin; induce, persuade 375.23, jawbone and twist one's arm and hold one's feet to the fire <all nonformal>, work, work or bend to one's will; lead by the nose <nonformal>, wear down, soften up; win friends and influence people, ingratiate oneself

8 <exercise influence over> govern 612.12, rule, control 612.13, order, regulate, di-

rect, guide; **determine,** decide, dispose; have the say *or* say-so, have veto power over, have the last word, call the shots *and* be in the driver's seat *and* wear the pants <all nonformal>; charismatize

9 **exercise** *or* **exert influence, use one's influence, bring pressure to bear upon,** lean on <nonformal>, act on, **work on,** bear upon, throw one's weight around *or* into the scale, say a few words to the right person *or* in the right quarter; charismatize; draw, draw on, lead on, magnetize; **approach,** go up to with hat in hand, make advances *or* overtures, make up to *or* get cozy with <both nonformal>; get at *or* get the ear of <nonformal>; **pull strings** *or* **wires** *or* **ropes,** wire-pull <nonformal>; lobby, lobby through

10 **have influence, be influential, carry weight, weigh, tell, count,** cut ice, throw a lot of weight <nonformal>, have a lot to do with *or* say about <nonformal>; be the decisive factor *or* the one that counts, have pull *or* suction *or* drag *or* leverage <nonformal>; have a way with one, have personality *or* magnetism *or* charisma, charm the birds out of the trees, charm the pants off one <nonformal>, be persuasive; have an in <nonformal>, have the inside track <nonformal>; have full play

11 have influence *or* power *or* a hold over, have pull *or* clout with <nonformal>; **lead by the nose, twist** *or* **turn** *or* **wind around one's little finger,** have in one's pocket, keep under one's thumb, make sit up and beg *or* lie down and roll over; hypnotize, mesmerize, **dominate** 612.15

12 gain influence, **get in with** <nonformal>, ingratiate oneself with, get cozy with <nonformal>; make peace, **mend fences;** gain a footing, take hold, move in, take root, strike root in, make a dent in; gain a hearing, make one's voice heard, make one sit up and take notice, be listened to, be recognized; get the mastery *or* control of, get the inside track <nonformal>, gain a hold upon; change the preponderance, turn the scale *or* balance, turn the tables

ADJS 13 **influential, powerful** 18.12, affluential, potent, strong, to be reckoned with; **effective,** effectual, efficacious, telling; **weighty,** momentous, important, consequential, substantial, **prestigious,** estimable, authoritative, reputable; **persuasive,** suasive, personable, **winning,** magnetic, charming, enchanting, charismatic

14 <in a position of influence> **well-connected,** favorably situated, near the seat of power; **dominant** 612.18, **predominant,** preponderant, prepotent, prepollent, regnant, ruling, swaying, prevailing, on the throne, in the driver's seat <nonformal>; **ascendant,** in the ascendant, in ascendancy

15 **influenceable, swayable, movable; persuadable,** persuasible, suasible, open, open-minded, pervious, accessible, receptive, responsive, amenable; **under one's thumb,** in one's pocket, on one's payroll; coercible, bribable, compellable, vulnerable; **plastic, pliant,** pliable, malleable; **suggestible, susceptible, impressionable,** weak 16.12

894 ABSENCE OF INFLUENCE

NOUNS 1 **lack of influence** *or* **power** *or* **force,** uninfluentiality, **unauthoritativeness,** powerlessness, forcelessness, impotence 19, impotency; **ineffectiveness,** inefficaciousness, inefficacy, ineffectuality; **no say,** no say-so, nothing to do with *or* say about <nonformal>; unpersuasiveness, lack of personality *or* charm, lack of magnetism *or* charisma; **weakness** 16, wimpiness *or* wimpishness <nonformal>

2 **uninfluenceability,** unswayableness, unmovability; **unpersuadability,** impersuadability, impersuasibility, unreceptiveness, imperviousness, unresponsiveness; unsuggestibility, **unsusceptibility,** unimpressionability; invulnerability; **obstinacy** 361

ADJS 3 **uninfluential, powerless,** forceless, impotent 19.13; **weak** 16.12, wimpy *or* wimpish <nonformal>; unauthoritative; **ineffective,** ineffectual, inefficacious; **of no account,** no-account, without any weight, featherweight, lightweight

4 **uninfluenceable, unswayable, unmovable; unpliable,** unyielding, inflexible; **unpersuadable** 361.13, impersuadable, impersuasible, unreceptive, unresponsive, unamenable; impervious, closed to; **unsuggestible, unsusceptible,** unimpressionable; invulnerable; **obstinate** 361.8

5 **uninfluenced, unmoved, unaffected, unswayed**

895 TENDENCY

NOUNS 1 **tendency, inclination, leaning,** penchant, proneness, conatus, weakness, susceptibility; liability 896, readiness, willingness, eagerness, aptness, aptitude, disposition, proclivity, propensity, predisposition, **predilection,** a thing for <nonformal>, affinity, prejudice, **liking,** delight, soft spot; **yen,** lech <nonformal>, hunger, thirst; instinct *or* feeling for, sensitivity to; **bent, turn, bias,** slant, tilt, spin <nonformal>, cast, warp, twist; probability 967; diathesis <medicine>, tropism <biology>

2 **trend, drift, course, current,** *Tendenz* <Ger>, flow, stream, mainstream, main current, movement, glacial movement, motion, run, **tenor,** tone, **set,** set of the current, swing, bearing, line, direction, the general tendency *or* drift, the main course, the course of events, the way the wind blows, **the way things go,** trend of the times, spirit of the age *or* time, time spirit, *Zeitgeist* <Ger>; the way it looks

VERBS 3 **tend,** have a tendency, **incline,** be disposed, **lean, trend,** have a penchant, set, **go,** head, lead, point, verge, turn, warp, tilt, bias, bend to, work *or* gravitate *or* set toward; show a tendency *or* trend *or* set *or* direction, swing toward, point to, look to; **conduce,** contribute, serve, redound to

ADJS 4 **tending;** tendentious *or* tendential; **leaning, inclining,** inclinatory, inclinational; **mainstream,** main-current, mainline

PREPS 5 **tending to, conducive to,** leading to, inclined toward, inclining toward, heading *or* moving *or* swinging *or* working toward

6 **inclined to, leaning to, prone to, disposed to,** drawn to, predisposed to, given to; **apt to, likely to, liable to** 896.6, calculated to, minded to, ready to, in a fair way to

896 LIABILITY

NOUNS 1 **liability, likelihood** *or* **likeliness; probability** 967, contingency, chance 971, eventuality 830.1; weakness, **proneness** 895.1; **possibility** 965; **responsibility** 641.2, legal responsibility; **indebtedness** 623.1, financial commitment, pecuniary obligation

2 **susceptibility, liability,** susceptivity, liableness, **openness, exposure; vulnerability** 1005.4

VERBS 3 **be liable; be subjected** *or* **subjected to,** be a pawn *or* plaything of, be the prey of, lie under; **expose oneself to, lay** *or* **leave oneself open to,** open the door to; **gamble,** stand to lose *or* gain, stand a chance, **run the chance** *or* **risk,** let down one's guard *or* defenses; **admit of,** open

the possibility of, be in the way of, bid *or* stand fair to; **owe,** be in debt *or* indebted for

4 **incur, contract, invite,** welcome, run, **bring on, bring down,** bring upon *or* down upon, bring upon *or* down upon oneself; **be responsible for** 641.6; fall into, fall in with; get, gain, acquire

ADJS 5 **liable, likely, prone; probable; responsible,** legally responsible, answerable; **in debt, indebted,** financially burdened, heavily committed, overextended; **exposed, susceptible, at risk,** overexposed, open, like a sitting duck, **vulnerable**

6 **liable to, subject to,** standing to, in a position to, incident to, dependent on; **susceptible** *or* **prone to,** susceptive to, **open** *or* vulnerable *or* **exposed to,** naked to, in danger of, within range of, at the mercy of; **capable of,** ready for; **likely to, apt to** 895.6; obliged to, responsible *or* answerable for

CONJS 7 **lest,** that, **for fear that**

897 INVOLVEMENT

NOUNS 1 **involvement,** involution, **implication, entanglement,** enmeshment, engagement, involuntary presence *or* cooperation, embarrassment; relation 774; **inclusion** 771; **absorption** 982.3

VERBS 2 **involve, implicate,** tangle, **entangle,** embarrass, enmesh, engage, **draw in,** drag *or* hook *or* suck into, catch up in, **make a party to;** interest, concern; **absorb** 982.13

3 **be involved, be into** <nonformal>, partake, participate, take an interest, interest oneself, have a role *or* part

ADJS 4 **involved, implicated;** interested, concerned, a party to; **included** 771.5

5 **involved in, implicated in,** tangled *or* entangled in, enmeshed in, **caught up in,** tied up in, wrapped up in, all wound up in, dragged *or* hooked *or* sucked into; in deep, deeply involved, **up to one's neck** *or* **ears in,** up to one's elbows *or* ass in, head over heels in, **absorbed in** 982.17, immersed *or* submerged in, far-gone

898 CONCURRENCE

NOUNS 1 **concurrence, collaboration,** coaction, **co-working,** collectivity, combined effort *or* operation, united *or* concerted action, concert, synergy; **cooperation** 450; **agreement** 787; me-tooism; **coincidence,** simultaneity 835, synchronism;

concomitance, accompaniment 768;
union, junction 799.1, **conjunction,** combination 804, association, alliance,
consociation; conspiracy, collusion,
cahoots <nonformal>; concourse,
confluence; **accordance** 455.1, concordance, correspondence, consilience;
symbiosis, parasitism; saprophytism

VERBS **2 concur, collaborate,** coact, **co-
work,** synergize; **cooperate** 450.3; conspire, collude, connive, be in cahoots
<nonformal>; **combine** 804.3, **unite, as-
sociate** 804.4, coadunate, join, conjoin;
harmonize; **coincide,** synchronize, happen together; **accord** 455.2, correspond,
agree 787.6

3 go with, **go along with, go hand in hand
with,** be hand in glove with, team or join
up with, buddy up with <nonformal>;
keep pace with, run parallel to

ADJS **4 concurrent,** concurring; **coacting,** coactive, **collaborative,** collective, **co-
working,** cooperant, synergetic or synergic or synergistic; **cooperative** 450.5;
conspiratorial, collusive; **united, joint,**
conjoint, **combined, concerted,** associated, associate, coadunate; **coincident,**
synchronous, synchronic, in sync, coordinate; concomitant, accompanying 768.9;
meeting, uniting, combining; **accordant,
agreeing** 787.9, concordant, harmonious,
consilient, at one with; symbiotic, parasitic, saprophytic

ADVS **5 concurrently,** coactively, **jointly,
conjointly, concertedly,** in concert, in
harmony or unison with, synchronously,
together; with one accord, with one voice,
as one, as one man; hand in hand, hand in
glove, shoulder to shoulder, cheek by jowl

899 COUNTERACTION

NOUNS **1 counteraction, counterworking;
opposition** 451, opposure, counterposition or contraposition, confutation,
contradiction; antagonism, repugnance,
oppugnance or oppugnancy, **antipathy,
conflict, friction,** interference, clashing,
collision; reaction, repercussion, **backlash, recoil,** kick, backfire; resistance,
recalcitrance, dissent 333, revolt 327.4,
perverseness, nonconformity 867, crankiness, crotchetiness, orneriness <nonfor-
mal>, renitency; going against the current or against the tide, swimming upstream; **contrariety** 778

2 neutralization, nullification, annulment,
cancellation, voiding, invalidation, vitiation, frustration, thwarting, undoing;

offsetting, counterbalancing, countervailing, balancing

3 counteractant, counteractive, **counter-
agent;** counterirritant; **antidote,** remedy,
preventive or preventative, prophylactic;
neutralizer, nullifier, offset; antacid,
buffer

4 counterforce, countervailing force, coun-
terinfluence, counterpressure; counterpoise, counterbalance, counterweight;
countercurrent, crosscurrent, undercurrent; counterblast; head wind, foul wind,
cross wind

5 countermeasure, counterattack, counter-
step; **counterblow** or counterstroke or
countercoup or counterblast, counterfire;
counterrevolution, counterinsurgency;
counterterrorism; counterculture; **retort,**
comeback <nonformal>; defense 460

VERBS **6 counteract,** counter, counterwork,
counterattack, countervail; counterpose
or contrapose, **oppose,** antagonize, **go in
opposition to,** go or **run counter to, go**
or **work against,** go clean counter to,
go or fly in the face of, run against, beat
against, militate against; **resist,** fight
back, bite back, lift a hand against, defend oneself; **dissent,** dissent from; **cross,**
confute, **contradict,** contravene, oppugn,
conflict, be antipathetic or hostile or inimical, interfere or conflict with, come in
conflict with, **clash,** collide, meet head-
on, lock horns; rub or go against the
grain; swim upstream or against the tide
or against the current

7 neutralize, nullify, annul, cancel, cancel
out, negate, negative, negativate, invalidate, vitiate, void, frustrate, stultify,
thwart, come or bring to nothing, undo;
offset, counterbalance 338.5; buffer

ADJS **8** counteractive or counteractant,
**counteracting, counterworking, counter-
productive,** countervailing; **opposing,**
oppositional; contradicting, contradictory; **antagonistic,** hostile, antipathetic,
inimical, oppugnant, repugnant, **conflicting, clashing;** reactionary; resistant,
recalcitrant, dissentient, dissident, revolutionary, breakaway, nonconformist,
perverse, cranky, crotchety, ornery
<nonformal>, renitent

9 neutralizing, nullifying, stultifying, an-
nulling, canceling, negating, invalidating,
vitiating, voiding; **balanced,** counter-
balanced, poised, in poise, offset, **zero-
sum; offsetting,** counterbalancing, countervailing; antacid, buffering

ADVS **10** counteractively, antagonistically,
opposingly, **in opposition to, counter to**

WORD ELEMENTS **11** ant—, anti—, anth—, contra—, counter—

900 SUPPORT

NOUNS **1 support, backing, aid** 449; **upholding, upkeep,** carrying, carriage, maintenance, **sustaining,** sustainment, sustenance, sustentation; **reinforcement,** backup; subsidy, subvention; **support services, infrastructure; moral support;** emotional *or* psychological support, security blanket <nonformal>; **power base, constituency, party;** supportive relationship, supportive therapy; strokes <nonformal>; **approval** 509; **assent, concurrence** 332; **reliance** 952.1; life-support, life-sustainment

2 supporter, support; upholder, bearer, carrier, sustainer, maintainer; staff 273.2, stave, cane, stick, walking stick, alpenstock, crook, crutch; **advocate** 616.9; **stay, prop,** fulcrum, **bracket, brace,** bracer, guy, guywire *or* guyline, shroud, rigging, standing rigging; buttress, shoulder, arm, good right arm; mast, sprit, yard, yardarm; **mainstay,** backbone, spine, neck, cervix; athletic supporter, jock *and* jockstrap <both nonformal>, G-string <nonformal>; brassiere, bra <nonformal>, bandeau, corset, girdle, foundation garment; **reinforcement,** reinforce, reinforcing, reinforcer, strengthener, stiffener; back, backing; rest, resting place

3 <mythology> Atlas, Hercules, Telamon, the tortoise that supports the earth

4 buttress, buttressing; abutment, shoulder; **bulwark,** rampart; **embankment,** bank, retaining wall, bulkhead, bulkheading, plank buttress, piling; **breakwater,** seawall, mole, **jetty,** jutty, groin; **pier,** pier buttress, buttress pier; flying buttress, *arc-boutant* <Fr>, arch buttress; hanging buttress; **beam**

5 footing, foothold, toehold, hold, perch, **purchase** 905; **standing,** stand, stance, standing place, pou sto, *point d'appui* <Fr>, *locus standi* <L>; footrest, footplate, footrail

6 foundation, *fond* <Fr>, firm foundation, **base, basis, footing,** basement, pavement, **ground,** grounds, **groundwork, seat,** sill, floor *or* flooring, fundament; bed, bedding; **substructure,** substruction, substratum; infrastructure; **understructure,** understruction, underbuilding, undergirding, undercarriage, underpinning, bearing wall; stereobate, stylobate; firm

or solid ground, *terra firma* <L>; solid rock *or* bottom, rock bottom, bedrock; hardpan; riprap; **fundamental** 996.6, **principle, premise** 956.1; root, radical; rudiment

7 foundation stone, footstone; **cornerstone, keystone,** headstone, first stone, quoin

8 base, pedestal; stand, standard; **shaft** 273, **upright, column, pillar, post,** jack, pole, staff, stanchion, pier, pile *or* piling, king-post, queen-post, pilaster, newel-post, banister, baluster, balustrade, colonnade, caryatid; dado, die; plinth, subbase; surbase; socle; **trunk,** stem, **stalk,** pedicel, peduncle, footstalk

9 sill, groundsel; mudsill; window sill; doorsill, threshold; doorstone

10 frame, underframe, infrastructure, chassis, **skeleton;** armature; **mounting,** mount, **backing, setting;** surround

11 handle, hold, grip, grasp, haft, helve

12 scaffold, scaffolding, *échafaudage* <Fr>; stage, staging

13 platform; stage, estrade, dais, floor; **rostrum, podium, pulpit,** speaker's platform *or* stand, **soapbox** <nonformal>; hustings, **stump;** tribune, tribunal; emplacement; catafalque; landing stage, landing; heliport, landing pad; launching pad; **terrace,** step terrace, deck; **balcony, gallery**

14 shelf, ledge, shoulder, corbel, beam-end; mantel, mantelshelf, mantelpiece; retable, superaltar, gradin, *gradino* <Ital>, predella; hob

15 table, board, **stand; bench,** workbench; **counter,** bar, buffet; **desk,** writing table, **secretary,** *secrétaire* <Fr>, escritoire; **lectern,** reading stand, ambo, reading desk

16 trestle, horse; sawhorse, buck *or* sawbuck; clotheshorse; trestle board *or* table, trestle and table; trestlework, trestling; A-frame

17 seat, chair; saddle

18 <saddle parts> **pommel,** horn; jockey; girth, girt, surcingle, bellyband; cinch, stirrup

19 sofa, **bed; couch;** the sack *and* the hay *and* kip *and* doss <all nonformal>; bedstead; **litter, stretcher,** gurney

20 bedding, underbed, underbedding; **mattress,** paillasse, pallet; air mattress, foam-rubber mattress, innerspring mattress; sleeping bag; pad, mat, rug; litter, bedstraw; **pillow,** cushion, bolster; **springs,** bedsprings, box springs

VERBS **21 support, bear,** carry, **hold, sustain, maintain, bolster, reinforce,** back, back up, shoulder, give *or* furnish *or* afford *or* supply *or* lend support; go to bat for

<nonformal>; **hold up, bear up,** bolster up, keep up, buoy up, keep afloat, back up; **uphold,** upbear, upkeep; **brace, prop,** crutch, buttress; shore, **shore up;** stay, mainstay; underbrace, undergird, underprop, underpin, underset; **underlie,** be at the bottom of, form the foundation of; cradle; cushion, pillow; **subsidize;** subvene; assent 332.8; concur 332.9; **approve** 509.9

22 **rest on, stand on, lie on,** recline on, repose on, bear on, **lean on,** abut on; **sit on,** perch, ride, piggyback on; **straddle,** bestraddle, stride, bestride; be based on, rely on

ADJS 23 **supporting, supportive, bearing,** carrying, burdened; **holding,** upholding, maintaining, sustaining, sustentative, suspensory; bracing, propping, shoring, bolstering, buttressing; life-sustaining

24 **supported, borne,** upborne, held, buoyed-up, **upheld, sustained,** maintained; **braced,** guyed, stayed, propped, shored or shored up, bolstered, buttressed; based or founded or grounded on

ADVS 25 **on, across, astride, astraddle,** straddle, straddle-legged, straddleback, on the back of; horseback, on horseback; pickaback or piggyback

901 IMPULSE, IMPACT
<driving and striking force>

NOUNS 1 **impulse,** impulsion, impelling force, impellent; **drive,** driving force or power; **motive power, power** 18; **force,** irresistible force; clout <nonformal>; **impetus; momentum;** moment, moment of force; propulsion 903.1; incitement 375.4, incentive 375.7, compulsion 424

2 **thrust, push, shove,** boost <nonformal>; **pressure; stress;** press; **prod, poke, punch, jab,** dig, nudge; **bump,** jog, joggle, jolt; **jostle,** hustle; **butt,** bunt; head <of water, steam, etc>

3 **impact, collision, clash,** appulse, **encounter,** meeting, impingement, **bump, crash,** crump, whomp; **carom,** carambole, cannon; sideswipe <nonformal>; smash and crunch <both nonformal>; **shock, brunt; concussion,** percussion; **thrusting, ramming,** bulling, **bulldozing,** shouldering, muscling, steamrollering, railroading; hammering, smashing, mauling, sledgehammering; onslaught 459.1

4 **hit, blow, stroke, knock, rap, pound,** slam, bang, crack, **whack, smack, thwack,** smash, dash, swipe, swing, **punch, poke, jab,** dig, drub, thump, pelt, cut, chop, dint, slog; drubbing, drumming, tattoo, fusillade; beating 604.4

5 <nonformal terms> **sock,** bang, bash, bat, belt, bonk, bust, clip, clout, duke, swat, yerk , plunk larrup, paste, lick, biff, clump, clunk, clonk, wallop, whop, bonk, slam, slug

6 **punch, boxing punch,** blow, belt, sock

7 **tap, rap, pat,** dab, chuck, touch, tip; lovetap; **snap, flick, flip,** fillip, flirt, whisk, brush; **peck,** pick

8 **slap, smack,** flap, box, **cuff,** buffet; **spank;** whip, **lash,** cut, stripe

9 **kick, boot;** punt, drop kick, place kick, kicking, calcitration <old>

10 **stamp,** stomp <nonformal>, drub, clump, clop

VERBS 11 **impel,** give an impetus, **set going** or agoing, put or set in motion, give momentum; **drive, move,** animate, actuate, forward; **thrust,** power; drive or whip on; goad; **propel;** motivate, incite 375.17; compel 424.4

12 **thrust, push, shove,** boost <nonformal>; press, stress, **bear,** bear upon, bring pressure to bear upon; **ram,** ram down, tamp, pile drive, jam, crowd, cram; bull, bulldoze, muscle, steamroller, railroad; **drive, force,** run; **prod, goad, poke, punch, jab,** dig, nudge; **bump,** jog, joggle, jolt, shake, rattle; **jostle,** hustle, hurtle; elbow, shoulder; **butt,** bunt, buck <nonformal>, run or bump or butt against, bump up against, knock or run one's head against; assault

13 **collide,** come into collision, be on a collision course, **clash,** meet, encounter, confront each other, impinge; percuss, concuss; **bump, hit, strike, knock, bang; run into, bump into,** bang into, slam into, smack into, **crash into, impact,** smash into, dash into, carom into, cannon into <Brit>; rear-end; **hit against,** strike against, knock against; foul, fall or run foul or afoul of; hurtle, hurt; **carom,** cannon <chiefly Brit>; **sideswipe** <nonformal>; **crash,** smash, crump, whomp; smash up or crack up or crunch <all nonformal>

14 **hit, strike, knock,** knock down or out, smite; land a blow, draw blood; **poke, punch, jab,** thwack, **smack,** clap, crack, swipe, **whack;** deal, fetch, swipe at, take a punch at, throw one at <nonformal>; deal or fetch a blow, hit a clip <nonformal>, let have it; **thump,** snap; strike at 459.16

15 <nonformal terms> **belt,** bat, clout, bang, slam, bash, biff, paste, wham,

whop, clump, bonk, wallop, clip, cut, plunk, swat, soak, sock, slog, slug, yerk <old>, clunk, clonk

16 **pound, beat, hammer, maul,** sledgehammer, **knock, rap, bang,** thump, **drub,** buffet, **batter,** pulverize, paste <nonformal>, patter, pommel, pummel, pelt, baste, lambaste; thresh, thrash; flail; spank, flap; whip

17 <nonformal terms> **clobber,** knock for a loop, marmelize <Brit>, knock cold, dust off, bash up, punch out, rough up, slap down, smack down, sandbag, work over, deck, coldcock, wallop, larrup

18 **tap, rap, pat,** dab, chuck, touch, tip; **snap, flick, flip,** fillip, tickle, flirt, whisk, **graze,** brush; bunt; **peck,** pick, beak

19 **slap, smack,** flap; **box, cuff,** buffet; **spank;** whip

20 **club,** cudgel, blackjack, sandbag, cosh <Brit>

21 **kick,** boot, kick about or around, calcitrate <old>; kick downstairs <old>; kick out; knee

22 **stamp,** stomp <nonformal>, trample, tread, drub, clump, clop

ADJS 23 **impelling,** impellent; impulsive, pulsive, **moving,** motive, animating, actuating, **driving;** thrusting

24 concussive, percussive, crashing, smashing

902 REACTION

NOUNS 1 **reaction, response,** respondence, feedback; reply, answer 939.1, **rise** <nonformal>; **reflex,** reflection, **reflex action;** echo, bounce back, reverberation, resonance, sympathetic vibration; return; reflux, refluence; action and reaction; opposite response, negative response, retroaction, revulsion; predictable response, automatic or autonomic reaction, knee-jerk and knee-jerk response <both nonformal>, spontaneous or unthinking response, spur-of-the-moment response; conditioned reflex

2 **recoil, rebound,** resilience, repercussion, contrecoup <Fr>; **bounce, bound, spring,** bounce-back; **repulse, rebuff; backlash,** backlashing, kickback, **kick,** a kick like a mule <nonformal>, recalcitration <old>; **backfire, boomerang;** ricochet, carom, cannon <Brit>

3 <a drawing back or aside> **retreat,** recoil, fallback, pullout, pullback, contingency plan, backup plan; evasion, avoidance, sidestepping; **flinch,** wince, cringe; **side step,** shy; **dodge, duck** <nonformal>

4 **reactionary,** reactionist, recalcitrant

VERBS 5 **react, respond,** reply, answer, riposte, snap back, come back at <nonformal>; rise to the fly, take the bait; go off half-cocked or at half cock

6 **recoil, rebound,** resile; **bounce, bound, spring; spring** or **fly back,** bounce or bound back, snap back; repercuss, have repercussions; **kick,** kick back, kick like a mule <nonformal>, recalcitrate <old>; **backfire, boomerang;** backlash, lash back; ricochet, carom, cannon and cannon off <both Brit>

7 **pull** or **draw back,** retreat, recoil, fade, **fall back,** reel back, hang back, start back, shrink back, give ground; **shrink, flinch, wince, cringe,** blink, blench, quail; **shy,** shy away, start or turn aside, evade, avoid, sidestep, weasel, weasel out, cop out <nonformal>; **dodge, duck** <nonformal>; jib, swerve, sheer off, give a wide berth

8 get a reaction, get a response, evoke a response, ring a bell, strike a responsive chord, strike fire, strike or hit home, hit a nerve, get a rise out of <nonformal>

ADJS 9 **reactive,** reacting, merely reactive; **responsive,** respondent, responding, antiphonal; **quick on the draw** or trigger or uptake; **reactionary;** retroactionary, retroactive; revulsive; **reflex,** reflexive, knee-jerk <nonformal>; refluent

10 recoiling, rebounding, **resilient; bouncing,** bouncy, bounding, springing; springy; repercussive; recalcitrant

ADVS 11 **on the rebound,** on the return, on the bounce; on the spur of the moment, off the top of the head

903 PUSHING, THROWING

NOUNS 1 **pushing, propulsion, propelling; shoving,** butting; **drive, thrust,** motive power, driving force, means of propulsion <see list>; **push, shove,** butt, bunt; shunt, impulsion 901.1

2 **throwing, projection,** jaculation, ejaculation, flinging, slinging, **pitching, tossing,** casting, hurling, lobbing, chucking, chunking <nonformal>, heaving, firing and burning and pegging <all nonformal>; bowling, rolling; **shooting,** firing, gunnery, gunning, musketry; trapshooting, skeet or skeet shooting; archery

3 **throw, toss, fling, sling, cast, hurl,** chuck, chunk <nonformal>, lob, **heave,** shy, **pitch, toss,** peg <nonformal>; **flip;** put, shot-put; <football> pass, forward pass,

lateral pass, lateral; <tennis> serve, service; bowl; <baseball> pitch

4 shot, discharge; ejection 908; detonation 56.3; gunfire; gun, cannon; bullet; **salvo, volley**, fusillade, tattoo, spray; bowshot, gunshot, stoneshot, potshot

5 projectile; ejecta, ejectamenta; **missile**; ball; discus, quoit

6 propeller, prop <nonformal>, airscrew, prop-fan; propellant, propulsor, driver; screw, wheel, screw propeller, twin screws; bow thruster; paddle wheel; turbine; fan, impeller, rotor; piston

7 thrower, pitcher, hurler, bowler <cricket>, chucker, chunker <nonformal>, **heaver, tosser**, flinger, slinger, caster, jaculator, ejaculator; bowler; shot-putter; javelin thrower; discus thrower, discobolus

8 shooter, shot; **gunner**, gun, **gunman; rifleman**, musketeer, carabineer; cannoneer, artilleryman; Nimrod, hunter 382.5; trapshooter; archer, bowman, toxophilite; **marksman, markswoman**, targetshooter, **sharpshooter**, sniper; good shot, dead shot, deadeye, **crack shot**

VERBS **9 push, propel**, impel, **shove**, thrust 901.11; **drive, move**, forward, advance; sweep, sweep along; butt, bunt; shunt; pole, row; pedal, treadle; **roll**, troll, bowl, trundle

10 throw, fling, sling, pitch, toss, cast, hurl, heave, chuck, chunk *and* peg <both non-formal>, lob, shy, fire, burn, pepper <nonformal>, launch, dash, let fly, let go, let rip, let loose; catapult; **flip**, snap, jerk; bowl; pass; serve; put, put the shot; dart, lance, tilt; fork, pitchfork; pelt 459.27

11 project, jaculate, ejaculate

12 shoot, fire, fire off, let off, let fly, **discharge**, eject 908.13; detonate 56.8; gun <nonformal>; pistol; sharpshoot; shoot at 459.22, gun for <nonformal>; strike, hit, plug <nonformal>; shoot down, fell, drop, stop in one's tracks; **riddle, pepper**, pelt, pump full of lead <nonformal>; snipe, pick off; torpedo; pot; potshoot, potshot, take a potshot; load, prime, charge; cock

13 start, start off, start up, give a start, crank up, give a push *or* shove <nonformal>, jump-start, kick-start, **put** *or* **set in motion, set on foot**, set going *or* agoing, start going; **kick off** *and* **start the ball rolling** <both nonformal>; get off the ground *or* off the mark, **launch**, launch forth *or* out, float, set afloat; send, send off *or* forth; bundle off

ADJS **14 propulsive**, propulsory, **propellant**, propelling; **motive; driving, pushing, shoving**

15 projectile, trajectile, jaculatory, ejaculatory; **ballistic**, missile; ejective

16 jet-propelled, rocket-propelled, steam-propelled, gasoline-propelled, gas-propelled, diesel-propelled, wind-propelled, self-propelled, etc

17 means of propulsion

battery propulsion	pulse-jet propulsion
diesel propulsion	ram-jet propulsion
diesel-electric propulsion	reaction propulsion
	resojet propulsion
electric propulsion	rocket propulsion
gas propulsion	spring propulsion
gasoline propulsion	steam propulsion
gravity propulsion	turbofan propulsion
jet propulsion	turbojet propulsion
plasma-jet propulsion	turbopropeller *or* turboprop propulsion
prop-fan propulsion	wind propulsion

904 PULLING

NOUNS **1 pulling, traction, drawing**, draft, dragging, heaving, tugging, towing; pulling *or* tractive power, **pull**; tug-of-war; towing, towage; towrope, towbar, towing cable *or* hawser; tow car, wrecker; **hauling**, haulage, drayage; man-hauling, man-haulage; attraction 906; extraction 192

2 pull, draw, heave, haul, tug, a long pull and a strong pull, strain, drag

3 jerk, yank <nonformal>, quick *or* sudden pull; **twitch**, tweak, pluck, hitch, wrench, snatch, start, bob; **flip**, flick, flirt, flounce; jig, **jiggle**; jog, joggle

VERBS **4 pull, draw, heave, haul**, hale, lug, **tug, tow**, take in tow; trail, train; **drag**, man-haul, draggle, snake <nonformal>; troll, trawl

5 jerk, yerk <nonformal>, **yank** <nonformal>; **twitch**, tweak, pluck, snatch, hitch, wrench, snake <nonformal>; **flip**, flick, flirt, flounce; **jiggle**, jig, jigget, jigger; jog, joggle

ADJS **6 pulling, drawing**, tractional, tractive, hauling, tugging, towing, towage; man-hauled

905 LEVERAGE, PURCHASE
<mechanical advantage applied to moving or raising>

NOUNS **1 leverage**, fulcrumage; **pry**, prize <nonformal>

2 purchase, hold, advantage; **foothold**, toehold, footing; differential purchase; collier's purchase; traction

3 **fulcrum, axis, pivot,** bearing, rest, resting point, *point d'appui* <Fr>; thole, thole-pin, rowlock, oarlock

4 **lever; pry,** prize <nonformal>; **bar,** pinch bar, **crowbar,** crow, pinchbar, iron crow, wrecking bar, ripping bar, claw bar; cant hook, peavey; **jimmy;** hand-spike, marlinespike; boom, spar, beam, outrigger; pedal, treadle, crank; limb

5 **arm;** forearm; wrist; elbow; upper arm, biceps

6 **tackle,** purchase

7 **windlass; capstan** <nautical>; **winch,** crab; reel; Chinese windlass, Spanish windlass

VERBS 8 get a purchase, get leverage, get a foothold; **pry,** prize, **lever,** wedge; pry or prize out; **jimmy,** crowbar, pinchbar

9 **reel in,** wind in, bring in, draw in, pull in, crank in, trim, tighten, tauten, draw taut, take the strain; windlass, winch, crank, reel; tackle

906 ATTRACTION
<a drawing toward>

NOUNS 1 **attraction,** traction 904.1, attrac-tiveness, attractivity; mutual attraction or magnetism; pulling power, **pull,** drag, draw, tug; magnetism 1031.7; gravity, gravitation; centripetal force; capillarity, capillary attraction; adduction; **affinity, sympathy; allurement** 377

2 attractor, attractant, attrahent; adduc-tor; cynosure, focus, center, center of attraction or attention; crowd-pleaser or drawer, charismatic figure; lure 377.2

3 **magnet,** artificial magnet, field magnet, bar magnet, horseshoe magnet, electro-magnet, solenoid, paramagnet, electro-magnetic lifting magnet, magnetic nee-dle; lodestone, magnetite; magnetic pole, magnetic north

VERBS 4 **attract, pull, draw,** drag, tug, pull or draw towards, have an attraction; **mag-netize,** magnet, be magnetic; **lure;** adduct

ADJS 5 attracting, drawing, pulling, drag-ging, tugging; eye-catching; **attractive, magnetic;** charismatic; magnetized, at-trahent; sympathetic; **alluring;** adduc-tive, adducent

ADVS 6 attractionally, attractively; magnet-ically; charismatically

907 REPULSION
<a thrusting away>

NOUNS 1 **repulsion,** repellence or repellency, **repelling;** mutual repulsion, polarization; disaffinity; centrifugal force; magnetic repulsion, diamagnetism; antigravity; ejection 908

2 **repulse, rebuff; dismissal,** cold shoulder, snub, spurning, brush-off, cut; kiss-off <nonformal>; turn-off <nonformal>; re-fusal; discharge 908.5

VERBS 3 **repulse, repel, rebuff, turn back,** put back, beat back, drive or push or thrust back; drive away, chase, chase off or away; send off or away, send about one's business, **send packing,** pack off, dismiss; snub, cut, brush off, drop; kiss off <nonformal>; spurn, refuse; **ward off,** hold off, keep off, fend off, fight off, push off, keep at arm's length; slap or smack down <nonformal>; eject 908.13, discharge 908.19

ADJS 4 **repulsive,** repellent, **repelling;** di-amagnetic, of opposite polarity

ADVS 5 repulsively, repellently

908 EJECTION

NOUNS 1 **ejection,** ejectment, throwing out, **expulsion, discharge,** extrusion, obtru-sion, detrusion, **ousting, ouster,** removal, kicking or booting or chucking out <all nonformal>; throwing or kicking down-stairs; the boot and the bounce and the bum's rush and the old heave-ho <all nonformal>, the chuck <Brit nonfor-mal>; defenestration; **rejection** 372; jettison

2 **eviction,** ousting, dislodgment, dispossces-sion; **ouster**

3 **depopulation,** dispeoplement, unpeo-pling; devastation, desolation

4 **banishment,** relegation, exclusion 772; **excommunication,** disfellowship; **disbar-ment,** unfrocking, defrocking; **expatria-tion, exile,** exilement; outlawing or out-lawry, fugitation <Scots law>; **ostra-cism,** ostracization, thumbs-down, thumbing-down, *pollice verso* <L>, blackballing, silent treatment, sending to Coventry, cold shoulder; **deportation,** transportation, **extradition;** rustication; degradation, **demotion** 447, stripping, de-pluming, displuming; deprivation

5 **dismissal, discharge,** forced separation, *congé* <Fr>; outplacement; **firing** and canning <both nonformal>, **cashiering,** drumming out, dishonorable discharge, rogue's march; disemployment, **layoff,** removal, surplusing, displacing, fur-loughing; suspension; **retirement;** the bounce, **the sack** and the chuck <both Brit nonformal>; the boot and the gate

and the ax <all nonformal>; walking papers *or* ticket <nonformal>, pink slip <nonformal>; deposal 447

6 **evacuation, voidance,** voiding; **elimination,** removal; **clearance, clearing,** clearage; unfouling, freeing; scouring *or* cleaning out, unclogging; exhaustion, exhausting, venting, emptying, depletion; **unloading,** off-loading, discharging cargo *or* freight; draining, drainage; egress 190.2; **excretion,** defecation 12.2,4

7 **disgorgement,** disemboguement, **expulsion,** ejaculation, **discharge,** emission; **eruption,** eructation, extravasation, **blowout, outburst;** outpour, jet, spout, squirt, spurt

8 **vomiting,** vomition, **disgorgement, regurgitation,** egestion, emesis, the pukes *and* the heaves <both nonformal>; **retching,** heaving, gagging; nausea; **vomit,** vomitus, puke *and* barf <both nonformal>, spew, egesta; the dry heaves <nonformal>; vomiturition

9 **belch, burp** <nonformal>, belching, wind, gas, eructation; **hiccup**

10 **fart** <nonformal>, **flatulence** *or* flatulency, flatuosity, flatus, gas, wind

11 **ejector,** expeller, —fuge; **ouster,** evictor; **bouncer** *and* chucker <both nonformal>, chucker-out <Brit nonformal>

12 **dischargee,** expellee; ejectee; evictee

VERBS 13 **eject, expel, discharge,** extrude, obtrude, detrude, exclude, **reject,** cast, remove; **oust, bounce** *and* give the hook <both nonformal>, **put out, turn out,** thrust out; **throw out,** run out <nonformal>, cast out, chuck out, give the chuck to <Brit nonformal>, toss out, heave out, throw *or* kick downstairs; kick *or* boot out <nonformal>; give the bum's rush *or* give the old heave-ho *or* throw out on one's ear <all nonformal>; defenestrate; jettison, throw overboard, discard, junk, throw away; **be rid of,** be shut of, see the last of

14 **drive out, run out,** chase out, chase away, run off, **rout out;** drum out, read out; freeze out <nonformal>, push out, force out, send packing, send about one's business; **hunt out,** harry out; **smoke out,** drive into the open; run out of town, ride on a rail

15 **evict, oust,** dislodge, dispossess, put out, turn out, **turn out of doors,** turn out of house and home, turn *or* put out bag and baggage, throw into the street; unhouse, unkennel

16 **depopulate,** dispeople, unpeople; devastate, desolate

17 **banish, expel, cast out,** thrust out, relegate, **ostracize,** disfellowship, exclude, send down, **blackball,** spurn, thumb down, turn thumbs down on, snub, cut, give the cold shoulder, send to Coventry, give the silent treatment; **excommunicate; exile, expatriate, deport,** transport, send away, **extradite; deport; outlaw,** fugitate <Scots law>, ban, proscribe; rusticate

18 **dismiss, send off** *or* **away, turn off** *or* **away,** bundle, bundle off *or* out, hustle out, pack off, **send packing,** send about one's business, send to the showers <nonformal>; bow out, **show the door,** show the gate; **give the gate** *or* the air <nonformal>

19 **dismiss, discharge, expel, cashier,** drum out, disemploy, outplace, separate forcibly *or* involuntarily, **lay off,** suspend, surplus, furlough, turn off, make redundant, riff <nonformal>, turn out, release, let go, let out, remove, displace, replace, strike off the rolls, give the pink slip ; unfrock, defrock; degrade, demote, strip, deplume, displume, deprive; depose, disbar 447.4; break, bust <nonformal>; **retire,** put on the retired list; pension off, superannuate, put out to pasture; read out of; kick upstairs

20 <nonformal terms> **fire, can, sack, bump,** bounce, kick, boot, give the ax, give the gate, give one the sack *or* the ax *or* the boot *or* the gate *or* the air *or* one's walking papers, send one to the showers, show one the door *or* gate

21 **do away with, exterminate, annihilate;** purge, liquidate; **shake off,** shoo, dispel; **throw off,** fling off, cast off; **eliminate, get rid of** 772.5; throw away 390.7

22 **evacuate, void; eliminate,** remove; **empty,** empty out, deplete, **exhaust,** vent, drain; **clear, purge,** clean *or* scour out, clear off *or* out *or* away, clear, unfoul, unclog, flush out, blow, blow out, sweep out, make a clean sweep, clear the decks; defecate 12.13

23 **unload,** off-load, unlade, unpack, disburden, unburden, **discharge, dump;** unship, break bulk; pump out

24 **let out, give vent to,** give out *or* off, throw off, blow off, **emit, exhaust,** evacuate, let go; **exhale,** expire, breathe out, let one's breath out, blow, puff; fume, steam, vapor, smoke, reek; open the sluices *or* floodgates, turn on the tap

25 **disgorge,** debouch, disembogue, **discharge, exhaust, expel,** ejaculate, throw out, **cast forth,** send out *or* forth; **erupt,**

eruct, **blow out**, extravasate; **pour out** *or* **forth**, pour, outpour, decant; **spew**, jet, spout, squirt, **spurt**

26 **vomit**, spew, **disgorge, regurgitate**, egest, **throw up**, bring up, be sick <Brit>, sick up <Brit nonformal>, cast *or* heave the gorge; **retch**, keck, **heave, gag**; reject; be seasick, feed the fish

27 <nonformal terms> **puke**, upchuck, chuck up, urp, oops, oops up, shoot *or* blow *or* toss one's cookies *or* lunch, barf, ralph, ralph up, blow grits

28 **belch, burp** <nonformal>, eruct, eructate; **hiccup**

29 **fart** <nonformal>, let *or* lay *or* cut a fart <nonformal>, let *or* break wind

ADJS 30 **ejective, expulsive**, ejaculative, emissive, extrusive; eliminant; vomitive, vomitory; eructative; flatulent, flatuous; **rejected** 372.3, rejective

INTERJS 31 **go away!**, begone!, get you gone!, go along!, get along!, **run along!**, **get along with you!**, away!, away with you!, **off with you!**, off you go!, on your way!, go about your business!, be off!, **get out of here!**, get out!, clear out!, leave!, *allez!* <Fr>, *allez-vous-en!* <Fr>, *va-t'-en!* <Fr>, *raus mit dir!* <Ger>, *heraus!* <Ger>, *¡váyase!* <Sp>, *via!* or *va' via!* <Ital>, shoo!, scat!, git! <nonformal>, "stand not on the order of your going, but go at once"—Shakespeare, "go and hang yourself"—Plautus

32 <nonformal terms> **beat it!, scram!**, buzz off!, bug off!, shoo!, skiddoo!, skedaddle!, vamoose!, cheese it!, make yourself scarce!, **get lost!**, take a walk!, take a hike!, go chase yourself!, go play in the traffic!, get the hell out!, push off!, shove off!, take a powder!, blow!

909 OVERRUNNING

NOUNS 1 **overrunning, overgoing, overpassing**; overrun, overpass; **overspreading**, overgrowth; inundation, whelming, overwhelming; burying, burial; seizure, taking 480; overflowing 238.6; exaggeration 355; surplus, excess 992; superiority 249

2 **infestation**, infestment; **invasion**, swarming, swarm, teeming, ravage, plague; **overrunning, overswarming**, overspreading; lousiness, pediculosis

3 **overstepping, transgression, trespass,** inroad, usurpation, incursion, intrusion, **encroachment,** infraction, **infringement**

VERBS 4 **overrun, overgo, overpass**, overreach, go beyond; overstep, overstride; overleap, overjump; **overshoot**, overshoot

the mark, overshoot the field; exaggerate 355.3; superabound, exceed, **overdo** 992.10

5 **overspread**, bespread, spread over; **overgrow**, grow over, run riot, cover, swarm over, teem over

6 **infest, beset,** invade, swarm, ravage, plague; **overrun, overswarm**, overspread; **creep with, crawl with**, swarm with; seize 480.14

7 **run over**, overrun; **ride over**, override, **run down**, ride down; **trample, trample on** *or* **upon**, trample down, tread upon, step on, walk on *or* over, trample underfoot, **ride roughshod over;** hit-and-run; **inundate, whelm, overwhelm;** overflow 238.17; shout down

8 **pass, go** *or* **pass by**, get *or* shoot ahead of; bypass; **pass over, cross,** go across, ford; step over, overstride, bestride, straddle

9 **overstep, transgress, trespass**, intrude, break bounds, overstep the bounds, go too far, know no bounds, **encroach, infringe**, invade, irrupt, make an inroad *or* incursion *or* intrusion, advance upon; usurp

ADJS 10 **overrun, overspread**, overpassed, bespread; overgrown; inundated, whelmed, overwhelmed; buried

11 **infested**, beset, ravaged, teeming, lagued; lousy, pediculous, pedicular; wormy, grubby; ratty

910 SHORTCOMING
<motion or action short of>

NOUNS 1 **shortcoming**, falling short, not measuring up, coming up short, **shortfall; shortage**, short measure, underage, deficit; **inadequacy** 794.1; insufficiency 991; delinquency; **default**, defalcation; arrear, **arrears**, arrearage; decline, slump; defectiveness, imperfection 1002; **inferiority** 250; **undercommitment; failure** 410

VERBS 2 **fall short, come short, run short**, stop short, not make the course, not reach; not measure up, not hack it *and* not make the grade *and* not make the cut <all nonformal>, not make it, not make out; want, want for, lack, not have it <nonformal>, **be found wanting**, not answer, not fill the bill, not suffice; not reach to, not stretch; decline, lag, lose ground, slump, collapse, fall away, run out of gas *or* steam; **lose out, fail** 410.9

3 **fall through**, fall down, **fall to the ground**, fall flat, **collapse**, break down; get bogged down, get mired, get mired down, get hung up, come to nothing, come to

naught, end up *or* go up in smoke; **fizzle** *or* peter *or* poop out <nonformal>; fall *or* drop by the wayside, end "not with a bang but a whimper"—T S Eliot

4 **miss, miscarry, go amiss,** go astray, **miss the mark,** miss by a mile <nonformal>; misfire; **miss out,** miss the boat *or* bus; miss stays, miss one's mooring

ADJS 5 **short of,** short, fresh *or* clean out of <nonformal>, not all *or* what it is cracked up to be; **deficient, inadequate** 794.4; **insufficient** 991.9; undercommitted; **inferior** 250.6; **lacking,** wanting, minus; unreached

ADVS 6 **behind, behindhand, in arrears** *or* arrear

7 **amiss, astray, beside the mark,** below the mark, beside the point, far from it, to no purpose, in vain, vainly, fruitlessly, bootlessly

911 ELEVATION
<act of raising>

NOUNS 1 **elevation, raising, lifting,** upping, boosting *and* hiking <both nonformal>; **rearing,** escalation, **erection;** uprearing, uplifting; upbuoying; **uplift,** upheaval, upthrow, upcast, upthrust; **exaltation;** apotheosis, deification; beatification, canonization; enshrinement, assumption; *sursum corda* <L>; height 272; ascent 193; increase 251

2 **lift, boost** *and* **hike** <both nonformal>, hoist, heave; a leg up

3 **lifter, erector;** crane, derrick, gantry crane, crab; **jack,** jackscrew; **hoist,** lift, hydraulic lift; forklift; hydraulic tailgate; lever 905.4; windlass 905.7; tackle

4 **elevator,** *ascenseur* <Fr>, **lift** <Brit>; escalator, moving staircase *or* stairway; dumbwaiter

VERBS 5 **elevate, raise, rear,** escalate, up, boost *and* hike <both nonformal>; **erect, heighten, lift,** levitate, boost <nonformal>, **hoist,** heist <nonformal>, heft, heave; raise up, rear up, lift up, hold up, set up; stick up, cock up, perk up; buoy up, upbuoy; **upraise, uplift,** uphold, uprear, uphoist; upheave, upthrow, upcast; throw up, cast up; jerk up, hike <nonformal>; knock up, lob, loft; sky <nonformal>

6 **exalt,** elevate, ensky; deify, apotheosize; beatify, canonize; enshrine; put on a pedestal

7 **give a lift,** give a boost, give a leg up <nonformal>, **help up,** put on; mount, horse

8 **pick up,** take up, pluck up, **gather up;** draw up, fish up, haul up, drag up; dredge, dredge up

ADJS 9 **raised, lifted, elevated;** upraised, **uplifted,** upcast; **reared,** upreared; rearing, rampant; upthrown, upflung; **exalted, lofty;** deified, apotheosized; canonized, sainted, beatified; enshrined, sublime; stilted, on stilts; erect, upright 200.11; high 272.19

10 **elevating,** elevatory, escalatory; lifting; **uplifting;** erective, erectile

912 DEPRESSION
<act of lowering>

NOUNS 1 **depression, lowering; sinking;** ducking, submergence, pushing *or* thrusting under, down-thrust, down-thrusting, detrusion, pushing *or* pulling *or* hauling down; reduction, de-escalation, diminution; demotion 447, debasement, degradation; concavity, hollowness 284.1; descent 194; decrease 252

2 **downthrow,** downcast; **overthrow,** overturn 205.2; **precipitation,** fall, downfall; downpour, downpouring

3 **crouch, stoop,** bend, squat; **bow,** genuflection, kneeling, kowtow, kowtowing, salaam, reverence, obeisance, **curtsy;** bob, duck, nod; prostration, supination; crawling, groveling; abasement, self-abasement

VERBS 4 **depress, lower,** let *or* take down, debase, de-escalate, **sink,** bring low, reduce, couch; pull *or* haul down, take down a peg <nonformal>; bear down, downbear; thrust *or* press *or* push down, detrude; indent 284.14

5 **fell, drop, bring down,** fetch down, down <nonformal>, take down, take down a peg, lay low; **raze,** rase, raze to the ground; **level,** lay level; pull down, pull about one's ears; **cut down,** chop down, hew down, whack down <nonformal>, mow down; **knock down,** dash down, send headlong, **floor,** deck *and* lay out <both nonformal>, lay by the heels, ground, **bowl down** *or* **over** <nonformal>; trip, trip up, topple, tumble; **prostrate,** supinate; **throw,** throw *or* fling *or* cast down, **precipitate;** bulldog; spread-eagle <nonformal>, pin, pin down; blow over *or* down

6 **overthrow,** overturn 205.6; depose 447.4; demote 447.3

7 **drop, let go of,** let drop *or* fall

8 **crouch, duck,** cringe, **cower; stoop, bend, stoop down, squat,** squat down, get

down, hunker *and* hunker down *and* get
down on one's hunkers <all nonformal>;
hunch, hunch down, hunch over, scrooch
or scrouch down <nonformal>

9 **bow, bend, kneel,** genuflect, bend the
knee, **curtsy,** make a low bow, make a leg,
make a reverence *or* an obeisance,
salaam, bob, duck, **kowtow,** prostrate
oneself; crawl, grovel; wallow, welter

10 **sit down,** seat oneself, **be seated** 173.10

11 **lie down,** couch, drape oneself, **recline**
201.5; prostrate, supinate, prone <non-
formal>; flatten oneself, prostrate oneself; hit the ground *or* the dirt <nonfor-
mal>

ADJS 12 **depressed, lowered,** debased, reduced, **fallen;** sunk, **sunken,** submerged;
downcast, downthrown; prostrated, prostrate 201.8; low, at a low ebb

913 CIRCUITOUSNESS

NOUNS 1 **circuitousness,** circuity, circuition
<old>; **roundaboutness,** indirection, am-
bagiousness <old>, meandering, deviance *or* deviancy, **deviation** 164; deviousness, **digression,** circumlocution 538.5;
excursion, excursus; **circling, wheeling,**
circulation, rounding, orbit, **orbiting; spiraling,** spiral, gyring, gyre; circumambu-
lation, circumambience *or* circumambiency, circumflexion, circumnavigation,
circummigration; turning, **turn** 164.1;
circularity 280; convolution 281

2 **circuit, round,** revolution, **circle,** full circle, go-round, **cycle,** orbit, ambit; pass;
round trip, *aller-retour* <Fr>; **beat,**
rounds, **walk,** tour, turn, lap, loop; round
robin

3 **detour, bypass, roundabout way,** roundabout, ambages <old>, circuit, circumbendibus <nonformal>, the long way
around, digression, deviation, excursion

VERBS 4 **go roundabout,** meander, deviate,
go around Robin Hood's barn, take *or* go
the long way around, twist and turn; **detour,** make a detour, **go around,** go round
about, go out of one's way, **bypass;** deviate 164.3; digress 538.9; **talk in circles,**
say in a roundabout way; equivocate
935.9, shilly-shally; dodge 368.8

5 **circle, circuit,** describe a circle, make a
circuit, move in a circle, **circulate; go
round** *or* **around,** go about; **wheel,** orbit,
round; make a pass; come full circle,
close the circle, make a round trip, return
to the starting point; cycle; spiral, gyre;
go around in circles, chase one's tail, go

round and round; revolve 914.9; **compass,** encompass, encircle, surround;
skirt, flank; go the round, make the round
of, make one's rounds, circuiteer <old>;
lap; circumambulate, circummigrate;
circumnavigate, girdle, girdle the globe,
"put a girdle round about the earth"—
Shakespeare

6 **turn, go around, round,** turn *or* round a
corner, corner, round a bend, double *or*
round a point

ADJS 7 **circuitous, roundabout, out-of-the-
way, devious, oblique, indirect,** ambagious <old>, meandering, backhanded;
deviative 164.7, **deviating,** digressive, discursive, excursive; equivocatory 935.14;
evasive 368.15; vacillating 362.10; **circular** 280.11, **round,** wheel-shaped,
O-shaped; spiral, helical; orbital; rotary
914.15

8 circumambient, circumambulatory, circumforaneous, circumfluent, circumvo-
lant, circumnavigatory, circumnavi-
gable

ADVS 9 **circuitously, deviously, obliquely,**
ambagiously <old> **indirectly, round
about,** about it and about, round Robin
Hood's barn, in a roundabout way, by a
side door, by a side wind; circlewise,
wheelwise

914 ROTATION

NOUNS 1 **rotation, revolution,** roll, **gyration,
spin,** circulation; axial motion, rotational
motion, angular motion, angular momentum, angular velocity; circumrotation,
circumgyration, full circle; **turning,
whirling,** swirling, **spinning,** wheeling,
reeling, whir; **spiraling,** twisting upward
or downward, gyring, volution, turbina-
tion; centrifugation; swiveling, pivoting,
swinging; **rolling,** trolling, trundling,
bowling, volutation <old>

2 **whirl,** wheel, reel, **spin, turn,** round; spiral, helix, helicoid, gyre; pirouette; **swirl,**
twirl, **eddy,** gurge, surge; vortex, **whirlpool,** maelstrom, Charybdis; dizzy round,
rat race; tourbillion, **whirlwind** 318.14

3 revolutions, **revs** <nonformal>; revolutions per minute *or* rpm

4 **rotator, rotor; roller,** rundle; **whirler,**
whirligig, **top,** whirlabout; **merry-go-
round,** carousel, roundabout; **wheel,** disk;
Ixion's wheel; rolling stone

5 **axle, axis; pivot,** gudgeon, trunnion,
swivel, spindle, arbor, pole, radiant; fulcrum 900.2; pin, pintle; **hub,** nave; axle
shaft, axle spindle, axle bar, axle-tree;

distaff; mandrel; gimbal; **hinge,** hingle
<nonformal>; rowlock, oarlock

6 **axle box,** journal, journal box; hotbox

7 **bearing,** ball bearing, journal bearing,
saw bearing, tumbler bearing, main bearing, needle bearing, roller bearing, thrust
bearing, bevel bearing, bushing; jewel;
headstock

8 <science of rotation> trochilics, gyrosta-
tics

VERBS 9 **rotate, revolve, spin, turn,** round,
go round or **around,** turn round or
around; **spiral, gyrate,** gyre; circumro-
tate, circumvolute; circle, circulate;
swivel, pivot, wheel, swing; pirouette,
turn a pirouette; wind, twist, screw,
crank; wamble

10 **roll,** trundle, troll, **bowl;** roll up, **furl**

11 **whirl,** whirligig, twirl, **wheel, reel, spin,**
spin like a top or teetotum, whirl like a
dervish; centrifuge, centrifugate; **swirl,**
gurge, surge, **eddy,** whirlpool

12 <move around in confusion> **seethe,**
mill, mill around or about, stir, roil, moil,
be turbulent

13 <roll about in> **wallow, welter,** grovel,
roll, flounder, tumble

ADJS 14 **rotating, revolving, turning,** gyrat-
ing; **whirling, swirling,** twirling, **spin-**
ning, wheeling, **reeling; rolling,** trolling,
bowling

15 **rotary, rotational,** rotatory, rotative;
trochilic, vertiginous; circumrotatory,
circumvolutory, circumgyratory; spiral,
spiralling, helical, gyral, gyratory, gyrational, gyroscopic, gyrostatic; whirly,
swirly, gulfy; whirlabout, whirligig; vortical, cyclonic, tornadic, whirlwindy,
whirlwindish

ADVS 16 **round, around,** round about, **in a**
circle; round and round, in circles, like a
horse in a mill; in a whirl, in a spin; head
over heels, heels over head; clockwise,
counterclockwise, anticlockwise, widdershins

915 OSCILLATION
<motion to and fro>

NOUNS 1 **oscillation, vibration,** vibrancy; to-
and-fro motion; harmonic motion, simple
harmonic motion; libration, nutation;
pendulation; **fluctuation,** vacillation, wavering 362.2; libration of the moon, libration in latitude or longitude; vibratility;
frequency, frequency band or spectrum;
resonance, resonant or resonance frequency; **periodicity** 849.2

2 **waving,** wave motion, **undulation,** undu-

lancy; **brandishing, flourishing,** flaunting, shaking; brandish, flaunt, flourish;
wave 238.14

3 **pulsation, pulse, beat, throb;** beating,
throbbing; systole, diastole; rat-a-tat,
staccato, rataplan, drumming 55.1;
rhythm, tempo 709.24; **palpitation,** flutter, arrhythmia, pitter-patter, pit-a-pat;
fibrillation, ventricular fibrillation, tachycardia, ventricular tachycardia <all
medicine>; **heartbeat,** heartthrob

4 **wave,** wave motion, **ray;** transverse
wave, longitudinal wave; electromagnetic wave, electromagnetic radiation; **light**
1024; **radio wave** 1033.11; mechanical
wave; acoustic wave, **sound wave** 50.1;
seismic wave, **shock wave;** de Broglie
wave; diffracted wave, guided wave; one-
or two- or three-dimensional wave; periodic wave; standing wave, node, anti-
node; surface wave, **tidal wave,** tsunami;
traveling wave; surge, storm surge; amplitude, crest, trough; scend; **surf,** roller,
curler, comber, whitecap, white horse;
tube; wavelength; frequency, frequency
band or spectrum; resonance, resonant or
resonance frequency; period; wave number; diffraction; reinforcement, interference; in phase, out of phase; wave equation, Schrödinger equation; Huygens'
principle

5 **alternation, reciprocation;** regular or
rhythmic play, **coming and going,** to-and-
fro, back-and-forth, ebb and flow, *va-et-*
vien <Fr>, flux and reflux, systole and diastole, ups and downs; sine wave, Lissajous figure or curve; **seesawing,** teetering, tottering, **teeter-tottering;** seesaw,
teeter, teeter-totter, wigwag; zig-zag, zig-
zagging, zig, zag

6 **swing,** swinging, **sway,** swag; **rock, lurch,**
roll, reel, careen; wag, waggle, wave, waver

7 seismicity, seismism; seismology, seis-
mography, seismometry

8 <instruments> oscilloscope, oscillo-
graph, oscillometer; wavemeter; har-
monograph; vibroscope, vibrograph;
kymograph; seismoscope, seismograph,
seismometer; wave gauge

9 **oscillator, vibrator;** pendulum, pendulum wheel; metronome; swing; seesaw, teeter, teeter-totter, teeterboard,
teetery-bender; rocker, rocking chair;
rocking stone, logan stone, shuttle; shuttlecock

VERBS 10 **oscillate, vibrate,** librate, nutate;
pendulate; **fluctuate,** vacillate, waver,
wave; resonate; **swing, sway,** swag, dan-

gle, **reel, rock, lurch, roll**, careen, toss, pitch; **wag**, waggle; **wobble**, coggle <Scots>, wamble; **bob**, bobble; shake, flutter 916.10,12

11 **wave, undulate; brandish, flourish,** flaunt, shake, swing, wield; float, fly; **flap, flutter;** wag, wigwag

12 **pulsate, pulse, beat, throb**, not miss a beat; **palpitate**, go pit-a-pat; miss a beat; beat time, beat out, tick, ticktock; drum 55.4

13 **alternate**, reciprocate, swing, **go to and fro**, to-and-fro, **come and go**, pass and repass, ebb and flow, wax and wane, ride and tie, hitch and hike, back and fill; **seesaw**, teeter, **teeter-totter;** shuttle, shuttlecock, battledore and shuttlecock; **wigwag**, wibble-wabble; zigzag

14 <move up and down> **pump, shake,** bounce

ADJS 15 **oscillating**, oscillatory; **vibrating**, vibratory, harmonic; vibratile; librational, libratory; nutational; **periodic**, pendular, pendulous; **fluctuating**, fluctuational, fluctuant; wavering; vacillating, vacillatory; resonant

16 **waving, undulating**, undulatory, undulant

17 **swinging, swaying**, dangling, **reeling, rocking, lurching**, careening, **rolling**, tossing, pitching

18 pulsative, pulsatory, pulsatile; **pulsating, pulsing, beating, throbbing, palpitating**, palpitant, pit-a-pat, staccato; rhythmic 709.28

19 **alternate, reciprocal**, reciprocative; sinewave; **back-and-forth, to-and-fro**, up-and-down, seesaw

20 seismatical, seismological, seismographic, seismometric; successive, succussatory, sussultatory

ADVS 21 **to and fro, back and forth**, backward and forward, backwards and forwards, **in and out, up and down**, seesaw, shuttlewise, from side to side, from pillar to post, off and on, ride and tie, hitch and hike, round and round, like buckets in a well

916 AGITATION
<irregular motion>

NOUNS 1 **agitation, perturbation**, hecticness, conturbation <old>; **frenzy, excitement** 105; **trepidation** 127.5, trepidity, fidgets *and* jitters *and* ants in the pants <all nonformal>, antsiness *and* jitteriness <both nonformal>, jumpiness, nervousness, yips <nonformal>, nervi-

ness <Brit>, nervosity, twitter, upset; **unrest, malaise, unease**, restlessness; fever, feverishness, febrility; **disquiet**, disquietude, inquietude, discomposure; **stir, churn, ferment**, fermentation, foment; seethe, seething, ebullition, boil, boiling; embroilment, roil, turbidity, fume, **disturbance, commotion**, moil, **turmoil, turbulence** 671.2, **swirl, tumult**, tumultuation, hubbub, shemozzle <Brit nonformal>, rout, fuss, row, to-do, bluster, fluster, flurry, flutteration, hoo-ha *and* flap <both nonformal>, bustle, brouhaha, bobbery, hurly-burly; maelstrom; **disorder** 809

2 **shaking, quaking**, palsy, **quivering, quavering, shivering, trembling**, tremulousness, **shuddering, vibration**; juddering <Brit>, succussion; jerkiness, fits and starts, spasms; jactation, jactitation; joltiness, bumpiness, the shakes *and* the shivers *and* the cold shivers <all nonformal>, ague, chattering; chorea, St Vitus's dance; delirium tremens *or* the DT's

3 **shake, quake, quiver, quaver**, falter, **tremor, tremble, shiver, shudder**, twitter, didder, dither; **wobble; bob**, bobble; **jog**, joggle; **shock, jolt**, jar, jostle; **bounce**, bump; **jerk, twitch**, tic, grimace, rictus; jig, jiggle

4 **flutter**, flitter, flit, **flicker, waver**, dance; shake, quiver 916.3; **sputter, splutter; flap**, flop <nonformal>; **beat**, beating; **palpitation**, throb, pit-a-pat, pitter-patter

5 **twitching, jerking**, vellication; **fidgets**, fidgetiness; itchiness, formication, pruritus

6 **spasm, convulsion**, cramp, **paroxysm**, throes; **orgasm**, sexual climax; epitasis, eclampsia; **seizure**, grip, attack, **fit**, access, ictus; epilepsy, falling sickness; stroke, apoplexy

7 **wiggle, wriggle;** wag, waggle; writhe, **squirm**

8 **flounder**, flounce, stagger, totter, stumble, falter; wallow, welter; **roll, rock, reel, lurch**, careen, **swing, sway; toss, tumble**, pitch, plunge

9 <instruments> **agitator**, shaker, jiggler, vibrator; beater, stirrer, paddle, whisk, eggbeater; churn; blender

VERBS 10 **agitate, shake, disturb, perturb**, shake up, perturbate, **disquiet, discompose, upset, trouble, unsettle, stir**, swirl, flurry, flutter, flutter the dovecot, fret, roughen, ruffle, rumple, ripple, ferment, convulse; **churn**, whip, whisk, beat, paddle; **excite** 105.11; **stir up**, cause a stir *or*

commotion, shake up a hornet's nest
<nonformal>; work up, shake up, churn
up, whip up, beat up; roil, rile <nonfor-
mal>; disarrange 810.2

11 **shake, quake, vibrate,** jactitate; **tremble,
quiver, quaver,** falter, **shudder, shiver,**
twitter, didder, chatter; shake in one's
boots *or* shoes, quake *or* shake *or* tremble
like an aspen leaf, have the jitters *or* the
shakes <nonformal>, have ants in one's
pants <nonformal>; have an ague; **wobble; bob,** bobble; **jog, joggle; shock, jolt,**
jar, jostle, hustle, jounce, **bounce,** jump,
bump

12 **flutter,** flitter, flit, flick, **flicker,** gutter,
bicker, wave, **waver,** dance; **sputter,
splutter; flap,** flop <nonformal>, flip,
beat, slat; **palpitate,** pulse, throb, pitter-
patter, go pit-a-pat

13 **twitch, jerk,** vellicate; itch; **jig, jiggle,**
jigger *or* jigget <nonformal>; **fidget,**
have the fidgets

14 **wiggle, wriggle;** wag, waggle; **writhe,
squirm,** twist and turn; have ants in one's
pants <nonformal>

15 **flounder,** flounce, **stagger,** totter, stumble, falter, blunder, wallop; **struggle,**
labor; **wallow, welter; roll, rock, reel,**
lurch, careen, career, **swing, sway; toss,
tumble,** thrash about, **pitch, plunge,**
pitch and plunge, toss and tumble, toss
and turn, be the sport of winds and
waves; **seethe**

ADJS 16 **agitated, disturbed, perturbed, disquieted, discomposed, troubled, upset,
ruffled,** flurried, flustered, unsettled;
stirred up, shaken, shaken up, all worked
up, all shook up <nonformal>; troublous, feverish, fidgety *and* jittery *and*
antsy <all nonformal>, jumpy, nervous,
nervy <Brit>, restless, **uneasy,** unquiet,
unpeaceful; all of a twitter <nonfor-
mal>, all of a flutter; **turbulent;** excited
105.18,20,22

17 **shaking, vibrating,** chattering; **quivering,
quavering, quaking, shivering, shuddering, trembling, tremulous,** palsied,
aspen; successive, succussatory; **shaky,**
quivery, quavery, shivery, trembly; wobbly

18 **fluttering, flickering, wavering,** guttering, dancing; sputtering, spluttering,
sputtery; fluttery, flickery, bickering,
flicky, wavery, unsteady, desultory

19 **jerky,** herky-jerky <nonformal>, twitchy
or twitchety, jerking, **twitching, fidgety,
jumpy,** jiggety <nonformal>, vellicative;
spastic, spasmodic, eclamptic, orgasmic,
convulsive; fitful, saltatory

20 **jolting,** jolty, **joggling,** joggly, jogglety,
jouncy, **bouncy, bumpy,** choppy, rough;
jarring, bone-bruising

21 **wriggly,** wriggling, crawly, creepy-
crawly <nonformal>; **wiggly,** wiggling;
squirmy, squirming; writhy, writhing,
antsy <nonformal>

ADVS 22 **agitatedly, troublously, restlessly,**
uneasily, unquietly, unpeacefully, nervously, feverishly; **excitedly**

23 **shakily,** quiveringly, quaveringly, quakingly, **tremblingly,** shudderingly, tremulously; flutteringly, waveringly, unsteadily, desultorily; **jerkily,** spasmodically, fitfully, by jerks, by snatches, salta-
torily, by fits and starts, "with many a
flirt and flutter"—Pope

917 SPECTATOR

NOUNS 1 **spectator, observer; looker, onlooker,** looker-on, **watcher,** gazer, gazer-
on, gaper, goggler, **viewer,** seer, beholder,
perceiver, percipient; spectatress, spec-
tatrix; **witness, eyewitness; bystander,**
passerby; innocent bystander; sidewalk
superintendent; kibitzer; girl-watcher,
ogler, drugstore cowboy <nonformal>;
bird-watcher; **viewer,** television-viewer,
televiewer, video-gazer, TV-viewer,
couch potato <nonformal>

2 **attender** 221.5, attendee; theatergoer; **audience** 48.6, house, crowd, gate, fans

3 **sightseer,** excursionist, **tourist,** rubberneck *or* **rubbernecker** <nonformal>;
slummer; tour group

4 **sight-seeing,** rubbernecking <nonfor-
mal>, lionism <Brit nonformal>; **tour,**
walking tour, bus tour, sightseeing tour
or excursion, **rubberneck tour** <nonfor-
mal>

VERBS 5 spectate <nonformal>, witness,
see 27.12, look on, eye, **ogle, gape;** take in,
look at, watch; attend 221.8

6 **sight-see,** see the sights, take in the
sights, lionize *or* see the lions <both Brit
nonformal>; **rubberneck** <nonformal>;
go slumming; go on a tour, join a tour

ADJS 7 **spectating, spectatorial;** onlooking;
sight-seeing, rubberneck <nonformal>;
passing by, caught in the cross-fire *or* in
the middle

918 INTELLECT
<*mental faculty*>

NOUNS 1 **intellect, mind,** *mens* <L>; mental
or intellectual faculty, nous, **reason, rationality,** rational *or* reasoning faculty,

power of reason, *Vernunft* <Ger>, *esprit* <Fr>, *raison* <Fr>, ratio, discursive reason, "discourse of reason"—Shakespeare, **intelligence,** mentality, mental capacity, **understanding,** reasoning, intellection, conception; **brain, brains,** brainpower, smarts *and* gray matter <both nonformal>; **thought** 930; head, headpiece

2 **wits, senses, faculties,** parts, capacities, intellectual gifts *or* talents, mother wit; intellectuals <old>; consciousness 927.2

3 **inmost mind,** inner recesses of the mind, mind's core, deepest mind, center of the mind; inner man; subconscious, subconscious mind; inmost heart

4 **psyche, spirit,** spiritus, **soul,** *âme* <Fr>, **heart, mind,** anima, *anima humana* <L>; shade, shadow, manes; breath, pneuma, breath of life, divine breath; *atman and purusha and buddhi and jiva* and *jivatma* <all Skt>; *ba and khu* <both Egyptian myth>; *ruach and nephesh* <both Hebrew>; spiritual being, inner man, "the Divinity that stirs within us"—Addison; **ego,** the self, the I

5 **life principle,** vital principle, vital spirit *or* soul, *élan vital*—<Henri Bergson> <Fr>, **vital force,** prana <Hinduism>; essence *or* substance of life, individual essence, *ousia* <Gk>; divine spark, vital spark *or* flame

6 **brain** 2.13, seat *or* organ of thought; sensory, sensorium; encephalon; gray matter, head, pate *and* sconce *and* noddle <all nonformal>; noodle *or* noggin *or* bean *or* upper story <all nonformal>; sensation 24

ADJS 7 **mental, intellectual, rational, reasoning, thinking,** noetic, conceptive, conceptual, phrenic; intelligent 919.12; noological; endopsychic, psychic, psychical, psychologic, psychological, spiritual; cerebral; subjective, internal

919 INTELLIGENCE, WISDOM
<mental capacity>

NOUNS 1 **intelligence, understanding,** *Verstand* <Ger>, **comprehension,** apprehension, mental *or* intellectual grasp, prehensility of mind, intellectual power, brainpower, thinking power, power of mind *or* thought; ideation, conception; integrative power, esemplastic power; rationality, reasoning *or* deductive power, ratiocination; **sense, wit,** mother wit, natural *or* native wit; **intellect** 918; **intellectuality,** intellectualism; capacity,

mental capacity, **mentality,** caliber, reach *or* compass *or* scope of mind; **IQ** *or* intelligence quotient, mental ratio, mental age; sanity 924; knowledge 927

2 **smartness, braininess,** smarts *and* savvy <both nonformal>, **brightness, brilliance, cleverness,** aptness, aptitude, native cleverness, mental alertness, nous, **sharpness, keenness,** acuity, acuteness; **mental ability** *or* **capability,** gift, gifts, giftedness, **talent, flair, genius;** quickness, nimbleness, quickness *or* nimbleness of wit, adroitness, dexterity; sharp-wittedness, keen-wittedness, quick-wittedness, nimble-wittedness; nimble mind, mercurial mind, quick parts, clear *or* quick thinking; ready wit, quick wit, sprightly wit, *esprit* <Fr>

3 **shrewdness, artfulness, cunning,** cunningness, canniness, **craft, craftiness,** wiliness, guilefulness, slickness <nonformal>, **slyness,** pawkiness <Brit>, foxiness <nonformal>, peasant *or* animal cunning, low cunning; subtility, subtilty, **subtlety;** insinuation, insidiousness, deviousness

4 **sagacity,** sagaciousness, **astuteness, acumen,** longheadedness; **foresight,** foresightedness, providence; **farsightedness,** farseeingness, longsightedness; **discernment, insight,** penetration, acuteness, acuity; perspicacity, perspicaciousness, perspicuity, perspicuousness; incisiveness, trenchancy, cogency; **percipience** *or* percipiency, **perception,** apperception; **sensibility** 24.2

5 **wisdom,** ripe wisdom, seasoned understanding, mellow wisdom, wiseness, sageness, sapience, good *or* sound understanding; Sophia <female personification of wisdom>; erudition 927.5; **profundity,** profoundness, depth; broad-mindedness 978; **conventional wisdom,** received wisdom, prudential judgment

6 **sensibleness, reasonableness,** reason, rationality, sanity, saneness, **soundness; practicality,** practical wisdom, practical mind; **sense,** good *or* common *or* plain sense, **horse sense** <nonformal>; due sense of; level head, cool head, **levelheadedness,** balance, coolheadedness, coolness; soberness, sobriety, **sobermindedness**

7 **judiciousness, judgment,** good *or* sound judgment, cool judgment, soundness of judgment; **prudence,** prudentialism, providence, policy, polity; weighing, consideration, circumspection, circumspectness, reflection, reflectiveness, **thought-**

fulness; **discretion**, discreetness; **discrimination**

8 **genius**, *Geist* <Ger>, spirit, soul; daimonion, demon, daemon; **inspiration**, afflatus, divine afflatus; Muse; fire of genius; **creativity**; talent 413.4; creative thought 985.2

9 <intelligent being> **intelligence**, **intellect**, head, brain, mentality, consciousness; wise man 920

VERBS 10 **have all one's wits about one**, have all one's marbles *and* have smarts *or* savvy <all nonformal>, have a head on one's shoulders *and* have one's head screwed on right <both nonformal>; have method in one's madness; use one's head *or* wits, get *or* keep one's wits about one; know what's what, be wise as a serpent *or* an owl; be reasonable, listen to reason

11 be brilliant, **scintillate**, sparkle, coruscate

ADJS 12 **intelligent**, intellectual <old>; ideational, conceptual, conceptive, discursive; sophic, noetic; **knowing, understanding, reasonable, rational, sensible, bright**; sane 924.4; not so dumb <nonformal>, strong-minded

13 **clear-witted**, clearheaded, clear-eyed, clear-sighted; no-nonsense; awake, **wideawake**, alive, **alert**, on the ball <nonformal>

14 **smart, brainy** <nonformal>, **bright, brilliant**, scintillating; **clever**, apt, **gifted**, talented; **sharp**, keen; **quick**, nimble, adroit, dexterous; **sharp-witted**, keen-witted, needle-witted, **quick-witted**, quick-thinking, steel-trap, nimble-witted, quick on the trigger *or* uptake <nonformal>; smart as a whip, sharp as a tack <nonformal>; nobody's fool *and* no dumbbell *and* not born yesterday <all nonformal>

15 **shrewd, artful, cunning, knowing, crafty, wily**, guileful, canny, slick, sly, pawky <Brit>, smart as a fox, foxy *and* crazy like a fox <both nonformal>; **subtle**, subtile; insinuating, insidious, devious, Byzantine, calculating

16 **sagacious, astute**, longheaded, argute; **understanding, discerning**, penetrating, incisive, acute, trenchant, cogent, piercing; **foresighted**, foreseeing; forethoughted, forethoughtful, provident; **farsighted**, farseeing, longsighted; **perspicacious**, perspicuous; **perceptive, percipient**, apperceptive, apperceptient

17 **wise, sage**, sapient, seasoned, **knowing**; learned 927.21; **profound**, deep; wise as

an owl *or* a serpent, wise as Solomon; wise beyond one's years, in advance of one's age, wise in one's generation; broad-minded 978.8

18 **sensible, reasonable, rational, logical; practical**, pragmatic; philosophical; commonsense, commonsensical <nonformal>; **levelheaded**, balanced, coolheaded, cool, **sound, sane**, sober, **soberminded**, well-balanced

19 **judicious**, judicial, judgmatic, judgmatical, **prudent**, prudential, politic, careful, provident, **considerate**, circumspect, **thoughtful**, reflective, reflecting; **discreet**; discriminative, discriminating; **well-advised**, well-judged, enlightened

ADVS 20 **intelligently, understandingly**, knowingly, discerningly; **reasonably**, rationally, sensibly; **smartly, cleverly; shrewdly**, artfully, cunningly; **wisely**, sagaciously, astutely; **judiciously, prudently**, discreetly, providently, considerately, circumspectly, thoughtfully

920 WISE PERSON

NOUNS 1 **wise man, wise woman, sage**, sapient, man *or* woman of wisdom; **master, mistress**, authority, mastermind, master spirit of the age, oracle; **philosopher**, thinker, lover of wisdom; "he who, seeing the furthest, has the deepest love for mankind"—Maurice Maeterlinck, "the mouth of a wise man is in his heart"—Benjamin Franklin; rabbi; doctor; great soul, mahatma, guru, rishi; *starets* <Russ>, elder, wise old man, elder statesman; illuminate; seer; mentor; **intellect**, man of intellect; mandarin, **intellectual** 928; savant, **scholar** 928.3

2 Solomon, Socrates, Plato, Mentor, Nestor, Confucius, Buddha, Gandhi, Albert Schweitzer, Martin Luther King Jr

3 **the wise**, the intelligent, the sensible, the prudent, the knowing, the understanding

4 Seven Wise Men of Greece, Seven Sages, Seven Wise Masters; Solon, Chilon, Pittacus, Bias, Periander, Epimenides, Cleobulus, Thales

5 Magi, Three Wise Men, Wise Men of the East, Three Kings; Three Kings of Cologne; Gaspar *or* Caspar, Melchior, Balthasar

6 **wiseacre**, wisehead, wiseling, **witling**, wisenheimer <nonformal>, wise guy, smart ass <nonformal>; wise fool; Gothamite, wise man of Gotham, wise man of Chelm

921 UNINTELLIGENCE

NOUNS **1 unintelligence,** unintellectuality <old>, unwisdom, unwiseness, intellectual *or* mental weakness; **senselessness, witlessness, mindlessness,** brainlessness, primal stupidity, *Urdummheit* <Ger>, reasonlessness, lackwittedness, lackbrainedness, slackwittedness, slackmindedness; **irrationality; ignorance** 929; **foolishness** 922; incapacity, ineptitude; low IQ

2 unperceptiveness, imperceptiveness, insensibility, impercipience *or* impercipiency, undiscerningness, unapprehendingness, **incomprehension,** nonunderstanding; **blindness,** mindblindness, purblindness; **unawareness,** lack of awareness, unconsciousness, lack of consciousness; **shortsightedness,** nearsightedness, dimsightedness

3 stupidity, stupidness, *bêtise* <Fr>, **dumbness** <nonformal>, **doltishness,** boobishness, duncery <old>, dullardism, blockishness, cloddishness, lumpishness, sottishness, **asininity,** ninnyism, simpletonianism; oafishness, oafdom, yokelism, loutishness; **density,** denseness, opacity; grossness, crassness, crudeness, boorishness; **dullness,** dopiness <nonformal>, **obtuseness,** sluggishness, bovinity, cowishness, slowness, lethargy, stolidity, hebetude; **dim-wittedness,** dimness, **dullwittedness,** slow-wittedness, beefwittedness, dull-headedness, **thickwittedness,** thick-headedness, unteachability, ineducability; wrongheadedness

4 <nonformal terms> **blockheadedness,** woodenheadedness, klutziness, dunderheadedness, goofiness, jolterheadedness *or* joltheadedness <both Brit>, chowderheadedness, chuckleheadedness, beetleheadedness, chumpiness, numskulledness *or* numskullery, cabbageheadedness, sapheadedness, muttonheadedness, meatheadedness, fatheadedness, boneheadedness, knuckleheadedness, blunderheadedness

5 muddleheadedness, addleheadedness, addlepatedness, puzzleheadedness

6 empty-headedness, empty-mindedness, absence of mind, airheadedness *and* bubbleheadedness <both nonformal>; **vacuity,** vacuousness, vacancy, vacuum, emptiness, mental void, blankness, hollowness, inanity, vapidity, jejunity

7 superficiality, shallowness, unprofundity, lack of depth, unprofoundness, thinness; shallow-wittedness, shallow-

mindedness; **frivolousness,** flightiness, lightness, fluffiness, frothiness, volatility, dizziness *and* ditziness <both nonformal>

8 feeblemindedness, weak-mindedness; infirmity, weakness, feebleness, softness, mushiness <nonformal>

9 mental deficiency, mental retardation, amentia, mental handicap, subnormality, mental defectiveness; **arrested development,** infantilism, retardation, retardment, backwardness; **simplemindedness,** simple-wittedness, simpleness, simplicity; **idiocy,** idiotism <old>, profound idiocy, **imbecility, half-wittedness,** blithering idiocy; moronity, moronism, **cretinism;** mongolism, mongolianism, mongoloid idiocy, Down's syndrome; insanity 925

10 senility, senilism, senile weakness, senile debility, caducity, decrepitude, senectitude, decline; **childishness, second childhood, dotage, dotardism;** anility; senile dementia, senile psychosis, Alzheimer's disease

11 puerility, puerilism, immaturity, **childishness; infantilism,** babyishness

VERBS **12 be stupid,** not have all one's marbles; drool, slobber, drivel, dither, blither, blather, maunder, dote, burble; not see an inch beyond one's nose, not have enough sense to come in out of the rain, not find one's way to first base; lose one's mind *or* marbles

ADJS **13 unintelligent,** unintellectual <old>, **unthinking, unreasoning, irrational,** unwise, inept, **not bright;** ungifted, untalented; **senseless,** insensate; **mindless, witless, reasonless, brainless,** pinbrained, pea-brained, of little brain, headless; **lackwitted,** lackbrained, slackwitted, slackminded, lean-minded, leanwitted, short-witted; **foolish** 922.8; **ignorant** 929.12

14 undiscerning, unperceptive, imperceptive, impercipient, insensible, unapprehending, uncomprehending, nonunderstanding; **shortsighted,** myopic, nearsighted, dim-sighted; **blind,** purblind, mind-blind, blind as a bat; blinded, blindfold, blindfolded

15 stupid, dumb, dullard, **doltish,** blockish, klutzy *and* klutzish <both nonformal>, duncish, duncical, cloddish, clottish <Brit>, chumpish <nonformal>, lumpish, **oafish,** boobish, sottish, **asinine,** lamebrained, Boeotian; **dense,** thick <nonformal>, opaque, gross, crass, fat; bovine, cowish, beef-witted, beef-brained, beefheaded; unteachable, ineducable; wrongheaded

16 **dull, dull of mind, dopey** <nonformal>, **obtuse,** blunt, dim, wooden, heavy, sluggish, slow, **slow-witted,** hebetudinous, **dim-witted, dull-witted,** blunt-witted, dull-brained, dull-headed, dull-pated, **thick-witted,** thick-headed, thick-pated, thick-skulled, thick-brained, fat-witted, gross-witted, gross-headed

17 <nonformal terms> **blockheaded,** woodenheaded, stupidheaded, dumbheaded, dunderheaded, blunderheaded, clueless *or* jolterheaded *or* joltheaded *or* jinglebrained <all Brit>, chowderheaded, chuckleheaded, beetleheaded, nitwitted, numskulled, cabbageheaded, pumpkinheaded, sapheaded, lunkheaded, muttonheaded, meatheaded, fatheaded, boneheaded, knuckleheaded, clodpated; dead from the neck up, dead above *or* between the ears, muscle-bound between the ears; featherheaded, airheaded, bubbleheaded, out to lunch, lunchy, dufus, dufus-assed, spastic, spazzy, three bricks shy of a load, without brain one, not playing with a full deck

18 **muddleheaded, fuddlebrained** *and* scramblebrained <both nonformal>, mixed-up, muddled, addled, addleheaded, **addlepated,** addlebrained, muddybrained, puzzleheaded, blearwitted; dizzy <nonformal>, muzzy, foggy

19 **empty-headed,** empty-minded, emptynoddled, empty-pated, empty-skulled; **vacuous,** vacant, empty, hollow, inane, vapid, jejune, blank, airheaded *and* bubbleheaded <both nonformal>; **rattlebrained,** rattleheaded; scatterbrained 984.16

20 **superficial, shallow, unprofound;** shallow-witted, shallow-minded, shallow-brained, shallow-headed, shallow-pated; **frivolous,** dizzy *and* ditzy <both nonformal>, flighty, light, volatile, frothy, fluffy, **featherbrained, birdwitted, birdbrained**

21 **feebleminded, weak-minded,** weak, feeble, infirm, soft, soft in the head, weak in the upper story <nonformal>

22 **mentally deficient,** mentally defective, mentally handicapped, retarded, **mentally retarded,** backward, arrested, subnormal, not right in the head, **not all there** <nonformal>; **simpleminded,** simplewitted, simple, simpletonian; **halfwitted,** half-baked <nonformal>; **idiotic, moronic, imbecile,** imbecilic, cretinous,

cretinistic, mongoloid, spastic <nonformal>; crackbrained, cracked, crazy; babbling, driveling, slobbering, drooling, blithering, dithering, maundering, burbling

23 **senile,** decrepit, doddering, doddery; **childish,** childlike, in one's second childhood, **doting,** doited <Scots>

24 **puerile,** immature, **childish;** childlike; **infantile,** infantine; **babyish,** babish

ADVS 25 **unintelligently, stupidly;** insensately, foolishly

922 FOOLISHNESS

NOUNS 1 **foolishness, folly,** foolery, foolheadedness, **stupidity, asininity,** *niaiserie* <Fr>; *bêtise* <Fr>; **inanity, fatuity,** fatuousness; ineptitude; **silliness; frivolousness,** frivolity, giddiness, triviality, triflingness, nugacity, desipience; **nonsense,** tomfoolery, poppycock; **senselessness, insensateness, witlessness, thoughtlessness,** brainlessness, mindlessness; **idiocy, imbecility; craziness, madness,** lunacy, **insanity; eccentricity, queerness,** crankiness, crackpottedness; weirdness; screwiness *and* nuttiness *and* wackiness *and* goofiness *and* daffiness *and* battiness *and* sappiness <all nonformal>; zaniness, zanyism, **clownishness, buffoonery,** clowning, fooling *or* horsing *or* dicking around <nonformal>

2 **unwiseness,** unwisdom, **injudiciousness, imprudence;** indiscreetness, **indiscretion,** inconsideration, thoughtlessness, witlessness, inattention, unthoughtfulness, lack of sensitivity; **unreasonableness, unsoundness, unsensibleness,** senselessness, reasonlessness, **irrationality, unreason,** inadvisability; recklessness; childishness, immaturity, puerility, callowness; gullibility, bamboozlability <nonformal>; inexpedience 995; unintelligence 921; pompousness, stuffiness

3 **absurdity,** absurdness, **ridiculousness;** ludicrousness 488.1; **nonsense,** nonsensicality, stuff and nonsense, codswallop <Brit nonformal>, horseshit *and* bullshit <both nonformal>; **preposterousness,** fantasticalness, monstrousness, wildness, **outrageousness**

4 <foolish act> **folly, stupidity,** act of folly, absurdity, *sottise* <Fr>, foolish *or* stupid thing, dumb thing to do <nonformal>; fool *or* fool's trick, dumb trick <nonformal>; **imprudence, indiscretion,** imprudent *or* unwise step; blunder 974.5

5 stultification; infatuation; trivialization

VERBS 6 be foolish; be stupid 921.12; **act** *or*
play the fool; get funny, do the crazy act
or bit *or* shtick <nonformal>; **fool,** tomfool <nonformal>, **trifle,** frivol; **fool** *or*
horse around <nonformal>, dick around
<nonformal>, clown, clown around;
make a fool of oneself, make a monkey of
oneself <nonformal>, stultify oneself, invite ridicule, put oneself out of court, play
the buffoon; **lose one's head, take leave of
one's senses,** go haywire; pass from the
sublime to the ridiculous; strain at a gnat
and swallow a camel; tilt at windmills
  7 stultify, infatuate, turn one's head, befool; gull, dupe; **make a fool of,** make a
monkey of *and* play for a sucker *and* put
on <all nonformal>
ADJS 8 foolish, fool <nonformal>, fool-
headed <nonformal>, **stupid, dumb**
<nonformal>, clueless <Brit nonfor-
mal>, **asinine,** wet <Brit>; buffoonish;
silly, apish, dizzy <nonformal>; **fatuous,**
fatuitous, inept, **inane;** futile; **senseless,
witless, thoughtless,** insensate, brainless;
idiotic, moronic, imbecile, imbecilic,
spastic <nonformal>; **crazy, mad,** daft,
insane; infatuated, besotted, credulous,
gulled, befooled, beguiled, fond, doting,
gaga; sentimental, maudlin; dazed, fuddled
  9 <nonformal terms> **screwy, nutty,** cockeyed, wacky, goofy, daffy, loony, batty,
sappy, kooky, flaky, damn-fool, out of
it, out to lunch, lunchy, dorky, dippy,
doodle-brained, lame, ditzy, dizzy, loony,
loony-tune, dopey, fluffheaded, loopy,
scatty, zerking
 10 unwise, injudicious, **imprudent,** unpolitic, impolitic, contraindicated, **counterproductive;** indiscreet; inconsiderate,
thoughtless, mindless, witless, unthoughtful, unthinking, unreflecting,
unreflective; **unreasonable, unsound, un-
sensible,** senseless, insensate, reasonless,
irrational, reckless, inadvisable; inexpedient 995.5; **ill-advised, ill-considered,** ill-
gauged, ill-judged, ill-imagined, ill-
contrived, ill-devised, on the wrong track,
unconsidered; unadvised, misadvised,
misguided; undiscerning; unforseeing,
unseeing, shortsighted, myopic; suicidal,
self-defeating
 11 absurd, nonsensical, insensate, ridiculous, laughable, ludicrous 488.4; **foolish,
crazy;** preposterous, cockamamie <non-
formal>, fantastic, fantastical, grotesque, monstrous, wild, weird, **outrageous,** incredible, beyond belief, *outré*
<Fr>, extravagant, **bizarre;** high-flown

 12 foolable, befoolable, gullible, bamboozlable <nonformal>; naive, artless, guileless, inexperienced, impressionable; malleable, like putty; persuasible, biddable
ADVS 13 foolishly, stupidly, sillily, idiot-
ically; **unwisely,** injudiciously, imprudently, indiscreetly, inconsiderately;
myopically, blindly, senselessly, unreasonably, thoughtlessly, witlessly, insensately, unthinkingly; absurdly, ridiculously

923 FOOL

NOUNS 1 fool, damn fool, tomfool, perfect
fool, born fool; *schmuck* <Yiddish>; **ass,**
jackass, stupid ass, egregious ass; zany,
clown, buffoon, doodle, sop, milksop;
mome <old>, mooncalf, softhead; figure
of fun; **lunatic** 925.15; **ignoramus** 929.8
  2 stupid person, dolt, dunce, clod, Boeotian, **dullard,** *niais* <Fr>, donkey, yahoo,
thickwit, **dope, nitwit,** dimwit, lackwit,
half-wit, lamebrain, putz, lightweight,
witling
  3 <nonformal terms> **chump, boob,**
booby, sap, prize sap, klutz, basket case,
dingbat, dingdong, ding-a-ling, **ninny,**
ninnyhammer, **nincompoop,** looby,
noddy, saphead, mutt, jerk, jerk-off, asshole, goof, schlemiel, sawney <Brit>,
galoot, gonzo, dumbo, dweeb, dropshop,
dipshit, nerd, twerp, yo-yo
  4 <nonformal terms> **blockhead, airhead,**
bubblehead, fluffhead, featherhead,
woodenhead, dolthead, dumbhead,
dummy, dum-dum, dumbo, dumb cluck,
dodo head, doodoohead, dumbbell, dumb
bunny, stupidhead, dullhead, bufflehead,
bonehead, jughead, thickhead, thickskull,
numskull, putz, lunkhead, chucklehead,
knucklehead, chowderhead, headbanger
and jolterhead <both Brit>, muttonhead,
beefhead, meathead, noodlehead, thim-
blewit, pinhead, pinbrain, peabrain,
cabbagehead, pumpkin head, fathead,
blubberhead, muddlehead, puzzlehead,
addlebrain, addlehead, addlepate, tot-
tyhead <old>, puddinghead, stupe,
mushhead, blunderhead, dunderhead,
dunderpate, clodpate, clodhead, clodpoll,
jobbernowl *and* gaby *and* gowk <all
Brit>
  5 oaf, lout, boor, lubber, oik <Brit>, **gawk,**
gawky, **lummox,** yokel, rube, hick, hayseed, bumpkin, clod, clodhopper
  6 silly, silly Billy <nonformal>, **silly ass,
goose**
  7 scatterbrain, scatterbrains *and* shat-

terbrain *or* shatterplate <both old>, ditz <nonformal>, **rattlebrain**, rattlehead, rattlepate, **harebrain**, featherbrain, shallowbrain, shallowpate <old>, featherhead, giddybrain, giddyhead, giddypate, **flibbertigibbet**

8 **idiot**, driveling *or* blithering *or* adenoidal *or* congenital idiot; **imbecile, moron, half-wit**, natural, natural idiot, born fool, natural-born fool, mental defective, defective; cretin, mongolian *or* mongoloid idiot, basket case *and* spastic *and* spaz <all nonformal>; **simpleton**, simp <nonformal>, juggins *and* jiggins <both nonformal>, clot *and* berk <both Brit nonformal>, golem

9 **dotard**, senile; fogy, **old fogy**, fuddy-duddy, old fart *or* fud

924 SANITY

NOUNS 1 **sanity, saneness**, sanemindedness, soundness, **soundness of mind**, soundmindedness, sound mind, healthy mind, right mind <nonformal>, senses, reason, **rationality**, reasonableness, lucidity, balance, wholesomeness; normalness, normality, normalcy; **mental health;** mental hygiene; mental balance *or* poise *or* equilibrium; sobriety, sober senses; a sound mind in a sound body, *"mens sana in corpore sano"*—Juvenal <L, a healthy mind in a healthy body>; contact with reality; lucid interval; knowing right from wrong

VERBS 2 **come to one's senses**, sober down *or* up, recover one's sanity *or* balance *or* equilibrium, get things into proportion; see in perspective; have all one's marbles <nonformal>; have a good head on one's shoulder

3 **bring to one's senses**, bring to reason

ADJS 4 **sane**, sane-minded, **rational**, reasonable, sensible, **lucid,** normal, wholesome, clearheaded, clearminded, balanced, **sound**, mentally sound, of sound mind, *compos mentis* <L>, sound-minded, healthy-minded, right, right in the head, **in one's right mind**, in possession of one's faculties *or* senses, together *and* all there <both nonformal>; in touch with reality

925 INSANITY, MANIA

NOUNS 1 **insanity**, insaneness, unsaneness, **lunacy, madness**, *folie* <Fr>, **craziness, daftness,** oddness, strangeness, queerness, abnormality; loss of touch *or* contact with reality, loss of mind *or* reason; dementedness, dementia, athymia,

brainsickness, mindsickness, mental sickness, sickness; **criminal insanity,** homicidal mania, hemothymia; **mental illness, mental disease;** brain damage; rabidness, **mania,** furor; alienation, aberration, mental disturbance, **derangement,** distraction, disorientation, mental derangement *or* disorder, unbalance, mental instability, unsoundness, **unsoundness of mind;** unbalanced mind, diseased *or* unsound mind, **sick mind,** disturbed *or* troubled *or* clouded mind, shattered mind, mind overthrown *or* unhinged, darkened mind, disordered mind *or* reason; senselessness, witlessness, reasonlessness, irrationality; possession, pixilation; mental deficiency 921.9

2 <nonformal terms> **nuttiness**, craziness, daffiness, battiness, screwiness, goofiness, kookiness, wackiness, dottiness, pottiness, *mishegas* <Yiddish>, looniness, lunchiness, balminess; bats in the belfry, a screw loose, one wheel in the sand, one sandwich short of a picnic; lame brains

3 **psychosis**, psychopathy, psychopathology, psychopathic condition; certifiability; **neurosis;** psychopathia sexualis, sexual pathology 75.18; pathological drunkenness *or* intoxication, dipsomania; pharmacopsychosis, drug addiction 87.1; moral insanity, psychopathic personality, *folie du doute* <Fr>, abulia 362.4

4 **schizophrenia, dementia praecox,** mental dissociation, dissociation of personality; catatonic schizophrenia, catatonia, hebephrenia, hebephrenic schizophrenia; schizothymia; schizophasia; thought disorder; schizotypal personality; **paranoia,** paraphrenia, paranoiac *or* paranoid psychosis; paranoid schizophrenia

5 **depression, melancholia,** depressive psychosis, dysthymia, barythymia, lypothymia, "moping, melancholy and moonstruck madness"—Milton; melancholia hypochrondriaca; involutional melancholia *or* psychosis; stuporous melancholia, melancholia attonita; flatuous melancholia; melancholia religiosa; postpartum depression; **manic-depressive disorder, bipolar disorder;** cyclothymia, poikilothymia, mood swings

6 **rabies, hydrophobia,** lyssa, canine madness; dumb *or* sullen rabies, paralytic rabies; furious rabies

7 **frenzy, furor,** fury, maniacal excitement, fever, **rage; seizure,** attack, acute episode, episode, **fit,** paroxysm, spasm, **convulsion; snit,** *crise* <Fr>; amok, murderous

<erotic literature>
erotographomania
<ether>
etheromania
<falsities>
pseudomania
<female lust>
nymphomania
<fires> pyromania
<fish>
ichthyomania
<flowers>
anthomania
<food; eating>
phagomania
<food> sitomania
<foreigners>
xenomania
<foul speech>
coprolalomania
<France>
Francomania *or*
Gallomania
<freedom>
eleuthromania
<fur> doramania
<gaiety>
cheromania
<genitals>
edeomania
<Germany>
Germanomania *or*
Teutonomania
<great wealth>
cresomania *or*
plutomania
<Greece>
Grecomania
<grinding one's
teeth>
bruxomania
<hair>
trichomania
<home>
oikomania
<homesickness>
philopatridomania
<horses>
hippomania
<hypnosis>
mesmeromania
<icons> iconomania
<idols> idolomania
<imagined disease>
nosomania
<incurable
insanity>
acromania
<insects>
entomomania
<Italy> Italomania
<joy in complaints>
paramania

<lies;
exaggerations>
mythomania
<light> photomania
<liquor>
dipsomania
<lycanthropy>
lycomania
<male lust>
satyromania
<marriage>
gamomania
<medicines>
pharmacomania
<melancholia>
tristimania
<men> andromania
<mice> musomania
<Mikhail S
Gorbachev>
Gorbymania
<mild mania>
hypomania *or*
submania
<money>
chrematomania
<moral insanity>
pathomania
<movement>
kinesomania
<murder>
homicidomania
<music> melomania
or musicomania
<nakedness>
gymnomania
<narcotics>
letheomania
<night> noctimania
<noise>
phonomania
<novelty>
kainomania
<nudity>
nudomania
<nymphomania>
hysteromania *or*
oestromania *or*
uteromania
<one's own
wisdom>
sophomania
<one's self>
egomania
<one subject>
monomania
<open spaces>
agoramania
<opium> opiomania
<own importance>
megalomania
<penis>
mentulomania

<picking at
growths>
phaneromania
<pinching off one's
hair>
trichorrhexomania
<plants>
florimania
<pleasing
delusions>
amenomania
<pleasure>
hedonomania
<plucking one's
hair>
trichotillomania
<politics>
politicomania
<pornography>
pornographomania
<postage
stamps>
timbromania
<priests>
hieromania
<public
employment>
empleomania
<railroad travel>
siderodromomania
<religion>
entheomania
<reptiles>
ophidiomania
<return home>
nostomania
<running away>
drapetomania
<Russia>
Russomania
<satyriasis>
gynecomania
<sea>
thalassomania
<second coming of
Christ>
parousiamania
<sexual pleasure>
aphrodisiomania *or*
erotomania
<sin>
hamartomania
<sitting>
kathisomania
<sleep>
hypnomania
<snow>
chionomania

37 manias by name
ablutomania
<washing,
bathing>

<solitude>
automania
<speech> lalomania
<spending>
squandermania
<stealing>
kleptomania
<stillness>
eremiomania
<suicide>
autophonomania
<sun> heliomania
<surgery>
tomomania
<symmetry>
symmetromania
<talking>
logomania
<testicles>
orchidomania
<that one is God>
theomania
<theater>
theatromania
phronemomania
<travel> hodomania
<traveling>
dromomania
<tuberculosis>
phthisiomania
<Turkey>
Turkomania
<United States>
Americamania
<wandering>
ecdemiomania
<wanderlust>
poriomania
<washing, bathing>
ablutomania
<water>
hydromania
<wine> enomania *or*
oinomania
<woods> hylomania
<words>
verbomania
<work> ergomania
<writing for
publication>
typomania
<writing verse>
metromania
<writing>
graphomania *or*
scribblemania *or*
scribomania

acromania
<incurable
insanity>

agoramania <open spaces>

agyiomania <streets>

ailuromania <cats>

alcoholomania <alcohol>

amaxomania <being in vehicles>

amenomania <pleasing delusions>

Americamania <United States>

andromania <men>

Anglomania <England>

anthomania <flowers>

aphrodisiomania or erotomania <sexual pleasure>

apimania <bees>

arithmomania <counting>

automania <solitude>

autophonomania <suicide>

ballistomania <bullets>

Beatlemania <the Beatles>

bibliomania <books>

bibliokleptomania <book theft>

bruxomania <grinding one's teeth>

cacodemonomania <demonic possession>

cheromania <gaiety>

Chinamania <China>

chionomania <snow>

choreomania <dancing>

chrematomania <money>

clinomania <bed rest>

coprolalomania <foul speech>

cremnomania <cliffs>

cresomania <great wealth>

cynomania <dogs>

Dantomania <Dante>

demomania <crowds>

dipsomania <liquor>

doramania <fur>

drapetomania <running away>

dromomania <traveling>

ecdemiomania <wandering>

edeomania <genitals>

egomania <one's self>

eleuthromania <freedom>

empleomania <public employment>

enomania <wine>

entheomania <religion>

entomomania <insects>

eremiomania <stillness>

ergasiomania <activity>

ergomania <work>

eroticomania <erotica>

erotographomania <erotic literature>

erythromania <blushing>

etheromania <ether>

florimania <plants>

Francomania <France>

Gallomania <France>

gamomania <marriage>

gephyromania <crossing bridges>

Germanomania <Germany>

Gorbymania <Mikhail S Gorbachev>

graphomania <writing>

Grecomania <Greece>

gymnomania <nakedness>

gynecomania <satyriasis>

hamartomania <sin>

hedonomania <pleasure>

heliomania <sun>

hieromania <priests>

hippomania <horses>

hodomania <travel>

homicidomania <murder>

hydrodipsomania <drinking water>

hydromania <water>

hylomania <woods>

hypermania <acute mania>

hypnomania <sleep>

hypomania <mild mania>

hysteromania <nymphomania>

ichthyomania <fish>

iconomania <icons>

idolomania <idols>

Italomania <Italy>

kainomania <novelty>

kathisomania <sitting>

kinesomania <movement>

kleptomania <stealing>

lalomania <speech>

letheomania <narcotics>

logomania <talking>

lycomania <lycanthropy>

lypemania <deep melancholy>

macromania <becoming larger>

megalomania <own importance>

melomania <music>

mentulomania <the penis>

mesmeromania <hypnosis>

metromania <writing verse>

micromania <becoming smaller>

monomania <one subject>

musicomania <music>

musomania <mice>

mythomania <lies; exaggerations>

necromania <death; the dead>

noctimania <night>

nosomania <imagined disease>

nostomania <return home>

nudomania <nudity>

nymphomania <female lust>

ochlomania <crowds>

oestromania <nymphomania>

oikomania <home>

oinomania <wine>

oligomania <a few subjects>

oniomania <buying>

ophidiomania <reptiles>

opiomania <opium>

opsomania <a special food>

orchidomania <testicles>

ornithomania <birds>

paramania <joy in complaints>

parousiamania <second coming of Christ>

pathomania <moral insanity>

phagomania <food; eating>

phaneromania <picking at growths>

pharmacomania <medicines>

philopatridomania <homesickness>

phonomania <noise>

photomania <light>

phronemomania <thinking>

phthisiomania
<tuberculosis>
plutomania <great
wealth>
politicomania
<politics>
poriomania
<wanderlust>
pornographomania
<pornography>
potomania
<drinking;
delirium tremens>
pseudomania
<falsities>
pyromania <fires>
Russomania
<Russia>
satyromania <male
lust>
scribblemania
<writing>
scribomania
<writing>
siderodromomania
<railroad travel>
sitomania <food>
sophomania <one's
own wisdom>
squandermania
<spending>
submania <mild
mania>
symmetromania
<symmetry>
Teutonomania
<Germany>

thalassomania <the
sea>
thanatomania
<death>
theatromania
<theater>
theomania <that one
is God>
timbromania
<postage stamps>
tomomania
<surgery>
trichomania <hair>
trichorrhexomania
<pinching off one's
hair>
trichotillomania
<plucking one's
hair>
tristimania
<melancholia>
tromomania
<delirium
tremens>
Turkomania
<Turkey>
typomania
<writing for
publication>
uteromania
<nymphomania>
verbomania
<words>
xenomania
<foreigners>
zoomania
<animals>

926 ECCENTRICITY

NOUNS **1 eccentricity, idiosyncrasy,** idiocrasy, **erraticism,** erraticness, **queerness, oddity, peculiarity,** strangeness,
singularity, freakishness, freakiness,
quirkiness, crotchetiness, dottiness,
crankiness, crankism, crackpotism;
whimsy, whimsicality; abnormality,
anomaly, unnaturalness, irregularity,
deviation, deviancy, differentness, divergence, aberration; **nonconformity,**
unconventionality 867.2
2 quirk, twist, kink, crank, quip, trick,
mannerism, **crotchet,** conceit, whim,
maggot, maggot in the brain, bee in one's
bonnet or head <nonformal>
3 eccentric, erratic, character; odd person
869.4; **nonconformist** 867.3, recluse 584.5
4 freak, character, crackpot, nut, screwball, weirdie, weirdo, kook, queer potato,
oddball, flake, strange duck, odd fellow,
crank, bird, goofus, wack, wacko

ADJS **5 eccentric, erratic,** idiocratic, id-
iocratical, idiosyncratic, idiosyncratical,
queer, queer in the head, **odd, peculiar,**
strange, fey, singular, anomalous, freakish, funny; unnatural, abnormal, irregular, divergent, deviative, deviant, different, exceptional; unconventional 867.6;
crotchety, quirky, dotty, maggoty
<Brit>, cranky, crank, crankish, whimsical, twisted; solitary, reclusive, antisocial
6 <nonformal terms> **kooky, goofy,** birdy,
funny, kinky, loopy, goofus, haywire,
squirrely, screwy, screwball, nutty,
wacky, flaky, oddball, wacky, wacko,
lunch, out to lunch, nobody home, weird

927 KNOWLEDGE

NOUNS **1 knowledge,** knowing, knowing-
ness, ken; **command,** reach; **acquaintance, familiarity,** intimacy; private
knowledge, privity; **information,** data,
database, datum, items, facts, factual
base, corpus; **certainty, sure** or **certain
knowledge** 969; protocol, protocol statement or sentence or proposition; intelligence; practical knowledge, **experience,
know-how, expertise;** technic, technics,
technique; self-knowledge; *ratio cogno-
scendi* <L>
2 cognizance; cognition, noesis; **recognition, realization; perception,** insight,
apperception, sudden insight, illumination, dawning, aha reaction, flashing
<nonformal>; **consciousness, awareness,**
mindfulness, note, notice; altered state of
consciousness or ASC; **sense,** sensibility;
appreciation, appreciativeness
**3 understanding, comprehension, ap-
prehension,** intellection, prehension;
conception, conceptualization, ideation;
hipness *and* savvy <both nonformal>;
grasp, mental grasp, grip, **command,**
mastery; precognition, foreknowledge
960.3, clairvoyance 689.8; intelligence,
wisdom 919
**4 learning, enlightenment, education,
schooling, instruction,** edification, illumination; acquirements, acquisitions,
attainments, accomplishments, skills; sophistication; store of knowledge; liberal
education; acquisition of knowledge 570
5 scholarship, erudition, eruditeness,
learnedness, reading, letters; **intellectuality,** intellectualism; **literacy;** computer literacy, computeracy, numer-
acy; **culture, literary culture, high culture,** book learning, booklore; **bookish-**

ness, bookiness, **pedantry**, pedantism, donnishness <Brit>; bluestockingism; bibliomania, book madness, bibliolatry, bibliophilism; classicism, classical scholarship, humanism, humanistic scholarship

6 **profound knowledge**, deep knowledge, total command *or* mastery; specialism, specialized *or* special knowledge; expertise, proficiency 413.1; wide *or* vast *or* extensive knowledge, generalism, general knowledge, interdisciplinary *or* cross-disciplinary knowledge; **encyclopedic knowledge**, polymathy, polyhistory, pansophy; **omniscience**, all-knowingness

7 slight knowledge 929.6

8 tree of knowledge, tree of knowledge of good and evil; forbidden fruit; bo *or* bodhi tree

9 **lore, body of knowledge**, corpus, body of learning, store of knowledge, system of knowledge, treasury of information; **canon**; literature, literature of the field, publications, materials; bibliography; encyclopedia, cyclopedia

10 **science**, ology <see list>, **art, study, discipline; field**, field of inquiry, concern, province, domain, area, arena, sphere, branch *or* field of study, branch *or* department of knowledge, specialty, academic specialty, academic discipline; **technology, technics**, technicology, high technology, high-tech *or* hi-tech <nonformal>; social science, natural science; applied science, pure science, experimental science; Big Science

11 **scientist**, man of science; **technologist**; practical scientist, experimental scientist; boffin <Brit>; savant, **scholar** 928.3; authority, expert, maven <nonformal>; technocrat; intellectual

VERBS 12 **know, perceive, apprehend**, prehend, cognize, recognize, discern, see, make out; conceive, conceptualize; **realize, appreciate, understand, comprehend**, fathom; dig *and* savvy <both nonformal>; wot *or* wot of <Brit nonformal>, ken <Scots>; have, possess, **grasp**, seize, have hold of; have knowledge of, be informed, be apprised of, have a good command of, have information about, be acquainted with, be conversant with, be cognizant of, be conscious *or* aware of; know something by heart *or* by rote *or* from memory

13 **know well, know full well**, know damn well *or* darn well <nonformal>, have a good *or* thorough knowledge of, be

well-informed, be learned in, **be up on** <nonformal>, be master of, command, be thoroughly grounded in, **have down pat *or* cold** <both nonformal>, have it taped <Brit nonformal>, have at one's fingers' ends *or* fingertips, have in one's head, **know by heart *or* rote, know like a book**, know like the back of one's hand, **know backwards**, know backwards and forwards, **know inside out**, know down to the ground <nonformal>, **know one's stuff** *and* know one's onions <both nonformal>, know a thing or two, know one's way around; be expert in; **know the ropes**, know all the ins and outs, know the score <nonformal>, know all the answers <nonformal>; know what's what

14 learn <acquire knowledge> 570.6,9–11; come to one's knowledge 551.15

ADJS 15 **knowing**, knowledgeable, informed; **cognizant, conscious, aware, mindful, sensible**; intelligent 919.12; **understanding, comprehending**, apprehensive, apprehending; **perceptive**, insightful, apperceptive, percipient, perspicacious, appercipient, prehensile; shrewd, sagacious, wise 919.17; omniscient, all-knowing

16 **cognizant of, aware of, conscious of, mindful of, sensible to *or* of, appreciative of**, appreciatory of, no stranger to, seized of <Brit>; privy to, in the secret, let into, in the know <nonformal>, behind the scenes *or* curtain; alive to, awake to; **wise to** <nonformal>, hep to *and* on to <both nonformal>; streetwise; apprised of, informed of; undeceived, undeluded

17 <nonformal terms> **hep, hip**, on the beam, go-go, **with it**, into, really into, groovy; chic, clued-up, clued in, in the know, trendy

18 **informed, enlightened, instructed**, versed, well-versed, educated, schooled, **taught**; posted, briefed, primed, trained; **up on**, up-to-date, abreast of, *au courant* <Fr>

19 **versed in, informed in**, read *or* well-read in, up on, strong in, at home in, master of, expert *or* authoritative in, proficient in, **familiar with**, at home with, **conversant with, acquainted with**, intimate with

20 **well-informed**, well-posted, well-educated, **well-grounded, well-versed, well-read**, widely read

21 **learned, erudite, educated, cultured**, cultivated, lettered, literate, civilized, **scholarly**, scholastic, studious; wise 919.17; **profound**, deep, abstruse; **ency-**

clopedic, pansophic, polymath *or* polymathic, polyhistoric

22 **book-learned, literary,** book-taught, book-fed, book-wise, book-smart, **bookish,** booky, book-minded; book-loving, bibliophilic, bibliophagic; **pedantic,** donnish <Brit>, scholastic, inkhorn; **bluestocking**

23 **intellectual,** intellectualistic; **highbrow** *and* highbrowed *and* highbrowish <all nonformal>; elitist

24 **self-educated,** self-taught, autodidactic

25 **knowable,** cognizable, recognizable, **understandable, comprehensible,** apprehendable, apprehensible, prehensible, graspable, seizable, discernible, conceivable, appreciable, perceptible, distinguishable, ascertainable, discoverable

26 **known, recognized,** ascertained, conceived, grasped, apprehended, prehended, seized, perceived, discerned, appreciated, **understood, comprehended,** realized; pat *and* **down pat** <both nonformal>

27 **well-known,** well-kenned <Scots>, well-understood, well-recognized, **widely known,** commonly known, universally recognized, generally *or* universally admitted; **familiar,** familiar as household words, household, **common, current; proverbial;** public, notorious; known by every schoolboy; talked-of, talked-about, in everyone's mouth, **on everyone's tongue** *or* **lips;** commonplace, trite 117.9, hackneyed, platitudinous, truistic

28 **scientific; technical, technological,** technicological; high-tech *or* hi-tech <nonformal>; **scholarly;** disciplinary

ADVS 29 **knowingly, consciously, wittingly,** with forethought, understandingly, intelligently, studiously, learnedly, eruditely, as every schoolboy knows

30 to one's knowledge, **to the best of one's knowledge,** as far as one can see *or* tell, as far as one knows, as well as can be said

31 **-ologies by name**

abiology <inanimate things>
acarology <lice and ticks>
acology <therapeutic agents>
acrology <initial sounds or signs>
adenology <glands>
aesthology <sensory organs>
alethology <truth>
algology *or* phycology <seaweeds>
ambrology <amber>
anatripsology <friction>
andrology <male diseases>
angiology <blood vessels>
anorganology <inorganic things>
anthropology <mankind>
apiology *or* melittology <bees>
arachnology *or* araneology <spiders>
archeology <ancient or historical artifacts>
archology <government>
areology <the planet Mars>
argyrology <money boxes>
aristology <dining>
arthrology <joints>
asthenology <diseases of debility>
astrolithology <meteorites>
astrology <stellar and planetary influence>
atmology <water vapor>
audiology <hearing disorders>
auxology <growth>
azoology <inanimate things>
balneology <therapeutic baths>
barology <weight>
batology <brambles>
bibliology <books>
bioecology <biological interrelationships>
biology <life, living things>
biometeorology <organic-atmospheric interrelationships>
bromatology <food>
brontology <thunder>
bryology *or* muscology <mosses>
caliology <bird nests>
campanology <bells; bell-ringing>
carcinology <crustaceans>
cardiology <the heart>
carpology *or* pomology <fruits>
cartology <maps>
cephalology <the head>
cetology <whales and dolphins>
chololology *or* choledology <bile>
chorology <boundaries>
choreology <dance notation>
chrondrology <cartilage>
chronology <dates; dating>
coleopterology <beetles>
conchology <shells>
cosmology <the universe>
craniology <the skull>
crustaceology <crustaceans>
cryptology <codes and ciphers>
curiology <picture writing>
cyesiology <pregnancy>
cytology <cells>
cytopathology <cell pathology>
dactyliology <finger-rings>
dactylology <fingers>
deltiology <picture postcards>
demology <human activities>
dendrochronology <tree-ring dating>
dendrology <trees>
deontology <moral obligation>
dermatology <the skin>
desmology <ligaments>
diabiology <the devil, devils>
dipteriology <flies>
dittology <double interpretation>

docimology <metal assaying>
dolorology <pain>
dosiology <dosage>
dysteleology <purposeless-ness>
ecclesiology <churches; church history>
ecology and environmentology <the enviroment>
edaphology <soils>
eidology <mental imagery>
electrology <electricity>
embryology <embryos>
endocrinology <the endocrine glands>
enterology <internal organs>
entomology <insects>
epiphuytology <plant diseases>
epistemology <human knowledge>
eremology <deserts>
ergology <work and its effects>
eschatology <last things, esp death and final judgment>
ethnology <races and peoples>
ethology <animal behavior>
etiology <the causes of disease>
etymology <derivation and history of linguistic forms>
exobiology <life on other planets>
faunology <animal distribution>
fetology <the fetus>
garbology or garbageology <garbage, refuse>
gastrology <the stomach>
geology <the crust of the Earth>
geratology <extinction>

gerontology <old age>
glossology <language>
gnomology <didactic literature>
gnotobiology <germ-free biology>
graphology <handwriting>
gynecology <female health and disease>
hagiology <saints>
hamartiology <sin>
helcology <ulcers>
heliology <the sun>
helminthology <worms, esp parasitic worms>
hematology <the blood>
heortology <religious festivals>
hepatology <the liver>
heresiology <heresies>
herpetology <reptiles>
hierology <sacred things>
hippology <horses>
hippopathology <diseases of the horse>
histology or histiology <tissues and organs>
historology <history>
horology <time, clocks>
hydrology <water>
hyetology <rainfall>
hygiology <health and hygiene>
hygrology <humidity>
hymenology <membranes>
hymenopterology <wasps, bees, ants>
hypnology <sleep>
hysterology <the uterus>
iatrology <healing, medicine>
ichnolithology or ichnology <fossil footprint>

ichthyology or piscology <fishes>
immunology <immunity to diseases>
irenology <peace>
journology <newspapers>
kalology <beauty>
laryngology <the larynx>
lexicology <words and meanings>
limnology <lakes and ponds>
lithology or lithoidology <rock, stone>
loimology <infectious diseases>
malacostracology <crustaceology>
mallacology <molluscs>
mantology <divination>
mastology <mammals>
meteorology <the atmosphere and weather>
metrology <weights and measures>
microbiology <microorgan-isms>
micrology <tiny things>
microseismology <earthquake tremors>
morphology <form, shape>
mycology <fungi>
myology <muscles>
myrmecology <ants>
naology <church buildings>
nasology or rhinology <the nose>
nephology <clouds>
neurology <the nervous system>
neuropathology <pathology of the nervous system>
neurophysology <physiology of the nervous system>
neurypnology <hypnotism>

nomology <law>
noology <intuition>
nosology <classification of diseases>
nostology <old age, geriatrics>
numismatology <coins>
odontology <the teeth>
oenology or enology <wine>
olfactology <smells>
ombrology <rain>
oncology <tumors>
oneirology <dreams>
onomatology <names, naming>
ontology <being, as such>
oology <eggs>
ophiology <snakes>
ophthalmology <the eyes>
organology <body organs>
orismology <terminology>
ornithology <birds>
orology or oreology <mountains>
oryctology <fossils>
osmology <odors>
osteology <bones>
otology <the ear>
paleobiology <fossil life>
paleoethnology <prehistoric mankind>
paleoichtyology <fossil fishes>
paleontology <early history of life>
paleoornithology <fossil birds>
paleopedology <early soils>
paleoetiology <explanation of past phenomena>
paleozoology or zoogeolology <fossil animals>
palynology <pollen>
paroemiology <proverbs>
pathology <diseases>

pedology <soils; children>

penology <punishment of crime>

petrology or stromatology <rocks>

pharmacology <drugs>

phenology <natural cycles>

philology <languages>

phitology <political economy>

phlebology <blood vessels>

phonology <vocal sounds>

photology <light and optics>

phrenology <skull shape>

physicotheology <natural theology>

physiology <the living body>

phytology <plants>

phytopathology <plant diseases>

phytophysiology <plant physiology>

phytoserology <plant viruses>

piscatology <fishing>

pistology <religious faith>

pleology <running water>

pneumatology <spirit>

ponerology <evil>

potamology <rivers>

proctology <anus, rectum>

promorphology <fundamental shapes and forms>

psephology <election statistics>

psychology <the mind>

psychonosology <mental diseases>

psychopathology <insanity>

psychophysiology <body and mind>

pteridology <ferns>

pterology <insect wings>

pterylology <feathers>

pyretology <fever>

pyrgology <towers>

pyrology <fire and heat>

radiology or Röntgenology <X-rays>

rheology <flow and deformation of matter>

runology <runes>

satanology <devil worship>

scatology <fossil excrement>

seismology <earthquakes>

selenology <the moon>

semasiology <language meaning>

sematology or semeiology <symptoms>

serology <serums>

silphology <larval forms>

sinology <China>

siphonapterology <fleas>

sitiology <diet>

sociology <society>

somatology <organic bodies>

sophiology <ideas>

soteriology <salvation>

speciology <species>

spectrology <spectroscopic analysis>

speleology <caves>

spermatology <sperm>

sphygmoology <the pulse>

splanchnology <the viscera>

splenology <the spleen>

stoichiology <fundamental laws>

stomatology <mouth diseases>

storiology <folklore>

suicidology <suicide>

synchronology <comparative chronology>

systematology <ordered arrangements>

taxology <scientific classification>

technology <mechanical and manufacturing arts>

tectology <structural morphology>

teleology <aims, determined ends>

teratology <monsters>

terminology <system of names or terms>

thanatology <death>

thaumatology <miracles>

theology <divinity>

thermology or thermatology <heat>

therology <mammals>

thremmatology <plant or animal breeding>

threpsology <nutrition>

tidology <tides>

32 -ologies by subject

<aims, determined ends> teleology

<amber> ambrology

<ancient or historical artifacts> archeology

<animal behavior> ethology

<animal diseases> zoonosology

<animal distribution> faunology

<animal life> zoology

<animal physiology> zoophysiology

<ants> myrmecology

timbrology <stamps, stamp-collecting>

timology <values>

tocology <obstetrics>

toxicology <poisons>

traumatology <wounds; shock>

tribology <interacting surfaces>

trichology <hair>

typhology <blindness>

uranology <astronomy>

urbanology <cities>

urology <urogenital organs and diseases>

vermiology <worms>

vexillology <flags>

victimology <victims>

vulcanology <volcanoes>

xyloology <the structure of wood>

zoology <animal life>

zoonosology <animal diseases>

zoophysiology <animal physiology>

zymology or zymotechnology <fermentation>

<anus, rectum> proctology

<astronomy> uranology

<beauty> kalology

<bees> apiology or melittology

<beetles> coleopterology

<being, as such> ontology

<bells; bell-ringing> campanology

<bile> chology or choledology

<biological interrelation- ships> bioecology

<bird nests> caliology

<birds> ornithology

<blindness>
typhology
<blood vessels>
angiology
<blood vessels>
phlebology
<body and mind>
psychophysiology
<body organs>
organology
<bones> osteology
<books> bibliology
<brambles>
batology
<cartilage>
chrondrology
<caves> speleology
<cell pathology>
cytopathology
<cells> cytology
<China> sinology
<church buildings>
naology
<churches; church
history>
ecclesiology
<cities> urbanology
<classification of
diseases> nosology
<clouds> nephology
<codes and ciphers>
cryptology
<coins>
numismatology
<comparative
chronology>
synchronology
<crustaceans>
carcinology or
crustaceology
<crustaceology>
malacostracology
<dance notation>
choreology
<dates, dating>
chronology
<death>
thanatology
<derivation and
history of linguistic
forms> etymology
<deserts>
eremology
<devil worship>
satanology
<didactic
literature>
gnomology
<diet> sitiology
<dining> aristology
<diseases of
debility>
asthenology

<diseases of the
horse>
hippopathology
<diseases>
pathology
<divination>
mantology
<divinity> theology
<dosage> dosiology
or dosology or
posology
<double
interpretation>
dittology
<dreams>
oneirology
<drugs>
pharmacology
<early history of
life> paleontology
<early soils>
paleopedology
<earthquake
tremors>
microseismology
<earthquakes>
seismology
<eggs> oology
<election statistics>
psephology
<electricity>
electrology
<embryos>
embryology
<evil> ponerology
<explanation of past
phenomena>
paleoetiology
<extinction>
geratology
<feathers>
pterylology
<female health and
disease>
gynecology
<fermentation>
zymology or
zymotechnology
<ferns> pteridology
<fever> pyretology
<finger-rings>
dactyliology
<fingers>
dactylology
<fire and heat>
pyrology
<fishes> ichthyology
or piscology
<fishing>
piscatology
<flags> vexillology
<fleas>
siphonapterology

<flies> dipteriology
<flow and
deformation of
matter> rheology
<folklore>
storiology
<food> bromatology
<form, shape>
morphology
<fossil animals>
paleozoology or
zoogeolology
<fossil birds>
paleoornithology
<fossil excrement>
scatology
<fossil fishes>
paleoichtyology
<fossil footprint>
ichnolithology or
ichnology
<fossil life>
paleobiology
<fossils> oryctology
<friction>
anatripsology
<fruits> carpology
or pomology
<fundamental
laws> stoichiology
<fundamental
shapes and forms>
promorphology
<fungi> mycology
<garbage, refuse>
garbology or
garbageology
<geographical
boundaries>
chorology
<germ-free biology>
gnotobiology
<glands> adenology
<government>
archology
<growth> auxology
<hair> trichology
graphology
<healing, medicine>
iatrology
<health and
hygiene>
hygiology
<hearing disorders>
audiology
<heat> thermology
or thermatology
<heresies>
heresiology
<history>
historology
<horses> hippology

<human activities>
demology
<human
knowledge>
epistemology
<humidity>
hygrology
<hypnotism>
neurypnolohy
<ideas>
sophiology
<immunity to
diseases>
immunology
<inanimate things>
abiology
<inanimate things>
azoology
<infectious
diseases>
loimology
<initial sounds or
signs> acrology
<inorganic things>
anorganology
<insanity>
psychopathology
<insect wings>
pterology
<insects>
entomology
<interacting
surfaces>
tribology
<internal organs>
enterology
<intuition> noology
<joints> arthrology
<lakes and ponds>
limnology
<language
meaning>
semasiology
<language>
glossology
<languages>
philology
<larval forms>
silphology
<last things, esp
death and final
judgment>
eschatology
<law> nomology
<lice and ticks>
acarology
<life on other
planets>
exobiology
<life, living things>
biology
<ligaments>
desmology

<light and optics>
photology
<male diseases>
andrology
<mammals>
mastology
<mammals>
therology
<mankind>
anthropology
<maps> cartology
<mechanical and
manufacturing
arts> technology
<membranes>
hymenology
<mental diseases>
psychonosology
<mental imagery>
eidology
<metal assaying>
docimology
<meteorites>
astrolithology
<microorganisms>
microbiology
<miracles>
thaumatology
<molluscs>
mallacology
<money boxes>
argyrology
<monsters>
teratology
<moral obligation>
deontology
<mosses> bryology
or muscology
<mountains>
orology or oreology
<mouth diseases>
stomatology
<muscles> myology
<names, naming>
onomatology
<natural cycles>
phenology
<natural theology>
physicotheology
<newspapers>
journology
<nutrition>
threpsology
<obstetrics>
tocology
<odors> osmology
<old age, geriatrics>
nostology
<old age>
gerontology
<ordered
arrangements>
systematology

<organic bodies>
somatology
<organic-
atmospheric
interrelation-
ships>
biometeorology
<pain> dolorology
<pathology of the
nervous system>
neuropathology
<peace> irenology
<physiology of the
nervous system>
neurophysology
<picture postcards>
deltiology
<picture writing>
curiology
<plant diseases>
epiphuytology
<plant diseases>
phytopathology
<plant or animal
breeding>
thremmatology
<plant physiology>
phytophysiology
<plant viruses>
phytoserology
<plants> phytology
<poisons>
toxicology
<political economy>
phitology
<pollen> palynology
<pregnancy>
cyesiology
<prehistoric
mankind>
paleoethnology
<proverbs>
paroemiology
<punishment of
crime> penology
<purposelessness>
dysteleology
<races and peoples>
ethnology
<rain> ombrology
<rainfall>
hyetology
<religious faith>
pistology
<religious festivals>
heortology
<reptiles>
herpetology
<rivers>
potamology
<rock, stone>
lithology or
lithoidology

<rocks> petrology or
stromatology
<runes> runology
<running water>
pleology
<sacred things>
hierology
<saints> hagiology
<salvation>
soteriology
<scientific
classification>
taxology
<seaweeds>
algology or
phycology
<sensory organs>
aesthology
<serums> serology
<shells> conchology
<sin> hamartiology
<skull shape>
phrenology
<sleep> hypnology
<smells>
olfactology
<snakes> ophiology
<society> sociology
<soils; children>
pedology
<soils> edaphology
<species>
speciology
<spectroscopic
analysis>
spectrology
<sperm>
spermatology
<spiders>
arachnology or
araneology
<spirit>
pneumatology
<stamps, stamp-
collecting>
timbrology
<stellar and
planetary
influence>
astrology
<structural
morphology>
tectology
<suicide>
suicidology
<symptoms>
sematology or
semeiology
<system of names or
terms>
terminology
<terminology>
orismology

<the atmosphere and
weather>
meteorology
<the blood>
hematology
<the causes of
disease> etiology
<the crust of the
Earth> geology
<the devil, devils>
diabiology
<the ear> otology
<the endocrine
glands>
endocrinology
<the environment>
ecology or
environmentology
<the eyes>
ophthalmology
<the fetus> fetology
<the head>
cephalology
<the heart>
cardiology
<the larynx>
laryngology
<the liver>
hepatology
<the living body>
physiology
<the mind>
psychology
<the moon>
selenology
<the nervous
system> neurology
<the nose> nasology
or rhinology
<the planet Mars>
areology
<the pulse>
sphygmoology
<the skin>
dermatology
<the skull>
craniology
<the spleen>
splenology
<the stomach>
gastrology
<the structure of
wood> xyloology
<the sun>
heliology
<the teeth>
odontology
<the universe>
cosmology
<the uterus>
hysterology
<the viscera>
splanchnology

<therapeutic agents> acology
<therapeutic baths> balneology
<thunder> brontology
<tides> tidology
<time, clocks> horology
<tiny things> micrology
<tissues and organs> histology *or* histiology
<towers> pyrgology
<tree-ring dating> dendrochronology
<trees> dendrology
<truth> alethology
<tumors> oncology
<ulcers> helcology
<urogenital organs and diseases> urology
<values> timology
<victims> victimology
<vocal sounds> phonology

<volcanoes> vulcanology
<wasps, bees, ants> hymenopterology
<water vapor> atmology
<water> hydrology
<weight> barology
<weights and measures> metrology
<whales and dolphins> cetology
<wine> oenology *or* enology
<words and meanings> lexicology
<work and its effects> ergology
<worms, esp parasitic worms> helminthology
<worms> vermiology
<wounds, shock> traumatology
<X-rays> radiology *or* Röntgenology

928 INTELLECTUAL

NOUNS **1 intellectual, intellect,** intellectualist, literate, member of the intelligentsia, white-collar intellectual; "someone whose mind watches itself"—Camus; brainworker, thinker; **brain** *and* rocket scientist *and* brain surgeon <all nonformal>; **pundit, Brahmin, mandarin,** egghead *and* pointy-head <both nonformal>; **highbrow** <nonformal>; wise man 920

2 intelligentsia, literati, illuminati; intellectual elite; clerisy; literati

3 scholar, scholastic <old>, clerk *or* learned clerk <both archaic>; a gentleman and a scholar; student 572; **learned man,** man of learning, giant of learning, colossus of knowledge, mastermind, **savant,** pundit; genius 413.12; polymath, polyhistor *or* polyhistorian, **mine of information, walking encyclopedia;** literary man, *littérateur* <Fr> *or* litterateur, **man of letters;** philologist, philologue; philomath, lover of learning; philosopher, philosophe; bookman; **academician,** schoolman; classicist, classicalist, Latinist, humanist

4 bookworm, bibliophage; **grind** *and* greasy grind <both nonformal>; **booklover, bibliophile,** bibliophilist, philo-

biblist, bibliolater, bibliolatrist; bibliomaniac, bibliomane

5 pedant; formalist, precisionist, precisian, purist, *précieux* <Fr>, **bluestocking,** *bas bleu* <Fr>, *précieuse* <Fr fem>; Dr Pangloss <Voltaire>, Dryasdust <Rev Dr Carlyle>

6 dilettante, half scholar, sciolist, **dabbler,** dabster, amateur, trifler, smatterer; grammaticaster, philologaster, criticaster, philosophaster, Latinitaster

929 IGNORANCE

NOUNS **1 ignorance,** ignorantness, **unknowingness,** unknowing, nescience; lack of information, knowledge-gap, hiatus of learning; empty-headedness, blankmindedness, vacuousness, vacuity, inanity; tabula rasa; **unintelligence 921; unacquaintance, unfamiliarity; greenness,** greenhornism, rawness, callowness, unripeness, green in the eye, **inexperience 414.2;** innocence, ingenuousness, simpleness, simplicity; crass *or* gross *or* primal *or* pristine ignorance; ignorantism, knownothingism, obscurantism; agnosticism

2 "blind and naked Ignorance"—Tennyson, "the mother of devotion"— Robert Burton, "the mother of prejudice"—John Bright, "the dominion of absurdity"—J A Froude

3 incognizance, unawareness, unconsciousness, insensibility, unwittingness, nonrecognition; deniability; nonrealization, incomprehension; **unmindfulness;** mindlessness; blindness 30, deafness 49

4 unenlightenment, benightedness, benightment, dark, darkness; savagery, barbarism, paganism, heathenism, Gothicism; age of ignorance, dark age; rural idiocy

5 unlearnedness, inerudition, ineducation, unschooledness, unletteredness; **unscholarliness,** unstudiousness; **illiteracy,** illiterateness, functional illiteracy; **unintellectuality,** unintellectualism, Philistinism, bold ignorance

6 slight knowledge, vague notion, imperfect knowledge, a little learning, glimmering, glimpse <old>, smattering, **smattering of knowledge,** smattering of ignorance, **half-learning,** semi-learning, semi-ignorance, sciolism; **superficiality,** shallowness, surface-scratching; **dilettantism,** dilettantship, amateurism

7 the unknown, the unknowable, the strange, the unfamiliar, the incalculable; **matter of ignorance,** sealed book, riddle, enigma, mystery, puzzle 970.3; *terra incognita* <L>, unexplored ground *or* territory; frontier, frontiers of knowledge, **unknown quantity,** x, y, z, n; dark horse

8 **ignoramus, know-nothing;** no scholar, puddinghead, dunce, fool 923; **illiterate; lowbrow** <nonformal>; unintelligentsia, illiterati; **greenhorn,** greeny <nonformal>, tenderfoot, neophyte, novice; **dilettante,** dabbler 928.6; **middlebrow** <nonformal>

VERBS 9 **be ignorant,** be green, have everything to learn, **know nothing,** know from nothing <nonformal>; wallow in ignorance; not know any better; **not know what's what,** not know what it is all about, not know the score <nonformal>, not be with it <nonformal>, not know any of the answers; not know the time of day *or* what o'clock it is, not know beans, not know the first thing about, not know one's ass from one's elbow <nonformal>, not know the way home, not know enough to come in out of the rain, not know chalk from cheese, **not know up from down,** not know which way is up

10 **be in the dark,** be blind, labor in darkness, walk in darkness, be benighted, grope in the dark, "see through a glass, darkly"—Bible

11 **not know,** not rightly know <nonformal>, know not, know not what, know nothing of, wot not of <Brit nonformal>, be innocent of, have no idea *or* notion *or* conception, **not have the first idea, not have the least *or* remotest idea,** be clueless *and* not have a clue <both Brit nonformal> not have idea one, not have the foggiest <nonformal>, **not pretend to say,** not take upon oneself to say; not know the half of it; not know from Adam, not know from the man in the moon; wonder, wonder whether; half-know, have a little learning, scratch the surface, know a little, smatter, dabble, toy with, coquet with; pass, give up

ADJS 12 **ignorant,** nescient, **unknowing,** uncomprehending, **know-nothing;** simple, **dumb** <nonformal>, empty, empty-headed, blankminded, vacuous, inane, **unintelligent** 921.13; **ill-informed, uninformed, unenlightened,** unilluminated, unapprized, unposted <nonformal>, clueless *or* pig-ignorant <both Brit nonformal>; **unacquainted, unconversant,** unversed, uninitiated, **unfamiliar,** strange to; **inexperienced** 414.17; **green,** callow, innocent, ingenuous, gauche, awkward, naive, unripe, raw; groping, tentative, unsure

13 **unaware, unconscious, insensible, unknowing, incognizant;** mindless, witless; unprehensive, unrealizing, nonconceiving, **unmindful,** unwitting, unsuspecting; unperceiving, impercipient, unhearing, unseeing, uninsightful; unaware of, in ignorance of, unconscious of, unmindful of, insensible to, out of it <nonformal>, not with it <nonformal>; **blind to, deaf to,** dead to, a stranger to; asleep, napping, **off one's guard,** caught napping, caught tripping

14 **unlearned, inerudite,** unerudite, **uneducated,** unschooled, uninstructed, untutored, unbriefed, untaught, unedified, unguided; ill-educated, misinstructed, misinformed, mistaught, led astray; hoodwinked, deceived; **illiterate,** functionally illiterate, unlettered, grammarless; **unscholarly,** unscholastic, unstudious; **unliterary, unread,** unbookish, unbook-learned, bookless <old>, unbooked; **uncultured,** uncultivated, unrefined, rude, Philistine; barbarous, pagan, heathen; Gothic; nonintellectual, **unintellectual; lowbrow** *and* lowbrowed *and* lowbrowish <all nonformal>

15 **half-learned,** half-baked <nonformal>, half-cocked *and* half-assed <both nonformal>, sciolistic; **shallow, superficial;** immature, sophomoric, sophomorical; **dilettante,** dilettantish, smattering, dabbling, amateur, amateurish; **wise in one's own conceit**

16 **benighted, dark,** in darkness, in the dark

17 **unknown,** unbeknown <nonformal>, unheard <old>, **unheard-of,** unapprehended, unapparent, unperceived, unsuspected; unexplained, unascertained; uninvestigated, unexplored; unidentified, unclassified, uncharted, unfathomed, unplumbed, virgin, untouched; undisclosed, unrevealed, undivulged, undiscovered, unexposed, sealed; **unfamiliar,** strange; incalculable, **unknowable,** incognizable, undiscoverable; enigmatic 522.17, mysterious, puzzling

ADVS 18 **ignorantly, unknowingly,** unmindfully, unwittingly, witlessly, unsuspectingly, **unawares;** unconsciously, insensibly; for anything *or* aught one knows, not that one knows

INTERJS 19 **God knows!,** God only knows! Lord knows!, Heaven knows!, nobody knows!, damned if I know!, search me!, **beats me!,** beats the hell *or* heck *or* shit out of me!, your guess is as good as mine!, it has me guessing!, it's Greek to me!; **search me!**, you've got me!, I give up!, I pass!, **who knows?**, how should I know?, I don't know what!

930 THOUGHT
<exercise of the intellect>

NOUNS **1 thought, thinking, cogitation,** cerebration, ideation, noesis, mentation, intellection, intellectualization, ratiocination; using one's head *or* noodle <nonformal>; workings of the mind; **reasoning 934; brainwork, headwork,** mental labor *or* effort, mental act *or* process, act of thought, mental *or* intellectual exercise; **deep-think** <nonformal>; **way of thinking,** habit of thought *or* mind, thought-pattern; heavy thinking, straight thinking; conception, conceit <old>, conceptualization; abstract thought, imageless thought; excogitation, thinking out *or* through; thinking aloud; **idea** 931; creative thought 985.2

2 consideration, contemplation, reflection, speculation, meditation, musing, rumination, deliberation, lucubration, brooding, study, **pondering,** weighing, revolving, turning over in the mind, looking at from all angles, noodling *or* noodling around <nonformal>; lateral thought *or* thinking; advisement, counsel

3 thoughtfulness, contemplativeness, speculativeness, reflectiveness; **pensiveness,** wistfulness, reverie, musing, melancholy; **preoccupation, absorption, engrossment,** abstraction, brown study, intense *or* deep *or* profound thought; **concentration,** study, close study

4 thoughts, burden of one's mind, mind's content; inmost *or* innermost thoughts *or* mind, secret thoughts, mind's core, one's heart of hearts; **train of thought,** current *or* flow of thought *or* ideas, succession *or* sequence *or* chain of thought *or* ideas; **stream of consciousness; association,** association of ideas

5 mature thought, developed thought, ripe idea; **afterthought,** *arrière-pensée* <Fr>, *esprit d'escalier* <Fr>, second thought *or* thoughts; **reconsideration,** reappraisal, revaluation, rethinking, re-examination, review, thinking over

6 introspection, self-communion, self-counsel, self-consultation, subjective inspection *or* speculation, head trip <nonformal>

7 subject for thought, food for thought, something to chew on, something to get one's teeth into

VERBS **8 think, cogitate,** cerebrate, put on one's thinking *or* considering cap <nonformal>, intellectualize, ideate, conceive, conceptualize, form ideas, entertain ideas; **reason** 934.15; **use one's head,** use one's noodle *or* noggin <nonformal>, use *or* exercise the mind, set the brain *or* wits to work, bethink oneself, have something on one's mind, have a lot on one's mind

9 think hard, think one's head off, **rack** *or* **ransack one's brains,** crack one's brains <nonformal>, **beat** *or* **cudgel one's brains,** work one's head to the bone, do some heavy thinking, bend *or* apply the mind, knit one's brow; sweat *or* stew over <nonformal>, hammer *or* hammer away at; puzzle, **puzzle over**

10 concentrate, concentrate the mind *or* thoughts, concentrate on *or* upon, attend closely to, brood on, **focus on** *or* **upon,** give *or* devote the mind to, glue the mind to, cleave to the thought of, fix the mind *or* thoughts upon, bend the mind upon, bring the mind to bear upon; get to the point; gather *or* collect one's thoughts, pull one's wits together, focus *or* fix one's thoughts, marshal *or* arrange one's thoughts *or* ideas

11 think about, cogitate, **give** *or* **apply the mind to,** put one's mind to, apply oneself to, bend *or* turn the mind *or* thoughts to, direct the mind upon, **give thought to, trouble one's head about,** occupy the mind *or* thoughts with; think through *or* out, puzzle out, sort out, reason out, excogitate

12 consider, contemplate, speculate, reflect, study, ponder, perpend, **weigh, deliberate, debate, meditate, muse, brood, ruminate,** chew the cud <nonformal>, digest; introspect, be abstracted; wrinkle one's brow; fall into a brown study, retreat into one's mind *or* thoughts; **toy with, play with,** play around with, flirt *or* coquet with the idea

13 think over, ponder over, brood over, muse over, mull over, reflect over, con over, **deliberate over,** run over, **meditate over,** ruminate over, chew over, digest, turn over, **revolve,** revolve *or* turn over in the mind, deliberate upon, meditate upon, muse on *or* upon, bestow thought *or* consideration upon, noodle *or* noodle around <nonformal>

14 take under consideration, entertain, take under advisement, take under active consideration, inquire into, **think it over,**

have a look at *and* see about <both non-formal>; **sleep upon,** consult with *or* advise with *or* take counsel of one's pillow

15 **reconsider, re-examine,** review; revise one's thoughts, reappraise, revaluate, rethink; view in a new light, have second thoughts, think better of

16 **think of,** bethink oneself of, seize on, flash on <nonformal>; tumble to <nonformal>; **entertain the idea of,** entertain thoughts of; have an idea of, have thoughts about; **have in mind, contemplate, consider, have under consideration;** take it into one's head; **bear in mind, keep in mind,** hold the thought; harbor an idea, keep *or* hold an idea, cherish *or* foster *or* nurse *or* nurture an idea

17 <look upon mentally> **contemplate, look upon, view, regard,** see, view with the mind's eye, **envisage,** envision, **visualize** 985.15, imagine, image

18 **occur to,** occur to one's mind, occur, **come to mind,** rise to mind, rise in the mind, come into one's head, impinge on one's consciousness, claim one's mind *or* thoughts, pass through one's head *or* mind, dawn upon one, **enter one's mind,** pass in the mind *or* thoughts, **cross one's mind,** race *or* tumble through the mind, flash on *or* across the mind; **strike,** strike one, strike the mind, grab one <nonformal>, **suggest itself,** present itself, offer itself, present itself to the mind *or* thoughts, give one pause

19 **impress, make an impression, strike,** grab <nonformal>, hit; catch the thoughts, arrest the thoughts, seize one's mind, sink *or* penetrate into the mind, embed itself in the mind, lodge in the mind, **sink in** <nonformal>

20 **occupy the mind** *or* **thoughts,** engage the thoughts, monopolize the thoughts, fasten itself on the mind, seize the mind, fill the mind, take up one's thoughts; **preoccupy,** occupy, **absorb, engross,** absorb *or* enwrap *or* engross the thoughts, obsess the mind, run in the head; foster in the mind; come uppermost, be uppermost in the mind; have in *or* on one's mind, **have on the brain** <nonformal>, have constantly in one's thoughts

ADJS 21 **cognitive,** prehensive, **thought,** conceptive, conceptual, conceptualized, ideative, ideational, noetic, **mental; rational** 934.18, logical, ratiocinative; **thoughtful,** cogitative, **contemplative, reflective, speculative, deliberative, meditative, ruminative,** ruminant, museful <old>; **pensive,** wistful; introspective; thinking, reflecting, contemplating, pondering, deliberating, excogitating, excogitative, meditating, ruminating, musing; sober, serious, deepthinking; concentrating, concentrative

22 absorbed *or* engrossed in thought, **absorbed, engrossed,** introspective, rapt, **wrapped in thought, lost in thought,** abstracted, immersed in thought, buried in thought, engaged in thought, occupied, **preoccupied**

ADVS 23 **thoughtfully,** contemplatively, reflectively, meditatively, ruminatively, musefully <old>; **pensively,** wistfully; on reconsideration, on second thought

24 **on one's mind, on the brain** *and* on one's chest <both nonformal>, in the thoughts; in the heart, *in petto* <Ital>, in one's inmost *or* innermost thoughts

931 IDEA

NOUNS 1 **idea; thought,** mental *or* intellectual object, **notion, concept,** conception, conceit, fancy; **perception, sense, impression,** mental impression, image, **mental image,** picture in the mind, mental picture, representation, recept; imago; memory trace; **sentiment,** apprehension; reflection, observation; **opinion** 952.6; supposition, **theory** 950

2 <philosophy> ideatum, ideate; noumenon; universal, universal concept *or* conception; idée-force; Platonic idea *or* form, archetype, prototype, subsistent form, eternal object, transcendent universal, eternal universal, pattern, model, exemplar, ideal, transcendent idea *or* essence, universal essence, innate idea; Aristotelian form, form-giving cause, formal cause; complex idea, simple idea; percept; construct of memory and association; Kantian idea, supreme principle of pure reason, regulative first principle, highest unitary principle of thought, transcendent nonempirical concept; Hegelian idea, highest category, the Absolute, the Absolute Idea, the Self-determined, the realized ideal; logical form *or* category; noosphere <Teilhard de Chardin>; history of ideas, *Geistesgeschichte* <Ger>; **idealism** 1051.3

3 **abstract idea, abstraction,** general idea, generality, abstract

4 **main idea,** intellectual *or* philosophical basis, leading *or* principal idea, fundamental *or* basic idea, *idée-maitresse* <Fr>, guiding principle, crowning principle, **big idea** <nonformal>

5 **novel idea,** intellectual *or* conceptual
breakthrough, new *or* **latest wrinkle**
<nonformal>, new slant *or* twist *or* take
<nonformal>

6 **good idea, great idea,** not a bad idea;
bright thought, bright *or* brilliant idea,
insight; brainchild *and* **brainstorm**
<both nonformal>, **inspiration**

7 **absurd idea,** crazy idea, fool notion *and*
brainstorm <both nonformal>

8 **ideology,** system of ideas, body of ideas,
system of theories; world view, *Weltanschauung* <Ger>; philosophy; **ethos**

ADJS 9 ideational, ideal, **conceptual, notional,** fanciful; **intellectual; theoretical**
950.13; **ideological**

10 ideaed, notioned, thoughted

932 ABSENCE OF THOUGHT

NOUNS 1 **thoughtlessness,** thoughtfreeness;
vacuity, vacancy, **emptiness of mind,
empty-headedness,** blankness, mental
blankness, blankmindedness; fatuity,
inanity, foolishness 922; tranquillity,
calm of mind; **nirvana,** ataraxia, calm *or*
tranquillity of mind; **oblivion,** forgetfulness, lack *or* loss of memory, amnesia;
quietism, passivity, apathy; blank mind,
fallow mind, tabula rasa; unintelligence
921

VERBS 2 **not think, make the mind a blank,**
let the mind lie fallow; **not think of,** not
consider, be unmindful of; **not enter one's
mind** *or* **head,** be far from one's mind *or*
head *or* thoughts; pay no attention *or*
mind

3 **get it off one's mind, get it off one's chest**
<nonformal>, clear the mind, relieve
one's mind; **put it out of one's thoughts,**
dismiss from the mind *or* thoughts, push
from one's thoughts, put away thought

ADJS 4 **thoughtless, thoughtfree,** incogitant,
unthinking, unreasoning; unideaed; unintellectual; **vacuous,** vacant, blank,
blankminded, relaxed, empty, **empty-
headed,** fatuous, inane 921.19; unoccupied; calm, tranquil; nirvanic; oblivious; quietistic, passive

5 **unthought-of, undreamed-of,** unconsidered, unconceived, unconceptualized;
unimagined, unimaged; imageless

933 INTUITION, INSTINCT

NOUNS 1 **intuition, intuitiveness, sixth
sense;** intuitive reason *or* knowledge,
direct perception *or* apprehension,
immediate apprehension *or* perception,

unmediated perception *or* apprehension,
subconscious perception, unconscious *or*
subconscious knowledge, immediate cognition, knowledge without thought *or*
reason, flash of insight; *"l'esprit de tact"*—
Pascal, intuitive understanding, tact,
spontaneous sense; **revelation,** epiphany,
moment of illumination; **insight,** inspiration, aperçu; anticipation, a priori
knowledge; *satori* <Japanese>, *buddhi*
<Skt>; woman's intuition; second sight,
second-sightedness, precognition 960.3,
clairvoyance 689.8; intuitionism, intu-
itivism

2 **instinct,** natural instinct, unlearned capacity, innate *or* inborn proclivity, native
or natural tendency, **impulse,** blind *or* unreasoning impulse, vital impulse; **libido,
id,** primitive self; archetype, archetypal
pattern *or* idea; unconscious *or* subconscious urge *or* drive; collective unconscious, race memory; "the *not ourselves,* which is in us and all around us"—
Matthew Arnold, "an unfathomable
Somewhat, which is *Not we*"—Carlyle,
"that which is imprinted upon the spirit
of man by an inward instinct"—Francis
Bacon; **reflex,** spontaneous reaction, unthinking response, knee-jerk

3 **hunch** <nonformal>, sense, **presentiment, premonition,** preapprehension,
intimation, foreboding; suspicion, **impression,** intuition, intuitive impression,
feeling, forefeeling, vague feeling *or* idea,
funny feeling <nonformal>, feeling in
one's bones

VERBS 4 **intuit, sense, feel,** feel intuitively,
feel *or* **know in one's bones** <nonfor-
mal>, **have a feeling,** have a funny feeling
<nonformal>, **get** *or* **have the impres-
sion, have a hunch** <nonformal>, just
know, know instinctively; grok <nonfor-
mal>

ADJS 5 **intuitive,** intuitional, sensing, feeling; second-sighted, precognitive 960.7,
clairvoyant

6 **instinctive,** natural, **inherent, innate,**
unlearned; unconscious, subliminal;
involuntary, automatic, spontaneous,
impulsive; **instinctual,** libidinal

ADVS 7 **intuitively,** by intuition; **instinctively,** automatically, spontaneously,
on *or* by instinct, **instinctually**

934 REASONING

NOUNS 1 **reasoning, reason,** logical thought,
discursive reason, rationalizing, rationalization, ratiocination; the divine faculty,

"the homage we pay for not being beasts"—Sir Thomas Browne, "a harmony among irrational impulses"—Santayana; **rationalism, rationality,** discourse *or* discourse of reason <both old>; sweet reason, reasonableness; demonstration, proof 956; specious reasoning, sophistry 935; philosophy 951

2 **logic,** logics; **dialectics,** dialectic, dialecticism; art of reason, science of discursive thought, "the art of making truth prevail"—La Bruyère, "the ruin of the spirit"—Saint-Exupéry; formal logic, material logic; doctrine of terms, doctrine of the judgment, doctrine of inference, traditional *or* Aristotelian logic, Ramist *or* Ramistic logic, modern *or* epistemological logic, pragmatic *or* instrumental *or* experimental logic; psychological logic, psychologism; symbolic *or* mathematical logic, logistic; propositional calculus, calculus of individuals, functional calculus, combinatory logic, algebra of relations, algebra of classes, set theory, Boolean algebra

3 <methods> a priori reasoning, a fortiori reasoning, a posteriori reasoning; discursive reasoning; **deduction, deductive reasoning,** syllogism, syllogistic reasoning; hypothetico-deductive method; **induction, inductive reasoning,** epagoge; philosophical induction, inductive *or* Baconian method; **inference; generalization,** particularization; synthesis, analysis; hypothesis and verification

4 **argumentation, argument, controversy, dispute, disputation, polemic, debate,** disceptation <old>, eristic; **contention, wrangling, bickering,** hubbub 53.3, bicker, setto <nonformal>, rhubarb *and* hassle <both nonformal>, passage of arms; war of words, verbal engagement *or* contest, logomachy, flyting; paper war, *guerre de plume* <Fr>; adversarial procedure, confrontational occasion; academic disputation, defense of a thesis; defense, apology, apologia, apologetics; pilpul, casuistry; polemics; litigation; examination, cross-examination

5 **argument,** *argumentum* <L>; **case, plea,** pleading, *plaidoyer* <Fr>, brief; special pleading; **reason, consideration; refutation,** elenchus, ignoratio elenchi; pros, cons, **pros and cons;** talking point; **dialogue,** reasoning together, dialectic

6 **syllogism;** prosyllogism; mode; figure; mood; pseudosyllogism, paralogism; sorites, progressive *or* Aristotelian sorites, regressive *or* Goclenian sorites; categori-

cal syllogism; enthymeme; dilemma; **rule,** rule of deduction, transformation rule; modus ponens, modus tollens

7 **premise, proposition, position,** assumed position, sumption, **assumption,** supposal, presupposition, **hypothesis, thesis, theorem,** lemma, **statement,** affirmation, categorical proposition, assertion, basis, ground, foundation; **postulate, axiom, postulation,** postulatum; data; major premise, minor premise; first principles; a priori principle, apriorism; philosophical proposition, philosopheme; hypothesis ad hoc; sentential *or* propositional function, truth-function, truth table, truth-value

8 **conclusion** 945.4

9 **reasonableness,** reasonability, **logicalness,** logicality, **rationality, sensibleness, soundness,** justness, justifiability, admissibility, cogency; **sense,** common sense, sound sense, sweet reason, **logic, reason;** plausibility 967.3

10 **good reasoning, right thinking,** sound reasoning, ironclad reasoning, irrefutable logic; cogent argument, **cogency;** strong argument, knockdown argument; good case, good reason, sound evidence, strong point

11 **reasoner,** ratiocinator, **thinker; rationalist;** rationalizer; synthesizer; **logician,** logistician; logicaster; dialectician; syllogist, syllogizer; sophist 935.6; philosopher 951.6

12 **arguer, controversialist, disputant, debater,** eristic, argufier <nonformal>, advocate, wrangler, mooter, Philadelphia lawyer <nonformal>, guardhouse *or* latrine *or* forecastle lawyer <all nonformal>, disceptator <old>, pilpulist, casuist; polemic, polemist, polemicist; logomacher, logomachist; apologist

13 **contentiousness,** litigiousness, **quarrelsomeness,** argumentativeness, disputatiousness, testiness, feistiness <nonformal>, combativeness; ill humor 110

14 **side,** interest; **the affirmative,** pro, yes, aye, yea; **the negative,** con, no, nay

VERBS 15 **reason;** logicalize, logicize; rationalize, provide a rationale; intellectualize; bring reason to bear, apply *or* use reason, put two and two together; **deduce, infer, generalize; synthesize, analyze; theorize,** hypothesize; philosophize; syllogize

16 **argue,** argufy <nonformal>, **dispute,** discept <old>, logomachize, polemize, polemicize, moot, **bandy words, chop**

logic, **plead**, pettifog <nonformal>, join issue, give and take, cut and thrust, try conclusions, cross swords, lock horns, **contend, contest**, spar, **bicker, wrangle,** hassle <nonformal>, have it out; thrash out; take one's stand upon, **put up an argument** <nonformal>; take sides, take up a side; argue to no purpose; **quibble, cavil** 935.9

17 **be reasonable, be logical, make sense,** figure <nonformal>, **stand to reason,** be demonstrable, be irrefutable; hold good, hold water <nonformal>; have a leg to stand on

ADJS **18 reasoning, rational,** ratiocinative *or* ratiocinatory; analytic, analytical

19 **argumentative, argumental, dialectic, dialectical, controversial, disputatious, contentious, quarrelsome,** litigious, combative, testy, feisty <nonformal>, illhumored 110.18, eristic, eristical, polemic, polemical, logomachic, logomachical, pilpulistic, pro and con

20 **logical, reasonable, rational, cogent, sensible, sane, sound,** well-thought-out, legitimate, just, justifiable, admissible; credible 952.24; plausible 967.7; as it should be, as it ought to be; well-argued, **well-founded, well-grounded**

21 **reasoned, advised, considered, calculated,** meditated, contemplated, deliberated, studied, weighed, thought-out

22 **dialectic, dialectical, maieutic;** syllogistic, syllogistical, enthymematic, enthymematical, soritical, epagogic, inductive, deductive, inferential, synthetic, synthetical, analytic, analytical, discursive; a priori, a fortiori, a posteriori; categorical, hypothetical, conditional

23 **deducible, derivable, inferable;** sequential, following

ADVS **24 reasonably, logically, rationally,** by the rules of logic, **sensibly,** sanely, soundly; syllogistically, analytically; **in reason,** in all reason, within reason, within the bounds *or* limits of reason, within reasonable limitations, **within bounds,** within the bounds of possibility, as far as possible, in all conscience

935 SOPHISTRY

<specious reasoning>

NOUNS **1 sophistry,** sophistication, sophism, philosophism, **casuistry,** Jesuitry, Jesuitism, subtlety, oversubtlety; **false** *or* **specious reasoning, rationalization,** evasive reasoning, vicious reasoning, sophistical reasoning, special pleading; **fallacy,** falla-

ciousness; **speciousness,** speciosity, superficial *or* apparent soundness, plausibleness, plausibility; **insincerity, disingenuousness; equivocation,** equivocalness; fudging *and* waffling <both nonformal>, fudge and mudge <Brit nonformal>; perversion, distortion, misapplication; vicious circle, circularity; mystification, obfuscation, obscurantism; reduction, trivialization

2 **illogicalness,** illogic, illogicality, **unreasonableness, irrationality, reasonlessness, senselessness, unsoundness,** unscientificness, invalidity, untenableness, inconclusiveness; **inconsistency,** incongruity, antilogy

3 <specious argument> **sophism,** sophistry, insincere argument, mere rhetoric, philosophism, solecism; paralogism, pseudosyllogism; claptrap, moonshine, empty words, doubletalk, doublespeak, "sound and fury, signifying nothing"— Shakespeare; bad case, weak point, flaw in an argument, "lame and impotent conclusion"—Shakespeare; **fallacy,** logical fallacy, formal fallacy, material fallacy, verbal fallacy; *argumentum ad hominem, argumentum ad baculum, argumentum ad captandum, argumentum ad captandum vulgus* <all L>, crowdpleasing argument, argument by analogy, *tu quoque* <L>, argument, *petitio principii* <L>, begging the question, **circular argument,** undistributed middle, *non sequitur* <L>, *hysteron proteron* <Gk>, *post hoc, ergo propter hoc* <both L>

4 **quibble,** quiddity, quodlibet, quillet <old>, Jesuitism, **cavil;** quip, quirk, shuffle, dodge

5 **quibbling, caviling,** boggling, captiousness, nit-picking, **bickering; logicchopping, hairsplitting,** trichoschistism; subterfuge, chicane, chicanery, pettifoggery; **equivocation,** tergiversation, prevarication, **evasion, hedging, pussyfooting** <nonformal>, **sidestepping,** dodging, shifting, shuffling, fencing, parrying, boggling, paltering

6 **sophist,** sophister, philosophist <old>, **casuist,** Jesuit; choplogic <old>, logichopper; paralogist

7 **quibbler, caviler,** pettifogger, hairsplitter, captious *or* picayune critic, nitpicker; **equivocator,** Jesuit, mystifier, mystificator, obscurantist, prevaricator, palterer, tergiversator, shuffler, mudger <Brit nonformal>; **hedger;** pussyfoot *or* **pussyfooter** <nonformal>

VERBS **8** reason speciously, reason ill, par-
alogize, reason in a circle, argue insincerely, pervert, distort, misapply; explain
away, rationalize; prove that black is
white and white black; not have a leg to
stand on

9 quibble, cavil, bicker, boggle, chop logic,
split hairs, nitpick, pick nits; Jesuitize;
equivocate, mystify, obscure, prevaricate, tergiversate, doubletalk, doublespeak, tap-dance <nonformal>, palter,
fence, parry, shift, **shuffle, dodge,** shy,
evade, sidestep, hedge, skate around
<Brit nonformal>, pussyfoot <nonfor-
mal>, evade the issue; **beat about** or
around the bush, not come to the point,
beg the question; pick holes in, pick to
pieces; blow hot and cold; strain at a gnat
and swallow a camel

ADJS **10 sophistical,** sophistic, philosophis-
tic, philosophistical <old>, casuistic, ca-
suistical, Jesuitic, Jesuitical, **fallacious,
specious,** colorable, plausible, hollow,
superficially or apparently sound; deceptive, illusive, empty; overrefined, oversubtle, **insincere, disingenuous**

**11 illogical, unreasonable, irrational, rea-
sonless,** contrary to reason, **senseless,**
without reason, **without rhyme or reason;
unscientific,** nonscientific, unphilosophi-
cal; **invalid,** inauthentic, unauthentic,
faulty, flawed, paralogical, fallacious; inconclusive, inconsequent, inconsequential, not following; **inconsistent,** incongruous, absonant <old>, loose, unconnected; contradictory, **self-contradictory,** self-annulling, self-refuting, oxymoronic

12 unsound, unsubstantial, insubstantial,
weak, feeble, poor, flimsy, unrigorous, inconclusive, unproved, unsustained,
poorly argued

13 baseless, groundless, ungrounded, **unfounded,** ill-founded, unbased, **unsupported,** unsustained, **without foundation,** without basis or sound basis; **untenable, unsupportable,** unsustainable;
unwarranted, idle, empty, vain

14 quibbling, caviling, equivocatory, captious, nitpicky and nit-picking <both
nonformal>, bickering; picayune, petty,
trivial, trifling; paltering, shuffling, hedging, pussyfooting <nonformal>, **evasive;
hairsplitting,** trichoschistic, logic-
chopping, choplogic or choplogical
<old>

ADVS **15 illogically, unreasonably, irra-
tionally, reasonlessly, senselessly;** base-
lessly, groundlessly; untenably, unsup-

portably, unsustainably; out of all reason, out of all bounds

936 TOPIC

NOUNS **1 topic, subject,** subject of thought,
matter, subject matter, what it is about,
concern, focus of interest or attention,
discrete matter, category; **theme,** burden,
text, motif, motive, business at hand,
case, matter in hand, **question, problem, issue; point,** point at issue, point
in question, main point, gist 996.6; item
on the agenda; head, heading, chapter,
rubric; substance, meat, essence, material part, basis; living issue, topic of
the day

2 caption, title, heading, head, superscription, rubric; **headline;** overline; banner,
banner head or line, streamer; **scarehead,**
screamer; spread, spreadhead; drop
head, dropline, hanger; running head or
title, jump head; **subhead, subheading,**
subtitle; legend, motto, epigraph; title
page

VERBS **3** focus on, have regard to, distinguish, lift up, set forth, specify, zero in on
<nonformal>; caption, title, head, head
up <nonformal>; **headline;** subtitle, subhead

ADJS **4 topical, thematic**

937 INQUIRY

NOUNS **1 inquiry,** inquiring, probing, **inquest** 307.18, inquirendo; inquisition; inquiring mind; analysis 800

2 examination, school examination, ex-
amen, **exam** <nonformal>, **test, quiz;**
oral examination, oral, doctor's oral,
master's oral, viva voce examination,
viva <nonformal>; catechesis, catchiza-
tion; **audition, hearing;** multiple-choice
test, multiple-guess test <nonformal>;
written examination, written <nonfor-
mal>, blue book <nonformal>, test
paper; course examination, midterm,
midyear, midsemester; qualifying examination, preliminary examination, prelim
<nonformal>; take-home examination;
unannounced examination, pop or shotgun or surprise quiz <nonformal>; final
examination, **final** <nonformal>, comprehensive examination, comps <non-
formal>, great go <old> or greats
<Oxford>; honors <Brit>, tripos
<Cambridge>

**3 examination, inspection, scrutiny; sur-
vey, review, perusal,** look-over, once over

and look-see <both nonformal>, perlustration, **study**, look-through, scan, run-through; visitation; overhaul, overhauling; quality control; confirmation, cross-check

4 **investigation**, indagation <old>, **research**, legwork <nonformal>, inquiry into; data-gathering, gathering *or* amassing evidence; perscrutation, **probe**, searching investigation, close inquiry, exhaustive study; police inquiry *or* investigation, criminal investigation, detective work, detection, sleuthing; investigative bureau *or* agency, bureau *or* department of investigation; legislative investigation, Congressional investigation, hearing; witch-hunt, fishing expedition, Inquisition

5 preliminary *or* tentative examination; quick *or* cursory inspection, glance, quick look, first look, once-over-lightly <nonformal>

6 **checkup, check**; spot check; physical examination, **physical**, physical checkup, health examination; self-examination; exploratory examination; testing, drug testing, alcohol testing, random testing

7 **re-examination**, reinquiry, recheck, **review**, reappraisal, revaluation, rethinking, revision, rebeholding, second *or* further look

8 **reconnaissance**; recce *and* recco *and* recon <all nonformal>; **reconnoitering**, reconnoiter, exploration, **scouting**

9 **surveillance**, shadowing, following, trailing, tailing <nonformal>, 24-hour surveillance, observation, stakeout <nonformal>; **spying, espionage**, espial, **intelligence**, military intelligence, intelligence work, cloak-and-dagger work <nonformal>; intelligence agency, secret service, secret police; counterespionage, counterintelligence; wiretap, wiretapping, bugging <nonformal>, electronic surveillance

10 **question, query, inquiry, demand** <old>, **interrogation**, interrogatory; interrogative; **problem, issue, topic** 936, case *or* point in question, bone of contention, controversial point, question before the house, debating point, question *or* point at issue, **moot point** *or* case, question mark, *quodlibet* <L>; vexed *or* knotty question, burning question; leader, leading question; feeler, trial balloon, fishing question; cross-question, rhetorical question; cross-interrogatory; catechism, catechizing

11 **interview**, press conference, press opportunity, photo opportunity, photo op <nonformal>

12 **questioning, interrogation, querying**, asking, seeking, pumping, probing, inquiring; **quiz**, quizzing, **examination**; challenge, dispute; interpellation, bringing into question; catechizing, catechization; catechetical method, Socratic method *or* induction

13 **grilling**, the grill <nonformal>, inquisition; police interrogation; **the third-degree** <nonformal>; direct examination, redirect examination, **cross-examination**, cross-interrogation, **cross-questioning**

14 **canvass, survey, inquiry, questionnaire**, questionary; exit poll; **poll, public-opinion poll**, opinion poll *or* survey, statistical survey, opinion sampling, voter-preference survey; consumer-preference survey, market-research survey; consumer research, market research

15 **search**, searching, **quest, hunt**, hunting, stalk, stalking, still hunt, dragnet, posse, search party; search warrant; search-and-destroy operation *or* mission; **rummage, ransacking**, turning over *or* upside down; **forage**; house-search, perquisition, domiciliary visit; exploration, probe; **body search**, frisk *and* toss *and* shake *and* shakedown *and* skin-search *and* body-shake *and* pat-down search <all nonformal>

16 **inquirer, asker, prober**, querier, querist, **questioner**, questionist, interrogator; interviewer; interrogatrix; interpellator; **quizzer**, examiner, catechist; inquisitor, inquisitionist; cross-questioner, cross-interrogator, **cross-examiner**; interlocutor; **pollster**, poller, sampler, opinion sampler; **interviewer**; **detective** 576.10; **secret agent** 576.9; quiz-master

17 **examiner**, examinant, **tester; inspector**, scrutinizer, scrutator, scrutineer, quality-control inspector; **monitor**, reviewer; fact-checker; check-out pilot; observer; visitor, visitator; **investigator**, indagator <old>; editor, copy editor, proofreader

18 seeker, hunter, searcher, perquisitor; rummager, ransacker; digger, delver; zetetic; **researcher, fact finder**, researchist, research worker

19 **examinee**, examinant, examinate, questionee, quizzee; interviewee; informant, subject, interviewee; witness

VERBS 20 inquire, ask, **question, query**; **make inquiry**, take up *or* institute *or* pursue *or* follow up *or* conduct *or* carry on an inquiry, ask after, inquire after, ask about, ask questions, put queries; inquire of, require an answer, ask a question, put a question to, pose *or* set *or* propose *or* propound a question; bring into question, interpellate; **demand** <old>, **want to know**

21 **interrogate, question, query, quiz, test, examine;** catechize; **pump,** pump for information, shoot questions at, pick the brains of, worm out of; interview; draw one out

22 **grill,** put on the grill <nonformal>, inquisition, make inquisition; roast <nonformal>, put the pressure on *and* put the screws to *and* go over <all nonformal>; **cross-examine, cross-question,** cross-interrogate; third-degree <nonformal>, give *or* put through the third degree <nonformal>; put to the question; extract information, pry *or* prize out

23 **investigate,** indagate <old>, sift, **explore, look into,** peer into, **search into, go into, delve into,** dig into, poke into, pry into; **probe, sound, plumb, fathom; check into, check on, check out,** nose into, see into; poke about, root around *or* about, scratch around *or* about, cast about *or* around

24 **examine, inspect, scrutinize, survey,** canvass, **look at,** peer at, eyeball <nonformal>, **observe, scan, peruse, study; look over,** give the once-over <nonformal>, run the eye over, cast *or* pass the eyes over, scope out <nonformal>; go over, run over, pass over, pore over; overlook, overhaul; **monitor, review,** pass under review; set an examination, give an examination; **take stock of,** size *or* **size up,** take the measure <nonformal>; **check, check out, check over *or* through; check up on;** autopsy, postmortem 307.18

25 **make a close study of, scrutinize,** examine thoroughly, vet <Brit>, **go deep into,** look closely at; examine point by point, go over with a fine-tooth comb, go over step by step, subject to close scrutiny, view *or* try in all its phases, get down to nuts and bolts <nonformal>; perscrutate, perlustrate

26 **examine cursorily,** take a cursory view of, give a quick *or* cursory look, give a once-over-lightly <nonformal>, give a dekko <Brit nonformal>, **scan, skim, skim over *or* through,** slur, slur over, slip *or* skip over *or* through, **glance at,** give the once-over <nonformal>, pass over lightly, zip through, **dip into, touch upon,** touch upon lightly *or* in passing, **hit the high spots; thumb through,** flip through the pages, turn over the leaves, leaf *or* page *or* flick through

27 **re-examine,** recheck, reinquire, **reconsider,** reappraise, revaluate, rethink, **review,** revise, rebehold, take another *or* a second *or* a further look; retrace, retrace one's steps, go back over; rejig *or* rejigger <nonformal>; take back to the old drawing board

28 **reconnoiter,** make a reconnaissance, case <nonformal>, scout, **scout out,** spy, **spy out,** play the spy, peep; **watch,** put under surveillance, stake out <nonformal>; bug <nonformal>; check up on, check up

29 **canvass, survey,** make a survey; **poll,** conduct a poll, sample, **questionnaire** <nonformal>

30 **seek, hunt,** look <old>, **quest, pursue,** go in pursuit of, follow, go in search of, prowl after, see to, try to find; **look up, hunt up; look for,** look around *or* about for, look for high and low, look high and low, search out, **search for,** seek for, **hunt for,** cast *or* beat about for; shop around for; **fish for, angle for,** bob for, dig for, delve for, go on a fishing expedition; **ask for,** inquire for; **gun for,** go gunning for; still-hunt <nonformal>

31 **search, hunt, explore;** research; read up on; **hunt through, search through, look through, go through;** dig, delve, burrow, root, pick over, poke, pry; look round *or* around, poke around, nose around, smell around; beat the bushes; forage; frisk <nonformal>

32 **grope,** grope for, **feel for,** fumble, grabble, scrabble, feel around, poke around, pry around, beat about, grope in the dark; **feel *or* pick one's way**

33 **ransack, rummage, rake, scour, comb;** rifle; **look everywhere,** look into every hole and corner, **look high and low,** look upstairs and downstairs, **look all over,** look all over hell <nonformal>, search high heaven, turn upside down, turn inside out, **leave no stone unturned;** shake down *and* shake *and* toss <all nonformal>

34 **search out, hunt out, spy out,** scout out, **ferret out,** fish out, pry out, winkle out <Brit nonformal>, dig out, root out, grub up

35 **trace, stalk, track, trail; follow,** follow up, shadow, tail <nonformal>, dog the footsteps of, have *or* keep an eye on; nose, nose out, **smell *or* sniff out,** follow the trail *or* scent *or* spoor of; follow a clue; **trace down, hunt down, track down, run down, run to earth**

ADJS **36 inquiring, questioning, querying,**
quizzing; **quizzical, curious; interrogatory,** interrogative, interrogational;
inquisitorial, inquisitional; visitatorial,
visitorial; catechistic, catechistical, cate-
chetic, catechetical

37 examining, examinational; scrutatorial,
examinatorial; **testing,** trying, **tentative;**
groping, feeling; **inspectional;** inspec-
torial; **investigative,** indagative <old>;
zetetic; heuristic, investigatory, investi-
gational; **exploratory,** explorative, explo-
rational; fact-finding; analytic, analytical

38 searching, probing, prying, nosy
<nonformal>; poking, digging, fishing,
delving; in search or quest of, looking for,
out for, on the lookout for, **in the market
for,** loaded or out for bear <nonformal>;
all-searching

ADVS **39 in question, at issue,** in debate or
dispute, **under consideration,** under active consideration, **under advisement,**
subjudice <L>, under examination, under investigation, under surveillance, up
or open for discussion; **before the house,
on the docket, on the agenda, on the table, on the floor**

938 ANSWER

NOUNS **1 answer, reply, response,** respon-
sion, replication; answering, respondence; riposte, **uptake** <nonformal>,
retort, rejoinder, reaction 902, return,
comeback and **take** <both nonformal>,
back answer, short answer, back talk;
repartee, backchat, clever or ready or
witty reply or retort, snappy comeback
<nonformal>; yes-and-no answer, eva-
sive reply; **acknowledgment,** receipt;
rescript, rescription; antiphon; **echo,** reverberation 54.2

2 rebuttal, counterstatement, counter-
reply, counterclaim, counterblast,
counteraccusation, countercharge, *tu
quoque* <L, you too>, contraremon-
strance; **rejoinder,** replication, defense,
rebutter, surrebutter or surrebuttal, sur-
rejoinder; confutation, refutation

3 answerer, replier, responder, **respondent,**
responser

VERBS **4 answer,** make or give answer, return answer, return for answer, offer,
proffer, **reply, respond,** say, say in reply;
retort, riposte, **rejoin,** return, throw back,
flash back; come back *and* come back at
and come right back at <all nonformal>,
answer back *and* talk back *and* shoot back
<all nonformal>; **react; acknowledge,**

make or give acknowledgement; echo,
reecho, reverberate 54.7

5 rebut, make a rebuttal; **rejoin,** surrebut,
surrejoin; counterclaim, countercharge;
confute, refute

ADJS **6 answering, replying, responsive,** respondent, responding; rejoining, returning; antiphonal; echoing, echoic,
reechoing 54.11; confutative, refutative

ADVS **7** in answer, in reply, in response, in
return, in rebuttal

939 SOLUTION
<answer to a problem>

NOUNS **1 solution,** resolution, **answer, reason, explanation** 341.4; **finding,** conclusion, determination, ascertainment,
verdict, judgment; **outcome, upshot,** denouement, **result,** issue, end 819, end
result; accomplishment 407; **solving,**
working, **working-out,** finding-out, re-
solving, **clearing up,** cracking; **unrid-
dling,** riddling, unscrambling, unraveling, sorting out, untwisting, unspinning,
unweaving, untangling, disentanglement; **decipherment, deciphering, decoding,** decryption; interpretation 341;
happy ending or outcome, the answer to
one's prayers, the light at the end of the
tunnel; possible solution, **scenario**

VERBS **2 solve, resolve,** find the solution or
answer, **clear up,** get, get right, do, work,
work out, find out, figure out, dope *and*
dope out <both nonformal>; **straighten
out, iron out,** sort out, puzzle out; debug;
psych *and* psych out <both nonformal>;
unriddle, riddle, unscramble, undo, untangle, disentangle, untwist, unspin, unweave, **unravel,** ravel, ravel out; **decipher,
decode,** decrypt, crack; **make out,** interpret 341.9; **answer, explain** 341.10; unlock,
pick or open the lock; find the key of, find
a clue to; **get to the bottom** or **heart of,
fathom,** plumb, bottom; have it, hit it, hit
upon a solution, hit the nail on the head, hit
it on the nose <nonformal>; guess, divine,
guess right; end happily, work out right
and come up roses <both nonformal>

ADJS **3 solvable,** soluble, **resolvable,** open to
solution, capable of solution, workable,
doable, answerable; explainable, explicable, determinable, ascertainable;
decipherable, decodable

940 DISCOVERY

NOUNS **1 discovery, finding, detection,** spotting, catching, catching sight of, sighting,

espial; recognition, determination, distinguishment; **locating, location; disclosure, exposure, uncovering, unearthing,** digging up, exhumation, excavation, bringing to light *or* view; **find,** trove, treasure trove, *trouvaille* <Fr>, strike, lucky strike; accidental *or* chance discovery, happening *or* stumbling upon, tripping over, casual discovery; serendipity; **learning, finding out,** determining, becoming conscious *or* cognizant of, becoming aware of; self-discovery; rediscovery; invention

VERBS **2 discover, find,** get; strike, hit; put *or* lay one's hands on, lay one's fingers on, **locate** 159.10; **hunt down,** search out, trace down, track down, **run down, run** *or* **bring to earth;** trace; **learn, find out,** determine, become cognizant *or* conscious of, become aware of; discover *or* find out the hard way, discover to one's cost; discover *or* find oneself; rediscover; invent

3 come across, run across, meet with, meet up with <nonformal>, fall in with, **encounter, run into,** bump into <nonformal>, come *or* run up against <nonformal>, **come on** *or* **upon, hit on** *or* **upon,** strike on, light on *or* upon, alight on *or* upon, fall on, tumble on *or* upon; **chance on** *or* **upon,** happen on *or* upon *or* across, **stumble on** *or* **upon,** *or* across *or* into, stub one's toe on *or* upon, trip over, bump up against, blunder upon, discover serendipitously

4 uncover, unearth, dig up, disinter, exhume, excavate; **disclose, expose, reveal,** blow the lid off, crack wide open, **bring to light; turn up,** root up, rootle up <Brit>, fish up; worm out, ferret out, winkle out <Brit>, pry out

5 detect, spot, <nonformal>, **see, lay eyes on,** catch sight of, **spy,** espy, descry, sense, pick up, notice, discern, **perceive, make out, recognize,** distinguish, identify

6 scent, catch the scent of, sniff, smell, get a whiff of <nonformal>, **get wind of;** sniff *or* scent *or* smell out, nose out; be on the right scent, be near the truth, be warm <nonformal>, burn <nonformal>, have a fix on

7 catch, catch out; catch off side, catch off base; catch tripping, **catch napping, catch off-guard,** catch asleep at the switch; **catch at,** catch in the act, **catch red-handed,** catch in *flagrante delicto,* **catch with one's pants down** <nonformal>, catch flat-footed, have the goods on <nonformal>

8 <detect the hidden nature of> **see**

through, penetrate, see as it really is, see in its true colors, see the inside of, read between the lines, see the cloven hoof; open the eyes to, tumble to, catch on to, wise up to <nonformal>; **be on to, be wise to, be hep to** <nonformal>, have one's measure, **have one's number,** have dead to rights <nonformal>, read someone like a book

9 turn up, show up, be found; discover itself, expose *or* betray itself; hang out <nonformal>; materialize, **come to light,** come out; come along, come to hand

ADJS **10** on the right scent, **on the right track,** on the trail of; **hot** *and* **warm** <both nonformal>; **discoverable,** determinable, findable, **detectable,** spottable, disclosable, exposable, locatable, **discernible**

INTERJS **11 eureka!,** I have it!, at last!, at long last!, finally!, *thalassa!, thalatta!* <both Gk>; ah hah!

941 EXPERIMENT

NOUNS **1 experiment, experimentation;** experimental method; testing, trying, trying-out, **trial;** research and development *or* R and D; running it up the flagpole <nonformal>, trying it on *or* out <nonformal>; **trial and error,** hit and miss, cut and try <nonformal>; empiricism, experimentalism, pragmatism, instrumentalism; **rule of thumb;** tentativeness, tentative method; control experiment, controlled experiment, **control;** experimental design; experimental proof *or* verification; noble experiment; single-blind experiment, double-blind experiment

2 test, trial, try; essay; docimasy <old>, assay; determination, blank determination; **proof,** verification; touchstone, standard, criterion 300.2; crucial test; acid test, litmus *or* litmus-paper test; ordeal, crucible; probation; **feeling out, sounding out;** test case; first *or* rough draft, *brouillon* <Fr>; rough sketch

3 tryout, workout, **rehearsal,** practice; pilot plan *or* program; **dry run,** dummy run; *Gedankenexperiment* <Ger>; road test; **trial run,** practical test; shakedown, shakedown cruise, bench test; flight test, test flight *or* run; audition, hearing

4 feeler, probe, sound, sounder; **trial balloon,** *ballon d'essai* <Fr>, pilot balloon, barometer; weather vane, weathercock; straw to show the wind, straw vote; sample, random sample, experimental sample

5 **laboratory, lab** <nonformal>, research laboratory, research establishment *or* facility *or* institute, experiment station, field station, research and development *or* R and D establishment; **proving ground**; think tank <nonformal>

6 **experimenter,** experimentist, experimentalist, bench scientist, **researcher,** research worker, R and D worker; experimental engineer; **tester,** tryer-out, test driver, test pilot; essayer; assayer; analyst, analyzer

7 **subject, experimental subject,** experimentee, testee, patient, sample; laboratory animal, experimental *or* test animal, **guinea pig**

VERBS 8 **experiment,** experimentalize, **research,** make an experiment, **run an experiment,** run a sample *or* specimen; **test, try,** essay, cut and try <nonformal>, **test** *or* **try out,** have a dry run *or* dummy run *or* rehearsal *or* test run; run it up the flagpole and see who salutes <nonformal>; put to the test, **put to the proof, prove, verify,** validate, substantiate, confirm, put to trial, bring to test, make a trial of, give a trial to; **give a try,** have a go, give it a go <nonformal>, have *or* take a stab <nonformal>; sample, taste; assay; play around *or* fool around with <nonformal>; try out under controlled conditions; give a tryout *or* workout <nonformal>, **road-test,** shake down; try one out, put one through his paces; experiment *or* practice upon; try it on; try on, try it for size <nonformal>; try one's strength, see what one can do

9 **sound out, feel out, sound,** get a sounding *or* reading *or* sense, probe, **feel the pulse,** read; **put** *or* **throw out a feeler,** put out feelers, send up a trial balloon, fly a kite; **see which way the wind blows,** see how the land lies, test out, test the waters; take a straw vote, take a random sample, use an experimental sample

10 **stand the test, stand up, hold up, hold up in the wash,** pass, **pass muster,** get by <nonformal>, make it *and* hack it *and* cut the mustard <all nonformal>, meet *or* satisfy requirements

ADJS 11 **experimental, test, trial;** pilot; testing, proving, trying; probative, probatory, verificatory; probationary; **tentative,** provisional; empirical; trial-and-error, hit-or-miss, cut-and-try; heuristic

12 **tried, well-tried, tested, proved,** verified, confirmed, tried and true

ADVS 13 **experimentally,** by rule of thumb, by trial and error, by hit and miss, hit or miss, by guess and by God

14 **on trial,** under examination, **on** *or* **under probation,** under suspicion, **on approval**

942 COMPARISON

NOUNS 1 **comparison,** compare, examining side by side, matching, matchup, holding up together, proportion <old>, comparative judgment *or* estimate; **likening, comparing, analogy;** parallelism; comparative relation; weighing, balancing; opposing, opposition, **contrast;** contrastiveness, distinctiveness, distinction 943.3; confrontment, confrontation; **relation** 774, relating, relativism; correlation 776; simile, similitude, metaphor, allegory, figure *or* trope of comparison; comparative degree; comparative method; comparative linguistics, comparative grammar, comparative literature, comparative anatomy, etc

2 **collation,** comparative scrutiny, point-by-point comparison; **verification, confirmation, checking;** check, cross-check

3 **comparability,** comparableness, comparativeness; analogousness, equivalence, **commensurability;** proportionateness *or* proportionability <both old>; ratio, proportion, balance; **similarity** 783

VERBS 4 **compare, liken,** assimilate, similize, liken to, compare with; **make** *or* **draw a comparison,** run a comparison, do a comparative study, bring into comparison; **analogize,** bring into analogy; **relate** 774.6; metaphorize; **draw a parallel,** parallel; **match,** match up; examine side by side, view together, hold up together; weigh *or* measure against; confront, bring into confrontation; **contrast, oppose,** set in opposition, set off against, set in contrast, **put** *or* **set over against,** set *or* place against, counterpose; compare and contrast, note similarities and differences; **weigh,** balance

5 **collate,** scrutinize comparatively, compare point by point, painstakingly match; **verify, confirm, check, cross-check**

6 **compare notes,** exchange views *or* observations, match data *or* findings, put heads together <nonformal>

7 **be comparable, compare, compare to** *or* **with,** not compare with 786.2, admit of comparison, be commensurable, be of the same order *or* class, be worthy of compar-

ison, be fit to be compared; **measure up to, come up to,** match up with, stack up with <nonformal>, hold a candle to <nonformal>; **match, parallel;** vie, vie with, rival; **resemble** 783.7

ADJS **8 comparative, relative** 774.7, **comparable,** commensurate, commensurable, parallel, matchable, **analogous;** analogical; collatable; **correlative;** much at one, much of a muchness <nonformal>; **similar** 783.10; something of the sort *or* to that effect

9 incomparable, incommensurable, not to be compared, of different orders; apples and oranges; **unlike, dissimilar** 786.4

ADVS **10 comparatively, relatively;** comparably; dollar for dollar, pound for pound, ounce for ounce, etc; on the one hand, on the other hand

PREPS **11 compared to, compared with,** as compared with, by comparison with, **in comparison with, beside,** over against, taken with; than

943 DISCRIMINATION

NOUNS **1 discrimination,** discriminateness, discriminatingness, discriminativeness; seeing *or* making distinctions, appreciation of differences; analytic power *or* faculty; **criticalness; finesse,** refinement, delicacy; niceness of distinction, nicety, subtlety, refined discrimination, critical niceness; **tact, tactfulness,** feel, feeling, sense, **sensitivity** 24.3, **sensibility** 24.2; intuition, instinct 933; appreciation, appreciativeness; judiciousness 919.7; taste, discriminating taste, aesthetic *or* artistic judgment; palate, fine *or* refined palate; ear, good ear, educated ear; eye, good eye; connoisseurship, savvy <nonformal>, selectiveness, fastidiousness 495

2 discernment, critical discernment, penetration, **perception,** perceptiveness, **insight,** perspicacity; **flair; judgment,** acumen 919.4; analysis 800

3 distinction, contradistinction, distinctiveness <old>; **distinguishment, differentiation** 779.4, winnowing, shakeout, separation, separationism, division, segregation, segregationism, demarcation; nice *or* subtle *or* fine distinction, **nuance,** shade of difference, microscopic distinction; hairsplitting, trichoschistism

VERBS **4 discriminate, distinguish,** draw *or* make distinctions, contradistinguish, secern, distinguish in thought, **separate,** separate out, divide, analyze 800.6, sub-

divide, **segregate,** sever, severalize, **differentiate,** demark, demarcate, mark the interface, set off, **set apart,** sift, sift out, sieve, sieve out, winnow, screen, screen out, sort, classify, sort out; **pick out, select** 371.14; separate the sheep from the goats, separate the men from the boys, separate the wheat from the tares *or* chaff, winnow the chaff from the wheat; **draw the line,** fix *or* set a limit; **split hairs,** draw *or* make a fine *or* overfine *or* nice *or* subtle distinction, subtilize

5 be discriminating, discriminate, exercise discrimination, tell which is which; **be tactful,** show *or* exercise tact; be tasteful, use one's palate; shop around, pick and choose; use advisedly

6 distinguish between, make *or* **draw a distinction,** appreciate differences, see nuances *or* shades of difference, see the difference, tell apart, tell one thing from another, know which is which, know what's what <nonformal>, not confound *or* mix up; "know a hawk from a handsaw"—Shakespeare, know one's ass from one's elbow <nonformal>

ADJS **7 discriminating, discriminate,** discriminative, selective; discriminatory; **tactful, sensitive;** appreciative, appreciatory; **critical;** distinctive <old>, **distinguishing;** differential; precise, accurate, exact; nice, fine, delicate, subtle, subtile, refined; fastidious 495.9; distinctive, contrastive

8 discerning, perceptive, perspicacious, insightful; **astute, judicious** 919.19

9 discriminable, distinguishable, separable, differentiable, contrastable, opposable

ADVS **10 discriminatingly,** discriminatively, discriminately; with finesse; **tactfully; tastefully**

944 INDISCRIMINATION

NOUNS **1 indiscrimination,** indiscriminateness, undiscriminatingness, undiscriminativeness, unselectiveness, **uncriticalness, unparticularness;** syncretism; unfastidiousness; lack of refinement, coarseness *or* crudeness *or* crudity of intellect; **casualness,** promiscuousness, **promiscuity; indiscretion,** indiscreetness, **imprudence** 922.2; **untactfulness,** tactlessness, lack of feeling, **insensitivity,** insensibility 25, unmeticulousness, unpreciseness 340.4; **generality** 863, catholicity

2 indistinction, indistinctness, vagueness

32.2; **indefiniteness** 970.4; uniformity 780; facelessness, impersonality; **indistinguishableness,** undistinguishableness, indiscernibility; a distinction without a difference

VERBS **3 confound, confuse,** mix, mix up, muddle, tumble, jumble, jumble together, **blur,** blur distinctions, overlook distinctions

4 use loosely, use unadvisedly

ADJS **5 undiscriminating, indiscriminate,** indiscriminative, undiscriminative, undifferentiating, unselective; wholesale, **general** 863.11, **blanket; uncritical,** uncriticizing, undemanding, nonjudgmental; **unparticular,** unfastidious; unsubtle; **casual, promiscuous,** unexacting, unmeticulous 340.13; **indiscreet,** undiscreet, **imprudent; untactful,** tactless, insensitive

6 indistinguishable, undistinguishable, undistinguished, indiscernible, **indistinct,** indistinctive, **without distinction,** not to be distinguished, undiscriminated, unindividual, unindividualized, undifferentiated, **alike,** six of one and half a dozen of the other <nonformal>; **indefinite;** faceless, impersonal; standard, interchangeable, stereotyped, uniform 780.5

945 JUDGMENT

NOUNS **1 judgment,** judging, adjudgment, adjudication, judicature, deeming <old>; judgment call <nonformal>; arbitrament, arbitration 466.2; **resolution** 359; good judgment 919.7; **choice** 371; **discrimination** 943

2 criticism; censure 510.3; **approval** 509; **critique,** review, notice, critical notice, report, comment; book review, critical review, thumbnail review; literary criticism, art criticism, music criticism, etc, critical journal, critical bibliography

3 estimate, estimation; view, opinion 952.6; **assessment,** assessing, **appraisal,** appraisement, appraising, appreciation, reckoning, **stocktaking,** valuation, valuing, **evaluation,** evaluating, value judgment, evaluative criticism, analyzing, weighing, weighing up, gauging, ranking, rank-ordering, **rating;** measurement 300; comparison 942

4 conclusion, deduction, inference, consequence, consequent, corollary; derivation, illation; induction

5 verdict, decision, resolution <old>, **determination, finding,** holding; diagnosis, prognosis; **decree, ruling,** consideration,

order, **pronouncement,** deliverance; **award,** action, **sentence; condemnation,** doom; dictum; precedent

6 judge, judger, adjudicator, justice; arbiter 596.1; referee, umpire

7 critic, criticizer; connoisseur, *cognoscente* <Ital>; literary critic, man of letters; textual critic; editor; social critic, muckraker; captious critic, smellfungus, caviler, carper, faultfinder; criticaster, criticule, critickin; **censor,** censurer; **reviewer, commentator,** commenter; scholiast, annotator

VERBS **8 judge,** exercise judgment *or* the judgment; make a judgment call <nonformal>; adjudge, adjudicate; be judicious *or* judgmental; **consider, regard,** hold, **deem, esteem, count, account,** think of; allow <nonformal>, **suppose, presume** 950.10, opine, form an opinion, give *or* pass *or* express an opinion, weigh in *and* put in one's two cents worth <both nonformal>

9 estimate, form an estimate, make an estimation; **reckon,** call, guess, figure <nonformal>; **assess, appraise,** give an appreciation, **gauge, rate, rank,** rank-order, put in rank order, class, mark, **value, evaluate,** valuate, place *or* set a value on, weigh, weigh up, prize, appreciate; size up *or* take one's measure <nonformal>, **measure** 300.11

10 conclude, draw a conclusion, be forced to conclude, **come to *or* arrive at a conclusion, come up with a conclusion** *and* **end up** <both nonformal>; find, hold; deduce, derive, take as proved *or* demonstrated, extract, **gather,** collect, glean, fetch; **infer,** draw an inference; induce; **reason,** reason that; put two and two together

11 decide, determine; find, hold, ascertain; **resolve** 359.7, **settle,** fix; make a decision, come to a decision, **make up one's mind,** settle one's mind, come down <nonformal>

12 sit in judgment, hold the scales, hold court; **hear,** give a hearing to; **try** 598.17; **referee, umpire,** officiate; arbitrate 466.6

13 pass judgment, pronounce judgment, utter a judgment, deliver judgment; agree on a verdict, return a verdict, hand down a verdict, **bring in a verdict, find,** find for *or* against; pronounce on, act on, **pronounce,** report, **rule,** decree, order; **sentence,** pass sentence, hand down a sentence, doom, condemn

14 criticize, critique; **censure** 510.13, pick holes in, pick to pieces; **approve** 509.9; **re-**

view; comment upon, annotate; moralize upon; pontificate

15 **rank, rate,** count, be regarded, be thought of, be in one's estimation

ADJS **16 judicial, judiciary,** judicative, judgmental; juridic, juridical, juristic, juristical; **judicious** 919.19; **evaluative; critical; approbatory** 509.16

ADVS **17 all things considered, on the whole, taking one thing with another,** on balance, taking everything into consideration *or* account; everything being equal, other things being equal, *ceteris paribus* <L>, taking into account, considering, after all, this being so; therefore, wherefore; on the one hand, on the other hand, having said that; *sub judice* <L>, in court, before the bench *or* bar *or* court

946 PREJUDGMENT

NOUNS **1 prejudgment,** prejudication, forejudgment; **preconception, presumption, supposition, presupposition,** presupposal, presurmise, preapprehension, prenotion, **prepossession; predilection,** predisposition; preconsideration, **predetermination,** predecision, preconclusion, premature judgment; ulterior motive, hidden agenda, *parti pris* <Fr>, an ax to grind, **prejudice** 979.3

VERBS **2 prejudge,** forejudge; **preconceive, presuppose, presume,** presurmise; **be predisposed;** predecide, predetermine, preconclude, judge beforehand *or* prematurely, judge before the evidence is in, have one's mind made up; **jump to a conclusion,** go off half-cocked *or* at half cock *and* beat the gun *and* jump the gun *and* shoot from the hip <all nonformal>

ADJS **3 prejudged,** forejudged, **preconceived,** preconceptual, **presumed, presupposed,** presurmised; predetermined, predecided, preconcluded, judged beforehand *or* prematurely; **predisposed,** predispositional; prejudicial, prejudging, prejudicative

947 MISJUDGMENT

NOUNS **1 misjudgment,** poor judgment, error in judgment, warped *or* flawed *or* skewed judgment; **miscalculation,** miscomputation, **misreckoning, misestimation,** misappreciation, misperception, misevaluation, misvaluation, misconjecture, wrong impression; **misreading,** wrong construction, misconstruction,

misinterpretation 342; **inaccuracy, error** 974; unmeticulousness 340.4; injudiciousness 922.2

VERBS **2 misjudge,** judge amiss, **miscalculate, misestimate, misreckon,** misappreciate, misperceive, get a wrong impression, misevaluate, misvalue, miscompute, misdeem, misesteem, misthink, misconjecture; **misread,** misconstrue, put the wrong construction on things, misread the situation *or* case; **misinterpret** 342.2; err 974.9; fly in the face of facts

948 OVERESTIMATION

NOUNS **1 overestimation,** overestimate, **overreckoning,** overcalculation, **overrating,** overassessment, overvaluation, overappraisal; overreaction; **overstatement, exaggeration** 355

VERBS **2 overestimate, overreckon,** overcalculate, overcount, overmeasure, see more than is there; **overrate,** overassess, overappraise, overesteem, **overvalue,** overprize, think *or* make too much of, put on a pedestal, idealize, see only the good points of; overreact to; **overstate, exaggerate** 355.3; pump up *and* jump up *and* make a big deal *or* Federal case <all nonformal>

ADJS **3 overestimated, overrated,** puffed up, pumped up <nonformal>, overvalued, on the high side; **exaggerated** 355.4

949 UNDERESTIMATION

NOUNS **1 underestimation,** misestimation, underestimate, **underrating,** underreckoning, undervaluation, misprizing, misprizal, misprision; **belittlement, depreciation,** deprecation, **minimization,** disparagement 512

VERBS **2 underestimate,** misestimate, **underrate,** underreckon, **undervalue,** underprize, **misprize; make little of,** set at little, set at naught, set little by, attach little importance to, not do justice to, sell short, think little of, make *or* think nothing of, see less than is there, miss on the low side, set no store by, make light of, shrug off; **depreciate, deprecate,** minimize, belittle, bad-mouth *and* poor-mouth *and* put down *and* run down <all nonformal>, take someone for an idiot *or* a fool; disparage 512.8

ADJS **3 underestimated, underrated,** undervalued, on the low side; unvalued, unprized, misprized

950 THEORY, SUPPOSITION

NOUNS **1 theory,** theorization, *theoria*
<Gk>; theoretics, theoretic, theoric
<old>; **hypothesis,** hypothecation, hy-
pothesizing; **speculation,** mere theory;
doctrinairism, doctrinality, doctrinarity;
analysis, **explanation,** abstraction; theoretical basis *or* justification; body of
theory, theoretical structure *or* construct;
unified theory

2 theory, explanation, proposed *or* tentative explanation, proposal, proposition,
statement covering the facts or evidence;
hypothesis, working hypothesis

3 supposition, supposal, supposing; **presupposition,** presupposal; **assumption,
presumption, conjecture, inference,** surmise, guesswork; **postulate,** postulation,
postulatum <L>, set of postulates; **proposition, thesis, premise 934.7; axiom** 973.2

4 guess, conjecture, unverified supposition,
perhaps, speculation, guesswork, surmise, educated guess; guesstimate *and*
hunch *and* shot *and* stab <all nonfor-
mal>; rough guess, wild guess, blind
guess, bold conjecture, shot in the dark
<nonformal>

5 <vague supposition> **suggestion,** bare
suggestion, **suspicion, inkling, hint,
sense, feeling, feeling in one's bones,** intuition 933, intimation, impression, **notion,**
mere notion, hunch *and* sneaking suspicion <both nonformal>, trace of an idea,
half an idea, vague idea, hazy idea, **idea**
931

6 supposititiousness, presumptiveness,
presumableness, theoreticalness, hypo-
theticalness, conjecturableness, speculativeness

7 theorist, theorizer, theoretic, **theoretician,** notionalist <old>; **speculator;**
hypothesist, hypothesizer; doctrinaire,
doctrinarian; synthesizer; armchair authority *or* philosopher

8 supposer, assumer, surmiser, **conjec-
turer, guesser,** guessworker

VERBS **9 theorize, hypothesize, hypothecate,
speculate,** have *or* entertain a theory, espouse a theory

10 suppose, assume, presume, surmise, expect, **suspect, infer, understand, gather,
conclude, deduce, consider,** reckon, divine, imagine, **fancy,** dream, conceive,
believe, deem, repute, feel, **think,** be inclined to think, opine, say, daresay, be
afraid <nonformal>; take, take it, take it
into one's head, take for, take to be, take
for granted, take as a precondition, **pre-**
suppose, presurmise, prefigure; provisionally accept *or* admit *or* agree to, take
one up on <nonformal>, grant, stipulate,
take it as given, let, let be, say *or* assume
for argument's sake, say for the hell of it
<nonformal>

11 conjecture, guess, guesstimate <nonfor-
mal>, give a guess, talk off the top of
one's head <nonformal>, hazard a conjecture, venture a guess, risk assuming *or*
stating, tentatively suggest, go out on a
limb <nonformal>

12 postulate, predicate, posit, set forth, lay
down, assert; pose, advance, **propose,
propound** 439.5

ADJS **13 theoretical, hypothetical,** hypo-
thetic; postulatory, notional; **speculative,
conjectural;** impressionistic, intuitive
933.5; general, generalized, abstract,
ideal; merely theoretical, academic,
moot; impractical, armchair

**14 supposed, suppositive, assumed, pre-
sumed, conjectured, inferred,** understood, deemed, **reputed,** putative, alleged, accounted as; suppositional, sup-
positious; assumptive, **presumptive;**
given, granted, taken as *or* for granted,
agreed, stipulated; **postulated,** postula-
tional, premised

15 supposable, presumable, assumable, con-
jecturable, surmisable, imaginable,
premissable

ADVS **16 theoretically, hypothetically,** *ex hy-
pothesi* <L>, ideally; **in theory,** in idea, in
the ideal, in the abstract, on paper, in
Never-Neverland <nonformal>

17 supposedly, supposably, presumably,
presumedly, assumably, assumedly, presumptively, assumptively, reputedly;
suppositionally, suppositiously; **seemingly,** in seeming, quasi; as it were

18 conjecturably, **conjecturally;** to guess, to
make a guess, **as a guess,** as a rough guess
or an approximation

CONJS **19 supposing,** supposing that, **assuming that,** allowing that, if we assume that,
let's say that, granting *or* granted that,
given that, on the assumption *or* supposition that; if, as if, as though, by way of
hypothesis

951 PHILOSOPHY

NOUNS **1 philosophy,** "life's guide"—Cicero,
"a handmaid to religion"—Francis Bacon; philosophical inquiry *or* investigation, philosophical speculation; inquiry
or investigation into first causes; branch
of philosophy <see list>, department *or*

division of philosophy; school of philosophy <see list>, philosophic system, school of thought; philosophic doctrine, philosophic theory; philosophastry, philosophastering; sophistry 935

2 Platonic philosophy, Platonism, philosophy of the Academy; Aristotelian philosophy, Aristotelianism, philosophy of the Lyceum, Peripateticism, Peripatetic school; Stoic philosophy, Stoicism, philosophy of the Porch or Stoa; Epicureanism, philosophy of the Garden

3 **materialism; idealism** 1051.3

4 monism, philosophical unitarianism, mind-stuff theory; pantheism, cosmotheism; hylozoism

5 pluralism; dualism, mind-matter theory

6 **philosopher,** philosophizer, philosophe; philosophaster; **thinker,** speculator; casuist; metaphysician, cosmologist; sophist 935.6

VERBS 7 **philosophize,** reason 934.15, probe

ADJS 8 **philosophical,** philosophic, sophistical 935.10; philosophicohistorical, philosophicolegal, philosophicojuristic, philosophicopsychological, philosophicoreligious, philosophicotheological

9 absurdist, acosmistic, aesthetic, African, agnostic, Alexandrian, analytic, animalistic, animist or animistic, atomistic, etc <see list of schools and doctrines>

10 Aristotelian, Peripatetic; Augustinian, Averroist or Averroistic, Bergsonian, Berkeleian, Cartesian, Comtian, Hegelian, Neo-Hegelian, Heideggerian, Heraclitean, Humean, Husserlian, Kantian, Leibnizian, Parmenidean, Platonic, Neoplatonic, pre-Socratic, Pyrrhonic, Pyrrhonian, Pythagorean, Neo-Pythagorean, Sartrian, Schellingian, Schopenhauerian, Scotist, Socratic, Spencerian, Thomist or Thomistic, Viconian, Wittgensteinian

11 **branches or departments of philosophy**

aesthetics or theory of beauty or philosophy of art
axiology or value theory
cosmology
ethics
logic
metaphysics or first philosophy
ontology or science of being
philosophy of biology
philosophy of education
philosophy of history
philosophy of law
philosophy of logic
philosophy of nature
philosophy of physics
philosophy of religion
philosophy of science
political philosophy
theory of knowledge or epistemology or gnosiology

12 **schools and doctrines of philosophy**

Augustinianism
Averroism
Bergsonism
Berkeleianism
Bonaventurism
Bradleianism
Buddhism
Cartesianism
Comtism
Confucianism
cosmotheism
criticism or critical philosophy
Cynicism
Cyrenaic hedonism or Cyrenaicism
deconstructionism
deism
dialectical materialism
dualism
eclecticism
egoism
egoistic hedonism
Eleaticism or the Elean school
empiricism
Epicureanism
Eretrian school
eristic school
essentialism
ethicism
ethics
eudaemonism
existentialism or existential philosophy
Fichteanism
hedonism
Hegelianism
Heideggerianism
Heracliteanism
Herbartianism
Hinduism
humanism
Humism
hylomorphism
hylotheism
hylozoism
idealism
immaterialism
individualism
instrumentalism
intuitionism
Ionian school
Jainism
Kantianism
Leibnizianism
linguistic philosophy
logical empiricism or logical positivism
Marxism
materialism
mechanism
Megarianism
mentalism
Mimamsa
monism
mysticism
naturalism
Neo-Hegelianism
Neo-Pythagoreanism
neo-scholasticism
neocriticism
Neoplatonism
new ethical movement
nominalism
noumenalism
Nyaya
ontologism
ontology
optimism
ordinary language philosophy
organic mechanism
organicism
panlogism
panpneumatism
panpsychism
pantheism
panthelism
Parmenidean school
patristic philosophy
patristicism
Peripateticism
pessimism
phenomenalism
phenomenology
philosophy of organism
philosophy of signs
philosophy of the ante-Nicene Fathers
philosophy of the post-Nicene Fathers
physicalism
physicism
Platonism
pluralism
positivism
pragmatism or pragmaticism
probabilism
psychism
psychological hedonism
Purva Mimamsa
Pyrrhonism
Pythagoreanism
rationalism
realism
Sankhya
Sartrianism
Schellingism
Scholasticism
Schopenhauerism
Scotism
secular humanism

semiotic *or* semiotics
or semi-idiotics
<nonformal>
sensationalism
sensism
Shinto
Sikhism
skepticism
Socratism
solipsism
Sophism *or* Sophistry
Spencerianism
Spinozism
Stoicism

substantialism
syncretism
theism
Thomism
Toaism
transcendentalism
universalistic hedo-
nism
utilitarianism
Uttara Mimamsa
Valsheshika
vitalism
voluntarism
zetetic philosophy

952 BELIEF

NOUNS 1 **belief,** credence, credit, faith, trust; hope; **confidence,** assuredness, convincedness, persuadedness, **assurance;** sureness, surety, **certainty** 969; **reliance, dependence,** reliance on *or* in, dependence on, stock *and* store <both nonformal>; acceptation, acception, reception, acquiescence; full faith and credit; suspension of disbelief; fideism; **credulity** 953

2 **a belief, tenet, dogma,** precept, **principle, principle** *or* **article of faith,** canon, maxim, axiom; **doctrine,** teaching

3 **system of belief; religion, faith** 675.1, belief-system; **school, cult, ism, ideology,** *Weltanschauung* <Ger>, world view; political faith *or* belief *or* philosophy; **creed, credo,** credenda; articles of religion, articles of faith, creedal *or* doctrinal statement, formulated *or* stated belief; gospel; catechism

4 **statement of belief** *or* **principles, manifesto,** position paper; solemn declaration; deposition, affidavit, sworn statement

5 **conviction, persuasion, certainty; firm belief,** moral certainty, implicit *or* staunch belief, settled judgment, mature judgment *or* belief, fixed opinion, unshaken confidence, steadfast faith, rooted *or* deep-rooted belief

6 **opinion, sentiment, feeling, sense, impression,** reaction, **notion, idea, thought,** mind, thinking, **way of thinking, attitude,** stance, posture, position, mindset, **view,** point of view, eye, sight, lights, observation, **conception,** concept, conceit, **estimation,** estimate, consideration, **theory** 950, assumption, presumption, **conclusion, judgment** 945, personal judgment; **point of view** 977.2; public opinion, public belief, general belief, prevailing belief *or* sentiment, *consensus gentium* <L>, common belief, commu-

nity sentiment, popular belief, conventional wisdom, vox pop, *vox populi* <L>, climate of opinion; ethos; mystique

7 **profession, confession,** declaration, **profession** *or* **confession** *or* **declaration of faith**

8 **believability, persuasiveness** believableness, convincingness, **credibility, credit, trustworthiness, plausibility,** tenability, acceptability, conceivability; **reliability** 969.4

9 **believer, truster;** religious believer; true believer; the assured, the faithful, the believing; fideist; ideologist, ideologue

VERBS 10 **believe, credit, trust, accept,** receive, buy <nonformal>; give credit *or* credence to, give faith to, put faith in, take stock in *or* set store by <nonformal>, take to heart, attach weight to; be led to believe; accept implicitly, believe without reservation, take for granted, take *or* accept for gospel, take as gospel truth <nonformal>, take on faith, take on trust *or* credit, pin one's faith on; take at face value; **take one's word for,** trust one's word, take at one's word; **buy** *and* **buy into** <both nonformal>, **swallow** 953.6; **be certain** 969.9

11 **think, opine, be of the opinion, be persuaded, be convinced;** be afraid <nonformal>, **have the idea,** have an idea, **suppose, assume, presume, judge** 945.8, **guess, surmise, suspect,** have a hunch <nonformal>, have an inkling, expect <nonformal>, have an impression, be under the impression, have a sense *or* the sense, conceive, ween *and* trow <both archaic>, **imagine, fancy,** daresay; **deem, esteem, hold, regard, consider, maintain,** reckon, estimate; hold as, account as, set down as *or* for, view as, look upon as, take for, take, take it

12 **state, assert,** swear, swear to God <nonformal>, declare, **affirm,** vow, avow, avouch, warrant, asseverate, confess, be under the impression, profess, express the belief, swear to a belief; depose, make an affidavit *or* a sworn statement

13 **hold the belief, have the opinion,** entertain a belief *or* an opinion, adopt *or* embrace a belief, take as an article of faith; foster *or* nurture *or* cherish a belief, be wedded to *or* espouse a belief; get hold of an idea, get it into one's head, form a conviction

14 **be confident,** have confidence, **be satisfied, be convinced, be certain,** be easy in one's mind about, be secure in the belief,

feel sure, **rest assured,** rest in confidence; doubt not, **have no doubt,** have no misgivings *or* diffidence *or* qualms, have no reservations, have no second thoughts

15 **believe in, have faith in,** pin one's faith to, confide in, **have confidence in,** place *or* repose confidence in, place reliance in, put onself in the hands of, **trust in,** put trust in, have simple *or* childlike faith in, rest in, repose in *or* hope in <both old>; give *or* get the benefit of the doubt

16 **rely on** *or* **upon, depend on** *or* **upon,** place reliance on, rest on *or* upon, repose on, lean on, **count on,** calculate on, reckon on, **bank on** *or* **upon** <nonformal>; **trust to** *or* **unto, swear by,** take one's oath upon; **bet on** *and* gamble on *and* lay money on *and* bet one's bottom dollar on *and* make book on <all nonformal>; take one's word for

17 **trust, confide in, rely on, depend on,** repose, place trust *or* confidence in, have confidence in, **trust in** 952.15, trust utterly *or* implicitly, deem trustworthy, think reliable *or* dependable, take one's word, take at one's word

18 **convince; convert, win over,** lead one to believe, bring over, bring round, talk over, talk around, bring to reason, bring to one's senses, **persuade, lead to believe, give to understand; satisfy, assure;** put one's mind at rest on; sell *and* sell one on <both nonformal>; make *or* carry one's point, bring *or* drive home to; cram down one's throat *and* beat into one's head <both nonformal>; be convincing, carry conviction; inspire belief *or* confidence

19 **convince oneself, persuade oneself,** sell oneself <nonformal>, make oneself easy about, make oneself easy on that score, satisfy oneself on that point, make sure of, make up one's mind

20 **find credence, be believed,** be accepted, be received; be swallowed *and* **go down** *and* pass current <all nonformal>; produce *or* carry conviction; have the ear of, gain the confidence of

ADJS 21 **belief,** of belief, preceptive, principled; attitudinal; **believing, undoubting, undoubtful,** doubtless <old>; faithful <old>, God-fearing, pious, pietistic, observant, **devout;** under the impression, impressed with; **convinced, confident,** positive, dogmatic, secure, **persuaded,** sold on, **satisfied, assured; sure, certain** 969.13,20; fideistic

22 **trusting, trustful,** trusty <old>, **confiding, unsuspecting, unsuspicious,** without suspicion; childlike, innocent, guileless,

naive 416.5; **knee-jerk, credulous** 953.8; relying, depending, reliant, dependent

23 **believed, credited, held, trusted, accepted;** received, of belief; **undoubted,** unsuspected, **unquestioned,** undisputed, uncontested

24 **believable, credible; tenable,** conceivable, **plausible,** colorable; worthy of faith, trustworthy, trusty; fiduciary; reliable 969.17; unimpeachable, unexceptionable, **unquestionable** 969.15

25 fiducial, fiduciary; convictional

26 **convincing,** convictional, well-founded, **persuasive,** assuring, impressive, satisfying, satisfactory, confidence-building; decisive, absolute, conclusive, determinative; authoritative

27 **doctrinal, creedal,** preceptive, canonical, dogmatic, confessional, mandatory, of faith

ADVS 28 **believingly, undoubtingly,** undoubtfully, without doubt *or* question *or* quibble, unquestioningly; **trustingly,** trustfully, unsuspectingly, unsuspiciously; piously, devoutly; with faith; **with confidence,** on *or* upon trust, on faith, on one's say-so

29 **in one's opinion, to one's mind,** in one's thinking, **to one's way of thinking,** the way one thinks, **in one's estimation,** according to one's lights, **as one sees it, to the best of one's belief;** in the opinion of, in the eyes of

953 CREDULITY

NOUNS 1 **credulity, credulousness,** inclination *or* disposition to believe, ease of belief, will *or* willingness to believe, wishful belief *or* thinking; **blind faith,** unquestioning belief, knee-jerk response *or* agreement <nonformal>; uncritical acceptance, premature *or* unripe acceptation, hasty *or* rash conviction; **trustfulness, trustingness, unsuspiciousness,** unsuspectingness; uncriticalness, unskepticalness; overcredulity, overcredulousness, overtrustfulness, overopenness to conviction *or* persuasion, gross credulity; infatuation, fondness, dotage; one's blind side

2 **gullibility, dupability,** bamboozlability <nonformal>, cullibility <old>, **deceivability,** seduceability, persuadability, hoaxability; biddability; easiness <nonformal>, softness, weakness; **simpleness,** simplicity, **ingenuousness, unsophistication; greenness,** naïveness, **naïveté,** naivety

3 superstition, superstitiousness; popular belief, **old wives' tale;** tradition, lore, folklore; charm, spell 691

4 trusting soul; **dupe** 358; sucker *and* patsy *and* easy mark *and* pushover<all nonformal>

VERBS **5 be credulous,** accept unquestioningly; not boggle at anything, **believe anything,** be easy of belief *or* persuasion, be uncritical, believe at the drop of a hat, be a dupe, think the moon is made of green cheese, buy a pig in a poke

6 <nonformal or nonformal terms> kid oneself, fall for, swallow, swallow anything, swallow whole, not choke *or* gag on; swallow hook, line, and sinker; eat up, lap up, devour, gulp down, gobble up *or* down, buy, buy into, bite, nibble, rise to the fly, take the bait, swing at, go for, tumble for, be taken in, be suckered, be a sucker *or* a patsy *or* an easy mark

7 be superstitious; knock on wood, keep one's fingers crossed

ADJS **8 credulous, knee-jerk** <nonformal>, easy of belief, ready *or* inclined to believe, easily taken in; **undoubting** 952.21; **trustful, trusting; unsuspicious, unsuspecting;** unthinking, uncritical, unskeptical; overcredulous, overtrustful, overtrusting, overconfiding; fond, infatuated, doting; **superstitious**

9 gullible, dupable, bamboozlable <nonformal>; cullible <old>, **deceivable, foolable, deludable, exploitable,** victimizable, seduceable, persuadable, hoaxable, humbugable, hoodwinkable; biddable; soft, easy <nonformal>, **simple; ingenuous, unsophisticated, green, naive** 416.5

954 UNBELIEF

NOUNS **1 unbelief, disbelief,** nonbelief, unbelievingness, discredit; refusal *or* inability to believe; **incredulity** 955; **unpersuadedness,** unconvincedness, lack of conviction; **denial** 335.2, **rejection** 372; misbelief, heresy 688.2; infidelity, atheism, **agnosticism** 695.6; minimifidianism, nullifidianism

2 doubt, doubtfulness, dubiousness, dubiety; half-belief; **reservation, question,** question in one's mind; **skepticism,** skepticalness; total skepticism, Pyrrhonism; **suspicion,** suspiciousness, wariness, leeriness, **distrust, mistrust, misdoubt,** distrustfulness, mistrustfulness; **misgiving,** self-doubt, diffidence; scruple, scrupulousness <both old>; apprehen-

sion 127.4; **uncertainty** 970; shadow of doubt

3 unbelievability, unbelievableness, **incredibility, implausibility,** inconceivability, untenableness; unpersuasiveness, unconvincingness; **doubtfulness, questionableness;** credibility gap; unreliability 970.6

4 doubter, doubting Thomas; scoffer, skeptic, cynic, pooh-pooher, nay-sayer, unbeliever 695.11

VERBS **5 disbelieve,** unbelieve, misbelieve, **not believe,** find hard to believe, not admit, refuse to admit, not buy <nonformal>, take no stock in *and* set no store by <both nonformal>; **discredit,** refuse to credit, refuse to credit *or* give credence to, give no credit *or* credence to; gag on, **not swallow** 955.3; negate, **deny** 335.4, naysay, say nay; scoff at, pooh-pooh; **reject** 372.2

6 doubt, be doubtful, be dubious, be skeptical, doubt the truth of, beg leave to doubt, **have one's doubts,** have *or* harbor *or* entertain doubts *or* suspicions, half believe, have reservations, **take with a grain of salt,** be from Missouri <nonformal>, scruple <old>, **distrust, mistrust,** misgive, cross one's fingers; **be uncertain** 970.9; **suspect,** smell a rat *and* see something funny <both nonformal>; **question,** query, **challenge, contest, dispute,** cast doubt on, greet with skepticism, keep one's eye on, treat with reserve, bring *or* call into question, raise a question, throw doubt upon, awake a doubt *or* suspicion; **doubt one's word,** give one the lie; doubt oneself, be diffident

7 be unbelievable, be incredible, be hard to swallow, defy belief, pass belief, be hard to believe, strain one's credulity, **stagger belief;** shake one's faith, undermine one's faith; perplex, boggle the mind, stagger, fill with doubt

ADJS **8 unbelieving, disbelieving,** nonbelieving; faithless, without faith; unconfident, unconvinced, unconverted; nullifidian, minimifidian, creedless; **incredulous** 955.4; repudiative; **heretical** 688.9; **irreligious** 695.17

9 doubting, doubtful, in doubt, dubious; questioning; skeptical, Pyrrhonic, from Missouri <nonformal>; **distrustful, mistrustful, untrustful,** mistrusting, untrusting; **suspicious,** suspecting, scrupulous <old>, shy, wary, leery; **agnostic; uncertain**

10 unbelievable, incredible, unthinkable, **implausible,** unimaginable, inconceiv-

able, not to be believed, **hard to believe,**
hard of belief, beyond belief, unworthy of
belief, not meriting *or* not deserving belief, tall <nonformal>; **defying belief,**
staggering belief, passing belief; **mind-
boggling,** preposterous, absurd, ridiculous, unearthly, ungodly; **doubtful, dubious,** doubtable, dubitable, **questionable,**
problematic, problematical, **unconvinc-
ing,** open to doubt *or* suspicion; **suspicious,** suspect, funny; thin *and* a bit thin
<both nonformal>; thick *and* a bit thick
and a little too thick <all nonformal>

11 under a cloud, unreliable

12 **doubted, questioned,** disputed, contested, moot; **distrusted,** mistrusted;
suspect, suspected, **under suspicion,** under a cloud; **discredited,** exploded,
rejected, **disbelieved**

ADVS 13 **unbelievingly,** doubtingly, **doubtfully, dubiously,** questioningly, **skep-
tically,** suspiciously; **with a grain of salt,**
with reservations, with some allowance,
with caution

14 **unbelievably, incredibly,** unthinkably,
implausibly, inconceivably, unimaginably, staggeringly

955 INCREDULITY

NOUNS 1 **incredulity, incredulousness,** un-
credulousness, refusal *or* disinclination to
believe, resistance *or* resistiveness to belief, tough-mindedness, hardheadedness,
inconvincibility, unconvincibility, unpersuadability, unpersuasibility; **suspiciousness,** suspicion, wariness, leeriness,
guardedness, cautiousness, caution;
skepticism 954.2

2 **ungullibility,** uncullibility <old>, **un-
dupability, undeceivability,** unhoax-
ability, unseduceability; **sophistication**

VERBS 3 **refuse to believe,** resist believing,
not allow oneself to believe, be slow to
believe *or* accept; not kid oneself
<nonformal>; **disbelieve** 954.5; **be skep-
tical** 954.6; **not swallow,** not be able to
swallow *or* down <nonformal>, not go
for *and* **not fall for** <both nonformal>,
not be taken in by; **not accept, not buy** *or*
buy into <nonformal>, **reject** 372.2

ADJS 4 **incredulous,** uncredulous, **hard of
belief,** shy of belief, disposed to doubt,
indisposed *or* disinclined to believe,
unwilling to accept; impervious to
persuasion, **inconvincible,** unconvincible,
unpersuadable, unpersuasible; **suspicious, suspecting,** wary, leery, cautious,
guarded; **skeptical** 954.9

5 **ungullible,** uncullible <old>, **undupable,
undeceivable, unfoolable, undeludable,**
unhoaxable, unseduceable, hoaxproof;
sophisticated, wise, hardheaded, practical, realistic, tough-minded; nobody's
fool, not born yesterday, nobody's sucker
or patsy <nonformal>

956 EVIDENCE, PROOF

NOUNS 1 **evidence, proof; reason to believe,**
grounds for belief; **ground, grounds,** material grounds, **facts, data,** premises,
basis for belief; piece *or* item of evidence,
fact, datum, relevant fact; **indication,
manifestation, sign, symptom,** mark, token, mute witness; body of evidence,
documentation; muniments, title deeds
and papers; chain of evidence; **clue;** exhibit

2 **testimony, attestation,** attest <old>, **witness;** testimonial, testimonium <old>;
statement, declaration, assertion, asseveration, affirmation 334, avouchment,
avowal, averment, allegation, admission,
disclosure 351, profession, word; **deposition,** legal evidence, sworn evidence *or*
testimony; *procès-verbal* <Fr>; compurgation; affidavit, sworn statement;
instrument in proof, *pièce justificative*
<Fr>

3 **proof, demonstration,** ironclad proof,
incontrovertible proof; **determination,
establishment, settlement; conclusive
evidence,** indisputable evidence, incontrovertible evidence, damning evidence, unmistakable sign, sure sign, absolute indication, smoking gun <nonfor-
mal>; open-and-shut case; burden of
proof, onus, *onus probandi* <L>; the
proof of the pudding

4 **confirmation, substantiation,** proof,
proving, proving out, bearing out,
affirmation, attestation, **authentication,
validation, certification,** ratification,
verification; corroboration, support,
supporting evidence, corroboratory
evidence, fortification, buttressing,
bolstering, backing, backing up, reinforcement, undergirding, strengthening,
circumstantiation, fact sheet; **documentation**

5 **citation, reference,** quotation; **exemplification,** instance, example, case, case
in point, particular, item, illustration,
demonstration; cross reference

6 **witness, eyewitness,** spectator, earwit-
ness; **bystander,** passerby; **deponent,
testifier,** attestant, attester, attestator,

voucher, swearer; **informant,** informer; character witness; cojuror, compurgator

7 **provability, demonstrability,** determinability; confirmability, supportability, verifiability

VERBS 8 **evidence, evince,** furnish evidence, **show, go to show, mean,** tend to show, witness to, testify to; **demonstrate, illustrate,** exhibit, manifest, display, express, set forth; approve; **attest; indicate, signify,** signalize, symptomatize, mark, **denote, betoken, point to,** give indication of, show signs of, bear on, touch on; **connote, imply, suggest,** involve; argue, breathe, tell, bespeak; **speak for itself,** speak volumes

9 **testify, attest, give evidence,** witness, witness to, **give** or **bear witness; disclose** 351.4; **vouch,** state one's case, **depose,** depone, **warrant, swear,** take one's oath, acknowledge, avow, **affirm,** avouch, aver, allege, asseverate, **certify, give one's word**

10 **prove, demonstrate, show,** afford proof of, prove to be, prove true; **establish,** fix, **determine, ascertain,** make out, remove all doubt; **settle,** settle the matter; **set at rest;** clinch and cinch and nail down <all nonformal>; **prove one's point,** make one's case, bring home to, make good, have or make out a case; hold good, hold water; follow, follow from, follow as a matter of course

11 **confirm,** affirm, **attest,** warrant, uphold <Brit nonformal>, **substantiate, authenticate, validate, certify,** ratify, **verify;** circumstantiate, **corroborate, bear out,** support, buttress, **sustain,** fortify, bolster, back, back up, reinforce, undergird, strengthen; **document;** probate, prove

12 **adduce,** produce, **advance, present,** bring to bear, **offer,** proffer, invoke, obtest, allege <old>, plead, **bring forward,** bring on; rally, marshal, deploy, array; call to witness, call to or put in the witness box

13 **cite, name,** call to mind; **instance,** cite a particular or particulars, cite cases or a case in point, itemize, particularize, produce an instance, give a for-instance <nonformal>; **exemplify,** example <old>, **illustrate,** demonstrate; **document; quote,** quote chapter and verse

14 **refer to,** direct attention to, **appeal to,** invoke; make reference to; cross-refer, make a cross-reference; reference, crossreference

15 **have evidence** or **proof,** have a case, possess incriminating evidence, **have something on** <nonformal>; **have the goods on** and have dead to rights or bang to rights <all nonformal>

ADJS 16 **evidential,** evidentiary, **factual,** symptomatic, **significant, indicative,** attestative, attestive, probative; founded on, grounded on, based on; implicit, suggestive; material, telling, convincing, weighty; overwhelming, damning; **conclusive,** determinative, **decisive,** final, incontrovertible, irresistible, indisputable, irrefutable, sure, certain, absolute, documented, documentary; **valid, admissible;** adducible; firsthand, authentic, reliable 969.17, eye-witness; hearsay, circumstantial, presumptive, nuncupative, cumulative, ex parte

17 **demonstrative,** demonstrating, demonstrational; evincive, apodictic

18 **confirming,** confirmatory, confirmative, certificatory; substantiating, **verifying,** verificative; **corroborating,** corroboratory, **corroborative,** supportive, **supporting**

19 **provable, demonstrable,** demonstratable, apodictic, evincible, attestable, **confirmable,** checkable, **substantiatable, establishable,** supportable, sustainable, **verifiable,** validatable, authenticatable

20 **proved, proven, demonstrated,** shown; **established,** fixed, **settled, determined,** nailed down <nonformal>, ascertained; **confirmed, substantiated,** attested, **authenticated, certified, validated, verified;** circumstantiated, **corroborated,** borne out

21 **unrefuted,** unconfuted, unanswered, uncontroverted, uncontradicted, **undenied; unrefutable** 969.15

ADVS 22 **evidentially,** according to the evidence, on the evidence, as attested by, judging by; **in confirmation, in corroboration of, in support of;** at first hand, at second hand; dead to rights or bang to rights and with a smoking gun and with one's pants down <all nonformal>

23 **to illustrate,** to prove the point, as an example, as a case in point, to name an instance, by way of example, **for example, for instance,** to cite an instance, as an instance, e.g., exempli gratia <L>; as, **thus**

24 **which see, q.v.,** quod vide <L>; loco citato <L>, loc cit; opere citato <L>, op cit

25 PHRS **it is proven,** probatum est <L>, there is nothing more to be said, it must follow; QED, quod erat demonstrandum <L>

957 DISPROOF

NOUNS **1 disproof,** disproving, disproval, **invalidation,** disconfirmation, explosion, negation, redargution <old>; exposure, exposé; *reductio ad absurdum* <L>

2 refutation, confutation, confounding, refutal, **rebuttal, answer,** complete answer, crushing *or* effective rejoinder, squelch; discrediting; **overthrow,** overthrowal, upset, upsetting, subversion, undermining, demolition; **contradiction,** controversion, **denial** 335.2

3 conclusive argument, knockdown argument, floorer, sockdolager <nonformal>; **clincher** *or* crusher *or* **settler** *and* finisher *and* squelcher <all nonformal>

VERBS **4 disprove, invalidate,** disconfirm, discredit, prove the contrary, belie, give the lie to, redargue <old>; **negate,** negative; **expose, show up; explode,** blow up, blow sky-high, **puncture,** deflate, **shoot** *or* **poke full of holes, cut to pieces, cut the ground from under; knock the bottom out of** <nonformal>, knock the props *or* chocks out from under, take the ground from under, undercut, cut the ground from under one's feet, not leave a leg to stand on, have the last word, leave nothing to say, put *or* lay to rest

5 refute, confute, confound, rebut, parry, answer, **answer conclusively,** dismiss, dispose of; **overthrow,** overturn, overwhelm, upset, subvert, defeat, demolish, undermine; argue down; floor *and* finish *and* settle *and* squash *and* squelch <all nonformal>, crush, smash all opposition; silence, put *or* reduce to silence, shut up, stop the mouth of; nonplus, take the wind out of one's sails; **contradict,** controvert, counter, run counter, **deny** 335.4

ADJS **6 refuting, confuting,** confounding, confutative, refutative, refutatory, disconfirmatory; contradictory, contrary 335.5

7 disproved, disconfirmed, **invalidated,** negated, negatived, discredited, belied; **exposed,** shown up; **punctured,** deflated, **exploded; refuted,** confuted, confounded; upset, **overthrown,** overturned; **contradicted,** disputed, denied, impugned; dismissed, discarded, rejected 372.3

8 unproved, not proved, unproven, **undemonstrated,** unshown, not shown; **untried,** untested; **unestablished,** unfixed, **unsettled, undetermined,** unascertained; **unconfirmed, unsubstantiated,** unattested, **unauthenticated,** unvalidated, uncertified, **unverified; uncorroborated,** unsustained, **unsupported,** unsupported by evidence, **groundless,** without grounds *or* basis, **unfounded** 935.13; **inconclusive,** indecisive; **moot,** sub judice; not following

9 unprovable, controvertible, **undemonstrable,** undemonstratable, unattestable, unsubstantiatable, **unsupportable,** unconfirmable, unsustainable, unverifiable

10 refutable, confutable, **disprovable,** defeasible

958 QUALIFICATION

NOUNS **1 qualification, limitation, limiting, restriction,** circumscription, **modification,** hedge, hedging; setting conditions, conditionality, provisionality, circumstantiality; specification; **allowance, concession,** cession, grant; grain of salt; **reservation, exception,** waiver, exemption; **exclusion,** ruling out, including out <nonformal>; specialness, special circumstance, special case, special treatment; **mental reservation,** salvo <old>, *arrière-pensée* <Fr>, crossing one's fingers; extenuating circumstances

2 condition, provision, proviso, stipulation, whereas; **specification,** parameter, given, *donnée* <Fr>, **limitation,** limiting condition, boundary condition; **contingency, circumstance** 765; **catch** *and* joker *and* kicker *and* string *and* a string to it <all nonformal>; **requisite, prerequisite,** obligation; *sine qua non* <L>, *conditio sine qua non* <L>; clause, escape clause, escapeway, escape hatch, saving clause; escalator clause; **terms,** provisions; grounds; small *or* fine print *and* fine print at the bottom <all nonformal>; ultimatum

VERBS **3 qualify, limit,** condition <old>, hedge, hedge about, **modify, restrict,** restrain, circumscribe, set limits *or* conditions, box in <nonformal>, narrow; adjust to, regulate by; alter 851.6; **temper, season,** leaven, soften, modulate, moderate, assuage, **mitigate,** palliate, abate, reduce, diminish

4 make conditional, make contingent, **condition;** make it a condition, attach a condition *or* proviso, **stipulate;** insist upon, make a point of; **have a catch** *and* have a joker *or* kicker *and* have a joker in the deck *and* have a string attached <all nonformal>; cross one's fingers behind one's back

5 allow for, make allowance for, make room for, provide for, open the door to, take account of, **take into account** *or* **consideration, consider,** consider the circumstances; allow, **grant, concede,** admit, admit exceptions, see the special circumstances; **relax,** relax the condition, **waive, set aside,** ease, lift temporarily, pull one's punches <nonformal>; disregard, **discount,** leave out of account; consider the source, take with a grain of salt

6 **depend,** hang, rest, hinge; **depend on** *or* **upon, hang on** *or* **upon, rest on** *or* **upon,** rest with, repose upon, lie on, lie with, stand on *or* upon, be based on, be bounded *or* limited by, be dependent on, be predicated on, **be contingent** *or* **conditional on; hinge on** *or* **upon, turn on** *or* **upon, revolve on** *or* **upon,** have as a fulcrum

ADJS 7 **qualifying,** qualificative, qualificatory, **modifying,** modificatory, altering; **limiting, limitational, restricting,** limitative, restrictive, bounding; circumstantial, contingent; **extenuating,** extenuatory, **mitigating,** mitigative, mitigatory, modulatory, palliative, assuasive, lenitive, softening

8 **conditional, provisional,** provisory, stipulatory; specificative; **specified, stipulated,** fixed, stated, given; **temporary,** expedient

9 **contingent, dependent, depending;** contingent on, **dependent on, depending on,** predicated on, based on, hanging *or* hinging on, turning on, revolving on; depending on circumstances; circumscribed by, hedged *or* hedged about by; boxed in <nonformal>; **subject to,** incidental to, incident to

10 **qualified, modified, conditioned, limited, restricted,** hedged, hedged about; **tempered, seasoned,** leavened, softened, **mitigated,** modulated

ADVS 11 **conditionally, provisionally, with qualifications,** with a string *or* catch *or* joker *or* kicker to it <all nonformal>; with a reservation *or* an exception, with a grain of salt; **temporarily,** for the time being

CONJS 12 **provided,** provided that, provided always, **providing,** with this proviso, it being provided; **on condition,** on condition that, **with the stipulation,** with the understanding, according as, subject to

13 **granting, admitting, allowing,** admitting that, allowing that, seeing that; exempting, waiving

14 **if,** an *or* an' <both old>, if and when, only if, if only, if and only if, if it be so, if

it be true that, if it so happens *or* turns out

15 **so,** just so, so that <old>, so as, **so long as, as long as**

16 **unless,** unless that, **if not, were it not,** were it not that; **except, excepting,** except that, with the exception that, save, **but; without,** absent

959 NO QUALIFICATIONS

NOUNS 1 **unqualifiedness,** unlimitedness, **unconditionality,** unrestrictedness, **unreservedness,** uncircumscribedness; categoricalness; **absoluteness,** definiteness, **explicitness;** decisiveness

ADJS 2 **unqualified, unconditional,** unconditioned, **unrestricted,** unhampered, **unlimited,** uncircumscribed, unmitigated, **categorical,** straight, **unreserved,** without reserve; unaltered, unadulterated, intact; **implicit,** unquestioning, undoubting, unhesitating; **explicit, express, unequivocal,** clear, unmistakable; **peremptory,** indisputable, inappealable; **without exception,** admitting no exception, unwaivable; **positive, absolute, flat,** definite, definitive, determinate, decided, decisive, fixed, final, conclusive; **complete, entire, whole, total,** global; **utter,** perfect, downright, outright, out-and-out, straight-out <nonformal>, all-out, flat-out <nonformal>

ADVS 3 <nonformal terms> **no ifs, ands, or buts; no strings attached,** no holds barred, no catch *or* joker *or* kicker, no joker in the deck, no small print *or* fine print, no fine print at the bottom; downright, that's that, what you see is what you get

960 FORESIGHT

NOUNS 1 **foresight,** foreseeing, looking ahead, **prevision,** divination 961.2, forecast; **prediction** 961; **foreglimpse,** foreglance, foregleam; preview, prepublication; **prospect,** prospection; **anticipation,** contemplation, envisionment, envisagement; **foresightedness; farsightedness,** longsightedness, farseeingness; sagacity, providence, discretion, preparation, provision, forehandedness, readiness, prudence 919.7

2 **forethought, premeditation,** predeliberation, preconsideration 380.3; caution 494; lead time, advance notice; run-up

3 **foreknowledge,** foreknowing, forewisdom, **precognition,** prescience, presage,

presentiment, foreboding; clairvoyance 689.8; foreseeability 961.8

4 foretaste, antepast <old>, prelibation

VERBS **5 foresee,** see beforehand *or* ahead, foreglimpse, foretaste, **anticipate,** contemplate, envision, envisage, **look forward to,** look ahead, look beyond, look *or* pry *or* peep into the future; **predict** 961.9; think ahead *or* beforehand

6 foreknow, know beforehand, precognize; smell in the wind, scent from afar; **have a presentiment, have a premonition** 133.11; see the handwriting on the wall, have a hunch *or* feel in one's bones <nonformal>, just know, intuit 933.4

ADJS **7 foreseeing, foresighted; foreknowing, precognizant,** precognitive, prescient; divinatory 961.11; **forethoughted,** forethoughtful; anticipant, anticipatory; **farseeing, farsighted,** longsighted; sagacious, provident, providential, forehanded, prepared, ready, prudent 919.19; intuitive 933.5; clairvoyant

8 foreseeable 961.13; foreseen 961.14; intuitable

ADVS **9 foreseeingly, foreknowingly,** with foresight; against the time when, for a rainy day

961 PREDICTION

NOUNS **1 prediction, foretelling,** foreshowing, forecasting, **prognosis,** prognostication, presage <old>, presaging; **prophecy,** prophesying, vaticination; **soothsaying,** soothsay; prefiguration, prefigurement, prefiguring; preshowing, presignifying, presigning <old>; **forecast, promise;** apocalypse; prospectus; foresight 960; presentiment, foreboding; omen 133.3,6; **guesswork,** speculation, guestimation <nonformal>; **probability** 967, statistical prediction, actuarial prediction; improbability 968

2 divination, divining; **augury,** haruspication, haruspicy, pythonism, mantic, mantology <old>; **fortunetelling,** crystal gazing, palm-reading, palmistry; crystal ball; horoscopy, astrology 1070.20; sorcery 690; clairvoyance 689.8

3 dowsing, witching, water witching; **divining rod** *or* stick, wand, witch *or* witching stick, dowsing rod, doodlebug; water diviner, dowser, water witch *or* witcher

4 predictor, foreteller, prognosticator, seer, foreseer, foreshower, foreknower, presager <old>, prefigurer; **forecaster;** prophet, prophesier, soothsayer, *vates*

<L>; **diviner,** divinator; augur; psychic 689.13; prophetess, seeress, divineress, pythoness; Druid; **fortuneteller;** crystal gazer; palmist; geomancer; haruspex *or* aruspex, astrologer 1070.23; weather prophet 317.6; prophet of doom, calamity howler, Cassandra; religious prophets 684

5 <nonformal terms> **dopester, tipster, tout** *or* touter

6 sibyl; Pythia, Pythian, Delphic sibyl; Babylonian *or* Persian sibyl, Cimmerian sibyl, Cumaean sibyl, Erythraean sibyl, Hellespontine *or* Trojan sibyl, Libyan sibyl, Phrygian sibyl, Samian sibyl, Tiburtine sibyl

7 oracle; Delphic *or* Delphian oracle, Python, Pythian oracle; Delphic tripod, tripod of the Pythia; Dodona, oracle *or* oak of Dodona

8 predictability, divinability, foretellableness, **calculability, foreseeability,** foreknowableness

VERBS **9 predict,** make a prediction, **foretell, soothsay,** prefigure, **forecast, prophesy, prognosticate,** call <nonformal>, make a prophecy *or* prognosis, vaticinate, forebode, presage, see ahead, see *or* tell the future, read the future, see in the crystal ball; **foresee** 960.5; dope *and* dope out <both nonformal>; call the turn *and* call one's shot <both nonformal>; **divine;** witch *or* dowse for water; **tell fortunes,** fortune-tell, cast one's fortune; read one's hand, read palms, read tea leaves, cast a horoscope *or* nativity; **guess,** speculate, guestimate <nonformal>; **bet, bet on, gamble**

10 portend, foretoken 133.12

ADJS **11 predictive,** predictory, predictional; **foretelling,** forewarning, forecasting; prefiguring, prefigurative, presignifying, presignificative; **prophetic,** prophetical, fatidic, fatidical, apocalyptic, apocalyptical; vatic, vaticinatory, vaticinal, mantic, sibyllic, sibylline; **divinatory, oracular,** auguring, augural; haruspical; **foreseeing** 960.7; presageful, presaging; **prognostic,** prognosticative, prognosticatory; fortunetelling; weather-wise

12 ominous, premonitory, foreboding 133.17

13 predictable, divinable, foretellable, calculable, anticipatable; **foreseeable, foreknowable,** precognizable; **probable** 967.6; improbable 968.3

14 predicted, prophesied, presaged, **foretold, forecast,** foreshown; foreseen, foreglimpsed, **foreknown**

962 NECESSITY

NOUNS **1 necessity,** necessariness, necessitude <old>, necessitation, entailment; mandatoriness, mandatedness, obligatoriness, **obligation,** obligement; compulsoriness, **compulsion, duress** 424.3

2 requirement, requisite, requisition; **necessity, need, want,** occasion; need for, **call for, demand,** demand for; desideratum, desideration; **prerequisite,** prerequirement; **must,** must item; **essential,** indispensable; the necessary, the needful; necessities, necessaries, essentials, bare necessities

3 needfulness, requisiteness; **essentiality,** essentialness, vitalness; **indispensability,** indispensableness; irreplaceability; irreducibleness, irreducibility

4 urgent need, dire necessity; exigency or exigence, **urgency,** imperative, imperativeness, immediacy, pressingness, pressure; "necessity's sharp pinch"— Shakespeare; matter of necessity, case of need or emergency, **matter of life and death; predicament** 1012.4

5 involuntariness, unwilledness, **instinctiveness;** compulsiveness; reflex action, conditioning, automatism; echolalia, echopraxia; automatic writing; **instinct,** impulse 365; blind impulse or instinct, sheer chemistry

6 choicelessness, no choice, no alternative, **Hobson's choice,** only choice, zero option; that or nothing; not a pin to choose, six of one and half a dozen of the other, distinction without a difference; indiscrimination 944

7 inevitability, inevitableness, **unavoidableness,** necessity, inescapableness, inevasibleness, unpreventability, undeflectability, ineluctability; irrevocability, indefeasibility; uncontrollability; relentlessness, inexorability, unyieldingness, inflexibility; fatedness, fatefulness, **certainty,** sureness; force majeure <Fr>, vis major, act of God, inevitable accident, unavoidable casualty; **predetermination, fate** 963.2

VERBS **8 necessitate, oblige,** dictate, **constrain;** insist upon, **compel** 424.4

9 require, need, want, feel the want of, have occasion for, be in need of, be hurting for <nonformal>, stand in need of, not be able to dispense with, not be able to do without; **call for,** cry for, cry out for, clamor for; **demand,** ask, claim, exact; prerequire <old>; need or want doing, take doing <nonformal>, be indicated

10 be necessary, lie under a necessity, be one's fate; be a must <nonformal>; can't be avoided, can't be helped; be under the necessity of, be in for; be obliged, **must,** need or needs must <old>, **have to,** have got to <nonformal>, should, need, **need to,** have need to; not able to keep from, not able to help, **cannot help but,** cannot do otherwise; be forced or driven

11 have no choice or **alternative,** have one's options reduced or closed or eliminated, have no option but, cannot choose but, be robbed or relieved of choice; be pushed to the wall, be driven into a corner; take it or leave it and like it or lump it <both nonformal>, have that or nothing

ADJS **12 necessary, obligatory, compulsory,** entailed, mandatory; **exigent, urgent,** necessitous, importunate, **imperative;** choiceless, without choice, out of one's hands or control

13 requisite, needful, required, needed, necessary, **wanted, called for,** indicated; **essential, vital, indispensable,** unforgoable, irreplaceable; irreducible, irreductible; prerequisite

14 involuntary, instinctive, automatic, mechanical, reflex, reflexive, knee-jerk <nonformal>, conditioned; **unconscious,** unthinking, blind; **unwitting,** unintentional, independent of one's will, unwilling, unwilled, against one's will; **compulsive;** forced; **impulsive** 365.9

15 inevitable, unavoidable, necessary, **inescapable,** inevasible, unpreventable, undeflectable, ineluctable, irrevocable, indefeasible; uncontrollable, unstoppable; relentless, inexorable, unyielding, inflexible; irresistible, resistless; **certain,** fateful, **sure,** sure as fate, sure as death, sure as death and taxes; **destined, fated** 963.9

ADVS **16 necessarily, needfully,** requisitely; **of necessity,** from necessity, need or needs <both old>, perforce; without choice; **willy-nilly,** nolens volens <L>, willing or unwilling, bon gré mal gré <Fr>, whether one will or not; come what may; compulsorily

17 if necessary, if need be, if worst comes to worst; for lack of something better, faute de mieux <Fr>

18 involuntarily, instinctively, automatically, mechanically, by reflex, reflexively; blindly, **unconsciously,** unthinkingly, without premeditation; **unwittingly,** unintentionally; **compulsively; unwillingly** 325.8

19 inevitably, unavoidably, necessarily,

inescapably, come hell or high water
<nonformal>, inevasibly, unpreventa-
bly, ineluctably; irrevocably, indefea-
sibly; uncontrollably; relentlessly, inexorably, unyieldingly, inflexibly; fatefully,
certainly, surely

PHRS **20 it is necessary, it must be,** it needs
must be *or* it must needs be <both old>,
it will be, there's no two ways about it, it
must have its way; it cannot be helped,
there is no helping it *or* help for it, that's
the way the cookie crumbles *or* the ball
bounces <nonformal>, what will be will
be, it's God's will; the die is cast; it is
fated 963.11

963 PREDETERMINATION

NOUNS **1 predetermination, predestination,**
foredestiny, **preordination,** foreordina-
tion, foreordainment; decree; foregone
conclusion, par for the course <nonfor-
mal>; **necessity** 962; foreknowledge,
prescience 960.3

2 fate, fatality, fortune, lot, cup, **portion,**
appointed lot, karma, kismet, weird,
moira <Gk>, future 838; **destiny,** destination, **end,** final lot; **doom,** foredoom
<old>, God's will, will of Heaven; **inev-
itability** 962.7; "a tyrant's authority for
crime and a fool's excuse for failure"—
Ambrose Bierce; the handwriting on the
wall; book of fate; Fortune's wheel, wheel
of fortune *or* chance; astral influences,
stars, planets, constellation, astrology
1070.20; unlucky day, ides of March, Friday, Friday the thirteenth, *dies funestis*
<L>

3 Fates, *Fata* <L>, Parcae, *Moirai* <Gk>,
Clotho, Lachesis, Atropos; Nona, De-
cuma, Morta; Weird Sisters, Weirds;
Norns; Urdur, Verthandi, Skuld; Fortuna, Lady *or* Dame Fortune, *Tyche*
<Gk>; Providence, Heaven, "a divinity
that shapes our ends, rough-hew them
how we will"—Shakespeare

4 determinism, fatalism, necessitarianism,
necessarianism, predeterminism; predes-
tinarianism, Calvinism, election

5 determinist, fatalist, necessitarian, necessarian; predestinationist, predestinar-
ian, Calvinist

VERBS **6 predetermine, predecide,** pre-
establish; **predestine,** predestinate, **pre-
ordain,** foreordain

7 destine, predestine, necessitate 962.8,
destinate <old>, **ordain,** fate, mark, appoint; come with the territory <nonfor-
mal>; have in store for; **doom,** foredoom

ADJS **8 determined, predetermined, predecided,** preestablished, **predestined,** predestinate, **preordained,** foreordained;
foregone

9 destined, fated, fateful, fatal <old>, ordained, written, in the cards, marked,
appointed <old>, in store; **doomed,**
foredoomed, devoted; inevitable
962.15

10 deterministic, fatalistic, necessitarian,
necessarian

PHRS **11 it is fated, it is written,** it's in the
cards; what will be will be, *che sarà sarà*
<Ital>, *que sera sera* <Sp>; *c'est la vie*
and *c'est la guerre* <both Fr>

964 PREARRANGEMENT

NOUNS **1 prearrangement,** preordering,
preconcertedness; premeditation, plotting, planning, scheming; directed verdict; **reservation,** booking; overbook-
ing

2 <nonformal terms> **put-up job,** packed
or rigged game *or* jury, packed deal,
stacked deck, cold deck, boat race, tank
job; **frame-up,** frame, setup

3 schedule, program, programma, **bill,**
card, **calendar,** docket, slate; playbill; batting order, **lineup, roster,** rota <chiefly
Brit>; blueprint, budget; **prospectus;**
schedule *or* program of operation, **order
of the day,** things to be done, **agenda,** list
of agenda; protocol; laundry list *and* wish
list <both nonformal>; **bill of fare,
menu,** *carte du jour* <Fr>

VERBS **4 prearrange,** precontrive, predesign
<old>, preorder, preconcert; premedi-
tate, plot, plan, scheme; **reserve,** book,
overbook

5 <nonformal terms> **fix, rig,** pack, cook,
cook up; **stack the cards,** cold-deck, pack
the deal; put in the bag, sew up; frame,
frame-up, set up; **throw,** tank, go in the
tank, hold a boat race

6 schedule, line up <nonformal>, **slate,
book,** book in, bill, program, calendar,
docket, budget, put on the agenda

ADJS **7 prearranged,** precontrived, pre-
designed <old>, preordered, precon-
certed, cut out; premeditated, plotted,
planned, schemed; cut-and-dried, cut-
and-dry

8 <nonformal terms> **fixed, rigged, put-
up,** packed, stacked, cooked, cooked-up;
in the bag, on ice, iced, cinched, sewed
up; **framed, framed-up,** set-up

9 scheduled, slated, booked, billed, booked-
in, to come

965 POSSIBILITY

NOUNS **1 possibility**, possibleness, **the realm of possibility,** the domain of the possible, conceivableness, **conceivability,** thinkability, thinkableness, imaginability; **probability, likelihood** 967; what may be, what might be, what is possible, what one can do, what can be done, the possible, the attainable, the feasible; **potential, potentiality,** virtuality; contingency, eventuality; **chance, prospect; outside chance** <nonformal>, off chance, remote possibility, ghost of a chance; hope, outside hope, slim hope, slim odds; **good possibility, good chance,** even chance 971.7; bare possibility 971.9

2 practicability, practicality, feasibility; workability, operability, actability, performability, realizability, negotiability; **viability,** viableness; **achievability,** doability, compassability, **attainability;** surmountability, superability

3 accessibility, access, **approachability, openness,** reachableness, come-at-ableness *and* get-at-ableness <both nonformal>; **penetrability,** perviousness; **obtainability,** obtainableness, **availability, donability, procurability,** procurableness, securableness, getableness, acquirability

VERBS **4 be possible,** could be, might be, **have** *or* **stand a chance** *or* **good chance, bid fair to**

5 make possible, **enable,** permit, permit of, clear the road *or* path for, smooth the way for, open the way for, open the door to, open up the possibility of

ADJS **6 possible,** within the bounds *or* realm *or* range *or* domain of possibility, in one's power, in one's hands, humanly possible; **probable, likely** 967.6; **conceivable,** conceivably possible, **imaginable, thinkable,** cogitable; plausible 967.7; **potential;** contingent

7 practicable, practical, feasible; workable, actable, performable, effectible <old>, realizable, compassable, operable, negotiable, doable, swingable, bridgeable; **viable; achievable, attainable;** surmountable, superable, overcomable

8 accessible, approachable, come-at-able *and* get-at-able <both nonformal>, **reachable,** within reach; **open,** open to; **penetrable,** get-in-able <nonformal>, pervious; **obtainable, attainable, available,** procurable, securable, findable, easy to come by, getable, to be had, donable

ADVS **9 possibly, conceivably,** imaginably, feasibly; within the realm of possibility; **perhaps,** perchance, haply; **maybe,** it may be, for all *or* aught one knows

10 by any possibility, by any chance, by any means, **by any manner of means;** in any way, in any possible way, **at any cost, at all,** if at all, ever; on the bare possibility, on the off chance, by merest chance

11 if possible, if humanly possible, **God willing,** *Deo volente* <L>, wind and weather permitting, Lord willing and the creek don't rise

966 IMPOSSIBILITY

NOUNS **1 impossibility,** impossibleness, the realm *or* domain of the impossible, **inconceivability,** unthinkability, unimaginability, what cannot be, what can never be, what cannot happen, hopelessness, Chinaman's chance *and* a snowball's chance in hell <both nonformal>, **no chance** 971.10; **self-contradiction,** absurdity, paradox, oxymoron, logical impossibility; impossible, the impossible, impossibilism

2 impracticability, unpracticability, **impracticality, unfeasibility; unworkability,** inoperability, unperformability; **unachievability, unattainability;** unrealizability, uncompassability; insurmountability, **insuperability**

3 inaccessibility, unaccessibility; **unapproachability,** un-come-at-ableness <nonformal>, unreachableness; **impenetrability,** imperviousness; **unobtainability,** unobtainableness, **unattainability, unavailability,** unprocurableness, unsecurableness, ungettableness <nonformal>, unacquirability; undiscoverability, unascertainableness

VERBS **4 be impossible,** be an impossibility, **not have a chance,** be a waste of time; **contradict itself,** be a logical impossibility, be a paradox; fly in the face of reason

5 attempt the impossible, try for a miracle, look for a needle in a haystack *or* in a bottle of hay, try to be in two places at once, try to fetch water in a sieve *or* catch the wind in a net *or* weave a rope of sand *or* get figs from thistles *or* gather grapes from thorns *or* make bricks from straw *or* make cheese of chalk *or* make a silk purse out of a sow's ear *or* change the leopard's spots *or* get blood from a turnip; ask the impossible, cry for the moon

6 make impossible, rule out, disenable, disqualify, close out, **bar**, prohibit, put out of reach, leave no chance

ADJS **7 impossible, not possible,** beyond the bounds of possibility *or* reason, contrary to reason, at variance with the facts; **inconceivable, unimaginable, unthinkable, not to be thought of, out of the question;** hopeless; **absurd,** ridiculous, preposterous; **self-contradictory,** paradoxical, oxymoronic, logically impossible; **ruledout,** excluded, closed-out, **barred,** prohibited

8 impracticable, impractical, unpragmatic, unfeasible; unworkable, unperformable, inoperable, undoable, unnegotiable, unbridgeable; **unachievable, unattainable,** uneffectible <old>; unrealizable, uncompassable; insurmountable, unsurmountable, **insuperable,** unovercomable; **beyond one,** beyond one's power, beyond one's control, out of one's depth, too much for

9 inaccessible, unaccessible; **unapproachable,** un-come-at-able <nonformal>; **unreachable,** beyond reach, out of reach; **impenetrable,** impervious; closed to, denied to, lost to, closed forever to; **unobtainable, unattainable, unavailable,** unprocurable, unsecurable, ungettable <nonformal>, unacquirable; not to be had, **not to be had for love or money;** undiscoverable, unascertainable

ADVS **10 impossibly, inconceivably,** unimaginably, unthinkably; not at any price

PHRS **11** no can do, no way, no way José <nonformal>

967 PROBABILITY

NOUNS **1 probability, likelihood,** likeliness, liability, aptitude, verisimilitude; **chance, odds; expectation, outlook,** prospect; favorable prospect, well-grounded hope, some *or* reasonable hope, fair expectation; **good chance** 971.8; presumption, presumptive evidence; tendency; probable cause, reasonable ground *or* presumption; probabilism; possibility 965

2 mathematical probability, statistical probability, statistics, **predictability;** probability theory, game theory, theory of games; operations research; probable error, standard deviation; stochastic *or* statistical independence, stochastic variable; probability curve, frequency curve, frequency polygon, frequency distribution, probability function, probability density function, probability distribu-

tion, cumulative distribution function; **statistical mechanics,** quantum mechanics, uncertainty *or* indeterminancy principle, Maxwell-Boltzmann distribution law, Bose-Einstein statistics, Fermi-Dirac statistics; **mortality table,** actuarial table, life table, combined experience table, Commissioners Standard Ordinary table

3 plausibility; reasonability 934.9; **credibility** 952.8

VERBS **4 be probable, seem likely,** could be, offer a good prospect, offer the expectation, have *or* run a good chance; **promise,** be promising, make fair promise, **bid fair to,** stand fair to, show a tendency, be in the cards, have the makings of, have favorable odds, lead one to expect; **make probable,** probabilize, make more likely, smooth the way for; increase the chances

5 think likely, daresay, venture to say; **presume,** suppose 950.10

ADJS **6 probable, likely, liable, apt,** verisimilar, in the cards, odds-on; **promising, hopeful,** fair, in a fair way; foreseeable, **predictable; presumable,** presumptive; **statistical,** actuarial; mathematically *or* statistically probable, predictable within limits

7 plausible, colorable, apparent <old>; **reasonable** 934.20; credible 952.24; **conceivable** 965.6

ADVS **8 probably, in all probability** *or* **likelihood,** likely, **most likely, very likely;** as likely as not, very like *and* like enough *and* like as not <all nonformal>; **doubtlessly,** doubtless, **no doubt,** indubitably; **presumably,** presumptively; by all odds, ten to one, a hundred to one, dollars to doughnuts

9 PHRS there is reason to believe, I am led to believe, it can be supposed, it would appear, it stands to reason, it might be thought, one can assume, appearances are in favor of, the chances *or* odds are, you can bank on it, you can make book on it, you can bet on it, you can bet your bottom dollar, you can just bet, you can't go wrong; I daresay, I venture to say

968 IMPROBABILITY

NOUNS **1 improbability, unlikelihood,** unlikeliness; **doubtfulness,** dubiousness, **questionableness; implausibility,** incredibility 954.3; little expectation, low order of probability, poor possibility, bare possibility, faint likelihood, poor prospect, poor outlook, a ghost of a chance, fat

chance <nonformal>; **small chance**
971.9
VERBS **2 be improbable, not be likely,** be a
stretch of the imagination, strain one's
credulity, go beyond reason, go far afield,
go beyond the bounds of reason *or* probability, be far-fetched *or* fetched from afar
ADJS **3 improbable, unlikely,** unpromising,
hardly possible, logic-defying, scarcely to
be expected *or* anticipated; statistically
improbable; **doubtful,** dubious, **questionable,** doubtable, dubitable, more than
doubtful; **implausible,** incredible 954.10;
unlooked-for, unexpected, unpredictable
4 PHRS **not likely!,** no fear!, never fear!, I
ask you!, you should live so long! <non-
formal>, don't hold your breath!, don't
bet *or* make book on it <nonformal>

969 CERTAINTY

NOUNS **1 certainty, certitude,** certainness,
sureness, surety, **assurance, assuredness,**
certain knowledge; **positiveness, absoluteness, definiteness,** dead *or* moral *or*
absolute certainty; unequivocalness, unmistakableness, unambiguity, nonambi-
guity, univocity, univocality; **infallibility,** infallibilism, inerrability, inerrancy;
necessity, determinacy, determinateness,
noncontingency, Hobson's choice, ineluctability, predetermination, predestination, **inevitability** 962.7; **truth** 972;
proved fact, probatum
2 <nonformal terms> **sure thing,** dead certainty, dead-sure thing, sure bet, sure
card, aces wired, cinch, lead-pipe cinch,
dead cinch, lock, mortal lock, shoo-in,
open-and-shut case
3 unquestionability, undeniability, indu-
bitability, indubitableness, **indisput-
ability,** incontestability, incontrover-
tibility, **irrefutability,** unrefutability,
unconfutability, irrefragability, unimpeachability; **doubtlessness, question-
lessness; demonstrability,** provability,
verifiability, confirmability; factuality,
reality, actuality 760.2
**4 reliability, dependability, dependable-
ness, validity, trustworthiness,** faithworthiness; unerringness; predictability,
calculability; stability, substantiality,
firmness, **soundness,** solidity, staunchness, steadiness, **steadfastness;** secureness, **security;** invincibility 15.4; **authoritativeness, authenticity**
5 confidence, confidentness, conviction, belief 952, fixed *or* settled belief, **sureness,
assurance, assuredness,** surety, security,

certitude; **faith,** subjective certainty;
trust 952.1; **positiveness, cocksureness;
self-confidence, self-assurance, self-
reliance;** poise 106.3; courage 492; **overconfidence, oversureness,** overweening
<old>, overweeningness, hubris; pride
136, arrogance 141, pomposity 501.7, self-
importance 140.1
6 dogmatism, dogmaticalness, pontification, **positiveness,** positivism, peremptoriness, **opinionatedness,** self-
opinionatedness; bigotry; infallibilism
7 dogmatist, dogmatizer, opinionist, doctrinaire, bigot; positivist; infallibilist
8 ensuring, assurance; reassurance, reas-
surement; **certification;** ascertainment,
determination, establishment; **verification, corroboration,** substantiation,
validation, collation, check, cross-check,
double-check, checking; independent *or*
objective witness; **confirmation**
VERBS **9 be certain, be confident,** feel sure,
rest assured, have sewed up <nonfor-
mal>, **have no doubt,** doubt not; know,
just know, know for certain; **bet on** *and*
gamble on *and* bet one's bottom dollar on
and bet the ranch on <all nonformal>;
admit of no doubt; **go without saying,**
aller sans dire <Fr>, be axiomatic *or*
apodictic
10 dogmatize, lay down the law, pontificate,
oracle, oraculate, proclaim
11 make sure, make certain, make sure of,
make no doubt, make no mistake; remove
or dismiss *or* expunge *or* erase all doubt;
assure, ensure, insure, **certify; ascertain,
get a fix** *or* **lock on** <nonformal>; **find
out,** get at, see to it, see that; **determine,**
decide, **establish,** settle, fix, lock in *and*
nail down *and* clinch *and* cinch <all non-
formal>, clear up, sort out, set at rest;
assure *or* satisfy oneself, make oneself
easy about *or* on that score; **reassure**
12 verify, confirm, test, prove, audit, **collate,**
validate, **check,** check up *or* on *or* out
<nonformal>, check over *or* through,
double-check, triple-check, cross-check,
recheck, check and doublecheck, check
up and down, check over and through,
check in and out, "make assurance double sure"—Shakespeare, measure twice
cut once
ADJS **13 certain, sure,** sure-enough <nonfor-
mal>; bound; **positive, absolute, definite,**
perfectly sure, apodictic; decisive, conclusive; clear, clear as day, clear and distinct, unequivocal, unmistakable, unambiguous, nonambiguous, univocal; **necessary,** determinate, ineluctable, predeter-

mined, predestined, **inevitable** 962.15; **true** 972.12

14 <nonformal or nonformal terms> dead sure, sure as death, sure as death and taxes, sure as fate, sure as can be, sure as shooting, sure as God made little green apples, sure as hell *or* the devil, shit-sure, as sure as I live and breathe

15 **obvious, patent, unquestionable, unexceptionable, undeniable, self-evident,** axiomatic; indubitable, unarguable, indisputable, incontestable, **irrefutable,** unrefutable, unconfutable, incontrovertible, irrefragable, unanswerable, inappealable, unimpeachable, absolute; admitting no question *or* dispute *or* doubt *or* denial; **demonstrable,** demonstratable, provable, verifiable, testable, confirmable; well-founded, well-established, well-grounded; factual, **real,** historical, actual 760.15

16 **undoubted,** not to be doubted, indubious, **unquestioned, undisputed, uncontested,** uncontradicted, unchallenged, uncontroverted, uncontroversial; **doubtless, questionless,** beyond a shade *or* shadow of doubt, past dispute, beyond question

17 **reliable, dependable, sure,** surefire <nonformal>, **trustworthy, trusty,** faithworthy, **to be depended** *or* **relied upon,** to be counted *or* reckoned on; predictable, calculable; **secure, solid, sound, firm,** fast, **stable, substantial,** staunch, steady, **steadfast, faithful, unfailing;** true to one's word; invincible

18 **authoritative, authentic,** magisterial, **official;** cathedral, ex cathedra; standard, approved, accepted, received, pontific; from *or* straight from the horse's mouth

19 **infallible, inerrable,** inerrant, unerring

20 **assured,** made sure; **determined, decided, ascertained; settled, established,** fixed, cinched *and* iced *and* sewed up *and* taped <all nonformal>, set, stated, determinate, secure; **certified,** attested, guaranteed, warranted, tested, tried, proved; wired *and* cinched *and* open-and-shut *and* nailed down *and* in the bag *and* on ice <all nonformal>

21 **confident, sure,** secure, **assured,** reassured, decided, determined; **convinced,** persuaded, positive, **cocksure; unhesitating,** unfaltering, unwavering; **undoubting** 952.21; **self-confident, self-assured, self-reliant,** sure of oneself; poised 106.13; unafraid; **overconfident, oversure,** overweening, hubristic; proud 136.8, arrogant 141.9, pompous 501.22, self-important 140.8

22 **dogmatic, dogmatical,** dogmatizing, pronunciative, didactic, **positive,** positivistic, peremptory, pontifical, oracular; **opinionated,** opinioned, opinionative, conceited 140.11; **self-opinionated,** self-opinioned; doctrinarian, doctrinaire; bigoted

ADVS **23** **certainly, surely, assuredly, positively, absolutely, definitely,** decidedly; without batting an eye <nonformal>; decisively, distinctly, clearly, unequivocally, unmistakably; **for certain,** for sure *and* for a fact <both nonformal>, in truth, certes *or* forsooth <both old>, and no mistake <nonformal>; **for a certainty,** to a certainty, *à coup sûr* <Fr>; **most certainly,** most assuredly; **indeed,** indeedy <nonformal>; truly; **of course,** as a matter of course; **by all means,** by all manner of means; at any rate, at all events; nothing else but <nonformal>, no two ways about it, no buts about it <nonformal>; no ifs, ands, or buts

24 **surely, sure, to be sure,** sure enough, for sure <nonformal>; sure thing *and* surest thing you know <both nonformal>

25 **unquestionably, without question, undoubtedly, beyond the shadow of a doubt, beyond a reasonable doubt, indubitably, admittedly, undeniably,** unarguably, indisputably, incontestably, incontrovertibly, irrefutably, irrefragably; **doubtlessly,** doubtless, **no doubt, without doubt,** beyond doubt *or* question, out of question

26 **without fail,** unfailingly, whatever may happen, **come what may,** come hell or high water <nonformal>; cost what it may, *coûte que coûte* <Fr>; rain or shine, live or die, sink or swim

27 PHRS **it is certain,** there is no question, there is not a shadow of doubt, that's for sure <nonformal>; that goes without saying, *cela va sans dire* <Fr>; that is evident, that leaps to the eye, *cela saute aux yeux* <Fr>

970 UNCERTAINTY

NOUNS **1** **uncertainty, incertitude, unsureness,** uncertainness; indemonstrability, unverifiability, unprovability, unconfirmability; **unpredictability,** unforeseeableness, incalculability, unaccountability; **indetermination,** indeterminacy, indeterminism; **relativity,** relativism, contingency, conditionality; **randomness, chance,** chanciness, hit-or-missness, **luck;** entropy; **indecision,** indecisiveness, undecidedness, undeterminedness; **hesitation, hesitancy; suspense,** suspensefulness, agony *or* state of suspense; **fickleness, capriciousness,** whimsicality, **erraticness,** erraticism, **changeableness** 853; **vacillation, irresolution** 362; trendlessness; Heisenberg *or* indeterminacy *or* uncertainty principle

2 **doubtfulness, dubiousness, doubt,** dubiety, dubitancy, dubitation <old>; **questionableness, disputability,** contestability, controvertibility, refutability, confutability, deniability; disbelief 954.1

3 **bewilderment,** disconcertion, disconcertedness, disconcert, disconcertment, **embarrassment, confoundment,** discomposure, unassuredness, **confusion,** cognitive dissonance; **perplexity, puzzlement,** baffle, **bafflement,** predicament, plight, **quandary, dilemma,** horns of a dilemma, nonplus; **puzzle,** problem, riddle, conundrum, mystery, enigma; fix *and* jam *and* pickle *and* scrape *and* stew <all nonformal>; perturbation, **disturbance, upset, bother,** pother

4 **vagueness, indefiniteness, indecisiveness,** indeterminateness, indeterminableness, indefinableness, **unclearness, indistinctness,** haziness, fogginess, mistiness, murkiness, blurriness, fuzziness; **obscurity,** obscuration; **looseness, laxity, inexactness,** inaccuracy, imprecision; **broadness, generality,** sweepingness; ill-definedness, amorphousness, shapelessness, blobbiness; inchoateness, disorder, incoherence

5 **equivocalness,** equivocality, polysemousness, ambiguity 539

6 **unreliability, undependability, untrustworthiness,** unfaithworthiness, treacherousness, treachery; **unsureness, insecurity, unsoundness, infirmity,** insolidity, unsolidity, **instability,** insubstantiality, unsubstantiality, **unsteadfastness,** unsteadiness, desultoriness, shakiness; **precariousness,** hazard, danger, risk, riskiness, diceyness *and* dodginess <Brit nonformal>, knife-edge, moment of truth, tightrope walking, peril, perilousness, ticklishness, slipperiness, shiftiness, shiftingness; speculativeness; **unauthoritativeness,** unauthenticity

7 **fallibility,** errability, errancy, liability to error

8 <an uncertainty> **gamble, guess,** piece of guesswork, estimate, guesstimate *and* ball-park figure <nonformal>; **chance, wager; toss-up** *and* **coin-toss** <both nonformal>, **touch and go;** contingency, double contingency, possibility upon a possibility; **question, open question;** undecided issue, loose end; **gray area,** twilight zone, borderline case; blind bargain, pig in a poke, sight-unseen transaction; leap in the dark

VERBS 9 **be uncertain, feel unsure; doubt,** have one's doubts, **question,** puzzle over, agonize over; **wonder,** wonder whether, wrinkle one's brow; not know what to make of, not be able to make head or tail of; be at sea, float in a sea of doubt; be at one's wit's end, **not know which way to turn,** be of two minds, be at sixes and sevens, not know where one stands, have mixed feelings feelings, not know whether one stands on one's head or one's heels, be in a dilemma *or* quandary, flounder, grope, beat about, thrash about, not know whether one is coming or going, go around in circles; go off in all directions at once

10 **hang in doubt,** stop to consider, think twice; **falter,** dither, **hesitate, vacillate** 362.8

11 **depend,** all depend, be contingent *or* conditional on, hang on *or* upon; **hang, hang in the balance,** be touch and go, tremble in the balance, **hang in suspense; hang by a thread,** cliffhang, hang by a hair, hang by the eyelids

12 **bewilder, disconcert,** discompose, **upset,** perturb, **disturb, dismay,** tie one in knots; abash, **embarrass, put out,** pother, **bother,** moider <Brit nonformal>, flummox <nonformal>, keep one on tenterhooks

13 **perplex, baffle, confound,** daze, amaze <old>, maze, addle, fuddle, muddle, **mystify, puzzle,** nonplus, put to one's wit's end; keep one guessing, keep in suspense

14 <nonformal terms> **stump,** boggle <Brit>, buffalo, bamboozle, stick, floor, throw, get, beat, beat the shit out of, lick

15 **make uncertain, obscure, muddle, muddy,** fuzz, fog, **confuse** 984.7

ADJS 16 **uncertain, unsure; doubting,** agnostic, **skeptical,** unconvinced, unpersuaded; chancy, dicey <Brit>, touch-and-go; **unpredictable,** unforeseeable, incalculable, uncountable, unreckonable, unaccountable, undivinable; indemonstrable, unverifiable, unprovable, unconfirmable; **equivocal,** polysemous, inexplicit, imprecise, ambiguous; **fickle, capricious,** whimsical, **erratic,** variable, wavering, **changeable** 853.6; **hesitant,** hesitating; **indecisive, irresolute** 362.9

17 **doubtful,** iffy <nonformal>; **in doubt,** *in
dubio* <L>; dubitable, doubtable, **dubious, questionable, problematic, problematical, speculative,** conjectural, suppositional; **debatable,** moot, arguable, disputable, contestable, controvertible, **controversial,** refutable, confutable, deniable;
mistakable; **suspicious,** suspect; open to
question *or* doubt; in question, in dispute,
at issue

18 **undecided, undetermined, unsettled,** unfixed, unestablished; untold, uncounted;
pendent, dependent, **pending,** depending,
contingent, conditional, conditioned;
open, in question, at issue, **in the balance,
up in the air,** up for grabs <nonformal>,
in suspense, in a state of suspense, suspenseful

19 **vague, indefinite, indecisive, indeterminate,** indeterminable, **undetermined,**
unpredetermined, undestined; **random,**
stochastic, entropic, **chance,** chancy
<nonformal>, dicey *and* dodgy <Brit
nonformal>, aleatory *or* aleatoric, hit-or-
miss; indefinable, undefined, ill-defined,
unclear, unplain, **indistinct,** fuzzy, **obscure, confused, hazy,** shadowy, shadowed forth, misty, foggy, fog-bound,
murky, blurred, blurry, veiled; **loose, lax,
inexact,** inaccurate, imprecise; nonspecific, unspecified; **broad, general,**
sweeping; amorphous, shapeless, blobby;
inchoate, disordered, orderless, chaotic,
incoherent

20 **unreliable, undependable, untrustworthy,** unfaithworthy, treacherous, **unsure,**
not to be depended *or* relied on; **insecure,
unsound, infirm,** unsolid, **unstable,** unsubstantial, insubstantial, **unsteadfast,**
unsteady, desultory, shaky; **precarious,**
hazardous, dangerous, perilous, risky,
ticklish; shifty, shifting, slippery, slippery as an eel; provisional, tentative,
temporary

21 **unauthoritative, unauthentic, unofficial,**
nonofficial, apocryphal; **uncertified, unverified,** unchecked, unconfirmed, uncorroborated, unauthenticated, unvalidated,
unattested, unwarranted; **undemonstrated, unproved**

22 **fallible, errable,** errant, liable *or* open to
error, error-prone

23 **unconfident, unsure, unassured, insecure,**
unsure of oneself; unselfconfident, un-
selfassured, unselfreliant

24 **bewildered, dismayed,** distracted, distraught, abashed, **disconcerted, embarrassed,** discomposed, **put-out, disturbed,
upset,** perturbed, **bothered,** all hot and

bothered <nonformal>; **confused** 984.12;
clueless, without a clue, guessing, mazed,
in a maze; turned around, going around
in circles, like a chicken with its head-
cut off <nonformal>; in a fix *or* stew *or*
pickle *or* jam *or* scrape <nonformal>;
lost, astray, abroad, adrift, **at sea,** off the
track, out of one's reckoning, out of one's
bearings, disoriented

25 **in a dilemma,** on the horns of a dilemma;
**perplexed, confounded, mystified, puz-
zled, nonplussed, baffled,** bamboozled
<nonformal>, buffaloed <nonformal>;
at a loss, at one's wit's end, fuddled, addled, muddled, dazed; **on tenterhooks,** in
suspense

26 <nonformal terms> **beat,** licked, stuck,
floored, stumped, thrown, buffaloed, bog-
gled <Brit>

27 **bewildering, confusing, distracting, disconcerting,** discomposing, **dismaying,
embarrassing,** disturbing, **upsetting,** perturbing, bothering; **perplexing, baffling,
mystifying, mysterious, puzzling,** funny,
funny peculiar, confounding; **problematic** *or* problematical; intricate 798.4;
enigmatic 522.17

ADVS 28 **uncertainly,** in an uncertain state,
unsurely; doubtfully, dubiously; in suspense, at sea, on the horns of a dilemma,
at sixes and sevens; perplexedly, discon-
certedly, confusedly, dazedly, mazedly,
in a daze, in a maze, around in circles

29 **vaguely, indefinitely,** indeterminably,
indefinably, **indistinctly,** indecisively,
obscurely; broadly, generally, in broad *or*
general terms

971 CHANCE
<absence of assignable cause>

NOUNS **1 chance,** happenstance, hap, "heedless hap"—Spenser; **luck;** good luck *or*
fortune, serendipity, happy chance,
dumb luck <nonformal>, rotten *and*
tough luck <both nonformal>; **fortune,**
fate, **destiny,** whatever comes, *moira*
<Gk>, lot 963.2; **fortuity, randomness,**
randomicity, fortuitousness, adven-
titiousness, indeterminateness *or* indeterminacy, problematicness, uncertainty 970, flukiness <nonformal>,
casualness, flip of a coin, crazy quilt, pat-
ternlessness, trendlessness, accidentality;
break <nonformal>, the breaks <nonfor-
mal>, run of luck, the luck of the draw,
the rub of the green, run *or* turn of the
cards, fall *or* throw of the dice, the way
things fall, the way the cards fall, how

they fall, the way the cookie crumbles *or* the ball bounces <both nonformal>; uncertainty principle, principle of indeterminacy, Heisenberg's principle; **probability** 967, stochastics, theory of probability, law of averages, statistical probability, actuarial calculation; random sample, **risk, risk-taking, chancing, gamble** 759; **opportunity** 842.2

2 Chance, Fortune, Lady *or* Dame Fortune, wheel of fortune, Fortuna, the fickle finger of fate <nonformal>; Luck, Lady Luck; "a nickname of Providence"—de Chamfort, "blind Chance"—Lucan, "fickle Chance"—Milton, "that Power which erring men call Chance"—Milton, "the pseudonym of God when He did not want to sign"—Anatole France

3 **purposelessness, causelessness,** aimlessness, randomness, dysteleology, **unpredictability** 970.1, designlessness, **aimlessness**

4 **haphazard,** chance-medley <law>, **random;** random shot; potluck

5 **vicissitudes,** vicissitudes of fortune, ins and outs, **ups and downs,** ups and downs of life, chapter of accidents, feast and famine, "the various turns of chance"—Dryden; **chain of circumstances,** concatenation of events, chain reaction, vicious circle, causal nexus, **domino effect**

6 <chance event> **happening,** hap, happenstance; **fortuity, accident,** casualty, adventure, hazard; contingent, contingency; **fluke** <nonformal>, freak, freak occurrence *or* accident; chance hit, lucky shot, long shot, one in a million, long odds

7 **even chance,** even break *and* fair shake <both nonformal>, even *or* square odds, level playing field, touch and go, odds; **half a chance,** fifty-fifty; toss, **toss-up,** standoff <nonformal>

8 **good chance, sporting chance,** good opportunity, good possibility; odds-on, odds-on chance, **likelihood, possibility** 965, probability 967, favorable prospect, well-grounded hope; **sure bet,** sure thing *and* dollars to doughnuts <both nonformal>; **best bet,** main chance, winning chance

9 **small chance,** little chance, dark horse, **poor prospect** *or* prognosis, poor lookout <nonformal>, little opportunity, poor possibility, **unlikelihood, improbability** 968, hardly a chance, not half a chance; **off chance, outside chance** <nonformal>, **remote possibility,** bare possibility, a ghost of a chance, slim chance, gambling

chance, **fighting chance** <nonformal>; poor bet, long odds, long shot <nonformal>, hundred-to-one shot <nonformal>

10 **no chance,** not a Chinaman's chance *and* not a snowball's chance in hell <both nonformal>, Buckley's chance <Austral nonformal>, not a prayer; **impossibility** 966, hopelessness

VERBS 11 **chance,** bechance, betide, come *or* happen by chance, hap, hazard, **happen** 830.5, happen *or* fall on, come, come *or* happen along, **turn up,** pop up <nonformal>, **befall;** fall to one's lot, be one's fate

12 **risk,** take a chance, run a risk, push *or* press one's luck, lay one's ass on the line *and* put one's money where one's mouth is <both nonformal>, **gamble, bet** 759.19; risk one's neck *and* shoot the works *and* go for broke <all nonformal>; **predict** 961.9, prognosticate, make book <nonformal>; call someone's bluff

13 have a chance *or* an opportunity, **stand a chance, run a good chance, bid** *or* **stand fair to,** admit of; be in it *or* in the running <nonformal>; have *or* take a chance at, have a fling *or* shot at <nonformal>; have a small *or* slight chance, be a dark horse, barely have a chance

14 **not have** *or* **stand a chance,** have no chance *or* opportunity, not have a prayer, not have a Chinaman's chance <nonformal>, not stand a snowball's chance in hell <nonformal>; not be in it <nonformal>, be out of it <nonformal>, **be out of the running**

ADJS 15 **chance;** chancy <nonformal>, dicey <Brit nonformal>, **risky** <nonformal>; **fortuitous, accidental,** aleatory; **lucky,** fortunate, blessed by fortune, serendipitous; **casual,** adventitious, incidental, contingent, iffy <nonformal>; **causeless,** uncaused; indeterminate, undetermined; **unexpected** 131.10, **unpredictable,** unforeseeable, unlooked-for, **unforeseen; fluky** <nonformal>; fatal, fatidic, destinal

16 **purposeless, causeless,** designless, **aimless,** driftless, undirected, objectless, unmotivated, mindless; **haphazard, random,** dysteleological, stochastic, stray, inexplicable, unaccountable, promiscuous, indiscriminate, casual, leaving much to chance

17 **unintentional,** unintended, **unmeant, unplanned,** undesigned, unpurposed, unthought-of; **unpremeditated,** unmeditated, unprompted, unguided,

unguarded; **unwitting, unthinking,** unconscious, involuntary

18 impossible 966.7; **improbable** 968.3; certain 969.13; **probable** 967.6

ADVS **19 by chance,** perchance, **by accident, accidentally, casually,** incidentally, by coincidence, **unpredictably, fortuitously, out of a clear blue sky;** by a piece of luck, by a fluke <nonformal>, by good fortune; **as it chanced, as luck would have it,** by hazard, as it may happen, as it may be, as the case may be, as it may chance, as it may turn up *or* out; somehow, in some way, in some way or other, somehow or other, for some reason

20 purposelessly, aimlessly; haphazardly, randomly, dysteleologically, stochastically, inexplicably, unaccountably, promiscuously, indiscriminately, casually, **at haphazard, at random,** at hazard

21 unintentionally, without design, unwittingly, unthinkingly, unexpectedly, unconsciously, involuntarily

INTERJS **22** break a leg!, best of luck! good luck!

PHR **23** it's a crapshoot

972 TRUTH
<conformity to fact or reality>

NOUNS **1 truth, trueness, verity,** veridicality, conformity to fact *or* reality *or* the evidence *or* the data, simple *or* unadorned truth, very truth, sooth *or* good sooth <both archaic>; more truth than poetry; **unerroneousness, unfalseness,** unfallaciousness; historical truth, **objective truth, actuality,** historicity, impersonality; **fact, actuality, reality** 760.2, the real world; the true, ultimate truth; eternal verities; truthfulness, veracity 644.3

2 a truth, a self-evident truth, an axiomatic truth, an axiom; a premise, a given, a donnée *or* donné, an accomplished fact *or* fait accompli <Fr>

3 the truth, the truth of the matter, the case; the home truth, the unvarnished truth, the simple truth, the unadorned truth, the naked truth, the plain truth, the unqualified truth, the honest truth, the sober truth, the exact truth, the straight truth; the absolute truth, the intrinsic truth, the unalloyed truth, the cast-iron truth, the hard truth, the stern truth, gospel, gospel truth, Bible truth, revealed truth; the truth, the whole truth, and nothing but the truth

4 <nonformal terms> **what's what,** how it is, how things are, like it is, where it's at,

dinkum oil <Austral>, the straight of it, the straight goods *or* skinny *or* scoop, the honest-to-God truth, God's truth, the real thing, the very model, the genuine article, the very thing, it, the article, the goods, the McCoy, the real McCoy, chapter and verse, the gospel, the gospel truth, the lowdown, the skinny

5 accuracy, correctness, care for truth, attention to fact, right, subservience to the facts *or* the data, **rightness, rigor, rigorousness, exactness, exactitude; preciseness, precision;** mathematical precision, pinpoint accuracy *or* precision, scientific exactness *or* exactitude; **faultlessness,** perfection, absoluteness, flawlessness, impeccability, unimpeachability; **faithfulness, fidelity;** literalness, literality, literalism, textualism, the letter; strictness, severity, rigidity; niceness, nicety, delicacy, subtlety, fineness, refinement; **meticulousness** 339.3; laboratory conditions

6 validity, soundness, solidity, substantiality, **justness;** authority, **authoritativeness; cogency,** weight, force, persuasiveness

7 genuineness, authenticity, bona fides, bona fideness, **legitimacy; realness, realism,** photographic realism, absolute realism, realistic representation, **naturalism,** naturalness, truth to nature, **lifelikeness,** truth to life, slice of life, *tranche de vie* <Fr>, kitchen sink, true-to-lifeness, verisimilitude, *vraisemblance* <Fr>, verism, verismo; absolute likeness, **literalness,** literality, literalism, truth to the letter; socialist realism; inartificiality, unsyntheticness; **unspuriousness,** unspeciousness, unfictitiousness, artlessness, unaffectedness; **honesty, sincerity;** unadulteration 797.1

VERBS **8 be true,** be the case; conform to fact, square *or* chime with the facts *or* evidence; **prove true,** prove to be, **prove out,** be so in fact; **hold true, hold good, hold water** <nonformal>, hold *or* stick together <nonformal>, **hold up, hold up in the wash** <nonformal>, wash <nonformal>, **stand up,** stand the test, be consistent *or* self-consistent, **hold,** remain valid; **be truthful**

9 seem true, ring true, sound true, **carry conviction,** convince, persuade, win over, hold *or* have the ring of truth

10 be right, be correct, be just right, get it straight; be OK <nonformal>, add up; **hit the nail on the head,** hit it on the nose *or* on the money *and* say a mouthful <all

nonformal>, hit the bull's-eye, score a bull's-eye

11 **be accurate, dot one's i's and cross one's t's,** draw *or* cut it fine <nonformal>, be precise; make precise, precise, particularize

12 **come true, come about,** attain fulfillment, **turn out, come to pass** *or* **to be,** happen as expected

ADJS 13 **true, truthful; unerroneous,** not in error, in conformity with the facts *or* the evidence *or* reality, on the up-and-up *or* strictly on the up-and-up <nonformal>; gospel, **hard,** cast-iron; unfalse, unfallacious, unmistaken; **real, veritable,** sureenough <nonformal>, objective, true to the facts, in conformity with the facts *or* the evidence *or* the data *or* reality, **factual, actual** 760.15, effectual, **historical,** documentary; objectively true; **certain,** undoubted, unquestionable 969.15; unrefuted, unconfuted, undenied; **ascertained, proved, proven, verified,** validated, **certified,** demonstrated, confirmed, determined, established, attested, substantiated, **authenticated,** corroborated; true as gospel; substantially true, categorically true; **veracious** 644.16

14 **valid, sound, well-grounded, well-founded,** conforming to the facts *or* the data *or* the evidence *or* reality, hard, solid, substantial; consistent, self-consistent, logical; **good, just,** sufficient; **cogent, weighty, authoritative; legal, lawful,** legitimate, **binding**

15 **genuine, authentic,** veridic, veridical, **real, natural, realistic, naturalistic,** true to reality, **true to nature, lifelike,** true to life, verisimilar, veristic; **literal,** following the letter, letter-perfect, *au pied de la lettre* <Fr>, true to the letter; verbatim, verbal, word-perfect, **word-for-word;** true to the spirit; **legitimate,** rightful, lawful; **bona fide,** card-carrying <nonformal>, **good,** sure-enough <nonformal>, **sincere, honest;** candid, honest-to-God <nonformal>, dinkum <Austral nonformal>; **inartificial, unsynthetic;** unspurious, unspecious, unsimulated, unfaked, unfeigned, **undisguised, uncounterfeited, unpretended, unaffected, unassumed; unassuming, simple,** unpretending, unfeigning, undisguising; **unfictitious,** unfanciful, unfabricated, unconcocted, uninvented, unimagined; unromantic; **original,** unimitated, uncopied; unexaggerated, undistorted; unflattering, unvarnished, uncolored, unqualified; **unadulterated** 797.7; **pure,** simon-pure; **sterling,**

twenty-four carat, all wool and a yard wide <nonformal>

16 **accurate, correct, right,** proper, just; all right *or* OK *or* okay <all nonformal>, just right as rain, right, dead right, on target *and* on the money *and* on the nose <all nonformal>, bang on <Brit nonformal>, straight, straight-up-and-down; **faultless,** flawless, impeccable, unimpeachable, unexceptionable; **absolute, perfect; meticulous** 339.12

17 **exact, precise,** express; even, square; absolutely *or* definitely *or* positively right; **faithful;** direct; **unerring,** undeviating, constant; **infallible,** inerrant, inerrable; **strict,** close, severe, **rigorous,** rigid; mathematically exact, mathematical; mechanically *or* micrometrically precise; scientifically exact, scientific; religiously exact, religious; **nice,** delicate, subtle, **fine,** refined; pinpoint, microscopic

ADVS 18 **truly, really,** really-truly <nonformal>, **verily,** veritably, forsooth *or* in very sooth <both old>, **in truth,** in good *or* very truth, **actually,** historically, objectively, impersonally, rigorously, strictly, strictly speaking, unquestionably, without question, **in reality, in fact,** factually, technically, in point of fact, as a matter of fact, for that matter, for the matter of that, to tell the truth, if you want to know the truth, to state the fact *or* truth, of a truth, with truth; **indeed,** indeedy <nonformal>; **certainly; indubitably, undoubtedly** 969.25; no buts about it <nonformal>, nothing else but

19 **genuinely, authentically, really,** naturally, **legitimately, honestly,** veridically; warts and all; unaffectedly, unassumedly, from the heart, in one's heart of hearts, with all one's heart and soul

20 **accurately, correctly,** rightly, properly, straight; **perfectly, faultlessly,** flawlessly, impeccably, unimpeachably, unexceptionally; **just right,** just so; **so,** sic

21 **exactly, precisely,** to a T, expressly; **just, dead,** right, straight, even, square, **plumb,** directly, squarely, point-blank; unerringly, undeviatingly; verbatim, **literally,** *literatim* <L>, verbally, word-perfectly, word for word, word by word, word for word and letter for letter, *verbatim et litteratim* <L>, in the same words, *ipsissimis verbis* <L>, to the letter, according to the letter, *au pied de la lettre* <Fr>; **faithfully, strictly, rigorously,** rigidly; **definitely, positively,**

absolutely; in every respect, in all respects, for all the world, neither more nor less

22 **to be exact, to be precise, strictly, technically, strictly speaking,** not to mince the matter, by the book

23 **to a nicety,** to a T *or* tittle, to a turn, to a hair, to *or* within an inch

24 PHRS **right!, that's right, that is so,** amen!, that's it, that's just it, just so, it is that, *c'est ça* <Fr>; **you are right,** right you are, right as rain, it is for a fact, you speak truly, as you say, **right;** believe it or not; touché!

25 <nonformal terms> **right on!,** you better believe it!, you've got something there, I'll say, I'll tell the world, I'll drink to that, righto, quite, rather!, you got it!, you said it, you said a mouthful, now you're talking, you can say that again, you're not kidding, that's for sure, ain't it the truth?, you're damn tootin', don't I know it?, you're telling me?, you're not just whistling Dixie, bet your ass *or* sweet ass *or* bippy *or* boots *or* life *or* you bet the rent, fucking ay, fucking ay right

973 WISE SAYING

NOUNS 1 **maxim, aphorism, apothegm, epigram, dictum, adage, proverb,** gnome, words of wisdom, **saw, saying,** witticism, sentence, expression, phrase, catchword, catchphrase, word, byword, mot, motto, moral; **precept,** prescript, teaching, text, verse, sutra, distich, sloka; golden saying, proverbial saying; common *or* current saying, stock saying, pithy saying, wise saying *or* expression, oracle, sententious expression *or* saying; **conventional wisdom, common knowledge; ana, analects, proverbs, wisdom, wisdom literature, collected sayings**

2 **axiom, truth,** a priori truth, postulate, **truism,** self-evident truth, general *or* universal truth, home truth, obvious truth; theorem; **proposition;** brocard, **principle,** *principium* <L>, settled principle; **formula; rule, law,** dictate <old>, **dictum;** golden rule

3 **platitude, cliché, saw, old saw, commonplace, banality,** bromide, **chestnut** <nonformal>, corn <nonformal>, triticism <old>, tired phrase, trite saying, hackneyed *or* stereotyped saying, commonplace expression, *lieu commun* <Fr>, *locus communis* <L>, **familiar tune *or* story, old song *or* story,** old song and dance <nonformal>; twice-told tale, re-

told story; reiteration 848.2; prosaicism, prosaism; prose; old joke 489.9

4 **motto, slogan,** watchword, catchword, catchphrase, tag line; **device;** epithet; inscription, epigraph

VERBS 5 aphorize, apothegmatize, epigrammatize, coin a phrase; proverb

ADJS 6 **aphoristic, proverbial,** epigrammatic, epigrammatical, **axiomatical; sententious, pithy,** gnomic, pungent, succinct, terse, crisp, pointed; formulistic, formulaic; **cliché,** banal, tired, trite, tritical <old>, **platitudinous** 117.9

ADVS 7 **proverbially, as the saying is *or* goes,** as they say, as the fellow says <nonformal>, as it has been said, as it was said of old

974 ERROR

NOUNS 1 **error, erroneousness; untrueness,** untruthfulness, **untruth; wrongness, wrong; falseness, falsity; fallacy, fallaciousness,** self-contradiction; fault, **faultiness,** defectiveness; **sin** 655, sinfulness, peccancy, flaw, flawedness, *hamartia* <Gk>; misdoing, misfeasance; errancy, aberrancy, aberration, **deviancy; heresy,** unorthodoxy, heterodoxy; perversion, **distortion; mistaking,** misconstruction, misapplication, misprision <old>; **delusion, illusion** 975; misjudgment 947; **misinterpretation** 342

2 **inaccuracy,** inaccurateness, **incorrectness, uncorrectness, inexactness,** unfactualness, inexactitude, **unpreciseness,** imprecision, unspecificity, looseness, laxity, unrigorousness; tolerance, allowance; negligence; approximation; **deviation,** standard deviation, probable error, predictable error, range of error; uncertainty 970

3 **mistake, error,** *erratum* <L>, *corrigendum* <L>; **fault,** *faute* <Fr>; gross error, bevue; human error; **misconception, misapprehension, misunderstanding;** misstatement, misquotation; misreport; **misprint, typographical error,** typo <nonformal>, printer's error, typist's error; clerical error; misidentification; **misjudgment, miscalculation** 947.1; misplay; misdeal; miscount; misuse; failure, miss, miscarriage

4 **slip,** slipup *and* miscue <both nonformal>; **lapse,** *lapsus* <L>, **oversight,** omission, balk <old>, inadvertence *or* inadvertency, loose thread; **misstep,** trip, stumble, false *or* wrong step, wrong *or* bad *or* false move; false note; **slip of the**

tongue, *sus linguae* <L>; **slip of the pen,** *lapsus calami* <L>

5 **blunder, faux pas,** gaffe, solecism; stupidity, indiscretion 922.4; **botch, bungle** 414.5

6 <nonformal terms> **goof, boo-boo,** muff, flub, foozle, bloomer, bloop, blooper, boot, bobble, boner, bonehead play *or* trick, dumb trick, boob stunt, fool mistake; howler, clanger <Brit>, screamer; fuck-up, screw-up, foul-up, snafu, muck-up, balls-up <Brit>, louse-up; pratfall, whoops

7 **grammatical error, solecism,** anacoluthon, misusage, missaying, mispronunciation; **bull, Irish bull,** fluff, **malapropism,** malaprop, Mrs Malaprop <R B Sheridan>; Pickwickian sense; spoonerism, marrow-sky; hypercorrection, hyperform; folk etymology; catachresis

VERBS **8** **not hold water** *and* not hold together <both nonformal>, not stand up, not square, not figure <nonformal>, not add up, **not hold up, not hold up in the wash** *and* not wash <both nonformal>

9 **err,** fall into error, **go wrong, go amiss,** go astray, go *or* get out of line, go awry, stray, get off-base <nonformal>, **deviate,** wander; **lapse, slip, slip up,** trip, stumble; **miscalculate** 947.2

10 **be wrong, mistake oneself, be mistaken, be in error, be at fault,** be out of line, be off the track, be in the wrong, miss the truth, miss the point, miss by a mile <nonformal>, have another think coming <nonformal>; take wrong, receive a false impression, take the shadow for the substance, be misled, be misguided; deceive oneself, be deceived, delude oneself; labor under a false impression

11 bark up the wrong tree, back the wrong horse, count one's chickens before they are hatched

12 **misdo,** do amiss; misuse, misemploy, misapply; misconduct, mismanage; miscall, miscount, misdeal, misplay, misfield; misprint, miscite, misquote, misread, misreport, misspell

13 **mistake, make a mistake;** miscue *and* make a miscue <both nonformal>; **misidentify; misunderstand,** misapprehend, misconceive, **misinterpret** 342.2; **confuse** 810.3, mix up, not distinguish

14 **blunder, make a blunder, make a faux pas,** blot one's copy book, make a colossal blunder, make a false *or* wrong step, make a misstep; **misspeak** oneself, misspeak oneself, trip over one's tongue; embarrass oneself, have egg on one's face <nonfor-

mal>; blunder into; **botch, bungle** 414.11

15 <nonformal terms> **make** *or* **pull a boner** *or* boo-boo *or* blooper; drop a brick <Brit>, goof, fluff, duff <Brit>, foozle, boot, bobble, blow, blow it, drop the ball; fuck-up, screw-up, foul-up, muck-up, louse-up; put *or* stick one's foot in it *or* in one's mouth; muff one's cue, muff *or* blow *or* fluff one's lines, fall flat on one's face *or* ass, step on one's dick, trip up

ADJS **16** **erroneous, untrue,** not true, **not right;** unfactual, **wrong,** all wrong; peccant, perverse, corrupt; **false, fallacious,** self-contradictory; **illogical** 935.11; **unproved** 957.8; **faulty,** faultful, flawed, defective, **at fault;** out, off, all off, off the track *or* rails; wide <old>, wide of the mark, beside the mark; amiss, awry, askew, deviant, deviative, deviational; erring, errant, **aberrant;** straying, astray, adrift; **heretical,** unorthodox, heterodox; abroad, all abroad; perverted, **distorted; delusive,** deceptive, **illusory**

17 **inaccurate, incorrect, inexact,** unfactual, **unprecise,** imprecise, unspecific, loose, lax, unrigorous; negligent; **vague;** approximate, approximative; out of line, out of plumb, out of true, out of square; off-base <nonformal>

18 **mistaken, in error, erring,** under an error, **wrong, all wet** <nonformal>, full of bull *or* shit *or* hot air *or* it *or* prunes *or* crap *or* beans <all nonformal>; off *or* out in one's reckoning; in the wrong box, in the right church but the wrong pew

19 **unauthentic** *or* **inauthentic, unauthoritative, unreliable** 970.20; **misstated,** misreported, miscited, misquoted, **garbled;** unfounded 935.13; spurious

ADVS **20** **erroneously, falsely,** by mistake, fallaciously; faultily, faultfully; **untrue** <old>, untruly; **wrong,** wrongly; **mistakenly;** amiss, astray, on the wrong track

21 **inaccurately, incorrectly,** inexactly, unprecisely, by guess and by God *or* by golly <nonformal>

INTERJS **22** whoops! *and* sorry about that <both nonformal>

PHRS **23** **you are wrong, you are mistaken,** you're all wet *or* you're way off *or* you have another guess coming *or* don't kid yourself <all nonformal>

975 ILLUSION

NOUNS **1** **illusion, delusion,** deluded belief; **deception** 356, **trick;** self-deception, self-deceit, self-delusion; dereism, autism; **misconception, misbelief,** false belief, wrong impression, warped *or* distorted conception; **bubble, chimera,** vapor, "airy nothing"—Shakespeare; *ignis fatuus* <L>, will-o'-the-wisp; **dream,** dream vision; dreamworld, dreamland, dreamscape; **daydream;** pipe dream *and* trip <nonformal>; fool's paradise, castle in the air dreamscape; maya

2 **illusoriness,** illusiveness, delusiveness; **falseness,** fallaciousness; **unreality,** unactuality; unsubstantiality, airiness, immateriality; **idealization** 985.7; **seeming,** semblance, simulacrum, **appearance,** false *or* specious appearance, show, false show, false light; **magic, sorcery** 690, illusionism, sleight of hand, prestidigitation, magic show, magic act; magician, **sorcerer** 690.5, illusionist, Prospero <Shakespeare>; Mahamaya <Hinduism>

3 **fancy, phantasy, imagination** 985

4 **phantom, phantasm,** phantasma, wraith, specter; shadow, shade; phantasmagoria; **fantasy,** wildest dream; **figment of the imagination** 985.5, phantom of the mind; **apparition, appearance; vision,** waking dream, image <old>; shape, form, figure, presence; eidolon, idolum; "such stuff as dreams are made on"—Shakespeare

5 **optical illusion, trick of eyesight;** afterimage, spectrum, ocular spectrum

6 **mirage,** fata morgana, will-o'-the-wisp, looming

7 **hallucination;** hallucinosis; tripping <nonformal>, mind-expansion; consciousness-expansion; delirium tremens 925.9,10; dream 985.9

VERBS 8 **go on a trip** *and* **blow one's mind** <both nonformal>, freak out <nonformal>; **hallucinate;** expand one's consciousness; make magic, prestidigitate

ADJS 9 **illusory,** illusive; illusional, illusionary; Barmecide *or* Barmecidal; **delusory,** delusive; delusional, delusionary, deluding; dereistic, autistic; **dreamy, dreamlike; visionary; imaginary** 985.19; **erroneous** 974.16; **deceptive;** self-deceptive, self-deluding; **chimeric, chimerical, fantastic; unreal,** unactual, unsubstantial 763.5, airy; unfounded 935.13; **false,** fallacious, misleading; **specious, seeming,** apparent, ostensible, supposititious, all in the mind; spectral, apparitional, phantom, phantasmal; phantasmagoric, surreal

10 **hallucinatory,** hallucinative, hallucinational; hallucinogenic, psychedelic, con-

sciousness-expanding, mind-expanding, mind-blowing <nonformal>

976 DISILLUSIONMENT

NOUNS 1 **disillusionment,** disillusion, **disenchantment,** undeception, unspelling, return to reality, loss of one's illusions, loss of innocence, cold light of reality, enlightenment, bursting of the bubble; awakening, rude awakening, bringing back to earth; disappointment 132; debunking <nonformal>

VERBS 2 **disillusion,** disillude, disillusionize; **disenchant,** unspell, uncharm, break the spell *or* charm; **disabuse, undeceive;** correct, **set right** *or* **straight,** put straight, tell the truth, enlighten, let in on, put one wise <nonformal>; clear the mind of; open one's eyes, awaken, wake up, unblindfold; disappoint 132.2; dispel *or* dissipate one's illusions, rob *or* strip one of one's illusions; bring one back to earth, let down easy <nonformal>; **burst** *or* **prick the bubble,** puncture one's balloon <nonformal>; let the air out of, take the wind out of; knock the props out from under, take the ground from under; debunk <nonformal>; expose, show up 351.4

3 **be disillusioned,** be disenchanted, get back to earth, get one's feet on the ground, have one's eyes opened, return to *or* embrace reality; charge to experience; have another thing *or* guess coming <nonformal>

ADJS 4 **disillusioning,** disillusive, disillusionary, **disenchanting,** disabusing, undeceiving, enlightening

5 **disillusioned, disenchanted,** unspelled, uncharmed, **disabused,** undeceived, stripped *or* robbed of illusion, enlightened, set right, put straight; with one's eyes open, sophisticated, **blasé;** disappointed 132.5

977 MENTAL ATTITUDE

NOUNS 1 **attitude,** mental attitude; psychology; **position, posture,** stance; **way of thinking; feeling, sentiment,** the way one feels; feeling tone, affect, affectivity, emotion, emotivity; opinion 952.6

2 **outlook,** mental outlook; *Anschauung* <Ger>, **point of view, viewpoint, standpoint, perspective,** *optique* <Fr>; position, stand, place, situation; side; footing, basis; where one is *or* sits *or* stands; **view,** sight, light, eye; respect, regard; angle, angle of vision, slant, way of

looking at things, slant on things, where one is coming from <nonformal>; **frame of reference,** intellectual *or* ideational frame of reference, framework, arena, world, universe, world *or* universe of discourse, system, reference system; phenomenology

3 **disposition, character, nature, temper, temperament,** mettle, constitution, complexion *and* humor <both old>, make-up, stamp, type, stripe, kidney, make, mold; **turn of mind, inclination,** mind, tendency, grain, vein, set, mental set, mindset, **leaning,** animus, propensity, proclivity, predilection, preference, predisposition; **bent, turn, bias,** slant, cast, warp, twist; idiosyncrasy, eccentricity, individualism; diathesis, aptitude; strain, streak

4 **mood, humor, feeling, feelings, temper, frame of mind, state of mind, morale,** cue *or* frame <both old>, tone, note, **vein; mind,** heart, spirit *or* spirits

5 <pervading attitudes> **climate,** mental *or* intellectual climate, spiritual climate, moral climate, mores, norms, climate of opinion, **ethos,** ideology, *Weltanschauung* <Ger>, world view; *Zeitgeist* <Ger>, spirit of the time *or* the age

VERBS 6 **take the attitude,** feel about it, look at it, **view,** look at in the light of; **be disposed to,** tend *or* incline toward, prefer, lean toward, be bent on

ADJS 7 **attitudinal; temperamental, dispositional,** inclinational, constitutional; emotional, affective; mental, intellectual, ideational, ideological; spiritual; characteristic 864.13; innate

8 **disposed,** dispositioned, **predisposed, prone, inclined, given,** bent, bent on, apt, likely, **minded, in the mood** *or* humor

ADVS 9 **attitudinally; temperamentally, dispositionally,** constitutionally; emotionally; mentally, intellectually, ideationally, ideologically; morally, spiritually; **by temperament** *or* **disposition,** by virtue of mind-set, by the logic of character *or* temperament; from one's standpoint *or* viewpoint *or* angle, from where one stands *or* sits, from where one is; within the frame of reference *or* framework *or* reference system *or* universe of discourse

978 BROAD-MINDEDNESS

NOUNS 1 **broad-mindedness,** wide-mindedness, large-mindedness, "the result of flattening high-mindedness out"— George Saintsbury; **breadth,** broadness,

broad gauge, latitude; **unbigotedness,** unhideboundness, unprovincialism, noninsularity, unparochialism, cosmopolitanism; ecumenicity, ecumenicism, ecumenicalism, ecumenism; broad mind, spacious mind

2 **liberalness, liberality,** catholicity, **liberalmindedness;** liberalism, libertarianism, latitudinarianism; freethinking, free thought

3 **open-mindedness, openness,** receptiveness, receptivity; persuadableness, persuadability, persuasibility; open mind

4 **tolerance,** toleration; **indulgence,** lenience *or* **leniency** 427, condonation, lenity; **forbearance, patience,** long-suffering; easiness, **permissiveness; charitableness,** charity, **generousness, magnanimity** 652.2; **compassion** 427.1, sympathy; sensitivity

5 **unprejudicedness, unbiasedness; impartiality** 649.4, evenhandedness, equitability, **justice** 649, **fairness** 649.3, justness, **objectivity, detachment, dispassionateness, disinterestedness,** impersonality; indifference, neutrality; unopinionatedness

6 **liberal,** liberalist; libertarian; freethinker, latitudinarian, ecumenist, ecumenicist; big person, broad-gauge person; bleeding heart, bleeding-heart liberal

VERBS 7 **keep an open mind,** be big <nonformal>, judge not, not write off, suspend judgment, listen to reason, open one's mind to, see both sides, judge on the merits; **live and let live;** lean over backwards, **tolerate** 134.5; **accept,** be easy with, **view with indulgence, condone,** brook, abide with, be content with; **live with** <nonformal>; shut one's eyes to, look the other way, wink at, blink at, **overlook, disregard, ignore;** "swear allegiance to the words of no master"— Horace

ADJS 8 **broad-minded,** wide-minded, large-minded, **broad, wide,** wide-ranging, broad-gauged, catholic, spacious of mind; **unbigoted,** unfanatical, **unhidebound,** unprovincial, cosmopolitan, noninsular, unparochial; ecumenistic, ecumenical

9 **liberal, liberal-minded,** liberalistic; libertarian; freethinking, latitudinarian; bleeding-heart

10 **open-minded, open, receptive,** rational, admissive; **persuadable,** persuasible; **unopinionated,** unopinioned, unwedded to an opinion; **unpositive, undogmatic;** uninfatuated, unbesotted, unfanatical

11 **tolerant** 134.9, tolerating; **indulgent, lenient** 427.7, **condoning;** forbearing, forbearant <old>, **patient, long-suffering; charitable, generous, magnanimous** 652.6; compassionate 427.7, sympathetic, sensitive

12 **unprejudiced, unbiased, unprepossessed, unjaundiced; impartial,** evenhanded, **fair, just** 649.8, equitable, **objective, dispassionate, impersonal, detached, disinterested;** indifferent, neutral; **unswayed, uninfluenced,** undazzled

13 **liberalizing, liberating, broadening,** enlightening

979 NARROW-MINDEDNESS

NOUNS 1 **narrow-mindedness,** narrowness, illiberality, uncatholicity; littlemindedness, **small-mindedness, smallness, littleness, meanness, pettiness; bigotry,** bigotedness, fanaticism, *odium theologicum* <L>; insularity, insularism, provincialism, parochialism; **hideboundness,** straitlacedness, stuffiness <nonformal>; authoritarianism; **shortsightedness,** nearsightedness, purblindness; blind side, blind spot, tunnel vision, blinders; closed mind, mean mind, petty mind, shut mind; narrow views *or* sympathies, cramped ideas; *parti pris* <Fr>, an ax to grind

2 **intolerance,** intoleration; **uncharitableness,** ungenerousness; **unforbearance;** noncompassion, insensitivity

3 **prejudice,** prejudgment, forejudgment, **predilection, prepossession,** preconception; **bias,** bent, leaning, inclination, twist; **jaundice,** jaundiced eye; **partiality,** partialism, partisanship, favoritism, onesidedness, undispassionateness, undetachment

4 **discrimination,** social discrimination, minority prejudice; xenophobia, knownothingism; **chauvinism,** ultranationalism, superpatriotism; fascism; **class consciousness,** class prejudice, class distinction, class hatred, class war; anti-Semitism; redbaiting <nonformal>; **racism,** racialism, race hatred, **race prejudice,** race snobbery, racial discrimination; white *or* black supremacy, white *or* black power; **color line,** color bar; **social barrier,** Jim Crow, Jim Crow law; **segregation,** apartheid; sex discrimination, sexism, manism, masculism, male chauvinism, feminism, womanism; ageism, age discrimination; class prejudice, class hatred, social prejudice

5 **bigot,** intolerant, illiberal, little person; **racist,** racialist, racial supremacist, white *or* black supremacist, pig <nonformal>; **chauvinist,** ultranationalist, jingo, superpatriot; **sexist,** male chauvinist, male chauvinist pig *or* MCP <nonformal>, manist, masculist, feminist, female chauvinist, womanist, **dogmatist, doctrinaire** 969.7; fanatic

VERBS 6 **close one's mind,** shut the eyes of one's mind, take narrow views, put on blinders, blind oneself, have a blind side *or* spot, have tunnel vision, constrict one's views; not see beyond one's nose *or* an inch beyond one's nose; **view with a jaundiced eye,** see but one side of the question, look only at one side of the shield

7 **prejudge,** forejudge, judge beforehand, precondemn, prejudicate <old>, take one's opinions ready-made, accede to prejudice

8 **discriminate against, draw the line,** draw the color line; bait, **bash;** red-bait

9 **prejudice,** prejudice against, prejudice the issue, prepossess, **jaundice, influence, sway, bias,** bias one's judgment; warp, twist, bend, distort

ADJS 10 **narrow-minded,** narrow, narrow-gauged, closed, closed-minded, cramped, constricted, po-faced <Brit>, *borné* <Fr>, little-minded, small-minded, mean-minded, petty-minded, narrowhearted, narrow-souled, narrow-spirited, mean-spirited, small-souled; **small, little, mean, petty;** uncharitable, ungenerous; bigot, **bigoted,** fanatical; **illiberal,** unliberal, uncatholic; provincial, insular, parochial; **hidebound,** creedbound, **straitlaced,** stuffy <nonformal>; authoritarian; **shortsighted,** nearsighted, purblind; deaf, deaf-minded, deaf to reason

11 **intolerant,** untolerating; **unindulgent,** uncondoning, unforbearing

12 **discriminatory; prejudiced,** prepossessed, **biased, jaundiced,** colored; **partial,** one-sided, partisan; influenced, swayed, warped, twisted; interested, nonobjective, **undetached,** undispassionate; xenophobic, know-nothing; **chauvinistic,** ultranationalist, superpatriotic; **racist,** racialist, anti-Negro, antiblack, antiwhite; anti-Semitic; sexist; dogmatic, doctrinaire, **opinionated** 969.22

980 CURIOSITY

NOUNS 1 **curiosity,** curiousness, **inquisitiveness; interest,** interestedness, lively interest; thirst *or* desire *or* lust *or* itch for knowledge, mental acquisitiveness, inquiring *or* curious mind; **attention** 982; **alertness, watchfulness**, vigilance; **nosiness** *and* snoopiness <both nonformal>, prying; eavesdropping; officiousness, meddlesomeness 214.2; **morbid curiosity, ghoulishness;** voyeurism, scopophilia, prurience, prurient interest

2 inquisitive person, quidnunc; **inquirer**, questioner, querier, querist, inquisitor, inquisitress; **busybody**, gossip, *yenta* <Yiddish>, **pry**, Paul Pry, **snoop**, snooper, nosy Parker <nonformal>; eavesdropper; sightseer; rubbernecker *or* rubberneck <nonformal>; watcher, Peeping Tom, voyeur, scopophiliac; Lot's wife

VERBS **3 be curious, want to know, take an interest in**, take a lively interest, burn with curiosity; be alert, alert oneself, watch, be watchful, be vigilant; prick up one's ears, keep one's ear to the ground; eavesdrop; interrogate, quiz, question, inquire, query; keep one's eyes open, keep one's eye on, stare, gape, peer, gawk, rubber *and* rubberneck <both nonformal>; seek, dig up, dig around for, nose out, nose around for

4 **pry, snoop**, peep, peek, spy, nose, nose into, have a long *or* big nose, poke *or* stick one's nose in; meddle 214.7

ADJS **5 curious, inquisitive**, inquiring, interested, quizzical; **alert**, tuned in <nonformal>, **attentive** 982.15; burning with curiosity, eaten up *or* consumed with curiosity, curious as a cat; agape, agog, all agog, openmouthed, open-eyed; gossipy; overcurious, supercurious; morbidly curious, **morbid, ghoulish; prurient**, itchy, voyeuristic, scopophiliac

6 **prying**, snooping, **nosy** *and* **snoopy** <both nonformal>; meddlesome 214.9

981 INCURIOSITY

NOUNS **1 incuriosity**, incuriousness, **uninquisitiveness;** boredom; **inattention** 983; **uninterestedness,** disinterest, disinterestedness, **unconcern,** uninvolvement, **indifference** 102, indifferentness, indifferentism, uncaring, **apathy,** passivity, passiveness, impassivity, impassiveness, listlessness, stolidity, **lack of interest;** carelessness, heedlessness, regardlessness, insouciance, unmindfulness; aloofness, detachment, withdrawal, reclusiveness; intellectual inertia; catatonia, autism

VERBS **2 take no interest in, not care;** mind one's own business, pursue the even tenor of one's way, glance neither to the right nor to the left, keep one's nose out; be indifferent, not care less <nonformal>

ADJS **3 incurious, uninquisitive**, uninquiring; bored; **inattentive** 983.6; **uninterested**, unconcerned, disinterested, uninvolved, **indifferent, apathetic,** passive, impassive, stolid, phlegmatic, listless; careless, heedless, regardless, insouciant, mindless, unmindful; aloof, detached, distant, withdrawn, reclusive, sequestered, eremitic; catatonic, autistic

982 ATTENTION

NOUNS **1 attention, attentiveness,** mindfulness, regardfulness, heedfulness; **attention span; heed,** ear; consideration, thought, mind; **awareness, consciousness, alertness** 339.5; **observation,** observance, advertence, advertency, **note, notice,** remark, put one's finger on, **regard**, respect; **intentness**, intentiveness, concentration; diligence, assiduity, assiduousness, earnestness; **care** 339.1; **curiosity** 980

2 **interest, concern,** concernment; **curiosity** 980; **enthusiasm**, passion, ardor, zeal; cathexis; matter of interest, special interest

3 **engrossment, absorption, intentness,** single-mindedness, **concentration, application,** study, studiousness, **preoccupation,** engagement, **involvement, immersion,** submersion; obsession, monomania; rapt attention, absorbed attention *or* interest; deep study, deep *or* profound thought, contemplation, meditation

4 **close attention,** close study, scrutiny, fixed regard, rapt *or* fascinated attention, whole *or* total *or* undivided attention; minute *or* meticulous attention, attention to detail, microscopic *or* microscopical scrutiny, finicalness, finickiness; constant *or* unrelenting attention, harping, strict attention; special consideration

VERBS **5 attend to,** look to, **see to,** advert to, be aware of; **pay attention to,** pay regard to, give mind to, pay mind to <nonformal>, not forget, spare a thought for, **give heed to;** bethink, bethink oneself; have a look at; **turn to,** give thought to, trouble one's head about; give one's mind to, direct one's attention to, turn *or* bend *or* set the mind *or* attention to; **devote oneself to,** devote the mind *or* thoughts to, fix or rivet or focus the mind or thoughts on, set one's thoughts on, apply the mind or attention to, apply oneself to, **occupy oneself with, concern oneself with,** give oneself up to, be absorbed or engrossed in, be into <nonformal>; sink one's teeth, take an interest in, take hold of; **have a lot on one's mind or plate;** be preoccupied with; **lose oneself in; hang on one's words,** hang on the lips; **drink in,** drink in with rapt attention

6 **heed, attend,** be heedful, tend, **mind, watch, observe, regard,** look, see, view, mark, remark, animadvert <old>, **note, notice,** take note or notice, get a load of <nonformal>

7 **hearken to,** hark, **listen, hear,** give ear to, lend an ear to, incline or bend an ear to, prick up the ears, strain one's ears, **keep one's ears open,** unstopper one's ears, have or keep an ear to the ground, listen with both ears, **be all ears**

8 **pay attention** or **heed, take heed,** give heed, **look out, watch out** <nonformal>, **take care** 339.7; look lively or alive, **look sharp,** stay or be alert, sit up and take notice; be on the ball or keep one's eye on the ball or not miss a trick or not overlook a bet <all nonformal>, keep a weather eye out or on; miss nothing; get after, seize on, keep one's eyes open 339.8; attend to business, mind one's business; pay close or strict attention, strain one's attention, not relax one's concern, give one's undivided attention, give special attention to; keep in the center of one's attention, keep uppermost in one's thought; **concentrate on,** focus or fix on; **study,** scrutinize; be obsessed with; cathect

9 **take cognizance of,** take note or **notice of,** take heed of, **take account of, take into consideration** or **account, bear in mind,** keep or hold in mind, reckon with, keep in sight or view, not lose sight of, have in one's eye, have an eye to, have regard for

10 **call attention to,** direct attention to, **bring under** or **to one's notice,** hold up to notice, bring to attention, **mention,** mention in passing, touch on; **single out,** pick out, lift up, focus on, call or bring to notice, direct to the attention, **feature,** highlight, brightline; **direct to,** address to; **mention,** specify, mention in passing, touch on, cite, **refer to,** allude to; **alert one,** call to one's attention, put one wise and put one on <both nonformal>; **point out, point to,** point at, put or lay one's fin-

ger on; **excite** or **stimulate attention,** drum up attention

11 **meet with attention,** fall under one's notice; **catch the attention,** strike one, impress one, draw or hold or focus the attention, take or catch or meet or strike the eye, get or catch one's ear, attract notice or attention, arrest or engage attention, fix or rivet one's attention, arrest the thoughts, awaken the mind or thoughts, **excite notice,** arouse notice, arrest one's notice, invite or solicit attention, claim or demand attention

12 **interest, concern,** involve in or with, affect the interest, give pause; **pique, titillate,** tantalize, tickle, tickle one's fancy, **attract,** invite, **fascinate, provoke, stimulate, arouse, excite,** pique one's interest, excite interest, excite or whet one's interest, arouse one's passion or enthusiasm, turn one on <nonformal>

13 **engross, absorb,** immerse, **occupy, preoccupy, engage,** involve, monopolize, exercise, take up; **obsess; grip, hold, arrest, hold the interest, fascinate, enthrall,** spellbind, **hold spellbound,** grab <nonformal>, charm, enchant, mesmerize, hypnotize, catch; absorb the attention, claim one's thoughts, engross the mind or thoughts, engage the attention, involve the interest, occupy the attention, monopolize one's attention, engage the mind or thoughts

14 **come to attention,** stand at attention

ADJS 15 **attentive, heedful, mindful, regardful,** advertent; intent, intentive, on top of <nonformal>, diligent, assiduous, intense, earnest, concentrated; **careful** 339.10; **observing,** observant; watchful, aware, conscious, alert 339.14; **curious** 980.5; agog, openmouthed; open-eared, open-eyed, **all eyes, all ears,** all eyes and ears; on the job <nonformal>, on the ball and Johnny-on-the-spot <both nonformal>; **meticulous** 339.12, nice, finical, finicky, finicking, niggling

16 **interested,** concerned; **alert to, sensitive to, on the watch; curious** 980.5; tantalized, piqued, titillated, tickled, **attracted,** fascinated, excited, turned-on <nonformal>; keen on or about, enthusiastic, passionate; fixating, cathectic

17 **engrossed, absorbed,** totally absorbed, single-minded, **occupied, preoccupied, engaged,** devoted, devoted to, intent, intent on, monopolized, obsessed, monomaniacal, swept up, taken up with, **involved, caught up in,** wrapped in, **wrapped up in,** engrossed in, **absorbed in**

or with *or* by, **lost in, immersed in,** submerged in, buried in; over head and ears in, head over heels in <nonformal>, up to one's elbows in, up to one's ears in; contemplating, contemplative, studying, studious, meditative, meditating

18 **gripped, held, fascinated, enthralled, rapt, spellbound,** charmed, enchanted, mesmerized, **hypnotized,** fixed, caught, riveted, **arrested,** switched on <nonformal>

19 **interesting, stimulating, provocative,** provoking, thought-provoking, thought-challenging, thought-inspiring; **titillating,** tickling, **tantalizing, inviting, exciting; piquant,** lively, racy, juicy, succulent, spicy, rich; readable

20 **engrossing, absorbing,** consuming, **gripping,** riveting, holding, **arresting,** engaging, attractive, **fascinating, enthralling, spellbinding,** enchanting, magnetic, hypnotic, mesmerizing, mesmeric; obsessive, obsessing

ADVS 21 **attentively,** with attention; **heedfully,** mindfully, regardfully, advertently; observingly, observantly; **interestedly,** with interest; **raptly,** with rapt attention; engrossedly, absorbedly, preoccupiedly; devotedly, **intently,** without distraction, **with undivided attention**

INTERJS 22 **attention!, look!,** see!, look you!, look here!, looky! <nonformal>, witness!; tah-dah! <nonformal>, presto!, hey presto! <Brit>, voilà!; lo!, behold!, lo and behold!; **hark!,** listen!, listen up! <nonformal>, hark ye!, hear ye!, oyez!; *nota bene* <L, note well>, NB; mark my words

23 **hey!, hail!, ahoy!, hello!,** hollo!, hallo!, halloo!, halloa!, ho!, heigh!, hi!, hist!; hello there!, ahoy there!, yo!

983 INATTENTION

NOUNS 1 **inattention,** inattentiveness, **heedlessness, unheedfulness, unmindfulness, thoughtlessness,** inconsideration; **incuriosity** 981, **indifference** 102; inadvertence *or* inadvertency; unintentness, unintentiveness; disregard, disregardfulness, regardlessness; **flightiness** 984.5, giddiness 984.4, lightmindedness, dizziness *and* ditziness <both nonformal>, scattiness <Brit nonformal>; levity, frivolousness, flippancy; shallowness, superficiality; **inobservance,** unobservance, nonobservance; **unalertness,** unwariness, unwatchfulness; **obliviousness,** unconsciousness, unawareness; **carelessness,**

negligence 340.1; distraction, **absentmindedness, woolgathering, daydreaming** 984.2

VERBS 2 **be inattentive, pay no attention, pay no mind** <nonformal>, not attend, not notice, **take no note *or* notice of,** take no thought *or* account of, miss, not heed, give no heed, pay no regard to, not listen, hear nothing, not hear a word; **disregard, overlook, ignore,** pass over *or* by, have no time for, let pass *or* get by *or* get past; think little of, think nothing of, **slight,** make light of; **close *or* shut one's eyes to,** see nothing, be blind to, turn a blind eye, **look the other way, blink at, wink at,** connive at; stick *or* bury *or* hide one's head in the sand; **turn a deaf ear to,** stop one's ears, let come in one ear and go out the other, tune out <nonformal>; let well enough alone; not trouble oneself with, not trouble one's head with *or* about; **be unwary,** be off one's guard, be caught out

3 **wander, stray,** divagate, wander from the subject, ramble; have no attention span, have a short attention span, let one's attention wander, get off the track <nonformal>; **fall asleep at the switch** <nonformal>, woolgather, **daydream** 984.9

4 **dismiss,** dismiss *or* drive from one's thoughts; **put out of mind,** put out of one's head *or* thoughts, wean *or* force one's thoughts from, **think no more of, forget, forget it,** forget about it, **let it go** <nonformal>, let slip, not give it another *or* a second thought, **drop the subject,** give it no more thought; turn one's back upon, turn away from, turn one's attention from, walk away, abandon, leave out in the cold <nonformal>; put *or* set *or* lay aside, push *or* thrust aside *or* to one side, wave aside; put on the back burner *or* on hold <nonformal>; **turn up one's nose at,** sneeze at; **shrug off, brush off *or* aside *or* away,** blow off *and* laugh off *or* away <both nonformal>, dismiss with a laugh; **slight** 157.6, kiss off *and* slap *or* smack down <all nonformal>

5 **escape notice *or* attention,** escape one, get by, be missed, pass one by, not enter one's head, never occur to one, fall on deaf ears, not register, go over one's head

ADJS 6 **inattentive, unmindful,** inadvertent, thoughtless, **incurious** 981.3, **indifferent** 102.6; **heedless,** unheeding, unheedful, regardless, *distrait* <Fr>, **disregardful,** disregardant; **unobserving,** inobservant, unobservant, unnoticing, unnoting, unremarking, unmarking; **distracted** 984.10; **careless, negligent** 340.10; **scatter-**

brained, giddy 984.16, **ditzy** <nonformal>, **scatty** <Brit nonformal>, **flighty**

7 oblivious, unconscious, insensible, dead to the world, out of it *and* not with it <both nonformal>; blind, deaf; **preoccupied** 984.11

8 unalert, unwary, unwatchful, unvigilant, uncautious, incautious; **unprepared,** unready; unguarded, **off one's guard,** offguard; **asleep,** sleeping, nodding, napping, **asleep at the switch** *and* asleep on the job *and* **not on the job** *and* goofing off *and* looking out the window <all nonformal>; daydreaming, woolgathering

984 DISTRACTION, CONFUSION

NOUNS 1 distraction, distractedness, **diversion,** separation *or* withdrawal of attention, divided attention, competing stimuli; too much on one's mind *or* on one's plate, cognitive dissonance, sensory overload; **inattention** 983

2 abstractedness, abstraction, preoccupation, absorption, engrossment, depth of thought, fit of abstraction; **absentmindedness, absence of mind; bemusement,** musing, musefulness <old>; **woolgathering,** mooning <nonformal>, moonraking <old>, stargazing, **dreaming, daydreaming,** fantasying, pipe-dreaming <nonformal>, castle-building; **brown study,** study, reverie, muse, dreamy abstraction, quiet *or* muted ecstasy, trance; dream, **daydream,** fantasy, pipe dream <nonformal>; daydreamer, Walter Mitty

3 confusion, fluster, flummox <nonformal>, **flutter,** flurry, ruffle; disorientation, **muddle, muddlement,** fuddle *and* fuddlement <both nonformal>, befuddlement, muddleheadedness, daze, maze <nonformal>; unsettlement, disorganization, **disorder,** chaos, **mess** *and* mix-up *and* snafu <all nonformal>, balls-up *and* shemozzle <both Brit nonformal>, shuffle, jumble, **discomfiture, discomposure, disconcertion,** discombobulation <nonformal>, **bewilderment, embarrassment, disturbance,** perturbation, **upset,** frenzy, pother, bother, botheration *and* stew <both nonformal>, pucker <old>; tizzy *and* swivet *and* sweat <all nonformal>; haze, fog, mist, cloud; maze; **perplexity** 970.3

4 dizziness, vertigo, vertiginousness, spinning head, swimming, swimming of the head, **giddiness,** wooziness <nonformal>, **lightheadedness;** tiddliness <Brit nonformal>, **drunkenness** 88.1,3

5 flightiness, giddiness, volatility, mercuriality; **thoughtlessness,** witlessness, brainlessness, empty-headedness, frivolity, frivolousness, dizziness *and* ditziness <both nonformal>, scattiness <Brit nonformal>, foolishness 922; **scatterbrain, flibbertigibbet** 923.7

VERBS 6 distract, divert, detract, distract the attention, divert *or* detract attention, divert the mind *or* thoughts, draw off the attention, call away, take the mind off of, relieve the mind of, cause the mind to stray *or* wander, put off the track, derail, throw off the scent, lead the mind astray, beguile; throw off one's guard, catch off balance, put off one's stride, trip up

7 confuse, throw into confusion *or* chaos, entangle, **mix up, fluster;** flummox <nonformal>, **flutter,** put into a flutter, **flurry, rattle, ruffle,** moider <Brit nonformal>; **muddle,** fuddle <nonformal>, **befuddle, addle,** addle the wits, **daze,** maze, **dazzle,** bedazzle; **upset, unsettle,** raise hell, disorganize; throw into a tizzy *or* swivet; **disconcert, discomfit, discompose,** discombobulate <nonformal>, disorient, disorientate, **bewilder, embarrass, put out, disturb, perturb, bother,** pother, bug <nonformal>; fog, mist, cloud, becloud; **perplex** 970.13

8 dizzy, make one's head swim, cause vertigo, send one spinning, whirl the mind, swirl the senses, make one's head reel *or* whirl *or* spin *or* revolve, go to one's head; **intoxicate** 88.22

9 muse, moon <nonformal>, **dream, daydream,** pipe-dream <nonformal>, fantasy; abstract oneself, be lost in thought, let one's attention wander, let one's mind run on other things, dream of *or* muse on other things; **wander, stray, ramble,** divagate, let one's thoughts *or* mind wander, give oneself up to reverie, **woolgather, go woolgathering,** let one's wits go bird's nesting, **be in a brown study,** be absent, be somewhere else, stargaze, be out of it *and* be not with it <both nonformal>

ADJS 10 distracted, distraught, *distrait* <Fr>; **wandering, rambling; wild, frantic, beside oneself**

11 abstracted, bemused, museful <old>, **musing, preoccupied, absorbed, engrossed,** taken up; **absentminded, absent,** faraway, elsewhere, somewhere else, not there; pensive, meditative; lost, **lost in thought,** wrapped in thought; rapt, transported, ecstatic; dead to the world, **unconscious, oblivious; dreaming, dreamy,**

drowsing, dozing, nodding, half-awake, betwixt sleep and waking, napping; **daydreaming**, daydreamy, pipe-dreaming <nonformal>; **woolgathering**, mooning *and* moony <both nonformal>, moonraking <old>, castle-building, in the clouds, off in the clouds, stargazing, in a reverie

12 **confused, mixed-up**, crazy mixed-up <nonformal>; **flustered**, fluttered, **ruffled, rattled**, fussed <nonformal>; **upset, unsettled**, off-balance, off one's stride; **disorganized, disordered**, disoriented, disorientated, chaotic, jumbled, in a jumble, shuffled; shaken, shook <nonformal>, **disconcerted, discomposed**, discombobulated <nonformal>, **embarrassed, put-out, disturbed, perturbed**, bothered, all hot and bothered <nonformal>; in a stew *or* botheration <nonformal>, in a pucker <old>; in a tizzy *or* swivet *or* sweat <nonformal>, in a pother; **perplexed**

13 **muddled**, in a muddle; fuddled <nonformal>, **befuddled**; muddleheaded, fuddlebrained <nonformal>; puzzleheaded, puzzlepated; **addled**, addleheaded, addlepated, addlebrained; adrift, at sea, foggy, fogged, in a fog, hazy, muzzy <nonformal>, misted, misty, cloudy, beclouded

14 **dazed**, mazed, **dazzled**, bedazzled, in a daze; **silly**, knocked silly, cockeyed <nonformal>; **groggy** <nonformal>, **dopey** <nonformal>, woozy <nonformal>; **punch-drunk** *and* punchy *and* **slap-happy** <all nonformal>

15 **dizzy, giddy**, vertiginous, spinning, swimming, turned around, going around in circles; lightheaded, tiddly <Brit nonformal>, **drunk, drunken** 88.31

16 **scatterbrained**, shatterbrained *or* shatterpated <both old>, rattlebrained, rattleheaded, rattlepated, scramblebrained, harebrain, harebrained, **giddy, dizzy** *and* ditzy *and* gaga <all nonformal>, scatty <Brit nonformal>, giddy-brained, giddy-headed, giddy-pated, giddy-witted, giddy as a goose, fluttery, frivolous, featherbrained, featherheaded; **thoughtless, witless, brainless, empty-headed** 921.19

17 **flighty**, volatile, mercurial

985 IMAGINATION

NOUNS 1 **imagination**, imagining, imaginativeness, **fancy, fantasy**, conceit <old>; mind's eye, "that inward eye

which is the bliss of solitude"—Wordsworth, "the mad boarder"—Malebranche; flight of fancy, fumes of fancy; fantasticism

2 **creative thought**, conception; lateral thinking; productive *or* constructive *or* creative imagination, creative power *or* ability, esemplastic imagination *or* power, shaping imagination, poetic imagination, artistic imagination; mythopoeia, *mythopoesis* <Gk>; mythification, mythicization; inspiration, muse; Muses: Calliope <epic poetry>, Clio <history>, Erato <lyric and love poetry>, Euterpe <music>, Melpomene <tragedy>, Polyhymnia <sacred song>, Terpsichore <dancing and choral song>, Thalia <comedy>, Urania <astronomy>; genius 919.8

3 **invention, inventiveness, originality, creativity, fabrication**, creativeness, **ingenuity**; productivity, prolificacy, **fertility**, fecundity; rich *or* teeming imagination, fertile *or* pregnant imagination, seminal *or* germinal imagination, fertile mind; imagineering; **fiction**, fictionalization

4 **lively imagination**, active fancy, **vivid imagination**, colorful *or* highly colored *or* lurid imagination, warm *or* ardent imagination, fiery *or* heated imagination, excited imagination, bold *or* daring *or* wild *or* fervent imagination; verve, vivacity of imagination

5 **figment of the imagination**, creature of the imagination, creation *or* coinage of the brain, fiction of the mind, maggot, whim, whimsy, figment, imagination, invention; brainchild; **imagining**, fancy, idle fancy, vapor, "thick-coming fancies"—Shakespeare, imagery; **fantasy, make-believe**; phantom, vision, apparition, insubstantial image, eidolon, **phantasm** 975.4; **fiction**, myth, romance; wildest dreams, stretch of the imagination; **chimera, bubble, illusion** 975; hallucination, delirium, sick fancy; trip *or* drug trip <both nonformal>

6 **visualization, envisioning**, envisaging, picturing, objectification, imaging, calling to *or* before the mind's eye, figuring *or* portraying *or* representing in the mind; depicting *or* delineating in the imagination; conceptualization; **picture, vision, image**, mental image, mental picture, visual image, vivid *or* lifelike image, eidetic image, concept, **conception**, mental representation *or* presentation, *Vorstellung* <Ger>; **imagery**, word-painting; poetic

image, poetic imagery; imagery study; imagism, imagistic poetry

7 idealism, idealization; ideal, ideality; rose-colored glasses; visionariness, **utopianism;** flight of fancy, play of fancy, imaginative exercise; **romanticism,** romanticizing, romance; **quixotism,** quixotry; dreamery; **impracticality,** unpracticalness, **unrealism,** unreality; **wishful thinking,** wish fulfillment, wish-fulfillment fantasy, dream come true; autistic thinking, dereistic thinking, autism, dereism, autistic distortion

8 dreaminess, dreamfulness, musefulness, pensiveness; dreamlikeness; **dreaming, musing; daydreaming,** pipe-dreaming <nonformal>, dreamery, fantasying, castlebuilding

9 dream; reverie, daydream, pipe dream <nonformal>; **brown study** 984.2; **vision; nightmare,** incubus, bad dream

10 air castle, castle in the air, castle in the sky or skies, castle in Spain; Xanadu and pleasure dome of Kubla Khan <both Coleridge>

11 utopia or Utopia <Sir Thomas More>, **paradise, heaven** 681, **heaven on earth;** millennium, kingdom come; dreamland, lotus land, land of dreams, land of enchantment, land of heart's desire, wonderland, cloudland, fairyland, land of faerie, faerie; Eden, Garden of Eden; the Promised Land, land of promise, land of plenty, land of milk and honey, Canaan, Goshen; Shangri-la, New Atlantis <Francis Bacon>, Arcadia, Agapemone, Happy Valley <Samuel Johnson>, land of Prester John, Eldorado, Seven Cities of Cibola, Quivira; Laputa <Swift>; Cockaigne, Big Rock-Candy Mountain, Fiddler's Green, never-never land <J M Barrie>, Never-land, Cloudcuckooland or Nephelococcygia <Aristophanes>, Erewhon <Samuel Butler>, Land of Youth, Tir-na-n'Og <Irish>; dystopia or kakotopia; Pandemonium

12 imaginer, fancier, fantast; fantasist; mythmaker, mythopoet; mythifier, mythicizer; **inventor; creative artist,** poet; imagineer

13 visionary, idealist; prophet, **seer; dreamer, daydreamer,** dreamer of dreams, castle-builder, lotus-eater; **wishful thinker; romantic,** romanticist; romancer; Quixote, Don Quixote; utopian, utopianist, utopianizer; escapist; enthusiast, rhapsodist

VERBS **14 imagine, fancy, conceive,** conceit <old>, conceptualize, ideate, figure to oneself; **invent, create, originate, make,** think up, dream up, shape, mold, coin, hatch, concoct, fabricate, produce; **suppose** 950.10; **fantasize;** fictionalize; give free rein to the imagination, let one's imagination riot or run riot or run wild, allow one's imagination to run away with one; experience imaginatively or vicariously

15 visualize, vision, **envision, envisage, picture, image,** objectify; picture in one's mind, picture to oneself, **view with the mind's eye,** contemplate in the imagination, form a mental picture of, represent, **see,** just see, have a picture of; **call up,** summon up, conjure up, **call to mind,** realize

16 idealize, utopianize, quixotize, rhapsodize; **romanticize,** romance; paint pretty pictures of, paint in bright colors; see through rose-colored glasses; **build castles in the air** or **Spain**

17 dream; dream of, dream on; **daydream,** pipe-dream <nonformal>, get or have stars in one's eyes, have one's head in the clouds, indulge in wish fulfillment; fantasy, conjure up a vision, "see visions and dream dreams"—Bible; blow one's mind and go on a trip and trip and freak out <all nonformal>

ADJS **18 imaginative,** conceptual, conceptive, ideational, ideative, notional; **inventive, original,** originative, esemplastic, shaping, **creative, ingenious; productive, fertile,** fecund, prolific, seminal, germinal, teeming, pregnant; **inspired,** visioned

19 imaginary, imaginational, notional; **imagined, fancied; unreal,** unrealistic, airy-fairy <Brit>, unactual, nonexistent, never-never; visional, supposititious, **all in the mind; illusory**

20 fanciful, notional, notiony <nonformal>, whimsical, maggoty <Brit>; brain-born; fancy-bred, fancy-born, fancy-built, fancy-framed, fancy-woven, fancy-wrought; dream-born, dream-built, dream-created; **fantastic, fantastical,** fantasque, extravagant, preposterous, outlandish, wild, baroque, rococo, florid; Alice-in-Wonderland, bizarre, grotesque, Gothic

21 fictitious, make-believe, figmental, fictional, fictive, fabricated, fictionalized; nonhistorical, nonfactual, nonactual, nonrealistic; **fabulous, mythic, mythical,** mythological, legendary; mythified, mythicized

22 chimeric, chimerical, aerial, ethereal,

phantasmal; vaporous, vapory; gossamer; air-built, cloud-built, cloud-born, cloud-woven

23 **ideal, idealized;** utopian, Arcadian, Edenic, paradisal; pie in the sky <nonformal>; heavenly, celestial; millennial

24 **visionary, idealistic, quixotic; romantic, romanticized,** romancing, romanticizing; poetic or poetical; storybook; **impractical, unpractical, unrealistic;** wishfulfilling, autistic, dereistic; starry-eyed, dewy-eyed; in the clouds, with one's head in the clouds; airy, **otherworldly,** transmundane, transcendental

25 **dreamy, dreamful; dreamy-eyed,** dreamy-minded, dreamy-souled; dreamlike; day-dreamy, **dreaming, daydreaming,** pipe-dreaming <nonformal>, castle-building; **entranced,** tranced, in a trance, dream-stricken, enchanted, spellbound, spelled, charmed

26 **imaginable, fanciable, conceivable, thinkable,** cogitable; **supposable** 950.15

986 UNIMAGINATIVENESS

NOUNS 1 **unimaginativeness,** unfancifulness; **prosaicness,** prosiness, prosaism, prosaicism, unpoeticalness; **staidness, stuffiness** <nonformal>; stolidity; **dullness, dryness;** aridness, aridity, barrenness, infertility, infecundity; **unoriginality,** uncreativeness, uninventiveness, dearth of ideas

2 <practical attitude> **realism,** realisticness, **practicalness, practicality, practical-mindedness,** sober-mindedness, sobersidedness, **hardheadedness, matter-of-factness;** down-to-earthness, earthiness, worldliness, secularism; real world, the here and now; nuts and bolts, no nonsense, no frills; **pragmatism,** pragmaticism, positivism, scientism; unidealism, unromanticalness, unsentimentality; sensibleness, saneness, reasonableness, rationality; freedom from illusion, lack of sentimentality; lack of feelings 94

3 **realist,** pragmatist, positivist, practical person, hardhead

VERBS 4 **keep both feet on the ground,** stick to the facts, call a spade a spade; **come down to earth,** come down out of the clouds, know when the honeymoon is over

ADJS 5 **unimaginative, unfanciful;** unidealized, unromanticized; **prosaic,** prosy, prosing, unpoetic, unpoetical; **literal,** literal-minded; earthbound, mundane; **staid, stuffy** <nonformal>; stolid; **dull,**

dry; arid, barren, infertile, infecund; **unoriginal,** uninspired; hedged, undaring, unaspiring, **uninventive** 890.5

6 **realistic,** realist, **practical;** pragmatic, pragmatical, scientific, scientistic, positivistic; **unidealistic,** unideal, **unromantic, unsentimental, practical-minded,** sober-minded, sobersided, **hardheaded,** straight-thinking, **matter-of-fact, down-to-earth, with both feet on the ground;** worldly, earthy, secular; sensible, sane, reasonable, rational, sound, sound-thinking; **reductive, simplistic**

987 SPECTER

NOUNS 1 **specter, ghost,** spectral ghost, **spook** <nonformal>, **phantom,** phantasm, phantasma, **wraith, shade,** shadow, fetch, **apparition,** appearance, presence, shape, form, eidolon, idolum, revenant, larva; **spirit;** sprite, shrouded spirit, disembodied spirit, departed spirit, restless or wandering spirit or soul, soul of the dead, dybbuk; oni; Masan; astral spirit, astral; unsubstantiality, immateriality, incorporeal, incorporeity, incorporeal being or entity; walking dead man, zombie; duppy; vision, theophany; materialization; haunt or hant <both nonformal>; banshee; poltergeist; control, guide; manes, lemures; grateful dead

2 White Lady, White Lady of Avenel <Scots>, White Ladies of Normandy; Brocken specter; Wild Hunt; Flying Dutchman

3 **double,** etheric double or self, co-walker, Doppelgänger <Ger>, doubleganger, fetch, wraith

4 **eeriness, ghostliness, weirdness, uncanniness, spookiness** <nonformal>

5 **possession,** spirit control; obsession,

VERBS 6 **haunt,** hant <nonformal>, spook <nonformal>; **possess,** control; obsess

ADJS 7 **spectral,** specterlike; **ghostly,** ghostish, ghosty, ghostlike; **spiritual, psychic,** psychical; **phantomlike,** phantom, phantomic or phantomical, phantasmal, phantasmic, **wraithlike,** wraithy, shadowy; etheric, ectoplasmic, astral, ethereal 763.6; incorporeal 1051.7; **occult, supernatural** 869.15

8 **disembodied,** bodiless, immaterial 1051.7, discarnate, decarnate, decarnated

9 **weird, eerie,** eldritch, **uncanny,** unearthly, macabre; **spooky** and spookish and hairy <all nonformal>

10 haunted, spooked *and* spooky <both non-formal>, spirit-haunted, ghost-haunted, specter-haunted; **possessed,** ghost-ridden; obsessed

988 MEMORY

NOUNS **1 memory, remembrance, recollection,** mind, *souvenir* <Fr>; memory trace, engram; mind's eye, eye of the mind, mirror of the mind, tablets of the memory; corner *or* recess of the memory, inmost recesses of the memory; Mnemosyne, mother of the Muses; short-term memory, long-term memory, anterograde memory; computer memory, information storage; group memory, collective memory, mneme, race memory; atavism; cover *or* screen memory, affect memory; eye *or* visual memory, kinesthetic memory; skill, verbal response, emotional response

2 "that inward eye"—Wordsworth, "the warder of the brain"—Shakespeare, "the treasury and guardian of all things"—Cicero, "storehouse of the mind, garner of facts and fancies"—M F Tupper, "the hearing of deaf actions, and the seeing of blind"—Plutarch, "the diary that we all carry around with us"—Oscar Wilde

3 retention, retentiveness, retentivity, memory span; good memory, retentive memory *or* mind; total memory, eidetic memory *or* imagery, photographic memory, total recall; camera-eye

4 remembering, remembrance, recollection, recollecting, exercise of memory, **recall,** recalling; reflection, reconsideration; **retrospect,** retrospection, hindsight, looking back; flashback, **reminiscence,** review, contemplation of the past, review of things past; **memoir; memorization,** memorizing, **rote,** rote memory, rote learning, learning by heart, commitment to memory

5 recognition, identification, reidentification, distinguishment; realization 927.2

6 reminder, remembrance, remembrancer; **prompt,** prompter, tickler; prompting, cue, hint; jogger <nonformal>, flapper; *aide-mémoire* <Fr>, **memorandum** 549.4

7 memento, remembrance, token, trophy, souvenir, keepsake, relic, favor, token of remembrance; commemoration, memorial 549.12; *memento mori* <L>; **memories, memorabilia,** memorials

8 memorability, rememberability

9 mnemonics, memory training, mnemotechny, mnemotechnics, mnemonization; mnemonic, mnemonic device, *aide-mémoire* <Fr>

VERBS **10 remember, recall, recollect,** flash on *and* mind <both nonformal>; have a good *or* ready memory, remember clearly, remember as if it were yesterday; have total recall, remember everything; reflect; **think of,** bethink oneself <old>; **call** *or* **bring to mind,** recall to mind, call up, summon up, conjure up, evoke, reevoke, revive, recapture, call back, bring back, "call back yesterday, bid time return"—Shakespeare; **think back,** go back, **look back,** cast the eyes back, carry one's thoughts back, look back upon things past, use hindsight, retrospect, **see in retrospect,** go back over, hark back, retrace; review, review in retrospect

11 reminisce, rake *or* dig up the past

12 recognize, know, tell, distinguish, make out; identify, place, have; spot *and* nail *and* peg *and* cotton on <all nonformal>, **reidentify,** know again, recover *or* recall knowledge of, know by sight; realize 927.12

13 keep in memory, bear in mind, keep *or* hold in mind, hold *or* retain the memory of, **keep in view,** have in mind, hold *or* carry *or* retain in one's thoughts, store in the mind, **retain, keep;** tax *or* burden the memory, **treasure, cherish,** treasure up in the memory, enshrine *or* embalm in the memory, cherish the memory of; keep up the memory of, keep the memory alive, keep alive in one's thoughts; brood over, dwell on *or* upon, fan the embers, let fester in the mind, let rankle in the breast

14 be remembered, sink in, penetrate, make an impression; live *or* dwell in one's memory, be easy to recall, remain in one's memory, be green *or* fresh in one's memory, stick in the mind, remain indelibly impressed on the memory, be stamped on one's memory, **never be forgotten; haunt one's thoughts,** obsess, run in the head, be in one's thoughts, be on one's mind; be burnt into one's memory, plague one; be like King Charles's head; **rankle,** rankle in the breast, fester in the mind

15 recur, recur to the mind, return to mind, come back, resurface, reenter

16 come to mind, pop into one's head, come to me, come into one's head, flash on the mind, pass in review

17 memorize, commit to memory, con; study; **learn by heart,** get by heart, learn *or* get by rote, get word-perfect *or* letter-perfect, learn word for word, learn verbatim; know by heart or from memory, have by heart or rote, have at one's fingers' ends or tips; repeat by heart or rote, give word for word, recite, repeat, parrot, repeat like a parrot, say one's lesson, rattle or reel off; be a quick study

18 **fix in the mind** or memory, instill, infix, inculcate, impress, imprint, stamp, inscribe, etch, grave, engrave; **impress on the mind, get into one's head,** drive or hammer into one's head, get across, get into one's thick head or skull <nonformal>; **burden the mind with,** task the mind with, load or stuff or cram the mind with; inscribe or stamp or rivet in the memory, set in the tablets of memory, etch indelibly in the mind

19 **refresh the memory, review,** restudy, **brush up, rub up,** polish up and bone up <both nonformal>, get up on; **cram** <nonformal>, swot up <Brit nonformal>

20 **remind, put in mind,** remember, put in remembrance, bring back, bring to recollection, refresh the memory of; **remind one of, recall,** suggest, **put one in mind of; take one back,** carry back, carry back in recollection; **jog the memory,** awaken or arouse the memory, flap the memory, give a hint or suggestion; **prompt,** prompt the mind, give the cue, hold the promptbook; nudge, pull by the sleeve, nag

21 **try to recall,** think hard, rack or ransack one's brains, **cudgel one's brains,** crack one's brains <nonformal>; have on the tip of one's tongue, have on the edge of one's memory or consciousness

ADJS 22 **recollective, memoried;** mnemonic; retentive; **retrospective,** in retrospect; **reminiscent, mindful, remindful, suggestive,** redolent, evocative

23 **remembered, recollected, recalled; retained,** pent-up in the memory, kept in remembrance, enduring, lasting, **unforgotten;** present to the mind, lodged in one's mind, stamped on the memory; vivid, eidetic, fresh, green, alive

24 **remembering, mindful,** keeping or bearing in mind, holding in remembrance; unable to forget, haunted, plagued, obsessed, nagged, rankled

25 **memorable, rememberable, recollectable;** notable

26 **unforgettable, never to be forgotten,** never to be erased from the mind, **indelible,** indelibly impressed on the mind, fixed in the mind; haunting, persistent, recurrent, nagging, plaguing, rankling, festering; obsessing, obsessive

27 **memorial, commemorative**

ADVS 28 **by heart,** par cœur <Fr>, **by rote, by** or **from memory,** without book; **memorably;** rememberingly

29 **in memory of,** to the memory of, in remembrance or commemoration, *in memoriam* <L>; *memoria in aeterna* <L>, in perpetual remembrance

989 FORGETFULNESS

NOUNS 1 **forgetfulness,** unmindfulness, absentmindedness, **memorylessness;** short memory, short memory span, little retentivity or recall, mind or memory like a sieve; loose memory, vague or fuzzy memory, dim or hazy recollection; **lapse of memory,** decay of memory; **obliviousness, oblivion,** nirvana; obliteration; Lethe, Lethe water, waters of Lethe or oblivion, river of oblivion; nepenthe; **forgetting;** heedlessness 340.2; forgiveness 148

2 **loss of memory, memory loss, amnesia,** failure; **memory gap,** blackout <nonformal>; fugue; agnosia, unrecognition, body-image agnosia, ideational agnosia, astereognosis or astereocognosy; paramnesia, retrospective falsification, false memory, misremembrance; amnesiac

3 **block,** blocking, **mental block,** memory obstruction; repression, suppression, defense mechanism, conversion, sublimation, symbolization

VERBS 4 **be forgetful,** suffer memory loss, be absentminded, have a short memory, have a mind or memory like a sieve, have a short memory span, be unable to retain, have little recall, forget one's own name

5 **forget,** clean forget <nonformal>; **not remember,** disremember and disrecollect <both nonformal>, fail to remember, forget to remember, **have no remembrance** or **recollection of,** be unable to recollect or recall, draw a blank <nonformal>; lose, lose sight of, lose one's train of thought, lose track of what one was saying; have on the tip of the tongue; blow or go up in or fluff one's lines; misremember, misrecollect

6 efface or erase from the memory, consign to oblivion, unlearn, obliterate, **dismiss from one's thoughts** 983.4; **forgive** 148.3,5

7 **be forgotten, escape one, slip one's mind,** fade or die away from the memory, slip or escape the memory, drop from one's thoughts; fall or sink into oblivion, go in one ear and out the other

ADJS **8 forgotten,** clean forgotten <nonformal>, **unremembered,** disremembered *and* disrecollected <both nonformal>, **unrecollected, unretained, unrecalled,** past recollection *or* recall, out of the mind, lost, erased, effaced, obliterated, gone out of one's head *or* recollection, consigned to oblivion, buried *or* sunk in oblivion; out of sight out of mind; misremembered, misrecollected

9 forgetful, forgetting, inclined to forget, **memoryless, unremembering, unmindful,** absentminded, **oblivious,** insensible to the past, with a mind *or* memory like a sieve; suffering from *or* stricken with amnesia, amnesic, amnestic; blocked, repressed, suppressed, sublimated, converted; heedless 340.11; Lethean

10 forgettable, unrememberable, unrecollectable; effaceable, eradicable, erasable

ADVS **11 forgetfully,** forgettingly, unmindfully, absentmindedly, **obliviously**

990 SUFFICIENCY

NOUNS **1 sufficiency,** sufficientness, **adequacy,** adequateness, **enough,** a competence *or* competency; satisfactoriness, satisfaction, satisfactory amount, enough to go around; good *or* adequate supply; exact measure, right amount, no more and no less; bare sufficiency, minimum, bare minimum, just enough, enough to get by on

2 plenty, plenitude, plentifulness, plenteousness, muchness <old>; myriad, myriads, numerousness 883; **amplitude,** ampleness; substantiality, substantialness; **abundance, copiousness;** exuberance, riotousness; **bountifulness,** bounteousness, liberalness, **liberality,** generousness, **generosity; lavishness, extravagance, prodigality;** luxuriance, fertility, teemingness, productiveness 889; **wealth, opulence** *or* opulency, richness, affluence; more than enough; maximum; **fullness,** full measure, repletion, repleteness; **overflow, outpouring,** flood, inundation, flow, shower, spate, stream, gush, avalanche; landslide; **prevalence,** profuseness, **profusion,** riot; **superabundance** 992.2; **overkill;** no end of, great abundance, great plenty, "God's plenty"—Dryden, quantities, much, as much as one could wish, more than one can shake a stick at, lots, a fistful <nonformal>, **scads** 247.4; bumper crop, rich harvest, foison <old>; rich vein, bonanza, luau <nonformal>; an ample

sufficiency, enough and to spare, enough and then some; fat of the land

3 cornucopia, horn of plenty, horn of Amalthea, endless supply, bottomless well

VERBS **4 suffice, do,** just do, serve, **answer;** work, be equal to, **avail;** answer *or* serve the purpose, do the trick <nonformal>, **suit;** qualify, meet, fulfill, **satisfy,** meet requirements; **pass muster,** make the grade *or* the cut *and* hack it *and* cut the mustard *and* **fill the bill** <all nonformal>; get by *and* scrape by <both nonformal>, do it, do'er <nonformal>, do in a pinch, **pass,** pass in the dark <nonformal>; hold, stand, stand up, take it, bear; stretch <nonformal>, reach, go around

5 abound, exuberate <old>, teem, **teem with,** creep with, crawl with, swarm with, be lousy with <nonformal>, bristle with; proliferate 889.7; **overflow,** run over, flood; flow, stream, rain, **pour,** shower, gush

ADJS **6 sufficient,** sufficing; **enough, ample,** substantial, **plenty, satisfactory, adequate,** decent, due; competent, up to the mark; commensurate, proportionate, corresponding 787.9; suitable, fit 787.10; good, **good enough,** plenty good enough <nonformal>; sufficient for *or* to *or* unto, up to, equal to; barely sufficient, minimal, minimum

7 plentiful, plenty, **plenteous,** plenitudinous, "plenty as blackberries"— Shakespeare; **galore** *and* a gogo *and* up the gazoo *or* kazoo *and* up to the ass in <all nonformal>, in plenty, in quantity *or* quantities, aplenty <nonformal>; numerous 883.6; beaucoup <nonformal>, much, many 247.8; **ample,** all-sufficing; wholesale; well-stocked, well-provided, well-furnished, well-found; abundant, **copious,** exuberant, riotous; flush; **bountiful,** bounteous, **lavish, generous, liberal, extravagant, prodigal; luxuriant,** fertile, productive 889.9, **rich,** fat, **wealthy, opulent, affluent;** maximal; **full,** replete, well-filled, running over, overflowing; inexhaustible, exhaustless, bottomless; **profuse,** profusive, effuse, diffuse; **prevalent,** prevailing, rife, rampant, epidemic; lousy with <nonformal>, teeming 883.9; **superabundant** 992.19; a dime a dozen

ADVS **8 sufficiently, amply,** substantially, **satisfactorily, enough;** competently, **adequately;** minimally

9 plentifully, plenteously, **aplenty** <nonformal>, **in plenty,** in quantity *or* quantities, in good supply; **abundantly**, in abundance, copiously, no end <nonformal>; **superabundantly** 992.24; **bountifully**, bounteously, **lavishly, generously, liberally, extravagantly, prodigally**; maximally; **fully**, in full measure, to the full, overflowingly; inexhaustibly, exhaustlessly, bottomlessly; exuberantly, luxuriantly, riotously; richly, opulently, affluently; **profusely**, diffusely, effusely; beyond one's wildest dreams, beyond the dreams of avarice

991 INSUFFICIENCY

NOUNS **1 insufficiency, inadequacy,** insufficientness, inadequateness; short supply, seller's market; none to spare; nonsatisfaction, nonfulfillment, coming *or* falling short *or* shy; **undercommitment;** too little too late; a band-aid <nonformal>, a drop in the bucket *or* the ocean, a lick and a promise, a cosmetic measure; **incompetence**, incompetency, unqualification, unsuitability 788.3

2 meagerness, exiguousness, exiguity, scrimpiness, skimpiness, scantiness, spareness; meanness, miserliness, niggardliness, narrowness <nonformal>, stinginess, parsimony; smallness, slightness, puniness, paltriness; thinness, leanness, slimness, slim pickings <nonformal>, slenderness, scrawniness; jejuneness, jejunity; austerity; Lenten fare; skeleton crew, corporal's guard

3 scarcity, scarceness; **sparsity,** sparseness; **scantiness,** scant sufficiency; **dearth, paucity,** poverty; **rarity,** rareness, uncommonness

4 want, lack, need, deficiency, deficit, shortage, shortfall, wantage, **incompleteness,** defectiveness, shortcoming 910, imperfection; **absence** 222, omission; **destitution,** impoverishment, beggary, deprivation; starvation, famine, drought, drying-up

5 pittance, dole, scrimption <nonformal>; drop in the bucket *or* the ocean; **mite,** bit 248.2; short allowance, short commons, half rations, cheeseparings and candle ends; mere subsistence, starvation wages; widow's mite

6 dietary deficiency, vitamin deficiency; undernourishment, undernutrition, **malnutrition**

VERBS **7 want, lack, need, require;** miss, feel the want of, be sent away empty-handed; run short of

8 be insufficient, not qualify, be found wanting, leave a lot to be desired, kick the beam, not make it *and* not hack it *and* not make the cut *and* not cut it *and* not cut the mustard <all nonformal>, be beyond one's depth *or* ken, be in over one's head, **fall short,** fall shy, come short, not come up to; run short; want, want for, lack, fail, fail of *or* in

ADJS **9 insufficient,** unsufficing, **inadequate;** found wanting, defective, incomplete, imperfect, deficient, lacking, failing, wanting; **too few,** undersupplied; **too little,** not enough, precious little, a trickle *or* mere trickle; **unsatisfactory,** unsatisfying; cosmetic, merely cosmetic, surface, superficial, symptomatic, merely symptomatic; **incompetent,** unequal to, unqualified, not up to snuff, beyond one's depth *or* over one's head, outmatched; short-staffed, understaffed, shorthanded

10 meager, slight, scrimpy, skimp, skimpy, exiguous; scant, **scanty,** spare; miserly, niggardly, stingy, narrow <nonformal>, parsimonious, mean; austere, Lenten, Spartan, abstemious, ascetic; stinted, frugal, sparing; poor, impoverished; small, puny, paltry; thin, lean, slim, slender, scrawny; dwarfish, dwarfed, stunted, undergrown; straitened, limited; jejune, watered, watery, unnourishing, unnutritious; subsistence, starvation

11 scarce, sparse, scanty; in short supply, at a premium; **rare,** uncommon; scarcer than hen's teeth <nonformal>; not to be had, not to be had for love or money, not to be had at any price; out of print, out of stock *or* season

12 ill-provided, ill-furnished, ill-equipped, ill-found, ill off; **unprovided,** unsupplied, unreplenished; bare-handed; unfed, underfed, undernourished; shorthanded, undermanned; **empty-handed, poor,** pauperized, impoverished, beggarly; starved, half-starved, on short commons, starving, starveling, famished

13 wanting, lacking, needing, missing, in want of; for want of, in default of, in the absence of; short, **short of,** scant of; shy, **shy of** *or* **on; out of,** clean *or* fresh out of <nonformal>, destitute of, bare of, void of, empty of, devoid of, forlorn of, bereft of, deprived of, denuded of, unpossessed of, unblessed with, bankrupt in; out of pocket; at the end of one's rope *or* tether

ADVS **14 insufficiently; inadequately,** unsubstantially, incompletely

15 meagerly, slightly, sparely, punily, scantily, poorly, frugally, sparingly

16 scarcely, sparsely, scantily, skimpily, scrimpily; **rarely,** uncommonly
PREPS **17 without,** minus, less, sans, absent
WORD ELEMENTS **18** hyp—, hypo—, under—, mal—, ill—, sub—

992 EXCESS

NOUNS **1 excess, excessiveness, inordinance,** inordinateness, nimiety, **immoderateness,** immoderacy, immoderation, **extravagance** or extravagancy, intemperateness, incontinence, overindulgence, **intemperance** 669; unrestrainedness, abandon; gluttony 672; **extreme,** extremity, **extremes; boundlessness** 822.1; overlargeness, overgreatness, monstrousness, enormousness 247.1; overgrowth, overdevelopment, hypertrophy, gigantism, giantism, elephantiasis; **overmuch,** overmuchness, too much, too-muchness; **exorbitance** or exorbitancy, undueness, **outrageousness,** unconscionableness, **unreasonableness;** radicalism, extremism 611.4; egregiousness; fabulousness, hyperbole, **exaggeration** 355

2 superabundance, overabundance, superflux, **plethora,** redundancy, overprofusion, too many, too much, too much of a good thing, **overplentifulness,** overplenteousness, overplenty, **oversupply,** overstock, overaccumulation, **oversufficiency,** overmuchness, overcopiousness, overlavishness, overluxuriance, overbounteousness, overnumerousness; lavishness, **extravagance** or extravagancy, **prodigality; plenty** 990.2; **more than enough, enough and to spare,** enough in all conscience; **overdose,** overmeasure, "enough, with over-measure"—Shakespeare; too much of a good thing, egg in one's beer <nonformal>; more than one knows what to do with, drug on the market; spate, avalanche, landslide, deluge, flood, inundation; embarras de richesses <Fr>, money to burn <nonformal>; overpopulation

3 overfullness, plethora, **surfeit, glut;** satiety 993; engorgement, repletion, congestion; hyperemia; **saturation,** supersaturation; **overload,** overburden, overcharge, surcharge, overfreight, overweight; **overflow,** overbrimming, overspill; **insatiability,** insatiableness

4 superfluity, superfluousness, fat; **redundancy,** redundance; unnecessariness, needlessness; fifth wheel and tits on a boar <both nonformal>; featherbedding, payroll padding; duplication, duplication

of effort, overlap; **luxury,** extravagance, frill and **frills** and bells and whistles and gimcrackery <all nonformal>; frippery, froufrou, overadornment, bedizenment, gingerbread; **ornamentation, embellishment** 498.1; expletive, **padding, filling;** pleonasm, tautology; verbosity, prolixity 538.2; more than one really wants to know

5 surplus, surplusage, leftovers, plus, **overplus,** overstock, **overage,** overset, overrun, **overmeasure, oversupply;** margin; **remainder, balance, leftover, extra, spare,** something extra or to spare; bonus, dividend; lagniappe <nonformal>; gratuity, tip, pourboire <Fr>

6 overdoing, overcarrying, **overreaching,** supererogation; **overkill;** piling on <nonformal>, overimportance, overemphasis; overuse; overreaction; **overwork, overexertion,** overexercise, overexpenditure, overtaxing, overstrain, tax, strain; too much on one's plate, too many irons in the fire, too much at once; **overachievement,** overachieving

7 overextension, overdrawing, drawing or spreading too thin, **overstretching,** overstrain, overstraining, stretching, straining, stretch, strain, tension, extreme tension, snapping or breaking point; **overexpansion;** inflation, distension, overdistension, edema, turgidity, swelling, bloat, bloating 259.2

VERBS **8 superabound,** overabound, **know no bounds, swarm,** pullulate, run riot, luxuriate, **teem;** overflow, flood, overbrim, overspill, spill over, overrun, overspread, overswarm, overgrow, fill; meet one at every turn; hang heavy on one's hands, remain on one's hands

9 exceed, surpass, pass, top, transcend, go beyond; overpass, overstep, overrun, **overreach,** overshoot, overshoot the mark

10 overdo, go too far, do it to death <nonformal>, pass all bounds, know no bounds, overact, **carry too far,** overcarry, go to an extreme, **go to extremes,** go overboard, go or jump off the deep end; **run or drive into the ground; make a big deal of** and **make a Federal case of** <both nonformal>; overemphasize, overstress; overplay, overplay one's hand <nonformal>; **overreact,** protest too much; overreach oneself; **overtax,** overtask, overexert, overexercise, overstrain, overdrive, overspend, exhaust, overexpend, overuse; overtrain; **overwork,** overlabor; overelaborate, overdevelop, tell more than one wants to know; overstudy; burn the

candle at both ends; **spread oneself too
thin**, **take on too much**, have too much on
one's plate, have too many irons in the
fire, do too many things at once; **exaggerate** 355.3; **overindulge** 669.5

11 **pile it on**, lay it on, **lay it on thick**, lay it
on with a trowel <nonformal>

12 **carry coals to Newcastle**, teach fishes to
swim, teach one's grandmother to suck
eggs, kill the slain, beat *or* flog a dead
horse, labor the obvious, butter one's
bread on both sides, preach to the converted, paint *or* gild the lily, "to gild
refined gold, to paint the lily, to throw a
perfume on the violet"—Shakespeare

13 **overextend, overdraw, overstretch, overstrain,** stretch, strain; reach the breaking *or* snapping point; **overexpand,** over-
distend, overdevelop, inflate, swell
259.4

14 **oversupply, overprovide,** overlavish,
overfurnish, overequip; **overstock;** over-
provision, overprovender; overdose; flood
the market, oversell; **flood, deluge,** inundate, engulf, swamp, whelm, overwhelm;
lavish with, be prodigal with

15 **overload,** overlade, **overburden,** overweight, **overcharge,** surcharge; **overfill,**
stuff, crowd, cram, jam, pack, jam-pack,
congest, choke; **overstuff,** overfeed; gluttonize 672.4; **surfeit, glut, gorge,** satiate
993.4; **saturate,** soak, drench, supersaturate, supercharge

ADJS 16 **excessive, inordinate, immoderate,**
overweening, hubristic, **intemperate, extravagant,** incontinent; unrestrained,
unbridled, abandoned; gluttonous 672.6;
extreme; overlarge, overgreat, overbig,
larger than life, monstrous, enormous,
jumbo, elephantine, gigantic 247.7; overgrown, overdeveloped, hypertrophied;
overmuch, too much, a bit much; **exorbitant, undue, outrageous,** unconscionable, **unreasonable;** fancy *and* high *and*
stiff *and* steep <all nonformal>; **out
of bounds** *or* **all bounds,** out of sight *and*
out of this world <both nonformal>,
boundless 822.3; egregious; fabulous, hyperbolic, hyperbolical, **exaggerated** 355.4

17 **superfluous, redundant; excess, in excess;**
unnecessary, unessential, nonessential,
expendable, dispensable, **needless,** unneeded, gratuitous, uncalled-for; expletive; pleonastic, tautologous, tautological; verbose, prolix 538.12; *de trop* <Fr>,
supererogatory, supererogative; spare, to
spare; on one's hands

18 **surplus,** overplus; **remaining,** unused,
leftover; over, **over and above; extra,**

spare, supernumerary, for lagniappe
<nonformal>, as a bonus

19 **superabundant,** overabundant, plethoric,
overplentiful, overplenteous, overplenty,
**oversufficient, overmuch; lavish, prodi-
gal,** overlavish, overbounteous, overgenerous, overliberal; overcopious, overlux-
uriant, riotous, overexuberant; overpro-
lific, overnumerous; **swarming,** pullulat-
ing, **teeming,** overpopulated, overpopu-
lous; plentiful 990.7

20 **overfull, overloaded, overladen, overburdened,** overfreighted, overfraught, overweighted, **overcharged,** surcharged, **saturated,** drenched, soaked, supersaturated,
supercharged; **surfeited, glutted,** gorged,
overfed, bloated, replete, swollen, **satiated** 993.6, **stuffed,** overstuffed, **crowded,
overcrowded, crammed,** jammed,
packed, jam-packed, like sardines in a
can *or* tin, bumper-to-bumper <nonfor-
mal>; choked, **congested,** stuffed up;
overstocked, oversupplied; overflowing,
in spate, running over, filled to overflowing; plethoric, hyperemic; **bursting,**
ready to burst, bursting at the seams, at
the bursting point, overblown, distended,
swollen, bloated 259.13

21 **overdone,** overwrought; overdrawn,
overstretched, overstrained; overwritten,
overplayed, overacted

ADVS 22 **excessively, inordinately, immoderately, intemperately,** overweeningly,
hubristically, **overly,** over, **overmuch,** too
much; **too,** too-too <nonformal>; **exorbitantly, unduly, unreasonably,** unconscionably, **outrageously**

23 **in** *or* **to excess, to extremes,** to the extreme, all out *and* to the max <both
nonformal>, flat out <Brit nonformal>,
to a fault, too far, out of all proportion

24 **superabundantly,** overabundantly, **lavishly, prodigally, extravagantly;** more
than enough, plentifully 990.9; without
measure, out of measure, beyond measure

25 **superfluously, redundantly,** super-
erogatorily; tautologously; unnecessarily, needlessly, beyond need, beyond reason, to a fare-thee-well <nonformal>

PREPS 26 **in excess of,** over, beyond, past,
above, **over and above,** above and beyond

WORD ELEMENTS 27 arch—, hyper—,
over—, super—, sur—, ultra—, extra—

993 SATIETY

NOUNS 1 **satiety, satiation, satisfaction, fullness, surfeit, glut,** repletion, engorge-

ment; contentment; **fill, bellyful** *and* skinful <both nonformal>; **saturation,** oversaturation, saturatedness, supersaturation; saturation point; more than enough, enough in all conscience, all one can stand *or* take; too much of a good thing, much of a muchness <nonformal>

2 **satedness,** surfeitedness, cloyedness, jadedness; overfullness, fed-upness <nonformal>

3 cloyer, surfeiter, sickener; **overdose;** a diet of cake; warmed-over cabbage, "cabbage repeatedly"—Juvenal

VERBS 4 **satiate, sate, satisfy,** slake, allay; **surfeit, glut, gorge,** engorge; **cloy,** jade, pall; **fill,** fill up; saturate, oversaturate, supersaturate; **stuff,** overstuff, cram; **overfill,** overgorge, overdose, overfeed

5 **have enough,** have about enough of, have quite enough, **have one's fill;** have too much, have too much of a good thing, **have a bellyful** *or* skinful <nonformal>, have an overdose, **be fed up** <nonformal>, have all one can take *or* stand, have it up to here *and* up the gazoo *or* kazoo <all nonformal>, have had it

ADJS 6 **satiated, sated, satisfied,** slaked, allayed; **surfeited, gorged,** replete, engorged; **glutted; cloyed,** jaded; **full,** full of, with one's fill of, **overfull,** saturated, oversaturated, supersaturated; **stuffed,** overstuffed, crammed, overgorged, overfed; **fed up** *and* fed to the gills *or* fed to the teeth *and* stuffed to the gills <all nonformal>; **with a bellyful** *or* skinful <nonformal>, with enough of; disgusted, **sick of,** tired of, sick and tired of

7 **satiating,** sating, satisfying, filling; surfeiting, overfilling; jading, **cloying,** cloysome

INTERJS 8 enough!, *basta* <Ital>, *genug!* and *genug shayn!* <both Yiddish>, all right already!, enough already!

994 EXPEDIENCE

NOUNS 1 **expedience** *or* **expediency, advisability,** politicness, **desirability,** recommendability; **fitness, fittingness, appropriateness,** propriety, decency <old>, seemliness, **suitability,** rightness, feasibility, **convenience;** seasonableness, timeliness, **opportuneness; usefulness** 387.3; **advantage, advantageousness,** beneficialness, **profit,** profitability, percentage *and* mileage <both nonformal>, worthwhileness, fruitfulness; wisdom, prudence 919.7; **temporariness, provisionality**

2 **expedient, means,** means to an end, **provision, measure, step, action,** effort, **stroke,** stroke of policy, coup, **move,** countermove, **maneuver,** demarche, course of action; tactic, **device,** contrivance, artifice, stratagem, **shift; gimmick** *and* dodge *and* trick <all nonformal>; **resort,** resource; answer, solution; quick-and-dirty solution <nonformal>; working proposition, working hypothesis; **temporary expedient, improvisation,** ad hoc measure, ad hoc *or* ad hockery *or* ad hocism; **fix** *and* **quick fix** <both nonformal>, jury-rigged expedient, **makeshift,** stopgap, shake-up, jury-rig; last expedient, **last resort** *or* resource, *pis aller* <Fr>, last shift, trump

VERBS 3 **expedite one's affair,** work to one's advantage, not come amiss, come in handy, be just the thing, be just what the doctor ordered <nonformal>, fit to a T *or* like a glove *or* like a second skin; forward, advance, promote, profit, advantage, benefit; **work, serve,** answer, answer *or* serve one's purpose, fill the bill *and* do the trick <both nonformal>; suit the occasion, **be fitting,** fit, befit, be right

4 **make shift, make do,** make out <nonformal>, rub along <Brit>, cope, manage, manage with, get along on, get by on, do with; do as well as *or* the best one can; use a last resort, scrape the bottom of the barrel

ADJS 5 **expedient, desirable,** to be desired, much to be desired, **advisable, politic,** recommendable; **appropriate, meet, fit, fitting,** befitting, **right, proper,** good, decent <old>, **becoming,** seemly, likely, congruous, **suitable,** sortable, feasible, doable, swingable <nonformal>, **convenient,** happy, heaven-sent, felicitous; timely, seasonable, opportune, well-timed, in the nick of time; **useful** 387.18; **advantageous,** favorable; **profitable,** fructuous, worthwhile, worth one's while; **wise** 919.17

6 **practical,** practicable, pragmatic *or* pragmatical, banausic; feasible, workable, operable, realizable; **efficient,** effective, **effectual**

7 **makeshift,** makeshifty, **stopgap,** band-aid <nonformal>, improvised, improvisational, **jury-rigged; last-ditch; ad hoc;** quick and dirty <nonformal>; temporary, provisional, tentative

ADVS 8 **expediently, fittingly,** fitly, **appropriately, suitably,** sortably, congruously, rightly, properly, decently <old>, feasibly, conveniently; practically; seasonably, opportunely; desirably, advisably; advantageously, to advantage, all to the good; as a last resort

PHRS **9** there's more than one way to skin a cat, where there's a will there's a way

995 INEXPEDIENCE

NOUNS **1 inexpedience** or inexpediency, **undesirability, inadvisability,** impoliticness or impoliticalness; **unwiseness** 922.2; **unfitness, unfittingness, inappropriateness, unaptness, unsuitability,** incongruity, **unmeetness,** wrongness, unseemliness; **inconvenience** or inconveniency, awkwardness; ineptitude, inaptitude; unseasonableness, untimeliness, inopportuneness; unfortunateness, infelicity; disadvantageousness, unprofitableness, unprofitability, worthlessness, futility, uselessness 391

2 disadvantage, drawback, liability; detriment, impairment, prejudice, loss, damage, hurt, harm, mischief, injury; **a step back** or **backward,** a loss of ground; **handicap** 1011.6, disability; drag, millstone around one's neck

3 inconvenience, discommodity, incommodity, disaccommodation <old>, **trouble, bother;** inconvenientness, inconveniency, **unhandiness,** awkwardness, clumsiness, unwieldiness, troublesomeness, clunkiness <nonformal>; gaucheness, gaucherie

VERBS **4 inconvenience,** put to inconvenience, **put out, discommode,** incommode, disaccommodate <old>, disoblige, **burden, embarrass; trouble, bother,** put to trouble, put to the trouble of, **impose upon;** harm, disadvantage 999.6

ADJS **5 inexpedient, undesirable, inadvisable, counterproductive,** impolitic, impolitical, unpolitic, not to be recommended, contraindicated; **impractical, impracticable,** dysfunctional, unworkable; **ill-advised, ill-considered, unwise; unfit, unfitting,** unbefitting, **inappropriate, unsuitable,** unmeet, inapt, inept, unseemly, **improper, wrong,** bad, out of place, out of order, incongruous, ill-suited; malapropos, mal à propos <Fr>, inopportune, untimely, ill-timed, badly timed, unseasonable; infelicitous, unfortunate, unhappy; unprofitable 391.12; futile 391.13

6 disadvantageous, unadvantageous, **unfavorable;** unprofitable, profitless, unrewarding, worthless, useless 391.9;

detrimental, deleterious, injurious, harmful, prejudicial, disserviceable

7 inconvenient, incommodious, discommodious; **unhandy, awkward,** clumsy, unwieldy, troublesome; gauche

ADVS **8 inexpediently, inadvisably,** impoliticly or impolitically, **undesirably; unfittingly, inappropriately, unsuitably,** ineptly, inaptly, incongruously; inopportunely, unseasonably; infelicitously, unfortunately, unhappily

9 disadvantageously, unadvantageously, unprofitably, unrewardingly; uselessly 391.15; **inconveniently,** unhandily, with difficulty, ill

996 IMPORTANCE

NOUNS **1 importance, significance, consequence,** consideration, **import,** note, mark, **moment, weight, gravity;** materiality; concern, concernment, interest; **first order,** high order, high rank; **priority,** primacy, precedence, preeminence, paramountcy, superiority, **supremacy;** value, worth, merit, excellence 998.1; self-importance 140.1

2 notability, noteworthiness, remarkableness, salience, memorability; **prominence, eminence, greatness,** distinction; prestige, esteem, repute, reputation, honor, glory, renown, dignity, **fame** 662.1; **stardom,** celebrity, celebrityhood, superstardom; semicelebrity

3 gravity, graveness, seriousness, solemnity, weightiness; gravitas <L>; no joke, no laughing matter, hardball <nonformal>

4 urgency, imperativeness, exigence or exigency; **momentousness, crucialness, cruciality;** consequentiality, consequentialness; **press,** pressure, high pressure, **stress,** tension, **pinch;** clutch and crunch <both nonformal>; **crisis, emergency;** moment of truth, turning point, climax, defining moment

5 matter of importance or **consequence,** thing of interest, point of interest, matter of concern, object of note, one for the book and something to write home about <both nonformal>, something special, no tea party, no picnic; vital concern or interest, matter of life or death; notabilia, memorabilia, great doings

6 salient point, cardinal point, high point, great point; important thing, chief thing, **the point, main point,** main thing, essential matter, **essence,** the name of the game and the bottom line and what it's all about *and* where it's at <all nonformal>, substance, gravamen, *sine qua non* <L>, issue, real issue, front-burner issue <nonformal>, prime issue; **essential,** fundamental, substantive point, material point; **gist, nub** <nonformal>, **heart,** meat, pith, kernel, **core; crux,** crucial *or* pivotal *or* critical point, pivot; turning point, **climax, cusp, crisis;** keystone, cornerstone; landmark, milestone, bench mark; linchpin

7 **feature, highlight,** high spot, main attraction, centerpiece, pièce de résistance; outstanding feature

8 **personage, important person,** person of importance *or* consequence, **great man** *or* **woman,** man *or* woman of mark *or* note, **somebody, notable,** notability, figure; **celebrity,** famous person, person of renown, personality; name, big name, nabob, **mogul,** panjandrum, person to be reckoned with, very important person; sachem; mover and shaker, lord of creation; **worthy,** pillar of society, elder, father; **dignitary,** dignity; **magnate;** tycoon <nonformal>, baron; power; power elite, Establishment; interests; brass, top brass; top people, the great; ruling circle, lords of creation, "the choice and master spirits of the age"—Shakespeare; the top, the summit

9 <nonformal terms> **big shot,** wheel, **big wheel,** big boy, big cat, big fish, big shot, biggie, big cheese, big noise, big-timer, big-time operator, **bigwig,** big man, big gun, **high-muck-a-muck** *or* high-muckety-muck, lion, something, **VIP,** brass hat, high man on the totem pole, suit; sacred cow, little tin god, tin god; big man on campus *or* BMOC; 800-pound gorilla; queen bee, heavy momma

10 **chief, principal,** chief executive, chief executive officer *or* CEO, paramount, overlord, **king,** electronics king, etc; leading light, luminary, master spirit, **star,** superstar, prima donna, lead 707.6

11 <nonformal terms> **boss, honcho,** big enchilada, biggest frog in the pond, top *or* high man on the totem pole, top dog, Mr Big, head cheese, his nibs, himself, man upstairs

VERBS 12 **matter,** import <old>, signify, **count, tell, weigh, carry weight,** cut ice *and* cut some ice <both nonformal>, be prominent, stand out, mean much; be something, be somebody, amount to something; have a key to the executive washroom; be featured, star, get top billing

13 **value, esteem, treasure, prize,** appreciate, **rate highly,** think highly of, think well of, **think much of,** set store by; give *or* attach *or* ascribe importance to; make much of, make a fuss *or* stir about, make an ado *or* much ado about; hold up as an example

14 **emphasize, stress,** lay emphasis *or* stress upon, feature, highlight, brightline, place emphasis on, give emphasis to, **accent, accentuate, punctuate, point up,** bring to the fore, put in the foreground; prioritize; **highlight,** spotlight; **star, underline, underscore,** italicize; overemphasize, overstress, overaccentuate, rub in; harp on; dwell on, belabor; attach too much importance to, make a big deal *or* Federal case of <nonformal>, make a mountain out of a molehill

15 **feature,** headline <nonformal>; **star,** give top billing to

16 **dramatize, play up** <nonformal>, splash, make a production of

ADJS 17 **important, major, consequential, momentous, significant, considerable,** substantial, material, **great,** grand, big; superior, world-shaking, earthshaking; big-time *and* big-league *and* major-league *and* heavyweight <all nonformal>; high-powered <nonformal>, double-barreled <nonformal>; bigwig *and* bigwigged <both nonformal>; name *and* big-name <both nonformal>, self-important 140.8

18 **of importance, of significance, of consequence,** of note, of moment, of weight; of concern, of concernment, of interest, not to be overlooked *or* despised, not hay *and* not chopped liver *and* not to be sneezed at <all nonformal>; viable

19 **notable, noteworthy, celebrated, remarkable, marked, standout** <nonformal>, of mark, signal; **memorable,** rememberable, unforgettable, never to be forgotten; striking, telling, salient; **eminent, prominent,** conspicuous, noble, **outstanding, distinguished;** prestigious, esteemed, estimable, reputable 662.15; **extraordinary,** *extraordinaire* <Fr>, out of the ordinary, **exceptional, special,** rare

20 **weighty,** heavy, **grave,** sober, sobering, **solemn, serious,** earnest; portentous, fateful, fatal; formidable, awe-inspiring, imposing, larger than life

21 **emphatic, decided, positive, forceful,** forcible; **emphasized, stressed,** accented, accentuated, punctuated, pointed; underlined, underscored, starred, italicized; red-letter, in red letters, in letters of fire

22 **urgent, imperative,** imperious, **compelling, pressing,** high-priority, high-

pressure, crying, clamorous, insistent, instant, exigent; crucial, critical, pivotal, acute

23 **vital, all-important,** crucial, of vital importance, life-and-death *or* life-or-death; earth-shattering, epoch-making; **essential,** fundamental, indispensable, basic, substantive, bedrock, material; **central,** focal; bottom-line *and* meat-and-potatoes *and* gut <all nonformal>

24 **paramount, principal, leading, foremost, main, chief,** number one <nonformal>, premier, **prime, primary,** preeminent, **supreme,** capital <old>, cardinal; highest, uppermost, topmost, toprank, ranking, of the first rank, world-class, **dominant,** predominant, master, controlling, **overruling,** overriding, all-absorbing

ADVS 25 **importantly, significantly,** consequentially, materially, momentously, greatly, grandly; eminently, prominently, conspicuously, outstandingly, saliently, signally, notably, markedly, remarkably

26 **at the decisive moment,** in the clutch *and* when the chips are down *and* when push comes to shove <all nonformal>

997 UNIMPORTANCE

NOUNS 1 **unimportance, insignificance,** inconsequence, inconsequentiality, indifference, **immateriality;** inessentiality; ineffectuality; unnoteworthiness, unimpressiveness; inferiority, secondariness, low order of importance, low priority, dispensability, expendability, marginality; **smallness,** littleness, slightness, inconsiderableness, negligibility; irrelevancy, meaninglessness; **pettiness,** puniness, pokiness, picayune, picayunishness; irrelevance 775.1

2 **paltriness,** poorness, **meanness,** sorriness, sadness, pitifulness, contemptibleness, pitiableness, despicableness, miserableness, wretchedness, vileness, crumminess <nonformal>, shabbiness, shoddiness, cheapness, cheesiness, beggarliness, worthlessness, unworthiness, meritlessness; tawdriness, meretriciousness, gaudiness 501.3

3 **triviality,** trivialness, triflingness, nugacity, nugaciousness; **superficiality,** shallowness; slightness, slenderness, slimness, flimsiness, **frivolity,** frivolousness, lightness, levity; **foolishness,** silliness; inanity, emptiness, vacuity; triteness, vapidity; vanity, idleness, futility; **much ado about nothing,** tempest *or*

storm in a teacup *or* teapot, much cry and little wool, piss and wind *and* big deal <both nonformal>

4 **trivia, trifles; trumpery,** nugae <L>, gimcrackery, knickknackery, bric-a-brac; **rubbish,** trash, chaff; peanuts *and* chicken feed *and* chickenshit *and* Mickey Mouse <all nonformal>, small change; small beer; froth, "trifles light as air"— Shakespeare; minutiae, details, minor details

5 **trifle, triviality, oddment, bagatelle,** fribble, **gimcrack, gewgaw,** frippery, **trinket,** bibelot, curio, **bauble,** gaud, toy, **knick-knack,** knickknackery, kickshaw, minikin <old>, whim-wham, folderol; pin, button, hair, straw, rush, feather, fig, bean, hill of beans <nonformal>, molehill, row of pins *or* buttons <nonformal>, sneeshing <Brit nonformal>, pinch of snuff; bit, snap; a curse, a continental, a hoot *and* a damn *and* a darn *and* a shit <all nonformal>, a tinker's damn; picayune, rap, sou, halfpenny, farthing, brass farthing, cent, red cent, two cents, twopence *or* tuppence <both Brit>; peppercorn; drop in the ocean *or* the bucket; fleabite, pinprick; joke, jest, farce, mockery, child's play

6 **an insignificancy,** an inessential, a marginal matter *or* affair, a trivial *or* paltry affair, a small *or* trifling *or* minor matter, **no great matter;** a little thing, *peu de chose* <Fr>, hardly *or* scarcely anything, matter of no importance *or* consequence, matter of indifference; **a nothing, a big nothing, a naught,** a mere nothing, nothing in particular, nothing to signify, nothing to speak *or* worth speaking of, nothing to think twice about, nothing to boast of, nothing to write home about, thing of naught, *rien du tout* <Fr>, nullity, nihility; **technicality,** mere technicality

7 **a nobody, insignificancy,** hollow man, jackstraw <old>, **nonentity,** empty suit *and* nebbish <both nonformal>, an obscurity, a nothing, cipher, "an O without a figure"—Shakespeare, little man, nobody one knows; lightweight, mediocrity; whippersnapper *and* whiffet *and* pipsqueak *and* squirt *and* shrimp *and* scrub *and* runt <all nonformal>; squit <Brit nonformal>, punk <nonformal>; small potato, small potatoes; **the little fellow,** the little guy <nonformal>, **the man in the street;** common man 863.3; man of straw, dummy, figurehead; **small fry,** Mr and Mrs Nobody, John Doe and Richard

Roe *or* Mary Roe; Tom, Dick, and Harry; Brown, Jones, and Robinson

8 trifling, dallying, **dalliance,** flirtation, flirtiness, coquetry; toying, fiddling, playing, fooling, **puttering,** tinkering, pottering, piddling; dabbling, smattering; loitering, idling 331.4

9 <nonformal terms> **monkeying, monkeying around,** buggering around, diddling around, fiddling around, frigging around, horsing around, fooling around, kidding around, messing around, pissing around, playing around, screwing around, mucking around, farting around; jerking off

10 trifler, dallier, fribble; **putterer,** potterer, piddler, tinkerer, smatterer, dabbler; amateur, dilettante, Sunday painter; **flirt, coquet**

VERBS **11 be unimportant,** be of no importance, not signify, **not matter,** not count, signify nothing, matter little, **not make any difference; cut no ice, not amount to anything,** make no never mind *and* not amount to a hill of beans *or* a damn <all nonformal>

12 attach little importance to, give little weight to; make little of, underplay, de-emphasize, downplay, play down, **minimize, make light of,** think little of, throw away, **make** *or* **think nothing of,** take no account of, set little by, set no store by, set at naught; snap one's fingers at; not care a straw about; not give a shit *or* a hoot *or* two hoots for <nonformal>, not give a damn about, not give a dime a dozen for; bad-mouth <nonformal>, deprecate, depreciate 512.8; **trivialize**

13 make much ado about nothing, make mountains out of molehills, have a storm *or* tempest in a teacup *or* teapot

14 trifle, dally; flirt, coquet; toy, fribble, **play, fool,** play at, **putter, potter,** tinker, **piddle; dabble,** smatter; toy with, fiddle with, fool with, play with; idle, loiter 331.12,13; nibble, niggle, nickel-and-dime <nonformal>

15 <nonformal terms> **monkey, monkey around,** fiddle, fiddle around, fiddle-faddle, frivol, horse around, fool around, play around, mess around, kid around, **screw around,** muck around, muck about <Brit>, fart around, piss around, bugger around, diddle around, frig around, mess around; jerk off

ADJS **16 unimportant, of no importance,** of little *or* small importance, of no great importance, **of no account,** of no significance, of no concern, of no matter, of lit-

tle *or* no consequence, no great shakes <nonformal>; no skin off one's nose *or* elbow *or* ass <nonformal>; inferior, secondary, of a low order of importance, low-priority, expendable; marginal; one-dimensional, two-dimensional

17 insignificant 248.6, **inconsequential, immaterial;** nonessential, unessential, inessential, **not vital,** back-burner <nonformal>, dispensable; unnoteworthy, unimpressive; **inconsiderable,** inappreciable, negligible; **small, little,** minute, footling, petit <old>, minor, inferior; technical; irrelevant

18 <nonformal terms> **measly, small-time, two-bit,** Mickey Mouse, chickenshit, nickel-and-dime, low-rent, piddly, pissy-ass, dinky, poky <Brit>, tinhorn, punk; not worth a dime *or* a red cent *or* beans *or* a hill of beans *or* bubkes *or* shit; **one-horse, two-by-four,** jerkwater

19 trivial, trifling; fribble, fribbling, nugacious, nugatory; catchpenny; **slight,** slender, flimsy; **superficial, shallow; frivolous, light,** windy, airy, frothy; idle, futile, vain, otiose; **foolish,** fatuous, asinine, **silly; inane,** empty, vacuous; trite, vapid; unworthy of serious consideration

20 petty, puny, piddling, piffling, niggling, pettifogging, picayune, picayunish; small-beer

21 paltry, poor, common, **mean, sorry, sad, pitiful,** pitiable, pathetic, **despicable, contemptible,** beneath contempt, **miserable, wretched,** beggarly, vile, **shabby,** scrubby, scruffy, shoddy, scurvy, scuzzy <nonformal>, scummy, **crummy** *and* cheesy <both nonformal>, **trashy,** rubbishy, garbagey <nonformal>, trumpery, gimcracky <nonformal>; tinpot <nonformal>; **cheap,** worthless, valueless, twopenny *or* twopenny-halfpenny <both Brit>, two-for-a-cent *or* -penny, dime-a-dozen; tawdry, meretricious, gaudy 501.20

22 unworthy, worthless, meritless, unworthy of regard *or* consideration, beneath notice

ADVS **23 unimportantly, insignificantly, inconsequentially,** immaterially, unessentially; **pettily,** paltrily; **trivially,** triflingly; superficially, shallowly; frivolously, lightly, idly

PHRS **24 it does not matter,** it matters not, it does not signify, mox nix <nonformal>, **it is of no consequence** *or* **importance, it makes no difference,** it makes no never mind <nonformal>, it cannot be helped, it is all the same; *n'importe, de rien, ça ne* *fait rien* <all Fr>; it will all come out in the wash <nonformal>, it will be all the same a hundred years from now

25 no matter, never mind, think no more of it, do not give it another *or* a second thought, don't lose any sleep over it, let it pass, let it go <nonformal>, ignore it, forget it <nonformal>, skip it *and* drop it <both nonformal>; fiddle-dee-dee

26 what does it matter?, what matter?, what's the difference?, what's the diff? <nonformal>, what do I care?, what of it?, what boots it?, what's the odds?, so what?, what else is new?; for aught one cares, big deal <nonformal>

998 GOODNESS

NOUNS 1 goodness, excellence, quality, class <nonformal>; **virtue,** grace; **merit,** desert; **value, worth; fineness,** goodliness, fairness, niceness; **superiority,** firstrateness, **skillfulness** 413.1; wholeness, **soundness,** healthiness 81.1; **virtuousness** 653.1; **kindness, benevolence,** benignity 143.1; beneficialness, helpfulness 449.10; favorableness, auspiciousness 133.9; expedience, advantageousness 994.1; **usefulness** 387.3; pleasantness, agreeableness 97.1; cogency, validity; profitableness, rewardingness 472.4

2 superexcellence, supereminence, preeminence, supremacy, primacy, paramountcy, peerlessness, unsurpassedness, matchlessness, superfineness; **superbness,** exquisiteness, **magnificence,** splendidness, splendiferousness, marvelousness

3 tolerableness, tolerability, goodishness, passableness, fairishness, **adequateness, satisfactoriness,** acceptability, admissibility; sufficiency 990

4 good, welfare, well-being, **benefit; interest, advantage; behalf,** behoof; **blessing,** benison, boon; **profit,** avail <old>, gain; world of good

5 good thing, a thing to be desired, "a consummation devoutly to be wish'd"— Shakespeare; **treasure,** gem, jewel, diamond, pearl; boast, pride, **pride and joy;** prize, trophy, plum; winner *and* no slouch *and* nothing to sneeze at <all nonformal>; catch, find <nonformal>, *trouvaille* <Fr>; godsend, windfall

6 first-rater, topnotcher, world-beater; wonder, prodigy, genius, virtuoso, **star, superstar;** luminary, leading light, one in

a thousand *or* a million; hard *or* tough act to follow <nonformal>

7 <nonformal terms> **dandy, jim dandy, dilly, humdinger, pip,** pippin, **peach,** ace, beaut, **lulu, daisy,** darb, doozy, honey, sweetheart, dream, lollapaloosa, bitch, crackerjack, hot shit *or* poo, pisser, pistol, corker, whiz, blinger, **crackerjack,** knockout, something else, something else again, barn-burner, killer, killer-diller, the nuts, the cat's pajamas *or* balls *or* meow, bitch-kitty, whiz, whizbang, wow, wowser

8 the best, the very best, the best ever, the top of the heap *or* the line <nonformal>, the tops <nonformal>; **quintessence,** prime, optimum, superlative; **choice, pick, select, elect, elite,** *corps d'élite* <Fr>, chosen; **cream, flower,** fat; cream of the crop, *crème de la crème* <Fr>, salt of the earth; *pièce de résistance* <Fr>; prize, champion, queen; nonesuch, paragon, nonpareil; gem of the first water

9 harmlessness, hurtlessness, uninjuriousness, **innocuousness,** benignity, benignancy; unobnoxiousness, inoffensiveness, innocence; heart of gold, kindness of heart, milk of human kindness

VERBS 10 do good, profit, avail; do a world of good; **benefit, help, serve,** be of service, advance, advantage, favor 449.11,14,17,19; be the making of, make a man *or* woman of; do no harm, break no bones

11 excel, surpass, outdo, pass, do *or* go one better; do up brown *or* in spades <nonformal>, do with a vengeance; be as good as, equal, emulate, rival, vie, vie with, challenge comparison, go one-on-one with <nonformal>; **make the most of, optimize;** cream off <Brit>, skim off the cream

ADJS 12 good, excellent, *bueno* <Sp>, *bon* <Fr>, bonny <Brit>, **fine, nice,** goodly, fair; **splendid, capital, grand,** elegant <nonformal>, braw <Scots>, famous <nonformal>, noble; royal, regal, fit for a king; very good, *très bon* <Fr>; commendable, laudable, **estimable** 509.20; skillful 413.22; **sound,** healthy 81.5; virtuous; kind, benevolent 143.15; beneficial, helpful 449.21; profitable; favorable, auspicious 133.18; expedient, advantageous 994.5; useful 387.18; pleasant 97.6; cogent, valid 972.13

13 <nonformal terms> **great,** swell, dandy, bitchin', jim dandy, neat, cool, super, super-duper, bully <old>, tough, mean, gnarly, heavy, bad, groovy, out of sight, fab, fantabulous, marvy, gear, something else, ducky, dynamite, keen, killer, hot, nifty, sexy, spiffy, spiffing, ripping, nobby, peachy, peachy-keen, delicious, scrumptious, not too shabby, tits, out of this world, hunky-dory, crackerjack, boss, stunning, corking, smashing, solid, all wool and a yard wide; rum *or* wizard <both Brit>, bonzer <Austral>; bang-up, jam-up, slap-up, ace-high, fine and dandy, just dandy, but good, OK, okay, A-OK

14 **superior,** above par, head and shoulders above, **crack** <nonformal>; **high-grade, high-class,** high-quality, high-caliber, high-test, **world-class**

15 **superb,** super <nonformal>, **superexcellent, supereminent,** superfine, **exquisite; magnificent,** splendid, splendiferous, tremendous, immense, **marvelous, wonderful,** glorious, divine, heavenly, terrific, sensational; sterling, golden; gilt-edged *and* gilt-edge, blue-chip; of the highest type, of the best sort, of the first water, as good as good can be, as good as they come, as good as they make 'em *and* out of this world <both nonformal>

16 **best,** very best, greatest *and* top-of-the-line <both nonformal>, **prime,** optimum, optimal; **choice, select, elect,** elite, **picked,** handpicked; **prize, champion; supreme,** paramount, **unsurpassed,** surpassing, unparalleled, unmatched, unmatchable, matchless, makeless <old>, **peerless;** quintessential; for the best, all for the best

17 **first-rate, first-class,** in a class by itself; of the first *or* highest degree; unmatched, matchless; champion, record-breaking

18 <nonformal terms> **A-1, A number one,** primo, first-chop, tip-top, top-notch, top-flight, top-drawer, tops; topping *or* top-hole <both Brit>

19 **up to par,** up to standard, **up to snuff** <nonformal>; **up to the mark,** up to the notch *and* **up to scratch** <both nonformal>

20 **tolerable, goodish, fair, fairish,** moderate, tidy <nonformal>, **decent,** respectable, presentable, good enough, **pretty good, not bad,** not amiss, not half bad, not so bad, **adequate, satisfactory, all right,** OK *or* okay <nonformal>; better than nothing; **acceptable,** admissible, **passable,** unobjectionable, unexceptionable; workmanlike; sufficient 990.6

21 **harmless,** hurtless, unhurtful; well-meaning, well-meant; **uninjurious,** un-

damaging, **innocuous,** innoxious, innocent; unobnoxious, inoffensive; non-malignant, **benign;** nonpoisonous, nontoxic, nonvirulent, nonvenomous

ADVS 22 **excellently, nicely,** finely, **capitally, splendidly, famously,** royally; **well,** very well, **fine** <nonformal>, right, aright; one's best, at one's best, at the top of one's bent

23 **superbly,** exquisitely, **magnificently,** tremendously, immensely, terrifically, **marvelously, wonderfully,** gloriously, divinely

24 **tolerably, fairly,** fairishly, moderately, respectably, **adequately, satisfactorily,** passably, **acceptably,** unexceptionably, presentably, decently; fairly well, well enough, pretty well; **rather, pretty**

999 BADNESS

NOUNS 1 **badness, evil,** evilness, viciousness, damnability, reprehensibility; moral badness, dereliction, peccancy, iniquity, sinfulness, wickedness 654.4; unwholesomeness, unhealthiness 82.1; inferiority 1004.3; unskillfulness 414.1; unkindness, malevolence 144; inauspiciousness, unfavorableness 133.8; inexpedience 995; unpleasantness 98; invalidity 19.3; inaccuracy 974.2; improperness 638.1

2 **terribleness, dreadfulness,** direness, **awfulness** <nonformal>, horribleness; **atrociousness, outrageousness,** heinousness, nefariousness; **notoriousness, egregiousness,** scandalousness, shamefulness, **infamousness; abominableness,** odiousness, **loathsomeness, detestableness,** despicableness, contemptibleness, hatefulness; **offensiveness,** grossness, obnoxiousness; squalor, squalidness, sordidness, **wretchedness,** filth, **vileness,** fulsomeness, **nastiness,** rankness, **foulness,** noisomeness; disgustingness, repulsiveness; uncleanness 80; beastliness, bestiality, brutality; **rottenness** *and* lousiness <both nonformal>; the pits <nonformal>; shoddiness, shabbiness; scurviness, **baseness** 661.3; **worthlessness** 997.2

3 **evil, bad, wrong, ill; harm, hurt, injury, damage, detriment; destruction** 395; despoliation; mischief, havoc; outrage, atrocity; abomination, grievance, vexation, woe, crying evil; poison 1000.3; blight, venom, toxin, **bane** 1000; **corruption,** pollution, infection, befoulment, defilement; environmental pollution, fly

in the ointment, worm in the apple *or* rose; skeleton in the closet; snake in the grass; "something rotten in the state of Denmark"—Shakespeare; ills the flesh is heir to, "all ills that men endure"—Abraham Cowley; the worst

4 **bad influence,** malevolent influence, evil star, **ill wind;** evil genius, **hoodoo** *and* **jinx** <both nonformal>, **Jonah; curse,** enchantment, whammy *and* double *or* triple whammy <all nonformal>, spell, hex, voodoo; **evil eye,** *malocchio* <Ital>

5 **harmfulness, hurtfulness,** injuriousness, banefulness, balefulness, detrimentalness, deleteriousness, perniciousness, mischievousness, noxiousness, venomousness, poisonousness, toxicity, virulence, noisomeness, **malignance** *or* **malignancy, malignity, viciousness;** unhealthiness 82.1; disease 85; deadliness, lethality 308.8; ominousness 133.7

VERBS 6 **work evil,** do ill; **harm, hurt; injure,** scathe, wound, **damage; destroy** 395.10; despoil, prejudice, disadvantage, impair, disserve, distress; **wrong,** do wrong, do wrong by, aggrieve, do evil, do a mischief, do an ill office to; **molest,** afflict; lay a hand on; get into trouble; **abuse,** bash <nonformal>, batter, outrage, violate, maltreat, mistreat 389.5; torment, **harass,** hassle <nonformal>, persecute, savage, crucify, torture 96.18; play mischief *or* havoc with, wreak havoc on, play hob with <nonformal>; **corrupt,** deprave, taint, pollute, infect, befoul, defile; poison, envenom, blight; **curse,** put a whammy on <nonformal>, give the evil eye, hex, jinx, bewitch; spell *or* mean trouble, threaten, menace 514.2; doom; condemn 602.3

ADJS 7 **bad, evil, ill,** untoward, black, sinister; **wicked, wrong,** peccant, iniquitous, **vicious; sinful** 654.16; criminal; unhealthy 82.5; **inferior** 1004.9; unskillful 414.15; unkind, malevolent 144.19; inauspicious, unfavorable 133.17; inexpedient 995.5; unpleasant 98.17; invalid 19.15; inaccurate 974.17; improper 638.3

8 <nonformal terms> **lousy,** punk, bum, badass, shitty, crappy, cruddy, cheesy, dog-ass, gnarly, gross, raunchy, pisspoor, rat-ass, **crummy,** grim, low-rent, low-ride, putrid, icky, skanky, yecchy, vomity, barfy, stinking, stinky, creepy, hairy, god-awful, gosh-awful

9 **terrible, dreadful,** awful <nonformal>, dire, horrible, horrid; atrocious, outrageous, heinous, villainous, nefarious; enormous, monstrous; **deplorable,** lamentable, regrettable, pitiful, pitiable, woeful, woesome <old>, grievous, sad 98.20; flagrant; **scandalous,** shameful, **shocking,** infamous, **notorious,** arrant, **egregious;** unclean 80.20; shoddy, schlocky <nonformal>, shabby, scurvy, **base** 661.12; **odious, obnoxious,** offensive, gross, **disgusting,** repulsive, loathsome, **abominable, detestable, despicable, contemptible,** beneath contempt, hateful; blameworthy, **reprehensible;** rank, fetid, foul, filthy, vile, fulsome, noisome, **nasty,** squalid, sordid, **wretched;** beastly, brutal; as bad as they come, as bad as they make 'em <nonformal>, as bad as bad can be; worst; too bad; below par, subpar, not up to scratch *or* snuff *or* the mark, poor-quality, **worthless**

10 **execrable, damnable;** damned, accursed, cursed 513.9; infernal, hellish, devilish, fiendish, satanic, ghoulish, demoniac, demonic, demonical, diabolic, diabolical, unholy, ungodly

11 **evil-fashioned,** ill-fashioned, evil-shaped, ill-shaped, evil-qualitied, evil-looking, ill-looking, evil-favored, ill-favored, evil-hued, evil-faced, evil-minded, evil-eyed, ill-affected <old>, evil-gotten, ill-gotten, ill-conceived

12 **harmful, hurtful,** scatheful, **baneful,** baleful, distressing, **injurious, damaging, detrimental,** deleterious, counterproductive, **pernicious,** mischievous; noxious, mephitic, venomous, venenate, poisonous, venenous, veneniferous, toxic, virulent, noisome; **malignant,** malign, malevolent, malefic, vicious; prejudicial, disadvantageous, disserviceable; corruptive, corrupting, corrosive, corroding; deadly, lethal; ominous 133.17

ADVS 13 **badly,** bad <nonformal>, **ill,** evil, evilly, wrong, wrongly, amiss; to one's cost

14 **terribly, dreadfully,** dreadful <nonformal>, **horribly,** horridly, **awfully** <nonformal>, **atrociously, outrageously;** flagrantly, scandalously, shamefully, shockingly, infamously, notoriously, egregiously, grossly, offensively, nauseatingly, fulsomely, odiously, **vilely,** obnoxiously, **disgustingly,** loathsomely; wretchedly, sordidly, shabbily, basely, abominably, detestably, despicably, contemptibly, foully, nastily; brutally, bestially, savagely, viciously; something fierce *or* terrible <nonformal>

15 **harmfully, hurtfully, banefully,** balefully, **injuriously, damagingly, detrimentally,** deleteriously, counterpro-

ductively, **perniciously,** mischievously; noxiously, venomously, poisonously, toxically, virulently, noisomely; **malignantly,** malignly, malevolently, malefically, **viciously;** prejudicially, disadvantageously, disserviceably; corrosively, corrodingly

1000 BANE

NOUNS **1 bane, curse, affliction,** infliction, visitation, **plague, pestilence,** pest, calamity, scourge, **torment,** open wound, running sore, grievance, woe, burden, crushing burden; disease 85; death 307; evil, harm 999.3; destruction 395; vexation 96.2; thorn, thorn in the flesh *or* side, pea in the shoe; bugbear, *bête noire* <Fr>, bogy, bogeymen, nemesis, arch-nemesis

2 blight, blast; canker, cancer; mold, fungus, mildew, smut, must, rust; rot, dry rot; **pest;** worm, worm in the apple *or* rose; moth <old>, "moth and rust"— Bible

3 poison, venom, venin, virus <old>, toxic, toxin, toxicant; eradicant, **pesticide; insecticide,** insect powder, bug bomb <nonformal>; roach powder, roach paste; stomach poison, contact poison, systemic insecticide *or* systemic, fumigant, chemosterilant; chlorinated hydrocarbon insecticide, organic chlorine; organic phosphate insecticide; carbamate insecticide, sheepdip; termiticide, miticide, acaricide, vermicide, anthelminthic; rodenticide, rat poison; **herbicide,** defoliant, Agent Orange, paraquat, **weed killer;** fungicide; microbicide, germicide, antiseptic, disinfectant, antibiotic; **toxicology;** toxic waste, **environmental pollutant**

4 miasma, mephitis, malaria <old>; effluvium, exhaust, exhaust gas; coal gas, chokedamp, blackdamp, firedamp; air *or* atmospheric pollution, smog

5 sting, stinger, dart; fang, tang <nonformal>; beesting, snakebite

6 poisonous plants

aconite	death cup *or* angel
amanita	ergot
banewort	foxglove
bearded darnel	gastrolobium
belladonna	hellebore
black henbane	hemlock
black nightshade	henbane
castor-oil plant	horsetail
corn cackle	jequirity *or* jequirity
datura	bean
deadly nightshade	jimsonweed
death camas	larkspur

locoweed	poison ivy
mayapple	poison oak
mescal bean	poison rye grass
monkshood	poison sumac
nightshade	poison tobacco
nux vomica	poisonweed
ordeal tree	pokeweed
poison bean	sheep laurel
poisonberry	upas
poison bush	water hemlock
poison hemlock *or*	white snakeroot
parsley	wolfsbane

1001 PERFECTION

NOUNS **1 perfection, faultlessness, flawlessness,** defectlessness, indefectibility, impeccability, absoluteness; infallibility; spotlessness, stainlessness, taintlessness, purity, immaculateness; sinlessness; chastity 664

2 soundness, integrity, intactness, wholeness, entireness, completeness; **fullness,** plenitude; finish

3 acme of perfection, pink, pink of perfection, culmination, perfection, height, top, acme, ultimate, summit, pinnacle, peak, highest pitch, climax, consummation, *ne plus ultra* <L>, **the last word,** a dream come true

4 pattern *or* standard *or* mold *or* norm of perfection, very model, quintessence; archetype, prototype, exemplar, mirror, **epitome;** perfect specimen, highest type; **classic,** masterwork, masterpiece, *chef d'œuvre* <Fr>, showpiece; **ideal** 785.4; role model; **paragon** 659.4

VERBS **5 perfect,** develop, flesh out, ripen, mature; improve 392.7; crown, culminate; lick *or* whip into shape, fine-tune; complete 407.6; do to perfection 407.7

ADJS **6 perfect, ideal, faultless, flawless,** unflawed, defectless, not to be improved, **impeccable,** absolute; **just right;** spotless, stainless, taintless, unblemished, untainted, unspotted, immaculate, **pure,** uncontaminated, unadulterated, unmixed; sinless; chaste 664.4; indefective <old>, indefectible, trouble-free; infallible; beyond all praise, irreproachable, unfaultable, *sans peur et sans reproche* <Fr>, **matchless, peerless** 249.15

7 sound, intact, whole, entire, complete, integral; **full;** total, utter, unqualified 959.2

8 undamaged, unharmed, unhurt, uninjured, unscathed, **unspoiled,** virgin, inviolate, **unimpaired;** harmless, scatheless; **unmarred,** unmarked, unscarred, unscratched, undefaced, unbruised; **unbroken,** unshattered, untorn; undemolished, undestroyed; undeformed, unmutilated, unmangled, unmaimed; unfaded, unworn, unwithered, bright, fresh, untouched, pristine, mint; none the worse for wear

9 **perfected, finished,** polished, refined; done to a T *or* to a turn; **classic, classical,** masterly, masterful, expert, proficient; ripened, ripe, matured, mature, developed, fully developed; thorough-going, thorough-paced; **consummate,** quintessential, archetypical, exemplary, model

ADVS 10 **perfectly,** ideally; **faultlessly, flawlessly, impeccably; just right;** spotlessly; immaculately, purely; infallibly; **wholly, entirely, completely, fully,** thoroughly, totally, absolutely 793.15

11 **to perfection, to a turn, to a T,** to a finish, to a nicety; to a fare-thee-well *or* fare-youwell *or* fare-ye-well <nonformal>; to beat the band <nonformal>

1002 IMPERFECTION

NOUNS 1 **imperfection,** imperfectness; **unperfectedness; faultiness, defectiveness,** defectibility; **shortcoming, deficiency,** lack, want, shortage, **inadequacy,** inadequateness; erroneousness, **fallibility;** inaccuracy, inexactness, inexactitude 974.2; **unsoundness,** incompleteness, patchiness, sketchiness, unevenness; **impairment** 393; **mediocrity** 1004; immaturity, undevelopment 406.4; impurity, adulteration 796.3

2 **fault,** *faute* <Fr>, **defect, deficiency, inadequacy,** imperfection, kink, defection <old>; **flaw,** hole, bug <nonformal>; something missing; catch <nonformal>, fly in the ointment, problem, little problem, curate's egg <Brit>, snag, drawback; **crack,** rift; **weakness,** frailty, infirmity, failure, **failing, foible, shortcoming;** weak point, Achilles' heel, vulnerable place, chink in one's armor, weak link; **blemish,** taint 1003.3; **malfunction,** glitch <nonformal>

VERBS 3 **fall short,** come short, miss, miss out, miss the mark, miss by a mile <nonformal>, not qualify, fall down <nonformal>, **not measure up,** not come up to par, not come up to the mark, not come up to scratch *or* to snuff <nonformal>, not pass muster, not bear inspection, not hack it *and* not make it *and* not cut it *and* not make the cut <all nonformal>; not make the grade

ADJS 4 **imperfect,** not perfect; unperfected; **defective, faulty, inadequate, deficient,**

short, not all it's cracked up to be <nonformal>, lacking, wanting, found wanting, "weighed in the balance and found wanting"—Bible; off; erroneous, **fallible;** inaccurate, inexact, imprecise 974.17; **unsound, incomplete,** unfinished, partial, patchy, sketchy, uneven, unthorough; makeshift 994.7; **damaged, impaired** 393.27; mediocre 1004.7; **blemished** 1003.8; half-baked <nonformal>, immature, undeveloped 406.12; impure, adulterated, mixed

ADVS 5 **imperfectly, inadequately,** deficiently; **incompletely,** partially; **faultily, defectively**

1003 BLEMISH

NOUNS 1 **blemish, disfigurement,** disfiguration, **defacement;** scar, keloid, cicatrix; needle scar, track *or* crater <both nonformal>; scratch; scab; blister, vesicle, bulla, bleb; weal, wale, welt, wen, sebaceous cyst; port-wine stain *or* mark, hemangioma, strawberry mark; pock, pustule; pockmark, pit; nevus, birthmark, mole; freckle, lentigo; milium, whitehead, blackhead, comedo, pimple, hickey, sty; wart, verruca; **crack,** craze, check, rift, split; **deformity,** deformation, warp, twist, kink, **distortion; flaw, defect, fault** 1002.2

2 **discoloration,** discolorment, discolor <old>; bruise

3 **stain, taint, tarnish;** mark, brand, **stigma;** maculation, macule, macula; **spot, blot,** blur, **blotch,** patch, speck, speckle, fleck, flick, flyspeck; daub, dab; **smirch, smudge,** smutch *or* smouch, smut, **smear;** splotch, splash, splatter, spatter; bloodstain; eyesore

VERBS 4 **blemish, disfigure,** deface, **flaw, mar;** scab; scar, cicatrize, scarify; **crack,** craze, check, split; **deform,** warp, twist, kink, **distort**

5 **spot,** bespot, **blot, blotch, speck, speckle,** bespeckle, maculate <old>; freckle; flyspeck; **spatter, splatter,** splash, splotch

6 **stain,** bestain, **discolor,** smirch, besmirch, **taint,** attaint, **tarnish; mark, stigmatize,** brand; smear, besmear, daub, bedaub, slubber <Brit nonformal>; blur, slur <nonformal>; **darken, blacken;** smoke, besmoke; scorch, singe, sear; dirty, **soil** 80.16

7 **bloodstain, bloody,** ensanguine

ADJS 8 **blemished, disfigured,** defaced, **marred,** scarred, keloidal, cicatrized, scarified, scabbed, scabby; pimpled, pimply; cracked, crazed, checked, split; deformed, warped, twisted, kinked, distorted; **faulty, flawed, defective** 1002.4

9 **spotted, spotty,** maculate, maculated, macular, blotched, **blotchy,** splotched, splotchy; **speckled,** speckly, bespeckled; freckled, freckly, freckle-faced; spattered, splattered, splashed

10 **stained, discolored,** foxed, foxy, **tainted, tarnished,** smirched, besmirched; stigmatized, stigmatic, stigmatiferous; darkened, blackened, murky, smoky, inky; **soiled** 80.21

11 **bloodstained,** blood-spattered, **bloody,** sanguinary, **gory,** ensanguined

1004 MEDIOCRITY

NOUNS 1 **mediocrity,** mediocreness, fairishness, modestness, modesty, moderateness, middlingness, **indifference;** respectability, passableness, **tolerableness** 998.3; **dullness,** lackluster, tediousness 117.1

2 **ordinariness,** averageness, normalness, normality, **commonness, commonplaceness;** unexceptionality, unremarkableness, unnoteworthiness; conventionality

3 **inferiority,** inferiorness, **poorness,** lowliness, humbleness, **baseness, meanness, commonness,** coarseness, tackiness, tack; **second-rateness,** third-rateness, fourthrateness

4 **low grade,** low class, low quality, poor quality; second best, next best

5 **mediocrity, second-rater,** third-rater, fourth-rater, nothing or nobody special, no great shakes <nonformal>, no prize, no prize package, no brain surgeon, no rocket scientist, not much of a bargain, small potatoes and small beer <both nonformal>; tinhorn <nonformal>; **nobody, nonentity** 997.7; middle class, bourgeoisie, burgherdom; suburbia, the burbs <nonformal>; Middle America, silent majority

6 **irregular,** second, third; schlock <nonformal>

ADJS 7 **mediocre, middling, indifferent, fair, fairish,** fair to middling <nonformal>, moderate, modest, medium, betwixt and between; respectable, passable, **tolerable; so-so,** comme ci comme ça <Fr>; of a kind, of a sort, of sorts <nonformal>; nothing to brag about, not much to boast of, nothing to write home about; "not below mediocrity nor above it"—Johnson; bush-league; dull, lackluster, tedious

117.6; insipid, vapid, wishy-washy, namby-pamby

8 **ordinary, average,** normal, **common, commonplace,** garden and gardenvariety <both nonformal>, run-of-mine or -mill, run-of-the-mine or -mill; **unexceptional, unremarkable, unnoteworthy,** unspectacular, nothing or nobody special and no great shakes <all nonformal>, no prize, no prize package, no brain surgeon, no rocket scientist; conventional; middle-class, bourgeois, plastic <nonformal>; suburban; usual, regular

9 **inferior, poor,** punk <nonformal>, **base, mean, common,** coarse, cheesy and tacky <both nonformal>, tinny; shabby, seedy; cheap, Mickey Mouse <nonformal>, paltry; irregular; second-best; **second-rate,** third-rate, fourth-rate; **second-class,** third-class, fourth-class, etc; **low-grade, low-class,** low-quality, low-test, low-rent and low-ride <both nonformal>

10 **below par,** below standard, **below the mark** <nonformal>, substandard, **not up to scratch** or snuff or the mark <nonformal>, not up to sample or standard or specification, off

ADVS 11 **mediocrely, middlingly,** fairly, fairishly, middling well, fair to middling <nonformal>, moderately, modestly, **indifferently, so-so;** passably, **tolerably**

12 **inferiorly, poorly,** basely, meanly, commonly

1005 DANGER

NOUNS 1 **danger, peril, endangerment, imperilment, jeopardy, hazard, risk,** cause for alarm, **menace, threat** 514; **crisis, emergency,** hot spot, nasty or tricky spot, pass, pinch, strait, plight, predicament 1012.4; powder keg, time bomb; dangerous or unpredictable or uncontrollable person, loose cannon <nonformal>; rocks or breakers or white water ahead, gathering clouds, storm clouds; dangerous ground, yawning or gaping chasm, quicksand, thin ice; hornet's nest; house of cards, cardhouse; hardball <nonformal>, no tea party, no picnic

2 **dangerousness, hazardousness, riskiness, precariousness** 970.6, chanciness, dodginess <chiefly Brit nonformal>, diceyness <nonformal>, **perilousness; unsafeness,** unhealthiness <nonformal>; criticalness; **ticklishness,** slipperiness, touchiness, delicacy, ticklish business and shaky ground <both nonformal>; **in-**

security, unsoundness, instability, unsteadiness, shakiness, totteriness, wonkiness <Brit nonformal>; sword of Damocles; **unreliability,** undependability, untrustworthiness 970.6; **unsureness,** unpredictability, **uncertainty,** doubtfulness, dubiousness 970.2

3 **exposure, openness,** liability, nonimmunity, susceptibility; **unprotectedness, defenselessness,** nakedness, helplessness; lamb, sitting duck

4 **vulnerability,** pregnability, penetrability, assailability, vincibility; weakness 16; vulnerable point, **weak link, weak point, soft spot,** heel of Achilles, chink, chink in one's armor, soft spot, "the soft underbelly"—Sir Winston Churchill

5 <hidden danger> snags, rocks, reefs, ledges; coral heads; shallows, shoals; sandbank, sandbar, sands; quicksands; crevasses; rockbound or ironbound coast, lee shore; undertow, undercurrent; **pitfall;** snake in the grass; trap, booby trap, springe, snare, tripwire, pitfall

VERBS 6 **endanger, imperil,** peril; **risk, hazard, gamble, gamble with; jeopardize,** jeopard, jeopardy, compromise, put in danger, **put in jeopardy,** put on the spot *and* lay on the line <both nonformal>; **expose,** lay open; incur danger, run into *or* encounter danger

7 **take chances, take a chance, chance, risk, gamble,** hazard, press *or* push one's luck, **run the chance** *or* **risk** *or* **hazard;** risk one's neck, run a risk, go out on a limb, stick one's neck out<nonformal>, **expose oneself,** bare one's breast, lower one's guard, **lay oneself open to,** leave oneself wide open, open the door to, let oneself in for; **tempt Providence** *or* fate, forget the odds, **defy danger,** skate on thin ice, court destruction, dance on the razor's edge, go in harm's way, hang by a hair *or* a thread, stand *or* sleep on a volcano, sit on a barrel of gunpowder, build a house of cards, put one's head in the lion's mouth, "beard the lion in his den"—Sir Walter Scott, march up to the cannon's mouth, play with fire, go through fire and water, go out of one's depth, go to sea in a sieve, carry too much sail, sail too near the wind; risk one's life, throw caution to the wind, **take one's life in one's hand, dare, face up to, brave** 492.11

8 **be in danger,** be in peril, be *in extremis,* be in a desperate case, have one's name on the danger list, have the chances *or* odds against one, have one's back to the wall, have something hanging over one's head;

be despaired of; hang by a thread; tremble on the verge, totter on the brink; feel the ground sliding from under one; have to run for it; race against time *or* the clock; be threatened, be on the spot *or* in a bind <both nonformal>

ADJS 9 **dangerous,** dangersome <nonformal>, **perilous,** periculous, parlous, jeopardous, bad, ugly, serious, critical, explosive, attended *or* beset *or* fraught with danger; alarming, too close for comfort *or* words, **menacing, threatening** 514.3

10 **hazardous, risky, chancy,** dodgy <chiefly Brit nonformal>, dicey <nonformal>, aleatory, riskful, full of risk; **adventurous,** venturous, venturesome; **speculative,** wildcat

11 **unsafe,** unhealthy <nonformal>; **unreliable, undependable, untrustworthy,** treacherous, **insecure, unsound,** unstable, unsteady, shaky, tottery, wonky <Brit nonformal>, rocky; **unsure, uncertain,** unpredictable, doubtful, dubious

12 **precarious, ticklish, touchy,** touch-and-go, **critical, delicate;** slippery, slippy; on thin ice, on slippery ground; hanging by a thread, trembling in the balance

13 **in danger, in jeopardy, in peril, at risk,** in a bad way; **endangered, imperiled, jeopardized,** *in periculo* <L>, at the last extremity, *in extremis* <L>, in deadly peril, *in periculo mortis* <L>, in desperate case; threatened, up against it, on the spot *and* on *or* in the hot seat <both nonformal>; sitting on a powder keg; between the hammer and the anvil, between Scylla and Charybdis, between two fires, between the devil and the deep blue sea, between a rock and a hard place <nonformal>; in a predicament 1012.21; cornered

14 **unprotected, unshielded, unsheltered,** uncovered, unscreened, **unguarded, undefended,** unattended, unwatched, unfortified; armorless, unarmored, **unarmed,** bare-handed, weaponless; guardless, ungarrisoned, **defenseless, helpless;** unwarned, unsuspecting

15 **exposed, open,** out in the open, naked; out on a limb <nonformal>; liable, susceptible, nonimmune

16 **vulnerable, pregnable,** penetrable, expugnable; assailable, attackable, surmountable; conquerable, beatable <nonformal>; vincible; weak 16.12–14

ADVS 17 **dangerously, perilously, hazardously, riskily,** critically, unsafely; **precariously,** ticklishly; at gun point

1006 SAFETY

NOUNS **1 safety**, safeness, **security**, surety
<old>, assurance; risklessness, immu-
nity, clear sailing; **protection**, safeguard
1007.3; harmlessness 998.9; airworthi-
ness, crashworthiness, roadworthiness,
seaworthiness; invulnerability 15.4

VERBS **2 be safe, be on the safe side; keep
safe, come through;** weather, ride out,
weather the storm; keep one's head above
water, tide over; land on one's feet; save
one's bacon <nonformal>, save one's
neck; lead a charmed life, have nine lives

 3 play safe <nonformal>, **keep on the safe
side,** give danger a wide berth, watch
oneself, watch out, take precautions
494.6; assure oneself, make sure, keep an
eye or a weather eye out, look before one
leaps; **save, protect** 1007.18

ADJS **4 safe, secure, safe and sound;** immune, immunized; insured; **protected**
1007.21; on the safe side; unthreatened,
unmolested; unhurt, unharmed, unscathed, intact, untouched, with a whole
skin, undamaged

 **5 unhazardous, undangerous, unperilous,
unrisky,** riskless, **unprecarious;** fail-safe,
trouble-free; recession-proof; guaranteed,
warranteed; dependable, reliable, trustworthy, sound, stable, steady, firm
969.17; "founded upon a rock"—Bible; as
safe as houses; harmless; invulnerable

 6 in safety, out of danger, past danger, out
of the meshes or toils, in, home, out of the
woods and over the hump or home free
<all nonformal>, free and dry <Brit non-
formal>, **in the clear, out of harm's reach**
or **way;** under cover, under lock and key;
in shelter, in harbor or port, at anchor or
haven, in the shadow of a rock; on sure or
solid ground, on terra firma, high and dry,
above water

 7 snug, cozy; crashworthy, roadworthy,
airworthy, seaworthy, seakindly

ADVS **8 safely, securely,** reliably, dependably; with safety, **with impunity**

INTERJS **9 all's well!,** all clear!, all serene!,
A-OK!; ally-ally out'n free!

PHRS **10 the danger is past,** the storm has
blown over, the coast is clear

1007 PROTECTION

NOUNS **1 protection, guard, shielding, safekeeping; policing, law enforcement; patrol, patroling,** community policing,
professional or bureaucratic policing;
eye, protectiveness, watchfulness, vigilance, watchful eye, shepherding; house-
sitting <nonformal>; protective custody;
safeguarding, security, security industry,
public safety, **safety** 1006; **shelter, cover,**
shade, shadow <old>, windbreak, lee;
refuge 1008; preservation 397; **defense**
460; protective coating, Teflon coating
<trademark>

 2 protectorship, guardianship, stewardship, custodianship; **care, charge, keeping, nurture, nurturing, nurturance,**
custody, **fostering, fosterage; hands,**
safe hands, wing; **auspices, patronage,
tutelage, guidance; ward,** wardship,
wardenship, watch and ward; cure,
pastorship, pastorage, pastorate; **oversight,** jurisdiction, management, ministry, administration, government, governance; **child care,** infant care, day-care,
family service; baby-sitting, baby-
minding <Brit>

 3 safeguard, palladium, **guard; shield,
screen,** aegis; umbrella, protective umbrella; patent, copyright; **bulwark** 460.4;
backstop; **fender,** mudguard, **bumper,
buffer, cushion,** pad, padding; seat or
safety belt; protective clothing; shin
guard, knuckle guard, knee guard, nose
guard, hand guard, arm guard, ear guard,
finger guard, foot guard; goggles, mask,
face mask, welder's mask, fencer's mask;
safety shoes; helmet, hard hat <non-
formal>, crash helmet, sun helmet;
cowcatcher, pilot; dashboard; windshield, windscreen <Brit>; dodger
and cockpit dodger <both Brit>; life
preserver 397.6; lifeline, safety rail,
guardrail, handrail; governor; safety,
safety switch, interlock; safety valve,
safety plug; fuse, circuit breaker; insulation; safety glass, laminated glass;
lightning rod, lightning conductor; **anchor,** bower, sea anchor, sheet anchor,
drogue; **parachute; safety net;** prophylactic, preventive 86.20; contraceptive 86.23

 4 insurance, assurance <Brit>; **annuity,**
variable annuity; **social security** 611.7;
insurance company, stock company, mutual company; **insurance policy,** policy,
certificate of insurance; deductible; insurance man, underwriter, insurance
broker, insurance agent, insurance ad-
juster, actuary

 5 protector, keeper, protectress, safekeeper; patron, patroness; tower, pillar,
strong arm, tower of strength, rock;
champion, **defender** 460.7

 6 guardian, warden, governor; **custodian,**
steward, **keeper, caretaker,** warder

<Brit>, attendant; caregiver; next friend, prochein ami, guardian *ad litem;* **curator,** conservator; janitor; castellan; **shepherd,** herd, cowherd; **game warden,** gamekeeper; **ranger,** forest ranger, forester; lifeguard, lifesaver <Brit>; air warden; guardian angel

7 **chaperon,** duenna; **governess;** escort

8 **nurse, nursemaid,** nurserymaid, nanny <chiefly Brit>, amah, ayah, mammy <nonformal>; dry nurse, wet nurse; **baby-sitter,** baby-minder <Brit>, sitter <nonformal>

9 **guard,** guarder, guardsman <old>, warder; **outguard, outpost; picket,** outlying picket, inlying picket, outrider; advance guard, **vanguard,** van; **rear guard;** coast guard; armed guard, security guard; jailer 429.10; bank guard; railway *or* train guard; goalkeeper, goaltender, goalie <nonformal>; **garrison;** cordon, *cordon sanitaire* <Fr>

10 **watchman, watch,** watcher; watchkeeper; **lookout,** lookout man; **sentinel,** picket, **sentry; scout,** vedette; **point,** forward observer, spotter; **patrol, patrolman,** patroller, roundsman; night watchman, Charley <nonformal>; fireguard, fire patrolman, fire warden; airplane spotter; Argus

11 **watchdog,** bandog, guard dog, attack dog; sheep dog; Cerberus

12 **doorkeeper, doorman, gatekeeper,** Cerberus, warden, **porter, janitor,** commissionaire <Brit>, *concierge* <Fr>, ostiary, usher; receptionist

13 **picket, picketer,** demonstrator, picket line; counterdemonstrator

14 **bodyguard,** safeguard; **convoy, escort;** guards, praetorian guard; guardsman; yeoman *or* yeoman of the guard *or* beefeater, gentleman-at-arms, Life Guardsman <all England>

15 **policeman, constable, officer, police officer,** *flic* <Fr nonformal>, *gendarme* <Fr>, *carabiniere* <Ital>; peace officer, law enforcement agent, arm of the law; military policeman *or* MP; detective 576.10; policewoman, police matron; patrolman, police constable <England>; trooper, mounted policeman; reeve, portreeve; **sheriff, marshal;** deputy sheriff, deputy, bound bailiff, catchpole, beagle <nonformal>; bombailiff <Brit nonformal>; sergeant, police sergeant; roundsman; lieutenant, police lieutenant; captain, police captain; inspector, police inspector; superintendent, chief of police; commissioner, police commissioner;

government man, federal, fed *and* G-man <both nonformal>; narc <nonformal>; **bailiff,** tipstaff, tipstaves <pl>; macebearer, lictor, sergeant at arms; beadle; traffic officer, meter maid

16 <nonformal terms> cop, copper, John Law, bluecoat, bull, flatfoot, gumshoe, gendarme, shamus, dick, pig, flattie, bizzy *and* bobby *and* peeler <all Brit>, Dogberry; the cops, the law, the fuzz; New York's finest; tec, op

17 **police, police force,** law enforcement agency; **constabulary;** state police, troopers *or* state troopers, highway patrol, county police, provincial police; security force; special police; tactical police, riot police; SWAT *or* special weapons and tactics, SWAT team, **posse,** *posse comitatus* <L>; **vigilantes,** vigilance committee; secret police, political police; Federal Bureau of Investigation *or* FBI; military police *or* MP; shore patrol *or* SP; Scotland Yard <England>; Sûreté <France>; Cheka, NKVD, MVD, OGPU <all USSR>; Gestapo <Germany>; Royal Canadian Mounted Police *or* RCMP, Mounties <all Canada>; Interpol, International Criminal Police Commission

VERBS 18 **protect, guard, safeguard, secure, keep,** bless, make safe, **police, enforce the law;** keep from harm; **insure,** underwrite; ensure, guarantee 438.9; patent, copyright, register; **cushion;** champion, go to bat for <nonformal>; ride shotgun <nonformal>, fend, defend 460.8; **shelter, shield, screen, cover,** cloak, shroud <old>, temper the wind to the shorn lamb; **harbor, haven;** nestle; compass about, fence; arm, armor

19 **care for, take care of;** preserve, conserve; provide for, support; take charge of, **take under one's wing,** make one a *protégé;* **look after,** see after, **attend to, minister to,** look *or* see to, look *or* watch out for <nonformal>, have *or* keep an eye on *or* upon, keep a sharp eye on *or* upon, **watch over,** keep watch over, **watch, mind, tend;** keep tab *or* tabs on <nonformal>; **shepherd,** ride herd on <nonformal>; **chaperon,** matronize; baby-sit <nonformal>; **foster, nurture, cherish, nurse; mother,** be a mother *or* father to

20 **watch, keep watch, keep guard,** keep watch over, keep vigil, keep watch and ward; stand guard, stand sentinel; be on the lookout 339.8; mount guard; **police,** patrol, pound a beat <nonformal>, go on one's beat

ADJS 21 protected, guarded, safeguarded, defended; safe 1006.4–6; patented, copyrighted; **sheltered, shielded,** screened, covered, cloaked; policed; armed 460.14; invulnerable

22 under the protection of, under the shield of, under the auspices of, under the aegis of, **under one's wing,** under the wing of, under the shadow of one's wing

23 protective, custodial, guardian, tutelary; curatorial, vigilant, watchful, on the watch, on top of; prophylactic, preventive; immunizing; protecting, guarding, safeguarding, sheltering, **shielding,** screening, covering; fostering, parental; defensive 460.11; Teflon-coated <trademark>

1008 REFUGE

NOUNS 1 refuge, sanctuary, safehold, **asylum, haven, port,** harborage, **harbor;** harbor of refuge, port in a storm, snug harbor, safe haven; game sanctuary, bird sanctuary, preserve, forest preserve, game preserve; stronghold 460.6; **political asylum**

2 **recourse, resource, resort;** last resort *or* resource, *dernier ressort* and *pis aller* <both Fr>; **hope; expedient** 994.2

3 **shelter, cover, covert,** coverture; concealment 346; *abri* <Fr>, dugout, cave, earth, funk hole <Brit nonformal>, foxhole; **bunker;** trench; storm cellar, storm cave, cyclone cellar; air-raid shelter, bomb shelter, bombproof, fallout shelter, safety zone *or* isle *or* island

4 **asylum, home,** retreat; **poorhouse,** almshouse, workhouse <Brit>, poor farm; **orphanage; hospice,** hospitium; old folks' home, rest home, nursing home, old soldiers' home, sailors' snug harbor; foster home; halfway house; retirement home *or* village *or* community, life-care home, continuing-care retirement community *or* CCRC

5 **retreat,** recess, hiding place, **hideaway,** hideout, hidey-hole <nonformal>; **sanctum, inner sanctum, sanctum sanctorum,** holy ground, holy of holies, adytum; private place, privacy <old>, secret place; **den,** lair, mew; safe house; **cloister,** hermitage, ashram, cell; **ivory tower;** study, library

6 **harbor, haven, port, seaport,** port of call, free port, treaty port, home port; hoverport; harborage, **anchorage,** anchorage ground, protected anchorage, moorage, moorings; **roadstead,** road, roads; berth,

slip; **dock,** dockage, marina, basin; dry dock; shipyard, dockyard; **wharf, pier,** quay; harborside, dockside, pierside, quayside, landing, landing place *or* stage, jetty, jutty <old>; breakwater, mole, groin; seawall, embankment, bulkhead

VERBS 7 take refuge, take shelter, seek refuge, **claim sanctuary,** claim refugee status; run into port; fly to, throw oneself into the arms of; bar the gate, lock *or* bolt the door, raise the drawbridge, let the portcullis down; take cover 346.8

8 **find refuge** *or* sanctuary, make port, reach safety; seclude *or* sequester oneself, dwell *or* live in an ivory tower

1009 PROSPERITY

NOUNS 1 prosperity, prosperousness, thriving *or* flourishing condition; **success** 409; **welfare, well-being,** weal, happiness, felicity; quality of life; comfortable *or* easy circumstances, **comfort, ease,** security; **life of ease,** the life of Riley <nonformal>, **the good life; clover** *and* velvet <both nonformal>, **bed of roses, luxury,** lap of luxury, Easy Street *and* Fat City *and* hog heaven <all nonformal>; the affluent life, gracious life, gracious living; fat of the land; fleshpots, fleshpots of Egypt; milk and honey, loaves and fishes; a chicken in every pot, a car in every garage; purple and fine linen; high standard of living; upward mobility; **affluence, wealth** 618

2 **good fortune** *or* **luck,** happy fortune, **fortune, luck,** the breaks <nonformal>; **fortunateness, luckiness,** felicity <old>; blessing, smiles of fortune, fortune's favor

3 **stroke of luck,** piece of good luck; blessing; **fluke** *and* lucky strike *and* scratch hit *and* **break** <all nonformal>, **good** *or* **lucky break** <nonformal>; **run** *or* **streak of luck** <nonformal>

4 **good times,** piping times, bright *or* palmy *or* halcyon days, days of wine and roses, rosy era; heyday; prosperity, era of prosperity; fair weather, sunshine; golden era, **golden age,** golden time, Saturnian age, reign of Saturn, *Saturnia regna* <L>; age of Aquarius, millennium; **utopia** 985.11; **heaven** 681

5 **roaring trade, land-office business** <nonformal>, bullishness, bull market, seller's market; **boom,** booming economy, expanding economy

6 **lucky dog** <nonformal>, fortune's favorite, favorite of the gods, fortune's child, destiny's darling

VERBS **7 prosper,** enjoy prosperity, **fare
well,** get on well, do well, have it made *or*
hacked <nonformal>, have a good thing
going, have everything going one's way,
get on swimmingly, go great guns
<nonformal>; **turn out well, go well,**
take a favorable turn; **succeed;** come on
or along <nonformal>, come a long way,
get on <nonformal>; **advance,** progress,
make progress, make headway, get ahead
<nonformal>, move up in the world, pull
oneself up by one's own boot-straps

8 thrive, flourish, boom; blossom, bloom,
flower; batten, fatten, grow fat; be fat,
dumb, and happy <nonformal>

**9 be prosperous, make good, make one's
mark,** rise *or* get on in the world, make a
noise in the world <nonformal>, do all
right by oneself <nonformal>, **make
one's fortune;** grow rich; drive a roaring
trade, do a land-office business <nonfor-
mal>, rejoice in a seller's market

10 live well, live in clover *or* on velvet
<nonformal>, **live a life of ease,** live *or*
lead the life of Riley, **live high, live high
on the hog** <nonformal>, live on *or* off
the fat of the land, ride the gravy train
and piss on ice <both nonformal>, roll in
the lap of luxury; bask in the sunshine,
have one's place in the sun; have a good
or fine time of it

11 be fortunate, be lucky, be in luck, luck
out <nonformal>, have all the luck, have
one's moments <nonformal>, **lead** *or*
have a charmed life; fall into the shithouse and come up with a five-dollar gold
piece <nonformal>; **get a break** *and* get
the breaks <both nonformal>; hold aces
and turn up trumps *or* roses <all nonfor-
mal>; have a run of luck *and* hit a streak
of luck <both nonformal>; have it break
good for one <nonformal>, have a stroke
of luck; strike it lucky *and* make a lucky
strike *and* strike oil <all nonformal>,
strike it rich <nonformal>, hit it big
<nonformal>, strike a rich vein, come
into money, drop into a good thing

ADJS **12 prosperous,** in good case; **successful,**
rags-to-riches; **well-paid, high-income,**
higher-income, well-heeled *and* upscale
<both nonformal>; **affluent, wealthy;
comfortable,** comfortably situated, **easy;**
on Easy Street *and* in Fat City *and* in hog
heaven <all nonformal>, **in clover** *and*
on velvet <both nonformal>, on a bed of
roses, in luxury, high on the hog <nonfor-
mal>; up in the world, on top of the heap
<nonformal>

13 thriving, flourishing, prospering, boom-
ing <nonformal>; vigorous, exuberant;
in full swing, going strong <nonformal>;
halcyon, palmy, balmy, rosy, piping,
clear, fair; blooming, blossoming, flowering, fruiting; fat, sleek, in good case; fat,
dumb, and happy <nonformal>

**14 fortunate, lucky, providential; in luck;
blessed,** blessed with luck, favored; born
under a lucky star, born with a silver
spoon in one's mouth, born on the sunny
side of the hedge; out of the woods, over
the hump; **auspicious**

ADVS **15 prosperously, thrivingly, flour-
ishingly,** boomingly, swimmingly
<nonformal>

16 fortunately, luckily, providentially

1010 ADVERSITY

NOUNS **1 adversity,** adverse circumstances,
difficulties, hard knocks *and* rough going <both nonformal>, **hardship,
trouble,** troubles, "sea of troubles"—
Shakespeare, **rigor,** vicissitude, care,
stress, pressure, stress of life; hard case
or plight, **hard life,** dog's life, vale of
tears; wretched *or* miserable *or* hard *or*
unhappy lot, tough *or* hard row to hoe
<nonformal>, ups and downs of life,
things going against one; bummer *and*
downer <both nonformal>; the bad part,
the downside <nonformal>; annoyance,
irritation, aggravation; **difficulty** 1012;
trial, tribulation, cross, curse, blight,
affliction 96.8; plight, predicament
1012.4

2 misfortune, mishap, ill hap, **misadventure, mischance,** *contretemps* <Fr>, grief;
disaster, calamity, catastrophe, meltdown, cataclysm; **tragedy; shock, blow,**
hard *or* nasty *or* staggering blow; **accident,** casualty, collision, crash, plane *or*
car crash; **wreck,** shipwreck; smash *and*
smashup *and* crack-up *and* pileup <all
nonformal>

3 reverse, reversal, reversal of fortune, **setback,** check, severe check, backset *and*
throwback <both nonformal>; **comedown,** descent, down

4 unfortunateness, unluckiness, luckless-
ness, ill success; unprosperousness;
starcrossed *or* ill-fated life; "the slings
and arrows of outrageous fortune"—
Shakespeare; inauspiciousness 133.8

5 bad luck, ill luck, hard luck, hard lines
<Brit>, **tough** *or* **rotten luck** <nonfor-
mal>, raw deal <nonformal>, bad *or*
tough *or* rotten break <nonformal>,
devil's own luck; **ill fortune,** bad fortune,

evil fortune, evil star, ill wind, evil dispensation; frowns of fortune

6 hard times, bad times, sad times; evil day, ill day; rainy day; hard *or* stormy *or* heavy weather; **depression,** recession, **slump,** economic stagnation, **bust** <nonformal>

7 unfortunate, poor unfortunate, the plaything *or* toy *or* sport of fortune, fortune's fool; **loser** *and* sure loser *and* non-starter <all nonformal>; hard case *and* sad sack *and* hard-luck guy <all nonformal>; *schlemiel, schlimazel* <both Yiddish>; odd man out; the underclass, the dispossessed, the homeless, the wretched of the earth; victim 96.11

VERBS **8 go hard with,** go ill with; run one hard; **oppress, weigh on** *or* **upon,** weigh heavy on, weigh down, **burden,** overburden, load, overload, bear hard upon, lie on, lie hard *or* heavy upon; try one, put one out

9 have trouble; be born to trouble, be born under an evil star, be "born unto trouble, as the sparks fly upward"—Bible; **have a hard time of it,** be up against it <nonformal>, make heavy weather of it, meet adversity, have a bad time, lead *or* live a dog's life, have a tough *or* hard row to hoe; bear the brunt, bear more than one's share; be put to one's wit's end, not know which way to turn; **be unlucky, have bad** *or* **rotten luck,** be misfortuned, get the short *or* shitty end of the stick <nonformal>

10 come to grief, have a mishap, suffer a misfortune, fall, be stricken, be staggered, be shattered, be poleaxed, be felled, come a cropper <Brit nonformal>, be clobbered <nonformal>; run aground, go on the rocks *or* shoals, split upon a rock; sink, drown; **founder**

11 fall on evil days, go *or* **come down in the world,** go downhill, slip, be on the skids <nonformal>, come down, have a comedown, fall from one's high estate; **deteriorate,** degenerate, run *or* go to seed, sink, decline; **go to pot** <nonformal>, go to the dogs; reach the depths, touch bottom, hit rock bottom; have seen better days

12 bring bad luck; hoodoo *and* hex *and* jinx *and* Jonah *and* put the jinx on <all nonformal>; put the evil eye on, whammy <nonformal>

ADJS **13 adverse, untoward, detrimental, unfavorable;** sinister; hostile, antagonistic, inimical; contrary, counter, counteractive, conflicting, opposing, opposed, opposite, in opposition; **difficult, trouble-**

some, **troublous, hard,** trying, rigorous, stressful; wretched, miserable 96.26; **not easy;** harmful 999.12

14 unfortunate, unlucky, unprovidential, unblessed, **unprosperous,** sad, unhappy, hapless, fortuneless, misfortuned, luckless, donsie <Brit nonformal>; **out of luck,** short of luck; **down on one's luck** <nonformal>, badly *or* ill off, down in the world, in adverse circumstances; underprivileged, depressed; ill-starred, evil-starred, born under a bad sign, born under an evil star, planet-stricken, planet-struck, star-crossed; fatal, dire, doomful, funest <old>, **ominous, inauspicious** 133.17; **in a jam** *and* in a pickle *or* pretty pickle *and* in a tight spot *and* between a rock and a hard place <all nonformal>, between the devil and the deep blue sea, caught in the crossfire *or* middle; up a tree *and* up the creek *or* up shit creek without a paddle *and* up to one's ass in alligators <all nonformal>

15 disastrous, calamitous, catastrophic, cataclysmic, cataclysmal, **tragic,** ruinous, wreckful <old>, fatal, dire, black, woeful, sore, baneful, grievous; destructive 395.26; **life-threatening, terminal**

ADVS **16 adversely, untowardly,** detrimentally, **unfavorably;** contrarily, conflictingly, opposingly, oppositely

17 unfortunately, unluckily, unprovidentially, sadly, unhappily, **as ill luck would have it;** by ill luck, by ill hap; in adverse circumstances, if worse comes to worse

18 disastrously, calamitously, catastrophically, cataclysmically, grievously, woefully, sorely, banefully, tragically, crushingly, shatteringly

INTERJS **19 tough luck!,** tough tiddy! *and* tough shit! *and* tough darts! <all nonformal>

1011 HINDRANCE

NOUNS **1 hindrance,** hindering, **hampering,** let, let or hindrance; **check, arrest,** arrestment, arrestation; fixation; **impediment,** holdback; **resistance, opposition** 451; suppression, **repression, restriction, restraint** 428; **obstruction,** blocking, blockage, clogging, occlusion; **bottleneck,** traffic jam, gridlock; speed bump, sleeping policeman <Brit>; **interruption,** interference; **retardation,** retardment, **detention,** detainment, **delay,** holdup, setback; **inhibition;** constriction, squeeze, stricture, cramp, stranglehold; **closure,** closing up *or* off; obstructionism, bloody-mindedness <Brit>, negativism, foot-dragging <nonformal>; nuisance value

2 **prevention, stop, stoppage, stopping**, arrestation, estoppel; stay, staying, halt, halting; **prohibition**, forbiddance; debarment; **determent**, deterrence, **discouragement; forestalling, preclusion, obviation**, foreclosure

3 **frustration, thwarting, balking, foiling; discomfiture, disconcertion**, bafflement, confounding; **defeat**, upset; check, checkmate, balk, foil <old>; derailing, derailment

4 **obstacle, obstruction**, obstructer; **hang-up** <nonformal>; **block**, blockade, cordon, curtain; **difficulty**, hurdle, hazard; **deterrent**, determent; **drawback**, objection; **stumbling block**, stumbling stone, stone in one's path; fly in the ointment, one small difficulty, **hitch, catch**, joker <nonformal>, a "but," a "however"

5 **barrier, bar**; gate, portcullis; **fence, wall**, stone wall, brick wall, impenetrable wall; seawall, jetty, groin, mole, breakwater; **bulwark, rampart**, defense, buffer, bulkhead, parapet, breastwork, work, earthwork, mound; bank, embankment, levee, dike; ditch, moat; dam, weir, leaping weir, barrage, milldam, beaver dam, cofferdam, wicket dam, shutter dam, beartrap dam, hydraulic-fill dam, rock-fill dam, arch dam, arch-gravity dam, gravity dam; boom, jam, logjam; roadblock; backstop; iron curtain, bamboo curtain

6 **impediment**, embarrassment, hamper; encumbrance, cumbrance; **trouble**, difficulty 1012; **handicap**, disadvantage, inconvenience, penalty; white elephant; **burden**, burthen <old>, imposition, onus, cross, weight, deadweight, ball and chain, millstone around one's neck; **load**, pack, cargo, freight, charge; impedimenta, lumber

7 **curb, check**, countercheck, arrest, **stay, stop**, damper, holdback; **brake**, clog, drag, drogue, remora; chock, scotch, spoke, spoke in one's wheel; doorstop; check-rein, bearing rein, martingale; bit, snaffle, pelham, curb bit; shackle, chain, fetter, trammel 428.4; sea anchor, drift anchor, drift sail, drag sail or sheet

8 **hinderer**, impeder, **marplot**, obstructer; frustrater, thwarter; obstructionist, negativist; filibuster, filibusterer

9 **spoilsport**, wet blanket, **killjoy**, grouch, grinch and sourpuss <both nonformal>, malcontent, **dog in the manger** <nonformal>

VERBS 10 **hinder, impede, inhibit, arrest, check**, countercheck, scotch, **curb**, snub; **resist, oppose** 451.3; stonewall <nonformal>, stall, stall off; **suppress, repress** 428.8; **interrupt**, intercept <old>; intervene, interfere, intermeddle, meddle 214.7; damp, dampen, pour or dash or throw cold water; **retard**, slacken, **delay**, detain, **hold back, keep back**, set back, hold up <nonformal>; **restrain** 428.7; keep or hold in check, bottle up, dam up

11 **hamper, impede, cramp**, embarrass; trammel, entrammel, enmesh, entangle, ensnarl, entrap, entwine, involve, entoil, toil, net, lime, tangle, snarl; fetter, shackle; **handcuff**, tie one's hands; **encumber**, cumber, **burden**, lumber, **saddle with**, weigh or weight down, press down; hang like a millstone round one's neck; **handicap**, put at a disadvantage; lame, cripple, hobble, hamstring

12 **obstruct**, get or stand in the way; dog, **block**, block the way, put up a roadblock, blockade, block up, occlude; **jam**, crowd, pack; **bar**, barricade, bolt, lock; **debar**, shut out; shut off, **close**, close off or up, close tight, shut tight; constrict, squeeze, squeeze shut, **strangle**, strangulate, **stifle**, suffocate, **choke**, choke off, chock; stop up 293.7

13 **stop, stay, halt**, bring to a stop, put a stop or end to, bring to a shuddering or screeching halt <nonformal>; **brake**, slow down, put on the brakes, hit the brakes <nonformal>; **block, stall, stymie**, deadlock; nip in the bud

14 **prevent, prohibit, forbid, bar**, estop; save, help, **keep from; deter, discourage**, dishearten; **avert, parry, keep off, ward off, stave off, fend off**, fend, repel, deflect, turn aside; **forestall**, foreclose, **preclude**, exclude, debar, **obviate**, anticipate; rule out

15 **thwart, frustrate, foil, cross, balk**; spike, scotch, checkmate; **counter**, contravene, counteract, countermand, counterwork; stand in the way of, confront, brave, defy, challenge; **defeat** 412.6,8,9; **discomfit**, upset, **disrupt, confound**, flummox <nonformal>, discountenance, put out of countenance, **disconcert, baffle**, nonplus, perplex, stump <nonformal>; throw on one's beam ends, trip one up, throw one for a loss <nonformal>; **circumvent**, elude; sabotage, **spoil, ruin**, dish <nonformal>, dash, blast; **destroy** 395.10; throw a wrench in the machinery, **throw a monkey wrench or spanner** <Brit> **into the works** <nonformal>; put a spoke in

one's wheel, scotch one's wheel, spike one's guns, put one's nose out of joint <nonformal>, upset one's applecart; **derail;** take the wind out of one's sails, steal one's thunder, cut the ground from under one, knock the chocks *or* props from under one, knock the bottom out of <nonformal>; tie one's hands, clip one's wings

16 <nonformal terms> **queer, crab, foul up, louse up,** snafu, bollix *or* bollix up, gum, **gum up,** gum up the works; crimp, cramp, **put a crimp in,** cramp one's style; cook one's goose, cut one down to size; give one a hard time

ADJS 17 **hindering,** troublesome; **inhibitive,** inhibiting, suppressive, repressive; constrictive, strangling, stifling, choking; restrictive 428.12; **obstructive,** obstructing, occlusive, obstruent <old>; cantankerous <nonformal>, bloody-minded <Brit>, contrary, crosswise; interruptive, interrupting; in the way

18 **hampering, impeding, counterproductive,** impedimental, impeditive; onerous, oppressive, burdensome, cumbersome, cumbrous, encumbering

19 **preventive,** preventative, avertive, prophylactic; **prohibitive, forbidding; deterrent,** deterring, **discouraging;** preclusive, forestalling

20 **frustrating,** confounding, disconcerting, baffling, defeating

ADVS 21 **under handicap,** at a disadvantage, on the hip <old>, with everything against one

1012 DIFFICULTY

NOUNS 1 **difficulty,** difficultness; "the nurse of greatness"—William Cullen Bryant; **hardness, toughness** <nonformal>, the hard way <nonformal>, **rigor,** rigorousness, ruggedness; **arduousness,** laboriousness, strenuousness, toilsomeness; **troublesomeness,** bothersomeness; onerousness, oppressiveness, burdensomeness; formidability, hairiness <nonformal>; complication, intricacy, **complexity** 798; abstruseness 522.2

2 **tough proposition** *and* tough one *and* toughie <all nonformal>, large *or* tall order <nonformal>; **hard job, tough job** *and* heavy lift <both nonformal>, backbreaker, ballbuster <nonformal>, **chore,** man-sized job; brutal task, Herculean task, Augean task; **uphill work** *or* **going,** rough go <nonformal>, **heavy sledding,** hard pull <nonformal>, dead lift <old>; tough lineup to buck <nonformal>, hard

road to travel; hard *or* tough nut to crack *and* hard *or* tough row to hoe *and* hard row of stumps <all nonformal>; bitch <nonformal>; **handful** <nonformal>, all one can manage

3 **trouble, the matter;** headache <nonformal>, problem, besetment, **inconvenience,** disadvantage; the bad part, the downside <nonformal>; **ado,** great ado; peck of troubles, "sea of troubles"—Shakespeare; hornet's nest, Pandora's box, can of worms <nonformal>; **evil** 999.3; **bother, annoyance** 98.7; **anxiety, worry** 126.2

4 **predicament, plight,** spot of trouble, **strait,** straits, parlous straits, tightrope, knife-edge, thin edge; **pinch, bind,** pass, clutch, situation, emergency; pretty pass, nice *or* pretty predicament, pretty *or* fine state of affairs, **sorry plight;** slough, quagmire, morass, swamp, quicksand; **embarrassment,** embarrassing position *or* situation; **complication,** imbroglio; the devil to pay

5 <nonformal terms> **pickle,** crunch, hobble, pretty pickle, fine kettle of fish, how-do-you-do, fine how-do-you-do; **spot, tight spot; squeeze, tight squeeze,** ticklish *or* tricky spot, hot spot, hot seat, sticky wicket <Brit>; **scrape, jam, hot water,** tail in a gate, tit in the wringer; **mess,** holy *or* unholy mess, mix, stew; hell to pay

6 **impasse, corner** *and* **box** *and* **hole** <all nonformal>, cleft stick; **cul-de-sac, blind alley, dead end,** dead-end street; **extremity, end of one's rope** *or* **tether,** wit's end, nowhere to turn; **stalemate,** deadlock; stand, standoff, standstill, halt, stop

7 **dilemma,** horns of a dilemma, double bind, damned-if-you-do-and-damned-if-you-don't, no-win situation, **quandary,** nonplus; **vexed question,** thorny problem, knotty point, knot, crux, node, nodus, Gordian knot, poser, teaser, perplexity, puzzle, enigma 522.8; paradox, oxymoron; asses' bridge, *pons asinorum* <L>

8 **crux, hitch, pinch, rub,** snag, catch, joker <nonformal>, where the shoe pinches

9 **unwieldiness, unmanageability; unhandiness,** inconvenience, impracticality; **awkwardness, clumsiness; cumbersomeness,** ponderousness, bulkiness, hulkiness

VERBS 10 **be difficult, present difficulties, take some doing** <nonformal>

11 **have difficulty, have trouble,** have a rough time <nonformal>, hit a snag, have a hard time of it, have one's hands

full, get off to a bad start *or* on the wrong foot; be hard put, have much ado with; labor under difficulties, labor under a disadvantage, have the cards stacked against one *and* have two strikes against one <both nonformal>; struggle, **flounder,** beat about, make heavy weather of it; have one's back to the wall, not know where to turn, come to a dead end *or* standstill, not know whether one is coming or going, go around in circles, swim against the current; walk a tightrope, walk on eggshells *or* hot coals, dance on a hot griddle

12 **get into trouble,** plunge into difficulties; **let oneself in for, put one's foot in it** <nonformal>; **get in a jam** *or* **hot water** *or* **the soup** <nonformal>, **get into a scrape** <nonformal>, **get in a mess** *or* **hole** *or* **box** *or* **bind** <nonformal>; paint oneself into a corner <nonformal>, get one's ass in a bind *and* put oneself in a spot <both nonformal>, put one's foot in one's mouth; have a tiger by the tail; burn one's fingers; get all tangled *or* snarled *or* wound up, get all balled *or* bollixed up <nonformal>

13 **trouble,** beset; **bother,** pother, get one down, <nonformal>, **disturb, perturb,** irk, plague, **torment,** drive one up the wall <nonformal>, give one gray hair, make one lose sleep; **harass, vex, distress** 96.16; inconvenience, **put out,** put out of the way, discommode 995.4; **concern, worry** 126.3; **puzzle, perplex** 970.13; put to it, give one trouble, complicate matters; give one a hard time *and* give one a bad time *and* make it tough for <all nonformal>; be too much for; ail, be the matter

14 **cause trouble,** bring trouble, "sow the wind and reap the whirlwind"—Bible; ask for trouble, ask for it <nonformal>, bring down upon one, bring down upon one's head, bring down around one's ears; **stir up a hornet's nest,** kick up *or* piss up a fuss *or* storm *or* row <nonformal>; bring a hornet's nest about one's ears, open Pandora's box, open a can of worms <nonformal>, put fire to tow; **raise hob** *or* **hell** <nonformal>; raise merry hell *and* play hob *and* play hell <all nonformal>, play the deuce *or* devil <nonformal>

15 **put in a hole** <nonformal>, put in a spot <nonformal>; **embarrass; involve,** enmesh, entangle

16 **corner,** run *and* drive into a corner <both nonformal>, **tree** <nonformal>, chase up

a tree *or* stump <nonformal>, drive *or* force to the wall, push one to the wall, put one's back to the wall, have one on the ropes <nonformal>

ADJS 17 **difficult,** difficile; **not easy,** no picnic; **hard, tough** *and* **rough** *and* **rugged** <all nonformal>, rigorous, brutal, severe; wicked *and* mean *and* **hairy** <all nonformal>, **formidable; arduous, strenuous, toilsome, laborious,** operose, Herculean; steep, uphill; hard-fought; hard-earned; jawbreaking; knotty, knotted; thorny, spiny, set with thorns; delicate, ticklish, tricky, sticky <nonformal>, critical, easier said than done, like pulling teeth; exacting, demanding; intricate, complex 798.4; abstruse 522.16

18 **troublesome,** besetting; **bothersome,** irksome, vexatious, painful, plaguey <nonformal>, annoying 98.22; **burdensome,** oppressive, onerous, heavy *and* hefty <both nonformal>, crushing, backbreaking; **trying,** grueling

19 **unwieldy, unmanageable, unhandy;** inconvenient, impractical; **awkward, clumsy, cumbersome,** unmaneuverable; contrary, perverse, crosswise; ponderous, bulky, hulky, hulking

20 **troubled,** trouble-plagued, beset, sore beset; **bothered, vexed,** irked, annoyed 96.21; plagued, **harassed** 96.24; distressed, perturbed 96.22; inconvenienced, embarrassed; put to it *and* hard put to it <both nonformal>; **worried, anxious** 126.6,7; puzzled

21 **in trouble, in deep trouble, in a predicament, in a sorry plight,** in a pretty pass; in deep water, out of one's depth

22 <nonformal terms> **in deep shit** *or* doo-doo, in a jam, in a pickle, in a pretty pickle, in a spot, in a tight spot, in a fix, in a hole, in a bind, in a box; in a mess, in a scrape, in hot water, in the soup; up a tree, up to one's ass in alligators, up the creek, up shit creek without a paddle, in Dutch, on the spot, behind the eight ball, on Queer Street, out on a limb, on the hot seat

23 **in a dilemma,** on the horns of a dilemma, **in a quandary;** between two stools; between Scylla and Charybdis, between the devil and the deep blue sea, between a rock and a hard place <nonformal>

24 **at an impasse, at one's wit's end, at a loss,** at a stand *or* standstill; **nonplussed,** at a nonplus; **baffled, perplexed, bewildered,** mystified, stuck *and* stumped <both nonformal>, stymied

25 **cornered,** in a corner, with one's back to

the wall; **treed** *and* **up a tree** *and* up a
stump <all nonformal>; **at bay,** *aux
abois* <Fr>

26 **straitened,** reduced to dire straits, in desperate straits, **pinched,** sore *or* sorely
pressed, **hard-pressed, hard up** <nonfor-
mal>, **up against it** <nonformal>; driven
from pillar to post; **desperate, in extremi-
ties,** *in extremis* <L>, **at the end of one's
rope** *or* **tether**

27 **stranded, grounded,** aground, **on the
rocks,** high and dry; **stuck,** stuck *or* set
fast; foundered, swamped; castaway,
marooned, wrecked, shipwrecked

ADVS 28 **with difficulty,** difficultly, with
much ado; hardly, painfully; the hard
way, **arduously, strenuously, laboriously,**
toilsomely

29 **unwieldily, unmanageably, unhandily,**
inconveniently; **awkwardly, clumsily,
cumbersomely;** ponderously

1013 FACILITY

NOUNS **1 facility, ease, easiness,** facileness,
effortlessness; lack of hindrance, **smoothness,** freedom; clear coast, clear road *or*
course; smooth road, royal road, highroad; easy going, plain sailing, smooth *or*
straight sailing; clarity, intelligibility
521; uncomplexity, uncomplicatedness,
simplicity 797

2 **handiness, wieldiness,** wieldableness,
handleability, **manageability,** man-
ageableness, maneuverability; **convenience,** practicality, untroublesome-
ness; **flexibility,** pliancy, **pliability,** ductility, malleability; adaptability, feasibility

3 **easy thing,** mere child's play, simple matter, mere twist of the wrist; easy target,
sitting duck <nonformal>; sinecure

4 <nonformal terms> **cinch, snap,** pushover, breeze, waltz, duck soup, velvet,
picnic, pie, cherry pie, apple pie, cake-
walk, piece of cake <Brit>, kid stuff,
turkey shoot, no-brainer, setup

5 **facilitation, facilitating, easing,** smoothing, smoothing out, smoothing the way;
speeding, expediting, expedition, quickening, hastening; streamlining; lubricating, greasing, oiling

6 **disembarrassment, disentanglement,
disencumbrance,** disinvolvement, uncluttering, uncomplicating, unscrambling, unsnarling, disburdening, unham-
pering; **extrication,** disengagement,
freeing, clearing; deregulation; **simplification** 797.2

VERBS **7 facilitate, ease; grease the wheels**
<nonformal>; **smooth, smooth** *or* **pave
the way,** ease the way, grease *or* soap the
ways <both nonformal>, prepare the
way, **clear the way,** make all clear for,
make way for; run interference for
<nonformal>, open the way, open the
door to; **open up, unclog,** unblock, unjam,
unbar, loose 431.6; **lubricate,** make frictionless *or* dissipationless, remove
friction, grease, oil; **speed, expedite,**
quicken, hasten; **help along,** help on its
way; **aid** 449.11; **explain,** make clear
521.6; **simplify** 797.4

8 **do easily,** make short work of, do with
one's hands tied behind one's back, do
with both eyes shut, do standing on one's
head, do hands down, sail *or* dance *or*
waltz through, wing it <nonformal>

9 **disembarrass, disencumber, unload,** relieve, disburden, unhamper, get out from
under; **disentangle,** disembroil, disinvolve, unclutter, unscramble, unsnarl;
extricate, disengage, **free,** free up, clear;
liberate 431.4

10 **go easily, run smoothly,** work well, work
like a machine, go like clockwork *or* a
sewing machine; present no difficulties,
give no trouble, be painless, be effortless;
flow, roll, glide, slide, coast, sweep, sail

11 **have it easy, have it soft** <nonformal>,
have it all one's own way, have the game
in one's hands; win easily; breeze in
<nonformal>, walk over the course
<nonformal>, win in a walk *or* in a can-
ter *or* hands down <nonformal>

12 **take it easy** *and* **go easy** <both nonfor-
mal>, swim with the stream, drift with
the current, go with the tide; cool it *and*
not sweat it <both nonformal>; take it in
one's stride, make little *or* light of, think
nothing of

ADJS **13 easy, facile, effortless,** smooth, painless; soft <nonformal>, cushy <nonfor-
mal>; plain, uncomplicated, straightforward, **simple** 797.6, Mickey Mouse
<nonformal>, simple as ABC <nonfor-
mal>, easy as pie *and* easy as falling off a
log <both nonformal>, downhill all the
way, like shooting fish in a barrel, like
taking candy from a baby; **clear;** glib;
light, unburdensome; nothing to it; casual, throwaway <nonformal>

14 **smooth-running,** frictionless, dissipationless, easy-running, easy-flowing; well-
lubricated, well-oiled, well-greased

15 **handy, wieldy,** wieldable, handleable;
tractable; flexible, pliant, yielding, malleable, ductile, pliable, **manageable,**

maneuverable; **convenient,** foolproof, goofproof <nonformal>, practical, untroublesome, user-friendly; adaptable, feasible

ADVS **16 easily,** facilely, **effortlessly, readily, simply,** lightly, swimmingly <nonformal>, without difficulty; no sweat *and* like nothing *and* slick as a whistle <all nonformal>; hands down <nonformal>, with one hand tied behind one's back, with both eyes closed, standing on one's head; like a duck takes to water; **smoothly,** frictionlessly, like clockwork; on easy terms

1014 UGLINESS

NOUNS **1 ugliness, unsightliness, unattractiveness,** uncomeliness, unhandsomeness, unbeautifulness, unprettiness, unloveliness, unaestheticness, unpleasingness 98.1; unprepossessingness, illfavoredness, inelegance; **homeliness,** plainness; unshapeliness, shapelessness; ungracefulness, gracelessness, clumsiness, ungainliness 414.3; **uglification, uglifying, disfigurement,** defacement; dysphemism; cacophony

2 hideousness, horridness, horribleness, frightfulness, dreadfulness, terribleness, awfulness <nonformal>; **repulsiveness** 98.2, repugnance, repugnancy, repellence, repellency, offensiveness, forbiddingness, loathsomeness; ghastliness, gruesomeness, grisliness; **deformity,** misshapenness

3 forbidding countenance, vinegar aspect, wry face, face that would stop a clock

4 eyesore, blot, blot on the landscape, blemish, **sight** <nonformal>, **fright, horror, mess,** no beauty, no beauty queen, ugly duckling; baboon; **scarecrow,** gargoyle, monster, **monstrosity,** teratism; witch, bag *and* dog <both nonformal>, **hag,** harridan; Loathly Lady

VERBS **5 offend,** offend the eye, offend one's aesthetic sensibilities, **look bad;** look something terrible *and* look like hell *and* look like the devil *and* look a sight *or* a fright *or* a mess *or* like something the cat dragged in <all nonformal>; **uglify, disfigure,** deface, blot, blemish, mar, spoil; dysphemize

ADJS **6 ugly, unsightly, unattractive, unhandsome, unpretty, unlovely,** uncomely, inelegant; **unbeautiful,** unbeauteous, beautiless, unaesthetic, unpleasing 98.17; **homely, plain;** not much to look at, not much for looks, short on looks <nonfor-

mal>, hard on the eyes <nonformal>; ugly as sin, ugly as the wrath of God, ugly as hell, homely as a mud fence, homely enough to sour milk, homely enough to stop a clock, not fit to be seen; **uglified, disfigured,** defaced, blotted, blemished, marred, spoiled; dysphemized, dysphemistic; cacophonous, cacophonic

7 unprepossessing, ill-favored, hardfavored, evil-favored, ill-featured; illlooking, evil-looking; hard-featured, hard-visaged; grim, grim-faced, grimvisaged; hatchet-faced, horse-faced

8 unshapely, shapeless, **ill-shaped,** illmade, ill-proportioned; **deformed,** misshapen, misproportioned, malformed, misbegotten; grotesque, scarecrowish, gargoylish; monstrous, teratic, cacogenic

9 ungraceful, ungraced, graceless; clumsy, clunky <nonformal>, **ungainly** 414.20

10 inartistic, unartistic, **unaesthetic; unornamental, undecorative**

11 hideous, horrid, horrible, frightful, dreadful, terrible, awful <nonformal>; **repulsive** 98.18, repellent, repelling, rebarbative, **repugnant,** offensive, foul, forbidding, loathsome, loathly <old>, revolting; **ghastly,** gruesome, grisly

ADVS **12 uglily,** homelily, uncomelily, **unattractively, unhandsomely, unbeautifully, unprettily**

13 hideously, horridly, horribly, frightfully, dreadfully, terribly, awfully <nonformal>; **repulsively, repugnantly,** offensively, forbiddingly, loathsomely, revoltingly; gruesomely, ghastly

1015 BEAUTY

NOUNS **1 beauty, beautifulness,** beauteousness, **prettiness, handsomeness, attractiveness** 97.2, wellfavoredness, **loveliness, pulchritude, charm,** grace, elegance, exquisiteness; bloom, glow; the beautiful; source of aesthetic pleasure *or* delight; beauty unadorned

2 "truth's smile when she beholds her own face in a perfect mirror"—Tagore, "the sensible image of the Infinite"—Bancroft, "God's handwriting"—Emerson, "a form of genius"—Oscar Wilde, "the power by which a woman charms a lover and terrifies a husband"—Ambrose Bierce

3 comeliness, fairness, sightliness, personableness, becomingness, pleasingness 97.1, goodliness, bonniness, agreeability, agreeableness

4 good looks, good appearance, good effect; good proportions, aesthetic proportions;

shapeliness, good figure, good shape, *belle tournure* <Fr>, nice body, lovely build, physical *or* bodily charm, curvaceousness, curves <nonformal>, pneumaticness, sexy body; bodily grace, **gracefulness,** gracility; good points, **beauties, charms, delights,** perfections, good features

5 **daintiness, delicacy,** delicateness; **cuteness** *or* cunningness <both nonformal>

6 **gorgeousness,** ravishingness; **gloriousness,** heavenliness, sublimity; **splendor,** splendidness, splendiferousness, splendorousness *or* splendrousness, resplendence; **brilliance,** brightness, radiance, luster; **glamour** 377.1

7 **thing of beauty,** vision, picture <nonformal>, poem, eyeful <nonformal>, **sight** *or* **treat for sore eyes** <nonformal>

8 **beauty, charmer,** *charmeuse* <Fr>; beauty queen, beauty contest winner, Miss America, bathing beauty; **glamor girl,** cover girl, model; sex goddess; **belle,** reigning beauty, great beauty, lady fair; beau ideal, paragon; enchantress; "the face that launch'd a thousand ships"— Marlowe

9 <nonformal terms> **doll, dish, cutie,** angel, angelface, babyface, beaut, honey, dream, looker, good-looker, stunner, dazzler, dreamboat, fetcher, bird *and* crumpet <both Brit>, peach, knockout, raving beauty, centerfold, pinup girl, pinup, bunny, cutie *or* cutesy pie, cute *or* slick chick, pussycat, sex kitten, ten

10 <famous beauties> Venus, Venus de Milo; Aphrodite, Hebe; Adonis, Appollo, Apollo Belvedere, Hyperion, Antinoüs, Narcissus; Astarte; Balder, Freya; Helen of Troy, Cleopatra; the Graces, houri, peri

11 **beautification,** prettification, cutification <nonformal>, **adornment;** decoration 498.1; **beauty care,** beauty treatment, cosmetology; facial <nonformal>; manicure; hairdressing

12 **makeup, cosmetics, beauty products, beauty-care products;** war paint *and* drugstore complexion <both nonformal>; pancake makeup; powder, talcum, talcum powder; rouge, paint; lip rouge, **lipstick; nail polish;** greasepaint, clown white; eye makeup, eyeliner, mascara, eye shadow, kohl; cold cream, hand cream *or* lotion, vanishing cream, foundation cream; foundation, base; mudpack; eyebrow pencil; puff, powder puff; compact, vanity case

13 **beautician,** beautifier, cosmetologist; hairdresser, *coiffeur, coiffeuse* <both Fr>; barber; manicurist

14 **beauty parlor** *or* salon *or* shop, *salon de beauté* <Fr>; barbershop

VERBS 15 **beautify, prettify,** cutify <nonformal>, pretty up *or* gussy up *or* doll up <all nonformal>, grace, **adorn; decorate** 498.8; set off, set off to advantage *or* good advantage, become one; **glamorize; make up,** paint *and* put on one's face <both nonformal>, titivate, cosmetize, cosmeticize

16 **look good;** look like a million *and* look fit to kill *and* knock dead *and* knock one's eyes out <all nonformal>; take the breath away, beggar description; shine, beam, **bloom, glow**

ADJS 17 **beautiful, beauteous,** endowed with beauty; **pretty, handsome, attractive** 97.7, pulchritudinous, **lovely, graceful,** gracile; elegant; esthetic, aesthetically appealing; **cute;** pretty as a picture, "lovely as the day"—Longfellow, "fair as is the rose in May"—Chaucer; tall dark and handsome

18 **comely, fair, good-looking, nice-looking,** well-favored, **personable,** presentable, agreeable, becoming, pleasing 97.6, goodly, bonny, likely <nonformal>, **sightly,** braw <Scots>; pleasing to the eye, lovely to behold; **shapely,** well-built, built, well-shaped, well-proportioned, well-made, well-formed, stacked *or* well-stacked <both nonformal>, curvaceous, curvy <nonformal>, pneumatic, amply endowed, built for comfort *or* built like a brick shithouse <both nonformal>, buxom, callipygian, callipygous; Junoesque, statuesque, goddess-like; slender 270.16; Adonis-like, hunky <nonformal>

19 **fine, exquisite,** flowerlike, **dainty, delicate;** *mignon* <Fr>

20 **gorgeous, ravishing; glorious,** heavenly, divine, sublime; **resplendent,** splendorous *or* splendrous, splendiferous, **splendid,** resplendently beautiful; **brilliant,** bright, radiant, shining, beaming, glowing, blooming, abloom, sparkling, **dazzling; glamorous**

21 <nonformal terms> **eye-filling, easy on the eyes,** not hard to look at, long on looks, looking fit to kill, dishy <chiefly Brit>; cutesy, cutesy-poo; **raving,** devastating, **stunning,** killing

22 **beautifying,** cosmetic; decorative 498.10; cosmetized, cosmeticized, beautified, made-up, mascaraed, titivated

ADVS 23 **beautifully,** beauteously, **prettily, handsomely, attractively, becomingly,** comelily; elegantly, exquisitely; charmingly, enchantingly

24 daintily, delicately; cutely

25 gorgeously, ravishingly; ravingly *and* devastatingly *and* stunningly <all nonformal>; **gloriously,** divinely, sublimely; **resplendently,** splendidly, splendorously, splendrously; **brilliantly,** brightly, radiantly, glowingly, **dazzlingly**

WORD ELEMENTS **26** cal—, calo—, callo—, cali—, calli—

1016 MATHEMATICS

NOUNS **1 mathematics** <see list>, math <US nonformal>, maths <Brit nonformal>, mathematic, **numbers, figures;** pure mathematics, abstract mathematics, applied mathematics, higher mathematics, elementary mathematics; algorithm; mathematical element <see list>

2 <mathematical operations> notation, **addition** 253, **subtraction** 255, **multiplication, division,** proportion, practice, equation, extraction of roots, inversion, reduction, involution, evolution, approximation, interpolation, extrapolation, transformation, differentiation, integration

3 number <see list>, **numeral,** *numero* <Sp and Ital>, no *or* n, digit, binary digit *or* bit, **cipher,** character, symbol, sign, notation

4 <number systems> **Arabic numerals,** algorism *or* algorithm, Roman numerals; **decimal system,** binary system, octal system, duodecimal system, hexadecimal system

5 large number, astronomical number, boxcar number <nonformal>, zillion *and* jillion <both nonformal>; googol, googolplex; infinity, infinitude 822.1; billion, trillion, etc 881.13

6 sum, summation, difference, product, **number, count,** x number, n number; account, cast, **score, reckoning, tally,** tale, the story *and* whole story *and* all she wrote <all nonformal>, the bottom line <nonformal>, **aggregate, amount,** quantity 244; **whole** 791, **total** 791.2; box score <nonformal>

7 ratio, rate, proportion; quota, quotum; **percentage,** percent; **fraction,** proper fraction, improper fraction, compound fraction, continued fraction; geometric ratio *or* proportion, arithmetical proportion, harmonic proportion; rule of three

8 series, progression; arithmetical progression, geometrical progression, harmonic progression; Fibonacci numbers

9 numeration, enumeration, numbering, counting, accounting, census, inventorying, telling, tallying; page numbering, pagination, foliation; counting on the fingers, dactylonomy; **measurement** 300; quantification, quantization

10 calculation, computation, estimation, reckoning, calculus; adding, footing, casting, ciphering, totaling, toting *or* totting <nonformal>

11 summation, summary, summing, summing up, recount, recounting, rehearsal, capitulation, **recapitulation,** recap *and* rehash <both nonformal>, statement, **reckoning, count,** bean-counting <nonformal>, repertory, census, inventory, head count, nose count, body count; account, accounts; **table,** reckoner, ready reckoner

12 account of, count of, a reckoning of, **tab** *or* **tabs of** <nonformal>, tally of, check of, track of

13 figures, statistics, indexes *or* indices; vital statistics

14 calculator <see list>, **computer** 1041.2, estimator, figurer, reckoner, abacist; statistician, actuary; accountant, bookkeeper 628.7

15 mathematician, arithmetician; geometer, geometrician; algebraist, trigonometrician, statistician, geodesist, mathematical physicist

VERBS **16 number,** numerate, number off, **enumerate, count, tell, tally,** give a figure to, put a figure on, call off, name, call over, run over; **count noses** *or* **heads** <nonformal>, call the roll; census, poll; page, paginate, foliate; **measure** 300.11; **round,** round out *or* off *or* down; quantify, quantitate, quantize

17 calculate, compute, estimate, reckon, figure, reckon at, put at, cipher, cast, tally, score; **figure out,** work out, dope out <nonformal>; take account of, figure in *and* figure on <both nonformal>; **add, subtract, multiply, divide,** multiply out, algebraize, extract roots; factor, factor out, factorize; **measure** 300.11

18 sum up, sum, summate, say it all <nonformal>; **figure up,** cipher up, reckon up, **count up, add up,** foot up, cast up, score up, **tally up; total,** total up, tote *or* tot up <nonformal>; **summarize, recapitulate,** recap *and* rehash <both nonformal>, **recount,** rehearse, recite, relate; detail, itemize, inventory

19 keep account of, keep count of, **keep**

track of, keep tab *or* **tabs** <nonformal>, keep tally, keep a check on *or* of

20 **check, verify** 969.12, double-check, check on *or* out; **prove,** demonstrate; balance, balance the books; **audit,** overhaul; take stock, inventory

ADJS 21 **mathematical,** numeric *or* numerical, numerary, arithmetic *or* arithmetical, algebraic *or* algebraical, geometric *or* geometrical, trigonometric *or* trigonometrical, analytic *or* analytical

22 **numeric** *or* **numerical,** numeral, numerary, numerative; **odd,** impair, **even,** pair; arithmetical, algorismic *or* algorithmic; **cardinal, ordinal;** figural, **figurate,** figurative, **digital;** aliquot, submultiple, **reciprocal,** prime, fractional, decimal, exponential, **logarithmic,** logometric, differential, integral; positive, negative; rational, irrational, transcendental; surd, radical; real, imaginary; possible, impossible, finite, infinite, transfinite

23 **numerative, enumerative; calculative,** computative, estimative; **calculating,** computing, computational, estimating; statistical; quantifying, quantizing

24 **calculable,** computable, **reckonable,** estimable, countable, numberable; **measurable,** mensurable, quantifiable

25 **kinds of mathematics**

addition algebra
affine geometry
algebra
algebraic geometry
analysis
analytic geometry
arithmetic
associative algebra
binary arithmetic
Boolean algebra
calculus
calculus of differences
circle geometry
combinatorial mathematics
combinatorial topology
commutative algebra
complex *or* double algebra
denumerative geometry
descriptive geometry
differential calculus
division algebra
elementary arithmetic
elementary *or* ordinary algebra
equivalent algebras
Euclidean geometry
Fourier analysis
game theory
geodesic geometry
geodesy
geometry
Gödel's proof
graphic algebra
group theory
higher algebra
higher arithmetic
hyperalgebra
hyperbolic geometry
infinitesimal calculus
integral calculus
intuitional geometry
invariant subalgebra
inverse geometry
Lagrangian function
Laplace's equation
linear algebra
line geometry
mathematical physics
matrix algebra
metageometry
modular arithmetic
multiple algebra
natural geometry
nilpotent algebra
noncommutative algebra
non-Euclidean geometry
n-tuple linear algebra
number theory
plane geometry
plane trigonometry
point-set topology
political arithmetic
projective geometry
proper subalgebra
quadratics
quaternian algebra
reducible algebra
Riemannian geometry
semisimple algebra
set theory
simple algebra
solid geometry
speculative geometry
sphere geometry
spherical trigonometry
statistics
subalgebra
systems analysis
topology
trigonometry *or* trig <nonformal>
universal algebra
universal geometry
vector algebra
zero algebra

26 **mathematical elements**

addend
algorithm
aliquot
antilogarithm
argument
auxiliary equation
base
Bessel function
binomial
characteristic
characteristic equation
characteristic function
characteristic polynomial
characteristic root *or* characteristic value *or* eigenvalue *or* latent root *or* proper value
characteristic vector
coefficient
combination
common divisor *or* measure
complement
congruence
constant
cosecant
cosine
cotangent
cube
cube root
decimal
denominator
derivative
determinant
difference *or* remainder
differential
discriminate
dividend
division sign
divisor
e
elliptical function
empty set *or* null set
equal sign
equation
exponent
exponential
factor
factorial
formula
fraction
function
greatest common divisor *or* GCD
haversine
hyperbolic
i
increment
index
integral
Laplace transform
least common denominator *or* LCD
least common multiple *or* LCM
logarithm
mantissa
matrix
minuend
minus sign
mixed decimal
modulus
monomial
multiple
multiplicand
multiplicator
multiplier
norm
numerator
parameter
part
permutation
pi <π>

plus sign
polynomial
power
quadratic equation
quaternion
quotient
radical
radix
reciprocal
repeating *or* circulating decimal
root
secant
set
simultaneous equations

sine
square root
submultiple
subtrahend
summand
tangent
tensor
topological group
topological space
variable
vector
vector product
vector sum
versed sine *or* versine
vulgar fraction

27 kinds of numbers

abundant number
algebraic number
cardinal number *or* cardinal
complex *or* Gaussian integer
complex number
composite *or* rectangular number
deficient *or* defective number
even number *or* pair
Fermat number
figurate number
finite number
fraction
imaginary number *or* pure imaginary
infinity
integer *or* whole number

irrational number *or* irrational
Mersenne number
mixed number
odd number *or* impair
ordinal number *or* ordinal
perfect number
polygonal number
prime *or* rectilinear number
pyramidal number
rational number *or* rational
real number *or* real
round *or* rounded number
serial number
surd *or* surd quantity
transcendental number
transfinite number

28 calculators

abacus
adding machine
analog computer
arithmograph
arithmometer
calculating machine
cash register
Comptometer <trademark>
computer *or* electronic computer
counter
difference engine
digital computer

listing machine
Napier's bones *or* rods
pari-mutuel machine
pocket calculator
quipu
rule
slide rule *or* sliding scale
suan pan <Chin>
tabulator
totalizator
Turing machine

1017 PHYSICS

NOUNS **1 physics;** natural *or* physical science; philosophy *or* second philosophy *or* natural philosophy *or* physic <all old>; **branch of physics** <see list>; physical theory, quantum theory, relativity theory, special relativity theory, general relativity theory, unified field theory, grand unified theory *or* GUT, superunified theory *or* theory of everything *or* TOE, eightfold way, superstring theory

2 physicist, aerophysicist, astrophysicist, biophysicist, etc

ADJS **3 physical;** aerophysical, astrophysical, biophysical, etc

4 branches of physics

acoustics
aerophysics
applied physics
astrophysics
basic conductor physics
biophysics
chaos theory *or* chaos dynamics *or* chaology
chemical physics *or* chemicophysics
classical physics *or* Newtonian physics
condensed-matter physics
cryogenics
crystallography
cytophysics
electron optics
electronics *or* electron physics
electrophysics
geophysics
high-energy physics
hyperphysics
hypophysics
iatrophysics
macrophysics

mathematical physics
mechanics
medicophysics
microphysics
molecular physics
morphophysics
myophysics
nuclear physics
optics
organismic physics
physical chemistry *or* physicochemistry
physicomathematics
plasma physics
psychophysics
quantum physics
radiation physics
radionics
solar physics
solid-state physics
statics
stereophysics
theoretical physics
thermodynamics
X-ray crystallography
zoophysics

1018 HEAT

NOUNS **1 heat, hotness,** heatedness; superheat, superheatedness; calidity *or* caloric <both old>; **warmth,** warmness; incalescence; radiant heat, thermal radiation, induction heat, convector *or* convected heat, coal heat, gas heat, oil heat, hot-air heat, steam heat, electric heat, solar heat, dielectric heat, ultraviolet heat, atomic heat, molecular heat; animal heat, body heat, blood heat, hypothermia; fever heat, fever; heating, burning 1019.5

2 <metaphors> **ardor,** ardency, **fervor,** fervency, fervidness, fervidity; eagerness 101; excitement 105; **anger** 152.5,8,9; **sexual desire** 75.5; love 104

3 temperature, temp <nonformal>; room temperature, comfortable temperature; comfort index, temperature-humidity index *or* THI; flash point; boiling point;

melting point, freezing point; dew point; recalescence point; zero, absolute zero

4 **lukewarmness,** tepidness, tepidity; tepidarium

5 **torridness,** torridity; extreme heat, intense heat, torrid heat, red heat, white heat, tropical heat, sweltering heat, Afric heat, Indian heat, Bengal heat, summer heat, oppressive heat; "where the sun beats, and the dead tree gives no shelter, the cricket no relief"—T S Eliot; **hot wind** 318.7

6 **sultriness, stuffiness, closeness,** oppressiveness; **humidity, humidness, mugginess,** stickiness <nonformal>, swelter

7 **hot weather,** sunny or sunshiny weather; sultry weather, stuffy weather, humid weather, muggy weather, sticky weather <nonformal>; summer, midsummer, high summer; Indian Summer, **dog days,** canicular days, canicule; **heat wave,** hot wave; broiling sun, midday sun; vertical rays; warm weather, fair weather

8 **hot day,** summer day; **scorcher** and **roaster** and broiler and sizzler and swelterer <all nonformal>

9 **hot air,** superheated air; thermal; firestorm

10 **hot water,** boiling water; **steam,** vapor; volcanic water; hot or warm or thermal spring, thermae; geyser, Old Faithful

11 <hot place> **oven, furnace,** fiery furnace, inferno, hell; steam bath; **tropics,** subtropics, Torrid Zone; equator

12 **glow,** incandescence, fieriness; **flush, blush, bloom,** redness 41, rubicundity, rosiness; whiteness 37; thermochromism; hectic, hectic flush

13 **fire; blaze, flame,** ingle, devouring element; **combustion, ignition,** ignition temperature or point, flash or flashing point; **conflagration;** flicker 1024.8, wavering or flickering flame, "lambent flame"—Dryden; smoldering fire, sleeping fire; marshfire, fen fire, ignis fatuus, will-o'-the-wisp; fox fire; witch fire, St Elmo's fire, corposant; **cheerful fire,** cozy fire, crackling fire, "bright-flaming, heatfull fire"—Du Bartas; **roaring fire,** blazing fire; **raging fire,** sheet of fire, sea of flames, "whirlwinds of tempestuous fire"—Milton; bonfire, balefire; beacon fire, beacon, signal beacon, watch fire; alarm fire, two-alarm fire, three-alarm fire, etc; wildfire, prairie fire, forest fire; backfire; brushfire; open fire; campfire; smudge fire; death fire, pyre, funeral pyre, crematory; burning ghat

14 **flare,** flare-up, **flash,** flash fire, **blaze,** burst, outburst; deflagration

15 **spark,** sparkle; **scintillation,** scintilla; ignescence

16 **coal,** live coal, brand, firebrand, **ember,** burning ember; **cinder**

17 **fireworks** <see list>, **pyrotechnics** or pyrotechny

18 <perviousness to heat> transcalency; adiathermancy, athermancy

19 **thermal unit;** British thermal unit or BTU; Board of Trade unit or BOT; centigrade thermal unit; centigrade or Celsius scale, Fahrenheit scale; **calorie,** mean calorie, centuple or rational calorie, small calorie, large or great calorie, kilocalorie, kilogram-calorie; therm

20 **thermometer,** thermal detector; mercury, glass; thermostat

21 <science of heat> thermochemistry, thermology, thermotics, thermodynamics; volcanology; pyrology, pyrognostics; pyrotechnics or pyrotechny, ebulliometry; calorimetry

VERBS 22 <be hot> **burn** 1019.24, **scorch,** parch, scald, **swelter, roast,** toast, cook, bake, fry, broil, boil, seethe, simmer, stew; **be in heat;** shimmer with heat, give off waves of heat, radiate heat; **blaze,** combust, spark, **catch fire, flame** 1019.23, flame up, **flare,** flare up; **flicker** 1024.25; **glow,** incandesce, flush, bloom; smolder; steam; sweat 12.16; gasp, pant; **suffocate, stifle,** smother, choke

23 **smoke, fume,** reek; smudge

ADJS 24 **warm,** calid <old>, **thermal,** thermic; **toasty** <nonformal>, warm as toast; **sunny,** sunshiny; fair, mild, genial; summery, aestival; **temperate,** warmish; **tropical,** equatorial, subtropical; semitropical; **tepid, lukewarm,** luke; room-temperature; blood-warm, blood-hot; unfrozen

25 **hot, heated, torrid; sweltering,** sweltry, canicular; **burning,** parching, scorching, searing, scalding, blistering, baking, roasting, toasting, broiling, grilling, simmering; **boiling,** seething, ebullient; **piping hot,** scalding hot, burning hot, roasting hot, scorching hot, sizzling hot, smoking hot; **red-hot,** white-hot; ardent; flushed, sweating, sweaty, sudorific; overwarm, overhot, overheated; hot as fire, hot as a three-dollar pistol <nonformal>, hot as hell or blazes, hot as the hinges of hell, hot enough to roast an ox, so hot you can fry eggs on the sidewalk <nonformal>, like a furnace or an oven; feverish

26 **fiery,** igneous, firelike, pyric; combustive, conflagrative

27 **burning, ignited,** kindled, enkindled, **blazing,** ablaze, ardent, flaring, flaming, aflame, inflamed, alight, **afire, on fire,** in flames, in a blaze, flagrant <old>; conflagrant, comburent; live, living; **glowing,** aglow, in a glow, incandescent, candescent, candent; sparking, scintillating, scintillant, ignescent; **flickering,** aflicker, guttering; unquenched, unextinguished; slow-burning; **smoldering; smoking,** fuming, reeking

28 **sultry, stifling, suffocating, stuffy, close,** oppressive; **humid, sticky** <nonformal>, **muggy**

29 **warm-blooded,** hot-blooded

30 **isothermal,** isothermic; centigrade, Fahrenheit

31 **diathermic,** diathermal, transcalent; adiathermic, adiathermal, athermanous

32 **pyrological,** pyrognostic, pyrotechnic *or* pyrotechnical; pyrogenic *or* pyrogenous *or* pyrogenetic; thermochemical; thermodynamic, thermodynamical

WORD ELEMENTS 33 igni—, pyr—, pyro—; therm—, thermo—, —thermous

34 **fireworks**

bomb	girandole
candlebomb	ladyfinger
cannon cracker	pinwheel
cap	rocket
Catherine wheel	Roman candle
cherry bomb	serpent
cracker	skyrocket
cracker bonbon	snake
firecracker	sparkler
fizgig	squib
flare	torpedo
flowerpot	whiz-bang

1019 HEATING

NOUNS 1 **heating, warming,** calefaction, torrefaction, increase *or* raising of temperature; superheating; pyrogenesis; decalescence, recalescence; preheating; **heating system** <see list>, heating method; solar radiation, insolation; dielectric heating; induction heating; heat exchange; cooking 11

2 **boiling,** seething, **stewing,** ebullition, ebullience *or* ebulliency, coction; decoction; **simmering;** boil; simmer

3 **melting, fusion,** liquefaction, liquefying, liquescence, running; **thawing,** thaw; liquation; fusibility; thermoplasticity

4 **ignition, lighting,** lighting up *or* off, **kindling,** firing; reaching flash point *or* flashing point

5 **burning, combustion,** blazing, flaming; **scorching,** parching, singeing; **searing,** branding; **blistering,** vesication; **cauterization,** cautery; **incineration; cremation;** suttee, self-cremation, self-immolation; the stake, burning at the stake, *auto da fé* <Pg>; scorification; carbonization; oxidation, oxidization; calcination; cupellation; deflagration; distilling, distillation; refining, smelting; pyrolysis; cracking, thermal cracking, destructive distillation; **spontaneous combustion,** thermogenesis

6 **burn,** scald, scorch, singe; sear; brand; sunburn, sunscald; windburn; mat burn; first- *or* second- *or* third-degree burn

7 **incendiarism, arson,** torch job <nonformal>, fire-raising <Brit>; **pyromania;** pyrophilia; pyrolatry, fire worship

8 **incendiary, arsonist,** torcher <nonformal>; pyromaniac, firebug <nonformal>; pyrophile, fire buff <nonformal>; pyrolater, fire worshiper

9 **flammability, inflammability,** combustibility

10 **heater, warmer; stove, furnace; cooker,** cookery; firebox; tuyere, tewel <old>; burner, jet, gas jet, pilot light *or* burner, element, heating element; heating pipe, steam pipe, hot-water pipe; heating duct, caliduct

11 **fireplace, hearth,** ingle; **fireside,** hearthside, ingleside, inglenook, ingle cheek <Scots>, chimney corner; hearthstone; hob, hub; fireguard, fireboard, fire screen, fender; chimney, chimney piece, chimney-breast, chimney-pot, chimney-stack, flue; smokehole

12 **fire iron; andiron,** firedog; tongs, pair of tongs, fire tongs, coal tongs; poker, stove poker, salamander, fire hook; lifter, stove lifter; pothook, crook, crane, chain; trivet, tripod; spit, turnspit; grate, grating; gridiron, grid, griddle, grill, griller; damper

13 **incinerator,** cinerator, burner; solid-waste incinerator, garbage incinerator; **crematory,** cremator, crematorium, burning ghat; calcinatory

14 **blowtorch,** blowlamp <Brit>, blast lamp, torch, alcohol torch, butane torch; soldering torch; blowpipe; **burner; welder;** acetylene torch *or* welder, cutting torch *or* blowpipe, oxyacetylene blowpipe *or* torch, welding blowpipe *or* torch

15 **cauterant,** cauterizer, cauter, cautery, thermocautery, actual cautery; hot iron, **branding iron,** brand iron, brand; moxa; electrocautery; **caustic, corrosive,** mordant, escharotic, potential cautery; acid; lunar caustic; radium

16 <products of combustion> scoria, sul-
lage, slag, dross; **ashes,** ash; **cinder,**
clinker, coal; coke, charcoal, brand, lava,
carbon, calx; **soot,** smut, coom <Brit non-
formal>; **smoke,** smudge, fume, reek

VERBS **17 heat,** raise or increase the temperature, hot or hot up <both Brit>,
warm, warm up, fire, fire up, stoke up;
chafe; take the chill off; tepefy; gas-heat,
oil-heat, hot-air-heat, hot-water-heat,
steam-heat, electric-heat, solar-heat; superheat; overheat; preheat; **reheat,**
recook, warm over; mull; steam; foment;
cook 11.4

18 <metaphors> **excite, inflame;** incite, **kindle, arouse** 375.17,19; anger, **enrage**

19 insolate, sun-dry; **sun,** bask, bask in the
sun, sun oneself, sunbathe

20 boil, stew, simmer, seethe; distill

21 melt, melt down, liquefy; **run,** colliquate,
fuse, flux; refine, smelt; render; **thaw,**
thaw out, unfreeze; defrost, deice

22 ignite, set fire to, fire, set on fire, kindle,
enkindle, inflame, **light,** light up, strike a
light, apply the match or torch to, torch
<nonformal>, touch off, **burn,** confla-
grate; **build a fire;** rekindle, relight,
relume; feed, feed the fire, **stoke,** stoke the
fire, add fuel to the flame; bank; poke or
stir the fire, blow up the fire, fan the
flame; open the draft

23 catch fire, catch on fire, catch, take fire,
burn, flame, combust, blaze, **blaze up,
burst into flame**

24 burn, torrefy, **scorch, parch, sear; singe,**
swinge; **blister,** vesicate, **cauterize,**
brand, burn in; **char,** coal, carbonize;
scorify; calcine; pyrolyze, crack; solder,
weld; vulcanize; cast, found; oxidize, oxi-
date; deflagrate; cupel; burn off; blaze,
flame 1018.22

25 burn up, incendiarize, **incinerate, cremate,** consume, burn or reduce to ashes,
burn to a crisp, burn to a cinder; **burn
down,** burn to the ground, **go up in smoke**

ADJS **26 heating, warming,** chafing, calorific;
calefactory, calefactive, calefacient, calo-
rificacient, calorigenic; fiery, burning
1018.25,27; cauterant, cauterizing; calcinatory

27 inflammatory, inflammative, **inflaming,
kindling,** enkindling, lighting; **incendiary,** incendive; arsonous

28 flammable, inflammable, combustible,
burnable

29 heated, het or het up <both nonformal>,
hotted up <Brit>, **warmed,** warmed up,
centrally heated, gas-heated, oil-heated,
kerosene-heated, hot-water-heated, hot-
air-heated, steam-heated, solar-heated,
electric-heated, baseboard-heated; superheated; overheated; **reheated,** recooked,
warmed-over, réchauffé <Fr>; hot
1018.25

30 burned, burnt, burned to the ground, in-
cendiarized, torched <nonformal>,
burned-out or -down, gutted; **scorched,
blistered, parched, singed, seared,
charred,** pyrographic, adust; sunburned;
burnt-up, incinerated, cremated, consumed, consumed by fire; ashen, ashy,
carbonized, pyrolyzed, pyrolytic

31 molten, melted, fused, liquefied; li-
quated; meltable, fusible; thermoplastic

32 heating systems

baseboard heating	kerosene heating
central heating	oil heating
electric heating	panel heating
furnace heating	radiant heating
gas heating	solar heating
heat pump	steam heating
hot-air heating	stove heating
hot-water heating	

1020 FUEL

NOUNS **1 fuel** <see list>, energy source;
heat source, firing, combustible or inflammable or flammable material,
burnable, combustible, inflammable,
flammable; fossil fuel, nonrenewable energy or fuel source; alternate or
alternative energy source, renewable energy or fuel source; solar energy, solar
radiation, insolation; wind energy; geothermal energy, geothermal heat,
geothermal gradient; synthetic fuels or
synfuels; fuel additive, dope, fuel dope;
propellant; **oil** 1054; gas 1065

2 slack, coal dust, coom or comb <both
Brit nonformal>, culm

3 firewood, stovewood, wood; woodpile;
kindling, kindlings, kindling wood;
brush, brushwood; fagot, bavin <Brit>;
log, backlog, yule log or yule clog <old>

4 lighter, light, igniter, sparker; pocket
lighter, cigar or cigarette lighter, butane
lighter; **torch,** flambeau, taper, spill;
brand, **firebrand;** portfire; **flint,** flint and
steel; **detonator**

5 match, matchstick, lucifer; friction
match, locofoco and vesuvian and vesta
and fusee and Congreve or Congreve
match <all old>; safety match; match-
book

6 tinder, touchwood; **punk,** spunk, German
tinder, amadou; tinder fungus; pyrotechnic sponge; tinderbox

VERBS **7 fuel,** fuel up; fill up, top off; refuel; coal, oil; **stoke, feed,** add fuel to the flame; detonate, explode

ADJS **8 fuel,** energy, heat; fossil-fuel; alternate- *or* alternative-energy; oil-fired, coal-fired, etc; gas-powered, oil-powered, etc; coaly, carbonaceous, carboniferous; anthracite; clean-burning; bituminous; high-sulfur; lignitic; peaty

9 fuels

alcohol	heptane
anthracite *or* hard	hexane
coal	high-octane gasoline
aviation gasoline *or*	isooctane
avgas	jet fuel
benzine	kerosene *or* paraffin
bituminous *or* soft	<Brit>
coal	leaded gasoline
blind coal	lignite *or* brown coal
briquette	lump coal
broken coal	methane
buckwheat coal	methanol
butane	motor fuel
cannel *or* cannel coal	mustard-seed coal
carbon	natural gas
charcoal	nut coal
chestnut coal	octane
coal	pea coal
coke	peat *or* turf
diesel fuel *or* diesel *or*	pentane
diesel oil *or* derv	petrol <Brit>
<Brit>	premium *or* high-test
egg coal	gasoline
ethane	propane
ethanol	regular gasoline
ethyl gasoline	rocket fuel
flaxseed coal	sea coal
gas carbon	steamboat coal
gasohol	stove coal
gasoline	unleaded *or* lead-free
glance coal	gasoline
grate coal	white gasoline

1021 INCOMBUSTIBILITY

NOUNS **1 incombustibility, uninflammability,** noninflammability, **nonflammability;** unburnableness; fire resistance

2 extinguishing, extinguishment, extinction, **quenching,** dousing <nonformal>, **snuffing,** putting out; **choking, damping, stifling, smothering,** smotheration; controlling; fire fighting; going out, dying, burning out, flame-out, burnout

3 extinguisher, fire extinguisher; fire apparatus, fire engine, hook-and-ladder, ladder truck; ladder pipe, snorkel, deluge set, deck gun; pumper, super-pumper; **foam,** carbon-dioxide foam, Foamite <trademark>, foam extinguisher; dry-powder extinguisher; carbon tetrachlo-

ride, carbon tet; water, soda, acid, wet blanket; sprinkler, automatic sprinkler, sprinkler system, sprinkler head; hydrant, fire hydrant, fireplug; fire hose

4 fire fighter, fireman, fire-eater <nonformal>; pumpman; forest fire fighter, fire warden, fire-chaser, smokechaser, smoke-jumper; volunteer fireman, vamp <nonformal>; fire department, fire brigade <chiefly Brit>

5 fireproofing; fire resistance; fireproof *or* fire-resistant *or* fire-resisting *or* fire-resistive *or* fire-retardant material, fire retardant; asbestos; amianthus, earth flax, mountain flax; asbestos curtain, fire wall; fire break, fire line

VERBS **6 fireproof,** flameproof

7 fight fire; extinguish, put out, quench, out, douse <nonformal>, **snuff,** snuff out; blow out, stamp out; stub out, dinch <nonformal>; **choke, damp, smother, stifle,** slack; bring under control, contain

8 burn out, go out, die, die out *or* down *or* away; fizzle *and* **fizzle out** <both nonformal>; flame out

ADJS **9 incombustible, noncombustible, uninflammable, noninflammable,** noncombustive, **nonflammable,** unburnable; asbestine, asbestous, asbestoid, asbestoidal; amianthine

10 fireproof, flameproof, fireproofed, fire-retarded, fire-resisting *or* -resistant *or* -resistive, fire-retardant

11 extinguished, quenched, snuffed, **out;** contained, under control

1022 COLD

NOUNS **1 cold, coldness; coolness,** coolth, freshness; low temperature, arctic temperature, drop *or* decrease in temperature; **chilliness,** nippiness, crispness, briskness, sharpness, bite; **chill, nip,** sharp air; **frigidity, iciness,** frostiness, extreme *or* intense cold, gelidity, algidity, algidness; **rawness,** bleakness, keenness, sharpness, bitterness, severity, inclemency, rigor, "a hard, dull bitterness of cold"—Whittier; freezing point; cryology; cryogenics; absolute zero

2 <sensation of cold> **chill,** chilliness, chilling; shivering, **shivers,** cold shivers, shakes, didders <Brit nonformal>, dithers, chattering of the teeth; creeps, **cold creeps** <nonformal>; **gooseflesh, goose pimples,** goose *or* duck bumps <nonformal>, horripilation; **frostbite, chilblains,** kibe, cryopathy; ache, aching

3 cold weather, bleak weather, raw

weather, bitter weather, wintry weather,
arctic weather, **freezing weather,** zero
weather, subzero weather; **cold wave,**
snap, **cold snap; freeze,** frost, hard frost,
deep freeze, arctic frost; winter, depth of
winter, hard winter; "The ways deep and
the weather sharp, / The very dead of
winter"—T S Eliot; "When icicles hang
by the wall"—Shakespeare, "Stern
winter"—Wordsworth; wintry wind
318.8

4 <cold place> Siberia, Hell, Novaya
Zemlya, Alaska, Iceland, the Hebrides,
Greenland, "Greenland's icy moun-
tains"—Reginald Heber, the Yukon,
Tierra del Fuego, Lower Slobbovia <Al
Capp>; North Pole, South Pole; Frigid
Zones; the Arctic, Arctic Circle *or* Zone;
Antarctica, the Antarctic; Antarctic Cir-
cle *or* Zone; tundra; the freezer, the deep-
freeze

5 **ice,** frozen water; ice needle *or* crystal;
icicle, iceshockle <Brit nonformal>;
cryosphere; ice sheet, ice field, ice barrier, ice front; **floe, ice floe,** sea ice, ice
island, ice raft, ice pack; ice foot, ice belt;
shelf ice, sheet ice, pack ice, bay ice, berg
ice, field ice; **iceberg,** berg, growler; calf;
snowberg; **icecap,** *jokul* <Iceland>; ice
pinnacle, serac, nieve penitente; **glacier,**
glacieret, glaciation, ice dike, "motionless torrents, silent cataracts"—Samuel
Taylor Coleridge; piedmont glacier; ice-
fall; ice banner; ice cave; **sleet,** glaze,
glazed frost, verglasblack ice; snow ice;
névé, granular snow, firn; ground ice, anchor ice, frazil; lolly; sludge, slob *or* slob
ice <chiefly Can>; ice cubes; crushed
ice; Dry Ice <trademark>, solid carbon
dioxide; icequake; ice storm, freezing
rain

6 **hail,** hailstone; soft hail, graupel, snow
pellets, tapioca snow; **hailstorm**

7 **frost,** Jack Frost; **hoarfrost,** hoar, rime,
rime frost, white frost; black frost; hard
frost, sharp frost; killing frost; frost
smoke; frost line

8 **snow;** granular snow, corn snow, spring
corn, spring snow, powder snow, wet
snow, tapioca snow; "a pure and grandfather moss"—Dylan Thomas, "White
petals from the flowers that grow in the
cold atmosphere"—George W Bungay;
snowfall, "feather'd rain"—William
Strode, "the whitening shower"—James
Thomson; **snowstorm,** snow blast, snow
squall, snow flurry, flurry, blizzard;
snowflake, snow-crystal, flake, crystal;
snow dust; **snowdrift,** snowbank, snow

wreath <Brit nonformal>, driven snow,
"the frolic architecture of the snow"—
Emerson; snowcap; snow banner; snow
blanket; snow bed, snowpack, snowfield;
mantle of snow; snowscape; snowland;
snowshed; snow line; snowball, snowman; snowslide, snowslip, avalanche;
snow slush, **slush,** slosh; snowbridge;
snow fence; snowhouse, igloo; mogul

VERBS 9 freeze, be cold, grow cold, lose
heat; **shiver, quiver,** shiver to death,
quake, shake, tremble, shudder, didder
<Brit nonformal>, dither; **chatter; chill,**
have a chill, have the cold shivers; **freeze,**
freeze to death, freeze one's balls off
<nonformal>, die *or* perish with the
cold, horripilate, have goose pimples,
have goose *or* duck bumps <nonformal>;
have chilblains

10 <make cold> **freeze, chill,** chill to the
bone *or* marrow, make one shiver, make
one's teeth chatter; **nip,** bite, cut, **pierce,**
penetrate, penetrate to the bone, go
through *or* right through; **freeze** 1023.11;
frost, frostbite; numb, benumb; **refrigerate** 1023.10

11 **hail, sleet, snow;** snow in; snow under;
frost, ice, ice up, ice over, glaze, glaze
over

ADJS 12 **cool,** coolish, temperate; chill,
chilly, parky <Brit nonformal>; **fresh,**
brisk, crisp, bracing, sharpish, **invigorating,** stimulating

13 **unheated,** unwarmed; unmelted, unthawed

14 **cold, freezing,** freezing cold, **crisp, brisk,**
nipping, **nippy, snappy** <nonformal>,
raw, bleak, keen, sharp, bitter, biting,
pinching, cutting, **piercing,** penetrating;
inclement, severe, rigorous; snowcold;
sleety; slushy; **icy,** icelike, **ice-cold,** glacial, ice-encrusted; cryospheric;
supercooled; **frigid,** bitter *or* bitterly
cold, gelid, algid; below zero, subzero;
numbing; **wintry,** wintery, winterlike,
winterbound, hiemal, brumal, hibernal;
arctic, Siberian, boreal, hyperborean;
stone-cold, cold as death, cold as ice, cold
as marble, cold as charity, "cold as the
north side of a gravestone in winter"—
Anon

15 <nonformal terms> **cold as hell,** cold as
a welldigger's ass, cold as a witch's tit *or*
kiss, cold enough to freeze the tail *or* balls
off a brass monkey, cold as a bastard *or* a
bitch, colder than hell *or* the deuce *or* the
devil

16 <feeling cold> **cold, freezing; cool,
chilly; shivering,** shivery, shaky, dithery;

algid, aguish, aguey; chattering, with chattering teeth; **frozen** 1023.14, half-frozen, frozen to death, chilled to the bone, blue with cold, *figé de froid* <Fr>, so cold one could spit ice cubes

17 **frosty,** frostlike; **frosted,** frosted-over, frost-beaded, frost-covered, frost-chequered, rimed, **hoary,** hoar-frosted, rime-frosted; frost-riven, frost-rent; frosty-faced, frosty-whiskered; frost-bound, frost-fettered

18 **snowy,** snowlike, niveous, nival; snow-blown, snow-drifted, snow-driven; **snow-covered,** snow-clad, snow-mantled, snow-robed, snow-blanketed, snow-sprinkled, snow-lined, snow-encircled, snow-laden, snow-loaded, snow-hung; **snow-capped,** snow-peaked, snow-crested, snow-crowned, snow-tipped, snow-topped; snow-bearded; snow-feathered; snow-still

19 frozen out *or* in, **snowbound,** snowed-in, **icebound**

20 **cold-blooded,** hypothermic, heterothermic, poikilothermic; cryogenic; cryological

WORD ELEMENTS 21 cryo— *or* kryo—, frigo—, psychro—; glacio—; chio—, chion—

1023 REFRIGERATION

NOUNS 1 **refrigeration,** infrigidation, reduction of temperature; **cooling, chilling; freezing,** glacification, glaciation, congelation, congealment; refreezing, regelation; mechanical refrigeration, electric refrigeration, electronic refrigeration, gas refrigeration; food freezing, quick freezing, deep freezing, sharp freezing, blast freezing, dehydrofreezing; adiabatic expansion, adiabatic absorption, adiabatic demagnetization; cryogenics; super-cooling; **air conditioning,** air cooling, *climatisation* <Fr>; climate control

2 refrigeration anesthesia, crymoanesthesia, hypothermia *or* hypothermy; crymotherapy, cryo-aerotherapy; cold cautery, cryocautery; cryopathy

3 **cooler,** chiller; water cooler, air cooler; ventilator; fan; surface cooler; ice cube, ice pail *or* bucket, wine cooler; ice bag, ice pack, cold pack

4 **refrigerator,** refrigeratory, **icebox,** ice chest; Frigidaire <trademark>, fridge <nonformal>, electric refrigerator, electronic refrigerator, gas refrigerator;

refrigerator car, refrigerator truck, reefer <nonformal>; freezer ship

5 **freezer, deep freeze,** deep-freezer, quick-freezer, sharp-freezer; ice-cream freezer; ice machine, ice-cube machine, freezing machine, refrigerating machine *or* engine; **ice plant,** icehouse, refrigerating plant

6 **cold storage; frozen-food locker,** locker, freezer locker, locker plant; coolhouse; coolerman; frigidarium

7 <cooling agent> **coolant; refrigerant;** cryogen; ice, Dry Ice <trademark>, ice cubes; freezing mixture, liquid air, ammonia, carbon dioxide, Freon <trademark>, ether; ethyl chloride; liquid air, liquid oxygen *or* lox, liquid nitrogen, liquid helium, etc

8 **antifreeze,** coolant, radiator coolant, alcohol, ethylene glycol

9 refrigerating engineering, refrigerating engineer

VERBS 10 **refrigerate; cool, chill;** refresh, freshen; ice, ice-cool; water-cool, air-cool; **air-condition;** ventilate

11 **freeze** 1022.9,10, ice, glaciate, congeal; **deep-freeze,** quick-freeze, sharp-freeze, blast-freeze; freeze solid; freeze-dry; **nip,** blight, blast; refreeze, regelate

ADJS 12 **refrigerative,** refrigeratory, refrigerant, frigorific, algific; **cooling, chilling; freezing,** congealing; quick-freezing, deep-freezing, sharp-freezing, blast-freezing; freezable, glaciable

13 **cooled, chilled; air-conditioned;** iced, ice-cooled; air-cooled, water-cooled; super-cooled

14 **frozen,** frozen solid, glacial, gelid, congealed; **icy,** ice-cold, icy-cold, ice, icelike; deep-frozen, quick-frozen, sharp-frozen, blast-frozen; frostbitten, frostnipped

15 antifreeze, antifreezing

1024 LIGHT

NOUNS 1 **light,** radiant *or* luminous energy, visible radiation, radiation in the visible spectrum, **illumination, radiation, radiance** *or* radiancy, irradiance *or* irradiancy, irradiation, emanation; "God's first creature"—Francis Bacon, "God's eldest daughter"—Thomas Fuller, "offspring of Heav'n firstborn"—Milton, "the first of painters"—Emerson, "the prime work of God"—Milton, "the white radiance of eternity"—Shelley; highlight; sidelight; photosensitivity; light source 1025; **invisible light,** black light, infrared light, ultraviolet light

2 shine, shininess, **luster, sheen, gloss, glint; glow, gleam,** flush, sunset glow; lambency; **incandescence,** candescence; shining light; afterglow; skylight, air glow, night glow, day glow, twilight glow

3 lightness, luminousness, lightedness, luminosity; **lucidity,** lucence *or* lucency, translucence *or* translucency; backlight

4 brightness, brilliance *or* brilliancy, **splendor,** radiant splendor, **glory, radiance** *or* radiancy, **resplendence** *or* resplendency, **vividness,** flamboyance *or* flamboyancy; effulgence, refulgence *or* refulgency, fulgentness, fulgidity, fulgor; **glare,** blare, blaze; bright light, brilliant light, blazing light, glaring light, dazzling light, blinding light; TV lights, Klieg light; streaming light, flood of light, burst of light

5 ray, radiation 1036, **beam, gleam,** leam <Scots>, **stream, streak, pencil, patch,** ray of light, beam of light; "slant of light"—Emily Dickinson; ribbon, ribbon of light, streamer, stream of light; violet ray, ultraviolet ray, infrared ray, X ray, gamma ray, invisible radiation; actinic ray *or* light, actinism; atomic beam, atomic ray; laser beam; solar rays; photon

6 flash, blaze, flare, flame, gleam, glint, glance; blaze *or* flash *or* gleam of light; green flash; solar flare, solar prominence, facula; Bailey's beads

7 glitter, glimmer, shimmer, twinkle, blink; sparkle, spark; **scintillation,** scintilla; coruscation; **glisten,** glister, spangle, tinsel, glittering, glimmering, shimmering, twinkling; "shining from shook foil"—G M Hopkins; stroboscopic *or* strobe light <nonformal>, blinking; firefly, glowworm

8 flicker, flutter, dance, quiver; flickering, fluttering, bickering, guttering, dancing, quivering, lambency; wavering *or* flickering light, play, play of light, dancing *or* glancing light; light show; "the lambent easy light"—Dryden

9 reflection; reflected *or* incident light; reflectance, albedo; blink, iceblink, ice sky, snowblink, waterblink, water sky

10 daylight, dayshine, day glow, light of day; day, daytime, daytide; **natural light; sunlight, sunshine,** shine; noonlight, white light, midday sun, noonday *or* noontide light, "the blaze of noon"—Milton; broad day *or* daylight, full sun; bright time; dusk, twilight 315.3; the break *or* crack of dawn, cockcrow, dawn

314.4; sunburst, sunbreak; **sunbeam,** sun spark, ray of sunshine; green flash

11 moonlight, moonshine, moonglow; **moonbeam**

12 starlight, starshine; earthshine

13 luminescence; luciferin, luciferase; phosphor, luminophor; **ignis fatuus, will-o'-the-wisp,** will-with-the-wisp, wisp, jack-o'-lantern, marshfire, spunkie <Scots>; friar's lantern; fata morgana; fox fire; St Elmo's light *or* fire, wild fire, witch fire, corposant; double corposant

14 halo, nimbus, aura, **aureole,** circle, ring, glory; **rainbow,** solar halo, lunar halo, ring around the sun *or* moon; white rainbow *or* fogbow; **corona,** solar corona, lunar corona; parhelion, parhelic circle *or* ring, mock sun, sun dog; anthelion, antisun, countersun; paraselene, mock moon, moon dog

15 <nebulous light> nebula 1070.7; zodiacal light, gegenschein, counterglow

16 polar lights, **aurora; northern lights, aurora borealis,** merry dancers; southern lights, **aurora australis;** aurora polaris; aurora glory; streamer *or* curtain *or* arch aurora; polar ray

17 lightning, flash *or* **stroke of lightning,** fulguration, fulmination, bolt, lightning strike, **bolt of lightning,** bolt from the blue, **thunderbolt,** thunderstroke, thunderball, fireball, firebolt, levin bolt *or* brand; "flying flame"—Tennyson, "the lightning's gleaming rod"—Joaquin Miller, "oak-cleaving thunderbolts"—Shakespeare; fork *or* forked lightning, chain lightning, globular *or* ball lightning, summer *or* heat lightning, sheet lightning, dark lightning; Jupiter Fulgur *or* Fulminator; Thor

18 iridescence, opalescence, nacreousness, pearliness; **rainbow;** nacre, mother-of-pearl; nacreous *or* mother-of-pearl cloud

19 lighting, illumination, artificial light *or* lighting; arc light, calcium light, candlelight, electric light, fluorescent light, gaslight, incandescent light, mercury-vapor light, neon light, sodium light, strobe light, torchlight, floodlight, spotlight; tonality; light and shade, black and white, chiaroscuro, clairobscure, contrast, highlights

20 illuminant, luminant; electricity; gas, illuminating gas; oil, petroleum, benzine; gasoline, petrol <Brit>; kerosene, paraffin <Brit>, coal oil; light source 1025

21 <measurement of light> **candle power,** luminous intensity, luminous power, luminous flux, flux, intensity, light;

quantum, **light quantum, photon;** unit of light <see list>, unit of flux; lux, candle-meter, lumen meter, lumeter, lumen, candle lumen; **exposure meter,** light meter, ASA scale, Scheiner scale

22 <science of light> photics, photology, photometry; **optics,** geometrical optics, physical optics; dioptrics, catoptrics, fiber optics; actinology, actinometry; heliology, heliometry, heliography

VERBS **23 shine,** shine forth, **burn, give light,** incandesce; **glow, beam, gleam,** glint, luster, glance; **flash, flare, blaze, flame,** fulgurate; **radiate,** shoot, shoot out rays, send out rays; spread *or* diffuse light; be bright, shine brightly, beacon; **glare;** daze, blind, dazzle, bedazzle

24 glitter, glimmer, shimmer, twinkle, blink, spangle, tinsel, coruscate; **sparkle,** spark, **scintillate; glisten,** glister, glisk <Scots>

25 flicker, bicker, gutter, **flutter, waver, dance,** play, quiver

26 luminesce, phosphoresce, fluoresce; iridesce, opalesce

27 grow light, grow bright, light, **lighten,** brighten; dawn, break

28 illuminate, illumine, illume, luminate, **light, light up, lighten,** enlighten, brighten, brighten up, irradiate; bathe *or* flood with light; relumine, relume; **shed light upon,** cast *or* throw light upon, shed luster on, shine upon, overshine; spotlight, highlight; floodlight; beacon

29 strike a light, light, **turn** *or* **switch on the light,** open the light <nonformal>, make a light, shine a light

ADJS **30 luminous,** luminant, luminative, luminificent, luminiferous, luciferous *or* lucific <both old>, luciform, illuminant; **incandescent,** candescent; **lustrous,** orient; **radiant,** irradiative; **shining,** shiny, burning, lamping, streaming; **beaming,** beamy; **gleaming,** gleamy, glinting; **glowing,** aglow, suffused, blushing, flushing; rutilant, rutilous; **sunny, sunshiny,** bright and sunny, light as day; starry, starlike, starbright

31 light, lightish, lightsome; **lucid,** lucent, luculent, relucent; translucent, translucid, pellucid, diaphanous, transparent; **clear,** serene; **cloudless,** unclouded, unobscured

32 bright, brilliant, vivid, splendid, splendorous, splendent, **resplendent,** bright and shining; fulgid <old>, fulgent, effulgent, refulgent; **flamboyant,** flaming; **glaring,** glary, garish; **dazzling,** bedazzling, blinding, pitiless; shadowless, shadeless

33 shiny, shining, **lustrous, glossy,** glassy, *glacé* <Fr>, bright as a new penny, **sheeny, polished,** burnished, shined

34 flashing, flashy, **blazing, flaming, flaring, burning,** fulgurant, fulgurating; aflame, ablaze; meteoric

35 glittering, glimmering, shimmering, twinkling, blinking, glistening, glistering; glittery, glimmery, glimmerous, shimmery, twinkly, blinky, spangly, tinselly; **sparkling, scintillating,** scintillant, scintillescent, coruscating, coruscant

36 flickering, bickering, **fluttering, wavering, dancing,** playing, quivering, lambent; flickery, flicky <nonformal>, aflicker, fluttery, wavery, quivery; blinking, flashing, stroboscopic

37 iridescent, opalescent, nacreous, pearly, pearl-like; rainbowlike

38 luminescent, photogenic; autoluminescent, bioluminescent

39 illuminated, luminous, **lightened,** enlightened, brightened, **lighted,** lit, **lit up,** flooded *or* bathed with light, floodlit; irradiated, irradiate; **alight, glowing,** aglow, lambent, suffused with light; ablaze, blazing, in a blaze, fiery; lamplit, lanternlit, candlelit, torchlit, gaslit, firelit; sunlit, moonlit, starlit; spangled, bespangled, tinseled, studded; star-spangled, star-studded

40 illuminating, illumining, **lighting, lightening,** brightening

41 luminary, photic; photologic *or* photological; photometric *or* photometrical; heliological, heliographic; actinic, photoactinic; catoptric *or* catoptrical; luminal

42 photosensitive; photophobic; phototropic

WORD ELEMENTS **43** phot—, photo—, lumin—, lumino—, lumini—; fluoro— *or* fluori—; irido—; actino—, actini—

44 units of light and lighting

bougie décimale <Fr>	decimal candle
	foot-candle
British candle	Hefner candle
candle	international candle
candle-foot	lamp-hour
candle-hour	lumen-hour

1025 LIGHT SOURCE

NOUNS **1 light source,** source of light, **luminary,** illuminator, luminant, illuminant, incandescent body *or* point, **light,** glim; **lamp,** light bulb, electric light bulb, lantern, candle, taper, torch, flame; match; **fluorescent light, fluorescent tube,** fluorescent lamp; starter, ballast; "a lamp

unto my feet, and a light unto my path"—
Bible; fire 1018.13; sun, moon, stars
1070.4

2 **candle,** taper; dip, farthing dip, tallow
dip; tallow candle; wax candle, bougie;
bayberry candle; rush candle, rushlight;
corpse candle; votary candle

3 **torch,** flaming torch, flambeau, cresset,
link <old>; **flare,** signal flare, fusee; beacon

4 **traffic light,** stop-and-go light; stop *or* red
light, go *or* green light, caution *or* amber
light

5 **firefly,** lightning bug, lampyrid, **glowworm,** fireworm; fire beetle; lantern fly,
candle fly; luciferin, luciferase; phosphor,
luminophor

6 **chandelier,** gasolier, electrolier, hanging
or ceiling fixture, luster; corona, corona
lucis, crown, circlet; light holder, light
fixture, candlestick

7 **wick,** taper; candlewick, lampwick

1026 DARKNESS, DIMNESS

NOUNS 1 **darkness, dark, lightlessness; obscurity,** obscure, tenebrosity, tenebrous-
ness; **night** 315.4, dead of night, deep
night; sunlessness, moonlessness, star-
lessness; **pitch-darkness,** pitch-blackness,
pitchy darkness, utter *or* thick *or* total
darkness, intense darkness, velvet darkness, Cimmerian *or* Stygian *or* Egyptian
darkness, Erebus; "obscure darkness"—
Bible, "the palpable obscure"—Milton,
"darkness visible"—Milton, "a fabulous,
formless darkness"—Yeats, "the suit of
night"—Shakespeare, "darkness which
may be felt"—Bible; **blackness,** swarthiness 38.2

2 **darkishness,** darksomeness, **duskiness,**
duskness; **murkiness, murk; dimness,**
dim; **semidarkness,** semidark, partial
darkness, bad light, dim light, half-light,
demi-jour <Fr>; gloaming, crepuscular
light, **dusk,** twilight 314.4/315.3

3 **shadow, shade, shadiness;** umbra, umbrage, umbrageousness; thick *or* dark
shade, gloom; mere shadow, "the shadow
of a shade"—Aeschylus; penumbra; silhouette; skiagram, skiagraph

4 **gloom, gloominess, somberness,**
sombrousness, somber; lowering, lower

5 **dullness, flatness,** lifelessness, **drabness,
deadness,** somberness, **lackluster, luster-
lessness,** lack of sparkle *or* sheen; matte,
matte finish

6 **darkening, dimming, bedimming; obscuration,** obscurement, obumbration,

obfuscation; eclipsing, occulting, blocking the light; **shadowing, shading,**
overshadowing, overshading, over-
shadowment, **clouding,** overclouding,
obnubilation, gathering of the clouds,
overcast; blackening 38.5; extinguishment 1021.2

7 **blackout,** dimout, brownout

8 **eclipse,** occultation; total eclipse, partial
eclipse, central eclipse, annular eclipse;
solar eclipse, lunar eclipse

VERBS 9 **darken,** bedarken; **obscure,** obfuscate, obumbrate; **eclipse,** occult, occul-
tate, block the light; **black out,** brown
out; black, brown; blot out; **overcast,**
darken over; **shadow, shade,** cast a
shadow, spread a shadow *or* shade over,
encompass with shadow, overshadow;
cloud, becloud, encloud, cloud over, overcloud, obnubilate; gloom, begloom,
somber, cast a gloom over, murk; **dim,
bedim,** dim out; blacken 38.7

10 **dull,** mat, deaden; **tone down**

11 turn *or* switch off the light, close the light
<nonformal>; extinguish 1021.7

12 **grow dark, darken,** darkle, lower; gloom
<old>, gloam <Scots>; dusk; **dim, grow
dim**

ADJS 13 **dark, black,** darksome, darkling;
lightless, beamless, rayless, unlighted,
unilluminated, unlit; **obscure,** caliginous,
obscured, obfuscated, eclipsed, occulted,
clothed *or* shrouded *or* veiled *or* cloaked
or mantled in darkness; tenebrous, ten-
ebrific, tenebrious, tenebrose; Cimmerian, Stygian; **pitch-dark,** pitch-black,
pitchy, dark as pitch, "dark as a wolf's
mouth"—Sir Walter Scott, dark as
the inside of a black cat; ebon, ebony;
night-dark, night-black, dark *or* black as
night; night-clad, night-cloaked, night-
enshrouded, night-mantled, night-veiled,
night-hid, night-filled; sunless, moonless,
starless

14 **gloomy,** gloomful <old>, glooming, dark
and gloomy, Acheronian, Acherontic,
somber, sombrous; lowering; **funereal;**
stormy, cloudy, clouded, overcast; ill-
lighted, ill-lit

15 **darkish,** darksome, **semidark; dusky,**
dusk; fuscous, subfuscous, subfusc;
murky, murksome, murk <old>; **dim,**
dimmed, bedimmed, dimmish, dimpsy
<Brit nonformal>; dark-colored 38.9

16 **shadowy, shady, shadowed, shaded,**
darkling, umbral, umbrageous; over-
shadowed, overshaded, obumbrate,
obumbrated; penumbral

17 **lackluster, lusterless; dull, dead,** dead-

ened, **lifeless,** somber, **drab,** wan, **flat,**
mat

18 obscuring, obscurant

ADVS **19 in the dark,** darkling, in darkness;
in the night, in the dark of night, in the
dead of night, at *or* by night; dimly,
wanly

1027 SHADE

NOUNS **1 shade,** shader, **screen, light
shield, curtain,** drape, drapery, blind,
veil; **awning,** sunblind <Brit>; **sunshade,** parasol, **umbrella,** beach umbrella; cover 295.2; shadow 1026.3

2 **eyeshade,** eyeshield, visor, bill; goggles,
colored spectacles, smoked glasses, dark
glasses, **sunglasses,** shades <nonformal>

3 **lamp shade;** moonshade; globe, light
globe

4 **light filter,** filter, diffusing screen;
smoked glass, frosted glass, ground glass;
stained glass; butterfly; gelatin filter, celluloid filter; frosted lens; lens hood;
sunscreen

VERBS **5 shade, screen,** veil, curtain, shutter,
draw the curtains, put up *or* close the
shutters; cover 295.19; **shadow** 1026.9

ADJS **6 shading, screening,** veiling, curtaining; shadowing; covering

7 **shaded, screened,** veiled, curtained;
sunproof; visored; shadowed, shady
1026.16

1028 TRANSPARENCY

NOUNS **1 transparency,** transparence, trans-
picuousness, show-through, transmission
or admission of light; **lucidity,** pellucidity, **clearness, clarity,** limpidity; nonopacity, uncloudedness; **crystallinity,**
crystal-clearness; **glassiness,** glasslike-
ness, vitreousness, vitrescence; vitreos-
ity, hyalescence; **diaphanousness,** di-
aphaneity, sheerness, thinness, **gossameriness,** filminess, gauziness

2 transparent substance, diaphane; **glass**
<see list>, glassware, glasswork; vitrics;
stemware; pane, windowpane, light, win-
dowlight, shopwindow; vitrine; showcase, display case; watch crystal *or* glass

VERBS **3 be transparent,** show through;
pass light; vitrify

ADJS **4 transparent,** transpicuous, light-
pervious; show-through, see-through,
peekaboo, revealing; **lucid,** pellucid,
clear, limpid; nonopaque, unclouded,
crystalline, crystal, **crystal-clear,** clear as
crystal; **diaphanous,** diaphane <old>,

sheer, thin; **gossamer,** gossamery, filmy,
gauzy

5 **glass, glassy,** glasslike, clear as glass, vit-
ric, vitreous, vitriform, hyaline, hyales-
cent; hyalinocrystalline

WORD ELEMENTS **6** vitri—

7 glass

agate glass	ice glass
antimony glass	lace glass
arsenic glass	Lalique glass
basalt glass	laminated glass *or*
Bilbao glass	laminated safety
borax glass	glass
lead glass	lead glass
barley-pattern glass	milk glass
blown glass	opal glass
bone glass	opaline
bottle glass	optical glass
bullet-proof glass	ornamental glass
bullet-resisting glass	Orrefors glass
camphor glass	photosensitive glass
carnival glass	plastic glass
Cel-o-Glass	plate glass
<trademark>	porcelain glass
CM-glass	pressed glass
coralene	prism glass
cranberry glass	Pyrex <trademark>
CR-glass	quartz glass
crown glass	rhinestone
cryolite glass	ruby glass
crystal *or* crystal	safety glass
glass	Sandwich glass
custard glass	satin glass
cut glass	sheet glass
end-of-day glass	show glass
etched glass	stained glass
Fiberglas	Steuben glass
<trademark>	Swedish glass
flashed glass	Syracuse watch glass
flat glass	tempered glass *or*
flint glass	tempered safety
float glass	glass
Fostoria <trade-	uranium glass
mark>	uviol glass
frosted glass	Venetian glass
fused quartz	Vitaglass <trade-
glass bead	mark>
glass brick	vitreous silica
glass wool	Waterford glass
ground glass	window glass
hobnail glass	wire *or* wired glass

1029 SEMITRANSPARENCY

NOUNS **1 semitransparency,** semipellucid-
ity, semidiaphaneity; semiopacity

2 **translucence, translucency,** lucence, lucency, translucidity, pellucidity, lucidity;
transmission *or* admission of light

VERBS **3 frost,** frost over

ADJS **4 semitransparent,** semipellucid, semi-
diaphanous, semiopaque; frosty, frosted

5 translucent, lucent, translucid, lucid, pellucid; semitranslucent, semipellucid

1030 OPAQUENESS

NOUNS **1 opaqueness,** opacity, intransparency, nontranslucency, imperviousness to light, adiaphanousness; roil, roiledness, turbidity, turbidness; cloudiness; **darkness, obscurity, dimness** 1026

VERBS **2** opaque, **darken, obscure** 1026.9; **cloud,** becloud

ADJS **3 opaque,** intransparent, nontranslucent, adiaphanous, impervious to light; **dark, obscure** 1026.13, **cloudy,** roiled, roily, grumly <Scots>, turbid

1031 ELECTRICITY, MAGNETISM

NOUNS **1 electricity; electrical science** <see list>; **electrical** or **electric unit,** unit of measurement

2 current, electric current <see list>, current flow, amperage, electric stream or flow, juice <nonformal>

3 electric or **electrical field,** static field, electrostatic field, field of electrical force; tube of electric force, electrostatic tube of force; **magnetic field,** magnetic field of currents; **electromagnetic field;** variable field

4 circuit, electrical circuit, path

5 charge, electric or **electrical charge,** positive charge, negative charge; live wire

6 discharge, arc, electric discharge; **shock,** electroshock, galvanic shock

7 magnetism, magnetic attraction; **electromagnetism;** magnetization; diamagnetism, paramagnetism, ferromagnetism; residual magnetism, magnetic remanence; magnetic memory, magnetic retentiveness; magnetic elements; magnetic dip or inclination, magnetic variation or declination; hysteresis, magnetic hysteresis, hysteresis curve, magnetic friction, magnetic lag or retardation, magnetic creeping; permeability, magnetic permeability, magnetic conductivity; magnetic circuit, magnetic curves, magnetic figures; magnetic flux, gilbert, weber, maxwell; magnetic moment; magnetic potential; magnetic viscosity; magnetics

8 polarity, polarization; **pole, positive pole, anode, negative pole, cathode,** magnetic pole, magnetic axis; north pole, N pole; south pole, S pole

9 magnetic force or **intensity,** magnetic flux density, gauss, oersted; magnetomo-

tive force; magnetomotivity; magnetic tube of force; line of force; **magnetic field, electromagnetic field**

10 electroaffinity, electric attraction; electric repulsion

11 voltage, volt, **electromotive force** or EMF, electromotivity, potential difference; **potential, electric potential;** tension, high tension, low tension

12 resistance, ohm, ohms, ohmage, ohmic resistance, electric resistance; surface resistance, skin effect, volume resistance; insulation resistance; **reluctance,** magnetic reluctance or resistance; specific reluctance, reluctivity; **reactance,** inductive reactance, capacitive reactance; **impedance**

13 conduction, electric conduction; **conductance,** conductivity, mho; superconductivity; gas conduction, ionic conduction, metallic conduction, liquid conduction, photoconduction; **conductor,** semiconductor, superconductor; **nonconductor,** dielectric, insulator

14 induction; electrostatic induction, magnetic induction, electromagnetic induction, electromagnetic induction of currents; self-induction, mutual induction; **inductance,** inductivity, henry

15 capacitance, capacity, farad; collector junction capacitance, emitter junction capacitance, resistance capacitance

16 gain, available gain, current gain, operational gain

17 electric power, wattage, watts; electric horsepower; hydroelectric power, hydroelectricity; power load

18 powerhouse, power station, power plant, central station; oil-fired power plant, coal-fired power plant; hydroelectric plant; nuclear or atomic power plant; power grid, distribution system

19 blackout, power failure, power cut, power loss; **brownout,** voltage drop, voltage loss

20 electrical device, electrical appliance; **battery** <see list>, accumulator, storage battery, storage device; **electric meter,** meter; **wire, cable,** electric wire, electric cord, cord, power cord, power cable

21 electrician, electrotechnician; radio technician 1033.24; wireman; **lineman,** linesman; rigger; groundman; power worker

22 electrotechnologist, electrobiologist, electrochemist, electrometallurgist, electrophysicist, electrophysiologist, **electrical engineer**

23 electrification, electrifying, supplying electricity

24 electrolysis; ionization; galvanization, electrogalvanization; electrocoating, electroplating, electrogilding, electrograving, electroetching; ion, cation, anion; electrolyte, ionogen; nonelectrolyte

VERBS **25 electrify, galvanize,** energize, **charge;** wire, wire up; shock; **generate,** step up, amplify, stiffen; step down; plug in, loop in; switch on or off, turn on or off, turn on or off the juice <nonformal>; short-circuit, short

26 magnetize; electromagnetize; demagnetize, degauss

27 electrolyze; ionize; galvanize, electrogalvanize; electroplate, electrogild

28 insulate, isolate; **ground**

ADJS **29 electric, electrical, electrifying;** galvanic, voltaic; dynamoelectric, hydroelectric, photoelectric, piezoelectric, etc; electrothermal, electrochemical, electromechanical, electropneumatic, electrodynamic, static, electrostatic; electromotive; electrokinetic; electroscopic, galvanoscopic; electrometric, galvanometric, voltametric; **electrified,** electric-powered, battery-powered, cordless; solar-powered

30 magnetic, electromagnetic; diamagnetic, paramagnetic, ferromagnetic; **polar**

31 electrolytic; hydrolytic; ionic, anionic, cationic; ionogenic

32 electrotechnical; electroballistic, electrobiological, electrochemical, electrometallurgical, electrophysiological

33 charged, electrified, live, hot; high-tension, low-tension

34 positive, plus, electropositive; **negative,** minus, electronegative

35 nonconducting, nonconductive, insulating, dielectric

WORD ELEMENTS **36 electr—,** electro—; rheo—; magnet—, magneto—

37 electrical sciences

electrical engineering	electro-
electroballistics	photomicrography
electrobiology	electrophysics
electrochemistry	electrophysiology
electrodynamics	electrostatics
electrokinematics	electrotechnology or
electrokinetics	electrotechnics
electromechanics	electrothermics
electrometallurgy	galvanism
electrometry	magnetics
electronics	magnetometry
electrooptics	thermionics

38 electric currents

absorption current	alternating current or
active current	AC
conduction current	magnetizing current
convection current	multiphase current
delta current	oscillating current
dielectric displace-	pulsating direct cur-
ment current	rent
direct current or DC	reactive current
displacement current	rotary current
eddy current	single-phase alternat-
emission current	ing current
exciting current	stray current
free alternating cur-	thermionic current
rent	thermoelectric cur-
galvanic current	rent
high-frequency cur-	three-phase alternat-
rent	ing current
induced current	voltaic current
induction current	watt current
ionization current	wattless or idle cur-
low-frequency cur-	rent
rent	

39 batteries

accumulator	nickel-cadmium bat-
alkaline cell	tery
atomic battery	primary battery
cell	secondary battery
dry battery	solar battery
dry cell	solar cell
electronic battery	storage battery
fuel cell	storage cell
lead-acid battery	voltaic battery
Leyden battery	voltaic cell
Leyden jar	voltaic pile
mercury cell	wet cell

1032 ELECTRONICS

NOUNS **1 electronics,** radionics, radio-electronics; electron physics, electro-physics, electron dynamics; electron optics; semiconductor physics, transistor physics; photoelectronics, photoelectricity; microelectronics; electronic engineering; avionics; electron microscopy; nuclear physics 1037; radio 1033; television 1034; radar 1035; automation 1040

2 <electron theory> electron theory of atoms, electron theory of electricity, electron theory of solids, free electron theory of metals, band theory of solids

3 electron <see list>, negatron, cathode particle, beta particle; thermion; electron capture, electron transfer; electron spin; electron state, energy level; ground state, excited state; electron pair, lone pair, shared pair, electron-positron pair, duplet, octet; electron cloud; shells, electron layers, electron shells, valence shell, valence electrons, subvalent electrons; electron affinity, relative electron affinity

4 electronic effect; Edison effect, thermionic effect, photoelectric effect

5 electron emission; thermionic emission; photoelectric emission, photoemission; collision emission, bombardment emission, secondary emission; field emission; grid emission, thermionic grid emission; electron ray, electron beam, cathode ray, anode ray, positive ray, canal ray; glow discharge, cathode glow, cathodoluminescence, cathodofluorescence; electron diffraction

6 electron flow, electron stream, electron *or* **electronic current;** electric current 1031.2; electron gas, electron cloud, space charge

7 electron volt; ionization potential; input voltage, output voltage; base signal voltage, collector signal voltage, emitter signal voltage; battery supply voltage; screen-grid voltage; inverse peak voltage; voltage saturation

8 electronic circuit <see list>, transistor circuit, semiconductor circuit; vacuum-tube circuit, thermionic tube circuit; **printed circuit, microcircuit; chip, silicon chip,** microchip; **circuitry**

9 conductance, electronic conductance; **resistance,** electronic resistance

10 electron tube, vacuum tube, tube, valve <Brit>, thermionic tube; radio tube, television tube; **special-purpose tube; vacuum tube component**

11 photoelectric tube *or* **cell, phototube,** photocell; electron-ray tube, **electric eye;** photosensitivity, **photosensitive devices**

12 transistor <see list>, semiconductor *or* solid-state device

13 electronic device, electronic meter, electronic measuring device; **electronic tester,** electronic testing device

14 electronics engineer, electronics physicist

ADJS **15 electronic;** photoelectronic, **photoelectric;** autoelectronic; microelectronic; thermoelectronic; thermionic; anodic, cathodic; transistorized

16 electrons

bonding electron	planetary electron
bound electron	positive electron
conduction electron	primary electron
excess electron	recoil electron
extranuclear electron	secondary electron
free electron	spinning electron
nuclear electron	surface-bound electron
orbital electron	tron
peripheral electron	valence electron
photoelectron	wandering electron

17 electronic circuits

amplifier circuit	shunt circuit
astable circuit	sinusoidal circuit
back-to-back switching circuit	small signal hybrid open circuit
bistable circuit	small signal hybrid short circuit
coupling circuit	small signal open circuit
equivalent circuit	cuit
flip-flop circuit	small signal short circuit
gate *or* logic gate	cuit
monostable circuit	
mu circuit	trigger circuit
nonsinusoidal circuit	tuned circuit
rectifier circuit	

18 transistors

base	melt-quench transistor
collector	tor
conductivity-modulation transistor	meltback transistor
	mesa transistor
tor	microalloy transistor
diffused-base transistor	phototransistor
tor	point-contact transistor
diffusion transistor	tor
drift transistor	point-junction transistor
emitter	sistor
field-effect transistor	power transistor
filamentary transistor	rate-grown transistor
tor	spacistor
germanium crystal triode	symmetrical transistor
	tor
germanium diode	tandem transistor
germanium triode	tetrode transistor
hook transistor	unijunction transistor
hook-collector transistor	tor
sistor	unipolar transistor
junction transistor	

1033 RADIO

NOUNS **1 radio, wireless** <Brit>; radiotelephony, radiotelegraphy; communications, telecommunication 347.1

2 radiotechnology, radio engineering, communication engineering; radio electronics, radioacoustics; radiogoniometry; conelrad *or* Control of Electromagnetic Radiation for Civil Defense <old>, emergency warning network

3 radio, radio receiver <see list>; radio telescope; **radio set, receiver,** receiving set, **wireless** *and* wireless set <both Brit>, set; cabinet, console, housing; chassis; receiver part

4 radio transmitter <see list>, **transmitter;** transmitter part; microphone 50.9, radiomicrophone; **antenna,** aerial

5 radiomobile, mobile transmitter, remote-pickup unit

6 radio station, transmitting station, **studio,** studio plant; AM station, FM station, shortwave station, ultrahigh-frequency station, clear-channel station; direction-finder station, RDF station; relay station, radio relay station, microwave relay station; amateur station, ham station <nonformal>, ham shack <nonformal>; pirate radio station, offshore station

7 control room, mixing room, monitor room, monitoring booth; **control desk,** console, master control desk, instrument panel, control panel or board, jack field, mixer <nonformal>

8 network, net, radio links, **hookup,** communications net, circuit, network stations, network affiliations, affiliated stations; coaxial network, circuit network, coast-to-coast hookup

9 radio circuit, radio-frequency circuit, audio-frequency circuit, superheterodyne circuit, amplifying circuit; electronic circuit 1032.8

10 radio signal, radio-frequency or RF signal, direct signal, shortwave signal, AM signal, FM signal; reflected signal, bounce; unidirectional signal, beam; signal-noise ratio; **radio-frequency or RF amplifier,** radio-frequency or RF stage

11 radio wave, electric wave, electromagnetic wave, hertzian wave; shortwave, long wave, microwave, high-frequency wave, low-frequency wave; ground wave, sky wave; carrier, carrier wave; **wavelength**

12 frequency; radio frequency or RF, intermediate frequency or IF, audio frequency or AF; high frequency or HF; very high frequency or VHF; ultrahigh frequency or UHF; superhigh frequency or SHF; extremely high frequency or EHF; medium frequency or MF; low frequency or LF; very low frequency or VLF; upper frequencies, lower frequencies; **carrier frequency;** spark frequency; spectrum, frequency spectrum; cycles, CPS, hertz, Hz, **kilohertz, kilocycles; megahertz, megacycles**

13 band, frequency band, standard band, broadcast band, amateur band, citizens band, police band, shortwave band, FM band; **channel,** radio channel, broadcast channel

14 modulation; amplitude modulation or AM; frequency modulation or FM; phase modulation or PM; sideband, side frequency, single sideband, double sideband

15 amplification, radio-frequency or RF amplification, audio-frequency or AF amplification, intermediate-frequency or IF amplification, high-frequency amplification

16 radio broadcasting, broadcasting, the air

waves, radiocasting; **airplay, airtime;** commercial radio, public radio; AM broadcasting, FM broadcasting, shortwave broadcasting; **transmission, radio transmission;** direction or beam transmission, asymmetric or vestigial transmission; multipath transmission, multiplex transmission; mixing, volume control, sound or tone control, fade-in, fadeout; broadcasting regulation, Federal Communications Commission or FCC

17 pickup, outside pickup, **remote pickup,** spot pickup

18 radiobroadcast, broadcast, radiocast, **radio program;** rebroadcast, rerun; simulcast; electronic or broadcast journalism, broadcast news, newscast, newsbreak, newsflash; all-news radio or format; sportscast; **talk radio;** talk show, audience-participation show, call-in or phone-in show, interview show; network show; commercial program, commercial; sustaining program, sustainer; serial, soap opera <nonformal>; taped program, canned show <nonformal>, electrical transcription; sound effects

19 signature, station identification, call letters; theme song; **station break,** pause for station identification

20 commercial, commercial announcement, commercial message, message, **spot announcement,** spot and plug <both nonformal>

21 reception; fading, fade-out; **drift,** creeping, crawling; **interference,** noise interference, station interference; **static,** atmospherics, noise; blasting, blaring; blind spot; **jamming,** deliberate interference

22 radio listener, listener-in and tuner-inner <both nonformal>; radio audience, listeners, **listenership**

23 broadcaster, radiobroadcaster, radiocaster; newscaster, sportscaster; commentator, news commentator; anchor, news anchor, anchor man or woman; host, talk-show host, talk jockey <nonformal>; announcer; disk jockey or DJ <both nonformal>; master of ceremonies, MC or emcee <both nonformal>; program director, programmer; sound-effects man, sound man; American Federation of Radio and Television Artists or AFTRA

24 radioman, radio technician, radio engineer; radiotrician, radio electrician, radio repairman; **radio operator;** control engineer, volume engineer; mixer; **amateur radio operator, ham** and ham opera-

tor <both nonformal>, radio amateur;
Amateur Radio Relay League *or* ARRL;
monitor; radiotelegrapher 347.16

VERBS 25 broadcast, radiobroadcast, radiocast, simulcast, **radio, wireless** <Brit>,
radiate, **transmit,** send; narrowcast;
shortwave; beam; newscast, sportscast,
put *or* go on the air, sign on; go off the air,
sign off

26 monitor, check

27 listen in, tune in; tune up, tune down,
tune out, tune off

ADJS 28 radio, wireless <Brit>; radiosonic;
neutrodyne; heterodyne; superheterodyne; shortwave; radio-frequency, audio-
frequency; high-frequency, low-
frequency, etc; radiogenic

29 radio receivers

all-wave receiver	radio-record player
AM receiver	radiophone
AM tuner	railroad radio
AM-FM receiver	receiver
AM-FM tuner	rechargeable-battery
auto radio *or* car	radio
radio	regenerative receiver
aviation radio	relay receiver
battery radio	scanner
citizens band *or* CB	ship-to-shore radio
radio *or* CB	shortwave receiver
clock radio	single-signal receiver
communications re-	six-band receiver
ceiver	stereo receiver
crystal set	superheterodyne
facsimile receiver *or*	table radio
fax	three-way *or* three-
FM receiver	power receiver
FM tuner	transceiver
ghetto box *or* blaster	transistor radio
or beat box *or* box	transmit-receiver
headband receiver	tuner
mobile radio	two-way radio
multiplex receiver	universal receiver
pocket radio	VHF-FM receiver
portable radio	walkie-talkie
radar receiver	Walkman
radio direction finder	<trademark>
or RDF	weather radio
radio-phonograph	

30 radio transmitters

AM transmitter	picture transmitter
amateur *or* ham	portable transmitter
transmitter *or* rig	pulse transmitter
<nonformal>	radio beacon
arc *or* spark trans-	radio marker
mitter	radio range
continuous-wave *or*	beacon
CW transmitter	radiometeorograph
facsimile transmitter	radiosonde
or fax	radiotelephone trans-
fan marker	mitter
FM transmitter	relay transmitter
link transmitter	RT transmitter

shortwave trans-	transmitter receiver
mitter	*or* transceiver
standby transmitter	vacuum-tube trans-
tape transmitter	mitter
television transmitter	VHF-FM transmitter

1034 TELEVISION

NOUNS 1 television, TV, video, telly <Brit
nonformal>; the small screen *or* the tube
<both nonformal>, the boob tube <non-
formal>; **network television,** free television; the dream factory; subscription
television, pay TV; cable television, cable
TV, cable-television system *or* cable system; closed-circuit television *or* closed
circuit TV; public-access television *or*
public-access TV

2 television broadcast, telecast, TV show;
direct broadcast, live show <nonfor-
mal>; taped show, canned show <non-
formal>; prime time, prime-time
show *or* attraction; television drama *or*
play, teleplay; telefilm; dramatic series,
miniseries; situation comedy *or* sitcom
<nonformal>; game-show; **serial,** day-
time serial, soap opera *or* soap <non-
formal>; quiz show; giveaway show;
panel show; electronic *or* broadcast journalism, broadcast news, newscast, news
show; documentary, docudrama; edu-
tainment, infotainment; film pickup;
colorcast; simulcast; childrens' television, kidvid <nonformal>; television *or*
TV performer, television *or* TV personality; news anchor, anchor, anchor
man, anchor woman, anchor person; ratings, Nielsen rating; people meter

3 televising, telecasting; facsimile broadcasting; monitoring, mixing, shading,
blanking, switching; scanning, parallel-
line scanning, interlaced scanning

4 <transmission> photoemission, audio-
emission; television channel, TV band;
video *or* picture channel, audio *or* sound
channel, video frequency; picture carrier,
sound carrier; beam, scanning beam, return beam; triggering pulse, voltage
pulse, output pulse, timing pulse, equalizing pulse; synchronizing pulse, vertical
synchronizing pulse, horizontal synchronizing pulse; video signal, audio signal;
IF video signal, IF audio signal; synchronizing signal, blanking signal

5 <reception> **picture, image; color television,** dot-sequential *or* field-sequential *or*
line-sequential color television; **black-
and-white television;** HDTV *or* high-
definition television; definition, blacker

than black synchronizing; shading, black spot, hard shadow; test pattern, scanning pattern, grid; vertical interference, rain; granulation, scintillation, snow, snowstorm; flare, bloom, woomp; picture shifts, blooping, rolling; double image, multiple image, ghost; video static, noise, picture noise; signal-to-noise ratio; fringe area

6 television studio, TV station

7 mobile unit, TV mobile; video truck, audio truck, transmitter truck

8 transmitter, televisor; audio transmitter, video transmitter; transmitter part <see list>

9 relay links, boosters, booster amplifiers, relay transmitters, **booster** or **relay stations;** microwave link; aeronautical relay, stratovision; communication satellite, satellite relay; Telstar, Intelsat, Syncom; Comsat

10 television camera, telecamera, pickup camera, pickup; **camera tube** <see list>; camcorder; mobile camera

11 television receiver, television or **TV set,** TV, telly <Brit nonformal>, televisor, boob tube and idiot box <both nonformal>; **picture tube** <see list>; receiver part <see list>; portable television or TV set; **screen,** telescreen, videoscreen; raster; **video-cassette recorder** or **VCR,** videorecorder, video-tape recorder; video tape, video-cassette; videophone, Picturephone <trademark>

12 televiewer, viewer; television or viewing audience; viewership

13 television technician, TV man or woman, television or TV repairman or repairwoman, television engineer; monitor, sound or audio monitor, picture or video monitor; pickup unit man, cameraman, camerawoman, sound man, sound woman

VERBS **14 televise, telecast;** colorcast; simulcast

15 teleview, watch television or TV; telerecord, record, tape

ADJS **16 televisional,** televisual, televisionary, **video;** telegenic, videogenic; in synchronization, in sync <nonformal>, locked in

WORD ELEMENTS **17** tele—, video—, TV—

18 transmitter parts

adder	exploring element
antenna filter	monitor screen
camera deflection generator	reproducing element
channel filter	signal generator
encoder	sound unit

synchronizing generator — Tel-Eye
TV-Eye

19 camera tubes

iconoscope	orthicon
image dissector or dissector tube	pickup tube
	Saticon <trademark>
image iconoscope	vidicon
image orthicon	

20 picture tubes

cathode-ray tube	Oscilight
color kinescope	projection tube
direct-viewing tube	shadow-mask kinescope
kinescope	
monoscope	

21 receiver parts

audio amplifier	photocathode
audio detector	photoelectric cells
audio-frequency detector	picture control
	picture detector
blanking amplifier	radio units
contrast control	screen
converter	shading amplifier
deflection generator	signal separator
electron tubes	sound limiter
FM detector	synchronizing separator
horizontal deflector	
horizontal synchronizer	vertical deflector
	vertical synchronizer
limiter	video amplifier
mixer	video detector

1035 RADAR, RADIOLOCATORS

NOUNS **1 radar,** radio detection and ranging; **radar set,** radiolocator <Brit>; radar part; oscilloscope, radarscope; radar antenna; radar reflector

2 airborne radar, aviation radar; **navar,** navigation and ranging; **teleran,** television radar air navigation; radar bombsight, K-1 bombsight; radar dome, radome

3 loran, long range aid to navigation; **shoran,** short range aid to navigation; GEE navigation, consolan

4 radiolocator; direction finder, radio direction finder or RDF; radiogoniometer, high-frequency direction finder or HFDF; huff-duff <nonformal>; radio compass, wireless compass <Brit>

5 radar speed meter, electronic cop <nonformal>; radar highway patrol; radar detector, Fuzzbuster <trademark>

6 radar station, control station; Combat Information Center or CIC; Air Route Traffic Control Center or ARTCC; beacon station, display station; fixed station, home station; portable field unit, mobile trailer unit; tracking station; direction-finder station, radio compass station; triangulation stations

7 radar beacon, racon; transponder; radar beacon buoy, marker buoy, radar marked beacon, ramark

8 <radar operations> data transmission, scanning, scan conversion, flector tuning, signal modulation, triggering signals; phase adjustment, locking signals; triangulation, three-pointing; mapping; range finding; tracking, automatic tracking, locking on; precision focusing, pinpointing; radar-telephone relay; radar navigation

9 <applications> detection, interception, ranging, ground control of aircraft, air-traffic control, blind flying, blind landing, storm tracking, hurricane tracking; radar fence *or* screen; radar astronomy

10 pulse, radio-frequency *or* RF pulse, high-frequency *or* HF pulse, intermediate-frequency *or* IF pulse, trigger pulse, echo pulse

11 signal, radar signal; transmitter signal, output signal; return signal, echo signal, video signal, reflection, picture, target image, display, signal display, trace, reading, return, **echo, bounces, blips, pips;** spot, CRT spot; three-dimensional *or* 3-D display, double-dot display; deflection-modulated *or* DM display, intensity-modulated *or* IM display; radio-frequency *or* RF echoes, intermediate-frequency *or* IF signal; beat signal, Doppler signal, local oscillator signal; beam, beavertail beam

12 radar interference, deflection, refraction, superrefraction; atmospheric attenuation, signal fades, blind spots, false echoes; clutter, ground clutter, sea clutter

13 <radar countermeasure> **jamming, radar jamming;** tinfoil, aluminum foil, chaff, window <Brit>

14 radar technician, radar engineer, radarman; air-traffic controller; jammer

VERBS **15 transmit, send,** radiate, beam; **jam**

16 reflect, return, echo, bounce back

17 receive, tune in, pick up, spot, home on; pinpoint; identify, trigger; lock on; sweep, scan; map

1036 RADIATION, RADIOACTIVITY

NOUNS **1 radiation,** radiant energy; ionizing radiation; **radioactivity,** activity, radioactive radiation *or* emanation, atomic *or* nuclear radiation; natural radioactivity, artificial radioactivity; curiage; specific activity, high-specific activity; actinic ra-

diation, ultra-violet *or* violet radiation; radiotransparency, radiolucence *or* radiolucency; radiopacity; radiosensitivity, radiosensibility; half-life; radiocarbon dating; contamination, decontamination; saturation point; radiac *or* radioactivity detection identification and computation; fallout 1037.16

2 radioluminescence, autoluminescence; cathode luminescence; Cerenkov radiation, synchrotron radiation

3 ray, radiation, <see list>, cosmic ray bombardment, electron shower; electron emission 1032.5

4 radioactive particle; alpha particle, beta particle; heavy particle; high-energy particle; meson, mesotron; cosmic particle, solar particle, aurora particle, V-particle

5 <radioactive substance> **radiator;** alpha radiator, beta radiator, gamma radiator; fluorescent paint, radium paint; radium nonformal; fission products; radiocarbon, radiocopper, radioiodine, radiothorium, etc; mesothorium; **radioactive element** <see list>, radioelement; radioisotope; tracer, tracer element, tracer atom; radioactive waste

6 counter, radioscope, radiodetector, **atom-tagger;** ionization chamber; ionizing event; X-ray spectrograph, X-ray spectrometer

7 radiation physics, radiological physics; radiobiology, radiochemistry, radio-metallography, radiography, roentgenography, roentgenology, radiometry, spectroradiometry, radiotechnology, radiopathology; radiology; radiotherapy; radioscopy, curiescopy, roentgenoscopy, radiostereoscopy, fluoroscopy, photofluorography, orthodiagraphy; X-ray photometry, X-ray spectrometry; tracer investigation, atom-tagging; **unit of radioactivity** <see list>; exposure, dose, absorbed dose

8 radiation physicist; radiobiologist, radiometallographer, radiochemist, etc; radiologist

VERBS **9 radioactivate,** activate, **irradiate,** charge; radiumize; **contaminate,** poison, infect

ADJS **10 radioactive,** activated, radioactivated, irradiated, charged, **hot; contaminated,** infected, poisoned; exposed; radiferous; radioluminescent, autoluminescent

11 radiable; radiotransparent, radioparent, radiolucent; radiopaque, radium-proof; radiosensitive

12 rays, radiation

actinic ray	gamma ray *or* radia-
alpha ray *or* radiation	tion
anode ray	Grenz ray
Becquerel ray	infraroentgen ray
beta ray *or* radiation	Leonard ray
canal ray	nuclear radiation
cathode ray	positive ray
cosmic ray *or* radia-	Roentgen ray
tion	X ray *or* radiation

13 radioactive elements

actinium	nobelium
americium	plutonium
astatine	polonium
berkelium	promethium
californium	protactinium
curium	radium
einsteinium	radon *or* radium ema-
fermium	nation
francium	technetium
hahnium	thorium
mendelevium	uranium
neptunium	

14 units of radioactivity

curie	microcurie
dose equivalent	millicurie
gray	multicurie
half-life	rad
megacurie	roentgen

1037 NUCLEAR PHYSICS

NOUNS **1 nuclear physics,** particle physics, nucleonics, atomics, atomistics, atomology, atomic science; quantum mechanics, wave mechanics; molecular physics; thermionics; mass spectrometry, mass spectrography; radiology 1036.7

  2 <atomic theory> quantum theory, Bohr theory, Dirac theory, Rutherford theory, Schrödinger theory, Lewis-Langmuir *or* octet theory, Thomson's hypothesis; law of conservation of mass, law of definite proportions, law of multiple proportions, law of Dulong and Petit, law of parity, correspondence principle; Standard Model; supersymmetry theory, unified field theory; atomism; quark model

  3 atomic scientist, nuclear physicist, particle physicist; radiologist 1036.8

  4 atom <see lists>; tracer, tracer atom, tagger atom; atomic model, nuclear atom; nuclide; **ion; shell,** subshell, planetary shell, valence shell; **atomic unit;** atomic constant

  5 isotope; protium, deuterium *or* heavy hydrogen *and* tritium <all isotopes of hydrogen>; radioactive isotope, **radioisotope;** carbon 14, strontium 90, uranium 235; artificial isotope; isotone; isobar, isomer, nuclear isomer

  6 elementary particle, atomic particle, **subatomic particle** <see list>, subnuclear particle, ultraelementary particle; **atomic nucleus, nucleus,** *Kern* <Ger>; **nuclear particle,** nucleon; proton, neutron <see list>; deuteron *or* deuterium nucleus, triton *or* tritium nucleus, alpha particle *or* helium nucleus; **nuclear force,** weak force *or* weak nuclear force, strong force *or* strong nuclear force; weak interaction, strong interaction; fifth force; nucleosynthesis; nuclear resonance, Mössbauer effect, nuclear magnetic resonance *or* NMR; strangeness; charm

  7 atomic cluster, molecule; radical, simple radical, compound radical, chain, straight chain, branched chain, side chain; ring, closed chain, cycle; homocycle, heterocycle; benzene ring *or* nucleus, Kekulé formula; lattice, space-lattice

  8 fission, nuclear fission, fission reaction; **atom-smashing,** atom-chipping, **splitting the atom;** atomic reaction; atomic disintegration *or* decay, alpha decay, beta decay, gamma decay; stimulation, dissociation, photodisintegration, ionization, nucleization, cleavage; neutron reaction, proton reaction, etc; reversible reaction, nonreversible reaction; thermonuclear reaction; **chain reaction;** exchange reaction; breeding; disintegration series; bombardment, atomization; bullet, target; proton gun

  9 fusion, nuclear fusion, fusion reaction, thermonuclear reaction, thermonuclear fusion, laser-induced fusion, cold fusion

10 fissionable material, nuclear fuel; fertile material; **critical mass,** noncritical mass; parent element, daughter element; end product

11 accelerator <see list>, **particle accelerator,** atomic accelerator, atom smasher, atomic cannon

12 mass spectrometer, mass spectrograph

13 reactor <see list>, **nuclear reactor, pile,** atomic pile, reactor pile, chain-reacting pile, chain reactor, **furnace,** atomic *or* nuclear furnace, neutron factory; fast pile, intermediate pile, slow pile; lattice; bricks; rods; radioactive waste

14 atomic engine, **atomic** *or* **nuclear power plant,** reactor engine

15 atomic energy, nuclear energy *or* **power,** thermonuclear power; activation energy, binding energy, mass energy; energy level; atomic research, atomic project; Atomic Energy Commission *or* AEC

16 atomic explosion, atom blast, A-blast; thermonuclear explosion, hydrogen blast, **H-blast;** ground zero; blast wave, Mach stem; Mach front; mushroom cloud; **fallout,** airborne radioactivity, fission particles, dust cloud, radioactive dust; flash burn; **atom bomb** or **atomic bomb** or **A-bomb, hydrogen bomb,** thermonuclear bomb, nuke <nonformal>; A-bomb shelter, fallout shelter

VERBS **17 atomize,** nucleize; activate, accelerate; bombard, cross-bombard; cleave, fission, **split** or **smash the atom**

ADJS **18 atomic;** atomistic; atomiferous; monatomic, diatomic, triatomic, tetratomic, pentatomic, hexatomic, heptatomic; heteratomic, heteroatomic; subatomic, subnuclear, ultraelementary; dibasic, tribasic; cyclic, isocyclic, homocyclic, heterocyclic; isotopic, isobaric, isoteric

19 nuclear, thermonuclear, isonuclear, homonuclear, heteronuclear, extranuclear

20 fissionable, fissile, scissile

21 atoms

acceptor atom	isotopic isobar
asymmetric carbon atom	labeled atom
	neutral atom
discrete atom	normal atom
excited atom	nuclear isomer
hot atom	radiation atom
impurity atom	recoil atom
isobar	stripped atom
isotere	

22 subatomic particles

antibaryon	kaon or K-meson or
antielectron	K-particle
antilepton	lambda particle
antimeson	lepton
antineutrino	magnetic monopole
antineutron	matter particle
antiparticle	meson or mesotron
antiproton	muon or mu-meson
antiquark	neutrino
b or bottom quark	neutron
baryon	omega or omega-zero
beta particle	or omega nought
boson	particle
electron	phi-meson
energy particle	photino
fermion	photon
flavor	pion or pi-meson
gauge boson	positron or positive
gluino	electron
gravitino	proton
graviton	quark
hadron	quarkonium
Higgs boson	rho particle
hyperon	s or strange quark
intermediate-vector boson	sigma particle
	slepton
J or J particle or psi particle	squark
	strange particle

superstring	u or up quark
tachyon	weakon
tardyon	WIMP or weakly interactive massive particle
tau or tauon or tau lepton	
tau-meson	w particle
tau neutrino or tauonic neutrino	xi-particle
	zino
technifermion	z particle
t or top quark	z-zero

23 neutrons

fast neutron	resonance neutron
monoenergetic neutron	slow neutron
	thermal neutron
photoneutron	

24 accelerators

betatron	linear accelerator
bevatron	microwave linear accelerator
cascade transformer	
charge-exchange accelerator	positive-ion accelerator
Cockcroft-Walton voltage multiplier	superconducting supercollider or SSC
collider	synchrocyclotron
cosmotron	synchrotron
cyclotron	tokamak
electron accelerator	Van de Graaff generator
electrostatic generator	
induction accelerator	wake-field accelerator

25 reactors

boiling water reactor	plutonium reactor
breeder reactor	power-breeder reactor
CANDU or Canada deuterium oxide-uranium reactor	power reactor
gas-cooled reactor	pressurized-water reactor
heterogeneous reactor	stellarator
homogeneous reactor	uranium reactor

1038 MECHANICS

NOUNS **1 mechanics** <see list>; leverage 905; tools and machinery 1039

2 statics <see list>

3 dynamics <see list>, **kinetics,** energetics

4 hydraulics, fluid dynamics, hydromechanics, hydrokinetics, fluidics, hydrodynamics, hydrostatics; hydrology, hydrography, hydrometry, fluviology

5 pneumatics, pneumatostatics; aeromechanics, aerophysics, aerology, aerometry, aerography, aerotechnics, aerodynamics, aerostatics

6 engineering, mechanical engineering, jet engineering, etc; engineers

ADJS **7 mechanical,** mechanistic; locomotive, locomotor; zoomechanical, biomechanical, aeromechanical, hydromechanical, etc

8 **static;** biostatic, electrostatic, geostatic, etc

9 **dynamic, dynamical, kinetic, kinetical, kinematic, kinematical;** geodynamic, radiodynamic, electrodynamic, etc

10 **pneumatic,** pneumatological; aeromechanical, aerophysical, aerologic, aerological, aerotechnical, aerodynamic, aerostatic, aerographic, aerographical

11 hydrologic, hydrometric, hydrometrical, hydromechanic, hydromechanical, hydrodynamic, hydrostatic, hydraulic

12 **kinds and branches of mechanics**

aeromechanics	mechanical arts
animal mechanics	micromechanics
applied mechanics	practical mechanics
atomechanics	pure *or* abstract me-
auto mechanics	chanics
celestial mechanics	quantum mechanics
electromechanics	rational mechanics
fluid mechanics	servomechanics
hydromechanics *or*	statistical mechanics
hydrodynamics	telemechanics
kinematics	theoretical *or* analyti-
magneto-	cal mechanics
hydrodynamics	wave mechanics
or MHD	zoomechanics *or* bio-
matrix mechanics	mechanics

13 **statics**

aerostatics	hemastatics *or*
biostatics	hematostatics
electrostatics	hydrostatics
geostatics	hygrostatics
gnathostatics	rheostatics
graphostatics	stereostatics
gyrostatics	thermostatics

14 **dynamics**

aerodynamics	magneto-
astrodynamics	hydrodynamics
barodynamics	megadynamics
biodynamics	myodynamics
cardiodynamics	pharmacodynamics
electrodynamics	photodynamics
fluid dynamics	phytodynamics
geodynamics	pneodynamics
gnathodynamics	pneumodynamics
hemadynamics *or*	radiodynamics
hematodynamics	thermodynamics
hydrodynamics	trophodynamics
kinesiology	zoodynamics

1039 TOOLS, MACHINERY

NOUNS 1 **tool, instrument, implement, utensil; apparatus, device,** mechanical device, contrivance, contraption <nonformal>, gadget, gizmo, gimcrack, gimmick <nonformal>, means, mechanical means; gadgetry; **hand tool;** hammer; wrench; **power tool;** machine tool; speed tool; pre-cision tool *or* instrument; **mechanization,** mechanizing; motorizing

2 **cutlery,** edge tool; **knife, ax,** dagger, sword, blade, cutter, whittle; steel, cold steel, naked steel; shiv *and* pigsticker *and* toad stabber *and* toad sticker <all nonformal>; perforator, piercer, puncturer, point; sharpener; **saw;** trowel; shovel; plane; drill; valve 239.10

3 **machinery,** enginery; **machine, mechanism,** mechanical device; heavy machinery, earthmoving machinery, earthmover; farm machinery; mill; welder; pump; **engine,** motor; engine part; power plant, **power source,** drive, motive power, prime mover; **appliance,** convenience, facility, utility, home appliance, mechanical aid; fixture; labor-saving device

4 **mechanism,** machinery, **movement,** movements, **action, motion, works,** workings, inner workings, what makes it work, innards, what makes it tick; drive train, power train; wheelwork, **wheelworks,** wheels, gear, wheels within wheels, epicyclic train; clockworks, watchworks, servomechanism 1040.13

5 **gear,** gearing, gear train; gearwheel, cogwheel, rack; **gearshift;** low, intermediate, high, neutral, reverse; differential, differential gear *or* gearing; **transmission,** gearbox; automatic transmission; selective transmission; standard transmission, stick shift; synchronized shifting, synchromesh

6 **clutch,** cone clutch, plate clutch, dog clutch, disk clutch, multiple-disk clutch, rim clutch, friction clutch, cone friction clutch, slip friction clutch, spline clutch, rolling-key clutch

7 **tooling,** tooling up; **retooling;** instrumentation, industrial instrumentation; servo instrumentation

8 **mechanic,** mechanician; grease monkey <nonformal>; artisan, artificer; **machinist,** machiner; auto mechanic, aeromechanic, etc

VERBS 9 **tool,** tool up, instrument; retool; **machine,** mill; **mechanize,** motorize; sharpen

ADJS 10 **mechanical;** machinelike; power, powered, power-driven, motor-driven, motorized; **mechanized**

1040 AUTOMATION

NOUNS 1 **automation,** automatic control; robotization, cybernation; **self-action,** self-activity; self-movement, self-motion, **self-propulsion;** self-direction, self-determination, self-government, automatism, self-regulation; automaticity, automatization; servo instrumentation; computerization

2 autonetics, automatic *or* automation technology, automatic electronics, automatic engineering, automatic control engineering, servo engineering, **servomechanics,** system engineering, systems analysis, feedback system engineering; **cybernetics;** telemechanics; radiodynamics, radio control; systems planning, systems design; circuit analysis; bionics; communication *or* communications theory, information theory

3 **automatic control,** cybernation, servo control, robot control, robotization; cybernetic control; electronic control, electronic-mechanical control; feedback control, digital feedback control, analog feedback control; cascade control, piggyback control <nonformal>; supervisory control; action, control action; derivative *or* rate action, reset action; control agent; control means

4 semiautomatic control; **remote control,** push-button control, remote handling, tele-action; radio control; telemechanics; telemechanism; telemetry, telemeter, telemetering; transponder; bioinstrument, bioinstrumentation

5 control system, **automatic control system,** servo system, robot system; closed-loop system; open-sequence system; linear system, nonlinear system; carrier-current system; integrated system, complex control system; data system, data-handling system, data-reduction system, data-input system, data-interpreting system, digital data reducing system; process-control system, annunciator system, flow-control system, motor-speed control system; automanual system; automatic telephone system; electrostatic spraying system; automated factory, automatic *or* robot factory, push-button plant; servo laboratory, servolab

6 **feedback,** closed sequence, feedback loop, closed loop; multiple-feed closed loop; process loop, quality loop; feedback circuit, current-control circuit, direct-current circuit, alternating-current circuit, calibrating circuit, switching circuit, flip-flop circuit, peaking circuit; multiplier channels; open sequence, linear operation; positive feedback, negative feedback; reversed feedback, degeneration

7 <functions> accounting, analysis, automatic electronic navigation, automatic guidance, braking, comparison of variables, computation, coordination, corrective action, fact distribution, forecasts, impedance matching, inspection, linear *or* nonlinear calibrations, manipulation, measurement of variables, missile guidance, output measurement, processing, rate determination, record keeping, statistical communication, steering, system stabilization, ultrasonic *or* supersonic flow detection

8 **process control,** bit-weight control, color control, density control, dimension control, diverse control, end-point control, flavor control, flow control, fragrance control, hold control, humidity control, light-intensity control, limit control, liquid-level control, load control, pressure control, precision-production control, proportional control, quality control, quantity control, revolution control, temperature control, time control, weight control

9 variable, process variable; simple variable, complex variable; manipulated variable; steady state, transient state

10 values, target values; set point; differential gap; proportional band; dead band, dead zone; neutral zone

11 time constants; time lead, gain; time delay, dead time; lag, process lag, hysteresis, holdup, output lag; throughput

12 automatic device <see list>, automatic; semi-automatic; self-actor, self-mover; **robot, automation,** mechanical man; cyborg; bionic man, bionic woman

13 **servomechanism,** servo; cybernion, automatic machine; **servomotor;** synchro, selsyn, autosyn; synchronous motor, synchronous machine

14 **system component; control mechanism; regulator, control,** controller, **governor;** servo control, servo regulator; control element

15 **automatic detector;** automatic analyzer; automatic indicator

16 **control panel,** console; coordinated panel, graphic panel; panelboard, set-up board

17 **computer, computer science** 1041, electronic computer, electronic brain; information machine, thinking machine; computer unit, hardware, computer hardware

18 **control engineer,** servo engineer, system engineer, systems analyst, automatic control system engineer, feedback system

engineer, automatic technician, robot specialist; computer engineer, computer technologist, computer technician, **computer programmer;** cybernetic technologist, cyberneticist

VERBS **19 automate,** automatize, robotize; robot-control, servo-control; program; computerize

20 self-govern, self-control, **self-regulate,** selfdirect

ADJS **21 automated,** cybernated, robotized; **automatic,** automatous, **spontaneous; self-acting,** self-active; **self-operating,** self-operative, self-working; **self-regulating,** self-regulative, self-governing, self-directing; **self-regulated, self-controlled,** self-governed, self-directed, self-steered; self-adjusting, self-closing, self-cocking, self-cooking, self-dumping, self-emptying, self-lighting, self-loading, self-opening, self-priming, self-rising, self-sealing, self-starting, self-winding, automanual; semiautomatic; computerized, computer-controlled

22 self-propelled, self-moved, horseless; **self-propelling,** self-moving, self-propellent; self-driven, self-drive; **automotive,** automobile, automechanical; **locomotive,** locomobile

23 servomechanical, servo-controlled; **cybernetic;** isotronic

24 remote-control, remote-controlled, telemechanic; telemetered, telemetric; by remote control

WORD ELEMENTS **25** aut—, auto—, automat—, automato—, self—

26 automatic devices

airborne controls	automatic stop
antiaircraft gun positioner	automatic telegraph
	automatic telephone
artificial feedback kidney	automatic telephone exchange
automatic block signal	automaton
	chess-playing machine
automatic gun	guided missile
automatic gun director	gyroscopic pilot
automatic heater	lever pilot
automatic iron	mechanical heart
automatic piano	multiple-stylus electronic printer
automatic pilot or autopilot or	radar controls
automatic or gyropilot or robot	robot pilot
	robot plane
automatic pinspotter	robot submarine
automatic pistol	self-starter
automatic printer	semiautomatic pistol or rifle
automatic rifle	
automatic sight	speedometer
automatic sprinkler	

1041 COMPUTER SCIENCE

NOUNS **1 computer science** <see list>, computer systems and applications, computer hardware and software, computers, digital computers, computing, machine computation, number-crunching <nonformal>; **computerization,** digitization; **data processing,** electronic data processing or EDP, data storage and retrieval; data bank; **information science,** information processing, informatics; computer security; computer crime or fraud, computer virus or worm; hacking

2 computer, electronic data processor, information processor, electronic brain, digital computer, general purpose computer, analog computer, hybrid computer, machine, **hardware,** computer hardware, microelectronics device; **processor,** central processing unit or CPU, multiprocessor, microprocessor, mainframe computer or mainframe, dataflow computer, work station, minicomputer, microcomputer, personal computer or PC, home computer, laptop computer, briefcase computer, pocket computer, minisupercomputer, superminicomputer, supermicrocomputer, supercomputer, graphoscope, array processor, neurocomputer; neural net or network, semantic net or network

3 circuitry, circuit, integrated circuit, logic circuit, **chip,** silicon chip, gallium arsenide chip, semiconductor chip, hybrid chip, wafer chip, superchip, microchip, neural network chip, transputer, **board,** printed circuit board or PCB, motherboard; **peripheral,** peripheral device or unit, input device, output device; **port,** channel interface, serial interface, serial port; **read-write head**

4 input device, keyboard; reader, tape reader, scanner, optical scanner, optical character reader, optical character recognition or OCR device, light pen, mouse

5 drive, disk drive, floppy disk drive, hard disk drive or Winchester drive, tape drive

6 disk, magnetic disk, floppy disk or floppy <nonformal> or diskette, minifloppy, microfloppy, hard or fixed or Winchester disk, disk pack; magnetic tape or mag tape <nonformal>, magnetic tape unit, magnetic drum

7 memory, storage, memory bank, memory chip, firmware; **main memory,** main storage or store, random access memory or RAM, core, core storage or store, disk pack, magnetic disk, primary storage, backing store, read/write memory, optical disk memory, bubble memory; read-only memory or ROM, programmable read-only memory or PROM

8 **retrieval, access,** random access, sequential access, direct access

9 **output device,** terminal, workstation, video terminal, video display terminal or VDT, video display unit or VDU, visual display unit or VDU, graphics terminal, **monitor,** cathode ray tube or CRT, monochrome monitor, color monitor, RGB monitor, **printer, serial printer,** character printer, impact printer, dot-matrix printer, daisy-wheel or printwheel printer, drum printer, **line printer,** line dot-matrix printer, chain printer, **page printer,** nonimpact printer, laser printer, electronic printer, graphics printer, color graphics printer; **modem** or modulator-demodulator

10 **forms, computer forms, computer paper,** continuous stationery

11 **software, program,** computer program, source program, object program, binary file, binary program, software package, software support, courseware, groupware, routine, subroutine

12 **systems program, operating system** or **OS,** disk operating system or DOS; Microsoft <trademark> disk operating system or MS-DOS <trademark>; UNIX; control program monitor or CPM; **word processor,** text editor, editor, print formatter, WYSIWYG or what-you-see-is-what-you-get word processor, postformatted word processor; spreadsheet, electronic spreadsheet, desktop publishing program, database management system or DBMS; **computer application** <see list>, applications program, bootloader or bootstrap loader

13 **language** <see list>, assembler or assemblage language, programming language, machine language, machine-readable language, conventional programming language, computer language, high-level language, interpreter, low-level language, application development language, assembly language, object code, job-control language or JCL, procedural language, problem-oriented language, query language; **computer** or **electronic virus,** computer worm, phantom bug, Trojan horse, logic bomb

14 **bit, binary digit,** infobit, kilobit, megabit, gigabit, terbit; **byte,** kilobyte, megabyte

15 **data, information,** database, data capture, database management, file, record, data bank, input, input-output or I/O; **file,** data set, record, data record, data file, text file

16 **network, computer network,** communications network, local area network or LAN, workgroup computing, mesh; **on-line system,** interactive system, on-line service

17 **liveware, programmer,** systems programmer, system software specialist, application programmer, systems analyst, systems engineer, computer designer, computer architect, operator, technician, key puncher; hacker <nonformal>

VERBS 18 **computerize,** digitize; **program,** boot, boot up, initialize, log in, log out, run, load, download, **compute,** crunch numbers <nonformal>; **keyboard,** key in, input

ADJS 19 **computerized;** machine-usable, computer-usable; computer-aided, computer-assisted; computer-driven, computer-guided, computer-controlled, computer-governed

20 **branches of computer science**

analysis of algorithms	nonnumerical applications
artificial intelligence	numerical analysis
automata theory	numerical applications
combinatorial processes	operating systems
compiler design	optimization
computer applications	programming
computer architecture	programming languages
computer graphics	robotics
computer systems	simulation
information storage and retrieval	switching theory
language processing	symbol manipulation
logical design	theory of computation
machine organization	theory of formal languages
	utility programs

21 **computer applications**

batch processing	computer-aided design
computer art	
computer bulletin boards	computer-aided engineering
computer conferencing	computer-aided manufacturer
computer crime	computer-aided radiology
computer games	
computer graphics	computer-assisted instruction
computer or interactive fiction	
computer or synthesized music	desktop publishing or DTP
computer typesetting	electronic publishing
	image enhancement
	inventory control

linguistic analysis
quality control
sales report program

simulation
time-sharing

22 computer languages

ADA	FORTRAN *or* formula
ALGOL *or*	translator
algorithmic-	FORTRAN 77
oriented	GPSS
language	IPL-V
APL *or* a program-	JOSS
ming language	JOVIAL
APT *or* automatic	lex
programmed	LISP *or* list-
tools	processing
awk *or* Aho Wein-	LOGO
berger and	make
Kernighan	MUMPS
BAL *or* basic assem-	OCCAM
bly language	PASCAL
BASIC *or* beginners	pic
all-purpose sym-	PILOT *or* pro-
bolic instruction	grammed inquiry
code	learning or teach-
BCPL	ing
C	PL/1 *or* programming
COBOL *or* common	language 1
business-oriented	Ratfor
language	RPG II
COMIT	sh
COMPACT II	SNOBOL *or* sno *or*
efl	string-oriented
eqn	symbolic language
FLOWMATIC	SOL
FORMAC	yacc *or* yet another
FORTH	computer compiler

1042 FRICTION

NOUNS **1 friction, rubbing,** rub, frottage;
frication *and* confrication *and* perfrica-
tion <all old>; **drag,** skin friction; **resistance,** frictional resistance

**2 abrasion, attrition, erosion, wearing
away, wear,** detrition, ablation; ruboff;
erasure, erasing, rubbing away *or* off *or*
out; **grinding, filing,** rasping, limation;
fretting; galling; **chafing, chafe; scraping,** grazing, scratching, scuffing; **scrape,**
scratch, **scuff;** scrubbing, scrub; scouring, scour; **polishing,** burnishing, sanding, smoothing, dressing, buffing, shining; sandblasting; abrasive; brass-
rubbing, heelball rubbing, graphite
rubbing

3 massage, massaging, stroking, kneading;
rubdown; massotherapy; whirlpool bath,
Jacuzzi <trademark>; vibrator; facial
massage, facial

4 massager, **masseur, masseuse;** masso-
therapist

5 <mechanics> force of friction; force of

viscosity; coefficient of friction; friction
head; friction clutch, friction drive, friction gearing, friction pile, friction saw,
friction welding

VERBS **6 rub,** frictionize; **massage,** knead,
rub down; caress, pet, stroke 73.8

7 abrade, abrase, gnaw, gnaw away; **erode,**
erode away, ablate, wear, wear away;
erase, rub away *or* off *or* out; **grind, rasp,
file, grate; chafe,** fret, gall; **scrape, graze,**
raze <old>, **scuff,** bark, skin; **fray,** frazzle; **scrub, scour**

8 buff, burnish, polish, rub up, sandpaper,
sand, smooth, dress, shine, furbish, sandblast

ADJS **9 frictional,** friction; fricative; **rubbing**

10 abrasive, abradant, attritive, gnawing,
erosive, ablative; scraping; **grinding,**
rasping; chafing, fretting, galling

1043 DENSITY

NOUNS **1 density,** denseness, **solidity, solidness,** firmness, **compactness, closeness,**
spissitude <old>; **congestion,** congested-
ness, crowdedness, jammedness; **impenetrability,** impermeability, imporosity;
hardness 1044; incompressibility; specific gravity, relative density; **consistency,** consistence, thick consistency,
thickness; viscidity, viscosity, **viscousness, thickness,** gluiness, ropiness

2 indivisibility, inseparability, impartibil-
ity, infrangibility, indiscerptibility; in-
dissolubility; cohesion, coherence 802;
unity 791; insolubility, infusibility

**3 densification, condensation, compres-
sion, concentration,** inspissation, concretion, consolidation, conglobulation;
hardening, **solidification** 1044.5; agglutination, clumping, clustering

4 thickening, inspissation; congelation,
congealment, coagulation, clotting, **setting,** concretion; gelatinization, gelati-
nation, jellification, jellying, **jelling,**
gelling; **curdling,** clabbering; **distillation**

5 precipitation, deposit, sedimentation;
precipitate

6 solid, solid body, body, mass; lump,
clump, cluster; block, cake; node, knot;
concrete, concretion; conglomerate, conglomeration

7 clot, coagulum, coagulate; blood clot,
grume, embolus, crassamentum; **coagulant,** coagulator, clotting factor, coagu-
lase, coagulose, thromboplastin *or* coagu-
lin; casein, caseinogen, paracasein, legu-
min; **curd,** clabber, loppered milk *and*

bonnyclabber <both nonformal>, clotted cream, Devonshire cream

8 <instruments> densimeter, densitometer; aerometer, hydrometer, lactometer, urinometer, pycnometer

VERBS 9 **densify,** inspissate, densen; **condense, compress,** compact, **consolidate, concentrate,** come to a head; **congest; squeeze, press, crowd,** cram, jam, ram down; steeve; pack or jam in; **solidify** 1044.8

10 **thicken,** thick <old>; inspissate, incrassate; **congeal, coagulate, clot,** set, concrete; gelatinize, gelatinate, jelly, jellify, **jell,** gel; **curdle,** curd, clabber, lopper <nonformal>; cake, lump, clump, cluster, knot

11 **precipitate,** deposit, sediment, sedimentate

ADJS 12 **dense, compact, close;** close-textured, close-knit, close-woven, tight-knit; serried, **thick, heavy,** thickset, thick-packed, thick-growing, thick-spread, thick-spreading; **condensed, compressed,** compacted, concrete, consolidated, concentrated; **crowded, jammed,** packed, jam-packed, packed or jammed in, packed or jammed in like sardines; **congested,** crammed, crammed full; **solid,** firm, substantial, massive; impenetrable, impermeable, imporous, nonporous; hard 1044.10; incompressible; viscid, viscous, ropy, gluey

13 **indivisible,** nondivisible, undividable, **inseparable,** impartible, infrangible, indiscerptible, indissoluble; cohesive, coherent 802.10; unified; insoluble, indissolvable, infusible

14 **thickened,** inspissate or inspissated, incrassate; **congealed, coagulated, clotted,** grumous; **curdled,** curded, clabbered; **jellied,** jelled, gelatinized; lumpy, lumpish; caked, cakey; coagulant, coagulating

ADVS 15 **densely,** compactly, **close,** closely, **thick,** thickly, heavily; solidly, firmly

1044 HARDNESS, RIGIDITY

NOUNS 1 **hardness,** durity <old>, induration; **callousness,** callosity; stoniness, rock-hardness, flintiness, steeliness; **strength, toughness** 1047; solidity, impenetrability, density 1043; restiveness, resistance 453; obduracy 361.1; hardness of heart 94.3

2 **rigidity, rigidness,** rigor <old>; **firmness,** renitence or renitency, incompressibility; nonresilience or nonresiliency, inelasticity; **tension,** tensity, **tenseness,** tautness, tightness

3 **stiffness, inflexibility,** unpliability, unmalleability, intractability, unbendingness, unlimberness, starchiness; **stubbornness,** unyieldingness 361.2; **unalterability,** immutability; immovability 854.3; inelasticity, irresilience or irresiliency; inextensibility or unextensibility, unextendibility, inductility

4 **temper,** tempering; chisel temper, die temper, razor temper, saw file temper, set temper, spindle temper, tool temper; precipitation hardening, heat treating; hardness test, Brinell test; hardness scale, Brinell number or Brinell hardness number or Bhn; indenter; hardener, hardening, hardening agent

5 **hardening, toughening,** induration, firming; **strengthening; tempering,** case hardening, steeling; seasoning; **stiffening,** rigidification, starching; **solidification, setting,** curing, caking, concretion; crystallization, granulation; callusing; sclerosis, arteriosclerosis, atherosclerosis; lithification; lapidification <old>; **petrification,** fossilization, ossification; cornification, hornification; calcification; vitrification, vitrifaction

6 <comparisons> stone, rock 1057, adamant, granite, flint, marble, diamond; steel, iron, nails; concrete, cement; brick; oak, heart of oak; bone

VERBS 7 **harden,** indurate, firm, **toughen** 1047.3; **callous; temper,** anneal, oil-temper, heat-temper, **case-harden,** steel; season; **petrify,** lapidify <old>, fossilize; lithify; vitrify; calcify; ossify; cornify, hornify

8 **solidify,** concrete, **set,** take a set, cure, cake; condense, thicken 1043.10; **crystallize,** granulate, candy

9 **stiffen,** rigidify, starch; **strengthen, toughen** 1047.3; back, brace, reinforce, shore up; **tense, tighten,** tense up, tension; trice up, screw up

ADJS 10 **hard, solid,** dure <old>, lacking give, **tough** 1047.4; resistive, resistant, steely, steellike, iron-hard, ironlike; **stony,** rocky, stonelike, rock-hard, rocklike, lapideous, lapidific, lapidifical, lithoid or lithoidal; diamondlike, adamant, adamantine; flinty, flintlike; marble, marblelike; granitic, granitelike; gritty; concrete, cement, cemental; horny, bony, osseous; hard-boiled; hard as nails or a rock, etc 1044.6; "as firm as a stone; yea, as hard as a piece of the nether millstone"—Bible; dense 1043.12; obdurate 361.10; hard-hearted 94.12

11 **rigid, stiff, firm,** renitent, incompressible; **tense, taut, tight,** unrelaxed; nonresilient, inelastic; **rodlike,** virgate; ramrod-stiff, ramrodlike, pokerlike; stiff as a poker *or* rod, stiff as buckram; starched, starchy

12 **inflexible,** unflexible, **unpliable, unpliant, unmalleable, intractable,** untractable, intractile, **unbending,** unlimber, **unyielding** 361.9, ungiving, **stubborn, unalterable,** immutable; **immovable** 854.15; **adamant,** adamantine; **inelastic,** nonelastic, irresilient; inextensile, inextensible, unextensible, inextensional, unextendible, nonstretchable, inductile

13 **hardened, toughened,** steeled, indurate, indurated; **callous,** calloused; **solidified,** set; crystallized, granulated; petrified, lapidified <old>, fossilized; vitrified; sclerotic; ossified; cornified, hornified; calcified; crusted, crusty, incrusted; **stiffened, strengthened,** rigidified, backed, reinforced

14 **hardening, toughening,** indurative; petrifying, petrifactive

15 **tempered, case-hardened,** heat-treated, **annealed,** oil-tempered, heat-tempered, tempered in fire; seasoned

1045 SOFTNESS, PLIANCY

NOUNS 1 **softness,** give, nonresistiveness, insolidity, unsolidity, nonrigidity; **gentleness,** easiness, delicacy, tenderness; *morbidezza* <Ital>; lenity, leniency 427; mellowness; fluffiness, flossiness, downiness, featheriness; velvetiness, plushiness, satininess, silkiness; sponginess, pulpiness

2 **pliancy, pliability, plasticity, flexibility,** flexility, flexuousness, bendability, ductility, ductibility <old>, tensileness, tensility, tractility, **tractability,** amenability, adaptability, facility, give, **suppleness,** willowiness, **litheness, limberness; elasticity** 1046, **resilience,** springiness, resiliency; malleability, moldability, fictility, sequacity <old>; **impressionability,** susceptibility, responsiveness, receptiveness, sensibility, sensitiveness; formability, formativeness; extensibility, extendibility; agreeability 324.1; submissiveness 433.3

3 **flaccidity,** flaccidness, **flabbiness, limpness,** rubberiness, floppiness; **looseness,** laxness, laxity, laxation, relaxedness, relaxation

4 <comparisons> putty, clay, dough, blubber, rubber, wax, butter, pudding; velvet, plush, satin, silk; wool, fleece; pillow, cushion; kapok; baby's bottom; puff; fluff, floss, flue; down, feathers, feather bed, eiderdown, swansdown, thistledown; breeze, zephyr; foam

5 **softening,** softening-up; **easing,** padding, cushioning; mollifying, mollification; **relaxation,** laxation; mellowing; tenderizing

VERBS 6 **soften,** soften up; unsteel; **ease,** cushion; gentle, mollify, milden; **subdue,** tone *or* tune down; mellow; tenderize; **relax,** laxate, loosen; **limber,** limber up, supple; massage, knead, plump, plump up, fluff, fluff up, shake up; **mash, smash,** squash, pulp

7 **yield, give,** relent, relax, bend, unbend, give way; submit 433.6,9

ADJS 8 **soft,** nonresistive, nonrigid; mild, **gentle, easy, delicate, tender;** complaisant 427.8; mellow, mellowy <old>; **softened,** mollified; whisper-soft, soft as putty *or* clay *or* dough, etc 1045.4, soft as a kiss *or* a sigh *or* a baby's bottom, "soft as sinews of the new-born babe"— Shakespeare

9 **pliant, pliable, flexible,** flexile, flexuous, **plastic, elastic** 1046.7, **ductile,** sequacious *or* facile <both old>, tractile, **tractable, yielding,** giving, bending; adaptable, **malleable,** moldable, shapable, fabricable, fictile; compliant 324.5, submissive 433.12; **impressionable,** impressible, susceptible, responsive, receptive, sensitive; **formable,** formative; **bendable; supple,** willowy, **limber; lithe,** lithesome, lissome, "as lissome as a hazel wand"— Tennyson, double-jointed, loose-limbed, whippy; **elastic,** resilient, springy; extensile, extensible, extendible; like putty *or* wax *or* dough, etc

10 **flaccid, flabby, limp,** rubbery, flimsy, floppy; **loose,** lax, relaxed

11 **spongy,** pulpy, pithy, medullary; edematous

12 **pasty, doughy;** loamy, clayey, argillaceous

13 **squashy,** squishy, squushy, squelchy

14 **fluffy,** flossy, **downy,** pubescent, feathery; fleecy, woolly, lanate; furry

15 **velvety,** velvetlike, velutinous; plushy, plush; **satiny,** satinlike; cottony; **silky,** silken, silklike, sericeous, soft as silk

16 **softening, easing;** subduing, mollifying, emollient; demulcent; **relaxing,** loosening

ADVS 17 **softly, gently,** easily, delicately, tenderly; compliantly 324.9, submissively 433.17

1046 ELASTICITY

NOUNS **1 elasticity, resilience** or resiliency, **give; snap, bounce,** bounciness; **stretch, stretchiness,** stretchability; extensibility; tone, tonus, tonicity; **spring, springiness;** rebound 902.2; **flexibility** 1045.2; **adaptability,** responsiveness; **buoyancy** or buoyance; **liveliness** 330.2

  2 stretching; extension; distension 259.2; **stretch, tension, strain**

  3 elastic; elastomer; **rubber,** gum elastic; stretch fabric, Lastex <trademark>, spandex; gum, chewing gum 1060.6; whalebone, baleen; rubber band, rubber ball, handball, tennis ball; spring; springboard; trampoline; racket, battledore; jumping jack

VERBS **4 stretch;** extend; distend 259.4

  5 give, yield 1045.7; bounce, spring, spring back 902.6

  6 elasticize; rubberize, rubber; vulcanize

ADJS **7 elastic, resilient, springy,** bouncy; **stretchable, stretchy,** stretch; extensile; **flexible** 1045.9; flexile; **adaptable,** adaptive, responsive; buoyant; lively 330.17

  8 rubber, **rubbery,** rubberlike; rubberized

1047 TOUGHNESS

NOUNS **1 toughness, resistance; strength, hardiness, vitality, stamina** 15.1; stubbornness, **stiffness; unbreakableness** or **unbreakability,** infrangibility; cohesiveness, **tenacity,** viscidity 802.3; **durability,** lastingness 826.1; **hardness** 1044; **leatheriness,** leatherlikeness; stringiness

  2 <comparisons> leather; gristle, cartilage

VERBS **3 toughen,** harden, stiffen, workharden, **temper,** strengthen; season; be tough; **endure, hang tough** <nonformal>

ADJS **4 tough, resistant;** shockproof, shockresistant, impactproof, impact-resistant; stubborn, stiff; **heavy-duty;** hard or tough as nails; **strong, hardy,** vigorous; cohesive, **tenacious,** viscid; **durable,** lasting 826.10; untiring; **hard** 1044.10; chewy <nonformal>; leathery, leatherlike, coriaceous, tough as leather; sinewy, wiry; gristly, cartilaginous; stringy, fibrous

  5 unbreakable, nonbreakable, infrangible, unshatterable, shatterproof, chip-proof, fractureproof

  6 toughened, hardened, tempered, annealed; seasoned

1048 BRITTLENESS, FRAGILITY

NOUNS **1 brittleness, crispness,** crispiness; **fragility, frailty,** damageability, delicacy 16.2, flimsiness, **breakability,** breakableness, frangibility, fracturableness, crackability, crackableness, crunchability, crushability, crushableness; lacerability; fissility; friability, crumbliness 1049; vulnerableness, **vulnerability** 1005.4

  2 <comparisons> eggshell, matchwood, old paper, piecrust, glass, glass jaw, china, parchment, ice, bubble, glass house, house of cards, hothouse plant

VERBS **3 break, shatter,** fragment, fragmentize, fragmentate, fall to pieces, shard, **disintegrate** 805

ADJS **4 brittle, crisp,** crispy; **fragile, frail,** delicate 16.14, flimsy, **breakable,** frangible, crushable, crackable, crunchable, fracturable; lacerable; **shatterable,** shattery, shivery, splintery; friable, crumbly 1049.13; fissile, scissile; brittle as glass; **vulnerable** 1005.16

1049 POWDERINESS, CRUMBLINESS

NOUNS **1 powderiness,** pulverulence, **dustiness;** chalkiness; **mealiness,** flouriness, branniness; efflorescence

  2 granularity, graininess, granulation; **sandiness, grittiness,** gravelliness, sabulosity

  3 friability, pulverableness, crispness, crumbliness; brittleness 1048

  4 pulverization, comminution, trituration, attrition, detrition; levigation; reduction to powder or dust, pestling; fragmentation, sharding; brecciation; atomization, micronization; **powdering, crumbling;** abrasion 1042.2; **grinding,** milling, grating, shredding; granulation, granulization; **beating, pounding, shattering,** flailing, mashing, smashing, crushing; disintegration 805

  5 powder, dust; dust ball, pussies, kittens, slut's wool, lint; efflorescence; **crumb,** crumble; **meal,** bran, flour, farina; grits, groats; filings, raspings, sawdust; soot, smut; **particle, particulate,** particulates, airborne particles, air pollution; fallout; cosmic dust

  6 grain, granule, granulet; **grit, sand; gravel,** shingle; detritus, debris; breccia, collapse breccia

  7 pulverizer, comminutor, triturator, levigator; **crusher; mill; grinder;** granulator, pepper grinder, pepper mill; **grater,** nutmeg grater, cheese grater; **shredder;** pestle, **mortar and pestle; masher;** millstone, quern, quernstone; roller, steamroller

8 koniology; konimeter

VERBS **9 pulverize, powder,** comminute, triturate, contriturate, levigate, bray, pestle, disintegrate, reduce to powder *or* dust, grind to powder *or* dust, grind up; **fragment,** shard, shatter; brecciate; atomize, micronize; **crumble,** crumb; **granulate,** granulize, grain; **grind, grate, shred,** abrade 1042.7; **mill,** flour; **beat, pound, mash, smash, crush,** crunch, flail, squash, scrunch <nonformal>

10 <be reduced to powder> **powder,** come *or* fall to dust, **crumble,** crumble to *or* into dust, **disintegrate** 805, fall to pieces, break up; effloresce; granulate, grain

ADJS **11 powdery, dusty,** powder, pulverulent, pulverous, lutose; **pulverized,** pulverant, powdered, disintegrated, comminute, gone to dust, reduced to powder; **particulate; ground, grated,** pestled, milled, stone-ground, comminuted, triturated, levigated; sharded, **crushed; fragmented; shredded; fine,** impalpable; **chalky,** chalklike; **mealy,** floury, farinaceous; branny; furfuraceous, scaly, scurfy; flaky 296.7; detrited, detrital; scobiform, scobicular; efflorescent

12 **granular, grainy,** granulate, **granulated; sandy, gritty,** sabulous, arenarious, arenaceous; shingly, shingled, pebbled, pebbly; **gravelly;** breccial, brecciated

13 **pulverable, pulverizable,** pulverulent, triturable; **friable,** crimp <old>, crisp, **crumbly**

1050 MATERIALITY

NOUNS **1 materiality,** materialness; **corporeity,** corporality, corporeality, corporealness, bodiliness, embodiment; **substantiality** 762, concreteness 762.1; **physicalness,** physicality

2 **matter, material,** materiality, **substance** 762, **stuff,** hyle; **primal matter,** initial substance, xylem; brute matter; **element;** chemical element 1058.1; the four elements; earth, air, fire, water; elementary particle, fundamental particle; elementary unit, building block, unit of being, monad; constituent, component; **atom** 1037.4; atomic particles 1037.6; **molecule;** material world, physical world, nature, natural world; hypostasis, substratum; plenum; antimatter

3 **body,** physical body, material body,

corpus <nonformal>, anatomy <nonformal>, person, **figure, form,** frame, **physique,** carcass <nonformal>, bones, flesh, clay, clod, hulk; soma; **torso, trunk;** warm body <nonformal>

4 **object, article, thing,** material thing, affair, something; whatsit <nonformal>, what's-its-name 528.2; something or other, *etwas* <Ger>, *eppes* <Yiddish>, *quelque chose* <Fr>; artifact

5 <nonformal terms> gadget 1039.1; thingum, **thingumabob,** thingumadad, thingy, thingumadoodle, **thingumajig,** thingumajigger, thingumaree, thingummy, **doodad,** dofunny, **dojigger,** dojiggy, domajig, domajigger, **dohickey,** dowhacky, flumadiddle, gigamaree, **gimmick, gizmo,** dingus, hickey, jigger, hootmalalie, hootenanny, whatchy, widget

6 **materialism,** physicism, epiphenomenalism, identity theory of mind, atomism, mechanism; physicalism, behaviorism, instrumentalism, pragmatism, pragmaticism; historical materialism, dialectical materialism, Marxism; **positivism,** logical positivism, positive philosophy, empiricism, **naturalism;** realism, natural realism, commonsense realism, commonsense philosophy, naïve realism, new realism, critical realism, representative realism, epistemological realism; substantialism; hylomorphism; hylotheism; hylozoism; worldliness, earthliness, animalism, secularism, temporality

7 **materialist,** physicist, atomist; historical *or* dialectical materialist, Marxist; **naturalist;** realist, natural realist, commonsense realist, commonsense philosopher, epistemological realist

8 **materialization,** corporealization; substantialization, substantiation; **embodiment, incorporation,** personification, **incarnation; reincarnation,** reembodiment, transmigration, metempsychosis

VERBS **9 materialize** 762.5, corporalize; substantialize, substantify, substantiate; **embody** 762.5, body, **incorporate,** corporify, personify, **incarnate; reincarnate,** reembody, transmigrate

ADJS **10 material,** materiate, hylic, **substantial** 762.6; **corporeal,** corporeous, corporal, **bodily; physical,** somatic, somatical, somatous; **fleshly;** worldly, earthly, here-and-now, **secular,** temporal, **unspiritual,** nonspiritual

11 **embodied,** bodied, **incorporated, incarnate**

12 **materialist** *or* **materialistic,** atomistic, mechanist, mechanistic; Marxian, Marx-

ist; **naturalist, naturalistic, positivist, positivistic;** commonsense, **realist,** realistic; hylotheistic; hylomorphous; hylozoic, hylozoistic

1051 IMMATERIALITY

NOUNS **1 immateriality,** immaterialness; incorporeity, incorporeality, incorporealness, **bodilessness; unsubstantiality** 763, unsubstantialness; **intangibility,** impalpability, imponderability; inextension, nonextension; nonexteriority, nonexternality; **unearthliness, unworldliness; supernaturalism** 689.2; **spirituality,** spiritualness, spirituousness <old>, otherworldliness, ghostliness, shadowiness; occultism 689, the occult, occult phenomena; ghost-raising, ghost-hunting, ghostbusting <nonformal>; psychism, psychics, psychic *or* psychical research, psychicism; spirit world, astral plane

2 incorporeal, incorporeity, immateriality, unsubstantiality 763

3 immaterialism, idealism, philosophical idealism, metaphysical idealism; objective idealism; absolute idealism; epistemological idealism; monistic idealism, pluralistic idealism; critical idealism; transcendental idealism; subjectivism; solipsism; subjective idealism; **spiritualism;** personalism; panpsychism, psychism, animism, hylozoism, animatism; Platonism, Platonic realism, Berkeleianism, Cambridge Platonism, Kantianism, Hegelianism, New England Transcendentalism; Neoplatonism; Platonic idea *or* ideal *or* form, pure form, form, universal; transcendental object; transcendental

4 immaterialist, **idealist;** Berkeleian, Platonist, Hegelian, Kantian; Neoplatonist; **spiritualist;** psychist, panpsychist, animist; **occultist** 689.11; medium; ghost-raiser, ghost-hunter, ghost-buster <nonformal>

5 dematerialization; **disembodiment,** disincarnation; **spiritualization**

VERBS **6** dematerialize, immaterialize, unsubstantialize, insubstantialize, desubstantialize, **disembody,** disincarnate; **spiritualize,** spiritize

ADJS **7 immaterial,** nonmaterial; **unsubstantial** 763.5, insubstantial, **intangible,** impalpable, imponderable; unextended, extensionless; **incorporeal,** incorporate, incorporeous; **bodiless,** unembodied, without body, asomatous; **disembodied,** disbodied, discarnate, decarnate, decarnated; **unphysical,** nonphysical;

unfleshly; airy, ghostly, spectral, phantom, shadowy, ethereal; **spiritual,** astral, psychic *or* psychical; **unearthly, unworldly, otherworldly,** extramundane, transmundane; supernatural; **occult**

8 idealist, idealistic, immaterialist, immaterialistic; solipsistic; spiritualist, spiritualistic; panpsychist, panpsychistic; animist, animistic; Platonic, Platonistic, Berkeleian, Hegelian, Kantian; Neoplatonic, Neoplatonistic

1052 MATERIALS

NOUNS **1 materials,** substances, stuff; **raw material, staple, stock;** material resources *or* means; store, supply 386; strategic materials; matériel

2 <building materials> sticks and stones, lath and plaster, bricks and mortar, wattle and daub; **roofing,** roofage, tiles, shingles; walling, siding; **flooring,** pavement, paving material, paving, paving stone; masonry, stonework, flag, flagstone, ashlar, stone 1057.1; covering materials; mortar, plasters; **cement, concrete,** cyclopean concrete, ferroconcrete, prestressed concrete, reinforced concrete, slag concrete, cinder concrete; brick, firebrick; cinder block, concrete block; clinker, adobe; **tile,** tiling

3 wood <see list>, **lumber, timber,** forestproduct; hardwood, softwood; stick, stick of wood, stave; billet; pole, post, beam 273.3, **board,** plank; deal; two-by-four, three-by-four, etc; slab, puncheon; slat, splat, lath; boarding, timbering, timberwork, planking; lathing, lathwork; sheeting; paneling, panelboard, panelwork; plywood, plyboard; sheathing, sheathing board; siding, sideboard; weatherboard, clapboard; shingle, shake; log; driftwood; firewood, stovewood; cordwood; cord

4 cane, bamboo, rattan

5 paper, paper stock, stock; sheet, leaf, page; quire, ream, stationery; cardboard

6 plastic <see list>; thermoplastic; thermosetting plastic; resin plastic; cellulose plastic; protein plastic; cast plastic, molded plastic, extruded plastic; molding compounds; laminate; adhesive; plasticizer; polymer; **synthetic;** synthetic fabric *or* textile *or* cloth; synthetic rubber

VERBS **7** gather *or* procure materials; **store, stock,** stock up 386.11, lay in, restock; **process,** utilize

8 woods

acacia	applewood
alder	ash

balsa
balsam
banyan
bass or basswood
beech or beechwood
birch
brierwood
burl
buttonwood
cedar or cedarwood
cherry
chestnut
cork
cottonwood
cypress
dogwood
ebony
elm or elmwood
eucalyptus
fir
fruit wood
gum or gumwood
hazel or hazelwood
hemlock
hickory
incense wood
ironwood
juniper
knotty pine
lancewood
larch

lemonwood
lignum vitae
linden
loblolly pine
locust
logwood
magnolia
mahogany
maple
oak
olive
orangewood
peachwood
pecan
Philippine mahogany
pine
poplar
Port Orford cedar
redwood
rosewood
sandalwood
satinwood
spruce
sumac
sycamore
teak or teakwood
tulipwood
tupelo
walnut
yew
zebrawood

9 plastics

acetate
acetate nitrate
acrylic
alkyd
aminoplast
Bakelite <trademark>
Buna <trademark>
casein plastic
cellophane
celluloid
cellulose acetate
cellulose ether
cellulose nitrate
cellulosic
coumarone-indene
epoxy
fluorocarbon plastic
Formica <trademark>
furane
lignin
Lucite <trademark>
melamine
multiresin
Mylar <trademark>
neoprene
nitrate
nylon

Perspex <trademark>
phenolic
phenolic urea
Plexiglas <trademark>
polyester
polyethylene
polymeric amide
polypropylene
polystyrene
polyurethane
polyvinyl chloride or PVC
polyvinyl-formaldehyde
resinoid
silicone resin
Styrofoam <trademark>
Teflon <trademark>
terpene
tetrafluoroethylene
urea
urea formaldehyde
vinyl
Vinylite <trademark>

1053 INORGANIC MATTER

NOUNS **1 inorganic matter,** nonorganic matter; inanimate or lifeless or nonliving matter, inorganized or unorganized matter, inert matter, dead matter, **brute matter;** mineral kingdom or world; matter, mere matter

2 inanimateness, inanimation, **lifelessness,** inertness; **insensibility,** insentience, insensateness, senselessness, unconsciousness, unfeelingness

3 inorganic chemistry; chemicals 1058

ADJS **4 inorganic,** unorganic, nonorganic; **mineral,** nonbiological; unorganized, inorganized; material 1050.9

5 inanimate, inanimated, unanimated, exanimate, azoic, nonliving, dead, **lifeless,** soulless; inert; insentient, unconscious, nonconscious, **insensible,** insensate, senseless, unfeeling; dumb, mute

1054 OILS, LUBRICANTS

NOUNS **1 oil,** oleum <L>; **fat,** lipid, **grease;** sebum, tallow, vegetable oil, animal oil; **ester,** glyceryl ester; fixed oil, fatty oil, nonvolatile oil, volatile oil, essential oil; saturated fat, hydrogenated fat, unsaturated fat, polyunsaturated fat; drying oil, semidrying oil, nondrying oil

2 lubricant, lubricator, lubricating oil, lubricating agent, antifriction; graphite, plumbago, black lead; silicone; glycerin; wax, cerate; mucilage, mucus, synovia; Vaseline <trademark>, petroleum jelly, K-Y <trademark>

3 ointment, balm, salve, lotion, cream, unguent, unguentum, inunction, inunctum, unction, chrism; soothing syrup, lenitive, embrocation, demulcent, emollient; spikenard, nard; balsam; **pomade,** pomatum, brilliantine; cold cream, hand lotion, face cream, lanolin; eye-lotion, eyewash, collyrium; sun-block, sun-tan lotion, tanning cream

4 petroleum, rock oil, fossil oil; **fuel;** fuel oil; mineral oil; crude oil, crude; motor oil

5 oiliness, greasiness, unctuousness, unctiousness, unctuosity; **fattiness,** fatness, pinguidity; richness; sebaceousness; adiposis, adiposity; **soapiness,** saponacity or saponaceousness; smoothness, slickness, sleekness, **slipperiness,** lubricity

6 lubrication, lubricating, **oiling, greasing,** lubrification <old>; grease or lube job <nonformal>; **anointment,** unction, inunction; chrismatory, chrismation

7 lubritorium, lubritory; grease rack, grease pit

VERBS 8 **oil**, grease; **lubricate**, lubrify <old>; **anoint**, salve, unguent, embrocate, dress, pour oil or balm upon; smear, daub; slick, slick on <nonformal>; pomade; lard; glycerolate, glycerinate, glycerinize; wax, beeswax; smooth the way and soap the way and grease the wheels <all nonformal>

ADJS 9 **oily, greasy; unctuous**, unctional; unguinous; **oleaginous**, oleic; unguentary, **unguent**, unguentous; chrismal, chrismatory; **fat, fatty,** adipose; pinguid, pinguedinous, pinguescent; rich; sebaceous; blubbery, tallowy, suety; lardy, lardaceous; buttery, butyraceous; soapy, saponaceous; paraffinic; mucoid; smooth, slick, sleek, **slippery**

10 **lubricant**, lubricating, **lubricative**, lubricatory, lubricational; lenitive, emollient, soothing

WORD ELEMENTS 11 ole—, oleo—, oli—; lip—, lipo—, lipar—, liparo—; cer—, cero—; sebo—, sebi—; steat—, steato—; petr—, petro—, petri—

1055 RESINS, GUMS

NOUNS 1 **resin; gum,** gum resin; oleoresin; hard or varnish resin, vegetable resin; synthetic resin, plastic, resinoid; resene; **rosin,** colophony, colophonium, colophonone, resinate

VERBS 2 resin, resinize, resinate; rosin

ADJS 3 **resinous**, resinic, resiny; resinoid; rosiny; **gummy,** gummous, gumlike; pitchy

1056 MINERALS, METALS

NOUNS 1 **mineral** <see list>; inorganic substance, lifeless matter found in nature; extracted matter or material; **mineral world** or **kingdom;** mineral resources; mineraloid, gel mineral; mineralization

2 **ore** <see list>, mineral; mineral-bearing material; unrefined or untreated mineral; natural or native mineral

3 **metal,** elementary metal <see list>; metallics; native metals, alkali metals, earth metals, alkaline-earth metals, noble metals, precious metals, base metals, rare metals, rare-earth metals or elements; metalloid, semimetal, nonmetal; gold or silver bullion; gold dust; leaf metal, metal leaf, metal foil; metalwork, metalware; metallicity, metalleity

4 **alloy,** alloyage, fusion, compound; **amalgam**

5 **cast, casting; ingot, bullion;** pig, sow; sheet metal; button, gate, regulus

6 **mine,** pit; **quarry; diggings, workings;** open cut, opencast; bank; shaft; coal mine, colliery; strip mine; gold mine, silver mine, etc

7 **deposit,** mineral deposit, pay dirt; **vein, lode,** seam, dike, ore bed; shoot or chute, ore shoot or chute; chimney; stock; placer, placer deposit, placer gravel; country rock; lodestuff, gangue, matrix, veinstone

8 **mining;** coal mining, gold mining, etc; long-wall mining; room-and-pillar mining; strip mining; placer mining; hydraulic mining; prospecting; mining claim, lode claim, placer claim; gold fever; gold rush

9 **miner,** mineworker, pitman; coal miner, collier <Brit>; gold miner, gold digger; gold panner; placer miner; quarry miner; **prospector,** desert rat <nonformal>, sourdough; wildcatter; **forty-niner;** hand miner, rockman, powderman, driller, draw man; butty

10 **mineralogy;** mineralogical chemistry; crystallography; **petrology,** petrography, micropetrography; **geology;** mining geology, mining engineering

11 **metallurgy;** metallography, metallurgical chemistry, metallurgical engineering, physical metallurgy, powder metallurgy, electrometallurgy, hydrometallurgy, pyrometallurgy

12 **mineralogist; metallurgist,** electrometallurgist, metallurgical engineer; **petrologist,** petrographer; **geologist;** mining engineer

VERBS 13 mineralize; petrify 1044.7

14 **mine;** quarry; pan, pan for gold; prospect; hit pay dirt; mine out

ADJS 15 **mineral;** inorganic 1053.4; mineralized, petrified; asbestine, carbonous, graphitic, micaceous, alabastrine, quartzose, silicic; sulfurous, sulfuric; ore-bearing, ore-forming

16 **metal, metallic,** metallike, metalline, metalloid or metalloidal, metalliform; semimetallic; nonmetallic; metalloorganic or metallorganic, organometallic; bimetallic, trimetallic; metalliferous, metalbearing

17 brass, brassy, brazen; bronze, bronzy; copper, coppery, cuprous, cupreous; gold, golden, gilt, aureate; nickel, nickelic, nickelous, nickeline; silver, silvery; iron, ironlike, ferric, ferrous, ferruginous;

steel, steely; tin, tinny; lead, leaden;
pewter, pewtery; mercurial, mercurous,
quicksilver; gold-filled, gold-plated,
silver-plated, etc

18 mineralogical, metallurgical, petrologi-
cal, crystallographic

19 minerals

alabaster	lime
antimony	magnesite
amphibole	malachite
apatite	maltha
aplite	marcasite
argillite	marl
arsenic	meerschaum
asbestos	mica
asphalt	mineral charcoal
azurite	mineral coal
barite	mineral oil
bauxite	mineral salt
bitumen	mineral tallow
boron	mineral tar
brimstone	mineral wax
bromine	molybdenite
brookite	monazite
brucite	obsidian
calcite	olivine
carbon	orthoclase
celestite	ozokerite
chalcedony	peat
chlorite	perlite
chromite	phosphate rock
clay	phosphorus
coal	pitchblende
coke	pumice
corundum	pumicite
cryolite	pyrite
diatomite	pyrites
elaterite	pyroxene
emery	quartz
epidote	realgar
epsomite	red clay
feldspar	rhodonite
fluorite	rock
fluorspar	siderite
fool's gold	silica
garnet	silicate
glauconite	silicon
graphite	spar
gypsum	spinel
hatchettine	spodumene
holosiderite	sulfur
hornblende	talc
ilmenite	tellurium
iolite	tourmaline
iron pyrites	tripoli
jet	vermiculite
kaolinite	wollastonite
kyanite	wulfenite
lazurite	zeolite
lignite	

20 ores

argentite	bauxite
arsenopyrite	cassiterite

chalcocite	lodestone
chalcopyrite	magnetite
cinnabar	mispickel
galena	pyrite
göthite	siderite
hematite	stibnite
iron ore	tinstone
ironstone	turgite
limonite	zincite

21 elementary metals

aluminum	osmium
americium	palladium
barium	phosphorus
beryllium	platinum
bismuth	polonium
cadmium	potassium
calcium	praseodymium
cerium	promethium
cesium	protactinium
chromium	radium
copper	rhenium
dysprosium	rubidium
erbium	ruthenium
europium	samarium
gadolinium	scandium
gallium	silver
germanium	sodium
gold	strontium
hafnium	tantalum
holmium	technetium
indium	terbium
iridium	thallium
iron	thorium
lanthanum	thulium
lead	tin
lithium	titanium
lutetium	tungsten
magnesium	uranium
mercury	vanadium
molybdenum	ytterbium
neodymium	yttrium
nickel	zinc
niobium	zirconium

1057 ROCK

NOUNS **1 rock, stone** <see list>; living rock;
igneous rock, plutonic *or* abyssal rock,
hypabyssal rock; volcanic rock, extrusive
or effusive rock, scoria; magma, intrusive
rock; granite, basalt, porphyry, **lava,,** aa
and pahoehoe <both Hawaiian>; **sedimentary rock;** limestone, sandstone;
metamorphic rock, schist, gneiss; conglomerate, pudding stone, breccia, rubble, rubblestone, scree, talus, tuff, tufa,
brash; sarsen, sarsen stone, druid stone;
monolith; crag, craig <Scots>; bedrock;
mantlerock, regolith; saprolite, geest, lat-
erite; building stone

2 sand; grain of sand; sands of the sea; sand

pile, sand dune, sand hill; sand reef, sandbar

3 gravel, shingle, chesil <Brit>

4 pebble, pebblestone, gravelstone, chuckie
<Scots>; jackstone *and* checkstone
<both nonformal>; fingerstone; sling-
stone; drakestone; spall

5 boulder, river boulder, shore boulder,
glacial boulder

6 precious stone, gem, gemstone <see
list>; stone: crystal; semiprecious stone;
gem of the first water; birthstone

7 petrification, petrifaction, lithification,
crystallization

8 geology, petrology, crystallography; pet-
rochemistry

VERBS **9** petrify, lithify, crystallize, turn to
stone; harden 1044.7

ADJS **10 stone, rock,** lithic; petrified; petro-
genic, petrescent; adamant, adamantine;
flinty, flintlike; marbly, marblelike; granitic, granitelike; slaty, slatelike

11 stony, rocky, lapideous; stonelike, rock-
like, lithoid *or* lithoidal; sandy, gritty
1049.12; gravelly, shingly, shingled; pebbly, pebbled; porphyritic, trachytic;
crystal, crystalline; bouldery, rock- *or*
boulder-strewn, rock-studded, rock-
ribbed; craggy; monolithic

WORD ELEMENTS **12** petr—, petro—,
petri—, saxi—, lith—, litho—, —lith;
grano—; blast—, blasto—, —blast,
orth—, ortho—, par—; para—; —clast;
—lithic, litic; —clastic; crystall—,
crystallo—

13 stones

anthraconite	floatstone
aplite	freestone
aventurine	geode
basalt	gneiss
basanite	goldstone
beetlestone	granite
brimstone	granulite
brownstone	graywacke
buhr *or* buhrstone	greenstone
cairngorm	grit
chalk	gritrock *or* gritstone
clinkstone	hairstone
corundophilite	ironstone
dendrite	lava
diabase	limestone
diorite	lodestone
dolerite	Lydian stone
dolomite	marble
dripstone	milkstone
eaglestone	mudstone
emery rock	obsidian
fieldstone	phonolite
flag *or* flagstone	pitchstone
flint	porphyry

pumice	snakestone
quarrystone	soapstone
quartz	stalactite
quartzite	stalagmite
rance	starstone
rottenstone	steatite
sandstone	stinkstone
serpentine	tinstone
shale	touchstone
slab	trap *or* traprock
stone	tufa
slate	wacke
smokestone	whitestone

14 gemstones

adamant <old>	hyacinth
adder stone	jacinth
agate	jade *or* jadestone
alexandrite	jargoon
amethyst	jasper
aquamarine	kunzite
beryl	lapis lazuli
black opal	moonstone
bloodstone	morganite
brilliant	onyx
carbuncle	opal
carnelian	peridot
cat's-eye	plasma
chalcedony	rose quartz
chrysoberyl	ruby
chrysolite	sapphire
chrysoprase	sard
citrine	sardonyx
coral	spinel *or* spinel ruby
demantoid	star
diamond	sunstone
emerald	topaz
fire opal	tourmaline
garnet	turquoise
girasol	water sapphire
harlequin opal	white sapphire
heliotrope	zircon

1058 CHEMISTRY, CHEMICALS

NOUNS **1 chemistry,** chemical science, science of substances, science of matter;
branch of chemistry <see list>

2 element <see list>, chemical element;
table of elements, periodic table; rare
earth element, rare gas element; **radical**
group; free radical, diradical; **ion,** anion,
cation; atom 1037.4; **molecule,** macro-
molecule; trace element, microelement,
micronutrient, minor element; **chemical,
chemical compound;** organic chemical,
biochemical, inorganic chemical; fine
chemicals, heavy chemicals; agent, **re-
agent**

3 acid; hydracid, oxyacid, sulfacid; acidity;
base, alkali, nonacid; pH; neutralizer, antacid; alkalinity

4 valence, valency <Brit>, positive valence, negative valence; monovalence, univalence, bivalence, trivalence, tervalence, quadrivalence, tetravalence, etc, multivalence, polyvalence; covalence, electrovalence

5 **atomic weight,** atomic mass, atomic volume, mass number; **molecular weight,** molecular mass, molecular volume; atomic number, valence number

6 **chemicalization,** chemical process <see list>, chemical action, chemism; **chemical apparatus,** beaker, Bunsen burner, burette, centrifuge, condenser, crucible, graduated cylinder *or* graduate, pipette, test tube

VERBS 7 **chemicalize,** chemical; alkalize, alkalinize, alkalify; acidify, acidulate, acetify; borate, carbonate, chlorinate, hydrate, hydrogenate, hydroxylate, nitrate, oxidize, reduce, pepsinate, peroxidize, phosphatize, sulfate, sulfatize, sulfonate; isomerize, metamerize, polymerize, copolymerize, homopolymerize; ferment, work; catalyze 805.4; electrolyze

ADJS 8 **chemical;** biochemical, chemicobiologic; physicochemical, physiochemical, chemicophysical, chemicobiological, chemicophysiologic *or* chemicophysiological, chemicodynamic, chemicoengineering, chemicomechanical, chemicomineralogical, chemicopharmaceutical, chemurgic, electrochemical, iatrochemical, chemotherapeutic *or* chemotherapeutical, chemophysiologic *or* chemophysiological, macrochemical, microchemical, phytochemical, photochemical, radiochemical, thermochemical, zoochemical; elemental, elementary; acid; alkaline, alkali, nonacid, basic; isomeric, isomerous, metameric, metamerous, heteromerous, polymeric, polymerous, copolymeric, copolymerous, monomeric, monomerous, dimeric, dimerous, etc

9 valent; univalent, monovalent, monatomic, bivalent, trivalent, tervalent, quadrivalent, tetravalent, etc, multivalent, polyvalent; covalent, electrovalent

WORD ELEMENTS 10 chem—, chemo—, chemi—, chemic—, chemico—; —mer, —merous, —meric; —valent

11 **branches of chemistry**

actinochemistry	biochemistry
alchemy *or* alchemistry	biogeochemistry
analytical chemistry	business chemistry
applied chemistry	capillary chemistry
astrochemistry	chemiatry
atomic chemistry	chemical dynamics
	chemical engineering

chemicobiology	organic chemistry
chemicoengineering	pathological chemistry *or*
chemicophysics	pathochemistry
chemophysiology	petrochemistry
chemurgy	pharmacochemistry
colloid chemistry	phonochemistry
colorimetry *or* colorimetric analysis	photochemistry
crystallochemistry	physical chemistry *or* physiochemistry
cytochemistry	physiological chemistry *or*
electrochemistry	physiochemistry
engineering chemistry	phytochemistry
galactochemistry	piezochemistry
galvanochemistry	pneumatochemistry
geological chemistry *or* geochemistry	psychobiochemistry *or* psychochemistry
histochemistry	pure chemistry
hydrochemistry	radiochemistry
iatrochemistry	soil chemistry
immunochemistry	spectrochemistry
industrial chemistry	stereochemistry
inorganic chemistry	structural chemistry
lithochemistry	synthetic chemistry
macrochemistry	technochemistry
magnetochemistry	theoretical chemistry
metachemistry	thermochemistry
metallurgical chemistry	topochemistry
microchemistry	ultramicrochemistry
mineralogical chemistry	zoochemistry *or* zoochemy
neurochemistry	zyochemistry *or* zymurgy
nuclear chemistry	

12 **chemical elements**

actinium *or* Ac	europium *or* Eu
aluminum *or* Al	fermium *or* Fm
americium *or* Am	fluorine *or* F
antimony *or* Sb	francium *or* Fr
argon *or* Ar *or* A	gadolinium *or* Gd
arsenic *or* As	gallium *or* Ga
astatine *or* At	germanium *or* Ge
barium *or* Ba	gold *or* Au
berkelium *or* Bk	hafnium *or* Hf
beryllium *or* Be	hahnium *or* Ha
bismuth *or* Bi	helium *or* He
boron *or* B	holmium *or* Ho
bromine *or* Br	hydrogen *or* H
cadmium *or* Cd	indium *or* In
calcium *or* Ca	iodine *or* I
californium *or* Cf	iridium *or* Ir
carbon *or* C	iron *or* Fe
cerium *or* Ce	krypton *or* Kr
cesium *or* Cs	lanthanum *or* La
chlorine *or* Cl	lawrencium *or* Lw
chromium *or* Cr	lead *or* Pb
cobalt *or* Co	lithium *or* Li
columbium *or* Cb	lutetium *or* Lu
copper *or* Cu	magnesium *or* Mg
curium *or* Cm	manganese *or* Mn
dysprosium *or* Dy	mendelevium *or* Md *or* Mv
einsteinium *or* Es *or* E	
erbium *or* Er	mercury *or* Hg

molybdenum *or* Mo
neodymium *or* Nd
neon *or* Ne
neptunium *or* Np
nickel *or* Ni
niobium *or* Nb
nitrogen *or* N
nobelium *or* No
osmium *or* Os
oxygen *or* O
palladium *or* Pd
phosphorus *or* P
platinum *or* Pt
plutonium *or* Pu
polonium *or* Po
potassium *or* K
praseodymium *or* Pr
promethium *or* Pm
protactinium *or* Pa
radium *or* Ra
radon *or* Rn
rhenium *or* Re
rhodium *or* Rh
rubidium *or* Rb
ruthenium *or* Ru
rutherfordium *or* Rf

samarium *or* Sm
scandium *or* Sc
selenium *or* Se
silicon *or* Si
silver *or* Ag
sodium *or* Na
strontium *or* Sr
sulfur *or* S
tantalum *or* Ta
technetium *or* Tc
tellurium *or* Te
terbium *or* Tb
thallium *or* Tl
thorium *or* Th
thulium *or* Tm
tin *or* Sn
titanium *or* Ti
tungsten *or* wolfram
     or W
uranium *or* U
vanadium *or* V
xenon *or* Xe
ytterbium *or* Yb
yttrium *or* Y
zinc *or* Zn
zirconium *or* Zr

13 chemical processes

acetification
acidification *or* acid-
     ulation
alkalization *or* alkali-
     nization
carbonation
catalysis
chlorination
copolymerization
electrolysis
fermentation *or* fer-
     ment
geometric isomeriza-
     tion
homopolymerization
hydration
hydrogenation

hydroxylation
isomerization
metamerization
nitration
optical isomerization
oxidation
oxidization
phosphatization
polymerization
position isomeriza-
     tion
reduction
saturization
sulfation
sulfatization
sulfonation
tautoisomerization

1059 LIQUIDITY

NOUNS **1 liquidity, fluidity,** fluidness, liq-
uidness, liquefaction 1062; wateriness;
rheuminess; **juiciness,** sappiness, succulence; milkiness, lactescence; lactation; chylifaction, chylification; serosity;
suppuration; **moisture, wetness** 1063.1;
fluency, flow, flowage, flux, fluxion, flux-
ility <old>; **circulation;** turbulence, turbidity, turbulent flow; streamline flow
  2 fluid, liquid; liquor 10.47, drink, beverage; liquid extract, fluid extract; **juice,
sap,** latex; milk, whey; water 1063.3;
body fluid, blood; semiliquid 1060.5;
fluid mechanics, hydraulics, etc 1038.4
  3 flowmeter, fluidmeter, hydrometer

ADJS **4 fluid,** fluidal, fluidic, **fluent, flowing,**
fluxible *or* fluxile <both old>, fluxional,
fluxionary, runny; **circulatory,** circulation, turbid; **liquid,** liquidy; watery
1063.16; **juicy,** sappy, succulent; **wet**
1063.15
  5 milky, lacteal, lacteous, **lactic;** lactescent, lactiferous; milk, milch

1060 SEMILIQUIDITY

NOUNS **1 semiliquidity,** semifluidity;
butteriness, creaminess; pulpiness
1061
  2 viscosity, viscidity, viscousness, slabbiness, lentor <old>; thickness, spissitude
<old>, heaviness, stodginess, **stickiness,
tackiness,** glutinousness, glutinosity,
toughness, tenaciousness, tenacity, **adhesiveness,** clinginess, clingingness, **gumminess,** gauminess <nonformal>, gum-
likeness; **ropiness, stringiness;** clammi-
ness, sliminess, mucilaginousness; gooey-
ness *and* gunkiness <both nonformal>;
gluiness, gluelikeness; syrupiness, trea-
cliness <Brit>; gelatinousness, jellylike-
ness, gelatinity; colloidality; doughiness,
pastiness; **thickening,** curdling, clotting,
coagulation, incrassation, inspissation,
clabbering *and* loppering <both nonfor-
mal>, jellification
  3 mucosity, mucidness, mucousness, pitu-
itousness <old>, snottiness <nonfor-
mal>; **sliminess**
  4 muddiness, muckiness, miriness, **slushi-
ness,** sloshiness, sludginess, **sloppiness,**
slobbiness, slabbiness <old>, squashiness, squelchiness, **ooziness,** miriness;
turbidity, turbidness, dirtiness
  5 semiliquid, semifluid; **goo** *and* goop *and*
gook *and* gunk *and* glop <all nonfor-
mal>, sticky mess, gaum <nonformal>;
paste, pap, pudding, putty, **butter,**
cream; **pulp** 1061.2; **jelly,** gelatin, jell,
gel, jam, rob; **glue;** size; **gluten;** mucilage; mucus; **dough,** batter; **syrup,** molasses, treacle <Brit>; egg white, albumen,
glair; starch, cornstarch; **curd,** clabber,
bonnyclabber; gruel, porridge, loblolly
<nonformal>; soup, gumbo, purée
  6 gum 1055, chewing gum, bubble gum;
chicle, chicle gum
  7 emulsion, emulsoid; emulsification;
emulsifier; **colloid,** colloider
  8 mud, muck, mire, slush, slosh, sludge,
slob <Ir>, squash, swill, **slime; slop,
ooze, mire;** clay, slip; gumbo
  9 mud puddle, puddle, loblolly <nonfor-
mal>, slop; **mudhole,** slough, muckhole,

chuckhole, chughole <nonformal>; hog wallow

VERBS **10 emulsify,** emulsionize; colloid, colloidize; cream; churn, whip, beat up; **thicken,** inspissate, incrassate, curdle, clot, coagulate, clabber *and* lopper <both nonformal>; jell, jelly, jellify

ADJS **11 semiliquid,** semifluid, semifluidic; buttery; creamy; emulsive, colloidal; **pulpy** 1061.6; half-frozen, half-melted

12 viscous, viscid, viscose, slabby; **thick,** heavy, stodgy, soupy, thickened, inspissated, incrassated; curdled, clotted, grumous, coagulated, clabbered *and* loppered <both nonformal>; **sticky, tacky,** tenacious, adhesive, clingy, clinging, tough; gluey, gluelike, glutinous, glutenous, glutinose; gumbo, gumbolike; **gummy,** gaumy <nonformal>, gummous, gumlike, **syrupy;** treacly <Brit>; ropy, stringy; mucilaginous, clammy, slimy, slithery; gooey *and* gunky *and* gloppy *and* goopy *and* gooky <all nonformal>; **gelatinous,** jellylike, jellied, jelled; tremelloid *or* tremellose; glairy; **doughy, pasty;** starchy, amylaceous

13 mucous, muculent, mucoid, mucinous, pituitous <old>; phlegmy, snotty <nonformal>; mucific, muciferous

14 slimy; muddy, miry, mucky, **slushy, sloshy,** sludgy, **sloppy,** slobby, slabby <old>, splashy, **squashy,** squishy, **squelchy, oozy,** soft, sloughy, plashy, sposhy <nonformal>; **turbid, dirty**

1061 PULPINESS

NOUNS **1 pulpiness,** pulpousness; **softness** 1045; flabbiness; **mushiness,** mashiness, squashiness; **pastiness,** doughiness; **sponginess,** pithiness; fleshiness, succulence

2 pulp, paste, mash, mush, smash, squash, crush; tomato paste *or* pulp; pudding, porridge, sponge; sauce, butter; poultice, cataplasm, plaster; pith; paper pulp, wood pulp, sulfate pulp, sulfite pulp, rag pulp; pulpwood; pulp lead, white lead; dental *or* tooth pulp

3 pulping, pulpification, pulpefaction; blending; digestion; **maceration,** mastication

4 pulper, pulpifier, macerator, pulp machine *or* engine, digester; **masher,** smasher, potato masher, beetle

VERBS **5 pulp,** pulpify; **macerate,** masticate, chew; regurgitate; **mash,** smash, squash, crush

ADJS **6 pulpy,** pulpous, pulpal, pulpar, pulplike, pulped; **pasty,** doughy; pultaceous; **mushy;** macerated, masticated, chewed; regurgitated; **squashy,** squelchy, squishy; soft, flabby; fleshy, succulent; **spongy,** pithy

1062 LIQUEFACTION

NOUNS **1 liquefaction,** liquefying, liquidizing, liquidization, fluidification, fluidization; liquescence *or* liquescency, deliquescence, deliquiation *and* deliquium <both old>; **solution,** dissolution, dissolving; **infusion,** soaking, steeping, brewing; **melting,** thawing, running, fusing, fusion; decoagulation, unclotting; solubilization; colliquation; lixiviation, percolation, leaching

2 solubility, solubleness, dissolvability, dissolvableness, dissolubility, dissolubleness; meltability, fusibility

3 solution; decoction, infusion, mixture; chemical solution; lixivium, leach, leachate; **suspension,** colloidal suspension; **emulsion,** gel, aerosol

4 solvent <see list>, dissolvent, dissolver, dissolving agent, resolvent, resolutive, **thinner,** diluent; anticoagulant; liquefier, liquefacient; menstruum; universal solvent, alkahest; flux

VERBS **5 liquefy,** liquidize, liquesce, fluidify, fluidize; **melt, run,** thaw, colliquate; melt down; fuse, flux; deliquesce; **dissolve,** solve; thin, cut; solubilize; hold in solution; unclot, decoagulate; leach, lixiviate, percolate; **infuse,** decoct, steep, soak, brew

ADJS **6 liquefied, melted, molten,** thawed; unclotted, decoagulated; in solution, in suspension, liquescent, deliquescent; colloidal

7 liquefying, liquefactive; colliquative, **melting,** fusing, thawing; **dissolving,** dissolutive, dissolutional

8 solvent, dissolvent, resolvent, resolutive, thinning, cutting, diluent; alkahestic

9 liquefiable; meltable, fusible, thawable; **soluble, dissolvable,** dissoluble; water-soluble

10 solvents

acetone	carbon tetrachloride
alcohol	*or* carbon tet
aqua regia	<nonformal>
benzene *or* benzol	chloroform
benzine	ether
carbolic acid	ethyl acetate
carbon disulfide	furfural

gasoline	toluene
kerosene	turpentine
naphtha	water
phenol	xylene *or* xylol

1063 MOISTURE

NOUNS **1 moisture**, damp, wet; **dampness, moistness**, moistiness, **wetness**, wettedness, wettishness, **wateriness**, humor *or* humectation <both old>; soddenness, soppiness, soppingness, sogginess; swampiness, bogginess, marshiness; dewiness; mistiness, fogginess 319.3; raininess, pluviosity, showeriness; rainfall; exudation 190.6; secretion 13

2 humidity, humidness, **dankness**, dankishness, **mugginess**, stickiness, sweatiness; absolute humidity, relative humidity; dew point; humidification

3 water, aqua <L>, agua <Sp>, *eau* <Fr>; Adam's ale *or* wine, **H₂O**; hydrol; hard water, soft water; heavy water; water supply, water system, waterworks; drinking water, tap water; rain water, rain 316; snowmelt, melt water; **groundwater**, underground water; water table, aquifer; spring water, well water; seawater, salt water; limewater; mineral water *or* waters; steam, water vapor; hydrosphere; hydrometeor; head, hydrostatic head; hydrothermal water; wetting agent, wetting-out agent, liquidizer, moisturizer; humidifier; bottled water, commercially bottled water, designer water <nonformal>

4 dew, dewdrops, dawn *or* morning dew, night dew, evening damp; fog drip, false dew

5 sprinkle, spray, sparge, shower; spindrift, spume, froth, foam; **splash**, plash, swash, slosh; **splatter**, spatter

6 wetting, moistening, dampening, damping; humidification; dewing, bedewing; **watering, irrigation**; hosing, wetting *or* hosing down; **sprinkling, spraying**, spritzing <nonformal>, sparging, aspersion, aspergation; **splashing**, swashing, splattering, spattering; affusion, baptism; bath, bathing, rinsing, laving; **flooding**, drowning, inundation, deluge; **immersion, submersion** 367.2

7 soaking, soakage, soaking through, sopping, **drenching**, imbruement, sousing; ducking, dunking <nonformal>; soak, drench, souse; **saturation**, permeation; waterlogging; **steeping**, maceration, seething, infusion, brewing, imbuement; injection, impregnation; infiltration, per-

colation, leaching, lixiviation; pulping 1061.3

8 sprinkler, sparger, sparge, sprayer, speed sprayer, concentrate sprayer, mist concentrate sprayer, spray, spray can, atomizer, aerosol; nozzle; aspergil, aspergillum; **shower**, shower bath, shower head, needle bath; syringe, fountain syringe, douche, enema, clyster; sprinkling *or* watering can, watering pot, watercart; lawn sprinkler; sprinkling system, sprinkler head

9 <science of humidity> hygrology, hygrometry, psychrometry

10 <instruments> hygrometer, hair hygrometer, hygrograph, hygrodeik, hygroscope, hygrothermograph; psychrometer, sling psychrometer; humidor; hygrostat

VERBS **11 be damp**, not have a dry thread; **drip**, weep; **seep, ooze**, percolate; exude 190.15; sweat; secrete 13.5

12 moisten, dampen, moisturize, damp, **wet**, wet down; humidify, humect *or* humectate <both old>; **water, irrigate**; dew, bedew; **sprinkle**, besprinkle, **spray**, spritz <nonformal>, sparge, asperge; bepiss; **splash**, dash, **swash, slosh, splatter, spatter**, bespatter; dabble, paddle; slop, slobber; hose, hose down; syringe, douche; sponge

13 soak, drench, drouk <Scots>, imbrue, **souse, sop**, sodden; **saturate**, permeate; **bathe**, lave, wash, rinse, douche, flush; water-soak, waterlog; **steep**, seethe, macerate, infuse, imbue, brew, impregnate, inject; infiltrate, percolate, leach, lixiviate

14 flood, float, **inundate, deluge**, turn to a lake *or* sea, swamp, whelm, overwhelm, drown; duck, dip, dunk <nonformal>; **submerge** 367.7; sluice, pour on, flow on; rain 316.9

ADJS **15 moist**, moisty; **damp**, dampish; **wet**, wettish; undried, tacky; **humid, dank, muggy, sticky**; dewy, bedewed, roric *and* roriferous <both old>; rainy 316.10; marshy, swampy, fenny, boggy

16 watery, waterish, **aqueous, aquatic**; liquid; **splashy**, plashy, sloppy, swashy <Brit>; hydrous, hydrated; hydraulic

17 soaked, drenched, soused, bathed, steeped, macerated; **saturated**, permeated; **watersoaked, waterlogged; soaking, sopping, wringing wet**, soaking wet, sopping wet, wet to the skin, like a drowned rat; **sodden**, soppy, **soggy**, soaky; dripping, **dripping wet**; dribbling, seeping, weeping, oozing; flooded, overflowed, whelmed, swamped, engulfed, inundated, deluged, drowned, submerged, submersed, immersed, dipped, dunked <nonformal>; awash, weltering

18 wetting, dampening, moistening, watering, humectant; **drenching, soaking,** sopping; **irrigational,** irriguous <old>

19 hygric, hygrometric, hygroscopic, hygrophilous, hygrothermal

WORD ELEMENTS 20 hydr—, hydro—, hydrat—, hydrato—, aqui—, aqua—; hygr—, hygro—

1064 DRYNESS

NOUNS 1 **dryness, aridness,** aridity, waterlessness; **drought;** juicelessness, saplessness; **thirst,** thirstiness; corkiness; watertightness, watertight integrity

2 <comparisons> desert, dust, bone, parchment, stick, mummy, biscuit, cracker

3 **drying, desiccation,** drying up; **dehydration,** anhydration; evaporation; airdrying; blow-drying; freeze-drying; insolation; drainage; withering, mummification; dehumidification

4 **drier,** desiccator, desiccative, siccative, exsiccative, exsiccator, **dehydrator,** dehydrant; dehumidifier; evaporator; hairdrier, blow-dryer; clothes-drier; tumblerdryer

VERBS 5 thirst; drink up, soak up, sponge up

6 **dry, desiccate,** exsiccate, dry up, **dehydrate,** anhydrate; evaporate; dehumidify; air-dry; drip-dry; insolate, sun, sun-dry; spin-dry, tumbler-dry; blow-dry; freeze-dry; smoke, smoke-dry; cure; torrefy, burn, fire, kiln, **bake, parch,** scorch, sear; **wither, shrivel;** wizen, weazen; mummify; sponge, blot, soak up; **wipe,** rub, swab, brush; towel; drain 192.12

ADJS 7 **dry, arid; waterless,** unwatered, undamped, anhydrous; **bone-dry,** dry as dust, dry as a bone; like parchment; droughty; juiceless, sapless; **thirsty,** thirsting, athirst; high and dry; sandy, dusty; desert, Saharan

8 rainless, fine, fair, bright and fair, pleasant

9 **dried, dehydrated, desiccated,** dried-up, exsiccated; evaporated; **parched, baked,** sunbaked, burnt, scorched, **seared,** sere, sun-dried, adust; wind-dried, air-dried; drip-dried; blow-dried; freeze-dried; **withered, shriveled,** wizened, weazened; corky; mummified

10 **drying, dehydrating, desiccative,** desic-

cant, exsiccative, exsiccant, siccative, siccant; evaporative

11 **watertight, waterproof,** moistureproof, dampproof, leakproof, seepproof, dripproof, stormproof, stormtight, rainproof, raintight, showerproof, floodproof

1065 VAPOR, GAS

NOUNS 1 **vapor,** volatile; **fume, reek,** exhalation, breath, effluvium; fluid; **miasma,** mephitis, malaria <old>, fetid air; **smoke,** smudge; wisp or plume or puff of smoke; **damp,** chokedamp, blackdamp, firedamp, afterdamp; **steam,** water vapor; **cloud** 319

2 **gas** <see list>; rare or noble or inert gas, halogen gas; fluid; **atmosphere, air** 317; pneumatics, aerodynamics 1038.5

3 **vaporousness,** vaporiness; vapor pressure or tension; **aeriness; ethereality,** etherialism; **gaseousness,** gaseous state, gassiness, gaseity; **gas,** stomach gas, gassiness, flatulence, flatus, windiness, farting <nonformal>, flatuosity <old>; fluidity

4 **volatility,** vaporability, vaporizability, evaporability

5 **vaporization, evaporation,** volatilization, gasification; sublimation; distillation, fractionation; etherification; aeration, aerification; fluidization; atomization; exhalation; fumigation; smoking; steaming; etherealization

6 **vaporizer, evaporator;** atomizer, aerosol, spray; still, retort

7 vaporimeter, manometer, pressure gauge; gas meter, gasometer; pneumatometer, spirometer; aerometer; airometer; eudiometer

VERBS 8 **vaporize, evaporate,** volatilize, **gasify;** sublimate, sublime; distill, fractionate; etherify; **aerate,** aerify; carbonate, oxygenate, hydrogenate, chlorinate, halogenate, etc; atomize, spray; fluidize; **reek, fume;** exhale, give off, emit, send out; **smoke; steam;** fumigate, perfume; **etherize**

ADJS 9 **vaporous,** vaporish, vapory, vaporlike; **airy, aerial, ethereal; gaseous,** in the gaseous state, gasified, gassy, gaslike, gasiform; vaporing; **reeking,** reeky; miasmic or miasmal or miasmatic, mephitic; **fuming,** fumy; smoky, smoking, steamy, steaming; ozonic; oxygenous; oxyacetylene; pneumatic, aerostatic, aerodynamic

10 **volatile,** volatilizable; **vaporable,** vaporizable, vaporescent; **evaporative,** evaporable

WORD ELEMENTS 11 vapo—, vapori—,

atm—, atmo—; aer—, aero—, mano—,
pneum—, pneumo—, pneumat—,
pneumato—

12 gases

acetylene *or* ethyne	illuminating gas
air gas	krypton
ammonia	lewisite
argon	marsh *or* swamp gas
asphyxiating gas	methane
butane	mustard gas
carbon dioxide	natural gas
carbon monoxide	neon
carbonic-acid gas	nerve gas
carbureted-hydrogen	nitric oxide
gas	nitrogen
chlorine	nitrogen dioxide
chlorofluorocarbon	nitrous oxide *or*
coal gas	laughing gas
ethane	oil gas
ether *or* ethyl ether	oxygen
ethyl chloride	ozone
ethylene *or* ethene *or*	phosgene *or* carbon
olefiant gas	oxychloride
ethylene oxide	poison gas
fluorocarbon	propane
fluorine	radon
formaldehyde	refrigerator gas
Freon <trademark>	sewer gas
helium	sneeze gas
hydrogen	tear gas *or* lachryma-
hydrogen bromide	tory gas
hydrogen chloride	vesicatory gas
hydrogen cyanide	vomiting gas
hydrogen fluoride	war gas
hydrogen iodide	water gas
hydrogen sulfide	xenon

1066 BIOLOGY

NOUNS **1 biology** <see list>, biological science, life science, the science of life, the
study of living things; **botany** <see list>,
plant biology, phytobiology, phytology,
plant science; **plant kingdom**, vegetable
kingdom; **plants** 310, flora plantlife; **zoology** <see list>, animal biology, animal
science; **animal kingdom**, kingdom Animalia, phylum, class, order, family, genus,
species; **animals** 311, fauna, animal life
  2 biologist, naturalist, life scientist; **bota-
nist,** plant scientist, plant biologist, phy-
tobiologist, phytologist; **zoologist,** animal biologist, animal scientist <for other
agent NOUNS add -ist or -er to names of
branches listed>
ADJS **3 biological**, biologic; **botanical**, botanic, plant, phytological, phytologic,
phytobiological; **zoological**, zoologic, fau-
nal <for other ADJS add -ic or -ical to the
names of branches listed>

4 branches of biology

aerobiology	genetics
agrobiology	histology
anatomy	human ecology
aquatic biology	hydrobiology
aquatic microbiology	hydrology *or* hydro-
autoecology	geology *or*
bacteriology	geohydrology
biobehavioral science	mathematical biol-
biochemical genetics	ogy
biochemistry	microbiology
biometry *or* bio-	molecular biology
metrics *or*	morphology
biostatistics	natural classification
bionics	natural history
biotechnology *or* bio-	neurobiology
tech <nonformal>	neurochemistry
biothermodynamics	neuroendocrin-
biophysics	ology
botany	neurogenetics
cell biology	neuroscience
cell physiology	paleontology
chronobiology	palynology
cryobiochemistry	parasitology
cryobiology	phylogenetic classi-
cytogenetics	fication *or* phyletic
cytology	classification *or*
cytotaxonomy	phyletics
ecology *or* bioecology	physiology
or bionomics	radiobiology
electrobiology	sociobiology
electrophysiology	somatology
embryology	synecology
enzymology	taxonomy *or* systema-
ethnobiology	tics
exobiology *or* astro-	virology
biology *or*	zoogeography *or*
bioastronautics *or*	animal
space biology *or*	geography
space bioscience	zoology

5 branches of botany

agriculture	mycology
agrobiology	olericulture
agronomy	paleobotany
algology	palynology
applied botany	phycology
aquiculture	physiological
bacteriology	phytography
botanical histo-	phytosociology
chemistry	plant anatomy *or*
bryology	phytotomy
dendrology	plant biochemistry *or*
economic botany	phytochemistry
ethnobotany	plant cytology
evolution	plant ecology *or* phy-
floriculture	toecology
forestry	plant geography *or*
fungology	phytogeography
genetics	plant morphology
gnotobiology	plant pathology *or*
histology	phytopathology
horticulture	plant physiology
hydroponics	pomology

pteridology
seed biology
silviculture

systematic
botany *or*
taxonomy

6 branches of zoology

anatomy
animal behavior
animal chemistry *or*
zoochemistry
animal pathology *or*
zoopathology
animal physiology *or*
zoonomy
animal psychology
behavioral ecology
biochemistry
biometrics
biophysics
comparative anat-
omy *or* zootomy
comparative embry-
ology
comparative psychol-
ogy
conchology
cytogenetics
cytology
ecology
embryology
endocrinology
entomology
ethology

evolution
genetics
helminthology
herpetology
histology
ichthyology
invertebrate zoology
malacology
mammalogy
marine biology
morphology
ophiology
ornithology
paleontology
parasitology
physiological chemis-
try
physiology
protozoology
sociobiology
systematic zoology *or*
systematics *or* tax-
onomy
vertebrate zoology
zoogeography
zoography

1067 AGRICULTURE

NOUNS **1 agriculture, farming** <see list>,
husbandry; cultivation, culture, geo-
ponics, tillage, tilth; green revolution;
agrology, agronomy, agronomics, agro-
technology; thremmatology; agroeco-
system; agrogeology, agricultural geology; agrochemistry; agricultural engineering; agricultural economics; rural
economy *or* economics, farm economy *or*
economics, agrarian economy *or* economics, agrarianism; agribusiness *or*
agrobusiness, agribiz <nonformal>,
agroindustry; sharecropping
2 horticulture, gardening; landscape gardening, landscape architecture, grounds-
keeping; truck gardening, market gardening, olericulture; flower gardening,
flower-growing, floriculture; viniculture;
viticulture; orcharding, fruit-growing,
pomiculture, citriculture
3 forestry, arboriculture, tree farming, silviculture, forest management; Christmas
tree farming; forestation, afforestation,
reforestation; lumbering, logging; deforestation; woodcraft
4 <agricultural deities> vegetation spirit
or daemon, fertility god *or* spirit, year-

daemon, forest god *or* spirit, green man,
corn god, Ceres, Demeter, Gaea, Trip-
tolemus, Dionysus, Persephone, Kore,
Flora, Aristaeus, Pomona, Frey
5 agriculturist, agriculturalist; agrolo-
gist, agronomist; **farmer,** granger, hus-
bandman, **yeoman,** cultivator, tiller,
sodbuster, **tiller of the soil;** boutique
farmer, contour farmer, crop-farmer, dirt
farmer <nonformal>, etc; gentleman-
farmer; **peasant,** *campesino* <Sp>, *Bauer*
<Ger>, countryman, rustic; **grower,**
raiser; **planter,** tea-planter, coffee-
planter, etc; peasant holder *or* proprietor, *kulak, muzhik* <both Russ>; tenant
farmer, crofter <Brit>; sharecropper,
cropper, collective farm worker, *ko-
lkhoznik* <Russ>, *kibbutznik* <Yiddish>;
agricultural worker, farm worker, farm-
hand, farm laborer, migrant *or* migratory
worker *or* laborer, bracero, picker; plow-
man, plowboy; farmboy, farmgirl;
planter, sower; reaper, harvester, harvestman; haymaker
6 horticulturist, nurseryman, gardener;
landscape gardener, landscapist, landscape architect; truck gardener, market
gardener, olericulturist; **florist,** flo-
riculturist; vinegrower, viniculturist,
viticulturist, vintager; *vigneron* <Fr>;
vinedresser; orchardist, orchardman,
fruitgrower
7 forester; arboriculturist, silviculturist,
tree farmer; conservationist; **ranger,**
forest ranger; woodsman, woodman
<Brit>, woodcraftsman; **logger, lumber-
man,** timberman, lumberjack; wood-
cutter, wood chopper
8 farm, farmplace, farmstead, farmhold
<old>, farmery <Brit>, **grange,** location
<Austral>, pen <Jamaica>; boutique
farm, crop farm, dirt farm, tree farm, etc;
plantation, cotton plantation, etc, *hacienda* <Sp>; croft, homecroft <Brit>;
homestead, steading; toft <Brit>; mains
<Brit nonformal>; demesne, homefarm,
demesne farm, manor farm; **barnyard,**
farmyard, barton <Brit nonformal>; collective farm, *kolkhoz* <Russ>, *kibbutz*
<Heb>; farmland, cropland, arable land,
plowland, fallow; grassland, pasture 310.8
9 field, tract, plat, **plot, patch,** piece *or* parcel of land; cultivated land; clearing;
hayfield, corn field, wheat field, etc;
paddy, paddy field, rice paddy
10 garden, *jardin* <Fr>; bed, **flower bed,**
border, ornamental border; paradise;
garden spot, **vineyard,** vinery, grapery,
grape ranch

11 **nursery; conservatory, greenhouse**, glass-house <Brit>, forcing house, summer-house, lathhouse, **hothouse**, coolhouse; potting shed; force or forcing bed, forcing pit, **hotbed**, cold frame; seedbed; cloche; pinery, orangery

12 **growing, raising**, rearing, cultivation; **green thumb**

13 **cultivation**, cultivating, culture, **tilling**, dressing, working; harrowing, plowing, contour plowing, furrowing, listing, fallowing, weeding, hoeing, pruning, thinning; overcropping, overcultivation; irrigation, overirrigation

14 **planting**, setting; **sowing, seeding**, semination, insemination; breeding, hydridizing; **dissemination**, broadcast, broadcasting; transplantation, resetting; retimbering, reforestation

15 **harvest**, harvesting, **reaping, gleaning**, gathering, cutting; nutting; cash crop, root crop, **crop** 472.5

VERBS 16 **farm, ranch; grow, raise**, rear; crop; dryfarm; sharecrop; **garden; have a green thumb**

17 **cultivate**, culture, **dress, work, till**, till the soil, dig, delve, spade; mulch; **plow**, plow in, plow under, plow up, list, fallow, backset <W US>; **harrow**, rake; **weed**, weed out, hoe, cut, prune, thin, thin out; force; overcrop, overcultivate; slash and burn; fertilize 889.8

18 **plant**, implant <old>, **set**, put in; **sow, seed**, seed down, seminate, inseminate; **disseminate**, broadcast, sow broadcast, scatter seed; drill; bed; dibble; **transplant**, reset, pot; vernalize; **forest**, afforest; deforest; retimber, reforest

19 **harvest, reap**, crop, **glean, gather**, gather in, bring in, get in the harvest, reap and carry; **pick**, pluck; dig, grabble <S US>; mow, cut; hay; nut; crop herbs

ADJS 20 **agricultural, agrarian**, agro—, geoponic, geoponical, agronomic, agronomical; farm, **farming**; arable; **rural** 233.6

21 **horticultural**; olericultural; vinicultural; viticultural; arboricultural, silvicultural

22 **types of farming**

boutique farming	hydroponics or tank farming
contour farming	intensive farming
crop-farming	mixed farming
dirt farming <nonformal>	slash-and-burn farming
dry farming	strip farming
dryland farming	stubble-mulch farming or trash farming
fen farming	
fruit farming	subsistence farming
grain farming	truck farming

1068 ANIMAL HUSBANDRY

NOUNS 1 **animal husbandry**, animal rearing or raising or culture, stock raising, **ranching**; zooculture, zootechnics, zootechny; thremmatology; gnotobiotics; herding, grazing, keeping flocks and herds, running livestock; transhumance; breeding, stockbreeding, stirpiculture; horse training, dressage, manège; horsemanship; pisciculture, fish culture; apiculture, bee culture, beekeeping; cattle raising; sheepherding; stock farming, fur farming; factory farming; pig-keeping; dairy-farming, chicken-farming, pig-farming, etc; cattle-ranching, mink-ranching, etc

2 **stockman**, stock raiser, stockkeeper <Austral>; breeder, stockbreeder; sheepman; cattleman, cow keeper, cowman, grazier <Brit>; **rancher**, ranchman, ranchero; ranchhand; dairyman, dairy farmer; milkmaid; **stableman**, stableboy, **groom**, hostler, equerry; trainer, breaker, tamer; broncobuster and buckaroo <both nonformal>; **blacksmith**, horseshoer, farrier

3 **herder, drover, herdsman**, herdboy; **shepherd**, shepherdess, **sheepherder**, sheepman; goatherd; swineherd, pigman, pigherd, hogherd; gooseherd, gooseboy, goosegirl; swanherd; cowherd, neatherd <Brit>; **cowboy**, cowgirl, cowhand, puncher and **cowpuncher** and cowpoke <all nonformal>, waddy <W US>, cowman, cattleman, vaquero <Sp>, gaucho; horseherd, **wrangler**, horse wrangler

4 **apiarist**, apiculturist, **beekeeper**, beeherd

5 **farm**, stock farm, animal farm; **ranch**, rancho, rancheria; station <Austral>; horse farm, stable, stud farm; **cattle ranch**; dude ranch; pig farm, piggery; chicken farm or ranch, turkey farm, duck farm, poultry farm; sheep farm or ranch; fur farm or ranch, mink farm or ranch; **dairy farm**; factory farm; animal enclosure

VERBS 6 **raise, breed**, rear, grow, hatch, feed, nurture, fatten; keep, run; ranch; farm; culture; back-breed

7 **tend; groom**, rub down, brush, curry, currycomb; water, drench, feed, fodder; bed, bed down, litter; milk; harness, saddle, hitch, bridle, yoke; gentle, handle, manage; tame, train, break

8 **drive, herd**, drove <Brit>, herd up, punch cattle, **shepherd**, ride herd on; spur, goad, prick, lash, whip; wrangle, round up; corral, cage

1069 EARTH SCIENCE

NOUNS **1 earth science, earth sciences** <see list>; geoscience; geography, geology, rock hunting *and* rock hounding <both nonformal>, geological science, oceanography, oceanographic science, meteorology, atmospheric science, planetary science, space science

2 earth scientist, geoscientist; **geologist,** rock hound *and* rock hunter <both nonformal>, **geographer, oceanographer, astronomer,** star-gazer <nonformal>, **meteorologist,** weather man <for other agent NOUNS, add -ist or -er to names of branches listed below>

3 earth sciences

aerology	oceanology
aeronomy	paleobiogeography
bathymetry	paleoclimatology
biogeography	paleogeography
biostratigraphy	paleogeophysics
chronostratigraphy	paleolimnology
climatology	paleomagnetism
crystallography	paleontology
geochemistry	paleopedology
geochronology	pedology *or* soil sci-
geochronometry	ence
geodesy	petrochemistry
geodynamics	petrogenesis
geography	petrography
geological cartogra-	petrology *or* lithology
phy	physical climatology
geology	physical geography *or*
geomagnetism	physiography
geomorphology	planetology
geophysics	plate *or* global tec-
glaciology	tonics
historical geology	sedimentology
hydrography	seismology
hydrology *or* geo-	submarine geology
hydrology *or*	tectonic *or* geotec-
hydrogeology	tonic *or* structural
lithostratigraphy	geology
magnetostratigraphy	tectonophysics
meteorology	thalassography
mineralogy	topography
mining geology	volcanology
oceanography	

1070 THE UNIVERSE, ASTRONOMY

NOUNS **1 universe, world, cosmos;** creation, created universe, created nature, all, **all creation,** all tarnation <nonformal>, all *or* everything that is, all being, totality, totality of being, sum of things; omneity, allness; nature, system; wide world, whole wide world, "world without end"—Bible; plenum; **macrocosm,** macrocosmos, megacosm; metagalaxy; open universe, closed universe, oscillating universe, steady-state universe, expanding universe, pulsating universe; Einsteinian universe, Newtonian universe, Friedmann universe; Ptolemaic universe, Copernican universe; sidereal universe

2 the heavens, heaven, **sky, firmament;** empyrean, welkin, *caelum* <L>, lift *or* lifts <nonformal>; **the blue,** blue sky, azure, cerulean, the blue serene; **ether, air,** hyaline, "the clear hyaline, the glassy sea"—Milton, "an infinite grace"—Albert Camus; vault, cope, canopy, vault *or* canopy of heaven, "the arch of heaven"—Vergil, "that inverted bowl they call the sky"—Omar Khayyám, "heaven's ebon vault"—Shelley, starry sphere, celestial sphere, starry heaven *or* heavens, "this majestical roof fretted with golden fire"—Shakespeare; Caelus

3 space, outer space, cosmic space, empty space, ether space, pressureless space, celestial spaces, interplanetary *or* interstellar *or* intergalactic *or* intercosmic space, metagalactic space, **the void,** the void above, ocean of emptiness; chaos; outermost reaches of space; astronomical unit, light-year, parsec; interstellar medium

4 stars, fixed stars, starry host, "living sapphires"—Milton, "all the fire-folk sitting in the air"—G M Hopkins, "the burning tapers of the sky"—Shakespeare, "the mystical jewels of God"—Robert Buchanan, "golden fruit upon a tree all out of reach"—George Eliot, "bright sentinels of the sky"—William Habington, "the pale populace of Heaven"—R Browning; music *or* harmony of the spheres; orb, sphere; **heavenly body,** celestial body *or* sphere; **comet; comet cloud; morning star,** daystar, Lucifer, Phosphor, Phosphorus; **evening star,** Vesper, Hesper, Hesperus, Venus; **North Star,** polestar, polar star, lodestar, Polaris; Dog Star, Sirius, Canicula; Bull's Eye, Aldebaran

5 constellation <see list>, **configuration,** asterism; zodiacal constellation; **star cluster,** galactic cluster, open cluster, globular cluster, stellar association, supercluster; Magellanic clouds

6 galaxy, island universe, galactic nebula; spiral galaxy *or* nebula, spiral; barred spiral galaxy *or* nebula, barred spiral; elliptical *or* spheroidal galaxy; disk galaxy; irregular galaxy; radio galaxy; **the Local Group; the Galaxy, the Milky Way,** the galactic circle, *Via Lactea* <L>; galactic

cluster, supergalaxy; great attractor; chaotic attractor; continent of galaxies, great
wall *or* sheet of galaxies; galactic coordinates, galactic pole, galactic latitude,
galactic longitude; galactic noise, cosmic
noise; galactic nucleus, active galactic
nucleus; cosmic string

7 nebula, nebulosity; gaseous nebula; hydrogen cloud; dark nebula; dust cloud;
dark matter; planetary nebula; whirlpool
nebula; cirro-nebula; ring nebula; diffuse
nebula; bright diffuse nebula; dark nebula, dark cloud, coalsack; Nebula of Lyra
or Orion, Crab Nebula, the Coalsack,
Black Magellanic Cloud; nebulous stars;
nebular hypothesis

8 star <see list>; **quasar,** quasi-stellar
radio source; **pulsar,** pulsating star,
eclipsing binary X-ray pulsar; Nemesis,
the Death Star; **black hole,** gravitational
collapse, giant black hole, mini-black
hole, starving black hole, supermassive
black hole, frozen black hole, white hole,
active galactic nucleus; Hawking radiation; **magnitude,** stellar magnitude,
visual magnitude; relative magnitude,
absolute magnitude; star *or* stellar popu-
lations; mass-luminosity law; spectrum-
luminosity diagram, Hertzsprung-
Russell diagram; star catalog, star chart,
sky atlas, Messier catalog, Dreyer's New
General Catalog *or* NGC; star cloud, star
cluster, globular cluster, open cluster;
Pleiades *or* Seven Sisters, Hyades, Beehive

9 planet, wanderer, terrestrial planet, inferior planet, superior planet, secondary
planet, major planet; minor planet, plan-
etoid, asteroid; asteroid belt; Earth;
Jupiter; Mars, the Red Planet; Mercury;
Neptune; Pluto; Saturn; Uranus; Venus;
solar system

10 Earth, the world, *terra* <L>; **globe,** terrestrial globe, Spaceship Earth, the blue
planet; geosphere, biosphere, magneto-
sphere; vale, vale of tears; "this pendent
world, "the little O, the earth, "this goodly
frame, the earth, "a stage where every
man must play a part"—all Shakespeare,
"a seat where gods might dwell"—Milton; Mother Earth, Ge *or* Gaea, Tellus *or*
Terra; whole wide world, four corners of
the earth, "the round earth's imagined
corners"—Donne, the length and breadth
of the land; geography; Gaia hypothesis

11 moon, satellite; orb of night, queen of
heaven, queen of night, "that orbèd
maiden"—Shelley, "the wat'ry star,
"the governess of floods, "sovereign mis-

tress of the true melancholy"—all Shakespeare, "a ghostly galleon tossed upon
cloudy seas"—Alfred Noyes, "Maker of
sweet poets"—Keats, "the wandering
Moon"—Milton, "bright wanderer, fair
coquette of Heaven"—Shelley, "Queen
and huntress, chaste and fair"—Ben Jonson, "a ruined world, a globe burnt out, a
corpse upon the road of night"—Robert
Burton; silvery moon; **new moon,** wet
moon; **crescent moon,** crescent, increscent moon, increscent, waxing moon,
waxing crescent moon; decrescent moon,
decrescent, waning moon, waning crescent moon; gibbous moon; **half-moon,**
demilune; **full moon, harvest moon,**
hunter's moon; **eclipse,** lunar eclipse,
eclipse of the moon; artificial satellite
1073.6,14

12 <moon goddess, the moon personified>
Diana, Phoebe, Cynthia, Artemis, Hecate,
Selene, Luna, Astarte, Ashtoreth; man in
the moon

13 sun; orb of day, daystar; "the glorious
lamp of Heav'n, the radiant sun"—
Dryden, "that orbèd continent, the fire
that severs day from night"—Shakespeare, "of this great world both eye and
soul"—Milton, "the God of life and poesy
and light"—Byron; photosphere, chro-
mosphere, corona; sunspot; sunspot cycle;
solar flare, solar prominence; solar wind;
eclipse, eclipse of the sun, solar eclipse,
total eclipse, partial eclipse, central
eclipse, annular eclipse; corona, solar
corona, Baily's beads

14 <sun god or goddess, the sun personi-
fied> Sol, Helios, Hyperion, Titan,
Phaëthon, Phoebus, Phoebus Apollo,
Apollo, Ra *or* Amen-Ra, Shamash,
Surya, Savitar, Amaterasu

15 meteor; falling *or* shooting star, mete-
oroid, fireball, bolide; **meteorite,** mete-
orolite; micrometeoroid, micrometeorite;
aerolite; chondrite; siderite; siderolite;
tektite; meteor dust, cosmic dust; meteor
trail, meteor train; meteor swarm; meteor *or* meteoric shower; radiant, radiant
point; meteor crater

16 orbit, circle, trajectory; circle of the
sphere, great circle, small circle; **ecliptic;**
zodiac; zone; meridian, celestial meridian; colures, equinoctial colure, solstitial
colure; equator, celestial equator, equinoctial, equinoctial circle *or* line; equinox, vernal equinox, autumnal equinox;
longitude, celestial longitude, geocentric
longitude, heliocentric longitude, galactic longitude, astronomical longitude,

geographic *or* geodetic longitude; apogee, perigee; aphelion, perihelion; period

17 **observatory,** astronomical observatory; radio observatory, orbiting astronomical observatory *or* OAO, orbiting solar observatory *or* OSO; **planetarium;** orrery; **telescope,** astronomical telescope; reflector, refractor, Newtonian telescope, Cassegrainian telescope; **radio telescope,** radar telescope; **spectroscope,** spectrograph; spectrohelioscope, spectroheliograph; coronagraph; heliostat, coelostat; **observation;** seeing, bright time, dark time

18 **cosmology,** cosmography, **cosmogony;** stellar cosmogony, astrogony; cosmism, cosmic philosophy, cosmic evolution; nebular hypothesis; **big bang** *or* expanding universe theory, oscillating *or* pulsating universe theory, steady state *or* continuous creation theory, plasma theory; creationism, creation science

19 **astronomy, stargazing,** uranology, astrognosy, astrography, uranography, uranometry; astrophotography, stellar photometry; spectrography, spectroscopy, radio astronomy, radar astronomy, X-ray astronomy; **astrophysics,** solar physics; celestial mechanics, gravitational astronomy; astrolithology; meteoritics; astrogeology

20 **astrology,** astromancy, **horoscopy;** astrodiagnosis; natural astrology; judicial *or* mundane astrology; genethliacism, genethlialogy, genethliacs, genethliac astrology; **horoscope,** nativity; zodiac, **signs of the zodiac; house,** mansion; house of life, mundane house, planetary house *or* mansion; aspect

21 **cosmologist;** cosmogonist, cosmogoner; cosmographer, cosmographist; cosmic philosopher, cosmist

22 **astronomer,** stargazer, uranologist, uranometrist, uranographer, uranographist, astrographer, astrophotographer; radio astronomer, radar astronomer; **astrophysicist,** solar physicist; astrogeologist

23 **astrologer,** astrologian, astromancer, stargazer, Chaldean, astroalchemist, horoscoper, horoscopist, genethliac <old>

ADJS 24 **cosmic,** cosmical, **universal;** cosmologic *or* cosmological, cosmogonal, cosmogonic *or* cosmogonical; cosmographic, cosomographical

25 **celestial, heavenly, empyrean,** empyreal; uranic; **astral, starry, stellar,** stellary, sphery; star-spangled, star-studded; sidereal; zodiacal; equinoctial; **astronomic** *or*

astronomical, astrophysical, astrologic *or* astrological, astrologistic, astrologous; **planetary,** planetarian, planetal, circumplanetary; planetoidal, planetesimal, asteroidal; **solar,** heliacal; terrestrial; **lunar,** lunular, lunate, lunulate, lunary, cislunar, translunar, Cynthian; semilunar; meteoric, meteoritic; extragalactic, anagalactic; galactic; nebular, nebulous, nebulose; interstellar, intersidereal; interplanetary; intercosmic

26 **extraterrestrial,** exterrestrial, extraterrene, extramundane, alien, space; **transmundane, otherworldly,** transcendental; extra-solar

ADVS 27 **universally,** everywhere

28 **star types**

A star	long-period variable
binary star	M star
black dwarf	main sequence star
blaze star	multiple star
brown dwarf	N star
C star	nautical star
carbon star	nebulous star
Cepheid *or* Cepheid variable	neutron star
	nova
comparison star	O-type star
dark star	R star
double star	radio star
dwarf star	red giant
early-type star	red supergiant
eclipsing binary	RR Lyrae star
eclipsing variable	runaway star
eruptive variable	semiregular variable
F star	silicon star
fixed star	solar *or* sun star
flare star	spectroscopic binary
giant star	standard star
gravity star	supermassive star
Greenwich star	supernova
G star	variable star
hydrogen star	visible binary
intrinsic variable	white dwarf
irregular star	x-ray star
K star	zenith star
late-type star	

29 **constellations**

Andromeda *or* the Chained Lady	Auriga *or* the Charioteer
Antlia *or* Antlia Pneumatica *or* the Air Pump	Big Dipper *or* Ursa Major *or* Charles' Wain
Apus *or* the Bird of Paradise	Boötes *or* the Herdsman
Aquarius *or* the Water Bearer	Caelum *or* Caela Sculptoris *or* the Sculptor's Tool
Aquila *or* the Eagle	
Ara *or* the Altar	Camelopardalis *or* Camelopardus *or* the Giraffe
Argo *or* Argo Navis *or* the Ship Argo	
Aries *or* the Ram	Cancer *or* the Crab

Canes Venatici *or* the Hunting Dogs
Canis Major the Larger Dog *or* Orion's Hound
Canis Minor *or* the Lesser Dog
Capricorn *or* the Horned Goat
Carina *or* the Keel
Cassiopeia *or* the Lady in the Chair
Centaurus *or* the Centaur
Cepheus *or* the Monarch
Cetus *or* the Whale
Chamaeleon *or* the Chameleon
Circinus *or* the Compasses
Columba *or* Columba Noae *or* Noah's Dove
Coma Berenices *or* Berenice's Hair
Corona Australis *or* the Wreath *or* the Southern Crown
Corona Borealis *or* the Northern Crown
Corvus *or* the Crow
Crater *or* the Cup
Crux *or* the Cross
Cygnus *or* the Swan
Delphinus *or* the Dolphin
Dorado *or* the Dorado Fish
Draco *or* the Dragon
Equuleus *or* the Foal
Eridanus *or* the River Po
Fornax *or* the Furnace
Gemini *or* the Twins
Grus *or* the Crane
Hercules
Horologium *or* the Clock
Hydra *or* the Sea Serpent
Hydrus *or* the Water Snake
Indus *or* the Indian
Lacerta *or* the Lizard
Leo *or* the Lion
Leo Minor *or* the Lesser Lion
Lepus *or* the Hare
Libra *or* the Balance
Little Dipper *or* Ursa Minor
Lupus *or* the Wolf
Lynx *or* the Lynx

Lyra *or* the Lyre
Malus *or* the Mast
Mensa *or* the Table
Microscopium *or* the Microscope
Monoceros *or* the Unicorn
Musca *or* the Fly
Norma *or* the Rule
Northern Cross
Octans *or* the Octant
Ophiuchus *or* the Serpent Bearer
Orion *or* the Giant Hunter
Orion's Belt
Orion's Sword
Pavo *or* the Peacock
Pegasus *or* the Winged Horse
Perseus
Phoenix *or* the Phoenix
Pictor *or* the Painter
Pisces *or* the Fishes
Piscis Australis *or* the Southern Fish
Puppis *or* the Stern
Reticulum *or* the Net
Sagitta *or* the Arrow
Sagittarius *or* the Archer
Scorpio *or* Scorpius *or* the Scorpion
Sculptor *or* the Sculptor
Scutum *or* the Shield
Serpens *or* the Serpent
Sextans *or* the Sextant
Southern Cross
Taurus *or* the Bull
Telescopium *or* the Telescope
Triangulum *or* the Triangle
Triangulum Australe *or* the Southern Triangle
Tucana *or* the Toucan
Ursa Major *or* the Great Bear *or* the Big Dipper
Ursa Minor *or* the Lesser Bear *or* the Little Dipper
Vela *or* the Sails
Virgo *or* the Virgin
Volans *or* Piscis Volans *or* the Flying Fish
Vulpecula *or* the Little Fox

1071 THE ENVIRONMENT

NOUNS **1 the environment,** the natural world, the ecology, global ecology, ecosystem, global ecosystem, the biosphere, the ecosphere, the balance of nature, macroecology, microecology; **ecology,** bioregion; **environmental protection,** environmental policy; **environmental control,** environmental management; environmental assessment, environmental auditing, environmental monitoring, environmental impact analysis; emission control; **environmental science** <see list>, environmentology

2 environmental destruction, ecocide, ecocatastrophe; environmental pollution, pollution, contamination; **air pollution,** atmospheric pollution, air quality; **water pollution,** stream pollution, lake pollution, ocean pollution, groundwater pollution, pollution of the aquifer; **environmental pollutant** <see list>; eutrophication; **biodegradation,** biodeterioration, microbial degradation

3 environmentalist, conservationist, preservationist, nature-lover, environmental activist, doomwatcher <Brit>, duck-squeezer *and* ecofreak *and* tree-hugger *and* eagle freak <all nonformal>; Green Panther

4 environmental sciences

autecology	environmental engineering
bioecology *or* bionomics	environmental health
ecology	
environmental archaeology	human ecology
environmental biology	land management
environmental chemistry	synecology
	wildlife management
	zoo-ecology

5 environmental pollutants

aerosol sprays	chlorine
aircraft noise	chlorobenzenes
aldrin	chloroethanes
arsenic	chlorofluorocarbons
asbestos	
automobile exhaust	chlorohydrocarbons
azo compounds	
benzene	chloromethane
beryllium	chlorophenol
bromo compounds	chloropropanones
calcium carbonates	chlorpropham
captan	chromium
carbon dioxide	coal smoke
carbon monoxide	dibromochloropropane *or* DBCP
carbon tetrachloride	
carcinogens	dichlorides
chemical waste	dichloroacetate
chlordane	dichlorobenzenes

dichlorodiphenyltri-
 chloroethane or
 DDT
dichloroethanes
dichlorophenol
dichloropropane
dieldrin
dioxin
dioxins
endosulfan
endrin
ethanes
ethylene
ethylene dibromide
 or EDB
ethylene glycol
ethylene oxide
fenoxaprop ethyl
fluorenes
fluorides
fluorocarbons
fluorohydrocarbons
formaldehyde
fungicides
gasoline
heptachlor
herbicides
hexachlorethane
hexone
hydrocarbons
industrial particulate
 matter
isocyanuric acid
kepone
lead
lead paint
leaded gasoline
leptophos
malathion
mercury

metalaxyl
methyl ethyl ketone
methyl parathion
mining waste
mirex
nabam
naphthalene
nitro compounds
nitrogen oxides
nitroso compounds
noise
nuclear waste
paraquat dichloride
parathion
pentachloraphenol or
 PCP
pesticides
polybrominated bi-
 phenyls or PBBs
polychlorinated bi-
 phenyls or PCBs
radionuclides
sewage
sewage sludge
solid waste
sulfur oxides
tobacco smoke
toxaphene
toxic waste
trichloroacetic acid
trichlorobenzene
trichloroethylene or
 TCE
trimethylbenzenes
triphenyltin hydrox-
 ide or DuTer
 <trademark>
ultraviolet radiation
vinyl chloride
wood smoke

1072 ROCKETRY, MISSILERY

NOUNS **1 rocketry,** rocket science or engineering or research or technology; **missilery,** missile science or engineering or
research or technology; rocket or missile
testing; ground test, firing test, static firing; rocket or missile project or program;
instrumentation; telemetry

2 rocket, rocket engine or **motor,** reaction engine or motor; rocket thruster,
thruster; retrorocket; rocket exhaust;
plasma jet, plasma engine; ion engine;
jetavator

3 rocket, missile <see list>, **ballistic missile, guided missile; torpedo;** projectile
rocket, ordnance rocket, combat or military or war rocket; bird <nonformal>;
payload; warhead, nuclear or thermonuclear warhead, atomic warhead;
multiple or multiple-missile warhead

4 rocket bomb, flying bomb or torpedo,
cruising missile; **robot bomb,** robomb,
Vergeltungswaffe <Ger>, V-weapon,
P-plane; **buzzbomb,** bumblebomb,
doodle-bug

5 multistage rocket, step rocket; two- or
three-stage rocket, two- or three-step
rocket; single-stage rocket, single-step
rocket, one-step rocket; **booster,** booster
unit, booster rocket, takeoff booster or
rocket; piggyback rocket

6 test rocket, research rocket, high-altitude
research rocket, registering rocket, instrument rocket, instrument carrier, test instrument vehicle, rocket laboratory; probe

7 proving ground, testing ground; firing
area; impact area; control center, mission control, bunker; radar tracking station, tracking station, visual tracking
station; meteorological tower

8 rocket propulsion, reaction propulsion,
jet propulsion, blast propulsion; **fuel,
propellant,** solid fuel, liquid fuel, hy-
drazine, liquid oxygen or lox; charge,
propelling or propulsion charge, powder
charge or grain, high-explosive charge;
thrust, constant thrust; **exhaust,** jet blast,
backflash

9 rocket launching or **firing,** ignition,
launch, shot, shoot; countdown; **lift-off,**
blast-off; guided or automatic control,
programming; flight, trajectory; **burn;
burnout,** end of burning; velocity peak,
Brennschluss <Ger>; altitude peak, ceiling; descent; airburst; impact

10 rocket launcher, projector; **launching** or
launch pad, launching platform or rack,
firing table; **silo;** takeoff ramp; tower
projector, launching tower; launching
mortar, launching tube, projector tube,
firing tube; rocket gun, bazooka, antitank rocket, *Panzerfaust* <Ger>; super-
bazooka; multiple projector, calliope,
Stalin organ, Katusha; antisubmarine
projector, Mark 10, hedgehog <nonfor-
mal>; Minnie Mouse launcher, mousetrap <nonformal>; Meilewagon

11 rocket scientist or technician, rocketeer
or rocketer, rocket or missile man, rocket
or missile engineer

VERBS **12 rocket, skyrocket**

13 launch, project, **shoot, fire,** blast off;
abort

14 rockets, missiles

AAM or air-to-air mis-
 sile
AA target rocket
ABM or antiballistic
 missile

airborne rocket
anchor rocket
antiaircraft rocket
antimine rocket
antimissile

antiradar rocket
antisubmarine or antisub rocket
antitank rocket
ASM or air-to-surface missile
ATA missile or air-to-air
ATG rocket or air-to-ground
atom-rocket
ATS or air-to-ship
AUM or air-to-underwater missile
barrage rocket
bat bomb
bazooka rocket
bombardment rocket
chemical rocket
combat high-explosive rocket
Congreve rocket
countermissile
demolition rocket
fin-stabilized rocket
fireworks rocket
flare rocket
flying tank
GAPA or ground-to-air pilotless aircraft
glide bomb
GTA rocket or ground-to-air
GTG rocket or ground-to-ground
guided missile
harpoon rocket
high-altitude rocket
homing rocket
HVAR or high velocity aircraft rocket
ICBM or intercontinental ballistic missile
incendiary anti-aircraft rocket
incendiary rocket
ion rocket
IRBM or intermediate range ballistic missile
line-throwing rocket
liquid-fuel rocket
long-range rocket

MIRV or multiple independently targetable re-entry vehicle
MRV or multiple re-entry vehicle
ram rocket
retro-float light
retro-rocket
rockoon
SAM or surface-to-air missile
scud
signal rocket
skyrocket
smart rocket
smokeless powder rocket
smoke rocket
snake or antimine
solid-fuel rocket
space rocket
spinner
spin-stabilized rocket
SSM or surface-to-surface missile
STS rocket or ship-to-shore
submarine killer
supersonic rocket
target missile
torpedo rocket
training rocket or missile
trajectory missile
transoceanic rocket
ullage rocket
vernier or vernier rocket
window rocket or antiradar
winged rocket
XAAM or experimental air-to-air missile
XASM or experimental air-to-surface missile
XAUM or experimental air-to-underwater missile
XSAM or experimental surface-to-air missile
XSSM or experimental surface-to-surface missile

1073 SPACE TRAVEL

NOUNS 1 space travel, astronautics, cosmonautics, **space flight,** navigation of empty space; interplanetary travel, space exploration; space walk; space navigation, astrogation; **space science,** space technology or engineering; **aerospace science,** aerospace technology or engineering; space or aerospace research; space or aerospace medicine, bioastronautics; astrionics; escape velocity; rocketry 1072; multistage flight, step flight, shuttle flights; trip to the moon, trip to Mars, grand tour; space terminal, target planet; science fiction

2 spacecraft <see list>, **spaceship, space rocket,** rocket ship, manned rocket, interplanetary rocket; **rocket** 1072.2; orbiter; **shuttle,** space shuttle; **capsule, space capsule,** ballistic capsule; **nose cone, heat shield,** heat barrier, thermal barrier; module, command module, lunar excursion module or LEM, lunar module or LM; moon ship, Mars ship, etc; deep-space ship; exploratory ship, reconnaissance rocket; ferry rocket, tender rocket, tanker ship, fuel ship; **multistage rocket** 1072.5, shuttle rocket, retrorocket, rocket thruster or thruster, attitude-control rocket, main rocket; **burn;** space docking, docking, docking maneuver; **orbit,** parking orbit, geostationary orbit; earth orbit, apogee, perigee; lunar or moon orbit, apolune, perilune, apocynthion, pericynthion; **guidance system,** terrestrial guidance; soft landing, hard landing; injection, insertion, lunar insertion, Earth insertion; **reentry, splashdown**

3 flying saucer, unidentified flying object or UFO

4 rocket engine 1072.2; atomic power plant; solar battery; power cell

5 space station, astro station, **space island,** island base, cosmic stepping-stone, halfway station, advance base; manned station; inner station, outer station, transit station, space airport, **spaceport,** spaceport station, space dock, launching base, research station, space laboratory, space observatory; tracking station, radar tracking station; radar station, radio station; radio relay station, radio mirror; space mirror, solar mirror; moon station, moon base, lunar base, lunar city, observatory on the moon

6 artificial satellite <see list>, **satellite,** space satellite, robot satellite, unmanned satellite, sputnik; communications satellite, active communications satellite, communications relay satellite, weather satellite, orbiting observatory, geophysical satellite, navigational satellite, geodetic satellite, research satellite, inter-

planetary monitoring satellite, automated satellite; **probe, space probe,** geo
probe, interplanetary explorer

7 <satellite telemetered recorders> micro-
instrumentation; aurora particle counter,
cosmic ray counter, gamma ray counter,
heavy particle counter, impulse recorder,
magnetometer, solar ultraviolet detector,
solar X-ray detector, telecamera

8 astronaut, astronavigator, cosmonaut,
spaceman, spacewoman, space crew
member, shuttle crew member, space
traveler, rocketeer, rocket pilot; space
doctor; space crew; planetary colony, lunar colony; extraterrestrial visitor, alien,
saucerman, man from Mars, Martian, little green man

9 rocket society, American Rocket Society,
American Interplanetary Society, British
Interplanetary Society, German Society
for Space Research

10 <space hazards> cosmic particles, intergalactic matter, aurora particles, radiation, cosmic ray bombardment; rocket
or satellite debris, space junk <nonfor-
mal>; meteors, meteorites; asteroids;
meteor dust impacts, meteoric particles,
space bullets; extreme temperatures; the
bends, blackout, weightlessness

11 space suit, pressure suit, G suit, anti-G
suit; space helmet

VERBS **12** travel in space, go into outer
space; orbit the earth, go into orbit, orbit
the moon, etc; navigate in space, astro-
gate; escape earth, break free, leave the
atmosphere, shoot into space; rocket to
the moon, park in space, hang *or* float in
space, space-walk

ADJS **13 astronautical,** cosmonautical,
spacetraveling, spacefaring; astroga-
tional; rocketborne, spaceborne

**14 spacecraft, artificial satellites, space
probes**

A-1	Cosmos
Alouette	Courier
Anik	D1-C
Anna	D2-D
Apollo	Diapason
Ariane	Discoverer
Ariel	Early Bird
ATDA	Echo
Atlas-Score	Elektron
ATS	ERS
Aurora 7 <Mercury>	ESSA *or* environ-
Biosatellite	mental survey
communications sat-	satellite
ellites *or* comsats	Explorer
Comsat	Explorer 760
cosmic background	Faith 7 <Mercury>
explorer *or* COBE	FR-1

Freedom 7	OSO *or* orbiting solar
<Mercury>	observatory
Friendship 7	OV1
<Mercury>	OV3
Galileo	Pageos
GATV	Pegasus
Gemini	Pioneer
Geostationary	Polyot
Operational	Proton
Environmental	Ranger
Satellite *or* GOES	Relay
Greb	Samos
Injun	San Marco
Intelsat	Secor
killersat	shuttle *or* space
Lageos *or* laser	shuttle
geodynamic	Sigma 7 <Mercury>
satellite	Skylab
Lani Bird	skylab
Liberty Bell 7	Solar Max
<Mercury>	Soyuz
Lofti	Spacelab
Luna	space station
Lunar Orbiter	Sputnik
Lunik	Surveyor
Mariner	Syncom
Mars probes	Telstar
Mercury	TIROS *or* television
Midas	and infrared obser-
Molniya	vation satellite
Nimbus	Transit
OAO *or* orbiting	Vanguard
astronomical	Venus probes
observatory	Viking
OGO *or* orbiting	Voskhod
geophysical	Vostok
observatory	WRESAT
orbiter	Zond

Index

How to Use This Index

Numbers after index entries refer to categories and paragraphs in the front section of this book, not to page numbers. The part of the number before the decimal point refers to the category in which synonyms and related words to the word you are looking up are found. The part of the number after the decimal point refers to the paragraph or paragraphs within the category. Look at the index entry for **abdomen** on the next page:

abdomen 2.16

This entry listing tells you that you can find words related to **abdomen** in paragraph 16 of category 2.

Words, of course, frequently have more than one meaning. Each of those meanings may have synonyms or associated related words. Look at the entry for **abhor**:

abhor dislike 99.3
hate 103.5

This tells you that you will find synonyms for **abhor** in the sense meaning "dislike" in category 99, paragraph 3. It also tells you that you will find synonyms for **abhor**, meaning "hate" in category 103, paragraph 5.

In many cases, words are spelled the same as nouns, verbs, adjectives, etc. Look at the entry for **abandon** and notice that here you are directed to **abandon** when it is used as a noun and when it is used as a verb in a variety of meanings. Here, as in the examples above, you are referred to the category and paragraph number.

Not all words in the main part of the book are included in the index. Many adverbs ending with **-ly** have been left out of the index; but you will find the common adverbs ending in **-ly** here, such as **lightly** or **easily**. If you can't find the adverb ending in **-ly** that you are looking for, look up the word in its adjective form and go to that category. Frequently, you can use the words in the adjective paragraphs you find and convert them into the adverb you are looking for by simply adding **-ly** to the adjective.

To make it easier to find phrases, we have indexed them according to their first word, unless that first word is an article such as **a**, **the** or **an**. You do not have to guess what the main word of the phrase is to find it in the index. Simply look up the first word in the phrase. For example, **hot air** will be found in the Hs, **fat cat** in the Fs and **let go** in the Ls.

abaft aft 182.69
  after 217.14
abandon
  n zeal 101.2
  fury 105.8
  carelessness 340.2
  unrestraint 430.3
  turpitude 654.5
  excess 992.1
  v quit 188.9
  leave undone 340.7
  desert 370.5
  break the habit
  374.3
  discard 390.7
  surrender 433.8
  disregard 435.3
  relinquish 475.3
  swear off 668.8
  cease 856.6
  dismiss 983.4
abandoned
  zealous 101.9
  frenzied 105.25
  available 222.15
  neglected 340.14
  forsaken 370.8
  disused 390.10
  unrestrained 430.24
  relinquished 475.5
  forlorn 584.12
  outcast 586.10
  corrupt 654.14
  profligate 665.25
  excessive 992.16
abase debase 137.5
  demote 447.3
abashed
  distressed 96.22
  humiliated 137.14
  bewildered 970.24
abate weaken 16.10
  relieve 120.5
  decrease 252.6
  bate 252.8
  subtract 255.9
  discount 631.2
  moderate 670.6
  relax 670.9
  qualify 958.3
abatement
  weakening 16.5
  relief 120.1
  decrease 252.1
  discount 631.1
  modulation 670.2
abattoir 308.11
abbé 699.2
abbess
  mistress 575.2
  nun 699.17
abbey 703.6
abbot 699.15
abbreviate
  delete 255.12
  contract 260.7
  shorten 268.6
  be brief 537.5
abbreviated
  short 268.8
  shortened 268.9
  concise 537.6

abbreviation
  deletion 255.5
  contraction 260.1
  shortening 268.3
  shortening 537.4
  abridgment 557.1
ABC's
  writing system 546.3
  elementary education
  568.5
  basics 817.6
abdicate give up 370.7
  cease to use 390.4
  resign 448.2
abdomen 2.16
abdominal 2.29
abduct seize 480.14
  abduce 482.20
abduction
  seizure 480.2
  kidnapping 482.9
abductor 483.10
abeam 218.11
abed 20.11
Abélard and Héloïse
  104.18
aberrant
  deviative 164.7
  wrong 638.3
  changed 851.10
  abnormal 869.9
  erroneous 974.16
aberration
  deviation 164.1
  divergence 171.1
  obliquity 204.1
  abnormality 869.1
  insanity 925.1
  eccentricity 926.1
  error 974.1
abet advance 162.5
  encourage 375.21
  aid 449.11
  encourage 449.14
abettor
  prompter 375.10
  accomplice 616.3
  supporter 616.9
abeyance
  inertness 173.4
  discontinuance 390.2
  pause 856.3
abhor dislike 99.3
  hate 103.5
abhorrent
  offensive 98.18
  unlikable 99.7
  hating 103.7
abide await 130.8
  endure 134.5
  inhabit 225.7
  endure 826.6
  wait 845.12
  remain 852.5
  continue 855.3
abide by
  assent 332.8
  observe 434.2
  execute 437.9
abide in 760.11
abiding
  n habitation 225.1

adj resident 225.13
  durable 826.10
  permanent 852.7
  continuing 855.7
ability
  capability 18.2
  means 384.2
  preparedness 405.4
  skill 413.1
  talent 413.4
abject penitent 113.9
  humblehearted 137.11
  obsequious 138.14
  submissive 433.12
  base 661.12
abjure
  n recant 363.8
  v deny 335.4
  give up 370.7
  reject 372.2
  cease to use 390.4
  relinquish 475.3
ablate decrease 252.6
  consume 388.3
  wear 393.20
  waste 473.5
  disintegrate 805.3
  abrade 1042.7
ablaze fervent 93.18
  burning 1018.27
  flashing 1024.34
  illuminated 1024.39
able
  capable 18.14
  fitted 405.17
  competent 413.24
able-bodied 15.16
abloom floral 310.35
  ripe 407.13
  gorgeous 1015.20
ablution 79.5
ably capably 18.16
  skillfully 413.31
abnormal wrong 638.3
  inconsistent 788.8
  unnatural 869.9
  insane 925.26
  eccentric 926.5
abnormality
  disease 85.1
  wrong 638.1
  unfitness 788.3
  unnaturalness 869
  fluke 869.1
  oddity 869.5
  insanity 925.1
  eccentricity 926.1
aboard here 159.23
  on board 182.62
abode location 159.1
  habitation 225.1
  dwelling 228
  living place 228.1
abolish nullify 395.13
  repeal 445.2
abolition
  extinction 395.6
  repeal 445.1
A-bomb 1037.16
abominable
  offensive 98.18
  wrong 638.3

  wicked 654.16
  base 661.12
  terrible 999.9
abominate 103.5
abomination
  defilement 80.4
  hostility 99.2
  hate 103.1
  hated thing 103.3
  horror 638.2
  iniquity 654.3
  evil 999.3
aborigine
  native 227.3
  ancient 841.7
abort miscarry 410.15
  end 819.5
  cease 856.6
  launch 1072.13
abortion
  miscarriage 410.5
  monstrosity 869.6
  unproductiveness
  890.1
abortive
  fruitless 391.12
  unsuccessful 410.18
abound
  teem with 883.5
  exuberate 990.5
about
  adv around 209.12
  near 223.20
  approximately 244.6
  prep around 223.26
  in relation to 774.13
about-face
  n reverse 163.3
  denial 335.2
  switch 363.1
  change 851.1
  conversion 857.1
  reversion 858.1
  v regress 163.10
  change 851.7
about to
  adj prepared 405.16
  prep at the point of
  838.13
above
  adj superior 249.12
  higher 272.19
  previous 833.4
  adv additionally
  253.11
  on high 272.21
  before 813.6
  prep on 295.37
  beyond 522.26
  in excess of 992.26
above all 249.17
above all that 141.12
above and beyond
  992.26
aboveboard
  adj straight 644.14
  adv openly 348.15
above it all 94.13
above suspicion 657.8
above water
  unindebted 624.23
  in safety 1006.6

ab ovo
  adj essential 766.9
  adv first 817.18
  newly 840.15
abracadabra 691.4
abrade subtract 255.9
  grind 287.8
  injure 393.13
  wear 393.20
  abrase 1042.7
  pulverize 1049.9
abrasion trauma 85.37
  subtraction 255.1
  roughness 288.1
  attrition 1042.2
  pulverization 1049.4
abrasive
  n smoother 287.4
  abrasion 1042.2
  adj unpleasant 98.17
  out of humor 110.17
  rugged 288.7
  abradant 1042.10
abreast
  in parallel 203.7
  beside 218.11
  informed 927.18
abridge reduce 252.7
  delete 255.12
  abbreviate 268.6
  take from 480.21
  shorten 557.5
abridged
  shortened 268.9
  concise 537.6
  condensed 557.6
abridgment
  decrease 252.1
  deletion 255.5
  shortening 268.3
  deprivation 480.6
  aphorism 537.3
  compendium 557.1
abroad
  adj nonresident
    222.12
  bewildered 970.24
  erroneous 974.16
  adv extensively 158.11
  outdoors 206.11
  far and wide 261.16
  wide 261.19
  in foreign parts 773.6
abrogate
  abolish 395.13
  repeal 445.2
abrupt steep 204.18
  blunt 286.3
  precipitate 401.10
  commanding 420.13
  gruff 505.7
  sudden 829.5
abruptly short 268.13
  precipitately 401.15
  gruffly 505.9
abscess
  symptom 85.9
  sore 85.36
abscissa 300.5
abscond quit 188.9
  flee 368.10
absconded 222.11

absconder 368.5
absence
  nonpresence 222.1
  nonattendance 222.4
  nonexistence 761.1
  want 991.4
absent
  adj not present 222.11
  abstracted 984.11
  prep lacking 222.19
  excluding 772.10
  without 991.17
  conj unless 958.16
absentee 222.5
absentee ballot 609.19
absentminded
  abstracted 984.11
  forgetful 989.9
absolute
  omnipotent 18.13
  downright 247.12
  affirmative 334.8
  authoritative 417.15
  imperious 417.16
  mandatory 420.12
  unrestricted 430.27
  governmental 612.17
  musical 708.47
  real 760.15
  thorough 793.10
  unmixed 797.7
  particular 864.12
  sole 871.9
  convincing 952.26
  evidential 956.16
  unqualified 959.2
  certain 969.13
  obvious 969.15
  accurate 972.16
  perfect 1001.6
absolutely
  adv extremely 247.22
  affirmatively 334.10
  really 760.16
  fully 793.15
  certainly 969.23
  exactly 972.21
  perfectly 1001.10
  inter yes 332.18
absoluteness 1001.1
absolve
  forgive 148.3
  exempt 430.14
  acquit 601.4
  declare a moratorium
    625.9
  confess 701.17
absorb digest 7.16
  adsorb 187.13
  consume 388.3
  understand 521.7
  acquire 570.7
  corner 737.26
  involve 897.2
  occupy the thoughts
    930.20
  engross 982.13
absorbed
  engrossed in thought
    930.22
  occupied 982.17
  abstracted 984.11

absorbent
  n sorption 187.6
  adj sorbent 187.17
absorbing
  deep-felt 93.24
  engrossing 982.20
absorption
  body function 2.15
  digestion 7.8
  sorption 187.6
  permeation 221.3
  consumption 388.1
  ingestion 570.2
  involvement 897.1
  thoughtfulness 930.3
  engrossment 982.3
  abstractedness 984.2
abstain refrain 329.3
  not use 390.5
  remain neutral 467.5
  deny oneself 667.3
  abstain from 668.7
abstainer ascetic 667.2
  abstinent 668.4
abstemious
  continent 664.6
  abstinent 668.10
  meager 991.10
abstention disuse 390.1
  neutrality 467.1
  abstinence 668.2
abstinence disuse 390.1
  fasting 515.1
  continence 664.3
  asceticism 667.1
  refraining 668.2
  moderation 670.1
abstract
  n shortening 268.3
  abridgment 557.1
  picture 712.11
  abstract idea 931.3
  v subtract 255.9
  shorten 268.6
  steal 482.13
  eliminate 772.5
  adj recondite 522.16
  general 863.11
  theoretical 950.13
abstracted
  shortened 268.9
  absorbed in thought
    930.22
  bemused 984.11
abstraction
  subtraction 255.1
  theft 482.1
  picture 712.11
  separation 801.1
  generalization 863.8
  thoughtfulness 930.3
  abstract idea 931.3
  theory 950.1
  abstractedness 984.2
abstruse
  concealed 346.11
  recondite 522.16
  learned 927.21
  difficult 1012.17
absurd vain 391.13
  humorous 488.4
  nonsensical 520.7

  inconsistent 788.8
  odd 869.11
  foolish 922.11
  unbelievable 954.10
  impossible 966.7
abulia weak will 362.4
  psychosis 925.3
abundance
  quantity 247.3
  store 386.1
  wordiness 538.2
  numerousness 883.1
  productiveness 889.1
  plenty 990.2
abundant much 247.8
  diffuse 538.11
  copious 883.8
  productive 889.9
  plentiful 990.7
abuse
  n misuse 389.1
  mistreatment 389.2
  berating 510.7
  vilification 513.2
  seduction 665.6
  v exploit 387.16
  misuse 389.4
  mistreat 389.5
  berate 510.19
  vilify 513.7
  seduce 665.20
  blaspheme 694.5
  work evil 999.6
abusive caustic 144.23
  insulting 156.8
  condemnatory 510.22
  disparaging 512.13
  cursing 513.8
  threatening 514.3
abut adjoin 223.9
  juxtapose 223.13
  rest on 900.22
abysmal huge 257.20
  abyssal 275.11
abyss crack 224.2
  something deep
    275.2
  ocean depths 275.4
  pit 284.4
  hell 682.1
academia 567.5
academic
  n teacher 571.1
  adj learning 567.13
  scholastic 568.19
  studious 570.17
  pedagogic 571.11
  theoretical 950.13
academician 928.3
academy school 567.1
  secondary school
    567.4
accede assent 332.8
  submit 433.6
  consent 441.2
  be instated 615.13
accelerate
  speed up 174.10
  intensify 251.5
  hasten 401.4
  drive 756.4
  atomize 1037.17

acceleration
quickening 174.4
intensification 251.2
hastening 401.3
accelerator 1037.11
accent
n regional accent
524.9
enunciation 524.11
notation 709.12
accentuation 709.25
meter 720.7
v emphasize 996.14
accept
take for granted 123.2
condone 134.7
forgive 148.4
assent 332.8
acknowledge 332.11
ratify 332.12
adopt 371.15
undertake 404.3
submit 433.6
consent 441.2
take 479.6
approve 509.9
receive 585.7
believe 952.10
keep an open mind
978.7
acceptable
desirable 100.30
admissible 107.12
eligible 371.24
welcome 585.12
tolerable 998.20
acceptance
composure 106.2
contentment 107.1
patience 134.1
admission 187.2
assent 332.1
acknowledgment
332.3
ratification 332.4
adoption 371.4
lenience 427.1
submission 433.1
consent 441.1
receiving 479.1
approval 509.1
usage 518.4
negotiable instrument
728.11
accepted
allowed 332.14
chosen 371.26
customary 373.14
undertaken 404.7
received 479.10
approved 509.19
conventional 579.5
orthodox 687.7
real 760.15
believed 952.23
authoritative 969.18
accepter
assenter 332.6
recipient 479.3
believer 692.4
accepting
content 107.7

patient 134.9
lenient 427.7
submissive 433.12
access
n seizure 85.6
outburst 152.9
approach 167.1
entree 187.3
ingress 189.1
entrance 189.5
increase 251.1
passageway 383.3
influence 893.6
spasm 916.6
accessibility 965.3
retrieval 1041.8
v arrive 186.6
enter 189.7
accessible
approachable 167.5
present 221.12
permeable 292.21
communicative
343.10
published 352.17
handy 387.20
obtainable 472.14
influenceable 893.15
possible 965.8
accession
approach 167.1
increase 251.1
addition 253.1
adjunct 254.1
assent 332.1
authority 417.12
acquisition 472.1
installation 615.3
accessory
n adjunct 254.1
belongings 471.2
participator 476.4
litigant 598.11
accomplice 616.3
nonessential 767.2
attendant 768.3
adj additional 253.10
helping 449.20
participating 476.8
unessential 767.4
accompanying 768.9
accident
nonessential 767.2
event 830.1
chance event 971.6
misfortune 1010.2
accidental
n note 709.14
nonessential 767.2
adj circumstantial
765.7
unessential 767.4
happening 830.9
incidental 842.11
chance 971.15
accident-prone
bungling 414.20
reckless 493.8
acclaim
n applause 509.2
repute 662.1
v assent 332.8

applaud 509.10
acclaimed
approved 509.19
distinguished 662.16
acclamation
unanimity 332.5
applause 509.2
acclimated 373.16
acclivity 204.6
accolade
praise 509.5
citation 646.4
accommodate
be kind 143.9
orient 161.11
accustom 373.10
provide 385.7
furnish
accommodations
385.10
arrange 437.8
oblige 449.19
reconcile 465.8
compromise 468.2
make agree 787.7
equalize 789.6
change 851.7
conform 866.3
accommodating
resigned 134.10
considerate 143.16
indulgent 427.8
courteous 504.14
accommodation
orientation 161.4
quarters 228.4
capacity 257.2
habituation 373.8
lodgings 385.3
compact 437.1
facility 449.9
appeasement 465.4
compromise 468.1
giving 478.1
loan 620.2
adjustment 787.4
equating 789.2
change 851.1
conformity 866.1
**accommodation
address**
hiding place 346.4
address 553.9
accommodation ladder
193.4
accompaniment
adjunct 254.1
part 708.22
togetherness 768
concomitance 768.1
simultaneity 835.1
concurrence 898.1
accompanist
player 710.3
accompanier 768.4
accompany play 708.39
keep one company
768.7
coincide 835.4
result 886.4
accompanying
attending 768.9

happening 830.9
simultaneous 835.5
concurrent 898.4
accomplice
participator 476.4
cohort 616.3
accomplice in crime
616.3
accomplish
arrive 186.6
do 328.6
perform 328.9
achieve 407.4
succeed with 409.11
complete 793.6
evolve 860.5
finish 891.11
accomplished
achieved 407.10
skilled 413.26
accomplishment
arrival 186.1
superiority 249.1
development 328.2
act 328.3
fulfillment 407
achievement 407.1
success 409.1
acquirement 413.8
completion 793.4
evolution 860.1
performance 891.5
learning 927.4
solution 939.1
accord
n unanimity 332.5
compact 437.1
consent 441.1
relationship 455
accordance 455.1
peace 464.1
harmony 708.3
relation 774.1
agreement 787.1
conformity 866.1
v consent 332.9
permit 443.9
get along 455.2
give 478.12
harmonize 708.35
agree 787.6
make agree 787.7
conform 866.3
concur 898.2
accordingly
in that case 765.11
consequently 886.7
hence 887.7
according to 866.9
according to Hoyle
adj right 637.3
adv according to rule
866.8
accordion 711.11
accost
n greeting 585.4
v approach 167.3
address 524.27
greet 585.10
account
n recounting 349.3
record 549.1

sharp 285.8
hostile 589.10
acrimonious
  acrid 17.14
  caustic 144.23
  resentful 152.26
  violent 671.16
acrimony acridity 17.5
  causticity 144.8
  bitterness 152.3
  berating 510.7
  animosity 589.4
  violence 671.1
acrobat 707.3
acrobatic
  n maneuvers 184.13
  adj sporting 743.30
acronym 526.4
across
  v come across 940.3
  adj crosswise 170.9
  transverse 204.19
  adv crosswise 170.13
  transversely 204.24
  on 900.25
  prep opposite to 215.7
  beyond 261.21
across the board
  comprehensive 771.7
  wholly 791.13
acrostic
  wordplay 489.8
  word form 526.4
act
  n doing 328.1
  action 328.3
  legislation 613.5
  law 673.3
  scene 704.7
  process 888.2
  v behave 321.4
  serve 328.4
  impersonate 349.12
  sham 354.20
  stage 704.29
  be operative 888.7
  perform 891.11
act as
  impersonate 349.12
  officiate 724.13
  function as 888.8
act for
  be instrumental 384.7
  represent 576.14
  substitute for 861.5
acting
  n action 328.1
  impersonation 349.4
  sham 354.3
  playing 704.8
  adj performing 328.10
  deputy 576.15
  operating 888.11
acting-out 92.25
actinic 1024.41
action behavior 321.1
  activity 328
  doing 328.1
  act 328.3
  activeness 330.1
  undertaking 404.1
  fight 457.4

military operation
  458.5
  lawsuit 598.1
  plot 722.4
  fun 743.2
  basketball game 747.3
  gambling 759.1
  operation 888.1
  verdict 945.5
  expedient 994.2
  mechanism 1039.4
  automatic control
  1040.9
actionable
  litigious 598.20
  legal 673.10
  illegal 674.6
activate
  reactivate 17.12
  militarize 458.20
  radioactivate 1036.9
  atomize 1037.17
active
  n voice 530.14
  adj energetic 17.13
  moving 172.7
  lively 330.17
  effectual 387.21
  observant 434.4
  operating 888.11
activist
  n man of action 330.8
  adj energetic 17.13
  active 330.17
  enterprising 330.23
activity animation 17.4
  motion 172.1
  behavior 321.1
  active 328.1
  movement 330
  action 330.1
  occupation 724.1
  cause 885.9
  radiation 1036.1
act of God 962.7
act of grace 143.7
act on
  take action 328.5
  operate on 888.6
  exercise influence
  893.9
  pass judgment 945.13
act on behalf of 576.14
actor deceiver 357.1
  phony 500.7
  role 704.10
  motion-picture studio
  706.3
  actress 707.2
  doer 726.1
actual real 760.15
  happening 830.9
  present 837.2
  obvious 969.15
  true 972.13
actuality
  reality 760.2
  the present 837.1
  unquestionability
  969.3
  truth 972.1
actualize 206.5

actually
  positively 247.19
  really 760.16
  truly 972.18
actuarial 967.6
actuary
  accountant 628.7
  insurance 1007.4
  calculator 1016.14
actuate
  set in motion 172.6
  motivate 375.12
  impel 901.11
act up 322.4
acuity sharpness 285.1
  alertness 339.5
  smartness 919.2
  sagacity 919.4
acumen sagacity 919.4
  discernment 943.2
acute energetic 17.13
  sensitive 24.13
  painful 26.10
  shrill 58.14
  deep-felt 93.24
  sharp 285.8
  pointed 285.9
  cunning 415.12
  violent 671.16
  sagacious 919.16
  urgent 996.22
acutely 247.20
ad advertisement 352.6
  game 748.2
AD 820.13
adage 973.1
adagio
  n music 708.25
  adj music 708.54
Adam's apple 524.19
adamant
  n hardness 1044.6
  adj unyielding 361.9
  immovable 854.15
  hard 1044.10
  inflexible 1044.12
  stone 1057.10
adapt orient 161.11
  accustom 373.10
  fit 405.8
  compose 708.46
  make agree 787.7
  change 851.7
  conform 866.3
adaptable
  handy 387.20
  versatile 413.25
  changeable 853.6
  conformable 866.5
  facile 1013.15
  pliant 1045.9
  elastic 1046.7
adaptation
  orientation 161.4
  fitting 405.2
  piece 708.5
  harmonization 709.2
  adjustment 787.4
  change 851.1
  evolution 860.3
  conformity 866.1
add plus 253.4

combine 804.3
  calculate 1016.17
added-in 771.5
addendum
  adjunct 254.1
  nonessential 767.2
  sequel 816.1
add fuel to the fire
  excite 105.12
  aggravate 119.2
  intensify 251.5
  sow dissension 456.14
addict
  drug addict 87.20
  desirer 100.12
  enthusiast 101.4
  addiction 373.9
addiction
  substance abuse 87.1
  addict 373.9
adding machine 253.3
add insult to injury
  aggravate 119.2
  offend 156.5
  impair 393.9
  pick a quarrel 456.13
addition increase 251.1
  attachment 253
  accession 253.1
  component 254.1
  adjunct 254.3
  expansion 259.1
  acquisition 472.1
  nonessential 767.2
  relation 774.1
  combination 804.1
  notation 1016.2
additional
  additive 253.8
  supplementary 253.10
  unessential 767.4
  fresh 840.8
additive
  n adjunct 254.1
  adj additional 253.8
addle intoxicate 88.22
  perplex 970.13
  confuse 984.7
addled
  intoxicated 88.31
  muddleheaded 921.18
  in a dilemma 970.25
  befuddled 984.13
address
  n abode 228.1
  behavior 321.1
  skill 413.1
  request 440.1
  remark 524.4
  speech 543.2
  name and address
  553.9
  greeting 585.4
  round 751.3
  v solicit 440.14
  speak to 524.27
  make a speech 543.9
  direct 553.13
  court 562.21
  greet 585.10
addressee
  inhabitant 227.2

recipient 479.3
correspondent 553.8
address oneself to
practice 328.8
undertake 404.3
busy oneself with
724.11
add to increase 251.4
augment 253.5
enlarge 259.4
adduction 906.1
add up compute 253.6
be right 972.10
sum up 1016.18
adenoidal 525.12
adept
n expert 413.11
occultist 689.11
adj skillful 413.22
adequacy ability 18.2
satisfactoriness 107.3
mean 246.1
sufficiency 990.1
adequate able 18.14
satisfactory 107.11
sufficient 990.6
tolerable 998.20
adhere
join 799.11
cohere 802.6
adherent
n hanger-on 138.6
associate 166.2
commender 509.8
follower 616.8
adhesive 802.4
adj adhesive 802.12
adhere to
observe 434.2
execute 437.9
hold 474.6
adhesion fidelity 644.7
cohesion 802.1
adhesive
n fastening 799.3
adherent 802.4
plastic 1052.6
adj adherent 802.12
viscous 1060.12
ad hoc
n transience 827.1
expedient 994.2
adj extemporaneous
365.12
transient 827.7
substitute 861.8
makeshift 994.7
ad hominem attack
512.2
adieu
n leave-taking 188.4
inter farewell! 188.22
ad infinitum
lengthily 267.10
throughout 793.17
continuously 811.10
infinitely 822.4
perpetually 828.10
adios! 188.22
adipose
corpulent 257.18
oily 1054.9

adiposity
corpulence 257.8
oiliness 1054.5
adit
entrance 189.5
channel 239.1
adjacent 223.16
adjective 530.3
adjoin
border 211.10
join 223.9
juxtapose 223.13
add 253.4
adjoining 223.16
adjourn 845.9
adjournment 845.4
adjudicate 945.8
adjunct
n thing added 253.1
addition 254.1
expansion 259.1
associate 616.1
nonessential 767.2
attendant 768.3
relation 774.1
part 792.1
component 795.2
adj added 253.9
adjure
administer an oath
334.7
entreat 440.11
adjust
orient 161.11
size 257.15
accustom 373.10
fit 405.8
arrange 437.8
reconcile 465.8
settle 466.7
compromise 468.2
make agree 787.7
equalize 789.6
organize 807.10
change 851.7
conform 866.3
adjustable
versatile 413.25
changeable 853.6
conformable 866.5
adjusted
accustomed
373.16
fitted 405.17
adjustment
rehabilitation
92.27
orientation 161.4
habituation 373.8
fitting 405.2
compact 437.1
accommodation 465.4
compromise 468.1
good condition 764.3
adaptation 787.4
equating 789.2
organization 807.2
change 851.1
conformity 866.1
adjutant 616.6
adjuvant
n adjunct 254.1

adj remedial 86.39
helping 449.20
ad lib
n improvisation 365.5
unpreparedness 406.1
adv at will 323.5
extemporaneously
365.15
ad-lib
v improvise 365.8
be unprepared 406.6
adj extemporaneous
365.12
unprepared 406.8
administer
execute 437.9
parcel out 477.8
give 478.12
administrate 573.11
administer justice
594.5
govern 612.12
give 643.6
administer to 577.13
administration
performance 328.2
governance 417.5
distribution 477.2
principal 571.8
executive function
573.3
government 612.1
giving 643.2
protectorship 1007.2
administrator
principal 571.8
director 574.1
admirable
endearing 104.25
praiseworthy 509.20
admiral 575.20
admire
cherish 104.21
respect 155.4
approve 509.9
admirer
enthusiast 101.4
lover 104.12
supporter 616.9
admissible
acceptable 107.12
receptive 187.16
eligible 371.24
permissible 443.15
justifiable 600.14
relevant 774.11
logical 934.20
evidential 956.16
tolerable 998.20
admission
admittance 187.2
entrance 189.1
naturalization 226.3
acknowledgment
332.3
confession 351.3
permission 443.1
receiving 479.1
fee 630.6
inclusion 771.1
testimony 956.2
admit receive 187.10

enter 189.7
naturalize 226.4
acknowledge 332.11
confess 351.7
permit 443.9
take in 479.6
welcome 585.7
include 771.3
allow for 958.5
admit of
be liable 896.3
have a chance 971.13
admitted
accepted 332.14
disclosive 351.10
permitted 443.16
received 479.10
approved 509.19
conventional 579.5
real 760.15
traditional 841.12
admixture
mixture 796.1
compound 796.5
admonish
dissuade 379.3
warn 399.5
exhort 422.6
reprove 510.17
admonition
dissuasion 379.1
warning 399.1
advice 422.1
reproof 510.5
ad nauseam
lengthily 267.10
at length 538.16
fully 765.13
repeatedly 848.16
ado
n agitation 105.4
bustle 330.4
commotion 809.4
trouble 1012.3
adj happening 830.9
adobe
n ceramic ware 742.2
building material
1052.2
adj earthy 234.5
adolescent
n youngster 302.1
adj grown 14.3
pubescent 301.13
immature 406.11
Adonis 1015.10
adopt naturalize 226.4
approve 371.15
use 384.5
appropriate 480.19
borrow 621.4
usurp 640.8
adoptive parent 560.8
adorable
desirable 100.30
endearing 104.25
adore enjoy 95.12
cherish 104.21
respect 155.4
worship 696.10
adorn
ornament 498.8

make grandiloquent
545.7
honor 662.12
beautify 1015.15
adrift
adj afloat 182.61
unfastened 801.22
inconstant 853.7
bewildered 970.24
erroneous 974.16
muddled 984.13
adv separately 801.27
adroit skillful 413.22
smart 919.14
adsorb 187.13
adsorption 187.6
adulation praise 509.5
flattery 511.1
adult
n grownup 304.1
adj grown 14.3
mature 303.12
lascivious 665.29
obscene 666.9
adulterate dilute 16.11
rarefy 299.3
tamper with 354.16
weaken 393.12
corrupt 796.12
adulterated
diluted 16.19
rare 299.4
imperfect 1002.4
adulterer 665.13
adulterous 665.27
adultery
copulation 75.7
love affair 104.6
illicit sex 665.7
adumbrate
foreshow 133.10
image 349.11
hint 551.10
advance
n progression 162.1
approach 167.1
course 172.2
increase 251.1
improvement 392.1
offer 439.1
promotion 446.1
furtherance 449.5
lending 620.1
loan 620.2
evolution 860.1
v progress 162.2
further 162.5
approach 167.3
move 172.5
grow 251.6
be instrumental 384.7
improve 392.7
make better 392.9
make good 409.10
propose 439.5
promote 446.2
be useful 449.17
lend 620.5
elapse 820.5
evolve 860.5
determine 885.12
push 903.9

postulate 950.12
adduce 956.12
expedite one's affair
994.3
do good 998.10
prosper 1009.7
advance! 459.32
advanced front 216.10
aged 303.16
improved 392.13
preceding 815.4
modern 840.13
premature 844.8
advancement
progression 162.1
improvement 392.1
promotion 446.1
furtherance 449.5
lending 620.1
evolution 860.1
advantage
n vantage 249.2
benefit 387.4
facility 449.9
game 748.2
purchase 905.2
expedience 994.1
good 998.4
v avail 387.17
be useful 449.17
expedite one's affair
994.3
do good 998.10
advantageous
useful 387.18
gainful 472.16
expedient 994.5
good 998.12
advent approach 167.1
arrival 186.1
coming 838.5
adventitious
circumstantial 765.7
unessential 767.4
chance 971.15
adventure
act 328.3
emprise 404.2
exploit 492.7
speculator 737.11
event 830.2
happening 971.6
adventurer
traveler 178.1
mercenary 461.17
daredevil 493.4
upstart 606.7
gambler 759.21
adventurous
dynamic 330.23
enterprising 404.8
daring 492.22
foolhardy 493.9
hazardous 1005.10
adverb 530.3
adverbial 530.3
adversarial
contrapositive 215.5
oppositional 451.8
contrary 778.6
adversarial procedure
934.4

adversary
n opponent 452.1
enemy 589.6
adj oppositional 451.8
adverse
oppositional 451.8
contrary 778.6
untoward 1010.13
adversity 1010
advertent 982.15
advertise
publish 352.10
publicize 352.15
flaunt 501.17
inform 551.8
advertisement 352.6
advertising 352.5
advice counsel 422
tip 551.3
news 552.1
message 552.4
advisable 994.5
advise warn 399.5
counsel 422.5
inform 551.8
advised
intentional 380.8
reasoned 934.21
advisement 930.2
adviser counsel 422.3
informant 551.5
advisory
recommendatory
422.8
conciliar 423.5
informative 551.18
advocacy
promotion 352.5
advice 422.1
patronage 449.4
recommendation
509.4
advocate
n defender 460.7
deputy 576.1
friend 588.1
lawyer 597.1
justifier 600.8
associate 616.9
supporter 900.2
arguer 934.12
v urge 375.14
advise 422.5
abet 449.14
defend 460.8
commend 509.11
defend 600.10
aegis patronage 449.4
safeguard 1007.3
aeon age 823.4
long time 826.4
aerate air 317.10
foam 320.5
vaporize 1065.8
aerial
n radio transmitter
1033.4
adj aviation 184.49
high 272.14
airy 317.11
chimeric 985.22
vaporous 1065.9

aerialist 707.3
aerification 1065.5
aerobe 85.41
aerobics 84.2
aerodynamic
aviation 184.49
pneumatic 1038.10
vaporous 1065.9
aerodynamics
pneumatics 1038.5
gas 1065.2
aerography
meteorology 317.5
pneumatics 1038.5
aerology
meteorology 317.5
pneumatics 1038.5
aerometer
density 1043.8
vaporimeter 1065.7
aerometry 1038.5
aeronaut aviator 185.1
balloonist 185.7
aeronautical 184.49
aeronautics 184.1
aeroplane
n aircraft 181.1
v fly 184.36
aerosol
solution 1062.3
sprinkler 1063.8
vaporizer 1065.6
aerospace
n atmosphere 184.32
adj aviation 184.49
aerospace technology
1073.1
aerostatic
aviation 184.49
pneumatic 1038.10
vaporous 1065.9
aerostatics 1038.5
aerotechnics 1038.5
aery 317.11
aesthete 496.6
aesthetic
tasteful 496.8
artistic 712.20
absurdist 951.9
aesthetician 723.4
aesthetics
artistic taste 496.5
criticism 723.1
aestival green 44.4
seasonal 313.9
warm 1018.24
aestivate
hibernate 22.15
lie idle 331.16
AF tone 50.2
frequency 1033.12
afar 261.15
afeared 127.22
affable pleasant 97.6
good-natured 143.14
indulgent 427.8
courteous 504.14
informal 581.3
sociable 582.22
cordial 587.16
affair
love affair 104.6

undertaking 404.1
social gathering
  582.10
occupation 724.1
concern 830.3
object 1050.4
affaire d'honneur 457.7
affairs action 328.1
occupation 724.1
relation 774.1
concerns 830.4
affect
n feeling 93.1
attitude 977.1
v wear 5.43
touch 93.14
impress 93.15
move 145.5
imitate 336.5
manifest 348.5
sham 354.20
assume 500.12
entail 771.4
relate to 774.5
operate on 888.6
influence 893.7
affectation
behavior 321.1
sham 354.3
pretension 500
airs 500.1
style 532.2
elegance 533.3
grandiloquence 545.1
sanctimony 693.1
affecting
touching 93.22
distressing 98.20
pitiful 145.8
affection
disease 85.1
feeling 93.1
liking 100.2
love 104.1
amorousness 104.3
friendship 587.1
affectionate
loving 104.27
kind 143.13
affective
emotional 93.17
attitudinal 977.7
affectless
insensible 25.6
unfeeling 94.9
affiance
n betrothal 436.3
v be engaged 436.6
affianced
n fiancé 104.17
adj promised 436.8
affidavit
deposition 334.3
certificate 549.6
declaration 598.7
statement of
  principles 952.4
testimony 956.2
affiliate
n branch 617.10
member 617.11
v naturalize 226.4

adopt 371.15
cooperate 450.3
join 617.14
league 804.4
adj related 774.9
leagued 804.6
affiliates 617.12
affiliation
naturalization 226.3
adoption 371.4
alliance 450.2
blood relationship
  559.1
lineage 560.4
association 582.6
sect 675.3
relation 774.1
combination 804.1
affinity
inclination 100.3
preference 371.5
accord 455.1
marriage relationship
  564.1
familiarity 587.5
relation 774.1
kinship 774.3
similarity 783.2
agreement 787.1
tendency 895.1
attraction 906.1
affirm
ratify 332.12
assert 334.5
announce 352.12
say 524.24
be pious 692.6
state 952.12
testify 956.9
confirm 956.11
affirmation
ratification 332.4
assertion 334
declaration 334.1
deposition 334.3
consent 441.1
remark 524.4
premise 934.7
testimony 956.2
confirmation 956.4
affirmative
n yes 332.2
consent 441.1
adj affirming 334.8
consenting 441.4
agreeing 787.9
affix
n added to writing
  254.2
morphology 526.3
v add 253.4
fasten 799.7
afflatus
inspiration 375.9
revelation 683.9
Muse 720.10
genius 919.8
afflict pain 26.7
disorder 85.49
distress 96.16
aggrieve 112.19
work evil 999.6

affliction
disease 85.1
infliction 96.8
bane 1000.1
adversity 1010.1
affluent
n tributary 238.3
adj flowing 238.24
wealthy 618.14
plentiful 990.7
prosperous 1009.12
afflux
approach 167.1
influx 189.2
flow 238.4
afford provide 385.7
give 478.12
furnish 478.15
have money 618.11
well afford 626.7
yield 627.4
affordable 633.7
afforestation
woodland 310.11
forestry 1067.3
affray 457.4
affright
n fear 127.1
v frighten 127.15
affront
n provocation 152.11
indignity 156.2
v offend 152.21
disrespect 156.5
confront 216.8
oppose 451.5
defy 454.3
brave 492.11
affusion
baptism 701.6
wetting 1063.6
afghan 295.10
aficionado
enthusiast 101.4
attender 221.5
supporter 616.9
specialist 865.3
fanatic 925.18
afield 261.19
afire
fervent 93.18
zealous 101.9
inspired 375.31
burning 1018.27
afloat
adj floating 182.60
adrift 182.61
flooded 238.25
afoot 405.23
reported 552.15
unfastened 801.22
happening 830.9
inconstant 853.7
adv on board 182.62
at sea 240.9
afoot
adj astir 330.19
on foot 405.23
existent 760.13
happening 830.9
adv walking 177.43
aforementioned 813.5

aforethought
n intentionality 380.3
adj premeditated
  380.9
afoul of sail into 182.41
collide 901.13
afraid scared 127.22
cowardly 491.10
weak-willed 362.12
afresh newly 840.15
repeated 848.17
again 873.7
African-American
  312.3
aft
adj rear 217.9
adv abaft 182.69
after 217.14
after
adj rear 217.9
subsequent 834.4
adv behind 166.6
aft 217.14
subsequently 834.6
like 336.12
in pursuit of 382.12
following 834.8
conformable to 866.9
because of 887.9
after a fashion
limited 248.10
somehow 384.11
after all
notwithstanding
  338.8
subsequently 834.6
all things considered
  945.17
afterglow
remainder 256.1
aftermath 816.3
aftereffect 886.3
shine 1024.2
afterimage
remainder 256.1
aftermath 816.3
aftereffect 886.3
optical illusion 975.5
afterlife 681.2
aftermath
yield 472.5
afterclap 816.3
event 830.1
sequel 834.2
result 886.1
aftereffect 886.3
afternoon
n post meridiem 315.1
adj post meridian
  315.7
aftertaste taste 62.1
aftermath 816.3
aftereffect 886.3
afterthought
change of mind 363.1
sequel 816.1
untimeliness 843.1
delay 845.2
mature thought 930.5
afterwards
subsequently 834.6
in the future 838.9

afterworld
the hereafter 681.2
destiny 838.2
aftmost 217.9
again
adv additionally
253.11
notwithstanding
338.8
then 820.11
newly 840.15
over 848.17
another time 873.7
inter encore! 848.18
again and again
continuously 811.10
frequently 846.6
repeatedly 848.16
against
adj disapproving
510.21
prep toward 161.26
contraposed 215.7
up against 223.25
in preparation for
405.24
opposed to 451.10
in disagreement with
788.10
against the grain
adj unlikable 99.7
adv backwards 163.13
crosswise 170.13
cross-grained 288.12
in opposition 451.9
contrarily 778.9
agape love 104.1
benevolence 143.4
accord 455.1
agape
wondering 122.9
expectant 130.11
gaping 292.18
curious 980.5
age
n time of life 303
years 303.1
generation 823.4
era 823.5
durability 826.1
long time 826.4
duration 826.5
oldness 841.1
v ripen 303.10
grow old 841.9
aged ripe 303.13
elderly 303.16
mature 304.7
durable 826.10
old-fogyish 841.17
agee 204.14
ageism 979.4
ageless
perpetual 828.7
old 841.10
agency
instrumentality 384.3
commission 615.1
trade 731.2
workplace 739.1
substitution 861.1
operation 888.1

agenda
record book 549.11
roll 870.6
schedule 964.3
agent
intermediary 213.4
instrument 384.4
mediator 466.3
director 574.1
representative 576
deputy 576.3
lawyer 597.1
assignee 615.9
assistant 616.6
advance man 704.25
doer 726.1
salesman 730.3
transformer 851.5
substitute 861.2
author 885.4
operator 888.4
element 1058.2
agent provocateur
shill 357.5
instigator 375.11
age-old 841.10
ages 826.4
agglomeration
accumulation 769.9
joining 799.1
cohesion 802.1
conglomeration 802.5
combination 804.1
agglutination
addition 253.1
joining 799.1
cohesion 802.1
densification 1043.3
agglutinative 802.10
aggrandize
increase 251.4
enlarge 259.4
exaggerate 355.3
promote 446.2
glorify 662.13
aggravate annoy 96.13
irritate 96.14
vex 98.15
worsen 119.2
provoke 152.24
intensify 251.5
impair 393.9
sow dissension 456.14
antagonize 589.7
aggravating
annoying 98.22
exasperating 119.5
aggravation annoyance
96.2
irritation 96.3
vexatiousness 98.7
excitation 105.11
worsening 119
increase 119.1
resentment 152.1
intensification 251.2
adversity 1010.1
aggregate
n accumulation 769.9
sum 1016.6
v assemble 769.18
total 791.8

adj assembled 769.21
whole 791.9
aggregation
accumulation 769.9
joining 799.1
combination 804.1
aggression
enterprise 330.7
warlikeness 458.11
attack 459.1
aggressive energetic
17.13
enterprising 330.23
partisan 456.17
warlike 458.21
offensive 459.30
gruff 505.7
aggressor 459.12
aggrieve pain 96.17
oppress 112.19
offend 152.21
work evil 999.6
aghast
wondering 122.9
terrified 127.26
agile fast 174.15
quick 330.18
alert 339.14
nimble 413.23
agility quickness 330.3
alertness 339.5
nimbleness 413.2
aging
n maturation 303.6
adj growing old
303.17
agitated
distressed 96.22
perturbed 105.23
anxious 126.7
jittery 128.12
bustling 330.20
disturbed 916.16
agitation
perturbation 105.4
excitation 105.11
anxiety 126.1
trepidation 127.5
nervousness 128.1
bustle 330.4
incitement 375.4
turbulence 671.2
violence 916
stimulation 916.1
agitator rebel 327.5
instigator 375.11
troublemaker 593.2
mixer 796.9
shaker 916.9
agitprop
instigator 375.11
propaganda 569.2
aglow burning 1018.27
luminous 1024.30
illuminated 1024.39
agnate
n kinfolk 559.2
lineage 560.4
adj related 559.6
lineal 560.18
kindred 774.10
akin 783.13

agnostic
n skeptic 695.12
adj skeptic 695.20
absurdist 951.9
doubting 954.9
uncertain 970.16
ago
adj past 836.7
adv since 836.15
agog eager 101.8
excited 105.20
wondering 122.9
expectant 130.11
curious 980.5
attentive 982.15
agonize pain 26.7
suffer 26.8
torture 96.18
cause upleasantness
96.19
excruciate 98.12
grieve 112.17
struggle 725.11
be uncertain 970.9
agony anguish 26.6
wretchedness 96.6
harshness 98.4
sorrow 112.10
moribundity 307.9
agrarian rustic 233.6
agricultural 1067.20
agree be willing 324.3
assent 332.8
concur 332.9
come to an agreement
332.10
contract 437.5
get along 455.2
relate to 774.5
be the same 777.4
accord 787.6
coincide 835.4
collaborate 898.2
agreeable tasty 63.8
pleasant 97.6
desirable 100.30
acceptable 107.12
good-natured 143.14
considerate 143.16
willing 324.5
indulgent 427.8
submissive 433.12
consenting 441.4
in accord 455.3
courteous 504.14
welcome 585.12
friendly 587.15
melodious 708.48
agreeing 787.9
comely 1015.18
agreed
adj assenting 332.13
contracted 437.11
supposed 950.14
inter so be it 332.20
agreement assent 332.1
unanimity 332.5
obligation 436.2
compact 437.1
consent 441.1
harmony 455.1
sameness 777.1

dangerous 1005.9
alarmist 127.8
alas 98.31
albeit 338.8
albinism
  faulty eyesight 28.1
  whiteness 37.1
albino
  n whiteness 37.1
  adj albinic 37.10
album
  record book 549.11
  compilation 554.7
albumen egg 305.15
  semiliquid 1060.5
albuminous 305.23
alchemist 690.5
alchemy sorcery 690.1
  conversion 857.1
alcohol sedative 86.12
  spirits 88.13
  antifreeze 1023.8
alcoholic
  n addict 87.20
  drinker 88.11
  adj spirituous 88.37
alcoholism
  substance abuse 87.1
  dipsomania 88.3
alcove nook 197.3
  summerhouse 228.12
  recess 284.7
alderman
  public official 575.17
  legislator 610.3
aleatory
  musical 708.47
  circumstantial 765.7
  unessential 767.4
  vague 970.19
  chance 971.15
  hazardous 1005.10
alee leeward 182.68
  downwind 218.9
alehouse 88.20
alert
  n warning sign 399.3
  alarm 400.1
  v warn 399.5
  alarm 400.3
  tip off 551.11
  adj awake 23.8
  wary 339.14
  prepared 405.16
  prompt 844.9
  clear-witted 919.13
  curious 980.5
  attentive 982.15
alfresco
  outdoor 206.8
  exterior 206.11
  airy 317.11
algae 310.4
algebraic 1016.21
algesia 26.4
algid
  cold 1022.14
  frigid 1022.16
algorithm
  mathematics 1016.1
  Arabic numerals
    1016.4

alias
  n pseudonym 527.8
  adj nominal 527.15
  adv otherwise 779.11
alibi
  n pretext 376.1
  justification 600.4
  v excuse 600.11
alien
  n exclusiveness 772.3
  stranger 773.3
  oddity 869.4
  astronaut 1073.8
  v transfer 629.3
  adj extraterritorial
    206.9
  oppositional 451.8
  extraneous 773.5
  unrelated 775.6
  extraterrestrial
    1070.26
alienate
  sow dissension 456.14
  antagonize 589.7
  transfer 629.3
  separate 801.8
  indoctrinate 857.15
alienation
  defense mechanism
    92.23
  dissent 333.1
  falling-out 456.4
  disaccord 589.2
  transfer 629.1
  extraneousness 773.1
  separation 801.1
  indoctrination 857.5
  aloneness 871.2
  insanity 925.1
alight
  v land 184.43
  arrive 186.8
  light upon 194.7
  adj burning 1018.27
  illuminated 1024.39
alight upon
  light upon 194.10
  meet 223.11
  come across 940.3
align level 201.6
  parallelize 203.5
  dispose 807.9
  line 811.5
alignment
  orientation 161.4
  parallelism 203.1
  affiliation 450.2
align oneself with
  back 449.13
  side with 450.4
alike identical 777.7
  congruent 777.9
  uniform 780.5
  similar 783.10
  equal 789.7
  indistinguishable
    944.6
alimentary 7.19
alimentation
  nutrition 7.1
  food 10.3
alimony 478.8

aliquot 1016.22
alive living 306.11
  active 330.17
  alert 339.14
  clear-witted 919.13
  remembered 988.23
alive and kicking
  healthy 83.9
  living 306.11
alive to sensible 24.11
  cognizant of 927.16
alkali
  n acid 1058.3
  adj chemical 1058.8
alkalinity 1058.3
alkalizer 86.25
all
  n the whole 791.3
  limit 793.5
  everyone 863.4
  universe 1070.1
  adj whole 791.9
  every 863.15
  adv wholly 791.13
the all 822.1
all aboard 182.62
all-absorbing 996.24
Allah 677.2
all along 828.11
all and sundry
  n all 791.3
  adj every 863.15
all around
  handy 387.20
  versatile 413.25
all-around event 755.2
all at once
  together 768.11
  abruptly 829.8
  suddenly 829.9
allay gratify 95.7
  relieve 120.5
  pacify 465.7
  moderate 670.6
  satiate 993.4
all but nearly 223.22
  on the whole 791.14
all clear
  n alarm 400.1
  adj unindebted 624.23
  inter all's well! 1006.9
all-consuming 395.27
all creation 1070.1
all ears listening 48.14
  vigilant 339.13
  attentive 982.15
allegation
  affirmation 334.1
  claim 376.2
  remark 524.4
  declaration 598.7
  accusation 599.1
  testimony 956.2
allege affirm 334.5
  pretext 376.3
  state 524.24
  accuse 599.7
  testify 956.9
  adduce 956.12
alleged affirmed 334.9
  pretexted 376.5
  attributable 887.6

supposed 950.14
allegiance
  obedience or
    obediency 326.1
  duty 641.1
  fidelity 644.7
allegorical
  meaningful 518.10
  symbolic 519.10
  fictional 722.7
allegorist 341.7
allegory symbol 517.2
  implication 519.2
  comparison 942.1
allegro
  n music 708.25
  adv actively 330.25
  music 708.55
alleluia
  n cheer 116.2
  paean 696.3
  inter hallelujah!
    696.16
all-embracing
  whole 791.9
  thorough 793.10
  universal 863.14
allergen allergy 85.33
  antitoxin 86.27
allergic sensitive 24.12
  anemic 85.60
  averse 99.8
allergy sensitivity 24.3
  allergic disorder 85.33
  hostility 99.2
alleviate relieve 120.5
  abate 252.8
  lighten 298.6
  moderate 670.6
alleviation relief 120.1
  decrease 252.1
  lightening 298.3
  modulation 670.2
alleviative
  n palliative 86.10
  moderator 670.3
  adj palliative 86.40
  relieving 120.9
  lightening 298.16
  sedative 670.16
alley
  passageway 383.3
  tennis 748.1
  field hockey 749.4
  bowling 750.1
all eyes and ears
  vigilant 339.13
  attentive 982.15
all for
  adj favorable 449.22
  prep in favor of 509.21
all fours 177.17
alliance treaty 437.2
  affiliation 450.2
  blood relationship
    559.1
  marriage 563.1
  association 617.1
  relation 774.1
  similarity 783.1
  combination 804.1
  concurrence 898.1

allied akin 559.6
related 774.9
joined 799.13
leagued 804.6
alligator 311.25
all in 21.8
all in all
on the average 246.5
on the whole 791.14
generally 863.17
all-inclusive
comprehensive 771.7
whole 791.9
infinite 822.3
universal 863.14
all in the mind
illusory 975.8
imaginary 985.19
alliteration
rhyme 720.8
assonance 783.6
repetitiousness 848.4
alliterative
rhyming 720.17
assonant 783.17
monotonous 848.15
all-knowing
almighty 677.18
knowing 927.15
allocate locate 159.11
allot 477.9
dispose 807.9
allocation
placement 159.6
allotment 477.3
arrangement 807.1
specification 864.6
allocution 543.2
all of a sudden
short 268.13
suddenly 829.9
all off ended 819.8
erroneous 974.16
all one's got 403.4
allopathic 90.15
allot quantify 244.4
lot 477.9
give 478.12
dispose 807.9
allotment rations 10.6
amount 244.2
assignment 477.3
portion 477.5
subsidy 478.8
arrangement 807.1
allottee 479.4
all out
at full speed 174.20
extremely 247.22
actively 330.25
utterly 793.16
thorough 793.10
unqualified 959.2
to excess 992.23
allover 863.14
all over
adj ended 819.8
adv everywhere
158.12
throughout 793.17
in disorder 809.17
universally 863.18

prep over 159.28
all over the place
adj dispersed 770.9
adv everywhere
158.12
in every direction
161.25
in disorder 809.17
all over with
completed 407.11
no more 761.11
allow
acknowledge 332.11
permit 443.9
give 478.12
discount 631.2
judge 945.8
qualify 958.5
allowable
permissible 443.15
giveable 478.23
justifiable 600.14
allowance
n rations 10.6
acknowledgment
332.3
permission 443.1
portion 477.5
subsidy 478.8
extenuation 600.5
fee 624.5
discount 631.1
qualification 958.1
inaccuracy 974.2
v budget 477.10
allowed
accepted 332.14
permitted 443.16
given 478.24
allow for
condone 148.4
extenuate 600.12
make allowance for
958.5
alloy
n compound 796.5
amalgam 1056.4
v corrupt 393.12
mix 796.10
all-pervading
thorough 793.10
universal 863.14
all-powerful
omnipotent 18.13
almighty 677.18
all-presence 221.2
all right
adj well 83.10
acceptable 107.12
accurate 972.16
tolerable 998.20
inter congratulations!
149.5
yes 332.18
all round
everywhere 158.12
in every direction
161.25
all about 209.13
all said and done
407.11
all-seeing 677.18

all set 405.16
all sorts 796.6
all sorts of 883.3
all the better for 392.14
all the more 249.17
all there 924.4
all the same
adj identical 777.7
equivalent 789.8
adv notwithstanding
338.8
all the time
regularly 780.8
always 828.11
constantly 846.7
all the way
through thick and
thin 360.10
utterly 793.16
to the end 819.13
all the worse for 393.27
all things considered
on the average 246.5
generally 863.17
on the whole 945.17
all through over 159.28
through 161.27
all thumbs 414.20
all together
unanimously 332.17
jointly 799.18
at once 829.8
simultaneously 835.7
allude to
designate 517.18
imply 519.4
remark 524.25
hint 551.10
call attention to
982.10
allurement
loveableness 104.7
inducement 375.3
enticement 377
allure 377.1
attraction 906.1
alluring
provocative 375.27
fascinating 377.8
attracting 906.5
allusion 519.2
allusive
suggestive 519.6
figurative 536.3
allusory 519.6
alluvium deposit 176.9
land 234.1
overflow 238.6
dregs 256.2
all wet 974.18
ally
n country 232.1
associate 616.1
v cooperate 450.3
come together 769.16
relate 774.6
league 804.4
alma mater 567.5
almanac
The Old Farmer's
Almanac 831.7
calendar 831.8

almighty
adj powerful 18.13
omnipotent 677.18
adv very 247.18
almost 223.22
alms 478.6
almsgiver
philanthropist 143.8
giver 478.11
almshouse 1008.4
almsman
beneficiary 479.4
poor man 619.4
aloft on board 182.62
on high 272.21
aloha
n leave-taking 188.4
inter farewell! 188.22
greetings! 585.15
alone
adj secluded 584.11
solitary 871.8
sole 871.9
adv independently
430.33
simply 797.11
singly 871.13
along
v walk 177.27
adv forward 162.8
lengthwise 267.11
alongside
adj side 218.6
adv board and board
182.70
in parallel 203.7
aside 218.10
prep beside 218.11
along with also 253.12
with 768.12
aloof
adj apathetic 94.13
unsociable 141.12
reticent 344.10
standoffish 583.6
incoherent 803.4
alone 871.8
incurious 981.3
adv at a distance
261.14
on high 272.21
aloud audibly 50.18
loudly 53.14
alp 237.6
alpen 272.18
alpha beginning 817.1
first 817.3
alphabet
n representation 349.1
symbols 546.3
writing 547.1
letter 547.9
basics 817.6
v letter 546.6
alphabetic
literal 546.8
ideographic 547.26
alphabetize letter 546.6
classify 808.6
alpine highland 237.8
hilly 272.18
alpinist traveler 178.1

climber 193.6
already
  previously 833.6
  until now 837.4
alright 107.12
also
  adv additionally
    253.11
  conj and 253.13
also-ran failure 410.8
  loser 412.5
  candidate 610.9
  jockey 757.2
altar 703.12
altarpiece altar 703.12
  picture 712.11
alter
  n self 864.5
  v castrate 255.11
  be changed 851.6
  change 851.7
  qualify 958.3
alterable 853.6
alteration
  differentiation 779.4
  change 851.1
altercation
  quarrel 456.5
  contention 457.1
alter ego
  deputy 576.1
  friend 588.1
  right-hand man 616.7
  likeness 783.3
  self 864.5
alterer 851.5
alternate
  n deputy 576.1
  substitute 861.2
  v vacillate 362.8
  take one's turn 824.5
  recur 849.5
  change 853.5
  interchange 862.4
  reciprocate 915.13
  adj periodic 849.7
  substitute 861.8
  reciprocal 915.19
alternating 853.7
alternation
  interaction 776.3
  periodicity 849.2
  changing 853.3
  interchange 862.1
  reciprocation 915.5
alternative
  n loophole 369.4
  option 371.2
  substitute 861.2
  adj elective 371.22
  substitute 861.8
although 338.8
altimeter 272.9
altitude
  height 272.1
  coordinates 300.5
alto
  n high voice 58.6
  part 708.22
  harmonics 709.5
  adj high 58.13
  vocal 708.50

altogether
  additionally 253.11
  wholly 791.13
  completely 793.14
  generally 863.17
the altogether 6.3
alto-rilievo
  protuberance 283.2
  relief 715.3
altruism
  benevolence 143.4
  public spirit 591.1
  unselfishness 652.1
altruist 143.8
altruistic
  benevolent 143.15
  unselfish 652.5
alum 260.6
alumna 572.8
alumnus 572.8
alveolar
  indented 284.17
  phonetic 524.31
alveolus
  cavity 284.2
  indentation 284.6
  speech organ 524.19
always regularly 780.8
  all along 828.11
  universally 863.18
  constantly 846.7
  permanently 852.9
AM morning 314.1
  modulation 1033.14
amalgam
  compound 796.5
  alloy 1056.4
amalgamate
  cooperate 450.3
  mix 796.10
  combine 804.3
amalgamation
  affiliation 450.2
  mixture 796.1
  combination 804.1
amanuensis
  writer 547.13
  recorder 550.1
  agent 576.3
amass store up 386.11
  collect 472.11
  assemble 769.18
  put together 799.5
amassed stored 386.14
  assembled 769.21
amateur
  n enthusiast 101.4
  connoisseur 496.7
  nonprofessional 726.5
  specialist 865.3
  dilettante 928.6
  trifler 997.10
  adj avocational 724.17
  half-learned 929.15
amateurish
  unskilled 414.16
  half-learned 929.15
amateurism
  inexperience 414.2
  avocation 724.7
  nonprofessionalism
    724.9

slight knowledge
    929.6
amatory
  amorous 104.26
  lovemaking 562.23
amaze
  n wonder 122.1
  v astonish 122.6
  perplex 970.13
amazement
  wonder 122.1
  marvel 122.2
amazing 122.12
amazon
  mannish female 76.9
  giantess 257.13
Amazon 461.6
ambages
  convolution 281.1
  circumlocution 538.5
  detour 913.3
ambassador 576.6
ambergris 70.2
ambidextrous
  ambidextral 219.6
  falsehearted 354.30
  versatile 413.25
  treacherous 645.21
ambience
  environment 209.1
  milieu 209.3
ambiguity
  unintelligibility 522.1
  complexity of
    meaning 539
  gray area 539.1
  equivoque 539.2
  self-contradiction
    778.3
  inconsistency 788.2
  doubleness 872.1
  equivocalness 970.5
ambiguous
  unintelligible
    522.13
  equivocal 539.4
  self-contradictory
    778.8
  mixed 796.14
  uncertain 970.16
ambition
  ambitiousness
    100.10
  desire 100.11
  motive 375.1
  intention 380.1
ambitious
  aspiring 100.28
  enterprising 330.23
  ostentatious 501.18
ambivalence
  psychological stress
    92.17
  irresolution 362.1
  self-contradiction
    778.3
  inconsistency 788.2
  doubleness 872.1
ambivalent
  irresolute 362.9
  self-contradictory
    778.8

mixed 796.14
amble
  n walk 177.10
  gait 177.12
  v go slowly 175.6
  stride 177.28
  go on horseback
    177.34
amblyopia 28.2
ambrosia
  delicacy 10.8
  sweetening 66.2
  perfumery 70.2
ambulance chaser
    597.3
ambulate 177.27
ambulatory
  n passageway 383.3
  adj traveling 177.36
ambush
  n trap 346.3
  v surprise 131.7
  ambuscade 346.10
  attack 459.14
ameliorate
  improve 392.7
  make better 392.9
  be changed 851.6
  change 851.7
amelioration
  improvement 392.1
  change 851.1
amen
  n affirmative 332.2
  v ratify 332.12
  adv right! 972.24
  inter yes 332.18
  so be it 332.20
amenable
  resigned 134.10
  willing 324.5
  consenting 441.4
  responsible 641.17
  influenceable 893.15
amend improve 392.7
  make better 392.9
  revise 392.12
  remedy 396.13
  re-form 857.12
amendment
  improvement 392.1
  revision 392.4
  new start 857.2
amends
  compensation 338.1
  reparation 396.6
  restitution 481.2
  recompense 624.3
  atonement 658.1
amenities
  creature comforts
    121.3
  courtesies 504.7
  etiquette 580.3
amenity
  pleasantness 97.1
  facility 449.9
  polite act 504.1
  courtesy 504.6
amentia 921.9
America
  world region 231.6

United States 232.3
American Indian 312.3
Americanism
language 523.8
patriotism 591.2
Americanize 226.4
amiable pleasant 97.6
good-natured 143.14
indulgent 427.8
sociable 582.22
hospitable 585.11
friendly 587.15
amicable pleasant 97.6
favorable 449.22
friendly 587.15
in accord 455.3
amicus curiae
deputy 576.1
lawyer 597.1
amid between 213.12
among 796.17
amidships
adj middle 818.4
adv midway 818.5
amidst between 213.12
among 796.17
amigo 588.3
amino acid 7.6
amiss
adj disorderly 809.13
erroneous 974.16
adv irrelevantly 775.9
astray 910.7
erroneously 974.20
badly 999.13
amity accord 455.1
friendship 587.1
ammonia
fertilizer 889.4
coolant 1023.7
ammunition 462.13
amnesia
trance 92.19
thoughtlessness 932.1
loss of memory 989.2
amnesty
n pardon 148.2
exemption 601.2
v forgive 148.3
acquit 601.4
amoeba 85.41
amoebic 258.15
amok
n frenzy 925.7
adj frenzied 105.25
rabid 925.30
among
v include 771.3
prep at 159.27
between 213.12
amongst 796.17
amor 104.9
Amor love god 104.1
deity 104.8
amoral
dishonest 645.16
vice-prone 654.11
amorality
unmorality 636.4
vice 654.1
amorous sexual 75.24
amatory 104.26

amorphous
formless 263.4
obscure 522.15
unordered 809.12
inconstant 853.7
abnormal 869.9
vague 970.19
amortization
payment 624.1
transfer 629.1
amount count 244.1
quantity 244.2
degree 245.1
price 630.1
sum 1016.6
amount to
cost 630.13
equal 789.5
total 791.8
amour 104.6
amperage power 18.1
current 1031.2.
amphibian
n seaplane 181.8
plant 310.3
creature 311.3
batrachian 311.27
adj reptile 311.46
amphibious
versatile 413.25
mixed 796.14
amphitheater
hall 197.4
arena 463.1
schoolroom 567.11
theater 704.14
ample
satisfactory 107.11
spacious 158.10
much 247.8
voluminous 257.17
broad 269.6
abundant 883.8
sufficient 990.6
plentiful 990.7
amplification
aggravation 119.1
increase 251.1
expansion 259.1
translation 341.3
exaggeration 355.1
expatiation 538.6
evolution 860.1
radio-frequency
amplification
1033.15
amplifier
listening device 48.8
audio 50.10
amplify
aggravate 119.2
increase 251.4
enlarge 259.4
exaggerate 355.3
expatiate 538.7
elaborate 860.6
electrify 1031.25
amplitude sound 50.1
loudness 53.1
spaciousness 158.5
quantity 244.1
greatness 247.1

size 257.1
breadth 269.1
wordiness 538.2
fullness 793.2
wave 915.4
plenty 990.2
amputate
excise 255.10
sever 801.11
amputation 255.3
amputee 85.44
amulet 691.5
amusement
pleasure 95.1
merriment 109.5
diversion 743
entertainment 743.1
amusing
humorous 488.4
witty 489.15
entertaining 743.27
ana archives 549.2
compilation 554.7
excerpts 557.4
collection 769.11
maxim 973.1
anabolism
body function 2.18
metabolism 7.10
transformation 851.3
anachronism
false estimation of
time 832
chronological error
832.1
anachronistic 832.3
anaerobe 85.41
anagram
wordplay 489.8
riddle 522.9
anal retentive 474.8
overfastidious 495.12
conformist 866.6
analects
compilation 554.7
excerpts 557.4
maxim 973.1
analeptic
n remedy 86.1
tonic 86.8
adj refreshing 9.3
remedial 86.39
tonic 86.44
restorative 396.22
analgesic
n anesthetic 25.3
sedative 86.12
adj deadening 25.9
sedative 86.45
relieving 120.9
analogy
parallelism 203.1
similarity 783.1
substitute 861.2
comparison 942.1
analysis
psychoanalysis 92.6
discussion 541.7
commentary 556.2
circumstantiation
765.5
differentiation 779.4

simplification 797.2
breaking down 800
analyzation 800.1
dissection 801.5
classification 808.1
reasoning 934.3
inquiry 937.1
discernment 943.2
theory 950.1
automation 1040.7
analyst
psychologist 92.10
critic 723.4
analyzer 800.5
experimenter 941.6
analytic
schematic 800.9
reasoning 934.18
dialectic 934.22
examining 937.36
absurdist 951.9
mathematical 1016.21
analyze
grammaticize 530.16
discuss 541.12
criticize 723.5
itemize 765.6
differentiate 779.6
diversify 781.2
separate 792.6
simplify 797.4
break down 800.6
dissect 801.17
classify 808.6
reason 934.15
discriminate 943.4
anaphylactic 24.12
anaphylaxis 24.3
anarchic
formless 263.4
lawless 418.6
turbulent 671.18
unruly 671.19
illegal 674.6
incoherent 803.4
confused 809.16
revolutionist 859.6
anarchist
law-breaker 418.3
radical 611.12
revolutionist 859.3
anarchy
formlessness 263.1
lawlessness 418.2
illegality 674.1
noncohesion 803.1
confusion 809.2
anathema
hated thing 103.3
censure 510.3
curse 513.1
anathematize
censure 510.13
curse 513.5
condemn 602.3
anatomical 266.6
anatomize
itemize 765.6
differentiate 779.6
analyze 800.6
dissect 801.17
anatomy body 2.1

human form 262.4
structure 266.1
anthropology 312.10
analysis 800.1
dissection 801.5
physical being 1050.3
ancestor parent 560.8
precursor 815.1
antecedent 833.2
ancestral
parental 560.17
beginning 817.15
primitive 841.11
ancestry
blood relationship
559.1
kinfolk 559.2
genealogy 560
progenitorship 560.1
nobility 608.2
anchor
n mooring 180.16
safeguard 1007.3
broadcaster 1033.23
television broadcast
1034.2
v settle 159.17
moor 182.15
land 186.8
bind 428.10
fasten 799.7
secure 854.8
anchorage
establishment 159.7
ship 180.16
destination 186.5
fee 630.6
harbor 1008.6
anchorite
recluse 584.5
ascetic 667.2
ancient
n man of old 841.7
adj aged 303.16
durable 826.10
former 836.10
old 841.10
ancient history 836.3
ancillary
additional 253.10
helping 449.20
and/or 371.29
and 253.13
andante
n slow motion 175.2
music 708.25
adj music 708.54
andiron 1019.12
andric 76.11
androgynous 75.30
androgyny
intersexuality 75.12
effeminacy 77.2
and so forth 253.14
anecdotal 722.8
anecdote 719.3
anemia
weakness 16.1
paleness 36.2
symptom 85.9
anemic weak 16.12
colorless 36.7

chlorotic 85.60
anemometer
speedometer 174.7
weather vane 318.17
anent 774.13
anesthesia
insensibility 25.1
unfeeling 94.1
numb 94.2
relief 120.1
anesthetic
n sleep-inducer 22.10
general anesthetic 25.3
drug 86.15
adj deadening 25.9
remedy 86.47
relieving 120.9
anesthetist 90.11
anesthetize
put to sleep 22.20
deaden 25.4
numb 94.8
relieve 120.5
anew newly 840.15
repeated 848.17
again 873.7
angel
n ladylove 104.15
giver 478.11
endearment term
562.6
benefactor 592.1
supporter 616.9
innocent 657.4
holy man 659.6
familiar spirit 678.12
celestial being 679
heaven figure 679.1
patron 704.26
financer 729.9
beauty 1015.9
v subsidize 478.19
finance 729.15
angelic
endearing 104.25
virtuous 653.6
innocent 657.6
seraphic 679.6
godly 692.9
anger
n darkness 38.2
ill humor 110.1
vexation 152
wrath 152.5
violence 671.1
heat metaphor 1018.2
v lose one's temper
152.17
make angry 152.22
heat 1019.18
angina 26.5
angle
n viewpoint 27.7
aspect 33.3
station 159.2
point 278.2
partiality 650.3
plot 722.4
cheating 759.13
particular 765.3
outlook 977.2
v deviate 164.3

oblique 204.9
go sideways 218.5
crook 278.5
plot 381.9
fish 382.10
maneuver 415.10
favor 650.8
angle for
solicit 440.14
seek 937.29
angler 382.6
Anglicism
language 523.8
patriotism 591.2
Anglicize 226.4
angry sore 26.11
dark 38.9
annoyed 96.21
out of humor 110.17
angered 152.28
stormy 318.23
turbulent 671.18
angst unpleasure 96.1
anxiety 126.1
anguish
n agony 26.6
unpleasure 96.1
wretchedness 96.6
sorrow 112.10
v feel discomfort 26.8
pain 96.17
suffer 96.19
aggrieve 112.19
angularity
inclination 204.2
having sharp angles
278
crookedness 278.1
anhydrous 1064.7
anima psyche 92.28
life force 306.3
mind 918.4
animadversion 510.4
animal
n beast 144.14
creature 311.2
barbarian 497.7
savage 593.5
bad person 660.7
glutton 672.3
adj cruel 144.26
animalian 311.38
unrefined 497.12
carnal 663.6
lascivious 665.29
animal enclosure
1068.5
animal husbandry
rearing 1068
animal culture 1068.1
animalistic
cruel 144.26
animal 311.38
carnal 663.6
absurdist 951.9
animality
cruelty 144.11
animal life 311.1
unrefinement 497.3
carnality 663.2
lasciviousness 665.5
violence 671.1

animal kingdom
animal life 311.1
race 559.4
hierarchy 808.4
biology 1066.1
animal magnetism 22.8
animal sounds 60
animal spirits
gaiety 109.4
life 306.1
animal worship 697.1
animate
n gender 530.10
v refresh 9.2
energize 17.10
stimulate 105.13
cheer 109.7
vivify 306.9
motivate 375.12
inspire 375.20
impel 901.11
adj organic 305.17
living 306.11
animated refreshed 9.4
energetic 17.13
eager 101.8
gay 109.14
living 306.11
active 330.17
moved 375.30
motion-picture 706.8
animation
vivacity 17.4
energizing 17.8
eagerness 101.1
excitation 105.11
gaiety 109.4
life 306.1
vivification 306.5
liveliness 330.2
motivation 375.2
inspiration 375.9
motion pictures 706.1
animism
animistic religion
675.6
paganism 688.4
immaterialism 1051.3
animosity
bad feeling 93.7
enmity 103.2
bitterness 152.3
animus 589.4
animus will 323.1
inspiration 375.9
intention 380.1
animosity 589.4
disposition 977.3
anion
electrolysis 1031.24
element 1058.2
ankle
n member 2.7
leg 177.14
joint 799.4
v walk 177.27
ankle-deep deep 275.10
shallow 276.5
annalist writer 547.15
genealogist 550.2
author 718.4
historian 719.4

chronologist 831.10
annals record 549.1
history 719.1
chronicle 831.9
annealed
tempered 1044.15
toughened 1047.6
annex
n addition 254.1
adjunct 254.3
v add 253.4
take possession 472.10
attach 480.20
rob 482.16
fasten 799.7
annexation
addition 253.1
adjunct 254.1
attachment 480.5
theft 482.1
fastening 799.3
annihilate
excise 255.10
kill 308.12
abolish 395.13
destroy 395.14
exterminate 761.7
do away with 908.21
annihilation
excision 255.3
death 307.1
extinction 395.6
anniversary 849.4
annotate
comment upon 341.11
criticize 945.14
annotation
comment 341.5
memorandum 549.4
announce
herald 133.14
affirm 334.5
annunciate 352.12
state 524.24
report 552.11
be prior 833.3
announcement
affirmation 334.1
communication 343.2
annunciation 352.2
information 551.1
announcer
harbinger 133.5
annunciator 353.3
informant 551.5
precursor 815.1
broadcaster 1033.23
annoy irk 96.13
vex 98.15
excite 105.12
aggravate 119.2
provoke 152.24
annoyance
displeasure 96.2
vexatiousness 98.7
aggravation 119.1
resentment 152.1
adversity 1010.1
trouble 1012.3
annoying
irritating 98.22
aggravating 119.5

troublesome 126.10
difficult 1012.18
annual
n plant 310.3
report 549.7
record book 549.11
periodical 555.1
adj momentary 849.8
annuity
subsidy 478.8
insurance 1007.4
annul abolish 395.13
repeal 445.2
neutralize 899.7
annular 280.11
annulment
denial 335.2
extinction 395.6
divorce 566.1
neutralization 899.2
annulus 280.2
annunciation
affirmation 334.1
announcement 352.2
anode 1031.8
anodic 1032.15
anodized 295.33
anodyne
n anesthetic 25.3
sedative 86.12
relief 120.1
moderator 670.3
adj sedative 86.45
relieving 120.9
palliative 670.16
anoint
medicate 91.25
install 615.12
minister 701.15
oil 1054.8
anointment
authority 417.12
lubrication 1054.6
anomalous
inconsistent 788.8
abnormal 869.9
eccentric 926.5
anomaly
unfitness 788.3
misfit 788.4
abnormality 869.1
oddity 869.5
eccentricity 926.1
anomie 674.1
anon
adj anonymous 528.3
adv then 820.11
in the future 838.9
soon 844.16
anonymity
privacy 345.2
namelessness 528
incognito 528.1
anonymous
private 345.13
anon 528.3
another
n a different thing
779.3
adj additional 253.10
other 779.8
fresh 840.8

answer
n communication
343.1
remark 524.4
letter 553.2
defense 600.2
paean 696.3
response 708.23
equal 789.4
reaction 902.1
retort 938
reply 938.1
solution 939.1
refutation 957.2
expedient 994.2
v communicate with
343.8
avail 387.17
reply 553.11
defend 600.10
reciprocate 776.7
suit 787.8
react 902.5
make answer 938.4
solve 939.2
refute 957.5
suffice 990.4
expedite one's affair
994.3
answerable
responsible 641.17
agreeing 787.9
liable 896.5
solvable 939.3
answer for
go for 349.10
commit 436.5
represent 576.14
be responsible for
641.6
take the responsibility
641.9
ant 311.32
antacid
n gastric antacid
86.25
counteractant 899.3
acid 1058.3
adj antidotal 86.41
neutralizing 899.9
antagonism
hostility 99.2
opposition 451.2
warlikeness 458.11
enmity 589.3
contrariety 778.1
disagreement 788.1
counteraction 899.1
antagonist
opponent 452.1
enemy 589.6
role 704.10
actor 707.2
antagonize
contend against 451.4
set against 589.7
counteract 899.6
ante
n bet 759.3
v pay over 624.15
bet 759.25
ante-bellum 833.5

antecede
precede 813.2
be prior 833.3
antecedent
n precursor 815.1
precedent 833.2
adj leading 165.3
preceding 813.4
previous 833.4
antecedents
ancestors 560.7
cause 885.1
antechamber 197.20
antedate
n date 831.4
previousness 833.1
v date 831.13
mistime 832.2
be prior 833.3
antediluvian
n ancient 841.7
back number 841.8
adj prewar 833.5
antiquated 841.13
antelope
swiftness 174.6
hoofed animal 311.5
antemeridian 314.6
antenna whiskers 3.10
feeler 73.4
radio transmitter
1033.4
anterior front 216.10
preceding 813.4
previous 833.4
anteroom 197.20
anthem
n paean 696.3
sacred music 708.17
v sing 708.38
anthill hill 237.4
pile 769.10
anthology
compilation 554.7
excerpts 557.4
book of verse 720.5
collection 769.11
anthrax 85.40
anthropocentric 312.13
anthropoid
n ancient 841.7
adj manlike 312.14
anthropological 312.13
anthropology 312.10
anthropomorphic
animal 311.38
manlike 312.14
religious 675.25
anti oppositional 451.8
contrary 778.6
antibiotic
n panacea 86.3
miracle drug 86.29
poison 1000.3
adj antidotal 86.41
antibody blood 2.23
immunity 83.4
antitoxin 86.27
antic
n prank 489.10
v play 743.23
adj gay 109.14

fantastic 869.12
antichrist 695.10
anticipate expect 130.5
be prior 833.3
come 838.6
foresee 844.6
predict 960.5
prevent 1011.14
anticipating
pregnant 78.18
expectant 130.11
anticipation
expectation 130.1
carefulness 339.1
anachronism 832.1
previousness 833.1
the future 838.1
earliness 844.1
intuition 933.1
foresight 960.1
anticipatory
expectant 130.11
previous 833.4
future 838.8
early 844.7
foreseeing 960.7
anticlimax 488.3
anticoagulant 1062.4
antidepressant
n drug 87.2
adj psychochemical
86.46
antidote
counterpoison 86.26
counteractant 899.3
antiestablishment
333.6
antifreeze
n coolant 1023.8
adj antifreezing
1023.15
antigen blood 2.23
immunity 83.4
antitoxin 86.27
antihero 704.10
antinomian
n anarchist 418.3
heretic 688.5
adj anarchic 418.6
unorthodox 688.9
antinomy
self-contradiction
778.3
inconsistency 788.2
antipasto 10.9
antipathetic
oppositional 451.8
hostile 589.10
contrary 778.6
disagreeing 788.6
counteractive 899.8
antipathy
dislike 99.2
loathing 103.1
hated thing 103.3
refusal 325.1
hostility 451.2
enmity 589.3
contrariety 778.1
counteraction 899.1
antiphon paean 696.3
response 708.23

answer 938.1
antipodes
opposites 215.2
remote region 261.4
poles 778.2
Antipodes 231.6
antipyretic
n febrifuge 86.14
adj antidotal 86.41
antiquarian
n antiquary 841.5
adj archaeological
841.20
antiquated
disused 390.10
past 836.7
grown old 841.13
antique
n relic 841.6
back number 841.8
adj disused 390.10
durable 826.10
past 836.7
old 841.10
antiquated 841.13
antiquity
durability 826.1
ancient times 836.3
oldness 841.1
antique 841.6
antireligious 695.22
anti-Semitism
hate 103.1
discrimination 979.4
antiseptic
n disinfectant 86.21
poison 1000.3
adj sanitary 79.27
disinfectant 86.43
antisocial
misanthropic 590.3
eccentric 926.5
antithesis
contraposition 215.1
contrariety 778.1
antithetical
contrapositive 215.5
oppositional 451.8
contrary 778.6
antitoxin
antitoxic serum 86.27
inoculation 91.16
antler 285.4
antonym word 526.1
the opposite 778.2
antrum 284.2
antsy
excited 105.23
restless 105.27
apprehensive 127.24
impatient 135.6
agitated 916.16
wriggly 916.21
anus
digestive system 2.16
asshole 292.5
anvil ear 2.10
instrument of
conversion 857.10
anxiety
unpleasure 96.1
eagerness 101.1

apprehensiveness 126
anxiousness 126.1
fear 127.4
suspense 130.3
impatience 135.1
trouble 1012.3
anxious
pleasureless 96.20
eager 101.8
concerned 126.7
apprehensive 127.24
in suspense 130.12
impatient 135.6
troubled 1012.20
any
n some 244.3
anything 863.5
adj quantitative 244.5
every 863.15
one 871.7
anybody 863.5
anyhow
carelessly 340.18
anyway 384.10
any kind 808.9
anyone any 863.5
whoever 863.7
any one
n any 863.5
adj one 871.7
anyplace 159.22
anything some 244.3
any 863.5
anytime
whenever 820.12
imminently 839.4
anyway 384.10
anywhere
adj addicted 87.24
adv wherever 159.22
aorta 2.21
apace swiftly 174.17
hastily 401.12
promptly 844.15
apart
adj distant 261.8
secluded 584.8
unrelated 775.6
separate 801.20
alone 871.8
adv away 261.17
privately 345.19
separately 801.27
singly 871.13
in half 874.8
apartheid
seclusion 584.1
exclusiveness 772.3
discrimination 979.4
apartment 228.13
apathy
insensibility 25.1
lack of feeling 94.4
unconcern 102.2
despair 125.2
inertness 173.4
languor 331.1
indifference 467.2
thoughtlessness 932.1
incuriosity 981.1
ape
n strong man 15.7

wild animal 311.23
imitator 336.4
ruffian 593.4
violent person 671.10
v mimic 336.6
impersonate 349.12
gesture 517.21
resemble 783.7
adj crazy 925.27
aperçu
treatise 556.1
abridgment 557.1
intuition 933.1
apéritif appetizer 10.9
drink 88.9
aperture
opening 292.1
passageway 383.3
apex summit 198.2
height 272.2
angle 278.2
speech organ 524.19
aphasia muteness 51.2
loss of speech 525.6
aphorism
witticism 489.7
epigram 537.3
maxim 973.1
aphrodisiac
love potion 75.6
aphroditous 75.25
Aphrodite Love 104.8
beauty 1015.10
apical 198.10
apiece 864.19
apish imitative 336.9
representational
349.13
foolish 922.8
aplenty
adj sufficient 990.7
adv plentifully 990.9
aplomb
equanimity 106.3
verticalness 200.1
self-control 359.5
stability 854.1
apnea 85.9
apocalypse
disclosure 351.1
revelation 683.9
prediction 961.1
Apocalypse 683.4
apocalyptic
ominous 133.17
scriptural 683.10
predictive 961.11
apocryphal
spurious 354.25
unorthodox 688.9
unauthoritative
970.21
apogee summit 198.2
boundary 211.3
long way 261.2
limit 793.5
orbit 1070.16
spacecraft 1073.2
Apollo
music 710.22
Muse 720.10
sun 1070.14

apologetic
  n apology 600.3
  justifier 600.8
  adj penitent 113.9
  justifying 600.13
  atoning 658.7
apologia apology 600.3
  argumentation 934.4
apologist
  defender 460.7
  justifier 600.8
  supporter 616.9
  arguer 934.12
apologize
  repent 113.7
  beg pardon 658.5
apology
  penitence 113.4
  pretext 376.1
  apologia 600.3
  excuse 658.2
  argumentation 934.4
apoplectic
  n sick person 85.42
  adj anemic 85.60
apoplexy seizure 85.6
  paralysis 85.27
  upheaval 671.5
  spasm 916.6
apostasy dissent 333.1
  denial 335.2
  recreancy 363.2
  desertion 370.2
  backsliding 394.2
  nonobservance 435.1
  Protestantism 675.10
  impiety 694.1
  change 851.1
  renunciation 857.3
apostate
  n dissenter 333.3
  turncoat 363.5
  backslider 394.3
  Protestant 675.20
  sacrilegist 694.3
  defector 857.8
  adj recreant 363.11
  relapsing 394.5
  Protestant 675.28
  impious 694.6
  treasonable 857.20
apostle disciple 572.2
  religion 684.2
  clergy 699.9
  converter 857.9
apostolic
  abstinent 668.10
  scriptural 683.10
  papal 698.15
apostrophe
  remark 524.4
  soliloquy 542.1
apothecary 86.35
apothegm
  witticism 489.7
  maxim 973.1
apotheosis
  respect 155.1
  praise 509.5
  glorification 662.8
  removal to heaven
    681.11

idolization 697.2
  ideal 785.4
  elevation 911.1
appall offend 98.11
  terrify 127.17
  dismay 127.19
appalling horrid 98.19
  terrible 127.30
  remarkable 247.10
apparatus
  equipment 385.4
  impedimenta 471.3
  tool 1039.1
apparel
  n clothing 5.1
  v outfit 5.38
apparent visible 31.6
  appearing 33.11
  exterior 206.7
  manifest 348.8
  specious 354.26
  plausible 967.7
  illusory 975.8
apparently visibly 31.8
  seemingly 33.12
  externally 206.10
  manifestly 348.14
  falsely 354.34
apparition ghost 33.1
  appearance 33.5
  phantom 975.4
  figment of the
    imagination 985.5
  specter 987.1
appeal
  n delightfulness 97.2
  desirability 100.13
  loveableness 104.7
  allurement 377.1
  entreaty 440.2
  appeal motion 598.10
  prayer 696.4
  v attract 377.6
  entreat 440.11
appealing
  delightful 97.7
  alluring 377.8
  imploring 440.17
  melodious 708.48
appeal to
  entreat 440.11
  address 524.27
  refer to 956.14
appear show 31.4
  become visible 33.8
  seem 33.10
  attend 221.8
  come out 348.6
  be revealed 351.8
  be published 352.16
  act 704.29
  turn up 830.6
appearance
  showing up 33
  appearing 33.1
  exterior 33.2
  apparition 33.5
  arrival 186.1
  front 206.1
  lineaments 262.3
  manifestation 348.1
  sham 354.3

illusoriness 975.2
  phantom 975.4
  specter 987.1
appear for 576.14
appease gratify 95.7
  relieve 120.5
  pacify 465.7
  calm 670.7
  propitiate 696.14
appeasement
  relief 120.1
  pacification 465.1
  foreign policy 609.5
  propitiation 696.6
appellate 595.7
appellation
  naming 527.2
  nomenclature 527.3
append add 253.4
  place after 814.3
appendage
  member 2.7
  hanger-on 138.6
  follower 166.2
  adjunct 254.1
  belongings 471.2
  nonessential 767.2
  attendant 768.3
  part 792.4
appendix
  digestive system 2.16
  added to writing
    254.2
  sequel 816.1
appertaining
  relative 774.7
  relevant 774.11
appertain to
  belong to 469.7
  relate to 774.5
appetite eating 8.1
  craving 100.6
  stomach 100.7
  eagerness 101.1
  will 323.1
  sensuality 663.1
appetizer 10.9
appetizing
  mouth-watering 63.10
  desirable 100.30
  alluring 377.8
applaud cheer 116.6
  congratulate 149.2
  assent 332.8
  acclaim 509.10
applause
  cheer 116.2
  congratulation 149.1
  plaudit 509.2
apple pie 1013.4
apple-polisher 138.4
appliance
  instrument 384.4
  use 387.1
  facility 449.9
  machinery 1039.3
applicable
  usable 387.23
  legal 673.10
  relevant 774.11
  apt 787.10
applicant 440.7

application
  dressing 86.33
  industry 330.6
  perseverance 360.1
  use 387.1
  request 440.1
  study 570.3
  administration 643.2
  relevance 774.4
  attribution 887.1
  engrossment 982.3
applied 387.24
appliqué 295.4
apply
  cover 295.19
  put to use 387.11
  petition 440.10
  administer 643.6
  relate 774.6
  attribute 887.3
apply for 440.9
apply oneself
  practice 328.8
  endeavor 403.5
  undertake 404.3
  study 570.12
  busy oneself with
    724.11
  exert oneself 725.9
  think about 930.11
  attend to 982.5
appoint
  elect 371.20
  equip 385.8
  prescribe 420.9
  allot 477.9
  assign 615.11
  destine 963.7
appointee 615.9
appointment
  election 371.9
  authority 417.12
  decree 420.4
  allotment 477.3
  engagement 582.8
  assignment 615.2
  commission 615.4
  holy orders 698.10
  position 724.5
appointments
  equipment 385.4
  belongings 471.2
Appollo 1015.10
apportion
  quantify 244.4
  share 476.6
  mete out 477.6
  separate 792.6
  portion 801.18
  dispose 807.9
apposite
  relevant 774.11
  apt 787.10
apposition 223.3
appraisal
  measurement 300.1
  valuation 630.3
  classification 800.3
  estimate 945.3
appreciable
  weighable 297.19
  measurable 300.14

substantial 762.6
knowable 927.25
appreciate
savor 63.5
enjoy 95.12
be grateful 150.3
respect 155.4
grow 251.6
measure 300.10
understand 521.7
know 927.12
estimate 945.9
value 996.13
appreciation
gratitude 150.1
respect 155.1
increase 251.1
acknowledgment
  332.3
commendation 509.3
cognizance 927.2
discrimination 943.1
estimate 945.3
appreciative
grateful 150.5
approbatory 509.16
aware of 927.16
discriminating 943.7
apprehend sense 24.6
fear 127.10
forebode 133.11
arrest 429.15
capture 480.18
understand 521.7
know 927.12
apprehension
anxiety 126.1
apprehensiveness
  127.4
suspense 130.3
foreboding 133.2
arrest 429.6
seizure 480.2
intelligence 919.1
understanding 927.3
idea 931.1
doubt 954.2
apprehensive
anxious 126.7
misgiving 127.24
nervous 128.11
in suspense 130.12
knowing 927.15
apprentice
n novice 572.9
skilled worker 726.6
beginner 817.2
producer 891.7
v train 568.13
indenture 615.18
adj indentured 615.21
apprised of 927.16
apprise 551.8
approach
n motion towards 167
access 167.1
convergence 169.1
landing 184.18
arrival 186.1
entrance 189.5
nearness 223.1
plan 381.1

manner 384.1
attempt 403.2
offer 439.1
game 750.2
similarity 783.1
imminence 839.1
v come close 167.3
converge 169.2
arrive 186.6
near 223.7
be around 223.8
communicate with
  343.8
bribe 378.3
use 384.5
attempt 403.6
make advances
  439.7
address 524.27
cultivate 587.12
resemble 783.7
turn up 830.6
be in the future 838.6
be imminent 839.2
exercise influence
  893.9
approachable
accessible 167.5
communicative
  343.10
bribable 378.4
possibility 965.8
approbation
respect 155.1
ratification 332.4
consent 441.1
approval 509.1
esteem 662.3
appropriate
v take possession
  472.10
adopt 480.19
steal 482.13
plagiarize 482.19
borrow 621.4
usurp 640.8
adj useful 387.18
decorous 496.10
fit 533.7
right 637.3
due 639.8
relevant 774.11
apt 787.10
timely 842.9
characteristic 864.13
expedient 994.5
appropriation
allotment 477.3
taking over 480.4
theft 482.1
plagiarism 482.8
adoption 621.2
usurpation 640.3
approval
respect 155.1
ratification 332.4
consent 441.1
high marks 509
approbation 509.1
esteem 662.3
support 900.1
criticism 945.2

approve
ratify 332.12
adopt 371.15
consent 441.2
accept 509.9
support 900.21
criticize 945.14
evidence 956.8
approved
accepted 332.14
chosen 371.26
received 479.10
favored 509.19
conventional 579.5
orthodox 687.7
authoritative 969.18
approximate
v be around 223.8
imitate 336.5
resemble 783.7
similarize 783.8
adj approaching 167.4
near 223.14
approximating 774.8
similar 783.14
inaccurate 974.17
v approach 167.3
approximately
also 223.23
nearly 244.6
on the whole 791.14
approximation
approach 167.1
nearness 223.1
measurement 300.1
reproduction 336.3
relation 774.1
similarity 783.1
likeness 783.3
inaccuracy 974.2
notation 1016.2
appurtenance
adjunct 254.1
equipment 385.4
facility 449.9
belongings 471.2
prerogative 642.1
nonessential 767.2
component 795.2
apron clothing 5.17
runway 184.23
stage 704.16
golf 751.1
apropos
relevant 774.11
apt 787.10
incidentally 842.13
apse arch 279.4
church 703.9
apt skillful 413.22
appropriate 533.7
teachable 570.18
apposite 787.10
prompt 844.9
smart 919.14
probable 967.6
disposed 977.8
aptitude
innate skill 413.5
teachableness 570.5
fitness 787.5
tendency 895.1

smartness 919.2
probability 967.1
disposition 977.3
apt to
adj liable to 896.6
prep inclined to 895.6
aquarium
vivarium 228.24
collection 769.11
aquatic
n creatures 311.3
adj water-dwelling
  182.58
watery 1063.16
aquatics 182.11
aqueduct
watercourse 239.2
trench 290.2
aqueous 1063.16
aquiline hooked 279.8
birdlike 311.47
aquiver 105.20
Arab 178.4
arabesque
n network 170.3
detailed design 498.2
ornament 709.18
adj ornate 498.12
Arabesque 554.15
Arabic numerals
  1016.4
arable 1067.20
arachnid 311.31
arbiter
arbitrator 466.4
connoisseur 496.7
referee 596.1
judge 945.6
arbitrage
n stocks 737.19
v trade 737.23
arbitrary
voluntary 324.7
capricious 364.5
unthinking 365.10
imperious 417.16
arbitration
arbitrament 466.2
unionism 727.1
adjustment 787.4
judgment 945.1
arbitrator arbiter 466.4
go-between 576.4
judge 596.1
arbor
summerhouse 228.12
axle 914.5
arboreal forked 171.10
arborical 310.36
arc
n curve 279.2
lights 704.18
discharge 1031.6
v curve 279.6
arcade corridor 197.18
fence 212.4
pillar 273.5
arch 279.4
passageway 383.3
Arcadian rustic 233.6
natural 416.6
ideal 985.23

arcane secret 345.11
  implied 519.7
  recondite 522.16
  supernatural 869.15
arch
  n foot 199.5
  span 279.4
  monument 549.12
  v curve 279.6
  adj chief 249.14
  mischievous 322.6
  cunning 415.12
archaeological 841.20
archaeologist 841.5
archaeology 841.4
archaism
  archaicism 526.12
  antiquity 841.6
archangel 679.1
archdiocese
  region 231.5
  diocese 698.8
arched bowed 279.10
  convex 283.13
archenemy
  opponent 452.1
  enemy 589.6
archer 903.8
archery ballistics 462.3
  sport 744.1
  throwing 903.2
archetype
  engram 92.29
  form 262.1
  original 337.2
  model 785.1
  philosophy 931.2
  instinct 933.2
  standard of perfection
    1001.4
archetypical
  unimitated 337.6
  prototypal 785.9
  perfected 1001.9
archipelago 235.2
architect planner 381.6
  draftsman 716.10
  landscape planner
    717.3
  doer 726.1
  producer 891.7
architectural
  structural 266.6
  design 717.6
  constructional 891.15
architecture
  structure 266.1
  design 717
  construction 717.1
  plot 722.4
  production 891.2
archives
  storehouse 386.6
  preserve 397.7
  public records 549.2
  registry 549.3
archivist 550.1
archway 279.4
arctic unfeeling 94.9
  northern 161.14
  seasonal 313.9
  cold 1022.14

ardent alcoholic 88.37
  fervent 93.18
  zealous 101.9
  amorous 104.26
  willing 324.5
  industrious 330.22
  vehement 544.13
  cordial 587.16
  fiery 671.22
  hot 1018.25
  burning 1018.27
ardor animation 17.4
  passion 93.2
  desire 100.1
  zeal 101.2
  love 104.1
  willingness 324.1
  industry 330.6
  vehemence 544.5
  interest 982.2
  heat 1018.2
arduous
  laborious 725.18
  difficult 1012.17
area space 158.1
  location 159.1
  region 231.1
  size 257.1
  study 568.8
  occupation 724.4
  specialty 865.1
  science 927.10
arear 163.13
arena space 158.1
  hall 197.4
  setting 209.2
  enclosed place 212.3
  sphere 231.2
  sports venue 463
  scene of action 463.1
  occupation 724.4
  track 755.1
  science 927.10
  outlook 977.2
argosy ship 180.1
  fleet 180.10
  navy 461.27
argot
  Greek 522.7
  jargon 523.9
arguable 970.17
argue
  affirm 334.5
  signify 517.17
  mean 518.8
  support 600.10
  reason 934.16
  evidence 956.8
argument
  quarrel 456.5
  contention 457.1
  pleadings 598.6
  testimony 598.8
  defense 600.2
  plot 722.4
  reason 934.4
  case 934.5
  specious argument
    935.3
aria
  air 708.4
  solo 708.15

arid
  dull 117.6
  unproductive 890.4
  unimaginative 986.5
  dry 1064.7
aright 998.22
arise
  get up 23.6
  appear 33.8
  emerge 190.11
  ascend 193.8
  rise 200.8
  revolt 327.7
  originate 817.13
  turn up 830.6
arise from 886.5
aristocracy
  the best 249.5
  mastership 417.7
  upper class 607.2
  social status 607.3
  noble rank 608
  nobility 608.1
  aristocracy 608.1
  blue blood 608.2
  government 612.4
aristocrat
  patrician 607.4
  nobleman 608.4
aristocratic
  dignified 136.12
  lordly 141.11
  imperious 417.16
  upper-class 607.10
  noble 608.10
  governmental 612.17
arithmetic 1016.21
arm
  n appendage 2.7
  inlet 242.1
  branch 617.10
  game 745.3
  member 792.4
  supporter 900.2
  forearm 905.5
  v empower 18.10
  equip 385.8
  fortify 460.9
  protect 1007.18
armada 461.27
armament
  provision 385.1
  equipment 385.4
  arms 462.1
  football 746.1
armchair 950.13
armed provided 385.13
  prepared 405.16
  embattled 458.23
  heeled 460.14
  protected 1007.21
armed forces 461.20
arm in arm
  adj near 223.14
  adv sociably 582.25
  amicably 587.22
  hand in hand 768.10
armistice 465.5
armor
  n callousness 94.3
  shell 295.15
  armature 460.3

  v fortify 460.9
  protect 1007.18
armory
  storehouse 386.6
  arsenal 462.2
  insignia 647.1
  heraldry 647.2
  plant 739.3
  track 755.1
arms
  military science 458.6
  materiel 462
  weapons 462.1
  heraldry 647.2
arms race 458.10
arm-twisting
  inducement 375.3
  coercion 424.3
  threat 514.1
army branch 461.21
  military units 461.22
  forces 461.23
  throng 769.4
  group of animals
    769.5
  multitude 883.3
aroma odor 69.1
  fragrance 70.1
  characteristic 864.4
aromatic
  n perfumery 70.2
  adj odorous 69.9
  fragrant 70.9
around
  adv in every direction
    161.25
  round 209.12
  near 223.20
  rotating 914.16
  prep through 161.27
  about 223.26
arousal
  awakening 23.2
  stimulation 105.1
  excitation 105.11
  elicitation 192.5
  incitement 375.4
arouse energize 17.10
  wake someone up 23.5
  excite 105.12
  provoke 152.24
  elicit 192.14
  incite 375.17
  rouse 375.19
  alarm 400.3
  interest 982.12
  heat 1019.18
arousing
  n excitation 105.11
  adj aphrodisiac 75.25
  extractive 192.17
arraignment
  censure 510.3
  indictment 598.3
  accusation 599.1
arrange
  plan 381.8
  prepare 405.6
  settle 437.8
  mediate 466.7
  compose 708.46
  order 806.4

align 807.8
classify 808.6
arranged
planned 381.12
contracted 437.11
orderly 806.6
composed 807.14
arrangement
form 262.1
structure 266.1
plan 381.1
preparation 405.1
compact 437.1
adjustment 465.4
compromise 468.1
ornamentation 498.1
appointment 582.8
piece 708.5
score 708.28
harmonization 709.2
music 709.11
treatment 712.9
order 806.1
configuration 807
organization 807.1
classification 808.1
arrant
downright 247.12
conspicuous 348.12
wicked 654.16
base 661.12
terrible 999.9
array
n clothing 5.1
army 461.23
order 806.1
arrangement 807.1
series 811.2
v clothe 5.38
ornament 498.8
order 806.4
dispose 807.9
align 811.5
adduce 956.12
arrayed clothing 5.44
embattled 458.23
arranged 807.14
arrears debt 623.2
shortcoming 910.1
arrest
n seizure 85.6
slowing 175.4
restraint 428.1
arrestment 429.6
confinement 480.2
stop 856.2
hindrance 1011.1
curb 1011.7
v slow 175.9
restrain 428.7
confine 429.15
capture 480.18
delay 845.8
put a stop to 856.11
engross 982.13
hinder 1011.10
arrested
retarded 175.12
undeveloped 406.12
restrained 428.13
incomplete 794.4
late 845.16

mentally deficient
921.22
gripped 982.18
arrested development
fixation 92.21
mental deficiency
921.9
arrival
landing 184.18
entrant 186.1
incomer 189.4
arrive
appear 33.8
arrive at 186.6
make good 409.10
arrivederci! 188.22
arriving
adj approaching 186.9
adv on arrival 186.10
arriviste
vulgarian 497.6
upstart 606.7
newcomer 773.4
modern 840.4
arrogant
vain 136.9
proud 140.9
overbearing 141.9
insolent 142.9
contemptuous 157.8
imperious 417.16
confident 969.21
defiant 454.7
arrogate
take command 417.14
appropriate 480.19
usurp 640.8
arrow
n swiftness 174.6
shaft 462.6
pointer 517.4
v be straight 277.4
arsenal
storehouse 386.6
armory 462.2
plant 739.3
arson 1019.7
arsonist
destroyer 395.8
incendiary 1019.8
art
representation 349.1
knack 413.6
science 413.7
cunning 415.1
stratagem 415.3
visual arts 712.1
artistry 712.7
vocation 724.6
science 927.10
arterial 2.31
arteriosclerosis 1044.5
artery duct 2.21
passageway 383.3
artful
falsehearted 354.30
deceitful 356.22
cunning 415.12
insincere 645.18
shrewd 919.15
arthritic
n sick person 85.42

adj anemic 85.60
article
n definite article 530.6
writing 547.10
news item 552.3
part 554.13
treatise 556.1
commodity 735.2
particular 765.3
part of grammar
792.2
individual 871.4
object 1050.4
v accuse 599.7
indenture 615.18
articulate
v say 524.23
put together 799.5
hook 799.8
adj audible 50.16
intelligible 521.10
speaking 524.32
eloquent 544.8
jointed 799.17
articulation
uttering 524.6
speech sound 524.13
word 526.1
joining 799.1
joint 799.4
series 811.2
artifact antiquity 841.6
product 892.1
object 1050.4
artifice
falseheartedness 354.4
chicanery 356.4
trick 356.6
intrigue 381.5
cunning 415.1
stratagem 415.3
affectation 533.3
expedient 994.2
artificial
spurious 354.25
put on 500.15
affected 533.9
artificial insemination
78.3
arithmetical 1016.21
artillery ballistics
462.3
cannon 462.11
artilleryman
artillerist 461.11
shooter 903.8
artisan expert 413.11
worker 607.9
artist 716.1
skilled laborer 726.6
mechanic 1039.8
artist expert 413.11
entertainer 707.1
musician 710.1
visual arts 712.1
creator 716
artiste 716.1
skilled worker 726.6
producer 891.7
artistic
skillful 413.22
tasteful 496.8

painterly 712.20
artistry skill 413.1
authorship 547.2
art 712.7
talent 718.2
artless natural 406.13
unskillful 414.15
simple 416.5
candid 644.17
foolable 922.12
artlessness
naturalness 406.3
simplicity 416
ingenuousness 416.1
candor 644.4
genuineness 972.7
arts and crafts 712.1
artsy-craftsy 712.20
artwork
visual arts 712.1
work of art 712.10
arty 712.20
as
adv how 384.9
equally 789.11
to illustrate 956.23
conj because 887.10
as a matter of course
finally 819.12
generally 863.17
normally 868.10
consequently 886.7
certainly 969.23
as a matter of fact
really 760.16
truly 972.18
as a rule
generally 863.17
normally 868.10
asbestos 1021.5
ascend move 172.5
climb 184.39
fly 193.8
rise 200.8
incline 204.10
tower 272.10
levitate 298.9
ascendancy
superiority 249.1
victory 411.1
dominance 417.6
influence 893.1
ascendant
rising 193.14
superior 249.12
victorious 411.7
authoritative 417.15
governing 612.18
influential 893.14
ascending
n course 172.2
rising 200.5
adj flowing 172.8
in the ascendant
193.14
sloping upward
204.17
high 272.14
ascension ascent 193.1
rising 200.5
removal to heaven
681.11

ascent course 172.2
motion upwards 193
ascension 193.1
rising 200.5
acclivity 204.6
increase 251.1
lightness 298.1
improvement 392.1
elevation 911.1
ascertain learn 570.6
decide 945.11
prove 956.10
make sure 969.11
ascertained
known 927.26
proved 956.20
assured 969.20
true 972.13
ascetic
n recluse 584.5
puritan 667.2
abstainer 668.4
religious 699.15
adj plain-speaking
535.3
atoning 658.7
austere 667.4
abstinent 668.10
meager 991.10
asceticism
penance 658.3
self-denial 667
austerity 667.1
abstinence 668.2
ascribable
due 639.10
attributable 887.6
ascribe accuse 599.7
attribute 887.3
aseptic 79.27
asexual 75.28
as far as to 261.20
when 820.16
as for 774.13
as good as 223.22
ash dregs 256.2
extract 892.3
combustion product
1019.16
ashamed
regretful 113.8
humiliated 137.14
ashen colorless 36.7
gray 39.4
terrified 127.26
burned 1019.30
ashes corpse 307.16
combustion product
1019.16
ashore 234.8
ashram
community 617.2
retreat 1008.5
aside
n interjection 213.2
byplay 490.1
soliloquy 542.1
adv in an undertone
52.22
laterally 218.8
on one side 218.10
apart 261.17

privately 345.19
in reserve 386.17
aside from
adv separately 801.27
prep excluding 772.10
as if 950.19
asinine
ungulate 311.44
stupid 921.15
foolish 922.8
trivial 997.19
as is
adj present 837.2
adv identically 777.9
as it were
by interpretation
341.18
figuratively 536.4
so to speak 783.19
supposedly 950.17
ask demand 421.5
request 440.9
invite 440.13
charge 630.12
inquire 937.19
require 962.9
ask about 937.19
askance
obliquely 204.14
askew 204.22
laterally 218.8
warily 494.13
disapprovingly 510.26
askew skew 204.14
awry 204.22
distorted 265.10
disorderly 809.13
erroneous 974.16
ask for
encourage 375.21
demand 421.5
request 440.9
seek 937.29
ask for it defy 454.3
be rash 493.5
cause trouble 1012.14
asking price offer 439.1
price 738.9
ask no quarter 430.20
aslant
adj inclining 204.15
adv slantingly 204.23
asleep sleeping 22.22
insensible 25.6
unconscious 25.8
dead 307.30
unaware 929.13
unalert 983.8
as long as
prep when 820.16
conj so 958.15
aslope
adj inclining 204.15
adv slantingly 204.23
as much as 244.7
as new 840.15
as of now 837.3
as one
unanimously 332.17
cooperatively 450.6
in step 787.11
jointly 799.18

simultaneously 835.7
concurrently 898.5
aspect look 33.3
navigation 159.3
perfective 530.13
particular 765.3
component 795.2
astrology 1070.20
as per 866.9
asperity
pungency 68.1
ill humor 110.1
causticity 144.8
bitterness 152.3
roughness 288.1
aspersion
indignity 156.2
criticism 510.4
slur 512.4
stigma 661.6
baptism 701.6
wetting 1063.6
asphalt
n ground covering
199.3
pavement 383.6
v floor 295.22
asphyxiate
suffocate 307.24
strangle 308.18
suppress 428.8
asphyxiation
symptom 85.9
violent death 307.6
suffocation 308.6
aspic 10.12
aspirant desirer 100.12
optimist 124.6
petitioner 440.7
candidate 610.9
aspiration
breathing 2.19
murmur 52.4
reaching high 100.9
hope 124.1
inhaling 187.5
drawing 192.3
motive 375.1
intention 380.1
speech sound 524.13
aspire
be ambitious 100.20
take off 193.10
aspiring
ambitious 100.28
hopeful 124.11
high 272.14
as regards 774.13
ass sex object 75.4
copulation 75.7
beast of burden 176.8
buttocks 217.5
donkey 311.16
obstinate person
361.6
fool 923.1
assail attack 459.14
criticize 510.20
incriminate 599.10
assailant
opponent 452.1
assailer 459.12

assailing
n attack 459.1
berating 510.7
adj attacking 459.29
assassin
alarmist 127.8
killer 308.10
assassination 308.2
assault
n attack 459.1
berating 510.7
incrimination 599.2
unruliness 671.3
v attack 459.14
rage 671.11
thrust 901.12
assay
n measurement 300.1
attempt 403.2
analysis 800.1
test 941.2
v measure 300.10
attempt 403.6
analyze 800.6
experiment 941.8
ass-backwards
adj backward 163.12
misinterpreted 342.3
botched 414.22
confused 809.16
adv backwards 163.13
clumsily 414.24
assemblage
association 617.1
picture 712.11
gathering 769
assembly 769.1
all 769.14
relation 774.1
composition 795.1
hodgepodge 796.6
assemble
collect 472.11
sculpture 715.5
come together 769.16
gather 769.18
compose 795.3
join 799.5
produce 891.8
assembly
council 423.1
legislature 613.1
the laity 700.1
assemblage 769.1
bunch 769.2
meeting 769.14
composition 795.1
production 891.2
assembly line
plant 739.3
assembly 769.14
industrial production
891.3
assembly-line 891.18
assemblyman 610.3
assent
n agreement 332
acquiescence 332.1
submission 433.1
consent 441.1
vote yes 787.1
support 900.1

v acquiesce 332.8
submit 433.6
consent 441.2
agree 787.6
support 900.21
assenting
agreeing 332.13
submissive 433.12
consenting 441.4
assert
affirm 334.5
insist 421.8
state 524.24
defend 600.10
postulate 950.12
maintain 952.12
assertative 334.8
assertion
affirmation 334.1
remark 524.4
premise 934.7
testimony 956.2
assertive 334.8
assert oneself 348.6
asseverate 524.24
assess
measure 300.10
price 630.11
charge 630.12
classify 800.8
estimate 945.9
assessment
measurement 300.1
fee 624.5
valuation 630.3
tax 630.9
Irish dividend 738.8
classification 800.3
estimate 945.3
assessor
measurer 300.9
tax collector 630.10
assets
supply 386.2
means 471.7
wealth 618.1
accounts 628.1
funds 728.14
asseverate
affirm 334.5
state 952.12
testify 956.9
asshole anus 292.5
bad person 660.6
fool 923.3
assiduous
industrious 330.22
painstaking 339.11
persevering 360.8
attentive 982.15
assign
n beneficiary 479.4
v locate 159.11
transfer 176.10
allot 477.9
commit 478.16
give homework 568.17
commission 615.10
appoint 615.11
transfer property
629.3
classify 808.6

specify 864.11
attribute 887.3
assignation
rendezvous 582.9
transfer 629.1
assembly 769.2
attribution 887.1
assignee
beneficiary 479.4
appointee 615.9
assignment
placement 159.6
authority 417.12
allotment 477.3
commitment 478.2
lesson 568.7
commission 615.1
appointment 615.2
transfer 629.1
duty 641.1
task 724.2
specification 864.6
attribution 887.1
assimilate digest 7.16
absorb 187.13
internalize 207.5
naturalize 226.4
consume 388.3
understand 521.7
conform 570.7
include 771.3
make uniform 780.4
similarize 783.8
make agree 787.7
combine 804.3
compare 942.4
assimilation
digestion 2.15
metabolism 2.18
nutrition 7.8
body function 7.10
sorption 187.6
naturalization 226.3
consumption 388.1
speech sound 524.13
absorption 570.2
inclusion 771.1
similarity 783.1
adjustment 787.4
combination 804.1
conversion 857.1
assist
n helping hand 449.2
baseball 745.3
basketball game 747.3
hockey 749.3
v be instrumental
384.7
aid 449.11
subsidize 478.19
benefit 592.3
assistance
remedy 86.1
aid 449.1
subsidy 478.8
assistant
n subordinate 432.5
helper 449.7
academic rank 571.3
employee 577.3
aid 616.6
adj helping 449.20

ass-kisser
yes-man 138.4
assenter 332.6
flatterer 511.4
associate
n academic rank
571.3
companion 588.3
partner 616
confederate 616.1
member 617.11
v cooperate 450.3
join 617.14
accompany 768.7
relate 774.6
put together 799.5
league 804.4
concur 898.2
adj related 774.9
leagued 804.6
concurrent 898.4
associate oneself with
undertake 404.3
back 449.13
participate 476.5
espouse 509.13
defend 600.10
join 617.14
association
association of ideas
92.33
council 423.1
affiliation 450.2
participation 476.1
social set 582.5
consociation 582.6
society 617
social grouping 617.1
company 768.2
relation 774.4
combination 804.1
concurrence 898.1
thoughts 930.4
assonance rhyme 720.8
repetitiousness 848.4
assonant
harmonious 708.49
rhyming 720.17
monotonous 848.15
assorted different 779.7
diversified 782.4
arranged 807.14
classified 808.8
assortment
miscellany 769.13
hodgepodge 796.6
grouping 807.3
assuage gratify 95.7
relieve 120.5
moderate 670.6
qualify 958.3
assuasive
n palliative 86.10
adj palliative 86.40
relieving 120.9
moderating 670.16
qualifying 958.7
as such 766.11
assume don 5.42
imitate 336.5
sham 354.20
undertake 404.3

take command 417.14
receive 479.6
appropriate 480.19
affect 500.12
imply 519.4
adopt 621.4
presume 640.6
usurp 640.8
entail 771.4
suppose 950.10
think 952.11
assumed
spurious 354.25
undertaken 404.7
put-on 500.16
implied 519.7
supposed 950.14
assumed name 527.8
assuming 141.10
assumption
hope 124.1
presumptuousness
141.2
authority 417.12
receiving 479.1
appropriation 480.4
implication 519.2
adoption 621.2
presumption 640.2
usurpation 640.3
removal to heaven
681.11
entailment 771.2
conversion 857.1
elevation 911.1
premise 934.7
supposition 950.3
opinion 952.6
assumptive 950.14
assurance
equanimity 106.3
consolation 121.4
hope 124.1
insolence 142.1
oath 334.4
promise 436.1
security 438.1
encouragement
492.9
belief 952.1
certainty 969.1
confidence 969.5
ensuring 969.8
safety 1006.1
insurance 1007.4
assure comfort 121.6
give hope 124.10
depose 334.6
promise 436.4
secure 438.9
encourage 492.16
convince 952.18
make sure 969.11
assured
composed 106.13
hopeful 124.11
insolent 142.9
promised 436.8
secured 438.11
belief 952.21
made sure 969.20
confident 969.21

atmospheric 317.11
at most 248.10
at odds
  adj unwilling 325.5
  oppositional 451.8
  at variance 456.16
  at outs 589.12
  different 779.7
  disagreeing 788.6
  adv in opposition
    451.9
atoll 235.2
atom modicum 248.2
  particle 258.8
  one 871.3
  tracer 1037.4
  matter 1050.2
  element 1058.2
atom bomb
  n atomic explosion
    1037.16
  v bomb 459.23
atomic
  infinitesimal 258.14
  one 871.7
  atomistic 1037.18
atomic energy 1037.15
atomic nucleus 1037.6
atomic number 1058.5
atomic scientist 1037.3
atomic weight
  unit of measure 297.5
  weight 297.8
  chemistry 1058.5
atomize
  demolish 395.17
  itemize 765.6
  differentiate 779.6
  analyze 800.6
  come apart 801.9
  shatter 801.13
  disintegrate 805.3
  nucleize 1037.17
  pulverize 1049.9
  vaporize 1065.8
atomizer perfume 70.6
  sprinkler 1063.8
  vaporizer 1065.6
atom smasher 1037.11
atonal 61.4
atonality 61.1
at once hastily 401.12
  together 768.11
  jointly 799.18
  at once 829.8
  promptly 844.15
atone
  compensate 338.4
  make restitution
    481.5
  repay 624.11
  make amends 658.4
  harmonize 708.35
  tune 708.36
at one
  unanimous 332.15
  in accord 455.3
  agreeing 787.9
at one's disposal
  at one's command
    326.4
  handy 387.20

possessed 469.8
at one's fingertips
  adj handy 387.20
  adv near 223.20
at one's mercy 432.14
at one's wit's end
  in a dilemma 970.25
  at an impasse 1012.24
atonement
  compensation 338.1
  restitution 481.2
  recompense 624.3
  reparation 658.1
  function of Christ
    677.15
  propitiation 696.6
at one with
  unanimous 332.15
  concurrent 898.4
atop on top 198.15
  on high 198.16
at par 789.7
at present 837.3
at random
  haphazardly 809.18
  irregularly 850.3
  purposelessly 971.20
at rest
  adj at ease 121.12
  quiescent 173.12
  dead 307.30
  adv at ease 20.11
  beneath the sod
    309.23
at risk
  liable 896.5
  in danger 1005.13
atrocious
  painful 26.10
  horrid 98.19
  cruel 144.26
  insulting 156.8
  wrong 638.3
  wicked 654.16
  base 661.12
  savage 671.21
  terrible 999.9
atrocity
  dreadfulness 98.3
  act of cruelty 144.12
  indignity 156.2
  mistreatment 389.2
  abomination 638.2
  injustice 650.4
  iniquity 654.3
  misdeed 655.2
  violence 671.1
  evil 999.3
atrophy
  n symptom 85.9
  shrinking 260.3
  emaciation 270.6
  waste 393.4
  v waste 393.19
at sea
  adj bewildered 970.24
  muddled 984.13
  adv under way 182.63
  on the water 240.9
at stake 438.12
attach add 253.4
  annex 480.20

fasten 799.7
  attribute 887.3
attaché expert 413.11
  diplomat 576.6
attached to 104.30
attachment
  love 104.1
  addition 253.1
  adjunct 254.1
  annexation 480.5
  fidelity 644.7
  fastening 799.3
  attribution 887.1
attack
  n seizure 85.6
  plan 381.1
  manner 384.1
  war 458.1
  assault 459
  accusation 459.1
  berating 510.7
  articulation 524.6
  incrimination 599.2
  unruliness 671.3
  team 749.5
  spasm 916.6
  frenzy 925.7
  v use 384.5
  undertake 404.3
  raise one's hand
    against 457.14
  make war on 458.15
  assault 459.14
  criticize 510.20
  incriminate 599.10
  rage 671.11
  set to work 725.15
  inter advance! 459.32
attacker 459.12
attain arrive 186.6
  accomplish 407.4
attainable
  approachable 167.5
  obtainable 472.14
  practicable 965.7
  accessible 965.8
attainder 602.2
attainment
  arrival 186.1
  accomplishment
    407.1
  skill 413.8
  acquisition 472.1
  learning 927.4
attempt
  n trial 403.2
  undertaking 404.1
  v try 403.6
  undertake 404.3
  presume 640.6
attend
  v listen 48.10
  be at 221.8
  aid 449.18
  serve 577.13
  accompany 768.7
  escort 768.8
  come after 834.3
  result 886.4
  spectate 917.5
  heed 982.6
  inter hark! 48.16

attendant
  n hospital staff
    90.11
  follower 166.2
  tender 577.5
  assistant 616.6
  concomitant 768.3
  accompanier 768.4
  guardian 1007.6
  adj present 221.12
  serving 577.14
  environmental 765.8
  accompanying 768.9
  subsequent 834.4
attending
  serving 577.14
  environmental 765.8
  accompanying 768.9
attend to
  listen 48.10
  observe 434.2
  punish 604.11
  look to 982.5
  care for 1007.19
attention
  n hearing 48.1
  audition 48.2
  carefulness 339.1
  alertness 339.5
  courtesy 504.6
  curiosity 980.1
  attentiveness 982
  respects 982.1
  inter hark! 48.16
  look! 982.22
attentive
  listening 48.14
  considerate 143.16
  respectful 155.8
  careful 339.10
  meticulous 339.12
  alert 339.14
  courteous 504.14
  curious 980.5
  heedful 982.15
attenuate
  v weaken 16.10
  dilute 16.11
  abate 252.8
  shrink 260.9
  thin 270.12
  rarefy 299.3
  spiritualize 763.4
  dissipate 770.5
  adj thin 270.16
  smooth 294.8
  rare 299.4
attenuated
  diluted 16.19
  reduced 252.10
  shrunk 260.13
  thin 270.16
  haggard 270.20
  smooth 294.8
  rare 299.4
attest
  n testimony 956.2
  v depose 334.6
  secure 438.9
  evidence 956.8
  testify 956.9
  confirm 956.11

attestation
deposition 334.3
certificate 549.6
testimony 956.2
confirmation 956.4
attested affirmed 334.9
proved 956.20
assured 969.20
true 972.13
at the bottom of
adj responsible 641.17
causal 885.13
conj resulting from
886.8
at the drop of a hat
willingly 324.8
quickly 829.7
at the end of one's rope
dying 307.33
poor 619.7
wanting 991.13
straitened 1012.26
at the mercy of 896.6
at the pleasure of
432.17
at the point of
near 223.24
about to 838.13
at the same time
additionally 253.11
notwithstanding
338.8
meanwhile 825.5
simultaneously 835.7
at the wheel 417.21
attic room 197.16
storehouse 386.6
Attic witty 489.15
tasteful 496.8
simple 499.6
elegant 533.6
Attila 144.14
at times 847.5
attire
n clothing 5.1
v clothe 5.38
attitude
navigation 159.3
opinion 952.6
mental disposition
977.1
attitudinal
belief 952.21
temperamental 977.7
attitudinize 500.13
attorney steward 574.4
deputy 576.1
lawyer 597.1
attract enamor 104.23
allure 377.6
pull 906.4
interest 982.12
attraction
desirability 100.13
allurement 377.1
lure 377.3
pulling 904.1
a drawing toward 906
traction 906.1
attractive
delightful 97.7
desirable 100.30

alluring 377.8
attracting 906.5
engrossing 982.20
beautiful 1015.17
attributable
adj due 639.10
assignable 887.6
conj resulting from
886.8
attribute
n syntax 530.2
insignia 647.1
characteristic 864.4
v assign 887.3
attribution
specification 864.6
assignment of cause
887
designation 887.1
attrition
weakening 16.5
regret 113.1
decrement 252.3
reduction 255.2
consumption 388.1
abrasion 1042.2
pulverization 1049.4
attune
n harmony 708.3
v fit 405.8
harmonize 708.35
tune 708.36
make agree 787.7
attuned in accord 455.3
harmonious 708.49
at variance
adj at odds 456.16
at outs 589.12
different 779.7
disagreeing 788.6
adv in opposition
451.9
at war
adj at odds 456.16
disagreeing 788.6
adv up in arms 458.24
at which 820.8
atwitter 105.20
at worst 248.10
atypical
nonconforming 867.5
unusual 869.10
auburn
reddish-brown 40.4
redheaded 41.10
au courant 927.18
auction
n sale 734.4
v sell 734.11
auctioneer
n auction agent 730,8
v sell 734.11
audacious
insolent 142.9
defiant 454.7
daring 492.22
foolhardy 493.9
audacity
insolence 142.1
defiance 454.1
daring 492.5
foolhardiness 493.3

audible auditory 48.13
hearable 50.16
audience audition 48.2
auditory 48.6
attender 221.5
recipient 479.3
conference 541.6
playgoer 704.27
spectator 917.2
audio 48.13
audio frequency
n tone 50.2
frequency 1033.12
adj radio 1033.28
audiologist 90.11
audio-visual 48.13
audit
n accounting 628.6
v be taught 570.11
take account of 628.9
verify 969.12
check 1016.20
audition recital 48.1
hearing 48.2
examination 937.2
tryout 941.3
auditor listener 48.5
recipient 479.3
student 572.1
superintendent 574.2
accountant 628.7
treasurer 729.11
auditorium hall 197.4
arena 463.1
schoolroom 567.11
theater 704.14
parquet 704.15
auditory
n audience 48.6
adj audio 48.13
auf Wiedersehen!
188.22
auger
n point 285.3
v perforate 292.15
aught some 244.3
nothing 761.2
any 863.5
augment
aggravate 119.2
increase 251.4
add to 253.5
enlarge 259.4
augur
n predictor 961.4
v hint 133.12
augur well 124.10
augury omen 133.3
divination 961.2
august dignified 136.12
venerable 155.12
eminent 247.9
aunt 559.3
au pair girl 577.8
aura milieu 209.3
illustriousness 662.6
ectoplasm 689.7
halo 1024.14
aural eye 2.26
auditory 48.13
aureole radiation 171.2
circle 280.2

halo 1024.14
au revoir! 188.22
auricle
the hearing sense 2.10
ear 310.27
auricular
auditory 48.13
confidential 345.14
aurora dawn 314.3
foredawn 314.4
polar lights 1024.16
Aurora 314.2
auscultate 48.10
auspices
patronage 449.4
supervision 573.2
protectorship 1007.2
auspicious
promising 124.13
of good omen 133.18
timely 842.9
good 998.12
fortunate 1009.14
austere harsh 144.24
strict 425.6
inornate 499.9
plain-speaking 535.3
ascetic 667.4
simple 797.6
meager 991.10
austerity
harshness 144.9
strictness 425.1
inornateness 499.4
plain speech 535.1
thrift 635.1
asceticism 667.1
meagerness 991.2
autarchy
independence 430.5
government 612.4
absolutism 612.9
auteur
theater man 704.23
motion-picture studio
706.3
authentic
original 337.5
straight 644.14
orthodox 687.7
real 760.15
evidential 956.16
authoritative 969.18
genuine 972.15
authenticate
ratify 332.12
confirm 956.11
authenticated
accepted 332.14
proved 956.20
true 972.13
authenticity
nonimitation 337.1
candor 644.4
orthodoxy 687.1
reality 760.2
reliability 969.4
genuineness 972.7
author
n writer 547.15
discourser 556.3
literary person 718.4

avoidance
working around 368
shunning 368.1
abstinence 668.2
retreat 902.3
avoidance mechanism
92.23
avoirdupois 297.1
avouch
n promise 436.1
v affirm 334.5
promise 436.4
state 952.12
testify 956.9
avow
n oath 334.4
v acknowledge 332.11
affirm 334.5
confess 351.7
pretext 376.3
state 952.12
testify 956.9
avowal
acknowledgment
332.3
affirmation 334.1
confession 351.3
testimony 956.2
avulsion 192.1
avuncular 559.6
await wait 130.8
come 838.6
be imminent 839.2
be in the future
845.12
awake
v get up 23.4
revive 23.5
excite 105.12
come to life 306.8
adj conscious 23.8
alert 339.14
clear-witted 919.13
awaken
get up 23.4
revive 23.5
excite 105.12
come to life 306.8
rouse 375.19
disillusion 976.2
awakening
wakening 23.2
disillusionment 976.1
awake to 927.16
award
n giving 478.1
gift 478.4
reward 646.2
verdict 945.5
v give 478.12
aware sensible 24.11
knowing 927.15
attentive 982.15
awash
floating 182.60
flooded 238.25
soaked 1063.17
away
adj gone 34.4
absent 222.11
distant 261.8
adv backwards 163.13

hence 188.20
aside 218.10
elsewhere 222.18
at a distance 261.14
apart 261.17
inter go away! 908.31
away from
adv separately 801.27
prep departed 188.21
awe
n wonder 122.1
fear 127.1
respect 155.1
v astonish 122.6
terrify 127.17
daunt 127.18
command respect
155.7
awe-inspiring
awesome 122.11
terrible 127.30
venerable 155.12
grandiose 501.21
weighty 996.20
awesome awful 122.11
terrible 127.30
venerable 155.12
large 247.7
grandiose 501.21
eminent 662.18
sacred 685.7
awestruck
wondering 122.9
terrified 127.26
reverent 155.9
awful horrid 98.19
awesome 122.11
terrible 127.30
venerable 155.12
remarkable 247.11
grandiose 501.21
sacred 685.7
ugly 999.9
hideous 1014.11
awfully
awesomely 122.15
frightfully 127.34
very 247.18
distressingly 247.21
terribly 999.14
hideously 1014.13
awhile 827.9
awkward
mortifying 98.21
bulky 257.19
bungling 414.20
stiff 534.3
ignorant 929.12
inconvenient 995.7
unwieldy 1012.19
awning 1027.1
AWOL
n absence 222.4
flight 368.4
adj truant 222.13
awry
adj askew 204.14
disorderly 809.13
erroneous 974.16
adv askew 204.22
ax
n blade 462.5

execution 605.5
cutlery 1039.2
v sever 801.11
axial
flowing 172.8
central 208.11
axiom fact 760.3
essence 766.2
premise 934.7
supposition 950.3
a belief 952.2
truth 973.2
axiomatic
manifest 348.8
real 760.15
obvious 969.15
aphoristic 973.6
axis center 208.2
straight line 277.2
stem 310.19
association 617.1
fulcrum 905.3
axle 914.5
axle 914.5
an ax to grind
prejudgment 946.1
narrow-mindedness
979.1
aye
n affirmative 332.2
vote 371.6
consent 441.1
side 934.14
adv forever 828.12
inter yes 332.18
azimuth
navigation 159.3
position 161.1
direction 161.2
horizon 201.4
coordinates 300.5
azure
n blueness 45.1
heraldry 647.2
the heavens 1070.2
v blue 45.2
adj blue 45.3
Babbitt
vulgarian 497.6
conformist 866.2
babble
n nonsense 520.2
Greek 522.7
chatter 540.3
v ripple 52.11
betray 351.6
talk nonsense 520.5
be incomprehensible
522.10
chatter 540.5
be insane 925.20
babbling
n divulgence 351.2
v chattering 540.10
adj rippling 52.19
mentally deficient
921.22
delirious 925.31
babe woman 77.6
gal 302.7
infant 302.9
dupe 358.1

simple soul 416.3
endearment term
562.6
innocent 657.4
Babel clash 61.2
Greek 522.7
confusion 809.2
commotion 809.4
pandemonium 809.5
baboon 1014.4
baby
n weakling 16.6
loved one 104.11
ladylove 104.15
miniature 258.6
youngster 302.1
gal 302.7
infant 302.9
simple soul 416.3
coward 491.5
endearment term
562.6
innocent 657.4
jockey 757.2
beginner 817.2
adj miniature 258.12
infant 301.12
baby boom
reproduction 78.1
intensification 251.2
babyish infant 301.12
puerile 921.24
Babylon 654.7
baby-sit 1007.19
baby-sitter 1007.8
baccalaureate 648.6
bacchanal spree 88.5
drinker 88.11
bacchic 925.30
Bacchus 88.2
bachelor
single man 565.3
knight 608.5
degree 648.6
bachelor girl
woman 77.5
single woman 565.4
bachelorhood 565.1
bacillus 85.41
back
n exterior 206.2
setting 209.2
rear 217.1
dorsum 217.3
speech organ 524.19
type 548.6
makeup 554.12
football team 746.2
soccer team 752.2
supporter 900.2
v reverse 163.7
move 172.5
backwater 182.34
mount 193.12
be behind 217.8
secure 438.9
back up 449.13
commend 509.11
benefit 592.3
support 609.41
finance 729.15
bet 759.25

subsidize 900.21
confirm 956.11
stiffen 1044.9
adj backward 163.12
flowing 172.8
rear 217.9
hinterland 233.9
phonetic 524.31
due 623.10
past 836.12
late 845.16
adv backwards 163.13
in compensation 338.7
in reserve 386.17
ago 836.15
backache
ache 26.5
symptom 85.9
back and forth
n alternation 915.5
adj alternate 915.19
adv reciprocally 776.12
changeably 853.8
to and fro 915.21
back away 163.7
backbiting
n slander 512.3
adj disparaging 512.13
backbone pluck 359.3
fearlessness 492.4
supporter 900.2
backbreaking
laborious 725.18
troublesome 1012.18
back burner
n discontinuance 390.2
adj insignificant 997.17
back country
n open space 158.4
hinterland 233.2
adj country 233.9
backdoor 345.12
back door rear 217.1
secret passage 346.5
byway 383.4
back down
n recant 363.8
v retreat 163.6
hesitate 362.7
yield 433.7
backdrop
setting 209.2
scenery 704.20
backer giver 478.11
friend 588.1
benefactor 592.1
supporter 616.9
patron 704.26
financer 729.9
backfire
n explosion 671.7
counteraction 899.1
recoil 902.2
fire 1018.13
v explode 671.14
recoil 902.6
backflow 238.12

background
setting 209.2
the distance 261.3
experience 413.9
arena 463.1
motif 498.7
plot 722.4
cause 885.1
source 885.5
backhanded
insulting 156.8
oblique 204.13
circuitous 913.7
backing
n regress 163.3
course 172.2
means 384.2
consent 441.1
patronage 449.4
bookbinding 554.14
film 714.10
financing 729.2
reversion 858.1
support 900.1
supporter 900.2
frame 900.10
confirmation 956.4
adj approving 509.17
benefitting 592.4
backlash
n retaliation 506.1
impact 886.2
counteraction 899.1
recoil 902.2
v recoil 902.6
backlist 558.4
backlog
n store 386.1
reserve 386.3
firewood 1020.3
v store up 386.11
back matter
added to writing 254.2
makeup 554.12
part of a book 792.2
sequel 816.1
back number
n edition 554.5
old man 841.8
adj trite 117.9
old-fashioned 841.16
back off retreat 163.6
reverse 163.7
hesitate 362.7
not interfere 430.17
drive 756.4
back out
n recant 363.8
v retreat 163.6
abandon 370.5
lose one's nerve 491.8
backpack 177.30
backpedal
reverse 163.7
slow 175.9
back scratching
n obsequiousness 138.2
political influence 609.29
trading 862.2

adj obsequious 138.14
back seat
rear 217.1
inferiority 250.1
subservience 432.2
backseat driver
traveler 178.10
meddler 214.4
adviser 422.3
back side
buttocks 217.5
rear 217.1
golf 751.1
back side forward 205.7
backslapper 511.4
backslide
regress 163.5
invert 205.5
relapse 394.4
go wrong 654.9
revert 858.4
backstage
n stage 704.16
adv on the boards 704.36
back stairs
n stairs 193.3
secret passage 346.5
byway 383.4
adj covert 345.12
backstop
baseball team 745.2
safeguard 1007.3
barrier 1011.5
backstroke 182.11
back talk sass 142.4
answer 938.1
back to back
following 166.5
opposite 215.6
behind 217.13
cooperatively 450.6
same 780.6
continuously 811.8
consecutively 811.9
ongoing 811.10
sequentially 811.11
backtrack
v reverse 163.7
n reverse 163.3
backup
n reverse 163.3
reserve 386.3
deputy 576.1
game 750.2
successor 816.4
substitute 861.2
support 900.1
adj substitute 861.8
back up
reverse 163.7
move 172.5
be behind 217.8
back 449.13
represent 576.14
second 609.41
support 900.21
confirm 956.11
backward
adj reserved 139.11
reversed 163.12

flowing 172.8
retarded 175.12
inverted 205.7
rear 217.9
reluctant 325.6
distorted 342.3
reticent 344.10
undeveloped 406.12
back 836.12
late 845.16
dilatory 845.17
conservative 852.8
mentally deficient 921.22
adv inversely 205.8
rearward 217.15
ago 836.15
late 845.19
backwater
n eddy 238.12
recant 363.8
v reverse 163.7
slow 175.9
back 182.34
back when 836.15
backwoods
n hinterland 233.2
adj country 233.9
bacteria 85.41
bacterial 258.15
bactericide 86.21
bad
n vice 593.1
iniquity 654.3
evil 999.3
adj nasty 64.7
malodorous 71.5
unhealthful 82.5
ill 85.55
diseased 85.59
ominous 133.17
dying 307.33
misbehaving 322.5
crippled 393.30
decayed 393.40
wicked 654.16
inexpedient 995.5
excellent 998.13
evil 999.7
dangerous 1005.9
adv badly 999.13
bad blood
bad feeling 93.7
malevolence 144.4
hostility 451.2
disaccord 456.1
animosity 589.4
bad chemistry 93.7
bad egg 660.5
bad faith
falseheartedness 354.4
violation 435.2
infidelity 645.5
bad for 82.5
badge sign 517.1
identification 517.11
insignia 647.1
military symbol 647.5
characteristic 864.4
badger
annoy 96.13
wrest 480.22

bad guy
evildoer 593.1
actor 707.2
bad hand
handwriting 547.6
poker 759.10
badinage 490.1
badlands 890.2
bad lot
reprobate 660.5
bad person 660.6
badly off poor 619.7
unfortunate 1010.14
bad-mouth
be disrespectful 156.6
defame 512.9
underestimate 949.2
attach little
importance to 997.12
bad move 974.4
bad name 661.1
bad news
good news 552.2
bad person 660.1
bad press 510.4
bad rap 650.4
bad taste
unsavoriness 64.1
vulgarity 497.1
inelegance 534.1
bad temper
ill humor 110.1
malevolence 144.4
temper 152.6
bad trip 87.1
bad turn 144.13
bad vibes 93.7
baffle
n silencer 51.4
bewilderment 970.3
v muffle 51.9
disappoint 132.2
be incomprehensible
522.10
perplex 970.13
thwart 1011.15
baffled
disappointed 132.5
in a dilemma 970.25
at an impasse 1012.24
bafflement
disappointment 132.1
discomfiture 412.2
bewilderment 970.3
frustration 1011.3
baffling
bewildering 970.27
frustrating 1011.20
bag
n genitals 2.11
contraceptive 86.23
dose 87.19
sack 195.2
hang 202.2
quantity 247.3
breast 283.6
old woman 304.3
preference 371.5
take 480.10
occupation 724.1
purse 729.14
baseball 745.1

mode 764.4
bundle 769.8
specialty 865.1
eyesore 1014.4
v load 159.15
hang 202.6
package 212.9
bulge 283.11
acquire 472.9
catch 480.17
rob 482.16
bundle 769.20
bag and baggage
n impedimenta 471.3
adv free and clear
469.12
completely 793.14
bagatelle
hardly anything 248.5
trifle 997.5
baggage
freight 176.6
container 195.1
impedimenta 471.3
strumpet 665.14
baggy
drooping 202.10
formless 263.4
bulging 283.15
loose 803.5
bag lady 619.4
bagman
traveling salesman
730.4
fence 732.6
bookmaker 759.20
baignoire 704.15
bail
n pledge 438.2
arraignment 598.3
v ladle 176.17
bailiff steward 574.4
policeman 1007.15
bailiwick area 231.2
region 231.5
arena 463.1
bureau 594.4
occupation 724.4
sphere of influence
893.4
bail out
n rescue 398.1
aid 449.1
v parachute 184.47
emerge 190.11
escape 369.6
pledge 438.10
aid 449.11
bait
n snare 356.13
incentive 375.7
lure 377.3
v annoy 96.13
lure 377.5
discriminate against
979.8
baited 96.24
bake cook 11.4
pot 742.6
be hot 1018.22
dry 1064.6
baker 11.2

baker's dozen
extra 254.4
gratuity 478.5
thirteen 881.7
bakery 11.3
baking
n cooking 11.1
adj hot 1018.25
balance
n equanimity 106.3
mean 246.1
difference 255.8
remainder 256.1
symmetry 264.1
offset 338.2
supply 386.2
harmony 533.2
account 628.2
justice 649.1
moderation 670.1
treatment 712.9
funds 728.14
correlation 776.1
equality 789.1
stability 854.1
sensibleness 919.6
sanity 924.1
comparability 942.3
surplus 992.5
v symmetrize 264.3
weigh 297.10
offset 338.5
hesitate 362.7
keep accounts 628.8
make uniform 780.4
equal 789.5
make the same 789.6
stabilize 854.7
compare 942.4
check 1016.20
balanced
composed 106.13
symmetric 264.4
harmonious 533.8
just 649.8
uniform 780.5
poised 789.9
stable 854.12
neutralizing 899.9
sensible 919.18
sane 924.4
balance sheet 628.4
balance the books
keep accounts 628.8
equalize 789.6
check 1016.20
balcony
gallery 197.22
auditorium 704.15
platform 900.13
bald hairless 6.17
uncovered 292.17
open 348.10
unadorned 499.8
plain-speaking 535.3
balderdash
nonsense 520.2
bombast 545.2
bale
n wretchedness 96.6
burden 297.7
bundle 769.8

v bundle 769.20
balk
n disappointment
132.1
discomfiture 412.2
game 745.3
slip 974.4
frustration 1011.3
v disappoint 132.2
refuse 325.3
stickle 361.7
thwart 1011.15
balky
reluctant 325.6
obstinate 361.8
ball
n sphere 282.2
shot 462.19
dance 705.2
fun 743.2
baseball 745.1
prolate spheroid 746.1
football team 746.2
basketball 747.1
tennis 748.1
field hockey 749.4
bowling 750.1
bocci 750.3
soccer 752.1
assembly 769.2
projectile 903.5
v copulate 75.21
snowball 282.7
have a party 582.21
ballad
n popular music 708.7
song 708.14
v sing 708.38
balladeer
minstrel 710.14
composer 710.20
balladry 708.11
ball and chain
wife 563.8
impediment 1011.6
ballast
n counterbalance
297.4
offset 338.2
light source 1025.1
v trim ship 182.49
weight 297.12
stabilize 854.7
ball bearing 914.7
ballerina 705.3
ballet
n musical theater
708.34
adj dramatic 704.33
balletic
dramatic 704.33
dancing 705.6
ballistic 903.15
ballistics 462.3
ball of fire
energizer 17.6
man of action 330.8
balloon
n aerostat 181.11
bag 195.2
sphere 282.2
bubble 320.1

v grow 14.2
fly 184.36
increase 251.6
enlarge 259.5
ball 282.7
bulge 283.11
ballooning
n aviation 184.1
increase 251.1
adj drooping 202.10
bulging 283.15
balloonist 185.7
ballot
n vote 371.6
slate 609.19
v vote 371.18
ballpark figure
measurement 300.1
gamble 970.8
ballroom hall 197.4
dance emporium
705.4
entertainment 743.13
balls genitals 2.11
fearlessness 492.4
bull 520.3
ballsy 492.19
ball up
n confusion 809.2
v spoil 393.11
complicate 798.3
confuse 810.3
ballyhoo
n publicity 352.4
exaggeration 355.1
sales talk 734.5
v publicize 352.15
exaggerate 355.3
balm anesthetic 25.3
perfumery 70.2
remedy 86.1
medicine 86.4
lotion 86.11
condolence 147.1
moderator 670.3
ointment 1054.3
balmy fragrant 70.9
palliative 86.40
bright 97.11
relieving 120.9
crazy 925.27
thriving 1009.13
baloney
humbug 354.14
bullshit 520.3
balsa 180.11
balsam perfumery 70.2
remedy 86.1
medicine 86.4
balm 86.11
ointment 1054.3
balsamic
palliative 86.40
relieving 120.9
balustrade fence 212.4
post 273.4
base 900.8
bambino 302.9
bamboo grass 310.5
cane 1052.4
bamboo curtain
frontier 211.5

veil of secrecy 345.3
barrier 1011.5
bamboozle
deceive 356.14
stump 970.14
ban
n prohibition 444.1
disapproval 510.1
curse 513.1
ostracism 586.3
exclusion 772.1
v excise 255.10
prohibit 444.3
disapprove 510.10
ostracize 586.6
exclude 772.4
banish 908.17
banal trite 117.9
medium 246.3
aphoristic 973.6
banality triteness 117.3
platitude 973.3
bananas 925.27
band
n stripe 47.5
dressing 86.33
strip 271.4
circle 280.3
layer 296.1
jewel 498.6
line 517.6
association 617.1
orchestra 710.12
tennis 748.1
company 769.3
frequency 1033.13
v variegate 47.7
encircle 209.7
cooperate 450.3
put together 799.5
bind 799.9
bandage
n dressing 86.33
strip 271.4
wrapper 295.18
v blind 30.7
treat 91.24
bind 799.9
Band-Aid 86.33
band-aid
n pretext 376.1
adj makeshift 994.7
bandeau brassiere 5.24
heraldry 647.2
supporter 900.2
banded 47.15
bandied about 552.15
bandit
military aircraft 181.9
brigand 483.4
banditry theft 482.3
plundering 482.6
bandmaster 710.17
bandstand 704.16
band together
cooperate 450.3
accompany 768.7
league 804.4
the bandwagon 578.5
bandy
n field hockey 749.4
v interchange 862.4

adj deformed 265.12
bowed 279.10
bandy about
publish 352.10
interchange 862.4
bandy-legged 265.12
bane death 307.1
killing 308.1
end 395.2
destroyer 395.8
enemy 589.6
evil 999.3
affliction 1000
curse 1000.1
baneful
unhealthful 82.5
horrid 98.19
ominous 133.17
deadly 308.22
harmful 999.12
disastrous 1010.15
bang
n tuft 3.6
energy 17.3
power 18.1
noise 53.3
report 56.1
detonation 56.3
dose 87.19
excitement 105.3
gunfire 459.8
explosion 671.7
production 892.2
hit 901.4
blow 901.5
v din 53.7
crack 56.6
blast 56.8
close 293.6
collide 901.13
strike 901.15
pound 901.16
adv suddenly 829.9
inter boom! 56.13
banging crashing 56.11
large 257.21
bangle 498.6
**bang one's head
against a brick wall**
be impotent 19.7
be useless 391.8
bangs 3.6
banish
ostracize 586.6
expel 908.17
banishment
ostracism 586.3
relegation 908.4
banister
post 273.4
base 900.8
bank
n incline 204.4
border 211.4
side 218.1
shore 234.2
slope 237.2
shoal 276.2
storehouse 386.6
preserve 397.7
lending institution
620.4

treasury 729.12
banking house
729.13
workplace 739.1
pot 759.5
pile 769.10
series 811.2
buttress 900.4
barrier 1011.5
mine 1056.6
v maneuver 184.40
incline 204.10
store 386.10
fortify 460.9
pile 769.19
ignite 1019.22
bank account
account 622.2
funds 728.14
bankbook 628.4
banker
lender 620.3
money dealer 729.10
businessman 730.1
bingo 759.15
bank holiday 20.4
banking
maneuvers 184.13
money dealing 729.4
bank note 728.5
bank on
hope 124.7
plan 380.6
rely upon 952.16
bankroll
n means 384.2
roll 728.17
v subsidize 478.19
finance 729.15
bankrupt
n failure 410.7
poor man 619.4
insolvent 625.4
v impoverish 619.6
ruin 625.8
adj ruined 395.28
destitute 619.9
insolvent 625.11
bankruptcy
impairment 393.1
failure 410.1
insolvency 625.3
bank upon
rely on 952.16
plan 380.6
banned
prohibited 444.7
excluded 772.7
banner
n poster 352.7
rallying device 458.12
sign 517.1
trophy 646.3
flag 647.6
caption 936.2
adj chief 249.14
banns
betrothal 436.3
wedding 563.3
banquet
n feast 8.9
festival 743.4

fence 212.4
partition 213.5
obstruction 293.3
lock 428.5
fortification 460.4
horse racing 757.1
bar 1011.5
barring
n exclusion 772.1
prep off 255.14
excluding 772.10
barrio 230.6
barrister 597.1
barroom 88.20
barrow hill 237.4
tomb 309.16
swine 311.9
monument 549.12
bartender
liquor dealer 88.19
waiter 577.7
barter
n transfer 629.1
commerce 731.2
trading 862.2
v transfer 629.3
trade 731.14
basal basic 199.8
essential 766.9
original 885.14
basalt 1057.1
base
n station 159.2
point of departure
188.5
basement 199.2
headquarters 208.6
bottom 274.4
baseball 745.1
cause 885.1
foundation 900.6
pedestal 900.8
makeup 1015.12
acid 1058.3
v establish 159.16
adj offensive 98.18
servile 138.13
inadequate 250.7
dastardly 491.12
vulgar 497.15
populational 606.8
knavish 645.17
wicked 654.16
low 661.12
terrible 999.9
inferior 1004.9
baseboard 199.2
baseborn
populational 606.8
illegitimate 674.7
based on
supported 900.24
evidential 956.16
contingent 958.9
baseless
unsubstantiated 763.8
groundless 935.13
baseline
point of departure
188.5
baseball 745.1
basketball 747.1

tennis 748.1
basement latrine 12.10
cellar 197.17
base 199.2
storehouse 386.6
foundation 900.6
base metals 1056.3
base pay 624.4
bash
n attempt 403.3
party 582.12
blow 901.5
v injure 393.13
censure 510.13
strike 901.15
discriminate against
979.8
work evil 999.6
bashful fearful 127.23
shy 139.12
demurring 325.7
unsociable 583.5
reticent 344.10
bashing
persecution 389.3
censure 510.3
basic basal 199.8
essential 766.9
simple 797.6
original 885.14
vital 996.23
chemical 1058.8
basics
elementary education
568.5
essentials 817.6
basic training
preparation 405.1
training 568.3
basilar 199.8
basilica 703.1
basin washbasin 79.12
container 195.1
bed 199.4
plain 236.1
valley 237.7
cavity 284.2
harbor 1008.6
basis
point of departure
188.5
motive 375.1
warrant 600.6
cause 885.1
foundation 900.6
premise 934.7
topic 936.1
outlook 977.2
bask 1019.19
basket
n genitals 2.11
container 195.1
basketball 747.1
score 747.3
v package 212.9
basket case
fool 923.3
idiot 923.8
basketwork 170.3
bask in 95.12
bas-relief
protuberance 283.2

relief 715.3
bass
n part 708.22
voice 709.5
adj deep 54.10
vocal 708.50
bassist 710.5
basso 709.5
basso continuo 708.22
bastard
n man 76.5
illegitimate 561.5
bad person 660.6
adj spurious 354.25
illegitimate 674.7
bastardize 796.12
baste cook 11.4
whip 604.13
pound 901.16
bastille 429.8
bastion 460.6
bat
n the blind 30.4
drinking spree 88.6
tennis 748.1
blow 901.5
v play 745.5
strike 901.15
batch
n amount 244.2
lot 247.4
lump 257.10
bunch 769.7
product 892.4
v assemble 769.18
bate decrease 252.6
abate 252.8
subtract 255.9
blunt 286.2
discount 631.2
relax 670.9
bated muffled 52.17
reduced 252.10
bath
n bathe 79.8
dip 79.9
shower 79.10
washbasin 79.12
wetting 1063.6
v wash 79.19
bathe
n bath 79.8
aquatics 182.11
v wash 79.19
treat 91.24
swim 182.56
soak 1063.13
bather 182.12
bathetic 93.21
bathhouse 79.10
bathing
balneation 79.7
aquatics 182.11
wetting 1063.6
bathing suit 5.29
bathos
sentimentality 93.8
sadness 112.1
anticlimax 488.3
bathroom
latrine 12.10
bathing place 79.10

lavatory 197.26
baths
bathing place 79.10
health resort 91.23
spa 228.27
bathtub 79.12
bathysphere 367.5
bat of an eye 829.3
baton staff 273.2
scepter 417.9
insignia 647.1
heraldry 647.2
stigma 661.6
illegitimacy 674.2
music 711.22
batrachian
n amphibian 311.27
adj reptile 311.46
bats 925.27
battalion
military unit 461.22
company 769.3
batten
n strip 271.4
scenery 704.20
v close 293.6
gluttonize 672.4
hook 799.8
secure 854.8
thrive 1009.8
batter
n baseball team 745.2
semiliquid 1060.5
v mistreat 389.5
injure 393.13
thrash soundly
604.14
rage 671.11
pound 901.16
work evil 999.6
battered 393.33
battering trauma 85.37
unruliness 671.3
battery
military unit 461.22
artillery 462.11
corporal punishment
604.4
baseball team 745.2
electrical device
1031.20
battle
n contention 457.4
war 458.1
operation 458.5
struggle 725.3
fight 754.3
v oppose 451.4
quarrel 456.11
contend 457.13
war 458.14
fortify 460.9
struggle 725.11
battle-ax 110.12
battle cry cry 59.1
challenge 454.2
call to arms 458.8
call 517.16
battledore
textbook 554.10
elastic 1046.3
battlefield 463.2

battlefront
vanguard 216.2
battlefield 463.2
battlement 289.3
battleship 180.7
batty foolish 922.9
crazy 925.27
bauble trinket 498.4
toy 743.16
trifle 997.5
bawd 665.18
bawdy
lascivious 665.29
obscene 666.9
bawdyhouse 665.9
bawl
n cry 59.1
lament 115.3
v sob 59.6
cry 60.2
weep 115.12
wail 115.13
speak 524.26
bawl out 510.18
bay
n blare 53.5
nook 197.3
shore 234.2
ocean 240.3
inlet 242.1
recess 284.7
horse 311.11
storehouse 386.6
v blare 53.10
cry 60.2
adj reddish-brown
40.4
bay at the moon
cry 60.2
wail 115.13
be useless 391.8
bayonet 459.25
bayou tributary 238.3
inlet 242.1
bayside
n shore 234.2
adj coastal 234.7
bay window 2.17
bazaar sale 734.3
marketplace 736.2
bazooka
weapon 462.21
rocket launcher
1072.10
BC 820.13
be be able 18.11
exist 760.8
beach
n shore 234.2
golf 751.1
v shipwreck 182.42
beachcomber
vagabond 178.3
bum 331.9
wretch 660.2
beachfront
n shore 234.2
adj coastal 234.7
beachhead
vanguard 216.2
stronghold 460.6
beachside 234.7

beacon
n observation post
27.8
flying marker 184.19
alarm 400.1
signal 517.15
fire 1018.13
torch 1025.3
v lead 165.2
shine 1024.23
illuminate 1024.28
bead
n drop 282.3
v ball 282.7
figure 498.9
beaded beady 282.10
ornamented 498.11
beaded brow 12.7
beading 211.7
beadle 1007.15
beads jewel 498.6
prayer 696.4
beagle detective 576.11
jockey 757.2
policeman 1007.15
beak
n prow 216.3
spout 239.8
nose 283.8
judge 596.1
v tap 901.18
beaked 279.8
be-all and end-all
end 819.1
supremacy 249.3
all 791.3
beam
n smile 116.3
flying marker 184.19
side 218.1
breadth 269.1
shaft 273.3
buttress 900.4
lever 905.4
ray 1024.5
radio wave 1033.10
television 1034.4
signal 1035.11
wood 1052.3
v be pleased 95.11
exude cheerfulness
109.6
smile 116.7
look good 1015.16
shine 1024.23
broadcast 1033.25
transmit 1035.15
be a man 492.10
beaming happy 95.15
cheerful 109.11
gorgeous 1015.20
luminous 1024.30
beam out 171.6
bean man 76.5
head 198.6
plant 310.4
brain 918.6
trifle 997.5
beanery 8.17
beanpole slim 270.8
longlegs 272.7
beans vegetables 10.34

mescaline 87.12
nothing 761.3
beanstalk 270.8
bear
n sorehead 110.11
wild animal 311.23
short 737.12
v give birth 1.3
endure 134.5
take direction 161.7
transport 176.12
submit 433.6
suffer 443.10
aid 449.12
hold 474.7
afford 626.7
exert oneself 725.9
manipulate the
market 737.25
engender 817.14
cause 885.10
yield 891.13
support 900.21
thrust 901.12
suffice 990.4
bearable 107.13
bear arms 458.18
beard
n genitals 2.11
whiskers 3.8
type 548.6
v defy 454.3
brave 492.11
beardless hairless 6.17
childish 301.11
bear down
aggrieve 112.19
work hard 725.13
depress 912.4
bear down on
approach 167.3
sail for 182.35
press 424.6
bearer carrier 176.7
mourner 309.7
supporter 900.2
bear false witness
swear falsely 354.19
trump up a charge
599.12
bear fruit ripen 407.8
evolve 860.5
bear 891.13
bear hug hold 474.2
wrestling 474.3
embrace 562.3
bearing
n looks 33.4
navigation 159.3
direction 161.1
transportation 176.3
behavior 321.1
yield 472.5
gesture 517.14
meaning 518.1
relevance 774.4
origin 817.4
producing 891.6
trend 895.2
fulcrum 905.3
ball bearing 914.7
adj born 1.4

yielding 889.10
supporting 900.23
bearings location 159.1
navigation 159.3
orientation 161.4
heraldry 647.2
state 764.1
bear in mind think of
930.16
take cognizance of
982.9
keep in memory
988.13
bearish
irascible 110.19
ursine 311.42
gruff 505.7
bear malice
harshen 144.15
bear ill will 589.8
bear market 737.5
bear on
weigh on 297.11
relate to 774.5
operate on 888.6
rest on 900.22
evidence 956.8
bear one's cross 134.5
bear out
support 449.12
confirm 956.11
bear the brunt
endure 134.5
have trouble 1010.9
bear up
not weaken 15.10
be of good cheer
109.10
comfort 121.6
approach 167.3
buoy 298.8
stay with it 360.4
support 449.12
resist 453.2
keep up one's courage
492.15
support 900.21
bear upon
exercise influence
893.9
thrust 901.12
bear with endure 134.5
condone 148.4
be easy on 427.5
suffer 443.10
bear witness
be pious 692.6
testify 956.9
beastly hoggish 80.24
offensive 98.18
horrid 98.19
cruel 144.26
animal 311.38
gruff 505.7
carnal 663.6
terrible 999.9
beast of burden
pack animal 176.8
drudge 726.3
beat
n staccato 55.1
parasite 138.5

sphere 231.2
routine 373.6
route 383.1
accent 524.11
news item 552.3
rhythm 709.22
tempo 709.24
throb 709.26
meter 720.7
occupation 724.4
periodicity 849.2
round 849.3
circuit 913.2
pulsation 915.3
flutter 916.4
v get tired 21.6
drum 55.4
sail near the wind
  182.25
change course 182.30
best 249.7
foam 320.5
deceive 356.19
hunt 382.9
injure 393.13
vanquish 411.5
defeat 412.9
whip 604.13
time 708.44
din 848.10
pound 901.16
pulsate 915.12
agitate 916.10
flutter 916.12
stump 970.14
pulverize 1049.9
adj tired 21.8
defeated 412.15
without money 619.10
unconventional 867.6
licked 970.26
beat about
change course 182.30
grope 937.31
be uncertain 970.9
have difficulty
  1012.11
beat a dead horse
be useless 391.8
dwell on 848.9
persist 855.5
carry coals to
  Newcastle 992.12
beat around the bush
dodge 368.8
circumlocute 538.10
quibble 935.9
beat back 907.3
beat down
sadden 112.18
raze 395.19
subdue 432.9
domineer 612.16
cheapen 633.6
bargain 731.17
beaten burnt-out 21.10
bubbly 320.6
habitual 373.15
defeated 412.14
beaten path
routine 373.6
path 383.2

beater hunter 382.5
mixer 796.9
agitator 916.9
beatific happy 95.15
blissful 97.9
heavenly 681.12
beatified happy 95.15
eminent 662.18
angelic 679.6
heavenly 681.12
sanctified 685.8
raised 911.9
beatify
gladden 95.8
glorify 662.13
sanctify 685.5
exalt 911.6
beating
n staccato 55.1
defeat 412.1
corporal punishment
  604.4
hit 901.4
pulsation 915.3
flutter 916.4
pulverization 1049.4
adj staccato 55.7
rhythmic 709.28
periodic 849.7
pulsative 915.18
beat into one's head
inculcate 568.12
convince 952.18
beat it
v depart 188.7
leave 222.10
flee 368.11
inter go away! 908.31
beatitude
happiness 95.2
sanctification 685.3
beatnik 867.3
beat one's brains 930.9
beat one's breast
  115.11
beat out best 249.7
pulsate 915.12
**beat someone to the
  punch** 844.6
beat the drum for
publicize 352.15
espouse 509.13
beat the rap
get off 369.7
go free 431.9
beat the system 409.13
beat time
keep rhythm 708.44
time 831.11
pulsate 915.12
beat up
v punish 604.15
agitate 916.10
emulsify 1060.10
adj tired 21.8
spoiled 393.29
dilapidated 393.33
slovenly 809.15
beau
n inamorato 104.13
dandy 500.9
v court 562.21

Beau Brummel
dandy 500.9
person of fashion
  578.7
beaucoup
adj much 247.8
plural 882.7
plentiful 990.7
adv greatly 247.15
beaut
first-rate 998.7
beauty 1015.9
beautician 1015.13
beautification
development 392.2
prettification 1015.11
beautified
improved 392.13
beautifying 1015.22
beautiful
adj artistic 712.20
beauteous 1015.17
inter bravo! 509.22
beautiful people 578.6
beautify
develop 392.10
ornament 498.8
prettify 1015.15
beauty harmony 533.2
attractiveness 1015
beautifulness 1015.1
charmer 1015.8
beauty parlor
workplace 739.1
salon de beauté
  1015.14
beauty queen 1015.8
beauty sleep 22.2
beaux arts 712.1
beaver
n beard 3.8
man of action 330.8
v work hard 725.13
bebop 708.9
becalm 173.11
becalmed 173.17
because 887.10
bechance 971.11
becharm
delight 95.9
enamor 104.23
fascinate 377.7
charm 691.8
beck and call 420.5
beckon
n gesture 517.14
v attract 377.6
gesture 517.21
becloud fog 319.6
conceal 346.6
confuse 984.7
darken 1026.9
opaque 1030.2
become behoove 641.4
come to be 760.12
originate 817.13
convert 857.11
change into 857.17
become of 886.4
become one
get married 563.15
beautify 1015.15

becoming
n conversion 857.1
adj decorous 496.10
rightful 639.8
decent 664.5
apt 787.10
expedient 994.5
comely 1015.18
bed
n bottom 199.1
floor 199.4
furniture 229.1
watercourse 239.2
layer 296.1
accommodations
  385.3
presswork 548.9
marriage 563.1
bowling 750.1
foundation 900.6
sofa 900.19
garden 1067.10
v rest 20.6
retire 22.17
put to bed 22.19
inset 191.5
house 225.10
fix 854.9
plant 1067.18
tend 1068.7
bed and board 385.3
bed and breakfast
  228.15
bedarken blacken 38.7
darken 1026.9
bedaub soil 80.16
coat 295.24
stain 1003.6
bedazzle blind 30.7
astonish 122.6
confuse 984.7
shine 1024.23
bedazzled
blinded 30.10
dazed 984.14
bedbug 311.36
bedchamber 197.7
bedding blanket 295.10
layer 296.1
foundation 900.6
underbed 900.20
bedecked clothing 5.44
ornamented 498.11
bedevil annoy 96.13
demonize 680.16
bewitch 691.9
bedeviled
tormented 96.24
possessed 925.29
bedew 1063.12
bedfast 85.58
bedfellow companion
  588.3
associate 616.1
bedim 1026.9
bedimming
inconspicuousness
  32.2
decoloration 36.3
darkening 1026.6
bedizen dress up 5.41
color 35.13

ornament 498.8

bedizened
ornamented 498.11
grandiloquent 545.8

bedlam
noise 53.3
pandemonium 809.5
insane asylum 925.14

bed of roses
comfort 121.1
prosperity 1009.1

Bedouin 178.4

bedpan 12.11

bedraggled
soiled 80.21
slovenly 809.15

bedrape 5.38

bedridden 85.58

bedrock
n bottom 199.1
base 274.4
stability 854.6
foundation 900.6
rock 1057.1
adj bottom 199.7
deepest 275.15
vital 996.23

bedroom
n boudoir 197.7
v restrict 428.9

bedsheet 295.10

bedsore 85.36

bedspread 295.10

bedsprings 900.20

bedstead 900.19

bedtime sleep 22.2
night 315.4

bedwarf 252.9

bee honeybee 311.33
quilting bee 582.14

beef
n food 10.13
muscularity 15.2
power 18.1
complaint 115.5
weight 297.1
cattle 311.6
objection 333.2
bone of contention
456.7
v be discontented
108.6
complain 115.16
object 333.5

beefcake 714.3

beefeater 1007.14

beefheaded 921.15

beefing
n complaint 115.5
adj discontented 108.8
complaining 115.20

beefsteak 10.17

beef up
strengthen 15.13
intensify 251.5
add to 253.5

beefy strong 15.15
corpulent 257.18

beehive nest 228.25
hive 739.2

bee in one's bonnet
926.2

beekeeper 1068.4

beekeeping 1068.1

beeline
shortcut 268.5
straight line 277.2

Beelzebub 680.4

beep
n noise 53.5
v blare 53.10

beeper
telephone 347.4
alarm 400.1

beer 88.16

beerbelly 2.17

beer garden 88.20

beery
intoxicated 88.31
sentimental 93.21

beeswax 1054.8

beetle
n insect 311.31
jockey 757.2
pulper 1061.4
v overhang 202.7
adj overhanging
202.11

beetle-browed
sullen 110.24
overhanging 202.11

befall occur 830.5
chance 971.11

befit behoove 641.4
expedite one's affair
994.3

befitting apt 787.10
timely 842.9
expedient 994.5

befog
cover 295.19
cloud 319.6
conceal 346.6

befool fool 356.15
stultify 922.7

before
adv in front 165.4
ahead 216.12
preferably 371.28
above 813.6
previously 833.6
formerly 836.13
early 844.11
prep in the presence of
221.18
prior to 833.7

beforehand
adj anachronistic
832.3
adv early 844.11

before long
in the future 838.9
soon 844.16

beforementioned 813.5

before one's eyes
adj visible 31.6
adv before 216.12
openly 348.15

before the bar
adv all things
considered 945.17
phrs in litigation
598.21

before the house 937.38

beforetime
adj early 844.7
adv formerly 836.13
early 844.11

befoul defile 80.17
misuse 389.4
work evil 999.6

befouling 393.2

befriend aid 449.11
make friends with
587.10
benefit 592.3

befrilled
ornamented 498.11
ornate 545.11

befringed 211.12

befuddle
intoxicate 88.22
confuse 984.7

befuddled 984.13

beg
n governor 575.13
v evade 368.7
find means 384.6
entreat 440.11
scrounge 440.15

beget procreate 78.8
engender 817.14
cause 885.10
produce 889.7
originate 891.12

begetter parent 560.8
author 885.4
producer 891.7

beggar
n vagabond 178.3
bum 331.9
nonworker 331.11
mendicant 440.8
poor man 619.4
wretch 660.2
v strip 480.24
impoverish 619.6

beggar description
stagger belief 122.8
look good 1015.16

beggarly
obsequious 138.14
low 497.15
indigent 619.8
ill-provided 991.12
paltry 997.21

begild color 35.13
yellow 43.3

begin 817.7

begin again 855.6

beginner novice 572.9
neophyte 817.2
author 885.4
producer 891.7

beginning
n start 817
commencement 817.1
source 885.5
production 891.1
adj simple 797.6
initial 817.15

beginnings
origin 817.4
earliness 844.1

beg off abandon 370.5

refuse 442.3

begone
v depart 188.6
inter go away! 908.31

beg pardon
repent 113.7
apologize 658.5

begrime 80.15

begrudge envy 154.3
refuse 325.3
deny 442.4
stint 484.5

beg the question
dodge 368.8
quibble 935.9

beg to differ 333.4

beguile
deceive 356.14
fascinate 377.7
amuse 743.21
distract 984.6

beguiled
wondering 122.9
foolish 922.8

beguiling
n allurement 377.1
adj wonderful 122.10
deceptive 356.21
alluring 377.8
amusing 743.27

be had 632.8

behalf benefit 387.4
good 998.4

behave act 321.4
conduct oneself 321.5
be good 328.4

behavior
conditioning 92.26
tendency 321
conduct 321.1
action 328.1

behavioral
behaviorist 321.7
acting 328.10

behaviorism
behavioral science
321.3
materialism 1050.6

behaviorist 321.7

behead 604.17

behemoth 257.14

behest 420.1

behind
n rear 217.1
buttocks 217.5
adj retarded 175.12
adv after 166.6
in the rear 217.13
late 845.19
short 910.6
prep back of 449.27
after 834.8

behindhand
adj defaulting 625.10
anachronous 832.3
late 845.16
adv late 845.19
in arrears 910.6

behind the eight ball
1012.22

behind the scenes
adj invisible 32.5

manipulation 415.4
causal 885.13
cognizant of 927.16
adv behind 217.13
secretly 345.17
on the stage 704.36
behind the times
841.16
behold
v see 27.12
inter attention! 982.22
beholden
grateful 150.5
obliged 641.16
beholder
recipient 479.3
spectator 917.1
behoof
benefit 387.4
good 998.4
behoove 641.4
beige brown 40.3
yellow 43.4
being
n heart 93.3
organism 305.2
person 312.5
existence 760.1
something 762.3
adj existent 760.13
present 837.2
being as how 887.10
be it so 332.20
bejeweled 498.11
belabor whip 604.13
dwell on 848.9
emphasize 996.14
belabored 848.15
belaboring 604.4
belated 845.16
belay fasten 799.7
secure 854.8
cease 856.6
bel canto 708.13
belch
n rasp 58.3
outburst 671.6
burp 908.9
v sound harshly 58.9
erupt 671.13
burp 908.28
beldam bitch 110.12
old woman 304.3
witch 593.7
violent person 671.9
beleaguer annoy 96.13
enclose 212.5
besiege 459.19
belfry 272.6
belie deny 335.4
misrepresent 350.3
falsify 354.15
contradict 451.6
disprove 957.4
belied 957.7
belief
n religion 675.1
trust 952
credence 952.1
confidence 969.5
adj of belief 952.21
believable 952.24

believe be pious 692.6
suppose 950.10
credit 952.10
have faith in 952.15
believer
religionist 675.15
truster 692.4
zealot 952.9
belittle minimize 252.9
disparage 512.8
underestimate 949.2
belittled 252.10
belittle oneself 137.7
bell
n gong 54.4
marker 517.10
signal 517.15
wind instrument
711.6
time of day 831.2
stop 856.2
v blare 53.10
cry 60.2
belle
fine lady 500.10
beauty 1015.8
belles lettres
writing 547.12
literature 718.1
bellhop
errand boy 353.4
attendant 577.5
bellicose
contentious 110.26
partisan 456.17
warlike 458.21
contrary 778.6
bellied
rotund 282.8
bulged 283.16
belligerent
n combatant 461.1
adj contentious 110.26
partisan 456.17
warlike 458.21
hostile 589.10
contrary 778.6
bellow
n cry 59.1
v roar 59.6
cry 60.2
be excitable 105.16
speak 524.26
bellowing 105.25
bellows lungs 2.20
blower 318.18
bell-shaped 279.13
bell the cat
brave 492.11
court danger 493.6
bellwether
n sheep 311.7
leader 574.6
precursor 815.1
adj original 337.5
belly
n digestive system
2.16
bottom 199.1
sphericity 282.1
type 548.6
v bulge 283.11

bellyache
n ache 26.5
complaint 115.5
v be discontented
108.6
complain 115.16
belly dancer 707.1
bellyful
full measure 793.3
satiety 993.1
bellying
n convexity 283.1
protuberance 283.2
adj bulging 283.15
bellyland 184.43
belly laugh
n laughter 116.4
joke 489.6
v laugh 116.8
belly up
v die 307.20
go bankrupt 625.7
adj ruined 395.29
insolvent 625.11
ended 819.9
belong .
have place 159.9
hold membership
617.15
belonging 774.11
belongings 471.2
belong to
pertain to 469.7
relate to 774.5
beloved
n sweetheart 104.10
adj loved 104.24
below
adv down 194.13
on earth 234.9
underneath 274.10
hellishly 682.9
prep under 274.11
subordinate to 432.17
after 834.8
below par
adj ill 85.55
terrible 999.9
sub-standard 1004.10
adv beneath norm
274.10
at a discount 631.3
below the belt 650.10
below the mark
below 274.10
amiss 910.7
belt
n waistband 5.19
stripe 47.5
excitement 105.3
region 231.1
inlet 242.1
strip 271.4
circle 280.3
layer 296.1
attempt 403.3
victory 411.1
slap 604.3
whip 605.1
trophy 646.3
fight 754.3
blow 901.5

punch 901.6
v encircle 209.7
whip 604.13
play 745.5
bind 799.9
strike 901.15
belt out 708.38
belt-tightening
strictness 425.1
thrift 635.1
asceticism 667.1
belvedere
observation post 27.8
cigar 89.4
bemingle 796.10
bemire dirty 80.15
mire 243.2
bemist 319.6
bemoan regret 113.6
lament 115.10
bemuse 88.22
bemused
intoxicated 88.31
abstracted 984.11
be my guest 440.20
bench
fitness 84.1
plateau 272.4
authority 417.10
council 423.1
seat of justice
595.5
team 617.7
workplace 739.1
hockey players 749.2
substitute 861.2
table 900.15
bench mark
location 159.1
marker 517.10
salient point 996.6
bend
n obeisance 155.2
deviation 164.1
bias 204.3
diagonal 204.7
angle 278.2
bending 279.3
heraldry 647.2
crouch 912.3
v bow 155.6
direct 161.5
deviate 164.3
deflect 164.5
oblique 204.9
distort 265.5
angle 278.5
curve 279.6
conquer 412.10
subdue 432.9
submit 433.10
bind 799.9
conform 866.3
influence 893.7
crouch 912.8
depress 912.9
prejudice 979.9
yield 1045.7
bend an ear
listen 48.10
hearken to 982.7
bender 88.6

bending
 n deflection 164.2
 bend 279.3
 deliberate falsehood
  354.9
 adj pliant 1045.9
bend one's ear 524.21
bend over backwards
 be willing 324.3
 make a special effort
  403.11
 jump at 101.6
 be careful 339.7
 be just 649.6
the bends 1073.10
bene! 509.22
beneath
 below 274.11
 under 432.17
beneath one's dignity
 inferior 250.6
 disgraceful 661.11
Benedict Arnold 357.10
benediction
 thanks 150.2
 blessing 696.5
benedictory 696.15
benefaction
 act of kindness 143.7
 benefit 478.7
benefactor helper 449.7
 philanthopist 592
 benefactress 592.1
benefice 698.9
beneficence 143.4
beneficent
 benevolent 143.15
 favorable 449.22
beneficial
 healthful 81.5
 useful 387.18
 helpful 449.21
 good 998.12
beneficiary
 proprietor 470.2
 allottee 479.4
 benefice-holder 699.7
beneficience 133.9
benefit
 n act of kindness
  143.7
 use 387.4
 aid 449.1
 estate 471.4
 benefaction 478.7
 theatrical
  performance 704.12
 good 998.4
 v do a favor 143.12
 avail 387.17
 aid 449.11
 help 592.3
 expedite one's affair
  994.3
 do good 998.10
benevolence
 auspiciousness 133.9
 good nature 143
 charity 143.4
 act of kindness 143.7
 pity 145.1
 forgiveness 148.1

compliance 427.2
 benefit 478.7
 magnanimity 652.2
 goodness 998.1
benevolent
 charitable 143.15
 forgiving 148.6
 favorable 449.22
 magnanimous 652.6
 indulgent 427.8
 good 998.12
benighted blind 30.9
 night-overtaken
  315.10
 dark 929.16
benign
 healthful 81.5
 auspicious 133.18
 kind 143.13
 indulgent 427.8
 favorable 449.22
 harmless 998.21
benignity
 auspiciousness 133.9
 kindness 143.1
 act of charity 143.7
 compliance 427.2
 goodness 998.1
 harmlessness 998.9
benison
 benediction 696.5
 good 998.4
bent
 n inclination 100.3
 direction 161.1
 bias 204.3
 preference 371.5
 aptitude 413.5
 tendency 895.1
 disposition 977.3
 prejudice 979.3
 adj high 87.23
 drunk 88.33
 distorted 265.10
 angular 278.6
 curved 279.7
 disposed 977.8
benthic 275.14
bent on
 desirous of 100.22
 determined upon
  359.16
 disposed 977.8
bent out of shape
 152.30
benumb deaden 25.4
 numb 94.8
 relieve 120.5
 freeze 1022.10
benumbed
 insensible 25.6
 apathetic 94.13
 languid 331.20
be off
 v depart 188.6
 set out 188.8
 race 757.5
 inter go away! 908.31
be on to 940.8
bequeath
 will 478.18
 transfer 629.3

bequeathal
 bequest 478.10
 inheritance 479.2
 transfer 629.1
bequest
 bequeathal 478.10
 inheritance 479.2
be quiet! 51.14
bereave leave 307.28
 take from 480.21
 widow 566.6
bereaved bereft 307.35
 sorrowful 473.8
 indigent 619.8
bereavement
 deathliness 307.11
 loss 473.1
 deprivation 480.6
bereft bereaved 307.35
 at a loss 473.8
 indigent 619.8
 wanting 991.13
berg 1022.5
beribboned 498.11
berm shore 234.2
 path 383.2
berry 310.29
berserk
 n violent person 671.9
 lunatic 925.15
 adj frenzied 105.25
 rabid 925.30
berth
 n anchor 180.16
 quarters 228.4
 position 724.5
 harbor 1008.6
 v inhabit 225.7
 house 225.10
beseech entreat 440.11
 pray 696.12
beset
 v annoy 96.13
 make anxious 126.5
 enclose 212.5
 persecute 389.7
 importune 440.12
 besiege 459.19
 infest 909.6
 obsess 925.25
 trouble 1012.13
 adj distressed 96.22
 tormented 96.24
 worried 126.8
 enclosed 212.10
 infested 909.11
 troubled 1012.20
besetting
 prevalent 863.12
 troublesome 1012.18
beside
 adj side 218.6
 adv in juxtaposition
  223.21
 additionally 253.11
 prep alongside 218.11
 excluding 772.10
 compared to 942.11
beside oneself
 overjoyed 95.16
 frenzied 105.25
 angry 152.28

rabid 925.30
 distracted 984.10
beside the point
 adj irrelevant 775.7
 adv amiss 910.7
besiege enclose 212.5
 importune 440.12
 lay siege to 459.19
besmear color 35.13
 soil 80.16
 coat 295.24
 stain 1003.6
besmirch blacken 38.7
 soil 80.16
 vilify 512.10
 stigmatize 661.9
 stain 1003.6
besmirched
 dingy 38.11
 soiled 80.21
 unchaste 665.23
 stained 1003.10
besot deaden 25.4
 intoxicate 88.22
besotted
 intoxicated 88.31
 foolish 922.8
 obsessed 925.33
bespangled
 spotted 47.13
 ornamented 498.11
 illuminated 1024.39
bespatter
 spatter 80.18
 vilify 512.10
 stigmatize 661.9
 moisten 1063.12
bespeak outfit 5.40
 request 440.9
 signify 517.17
 mean 518.8
 address 524.27
 employ 615.14
 evidence 956.8
bespeckle
 variegate 47.7
 spot 1003.5
bespoke tailored 5.47
 made 891.18
best
 v excel 249.6
 beat 249.7
 vanquish 411.5
 defeat 412.6
 adj superlative 249.13
 reduced 633.9
 the tops 998.16
 n creature comforts
  121.3
 the top of the line
  249.5
 choice 998.8
best bet 971.8
best case
 n hope 124.1
 adj promising 124.13
bestial
 cruel 144.26
 animal 311.38
 unrefined 497.12
 carnal 663.6
 savage 671.21

bestiality
perversion 75.11
cruelty 144.11
sadism 144.12
unrefinement 497.3
carnality 663.2
terribleness 999.2
be still 51.14
bestir oneself
stir 330.11
make haste 401.5
best man
wedding party 563.4
assistant 616.6
bestow spend 387.13
give 478.12
administer 643.6
bestraddle
mount 193.12
rise above 272.11
overlie 295.30
rest on 900.22
bestride mount 193.12
rise above 272.11
overlie 295.30
dominate 612.15
rest on 900.22
pass 909.8
best seller
great success 409.3
book 554.1
best wishes
congratulation 149.1
regards 504.8
greetings 585.3
bet
n gamble 759.2
wager 759.3
poker 759.10
v ante 759.25
predict 961.9
risk 971.12
betake oneself 177.18
beta particle
electron 1032.3
radioactive particle
1036.4
bête noire
frightener 127.9
enemy 589.6
bugbear 680.9
bane 1000.1
be that as it may 338.8
bethink oneself
think 930.8
attend to 982.5
remember 988.10
betide occur 830.5
chance 971.11
betimes early 844.11
soon 844.16
bêtise stupidity 921.3
foolishness 922.1
betoken augur 133.12
manifest 348.5
signify 517.17
mean 518.8
evidence 956.8
bet on bet 759.25
rely on 952.16
predict 961.9
be certain 969.9

betray inform 351.6
deceive 356.14
defect 370.6
rat on 551.12
double-cross 645.14
seduce 665.20
betrayal
divulgence 351.2
apostasy 363.2
desertion 370.2
betrayment 645.8
seduction 665.6
betrayed 132.5
betrothal 436.3
betrothed
n fiancé 104.17
adj promised 436.8
better
v excel 249.6
improve 392.9
change 851.7
adj superior 249.12
preferable 371.25
augmented 392.14
changed 851.10
better half
spouse 563.6
wife 563.8
betterment
improvement 392.1
change 851.1
better self
compunction 113.2
self 864.5
betting parlor 759.19
bettor 759.21
between 213.12
**between the devil and
the deep blue sea**
in danger 1005.13
unfortunate 1010.14
in a dilemma 1012.23
between the lines 519.5
betweentimes
meanwhile 825.5
occasionally 847.5
betwixt 213.12
betwixt and between
adj ambiguous 539.4
mediocre 1004.7
adv midway 818.5
prep between 213.12
bet your life 972.25
bevel
n incline 204.4
instrument 278.4
type 548.6
adj inclining 204.15
beveled 204.15
beverage liquid 8.4
drink 10.47
spirits 88.13
fluid 1059.2
bevy company 769.3
assemblage 769.6
multitude 883.3
bewail regret 113.6
lament 115.10
beware 494.7
bewhiskered
bearded 3.25
trite 117.9

bewilder
astonish 122.6
disconcert 970.12
confuse 984.7
bewildered
wondering 122.9
dismayed 970.24
at an impasse 1012.24
bewildering
wonderful 122.10
confusing 970.27
bewitch
delight 95.9
enamor 104.23
fascinate 377.7
demonize 680.16
cast a spell 690.13
witch 691.9
work evil 999.6
bewitched
enamored 104.28
wondering 122.9
witched 691.13
miraculous 869.16
bewitching
delightful 97.7
alluring 377.8
witching 691.11
bey
ruler 575.9
governor 575.13
beyond
adv additionally
253.11
prep distant 261.21
past 522.26
after 834.8
in excess of 992.26
the beyond 838.2
**beyond a shadow of
doubt** 969.16
beyond belief
absurd 922.11
unbelievable 954.10
beyond compare
adj peerless 249.15
adv extremely 247.22
beyond measure
extremely 247.22
superabundantly
992.24
beyond one
adj hard to
understand 522.14
impracticable 966.8
adv unrealistic 19.20
beyond question
adj undoubted 969.16
adv unquestionably
969.25
beyond recall 125.15
beyond the call of duty
492.1
beyond the pale
prohibited 444.7
unpraiseworthy
510.24
segregated 772.8
beyond words 98.19
biannual 849.8
bias
n inclination 100.3

deviation 164.1
bend 204.3
diagonal 204.7
preference 371.5
partiality 650.3
tendency 895.1
disposition 977.3
prejudice 979.3
v deflect 164.5
oblique 204.9
pervert 265.6
influence 893.7
tend 895.3
prejudice 979.9
adj inclining 204.15
transverse 204.19
adv diagonally 204.25
biaxial 874.7
bib
n apron 5.17
v drink 8.29
tipple 88.24
bibacious 88.35
bibelot trinket 498.4
trifle 997.5
Bible scripture 683.1
Holy Bible 683.2
Biblical 683.10
bibliographer
writer 547.15
author 718.4
bibliography
makeup 554.12
bibliology 554.19
Modern Language
Association
Bibliography 558.4
directory 574.10
catalog 870.3
lore 927.9
bibliolatry
strictness 687.5
zeal 692.3
scholarship 927.5
bibliophile
booklover 554.18
bookworm 928.4
bibliophilic 927.22
bibulous
bibacious 88.35
sorbent 187.17
intemperate 669.7
bicameral
legislative 613.11
bipartite 874.7
bicentenary 849.4
bicentennial
anniversary 849.4
hundred 881.8
biceps member 2.7
arm 905.5
bicker
n quarrel 456.5
argumentation 934.4
v quarrel 456.11
flutter 916.12
argue 934.16
quibble 935.9
flicker 1024.25
bickerer 461.1
bicolored 47.9
bicorn 279.11

binder
  dressing 86.33
  wrapper 295.18
  payment 624.1
binding
  n edging 211.7
  wrapper 295.18
  bookbinding 554.14
  fastening 799.3
  cohesion 802.1
  adj preceptive 419.4
  mandatory 420.12
  compulsory 424.11
  obligatory 641.15
  joining 799.16
  valid 972.14
bind up
  bundle 769.20
  bind 799.9
binge 88.6
bingo 759.15
binocular
  optic 29.9
  bipartite 874.7
binoculars 29.4
binomial
  terminological 527.17
  bipartite 874.7
biochemical
  n element 1058.2
  adj chemical 1058.8
biodegradable
  degradable 393.47
  disintegrative 805.5
bioethics 636.1
biographer 719.4
biographical 719.7
biography
  n history 719.1
  v chronicle 719.5
biohazard 85.32
biological
  organic 305.17
  related 559.6
  botanical 1066.3
biological clock 306.3
biological urge 75.5
biologist 1066.2
biology
  organic matter 305.1
  animal life 311.1
  the study of living
    things 1066
  biological science
    1066.1
biomechanical 1038.7
bionics 1040.2
biophysicist 1017.2
biopsy 91.12
biorhythm 306.3
biosphere
  organic matter 305.1
  ecosphere 306.6
  atmosphere 317.2
  Earth 1070.10
biotic 305.17
bipartisan
  partisan 609.44
  two 872.6
bipartisanship 450.1
bipartite
  separate 801.20

two 872.6
  bifid 874.7
biped
  n creature 311.3
  adj bipartite 874.7
birch
  n rod 605.2
  v whip 604.13
bird poultry 10.21
  man 76.5
  woman 77.6
  fowl 311.28
  oddity 869.4
  freak 926.4
  beauty 1015.9
  rocket 1072.3
bird's-eye view
  viewpoint 27.7
  appearance 33.6
  abridgment 557.1
birdbrained 921.20
birdcage
  gambling wheel
    759.16
  birdhouse 228.23
birdcall
  animal noise 60.1
  call 517.16
birdhouse 228.23
bird in hand 469.1
bird of passage
  wanderer 178.2
  bird 311.28
bird of prey
  hunter 311.28
  extortionist 480.12
bird sanctuary
  preserve 397.7
  refuge 1008.1
birds of a feather 783.5
bird-watcher 917.1
birth
  n genesis 1
  beginning 1.1
  generation 78.6
  life 306.1
  lineage 560.4
  heredity 560.6
  aristocracy 607.3
  nobility 608.2
  origin 817.4
  v engender 817.14
  adj related 559.6
birth control 890.1
birth control device
  86.23
birthday 849.4
birthday suit 6.3
birth defect 85.1
birthmark mark 517.5
  blemish 1003.1
birth parent 560.8
birthplace
  fatherland 232.2
  breeding place 885.8
birthright
  inheritance 479.2
  prerogative 642.1
birthstone 1057.6
biscuit sinker 10.29
  cookie 10.41
  ceramic ware 742.2

dryness 1064.2
bisect sever 801.11
  seek the middle 818.3
  double 872.5
  halve 874.4
bisector 874.3
bisexual
  n homosexual 75.14
  adj homosexual 75.29
  bipartite 874.7
bisexuality
  sexuality 75.2
  sexual preference 75.10
bishop clergy 699.9
  chessman 743.17
bishopric region 231.5
  mastership 417.7
  diocese 698.8
bison 311.6
bisque 742.2
bistro restaurant 8.17
  bar 88.20
bit short distance 223.2
  modicum 248.2
  point 285.3
  portion 477.5
  information theory
    551.7
  act 704.7
  role 704.10
  script 706.2
  piece 792.3
  shift 824.3
  short time 827.3
  pittance 991.5
  trifle 997.5
  curb 1011.7
  binary digit 1041.14
a bit to a degree 245.7
  scarcely 248.9
bit by bit
  by degrees 245.6
  piece by piece 792.9
bitch
  n woman 77.6
  female animal 77.9
  shrew 110.12
  complaint 115.5
  dog 311.17
  objection 333.2
  strumpet 665.14
  card 758.2
  first-rate 998.7
  tough proposition
    1012.2
  v be discontented
    108.6
  sulk 110.14
  complain 115.16
  object 333.5
  bungle 414.12
bitchy irascible 110.20
  malicious 144.20
  spiteful 144.21
  disparaging 512.13
bite
  n morsel 8.2
  light meal 8.7
  acrimony 17.5
  pang 26.2
  sip 62.2
  zest 68.2

modicum 248.2
  minute 258.7
  hold 474.2
  portion 477.5
  vigor 544.3
  round 751.3
  piece 792.3
  cold 1022.1
  v chew 8.27
  pain 26.7
  nip 68.5
  come to a point 285.6
  hold 474.6
  etch 713.10
  kid oneself 953.6
  freeze 1022.10
**bite off more than one
  can chew**
  overextend oneself
    404.6
  overindulge 669.5
bite one's tongue
  n change one's tune
    363.6
  v be silent 51.5
  regret 113.6
  be humiliated 137.9
  keep to oneself 344.6
bite the bullet
  endure 134.6
  submit 433.6
  brave 492.11
  seize the opportunity
    842.7
bite the dust die 307.20
  be destroyed 395.22
  lose 412.12
**bite the hand that
  feeds one**
  be ungrateful 151.3
  play one false 645.13
biting
  acrimonious 17.14
  painful 26.10
  pungent 68.6
  penetrating 105.31
  caustic 144.23
  witty 489.15
  vigorous 544.11
  cold 1022.14
a bit much
  insufferable 98.25
  excessive 992.16
bitter
  v sour 110.16
  adj acrimonious 17.14
  flavored 62.9
  galling 64.6
  pungent 68.6
  unpleasant 98.17
  distressing 98.20
  sour 110.23
  caustic 144.23
  resentful 152.26
  hostile 589.10
  cold 1022.14
bitter end 819.2
bitterly
  caustically 144.32
  distressingly 247.21
bitter pill
  acridness 64.2

blare 53.10
detonate 56.8
use 87.21
kill 308.13
blow 318.20
blow up 395.18
pull the trigger 459.22
curse 513.5
explode 671.14
thwart 1011.15
freeze 1023.11
inter damn! 513.12
blasted
high 87.23
disappointed 132.5
blighted 393.42
ruined 395.28
curse 513.10
blast off
v begin 817.7
launch 1072.13
n beginning 817.1
rocket launching
  1072.9
blat
n blare 53.5
rasp 58.3
v blare 53.10
sound harshly 58.9
cry 60.2
speak 524.26
blatant
noisy 53.13
vociferous 59.10
howling 60.6
conspicuous 348.12
gaudy 501.20
blatantly
distressingly 247.21
conspicuously 348.16
gaudily 501.27
blather
n nonsense 520.2
chatter 540.3
v talk nonsense 520.5
chatter 540.5
be stupid 921.12
blaze
n outburst 105.9
notch 289.1
pointer 517.4
mark 517.5
card 758.2
fire 1018.13
flare 1018.14
brightness 1024.4
flash 1024.6
v notch 289.4
proclaim 352.13
mark 517.19
be hot 1018.22
catch fire 1019.23
burn 1019.24
shine 1024.23
blaze up
flare up 152.19
catch fire 1019.23
blazon
n display 501.4
heraldry 647.2
v proclaim 352.13
ornament 498.8

bleach
n decoloration 36.3
bleacher 36.4
v decolor 36.5
pale 36.6
whiten 37.5
clean 79.18
bleached
decolored 36.8
clean 79.25
vacant 222.14
weatherworn 393.34
bleachers
observation post 27.8
baseball 745.1
bleak distressing 98.20
gloomy 112.24
hopeless 125.12
windblown 318.24
cold 1022.14
bleakness
distressfulness 98.5
gloom 112.7
vacancy 222.2
cold 1022.1
bleary-eyed 28.13
bleat 60.2
bleb sore 85.36
bulge 283.3
bubble 320.1
blemish 1003.1
bleed
hemorrhage 12.17
let blood 91.27
suffer 96.19
grieve 112.17
pity 145.3
exude 190.15
draw off 192.12
exploit 387.16
take from 480.21
strip 480.24
overprice 632.7
bleeding
n hemorrhage 12.8
decoloration 36.3
symptom 85.9
bloodletting 91.20
drawing 192.3
adj bloody 12.23
pained 96.23
pitying 145.7
bleeding heart
n sentimentality 93.8
wretchedness 96.6
heartache 112.9
philanthropist 143.8
compassionateness
  145.2
pietist 693.3
liberal 978.6
adj liberal 611.19
pious 978.9
bleed white
exploit 387.16
consume 388.3
strip 480.24
overprice 632.7
bleep out excise 255.10
suppress 428.8
blemish
n mark 517.5

intruder 773.2
fault 1002.2
disfigurement 1003
blot 1003.1
eyesore 1014.4
v deform 265.7
mark 517.19
disfigure 1003.4
offend 1014.5
injure 393.13
blemished
deformed 265.12
unvirtuous 654.12
imperfect 1002.4
disfigured 1003.8
ugly 1014.6
blench flinch 127.13
demur 325.4
pull back 902.7
blend
n hybrid word 526.11
automobile racing
  756.1
compound 796.5
combination 804.1
v harmonize 708.35
identify 777.5
mix 796.10
combine 804.3
blender mixer 796.9
agitator 916.9
blend in with 455.2
bless gladden 95.8
congratulate 149.2
thank 150.4
approve 509.9
praise 509.12
sanctify 685.5
glorify 696.11
give one's blessing
  696.13
protect 1007.18
blessed
happy 95.15
curse 513.10
heavenly 681.12
sanctified 685.8
fortunate 1009.14
blessed event 1.1
blessed with 469.9
blessing
n act of kindness
  143.7
congratulation 149.1
consent 441.1
godsend 472.7
benefit 478.7
approval 509.1
sanctification 685.3
benediction 696.5
good 998.4
good fortune 1009.2
stroke of luck 1009.3
adj worshipful 696.15
blight
n disease 85.1
evil 999.3
blast 1000.2
adversity 1010.1
v spoil 393.10
work evil 999.6
freeze 1023.11

blighted
disappointed 132.5
spoiled 393.28
blasted 393.42
ruined 395.28
blighter 660.2
blimp aerostat 181.11
heavyweight 257.12
stuffed shirt 501.9
blind
n aviation 184.1
ambush 346.3
trick 356.6
pretext 376.1
stratagem 415.3
round 751.3
shade 1027.1
v cover the eyes 30.7
conceal 346.6
hoodwink 356.17
shine 1024.23
adj insensible 25.6
poor-sighted 28.11
sightless 30.9
high 87.23
closed 293.9
concealed 346.11
unpersuadable 361.13
obscure 522.15
undiscerning 921.14
involuntary 962.14
oblivious 983.7
blind alley
n obstruction 293.3
impasse 1012.6
adj closed 293.9
blind date 582.8
blinders blindfold 30.5
narrow-mindedness
  979.1
blind faith 953.1
blindfold
n eye patch 30.5
v blind 30.7
hoodwink 356.17
adj blinded 30.10
undiscerning 921.14
blinding
n blindness 30.1
adj obscuring 30.11
garish 35.19
rainy 316.10
bright 1024.32
blindness
insensibility 25.1
faulty eyesight 28.1
sightlessness 30
total darkness 30.1
carelessness 340.2
unpersuadableness
  361.5
unperceptiveness
  921.2
incognizance 929.3
blind spot
blindness 30.1
narrow-mindedness
  979.1
reception 1033.21
blind to
insensible 94.10
unaware 929.13

blink
n glance 27.4
glitter 1024.7
reflection 1024.9
v wink 28.10
flinch 127.13
slight 340.8
pull back 902.7
glitter 1024.24
blink at
be blind 30.8
condone 148.4
suffer 443.10
keep an open mind 978.7
be inattentive 983.2
blinkers
spectacles 29.3
blindfold 30.5
signals 517.15
blinking
n winking 28.7
glitter 1024.7
adj poor-sighted 28.11
glittering 1024.35
flickering 1024.36
blintz 10.43
blips 1035.11
bliss happiness 95.2
pleasantness 97.1
heaven 681.5
blissful happy 95.15
pleasant 97.6
beatific 97.9
blister
n sore 85.36
bulge 283.3
bubble 320.1
blemish 1003.1
v criticize 510.20
burn 1019.24
blistering
n burning 1019.5
adj bubbly 320.6
hot 1018.25
blithe 109.11
blithering 921.22
blitz
n attack 459.1
game 746.3
v blow up 395.18
attack 459.14
pull the trigger 459.22
play 746.5
blitzkrieg 459.1
blizzard
windstorm 318.12
snow 1022.8
bloat
n oversize 257.5
distension 259.2
overextension 992.7
v grow 251.6
enlarge 259.4
expand 259.5
bloated
puffed up 136.10
increased 251.7
corpulent 257.18
distended 259.13
deformed 265.12
bulging 283.15

pompous 501.22
overfull 992.20
blob sphere 282.2
bulge 283.3
blobby formless 263.4
vague 970.19
bloc 617.1
block
n suppression 92.24
boundary 211.3
city block 230.7
plot 231.4
lump 257.10
obstruction 293.3
execution 605.5
print 713.5
auction 734.4
share 738.3
game 746.3
delay 845.2
mental state 989.3
obstacle 1011.4
solid 1043.6
v stop 293.7
cover 295.19
fend off 460.10
play 746.5
pick 747.4
check 749.7
fight 754.4
delay 845.8
cease 856.11
obstruct 1011.12
hinder 1011.13
blockade
n enclosure 212.1
closure 293.1
obstruction 293.3
siege 459.5
exclusion 772.1
obstacle 1011.4
v enclose 212.5
stop 293.7
besiege 459.19
fortify 460.9
exclude 772.4
obstruct 1011.12
blockage seizure 85.6
suppression 92.24
obstruction 293.3
delay 845.2
hindrance 1011.1
blockbuster 131.2
blockhead
bungler 414.8
fool 923.4
blockhouse 460.6
blockish 921.15
block out form 262.7
outline 381.11
itemize 800.7
blocks 743.16
blocky 268.10
bloke 76.5
blond
n hair color 35.9
adj flaxen-haired 37.9
yellow-haired 43.5
blood
n whole blood 2.23
life force 306.3
killing 308.1

dandy 500.9
relationship 559.1
kinfolk 559.2
race 559.4
lineage 560.4
offspring 561.1
nobility 608.2
class 808.2
kind 808.3
fluid 1059.2
adj circulatory 2.31
blood and thunder
n emotionalism 93.9
adj sensational 105.32
blood bank
transfusion 91.18
hospital room 197.25
bloodbath carnage 308.4
destruction 395.1
blood brother 559.3
bloodcurdling 127.29
bloodied 96.25
bloodless weak 16.12
colorless 36.7
dull 117.6
pacific 464.9
bloodletting
bleeding 91.20
drawing 192.3
killing 308.1
bloodline lineage 560.4
offspring 561.1
bloodlust
cruelty 144.11
violence 671.1
bloodmobile 91.18
blood money
recompense 624.3
fee 624.5
blood relationship
bond 559.2
kinship 774.3
bloodshed
killing 308.1
war 458.1
blood-sport 382.2
bloodstained 1003.11
bloodstream 2.23
bloodsucker
parasite 311.36
extortionist 480.12
bloodthirsty
cruel 144.26
murderous 308.23
warlike 458.21
blood vessel 2.21
bloody
v bleed 12.17
torture 96.18
injure 393.13
bloodstain 1003.7
adj circulatory 2.31
bleeding 12.23
sanguine 41.7
cruel 144.26
murderous 308.23
warlike 458.21
cursed 513.9
savage 671.21
bloodstained 1003.11
bloody hands 656.1

bloom
n reddening 41.3
health 83.1
youth 301.1
flower 310.22
budding 310.24
beauty 1015.1
glow 1018.12
television reception 1034.5
v enjoy good health 83.6
mature 303.9
flower 310.32
ripen 407.8
evolve 860.5
thrive 1009.8
look good 1015.16
be hot 1018.22
blooper game 745.3
goof 974.6
blossom
n plant 310.22
flowering 310.24
v grow 14.2
expand 259.7
mature 303.9
flower 310.32
ripen 407.8
evolve 860.5
thrive 1009.8
blot
n soil 80.5
obliteration 395.7
stigma 661.6
intruder 773.2
stain 1003.3
eyesore 1014.4
v blacken 38.7
absorb 187.13
obliterate 395.16
stigmatize 661.9
spot 1003.5
offend 1014.5
dry 1064.6
blotch
n spottiness 47.3
soil 80.5
mark 517.5
stain 1003.3
v blacken 38.7
variegate 47.7
mark 517.19
spot 1003.5
blotchy dingy 38.11
blemished 47.13
spotted 1003.9
blot out delete 255.12
kill 308.13
obliterate 395.16
darken 1026.9
blotter LSD 87.9
sorption 187.6
record book 549.11
blotto 88.33
blouse 5.15
blow
n feast 8.9
cocaine 87.6
pain 96.5
surprise 131.2
disappointment 132.1

plant 310.22
flowering 310.24
gust 318.6
windstorm 318.12
act 328.3
slap 604.3
fight 754.3
hit 901.4
punch 901.6
misfortune 1010.2
v burn out 21.5
blare 53.10
use 87.21
leave 222.10
flower 310.32
waft 318.20
flee 368.11
spoil 393.11
ripen 407.8
bungle 414.12
squander 486.3
boast 502.7
talk big 545.6
blow a horn 708.42
evacuate 908.22
let out 908.24
make a boner 974.15
inter go away! 908.31
blow about 352.16
blow a gasket
get excited 105.17
fly into a rage 152.20
blow-by-blow
description 349.3
blow down raze 395.19
fell 912.5
blower ventilator 317.9
bellows 318.18
fan 318.19
braggart 502.5
automobile racing
756.1
blow for blow 506.3
blowhard
n braggart 502.5
v boast 502.7
blowhole outlet 190.9
air passage 239.13
blow hot and cold
vacillate 362.8
keep off and on 364.4
change 853.5
quibble 935.9
blown
windblown 318.24
tainted 393.41
blighted 393.42
blow off steam 743.24
blow one's cool 105.17
blow one's cover 351.8
blow one's mind
use 87.21
lose self-control 128.8
go mad 925.22
freak out 975.8
dream 985.17
blow one's top
get excited 105.17
fly into a rage 152.20
go mad 925.22
blowout feast 8.9
party 582.12

explosion 671.7
festival 743.4
disgorgement 908.7
blow out
run out 190.13
erupt 671.13
explode 671.14
evacuate 908.22
disgorge 908.25
fight fire 1021.7
blow over
die down 318.20
come to an end 819.6
fell 912.5
blowpipe
blower 318.18
blowtorch 1019.14
blow the lid off
disclose 351.4
uncover 940.4
blow the whistle
have no patience with
135.5
inform on 551.13
play 746.5
blow to 624.19
blowtorch
jet plane 181.3
blowlamp 1019.14
blowup outburst 152.9
intensification 251.2
explosion 671.7
print 714.5
blow up excite 105.12
get pumped 105.17
fly into a rage 152.20
intensify 251.5
enlarge 259.4
strike dead 308.17
blow 318.20
misrepresent 350.3
blast 395.18
come to nothing
410.13
praise 509.12
explode 671.14
process 714.15
disprove 957.4
blowy 318.22
blowzy
red-complexioned
41.9
corpulent 257.18
slovenly 809.15
blubber
n softness 1045.4
v weep 115.12
bubble 320.4
speak 524.26
mumble 525.9
blubbery 1054.9
bludgeon
intimidate 127.20
coerce 424.7
threaten 514.2
blue
n blueness 45.1
proof 548.5
the heavens 1070.2
v azure 45.2
adj bluish 45.3
melancholy 112.23

deathly 307.29
obscene 666.9
blue blood
aristocracy 607.3
upper class 607.4
nobility 608.2
nobleman 608.4
blue-blooded
upper-class 607.10
wellborn 608.11
blue book
official document
549.8
register 549.9
information 551.1
examination 937.2
blue-chip 998.15
blue-collar worker
726.2
bluegrass 708.11
blue in the face
105.25
bluejacket
mariner 183.1
navy man 183.4
blue language 513.3
bluenose 500.11
blue-pencil
delete 255.12
revise 392.12
obliterate 395.16
blueprint
n representation 349.1
plan 381.1
diagram 381.3
proof 548.5
print 714.5
outline 800.4
schedule 964.3
v plot 381.10
process 714.15
blue ribbon
supremacy 249.3
victory 411.1
award 646.2
decoration 646.5
blues
sulks 110.10
mumps 112.6
folk music 708.11
bluestocking
n pedant 928.5
adj book-learned
927.22
blue streak 174.6
bluff
n precipice 200.3
slope 237.2
sham 354.3
trick 356.6
impostor 357.6
bluster 503.1
actor 503.2
v sham 354.20
deceive 356.14
bluster 503.3
adj impudent 142.10
steep 204.18
blunt 286.3
artless 416.5
gruff 505.7
candid 644.17

blunder
n bungle 414.5
foolish act 922.4
error 974.5
v miss 410.14
bungle 414.11
flounder 916.15
make an error 974.14
blunderheaded
bungling 414.20
unintelligent 921.17
blundering
n bungling 414.4
adj inept 414.20
blunder upon
bungle 414.11
come across 940.3
blunt
n money 728.2
v weaken 16.10
deaden 25.4
numb 94.7
dull 286.2
disincline 379.4
moderate 670.6
adj unfeeling 94.9
dull 286.3
artless 416.5
free-acting 430.23
gruff 505.7
candid 644.17
dim-witted 921.16
blunted 286.3
blur
n inconspicuousness
32.2
stigma 661.6
stain 1003.3
v dim 32.4
deform 263.3
confound 944.3
stain 1003.6
blurb
publicity 352.4
commendation 509.3
blurred
inconspicuous 32.6
formless 263.4
inarticulate 525.12
vague 970.19
blurt out
exclaim 59.7
betray 351.6
act on the spur of the
moment 365.7
remark 524.25
blush
n warmth 35.2
reddening 41.3
blushing 139.5
glow 1018.12
v redden 41.5
change color 105.19
flush 139.8
be guilty 656.2
blushing
n reddening 41.3
flushing 139.5
adj reddening 41.11
humiliated 137.14
blushful 139.13
luminous 1024.30

bluster
n boasting 502.1
swagger 503
loud talk 503.1
turbulence 671.2
agitation 916.1
v intimidate 127.20
be angry 152.15
blow 318.20
put up a bold front
454.5
boast 502.6
hector 503.3
blustering
n act 503.1
adj noisy 53.13
windy 318.22
blustery 503.4
threatening 514.3
turbulent 671.18
boar male animal 76.8
swine 311.9
board
n meal 8.5
food 10.1
rations 10.6
accommodations
385.3
council 423.1
governing board
567.12
directorate 574.11
tribunal 595.1
stage 704.16
stock exchange 737.7
card 758.2
table 900.15
circuitry 1041.3
wood 1052.3
v feed 8.18
dine 8.21
ship activity 182.48
embark 188.15
mount 193.12
face 295.23
provision 385.9
accommodate 385.10
raid 459.20
boarder eater 8.16
lodger 227.8
board game 743.9
boardinghouse 228.15
the boards
show business 704.1
stage 704.16
boardwalk 383.2
boast
n boasting 502.1
good thing 998.5
v be stuck on oneself
140.6
possess 469.4
brag 502.6
praise 509.12
boastful vain 136.9
proud 140.9
boasting 502.10
boat
n car 179.10
watercraft 180
ship 180.1
v navigate 182.13

boathouse 197.27
boating 182.1
boatload 196.2
boat person 368.5
boatswain
ship's officer 183.7
superintendent 574.2
boatyard 739.3
bob
n obeisance 155.2
float 180.11
instrument 200.6
weight 297.6
greeting 585.4
money 728.8
repeat 848.5
jerk 904.3
crouch 912.3
shake 916.3
v cut the hair 3.22
bow 155.6
excise 255.10
shorten 268.6
caper 366.6
fish 382.10
depress 912.9
oscillate 915.10
shake 916.11
bobble
n bungle 414.5
shake 916.3
goof 974.6
v bungle 414.12
mishandle 745.5
play 746.5
oscillate 915.10
shake 916.11
make a boner 974.15
bobby 1007.16
bobbysoxer 302.8
bobcat 311.22
bob up burst forth 33.9
be unexpected 131.6
arrive 186.6
shoot up 193.9
bode 133.11
bodice 5.15
bodiless
unsubstantial 763.5
disembodied 987.8
immaterial 1051.7
bodily
adj carnal 663.6
innate 766.8
material 1050.10
adv in person 221.17
wholly 791.13
body
n the one 2.1
man 76.5
population 227.1
size 257.1
human form 262.4
thickness 269.2
corpse 307.16
person 312.5
type 548.6
association 617.1
community 617.2
sect 675.3
automobile racing
756.1

substantiality 762.1
something 762.3
company 769.3
collection 769.11
major part 791.6
individual 871.4
solid 1043.6
physical being 1050.3
v materialize 1050.9
bodybuilding
exercise 84.2
sport 744.1
body count
obituary 307.14
summation 1016.11
bodyguard escort 768.5
safeguard 1007.14
body language 517.14
body politic
population 227.1
country 232.1
the people 606.1
body snatcher
thief 483.1
executive search
agency 615.5
boffo 409.4
bog
n receptacle of filth
80.12
marsh 243.1
v mire 243.2
bog down 243.2
bogey
n frightener 127.9
military aircraft 181.9
bugbear 680.9
round 751.3
v play 751.4
bogeyman
frightener 127.9
bugbear 680.9
bogeymen 1000.1
boggle
n demur 325.2
bungle 414.5
v astonish 122.6
start 127.12
demur 325.4
object 333.5
not know one's own
mind 362.6
bungle 414.11
lose one's nerve 491.8
quibble 935.9
stump 970.14
boggle the mind
astonish 122.6
be unbelievable 954.7
boggy marshy 243.3
moist 1063.15
bogus
spurious 354.25
substitute 861.8
Bohemian
n nomad 178.4
nonconformist 867.3
adj informal 581.3
unconventional 867.6
boil
n dish 10.7
sore 85.36

swelling 283.4
turbulence 671.2
agitation 916.1
heating 1019.2
v cook 11.4
sanitize 79.24
be angry 152.15
bubble 320.4
seethe 671.12
be hot 1018.22
stew 1019.20
boil down 268.6
boiler room
noisemaker 53.6
confidence game
356.10
stockbrokerage 737.9
boiling over
fervent 93.18
heated 105.22
boisterous noisy 53.13
turbulent 105.24
blustering 503.4
rampageous 671.20
bold insolent 142.9
brazen 142.11
seaworthy 180.18
steep 204.18
protruding 283.14
in relief 283.18
conspicuous 348.12
defiant 454.7
courageous 492.17
foolhardy 493.9
immodest 666.6
boldfaced
brazen 142.11
typographic 548.20
bole cylinder 282.4
stem 310.19
boll sphere 282.2
seed vessel 310.28
bollix up spoil 393.11
bungle 414.12
complicate 798.3
confuse 810.3
hinder 1011.16
Bolshevik
n radical 611.12
Communist 611.13
revolutionist 859.3
adj Communist 611.21
revolutionist 859.6
bolster
n bedding 900.20
v comfort 121.6
aid 449.12
encourage 492.16
support 900.21
confirm 956.11
bolt
n a length 267.2
apostasy 363.2
change one's mind
363.7
flight 368.4
desertion 370.2
lock 428.5
arrow 462.6
missile 462.18
bundle 769.8
lightning 1024.17

v gobble 8.23
refine 79.22
speed 174.8
close 293.6
flee 368.10
defect 370.6
gluttonize 672.4
segregate 772.6
hook 799.8
classify 807.11
obstruct 1011.12
bolt-hole
hiding place 346.4
secret passage 346.5
means of escape 369.3
bolt out of the blue
131.2
bolt upright
vertical 200.11
straight 200.13
bolus bite 8.2
pill 86.7
sphere 282.2
bomb
n marijuana 87.10
surprise 131.2
failure 410.2
bombshell 462.20
stage show 704.4
game 746.3
v fall flat 117.4
blow up 395.18
fail 410.10
attack 459.23
dramatize 704.28
bombardier crew 185.4
artilleryman 461.11
bombardment
bombing 459.7
fission 1037.8
bombast
n boasting 502.1
nonsense 520.2
bombastry 545.2
v talk big 545.6
bombastic
pompous 501.22
inflated 502.12
stiff 534.3
fustian 545.9
bombed out 87.23
bomber alarmist 127.8
destroyer 395.8
artilleryman 461.11
violent person 671.9
bombshell
surprise 131.2
bomb 462.20
bona fide
adj straight 644.14
genuine 972.15
adv faithfully 644.25
bonanza
source of supply 386.4
rich source 618.4
plenty 990.2
bon appetit! 8.35
bond
n shackle 428.4
compact 437.1
security 438.1
pledge 438.2

fidelity 644.7
nominal rate 738.5
relation 774.1
joining 799.1
fastening 799.3
v secure 438.9
pledge 438.10
put together 799.5
adj subjugated 432.14
bondage 432.1
bondholder 737.14
bondsman
subject 432.7
guarantor 438.6
bone
n the skeleton 2.2
whiteness 37.2
hardness 1044.6
dryness 1064.2
v study 570.12
adj skeleton 2.24
bonehead
bungler 414.9
fool 923.4
bone of contention
apple of discord 456.7
question 937.10
boner bungle 414.5
goof 974.6
bones heart 93.3
corpse 307.16
refuse 391.4
dice 759.8
body 1050.3
bone to pick
bone of contention
456.7
grudge 589.5
bone up
study up 570.14
refresh the memory
988.19
bonfire 1018.13
bonhomie
good nature 143.2
hospitality 585.1
cordiality 587.6
bon jour! 585.15
bonkers 925.27
bon mot 489.7
bonnet cloak 5.39
top 295.21
bonny good 998.12
comely 1015.18
bon ton custom 373.1
fashion 578.1
chic 578.2
upper class 607.2
bonus extra 254.4
find 472.6
gratuity 478.5
premium 624.6
surplus 992.5
bon vivant
eater 8.16
connoisseur 496.7
sociable person
582.16
boon companion
588.5
sensualist 663.3
bon voyage! 188.22

bony
skeleton 2.24
lean 270.17
hard 1044.10
boo
n marijuana 87.10
booing 508.3
v hiss 508.10
inter bah! 157.10
boob dupe 358.2
fool 923.3
boo-boo
bungle 414.5
goof 974.6
boobs 283.7
boob tube 1034.11
booby loser 412.5
fool 923.3
booby hatch 925.14
booby prize 646.2
booby trap
ambush 346.3
deception 356.12
hidden danger 1005.5
boodle bribe 378.2
booty 482.11
spoils of office 609.35
money 728.2
boogie-woogie 708.9
boo-hoo 115.12
book
n publication 352.1
volume 554
edition 554.1
printed product 554.3
part 554.13
periodical 555.1
playbook 704.21
script 706.2
poetry 720.9
casino 759.19
part of writing 792.2
v depose 334.6
flee 368.11
curse 513.5
record 549.15
accuse 599.7
employ 615.14
keep accounts 628.8
list 870.8
prearrange 964.4
schedule 964.6
bookbinding 554.14
bookcase
storehouse 386.6
bookbinding 554.14
bookholder 554.17
bookdealer 554.2
book end 554.17
bookie 759.20
booking
registration 549.14
engagement 615.4
show 704.11
prearrangement 964.1
bookish
learned 570.17
studentlike 572.12
book-smart 927.22
bookkeeper
recorder 550.1
accountant 628.7

treasurer 729.11
calculator 1016.14
bookkeeping
n accounting 628.6
adj recording 628.12
book learning 927.5
booklet 554.11
booklover
philobiblist 554.18
bookworm 928.4
bookmaker 759.20
bookmark 517.10
book review 945.2
book reviewer 556.4
books
account book 628.4
bill 870.5
bookseller 554.2
bookshelf 554.17
bookstore 554.16
book value 738.9
bookworm
booklover 554.18
nerd 572.10
bibliophage 928.4
boom
n noise 53.3
reverberation 54.2
volume 56.4
float 180.11
intensification 251.2
explosion 671.7
business cycle 731.9
lever 905.4
roaring trade 1009.5
barrier 1011.5
v hum 52.13
din 53.7
reverberate 54.7
thunder 56.9
speed 174.9
ship activity 182.48
grow 251.6
speak 524.26
thrive 1009.8
inter bang! 56.13
boomerang
n missile 462.18
retaliation 506.1
recoil 902.2
v return 902.6
booming
n hum 52.7
reverberation 54.2
explosion 56.4
adj humming 52.20
loud 53.11
reverberating 54.11
thundering 56.12
thriving 1009.13
boon
n godsend 472.7
benefit 478.7
good 998.4
adj convivial 582.23
boondocks
open space 158.4
hinterland 233.2
remote region 261.4
woodland 310.11
boor bungler 414.8
vulgarian 497.6

peasant 606.6
oaf 923.5
boorish insensible 25.6
countrified 233.7
bungling 414.20
churlish 497.13
ill-bred 505.6
boost
n increase 251.1
improvement 392.1
promotion 446.1
assist 449.2
theft 482.4
commendation 509.3
thrust 901.2
lift 911.2
v cheer 109.7
increase 251.4
publicize 352.15
make better 392.9
promote 446.2
be useful 449.17
rob 482.16
commend 509.11
thrust 901.12
elevate 911.5
booster dose 86.6
inoculation 91.16
enthusiast 101.5
publicist 352.9
thief 483.1
commender 509.8
multistage rocket
1072.5
boot
n excitement 105.3
navy man 183.4
recruit 461.18
novice 572.9
torture 605.4
kick 901.9
goof 974.6
v cloak 5.39
play 745.5
kick 901.21
dismiss 908.20
make a boner 974.15
computerize 1041.18
bootblack 577.5
booth
compartment 197.2
hut 228.9
stall 736.3
bootleg
v distill 88.30
illicit goods 732.7
adj illegal 674.6
bootlegger
liquor dealer 88.19
racketeer 732.4
bootless
ineffective 19.15
fruitless 391.12
unsuccessful 410.18
bootlicker
flatterer 138.4
assenter 332.6
bootmaker 5.37
boot out 908.13
booty gain 472.3
take 480.10
spoil 482.11

booze
n spirits 88.13
v imbibe 8.29
drink 88.25
use 87.21
bop 708.9
bordello
disapproved place
228.28
brothel 665.9
border
n exterior 206.2
limbus 211.4
frontier 211.5
partition 213.5
side 218.1
sphere 231.2
size 257.1
scenery 704.20
garden 1067.10
v edge 211.10
side 218.4
adjoin 223.9
adj final 819.11
bordering
n edging 211.7
adj environing
209.8
fringing 211.11
adjacent 223.16
borderland
frontier 211.5
sphere 231.2
hinterland 233.2
borderline 211.11
borderline case
lunatic 925.15
gamble 970.8
bore
n annoyance 96.2
crashing bore 118.4
wave 238.14
diameter 269.3
hole 292.3
v give no pleasure
96.12
leave one cold 118.7
excavate 284.15
perforate 292.15
boreal
northern 161.14
seasonal 313.9
windy 318.22
cold 1022.14
boredom
unpleasure 96.1
weariness 118.3
languor 331.6
incuriosity 981.1
borehole 292.3
borer 285.3
boring
n hole 292.3
adj irritating 26.13
wearying 118.10
same 780.6
born
given birth 1.4
innate 766.8
thorough 793.10
born-again
redeemed 685.9

regenerate 692.10
converted 857.19
borne 900.24
borne out 956.20
born for 413.29
born yesterday 416.5
borough town 230.1
region 231.5
election district
609.16
borrow
imitate 336.5
rob 482.16
plagiarize 482.19
take a loan of 621.3
go in debt 623.6
discount 728.27
play 751.4
borrowing
plagiarism 482.8
loan word 526.7
appropriation 621
money-raising 621.1
debt 623.1
money market 728.16
borscht circuit 704.11
borstal
prison 429.8
reform school 567.9
bos'n 183.7
bosh humbug 354.14
bullshit 520.3
bosom
n heart 93.3
interior 207.2
breast 283.6
inner nature 766.5
v keep secret 345.7
conceal 346.7
hold 474.7
embrace 562.18
bosom buddy 588.4
bosomy
corpulent 257.18
bulging 283.15
pectoral 283.19
boss
n superior 249.4
bulge 283.3
print 517.7
superintendent 574.2
master 575.1
politics 610.7
relief 715.3
important person
996.11
v emboss 283.12
roughen 288.4
direct 573.8
supervise 573.10
adj supervising 573.13
governing 612.18
excellent 998.13
bossism
authoritativeness
417.3
politics 609.1
bossy
n female animal 77.9
cattle 311.6
adj in relief 283.18
imperious 417.16

botanical
vegetable 310.33
biological 1066.3
botany biology 1066.1
plants 310.1
botch
n slipshodness 340.3
bad likeness 350.2
fiasco 410.6
bungle 414.5
blunder 974.5
v do carelessly 340.9
misdraw 350.4
spoil 393.10
miss 410.14
bungle 414.11
blunder 974.14
both
n two 872.2
adj the two 872.7
bother
n annoyance 96.2
dither 105.6
bustle 330.4
imposition 643.1
commotion 809.4
bewilderment 970.3
confusion 984.3
inconvenience 995.3
trouble 1012.3
v annoy 96.13
distress 96.16
vex 98.15
concern 126.4
presume upon 640.7
bewilder 970.12
confuse 984.7
inconvenience 995.4
trouble 1012.13
bothered
annoyed 96.21
distressed 96.22
anxious 126.7
bewildered 970.24
confused 984.12
troubled 1012.20
bothersome
annoying 98.22
troublesome 126.10
difficult 1012.18
bottle
n container 195.1
v package 212.9
put up 397.11
bottleneck
convergence 169.1
contraction 260.1
narrow place 270.3
obstruction 293.3
hindrance 1011.1
bottle up enclose 212.6
secrete 346.7
suppress 428.8
confine 429.12
retain 474.5
hinder 1011.10
bottom
n ship 180.1
lower surface 199
under side 199.1
bed 199.4
buttocks 217.4

violate 435.4
break 801.12
open 817.12
breach of confidence
645.5
bread
n food 10.1
pain 10.27
support 449.3
Eucharist 701.7
money 728.2
v feed 8.18
sprinkle 770.6
breadth space 158.1
size 257.1
width 269
expanse 269.1
extent 300.3
broad-mindedness
978.1
breadwinner 726.2
break
n respite 20.2
trauma 85.37
act of kindness 143.7
start 188.2
boundary 211.3
crack 224.2
escape 369.1
falling-out 456.4
cheapening 633.4
declining market
737.5
horse race 757.3
deficiency 794.2
breakage 801.4
interruption 812.2
interim 825.1
delay 845.2
revolution 851.2
pause 856.3
chance 971.1
stroke of luck 1009.3
v weaken 16.9
take a rest 20.8
change course 182.30
set out 188.8
cleave 224.4
billow 238.22
be published 352.16
accustom 373.10
injure 393.13
crack up 393.23
conquer 412.10
subdue 432.9
domesticate 432.11
violate 435.4
depose 447.4
train 568.13
domineer 612.16
go bankrupt 625.7
ruin 625.8
cheapen 633.6
fight 754.4
race 757.5
disagree 788.5
burst 801.12
discontinue 812.3
intervene 825.3
pause 856.9
interrupt 856.10
dismiss 908.19

grow light 1024.27
shatter 1048.3
tend 1068.7
breakable frail 16.14
brittle 1048.4
breakaway
n apostasy 363.2
desertion 370.2
scoring chance 749.3
game 752.3
adj rebellious 327.11
dissenting 333.6
repudiative 363.12
unconventional 867.6
unusual 869.10
counteractive 899.8
break away
n apostacize 363.7
v revolt 327.7
escape 369.6
defect 370.6
break bread with 8.21
breakdown
exhaustion 21.2
collapse 85.8
impairment 393.1
debacle 395.4
failure 410.3
analysis 800.1
dissection 801.5
disintegration 805.1
revolution 859.1
break down
burn out 21.5
aggrieve 112.19
weep 115.12
founder 393.24
be impaired 393.26
raze 395.19
subdue 432.9
diversify 781.2
analyze 800.6
dissect 801.17
classify 808.6
fall through 910.3
breakers
wave 238.14
foam 320.2
break even 789.5
breakfast
n meal 8.6
v dine 8.21
break for 161.9
break forth
burst forth 33.9
emerge 190.11
be revealed 351.8
break ground
weigh anchor 182.18
initiate 817.10
break in
n burglary 482.5
v enter 189.7
intrude 214.5
interrupt 214.6
breach 292.14
accustom 373.10
domesticate 432.11
train 568.13
make a beginning
817.8
breaking point 992.7

break loose
escape 369.6
extricate 431.7
breakneck fast 174.15
steep 204.18
precipitate 401.10
reckless 493.8
break off
n cessation 856.1
v disaccustom 374.2
disagree 788.5
discontinue 812.3
interrupt 856.10
break one's heart
112.19
break one's neck
be active 330.14
make haste 401.5
do one's best 403.14
break one up
make laugh 116.9
amuse 743.21
breakout escape 369.1
game 749.3
itemization 800.2
break out take ill 85.46
find vent 369.10
extricate 431.7
free oneself from
431.8
erupt 671.13
play 749.7
itemize 800.7
originate 817.13
break the ice
prepare the way
405.12
cultivate 587.12
initiate 817.10
break the news
divulge 351.5
report 552.11
breakthrough
improvement 392.1
attack 459.1
curtain-raiser 815.2
innovation 851.4
conversion 857.1
break through
breach 292.14
find vent 369.10
make good 409.10
breakup decay 393.6
destruction 395.1
debacle 395.4
disbandment 770.3
analysis 800.1
disruption 801.3
disintegration 805.1
revolution 859.1
break up laugh 116.8
decay 393.22
break 393.23
be destroyed 395.22
disband 770.8
diversify 781.2
analyze 800.6
come apart 801.9
shatter 801.13
part company 801.19
disintegrate 805.3
change 851.7

powder 1049.10
breakwater
point of land 283.9
buttress 900.4
harbor 1008.6
barrier 1011.5
break water
submarines 182.47
shoot up 193.9
break wind 908.29
break with 456.10
breast
n fowl part 10.22
heart 93.3
bosom 283.6
inner nature 766.5
v confront 216.8
contend against 451.4
breast-beating 658.2
breast-feed 8.19
breastwork 1011.5
breath breathing 2.19
respite 20.2
murmur 52.4
odor 69.1
touch 73.1
life 306.1
vitality 306.3
puff 318.4
spirit 763.3
instant 829.3
psyche 918.4
vapor 1065.1
breathe take a rest 20.8
murmur 52.10
have an odor 69.6
smell 69.8
live 306.7
tell confidentially
345.9
manifest 348.5
divulge 351.5
mean 518.8
say 524.23
speak 524.26
tip off 551.11
exist 760.8
imbue 796.11
evidence 956.8
breathe easy 120.8
breathing
n respiration 2.19
adj respiratory 2.30
living 306.11
lifelike 783.16
breathing spell
respite 20.2
truce 465.5
pause 856.3
breathless
winded 21.12
mute 51.12
fervent 93.18
eager 101.8
wondering 122.9
impatient 135.6
stuffy 173.16
dead 307.30
precipitate 401.10
breathtaking
exciting 105.30
astonishing 122.12

breathy 525.12
breech
  n bottom 199.1
  rear 217.1
  v cloak 5.39
breeches 5.18
breed
  n race 559.4
  lineage 560.4
  offspring 561.1
  kind 808.3
  v procreate 78.8
  be pregnant 78.12
  grow 251.6
  train 568.13
  cause 885.10
  originate 891.12
  raise 1068.6
breeding
  n procreation 78.2
  good breeding 504.4
  training 568.3
  fission 1037.8
  planting 1067.14
  animal husbandry 1068.1
  adj pregnant 78.18
breeding ground 885.8
breeze
  n light wind 318.5
  easy 1013.4
  softness 1045.4
  v speed 174.9
  blow 318.20
  race 757.5
breezeway 197.18
breezy
  lighthearted 109.12
  airy 317.11
  windy 318.22
  active 330.17
brethren brother 559.3
  the laity 700.1
brevet decree 420.4
  grant 443.5
  commission 615.1
brevity shortness 268.1
  taciturnity 344.2
  conciseness 537.1
  briefness 827.2
brew
  n spirits 88.13
  beer 88.16
  concoction 405.3
  v cook 11.4
  grow 14.2
  distill 88.30
  expand 259.7
  blow 318.20
  plot 381.9
  make up 405.7
  imbue 796.11
  be imminent 839.2
  liquefy 1062.5
  soak 1063.13
brewer 88.19
brewery
  distillery 88.21
  plant 739.3
bribable
  corruptible 378.4
  improbity 645.23

influenceable 893.15
bribe
  n incentive 375.7
  bribe money 378.2
  gratuity 478.5
  v throw a sop to 378.3
bribery
  graft 378
  bribing 378.1
bric-a-brac
  trinket 498.4
  work of art 712.10
  trivia 997.4
brick
  n pavement 383.6
  good person 659.2
  ceramic ware 742.2
  hardness 1044.6
  building material 1052.2
  v face 295.23
brickbat
  n indignity 156.2
  disrespect 156.3
  missile 462.18
  v pelt 459.27
brick wall 1011.5
brickyard 739.3
bridal
  n wedding 563.3
  adj matrimonial 563.18
bride 563.5
bridegroom 563.5
bridesmaid 563.4
bridge
  n observation post 27.8
  railway 383.7
  span 383.9
  stage 704.16
  passage 708.24
  violin family 711.5
  auction bridge 758.3
  v overlie 295.30
bridged 799.13
bridgehead
  vanguard 216.2
  stronghold 460.6
bridging
  n joining 799.1
  adj overlying 295.36
  joining 799.16
bridle
  n shackle 428.4
  v give oneself airs 141.8
  anger 152.17
  restrain 428.7
  bind 428.10
  mince 500.14
  yoke 799.10
  tend 1068.7
brief
  n airmanship 184.3
  report 549.7
  abridgment 557.1
  argument 934.5
  v give a briefing 184.48
  outline 381.11
  advise 422.5

inform 551.8
  give instructions 568.15
  employ 615.14
  adj short 268.8
  taciturn 344.9
  concise 537.6
  abridged 557.6
  transient 827.8
briefing
  airmanship 184.3
  preparation 405.1
  advice 422.1
  information 551.1
  instructions 568.6
  engagement 615.4
briefly
  shortly 268.12
  concisely 537.7
  transiently 827.10
brier thorn 285.5
  shrubbery 310.9
  adhesive 802.4
brig prison 429.8
  jail 429.9
brigade
  military unit 461.22
  company 769.3
brigadier 575.18
brigand 483.4
bright
  n tobacco 89.2
  adj colorful 35.18
  clean 79.25
  sunny 97.11
  cheerful 109.11
  optimistic 124.12
  auspicious 133.18
  alert 339.14
  teachable 570.18
  illustrious 662.19
  intelligent 919.12
  smart 919.14
  undamaged 1001.8
  gorgeous 1015.20
  brilliant 1024.32
bright and early 844.7
brighten
  make pleasant 97.5
  cheer 109.7
  grow light 1024.27
  illuminate 1024.28
bright side
  cheerfulness 97.4
  optimism 124.3
brilliant
  colorful 35.18
  skillful 413.22
  witty 489.15
  illustrious 662.19
  smart 919.14
  gorgeous 1015.20
  bright 1024.32
brim
  n border 211.4
  v fill 793.7
brimming 793.11
brim over 238.17
brimstone
  n bitch 110.12
  witch 593.7
  adj hellish 682.8

brindle 47.15
brine
  n saltiness 68.4
  preservative 397.4
  v preserve 397.9
bring fetch 176.16
  induce 375.22
  cost 630.13
  inflict 643.5
  be sold 734.12
  entail 771.4
  cause 885.11
bring about
  change course 182.30
  do 328.6
  prompt 375.13
  bring to pass 407.5
  cause 885.10
  perform 891.11
bring back fetch 176.16
  revive 396.16
  restore 481.4
  remember 988.10
  remind 988.20
bring down
  n disrespect 156.3
  v abase 137.5
  strike dead 308.17
  raze 395.19
  disparage 512.8
  incur 896.4
  fell 912.5
bring down the curtain 819.5
bring forth
  elicit 192.14
  manifest 348.5
  cause 885.10
  originate 891.12
  bear 891.13
bring forward
  confront 216.8
  manifest 348.5
  make better 392.9
  propose 439.5
  call to witness 598.16
  adduce 956.12
bring home to
  impress upon 93.16
  accuse of 599.9
  condemn 602.3
  attribute to 887.4
  convince 952.18
  prove 956.10
bring in
  introduce 187.14
  yield 627.4
  cost 630.13
  reel in 905.9
  harvest 1067.19
bring into play 387.14
bring into question
  inquire 937.19
  doubt 954.6
bring off do 328.6
  carry out 328.7
  bring about 407.5
  succeed with 409.11
bring on induce 885.11
  incur 896.4
  adduce 956.12
bring oneself 324.3

bring out
elicit 192.14
externalize 206.5
manifest 348.5
issue 352.14
print 548.14
bring pressure to bear
upon urge 375.14
press 424.6
exercise influence
893.9
thrust 901.12
bring round
change course 182.30
persuade 375.23
cure 396.15
revive 396.16
convince 952.18
bring to
sail against the wind
182.24
revive 396.16
put a stop to 856.11
convert 857.11
bring to a head
aggravate 119.2
focus 208.10
ripen 407.8
bring to bear upon
apply 387.11
relate 774.6
bring together
add 253.4
reconcile 465.8
collect 472.11
assemble 769.18
bring to light
elicit 192.14
disclose 351.4
uncover 940.4
bring to mind
imply 519.4
resemble 783.7
remember 988.10
bring to one's senses
persuade 375.23
bring to reason 924.3
convince 952.18
bring to pass do 328.6
bring about 407.5
cause 885.10
bring to terms
subdue 432.9
reconcile 465.8
settle 466.7
bring up
confront 216.8
propose 439.5
train 568.13
inaugurate 817.11
stop 856.7
vomit 908.26
bring upon inflict 643.5
incur 896.4
bring up the rear
follow 166.3
be behind 217.8
brink 211.4
brinkmanship
foolhardiness 493.3
foreign policy 609.5
brio 17.4

brisk
v refresh 9.2
adj refreshing 9.3
energetic 17.13
zestful 68.7
penetrating 105.31
windy 318.22
active 330.17
brief 827.8
cool 1022.12
cold 1022.14
bristle
n hair 3.2
thorn 285.5
barb 288.3
v anger 152.17
provoke 152.24
rise 200.8
ruffle 288.5
bristle with
come to a point 285.6
teem with 883.5
abound 990.5
bristling bristly 288.9
crowded 769.22
teeming 883.9
Britain 232.4
britches 5.18
brittle frail 16.14
wasted 393.35
transient 827.7
crisp 1048.4
broach
n hole 292.3
v draw off 192.12
open 292.11
perforate 292.15
make public 352.11
propose 439.5
inaugurate 817.11
broad
n woman 77.6
gal 302.7
strumpet 665.14
adj spacious 158.10
voluminous 257.17
wide 269.6
comic 488.6
burlesque 508.14
phonetic 524.31
candid 644.17
vulgar 666.8
extensive 863.13
vague 970.19
open-minded 978.8
broadcast
n publication 352.1
dispersion 770.1
radiobroadcast
1033.18
planting 1067.14
v communicate 343.7
publish 352.10
disperse 770.4
radiobroadcast
1033.25
plant 1067.18
adj published 352.17
dispersed 770.9
broaden
increase 251.4
grow 251.6

enlarge 259.4
expand 259.5
widen 269.4
generalize 863.9
broadening
n increase 251.1
expansion 259.1
adj liberalizing 978.13
broad humor 489.1
broadly
extensively 158.11
far and wide 261.16
humorously 488.7
candidly 644.23
generally 863.17
vaguely 970.29
broad-minded
nonrestrictive 430.25
wise 919.17
wide-minded 978.8
broadsheet 352.8
broad-shouldered
able-bodied 15.16
virile 76.12
broadside
n side 218.1
announcement 352.2
advertising matter
352.8
volley 459.9
information 551.1
adv laterally 218.8
breadthwise 269.9
Broadway 704.1
brochure 554.11
brogue 524.9
broil
n dish 10.7
cooking 11.1
quarrel 456.5
free-for-all 457.5
turbulence 671.2
commotion 809.4
v cook 11.4
quarrel 456.11
contend 457.13
be hot 1018.22
broke bereft 473.8
without money 619.10
insolvent 625.11
broken
domesticated 228.34
rough 288.6
impaired 393.27
in disrepair 393.37
ruined 395.28
conquered 412.17
subdued 432.15
meek 433.15
insolvent 625.11
busted 801.24
incoherent 803.4
discontinuous 812.4
irregular 850.3
broken-down
overcome 112.29
dilapidated 393.33
brokenhearted 112.29
broken-in 373.16
broker
intermediary 213.4
go-between 576.4

businessman 730.9
stockbroker 737.10
brokerage fee 630.6
trade 731.2
commerce 737.9
stockbroking 737.18
bromide
generalization 863.8
platitude 973.3
bronchial 2.30
bronco 311.10
broncobuster
rider 178.8
stockman 1068.2
Bronx cheer 508.3
bronze
n sculpture 715.2
v brown 40.2
adj reddish-brown
40.4
brass 1056.17
brooch 498.6
brood
n race 559.4
family 559.5
offspring 561.1
v be pregnant 78.12
consider 930.12
brooder
sourpuss 112.13
coop 228.22
poultry 311.29
birthplace 885.8
brood over
grieve 112.17
harbor revenge 507.5
think over 930.13
keep in memory
988.13
brook
n stream 238.1
v endure 134.5
submit 433.6
suffer 443.10
keep an open mind
978.7
broom 79.23
broomstick 270.8
brothel
disapproved place
228.28
sewer 654.7
house of prostitution
665.9
brother buddy 559.3
friend 588.1
associate 616.1
member 617.11
religious 699.15
layman 700.2
likeness 783.3
brotherhood
kindness 143.1
blood relationship
559.1
fellowship 587.2
association 617.3
brotherly love
love 104.1
benevolence 143.4
accord 455.1
brouhaha noise 53.3

outcry 59.4
excitement 105.4
turbulence 671.2
commotion 809.4
agitation 916.1
brow eyelashes 3.12
looks 33.4
summit 198.2
head 198.6
border 211.4
forehead 216.5
browbeat
intimidate 127.20
domineer 612.16
browbeaten 432.16
brown
n brownness 40.1
heroin 87.8
v cook 11.4
embrown 40.2
darken 1026.9
adj brownish 40.3
brownie flatterer 138.4
dwarf 258.5
fairy 678.8
Brownie points 662.3
brown-nose
n flatterer 138.4
assenter 332.6
v fawn 138.7
brownout
n darkness 1026.7
blackout 1031.19
v darken 1026.9
brown study
thoughtfulness 930.3
abstractedness 984.2
dream 985.9
browse feed on 8.28
scan 570.13
shop 733.8
bruise
n trauma 85.37
discoloration 1003.2
v pain 96.17
mistreat 389.5
injure 393.13
thrash soundly 604.14
bruiser ruffian 593.4
violent person 671.10
bruit
n report 552.6
v publish 352.10
bruit about 352.10
brumal seasonal 313.9
cold 1022.14
brunch 8.6
brunet
n hair color 35.9
adj black-haired 38.13
brown 40.3
brown-haired 40.5
brunt 901.3
brush
n plant beard 3.9
touch 73.1
tail 217.6
contact 223.5
hinterland 233.2
scrub 310.14
fight 457.4
art equipment 712.18

wasteland 890.2
tap 901.7
firewood 1020.3
v touch lightly 73.7
sweep 79.23
speed 174.9
contact 223.10
portray 712.19
tap 901.18
dry 1064.6
tend 1068.7
brush aside
dismiss 983.4
reject 372.2
brush off
n rejection 372.1
repulse 907.2
v sweep 79.23
repulse 907.3
dismiss 983.4
brush up groom 79.20
perfect 392.11
study up 570.14
refresh the memory
988.19
brusque taciturn 344.9
gruff 505.7
concise 537.6
candid 644.17
brutal cruel 144.26
deadly 308.22
animal 311.38
unrefined 497.12
carnal 663.6
savage 671.21
terrible 999.9
difficult 1012.17
brutality
cruelty 144.11
unkindness 144.12
unrefinement 497.3
carnality 663.2
violence 671.1
terribleness 999.2
brutalize callous 94.6
bear malice 144.15
rage 671.11
brute
n beast 144.14
animal 311.2
barbarian 497.7
savage 593.5
violent person 671.9
adj cruel 144.26
animal 311.38
carnal 663.6
brute force
power 18.1
force 424.2
bub boy 302.5
brother 559.3
bubble
n airy hope 124.5
structure 266.2
sphere 282.2
bulge 283.3
lightness 298.2
globule 320
bleb 320.1
race 756.3
spirit 763.3
ephemeron 827.5

illusion 975.1
figment of the
imagination 985.5
fragility 1048.2
v ripple 52.11
foam up 320.4
bubble over
be enthusiastic 101.7
carbonate 320.4
bubbly light 298.10
burbly 320.6
active 330.17
buccaneer
n mariner 183.1
hijacker 483.7
v pirate 482.18
buck
n male animal 76.8
boy 302.5
hoofed animal 311.5
goat 311.8
hare 311.24
leap 366.1
money 728.7
trestle 900.16
v leap 366.5
contend against 451.4
thrust 901.12
buckaroo
rider 178.8
stockman 1068.2
bucket
n ship 180.1
basketball game 747.3
v ladle 176.17
trade 737.23
buck for 375.14
buckle
n distortion 265.1
v distort 265.5
exert oneself 725.9
hook 799.8
buckled 265.10
buckle down to
undertake 404.3
set to work 725.15
buck-passing 415.5
bucks 728.2
buckskin 311.11
bucktooth 2.8
buck up
refresh 9.2
cheer up 109.9
take courage 492.14
encourage 492.16
bucolic rustic 233.6
natural 416.6
poetic 720.15
bud
n boy 302.5
burgeon 310.21
brother 559.3
friend 588.4
vital force 885.7
v graft 191.6
vegetate 310.31
Buddha Deity 677.4
religious founder
684.4
Solomon 920.2
budding
n bodily 14.1

growth 259.3
vegetation 310.30
adj grown 14.3
expanding 259.12
immature 301.10
beginning 817.15
buddy boy 302.5
brother 559.3
friend 588.4
henchman 610.8
partner 616.2
co-worker 616.5
buddy-buddy 587.20
budge 172.5
budget
n amount 244.2
store 386.1
portion 477.5
expenses 626.3
accounts 628.1
funds 728.14
bundle 769.8
schedule 964.3
v ration 477.10
spend 626.5
schedule 964.6
adj accounting 628.12
cheap 633.7
buenos días! 585.15
buff
n enthusiast 101.5
follower 166.2
attender 221.5
commender 509.8
supporter 616.9
specialist 865.3
fanatic 925.18
v polish 287.7
burnish 1042.8
adj yellow 43.4
the buff
nudity 6.3
skin 295.3
buffalo
n cattle 311.6
v stump 970.14
buffer
n partition 213.5
counteractant 899.3
safeguard 1007.3
barrier 1011.5
v neutralize 899.7
buffer zone 465.5
buffet restaurant 8.17
table 900.15
buffet
n disappointment
132.1
knock 604.3
slap 901.8
v mistreat 389.5
injure 393.13
contend against 451.4
slap 604.12
whip 604.13
struggle 725.11
pound 901.16
knock 901.19
buffoon
mischief-maker 322.3
buffo 707.10
fool 923.1

buffoonery
clownishness 489.5
acting 704.8
foolishness 922.1

bug
n microphone 50.9
germ 85.41
enthusiast 101.5
insect 311.31
bugbear 680.9
jockey 757.2
mania 925.12
fanatic 925.18
fault 1002.2
v listen 48.10
annoy 96.13
bulge 283.11
importune 440.12
nag 510.16
discompose 810.4
reconnoiter 937.27
confuse 984.7

bugbear
frightener 127.9
false alarm 400.2
bugaboo 680.9
bane 1000.1

bug-eyed
cross-eyed 28.12
bulged 283.16

bugger
n sexual pervert 75.16
man 76.5
mischief-maker 322.3
bad person 660.6
bugbear 680.9
v disable 19.9
masturbate 75.22
spoil 393.11
bungle 414.12

buggy
n car 179.10
adj insectile 311.50
crazy 925.27

bugle
n nose 283.8
v blare 53.10
blow a horn 708.42

bugle call
call to arms 458.8
signal 517.16

bug off! 908.32

build
n muscularity 15.2
frame 262.1
human form 262.4
structure 266.1
nature 766.4
v establish 159.16
increase 251.4
enlarge 259.4
construct 266.5
compose 795.3
produce 891.8

building
n house 228.5
structure 266.1
edifice 266.2
composition 795.1
production 891.2
adj constructional
891.15

building blocks
essential content
196.5
substance 762.2

build on 199.6

buildup
increase 251.1
promotion 352.5
commendation 509.3
composition 795.1

build up
aggravate 119.2
increase 251.4
enlarge 259.4
publicize 352.15
exaggerate 355.3
prepare oneself 405.13
compose 795.3

built made 891.18
comely 1015.18

built-in 771.5

bulb sphere 282.2
bulge 283.3
root 310.20

bulbous
spherical 282.9
bulging 283.15
vegetable 310.33

bulge
n goozle 2.17
advantage 249.2
bilge 283.3
v bilge 283.11

bulging
n convexity 283.1
protuberance 283.2
adj rotund 282.8
spherical 282.9
swelling 283.15
full 793.11

bulimia 672.1

bulk
n quantity 244.1
greatness 247.1
size 257.1
bulkiness 257.9
thickness 269.2
major part 791.6
majority 882.2
v loom 247.5
size 257.15
enlarge 259.4
expand 259.5
assemble 769.18

bulkhead
partition 213.5
buttress 900.4
harbor 1008.6
barrier 1011.5

bulky large 247.7
hulky 257.19
thick 269.8
sturdy 762.7
unwieldy 1012.19

bull
n male animal 76.8
cattle 311.6
humbug 354.14
decree 420.4
jailer 429.10
bullshit 520.3
long 737.13

card 758.2
grammatical error
974.7
police 1007.16
v talk nonsense 520.5
manipulate the
market 737.25
thrust 901.12
adj masculine 76.11

bull's-eye center 208.2
objective 380.2
score 409.5

bulldog
n brave person 492.8
adhesive 802.4
v fell 912.5

bulldoze
intimidate 127.20
raze 395.19
defeat 412.9
coerce 424.8
threaten 514.2
domineer 612.16
thrust 901.12

bulldozer
n strong man 15.6
tractor 179.18
adj coercive 424.12

bullet swiftness 174.6
round 462.19
game 745.3
card 758.2
shot 903.4
fission 1037.8

bulletin
n press release 352.3
report 549.7
information 551.1
news report 552.5
v publicize 352.15

bulletproof 15.20

bullfight 457.4

bullfighter 461.4

bullheaded
obstinate 361.8
adhesive 802.12

bullion
precious metals
728.20
cast 1056.5

bull market
rising market 737.4
roaring trade 1009.5

bull session 541.3

bullshit
n humbug 354.14
boasting 502.2
shit 520.3
absurdity 922.3
v boast 502.7
talk nonsense 520.5

bullwhack 605.1

bullwhacker 178.9

bully
n beef 10.13
strong man 15.7
tormentor 96.10
combatant 461.1
blusterer 503.2
ruffian 593.3
game 749.6
v intimidate 127.20

coerce 424.7
bluster 503.3
domineer 612.16
adj excellent 998.13

bulwark
n fortification 460.4
buttress 900.4
safeguard 1007.3
barrier 1011.5
v fortify 460.9

bum
n drunk 88.12
vagabond 178.3
buttocks 217.5
stiff 331.9
failure 410.8
beggar 440.8
wretch 660.2
transient 827.4
v hum 52.13
wander 177.23
beg 440.15
adj bad 999.8

the bum's rush 908.1

bum around 331.12

bumble 414.11

bumbledom 612.11

bumbler 414.8

bummer
substance abuse 87.1
vagabond 178.3
nonworker 331.11
beggar 440.8
wretch 660.2
adversity 1010.1

bump
n thud 52.3
report 56.1
atmosphere 184.32
bulge 283.3
swelling 283.4
talent 413.4
demotion 447.1
print 517.7
poker 759.10
thrust 901.2
impact 901.3
shake 916.3
v crack 56.6
demote 447.3
thrust 901.12
collide 901.13
dismiss 908.20
shake 916.11

bumper
n drink 8.4
partition 213.5
full measure 793.3
safeguard 1007.3
adj large 257.16

bump into meet 223.11
collide 901.13
come across 940.3

bumpkin peasant 606.6
oaf 923.5

bump off
n homicide 308.2
v kill 308.13

bumptious
conceited 140.11
insolent 142.9
defiant 454.7

immodest 666.6
bumpy bulging 283.15
  rough 288.6
  nappy 294.7
  jolting 916.20
bum steer 356.2
bun braid 3.7
  roll 10.30
bunch
  n amount 244.2
  bulge 283.3
  clique 617.6
  company 769.3
  group of animals
    769.5
  assemblage 769.7
  conglomeration 802.5
  multitude 883.3
  v come together
    769.16
  assemble 769.18
  cohere 802.6
  league 804.4
bunchy 283.15
bunco
  n fraud 356.8
  cheater 357.4
  v cheat 356.18
bundle
  n gain 472.3
  wealth 618.3
  bindle 769.8
  v snuggle 121.10
  way of walking 177.28
  package 212.9
  hasten 401.4
  move quickly 401.5
  cuddle 562.17
  swaddle 769.20
  bind 799.9
  dismiss 908.18
bundle off start 903.13
  dismiss 908.18
bundle up clothe 5.38
  bundle 769.20
bung
  n anus 292.5
  stopper 293.4
  v stop 293.7
  injure 393.13
bungalow 228.8
bungle
  n fiasco 410.6
  blunder 414.5
  error 974.5
  v do carelessly 340.9
  miss 410.14
  blunder 414.11
  fail 974.14
bunion sore 85.36
  swelling 283.4
bunk
  n humbug 354.14
  boasting 502.2
  bullshit 520.3
  v inhabit 225.7
  house 225.10
bunker
  n cellar 197.17
  cave 284.5
  storehouse 386.6
  entrenchment 460.5

stronghold 460.6
golf 751.1
shelter 1008.3
proving ground
  1072.7
v provision 385.9
bunkum
  humbug 354.14
  boasting 502.2
  flattery 511.1
  bullshit 520.3
  political jargon
    609.37
bunny hare 311.24
  beauty 1015.9
bunt
  n game 745.3
  thrust 901.2
  pushing 903.1
  v thrust 901.12
  tap 901.18
  push 903.9
bunting 647.6
buoy
  n float 180.11
  life preserver 397.6
  marker 517.10
  v lighten up 298.8
buoyant
  lighthearted 109.12
  floaty 298.14
  recuperative 396.23
  elastic 1046.7
buoy up
  cheer 109.7
  buoy 298.8
  support 900.21
  elevate 911.5
burble
  n flow 184.29
  v ripple 52.11
  bubble 320.4
  be stupid 921.12
burden
  n affliction 96.8
  load 196.2
  capacity 257.2
  burthen 297.7
  duty 641.1
  charge 643.3
  guilt 656.1
  part 708.22
  passage 708.24
  poetry 720.9
  repeat 848.5
  topic 936.1
  bane 1000.1
  impediment 1011.6
  v distress 96.16
  oppress 98.16
  load 159.15
  burthen 297.13
  task 725.16
  inconvenience 995.4
  go hard with 1010.8
  hamper 1011.11
burdened
  weighted 297.18
  fraught 793.12
  supporting 900.23
burden of proof 956.3

burdensome
  oppressive 98.24
  onerous 297.17
  laborious 725.18
  hampering 1011.18
  troublesome 1012.18
bureau 594.4
bureaucracy
  routine 373.6
  the authorities 575.15
  officialism 612.11
bureaucratic
  governmental 612.17
  executive 612.19
burg 230.1
burgeon
  n branch 310.18
  bud 310.21
  v grow 14.2
  expand 259.7
  vegetate 310.31
burgher
  townsman 227.6
  respectable citizen
    659.3
  conformist 866.2
burglar 483.3
burglary 482.5
burial interment 309.1
  funeral 309.5
  tomb 309.16
  concealment 346.1
  submergence 367.2
  overrunning 909.1
buried
  underground 275.12
  underwater 275.13
  concealed 346.11
  overrun 909.10
  engrossed 982.17
burl 283.3
burlesque
  n imitation 336.1
  reproduction 336.3
  bad likeness 350.2
  exaggeration 355.1
  wit 489.1
  lampoon 508.6
  disparagement 512.5
  show business 704.1
  similarity 783.1
  v misrepresent 350.3
  exaggerate 355.3
  ridicule 508.11
  lampoon 512.12
  adj comical 488.6
  farcical 508.14
burly
  able-bodied 15.16
  corpulent 257.18
burn
  n smart 26.3
  trauma 85.37
  stream 238.1
  deception 356.9
  theft 482.4
  scald 1019.6
  rocket launching
    1072.9
  spacecraft 1073.2
  v pain 26.7

brown 40.2
be angry 152.15
cremate 309.20
deceive 356.19
injure 393.13
rob 482.16
execute 604.17
rage 671.11
play 747.4
throw 903.10
scent 940.6
be hot 1018.22
ignite 1019.22
catch fire 1019.23
torrefy 1019.24
shine 1024.23
dry 1064.6
burner destroyer 395.8
  heater 1019.10
  incinerator 1019.13
  blowtorch 1019.14
burn in effigy 661.9
burning
  n smart 26.3
  cremation 309.2
  discard 390.3
  capital punishment
    604.7
  throwing 903.2
  heat 1018.1
  combustion 1019.5
  adj sore 26.11
  colorful 35.18
  zestful 68.7
  in heat 75.27
  feverish 85.57
  fervent 93.18
  zealous 101.9
  excited 105.22
  resentful 152.26
  seething 152.29
  near 223.14
  vehement 544.13
  hot 1018.25
  ignited 1018.27
  heating 1019.26
  luminous 1024.30
  flashing 1024.34
burnish
  n polish 287.2
  smoother 287.4
  v polish 287.7
  buff 1042.8
burn one's bridges
  leave home 188.17
  be determined 359.8
burnout fatigue 21.1
  apathy 94.4
  extinguishing 1021.2
  rocket launching
    1072.9
burn out fatigue 21.4
  get tired 21.5
  go out 1021.8
burnt
  red-complexioned
    41.9
  burned 1019.30
  dried 1064.9
burn the candle at both
  ends squander 486.3
  dissipate 669.6

overdo 992.10
burn the midnight oil
  study 570.12
  work hard 725.13
  be late 845.7
burn up annoy 96.13
  consume 388.3
  incendiarize 1019.25
burp
  n belch 908.9
  v expel 908.28
burr
  n rasp 58.3
  thorn 285.5
  seed vessel 310.28
  accent 524.9
  engraving 713.2
  adhesive 802.4
  v hum 52.13
  sound harshly 58.9
burro 311.16
burrow
  n lair 228.26
  cave 284.5
  v settle 159.17
  excavate 284.15
  hide 346.8
  search 937.30
bursar payer 624.9
  treasurer 729.11
burst
  n report 56.1
  detonation 56.3
  outburst 105.9
  resentment 152.9
  run 174.3
  bustle 330.4
  volley 459.9
  violence 671.6
  explosion 671.7
  separate 801.4
  flare 1018.14
  v blast 56.8
  break 393.23
  explode 671.14
  break 801.12
  adj impaired 393.27
  broken 801.24
burst forth
  break forth 33.9
  emerge 190.11
  vegetate 310.31
  erupt 671.13
  originate 817.13
burst in enter 189.7
  intrude 214.5
  breach 292.14
bursting
  n disruption 801.3
  adj banging 56.11
  excited 105.20
  explosive 671.24
  full 793.11
  teeming 883.9
  productive 889.9
  brimming 992.20
burst one's bubble
  sadden 112.18
  shatter one's hopes
    125.11
burst out erupt 671.13
  exclaim 59.7

laugh 116.8
bury inter 309.19
  secrete 346.7
  submerge 367.7
bury oneself in 570.12
bury the hatchet
  forget 148.5
  make peace 465.9
bus
  n car 179.10
  public vehicle 179.13
  v haul 176.13
  ride 177.33
busboy 577.7
bush
  marijuana 87.10
  lining 196.3
  hinterland 233.2
  shrubbery 310.9
  woodland 310.11
  brush 310.14
  wasteland 890.2
bushed 21.8
bush-league 1004.7
bushwhack
  surprise 131.7
  kill 308.13
  attack 459.15
bushwhacker
  irregular 461.16
  precursor 815.1
bushy hairy 3.24
  arboreal 310.36
  sylvan 310.37
business
  n action 328.1
  activity 330.1
  undertaking 404.1
  company 617.9
  duty 641.1
  acting 704.8
  occupation 724.1
  vocation 724.6
  commerce 731.1
  relation 774.1
  affair 830.3
  specialty 865.1
  adj occupational
    730.12
  commercial 731.21
the business 356.9
businesslike 806.6
businessman
  businessperson 730
  businesswoman 730.1
busman's holiday 20.3
buss
  n kiss 562.4
  v kiss 562.19
bust
  n drinking spree 88.6
  breast 283.6
  figure 349.6
  failure 410.2
  washout 410.8
  arrest 429.6
  demotion 447.1
  monument 549.12
  insolvency 625.3
  business cycle 731.9
  blow 901.5
  hard times 1010.6

v flunk 410.17
  arrest 429.16
  domesticate 432.11
  demote 447.3
  depose 447.4
  go under 625.7
  bankrupt 625.8
  explode 671.14
  break 801.12
  dismiss 908.19
busted impaired 393.27
  without money 619.10
  insolvent 625.11
  broken 801.24
bust in enter 189.7
  breach 292.14
bustle
  n excitement 105.4
  fuss 330.4
  haste 401.1
  bluster 503.1
  agitation 916.1
  v fuss 330.12
  hasten 401.4
  move quickly 401.5
bustling
  fussing 330.20
  eventful 830.10
bust out 431.8
busty
  corpulent 257.18
  pectoral 283.19
busy
  v occupy 724.10
  task 725.16
  adj meddlesome 214.9
  full of business 330.21
  ornate 498.12
  occupied 724.15
busybody
  n meddler 214.4
  newsmonger 552.9
  inquisitive person
    980.2
  v meddle 214.7
  adj meddlesome 214.9
busywork 724.2
but
  notwithstanding
    338.8
  unless 958.16
butch
  n mannish female
    76.9
  adj homosexual 75.29
butcher
  n killer 308.10
  vendor 730.5
  v slaughter 308.16
  misdraw 350.4
  bungle 414.11
  rage 671.11
  sever 801.11
butchered
  botched 414.21
  mutilated 794.5
butler steward 574.4
  man 577.4
  major-domo 577.10
butt
  n cigarette 89.5
  buttocks 217.5

remainder 256.1
  objective 380.2
  laughingstock 508.7
  piece 792.3
  joint 799.4
  extremity 819.2
  thrust 901.2
  pushing 903.1
  v adjoin 223.9
  hook 799.8
  thrust 901.12
  push 903.9
butte plateau 237.3
  hill 237.4
butter
  n suavity 504.5
  softness 1045.4
  semiliquid 1060.5
  pulp 1061.2
  v coat 295.24
  flatter 511.6
butterfingers 414.9
butterflies 128.2
buttery
  n storehouse 386.6
  larder 386.8
  adj slippery 287.11
  suave 504.18
  flattering 511.8
  oily 1054.9
  semiliquid 1060.11
butt in intrude 214.5
  mediate 466.6
  talk out of turn 843.4
buttinsky 422.3
buttocks
  bottom 199.1
  rump 217.4
button
  n chin 216.6
  runt 258.4
  bulge 283.3
  insignia 647.1
  trifle 997.5
  cast 1056.5
  v close 293.6
  hook 799.8
buttoned-down 866.6
buttonhole
  n bouquet 310.23
  v bore 118.7
  importune 440.12
  address 524.27
button up
  be silent 51.6
  close 293.6
  complete 407.6
butt out
  v not interfere 430.17
  phrs none of your
    business 214.10
buttress
  n supporter 900.2
  buttressing 900.4
  v strengthen 15.13
  help 449.12
  support 900.21
  confirm 956.11
buxom
  merry 109.15
  corpulent 257.18
  comely 1015.18

buy
n bargain 633.3
v assent 332.8
bribe 378.3
take advice 422.7
purchase 733.7
believe 952.10
kid oneself 953.6
buyer 733.5
buyers' market
cheapening 633.4
low price 633.2
commerce 731.1
sale 734.1
buy into
take advice 422.7
invest 729.16
purchase 733.7
believe 952.10
kid oneself 953.6
buyout
n trading 737.19
combination 804.1
v purchase 733.7
combine 804.3
buzz
n sibilation 57.1
rasp 58.3
tingle 74.1
substance abuse 87.1
telephone call 347.13
report 552.6
series 811.2
v hum 52.13
sibilate 57.2
sound harshly 58.9
flathat 184.42
telephone 347.18
publish 352.10
speak 524.26
tip off 551.11
buzzer 400.1
buzzing
n hum 52.7
flathatting 184.17
adj humming 52.20
buzz off
v depart 188.7
inter go away! 908.31
by
adj past 836.7
adv in reserve 386.17
prep at 159.27
through 161.27
beside 218.11
by means of 384.13
conformable to 866.9
by all means
adv certainly 969.23
inter yes 332.18
by all odds
by far 247.17
probably 967.8
by and by
in the future 838.9
soon 844.16
by and large
approximately 244.6
on the whole 791.14
generally 863.17
by any means
anyhow 384.10

by any possibility
965.10
by bits and pieces
incompletely 794.6
disjointedly 801.28
by chance
haphazardly 809.18
perchance 971.19
by degrees
degreewise 245.6
piece by piece 792.9
by design 380.10
by dint of
adv usefully 387.26
prep by virtue of
18.18
by means of 384.13
by ear 365.15
bye-bye 22.2
by far 247.17
by fits and starts
nonuniformly 781.4
disjointedly 801.28
haphazardly 809.18
discontinuously 812.5
irregularly 850.3
shakily 916.23
bygone 836.7
by hand 176.19
by heart 988.28
by hook or by crook
384.11
by inches
by degrees 245.6
piece by piece 792.9
bylaw 673.3
by law 673.12
by leaps and bounds
in progress 162.7
swiftly 174.17
by-line
avocation 724.7
acknowledgment
887.2
by means of
through the agency of
384.13
helped by 449.25
by nature 766.10
by no means
adv noway 248.11
inter by no manner of
means 335.9
God forbid! 510.27
phrs I refuse 442.7
by oneself
adj solitary 584.11
adv independently
430.33
singly 871.13
bypass
n byway 383.4
detour 913.3
v pass 909.8
go roundabout 913.4
by-product
aftermath 816.3
effect 886.1
extract 892.3
by proxy
indirectly 576.17
instead 861.11

by rights 637.4
bystander
neighbor 223.6
spectator 917.1
witness 956.6
by storm 18.17
byte 1041.14
by the board
adj lost 473.7
adv overboard 182.74
by the same token
additionally 253.11
accordingly 765.11
similarly 783.18
by the way
discursive 538.13
incidental 842.11
timely 842.13
by virtue of
by dint of 18.18
by means of 384.13
by authority of
417.20
because of 887.9
by virtue of office
417.18
byway
bypath 383.4
digression 538.4
by way of
through 161.27
by means of 384.13
byword
laughingstock 508.7
catchword 526.9
name 527.3
disgrace 661.5
maxim 973.1
Byzantine
n Aldine 554.15
adj convolutional
281.6
scheming 381.13
complex 798.4
shrewd 919.15
c'est la vie 963.11
cab 179.13
cabal
n intrigue 381.5
fellowship 617.3
clique 617.6
company 769.3
combination 804.1
v plot 381.9
league 804.4
cabalistic secret 345.11
occult 689.23
leagued 804.6
caballero beau 104.13
rider 178.8
knight 608.5
cabaret bar 88.20
theater 704.14
entertainment 743.13
cabbagehead 923.4
cabdriver driver 178.9
chauffeur 178.10
cabin
n stateroom 197.9
cottage 228.8
v confine 212.6
cabin boy hand 183.6

attendant 577.5
cabinet container 195.1
sanctum 197.8
furniture 229.1
council 423.1
directorate 574.11
ministry 613.3
office 739.7
radio 1033.3
cable
n cord 271.2
telegram 347.14
line 347.17
electrical device
1031.20
v telegraph 347.19
caboose kitchen 11.3
sequel 816.1
cache
n hiding place 346.4
reserve 386.3
v secrete 346.7
store 386.10
cachet
label 517.13
characteristic 864.4
cackle
n rasp 58.3
laughter 116.4
chatter 540.3
v sound harshly 58.9
bird sound 60.5
laugh 116.8
speak 524.26
cacophony
raucousness 58.2
discord 61.1
inelegance 534.1
turbulence 671.2
pandemonium 809.5
ugliness 1014.1
cactus mescaline 87.12
peyote 87.16
thorn 285.5
cad vulgarian 497.6
bounder 660.8
cadaver 307.16
cadaverous
tired-looking 21.9
colorless 36.7
haggard 270.20
deathly 307.29
caddie carrier 176.7
attendant 577.5
cadence sinkage 194.2
accent 524.11
passage 708.24
ornament 709.18
harmony 709.23
meter 720.7
cadenza
impromptu 708.27
ornament 709.18
cadet
n navy man 183.4
undergraduate 572.6
adj subsequent 834.4
cadger
nonworker 331.11
beggar 440.8
vendor 730.5
cadre frame 266.4

military unit 461.22
directorate 574.11
clique 617.6
caduceus 417.9
caesar ruler 575.9
tyrant 575.14
caesura
interval 224.1
meter 720.7
interruption 812.2
pause 856.3
grammar 856.4
café
restaurant 8.17
bar 88.20
cafeteria
restaurant 8.17
dining room 197.11
cage
n place of
confinement 429.7
hockey 749.1
gambling wheel
759.16
v enclose 212.5
confine 429.12
drive 1068.8
cagey evasive 368.15
cunning 415.12
wary 494.9
cahoots
affiliation 450.2
concurrence 898.1
Cain 308.10
cairn marker 517.10
monument 549.12
cajole deceive 356.14
urge 375.14
lure 377.5
importune 440.12
flatter 511.5
cake
n food 10.40
solid 1043.6
v thicken 1043.10
solidify 1044.8
caked 1043.14
calamitous
destructive 395.26
disastrous 1010.15
calamity fatality 308.7
bane 1000.1
misfortune 1010.2
calcify 1044.7
calcimine
n whitening agent
37.4
v color 35.13
whitewash 37.6
calculable
measurable 300.14
predictable 961.13
reliable 969.17
computable 1016.24
calculate
measure 300.10
intend 380.6
premeditate 380.7
plan 381.8
compute 1016.17
calculated
intentional 380.8

planned 381.12
reasoned 934.21
calculating
deceitful 356.22
scheming 381.13
sly 645.18
shrewd 919.15
numerative 1016.23
calculation
measurement 300.1
intentionality 380.3
plan 381.1
caution 494.1
computation 1016.10
calculator adding 253.3
strategist 415.7
accountant 628.7
computer 1016.14
calculus 1016.10
caldron 857.10
calefacient 1019.26
calendar
n record book 549.11
reference book 554.9
bill 613.9
calends 831.8
roll 870.6
schedule 964.3
v record 549.15
chronologize 831.14
list 870.8
schedule 964.6
calender 287.6
calf member 2.7
leg 177.14
fledgling 302.10
cattle 311.6
ice 1022.5
caliber ability 18.2
degree 245.1
size 257.1
diameter 269.3
talent 413.4
intelligence 919.1
calibrate
graduate 245.4
measure 300.10
calico 47.12
caliper 300.10
caliph 575.10
calisthenics
exercise 84.2
physical education
568.9
call
n audition 48.2
yell 59
cry 59.1
animal noise 60.1
telephone message
347.13
command 420.5
demand 421.1
entreaty 440.2
invitation 440.4
summons 517.16
visit 582.7
warrant 600.6
enlistment 615.7
the ministry 698.1
option 737.21
bridge 758.3

v cry 59.6
wail 60.2
bird sound 60.5
telephone 347.18
summon 420.11
invite 440.13
name 527.11
bill 628.11
gamble 759.23
estimate 945.9
predict 961.9
call a halt to 856.11
call a spade a spade
be frank 644.12
keep both feet on the
ground 986.4
call attention to
remark 524.25
direct attention to
982.10
call down 510.18
caller
telephoner 347.11
errand boy 353.4
guest 585.6
call for
n requirement 962.2
v fetch 176.16
summon 420.11
demand 421.5
oblige 424.5
request 440.9
entail 771.4
require 962.9
call forth excite 105.12
elicit 192.14
prompt 375.13
summon 420.11
induce 885.11
call girl 665.16
calligrapher
writer 547.13
limner 716.2
calligraphy
handwriting 547.3
fine writing 547.5
visual arts 712.1
calling motive 375.1
summons 420.5
invitation 440.4
naming 527.2
holy orders 698.10
vocation 724.6
calling card 517.11
call into question
contradict 451.6
doubt 954.6
call it a day
take a rest 20.8
complete 407.6
stop work 856.8
call names offend 156.5
vilify 512.10
curse 513.7
call off end 819.5
number 1016.16
call on urge 375.14
command 420.8
petition 440.10
entreat 440.11
visit 582.19
call one's bluff 454.6

callous
v harden 94.6
numb 1044.7
adj insensible 25.6
calloused 94.12
impenitent 114.5
heartless 144.25
hardened 654.17
unfeeling 1044.13
call out vociferate 59.8
elicit 192.14
summon 420.11
demand 421.5
defy 454.3
callow
immature 301.10
unprepared 406.11
inexperienced 414.17
incomplete 794.4
new 840.7
ignorant 929.12
call someone's bluff
confront 216.8
risk 971.12
call the shots
command 420.8
direct 573.8
control 612.13
exercise influence
893.8
call time 825.3
call to account
censure 510.13
reprove 510.17
punish 604.10
obligate 641.12
call up excite 105.12
elicit 192.14
telephone 347.18
prompt 375.13
summon 420.11
call to arms 458.19
enlist 615.17
conjure 690.11
resemble 783.7
visualize 985.15
remember 988.10
call-up
call to arms 458.8
enlistment 615.7
assemblage 769.1
call upon
petition 440.10
entreat 440.11
visit 582.19
urge 375.14
avail oneself of 387.14
command 420.8
callus 85.38
calm
n composure 106.2
unastonishment 123.1
lull 173.5
moderation 670.1
uniformity 780.1
v be cool 106.6
quiet 173.8
pacify 465.7
moderate 670.7
adj placid 106.12
unastonished 123.3
unnervous 129.2

quiescent 173.12
pacific 464.9
equable 670.13
thoughtless 932.4
calmative
  n sedative 86.12
  moderator 670.3
  adj sedative 86.45
  palliative 670.16
calming
  n pacification 465.1
  modulation 670.2
  adj tranquilizing
    670.15
calorie energy unit 17.7
  thermal unit 1018.19
calorific 1019.26
calumnious
  insulting 156.8
  disparaging 512.13
  cursing 513.8
calumny slander 512.3
  vilification 513.2
Calvinist
  n determinist 963.5
  adj Protestant 675.28
camaraderie
  affiliation 450.2
  fellowship 582.2
  companionship 587.2
camber arch 279.4
  convexity 283.1
camel
  beast of burden 176.8
  hoofed animal 311.5
camelback
  n deformity 265.3
  adj humpbacked
    265.13
cameo
  description 349.2
  script 706.2
  relief 715.3
camera lens 29.2
  Kodak 714.11
cameraman
  motion-picture
    photography 706.4
  photographer 716.5
  television technician
    1034.13
camisole 428.4
camouflage
  n cover 356.11
  dissimilarity 786.1
  v conceal 346.6
  misrepresent 350.3
  falsify 354.15
  disguise 786.3
camouflaged
  invisible 32.5
  disguised 346.13
camp
  n camping 225.4
  encampment 228.29
  settlement 463.3
  vulgarity 497.1
  political party 609.24
  association 617.4
  v settle 159.17
  encamp 225.11
  adj comic 704.35

campaign
  n journey 177.5
  war 458.4
  politics 609.13
  cause 885.9
  v journey 177.21
  undertake operations
    458.17
  electioneer 609.40
  go into politics 610.13
campaigner
  veteran 461.19
  electioneer 610.10
campaign for 509.13
campanile 272.6
camper traveler 178.1
  vehicle 179.19
  trailer 228.17
campfire 1018.13
camp follower
  follower 166.2
  associate 616.8
campground 463.3
campo plain 236.1
  grassland 310.8
campus arena 463.1
  schoolhouse 567.10
can
  n latrine 12.10
  toilet 12.11
  battleship 180.7
  buttocks 217.5
  jail 429.9
  marker 517.10
  v be able 18.11
  package 212.9
  put up 397.11
  may 443.13
  sink 747.4
  play 751.4
  dismiss 908.20
canal
  n duct 2.21
  channel 239.1
  watercourse 239.2
  inlet 242.1
  narrow place 270.3
  trench 290.2
  v furrow 290.3
canard
  fabrication 354.10
  report 552.6
canary
  n singer 710.13
  songbird 710.23
  adj yellow 43.4
cancel
  n obliteration 395.7
  repeal 445.1
  notation 709.12
  v excise 255.10
  delete 255.12
  abolish 395.13
  obliterate 395.16
  repeal 445.2
  declare a moratorium
    625.9
  equalize 789.6
  end 819.5
  cease 856.6
  neutralize 899.7
canceled forgiven 148.7

ended 819.8
cancellate 170.11
cancer
  growth 85.38
  blight 1000.2
cancerous 85.60
candescent
  burning 1018.27
  luminous 1024.30
candid
  v talkative 540.9
  adj communicative
    343.10
  artless 416.5
  free-acting 430.23
  natural 499.7
  plain-speaking 535.3
  frank 644.17
  genuine 972.15
candidacy 609.10
candidate
  desirer 100.12
  petitioner 440.7
  aspirant 610.9
  assignee 615.9
candle
  light source 1025.1
  taper 1025.2
candlelit 1024.39
can do
  v be able 18.11
  adj energetic 17.13
  active 330.17
candor
  communicativeness
    343.3
  artlessness 416.1
  plain speech 535.1
  talkativeness 540.1
  candidness 644.4
  fairness 649.3
candy
  n sweets 10.38
  amyl nitrate 87.4
  v sweeten 66.3
  solidify 1044.8
candy-stripe
  n stripe 47.5
  adj striped 47.15
cane
  n blind 30.6
  staff 273.2
  grass 310.5
  stem 310.19
  rod 605.2
  supporter 900.2
  bamboo 1052.4
  v whip 604.13
canicular
  seasonal 313.9
  hot 1018.25
canine
  n teeth 2.8
  creature 311.3
  dog 311.17
  adj doggish 311.40
canker
  n sore 85.36
  blight 1000.2
  v corrupt 393.12
  corrode 393.21
  decay 393.22

cankered
  diseased 85.59
  irascible 110.19
  decayed 393.40
cannibal
  n eater 8.16
  killer 308.10
  creature 311.3
  savage 593.5
  adj eating 8.31
cannibalize 365.8
cannon
  n artillery 462.11
  game 745.3
  impact 901.3
  recoil 902.2
  shot 903.4
  v pull the trigger
    459.22
  collide 901.13
  recoil 902.6
cannonade
  n boom 56.4
  volley 459.9
  v pull the trigger
    459.22
cannonball
  swiftness 174.6
  plunge 367.1
  shot 462.19
cannot 19.8
canny cunning 415.12
  cautious 494.8
  economical 635.6
  shrewd 919.15
canoe
  n roulette 759.12
  v navigate 182.13
can of worms
  hodgepodge 796.6
  complex 798.2
  trouble 1012.3
canon music 280.9
  measure 300.2
  precept 419.2
  literature 547.12
  compilation 554.7
  law 673.3
  Bible 683.2
  round 708.19
  scripture 718.1
  rule 868.4
  lore 927.9
  a belief 952.2
canonical
  preceptive 419.4
  theological 676.4
  scriptural 683.10
  orthodox 687.7
  ecclesiastic 698.13
  doctrinal 952.27
canonize
  glorify 662.13
  sanctify 685.5
  ordain 698.12
  exalt 911.6
canopy
  n the heavens 1070.2
  v cover 295.19
cant
  n inclination 204.2
  angle 278.2

hypocrisy 354.6
Greek 522.7
jargon 523.9
sanctimony 693.1
v change course
182.30
careen 182.43
incline 204.10
be hypocritical 354.22
speak 523.16
be sanctimonious
693.4
cantankerous
irascible 110.20
perverse 361.11
hindering 1011.17
cantata
sacred music 708.17
part music 708.18
canteen 8.17
canter
n run 174.3
hypocrite 357.8
pietist 693.3
v speed 174.8
go on horseback
177.34
canticle paean 696.3
song 708.14
sacred music 708.17
cantilever 202.3
cantina 8.17
canto air 708.4
part 708.22
poetry 720.9
fight 754.3
canton region 231.5
heraldry 647.2
cantor clergy 699.10
singer 710.13
choirmaster 710.18
canvas sail 180.14
tent 295.8
arena 463.1
painting 712.14
art equipment 712.18
boxing 754.1
canvass
n vote 371.6
solicitation 440.5
campaign 609.13
assemblage 769.1
survey 937.14
v vote 371.18
solicit 440.14
discuss 541.12
electioneer 609.40
examine 937.23
survey 937.28
canvasser
traveling salesman
730.4
solicitor 730.6
canyon 237.7
cap
n headdress 5.25
LSD 87.9
summit 198.2
top part 198.4
architectural topping
198.5
cover 295.5

fuse 462.15
type 548.6
v cloak 5.39
top 198.9
excel 249.6
cover 295.21
complete 407.6
give in kind 506.6
capability ability 18.2
preparedness 405.4
skill 413.1
talent 413.4
capable able 18.14
fitted 405.17
competent 413.24
liable to 896.6
capacious
spacious 158.10
voluminous 257.17
capacitate 405.8
capacities 918.2
capacity
n ability 18.2
spaciousness 158.5
volume 257.2
means 384.2
skill 413.1
talent 413.4
function 724.3
mode 764.4
full measure 793.3
intelligence 919.1
capacitance 1031.15
adj full 793.11
caparison
n wardrobe 5.2
horsecloth 295.11
harness 385.5
v outfit 5.40
cape 283.9
caper
n dido 366.2
prank 489.10
frolic 743.5
v exude cheerfulness
109.6
rejoice 116.5
leap 366.6
play 743.23
capillary
n duct 2.21
adj circulatory 2.31
hairlike 3.23
threadlike 271.7
capital
n architectural
topping 198.5
metropolis 208.7
city 230.4
means 384.2
supply 386.2
type 548.6
fund 728.15
adj top 198.10
chief 249.14
literal 546.8
monetary 728.30
paramount 996.24
good 998.12
capitalism
noninterference 430.9
political system 611.8

capitalist
n coupon-clipper
611.15
rich man 618.7
financier 729.8
adj bourgeois 611.23
capitalize letter 546.6
keep accounts 628.8
finance 729.15
capitalize on
take advantage of
387.15
profit 472.12
improve the occasion
842.8
capital punishment
condemnation 602.1
execution 604.7
capitol 613.4
capitulate 433.8
capitulation
surrender 433.2
treaty 437.2
summation 1016.11
a cappella 708.53
capping
topping 198.11
superior 249.12
ending 819.10
caprice whim 364
impulse 364.1
capriciousness 364.2
thoughtlessness 365.3
capricious
irresolute 362.9
whimsical 364.5
unthinking 365.10
unessential 767.4
nonuniform 781.3
unordered 809.12
transient 827.7
irregular 850.3
inconstant 853.7
uncertain 970.16
capriole
n leap 366.1
caper 366.2
v leap 366.5
caper 366.6
capsize
n overturn 205.2
v upset 182.44
tumble 194.8
overturn 205.6
capstone 407.3
capsule
n pill 86.7
hull 295.16
seed vessel 310.28
abridgment 557.1
spacecraft 1073.2
v package 212.9
abridge 557.5
adj shortened 268.9
captain
n ship's officer 183.7
aviator 185.1
governor 575.6
commissioned officer
575.18
naval officer 575.20
policeman 1007.15

v direct 573.8
govern 612.12
caption
n title 936.2
v focus on 936.3
captious
critical 510.23
quibbling 935.14
captivate delight 95.9
enamor 104.23
persuade 375.23
fascinate 377.7
charm 691.8
captivated
enamored 104.28
wondering 122.9
enchanted 691.12
captivating
delightful 97.7
alluring 377.8
captive
n prisoner 429.11
subject 432.7
adj subjugated 432.14
capture
n arrest 429.6
seizure 480.2
take 480.10
v triumph 411.3
arrest 429.15
acquire 472.8
apprehend 480.18
car
vehicle 179.9
railway car 179.15
automobile racing
756.1
carabineer
infantryman 461.9
shooter 903.8
caracole
n caper 366.2
v exude cheerfulness
109.6
rejoice 116.5
go on horseback
177.34
caper 366.6
play 743.23
carapace
shell 295.15
armor 460.3
caravan wagon 179.2
trailer 179.19
train 228.17
procession 811.3
carbohydrate 7.5
carbon
radiotherapy 91.8
transcript 784.4
combustion product
1019.16
isotope 1037.5
carbonated 320.6
carbon copy
the same 777.3
transcript 784.4
carboniferous 1020.8
carbonize 1019.24
carbonous 1056.15
carbuncle sore 85.36
swelling 283.4

carcass body 2.1
  corpse 307.16
  wreck 393.8
  dead thing 1050.3
carcinogen 85.41
carcinogenic 85.60
carcinoma 85.38
card
  n identification 517.11
  recording media
    549.10
  postcard 553.3
  playing card 758.2
  schedule 964.3
  v comb 79.21
cardboard 1052.5
card-carrying
  real 760.15
  genuine 972.15
card game game 743.9
  cardplaying 758.1
cardholder
  member 617.11
  unionist 727.4
cardinal red 41.6
  chief 249.14
  paramount 996.24
  numeric 1016.22
cardiovascular disease
    85.19
cardsharp cheat 357.3
  gambler 759.21
care
  n medicine 90.1
  affliction 96.8
  sorrow 112.10
  anxiety 126.1
  carefulness 339.1
  usage 387.2
  custody 429.5
  observance 434.1
  support 449.3
  patronage 449.4
  caution 494.1
  supervision 573.2
  commission 615.1
  thrift 635.1
  attention 982.1
  protectorship 1007.2
  adversity 1010.1
  v respond 93.11
  mind 339.6
  adj helping 449.20
careen
  n swing 915.6
  flounder 916.8
  v list 182.43
  tumble 194.8
  incline 204.10
  overturn 205.6
  oscillate 915.10
  flounder 916.15
career
  n progression 162.1
  course 172.2
  vocation 724.6
  v speed 174.8
  flounder 916.15
  adj skilled 413.26
careerism
  ambition 100.10
  selfishness 651.1

  vocation 724.6
care for treat 91.24
  love 104.19
  minister to 387.12
  foster 449.16
  serve 577.13
  protect 1007.19
carefree content 107.7
  lighthearted 109.12
careful
  adj heedful 339.10
  cautious 494.8
  economical 635.6
  conscientious 644.15
  judicious 919.19
  attentive 982.15
  inter be careful!
    494.14
caregiver nurse 90.10
  guardian 1007.6
care-giving
  n support 449.3
  adj helping 449.20
careless
  unconcerned 102.7
  heedless 340.11
  unthinking 365.10
  bungling 414.20
  lax 426.4
  reckless 493.8
  ungrammatic 531.4
  slovenly 809.15
  incurious 981.3
  inattentive 983.6
caress
  n touch 73.1
  contact 223.5
  endearment 562.5
  v stroke 73.8
  contact 223.10
  pet 562.16
  rub 1042.6
caretaker 1007.6
careworn
  sorrowful 112.26
  heavy-laden 126.9
carfare 630.6
cargo freight 176.6
  load 196.2
  burden 297.7
  charge 643.3
  impediment 1011.6
caricature
  n bad likeness 350.2
  exaggeration 355.1
  wit 489.1
  burlesque 508.6
  cartoon 712.16
  v misrepresent 350.3
  exaggerate 355.3
  burlesque 508.11
caries 85.39
carillon
  n bell 54.4
  chimes 711.18
  v blow a horn 708.42
caring
  n sympathy 93.5
  love 104.1
  carefulness 339.1
  support 449.3
  adj careful 339.10

  helping 449.20
carmine
  v make red 41.4
  adj red 41.6
carnage
  massacre 308.4
  destruction 395.1
carnal sexual 75.24
  unvirtuous 654.12
  sensual 663.6
  lascivious 665.29
  secularist 695.16
carnality sexuality 75.2
  amorousness 104.3
  vice 654.1
  sensuality 663.2
  lasciviousness 665.5
  secularism 695.2
carnival treat 95.3
  show business 704.1
  festival 743.4
  park 743.14
carnivore eater 8.16
  creature 311.3
carnivorous 8.31
carol
  n song 708.14
  v bird sound 60.5
  rejoice 116.5
  sing 708.38
carom
  n impact 901.3
  recoil 902.2
  v collide 901.13
  recoil 902.6
carouse
  n spree 88.5
  dissipation 669.2
  revel 743.6
  v go on a spree 88.28
  dissipate 669.6
  make merry 743.24
  riot 809.10
carousel
  merry-go-round
    743.15
  rotator 914.4
carp 510.15
carpet
  n ground covering
    199.3
  rug 295.9
  v floor 295.22
carpetbagger 357.3
carping
  n criticism 510.4
  adj critical 510.23
carriage looks 33.4
  transportation 176.3
  vehicle 179.1
  four-wheeler 179.4
  behavior 321.1
  gesture 517.14
  freightage 630.7
  support 900.1
carriage trade
  society 578.6
  market 733.3
carried away
  overjoyed 95.16
  excited 105.20
  frenzied 105.25

carrier infection 85.4
  vector 85.43
  conveyer 176.7
  vehicle 179.1
  aircraft ship 180.8
  messenger 353.1
  mail deliverer 353.6
  supporter 900.2
  radio wave 1033.11
carrion
  n filth 80.7
  offal 80.9
  corpse 307.16
  rot 393.7
  adj dead 307.30
carry
  n range 158.2
  transportation 176.3
  round 751.3
  v be pregnant 78.12
  use 87.21
  extend 158.8
  transport 176.12
  adopt 371.15
  induce 375.22
  triumph 411.3
  give credit 622.6
  keep accounts 628.8
  deal in 731.15
  support 900.21
carry a torch for 104.20
carry away delight 95.9
  enamor 104.23
  remove 176.11
  kill 308.12
  fascinate 377.7
  triumph 411.3
  abduct 482.20
  come apart 801.9
carry off
  remove 176.11
  kill 308.12
  carry out 328.7
  bring about 407.5
  succeed with 409.11
  triumph 411.3
  seize 480.14
  abduct 482.20
carry on
  be patient 134.4
  be angry 152.15
  misbehave 322.4
  practice 328.8
  keep going 330.15
  persevere 360.2
  direct 573.8
  rage 671.11
  play 743.23
  create disorder 809.11
  endure 826.6
  continue 855.3
  do the usual thing
    868.7
  operate 888.5
carry out
  reach out 261.5
  carry through 328.7
  apply 387.11
  bring about 407.5
  perform 434.3
  execute 437.9
  operate 888.5

incriminate 599.10
cast up erect 200.9
elevate 911.5
sum up 1016.18
casual
n irregular 461.16
poor man 619.4
worker 726.2
adj dressed up 5.45
in dishabille 5.46
unconcerned 102.7
nonchalant 106.15
careless 340.11
unpremeditated
365.11
informal 581.3
circumstantial 765.7
unessential 767.4
unordered 809.12
incidental 842.11
occasional 847.3
undiscriminating
944.5
chance 971.15
purposeless 971.16
easy 1013.13
casualty fatality 308.7
chance event 971.6
misfortune 1010.2
casuistry
insincerity 354.5
ethical philosophy
636.2
argumentation 934.4
sophistry 935.1
cat sharp vision 27.11
man 76.5
bitch 110.12
feline 311.21
whip 605.1
cat's-paw
sycophant 138.3
breeze 318.5
dupe 358.1
instrument 384.4
deputy 576.1
agent 576.3
follower 616.8
catabolism
the body 2.18
metabolism 7.10
transformation 851.3
cataclasm 801.3
cataclysm
overflow 238.6
debacle 395.4
upheaval 671.5
revolution 859.1
misfortune 1010.2
catacombs 309.16
catalepsy
stupor 22.6
unconsciousness 25.2
paralysis 85.27
trance 92.19
inertness 173.4
catalog
n description 349.2
record 549.1
book 549.11
reference 554.9
directory 574.10

account book 628.4
outline 800.4
classified list 870.3
v record 549.15
classify 800.8
represent 808.6
list 870.8
catalysis
dissociation 805.2
transformation 851.3
catalyst
instigator 375.11
dissociation 805.2
transformer 851.5
author 885.4
cataplexy
paralysis 85.27
trance 92.19
catapult
n takeoff 184.8
sling 462.9
toy 743.16
v throw 903.10
cataract
n blindness 30.1
descent 194.1
waterfall 238.11
v descend 194.5
overflow 238.17
catastrophe
debacle 395.4
upheaval 671.5
plot 722.4
end 819.1
revolution 859.1
misfortune 1010.2
catatonic
unconscious 25.8
unfeeling 94.9
inert 173.14
unsociable 583.5
psychotic 925.28
incurious 981.3
catcall
n noisemaker 53.6
boo 508.3
v boo 508.10
catch
n desire 100.11
lover 104.12
surprise 131.2
trick 356.6
proviso 421.3
lock 428.5
seizure 480.2
take 480.10
round 708.19
game 745.3
condition 958.2
good thing
998.5
fault 1002.2
obstacle 1011.4
crux 1012.8
v hear 48.11
take sick 85.46
jump at 101.6
row 182.53
attend 221.8
trap 356.20
acquire 472.8
hook 472.9

take 480.17
understand 521.7
play 745.5
fight 754.4
fix 854.10
discover 940.7
engross 982.13
flame up 1019.23
catch at straws
be hopeful 124.8
be rash 493.5
find fault 510.15
catcher taker 480.11
baseball team 745.2
catch fire
be excitable 105.16
succeed 409.7
catch on 578.8
be hot 1018.22
heat up 1019.23
catching
n seizure 480.2
discovery 940.1
adj poisonous 82.7
contagious 85.61
alluring 377.8
taking 480.25
catch it 604.20
catch on succeed 409.7
understand 521.7
become popular 578.8
catch one's breath
take a rest 20.8
recuperate 396.19
catch short 131.7
catch the eye show 31.4
appear 33.8
meet with attention
982.11
catch up
overtake 174.13
seize 480.14
catchword
call to arms 458.8
clue 517.9
phrase 526.9
makeup 554.12
maxim 973.1
motto 973.4
catchy
deceptive 356.21
melodious 708.48
irregular 850.3
catechism
question 937.10
system of belief 952.3
doctrine 676.2
catechize teach 568.10
inculcate 568.12
interrogate 937.20
catechumen
novice 572.9
believer 692.4
beginner 817.2
convert 857.7
categorical
classificational 808.7
dialectic 934.22
unqualified 959.2
categorize
analyze 800.8
arrange 807.11

classify 808.6
category class 808.2
topic 936.1
catenary
n sinkage 194.2
curve 279.2
adj consecutive 811.9
cater 385.9
catercorner
v cut 204.11
adj transverse 204.19
adv diagonally 204.25
catering cooking 11.1
provision 385.1
caterpillar larva 302.12
insect 311.31
cater to toady to 138.8
indulge 427.6
serve 449.18
caterwaul
n screech 58.4
cry 59.1
animal noise 60.1
v screech 58.8
cry 59.6
wail 60.2
catharsis
defecation 12.2
cleansing 79.2
purgation 92.25
release 120.2
cathartic
n cleanser 79.17
laxative 86.17
adj cleansing 79.28
laxative 86.48
relieving 120.9
cathedral
n church 703.1
adj authoritative
969.18
catheter 239.6
cathexis
cathection 92.34
feeling 93.1
interest 982.2
cathode 1031.8
cathode ray 1032.5
catholic
universal 863.14
broad-minded 978.8
Catholic
n Roman Catholic
675.19
adj religious
denomination 675.29
cathouse
disapproved place
228.28
brothel 665.9
cation
electrolysis 1031.24
element 1058.2
cat man 483.3
catnap
n nap 22.3
v sleep 22.13
cat-o'-nine-tails 605.1
cattle
animal life 311.1
kine 311.6
rabble 606.3

cattleman
stockman 1068.2
herder 1068.3
cattle rustler 483.8
catty peevish 110.22
spiteful 144.21
feline 311.41
disparaging 512.13
cattycorner
adj transverse 204.19
adv diagonally 204.25
catwalk 383.2
Caucasian race 312.2
white man 312.3
caucus
n legislative gathering
609.9
election 609.15
party 617.4
assembly 769.2
v politick 609.38
caudal tail 217.11
final 819.11
caught stuck 854.16
gripped 982.18
caught short
surprised 131.12
unprepared 406.8
caught up in
involved in 897.5
engrossed 982.17
caulk 293.7
cause
n motive 375.1
lawsuit 598.1
warrant 600.6
reason 885
occasion 885.1
principle 885.9
v prompt 375.13
compel 424.4
reason 885.10
perform 891.11
cause célèbre
report 552.6
affair 830.3
caused by 886.8
causeless
chance 971.15
purposeless 971.16
causerie chat 541.4
treatise 556.1
causeway 295.22
caustic
n curve 279.2
cauterant 1019.15
adj acrimonious 17.14
bitter 64.6
pungent 68.6
penetrating 105.31
out of humor 110.17
mordant 144.23
resentful 152.26
satiric 508.13
hostile 589.10
cauterant
n cauterizer 1019.15
adj heating 1019.26
cauterize 1019.24
caution
n wariness 339.1
hesitation 362.3

dissuasion 379.1
warning 399.1
advice 422.1
collateral 438.3
carefulness 494
cautiousness 494.1
tip-off 551.3
game 752.3
incredulity 955.1
forethought 960.2
v dissuade 379.3
warn 399.5
admonish 422.6
cautious slow 175.10
careful 339.10
hesitant 362.11
wary 494.8
incredulous 955.4
cavalcade 811.3
cavalier
n beau 104.13
rider 178.8
gallant 504.9
knight 608.5
escort 768.5
adj disdainful 141.13
gruff 505.7
cave
n lair 228.26
cavern 284.5
debacle 395.4
shelter 1008.3
v sink 194.6
collapse 260.10
hollow 284.13
caveat dissuasion 379.1
warning 399.1
advice 422.1
cave in weaken 16.9
sink 194.6
collapse 260.10
hollow 284.13
breach 292.14
break down 393.24
yield 433.7
cave-in collapse 260.4
debacle 395.4
caveman real man 76.6
ancient 841.7
cavern 284.5
cavernous
abysmal 275.11
concave 284.16
cavil
n criticism 510.4
quibble 935.4
v find fault 510.15
argue 934.16
quibble 935.9
cavity
compartment 197.2
crack 224.2
pit 275.2
concavity 284.2
opening 292.1
cavort
n caper 366.2
v caper 366.6
play 743.23
caw
n rasp 58.3
v sound harshly 58.9

bird sound 60.5
cay 235.2
cease
n cessation 856.1
v disappear 34.2
quiet 173.8
close shop 293.8
give up 370.7
perish 395.23
end 819.5
discontinue 856.6
inter stop! 856.13
cease-fire truce 465.5
pause 856.3
ceaseless nonstop 811.8
perpetual 828.7
constant 846.5
continuing 855.7
cede give up 370.7
yield 433.7
surrender 433.8
relinquish 475.3
transfer 629.3
ceiling
distinctness 31.2
atmosphere 184.32
boundary 211.3
height 272.1
roof 295.6
price index 630.4
limit 793.5
rocket launching
1072.9
celebrate party 487.2
praise 509.12
formalize 580.5
glorify 696.11
observe 701.14
make merry 743.24
celebrated
distinguished 662.16
notable 996.19
celebration
spree 88.5
treat 95.3
rejoicing 116.1
observance 487.1
ceremony 580.4
ritualism 701.1
revel 743.6
celebrity glory 247.2
publicity 352.4
repute 662.1
man of mark 662.9
notability 996.2
personage 996.8
celerity velocity 174.1
quickness 330.3
celestial
n angel 679.1
adj divine 677.17
angelic 679.6
heavenly 681.12
ideal 985.23
the universe 1070.25
celibate
n abstainer 565.2
religious 699.15
adj monastic 565.6
continent 664.6
abstinent 668.10
sole 871.9

unproductive 890.4
cell
compartment 197.2
bioplast 305.4
prison 429.8
refuge 584.6
clique 617.6
retreat 1008.5
cellar cellarage 197.17
storehouse 386.6
cellist 710.5
cellular 305.19
cellulose 305.6
Celsius scale 1018.19
cement
n pavement 383.6
ceramic ware 742.2
adhesive 802.4
hardness 1044.6
building material
1052.2
v floor 295.22
plaster 295.25
put together 799.5
fasten 799.7
stick together 802.9
adj hard 1044.10
cemetery 309.15
cenotaph tomb 309.16
monument 549.12
censer 70.6
censor
n restrictionist 428.6
faultfinder 510.9
conscience 636.5
critic 945.7
v delete 255.12
cover up 345.8
suppress 428.8
end 819.5
censorious averse 99.8
fastidious 495.9
prudish 500.19
disapproving 510.22
condemnatory 602.5
censorship
suppression 92.24
deletion 255.5
veil of secrecy 345.3
restraint 428.2
censure
n reprehension 510.3
incrimination 599.2
condemnation 602.1
stigma 661.6
criticism 945.2
v reprehend 510.13
incriminate 599.10
condemn 602.3
stigmatize 661.9
criticize 945.14
census
n contents 196.1
population 227.1
assemblage 769.1
table 807.4
roll 870.6
numeration 1016.9
summation 1016.11
v number 1016.16
cent money 728.7
trifle 997.5

centenarian
old man 304.2
hundred 881.8
centennial
n anniversary 849.4
hundred 881.8
adj momentary 849.8
hundredth 881.29
center
n interior 207.2
centrum 208.2
mean 246.1
middle course 467.3
moderatism 611.2
core 611.10
football team 746.2
basketball team 747.2
hockey team 749.2
essence 766.2
median 818.1
attractor 906.2
v converge 169.2
centralize 208.9
play 749.7
position 752.4
centerpiece
focus 208.4
feature 996.7
centigrade scale
1018.19
centipede
insect 311.31
hundred 881.8
central
n exchange 347.7
telephone operator
347.9
adj interior 207.6
centric 208.11
medium 246.3
chief 249.14
phonetic 524.31
middle 818.4
original 885.14
vital 996.23
centralize
converge 169.2
center 208.9
league 804.4
centrifugal 171.8
centrifugal force
centripetal force 18.6
repulsion 907.1
centrifuge
n separator 801.7
v whirl 914.11
centripetal
converging 169.3
focal 208.13
middle 818.4
centripetal force
centrifugal force 18.6
attraction 906.1
centrist
n nonpartisan
609.28
political follower
611.10
moderate 670.4
adj neutral 467.7
moderate 611.18
middle 818.4

centurion
Army
noncommissioned
officer 575.19
hundred 881.8
century money 728.7
moment 823.2
long time 826.4
eleven 881.7
hundred 881.8
cephalic 198.14
ceramic 742.7
ceramics
visual arts 712.1
pottery 742
earthenware 742.1
ceramic ware 742.2
cereal
n breakfast food 10.33
grass 310.5
adj vegetable 310.33
cerebral nerve 2.28
mental 918.7
cerebrate 930.8
ceremonial
n formality 580.1
ceremony 580.4
rite 701.3
adj solemn 580.8
ritualistic 701.18
ceremonious
respectful 155.8
gallant 504.15
solemn 580.8
ritualistic 701.18
ceremony
celebration 487.1
formality 580.1
function 580.4
rite 701.3
cerise 41.6
certain
expectant 130.11
quantitative 244.5
secured 438.11
particular 864.12
plural 882.7
evidential 956.16
inevitable 962.15
sure 969.13
impossible 971.18
true 972.13
belief 952.21
certainly 332.18
certainty
expectation 130.1
knowledge 927.1
belief 952.1
conviction 952.5
inevitability 962.7
sureness 969
certitude 969.1
certifiable 925.28
certificate
n certification 549.6
negotiable instrument
728.11
v authorize 443.11
certification
ratification 332.4
deposition 334.3
authorization 443.3

credential 549.6
confirmation 956.4
ensuring 969.8
certified
accepted 332.14
affirmed 334.9
secured 438.11
proved 956.20
assured 969.20
true 972.13
certify ratify 332.12
depose 334.6
secure 438.9
authorize 443.11
testify 956.9
confirm 956.11
make sure 969.11
cerulean
n the heavens 1070.2
adj blue 45.3
cervix genitals 2.11
contraction 260.1
joint 799.4
supporter 900.2
cessation
standstill 173.3
abandonment 370.1
disuse 390.2
interruption 812.2
end 819.1
close 819.3
stop 856
discontinuance 856.1
cession
abandonment 370.3
surrender 433.2
relinquishment 475.1
transfer 629.1
qualification 958.1
cesspool 80.12
chafe
n trauma 85.37
irritation 96.3
abrasion 1042.2
v pain 26.7
irritate 96.14
feel anxious 126.6
be impatient 135.4
be angry 152.15
provoke 152.24
injure 393.13
heat 1019.17
abrade 1042.7
chaff
n remainder 256.1
hull 295.16
lightness 298.2
refuse 391.4
rabble 606.3
trivia 997.2
radar 1035.13
v banter 490.5
scoff 508.9
chagrin
n distress 96.4
humiliation 137.2
v embarrass 96.15
chain
n mountain 237.6
jewel 498.6
insignia 647.1
series 811.2

curb 1011.7
fire iron 1019.12
atomic cluster 1037.7
v bind 428.10
put together 799.5
join 799.9
continue 811.4
secure 854.8
chain gang
prisoner 429.11
procession 811.3
chain reaction
series 811.2
vicissitudes 971.5
fission 1037.8
chains 428.4
chain-smoke
n smoking 89.10
v use 87.21
smoke 89.14
chair
n furniture 229.1
mastership 417.7
authority 417.10
instructorship 571.10
chairman 574.5
seat 900.17
v administer 573.11
govern 612.12
install 615.12
the chair
capital punishment
604.7
execution 605.5
chairmanship
mastership 417.7
directorship 573.4
chaise 179.4
chalet 228.8
chalice 703.11
chalk
n whiteness 37.2
art equipment 712.18
jockey 757.2
v whiten 37.5
mark 517.19
record 549.15
portray 712.19
chalky white 37.7
powdery 1049.11
challenge
n objection 333.2
opposition 451.1
resistance 453.1
dare 454.2
declaration of war
458.7
questioning 937.12
v confront 216.8
object 333.5
demand 421.5
claim 421.6
contradict 451.6
offer resistance 453.3
defy 454.3
compete 457.18
make war on 458.15
doubt 954.6
thwart 1011.15
challenging
provocative 375.27
defiant 454.7

chamber
 n toilet 12.11
 room 197.1
 compartment 197.2
 bedroom 197.7
 council 423.1
 v enclose 212.5
chamberlain
 major-domo 577.10
 treasurer 729.11
chambermaid 577.8
chamber of commerce
 617.9
chamber pot 12.11
chambers
 apartment 228.13
 office 739.7
chameleon
 variegation 47.6
 timeserver 363.4
 changeableness 853.4
champ
 n bite 8.2
 victor 411.2
 champion 413.15
 v chew 8.27
champ at the bit
 have energy 17.11
 be impatient 135.4
 wait impatiently
  845.13
champion
 n superior 249.4
 victor 411.2
 champ 413.15
 defender 460.7
 deputy 576.1
 justifier 600.8
 supporter 616.9
 the best 998.8
 protector 1007.5
 v back 449.13
 defend 460.8
 justify 600.10
 protect 1007.18
 adj peerless 249.15
 best 998.16
 first-rate 998.17
chance
 n gamble 759.2
 turn 824.2
 opportunity 842.2
 liability 896.1
 possibility 965.1
 probability 967.1
 uncertainty 970.1
 lottery 970.8
 absence of assignable
  cause 971
 happenstance 971.1
 v attempt 403.6
 risk 759.24
 turn up 830.6
 bechance 971.11
 take a gamble 1005.7
 adj circumstantial
  765.7
 unessential 767.4
 vague 970.19
 iffy 971.15
chancellery
 mastership 417.7

office 739.7
chancellor
 principal 571.8
 executive 574.3
 head of state 575.7
 public official 575.17
 diplomat 576.6
chancery registry 549.3
 office 739.7
chance upon 940.3
chancre 85.36
chandelier 1025.6
chandler
 provider 385.6
 merchant 730.2
change
 n custody 429.5
 money 728.2
 petty cash 728.19
 stock exchange 737.7
 differentiation 779.4
 alteration 851
 modification 851.1
 conversion 857.1
 substitution 861.1
 surrogate 861.2
 v don 5.42
 move 172.5
 vacillate 362.8
 trade 731.14
 differentiate 779.6
 alter 851.6
 make a change 851.7
 fluctuate 853.5
 convert 857.11
 substitute 861.4
 interchange 862.4
changeable
 wishy-washy 16.17
 irresolute 362.9
 fickle 364.6
 nonuniform 781.3
 transient 827.7
 changed 851.10
 alterable 853.6
 inconstant 853.7
 convertible 857.18
 interchangeable 862.5
 uncertain 970.16
change hands 629.4
changeless
 almighty 677.18
 permanent 852.7
 unchangeable 854.17
changeling 680.11
change of heart
 penitence 113.4
 conversion 851.1
 new start 857.2
change of life 303.7
change one's mind
 n sing a different tune
  363.6
 v repent 113.7
 vacillate 362.8
changing
 n fluctuation 853.3
 adj nonuniform 781.3
 inconstant 853.7
channel
 n seaway 182.10
 outlet 190.9

bed 199.4
 stream 238.1
 conduit 239
 pipe 239.1
 narrow place 270.3
 trench 290.2
 passageway 383.3
 informant 551.5
 communication
  theory 551.7
 band 1033.13
 v transport 176.14
 focus 208.10
 direct 239.15
 furrow 290.3
 guide 573.9
chant
 n paean 696.3
 repeat 848.5
 v speak 524.26
 sing 708.38
chanting 848.15
chaos
 formlessness 263.1
 anarchy 418.2
 turbulence 671.2
 noncohesion 803.1
 disorder 809.2
 confusion 984.3
 space 1070.3
chaotic formless 263.4
 anarchic 418.6
 turbulent 671.18
 incoherent 803.4
 disordered 809.16
 vague 970.19
 confused 984.12
chap man 76.5
 crack 224.2
chapel hall 197.4
 branch 617.10
 religious building
  703.3
chaperon
 n maid 577.8
 escort 768.5
 duenna 1007.7
 v escort 768.8
 care for 1007.19
chapfallen
 distressed 96.22
 glum 112.25
 disappointed 132.5
 humiliated 137.14
chaplain 699.2
chapter
 ecclesiastical council
  423.4
 part 554.13
 branch 617.10
 part of writing 792.2
 topic 936.1
char
 n cleaner 79.14
 v work 725.12
 burn 1019.24
character
 n man 76.5
 description 349.2
 recommendation
  509.4
 sign 517.1

letter 546.1
 phonetic symbol
  546.2
 heredity 560.6
 probity 644.1
 repute 662.1
 role 704.10
 actor 707.2
 notation 709.12
 plot 722.4
 function 724.3
 mode 764.4
 nature 766.4
 kind 808.3
 characteristic 864.4
 oddity 869.4
 eccentric 926.3
 freak 926.4
 disposition 977.3
 number 1016.3
 v represent 349.8
 describe 349.9
 letter 546.6
 engrave 713.9
character assassination
 defamation 512.2
 scandal 552.8
 smear campaign
  609.14
characteristic
 n habit 373.4
 sign 517.1
 nature 766.4
 peculiarity 864.4
 adj typical 349.15
 differentiative 779.9
 classificational 808.7
 peculiar 864.13
 attitudinal 977.7
characterization
 representation 349.1
 description 349.2
 impersonation 349.4
 indication 517.3
 acting 704.8
 plot 722.4
 distinction 864.8
characterless
 dull 117.6
 vacant 222.14
 formless 263.4
charade gesture 517.14
 riddle 522.9
charcoal
 n blackness 38.4
 blacking 38.6
 drawing 712.5
 sketching 712.13
 art equipment 712.18
 combustion product
  1019.16
 v blacken 38.7
 portray 712.19
charge
 n power 18.1
 cathexis 92.34
 excitement 105.3
 load 196.2
 burden 297.7
 precept 419.1
 injunction 420.2
 dependent 432.6

attack 459.1
load 462.16
supervision 573.2
arraignment 598.3
accusation 599.1
commission 615.1
price 630.1
fee 630.6
duty 641.1
imposition 643.3
heraldry 647.2
benefice 698.9
task 724.2
full measure 793.3
attribution 887.1
protectorship 1007.2
impediment 1011.6
electrical charge
  1031.5
rocket propulsion
  1072.8
v energize 17.10
burden 297.13
prime 405.9
command 420.8
admonish 422.6
rush 459.18
accuse 599.7
commission 615.10
receive credit 622.7
demand 630.12
impose 643.4
fill 793.7
shoot 903.12
electrify 1031.25
radioactivate 1036.9
inter attack! 459.32
charge card 622.3
chargé d'affaires 576.6
charge in 214.5
charge off
  n discount 631.1
  v forget 148.5
  keep accounts 628.8
  discount 631.2
charger animal 311.10
  war-horse 461.30
charisma power 18.1
  allurement 377.1
  illustriousness 662.6
  influence 893.1
charismatic
  alluring 377.8
  illustrious 662.19
  influential 893.13
  attracting 906.5
charitable
  loving 104.27
  kind 143.13
  benevolent 143.15
  pitying 145.7
  philanthropic 478.22
  gratuitous 634.5
  tolerant 978.11
charity love 104.1
  benevolence 143.4
  patronage 449.4
  accord 455.1
  almsgiving 478.3
  donation 478.6
  cardinal virtues 653.4
  tolerance 978.4

charity case 619.4
charlatan
  n impostor 357.6
  adj quack 354.27
charlatanism 354.7
charley horse 26.2
charm
  n delightfulness 97.2
  loveableness 104.7
  allurement 377.1
  lure 377.3
  jewel 498.6
  sorcery 690.1
  magic spell 691
  spell 691.1
  amulet 691.5
  assemblage 769.6
  influence 893.1
  superstition 953.3
  beauty 1015.1
  elementary particle
    1037.6
  v delight 95.9
  enamor 104.23
  persuade 375.23
  fascinate 377.7
  becharm 691.8
  engross 982.13
charmer deceiver 357.1
  tempter 377.4
  slyboots 415.6
  bewitcher 690.9
  beauty 1015.8
charming
  delightful 97.7
  endearing 104.25
  alluring 377.8
  bewitching 691.11
  influential 893.13
charnel house
  mortuary 309.9
  tomb 309.16
chart
  n map 159.5
  representation 349.1
  diagram 381.3
  statistics 757.4
  outline 800.4
  v locate 159.11
  represent 349.8
  plot 381.10
  itemize 800.7
  organize 807.10
charter
  n exemption 430.8
  permission 443.1
  grant 443.5
  rental 615.6
  v authorize 443.11
  commission 615.10
  hire 615.15
  rent out 615.16
chartreuse 44.4
chary wary 494.9
  economical 635.6
chase
  n furrow 290.1
  woodland 310.11
  pursuit 382.1
  hunting 382.2
  v follow 166.3
  emboss 283.12

pursue 382.8
hunt 382.9
make haste 401.5
court 562.21
sculpture 715.5
repulse 907.3
chase away
  repulse 907.3
  drive out 908.14
chaser drink 88.9
  pursuer 382.4
  act 704.7
  sculptor 716.6
chasm crack 224.2
  pit 275.2
  concavity 284.4
  opening 292.1
chassis base 199.2
  structure 266.4
  frame 900.10
  radio 1033.3
chaste tasteful 496.8
  celibate 499.6
  elegant 533.6
  immaculate 653.7
  virtuous 664.4
  abstinent 668.10
  simple 797.6
  perfect 1001.6
chasten
  simplify 499.5
  punish 604.10
  moderate 670.6
chastened meek 433.15
  restrained 670.11
chastise reprove 510.17
  punish 604.10
chastity elegance 533.1
  purity 653.3
  celibacy 664
  virtue 664.1
  abstinence 668.2
  perfection 1001.1
chat
  n talk 540.3
  cozy chat 541.4
  v chatter 540.5
  visit 541.10
château 228.7
chatelaine jewel 498.6
  mistress 575.2
  governor 575.6
chattel subject 432.7
  property 471.1
chatter
  n rattle 55.3
  speech 524.1
  jabber 540.3
  v rattle 55.6
  bird sound 60.5
  speak 524.20
  protract 538.8
  talk 540.5
  shake 916.11
  freeze 1022.9
chatty
  v talkative 540.9
  adj conversational
    541.13
  intimate 582.24
chauffeur
  n driver 178.10

man 577.4
v ride 177.33
chauvinist
  n militarist 461.5
  misanthrope 590.2
  patriot 591.3
  bigot 979.5
  adj militaristic 458.22
  public-spirited 591.4
cheap
  adj worthless 391.11
  stingy 484.9
  inexpensive 633.7
  disgraceful 661.11
  paltry 997.21
  inferior 1004.9
  adv cheaply 633.10
cheapen corrupt 393.12
  depreciate 633.6
  bargain 731.17
cheat
  n fake 354.13
  fraud 356.8
  cheater 357.3
  deceiver 759.22
  v victimize 356.18
  be dishonest 645.11
  be promiscuous
    665.19
  rook 759.26
check
  n plaid 47.4
  trauma 85.37
  slowing 175.4
  crack 224.2
  opening 292.1
  measure 300.2
  discomfiture 412.2
  restraint 428.1
  confinement 429.1
  mark 517.5
  label 517.13
  speech sound 524.13
  statement 628.3
  negotiable instrument
    728.11
  token 728.12
  game 749.3
  chip 759.18
  stop 856.2
  checkup 937.6
  collation 942.2
  ensuring 969.8
  blemish 1003.1
  reverse 1010.3
  hindrance 1011.1
  frustration 1011.3
  curb 1011.7
  v look 27.13
  variegate 47.7
  slow 175.9
  cleave 224.4
  injure 393.13
  thwart 412.11
  restrain 428.7
  confine 429.12
  fend off 460.10
  mark 517.19
  play 749.7
  ski 753.4
  bet 759.25
  agree 787.6

break 801.12
delay 845.8
put a stop to 856.11
specify 864.11
examine 937.23
collate 942.5
verify 969.12
blemish 1003.4
hinder 1011.10
recalculate 1016.20
monitor 1033.26
adj checked 47.14
checkered
checked 47.14
changeable 853.6
check in arrive 186.6
die 307.20
record 549.15
punch the clock
831.12
checking account
finances 622.2
funds 728.14
checklist
directory 574.10
list 870.1
roll 870.6
checkmate
n discomfiture 412.2
stop 856.2
frustration 1011.3
v defeat 412.11
put a stop to 856.11
thwart 1011.15
check out look 27.13
depart 188.7
clock out 188.13
die 307.20
qualify 405.15
punch out 831.12
investigate 937.22
examine 937.23
verify 969.12
check 1016.20
cheek impudence 142.3
side 218.1
rashness 493.1
cheek by jowl
adj near 223.14
adv hand in glove
768.10
concurrently 898.5
phrs side by side
218.12
cheeky
impudent 142.10
defiant 454.7
cheer
n food 10.1
cry 59.1
happiness 95.2
cheerfulness 109.1
hurrah 116.2
applause 509.2
conviviality 582.3
v refresh 9.2
cry 59.6
please 95.8
gladden 109.7
rejoice 116.6
comfort 121.6
give hope 124.10

assent 332.8
encourage 492.16
applaud 509.10
cheerful happy 95.15
pleasant 97.6
glad 109.11
cheering 109.16
homelike 228.33
optimistic 124.12
cheerless
pleasureless 96.20
distressing 98.20
unhappy 112.21
hopeless 125.12
cheese 10.46
cheesecake 714.3
cheeseparing
n parsimony 484.1
economizing 635.2
adj parsimonious
484.7
economical 635.6
sparse 884.5
cheesy base 661.12
paltry 997.21
bad 999.8
inferior 1004.9
chef 11.2
chef d'œuvre
masterpiece 413.10
work of art 712.10
product 892.1
standard of perfection
1001.4
chemical
n element 1058.2
v chemicalize 1058.7
adj biochemical
1058.8
chemist
pharmacist 86.35
drugstore 86.36
chemistry
science of matter 1058
chemical science
1058.1
cheque 728.11
cherish
hold dear 104.21
foster 449.16
retain 474.7
keep in memory
988.13
care for 1007.19
cherry bomb 53.6
cherub child 302.3
endearment term
562.6
angel 679.1
chessboard check 47.4
toy 743.16
chest
n breast 283.6
storehouse 386.6
treasury 729.12
adj pectoral 283.19
chestnut
n horse 311.11
old joke 489.9
platitude 973.3
adj reddish-brown
40.4

redheaded 41.10
chesty conceited 140.11
corpulent 257.18
pectoral 283.19
chevalier rider 178.8
gallant 504.9
knight 608.5
chevron zigzag 204.8
angle 278.2
heraldry 647.2
military insignia
647.5
chew
n bite 8.2
chewing tobacco 89.7
v masticate 8.27
smoke 89.14
disapprove 510.18
pulp 1061.5
chewed-up 393.27
chewing gum
elastic 1046.3
gum 1060.6
chew out 510.18
chew the fat 541.9
chewy delightful 97.8
tough 1047.4
chiaroscuro
drawing 712.13
lighting 1024.19
chic
n smartness 578.3
adj dressed up 5.45
smart 578.13
knowledgeable 927.17
chicanery
quackery 354.7
chicane 356.4
trick 356.6
stratagem 415.3
knavery 645.2
quibbling 935.5
chichi ornate 498.12
showy 501.19
ultrafashionable
578.14
chick woman 77.6
gal 302.7
fledgling 302.10
bird 311.28
poultry 311.29
endearment term
562.6
chicken
n weakling 16.6
homosexual 75.14
effeminate male 77.10
poultry 311.29
dupe 358.2
coward 491.5
military insignia
647.5
v lose one's nerve
491.8
adj weak 16.12
effeminate 77.14
irresolute 362.12
cowardly 491.10
chicken feed
feed 10.4
petty cash 728.19
trivia 997.4

chicken out
hesitate 362.7
compromise 468.2
lose one's nerve 491.8
defect 857.13
chide 510.17
chief
n superior 249.4
superintendent 574.2
master 575.1
head 575.3
potentate 575.8
heraldry 647.2
principal 996.10
adj leading 165.3
top 198.10
front 216.10
main 249.14
directing 573.12
governing 612.18
preceding 813.4
first 817.17
paramount 996.24
chiefly
mainly 249.17
on the whole 791.14
first 817.18
generally 863.17
normally 868.10
chieftain 575.8
chiffon
n finery 498.3
adj bubbly 320.6
chigger 311.35
chignon braid 3.7
false hair 3.13
chilblain sore 85.36
cold 1022.2
child one 302.3
person 312.5
simple soul 416.3
descendant 561.3
innocent 657.4
product 892.1
child's play 997.5
childbearing 1.1
childhood
preteens 301.2
origin 817.4
childishness
childlikeness 301.4
senility 921.10
puerility 921.11
unwiseness 922.2
childless 890.4
childlike
childish 301.11
artless 416.5
innocent 657.6
senile 921.23
puerile 921.24
trusting 952.22
children
young people 302.2
family 559.5
offspring 561.1
chill
n symptom 85.9
unfeeling 94.1
indifference 102.1
dejection 112.3
deterrent 379.2

aloofness 583.2
enmity 589.1
cold 1022.1
frost 1022.2
v disincline 379.4
freeze 1022.9
frost 1022.10
refrigerate 1023.10
adj unfeeling 94.9
unfriendly 589.9
cool 1022.12
chilling
n cold 1022.2
refrigeration 1023.1
adj frightening 127.28
refrigerative 1023.12
chilly unfeeling 94.9
aloof 141.12
reticent 344.10
unsociable 583.6
unfriendly 589.9
cool 1022.12
feeling cold 1022.16
chime
n ringing 54.3
harmony 708.3
repetitiousness 848.4
v ring 54.8
interrupt 214.6
say 524.23
harmonize 708.35
assonate 783.9
agree 787.6
chimera
airy hope 124.5
illusion 975.1
figment of the
imagination 985.5
chimerical
thin 763.6
illusory 975.8
imaginary 985.22
chimney valley 237.7
flue 239.14
fireplace 1019.11
deposit 1056.7
chimpanzee 311.23
chin
n point of the chin
216.6
v speak 524.21
converse 541.9
china
n tableware 8.12
ceramic ware 742.2
fragility 1048.2
adj ceramic 742.7
chink
n thud 52.3
ringing 54.3
crack 224.2
furrow 290.1
vulnerability 1005.4
v thud 52.15
ring 54.8
open 292.11
stop 293.7
chink in one's armor
weak point 16.4
fault 1002.2
vulnerability 1005.4
chinoiserie 498.2

chinook 318.7
chintzy stingy 484.9
vulgar 497.10
base 661.12
slovenly 809.15
sparse 884.5
chip
n trauma 85.37
scrap 248.3
flake 296.3
lightness 298.2
check 759.18
piece 792.3
break 801.4
electronic circuit
1032.8
component 1041.3
v use 87.21
injure 393.13
break 801.12
chip away at 252.7
chip in
interrupt 214.6
participate 476.5
contribute 478.14
pay for 624.18
a chip off the old block
descendant 561.3
likeness 783.3
duplicate 784.3
chip on one's shoulder
challenge 454.2
warlikeness 458.11
chipper healthy 83.9
pert 109.13
active 330.17
chippy
n strumpet 665.14
v use 87.21
chiropractor 90.4
chirp
n insect sound 58.5
v stridulate 58.7
bird sound 60.5
exude cheerfulness
109.6
rejoice 116.5
speak 524.26
sing 708.38
chisel
n sculpture tool
715.4
v form 262.7
furrow 290.3
deceive 356.19
engrave 713.9
sculpture 715.5
process 891.9
chiseler 357.4
chiseling
n fraud 356.8
engraving 713.2
adj deceitful 356.22
chit
runt 258.4
child 302.3
gal 302.7
letter 553.2
chitchat
conversation 541.5
gossip 552.7
chits 623.1

chivalry
military science 458.6
courage 492.1
gallantry 504.2
aristocracy 608.1
magnanimity 652.2
chivy
n hunting 382.2
v annoy 96.13
pursue 382.8
chlorinate
sanitize 79.24
chemicalize 1058.7
vaporize 1065.8
chloroform deaden
25.4
kill 308.12
chlorophyll 44.1
chock
n curb 1011.7
v fill 793.7
obstruct 1011.12
chock-full 793.11
chocolate 40.3
choice
n will 323.1
loophole 369.4
selection 371
option 371.1
free will 430.6
elegance 533.1
jockey 757.2
judgment 945.1
the best 998.8
adj tasteful 496.8
best 998.16
choicy 495.9
choir
n church 703.9
part music 708.18
chorus 710.16
keyboard 711.17
v sing 708.38
choirboy 710.15
choirmaster
leader 574.6
choral conductor
710.18
choke
n asphyxiation 307.6
suffocation 308.6
v silence 51.8
gag 99.4
contract 260.7
close 293.6
stop 293.7
asphyxiate 307.24
strangle 308.18
extinguish 395.15
overload 992.15
obstruct 1011.12
be hot 1018.22
fight fire 1021.7
choke back 106.8
choked raucous 58.15
contracted 260.12
closed 293.9
stopped 293.11
inarticulate 525.12
overfull 992.20
chokedamp
miasma 1000.4

vapor 1065.1
choked up mute 51.12
closed 293.9
stopped 293.11
choleric
n personality type
92.12
adj sour 110.23
resentful 152.26
cholesterol 7.7
chomp
n bite 8.2
v chew 8.27
chomp at the bit
845.13
choose desire 100.14
will 323.2
elect 371.13
choosing
n choice 371.1
adj selective 371.23
choosy selective 371.23
fastidious 495.9
chop
n feed 10.4
cutlet 10.18
side 218.1
wave 238.14
roughness 288.2
hit 901.4
v notch 289.4
play 745.5
sever 801.11
be changed 851.6
chop down raze 395.19
fell 912.5
chop logic
differentiate 779.6
argue 934.16
quibble 935.9
chopped-off 812.4
chopper cycle 179.8
rotor plane 181.5
game 745.3
choppy rough 288.6
nonuniform 781.3
discontinuous 812.4
irregular 850.3
jolting 916.20
chops mouth 292.4
wind instrument
711.6
choral 708.50
chorale paean 696.3
sacred music 708.17
part music 708.18
chorus 710.16
chord
n sympathy 93.5
straight line 277.2
concento 709.17
string 711.20
v harmonize 708.35
tune 708.36
play 708.39
chore
n task 724.2
tough proposition
1012.2
v serve 577.13
work 725.12
chorea 916.2

choreographer
dramatist 704.22
dancer 705.3
choreography
representation 349.1
dancing 705.1
chorister
choral singer 710.15
choirmaster 710.18
chorographic
locational 159.19
measuring 300.12
chortle
n laughter 116.4
v laugh 116.8
chorus
n unanimity 332.5
cast 707.11
part music 708.18
passage 708.24
chorale 710.16
poetry 720.9
agreement 787.1
sequel 816.1
repeat 848.5
v imitate 336.5
say 524.23
sing 708.38
chorus line 705.3
chosen
n legislator 610.3
the best 998.8
adj superior 249.12
selected 371.26
chow 10.2
chowder 10.11
chrismal
n unction 701.5
baptism 701.6
church 703.10
holy vessels 703.11
adj oily 1054.9
Christ 677.10
christen name 527.11
baptize 701.16
inaugurate 817.11
Christendom
Christianity 675.7
the believing 692.5
Christian
n respectable citizen
659.3
Nazarene 675.17
adj kind 143.13
honest 644.13
orthodox 687.7
Christianity 675.7
Christian name 527.4
Christian Scientist
675.24
Christlike
humblehearted 137.11
kind 143.13
divine 677.17
Christmas
n Yuletide 313.6
v vacation 20.9
chromatic
colorational 35.15
tonal 709.27
chromatics 35.10
chromatography 35.10

chromosome
allosome 305.8
heredity 560.6
chronic
confirmed 373.19
durable 826.10
chronicle
n record 549.1
history 719.1
annals 719.3
story 722.3
chronology 831.9
v record 549.15
write history 719.5
chronologize 831.14
chronicler annalist
550.2
historian 719.4
chronologist 831.10
chronological
historical 719.7
temporal 820.7
chronology
history 719.1
time 820.1
timekeeping 831.1
chronicle 831.9
chronometer
navigation 182.2
timepiece 831.6
chrysalis 302.12
chthonian
n Satanist 680.15
idolater 697.4
adj hellish 682.8
idolatrous 697.7
chubby
corpulent 257.18
stubby 268.10
chuck
n food 10.2
tap 901.7
throw 903.3
v bird sound 60.5
place violently 159.13
reject 372.2
discard 390.7
eliminate 772.5
tap 901.18
throw 903.10
chuckhole
pothole 284.3
mud puddle 1060.9
chuckle
n ripple 52.5
laughter 116.4
v laugh 116.8
chuck up 908.27
chug-a-lug 88.25
chum
n friend 588.4
v associate with
582.18
chummy 587.20
chump dupe 358.2
fool 923.3
chunk
n amount 244.2
lump 257.10
portion 477.5
bet 759.3
accumulation 769.9

piece 792.3
throw 903.3
v throw 903.10
chunky
corpulent 257.18
stubby 268.10
sturdy 762.7
church school 617.5
sect 675.3
divine service 696.8
kirk 703.1
the Church
the true church 687.3
the believing 692.5
the ministry 698.1
papacy 698.6
churchgoer
attender 221.5
believer 692.4
worshiper 696.9
the laity 700.1
churchly
ecclesiastic 698.13
churchish 703.15
churchman
believer 692.4
clergyman 699.2
layman 700.2
Church of England
675.11
churchyard 309.15
churlish
irascible 110.19
countrified 233.7
boorish 497.13
gruff 505.7
churn
n mixer 796.9
blend 916.1
agitator 916.9
v seethe 671.12
agitate 916.10
emulsify 1060.10
churn out write 547.21
pen 718.6
produce 891.8
chute parachute 181.13
outlet 190.9
incline 204.4
rapids 238.10
gutter 239.3
race 756.3
deposit 1056.7
chutzpah
impudence 142.3
rashness 493.1
fearlessness 492.4
CIA man 576.9
ciao! 188.22
cicatrix
mark 517.5
blemish 1003.1
cicerone
traveler 178.1
interpreter 341.7
guide 574.7
escort 768.5
cigar 89.4
cigarette 89.5
cilia
eyelashes 3.12
organelle 305.5

cinch
n dupe 358.2
sure success 409.2
poker 759.10
saddle parts 900.18
certainty 969.2
easy 1013.4
v fasten 799.7
bind 799.9
prove 956.10
make sure 969.11
cincture
n surrounding 209.5
enclosed place 212.3
circle 280.3
v encircle 209.7
cinder dregs 256.2
coal 1018.16
combustion product
1019.16
cinder block 1052.2
cinema
n motion-picture
theater 706.6
adj motion-picture
706.8
cinematic 706.8
cinematographer
motion-picture
photography 706.4
photographer 716.5
cinerary 309.22
cinereous colorless 36.7
gray 39.4
cipher
n discord 61.1
cryptography 345.6
symbol 517.2
Greek 522.7
signature 527.10
letter 546.1
nothing 761.2
thing of naught 763.2
a nobody 997.7
number 1016.3
v code 345.10
calculate 1016.17
circa
adv approximately
244.6
prep about 223.26
circadian
recurrent 848.13
momentary 849.8
circle
n environment 209.1
region 230.9
sphere 231.2
curve 279.2
circus 280.2
jewel 498.6
clique 617.6
round 849.3
circuit 913.2
halo 1024.14
orbit 1070.16
v move 172.5
encircle 209.7
round 280.10
recur 849.5
circuit 913.5
rotate 914.9

circuit
n journey 177.5
environment 209.1
sphere 231.2
circle 280.2
route 383.1
engagement
704.11
baseball 745.1
routine 849.3
round 913.2
detour 913.3
electrical circuit
1031.4
network 1033.8
circuitry 1041.3
v circle 913.5
circuitous
deviative 164.7
oblique 204.13
convolutional 281.6
circumlocutory
538.14
roundabout 913.7
circuitry
electronic circuit
1032.8
computer parts
1041.3
circular
n announcement
352.2
advertising matter
352.8
booklet 554.11
adj round 280.11
circuitous 913.7
circularity
curvature 279.1
roundness 280
orbit 280.1
circuitousness
913.1
sophistry 935.1
circulate
distribute 352.10
be published 352.16
deliver 478.13
monetize 728.26
circle 913.5
rotate 914.9
circulation
n blood 2.23
publication 352.1
monetization 728.23
circuitousness 913.1
rotation 914.1
liquidity 1059.1
adj fluid 1059.4
circumcise 701.16
circumcision 685.4
circumference
exterior 206.2
bounds 211.1
circle 280.2
circumferential
environing 209.8
outlining 211.14
circumlocution
convolution 281.1
roundaboutness 538.5
circuitousness 913.1

circumnavigate
navigate 182.13
circle 913.5
circumscribe
bound 210.4
limit 211.8
contract 260.7
restrict 428.9
qualify 958.3
circumscription
restriction 210
limiting 210.1
confines 211.1
boundary 211.3
enclosure 212.1
contraction 260.1
restraint 428.3
exclusion 772.1
qualification 958.1
circumspect
slow 175.10
careful 339.10
cautious 494.8
judicious 919.19
circumstance
pomp 501.6
fact 760.3
state 764.1
existing condition 765
occurrence 765.1
component 795.2
event 830.2
qualification 958.2
circumstances
environment 209.1
assets 471.7
total situation 765.2
affairs 830.4
circumstantial
conditional 765.7
unessential 767.4
happening 830.9
evidential 956.16
qualifying 958.7
circumstantiate
itemize 765.6
confirm 956.11
circumvent
deceive 356.14
avoid 368.6
evade 368.7
outwit 415.11
thwart 1011.15
circus town 230.9
circle 280.2
arena 463.1
show business 704.1
cirrous
threadlike 271.7
cloudy 319.7
cirrus filament 271.1
coil 281.2
cist 309.16
cistern 241.1
citadel 460.6
citation
incrimination 599.2
eulogy 646.4
acknowledgment
887.2
reference 956.5
Citation 311.15

cite summon 420.11
accuse 599.7
honor 646.8
itemize 765.6
name 956.13
call attention to
982.10
citified 230.11
citizen national 227.4
freeman 430.11
noncombatant 464.5
citizenry
population 227.1
the people 606.1
citizens band 1033.13
citizenship
native-born
citizenship 226.2
public spirit 591.1
citrus fruit 10.36
city
n metropolis 230
town 230.1
region 231.5
adj urban 230.11
city dweller 227.6
city father
public official 575.17
legislator 610.3
city hall
town hall 230.5
political party 609.24
capitol 613.4
city planner
artist 716.10
architect 717.3
city planning 230.10
city slicker
townsman 227.6
sophisticate 413.17
city-state 232.1
civic urban 230.11
public 312.16
public-spirited 591.4
political 609.43
governmental 612.17
civics 609.2
civil public 312.16
decorous 496.10
courteous 504.14
sociable 582.22
governmental 612.17
lay 700.3
civil ceremony 563.3
civil code 673.5
civil disobedience
327.1
civil disorder 327.4
civilian dress 5.8
civilian life 465.6
civility
cultivation 392.3
decorousness 496.3
courtesy 504.1
manners 504.6
amenities 504.7
social convention
579.1
etiquette 580.3
sociability 582.1
civilization
culture 373.3

cultivation 392.3
courtesy 504.1
civilize
humanize 312.12
make better 392.9
teach 568.10
civilized
improved 392.13
elegant 496.9
learned 927.21
civil liberties
freedom 430.2
human rights 642.3
civil rights
freedom 430.2
human rights 642.3
civil servant 575.16
civvies 5.8
clabber
n clot 1043.7
semiliquid 1060.5
v cohere 802.6
thicken 1043.10
emulsify 1060.10
clack
n noisemaker 53.6
rattle 55.3
snap 56.2
chatter 540.3
v rattle 55.6
snap 56.7
bird sound 60.5
chatter 540.5
clad 5.44
cladding exterior 206.2
plating 295.13
lamina 296.2
claim
n extortion 192.6
profession 376.2
demand 421.1
possession 469.1
estate 471.4
declaration 598.7
prerogative 642.1
v extort 192.15
pretext 376.3
demand 421.5
pretend to 421.6
possess 469.4
take 480.13
require 962.9
claimant
petitioner 440.7
accuser 599.5
clairvoyance ESP 689.8
the future 838.1
understanding 927.3
intuition 933.1
foreknowledge 960.3
divination 961.2
clam
n discord 61.1
marine animal 311.30
man of few words
344.5
v fish 382.10
clambake meal 8.6
party 582.12
electioneering 609.12
clamber
n ascent 193.1

v climb 193.11
clammy sweaty 12.22
  viscous 1060.12
clamor
  n noise 53.3
  outcry 59.4
  clash 61.2
  entreaty 440.2
  v be noisy 53.9
  vociferate 59.8
  complain 115.15
clamor for
  wish for 100.16
  demand 421.5
  entreat 440.11
  require 962.9
clamorous noisy 53.13
  vociferous 59.10
  turbulent 105.24
  demanding 421.9
  urgent 996.22
clamp
  n contractor 260.6
  hold 474.2
  v squeeze 260.8
  fasten 799.7
clampdown 428.1
clamp down on
  restrain 428.7
  suppress 428.8
  domineer 612.16
clam up
  v be silent 51.6
  keep to oneself 344.6
  keep secret 345.7
  inter silence! 51.14
clan race 559.4
  community 617.2
  clique 617.6
  class 808.2
  kind 808.3
clandestine 345.12
clangor
  n noise 53.3
  ringing 54.3
  rasp 58.3
  v be noisy 53.9
  ring 54.8
  sound harshly 58.9
clank
  n ringing 54.3
  rasp 58.3
  v ring 54.8
  sound harshly 58.9
  speak poorly 525.7
clannish
  contemptuous 157.8
  exclusive 495.13
  racial 559.7
  cliquish 617.18
clansman 559.2
clap
  n noise 53.3
  report 56.1
  applause 509.2
  v crack 56.6
  place violently 159.13
  close 293.6
  applaud 509.10
  hit 901.14
clapboard
  n wood 1052.3

v face 295.23
clapper
  noisemaker 53.6
  bell 54.4
claptrap
  humbug 354.14
  nonsense 520.2
  bull 520.3
  specious argument
    935.3
claque 509.8
clarification
  refinement 79.4
  explanation 341.4
clarify refine 79.22
  explain 341.10
  make clear 521.6
  disinvolve 797.5
clarinetist 710.4
clarion call 458.8
clarity
  distinctness 31.2
  clearness 521.2
  elegance 533.1
  facility 1013.1
  transparency 1028.1
clash
  n report 56.1
  rasp 58.3
  jangle 61.2
  disaccord 456.1
  fight 457.4
  hostility 589.3
  impact 901.3
  v conflict 35.14
  crack 56.6
  sound harshly 58.9
  strike a sour note 61.3
  disagree 456.8
  contend 457.13
  go contrary to 778.4
  fight 788.5
  counteract 899.6
  collide 901.13
clasp
  n hold 474.2
  embrace 562.3
  v stay near 223.12
  hold 474.6
  seize 480.14
  embrace 562.18
  hook 799.8
  cohere 802.6
class
  n rank 245.2
  nomenclature 527.1
  race 559.4
  form 572.11
  social class 607.1
  community 617.2
  school 617.5
  the laity 700.1
  category 808.2
  classifications 808.5
  goodness 998.1
  biology 1066.1
  v analyze 800.8
  classify 808.6
  estimate 945.9
classic
  n book 554.1
  classical music 708.6

work of art 712.10
  standard of perfection
    1001.4
  adj simple 499.6
  elegant 533.6
  model 785.8
  perfected 1001.9
classical
  downright 247.12
  tasteful 496.8
  simple 499.6
  elegant 533.6
  literary 547.24
  artistic 718.7
  antiquated 841.13
  perfected 1001.9
classicist purist 533.4
  antiquarian 841.5
  scholar 928.3
classification
  veil of secrecy 345.3
  nomenclature 527.1
  analysis 800.3
  grouping 807.3
  categorization 808
  listing 808.1
classify
  keep secret 345.7
  analyze 800.8
  group 807.11
  class 808.6
  discriminate 943.4
classmate
  schoolchild 572.3
  companion 588.3
classroom
  n schoolroom 567.11
  adj scholastic 567.13
classy
  ostentatious 501.18
  chic 578.13
clatter
  n noise 53.3
  rattle 55.3
  chatter 540.3
  v rattle 55.6
  chatter 540.5
  gossip 552.12
clause phrase 529.1
  part 554.13
  bill 613.9
  part of writing 792.2
  condition 958.2
clavichord 711.12
claw torture 96.18
  injure 393.13
  seize 480.14
clawed tortured 96.25
  pedal 199.9
  prehensile 474.9
claws governance 417.5
  clutches 474.4
  control 612.2
clay
  n pipe 89.6
  land 234.1
  corpse 307.16
  humankind 312.1
  person 312.5
  ceramics 742.3
  softness 1045.4
  body 1050.3

mud 1060.8
  adj ceramic 742.7
clayey earthy 234.5
  pasty 1045.12
clean
  v cleanse 79.18
  adj pure 79.25
  shapely 264.5
  skillful 413.22
  honest 644.13
  virtuous 653.7
  spotless 657.7
  chaste 664.4
  thorough 793.10
  adv cleanly 79.29
  absolutely 793.15
clean bill of health
  healthiness 83.2
  pass 443.7
  certificate 549.6
clean-cut distinct 31.7
  shapely 264.5
  clear 521.11
clean-limbed 264.5
cleanliness
  purity 79.1
  innocence 657.1
  chastity 664.1
clean out clean 79.18
  strip 480.24
  evacuate 908.22
cleanse clean 79.18
  release 120.6
  sanctify 685.5
cleanser
  sweeper 79.16
  cleaner 79.17
clean-shaven 6.17
cleansing
  n cleaning 79.2
  release 120.2
  adj cleaning 79.28
  relieving 120.9
  atoning 658.7
clean slate void 222.3
  innocence 657.1
  new start 857.2
  revolution 859.1
cleanup gain 472.3
  red-up 807.6
clean up clean 79.18
  complete 407.6
  triumph 411.3
  profit 472.12
  tidy 807.12
clear
  n clarity 521.2
  v refine 79.22
  take off 184.38
  rise above 272.11
  unclose 292.12
  leap 366.5
  manage 409.12
  extricate 431.7
  profit 472.12
  justify 600.9
  acquit 601.4
  pay in full 624.13
  pass 749.7
  play 752.4
  eliminate 772.5
  evacuate 908.22

disembarrass 1013.9
adj distinct 31.7
audible 50.16
vacant 222.14
open 292.17
manifest 348.8
free 430.21
unhampered 430.26
quit 430.31
crystal-clear 521.11
legible 521.12
elegant 533.6
unindebted 624.23
innocent 657.6
thorough 793.10
unmixed 797.7
unfastened 801.22
unqualified 959.2
certain 969.13
thriving 1009.13
easy 1013.13
light 1024.31
transparent 1028.4
adv wide 261.19
clearance room 158.3
open space 158.4
altitude 184.35
interval 224.1
distance 261.1
latitude 430.4
authorization 443.3
pass 443.7
justification 600.1
acquittal 601.1
payment 624.1
elimination 772.2
evacuation 908.6
clear-cut
distinct 31.7
lost 473.7
clear 521.11
clearheaded
sober 516.3
clear-witted 919.13
sane 924.4
clearing opening 292.1
extrication 431.3
justification 600.1
acquittal 601.1
evacuation 908.6
disembarrassment
1013.6
field 1067.9
clearing house 729.13
clearly visibly 31.8
audibly 50.18
positively 247.19
manifestly 348.14
intelligibly 521.13
certainly 969.23
clear out
v disappear 34.2
clean 79.18
depart 188.7
flee 368.11
eliminate 772.5
evacuate 908.22
inter go away! 908.31
clear sailing 1006.1
clear-sighted
clear-eyed 27.21
clear-witted 919.13

clear the air
explain 341.10
pacify 465.7
moderate 670.6
clear the decks
trim ship 182.49
prepare 405.6
take precautions
494.6
eliminate 772.5
tidy 807.12
evacuate 908.22
clear the way
prepare the way
405.12
facilitate 1013.7
clear up explain 341.10
disinvolve 797.5
tidy 807.12
solve 939.2
make sure 969.11
cleavage
falling-out 456.4
severance 801.2
fission 1037.8
cleave crack 224.4
open 292.11
demolish 395.17
sever 801.11
cohere 802.6
bisect 874.4
atomize 1037.17
cleft
n crack 224.2
notch 289.1
opening 292.1
falling-out 456.4
break 801.4
adj cut 224.7
severed 801.23
halved 874.6
cleft palate 265.3
clemency pity 145.1
leniency 427.1
clench
n hold 474.2
v hold 474.6
seize 480.14
clerestory floor 197.23
top 198.1
clergy priesthood 699
ministry 699.1
clerical
n clergyman 699.2
adj secretarial 547.28
ecclesiastic 698.13
clerk writer 547.13
recorder 550.1
agent 576.3
accountant 628.7
clergyman 699.2
salesman 730.3
scholar 928.3
clever skillful 413.22
well-laid 413.30
cunning 415.12
witty 489.15
teachable 570.18
smart 919.14
cliché
n triteness 117.3
catchword 526.9

generalization 863.8
platitude 973.3
adj aphoristic 973.6
click
n thud 52.3
snap 56.2
v thud 52.15
snap 56.7
succeed 409.7
befriend 587.11
clicking
n ticking 55.2
adj staccato 55.7
client
n advisee 422.4
dependent 432.6
customer 733.4
adj subject 432.13
clientele 733.3
cliff precipice 200.3
slope 237.2
climacteric
n change of life 303.7
crisis 842.4
adj critical 842.10
climactic top 198.10
critical 842.10
climate
milieu 209.3
zone 231.3
weather 317.3
mental climate 977.5
climatic 317.12
climatology 317.5
climax
n copulation 75.7
summit 198.2
finishing touch 407.3
upheaval 671.5
plot 722.4
limit 793.5
crisis 842.4
crucial moment 842.5
urgency 996.4
salient point 996.6
acme of perfection
1001.3
v come 75.23
top 198.9
complete 407.6
climb
n ascent 193.1
acclivity 204.6
v move 172.5
ascend 184.39
clamber 193.11
incline 204.10
climb down
n recant 363.8
v humble oneself
137.7
get down 194.7
climber
traveler 178.1
ascender 193.6
plant 310.4
upstart 606.7
clime zone 231.3
weather 317.3
clinch
n hold 474.2
joint 799.4

v hold 474.6
seize 480.14
fight 754.4
fasten 799.7
join 799.11
cohere 802.6
prove 956.10
make sure 969.11
clincher
finishing stroke 819.4
conclusive argument
957.3
cling
n hold 474.2
cohesion 802.1
v stay near 223.12
hold 474.6
retain 474.7
cohere 802.6
clinic facility 91.21
hospital room 197.25
clinical 90.15
clink
n thud 52.3
ringing 54.3
jail 429.9
rhyme 720.8
assonance 783.6
v thud 52.15
ring 54.8
clinker
discord 61.1
dregs 256.2
combustion product
1019.16
building material
1052.2
clip
n velocity 172.4
excerpt 557.3
piece 792.3
blow 901.5
v speed 174.9
excise 255.10
shorten 268.6
deceive 356.19
hold 474.6
retain 474.7
rob 482.16
abridge 557.5
overprice 632.7
hook 799.8
strike 901.15
clipper 181.8
clippings 557.4
clique
n social set 582.5
coterie 617.6
company 769.3
v associate with
582.18
cliquish
contemptuous 157.8
exclusive 495.13
clannish 617.18
clitoris 2.11
cloak
n overgarment 5.12
cover 295.2
pretext 376.1
robe 702.2
v mantle 5.39

tip-off 551.3
hint 551.4
evidence 956.1
clue one in 351.4
clump
  n thud 52.3
  lump 257.10
  bulge 283.3
  growth 310.2
  bunch 769.7
  blow 901.5
  stamp 901.10
  solid 1043.6
  v thud 52.15
  way of walking 177.28
  assemble 769.18
  strike 901.15
  stamp 901.22
  thicken 1043.10
clumsy
  n bungler 414.9
  adj bulky 257.19
  slipshod 340.12
  bungling 414.20
  inelegant 534.2
  inconvenient 995.7
  unwieldy 1012.19
  ungraceful 1014.9
clunk
  n thud 52.3
  blow 901.5
  v thud 52.15
  strike 901.15
cluster
  n throng 769.4
  bunch 769.7
  conglomeration 802.5
  solid 1043.6
  v come together
    769.16
  assemble 769.18
  cohere 802.6
  thicken 1043.10
clutch
  n amount 244.2
  hold 474.2
  offspring 561.1
  crisis 842.4
  urgency 996.4
  predicament 1012.4
  cone clutch 1039.6
  v hold 474.6
  seize 480.14
clutch at straws 124.8
clutches
  governance 417.5
  claws 474.4
  control 612.2
clutter
  n jumble 809.3
  multitude 883.3
  radar interference
    1035.12
  v disarrange 810.2
  teem with 883.5
coach
  n preparer 405.5
  tutor 571.5
  trainer 571.6
  baseball team 745.2
  v advise 422.5
  tutor 568.11

coach-and-four 179.5
coachman
  driver 178.9
  man 577.4
coact cooperate 450.3
  interact 776.6
  concur 898.2
coactive
  compulsory 424.10
  cooperative 450.5
  concurrent 898.4
coadjutant
  n assistant 616.6
  adj cooperative 450.5
coagulate
  n clot 1043.7
  v cohere 802.6
  thicken 1043.10
  emulsify 1060.10
coagulation
  thickening 1043.4
  viscosity 1060.2
coal
  n blackness 38.4
  live coal 1018.16
  combustion product
    1019.16
  v provision 385.9
  burn 1019.24
  fuel 1020.7
coalesce
  cooperate 450.3
  identify 777.5
  mix 796.10
  combine 804.3
coalescent 871.12
coalition
  affiliation 450.2
  front 609.33
  association 617.1
  combination 804.1
coarse raucous 58.15
  bitter 64.6
  offensive 98.18
  thick 269.8
  rough 288.6
  textured 294.6
  undeveloped 406.12
  gross 497.11
  ill-bred 505.6
  inelegant 534.2
  populational 606.8
  carnal 663.6
  vulgar 666.8
  inferior 1004.9
coarsened 94.12
coast
  n slide 194.4
  border 211.4
  side 218.1
  shore 234.2
  v be still 173.7
  glide 177.35
  navigate 182.13
  sail coast-wise 182.39
  slide 194.9
  do nothing 329.2
  take it easy 331.15
  go easily 1013.10
coastal
  bordering 211.11
  littoral 234.7

coast guard
  rescuer 398.2
  branch 461.21
  navy 461.27
  guard 1007.9
coastguardsman 183.4
coat
  n hair 3.2
  outerwear 5.13
  color 35.8
  cover 295.2
  blanket 295.12
  lamina 296.2
  card 758.2
  v cloak 5.39
  color 35.13
  spread on 295.24
coating
  n color 35.8
  painting 35.12
  covering 295.1
  blanket 295.12
  lamina 296.2
  adj covering 295.35
coat of arms 647.2
coattails 449.4
coauthor
  n writer 547.15
  collaborator 616.4
  author 718.4
  v write 547.21
  publish 718.6
coax
  n prompter 375.10
  v urge 375.14
  lure 377.5
  importune 440.12
coaxial 208.14
coaxial cable 347.17
cob ear 310.27
  race horse 311.14
cobalt 91.8
cobbler
  shoemaker 5.37
  mender 396.10
cobblestone
  n pavement 383.6
  v floor 295.22
cobelligerent 232.1
cobweb filament 271.1
  lightness 298.2
  snare 356.13
coccus 85.41
co-chairman 574.5
cochlear 281.8
cock
  n male animal 76.8
  valve 239.10
  stopper 293.4
  poultry 311.29
  weather vane 318.17
  pile 769.10
  v regress 163.5
  prime 405.9
  shoot 903.12
cock-a-doodle-doo 60.5
cockamamie 922.11
cock-and-bull story
    354.11
cockatrice
  traitor 357.10
  heraldry 647.2

cockeyed
  cross-eyed 28.12
  drunk 88.33
  askew 204.14
  distorted 265.10
  unbalanced 790.5
  disorderly 809.13
  foolish 922.9
  dazed 984.14
cockle
  n wrinkle 291.3
  marine animal 311.30
  v wrinkle 291.6
cockles of the heart
  heart 93.3
  inner nature 766.5
Cockney 523.7
cockpit 463.1
cockroach 311.35
cocksure 969.21
cocktail 88.9
cocktail lounge 88.20
cocky conceited 140.11
  impudent 142.10
  defiant 454.7
cocoa 40.3
coconspirator
  schemer 381.7
  accomplice 616.3
cocoon 302.12
coction 1019.2
coda adjunct 254.1
  added to writing
    254.2
  passage 708.24
  sequel 816.1
  end 819.1
coddle cook 11.4
  indulge 427.6
  foster 449.16
  caress 562.16
code
  n cryptography 345.6
  telegraph 347.2
  precept 419.2
  Greek 522.7
  ethics 636.1
  digest 673.5
  table 807.4
  rule 868.4
  v encode 345.10
codependency 776.3
code word
  implication 519.2
  cryptography 345.6
  catchword 526.9
codex
  manuscript 547.11
  rare book 554.6
codicil
  added to writing
    254.2
  bequest 478.10
  sequel 816.1
codify digest 673.9
  organize 807.10
  classify 808.6
  normalize 868.6
co-ed 572.5
coeducational 568.18
coequal
  n equal 789.4

v reciprocate 776.7
adj symmetric 264.4
reciprocal 776.10
coinciding 777.8
equivalent 789.8
coerce
use violence 424.7
domineer 612.16
coercion 424.3
coercive 424.12
coeternal
perpetual 828.7
simultaneous 835.5
coeval
n contemporary 835.2
adj innate 766.8
simultaneous 835.5
coexistence
foreign policy 609.5
simultaneity 835.1
coexisting
agreeing 787.9
simultaneous 835.5
coextend parallel 203.4
coincide 835.4
coextensive
parallel 203.6
coinciding 777.8
coffee 40.3
coffee break meal 8.6
respite 20.2
interim 825.1
coffee shop 8.17
coffer
n treasury 729.12
v store 386.10
coffin
n casket 309.11
v confine 212.6
inter 309.19
cofounder 891.7
cog
n inferior 250.2
projection 285.4
v cheat 356.18
cogent powerful 18.12
relevant 774.11
sagacious 919.16
logical 934.20
valid 972.14
good 998.12
cogitate
ruminate 930.8
think about 930.11
cognate
n root 526.2
kinfolk 559.2
lineage 560.4
likeness 783.3
adj related 559.6
lineal 560.18
kindred 774.10
akin 783.13
cognition 927.2
cognitive 930.21
cognizance
thanks 150.2
due 639.2
cognition 927.2
cognizant
sensible 24.11
knowing 927.15

cognomen name 527.3
surname 527.5
nomenclature 527.6
nickname 527.7
cognoscente
connoisseur 496.7
critic 945.7
cogwheel 1039.5
cohabit copulate 75.21
inhabit 225.7
live together 563.17
cohere agree 787.6
join 799.11
adhere 802.6
coherent clear 521.11
agreeing 787.9
clinging 802.10
indivisible 1043.13
cohesion adhesion 802
sticking 802.1
indivisibility 1043.2
cohesive
cohering 802.10
indivisible 1043.13
tough 1047.4
cohort hanger-on 138.6
military unit 461.22
henchman 610.8
associate 616.1
accomplice 616.3
attendance 768.6
company 769.3
coif
n hairdo 3.15
v cut the hair 3.22
cloak 5.39
top 295.21
coiffure
n hairdo 3.15
v cut the hair 3.22
coil
n braid 3.7
a length 267.2
whorl 281.2
v curl 281.5
coin
n angle 278.2
money 728.2
specie 728.4
v mint 728.28
innovate 840.5
change 851.9
originate 891.12
imagine 985.14
coinage
neologism 526.8
money 728.1
coining 728.24
innovation 851.4
production 891.1
result 892.1
coin a phrase 973.5
coincide assent 332.9
correspond 777.4
agree 787.6
co-occur 835.4
concur 898.2
coincidence
accompaniment 768.1
sameness 777.1
agreement 787.1
simultaneity 835.1

concurrence 898.1
coincidental 777.8
coital 75.24
coitus 75.7
coke cocaine 87.6
combustion product
1019.16
col ridge 237.5
valley 237.7
colander refinery 79.13
porousness 292.8
arranger 807.5
cold
n low temperature
1022
chilliness 1022.1
adj unconscious 25.8
chromatic 35.15
unsexual 75.28
unfeeling 94.9
indifferent 102.6
dull 117.6
insolent 142.9
heartless 144.25
stone-dead 307.31
reticent 344.10
aloof 583.6
unfriendly 589.9
speculative 759.27
freezing 1022.14
chilly 1022.16
cold blood 94.1
cold-blooded
unfeeling 94.9
heartless 144.25
hypothermic 1022.20
cold comfort 108.1
cold cream
cleanser 79.17
makeup 1015.12
ointment 1054.3
cold feet 491.4
coldhearted
unfeeling 94.9
heartless 144.25
cold shoulder
n aloofness 583.2
repulse 907.2
banishment 908.4
v snub 157.5
slight 340.8
cold sore allergy 85.33
sore 85.36
cold storage
storage 386.5
discontinuance 390.2
frozen-food locker
1023.6
cold sweat sweat 12.7
hostility 99.2
trepidation 127.5
nervousness 128.2
cold turkey 87.1
cold water 379.2
colic ache 26.5
symptom 85.9
colicky aching 26.12
anemic 85.60
coliseum 463.1
collaborate
be willing 324.3
cooperate 450.3

write 547.21
act the traitor 645.15
co-author 718.6
concur 898.2
collaborator
subversive 357.11
apostate 363.5
author 547.15
cooperator 616.4
author 718.4
collage 712.11
collapse
n weakness 16.1
exhaustion 21.2
breakdown 85.8
descent 194.1
decline 252.2
prostration 260.4
impairment 393.1
debacle 395.4
crash 410.3
defeat 412.1
insolvency 625.3
v weaken 16.9
burn out 21.5
take sick 85.46
descend 194.5
cave 260.10
break down 393.24
fail 410.12
go bankrupt 625.7
fall short 910.2
fall through 910.3
collapsible 260.11
collar
n circle 280.3
foam 320.2
shackle 428.4
arrest 429.6
insignia 647.1
golf 751.1
v arrest 429.16
acquire 472.9
capture 480.18
collate classify 807.11
scrutinize
comparatively 942.5
verify 969.12
collateral
n security 438.3
kinfolk 559.2
nonessential 767.2
adj parallel 203.6
additional 253.10
related 559.6
unessential 767.4
accompanying 768.9
related 774.9
eventual 830.11
simultaneous 835.5
collation
light meal 8.7
arrangement 807.1
comparative scrutiny
942.2
ensuring 969.8
colleague
companion 588.3
associate 616.1
equal 789.4
collect
n prayer 696.4

v store up 386.11
gather 472.11
come together 769.16
assemble 769.18
put together 799.5
conclude 945.10
collected
composed 106.13
stored 386.14
assembled 769.21
joined 799.13
collection
store 386.1
gathering 472.2
donation 478.6
edition 554.5
compilation 554.7
excerpts 557.4
oblation 696.7
book of verse 720.5
assemblage 769.1
collector's items
769.11
collective
cooperative 450.5
communal 476.9
concurrent 898.4
collective bargaining
unionism 727.1
labor union 727.2
negotiation 731.3
collectivism
cooperation 450.1
communion 476.2
socialism 611.6
government 612.8
collectivize
communize 476.7
attach 480.20
collect oneself 106.7
collector desirer 100.12
enthusiast 101.4
connoisseur 496.7
governor 575.13
gatherer 769.15
collector's items 769.11
colleen 302.6
college university 567.5
association 617.1
collegiality
affiliation 450.2
communion 476.2
social life 582.4
collegiate
n college student
572.5
adj scholastic 567.13
studentlike 572.12
collide clash 35.14
sail into 182.41
disagree 456.8
contend 457.13
argue 788.5
counteract 899.6
come into collision
901.13
collier 1056.9
collimation
orientation 161.4
parallelism 203.1
collision
crash 184.20

opposition 451.2
hostility 589.3
contrariety 778.1
counteraction 899.1
impact 901.3
misfortune 1010.2
collision course
convergence 169.1
meeting 223.4
collocation
placement 159.6
assemblage 769.1
arrangement 807.1
colloid
n emulsion 1060.7
v emulsify 1060.10
colloquial
vernacular 523.18
conversational 541.13
colloquialism
nonformal language
523.5
barbarism 526.6
colloquium
forum 423.3
discussion 541.7
assembly 769.2
colloquy 541.1
collusion
chicanery 356.4
intrigue 381.5
cooperation 450.1
concurrence 898.1
cologne 70.3
colon
digestive system 2.16
meter 720.7
grammar 856.4
colonel 575.18
colonial 227.9
colonialism
foreign policy 609.5
government 612.4
colonist 227.9
colonization
establishment 159.7
peopling 225.2
appropriation 480.4
voting 609.18
colonnade
corridor 197.18
pillar 273.5
passageway 383.3
base 900.8
colony country 232.1
possession 469.1
community 617.2
group of animals
769.5
colophon print 517.7
label 517.13
makeup 554.12
sequel 816.1
color
n looks 33.4
hue 35
shade 35.1
colorfulness 35.4
dye 35.8
redness 41.1
timbre 50.3
milieu 209.3

sham 354.3
pretext 376.1
ornamentation 498.1
extenuation 600.5
motion-picture
photography 706.4
treatment 712.9
kind 808.3
v hue 35.13
redden 41.5
change color 105.19
blush 139.8
show resentment
152.14
pervert 265.6
misrepresent 350.3
falsify 354.15
ornament 498.8
name 527.11
extenuate 600.12
portray 712.19
imbue 796.11
influence 893.7
coloration
color 35.1
applying color 35.11
implication 519.2
coloratura
n vocal music 708.13
aria 708.16
ornament 709.18
adj vocal 708.50
color-blind 30.9
colored hued 35.16
dark-skinned 38.10
spurious 354.25
specious 354.26
ornate 545.11
discriminatory 979.12
colored person 312.3
colorfast 35.17
colorful colory 35.18
variegated 47.9
gaudy 501.20
colorful imagination
985.4
colorize 706.7
colorless hueless 36.7
dull 117.6
color line 979.4
colors
rallying device 458.12
ornateness 545.4
flag 647.6
colossal large 247.7
huge 257.20
high 272.14
giant 272.16
colosseum 463.1
colossus
strong man 15.6
giant 257.13
tower 272.6
colt boy 302.5
fledgling 302.10
horse 311.10
jockey 757.2
coltish gay 109.14
childish 301.11
column tower 272.6
pillar 273.5
cylinder 282.4

military unit 461.22
monument 549.12
part 554.13
roulette 759.12
procession 811.3
base 900.8
columnar 282.11
columnist
writer 547.15
journalist 555.4
author 718.4
coma stupor 22.6
unconsciousness 25.2
apathy 94.4
permanence 852.1
comatose sleepy 22.21
asleep 22.22
unconscious 25.8
apathetic 94.13
permanent 852.7
comb
n ridge 237.5
wave 238.14
projection 285.4
slack 1020.2
v curry 79.21
billow 238.22
ransack 937.32
combat
n contention 457.1
fight 457.4
war 458.1
v oppose 451.4
contend 457.13
combatant
opponent 452.1
fighter 461
contender 461.1
combative
partisan 456.17
warlike 458.21
offensive 459.30
contrary 778.6
argumentative 934.19
combination
concoction 405.3
affiliation 450.2
association 617.1
assemblage 769.1
relation 774.1
identification
777.2
composition 795.1
mixture 796.1
compound 796.5
joining 799.1
consolidation 804
combine 804.1
oneness 871.1
concurrence 898.1
combine
n association 617.1
company 617.9
combination 804.1
v cooperate 450.3
join 617.14
accompany 768.7
assemble 769.18
identify 777.5
compose 795.3
mix 796.10
put together 799.5

unite 804.3
concur 898.2
combo
orchestra 710.12
compound 796.5
combination 804.1
combustible
n fuel 1020.1
adj hot-tempered
110.25
flammable 1019.28
combustion
fire 1018.13
burning 1019.5
come
n sperm 305.11
v appear 33.8
climax 75.23
approach 167.3
sail into 182.41
arrive 186.6
emerge 190.11
occur 830.5
come on 838.6
chance 971.11
come about
turn around 163.9
change course 182.30
rally 392.8
occur 830.5
be changed 851.6
result 886.4
come true 972.12
come across
meet 223.11
be manifest 348.7
pay 624.16
run across 940.3
come after follow 166.3
be behind 217.8
succeed 814.2
replace 816.5
follow 834.3
come along
progress 162.2
improve 392.7
manage 409.12
be in a certain state
764.5
turn up 830.6
discover 940.9
chance 971.11
prosper 1009.7
come apart
weaken 16.9
be excitable 105.16
lose self-control 128.7
break 393.23
spring apart 801.9
disintegrate 805.3
lapse into disorder
809.8
come at arrive at 186.7
attack 459.14
comeback
recovery 396.8
retaliation 506.1
gibe 508.2
countermeasure 899.5
answer 938.1
come back
turn back 163.8

recover 396.20
race 757.5
answer 938.4
recur 988.15
come back at
retaliate 506.4
react 902.5
answer 938.4
come between
intrude 214.5
sow dissension 456.14
come by acquire 472.8
receive 479.6
inherit 479.7
come clean 351.7
comedian
humorist 489.12
dramatist 704.22
comedienne 707.9
comedown
disappointment 132.1
humiliation 137.2
descent 194.1
deterioration 393.3
collapse 410.3
bathos 488.3
disparagement 512.1
infamy 661.4
reverse 1010.3
come down use 87.21
land 184.43
descend 194.5
occur 830.5
decide 945.11
fall on evil days
1010.11
come down on
light upon 194.10
attack 459.14
disapprove 510.18
punish 604.11
come down to 789.5
come down with
take ill 85.46
pay 624.16
comedy wit 489.1
comic relief 704.6
come forth appear 33.8
emerge 190.11
come out 348.6
be published 352.16
find vent 369.10
originate 817.13
turn up 830.6
come forward
appear 33.8
approach 167.3
volunteer 439.10
thrust oneself forward
501.12
come-hither
n allurement 377.1
adj alluring 377.8
amatory 562.23
come-hither look
gaze 27.5
flirtation 562.9
come in lust 75.20
land 184.43
arrive 186.6
enter 189.7
be received 479.8

come into
acquire 472.8
inherit 479.7
join 617.14
comely shapely 264.5
appropriate 533.7
fair 1015.18
come of 886.4
come of age grow 14.2
expand 259.7
mature 303.9
develop 392.10
come off
cease to use 390.4
succeed 409.7
come apart 801.9
occur 830.5
come on to lure 377.5
make advances 439.8
come out appear 33.8
emerge 190.11
come into the open
348.6
be revealed 351.8
be published 352.16
find vent 369.10
be printed 548.18
act 704.29
be in a certain state
764.5
originate 817.13
result 886.4
turn up 940.9
come out for 609.41
come out with
divulge 351.5
act on the spur of the
moment 365.7
propose 439.5
say 524.23
comer incomer 189.4
successful person
409.6
modern 840.4
come round
n change one's tune
363.6
v rally 392.8
recover 396.20
acquiesce 441.3
make up 465.10
recur 849.5
be changed 851.6
come round to 857.17
comestibles 10.1
comet 1070.4
come through
carry out 328.7
accomplish 407.4
succeed 409.7
make good 409.10
win through 409.13
get over 521.5
be in a certain state
764.5
be safe 1006.2
come to arrive 186.6
attend 221.8
extend to 261.6
come to life 306.8
recover 396.20
acquiesce 441.3

cost 630.13
equal 789.5
total 791.8
come to a head
fester 12.15
focus 208.10
ripen 407.8
densify 1043.9
come together
copulate 75.21
converge 169.2
kiss and make up
465.10
assemble 769.16
join 799.11
combine 804.3
league 804.4
form 806.5
come to grips with
confront 216.8
treat 387.12
endeavor 403.5
attempt 403.6
brave 492.11
exert oneself 725.9
come to light
appear 33.8
be revealed 351.8
turn up 940.9
come to mind
occur to 930.18
pop into one's head
988.16
come to nothing
be disappointing
132.3
perish 395.23
hang up and get
nowhere 410.13
go to waste 473.6
be unproductive 890.3
neutralize 899.7
fall through 910.3
come to one's senses
924.2
come to pass
occur 830.5
come true 972.12
come to terms
come to an agreement
332.10
surrender 433.8
make up 465.10
strike a bargain
731.18
come to the point
speak plainly 535.2
be brief 537.5
particularize 864.9
come true occur 830.5
come about 972.12
come up against
meet 223.11
encounter 457.15
come across 940.3
come upon
be unexpected 131.6
arrive at 186.7
meet 223.11
come across 940.3
comeuppance
reprisal 506.2

simple 499.6
vernacular 523.18
plain-speaking 535.3
populational 606.8
prosaic 721.5
mutual 776.11
frequent 846.4
prevalent 863.12
usual 868.9
well-known 927.27
paltry 997.21
ordinary 1004.8
inferior 1004.9
common denominator
776.1
commoner
student 572.7
common man 606.5
common knowledge
n publicity 352.4
information 551.1
maxim 973.1
adj published 352.17
common-law wife
563.8
common man
commoner 606.5
average 863.3
a nobody 997.7
commonplace
n generalization 863.8
platitude 973.3
adj dull 117.9
common 497.14
simple 499.6
plain-speaking 535.3
populational 606.8
prosaic 721.5
trite 863.16
usual 868.9
well-known 927.27
ordinary 1004.8
common practice 373.5
commons
nutriment 10.3
rations 10.6
dining room 197.11
the people 606.1
park 743.14
common sense
sensibleness 919.6
reasonableness 934.9
common touch 581.1
commonweal
welfare 143.5
country 232.1
commonwealth
population 227.1
country 232.1
government 612.4
community 617.2
commotion
noise 53.3
excitement 105.4
bustle 330.4
turbulence 671.2
hubbub 809.4
agitation 916.1
communal
public 312.16
cooperative 450.5
common 476.9

associational 617.17
mutual 776.11
commune region 231.5
participation 476.1
community 617.2
commune with
communicate 343.6
converse 541.9
communicable
poisonous 82.7
contagious 85.61
transferable 176.18
impartable 343.11
giveable 478.23
communicant
informant 551.5
believer 692.4
worshiper 696.9
layman 700.2
communicate
transfer 176.10
be in touch 343.6
impart 343.7
give 478.12
say 524.23
converse 541.9
inform 551.8
celebrate 701.14
join 799.11
communication
n transferal 176.1
intercourse 343
communion 343.1
passageway 383.3
giving 478.1
speech 524.1
conversation 541.1
information 551.1
message 552.4
letter 553.2
social life 582.4
joining 799.1
adj telephonic
347.20
communications
n electronic
communications
343.5
shortwave 347
signaling 347.1
the press 555.3
radio 1033.1
adj telephonic 347.20
communicative
v talkative 540.9
adj talkative 343.10
conversational 541.13
informative 551.18
sociable 582.22
communion
communication 343.1
accord 455.1
community 476.2
conversation 541.1
social life 582.4
school 617.5
sect 675.3
prayer 696.4
correlation 776.1
communiqué
announcement 352.2
information 551.1

message 552.4
communism
cooperation 450.1
communion 476.2
Bolshevism 611.5
participation 612.4
government 612.8
Communist
n Bolshevist 611.13
revolutionist 859.3
adj cooperative 450.5
communistic 611.21
Marxist 859.6
community
population 227.1
humankind 312.1
cooperation 450.1
accord 455.1
communion 476.2
social life 582.4
the people 606.1
society 617.2
sect 675.3
company 768.2
correlation 776.1
similarity 783.1
community center
230.5
communize
communalize 476.7
attach 480.20
politicize 611.16
commutation
travel 177.1
compensation 338.1
substitution 861.1
interchange 862.1
commute travel 177.18
substitute 861.4
interchange 862.4
commuter
traveler 178.1
worker 726.2
compact
n contract 437
pact 437.1
understanding 787.2
makeup 1015.12
v contract 260.7
squeeze 437.5
densify 1043.9
adj miniature 258.12
contracted 260.12
short 268.8
close 293.12
concise 537.6
crowded 769.22
joint 799.12
dense 1043.12
compacted
contracted 260.12
crowded 437.11
cohesive 802.10
dense 1043.12
companion
n lover 104.12
stairs 193.3
image 349.5
maid 577.8
fellow 588.3
knight 608.5
associate 616.1

accompanier 768.4
escort 768.5
likeness 783.3
v accompany 768.7
companionable 582.22
companionship
association 582.6
fellowship 587.2
company 768.2
company
military unit
461.22
association 582.6
guest 585.6
companion 588.3
team 617.7
firm 617.9
cast 707.11
workplace 739.1
association 768.2
actors 769.3
comparable
approximate 774.8
analogous 783.11
comparative 942.8
comparative 942.8
compare
n comparison 942.1
v assemble 769.18
liken 942.4
be comparable 942.7
comparison
assemblage 769.1
similarity 783.1
substitute 861.2
examining side by
side 942
compare 942.1
estimate 945.3
compartment 197.2
compartmentalize
801.18
compass
n range 158.2
environment 209.1
bounds 211.1
boundary 211.3
degree 245.1
distance 261.1
magnetic compass
574.9
scale 709.6
v surround 209.6
enclose 212.5
accomplish 407.4
succeed with 409.11
circle 913.5
compassion
sensitivity 24.3
kindness 143.1
pity 145.1
leniency 427.1
tolerance 978.4
compatible
pleasant 97.6
in accord 455.3
sociable 582.22
related 774.9
agreeing 787.9
compatriot
fellow citizen 227.5
associate 616.1

compeer
companion 588.3
associate 616.1
equal 789.4
compel
motivate 375.12
force 424.4
domineer 612.16
impel 901.11
obsess 925.25
necessitate 962.8
compelling
motivating 375.25
commanding 420.13
compulsory 424.10
obsessive 925.34
urgent 996.22
compendious
short 268.8
concise 537.6
abridged 557.6
comprehensive 771.7
compendium 557.1
compensate
symmetrize 264.3
make compensation
338.4
remedy 396.13
make restitution
481.5
requite 506.5
pay 624.10
atone 658.4
equalize 789.6
interchange 862.4
compensation
defense mechanism
92.23
symmetrization 264.2
repayment 338
recompense 338.1
reparation 396.6
reimbursement 481.2
reprisal 506.2
penalty 603.1
damages 624.3
pay 624.4
atonement 658.1
compete
contend 457.18
play 744.2
competence
power 18.1
ability 18.2
preparedness 405.4
skill 413.1
authority 417.1
competent able 18.14
fitted 405.17
capable 413.24
authoritative 417.15
legal 673.10
sufficient 990.6
competitive
oppositional 451.8
competitory 457.23
competitor
contestant 452.2
combatant 461.1
athlete 743.19
compilation
omnibus 554.7

code 673.5
collection 769.11
compile codify 673.9
assemble 769.18
complacent
bovine 107.10
vain 140.8
complain
dissatisfy 108.5
groan 115.15
object 333.5
offer resistance 453.3
accuse 599.7
complainer
malcontent 108.3
lamenter 115.8
faultfinder 510.9
complaint disease 85.1
grievance 115.4
objection 333.2
resistance 453.1
disapproval 510.1
arraignment 598.3
declaration 598.7
accusation 599.1
complaisant
pleasant 97.6
considerate 143.16
indulgent 427.8
submissive 433.12
courteous 504.14
conformable 866.5
soft 1045.8
complement
n hand 183.6
adjunct 254.1
syntax 530.2
team 617.7
company 769.3
likeness 783.3
all 791.3
full measure 793.3
v reciprocate 776.7
complementary
reciprocal 776.10
completing 793.13
complete
v perform 328.9
perfect 407.6
execute 437.9
include 771.3
bring to fruition 793.6
end 819.7
elaborate 860.6
develop 1001.5
adj downright 247.12
perfect 407.12
comprehensive 771.7
undivided 791.11
whole 793.9
ended 819.8
unqualified 959.2
sound 1001.7
completely 765.13
completion
performance 328.2
completing 407.2
execution 437.4
fulfillment 793.4
complex
n inferiority complex
92.22

culture 373.3
whole 791.1
perplex 798.2
obsession 925.13
adj hard to
understand 522.14
mixed 796.14
complicated 798.4
difficult 1012.17
complexion
n looks 33.4
color 35.1
personality 92.11
mode 764.4
nature 766.4
disposition 977.3
v color 35.13
complexity
convolution 281.1
abstruseness 522.2
complication 798.1
difficulty 1012.1
compliance
resignation 134.2
willingness 324.1
obedience 326.1
assent 332.1
complaisance 427.2
submission 433.1
observance 434.1
consent 441.1
conformity 866.1
complicate
intensify 251.5
add 253.4
make unintelligible
522.12
involve 798.3
complication
disease 85.1
abstruseness 522.2
plot 722.4
complexity 798.1
difficulty 1012.1
predicament 1012.4
complicity
intrigue 381.5
cooperation 450.1
participation 476.1
guilt 656.1
compliment
n congratulation
149.1
regards 504.8
polite commendation
509.6
flattery 511.1
v congratulate 149.2
pay a compliment
509.14
flatter 511.5
complimentary
congratulatory 149.3
approbatory 509.16
flattering 511.8
gratuitous 634.5
comply
obey 326.2
assent 332.8
submit 433.6
acquiesce 441.3
conform 866.3

component
n part 792.1
constituent 795.2
matter 1050.2
adj constituent 795.5
components
contents 196.1
substance 762.2
comportment 321.1
compose
make up 405.7
arrange 437.8
reconcile 465.8
settle 466.7
compromise 468.2
pen 547.21
set 548.16
calm 670.7
write 708.46
author 718.6
constitute 795.3
mix 796.10
dispose 807.9
conform 866.3
produce 891.8
composed
collected 106.13
content 107.7
unastonished
123.3
arranged 807.14
composer
songwriter 547.15
scorer 710.20
author 718.4
composite
n compound 796.5
adj mixed 796.14
unitary 871.10
plural 882.7
composition
contents 196.1
form 262.1
structure 266.1
concoction 405.3
compromise 468.1
diction 532.1
written piece
547.2
writing 547.10
typesetting 548.2
atonement 658.1
piece 708.5
treatment 712.9
work of art 712.10
authorship 718.2
nature 766.4
construction 795
constitution 795.1
mixture 796.1
compound 796.5
combination 804.1
production 891.2
product 892.1
compost 889.4
composure
countenance 106.2
contentment 107.1
unastonishment
123.1
quiescence 173.1
self-control 359.5

compound
  n word form 526.4
  composition 795.1
  mixture 796.5
  combination 804.2
  alloy 1056.4
  v make up 405.7
  compromise 468.2
  mix 796.10
  combine 804.3
  produce 891.8
  adj mixed 796.14
comprehend
  understand 521.7
  include 771.3
  know 927.12
comprehension
  inclusion 771.1
  intelligence 919.1
  understanding 927.3
comprehensive
  great 247.6
  voluminous 257.17
  broad 269.6
  sweeping 771.7
  whole 791.9
  thorough 793.10
  joint 799.12
compress
  n dressing 86.33
  v reduce 252.7
  contract 260.7
  squeeze 260.8
  shorten 268.6
  densify 1043.9
compressed
  contracted 260.12
  shortened 268.9
  concise 537.6
  dense 1043.12
comprise
  internalize 207.5
  include 771.3
  entail 771.4
  total 791.8
  put together 799.5
  combine 804.3
compromise
  n adjustment 465.4
  middle course 467.3
  mutual concession
    468
  composition 468.1
  foreign policy 609.5
  atonement 658.1
  agreement 787.4
  interchange 862.1
  v reconcile 465.8
  reach an agreement
    468.2
  interchange 862.4
  endanger 1005.6
compromise oneself
  661.7
comptroller
  superintendent 574.2
  accountant 628.7
  treasurer 729.11
compulsion power 18.1
  urge 375.6
  obligation 424
  duty 424.1

  impulse 901.1
  obsession 925.13
  necessity 962.1
compulsive
  driving 424.10
  overfastidious 495.12
  conformist 866.6
  obsessive 925.34
  involuntary 962.14
compulsory
  mandatory 420.12
  driving 424.10
  obligatory 424.11
  necessary 962.12
compunction
  qualm 113.2
  demur 325.2
  objection 333.2
computation
  adding 253.3
  measurement 300.1
  calculation 1016.10
  automation 1040.7
compute
  add up 253.6
  measure 300.10
  calculate 1016.17
  computerize 1041.18
computer
  calculator 1016.14
  computer science
    1040.17
  electronic data
    processor 1041.2
computerized
  automated 1040.21
  machine-usable
    1041.19
computer program
  1041.11
comrade
  companion 588.3
  associate 616.1
  member 617.11
comradeship
  affiliation 450.2
  camaraderie 582.2
  fellowship 587.2
con
  n prisoner 429.11
  cheating 759.13
  side 934.14
  v cheat 356.18
  persuade 375.23
  study 570.12
  memorize 988.17
  adj oppositional 451.8
  disapproving 510.21
  prep opposed to
    451.10
con artist 357.4
concatenation
  association 92.33
  joining 799.1
  series 811.2
concave
  n cavity 284.2
  v hollow 284.13
  adj bowed 279.10
  concaved 284.16
concavity
  compartment 197.2

  crack 224.2
  curvature 279.1
  hollowness 284
  imprint 284.1
  cavity 284.2
  print 517.7
  depression 912.1
conceal
  keep secret 345.7
  hide 346.6
concealment
  invisibility 32.1
  secrecy 345.1
  hiding 346
  veil 346.1
  hiding place 346.4
  shelter 1008.3
concede
  acknowledge 332.11
  confess 351.7
  play 751.4
  allow for 958.5
conceit
  n pride 136.1
  conceitedness 140.4
  caprice 364.1
  witticism 489.7
  foppery 500.4
  boasting 502.1
  quirk 926.2
  thought 930.1
  idea 931.1
  opinion 952.6
  imagination 985.1
  v flatter 511.5
  imagine 985.14
conceited
  vain 136.9
  self-proud 140.11
  contemptuous 157.8
  foppish 500.17
  boastful 502.10
  dogmatic 969.22
conceivable
  knowable 927.25
  believable 952.24
  possible 965.6
  plausible 967.7
  imaginable 985.26
conceive
  get in the family way
    78.11
  vivify 306.9
  understand 521.7
  phrase 532.4
  cause 885.10
  originate 891.12
  know 927.12
  think 930.8
  suppose 950.10
  believe 952.11
  imagine 985.14
concentrate
  n extract 192.8
  v converge 169.2
  extraction 192.16
  focus 208.10
  intensify 251.5
  contract 260.7
  narrow thoughts
    930.10
  densify 1043.9

concentration
  convergence 169.1
  extract 192.7
  formula 192.8
  centralization 208.8
  intensification 251.2
  contraction 260.1
  industry 330.6
  firmness 359.2
  perseverance 360.1
  thoughtfulness 930.3
  attention 982.1
  engrossment 982.3
  densification 1043.3
concentration camp
  camp 228.29
  place of killing 308.11
  prison 429.8
concentric 208.14
concept
  idea 931.1
  opinion 952.6
  visualization 985.6
conception
  conceiving 78.4
  plan 381.1
  source 885.5
  production 891.1
  intellect 918.1
  intelligence 919.1
  understanding 927.3
  thought 930.1
  idea 931.1
  opinion 952.6
  creative thought
    985.2
  visualization 985.6
conceptual
  mental 918.7
  intelligent 919.12
  cognitive 930.21
  ideational 931.9
  imaginative 985.18
conceptualize
  know 927.12
  think 930.8
  imagine 985.14
concern
  n sensitivity 24.3
  sympathy 93.5
  anxiety 126.1
  considerateness 143.3
  carefulness 339.1
  undertaking 404.1
  company 617.9
  occupation 724.1
  workplace 739.1
  relevance 774.4
  affair 830.3
  science 927.10
  topic 936.1
  interest 982.2
  importance 996.1
  v give anxiety 126.4
  relate to 774.5
  involve 897.2
  interest 982.12
  trouble 1012.13
concerning 774.13
concert
  n unanimity 332.5
  cooperation 450.1

harmony 708.3
performance 708.33
agreement 787.1
concurrence 898.1
v plan 381.8
cooperate 450.3
adj instrumental
708.51
concerted
cooperative 450.5
concurrent 898.4
concert hall hall 197.4
theater 704.14
concession
acknowledgment
332.3
confession 351.3
grant 443.5
compromise 468.1
giving 478.1
discount 631.1
merchant 730.2
market 736.1
qualification 958.1
concierge 1007.12
conciliate 465.7
conciliatory
forgiving 148.6
unbelligerent 464.10
pacificatory 465.12
concise short 268.8
taciturn 344.9
brief 537.6
conclave council 423.1
ecclesiastical council
423.4
conference 541.6
political convention
609.8
assembly 769.2
conclude resolve 359.7
complete 407.6
arrange 437.8
end 819.5
draw a conclusion
945.10
suppose 950.10
conclusion
affirmation 334.1
completion 407.2
signing 437.3
sequel 816.1
end 819.1
reasonableness 934.8
solution 939.1
deduction 945.4
opinion 952.6
conclusive
completing 407.9
mandatory 420.12
final 819.11
convincing 952.26
evidential 956.16
unqualified 959.2
certain 969.13
concoct
fabricate 354.17
plot 381.9
make up 405.7
mix 796.10
produce 891.8
originate 891.12

imagine 985.14
concoction
fabrication 354.10
decoction 405.3
compound 796.5
production 891.1
product 892.1
concomitant
n adjunct 254.1
attendant 768.3
contemporary 835.2
adj accompanying
768.9
simultaneous 835.5
concurrent 898.4
concord
n unanimity 332.5
treaty 437.2
cooperation 450.1
accord 455.1
harmony 708.3
agreement 787.1
order 806.1
v cooperate 450.3
concordance
unanimity 332.5
cooperation 450.1
accord 455.1
reference book 554.9
harmony 708.3
agreement 787.1
concurrence 898.1
concordant
unanimous 332.15
cooperative 450.5
in accord 455.3
pacific 464.9
harmonious 708.49
agreeing 787.9
conformist 866.6
concurrent 898.4
concourse
convergence 169.1
flow 238.4
assemblage 769.1
assembly 769.2
joining 799.1
concurrence 898.1
concrete
n ground covering
199.3
pavement 383.6
conglomeration 802.5
solid 1043.6
hardness 1044.6
building material
1052.2
v floor 295.22
plaster 295.25
thicken 1043.10
solidify 1044.8
adj substantial 762.6
cohesive 802.10
particular 864.12
dense 1043.12
hard 1044.10
concubine
subject 432.7
wife 563.8
mistress 665.17
concupiscence
sexual desire 75.5

desire 100.1
lasciviousness 665.5
concur accord 332.9
cooperate 450.3
agree 787.6
coincide 835.4
collaborate 898.2
support 900.21
concurrence
convergence 169.1
parallelism 203.1
assent 332.1
unanimity 332.5
cooperation 450.1
accompaniment 768.1
assemblage 769.1
interaction 776.3
joining 799.1
simultaneity 835.1
collaboration 898
agreement 898.1
support 900.1
concussion
trauma 85.37
shock 671.8
impact 901.3
condemn
destroy 395.10
censure 510.13
damn 602.3
pass judgment 945.13
work evil 999.6
condemnation
censure 510.3
judgment 598.9
conviction 602
damnation 602.1
verdict 945.5
condemnatory
censorious 510.22
accusing 599.13
damnatory 602.5
condense trickle 238.18
intensify 251.5
contract 260.7
shorten 268.6
be brief 537.5
abridge 557.5
densify 1043.9
solidify 1044.8
condescend deign 137.8
give oneself airs 141.8
consent 441.2
condescending 141.9
condescension
humility 137.3
arrogance 141.1
condign right 637.3
due 639.8
condiment
cooking 11.1
flavoring 63.3
condition
n fitness 84.1
disease 85.1
rank 245.2
preparedness 405.4
stipulation 421.2
state 764.1
circumstance 765.1
provision 958.2
v limit 210.5

accustom 373.10
repair 396.14
fit 405.8
inculcate 568.12
train 568.13
qualify 958.3
make conditional
958.4
conditional
n mood 530.11
adj modal 764.6
circumstantial 765.7
dialectic 934.22
provisional 958.8
undecided 970.18
conditioning
n classical
conditioning 92.26
habituation 373.8
fitting 405.2
inculcation 568.2
training 568.3
involuntariness 962.5
adj healthful 81.5
condolence
comfort 121.4
pity 145.1
consolation 147
reassurance 147.1
condom 86.23
condominium
apartment house
228.14
participation 476.1
condone accept 134.7
overlook 148.4
suffer 443.10
keep an open mind
978.7
conducive
adj modal 384.8
helpful 449.21
prep tending to 895.5
conduct
n behavior 321.1
performance 328.2
direction 573.1
operation 888.1
v transport 176.12
channel 239.15
practice 328.8
perform 328.9
direct 573.8
lead an orchestra
708.45
escort 768.8
operate 888.5
conduction
transferal 176.1
electric conduction
1031.13
conductor
trainman 178.13
director 574.1
leader 574.6
musician 710.17
escort 768.5
conduction
1031.13
conduit
channel 239.1
passageway 383.3

congenital innate 766.8
thorough 793.10
congested
diseased 85.59
stopped 293.11
full 793.11
late 845.16
stuck 854.16
overfull 992.20
dense 1043.12
congestion
obstruction 293.3
fullness 793.2
overfullness 992.3
density 1043.1
conglomerate
n accumulation 769.9
miscellany 769.13
cohesive object 802.5
solid 1043.6
rock 1057.1
v assemble 769.18
mix 796.10
cohere 802.6
adj assembled 769.21
mixed 796.14
conglomeration
accumulation 769.9
miscellany 769.13
hodgepodge 796.6
joining 799.1
cohesion 802.1
conglomerate 802.5
combination 804.1
solid 1043.6
congratulate
gratulate 149.2
compliment 509.14
congratulations
n appplause 149.1
inter take a bow!
149.4
bravo! 509.22
congregate
v come together
769.16
adj assembled 769.21
congregation
audience 48.6
ecclesiastical council
423.4
worshiper 696.9
the laity 700.1
assemblage 769.1
assembly 769.2
congress
copulation 75.7
convergence 169.1
communication 343.1
council 423.1
conference 541.6
social life 582.4
legislature 613.1
assembly 769.2
congressional 613.11
congressman 610.3
congruent
in accord 455.3
coinciding 777.8
agreeing 787.9
congruity
symmetry 264.1

agreement 787.1
conformity 866.1
congruous
in accord 455.3
agreeing 787.9
expedient 994.5
conic 282.12
conjectural
theoretical 950.13
doubtful 970.17
conjecture
n supposition 950.3
guess 950.4
v guess 950.11
conjoined added 253.9
environmental 765.8
related 774.9
joined 799.13
conjoint
communal 476.9
accompanying 768.9
related 774.9
mutual 776.11
joint 799.12
combined 804.5
concurrent 898.4
conjugal loving 104.27
matrimonial 563.18
conjugate
n word form 526.4
v grammaticize
530.16
put together 799.5
double 872.5
adj lexical 526.19
related 774.9
joint 799.12
combined 804.5
coupled 872.8
conjugation
fertilization 78.3
juxtaposition 223.3
morphology 526.3
joining 799.1
combination 804.1
doubleness 872.1
conjunction
juxtaposition 223.3
part of speech 530.3
joining 799.1
combination 804.1
concurrence 898.1
conjure deceive 356.14
summon 420.11
entreat 440.11
make up 690.11
conjurer
trickster 357.2
sorcerer 690.5
entertainer 707.1
conjure up
summon 420.11
make appear 690.11
visualize 985.15
remember 988.10
conk out weaken 16.9
stall 184.45
die 307.20
be impaired 393.26
perish 395.23
fail 410.16
con man cheater 357.4

thief 483.1
connate innate 766.8
kindred 774.10
akin 783.13
connect use 87.21
converge 169.2
adjoin 223.9
succeed 409.7
play 745.5
apply to 774.5
relate 774.6
put together 799.5
join 799.11
be consistent 802.7
combine 804.3
continue 811.4
connection
copulation 75.7
addict 87.20
intermediary 213.4
juxtaposition 223.3
communication 343.1
passageway 383.3
mediator 466.3
blood relationship
559.1
marriage 564.1
go-between 576.4
relation 774.1
relevance 774.4
joining 799.1
joint 799.4
consistency 802.2
series 811.2
connections
kinfolk 559.2
favor 893.2
conniption 152.8
connivance
chicanery 356.4
intrigue 381.5
consent 441.1
sufferance 443.2
connive plot 381.9
concur 898.2
connive at
condone 148.4
consent 441.2
suffer 443.10
be inattentive 983.2
conniving
scheming 381.13
cooperative 450.5
connoisseur
expert 413.11
judge 496.7
collector 769.15
specialist 865.3
critic 945.7
connoisseurship
aesthetic taste 496.5
discrimination 943.1
connotation
meaning 518.1
implication 519.2
connote signify 517.17
mean 518.8
imply 519.4
evidence 956.8
connubial 563.18
conquer
vanquish 412.10

subdue 432.9
appropriate 480.19
conqueror 411.2
consanguinity
blood relationship
559.1
lineage 560.4
kinship 774.3
conscience
n psyche 92.28
grace 636.5
v confess 351.7
conscience-stricken
113.8
conscientious
meticulous 339.12
observant 434.4
fastidious 495.9
dutiful 641.13
proper 644.15
conscientious objector
464.6
conscious awake 23.8
sensible 24.11
shy 139.12
living 306.11
intentional 380.8
knowing 927.15
attentive 982.15
consciousness
wakefulness 23.1
sensation 24.1
wits 918.2
intelligence 919.9
cognizance 927.2
attention 982.1
**consciousness-
expanding** 975.10
conscript
n recruit 461.18
v call to arms 458.19
enlist 615.17
consecrate
dedicate 477.11
sanctify 685.5
ordain 698.12
consecration
authority 417.12
dedication 477.4
unselfishness 652.1
sanctification 685.3
holy orders 698.10
consecutive
following 166.5
consistent 802.11
successive 811.9
subsequent 834.4
consensus
n unanimity 332.5
cooperation 450.1
agreement 787.3
adj cooperative
450.5
consent
n willingness 324.1
obedience 326.1
assent 332.1
unanimity 332.5
submission 433.1
approval 441
authorization 441.1
permission 443.1

v be willing 324.3
assent 332.8
submit 433.6
approve 441.2
permit 443.9
consequence
glory 247.2
prestige 417.4
meaning 518.1
distinction 662.5
sequel 816.1
event 830.1
subsequence 834.2
effect 886.1
influence 893.1
conclusion 945.4
importance 996.1
consequential
vain 140.8
great 247.6
authoritative 417.15
prominent 662.17
resultant 886.6
influential 893.13
important 996.17
consequently
accordingly 765.11
as a result 886.7
hence 887.7
conservation
storage 386.5
preservation 397.1
maintenance 852.2
conservationist
n preserver 397.5
conservative 852.4
forester 1067.7
environmentalist 1071.3
adj preservative 397.12
conservative
n right side 219.1
political party 611.9
moderate 670.4
back number 841.8
conservatist 852.4
adj right 219.4
preservative 397.12
right-wing 611.17
unexcessive 670.12
permanence 852.8
conservatory
n summerhouse 228.12
storehouse 386.6
nursery 1067.11
adj preservative 397.12
conserve
n sweets 10.38
v reserve 386.12
preserve 397.8
care for 1007.19
consider
be considerate 143.10
care 339.6
discuss 541.12
contemplate 930.12
think of 930.16
judge 945.8
suppose 950.10

believe 952.11
allow for 958.5
considerable
n lot 247.4
adj great 247.6
large 257.16
authoritative 417.15
numerous 883.6
important 996.17
adv greatly 247.15
considerate
sensitive 24.12
thoughtful 143.16
careful 339.10
courteous 504.14
judicious 919.19
consideration
thoughtfulness 143.3
respect 155.1
offset 338.2
carefulness 339.1
motive 375.1
gratuity 478.5
courtesy 504.1
discussion 541.7
recompense 624.3
esteem 662.3
judiciousness 919.7
contemplation 930.2
argument 934.5
verdict 945.5
opinion 952.6
attention 982.1
importance 996.1
considered
intentional 380.8
reasoned 934.21
considering
adv all things considered 945.17
prep because of 887.9
consign transfer 176.10
send 176.15
commit 429.17
give 478.16
commission 615.10
transfer 629.3
consignment
freight 176.6
confinement 429.4
commitment 478.2
commission 615.1
transfer 629.1
consistency
symmetry 264.1
clearness 521.2
uniformity 780.1
agreement 787.1
connection 802.2
tenacity 802.3
conformity 866.1
density 1043.1
consistent
clear 521.11
faithful 644.20
uniform 780.5
agreeing 787.9
connected 802.11
valid 972.14
consist of 795.3
consolation
solace 121.4

condolence 147.1
function of Holy Ghost 677.16
console
n keyboard 711.17
radio 1033.3
control room 1033.7
panel 1040.16
v comfort 121.6
condole with 147.2
consolidate
intensify 251.5
contract 260.7
cooperate 450.3
combine 804.3
densify 1043.9
consolidation
intensification 251.2
contraction 260.1
affiliation 450.2
cohesion 802.1
combination 804.1
densification 1043.3
consonance
harmony 708.3
rhyme 720.8
uniformity 780.1
agreement 787.1
consonant
n speech sound 524.13
adj phonetic 524.31
harmonious 708.49
uniform 780.5
agreeing 787.9
consort spouse 563.6
companion 588.3
associate 616.1
harmony 708.3
accompanier 768.4
agreement 787.1
consortium
compact 437.1
company 617.9
understanding 787.2
consort with
associate with 582.17
accompany 768.7
conspicuous
distinct 31.7
remarkable 247.10
noticeable 348.12
prominent 662.17
notable 996.19
conspiracy
chicanery 356.4
intrigue 381.5
stratagem 415.3
combination 804.1
concurrence 898.1
conspirator
traitor 357.10
schemer 381.7
conspire plot 381.9
cooperate 450.3
league 804.4
concur 898.2
constable 1007.15
constabulary
bureau 594.4
police 1007.17
constant
deep-dyed 35.17

firm 359.12
persevering 360.8
habitual 373.15
observant 434.4
devoted 587.21
faithful 644.20
uniform 780.5
continuous 811.8
durable 826.10
perpetual 828.7
continual 846.5
regular 849.6
permanent 852.7
unchangeable 854.17
exact 972.17
constantly
faithfully 644.25
uniformly 780.8
perpetually 828.10
continually 846.7
regularly 849.9
constellation
celebrity 662.9
fate 963.2
configuration 1070.5
consternation 127.1
constipated 293.11
constipation
symptom 85.9
obstruction 293.3
constituency
population 227.1
means 384.2
electorate 609.22
membership 617.12
sphere of influence 893.4
support 900.1
constituent
n piece 792.1
part of writing 792.2
component 795.2
matter 1050.2
adj selective 371.23
essential 766.9
component 795.5
constitute
legislate 613.10
legalize 673.8
compose 795.3
establish 891.10
constitution
structure 266.1
legislation 613.5
written document 673.6
nature 766.4
composition 795.1
arrangement 807.1
establishment 891.4
disposition 977.3
constitutional
n exercise 84.2
walk 177.10
fitness 725.6
adj healthful 81.5
governmental 612.17
legal 673.10
innate 766.8
attitudinal 977.7
constrain compel 424.4
restrain 428.7

confine 429.12
moderate 670.6
necessitate 962.8
constraint
reserve 139.3
reticence 344.3
self-control 359.5
urge 375.6
compulsion 424.1
restraint 428.1
confinement 429.1
temperance 668.1
moderation 670.1
constrict
contract 260.7
narrow 270.11
close 293.6
obstruct 1011.12
constricted
contracted 260.12
narrow 270.14
closed 293.9
narrow-minded
979.10
construct
n structure 266.2
v build 266.5
compose 795.3
produce 891.8
construction
structure 266.1
frame 266.2
interpretation 341.1
explanation 518.3
word form 526.4
phrase 529.1
composition 795.1
production 891.2
constructive
interpretative 341.14
helpful 449.21
creative 891.16
construe
interpret 341.9
translate 341.12
consular 576.16
consulate house 228.5
mastership 417.7
office 739.7
consult 541.11
consultant
expert 413.11
adviser 422.3
consultation
advice 422.1
conference 541.6
consume devour 8.22
decrease 252.6
shrink 260.9
use 387.13
spend 388.3
impair 393.19
destroy 395.10
lose 473.5
waste 486.4
expend 626.5
disintegrate 805.3
burn up 1019.25
consumer
eater 8.16
user 387.9
buyer 733.5

consuming
n consumption 388.1
adj agonizing 98.23
destructive 395.26
engrossing 982.20
consummate
v top 198.9
accomplish 407.4
adj top 198.10
downright 247.12
complete 407.12
thorough 793.10
perfected 1001.9
consumption
eating 8.1
tuberculosis 85.17
decrement 252.3
shrinking 260.3
use 387.1
using up 388
consuming 388.1
impairment 393.4
destruction 395.1
waste 473.2
expenditure 626.1
contact
n touch 73.1
addict 87.20
nearness 223.5
communication 343.1
go-between 576.4
v be heard 48.12
come near 223.10
communicate with
343.8
contagious
poisonous 82.7
infectious 85.61
transferable 176.18
communicable 343.11
contain
internalize 207.5
limit 210.5
enclose 212.5
close 293.6
restrain 428.7
include 771.3
entail 771.4
total 791.8
compose 795.3
fight fire 1021.7
container
receptacles 195
can 195.1
enclosed place 212.3
cavity 284.2
containment
surrounding 209.5
enclosure 212.1
foreign policy 609.5
contaminate
defile 80.17
infect 85.50
corrupt 393.12
blaspheme 694.5
adulterate 796.12
radioactivate 1036.9
contamination
defilement 80.4
unhealthfulness 82.1
infection 85.4
corruption 393.2

hybrid word 526.11
sacrilege 694.2
adulteration 796.3
radiation 1036.1
environmental
destruction 1071.2
contemn disdain 157.3
reject 372.2
contemplate
scrutinize 27.14
expect 130.5
meditate 380.5
study 570.12
consider 930.12
think of 930.16
mull over 930.17
foresee 960.5
contemplation
scrutiny 27.6
expectation 130.1
quiescence 173.1
inaction 329.1
study 570.3
revelation 683.9
trance 691.3
prayer 696.4
consideration 930.2
foresight 960.1
engrossment 982.3
contemporary
n coeval 835.2
adj simultaneous
835.5
present 837.2
modern 840.13
contempt
hate 103.1
insolence 142.1
indignity 156.2
disdain 157
disrespect 157.1
rejection 372.1
defiance 454.1
deprecation 510.2
disparagement 512.1
contemptible
offensive 98.18
base 661.12
paltry 997.21
terrible 999.9
hateful 103.8
contemptuous
hating 103.7
arrogant 141.13
insolent 142.9
insulting 156.8
disdainful 157.8
rejective 372.4
defiant 454.7
condemnatory 510.22
disparaging 512.13
contend
contrapose 215.4
affirm 334.5
insist 421.8
contest 457.13
compete 457.18
struggle 725.11
argue 934.16
contender
competitor 452.2
combatant 461.1

contend for
try for 403.9
strive for 457.20
defend 600.10
contend with
treat 387.12
offer resistance
453.3
engage with 457.17
content
n components 196
material within 196.1
stuffing 196.1
capacity 257.2
makeup 554.12
table 870.2
content
n pleasure 95.1
contentment 107.1
v satisfy 107.4
adj pleased 95.14
contented 107.7
willing 324.5
assenting 332.13
consenting 441.4
contention
contraposition 215.1
opposition 451.1
disaccord 456.1
quarrel 456.5
contest 457
fight 457.1
hostility 589.3
argumentation 934.4
contentious
quarrelsome 110.26
aggravating 119.5
warlike 458.21
argumentative 934.19
contest
n contention 457.1
engagement 457.3
game 743.9
sport 744.1
v deny 335.4
contend against
451.4
contradict 451.6
oppose 457.13
dispute 457.21
argue 934.16
doubt 954.6
contestant
n competitor 452.2
combatant 461.1
player 743.18
adj contending 457.22
context
environment 209.1
circumstances 765.2
contiguity
juxtaposition 223.3
relation 774.1
contiguous
adjacent 223.16
consistent 802.11
continence
limitation 210.2
celibacy 565.1
abstemiousness 664.3
abstinence 668.2
moderation 670.1

continent
n world region 231.6
mainland 235.1
adj abstemious 664.6
abstinent 668.10
contingency
circumstance 765.1
nonessential 767.2
relativity 774.2
event 830.1
liability 896.1
condition 958.2
possibility 965.1
uncertainty 970.1
gamble 970.8
chance event 971.6
contingent
n portion 477.5
nonessential 767.2
company 769.3
part 792.1
event 830.1
chance event 971.6
adj in contact 223.17
substantial 762.6
circumstantial 765.7
unessential 767.4
eventual 830.11
qualifying 958.7
dependent 958.9
possible 965.6
undecided 970.18
chance 971.15
contingent on 886.8
continual
continuous 811.8
perpetual 828.7
constant 846.5
continuation
adjunct 254.1
payment 624.1
sequence 814.1
sequel 816.1
protraction 826.2
postponement 845.4
continuance 855.1
continue lengthen 267.6
persevere 360.2
be continuous 811.4
elapse 820.5
endure 826.6
protract 826.9
postpone 845.9
be frequent 846.3
stay with it 855.3
continuing
persevering 360.8
continuous 811.8
durable 826.10
permanent 852.7
abiding 855.7
continuity
playbook 704.21
plot 722.4
uniformity 780.1
consistency 802.2
logical order 806.2
uninterruption 811
cohesion 811.1
sequence 814.1
time 820.1
constancy 846.2

change 851.1
continuance 855.1
continuous
omnipresent 221.13
uniform 780.5
consistent 802.11
continued 811.8
temporal 820.7
perpetual 828.7
recurrent 848.13
continuing 855.7
continuum space 158.1
omnipresence 221.2
series 811.2
contort deflect 164.5
distort 265.5
convolve 281.4
misinterpret 342.2
contortion
n deflection 164.2
distortion 265.1
adj torsional 265.9
contour
n outline 211.2
tournure 262.2
v outline 211.9
contra
n oppositionist 452.3
adj negative 335.5
oppositional 451.8
adv in opposition
  451.9
prep opposed to
  451.10
opposite 778.10
contraband
n prohibition 444.1
smuggling 732.2
illicit goods 732.3
adj prohibited 444.7
illegal 674.6
contraceptive
birth control device
  86.23
safeguard 1007.3
contract
n make small 258.9
undertaking 404.1
obligation 436.2
compact 437.1
v take sick 85.46
compress 260.7
shorten 268.6
narrow 270.11
close 293.6
commit 436.5
be engaged 436.6
compact 437.5
acquire 472.8
incur 896.4
contraction
decrease 252.1
shrink in size 260
compression 260.1
narrowing 270.2
abbreviation 537.4
stenography 547.8
contractive
decreasing 252.11
compressible 260.11
contractual 437.10
contradict deny 335.4

reject 372.2
cross 451.6
go contrary to 778.4
disagree 788.5
counteract 899.6
refute 957.5
contradiction
denial 335.2
rejection 372.1
refusal 442.1
opposition 451.1
ambiguity 539.1
contrariety 778.1
disagreement 788.1
counteraction 899.1
refutation 957.2
contradictory
negative 335.5
oppositional 451.8
contrary 778.6
disagreeing 788.6
counteractive 899.8
illogical 935.11
refuting 957.6
contradistinction
contrariety 778.1
distinction 943.3
contraindicated
prohibited 444.7
unwise 922.10
inexpedient 995.5
contralto
n part 708.22
voice 709.5
adj deep 54.10
contraposition
opposition 215
anteposition 215.1
contrast 451.1
contrariety 778.1
counteraction 899.1
contraption
novelty 840.2
tool 1039.1
contrariety
offensiveness 98.2
contraposition 215.1
hostility 451.2
relation 774.1
oppositeness 778
difference 779.1
inequality 790.1
nonconformity 867.1
counteraction 899.1
contrary
adj negative 335.5
perverse 361.11
oppositional 451.8
contrarious 778.6
different 779.7
disagreeing 788.6
nonconforming 867.5
refuting 957.6
adverse 1010.13
hindering 1011.17
unwieldy 1012.19
adv opposite 215.6
contrast
n contraposition 215.1
contrariety 778.1
difference 779.1
dissimilarity 786.1

comparison 942.1
lighting 1024.19
v contrapose 215.4
compare 942.4
contravene deny 335.4
violate 435.4
contradict 451.6
break the law 674.5
go contrary to 778.4
counteract 899.6
thwart 1011.15
contretemps
wrong time 843.2
misfortune 1010.2
contribute
provide 385.7
participate 476.5
subscribe 478.14
tend 895.3
contribute to
advance 162.5
be useful 449.17
subscribe 478.14
determine 885.12
contribution
demand 421.1
participation 476.1
giving 478.1
donation 478.6
treatise 556.1
tax 630.9
contributor 478.11
contributory
additional 253.10
helpful 449.21
donative 478.25
contrite 113.9
contrition regret 113.1
apology 658.2
contrivance
plan 381.1
intrigue 381.5
instrument 384.4
stratagem 415.3
plot 722.4
production 891.1
expedient 994.2
tool 1039.1
contrive plan 381.8
manage 409.12
maneuver 415.10
fare 764.5
induce 885.11
originate 891.12
control
n supremacy 249.3
self-control 359.5
skill 413.1
governance 417.5
restraint 428.1
subjection 432.1
direction 573.1
mastery 612.2
moderation 670.1
familiar spirit
  678.12
influence 893.1
experiment 941.1
specter 987.1
system component
  1040.14
v pilot 184.37

possess authority
417.13
restrain 428.7
direct 573.8
hold in hand 612.13
moderate 670.6
exercise influence
893.8
haunt 987.6
controller
superintendent 574.2
accountant 628.7
treasurer 729.11
system component
1040.14
controlling
n extinguishing
1021.2
adj authoritative
417.15
restraining 428.11
directing 573.12
governing 612.18
paramount 996.24
control oneself
compose oneself 106.7
restrain oneself 668.6
controversial
contentious 110.26
argumentative 934.19
doubtful 970.17
controversy
quarrel 456.5
contention 457.1
disagreement 788.1
argumentation 934.4
controvert deny 335.4
contradict 451.6
discuss 541.12
go contrary to 778.4
refute 957.5
controvertible
unprovable 957.9
doubtful 970.17
contumacious
defiant 327.10
ungovernable 361.12
contumely
insolence 142.1
indignity 156.2
contempt 157.1
berating 510.7
vilification 513.2
contusion 85.37
conundrum
riddle 522.9
bewilderment 970.3
convalescence 396.8
convalescent 396.23
convection 176.1
convene
summon 420.11
meet 769.17
convenience
latrine 12.10
comfortableness
121.2
benefit 387.4
leisure 402.1
facility 449.9
timeliness 842.1
expedience 994.1

handiness 1013.2
machinery 1039.3
convenient
comfortable 121.11
nearby 223.15
handy 387.20
timely 842.9
expedient 994.5
convent 703.6
convention
custom 373.1
rule 419.2
ecclesiastical council
423.4
compact 437.1
treaty 437.2
conference 541.6
fashion 578.1
social rule 579.1
etiquette 580.3
political convention
609.8
assembly 769.2
conventional
customary 373.14
preceptive 419.4
contractual 437.10
decorous 579.5
ceremonious 580.8
orthodox 687.7
traditional 841.12
conformist 866.6
usual 868.9
ordinary 1004.8
converge
come together 169.2
focus 208.10
near 223.7
assemble 769.16
join 799.11
convergence
coming together 169
meeting 169.1
centralization 208.8
nearness 223.1
assemblage 769.1
joining 799.1
conversant with
used to 373.17
versed in 927.19
conversation
communication 343.1
speech 524.1
interchange of speech
541
converse 541.1
social life 582.4
conversational
v talkative 540.9
adj communicational
343.9
vernacular 523.18
colloquial 541.13
conversation piece
869.5
converse
v communicate 343.6
speak 524.20
talk together 541.9
converse
n inverse 205.4
opposite side 215.3

communication 343.1
conversation 541.1
social life 582.4
adj contrapositive
215.5
contrary 778.6
convert
n apostate 363.5
disciple 572.2
believer 692.4
proselyte 857.7
v invert 205.5
misuse 389.4
redeem 685.6
sell 737.24
change 851.7
reconvert 857.11
interchange 862.4
process 891.9
convince 952.18
converted
improved 392.13
redeemed 685.9
regenerate 692.10
altered 851.10
changed 857.19
forgetful 989.9
convertible
liquid 728.31
equivalent 789.8
changeable 857.18
interchangeable 862.5
convex
n bulge 283.3
adj bowed 279.10
rotund 282.8
convexed 283.13
convey
transport 176.12
channel 239.15
communicate 343.7
say 524.23
transfer 629.3
conveyability
transferability
176.2
communicability
343.4
conveyable
transferable 176.18
communicable 343.11
moveable 629.5
conveyance
transportation 176.3
vehicle 179.1
informing 343.2
theft 482.1
transfer 629.1
conveyor 176.7
convict
n prisoner 429.11
criminal 660.10
v bring in a verdict
598.19
condemn 602.3
conviction
hope 124.1
condemnation 602.1
persuasion 952.5
confidence 969.5
convince
persuade 375.23

cause to believe
857.16
convert 952.18
seem true 972.9
convinced belief 952.21
confident 969.21
convincing
convictional 952.26
evidential 956.16
conviviality
joviality 582.3
festivity 743.3
convocation
summons 420.5
ecclesiastical council
423.4
ceremony 580.4
assembly 769.2
convolution
curvature 279.1
brain 281
involution 281.1
grandiloquence 545.1
complexity 798.1
circuitousness 913.1
convoy
n escort 768.5
bodyguard 1007.14
v maneuver 182.46
escort 768.8
convulse pain 26.7
torture 96.18
amuse 743.21
discompose 810.4
agitate 916.10
convulsion seizure 85.6
symptom 85.9
outburst 105.9
laughter 116.4
fit 152.8
fall 395.3
upheaval 671.5
disarrangement 810.1
revolution 859.1
spasm 916.6
frenzy 925.7
coo murmur 52.10
bird sound 60.5
speak 524.26
co-occurrence 835.1
cook
n chef 11.2
maid 577.8
v prepare food 11.4
tamper with 354.16
spoil 393.11
do for 395.11
prearrange 964.5
be hot 1018.22
heat 1019.17
cookery
cooking 11.1
kitchen 11.3
heater 1019.10
cookie biscuit 10.41
man 76.5
cookout 8.6
cook up cook 11.4
fabricate 354.17
improvise 365.8
plot 381.9
originate 891.12

prearrange 964.5
cool
  n composure 106.2
  unastonishment 123.1
  moderation 670.1
  uniformity 780.1
  stability 854.1
  v disincline 379.4
  restrain 428.7
  pacify 465.7
  calm 670.7
  refrigerate 1023.10
  adj chromatic 35.15
  unfeeling 94.9
  indifferent 102.6
  calm 106.12
  unastonished 123.3
  aloof 141.12
  insolent 142.9
  quiescent 173.12
  reticent 344.10
  cautious 494.8
  unsociable 583.6
  unfriendly 589.9
  equable 670.13
  stable 854.12
  sensible 919.18
  excellent 998.13
  chilly 1022.12
  feeling cold 1022.16
coolant
  refrigerant 1023.7
  antifreeze 1023.8
cooler jail 429.9
  jockey 757.2
  chiller 1023.3
coolheaded
  calm 106.12
  unnervous 129.2
  sensible 919.18
coolie 176.7
cool off
  compose oneself 106.7
  restrain 428.7
  order 806.4
cool one's heels
  await 130.8
  do nothing 329.2
  be kept waiting
    845.14
coop
  n enclosed place 212.3
  chicken house 228.22
  place of confinement
    429.7
  jail 429.9
  participation 476.1
  v enclose 212.5
  confine 429.12
co-op
  apartment house
    228.14
  market 736.1
cooperation
  working together 450
  collaboration 450.1
  communion 476.2
  association 582.6
  interaction 776.3
  agreement 787.1
  interchange 862.1
  concurrence 898.1

cooperative
  n participation 476.1
  association 617.1
  market 736.1
  adj willing 324.5
  favorable 449.22
  collaborative 450.5
  communal 476.9
  interacting 776.9
  agreeing 787.9
  joint 799.12
  concurrent 898.4
co-opt 371.13
co-option 371.1
coordinate
  n likeness 783.3
  v symmetrize 264.3
  make agree 787.7
  equalize 789.6
  organize 807.10
  adj symmetric 264.4
  equivalent 789.8
  concurrent 898.4
coordinated 413.22
coordinates
  bounds 211.1
  Cartesian coordinates
    300.5
cop
  n cone 282.5
  police 1007.16
  v acquire 472.9
  rob 482.16
cop a plea
  confess 351.7
  get off 369.7
cope
  n the heavens 1070.2
  v cover 295.19
  support oneself 385.12
  compete 457.18
  make shift 994.4
cope with treat 321.6
  perform 328.9
  deal 387.12
  contend with 457.17
copious much 247.8
  voluminous 257.17
  diffuse 538.11
  abundant 883.8
  productive 889.9
  plentiful 990.7
cop out
  hesitate 362.7
  get off 369.7
  remain neutral 467.5
  compromise 468.2
  seclude oneself 584.7
  defect 857.13
  pull back 902.7
cop-out
  neutrality 467.1
  compromise 468.1
  excuse 600.4
copper
  n money 728.7
  precious metals
    728.20
  police 1007.16
  adj reddish-brown
    40.4
  brass 1056.17

copse
  grove 310.12
  thicket 310.13
  bunch 769.7
copulate
  v couple 75.21
  procreate 78.8
  make love 562.14
  come together 769.16
  join 799.5
  adj joined 799.13
copy
  n duplicate 78.1
  imitation 336.3
  image 349.5
  diagram 381.3
  writing 547.10
  printer's copy 548.4
  news item 552.3
  edition 554.5
  score 708.28
  picture 712.11
  the same 777.3
  reproduction 784
  representation 784.1
  iteration 848.2
  substitute 861.2
  v reproduce 78.7
  imitate 336.5
  impersonate 349.12
  write 547.19
  adopt 621.4
  portray 712.19
  mimic 777.6
  resemble 783.7
  substitute 784.8
  repeat 848.7
  duplicate 873.3
copycat
  n imitator 336.4
  v mimic 336.6
copy-edit 548.17
copyreader
  proofreader 548.13
  journalist 555.4
copyright
  n patent 210.3
  privilege 642.2
  safeguard 1007.3
  v limit 210.5
  preserve 397.8
  protect 1007.18
copywriter
  publicist 352.9
  writer 547.15
  author 718.4
coquette lover 104.12
  tempter 377.4
  flirt 562.11
coquettish fickle 364.6
  alluring 377.8
  amatory 562.23
coral 41.8
coral reef island 235.2
  shoal 276.2
  point of land 283.9
cord line 271.2
  electrical device
    1031.20
  wood 1052.3
cordage capacity 257.2
  cording 271.3

cordial
  n refreshment 9.1
  tonic 86.8
  liqueur 88.15
  adj refreshing 9.3
  fervent 93.18
  pleasant 97.6
  good-natured 143.14
  receptive 187.16
  informal 581.3
  hospitable 585.11
  genial 587.16
cordless 1031.29
cordon
  n quarantine 429.2
  decoration 646.5
  guard 1007.9
  obstacle 1011.4
  v enclose 212.5
  quarantine 429.13
  segregate 772.6
cordon bleu
  expert 413.11
  decoration 646.5
corduroy
  n roughness 288.2
  adj furrowed 290.4
core
  n essential content
    196.5
  interior 207.2
  center 208.2
  city district 230.6
  summary 557.2
  essence 766.2
  middle 818.1
  salient point 996.6
  memory 1041.7
  adj urban 230.11
  middle 818.4
cork
  n float 180.11
  stopper 293.4
  skin 295.3
  lightness 298.2
  v blacken 38.7
  stop 293.7
  top 295.21
  suppress 428.8
corkscrew
  n extractor 192.9
  coil 281.2
  opener 292.10
  v convolve 281.4
  adj spiral 281.8
corn
  n feed 10.4
  growth 85.38
  swelling 283.4
  grass 310.5
  old joke 489.9
  platitude 973.3
  v preserve 397.9
corncob pipe 89.6
  ear 310.27
cornea 2.9
corner
  n deviation 164.1
  nook 197.3
  small space 258.3
  angle 278.2
  recess 284.7

hiding place 346.4
monopoly 469.3
manipulation 737.20
boxing 754.1
race 756.3
impasse 1012.6
v monopolize 469.6
purchase 733.7
get a corner on 737.26
turn 913.6
run into a corner
1012.16
cornerstone
foundation 900.7
salient point 996.6
corn-fed 257.18
cornice 198.5
cornified pointed 285.9
hardened 1044.13
cornucopia store 386.1
source of supply 386.4
horn of plenty 990.3
corny trite 117.9
old-fogyish 841.17
corollary adjunct 254.1
attendant 768.3
effect 886.1
conclusion 945.4
corona
n cigar 89.4
radiation 171.2
circle 280.2
flower 310.26
halo 1024.14
chandelier 1025.6
sun 1070.13
adj circular 280.11
coronation
authority 417.12
installation 615.3
coroner doctor 90.4
autopsy 307.18
coronet circle 280.2
jewel 498.6
heraldry 647.2
royal insignia 647.3
corporal
n Army
noncommissioned
officer 575.19
naval officer 575.20
church 703.10
adj material 1050.10
corporate
associated 617.16
joint 799.12
leagued 804.6
corporation goozle 2.17
workplace 739.1
corporeal 1050.10
corps branch 461.21
military unit 461.22
association 617.1
company 769.3
corpse slim 270.8
dead body 307.16
corpulent stout 257.18
thick 269.8
corpus capital 728.15
collection 769.11
knowledge 927.1
lore 927.9

body 1050.3
corpuscle blood 2.23
cell 305.4
corpus delicti 307.16
corral enclose 212.5
acquire 472.9
assemble 769.18
drive 1068.8
correct
v revise 392.12
remedy 396.13
reprove 510.17
punish 604.10
conform 866.3
disillusion 976.2
adj meticulous 339.12
mannerly 504.16
grammatical 530.17
appropriate 533.7
conventional 579.5
right 637.3
orthodox 687.7
accurate 972.16
correction
measurement 300.1
revision 392.4
reparation 396.6
reproof 510.5
punishment 604.1
corrective
n remedy 86.1
adj remedial 86.39
emendatory 392.16
punishing 604.23
correlation
relativity 774.2
reciprocal relation
776
mutuality 776.1
comparison 942.1
correlative
n correspondent 776.4
likeness 783.3
adj accompanying
768.9
approximate 774.8
correlative 776.8
akin 783.13
comparative 942.8
correspondence
symmetry 264.1
communication 343.1
accord 455.1
record 549.1
written
communications 553
letter writing 553.1
correlation 776.1
sameness 777.1
uniformity 780.1
similarity 783.1
agreement 787.1
equality 789.1
conformity 866.1
concurrence 898.1
correspondent
n letter writer 553.8
journalist 555.4
correlate 776.4
likeness 783.3
adj reciprocal 776.10
coinciding 777.8

uniform 780.5
analogous 783.11
agreeing 787.9
equivalent 789.8
corridor airway 184.33
entrance 189.5
hall 197.18
region 231.1
passageway 383.3
corrigible
improvable 392.17
remediable 396.25
manageable 433.14
corroborate 956.11
corrode
decrease 252.6
erode 393.21
etch 713.10
disintegrate 805.3
corrosion
decrement 252.3
decay 393.6
disintegration 805.1
corrosive
n cauterant 1019.15
adj acid 110.17
caustic 144.23
corrupting 393.44
vigorous 544.11
disintegrative 805.5
harmful 999.12
corrugated rough 288.6
rugged 288.7
furrowed 290.4
wrinkled 291.8
corrupt
v defile 80.17
bribe 378.3
debase 393.12
decay 393.22
misteach 569.3
sully 654.10
adulterate 796.12
indoctrinate 857.15
work evil 999.6
adj bribable 378.4
decayed 393.40
dishonest 645.16
corrupted 654.14
erroneous 974.16
corruptible
bribable 378.4
venal 645.23
transient 827.7
corruption filth 80.7
perversion 265.2
bribery 378.1
pollution 393.2
decay 393.6
wordplay 489.8
mispronunciation
525.5
barbarism 526.6
solecism 531.2
misteaching 569.1
improbity 645.1
turpitude 654.5
adulteration 796.3
indoctrination 857.5
evil 999.3
corsage shirt 5.15
bouquet 310.23

corsair 483.7
corset stays 5.23
supporter 900.2
cortege funeral 309.5
attendance 768.6
procession 811.3
cortex exterior 206.2
skin 295.3
shell 295.15
armor 460.3
cosmetic
exterior 206.7
shallow 276.5
hasty 401.9
insufficient 991.9
beautifying 1015.22
cosmetics
appearance 33.2
exteriority 206.1
pretext 376.1
notions 735.6
dissimilarity 786.1
makeup 1015.12
cosmic large 247.7
universal 863.14
cosmologic 1070.24
cosmology 1070.18
cosmonaut 1073.8
cosmopolitan
n citizen 227.4
sophisticate 413.17
adj traveled 177.40
public 312.16
experienced 413.28
chic 578.13
universal 863.14
broad-minded 978.8
cosmos
completeness 793.1
universe 1070.1
cossack 461.12
cosset
n favorite 104.16
v indulge 427.6
foster 449.16
caress 562.16
cost
n loss 473.1
expenses 626.3
value 630.1
high price 632.3
v spend 626.5
sell for 630.13
cost-effective
635.6
costive 293.11
costly 632.11
cost of living
expenses 626.3
standard of living
731.8
costume
n clothing 5.1
suit 5.6
costumery 5.9
theater 704.17
v outfit 5.40
cot 228.8
coterie
social set 582.5
clique 617.6
company 769.3

instant 829.3
expedient 994.2
coup d'état revolt 327.4
seizure 480.2
revolution 859.1
couple
n set 783.5
two 872.2
v copulate 75.21
wed 563.14
get married 563.15
come together 769.16
relate 774.6
put together 799.5
combine 804.3
league 804.4
double 872.5
couplet poetry 720.9
two 872.2
coupon token 728.12
stock certificate 738.4
courage pluck 359.3
fortitude 492
bravery 492.1
confidence 969.5
courageous
resolute 359.14
plucky 492.17
courier
messenger 353.1
guide 574.7
course
n serving 8.10
dish 10.7
direction 161.1
progression 162.1
career 172.2
travel 177.1
journey 177.5
voyage 182.6
heading 184.34
flow 238.4
channel 239.1
layer 296.1
policy 381.4
route 383.1
manner 384.1
arena 463.1
track 517.8
study 568.8
golf 751.1
skiing 753.1
horse racing 757.1
series 811.2
round 849.3
process 888.2
trend 895.2
v travel 177.18
traverse 177.20
flow 238.16
hunt 382.9
adv under way 182.63
course of action 994.2
courser swiftness 174.6
horse 311.10
hunter 382.5
war-horse 461.30
court
n enclosed place 212.3
estate 228.7
council 423.1
courtship 562.7

judiciary 594.2
law court 595.2
courthouse 595.6
legislature 613.1
playground 743.11
basketball 747.1
tennis 748.1
attendance 768.6
influence 893.6
v curry favor 138.9
solicit 440.14
woo 562.21
cultivate 587.12
adj tribunal 595.7
courteous
sensitive 24.12
respectful 155.8
polite 504.14
sociable 582.22
courtesan 665.15
courtesy
sensitivity 24.3
act of kindness 143.7
respect 155.1
good behavior 321.2
politeness 504
courteousness 504.1
civility 504.6
sociability 582.1
courthouse
town hall 230.5
court 595.6
capitol 613.4
courtier
sycophant 138.3
follower 166.2
flatterer 511.4
courtliness
proud bearing 136.2
gallantry 504.2
courtesy 504.6
etiquette 580.3
courtly
dignified 136.12
gallant 504.15
flattering 511.8
court-martial
military court 595.4
trial 598.5
courtroom 595.6
courtship 562.7
courtyard 212.3
cousin 559.3
couturier
dressmaker 5.35
designer 716.9
cove man 76.5
nook 197.3
inlet 242.1
arch 279.4
cave 284.5
recess 284.7
coven 690.8
covenant
n compact 437.1
v come to an
agreement 332.10
contract 437.5
cover
n serving 8.10
food service 8.11
dish 10.7

Air Force mission
184.11
ground covering 199.3
covering 295.2
lid 295.5
blanket 295.10
concealment 346.1
veil 346.2
hiding place 346.4
disguise 356.11
pretext 376.1
anonymity 528.1
bookbinding 554.14
protection 1007.1
shelter 1008.3
shade 1027.1
v color 35.13
copulate 75.21
be pregnant 78.12
extend 158.8
traverse 177.20
close 293.6
stop 293.7
cover up 295.19
compensate 338.4
explain 341.10
conceal 346.6
hide under 376.4
bet 759.25
include 771.3
put together 799.5
take one's turn 824.5
overspread 909.5
protect 1007.18
shade 1027.5
coverage size 257.1
scope 295.1
protection 295.2
news 552.1
inclusion 771.1
cover charge
food service 8.11
fee 630.6
cover for 861.5
cover girl 1015.8
covert
n plumage 3.18
lair 228.26
cover 295.2
thicket 310.13
hiding place 346.4
shelter 1008.3
adj covered 295.31
clandestine 345.12
concealed 346.11
latent 519.5
cover-up
veil of secrecy 345.3
pretext 376.1
covet crave 100.18
envy 154.3
covey company 769.3
assemblage 769.6
multitude 883.3
cow
n female animal 77.9
cattle 311.6
v intimidate 127.20
domineer 612.16
coward
n jellyfish 491.5
adj cowardly 491.10

cowardice frailty 16.2
fear 127.1
weak will 362.4
submission 433.1
spinelessness 491
cowardliness 491.1
cowardly weak 16.12
fearful 127.23
weak-willed 362.12
coward 491.10
cowboy rider 178.8
violent person 671.10
card 758.2
herder 1068.3
cower be weak 16.8
fawn 138.7
quail 491.9
crouch 912.8
cowl
n cover 295.2
v hood 295.19
cowlick 3.6
co-worker 616.5
coxcomb dandy 500.9
comedy 704.6
coxswain
n steersman 183.8
guide 574.7
v pilot 182.14
coy shy 139.12
amatory 562.23
coyote 311.20
cozen 356.18
cozy pleased 95.14
comfortable 121.11
homelike 228.33
conversational 541.13
intimate 582.24
snug 1006.7
crab
n malcontent 108.4
complainer 115.9
marine animal 311.30
vermin 311.35
windlass 905.7
lifter 911.3
v be discontented
108.6
complain 115.16
maneuver 184.40
hinder 1011.16
adj sour 67.5
crabbed sour 67.5
irascible 110.19
stricken in years
303.18
hard to understand
522.14
stiff 534.3
complex 798.4
crack
n stripe 47.5
report 56.1
snap 56.2
detonation 56.3
trauma 85.37
cocaine 87.6
cleft 224.2
furrow 290.1
opening 292.1
attempt 403.3
witticism 489.7

remark 524.4
break 801.4
instant 829.3
hit 901.4
fault 1002.2
blemish 1003.1
v clap 56.6
snap 56.7
blast 56.8
lose self-control 128.8
cleave 224.4
furrow 290.3
open 292.11
unclose 292.12
explain 341.10
injure 393.13
break 393.23
separate 801.12
hit 901.14
solve 939.2
blemish 1003.4
burn 1019.24
adj skillful 413.22
superior 998.14
crack down on
restrain 428.7
suppress 428.8
attack 459.15
cracked raucous 58.15
dissonant 61.4
cleft 224.7
gaping 292.18
impaired 393.27
severed 801.23
mentally deficient
  921.22
crazy 925.27
blemished 1003.8
cracker
biscuit 10.29
noisemaker 53.6
wilderness settler
  227.10
dryness 1064.2
crackerjack
n skillful person
  413.14
good person 659.2
first-rate 998.7
adj skillful 413.22
excellent 998.13
crackle
n snap 56.2
trauma 85.37
v pop 56.7
crackpot oddity 869.4
lunatic 925.16
freak 926.4
crack up
n exhaustion 21.2
collapse 85.8
mental disorder 92.14
frayed nerves 128.4
crash 184.20
impairment 393.1
debacle 395.4
disruption 801.3
misfortune 1010.2
v burn out 21.5
laugh 116.8
lose self-control 128.8
crash 184.44

disintegrate 805.3
collide 901.13
go mad 925.21
cradle
n refinery 79.13
fatherland 232.2
infancy 301.5
origin 817.4
birthplace 885.8
v put to bed 22.19
foster 449.16
calm 670.7
support 900.21
craft ship 180.1
deceit 356.3
skill 413.1
art 413.7
cunning 415.1
stratagem 415.3
manual work 712.3
vocation 724.6
shrewdness 919.3
crafted 891.18
craftsman
expert 413.11
artist 716.1
skilled worker 726.6
producer 891.7
crafty
falsehearted 354.30
deceitful 356.22
cunning 415.12
cautious 494.8
sly 645.18
shrewd 919.15
crag
precipice 200.3
mountain 237.6
projection 285.4
rock 1057.1
craggy rugged 288.7
stony 1057.11
cram
n study 570.3
full measure 793.3
v stuff 8.25
tutor 568.11
study up 570.14
gluttonize 672.4
assemble 769.18
fill 793.7
thrust 901.12
refresh the memory
  988.19
overload 992.15
satiate 993.4
densify 1043.9
cramp
n pang 26.2
seizure 85.6
pain 96.5
restriction 428.3
spasm 916.6
hindrance 1011.1
v weaken 16.10
confine 212.6
contract 260.7
squeeze 260.8
restrict 428.9
fasten 799.7
hamper 1011.11
hinder 1011.16

adj narrow 270.14
hard to understand
  522.14
cramped limited 210.7
enclosed 212.10
little 258.10
contracted 260.12
constricted 270.14
restricted 428.15
stiff 534.3
narrow-minded
  979.10
cramp one's style
  1011.16
crane
n lifter 911.3
fire iron 1019.12
v gaze 27.15
be long 267.5
demur 325.4
cranium 198.7
crank
n amphetamines 87.3
malcontent 108.4
sorehead 110.11
complainer 115.9
angle 278.2
caprice 364.1
punishment 605.3
oddity 869.4
lever 905.4
fanatic 925.18
quirk 926.2
freak 926.4
v zigzag 204.12
angle 278.5
reel in 905.9
rotate 914.9
adj eccentric 926.5
cranky
discontented 108.8
irascible 110.19
complaining 115.20
capricious 364.5
disagreeing 788.6
counteractive 899.8
eccentric 926.5
cranny nook 197.3
crack 224.2
furrow 290.1
hiding place 346.4
crap
n defecation 12.2
feces 12.4
heroin 87.8
humbug 354.14
bull 520.3
v defecate 12.13
crape 115.7
craps dice 759.8
deuce 872.3
crapulent
intoxicated 88.31
intemperate 669.7
gluttonous 672.6
crash
n noise 53.3
report 56.1
substance abuse 87.1
crack-up 184.20
descent 194.1
decline 252.2

impairment 393.1
debacle 395.4
collapse 410.3
defeat 412.1
insolvency 625.3
declining market
  737.5
impact 901.3
misfortune 1010.2
v sleep 22.14
go to bed 22.18
din 53.7
boom 56.6
use 87.21
crack up 184.44
penetrate 189.8
descend 194.5
intrude 214.5
inhabit 225.7
billow 238.22
break down 393.24
fall 410.12
go bankrupt 625.7
cheapen 633.6
collide 901.13
adv at top speed 756.5
crass downright 247.12
thick 269.8
coarse 497.11
ill-bred 505.6
stupid 921.15
crate
n car 179.10
storehouse 386.6
v package 212.9
wrap 295.20
crater valley 237.7
pit 275.2
cavity 284.2
blemish 1003.1
crave covet 100.18
request 440.9
entreat 440.11
craven
n dastard 491.6
adj cowardly 491.12
craving
n coveting 100.6
adj desiring 100.24
craw
digestive system 2.16
narrow place 270.3
crawl
n slow motion 175.2
creeping 177.17
aquatics 182.11
v feel creepy 74.7
fawn 138.7
go slow 175.6
creep 177.26
lie 201.5
get low 274.5
linger on 826.7
bow 912.9
crawl with
pervade 221.7
teem with 883.5
infest 909.6
abound 990.5
crayon
n drawing 712.13
art equipment 712.18

v portray 712.19
craze
  n stripe 47.5
  trauma 85.37
  greed 100.8
  eagerness 101.1
  fury 105.8
  crack 224.2
  caprice 364.1
  fad 578.5
  mania 925.12
  blemish 1003.1
  v cleave 224.4
  injure 393.13
  break 801.12
  madden 925.24
  blemish 1003.4
crazy
  n lunatic 925.16
  adj variegated 47.9
  distorted 265.10
  mentally deficient
    921.22
  foolish 922.8
  absurd 922.11
  nutty 925.27
  adv swiftly 174.18
crazy about
  enthusiastic 101.11
  nuts about 104.31
creak
  n screech 58.4
  insect sound 58.5
  v stridulate 58.7
  screech 58.8
cream
  n whiteness 37.2
  cleanser 79.17
  superior 249.5
  upper class 607.2
  the best 998.8
  ointment 1054.3
  semiliquid 1060.5
  v foam 320.5
  defeat 412.9
  emulsify 1060.10
  adj whitish 37.8
  yellow 43.4
crease
  n fold 291.1
  wrinkle 291.3
  hockey 749.1
  v fold 291.5
  wrinkle 291.6
  engrave 713.9
create form 262.7
  originate 337.4
  initiate 817.10
  cause 885.10
  produce 891.8
  imagine 985.14
creation
  forming 262.5
  structure 266.1
  divine function 677.14
  work of art 712.10
  beginning 817.1
  production 891.1
  work 892.1
  universe 1070.1
creative
  nonimitative 337.5

falsehearted 354.30
  wrong 638.3
  dishonest 645.16
  illegal 674.6
  almighty 677.18
  beginning 817.15
  productive 889.9
  originative 891.16
  imaginative 985.18
creativity
  nonimitation 337.1
  genius 919.8
  invention 985.3
creator artist 716.1
  doer 726.1
  author 885.4
  producer 891.7
creature
  sycophant 138.3
  inferior 250.2
  organism 305.2
  animal 311.2
  person 312.5
  assenter 332.6
  instrument 384.4
  dependent 432.6
  figurehead 575.5
  deputy 576.1
  retainer 577.1
  follower 616.8
  something 762.3
  product 892.1
credence altar 703.12
  belief 952.1
credential
  preparedness 405.4
  recommendation
    509.4
  identification 517.11
  certificate 549.6
credibility
  honesty 644.3
  believability 952.8
  plausibility 967.3
credibility gap
  untruthfulness 354.8
  deceitfulness 645.3
  unbelievability 954.3
credible logical 934.20
  believable 952.24
  plausible 967.7
credit
  n thanks 150.2
  difference 255.8
  trust 622.1
  receipts 627.1
  entry 628.5
  due 639.2
  honor 646.1
  esteem 662.3
  attribution 887.1
  influence 893.1
  belief 952.1
  credible 952.8
  v thank 150.4
  pay 622.5
  keep accounts 628.8
  believe 952.10
creditable
  praiseworthy 509.20
  honest 644.13
  reputable 662.15

creditor 622.4
credit union
  association 617.1
  lending institution
    620.4
  credit 622.1
credo religion 675.1
  doctrine 676.2
  system of belief 952.3
credulous foolish 922.8
  trusting 952.22
  knee-jerk 953.8
creed affirmation 334.1
  policy 381.4
  religion 675.1
  doctrine 676.2
  system of belief 952.3
creedbound strict 687.8
  narrow-minded
    979.10
creek stream 238.1
  inlet 242.1
creep
  n slow motion 175.2
  crawling 177.17
  bad person 660.6
  v feel creepy 74.7
  fawn 138.7
  go slow 175.6
  crawl 177.26
  lurk 346.9
  linger on 826.7
creep in enter 189.7
  intrude 214.5
  join 617.14
creeps
  creeping of the flesh
    74.4
  trepidation 127.5
  nervousness 128.2
  cold 1022.2
creep with
  pervade 221.7
  teem with 883.5
  infest 909.6
  abound 990.5
creepy crawly 74.11
  spooky 127.31
  bad 999.8
cremation
  incineration 309.2
  burning 1019.5
crematorium
  mortuary 309.9
  incinerator 1019.13
crenellated
  notched 289.5
  fortified 460.12
creole 523.11
crêpe 10.43
crepitant 56.10
crepuscular 315.8
crepuscule
  foredawn 314.4
  dusk 315.3
crescendo
  n loudness 53.1
  increase 251.1
  expansion 259.1
  music 708.25
  v din 53.7
  grow 251.6

enlarge 259.4
  increase 259.5
  adj music 708.53
crescent
  n circle 230.9
  curve 279.5
  semicircle 280.8
  heraldry 647.2
  moon 1070.11
  adj grown 14.3
  increasing 251.8
  expanding 259.12
  curving 279.11
crest
  n feather 3.16
  summit 198.2
  top part 198.4
  mountain 237.6
  notching 289.2
  heraldry 647.2
  wave 915.4
  v top 198.9
crestfallen glum 112.25
  disappointed 132.5
  humiliated 137.14
cretin 923.8
cretinism 921.9
crevasse
  n valley 237.7
  pit 275.2
  v open 292.11
crevice 224.2
crew aircrew 185.4
  staff 577.11
  clique 617.6
  team 617.7
  motion-picture studio
    706.3
  baseball team 745.2
  company 769.3
crib
  n compartment 197.2
  quarters 228.4
  hut 228.9
  translation 341.3
  storehouse 386.6
  garner 386.7
  brothel 665.9
  casino 759.19
  v enclose 212.6
  imitate 336.5
  cheat 356.18
  confine 429.12
  rob 482.16
  plagiarize 482.19
crick
  n pang 26.2
  insect sound 58.5
  stream 238.1
  v stridulate 58.7
cricket
  noisemaker 53.6
  locust 311.34
  propriety 637.2
  fairness 649.3
crier 353.3
crime
  wrongdoing 655.1
  misdeed 655.2
  offense 674.4
criminal
  n evildoer 593.1

perpetrator 645.10
felon 660.10
adj wrong 638.3
dishonest 645.16
wicked 654.16
evil 655.5
guilty 656.3
illegal 674.6
bad 999.7
criminology 673.7
crimp
n lock 3.5
trench 290.2
fold 291.1
wrinkle 291.3
cheat 357.3
abductor 483.10
v curl 281.5
notch 289.4
furrow 290.3
fold 291.5
wrinkle 291.6
abduct 482.20
hinder 1011.16
adj pulverable
1049.13
crimson
v color 41.4
redden 41.5
change color
105.19
blush 139.8
adj red 41.6
cringe
n retreat 902.3
v be weak 16.8
flinch 127.13
fawn 138.7
retract 168.3
cower 491.9
pull back 902.7
crouch 912.8
crinkle
n convolution 281.1
wrinkle 291.3
v rustle 52.12
convolve 281.4
ruffle 288.5
wrinkle 291.6
cripple
n defective 85.44
v weaken 16.10
disable 19.9
lame 393.14
hamper 1011.11
crisis
financial trouble
729.7
business cycle 731.9
critical point 842.4
urgency 996.4
salient point 996.6
danger 1005.1
crisp
v curl 281.5
fold 291.5
adj refreshing 9.3
curly 281.9
clear 521.11
concise 537.6
aphoristic 973.6
cool 1022.12

cold 1022.14
brittle 1048.4
pulverable 1049.13
crisscross
v cross 170.6
adj cross 170.8
adv crosswise 170.13
criterion
measure 300.2
model 785.1
rule 868.4
test 941.2
critic
opinion maker 341.7
connoisseur 496.7
faultfinder 510.9
columnist 547.15
commentator 556.4
judge 596.1
author 718.4
interpreter 723.4
specialist 865.3
criticizer 945.7
critical
meticulous 339.12
explanatory 341.15
fastidious 495.9
faultfinding 510.23
dissertational 556.6
evaluative 723.6
crucial 842.10
discriminating 943.7
judicial 945.16
urgent 996.22
dangerous 1005.9
precarious 1005.12
difficult 1012.17
criticism
exegetics 341.8
adverse reaction 510.4
commentary 556.2
review of the arts
723.1
censure 945.2
criticize pan 510.14
write upon 556.5
critique 723.5
judge 945.14
critter animal 311.2
cattle 311.6
horse 311.10
croak
n rasp 58.3
speech defect 525.1
v sound harshly 58.9
bird sound 60.5
complain 115.15
forebode 133.11
die 307.20
kill 308.13
speak poorly 525.7
crock
n horse 311.12
ceramic ware 742.2
v intoxicate 88.23
crocodile 311.25
Croesus 618.8
croft 231.4
Cronus 820.2
crony
companion 588.3
associate 616.1

cronyism 609.35
crook
n deviation 164.1
bias 204.3
shaft 273.2
angle 278.2
curve 279.2
cheater 357.4
scepter 417.9
thief 483.1
evildoer 593.1
ecclesiastical insignia
647.4
criminal 660.10
staff 702.3
supporter 900.2
fire iron 1019.12
v deflect 164.5
oblique 204.9
distort 265.5
angle 278.5
curve 279.6
crooked askew 204.14
zigzag 204.20
distorted 265.10
fake 265.11
angular 278.6
hooked 279.8
falsehearted 354.30
dishonest 645.16
crooner 710.13
crop
n digestive system
2.16
head of hair 3.4
breast 283.6
growth 310.2
yield 472.5
whip 605.1
bunch 769.7
effect 886.1
production 892.2
harvest 1067.15
v feed on 8.28
excise 255.10
shorten 268.6
farm 1067.16
harvest 1067.19
crop out
be exposed 31.5
appear 33.8
crop up
originate 817.13
turn up 830.6
crosier shaft 273.2
scepter 417.9
ecclesiastical insignia
647.4
staff 702.3
cross
n affliction 96.8
crux 170.4
staff 273.2
signature 527.10
monument 549.12
execution 605.5
insignia 647.1
heraldry 647.2
rood 702.3
hybrid 796.8
adversity 1010.1
impediment 1011.6

v disappoint 132.2
converge 169.2
crisscross 170.6
traverse 177.20
navigate 182.13
deny 335.4
oppose 451.3
contradict 451.6
bless 696.13
hybridize 796.13
counteract 899.6
pass 909.8
thwart 1011.15
adj irascible 110.19
angry 152.28
crossing 170.8
transverse 170.9
cruciform 170.10
oppositional 451.8
disagreeing 788.6
hybrid 796.15
adv crosswise 170.13
in opposition 451.9
crossbow 462.7
crossbreed
n hybrid 796.8
v procreate 78.8
hybridize 796.13
cross-check
n examination 937.3
collation 942.2
ensuring 969.8
v collate 942.5
verify 969.12
crosscurrent flow 238.4
wind 318.1
opposition 451.1
counterforce 899.4
crossed
disappointed 132.5
cross 170.8
cruciform 170.10
hybrid 796.15
cross-examination
trial 598.5
argumentation 934.4
grilling 937.13
cross-eyed 28.12
cross-fertilization 78.3
cross-fertilize
reproduce 78.10
fertilize 889.8
cross fire 862.1
crossgrained
adj irascible 110.19
rough 288.6
coarse 294.6
negative 335.5
perverse 361.11
adv crosswise 170.13
against the grain
288.12
cross-hatching
network 170.3
line 517.6
engraving 713.2
crossing-over 857.3
cross-interrogation
937.13
cross one's fingers
be hopeful 124.8
await 130.8

doubt 954.6
cross one's heart
depose 334.6
promise 436.4
cross one's mind
930.18
cross out delete 255.12
obliterate 395.16
crosspatch
sorehead 110.11
misfit 788.4
crosspiece 170.5
cross purposes
hostility 451.2
disagreement 456.2
contrariety 778.1
crossroads
convergence 169.1
village 230.2
crisis 842.4
cross section
crossing 170.1
representative 349.7
part 792.1
crosswise
adj transverse 170.9
oblique 204.19
hindering 1011.17
unwieldy 1012.19
adv decussatively
170.13
transversely 204.24
crotch genitals 2.11
fork 171.4
crotchet angle 278.2
caprice 364.1
note 709.14
quirk 926.2
crotchety
capricious 364.5
counteractive 899.8
eccentric 926.5
crouch
n stoop 912.3
v fawn 138.7
lie low 274.5
bow down 433.10
cower 491.9
duck 912.8
crow
n blackness 38.4
laughter 116.4
speech defect 525.1
lever 905.4
v bird sound 60.5
laugh 116.8
put up a bold front
454.5
exult 502.9
speak 524.26
crow's-feet 291.3
crowbar
n extractor 192.9
lever 905.4
v get a purchase 905.8
crowd
n audience 48.6
social circle 582.5
the masses 606.2
clique 617.6
company 769.3
throng 769.4

attender 917.2
v make one's way
162.4
hurry 401.4
make haste 401.5
come together 769.16
fill 793.7
teem with 883.5
thrust 901.12
overload 992.15
obstruct 1011.12
densify 1043.9
crowd in enter 189.7
thrust in 191.7
intrude 214.5
crown
n summit 198.2
top part 198.4
architectural topping
198.5
head 198.6
supremacy 249.3
circle 280.2
finishing touch 407.3
victory 411.1
jewel 498.6
volume 554.4
trophy 646.3
heraldry 647.2
royal insignia 647.3
specie 728.4
money 728.8
tennis 748.1
limit 793.5
chandelier 1025.6
v top 198.9
cover 295.21
complete 407.6
take command 417.14
install 615.12
honor 646.8
glorify 662.13
perfect 1001.5
the Crown
sovereignty 417.8
the government 612.3
crowning
topping 198.11
chief 249.14
completing 407.9
ending 819.10
crown of thorns 96.8
crucial critical 842.10
original 885.14
urgent 996.22
vital 996.23
crucible mixer 796.9
instrument of
conversion 857.10
test 941.2
crucifix 170.4
crucifixion
agony 26.6
torment 96.7
capital punishment
604.7
crucify
pain 26.7
torture 96.18
execute 604.17
stigmatize 661.9
work evil 999.6

crude
n raw material 406.5
petroleum 1054.4
adj garish 35.19
offensive 98.18
raw 406.10
undeveloped 406.12
coarse 497.11
gaudy 501.20
ill-bred 505.6
inelegant 534.2
base 661.12
crudity
undevelopment 406.4
coarseness 497.2
baseness 661.3
cruel painful 26.10
cruel-hearted 144.26
pitiless 146.3
murderous 308.23
savage 671.21
cruelty
cruelness 144.11
unkindness 144.12
pitilessness 146.1
cruise
n journey 177.5
voyage 182.6
v journey 177.21
navigate 182.13
fly 184.36
make good 409.10
cruiser traveler 178.1
police car 179.11
motorboat 180.4
battleship 180.7
cruller 10.42
crumb
n scrap 248.3
minute 258.7
piece 792.3
powder 1049.5
v sprinkle 770.6
pulverize 1049.9
crumble
n powder 1049.5
v weaken 16.9
decrease 252.6
decay 393.22
be destroyed 395.22
disintegrate 805.3
pulverize 1049.9
powder 1049.10
crumbly frail 16.14
brittle 1048.4
pulverable 1049.13
crummy base 661.12
paltry 997.21
bad 999.8
crumple
n wrinkle 291.3
v distort 265.5
ruffle 288.5
wrinkle 291.6
crunch
n rasp 58.3
poverty 619.1
concussion 671.8
crisis 842.4
crucial moment 842.5
impact 901.3
urgency 996.4

predicament 1012.5
v grate 58.10
shatter 801.13
collide 901.13
pulverize 1049.9
crunched 265.10
crusade
n campaign 458.4
cause 885.9
v espouse 509.13
crush
n liking 100.2
infatuation 104.4
squeezing 260.2
throng 769.4
full measure 793.3
pulp 1061.2
v sadden 112.18
aggrieve 112.19
unnerve 128.10
abase 137.5
squeeze 260.8
conquer 412.10
suppress 428.8
subdue 432.9
shatter 801.13
refute 957.5
pulverize 1049.9
pulp 1061.5
crushing
n wretchedness 96.6
suppression 428.2
subdual 432.4
pulverization 1049.4
adj mortifying 98.21
oppressive 98.24
humiliating 137.15
laborious 725.18
troublesome 1012.18
crust
n bread 10.27
impudence 142.3
exterior 206.2
land 234.1
incrustation 295.14
upper class 607.2
v incrust 295.27
crustacean
n marine animal
311.30
adj invertebrate
311.49
crusty
irascible 110.20
impudent 142.10
gruff 505.7
hardened 1044.13
crutch
n genitals 2.11
fork 171.4
staff 273.2
aid 900.2
v support 449.12
help 900.21
crux cross 170.4
enigma 522.8
salient point 996.6
dilemma 1012.7
hitch 1012.8
cry
n yell 59
call 59.1

animal noise 60.1
weeping 115.2
lament 115.3
cheer 116.2
publicity 352.4
entreaty 440.2
catchword 526.9
report 552.6
v call 59.6
yelp 60.2
weep 115.12
wail 115.13
cheer 116.6
proclaim 352.13
crybaby 16.6
cry for wish for 100.16
demand 421.5
entreat 440.11
require 962.9
cry havoc warn 399.5
alarm 400.3
crying
n weeping 115.2
adj vociferous 59.10
howling 60.6
tearful 115.21
demanding 421.9
urgent 996.22
cryogenics cold 1022.1
refrigeration 1023.1
crypt compartment
197.2
understructure 266.3
cavity 284.2
tomb 309.16
church 703.9
cryptic secret 345.11
latent 519.5
implied 519.7
enigmatic 522.17
cryptography
exegetics 341.8
cryptoanalysis 345.6
writing 547.1
crystal
n amphetamines 87.3
snow 1022.8
adj transparent 1028.4
stony 1057.11
crystal ball
the future 838.1
divination 961.2
crystallize form 806.5
solidify 1044.8
petrify 1057.9
crystallography
mineralogy 1056.10
geology 1057.8
cry uncle weaken 16.9
flinch 127.13
cry wolf 400.3
cub
n boy 302.5
fledgling 302.10
adj unaccustomed
374.4
immature 406.11
cubbyhole nook 197.3
small space 258.3
hiding place 346.4
cube triplicate 876.2
square 878.3

cubes 759.8
cubic spatial 158.9
quadrangular 278.9
cubicle nook 197.3
bedroom 197.7
cuckold 665.22
cuckoldry
love affair 104.6
illicit sex 665.7
cuckoo
n imitator 336.4
songbird 710.23
v bird sound 60.5
adj crazy 925.27
cud bite 8.2
chewing tobacco 89.7
cuddle comfort 121.10
snuggle 562.17
cuddly 104.25
cudgel whip 604.13
club 901.20
cue braid 3.7
tail 217.6
clue 517.9
tip 551.3
hint 551.4
role 704.10
playbook 704.21
mood 977.4
reminder 988.6
cuff
n slap 604.3
punishment 901.8
v slap 604.12
hit 901.19
cuffs 428.4
cuisine food 10.1
cooking 11.1
kitchen 11.3
cul-de-sac
obstruction 293.3
impasse 1012.6
culinary 11.5
cull excise 255.10
select 371.14
collect 472.11
culling
elimination 772.2
grouping 807.3
culmination
summit 198.2
completion 407.2
accomplishment
793.4
end 819.1
acme of perfection
1001.3
culpable
blameworthy 510.25
guilty 656.3
culprit 660.9
cult ism 675.2
worship 696.1
ritualism 701.1
system of belief 952.3
cultist
n religionist 675.15
adj pious 692.8
cultivate
sensitize 24.7
develop 392.10
foster 449.16

train 568.13
nurture 587.12
process 891.9
culture 1067.17
cultivated
improved 392.13
elegant 496.9
well-bred 504.17
learned 927.21
cultural 568.18
culture
n humankind 312.1
society 373.3
cultivation 392.3
taste 496.1
good breeding 504.4
scholarship 927.5
agriculture 1067.1
cultivation 1067.13
v growth 1067.17
raise 1068.6
cultured
improved 392.13
elegant 496.9
well-bred 504.17
learned 927.21
culvert 239.2
cumbersome
bulky 257.19
onerous 297.17
bungling 414.20
hampering 1011.18
unwieldy 1012.19
cumbrous
bulky 257.19
onerous 297.17
stiff 534.3
hampering 1011.18
cum laude 646.11
cumulate
v store up 386.11
assemble 769.18
adj assembled 769.21
cumulative
additive 253.8
accumulative 769.23
evidential 956.16
cuneiform
n phonetic symbol
546.2
adj triangular 278.8
cunning
n falseheartedness
354.4
deceit 356.3
skill 413.1
craftiness 415
artfulness 415.1
shrewdness 919.3
adj falsehearted
354.30
deceitful 356.22
skillful 413.22
well-laid 413.30
crafty 415.12
shrewd 919.15
cup
n container 195.1
cupful 196.4
cavity 284.2
victory 411.1
monument 549.12

trophy 646.3
hockey 749.1
golf 751.1
soccer 752.1
skiing 753.1
track 755.1
fate 963.2
v bleed 91.27
ladle 176.17
be concave 284.12
hollow 284.13
cupboard
container 195.1
storehouse 386.6
Cupid symbol 104.9
Love 104.8
cupidity 100.8
cupola tower 272.6
arch 279.4
roof 295.6
cupping
bloodletting 91.20
drawing 192.3
cur mongrel 311.19
beast 660.7
curable 396.25
curate 699.2
curative
remedial 86.39
tonic 396.22
curator steward 574.4
treasurer 729.11
guardian 1007.6
curb
n kerb 211.6
pavement 383.6
restraint 428.1
stock exchange 737.7
check 1011.7
v slow 175.9
restrain 428.7
hinder 1011.10
curd
n clot 1043.7
semiliquid 1060.5
v thicken 1043.10
curdle thicken 1043.10
emulsify 1060.10
cure
n remedy 86.1
treatment 91.14
curing 396.7
commission 615.1
benefice 698.9
protectorship 1007.2
v remedy 86.38
treat 91.24
disaccustom 374.2
restore 396.15
preserve 397.9
prepare 405.6
solidify 1044.8
dry 1064.6
curé 699.5
cure-all 86.3
curfew 315.5
curio oddity 869.5
trifle 997.5
curiosity desire 100.1
marvel 122.2
oddity 869.5
inquisitiveness 980

alertness 980.1
attention 982.1
interest 982.2
curious careful 339.10
odd 869.11
inquiring 937.35
inquisitive 980.5
attentive 982.15
interested 982.16
curl
n lock 3.5
exercise 84.2
curve 279.2
coil 281.2
v curve 279.6
coil 281.5
curler
curling iron 281.3
wave 915.4
curlicue 281.2
curl up rest 20.6
snuggle 121.10
curly 281.9
curmudgeon
sorehead 110.11
niggard 484.4
currency
publicity 352.4
fashionableness 578.2
money 728.1
prevalence 863.2
usualness 868.2
current
n direction 161.1
course 172.2
flow 238.4
wind 318.1
trend 895.2
thoughts 930.4
electricity 1031.2
v follow the rule 866.4
adj published 352.17
customary 373.14
reported 552.15
fashionable 578.11
existent 760.13
happening 830.9
present 837.2
prevalent 863.12
usual 868.9
well-known 927.27
curriculum 568.8
curried cooked 11.6
zestful 68.7
curry
n stew 10.11
v cook 11.4
comb 79.21
tend 1068.7
curry favor 138.9
curse
n affliction 96.8
malediction 513
hex 513.1
oath 513.4
spell 691.1
bad influence 999.4
bane 1000.1
adversity 1010.1
v accurse 513.5
swear 513.6
blaspheme 694.5

work evil 999.6
cursed
accursed 513.9
execrable 999.10
cursive 547.22
cursory
insignificant 248.6
shallow 276.5
unwilling 325.5
careless 340.11
hasty 401.9
curt short 268.8
taciturn 344.9
gruff 505.7
concise 537.6
curtail reduce 252.7
subtract 255.9
contract 260.7
shorten 268.6
restrain 428.7
take from 480.21
curtain
n cover 295.2
partition 345.3
veil 346.2
act 704.7
stage 704.16
scenery 704.20
end 819.1
obstacle 1011.4
shade 1027.1
v cover 295.19
conceal 346.6
shade 1027.5
curtain call 704.7
curtain raiser act 704.7
overture 708.26
inauguration 817.5
countdown 815.2
curtains death 307.1
end 819.1
curtsy
n obeisance 155.2
greeting 585.4
crouch 912.3
v bow 155.6
show respect 433.10
greet 585.10
be polite 912.9
curvaceous
curved 279.7
comely 1015.18
curvature curving 279
turn 279.1
curve
n deviation 164.1
angle 278.2
sinus 279.2
trick 356.6
race 756.3
v deviate 164.3
deflect 164.5
angle 278.5
turn 279.6
adj curved 279.7
curvy crooked 204.20
wavy 279.7
comely 1015.18
cushion
n silencer 51.4
partition 213.5
moderator 670.3

bedding 900.20
safeguard 1007.3
softness 1045.4
v muffle 51.9
relieve 120.5
absorb the shock 670.8
support 900.21
protect 1007.18
soften 1045.6
cushioned 121.11
cushy
comfortable 121.11
easy 1013.13
cusp point 285.3
crisis 842.4
salience 996.6
cuss
n oath 513.4
v curse 513.6
cussedness
ill humor 110.3
malice 144.5
perversity 361.3
custodian cleaner 79.14
hospital staff 90.11
jailer 429.10
steward 574.4
guardian 1007.6
custodianship
vigilance 339.4
usage 387.2
preservation 397.1
custody 429.5
thrift 635.1
protectorship 1007.2
custody vigilance 339.4
storage 386.5
preservation 397.1
custodianship 429.5
directorship 573.4
protectorship 1007.2
custom
n behavior 321.1
convention 373
rite 373.1
habit 373.4
fashion 578.1
social more 579.1
patronage 731.6
market 733.3
tradition 841.2
adj made 891.18
customary
wonted 373.14
conventional 579.5
orthodox 687.7
traditional 841.12
usual 868.9
customer man 76.5
client 733.4
custom-made
tailored 5.47
made 891.18
customs 630.10
cut
n trauma 85.37
pain 96.5
indignity 156.2
snub 157.2
absence 222.4
crack 224.2

degree 245.1
gains 251.3
curtailment 252.4
reduction 255.2
form 262.1
shortcut 268.5
notch 289.1
furrow 290.1
trench 290.2
lamina 296.2
attempt 403.3
thrust 459.3
portion 477.5
gibe 508.2
mark 517.5
dividend 624.7
discount 631.1
cheapening 633.4
print 713.5
part 792.1
piece 792.3
break 801.4
characteristic 864.4
hit 901.4
slap 901.8
repulse 907.2
v dilute 16.11
pain 26.7
bite 68.5
hurt 96.17
offend 152.21
snub 157.5
slant across 204.11
leave 222.10
cleave 224.4
reduce 252.7
excise 255.10
delete 255.12
form 262.7
shorten 268.6
come to a point 285.6
notch 289.4
furrow 290.3
open 292.11
rarefy 299.3
leave undone 340.7
injure 393.13
discard 442.5
apportion 477.6
record 549.15
abridge 557.5
whip 604.13
discount 631.2
cheapen 633.6
engrave 713.9
sculpture 715.5
shuffle 758.4
separate 792.6
adulterate 796.12
sever 801.11
turn off 856.12
strike 901.15
repulse 907.3
banish 908.17
freeze 1022.10
liquefy 1062.5
cultivate 1067.17
harvest 1067.19
adj diluted 16.19
pained 96.23
cleft 224.7
formative 262.9

furrowed 290.4
rare 299.4
impaired 393.27
concise 537.6
reduced 633.9
engraved 713.11
severed 801.23
cut across
　v cross 170.6
　slice 204.11
　take a short cut 268.7
　adj cross 170.8
cut-and-dried
　trite 117.9
　ready-made 405.19
　prearranged 964.7
cutaneous
　n injection 91.17
　adj cuticular 2.25
　covering 295.32
cutback
　n curtailment 252.4
　economizing 635.2
　adj reduced 252.10
cut back reduce 252.7
　shorten 268.6
　retrench 635.5
cut corners
　take a short cut 268.7
　slight 340.8
　retrench 635.5
cut down reduce 252.7
　shorten 268.6
　kill 308.12
　strike dead 308.17
　raze 395.19
　retrench 635.5
　fell 912.5
cute deceitful 356.22
　skillful 413.22
　cunning 415.12
　tricky 645.18
　beautiful 1015.17
cuticle 295.3
cutie gal 302.7
　beauty 1015.9
cut in intrude 214.5
　interrupt 214.6
　include 771.3
cut it be able 18.11
　do 328.6
cut it out
　v cease 856.6
　inter stop! 856.13
cutlery tableware 8.12
　edge tool 1039.2
cutlet 10.18
cut loose release 120.6
　ship activity 182.48
　escape 369.6
　let oneself go 430.19
　loose 431.6
　extricate 431.7
　run amok 671.15
　make merry 743.24
　separate 801.8
　sever 801.11
　riot 809.10
cutoff boundary 211.3
　shortcut 268.5
　end 395.2
　stop 856.2

cut off
　v excise 255.10
　kill 308.12
　put an end to 395.12
　take from 480.21
　dispossess 480.23
　exclude 772.4
　separate 801.8
　sever 801.11
　interrupt 856.10
　adj bereft 473.8
cut out
　v depart 188.7
　extract 192.10
　leave 222.10
　excise 255.10
　reject 372.2
　plan 381.8
　cease to use 390.4
　exterminate 395.14
　exclude 772.4
　eliminate 772.5
　separate 801.8
　substitute for 861.5
　adj talented 413.29
　prearranged 964.7
cut-rate 633.9
cut short
　v shorten 268.6
　destroy 395.12
　put a stop to 856.11
　adj shortened 268.9
　mutilated 794.5
cutter teeth 2.8
　garmentmaker 5.33
　shortener 268.4
　separator 801.7
　cutlery 1039.2
cut the mustard
　be able 18.11
　do 328.6
　manage 409.12
　suit 787.8
　stand the test 941.10
　suffice 990.4
cutthroat
　n killer 308.10
　ruffian 593.3
　adj murderous 308.23
　competitive 457.23
　overpriced 632.12
cutting
　n reduction 255.2
　plant 310.3
　apportionment 477.1
　morphology 526.3
　syntax 530.2
　abbreviation 537.4
　motion-picture
　　editing 706.5
　piece 792.3
　adulteration 796.3
　severance 801.2
　harvest 1067.15
　adj acrimonious 17.14
　pungent 68.6
　penetrating 105.31
　caustic 144.23
　sharp 285.8
　vigorous 544.11
　violent 671.16
　cold 1022.14

solvent 1062.8
cutting edge
　leading 165.1
　border 211.4
　vanguard 216.2
　sharp 285.2
　beginning 817.1
cutting remark 508.2
cutup
　mischief-maker 322.3
　humorist 489.12
　player 743.18
cut up
　v pain 96.17
　aggrieve 112.19
　misbehave 322.4
　apportion 477.6
　find fault 510.15
　play 743.23
　separate 792.6
　divide 801.18
　create disorder 809.11
　adj wretched 96.26
　sorrowful 112.26
　overcome 112.29
cyanosis blueness 45.1
　symptom 85.9
cybernetic
　n autonetic 1040.2
　adj servomechanical
　　1040.23
cycle
　n wheel 179.8
　circle 280.2
　series 811.2
　age 823.4
　round 849.3
　circuit 913.2
　atomic cluster 1037.7
　v ride 177.33
　recur 849.5
　circle 913.5
cycles 1033.12
cyclical circular 280.11
　continuous 811.8
　recurrent 848.13
　periodic 849.7
cyclist 178.11
cyclone outburst 105.9
　weather map 317.4
　whirlwind 318.14
　storm 671.4
cyclonic
　climatal 317.12
　stormy 318.23
　rotary 914.15
cyclopedia reference
　book 554.9
　lore 927.9
Cyclops 15.6
cygnet 311.28
cylinder 282.4
cylindrical
　tubular 239.16
　columnar 282.11
cynic pessimist 125.7
　disparager 512.6
　misanthrope 590.2
　doubter 954.4
cynical
　pessimistic 125.16
　satiric 508.13

critical 510.23
　misanthropic 590.3
cynosure focus 208.4
　guiding star 574.8
　celebrity 662.9
　ideal 785.4
　attractor 906.2
cyst growth 85.38
　swelling 283.4
cytoplasm 305.4
czar ruler 575.9
　tyrant 575.14
dab
　n fish 10.23
　modicum 248.2
　tap 901.7
　stain 1003.3
　v color 35.13
　smooth 287.5
　coat 295.24
　tap 901.18
dabble spatter 80.18
　waste time 331.13
　not know 929.11
　trifle 997.14
　moisten 1063.12
dabbler
　dilettante 928.6
　ignoramus 929.8
　trifler 997.10
da capo 848.17
dactylic 720.16
dad father 560.10
　patriarch 841.8
dado
　n base 199.2
　furrow 290.1
　support 900.8
　v furrow 290.3
daedal variegated 47.9
　skillful 413.22
　complex 798.4
daemon spirit 678.5
　familiar 678.12
　genius 919.8
　agricultural deity
　　1067.4
daft foolish 922.8
　insane 925.26
dagger
　n cross 170.4
　sword 462.5
　cutlery 1039.2
　v stab 459.25
daguerreotype
　n tintype 714.4
　v photograph 714.14
daily
　n cleaner 79.14
　periodical 555.1
　newspaper 555.2
　adj recurrent 848.13
　momentary 849.8
dainty
　n delicacy 10.8
　adj edible 8.33
　frail 16.14
　tasty 63.8
　clean 79.25
　delicate 248.7
　smooth 294.8
　light 298.12

nice 495.11
elegant 496.9
fine 1015.19
dairy larder 386.8
plant 739.3
dairyman 1068.2
dais authority 417.10
platform 900.13
daisy 998.7
dale valley 237.7
concavity 284.9
dalliance
love affair 104.6
dawdling 175.3
lovemaking 562.1
flirtation 562.9
waiting 845.3
trifling 997.8
dally dawdle 175.8
dillydally 331.14
make love 562.14
wait 845.12
trifle 997.14
dam
n lake 241.1
mother 560.11
jockey 757.2
barrier 1011.5
v close 293.7
put a stop to 856.11
damage
n impairment 393.1
loss 473.1
price 630.1
disadvantage 995.2
evil 999.3
v impair 393.9
work evil 999.6
damages fine 603.3
recompense 624.3
dame female 77.5
damsel 77.6
woman 77.8
gal 302.7
old woman 304.3
teacher 571.2
mistress 575.2
noblewoman 608.6
damn
n trifle 997.5
v destroy 395.10
censure 510.13
curse 513.5
vilify 513.7
condemn 602.3
doom 682.6
adj cursed 513.9
inter damn it! 513.11
damnable cursed 513.9
wicked 654.16
execrable 999.10
damnation
destruction 395.1
censure 510.3
curse 513.1
condemnation 602.1
damndest 403.16
damned
n evil spirits 680.1
adj cursed 513.9
demoniac 680.17
unregenerate 695.18

execrable 999.10
damning 956.16
damp
n silencer 51.4
killjoy 112.14
deterrent 379.2
moisture 1063.1
vapor 1065.1
v weaken 16.10
muffle 51.9
sadden 112.18
reduce 252.7
disincline 379.4
moderate 670.6
cushion 670.8
make uniform 780.4
hinder 1011.10
fight fire 1021.7
moisten 1063.12
adj moist 1063.15
damp down 428.8
damper silencer 51.4
killjoy 112.14
deterrent 379.2
curb 1011.7
fire iron 1019.12
damsel 302.6
dance
n dancing 705
ball 705.1
hop 705.2
assembly 769.2
flutter 916.4
flicker 1024.8
v exude cheerfulness
109.6
rejoice 116.5
trip the light fantastic
705.5
play 743.23
flutter 916.12
flicker 1024.25
adj dancing 705.6
dance hall
hall 197.4
ballroom 705.4
entertainment 743.13
dancer
performer 705.3
entertainer 707.1
dander 152.6
dandified
foppish 500.17
ultrafashionable
578.14
dandruff filth 80.7
flake 296.3
dandy
n fop 500.9
person of fashion
578.7
first-rate 998.7
adj foppish 500.17
excellent 998.13
danger
unreliability 970.6
peril 1005
hazard 1005.1
dangerous
unreliable 970.20
perilous 1005.9
danger sign 399.3

dangle
n hang 202.2
v attach oneself to
138.11
hang 202.6
manifest 348.5
flaunt 501.17
oscillate 915.10
dangling
n pendency 202.1
adj pendent 202.9
loose 803.5
swinging 915.17
dank 1063.15
dankness 1063.2
dapper 578.13
dapple
n spottiness 47.3
mark 517.5
v variegate 47.7
mark 517.19
adj mottled 47.12
dare
n challenge 454.2
v have the audacity
142.7
confront 216.8
defy 454.3
venture 492.10
presume 640.6
take chances
1005.7
daredevil
n devil 493.4
adj foolhardy 493.9
daresay
suppose 950.10
believe 952.11
think likely 967.5
dare to 403.8
daring
n defiance 454.1
derring-do 492.5
foolhardiness 493.3
display 501.4
adj defiant 454.7
audacious 492.22
foolhardy 493.9
showy 501.19
dark
n obscurity 522.3
unenlightenment
929.4
night 1026.1
adj blind 30.9
inconspicuous 32.6
black 38.8
dark-colored 38.9
sullen 110.24
gloomy 112.24
ominous 133.17
cloudy 319.7
secret 345.11
clandestine 345.15
obscure 522.15
dishonest 645.16
wicked 654.16
benighted 929.16
pitch 1026.13
opaque 1030.3
dark age 929.4
Dark Ages 823.5

darken blind 30.7
blacken 38.7
change color 105.19
sadden 112.18
cloud 319.6
stain 1003.6
bedarken 1026.9
grow dark 1026.12
opaque 1030.2
dark horse
candidate 610.9
the unknown 929.7
small chance 971.9
darkness
blindness 30.1
inconspicuousness
32.2
blackness 38.1
duskiness 38.2
gloom 112.7
night 315.4
obscurity 522.3
unenlightenment
929.4
lightlessness 1026
opaqueness 1030.1
dark-skinned 38.10
darling
n sweetheart 104.10
favorite 104.16
child 302.3
endearment term
562.6
adj beloved 104.24
darn
v repair 396.14
curse 513.5
inter damn! 513.12
a darn 997.5
dart
n swiftness 174.6
arrow 462.6
sting 1000.5
v speed 174.8
throw 903.10
Darwinism 860.4
dash
n vim 17.2
disappointment
132.1
run 174.3
hint 248.4
haste 401.1
showiness 501.3
display 501.4
line 517.6
spirit 544.4
admixture 796.7
hit 901.4
v sadden 112.18
unnerve 128.10
disappoint 132.2
speed 174.8
billow 238.22
make haste 401.5
defeat 412.11
mark 517.19
throw 903.10
thwart 1011.15
moisten 1063.12
adv suddenly 829.9
inter damn! 513.12

dashing
fast 174.15
showy 501.19
chic 578.13
dash off
hasten off 188.10
do carelessly 340.9
improvise 365.8
make haste 401.5
write 547.21
portray 712.19
transcribe 718.6
dash one's hope
shatter 125.11
disappoint 132.2
dastardly 491.12
data records 551.1
the facts 760.4
collection 769.11
knowledge 927.1
premise 934.7
evidence 956.1
information 1041.15
data processing 1041.1
date
n lover 104.12
appointment 582.8
engagement 704.11
assembly 769.2
age 823.4
point of time 831.4
v come together
769.16
be dated 831.13
age 841.9
dated chronologic
831.15
anachronous 832.3
past 836.7
old-fashioned 841.16
dateless timeless 821.3
perpetual 828.7
old 841.10
datum particular 765.3
knowledge 927.1
evidence 956.1
daub
n bad likeness 350.2
picture 712.11
stain 1003.3
v color 35.13
soil 80.16
coat 295.24
misdraw 350.4
portray 712.19
stain 1003.6
oil 1054.8
daughter
brother 559.3
descendant 561.3
daunt deter 127.18
dissuade 379.3
domineer 612.16
daunting 127.28
dauntless
plucky 359.14
unafraid 492.20
dawdle
n slowpoke 175.5
idler 331.8
v lag 166.4
linger 175.8

dally 331.14
protract 826.9
wait 845.12
dawn
n morning 314.3
beginning 817.1
daylight 1024.10
v grow light 1024.27
adj morning 314.6
dawn on 521.5
dawn upon one 930.18
day period 823.1
moment 823.2
age 823.4
date 831.4
daylight 1024.10
day after day
for a long time 826.14
constantly 846.7
repeatedly 848.16
daybook
record book 549.11
periodical 555.1
account book 628.4
chronicle 831.9
daybreak 314.3
day-care center 567.2
daydream
n wistfulness 100.4
illusion 975.1
abstractedness 984.2
dream 985.9
v wander 983.3
muse 984.9
dream 985.17
day in day out
regularly 780.8
for a long time 826.14
constantly 846.7
daylight dawn 314.3
publicity 352.4
dayshine 1024.10
daylong 826.12
day off vacation 20.3
holiday 20.4
absence 222.4
pause 856.3
day of reckoning 838.3
day of rest 20.5
daytime 1024.10
daze
n trance 92.19
confusion 984.3
v blind 30.7
astonish 122.6
perplex 970.13
confuse 984.7
shine 1024.23
dazed stupefied 25.7
blinded 30.10
foolish 922.8
in a dilemma 970.25
mazed 984.14
dazzle
n showiness 501.3
v blind 30.7
astonish 122.6
cut a dash 501.13
confuse 984.7
shine 1024.23
dazzling
blinding 30.11

gorgeous 1015.20
bright 1024.32
D-day zero hour 459.13
crucial moment 842.5
deacon
holy orders 699.4
clergy 699.9
deactivate
disarm 465.11
disband 770.8
dead
n silence 51.1
corpse 307.16
the majority 307.17
adj tired 21.8
asleep 22.22
insensible 25.6
unconscious 25.8
colorless 36.7
muffled 52.17
insipid 65.2
dull 117.6
inert 173.14
closed 293.9
lifeless 307.30
languid 331.20
no more 761.11
ended 819.8
past 836.7
obsolete 841.15
lackluster 1026.17
inanimate 1053.5
adv directly 161.23
extremely 247.22
exactly 972.21
deadbeat 138.5
dead duck 125.8
deaden weaken 16.10
desensitize 25.4
muffle 51.9
numb 94.8
relieve 120.5
moderate 670.6
cushion 670.8
dull 1026.10
dead end
n obstruction 293.3
impasse 1012.6
adj closed 293.9
deadening
n weakening 16.5
relief 120.1
modulation 670.2
adj numbing 25.9
anesthetic 86.47
relieving 120.9
mitigating 670.14
deadeye 903.8
dead giveaway 351.2
deadhead
freeloader 634.3
playgoer 704.27
dead letter 520.1
deadline
boundary 211.3
plan 381.1
crucial moment 842.5
deadlock
n standstill 173.3
the same 789.3
stop 856.2
impasse 1012.6

v put a stop to 856.11
halt 1011.13
deadly
poisonous 82.7
remarkable 247.11
deathly 307.29
lethal 308.22
destructive 395.26
harmful 999.12
dead march dirge 115.6
slow motion 175.2
funeral 309.5
march 708.12
dead of night
silence 51.1
midnight 315.6
darkness 1026.1
deadpan
adj inexpressive
522.20
adv unfeelingly 94.14
dead reckoning
location 159.3
navigation 182.2
dead ringer
image 349.5
the same 777.3
dead set against
unwilling 325.5
oppositional 451.8
disapproving 510.21
dead set on 359.16
dead to the world
asleep 22.22
unconscious 25.8
oblivious 983.7
abstracted 984.11
deadweight
n impediment 1011.6
weight 297.1
onerousness 297.2
burden 297.7
adj heavy 297.16
deadwood
branch 310.18
refuse 391.4
deaf
hard of hearing 49.6
unpersuadable 361.13
narrow-minded
979.10
oblivious 983.7
deafen stun 49.5
muffle 51.9
din 53.7
deafening intense 15.22
loud 53.11
deaf-mute
n the deaf 49.2
mute 51.3
adj deaf 49.6
deafness
hardness of hearing
49
handicap 49.1
ear disease 85.15
unpersuadableness
361.5
incognizance 929.3
deaf to insensible 94.10
unconsenting 442.6
unaware 929.13

deal
n amount 244.2
lot 247.4
lamina 296.2
act 328.3
undertaking 404.1
compact 437.1
compromise 468.1
portion 477.5
transaction 731.4
bargain 731.5
blackjack 759.11
wood 1052.3
v use 87.21
parcel out 477.8
give 478.12
trade 731.1
bargain 731.17
shuffle 758.4
dispose 807.9
hit 901.14
dealer merchant 730.2
racketeer 732.4
stockbroker 737.10
dealings act 328.3
communication 343.1
commerce 731.1
relation 774.1
affairs 830.4
deal one in 477.6
deal with treat 321.6
perform 328.9
communicate 343.6
use 387.12
accomplish 407.4
discuss 541.12
write upon 556.5
punish 604.10
trade with 731.16
relate to 774.5
operate 888.5
dean
n superior 249.4
senior 304.5
principal 571.8
executive 574.3
chief 575.3
gambler 759.21
adj older 841.19
dear
n sweetheart 104.10
endearment term
562.6
adj beloved 104.24
precious 632.10
expensive 632.11
adv dearly 632.13
inter my! 122.21
dearth
unproductiveness
890.1
scarcity 991.3
death fatal disease 85.2
dying 307
finality 307.1
destruction 395.2
end 819.1
transience 827.1
bane 1000.1
deathbed
n moribundity 307.9
adj later 845.18

deathblow
early death 307.5
death stroke 308.9
end 395.2
defeat 412.1
finishing stroke 819.4
death-defying 493.9
death grip 474.2
death knell dirge 115.6
death 307.1
end 395.2
deathless
immortal 828.9
indestructible 854.18
deathly
deathlike 307.29
deadly 308.22
death penalty 602.1
death song dirge 115.6
swan song 307.10
death struggle
moribundity 307.9
life-and-death
struggle 457.6
deathwatch
moribundity 307.9
last offices 309.4
debacle descent 194.1
disaster 395.4
defeat 412.1
revolution 859.1
debar prohibit 444.3
exclude 772.4
obstruct 1011.12
prevent 1011.14
debarkation 186.2
debase abase 137.5
lower 274.6
misuse 389.4
corrupt 393.12
demote 447.3
disparage 512.8
disgrace 661.8
adulterate 796.12
depress 912.4
debased low 274.7
corrupt 654.14
base 661.12
depressed 912.12
debatable 970.17
debate
n contention 457.1
discussion 541.7
speech 543.2
legislative procedure
613.6
argumentation 934.4
v hesitate 362.7
discuss 541.12
declaim 543.10
consider 930.12
debauch
n spree 88.5
dissipation 669.2
v go on a spree
88.28
corrupt 393.12
be promiscuous
665.19
seduce 665.20
dissipate 669.6
make merry 743.24

debauchery
profligacy 665.3
dissipation 669.2
debenture 728.11
debilitated weak 16.12
ineffective 19.15
unmanned 19.19
tired 21.7
unhealthy 85.53
stricken in years
303.18
languid 331.20
debility weakness 16.1
fatigue 21.1
unhealthiness 85.3
old age 303.5
debit
n loss 473.1
expenditure 626.1
entry 628.5
v keep accounts 628.8
debonair 109.12
debouch
n outlet 190.9
v burst forth 33.9
emerge 190.11
find vent 369.10
disgorge 908.25
debrief brief 184.48
disband 770.8
debris deposit 176.9
remainder 256.1
rubbish 391.5
grain 1049.6
debt borrowing 621.1
liability 623
indebtedness 623.1
debtor borrowing 621.1
borrower 623.4
debug 939.2
debunk 976.2
debunker 512.6
debut
n coming out 582.15
theatrical
performance 704.12
inauguration 817.5
v act 704.29
enter 817.9
debutante 578.7
decade moment 823.2
ten 881.6
decadent
deteriorating 393.45
corrupt 654.14
decal
stencil printing 713.4
adhesive 802.4
decalogue 636.1
decamp depart 188.6
break camp 188.14
flee 368.10
decant ladle 176.17
draw off 192.12
disgorge 908.25
decapitate 604.17
decathlon sport 744.1
track meet 755.2
decay
n filth 80.7
decomposition 393.6
rot 393.7

disintegration 805.1
dissociation 805.2
v decompose 393.22
disintegrate 805.3
decease
n death 307.1
end 819.1
v die 307.19
deceased
n corpse 307.16
adj dead 307.30
past 836.7
deceit
falseness 356.3
stratagem 415.3
deceitful
falsehearted 354.30
false 356.22
cunning 415.12
improper 645.18
deceive lie 354.18
beguile 356.14
outwit 415.11
impose on 643.7
be dishonest 645.11
seduce 665.20
live by one's wits
415.9
deceiver imitator 336.4
misleader 357
deluder 357.1
evildoer 593.1
con man 645.10
criminal 660.10
seducer 665.12
cheater 759.22
deceleration
slowing 175.4
decline 252.2
restraint 428.1
decent kind 143.13
indulgent 427.8
decorous 496.10
conventional 579.5
right 637.3
honest 644.13
modest 664.5
sufficient 990.6
expedient 994.5
tolerable 998.20
decentralization
divergence 171.1
deconcentration
770.2
deception
concealment 346.1
sham 354.3
falseness 356
calculated lie 356.1
hoax 356.7
cheating 759.13
illusion 975.1
deceptive
deceiving 356.21
sophistical 935.10
erroneous 974.16
illusory 975.8
decibel 50.7
decide
resolve 359.7
induce 375.22
determine 885.12

exercise influence
  893.8
judge 945.11
make sure 969.11
will 323.2
decide against 444.5
decided
  downright 247.12
  affirmative 334.8
  resolute 359.11
  ended 819.8
  unqualified 959.2
  assured 969.20
  confident 969.21
  emphatic 996.21
decide upon 371.16
deciduous
  descending 194.11
  arboreal 310.36
  perennial 310.41
  transient 827.7
decimal tenth 881.22
  numeric 1016.22
decimate
  slaughter 308.16
  destroy 395.10
decipher
  explain 341.10
  make clear 521.6
  solve 939.2
decipherable
  intelligible 521.10
  legible 521.12
  solvable 939.3
decision will 323.1
  resolution 359.1
  choice 371.1
  judgment 598.9
  fight 754.3
  verdict 945.5
decisive
  resolute 359.11
  mandatory 420.12
  critical 842.10
  prompt 844.9
  causal 885.13
  convincing 952.26
  evidential 956.16
  unqualified 959.2
  certain 969.13
deck
  n dose 87.19
  ground covering
    199.3
  layer 296.1
  card 758.2
  bundle 769.8
  platform 900.13
  v clothe 5.38
  overcome 412.7
  ornament 498.8
  beat 901.17
  fell 912.5
deckhand 183.6
declaim
  proclaim 352.13
  speak 524.20
  hold forth 543.10
  overact 704.31
declamatory
  elocutionary 543.12
  grandiloquent 545.8

declaration
  acknowledgment
    332.3
  affirmation 334.1
  announcement 352.2
  decree 420.4
  remark 524.4
  statement 598.7
  profession 952.7
  testimony 956.2
declare affirm 334.5
  announce 352.12
  command 420.8
  speak 524.24
  state 952.12
declare war
  contend 457.13
  make war on 458.15
déclassé
  n outcast 586.4
  adj upper-class 607.10
decline
  n sinkage 194.2
  declivity 204.5
  declension 252.2
  deterioration 393.3
  ·cheapening 633.4
  price 738.9
  close 819.3
  shortcoming 910.1
  senility 921.10
  v weaken 16.9
  fail 85.47
  recede 168.2
  sink 194.6
  slope 204.10
  decrease 252.6
  age 303.10
  reject 372.2
  sink 393.17
  refuse 442.3
  grammaticize 530.16
  cheapen 633.6
  fall short 910.2
  fall on evil days
    1010.11
declivity descent 204.5
  slope 237.2
decoction
  extract 192.7
  product 192.8
  concoction 405.3
  imbuement 796.2
  boiling 1019.2
  solution 1062.3
decode
  make clear 521.6
  solve 939.2
decoding
  translation 341.3
  explanation 341.4
  information theory
    551.7
  solution 939.1
décolleté
  n nudity 6.3
  adj unclad 6.13
decoloration 36.3
decommission 465.11
decompose
  decay 393.22
  disintegrate 805.3

decompression
  rest 20.1
  composure 106.2
  relief 120.1
  rarefaction 299.2
deconcentrate 770.7
deconsecrate
  depose 447.4
  disbelieve 695.14
decontamination
  sanitation 79.3
  extenuation 600.5
  radiation 1036.1
decontrolled 430.27
decor furniture 229.1
  ornamentation 498.1
  scenery 704.20
decorate add 253.4
  trim 498.8
  ornament 545.7
  honor 646.8
  beautify 1015.15
decoration extra 254.4
  ornamentation 498.1
  honor 646.5
  insignia 647.1
  visual arts 712.1
  beautification 1015.11
decorative
  ornamental 498.10
  artistic 712.20
  beautifying 1015.22
decorator 716.11
decorous solemn 111.3
  tasteful 496.10
  conventional 579.5
  ceremonious 580.8
  right 637.3
  decent 664.5
decorum
  decorousness 496.3
  social convention
    579.1
  etiquette 580.3
  propriety 637.2
  decency 664.2
decoy
  n trap 356.12
  shill 357.5
  lure 377.3
  by-bidder 733.6
  v trap 356.20
  lure 377.5
decrease
  n descent 194.1
  lessening 252
  decrescence 252.1
  reduction 255.2
  contraction 260.1
  deterioration 393.3
  waste 473.2
  depression 912.1
  v quantify 244.4
  graduate 245.4
  diminish 252.6
  reduce 252.7
  subtract 255.9
  contract 260.7
  waste 473.5
decree
  n command 420.4
  law 673.3

  verdict 945.5
  predetermination
    963.1
  v will 323.2
  command 420.8
  legislate 613.10
  legalize 673.8
  pass judgment 945.13
decrepit unsound 16.15
  stricken in years
    303.18
  dilapidated 393.33
  senile 921.23
decrescendo
  n faintness 52.1
  decline 252.2
  music 708.25
  adj faint 52.16
  decreasing 252.11
  music 708.53
  adv decreasingly
    252.12
decriminalize
  authorize 443.11
  legalize 673.8
decry
  censure 510.13
  disparage 512.8
dedicate
  commit 477.11
  sanctify 685.5
dedicated
  zealous 101.9
  resolute 359.11
  devoted 587.21
  unselfish 652.5
  sanctified 685.8
dedicate oneself to
  be determined 359.8
  espouse 509.13
dedication
  zeal 101.2
  resolution 359.1
  commitment 477.4
  makeup 554.12
  devotion 587.7
  duty 641.1
  unselfishness 652.1
  sanctification 685.3
deduce elicit 192.14
  reason 934.15
  conclude 945.10
  suppose 950.10
deduct
  reduce 252.7
  subtract 255.9
  discount 631.2
deductible
  n insurance 1007.4
  adj tax-free 630.16
deduction
  decrease 252.1
  subtraction 255.1
  decrement 255.7
  tax 630.9
  discount 631.1
  relation 774.1
  reasoning 934.3
  conclusion 945.4
deductive
  subtractive 255.13
  dialectic 934.22

deed
  n act 328.3
  exploit 492.7
  v transfer 629.3
deedholder 470.2
deem judge 945.8
  suppose 950.10
  think 952.11
de-emphasize
  minimize 252.9
  moderate 670.6
  attach little
    importance to 997.12
deep
  n pit 275.2
  secret 345.5
  adj colored 35.16
  resonant 54.10
  heart-felt 93.24
  spacious 158.10
  interior 207.6
  great 247.6
  broad 269.6
  profound 275.10
  cunning 415.12
  recondite 522.16
  wise 919.17
  learned 927.21
  adv beyond one's
    depth 275.16
the deep sea 240.1
  ocean depths 275.4
deep-dyed
  fast-dyed 35.17
  confirmed 373.19
  thorough 793.10
  established 854.13
deepen aggravate 119.2
  intensify 251.5
  broaden 269.4
  lower 275.8
deep-felt 93.24
deep-freezer 1023.5
deep-fry 11.4
deep-rooted deep 275.10
  confirmed 373.19
  established 854.13
deep-sea
  aquatic 182.58
  oceanic 240.8
  deep-water 275.14
deep-seated
  deep 275.10
  confirmed 373.19
  intrinsic 766.7
  established 854.13
deep-set deep 275.10
  confirmed 373.19
  established 854.13
deep-six abandon 370.5
  discard 390.7
deep sleep 22.5
the Deep South 231.7
deep thought
  thoughtfulness 930.3
  engrossment 982.3
deer 311.5
de-escalation
  decrease 252.1
  modulation 670.2
  depression 912.1
deface deform 265.7

blemish 1003.4
  offend 1014.5
de facto
  adj existent 760.13
  real 760.15
  adv really 760.16
defame malign 512.9
  stigmatize 661.9
default
  n absence 222.4
  disobedience 327.1
  neglect 340.1
  nonobservance 435.1
  arrears 623.2
  nonpayment 625.1
  shortcoming 910.1
  v be absent 222.7
  neglect 340.6
  lose 473.4
  not pay 625.6
  play 751.4
defeat
  n disappointment
    132.1
  failure 410.1
  overcome 412
  beating 412.1
  frustration 1011.3
  v disappoint 132.2
  best 249.7
  do for 395.11
  triumph over 411.5
  worst 412.6
  refute 957.5
  thwart 1011.15
defeatist
  n pessimist 125.7
  adj pessimistic 125.16
defecate
  have a bowel
    movement 12.13
  evacuate 908.22
defect
  n disease 85.1
  apostatize 363.7
  deficiency 794.2
  fault 1002.2
  blemish 1003.1
  v leave home 188.17
  emigrate 190.16
  deny 335.4
  secede 370.6
  disregard 435.3
  renege 857.13
defection
  departure 188.1
  emigration 190.7
  denial 335.2
  apostasy 363.2
  desertion 370.2
  nonpayment 625.1
  change 851.1
  conversion 857.3
  fault 1002.2
defective
  n cripple 85.44
  idiot 923.8
  adj incomplete 794.4
  erroneous 974.16
  insufficient 991.9
  imperfect 1002.4
  blemished 1003.8

defend guard 460.8
  offer in defense 600.10
  protect 1007.18
defendant
  oppositionist 452.3
  litigant 598.11
  accused 599.6
defender
  champion 460.7
  justifier 600.8
  supporter 616.9
  team 752.2
  protector 1007.5
defense protection 460
  front 460.1
  pleadings 598.6
  plea 600.2
  basketball game 747.3
  hockey strategy 749.2
  team 749.5
  fight 754.3
  countermeasure 899.5
  argumentation 934.4
  rebuttal 938.2
  wall 1007.1
  barrier 1011.5
defenseless
  helpless 19.18
  forlorn 584.12
  unprotected 1005.14
defense mechanism
  reaction 92.23
  avoidance 368.1
  instinct 460.1
  block 989.3
defensive
  defending 460.11
  protective 1007.23
defer retreat 163.6
  retract 168.3
  postpone 845.9
deference respect 155.1
  obedience 326.1
  submission 433.1
  observance 434.1
  courtesy 504.1
  duty 641.1
deferential
  respectful 155.8
  obedient 326.3
  obeisant 433.16
  courteous 504.14
  dutiful 641.13
defer to respect 155.4
  obey 326.2
  submit to 433.9
  observe 434.2
defiance
  impenitence 114.2
  refractoriness 327.2
  ungovernability 361.4
  resistance 453.1
  defying 454
  disobedience 454.1
  declaration of war
    458.7
defiant
  impenitent 114.5
  disobedient 327.8
  refractory 327.10
  ungovernable 361.12
  defying 454.7

deficiency
  inadequacy 250.3
  incompleteness 794.1
  want 794.2
  lack 991.4
  imperfection 1002.1
  fault 1002.2
deficient
  inadequate 250.7
  slipshod 340.12
  incomplete 794.4
  short of 910.5
  insufficient 991.9
  imperfect 1002.4
deficit difference 255.8
  debt 623.1
  arrears 623.2
  deficiency 794.2
  shortcoming 910.1
  want 991.4
defile
  n valley 237.7
  narrow place 270.3
  passageway 383.3
  v foul 80.17
  march 177.30
  misuse 389.4
  corrupt 393.12
  vilify 512.10
  impair 654.10
  stigmatize 661.9
  seduce 665.20
  file 811.7
  work evil 999.6
define
  circumscribe 210.4
  interpret 341.9
  mark 517.19
  name 527.11
  fix 854.9
  characterize 864.10
defined distinct 31.7
  circumscribed 210.6
  clear 521.11
  particular 864.12
defining
  limiting 210.9
  classificational 808.7
definite distinct 31.7
  audible 50.16
  circumscribed 210.6
  resolute 359.11
  clear 521.11
  particular 864.12
  unqualified 959.2
  certain 969.13
definite article 530.6
definition
  distinctness 31.2
  circumscription 210.1
  interpretation 341.1
  explanation 518.3
  clearness 521.2
  naming 527.2
  characterization 864.8
  television reception
    1034.5
definitive
  limiting 210.9
  downright 247.12
  ending 819.10
  final 819.11

unqualified 959.2
deflate disable 19.10
  humiliate 137.4
  reduce 252.7
  collapse 260.10
  cheapen 633.6
  disprove 957.4
deflation
  humiliation 137.2
  decrease 252.1
  contraction 260.4
  collapse 410.3
  cheapening 633.4
  business cycle 731.9
deflect deviate 164.5
  oblique 204.9
  curve 279.6
  disincline 379.4
  prevent 1011.14
deflection
  bending 164.2
  obliquity 204.1
  angle 278.2
  curve 279.3
  radar interference
    1035.12
deflower
  corrupt 393.12
  possess sexually
    480.15
  seduce 665.20
defluxion outflow 190.4
  descent 194.1
  stream 238.4
defoliant 1000.3
defoliate 801.14
deforestation 1067.3
deform distort 263.3
  misshape 265.7
  change 851.7
  blemish 1003.4
deformation
  disfigurement 265.3
  misrepresentation
    350.1
  deterioration 393.3
  blemish 1003.1
deformed
  malformed 265.12
  freakish 869.13
  blemished 1003.8
  unshapely 1014.8
deformity disease 85.1
  cripple 85.44
  deformation 265.3
  oddity 869.3
  blemish 1003.1
  hideousness 1014.2
defraud cheat 356.18
  steal 482.13
defray 624.18
defrock depose 447.4
  disgrace 661.8
  dismiss 908.19
defrost 1019.21
deft 413.22
defunct dead 307.30
  no more 761.11
  ended 819.8
  past 836.7
defuse relieve 120.5
  keep the peace 464.7

pacify 465.7
  moderate 670.6
defy
  n challenge 454.2
  v confront 216.8
  disobey 327.6
  violate 435.4
  bid defiance 454.3
  dare 492.10
  thwart 1011.15
  resist 453.2
  make war on 458.15
dégagé
  nonchalant 106.15
  careless 340.11
  informal 581.3
degenerate
  n reprobate 660.5
  v corrupt 393.12
  deteriorate 393.16
  go wrong 654.9
  lapse into disorder
    809.8
  be changed 851.6
  defect 857.13
  evolve 860.5
  fall on evil days
    1010.11
  adj deteriorating
    393.45
  corrupt 654.14
  changed 851.10
  apostate 857.20
degradable
  biodegradable 393.47
  disintegrative 805.5
degradation
  deterioration 393.3
  decay 393.6
  demotion 447.1
  knavery 645.2
  turpitude 654.5
  baseness 661.3
  infamy 661.4
  disintegration 805.1
  banishment 908.4
  depression 912.1
degrade abase 137.5
  corrupt 393.12
  demote 447.3
  disparage 512.8
  disgrace 661.8
  dismiss 908.19
degree grade 245
  rank 245.1
  measure 300.2
  extent 300.3
  class 607.1
  academic honor 648.6
  staff 708.29
  interval 709.20
  continuity 806.2
degrees
  points of the compass
    161.3
  graduate 572.8
dehumanize 144.15
dehumidify 1064.6
dehydrate
  preserve 397.9
  dry 1064.6
deice 1019.21

deification
  respect 155.1
  praise 509.5
  glorification 662.8
  idolization 697.2
  elevation 911.1
deify respect 155.4
  praise 509.12
  glorify 662.13
  idolatrize 697.5
  exalt 911.6
deign condescend 137.8
  give oneself airs 141.8
  consent 441.2
deism 675.5
deist 675.16
deity divinity 677
  spirit 677.1
  god 678.2
deject 112.18
dejected sullen 110.24
  depressed 112.22
dejection
  defecation 12.2
  excrement 12.3
  sullenness 110.8
  depression 112.3
de jure 673.12
delay
  n slowing 175.4
  stoppage 845.2
  hindrance 1011.1
  v dawdle 175.8
  slow 175.9
  do nothing 329.2
  put away 390.6
  retard 845.8
  postpone 845.9
  wait 845.12
  hinder 1011.10
delectable tasty 63.8
  delicious 97.10
delectation 95.2
delegate
  n legate 576.2
  v commit 478.16
  commission 615.10
  deputize 861.7
delegation
  authority 417.12
  commitment 478.2
  deputation 576.13
  commission 615.1
  substitution 861.1
delete erase 255.12
  obliterate 395.16
  separate 801.8
  end 819.5
deleted absent 222.11
  ended 819.8
deleterious
  disadvantageous
    995.6
  harmful 999.12
deliberate
  v hesitate 362.7
  confer 541.11
  discuss 541.12
  consider 930.12
  adj slow 175.10
  intentional 380.8
  leisurely 402.6

cautious 494.8
deliberated
  intentional 380.8
  reasoned 934.21
deliberation
  slowness 175.1
  intentionality 380.3
  leisureliness 402.2
  caution 494.1
  discussion 541.7
  legislative procedure
    613.6
  consideration 930.2
deliberative
  conciliar 423.5
  legislative 613.11
  cognitive 930.21
delicacy tidbit 10.8
  frailty 16.2
  sensitivity 24.3
  unhealthiness 85.3
  sensibility 93.4
  tenderness 93.6
  considerateness 143.3
  insignificance 248.1
  thinness 270.4
  smoothness 294.3
  lightness 298.1
  meticulousness 339.3
  nicety 495.3
  taste 496.1
  decency 664.2
  margin 779.2
  discrimination 943.1
  accuracy 972.5
  dangerousness 1005.2
  daintiness 1015.5
  softness 1045.1
  brittleness 1048.1
delicate frail 16.14
  sensitive 24.12
  soft-colored 35.21
  tasty 63.8
  feeling 93.20
  considerate 143.16
  dainty 248.7
  thin 270.16
  smooth 294.8
  light 298.12
  meticulous 339.12
  nice 495.11
  elegant 496.9
  decent 664.5
  discriminating 943.7
  exact 972.17
  precarious 1005.12
  difficult 1012.17
  fine 1015.19
  soft 1045.8
  brittle 1048.4
delicious edible 8.33
  tasty 63.8
  delightful 97.7
  delectable 97.10
  excellent 998.13
delight
  n happiness 95.2
  tendency 895.1
  v delectate 95.9
  be pleased 95.11
  rejoice 116.5
  exult 502.9

amuse 743.21

delighted pleased 95.14
  amused 743.26

delightful tasty 63.8
  exquisite 97.7
  amusing 743.27

Delilah 665.15

delimit
  circumscribe 210.4
  mark 517.19

delimitation
  circumscription 210.1
  boundary 211.3

delineate outline 211.9
  represent 349.8
  describe 349.9
  plan 381.11
  portray 712.19

delineation
  outline 211.2
  representation 349.1
  description 349.2
  diagram 381.3
  line 517.6
  drawing 712.5
  sketch 712.13
  fiction 722.1

delineator limner 716.2
  draftsman 716.3

delinquency
  misbehavior 322.1
  disobedience 327.1
  nonobservance 435.1
  nonpayment 625.1
  wrong 638.1
  vice 654.1
  misdeed 655.2
  lawbreaking 674.3
  shortcoming 910.1

delinquent
  n evildoer 593.1
  defaulter 625.5
  wrongdoer 660.9
  adj defaulting 625.10
  wrong 638.3

deliquescent
  decreasing 252.11
  liquefied 1062.6

delirious feverish 85.57
  fervent 93.18
  overzealous 101.12
  frenzied 105.25
  out of one's head
    925.31

delirium fever 85.7
  fury 105.8
  deliriousness 925.8
  figment of the
    imagination 985.5

delirium tremens
  alcoholism 88.3
  shaking 916.2
  mania 925.9
  hallucination 975.7

deliver release 120.6
  transfer 176.10
  do 328.6
  rescue 398.3
  accomplish 407.4
  succeed 409.7
  liberate 431.4
  hand 478.13

say 524.23
  send 629.3
  play 745.5
  perform 891.11

deliverance
  release 120.2
  escape 369.1
  rescue 398.1
  liberation 431.1
  giving 478.1
  transfer 629.1
  verdict 945.5

deliverer
  preserver 397.5
  savior 592.2

delivery birth 1.1
  transportation 176.3
  escape 369.1
  rescue 398.1
  liberation 431.1
  giving 478.1
  articulation 524.6
  transfer 629.1
  pitch 745.3
  game 750.2

dell highland 237.7
  valley 284.9

delocalize 176.11

delouse 79.24

Delphic oracle 961.7

delta fork 171.4
  plain 236.1
  point of land 283.9

deltoid
  diverging 171.8
  spread 259.11
  triangular 278.8
  three 875.3
  tripartite 877.4

delude deceive 356.10
  be mistaken 974.10

deluded 925.26

deluge
  n torrent 238.5
  overflow 238.6
  rainstorm 316.2
  throng 769.4
  superabundance 992.2
  wetting 1063.6
  v overflow 238.17
  submerge 367.7
  oversupply 992.14
  flood 1063.14

delusion sham 354.3
  deception 356.1
  error 974.1
  illusion 975.1

deluxe 501.21

delve
  excavate 284.15
  search 937.30
  cultivate 1067.17

demagnetize 1031.26

demagogue
  n instigator 375.11
  speaker 543.4
  v declaim 543.10

demand
  n extortion 192.6
  stipulation 421
  claim 421.1
  request 440.1

fee 630.6
  prerogative 642.1
  imposition 643.1
  sale 734.1
  question 937.10
  requirement 962.2
  v extort 192.15
  prescribe 420.9
  summon 420.11
  ask 421.5
  oblige 424.5
  request 440.9
  charge 630.12
  impose 643.4
  inquire 937.19
  require 962.9

demanding
  meticulous 339.12
  exacting 421.9
  strict 425.6
  importunate 440.18
  difficult 1012.17

demarcate
  circumscribe 210.4
  mark 517.19
  differentiate 779.6
  characterize 864.10
  discriminate 943.4

demarcation
  circumscription 210.1
  exclusion 772.1
  differentiation 779.4
  distinction 943.3

demasculinize
  unman 19.12
  feminize 77.12

demean 137.5

demeaning
  inferior 250.6
  disgraceful 661.11

demeanor
  looks 33.4
  behavior 321.1

demented
  turbulent 671.18
  insane 925.26

dementia 925.1

demesne
  sphere 231.2
  real estate 471.6
  farm 1067.8

Demeter
  fertility 889.5
  agricultural deity
    1067.4

demigod
  brave person 492.8
  hero 659.5
  godling 678.3

demilitarize 465.11

demimonde 665.15

demise
  n death 307.1
  transfer 629.1
  v transfer 629.3

demobilize
  release 431.5
  disarm 465.11
  disband 770.8

democracy
  communion 476.2
  government 612.4

democratic centralism
  611.5

demographic
  human 312.13
  populational 606.8

demography
  population 227.1
  anthropology 312.10
  the people 606.1

demolish
  wreck 395.17
  shatter 801.13
  disassemble 801.15
  refute 957.5

demolition
  demolishment 395.5
  refutation 957.2

demon
  enthusiast 101.5
  monster 593.6
  violent person 671.9
  spirit 678.5
  familiar spirit 678.12
  fiend 680.6
  genius 919.8

demonic
  frenzied 105.25
  diabolic 654.13
  demoniac 680.17
  possessed 925.29
  execrable 999.10

demonism
  Satanism 680.14
  black magic 690.2
  idolatry 697.1

demonstrable
  manifested 348.13
  real 760.15
  provable 956.19
  obvious 969.15

demonstrate
  object 333.5
  explain 341.10
  manifest 348.5
  image 349.11
  flaunt 501.17
  teach 568.10
  evidence 956.8
  prove 956.10
  cite 956.13
  check 1016.20

demonstrated
  manifested 348.13
  proved 956.20
  true 972.13

demonstration
  objection 333.2
  explanation 341.4
  manifestation 348.2
  representation 349.1
  display 501.4
  assembly 769.2
  example 785.2
  reasoning 934.1
  proof 956.3
  citation 956.5

demonstrative
  emotional 93.17
  loving 104.27
  explanatory 341.15
  communicative
    343.10

manifesting 348.9
indicative 517.23
evincive 956.17
demonstrator
interpreter 341.7
picket 1007.13
demoralize
intimidate 127.20
unnerve 128.10
corrupt 654.10
demos 606.1
Demosthenes 543.6
demote degrade 447.3
dismiss 908.19
overthrow 912.6
demotion
deterioration 393.3
downgrading 447
degrading 447.1
infamy 661.4
banishment 908.4
depression 912.1
demulcent
n balm 86.11
ointment 1054.3
adj palliative 86.40
relieving 120.9
moderate 670.16
softening 1045.16
demur
n scruple 325.2
objection 333.2
resistance 453.1
v scruple 325.4
object 333.5
hesitate 362.7
demure solemn 111.3
shy 139.12
prudish 500.19
demurrer
objection 333.2
dissenter 333.3
pleadings 598.6
defense 600.2
demystify 521.6
demythologize 341.10
den sanctum 197.8
lair 228.26
disapproved place
228.28
hiding place 346.4
sewer 654.7
office 739.7
retreat 1008.5
denature
corrupt 393.12
adulterate 796.12
change 851.7
deniability
incognizance 929.3
doubtfulness 970.2
denial
disaffirmation 335
disavowal 335.2
recantation 363.3
rejection 372.1
refusal 442.1
prohibition 444.1
opposition 451.1
loss 473.1
defense 600.2
temperance 668.1

unbelief 954.1
refutation 957.2
denied rejected 372.3
disproved 957.7
denied to 966.9
denigrate blacken 38.7
deprecate 510.12
vilify 512.10
denizen
n inhabitant 227.2
v people 225.9
den of iniquity
sewer 654.7
brothel 665.9
denomination
indication 517.3
naming 527.2
name 527.3
school 617.5
sect 675.3
kind 808.3
specification 864.6
denotation
indication 517.3
meaning 518.1
denote signify 517.17
designate 517.18
mean 518.8
evidence 956.8
denouement plot 722.4
end 819.1
solution 939.1
denounce
censure 510.13
threaten 514.2
accuse 599.7
condemn 602.3
dense thick 269.8
luxuriant 310.40
sturdy 762.7
crowded 769.22
stupid 921.15
compact 1043.12
hard 1044.10
density
substantiality 762.1
stupidity 921.3
solidness 1043
compactness 1043.1
hardness 1044.1
dent
n indentation 284.6
print 517.7
v indent 284.14
dental hygienist 81.3
dentate notched 289.5
prehensile 474.9
dentist 90.6
dentistry 90.3
denude divest 6.5
strip 480.24
tear apart 801.14
denuded
divested 6.12
bereft 473.8
denuded of 991.13
denunciation
censure 510.3
curse 513.1
threat 514.1
accusation 599.1
condemnation 602.1

deny
n recant 363.8
v not admit 335.4
reject 372.2
withhold 442.4
prohibit 444.3
contradict 451.6
disbelieve 954.5
refute 957.5
deny oneself
abstain 667.3
restrain oneself 668.6
detemperate 668.7
deodorant 72.3
deodorize
fumigate 72.4
falsify 354.15
Deo volente 965.11
depart disappear 34.2
deviate 164.3
make off 188.6
exit 190.12
absent oneself 222.8
die 307.19
flee 368.10
abandon 370.5
digress 538.9
differ 779.5
separate 801.8
departed
left 188.19
absent 222.11
dead 307.30
past 836.7
department
region 231.1
sphere 231.2
bureau 594.4
occupation 724.4
department store 736.1
departure
disappearance 34.1
deviation 164.1
leaving 188.1
leave-taking 188.4
egress 190.2
absence 222.4
death 307.1
digression 538.4
difference 779.1
depend pend 202.6
hang 958.6
all depend 970.11
dependability
trustworthiness 644.6
reliability 969.4
dependable
trustworthy 644.19
reliable 969.17
unhazardous 1006.5
dependence
hope 124.1
pendency 202.1
tutelage 432.3
supporter 616.9
relativity 774.2
belief 952.1
dependency
pendency 202.1
tutelage 432.3
dependent 432.6
possession 469.1

dependent
n hanger-on 138.6
follower 166.2
charge 432.6
retainer 577.1
adj pendent 202.9
subject 432.13
trusting 952.22
contingent 958.9
undecided 970.18
depend on
be at the mercy of
432.12
result from 886.5
rely on 952.16
trust 952.17
depend 958.6
depersonalization
92.20
depict
represent 349.8
describe 349.9
enact 704.30
portray 712.19
depiction
representation 349.1
description 349.2
depilatory 6.4
deplane 186.8
deplete consume 388.3
waste 473.5
evacuate 908.22
depletion
decrement 252.3
reduction 255.2
consumption 388.1
waste 473.2
evacuation 908.6
deplorable
distressing 98.20
regrettable 113.10
disgraceful 661.11
terrible 999.9
deplore
regret 113.6
lament 115.10
deploy locate 159.11
diverge 171.5
spread 259.6
prepare 405.6
order 806.4
adduce 956.12
deployment
placement 159.6
divergence 171.1
expansion 259.1
battle array 458.3
order 806.1
arrangement 807.1
deplume
demote 447.3
strip 480.24
disgrace 661.8
dismiss 908.19
depopulate
slaughter 308.16
dispeople 908.16
deport transfer 176.10
emigrate 190.16
eliminate 772.5
banish 908.17
deportment 321.1

depose dislodge 160.6
depone 334.6
remove from office
 447.4
dismiss 908.19
overthrow 912.6
state 952.12
testify 956.9
deposit
 n placement 159.6
sediment 176.9
collateral 438.3
payment 624.1
precipitation 1043.5
mineral deposit
 1056.7
 v lay 78.9
repose 159.14
secrete 346.7
store 386.10
pledge 438.10
precipitate 1043.11
deposition
placement 159.6
dregs 256.2
sworn statement
 334.3
deposal 447.2
certificate 549.6
declaration 598.7
statement of belief
 952.4
testimony 956.2
depository
storehouse 386.6
trustee 470.5
treasurer 729.11
treasury 729.12
depot 386.6
deprave
corrupt 393.12
work evil 999.6
depravity
turpitude 654.5
baseness 661.3
deprecate
discommend 510.12
underestimate 949.2
attach little
 importance to 997.12
deprecatory
self-effacing 139.10
condemnatory 510.22
disparaging 512.13
depreciate
reduce 252.7
subtract 255.9
 waste 473.5
deprecate 510.12
disparage 512.8
discount 631.2
cheapen 633.6
underestimate 949.2
attach little
 importance to 997.12
depreciation
decrease 252.1
reduction 255.2
deterioration 393.3
waste 473.2
deprecation 510.2
disparagement 512.1

discount 631.1
cheapening 633.4
underestimation
 949.1
depredate
destroy 395.10
plunder 482.17
depress
sadden 112.18
reduce 252.7
lower 274.6
deepen 275.8
indent 284.14
press down 912.4
depressant
 n sedative 86.12
drug 87.2
 adj sedative 86.45
depressing 112.30
depressed
pleasureless 96.20
dejected 112.22
low 274.7
indented 284.17
lowered 912.12
unfortunate 1010.14
depression
mental disorder 92.14
wretchedness 96.6
distressfulness 98.5
dejection 112.3
decrease 252.1
lowness 274.1
deepening 275.7
concavity 284.1
cavity 284.2
notch 289.1
business cycle 731.9
lowering 912.1
melancholia 925.5
hard times 1010.6
Depression Era 823.5
deprivation
absence 222.1
refusal 442.1
deposal 447.2
loss 473.1
divestment 480.6
indigence 619.2
nonexistence 761.1
disassembly 801.6
banishment 908.4
want 991.4
deprive
take from 480.21
dismiss 908.19
deprived limited 210.7
bereaved 307.35
indigent 619.8
deprived of
bereft 473.8
wanting 991.13
depth space 158.1
interiority 207.1
size 257.1
thickness 269.2
deepness 275.1
pit 275.2
pitch 709.4
wisdom 919.5
deputation
authority 417.12

delegation 576.13
commission 615.1
substitution 861.1
deputize
empower 18.10
represent 576.14
commission 615.10
delegate 861.7
deputy
 n mediator 466.3
director 574.1
representative 576
proxy 576.1
lawyer 597.1
assignee 615.9
assistant 616.6
substitute 861.2
policeman 1007.15
 adj deputative 576.15
deracinate
dislodge 160.6
extract 192.10
exterminate 395.14
derail miscarry 410.15
distract 984.6
thwart 1011.15
derange afflict 85.49
disarrange 810.2
madden 925.24
derangement
disorder 809.1
disarrangement 810.1
abnormality 869.1
insanity 925.1
derby contest 457.3
race 457.12
Derby 757.1
deregulate
not interfere 430.16
politicize 611.16
deregulation
noninterference 430.9
disembarrassment
 1013.6
derelict
 n bum 331.9
castoff 370.4
outcast 586.4
wretch 660.2
transient 827.4
 adj negligent 340.10
abandoned 370.8
dilapidated 393.33
outcast 586.10
unfaithful 645.20
dereliction
disobedience 327.1
neglect 340.1
desertion 370.2
nonobservance 435.1
infidelity 645.5
misdeed 655.2
badness 999.1
deride
disdain 157.3
flout 454.4
ridicule 508.8
have the audacity
 142.7
de rigueur
conventional 579.5
obligatory 641.15

derisive
impudent 142.10
disrespectful 156.7
defiant 454.7
ridiculing 508.12
condemnatory 510.22
disparaging 512.13
derivation
receiving 479.1
root 526.2
morphology 526.3
etymology 526.15
lineage 560.4
adoption 621.2
source 885.5
effect 886.1
conclusion 945.4
derivative
 n root 526.2
effect 886.1
 adj resultant 886.6
attributable 887.6
uncreative 890.5
derive elicit 192.14
acquire 472.8
receive 479.6
conclude 945.10
derive from
receive 479.6
adopt 621.4
result from 886.5
trace to 887.5
dermal
cutaneous 2.25
covering 295.32
dermis the skin 2.4
skin 295.3
dernier cri 840.2
derogation
reduction 255.2
deterioration 393.3
disparagement 512.1
derogatory
disparaging 512.13
disreputable 661.10
derrick tower 272.6
lifter 911.3
derrière 217.4
derring-do 492.5
dervish
ascetic 667.2
Muslim 675.23
clergy 699.11
désœuvré 331.18
descant
 n treatise 556.1
air 708.4
part 708.22
overture 708.26
 v amplify 538.7
write upon 556.5
sing 708.38
descend
condescend 137.8
give oneself airs 141.8
move 172.5
land 184.43
go down 194.5
incline 204.10
gravitate 297.15
change hands 629.4
incur disgrace 661.7

descendant
offspring 561.3
successor 816.4
sequel 834.2
descending
n course 172.2
descent 194.1
adj flowing 172.8
descendant 194.11
sloping downward
204.16
descend upon
light upon 194.10
attack 459.14
descent
humiliation 137.2
course 172.2
motion downwards
194
descending 194.1
declivity 204.5
deterioration 393.3
lineage 560.4
offspring 561.1
series 811.2
sequence 814.1
conversion 857.1
depression 912.1
reverse 1010.3
rocket launching
1072.9
describe
interpret 341.9
portray 349.9
characterize 864.10
description
interpretation 341.1
portrait 349
portrayal 349.2
fiction 722.1
kind 808.3
characterization 864.8
descriptive
interpretative 341.14
depictive 349.14
linguistic 523.17
descry see 27.12
perceive 521.9
detect 940.5
desecrate misuse 389.4
corrupt 393.12
profane 694.4
desecration
misuse 389.1
abomination 638.2
sacrilege 694.2
desensitize deaden 25.4
dull 94.7
desert
n open space 158.4
plain 236.1
wasteland 890.2
dryness 1064.2
adj unproductive
890.4
dry 1064.7
desert
n reprisal 506.2
goodness 998.1
v quit 188.9
apostatize 363.7
flee 368.10

abandon 370.5
be unfaithful 645.12
defect 857.13
deserted available 222.15
neglected 340.14
abandoned 370.8
disused 390.10
forlorn 584.12
deserter
apostate 363.5
desertion 370.2
sacrilegist 694.3
apostate 857.8
desertion
departure 188.1
apostasy 363.2
flight 368.4
defection 370.2
forlornness 584.4
impiety 694.1
apostasy 857.3
deserts reprisal 506.2
just deserts 639.3
deserve 639.5
deserved
warranted 639.9
just 649.8
deserving
praiseworthy 509.20
due 639.10
desex 19.12
déshabillé 5.20
desiccate
languish 393.18
preserve 397.9
dry 1064.6
desideratum
desire 100.11
intention 380.1
requirement 962.2
design
n trick 356.6
intention 380.1
plan 381.1
diagram 381.3
stratagem 415.3
motif 498.7
intent 518.2
makeup 554.12
form 709.11
visual arts 712.1
treatment 712.9
work of art 712.10
drawing 712.13
architectural design
717
styling 717.4
plot 722.4
production 891.2
v intend 380.4
plan 381.8
portray 712.19
produce 891.8
originate 891.12
designate
nominate 371.19
commit 436.5
specify 517.18
name 527.11
appoint 615.11
classify 808.6
specify 864.11

designation
nomination 371.8
obligation 436.2
indication 517.3
naming 527.2
name 527.3
appointment 615.2
kind 808.3
specification 864.6
designer planner 381.6
theater man 704.23
stylist 716.9
architect 717.5
producer 891.7
designing
n visual arts 712.1
adj scheming 381.13
cunning 415.12
desirable sexual 75.24
pleasant 97.6
sought-after 100.30
eligible 371.24
welcome 585.12
expedient 994.5
desire
n sexual desire 75.5
want 100
wish 100.1
heart's desire 100.11
love 104.1
hope 124.1
will 323.1
intention 380.1
request 440.1
v lust 75.20
desiderate 100.14
jump at 101.6
hope 124.7
will 323.2
intend 380.4
request 440.9
desired wanted 100.29
welcome 585.12
future 838.8
normal 868.8
desirous
keen on 100.21
eager 101.8
amorous 104.26
desirous of
keen on 100.22
envious 154.4
desist
v cease to use 390.4
cease 856.6
inter cease! 856.13
desk furniture 229.1
pulpit 703.13
workplace 739.1
table 900.15
desktop publishing
program 1041.12
desolate
v agonize 98.12
aggrieve 112.19
destroy 395.10
depopulate 908.16
adj wretched 96.26
distressing 98.20
disconsolate 112.28
forlorn 584.12
unproductive 890.4

desolation
wretchedness 96.6
harshness 98.4
disconsolateness
112.12
destruction 395.1
forlornness 584.4
wasteland 890.2
depopulation 908.3
despair
n wretchedness 96.6
dejection 112.3
desperation 125.2
v lose heart 112.16
despair of 125.10
desperado
killer 308.10
ruffian 593.3
criminal 660.10
desperate
hopeless 125.12
reckless 493.8
rabid 925.30
straitened 1012.26
desperation 125.2
despicable
offensive 98.18
base 661.12
paltry 997.21
terrible 999.9
despise hate 103.5
disdain 157.3
reject 372.2
flout 454.4
deprecate 510.12
despite
n hate 103.1
spite 144.6
indignity 156.2
contempt 157.1
defiance 454.1
adv in spite of 338.9
despoil
corrupt 393.12
destroy 395.10
strip 480.24
plunder 482.17
seduce 665.20
work evil 999.6
despoliation
destruction 395.1
loss 473.1
plundering 482.6
evil 999.3
despondency
n wretchedness 96.6
dejection 112.3
despair 125.2
v lose heart 112.16
despondent
dejected 112.22
hopeless 125.12
despot 575.14
despotic
imperious 417.16
governmental 612.17
despotism
absolutism 612.9
tyranny 612.10
dessert serving 8.10
delicacy 10.8
desserts 604.1

destabilize 809.9
destigmatize
justify 600.9
acquit 601.4
destination goal 186.5
objective 380.2
address 553.9
end 819.1
fate 963.2
destined future 838.8
inevitable 962.15
fated 963.9
destiny portion 477.5
end 819.1
predestiny 838.2
fate 963.2
chance 971.1
destitute bereft 473.8
down-and-out 619.9
insolvent 625.11
destitution
indigence 619.2
want 991.4
destroy
excise 255.10
kill 308.12
spoil 393.10
deal destruction
  395.10
defeat 412.6
rage 671.11
thwart 1011.15
work evil 999.6
destroyer
battleship 180.7
ruiner 395.8
savage 593.5
destructible 16.14
destruction
excision 255.3
killing 308.1
impairment 393.1
ruin 395.1
defeat 412.1
loss 473.1
violence 671.1
disintegration 805.1
evil 999.3
bane 1000.1
destructive
poisonous 82.7
deadly 308.22
destroying 395.26
violent 671.16
disintegrative 805.5
disastrous 1010.15
desuetude
abandonment 370.1
disuse 390.1
desultory
deviative 164.7
discursive 538.13
unordered 809.12
irregular 850.3
inconstant 853.7
fluttering 916.18
unreliable 970.20
detach
commission 615.10
enlist 615.17
disband 770.8
remove 801.10

detached
apathetic 94.13
reticent 344.10
free 430.21
aloof 583.6
secluded 584.8
impartial 649.10
unrelated 775.6
distinct 801.20
separated 801.21
incoherent 803.4
alone 871.8
unprejudiced 978.12
incurious 981.3
detachment
apathy 94.4
unconcern 102.2
reticence 344.3
military unit 461.22
aloofness 583.2
seclusion 584.1
impartiality 649.4
company 769.3
disbandment 770.3
elimination 772.2
part 792.1
separation 801.1
aloneness 871.2
unprejudicedness
  978.5
incuriosity 981.1
detail
n meticulousness
  339.3
military unit
  461.22
motif 498.7
particular 765.3
company 769.3
part 792.1
component 795.2
v allot 477.9
amplify 538.7
commission 615.10
itemize 765.6
analyze 800.7
elaborate 860.6
particularize 864.9
sum up 1016.18
details
description 349.2
trivia 997.4
detain
slow 175.9
confine 429.12
delay 845.8
hinder 1011.10
detect 940.5
detectable
visible 31.6
discoverable 940.10
detection
investigation 937.4
discovery 940.1
radar 1035.9
detective
operative 576.10
inquirer 937.16
policeman 1007.15
détente
pacification 465.1
foreign policy 609.5

detention
slowing 175.4
imprisonment 429.3
delay 845.2
hindrance 1011.1
deter daunt 127.18
disincline 379.4
prevent 1011.14
detergent 79.17
deteriorate
aggravate 119.2
impair 393.9
sicken 393.16
be changed 851.6
degenerate 1010.11
determinant
n boundary 211.3
heredity 560.6
cause 885.1
adj bordering 211.11
determinate
circumscribed 210.6
particular 864.12
unqualified 959.2
certain 969.13
assured 969.20
determination
circumscription 210.1
measurement 300.1
will 323.1
resolution 359.1
obstinacy 361.1
intention 380.1
endeavor 403.1
solution 939.1
discovery 940.1
test 941.2
verdict 945.5
proof 956.3
ensuring 969.8
determine
direct 161.5
circumscribe 210.4
will 323.2
resolve 359.7
induce 375.22
intend 380.4
learn 570.6
end 819.5
specify 864.11
decide 885.12
exercise influence
  893.8
discover 940.2
decide 945.11
prove 956.10
make sure 969.11
determined
circumscribed 210.6
resolute 359.11
trial 403.16
future 838.8
proved 956.20
predetermined 963.8
assured 969.20
confident 969.21
true 972.13
determinism
the future 838.1
fatalism 963.4
deterrent
n determent 379.2

obstacle 1011.4
adj frightening 127.28
dissuasive 379.5
warning 399.7
preventive 1011.19
detest dislike 99.3
hate 103.5
detestable
offensive 98.18
hateful 103.8
terrible 999.9
dethrone 447.4
detonate blast 56.8
explode 671.14
shoot 903.12
fuel 1020.7
detour
n deviation 164.1
byway 383.4
bypass 913.3
v deviate 164.3
go roundabout 913.4
detoxification 87.1
detract subtract 255.9
distract 984.6
detraction
minimization 252.5
reduction 255.2
disparagement 512.1
detrain 186.8
detriment
impairment 393.1
loss 473.1
disadvantage 995.2
evil 999.3
detrimental
disadvantageous
  995.6
harmful 999.12
adverse 1010.13
detritus deposit 176.9
remainder 256.1
grain 1049.6
de trop
excessive 992.16
superfluous 992.17
deuce game 748.2
card 758.2
pair 872.3
deuced 513.10
deus ex machina 722.4
devaluate
cheapen 633.6
monetize 728.26
devalue corrupt 393.12
monetize 728.26
devastate
destroy 395.10
depopulate 908.16
devastation
destruction 395.1
depopulation 908.3
develop
age 14.2
grow 251.6
enlarge 259.4
become larger 259.5
expand 259.7
mature 303.9
manifest 348.5
disclose 351.4
improve 392.7

bisector 874.3
diametric 778.7
diamond
  n good person 659.1
  playground 743.11
  baseball 745.1
  good thing 998.5
  hardness 1044.6
  v figure 498.9
Diana 1070.12
diapason range 158.2
  harmony 708.3
  scale 709.6
  interval 709.20
  music 711.22
diaper 5.19
diaphanous
  dainty 248.7
  thin 270.16
  light 1024.31
  transparent 1028.4
diaphragm
  digestive system 2.16
  loudspeaker 50.8
  contraceptive 86.23
  partition 213.5
  middle 818.1
diarist writer 547.15
  author 718.4
  historian 719.4
  chronologist 831.10
diarrhea
  defecation 12.2
  symptom 85.9
diary
  record book 549.11
  periodical 555.1
  history 719.1
  chronicle 831.9
diaspora 770.3
diastole
  distension 259.2
  round 849.3
  pulsation 915.3
diatonic scale 709.6
diatribe berating 510.7
  speech 543.2
dice
  n gambling device
    759.8
  v square 878.3
dicey
  speculative 759.27
  uncertain 970.16
  vague 970.19
  chance 971.15
  hazardous 1005.10
dichotomy
  severance 801.2
  doubleness 872.1
  bisection 874.1
dichromatic
  chromatic 35.15
  variegated 47.9
dick detective 576.10
  gumshoe 576.11
  police 1007.16
dick around 922.6
dicker
  n compact 437.1
  bargain 731.5
  v bargain 731.17

Dick Turpin 483.11
dictate
  n precept 419.1
  command 420.1
  law 673.3
  axiom 973.2
  v command 420.8
  prescribe 420.9
  oblige 424.5
  dominate 612.15
  necessitate 962.8
dictator 575.14
dictatorial
  lordly 141.11
  imperious 417.16
  governmental 612.17
dictatorship
  mastership 417.7
  directorship 573.4
  government 612.4
  absolutism 612.9
diction phrasing 529.2
  word-usage 532
  words 532.1
dictionary
  reference book 554.9
  word list 870.4
dictum
  affirmation 334.1
  rule 419.2
  decree 420.4
  remark 524.4
  verdict 945.5
  maxim 973.1
  axiom 973.2
didactic
  preceptive 419.4
  advisory 422.8
  educational 568.18
  poetic 720.15
  dogmatic 969.22
diddle
  n deception 356.9
  v copulate 75.21
  waste time 331.13
  dally 331.14
  deceive 356.14
  fake 356.19
die
  n engraving tool 713.8
  cast 784.6
  mold 785.6
  base 900.8
  v disappear 34.2
  decease 307.19
  decline 393.17
  perish 395.23
  stall 410.16
  cease to exist 761.6
  come to an end 819.6
  pass 836.6
  burn out 1021.8
die away
  disappear 34.2
  recede 168.2
  decrease 252.6
  cease to exist 761.6
  come to an end 819.6
  burn out 1021.8
die down quiet 173.8
  decrease 252.6
  burn out 1021.8

die for 100.14
diehard
  n obstinate person
    361.6
  rightwinger 611.9
  conservative 852.4
  adj conservative 852.8
the die is cast 962.20
die laughing 116.8
die out disappear 34.2
  be dying 307.26
  cease to exist 761.6
  burn out 1021.8
diet
  n dieting 7.11
  council 423.1
  legislature 613.1
  assembly 769.2
  v go on a diet 7.17
  eat 8.20
  slenderize 270.13
dietary
  n diet 7.11
  adj dietetic 7.21
dietitian
  nutritionist 7.13
  hospital staff 90.11
differ dissent 333.4
  argue 456.8
  vary 779.5
  diversify 781.2
  not resemble 786.2
  disagree 788.5
difference
  n remainder 255.8
  dissent 333.1
  disagreement 456.2
  heraldry 647.2
  dissimilarity 779
  otherness 779.1
  nonuniformity 781.1
  dissimilarity 786.1
  argument 788.1
  inequality 790.1
  change 851.1
  abnormality 869.1
  sum 1016.6
  v differentiate 779.6
different
  differing 779.7
  nonuniform 781.3
  dissimilar 786.4
  novel 840.11
  particular 864.12
  abnormal 869.9
  eccentric 926.5
differential
  n margin 779.2
  characteristic 864.4
  gear 1039.5
  adj differentiative
    779.9
  classificational
    808.7
  discriminating 943.7
  numeric 1016.22
differentiate
  signify 517.17
  difference 779.6
  diversify 781.2
  characterize 864.10
  discriminate 943.4

differentiation
  indication 517.3
  differencing 779.4
  nonuniformity 781.1
  particularity 864.1
  characterization 864.8
  distinction 943.3
  notation 1016.2
difficult perverse 361.11
  finical 495.10
  hard to understand
    522.14
  adverse 1010.13
  difficile 1012.17
difficulties
  poverty 619.1
  adversity 1010.1
difficulty
  annoyance 96.2
  disagreement 456.2
  abstruseness 522.2
  adversity 1010.1
  obstacle 1011.4
  impediment 1011.6
  difficultness 1012.1
diffidence
  fearfulness 127.3
  self-effacement 139.2
  demur 325.2
  hesitation 362.3
  doubt 954.2
diffraction
  deflection 164.2
  dispersion 770.1
  wave 915.4
diffuse
  v deflect 164.5
  radiate 171.6
  transfer 176.10
  pervade 221.7
  rarefy 299.3
  publish 352.10
  disperse 770.4
  shatter 801.13
  loosen 803.3
  adj deflective 164.8
  rare 299.4
  formless 538.11
  dispersed 770.9
  extensive 863.13
  plentiful 990.7
diffusion
  deflection 164.2
  radiation 171.2
  transferal 176.1
  permeation 221.3
  rarefaction 299.2
  publication 352.1
  waste 473.2
  diffuseness 538.1
  dispersion 770.1
  disruption 801.3
  noncohesion 803.1
diffusive
  formless 538.11
  dispersive 770.11
dig
  n disrespect 156.3
  pit 284.4
  thrust 901.2
  hit 901.4
  v respond 93.11

deepen 275.8
excavate 284.15
read one loud and
  clear 521.8
study 570.12
drudge 725.14
play 749.7
thrust 901.12
know 927.12
search 937.30
cultivate 1067.17
harvest 1067.19
digest
n abridgment 557.1
code 673.5
table 807.4
v assimilate 7.16
take 134.8
absorb 187.13
consume 388.3
understand 521.7
learn 570.7
codify 673.9
classify 808.6
consider 930.12
think over 930.13
digestion
ingestion 2.15
assimilation 7.8
sorption 187.6
consumption 388.1
absorption 570.2
pulping 1061.3
dig in
remain firm 359.9
fortify 460.9
digit finger 73.5
foot 199.5
number 1016.3
digital
prehensile 474.9
numeric 1016.22
dignified solemn 111.3
stately 136.12
lofty 544.14
dignify formalize 580.5
honor 662.12
dignitary 996.8
dignity solemnity 111.1
proud bearing 136.2
elegance 533.1
loftiness 544.6
formality 580.1
prestige 662.4
ecclesiastical office
  698.5
notability 996.2
personage 996.8
digression
deviation 164.1
obliquity 204.1
departure 538.4
circuitousness 913.1
detour 913.3
digs 228.4
dig up
extract 192.10
disinter 192.11
acquire 472.9
assemble 769.18
uncover 940.4
be curious 980.3

dike
n crack 224.2
lake 241.1
trench 290.2
barrier 1011.5
deposit 1056.7
v excavate 284.15
furrow 290.3
dilapidated
unsteady 16.16
ramshackle 393.33
disintegrative 805.5
slovenly 809.15
stale 841.14
dilate enlarge 259.4
make larger 259.5
bulge 283.11
amplify 538.7
dilation
distension 259.2
swelling 283.4
exaggeration 355.1
amplification 538.6
dilatory
dawdling 175.11
reluctant 325.6
indolent 331.19
delaying 845.17
dilemma
no choice 371.3
syllogism 934.6
bewilderment 970.3
horns of a dilemma
  1012.7
dilettante
enthusiast 101.4
connoisseur 496.7
specialist 865.3
half scholar 928.6
ignoramus 929.8
trifler 997.10
diligence
industry 330.6
painstakingness 339.2
perseverance 360.1
studiousness 570.4
attention 982.1
diligent
industrious 330.22
painstaking 339.11
persevering 360.8
studious 570.17
attentive 982.15
dillydally dawdle 175.8
dally 331.14
wait 845.12
dilute
v cut 16.11
abate 252.8
thin 270.12
rarefy 299.3
dissipate 770.5
adulterate 796.12
adj insipid 65.2
rare 299.4
diluvium deposit 176.9
dregs 256.2
dim
n darkishness 1026.2
v blind 30.7
blur 32.4
decolor 36.5

darken 1026.9
grow dark 1026.12
adj dim-sighted 28.13
inconspicuous 32.6
colorless 36.7
faint 52.16
obscure 522.15
dull 921.16
darkish 1026.15
dime
n money 728.7
v inform on 551.13
dime-a-dozen
dirt cheap 633.8
plentiful 990.7
common 997.21
dimension space 158.1
size 257.1
dime store 736.1
diminish relieve 120.5
abase 137.5
recede 168.2
decrease 252.6
reduce 252.7
subtract 255.9
narrow 270.11
languish 393.18
extenuate 600.12
moderate 670.6
qualify 958.3
diminution relief 120.1
decrease 252.1
reduction 255.2
modulation 670.2
depression 912.1
diminutive
n runt 258.4
nickname 527.7
adj miniature 258.12
nominal 527.15
dimple
n indentation 284.6
v indent 284.14
dim view 510.1
dimwit 923.2
din
n noise 53.3
pandemonium 809.5
v boom 53.7
ding 848.10
dine feed 8.18
dinner 8.21
diner meal 8.6
eater 8.16
restaurant 8.17
dining room 197.11
ding
n ringing 54.3
disrespect 156.3
v ring 54.8
din 848.10
ding-a-ling
ringing 54.3
fool 923.3
dingdong
n ringing 54.3
regularity 780.2
repetitiousness 848.4
fool 923.3
v ring 54.8
adj monotonous
  848.15

dingy colorless 36.7
grimy 38.11
gray 39.4
dirty 80.22
dining room
restaurant 8.17
cafeteria 197.11
dinky inferior 250.6
little 258.10
tidy 806.8
insignificant 997.18
dinner
n meal 8.6
v dine 8.21
dinnerware 735.4
dinosaur
behemoth 257.14
reptile 311.25
dint
n power 18.1
indentation 284.6
print 517.7
hit 901.4
v indent 284.14
diocese region 231.5
see 698.8
Dionysus
bibulousness 88.2
patron 704.26
fertility 889.5
agricultural deity
  1067.4
diorama spectacle 33.7
scene 712.12
dip
n bath 79.9
declivity 204.5
cavity 284.2
submergence 367.2
pickpocket 483.2
candle 1025.2
v color 35.13
ladle 176.17
maneuver 184.40
incline 204.10
submerge 367.7
signal 517.22
baptize 701.16
flood 1063.14
diphthong 524.13
diploma grant 443.5
certificate 549.6
diplomacy skill 413.1
Machiavellianism
  415.2
foreign policy 609.5
diplomat
expert 413.11
Machiavellian 415.8
diplomatist 576.6
diplomatic
n diplomat 576.6
foreign policy 609.5
adj skillful 413.22
cunning 415.12
ambassadorial 576.16
political 609.43
diplomatic agent 576.6
dipsomania
substance abuse 87.1
alcoholism 88.3
psychosis 925.3

diptych
record book 549.11
picture 712.11
dire horrid 98.19
terrible 127.30
ominous 133.17
bad 999.9
unfortunate 1010.14
disastrous 1010.15
direct
exercise influence
  893.8
adj directional 161.12
straight 277.6
artless 416.5
free-acting 430.23
natural 499.7
clear 521.11
elegant 533.6
plain-speaking 535.3
lineal 560.18
candid 644.17
continuous 811.8
exact 972.17
adv directly 161.23
direction bearing 161
directionality 161.1
motivation 375.2
precept 419.1
directive 420.3
advice 422.1
pointer 517.4
address 553.9
teaching 568.1
supervision 573
management 573.1
government 612.1
production 704.13
operation 888.1
trend 895.2
directive
n direction 420.3
adj directable 161.13
motivating 375.25
commanding 420.13
advisory 422.8
directing 573.12
director librarian 558.3
person in charge 574
directeur 574.1
governor 575.6
theater man 704.23
motion-picture studio
  706.3
conductor 710.17
businessman 730.1
directory
n council 423.1
register 549.9
information 551.1
reference book 554.9
guidebook 574.10
directorate 574.11
adj directing 573.12
dirge
n funeral song 115.6
last offices 309.4
funeral 309.5
v lament 115.10
dirigible
n aerostat 181.11
adj directable 161.13

dirt
n grime 80.6
land 234.1
scandal 552.8
obscenity 666.4
v dirty 80.15
dirt cheap 633.8
dirty
v dirty up 80.15
stain 1003.6
adj dingy 38.11
grimy 80.22
stormy 318.23
cloudy 319.7
cursing 513.8
unfair 650.10
evil-minded 654.15
base 661.12
lascivious 665.29
obscene 666.9
slimy 1060.14
dirty pool
juggling 356.5
smear campaign
  609.14
treachery 645.6
unfairness 650.2
dirty trick trick 356.6
treachery 645.6
dirty word oath 513.4
barbarism 526.6
disability
inability 19.2
disease 85.1
handicap 603.2
disadvantage 995.2
disable
disenable 19.9
afflict 85.49
cripple 393.14
disabled
weakened 16.18
incapacitated 19.16
crippled 393.30
ended 819.8
disabuse 976.2
disaccord
n dissent 333.1
hostility 451.2
unharmonious
  relationship 456
discord 456.1
ruffled feelings 589.2
difference 779.1
disagreement 788.1
nonconformity 867.1
v discord 456.8
disagree 788.5
disaccustomed 374.4
disadvantage
n handicap 603.2
drawback 995.2
impediment 1011.6
trouble 1012.3
v inconvenience 995.4
work evil 999.6
disadvantaged
inferior 250.6
indigent 619.8
the disadvantaged
the underprivileged
  606.4

the poor 619.3
disaffected
averse 99.8
alienated 589.11
unfaithful 645.20
disaffirm 335.4
disagree dissent 333.4
refuse 442.3
differ 456.8
dispute 788.5
disagreeable
unsavory 64.5
unpleasant 98.17
irascible 110.19
unkind 144.16
disagreeing 788.6
disagreement
dissent 325.1
dissidence 333.1
refusal 442.1
difficulty 456.2
disapproval 510.1
relation 774.1
contrariety 778.1
difference 779.1
disaccord 788
discord 788.1
nonconformity 867.1
disagree with
not be good for 82.4
dissent 333.4
differ 779.5
disallow deny 335.4
refuse 442.3
prohibit 444.3
disapprove 510.10
not pay 625.6
disappear
be invisible 32.3
vanish 34.2
quit 188.9
absent oneself 222.8
hide 346.8
perish 395.23
cease to exist 761.6
flit 827.6
pass 836.6
disappearance
invisibility 32.1
vanishing 34
disappearing 34.1
absence 222.4
flight 368.4
disappoint
dissatisfy 108.5
shatter one's hopes
  125.11
defeat expectation
  132.2
disillusion 976.2
disappointed
discontented 108.7
bitterly disappointed
  132.5
unaccomplished 408.3
disapproving 510.21
disillusioned 976.5
disapprobation
dislike 99.1
resentment 152.1
dissent 333.1
disapproval 510.1

disrepute 661.1
disapproval
dislike 99.1
resentment 152.1
dissent 333.1
rejection 372.1
disapprobation 510.1
disparagement 512.1
disapprove reject 372.2
disfavor 510.10
stigmatize 661.9
disarm disable 19.9
lay down one's arms
  465.11
disarmament 465.6
disarming 504.18
disarrange
dislocate 160.5
disorder 809.9
derange 810.2
discontinue 812.3
agitate 916.10
disarray
n disorder 809.1
v undress 6.7
disarrange 810.2
disassemble
demolish 395.17
take apart 801.15
disassociation
unrelatedness 775.1
separation 801.1
disaster
fatality 308.7
debacle 395.4
upheaval 671.5
misfortune 1010.2
disastrous
destructive 395.26
convulsive 671.23
calamitous 1010.15
disavow
n recant 363.8
v deny 335.4
disavowal denial 335.2
recantation 363.3
rejection 372.1
disband disarm 465.11
disperse 770.8
part company 801.19
disbar depose 447.4
dismiss 908.19
disbelief
nonreligious 695.5
unbelief 954.1
doubtfulness 970.2
disbelieve doubt 695.14
unbelieve 954.5
refuse to believe 955.3
disburden ease 120.7
lighten 298.6
confess 351.7
unload 908.23
disembarrass 1013.9
disburse
parcel out 477.8
spend 626.5
disc record 50.12
recording media
  549.10
discard
n derelict 370.4

rejection 372.1
discarding 390.3
elimination 772.2
v abandon 370.5
reject 372.2
eliminate 390.7
eject 908.13
discern see 27.12
perceive 521.9
know 927.12
detect 940.5
discernible visible 31.6
manifest 348.8
knowable 927.25
on the right scent 940.10
discerning
sagacious 919.16
perceptive 943.8
discharge
n humor 2.22
excretion 12.1
excrement 12.3
detonation 56.3
release 120.2
emergence 190.1
outflow 190.4
performance 328.2
accomplishment 407.1
exemption 430.8
freedom 431.2
observance 434.1
execution 437.4
acquittal 601.1
payment 624.1
acknowledgment 627.2
explosion 671.7
shot 903.4
repulse 907.2
ejection 908.1
dismissal 908.5
disgorgement 908.7
arc 1031.6
v excrete 12.12
blast 56.8
exude 190.15
perform 328.9
accomplish 407.4
exempt 430.14
release 431.5
perform 434.3
execute 437.9
acquit 601.4
pay in full 624.13
erupt 671.13
explode 671.14
disband 770.8
shoot 903.12
repulse 907.3
eject 908.13
dismiss 908.19
unload 908.23
disgorge 908.25
disciple
enthusiast 101.4
follower 166.2
protégé 572.2
associate 616.8
religion 684.2
believer 692.4

convert 857.7
disciplinarian 575.14
discipline
n limitation 210.2
self-control 359.5
strictness 425.1
training 568.3
study 568.8
punishment 604.1
government 612.1
temperance 668.1
occupation 724.4
orderliness 806.3
science 927.10
v limit 210.5
hold a tight hand upon 425.4
train 568.13
punish 604.10
govern 612.12
conform 866.3
disclaim
n recant 363.8
v deny 335.4
reject 372.2
refuse 442.3
disclose unclose 292.12
manifest 348.5
reveal 351.4
signify 517.17
say 524.23
uncover 940.4
inform 551.8
testify 956.9
disclosure
appearance 33.1
opening 292.1
informing 343.2
manifestation 348.1
revelation 351
publicizing 351.1
indication 517.3
discovery 940.1
testimony 956.2
disco 743.13
discolor
n discoloration 1003.2
v decolor 36.5
mark 517.19
stain 1003.6
discombobulate
agitate 105.14
confuse 984.7
discomfit
chagrin 96.15
dismay 127.19
overwhelm 412.8
confuse 984.7
thwart 1011.15
discomfiture
chagrin 96.4
disappointment 132.1
rout 412.2
disorder 809.1
confusion 984.3
frustration 1011.3
discomfort
n pain 26.1
unpleasure 96.1
distressfulness 98.5
v chagrin 96.16
distress 98.14

disconcert
n bewilderment 970.3
v chagrin 96.15
mortify 98.13
agitate 105.14
dismay 127.19
bewilder 970.12
confuse 984.7
thwart 1011.15
disconnect 801.8
disconnected
unrelated 775.6
separated 801.21
incoherent 803.4
discontinuous 812.4
irregular 850.3
disconsolate
wretched 96.26
inconsolable 112.28
hopeless 125.12
discontent
n unpleasure 96.1
dissatisfaction 108
discontentment 108.1
ill humor 110.1
unhappiness 112.2
resentment 152.1
disapproval 510.1
v give no pleasure 96.12
dissatisfy 108.5
discontinue
break the habit 374.3
cease to use 390.4
swear off 668.8
interrupt 812.3
cease 856.6
discontinuity
dislocation 160.1
interval 224.1
deficiency 794.2
separation 801.1
noncohesion 803.1
interrupted sequence 812
discontinuousness 812.1
irregularity 850.1
revolution 851.2
discontinuous
separate 801.20
incoherent 803.4
unordered 809.12
noncontinuous 812.4
irregular 850.3
discord
noise 53.3
raucousness 58.2
dissonant sounds 61
discordance 61.1
disaccord 456.1
disagreement 788.1
discordance
dissonance 61.1
disaccord 456.1
difference 779.1
disagreement 788.1
discordant
off-color 35.20
dissonant 61.4
disaccordant 456.15
contrary 778.6

different 779.7
disagreeing 788.6
discotheque 743.13
discount
n deduction 631
cut 631.1
v reject 372.2
price 630.11
cut 631.2
discount notes 728.27
allow for 958.5
discourage
sadden 112.18
daunt 127.18
disincline 379.4
prevent 1011.14
discouragement
dejection 112.3
deterrent 379.2
prevention 1011.2
discourse
n speech 524.1
conversation 541.1
lecture 543.3
treatise 556.1
lesson 568.7
reasoning 934.1
v make a speech 543.9
write upon 556.5
expound 568.16
discourteous
disrespectful 156.7
uncourteous 505.4
discourtesy
insensibility 25.1
disrespect 156.1
bad behavior 321.2
misbehavior 322.1
impoliteness 505
discourteousness 505.1
discover see 27.12
disclose 351.4
learn 570.6
innovate 851.9
originate 891.12
find 940.2
discovery
disclosure 351.1
find 472.6
innovation 851.4
finding 940.1
discredit
n disrepute 661.1
unbelief 954.1
v disparage 512.8
disgrace 661.8
disbelieve 954.5
disprove 957.4
discreet reticent 344.10
secretive 345.15
cautious 494.8
judicious 919.19
discrepancy
difference 255.8
contrariety 778.1
differentness 779.1
disagreement 788.1
discrete
dispersed 770.9
unrelated 775.6
different 779.7

separate 801.20
incoherent 803.4
discontinuous 812.4
discretion
will 323.1
reticence 344.3
secrecy 345.1
option 371.2
free will 430.6
caution 494.1
judiciousness 919.7
foresight 960.1
discriminate
favor 650.8
differentiate 779.6
distinguish 943.4
be discriminating
943.5
discriminate against
979.8
discriminating
selective 371.23
fastidious 495.9
elegant 496.9
differentiative 779.9
judicious 919.19
discriminate 943.7
discrimination
selectivity 371.10
fastidiousness 495.1
taste 496.1
elegance 533.1
partiality 650.3
differentiation 779.4
judiciousness 919.7
critical discernment
943
discriminateness
943.1
judgment 945.1
social discrimination
979.4
discursive
deviative 164.7
wandering 177.37
aimless 538.13
circuitous 913.7
intelligent 919.12
dialectic 934.22
discuss confer 541.11
debate 541.12
write upon 556.5
discussion
conference 541.6
debate 541.7
treatise 556.1
disdain
n disdainfulness 141.5
insolence 142.1
contempt 157.1
rejection 372.1
defiance 454.1
v scorn 157.3
reject 372.2
flout 454.4
be hard to please
495.8
deprecate 510.12
disease
n illness 85.1
harmfulness 999.5
bane 1000.1

v infect 85.50
disembark
anchor 182.15
land 186.8
disembarrass
lighten 120.7
extricate 431.7
disencumber 1013.9
disembody
spiritualize 689.20
unsubstantiate 763.4
dematerialize 1051.6
disembowel 192.13
disembroil
extricate 431.7
disinvolve 797.5
disembarrass 1013.9
disenchanted
averse 99.8
disapproving 510.21
disillusioned 976.5
disencumber
relieve 120.7
lighten 298.6
disembarrass 1013.9
disenfranchise 432.8
disengage
retreat 163.6
extricate 431.7
separate 801.8
detach 801.10
disembarrass 1013.9
disentangle
extract 192.10
straighten 277.5
extricate 431.7
disinvolve 797.5
solve 939.2
disembarrass 1013.9
disfavor
n dislike 99.1
falling-out 456.4
disapproval 510.1
disrepute 661.1
v dislike 99.3
disapprove 510.10
disfigure
deform 265.7
blemish 1003.4
offend 1014.5
disfranchise 432.8
disgorge
relinquish 475.3
erupt 671.13
debouch 908.25
vomit 908.26
disgrace
n humiliation 137.2
disparagement 512.1
abomination 638.2
iniquity 654.3
scandal 661.5
v humiliate 137.4
disparage 512.8
dishonor 661.8
disgraceful
wrong 638.3
wicked 654.16
shameful 661.11
disgruntled
discontented 108.7
disapproving 510.21

disguise
n costume 5.9
veil 346.2
sham 354.3
cover 356.11
dissimilarity 786.1
v conceal 346.6
misrepresent 350.3
falsify 354.15
dissimilate 786.3
disgust
n hostility 99.2
v repel 64.4
offend 98.11
displeases 99.6
disgusted
pleasureless 96.20
hating 103.7
satiated 993.6
disgusting filthy 80.23
offensive 98.18
horrid 98.19
base 661.12
terrible 999.9
dish
n serving 8.10
tableware 8.12
culinary preparation
10.7
cooking 11.1
baseball 745.1
basketball game 747.3
beauty 1015.9
v ladle 176.17
be concave 284.12
hollow 284.13
do for 395.11
play 747.4
thwart 1011.15
dishabille 5.20
disharmony
discord 61.1
disaccord 456.1
disagreement 788.1
disorder 809.1
dishearten
dissatisfy 108.5
sadden 112.18
daunt 127.18
prevent 1011.14
dishevel
disorder 809.9
disarrange 810.2
dishonest
falsehearted 354.30
insincere 354.31
untruthful 354.33
dishonorable 645.16
dishonesty
falseheartedness 354.4
untruthfulness 354.8
fraud 356.8
improbity 645.1
dishonor
n disrespect 156.1
nonpayment 625.1
improbity 645.1
disrepute 661.1
v offend 156.5
not pay 625.6
disgrace 661.8
desecrate 694.4

dish out
ladle 176.17
parcel out 477.8
give 478.12
administer 643.6
dishpan 79.12
dish up
ladle 176.17
provide 385.7
propose 439.5
dishwasher
washbasin 79.12
washer 79.15
dishwater
symbol of weakness
16.7
offal 80.9
refuse 391.4
dishy delightful 97.8
desirable 100.30
alluring 377.8
beautiful 1015.21
disillusion
n disapproval 510.1
disillusionment 976.1
v disappoint 132.2
disillude 976.2
disincentive 379.2
disinclination
dislike 99.1
refusal 325.1
disinfect 79.24
disinfectant
n cure 86.21
poison 1000.3
adj antiseptic 86.43
disingenuous
insincere 354.31
deceitful 645.18
sophistical 935.10
disinherit 480.23
disintegrate
weaken 16.9
strike dead 308.17
decay 393.22
break 393.23
demolish 395.17
be destroyed 395.22
disband 770.8
come apart 801.9
decompose 805.3
lapse into disorder
809.8
be brittle 1048.3
pulverize 1049.9
powder 1049.9
disintegration
frailty 16.2
decay 393.6
destruction 395.1
disbandment 770.3
disruption 801.3
coming-apart 805
decomposition 805.1
disorder 809.1
pulverization 1049.4
disinterest
n apathy 94.4
unconcern 102.2
impartiality 649.4
unselfishness 652.1
incuriosity 981.1

v disincline 379.4
disinterested
  apathetic 94.13
  unconcerned 102.7
  impartial 649.10
  unselfish 652.5
  unprejudiced 978.12
  incurious 981.3
disinvolve
  extricate 431.7
  disintricate 797.5
  disembarrass 1013.9
disjoin
  differentiate 779.6
  separate 801.8
  loosen 803.3
  disintegrate 805.3
  discontinue 812.3
disjointed
  dislocated 160.9
  separated 801.21
disjunction
  elimination 772.2
  relation 774.1
  unrelatedness 775.1
  differentiation 779.4
  separation 801.1
  noncohesion 803.1
  disintegration 805.1
  disorder 809.1
  discontinuity 812.1
disk circle 280.2
  lamina 296.2
  recording media
    549.10
  rotator 914.4
  magnetic disk 1041.6
diskette
  recording media
    549.10
  disk 1041.6
disk jockey 1033.23
dislike
  n unpleasure 96.1
  distaste 99.1
  hate 103.1
  v mislike 99.3
  have it in for 103.6
dislocate
  displace 160.5
  disjoint 801.16
  disarrange 810.2
dislocation
  displacement 160.1
  separation 801.1
  noncohesion 803.1
  disarrangement 810.1
dislodge
  unplace 160.6
  remove 176.11
  extricate 431.7
  evict 908.15
disloyal
  apostate 363.11
  unfaithful 645.20
dismal gray 39.4
  distressing 98.20
  gloomy 112.24
  dull 117.6
  hopeless 125.12
  pessimistic 125.16
  funereal 309.22

dismantle
  demolish 395.17
  disassemble 801.15
dismay
  n fear 127.1
  v distress 98.14
  disconcert 127.19
  bewilder 970.12
dismayed
  frightened 127.25
  cowardly 491.10
  bewildered 970.24
dismember
  torture 604.16
  tear apart 801.14
  loosen 803.3
dismiss slight 157.6
  reject 372.2
  release 431.5
  depose 447.4
  acquit 601.4
  disband 770.8
  repulse 907.3
  send off 908.18
  discharge 908.19
  refute 957.5
  dismiss from one's
    thoughts 983.4
dismissal snub 157.2
  rejection 372.1
  release 431.2
  deposal 447.2
  acquittal 601.1
  disbandment 770.3
  repulse 907.2
  discharge 908.5
dismount
  dislodge 160.6
  get down 194.7
  disassemble 801.15
disobedience
  refusal 325.1
  noncompliance 327
  nonobedience 327.1
  lawlessness 418.1
  refusal 442.1
disoblige offend 156.5
  inconvenience 995.4
disorder
  n disease 85.1
  formlessness 263.1
  misbehavior 322.1
  anarchy 418.2
  nonuniformity 781.1
  noncohesion 803.1
  disarrangement 809
  disorderliness 809.1
  disarrangement 810.1
  change 851.1
  agitation 916.1
  vagueness 970.4
  confusion 984.3
  v afflict 85.49
  deform 263.3
  disorganize 809.9
  disarrange 810.2
disorganization
  decay 393.6
  destruction 395.1
  anarchy 418.2
  disbandment 770.3
  disintegration 805.1

  disorder 809.1
  disarrangement 810.1
  confusion 984.3
disorientation
  orientation 161.4
  insanity 925.1
  confusion 984.3
disoriented
  insane 925.26
  bewildered 970.24
  confused 984.12
disown
  n recant 363.8
  v deny 335.4
  reject 372.2
  dispossess 480.23
disparage
  disrespect 156.4
  disdain 157.3
  subtract 255.9
  deprecate 510.12
  depreciate 512.8
  stigmatize 661.9
  underestimate 949.2
disparaging
  disrespectful 156.7
  condemnatory 510.22
  derogatory 512.13
disparate
  different 779.7
  dissimilar 786.4
  unequal 790.4
disparity dissent 333.1
  lack of agreement
    456.2
  difference 779.1
  dissimilarity 786.1
  disagreement 788.1
  inequality 790.1
dispassion
  unfeeling 94.1
  apathy 94.4
  unconcern 102.2
  inexcitability 106.1
  impartiality 649.4
  moderation 670.1
dispatch
  n velocity 174.1
  killing 308.1
  performance 328.2
  quickness 330.3
  accomplishment
    407.1
  information 551.1
  message 552.4
  letter 553.2
  promptness 844.3
  v devour 8.22
  send 176.15
  kill 308.12
  perform 328.9
  hasten 401.4
  accomplish 407.4
  mail 553.12
dispel disappear 34.2
  dissipate 770.5
  part company 801.19
  do away with 908.21
dispensable
  apportioned 477.12
  justifiable 600.14
  superfluous 992.17

  insignificant 997.17
dispensary
  drugstore 86.36
  hospital room 197.25
dispensation
  permission 443.1
  relinquishment 475.1
  distribution 477.2
  administration 573.3
  government 612.1
  privilege 642.2
  divine function 677.14
  dispersion 770.1
dispense
  exempt 430.14
  permit 443.9
  parcel out 477.8
  give 478.12
  vend 734.9
  disperse 770.4
dispense with
  not use 390.5
  exempt 430.14
  relinquish 475.3
disperse
  disappear 34.2
  deflect 164.5
  radiate 171.6
  spread 259.6
  rarefy 299.3
  parcel out 477.8
  scatter 770.4
  disband 770.8
  shatter 801.13
  part company 801.19
  loosen 803.3
dispersion
  deflection 164.2
  radiation 171.2
  expansion 259.1
  rarefaction 299.2
  distribution 477.2
  scattering 770.1
  disbandment 770.3
  noncohesion 803.1
dispirited
  dejected 112.22
  weary 118.11
displace
  dislocate 160.5
  remove 176.11
  depose 447.4
  come after 834.3
  substitute for 861.5
  dismiss 908.19
displaced person
  stateless person 160.4
  migrant 178.5
  fugitive 368.5
  outcast 586.4
display
  n appearance 33.2
  spectacle 33.7
  externalization 206.4
  front 216.1
  demonstration 348.2
  publication 352.1
  show 501.4
  signal 1035.11
  v externalize 206.5
  manifest 348.5
  make public 352.11

flaunt 501.17
signify 517.17
evidence 956.8
displeased averse 99.8
discontented 108.7
disapproving 510.21
displeasing
unsavory 64.5
unpleasant 98.17
unlikable 99.7
unsatisfactory 108.9
displeasure
unpleasure 96.1
unpleasantness 98.1
dislike 99.1
unhappiness 112.2
resentment 152.1
disapproval 510.1
disposal
placement 159.6
discard 390.3
relinquishment 475.1
distribution 477.2
administration 573.3
transfer 629.1
elimination 772.2
order 806.1
arrangement 807.1
dispose locate 159.11
take direction 161.7
induce 375.22
parcel out 477.8
order 806.4
distribute 807.9
influence 893.7
exercise influence
893.8
disposed
adj willing 324.5
arranged 807.14
dispositioned 977.8
prep inclined to 895.6
dispose of devour 8.22
kill 308.12
perform 328.9
discard 390.7
put an end to 395.12
accomplish 407.4
relinquish 475.3
give away 478.21
eliminate 772.5
end 819.5
refute 957.5
disposition
placement 159.6
will 323.1
plan 381.1
governance 417.5
battle array 458.3
relinquishment 475.1
distribution 477.2
administration 573.3
government 612.1
transfer 629.1
nature 766.4
elimination 772.2
order 806.1
arrangement 807.1
tendency 895.1
character 977.3
dispossess
foreclose 480.23

evict 908.15
dispossession
loss 473.1
reclaiming 480.7
eviction 908.2
disproportion
n distortion 265.1
inconsistency 788.2
inequality 790.1
disorder 809.1
v deform 265.7
unequalize 790.2
disproportionate
exaggerated 355.4
disagreeing 788.6
inconsistent 788.8
unequal 790.4
unordered 809.12
disprove deny 335.4
invalidate 957.4
disputable 970.17
disputatious
contentious 110.26
resistant 453.5
partisan 456.17
argumentative 934.19
dispute
n resistance 453.1
quarrel 456.5
contention 457.1
argumentation 934.4
questioning 937.12
v object 333.5
deny 335.4
offer resistance 453.3
quarrel 456.11
contest 457.21
argue 934.16
doubt 954.6
disqualification
inability 19.2
unpreparedness 406.1
disqualify
invalidate 19.11
make impossible
966.6
disquiet
n unpleasure 96.1
trepidation 105.5
anxiety 126.1
fearfulness 127.5
nervousness 128.1
impatience 135.1
agitation 916.1
v give no pleasure
96.12
distress 96.16
excite 105.14
concern 126.4
frighten 127.15
agitate 916.10
disquisition
treatise 556.1
lesson 568.7
disregard
n unconcern 102.2
forgiveness 148.1
snub 157.2
neglect 340.1
rejection 372.1
nonobservance 435.1
defiance 454.1

inattention 983.1
v take 134.8
condone 148.4
slight 157.6
disobey 327.6
neglect 340.6
reject 372.2
lose sight of 435.3
flout 454.4
allow for 958.5
keep an open mind
978.7
be inattentive
983.2
disrepair
uselessness 391.1
impairment 393.1
disreputable
n bad person 660.1
adj discreditable
661.10
disrepute 661.1
disrespect
n impudence 142.2
irreverence 156
low esteem 156.1
disobedience 327.1
discourteousness
505.2
disapproval 510.1
v not respect 156.4
disrobe 6.7
disrupt shatter 801.13
thwart 1011.15
disruption
misbehavior 322.1
destruction 395.1
anarchy 418.2
falling-out 456.4
dissolution 801.3
disorder 809.1
dissatisfaction
unpleasure 96.1
discontent 108.1
disappointment 132.1
resentment 152.1
dissent 333.1
disapproval 510.1
dissatisfied
discontented 108.7
disappointed 132.5
disapproving 510.21
dissect analyze 800.6
separate 801.17
dissemblance sham
354.3
dissimilarity 786.1
dissemble conceal 346.6
sham 354.20
dissembler
imitator 336.4
deceiver 357.1
pietist 693.3
disseminate
transfer 176.10
communicate 343.7
publish 352.10
disperse 770.4
plant 1067.18
dissension
dissent 333.1
hostility 451.2

dissent 456.3
disagreement 788.1
dissent
n complaint 115.4
dissension 325.1
quarrel 333
dissidence 333.1
refusal 442.1
resistance 453.4
dissension 456.3
disapproval 510.1
Protestantism 675.10
difference 779.1
disagreement 788.1
nonconformity 867.1
counteraction 899.1
v dissent from 333.4
refuse 442.3
offer resistance 453.3
diversify 781.2
disagree 788.5
not conform 867.4
counteract 899.6
dissertation 556.1
disservice
bad deed 144.13
injustice 650.4
dissident
n dissenter 333.3
oppositionist 452.3
adj dissenting 333.6
disaccordant 456.15
disagreeing 788.6
nonconforming 867.5
counteractive 899.8
dissimilar
different 779.7
unsimilar 786.4
incomparable 942.9
dissimilitude 786.1
dissimulate 354.20
dissimulator
imitator 336.4
deceiver 357.1
pietist 693.3
dissipate
disappear 34.2
spend 387.13
waste 473.5
go to waste 473.6
squander 486.3
be promiscuous
665.19
plunge into
dissipation 669.6
dispel 770.5
dissociate
separate 801.8
chemical terms 805.4
dissociated 775.6
dissociate oneself from
510.10
dissoluble
separable 801.26
liquefiable 1062.9
dissolute
corrupt 654.14
profligate 665.25
licentious 669.8
dissolution
disappearance 34.1
decrement 252.3

death 307.1
decay 393.6
destruction 395.1
disbandment 770.3
disruption 801.3
noncohesion 803.1
disintegration 805.1
liquefaction 1062.1

dissolvable
separable 801.26
liquefiable 1062.9

dissolve
n motion-picture
   editing 706.5
v disappear 34.2
destroy 395.10
cease to exist 761.6
dissipate 770.5
disband 770.8
disintegrate 805.3
flit 827.6
liquefy 1062.5

dissonant
discordant 61.4
different 779.7
disagreeing 788.6

dissuade 379.3

distaff
n woman 77.5
axle 914.5
adj feminine 77.13

distance
n station 159.2
setting 209.2
farness 261
remoteness 261.1
length 267.1
extent 300.3
reticence 344.3
aloofness 583.2
round 751.3
v outdistance 249.10

distant faint 52.16
aloof 141.12
distal 261.8
reticent 344.10
aloof 583.6
farfetched 775.8
incurious 981.3

distaste dislike 99.1
refusal 325.1
disapproval 510.1

distasteful
unsavory 64.5
unpleasant 98.17
unlikable 99.7

distemper
n color 35.8
illness 85.1
disease 85.40
v color 35.13
annoy 96.13

distended
corpulent 257.18
dilated 259.13
bulging 283.15
overfull 992.20

distension
expanding 259.2
swelling 283.4
overextension 992.7
stretching 1046.2

distich poetry 720.9
two 872.2
maxim 973.1

distill refine 79.22
brew 88.30
leak 190.14
extraction 192.16
trickle 238.18
simplify 797.4
boil 1019.20
vaporize 1065.8

distillation
refinement 79.4
leakage 190.5
take out 192.7
extract 192.8
essential content
   196.5
trickle 238.7
simplification 797.2
product 892.3
burning 1019.5
thickening 1043.4
vaporization 1065.5

distinct plain 31.7
audible 50.16
manifest 348.8
clear 521.11
different 779.7
separate 801.20
particular 864.12

distinction glory 247.2
elegance 533.1
nobility 608.2
honor 646.1
mark 662.5
difference 779.1
margin 779.2
differentiation 779.4
characterization 864.8
comparison 942.1
contradistinction
   943.3
notability 996.2

distinctive
audible 50.16
typical 349.15
differentiative 779.9
classificational 808.7
characteristic 864.13
discriminating 943.7

distinguish see 27.12
honor 662.12
differentiate 779.6
characterize 864.10
focus on 936.3
detect 940.5
discriminate 943.4
recognize 988.12

distinguished
eminent 247.9
superior 249.12
honored 646.9
distingué 662.16
different 779.7
particular 864.12
characteristic 864.13
notable 996.19

distort deflect 164.5
deform 263.3
contort 265.5
misinterpret 342.2

misrepresent 350.3
falsify 354.15
corrupt 393.12
reason speciously
   935.8
prejudice 979.9
blemish 1003.4

distortion
audio distortion 50.13
deflection 164.2
twistedness 265
torsion 265.1
misinterpretation
   342.1
misrepresentation
   350.1
bad likeness 350.2
deliberate falsehood
   354.9
sophistry 935.1
error 974.1
blemish 1003.1

distract
disincline 379.4
discompose 810.4
madden 925.24
divert 984.6

distracted
frenzied 105.25
bewildered 970.24
inattentive 983.6
distraught 984.10

distraught
insane 925.26
bewildered 970.24
distracted 984.10

distress
n pain 26.1
chagrin 96.4
unpleasantness 96.5
affliction 96.8
distressfulness 98.5
anxiety 126.1
attachment 480.5
fine 603.3
v pain 26.7
afflict 96.16
dismay 98.14
concern 126.4
work evil 999.6
trouble 1012.13

distribute
publish 352.10
parcel out 477.8
give 478.12
deliver 478.13
disperse 770.4
separate 792.6
dispose 807.9

distributor
intermediary 213.4
merchant 730.2

district
n location 159.1
area 231.1
region 231.5
v apportion 801.18

distrust
n suspiciousness
   153.2
wariness 494.2
doubt 954.2

v suffer pangs of
   jealousy 153.3
doubt 954.6

disturb
annoy 96.13
distress 96.16
mortify 98.13
excite 105.14
concern 126.4
disorder 809.9
discompose 810.4
agitate 916.10
bewilder 970.12
confuse 984.7
trouble 1012.13

disturbed
neurotic 92.38
annoyed 96.21
distressed 96.22
excited 105.23
anxious 126.7
disorderly 809.13
agitated 916.16
psychotic 925.28
bewildered 970.24
confused 984.12

disunity
falling-out 456.4
disagreement 788.1

ditch
n crack 224.2
channel 239.1
trench 290.2
entrenchment 460.5
lawn bowling 750.3
barrier 1011.5
v land 184.43
cleave 224.4
furrow 290.3
evade 368.7
discard 390.7

dither
n tizzy 105.6
shake 916.3
v vacillate 362.8
chatter 540.5
be stupid 921.12
hang in doubt 970.10
freeze 1022.9

ditto
n the same 777.3
duplicate 784.3
equal 789.4
repeat 848.5
v concur 332.9
imitate 336.5
reproduce 777.6
copy 784.8
equal 789.5
repeat 848.7
duplicate 873.3
adv identically 777.9
again 848.17

ditty 708.14

ditzy inconstant 853.7
superficial 921.20
foolish 922.9
inattentive 983.6
scatterbrained 984.16

diuretic
n cleanser 79.17
laxative 86.17

adj cleansing 79.28
cathartic 86.48
diurnal 849.8
diva lead 707.6
singer 710.13
divaricate
v deviate 164.3
diverge 171.5
fork 171.7
open 292.11
diversify 781.2
adj diverging 171.8
nonuniform 781.3
dive
n bar 88.20
submarines 182.8
maneuvers 184.13
tumble 194.3
disapproved place
228.28
decline 252.2
plunge 367.1
cheapening 633.4
brothel 665.9
casino 759.19
v submarines 182.47
swim 182.56
nose-dive 184.41
decrease 252.6
deepen 275.8
plunge 367.6
cheapen 633.6
dive into
rush into 401.7
set to work 725.15
diverge deviate 164.3
deflect 164.5
divaricate 171.5
oblique 204.9
fall out 456.10
disperse 770.4
differ 779.5
diversify 781.2
part company 801.19
be changed 851.6
divergence
deviation 164.1
divarication 171.1
obliquity 204.1
distance 261.1
falling-out 456.4
dispersion 770.1
difference 779.1
nonuniformity 781.1
dissimilarity 786.1
disagreement 788.1
change 851.1
abnormality 869.1
eccentricity 926.1
diverse different 779.7
diversified 782.4
dissimilar 786.4
diversify
differentiate 779.6
diverge 781.2
vary 782.2
be changed 851.6
change 851.7
diversion
deviation 164.1
misuse 389.1
attack 459.1

amusement 743.1
change 851.1
distraction 984.1
diversity dissent 333.1
difference 779.1
nonuniformity 781.1
multiformity 782.1
dissimilarity 786.1
disagreement 788.1
change 851.1
divert deflect 164.5
disincline 379.4
misuse 389.4
amuse 743.21
distract 984.6
divest strip 6.5
take from 480.21
take 480.24
divested stripped 6.12
bereft 473.8
divestment
unclothing 6.1
loss 473.1
deprivation 480.6
investment 729.3
disassembly 801.6
divide
n watershed 272.5
v diverge 171.5
bound 211.8
partition 213.8
quantify 244.4
open 292.11
measure 300.10
vote 371.18
fall out 456.10
sow dissension 456.14
apportion 477.6
segregate 772.6
differentiate 779.6
part 792.6
analyze 800.6
separate 801.8
apportion 801.18
arrange 807.11
classify 808.6
bisect 874.4
discriminate 943.4
calculate 1016.17
dividend portion 477.5
royalty 624.7
receipts 627.1
regular dividend
738.7
surplus 992.5
divination
sorcery 689.10
augury 690.1
the future 838.1
foresight 960.1
divining 961.2
divine
n theologian 676.3
clergyman 699.2
v augur 133.12
solve 939.2
suppose 950.10
predict 961.9
adj blissful 97.9
theological 676.4
heavenly 677.17
godlike 678.16

sacred 685.7
superb 998.15
gorgeous 1015.20
divinity theology 676.1
deity 677.1
god 678.2
sanctity 685.1
division
divergence 171.1
partition 213.5
region 231.1
vote 371.6
disagreement 456.2
falling-out 456.4
military unit 461.22
navy 461.27
apportionment 477.1
class 607.1
legislative procedure
613.6
party 617.4
branch 617.10
sect 675.3
passage 708.24
ornament 709.18
boxer 754.2
company 769.3
exclusiveness 772.3
differentiation 779.4
part 792.1
analysis 800.1
separation 801.1
classification 808.1
class 808.2
bisection 874.1
distinction 943.3
notation 1016.2
divorce
n dissolution of
marriage 566
divorcement 566.1
separation 801.1
v separate 566.5
sever 801.8
divot wig 3.14
turf 310.6
divulge
manifest 348.5
divulgate 351.5
make public 352.11
divvy
n apportionment
477.1
v apportion 477.6
separate 801.18
Dixie 231.7
dizzy
v make one's head
swim 984.8
adj weak 16.12
intoxicated 88.31
inconstant 853.7
muddleheaded 921.18
superficial 921.20
giddy 922.8
foolish 922.9
delirious 925.31
giddy 984.15
scatterbrained 984.16
DJ 1033.23
DNA
genetic material 305.9

heredity 560.6
DNA double helix
305.9
DNA print 517.11
do
n party 582.12
festival 743.4
assembly 769.2
v cook 11.4
be satisfactory 107.6
travel 177.19
traverse 177.20
attend 221.8
average 246.2
behave 321.4
effect 328.6
practice 328.8
imitate 336.5
impersonate 349.12
deceive 356.19
avail 387.17
accomplish 407.4
perform 434.3
play 708.39
busy oneself with
724.11
suit 787.8
cause 885.10
perform 891.11
solve 939.2
suffice 990.4
inter please 440.20
do all right by oneself
make good 409.10
grow rich 618.10
be prosperous 1009.9
do a number on
deceive 356.19
defame 512.9
do away with
kill 308.12
commit suicide
308.21
put an end to 395.12
repeal 445.2
exterminate 908.21
do business
cooperate 450.3
work 724.12
trade 731.14
docile willing 324.5
tractable 433.13
teachable 570.18
dock
n hangar 184.24
tail 217.6
storehouse 386.6
courthouse 595.6
stage 704.16
harbor 1008.6
v anchor 182.15
land 186.8
excise 255.10
shorten 268.6
docket
n label 517.13
memorandum 549.4
document 549.5
record book 549.11
roll 870.6
schedule 964.3
v record 549.15

keep accounts 628.8
schedule 964.6
doctor
  n physician 90.4
  mender 396.10
  degree 648.6
  dramatist 704.22
  professional 726.4
  wise man 920.1
  v practice medicine
    90.14
  treat 91.24
  undergo treatment
    91.29
  tamper with 354.16
  repair 396.14
  aid 449.11
  adulterate 796.12
doctorate 648.6
doctrinaire
  n theorist 950.7
  dogmatist 969.7
  bigot 979.5
  adj dogmatic 969.22
  discriminatory 979.12
doctrine religion 675.1
  dogma 676.2
  a belief 952.2
document
  n writing 547.10
  official document
    549.5
  v itemize 765.6
  confirm 956.11
  cite 956.13
documentary
  n television broadcast
    1034.2
  adj documentational
    549.18
  evidential 956.16
  true 972.13
documentation
  record 549.1
  evidence 956.1
  confirmation 956.4
doddering
  unsteady 16.16
  stricken in years
    303.18
  senile 921.23
dodge
  n trick 356.6
  fraud 356.8
  avoidance 368.1
  stratagem 415.3
  retreat 902.3
  quibble 935.4
  expedient 994.2
  v avoid 157.7
  deviate 164.6
  slight 340.8
  prevaricate 344.7
  duck 368.8
  shirk 368.9
  live by one's wits
    415.9
  pull back 902.7
  go roundabout 913.4
  quibble 935.9
doe
  female animal 77.9

hoofed animal 311.5
goat 311.8
hare 311.24
dog
  n member 2.7
  male animal 76.8
  foot 199.5
  horse 311.12
  canine 311.17
  telephone 347.4
  beast 660.7
  eyesore 1014.4
  v annoy 96.13
  make anxious 126.5
  follow 166.3
  pursue 382.8
  hunt 382.9
  obstruct 1011.12
dog days summer 313.3
  hot weather 1018.7
dog-eared eared 48.15
  folded 291.7
  worn 393.31
dog-eat-dog 146.3
dogged
  tormented 96.24
  worried 126.8
  persevering 360.8
  obstinate 361.8
doggerel
  n bad poetry 720.3
  adj burlesque 508.14
  inelegant 534.2
doghouse
  kennel 228.21
  small space 258.3
dog in the manger
  self-seeker 651.3
  spoilsport 1011.9
dog-in-the-manger
  108.7
dog it shirk 368.9
  flee 368.11
dogma
  doctrine 676.2
  a belief 952.2
dogmatic
  obstinate 361.8
  unpersuadable 361.13
  strict 687.8
  belief 952.21
  doctrinal 952.27
  positive 969.22
  discriminatory 979.12
do good
  do a favor 143.12
  aid 449.11
  profit 998.10
dog tag 517.11
dog-tired 21.10
doohickey 1050.5
do in fatigue 21.4
  get tired 21.6
  kill 308.13
  do for 395.11
  put an end to 395.12
  defeat 412.9
do it yourself 891.18
do justice to
  feast 8.24
  savor 63.5
  enjoy 95.12

observe 434.2
justify 600.9
do one's duty 641.10
be just 649.6
doldrums
  blues 112.6
  calm 173.5
  prevailing wind
    318.10
dole
  n modicum 248.2
  distribution 477.2
  portion 477.5
  donation 478.6
  subsidy 478.8
  part 792.1
  pittance 991.5
  v parcel out 477.8
  give 478.12
the dole 143.5
doleful
  sorrowful 112.26
  pitiful 145.8
doll woman 77.6
  ladylove 104.15
  miniature 258.6
  gal 302.7
  figure 349.6
  endearment term
    562.6
  good person 659.2
  toy 743.16
  beauty 1015.9
dollar currency 728.7
  money 728.8
dollars to doughnuts
  n good chance 971.8
  adv probably 967.8
dollhouse
  small space 258.3
  toy 743.16
dollop 792.3
doll up dress up 5.41
  ornament 498.8
  beautify 1015.15
dolorous
  distressing 98.20
  sorrowful 112.26
dolphin 311.30
dolt bungler 414.8
  stupid person 923.2
domain
  sphere 231.2
  country 232.1
  real estate 471.6
  occupation 724.4
  hierarchy 808.4
  science 927.10
dome
  n hall 197.4
  head 198.6
  highlands 237.1
  mountain 237.6
  tower 272.6
  arch 279.4
  football 746.1
  v curve 279.6
  top 295.21
domestic
  n servant 577.2
  adj residential 228.32
  recluse 584.10

domesticate
  settle 159.17
  accustom 373.10
  tame 432.11
domicile
  n abode 228.1
  v inhabit 225.7
  house 225.10
dominance
  dominion 417.6
  influence 893.1
dominant
  n note 709.14
  key 709.15
  adj chief 249.14
  victorious 411.7
  authoritative 417.15
  governing 612.18
  prevalent 863.12
  influential 893.14
  paramount 996.24
dominate show 31.4
  rise above 272.11
  subjugate 432.8
  predominate 612.15
  prevail 863.10
  have influence over
    893.11
domineering
  n arrogance 141.1
  authoritativeness
    417.3
  despotism 612.10
  adj arrogant 141.9
  imperious 417.16
dominion
  sphere 231.2
  country 232.1
  supremacy 249.3
  governance 417.5
  dominance 417.6
  ownership 469.2
  control 612.2
  precedence 813.1
domino effect
  immediate cause
    885.3
  aftereffect 886.3
  vicissitudes 971.5
don
  n man 76.7
  teacher 571.1
  v put on 5.42
donate provide 385.7
  give 478.12
done
  adj well-done 11.7
  tired 21.8
  worn-out 393.36
  completed 407.11
  ended 819.8
  produced 891.17
  inter so be it 332.20
done deal act 328.3
  accomplishment
    407.1
done for dead 307.30
  dying 307.33
  spoiled 393.29
  ruined 395.29
  defeated 412.14
  no more 761.11

ended 819.9
done with
disused 390.10
completed 407.11
ended 819.8
Don Juan
beau 104.13
deceiver 357.1
tempter 377.4
philanderer 562.12
libertine 665.10
donkey ass 311.16
obstinate person
361.6
stupid person 923.2
donnybrook noise 53.4
quarrel 456.5
commotion 809.4
donor provider 385.6
giver 478.11
do-nothing
passive 329.6
indolent 331.19
Don Quixote
knight 608.5
visionary 985.13
doodle
n drawing 712.13
fool 923.1
v waste time 331.13
dally 331.14
scribble 547.20
blow a horn 708.42
portray 712.19
doom
n death 307.1
destruction 395.2
condemnation 602.1
end 819.1
destiny 838.2
doomsday 838.3
verdict 945.5
fate 963.2
v condemn 602.3
damn 682.6
pass judgment 945.13
destine 963.7
work evil 999.6
do one's bit
lay down one's life for
one's country 307.25
be willing 324.3
do one's duty 641.10
do one's duty feast 8.24
perform 434.3
perform one's duty
641.10
do one's heart good
please 95.5
gratify 95.7
make proud 136.6
do one's part
be willing 324.3
do 328.6
share 476.6
do one's duty 641.10
door entrance 189.5
porch 189.6
outlet 190.9
doorway 292.6
doormat wig 3.14
weakling 16.6

dupe 358.2
doorstep 193.5
doorway porch 189.6
door 292.6
do out of cheat 356.18
take from 480.21
do over
reproduce 78.7
repeat 848.7
convert 857.11
dope
n anesthetic 25.3
drug 87.2
film 714.10
contraband 732.3
stupid person 923.2
fuel 1020.1
v put to sleep 22.20
deaden 25.4
medicate 91.25
relieve 120.5
solve 939.2
predict 961.9
the dope
information 551.1
the facts 760.4
dopey inert 173.14
languid 331.20
dull 921.16
foolish 922.9
dazed 984.14
Doppelgänger
the same 777.3
double 987.3
do right by 143.9
dormant
asleep 22.22
inert 173.14
passive 329.6
languid 331.20
latent 519.5
dormitory
bedroom 197.7
inn 228.15
dorsal 217.10
DOS 1041.12
dose
n venereal disease
85.18
draft 86.6
hit 87.19
amount 244.2
portion 792.5
radiation physics
1036.7
v medicate 91.25
administer 643.6
**a dose of one's own
medicine** 506.2
dossier 549.5
dot
n spottiness 47.3
modicum 248.2
minute 258.7
endowment 478.9
mark 517.5
notation 709.12
v variegate 47.7
interspace 224.3
mark 517.19
disperse 770.4
sprinkle 770.6

dotage old age 303.5
senility 921.10
credulity 953.1
dote on 104.19
do the honors
extend courtesy
504.12
entertain 585.8
introduce 587.14
do the right thing
behave oneself 321.5
do one's duty 641.10
be good 653.5
do the right thing by
observe 434.2
be just 649.6
do the trick do 328.6
avail 387.17
accomplish 407.4
succeed with 409.11
suit 787.8
suffice 990.4
expedite one's affair
994.3
do time
be imprisoned 429.18
take one's turn 824.5
dotty
spotted 47.13
crazy 925.27
eccentric 926.5
double
n deviation 164.1
fold 291.1
image 349.5
game 745.3
string 750.2
the same 777.3
duplicate 784.3
substitute 861.2
etheric double 987.3
v turn back 163.8
intensify 251.5
fold 291.5
play 745.5
copy 784.8
seek the middle
818.3
repeat 848.7
double 872.5
duplicate 873.3
adj falsehearted
354.30
treacherous 645.21
two 872.6
doubled 873.4
double agent
traitor 357.10
secret agent 576.9
double-check
n ensuring 969.8
v verify 969.12
check 1016.20
double-cross
deceive 356.14
betray 645.14
double-dealing
n falseheartedness
354.4
treachery 645.6
adj falsehearted
354.30

treacherous 645.21
double-edged
acrimonious 17.14
sharp 285.8
double entendre
joke 489.6
ambiguity 539.1
equivocation 539.2
double meaning 539.1
double or nothing
759.3
doubles 748.1
double standard 354.4
doublet root 526.2
two 872.2
double take
sequel 816.1
delay 845.2
double-talk
n nonsense 520.2
speech sound 524.13
specious argument
935.3
v quibble 935.9
double vision 28.1
doubt
n apprehension 127.4
suspiciousness 153.2
agnosticism 695.6
doubtfulness 954.2
uncertainty 970.2
v suffer pangs of
jealousy 153.3
disbelieve 695.14
be doubtful 954.6
be uncertain 970.9
doubtful
dishonest 645.16
agnostic 695.20
doubting 954.9
unbelievable 954.10
improbable 968.3
iffy 970.17
unsafe 1005.11
doubting Thomas
agnostic 695.12
doubter 954.4
doubtless
adj belief 952.21
undoubted 969.16
adv probably 967.8
unquestionably
969.25
douche
n washing 79.5
bath 79.8
sprinkler 1063.8
v wash 79.19
moisten 1063.12
soak 1063.13
dough soldier 461.7
money 728.2
softness 1045.4
semiliquid 1060.5
doughboy 461.7
doughnut 10.42
doughty strong 15.15
courageous 492.17
doughy pasty 1045.12
viscous 1060.12
pulpy 1061.6
dour sullen 110.24

harsh 144.24
unyielding 361.9
strict 425.6
firm 425.7
douse take off 6.6
submerge 367.7
fight fire 1021.7
dove bird 311.28
simple soul 416.3
pacifist 464.6
innocent 657.4
dovecote 228.23
dovetail
  n joint 799.4
  v interact 776.6
agree 787.6
hook 799.8
dowager woman 77.5
old woman 304.3
widow 566.4
mistress 575.2
aristocrat 607.4
dowdiness 809.6
dowdy
  n pastry 10.39
  adj shabby 393.32
dowel 283.3
do well 1009.7
dower
  n talent 413.4
endowment 478.9
  v endow 478.17
  adj endowed 478.26
do without
not use 390.5
relinquish 475.3
abstain 668.7
Dow-Jones Industrial
  Average 737.1
down
  n beard 3.8
fluff 3.19
descent 194.1
plain 236.1
hill 237.4
smoothness 294.3
lightness 298.2
game 746.3
reverse 1010.3
softness 1045.4
  v devour 8.22
tipple 88.24
take 134.8
descend 194.5
thin 270.12
change 851.7
fell 912.5
  adj ill 85.55
laid up 85.58
dejected 112.22
motionless 173.13
descending 194.11
lower 274.8
defeated 412.14
recorded 549.17
  adv downward 194.13
cash 624.25
Down's syndrome
  921.9
down-and-out
  n poor man 619.4
  adj ruined 395.28

destitute 619.9
ended 819.9
down-at-the-heel
shabby 393.32
indigent 619.8
slovenly 809.15
downbeat
  n beat 709.26
round 849.3
  adj depressing 112.30
pessimistic 125.16
downcast
  n downthrow 912.2
  adj dejected 112.22
downturned 194.12
depressed 912.12
downer annoyance 96.2
dejection 112.3
adversity 1010.1
downers 87.4
downfall descent 194.1
rainstorm 316.2
fall 395.3
collapse 410.3
defeat 412.1
downthrow 912.2
downgrade
  n descent 194.1
declivity 204.5
  v reduce 252.7
demote 447.3
  adj sloping downward
    204.16
  adv down 194.13
slantingly 204.23
downhearted 112.22
downhill
  n declivity 204.5
  adj descending 194.11
sloping downward
  204.16
  adv down 194.13
slantingly 204.23
down-home
comfortable 121.11
informal 581.3
simple 797.6
down in the dumps
  112.22
download 1041.18
down on averse 99.8
disapproving 510.21
down on one's luck
  1010.14
down pat 927.26
down payment 624.1
downplay
minimize 252.9
moderate 670.6
attach little
  importance to 997.12
downpour
descent 194.1
flow 238.4
rainstorm 316.2
downthrow 912.2
downright
  adj vertical 200.11
outright 247.12
candid 644.17
thorough 793.10
unqualified 959.2

  adv down 194.13
extremely 247.22
no ifs, ands, or buts
  959.3
the downside
adversity 1010.1
trouble 1012.3
downsize 252.7
downstage
  n stage 704.16
  adv on the stage
    704.36
downstairs
down 194.13
below 274.10
down the drain
lost 473.7
wasted 486.9
no more 761.11
down the hatch! 88.38
down the tube
ruined 395.29
lost 473.7
no more 761.11
downtime respite 20.2
leisure 402.1
interim 825.1
delay 845.2
down-to-earth 986.6
downtown
  n city district 230.6
  adj urban 230.11
  adv down 194.13
downtrodden 432.16
downturn
descent 194.1
decline 252.2
deterioration 393.3
business cycle 731.9
down under 231.6
downward
  adj flowing 172.8
descending 194.11
  adv down 194.13
downward mobility
deterioration 393.3
class 607.1
change 851.1
downy feathery 3.27
smooth 287.9
smooth-textured
  294.8
light 298.10
fluffy 1045.14
do wonders 409.7
dowry
  n talent 413.4
endowment 478.9
  adj endowed 478.26
doxology paean 696.3
sacred music 708.17
doyen senior 304.5
chief 575.3
doze
  n sleep 22.2
  v sleep 22.13
dozen 881.7
drab
  n strumpet 665.14
slob 809.7
  adj brown 40.3
same 780.6

lackluster 1026.17
Draconian 144.26
Dracula 127.9
draft
  n beverage 8.4
dose 86.6
drink 88.7
submergence 275.6
wind 318.1
diagram 381.3
demand 421.1
recruit 461.18
writing 547.10
abridgment 557.1
enlistment 615.7
score 708.28
drawing 712.13
negotiable instrument
  728.11
pulling 904.1
  v draw off 192.12
outline 381.11
write 547.19
enlist 615.17
portray 712.19
drive 756.4
drag
  n substance abuse
    87.1
smoking 89.10
annoyance 96.2
killjoy 112.14
tedious person
  118.5
slowing 175.4
gait 177.12
resistance 184.27
burden 297.7
favor 893.2
pull 904.2
attraction 906.1
disadvantage 995.2
curb 1011.7
friction 1042.1
  v use 87.21
smoke 89.14
lag 166.4
go slow 175.6
dawdle 175.8
way of walking 177.28
hang 202.6
smooth 287.5
linger on 826.7
delay 845.8
pull 904.4
attract 906.4
drag in
interpose 213.6
foist 775.5
drag into 897.2
dragnet
snare 356.13
seizure 480.2
search 937.15
dragon
sorehead 110.11
violent person 671.9
drag on
be tedious 118.6
persist 780.3
linger on 826.7
continue 855.3

drag one's feet
go slow 175.6
hesitate 362.7
protract 826.9
delay 845.8
procrastinate 845.11
dragoon
n cavalryman 461.12
v intimidate 127.20
compel 424.4
coerce 424.7
drag out go slow 175.6
elicit 192.14
lengthen 267.6
diffuse 538.8
protract 826.9
postpone 845.9
drag queen 75.15
drain
n receptacle of filth
80.12
outflow 190.4
sough 239.5
consumption 388.1
demand 421.1
waste 473.2
v disable 19.9
decolor 36.5
run out 190.13
draw off 192.12
subtract 255.9
exploit 387.16
consume 388.3
waste 473.5
take from 480.21
strip 480.24
evacuate 908.22
dry 1064.6
drake
male animal 76.8
poultry 311.29
dram
n beverage 8.4
drink 88.7
modicum 248.2
dose 792.5
v tipple 88.24
drama
show business 704.1
representation 349.1
dramatic
emotionalistic 93.19
theatrical 501.24
thespian 704.33
vocal 708.50
poetic 720.15
dramatist
author 547.15
playwright 704.22
writer 718.4
dramatize
manifest 348.5
affect 500.12
theatricalize 704.28
play up 996.16
drape
n pendant 202.4
cover 295.2
shade 1027.1
v clothe 5.38
hang 202.6
drastic 671.16

drat! 513.12
draw
n attendance 221.4
valley 237.7
lure 377.3
poker 759.10
the same 789.3
tie 835.3
pull 904.2
attraction 906.1
v smoke 89.14
extract 192.10
draw off 192.12
contract 260.7
lengthen 267.6
represent 349.8
describe 349.9
lure 377.5
acquire 472.8
receive 479.6
portray 712.19
play 751.4
equal 789.5
exercise influence
893.9
pull 904.4
attract 906.4
draw a blank
fail 410.10
forget 989.5
draw and quarter
torture 604.16
tear apart 801.14
draw apart
antagonize 589.7
separate 801.8
drawback
discount 631.1
disadvantage 995.2
fault 1002.2
obstacle 1011.4
drawer lure 377.3
storehouse 386.6
draftsman 716.3
draw in retract 168.3
suck 187.12
contract 260.7
narrow 270.11
lure 377.5
portray 712.19
involve 897.2
reel in 905.9
drawing
n extraction 192.1
drafting 192.3
representation 349.1
diagram 381.3
draftsmanship 712.5
delineation 712.13
graphic arts 713.1
lottery 759.14
pulling 904.1
adj pulling 904.6
attracting 906.5
drawing card 377.3
drawing room
parlor 197.5
room on train 197.10
society 578.6
drawl
n slowness 175.1
accent 524.9

v speak 524.26
speak poorly 525.7
draw lots 759.23
drawn
tired-looking 21.9
lengthened 267.8
equal 789.7
draw out
extract 192.10
elicit 192.14
lengthen 267.6
diffuse 538.8
protract 826.9
draw the line at 325.3
draw up
write 547.19
form 806.5
stop 856.7
pick up 911.8
dray 179.2
dread
n unpleasure 96.1
anxiety 126.1
fear 127.1
suspense 130.3
v fear 127.10
expect 130.5
adj terrible 127.30
dreadful
adj horrid 98.19
terrible 127.30
venerable 155.12
remarkable 247.11
bad 999.9
hideous 1014.11
adv terribly 999.14
dream
n aspiration 100.9
airy hope 124.5
illusion 975.1
hallucination 975.7
abstractedness 984.2
reverie 985.9
first-rate 998.7
beauty 1015.9
v suppose 950.10
muse 984.9
dream of 985.17
dreamland sleep 22.2
illusion 975.1
utopia 985.11
dream up
originate 891.12
imagine 985.14
dreamy sleepy 22.21
tranquilizing 670.15
illusory 975.8
abstracted 984.11
dreamful 985.25
dreary gray 39.4
distressing 98.20
gloomy 112.24
dull 117.6
tedious 118.9
ominous 133.17
dredge
n excavator 284.10
v extract 192.10
excavate 284.15
sprinkle 770.6
imbue 796.11
pick up 911.8

dredge up
extract 192.10
assemble 769.18
pick up 911.8
dregs grounds 256.2
refuse 391.4
rabble 606.3
extract 892.3
drench
n inhibition 8.4
drink 88.7
soaking 1063.7
v overload 992.15
soak 1063.13
tend 1068.7
dress
n clothing 5.1
suit 5.6
gown 5.16
insignia 647.1
v clothe 5.38
groom 79.20
smooth 287.5
equip 385.8
prepare 405.6
ornament 498.8
fertilize 889.8
buff 1042.8
oil 1054.8
cultivate 1067.17
adj clothing 5.44
dressage 1068.1
dress down
dress up 5.41
disapprove 510.18
punish 604.15
dressed to kill
dressed up 5.45
chic 578.13
dressing clothing 5.1
stuffing 10.26
application 86.33
disapproval 510.6
fertilizer 889.4
abrasion 1042.2
cultivation 1067.13
dressing room
closet 197.15
stage 704.16
dress rehearsal 704.13
dried-up shrunk 260.13
wasted 393.35
unproductive 890.4
dried 1064.9
drift
n direction 161.1
deviation 164.1
course 172.2
deposit 176.9
drift angle 184.28
flow 238.4
meaning 518.1
race 756.3
group of animals
769.5
pile 769.10
trend 895.2
reception 1033.21
v stray 164.4
wander 177.23
drift off course 182.29
float 182.54

fly 184.36
do nothing 329.2
take it easy 331.15
pile 769.19
drifter
displaced person
160.4
wanderer 178.2
bum 331.9
fisher 382.6
wretch 660.2
transient 827.4
drift off 22.16
driftwood 1052.3
drill
n exercise 84.2
point 285.3
action 328.1
rule 373.5
training 568.3
study 570.3
exercise 725.6
cutlery 1039.2
v deepen 275.8
excavate 284.15
perforate 292.15
train 568.13
study 570.12
plant 1067.18
drink
n potation 8.4
beverage 10.47
dram 88.7
cocktail 88.9
spirits 88.13
ocean 240.1
fluid 1059.2
v drink in 8.29
use 87.21
tipple 88.24
ingest 187.11
absorb 187.13
drink in drink 8.29
absorb 187.13
learn 570.7
attend to 982.5
drinking habit 87.1
drink to drink 8.29
toast 88.29
drink up drink 8.29
tipple 88.24
absorb 187.13
thirst 1064.5
drip
n tedious person 118.5
leakage 190.5
trickle 238.7
v leak 190.14
trickle 238.18
be damp 1063.11
drive
n vim 17.2
power 18.1
desire 100.1
acceleration 174.4
ride 177.7
enterprise 330.7
motive 365.1
urge 375.6
haste 401.1
campaign 458.4
attack 459.1

vigor 544.3
group of animals
769.5
cause 885.9
impulse 901.1
pushing 903.1
machinery enginery
1039.3
disk drive 1041.5
v set in motion 172.6
ride 177.33
drift off course 182.29
pilot 184.37
excavate 284.15
hustle 330.13
hunt 382.9
compel 424.4
launch an attack
459.17
guide 573.9
task 725.16
play tennis 748.3
play 751.4
race 756.4
ride 757.5
impel 901.11
thrust 901.12
push 903.9
obsess 925.25
herd 1068.8
drive a bargain 731.17
drive at 380.4
drive away
dissipate 770.5
repulse 907.3
drive crazy 925.24
drive home to 952.18
drive-in movie 706.6
drive insane 925.24
drive-in theater 706.6
drivel
n saliva 13.3
nonsense 520.2
v salivate 13.6
talk nonsense 520.5
be incomprehensible
522.10
be stupid 921.12
be insane 925.20
drive on
make one's way 162.4
hustle 330.13
urge on 375.16
hasten 401.4
impel 901.11
driver reinsman 178.9
motorist 178.10
tyrant 575.14
man 577.4
race driving 756.2
operator 888.4
propeller 903.6
driver's license 443.6
driver's seat 417.10
drive up the wall
annoy 96.13
madden 925.24
driving
n riding 177.6
race 756.3
adj moving 172.7
rainy 316.10

enterprising 330.23
motivating 375.25
compulsory 424.10
attacking 459.29
vigorous 544.11
impelling 901.23
propulsive 903.14
obsessive 925.34
drizzle
n rain 316.1
v rain 316.9
droit 642.1
droll
humorous 488.4
witty 489.15
dromedary
beast of burden 176.8
hoofed animal 311.5
drone
n slowpoke 175.5
bee 311.33
nonworker 331.11
mumbling 525.4
part 708.22
bagpipes 711.9
regularity 780.2
series 811.2
repetitiousness 848.4
v hum 52.13
mumble 525.9
persist 780.3
drool
n saliva 13.3
nonsense 520.2
v salivate 13.6
talk nonsense 520.5
be stupid 921.12
be insane 925.20
droop
n gait 177.12
sinkage 194.2
hang 202.2
v weaken 16.9
burn out 21.5
fail 85.47
lose heart 112.16
sink 194.6
hang 202.6
languish 393.18
drooping weak 16.12
languishing 16.21
tired 21.7
dejected 112.22
descending 194.11
limp 202.10
deteriorating 393.45
loose 803.5
drop
n drink 88.7
leakage 190.5
descent 194.1
declivity 204.5
trickle 238.7
modicum 248.2
advantage 249.2
decline 252.2
minute 258.7
droplet 282.3
hiding place 346.4
plunge 367.1
deterioration 393.3
address 553.9

execution 605.5
scenery 704.20
skiing 753.1
pause 856.3
v give birth 1.3
take off 6.6
weaken 16.9
burn out 21.5
faint 25.5
lay 78.9
snub 157.5
leak 190.14
descend 194.5
incline 204.10
trickle 238.18
decrease 252.6
gravitate 297.15
strike dead 308.17
plunge 367.6
give up 370.7
break the habit 374.3
cease to use 390.4
lose 473.4
relinquish 475.3
cheapen 633.6
shoot 903.12
repulse 907.3
fell 912.5
let go of 912.7
drop a hint 551.10
drop a line
communicate with
343.8
correspond 553.10
drop anchor
settle 159.17
land 186.8
drop by go to 177.25
enter 189.7
visit 582.19
drop cloth 295.9
drop dead 307.22
drop in go to 177.25
enter 189.7
visit 582.19
drop in on 131.7
drop in the bucket
pittance 991.5
trifle 997.5
drop off
go to sleep 22.16
descend 194.5
decrease 252.6
die 307.20
drop out
dissent 333.4
abandon 370.5
not conform 867.4
drops 86.4
dropsy symptom 85.9
distension 259.2
drop the ball
fail 410.10
bungle 414.12
make a boner 974.15
drop the other shoe
816.5
drop the subject
983.4
dross dregs 256.2
combustion product
1019.16

drought
appetite 100.7
want 991.4
dryness 1064.1

drove
n group of animals 769.5
v drive 1068.8

drown choke 307.24
strangle 308.18
submerge 367.7
suppress 428.8
come to grief 1010.10
flood 1063.14

drown out 53.8

drowsy sleepy 22.21
tranquilizing 670.15

drub
n hit 901.4
stamp 901.10
v defeat 412.9
whip 604.13
pound 901.16
stamp 901.22

drudge
n servant 577.2
grub 726.3
v keep doggedly at 360.3
serve 577.13
grind and dig 725.14
be busy 330.10

drug
n anesthetic 25.3
medicine 86.4
narcotic drug 86.5
narcotic 87.2
moderator 670.3
commodity 735.2
v put to sleep 22.20
deaden 25.4
medicate 91.25
numb 94.8
moderate 670.6

drug abuse 87.1
drug addict 87.20
drugged 25.8
drug habit 87.1
drug pusher 732.4
drugstore 86.36

Druid
idolater 697.4
pagan clergy 699.14
predictor 961.4

drum
n staccato 55.1
cylinder 282.4
percussion instrument 711.16
v thrum 55.4
bird sound 60.5
rain 316.9
beat time 708.44
din 848.10
pulsate 915.12

drum out
depose 447.4
exclude 772.4
drive out 908.14
dismiss 908.19

drumstick
fowl part 10.22

leg 177.14
percussion instrument 711.16

drum up acquire 472.9
assemble 769.18

drunk
n drinking spree 88.6
drinker 88.11
lush 88.12
adj intoxicated 88.31
fervent 93.18
dizzy 984.15

druthers
preference 371.5
free will 430.6

dry
n conservative 611.9
prohibitionist 668.5
v preserve 397.9
strip 480.24
desiccate 1064.6
adj raucous 58.15
sour 67.5
thirsty 100.26
dull 117.6
tedious 118.9
right 219.4
satiric 508.13
sober 516.3
plain-speaking 535.3
conservative 611.17
prohibitionist 668.11
unproductive 890.4
unimaginative 986.5
arid 1064.7

dry-clean 79.18
dry goods 735.3
dry goods dealer 5.32

drying
n shrinking 260.3
food preservation 397.2
desiccation 1064.3
adj dehydrating 1064.10

dry land 234.1
dry out use 87.21
sober up 516.2
swear off 668.8

dry run
Air Force mission 184.11
preparation 405.1
operation 458.5
tryout 941.3

dry up
v shrink 260.9
be consumed 388.4
languish 393.18
dry 1064.6
inter silence! 51.14

dual
n number 530.8
adj two 872.6

dualism theism 675.5
doubleness 872.1
pluralism 951.5

dualist 675.16

dub
n bungler 414.9
golfer 751.2
v smooth 287.5

name 527.11
dub in 861.4
dubious
deceptive 356.21
irresolute 362.9
dishonest 645.16
agnostic 695.20
doubting 954.9
unbelievable 954.10
improbable 968.3
doubtful 970.17
unsafe 1005.11

ducal 608.10
ducat 728.4
duchess 608.6
duchy region 231.5
country 232.1

duck
n man 76.5
poultry 311.29
submergence 367.2
avoidance 368.1
loser 412.5
endearment term 562.6
card 758.2
retreat 902.3
crouch 912.3
v avoid 164.6
retract 168.3
prevaricate 344.7
submerge 367.7
dodge 368.8
shirk 368.9
fight 754.4
pull back 902.7
crouch 912.8
bow 912.9
flood 1063.14

duck out
absent oneself 222.8
flee 368.11
slip away 368.12

duck soup 1013.4
ducky
n ladylove 104.15
adj excellent 998.13

duct vessel 2.21
channel 239.1

ductile docile 433.13
handy 1013.15
pliant 1045.9

dud
n impotent 19.6
false alarm 400.2
failure 410.2
abortion 410.5
flop 410.8
candidate 610.9
thing of naught 763.2
v clothe 5.38

dude man 76.5
dandy 500.9

dudgeon 152.7
duds clothing 5.1
garment 5.3

due
n debt 623.1
one's due 639.2
prerogative 642.1
adj expected 130.13
owed 623.10

right 637.3
payable 639.7
entitled to 639.10
attributable 887.6
sufficient 990.6
adv directly 161.23
adj just 649.8

duel
n single combat 457.7
fight 754.3
v contend 457.13

duelist 461.1
dues debt 623.1
fee 630.6
deserts 639.3

duet cooperation 450.1
part music 708.18
two 872.2

due to
conj resulting from 886.8
prep because of 887.9

duffel equipment 385.4
impedimenta 471.3

duffer
incompetent 414.7
bungler 414.9
golfer 751.2

dugout cave 284.5
hiding place 346.4
entrenchment 460.5
baseball 745.1
shelter 1008.3

dugs 283.6
duke nobleman 608.4
poker 759.10
blow 901.5

duke it out 457.17
dulcet pleasant 97.6
melodious 708.48

dulcify sweeten 66.3
pacify 465.7
calm 670.7

dull
v weaken 16.10
deaden 25.4
decolor 36.5
muffle 51.9
blunt 94.7
relieve 120.5
blunt 286.2
moderate 670.6
mat 1026.10
adj weak 16.12
insensible 25.6
colorless 36.7
gray 39.4
muffled 52.17
unfeeling 94.9
apathetic 94.13
inexcitable 106.10
dry 117.6
tedious 118.9
inert 173.14
blunt 286.3
languid 331.20
plain-speaking 535.3
prosaic 721.5
dull of mind 921.16
unimaginative 986.5
mediocre 1004.7
lackluster 1026.17

dullard 923.2
dumb
  v thrive 1009.8
  adj mute 51.12
  animal 311.38
  taciturn 344.9
  stammering 525.13
  stupid 921.15
  foolish 922.8
  ignorant 929.12
  inanimate 1053.5
dumbbell
  exerciser 725.7
  fool 923.4
dumbfound
  silence 51.8
  astonish 122.6
dumbstruck
  mute 51.12
  wondering 122.9
dumbwaiter 911.4
dummy
  n mute 51.3
  reproduction 336.3
  figure 349.6
  fake 354.13
  instrument 384.4
  composition 548.2
  figurehead 575.5
  deputy 576.1
  follower 616.8
  bridge 758.3
  thing of naught 763.2
  artist's model 785.5
  substitute 861.2
  fool 923.4
  a nobody 997.7
  adj spurious 354.25
  substitute 861.8
dump
  n sty 80.11
  receptacle of filth
    80.12
  humiliation 137.2
  disrespect 156.3
  hovel 228.11
  disapproved place
    228.28
  derelict 370.4
  store 386.1
  storehouse 386.6
  trash pile 391.6
  armory 462.2
  v abase 137.5
  place 159.12
  load 159.15
  discard 390.7
  relinquish 475.3
  sell 734.8
  divest 737.24
  unload 908.23
dumpling 10.32
dump on
  abase 137.5
  be disrespectful 156.6
  disdain 157.3
dumps
  sulks 110.10
  blues 112.6
dumpy
  corpulent 257.18
  dwarf 258.13

  stubby 268.10
dun
  n horse 311.11
  creditor 622.4
  statement 628.3
  v importune 440.12
  bill 628.11
  adj brown 40.3
dunce
  stupid person 923.2
  ignoramus 929.8
dunderhead 923.4
dune hill 237.4
  pile 769.10
dung
  n feces 12.4
  fertilizer 889.4
  v defecate 12.13
dungeon 429.8
dunghill
  n manure pile 80.10
  adj dastardly 491.12
dunk
  submerge 367.7
  play 751.4
  flood 1063.14
duo
  part music 708.18
  two 872.2
duodecimal system
  1016.4
duodenal 881.24
dupe
  n sycophant 138.3
  dupable person 358
  gull 358.1
  instrument 384.4
  simple soul 416.3
  laughingstock 508.7
  agent 576.3
  cheater 759.22
  duplicate 784.3
  trusting soul 953.4
  v deceive 356.14
  copy 784.8
  duplicate 873.3
  stultify 922.7
duplex
  n apartment house
    228.14
  adj two 872.6
duplicate
  n image 349.5
  the same 777.3
  replica 784.3
  duplication 873.1
  v reproduce 78.7
  re-create 777.6
  copy 784.8
  repeat 848.7
  double 872.5
  dupe 873.3
  multiply 882.6
  adj identical 777.7
  analogous 783.11
  double 873.4
duplication
  remake 78.1
  replica 336.3
  reproduction 784.2
  clone 784.3
  repetition 848.1

  doubleness 872.1
  replication 873
  reduplication 873.1
  multiplication 882.4
  superfluity 992.4
duplicity
  falseheartedness 354.4
  deceit 356.3
  treachery 645.6
  doubleness 872.1
durable sturdy 762.7
  perdurable 826.10
  permanent 852.7
  tough 1047.4
duration time 820.1
  term 823.3
  lastingness 826
  durability 826.1
  perpetuity 828.1
  permanence 852.1
duress power 18.1
  coercion 424.3
  imprisonment 429.3
  necessity 962.1
during 820.14
dusk
  n dusking time 315.3
  daylight 1024.10
  darkishness 1026.2
  v grow dark 1026.12
  adj dark 38.9
  evening 315.8
  darkish 1026.15
dust
  n dirt 80.6
  cocaine 87.6
  drugs 87.17
  land 234.1
  lightness 298.2
  corpse 307.16
  refuse 391.4
  rubbish 391.5
  powder 1049.5
  dryness 1064.2
  v clean 79.18
  dirty 80.15
  sprinkle 770.6
dust bowl
  the country 233.1
  wasteland 890.2
dust jacket
  wrapper 295.18
  bookbinding 554.14
dusty gray 39.4
  dirty 80.22
  dull 117.6
  tedious 118.9
  wayworn 177.41
  stale 841.14
  powdery 1049.11
  dry 1064.7
Dutch uncle 422.3
dutiful respectful 155.8
  obedient 326.3
  observant 434.4
  duteous 641.13
  pious 692.8
duty respect 155.1
  function 387.5
  demand 421.1
  tax 630.9
  obligation 641.1

  charge 643.3
  divine service 696.8
  rite 701.3
  task 724.2
  job 724.3
duty-free 630.16
duvet 295.10
dwarf
  n modicum 248.2
  dwarfling 258.5
  fairy 678.8
  v minimize 252.9
  adj dwarfed 258.13
dwell inhabit 225.7
  endure 826.6
dwell in
  be present 221.6
  exist in 760.11
dwelling
  n habitation 225.1
  abode 228.1
  house 228.5
  adj resident 225.13
dwell on
  harp on 118.8
  harbor revenge 507.5
  protract 826.9
  insist upon 848.9
  keep in memory
    988.13
  emphasize 996.14
dwindle disappear 34.2
  fail 85.47
  recede 168.2
  quiet 173.8
  decrease 252.6
dyad 872.2
dybbuk demon 680.6
  specter 987.1
dye
  n color 35.8
  v infuse 35.13
  imbue 796.11
dyed-in-the-wool
  deep-dyed 35.17
  confirmed 373.19
  thorough 793.10
  established 854.13
dying
  n decrease 252.1
  death 307.1
  terminal case 307.15
  deterioration 393.3
  extinguishing 1021.2
  adj unhealthy 85.53
  impatient 135.6
  receding 168.5
  terminal 307.33
  transient 827.7
dying breath 307.9
dying to
  wanting 100.21
  desirous of 100.22
  eager 101.8
dying words
  sequel 816.1
  end 819.1
dyke 76.9
dynamic
  energetic 17.13
  powerful 18.12
  enterprising 330.23

consume 388.3
kid oneself 953.6
inter chow down! 8.35
eau de Cologne 70.3
eaves 295.6
eavesdrop
  listen 48.10
  be curious 980.3
eaves trough 239.3
ebb
  n standstill 173.3
  tide 238.13
  decline 252.2
  deterioration 393.3
  v recede 168.2
  move 172.5
  quiet 173.8
  flow 238.16
  decrease 252.6
  decline 393.17
ebb and flow
  n tide 238.13
  alternation 915.5
  v billow 238.22
  change 853.5
  alternate 915.13
ebony
  n blackness 38.1
  darkness 38.4
  adj black 38.8
  dark 1026.13
ebullient
  excited 105.20
  bubbly 320.6
  active 330.17
  hot 1018.25
eccentric
  n nonconformist 867.3
  oddity 869.4
  erratic 926.3
  adj off-center 160.12
  humorous 488.4
  irregular 850.3
  inconstant 853.7
  unconventional 867.6
  abnormal 869.9
  odd 869.11
  erratic 926.5
eccentricity
  humorousness 488.1
  irregularity 850.1
  inconstancy 853.2
  abnormality 869.1
  foolishness 922.1
  idiosyncrasy 926.1
  disposition 977.3
ecclesiastic
  n clergyman 699.2
  adj ministerial 698.13
ecdysiast
  nudity 6.3
  entertainer 707.1
ECG 91.9
echelon
  flight formation
    184.12
  rank 245.2
  battle array 458.3
echo
  n reverberation 54.2
  sympathy 93.5
  imitator 336.4

response 708.23
keyboard 711.17
reflection 784.7
repetition 848.1
repeat 848.5
duplicate 873.2
reaction 902.1
answer 938.1
signal 1035.11
v reverberate 54.7
respond 93.11
concur 332.9
imitate 336.5
repeat 848.7
recurrence 848.11
answer 938.4
reflect 1035.16
éclat publicity 352.4
  display 501.4
  applause 509.2
  repute 662.1
eclectic
  selective 371.23
  mixed 796.14
  combined 804.5
eclecticism
  selectivity 371.10
  sectarianism 675.4
  mixture 796.1
eclipse
  n disappearance 34.1
  covering 295.1
  occultation 1026.8
  moon 1070.11
  sun 1070.13
  v blind 30.7
  overshadow 249.8
  cover 295.19
  conceal 346.6
  darken 1026.9
ecological 209.9
ecology 1071.1
economic cheap 633.7
  thrifty 635.6
  socio-economic 731.22
economics
  finance 729.1
  trade 731
  eco 731.10
economist
  economizer 635.3
  financier 729.8
  economic expert
    731.11
economy
  n parsimony 484.1
  thrift 635.1
  economic system
    731.7
  adj cheap 633.7
ecosphere
  organic matter 305.1
  biosphere 306.6
  atmosphere 317.2
  the environment
    1071.1
ecosystem 1071.1
ecru brown 40.3
  yellow 43.4
ecstasy
  amphetamines 87.3
  passion 93.2

happiness 95.2
amorousness 104.3
fury 105.8
revelation 683.9
trance 691.3
ecstatic
  n psychic 689.13
  adj overjoyed 95.16
  frenzied 105.25
  abstracted 984.11
ectomorph 92.12
ectoplasm cell 305.4
  exteriorized
    protoplasm 689.7
ecumenical
  cooperative 450.5
  universal 863.14
  broad-minded 978.8
ecumenism
  cooperation 450.1
  moderation 670.1
  combination 804.1
  broad-mindedness
    978.1
eczema 85.33
eddy
  n agitation 105.4
  back stream 238.12
  whirl 914.2
  v gurge 238.21
  whirl 914.11
edema symptom 85.9
  increase 251.1
  distension 259.2
  swelling 283.4
  overextension 992.7
Eden 985.11
edge
  n acrimony 17.5
  pungency 68.1
  summit 198.2
  border 211.4
  advantage 249.2
  straight line 277.2
  sharpness 285.1
  sharp edge 285.2
  v border 211.10
  side 218.4
  go sideways 218.5
  sharpen 285.7
edge in enter 189.7
  interpose 213.6
  intrude 214.5
edge out outdo 249.9
  triumph 411.3
  defeat 412.6
edgy
  excitable 105.28
  nervous 128.11
  impatient 135.6
edible 8.33
edict
  announcement 352.2
  decree 420.4
  law 673.3
edification
  teaching 568.1
  learning 927.4
edifice house 228.5
  structure 266.2
edify
  make better 392.9

teach 568.10
edit delete 255.12
  comment upon 341.11
  revise 392.12
  write 547.19
edition rendering 341.2
  issue 554.5
  score 708.28
editor interpreter 341.7
  publisher 554.2
  journalist 555.4
  commentator 556.4
  motion-picture studio
    706.3
  examiner 937.17
  critic 945.7
  systems program
    1041.12
editorial
  n commentary 556.2
  adj explanatory
    341.15
  journalistic 555.5
educate
  make better 392.9
  teach 568.10
educated
  improved 392.13
  learned 570.16
  informed 927.18
  scholarly 927.21
educated guess 950.4
education
  cultivation 392.3
  teaching 568.1
  learning 570.1
  erudition 927.4
educational 551.18
educe 192.14
EEG 91.9
eel 10.23
eerie awesome 122.11
  creepy 127.31
  deathly 307.29
  supernatural 869.15
  weird 987.9
efface 395.16
effect
  n power 18.1
  aspect 33.3
  intention 380.1
  meaning 518.1
  relevance 774.4
  end 819.1
  event 830.1
  sequel 834.2
  consequence 886
  result 886.1
  product 892.1
  influence 893.1
  v do 328.6
  use 384.5
  accomplish 407.4
  execute 437.9
  cause 885.10
  induce 885.11
  establish 891.10
effective
  powerful 18.12
  able 18.14
  effectual 387.21
  vigorous 544.11

electric
  n streetcar 179.17
  adj exciting 105.30
  provocative 375.27
  galvanic 1031.29
electric chair 605.5
electric current
  current 1031.2
  electron flow 1032.6
electric field 1031.3
electrician
  stage technician
    704.24
  electrotechnician
    1031.21
electricity
  swiftness 174.6
  telegraph 347.2
  illuminant 1024.20
  electrical science
    1031.1
electric power
  manpower 18.4
  wattage 1031.17
electrify energize 17.10
  agitate 105.14
  startle 131.8
  galvanize 1031.25
electrolysis 1031.24
electromagnetic field
  electric field 1031.3
  magnetic force 1031.9
electron atom 258.8
  negatron 1032.3
electronic device
  1032.13
electronic media 551.5
electronics radio 347.3
  electron physics 1032
  radionics 1032.1
electron theory of
  atoms 1032.2
electrostatic
  electric 1031.29
  static 1038.8
eleemosynary
  benevolent 143.15
  philanthropic 478.22
  gratuitous 634.5
elegance
  parsimony 484.1
  taste 496.1
  ornateness 498.2
  overniceness 500.5
  grandeur 501.5
  good breeding 504.4
  refinement 533
  grace 533.1
  fluency 544.2
  smartness 578.3
  etiquette 580.3
  decency 664.2
  beauty 1015.1
elegant graceful 496.9
  ornate 498.12
  overnice 500.18
  grandiose 501.21
  tasteful 533.6
  fluent 544.9
  chic 578.13
  decent 664.5
  good 998.12

  beautiful 1015.17
elegiac
  n meter 720.7
  adj dirgelike 115.22
  poetic 720.15
elegy 115.6
element
  natural environment
    209.4
  particular 765.3
  component 795.2
  cause 885.1
  heater 1019.10
  matter 1050.2
  chemical element
    1058.2
elemental
  n elemental spirit
    678.6
  adj basic 199.8
  climatal 317.12
  essential 766.9
  beginning 817.15
  original 885.14
  chemical 1058.8
elementary basic 199.8
  essential 766.9
  component 795.5
  simple 797.6
  beginning 817.15
  original 885.14
  chemical 1058.8
elementary school
  567.3
elements
  contents 196.1
  elementary education
    568.5
  Eucharist 701.7
  substance 762.2
  basics 817.6
the elements 317.3
elephant drugs 87.17
  beast of burden 176.8
  behemoth 257.14
  pachyderm 311.4
elephantine dull 117.6
  bulky 257.19
  huge 257.20
  elephantlike 311.45
  stiff 534.3
  excessive 992.16
elevate elate 109.8
  erect 200.9
  heighten 272.13
  make better 392.9
  promote 446.2
  glorify 662.13
  raise 911.5
  exalt 911.6
elevated
  n train 179.14
  adj drunk 88.33
  lofty 136.11
  eminent 247.9
  increased 251.7
  high 272.14
  lofty 544.14
  grandiloquent 545.8
  magnanimous 652.6
  eminent 662.18
  raised 911.9

elevation ascent 193.1
  erection 200.4
  increase 251.1
  height 272.1
  steep 272.2
  diagram 381.3
  promotion 446.1
  loftiness 544.6
  magnanimity 652.2
  distinction 662.5
  glorification 662.8
  raising 911.1
elevator
  people mover 176.5
  garner 386.7
  ascensor 911.4
eleven team 617.7
  football team 746.2
  twelve 881.7
eleventh hour
  curfew 315.5
  crucial moment 842.5
  lateness 845.1
elf dwarf 258.5
  brat 302.4
  mischief-maker 322.3
  fairy 678.8
  imp 680.7
elfish
  mischievous 322.6
  fairy 678.17
  impish 680.18
elicit educe 192.14
  prompt 375.13
  induce 885.11
elide shorten 268.6
  eliminate 772.5
eligibility
  qualification 371.11
  inclusion 771.1
eligible
  n eligibility 371.11
  adj qualified 371.24
eliminate excrete 12.12
  excise 255.10
  murder 308.15
  discard 390.7
  exterminate 395.14
  annihilate 761.7
  get rid of 772.5
  do away with 908.21
  evacuate 908.22
elimination
  excretion 12.1
  disappearance 34.1
  excision 255.3
  homicide 308.2
  discard 390.3
  extinction 395.6
  riddance 772.2
  evacuation 908.6
elision
  shortening 268.3
  abbreviation 537.4
elite
  n superior 249.5
  elect 371.12
  society 578.6
  upper class 607.2
  aristocracy 608.1
  clique 617.6
  the best 998.8

  adj exclusive 495.13
  socially prominent
    578.16
  best 998.16
elixir panacea 86.3
  medicine 86.4
  extract 192.8
  essential content
    196.5
  essence 766.2
elk 311.5
ell adjunct 254.3
  angle 278.2
ellipse curve 279.2
  oval 280.6
ellipsis
  shortening 268.3
  abbreviation 537.4
ellipsoid
  n sphere 282.2
  adj parabolic 279.13
  spherical 282.9
elliptical
  oblong 267.9
  shortened 268.9
  parabolic 279.13
elocution speech 524.1
  public speaking 543.1
elongated
  lengthened 267.8
  oblong 267.9
elope 368.10
elopement
  flight 368.4
  wedding 563.3
eloquence
  articulateness 524.5
  public speaking 543.1
  rhetoric 544.1
else
  adj other 779.8
  adv additionally
    253.11
  otherwise 779.11
elsewhere
  adj abstracted 984.11
  adv away 222.18
elucidate
  explain 341.10
  make clear 521.6
elude evade 368.7
  outwit 415.11
  thwart 1011.15
elvish
  mischievous 322.6
  impish 680.18
Elysian blissful 97.9
  heavenly 681.12
Elysian Fields
  mythological 681.9
  destiny 838.2
emaciate
  v shrink 260.9
  thin 270.12
  waste 393.19
  adj haggard 270.20
emaciation
  symptom 85.9
  shrinking 260.3
  emaceration 270.6
  waste 393.4
emanate radiate 171.6

emerge 190.11
come after 834.3
emanation odor 69.1
radiation 171.2
emergence 190.1
ectoplasm 689.7
light 1024.1
emancipated
free 430.21
liberated 431.10
emasculate
v unman 19.12
feminize 77.12
castrate 255.11
cripple 393.14
adj unmanned 19.19
embalm perfume 70.8
lay out 309.21
mummify 397.10
perpetuate 828.5
embankment
shore 234.2
railway 383.7
pile 769.10
buttress 900.4
harbor 1008.6
barrier 1011.5
embargo
n closure 293.1
prohibition 444.1
exclusion 772.1
v stop 293.7
prohibit 444.3
exclude 772.4
embark send 176.15
get under way 182.19
go aboard 188.15
embark on 817.9
embarrass
chagrin 96.15
mortify 98.13
humiliate 137.4
involve 897.2
bewilder 970.12
confuse 984.7
inconvenience 995.4
hamper 1011.11
put in a hole 1012.15
embarrassed
distressed 96.22
humiliated 137.14
blushing 139.13
indebted 623.8
bewildered 970.24
confused 984.12
troubled 1012.20
embarrassment
chagrin 96.4
mortification 98.6
humiliation 137.2
shyness 139.4
involvement 897.1
bewilderment 970.3
confusion 984.3
impediment 1011.6
predicament 1012.4
embassy
house 228.5
message 552.4
foreign office 576.7
commission 615.1
office 739.7

embattled
battled 458.23
fortified 460.12
embed inset 191.5
internalize 207.5
fix 854.9
embellish falsify 354.15
develop 392.10
ornament 498.8
bombast 545.7
embellishment
development 392.2
ornamentation 498.1
ornateness 545.4
ornament 709.18
superfluity 992.4
ember dregs 256.2
coal 1018.16
embezzle misuse 389.4
steal 482.13
embitter sour 110.16
aggrieve 112.19
aggravate 119.2
provoke 152.24
impair 393.9
antagonize 589.7
embittered sour 110.23
aggravated 119.4
resentful 152.26
impaired 393.27
emblazon color 35.13
ornament 498.8
flaunt 501.17
praise 509.12
emblem symbol 517.2
insignia 647.1
example 785.2
embodiment
manifestation 348.1
impersonation 349.4
representative 349.7
incarnation 762.4
essence 766.2
inclusion 771.1
whole 791.1
composition 795.1
materiality 1050.1
materialization
1050.8
embody manifest 348.5
image 349.11
incarnate 762.5
include 771.3
compose 795.3
materialize 1050.9
embolden
encourage 375.21
abet 449.14
motivate 492.16
embolism 293.3
embossed
in relief 283.18
sculptured 715.7
established 854.13
embouchure
mouth 292.4
wind instrument
711.6
embrace
n hold 474.2
hug 562.3
welcome 585.2

greeting 585.4
joint 799.4
v surround 209.6
wrap 295.20
adopt 371.15
hold 474.6
retain 474.7
seize 480.14
hug 562.18
welcome 585.9
include 771.3
put together 799.5
join 799.11
cohere 802.6
embroider
falsify 354.15
ornament 498.8
grandiloquent 545.7
embroilment
agitation 105.4
quarrel 456.5
fight 457.4
turbulence 671.2
commotion 809.4
agitation 916.1
embryo
zygote 305.14
vital force 885.7
embryonic
infinitesimal 258.14
germinal 305.22
undeveloped 406.12
incomplete 794.4
beginning 817.15
original 885.14
emcee steward 574.4
theater man 704.23
master of ceremonies
743.20
broadcaster 1033.23
emend
make better 392.9
revise 392.12
remedy 396.13
emendation
explanation 341.4
revision 392.4
emerald 44.4
emerge
show 31.4
appear 33.8
come out 190.11
find vent 369.10
emergency
hospital room 197.25
crisis 842.4
urgency 996.4
danger 1005.1
predicament 1012.4
emergent
emerging 190.18
future 838.8
critical 842.10
emeritus
n academic rank
571.3
adj retired 448.3
emery 287.8
emetic
n nastiness 64.3
cleanser 79.17
vomitive 86.18

adj cleansing 79.28
vomitive 86.49
emigrant
migrant 178.5
goer 190.10
newcomer 773.4
emigrate
migrate 177.22
leave home 188.17
out-migrate 190.16
eminence
hill 237.4
glory 247.2
height 272.1
steep 272.2
protuberance 283.2
prestige 417.4
distinction 662.5
influence 893.1
notability 996.2
éminence grise
Machiavellian 415.8
politics 610.6
influence 893.6
eminent
prominent 247.9
superior 249.12
high up 272.14
protruding 283.14
authoritative 417.15
high 662.18
notable 996.19
emir
Muslim ruler 575.10
prince 608.7
Sir 648.3
emissary
messenger 353.1
delegate 576.2
diplomat 576.6
emit excrete 12.12
exude 190.15
issue 352.14
say 524.23
let out 908.24
vaporize 1065.8
emollient
n balm 86.11
ointment 1054.3
adj palliative 86.40
relieving 120.9
softening 1045.16
lubricant 1054.10
emote
emotionalize 93.13
affect 500.12
act 704.29
emotion feeling 93.1
excitement 105.1
attitude 977.1
emotional
affective 93.17
excitable 105.28
attitudinal 977.7
emotive
feeling 93.17
emotionalistic 93.19
affecting 93.22
empathic
sensitive 24.12
condoling 147.3
in accord 455.3

empathize with
respond 93.11
condole with 147.2
empathy
sensitivity 24.3
sympathy 93.5
accord 455.1
emperor 575.8
emphasis
impressiveness 524.11
accent 709.25
meter 720.7
emphasize 996.14
emphatic
affirmative 334.8
vehement 544.13
decided 996.21
empire country 232.1
dominion 417.5
sovereignty 417.8
government 612.1
empirical
real 760.15
experimental 941.11
empiricism
ethical philosophy
636.2
experiment 941.1
materialism 1050.6
emplacement
location 159.1
placement 159.6
platform 900.13
emplane 188.15
employ
n use 387.1
service 577.12
occupation 724.1
v practice 328.8
use 387.10
spend 387.13
hire 615.14
occupy 724.10
exert 725.8
employee
subordinate 432.5
hireling 577
pensioner 577.3
assistant 616.6
worker 726.2
emporium
market 736.1
marketplace 736.2
empower
enable 18.10
authorize 443.11
commission 615.10
empty
v run out 190.13
draw off 192.12
evacuate 908.22
adj ineffective 19.15
hungry 100.25
dull 117.6
vacant 222.14
concave 284.16
insincere 354.31
vain 391.13
meaningless 520.6
inexpressive 522.20
nonexistent 761.8
empty-headed 921.19

ignorant 929.12
thoughtless 932.4
sophistical 935.10
baseless 935.13
trivial 997.19
empty-headed
empty-minded 921.19
ignorant 929.12
thoughtless 932.4
scatterbrained 984.16
emulate follow 336.7
compete 457.18
set an example 785.7
excel 998.11
emulsify mix 796.10
emulsionize 1060.10
emulsion film 714.10
emulsoid 1060.7
solution 1062.3
enable
empower 18.10
fit 405.8
authorize 443.11
include 771.3
make possible 965.5
enact perform 328.9
manifest 348.5
impersonate 349.12
accomplish 407.4
legislate 613.10
legalize 673.8
act out 704.30
enamel
n blanket 295.12
v color 35.13
coat 295.24
adj ceramic 742.7
enamored 104.28
enate
n kinfolk 559.2
lineage 560.4
adj related 559.6
lineal 560.18
kindred 774.10
akin 783.13
encampment
camping 225.4
camp 228.29
campground 463.3
encapsulate
shorten 268.6
wrap 295.20
abridge 557.5
iterate 848.8
encase
confine 212.6
package 212.9
wrap 295.20
enchant
delight 95.9
fascinate 377.7
charm 691.8
engross 982.13
enchanted
overjoyed 95.16
enamored 104.28
wondering 122.9
charmed 691.12
miraculous 869.16
gripped 982.18
dreamy 985.25
encipher 345.10

encircle
surround 209.7
enclose 212.5
circle 280.10
besiege 459.19
include 771.3
enclose 913.5
enclave
enclosed place 212.3
plot 231.4
enclitic
added to writing
254.2
morphology 526.3
enclose
internalize 207.5
surround 209.6
circumscribe 210.4
bound 211.8
close in 212.5
confine 429.12
include 771.3
enclosure
the enclosed 196.6
surrounding 209.5
confinement 212.1
enclosed place 212.3
place of confinement
429.7
fortification 460.4
encode 345.10
encomiastic 509.16
encompass
extend 158.8
surround 209.6
enclose 212.5
circle 280.10
wrap 295.20
besiege 459.19
include 771.3
total 791.8
put together 799.5
combine 804.3
encircle 913.5
encore
n repeat performance
848.6
repeat 873.2
v applaud 509.10
adv recurrently 848.17
again 873.7
inter bravo! 509.22
bis! 848.18
encounter
n meeting 223.4
contest 457.3
impact 901.3
v approach 167.3
confront 216.8
meet 223.11
oppose 451.5
come up against
457.15
experience 830.8
collide 901.13
come across 940.3
encourage cheer 109.7
comfort 121.6
hearten 375.21
admonish 422.6
abet 449.14
be useful 449.17

hearten 492.16
encouraging
cheering 109.16
comforting 121.13
promising 124.13
provocative 375.27
encroach intrude 214.5
usurp 640.8
overstep 909.9
encroachment
intrusion 214.1
impairment 393.1
usurpation 640.3
overstepping 909.3
encrust 295.27
encumber add 253.4
burden 297.13
hamper 1011.11
encumbered
weighted 297.18
indebted 623.8
encyclical 352.2
encyclopedia
reference book 554.9
lore 927.9
encyclopedic
comprehensive 771.7
learned 927.21
end
n boundary 211.3
remainder 256.1
death 307.1
motive 375.1
objective 380.2
fatality 395.2
completion 407.2
gain 472.3
portion 477.5
football team 746.2
piece 792.3
limit 793.5
end point 819.1
stop 856.2
immediate cause
885.3
solution 939.1
fate 963.2
v kill 308.12
put an end to 395.12
perish 395.23
complete 407.6
terminate 819.5
cease 856.6
result 886.4
endanger 1005.6
endearing
delightful 97.7
lovable 104.25
endeavor
n act 328.3
effort 403.1
attempt 403.2
exertion 725.1
v strive 403.5
undertake 404.3
exert oneself 725.9
endemic
contagious 85.61
native 226.5
endless wordy 538.12
continuous 811.8
infinite 822.3

perpetual 828.7
continuing 855.7
innumerable 883.10
endocrine
n digestive secretion
13.2
adj glandular 13.8
endomorph 92.12
endorse ratify 332.12
adopt 371.15
secure 438.9
consent 441.2
abet 449.14
approve 509.9
support 609.41
endow empower 18.10
provide 385.7
invest 478.17
establish 891.10
endowed
provided 385.13
talented 413.29
dowered 478.26
end up arrive 186.6
end 819.5
come to an end 819.6
result 886.4
conclude 945.10
endurance
strength 15.1
patience 134.1
perseverance 360.1
durability 826.1
permanence 852.1
continuance 855.1
endure bear 134.5
condone 148.4
keep alive 306.10
persevere 360.2
suffer 443.10
resist 453.2
afford 626.7
live on 760.9
elapse 820.5
last 826.6
experience 830.8
remain 852.5
continue 855.3
toughen 1047.3
enema washing 79.5
cleanser 79.17
clyster 86.19
sprinkler 1063.8
enemy
n opponent 452.1
foe 589.6
adj oppositional 451.8
warlike 458.21
energetic
vigorous 17.13
powerful 18.12
active 330.17
industrious 330.22
energize
dynamize 17.10
vivify 306.9
motivate 375.12
electrify 1031.25
energy
n strength 15.1
vigor 17.1
power 18.1

liveliness 330.2
industry 330.6
exertion 725.1
adj fuel 1020.8
enervate weaken 16.10
unman 19.12
fatigue 21.4
afflict 85.49
spiritualize 763.4
enervation
weakening 16.5
helplessness 19.4
fatigue 21.1
unhealthiness 85.3
languor 331.6
enfant terrible
brat 302.4
mischief-maker 322.3
spoiled child 427.4
enfeeble weaken 16.10
disable 19.9
afflict 85.49
enfeebled
weakened 16.18
tired 21.7
enflame 375.18
enfold
internalize 207.5
surround 209.6
fold 291.5
wrap 295.20
embrace 562.18
enforce apply 387.11
compel 424.4
execute 437.9
legalize 673.8
enfranchise
liberate 431.4
authorize 443.11
include 771.3
enfranchisement
empowerment 18.8
vote 371.6
liberation 431.1
authorization 443.3
inclusion 771.1
engage induce 375.22
attract 377.6
attempt 403.6
commit 436.5
contract 437.5
take on 457.16
employ 615.14
occupy 724.10
interact 776.6
involve 897.2
engross 982.13
engage in
practice 328.8
undertake 404.3
busy oneself with
724.11
engagement
inducement 375.3
undertaking 404.1
obligation 436.2
betrothal 436.3
contest 457.3
participation 476.1
proposal 562.8
appointment 582.8
employment 615.4

playing engagement
704.11
position 724.5
interaction 776.3
involvement 897.1
engrossment 982.3
engaging
delightful 97.7
alluring 377.8
engrossing 982.20
engender
procreate 78.8
beget 817.14
cause 885.10
produce 889.7
originate 891.12
engine
instrument of
conversion 857.10
machinery enginery
1039.3
engineer
n engineman 178.12
planner 381.6
combat engineer
461.14
professional engineer
726.7
producer 891.7
v plot 381.9
manage 409.12
maneuver 415.10
direct 573.8
perform 891.11
English 341.12
English-speaking
524.32
engorge stuff 8.25
ingest 187.11
destroy 395.10
gluttonize 672.4
satiate 993.4
engrave
impress upon 93.16
indent 284.14
furrow 290.3
figure 498.9
mark 517.19
print 548.14
record 549.15
grave 713.9
sculpture 715.5
fix 854.9
fix in the mind 988.18
engross
absorb 187.13
fatten 259.8
monopolize 469.6
write 547.19
purchase 733.7
corner 737.26
occupy the mind
930.20
take in 982.13
engrossed in 982.17
engulf ingest 187.11
overflow 238.17
submerge 367.7
overwhelm 395.21
oversupply 992.14
enhance
aggravate 119.2

intensify 251.5
make better 392.9
enhancement
aggravation 119.1
intensification 251.2
exaggeration 355.1
improvement 392.1
enigma secret 345.5
mystery 522.8
the unknown 929.7
bewilderment 970.3
dilemma 1012.7
enigmatic
wonderful 122.10
secret 345.11
cryptic 522.17
unknown 929.17
bewildering 970.27
ambiguous 539.4
enjoin command 420.8
admonish 422.6
restrain 428.7
prohibit 444.3
impose 643.4
enjoy savor 63.5
pleasure in 95.12
possess 469.4
enjoyment
pleasure 95.1
amusement 743.1
enkindle
excite 105.12
kindle 375.18
ignite 1019.22
enlace 740.6
enlarge
aggravate 119.2
increase 251.4
size 257.15
expand 259.4
grow 259.5
amplify 538.7
process 714.15
elaborate 860.6
enlargement
aggravation 119.1
increase 251.1
expansion 259.1
exaggeration 355.1
amplification 538.6
print 714.5
photoprint 784.5
evolution 860.1
enlighten
explain 341.10
make better 392.9
inform 551.8
teach 568.10
disillusion 976.2
illuminate 1024.28
enlightening
explanatory 341.15
informative 551.18
educational 568.18
disillusioning 976.4
liberalizing 978.13
enlightenment
explanation 341.4
cultivation 392.3
information 551.1
teaching 568.1
learning 927.4

entwine
weave 740.6
hamper 1011.11
enumerate
quantify 244.4
itemize 800.7
list 870.8
number 1016.16
enunciate affirm 334.5
announce 352.12
say 524.23
envelop clothe 5.38
surround 209.6
wrap 295.20
conceal 346.6
envelope
n exterior 206.2
wrapper 295.18
illustriousness 662.6
v besiege 459.19
enviable 100.30
envious
discontented 108.7
jealous 153.5
envying 154.4
environment
neighborhood 209.1
natural environment
209.4
surrounding 209.5
circumstances 765.2
the natural world
1071.1
environs
environment 209.1
nearness 223.1
region 231.1
envision expect 130.5
contemplate 380.5
come 838.6
think of 930.17
foresee 960.5
visualize 985.15
envoy delegate 576.2
diplomat 576.6
envoy extraordinary
576.6
envy
n discontent 108.1
jealousy 153.1
resentfulness 154
enviousness 154.1
v be envious of 154.3
enwrap clothe 5.38
surround 209.6
package 212.9
wrap 295.20
enzyme 7.9
eon 823.4
epaulet 647.5
ephemeral
n plant 310.3
ephemeron 827.5
adj mortal 307.34
perennial 310.41
unsubstantial 763.5
transient 827.7
epic
n story 719.3
adj huge 257.20
poetic 720.15
narrative 722.8

epicedium 115.6
epicentre 671.5
epicureanism
gastronomy 8.15
pleasure-loving 95.4
aesthetic taste 496.5
sensuality 663.1
epicurism 672.2
epidemic
n plague 85.5
adj contagious 85.61
prevalent 863.12
plentiful 990.7
epidermic
epidermal 2.25
exterior 206.7
cutaneous 295.32
epigram
witticism 489.7
aphorism 537.3
maxim 973.1
epigrammatic
concise 537.6
aphoristic 973.6
epigraph
lettering 546.5
caption 936.2
motto 973.4
epigraphy 341.8
epilepsy seizure 85.6
spasm 916.6
epilogue
added to writing
254.2
act 704.7
part of writing 792.2
sequel 816.1
end 819.1
epiphany visibility 31.1
appearance 33.1
manifestation 348.1
revelation 683.9
intuition 933.1
episcopal 698.13
episode
interjection 213.2
digression 538.4
plot 722.4
discontinuity 812.1
event 830.2
frenzy 925.7
epistle 553.2
epitaph 309.18
epithalamium 563.3
epithet
n oath 513.4
name 527.3
nickname 527.7
motto 973.4
v vilify 513.7
epitome
shortening 268.3
abridgment 557.1
paragon 659.4
essence 766.2
ideal 785.4
pattern of perfection
1001.4
epitomize
shorten 268.6
set an example 785.7
epoch 823.5

epode 720.9
eponym root 526.2
name 527.3
equal
n match 789.4
substitute 861.2
v parallel 203.4
match 789.5
excel 998.11
adj parallel 203.6
symmetric 264.4
proportionate 477.13
coinciding 777.8
uniform 780.5
equalized 789.7
interchangeable
862.5
equality
symmetry 264.1
justice 649.1
sameness 777.1
parity 789.1
equalize level 201.6
symmetrize 264.3
smooth 287.5
make uniform 780.4
make agree 787.7
equate 789.6
equal opportunity
equating 789.2
opportunity 842.2
equanimity
equilibrium 106.3
uniformity 780.1
equate
parallelize 203.5
relate 774.6
equalize 789.6
equator zone 231.3
circle 280.3
middle 818.1
bisector 874.3
hot place 1018.11
orbit 1070.16
equestrian
n rider 178.8
adj ungulate 311.44
equidistant
parallel 203.6
central 208.11
middle 818.4
equilibrium
equanimity 106.3
symmetry 264.1
inaction 329.1
harmony 533.2
moderation 670.1
correlation 776.1
uniformity 780.1
equality 789.1
continuity 811.1
stability 854.1
equine
n horse 311.10
adj ungulate 311.44
equinox
vernal equinox 313.7
orbit 1070.16
equip outfit 5.40
furnish 385.8
fit 405.8
establish 891.10

equipment
supplies 385
provision 385.1
matériel 385.4
preparation 405.1
fitting 405.2
talent 413.4
baseball 745.1
football 746.1
hockey 749.1
field hockey 749.4
bowling 750.1
golf 751.1
soccer 752.1
skiing 753.1
boxing 754.1
equitable just 649.8
impartial 649.10
unprejudiced 978.12
equity estate 471.4
justice 649.1
stock 738.2
equality 789.1
equivalence
correlation 776.1
sameness 777.1
agreement 787.1
equality 789.1
comparability 942.3
equivalent
n offset 338.2
the same 777.3
likeness 783.3
equal 789.4
substitute 861.2
adj reciprocal 776.10
coinciding 777.8
analogous 783.11
agreeing 787.9
tantamount 789.8
substitute 861.8
interchangeable 862.5
equivocal
n ambiguity 539.2
adj prevaricating
344.11
untruthful 354.33
ambiguous 539.4
self-contradictory
778.8
mixed 796.14
uncertain 970.16
equivocate
prevaricate 344.7
lie 354.18
vacillate 362.8
dodge 368.8
weasel 539.3
go roundabout 913.4
quibble 935.9
era 823.5
eradicate
extract 192.10
excise 255.10
exterminate 395.14
annihilate 761.7
eliminate 772.5
erase delete 255.12
kill 308.13
obliterate 395.16
end 819.5
abrade 1042.7

Erato music 710.22
Muse 720.10
creative thought 985.2
Erebus
nether world deity
682.5
darkness 1026.1
erect
v elevate 200.9
produce 891.8
elevate 911.5
adj proud 136.8
vertical 200.11
honest 644.13
raised 911.9
erection
sexual desire 75.5
erecting 200.4
house 228.5
structure 266.2
production 891.2
elevation 911.1
eremite 584.5
erg 17.7
ergo 887.7
eristic
n argumentation
934.4
arguer 934.12
adj partisan 456.17
argumentative 934.19
ermine heraldry 647.2
royal insignia 647.3
erode disappear 34.2
recede 168.2
decrease 252.6
subtract 255.9
consume 388.3
wear 393.20
corrode 393.21
waste 473.5
disintegrate 805.3
abrade 1042.7
erogenous 75.24
Eros god 104.1
Love 104.8
erose notched 289.5
nonuniform 781.3
erosion
decrement 252.3
subtraction 255.1
consumption 388.1
wear 393.5
waste 473.2
disintegration 805.1
abrasion 1042.2
erotic sexual 75.24
amorous 104.26
lascivious 665.29
erotica
literature 547.12
pornographic
literature 718.1
err stray 164.4
miss 410.14
go wrong 654.9
do wrong 655.4
misbelieve 688.8
misjudge 947.2
fall into error 974.9
errand
commission 615.1

task 724.2
errant
deviative 164.7
wandering 177.37
fallible 970.22
erroneous 974.16
errata 554.12
erratic
n eccentric 926.3
adj deviative 164.7
nonuniform 781.3
unordered 809.12
irregular 850.3
inconstant 853.7
abnormal 869.9
eccentric 926.5
uncertain 970.16
erratum 974.3
erroneous false 354.24
ungrammatic 531.4
unorthodox 688.9
untrue 974.16
illusory 975.8
imperfect 1002.4
error
misinterpretation
342.1
miss 410.4
bungle 414.5
iniquity 654.3
misdeed 655.2
heresy 688.2
muff 745.3
game 748.2
misjudgment 947.1
erroneousness 974.1
mistake 974.3
ersatz
n substitute 861.2
adj imitation 336.8
spurious 354.25
similar 783.10
substitute 861.8
erstwhile 836.10
eruct erupt 671.13
disgorge 908.25
belch 908.28
erudition
learning 570.1
wisdom 919.5
scholarship 927.5
erupt
burst forth 33.9
take sick 85.46
emerge 190.11
find vent 369.10
burst out 671.13
originate 817.13
disgorge 908.25
escalator
people mover 176.5
elevator 911.4
escapade 743.6
escape
n defense mechanism
92.23
departure 188.1
outlet 190.9
absence 222.4
avoidance 368.1
getaway 369.1
v absent oneself 222.8

evade 368.7
make one's escape
369.6
free oneself from
431.8
escape clause
loophole 369.4
condition 958.2
escape one
be incomprehensible
522.10
not understand 522.11
escape notice 983.5
be forgotten 989.7
escapism
defense mechanism
92.23
escape 369.1
escargot 10.24
escarpment
precipice 200.3
slope 237.2
eschatology
end 819.1
doomsday 838.3
eschew 668.7
escort
n lover 104.12
conductor 768.5
chaperon 1007.7
bodyguard 1007.14
v conduct 768.8
escrow
storage 386.5
pledge 438.2
esker 237.5
esophagus 2.16
esoteric
n occultist 689.11
adj secret 345.11
confidential 345.14
latent 519.5
implied 519.7
recondite 522.16
occult 689.23
intrinsic 766.7
particular 864.12
supernatural 869.15
ESP
communication 343.1
clairvoyance 689.8
espionage
observation 27.2
surveillance 937.9
esplanade 383.2
espousal
adoption 371.4
betrothal 436.3
espouse
adopt 371.15
join with 509.13
get married 563.15
defend 600.10
esprit heart 93.3
gaiety 109.4
cooperation 450.1
accord 455.1
wit 489.1
intellect 918.1
smartness 919.2
espy see 27.12
detect 940.5

esquire
n beau 104.13
nobleman 608.4
escort 768.5
v court 562.21
escort 768.8
essay
n attempt 403.2
writing 547.10
treatise 556.1
test 941.2
v attempt 403.6
experiment 941.8
essence odor 69.1
perfumery 70.2
extract 192.8
essential content
196.5
meaning 518.1
summary 557.2
existence 760.1
substance 766.2
major part 791.6
intrinsicalness 892.3
topic 936.1
salient point 996.6
essential
n essence 766.2
requirement 962.2
adj quintessential
192.18
basic 199.8
of the essence 766.9
simple 797.6
requisite 962.13
vital 996.23
establish fix 159.16
publicize 352.15
accustom 373.10
legalize 673.8
inaugurate 817.11
stable 854.9
cause 885.10
found 891.10
prove 956.10
make sure 969.11
establishment
foundation 159.7
the best 249.5
structure 266.2
organization 617.8
market 736.1
workplace 739.1
hierarchy 808.4
beginning 817.1
fixity 854.2
foundation 891.4
proof 956.3
ensuring 969.8
the Establishment
the authorities 575.15
the government 612.3
influence 893.6
estate
mansion 228.7
rank 245.2
interest 471.4
class 607.1
state 764.1
category 808.2
esteem
n respect 155.1

approval 509.1
estimation 662.3
influence 893.1
notability 996.2
v cherish 104.21
respect 155.4
approve 509.9
judge 945.8
think 952.11
value 996.13
esthetic 1015.17
estimable
venerable 155.12
measurable 300.14
praiseworthy 509.20
honest 644.13
reputable 662.15
influential 893.13
notable 996.19
good 998.12
calculable 1016.24
estimate
n measurement 300.1
estimation 945.3
opinion 952.6
gamble 970.8
v measure 300.10
form an estimate
945.9
think 952.11
calculate 1016.17
estrange
sow dissension 456.14
antagonize 589.7
separate 801.8
estuary outlet 190.9
inlet 242.1
et al
adv in the majority
882.10
phrs et cetera 253.14
et cetera
adv in the majority
882.10
phrs and so forth
253.14
etch eat 713.10
fix 854.9
etching 713.2
eternal
mandatory 420.12
almighty 677.18
infinite 822.3
perpetual 828.7
eternity
timelessness 821.1
infinity 822.1
long time 826.4
perpetuity 828.1
an eternity 828.2
ether height 272.2
lightness 298.2
air 317.1
spirit 763.3
coolant 1023.7
the heavens 1070.2
ethereal thin 270.16
high 272.14
light 298.10
rare 299.4
airy 317.11
heavenly 681.12

unsubstantial 763.6
chimeric 985.22
spectral 987.7
immaterial 1051.7
vaporous 1065.9
ethical moral 636.6
dutiful 641.13
honest 644.13
ethics principles 636.1
duty 641.1
ethnic
n person 312.5
adj racial 559.7
ethnicity
humankind 312.1
race 559.4
exclusiveness 772.3
ethos culture 373.3
ethics 636.1
nature 766.4
ideology 931.8
opinion 952.6
climate 977.5
etiology cause 885.1
attribution 887.1
etiquette
good behavior 321.2
custom 373.1
mannerliness 504.3
social convention
579.1
social code 580.3
etymologist 523.13
etymology 526.15
eugenics
improvement 392.1
heredity 560.6
euhemeristic 341.15
eulogy dirge 115.6
last offices 309.4
praise 509.5
speech 543.2
citation 646.4
eunuch impotent 19.6
sexlessness 75.9
euphemism
overniceness 500.5
catchword 526.9
affectation 533.3
euphonious
harmonious 533.8
melodious 708.48
euphoric pleased 95.14
content 107.7
cheerful 109.11
euphuistic
overnice 500.18
affected 533.9
grandiloquent 545.8
eureka! 940.11
Europe
world region 231.6
continent 235.1
eurythmic 264.4
Euterpe music 710.22
Muse 720.10
creative thought 985.2
euthanasia
natural death 307.7
killing 308.1
evacuate defecate 12.13
quit 188.9

abandon 370.5
void 908.22
let out 908.24
evade avoid 164.6
prevaricate 344.7
elude 368.7
escape 369.6
outwit 415.11
remain neutral 467.5
be dishonest 645.11
pull back 902.7
quibble 935.9
evaluate
measure 300.10
price 630.11
criticize 723.5
classify 800.8
estimate 945.9
evanescence
disappearance 34.1
recession 168.1
infinitesimalness
258.2
unsubstantiality 763.1
transience 827.1
evanescent
infinitesimal 258.14
thin 763.6
transient 827.7
evangelical
scriptural 683.10
orthodox 687.7
strict 687.8
evangelist herald 353.2
lecturer 543.5
religion 684.2
worshiper 696.9
revivalist 699.6
converter 857.9
evangelistic
scriptural 683.10
ecclesiastic 698.13
evaporate
disappear 34.2
preserve 397.9
cease to exist 761.6
dissipate 770.5
flit 827.6
dry 1064.6
vaporize 1065.8
evasion
prevarication 344.4
secrecy 345.1
avoidance 368.1
escape 369.1
circumvention 415.5
neutrality 467.1
retreat 902.3
quibbling 935.5
Eve 77.5
even
n evening 315.2
v level 201.6
symmetrize 264.3
smooth 287.5
make uniform 780.4
equalize 789.6
adj horizontal 201.7
parallel 203.6
symmetric 264.4
straight 277.6
smooth 287.9

neutral 467.7
just 649.8
equable 670.13
uniform 780.5
equal 789.7
periodic 849.7
interchangeable 862.5
exact 972.17
numeric 1016.22
adv chiefly 249.17
notwithstanding
338.8
interchangeably
862.6
exactly 972.21
even break
gambling odds 759.6
equating 789.2
opportunity 842.2
even chance 971.7
evenhanded
just 649.8
impartial 649.10
unprejudiced 978.12
evening
symmetrization 264.2
equating 789.2
evening
n post meridiem 315
eve 315.2
adj evensong 315.8
event game 743.9
circumstance 765.1
eventuality 830.1
occurrence 830.2
effect 886.1
even-tempered
inexcitable 106.10
equable 670.13
eventuality
circumstance 765.1
event 830.1
the future 838.1
futurity 838.4
effect 886.1
liability 896.1
possibility 965.1
ever forever 828.12
constantly 846.7
by any possibility
965.10
everglade 243.1
evergreen
n plant 310.3
tree 310.10
adj arboreal 310.36
perennial 310.41
durable 826.10
perennial 828.8
new 840.7
everlasting
tedious 118.9
almighty 677.18
perpetual 828.7
immortal 828.9
ever so greatly 247.15
chiefly 249.17
ever so little 248.9
every 863.15
everybody
the people 606.1
all 863.4

exchange
n communication 343.1
telephone number 347.12
banter 490.1
retaliation 506.1
conversation 541.1
transfer 629.1
trade 731.2
stock exchange 737.7
changing 853.3
substitution 861.1
substitute 861.2
transpose 862.1
v transfer 629.3
trade 731.14
change 851.7
interchange 853.5
substitute 861.4
transpose 862.4
exchange rate 728.9
exchequer
storehouse 386.6
funds 728.14
treasury 729.12
excise
extract 192.10
cut out 255.10
sever 801.11
excitable
emotional 105.28
irascible 110.19
nervous 128.11
excitation
arousal 105.11
incitement 375.4
excite sensitize 24.7
impassion 105.12
incite 375.17
agitate 916.10
interest 982.12
heat 1019.18
excitement
passion 93.2
stimulation 105
emotion 105.1
excitation 105.11
impatience 135.1
incitement 375.4
agitation 916.1
heat metaphor 1018.2
exciting
desirable 100.30
thrilling 105.30
provocative 375.27
alluring 377.8
vehement 544.13
interesting 982.19
exclaim
give an exclamation 59.7
remark 524.25
speak 524.26
exclaim at
object 333.5
offer resistance 453.3
exclamation
ejaculation 59.2
remark 524.4
exclude excise 255.10
close 293.6

reject 372.2
prohibit 444.3
disapprove 510.10
bar 772.4
eject 908.13
banish 908.17
prevent 1011.14
exclusion
excision 255.3
closure 293.1
rejection 372.1
prohibition 444.1
disapproval 510.1
barring 772.1
banishment 908.4
qualification 958.1
exclusive
n news item 552.3
adj contemptuous 157.8
limiting 210.9
closed 293.9
selective 371.23
prohibitive 444.6
selective 495.13
aloof 583.6
cliquish 617.18
excluding 772.9
one 871.7
exclusivity
contempt 157.1
selectness 495.5
seclusiveness 583.3
partisanism 617.13
exclusion 772.1
excogitate 930.11
excommunication
deposal 447.2
curse 513.1
condemnation 602.1
banishment 908.4
excoriation
unclothing 6.1
torment 96.7
censure 510.3
excrement
dejection 12.3
filth 80.7
excretion discharge 12
egestion 12.1
secretion 13.1
exuding 190.6
evacuation 908.6
excruciating
sensitive 24.13
painful 26.10
agonizing 98.23
exculpate
forgive 148.3
justify 600.9
acquit 601.4
excursion
deviation 164.1
journey 177.5
obliquity 204.1
digression 538.4
circuitousness 913.1
detour 913.3
excursus
deviation 164.1
digression 538.4
treatise 556.1

circuitousness 913.1
excuse
n pardon 148.2
pretext 376.1
cop-out 600.4
acquittal 601.1
apology 658.2
reason 885.2
v forgive 148.3
exempt 430.14
alibi 600.11
acquit 601.4
execrable
offensive 98.18
cursed 513.9
wicked 654.16
base 661.12
damnable 999.10
execration hate 103.1
hated thing 103.3
berating 510.7
curse 513.1
execute kill 308.12
perform 328.9
accomplish 407.4
perform 434.3
complete 437.9
put to death 604.17
play 708.39
produce 891.11
execution
killing 308.1
action 328.2
accomplishment 407.1
observance 434.1
completion 437.4
attachment 480.5
capital punishment 604.7
performance 708.30
operation 888.1
performance 891.5
executive
n officer 574.3
governor 575.6
operator 888.4
adj grandiose 501.21
officiating 573.14
administrative 612.19
expensive 632.11
the executive 574.11
executor doer 726.1
producer 891.7
exegesis
explanation 341.4
comment 341.5
exegetic
interpretative 341.14
explanatory 341.15
exemplar
representative 349.7
paragon 659.4
example 785.2
rule 868.4
philosophy 931.2
pattern of perfection 1001.4
exemplary
typical 349.15
warning 399.7
praiseworthy 509.20

model 785.8
perfected 1001.9
exemplify
explain 341.10
image 349.11
set an example 785.7
cite 956.13
exempt
v free 430.14
acquit 601.4
adj immune 430.30
exemption
pardon 148.2
exception 430.8
immunity 601.2
qualification 958.1
exercise
n physical conditioning 84
motion 84.2
action 328.1
use 387.1
training 568.3
lesson 568.7
study 570.3
ceremony 580.4
task 724.2
exercising 725.6
operation 888.1
v work out 84.4
annoy 96.13
practice 328.8
use 387.10
train 568.13
exert 725.8
engross 982.13
exert use 387.10
exercise 725.8
exertion use 387.1
endeavor 403.1
effort 725.1
exfoliate scale 6.11
layer 296.5
break 801.12
exfoliation
unclothing 6.1
stratification 296.4
disruption 801.3
exhalation
breathing 2.19
murmur 52.4
odor 69.1
outflow 190.4
cloud 1065.1
vaporization 1065.5
exhaust
n wash 184.30
outflow 190.4
outlet 190.9
miasma 1000.4
rocket propulsion 1072.8
v weaken 16.10
unman 19.12
fatigue 21.4
oppress 98.16
run out 190.13
draw off 192.12
spend 387.13
consume 388.3
strip 480.24
waste 486.4

evacuate 908.22
let out 908.24
disgorge 908.25
overdo 992.10
exhaustion
weakness 16.1
debilitation 16.5
draining 21.2
unhealthiness 85.3
collapse 85.8
decrement 252.3
consumption 388.1
waste 473.2
evacuation 908.6
exhaustive great 247.6
broad 269.6
complete 407.12
whole 791.9
thorough 793.10
exhibit
n display 348.2
theatrical
　performance 704.12
evidence 956.1
v externalize 206.5
manifest 348.5
flaunt 501.17
evidence 956.8
exhibition
spectacle 33.7
demonstration 348.2
display 501.4
theatrical
　performance 704.12
exhibitionism
unclothing 6.1
perversion 75.11
display 501.4
immodesty 666.2
exhilarate refresh 9.2
energize 17.10
stimulate 105.13
cheer 109.7
inspire 375.20
amuse 743.21
exhilaration
refreshment 9.1
energizing 17.8
happiness 95.2
excitement 105.1
excitation 105.11
good humor 109.2
inspiration 375.9
exhortation
inducement 375.3
advice 422.1
call to arms 458.8
speech 543.2
exhumation
disinterment 192.2
discovery 940.1
exigency
insistence 421.4
crisis 842.4
urgent need 962.4
urgency 996.4
exigent
meticulous 339.12
demanding 421.9
strict 425.6
critical 842.10
necessary 962.12

urgent 996.22
exiguous little 258.10
sparse 884.5
meager 991.10
exile
n displaced person
　160.4
migrant 178.5
emigration 190.7
outcast 586.4
elimination 772.2
alien 773.3
banishment 908.4
v emigrate 190.16
ostracize 586.6
eliminate 772.5
banish 908.17
exist be present 221.6
live 306.7
be 760.8
endure 826.6
existence
presence 221.1
life 306.1
being 760.1
existentialism 760.7
exit
n departure 188.1
egress 190.2
outlet 190.9
channel 239.1
death 307.1
flight 368.4
passageway 383.3
v disappear 34.2
depart 188.6
make an exit 190.12
absent oneself 222.8
find vent 369.10
exodus departure 188.1
egress 190.2
act 704.7
exonerate 601.4
exorbitant
exaggerated 355.4
demanding 421.9
overpriced 632.12
violent 671.16
excessive 992.16
exorcism
conjuration 690.4
spell 691.1
exorcist shaman 690.7
holy orders 699.4
exotic
n plant 310.3
adj colorful 35.18
distant 261.8
alluring 377.8
extraneous 773.5
unrelated 775.6
expand
increase 251.4
grow 259.4
enlarge 259.5
spread 259.6
broaden 269.4
rarefy 299.3
amplify 538.7
disperse 770.4
elaborate 860.6
generalize 863.9

expand on
amplify 538.7
elaborate 860.6
expanse space 158.1
spaciousness 158.5
greatness 247.1
size 257.1
breadth 269.1
expansion
space 158.1
increase 251.1
size 257.1
increase in size 259
extension 259.1
exaggeration 355.1
amplification 538.6
business cycle 731.9
dispersion 770.1
evolution 860.1
expansive
v talkative 540.9
adj spacious 158.10
voluminous 257.17
extensive 259.9
broad 269.6
communicative
　343.10
expatriate
n migrant 178.5
outcast 586.4
v migrate 177.22
leave home 188.17
emigrate 190.16
eliminate 772.5
banish 908.17
expect hope 124.7
be expectant 130.5
come 838.6
suppose 950.10
think 952.11
expectation
unastonishment 123.1
hope 124.1
anticipation 130
expectance 130.1
dueness 639.1
the future 838.1
probability 967.1
expecting
pregnant 78.18
unastonished 123.3
expectant 130.11
expectorate 13.6
expedience
transience 827.1
timeliness 842.1
advisability 994.1
goodness 998.1
expedient
n instrumentality
　384.3
stratagem 415.3
means 994.2
recourse 1008.2
adj useful 387.18
transient 827.7
timely 842.9
conditional 958.8
desirable 994.5
good 998.12
expedite
advance 162.5

send 176.15
hasten 401.4
be useful 449.17
facilitate 1013.7
expedition
velocity 174.1
journey 177.5
quickness 330.3
adventure 404.2
furtherance 449.5
campaign 458.4
promptness 844.3
facilitation 1013.5
expeditious fast 174.15
quick 330.18
hasty 401.9
prompt 844.9
expel
transfer 176.10
depose 447.4
eliminate 772.5
separate 801.8
eject 908.13
banish 908.17
dismiss 908.19
disgorge 908.25
expend
spend 387.13
consume 388.3
waste 486.4
pay out 624.14
spend 626.5
expendable
consumable 388.6
replaceable 861.10
superfluous 992.17
unimportant 997.16
expenditure use 387.1
consumption 388.1
waste 473.2
spending 626.1
price 630.1
expense loss 473.1
expenditure 626.1
charges 626.3
price 630.1
expensive 632.11
experience
n sensation 24.1
practice 413.9
event 830.2
knowledge 927.1
v sense 24.6
feel 93.10
have 830.8
experienced
accustomed 373.16
practiced 413.28
experiment
n attempt 403.2
testing 941
trial 941.1
v see what one can do
　403.10
experimentalize 941.8
expert
n adept 413.11
adviser 422.3
connoisseur 496.7
specialist 865.3
scientist 927.11
adj skillful 413.22

specialized 865.5
perfected 1001.9
expertise skill 413.1
aesthetic taste 496.5
knowledge 927.1
profound knowledge
927.6
expiate
compensate 338.4
atone 658.4
expiration
breathing 2.19
death 307.1
end 819.1
expire die 307.19
perish 395.23
cease to exist 761.6
come to an end 819.6
elapse 820.5
let out 908.24
explain
explicate 341.10
make clear 521.6
expound 568.16
justify 600.9
excuse 600.11
solve 939.2
facilitate 1013.7
explain away
explain 341.10
extenuate 600.12
reason speciously
935.8
explainer 341.7
explain oneself 341.10
explanation
explication 341.4
definition 518.3
justification 600.1
example 785.2
reason 885.2
solution 939.1
theory 950.1
theorization 950.2
expletive
n exclamation 59.2
oath 513.4
redundancy 848.3
superfluity 992.4
adj superfluous 992.17
explicable
interpretable 341.17
attributable 887.6
solvable 939.3
explicate
explain 341.10
make clear 521.6
amplify 538.7
criticize 723.5
explicit manifest 348.8
clear 521.11
candid 644.17
unqualified 959.2
explode blast 56.8
be excitable 105.16
fly into a rage 152.20
grow 251.6
destruct 395.18
come to nothing
410.13
blow up 671.14
disprove 957.4

fuel 1020.7
exploit
n act 328.3
feat 492.7
v take advantage of
387.15
use 387.16
overprice 632.7
exploration
adventure 404.2
reconnaissance 937.8
search 937.15
exploratory
preceding 815.4
examining 937.36
explore
investigate 937.22
search 937.30
explosion
detonation 56.3
outbreak 105.9
outburst 152.9
intensification 251.2
discharge 671.7
disproof 957.1
explosive
n high explosive
462.14
speech sound 524.13
adj banging 56.11
excitable 105.28
hot-tempered 110.25
bursting 671.24
dangerous 1005.9
exponent
interpreter 341.7
representative 349.7
deputy 576.1
supporter 616.9
example 785.2
export
n transferal 176.1
exporting 190.8
v transfer 176.10
send 176.15
send abroad 190.17
expose
divest 6.5
unclose 292.12
disclose 351.4
stigmatize 661.9
uncover 940.4
disprove 957.4
disillusion 976.2
endanger 1005.6
exposé
disclosure 351.1
disproof 957.1
expose oneself to 896.3
exposition
spectacle 33.7
explanation 341.4
display 348.2
disclosure 351.1
treatise 556.1
lesson 568.7
passage 708.24
marketplace 736.2
expository
explanatory 341.15
manifesting 348.9
dissertational 556.6

expostulate
object 333.5
dissuade 379.3
admonish 422.6
exposure
unclothing 6.1
visibility 31.1
distinctness 31.2
appearance 33.1
navigation 159.3
display 348.2
disclosure 351.1
publicity 352.4
repute 662.1
time exposure 714.9
susceptibility 896.2
discovery 940.1
disproof 957.1
openness 1005.3
radiation physics
1036.7
expound
explain 341.10
exposit 568.16
express
n carrier 176.7
train 179.14
messenger 353.1
message 552.4
v send 176.15
extraction 192.16
affirm 334.5
manifest 348.5
describe 349.9
signify 517.17
say 524.23
phrase 532.4
evidence 956.8
adj fast 174.15
manifest 348.8
clear 521.11
particular 864.12
unqualified 959.2
exact 972.17
adv posthaste 401.13
expression
extraction 192.1
extract 192.7
manifestation 348.1
indication 517.3
remark 524.4
word 526.1
phrase 529.1
diction 532.1
eloquence 544.1
execution 708.30
maxim 973.1
expressive
manifesting 348.9
descriptive 349.14
indicative 517.23
meaningful 518.10
graphic 544.10
expropriate
attach 480.20
dispossess 480.23
expulsion
transferal 176.1
deposal 447.2
elimination 772.2
ejection 908.1
disgorgement 908.7

expunge
delete 255.12
obliterate 395.16
end 819.5
expurgate clean 79.18
delete 255.12
exquisite
n dandy 500.9
adj sensitive 24.13
painful 26.10
tasty 63.8
delightful 97.7
meticulous 339.12
nice 495.11
overnice 500.18
chic 578.13
superb 998.15
fine 1015.19
exsanguineous 36.7
exsiccated 1064.9
extant remaining 256.7
existent 760.13
present 837.2
extemporaneous
extemporary 365.12
unprepared 406.8
extemporize
improvise 365.8
be unprepared 406.6
extend reach 158.8
increase 251.4
enlarge 259.4
grow 259.5
spread 259.6
reach out 261.5
be long 267.5
lengthen 267.6
broaden 269.4
straighten 277.5
offer 439.4
give 478.12
diffuse 538.8
race 757.5
endure 826.6
protract 826.9
postpone 845.9
sustain 855.4
generalize 863.9
stretch 1046.4
extension
space 158.1
increase 251.1
adjunct 254.1
addition 254.3
size 257.1
expansion 259.1
length 267.1
lengthening 267.4
telephone 347.4
meaning 518.1
sequence 814.1
protraction 826.2
continuance 855.1
stretching 1046.2
extensive
spacious 158.10
large 247.7
voluminous 257.17
expansive 259.9
long 267.7
broad 269.6
general 863.13

flirt 562.20
spectate 917.5
adj optic 2.26
visual 27.20
the eye 27.3
eyeball
n eye 2.9
visual organ 27.9
v look 27.13
examine 937.23
adj visual 27.20
eyeball to eyeball
contrapositive 215.5
opposite 215.6
front 216.10
in opposition 451.9
contrary 778.6
eyebrows 3.12
eye-catching
alluring 377.8
attracting 906.5
an eye for 413.5
an eye for an eye
tit for tat 506.3
interchange 862.1
eyeglasses 29.3
eyelashes 3.12
eyelet 280.5
eyelid eye 2.9
visual organ 27.9
eye of the storm
center 208.2
storm 671.4
eye-opening
astonishing 122.12
surprising 131.11
disclosive 351.10
eyesight vision 27.1
field of view 31.3
eyesore stain 1003.3
blot 1014.4
eyewitness
spectator 917.1
witness 956.6
eyrie 228.23
Fabianism
reform 392.5
socialism 611.6
fable
n fabrication 354.10
plot 722.4
v narrate 722.6
fabled 662.16
fabric material 4.1
essential content 196.5
house 228.5
structure 266.1
building 266.2
frame 266.4
weaving 740.1
substance 762.2
fabricate invent 354.17
compose 795.3
produce 891.8
originate 891.12
imagine 985.14
fabrication
structure 266.1
falsehood 354.10
composition 795.1
production 891.1

manufacture 891.2
invention 985.3
fabricator liar 357.9
doer 726.1
fabulous
wonderful 122.10
remarkable 247.10
fabricated 354.28
mythic 678.15
fictional 722.7
extraordinary 869.14
fictitious 985.21
excessive 992.16
facade appearance 33.2
exterior 206.2
front 216.1
sham 354.3
pretext 376.1
affectation 500.1
face
n looks 33.4
pride 136.1
impudence 142.3
precipice 200.3
exterior 206.2
front 216.1
facies 216.4
slope 237.2
sham 354.3
rallying device 458.12
type 548.6
worth 630.2
reputability 662.2
prestige 662.4
v color 35.13
expect 130.5
fill 196.7
contrapose 215.4
confront 216.8
veneer 295.23
plaster 295.25
oppose 451.5
defy 454.3
brave 492.11
be imminent 839.2
faceless uniform 780.5
indistinguishable 944.6
face-lift
n renovation 396.4
v renovate 396.17
face mask 1007.3
facet aspect 33.3
exterior 206.2
front 216.1
particular 765.3
face the music
submit 433.6
brave 492.11
take one's
punishment 604.21
facetious 489.15
face-to-face
adj adjacent 223.16
adv opposite 215.6
openly 348.15
facial
beautification 1015.11
massage 1042.3
facile docile 433.13
eloquent 544.8
fluent 544.9

teachable 570.18
easy 1013.13
pliant 1045.9
facilitate
advance 162.5
be instrumental 384.7
be useful 449.17
ease 1013.7
facilitator
planner 381.6
instrument 384.4
helper 449.7
agent 576.3
producer 891.7
facility ability 18.2
equipment 385.4
skill 413.1
submissiveness 433.3
accommodation 449.9
fluency 544.2
teachableness 570.5
workplace 739.1
ease 1013.1
machinery 1039.3
pliancy 1045.2
facing
n lining 196.3
blanket 295.12
adj contrapositive 215.5
fronting 216.11
adv frontward 216.13
prep opposite to 215.7
facsimile
n reproduction 336.3
Telephoto 347.15
the same 777.3
copy 784.1
duplicate 784.3
print 784.5
v copy 784.8
adj communicational 347.20
fact the case 760.3
particular 765.3
event 830.2
evidence 956.1
truth 972.1
faction
dissension 456.3
party 617.4
partisanism 617.13
sect 675.3
company 769.3
disagreement 788.1
factitious 354.25
factor
n heredity 560.6
steward 574.4
agent 576.3
particular 765.3
component 795.2
cause 885.1
v classify 800.8
calculate 1016.17
factory 739.3
factotum 577.9
facts
information 551.1
knowledge 927.1
evidence 956.1
the facts 760.4

factual real 760.15
evidential 956.16
obvious 969.15
true 972.13
faculty
ability 18.2
talent 413.4
authority 417.1
staff 571.9
prerogative 642.1
intellect 918.2
fad
caprice 364.1
great success 409.3
craze 578.5
fade
n motion-picture editing 706.5
v weaken 16.9
disappear 34.2
decolor 36.5
lose color 36.6
fail 85.47
recede 168.2
age 303.10
decline 393.17
languish 393.18
play 751.4
race 757.5
bet 759.25
cease to exist 761.6
flit 827.6
pass 836.6
age 841.9
pull back 902.7
adj insipid 65.2
trite 117.9
fag
n homosexual 75.15
cigarette 89.5
work 725.4
drudge 726.3
v get tired 21.6
drudge 725.14
task 725.16
fail weaken 16.9
lose strength 85.47
be inferior 250.4
age 303.10
neglect 340.6
decline 393.17
neglect 408.2
be unsuccessful 410.9
flunk 410.17
go bankrupt 625.7
be unfaithful 645.12
dramatize 704.28
fall short 910.2
be insufficient 991.8
failing
n deterioration 393.3
vice 654.2
fault 1002.2
adj languishing 16.21
unhealthy 85.53
deteriorating 393.45
unsuccessful 410.18
incomplete 794.4
insufficient 991.9
fail-safe 1006.5
failure
ineffectiveness 19.3

disappointment 132.1
inadequacy 250.3
neglect 340.1
deterioration 393.3
nonaccomplishment
  408.1
unsuccessfulness
  410.1
flash in the pan 410.7
defeat 412.1
nonobservance 435.1
bankruptcy 625.3
insolvent 625.4
vice 654.2
misdeed 655.2
stage show 704.4
shortcoming 910.1
mistake 974.3
loss of memory 989.2
fault 1002.2
faint
  n unconsciousness
    25.2
  v weaken 16.9
burn out 21.5
swoon 25.5
  adj weak 16.12
tired 21.7
inconspicuous 32.6
colorless 36.7
low 52.16
ill 85.55
weak-willed 362.12
fainthearted
weak-willed 362.12
cowardly 491.10
fair
  n marketplace 736.2
festival 743.4
  adj whitish 37.8
clean 79.25
pleasant 97.6
bright 97.11
auspicious 133.18
courteous 504.14
legible 521.12
rightful 639.8
honest 644.13
just 649.8
probable 967.6
unprejudiced 978.12
good 998.12
tolerable 998.20
mediocre 1004.7
thriving 1009.13
comely 1015.18
warm 1018.24
rainless 1064.8
  adv pleasantly 97.12
justly 649.11
fair game
laughingstock 508.7
opportunity 842.2
fair-haired boy 104.16
fairly to a degree 245.7
limited 248.10
legibly 521.14
justly 649.11
tolerably 998.24
mediocrely 1004.11
fair-minded 649.9
fair name 662.2

fairway seaway 182.10
runway 184.23
green 310.7
playground 743.11
golf 751.1
fair-weather friend
  357.8
fairy
  n homosexual 75.15
lightness 298.2
sprite 678.8
  adj elfin 678.17
fairy tale 354.11
fait accompli
act 328.3
accomplishment
  407.1
fact 760.3
a truth 972.2
faith zeal 101.2
hope 124.1
obedience 326.1
observance 434.1
promise 436.1
school 617.5
fidelity 644.7
cardinal virtues 653.4
religion 675.1
piety 692.1
cause 885.9
belief 952.1
system of belief 952.3
confidence 969.5
the faith 687.2
faithful
  n person of honor
    644.8
  adj zealous 101.9
loving 104.27
obedient 326.3
descriptive 349.14
persevering 360.8
observant 434.4
devoted 587.21
loyal 644.20
orthodox 687.7
pious 692.8
lifelike 783.16
permanent 852.7
belief 952.21
reliable 969.17
exact 972.17
the faithful
the believing 692.5
believer 952.9
faith healer 90.9
faithless
falsehearted 354.30
apostate 363.11
unfaithful 645.20
atheistic 695.19
unbelieving 954.8
fake
  n fakement 354.13
hoax 356.7
impostor 357.6
affecter 500.7
basketball game 747.3
copy 784.1
substitute 861.2
  v imitate 336.5
tamper with 354.16

fabricate 354.17
sham 354.20
improvise 365.8
affect 500.12
play 747.4
  adj imitation 336.8
spurious 354.25
assumed 500.16
similar 783.10
substitute 861.8
faker imitator 336.4
deceiver 357.1
impostor 357.6
fakir ascetic 667.2
clergy 699.11
falafel 10.9
falcate 279.11
falcon
  n bird 311.28
heraldry 647.2
  v hunt 382.9
fall
  n false hair 3.13
descent 194.1
tumble 194.3
hang 202.2
declivity 204.5
waterfall 238.11
decline 252.2
autumn 313.4
rain 316.1
plunge 367.1
deterioration 393.3
backsliding 394.2
downfall 395.3
collapse 410.3
defeat 412.1
original sin 655.3
downthrow 912.2
  v descend 194.5
tumble 194.8
incline 204.10
decrease 252.6
die 307.19
rain 316.9
plunge 367.6
decline 393.17
relapse 394.4
be destroyed 395.22
fall down 410.12
lose 412.12
cheapen 633.6
go wrong 654.9
occur 830.5
collide 901.13
come to grief 1010.10
fallacious false 354.24
deceptive 356.21
unorthodox 688.9
sophistical 935.10
illogical 935.11
erroneous 974.16
illusory 975.8
fallacy
falseness 354.1
deception 356.1
heresy 688.2
sophistry 935.1
specious argument
  935.3
error 974.1

fall all over 138.9
fall all over oneself
jump at 101.6
be willing 324.3
make haste 401.5
make a special effort
  403.11
fall apart
lose self-control 128.7
break 393.23
come apart 801.9
fall asleep
go to sleep 22.16
die 307.19
fall away
  n apostatize 363.7
  v incline 204.10
decrease 252.6
decline 393.17
fall short 910.2
fall back
retreat 163.6
be behind 217.8
deteriorate 393.16
relapse 394.4
pull back 902.7
fall behind
regress 163.5
lag 166.4
be behind 217.8
fall down
drift off course 182.29
descend 194.5
tumble 194.8
fall 410.12
fall through 910.3
fall short 1002.3
fallen underdone 11.8
reduced 252.10
dead 307.30
ruined 395.28
defeated 412.14
unvirtuous 654.12
carnal 663.6
prostitute 665.28
impious 694.6
unregenerate 695.18
depressed 912.12
fall flat
fall flat as a pancake
  117.4
tumble 194.8
fall 410.12
fall through 910.3
fall for
fall in love 104.22
kid oneself 953.6
fall from grace
  n backsliding 394.2
original sin 655.3
impiety 694.1
  v relapse 394.4
fall guy dupe 358.2
loser 412.5
scapegoat 861.3
fall in
collapse 260.10
obey 326.2
break down 393.24
fall 410.12
form 806.5
fall in love 104.22

fall into place 806.5
fall in with
  converge 169.2
  concur 332.9
  acquiesce 441.3
  side with 450.4
  get along 455.2
  associate with 582.17
  conform 866.3
  follow the rule 866.4
  incur 896.4
  come across 940.3
fall off
  n apostatize 363.7
  v descend 194.5
  incline 204.10
  decrease 252.6
  decline 393.17
  come apart 801.9
fall on
  light upon 194.10
  attack 459.14
  come across 940.3
  chance 971.11
fallout
  radiation 1036.1
  atomic explosion
    1037.16
  powder 1049.5
fall out
  have a falling-out
    456.10
  result 886.4
fallow
  n farm 1067.8
  v cultivate 1067.17
  adj colorless 36.7
  yellow 43.4
  idle 331.18
  untilled 406.14
  unproductive 890.4
falls 238.11
fall short
  be disappointing
    132.3
  be inferior 250.4
  fall 410.12
  lack 794.3
  come short 910.2
  be insufficient 991.8
  come short 1002.3
fall to eat 8.20
  undertake 404.3
  set to work 725.15
  begin 817.7
fall upon
  be unexpected 131.6
  arrive at 186.7
  meet 223.11
  attack 459.14
false
  untrue 354.24
  falsehearted 354.30
  deceptive 356.21
  deceitful 356.22
  unfaithful 645.20
  illegitimate 674.7
  sanctimonious 693.5
  erroneous 974.16
  illusory 975.8
false alarm
  cry of wolf 400.2

failure 410.8
falsehood
  falseness 354.1
  untruthfulness 354.8
  lie 354.11
falsetto
  n high voice 58.6
  speech defect 525.1
  voice 709.5
  adj high 58.13
  vocal 708.50
falsify
  pervert 265.6
  belie 354.15
  lie 354.18
  be dishonest 645.11
  misrepresent 350.3
falter
  n demur 325.2
  hesitation 362.3
  trill 709.19
  shake 916.3
  flounder 916.8
  v despair 125.10
  dawdle 175.8
  demur 325.4
  hesitate 362.7
  lose one's nerve
    491.8
  stammer 525.8
  shake 916.11
  flounder 916.15
  hang in doubt 970.10
fame glory 247.2
  publicity 352.4
  repute 662.1
  notability 996.2
familiar
  n friend 588.1
  familiar spirit 678.12
  adj trite 117.9
  insolent 142.9
  customary 373.14
  vernacular 523.18
  informal 581.3
  intimate 582.24
  friendly 587.19
  usual 868.9
  well-known 927.27
familiarity
  informality 581.1
  sociability 582.1
  intimacy 587.5
  presumption 640.2
  knowledge 927.1
familiarize
  accustom 373.10
  inform 551.8
familiar with
  used to 373.17
  versed in 927.19
family
  n nomenclature 527.1
  kinfolk 559.2
  race 559.4
  brood 559.5
  lineage 560.4
  offspring 561.1
  community 617.2
  classifications 808.5
  sequel 834.2
  biology 1066.1

adj racial 559.7
  lineal 560.18
family tree 560.5
famine
  unproductiveness
    890.1
  want 991.4
famine price 632.3
famished
  hungry 100.25
  ill-provided 991.12
famous eminent 247.9
  distinguished 662.16
  good 998.12
fan
  n enthusiast 101.5
  follower 166.2
  fork 171.4
  attender 221.5
  ventilator 317.9
  flabellum 318.19
  commender 509.8
  supporter 616.9
  specialist 865.3
  propeller 903.6
  fanatic 925.18
  cooler 1023.3
  v excite 105.12
  spread 259.6
  air 317.10
  incite 375.17
  fail 410.10
  play 745.5
  shuffle 758.4
fanatic
  n enthusiast 101.4
  obstinate person
    361.6
  believer 692.4
  oddity 869.4
  lunatic 925.15
  infatuate 925.18
  bigot 979.5
  adj obstinate 361.8
  fiery 671.22
  fanatical 925.32
fanaticism
  overzealousness 101.3
  obstinacy 361.1
  turbulence 671.2
  zeal 692.3
  cause 885.9
  rabidness 925.11
  narrow-mindedness
    979.1
fanciful
  capricious 364.5
  unreal 761.9
  thin 763.6
  fantastic 869.12
  ideational 931.9
  notional 985.20
fancy
  n desire 100.1
  inclination 100.3
  love 104.1
  will 323.1
  caprice 364.1
  impulse 365.1
  preference 371.5
  idea 931.1
  phantasy 975.3

imagination 985.1
  figment of the
    imagination 985.5
  v desire 100.14
  love 104.19
  suppose 950.10
  think 952.11
  imagine 985.14
  adj edible 8.33
  skillful 413.22
  ornate 498.12
  ostentatious 501.18
  grandiose 501.21
  grand 545.11
  expensive 632.11
  overpriced 632.12
  excessive 992.16
  inter imagine! 122.22
fancy that! 122.22
fanfare blare 53.5
  celebration 487.1
  Aldine 554.15
fang teeth 2.8
  sting 1000.5
fanged toothlike 285.14
  prehensile 474.9
fangs 474.4
fan mail 553.4
fanny 217.5
fan out diverge 171.5
  spread 259.6
  disperse 770.4
fantasize
  fabricate 354.17
  imagine 985.14
fantastic
  wonderful 122.10
  remarkable 247.10
  fabricated 354.28
  capricious 364.5
  unreal 761.9
  unbelievable 869.12
  absurd 922.11
  illusory 975.8
  fanciful 985.20
fantasy
  n defense mechanism
    92.23
  desire 100.1
  caprice 364.1
  miracle 869.8
  phantom 975.4
  abstractedness 984.2
  imagination 985.1
  figment of the
    imagination 985.5
  v muse 984.9
  dream 985.17
fan the flame
  excite 105.12
  incite 375.17
  sow dissension 456.14
  ignite 1019.22
far
  adj distant 261.8
  adv by far 247.17
  far off 261.15
far and away
  by far 247.17
  superlatively 249.16
farce stuffing 10.26
  wit 489.1

burlesque 508.6
trifle 997.5
farcical comic 488.6
witty 489.15
burlesque 508.14
comic 704.35
fare
n food 10.1
traveler 178.1
fee 630.6
v eat 8.20
travel 177.18
journey 177.21
be in a certain state
764.5
result 886.4
farewell
n leave-taking 188.4
v take leave 188.16
adj departing 188.18
inter good-bye! 188.22
fare well succeed 409.7
prosper 1009.7
farfetched 775.8
far-flung long 267.7
extensive 863.13
far from it
adj nothing like 786.5
adv amiss 910.7
inter no 335.8
by no means 335.9
far-gone
intoxicated 88.31
worn-out 393.36
involved in 897.5
farm
n house 228.5
baseball 745.1
farmplace 1067.8
stock farm 1068.5
v ruralize 233.5
die 307.20
rent out 615.16
ranch 1067.16
raise 1068.6
adj rustic 233.6
agricultural 1067.20
farmer
peasant 606.6
tax collector 630.10
agriculturist 1067.5
farm out 615.16
far out
extreme 247.13
modern 840.13
unconventional 867.6
farrow
n offspring 561.1
v give birth 1.3
farsighted
clear-sighted 27.21
poor-sighted 28.11
sagacious 919.16
foreseeing 960.7
fart
n stinker 71.3
bad person 660.6
zilch 761.3
flatulence 908.10
v let a fart 908.29
farther
adj additional 253.10

thither 261.10
adv additionally
253.11
farthing
modicum 248.2
money 728.8
fourth 880.2
trifle 997.5
fasces scepter 417.9
insignia 647.1
bundle 769.8
fascinate
delight 95.9
enamor 104.23
thrill 105.15
captivate 377.7
charm 691.8
interest 982.12
engross 982.13
fascinating
delightful 97.7
wonderful 122.10
alluring 377.8
bewitching 691.11
engrossing 982.20
fascination
delightfulness 97.2
inclination 100.3
eagerness 101.1
amazement 122.1
wonderfulness 122.3
allurement 377.1
bewitchment 691.2
mania 925.12
obsession 925.13
fascism
government 612.4
despotism 612.8
discrimination 979.4
fashion
n aspect 33.3
form 262.1
structure 266.1
custom 373.1
manner 384.1
mode 532.2
style 578.1
mode 764.4
v form 262.7
produce 891.8
fast
n lack of food 515.2
abstinence 668.2
holy day 701.11
v not eat 515.4
adj deep-dyed 35.17
swift 174.15
close 293.12
confirmed 373.19
devoted 587.21
profligate 665.25
fastened 799.14
stable 854.12
stuck 854.16
reliable 969.17
adv swiftly 174.17
securely 799.19
fasten
close 293.6
bind 428.10
fix 799.7
secure 854.8

fasten upon
seize on 480.16
blame 599.8
impose 643.4
attribute to 887.4
fast food 10.1
fast-food restaurant
8.17
fast-forward
run 174.3
hastening 401.3
fastidious
clean 79.25
particular 495.9
elegant 496.9
conscientious 644.15
discriminating 943.7
fasting
n abstinence from
food 515.1
penance 658.3
asceticism 667.1
adj hungry 100.25
uneating 515.5
fast track 174.3
fat
n glyceride 7.7
superfluity 992.4
the best 998.8
oil 1054.1
v fatten 259.8
adj corpulent 257.18
distended 259.13
stubby 268.10
thick 269.8
heavy 297.16
gainful 472.16
wealthy 618.14
stupid 921.15
plentiful 990.7
thriving 1009.13
oily 1054.9
fatal
deadly 308.22
destructive 395.26
future 838.8
destined 963.9
chance 971.15
weighty 996.20
unfortunate 1010.14
disastrous 1010.15
fatalism
composure 106.2
resignation 134.2
determinism 963.4
fatality
ominousness 133.7
inauspiciousness
133.8
fatal accident 308.7
deadliness 308.8
fate 963.2
fat cat 618.7
fat chance
n improbability 968.1
inter nope 335.10
fate
n doom 395.2
portion 477.5
end 819.1
destiny 838.2
inevitability 962.7

fatality 963.2
chance 971.1
v allot 477.9
destine 963.7
fateful
ominous 133.17
destructive 395.26
inevitable 962.15
destined 963.9
weighty 996.20
fathead 923.4
father
n senior 304.5
brother 559.3
sire 560.9
priest 699.5
author 885.4
producer 891.7
personage 996.8
v procreate 78.8
engender 817.14
cause 885.10
trace to 887.5
fatherland 232.2
fathom
sound 275.9
measure 300.10
understand 521.7
know 927.12
investigate 937.22
solve 939.2
fatigue
n weakness 16.1
weakening 16.5
tiredness 21.1
symptoms 85.9
languor 331.6
work 725.4
v tire 21.4
burn out 21.5
be tedious 118.6
fatten nourish 8.19
increase 251.4
size 257.15
fat 259.8
thicken 269.5
make better 392.9
fertilize 889.8
thrive 1009.8
raise 1068.6
fatuous
ineffective 19.15
vain 391.13
thin 763.6
foolish 922.8
thoughtless 932.4
trivial 997.19
faucet
valve 239.10
stopper 293.4
fault
n crack 224.2
vice 654.2
misdeed 655.2
game 748.2
error 974.1
mistake 974.3
defect 1002.2
blemish 1003.1
v complain 115.15
deprecate 510.12
play tennis 748.3

faultfinding
  n complaint 115.4
  critisism 510.4
  disparagement 512.1
  adj discontented 108.7
  plaintive 115.19
  critical 510.23
faultless
  innocent 657.6
  accurate 972.16
  perfect 1001.6
faulty
  ungrammatic 531.4
  guilty 656.3
  illogical 935.11
  erroneous 974.16
  imperfect 1002.4
  blemished 1003.8
fauna
  animal life 311.1
  biology 1066.1
Faust 690.5
faux pas 974.5
favor
  n looks 33.4
  inclination 100.3
  act of kindness 143.7
  pity 145.1
  respect 155.1
  face 216.4
  superiority 249.1
  preference 371.5
  patronage 449.4
  benefit 478.7
  approval 509.1
  letter 553.2
  good terms 587.3
  privilege 642.2
  esteem 662.3
  influence 893.1
  special favor 893.2
  memento 988.7
  v desire 100.14
  be kind 143.9
  respect 155.4
  choose 371.17
  make better 392.9
  indulge 427.6
  aid 449.11
  abet 449.14
  be useful 449.17
  oblige 449.19
  approval 509.9
  prefer 650.8
  resemble 783.7
  do good 998.10
favorable
  promising 124.13
  auspicious 133.18
  willing 324.5
  consenting 441.4
  propitious 449.22
  approving 509.17
  friendly 587.15
  timely 842.9
  expedient 994.5
  good 998.12
favorite
  n preference 104.16
  jockey 757.2
  adj beloved 104.24
  approved 509.19

favoritism
  partiality 650.3
  prejudice 979.3
fawn
  n fledgling 302.10
  hoofed animals 311.5
  v give birth 1.3
  truckle 138.7
  adj brown 40.3
fawning
  n obsequiousness
    138.2
  flattery 511.1
  adj obsequious 138.14
  flattering 511.8
fax
  n Telephoto 347.15
  print 784.5
  v copy 784.8
fay
  n fairy 678.8
  adj fairy 678.17
faze 127.18
FBI detective 576.10
  police 1007.17
FBI agent 576.10
fealty
  obedience 326.1
  duty 641.1
  fidelity 644.7
fear
  n anxiety 126.1
  terror 127
  fright 127.1
  nervousness 128.1
  weak will 362.4
  cowardice 491.1
  v be afraid 127.10
  hesitate 362.7
fearful
  anxious 126.7
  fearing 127.23
  frightening 127.28
  nervous 128.11
  remarkable 247.11
  cowardly 491.10
fearsome
  fearful 127.23
  frightening 127.28
feasible
  workable 888.10
  practicable 965.7
  expedient 994.5
  practical 994.6
  handy 1013.15
feast
  n banquet 8.9
  food 10.1
  holiday 20.4
  treat 95.3
  holy day 701.11
  festival 743.4
  v banquet 8.24
  gratify 95.7
feat act 328.3
  masterpiece 413.10
  exploit 492.7
feather
  n quill 3.16
  plumage 3.18
  lightness 298.2
  kind 808.3

  trifle 997.5
  v fledge 3.21
  row 182.53
  maneuver 184.40
  fill 196.7
  figure 498.9
featherbrained
  superficial 921.20
  scatterbrained 984.16
feather in one's cap
  victory 411.1
  trophy 646.3
featherweight
  n runt 258.4
  weight 297.3
  adj lightweight 298.13
  uninfluential 894.3
feature
  n aspect 33.3
  looks 33.4
  treatise 556.1
  motion pictures 706.1
  commodity 735.2
  component 795.2
  characteristic 864.4
  special 865.2
  highlight 996.7
  v manifest 348.5
  dramatize 704.28
  specify 864.11
  specialize 865.4
  call attention to
    982.10
  emphasize 996.14
  headline 996.15
  adj specialized 865.5
febrile feverish 85.57
  fervent 93.18
  overzealous 101.12
  heated 105.22
fecal
  excremental 12.20
  malodorous 71.5
  filthy 80.23
feces feculence 12.4
  dregs 256.2
feckless
  ineffective 19.15
  useless 391.9
  improvident 406.15
fecund
  diffuse 538.11
  productive 889.9
  invention 985.18
fecundity
  wordiness 538.2
  productiveness 889.1
  invention 985.3
federal
  n policeman 1007.15
  adj governmental
    612.17
  combining 804.7
federation
  affiliation 450.2
  government 612.4
  association 617.1
  combination 804.1
fed up weary 118.11
  satiated 993.6
fee
  n gratuity 478.5

  stipend 624.5
  charge 630
  dues 630.6
  v pay 624.10
feeble weak 16.12
  impotent 19.13
  inconspicuous 32.6
  faint 52.16
  unhealthy 85.53
  stricken in years
    303.18
  weak-willed 362.12
  feebleminded 921.21
  unsound 935.12
feebleminded
  weak-willed 362.12
  weak-minded 921.21
feed
  n meal 8.5
  fodder 10.4
  basketball game 747.3
  game 749.3
  v nourish 7.15
  dine 8.18
  eat 8.20
  gratify 95.7
  encourage 375.21
  provision 385.9
  foster 449.16
  fertilize 889.8
  ignite 1019.22
  fuel 1020.7
  raise 1068.6
  tend 1068.7
feedback
  audio distortion 50.13
  reaction 902.1
  closed sequence
    1040.6
feeder eater 8.16
  tributary 238.3
  role 704.10
  actor 707.2
feed the fire
  excite 105.12
  incite 375.17
  vomit 908.26
  ignite 1019.22
feel
  n touch 73.1
  milieu 209.3
  texture 294.1
  knack 413.6
  discrimination 943.1
  v sense 24.6
  appear to be 33.10
  touch 73.6
  entertain a feeling
    93.10
  contact 223.10
  caress 562.16
  experience 830.8
  intuit 933.4
  suppose 950.10
feeler
  tactile organ 73.4
  offer 439.1
  question 937.10
  probe 941.4
feel for
  pity 145.3
  grope 937.31

feel good
  enjoy good health
    83.6
  please 95.5
  be pleased 95.11
feeling
  n sensation 24.1
  touch 73.1
  handling 73.2
  emotion 93.1
  pity 145.1
  milieu 209.3
  hunch 933.3
  discrimination 943.1
  suggestion 950.5
  opinion 952.6
  attitude 977.1
  mood 977.4
  adj emotional 93.17
  intuitive 933.5
  examining 937.36
feelings emotion 93.1
  mood 977.4
feel in one's bones
  feel 93.10
  foreshow 133.10
  intuit 933.4
  foreknow 960.6
feel one's way
  be blind 30.8
  make one's way 162.4
  be careful 339.7
  see what one can do
    403.10
  be cautious 494.5
  grope 937.31
feign sham 354.20
  affect 500.12
feint
  n sham 354.3
  trick 356.6
  pretext 376.1
  stratagem 415.3
  thrust 459.3
  game 746.3
  fight 754.3
  v lash out at 459.16
  fight 754.4
feisty
  hot-tempered 110.25
  defiant 327.10
  plucky 359.14
  perverse 361.11
  partisan 456.17
  argumentative 934.19
felicitation 149.1
felicitous pleasant 97.6
  decorous 496.10
  appropriate 533.7
  eloquent 544.8
  apt 787.10
  timely 842.9
  expedient 994.5
felicity
  happiness 95.2
  aptitude 413.5
  decorousness 496.3
  elegance 533.1
  eloquence 544.1
  fitness 787.5
  prosperity 1009.1
  good fortune 1009.2

feline
  n creature 311.3
  cat 311.21
  adj felid 311.41
  covert 345.12
  cunning 415.12
fell
  n fur 4.2
  plain 236.1
  plateau 237.3
  hill 237.4
  skin 295.3
  v level 201.6
  strike dead 308.17
  raze 395.19
  conquer 412.10
  shoot 903.12
  drop 912.5
  adj terrible 127.30
  cruel 144.26
fellatio 75.7
fellow
  n man 76.5
  doctor 90.4
  beau 104.13
  boy 302.5
  person 312.5
  image 349.5
  teacher 571.1
  friend 588.1
  companion 588.3
  associate 616.1
  member 617.11
  accompanier 768.4
  likeness 783.3
  equal 789.4
  adj cooperative 450.5
  accompanying 768.9
fellowship
  n cooperation 450.1
  affiliation 450.2
  accord 455.1
  subsidy 478.8
  instructorship 571.10
  camaraderie 582.2
  social life 582.4
  association 582.6
  companionship 587.2
  sodality 617.3
  scholarship 646.7
  sect 675.3
  company 768.2
  v associate with
    582.17
felon sore 85.36
  evildoer 593.1
  criminal 660.10
felony
  misdeed 655.2
  offense 674.4
felt 4.1
female
  n female being 77.4
  adj feminine 77.13
feminine
  n gender 530.10
  adj female 77.13
feminine caesura 720.7
femininity
  femaleness 77
  feminality 77.1
  womankind 77.3

  maturity 303.2
feminism
  effeminacy 77.2
  women's rights 642.4
  discrimination 979.4
femme fatale
  tempter 377.4
  demimonde 665.15
fen 243.1
fence
  n wall 212.4
  fortification 460.4
  receiver 732.6
  barrier 1011.5
  v wall 212.7
  dodge 368.8
  contend 457.13
  fortify 460.9
  illicit goods 732.7
  quibble 935.9
  protect 1007.18
fence in enclose 212.5
  fence 212.7
  confine 429.12
fencer 461.1
fence-sitting
  n irresolution 362.1
  neutrality 467.1
  adj irresolute 362.9
  repudiative 363.12
fend fend off 460.10
  protect 1007.18
  prevent 1011.14
fender partition 213.5
  safeguard 1007.3
  fireplace 1019.11
fend off
  ward off 460.10
  repulse 907.3
  prevent 1011.14
feral frenzied 105.25
  cruel 144.26
  deadly 308.22
  funereal 309.22
  animal 311.38
  savage 671.21
ferment
  n bread 10.27
  agitation 105.4
  dudgeon 152.7
  leavening 298.4
  bubbling 320.3
  bustle 330.4
  turbulence 671.2
  transformer 851.5
  agitation 916.1
  v sour 67.4
  leaven 298.7
  bubble 320.4
  incite 375.17
  seethe 671.12
  agitate 916.10
  chemicalize 1058.7
fermentation
  souring 67.3
  commotion 105.4
  leavening 298.4
  bubbling 320.3
  agitation 916.1
fern 310.4
ferocious
  frenzied 105.25

  cruel 144.26
  warlike 458.21
  savage 671.21
ferret
  sharp vision 27.11
  wild animal 311.23
ferret out
  search out 937.33
  uncover 940.4
Ferris wheel 743.15
ferrous 1056.17
ferry
  n passageway 383.3
  v haul 176.13
  fly 184.36
fertile productive 889.9
  imaginative 985.18
  plentiful 990.7
fertility
  wordiness 538.2
  productiveness 889.1
  invention 985.3
  plenty 990.2
fertilize fructify 78.10
  enrich 889.8
  cultivate 1067.17
fervent fervid 93.18
  zealous 101.9
  heated 105.22
  industrious 330.22
  vehement 544.13
fervid craving 100.24
  zealous 101.9
  heated 105.22
fervor zeal 101.2
  love 104.1
  industry 330.6
  vehemence 544.5
  heat metaphor 1018.2
festal vacational 20.10
  festive 743.28
festering
  n pus 12.6
  soreness 26.4
  sore 85.36
  corruption 393.2
  adj suppurative 12.21
  sore 26.11
  decayed 393.40
  unforgettable 988.26
festination 401.3
festival
  musical occasion
    708.32
  festivity 743.4
festive
  convivial 582.23
  festal 743.28
festivity treat 95.3
  rejoicing 116.1
  celebration 487.1
  conviviality 582.3
  merrymaking 743.3
  festival 743.4
  assembly 769.2
festoon
  n curve 279.2
  bouquet 310.23
  v ornament 545.7
Festschrift
  compilation 554.7
  collection 769.11

celebrity 662.9
passage 708.24
card 758.2
characteristic 864.4
syllogism 934.6
phantom 975.4
personage 996.8
body 1050.3
v form 262.7
image 349.11
plan 381.8
filigree 498.9
designate 517.18
metaphorize 536.2
be somebody 662.10
be reasonable 934.17
estimate 945.9
calculate 1016.17
figurehead prow 216.3
figure 349.6
nominal head 575.5
deputy 576.1
follower 616.8
insignia 647.1
a nobody 997.7
figure in
participate 476.5
calculate 1016.17
figure of speech
turn of expression 536
figure 536.1
ornateness 545.4
figure on plan 380.6
calculate 1016.17
figure out
plan 380.6
solve 939.2
calculate 1016.17
figurine 349.6
filament
feather part 3.17
thread 271
fiber 271.1
filch 482.13
file
n military unit 461.22
document 549.5
recording media
549.10
heraldry 647.2
series 811.2
catalog 870.3
data 1041.15
v march 177.30
sharpen 285.7
grind 287.8
store 386.10
record 549.15
classify 808.6
defile 811.7
list 870.8
abrade 1042.7
filial
loving 104.27
sonly 561.7
filibuster
n legislative
procedure 613.6
hinderer 1011.8
v outtalk 540.7
legislate 613.10
procrastinate 845.11

filigree
n extra 254.4
v figure 498.9
filing
legislative procedure
613.6
classification 808.1
index 870.7
abrasion 1042.2
filing card 549.10
filing clerk 550.1
filings remainder 256.1
refuse 391.4
powder 1049.5
fill
n full measure 793.3
satiety 993.1
v load 159.15
pack 196.7
top 198.9
pervade 221.7
stop 293.7
provide 385.7
observe 434.2
possess 469.4
include 771.3
charge 793.7
iterate 848.8
superabound 992.8
satiate 993.4
filler lining 196.3
hunter 311.13
syntax 530.2
fillet strip 271.4
circle 280.3
fill in for
take one's turn 824.5
substitute for 861.5
filling
n lining 196.3
extra 254.4
warp 740.3
redundancy 848.3
superfluity 992.4
adj completing 793.13
satiating 993.7
fill out increase 251.4
enlarge 259.5
round 282.6
execute 437.9
protract 538.8
record 549.15
include 771.3
complete 793.6
fill up shoal 276.3
stop 293.7
provide 385.7
provision 385.9
fill 793.7
satiate 993.4
fuel 1020.7
filly
female animal 77.9
gal 302.7
horse 311.10
jockey 757.2
film
n blanket 295.12
lamina 296.2
fog 319.2
recording media
549.10

motion pictures 706.1
negative 714.10
v blur 32.4
cover 295.19
shoot 706.7
photograph 714.14
adj motion-picture
706.8
filmmaker 706.3
filmy smooth 294.8
transparent 1028.4
filo 10.39
filter
n refinery 79.13
light filter 1027.4
v refine 79.22
exude 190.15
extraction 192.16
trickle 238.18
filth muck 80.7
cursing 513.3
obscenity 666.4
terribleness 999.2
filthy obscene 666.9
terrible 999.9
filtration
refinement 79.4
exuding 190.6
fin money 728.7
five 881.1
finagle cheat 356.18
plot 381.9
maneuver 415.10
final
departing 188.18
completing 407.9
mandatory 420.12
terminal 819.11
eventual 830.11
resultant 886.6
evidential 956.16
unqualified 959.2
finale act 704.7
end 819.1
finalize
accomplish 407.6
complete 819.7
finally
adv in fine 819.12
eventually 830.12
consequently 886.7
inter eureka! 940.11
finance
n money matters 729
economics 729.1
v support 449.12
subsidize 478.19
pay for 624.18
back 729.15
financier
n moneyman 729.8
businessman 730.1
v invest 729.16
find
n finding 472.6
discovery 940.1
good thing 998.5
v arrive 186.6
provide 385.7
learn 570.6
discover 940.2
conclude 945.10

decide 945.11
pass judgment 945.13
finding find 472.6
solution 939.1
discovery 940.1
verdict 945.5
find oneself 940.2
find out learn 570.6
solve 939.2
discover 940.2
make sure 969.11
find time 820.6
find time for 449.13
fine
v mulct 603.5
spiritualize 763.4
adj edible 8.33
healthy 83.8
pleasant 97.6
tiny 258.11
narrow 270.16
sharp 285.8
smooth 294.8
rare 299.4
meticulous 339.12
nice 495.11
elegant 496.9
ornate 498.12
grandiose 501.21
thin 763.6
discriminating 943.7
exact 972.17
good 998.12
exquisite 1015.19
powdery 1049.11
rainless 1064.8
adv excellently 998.22
inter yeah 332.19
bravo! 509.22
fine arts 712.1
fine fettle
healthiness 83.2
orderliness 806.3
fine point 779.2
fine print 958.2
finery clothing 5.1
frippery 5.10
ornament 498.3
finesse
n skill 413.1
cunning 415.1
taste 496.1
discrimination 943.1
v plot 381.9
live by one's wits
415.9
fine-tune
improve 392.11
arrange 437.8
rearrange 807.13
change 851.7
perfect 1001.5
finger
n digit 73.5
v touch 73.6
condemn to death
308.19
designate 517.18
inform on 551.13
accuse 599.7
attribute to 887.4
finger bowl 79.12

change 851.7
conform 866.3
expedite one's affair
  994.3
adj healthy 83.8
hale 83.12
eligible 371.24
fitted 405.17
competent 413.24
appropriate 533.7
right 637.3
rightful 639.8
just 649.8
apt 787.10
timely 842.9
sufficient 990.6
expedient 994.5
fitful unordered 809.12
discontinuous 812.4
irregular 850.3
inconstant 853.7
jerky 916.19
fit in have place 159.9
implant 191.8
follow the rule 866.4
fit like a glove
interact 776.6
suit 787.8
expedite one's affair
  994.3
fitness ability 18.2
health 83.1
physical conditioning
  84
physical fitness 84.1
eligibility 371.11
preparedness 405.4
decorousness 496.3
propriety 637.2
suitability 787.5
timeliness 842.1
expedience 994.1
fit out outfit 5.40
equip 385.8
fitted eligible 371.24
provided 385.13
adapted 405.17
competent 413.24
apt 787.10
fitting
n checking the fit
  405.2
change 851.1
adj useful 387.18
decorous 496.10
appropriate 533.7
right 637.3
apt 787.10
timely 842.9
expedient 994.5
fit to be tied 152.30
five
basketball team 747.2
card 758.2
V 881.1
five 617.7
five-and-dime 736.1
five-card stud 759.10
fix
n navigation 159.3
circumnavigation
  182.2

state 764.1
bewilderment 970.3
expedient 994.2
v locate 159.11
establish 159.16
direct 161.5
circumscribe 210.4
quantify 244.4
castrate 255.11
form 262.7
perforate 292.15
kill 308.13
resolve 359.7
accustom 373.10
bribe 378.3
perfect 392.11
do for 395.11
repair 396.14
prepare 405.6
defeat 412.9
prescribe 420.9
arrange 437.8
get even with 506.7
punish 604.11
make agree 787.7
fasten 799.7
dispose 807.9
organize 807.10
define 854.9
specify 864.11
decide 945.11
prove 956.10
prearrange 964.5
make sure 969.11
fix and toke 87.19
fixate
psychologize 92.35
obsess 925.25
fixation
libido fixation 92.21
establishment 159.7
motionlessness 173.2
fixity 854.2
obsession 925.13
hindrance 1011.1
fixative perfumery 70.2
art equipment 712.18
fixer mender 396.10
lawyer 597.3
wire-puller 609.30
processing solution
  714.13
fixings 795.2
fixing to
adj prepared 405.16
prep in preparation
  for 405.24
fixity motionlessness
  173.2
fixedness 854.2
fixity of purpose 359.4
fix on direct 161.5
attribute to 887.4
pay attention 982.8
fixture adjunct 254.1
fixity 854.2
machinery 1039.3
fixtures equipment
  385.4
hard goods 735.4
fix up equip 385.8
repair 396.14

cure 396.15
prepare 405.6
make up 405.7
reconcile 465.8
ornament 498.8
tidy 807.12
fizz
n sibilation 57.1
bubbling 320.3
v sibilate 57.2
bubble 320.4
fizzle
n sibilation 57.1
disappointment 132.1
bubbling 320.3
failure 410.2
v sibilate 57.2
be disappointing
  132.3
bubble 320.4
come to nothing
  410.13
burn out 1021.8
fizzle out weaken 16.9
be disappointing
  132.3
come to nothing
  410.13
be unproductive 890.3
fall through 910.3
burn out 1021.8
fjord 242.1
flabbergast 122.6
flabby weak 16.12
impotent 19.13
flaccid 1045.10
pulpy 1061.6
flaccid weak 16.12
flabby 1045.10
flack appearance 33.2
promotion 352.5
publicist 352.9
flag
n leaf 310.17
pavement 383.6
trophy 646.3
banner 647.6
golf 751.1
building material
  1052.2
v weaken 16.9
fatigue 21.4
burn out 21.5
fail 85.47
dawdle 175.8
floor 295.22
languish 393.18
figure 498.9
signal 517.22
flag down
signal 517.22
play 745.5
put a stop to 856.11
flagellate oneself
regret 113.6
do penance 658.6
deny oneself 667.3
flagellation
corporal punishment
  604.4
penance 658.3
asceticism 667.1

flagging
n slowing 175.4
pavement 383.6
adj languishing 16.21
tired 21.7
slow 175.10
deteriorating 393.45
flagrant
downright 247.12
conspicuous 348.12
gaudy 501.20
wicked 654.16
base 661.12
immodest 666.6
terrible 999.9
burning 1018.27
flagship 817.17
flagstaff 273.1
flagstone
pavement 383.6
building material
  1052.2
flail whip 604.13
pound 901.16
pulverize 1049.9
flail at 459.16
flair ability 18.2
talent 413.4
aptitude 413.5
display 501.4
artistry 712.7
smartness 919.2
discernment 943.2
flak
dissension 456.3
artillery 462.11
criticism 510.4
flake
n cocaine 87.6
flock 296.3
lunatic 925.16
freak 926.4
snow 1022.8
v scale 6.11
variegate 47.7
layer 296.5
flaked-out 22.22
flake off scale 6.11
depart 188.7
flake out 22.14
flaky
n addict 87.20
adj flocculent 296.7
capricious 364.5
foolish 922.9
crazy 925.27
eccentric 926.6
powdery 1049.11
flamboyance
ornateness 498.2
showiness 501.3
brightness 1024.4
flamboyant
ornate 498.12
grandiloquent 545.8
bright 1024.32
flame
n love 104.1
beau 104.13
fire 1018.13
flash 1024.6
light source 1025.1

v redden 41.5
be hot 1018.22
catch fire 1019.23
burn 1019.24
shine 1024.23

flameproof
v fireproof 1021.6
adj resistant 15.20
fireproof 1021.10

flaming
n burning 1019.5
adj red 41.6
fervent 93.18
zealous 101.9
heated 105.22
grandiloquent 545.8
fiery 671.22
burning 1018.27
bright 1024.32
flashing 1024.34

flammable
n fuel 1020.1
adj inflammable
  1019.28

flange border 211.4
bulge 283.3

flank
n side 218.1
v side 218.4
launch an attack
  459.17
defend 460.8
circle 913.5

flank attack 459.1

flannels 5.22

flap
n noise 53.4
report 56.1
dither 105.6
bulge 283.3
overlayer 295.4
lamina 296.2
bustle 330.4
turbulence 671.2
slap 901.8
agitation 916.1
flutter 916.4
v crack 56.6
hang 202.6
pound 901.16
slap 901.19
wave 915.11
flutter 916.12

flare
n expansion 259.1
alarm 400.1
signal 517.15
explosion 671.7
flare-up 1018.14
flash 1024.6
torch 1025.3
television reception
  1034.5
v spread 259.6
be hot 1018.22
shine 1024.23

flare-up outbreak 105.9
outburst 152.9
explosion 671.7
flare 1018.14

flash
n glance 27.4

excitement 105.3
swiftness 174.6
impulse 365.1
skillful person 413.14
bulletin 552.5
explosion 671.7
instant 829.3
flare 1018.14
blaze 1024.6
v burst forth 33.9
telegraph 347.19
flaunt 501.17
signal 517.22
shine 1024.23

flashback 988.4

flashing
n unclothing 6.1
cognizance 927.2
adj showy 501.19
brief 827.8
flashy 1024.34
flickering 1024.36

flash in the pan
n impotent 19.6
false alarm 400.2
great success 409.3
abortion 410.5
failure 410.7
thing of naught 763.2
ephemeron 827.5
v come to nothing
  410.13
be unproductive 890.3

flash on think of 930.16
remember 988.10

flashy garish 35.19
showy 501.19
grandiloquent 545.8
flashing 1024.34

flat
n floor 197.23
horizontal 201.3
apartment 228.13
plain 236.1
shoal 276.2
smoothness 287.3
scenery 704.20
note 709.14
game 746.3
cheater 759.22
adj soft-colored 35.21
colorless 36.7
muffled 52.17
dissonant 61.4
insipid 65.2
dull 117.6
spatial 158.9
inert 173.14
horizontal 201.7
recumbent 201.8
champaign 236.2
deflated 260.14
lean 270.17
low 274.7
straight 277.6
smooth 287.9
phonetic 524.31
without money 619.10
prosaic 721.5
uniform 780.5
unqualified 959.2
lackluster 1026.17

adv horizontally 201.9

flatfoot
deformity 265.3
detective 576.11
police 1007.16

flatland
horizontal 201.3
plain 236.1

flat out
at full speed 174.20
extremely 247.22
at top speed 756.5
utterly 793.16
unqualified 959.2
in excess 992.23

flatten level 201.6
straighten 277.5
smooth 287.5
raze 395.19
conquer 412.10
make uniform 780.4

flatter fawn 138.7
congratulate 149.2
importune 440.12
praise 509.12
adulate 511.5

flatterer 509.8

flattering
obsequious 138.14
congratulatory 149.3
importunate 440.18
approbatory 509.16
adulatory 511.8

flattery
congratulation 149.1
praise 509.5
laudation 511
adulation 511.1

flatulence
distension 259.2
grandiloquence 545.1
fart 908.10
vaporousness 1065.3

flatulent
distended 259.13
pompous 501.22
bombastic 545.9
ejective 908.30

flatware tableware 8.12
hard goods 735.4

flaunt
n display 501.4
waving 915.2
v manifest 348.5
vaunt 501.17
wave 915.11

flaunting
n display 501.4
waving 915.2
adj garish 35.19
showy 501.19
gaudy 501.20
grandiloquent 545.8

flautist 710.4

flavor
n taste 62.1
flavoring 63.3
odor 69.1
characteristic 864.4
v savor 63.7
imbue 796.11

flavor control 1040.8

flavorless 65.2

flavorsome
flavorful 63.9
delectable 97.10

flaw
n crack 224.2
gust 318.6
vice 654.2
error 974.1
fault 1002.2
blemish 1003.1
v blemish 1003.4

flawed
unvirtuous 654.12
illegal 674.6
illogical 935.11
erroneous 974.16
blemished 1003.8

flawless
accurate 972.16
perfect 1001.6

flaxen 43.4

flay peel 6.8
strip 480.24
criticize 510.20
tear apart 801.14

flea vermin 311.35
jumper 366.4

fleabag 228.15

flea-bitten 47.13

flea in one's ear 399.1

a flea in one's ear
rejection 372.1
repulse 442.2
reproof 510.5

flea market sale 734.3
marketplace 736.2

fleck
n tuft 3.6
spottiness 47.3
modicum 248.2
minute 258.7
mark 517.5
stain 1003.3
v variegate 47.7
mark 517.19

fledgling
n youngster 302.1
boy 302.5
birdling 302.10
bird 311.28
novice 572.9
modern 840.4
adj immature 406.11
new 840.7

flee disappear 34.2
run off 188.12
fly 368.10
escape 369.6
cease to exist 761.6

fleece
n hair 3.2
head of hair 3.4
fur 4.2
whiteness 37.2
skin 295.3
softness 1045.4
v divest 6.5
cheat 356.18
strip 480.24
plunder 482.17
overprice 632.7

fleet
n ships 180.10
navy 461.27
company 769.3
v speed 174.8
flit 827.6
adj fast 174.15
agile 413.23
brief 827.8
fleeting
vanishing 34.3
receding 168.5
unsubstantial 763.5
transient 827.7
flesh meat 10.12
sexuality 75.2
skin 295.3
organic matter 305.1
humankind 312.1
kinfolk 559.2
carnality 663.2
body 1050.3
the flesh 663.2
flesh out amplify 538.7
elaborate 860.6
perfect 1001.5
fleshpots
disapproved place
228.28
sewer 654.7
prosperity 1009.1
fleshy corpulent 257.18
pulpy 1061.6
fleur-de-lis
insignia 647.1
heraldry 647.2
flex
n bend 279.3
v curve 279.6
flexible folded 291.7
versatile 413.25
unstrict 426.5
docile 433.13
changeable 853.6
conformable 866.5
handy 1013.15
pliant 1045.9
elastic 1046.7
flibbertigibbet
scatterbrain 923.7
flightiness 984.5
flick
n thud 52.3
touch 73.1
mark 517.5
motion pictures 706.1
tap 901.7
jerk 904.3
stain 1003.3
v touch 73.6
tap 901.18
jerk 904.5
flutter 916.12
flickering
n flicker 1024.8
adj brief 827.8
irregular 850.3
inconstant 853.7
fluttering 916.18
burning 1018.27
bickering 1024.36
flier speeder 174.5

train 179.14
aviator 185.1
advertising matter
352.8
circus artist 707.3
trading 737.19
gamble 759.2
flight
defense mechanism
92.23
course 172.2
velocity 174.1
migration 177.4
aviation 184.1
trip 184.9
departure 188.1
fugitation 368.4
escape 369.1
air force 461.29
arrow 462.6
ornament 709.18
assemblage 769.6
multitude 883.3
rocket launching
1072.9
flight attendant
crew 185.4
attendant 577.5
flight of fancy
imagination 985.1
idealism 985.7
flight path
airway 184.33
route 383.1
flighty fickle 364.6
inconstant 853.7
superficial 921.20
insane 925.26
inattentive 983.6
volatile 984.17
flimflam
n lie 354.11
humbug 354.14
deception 356.1
caprice 364.1
v deceive 356.19
flimsy
n writing 547.10
adj frail 16.14
thin 270.16
rare 299.4
fragile 763.7
unsound 935.12
trivial 997.19
flaccid 1045.10
brittle 1048.4
flinch
n retreat 902.3
v shrink 127.13
be startled 131.5
retract 168.3
demur 325.4
hesitate 362.7
pull back 902.7
fling
n attempt 403.3
revel 743.6
throw 903.3
v place violenty
159.13
speed 174.8
throw 903.10

fling off
flounce out 188.11
say 524.23
do away with 908.21
fling oneself at
make advances 439.7
court 562.21
flint lighter 1020.4
hardness 1044.6
flinty callous 94.12
pitiless 146.3
firm 359.12
unyielding 361.9
hard 1044.10
stone 1057.10
flip
n reverse 363.1
game 749.3
tap 901.7
throw 903.3
jerk 904.3
v get excited 105.17
lose self-control 128.8
talkative 540.9
reverse 778.5
tap 901.18
throw 903.10
jerk 904.5
flutter 916.12
adj impudent 142.10
flip-flop
n reverse 363.1
change 851.1
conversion 857.1
reversion 858.1
v change 851.7
turn back 858.5
flip of a coin
gamble 759.2
chance 971.1
flip out
get excited 105.17
get angry 152.18
go mad 925.22
flippant
impudent 142.10
careless 340.11
ridiculing 508.12
flipped 925.27
flipper aquatics 182.11
scenery 704.20
flip side 215.3
the flip side
inverse 205.4
the opposite 778.2
flirt
n lover 104.12
tempter 377.4
coquette 562.11
tap 901.7
jerk 904.3
trifler 997.10
v lure 377.5
coquet 562.20
tap 901.18
jerk 904.5
trifle 997.14
flirtation
love affair 104.6
allurement 377.1
flirtiness 562.9
trifling 997.8

flit
n homosexual 75.15
velocity 174.1
flutter 916.4
v speed 174.8
travel 177.18
migrate 177.22
wander 177.23
glide 177.35
elapse 820.5
fly 827.6
flutter 916.12
flitter
n flutter 916.4
v flutter 916.12
flitting
n wandering 177.3
adj wandering 177.37
transient 827.7
inconstant 853.7
float
n raft 180.11
v haul 176.13
ride 182.54
swim 182.56
take off 193.10
buoy 298.8
levitate 298.9
issue 738.12
inaugurate 817.11
start 903.13
wave 915.11
flood 1063.14
float a loan
lend 620.5
borrow 621.3
floater wanderer 178.2
voter 609.23
floating
n aquatics 182.11
voting 609.18
inauguration 817.5
adj wandering 177.37
afloat 182.60
buoyant 298.14
unfastened 801.22
flocculent hairy 3.24
flaky 296.7
flock tuft 3.6
flake 296.3
the laity 700.1
throng 769.4
group of animals
769.5
assemblage 769.6
multitude 883.3
flock to 450.4
flock together
associate with 582.17
accompany 768.7
come together 769.16
floe 1022.5
flog urge 375.14
whip 604.13
flood
n torrent 238.5
overflow 238.6
tide 238.13
quantity 247.3
increase 251.1
high tide 272.8
rainstorm 316.2

lights 704.18
throng 769.4
plenty 990.2
superabundance 992.2
v flow 238.16
overflow 238.17
abound 990.5
superabound 992.8
oversupply 992.14
float 1063.14
floodgate outlet 190.9
flood-hatch 239.11
floodlight
n lights 704.18
v illuminate 1024.28
flood tide tide 238.13
high tide 272.8
floor
n story 197.23
ground covering 199.3
bed 199.4
horizontal 201.3
boundary 211.3
layer 296.1
arena 463.1
price index 630.4
foundation 900.6
platform 900.13
v carpet 295.22
overcome 412.7
fell 912.5
refute 957.5
stump 970.14
floor it speed 174.9
be active 330.14
floorwalker
superintendent 574.2
salesman 730.3
floozy 665.14
flop
n report 56.1
tumble 194.3
failure 410.2
unsuccessful person
410.8
stage show 704.4
flutter 916.4
v go to bed 22.18
sink 194.6
hang 202.6
fail 410.10
dramatize 704.28
be changed 851.6
flutter 916.12
flophouse 228.15
floppy
n recording media
549.10
disk 1041.6
adj weak 16.12
drooping 202.10
flaccid 1045.10
floppy disk
recording media
549.10
disk 1041.6
flora 310.1
floral 310.35
florescent grown 14.3
mature 259.12
young 301.9
floral 310.35

florid
red-complexioned
41.9
floral 310.35
ornate 498.12
grandiloquent 545.11
fanciful 985.20
florilegium
compilation 554.7
excerpts 557.4
collection 769.11
florist 1067.6
floss down 3.19
softness 1045.4
flossy feathery 3.27
threadlike 271.7
ostentatious 501.18
fluffy 1045.14
flotation issue 738.6
inauguration 817.5
flotilla ships 180.10
navy 461.27
flotsam 370.4
flounce
n gait 177.12
edging 211.7
fold 291.1
jerk 904.3
flounder 916.8
v way of walking
177.28
fold 291.5
caper 366.6
figure 498.9
play 743.23
jerk 904.5
flounder 916.15
flounder
n fish 10.23
flounce 916.8
v pitch 182.55
tumble 194.8
bungle 414.11
change 853.5
wallow 914.13
flounce 916.15
be uncertain 970.9
have difficulty
1012.11
flour
n cereal 10.33
whiteness 37.2
powder 1049.5
v sprinkle 770.6
pulverize 1049.9
flourish
n extra 254.4
ornamentation 498.1
display 501.4
figure of speech 536.1
ornateness 545.4
impromptu 708.27
ornament 709.18
waving 915.2
v grow 14.2
have energy 17.11
enjoy good health
83.6
grow 259.7
mature 303.9
vegetate 310.31
manifest 348.5

ripen 407.8
flaunt 501.17
boast 502.6
ornament 545.7
be somebody 662.10
wave 915.11
thrive 1009.8
flourishing
n maturation 303.6
waving 915.2
adj maturing 14.3
increasing 251.8
grown 259.12
luxuriant 310.40
productive 889.9
thriving 1009.13
flout
n indignity 156.2
gibe 508.2
v offend 156.5
disobey 327.6
violate 435.4
disregard 454.4
scoff 508.9
flow
n excretion 12.1
course 172.2
gliding 177.16
air flow 184.29
flowing 238.4
tide 238.13
elegance 533.1
fluency 544.2
trend 895.2
plenty 990.2
liquidity 1059.1
v move 172.5
travel 177.18
glide 177.35
run out 190.13
hang 202.6
stream 238.16
elapse 820.5
abound 990.5
go easily 1013.10
flow chart
diagram 381.3
outline 800.4
flower
n posy 310.22
figure of speech 536.1
essence 766.2
the best 998.8
v mature 303.9
be in flower 310.32
figure 498.9
evolve 860.5
thrive 1009.8
flower bed 1067.10
flower child 867.3
flowering
n florescence 310.24
evolution 860.1
adj maturing 14.3
grown 259.12
young 301.9
floral 310.35
thriving 1009.13
flower power
power 18.1
benevolence 143.4
flowery fragrant 70.9

floral 310.35
ornate 498.12
figurative 536.3
grandiloquent 545.11
flowing
n gliding 177.16
flow 238.4
adj fluent 172.8
pendent 202.9
streaming 238.24
elegant 533.6
harmonious 533.8
eloquent 544.9
written 547.22
fluid 1059.4
flow on march on 162.3
coat 295.24
elapse 820.5
flood 1063.14
flub
n bungle 414.5
goof 974.6
v bungle 414.12
fluctuate
vacillate 362.8
blow hot and cold
364.4
intermit 850.2
change 853.5
oscillate 915.10
fluctuation
vacillation 362.2
irregularity 850.1
changing 853.3
oscillation 915.1
flue down 3.19
chimney 239.14
lightness 298.2
fireplace 1019.11
softness 1045.4
fluency flow 238.4
elegance 533.1
wordiness 538.2
talkativeness 540.1
flow 544.2
liquidity 1059.1
fluent
v talkative 540.9
adj flowing 172.8
streaming 238.24
elegant 533.6
harmonious 533.8
eloquent 544.9
fluid 1059.4
fluff
n down 3.19
smoothness 294.3
lightness 298.2
bungle 414.5
grammatical error
974.7
softness 1045.4
v make a boner 974.15
soften 1045.6
fluffy feathery 3.27
smooth 294.8
light 298.10
superficial 921.20
flossy 1045.14
fluid
n liquid 1059.2
vapor 1065.1

gas 1065.2
adj changeable 853.6
fluidal 1059.4
fluidity
changeableness 853.1
liquidity 1059.1
vaporousness 1065.3
fluke
n fish 10.23
chance event 971.6
stroke of luck 1009.3
v triumph 411.3
flume
n outlet 190.9
valley 237.7
watercourse 239.2
gutter 239.3
v transport 176.14
flummery 520.2
flummox
n confusion 984.3
v fail 410.10
bewilder 970.12
confuse 984.7
thwart 1011.15
flunk
n abortion 410.5
v fail 410.9
disappoint 410.17
flunky sycophant 138.3
pursuer 166.2
inferior 250.2
subordinate 432.5
retainer 577.1
lackey 577.6
follower 616.8
worker 726.2
fluorescent light
1025.1
flurry
n agitation 105.4
velocity 174.1
rain 316.1
gust 318.6
bustle 330.4
haste 401.1
bluster 503.1
price 738.9
agitation 916.1
confusion 984.3
snow 1022.8
v excite 105.14
agitate 916.10
confuse 984.7
flush
n warmth 35.2
reddening 41.3
washing 79.5
health 83.1
fever 85.7
thrill 105.2
blushing 139.5
jet 238.9
skiing 753.1
glow 1018.12
shine 1024.2
v redden 41.5
wash 79.19
change color 105.19
elate 109.8
make proud 136.6
blush 139.8

show resentment
152.14
level 201.6
flow 238.16
hunt 382.9
be hot 1018.22
soak 1063.13
adj red-complexioned
41.9
hale 83.12
fresh 83.13
horizontal 201.7
wealthy 618.14
full 793.11
plentiful 990.7
adv horizontally
201.9
flushed
red-complexioned
41.9
fresh 83.13
feverish 85.57
fervent 93.18
overjoyed 95.16
heated 105.22
cheerful 109.11
rejoicing 116.10
puffed up 136.10
blushing 139.13
crowing 502.13
hot 1018.25
fluster
n dither 105.6
bustle 330.4
bluster 503.1
agitation 916.1
confusion 984.3
v agitate 105.14
confuse 984.7
flute
n furrow 290.1
v furrow 290.3
fold 291.5
speak 524.26
blow a horn
708.42
flutist 710.4
flutter
n audio distortion
50.13
staccato 55.1
trepidation 105.5
dither 105.6
bustle 330.4
haste 401.1
trill 709.19
trading 737.19
price 738.9
pulsation 915.3
flitter 916.4
confusion 984.3
flicker 1024.8
v drum 55.4
excite 105.14
be excited 105.18
oscillate 915.10
wave 915.11
agitate 916.10
flitter 916.12
confuse 984.7
flicker 1024.25
fluvial 238.23

flux
n excretion 12.1
defecation 12.2
symptom 85.9
course 172.2
flow 238.4
tide 238.13
ceramics 742.3
measurement of light
1024.21
liquidity 1059.1
solvent 1062.4
v treat 91.24
combine 804.3
melt 1019.21
liquefy 1062.5
fly
n overlayer 295.4
insect 311.31
snare 356.13
game 745.3
v disappear 34.2
speed 174.8
transport 176.12
glide 177.35
be airborne 184.36
pilot 184.37
run off 188.12
take off 193.10
flee 368.10
play 745.5
cease to exist 761.6
elapse 820.5
flit 827.6
wave 915.11
fly at 459.18
flyblown filthy 80.23
blighted 393.42
fly-by-night
untrustworthy 645.19
transient 827.7
flying
n aviation 184.1
adj vanishing 34.3
high 87.23
flowing 172.8
fast 174.15
airborne 184.50
hasty 401.9
transient 827.7
flying buttress 900.4
Flying Dutchman
wanderer 178.2
mariner 183.1
White Lady 987.2
fly in the face of
disobey 327.6
deny 335.4
oppose 451.3
offer resistance 453.3
flout 454.4
go contrary to 778.4
counteract 899.6
fly in the ointment
evil 999.3
fault 1002.2
obstacle 1011.4
flyleaf 554.12
fly off at a tangent
fly into a rage 152.20
avoid 164.6
diverge 171.5

fly off the handle
get excited 105.17
fly into a rage 152.20
fly on the wall
viewpoint 27.7
listener 48.5
flytrap 356.12
FM signal 1033.10
foal
n fledgling 302.10
horse 311.10
jockey 757.2
v give birth 1.3
foam
n saliva 13.3
whiteness 37.2
lightness 298.2
froth 320.2
extinguisher 1021.3
softness 1045.4
sprinkle 1063.5
v bubble 320.4
froth 320.5
seethe 671.12
foam at the mouth
be angry 152.15
be insane 925.20
foamy light 298.10
foam-flecked 320.7
fob
n bag 195.2
jewel 498.6
v cheat 356.18
fob off on 643.7
focal converging 169.3
confocal 208.13
chief 249.14
vital 996.23
focus
n convergence 169.1
focal point 208.4
centralization 208.8
essence 766.2
attractor 906.2
v focalize 208.10
focus on
specify 864.11
operate on 888.6
concentrate 930.10
have regard to 936.3
pay attention 982.8
call attention to
982.10
fodder
n feed 10.4
v feed 8.18
tend 1068.7
foe
opponent 452.1
enemy 589.6
fog
n atmosphere 184.32
grass 310.5
pea soup 319.2
obscurity 522.3
confusion 984.3
v blur 32.4
cover 295.19
cloud 319.6
make uncertain
970.15
confuse 984.7

foggy
inconspicuous 32.6
soupy 319.9
obscure 522.15
muddleheaded 921.18
vague 970.19
muddled 984.13
foghorn
alarm 400.1
signal 517.15
fogy
old-timer 841.8
conservative 852.4
dotard 923.9
foible
vice 654.2
fault 1002.2
foil
n lamina 296.2
discomfiture 412.2
motif 498.7
actor 707.2
frustration 1011.3
v disappoint 132.2
outwit 415.11
thwart 1011.15
foist 775.5
foist oneself upon
214.5
fold
n enclosed place 212.3
cavity 284.2
crease 291
double 291.1
lamina 296.2
the laity 700.1
v collapse 260.10
fold on itself 291.5
close shop 293.8
fail 410.10
embrace 562.18
go bankrupt 625.7
seek the middle 818.3
folder
advertising matter
352.8
booklet 554.11
bookholder 554.17
folderol finery 498.3
nonsense 520.2
passage 708.24
trifle 997.5
fold in 291.5
folding
n mountain 237.6
creasing 291.4
bookbinding 554.14
adj folded 291.7
fold up
collapse 260.10
fold 291.5
close shop 293.8
fail 410.10
go bankrupt 625.7
end 819.5
foliage 310.16
foliation
stratification 296.4
foliage 310.16
numeration 1016.9
folio volume 554.4
makeup 554.12

bookholder 554.17
part of writing 792.2
folk
n population 227.1
race 559.4
family 559.5
the people 606.1
adj traditional 841.12
folklore
mythology 678.14
tradition 841.2
superstition 953.3
folk music 708.11
folks
kinfolk 559.2
family 559.5
the people 606.1
folk singer
singer 710.13
minstrel 710.14
folk singing 708.13
folksy 581.3
folktale 841.2
follicle 310.28
follow
n pursuit 382.1
v look 27.13
attach oneself to
138.11
go after 166.3
parallelize 203.5
be behind 217.8
be inferior 250.4
practice 328.8
emulate 336.7
pursue 382.8
take advice 422.7
observe 434.2
understand 521.7
court 562.21
play 744.2
resemble 783.7
set an example 785.7
be consistent 802.7
come next 814.2
succeed 816.5
come after 834.3
specialize 865.4
conform 866.3
result 886.4
seek 937.29
trace 937.34
prove 956.10
follower
enthusiast 101.4
lover 104.12
hanger-on 138.6
successor 166.2
inferior 250.2
pursuer 382.4
apostle 572.2
retainer 577.1
disciple 616.8
believer 692.4
follow from
result from 886.5
prove 956.10
following
n going behind 166
heeling 166.1
follower 166.2
imitation 336.1

pursuit 382.1
attendance 768.6
sequence 814.1
subsequence 834.1
surveillance 937.9
adj trailing 166.5
pursuing 382.11
similar 783.10
succeeding 814.4
subsequent 834.4
resultant 886.6
deducible 934.23
prep after 834.8
follow-through
game 750.2
round 751.3
sequel 816.1
follow up
prosecute to a
conclusion 360.5
pursue 382.8
be thorough 793.8
come after 834.3
trace 937.34
follow-up
case history 91.10
pursuit 382.1
news item 552.3
sequel 816.1
subsequence 834.2
folly
foolishness 922.1
foolish act 922.4
foment
n agitation 916.1
v excite 105.12
relieve 120.5
incite 375.17
heat 1019.17
fond
n foundation 900.6
adj loving 104.27
hopeful 124.11
foolish 922.8
credulous 953.8
fondle stroke 73.8
foster 449.16
hold 474.7
caress 562.16
fond of
desirous of 100.22
enamored of 104.30
font jet 238.9
source of supply 386.4
type 548.6
baptism 701.6
church vessels 703.11
fountainhead 885.6
food nutrient 7.3
sustenance 10
foodstuff 10.1
food for thought 930.7
foofaraw dither 105.6
bustle 330.4
finery 498.3
turbulence 671.2
commotion 809.4
foofooraw
noise 53.4
quarrel 456.6
fool
n dupe 358.1

laughingstock 508.7
buffoon 707.10
stupid person 923
damn fool 923.1
ignoramus 929.8
v befool 356.15
be foolish 922.6
trifle 997.14
adj foolish 922.8
fool around
banter 490.6
play 743.23
be foolish 922.6
trifle 997.15
fool around with
meddle 214.7
experiment 941.8
foolery
buffoonery 489.5
gibe 508.2
foolishness 922.1
foolhardy
daring 492.22
harebrained 493.9
fooling
n deception 356.1
buffoonery 489.5
banter 490.1
bantering 490.2
ridicule 508.1
trifling 997.8
adj bantering 490.7
ridiculing 508.12
foolish
mischievous 322.6
nonsensical 520.7
unintelligent 921.13
fool 922.8
absurd 922.11
trivial 997.19
foolproof
resistant 15.20
handy 1013.15
fool with meddle 214.7
trifle 997.14
foot
n member 2.7
sail 180.14
base 199.2
extremity 199.5
meter 720.7
v speed 174.8
walk 177.27
way of walking 177.28
make way 182.21
float 182.54
dance 705.5
footage length 267.1
motion-picture
photography 706.4
football sport 746.1
football team 746.2
soccer 752.1
foot-dragging
n slowness 175.1
refusal 325.1
delay 845.2
hindrance 1011.1
adj slow 175.10
dilatory 845.17
foothills
the country 233.1

highlands 237.1
foothold hold 474.2
  footing 900.5
  purchase 905.2
footing station 159.2
  base 199.2
  hold 474.2
  class 607.1
  fee 624.5
  horse racing 757.1
  state 764.1
  sphere of influence
    893.4
  foothold 900.5
  foundation 900.6
  purchase 905.2
  outlook 977.2
  calculation 1016.10
footlights
  show business 701.1
  illumination 701.18
footloose
  wandering 177.37
  free 430.21
footman 577.6
footnote
  comment 341.5
  memorandum 549.4
footprint 517.7
footrest step 193.5
  footing 900.5
foot soldier
  pedestrian 178.6
  infantryman 461.9
footstep stride 177.11
  step 193.5
  print 517.7
foot the bill 624.18
fop dandy 500.9
  person of fashion
    578.7
for
  prep to 380.11
  in preparation for
    405.24
  on behalf of 449.26
  in favor of 509.21
  instead of 861.12
  conj because 887.10
forage
  n feed 10.4
  search 937.15
  v feed 8.18
  provision 385.9
  plunder 482.17
  search 937.30
forage grass 310.5
forager 483.6
foray
  n raid 459.4
  plundering 482.6
  v raid 459.20
  plunder 482.17
forbear
  be patient 134.4
  have pity 145.4
  refrain 329.3
  not use 390.5
  abstain 668.7
forbearance
  patience 134.1
  pity 145.1

forgiveness 148.1
  avoidance 368.1
  discontinuance 390.2
  leniency 427.1
  temperance 668.1
  tolerance 978.4
forbid
  v prohibit 444.3
  prevent 1011.14
  adj prohibited 444.7
forbidden fruit
  desire 100.11
  lure 377.3
  prohibition 444.1
  tree of knowledge
    927.8
forbidding
  n prohibition 444.1
  adj offensive 98.18
  reticent 344.10
  prohibitive 444.6
  preventive 1011.19
  hideous 1014.11
force
  n strength 15.1
  energy 17.1
  power 18.1
  waterfall 238.11
  quantity 244.1
  enterprise 330.7
  ultima ratio 424.2
  meaning 518.1
  vigor 544.3
  staff 577.11
  violence 671.1
  impact 886.2
  influence 893.1
  impulse 901.1
  validity 972.6
  v motivate 375.12
  compel 424.4
  administer 643.6
  seduce 665.20
  thrust 901.12
  cultivate 1067.17
forced march
  walk 177.10
  hastening 401.3
force-feed 8.19
forceful strong 15.15
  energetic 17.13
  powerful 18.12
  enterprising 330.23
  vigorous 544.11
  emphatic 996.21
force of habit 373.4
forceps 192.9
forces work force 18.9
  army 461.23
force upon
  urge upon 439.9
  thrust upon 478.20
  administer 643.6
forcible strong 15.15
  energetic 17.13
  powerful 18.12
  coercive 424.12
  vigorous 544.11
  emphatic 996.21
forcible removal 160.1
forcible seizure
  seizure 480.2

unruliness 671.3
forcible shift 160.1
for crying out loud!
  122.21
ford
  n shoal 276.2
  passageway 383.3
  v pass 909.8
fore
  n front 216.1
  adj front 216.10
  previous 833.4
  former 836.10
  inter golf tournaments
    751.5
fore and aft
  aft 182.69
  from beginning to end
    793.18
forearm
  n member 2.7
  arm 905.5
  v prepare for 405.11
  take precautions
    494.6
forebear 815.1
forebears 560.7
forebode bode 133.11
  forewarn 399.6
  threaten 514.2
  predict 961.9
foreboding
  n feeling 93.1
  anxiety 126.1
  apprehension 127.4
  boding 133.2
  forewarning 399.2
  threat 514.1
  hunch 933.3
  foreknowledge 960.3
  prediction 961.1
  adj anxious 126.7
  ominous 133.17
  forewarning 399.8
  threatening 514.3
foreshadowing
  961.12
forecast
  n foresight 960.1
  prediction 961.1
  v plan 381.8
  predict 961.9
  adj predicted 961.14
forecasting
  n meteorology 317.5
  prediction 961.1
  adj predictive 961.11
foreclose
  dispossess 480.23
  prevent 1011.14
forecourt
  basketball 747.1
  tennis 748.1
forefathers 560.7
forefront
  leading 165.1
  border 211.4
  front 216.1
  vanguard 216.2
foregoing
  n leading 165.1
  adj leading 165.3

former 813.5
  previous 833.4
  aforegoing 836.11
foregone conclusion
  sure success 409.2
  predetermination
    963.1
foreground
  front 216.1
  nearness 223.1
forehand
  n front 216.1
  adj front 216.10
  early 844.7
forehead 216.5
foreign
  extraterritorial 206.9
  extrinsic 767.3
  extraneous 773.5
  unrelated 775.6
foreign affairs 609.5
foreign correspondent
  555.4
foreigner
  exclusiveness 772.3
  alien 773.3
  oddity 869.4
foreign exchange 728.9
foreign policy 609.5
foreknowledge
  understanding 927.3
  foreknowing 960.3
  predetermination
    963.1
foreman
  superintendent 574.2
  juror 596.7
foremost
  adj leading 165.3
  front 216.10
  chief 249.14
  preceding 813.4
  first 817.17
  paramount 996.24
  adv before 165.4
  frontal 216.12
forensic
  n speech 543.2
  adj declamatory
    543.12
  jurisprudent 673.11
foreordain 963.6
foreplay 75.7
forerunner
  harbinger 133.5
  herald 353.2
  preparer 405.5
  leader 574.6
  skier 753.2
  precursor 815.1
  antecedent 833.2
foresee
  expect 130.5
  look forward to 130.6
  come 838.6
  anticipate 844.6
  see beforehand 960.5
  predict 961.9
foreseeable
  foreseen 960.8
  predictable 961.13
  probable 967.6

foreseeing 960.1
foreshadow
  n omen 133.3
  v foreshow 133.10
  image 349.11
foreshorten 268.6
foreshortening 268.3
foresight plan 381.1
  precaution 494.3
  extrasensory
    perception 689.8
  the future 838.1
  earliness 844.1
  sagacity 919.4
  looking ahead 960
  foreseeing 960.1
  prediction 961.1
forest
  n woodland 310.11
  v plant 1067.18
  adj sylvan 310.37
forestall
  look forward to 130.6
  deceive 356.14
  monopolize 469.6
  anticipate 844.6
  prevent 1011.14
forestation 1067.3
forester
  guardian 1007.6
  arboriculturist 1067.7
forest ranger
  preserver 397.5
  guardian 1007.6
  forester 1067.7
forest reserve 397.7
forestry
  woodland 310.11
  arboriculture 1067.3
foretaste
  n appetizer 10.9
  antepast 960.4
  v anticipate 844.6
  foresee 960.5
foretell come 838.6
  predict 961.9
forethought
  carefulness 339.1
  intentionality 380.3
  plan 381.1
  precaution 494.3
  premeditation 960.2
foretold 961.14
forever
  n infinity 822.1
  an eternity 828.2
  adv for keeps 474.10
  infinitely 822.4
  forevermore 828.12
  permanently 852.9
forewarned 130.11
forewarning
  n warning 133.4
  prewarning 399.2
  adj premonitory
    133.16
  prewarning 399.8
  predictive 961.11
foreword
  front 216.1
  makeup 554.12
  part of writing 792.2

curtain-raiser 815.2
for example
  incidentally 842.13
  to illustrate 956.23
for fear that 896.7
forfeit
  n collateral 438.3
  loss 473.1
  fine 603.3
  v lose 473.4
  adj lost 473.7
for fun
  for the hell of it 95.19
  in fun 489.19
  for amusement 743.31
forge
  n foundry 739.4
  v form 262.7
  imitate 336.5
  fabricate 354.17
  coin 728.28
forge ahead
  make one's way 162.4
  be in front 216.7
  hustle 330.13
forgery
  imitation 336.1
  fabrication 354.10
  fake 354.13
  counterfeit 728.10
  coining 728.24
  copy 784.1
forget
  forgive and forget
    148.5
  dismiss 983.4
  clean forget 989.5
forget about it 983.4
forgetful
  inconsiderate 144.18
  careless 340.11
  forgetting 989.9
forget it
  v compose oneself
    106.7
  dismiss 983.4
  inter nope! 335.10
  cease! 856.13
  phrs no matter 997.25
forgive have pity 145.4
  pardon 148.3
  acquit 601.4
  declare a moratorium
    625.9
  efface from the
    memory 989.6
forgo refrain 329.3
  give up 370.7
  not use 390.5
  relinquish 475.3
  abstain 668.7
forgone
  relinquished 475.5
  determined 963.8
for good
  for keeps 474.10
  forever 828.12
forgotten
  forgiven 148.7
  unthanked 151.5
  past 836.7
  clean forgotten 989.8

for instance 956.23
fork
  n prong 171.4
  tributary 238.3
  angle 278.2
  branch 310.18
  v furcate 171.7
  ladle 176.17
  angle 278.5
  bisect 874.4
  throw 903.10
for keeps
  to keep 474.10
  forever 828.12
for kicks 743.31
forklift 911.3
fork out give 478.12
  pay out 624.14
  spend 626.5
fork over
  deliver 478.13
  pay out 624.14
forks 8.12
forlorn
  disconsolate 112.28
  hopeless 125.12
  lorn 584.12
form
  n aspect 33.3
  apparition 33.5
  lair 228.26
  shape 262.1
  human form 262.4
  grammar 262.6
  structure 266.1
  standard 373.5
  manner 384.1
  rule 419.2
  formula 419.3
  motif 498.7
  document 549.5
  class 572.11
  social convention
    579.1
  formality 580.1
  law 673.3
  rite 701.3
  piece 708.5
  arrangement 709.11
  statistics 757.4
  good condition 764.3
  mode 764.4
  mold 785.6
  ordering 807.1
  kind 808.3
  rule 868.4
  phantom 975.4
  specter 987.1
  body 1050.3
  immaterialism 1051.3
  v formalize 262.7
  be formed 262.8
  construct 266.5
  train 568.13
  compose 795.3
  order 806.4
  take form 806.5
  produce 891.8
  establish 891.10
formal
  n ceremony 580.4
  dance 705.2

adj formative 262.9
  structural 266.6
  gallant 504.15
  nominal 527.15
  grammatical 530.17
  stiff 534.3
  conventional 579.5
  formulary 580.7
  ritualistic 701.18
  conditional 764.6
  orderly 806.6
  solemn 111.3
  pompous 501.22
formalist
  n pietist 693.3
  ritualist 701.2
  conformist 866.2
  pedant 928.5
  adj formal 580.7
formalities
  amenities 504.7
  etiquette 580.3
formality
  solemnity 111.1
  overniceness 500.5
  pomp 501.6
  social convention
    579.1
  form 580.1
  ceremony 580.4
  law 673.3
  rite 701.3
  rule 868.4
formalize form 262.7
  sign 437.7
  ritualize 580.5
  normalize 868.6
format form 262.1
  structure 266.1
formation
  flight formation
    184.12
  form 262.1
  forming 262.5
  structure 266.1
  word form 526.4
  game 746.3
  composition 795.1
  order 806.1
  arrangement 807.1
  production 891.2
  establishment 891.4
formative
  n morphology 526.3
  adj formal 262.9
  component 795.5
  beginning 817.15
  causal 885.13
  creative 891.16
  pliant 1045.9
former foregoing 813.5
  previous 833.4
  past 836.10
  older 841.19
formidable
  terrible 127.30
  remarkable 247.10
  weighty 996.20
  difficult 1012.17
formless
  shapeless 263.4
  diffuse 538.11

unordered 809.12
abnormal 869.9
formula rule 419.2
  form 419.3
  law 673.3
  rite 701.3
  rule 868.4
  axiom 973.2
formulary
  n formula 419.3
  law 673.3
  rite 701.3
  norm 868.4
  adj preceptive 419.4
  formal 580.7
  ritualistic 701.18
formulate say 524.23
  phrase 532.4
  write 547.21
  legalize 673.8
  compose 718.6
  produce 891.8
fornicate
  copulate 75.21
  be promiscuous
    665.19
for real
  adj real 760.15
  adv positively 247.19
forsake abandon 370.5
  be unfaithful 645.12
forsaken unloved 99.10
  available 222.15
  abandoned 370.8
  forlorn 584.12
  outcast 586.10
forswear
  n recant 363.8
  v deny 335.4
  give up 370.7
  reject 372.2
  relinquish 475.3
  swear off 668.8
forsworn
  untruthful 354.33
  apostate 363.11
  rejected 372.3
  relinquished 475.5
  deceitful 645.18
fort 460.6
forte
  n talent 413.4
  music 708.25
  specialty 865.1
  adj loud 53.11
  music 708.53
  adv loudly 53.14
forth
  adv forward 162.8
  hence 188.20
  out 190.21
  prep out of 190.22
forthcoming
  n appearance 33.1
  approach 167.1
  imminence 839.1
  adj approaching 167.4
  emerging 190.18
  future 838.8
  imminent 839.3
  in preparation 405.22
for the birds 98.25

for the hell of it
for fun 95.19
  in fun 743.31
for the most part
  chiefly 249.17
  on the whole 791.14
  generally 863.17
  normally 868.10
for the nonce
  meanwhile 825.5
  temporarily 827.9
  now 837.3
for the period of 820.14
for the sake of
  on behalf of 380.11
  in order to 449.26
  because of 887.9
for the time being
  temporarily 827.9
  now 837.3
  conditionally 958.11
forthright
  adj candid 644.17
  adv directly 161.23
forthwith at once 829.8
  promptly 844.15
fortification
  vitaminization 7.12
  strengthening 15.5
  work 460.4
  confirmation 956.4
fortify vitaminize 7.18
  refresh 9.2
  strengthen 15.13
  add to 253.5
  embattle 460.9
  adulterate 796.12
  confirm 956.11
a fortiori
  adj dialectic 934.22
  adv chiefly 249.17
fortitude strength 15.1
  patience 134.1
  will power 359.4
  hardihood 492.6
  cardinal virtues 653.4
Fort Knox 729.12
fortnight
  moment 823.2
  eleven 881.7
fortress 460.6
fortuitous
  circumstantial 765.7
  unessential 767.4
  chance 971.15
fortuity chance 971.1
  chance event 971.6
fortunate
  auspicious 133.18
  successful 409.14
  timely 842.9
  chance 971.15
  lucky 1009.14
fortune wealth 618.1
  gamble 759.2
  fate 963.2
  chance 971.1
  good fortune 1009.2
fortune hunter 651.3
fortuneteller 961.4
forty plot 231.4
  eleven 881.7

forty-niner
  traveler 178.1
  miner 1056.9
forty winks 22.3
forum square 230.8
  conference 423.3
  arena 463.1
  discussion 541.7
  tribunal 595.1
  assembly 769.2
forward
  n team 752.2
  v advance 162.5
  send 176.15
  be instrumental 384.7
  make better 392.9
  hasten 401.4
  be useful 449.17
  deliver 478.13
  determine 885.12
  impel 901.11
  push 903.9
  expedite one's affair
    994.3
  adj eager 101.8
  insolent 142.9
  progressive 162.6
  meddlesome 214.9
  front 216.10
  willing 324.5
  strong-willed 359.15
  foolhardy 493.9
  immodest 666.6
  premature 844.8
  adv forwards 162.8
  frontward 216.13
forward-looking
  progressive 162.6
  modern 840.13
fosse trench 290.2
  entrenchment 460.5
fossil
  n remainder 256.1
  antiquity 841.6
  back number 841.8
  adj antiquated 841.13
fossilized
  stricken in years
    303.18
  antiquated 841.13
  hardened 1044.13
foster
  v nourish 8.19
  advance 162.5
  look after 339.9
  motivate 375.12
  encourage 375.21
  make better 392.9
  nurture 449.16
  hold 474.7
  train 568.13
  care for 1007.19
  adj related 559.6
foster-care 449.3
foster child
  dependent 432.6
  descendant 561.3
fostering
  n accommodations
    385.3
  support 449.3
  training 568.3

  protectorship 1007.2
  adj helping 449.20
  protective 1007.23
foul
  n unfairness 650.2
  baseball game 745.3
  football game 746.3
  basketball game 747.3
  hockey game 749.3
  game 749.6
  match 752.3
  fight 754.3
  v defile 80.17
  stop 293.7
  misuse 389.4
  catch 480.17
  play 747.4
  fix 854.10
  collide 901.13
  adj nasty 64.7
  malodorous 71.5
  filthy 80.23
  unhealthful 82.5
  offensive 98.18
  inert 173.14
  stopped 293.11
  stormy 318.23
  decayed 393.40
  cursing 513.8
  unfair 650.10
  wicked 654.16
  base 661.12
  vulgar 666.8
  obscene 666.9
  demoniac 680.17
  terrible 999.9
  hideous 1014.11
  adv afoul 182.72
foulmouthed
  caustic 144.23
  cursing 513.8
  obscene 666.9
foul play
  homicide 308.2
  chicanery 356.4
  treachery 645.6
  unfairness 650.2
foul up spoil 393.11
  bungle 414.12
  complicate 798.3
  confuse 810.3
  make a boner 974.15
  hinder 1011.16
foul-up
  bungler 414.9
  confusion 809.2
  goof 974.6
found
  establish 159.16
  form 262.7
  sculpture 715.5
  inaugurate 817.11
  fix 854.9
  cause 885.10
  set up 891.10
  burn 1019.24
foundation
  settlement 159.7
  base 199.2
  preparation 405.1
  endowment 478.9
  warrant 600.6

adj bizarre 869.13
freakish
  capricious 364.5
  inconstant 853.7
  freak 869.13
  eccentric 926.5
freak out delight 95.10
  lose self-control 128.8
  go mad 925.22
  go on a trip 975.8
  dream 985.17
freckle
  n spottiness 47.3
  mark 517.5
  blemish 1003.1
  v variegate 47.7
  mark 517.19
  spot 1003.5
free
  v release 120.6
  unclose 292.12
  rescue 398.3
  liberalize 430.13
  exempt 430.14
  liberate 431.4
  extricate 431.7
  acquit 601.4
  detach 801.10
  loosen 803.3
  disembarrass 1013.9
  adj available 222.15
  open 292.17
  voluntary 324.7
  idle 331.18
  communicative 343.10
  escaped 369.11
  leisure 402.5
  at liberty 430.21
  quit 430.31
  liberated 431.10
  liberal 485.4
  gratuitous 634.5
  candid 644.17
  profligate 665.25
  unfastened 801.22
  adv freely 430.32
  as a gift 478.27
  gratuitously 634.6
free and easy
  nonchalant 106.15
  lighthearted 109.12
  careless 340.11
  free 430.21
  informal 581.3
  convivial 582.23
  unconventional 867.6
free association 92.33
freebie
  n gift 478.4
  costlessness 634.1
  adj gratuitous 634.5
freedom
  leisure 402.1
  liberty 430.1
  liberality 485.1
  privilege 642.2
  candor 644.4
  facility 1013.1
free enterprise
  noninterference 430.9
  policy 609.4

capitalism 611.8
free-for-all noise 53.4
  knock-down-and-
    drag-out 457.5
  commotion 809.4
freehand
  free-acting 430.23
  pictorial 712.21
free hand
  latitude 430.4
  carte blanche 443.4
  liberality 485.1
freeholder
  householder 227.7
  landowner 470.3
  legislator 610.3
freeing
  n release 120.2
  escape 369.1
  rescue 398.1
  liberation 431.1
  freedom 431.2
  extrication 431.3
  evacuation 908.6
  disembarrassment
    1013.6
  adj benefiting 592.4
free lance
  free agent 430.12
  mercenary 461.17
  writer 547.15
  author 718.4
  worker 726.2
free-lance
  stand on one's own
    two feet 430.20
  author 547.21
  write 718.6
freeloader
  parasite 138.5
  nonworker 331.11
  guest 585.6
  free rider 634.3
free love
  sexology 75.18
  love 104.1
  illicit sex 665.7
freemasonry
  affiliation 450.2
  fellowship 587.2
free of
  adj quit 430.31
  prep absent 222.19
free ride
  costlessness 634.1
  game 745.3
free rider 634.3
free-standing
  independent 430.22
  separate 801.20
freestyle 182.11
freestyle skiing 753.1
freethinking
  n liberalism 430.10
  free thought 695.7
  liberalness 978.2
  adj nonrestrictive
    430.25
  latitudinarian 695.21
  liberal 978.9
free thought
  liberalism 430.10

freethinking 695.7
  liberalness 978.2
free throw 747.3
free time 402.1
free trade
  noninterference 430.9
  policy 609.4
  commerce 731.1
free up 1013.9
freewheeling 430.22
free will will 323.1
  voluntariness 324.2
  choice 371.1
  free choice 430.6
free with one's money
  485.4
freeze
  n cold weather 1022.3
  v deaden 25.4
  numb 94.8
  take fright 127.11
  terrify 127.17
  be still 173.7
  preserve 397.9
  speak poorly 525.7
  perpetuate 828.5
  stabilize 854.7
  fix 854.10
  stop 856.7
  put a stop to 856.11
  be cold 1022.9
  freeze 1022.9
  chill 1022.10
  ice up 1022.10
  ice 1023.11
  inter cease! 856.13
the freeze 589.1
freeze-dry
  preserve 397.9
  freeze 1023.11
  dry 1064.6
freeze out
  exclude 772.4
  drive out 908.14
freezing
  n food preservation
    397.2
  refrigeration 1023.1
  adj cold 1022.14
  feeling cold 1022.16
  refrigerative 1023.12
freight
  n transportation 176.3
  freightage 176.6
  train 179.14
  load 196.2
  burden 297.7
  haulage 630.7
  charge 643.3
  impediment 1011.6
  v load 159.15
  transport 176.12
  send 176.15
  burden 297.13
  fill 793.7
freighter
  carrier 176.7
  train 179.14
frenetic
  overzealous 101.12
  overactive 330.24
  rabid 925.30

frenzied
  overzealous 101.12
  frantic 105.25
  overactive 330.24
  turbulent 671.18
  rabid 925.30
frenzy
  n seizure 85.6
  overzealousness 101.3
  fury 105.8
  turbulence 671.2
  agitation 916.1
  furor 925.7
  confusion 984.3
  v excite 105.12
  enrage 152.25
  madden 925.24
frequency
  oftenness 846
  routineness 846.1
  oscillation 915.1
  wave 915.4
  radio frequency
    1033.12
frequent
  v haunt 221.10
  adj habitual 373.15
  oftentime 846.4
  recurrent 848.13
fresco
  n painting 35.12
  picture 712.11
  v color 35.13
fresh
  n stream 238.1
  torrent 238.5
  adj refreshing 9.3
  clean 79.25
  green 83.13
  impudent 142.10
  additional 253.10
  windy 318.22
  original 337.5
  unused 390.12
  inexperienced 414.17
  present 837.2
  new 840.7
  additional 840.8
  remembered 988.23
  undamaged 1001.8
  cool 1022.12
freshen refresh 9.2
  clean 79.18
  air 317.10
  blow 318.20
  perfect 392.11
  refrigerate 1023.10
freshet stream 238.1
  torrent 238.5
fresh-faced fresh 83.13
  young 301.9
freshman
  undergraduate 572.6
  novice 572.9
  beginner 817.2
fret
  n ache 26.5
  irritation 96.3
  dither 105.6
  dudgeon 152.7
  network 170.3
  heraldry 647.2

roulette 759.12
v pain 26.7
irritate 96.14
sulk 110.14
grieve 112.17
complain 115.15
make anxious 126.5
feel anxious 126.6
be impatient 135.4
be angry 152.15
provoke 152.24
injure 393.13
wear 393.20
agitate 916.10
abrade 1042.7
fretful
peevish 110.22
plaintive 115.19
impatient 135.6
bustling 330.20
fretting
n worry 126.2
impatience 135.1
abrasion 1042.2
adj irritating 26.13
troublesome 126.10
impatient 135.6
abrasive 1042.10
friable
brittle 1048.4
pulverable 1049.13
friar 699.15
fricassee
n stew 10.11
v cook 11.4
friction
n touching 73.2
opposition 451.2
disaccord 456.1
hostility 589.3
counteraction 899.1
rubbing 1042.1
adj frictional 1042.9
Friday abstinence
668.2
fate 963.2
Friday the thirteenth
963.2
fridge 1023.4
fried cooked 11.6
high 87.23
drunk 88.33
friend 588.1
friendless
helpless 19.18
forlorn 584.12
alone 871.8
friendly
comfortable 121.11
homelike 228.33
favorable 449.22
sociable 582.22
hospitable 585.11
friendlike 587.15
friendship
comradeship 587
friendliness 587.1
fright
n fear 127.1
eyesore 1014.4
v frighten 127.15
frighten fright 127.15

startle 131.8
alarm 400.3
frightening
n intimidation 127.6
adj frightful 127.28
frighten off
scare away 127.21
dissuade 379.3
frightful
frightening 127.28.
remarkable 247.11
hideous 1014.11
frigid unsexual 75.28
unfeeling 94.9
reticent 344.10
aloof 583.6
cold 1022.14
frill
n edging 211.7
extra 254.4
fold 291.1
finery 498.3
ornateness 545.4
superfluity 992.4
v fold 291.5
frilly ornate 498.12
showy 501.19
fringe
n tuft 3.6
exterior 206.2
border 211.4
edging 211.7
golf 751.1
adj exterior 206.7
fringe benefits 624.6
frippery finery 5.10
frills 498.3
superfluity 992.4
trifle 997.5
frisk
n caper 366.2
frolic 743.5
search 937.15
v rejoice 116.5
go on horseback
177.34
caper 366.6
play 743.23
search 937.30
frisky gay 109.14
active 330.17
fritter away 486.5
frivolity
merriment 109.5
lightness 298.1
waggishness 489.4
foolishness 922.1
flightiness 984.5
triviality 997.3
frivolous
merry 109.15
litigious 598.20
unordered 809.12
superficial 921.20
scatterbrained
984.16
trivial 997.19
frizz
n lock 3.5
v cook 11.4
frizzy 281.9
fro 163.13

frock
n garment 5.3
suit 5.6
dress 5.16
robe 702.2
v cloak 5.39
ordain 698.12
frog
derogatory names
232.7
amphibian 311.27
jumper 366.4
frogman
swimmer 182.12
navy man 183.4
diver 367.4
frolic
n prank 489.10
play 743.5
v exude cheerfulness
109.6
rejoice 116.5
play 743.23
from at 159.27
away from 188.21
out of 190.22
off 255.14
from A to Z
wholly 791.13
from beginning to end
793.18
from bad to worse
119.6
from scratch
first 817.18
newly 840.15
from soup to nuts
wholly 791.13
from beginning to end
793.18
from time to time
847.5
frond leaf 310.17
branch 310.18
front
n appearance 33.2
leading 165.1
atmosphere 184.32
exteriority 206.1
facade 206.2
forepart 216
fore 216.1
vanguard 216.2
weather map 317.4
sham 354.3
pretext 376.1
mediator 466.3
affectation 500.1
figurehead 575.5
movement 609.33
v contrapose 215.4
be in front 216.7
confront 216.8
oppose 451.5
offer resistance 453.3
defy 454.3
brave 492.11
precede 813.2
adj frontal 216.10
phonetic 524.31
first 817.17
the front 463.2

frontage
navigation 159.3
front 216.1
frontal
n fore 216.1
altar 703.12
adj anterior 216.10
front for
be in front 216.7
represent 576.14
take the place of 861.6
frontier
n boundary 211.3
border 211.5
front 216.1
hinterland 233.2
remote region 261.4
the unknown 929.7
adj bordering 211.11
frontispiece
front 216.1
curtain-raiser 815.2
front man front 216.1
mediator 466.3
figurehead 575.5
front matter
front 216.1
added to writing
254.2
makeup 554.12
part of writing 792.2
curtain-raiser 815.2
front page 216.1
front-page 552.13
front-runner
vanguard 216.2
jockey 757.2
precursor 815.1
frost
n failure 410.2
enmity 589.1
cold weather 1022.3
Jack Frost 1022.7
v whiten 37.5
top 198.9
freeze 1022.10
hail 1022.11
frost over 1029.3
frostbite
n cold 1022.2
v freeze 1022.10
frosted
n beverage 10.47
adj white 37.7
unfeeling 94.9
frosty 1022.17
semitransparent
1029.4
frosting
sweets 10.38
whitening 37.3
topping 198.3
frosty white 37.7
unfeeling 94.9
reticent 344.10
aloof 583.6
unfriendly 589.9
frostlike 1022.17
semitransparent
1029.4
froth
n saliva 13.3

dregs 256.2
lightness 298.2
foam 320.2
trivia 997.4
sprinkle 1063.5
v bubble 320.4
foam 320.5
froth at the mouth
  925.20
frothy light 298.10
foamy 320.7
showy 501.19
superficial 921.20
trivial 997.19
froward
disobedient 327.8
perverse 361.11
frown
n scowl 110.9
offense 152.2
reproving look 510.8
v look sullen 110.15
show resentment
  152.14
frozen unfeeling 94.9
terrified 127.26
fast 799.14
immortal 828.9
permanent 852.7
immovable 854.15
stuck 854.16
feeling cold 1022.16
frozen solid 1023.14
fructification
productiveness 889.1
proliferation 889.2
performance 891.5
bearing 891.6
fructuous 994.5
frugal
parsimonious 484.7
cheap 633.7
economical 635.6
temperate 668.9
meager 991.10
frugality
parsimony 484.1
thrift 635.1
temperance 668.1
fruit
n produce 10.36
homosexual 75.15
seed 310.29
yield 472.5
offspring 561.1
effect 886.1
product 892.1
v bear 891.13
fruitbearing 889.10
fruitcake
homosexual 75.15
lunatic 925.16
fruitful 889.9
fruition pleasure 95.1
accomplishment
  407.1
bearing 891.6
fruitless
ineffective 19.15
gainless 391.12
unsuccessful 410.18
fruits gain 472.3

receipts 627.1
fruity
flavorful 63.9
fragrant 70.9
vegetable 310.33
crazy 925.27
frump
old woman 304.3
slob 809.7
frustrate
disappoint 132.2
thwart 412.11
outwit 415.11
neutralize 899.7
hinder 1011.15
frustrated
unsexual 75.28
disappointed 132.5
frustration
psychological stress
  92.17
disappointment 132.1
discomfiture 412.2
circumvention 415.5
neutralization 899.2
thwarting 1011.3
fry
n dish 10.7
marine animal 311.30
offspring 561.1
v cook 11.4
brown 40.2
execute 604.17
be hot 1018.22
fuck copulate 75.21
deceive 356.19
mistreat 389.6
a fuck 761.3
fucked-up
botched 414.22
complex 798.4
confused 809.16
fuck off depart 188.7
leave 222.10
idle 331.12
fuck-off 331.8
fuck over 389.6
fuck up spoil 393.11
bungle 414.12
complicate 798.3
confuse 810.3
make a boner 974.15
fuck-up fiasco 410.6
bungle 414.5
bungler 414.9
complex 798.2
confusion 809.2
goof 974.6
fuddle
n intoxication 88.1
confusion 984.3
v intoxicate 88.23
perplex 970.13
confuse 984.7
fuddy-duddy
n fussbudget 495.7
back number 841.8
dotard 923.9
adj old-fogyish 841.17
fudge
n nonsense 520.2
v slight 340.8

falsify 354.15
fabricate 354.17
cheat 356.18
fuel
n automobile racing
  756.1
energy source 1020.1
petroleum 1054.4
rocket propulsion
  1072.8
v provision 385.9
fuel up 1020.7
adj energy 1020.8
fugitive
n fleer 368.5
escapee 369.5
criminal 660.10
adj vanishing 34.3
receding 168.5
wandering 177.37
runaway 368.16
escaped 369.11
unsubstantial 763.5
transient 827.7
fugue trance 92.19
round 708.19
loss of memory 989.2
führer leader 574.6
tyrant 575.14
fulcrum
supporter 900.2
axis 905.3
axle 914.5
fulfill
carry out 328.7
accomplish 407.4
observe 434.2
execute 437.9
complete 793.6
suffice 990.4
fulfillment
adjustment 92.27
contentment 107.1
accomplishment
  407.1
observance 434.1
execution 437.4
completion 793.4
fuliginous 38.11
full
n fullness 793.2
adj colored 35.16
loud 53.11
resonant 54.9
intoxicated 88.31
great 247.6
corpulent 257.18
broad 269.6
thick 269.8
stopped 293.11
unrestricted 430.27
detailed 765.9
crowded 769.22
complete 793.9
filled 793.11
plentiful 990.7
satiated 993.6
sound 1001.7
full-blooded
strong 15.15
red-complexioned
  41.9

upper-class 607.10
wellborn 608.11
full bloom
maturity 303.2
flowering 310.24
full-blown
full-sized 257.22
mature 303.13
full-bodied
flavorful 63.9
thick 269.8
full circle circuit 913.2
rotation 914.1
full-fledged
developed 14.3
full-sized 257.22
grown 259.12
mature 303.13
complete 793.9
full-grown
developed 14.3
full-sized 257.22
grown 259.12
mature 303.13
ripe 407.13
complete 793.9
full measure fill 793.3
plenty 990.2
full of beans
healthy 83.9
gay 109.14
full of holes 393.32
full of hope 124.11
full of hot air 974.18
full of it 974.18
full of oneself 140.12
full of piss and vinegar
energetic 17.13
healthy 83.9
gay 109.14
vigorous 544.11
full-scale
full-sized 257.22
complete 793.9
full tilt 330.25
full time 824.3
fulminate blast 56.8
explode 671.14
fulminate against
censure 510.13
berate 510.19
curse 513.5
fulsome nasty 64.7
malodorous 71.5
offensive 98.18
suave 504.18
uncritical 509.18
flattering 511.8
grandiloquent 545.8
bombastic 545.9
base 661.12
obscene 666.9
terrible 999.9
fumble
n bungle 414.5
game 746.3
v bungle 414.11
play 746.5
confuse 810.3
grope 937.31
fume
n odor 69.1

excitement 105.4
dudgeon 152.7
turbulence 671.2
agitation 916.1
combustion product
 1019.16
vapor 1065.1
v decolor 36.5
be angry 152.15
preserve 397.9
seethe 671.12
let out 908.24
smoke 1018.23
vaporize 1065.8
fumigate
perfume 70.8
deodorize 72.4
sanitize 79.24
vaporize 1065.8
fun
n pleasure 95.1
pleasantness 97.1
merriment 109.5
joke 489.6
action 743.2
v joke 489.13
adj delightful 97.8
amusing 743.27
function
n action 328.1
intention 380.1
use 387.5
syntax 530.2
ceremony 580.4
duty 641.1
rite 701.3
occupation 724.1
office 724.3
v act 328.4
officiate 724.13
operate 888.5
be operative 888.7
functional
psychological 92.36
acting 328.10
useful 387.18
grammatical 530.17
occupational 724.16
effective 888.9
working 888.11
operational 888.12
functionary
official 575.16
agent 576.3
operator 888.4
functioning
n action 328.1
operation 888.1
adj acting 328.10
operating 888.11
fund
n supply 386.2
finances 728.14
capital 728.15
collection 769.11
v provide 385.7
support 449.12
subsidize 478.19
pay for 624.18
finance 729.15
fundamental
n tone 50.2

essence 766.2
foundation 900.6
salient point 996.6
adj basic 199.8
essential 766.9
simple 797.6
beginning 817.15
original 885.14
vital 996.23
fundamentalism
firmness 425.2
Christianity 675.7
strictness 687.5
zeal 692.3
fundamentalist
n true believer 687.4
believer 692.4
adj firm 425.7
strict 687.8
fund-raise 769.18
fundraiser 729.9
funds means 384.2
assets 471.7
finances 728.14
funebrial
gloomy 112.24
funereal 309.22
funeral
n burial 309.5
procession 811.3
adj funereal 309.22
funeral march
dirge 115.6
slow motion 175.2
march 708.12
funeral oration
dirge 115.6
last offices 309.4
speech 543.2
funeral pyre 1018.13
funereal dark 38.9
sad 112.24
pessimistic 125.16
funeral 309.22
gloomy 1026.14
fungus growth 85.38
germ 85.41
plant 310.3
mold 310.4
blight 1000.2
funicular
n train 179.14
cableway 383.8
adj threadlike 271.7
funk
n stench 71.1
fear 127.1
coward 491.5
v take fright 127.11
flinch 127.13
frighten 127.15
lose one's nerve 491.8
funky malodorous 71.5
melancholy 112.23
cowardly 491.10
funnel
n convergence 169.1
tube 239.6
chimney 239.14
cone 282.5
v converge 169.2
transport 176.14

channel 239.15
funnies 712.16
funny humorous 488.4
witty 489.15
inexplicable 522.18
ambiguous 539.4
odd 869.11
eccentric 926.5
peculiar 926.6
unbelievable 954.10
bewildering 970.27
funny farm 925.14
funny feeling
apprehension 127.4
nervousness 128.1
forewarning 399.2
hunch 933.3
fur
n hair 3.2
down 3.19
pelt 4.2
skin 295.3
heraldry 647.2
v fill 196.7
furbish polish 287.7
perfect 392.11
renovate 396.17
ornament 498.8
buff 1042.8
furcate
v fork 171.7
angle 278.5
adj forked 171.10
angular 278.6
the Furies rage 152.10
avenger 507.3
Fury 680.10
furious
overzealous 101.12
frenzied 105.25
passionate 105.29
infuriated 152.32
hasty 401.9
reckless 493.8
violent 671.16
turbulent 671.18
rabid 925.30
furlough
n vacation 20.3
absence 222.4
unemployment 331.3
v dismiss 908.19
furnace foundry 739.4
kiln 742.5
hot place 1018.11
heater 1019.10
reactor 1037.13
furnish provide 385.7
equip 385.8
supply 478.15
bear 891.13
fit 405.8
furnishings
wardrobe 5.2
furniture 229.1
equipment 385.4
merchandise 735.5
furniture
home furnishings 229
furnishings 229.1
equipment 385.4
composition 548.2

merchandise 735.5
furor passion 93.2
greed 100.8
fury 105.8
rage 152.10
turbulence 671.2
insanity 925.1
frenzy 925.7
mania 925.12
furrier clothier 5.32
tailor 5.34
furrow
n crack 224.2
indentation 284.6
groove 290.1
wrinkle 291.3
v cleave 224.4
excavate 284.15
groove 290.3
wrinkle 291.6
engrave 713.9
furry hairy 3.24
feathery 3.27
cutaneous 295.32
fluffy 1045.14
further
v advance 162.5
be useful 449.17
adj additional 253.10
thither 261.10
fresh 840.8
adv additionally
 253.11
furtherance
progression 162.1
improvement 392.1
helping along 449.5
evolution 860.1
furthermore 253.11
further oneself 162.2
furthest
extreme 247.13
farthest 261.12
furtive covert 345.12
in hiding 346.14
deceitful 356.22
fury
n passion 93.2
overzealousness 101.3
furor 105.8
sorehead 110.11
bitch 110.12
rage 152.10
witch 593.7
turbulence 671.2
violent person 671.9
frenzy 925.7
adv swiftly 174.18
fuse
n detonator 462.15
safeguard 1007.3
v cooperate 450.3
come together 769.16
identify 777.5
mix 796.10
stick together 802.9
combine 804.3
melt 1019.21
liquefy 1062.5
fusillade
n detonation 56.3
volley 459.9

capital punishment
604.7
hit 901.4
shot 903.4
v pull the trigger
459.22
fusion affiliation 450.2
identification 777.2
mixture 796.1
combination 804.1
oneness 871.1
melting 1019.3
nuclear fusion 1037.9
alloy 1056.4
liquefaction 1062.1
fuss
n dither 105.6
bustle 330.4
quarrel 456.5
fussbudget 495.7
finery 498.3
bluster 503.1
turbulence 671.2
commotion 809.4
agitation 916.1
v agitate 105.14
complain 115.15
feel anxious 126.6
be impatient 135.4
bustle 330.12
be hard to please
495.8
fuss at 510.16
fussbudget 495.7
fussy restless 105.27
bustling 330.20
meticulous 339.12
finical 495.10
ornate 498.12
detailed 765.9
fustian
n nonsense 520.2
bombast 545.2
adj bombastic 545.9
fusty malodorous 71.5
trite 117.9
blighted 393.42
stale 841.14
futile ineffective 19.15
vain 125.13
useless 391.13
unsuccessful 410.18
foolish 922.8
inexpedient 995.5
trivial 997.19
futility
ineffectiveness 19.3
hopelessness 125.1
vanity 391.2
failure 410.1
meaninglessness
520.1
inexpedience 995.1
triviality 997.3
future
n fiancé 104.17
tense 530.12
the future 838.1
fate 963.2
adj later 838.8
imminent 839.3
the future 820.1

futures 738.11
fuzz
n down 3.19
smoothness 294.3
lightness 298.2
v cover 295.19
make uncertain
970.15
the fuzz 1007.16
gab
n speech 524.1
chatter 540.3
v speak 524.20
babble 524.21
chatter 540.5
Gabriel herald 353.2
Azrael 679.4
gad about
journey 177.21
wander 177.23
gadfly goad 375.8
prompter 375.10
gadget tool 1039.1
thing 1050.5
Gaea
agricultural deity
1067.4
Earth 1070.10
gaffe 974.5
gag
n silencer 51.4
shackle 428.4
joke 489.6
acting 704.8
v disable 19.10
silence 51.8
feel disgust 99.4
restrain 428.8
vomit 908.26
gaga 922.8
gage marijuana 87.10
pledge 438.2
challenge 454.2
gaggle
n assemblage 769.6
v bird sound 60.5
gaiety
colorfulness 35.4
happiness 95.2
gayness 109.4
finery 498.3
showiness 501.3
conviviality 582.3
festivity 743.3
gain
n increase 251.1
profit 472.3
game 746.3
good 998.4
available gain 1031.16
time constants
1040.11
v arrive 186.6
grow 251.6
persuade 375.23
improve 392.7
triumph 411.3
acquire 472.8
receive 479.6
incur 896.4
gainful valuable 387.22
productive 472.16

gain ground
progress 162.2
accelerate 174.10
improve 392.7
gain on 174.13
gains winnings 251.3
profit 472.3
receipts 627.1
gainsay deny 335.4
contradict 451.6
gait velocity 172.4
pace 177.12
gal woman 77.6
dame 302.7
person 312.5
gala
n festival 743.4
adj festive 743.28
galactic spatial 158.9
large 247.7
universal 863.14
innumerable 883.10
celestial 1070.25
galaxy celebrity 662.9
throng 769.4
island universe 1070.6
the Galaxy 1070.6
gale outburst 105.9
breeze 318.5
windstorm 318.12
gall
n digestive secretion
13.2
acridness 64.2
trauma 85.37
irritation 96.3
affliction 96.8
ill humor 110.1
impudence 142.3
rancor 144.7
bitterness 152.3
bulge 283.3
rashness 493.1
v pain 26.7
irritate 96.14
injure 393.13
abrade 1042.7
gallant
n beau 104.13
brave person 492.8
dandy 500.9
cavalier 504.9
libertine 665.10
adj courageous 492.17
showy 501.19
chivalrous 504.15
profligate 665.25
gallantry
courage 492.1
gallantness 504.2
courtship 562.7
profligacy 665.3
gallbladder 2.14
gallery
observation post 27.8
audience 48.6
hall 197.4
corridor 197.18
porch 197.21
balcony 197.22
showroom 197.24
layer 296.1

passageway 383.3
museum 386.9
entrenchment 460.5
auditorium 704.15
studio 712.17
platform 900.13
galley kitchen 11.3
sailboat 180.3
proof 548.5
galley slave
boatman 183.5
subject 432.7
drudge 726.3
Gallicism 523.8
gallivant
wander 177.23
flirt 562.20
gallop
n run 174.3
gait 177.12
v speed 174.8
go on horseback
177.34
gallows 605.5
the gallows 604.7
galore
adj plentiful 990.7
adv greatly 247.15
galvanize
energize 17.10
stimulate 105.13
plate 295.26
motivate 375.12
electrify 1031.25
electrolyze 1031.27
gambit trick 356.6
attempt 403.2
stratagem 415.3
first 817.3
gamble
n bet 759.2
guess 970.8
chance 971.1
v game 759.23
bet 759.25
be liable 896.3
predict 961.9
risk 971.12
endanger 1005.6
take chances 1005.7
gamble on
chance 759.24
rely on 952.16
be certain 969.9
gambling
illicit business 732.1
game 743.9
cardplaying 758.1
betting 759
playing 759.1
gambol
n caper 366.2
frolic 743.5
v exude cheerfulness
109.6
rejoice 116.5
caper 366.6
play 743.23
game
n meat 10.12
desire 100.11
sweetheart 104.10

animal life 311.1
objective 380.2
plan 381.1
intrigue 381.5
quarry 382.7
stratagem 415.3
contest 457.3
laughingstock 508.7
vocation 724.6
fun 743.2
card game 743.9
sport 744.1
ball game 745.3
artifice 746.3
basketball game 747.3
strategy 748.2
match 749.3
contest 749.6
frame 750.2
meet 752.3
cardplaying 758.1
bridge 758.3
gambling game 759.7
v gamble 759.23
adj willing 324.5
plucky 359.14
crippled 393.30
resolute 492.18
gamekeeper
guardian 1007.6
hunter 382.5
game plan
plan 381.1
project 381.2
game 746.3
game preserve
preserve 397.7
refuge 1008.1
game reserve 397.7
game room 197.12
game-show 1034.2
gamete 305.10
game warden
preserver 397.5
guardian 1007.6
gamin
vagabond 178.3
brat 302.4
gamut range 158.2
scale 709.6
series 811.2
gamy revolting 68.8
malodorous 71.5
tainted 393.41
gander
male animal 76.8
poultry 311.29
a gander 27.3
Gandhi 920.2
gang
n staff 577.11
association 617.1
company 769.3
group of animals
769.5
v league 804.4
gang bang
copulation 75.7
sexual possession
480.3
ganglord 660.11
gangly lean 270.17

giant 272.16
gangplank 189.5
gangrene
n filth 80.7
mortification 85.39
v decay 393.22
gangster bandit 483.4
evildoer 593.1
criminal 660.10
the underworld
660.11
gang up on 459.14
gang up with 582.18
gangway
n entrance 189.5
inter open up! 292.23
the gantlet 604.2
Ganymede
homosexual 75.14
carrier 176.7
attendant 577.5
gap
n interval 224.1
crack 224.2
ridge 237.5
valley 284.9
opening 292.1
difference 779.1
dissimilarity 786.1
deficiency 794.2
break 801.4
interruption 812.2
v cleave 224.4
gape 292.16
gape
n gaze 27.5
crack 224.2
opening 292.1
gaping 292.2
v gaze 27.15
wonder 122.5
gap 292.16
spectate 917.5
be curious 980.3
gaping
n yawning 292.2
adj wondering 122.9
expectant 130.11
cleft 224.7
spread 259.11
abysmal 275.11
yawning 292.18
gapless 811.8
garage carport 197.27
repair shop 739.5
garb
n clothing 5.1
looks 33.4
v clothe 5.38
garbage offal 80.9
heroin 87.8
refuse 391.4
bull 520.3
Greek 522.7
garbage dump
receptacle of filth
80.12
derelict 370.4
trash pile 391.6
garble
n Greek 522.7
v pervert 265.6

misinterpret 342.2
misrepresent 350.3
falsify 354.15
make unintelligible
522.12
confuse 810.3
garçon boy 302.5
man 577.4
garden
n compilation 554.7
horticulture 1067.10
v farm 1067.16
adj floral 310.35
simple 499.6
ordinary 1004.8
gardener man 577.4
horticulturist 1067.6
gardening
flower 310.22
horticulture 1067.2
Garden of Eden 985.11
garden variety 868.3
garden-variety
simple 499.6
ordinary 1004.8
Gargantuan large 247.7
huge 257.20
gargle
n dentifrice 86.22
drink 88.7
v wash 79.19
tipple 88.24
gargoyle spout 239.8
eyesore 1014.4
garish lurid 35.19
gaudy 501.20
grandiloquent 545.8
bright 1024.32
garland
n circle 280.2
bouquet 310.23
compilation 554.7
trophy 646.3
heraldry 647.2
book of verse 720.5
v figure 498.9
garment
n vestment 5.3
v clothe 5.38
garner
n granary 386.7
v store up 386.11
garnish
n ornamentation
498.1
v attach 480.20
ornament 498.8
garniture 498.1
garret 197.16
garrison
n stronghold 460.6
military unit 461.22
guard 1007.9
v fortify 460.9
garrote
n suffocation 308.6
capital punishment
604.7
v strangle 308.18
execute 604.17
garrulous 540.9
garter 646.5

gas
n success 409.4
boasting 502.2
poppycock 520.3
chatter 540.3
belch 908.9
fart 908.10
fuel 1020.1
illuminant 1024.20
volatile 1065
rare gas 1065.2
vaporousness 1065.3
v provision 385.9
talk nonsense 520.5
chatter 540.5
gas chamber
place of killing 308.11
execution 605.5
the gas chamber 604.7
gasconade
n boasting 502.1
v boast 502.6
bluster 503.3
gaseous rare 299.4
thin 763.6
vaporous 1065.9
gash
n trauma 85.37
crack 224.2
notch 289.1
furrow 290.1
refuse 391.4
mark 517.5
v cleave 224.4
notch 289.4
furrow 290.3
injure 393.13
mark 517.19
sever 801.11
gasket 293.5
gaslit 1024.39
gasoline 1024.20
gasp
n breathing 2.19
v burn out 21.5
speak 524.26
be hot 1018.22
gassiness
distension 259.2
talkativeness 540.1
vaporousness 1065.3
gassy
v talkative 540.9
adj distended 259.13
pompous 501.22
inflated 502.12
bombastic 545.9
vaporous 1065.9
gastric 2.29
gastronome 8.16
gastronomy
epicurism 8.15
aesthetic taste 496.5
gourmandise 672.2
gat opening 292.1
gun 462.10
gate entrance 189.5
porch 189.6
channel 239.4
valve 239.10
floodgate 239.11
receipts 627.1

horse racing 757.1
  attender 917.2
  barrier 1011.5
  cast 1056.5
the gate 908.5
gâteau 10.40
gate-crasher
  intruder 214.3
  guest 585.6
  newcomer 773.4
gatehouse 228.9
gatekeeper 1007.12
gather
  n fold 291.1
  v grow 14.2
  expand 259.7
  fold 291.5
  blow 318.20
  collect 472.11
  come together 769.16
  assemble 769.18
  put together 799.5
  be imminent 839.2
  conclude 945.10
  suppose 950.10
  harvest 1067.19
gathering
  n sore 85.36
  collection 472.2
  bookbinding 554.14
  social gathering
    582.10
  removal to heaven
    681.11
  assemblage 769.1
  assembly 769.2
  accumulation 769.9
  part of writing 792.2
  joining 799.1
  harvest 1067.15
  adj imminent 839.3
gauche
  bungling 414.20
  ignorant 929.12
  inconvenient 995.7
gaucho rider 178.8
  herder 1068.3
gaudy garish 35.19
  coarse 497.11
  tawdry 501.20
  grandiloquent 545.8
  paltry 997.21
gauge
  n size 257.1
  measure 300.2
  v size 257.15
  measure 300.10
  classify 800.8
  estimate 945.9
gaunt lean 270.17
  unproductive 890.4
gauntlet 454.2
gauze
  dressing 86.33
  fog 319.2
gauzy thin 270.16
  smooth 294.8
  unsubstantial 763.6
  transparent 1028.4
gavel 417.9
gawk
  n bungler 414.8

oaf 923.5
  v gaze 27.15
  wonder 122.5
  be curious 980.3
gawky
  n oaf 923.5
  adj lean 270.17
  bungling 414.20
gay colorful 35.18
  homosexual 75.29
  intoxicated 88.31
  happy 95.15
  gay as a lark 109.14
  showy 501.19
  convivial 582.23
  profligate 665.25
  festive 743.28
gaze
  n stare 27.5
  v gloat 27.15
  wonder 122.5
gazebo
  observation post 27.8
  summerhouse 228.12
gazelle
  swiftness 174.6
  hoofed animal 311.5
  jumper 366.4
gazette
  official document
    549.8
  periodical 555.1
  newspaper 555.2
gear
  n clothing 5.1
  rigging 180.12
  cordage 271.3
  equipment 385.4
  impedimenta 471.3
  baseball 745.1
  football 746.1
  hockey 749.1
  field hockey 749.4
  golf 751.1
  soccer 752.1
  skiing 753.1
  mechanism 1039.4
  gearing 1039.5
  v equip 385.8
  adj excellent 998.13
geared high 87.23
  apt 787.10
gee
  v avoid 164.6
  inter my! 122.21
geisha dancer 705.3
  entertainer 707.1
Geist 919.8
gel
  n lights 704.18
  semiliquid 1060.5
  solution 1062.3
  v thicken 1043.10
gelatin
  sweets 10.38
  lights 704.18
  semiliquid 1060.5
geld feminize 77.12
  castrate 255.11
gelded
  unmanned 19.19
  unproductive 890.4

gelding
  impotent 19.6
  sexlessness 75.9
  castration 255.4
  horse 311.10
  jockey 757.2
gelid cold 1022.14
  frozen 1023.14
gem
  n jewel 498.6
  good person 659.1
  good thing 998.5
  precious stone 1057.6
  v figure 498.9
geminate
  v duplicate 873.3
  adj double 873.4
Gemini 872.4
Gemütlichkeit
  pleasantness 97.1
  sociability 582.1
gendarme
  officer 1007.15
  police 1007.16
gender sex 75.1
  masculine 530.10
gene
  genetic material 305.9
  heredity 560.6
genealogy
  register 549.9
  pedigree 560.5
general
  n commissioned
    officer 575.18
  adj public 312.16
  communal 476.9
  common 497.14
  governing 612.18
  generalized 863.11
  normal 868.8
  undiscriminating
    944.5
  theoretical 950.13
  vague 970.19
generality mean 246.1
  major part 791.6
  universality 863.1
  usualness 868.2
  abstract idea 931.3
  indiscrimination
    944.1
  vagueness 970.4
generalization
  custom 373.1
  generality 863.1
  general idea 863.8
  reasoning 934.3
generally
  approximately 223.23
  on the average 246.5
  in general 863.17
  normally 868.10
  vaguely 970.29
general store 736.1
general strike
  revolt 327.4
  strike 727.5
generate procreate 78.8
  cause 885.10
  originate 891.12
  electrify 1031.25

generation
  procreation 78.2
  birth 78.6
  age 823.4
  lifetime 826.5
  production 891.1
generation gap 456.1
generator 885.4
generic 863.11
generosity
  benevolence 143.4
  liberality 485.1
  hospitality 585.1
  magnanimity 652.2
  plenty 990.2
generous
  benevolent 143.15
  forgiving 148.6
  much 247.8
  voluminous 257.17
  indulgent 427.8
  philanthropic 478.22
  liberal 485.4
  hospitable 585.11
  magnanimous 652.6
  productive 889.9
  tolerant 978.11
  plentiful 990.7
genesis birth 1.1
  reproduction 78.6
  origin 817.4
  evolution 860.3
  source 885.5
  production 891.1
genetic
  generative 78.16
  protoplasmic 305.18
  related 559.6
  racial 559.7
  hereditary 560.19
  innate 766.8
  evolutionary 860.8
  original 885.14
genetics 560.6
genial genetic 78.16
  pleasant 97.6
  cheerful 109.11
  good-natured 143.14
  sociable 582.22
  hospitable 585.11
  cordial 587.16
  warm 1018.24
geniality
  pleasantness 97.1
  cheerfulness 109.1
  good nature 143.2
  sociability 582.1
  hospitality 585.1
  cordiality 587.6
genie 680.6
genitalia
  n reproductive organs
    2.11
  sex 75.1
  adj phallic 2.27
  genetic 78.16
genius ability 18.2
  superior 249.4
  inspiration 375.9
  talent 413.4
  talented person
    413.12

giddy intoxicated 88.31
inconstant 853.7
delirious 925.31
inattentive 983.6
dizzy 984.15
scatterbrained 984.16
gift
n talent 413.4
present 478.4
costlessness 634.1
smartness 919.2
v give 478.12
contribute 478.14
gifted
talented 413.29
studentlike 572.12
smart 919.14
gift of the gab
style 532.2
eloquence 544.1
gig
n position 724.5
v fish 382.10
gigantic
herculean 15.17
large 247.7
huge 257.20
giant 272.16
excessive 992.16
gigantism
greatness 247.1
oversize 257.5
hugeness 257.7
excess 992.1
giggle
n laughter 116.4
v laugh 116.8
gigolo beau 104.13
procurer 665.18
gild color 35.13
yellow 43.3
make pleasant 97.5
coat 295.24
falsify 354.15
ornament 545.7
Gilded Age 823.5
gild the lily
make pleasant 97.5
ornament 545.7
carry coals to
Newcastle 992.12
gilt
n swine 311.9
sham 354.3
finery 498.3
money 728.2
adj yellow 43.4
brass 1056.17
gimmick trick 356.6
lure 377.3
stratagem 415.3
plot 722.4
gambling wheel
759.16
expedient 994.2
tool 1039.1
thing 1050.5
gimmickry
deception 356.1
machination 415.4
finery 498.3
showiness 501.3

gimmicky
deceitful 356.22
cunning 415.12
showy 501.19
gin
n trap 356.12
v trap 356.20
segregate 772.6
ginger energy 17.3
zest 68.2
gingerbread
n finery 498.3
superfluity 992.4
adj ornate 498.12
gingerbread man 349.6
gingerly
adj cautious 494.8
adv cautiously 494.12
giraffe 311.5
gird strengthen 15.13
encircle 209.7
bind 799.9
girdle
n corset 5.23
strip 271.4
circle 280.3
supporter 900.2
v encircle 209.7
surround 280.10
bind 799.9
circle 913.5
gird up one's loins
strengthen 15.13
prepare oneself 405.13
militarize 458.20
set to work 725.15
girl woman 77.5
cocaine 87.6
ladylove 104.15
girlie 302.6
old woman 304.3
maid 577.8
girl Friday 577.3
girlfriend
ladylove 104.15
companion 588.3
girlhood
childhood 301.2
young people 302.2
girlish feminine 77.13
thin 270.16
childish 301.11
immature 406.11
girt
n circle 280.3
saddle parts 900.18
v bind 799.9
adj encircled 209.11
girth
n size 257.1
circle 280.3
middle 818.1
saddle parts 900.18
v bind 799.9
gist
essential content
196.5
meaning 518.1
summary 557.2
essence 766.2
major part 791.6
topic 936.1

salient point 996.6
give
n softness 1045.1
pliancy 1045.2
elasticity 1046.1
v communicate 343.7
provide 385.7
donate 478.12
say 524.23
present 634.4
administer 643.6
attribute 887.3
soften 1045.7
yield 1046.5
transfer 629.3
give and take
compensate 338.4
contend 457.13
compromise 468.2
retaliate 506.4
be just 649.6
interchange 862.4
argue 934.16
give-and-take
n offset 338.2
compromise 468.1
banter 490.1
retaliation 506.1
conversation 541.1
justice 649.1
trade 731.2
interchange 862.1
adj interchangeable
862.5
giveaway
n divulgence 351.2
adj reduced 633.9
give away betray 351.6
discard 390.7
break 393.23
relinquish 475.3
dispose of 478.21
join in marriage
563.14
give back
restore 396.11
restitute 481.4
give birth bear 1.3
reproductive 78.13
vivify 306.9
give in bow to 250.5
yield 433.7
deliver 478.13
given
n fact 760.3
condition 958.2
a truth 972.2
adj allowed 478.24
gratuitous 634.5
real 760.15
supposed 950.14
conditional 958.8
disposed 977.8
give notice
herald 133.14
announce 352.12
warn 399.5
inform 551.8
given that 950.19
given to 895.6
give off excrete 12.12
exude 190.15

let out 908.24
vaporize 1065.8
give oneself airs
be stuck on oneself
140.6
hold one's nose in the
air 141.8
avoid 157.7
put on airs 501.14
give oneself up to
lose heart 112.16
be determined 359.8
undertake 404.3
indulge 669.4
attend to 982.5
give or take 223.26
give out secrete 13.5
weaken 16.9
burn out 21.5
divulge 351.5
make public 352.11
be consumed 388.4
be impaired 393.26
parcel out 477.8
give 478.12
deliver 478.13
let out 908.24
give over despair
125.10
give up 370.7
pass 387.13
cease to use 390.4
surrender 433.8
deliver 478.13
cease 856.6
give rise to
cause 885.10
originate 891.12
give room for 443.9
give up despair 125.10
waive 370.7
break the habit 374.3
cease to use 390.4
yield 433.7
surrender 433.8
resign 448.2
relinquish 475.3
not understand 522.11
swear off 668.8
not know 929.11
give way weaken 16.9
lose heart 112.16
despair 125.10
row 182.53
sink 194.6
break 393.23
yield 433.7
compromise 468.2
cheapen 633.6
come apart 801.9
soften 1045.7
give way
indulge 427.6
let oneself go 430.19
submit to 433.9
glabrous hairless 6.17
smooth 287.9
glacial cold 1022.14
frozen 1023.14
glacier 1022.5
glad pleased 95.14
happy 95.15

cheerful 109.11
cheering 109.16
glade
open space 158.4
marsh 243.1
gladiator 461.1
glamorous
alluring 377.8
illustrious 662.19
bewitching 691.11
gorgeous 1015.20
glamour
n delightfulness 97.2
allurement 377.1
illustriousness 662.6
sorcery 690.1
spell 691.1
gorgeousness 1015.6
v charm 691.8
glance
n glimpse 27.4
touch 73.1
contact 223.5
signal 517.15
preliminary
examination 937.5
flash 1024.6
v glimpse 27.17
touch lightly 73.7
avoid 164.6
contact 223.10
polish 287.7
signal 517.22
shine 1024.23
glancing
n touch 73.1
adj side 218.6
in contact 223.17
glandular
glandulous 13.8
emotional 93.17
glare
n gaze 27.5
offense 152.2
publicity 352.4
showiness 501.3
brightness 1024.4
v glower 27.16
blind 30.7
show 31.4
show resentment
152.14
be manifest 348.7
cut a dash 501.13
shine 1024.23
glaring distinct 31.7
garish 35.19
downright 247.12
conspicuous 348.12
gaudy 501.20
bright 1024.32
glass
n lens 29.2
telescope 29.4
mirror 29.6
container 195.1
smoothness 287.3
weather instrument
317.7
jewelry 498.5
ceramic ware 742.2
basketball 747.1

thermometer 1018.20
transparent substance
1028.2
fragility 1048.2
v face 295.23
adj glassy 1028.5
glasses tableware 8.12
spectacles 29.3
glassy sleek 287.10
inexpressive 522.20
shiny 1024.33
glass 1028.5
glaucoma 30.1
glaze
n sweets 10.38
polish 287.2
ceramics 742.3
ice 1022.5
v color 35.13
sweeten 66.3
polish 287.7
face 295.23
pot 742.6
hail 1022.11
glazed sleek 287.10
inexpressive 522.20
ceramic 742.7
gleam
n hint 248.4
shine 1024.2
ray 1024.5
flash 1024.6
v burst forth 33.9
be somebody 662.10
shine 1024.23
glean select 371.14
collect 472.11
conclude 945.10
harvest 1067.19
glebe land 234.1
benefice 698.9
parsonage 703.7
glee happiness 95.2
merriment 109.5
glee club
part music 708.18
chorus 710.16
glen
highland 237.7
valley 284.9
glib
v talkative 540.9
adj suave 504.18
eloquent 544.8
easy 1013.13
glide
n coasting 177.16
maneuvers 184.13
slide 194.4
speech sound 524.13
v coast 177.35
float 182.54
fly 184.36
slide 194.9
elapse 820.5
go easily 1013.10
adj phonetic 524.31
glider 181.12
glimmer
n hint 551.4
glitter 1024.7
v glitter 1024.24

glimmering
n hint 551.4
slight knowledge
929.6
glitter 1024.7
adj glittering 1024.35
glimpse
n glance 27.4
slight knowledge
929.6
v see 27.12
glance 27.17
glint
n shine 1024.2
flash 1024.6
v glance 27.17
shine 1024.23
glissade
n slide 194.4
v glide 177.35
slide 194.9
glisten
n glitter 1024.7
v glitter 1024.24
glitch
impairment 393.1
abortion 410.5
fault 1002.2
glitter
n showiness 501.3
glimmer 1024.7
v cut a dash 501.13
be somebody 662.10
glimmer 1024.24
glitz
appearance 33.2
garishness 35.5
finery 498.3
showiness 501.3
grandiloquence 545.1
gloat gaze 27.15
exult 502.9
glob lump 257.10
sphere 282.2
global
spherical 282.9
comprehensive 771.7
complete 793.9
universal 863.14
unqualified 959.2
global ecosystem
1071.1
globe
n sphere 282.2
lamp shade 1027.3
Earth 1070.10
v ball 282.7
globe-trotter 178.1
globule sphere 282.2
bubble 320.1
gloom
n gloominess 112.7
shadow 1026.3
somberness 1026.4
v look sullen 110.15
eclipse 1026.9
grow dark 1026.12
gloomy dismal 112.24
pessimistic 125.16
ominous 133.17
cloudy 319.7
gloomful 1026.14

gloppy filthy 80.23
viscous 1060.12
glorified
eminent 662.18
angelic 679.6
heavenly 681.12
sanctified 685.8
glorify approve 509.12
glamorize 662.13
sanctify 685.5
praise 696.11
glorious
intoxicated 88.31
eminent 247.9
grandiose 501.21
illustrious 662.19
almighty 677.18
superb 998.15
gorgeous 1015.20
glory
n radiation 171.2
eminence 247.2
circle 280.2
grandeur 501.5
praise 509.5
honor 646.1
repute 662.1
illustriousness 662.6
glorification 696.2
notability 996.2
brightness 1024.4
halo 1024.14
v rejoice 116.5
exult 502.9
gloss
n shallowness 276.1
polish 287.2
translation 341.3
comment 341.5
misinterpretation
342.1
sham 354.3
pretext 376.1
reference book 554.9
commentary 556.2
extenuation 600.5
shine 1024.2
v color 35.13
polish 287.7
coat 295.24
comment upon 341.11
misinterpret 342.2
falsify 354.15
adj soft-colored 35.21
glossal 62.10
glossary
translation 341.3
reference book 554.9
dictionary 870.4
gloss over
neglect 340.6
conceal 346.6
falsify 354.15
hide under 376.4
extenuate 600.12
glossy
n print 714.5
adj sleek 287.10
shiny 1024.33
glove
n challenge 454.2
v play 745.5

glow
n animation 17.4
warmth 35.2
reddening 41.3
health 83.1
foredawn 314.4
vehemence 544.5
beauty 1015.1
incandescence
1018.12
shine 1024.2
v redden 41.5
enjoy good health
83.6
be excited 105.18
change color 105.19
exude cheerfulness
109.6
be somebody 662.10
look good 1015.16
be hot 1018.22
shine 1024.23
glower
n offense 152.2
v glare 27.16
look sullen 110.15
show resentment
152.14
glowing
chromatic 35.15
red 41.6
red-complexioned
41.9
fervent 93.18
happy 95.15
enthusiastic 101.10
heated 105.22
cheerful 109.11
vehement 544.13
gorgeous 1015.20
burning 1018.27
luminous 1024.30
illuminated 1024.39
glue
n adhesive 802.4
semiliquid 1060.5
v put together 799.5
stick together 802.9
glum sullen 110.24
grum 112.25
glut
n performance 891.5
overfullness 992.3
satiety 993.1
v stuff 8.25
be tedious 118.6
gluttonize 672.4
overload 992.15
satiate 993.4
glutinous
adhesive 802.12
viscous 1060.12
glutton eater 8.16
wild animal 311.23
greedy eater 672.3
gluttonous eating 8.31
piggish 100.27
intemperate 669.7
greedy 672.6
excessive 992.16
G-man detective 576.10
policeman 1007.15

gnarl
n distortion 265.1
bulge 283.3
v growl 60.4
show resentment
152.14
distort 265.5
roughen 288.4
gnarled studded 283.17
gnarly 288.8
gnarly studded 283.17
gnarled 288.8
excellent 998.13
bad 999.8
gnash
n bite 8.2
v chew 8.27
gnash one's teeth
wring one's hands
115.11
show resentment
152.14
gnat 258.7
gnaw chew 8.27
pain 26.7
corrode 393.21
abrade 1042.7
gneiss 1057.1
gnocchi 10.32
gnome dwarf 258.5
elemental 678.6
fairy 678.8
maxim 973.1
gnu 311.5
go
n act 328.3
enterprise 330.7
attempt 403.3
contest 457.3
game 743.9
spell 824.1
turn 824.2
v disappear 34.2
extend 158.8
have place 159.9
take direction 161.7
progress 162.2
recede 168.2
move 172.5
travel 177.18
venture 177.19
depart 188.6
reach out 261.5
die 307.19
take action 328.5
perish 395.23
succeed 409.7
become 760.12
cease to exist 761.6
be operative 888.7
tend 895.3
adj operative 888.9
goad
n spur 375.8
v prod 375.15
impel 901.11
thrust 901.12
drive 1068.8
go after follow 166.3
fetch 176.16
pursue 382.8
succeed 814.2

come after 834.3
go aground 182.42
go ahead
progress 162.2
hustle 330.13
improve 392.7
begin 817.7
go-ahead
n progression 162.1
enterprise 330.7
endorsement 332.4
permission 443.1
adj progressive 162.6
enterprising 330.23
goal destination 186.5
motive 375.1
objective 380.2
score 409.5
hockey 749.1
field hockey 749.4
game 749.6
soccer 752.1
point 752.3
end 819.1
goalie
hockey team 749.2
team 752.2
guard 1007.9
goal line
football 746.1
hockey 749.1
field hockey 749.4
soccer 752.1
go all out speed 174.9
hustle 330.13
persevere 360.7
do one's best 403.14
do to perfection 407.7
let oneself go 430.19
exert oneself 725.9
be thorough 793.8
go all the way
copulate 75.21
prosecute to a
conclusion 360.5
go along
v progress 162.2
travel 177.18
depart 188.6
be willing 324.3
concur 332.9
consent 441.2
be in a certain state
764.5
continue 855.3
inter go away! 908.31
go along with
concur 332.9
acknowledge 332.11
take advice 422.7
submit 433.6
consent 441.2
suffer 443.10
side with 450.4
accompany 768.7
agree 787.6
coincide 835.4
go with 898.3
go around
move 172.5
surround 209.6
recur 849.5

go roundabout 913.4
circle 913.5
turn 913.6
rotate 914.9
suffice 990.4
go astray
stray 164.4
miscarry 410.15
digress 538.9
go wrong 654.9
misbelieve 688.8
miss 910.4
err 974.9
goat
he-goat 311.8
jumper 366.4
laughingstock 508.7
lecher 665.11
scapegoat 861.3
go at travel 177.19
undertake 404.3
attack 459.14
challenge 459.15
goatee 3.8
go away
v disappear 34.2
recede 168.2
diverge 171.5
depart 188.6
inter begone! 908.31
gob bite 8.2
navy man 183.4
amount 244.2
lump 257.10
sphere 282.2
mouth 292.4
accumulation 769.9
piece 792.3
go back on
abandon 370.5
repeal 445.2
be unfaithful 645.12
gobble gulp 8.23
bird sound 60.5
ingest 187.11
consume 388.3
destroy 395.10
gluttonize 672.4
gobbledygook
nonsense 520.2
Greek 522.7
jargon 523.9
bombast 545.2
political jargon
609.37
gobbler
male animal 76.8
poultry 311.29
glutton 672.3
gobble up
consume 388.3
destroy 395.10
monopolize 469.6
kid oneself 953.6
go between
interpose 213.6
be instrumental 384.7
mediate 466.6
go-between
intermediary 213.4
interpreter 341.7
messenger 353.1

instrument 384.4
mediator 466.3
middleman 576.4
goblin fairy 678.8
hobgoblin 680.8
gobs lot 247.4
wealth 618.3
go by be called 527.13
elapse 820.5
conform 866.3
pass 909.8
god hero 659.5
deus 678.2
goddesses 678.4
God 677.2
god-awful 999.8
God bless! 696.17
God bless me! 122.21
God bless you! 188.22
goddam it! 513.11
goddess hero 659.5
deity 678.2
god 678.4
God-fearing
godly 692.9
belief 952.21
God forbid
by no means 335.9
Heaven forbid! 510.27
O Lord! 696.17
godforsaken
available 222.15
out-of-the-way 261.9
forlorn 584.12
God knows! 929.19
godless ungodly 695.17
unregenerate 695.18
godlike great 247.9
eminent 662.18
superhuman 677.17
divine 678.16
godly 692.9
godliness
virtue 653.1
deity 677.1
sanctity 685.1
godlikeness 692.2
godly virtuous 653.6
divine 677.17
godlike 692.9
godown 386.6
go down
capsize 182.44
descend 194.5
sink 194.6
plunge 367.8
decline 393.17
fail 410.11
lose 412.12
play 745.5
fight 754.4
occur 830.5
find credence 952.20
go downhill
weaken 16.9
descend 194.5
incline 204.10
decline 393.17
sink 410.11
fall on evil days
1010.11
godparent 438.6

godsend boon 472.7
good thing 998.5
Godspeed
n leave-taking 188.4
inter farewell! 188.22
go Dutch
pay for 624.18
bisect 874.4
God willing 965.11
go easy
v swim with the
stream 1013.12
inter easy does it 175.15
phrs easy does it 175.15
go easy on 145.4
gofer
subordinate 432.5
attendant 577.5
go for love 104.20
head for 161.9
fetch 176.16
pass for 349.10
intend 380.4
abet 449.14
attack 459.15
kid oneself 953.6
go for broke
n call to arms 458.8
v be determined 359.8
persevere 360.7
do one's best 403.14
do to perfection 407.7
court danger 493.6
risk 971.12
go for it
attempt 403.7
do one's best 403.14
go-getter 330.8
go-getting 330.7
goggle
n gaze 27.5
v gaze 27.15
squint 28.9
bulge 283.11
adj bulged 283.16
goggles spectacles 29.3
safeguard 1007.3
eyeshade 1027.2
go in for practice 328.8
adopt 371.15
undertake 404.3
study to be 570.15
specialize 865.4
going-over
apostasy 363.2
iteration 848.2
disapproval 510.6
goings-on
behavior 321.1
activity 330.1
affairs 830.4
go into enter 189.7
undertake 404.3
participate 476.5
discuss 541.12
write upon 556.5
join 617.14
compose 795.3
embark on 817.9
elaborate 860.6
investigate 937.22

gold
n yellowness 43.1
wealth 618.1
money 728.1
precious metals
728.20
adj yellow 43.4
brass 1056.17
goldbrick
n slowpoke 175.5
idler 331.8
neglecter 340.5
confidence game
356.10
shirker 368.3
v leave undone 340.7
shirk 368.9
golden yellow 43.4
auspicious 133.18
precious 632.10
melodious 708.48
superb 998.15
brass 1056.17
Golden Age 823.5
golden mean
mean 246.1
middle course 467.3
temperance 668.1
moderation 670.1
golden rule
rule 419.2
ethical philosophy
636.2
axiom 973.2
gold mine
source of supply 386.4
rich source 618.4
mine 1056.6
gold-plated
plated 295.33
expensive 632.11
brass 1056.17
gold rush 1056.8
golf
n sports 751
the royal and ancient
751.1
v play 745.5
golf course
green 310.7
playground 743.11
golf 751.1
golly! 513.12
Gomorrah 654.7
gonads 2.11
gondolier 183.5
gone weak 16.12
tired 21.8
burnt-out 21.10
away 34.4
past hope 125.15
departed 188.19
absent 222.11
dead 307.30
used up 388.5
lost 473.7
no more 761.11
past 836.7
goner 125.8
gong
n bell 54.4
marker 517.10

v ring 54.8
goo sentimentality 93.8
semiliquid 1060.5
good
n utility 387.3
welfare 998.4
adj tasty 63.8
healthful 81.5
pleasant 97.6
auspicious 133.18
kind 143.13
skillful 413.22
praiseworthy 509.20
right 637.3
honest 644.13
just 649.8
virtuous 653.6
almighty 677.18
godly 692.9
solvent 729.17
valid 972.14
genuine 972.15
sufficient 990.6
expedient 994.5
excellent 998.12
adv kindly 143.18
inter yes! 332.18
bravo! 509.22
the good 692.5
good at 413.27
good-bye
n leave-taking 188.4
inter farewell! 188.22
good day 585.15
good enough
adj acceptable 107.12
sufficient 990.6
tolerable 998.20
inter yes! 332.18
bravo! 509.22
good faith 644.7
good for
healthful 81.5
useful 387.18
helpful 449.21
priced 630.14
solvent 729.17
good-for-nothing
n bum 331.9
wretch 660.2
adj indolent 331.19
worthless 391.11
good-looking 1015.18
good luck chance 971.1
happy fortune 1009.2
good-luck charm 691.5
goodly pleasant 97.6
large 257.16
good 998.12
comely 1015.18
good-natured 143.14
goodness
n savoriness 63.1
healthfulness 81.1
pleasantness 97.1
kindness 143.1
propriety 637.2
probity 644.1
virtue 653.1
godliness 692.2
good quality 998
excellence 998.1

deceive 356.19
overprice 632.7
gouge out
  extract 192.10
  excavate 284.15
  perforate 292.15
goulash 10.11
go under
  go to ruin 395.24
  sink 410.11
  lose 412.12
  go bankrupt 625.7
go up against
  encounter 457.15
  engage 457.16
go up in smoke
  disappear 34.2
  come to nothing
    410.13
  go to waste 473.6
  flit 827.6
  fall through 910.3
  burn up 1019.25
gourmand
  eater 8.16
  connoisseur 496.7
  sensualist 663.3
  glutton 672.3
gourmet
  n eater 8.16
  connoisseur 496.7
  sensualist 663.3
  adj edible 8.33
  tasty 63.8
gout 85.22
goût taste 62.1
  savor 63.2
govern
  restrain 428.7
  direct 573.8
  regulate 612.12
  exercise influence
    893.8
governance
  authority 417.5
  direction 573.1
  government 612.1
  protectorship 1007.2
governess
  teacher 571.2
  mistress 575.2
  chaperon 1007.7
government
  region 231.5
  authority 417.5
  direction 573.1
  political science 609.2
  administration 612
  governance 612.1
  protectorship 1007.2
governor
  jailer 429.10
  father 560.9
  director 574.1
  ruler 575.6
  administrator 575.13
  safeguard 1007.3
  guardian 1007.6
  system component
    1040.14
governor-general
  575.13

governorship
  mastership 417.7
  directorship 573.4
go with
  stay near 223.12
  take action 328.5
  concur 332.9
  choose 371.13
  undertake 404.3
  accompany 768.7
  agree 787.6
  go along with
    898.3
go without 668.7
go with the flow
  be content 107.5
  take it easy 331.15
  follow the fashion
    578.10
gown
  n garment 5.3
  dress 5.16
  robe 702.2
  v cloak 5.39
go wrong
  be disappointing
    132.3
  get out of order
    393.25
  go to ruin 395.24
  miscarry 410.15
  stray 654.9
  misbelieve 688.8
  err 974.9
goy 688.6
grab
  n seizure 480.2
  v jump at 101.6
  acquire 472.9
  seize 480.14
  capture 480.18
  usurp 640.8
  play 745.5
  impress 930.19
  engross 982.13
grab bag lottery 759.14
  hodgepodge 796.6
grace
  n delightfulness 97.2
  benevolence 143.4
  act of kindness 143.7
  pity 145.1
  pardon 148.2
  thanks 150.2
  skill 413.1
  benefit 478.7
  taste 496.1
  elegance 533.1
  fluency 544.2
  reprieve 601.3
  conscience 636.5
  function of Holy
    Ghost 677.16
  sanctification 685.3
  prayer 696.4
  ornament 709.18
  goodness 998.1
  beauty 1015.1
  v ornament 498.8
  honor 662.12
  beautify 1015.15
graceful skillful 413.22

agile 413.23
  tasteful 496.9
  courteous 504.14
  elegant 533.6
  fluent 544.9
  beautiful 1015.17
graceless
  bungling 414.20
  inelegant 534.2
  irreclaimable 654.18
  unregenerate 695.18
  ungraceful 1014.9
the Graces 1015.10
grace with 478.17
gracile thin 270.16
  tasteful 496.9
  elegant 533.6
  beautiful 1015.17
gracious
  adj pleasant 97.6
  kind 143.13
  indulgent 427.8
  liberal 485.4
  elegant 496.9
  courteous 504.14
  informal 581.3
  hospitable 585.11
  inter my! 122.21
gradation
  graduation 245.3
  phonetics 524.14
  class 607.1
  continuity 806.2
  grouping 807.3
  series 811.2
grade
  n incline 204.4
  degree 245.1
  student 572.11
  class 607.1
  category 808.2
  v level 201.6
  incline 204.10
  graduate 245.4
  size 257.15
  smooth 287.5
  order 806.4
  group 807.11
  classify 808.6
grade school 567.3
gradient rising 200.5
  incline 204.4
gradual slow 175.10
  gradational 245.5
graduate
  n expert 413.11
  alumnus 572.8
  v grade 245.4
  size 257.15
  measure 300.10
  improve 392.7
  succeed 409.7
  promote 446.2
  adj scholastic 568.19
  studentlike 572.12
graduation
  gradation 245.3
  promotion 446.1
  ceremony 580.4
graffito 546.5
graft
  n insertion 191.1

inlay 191.2
  fraud 356.8
  bribery 378.1
  theft 482.1
  booty 482.11
  politics 609.34
  spoils of office 609.35
  v engraft 191.6
  fasten 799.7
grain
  n feed 10.4
  modicum 248.2
  minute 258.7
  texture 294.1
  grass 310.5
  seed 310.29
  nature 766.4
  kind 808.3
  disposition 977.3
  granule 1049.6
  v color 35.13
  coarsen 294.4
  pulverize 1049.9
  powder 1049.10
grain of salt 958.1
grammar
  rules of language
    530.1
  diction 532.1
  textbook 554.10
  basics 817.6
grammarian 523.13
grammar school
  elementary school
    567.3
  secondary school
    567.4
grammatical
  linguistic 523.17
  syntactical 530.17
gramps old man 304.2
  grandfather 560.14
granary 386.7
grand
  n money 728.7
  thousand 881.10
  adj dignified 136.12
  great 247.6
  large 257.16
  grandiose 501.21
  lofty 544.14
  eminent 662.18
  important 996.17
  good 998.12
grandeur
  proud bearing 136.2
  greatness 247.1
  sizableness 257.6
  grandness 501.5
  loftiness 544.6
  distinction 662.5
grandfather
  n old man 304.2
  grandsire 560.13
  v exempt 430.14
grandfather clause
  430.8
grandiloquence
  exaggeration 355.1
  pompousness 501.7
  long word 526.10
  style 532.2

grandiosity 545
  magniloquence 545.1
grandiose grand 501.21
  grandiloquent 545.8
grandiosity
  sizableness 257.6
  grandeur 501.5
  grandiloquence 545.1
grand-juror 596.7
grandmother
  old woman 304.3
  grandam 560.15
grand slam score 409.5
  victory 411.1
  bridge 758.3
grandstand
  n observation post
    27.8
  baseball 745.1
  v exercise skill 413.20
  show off 501.16
grange farmstead 228.6
  farm 1067.8
granite
  hardness 1044.6
  rock 1057.1
granny
  old woman 304.3
  fussbudget 495.7
  grandmother 560.16
  back number 841.8
grant
  n concession 443.5
  giving 478.1
  subsidy 478.8
  privilege 642.2
  qualification 958.1
  v acknowledge 332.11
  confess 351.7
  consent 441.2
  permit 443.9
  give 478.12
  suppose 950.10
  allow for 958.5
granular
  infinitesimal 258.14
  rough 294.6
  grainy 1049.12
granulated
  unsmooth 288.6
  rough 294.6
  hardened 1044.13
  granular 1049.12
granulation
  unsmoothness 288.1
  roughness 294.2
  television reception
    1034.5
  hardening 1044.5
  granularity 1049.2
  pulverization 1049.4
granule
  modicum 248.2
  grain 1049.6
grapevine plant 310.4
  gossip 551.5
  report 552.6
  news channel 552.10
graph
  n diagram 381.3
  letter 546.1
  drawing 712.13

outline 800.4
  v plot 381.10
  itemize 800.7
graphic
  representational
    349.13
  descriptive 349.14
  expressive 544.10
  written 547.22
  pictorial 712.21
graphic arts
  printing 548.1
  visual arts 712.1
  graphics 713.1
graphite 1054.2
grapple
  n hold 474.2
  v contend 457.13
  hold 474.6
  seize 480.14
  fasten 799.7
grapple with
  contest 451.4
  contend 457.13
  engage with 457.17
  brave 492.11
grasp
  n hold 474.2
  control 612.2
  handle 900.11
  understanding 927.3
  v hold 474.6
  seize 480.14
  understand 521.7
  cohere 802.6
  know 927.12
grasping
  n greed 100.8
  adj greedy 100.27
  demanding 421.9
  acquisitive 472.15
  retentive 474.8
  rapacious 480.26
  selfish 651.5
graspy greedy 100.27
  acquisitive 472.15
  rapacious 480.26
  selfish 651.5
grass
  n marijuana 87.10
  gramineous plant
    310.5
  grassland 310.8
  tennis 748.1
  v feed 8.18
grasshopper
  n locust 311.34
  jumper 366.4
  adj improvident
    406.15
grassland
  the country 233.1
  land 234.1
  plain 236.1
  grass 310.8
  farm 1067.8
grass roots
  bottom 199.1
  the country 233.1
  source 885.5
grass-roots basic 199.8
  populational 606.8

simple 797.6
grassy green 44.4
  verdant 310.39
grate
  n network 170.3
  arranger 807.5
  fire iron 1019.12
  v pain 26.7
  rasp 58.10
  sound a sour note 61.3
  irritate 96.14
  net 170.7
  abrade 1042.7
  pulverize 1049.9
grateful pleasant 97.6
  thankful 150.5
  welcome 585.12
grate on jar on 58.11
  irritate 96.14
  get on one's nerves
    128.9
gratify feed 8.18
  satisfy 95.7
  content 107.4
  make proud 136.6
  indulge 427.6
gratifying
  pleasant 97.6
  welcome 585.12
grating
  n network 170.3
  arranger 807.5
  fire iron 1019.12
  pulverization 1049.4
  adj irritating 26.13
  jarring 58.16
  dissonant 61.4
  unnerving 128.15
  disagreeing 788.6
gratis
  adj gratuitous 634.5
  adv as a gift 478.27
  gratuitously 634.6
gratitude
  thankfulness 150
  gratefulness 150.1
gratuitous
  impudent 142.10
  voluntary 324.7
  given 478.24
  gratis 634.5
  unordered 809.12
  superfluous 992.17
gratuity bribe 378.2
  largess 478.5
  costlessness 634.1
  surplus 992.5
grave
  n death 307.1
  tomb 309.16
  monument 549.12
  v record 549.15
  engrave 713.9
  sculpture 715.5
  fix in the mind 988.18
  adj painful 26.10
  dark 38.9
  deep 54.10
  sedate 106.14
  solemn 111.3
  gloomy 112.24
  dignified 136.12

great 247.6
  heavy 297.16
  lofty 544.14
  ceremonious 580.8
  base 661.12
  weighty 996.20
the grave
  hell 682.1
  destiny 838.2
gravedigger 309.8
gravel
  n pavement 383.6
  grain 1049.6
  shingle 1057.3
  v irritate 96.14
graven
  engraved 713.11
  sculptured 715.7
  established 854.13
graveness
  darkness 38.2
  gravity 996.3
graveyard 309.15
gravidity 78.5
gravitate
  descend 194.5
  drop 297.15
  lean 895.3
gravitation
  descent 194.1
  weight 297.5
  attraction 906.1
gravity
  sedateness 106.4
  solemnity 111.1
  gloom 112.7
  proud bearing 136.2
  weight 297.5
  loftiness 544.6
  formality 580.1
  attraction 906.1
  importance 996.1
  graveness 996.3
  weight 297.1
gravy find 472.6
  gratuity 478.5
  bonus 624.6
gray
  n grayness 39.1
  horse 311.11
  v grizzle 39.3
  adj colorless 36.7
  ashen 39.4
  gloomy 112.24
  aged 303.16
  same 780.6
gray area
  middle course 467.3
  ambiguity 539.1
  gamble 970.8
graybeard
  silver-haired person
    39.2
  old man 304.2
gray-haired
  gray-headed 39.5
  aged 303.16
gray matter
  intellect 918.1
  brain 918.6
graze
  n touch 73.1

contact 223.5
v feed 8.18
feed on 8.28
touch lightly 73.7
contact 223.10
tap 901.18
abrade 1042.7
grazing
n eating 8.1
touch 73.1
grassland 310.8
abrasion 1042.2
animal husbandry
1068.1
adj in contact 223.17
grease
n gratuity 478.5
flattery 511.1
money 728.2
oil 1054.1
v smooth 287.5
bribe 378.3
facilitate 1013.7
oil 1054.8
grease monkey
aircraftsman 185.6
mechanic 1039.8
greasepaint
theater 704.17
makeup 1015.12
greaser 232.7
grease the palm
bribe 375.23
pay off 378.3
pay 624.16
grease the wheels
facilitate 1013.7
oil 1054.8
greasy
slippery 287.11
oily 1054.9
greasy spoon 8.17
great
n skillful person
413.14
keyboard 711.17
adj pregnant 78.18
grand 247.6
chief 249.14
large 257.16
authoritative
417.15
magnanimous 652.6
eminent 662.18
important 996.17
excellent 998.13
inter bravo! 509.22
the great 996.8
great-coat 5.13
Great Divide
middle of nowhere
261.4
watershed 272.5
greathearted
benevolent 143.15
liberal 485.4
courageous 492.17
magnanimous 652.6
greed
greediness 100.8
selfishness 651.1
gluttony 672.1

greedy
avaricious 100.27
acquisitive 472.15
selfish 651.5
gluttonous 672.6
Greek gibberish 522.7
member 617.11
green
n greenness 44.1
verdigris 44.3
lawn 310.7
money 728.2
lawn bowling 750.3
golf 751.1
adj virid 44.4
sour 67.5
fresh 83.13
jealous 153.5
young 301.10
immature 406.11
inexperienced 414.17
new 840.7
ignorant 929.12
gullible 953.9
remembered 988.23
greenbacks 728.6
Green Berets 461.15
greenery 310.1
greenhorn
n dupe 358.1
incompetent 414.7
novice 572.9
newcomer 773.4
beginner 817.2
ignoramus 929.8
adj unaccustomed
374.4
greenhouse
summerhouse 228.12
nursery 1067.11
Greenland
continent 235.1
remote region 261.4
cold place 1022.4
green light
permission 443.1
signal 517.15
traffic light 1025.4
the green light
start 188.2
ratification 332.4
greenroom
anteroom 197.20
stage 704.16
greens
vegetables 10.34
salad 10.35
plants 310.1
green thumb 1067.12
green with jealousy
153.5
greet
n weeping 115.2
v weep 115.12
address 524.27
hail 585.10
greeter 585.5
greeting remark 524.4
salutation 585.4
greetings
n welcome 186.4
regards 504.8

salutations 585.3
inter salutations!
585.15
gregarious
talkative 540.9
sociable 582.22
Gregorian chant 708.20
gremlin
fairy 678.8
imp 680.7
grenadier
longlegs 272.7
infantryman 461.9
greyhound 174.6
grid
n network 170.3
stage 704.16
fire iron 1019.12
television reception
1034.5
v net 170.7
griddle
n fire iron 1019.12
v cook 11.4
griddlecake 10.43
gridiron
network 170.3
stage 704.16
playground 743.11
football 746.1
fire iron 1019.12
gridlock
obstruction 293.3
hindrance 1011.1
grief pain 96.5
wretchedness 96.6
distressfulness 98.5
sorrow 112.10
regret 113.1
misfortune 1010.2
grievance
affliction 96.8
complaint 115.4
objection 333.2
injustice 650.4
evil 999.3
bane 1000.1
grieve
pain 96.17
distress 98.14
sorrow 112.17
aggrieve 112.19
lament 115.10
move 145.5
offend 152.21
grieving
n lamentation 115.1
adj lamenting 115.18
grievous
distressing 98.20
sorrowful 112.26
pitiful 145.8
terrible 999.9
disastrous 1010.15
griffin 647.2
grift fraud 356.8
stratagem 415.3
cheating 759.13
grill
n restaurant 8.17
dish 10.7
inquisition 937.13

fire iron 1019.12
v cook 11.4
torture 604.16
put on the grill 937.21
grille 170.3
grilling
n cooking 11.1
the grill 937.13
adj hot 1018.25
grim
pleasureless 96.20
horrid 98.19
sullen 110.24
solemn 111.3
unhappy 112.21
gloomy 112.24
hopeless 125.12
terrible 127.30
harsh 144.24
unyielding 361.9
strict 425.6
bad 999.8
unprepossessing
1014.7
grimace
n scowl 110.9
wry face 265.4
shake 916.3
v suffer 26.8
shudder at 99.5
look sullen 110.15
make a face 265.8
overact 704.31
grime
n dirt 80.6
v dirty 80.15
Grim Reaper 307.3
grimy dingy 38.11
dirty 80.22
grin
n smile 116.3
v smile 116.7
grin and bear it
be of good cheer
109.10
accept 134.7
submit 433.6
grinch
killjoy 112.14
spoilsport 1011.9
grind
n rasp 58.3
routine 373.6
study 570.3
swotter 572.10
work 725.4
drudge 726.3
bookworm 928.4
v chew 8.27
pain 26.7
grate 58.10
sharpen 285.7
file 287.8
study 570.12
domineer 612.16
drudge 725.14
shatter 801.13
abrade 1042.7
pulverize 1049.9
grind in
urge 375.14
inculcate 568.12

grinding
n study 570.3
abrasion 1042.2
pulverization 1049.4
adj irritating 26.13
grating 58.16
oppressive 98.24
imperious 417.16
laboring 725.17
abrasive 1042.10
grind one's teeth
152.14
gringo 773.3
grip
n acrimony 17.5
skill 413.1
governance 417.5
hold 474.2
control 612.2
game 748.2
game or string 750.2
handle 900.11
spasm 916.6
understanding 927.3
v hold 474.6
seize 480.14
obsess 925.25
engross 982.13
gripe
n ache 26.5
complaint 115.5
control 612.2
indigence 619.2
v pain 26.7
annoy 96.13
be discontented 108.6
complain 115.16
seize 480.14
gripped
obsessed 925.33
held 982.18
gripping
retentive 474.8
obsessive 925.34
engrossing 982.20
grisly
terrible 127.30
deathly 307.29
hideous 1014.11
grist 386.2
gristle 1047.2
grit
n pluck 359.3
fortitude 492.6
grain 1049.6
v irritate 96.14
grit one's teeth 359.8
grits food 10.2
powder 1049.5
gritty rough 294.6
plucky 359.14
fearless 492.19
hard 1044.10
granular 1049.12
stony 1057.11
grizzled white 37.7
gray 39.4
grizzly bear 110.11
groan
n rasp 58.3
lament 115.3
complaint 115.4

v sound harshly 58.9
wail 115.13
complain 115.15
sigh 318.21
groaning board 8.9
groceries
food 10.2
provisions 10.5
grocery 735.7
grog
n spirits 88.13
v tipple 88.24
groggy
unsteady 16.16
inert 173.14
dazed 984.14
groin fork 171.4
buttress 900.4
harbor 1008.6
barrier 1011.5
groom
n newlywed 563.5
stockman 1068.2
v dress 79.20
train 568.13
tidy 807.12
tend 1068.7
groomed 405.16
groomsman
wedding party 563.4
assistant 616.6
groove
n crack 224.2
furrow 290.1
routine 373.6
path 383.2
type 548.6
race 756.3
v cleave 224.4
excavate 284.15
furrow 290.3
engrave 713.9
groove on 95.12
groovy
adj knowledgeable
927.17
excellent 998.13
inter goody! 95.20
grope contact 223.10
feel one's way 937.31
be uncertain 970.9
gross
n gain 472.3
receipts 627.1
round 751.3
v profit 472.12
yield 627.4
adj nasty 64.7
filthy 80.23
offensive 98.18
downright 247.12
corpulent 257.18
thick 269.8
rough 294.6
luxuriant 310.40
coarse 497.11
ill-bred 505.6
inelegant 534.2
base 661.12
carnal 663.6
vulgar 666.8
whole 791.9

stupid 921.15
bad 999.8
terrible 999.9
gross out offend 98.11
repel 99.6
grotesque
n work of art 712.10
adj deformed 265.12
freakish 869.13
absurd 922.11
fanciful 985.20
unshapely 1014.8
grotto 284.5
grouch
n malcontent 108.4
sorehead 110.11
complainer 115.9
spoilsport 1011.9
v be discontented
108.6
sulk 110.14
complain 115.16
grouchy
discontented 108.8
irascible 110.20
complaining 115.20
ground
n color 35.8
station 159.2
ground covering 199.3
bed 199.4
horizontal 201.3
setting 209.2
enclosed place
(enclosure) 212.3
region 231.1
land 234.1
ocean depths 275.4
motive 375.1
arena 463.1
warrant 600.6
art equipment 712.18
cause 885.1
foundation 900.6
premise 934.7
evidence 956.1
v establish 159.16
shipwreck 182.42
limit 210.5
restrict 428.9
confine 429.12
teach 568.10
play 745.5
fix 854.9
fell 912.5
insulate 1031.28
adj bottom 199.7
powdery 1049.11
grounder 745.3
ground floor
floor 197.23
earliness 844.1
groundhog
black clouds 133.6
excavator 284.10
wild animal 311.23
grounding
preparation 405.1
elementary education
568.5
groundless
unsubstantial 763.8

baseless 935.13
unproved 957.8
grounds nearness 223.1
dregs 256.2
green 310.7
real estate 471.6
warrant 600.6
cause 885.1
foundation 900.6
evidence 956.1
condition 958.2
group
n amount 244.2
association 617.1
clique 617.6
sect 675.3
orchestra 710.12
company 769.3
bunch 769.7
set 783.5
class 808.2
v size 257.15
assemble 769.18
analyze 800.8
arrange 807.11
classify 808.6
groupie 101.5
grouping
association 617.1
treatment 712.9
company 769.3
bunch 769.7
analysis 800.3
arrangement 807.3
classification 808.1
class 808.2
grouse
n complaint 115.5
v be discontented
108.6
complain 115.16
grouser
malcontent 108.4
complainer 115.9
grout 295.25
grove
valley 284.9
woodlet 310.12
bunch 769.7
grovel fawn 138.7
creep 177.26
lie 201.5
lie low 274.5
bow down 433.10
be promiscuous
665.19
bow 912.9
wallow 914.13
grow develop 14.2
increase 251.6
expand 259.7
grow up 272.12
mature 303.9
vegetate 310.31
become 760.12
evolve 860.5
process 891.9
farm 1067.16
raise 1068.6
growl
n reverberation 54.2
boom 56.4

rasp 58.3
v boom 56.9
sound harshly 58.9
snarl 60.4
complain 115.15
show resentment
  152.14
sigh 318.21
speak 524.26
growling
n reverberation 54.2
adj reverberating
  54.11
discontented 108.7
irascible 110.19
grown mature 14.3
full-grown 259.12
adult 303.12
produced 891.17
made 891.18
grownup 304.1
grown-up
mature 14.3
grown 259.12
adult 303.12
grow on one
enamor 104.23
become a habit 373.11
grow out of
overdevelop 14.2
expand 259.7
result from 886.5
growth
bodily development
  14.1
symptom 85.9
neoplasm 85.38
gain 251.1
increase in size 259
development 259.3
maturation 303.6
stand 310.2
vegetation 310.30
business cycle 731.9
conversion 857.1
evolution 860.1
grow up mature 14.2
ascend 193.8
expand 259.7
grow 272.12
age 303.9
ripen 407.8
grub
n food 10.2
larva 302.12
drudge 726.3
v excavate 284.15
drudge 725.14
grubby dirty 80.22
slovenly 809.15
infested 909.11
grudge
n hostility 99.2
spite 589.5
v envy 154.3
refuse 325.3
deny 442.4
stint 484.5
grudging
n envy 154.1
adj envious 154.4
reluctant 325.6

niggardly 484.8
gruel
n symbol of weakness
  16.7
thinness 270.7
semiliquid 1060.5
v weaken 16.10
grueling
weakening 16.20
fatiguing 21.13
punishing 604.23
laborious 725.18
troublesome 1012.18
gruesome
terrible 127.30
deathly 307.29
hideous 1014.11
gruff
raucous 58.15
irascible 110.19
brusque 505.7
grumble
n reverberation 54.2
thunder 56.4
rasp 58.3
v boom 56.9
sound harshly 58.9
growl 60.4
complain 115.15
grumbling
n reverberation 54.2
complaint 115.4
adj discontented 108.7
irascible 110.19
grump
n malcontent 108.4
sorehead 110.11
v be discontented
  108.6
sulk 110.14
complain 115.16
Grundyism 579.1
grungy dirty 80.22
filthy 80.23
offensive 98.18
grunt
n animal noise 60.1
dogface 461.10
v snort 60.3
complain 115.15
speak 524.26
G string 711.5
G-string
waistband 5.19
supporter 900.2
guacamole 10.9
guano feces 12.4
fertilizer 889.4
guarantee
n oath 334.4
promise 436.1
security 438.1
guarantor 438.6
v depose 334.6
promise 436.4
secure 438.9
protect 1007.18
guarantor
endorser 332.7
warrantor 438.6
guaranty
n security 438.1

guarantor 438.6
v secure 438.9
guard
n trainman 178.13
vigilance 339.4
jailer 429.10
defense 460.1
defender 460.7
football team 746.2
escort 768.5
protection 1007.1
safeguard 1007.3
guarder 1007.9
v preserve 397.8
restrain 428.7
defend 460.8
play 747.4
escort 768.8
protect 1007.18
guard against
defend 460.8
take precautions
  494.6
guarded
vigilant 339.13
reticent 344.10
restrained 428.13
cautious 494.8
incredulous 955.4
protected 1007.21
guardian
n jailer 429.10
steward 574.4
familiar spirit 678.12
warden 1007.6
adj protective 1007.23
guardian angel
penitence 113.4
defender 460.7
conscience 636.5
familiar spirit 678.12
custodian 1007.6
gubernatorial 612.17
guerrilla
irregular 461.16
violent person 671.9
guess
n conjecture 950.4
gamble 970.8
v solve 939.2
estimate 945.9
conjecture 950.11
think 952.11
predict 961.9
guesswork
supposition 950.3
guess 950.4
prediction 961.1
guest
n visitor 585.6
v entertain 585.8
guest house 228.15
guest room 197.7
guff bull 520.3
chatter 540.3
guffaw
n laughter 116.4
v laugh 116.8
guidance
navigation 159.3
advice 422.1
patronage 449.4

teaching 568.1
direction 573.1
protectorship 1007.2
guide
n gutter 239.3
interpreter 341.7
adviser 422.3
pointer 517.4
teacher 571.1
guider 574.7
familiar spirit 678.12
escort 768.5
precursor 815.1
specter 987.1
v lead 165.2
pilot 182.14
advise 422.5
teach 568.10
steer 573.9
escort 768.8
go before 815.3
exercise influence
  893.8
guidebook
information 551.1
handbook 554.8
directory 574.10
guide dog blind 30.6
dog 311.17
guideline plan 381.1
law 419.2
rule 868.4
guidepost pointer 517.4
guide 574.7
guild 617.3
guile deceit 356.3
cunning 415.1
guileful deceitful 356.22
cunning 415.12
shrewd 919.15
guileless
undeceptive 644.18
foolable 922.12
trusting 952.22
guillotine
n capital punishment
  604.7
execution 605.5
legislative procedure
  613.6
cloture 856.5
v execute 604.17
guilt culpability 656
guiltiness 656.1
guiltless chaste 653.7
innocent 657.6
guilty
adj at fault 656.3
adv shamefacedly
  656.5
guinea pig
wild animal 311.23
subject 941.7
guise clothing 5.1
aspect 33.3
looks 33.4
cover 295.2
behavior 321.1
pretext 376.1
manner 384.1
mode 764.4
guitarist 710.5

gulag 429.8
gulch valley 237.7
  watercourse 239.2
gulf crack 224.2
  eddy 238.12
  ocean 240.3
  cove 242
  inlet 242.1
  hole 275.2
  pit 284.4
  opening 292.1
gull
  n dupe 358.1
  v deceive 356.14
  cheat 356.18
  stultify 922.7
gullible foolable 922.12
  dupable 953.9
gullible person 358.1
Gulliver 178.2
gully
  n valley 237.7
  watercourse 239.2
  v furrow 290.3
gulp
  n breathing 2.19
  drink 8.4
  ingestion 187.4
  v gobble 8.23
  ingest 187.11
  gluttonize 672.4
gum
  n elastic 1046.3
  resin 1055.1
  chewing gum 1060.6
  v chew 8.27
  stick together 802.9
  hinder 1011.16
gumbo
  n semiliquid 1060.5
  mud 1060.8
  adj earthy 234.5
  viscous 1060.12
gummy
  adhesive 802.12
  resinous 1055.3
  viscous 1060.12
gumption 330.7
gumshoe
  n detective 576.11
  police 1007.16
  v creep 177.26
  lurk 346.9
gum up disable 19.9
  spoil 393.11
  bungle 414.12
  hinder 1011.16
gun
  n killer 308.10
  artilleryman 461.11
  mercenary 461.17
  firearm 462.10
  ruffian 593.4
  game 746.3
  stop 856.2
  shot 903.4
  shooter 903.8
  v hunt 382.9
  shoot 903.12
gun down
  kill 308.13
  strike dead 308.17

gunfire fire 459.8
  shot 903.4
gung ho
  n call to arms 458.8
  adj energetic 17.13
  enthusiastic 101.10
gunk slime 80.8
  adhesive 802.4
  semiliquid 1060.5
gunky filthy 80.23
  viscous 1060.12
gunman killer 308.10
  mercenary 461.17
  ruffian 593.3
  shooter 903.8
gunner hand 183.6
  crew 185.4
  artilleryman 461.11
  basketball team 747.2
  shooter 903.8
gunrunning 732.2
gunshot
  detonation 56.3
  short distance 223.2
  shot 903.4
gun-shy fearful 127.23
  jittery 128.12
gunslinger 737.11
gurgle ripple 52.11
  trickle 238.18
  bubble 320.4
gurney 900.19
guru teacher 571.1
  master 575.1
  holy man 659.6
  clergy 699.12
  wise man 920.1
gush
  n outflow 190.4
  ascent 193.1
  flow 238.4
  jet 238.9
  increase 251.1
  unction 511.2
  wordiness 538.2
  outburst 671.6
  plenty 990.2
  v emotionalize 93.13
  be enthusiastic 101.7
  run out 190.13
  shoot up 193.9
  flow 238.16
  jet 238.20
  chatter 540.5
  abound 990.5
gushiness 540.1
gushing
  n wordiness 538.2
  adj sentimental 93.21
  flowing 238.24
  flattering 511.8
  diffuse 538.11
gushy
  v talkative 540.9
  adj diffuse 538.11
gusset 191.2
gussy up dress up 5.41
  ornament 498.8
  beautify 1015.15
gust taste 62.1
  liking 100.2
  eagerness 101.1

  outburst 105.9
  wind gust 318.6
  characteristic 864.4
gusto vim 17.2
  animation 17.4
  savor 63.2
  passion 93.2
  pleasure 95.1
  liking 100.2
  eagerness 101.1
  gaiety 109.4
gusty tasty 63.8
  windy 318.22
gut
  n goozle 2.17
  heart 93.3
  inlet 242.1
  v eviscerate 192.13
  destroy 395.10
  plunder 482.17
  adj emotional 93.17
  interior 207.6
  unpremeditated
    365.11
  essential 766.9
  vital 996.23
gutless weak 16.12
  uncourageous 491.11
gut reaction
  feeling 93.1
  impulse 365.1
guts viscera 2.14
  goozle 2.17
  strength 15.1
  zest 68.2
  heart 93.3
  contents 196.1
  insides 207.4
  pluck 359.3
  fearlessness 492.4
  nut and bolts 766.3
  inner nature 766.5
gut sensation 93.1
gutsy strong 15.15
  plucky 359.14
  fearless 492.19
gutter
  n trough 239.3
  drain 239.5
  trench 290.2
  pavement 383.6
  sewer 654.7
  bowling 750.1
  v flutter 916.12
  flicker 1024.25
  adj disgraceful 661.11
  vulgar 666.8
guttersnipe
  vagabond 178.3
  vulgarian 497.6
guttural raucous 58.15
  inarticulate 525.12
guy man 76.5
  supporter 900.2
guzzle
  n goozle 2.17
  drink 8.4
  drinking spree 88.6
  swig 88.7
  v drink 8.29
  tipple 88.24
  gluttonize 672.4

gym fitness 84.1
  arena 463.1
  playground 743.11
gymnasium
  fitness 84.1
  playroom 197.12
  arena 463.1
  playground 743.11
gymnastics
  exercise 84.2
  physical education
    568.9
  sport 744.1
gyp
  n female animal 77.9
  dog 311.17
  deception 356.9
  cheater 357.4
  v deceive 356.19
gypsy 178.4
gypsy cab 179.13
gyrate move 172.5
  rotate 914.9
ha'penny 728.8
haberdasher 5.32
habit
  n clothing 5.1
  suit 5.6
  substance abuse 87.1
  convention 373
  habitude 373.4
  mannerism 500.2
  nature 766.4
  v outfit 5.40
habitat
  environment 209.1
  habitation 225.1
  dwelling 228
  home 228.18
habitation
  occupancy 225
  inhabiting 225.1
  abode 228.1
habitual regular 373.15
  orderly 806.6
  frequent 846.4
  usual 868.9
habitué
  n attender 221.5
  guest 585.6
  adj habituated 373.18
hacienda
  farmstead 228.6
  farm 1067.8
hack
  n breathing 2.19
  driver 178.9
  coachman 178.10
  public vehicle 179.13
  notch 289.1
  horse 311.12
  hunter 311.13
  attempt 403.3
  mark 517.5
  hack writer 547.16
  politician 610.4
  scribbler 718.5
  drudge 726.3
  v go on horseback
    177.34
  accomplish 407.4
  sever 801.11

hacker
incompetent 414.7
golfer 751.2
liveware 1041.17
hack it
be able 18.11
do 328.6
achieve one's purpose
409.8
manage 409.12
stand the test 941.10
suffice 990.4
hackneyed
trite 117.9
habitual 373.15
hack writer
writing 547.16
hack 718.5
Hades hell 682.1
nether world 682.3
nether world deity
682.5
destiny 838.2
hag old woman 304.3
witch 593.7
sorceress 690.8
eyesore 1014.4
haggard
tired-looking 21.9
colorless 36.7
frenzied 105.25
dejected 112.22
poor 270.20
deathly 307.29
fanatic 925.32
haggle
n negotiation 731.3
v bargain 731.17
hagiography 719.1
ha-ha
n laughter 116.4
trench 290.2
v laugh 116.8
hail
n greeting 585.4
multitude 883.3
hailstone 1022.6
v cry 59.6
assent 332.8
applaud 509.10
signal 517.22
address 524.27
greet 585.10
sleet 1022.11
inter all hail! 509.23
greetings! 585.15
hey! 982.23
hair covering 3
pile 3.2
short distance 223.2
modicum 248.2
narrowness 270.1
filament 271.1
skin 295.3
theater man 704.23
trifle 997.5
haircut 3.15
hairdo 3.15
hairdresser 1015.13
hairdressing 1015.11
hair-drier 1064.4
hairless 6.17

hairpiece 3.14
hairpin
n deviation 164.1
zigzag 204.8
skiing 753.1
race 756.3
v deflect 164.5
adj crooked 204.20
hair-raiser 127.9
hair shirt
self-reproach 113.3
penance 658.3
hairsplitter 935.7
hairsplitting
n overfastidiousness
495.4
criticism 510.4
quibbling 935.5
distinction 943.3
adj overfastidious
495.12
critical 510.23
quibbling 935.14
hairstyle 3.15
hairy hirsute 3.24
threadlike 271.7
bristly 288.9
nappy 294.7
cutaneous 295.32
weird 987.9
bad 999.8
difficult 1012.17
hajj 177.5
halcyon bright 97.11
quiescent 173.12
pacific 464.9
thriving 1009.13
hale
v pull 904.4
adj strong 15.15
hearty 83.12
half
n portion 477.5
football game 746.3
basketball game 747.3
game 749.6
mid-distance 818.2
moiety 874.2
adj proportionate
477.13
part 874.5
adv o'clock 831.16
half a mind 323.1
half-assed
slipshod 340.12
unskillful 414.15
botched 414.22
half-learned 929.15
half-baked
immature 406.11
premature 844.8
mentally deficient
921.22
half-learned 929.15
imperfect 1002.4
half-breed
n hybrid 796.8
adj hybrid 796.15
half-cocked
immature 406.11
premature 844.8
half-learned 929.15

half-heard 52.16
halfhearted
wishy-washy 16.17
indifferent 102.6
half-mast 517.22
half-moon
crescent 279.5
heavenly body
1070.11
half nelson 474.3
half note 709.14
halftime game 746.3
shift 824.3
interim 825.1
halftone
color system 35.7
interval 709.20
half-truth 354.11
halfway
adj middle 818.4
half 874.5
adv midway 818.5
halfway house
mid-distance 818.2
asylum 1008.4
half-wit
stupid person 923.2
idiot 923.8
halitosis 71.1
hall entrance 189.5
assembly hall 197.4
corridor 197.18
house 228.5
arena 463.1
schoolhouse 567.10
theater 704.14
hallelujah
n cheer 116.2
paean 696.3
inter alleluia! 696.16
hallmark
n sign 517.1
label 517.13
characteristic 864.4
v label 517.20
hall of famer 413.15
halloo
n cry 59.1
v cry 59.6
address 524.27
inter oh! 122.20
hey! 982.23
hallow celebrate 487.2
sanctify 685.5
hallucinate 975.8
hallucination
deception 356.1
hallucinosis 975.7
figment of the
imagination 985.5
hallucinogen
psychoactive drug
86.13
drug 87.2
hallway
entrance 189.5
corridor 197.18
halo
radiation 171.2
circle 280.2
illustriousness 662.6
nimbus 1024.14

halt
n respite 20.2
standstill 173.3
delay 845.2
stop 856.2
prevention 1011.2
impasse 1012.6
v be weak 16.8
quiet 173.8
dawdle 175.8
way of walking 177.28
stammer 525.8
cease 856.6
stop 856.7
put a stop to 856.11
hinder 1011.13
adj crippled 393.30
inter cease! 856.13
halter
n shackle 428.4
execution 605.5
v yoke 799.10
halting
n cessation 856.1
prevention 1011.2
adj slow 175.10
crippled 393.30
stammering 525.13
stiff 534.3
irregular 850.3
halve share 476.6
sever 801.11
double 872.5
bisect 874.4
ham
n member 2.7
leg 177.14
village 230.2
acting 704.8
grimacer 707.5
radioman 1033.24
v affect 500.12
overact 704.31
adj dramatic 704.33
hamburger 10.13
hamburger joint 8.17
ham-fisted
bungling 414.20
inelegant 534.2
ham it up
emotionalize 93.13
affect 500.12
overact 704.31
hamlet village 230.2
region 231.5
Hamlet 542.2
hammer
n ear 2.10
tool 1039.1
v rage 671.11
drudge 725.14
din 848.10
pound 901.16
think hard 930.9
hammer away at
dwell on 848.9
think hard 930.9
hammer out
form 262.7
do carelessly 340.9
produce 891.8
ham operator 1033.24

hamper
n shackle 428.4
impediment 1011.6
v package 212.9
burden 297.13
bind 428.10
impede 1011.11
hamstring disable 19.9
render powerless
19.10
cripple 393.14
hamper 1011.11
hand
n member 2.7
deckhand 183.6
side 218.1
person 312.5
act 328.3
skill 413.1
governance 417.5
assist 449.2
applause 509.2
pointer 517.4
signature 527.10
handwriting 547.3
control 612.2
worker 726.2
bridge 758.3
member 792.4
v deliver 478.13
transfer 629.3
handbag 729.14
handball 1046.3
handbill 352.8
handbook
manual 554.8
directory 574.10
casino 759.19
handcrafted 891.18
handcuff
disable 19.10
bind 428.10
hamper 1011.11
hand down
bequeath 478.18
transfer 629.3
handful
modicum 248.2
a few 884.2
tough proposition
1012.2
handicap
n disease 85.1
burden 297.7
disability 603.2
round 751.3
inequality 790.1
disadvantage 995.2
impediment 1011.6
v burden 297.13
penalize 603.4
hamper 1011.11
handicraft craft 712.3
vocation 724.6
production 891.2
hand in glove
cooperative 450.5
cooperatively 450.6
sociably 582.25
familiar 587.19
amicably 587.22
accompanying 768.9

arm in arm 768.10
in step 787.11
joined 799.13
concurrently 898.5
hand in hand
near 223.14
cooperatively 450.6
sociably 582.25
familiar 587.19
amicably 587.22
accompanying 768.9
arm in arm 768.10
joined 799.13
concurrently 898.5
hand it to bow to 250.5
compliment 509.14
handiwork act 328.3
work 725.4
production 891.2
product 892.1
handkerchief 5.25
handle
n bulge 283.3
pretext 376.1
name 527.3
title 648.1
hold 900.11
v touch 73.6
pilot 182.14
behave 321.6
perform 328.9
use 387.10
treat 387.12
discuss 541.12
write upon 556.5
direct 573.8
deal in 731.15
operate 888.5
tend 1068.7
handle with kid gloves
be careful 339.7
be easy on 427.5
handling touching 73.2
performance 328.2
usage 387.2
utilization 387.8
treatise 556.1
direction 573.1
operation 888.1
handmade 891.18
handmaiden
instrument 384.4
maid 577.8
hand-me-down
clothing 5.5
used 841.18
handout
press release 352.3
advertising matter
352.8
donation 478.6
information 551.1
hand out
parcel out 477.8
give 478.12
deliver 478.13
hand over
transfer 176.10
give up 370.7
surrender 433.8
relinquish 475.3
deliver 478.13

pay over 624.15
assign 629.3
hand over fist
swiftly 174.17
hastily 401.12
hands work force 18.9
governance 417.5
clutches 474.4
control 612.2
protectorship 1007.2
hands down 1013.16
handshake
n signing 437.3
greeting 585.4
v curry favor 138.9
hand signal 517.14
hands-off
indulgent 427.8
nonrestrictive 430.25
permissive 443.14
conservative 852.8
handsome liberal 485.4
magnanimous 652.6
beautiful 1015.17
hand-to-mouth 406.15
hand-to-mouth
existence 619.2
handwriting 547.3
handwriting on the
wall warning 133.4
sign 399.3
fate 963.2
handy nearby 223.15
miniature 258.12
modal 384.8
convenient 387.20
skillful 413.22
wieldy 1013.15
hang
n droop 202.2
declivity 204.5
v take off 193.10
dangle 202.6
suspend 202.8
frequent 221.10
inhabit 225.7
hang by the neck
604.18
procrastinate 845.11
depend 958.6
pend 970.11
hangar housing 184.24
garage 197.27
repair shop 739.5
hang around
attach oneself to
138.11
frequent 221.10
stay near 223.12
idle 331.12
wait 845.12
hang by a thread
depend 970.11
take chances 1005.7
be in danger 1005.8
hanger-on
adherent 138.6
follower 166.2
retainer 577.1
henchman 610.8
associate 616.8

hang fire
stagnate 173.9
do nothing 329.2
come to nothing
410.13
postpone 845.9
procrastinate 845.11
stop 856.7
be unproductive 890.3
hang in
be strong 15.11
endure 134.6
keep alive 306.10
remain firm 359.9
keep up one's courage
492.15
last 826.6
persist 855.5
hanging
n pendency 202.1
pendant 202.4
declivity 204.5
cover 295.2
camaraderie 582.2
capital punishment
604.7
scenery 704.20
adj downcast 194.12
pendent 202.9
loose 803.5
hang in there 134.5
hangman 604.8
hang on
keep alive 306.10
stay with it 360.4
hold 474.6
blame 599.8
cohere 802.6
result from 886.5
attribute to 887.4
depend 958.6
pend 970.11
hangout 228.27
hang out
be exposed 31.5
overhang 202.7
frequent 221.10
inhabit 225.7
be manifest 348.7
wait 845.12
turn up 940.9
hangover
intoxication 88.1
subsequence 834.1
hang over one's head
839.2
hang together 802.6
hang tough
be strong 15.11
use 87.21
endure 134.6
confront 216.8
remain firm 359.9
persevere 360.7
offer resistance 453.3
keep up one's courage
492.15
last 826.6
stand fast 854.11
persist 855.5
toughen 1047.3
hang up suspend 202.8

telephone 347.18
come to nothing
  410.13
postpone 845.9
hang-up delay 845.2
obsession 925.13
obstacle 1011.4
hankering
n yearning 100.5
adj wistful 100.23
hanky-panky
love affair 104.6
juggling 356.5
haphazard
n chance-medley
  971.4
adj slipshod 340.12
unprepared 406.8
unordered 809.12
purposeless 971.16
hapless 1010.14
happen occur 830.5
chance 971.11
happening
n event 830.2
chance event 971.6
adj occurring 830.9
happen on
come across 940.3
chance 971.11
happy
intoxicated 88.31
glad 95.15
content 107.7
cheerful 109.11
auspicious 133.18
decorous 496.10
appropriate 533.7
apt 787.10
timely 842.9
expedient 994.5
happy-go-lucky 406.15
happy medium
mean 246.1
middle course 467.3
moderation 670.1
hara-kiri 308.5
harangue
n speech 543.2
lesson 568.7
v declaim 543.10
expound 568.16
harass
fatigue 21.4
annoy 96.13
vex 98.15
make anxious 126.5
intimidate 127.20
persecute 389.7
besiege 459.19
work evil 999.6
trouble 1012.13
harassment
annoyance 96.2
vexatiousness 98.7
worry 126.2
persecution 389.3
harbinger
n forerunner 133.5
herald 353.2
precursor 815.1
v herald 133.14

harbor
n destination 186.5
inlet 242.1
refuge 1008.1
haven 1008.6
v house 225.10
hold 474.7
doubt 954.6
protect 1007.18
harbor a grudge 589.8
harbor resentment
  152.12
hard
adj strong 15.15
painful 26.10
bitter 64.6
alcoholic 88.37
callous 94.12
impenitent 114.5
harsh 144.24
heartless 144.25
pitiless 146.3
industrious 330.22
unyielding 361.9
obdurate 361.10
firm 425.7
hard to understand
  522.14
phonetic 524.31
hardened 654.17
lascivious 665.29
real 760.15
sturdy 762.7
true 972.13
valid 972.14
adverse 1010.13
difficult 1012.17
dense 1043.12
solid 1044.10
tough 1047.4
adv near 223.20
laboriously 725.19
hard and fast
aground 182.73
preceptive 419.4
mandatory 420.12
hard as nails
strong 15.15
pitiless 146.3
resistant 1044.10
tough 1047.4
hardball reality 760.2
gravity 996.3
danger 1005.1
hard-boiled
firm 15.18
obdurate 361.10
hard 1044.10
hard copy 547.10
hard-core
unyielding 361.9
fiery 671.22
hardcover 554.3
hard disk
recording media
  549.10
disk 1041.6
hard-drinking 88.35
hard drug 87.2
hard-earned
laborious 725.18
difficult 1012.17

harden
strengthen 15.13
callous 94.6
accustom 373.10
indurate 1044.7
toughen 1047.3
petrify 1057.9
hardened callous 94.12
impenitent 114.5
heartless 144.25
accustomed 373.16
hard 654.17
toughened 1044.13
tough 1047.6
hard feelings
bad feeling 93.7
bitterness 152.3
animosity 589.4
hard hat patriot 591.3
conservative 611.9
safeguard 1007.3
hardheaded
obstinate 361.8
ungullible 955.5
realistic 986.6
hard-hearted
callous 94.12
heartless 144.25
hardened 654.17
hard 1044.10
hard knocks 1010.1
hard labor
punishment 604.2
backbreaking work
  725.5
hard line
unyieldingness 361.2
strictness 425.1
warlikeness 458.11
orthodoxy 687.5
hard-line
unyielding 361.9
strict 425.6
militaristic 458.22
fiery 671.22
hard liquor 88.13
hard-nosed 361.10
hard nut to crack
enigma 522.8
tough proposition
  1012.2
hard-of-hearing 49.6
hard on 223.24
hard-on 75.5
hard-pressed
straitened 1012.26
hurried 401.11
hard rock 708.10
hard sell
inducement 375.3
importunity 440.3
selling 734.2
hard up poor 619.7
straitened 1012.26
hardware
hard goods 735.4
computer hardware
  1040.17
central processing
  unit 1041.2
the hard way
n difficulty 1012.1

adv laboriously 725.19
with difficulty
  1012.28
hardwood
n basketball 747.1
wood 1052.3
adj arboreal 310.36
hardworking
industrious 330.22
laboring 725.17
hardy strong 15.15
hale 83.12
insolent 142.9
perennial 310.41
courageous 492.17
durable 826.10
tough 1047.4
hare
swiftness 174.6
leveret 311.24
harebrained
capricious 364.5
foolhardy 493.9
scatterbrained 984.16
harem 563.10
hark
v listen 48.10
hearken to 982.7
inter hark ye! 48.16
attention! 982.22
hark back
turn back 858.5
remember 988.10
harlequin
n check 47.4
variegation 47.6
buffoon 707.10
v variegate 47.7
adj variegated 47.9
harlot
n prostitute 665.16
adj prostitute 665.28
harm
n impairment 393.1
disadvantage 995.2
evil 999.3
bane 1000.1
v impair 393.9
inconvenience 995.4
work evil 999.6
harmful
unhealthful 82.5
malicious 144.20
disadvantageous
  995.6
hurtful 999.12
adverse 1010.13
harmless
hurtless 998.21
undamaged 1001.8
unhazardous 1006.5
harmonic
n tone 50.2
harmonic tone 709.16
adj harmonious
  708.49
oscillating 915.15
harmonica 711.10
harmonious
chromatic 35.15
pleasant 97.6
symmetric 264.4

cooperative 450.5
in accord 455.3
balanced 533.8
friendly 587.15
harmonic 708.49
agreeing 787.9
orderly 806.6
conformist 866.6
concurrent 898.4
harmonize
symmetrize 264.3
cooperate 450.3
get along 455.2
reconcile 465.8
be harmonious 708.35
compose 708.46
make uniform 780.4
agree 787.6
make agree 787.7
order 806.4
organize 807.10
conform 866.3
concur 898.2
harmony
symmetry 264.1
unanimity 332.5
cooperation 450.1
accord 455.1
peace 464.1
proportion 533.2
good terms 587.3
heaven 681.5
concord 708.3
harmonics 709.1
agreement 787.1
order 806.1
conformity 866.1
harness
n wardrobe 5.2
parachute 181.13
caparison 385.5
armor 460.3
v yoke 799.10
tend 1068.7
harp
n lyre 711.3
mouth organ 711.10
v persist 855.5
harp on dwell on 118.8
belabor 848.9
emphasize 996.14
harpoon 480.17
harpsichord 711.12
harpy
extortionist 480.12
monster 593.6
harridan
strumpet 665.14
eyesore 1014.4
harried
tormented 96.24
worried 126.8
harrow
n projection 285.4
v pain 26.7
torture 96.18
smooth 287.5
cultivate 1067.17
harrowing
n cultivation 1067.13
adj painful 26.10
agonizing 98.23

harry annoy 96.13
make anxious 126.5
persecute 389.7
attack 459.14
besiege 459.19
harsh
acrimonious 17.14
painful 26.10
off-color 35.20
raucous 58.15
dissonant 61.4
clashing 61.5
bitter 64.6
pungent 68.6
distressing 98.20
oppressive 98.24
rough 144.24
pitiless 146.3
rugged 288.7
strict 425.6
gruff 505.7
inarticulate 525.12
inelegant 534.2
hart male animal 76.8
hoofed animal 311.5
harum-scarum
adj reckless 493.8
boisterous 671.20
adv in disorder 809.17
harvest
n autumn 313.4
yield 472.5
effect 886.1
production 892.2
harvesting 1067.15
v acquire 472.8
process 891.9
reap 1067.19
has-been
n back number 841.8
adj past 836.7
old-fashioned 841.16
hash
n meat 10.12
hashish 87.7
fiasco 410.6
bungle 414.5
hodgepodge 796.6
jumble 809.3
v mix 796.10
hash house 8.17
hash over 541.12
Hasidic 675.30
hasp 799.8
hassle
n quarrel 456.6
struggle 725.3
commotion 809.4
argumentation 934.4
v vex 98.15
quarrel 456.12
nag 510.16
struggle 725.11
argue 934.16
work evil 999.6
haste
n impatience 135.1
velocity 174.1
impulsiveness 365.2
hurry 401.1
recklessness 493.2
prematurity 844.2

v speed 174.8
hasten 401.4
hasten
be impatient 135.4
advance 162.5
speed 174.8
accelerate 174.10
haste 401.4
make haste 401.5
be useful 449.17
facilitate 1013.7
hasty
hot-tempered 110.25
impatient 135.6
fast 174.15
impulsive 365.9
hurried 401.9
unprepared 406.8
reckless 493.8
sudden 829.5
premature 844.8
hat
n headdress 5.25
v cloak 5.39
top 295.21
hatch
n porch 189.6
offspring 561.1
v be born 1.2
be pregnant 78.12
fabricate 354.17
plot 381.9
mark 517.19
portray 712.19
engrave 713.9
originate 891.12
imagine 985.14
raise 1068.6
hatchet man
killer 308.10
combatant 461.1
disparager 512.6
ruffian 593.4
henchman 610.8
hate
n hostility 99.2
aversion 103
malice 103.1
hated thing 103.3
antagonism 589.3
v have deep feelings 93.12
dislike 99.3
detest 103.5
bear ill will 589.8
hateful
offensive 98.18
loathsome 103.8
malicious 144.20
hostile 589.10
terrible 999.9
hatred hostility 99.2
abhorrence 103.1
antagonism 589.3
haughty vain 136.9
arrogant 141.9
contemptuous 157.8
high 272.14
haul
n distance 261.1
take 480.10
booty 482.11

strain 725.2
pull 904.2
v cart 176.13
sail against the wind 182.24
ship activity 182.48
strain 725.10
pull 904.4
haunch 218.1
haunt
n resort 228.27
specter 987.1
v oppress 98.16
make anxious 126.5
frequent 221.10
hant 987.6
haunted worried 126.8
spooked 987.10
remembering 988.24
haunting
recurrent 848.13
unforgettable 988.26
hauteur arrogance 141.1
contempt 157.1
height 272.1
have give birth 1.3
affirm 334.5
deceive 356.19
compel 424.4
suffer 443.10
possess 469.4
hold 474.7
receive 479.6
understand 521.7
experience 830.8
know 927.12
doubt 954.6
recognize 988.12
have it in for
dislike 99.3
loathe 103.6
bear ill will 589.8
have it made
make good 409.10
prosper 1009.7
have it out
contend with 457.17
argue 934.16
haven
n destination 186.5
refuge 1008.1
harbor 1008.6
v protect 1007.18
have to
be compelled 424.9
be necessary 962.10
havoc
n evil 999.3
v destroy 395.10
haw avoid 164.6
stammer 525.8
hawk
n sharp vision 27.11
bird 311.28
militarist 461.5
patriot 591.3
v salivate 13.6
hunt 382.9
vend 734.9
the hawk 318.8
hawk-eyed
clear-sighted 27.21

vigilant 339.13
hay
  n feed 10.4
  marijuana 87.10
  v harvest 1067.19
the hay 900.19
haystack 769.10
haywire
  impaired 393.38
  disorderly 809.13
  crazy 925.27
  eccentric 926.6
hazard
  n golf 751.1
  gamble 759.2
  bet 759.3
  unreliability 970.6
  chance event 971.6
  danger 1005.1
  obstacle 1011.4
  v presume 640.6
  risk 759.24
  bet 759.25
  chance 971.11
  endanger 1005.6
  take chances 1005.7
haze
  n LSD 87.9
  fog 319.2
  confusion 984.3
  v cloud 319.6
  banter 490.5
hazel 40.3
hazy
  inconspicuous 32.6
  formless 263.4
  foggy 319.9
  obscure 522.15
  vague 970.19
  muddled 984.13
he male 76.4
  self 864.5
head
  n member 2.7
  head of hair 3.4
  latrine 12.10
  addict 87.20
  enthusiast 101.5
  sail 180.14
  top part 198.4
  architectural topping
    198.5
  headpiece 198.6
  front 216.1
  headwaters 238.2
  superior 249.4
  point of land 283.9
  plant 310.25
  person 312.5
  foam 320.2
  makeup 554.12
  abridgment 557.1
  superintendent 574.2
  portrait 712.15
  class 808.2
  source 885.5
  thrust 901.2
  intellect 918.1
  brain 918.6
  intelligence 919.9
  topic 936.1
  caption 936.2

water 1063.3
  v take direction 161.7
  lead 165.2
  top 198.9
  be in front 216.7
  gravitate 297.15
  direct 573.8
  govern 612.12
  play 752.4
  precede 813.2
  tend 895.3
  focus on 936.3
  adj top 198.10
  front 216.10
  directing 573.12
  governing 612.18
  first 817.17
headache
  ache 26.5
  annoyance 96.2
  tedious person 118.5
  trouble 1012.3
head and shoulders
  above
  superlative 249.13
  superior 998.14
headband 554.14
head count
  population 227.1
  roll 870.6
  summation 1016.11
headdress
  hairdo 3.15
  headgear 5.25
headfirst
  precipitately 401.15
  recklessly 493.11
headhunter
  executive search
    agency 615.5
  killer 308.10
heading
  n direction 161.1
  leading 165.1
  course 184.34
  top part 198.4
  front 216.1
  supervision 573.2
  class 808.2
  topic 936.1
  caption 936.2
  adj leading 165.3
  topping 198.11
headline
  n caption 936.2
  v dramatize 704.28
  focus on 936.3
  feature 996.15
headlong
  adj fast 174.15
  steep 204.18
  impulsive 365.9
  precipitate 401.10
  reckless 493.8
  sudden 829.5
  adv precipitately
    401.15
  recklessly 493.11
  impulsively 365.13
headmaster 571.8
head off 164.6
head office 739.7

head-on
  adj front 216.10
  adv afoul 182.72
  in opposition 451.9
head over heels
  inversely 205.8
  precipitately 401.15
  recklessly 493.11
  round 914.16
  inverted 205.7
headphone
  loudspeaker 50.8
  radiophone 347.5
headpiece
  headdress 5.25
  top part 198.4
  head 198.6
  intellect 918.1
headquarters
  central station
    208.6
  office 739.7
heads 215.3
heads or tails 759.2
head start
  advantage 249.2
  earliness 844.1
headstone 900.7
headstrong
  obstinate 361.8
  lawless 418.5
head up
  be in front 216.7
  direct 573.8
  precede 813.2
  initiate 817.10
  focus on 936.3
headway
  progression 162.1
  way 182.9
  improvement 392.1
headwear 5.25
head wind
  atmosphere 184.32
  wind 318.1
  nautical 318.11
  opposition 451.1
  counterforce 899.4
heady
  intoxicating 88.36
  exciting 105.30
  foamy 320.7
  lawless 418.5
heal treat 91.24
  cure 396.15
  heal over 396.21
health
  n well-being 83.1
  normality 868.1
  adj medical 90.15
health care
  health protection 83.5
  medical care 90
  medicine 90.1
health club
  health care 83.5
  fitness 84.1
health food
  nutrient 7.3
  food 10.1
health insurance
  health care 83.5

medicine 90.1
  welfarism 611.7
health spa 84.1
healthy
  wellness 81.5
  healthful 83.8
  large 257.16
  good 998.12
heap
  n car 179.10
  amount 244.2
  lot 247.4
  store 386.1
  throng 769.4
  pile 769.10
  v load 159.15
  give 478.12
  pile 769.19
heap up load 159.15
  store up 386.11
  collect 472.11
  pile 769.19
heap upon
  furnish 478.15
  give freely 485.3
hear
  v sense 24.6
  listen 48.10
  catch 48.11
  know 551.15
  try 598.17
  sit in judgment 945.12
  hearken to 982.7
  inter hark! 48.16
  bravo! 509.22
hear a different
  drummer
  disobey 327.6
  dissent 333.4
hearing
  n senses 24.5
  auditory 48
  audition 48.1
  aural sense 48.2
  earshot 48.4
  trial 598.5
  examination 937.2
  investigation 937.4
  tryout 941.3
  adj auditory 48.13
hearken 48.10
hearken to obey 326.2
  hark 982.7
hearsay
  n report 552.6
  adj evidential 956.16
hearse
  n funeral car 309.10
  v inter 309.19
heart
  n viscera 2.14
  food 10.19
  passion 93.2
  soul 93.3
  love 104.1
  essential content
    196.5
  interior 207.2
  center 208.2
  life force 306.3
  fortitude 492.6
  essence 766.2

inner nature 766.5
middle 818.1
psyche 918.4
mood 977.4
salient point 996.6
v confess 351.7
heartache
  wretchedness 96.6
  aching heart 112.9
heartbeat
  life force 306.3
  pulsation 915.3
heartbreak
  harshness 98.4
  heartache 112.9
heartbreaker 562.12
heartburn ache 26.5
  jealousy 153.1
hear tell of hear 48.11
  know 551.15
hearten energize 17.10
  cheer 109.7
  comfort 121.6
  motivate 375.21
  abet 449.14
  encourage 492.16
heartening
  n encouragement
    492.9
  adj cheering 109.16
  comforting 121.13
heartfelt 93.24
hearth home 228.2
  family 559.5
  fireplace 1019.11
heartland inland 207.3
  region 231.1
  middle America 231.7
heartless unfeeling 94.9
  apathetic 94.13
  dejected 112.22
  unkind 144.25
  pitiless 146.3
  uncourageous 491.11
  hardened 654.17
heartrending
  agonizing 98.23
  pitiful 145.8
hearts
  amphetamines 87.3
  card 758.2
heartsick
  wretched 96.26
  disconsolate 112.28
heartstrings 93.3
heartthrob
  loved one 104.11
  pulsation 915.3
heart-to-heart
  n chat 541.4
  adj candid 644.17
heartwarming
  delightful 97.7
  pleasant 97.6
  cheering 109.16
hearty
  n mariner 183.1
  boon companion
    588.5
  adj strong 15.15
  energetic 17.13
  hale 83.12

fervent 93.18
zealous 101.9
gay 109.14
convivial 582.23
hospitable 585.11
cordial 587.16
hear ye
  hark! 48.16
  attention! 982.22
heat
  n sexual desire 75.5
  fever 85.7
  passion 93.2
  zeal 101.2
  fever of excitement
    105.7
  anger 152.5
  race 457.12
  hotness 1018.1
  v cook 11.4
  excite 105.12
  incite 375.17
  raise the temperature
    1019.17
  adj fuel 1020.8
heated
  cooked 11.6
  fervent 93.18
  zealous 101.9
  passionate 105.22
  fiery 671.22
  hot 1018.25
  het 1019.29
heater gun 462.10
  warmer 1019.10
heath
  plain 236.1
  wasteland 890.2
heathen
  n pagan 688.7
  unbeliever 695.11
  adj pagan 688.11
  unbelieving 695.19
  idolatrous 697.7
  unlearned 929.14
heat up
  aggravate 119.2
  intensify 251.5
  incite 375.17
  antagonize 589.7
heat wave
  weather 317.3
  hot weather 1018.7
heave
  n wave 238.14
  strain 725.2
  throw 903.3
  pull 904.2
  lift 911.2
  v feel disgust 99.4
  be excited 105.18
  ship activity 182.48
  pitch 182.55
  billow 238.22
  strain 725.10
  throw 903.10
  pull 904.4
  vomit 908.26
  elevate 911.5
heaven
  happiness 95.2
  summit 198.2

height 272.2
utopia 985.11
good times 1009.4
the heavens 1070.2
Heaven
  abode of the deity and
    blessed dead 681
  destiny 838.2
  Fates 963.3
Heaven forbid! 510.27
Heaven knows! 929.19
heavenly
  blissful 97.9
  divine 677.17
  angelic 679.6
  otherworldly 681.12
  sacred 685.7
  godly 692.9
  ideal 985.23
  superb 998.15
  gorgeous 1015.20
  celestial 1070.25
heavenly body 1070.4
heaven-sent
  timely 842.9
  expedient 994.5
heave to
  sail against the wind
    182.24
  come to a stop 182.33
heaving
  n trepidation 105.5
  throwing 903.2
  pulling 904.1
  vomiting 908.8
  adj respiratory 2.30
heavy
  n heavyweight 257.12
  role 704.10
  actor 707.2
  adj sleepy 22.21
  deep 54.10
  pregnant 78.18
  oppressive 98.24
  sad 112.20
  dull 117.6
  inert 173.14
  great 247.6
  thick 269.8
  ponderous 297.16
  luxuriant 310.40
  cloudy 319.7
  languid 331.20
  phonetic 524.31
  stiff 534.3
  tragic 704.34
  laborious 725.18
  sturdy 762.7
  unintelligent 921.16
  weighty 996.20
  excellent 998.13
  troublesome 1012.18
  dense 1043.12
  viscous 1060.12
  adv heavily 297.21
heavy-duty 1047.4
heavy hand
  firm hand 425.3
  despotism 612.10
heavy-handed
  insensible 25.6
  bungling 414.20

inelegant 534.2
heavy heart
  wretchedness 96.6
  sadness 112.1
heavyset
  corpulent 257.18
  thick 269.8
heavyweight
  n pig 257.12
  weight 297.3
  influence 893.6
  adj heavy 297.16
  important 996.17
hebetude apathy 94.4
  languor 331.6
  stupidity 921.3
Hebrew
  n Jew 675.21
  adj Jewish 675.30
hecatomb
  butchery 308.3
  destruction 395.1
  oblation 696.7
  hundred 881.8
heck! 513.12
heckle comb 79.21
  annoy 96.13
hectic
  n reddening 41.3
  glow 1018.12
  adj red-complexioned
    41.9
  feverish 85.57
  overzealous 101.12
  heated 105.22
  overactive 330.24
hector
  n braggart 502.5
  blusterer 503.2
  v annoy 96.13
  intimidate 127.20
  bluster 503.3
hedge
  n boundary 211.3
  caution 494.1
  qualification 958.1
  v limit 210.5
  fence 212.7
  dodge 368.8
  take precautions
    494.6
  quibble 935.9
  qualify 958.3
hedgehog
  wild animal 311.23
  launcher 462.21
  rocket launcher
    1072.10
hedge in
  circumscribe 210.4
  enclose 212.5
  fence 212.7
hedge one's bets 494.6
hedging
  n limitation 210.2
  caution 494.1
  quibbling 935.5
  qualification 958.1
  adj demurring 325.7
  quibbling 935.14
hedonism
  pleasure-loving 95.4

ethical philosophy
636.2
selfishness 651.1
sensuality 663.1
hedonistic
pleasure-loving 95.17
selfish 651.5
sensual 663.5
heed
n carefulness 339.1
observance 434.1
caution 494.1
attention 982.1
v listen 48.10
obey 326.2
care 339.6
observe 434.2
attend 982.6
heedful
considerate 143.16
careful 339.10
cautious 494.8
attentive 982.15
heedless
unconcerned 102.7
inconsiderate 144.18
careless 340.11
unthinking 365.10
improvident 406.15
incurious 981.3
inattentive 983.6
forgetful 989.9
heel
n foot 199.5
rear 217.1
stern 217.7
bad person 660.6
v turn round 163.9
deviate 164.3
follow 166.3
careen 182.43
equip 385.8
fight 754.4
heeled addicted 87.24
provided 385.13
armed 460.14
heel of Achilles 1005.4
heft
n weight 297.1
v weigh 297.10
elevate 911.5
hefty strong 15.15
corpulent 257.18
heavy 297.16
laborious 725.18
troublesome 1012.18
Hegelian
n immaterialist
1051.4
adj Aristotelian 951.10
idealist 1051.8
hegemony
superiority 249.1
supremacy 249.3
dominance 417.6
mastership 417.7
hegira
departure 188.1
flight 368.4
heifer
female animal 77.9
gal 302.7

cattle 311.6
height
degree 245.1
supremacy 249.3
size 257.1
tallness 272
heighth 272.1
rise 272.2
pitch 709.4
elevation 911.1
acme of perfection
1001.3
heighten
increase 272.13
elevate 911.5
heightening
aggravation 119.1
intensification 251.2
exaggeration 355.1
heights
highlands 237.1
altitude 272.2
heinous offensive 98.18
wicked 654.16
base 661.12
terrible 999.9
heir survivor 256.3
heritor 479.5
successor 816.4
sequel 834.2
heirloom 479.2
heist
n theft 482.4
v rob 482.16
elevate 911.5
held reserved 386.15
possessed 469.8
stuck 854.16
supported 900.24
obsessed 925.33
believed 952.23
gripped 982.18
Helicon 720.10
helicopter 181.5
heliport airport 184.22
platform 900.13
hell blackness 38.4
torment 96.7
depths 275.3
place of confinement
429.7
abode of the damned
682
Hades 682.1
casino 759.19
pandemonium 809.5
hot place 1018.11
Hell
river of death 307.4
destiny 838.2
cold place 1022.4
hell-bent 174.17
hellcat
daredevil 493.4
ruffian 593.3
witch 593.7
violent person 671.9
hellfire 682.2
hellion
ruffian 593.4
violent person 671.9
demon 680.6

hellish
frightening 127.28
cruel 144.26
diabolic 654.13
turbulent 671.18
demoniac 680.17
infernal 682.8
execrable 999.10
hello! oh! 122.20
salutation 585.4
greetings! 585.15
hey! 982.23
helm
n authority 417.10
direction 573.1
reins 573.5
control 612.2
v pilot 182.14
helmet
heraldry 647.2
safeguard 1007.3
helmsman
steersman 183.8
guide 574.7
helot
sycophant 138.3
subject 432.7
help
n serving 8.10
remedy 86.1
aid 449.1
subsidy 478.8
servant 577.2
staff 577.11
benefactor 592.1
assistant 616.6
v do a favor 143.12
aid 449.11
subsidize 478.19
serve 577.13
do good 998.10
prevent 1011.14
helper
subordinate 432.5
assistant 449.7
benefactor 592.1
associate 616.6
helpful
considerate 143.16
modal 384.8
useful 387.18
of use 449.21
good 998.12
helping
n serving 8.10
portion 477.5
adj assisting 449.20
serving 577.14
helpless
defenseless 19.18
dead-drunk 88.32
forlorn 584.12
unprotected 1005.14
helpmeet
wife 563.8
assistant 616.6
helter-skelter
n haste 401.1
jumble 809.3
commotion 809.4
adj carelessly 340.18
hastily 401.12

recklessly 493.11
nonuniformly 781.4
separated 801.21
confused 809.16
in disorder 809.17
hem
n border 211.4
edging 211.7
v border 211.10
fence 212.7
restrict 428.9
stammer 525.8
hem and haw
prevaricate 344.7
hesitate 362.7
dodge 368.8
stammer 525.8
hem in
border 211.10
enclose 212.5
confine 429.12
hemisphere
sphere 231.2
member 792.4
half 874.2
hemlock 604.7
hemmed-in
restricted 428.15
enclosed 212.10
hemorrhage
n bleeding 12.8
symptom 85.9
v bleed 12.17
hemorrhoids 85.36
hemp
marijuana 87.10
execution 605.5
hen woman 77.6
female animal 77.9
old woman 304.3
poultry 311.29
card 758.2
hence thence 188.20
therefore 887.7
henceforth 838.10
henchman
hanger-on 138.6
follower 166.2
cohort 610.8
associate 616.8
henhouse 228.22
henna
v make red 41.4
adj reddish-brown
40.4
henpeck
nag 510.16
domineer 612.16
henpecked
tied to one's apron
strings 326.5
downtrodden 432.16
hep 927.17
Hephaestus 726.8
heptagonal
pentagonal 278.10
seventh 881.19
her female 77.4
cocaine 87.6
self 864.5
herald
n foreshadower 133.5

leading 165.1
harbinger 353.2
king of arms 575.21
delegate 576.2
spokesman 576.5
precursor 815.1
v harbinger 133.14
proclaim 352.13
go before 815.3
be prior 833.3
heraldry pomp 501.6
insignia 647.1
herb
remedy 86.4
marijuana 87.10
plant 310.4
herbicide 1000.3
herbivore eater 8.16
creature 311.3
Herculean
Briarean 15.17
huge 257.20
laborious 725.18
difficult 1012.17
Hercules
strong man 15.6
support 900.3
herd
n guide 574.7
the masses 606.2
guardian 1007.6
v guide 573.9
drive 1068.8
herd together
associate with 582.17
accompany 768.7
come together 769.16
here hereat 159.23
there 221.16
now 837.3
hereabouts
here 159.23
near 223.20
hereafter
n the future 838.1
adj future 838.8
adv in future 838.10
the hereafter
the afterworld 681.2
destiny 838.2
here and now
now 837.3
material 1050.10
the here and now
reality 760.2
the present 837.1
realism 986.2
here and there
in places 159.25
discontinuously 812.5
sparsely 884.8
hereby 384.12
hereditary
protoplasmic 305.18
patrimonial 560.19
innate 766.8
heredity
genetic material 305.9
heritage 560.6
herein 207.10
heresy
false doctrine 688.2

inconsistency 788.2
unconventionality
867.2
unbelief 954.1
error 974.1
heretical
unorthodox 688.9
nonconformist 788.9
unconventional 867.6
unbelieving 954.8
erroneous 974.16
hereto 159.23
heretofore
previously 833.6
formerly 836.13
until now 837.4
herewith
therewith 384.12
hand in hand 768.10
heritage
inheritance 479.2
heredity 560.6
hermaphrodite
n intersex 75.17
adj androgynal 75.30
hermeneutics
exegetics 341.8
criticism 723.1
Hermes 353.1
hermetically sealed
293.12
hermetics 345.5
hermit recluse 584.5
ascetic 667.2
religious 699.15
oddity 869.4
hero victor 411.2
brave person 492.8
god 659.5
celebrity 662.9
godling 678.3
role 704.10
lead 707.6
ideal 785.4
heroic eminent 247.9
huge 257.20
courageous 492.17
magnanimous 652.6
vocal 708.50
poetic 720.15
traditional 841.12
heroics
rashness 493.1
boasting 502.1
heroine
brave person 492.8
hero 659.5
celebrity 662.9
godling 678.3
role 704.10
lead 707.6
heroism
glory 247.2
courage 492.1
magnanimity 652.2
hero worship
love 104.1
respect 155.1
praise 509.5
idolatry 697.1
hero-worship
respect 155.4

praise 509.12
Herr 76.7
hesitancy demur 325.2
hesitation 362.3
caution 494.1
uncertainty 970.1
hesitant
demurring 325.7
tentative 362.11
cautious 494.8
uncertain 970.16
hesitate demur 325.4
pause 362.7
stammer 525.8
procrastinate 845.11
hang in doubt 970.10
hesitation demur 325.2
hesitance 362.3
caution 494.1
stammering 525.3
procrastination 845.5
uncertainty 970.1
heterodoxy
unorthodoxy 688.1
inconsistency 788.2
unconventionality
867.2
error 974.1
heterogeneity
difference 779.1
multiformity 782.1
inconsistency 788.2
inequality 790.1
heterogeneous
different 779.7
diversified 782.4
mixed 796.14
heterosexual 75.13
het up
excited 105.22
angry 152.30
heated 1019.29
heuristic
examining 937.36
experimental 941.11
hew form 262.7
sever 801.11
hex
n curse 513.1
sorceress 690.8
spell 691.1
bad influence 999.4
v curse 513.5
bewitch 691.9
work evil 999.6
bring bad luck
1010.12
hexagonal
pentagonal 278.10
sixth 881.18
hey oh! 122.20
greetings! 585.15
howdy! 585.16
hail! 982.23
hi greetings! 585.15
hey! 982.23
hiatus interval 224.1
opening 292.1
deficiency 794.2
interruption 812.2
hibernate
aestivate 22.15

do nothing 329.2
lie idle 331.16
be latent 519.3
hibernation sleep 22.2
inactivity 331.1
hiccup
n breathing 2.19
belch 908.9
v belch 908.28
hick
n bungler 414.9
simple soul 416.3
peasant 606.6
oaf 923.5
adj not urbane 233.8
hickey sore 85.36
blemish 1003.1
thing 1050.5
hidden invisible 32.5
secret 345.11
concealed 346.11
latent 519.5
implied 519.7
recondite 522.16
hide
n fur 4.2
lamina 296.2
v disappear 34.2
conceal 346.6
conceal oneself 346.8
store up 386.11
defeat 412.9
punish 604.15
hideaway
hiding place 346.4
sanctum 584.6
retreat 1008.5
hideous horrid 98.19
terrible 127.30
ugly 1014.11
hideout
hiding place 346.4
retreat 1008.5
hide out 346.8
hiding
n covering 295.1
concealment 346.1
hiding place 346.4
defeat 412.1
punishment 604.5
adj concealing 346.15
hiding place
hideaway 346.4
retreat 1008.5
hie speed 174.8
travel 177.18
hiemal
seasonal 313.9
cold 1022.14
hierarchy
rank 245.2
mastership 417.7
the authorities 575.15
class 607.1
government 612.4
hierocracy 698.7
continuity 806.2
class structure 808.4
hieroglyphic
representation 349.1
phonetic symbol
546.2

higgledy-piggledy
n jumble 809.3
adj confused 809.16
adv nonuniformly
781.4
in disorder 809.17
high
n stupor 22.6
substance abuse 87.1
intoxication 88.1
excitement 105.1
weather map 317.4
secondary school
567.4
price 738.9
gear 1039.5
adj high-pitched 58.13
nasty 64.7
strong 68.8
malodorous 71.5
bent 87.23
drunk 88.33
overjoyed 95.16
excited 105.20
cheerful 109.11
lofty 136.11
spacious 158.10
great 247.9
high-reaching 272.14
tainted 393.41
phonetic 524.31
noble 608.10
expensive 632.11
magnanimous 652.6
eminent 662.18
raised 911.9
excessive 992.16
adv on high 272.21
intemperately 669.10
high and dry
stuck 854.16
in safety 1006.6
stranded 1012.27
dry 1064.7
high and low 158.12
high-and-mighty
lordly 141.11
eminent 662.18
highball
n drink 88.9
poker 759.10
v speed 174.9
highborn
upper-class 607.10
wellborn 608.11
highbrow
snob 141.7
intellectual 928.1
high-class 998.14
high dudgeon 152.7
higher-up
superior 249.4
politics 610.7
highest
n supremacy 249.3
adj top 198.10
superlative 249.13
higher 272.19
almighty 677.18
paramount 996.24
highfalutin
n boasting 502.2

bombast 545.2
adj lofty 136.11
arrogant 141.9
ostentatious 501.18
inflated 502.12
grandiloquent 545.8
high-flown
lofty 136.11
arrogant 141.9
exaggerated 355.4
ostentatious 501.18
inflated 502.12
grandiloquent 545.8
absurd 922.11
high-flying
aspiring 100.28
ostentatious 501.18
grandiloquent 545.8
high frequency 1033.12
high-frequency 1033.28
high-handed 417.16
High Holy Day 20.4
high hopes 124.1
high horse 141.1
high jinks 743.4
highland
n highlands 237.1
uplands 272.3
adj rustic 233.6
upland 272.17
highlands
the country 233.1
high country 237
uplands 237.1
highland 272.3
high life
society 578.6
upper class 607.2
aristocracy 608.1
highlight
n feature 996.7
light 1024.1
v manifest 348.5
signify 517.17
specify 864.11
call attention to
982.10
emphasize 996.14
illuminate 1024.28
high-living 669.8
highly 247.15
high-minded
lofty 136.11
honest 644.13
magnanimous 652.6
Highness 648.2
high on the hog
intemperately
669.10
prosperous 1009.12
high-pitched
strident 58.13
high 272.14
high point 996.6
high-powered
powerful 18.12
important 996.17
high pressure
inducement 375.3
coercion 424.3
importunity 440.3
urgency 996.4

high-pressure
v urge 375.14
coerce 424.8
adj powerful 18.12
climatal 317.12
urgent 996.22
high profile 31.2
high-profile 31.7
high-quality 998.14
high-rise 272.14
high school 567.4
high society
society 578.6
upper class 607.2
aristocracy 608.1
high-society
socially prominent
578.16
upper-class 607.10
high-spirited
excitable 105.28
mischievous 322.6
high-strung
excitable 105.28
touchy 110.21
nervous 128.11
hightail speed 174.9
run off 188.12
high tech 927.10
high-tech 927.28
high time fun 743.2
good opportunity
842.3
lateness 845.1
highway 383.5
highway interchange
170.2
highwayman 483.5
highway robbery
theft 482.3
overcharge 632.5
hijack coerce 424.7
rob 482.16
hike
n walk 177.10
increase 251.1
lift 911.2
v march 177.30
increase 251.4
enlarge 259.4
elevate 911.5
hilarious merry 109.15
humorous 488.4
festive 743.28
hilarity
merriment 109.5
laughter 116.4
humorousness 488.1
hill
n down 237.4
plateau 272.4
bulge 283.3
baseball 745.1
pile 769.10
v pile 769.19
hillbilly
n wilderness settler
227.10
peasant 606.6
adj not urbane 233.8
hill of beans
zilch 761.3

trifle 997.5
hilly
rolling 237.8
knobby 272.18
hind
n female animal 77.9
hoofed animal 311.5
peasant 606.6
adj rear 217.9
hind end 217.1
hinder
v restrain 428.7
fend off 460.10
delay 845.8
impede 1011.10
adj rear 217.9
hindquarter 217.3
hindrance
restraint 428.1
delay 845.2
impediment 1011
hindering 1011.1
hindsight 988.4
hinge
n joint 799.4
crisis 842.4
axle 914.5
v hook 799.8
depend 958.6
hint
n tinge 62.3
soupçon 248.4
remainder 256.1
warning 399.1
piece of advice 422.2
indication 517.3
clue 517.9
implication 519.2
gentle hint 551.4
admixture 796.7
suggestion 950.5
memory 988.6
v augur 133.12
promise 133.13
signify 517.17
imply 519.4
intimate 551.10
hinterland
n inland 207.3
setting 209.2
region 231.1
back country 233.2
adj inland 207.7
back 233.9
hip
n side 218.1
joint 799.4
adj fashionable 578.11
knowledgeable 927.17
hippie
n nonconformist 867.3
adj unconventional
867.6
hippo
heavyweight 257.12
behemoth 257.14
pachyderm 311.4
hippopotamus
behemoth 257.14
pachyderm 311.4
hire
n rental 615.6

hold
  n cellar 197.17
  storehouse 386.6
  custody 429.5
  stronghold 460.6
  possession 469.1
  purchase 474.2
  seizure 480.2
  control 612.2
  notation 709.12
  influence 893.1
  footing 900.5
  handle 900.11
  purchase 905.2
  v use 87.21
  extend 158.8
  refrain 329.3
  affirm 334.5
  store up 386.11
  restrain 428.7
  confine 429.12
  possess 469.4
  grip 474.6
  keep 474.7
  exist 760.8
  include 771.3
  cohere 802.6
  endure 826.6
  remain 852.5
  stabilize 854.7
  sustain 855.4
  cease 856.6
  support 900.21
  obsess 925.25
  judge 945.8
  conclude 945.10
  decide 945.11
  think 952.11
  be true 972.8
  engross 982.13
  suffice 990.4
hold a candle to
  942.7
hold a grudge 152.12
hold back
  suppress 106.8
  slow 175.9
  reserve 386.12
  not use 390.5
  restrain 428.7
  deny 442.4
  withhold 484.6
  restrain oneself
  668.6
  abstain 668.7
  delay 845.8
  hinder 1011.10
hold down
  suppress 428.8
  subjugate 432.8
holder container 195.1
  possessor 470.1
  recipient 479.3
hold fast
  remain firm 359.9
  stay with it 360.4
  restrain 428.7
  hold 474.6
  stick close 802.8
  stand fast 854.11
hold forth offer 439.4
  declaim 543.10

expound 568.16
hold in restrain 428.7
  retain 474.5
holding
  n possession 469.1
  estate 471.4
  retention 474.1
  share 738.3
  verdict 945.5
  adj addicted 87.24
  possessing 469.9
  retentive 474.8
  supporting 900.23
  obsessive 925.34
  engrossing 982.20
holdings
  supply 386.2
  property 471.1
  stock 738.2
  share 738.3
  collection 769.11
hold it! 856.13
hold off demur 325.4
  not use 390.5
  fend off 460.10
  postpone 845.9
  procrastinate 845.11
  repulse 907.3
hold office
  hold a post 609.42
  fill an office 724.14
  take one's turn 824.5
hold on
  v direct 161.5
  stay with it 360.4
  hold 474.6
  trade 737.23
  cohere 802.6
  endure 826.6
  wait 845.12
  continue 855.3
  inter cease! 856.13
hold out
  not weaken 15.10
  remain firm 359.9
  stay with it 360.4
  balk 361.7
  offer 439.4
  resist 453.2
  stand fast 453.4
  strike 727.10
  endure 826.6
  stand fast 854.11
holdover
  remainder 256.1
  officeholder 610.11
hold together
  cooperate 450.3
  agree 787.6
  join 799.11
  cohere 802.6
  be true 972.8
holdup slowing 175.4
  theft 482.3
  overcharge 632.5
  delay 845.2
  hindrance 1011.1
  time constants
  1040.11
hold up
  not weaken 15.10
  slow 175.9

buoy 298.8
  stay with it 360.4
  restrain 428.7
  help 449.12
  resist 453.2
  rob 482.14
  flaunt 501.17
  overprice 632.7
  delay 845.8
  postpone 845.9
  stand fast 854.11
  support 900.21
  elevate 911.5
  stand the test 941.10
  be true 972.8
  hinder 1011.10
hole
  n sty 80.11
  atmosphere 184.32
  compartment 197.2
  cellar 197.17
  crack 224.2
  hovel 228.11
  lair 228.26
  disapproved place
  228.28
  small space 258.3
  pit 275.2
  cavity 284.2
  cave 284.5
  opening 292.1
  perforation 292.3
  hiding place 346.4
  score 409.5
  sewer 654.7
  golf 751.1
  deficiency 794.2
  fault 1002.2
  impasse 1012.6
  v perforate 292.15
the hole 429.8
hole in one
  score 409.5
  round 751.3
hole-in-the-wall
  nook 197.3
  hut 228.9
  small space 258.3
holiday
  n vacation 20.3
  day off 20.4
  absence 222.4
  celebration 487.1
  interim 825.1
  pause 856.3
  v vacation 20.9
  adj vacational 20.10
holier-than-thou
  hypocritical 354.32
  sanctimonious 693.5
holistic whole 791.9
  universal 863.14
holler
  n cry 59.1
  complaint 115.5
  valley 237.7
  v cry 59.6
  complain 115.16
  object 333.5
hollow
  n compartment 197.2
  valley 237.7

pit 275.2
  cavity 284.2
  opening 292.1
  hollow out 284.13
  adj deep 54.10
  dull 117.6
  vacant 222.14
  concave 284.16
  insincere 354.31
  vain 391.13
  empty-headed 921.19
  sophistical 935.10
holly 44.4
holocaust
  torment 96.7
  slaughter 308.1
  butchery 308.3
  destruction 395.1
  oblation 696.7
the Holocaust 308.4
holograph
  n autograph 337.3
  handwriting 547.3
  writing 547.10
  document 549.5
  adj written 547.22
holy almighty 677.18
  sacred 685.7
  godly 692.9
holy orders
  the ministry 698.1
  calling 698.10
  major orders 699.4
  seven sacraments
  701.4
holy table 703.12
holy terror
  frightener 127.9
  brat 302.4
  ruffian 593.4
  violent person 671.10
homage
  respect 155.1
  obeisance 155.2
  obedience 326.1
  submission 433.1
  praise 509.5
  duty 641.1
  fidelity 644.7
  worship 696.1
home
  n home sweet home
  228.2
  habitat 228.18
  fatherland 232.2
  asylum 1008.4
  adj residential 228.32
  in safety 1006.6
home economics
  cooking 11.1
  domestic
  management 573.6
home free 1006.6
the home front 232.2
homeland 232.2
homeless
  n poor man 619.4
  adj unplaced 160.10
  forlorn 584.12
  destitute 619.9
  alone 871.8

the homeless
the underprivileged
606.4
the poor 619.3
unfortunate 1010.7
homely
comfortable 121.11
humble 137.10
homelike 228.33
common 497.14
plain 499.6
plain-speaking 535.3
informal 581.3
populational 606.8
simple 797.6
ugly 1014.6
homemade 891.18
homemaker 575.2
homeopathic 90.15
homeowner 227.7
home plate 745.1
homer
n mail carrier 353.6
score 409.5
game 745.3
v play 745.5
Homeric huge 257.20
poetic 720.15
home run score 409.5
game 745.3
homesick
wistful 100.23
melancholy 112.23
homespun
n plain speech 535.1
adj rough 288.6
natural 416.6
common 497.14
plain 499.6
plain-speaking 535.3
simple 797.6
made 891.18
homestead home 228.2
farm 1067.8
homesteader
settler 227.9
tenant 470.4
homestretch 819.3
homeward
adj arriving 186.9
adv clockwise 161.24
homework
lesson 568.7
task 724.2
homey
comfortable 121.11
homelike 228.33
informal 581.3
homicidal 308.23
homicide
manslaughter 308.2
killer 308.10
homily lecture 543.3
treatise 556.1
lesson 568.7
homing pigeon 353.6
hominid
n ancient 841.7
adj manlike 312.14
homoerotic 75.29
homogeneity
sameness 777.1

uniformity 780.1
simplicity 797.1
homogeneous
identical 777.7
uniform 780.5
similar 783.10
simple 797.6
homogenized 811.8
homonym word 526.1
the same 777.3
homophone word 526.1
the same 777.3
Homo sapiens 312.1
homosexual
n gay person 75.14
adj homoerotic 75.29
homosexuality
sexuality 75.2
sexual preference
75.10
honcho superior 249.4
chief 575.4
important person
996.11
hone 285.7
hone for 100.16
honest natural 499.7
upright 644.13
veracious 644.16
genuine 972.15
virtuous 653.6
honesty
probity 644.1
veracity 644.3
genuineness 972.7
honey
n sweets 10.38
sweetening 66.2
loved one 104.11
endearment term
562.6
adhesive 802.4
first-rate 998.7
beauty 1015.9
v sweeten 66.3
flatter 511.6
honeybee 311.33
honeycomb
n sweetening 66.2
indentation 284.6
porousness 292.8
v pervade 221.7
perforate 292.15
undermine 393.15
overthrow 395.20
honeydew 66.2
honeyed
sweet 66.4
pleasant 97.6
flattering 511.8
melodious 708.48
honeymoon
n wedding 563.3
v go on a honeymoon
563.16
honk
n blare 53.5
v blare 53.10
quack 60.5
honky-tonk 88.20
honor
n respect 155.1

real estate 471.6
praise 509.5
probity 644.1
token of esteem 646
great honor 646.1
title 648.1
esteem 662.3
prestige 662.4
chastity 664.1
attribution 887.1
notability 996.2
v respect 155.4
execute 437.9
celebrate 487.2
pay in full 624.13
recognize 646.8
confer honor upon
662.12
worship 696.10
honorable
venerable 155.12
honest 644.13
honorary 646.10
reputable 662.15
the Honorable 648.8
honorarium
gratuity 478.5
subsidy 478.8
recompense 624.3
honorary
honorific 646.10
titular 648.7
honored
respected 155.11
distinguished 646.9
reputable 662.15
esteemed 662.16
honorific
n name 527.3
title 648.1
adj respectful
155.8
nominal 527.15
honorary 646.10
titular 648.7
hood
n cover 295.2
mischief-maker 322.3
combatant 461.1
ruffian 593.4
bad person 660.6
violent person 671.10
v cloak 5.39
cover 295.19
top 295.21
hooded clothing 5.44
covered 295.31
hoodlum
mischief-maker 322.3
combatant 461.1
bandit 483.4
ruffian 593.4
violent person 671.10
hoodwink blind 30.7
blindfold 356.17
hooey humbug 354.14
bull 520.3
hoof
n foot 199.5
v dance 705.5
hoofed pedal 199.9
ungulate 311.44

hoofer pedestrian 178.6
dancer 705.3
entertainer 707.1
hoo-ha noise 53.4
bustle 330.4
quarrel 456.6
confusion 809.2
agitation 916.1
hook
n anchor 180.16
angle 278.2
curve 279.2
point of land 283.9
snare 356.13
lure 377.3
v angle 278.5
curve 279.6
trap 356.20
persuade 375.23
acquire 472.9
catch 480.17
rob 482.16
play 751.4
hitch 799.8
hook, line, and sinker
791.13
hookah 89.6
hooked addicted 87.24
angular 278.6
crooked 279.8
hooker ship 180.1
prostitute 665.16
hookup
affiliation 450.2
joining 799.1
combination 804.1
network 1033.8
hook up
cooperate 450.3
yoke 799.10
hook up with 804.4
hooky 222.4
hooligan
mischief-maker 322.3
combatant 461.1
vulgarian 497.6
ruffian 593.4
bad person 660.6
hoop circle 280.3
toy 743.16
basketball 747.1
hoopla
rejoicing 116.1
publicity 352.4
festivity 743.3
hooray
n cheer 116.2
v cheer 116.6
hoot
n cry 59.1
boo 508.3
v cry 59.6
coo 60.5
boo 508.10
a hoot nothing 761.3
trifle 997.5
hootenanny
musical occasion
708.32
thing 1050.5
hop
n opium 87.15

step 177.11
flight 184.9
leap 366.1
dance 705.2
v speed 174.9
way of walking 177.28
fly 184.36
leap 366.5
dance 705.5
hope
n desire 100.1
wish 100.11
aspiration 124
hopefulness 124.1
sanguine expectation
130.2
cardinal virtues 653.4
belief 952.1
possibility 965.1
recourse 1008.2
v be in hopes 124.7
expect 130.5
come 838.6
hoped-for
desired 100.29
expected 130.13
future 838.8
hopeful
n desirer 100.12
optimist 124.6
youngster 302.1
candidate 610.9
adj cheerful 109.11
hoping 124.11
expectant 130.11
probable 967.6
hopeless
apathetic 94.13
unhopeful 125.12
dying 307.33
unskillful 414.15
impossible 966.7
hopped-up
high 87.23
excited 105.20
impatient 135.6
increased 251.7
hop to it
v make haste 401.6
set to work 725.15
inter make haste!
401.17
horde
n the masses 606.2
throng 769.4
v come together
769.16
horizon vision 27.1
field of view 31.3
skyline 201.4
the distance 261.3
horizontal
n plane 201.3
adj level 201.7
straight 277.6
hormone 13.2
horn
n loudspeaker 50.8
noisemaker 53.6
mountain 237.6
projection 285.4
telephone 347.4

alarm 400.1
wind instrument
711.6
saddle parts 900.18
v gore 459.26
horned
crescent-shaped
279.11
pointed 285.9
hornet 311.33
hornet's nest
nest 228.25
danger 1005.1
trouble 1012.3
horn in 214.5
horns of a dilemma
n bewilderment 970.3
dilemma 1012.7
adv uncertainly
970.28
horny lustful 75.26
pointed 285.9
lascivious 665.29
hard 1044.10
horology 831.1
horoscope 1070.20
horrendous
horrid 98.19
terrible 127.30
horrible horrid 98.19
terrible 127.30
remarkable 247.11
bad 999.9
hideous 1014.11
horrid horrible 98.19
terrible 127.30
bad 999.9
hideous 1014.11
horrific horrid 98.19
terrible 127.30
horrified 127.26
horrify offend 98.11
terrify 127.17
horrifying horrid 98.19
terrible 127.30
horripilation
trepidation 127.5
roughness 288.2
cold 1022.2
horror
torment 96.7
hostility 99.2
fear 127.1
frighteningness 127.2
frightener 127.9
abomination 638.2
eyesore 1014.4
horror-stricken 127.26
hors d'oeuvre 10.9
horse
n symbol of strength
15.8
heroin 87.8
beast of burden 176.8
horseflesh 311.10
exerciser 725.7
jockey 757.2
trestle 900.16
v give a lift 911.7
horse around
misbehave 322.4
play 743.23

create disorder 809.11
be foolish 922.6
trifle 997.15
horseback
n ridge 237.5
adv on horseback
177.44
astride 900.25
horseback riding 177.6
horsehair
hair 3.2
string 711.20
horseman 178.8
horsemanship
riding 177.6
skill 413.1
animal husbandry
1068.1
**horse of a different
color** 779.3
horseplay
misbehavior 322.1
buffoonery 489.5
horsepower 18.4
horse race
contest 457.3
challenge 457.12
election 609.15
race 757.3
horse-race 457.19
horse racing
the sport of kings 757
the turf 757.1
horse sense 919.6
horseshoe 279.5
hortatory
persuasive 375.29
advisory 422.8
educational 568.18
horticultural
floral 310.35
olericultural 1067.21
horticulture
flower 310.22
gardening 1067.2
hosanna
n cheer 116.2
paean 696.3
inter hallelujah!
696.16
hose
n hosiery 5.28
tube 239.6
v deceive 356.19
moisten 1063.12
hosiery 5.28
hosing deception 356.9
wetting 1063.6
hospice inn 228.15
asylum 1008.4
hospitable
comforting 121.13
receptive 187.16
liberal 485.4
sociable 582.22
welcoming 585.11
cordial 587.16
hospital 91.21
hospitality
comfortableness 121.2
receptivity 187.9
housing 225.3

liberality 485.1
sociability 582.1
cordiality 585
hospitableness 585.1
congeniality 587.6
hospitalize 85.49
host
n army 461.23
receptionist 585.5
master of ceremonies
743.20
throng 769.4
group of animals
769.5
multitude 883.3
broadcaster 1033.23
v entertain 585.8
Host 701.7
hostage 438.2
hostel 228.15
hostess crew 185.4
attendant 577.5
waiter 577.7
host 585.5
hostile dark 38.9
unpleasant 98.17
oppositional 451.8
warlike 458.21
antagonistic 589.10
contrary 778.6
disagreeing 788.6
counteractive 899.8
adverse 1010.13
dislike 99.8
hostility darkness 38.2
bad feeling 93.7
unpleasantness 98.1
malice 99.2
contraposition 215.1
antagonism 451.2
contention 457.1
warlikeness 458.11
hate 589.3
contrariety 778.1
hot
v heat 1019.17
adj red 41.6
zestful 68.7
lustful 75.26
in heat 75.27
feverish 85.57
fervent 93.18
zealous 101.9
passionate 105.22
hot-tempered 110.25
angry 152.30
near 223.14
fugitive 368.16
stolen 482.23
distinguished 662.16
lascivious 665.29
fiery 671.22
syncopated 709.29
speculative 759.27
brand-new 840.10
on the right scent
940.10
excellent 998.13
torrid 1018.25
heated 1019.29
charged 1031.33
radioactive 1036.10

hot air boasting 502.2
  bull 520.3
  chatter 540.3
  bombast 545.2
  superheated air
    1018.9
hotbed birthplace 885.8
  productiveness 889.6
  nursery 1067.11
hot-blooded
  lustful 75.26
  zealous 101.9
  warm-blooded
    1018.29
hot dog
  n show-off 501.11
  v grandstand 413.20
  showboat 501.16
  inter oh boy ! 95.20
hotel 228.15
hotheaded
  passionate 105.29
  hot-tempered 110.25
  reckless 493.8
  fiery 671.22
hothouse 1067.11
hot line
  telephone call 347.13
  line 347.17
hot seat
  capital punishment
    604.7
  execution 605.5
  predicament 1012.5
hot spot
  entertainment 743.13
  danger 1005.1
  predicament 1012.5
hot spring
  health resort 91.23
  hot water 1018.10
hot tub bath 79.8
  fitness 84.1
hot under the collar
  heated 105.22
  angry 152.30
hot water
  predicament 1012.5
  boiling water 1018.10
hound
  n enthusiast 101.5
  beast 660.7
  v annoy 96.13
  make anxious 126.5
  follow 166.3
  pursue 382.8
  hunt 382.9
  persecute 389.7
hour period 823.1
  moment 823.2
  time of day 831.2
  the present 837.1
hourglass 260.1
hourglass figure 260.1
house
  n audience 48.6
  cabin 197.9
  dwelling 228.5
  structure 266.2
  council 423.1
  race 559.4
  family 559.5

lineage 560.4
  company 617.9
  cloister 703.6
  theater 704.14
  market 736.1
  workplace 739.1
  casino 759.19
  attender 917.2
  astrology 1070.20
  v domicile 225.10
  accommodate 385.10
houseboat 228.5
housebreak
  accustom 373.10
  domesticate 432.11
  train 568.13
housebreaker 483.3
housebreaking
  habituation 373.8
  burglary 482.5
  training 568.3
housebroken
  accustomed 373.16
  subdued 432.15
  meek 433.15
  mannerly 504.16
household
  n home 228.2
  family 559.5
  adj residential
    228.32
  simple 499.6
  usual 868.9
  well-known 927.27
household effects
  furniture 229.1
  property 471.1
householder
  homeowner 227.7
  proprietor 470.2
housekeeper
  steward 574.4
  major-domo 577.10
housekeeping
  domesticity 228.3
  domestic
    management 573.6
house of cards
  weakness 16.1
  danger 1005.1
  fragility 1048.2
housewares 735.4
housewarming 769.2
housewife 575.2
housing
  n hangar 184.24
  domiciliation 225.3
  abode 228.1
  quarters 228.4
  cover 295.2
  horsecloth 295.11
  radio 1033.3
  adj constructional
    891.15
hovel sty 80.11
  dump 228.11
hover
  fly 184.36
  take off 193.10
  levitate 298.9
  hesitate 362.7
  be imminent 839.2

Hovercraft
  hovercar 179.22
  flying platform 181.7
how 384.9
how come 887.8
how do you do? 585.15
how-do-you-do
  greeting 585.4
  predicament 1012.5
however
  notwithstanding
    338.8
  anyhow 384.10
howl
  n noise 53.3
  screech 58.4
  cry 59.1
  animal noise 60.1
  lament 115.3
  complaint 115.5
  objection 333.2
  v screech 58.8
  cry 59.6
  grunt 60.2
  wail 115.13
  complain 115.16
  sigh 318.21
  object 333.5
howler joke 489.6
  goof 974.6
howling
  n audio distortion
    50.13
  animal noise 60.1
  lamentation 115.1
  adj shrill 58.14
  yowling 60.6
  frenzied 105.25
  plaintive 115.19
  remarkable 247.11
hoyden
  n mannish female
    76.9
  schoolgirl 302.8
  adj mannish 76.13
hub convergence 169.1
  center 208.2
  axle 914.5
  fireplace 1019.11
hubbub noise 53.3
  outcry 59.4
  bustle 330.4
  turbulence 671.2
  commotion 809.4
  agitation 916.1
  argumentation 934.4
hubris
  presumptuousness
    141.2
  insolence 142.1
  rashness 493.1
  presumption 640.2
  confidence 969.5
hubristic lordly 141.11
  insolent 142.9
  rash 493.7
  presumptuous 640.11
  confident 969.21
  excessive 992.16
huckster
  n publicist 352.9
  vendor 730.5

v bargain 731.17
  vend 734.9
huddle
  n conference 541.6
  v stay near 223.12
  come together 769.16
hue
  n color 35.1
  color quality 35.6
  nature 766.4
  v color 35.13
hue and cry noise 53.3
  outcry 59.4
  publicity 352.4
  pursuit 382.1
  alarm 400.1
huff
  n dudgeon 152.7
  v intimidate 127.20
  provoke 152.24
  enlarge 259.4
  blow 318.20
huffing 2.30
huffy irascible 110.20
  provoked 152.27
hug
  n hold 474.2
  embrace 562.3
  welcome 585.2
  greeting 585.4
  v stay near 223.12
  hold 474.6
  harbor 474.7
  seize 480.14
  embrace 562.18
  welcome 585.9
  cohere 802.6
huge
  herculean 15.17
  large 247.7
  immense 257.20
hula hoop 743.16
hulk ship 180.1
  largeness 257.11
  wreck 393.8
  body 1050.3
hulking bulky 257.19
  bungling 414.20
  unwieldy 1012.19
hull
  n ship 180.1
  shell 295.16
  seed vessel 310.28
  v husk 6.9
hullabaloo noise 53.4
  outcry 59.4
  bustle 330.4
hullo! 585.15
hum
  n audio distortion
    50.13
  humming 52.7
  vocal music 708.13
  series 811.2
  v thrum 52.13
  stammer 525.8
  sing 708.38
  persist 780.3
human
  n person 312.5
  adj kind 143.13
  pitying 145.7

hominal 312.13
human behavior 321.3
human being 312.5
hum and haw
prevaricate 344.7
hesitate 362.7
stammer 525.8
humane kind 143.13
pitying 145.7
lenient 427.7
humanism
naturalistic
humanism 312.11
freethinking 695.7
scholarship 927.5
humanist
freethinker 695.13
scholar 928.3
humanitarian
n philanthropist 143.8
adj benevolent 143.15
humanity
kindness 143.1
pity 145.1
humankind 312.1
human nature 312.6
humanness 312.8
leniency 427.1
humankind
human race 312
mankind 312.1
human nature
humanity 312.6
humanness 312.8
human race 312.1
humble
v humiliate 137.4
conquer 412.10
subdue 432.9
demote 447.3
adj penitent 113.9
resigned 134.10
lowly 137.10
modest 139.9
inferior 250.6
meek 433.15
populational 606.8
unselfish 652.5
humbled
penitent 113.9
reduced 137.13
humiliated 137.14
conquered 412.17
subdued 432.15
humbug
n sham 354.3
quackery 354.7
humbuggery 354.14
hoax 356.7
impostor 357.6
nonsense 520.2
v deceive 356.14
humdinger 998.7
humdrum
n tedium 118.1
repetitiousness 848.4
adj tedious 118.9
prosaic 721.5
same 780.6
monotonous 848.15
humectant 1063.18
humid sultry 1018.28

moist 1063.15
humidifier 1063.3
humidify 1063.12
humidity
sultriness 1018.6
humidness 1063.2
humiliate
mortify 98.13
humble 137.4
offend 156.5
subdue 432.9
demote 447.3
disgrace 661.8
humiliating
mortifying 98.21
humiliative 137.15
insulting 156.8
disgraceful 661.11
humiliation
chagrin 96.4
mortification 98.6
embarrassment 137.2
indignity 156.2
snub 157.2
subdual 432.4
demotion 447.1
disgrace 661.5
humility
resignation 134.2
humbleness 137
selflessness 137.1
modesty 139.1
inferiority 250.1
meekness 433.5
unselfishness 652.1
hummock 237.4
hummocky 283.15
humongous
remarkable 247.10
huge 257.20
humor
n lymph 2.22
blood 2.23
personality tendency
92.11
caprice 364.1
pleasantry 489
wit 489.1
nature 766.4
disposition 977.3
mood 977.4
moisture 1063.1
v indulge 427.6
humorist wit 489.12
writer 547.15
author 718.4
humorless 112.21
humorous funny 488.4
witty 489.15
amusing 743.27
hump
n mountain 237.6
bulge 283.3
v speed 174.9
curve 279.6
be active 330.14
make haste 401.6
exert oneself 725.9
humpbacked
hunchbacked 265.13
bowed 279.10
hun 395.8

hunch
n feeling 93.1
premonition 133.1
bulge 283.3
forewarning 399.2
sense 933.3
guess 950.4
suggestion 950.5
v curve 279.6
crouch 912.8
hunchbacked 265.13
hunch over 912.8
hundred region 231.5
century 881.8
hung 202.9
hunger
n eating 8.1
craving 100.6
appetite 100.7
tendency 895.1
v eat 8.20
hunger for 100.19
hung jury 596.6
hungry
craving 100.24
hungering 100.25
hung up
distressed 96.22
late 845.16
obsessed 925.33
hunk strong man 15.6
hulk 15.7
real man 76.6
amount 244.2
lump 257.10
accumulation 769.9
piece 792.3
hunker down 912.8
hunky
strong 15.15
virile 76.12
comely 1015.18
hunky-dory 998.13
hunt
n hunting 382.2
search 937.15
v pursue 382.8
go hunting 382.9
persecute 389.7
seek 937.29
search 937.30
hunter
stalking-horse
311.13
sporting dog 311.18
pursuer 382.4
huntsman 382.5
shooter 903.8
seeker 937.18
hunt for 937.29
hunting
n pursuit 382.1
gunning 382.2
search 937.15
adj pursuing 382.11
hurdle
n leap 366.1
obstacle 1011.4
v leap 366.5
hurdy-gurdy 711.14
hurl
n throw 903.3

v place violently
159.13
throw 903.10
hurler
baseball team 745.2
thrower 903.7
hurling
field hockey 749.4
throwing 903.2
hurly-burly
excitement 105.4
agitation 916.1
hurrah
n cry 59.1
cheer 116.2
v cheer 116.6
inter bravo! 509.22
hurricane
outburst 105.9
windstorm 318.12
storm 671.4
hurried
hasty 401.9
rushed 401.11
reckless 493.8
hurry
n agitation 105.4
velocity 174.1
haste 401.1
v move 172.5
speed 174.8
hasten 401.4
make haste 401.5
hurry up
v accelerate 174.10
hasten 401.4
make haste 401.5
inter make haste!
401.16
hurt
n pain 26.1
discomfort 96.5
impairment 393.1
disadvantage 995.2
evil 999.3
v pain 26.7
anguish 26.8
afflict 96.17
suffer 96.19
offend 152.21
impair 393.9
injure 393.13
collide 901.13
work evil 999.6
adj pained 26.9
in pain 96.23
impaired 393.27
hurting
n pain 26.1
impairment 393.1
adj pained 26.9
painful 26.10
hurtle
speed 174.8
thrust 901.12
collide 901.13
hurt one's feelings
pain 96.17
offend 152.21
husband
n married man 563.7
master 575.1

I'll say 972.25
iambic 720.16
ibid 777.9
ice
  n glace 10.45
  amphetamines 87.3
  smoothness 287.3
  jewelry 498.5
  frozen water 1022.5
  coolant 1023.7
  fragility 1048.2
  v top 198.9
  kill 308.13
  play 749.7
  hail 1022.11
  refrigerate 1023.10
  freeze 1023.11
  adj frozen 1023.14
iceberg 1022.5
icebox 1023.4
ice-cold cold 1022.14
  frozen 1023.14
ice cream 10.45
ice cubes ice 1022.5
  coolant 1023.7
iced prearranged 964.8
  assured 969.20
  cooled 1023.13
ice hockey 749.1
ice pack ice 1022.5
  cooler 1023.3
ice-skate 177.35
ice skates 179.21
ichor humor 2.22
  blood 2.23
  pus 12.6
icicle 1022.5
icing sweets 10.38
  topping 198.3
  game 749.3
the icing on the cake
  407.3
icky nasty 64.7
  filthy 80.23
  bad 999.8
icon aspect 33.3
  image 349.5
  symbol 517.2
  sign 518.6
  picture 712.11
  copy 784.1
  substitute 861.2
iconoclasm 695.9
iconoclast
  destroyer 395.8
  irreligionist 695.10
iconography 349.1
iconology 517.2
icterus yellow skin 43.2
  symptom 85.9
ictus seizure 85.6
  accentuation 524.11
  accent 709.25
  meter 720.7
  spasm 916.6
icy unfeeling 94.9
  seasonal 313.9
  reticent 344.10
  aloof 583.6
  unfriendly 589.9
  cold 1022.14
  frozen 1023.14

id psyche 92.28
  instinct 933.2
ID 517.11
idea hint 248.4
  intention 380.1
  plan 381.1
  advice 422.1
  meaning 518.1
  reason 885.2
  thinking 930.1
  notion 931
  thought 931.1
  suggestion 950.5
  opinion 952.6
ideal
  n motive 375.1
  paragon 659.4
  beau ideal 785.4
  rule 868.4
  philosophy 931.2
  idealism 985.7
  pattern of perfection
    1001.4
  adj model 785.8
  normal 868.8
  ideational 931.9
  theoretical 950.13
  idealized 985.23
  perfect 1001.6
idealism
  aspiration 100.9
  magnanimity 652.2
  philosophy 931.2
  materialism 951.3
  idealization 985.7
  immaterialism 1051.3
idealist
  n visionary 985.13
  immaterialist 1051.4
  adj idealistic 1051.8
idealization
  spiritualization
    689.19
  illusoriness 975.2
  idealism 985.7
idealize
  spiritualize 689.20
  overestimate 948.2
  utopianize 985.16
ideate
  n philosophy 931.2
  v think 930.8
  imagine 985.14
idée fixe 925.13
identical
  identic 777.7
  similar 783.10
  equivalent 789.8
  two 872.6
identification
  sensitivity 24.3
  association 92.33
  sympathy 93.5
  indication 517.3
  identification mark
    517.11
  naming 527.2
  likening 777.2
  recognition 988.5
identify
  signify 517.17
  name 527.11

  relate 774.6
  make one 777.5
  detect 940.5
  recognize 988.12
  receive 1035.17
identify with
  respond 93.11
  get along 455.2
identity accord 455.1
  sameness 777.1
  similarity 783.1
  equality 789.1
  particularity 864.1
  oneness 871.1
ideogram
  representation 349.1
  symbol 517.2
  phonetic symbol
    546.2
ideographic
  n letter 546.1
  adj representational
    349.13
  indicative 517.23
  literal 546.8
  alphabetic 547.26
ideological
  ideational 931.9
  attitudinal 977.7
ideology
  system of ideas 931.8
  system of belief 952.3
  climate 977.5
ides of March 963.2
id est 341.18
idiocy
  mental deficiency
    921.9
  foolishness 922.1
idiom language 523.1
  dialect 523.7
  phrase 529.1
  diction 532.1
idiosyncrasy
  mannerism 500.2
  sign 517.1
  characteristic 864.4
  eccentricity 926.1
  disposition 977.3
idiosyncratic
  personal 312.15
  indicative 517.23
  differentiative 779.9
  characteristic 864.13
  eccentric 926.5
idiot cripple 85.44
  imbecile 923.8
  lunatic 925.15
idiot box 1034.11
idiotic
  mentally deficient
    921.22
  foolish 922.8
idle
  v stagnate 173.9
  go slow 175.6
  slow 175.9
  do nothing 329.2
  while away 486.5
  trifle 997.14
  adj motionless 173.13
  slow 175.10

  passive 329.6
  inactive 331.17
  fallow 331.18
  vain 391.13
  leisure 402.5
  baseless 935.13
  trivial 997.19
idle fancy 985.5
idle rich 331.11
idle talk chatter 540.3
  gossip 552.7
idol
  n favorite 104.16
  image 349.5
  hero 659.5
  celebrity 662.9
  god 678.2
  fetish 697.3
  ideal 785.4
  v idolatrize 697.5
idolater
  enthusiast 101.4
  pagan 688.7
  worshiper 696.9
  idolatress 697.4
idolatrize 697.5
idolatrous
  reverent 155.9
  uncritical 509.18
  pagan 688.11
  idolatric 697.7
idolatry love 104.1
  respect 155.1
  praise 509.5
  overpraise 511.3
  paganism 688.4
  worship 696.1
  idol worship 697
  idolatrousness 697.1
idolization love 104.1
  respect 155.1
  fetishization 697.2
idolize
  cherish 104.21
  respect 155.4
  praise 509.12
  overpraise 511.7
  worship 696.10
  idolatrize 697.5
idol worship 697.1
idyllic pacific 464.9
  poetic 720.15
if
  in the event that
    830.13
  supposing 950.19
  if and when 958.14
iffy doubtful 970.17
  chance 971.15
if only 958.14
if possible 965.11
ifs, ands, and buts
  421.3
if worse comes to
  worse 1010.17
igloo house 228.10
  arch 279.4
  snow 1022.8
igneous 1018.26
ignis fatuus
  illusion 975.1
  fire 1018.13

luminescence 1024.13
ignite flare up 152.19
set fire to 1019.22
ignition fire 1018.13
lighting 1019.4
rocket launching
1072.9
ignoble
offensive 98.18
low 497.15
disreputable 661.10
ignominious
wrong 638.3
disreputable 661.10
ignominy
abomination 638.2
infamy 661.4
ignoramus
novice 572.9
fool 923.1
know-nothing 929.8
ignorance
unaccustomedness
374.1
inexperience 414.2
unintelligence 921.1
unknowingness 929
ignorantness 929.1
ignorant
unaccustomed 374.4
inexperienced 414.17
unintelligent 921.13
nescient 929.12
ignore take 134.8
condone 148.4
slight 157.6
disobey 327.6
neglect 340.6
reject 372.2
extenuate 600.12
exclude 772.4
keep an open mind
978.7
be inattentive 983.2
ignored
unthanked 151.5
neglected 340.14
rejected 372.3
excluded 772.7
ileum 2.16
ilk nature 766.4
kind 808.3
ill
n evil 999.3
adj ailing 85.55
ominous 133.17
unkind 144.16
bad 999.7
adv unkindly 144.27
disadvantageously
995.9
badly 999.13
ill-advised
unpremeditated
365.11
botched 414.21
unwise 922.10
inexpedient 995.5
ill at ease 96.22
ill-behaved 505.5
ill-bred
ungenteel 505.6

unrefined 497.12
ill-bred fellow 497.6
ill-conceived 999.11
ill-considered
unpremeditated
365.11
botched 414.21
untimely 843.6
premature 844.8
unwise 922.10
inexpedient 995.5
ill-defined
inconspicuous 32.6
vague 970.19
illegal prohibited 444.7
wrong 638.3
unjust 650.9
unlawful 674.6
illegal drug 87.2
illegality
wrong 638.1
injustice 650.1
crime 674
unlawfulness 674.1
offense 674.4
illegible 522.19
illegible handwriting
547.6
illegitimate
n bastard 561.5
adj fake 354.25
illegal 674.6
spurious 674.7
ill-equipped
unfitted 406.9
ill-provided 991.12
ill-fated 133.17
ill-favored
evil-fashioned 999.11
unprepossessing
1014.7
ill-founded 935.13
ill-gotten
dishonest 645.16
evil-fashioned 999.11
ill health 85.3
ill humor
discontent 108.1
bad temper 110
bad humor 110.1
contentiousness
934.13
ill-humored
bad-tempered 110.18
argumentative 934.19
illiberal
n bigot 979.5
adj stingy 484.9
ungenerous 651.6
narrow-minded
979.10
illicit prohibited 444.7
freeloving 665.27
illegal 674.6
illicit business
fraud 356.8
illegality 674.1
illegitimate business
732
scam 732.1
ill-informed 929.12
illiteracy 929.5

illiterate
n ignoramus 929.8
adj unlearned 929.14
ill nature
ill humor 110.1
malevolence 144.4
ill-natured
ill-humored 110.18
malevolent 144.19
illness 85.1
ill off poor 619.7
ill-provided 991.12
unfortunate 1010.14
illogic 935.2
illogical
unreasonable 935.11
erroneous 974.16
ill repute 661.1
ill-suited
inappropriate 788.7
inexpedient 995.5
ill-timed
inappropriate 788.7
untimely 843.6
inexpedient 995.5
illuminant
n luminant 1024.20
light source 1025.1
adj luminous
1024.30
illuminate
n wise man 920.1
v color 35.13
explain 341.10
manifest 348.5
figure 498.9
illumine 1024.28
illuminated
drunk 88.33
luminous 1024.39
illuminating
explanatory 341.15
educational 568.18
illumining 1024.40
illumination
coloring 35.11
explanation 341.4
ornamentation
498.1
teaching 568.1
picture 712.11
cognizance 927.2
learning 927.4
light 1024.1
lighting 1024.19
ill-use
n mistreatment
389.2
v exploit 387.16
mistreat 389.5
illusion
deception 356.1
bewitchment 691.2
spirit 763.3
error 974.1
deluded belief 975
delusion 975.1
figment of the
imagination 985.5
illusionary
bewitching 691.11
illusory 975.8

illusive
deceptive 356.21
bewitching 691.11
sophistical 935.10
illusory 975.8
illusory
deceptive 356.21
bewitching 691.11
unreal 761.9
thin 763.6
erroneous 974.16
illusive 975.8
imaginary 985.19
illustrate
explain 341.10
image 349.11
evidence 956.8
cite 956.13
illustration
explanation 341.4
representation
349.1
picture 712.11
example 785.2
citation 956.5
illustrative
explanatory 341.15
representational
349.13
illustrator 716.2
illustrious 662.19
ill will
malevolence 144.4
animosity 589.4
ill wind
windstorm 318.12
bad influence 999.4
bad luck 1010.5
image
n appearance 33.2
aspect 33.3
apparition 33.5
engram 92.29
description 349.2
likeness 349.5
affectation 500.1
sign 517.1
figure of speech 536.1
picture 712.11
copy 784.1
idea 931.1
phantom 975.4
visualization 985.6
television reception
1034.5
v mirror 349.11
think of 930.17
visualize 985.15
imagery
representation 349.1
description 349.2
figure of speech 536.1
figment of the
imagination 985.5
visualization 985.6
imaginable
supposable 950.15
possible 965.6
fanciable 985.26
imaginary unreal 761.9
thin 763.6
farfetched 775.8

illusory 975.8
imaginational 985.19
numeric 1016.22
imagination
fancy 975.3
creative thought 985
imagining 985.1
figment of the
  imagination 985.5
imaginative
original 337.5
expressive 544.10
conceptual 985.18
imagine
v think of 930.17
suppose 950.10
think 952.11
fancy 985.14
inter fancy! 122.22
imagined
unreal 761.9
imaginary 985.19
imaging
catharsis 92.25
representation 349.1
visualization 985.6
imagining
imagination 985.1
figment of the
  imagination 985.5
imbalance
distortion 265.1
inequality 790.1
imbecile
n cripple 85.44
idiot 923.8
adj weak 16.12
mentally deficient
  921.22
foolish 922.8
imbecility
inability 19.2
mental deficiency
  921.9
foolishness 922.1
imbibe
drink 8.29
tipple 88.24
ingest 187.11
receive 187.13
absorb 570.7
imbricate
v overlie 295.30
adj overlying 295.36
imbroglio
quarrel 456.5
predicament 1012.4
imbrue
imbue 796.11
soak 1063.13
imbue
color 35.13
pervade 221.7
inspire 375.20
inculcate 568.12
imbrue 796.11
soak 1063.13
imbuement
permeation 221.3
inculcation 568.2
impregnation 796.2
soaking 1063.7

imitate
copy 336.5
adopt 621.4
resemble 783.7
repeat 848.7
imitation
n reproduction 78.1
copying 336
simulation 336.1
re-creation 336.3
impersonation 349.4
fake 354.13
burlesque 508.6
adoption 621.2
similarity 783.1
copy 784.1
repetition 848.1
substitute 861.2
duplication 873.1
adj mock 336.8
spurious 354.25
similar 783.10
substitute 861.8
immaculate
clean 79.25
honest 644.13
virtuous 653.7
spotless 657.7
chaste 664.4
perfect 1001.6
immanence
presence 221.1
intrinsicality 766.1
immanent
present 221.12
intrinsic 766.7
immaterial
unreal 761.9
unsubstantial 763.5
irrelevant 775.7
disembodied 987.8
insignificant 997.17
nonmaterial 1051.7
immateriality
invisibility 32.1
rarity 299.1
unsubstantiality
  763.1
unrelatedness 775.1
illusoriness 975.2
specter 987.1
unimportance 997.1
incorporealness 1051
immaterialness
  1051.1
incorporeal 1051.2
immaterialize
spiritualize 689.20
dematerialize 1051.6
immature
unadult 301.10
unripe 406.11
inexperienced 414.17
incomplete 794.4
new 840.7
puerile 921.24
half-learned 929.15
imperfect 1002.4
immaturity
youthfulness 301.3
undevelopment 406.4
inexperience 414.2

incompleteness
  794.1
newness 840.1
puerility 921.11
unwiseness 922.2
imperfection 1002.1
immeasurable
large 247.7
infinite 822.3
innumerable 883.10
immediacy
presence 221.1
nearness 223.1
instantaneousness
  829.1
promptness 844.3
urgent need 962.4
immediate
adj present 221.12
adjacent 223.16
nearest 223.19
hasty 401.9
continuous 811.8
instantaneous 829.4
the present 837.2
imminent 839.3
prompt 844.9
inter make haste!
  401.16
immemorial
perpetual 828.7
former 836.10
old 841.10
traditional 841.12
immense large 247.7
huge 257.20
infinite 822.3
superb 998.15
immensity
greatness 247.1
hugeness 257.7
infinity 822.1
immerge 367.7
immerse
submerge 367.7
baptize 701.16
engross 982.13
immersed
underwater 275.13
soaked 1063.17
immersion
submergence 367.2
baptism 701.6
engrossment 982.3
wetting 1063.6
immigrant
migrant 178.5
incomer 189.4
citizen 227.4
settler 227.9
newcomer 773.4
immigrate
migrate 177.22
in-migrate 189.11
immigration
migration 177.4
in-migration 189.3
imminence
expectation 130.1
approach 167.1
threat 514.1
the future 838.1

forthcomingness 839
impendence 839.1
imminent
expected 130.13
approaching 167.4
threatening 514.3
future 838.8
impending 839.3
immobile
motionless 173.13
passive 329.6
permanent 852.7
immovable 854.15
immobility
motionlessness 173.2
inaction 329.1
inactivity 331.1
permanence 852.1
immovability 854.3
immoderate
unrestrained 430.24
overpriced 632.12
intemperate 669.7
violent 671.16
excessive 992.16
immodest
conceited 140.11
unmodest 666.6
immolate 308.12
immolation
killing 308.1
oblation 696.7
immoral
dishonest 645.16
vice-prone 654.11
immorality 654.1
immortal
n celebrity 662.9
god 678.2
adj peerless 249.15
eminent 662.18
almighty 677.18
everlasting 828.9
indestructible 854.18
immortality
life 306.1
posthumous fame
  662.7
eternal life 828.3
indestructibility 854.5
immortalize
glorify 662.13
chronicle 719.5
perpetuate 828.5
immovable
unfeeling 94.9
firm 359.12
unyielding 361.9
unmovable 854.15
inflexible 1044.12
immune
resistant 83.14
exempt 430.30
safe 1006.4
immunity
resistance 83.4
immunization 91.15
pardon 148.2
freedom 430.8
exemption 601.2
privilege 642.2
safety 1006.1

immunization
immunity 83.4
immunization
therapy 91.15
immunize 91.28
immunology 91.15
immure
enclose 212.6
confine 429.12
imprison 429.14
immured
enclosed 212.10
jailed 429.21
immutable
persevering 360.8
unyielding 361.9
almighty 677.18
uniform 780.5
durable 826.10
permanent 852.7
unchangeable 854.17
inflexible 1044.12
imp
n brat 302.4
mischief-maker 322.3
fairy 678.8
pixie 680.7
member 792.4
v graft 191.6
impact
n power 18.1
meaning 518.1
concussion 671.8
force 886.2
striking force 901
collision 901.3
rocket launching
1072.9
v thrust in 191.7
cause 885.10
operate on 888.6
collide 901.13
impacted 854.16
impair
v subtract 255.9
damage 393.9
work evil 999.6
adj sole 871.9
numeric 1016.22
impaired
damaged 393.27
imperfect 1002.4
impaired hearing 49.1
impaired vision 28.1
impairment
reduction 255.2
damage 393
flaw 393.1
disintegration 805.1
disadvantage 995.2
imperfection 1002.1
impale
torture 96.18
perforate 292.15
stab 459.25
punish 604.16
stigmatize 661.9
impalpable
infinitesimal 258.14
unsubstantial 763.5
powdery 1049.11
immaterial 1051.7

impanel
record 549.15
select a jury 598.15
list 870.8
impanelment
registration 549.14
jury selection 598.4
impart transfer 176.10
communicate 343.7
disclose 351.4
give 478.12
say 524.23
impartable
transferable 176.18
communicable 343.11
giveable 478.23
impartial
neutral 467.7
impersonal 649.10
unprejudiced 978.12
impartiality
neutrality 467.1
detachment 649.4
moderation 670.1
unprejudicedness
978.5
imparting 343.2
impasse
obstruction 293.3
the same 789.3
corner 1012.6
impassion
excite 105.12
incite 375.17
impassioned
fervent 93.18
zealous 101.9
amorous 104.26
excited 105.20
vehement 544.13
impassive
unfeeling 94.9
inexcitable 106.10
quiescent 173.12
reticent 344.10
inexpressive 522.20
stable 854.12
incurious 981.3
impatience
eagerness 101.1
restlessness 135
anxiety 135.1
impulsiveness 365.2
impatient
eager 101.8
anxious 135.6
impulsive 365.9
impeach
censure 510.13
arraign 598.14
accuse 599.7
impeachable
blameworthy 510.25
guilty 656.3
impeachment
deposal 447.2
censure 510.3
arraignment 598.3
accusation 599.1
impeccable
spotless 657.7
accurate 972.16

perfect 1001.6
impecunious 619.7
impedance 1031.12
impede
slow 175.9
delay 845.8
hinder 1011.10
hamper 1011.11
impediment
obstruction 293.3
hindrance 1011.1
embarrassment
1011.6
impedimenta
freight 176.6
equipment 385.4
luggage 471.3
impediment 1011.6
impel
set in motion 172.6
motivate 375.12
compel 424.4
give an impetus
901.11
push 903.9
obsess 925.25
impelling
moving 172.7
motivating 375.25
impellent 901.23
obsessive 925.34
impend
be as expected 130.10
overhang 202.7
be imminent 839.2
impending
overhanging 202.11
imminent 839.3
impenetrable
impregnable 15.19
impervious 293.13
luxuriant 310.40
unintelligible 522.13
inaccesible 966.9
dense 1043.12
impenitent 114.5
imperative
n rule 419.2
command 420.1
mood 530.11
duty 641.1
urgent need 962.4
adj authoritative
417.15
imperious 417.16
mandatory 420.12
commanding 420.13
compulsory 424.10
binding 424.11
vigorous 544.11
obligatory 641.15
necessary 962.12
urgent 996.22
imperceptible
invisible 32.5
infinitesimal 258.14
imperceptive
insensible 25.6
undiscerning 921.14
imperfect
n tense 530.12
adj inadequate 250.7

impaired 393.27
incomplete 794.4
insufficient 991.9
not perfect 1002.4
imperfection
inadequacy 250.3
vice 654.2
incompleteness 794.1
shortcoming 910.1
want 991.4
defectiveness 1002
imperfectness 1002.1
fault 1002.2
imperial
n beard 3.8
volume 554.4
adj imperious 417.16
sovereign 417.17
imperialism
sovereignty 417.8
foreign policy 609.5
government 612.8
imperialist 611.9
imperil 1005.6
imperiled 1005.13
imperious
lordly 141.11
imperial 417.16
sovereign 417.17
commanding 420.13
compulsory 424.10
obligatory 641.15
urgent 996.22
imperishable
immortal 828.9
indestructible 854.18
impermanence
transience 827.1
changeableness 853.1
impermanent
transient 827.7
changeable 853.6
impermeable
impervious 293.13
dense 1043.12
impersonal
reticent 344.10
formal 580.7
impartial 649.10
extrinsic 767.3
indistinguishable
944.6
unprejudiced 978.12
impersonate
mimic 336.6
image 349.11
personate 349.12
pose as 354.21
enact 704.30
impersonation
imitation 336.1
personation 349.4
acting 704.8
impersonator
imitator 336.4
impostor 357.6
masquerader 357.7
entertainer 707.1
impersuadable 894.4
impertinence
impudence 142.2
meddling 214.2

defiance 454.1
unrelatedness 775.1
impertinent
impudent 142.10
meddlesome 214.9
defiant 454.7
irrelevant 775.7
imperturbable
inexcitable 106.10
stable 854.12
impervious
resistant 15.20
callous 94.12
impenetrable 293.13
uninfluenceable
  894.4
inaccessible 966.9
impetration
request 440.1
entreaty 440.2
prayer 696.4
impetuous
energetic 17.13
passionate 105.29
impatient 135.6
impulsive 365.9
precipitate 401.10
reckless 493.8
transient 827.7
sudden 829.5
inconstant 853.7
impetus
animation 17.4
acceleration 174.4
impulse 901.1
impiety
irreverence 694
impiousness 694.1
sacrilege 694.2
ungodliness 695.3
impinge
intrude 214.5
contact 223.10
collide 901.13
impingement
intrusion 214.1
contact 223.5
impact 901.3
impious
irreverent 694.6
ungodly 695.17
impish
mischievous 322.6
puckish 680.18
implacable
unyielding 361.9
revengeful 507.7
implant graft 191.6
transplant 191.8
inculcate 568.12
fix 854.9
plant 1067.18
implantation
insertion 191.1
inculcation 568.2
fixity 854.2
implanted
confirmed 373.19
intrinsic 766.7
established 854.13
implausible
unbelievable 954.10

improbable 968.3
implement
n instrument 384.4
agent 576.3
tool 1039.1
v carry out 328.7
bring about 407.5
execute 437.9
implementation
performance 328.2
accomplishment
  407.1
impliable
unyielding 361.9
firm 425.7
implicate
imply 519.4
incriminate 599.10
entail 771.4
complicate 798.3
involve 897.2
implicated
participating 476.8
implied 519.7
accused 599.10
guilty 656.3
related 774.9
complex 798.4
involved 897.4
implication
connotation 519.2
hint 551.4
accusation 599.1
incrimination 599.2
guilt 656.1
entailment 771.2
involvement 897.1
meaning 518.1
implicative
indicative 517.23
suggestive 519.6
implicit
unspoken 51.11
tacit 519.8
intrinsic 766.7
evidential 956.16
unqualified 959.2
implied
meant 518.11
implicated 519.7
tacit 519.8
implode 260.10
implore
admonish 422.6
entreat 440.11
pray 696.12
imploring
n entreaty 440.2
adj entreating 440.17
worshipful 696.15
implosion 260.4
imply
promise 133.13
mean 518.8
implicate 519.4
hint 551.10
accuse 599.7
entail 771.4
evidence 956.8
impolite
unrefined 497.12
discourteous 505.4

impolitic
botched 414.21
unwise 922.10
inexpedient 995.5
imponderable
infinitesimal 258.14
unweighable 298.18
unsubstantial 763.5
immaterial 1051.7
import
n transferal 176.1
bringing in 187.7
entrance 189.1
meaning 518.1
implication 519.2
importance 996.1
v transfer 176.10
bring in 187.14
mean 518.8
imply 519.4
matter 996.12
importance
prestige 417.4
distinction 662.5
influence 893.1
significance 996
repute 996.1
important
authoritative 417.15
prominent 662.17
influential 893.13
major 996.17
important person
chief 575.3
celebrity 662.9
personage 996.8
importation
transferal 176.1
bringing in 187.7
entrance 189.1
importunate
annoying 98.22
strong-willed 359.15
demanding 421.9
teasing 440.18
necessary 962.12
importune
v motivate 375.14
make advances 439.7
urge 440.12
adj annoying 98.22
importunity
insistence 421.4
importunateness
  440.3
impose
intrude 214.5
prescribe 420.9
demand 421.5
oblige 424.5
compose 548.16
charge 630.12
impose on 643.4
minister 701.15
imposed
mandatory 420.12
inflicted 643.8
impose upon
presume on 640.7
impose 643.4
take advantage of
  643.7

intrude 214.5
exploit 387.16
inconvenience 995.4
imposing
dignified 136.12
corpulent 257.18
grandiose 501.21
weighty 996.20
imposition
intrusion 214.1
fraud 356.8
demand 421.1
composition 548.2
tax 630.9
presumption 640.2
inconsiderateness 643
infliction 643.1
injustice 650.4
impediment 1011.6
impossibility
hopelessness 125.1
unusualness 869.2
the realm of the
  impossible 966
inconceivability 966.1
no chance 971.10
impossible
n impossibility 966.1
adj unacceptable
  108.10
out of the question
  125.14
fantastic 869.12
not possible 966.7
improbable 971.18
numeric 1016.22
phrs I refuse 442.7
impost
demand 421.1
tax 630.9
impostor
imitator 336.4
fake 354.13
ringer 357.6
imposture
imitation 336.1
sham 354.3
quackery 354.7
fraud 356.8
impotence
weakness 16.1
powerlessness 19
feebleness 19.1
sexuality 75.2
sexlessness 75.9
futility 391.2
laxness 426.1
unproductiveness
  890.1
lack of influence 894.1
impotent
n weakling 19.6
adj weak 16.12
powerless 19.13
unsexual 75.28
unproductive 890.4
uninfluential 894.3
lax 426.4
useless 391.9
impound
enclose 212.5
confine 429.12

attach 480.20
impoverish
 consume 388.3
 strip 480.24
 reduce 619.6
 bankrupt 625.8
impoverished
 used up 388.5
 indigent 619.8
 meager 991.10
 ill-provided 991.12
impractical
 theoretical 950.13
 impracticable 966.8
 visionary 985.24
 inexpedient 995.5
 unwieldy 1012.19
impracticality
 impracticability 966.2
 idealism 985.7
 unwieldiness 1012.9
imprecation
 entreaty 440.2
 curse 513.1
imprecise lax 426.4
 ungrammatic 531.4
 uncertain 970.16
 vague 970.19
 inaccurate 974.17
 imperfect 1002.4
imprecision
 unmeticulousness
  340.4
 laxness 426.1
 vagueness 970.4
 inaccuracy 974.2
impregnable
 impenetrable 15.19
 indestructible 854.18
impregnate
 reproduce 78.10
 inculcate 568.12
 imbue 796.11
 fertilize 889.8
 soak 1063.13
impregnation
 reproduction 78.3
 inculcation 568.2
 imbuement 796.2
 fertilization 889.3
 soaking 1063.7
impresario
 director 574.1
 theater man 704.23
impress
 n indentation 284.6
 character 517.7
 etching 548.3
 print 713.5
 reprint 784.5
 characteristic 864.4
 impact 886.2
 v affect 93.15
 stamp 93.16
 indent 284.14
 attract 377.6
 avail oneself of 387.14
 attach 480.20
 abduct 482.20
 mark 517.19
 print 548.14
 inculcate 568.12

enlist 615.17
 be somebody 662.10
 fix 854.9
 make an impression
  930.19
 fix in the mind 988.18
impressed
 affected 93.23
 engraved 713.11
 established 854.13
impression aspect 33.3
 feeling 93.1
 form 262.1
 concavity 284.1
 indentation 284.6
 imitation 336.1
 description 349.2
 character 517.7
 etching 548.3
 edition 554.5
 inculcation 568.2
 print 713.5
 reprint 784.5
 characteristic 864.4
 impact 886.2
 idea 931.1
 hunch 933.3
 suggestion 950.5
 opinion 952.6
impressionable
 sensible 24.11
 sensitive 93.20
 teachable 570.18
 influenceable 893.15
 foolable 922.12
 pliant 1045.9
impressive
 sensible 24.11
 exciting 105.30
 grandiose 501.21
 vigorous 544.11
 convincing 952.26
imprimatur
 ratification 332.4
 permit 443.6
imprint
 n indentation 284.6
 character 517.7
 label 517.13
 etching 548.3
 makeup 554.12
 print 713.5
 impact 886.2
 v indent 284.14
 mark 517.19
 print 548.14
 fix 854.9
 fix in the mind 988.18
imprinted
 engraved 713.11
 established 854.13
imprison enclose 212.5
 incarcerate 429.14
imprisoned
 enclosed 212.10
 jailed 429.21
imprisonment
 enclosure 212.1
 jailing 429.3
 punishment 604.2
improbability
 inexpectation 131.1

oddity 869.5
 prediction 961.1
 unlikelihood 968.1
 small chance 971.9
improbable
 unexpected 131.10
 farfetched 775.8
 predictable 961.13
 unlikely 968.3
 impossible 971.18
improbity
 falseheartedness
  354.4
 dishonesty 645.1
impromptu
 n improvisation 365.5
 extempore 708.27
 adj extemporaneous
  365.12
 unprepared 406.8
 adv extemporaneously
  365.15
improper
 misbehaving 322.5
 vulgar 497.10
 ungrammatic 531.4
 inelegant 534.2
 wrong 638.3
 inapt 640.10
 wicked 654.16
 indecent 666.5
 inappropriate 788.7
 untimely 843.6
 inexpedient 995.5
 bad 999.7
impropriety
 misbehavior 322.1
 vulgarity 497.1
 barbarism 526.6
 inelegance 534.1
 wrong 638.1
 undueness 640.1
 injustice 650.1
 misdeed 655.2
 indecency 666.1
 unfitness 788.3
 untimeliness 843.1
improve
 take advantage of
  387.15
 grow better 392.7
 recuperate 396.19
 train 568.13
 be changed 851.6
 change 851.7
 perfect 1001.5
improved
 bettered 392.13
 changed 851.10
improvement
 progression 162.1
 betterment 392.1
 restoration 396.1
 training 568.3
 change 851.1
 new start 857.2
improvidence
 thriftlessness 406.2
 rashness 493.1
improvident
 prodigal 406.15
 rash 493.7

improvisation
 extemporization 365.5
 unpreparedness 406.1
 impromptu 708.27
 production 891.1
 expedient 994.2
improvise
 extemporize 365.8
 be unprepared 406.6
 produce 891.8
 originate 891.12
improvised
 extemporaneous
  365.12
 unprepared 406.8
 makeshift 994.7
imprudence
 rashness 493.1
 unwiseness 922.2
 foolish act 922.4
 indiscrimination
  944.1
imprudent rash 493.7
 unwise 922.10
 undiscriminating
  944.5
impudence
 impertinence 142.2
 disrespect 156.1
 defiance 454.1
 rashness 493.1
impudent
 impertinent 142.10
 disrespectful 156.7
 defiant 454.7
 rash 493.7
impugn deny 335.4
 censure 510.13
 incriminate 599.10
impugned
 accused 599.15
 disproved 957.7
impulse
 manpower 18.4
 sudden thought 365
 natural impulse 365.1
 urge 375.6
 prematurity 844.2
 impulsion 901.1
 instinct 933.2
 involuntariness 962.5
 driving force 901
impulsive fickle 364.6
 impetuous 365.9
 motivating 375.25
 precipitate 401.10
 nonuniform 781.3
 transient 827.7
 sudden 829.5
 premature 844.8
 inconstant 853.7
 impelling 901.23
 instinctive 933.6
 involuntary 962.14
impunity 601.2
impure
 unclean 80.20
 inelegant 534.2
 unvirtuous 654.12
 unchaste 665.23
 obscene 666.9
 imperfect 1002.4

impurity
uncleanness 80.1
inelegance 534.1
vice 654.1
unchastity 665.1
intruder 773.2
imperfection 1002.1
imputable
blameworthy 510.25
attributable 887.6
imputation
criticism 510.4
aspersion 512.4
accusation 599.1
stigma 661.6
attribution 887.1
impute accuse 599.7
attribute 887.3
in
n entrée 187.3
entrance 189.5
adj entering 189.12
participating 476.8
on good terms 587.18
modern 840.13
in safety 1006.6
adv inward 189.13
inside 207.10
by authority of 417.20
prep at 159.27
into 189.14
interior 207.13
in a bad way ill 85.55
worn-out 393.36
in danger 1005.13
inability
incapability 19.2
unskillfulness 414.1
in a bind
late 845.16
in trouble 1012.22
inaccessible
out-of-the-way 261.9
reticent 344.10
aloof 583.6
inaccordance
difference 779.1
disagreement 788.1
nonconformity 867.1
inaccordant
different 779.7
disagreeing 788.6
inaccuracy
unmeticulousness
340.4
misrepresentation
350.1
misjudgment 947.1
vagueness 970.4
inaccurateness 974.2
badness 999.1
imperfection 1002.1
inaccurate
unmeticulous 340.13
vague 970.19
incorrect 974.17
bad 999.7
imperfect 1002.4
in a class by itself
peerless 249.15
other 779.8
first-rate 998.17

inaction
motionlessness 173.2
passivity 329
passiveness 329.1
inactivity 331.1
in action acting 328.10
operating 888.11
inactivate 19.9
inactive inert 173.14
passive 329.6
unactive 331.17
leisurely 402.6
inactivity rest 20.1
motionlessness 173.2
passivity 329.1
inaction 331.1
leisureliness 402.2
in addition 253.11
inadequacy
inability 19.2
unsatisfactoriness
108.2
mediocrity 250.3
unskillfulness 414.1
inequality 790.1
incompleteness 794.1
shortcoming 910.1
insufficiency 991.1
imperfection 1002.1
fault 1002.2
inadequate
ineffective 19.15
unsatisfactory 108.9
mediocre 250.7
incompetent 414.19
unequal 790.4
incomplete 794.4
short of 910.5
insufficient 991.9
imperfect 1002.4
inadmissible
unacceptable 108.10
exclusive 772.9
irrelevant 775.7
inappropriate 788.7
in advance
ahead 165.4
before 216.12
on loan 620.7
early 844.11
inadvertence
neglect 340.1
slip 974.4
inattention 983.1
inadvertent
negligent 340.10
unthinking 365.10
unpremeditated
365.11
inattentive 983.6
inadvisable
unwise 922.10
inexpedient 995.5
in a fog
concealed 346.11
muddled 984.13
in agreement
adj unanimous
332.15
cooperative 450.5
agreeing 787.9
adv jointly 799.18

prep together with
787.12
conformable to 866.9
in a jam
bewildered 970.24
unfortunate 1010.14
in trouble 1012.22
in a jiffy
in short order 174.19
hastily 401.12
quickly 829.7
inalienable
intrinsic 766.7
inseparable 799.15
in all conscience
positively 247.19
rightly 637.4
candidly 644.23
in justice 649.12
reasonably 934.24
in all fairness 649.12
in all likelihood 967.8
in all respects
wholly 791.13
throughout 793.17
exactly 972.21
in all seriousness
resolutely 359.17
candidly 644.23
inalterable
persevering 360.8
permanent 852.7
**in a manner of
speaking**
limited 248.10
figuratively 536.4
so to speak 783.19
in a mess
adj confused 809.16
in trouble 1012.22
adv in disorder 809.17
inamorato 104.13
inane
ineffective 19.15
insipid 65.2
dull 117.6
vacant 222.14
vain 391.13
meaningless 520.6
nonexistent 761.8
thin 763.6
empty-headed 921.19
foolish 922.8
ignorant 929.12
thoughtless 932.4
trivial 997.19
inanimate
n gender 530.10
adj dead 307.30
languid 331.20
inanimated 1053.5
inanity
ineffectiveness 19.3
insipidness 65.1
dullness 117.1
void 222.3
futility 391.2
meaninglessness
520.1
nonexistence 761.1
empty-headedness
921.6

foolishness 922.1
ignorance 929.1
thoughtlessness 932.1
triviality 997.3
in anticipation
adj expectant 130.11
in readiness 405.21
adv early 844.11
in a nutshell
small 258.16
shortly 268.12
concisely 537.8
in brief 557.7
in any event
anyhow 384.10
notwithstanding
338.8
inappetence
apathy 94.4
undesirousness 102.3
inapplicable
unserviceable 391.14
irrelevant 775.7
inappropriate 788.7
inapposite
irrelevant 775.7
inappropriate 788.7
inappreciable
infinitesimal 258.14
insignificant 997.17
inapprehensible 522.13
inappropriate
vulgar 497.10
wrong 638.3
improper 640.10
indecent 666.5
irrelevant 775.7
inapt 788.7
untimely 843.6
inexpedient 995.5
inapt
unskillful 414.15
inappropriate 788.7
inexpedient 995.5
inaptitude
unskillfulness 414.1
unfitness 788.3
inexpedience 995.1
in arrears
adj due 623.10
defaulting 625.10
incomplete 794.4
adv behind 910.6
inarticulate
mute 51.12
shy 139.12
unintelligible 522.13
indistinct 525.12
inartificial
natural 406.13
artless 416.6
plain 499.7
genuine 972.15
inartistic 1014.10
in a rut
adj habituated 373.18
adv uniformly 780.7
inasmuch as 887.10
in a stew
adj in a dither 105.21
anxious 126.7
impatient 135.6

in a temper 152.31
bewildered 970.24
confused 984.12
adv excitedly 105.33
in a sweat
adj sweaty 12.22
in a dither 105.21
impatient 135.6
confused 984.12
adv excitedly 105.33
in a tizzy
adj in a dither 105.21
confused 984.12
adv excitedly 105.33
inattention
unconcern 102.2
neglect 340.1
nonobservance 435.1
unwiseness 922.2
incuriosity 981.1
inattentiveness 983.1
distraction 984.1
inattentive
unconcerned 102.7
negligent 340.10
unskillful 414.15
nonobservant 435.5
incurious 981.3
unmindful 983.6
inaudible 51.10
inaugural
n speech 543.2
ceremony 580.4
adj preceding 813.4
prior 815.4
beginning 817.15
inaugurate insert 191.4
install 615.12
institute 817.11
innovate 840.5
cause 885.10
establish 891.10
inauguration
location 159.7
admission 187.2
ceremony 580.4
installation 615.3
installment 817.5
establishment 891.4
inauspicious
ominous 133.17
untimely 843.6
bad 999.7
unfortunate 1010.14
inauthentic
illogical 935.11
unauthoritative 974.19
in a way
to a degree 245.7
limited 248.10
so to speak 783.19
in awe
adj wondering 122.9
reverent 155.9
adv in wonder 122.18
in fear 127.33
in bad taste
vulgar 497.10
inelegant 534.2
in behalf of
adv by proxy 576.17

prep for 449.26
instead of 861.12
in black and white 547.22
inborn 766.8
inbound arriving 186.9
entering 189.12
inbred bred 78.17
innate 766.8
inbreed 78.8
in brief
in short 537.8
in summary 557.7
in cahoots
adj leagued 804.6
adv in cooperation 450.7
incalculable
infinite 822.3
innumerable 883.10
unknown 929.17
uncertain 970.16
incalescence 1018.1
incandesce
be hot 1018.22
shine 1024.23
incandescence
glow 1018.12
shine 1024.2
incandescent
burning 1018.27
luminous 1024.30
incantation
conjuration 690.4
spell 691.4
incapable
n cripple 85.44
incompetent 414.7
adj unable 19.14
unfitted 406.9
incompetent 414.19
incapacitate
disable 19.9
afflict 85.49
cripple 393.14
incapacitated
weakened 16.18
disabled 19.16
crippled 393.30
incapacity
infirmity 16.3
inability 19.2
unskillfulness 414.1
unproductiveness 890.1
unintelligence 921.1
incarcerate
enclose 212.5
imprison 429.14
incarcerated
enclosed 212.10
jailed 429.21
incarceration
enclosure 212.1
imprisonment 429.3
punishment 604.2
incarnate
v manifest 348.5
image 349.11
embody 762.5
compose 795.3
materialize 1050.9

adj divine 677.17
embodied 1050.11
incarnation
appearance 33.1
manifestation 348.1
impersonation 349.4
embodiment 762.4
essence 766.2
composition 795.1
materialization 1050.8
in case 830.13
incautious rash 493.7
unalert 983.8
incendiarism 1019.7
incendiary
n instigator 375.11
violent person 671.9
arsonist 1019.8
adj incitive 375.28
inflammatory 1019.27
incense
n fragrance 70.1
joss stick 70.4
suavity 504.5
flattery 511.1
oblation 696.7
v perfume 70.8
excite 105.12
provoke 152.24
incite 375.17
incensory 70.6
incentive
n inducement 375.7
impulse 901.1
adj incitive 375.28
inception origin 817.4
source 885.5
establishment 891.4
incertitude 970.1
incessancy
continuity 811.1
perpetuity 828.1
constancy 846.2
incessant
continuous 811.8
perpetual 828.7
constant 846.5
recurrent 848.13
continuing 855.7
incest perversion 75.11
illicit sex 665.7
inch go slow 175.6
creep 177.26
in character
to be expected 130.14
characteristic 864.13
in charge
adj under arrest 429.22
supervising 573.13
governing 612.18
adv in authority 417.21
inchmeal
by degrees 245.6
piece by piece 792.9
inchoate formless 263.4
unordered 809.12
vague 970.19
inchoative
n aspect 530.13

adj beginning 817.15
in chorus
adj harmonious 708.49
adv unanimously 332.17
cooperatively 450.6
in step 787.11
simultaneously 835.7
incidence event 830.1
frequency 846.1
incident
plot 722.4
circumstance 765.1
event 830.2
incidental
n ornament 709.18
particular 765.3
nonessential 767.2
adj circumstantial 765.7
unessential 767.4
irrelevant 775.7
happening 830.9
occasional 842.11
infrequent 847.3
chance 971.15
incinerate
strike dead 308.17
cremate 309.20
destroy 395.10
burn up 1019.25
incineration
cremation 309.2
discard 390.3
burning 1019.5
incinerator 1019.13
incipience 817.4
incipient 817.15
incise cleave 224.4
notch 289.4
furrow 290.3
open 292.11
injure 393.13
record 549.15
engrave 713.9
sever 801.11
incised notched 289.5
furrowed 290.4
engraved 713.11
incision trauma 85.37
crack 224.2
notch 289.1
furrow 290.1
engraving 713.2
incisive energetic 17.13
acrimonious 17.14
caustic 144.23
vigorous 544.11
sagacious 919.16
incisor 2.8
incite
excite 105.12
instigate 375.17
admonish 422.6
impel 901.11
heat 1019.18
incitement
excitation 105.11
incitation 375.4
incentive 375.7
impulse 901.1

incivility
unrefinement 497.3
discourtesy 505.1
inclemency
harshness 144.9
pitilessness 146.1
violence 671.1
cold 1022.1
inclement harsh 144.24
pitiless 146.3
cold 1022.14
inclination
penchant 100.3
obeisance 155.2
direction 161.1
descent 194.1
leaning 204.2
incline 204.4
will 323.1
preference 371.5
aptitude 413.5
partiality 650.3
tendency 895.1
disposition 977.3
prejudice 979.3
incline
n stairs 193.3
inclination 204.4
slope 237.2
v take direction 161.7
lean 204.10
gravitate 297.15
be willing 324.3
induce 375.22
influence 893.7
tend 895.3
inclined
inclining 204.15
willing 324.5
moved 375.30
disposed 977.8
inclining
inclined 204.15
tending 895.4
in clover
adj pleased 95.14
prosperous 1009.12
adv in comfort 121.15
include
internalize 207.5
enclose 212.5
comprise 771.3
put together 799.5
combine 804.3
included
comprised 771.5
involved 897.4
including
adj inclusive 771.6
composed of 795.4
prep with 253.12
inclusion
surrounding 209.5
enclosure 212.1
affiliation 450.2
incorporation 771
comprisal 771.1
combination 804.1
involvement 897.1
inclusive
including 771.6
whole 791.9

joint 799.12
incognito
n privacy 345.2
cover 356.11
masquerader 357.7
anonymity 528.1
adj private 345.13
disguised 346.13
anonymous 528.3
incognizance 929.3
incoherence
dislocation 160.1
unintelligibility 522.1
inconsistency 788.2
separation 801.1
noncohesion 803.1
disintegration 805.1
disorder 809.1
discontinuity 812.1
delirium 925.8
vagueness 970.4
incoherent
unintelligible 522.13
inconsistent 788.8
separate 801.20
uncohesive 803.4
unordered 809.12
discontinuous 812.4
delirious 925.31
vague 970.19
in cold blood
unfeelingly 94.14
heartlessly 144.34
intentionally 380.10
incombustible 1021.9
income entrance 189.1
gain 472.3
pay 624.4
receipts 627.1
incoming
n entrance 189.1
adj arriving 186.9
entering 189.12
incommensurable
unrelated 775.6
uncomparable 786.6
inconsistent 788.8
unlike 942.9
incommensurate
unsatisfactory 108.9
uncomparable 786.6
inconsistent 788.8
incommodious
narrow 270.14
inconvenient 995.7
incommunicable
122.13
incommunicado
346.11
incommutable 854.17
incomparable
peerless 249.15
unrelated 775.6
uncomparable 786.6
incommensurable
942.9
incompatible
unsociable 583.5
unfriendly 589.9
different 779.7
disagreeing 788.6
inconsistent 788.8

incompetence
inability 19.2
inadequacy 250.3
unpreparedness 406.1
unskillfulness 414.1
insufficiency 991.1
incompetent
n impotent 19.6
incapable 414.7
adj unable 19.14
inadequate 250.7
unfitted 406.9
incapable 414.19
insufficient 991.9
incomplete
partial 792.7
uncompleted 794.4
insufficient 991.9
imperfect 1002.4
in compliance with
adv obediently 326.6
prep conformable to
866.9
incomprehensible
wonderful 122.10
unintelligible 522.13
infinite 822.3
fantastic 869.12
incomprehension
unperceptiveness
921.2
incognizance 929.3
incompressible
dense 1043.12
rigid 1044.11
inconceivable
wonderful 122.10
fantastic 869.12
unbelievable 954.10
impossible 966.7
in concert
adj cooperative 450.5
in accord 455.3
harmonious 708.49
adv unanimously
332.17
in step 787.11
concurrently 898.5
inconclusive
illogical 935.11
unsound 935.12
unproved 957.8
in condition
healthy 83.8
hale 83.12
out of order 764.7
in order 806.7
in conformity
adj obedient 326.3
adv in step 787.11
conformably 866.7
incongruity
humorousness 488.1
difference 779.1
inconsistency 788.2
nonconformity 867.1
illogicalness 935.2
inexpedience 995.1
incongruous
off-color 35.20
humorous 488.4
different 779.7

inconsistent 788.8
illogical 935.11
inexpedient 995.5
in conjunction with
additionally 253.12
with 768.12
inconsequence
unrelatedness 775.1
unimportance 997.1
inconsequent
irrelevant 775.7
inconsistent 788.8
illogical 935.11
inconsequential
insignificant 248.6
illogical 935.11
unimportant 997.17
inconsiderable
insignificant 248.6
unimportant 997.17
inconsiderate
unthoughtful 144.18
careless 340.11
unthinking 365.10
ill-bred 505.6
unwise 922.10
inconsistency
contrariety 778.1
difference 779.1
nonuniformity 781.1
incongruity 788.2
noncohesion 803.1
inconstancy 853.2
nonconformity 867.1
illogicalness
935.2
inconsistent
contrary 778.6
different 779.7
nonuniform 781.3
incongruous 788.8
incoherent 803.4
inconstant 853.7
illogical 935.11
inconsolable
sorrowful 112.26
disconsolate 112.28
inconsonant
different 779.7
inconsistent 788.8
inconspicuous 32.6
inconstancy
irresolution 362.1
fickleness 364.3
infidelity 645.5
nonuniformity 781.1
irregularity 850.1
instability 853.2
inconstant
fickle 364.6
nonobservant 435.5
unfaithful 645.20
nonuniform 781.3
transient 827.7
irregular 850.3
changeable 853.7
incontestable
impregnable 15.19
obvious 969.15
incontinence
greed 100.8
unrestraint 430.3

prodigality 486.1
uncontinence 665.2
intemperance 669.1
excess 992.1

incontinent
unrestrained 430.24
prodigal 486.8
uncontinent 665.24
intemperate 669.7
excessive 992.16

incontrovertible
evidential 956.16
obvious 969.15

inconvenience
n imposition 643.1
untimeliness 843.1
inexpedience 995.1
discommodity 995.3
impediment 1011.6
trouble 1012.3
unwieldiness 1012.9
v presume on 640.7
put to inconvenience
995.4
trouble 1012.13

inconvenient
untimely 843.6
incommodious 995.7
unwieldy 1012.19

inconvertible
unpayable 625.13
unchangeable 854.17

inconvincible 955.4

incorporate
include 771.3
compose 795.3
combine 804.3
materialize 1050.9

incorporated
associated 617.16
joined 799.13
combined 804.5
embodied 1050.11

incorporation
affiliation 450.2
inclusion 771.1
composition 795.1
combination 804.1
materialization
1050.8

incorporeal
n specter 987.1
incorporeity 1051.2
adj unsubstantial
763.5
spectral 987.7
immaterial 1051.7

incorrect
ungrammatic 531.4
inelegant 534.2
wrong 638.3
inaccurate 974.17

incorrigible
past hope 125.15
ungovernable 361.12
confirmed 373.19
irreclaimable 654.18

incorrupt
unsinful 653.8
innocent 657.6

incorruptible
trustworthy 644.19

immortal 828.9
indestructible
854.18

incrassate
v thicken 269.5
congeal 1043.10
emulsify 1060.10
adj distended 259.13
thickened 1043.14

increase
n aggravation 119.1
ascent 193.1
gain 251.1
addition 253.1
adjunct 254.1
expansion 259.1
improvement 392.1
multiplication 882.4
elevation 911.1
v develop 14.2
aggravate 119.2
quantify 244.4
graduate 245.4
enlarge 251.4
increase 251.6
add to 253.5
expand 259.4
develop 259.5
grow 259.7
multiply 882.6

increased
aggravated 119.4
heightened 251.7
expanded 259.10
multiple 882.8

incredible
wonderful 122.10
remarkable 247.10
fantastic 869.12
absurd 922.11
unbelievable 954.10
improbable 968.3

incredulity
agnosticism 695.6
unbelief 954.1
ungullibility 955
incredulousness 955.1

incredulous
agnostic 695.20
unbelieving 954.8
uncredulous 955.4

increment
increase 251.1
adjunct 254.1

incriminate 599.10

incrimination 599.2

incrustation
covering 295.1
crust 295.14

incubate 78.12

incubation 78.5

incubator 885.8

incubus
frightener 127.9
burden 297.7
demon 680.6
dream 985.9

inculcate
indoctrinate 568.12
fix in the mind 988.18

inculcated 373.19

inculcation 568.2

inculpable 657.8

inculpate 599.10

inculpated
accused 599.15
guilty 656.3

incumbency
burden 297.7
responsibility 641.2
benefice 698.9
position 724.5

incumbent
n inhabitant 227.2
tenant 470.4
officeholder 610.11
benefice-holder 699.7
adj overhanging
202.11
overlying 295.36
onerous 297.17

incur 896.4

incurable
n sick person 85.42
adj past hope 125.15

incuriosity
unconcern 102.2
uninquisitiveness 981
incuriousness 981.1
inattention 983.1

incurious
unconcerned 102.7
uninquisitive 981.3
inattentive 983.6

incursion influx 189.2
intrusion 214.1
raid 459.4
overstepping 909.3

incurve curve 279.6
be concave 284.12

incurved
curved 279.7
concave 284.16

indebted grateful 150.5
obliged 641.16
in debt 623.8
insolvent 729.18
liable 896.5

indecency
sexual desire 75.5
vulgarity 497.1
unchastity 665.1
immodesty 666
indelicacy 666.1

indecent vulgar 497.10
unchaste 665.23
indelicate 666.5

indecipherable 522.19

indecision
irresolution 362.1
uncertainty 970.1

indecisive
wishy-washy 16.17
formless 263.4
irresolute 362.9
inconstant 853.7
unproved 957.8
uncertain 970.16
vague 970.19

indecorous
vulgar 497.10
inelegant 534.2
wrong 638.3
indecent 666.5

indecorum
vulgarity 497.1
wrong 638.1
indecency 666.1

indeed
adv positively 247.19
chiefly 249.17
certainly 969.23
truly 972.18
inter astonishment
122.19
yes! 332.18

indefatigable
industrious 330.22
persevering 360.8
continuing 855.7

indefeasible
unchangeable 854.17
inevitable 962.15

indefensible
unacceptable 108.10
unjustifiable 650.12

indefinable
indescribable 122.13
inexplicable 522.18
vague 970.19

indefinite
inconspicuous 32.6
formless 263.4
general 863.11
indistinguishable
944.6
vague 970.19

indeliberate 365.11

indelible
deep-dyed 35.17
deep-felt 93.24
indestructible 854.18
unforgettable 988.26

indelicacy
vulgarity 497.1
indecency 666.1

in demand
desired 100.29
salable 734.14

indemnification
compensation 338.1
reparation 481.2
recompense 624.3
atonement 658.1

indemnify
compensate 338.4
make restitution
481.5
requite 506.5
pay 624.10

indemnity
pardon 148.2
compensation 338.1
security 438.1
exemption 601.2
recompense 624.3
atonement 658.1

indemonstrable 970.16

indent
n indentation 284.6
summons 420.5
demand 421.1
request 440.1
appropriation 480.4
print 517.7
v dent 284.14

individualism
egotism 140.3
independence 430.5
capitalism 611.8
selfishness 651.1
particularity 864.1
characteristic 864.4
disposition 977.3
individualist
n egotist 140.5
free agent 430.12
self-seeker 651.3
misfit 788.4
adj particular 864.12
individualistic
independent 430.22
capitalist 611.23
selfish 651.5
nonconformist 788.9
particular 864.12
individuality
person 312.5
particularity 864.1
oneness 871.1
individual 871.4
individualize
differentiate 779.6
particularize 864.9
indivisible
simple 797.6
inseparable 799.15
indestructible 854.18
one 871.7
nondivisible 1043.13
indocile
unwilling 325.5
insubordinate 327.9
ungovernable 361.12
indocility refusal 325.1
disobedience 327.1
ungovernability 361.4
indoctrinate
inculcate 568.12
propagandize 569.4
brainwash 857.15
indoctrinated 226.6
indoctrination
inculcation 568.2
propaganda 569.2
reindoctrination 857.5
indolence
inertness 173.4
slowness 175.1
inaction 329.1
laziness 331.5
indolent
n lazybones 331.7
adj slow 175.10
lazy 331.19
indomitable
impregnable 15.19
persevering 360.8
ungovernable 361.12
indoor
adj interior 207.6
adv indoors 207.12
indraft
influx 189.2
wind 318.1
in dribs and drabs
piece by piece 792.9
sparsely 884.8

indubitable
manifest 348.8
obvious 969.15
induce elicit 192.14
prompt 375.22
admonish 422.6
lead 885.11
influence 893.7
conclude 945.10
inducement reason 375
enlistment 375.3
incentive 375.7
allurement 377.1
gratuity 478.5
induct insert 191.4
install 615.12
enlist 615.17
inaugurate 817.11
inductee recruit 461.18
novice 572.9
inductile 1044.12
induction
admission 187.2
installation 615.3
enlistment 615.7
holy orders 698.10
inauguration 817.5
basics 817.6
reasoning 934.3
conclusion 945.4
electrostatic
induction 1031.14
in due course
in time 838.11
opportunely 842.12
soon 844.16
indulge humor 427.6
suffer 443.10
indulge oneself 669.4
indulged forgiven 148.7
pampered 427.9
indulgence
patience 134.1
considerateness 143.3
forgiveness 148.1
humoring 427.3
sufferance 443.2
privilege 642.2
intemperance 669.1
tolerance 978.4
indulgent patient 134.9
considerate 143.16
compliant 427.8
nonrestrictive 430.25
permissive 443.14
intemperate 669.7
tolerant 978.11
indulge oneself
reject authority 418.4
please oneself 651.4
indulge 669.4
indurate
v callous 94.6
harden 1044.7
adj hard 1044.13
indurated callous 94.12
heartless 144.25
obdurate 654.17
hardened 1044.13
induration
callousness 94.3
impenitence 114.2

heartlessness 144.10
pitilessness 146.1
hardness 1044.1
hardening 1044.5
industrial
occupational 724.16
commercial 731.21
productional 891.14
industrialist
businessman 730.1
producer 891.7
industrialization
commercialization
731.13
industrial production
891.3
industrialize
put on a business
basis 731.19
perform 891.11
industrious
assiduous 330.22
painstaking 339.11
persevering 360.8
industry
industriousness 330.6
painstakingness 339.2
perseverance 360.1
company 617.9
work 725.4
commerce 731.1
industrial production
891.3
indwell
be present 221.6
inhere 766.6
indwelling
n intrinsicality 766.1
adj present 221.12
intrinsic 766.7
inebriant
n spirits 88.13
adj intoxicating
88.36
inebriate
n drinker 88.11
v intoxicate 88.22
adj intoxicated 88.31
inebriation 88.1
inedible 64.8
ineducable 921.15
ineffable
indescribable 122.13
sacred 685.7
extraordinary 869.14
in effect
adj in use 387.25
existent 760.13
adv really 760.16
ineffective
unable 19.14
ineffectual 19.15
useless 391.9
unsuccessful 410.18
incompetent 414.19
uninfluential 894.3
ineffectual
ineffective 19.15
useless 391.9
unsuccessful 410.18
incompetent 414.19
unproductive 890.4

uninfluential 894.3
inefficacious
ineffective 19.15
unsuccessful 410.18
uninfluential 894.3
inefficacy
ineffectiveness 19.3
futility 391.2
lack of influence 894.1
inefficiency
inability 19.2
unskillfulness 414.1
inefficient unable 19.14
unskillful 414.15
inelastic
unyielding 361.9
rigid 1044.11
inflexible 1044.12
inelegance
clumsiness 414.3
vulgarity 497.1
unwieldiness 534
inelegancy 534.1
indecency 666.1
ugliness 1014.1
inelegant
bungling 414.20
vulgar 497.10
clumsy 534.2
indecent 666.5
ugly 1014.6
ineluctable
inevitable 962.15
certain 969.13
inenarrable
indescribable 122.13
sacred 685.7
inept unable 19.14
unskillful 414.15
inappropriate 788.7
unintelligent 921.13
foolish 922.8
inexpedient 995.5
ineptitude
inability 19.2
unintelligence 921.1
foolishness 922.1
inexpedience 995.1
inequality
roughness 288.1
class 607.1
injustice 650.1
partiality 650.3
difference 779.1
nonuniformity 781.1
disagreement 788.1
disparity 790
unevenness 790.1
inequity injustice 650.1
inequality 790.1
ineradicable 854.18
inerasable 854.18
inerrant
infallible 969.19
exact 972.17
inert inactive 173.14
passive 329.6
languid 331.20
unchangeable 854.17
inanimate 1053.5
inertia inertness 173.4
slowness 175.1

inaction 329.1
inactivity 331.1
indolence 331.5
immobility 854.3
inerudite 929.14
inescapable
real 760.15
inevitable 962.15
inessential
n nonessential 767.2
adj circumstantial
765.7
accessory 767.4
insignificant 997.17
inestimable 632.10
inevasible 962.15
in every respect
throughout 793.17
exactly 972.21
inevitable
obligatory 424.11
unavoidable 962.15
destined 963.9
certain 969.13
inexact
unmeticulous 340.13
vague 970.19
inaccurate 974.17
imperfect 1002.4
in excess
adj superfluous 992.17
adv intemperately
669.10
to extremes 992.23
inexcitable
unfeeling 94.9
unconcerned 102.7
imperturbable 106.10
dull 117.6
unastonished 123.3
unnervous 129.2
inexcusable 650.12
inexhaustible
infinite 822.3
innumerable 883.10
plentiful 990.7
inexorable
pitiless 146.3
unyielding 361.9
firm 425.7
inevitable 962.15
inexpectation
hopelessness 125.1
unexpectedness 131
nonexpectation 131.1
suddenness 829.2
inexpedience
mismanagement
414.6
untimeliness 843.1
unwiseness 922.2
inadvisablity 995
undesirability 995.1
badness 999.1
inexpedient
untimely 843.6
unwise 922.10
undesirable 995.5
bad 999.7
inexpensive 633.7
inexperience
immaturity 301.3

unaccustomedness
374.1
unfamiliarity 414.2
ignorance 929.1
inexperienced
immature 301.10
unaccustomed 374.4
unpracticed 414.17
foolable 922.12
ignorant 929.12
inexpiable 650.12
inexplicable
unexplainable 522.18
purposeless 971.16
inexplicit
ambiguous 539.4
uncertain 970.16
inexpressible
indescribable 122.13
sacred 685.7
inexpressive 522.20
inexpugnable
impregnable 15.19
indestructible 854.18
inextensible 1044.12
inextinguishable
854.18
in extremis
dying 307.33
in danger 1005.13
straitened 1012.26
inextricable
inexplicable 522.18
irreducible 798.5
stuck 854.16
in fact really 760.16
truly 972.18
infallibility
certainty 969.1
perfection 1001.1
infallible
inerrable 969.19
exact 972.17
perfect 1001.6
infamous wrong 638.3
knavish 645.17
wicked 654.16
disreputable 661.10
terrible 999.9
infamy
abomination 638.2
iniquity 654.3
infamousness 661.4
infancy
inability 19.2
immaturity 301.3
babyhood 301.5
origin 817.4
infant
n youngster 302.1
baby 302.9
simple soul 416.3
schoolchild 572.3
innocent 657.4
beginner 817.2
adj infantile 301.12
incomplete 794.4
beginning 817.15
infantile
infant 301.12
beginning 817.15
puerile 921.24

infantilism
mental deficiency
921.9
puerility 921.11
infantryman
pedestrian 178.6
foot soldier 461.9
infarction 293.3
infatuate
n enthusiast 101.4
lover 104.12
fanatic 925.18
v enamor 104.23
fascinate 377.7
stultify 922.7
obsess 925.25
adj enamored 104.28
infatuated
overzealous 101.12
enamored 104.28
foolish 922.8
obsessed 925.33
credulous 953.8
infatuation liking 100.2
overzealousness 101.3
infatuatedness 104.4
stultification 922.5
mania 925.12
credulity 953.1
in favor of
adj approving 509.17
prep for 449.26
approving of 509.21
infect defile 80.17
disease 85.50
inspire 375.20
corrupt 393.12
work evil 999.6
radioactivate 1036.9
infected unclean 80.20
diseased 85.59
radioactive 1036.10
infection
defilement 80.4
contagion 85.4
infectious disease
85.13
inspiration 375.9
corruption 393.2
evil 999.3
infectious
poisonous 82.7
contagious 85.61
infectious disease 85.13
infecund
unproductive 890.4
unimaginative 986.5
infelicitous
ungrammatic 531.4
inelegant 534.2
inappropriate 788.7
untimely 843.6
inexpedient 995.5
infelicity
wretchedness 96.6
unhappiness 112.2
solecism 531.2
inelegance 534.1
unfitness 788.3
untimeliness 843.1
inexpedience 995.1
infer imply 519.4

reason 934.15
conclude 945.10
suppose 950.10
inference
implication 519.2
reasoning 934.3
conclusion 945.4
supposition 950.3
inferential
suggestive 519.6
dialectic 934.22
inferior
n underling 250.2
subordinate 432.5
retainer 577.1
adj unable 19.14
subordinate 250.6
lower 274.8
subject 432.13
short of 910.5
unimportant 997.16
insignificant 997.17
bad 999.7
poor 1004.9
inferiority
inability 19.2
subordinacy 250.1
subservience 432.2
abnormality 869.1
shortcoming 910.1
unimportance 997.1
badness 999.1
inferiorness 1004.3
inferiority complex
complex 92.22
self-effacement 139.2
infernal cruel 144.26
diabolic 654.13
hellish 682.8
execrable 999.10
inferno hell 682.1
hot place 1018.11
inferred implied 519.7
supposed 950.14
infertile
unproductive 890.4
unimaginative 986.5
infertility
unproductiveness
890.1
unimaginativeness
986.1
infest 909.6
infestation 909.2
infidel
n gentile 688.6
unbeliever 695.11
adj infidelic 688.10
unbelieving 695.19
infidelity
love affair 104.6
unfaithfulness 645.5
infidelism 688.3
atheism 695.5
unbelief 954.1
infield playground
743.11
baseball 745.1
track 755.1
horse racing 757.1
infighting
dissension 456.3

contention 457.1
boxing 457.9
infiltrate absorb 187.13
filter in 189.10
intrude 214.5
launch an attack
459.17
imbue 796.11
soak 1063.13
infiltration
sorption 187.6
entrance 189.1
intrusion 214.1
attack 459.1
imbuement 796.2
soaking 1063.7
infiltrator 214.3
infinite
spacious 158.10
omnipresent 221.13
large 247.7
huge 257.20
almighty 677.18
boundless 822.3
perpetual 828.7
innumerable 883.10
numeric 1016.22
infinitesimal 258.14
infinity
omnipresence 221.2
greatness 247.1
distance 261.1
length 267.1
limitlessness 822
infiniteness 822.1
perpetuity 828.1
large number 1016.5
infirm
unsound 16.15
unhealthy 85.53
stricken in years
303.18
weak-willed 362.12
unvirtuous 654.12
fragile 763.7
inconstant 853.7
feebleminded 921.21
unreliable 970.20
infirmity
unsoundness 16.3
disease 85.1
unhealthiness 85.3
old age 303.5
weak will 362.4
vice 654.2
feeblemindedness
921.8
unreliability 970.6
fault 1002.2
infix
n interjection 213.2
added to writing
254.2
morphology 526.3
v implant 191.8
add 253.4
inculcate 568.12
fix 854.9
fix in the mind 988.18
infixed
confirmed 373.19
intrinsic 766.7

established 854.13
inflame energize 17.10
pain 26.7
make red 41.4
excite 105.12
provoke 152.24
incite 375.17
heat 1019.18
ignite 1019.22
inflamed sore 26.11
red 41.6
feverish 85.57
diseased 85.59
excited 105.20
fiery 671.22
burning 1018.27
inflammable
n fuel 1020.1
adj excitable 105.28
flammable 1019.28
inflammation
soreness 26.4
symptom 85.9
inflammatory disease
85.10
excitation 105.11
incitement 375.4
inflammatory
exciting 105.30
incitive 375.28
inflammative 1019.27
inflate puff up 140.7
increase 251.4
enlarge 259.4
exaggerate 355.3
talk big 545.6
heat the economy
632.9
overextend 992.13
inflated
increased 251.7
distended 259.13
exaggerated 355.4
pompous 501.22
swollen 502.12
bombastic 545.9
inflation increase 251.1
distension 259.2
exaggeration 355.1
pompousness 501.7
style 532.2
grandiloquence 545.1
price index 630.4
high price 632.3
business cycle 731.9
overextension 992.7
inflationary
expansive 259.9
overpriced 632.12
inflect curve 279.6
modulate 524.29
grammaticize 530.16
inflection angle 278.2
bend 279.3
intonation 524.7
morphology 526.3
inflexible firm 359.12
unyielding 361.9
strict 425.7
immovable 854.15
uninfluenceable 894.4
inevitable 962.15

intractable 1044.12
inflict do 328.6
wreak 643.5
infliction affliction 96.8
punishment 604.1
imposition 643.1
bane 1000.1
in flight
adj fugitive 368.16
adv on the wing
184.51
inflorescence 310.24
inflorescent 310.35
inflow influx 189.2
flow 238.4
wind 318.1
influence
n power 18.1
supremacy 249.3
motivation 375.2
machination 415.4
prestige 417.4
effectiveness 893
influentiality 893.1
good influence 893.6
v motivate 375.22
cause 885.10
induce 885.11
determine 885.12
operate on 888.6
make oneself felt
893.7
prejudice 979.9
influence peddler
Machiavellian 415.8
wire-puller 609.30
politician 610.5
influence 893.6
influential
authoritative 417.15
powerful 893.13
influx inflow 189.2
intrusion 214.1
in focus 31.7
in force powerful 18.12
in use 387.25
existent 760.13
operating 888.11
inform
v pervade 221.7
betray 351.6
inspire 375.20
tell 551.8
report 552.11
teach 568.10
adj formless 263.4
informality
unceremoniousness
581
informalness 581.1
informant
informer 551.5
examinee 937.18
witness 956.6
information
communication 343.1
facts 551
info 551.1
news 552.1
teaching 568.1
arraignment 598.3
accusation 599.1

knowledge 927.1
data 1041.15
information theory
communications
343.5
electronic
communications
347.1
data storage 551.7
autonetics 1040.2
informative
informing 551.18
educational 568.18
informed
prepared 405.16
clued-in 551.17
knowing 927.15
cognizant of 927.16
enlightened 927.18
up on 927.19
informer
traitor 357.10
informant 551.5
betrayer 551.6
accuser 599.5
witness 956.6
inform on
disclose 351.6
inform 551.12
accuse 599.7
betray 645.14
infra 274.10
infraction
disobedience 327.1
violation 435.2
wrong 638.1
lawbreaking 674.3
foul 746.3
basketball game 747.3
game 749.3
hockey game 749.6
overstepping 909.3
infrangible
firm 15.18
indivisible 1043.13
unbreakable 1047.5
infrared 41.6
infrastructure
inferior 250.2
understructure 266.3
directorate 574.11
support 900.1
foundation 900.6
frame 900.10
infrequency
seldomness 847
rarity 847.1
fewness 884.1
infrequent
rare 847.2
sparse 884.5
infringe
intrude 214.5
violate 435.4
adopt 621.4
usurp 640.8
break the law 674.5
overstep 909.9
infringement
intrusion 214.1
disobedience 327.1
impairment 393.1

violation 435.2
adoption 621.2
usurpation 640.3
lawbreaking 674.3
overstepping 909.3
in front
adj front 216.10
adv ahead 165.4
before 216.12
prep facing 215.7
in full at length 538.16
fully 765.13
completely 793.14
in full bloom 303.13
in full swing
adj unweakened 15.21
astir 330.19
thriving 1009.13
adv actively 330.25
in fun
mischievously 322.7
in sport 489.19
for amusement 743.31
infundibular
conical 282.12
concave 284.16
infuriate
v excite 105.12
enrage 152.25
antagonize 589.7
adj infuriated 152.32
turbulent 671.18
infuriated 152.32
infuse insert 191.3
extraction 192.16
inspire 375.20
inculcate 568.12
imbue 796.11
liquefy 1062.5
soak 1063.13
infusion
insertion 191.1
extract 192.7
distillation 192.8
inspiration 375.9
inculcation 568.2
baptism 701.6
imbuement 796.2
admixture 796.7
liquefaction 1062.1
solution 1062.3
soaking 1063.7
in general 863.17
ingenious
skillful 413.22
cunning 415.12
imaginative 985.18
ingenue
simple soul 416.3
role 704.10
script 706.2
actor 707.2
ingenuity
skill 413.1
invention 985.3
ingenuous
immature 301.10
artless 416.5
candid 644.17
ignorant 929.12
gullible 953.9
ingest devour 8.22

eat 187.11
consume 388.3
absorb 570.7
ingesta 10.1
ingestion
body function 2.15
digestion 7.8
eating 8.1
reception 187.4
consumption 388.1
absorption 570.2
ingle home 228.2
fire 1018.13
fireplace 1019.11
inglenook home 228.2
recess 284.7
fireplace 1019.11
ingleside home 228.2
fireplace 1019.11
inglorious
humble 137.10
disreputable 661.10
unrenowned 661.14
ingoing
n entrance 189.1
adj introverted 92.39
entering 189.12
in good shape
healthy 83.8
in order 806.7
ingot
precious metals
728.20
cast 1056.5
ingrain color 35.13
fix 854.9
ingrained
deep-dyed 35.17
confirmed 373.19
intrinsic 766.7
established 854.13
ingrate 151.2
ingratiate oneself
insinuate oneself
138.10
influence 893.7
gain influence 893.12
ingratiating
obsequious 138.14
suave 504.18
ingratitude
unthankfulness 151
ungratefulness 151.1
ingredient
particular 765.3
part 792.1
component 795.2
ingress
entrance 189.1
inlet 189.5
channel 239.1
ingroup clique 617.6
influence 893.6
ingrown 854.13
inhabit settle 159.17
occupy 225.7
people 225.9
exist in 760.11
inhabitant
dweller 227
population 227.1
inhabiter 227.2

inhalant medicine 86.4
drug 87.2
inhalation
breathing 2.19
drawing in 187.5
inhale smell 69.8
smoke 89.14
draw in 187.12
in hand unused 390.12
undertaken 404.7
in preparation 405.22
possessed 469.8
under control 612.20
restrained 670.11
orderly 806.6
happening 830.9
operating 888.11
in production 891.21
inharmonious
off-color 35.20
dissonant 61.4
disaccordant 456.15
different 779.7
disagreeing 788.6
in harmony
in accord 455.3
agreeing 787.9
jointly 799.18
in heat 75.27
inherence
presence 221.1
intrinsicality 766.1
inherent present 221.12
intrinsic 766.7
instinctive 933.6
inherit be heir to 479.7
inhere 766.6
succeed 814.2
inheritable
heritable 560.20
transferable 629.5
inheritance
property 471.1
bequest 478.10
heritance 479.2
heredity 560.6
inherited
hereditary 560.19
innate 766.8
inheritor heir 479.5
successor 816.4
sequel 834.2
inhibit suppress 106.8
restrain 428.7
confine 429.12
prohibit 444.3
retain 474.5
hinder 1011.10
inhibiting
restraining 428.11
hindering 1011.17
inhibition
suppression 92.24
restraint 428.1
prohibition 444.1
retention 474.1
hindrance 1011.1
inhibitive
restraining 428.11
prohibitive 444.6
hindering 1011.17
in honor of 487.4

inhospitable
unkind 144.16
unhospitable 586.7
unfriendly 589.9
inhospitality
unkindness 144.1
uncordialness 586
inhospitableness
586.1
enmity 589.1
inhuman
cruel 144.26
savage 671.21
demoniac 680.17
inhumane 144.26
inhumanity
cruelty 144.11
act of cruelty 144.12
violence 671.1
inhume 309.19
inimical
oppositional 451.8
warlike 458.21
unfriendly 589.9
contrary 778.6
counteractive 899.8
adverse 1010.13
inimitable 249.15
in installments
on credit 622.10
piece by piece 792.9
incompletely 794.6
iniquitous
malicious 144.20
unjust 650.9
wicked 654.16
wrongdoing 655.5
bad 999.7
iniquity
injustice 650.1
evil 654.3
misdeed 655.2
badness 999.1
initial
n first 817.3
v ratify 332.12
letter 546.6
adj beginning 817.15
initials
identification 517.11
signature 527.10
initiate
n novice 572.9
member 617.11
v install 191.4
preinstruct 568.14
originate 817.10
inaugurate 817.11
adj skilled 413.26
initiation
establishment
159.7
admission 187.2
elementary education
568.5
ceremony 580.4
first 817.3
inauguration 817.5
initiative
n vim 17.2
act 328.3
enterprise 330.7

established 854.13
in place of 861.12
in plain sight
  visible 31.6
  openly 348.15
inpouring 189.12
in power
  powerful 18.12
  in authority 417.21
in practice
  in use 387.25
  operating 888.11
in process 888.11
in production
  in preparation 405.22
  in the works 891.21
in progress
  in mid-progress 162.7
  undertaken 404.7
  in preparation 405.22
in public openly 348.15
  publicly 352.19
in pursuit of 382.12
input
  n entrance 189.1
  data 1041.15
  v computerize 1041.18
inquest autopsy 307.18
  jury 596.6
  trial 598.5
  inquiry 937.1
in question
  at issue 937.38
  doubtful 970.17
  undecided 970.18
inquietude
  unpleasure 96.1
  excitement 105.5
  anxiety 126.1
  trepidation 127.5
  agitation 916.1
inquire ask 937.19
  be curious 980.3
inquirer student 572.1
  asker 937.16
  inquisitive person
    980.2
inquiring
  n inquiry 937.1
  questioning 937.12
  adj questioning 937.35
  curious 980.5
inquiry trial 598.5
  examination 937
  inquiring 937.1
  question 937.10
  canvass 937.14
inquisition
  n tribunal 595.1
  trial 598.5
  inquiry 937.1
  grilling 937.13
  v grill 937.21
Inquisition 937.4
inquisitive
  meddlesome 214.9
  curious 980.5
inquisitor
  inquirer 937.16
  inquisitive person
    980.2
in rags shabby 393.32

indigent 619.8
slovenly 809.15
in reality
  really 760.16
  truly 972.18
in regard to 774.13
in repair
  out of order 764.7
  in order 806.7
in reserve back 386.17
  in readiness 405.21
  imminent 839.3
in return
  in compensation
    338.7
  in retaliation 506.9
  interchangeably 862.6
  in answer 938.7
inroad
  n intrusion 214.1
  impairment 393.1
  raid 459.4
  overstepping 909.3
  v raid 459.20
inrush influx 189.2
  wind 318.1
ins 610.11
insalubrious 82.5
ins and outs
  circumstances 765.2
  vicissitudes 971.5
insane
  turbulent 671.18
  foolish 922.8
  unsane 925.26
  overzealous 101.12
insanity
  mental disorder 92.14
  disarrangement 810.1
  mental deficiency
    921.9
  foolishness 922.1
  mental sickness 925
  insaneness 925.1
insatiable
  greedy 100.27
  rapacious 480.26
  gluttonous 672.6
inscribe letter 546.6
  write 547.19
  record 549.15
  engrave 713.9
  fix 854.9
  remember 988.18
inscribed
  written 547.22
  recorded 549.17
  engraved 713.11
inscription
  epitaph 309.18
  lettering 546.5
  writing 547.1
  monument 549.12
  registration 549.14
  makeup 554.12
  engraving 713.2
  motto 973.4
inscrutable 522.13
in season 313.9
insect bug 311.31
  invertebrate 311.31
  bad person 660.7

insecticide 1000.3
insectivore 311.3
insecure
  unreliable 970.20
  unconfident 970.23
  unsafe 1005.11
insecurity
  unreliability 970.6
  dangerousness 1005.2
in self-defense 460.16
inseminate
  reproduce 78.10
  fertilize 889.8
  plant 1067.18
insemination
  reproduction 78.3
  fertilization 889.3
  planting 1067.14
insensate
  insensible 25.6
  cruel 144.26
  turbulent 671.18
  savage 671.21
  unintelligent 921.13
  foolish 922.8
  unwise 922.10
  absurd 922.11
  inanimate 1053.5
insensibility
  physical unfeeling 25
  insensibleness 25.1
  callousness 94.2
  unperceptiveness
    921.2
  incognizance 929.3
  indiscrimination
    944.1
  inanimateness 1053.2
insensible
  unfeeling 25.6
  invisible 32.5
  unconscious 94.10
  undiscerning 921.14
  unaware 929.13
  oblivious 983.7
  inanimate 1053.5
insensitive
  insensible 25.6
  callous 94.12
  inconsiderate 144.18
  heartless 144.25
  ill-bred 505.6
  undiscriminating
    944.5
insensitivity
  insensibility 25.1
  callousness 94.3
  unconcern 102.2
  heartlessness 144.10
  discourtesy 505.1
  indiscrimination
    944.1
  intolerance 979.2
insentient
  insensible 25.6
  inanimate 1053.5
inseparability
  familiarity 587.5
  cohesion 802.1
  indivisibility 1043.2
inseparable
  familiar 587.19

impartible 799.15
cohesive 802.10
indivisible 1043.13
insert
  n insertion 191.2
  interjection 213.2
  v enter 189.7
  introduce 191.3
  record 549.15
insertion
  entrance 189.1
  putting in 191
  introduction 191.1
  insert 191.2
  interjection 213.2
  registration 549.14
  spacecraft 1073.2
in session
  in council 423.6
  assembled 769.21
inset
  n map 159.5
  insert 191.2
  v inlay 191.5
in shape
  healthy 83.8
  hale 83.12
  hearty 764.7
  in order 806.7
in short order
  in no time 174.19
  in a hurry 401.14
  quickly 829.7
inside
  n interior 207.2
  inner nature 766.5
  adj interior 207.6
  confidential 345.14
  adv in 207.10
  prep in 207.13
inside information
  secret 345.5
  private information
    551.2
inside out
  inverted 205.7
  completely 793.14
insider
  inside information
    551.2
  member 617.11
insides
  viscera 2.14
  contents 196.1
  inner parts 207.4
  inner nature 766.5
inside track
  advantage 249.2
  favor 893.2
insidious
  deceitful 356.22
  cunning 415.12
  dishonest 645.16
  shrewd 919.15
insight
  extrasensory
    perception 689.8
  sagacity 919.4
  cognizance 927.2
  good idea 931.6
  intuition 933.1
  discernment 943.2

insightful
knowing 927.15
discerning 943.8
insignia
sign 517.1
symbol 647
regalia 647.1
insignificance
triviality 248
inconsiderableness
248.1
meaninglessness
520.1
unimportance 997.1
insignificant
small 248.6
meaningless 520.6
inconsequential
997.17
insincere
uncandid 354.31
affected 500.15
flattering 511.8
deceitful 645.18
sanctimonious 693.5
sophistical 935.10
insincerity
uncandidness 354.5
affectation 500.1
unction 511.2
deceitfulness 645.3
sanctimony 693.1
sophistry 935.1
insinuate
insert 191.3
intrude 214.5
advise 422.5
imply 519.4
hint 551.10
accuse 599.7
insinuating
flattering 511.8
suggestive 519.6
shrewd 919.15
disparaging 512.13
insinuation
obsequiousness 138.2
entrance 189.1
insertion 191.1
interjection 213.2
intrusion 214.1
piece of advice 422.2
aspersion 512.4
hint 551.4
accusation 599.1
influence 893.1
shrewdness 919.3
insipid
wishy-washy 16.17
tasteless 65.2
dull 117.6
vacant 222.14
prosaic 721.5
mediocre 1004.7
insist
affirm 334.5
urge 375.14
demand 421.8
urge upon 439.9
dwell on 848.9
make conditional
958.4

necessitate 962.8
insistence
perseverance 360.1
urging 375.5
exigence 421.4
insistent
persevering 360.8
demanding 421.9
importunate
440.18
urgent 996.22
insobriety 88.1
insociable 583.5
insofar as 887.10
insolation
heatstroke 85.28
heating 1019.1
fuel 1020.1
drying 1064.3
insolence
impenitence 114.2
arrogance 141.2
effrontery 142
presumption 142.1
disrespect 156.1
defiance 454.1
rashness 493.1
impudence 505.2
insolent
presumptuous
141.10
impudent 142.9
disrespectful 156.7
insulting 156.8
defiant 454.7
rash 493.7
discourteous 505.4
impenitent 114.5
insoluble
inexplicable 522.18
indivisible 1043.13
insolvable 522.18
insolvency
poverty 619.1
credit 622.1
bankruptcy 625.3
insolvent
n insolvent debtor
625.4
adj destitute 619.9
bankrupt 625.11
unsound 729.18
insomnia
wakefulness 23.1
symptom 85.9
insomniac
n wakefulness 23.1
adj wakeful 23.7
insomuch as 887.10
insouciance
apathy 94.4
unconcern 102.2
carelessness 340.2
incuriosity 981.1
insouciant
apathetic 94.13
unconcerned 102.7
careless 340.11
incurious 981.3
inspect
scrutinize 27.14
examine 937.23

inspection
scrutiny 27.6
study 570.3
examination 937.3
automation 1040.7
inspector
superintendent 574.2
examiner 937.17
policeman 1007.15
inspiration
breathing 2.19
drawing in 187.5
impulse 365.1
motive 375.1
infusion 375.9
encouragement 492.9
function of Holy
Ghost 677.16
revelation 683.9
Muse 720.10
genius 919.8
good idea 931.6
intuition 933.1
creative thought 985.2
inspire cheer 109.7
give hope 124.10
draw in 187.12
prompt 375.13
inspirit 375.20
encourage 492.16
induce 885.11
inspired fired 375.31
appropriate 533.7
scriptural 683.10
imaginative 985.18
inspirer
prompter 375.10
author 885.4
inspiring
cheering 109.16
promising 124.13
inspirational 375.26
lofty 544.14
inspirit cheer 109.7
give hope 124.10
vivify 306.9
inspire 375.20
encourage 492.16
inspissate
v broaden 269.5
densify 1043.9
thicken 1043.10
emulsify 1060.10
adj thickened 1043.14
in spite of 338.9
instability
infirmity 16.3
irresolution 362.1
nonuniformity 781.1
transience 827.1
inconstancy 853.2
unreliability 970.6
dangerousness 1005.2
install locate 159.11
establish 159.16
insert 191.4
instate 615.12
inaugurate 817.11
produce 891.10
installation
foundation 159.7
admission 187.2

installment 615.3
holy orders 698.10
workplace 739.1
inauguration 817.5
establishment 891.4
installment
establishment 159.7
admission 187.2
book part 554.13
installation 615.3
payment 624.1
part 792.1
inauguration 817.5
installment plan
borrowing 621.1
credit 622.1
payment 624.1
instance
n urging 375.5
proposal 439.2
particular 765.3
example 785.2
sample 785.3
citation 956.5
v itemize 765.6
cite 956.13
instant
n period 823.1
short time 827.3
moment 829.3
adj hasty 401.9
demanding 421.9
instantaneous 829.4
imminent 839.3
prompt 844.9
urgent 996.22
instantaneous
short 268.8
instant 829.4
prompt 844.9
instate insert 191.4
install 615.12
instead 861.11
instead of 861.12
instep 199.5
in step
in concert 787.11
synchronous 835.6
conformist 866.6
instigate
incite 375.17
induce 885.11
instigation 375.4
instigator
inciter 375.11
author 885.4
producer 891.7
instill inculcate 568.12
imbue 796.11
fix in the mind 988.18
instilled 373.19
instillment
inculcation 568.2
imbuement 796.2
instinct
feeling 93.1
impulse 365.1
talent 413.4
intuitiveness 933
innateness 933.2
discrimination 943.1
involuntariness 962.5

instinctive
  animal 311.38
  innate 766.8
  natural 933.6
  involuntary 962.14
instinctual
  animal 311.38
  innate 766.8
  intuitive 933.6
institute
  n school 567.1
  organization 617.8
  v inaugurate 817.11
  cause 885.10
  establish 891.10
institution
  organization 617.8
  law 673.3
  holy orders 698.10
  rite 701.3
  workplace 739.1
  beginning 817.1
  establishment 891.4
institutionalize 429.17
in store
  in stock 386.16
  in readiness 405.21
  possessed 469.8
  imminent 839.3
  destined 963.9
instruct
  command 420.8
  advise 422.5
  inform 551.8
  teach 568.10
instruction
  precept 419.1
  direction 420.3
  advice 422.1
  information 551.1
  teaching 568.1
  orders 568.6
  lesson 568.7
  learning 927.4
instructive
  preceptive 419.4
  commanding 420.13
  advisory 422.8
  informative 551.18
  educational 568.18
instructor
  aviator 185.1
  preparer 405.5
  adviser 422.3
  teacher 571.1
  academic rank 571.3
instrument
  n surgery 91.19
  sycophant 138.3
  measure 300.2
  manner 384.4
  document 549.5
  agent 576.3
  tool 1039.1
  v compose 708.46
  tool 1039.9
instrumental
  n case 530.9
  adj modal 384.8
  helping 449.20
  orchestral 708.51
instrumentalist 710.3

instrumentation
  measurement 300.1
  harmonization 709.2
  tooling 1039.7
  rocketry 1072.1
insubordinate
  n rebel 327.5
  adj unsubmissive
    327.9
  lawless 418.5
insubordination
  disobedience 327.1
  lawlessness 418.1
insubstantial
  thin 270.16
  rare 299.4
  bodiless 763.5
  transient 827.7
  unsound 935.12
  unreliable 970.20
  immaterial 1051.7
insubstantiality
  thinness 270.4
  rarity 299.1
  immateriality 763.1
  unreliability 970.6
in succession
  in order 806.10
  continuously 811.11
insufferable 98.25
insufficiency
  inability 19.2
  unsatisfactoriness
    108.2
  insignificance 248.1
  inferiority 250.3
  shallowness 276.1
  inequality 790.1
  shortcoming 910.1
  inadequacy 991.1
insufficient
  unsatisfactory 108.9
  inadequate 250.7
  unequal 790.4
  short of 910.5
  unsufficing 991.9
insular
  n islander 235.4
  adj local 231.9
  insulated 235.7
  secluded 584.8
  exclusive 772.9
  unrelated 775.6
  separate 801.20
  alone 871.8
  narrow-minded
    979.10
insularity island 235.2
  exclusiveness 772.3
  narrow-mindedness
    979.1
insulate proof 15.14
  isolate 235.5
  segregate 772.6
  nonconduct 1031.28
insulated insular 235.7
  segregated 772.8
insulation
  exclusiveness 772.3
  safeguard 1007.3
insult
  n indignity 156.2

  contempt 157.1
  gibe 508.2
  v offend 156.5
  disdain 157.3
  ridicule 508.8
insulting
  insolent 142.9
  disrespectful 156.8
insuperable
  impregnable 15.19
  impracticable 966.8
insupportable 98.25
insuppressible 361.12
insurance
  security 438.1
  precaution 494.3
  assurance 1007.4
insurance company
  1007.4
insurance policy 1007.4
insure secure 438.9
  make sure 969.11
  protect 1007.18
insured
  secured 438.11
  safe 1006.4
insurer
  endorser 332.7
  guarantor 438.6
insurgence 327.4
insurgent
  n rebel 327.5
  adj rebellious 327.11
insurmountable 966.8
insurrection 327.4
insurrectionary
  n rebel 327.5
  adj rebellious 327.11
  revolutionary 859.5
insusceptible 94.9
in suspense
  on tenterhooks 130.12
  inert 173.14
  undecided 970.18
  in a dilemma 970.25
  uncertainly 970.28
in sync
  harmonious 708.49
  agreeing 787.9
  in step 787.11
  synchronous 835.6
  simultaneously 835.7
  concurrent 898.4
  televisional 1034.16
intact
  unpierced 293.10
  immature 301.10
  preserved 397.13
  continent 664.6
  untouched 791.10
  complete 793.9
  unmixed 797.7
  new 840.7
  permanent 852.7
  unqualified 959.2
  sound 1001.7
  safe 1006.4
intaglio
  engraving tool 713.8
  relief 715.3
  mold 785.6
intake entrance 189.1

  inlet 189.5
  receipts 627.1
intangibility
  infinitesimalness
    258.2
  unsubstantiality 763.1
  immateriality 1051.1
intangible
  infinitesimal 258.14
  unsubstantial 763.5
  immaterial 1051.7
intangibles 471.7
integer whole 791.1
  individual 871.4
integral whole 791.9
  component 795.5
  one 871.7
  unitary 871.10
  sound 1001.7
  numeric 1016.22
integrate
  symmetrize 264.3
  equalize 789.6
  form a whole 791.7
  mix 796.10
  combine 804.3
  unify 871.5
integrated
  whole 791.9
  joined 799.13
  combined 804.5
  unitary 871.10
integration
  symmetrization 264.2
  affiliation 450.2
  adjustment 787.4
  equating 789.2
  whole 791.1
  mixture 796.1
  combination 804.1
  oneness 871.1
  notation 1016.2
integrity
  artlessness 416.1
  probity 644.1
  wholeness 791.1
  completeness 793.1
  simplicity 797.1
  particularity 864.1
  oneness 871.1
  soundness 1001.2
integument
  exterior 206.2
  skin 295.3
intellect
  intellectual faculty
    918
  mind 918.1
  intelligence 919.1
  knowledge 919.9
  wise man 920.1
  intellectual 928.1
intellectual
  n wise man 920.1
  scientist 927.11
  learned person 928
  intellect 928.1
  adj mental 918.7
  intelligent 919.12
  knowledgeable 927.23
  ideational 931.9
  attitudinal 977.7

intellectuality
intelligence 919.1
scholarship 927.5
intellectualize
think 930.8
reason 934.15
intelligence
information 551.1
news 552.1
teachableness 570.5
secret service 576.12
spirit 678.5
intellect 918.1
mental grasp 919
understanding 919.1
mental capacity 919.9
knowledge 927.1
brains 927.3
surveillance 937.9
intelligence agent
576.9
intelligence quotient
919.1
intelligence service
576.12
intelligence testing
92.8
intelligence work 937.9
intelligent
teachable 570.18
mental 918.7
intellectual 919.12
knowing 927.15
intelligentsia 928.2
intelligibility
meaningfulness 518.5
comprehensibility
521.1
facility 1013.1
intelligible
meaningful 518.10
comprehensible
521.10
intemperance
bibulousness 88.2
unrestraint 430.3
prodigality 486.1
incontinence 665.2
indulgence 669
intemperateness 669.1
gluttony 672.1
excess 992.1
intemperate
unrestrained 430.24
prodigal 486.8
incontinent 665.24
indulgent 669.7
violent 671.16
gluttonous 672.6
excessive 992.16
intend purpose 380.4
plan 381.8
have in mind 518.9
intended
n fiancé 104.17
adj intentional 380.8
promised 436.8
meant 518.11
intense
penetrating 15.22
energetic 17.13
sensitive 24.13

colorful 35.18
fervent 93.18
zealous 101.9
great 247.6
violent 671.16
attentive 982.15
intensified
aggravated 119.4
increased 251.7
intensify pain 26.7
aggravate 119.2
heighten 251.5
grow 251.6
intensity energy 17.1
colorfulness 35.4
loudness 53.1
zeal 101.2
greatness 247.1
violence 671.1
measurement of light
1024.21
intensive
laborious 725.18
thorough 793.10
intent
n intention 380.1
meaning 518.2
adj zealous 101.9
attentive 982.15
engrossed 982.17
intention will 323.1
motive 375.1
aim 380
intent 380.1
plan 381.1
meaning 518.2
inter 309.19
interact 776.6
interacting
communicational
343.9
interactive 776.9
interaction
communication 343.1
interworking 776.3
inter alia 253.11
interassociation
interrelation 776.2
interconnection 799.2
interbreed 796.13
interbreeding 796.4
intercalate
interpose 213.6
chronologize 831.14
intercede 466.6
intercept
listen 48.10
hinder 1011.10
interception
game 746.3
radar 1035.9
intercession
mediation 466.1
function of Christ
677.15
prayer 696.4
intercessional
mediatory 466.8
divine 677.17
intercessor
mediator 466.3
lawyer 597.1

interchange
n crossing 170.2
transferal 176.1
communication 343.1
passageway 383.3
retaliation 506.1
trade 731.2
interaction 776.3
mutual transfer 862
exchange 862.1
v communicate 343.6
get along 455.2
trade 731.14
interact 776.6
exchange 862.4
interchangeable
transferable 176.18
exchangeable 862.5
indistinguishable
944.6
intercollegiate 567.13
intercom
sound reproduction
system 50.11
Interphone 347.6
intercommunicate
communicate 343.6
join 799.11
intercommunication
communication 343.1
social life 582.4
interaction 776.3
joining 799.1
intercommunicational
343.9
interconnect
relate 774.6
correlate 776.5
interjoin 799.6
interconnection
interrelation 776.2
interjoinder 799.2
intercosmic 1070.25
intercourse
copulation 75.7
communication 343.1
conversation 541.1
social life 582.4
commerce 731.1
relation 774.1
interaction 776.3
joining 799.1
interdenominational
675.27
interdependency 776.2
interdependent 776.8
interdict
n restraint 428.1
prohibition 444.1
v prohibit 444.3
interdigitation
interrelation 776.2
interconnection 799.2
interdisciplinary
scholastic 568.19
extensive 863.13
interest
n incentive 375.7
allurement 377.1
benefit 387.4
undertaking 404.1
patronage 449.4

estate 471.4
gain 472.3
portion 477.5
party 617.4
lending 620.1
premium 623.3
prerogative 642.1
partiality 650.3
selfishness 651.1
occupation 724.1
dividend 738.7
relevance 774.4
affair 830.3
cause 885.9
favor 893.2
side 934.14
curiosity 980.1
concern 982.2
importance 996.1
good 998.4
v attract 377.6
relate to 774.5
involve 897.2
concern 982.12
interested
partisan 617.19
partial 650.11
involved 897.4
discriminatory 979.12
curious 980.5
concerned 982.16
interest group
pressure group 609.31
party 617.4
interesting
alluring 377.8
stimulating 982.19
interest rate
lending 620.1
interest 623.3
interface
boundary 211.3
middle course 467.3
joint 799.4
interfere
intrude 214.5
hinder 1011.10
interference
intrusion 214.1
counteraction 899.1
wave 915.4
hindrance 1011.1
reception 1033.21
interfering 214.8
interfuse
intersperse 213.7
combine 804.3
interfusion
interspersion 213.3
mixture 796.1
interim
n interval 224.1
interruption 812.2
intermediate period
825
meantime 825.1
delay 845.2
pause 856.3
adj temporary 825.4
interior
n inside 207.2
inland 207.3

scene 712.12
middle 818.1
adj internal 207.6
inland 207.7
private 345.13
middle 818.4
interior decorating
498.1
interiority
inwardness 207
internalness 207.1
depth 275.1
interjacent 213.10
interject
insert 191.3
interpose 213.6
remark 524.25
interjection
insertion 191.1
interpolation 213.2
intrusion 214.1
remark 524.4
part of speech 530.3
interjoin
correlate 776.5
interconnect 799.6
interlace weave 740.6
interact 776.6
mix 796.10
interlaced
webbed 170.12
woven 740.7
interlacing
n weaving 740.1
interaction 776.3
adj weaving 740.8
interlard
intersperse 213.7
mix 796.10
interlining 196.3
interlink
correlate 776.5
interconnect 799.6
interlinked
related 774.9
correlative 776.8
interlock
n safeguard 1007.3
v correlate 776.5
agree 787.6
interconnect 799.6
interlocked
related 774.9
correlative 776.8
interlocking
interrelation 776.2
interconnection 799.2
interlocutory
mediatory 466.8
conversational 541.13
interlope 214.5
interloper
intruder 214.3
outsider 773.2
interloping 214.1
interlude
n respite 20.2
act 704.7
passage 708.24
interim 825.1
pause 856.3
v intervene 825.3

intermarriage 563.1
intermarry 563.15
intermeddle
meddle 214.7
hinder 1011.10
intermediary
n intermedium 213.4
instrument 384.4
mediator 466.3
go-between 576.4
adj intervening 213.10
medium 246.3
modal 384.8
mediatory 466.8
middle 818.4
intermediate
n instrument 384.4
mediator 466.3
go-between 576.4
gear 1039.5
v mediate 466.6
adj intervening 213.10
medium 246.3
mediatory 466.8
middle 818.4
intermediator 466.3
interment
burial 309.1
concealment 346.1
intermesh 776.6
intermezzo
act 704.7
passage 708.24
interim 825.1
pause 856.3
interminable 828.7
intermingle 796.10
intermission
respite 20.2
release 120.2
act 704.7
game 746.3
interruption 812.2
interim 825.1
pause 856.3
intermit
release 120.6
discontinue 812.3
recur 849.5
fluctuate 850.2
interrupt 856.10
intermittence
discontinuity 812.1
periodicity 849.2
irregularity 850.1
pause 856.3
intermittent
discontinuous 812.4
periodic 849.7
irregular 850.3
intermix 796.10
intern
n doctor 90.4
interior 207.2
teaching fellow 571.4
v practice medicine
90.14
imprison 429.14
internal
n interior 207.2
adj interior 207.6
intrinsic 766.7

mental 918.7
internalize 207.5
Internal Revenue
Service 630.10
international
public 312.16
universal 863.14
International Date
Line 831.4
internationalism
nationhood 232.6
foreign policy 609.5
generality 863.1
international relations
609.2
internecine
deadly 308.22
destructive 395.26
internecine struggle
457.4
interpersonal
communication 343.1
interplanetary 1070.25
interplay
n communication
343.1
interaction 776.3
interchange 862.1
v interact 776.6
Interpol 1007.17
interpolate 213.6
interpolation
insertion 191.1
interjection 213.2
added to writing
254.2
impromptu 708.27
notation 1016.2
interpose
interject 213.6
intrude 214.5
mediate 466.6
interposition
a putting between 213
interposing 213.1
intrusion 214.1
mediation 466.1
interpret
diagnose 341.9
play 708.39
criticize 723.5
solve 939.2
interpretable
construable 341.17
meaningful 518.10
intelligible 521.10
interpretation
way of understanding
341
construction 341.1
explanation 518.3
solution 939.1
interpreter
exegete 341.7
musician 710.1
critic 723.4
language 1041.13
interpretive
interpretative 341.14
critical 723.6
interrelated
related 774.9

correlative 776.8
interrogate
communicate with
343.8
question 937.20
be curious 980.3
interrogation
question 937.10
questioning 937.12
interrogative
n question 937.10
adj communicational
343.9
inquiring 937.35
interrogator 937.16
interrogatory
n question 937.10
adj communicational
343.9
inquiring 937.35
interrupt put in 214.6
discontinue 812.3
talk out of turn 843.4
suspend 856.10
hinder 1011.10
interruption
intrusion 214.1
interval 224.1
suspension 812.2
interim 825.1
untimeliness 843.1
pause 856.3
hindrance 1011.1
intersect
converge 169.2
crossing 170.6
agree 787.6
intersecting
n crossing 170.1
adj converging 169.3
cross 170.8
intersection
crossing 170.1
crossroad 170.2
passageway 383.3
agreement 787.1
interseptum 213.5
intersexuality 75.12
interspace
n interval 224.1
v space 224.3
intersperse 213.7
interstellar
spatial 158.9
celestial 1070.25
interstice 224.1
intertwine
weave 740.6
interact 776.6
mix 796.10
intertwined
webbed 170.12
woven 740.7
intertwining
n weaving 740.1
interaction 776.3
adj weaving 740.8
interval
n space between 224
gap 224.1
degree 245.1
opening 292.1

harmonics 709.20
deficiency 794.2
interruption 812.2
period 823.1
interim 825.1
pause 856.3
v intervene 825.3
intervene
interpose 213.6
intrude 214.5
mediate 466.6
interlude 825.3
hinder 1011.10
intervening
intervenient 213.10
mediatory 466.8
intervention
interposition 213.1
intrusion 214.1
mediation 466.1
interview
n audition 48.2
talk 541.3
conference 541.6
appointment 582.8
press conference
937.11
v interrogate 937.20
interviewer
journalist 555.4
inquirer 937.16
interweave
weave 740.6
interact 776.6
mix 796.10
interweaving
n weaving 740.1
interaction 776.3
adj weaving 740.8
interwork 776.6
interworking
n interaction 776.3
adj interacting 776.9
interwoven
webbed 170.12
woven 740.7
intestate 478.25
intestine
n digestive system
2.16
fight 457.4
adj interior 207.6
in that case
accordingly 765.11
then 820.11
in the act 656.4
in the air
on high 272.21
reported 552.15
in the bag
prearranged 964.8
assured 969.20
in the black 472.17
in the cards
imminent 839.3
destined 963.9
probable 967.6
in the clear
free 430.21
legible 521.12
innocent 657.6
in safety 1006.6

in the clouds
on high 272.21
abstracted 984.11
visionary 985.24
in the dark
secretly 345.17
benighted 929.16
darkling 1026.19
in the doghouse 661.13
in the dough 618.15
in the driver's seat
in authority 417.21
influential 893.14
in the dumps 112.22
in the flesh
in person 221.17
living 306.11
personally 864.16
in the gutter
poorly 250.9
destitute 619.9
corrupt 654.14
in the hole 623.8
in the know
informed 551.17
cognizant of 927.16
knowledgeable
927.17
in the limelight
publicly 352.19
prominent 662.17
on the stage 704.36
in the long run
on the average 246.5
on the whole 791.14
eventually 830.12
in time 838.11
generally 863.17
in the market for
adj searching 937.37
prep after 382.12
in the midst of
adv midway 818.5
prep at 159.27
between 213.12
among 796.17
in the mood
willing 324.5
disposed 977.8
in the neighborhood of
adv near 223.20
at a price 630.17
prep about 223.26
in the nick of time
opportunely 842.12
in time 844.12
expedient 994.5
in the pink
healthy 83.9
in order 806.7
in the red
at a loss 473.9
destitute 619.9
indebted 623.8
in the same boat 789.7
in the same breath
at once 829.8
simultaneously 835.7
in the swim 578.11
in the thick of
adv midway 818.5
prep between 213.12

among 796.17
in the wind
against the wind
182.65
happening 830.9
imminent 839.3
in the works
adj planned 381.12
undertaken 404.7
in preparation 405.22
operating 888.11
adv in production
891.21
intimacy
copulation 75.7
nearness 223.1
sociability 582.1
familiarity 587.5
relation 774.1
knowledge 927.1
intimate
n friend 588.1
v advise 422.5
imply 519.4
hint 551.10
adj interior 207.6
near 223.14
homelike 228.33
private 345.13
familiar 582.24
friendly 587.19
joined 799.13
particular 864.12
intimation
hint 248.4
piece of advice 422.2
sign 517.9
implication 519.2
clue 551.4
admixture 796.7
hunch 933.3
suggestion 950.5
in time
in tempo 709.30
synchronous 835.6
in due time 838.11
in good time 844.12
periodically 849.10
intimidate
cow 127.20
dissuade 379.3
coerce 424.7
bluster 503.3
threaten 514.2
domineer 612.16
intimidated
terrified 127.26
cowardly 491.10
intimidating
dissuasive 379.5
threatening 514.3
intimidation
frightening 127.6
dissuasion 379.1
coercion 424.3
bluster 503.1
threat 514.1
into
adj knowledgeable
927.17
prep in 189.14
inside 207.13

intolerable
insufferable 98.25
unlikable 99.7
unacceptable 108.10
downright 247.12
intolerance
intoleration 135.2
obstinacy 361.1
narrow-mindedness
979.2
intolerant
n bigot 979.5
adj unforbearing
135.7
obstinate 361.8
untolerating 979.11
intonate
inflect 524.29
sing 708.38
intonation tone 50.2
inflection 524.7
vocal music 708.13
execution 708.30
harmonization 709.2
intone 708.38
in toto fully 765.13
wholly 791.13
intoxicate
inebriate 88.22
thrill 105.15
dizzy 984.8
intoxicated
under the influence
87.22
inebriated 88.31
fervent 93.18
frenzied 105.25
intoxicating
intoxicative 88.36
exciting 105.30
intoxication
poisoning 85.31
inebriation 88.1
happiness 95.2
fury 105.8
intractable
insubordinate 327.9
ungovernable 361.12
inflexible 1044.12
intramural
intramarginal 207.8
scholastic 567.13
intransient 826.10
intransigence 361.2
intransigent
n obstinate person
361.6
oppositionist 452.3
adj unyielding 361.9
in transit
on the way 176.20
on the move 177.42
intransitive
n verb 530.4
adj grammatical
530.17
intransmutable 854.17
intraterritorial 207.8
intravenous 91.17
intrepid 492.17
intricacy
abstruseness 522.2

complexity 798.1
difficulty 1012.1
intricate
hard to understand
 522.14
mixed 796.14
complex 798.4
bewildering 970.27
difficult 1012.17
intrigue
n love affair 104.6
web of intrigue 381.5
stratagem 415.3
deceitfulness 645.3
v fascinate 377.7
plot 381.9
maneuver 415.10
intrigued 95.14
intriguing
delightful 97.7
alluring 377.8
scheming 381.13
intrinsic
interior 207.6
internal 766.7
characteristic 864.13
introduce
bring in 187.14
insert 191.3
propose 439.5
preinstruct 568.14
present 587.14
prefix 813.3
go before 815.3
inaugurate 817.11
innovate 851.9
introducer
transformer 851.5
producer 891.7
introduction
bringing in 187.7
entrance 189.1
insertion 191.1
interjection 213.2
makeup 554.12
elementary education
 568.5
acquaintance 587.4
legislative procedure
 613.6
act 704.7
overture 708.26
part of writing 792.2
curtain-raiser 815.2
inauguration 817.5
basics 817.6
innovation 851.4
introductory
introductive 187.18
educational 568.18
beginning 817.15
introit 708.17
Introit 696.3
intromission
admission 187.2
insertion 191.1
intromit receive 187.10
insert 191.3
introspect 930.12
introspection 930.6
introspective
cognitive 930.21

absorbed in thought
 930.22
introversion
personality tendency
 92.11
inversion 205.1
interiority 207.1
reticence 344.3
introvert
n personality type
 92.12
v invert 205.5
adj introverted 92.39
introverted
introvert 92.39
inverted 205.7
reticent 344.10
intrude enter 189.7
interpose 213.6
obtrude 214.5
talk out of turn 843.4
overstep 909.9
intruder incomer 189.4
interloper 214.3
foreign body 773.2
newcomer 773.4
intrusion
entrance 189.1
interposition 213.1
interference 214
obtrusion 214.1
extraneousness 773.1
intruder 773.2
untimeliness 843.1
overstepping 909.3
intrusive
entering 189.12
obtrusive 214.8
overactive 330.24
extraneous 773.5
untimely 843.6
intuit sense 933.4
foreknow 960.6
intuition
extrasensory
 perception 689.8
intuitiveness 933.1
hunch 933.3
discrimination 943.1
suggestion 950.5
intuitive
premonitory 133.16
intuitional 933.5
theoretical 950.13
foreseeing 960.7
intumescence
growth 85.38
distension 259.2
swelling 283.4
in tune in accord 455.3
harmonious 708.49
in turn in order 806.10
consecutively 811.11
interchangeably 862.6
inundate
aggrieve 112.19
overflow 238.17
submerge 367.7
overwhelm 395.21
raid 459.20
run over 909.7
oversupply 992.14

flood 1063.14
inundated
overcome 112.29
flooded 238.25
underwater 275.13
overrun 909.10
soaked 1063.17
inundation
overflow 238.6
submergence 367.2
wordiness 538.2
overrunning 909.1
plenty 990.2
superabundance 992.2
wetting 1063.6
in unison
unanimously 332.17
cooperatively 450.6
harmonious 708.49
in step 787.11
jointly 799.18
simultaneously 835.7
inure callous 94.6
accustom 373.10
inured callous 94.12
accustomed 373.16
hardened 654.17
invade intrude 214.5
raid 459.20
usurp 640.8
infest 909.6
overstep 909.9
invader intruder 214.3
assailant 459.12
in vain
unsuccessfully 410.19
amiss 910.7
invalid
n impotent 19.6
sick person 85.42
recluse 584.5
v afflict 85.49
adj ineffective 19.15
unhealthy 85.53
repealed 445.3
illogical 935.11
bad 999.7
invalidate
disqualify 19.11
abolish 395.13
repeal 445.2
neutralize 899.7
disprove 957.4
invalidated
disabled 19.16
disproved 957.7
invalidation
repeal 445.1
neutralization 899.2
disproof 957.1
invalidity
ineffectiveness 19.3
unhealthiness 85.3
illogicalness 935.2
badness 999.1
invaluable 632.10
invariable
tedious 118.9
uniform 780.5
unchangeable 854.17
invasion
intrusion 214.1

raid 459.4
usurpation 640.3
infestation 909.2
invasive
entering 189.12
intrusive 214.8
attacking 459.29
invective
n sarcasm 508.5
berating 510.7
vilification 513.2
speech 543.2
adj condemnatory
 510.22
inveigh against 510.13
inveigle trap 356.20
lure 377.5
inveiglement 377.1
invent originate 337.4
fabricate 354.17
initiate 817.10
innovate 840.5
change 851.9
produce 891.12
discover 940.2
imagine 985.14
invented
fabricated 354.28
originated 891.19
invention
fabrication 354.10
innovation 851.4
production 891.1
product 892.1
discovery 940.1
inventiveness 985.3
figment of the
 imagination 985.5
inventive
cunning 415.12
beginning 817.15
creative 891.16
imaginative 985.18
inventor
producer 891.7
imaginer 985.12
inventory
n contents 196.1
store 386.1
record 549.1
account book 628.4
merchandise 735.1
assemblage 769.1
table 807.4
list 870.1
summation 1016.11
v take account of
 628.9
list 870.8
sum up 1016.18
check 1016.20
inverse
n reverse 205.4
opposite side 215.3
v invert 205.5
adj contrapositive
 215.5
contrary 778.6
inversion
turning over 205
inverting 205.1
notation 1016.2

ironclad firm 425.7
  armored 460.13
iron curtain
  frontier 211.5
  veil of secrecy 345.3
  communism 611.5
  barrier 1011.5
iron grip 474.2
iron hand
  governance 417.5
  firm hand 425.3
  control 612.2
  despotism 612.10
ironic witty 489.15
  satiric 508.13
  suggestive 519.6
  ambiguous 539.4
  self-contradictory
    778.8
  mixed 796.14
iron out reconcile 465.8
  solve 939.2
irons 428.4
iron will 359.4
irony wit 489.1
  sarcasm 508.5
  ambiguity 539.1
  self-contradiction
    778.3
  doubleness 872.1
irradiate
  v radiumize 91.26
  preserve 397.9
  illuminate 1024.28
  radioactivate 1036.9
  adj illuminated
    1024.39
irradiated
  illuminated 1024.39
  radioactive 1036.10
irradiation
  food preservation
    397.2
  light 1024.1
irrational
  unintelligent 921.13
  unwise 922.10
  insane 925.26
  illogical 935.11
  numeric 1016.22
irrationality
  unintelligence 921.1
  unwiseness 922.2
  insanity 925.1
  illogicalness 935.2
irreclaimable
  past hope 125.15
  irredeemable 654.18
irreconcilable
  n oppositionist 452.3
  adj unyielding 361.9
  vengeful 507.7
  alienated 589.11
  different 779.7
  inconsistent 788.8
irrecoverable
  past hope 125.15
  past 836.7
irredeemable
  past hope 125.15
  unpayable 625.13
  irreclaimable 654.18

irreducible
  intrinsic 766.7
  simple 797.6
  inextricable 798.5
  one 871.7
  requisite 962.13
irreformable
  past hope 125.15
  irreclaimable 654.18
irrefutable
  evidential 956.16
  obvious 969.15
irregular
  n casual 461.16
  second 1004.6
  adj distorted 265.10
  rough 288.6
  informal 581.3
  illegal 674.6
  nonuniform 781.3
  unequal 790.4
  unordered 809.12
  discontinuous
    812.4
  unregular 850.3
  inconstant 853.7
  abnormal 869.9
  eccentric 926.5
  inferior 1004.9
irregularity
  distortion 265.1
  roughness 288.1
  unsmoothness 294.2
  informality 581.1
  nonuniformity 781.1
  inequality 790.1
  disorder 809.1
  discontinuity 812.1
  unmethodicalness
    850.1
  inconstancy 853.2
  abnormality 869.1
  eccentricity 926.1
irrelevance
  unrelatedness 775.1
  unfitness 788.3
  untimeliness 843.1
  unimportance 997.1
irrelevant
  unrelated 775.7
  inappropriate 788.7
  untimely 843.6
  insignificant 997.17
irreligion
  impiety 694.1
  ungodliness 695.3
irreligious
  impious 694.6
  ungodly 695.17
  unbelieving 954.8
irremediable
  past hope 125.15
  ruined 395.28
irremovable 854.15
irreparable 125,15
irreplaceable
  used up 388.5
  requisite 962.13
irreprehensible 657.8
irrepressible
  cheerful 109.11
  ungovernable 361.12

  unrestrained 430.24
irreproachable
  honest 644.13
  inculpable 657.8
  perfect 1001.6
irresistible
  impregnable 15.19
  powerful 18.12
  delightful 97.7
  great 247.6
  alluring 377.8
  overpowering 412.18
  compulsory 424.10
  evidential 956.16
  inevitable 962.15
irresolute
  wishy-washy 16.17
  irresolved 362.9
  inconstant 853.7
  uncertain 970.16
irresolution
  frailty 16.2
  indecision 362.1
  uncertainty 970.1
irrespective of 338.9
irresponsible
  lawless 418.5
  exempt 430.30
  untrustworthy 645.19
  inconstant 853.7
irretrievable
  past hope 125.15
  lost 473.7
  unchangeable 854.17
irreverence
  disrespect 156.1
  impiety 694.1
irreverent
  disrespectful 156.7
  impious 694.6
irreversible
  past hope 125.15
  directional 161.12
  confirmed 373.19
  unchangeable 854.17
irrevocable
  past hope 125.15
  mandatory 420.12
  unchangeable 854.17
  inevitable 962.15
irrigate dilute 16.11
  wash 79.19
  moisten 1063.12
irrigation washing 79.5
  wetting 1063.6
  cultivation 1067.13
irritability
  sensitivity 24.3
  excitability 105.10
  irascibility 110.2
  dissension 456.3
irritable sensitive 24.12
  excitable 105.28
  irascible 110.19
  nervous 128.11
  partisan 456.17
irritant
  n irritation 96.3
  adj irritating 26.13
irritate pain 26.7
  displease 96.14
  aggravate 119.2

  get on one's nerves
    128.9
  provoke 152.24
  impair 393.9
  sow dissension 456.14
irritated sore 26.11
  annoyed 96.21
  aggravated 119.4
  provoked 152.27
  impaired 393.27
irritating
  painful 26.13
  pungent 68.6
  annoying 98.22
  aggravating 119.5
irritation
  soreness 26.4
  annoyance 96.3
  excitation 105.11
  aggravation 119.1
  resentment 152.1
  incitement 375.4
  adversity 1010.1
irrupt
  burst forth 33.9
  enter 189.7
  intrude 214.5
  originate 817.13
  overstep 909.9
irruption
  outburst 105.9
  intrusion 214.1
  raid 459.4
irruptive
  entering 189.12
  attacking 459.29
Isis 889.5
Islam 675.13
Islamic 675.31
island
  n airport 184.22
  isle 235.2
  v insulate 235.5
  adj insular 235.7
islander 235.4
island-hop 235.5
isle 235.2
ism school 617.5
  cult 675.2
  system of belief 952.3
isobar
  weather map 317.4
  isotope 1037.5
isolate
  insulate 235.5
  excise 255.10
  quarantine 429.13
  segregate 772.6
  analyze 800.6
  separate 801.8
  nonconduct 1031.28
isolated
  quiescent 173.12
  insular 235.7
  private 345.13
  quarantined 429.20
  secluded 584.8
  segregated 772.8
  unrelated 775.6
  separate 801.20
  separated 801.21
  alone 871.8

isolation
defense mechanism 92.23
privacy 345.2
quarantine 429.2
seclusion 584.1
exclusiveness 772.3
itemization 800.2
separation 801.1
aloneness 871.2
isolationism
noninterference 430.9
seclusion 584.1
foreign policy 609.5
isolationist
free agent 430.12
recluse 584.5
isomer 1037.5
isometric
n weather map 317.4
adj climatal 317.12
equisized 789.10
isometrics 84.2
isotherm 317.4
isothermal 1018.30
isothermic 1018.30
isotope 1037.5
Israelite
n Jew 675.21
adj Jewish 675.30
issue
n emergence 190.1
amount 244.2
publication 352.1
escape 369.1
edition 554.5
family 559.5
offspring 561.1
platform 609.7
issuance 738.6
event 830.1
cause 885.9
effect 886.1
product 892.1
topic 936.1
question 937.10
solution 939.1
salient point 996.6
v be born 1.2
appear 33.8
set out 188.8
emerge 190.11
flow 238.16
quantify 244.4
bring out 352.14
be published 352.16
find vent 369.10
parcel out 477.8
give 478.12
print 548.14
monetize 728.26
float 738.12
disperse 770.4
originate 817.13
come after 834.3
result 886.4
issueless 890.4
issue price 738.9
issuing
n appearance 33.1
emergence 190.1
adj emerging 190.18

isthmus
contraction 260.1
narrow place 270.3
it self 864.5
what's what 972.4
italic
n type 548.6
adj written 547.22
italicize 996.14
italicized
written 547.22
emphatic 996.21
it beats me 522.27
itch
n itching 74.3
sexual desire 75.5
craving 100.6
v tingle 74.5
twitch 916.13
itch for lust 75.20
wish for 100.16
itching
n itch 74.3
symptom 85.9
craving 100.6
adj itchy 74.10
lustful 75.26
craving 100.24
lascivious 665.29
itchy sensitive 24.12
itching 74.10
lascivious 665.29
curious 980.5
item
n memorandum 549.4
entry 628.5
commodity 735.2
particular 765.3
part 792.1
component 795.2
individual 871.4
citation 956.5
adv additionally 253.11
itemization
description 349.2
circumstantiation 765.5
enumeration 800.2
particularization 864.7
list 870.1
index 870.7
itemize specify 765.6
enumerate 800.7
particularize 864.9
list 870.8
cite 956.13
sum up 1016.18
items contents 196.1
merchandise 735.1
list 870.1
knowledge 927.1
iterate
reiterate 848.8
persist 855.5
iteration
wordiness 538.2
reiteration 848.2
duplication 873.1
iterative
n aspect 530.13

adj diffuse 538.11
repetitious 848.14
itinerant
n wanderer 178.2
adj traveling 177.36
itinerary
n route 383.1
directory 574.10
adj traveling 177.36
itself 864.5
itsy-bitsy 258.11
IUD 86.23
ivied halls 567.5
ivories teeth 2.8
keyboard 711.17
dice 759.8
ivory
n whiteness 37.2
smoothness 287.3
adj whitish 37.8
ivory tower
seclusion 584.1
retreat 584.6
refuge 1008.5
ivy
n plant 310.4
adj green 44.4
Ivy League 746.1
izzard 819.1
jab
n attack 459.3
thrust 901.2
hit 901.4
v use 87.21
scoff 508.9
thrust 901.12
hit 901.14
jabber
n nonsense 520.2
mumbling 525.4
chatter 540.3
v talk nonsense 520.5
mumble 525.9
chatter 540.5
jabberer 540.4
jack
n mariner 183.1
ass 311.16
flag 647.6
money 728.2
lawn bowling 750.3
card 758.2
base 900.8
lifter 911.3
v hunt 382.9
jackal fox 311.20
follower 616.8
jackass ass 311.16
fool 923.1
jacket
n outerwear 5.13
skin 295.3
hull 295.16
wrapper 295.18
bookbinding 554.14
v cloak 5.39
jackknife 367.1
jack-of-all-trades 413.11
jackpot award 646.2
pot 759.5
jackrabbit hare 311.24

jumper 366.4
jacks 743.16
jack up increase 251.4
disapprove 510.18
jactitation
boasting 502.1
shaking 916.2
Jacuzzi bath 79.8
fitness 84.1
massage 1042.3
jade
n horse 311.12
strumpet 665.14
v fatigue 21.4
burn out 21.5
be tedious 118.6
satiate 993.4
jaded tired 21.7
weary 118.11
languid 331.20
worn-out 393.36
satiated 993.6
jag
n drinking spree 88.6
projection 285.4
notch 289.1
v notch 289.4
jagged angular 278.6
rugged 288.7
notched 289.5
nonuniform 781.3
discontinuous 812.4
jaguar variegation 47.6
wild cat 311.22
jail
n prison 429.8
v enclose 212.5
imprison 429.14
jailbird
prisoner 429.11
criminal 660.10
jailbreak 369.1
jailed
enclosed 212.10
jugged 429.21
jailer gaoler 429.10
penologist 604.9
guard 1007.9
jalopy 179.10
jam
n sweets 10.38
obstruction 293.3
state 764.1
throng 769.4
delay 845.2
multitude 883.3
bewilderment 970.3
barrier 1011.5
predicament 1012.5
semiliquid 1060.5
v drown out 53.8
stop 293.7
have a party 582.21
fill 793.7
hook 799.8
secure 854.8
fix 854.10
stop 856.7
teem with 883.5
thrust 901.12
overload 992.15
obstruct 1011.12

transmit 1035.15
densify 1043.9
jamb leg 177.14
post 273.4
jamboree 743.4
jam in enter 189.7
thrust in 191.7
jammed
stopped 293.11
fast 799.14
late 845.16
stuck 854.16
teeming 883.9
overfull 992.20
dense 1043.12
jamming
reception 1033.21
radar 1035.13
jam-packed
stopped 293.11
crowded 769.22
full 793.11
teeming 883.9
overfull 992.20
dense 1043.12
jam session 708.32
Jane Doe alias 527.8
common woman
606.5
average 863.3
jangle
n noise 53.3
ringing 54.3
rasp 58.3
clash 61.2
disaccord 456.1
v ring 54.8
sound harshly 58.9
grate on 58.11
sound a sour note 61.3
differ 456.8
disagree 788.5
jangling
grating 58.16
clashing 61.5
disagreeing 788.6
janitor
cleaner 79.14
guardian 1007.6
doorkeeper 1007.12
Janus 872.1
japanning 35.12
jape
n joke 489.6
gibe 508.2
v joke 489.13
banter 490.5
scoff 508.9
jar
n rasp 58.3
clash 61.2
start 131.3
disaccord 456.1
shake 916.3
v sound harshly 58.9
sound a sour note 61.3
agitate 105.14
startle 131.8
package 212.9
put up 397.11
differ 456.8
disagree 788.5

shake 916.11
jargon
n nonsense 520.2
Greek 522.7
lingo 523.9
argot 523.11
technical term 526.5
v speak 523.16
jarring
n disaccord 456.1
disagreement 788.1
adj grating 58.16
clashing 61.5
exciting 105.30
unnerving 128.15
surprising 131.11
disagreeing 788.6
jolting 916.20
jaundice
n yellow skin 43.2
symptom 85.9
jealousy 153.1
prejudice 979.3
v yellow 43.3
prejudice 979.9
jaundiced
yellow-faced 43.6
sour 110.23
jealous 153.5
discriminatory 979.12
jaunt
n journey 177.5
walk 177.10
v journey 177.21
wander 177.23
jaunty
lighthearted 109.12
showy 501.19
chic 578.13
javelin 462.8
jaw
n mouth 292.4
v berate 510.19
speak 524.21
chatter 540.5
jawbreaker
long word 526.10
high-sounding words
545.3
jawbreaking
sesquipedalian 545.10
difficult 1012.17
jaws 474.4
jaywalk 177.27
jaywalker 178.6
jazz
n energy 17.3
hot jazz 708.9
adj instrumental
708.51
syncopated 709.29
Jazz Age 823.5
jazz musician 710.2
jazz up energize 17.10
stimulate 105.13
intensify 251.5
jazzy showy 501.19
instrumental 708.51
syncopated 709.29
JD 302.4
jealous jaundiced 153.5
envious 154.4

jealousy
jealousness 153
resentment 153.1
envy 154.1
jeans 5.18
jeer
n indignity 156.2
gibe 508.2
v scoff 508.9
jeering
n indignity 156.2
ridicule 508.1
adj ridiculing 508.12
jejune insipid 65.2
dull 117.6
haggard 270.20
shallow 276.5
unproductive 890.4
empty-headed 921.19
meager 991.10
jell
n semiliquid 1060.5
v thicken 1043.10
emulsify 1060.10
jellied
thickened 1043.14
viscous 1060.12
jelling 1043.4
jelly
n sweets 10.38
semiliquid 1060.5
v thicken 1043.10
emulsify 1060.10
jellyfish weakling 16.6
vacillator 362.5
coward 491.5
jenny
female animal 77.9
spinner 271.5
ass 311.16
jeopardize 1005.6
jeopardy
n danger 1005.1
v endanger 1005.6
Jeremiah 399.4
jerk
n bad person 660.6
yank 904.3
shake 916.3
fool 923.3
v be excited 105.18
preserve 397.9
throw 903.10
yerk 904.5
twitch 916.13
jerking
n food preservation
397.2
twitching 916.5
adj jerky 916.19
jerkwater 997.18
jerky
n meat 10.12
beef 10.13
adj convulsive 671.23
nonuniform 781.3
discontinuous 812.4
irregular 850.3
herky-jerky 916.19
jerry-built 16.14
jest
n joke 489.6

gibe 508.2
laughingstock 508.7
trifle 997.5
v joke 489.13
banter 490.5
jester humorist 489.12
buffoon 707.10
jesting
n bantering 490.2
adj witty 489.15
Jesuit sophist 935.6
quibbler 935.7
jesuitic
insincere 354.31
sophistical 935.10
jet
n blackness 38.4
jet plane 181.3
ascent 193.1
spout 238.9
outburst 671.6
disgorgement 908.7
heater 1019.10
v fly 184.36
run out 190.13
shoot up 193.9
spout 238.20
disgorge 908.25
Jet Age 823.6
jet-black 38.8
jeté 366.1
jet flight 184.1
jet plane
swiftness 174.6
jet 181.3
jet power
manpower 18.4
propulsion 184.25
jet-propelled
flying 184.50
rocket-propelled
903.16
jet propulsion
propulsion 184.25
rocket propulsion
1072.8
jetsam 370.4
jet set traveler 178.1
society 578.6
jet-setter 178.1
jetstream 184.32
jettison
n abandonment 370.1
discard 390.3
ejection 908.1
v abandon 370.5
discard 390.7
eject 908.13
jetty
n buttress 900.4
harbor 1008.6
barrier 1011.5
adj black 38.8
jeu d'esprit 489.7
Jew 675.21
jewel
n favorite 104.16
bijou 498.6
good person 659.1
bearing 914.7
good thing 998.5
v figure 498.9

jewelry 498.5

Jewish 675.30

Jezebel
witch 593.7
strumpet 665.14
demimonde 665.15

jib start 127.12
avoid 164.6
hesitate 362.7
pull back 902.7

jibe
change course 182.30
agree 787.6
be changed 851.6

jiffy 829.3

jig
n snare 356.13
leap 366.1
jerk 904.3
shake 916.3
v jerk 904.5
twitch 916.13

jigger
n drink 88.7
vermin 311.35
fisher 382.6
thing 1050.5
v jerk 904.5
twitch 916.13

jiggle
n jerk 904.3
shake 916.3
v jerk 904.5
twitch 916.13

jillion
n trillion 881.13
large number 1016.5
adj numerous 883.6

jilt
n deceiver 357.1
v abandon 370.5
discard 390.7

jilted 99.10

jilter 357.1

Jim Crow
seclusion 584.1
exclusiveness 772.3
discrimination 979.4

jim-dandy 998.13

jimjams
trepidation 127.5
nervousness 128.2

jimmy
n lever 905.4
v get a purchase 905.8

jingle
n ringing 54.3
meter 720.7
assonance 783.6
repetitiousness 848.4
v ring 54.8
rhyme 720.14

jingling
n ringing 54.3
adj ringing 54.12
rhyming 720.17
assonant 783.17

jingo
n militarist 461.5
patriot 591.3
bigot 979.5
adj militaristic 458.22

jingoism
warlikeness 458.11
patriotism 591.2

jingoistic
militaristic 458.22
public-spirited 591.4

jinni 680.6

jinx
n spell 691.1
bad influence 999.4
v bewitch 691.9
work evil 999.6
bring bad luck 1010.12

jitney 179.13

jitters
nervousness 128.2
agitation 916.1

jittery
jumpy 128.12
agitated 916.16

jive
n bull 520.3
jazz 708.9
v banter 490.6
syncopate 708.43

job
n act 328.3
theft 482.4
occupation 724.1
task 724.2
function 724.3
position 724.5
affair 830.3
v rent 615.15
hire out 615.16
deal in 731.15
sell 734.8

Job 134.3

job action 727.5

jobber
intermediary 213.4
worker 726.2
merchant 730.2
stockbroker 737.10

jobbing
Machiavellianism 415.2
trade 731.2
selling 734.2
stockbroking 737.18

jobholder 726.2

jobless 331.18

job lot 735.1

jock real man 76.6
soldier 461.7
athlete 743.19
jockey 757.2
supporter 900.2

jockey
n speeder 174.5
rider 178.8
jock 757.2
saddle parts 900.18
v maneuver 415.10
compete 457.18

jocose 489.15

jocularity
merriment 109.5
wittiness 489.2

jog
n slow motion 175.2

gait 177.12
bulge 283.3
notch 289.1
thrust 901.2
jerk 904.3
shake 916.3
v exercise 84.4
plod 175.7
walk 177.27
trot 177.28
thrust 901.12
jerk 904.5
shake 916.11

jogger 988.6

joggle
n bulge 283.3
notch 289.1
thrust 901.2
jerk 904.3
shake 916.3
v thrust 901.12
jerk 904.5
shake 916.11

jog on march on 162.3
continue 855.3

jog the memory 988.20

jog trot run 174.3
slow motion 175.2
routine 373.6

jog-trot tedious 118.9
monotonous 848.15

john latrine 12.10
toilet 12.11
card 758.2
cheater 759.22

John Bull country 232.5
the government 612.3

John Doe alias 527.8
the people 606.1
common man 606.5
average 863.3

John Hancock
ratification 332.4
signature 527.10

johnny latrine 12.10
toilet 12.11
man 76.5

Johnny 461.7

johnnycake 10.28

Johnny-come-lately
newcomer 773.4
beginner 817.2
latecomer 845.6

Johnny-on-the-spot
n benefactor 592.1
adj prompt 844.9
attentive 982.15

John Q Public
the people 606.1
the man in the street 863.3

Johnsonian 545.8

joie de vivre
animation 17.4
pleasure 95.1

join
n joint 799.4
v adjoin 223.9
juxtapose 223.13
flow 238.16
cooperate 450.3
side with 450.4

participate 476.5
join in marriage 563.14
associate with 582.17
enlist 615.17
join up 617.14
assemble 769.18
identify 777.5
compose 795.3
put together 799.5
connect 799.11
be consistent 802.7
combine 804.3
continue 811.4
concur 898.2

join battle 457.16

joined
adjacent 223.16
accompanying 768.9
assembled 769.21
related 774.9
joint 799.12
united 799.13
consistent 802.11
combined 804.5
continuous 811.8

joiner
sociable person 582.16
member 617.11

join forces 804.4

joining
n meeting 223.4
addition 253.1
connection 799
junction 799.1
joint 799.4
adj connecting 799.16

joint
n meat 10.12
marijuana cigarette 87.11
crack 224.2
disapproved place 228.28
jail 429.9
sewer 654.7
brothel 665.9
casino 759.19
join 799.4
v hook 799.8
adj cooperative 450.5
communal 476.9
accompanying 768.9
assembled 769.21
mutual 776.11
connected 799.12
combined 804.5
concurrent 898.4

joint effort 450.1

joint operation 450.1

joint ownership 476.1

jointure
endowment 478.9
joining 799.1

joke
n jest 489.6
laughingstock 508.7
trifle 997.5
v jest 489.13
banter 490.5

joker man 76.5
surprise 131.2

mischief-maker 322.3
trick 356.6
deceiver 357.1
proviso 421.3
humorist 489.12
bill 613.9
card 758.2
condition 958.2
obstacle 1011.4
crux 1012.8
jokester
mischief-maker 322.3
deceiver 357.1
humorist 489.12
joking
n wittiness 489.2
bantering 490.2
adj witty 489.15
jollies
excitement 105.3
marines 461.28
jollity merriment 109.5
conviviality 582.3
festivity 743.3
jolly
n navy man 183.4
v banter 490.6
flatter 511.6
make merry 743.24
adj intoxicated 88.31
merry 109.15
convivial 582.23
festive 743.28
jollying
n bantering 490.3
adj bantering 490.7
Jolly Roger 647.6
jolt
n drink 88.7
excitement 105.3
start 131.3
thrust 901.2
shake 916.3
v agitate 105.14
startle 131.8
way of walking 177.28
thrust 901.12
shake 916.11
jolting
exciting 105.30
surprising 131.11
jolty 916.20
Jonah
n bad influence 999.4
v bring bad luck
1010.12
jongleur
minstrel 710.14
poet 720.11
josh joke 489.13
banter 490.6
joshing
n wittiness 489.2
bantering 490.3
ridicule 508.1
adj witty 489.15
ridiculing 508.12
joss 697.3
joss stick 70.4
jostle
n thrust 901.2
shake 916.3

v sound a sour note
61.3
differ 456.8
contend 457.13
rob 482.14
disagree 788.5
thrust 901.12
shake 916.11
jostling
n theft 482.3
adj clashing 61.5
jot modicum 248.2
minute 258.7
mark 517.5
jounce 916.11
journal
record book 549.11
periodical 555.1
account book 628.4
history 719.1
chronicle 831.9
axle box 914.6
journalese
n jargon 523.10
adj journalistic 555.5
journalism
authorship 547.2
news 552.1
the press 555.3
literature 718.2
journalist 555.4
journey
n trip 177.5
v travel 177.21
journeying
n travel 177.1
adj traveling 177.36
journeyman
n expert 413.11
skilled worker 726.6
producer 891.7
adj competent 413.24
joust
n contest 457.3
v contend 457.13
jovial merry 109.15
convivial 582.23
festive 743.28
joviality
merriment 109.5
conviviality 582.3
festivity 743.3
jowl 218.1
joy
n happiness 95.2
merriment 109.5
v be pleased 95.11
rejoice 116.5
exult 502.9
joyful happy 95.15
merry 109.15
cheering 109.16
festive 743.28
joyless
pleasureless 96.20
distressing 98.20
unhappy 112.21
joyous happy 95.15
merry 109.15
festive 743.28
joyride
n ride 177.7

v ride 177.33
joy stick 87.11
JP 596.1
Jr 301.15
jubilant
overjoyed 95.16
rejoicing 116.10
crowing 502.13
jubilate rejoice 116.5
celebrate 487.2
exult 502.9
jubilation treat 95.3
rejoicing 116.1
crowing 502.4
jubilee rejoicing 116.1
celebration 487.1
anniversary 849.4
Judaic 675.30
Judaism 675.12
Judas
traitor 357.10
criminal 660.10
judge
n arbitrator 466.4
connoisseur 496.7
adjudicator 596
magistrate 596.1
fight 754.3
judger 945.6
v mediate 466.6
administer justice
594.5
try 598.17
criticize 723.5
classify 800.8
exercise judgment
945.8
think 952.11
judgeship 594.3
judgment
judiciary 594.2
decision 598.9
condemnation 602.1
punishment 604.1
function of Christ
677.15
classification 800.3
judiciousness 919.7
solution 939.1
discernment 943.2
assessment 945
judging 945.1
opinion 952.6
judgmental
averse 99.8
fastidious 495.9
condemnatory 510.22
judicial 945.16
Judgment Day 838.3
judicature
judiciary 594.2
tribunal 595.1
court 595.2
judgment 945.1
judicial
jurisdictional 594.6
tribunal 595.7
legal 673.10
judicious 919.19
judiciary 945.16
judicial process
judiciary 594.2

lawsuit 598.1
judicial system 594.2
judiciary
n judicial system
594.2
tribunal 595.1
adj jurisdictional
594.6
tribunal 595.7
judicial 945.16
judicious
cautious 494.8
moderate 670.10
intelligent 919.19
discerning 943.8
judicial 945.16
jug
n jail 429.9
ceramic ware 742.2
v imprison 429.14
Juggernaut 697.3
juggle
n trick 356.6
v tamper with 354.16
deceive 356.14
juggler trickster 357.2
cheat 357.3
circus artist 707.3
juggling 356.5
jughead horse 311.12
fool 923.4
juice liquor 88.14
automobile racing
756.1
current 1031.2
fluid 1059.2
juiceless 1064.7
juicy tasty 63.8
delectable 97.10
immature 301.10
interesting 982.19
fluid 1059.4
juju animism 675.6
sorcery 690.1
charm 691.5
jukebox 50.11
juke joint 743.13
jumble
n Greek 522.7
hodgepodge 796.6
scramble 809.3
confusion 984.3
v deform 263.3
make unintelligible
522.12
mix 796.10
disorder 809.9
confuse 810.3
confound 944.3
jumbled
hard to understand
522.14
mixed 796.14
chaotic 809.16
confused 984.12
jumbo
n largeness 257.11
behemoth 257.14
adj huge 257.20
excessive 992.16
Jumbo 311.4
jumbo jet 181.3

jump
n progression 162.1
step 177.11
flight 184.9
ascent 193.1
interval 224.1
advantage 249.2
increase 251.1
leap 366.1
promotion 446.1
basketball game 747.3
v start 127.12
be startled 131.5
way of walking 177.28
parachute 184.47
leave undone 340.7
leap 366.5
flee 368.10
escape 369.6
promote 446.2
lift one's hand against 457.14
attack 459.15
seize on 480.16
drive 756.4
shake 916.11
jumper leaper 366.4
diver 367.4
jump in enter 189.7
mount 193.12
interrupt 214.6
jumping
n leaping 366.3
skiing 753.1
adj leaping 366.7
jumping-off place
small town 230.3
remote region 261.4
extremity 819.2
jump on
suppress 428.8
disapprove 510.18
jump ship quit 188.9
play truant 222.9
jump the gun
be impatient 135.4
anticipate 844.6
prejudge 946.2
jump to a conclusion 946.2
jump to it 725.15
jump up
shoot up 193.9
rise 200.8
increase 251.4
overestimate 948.2
jumpy fearful 127.23
jittery 128.12
bustling 330.20
agitated 916.16
jerky 916.19
junction
juxtaposition 223.3
addition 253.1
passageway 383.3
railway 383.7
assemblage 769.1
relation 774.1
composition 795.1
joining 799.1
consistency 802.2
combination 804.1

concurrence 898.1
juncture
pause 524.10
circumstance 765.1
joint 799.4
period 823.1
grammar 856.4
jungle 798.2
junior
n inferior 250.2
youngster 302.1
subordinate 432.5
undergraduate 572.6
adj inferior 250.6
Jr 301.15
subsequent 834.4
junk
n heroin 87.8
fake 354.13
derelict 370.4
rubbish 391.5
v abandon 370.5
scrap 390.8
eject 908.13
adj abandoned 370.8
worthless 391.11
junk dealer 730.10
junket
n journey 177.5
v journey 177.21
junk food 10.1
junkie addict 87.20
enthusiast 101.5
junking 390.3
junk mail 553.4
junkpile car 179.10
derelict 370.4
trash pile 391.6
junkyard 391.6
Juno 563.13
Junoesque 1015.18
junta council 423.1
clique 617.6
company 769.3
combination 804.1
Jupiter 1070.9
juridic
jurisdictional 594.6
judicial 945.16
jurisdiction
sphere 231.2
supremacy 249.3
governance 417.5
supervision 573.2
the confines of the law 594
legal authority 594.1
control 612.2
commission 615.1
legality 673.1
protectorship 1007.2
jurisprudence 673.7
jurist 597.2
juror 596.7
jury committee 596
panel 596.6
jury box 595.6
juryman 596.7
jury-rig
n improvisation 365.5
expedient 994.2
v do carelessly 340.9

improvise 365.8
jury-rigged
extemporaneous 365.12
makeshift 994.7
jury selection 598.4
jus 673.3
just
adj appropriate 533.7
fair 649.8
virtuous 653.6
almighty 677.18
logical 934.20
valid 972.14
accurate 972.16
unprejudiced 978.12
adv very 247.18
simply 797.11
exactly 972.21
adj rightful 639.8
honest 644.13
legal 673.10
just about
adv nearly 223.22
prep around 223.26
just around the corner
near 223.20
handy 387.20
in the future 838.9
imminent 839.3
just deserts
reprisal 506.2
deserts 639.3
juste-milieu
mean 246.1
temperance 668.1
moderation 670.1
justice judiciary 594.2
judge 596.1
dueness 639.1
probity 644.1
justness 649.1
cardinal virtues 653.4
legality 673.1
equality 789.1
magistrate 945.6
unprejudicedness 978.5
Justice 649.5
justiceship 594.3
justifiable
permissible 443.15
vindicable 600.14
just 649.8
logical 934.20
justification
composition 548.2
vindication 600.1
justice 649.1
sanctification 685.3
justified
warranted 639.9
just 649.8
redeemed 685.9
justify
compose 548.16
vindicate 600.9
acquit 601.4
just in case 830.13
just right apt 787.10
in step 787.11
accurately 972.20

perfect 1001.6
perfectly 1001.10
just so
adv how 384.9
thus 765.10
accurately 972.20
phrs right! 972.24
inter yes 332.18
conj so 958.15
jut overhang 202.7
protrude 283.10
overlie 295.30
jutting
n overhang 202.3
adj overhanging 202.11
protruding 283.14
jutty
buttress 900.4
harbor 1008.6
juvenescent 301.9
juvenile
n youngster 302.1
book 554.1
actor 707.2
jockey 757.2
adj young 301.9
immature 406.11
juvenile delinquent 302.4
juvenility 301.1
juxtapose
appose 223.13
assemble 769.18
juxtaposition
apposition 223.3
addition 253.1
assemblage 769.1
kaleidoscope 853.4
kama 689.18
Kama 104.8
kamikaze 181.9
kangaroo 366.4
kaolin 742.3
kapok 1045.4
kaput past hope 125.15
spoiled 393.29
ruined 395.29
defeated 412.14
no more 761.11
ended 819.9
karma destiny 838.2
fate 963.2
kayo
n unconsciousness 25.2
finishing stroke 819.4
v deaden 25.4
end 819.5
kazoo
n mouth organ 711.10
v teem with 883.5
keel
n ship 180.1
base 199.2
v faint 25.5
capsize 182.44
incline 204.10
overturn 205.6
keelhaul 604.16
keen
n screech 58.4

telegraph 347.2
clue 517.9
pitch 709.4
key signature 709.15
wind instrument
   711.6
basketball 747.1
influence 893.6
v close 293.6
adj central 208.11
keyboard
   n fingerboard 711.17
   input device 1041.4
   v autotype 548.15
   computerize 1041.18
keyed up 105.20
keyhole 747.1
keynote
   n sign 517.1
   key 709.15
   characteristic 864.4
   v characterize 864.10
keynoter 610.7
keys ecclesiastical
   insignia 647.4
   keyboard 711.17
key signature
   notation 709.12
   key 709.15
keystone arch 279.4
   baseball 745.1
   foundation stone
      900.7
   salient point 996.6
key up excite 105.12
   intensify 251.5
khaki 40.3
khan ruler 575.9
   Muslim ruler 575.10
   prince 608.7
   Sir 648.3
kibbutz
   communion 476.2
   farm 1067.8
kibitz meddle 214.7
   advise 422.5
kibitzer meddler 214.4
   adviser 422.3
   gambler 759.21
   spectator 917.1
kibosh disable 19.9
   end 819.5
kick
   n energy 17.3
   zest 68.2
   excitement 105.3
   complaint 115.5
   objection 333.2
   signal 517.15
   hint 551.4
   baseball 745.3
   football 746.3
   soccer 752.3
   poker 759.10
   counteraction 899.1
   boot 901.9
   recoil 902.2
   v use 87.21
   be discontented 108.6
   complain 115.16
   object 333.5
   break the habit 374.3

signal 517.22
swear off 668.8
football 746.5
soccer 752.4
boot 901.21
recoil 902.6
dismiss 908.20
kick around
   subdue 432.9
   discuss 541.12
   domineer 612.16
   kick 901.21
kick back relax 20.7
   compose oneself 106.7
   do nothing 329.2
   repay 624.11
   discount 631.2
   recoil 902.6
kicker
   malcontent 108.4
   complainer 115.9
   surprise 131.2
   proviso 421.3
   football team 746.2
   condition 958.2
kick in die 307.20
   provide 385.7
   contribute 478.14
   pay 624.16
   begin 817.7
kick in the teeth 442.2
kickoff
   n football 746.3
   soccer 752.3
   curtain-raiser 815.2
   beginning 817.1
   adj preceding 815.4
kick off die 307.20
   propose 439.5
   football 746.5
   soccer 752.4
   precede 813.2
   begin 817.7
   start 903.13
kick out kick 901.21
   eject 908.13
kickshaw
   delicacy 10.8
   trinket 498.4
   toy 743.16
   trifle 997.5
kick the bucket 307.20
kick the habit
   use 87.21
   overcome 412.7
   swear off 668.8
kick up a storm
   complain 115.16
   fly into a rage 152.20
   create disorder 809.11
kick upstairs
   promote 446.2
   depose 447.4
   dismiss 908.19
kid
   n child 302.3
   fledgling 302.10
   goat 311.8
   v fool 356.15
   joke 489.13
   banter 490.6
   trifle 997.15

kidder
   deceiver 357.1
   banterer 490.4
kidding
   n deception 356.1
   banter 490.1
   bantering 490.3
   adj bantering 490.7
   ridiculing 508.12
kidnap seize 480.14
   abduct 482.20
kidnapper 483.10
kidnapping
   seizure 480.2
   abduction 482.9
kidney viscera 2.14
   kind 808.3
   disposition 977.3
kill
   n stream 238.1
   killing 308.1
   quarry 382.7
   v make laugh 116.9
   excise 255.10
   delete 255.12
   slay 308.12
   cover up 345.8
   put an end to 395.12
   obliterate 395.16
   suppress 428.8
   veto 444.5
   legislate 613.10
   amuse 743.21
   end 819.5
   turn off 856.12
killer
   n slayer 308.10
   ruffian 593.3
   violent person 671.9
   first-rate 998.7
   adj excellent 998.13
killing
   n violent death 307.6
   slaying 308.1
   gain 472.3
   unruliness 671.3
   adj fatiguing 21.13
   deadly 308.22
   laborious 725.18
   beautiful 1015.21
killjoy
   spoilsport 112.14
   pessimist 125.7
   hinderer 1011.9
kill oneself 308.21
kill time
   waste time 331.13
   amuse oneself 743.22
   spend time 820.6
kiln
   n oven 742.5
   v dry 1064.6
kilo 881.10
kilocycle 881.10
kilogram 881.10
kilometer 881.10
kilowatt-hour 17.7
kin kinfolk 559.2
   class 808.2
   kind 808.3
kind
   n race 559.4

nature 766.4
sort 808.3
adj kindly 143.13
forgiving 148.6
indulgent 427.8
favorable 449.22
friendly 587.15
good 998.12
kindergarten 567.2
kindergartner 572.3
kindhearted 143.13
kindle energize 17.10
   excite 105.12
   flare up 152.19
   enkindle 375.18
   heat 1019.18
   ignite 1019.22
kindling
   n ignition 1019.4
   firewood 1020.3
   adj inflammatory
      1019.27
kind of
   to a degree 245.7
   so to speak 783.19
kindred
   n blood relationship
      559.1
   kinfolk 559.2
   adj related 559.6
   akin 774.10
kindred soul 783.3
kine 311.6
kinematograph
   camera 714.11
   projector 714.12
kinescope 714.8
kinesic 517.25
kinesis 172.1
kinetic energetic 17.13
   dynamic 1038.9
kinfolk 559.2
king potentate 575.8
   prince 608.7
   businessman 730.1
   chessman 743.17
   card 758.2
   chief 996.10
kingdom country 232.1
   biological
      classification 305.3
   nomenclature 527.1
   hierarchy 808.4
   classifications 808.5
kingfish 575.4
kingmaker
   Machiavellian 415.8
   politics 610.6
   influence 893.6
kingpin 575.4
kingship
   supremacy 249.3
   sovereignty 417.8
   aristocracy 608.9
king-size great 247.7
   large 257.16
   huge 257.20
   oversize 257.23
kink
   n pang 26.2
   coil 281.2
   caprice 364.1

quirk 926.2
fault 1002.2
blemish 1003.1
v curl 281.5
blemish 1003.4
kinked curly 281.9
blemished 1003.8
kinky curly 281.9
capricious 364.5
unconventional 867.6
eccentric 926.6
kinship
accord 455.1
blood relationship
559.1
common source 774.3
affinity 783.2
kinsmen 559.2
kiosk hut 228.9
summerhouse 228.12
booth 736.3
kipper
n fish 10.23
marine animal 311.30
v preserve 397.9
kirk 703.1
kishkes viscera 2.14
insides 207.4
inner nature 766.5
kismet destiny 838.2
fate 963.2
kiss
n touch 73.1
contact 223.5
buss 562.4
greeting 585.4
v touch lightly 73.7
contact 223.10
osculate 562.19
greet 585.10
kissable 104.25
kiss and make up
465.10
kiss and tell 351.6
kiss ass
bow down 433.10
flatter 511.5
kiss good-bye 473.4
kiss off
relinquish 475.3
repulse 907.3
dismiss 983.4
kit
fledgling 302.10
cat 311.21
equipment 385.4
impedimenta 471.3
set 769.12
kitchen
n restaurant 8.17
cookroom 11.3
storeroom 197.14
baseball 745.3
adj cooking 11.5
kitchen cabinet
council 423.1
cabinet 613.3
kitchen sink
washbasin 79.12
genuineness 972.7
kite
n aircraft 181.1

box kite 181.14
counterfeit 728.10
v take off 193.10
kith and kin 559.2
kitsch vulgarity 497.1
writing 547.12
work of art 712.10
literature 718.1
kitten
n child 302.3
fledgling 302.10
cat 311.21
v give birth 1.3
kittenish
feminine 77.13
gay 109.14
infant 301.12
feline 311.41
kitty cat 311.21
funds 728.14
lawn bowling 750.3
pot 759.5
kittycorner
adj transverse 204.19
adv diagonally 204.25
klutz bungler 414.9
fool 923.3
klutzy
inelegant 534.2
stupid 921.15
knack art 413.6
trinket 498.4
knave
mischief-maker 322.3
rascal 660.3
card 758.2
knavery
stratagem 415.3
roguery 645.2
iniquity 654.3
knavish
mischievous 322.6
roguish 645.17
wicked 654.16
knead stroke 73.8
form 262.7
mix 796.10
rub 1042.6
soften 1045.6
knee
n member 2.7
leg 177.14
angle 278.2
joint 799.4
v kick 901.21
knee-deep deep 275.10
shallow 276.5
knee-high
little 258.10
low 274.7
kneel fawn 138.7
bow 155.6
bend 912.9
kneeling
obeisance 155.2
submission 433.1
crouch 912.3
kneel to
bow down 433.10
entreat 440.11
knell
n ringing 54.3

dirge 115.6
death 307.1
passing bell 309.6
v ring 54.8
lament 115.10
knickknack
trinket 498.4
toy 743.16
trifle 997.5
knife
n sword 462.5
cutlery 1039.2
v stab 459.25
knife-edge
sharp edge 285.2
unreliability 970.6
predicament 1012.4
knight
n rider 178.8
combatant 461.1
gallant 504.9
cavalier 608.5
chessman 743.17
v promote 446.2
knight-errantry 652.2
knighthood
military science
458.6
aristocracy 608.9
knightly
adj courageous 492.17
gallant 504.15
noble 608.10
magnanimous 652.6
adv courageously
492.23
courteously 504.19
magnanimously 652.8
knit
v contract 260.7
wrinkle 291.6
heal 396.21
weave 740.6
fasten 799.7
join 799.11
adj woven 740.7
joined 799.13
knitted
contracted 260.12
wrinkled 291.8
joined 799.13
knitting
contraction 260.1
weaving 740.1
knob
n hill 237.4
sphere 282.2
bulge 283.3
v roughen 288.4
knobbed
studded 283.17
nappy 294.7
knobby
hilly 272.18
studded 283.17
knock
n report 56.1
criticism 510.4
hit 901.4
v crack 56.6
criticize 510.14
collide 901.13

hit 901.14
pound 901.16
knock about
wander 177.23
mistreat 389.5
knock around
wander 177.23
discuss 541.12
knock dead
delight 95.10
amuse 743.21
look good 1015.16
knock down
sadden 112.18
unnerve 128.10
raze 395.19
acquire 472.9
disparage 512.8
auction 734.11
fight 754.4
hit 901.14
fell 912.5
knock-down-and-drag-out
n quarrel 456.6
free-for-all 457.5
adj boisterous 671.20
knocker 512.6
knock for a loop
delight 95.10
beat 901.17
knock heads together
coerce 424.8
hold a tight hand
upon 425.4
punish 604.15
knockoff 336.3
knock off
take a rest 20.8
excise 255.10
die 307.20
kill 308.13
do carelessly 340.9
improvise 365.8
accomplish 407.4
defeat 412.9
rob 482.16
write 547.21
compose 718.6
stop work 856.8
knock one's socks off
delight 95.10
astonish 122.6
fascinate 377.7
knock on wood
be hopeful 124.8
be superstitious 953.7
knockout
unconsciousness 25.2
victory 411.1
fight 754.3
finishing stroke 819.4
first-rate 998.7
beauty 1015.9
knock out
disable 19.10
get tired 21.6
deaden 25.4
delight 95.10
form 262.7
do carelessly 340.9
do for 395.11

write 547.21
compose 718.6
fight 754.4
end 819.5
hit 901.14
knock over 395.19
knoll 237.4
knot
  n braid 3.7
  distortion 265.1
  sphere 282.2
  bulge 283.3
  enigma 522.8
  company 769.3
  bunch 769.7
  complex 798.2
  fastening 799.3
  dilemma 1012.7
  solid 1043.6
  v distort 265.5
  equal 789.5
  complicate 798.3
  put together 799.5
  thicken 1043.10
knotted studded 283.17
  gnarled 288.8
  wrinkled 291.8
  assembled 769.21
  related 774.9
  equal 789.7
  complex 798.4
  joined 799.13
  difficult 1012.17
knotty studded 283.17
  gnarled 288.8
  hard to understand
    522.14
  difficult 1012.17
know understand 521.7
  be informed 551.15
  be friends 587.9
  experience 830.8
  perceive 927.12
  be certain 969.9
  recognize 988.12
know all the answers
  know backwards and
    forwards 413.19
  know well 927.13
**know backwards and
  forwards**
  know all the answers
    413.19
  know well 927.13
know-how skill 413.1
  knowledge 927.1
knowing
  n knowledge 927.1
  adj intentional 380.8
  experienced 413.28
  cunning 415.12
  intelligent 919.12
  shrewd 919.15
  wise 919.17
  knowledgeable 927.15
know it all 140.6
know-it-all
  n egotist 140.5
  adj conceited 140.11
knowledge
  information 551.1
  learning 570.1

intelligence 919.1
cognizance 927
knowing 927.1
knowledgeable
  specialized 865.5
  knowing 927.15
known as 527.14
know no bounds
  overstep 909.9
  superabound 992.8
  overdo 992.10
know nothing 929.9
know-nothing
  n ignoramus 929.8
  adj ignorant 929.12
  discriminatory 979.12
know well know 551.15
  master 570.9
  know full well 927.13
know what's what
  know backwards and
    forwards 413.19
  have all one's wits
    about one 919.10
  know well 927.13
  distinguish between
    943.6
knub 294.1
knuckle
  n joint 799.4
  v exert oneself 725.9
knuckle down to
  undertake 404.3
  submit 433.6
  set to work 725.15
knucklehead 923.4
knuckleheaded 921.17
knuckles 462.4
knurl
  n bulge 283.3
  v notch 289.4
knurled
  studded 283.17
  gnarled 288.8
KO
  n unconsciousness
    25.2
  victory 411.1
  fight 754.3
  finishing stroke 819.4
  v deaden 25.4
  do for 395.11
  end 819.5
Kodak 714.11
kohl 1015.12
kook oddity 869.4
  lunatic 925.16
  freak 926.4
kooky odd 869.11
  foolish 922.9
  crazy 925.27
  eccentric 926.6
Koran 683.6
Kore
  nether world deity
    682.5
  agricultural deity
    1067.4
kosher edible 8.33
  clean 79.25
  right 637.3
  legal 673.10

conformist 866.6
kowtow
  n obeisance 155.2
  crouch 912.3
  v fawn 138.7
  kneel 155.6
  lie 201.5
  bow down 433.10
  bend 912.9
Kraut vegetables 10.34
  derogatory names
    232.7
  soldier 461.7
kudos praise 509.5
  citation 646.4
  repute 662.1
kvetch
  n malcontent 108.4
  complaint 115.5
  complainer 115.9
  faultfinder 510.9
  v be discontented
    108.6
  complain 115.16
L LSD 87.9
  adjunct 254.3
  angle 278.2
  stage 704.16
  eleven 881.7
lab workplace 739.6
  laboratory 941.5
label
  n tag 517.13
  name 527.3
  heraldry 647.2
  class 808.2
  kind 808.3
  v tag 517.20
  name 527.11
  generalize 863.9
labia 2.11
labial 211.13
labor
  n birth 1.1
  occupation 724.1
  task 724.2
  work 725.4
  v give birth 1.3
  be busy 330.10
  endeavor 403.5
  work 724.12
  exert oneself 725.12
  dwell on 848.9
  flounder 916.15
laboratory
  hospital room 197.25
  workplace 739.6
  lab 941.5
labor camp 429.8
labored ornate 498.12
  stiff 534.3
  laborious 725.18
  monotonous 848.15
laborer subject 432.7
  commoner 607.9
  worker 726.2
laboring
  n interpretation 341.1
  amplification 538.6
  adj working 725.17
labor in vain
  n labor lost 391.3

v be useless 391.8
  fail 410.9
laborious
  industrious 330.22
  toilsome 725.18
  difficult 1012.17
labor of love
  act of kindness 143.7
  costlessness 634.1
labor organizer 727.4
labor-saving 635.6
labor under ail 85.45
  experience 830.8
**labor under a
  disadvantage** 1012.11
labor union
  association 617.1
  trade unionism 727
  trade union 727.2
labor unionist 727.4
labyrinth 798.2
labyrinthine
  deviative 164.7
  distorted 265.10
  curved 279.7
  convolutional 281.6
  grandiloquent 545.8
  complex 798.4
lace
  n material 4.1
  network 170.3
  strip 271.4
  v whip 604.13
  weave 740.6
  adulterate 796.12
  bind 799.9
laced netlike 170.11
  woven 740.7
lacerate
  v pain 26.7
  torture 96.18
  injure 393.13
  tear apart 801.14
  adj notched 289.5
lacerated
  pained 26.9
  tortured 96.25
  notched 289.5
  impaired 393.27
laceration
  trauma 85.37
  torment 96.7
  severance 801.2
lachrymal
  circulatory 2.31
  secretory 13.7
  tearful 115.21
lachrymose
  secretory 13.7
  tearful 115.21
lacing
  network 170.3
  corporal punishment
    604.4
  weaving 740.1
  adulteration 796.3
lack
  n absence 222.1
  indigence 619.2
  deficiency 794.2
  want 991.4
  imperfection 1002.1

v be poor 619.5
be incomplete 794.3
fall short 910.2
want 991.7
be insufficient 991.8
lackadaisical
unconcerned 102.7
nonchalant 106.15
languid 331.20
dilatory 845.17
lackey
n retainer 577.1
flunky 577.6
follower 616.8
v serve 577.13
lacking
adj absent 222.11
bereft 473.8
nonexistent 761.8
incomplete 794.4
short of 910.5
insufficient 991.9
wanting 991.11
imperfect 1002.4
prep absent 222.19
lackluster
n colorlessness 36.1
mediocrity 1004.1
dullness 1026.5
adj colorless 36.7
mediocre 1004.7
lusterless 1026.17
lack of feeling
lack of emotion 94
unfeeling 94.1
unconcern 102.2
indiscrimination
  944.1
lackwitted 921.13
laconic
n man of few words
  344.5
adj taciturn 344.9
concise 537.6
lacquer
n blanket 295.12
v color 35.13
coat 295.24
lacquered 287.10
lactate nourish 8.19
secrete 13.5
lactation humor 2.22
secretion 13.1
liquidity 1059.1
lacteal secretory 13.7
milky 1059.5
lactose intolerance
  85.22
lacuna interval 224.1
cavity 284.2
opening 292.1
deficiency 794.2
interruption 812.2
lacustrian
n lake dweller 241.2
adj lakish 241.5
lacy netlike 170.11
thin 270.16
lad man 76.5
boy 302.5
ladder 193.4
lade load 159.15

burden 297.13
fill 793.7
laden weighted 297.18
fraught 793.12
la-di-da 500.15
ladies' man
beau 104.13
dandy 500.9
philanderer 562.12
lading placement 159.6
freight 176.6
load 196.2
burden 297.7
full measure 793.3
ladino 796.8
ladle
n container 195.1
v dip 176.17
lady woman 77.5
female 77.8
cocaine 87.6
ladylove 104.14
wife 563.8
aristocrat 607.4
noblewoman 608.6
person of honor 644.8
good person 659.1
card 758.2
Lady title 648.2
Chance 971.2
lady bountiful
humanitarian 143.8
donor 478.11
cheerful giver 485.2
lady-killer beau 104.13
dandy 500.9
philanderer 562.12
libertine 665.10
ladylike
feminine 77.13
well-bred 504.17
upper-class 607.10
noble 608.10
ladylove 104.14
Lady Luck 971.2
lag
n dawdling 175.3
slowing 175.4
delay 845.2
time constants
  1040.11
v lag behind 166.4
dawdle 175.8
be behind 217.8
dally 331.14
mistime 832.2
delay 845.8
fall short 910.2
laggard
n slowpoke 175.5
idler 331.8
adj reluctant 325.6
indolent 331.19
dilatory 845.17
lagging
n dawdling 175.3
delay 845.2
adj dawdling 175.11
dilatory 845.17
lagniappe extra 254.4
gratuity 478.5
bonus 624.6

surplus 992.5
lagoon 241.1
laic
n layman 700.2
amateur 726.5
adj lay 700.3
laid-back
nonchalant 106.15
at ease 121.12
quiescent 173.12
negligent 340.10
leisurely 402.6
unstrict 426.5
laid low ill 85.55
low 274.7
worn-out 393.36
laid up invalided 85.58
stored 386.14
lair den 228.26
disapproved place
  228.28
cave 284.5
hiding place 346.4
retreat 584.6
refuge 1008.5
laird proprietor 470.2
nobleman 608.4
laisser aller 329.4
laissez-faire
n inaction 329.1
neglect 340.1
noninterference 430.9
policy 609.4
capitalism 611.8
adj passive 329.6
negligent 340.10
conservative 852.8
lake 241.1
lake dweller 241.2
lakefront
n shore 234.2
adj coastal 234.7
lam depart 188.7
flee 368.11
lama 699.13
lamb
n mutton 10.15
child 302.3
fledgling 302.10
sheep 311.7
simple soul 416.3
endearment term
  562.6
innocent 657.4
cheater 759.22
exposure 1005.3
v give birth 1.3
lambaste defeat 412.9
attack 459.15
disapprove 510.18
punish 604.15
pound 901.16
lambent
lightly touching 73.12
flickering 1024.36
illuminated 1024.39
lame
v disable 19.9
cripple 393.14
hamper 1011.11
adj crippled 393.30
unsuccessful 410.18

foolish 922.9
lamebrain 923.2
lame duck
officeholder 610.11
insolvent 625.4
speculator 737.11
lame excuse
pretext 376.1
excuse 600.4
lamellate 296.6
lament
n plaint 115.3
v distress 98.14
mourn 115.10
lamentable
distressing 98.20
sorrowful 112.26
terrible 999.9
lamentation
distressfulness 98.5
sorrow 112.10
mourning 115
lamenting 115.1
lamenter griever 115.8
mourner 309.7
laminate
n plastic 1052.6
v layer 296.5
adj layered 296.6
lamination 296.4
lamp 1025.1
lampoon
n wit 489.1
burlesque 508.6
send-up 512.5
v burlesque 508.11
satirize 512.12
lampooner
humorist 489.12
lampoonist 512.7
lanai 197.21
lance
n cavalryman 461.12
v perforate 292.15
stab 459.25
sever 801.11
throw 903.10
Lancelot 608.5
lancinate 96.18
land
n region 231.1
country 232.1
earth 234
ground 234.1
real estate 471.6
v set her down 184.43
come to land 186.8
get down 194.7
meet one's Maker
  307.21
acquire 472.9
catch 480.17
landed
possessing 469.9
propertied 471.8
landed gentry
landowner 470.3
gentry 608.3
landfill
receptacle of filth
  80.12
derelict 370.4

trash pile 391.6
landholding
  n real estate 234.1
  ownership 469.2
  adj possessing 469.9
landing
  coming in 184.18
  airport 184.22
  landfall 186.2
  stairs 193.3
  platform 900.13
  harbor 1008.6
landlady 470.2
landless 619.9
landlocked 428.15
landloper 178.3
landloping 177.37
landlord
  proprietor 470.2
  host 585.5
landlubber
  mariner 183.2
  landsman 234.3
landmark
  marker 517.10
  salient point 996.6
landmark decision
  598.9
landmass
  world region 231.6
  land 234.1
  continent 235.1
land-office business
  demand 421.1
  roaring trade 1009.5
land on attack 459.15
  punish 604.11
landowner 470.3
landscape view 33.6
  scene 712.12
landscape architect
  artist 716.10
  architect 717.3
  horticulturist 1067.6
landscape gardener
  artist 716.10
  architect 717.3
  horticulturist 1067.6
land shark cheat 357.3
  thief 483.1
landslide slide 194.4
  victory 411.1
  returns 609.21
  plenty 990.2
  superabundance 992.2
landsman
  fellow citizen 227.5
  landman 234.3
  friend 588.4
landward
  clockwise 161.24
  coastward 182.67
lane airway 184.33
  passageway 383.3
  bowling 750.1
  track 755.1
lang syne 836.2
language
  n tongue 523
  communication 523.1
  speech 524.1
  diction 532.1

assembler language
  1041.13
  adj speech 524.30
languid weak 16.12
  tired 21.7
  sleepy 22.21
  apathetic 94.13
  inert 173.14
  slow 175.10
  languorous 331.20
languish weaken 16.9
  fail 85.47
  lose heart 112.16
  decrease 252.6
  pine 393.18
languishing
  n unhealthiness 85.3
  yearning 100.5
  adj drooping 16.21
  unhealthy 85.53
  wistful 100.23
  loving 104.27
  dejected 112.22
  decreasing 252.11
  deteriorating 393.45
  protracted 826.11
languor weakness 16.1
  fatigue 21.1
  sleepiness 22.1
  apathy 94.4
  inertness 173.4
  slowness 175.1
  languidness 331.6
languorous weak 16.12
  inert 173.14
  slow 175.10
  languid 331.20
lanky
  n slim 270.8
  adj lean 270.17
  tall 272.16
lanolin 1054.3
lantern tower 272.6
  roof 295.6
  light source 1025.1
lantern jaws 270.5
lap
  n drink 8.4
  touch 73.1
  front 216.1
  swash 238.8
  overlayer 295.4
  lamina 296.2
  race 457.12
  track 755.1
  car race 756.3
  circuit 913.2
  v clothe 5.38
  lap up 8.30
  ripple 52.11
  lick 73.9
  tipple 88.24
  lead 165.2
  overtake 174.13
  surround 209.6
  border 211.10
  overflow 238.17
  plash 238.19
  fold 291.5
  wrap 295.20
  overlie 295.30
  cuddle 562.17

circle 913.5
lap dog favorite 104.16
  sycophant 138.3
  dog 311.17
lapel 291.1
lapidary
  n printmaker 716.8
  adj elegant 533.6
  glyptic 713.12
lapin 311.24
lap of luxury 1009.1
lappet pendant 202.4
  fold 291.1
lapping
  n drinking 8.3
  lap 238.8
  adj rippling 52.19
  overlying 295.36
lapse
  n regression 163.1
  sinkage 194.2
  decline 252.2
  neglect 340.1
  deterioration 393.3
  relapse 394.1
  misdeed 655.2
  impiety 694.1
  close 819.3
  pause 856.3
  conversion 857.1
  reversion 858.1
  slip 974.4
  v regress 163.5
  sink 194.6
  invert 205.5
  neglect 340.6
  decline 393.17
  relapse 394.4
  go wrong 654.9
  come to an end 819.6
  elapse 820.5
  pass 836.6
  defect 857.13
  revert 858.4
  err 974.9
lapsed inverted 205.7
  nonobservant 435.5
  unvirtuous 654.12
  carnal 663.6
  impious 694.6
  unregenerate 695.18
  past 836.7
lapse of memory 989.1
lapse of time
  passage of time 820.4
  period 823.1
laptop computer
  1041.2
lap up
  sponge up 8.30
  tipple 88.24
  kid oneself 953.6
larboard
  n left side 220.1
  adj left 220.4
  adv leftward 220.6
larcenous 482.21
larceny 482.2
lard make better 392.9
  oil 1054.8
larder
  provisions 10.5

store 386.1
  pantry 386.8
lares and penates
  household deity
  228.30
  property 471.1
  familiar spirit 678.12
large immense 247.7
  sizable 257.16
  liberal 485.4
largehearted
  benevolent 143.15
  liberal 485.4
  magnanimous 652.6
large-minded 978.8
larger than life
  large 257.16
  huge 257.20
  full-sized 257.22
  excessive 992.16
  weighty 996.20
large-scale
  large 257.16
  extensive 863.13
largess gratuity 478.5
  liberality 485.1
largo
  n slow motion 175.2
  music 708.25
  tempo 709.24
  adj music 708.54
lariat 356.13
lark
  n ascent 193.7
  songbird 710.23
  revel 743.6
  v make merry 743.24
larrup punish 604.15
  beat 901.17
larva chrysalis 302.12
  embryo 305.14
  insect 311.31
  specter 987.1
larval 305.22
larynx 524.19
lascivious
  lustful 75.26
  desirous 100.21
  amorous 104.26
  lecherous 665.29
lash
  n goad 375.8
  whip 605.1
  slap 901.8
  v anchor 182.15
  goad 375.15
  bind 428.10
  criticize 510.20
  whip 604.13
  join 799.9
  drive 1068.8
lashing
  corporal punishment
  604.4
  fastening 799.3
lass woman 77.5
  ladylove 104.14
  girl 302.6
lassitude
  weakness 16.1
  fatigue 21.1
  languor 331.6

lasso
  n circle 280.2
  snare 356.13
  v catch 480.17
last
  n mold 785.6
  end 819.1
  v keep alive 306.10
  persevere 360.2
  stay with it 360.4
  live on 760.9
  elapse 820.5
  endure 826.6
  outlast 826.8
  remain 852.5
  adj departing 188.18
  completing 407.9
  final 819.11
  eventual 830.11
  foregoing 836.11
  state-of-the-art 840.14
  adv finally 819.12
last-ditch
  final 819.11
  makeshift 994.7
lasting
  persevering 360.8
  sturdy 762.7
  temporal 820.7
  durable 826.10
  protracted 826.11
  permanent 852.7
  unchangeable 854.17
  remembered 988.23
  tough 1047.4
last minute 845.1
last-minute
  hasty 401.9
  later 845.18
last name 527.5
last resort
  expedient 994.2
  recourse 1008.2
last rites
  last offices 309.4
  unction 701.5
last straw 885.3
Last Supper 701.7
last word
  supremacy 249.3
  ultimatum 439.3
  meaning 518.1
  administration 573.3
the last word
  the rage 578.4
  novelty 840.2
  influence 893.1
  acme of perfection 1001.3
latch close 293.6
  hook 799.8
late
  adj retarded 175.12
  dead 307.30
  anachronous 832.3
  former 836.10
  recent 840.12
  untimely 843.6
  belated 845.16
  adv behind 845.19
late bloomer 845.6
latecomer 845.6

late lamented
  n corpse 307.16
  adj dead 307.30
latent invisible 32.5
  inert 173.14
  secret 345.11
  concealed 346.11
  lurking 519.5
later
  adj subsequent 834.4
  future 838.8
  recent 840.12
  last-minute 845.18
  adv subsequently 834.6
  in the future 838.9
lateral
  n speech sound 524.13
  throw 903.3
  v go sideways 218.5
  adj side 218.6
  sided 218.7
  phonetic 524.31
latest present 837.2
  state-of-the-art 840.14
the latest thing
  the rage 578.4
  novelty 840.2
lath
  n thinness 270.7
  strip 271.4
  wood 1052.3
  v cover 295.23
lathe 857.10
lather
  n sweat 12.7
  dither 105.6
  impatience 135.1
  foam 320.2
  v wash 79.19
  get excited 105.17
  foam 320.2
  defeat 412.9
  punish 604.15
latitude
  room 158.3
  map 159.5
  zone 231.3
  breadth 269.1
  coordinates 300.5
  scope 430.4
  broad-mindedness 978.1
latitudinarian
  n free agent 430.12
  freethinker 695.13
  liberal 978.6
  adj nonrestrictive 430.25
  freethinking 695.21
  liberal 978.9
latrine
  convenience 12.10
  toilet 12.11
latter foregoing 836.11
  recent 840.12
lattice
  n network 170.3
  frame 266.4
  atomic cluster 1037.7
  reactor 1037.13
  v net 170.7

laud
  n thanks 150.2
  praise 509.5
  glorification 696.2
  paean 696.3
  v praise 509.12
  glorify 696.11
laudable
  praiseworthy 509.20
  good 998.12
laudatory 509.16
lauded 247.9
laugh
  n laughter 116.4
  joke 489.6
  v be pleased 95.11
  exude cheerfulness 109.6
  burst out laughing 116.8
laughable
  humorous 488.4
  absurd 922.11
laugh at flout 454.4
  ridicule 508.8
laughing
  n laughter 116.4
  adj happy 95.15
  cheerful 109.11
laughingstock 508.7
laugh it up laugh 116.8
  amuse oneself 743.22
laughs 743.2
laughter
  merriment 109.5
  laughing 116.4
launch
  n motorboat 180.4
  beginning 817.1
  rocket launching 1072.9
  v propose 439.5
  inaugurate 817.11
  throw 903.10
  start 903.13
  project 1072.13
launcher 462.21
launching
  beginning 817.1
  inauguration 817.5
  innovation 851.4
launching pad
  beginning 817.1
  platform 900.13
  rocket launcher 1072.10
launch into
  undertake 404.3
  set to work 725.15
launder 79.19
laundress 79.15
Laundromat 79.11
laundry
  laundering 79.6
  washery 79.11
laundry list list 870.1
  schedule 964.3
laureate
  n superior 249.4
  champion 413.15
  poet 720.11
  adj honored 646.9

laurels
  supremacy 249.3
  victory 411.1
  trophy 646.3
lava
  combustion product 1019.16
  rock 1057.1
lavatory latrine 12.10
  bathing place 79.10
  washbasin 79.12
  bathroom 197.26
lave wash 79.19
  soak 1063.13
lavender 46.3
lavish
  v give 478.12
  furnish 478.15
  spare no expense 485.3
  squander 486.3
  adj liberal 485.4
  prodigal 486.8
  ornate 545.11
  teeming 883.9
  plentiful 990.7
  superabundant 992.19
lavish with 992.14
law
  n rule 419.2
  decree 420.4
  prohibition 444.1
  lex 673.3
  legal system 673.4
  jurisprudence 673.7
  game 752.3
  norm 868.4
  axiom 973.2
  v sue 598.12
the Law 683.3
the law 1007.16
law-abiding
  obedient 326.3
  honest 644.13
law and order 464.2
lawbreaker
  evildoer 593.1
  criminal 660.10
lawbreaking
  disobedience 327.1
  wrongdoing 655.1
  violation 674.3
law enforcement agency 1007.17
law enforcement agent 1007.15
law firm 597.4
lawful
  permissible 443.15
  just 649.8
  legal 673.10
  valid 972.14
  genuine 972.15
lawgiver 610.3
lawless
  disobedient 327.8
  licentious 418.5
  illegal 674.6
lawmaker 610.3
lawmaking
  n legislation 613.5
  adj legislative 613.11

legal 673.10
lawn 310.7
law of averages 971.1
lawsuit suit 598.1
accusation 599.1
lawyer attorney 597.1
professional 726.4
lax indolent 331.19
negligent 340.10
slack 426.4
lenient 427.7
unrestrained 430.24
nonrestrictive 430.25
permissive 443.14
phonetic 524.31
wanton 665.26
loose 803.5
dilatory 845.17
vague 970.19
inaccurate 974.17
flaccid 1045.10
laxative
n cathartic 86.17
adj cathartic 86.48
laxity neglect 340.1
laxness 426.1
nonobservance 435.1
wantonness 665.4
looseness 803.2
vagueness 970.4
inaccuracy 974.2
flaccidity 1045.3
lay
n navigation 159.3
direction 161.1
air 708.4
song 708.14
bet 759.3
v copulate 75.21
reproduce 78.9
relieve 120.5
place 159.12
deposit 159.14
ship activity 182.48
lie 201.5
level 201.6
smooth 287.5
pacify 465.7
impose 643.4
moderate 670.6
exorcise 690.12
bet 759.25
adj laic 700.3
lay an egg
fall flat 117.4
fail 410.10
bungle 414.12
bomb 459.23
lay aside
remove 176.11
put away 390.6
segregate 772.6
postpone 845.9
dismiss 983.4
lay away store 386.10
put away 390.6
lay back relax 20.7
compose oneself 106.7
lay before
confront 216.8
propose 439.5
lay by lay to 182.17

lie idle 331.16
store 386.10
reserve 386.12
put away 390.6
prepare for 405.11
postpone 845.9
lay down
deposit 159.14
careen 182.43
level 201.6
layer 296.5
affirm 334.5
give up 370.7
store 386.10
prescribe 420.9
pledge 438.10
pay over 624.15
bet 759.25
postulate 950.12
lay down the law
put one's foot down
420.10
direct 573.8
dominate 612.15
dogmatize 969.10
layer
n tier 296
thickness 296.1
v lay down 296.5
layette 5.30
lay figure figure 349.6
figurehead 575.5
art equipment 712.18
thing of naught 763.2
artist's model 785.5
lay hands on
attack 459.14
seize 480.14
bless 696.13
minister 701.15
lay in sail for 182.35
store 386.10
gather materials
1052.7
lay into
lift one's hand against
457.14
attack 459.15
punish 604.11
lay it on
exaggerate 355.3
flatter 511.6
talk big 545.6
pile it on 992.11
lay it on thick
coat 295.24
exaggerate 355.3
affect 500.12
boast 502.7
commend 509.11
flatter 511.6
talk big 545.6
pile it on 992.11
lay low
weaken 16.10
level 201.6
lie low 274.5
strike dead 308.17
hide 346.8
fell 912.5
layman laic 700.2
amateur 726.5

layoff
unemployment 331.3
dismissal 908.5
lay off
v take a rest 20.8
circumscribe 210.4
measure off 300.11
lie idle 331.16
plot 381.10
cease to use 390.4
cease 856.6
dismiss 908.19
inter cease! 856.14
the lay of the land
764.2
lay on cover 295.19
coat 295.24
lift one's hand against
457.14
blame 599.8
whip 604.13
impose 643.4
administer 643.6
layout form 262.1
plan 381.1
composition 548.2
roulette 759.12
gambling wheel
759.16
order 806.1
lay out deaden 25.4
level 201.6
form 262.7
measure off 300.11
kill 308.13
embalm 309.21
plot 381.10
pledge 438.10
spend 626.5
order 806.4
fell 912.5
layover 225.5
lay over sojourn 225.8
cover 295.19
postpone 845.9
lay the foundation
establish 159.16
prepare the way
405.12
lay to lay by 182.17
lie idle 331.16
exert oneself 725.9
attribute to 887.4
lay to rest inter 309.19
abolish 395.13
end 819.5
disprove 957.4
lay up afflict 85.49
lay to 182.17
layer 296.5
store up 386.11
lay waste
destroy 395.10
raze 671.11
laze go slow 175.6
idle 331.12
lazy slow 175.10
indolent 331.19
careless 340.11
dilatory 845.17
lazybones 331.7
lea 310.8

leach
n solution 1062.3
v refine 79.22
exude 190.15
trickle 238.18
subtract 255.9
liquefy 1062.5
soak 1063.13
leached 890.4
lead
n instrument 200.6
weight 297.6
v weight 297.12
gravitate 297.15
adj brass 1056.17
lead
n superiority 249.1
hunter 311.13
shackle 428.4
pointer 517.4
clue 517.9
direction 573.1
role 704.10
script 706.2
leading man 707.6
notation 709.12
lawn bowling 750.3
bridge 758.3
chief 996.10
v take direction 161.7
head 165.2
be in front 216.7
rule 249.11
induce 375.22
direct 573.8
govern 612.12
conduct 708.45
escort 768.8
precede 813.2
go before 815.3
initiate 817.10
cause 885.11
influence 893.7
tend 895.3
lead by the nose
have subject 432.10
dominate 612.15
influence 893.7
have influence over
893.11
leaden
colorless 36.7
gray 39.4
dull 117.6
inert 173.14
heavy 297.16
languid 331.20
stiff 534.3
brass 1056.17
leader
vanguard 216.2
superior 249.4
hunter 311.13
commentary 556.2
director 574.6
chief 575.3
conductor 710.17
commodity 735.2
lawn bowling 750.3
precursor 815.1
special 865.2
question 937.10

leadership
supremacy 249.3
mastership 417.7
directorship 573.4
influence 893.1
leading
n preceding 165
heading 165.1
direction 573.1
adj heading 165.3
front 216.10
chief 249.14
authoritative 417.15
directing 573.12
governing 612.18
preceding 813.4
first 817.17
paramount 996.24
leading lady
role 704.10
lead 707.6
leading to 895.5
lead item
commodity 735.2
special 865.2
lead off
precede 813.2
initiate 817.10
lead on lure 377.5
direct 573.8
exercise influence
893.9
lead one to expect
give hope 124.10
be as expected 130.10
promise 133.13
be probable 967.4
lead the way lead 165.2
set an example 785.7
go before 815.3
initiate 817.10
lead time
preparation 405.1
earliness 844.1
forethought 960.2
lead to direct to 161.6
extend to 261.6
pave the way 405.12
entail 771.4
determine 885.12
**lead up the garden
path** 356.16
leaf
n tobacco 89.2
lamina 296.2
frond 310.17
advertising matter
352.8
makeup 554.12
paper 1052.5
v vegetate 310.31
leaflet leaf 310.17
advertising matter
352.8
booklet 554.11
leaf metal 1056.3
leaf through 937.25
leafy green 44.4
leaved 310.38
league
n treaty 437.2
affiliation 450.2

association 617.1
baseball 745.1
football 746.1
bowling 750.1
soccer 752.1
combination 804.1
v cooperate 450.3
come together 769.16
put together 799.5
ally 804.4
leagued
assembled 769.21
joined 799.13
enleagued 804.6
League of Nations
supranational
government 612.7
United Nations 614.1
leak
n leakage 190.5
opening 292.1
divulgence 351.2
escape 369.1
v leak out 190.14
communicate 343.7
disclose 351.4
betray 351.6
go to waste 473.6
hint 551.10
leakage entrance 189.1
leaking 190.5
escape 369.1
waste 473.2
leak in 189.10
leak out leak 190.14
be revealed 351.8
find vent 369.10
leakproof
resistant 15.20
watertight 1064.11
leaky
exudative 190.20
apertured 292.19
lean
n inclination 204.2
v incline 204.10
gravitate 297.15
be willing 324.3
tend 895.3
adj thin 270.17
plain-speaking 535.3
meager 991.10
leaning
n desire 100.3
inclination 204.2
preference 371.5
aptitude 413.5
partiality 650.3
tendency 895.1
disposition 977.3
prejudice 979.3
adj inclining 204.15
unbalanced 790.5
tending 895.4
lean on
coerce 424.8
threaten 514.2
exercise influence
893.9
rest on 900.22
rely on 952.16
lean-to 228.9

lean toward
desire 100.14
prefer 371.17
take the attitude
977.6
leap
n progression 162.1
ascent 193.1
interval 224.1
degree 245.1
increase 251.1
jump 366.1
curtain-raiser 815.2
innovation 851.4
v speed 174.8
jump 366.5
make haste 401.5
leap before one looks
401.7
leapfrog
n leap 366.1
v leap 366.5
leaping
n jumping 366.3
adj happy 95.15
ascending 193.14
jumping 366.7
leap year
moment 823.2
anniversary 849.4
learn
come to know 551.14
get 570.6
master 570.9
come to one's
knowledge 927.14
discover 940.2
understand 521.7
learn by heart 988.17
learned
studentlike 572.12
wise 919.17
erudite 927.21
educated 570.16
learner
student 572.1
beginner 817.2
learning
intellectual
acquirement 570.1
enlightenment 927.4
discovery 940.1
lease
n possession 469.1
rental 615.6
v inhabit 225.7
rent 615.15
rent out 615.16
leasehold
n possession 469.1
adj freehold 471.10
leaseholder 470.4
lease-lend
rent out 615.16
lend 620.5
leash
n shackle 428.4
three 875.1
v bind 428.10
join 799.9
least
n minority 884.3

adj humble 137.10
smallest 250.8
minority 884.7
leather
n fur 4.2
hide 4.3
toughness 1047.2
v punish 604.15
leatherneck 183.4
leave
n vacation 20.3
leave-taking 188.4
absence 222.4
consent 441.1
permission 443.1
game 750.2
v depart 188.6
leave over 256.6
bereave 307.28
vegetate 310.31
leave undone 340.7
abandon 370.5
permit 443.9
resign 448.2
bequeath 478.18
separate 801.8
inter go away! 908.31
leave alone
let alone 329.4
not interfere 430.16
give permission
443.12
be conservative 852.6
leave behind
overtake 174.13
outdistance 249.10
leave 256.6
bereave 307.28
abandon 370.5
leaved
green 44.4
leafy 310.38
leaven
n bread 10.27
leavening 298.4
transformer 851.5
v pervade 221.7
raise 298.7
imbue 796.11
qualify 958.3
leavening
n bread 10.27
fermentation 298.4
adj raising 298.17
**leave no stone
unturned**
prosecute to a
conclusion 360.5
make every effort
403.15
take precautions
494.6
be thorough 793.8
ransack 937.32
leave of absence
vacation 20.3
absence 222.4
leave off
v give up 370.7
break the habit 374.3
cease to use 390.4
cease 856.6

inter cease! 856.13
leave one cold
  not be affected by
    94.5
  fall flat 117.4
  bore 118.7
leave out 772.4
leave-taking 188.4
leave undone
  leave 340.7
  slight 340.8
  neglect 408.2
leave word
  communicate 343.7
  inform 551.8
leaving
  n departure 188.1
  absence 222.4
  abandonment 370.1
  adj departing 188.18
leaving out off 255.14
  excluding 772.10
leaving-out 772.1
leavings
  remainder 256.1
  refuse 391.4
  extract 892.3
lecher
  philanderer 562.12
  reprobate 660.5
  satyr 665.11
lechery
  philandering 562.10
  lasciviousness 665.5
lectern pulpit 703.13
  table 900.15
lection 341.2
lector lecturer 571.7
  holy orders 699.4
lecture
  n reproof 510.5
  prelection 543.3
  lesson 568.7
  v reprove 510.17
  prelect 543.11
  expound 568.16
lecturer
  praelector 543.5
  academic rank 571.3
  lector 571.7
lecturing
  n public speaking
    543.1
  adj educational 568.18
ledge
  horizontal 201.3
  border 211.4
  layer 296.1
  shelf 900.14
ledger
  record book 549.11
  account book 628.4
  bill 870.5
lee
  n lee side 218.2
  protection 1007.1
  adj side 218.6
leech
  n doctor 90.4
  parasite 138.5
  sail 180.14
  bloodsucker 311.36

extortionist 480.12
  adhesive 802.4
  v bleed 91.27
leeching 91.20
leer
  n look 27.3
  scornful laugh 508.4
  signal 517.15
  v scrutinize 27.14
  signal 517.22
leering
  n ridicule 508.1
  adj ridiculing
    508.12
leery wary 494.9
  doubting 954.9
  incredulous 955.4
lees dregs 256.2
  refuse 391.4
  extract 892.3
leeward
  n lee side 218.2
  adj side 218.6
  adv clockwise 161.24
  to leeward 182.68
  downwind 218.9
leeway room 158.3
  way 182.9
  drift 184.28
  interval 224.1
  distance 261.1
  latitude 430.4
left
  n left side 220.1
  liberalism 611.3
  liberal 611.11
  adj departed 188.19
  left-hand 220.4
  remaining 256.7
  abandoned 370.8
  adv leftward 220.6
left-handed
  insulting 156.8
  oblique 204.13
  sinistromanual 220.5
  bungling 414.20
left-hander
  southpaw 220.3
  baseball team 745.2
leftist
  n liberal 611.11
  adj liberal 611.19
left-out 772.7
leftover
  n surplus 992.5
  adj remaining 256.7
  surplus 992.18
leftward
  clockwise 161.24
  to the left 220.6
left wing
  left side 220.1
  liberalism 611.3
left-wing left 220.4
  liberal 611.19
left-winger
  left side 220.1
  liberal 611.11
lefty
  n left-hander 220.3
  baseball team 745.2
  adj left-handed 220.5

leg
  n body part 2.7
  fowl part 10.22
  limb 177.14
  voyage 182.6
  shank 273.6
  member 792.4
  v walk 177.27
legacy bequest 478.10
  inheritance 479.2
  effect 886.1
legal
  permissible 443.15
  recorded 549.17
  just 649.8
  legitimate 673.10
  valid 972.14
legal age 303.2
legal counselor 597.1
legalistic formal 580.7
  jurisprudent 673.11
  conformist 866.6
legality
  permissibility 443.8
  justice 649.1
  lawfulness 673
  legitimacy 673.1
legalization
  authorization 443.3
  legitimation 673.2
legalize
  authorize 443.11
  legitimize 673.8
legal system
  judiciary 594.2
  law 673.4
legal tender 728.1
legate
  delegate 576.2
  diplomat 576.6
legatee 479.4
legation
  foreign office 576.7
  commission 615.1
  office 739.7
legato
  n music 708.25
  execution 708.30
  note 709.14
  adj music 708.53
legend map 159.5
  posthumous fame
    662.7
  mythology 678.14
  history 719.1
  tradition 841.2
  caption 936.2
legendary
  fabricated 354.28
  distinguished 662.16
  mythic 678.15
  historical 719.7
  fictional 722.7
  traditional 841.12
  extraordinary 869.14
  fictitious 985.21
legible 521.12
legion
  military unit 461.22
  throng 769.4
  multitude 883.3
legionary 461.6

legislate
  make laws 613.10
  legalize 673.8
legislation
  lawmaking 613.5
  legalization 673.2
  law 673.3
legislative
  legislatorial 613.11
  legal 673.10
legislator
  public official 575.17
  lawmaker 610.3
legislature
  council 423.1
  legislative body 613.1
  legislation 613.5
legit
  n show business 704.1
  adj legal 673.10
legitimacy
  authority 417.1
  permissibility 443.8
  justifiability 600.7
  legality 673.1
  genuineness 972.7
legitimate
  v authorize 443.11
  legalize 673.8
  adj permissible 443.15
  justifiable 600.14
  legal 673.10
  dramatic 704.33
  logical 934.20
  valid 972.14
  genuine 972.15
leg man 555.4
legume plant 310.4
  seed vessel 310.28
legwork 937.4
lei 310.23
leisure
  n idleness 331.2
  ease 402.1
  pause 856.3
  adj idle 331.18
  leisured 402.5
leisure class 331.11
leisured
  idle 331.18
  leisure 402.5
leitmotiv 708.24
lemon
  n sour 67.2
  failure 410.2
  adj yellow 43.4
lend loan 620.5
  discount 728.27
lend a hand 449.11
lend an ear 48.10
lender 620.3
lending loaning 620.1
  money market 728.16
lend-lease
  n rental 615.6
  lending 620.1
  v rent out 615.16
  lend 620.5
length size 257.1
  distance 261.1
  longness 267.1
  extent 300.3

lengthen increase 251.4
  prolong 267.6
  protract 826.9
  sustain 855.4
lengthened
  prolonged 267.8
  protracted 826.11
lengthening
  n prolongation 267.4
  protraction 826.2
  continuance 855.1
  adj increasing 251.8
lengthy long 267.7
  giant 272.16
  wordy 538.12
leniency patience 134.1
  considerateness 143.3
  pity 145.1
  unstrictness 426.2
  mercifulness 427
  lenientness 427.1
  modulation 670.2
  tolerance 978.4
  softness 1045.1
lenient patient 134.9
  considerate 143.16
  pitying 145.7
  unstrict 426.5
  mild 427.7
  permissive 443.14
  tolerant 978.11
lenitive
  n palliative 86.10
  moderator 670.3
  ointment 1054.3
  adj palliative 86.40
  relieving 120.9
  moderating 670.16
  qualifying 958.7
  lubricant 1054.10
lens eye 2.9
  glass 29.6
Lent fast day 515.3
  penance 658.3
Lenten
  fasting 515.5
  abstinent 668.10
  meager 991.10
lentil 310.4
lento 708.54
leonine 311.41
leopard
  variegation 47.6
  wild cat 311.22
leper 586.4
leprechaun 678.8
lesbian
  n homosexual 75.14
  mannish female 76.9
  adj homosexual 75.29
lesion sore 85.36
  trauma 85.37
  pain 96.5
less
  adj inferior 250.6
  reduced 252.10
  fewer 884.6
  adv decreasingly
    252.12
  prep off 255.14
  without 991.17
lessee lodger 227.8

tenant 470.4
lessen relieve 120.5
  decrease 252.6
  reduce 252.7
  subtract 255.9
  extenuate 600.12
  moderate 670.6
lessening
  n relief 120.1
  decrease 252.1
  deterioration 393.3
  modulation 670.2
  adj decreasing 252.11
  mitigating 670.14
lesser inferior 250.6
  reduced 252.10
lesson warning 399.1
  reproof 510.5
  teaching 568.7
lest 896.7
let
  n rental 615.6
  game 748.2
  hindrance 1011.1
  v draw off 192.12
  permit 443.9
  rent 615.15
  rent out 615.16
  suppose 950.10
  adj employed 615.20
let alone
  v leave undone 340.7
  avoid 368.6
  not use 390.5
  abstain 668.7
  adv additionally
    253.11
  prep with 253.12
  excluding 772.10
let be let alone 329.4
  leave undone 340.7
  not interfere 430.16
  be conservative 852.6
  suppose 950.10
letdown
  disappointment 132.1
  humiliation 137.2
  slowing 175.4
  collapse 410.3
  modulation 670.2
let down
  v rest 20.7
  disappoint 132.2
  slow 175.9
  deceive 356.14
  deteriorate 393.16
  betray 645.14
  relax 670.9
  depress 912.4
  adj disappointed
    132.5
  discontented 108.7
let drop betray 351.6
  remark 524.25
  drop 912.7
let fly throw 903.10
  shoot 903.12
let go condone 148.4
  let pass 329.5
  neglect 340.6
  leave undone 340.7
  cease to use 390.4

exempt 430.14
  let oneself go 430.19
  release 431.5
  relinquish 475.4
  acquit 601.4
  make merry 743.24
  disband 770.8
  loosen 803.3
  throw 903.10
  dismiss 908.19
  let out 908.24
lethal deadly 308.22
  harmful 999.12
lethality
  deadliness 308.8
  harmfulness 999.5
lethargic sleepy 22.21
  apathetic 94.13
  languid 331.20
lethargy
  sleepiness 22.1
  stupor 22.6
  apathy 94.4
  languor 331.6
  stupidity 921.3
let in receive 187.10
  welcome 585.7
let in on divulge 351.5
  tip 551.11
  disillusion 976.2
let it all hang out
  lighten 120.7
  confess 351.7
  let oneself go 430.19
let it go
  v forget 148.5
  dismiss 983.4
  phrs no matter 997.25
let loose
  let oneself go 430.19
  release 431.5
  loose 431.6
  make merry 743.24
  throw 903.10
let off
  v exempt 430.14
  release 431.5
  acquit 601.4
  rent out 615.16
  explode 671.14
  shoot 903.12
  adj exempt 430.30
let on confess 351.7
  sham 354.20
let one's hair down
  lighten 120.7
  divulge 351.5
  let oneself go 430.19
  chat 541.10
  not stand on
    ceremony 581.2
  make merry 743.24
let one have it
  attack 459.15
  disapprove 510.18
  punish 604.11
let out
  draw off 192.12
  lengthen 267.6
  disclose 351.4
  divulge 351.5
  release 431.5

say 524.23
  rent out 615.16
  dismiss 908.19
  give vent to 908.24
let pass accept 134.7
  let go 329.5
  be inattentive 983.2
let slip let go 329.5
  neglect 340.6
  betray 351.6
  lose 473.4
  dismiss 983.4
letter
  n representation 349.1
  symbol 546.1
  written character
    547.9
  writing 547.10
  type 548.6
  message 552.4
  epistle 553.2
  v initial 546.6
  adj epistolary 553.14
letter carrier
  carrier 176.7
  postman 353.5
lettered literal 546.8
  learned 927.21
letterer 547.13
letterhead label 517.13
  address 553.9
lettering
  initialing 546.5
  writing 547.1
  handwriting style
    547.4
letter of credit
  credit instrument
    622.3
  negotiable instrument
    728.11
letter-perfect 972.15
letterpress
  printing 548.1
  print 548.3
  printed matter 548.10
letters
  writing system 546.3
  literary work 547.12
  record 549.1
  literature 718.1
  scholarship 927.5
letter writer 553.8
letter writing 553.1
letting go 475.1
letup slowing 175.4
  decrease 252.1
  modulation 670.2
  interruption 812.2
  interim 825.1
  pause 856.3
let-up 175.9
let up
  v relax 20.7
  decrease 252.6
  ease up 670.9
  loosen 803.3
  pause 856.9
  inter cease! 856.13
let well enough alone
  be content 107.5
  be inattentive 983.2

leukocyte 2.23
levant
  flee 368.10
  not pay 625.6
Levant 231.6
levanter
  north wind 318.9
  defaulter 625.5
levee
  social gathering
    582.10
  assembly 769.2
  barrier 1011.5
level
  n floor 197.23
  horizontal 201.3
  plain 236.1
  degree 245.1
  smoothness 287.3
  layer 296.1
  class 607.1
  classification 808.2
  v flatten 201.6
  smooth 287.5
  raze 395.19
  make uniform 780.4
  equalize 789.6
  fell 912.5
  adj horizontal 201.7
  straight 277.6
  smooth 287.9
  just 649.8
  uniform 780.5
  equal 789.7
  adv horizontally 201.9
level at 459.22
level head
  equanimity 106.3
  sensibleness 919.6
levelheaded
  composed 106.13
  equable 670.13
  sensible 919.18
level off
  land 184.43
  make uniform 780.4
  equalize 789.6
lever
  n instrument 384.4
  leverage 905.4
  lifter 911.3
  v get a purchase 905.8
leverage
  trading 737.19
  influence 893.1
  fulcrumage 905.1
  mechanics 1038.1
leviathan ship 180.1
  behemoth 257.14
Leviathan 311.30
levitate
  ascend 193.8
  rise 298.9
  elevate 911.5
levitation
  ascent 193.1
  lightness 298.1
  psychic phenomena
    689.6
levity
  lightheartedness
    109.3

  merriment 109.5
  lightness 298.1
  fickleness 364.3
  waggishness 489.4
  ridicule 508.1
  inattention 983.1
  triviality 997.3
levy
  n demand 421.1
  call to arms 458.8
  recruit 461.18
  attachment 480.5
  enlistment 615.7
  tax 630.9
  v demand 421.5
  call to arms 458.19
  attach 480.20
  enlist 615.17
  charge 630.12
  impose 643.4
lewd lascivious 665.29
  obscene 666.9
lex 673.3
lexeme sign 518.6
  word 526.1
lexicographer
  interpreter 341.7
  linguist 523.13
lexicography
  exegetics 341.8
  lexicology 526.14
lexicologist 523.13
lexicology
  semantics 518.7
  lexicography 526.14
lexicon
  vocabulary 526.13
  reference book 554.9
  dictionary 870.4
lexigraphic
  lexical 526.19
  literal 546.8
lexis 526.13
liabilities
  expenses 626.3
  accounts 628.1
liability debt 623.1
  responsibility 641.2
  tendency 895.1
  indebtedness 896
  likelihood 896.1
  susceptibility 896.2
  probability 967.1
  disadvantage 995.2
  exposure 1005.3
liable chargeable 623.9
  responsible 641.17
  likely 896.5
  probable 967.6
  exposed 1005.15
liable to
  adj subject to 896.6
  prep inclined to 895.6
liaison love affair 104.6
  intermediary 213.4
  instrument 384.4
  relation 774.1
  joining 799.1
liar 357.9
libation drink 8.4
  alcohol 88.7
  oblation 696.7

libel
  n monstrous lie
    354.12
  slander 512.3
  declaration 598.7
  v slander 512.11
liberal
  n left side 220.1
  free agent 430.12
  left-winger 611.11
  liberalist 978.6
  adj left 220.4
  nonrestrictive 430.25
  philanthropic 478.22
  free 485.4
  hospitable 585.11
  liberalistic 611.19
  magnanimous 652.6
  extensive 863.13
  liberal-minded 978.9
  plentiful 990.7
liberalism
  noninterference 430.9
  libertarianism 430.10
  progressivism 611.3
  liberalness 978.2
Liberalism 609.25
liberality
  giving 478.1
  gratuity 478.5
  generosity 485
  liberalness 485.1
  hospitality 585.1
  magnanimity 652.2
  liberalness 978.2
  plenty 990.2
liberalize 430.13
liberate
  rescue 398.3
  liberalize 430.13
  free 431.4
  detach 801.10
  disembarrass 1013.9
liberated free 430.21
  freed 431.10
liberation escape 369.1
  rescue 398.1
  liberalism 430.10
  freeing 431.1
  theft 482.1
liberator 592.2
libertarian
  n free agent 430.12
  liberal 978.6
  adj nonrestrictive
    430.25
  liberal 978.9
libertine
  n free agent 430.12
  philanderer 562.12
  swinger 665.10
  adj nonrestrictive
    430.25
libertinism
  liberalism 430.10
  profligacy 665.3
liberty vacation 20.3
  freedom 430.1
  exemption 430.8
  permission 443.1
  grant 443.5
  privilege 642.2

  opportunity 842.2
libidinal sexual 75.24
  desirous 100.21
  instinctive 933.6
libidinous lustful 75.26
  desirous 100.21
  lascivious 665.29
libido sexuality 75.2
  psyche 92.28
  desire 100.1
  love 104.1
  amorousness 104.3
  instinct 933.2
librarian
  recorder 550.1
  professional librarian
    558.3
  steward 574.4
library stacks 197.6
  storehouse 386.6
  preserve 397.7
  edition 554.5
  book depository 558.1
  collection 769.11
  retreat 1008.5
libration 915.1
librettist
  dramatist 704.22
  composer 710.20
  poet 720.11
libretto
  playbook 704.21
  score 708.28
license
  n lawlessness 418.1
  freedom 430.1
  exemption 430.8
  permission 443.1
  permit 443.6
  commission 615.1
  presumption 640.2
  privilege 642.2
  profligacy 665.3
  confusion 809.2
  v authorize 443.11
  commission 615.10
licensed exempt 430.30
  authorized 443.17
licentious lawless 418.5
  unrestrained 430.24
  presumptuous 640.11
  profligate 665.25
  dissipated 669.8
lichen 310.4
licit permissible 443.15
  legal 673.10
lick
  n sip 62.2
  touch 73.1
  velocity 172.4
  hint 248.4
  attempt 403.3
  impromptu 708.27
  work 725.4
  blow 901.5
  v lap up 8.30
  taste 62.7
  touch 73.9
  best 249.7
  defeat 412.9
  punish 604.15
  stump 970.14

licked defeated 412.15
  beaten 970.26
lickerish lustful 75.26
  desirous 100.21
  lascivious 665.29
lickety-split 174.17
licking eating 8.1
  defeat 412.1
  punishment 604.5
lid body part 2.9
  headdress 5.25
  eye 27.9
  stopper 293.4
  cover 295.5
lido 234.2
lie
  n navigation 159.3
  direction 161.1
  falsehood 354.11
  round 751.3
  v extend 158.8
  be located 159.10
  ride at anchor 182.16
  lie down 201.5
  be present 221.6
  tell a lie 354.18
  be dishonest 645.11
lie detector 92.8
lie down rest 20.6
  lie 201.5
  couch 912.11
lief 324.9
liege
  n subject 432.7
  master 575.1
  retainer 577.1
  adj subject 432.13
lie in give birth 1.3
  be located 159.10
  sail for 182.35
  exist in 760.11
lie in state 309.21
lie in wait 346.9
lie low squat 274.5
  do nothing 329.2
  hide 346.8
  beware 494.7
  be latent 519.3
lien mortgage 438.4
  general lien 438.5
  possession 469.1
lie on weigh on 297.11
  rest on 900.22
  depend 958.6
  go hard with 1010.8
lieu location 159.1
  place 159.4
lieutenant
  subordinate 432.5
  commissioned officer
    575.18
  Navy officer 575.20
  deputy 576.1
  assistant 616.6
  policeman 1007.15
life
  n animation 17.4
  energizer 17.6
  eagerness 101.1
  gaiety 109.4
  vitality 306
  living 306.1

person 312.5
liveliness 330.2
history 719.1
existence 760.1
something 762.3
lifetime 826.5
affairs 830.4
v meet one's Maker
  307.21
Life 677.6
life after death
  the hereafter 681.2
  destiny 838.2
life-and-death 996.23
lifeblood blood 2.23
  life force 306.3
lifeboat
  means of escape 369.3
  life preserver 397.6
  rescuer 398.2
life cycle 306.3
life force
  animation 17.4
  soul 306.3
  inner nature 766.5
life-giving
  reproductive 78.15
  animating 306.12
lifeguard rescuer 398.2
  guardian 1007.6
lifeless dull 117.6
  inert 173.14
  dead 307.30
  languid 331.20
  lackluster 1026.17
  inanimate 1053.5
lifelike
  descriptive 349.14
  similar 783.16
  genuine 972.15
lifeline
  means of escape 369.3
  life preserver 397.6
  safeguard 1007.3
lifelong 826.13
the life of Riley 1009.1
life of the party
  energizer 17.6
  mischief-maker 322.3
  humorist 489.12
  sociable person
    582.16
life preserver
  float 180.11
  life jacket 397.6
  safeguard 1007.3
lifer 429.11
lifesaver
  preserver 397.5
  rescuer 398.2
  guardian 1007.6
lifesaving 398.1
life savings 728.14
life size 257.3
life-size 257.16
life-style behavior 321.1
  preference 371.5
  custom 373.1
  mode 764.4
  specialty 865.1
life-threatening
  disease-causing 85.52

deadly 308.22
disastrous 1010.15
lifetime
  n life 306.1
  existence 826.5
  adj lifelong 826.13
lifework vocation 724.6
  cause 885.9
lift
  n excitement 105.3
  people mover 176.5
  ride 177.7
  lift ratio 184.26
  wave 238.14
  height 272.2
  atmosphere 317.2
  improvement 392.1
  assist 449.2
  skiing 753.1
  boost and hike 911.2
  lifter 911.3
  elevator 911.4
  the heavens 1070.2
  v elate 109.8
  transport 176.12
  billow 238.22
  imitate 336.5
  make better 392.9
  rob 482.16
  pay in full 624.13
  elevate 911.5
lifter thief 483.1
  erector 911.3
  fire iron 1019.12
lift-off 1072.9
lift up erect 200.9
  inaugurate 817.11
  elevate 911.5
  focus on 936.3
  call attention to
    982.10
lift weights 84.4
ligament 271.2
ligature
  cord 271.2
  type 548.6
  notation 709.12
  fastening 799.3
light
  n aspect 33.3
  swiftness 174.6
  window 292.7
  dawn 314.3
  explanation 341.4
  information 551.1
  wave 915.4
  outlook 977.2
  lighter 1020.4
  illumination 1024
  radiant energy 1024.1
  measurement of light
    1024.21
  light source 1025.1
  transparent substance
    1028.2
  v land 184.43
  get down 194.7
  ignite 1019.22
  grow light 1024.27
  illuminate 1024.28
  strike a light 1024.29
  adj frail 16.14

soft-colored 35.21
whitish 37.8
lighthearted 109.12
thin 270.16
shallow 276.5
unheavy 298.10
gentle 298.12
airy 317.11
fickle 364.6
agile 413.23
phonetic 524.31
wanton 665.26
comic 704.35
superficial 921.20
trivial 997.19
easy 1013.13
lightish 1024.31
light bulb 1025.1
lighten
  disburden 120.7
  make light 298.6
  moderate 670.6
  grow light 1024.27
  illuminate 1024.28
lightened
  bleached 36.8
  eased 298.11
  illuminated 1024.39
lightening
  n decoloration 36.3
  disburdening 120.3
  easing 298.3
  modulation 670.2
  adj easing 298.16
  illuminating 1024.40
lighter
  n light 1020.4
  v haul 176.13
lightface 548.20
light fingers 482.12
light-footed fast 174.15
  agile 413.23
lightheaded weak 16.12
  delirious 925.31
  dizzy 984.15
light heart 109.3
light holder 1025.6
lighthouse
  observation post 27.8
  tower 272.6
  alarm 400.1
  marker 517.10
lighting
  n ignition 1019.4
  illumination 1024.19
  adj inflammatory
    1019.27
  illuminating 1024.40
light into
  lift one's hand against
    457.14
  attack 459.15
  punish 604.11
  set to work 725.15
lightless 1026.13
light meter
  exposure 714.9
  measurement of light
    1024.21
lightness frailty 16.2
  color quality 35.6
  paleness 36.2

whiteness 37.1
lightheartedness
109.3
thinness 270.4
lack of weight 298
levity 298.1
fickleness 364.3
agility 413.2
wantonness 665.4
superficiality 921.7
triviality 997.3
luminousness 1024.3
lightning
swiftness 174.6
flash of lightning
1024.17
lightning rod 1007.3
light opera 708.34
light out 188.10
lights lungs 2.20
instruments 704.18
opinion 952.6
light show
spectacle 33.7
iridescence 47.2
flicker 1024.8
lightsome
lighthearted 109.12
light 1024.31
light source
light 1024.1
illuminant 1024.20
source of light 1025.1
light touch touch 73.1
lightness 298.1
light up excite 105.12
cheer up 109.9
ignite 1019.22
illuminate 1024.28
light upon
arrive at 186.7
alight upon 194.10
meet 223.11
come across 940.3
lightweight
n weakling 16.6
inferior 250.2
runt 258.4
weight 297.3
stupid person 923.2
a nobody 997.7
adj frail 16.14
bantamweight 298.13
uninfluential 894.3
light-year 1070.3
lignitic 1020.8
likable
tasty 63.8
pleasant 97.6
desirable 100.30
endearing 104.25
like
n love 104.1
likeness 783.3
equal 789.4
v savor 63.5
enjoy 95.12
desire 100.14
love 104.19
adj approximate 774.8
identical 777.7
similar 783.10

equal 789.7
adv how 384.9
similarly 783.18
prep in imitation of
336.12
like a bat out of hell
174.18
like a bump on a log
adj passive 329.6
adv inertly 173.20
like a fish out of water
160.11
like a thief in the night
unexpectedly 131.14
surreptitiously 345.18
deceitfully 356.24
dishonestly 645.24
like clockwork
smoothly 287.12
uniformly 780.8
methodically 806.9
regularly 849.9
easily 1013.16
likelihood
liability 896.1
possibility 965.1
probability 967.1
good chance 971.8
likely
adj apt 787.10
liable 896.5
possible 965.6
probable 967.6
disposed 977.8
expedient 994.5
comely 1015.18
adv probably 967.8
likely story 600.4
likely to
adj liable to 896.6
prep inclined to 895.6
like mad swiftly 174.18
excessively 247.23
recklessly 493.11
violently 671.25
like-minded
unanimous 332.15
in accord 455.3
agreeing 787.9
liken 942.4
likeness
aspect 33.3
image 349.5
picture 712.11
similarity 783.1
like 783.3
copy 784.1
equality 789.1
likewise
adv additionally
253.11
identically 777.9
similarly 783.18
inter yeah 332.19
liking
desire 100.2
love 104.1
will 323.1
tendency 895.1
Lilliputian
n dwarf 258.5
adj dwarf 258.13

lilt
n air 708.4
song 708.14
rhythm 709.22
meter 720.7
v exude cheerfulness
109.6
rejoice 116.5
speak 524.26
sing 708.38
lily whiteness 37.2
effeminate male 77.10
lily-livered
weak 16.12
cowardly 491.10
limb
member 2.7
leg 177.14
border 211.4
branch 310.18
body part 792.4
lever 905.4
limber
v soften 1045.6
adj weak 16.12
pliant 1045.9
limber up
prepare oneself 405.13
soften 1045.6
limbo
place of confinement
429.7
hell 682.1
lime
n whiteness 37.2
sour 67.2
snare 356.13
v trap 356.20
hamper 1011.11
limelight
publicity 352.4
lights 704.18
limen
sensibility 24.2
boundary 211.3
limit
n the last straw 135.3
summit 198.2
environment 209.1
limitation 210.2
bounds 211.1
boundary 211.3
capacity 257.2
end 793.5
extremity 819.2
v restrict 210.5
bound 211.8
narrow 270.11
restrain 428.9
specialize 865.4
qualify 958.3
adj bordering 211.11
limitation
limiting 210.2
boundary 211.3
narrowness 270.1
restriction 428.3
estate 471.4
qualification 958.1
condition 958.2
limited
n train 179.14

adj circumscribed
210.7
local 231.9
little 258.10
narrow 270.14
restricted 428.15
restrained 670.11
specialized 865.5
qualified 958.10
meager 991.10
limiting
n circumscription
210.1
limitation 210.2
differentiation 779.4
qualification 958.1
adj restricting 210.9
bordering 211.11
enclosing 212.11
restrictive 428.12
environmental 765.8
final 819.11
qualifying 958.7
limitless greedy 100.27
unrestricted 430.27
almighty 677.18
infinite 822.3
limn outline 211.9
represent 349.8
describe 349.9
portray 712.19
limner 716.2
limousine 179.13
limp
n slow motion 175.2
gait 177.12
v be weak 16.8
go slow 175.6
way of walking 177.28
adj weak 16.12
drooping 202.10
flaccid 1045.10
limpet 802.4
limpid clear 521.11
elegant 533.6
transparent 1028.4
limping slow 175.10
crippled 393.30
line
n direction 161.1
ships 180.10
boundary 211.3
vanguard 216.2
strip 267.3
cord 271.2
wire line 347.17
policy 381.4
route 383.1
railway 383.7
manner 384.1
battlefield 463.2
score 517.6
track 517.8
letter 553.2
race 559.4
lineage 560.4
endearment 562.5
policy 609.4
air 708.4
part 708.22
staff 708.29
treatment 712.9

engraving 713.2
poetry 720.9
plot 722.4
vocation 724.6
merchandise 735.1
baseball 745.1
sideline 746.1
linemen746.2
line of scrimmage
  746.3
hockey team 749.2
kind 808.3
series 811.2
procession 811.3
sequence 814.1
sequel 834.2
specialty 865.1
trend 895.2
v fill 196.7
border 211.10
plaster 295.25
outline 381.11
mark 517.19
engrave 713.9
dispose 807.9
align 811.5
lineage race 559.4
line 560.4
offspring 561.1
series 811.2
sequence 814.1
sequel 834.2
lineal straight 277.6
racial 559.7
family 560.18
consecutive 811.9
subsequent 834.4
lineaments aspect 33.3
looks 33.4
exterior 206.2
outline 211.2
face 216.4
appearance 262.3
linear straight 277.6
consecutive 811.9
linebacker 746.2
lineman
trainman 178.13
telephone man 347.10
soccer team 752.2
electrician 1031.21
linemen 746.2
linen clothing 5.1
shirt 5.15
underclothes 5.22
blanket 295.10
liner ocean liner 180.5
lining 196.3
game 745.3
lines looks 33.4
outline 211.2
camp 228.29
manner 384.1
role 704.10
playbook 704.21
style 712.8
lineup
plan 381.1
game 746.3
order 806.1
roll 870.6
schedule 964.3

line up
make parallel 203.5
order 806.4
dispose 807.9
align 811.5
get in line 811.6
schedule 964.6
linger lag 166.4
dawdle 175.8
dally 331.14
linger on 826.7
wait 845.12
continue 855.3
lingerer
slowpoke 175.5
idler 331.8
lingerie 5.22
lingering
n dawdling 175.3
idling 331.4
protraction 826.2
waiting 845.3
adj reverberating
  54.11
dawdling 175.11
protracted 826.11
dilatory 845.17
lingo language 523.1
jargon 523.9
lingua franca 523.11
lingual glossal 62.10
linguistic 523.17
speech 524.30
linguist
linguistic scientist
  523.13
polyglot 523.14
linguistic
communicational
  343.9
lingual 523.17
speech 524.30
liniment 86.11
lining liner 196.3
bookbinding 554.14
engraving 713.2
link
n intermediary 213.4
relation 774.1
joint 799.4
torch 1025.3
v way of walking
  177.28
come together 769.16
relate 774.6
put together 799.5
join 799.11
be consistent 802.7
combine 804.3
league 804.4
continue 811.4
linkage relation 774.1
joining 799.1
combination 804.1
linked related 774.9
joined 799.13
leagued 804.6
continuous 811.8
linking
n relation 774.1
joining 799.1
fastening 799.3

combination 804.1
adj grammatical
  530.17
relative 774.7
joining 799.16
linotype 548.15
lint down 3.19
dressing 86.33
powder 1049.5
lintel 189.6
lion
symbol of strength
  15.8
wild cat 311.22
brave person 492.8
heraldry 647.2
celebrity 662.9
important person
  996.9
lionhearted 492.17
lionize
praise 509.12
glorify 662.13
sightsee 917.6
lion tamer 707.3
lip
n back talk 142.4
border 211.4
bulge 283.3
lawyer 597.3
wind instrument
  711.6
golf 751.1
v sass 142.8
say 524.23
blow a horn 708.42
lipid fat 7.7
oil 1054.1
lip reader 49.2
lips genitals 2.11
mouth 292.4
vocal organ 524.19
lip service
hypocrisy 354.6
mouth honor 693.2
lipstick
n makeup 1015.12
v make red 41.4
liquefaction
melting 1019.3
liquidity 1059.1
fluidification 1062
liquefying 1062.1
liquefied
molten 1019.31
melted 1062.6
liquefy melt 1019.21
liquidize 1062.5
liquefying
n melting 1019.3
liquefaction 1062.1
adj liquefactive 1062.7
liqueur 88.15
liquid
n beverage 10.47
speech sound 524.13
fluid 1059.2
adj phonetic 524.31
convertible 728.31
fluid 1059.4
watery 1063.16
liquid air 1023.7

liquid assets
assets 471.7
cash 728.18
liquidate excise 255.10
kill 308.12
murder 308.15
exterminate 395.14
depose 447.4
pay in full 624.13
cash 728.29
sell 737.24
annihilate 761.7
eliminate 772.5
do away with 908.21
liquidated paid 624.22
excluded 772.7
liquidation
homicide 308.2
extinction 395.6
deposal 447.2
payment 624.1
trading 737.19
elimination 772.2
liquidator payer 624.9
treasurer 729.11
liquid oxygen
coolant 1023.7
rocket propulsion
  1072.8
liquor
n beverage 10.47
sedative 86.12
spirits 88.13
fluid 1059.2
v drink 88.25
lisp
n sibilation 57.1
speech defect 525.1
v sibilate 57.2
speak poorly 525.7
lisping
n speech defect 525.1
adj inarticulate 525.12
lissome 1045.9
list
n stripe 47.5
contents 196.1
inclination 204.2
border 211.4
edging 211.7
enclosed place 212.3
record 549.1
itemization 870
enumeration 870.1
v careen 182.43
tumble 194.8
incline 204.10
border 211.10
record 549.15
enlist 615.17
classify 808.6
enumerate 870.8
cultivate 1067.17
inter hark! 48.16
listen
v hark 48.10
hearken to 982.7
inter hark! 48.16
attention! 982.22
listener hearer 48.5
recipient 479.3
listen in listen 48.10

beggar 440.8
loafing 331.4
loamy earthy 234.5
pasty 1045.12
loan
n the lend 620.2
v lend 620.5
loaner 620.3
loaning 620.1
loan shark 620.3
loan-shark 620.5
loan-sharking
lending 620.1
illicit business 732.1
loathe dislike 99.3
hate 103.5
loathing
n hostility 99.2
hate 103.1
adj hating 103.7
loathsome
offensive 98.18
terrible 999.9
hideous 1014.11
lob
n throw 903.3
v play tennis 748.3
throw 903.10
elevate 911.5
lobar 202.12
lobby
n vestibule 197.19
bungler 414.8
legislative lobby
609.32
influence 893.6
v urge 375.14
exercise influence
893.9
lobbying
inducement 375.3
political influence
609.29
backstairs influence
893.3
lobbyist lobby 609.32
influence 893.6
lobe ear 2.10
pendant 202.4
member 792.4
lobo 311.20
lobster
n marine animal
311.30
cheater 759.22
v row 182.53
local
n bar 88.20
train 179.14
native 227.3
branch 617.10
labor union 727.2
adj localized 231.9
idiomatic 523.20
local color milieu 209.3
plot 722.4
locale location 159.1
area 209.2
arena 463.1
setting 704.19
plot 722.4
localism dialect 523.7

barbarism 526.6
policy 609.4
locality location 159.1
habitat 228.18
localize locate 159.11
restrict 428.9
local yokel 227.3
locate situate 159.11
settle 159.17
discover 940.2
locating
placement 159.6
discovery 940.1
location place 159
situation 159.1
placement 159.6
setting 704.19
motion-picture studio
706.3
state 764.1
discovery 940.1
farm 1067.8
loch lake 241.1
inlet 242.1
Loch Ness monster
311.30
lock
n tress 3.5
standstill 173.3
floodgate 239.11
bolt 428.5
wrestling 474.3
poker 759.10
sure thing 969.2
v close 293.6
agree 787.6
hook 799.8
obstruct 1011.12
locker storehouse 386.6
treasury 729.12
cold storage 1023.6
locket 498.6
lock horns
quarrel 456.12
contend with 457.17
counteract 899.6
argue 934.16
lock in imprison 429.14
retain 474.5
make sure 969.11
lockjaw 85.6
lockout exclusion 772.1
stop 856.2
lock out close 293.6
strike 727.10
exclude 772.4
lockup
confinement 429.1
prison 429.8
lock up enclose 212.5
close 293.6
secrete 346.7
imprison 429.14
loco
n disease 85.40
adj crazy 925.27
locomotion
mobility 172.3
travel 177.1
locomotive
traveling 177.36
vehicular 179.23

mechanical 1038.7
self-propelled 1040.22
locus 159.1
locust 311.34
locution
language 523.1
utterance 524.3
word 526.1
phrase 529.1
diction 532.1
lode
source of supply 386.4
rich source 618.4
deposit 1056.7
lodestar focus 208.4
motive 375.1
guiding star 574.8
stars 1070.4
lodestone desire 100.11
magnet 906.3
lodge
n house 228.5
cottage 228.8
lair 228.26
branch 617.10
v deposit 159.14
inhabit 225.7
house 225.10
accommodate 385.10
store 386.10
fix 854.9
repair 854.10
lodger roomer 227.8
tenant 470.4
lodging
n habitation 225.1
housing 225.3
abode 228.1
quarters 228.4
adj resident 225.13
loess deposit 176.9
dregs 256.2
loft
n library 197.6
attic 197.16
workplace 739.1
v play 751.4
elevate 911.5
lofty elevated 136.11
arrogant 141.9
eminent 247.9
high 272.14
ostentatious 501.18
eloquent 544.14
grandiloquent 545.8
impartial 649.10
magnanimous 652.6
renowned 662.18
raised 911.9
log
n speedometer 174.7
record book 549.11
accounts book 628.4
chronicle 831.9
firewood 1020.3
wood 1052.3
v ship activity 182.48
record 549.15
keep accounts 628.8
logarithmic 1016.22
log cabin 228.8
loge 704.15

logger 1067.7
loggia 197.18
logging
registration 549.14
forestry 1067.3
logic
analytic reasoning
934.2
reasonableness 934.9
logical sensible 919.18
cognitive 930.21
reasonable 934.20
valid 972.14
logic-chopping
n quibbling 935.5
adj quibbling 935.14
logician 934.11
logistics 385.1
logjam delay 845.2
barrier 1011.5
logo patent 210.3
symbol 517.2
label 517.13
insignia 647.1
logogram
representation 349.1
wordplay 489.8
symbol 517.2
phonetic symbol
546.2
logomachy
quarrel 456.5
contention 457.1
argumentation 934.4
logomania 540.2
logorrhea
wordiness 538.2
logomania 540.2
logotype patent 210.3
symbol 517.2
label 517.13
type 548.6
log out 1041.18
logroller
wire-puller 609.30
politics 610.6
logrolling
political influence
609.29
legislative procedure
613.6
trading 862.2
logy inert 173.14
languid 331.20
loin 217.3
loincloth 5.19
loins 885.7
loiter lag 166.4
dawdle 175.8
dally 331.14
wait 845.12
trifle 997.14
loiterer
slowpoke 175.5
idler 331.8
loitering
n dawdling 175.3
idling 331.4
trifling 997.8
adj dawdling 175.11
dilatory 845.17
Loki evil 680.5

nether world deity
682.5
loll
  n recumbency 201.2
  v rest 20.6
  lie 201.5
lollapaloosa 998.7
lolling
  n idling 331.4
  adj recumbent 201.8
lollygag dawdle 175.8
  dally 331.14
  make love 562.15
lollygagging
  n love affair 104.6
  dawdling 175.3
  lovemaking 562.2
  adj dawdling 175.11
lone solitary 584.11
  one 871.7
  alone 871.8
  sole 871.9
loneliness
  solitude 584.3
  aloneness 871.2
lonely solitary 584.11
  alone 871.8
loner recluse 584.5
  self-seeker 651.3
  oddity 869.4
lonesomeness
  solitude 584.3
  aloneness 871.2
lone wolf
  self-seeker 651.3
  oddity 869.4
long
  n bull 737.13
  long time 826.4
  adj lengthy 267.7
  giant 272.16
  wordy 538.12
  protracted 826.11
  adv for a long time
  826.14
long ago for a long
  time 826.14
  long since 836.16
longanimity
  patience 134.1
  forgiveness 148.1
  submission 433.1
long distance
  telephone operator
  347.9
  telephone call 347.13
long-distance 261.8
long-established
  confirmed 373.19
  traditional 841.12
  established 854.13
longevity haleness 83.3
  old age 303.5
  life 306.1
  durability 826.1
longhair 841.8
longhand 547.22
long haul 261.2
longing
  n yearning 100.5
  adj wistful 100.23
longitude map 159.5

zone 231.3
length 267.1
coordinates 300.5
orbit 1070.16
long-lasting 826.10
long-lived living 306.11
  durable 826.10
long-lost gone 34.4
  absent 222.11
  lost 473.7
long range 261.2
long-range 261.8
long shot
  motion picture 714.8
  bet 759.3
  gambling odds 759.6
  chance event 971.6
  small chance 971.9
longsighted
  poor-sighted 28.11
  sagacious 919.16
  foreseeing 960.7
long since
  for a long time 826.14
  long ago 836.16
  since 836.17
long-standing
  durable 826.10
  traditional 841.12
long-suffering
  n patience 134.1
  forgiveness 148.1
  submission 433.1
  tolerance 978.4
  adj patient 134.9
  forgiving 148.6
  submissive 433.12
  tolerant 978.11
long suit
  talent 413.4
  specialty 865.1
long-term 826.10
long time length 267.1
  long while 826.4
long way 261.2
long-winded
  tedious 118.9
  lengthened 267.8
  wordy 538.12
  protracted 826.11
long word
  hard word 526.10
  high-sounding words
  545.3
loo 12.10
looby vulgarian 497.6
  peasant 606.6
  fool 923.3
look
  n sight 27.3
  aspect 33.3
  looks 33.4
  hint 248.4
  information 551.4
  v peer 27.13
  gaze 27.15
  appear to be 33.10
  be vigilant 339.8
  seek 937.29
  heed 982.6
  inter attention! 982.22
look after look 27.13

nurture 339.9
serve 577.13
care for 1007.19
look ahead 960.5
look-alikes set 783.5
  twins 872.4
look alive
  v be vigilant 339.8
  pay attention 982.8
  inter make haste!
  401.16
look around 937.30
look at look 27.13
  spectate 917.5
  examine 937.23
look back 988.10
look down one's nose
  look askance 27.18
  shudder at 99.5
  give oneself airs 141.8
  be hard to please
  495.8
look down upon
  disdain 157.3
  rise above 272.11
looked-for
  expected 130.13
  future 838.8
looker recipient 479.3
  spectator 917.1
  beauty 1015.9
look for hope 124.7
  look forward to 130.6
  solicit 440.14
  come 838.6
  seek 937.29
look for trouble
  defy 454.3
  pick a quarrel 456.13
look forward to
  reckon on 130.6
  come 838.6
  foresee 960.5
look in enter 189.7
  visit 582.19
looking glass 29.6
looking up
  promising 124.13
  improving 392.15
look like
  appear to be 33.10
  augur 133.12
  resemble 783.7
look on see 27.12
  look 27.13
  attend 221.8
  spectate 917.5
lookout
  observation 27.2
  observation post 27.8
  view 33.6
  vigilance 339.4
  warner 399.4
  occupation 724.1
  watchman 1007.10
look out
  v be vigilant 339.8
  beware 494.7
  pay attention 982.8
  inter careful! 494.14
look over
  scrutinize 27.14

front on 216.9
examine 937.23
looks 33.4
look the other way
  be blind 30.8
  let alone 329.4
  keep an open mind
  978.7
  be inattentive 983.2
look through 937.30
look-through 937.3
look to
  look forward to 130.6
  avail oneself of 387.14
  prepare for 405.11
  tend 895.3
  attend to 982.5
  care for 1007.19
look up improve 392.7
  seek 937.29
look up to 155.4
loom
  n weaver 740.5
  imminence 839.1
  v appear 33.8
  ascend 193.8
  bulk 247.5
  threaten 514.2
  weave 740.6
  come 838.6
  be imminent 839.2
looming
  n mirage 975.6
  adj ominous 133.17
  imminent 839.3
loon 925.16
loony
  n lunatic 925.16
  adj foolish 922.9
  crazy 925.27
loonybin 925.14
loop
  n spiral loop 184.16
  circle 280.2
  bulge 283.3
  baseball 745.1
  circuit 913.2
  v maneuver 184.40
  encircle 209.7
  curve 279.6
  weave 740.6
loophole
  observation post 27.8
  outlet 190.9
  way out 369.4
loose
  n freedom 430.1
  v set free 431.6
  relax 670.9
  detach 801.10
  loosen 803.3
  facilitate 1013.7
  adj adrift 182.61
  drooping 202.10
  negligent 340.10
  escaped 369.11
  lax 426.4
  free 430.21
  unrestrained 430.24
  ungrammatic 531.4
  discursive 538.13
  informal 581.3

wanton 665.26
unfastened 801.22
slack 803.5
slovenly 809.15
illogical 935.11
vague 970.19
inaccurate 974.17
flaccid 1045.10
loose ends
slipshodness 340.3
nonaccomplishment
408.1
loosen
loose 431.6
relax 670.9
detach 801.10
slacken 803.3
soften 1045.6
loosening
n laxness 426.1
modulation 670.2
adj softening
1045.16
loosen up
amuse 743.21
amuse oneself 743.22
loose woman 665.14
loot
n booty 482.11
money 728.2
v seize 480.14
plunder 482.17
raze 671.11
looter 483.6
looting
n rapacity 480.9
plundering 482.6
unruliness 671.3
adj plunderous 482.22
lop
n wave 238.14
roughness 288.2
v hang 202.6
excise 255.10
adj drooping 202.10
lope
n run 174.3
v speed 174.8
go on horseback
177.34
lopped 794.5
loppy 202.10
lopsided
distorted 265.10
unbalanced 790.5
loquacity 540.1
loran
ship navigation 182.2
airplane navigation
184.6
long-range navigation
1035.3
lord proprietor 470.2
master 575.1
nobleman 608.4
Lord 648.2
lord it over 612.16
lordly dignified 136.12
arrogant 141.11
imperious 417.16
lordship
supremacy 249.3

mastership 417.7
ownership 469.2
aristocracy 608.9
Lordship 648.2
lore
mythology 678.14
tradition 841.2
body of knowledge
927.9
superstition 953.3
Lorelei 377.4
lorgnette 29.3
lorry 179.12
lose fail 410.9
lose out 412.12
incur loss 473.4
waste 486.4
forget 989.5
lose face
bow to 250.5
incur disgrace 661.7
lose ground
regress 163.5
slow 175.9
fall short 910.2
lose heart
despond 112.16
despair 125.10
lose one's head 922.6
lose one's mind
be stupid 921.12
go mad 925.21
loser
inferior 250.2
failure 410.2
disappointment 410.8
defeatee 412.5
loss 473.1
insolvent 625.4
unfortunate 1010.7
lose sight of
neglect 340.6
disregard 435.3
forget 989.5
lose track of 340.6
lose weight 270.13
losing streak 473.1
loss
disappearance 34.1
decrement 252.3
impairment 393.1
losing hold of 473
losing 473.1
game 746.3
disadvantage 995.2
loss of memory
thoughtlessness 932.1
amnesia 989.2
loss of speech 525.6
lost vanished 34.4
past hope 125.15
unwon 412.13
gone 473.7
wasted 486.9
irreclaimable 654.18
unregenerate 695.18
bewildered 970.24
abstracted 984.11
forgotten 989.8
the lost 680.1
lost cause 125.8
lost in 982.17

lost in thought
absorbed in thought
930.22
abstracted 984.11
lost soul 660.5
lot
n plot 231.4
amount 244.2
lots 247.4
real estate 471.6
portion 477.5
motion-picture studio
706.3
share 738.3
state 764.1
bunch 769.7
kind 808.3
amount made 892.4
fate 963.2
chance 971.1
v allot 477.9
gamble 759.23
the lot 791.3
Lothario beau 104.13
libertine 665.10
lotion toilet water 70.3
cleanser 79.17
balm 86.11
ointment 1054.3
lots lot 247.4
real estate 471.6
multitude 883.3
plenty 990.2
lottery 759.14
lotus-eater idler 331.8
visionary 985.13
loud
adj intense 15.22
garish 35.19
loud-sounding 53.11
demanding 421.9
coarse 497.11
gaudy 501.20
adv loudly 53.14
loud and clear
adj affirmative 334.8
clear 521.11
adv affirmatively
334.10
loudmouthed
loud-voiced 53.12
vociferous 59.10
loudness
garishness 35.5
sound 50.1
intensity of sound 53
intensity 53.1
coarseness 497.2
showiness 501.3
lounge
anteroom 197.20
v rest 20.6
lie 201.5
idle 331.12
lounger 331.8
lounging
n recumbency 201.2
idling 331.4
adj recumbent 201.8
louring 319.7
louse vermin 311.35
bad person 660.6

louse up spoil 393.11
bungle 414.12
complicate 798.3
goof 974.6
make a boner 974.15
hinder 1011.16
lousy infested 909.11
bad 999.8
lout bungler 414.8
simple soul 416.3
vulgarian 497.6
peasant 606.6
oaf 923.5
loutish
countrified 233.7
bungling 414.20
boorish 497.13
ill-bred 505.6
louver 239.13
lovable
desirable 100.30
endearing 104.25
love
n sexuality 75.2
liking 100.2
affection 104.1
sweetheart 104.10
benevolence 143.4
accord 455.1
regards 504.8
endearment term
562.6
friendship 587.1
cardinal virtues 653.4
game 748.2
heat metaphor 1018.2
v savor 63.5
have deep feelings
93.12
enjoy 95.12
desire 100.14
be fond of 104.19
Love Cupid 104.8
Deity 677.6
love affair 104.6
love child 561.5
loveless unloved 99.10
undesirous 102.8
love letter 562.13
love-life 75.2
lovelock 3.5
lovelorn unloved 99.10
loving 104.27
lovely delightful 97.7
endearing 104.25
beautiful 1015.17
lovemaking
sexuality 75.2
copulation 75.7
love 104.1
dalliance 562.1
love nest 582.9
love potion 75.6
lover desirer 100.12
admirer 104.12
endearment term
562.6
friend 588.1
supporter 616.9
lovesick 104.27
loving lovesome 104.27
kind 143.13

luminant 1024.30
illuminated 1024.39
lummox bungler 414.9
oaf 923.5
lump
n clump 257.10
bulge 283.3
swelling 283.4
bungler 414.9
print 517.7
accumulation 769.9
piece 792.3
solid 1043.6
v thicken 1043.10
lumpen
n the underprivileged
606.4
adj countrified 233.7
idle 331.18
base 661.12
slovenly 809.15
lumpish
countrified 233.7
bulky 257.19
formless 263.4
onerous 297.17
languid 331.20
bungling 414.20
boorish 497.13
stupid 921.15
thickened 1043.14
lump sum 728.13
lump together
assemble 769.18
put together 799.5
combine 804.3
lumpy bulky 257.19
formless 263.4
gnarled 288.8
nappy 294.7
thickened 1043.14
Luna 1070.12
lunacy
foolishness 922.1
insanity 925.1
lunar
crescent-shaped
279.11
celestial 1070.25
lunar eclipse
eclipse 1026.8
moon 1070.11
lunar module 1073.2
lunatic
n fool 923.1
madman 925.15
adj insane 925.26
lunatic fringe
radical 611.12
fanatic 925.18
lunch
n meal 8.6
v dine 8.21
adj eccentric 926.6
lunch counter 8.17
luncheon 8.6
lunchroom 8.17
lung
n viscera 2.14
adj respiratory 2.30
lunge
n thrust 459.3

v way of walking
177.28
lunkhead 923.4
lunkheaded 921.17
lupine
canine 311.40
rapacious 480.26
lurch
n gait 177.12
bias 204.3
swing 915.6
flounder 916.8
v way of walking
177.28
pitch 182.55
tumble 194.8
oscillate 915.10
flounder 916.15
lurching
irregular 850.3
swinging 915.17
lure
n snare 356.13
incentive 375.7
charm 377.3
attractor 906.2
v trap 356.20
induce 375.22
allure 377.5
attract 906.4
lurid garish 35.19
colorless 36.7
brown 40.3
red 41.6
sensational 105.32
deathly 307.29
gaudy 501.20
grandiloquent 545.8
obscene 666.9
lurk couch 346.9
be latent 519.3
lurking
in hiding 346.14
latent 519.5
imminent 839.3
luscious tasty 63.8
oversweet 66.5
delectable 97.10
lush
n drunk 88.12
v drink 88.25
adj tasty 63.8
luxuriant 310.40
ornate 545.11
productive 889.9
lust
n sexual desire 75.5
craving 100.6
greed 100.8
will 323.1
lasciviousness 665.5
v lust after 75.20
desire 100.14
crave 100.18
luster
n polish 287.2
illustriousness 662.6
moment 823.2
gorgeousness 1015.6
shine 1024.2
chandelier 1025.6
v polish 287.7

shine 1024.23
lusterless colorless 36.7
lackluster 1026.17
lustful prurient 75.26
desirous 100.21
lascivious 665.29
lustful leer 27.3
lustral cleansing 79.28
atoning 658.7
lustrous
illustrious 662.19
luminous 1024.30
shiny 1024.33
lusty strong 15.15
energetic 17.13
hale 83.12
corpulent 257.18
Lutheran 675.28
lux 1024.21
luxate dislocate 160.5
disjoint 801.16
luxuriant
flourishing 310.40
ornate 498.12
grandiloquent 545.11
productive 889.9
plentiful 990.7
luxuriate
vegetate 310.31
superabound 992.8
luxuriate in
enjoy 95.12
indulge 669.4
luxurious
delightful 97.7
comfortable 121.11
ornate 498.12
grandiose 501.21
wealthy 618.14
expensive 632.11
sensual 663.5
luxury pleasure 95.1
delightfulness 97.2
grandeur 501.5
sensuality 663.1
superfluity 992.4
prosperity 1009.1
lyceum hall 197.4
secondary school
567.4
lying
n recumbency 201.2
lowness 274.1
untruthfulness 354.8
adj recumbent 201.8
untruthful 354.33
lying-in 1.1
lymph 2.22
lymphatic
n duct 2.21
adj circulatory 2.31
secretory 13.7
languid 331.20
lynch kill 308.12
hang 604.18
lynching killing 308.1
capital punishment
604.7
lynch law 418.2
lynx
sharp vision 27.11
wild cat 311.22

lyre 711.3
lyric melodious 708.48
vocal 708.50
poetic 720.15
lyricist
composer 710.20
poet 720.11
lyric theater 708.34
lysis 395.1
ma 560.12
ma'am 77.8
Mab 678.8
macabre
terrible 127.30
deathly 307.29
weird 987.9
macadam
ground covering 199.3
pavement 383.6
macaroni
noodles 10.32
dandy 500.9
mace scepter 417.9
insignia 647.1
macerate
torture 96.18
shrink 260.9
pulp 1061.5
soak 1063.13
Mach 174.2
Machiavellian
n deceiver 357.1
schemer 381.7
Machiavel 415.8
politics 610.6
adj falsehearted
354.30
scheming 381.13
cunning 415.12
machinate plot 381.9
maneuver 415.10
machination
chicanery 356.4
intrigue 381.5
manipulation 415.4
machinator
traitor 357.10
schemer 381.7
strategist 415.7
politics 610.6
machine
n automobile 179.9
political party 609.24
association 617.1
machinery 1039.3
computer 1041.2
v process 891.9
tool 1039.9
n instrument of
conversion 857.10
machine gun 846.5
machine-made 891.18
machinery
instrumentality 384.3
equipment 385.4
instruments 1039
machine 1039.3
mechanism 1039.4
machine shop 739.3
machinist stage
technician 704.24
mechanic 1039.8

machismo
male sex 76.2
courage 492.1
macho
virile 76.12
courageous 492.17
macro 257.20
macrobiotic 826.10
macrocosm 1070.1
maculate
v variegate 47.7
spot 1003.5
adj spotted 47.13
unvirtuous 654.12
unchaste 665.23
spotted 1003.9
mad
n anger 152.5
v madden 925.24
adj frenzied 105.25
angry 152.30
reckless 493.8
turbulent 671.18
foolish 922.8
insane 925.26
rabid 925.30
mad about
enthusiastic 101.11
crazy about 104.31
madam woman 77.8
mistress 575.2
procurer 665.18
madame woman 77.8
Mrs 648.4
madcap
n humorist 489.12
daredevil 493.4
adj foolhardy 493.9
madden excite 105.12
enrage 152.25
antagonize 589.7
dement 925.24
maddening 105.30
madder 41.4
mad dog ruffian 593.3
violent person 671.9
made formative 262.9
successful 409.14
produced 891.17
man-made 891.18
mademoiselle
woman 77.8
girl 302.6
made of 795.4
made-up
fabricated 354.28
invented 891.19
beautified 1015.22
mad for 100.22
madhouse 925.14
madman 925.15
madness fury 105.8
foolishness 922.1
insanity 925.1
Madonna 679.5
madrigal 708.18
maelstrom eddy 238.12
bustle 330.4
whirl 914.2
agitation 916.1
maestro
teacher 571.1

musician 710.1
Mae West 397.6
maffick be noisy 53.9
celebrate 487.2
create disorder 809.11
Mafia
the underworld
660.11
illicit business 732.1
Mafioso
violent person 671.9
racketeer 732.4
magazine
storehouse 386.6
armory 462.2
periodical 555.1
magenta 46.3
maggot
whiteness 37.2
larva 302.12
insect 311.31
caprice 364.1
quirk 926.2
figment of the
imagination 985.5
maggoty
nasty 64.7
filthy 80.23
capricious 364.5
blighted 393.42
eccentric 926.5
fanciful 985.20
Magi 920.5
magic
n illustriousness
662.6
sorcery 690.1
illusoriness 975.2
v summon 420.11
adj illustrious 662.19
sorcerous 690.14
magical
illustrious 662.19
sorcerous 690.14
miraculous 869.16
magic carpet 691.6
magician
trickster 357.2
master 413.13
mage 690.6
entertainer 707.1
illusoriness 975.2
magic lantern 714.12
magic show 975.2
magic wand 691.6
magisterial
dignified 136.12
lordly 141.11
chief 249.14
skillful 413.22
imperious 417.16
jurisdictional 594.6
authoritative 969.18
magistracy
region 231.5
mastership 417.7
magistrature 594.3
magistrate
arbitrator 466.4
executive 574.3
public official 575.17
judge 596.1

Magna Charta 430.2
magna cum laude
646.11
magnanimity
ambition 100.10
forgiveness 148.1
glory 247.2
liberality 485.1
magnanimousness
652.2
tolerance 978.4
magnanimous
forgiving 148.6
eminent 247.9
liberal 485.4
great-souled 652.6
tolerant 978.11
magnate
nobleman 608.4
businessman 730.1
personage 996.8
magnet
n desire 100.11
focus 208.4
artificial magnet
906.3
v attract 906.4
magnetic
influential 893.13
attracting 906.5
engrossing 982.20
electromagnetic
1031.30
magnetic field
electric field 1031.3
magnetic force 1031.9
magnetic force 1031.9
magnetic pole
magnet 906.3
polarity 1031.8
magnetic tape
recording media
549.10
disk 1041.6
magnetism
desirability 100.13
allurement 377.1
influence 893.1
attraction 906.1
electrical science 1031
magnetic attraction
1031.7
magnetize
put to sleep 22.20
exercise influence
893.9
attract 906.4
electromagnetize
1031.26
magnification
aggravation 119.1
intensification 251.2
expansion 259.1
exaggeration 355.1
praise 509.5
glorification 662.8
adoration 696.2
magnificence
grandeur 501.5
superexcellence 998.2
magnificent
eminent 247.9

grandiose 501.21
superb 998.15
magnified
aggravated 119.4
increased 251.7
exaggerated 355.4
eminent 662.18
magnify
aggravate 119.2
intensify 251.5
enlarge 259.4
exaggerate 355.3
praise 509.12
glorify 662.13
adore 696.11
magnitude
quantity 244.1
greatness 247.1
size 257.1
star 1070.8
magpie chatterer 540.4
collector 769.15
magus 690.6
maharani
sovereign queen
575.11
princess 608.8
mahatma
master 413.13
holy man 659.6
occultist 689.11
wise man 920.1
mahogany
n smoothness 287.3
adj reddish-brown
40.4
maid
n girl 302.6
single woman 565.4
maidservant 577.8
v serve 577.13
maiden
n girl 302.6
single woman 565.4
execution 605.5
jockey 757.2
adj childish 301.11
unmarried 565.7
first 817.17
new 840.7
maidenhead
membrane 2.6
childhood 301.2
celibacy 565.1
continence 664.3
maiden lady 565.4
maiden name 527.5
maiden speech 817.5
mail
n plumage 3.18
shell 295.15
armor 460.3
post 553.4
v send 176.15
post 553.12
mailbox 553.6
mail carrier 353.5
mail coach 353.6
maillot 5.29
mailman
postman 353.5
postal service 553.7

mail-order 553.14
mail-order house 736.1
maim disable 19.9
  injure 393.13
  cripple 393.14
  tear apart 801.14
maiming
  emasculation 19.5
  impairment 393.1
main
  n continent 235.1
  water main 239.7
  ocean 240.1
  adj great 247.6
  chief 249.14
  first 817.17
  paramount 996.24
main dish 10.7
main idea 931.4
mainland
  n continent 235.1
  adj continental 235.6
mainlander 235.3
mainline
  v use 87.21
  adj tending 895.4
main office
  headquarters 208.6
  office 739.7
main point
  summary 557.2
  topic 936.1
  salient point 996.6
mainspring
  motive 375.1
  fountainhead 885.6
mainstay
  n supporter 616.9
  support 900.2
  v support 900.21
mainstream
  n trend 895.2
  adj tending 895.4
maintain affirm 334.5
  provide 385.7
  preserve 397.8
  insist 421.8
  aid 449.12
  retain 474.5
  defend 600.10
  treat 624.19
  endure 826.6
  sustain 855.4
  support 900.21
  think 952.11
maintenance
  reparation 396.6
  preservation 397.1
  aid 449.3
  retention 474.1
  treatment 624.8
  durability 826.1
  preservation 852.2
  continuance 855.1
  support 900.1
maintenance man
  396.10
maître d'hôtel
  waiter 577.7
  major-domo 577.10
majestic
  dignified 136.12

eminent 247.9
sovereign 417.17
grandiose 501.21
lofty 544.14
almighty 677.18
majesty
  proud bearing 136.2
  glory 247.2
  sovereignty 417.8
  grandeur 501.5
  loftiness 544.6
  potentate 575.8
Majesty 648.2
major
  n adult 304.1
  study 568.8
  commissioned officer
    575.18
  key 709.15
  adj older 841.19
  important 996.17
majordomo
  steward 574.4
  butler 577.10
major in
  study to be 570.15
  specialize 865.4
majority
  n maturity 303.2
  race 312.2
  major part 791.6
  plurality 882.2
  adj most 882.9
the majority
  dead 307.17
  the masses 606.2
majority leader 610.3
major league 745.1
make
  n form 262.1
  structure 266.1
  yield 472.5
  receipts 627.1
  composition 795.1
  kind 808.3
  amount made 892.4
  disposition 977.3
  v use 87.21
  travel 177.19
  sail for 182.35
  arrive 186.6
  flow 238.16
  act 328.4
  do 328.6
  perform 328.9
  make up 405.7
  accomplish 407.4
  compel 424.4
  execute 437.9
  acquire 472.8
  compose 795.3
  convert 857.11
  cause 885.10
  produce 891.8
  imagine 985.14
make a beeline
  go directly 161.10
  take a short cut 268.7
  be straight 277.4
make a bid
  offer 439.6
  bid 733.9

make a clean sweep
  revolutionize 859.4
  evacuate 908.22
make a deal
  contract 437.5
  compromise 468.2
  bargain 731.17
  strike a bargain
    731.18
make a dent in
  impress 93.15
  gain influence
    893.12
make advances
  communicate with
    343.8
  approach 439.7
  cultivate 587.12
  exercise influence
    893.9
make a face
  shudder at 99.5
  grimace 265.8
make a Federal case
  948.2
make a fool of
  fool 356.15
  outwit 415.11
  stultify 922.7
make a go of it
  succeed 409.7
  succeed with 409.11
make a killing
  score a success
    409.9
  triumph 411.3
  profit 472.12
  trade 737.23
make allowance for
  extenuate 600.12
  allow for 958.5
make amends
  compensate 338.4
  make restitution
    481.5
  requite 506.5
  repay 624.11
  atone 658.4
make an appearance
  appear 33.8
  arrive 186.6
  attend 221.8
  be manifest 348.7
make an example of
  604.10
make an impression
  be heard 48.12
  affect emotionally
    93.15
  impress 930.19
  be remembered
    988.14
make a point of
  resolve 359.7
  contend for 457.20
  make conditional
    958.4
make a scene 93.13
make a show of
  sham 354.20
  affect 500.12
make believe 354.20

make-believe
  n figment of the
    imagination 985.5
  adj spurious 354.25
  fictitious 985.21
make clear
  explain 341.10
  manifest 348.5
  make understandable
    521.6
  facilitate 1013.7
make do 994.4
make ends meet
  support oneself 385.12
  economize 635.4
make fun of
  joke 489.13
  ridicule 508.8
make good
  straighten 277.5
  compensate 338.4
  remedy 396.13
  come through 409.10
  observe 434.2
  make restitution
    481.5
  grow rich 618.10
  repay 624.11
  meet an obligation
    641.11
  keep faith 644.9
  atone 658.4
  complete 793.6
  prove 956.10
  be prosperous 1009.9
make haste
  v speed 174.8
  hasten 401.5
  inter make it quick!
    401.16
make hay while the
sun shines
  make the most of
    one's time 330.16
  improve the occasion
    842.8
make headway
  progress 162.2
  make way 182.21
  improve 392.7
  make good 409.10
  prosper 1009.7
make it
  be able 18.11
  arrive 186.6
  make good 409.10
  manage 409.12
  live on 838.7
  stand the test 941.10
make known
  communicate 343.7
  divulge 351.5
  make public 352.11
make light of
  underestimate 949.2
  be inattentive 983.2
  attach little
    importance to 997.12
  take it easy 1013.12
make love
  copulate 75.21
  procreate 78.8

bill and coo 562.14
make merry
celebrate 487.2
revel 743.24
make money
profit 472.12
grow rich 618.10
make no bones about
359.10
make nothing of
not understand 522.11
underestimate 949.2
attach little
importance to 997.12
make one's mark
make good 409.10
cut a dash 501.13
be somebody 662.10
be prosperous 1009.9
make one's way
work one's way 162.4
support oneself 385.12
make better 392.9
make good 409.10
make oneself at home
121.8
make out see 27.12
copulate 75.21
support oneself 385.12
manage 409.12
execute 437.9
perceive 521.9
write 547.19
record 549.15
make love 562.15
be in a certain state
764.5
persist 855.5
know 927.12
solve 939.2
detect 940.5
prove 956.10
recognize 988.12
make shift 994.4
make-out artist 562.12
make over
reproduce 78.7
transfer 176.10
transfer property
629.3
convert 857.11
make peace
cease hostilities 465.9
settle 466.7
gain influence 893.12
make plain
explain 341.10
manifest 348.5
make possible
permit 443.9
enable 965.5
make public 352.11
maker artist 716.1
poet 720.11
doer 726.1
skilled worker 726.6
author 885.4
producer 891.7
make sense
be understandable
521.4
be reasonable 934.17

makeshift
n improvisation
365.5
substitute 861.2
expedience 994.2
adj extemporaneous
365.12
unprepared 406.8
substitute 861.8
expedient 994.7
imperfect 1002.4
make sure
take precautions
494.6
secure 854.8
make certain 969.11
play safe 1006.3
make the best of it
be optimistic 124.9
accept 134.7
submit 433.6
make the grade
be able 18.11
manage 409.12
suffice 990.4
make the most of
take advantage of
387.15
excel 998.11
make the scene
appear 33.8
go to 177.25
arrive 186.6
make good 409.10
participate 476.5
make tracks
speed 174.9
run off 188.12
leave 222.10
flee 368.11
makeup
form 262.1
structure 266.1
design 554.12
theater 704.17
nature 766.4
composition 795.1
order 806.1
disposition 977.3
cosmetics 1015.12
make up
fabricate 354.17
improvise 365.8
get up 405.7
arrange 437.8
shake hands 465.10
print 548.16
shuffle 758.4
assemble 769.18
complete 793.6
compose 795.3
produce 891.8
originate 891.12
beautify 1015.15
make up one's mind
resolve 359.7
choose 371.16
persuade oneself
375.24
decide 945.11
convince oneself
952.19

make up to
curry favor 138.9
head for 161.9
communicate with
343.8
cultivate 587.12
repay 624.11
exercise influence
893.9
make waves
agitate 105.14
misbehave 322.4
oppose 451.3
offer resistance 453.3
not conform 867.4
make way
v gather way 182.21
make an opening
292.13
inter open up! 292.23
making
n reproduction 78.1
forming 262.5
structure 266.1
acquisition 472.1
production 891.1
manufacture 891.2
amount made 892.4
adj almighty 677.18
makings
gain 472.3
component 795.2
maladjusted
incompetent 414.19
wrong 638.3
inappropriate 788.7
maladjustment
mental disorder 92.14
unskillfulness 414.1
wrong 638.1
unfitness 788.3
maladroit
inadequate 250.7
bungling 414.20
malady 85.1
malaise
pain 26.1
disease 85.1
unpleasure 96.1
discontent 108.1
dejection 112.3
anxiety 126.1
nervousness 128.1
agitation 916.1
malapropism
wordplay 489.8
solecism 531.2
grammatical error
974.7
malapropos
inappropriate 788.7
untimely 843.6
inexpedient 995.5
malaria miasma 1000.4
vapor 1065.1
malarial 85.60
malarkey 520.3
malcontent
n maverick 108.3
lamenter 115.8
rebel 327.5
spoilsport 1011.9

adj discontented 108.7
mal de mer 85.30
male
n male being 76.4
adj masculine 76.11
male chauvinism
misanthropy 590.1
discrimination 979.4
male chauvinist
misanthrope 590.2
bigot 979.5
malediction 513.1
maledictory 513.8
malefactor
evildoer 593.1
wrongdoer 660.9
maleness sex 75.1
masculinity 76.1
maturity 303.2
male organs 2.11
male sex 76.2
malevolence
hate 103.1
inconsiderateness
144
ill will 144.4
hostility 589.3
badness 999.1
malevolent
n evildoer 593.1
adj ill-disposed 144.19
hostile 589.10
harmful 999.12
bad 999.7
malevolent influence
999.4
malfeasance
misbehavior 322.1
misuse 389.1
mismanagement
414.6
wrong 638.1
wrongdoing 655.1
misdeed 655.2
malformation
deformity 265.3
wrong 638.1
oddity 869.3
malformed
deformed 265.12
freakish 869.13
unshapely 1014.8
malfunction
n impairment 393.1
abortion 410.5
wrong 638.1
fault 1002.2
v get out of order
393.25
malice hate 103.1
maliciousness 144.5
hostility 589.3
malicious
maleficent 144.20
hostile 589.10
malign
v defame 512.9
adj poisonous 82.7
malicious 144.20
deadly 308.22
savage 671.21
harmful 999.12

malignancy
  poisonousness 82.3
  malice 144.5
  deadliness 308.8
  harmfulness 999.5
malignant
  poisonous 82.7
  anemic 85.60
  malicious 144.20
  deadly 308.22
  hostile 589.10
  savage 671.21
  harmful 999.12
malinger
  leave undone 340.7
  shirk 368.9
malingerer
  neglecter 340.5
  impostor 357.6
  shirker 368.3
malingering
  n shirking 368.2
  adj evasive 368.15
mall path 383.2
  marketplace 736.2
  workplace 739.1
malleable docile 433.13
  teachable 570.18
  changeable 853.6
  conformable 866.5
  influenceable 893.15
  foolable 922.12
  handy 1013.15
  pliant 1045.9
mallet 715.4
malnutrition 991.6
malocchio gaze 27.5
  malevolence 144.4
  curse 513.1
  spell 691.1
  bad influence 999.4
malodorous nasty 64.7
  bad-smelling 69.9
  fetid 71.5
  filthy 80.23
  offensive 98.18
malpractice
  misuse 389.1
  mismanagement
    414.6
  wrong 638.1
  wrongdoing 655.1
maltreat
  mistreat 389.5
  work evil 999.6
maltreatment 389.2
mama 560.12
mama's boy
  weakling 16.6
  effeminate male 77.10
  spoiled child 427.4
mammal 311.3
mammalian
  pectoral 283.19
  vertebrate 311.39
mammary gland 283.6
mammon wealth 618.1
  money 728.1
mammoth
  n behemoth 257.14
  pachyderm 311.4
  adj large 247.7

  huge 257.20
mammy
  mother 560.12
  nurse 1007.8
man
  n mankind 76.3
  male 76.4
  beau 104.13
  hanger-on 138.6
  adult 304.1
  humankind 312.1
  person 312.5
  husband 563.7
  manservant 577.4
  follower 616.8
  chessman 743.17
  v equip 385.8
  fortify 460.9
  inter goody! 95.20
the Man 312.3
mana power 18.1
  the gods 678.1
man-about-town
  sophisticate 413.17
  dandy 500.9
  person of fashion
    578.7
  sociable person
    582.16
manacle
  n shackle 428.4
  v disable 19.10
  bind 428.10
manacled 428.16
manage pilot 182.14
  perform 328.9
  support oneself 385.12
  use 387.10
  treat 387.12
  contrive 409.12
  direct 573.8
  govern 612.12
  economize 635.4
  be in a certain state
    764.5
  persist 855.5
  operate 888.5
  make shift 994.4
  tend 1068.7
  accomplish 407.4
manageability
  governability 433.4
  workability 888.3
  handiness 1013.2
manageable
  governable 433.14
  cheap 633.7
  workable 888.10
  handy 1013.15
management
  supremacy 249.3
  performance 328.2
  usage 387.2
  utilization 387.8
  supervision 573
  direction 573.1
  executive 574.3
  directorate 574.11
  the authorities 575.15
  government 612.1
  thrift 635.1
  operation 888.1

  protectorship 1007.2
manager director 574.1
  governor 575.6
  businessman 730.1
  baseball team 745.2
  boxer 754.2
  operator 888.4
managerial
  directing 573.12
  operational 888.12
mañana
  n the future 838.1
  adv in the future 838.9
man and wife 563.9
manchild 302.5
mandarin
  n snob 141.7
  official 575.16
  wise man 920.1
  intellectual 928.1
  adj studious 570.17
mandate
  n country 232.1
  authority 417.1
  injunction 420.2
  possession 469.1
  referendum 613.8
  commission 615.1
  v command 420.8
mandated 420.12
mandatory
  n country 232.1
  adj preceptive 419.4
  mandated 420.12
  obligatory 424.11
  required 641.15
  doctrinal 952.27
  necessary 962.12
mandibles mouth 292.4
  clutches 474.4
mandrake 22.10
mane 3.2
man-eater eater 8.16
  marine animal 311.30
  savage 593.5
manège riding 177.6
  animal husbandry
    1068.1
maneuver
  n exercise 84.2
  act 328.3
  stratagem 415.3
  operation 458.5
  race 753.3
  process 888.2
  expedient 994.2
  v execute a maneuver
    182.46
  take action 328.5
  plot 381.9
  manipulate 415.10
  direct 573.8
  operate 888.5
maneuverable
  workable 888.10
  handy 1013.15
maneuvering
  intrigue 381.5
  machination 415.4
man Friday
  employee 577.3
  right-hand man 616.7

mange 85.40
manger 197.2
mangle press 287.6
  tear apart 801.14
mangled
  impaired 393.27
  mutilated 794.5
manhandle
  exert strength 15.12
  remove 176.11
  transport 176.12
  mistreat 389.5
man-hater hater 103.4
  misanthrope 590.2
man-hating
  n misanthropy 590.1
  adj misanthropic
    590.3
manhood
  bodily development
    14.1
  masculinity 76.1
  mankind 76.3
  maturity 303.2
  courage 492.1
man-hour work 725.4
  moment 823.2
mania craving 100.6
  overzealousness 101.3
  mental sickness 925
  insanity 925.1
  delirium tremens
    925.9
  craze 925.12
maniac
  n lunatic 925.15
  adj frenzied 105.25
  rabid 925.30
maniacal
  frenzied 105.25
  rabid 925.30
manic excited 105.20
  insane 925.26
  psychotic 925.28
manic-depressive
  n psychotic 925.17
  adj psychotic 925.28
manic state 105.1
manicure
  n beautification
    1015.11
  v groom 79.20
manicurist 1015.13
manifest
  n statement 628.3
  bill 870.5
  v unclose 292.12
  show 348.5
  disclose 351.4
  flaunt 501.17
  signify 517.17
  evidence 956.8
  adj visible 31.6
  apparent 348.8
manifestation
  visibility 31.1
  appearance 33.1
  expression 348.1
  disclosure 351.1
  display 501.4
  indication 517.3
  evidence 956.1

manifested 348.13
manifesting 348.9
manifesto
  n affirmation 334.1
  announcement 352.2
  statement of belief
    952.4
  v affirm 334.5
manifold
  n transcript 784.4
  v copy 784.8
  adj multiform 782.3
  multiple 882.8
manikin dwarf 258.5
  figure 349.6
man in the street 606.5
manipulate touch 73.6
  pilot 184.37
  tamper with 354.16
  use 387.7
  exploit 387.16
  maneuver 415.10
  direct 573.8
  operate 888.5
manipulated 354.29
manipulation
  touching 73.2
  masturbation 75.8
  intrigue 381.5
  utilization 387.8
  machination 415.4
  direction 573.1
  rigging 737.20
  operation 888.1
  automation 1040.7
manipulative
  scheming 381.13
  using 387.19
  cunning 415.12
manipulator
  strategist 415.7
  operator 888.4
  influence 893.6
mankind man 76.3
  humankind 312.1
manlike
  masculine 76.11
  anthropoid 312.14
manly masculine 76.11
  courageous 492.17
  honest 644.13
man-made
  spurious 354.25
  made 891.18
manna delicacy 10.8
  support 449.3
  godsend 472.7
  benefit 478.7
manned
  provided 385.13
  armed 460.14
mannequin
  figure 349.6
  artist's model 785.5
manner aspect 33.3
  exteriority 206.1
  behavior 321.1
  custom 373.1
  mode 384
  way 384.1
  style 532.2
  state 764.4

kind 808.3
  specialty 865.1
mannered
  behavioral 321.7
  affected 500.15
  elegant 533.9
  figurative 536.3
mannerism sham 354.3
  affectation 500.1
  preciosity 500.2
  style 532.2
  elegance 533.3
  characteristic 864.4
  quirk 926.2
manner of speaking
  way of saying 524.8
  phrase 529.1
  style 532.2
  figure of speech 536.1
manners
  behavior 321.1
  custom 373.1
  mannerliness 504.3
  etiquette 580.3
mannish
  homosexual 75.29
  masculine 76.11
  mannified 76.13
man of action 330.8
man of the house 575.1
man of the world
  sophisticate 413.17
  person of fashion
    578.7
man-of-war 180.6
manor 471.6
manor house 228.5
manorial
  residential 228.32
  real 471.9
manpower 18.4
manqué 410.18
manse house 228.5
  parsonage 703.7
mansion
  estate 228.7
  astrology 1070.20
manslaughter 308.2
mantel 900.14
mantilla 5.26
mantle
  n cover 295.2
  scepter 417.9
  insignia 647.1
  robe 702.2
  v cloak 5.39
  redden 41.5
  change color 105.19
  blush 139.8
  show resentment
    152.14
  cover 295.19
  foam 320.5
  take command 417.14
mantled
  clothed 5.44
  covered 295.31
man-to-man
  plain-speaking 535.3
  intimate 582.24
  familiar 587.19
mantra 696.3

manual
  handbook 554.8
  textbook 554.10
  keyboard 711.17
manual art 712.3
manual labor 725.4
manufacture
  n structure 266.1
  preparation 405.1
  production 891.2
  product 892.1
  v fabricate 354.17
  produce 891.8
manufactured
  fabricated 354.28
  made 891.18
manufacturer 891.7
manufacturing
  n production 891.2
  adj productional
    891.14
manure
  n feces 12.4
  fertilizer 889.4
  v fertilize 889.8
manure pile 80.10
manuscript
  n handwriting 547.3
  writing 547.10
  copy 548.4
  rare book 554.6
  adj written 547.22
many much 247.8
  different 779.7
  diversified 782.4
  frequent 846.4
  plural 882.7
  numerous 883.6
  plentiful 990.7
many-sided sided 218.7
  versatile 413.25
  mixed 796.14
  changeable 853.6
Maoism
  communism 611.5
  revolutionism 859.2
Maoist
  n Communist 611.13
  revolutionist 859.3
  adj Communist 611.21
  revolutionist 859.6
map
  n chart 159.5
  face 216.4
  representation 349.1
  diagram 381.3
  v locate 159.11
  represent 349.8
  plot 381.10
  receive 1035.17
mapmaker
  charter 159.5
  measurer 300.9
mapped 300.13
mar deform 265.7
  spoil 393.10
  bungle 414.11
  blemish 1003.4
  offend 1014.5
marathon 826.11
maraud 482.17
marauder 483.6

marauding
  n plundering 482.6
  adj plunderous 482.22
marble
  n variegation 47.6
  smoothness 287.3
  sculpture 715.2
  toy 743.16
  hardness 1044.6
  v variegate 47.7
  adj white 37.7
  hard 1044.10
marbled mottled 47.12
  striped 47.15
marbleize 47.7
marbleized 47.15
marblelike
  hard 1044.10
  stone 1057.10
marcel
  n hairdo 3.15
  v cut the hair 3.22
march
  n progression 162.1
  walk 177.10
  quick gait 177.13
  boundary 211.3
  frontier 211.5
  sphere 231.2
  objection 333.2
  martial music 708.12
  v mush 177.30
  border 211.10
  object 333.5
marcher 178.6
march to a different
  drummer 333.4
Mardi Gras treat 95.3
  festival 743.4
mare
  female animal 77.9
  plain 236.1
  horse 311.10
  jockey 757.2
margin
  n room 158.3
  border 211.4
  interval 224.1
  distance 261.1
  latitude 430.4
  collateral 438.3
  thin margin 738.10
  wide margin 779.2
  surplus 992.5
  v border 211.10
marginal
  bordering 211.11
  unimportant 997.16
marginalia
  addition 254.2
  memorandum 549.4
marina 1008.6
marinate 397.9
marination 796.2
marine
  n navy man 183.4
  navy 461.27
  adj nautical 182.57
  oceanic 240.8
marine animal 311.30
marine biology 240.6
mariner traveler 178.1

seaman 183.1
marines
elite troops 461.15
sea soldiers 461.28
marionette figure 349.6
toy 743.16
marital 563.18
maritime
nautical 182.57
oceanic 240.8
mark
n boundary 211.3
degree 245.1
dupe 358.2
objective 380.2
sign 517.1
marking 517.5
marker 517.10
signature 527.10
distinction 662.5
notation 709.12
customer 733.4
game 750.2
cheater 759.22
kind 808.3
characteristic 864.4
impact 886.2
evidence 956.1
importance 996.1
stain 1003.3
v celebrate 487.2
signify 517.17
make a mark 517.19
grammaticize 530.16
letter 546.6
engrave 713.9
hockey 749.7
soccer 752.4
differentiate 779.6
characterize 864.10
specify 864.11
estimate 945.9
evidence 956.8
destine 963.7
heed 982.6
stain 1003.6
Mark 684.2
markdown 633.4
mark down
record 549.15
price 630.11
cheapen 633.6
marked
remarkable 247.10
superior 249.12
designated 517.24
distinguished 662.16
engraved 713.11
characteristic 864.13
destined 963.9
notable 996.19
marker mark 517.10
monument 549.12
recorder 550.1
round 751.3
market
n square 230.8
commerce 731.1
public 733.3
sale 734.1
place of trade 736
mart 736.1

marketplace 736.2
workplace 739.1
v deal in 731.15
shop 733.8
sell 734.8
adj sales 734.13
the market 737.1
marketable 734.14
market index 737.1
marketing
n commerce 731.1
purchase 733.1
selling 734.2
adj sales 734.13
marketplace
square 230.8
arena 463.1
mart 736.2
market research
selling 734.2
canvass 937.14
market value
worth 630.2
price 738.9
marking mark 517.5
insignia 647.1
engraving 713.2
game 749.6
characteristic 864.4
mark my words 982.22
mark off
circumscribe 210.4
measure off 300.11
plot 381.10
allot 477.9
mark 517.19
differentiate 779.6
characterize 864.10
marksman
expert 413.11
infantryman 461.9
shooter 903.8
marksmanship
skill 413.1
sport 744.1
mark time await 130.8
be still 173.7
time 831.11
wait 845.12
marmalade 10.38
maroon
v abandon 370.5
adj red 41.6
marooned
abandoned 370.8
stranded 1012.27
marquee poster 352.7
lights 704.18
marquis 608.4
marred
deformed 265.12
spoiled 393.28
blemished 1003.8
ugly 1014.6
marriage
sexuality 75.2
matrimony 563.1
wedding 563.3
joining 799.1
combination 804.1
marriageable
grown 14.3

adolescent 301.13
adult 303.12
nubile 563.20
marriage broker 563.12
marriage license 443.6
marriage vow 436.3
married
matrimonial 563.18
wedded 563.21
related 774.9
joined 799.13
leagued 804.6
marrow
food 10.19
essential content
196.5
center 208.2
essence 766.2
marry
join in marriage
563.14
get married 563.15
relate 774.6
put together 799.5
combine 804.3
league 804.4
Mars war-god 458.13
planet 1070.9
marsh
receptacle of filth
80.12
swamp 243
marshland 243.1
marshal
n commissioned
officer 575.18
master of ceremonies
743.20
policeman 1007.15
v prepare 405.6
escort 768.8
put together 799.5
order 806.4
dispose 807.9
adduce 956.12
marshland 243.1
marshy swampy 243.3
moist 1063.15
mart square 230.8
market 736.1
marketplace 736.2
martial 458.21
martial arts
wrestling 457.10
sports 744.1
martial law
militarization 458.10
government 612.4
Martian oddity 869.4
astronaut 1073.8
martinet 575.14
martyr
n sufferer 96.11
angel 679.1
v pain 26.7
torture 96.18
kill 308.12
martyrdom agony 26.6
torment 96.7
killing 308.1
punishment 604.2
martyred pained 26.9

dead 307.30
angelic 679.6
marvel
n wonder 122.1
phenomenon 122.2
v wonder 122.5
marvelous
wonderful 122.10
remarkable 247.10
extraordinary 869.14
superb 998.15
Marxism
communism 611.5
socialism 611.6
materialism 1050.6
Marxist
n Communist 611.13
socialist 611.14
revolutionist 859.3
materialist 1050.7
adj Communist 611.21
revolutionist 859.6
materialist 1050.12
mascara 1015.12
mascot 691.5
masculine
n male 76.4
gender 530.10
adj male 76.11
masculinity sex 75.1
maleness 76
masculineness 76.1
maturity 303.2
mash
n meal 8.6
feed 10.4
infatuation 104.4
pulp 1061.2
v make advances
439.8
soften 1045.6
pulverize 1049.9
pulp 1061.5
masher dandy 500.9
philanderer 562.12
pulverizer 1049.7
pulper 1061.4
mask
n cover 295.2
reticence 344.3
disguise 356.11
pretext 376.1
dance 705.2
relief 715.3
safeguard 1007.3
v cover 295.19
conceal 346.6
falsify 354.15
masked
covered 295.31
disguised 346.13
masochism 75.11
masochist 75.16
mason 716.6
masonry
sculpture 715.1
building material
1052.2
masque cover 356.11
dance 705.2
masquerade
n costume 5.9

impersonation 349.4
sham 354.3
cover 356.11
dance 705.2
v hide 346.8
masquerader 357.7
mass
n amount 244.1
quantity 247.3
size 257.1
lump 257.10
thickness 269.2
weight 297.5
store 386.1
sacred music 708.17
substantiality 762.1
throng 769.4
accumulation 769.9
major part 791.6
conglomeration 802.5
majority 882.2
solid 1043.6
v load 159.15
come together 769.16
assemble 769.18
put together 799.5
cohere 802.6
adj gravitational
297.20
populational 606.8
adv heavily 297.22
Mass
divine service 696.8
Missa 701.8
massacre
n carnage 308.4
unruliness 671.3
v slaughter 308.16
defeat 412.9
massage
n massaging 1042.3
v stroke 73.8
treat 91.24
rub 1042.6
soften 1045.6
masses lot 247.4
inferior 250.2
the masses 606.2
masseuse 1042.4
massive
large 247.7
bulky 257.19
thick 269.8
heavy 297.16
onerous 297.17
sturdy 762.7
dense 1043.12
mass market 734.1
mass murder
killing 308.1
carnage 308.4
mass-produced 891.18
mass production 891.3
mass spectrography
1037.1
mast spar 180.13
tower 272.6
supporter 900.2
master
n ship's officer 183.7
superior 249.4
boy 302.5

victor 411.2
past master 413.13
proprietor 470.2
teacher 571.1
principal 571.8
lord 575.1
chief 575.3
governor 575.6
degree 648.6
work of art 712.10
artist 716.1
skilled worker 726.6
producer 891.7
wise man 920.1
v conquer 412.10
subdue 432.9
understand 521.7
attain mastery of
570.9
dominate 612.15
adj chief 249.14
governing 612.18
paramount 996.24
Master man 76.7
Sir 648.3
mastered
conquered 412.17
subdued 432.15
masterful lordly 141.11
skillful 413.22
imperious 417.16
perfected 1001.9
mastermind
n master 413.13
wise man 920.1
scholar 928.3
v direct 573.8
master of ceremonies
steward 574.4
theater man 704.23
MC 743.20
broadcaster 1033.23
masterpiece
masterwork 413.10
work of art 712.10
product 892.1
pattern of perfection
1001.4
mastership
supremacy 249.3
skill 413.1
masterhood 417.7
directorship 573.4
control 612.2
mastery
supremacy 249.3
preparedness 405.4
victory 411.1
defeat 412.1
skill 413.1
mastership 417.7
learning 570.1
control 612.2
influence 893.1
understanding 927.3
profound knowledge
927.6
masthead
n label 517.13
v punish 604.10
masticate chew 8.27
pulp 1061.5

mastodon
behemoth 257.14
pachyderm 311.4
masturbate 75.22
masturbation
autoeroticism 75.8
vanity 140.1
mat
n head of hair 3.4
border 211.4
partition 213.5
rug 295.9
arena 463.1
lawn bowling 750.3
bedding 900.20
v weave 740.6
dull 1026.10
adj colorless 36.7
lackluster 1026.17
matador killer 308.10
bullfighter 461.4
match
n image 349.5
contest 457.3
marriage 563.1
amusement 743.9
tennis 748.1
game 749.3
hockey 749.6
round 751.3
soccer 752.3
fight 754.3
equal 789.4
two 872.2
matchstick 1020.5
light source 1025.1
v parallel 203.4
parallelize 203.5
contrapose 215.4
size 257.15
give in kind 506.6
join in marriage
563.14
assemble 769.18
be alike 777.4
resemble 783.7
agree 787.6
equal 789.5
coincide 835.4
double 872.5
compare 942.4
be comparable 942.7
matched
married 563.21
joined 799.13
two 872.6
coupled 872.8
matching
n contest 457.3
marriage 563.1
comparison 942.1
adj chromatic 35.15
analogous 783.11
matchless
peerless 249.15
best 998.16
first-rate 998.17
perfect 1001.6
matchmaker 563.12
mate
n ship's officer 183.7
image 349.5

spouse 563.6
companion 588.3
friend 588.4
partner 616.2
accompanier 768.4
likeness 783.3
equal 789.4
v copulate 75.21
get married 563.15
double 872.5
mated
married 563.21
joined 799.13
coupled 872.8
material
n fabric 4.1
material 4.1
essential content
196.5
store 386.1
substance 762.2
matter 1050.2
adj carnal 663.6
secularist 695.16
substantial 762.6
essential 766.9
relevant 774.11
evidential 956.16
important 996.17
vital 996.23
materiate 1050.10
inorganic 1053.4
materialism
carnality 663.2
secularism 695.2
idealism 951.3
physicism 1050.6
materialist
n irreligionist 695.10
physicist 1050.7
adj atomistic 1050.12
materialistic
carnal 663.6
secularist 695.16
occupied 724.15
atomistic 1050.12
materiality
existence 760.1
substantiality 762.1
relevance 774.4
importance 996.1
substance 1050
materialness 1050.1
matter 1050.2
materialize show 31.4
appear 33.8
be formed 262.8
manifest 348.5
come out 348.6
embody 762.5
happen 830.6
establish 891.10
turn up 940.9
corporalize 1050.9
matériel
equipment 385.4
store 386.1
arms 462.1
materials 1052.1
maternal loving 104.27
native 226.5
ancestral 560.17

maternity
blood relationship
559.1
motherhood 560.3
mathematical
exact 972.17
numeric 1016.21
mathematician 1016.15
mathematics
numbers 1016
math 1016.1
matinee 582.10
matinee idol
favorite 104.16
actor 707.2
mating copulation 75.7
fertilization 78.3
mating call
animal noise 60.1
endearment 562.5
matins morning 314.1
divine service 696.8
matriarch
mother 560.11
mistress 575.2
back number 841.8
matriarchal 612.17
matriarchy 612.5
matriculate
record 549.15
be taught 570.11
matriculation 549.14
matrilineage 559.1
matrimonial 563.18
matrimonial bureau
563.12
matrimony 563.1
matrix form 262.1
mold 785.6
vital force 885.7
deposit 1056.7
matron woman 77.5
wife 563.8
mistress 575.2
matronly
feminine 77.13
middle-aged 303.14
matte print 714.5
dullness 1026.5
matted hairy 3.24
complex 798.4
disheveled 809.14
matter
n humor 2.22
excrement 12.3
pus 12.6
essential content
196.5
quantity 244.1
motive 375.1
undertaking 404.1
writing 547.10
copy 548.4
occupation 724.1
substance 762.2
particular 765.3
affair 830.3
topic 936.1
material 1050.2
inorganic matter
1053.1
v fester 12.15

be important 996.12
matter of course 373.5
matter of fact
prosaicness 117.2
fact 760.3
event 830.2
matter-of-fact
prosaic 117.8
simple 499.6
plain-speaking 535.3
prosaic 721.5
realistic 986.6
**matter of life and
death**
urgent need 962.4
point of interest 996.5
mattress 900.20
maturation
bodily development
14.1
growth 259.3
adolescence 301.6
development 303.6
improvement 392.2
completion 407.2
evolution 860.1
mature
v grow 14.2
expand 259.7
grow up 303.9
grow old 304.6
develop 392.10
ripen 407.8
accrue 623.7
complete 793.6
evolve 860.5
produce 891.8
originate 891.12
perfect 1001.5
adj developed 14.3
grown 259.12
adult 303.12
grown old 303.13
middle-aged 304.7
prepared 405.16
ripe 407.13
experienced 413.28
due 623.10
complete 793.9
perfected 1001.9
matured
ripe 407.13
experienced 413.28
complete 793.9
perfected 1001.9
maturing
n bodily development
14.1
growth 259.3
adj evolutionary 860.8
maturity
adulthood 303.2
preparedness 405.4
completion 407.2
debt 623.1
maudlin
intoxicated 88.31
sentimental 93.21
foolish 922.8
maul mistreat 389.5
harm 393.13
injure 393.13

rage 671.11
fight 754.4
pound 901.16
mauled 96.23
mausoleum
tomb 309.16
monument 549.12
mauve 46.3
maven
expert 413.11
adviser 422.3
connoisseur 496.7
specialist 865.3
scientist 927.11
maverick
n cattle 311.6
rebel 327.5
obstinate person
361.6
nonconformist 867.3
oddity 869.4
adj unconventional
867.6
mavis 710.23
maw
digestive system 2.16
mouth 292.4
mawkish nasty 64.7
oversweet 66.5
sentimental 93.21
the max
n supremacy 249.3
adj extreme 247.13
maxim precept 419.2
rule 868.4
a belief 952.2
aphorism 973.1
maximal top 198.10
superlative 249.13
plentiful 990.7
maximize 251.4
maximum
n summit 198.2
supremacy 249.3
limit 793.5
plenty 990.2
adj top 198.10
great 247.6
superlative 249.13
may be able 18.11
can 443.13
maybe 965.9
Mayday 400.1
mayhem 393.1
mayor 575.17
mayoralty
mastership 417.7
magistracy 594.3
Mazda 677.5
maze
n complex 798.2
confusion 984.3
v perplex 970.13
confuse 984.7
mazy deviative 164.7
flowing 238.24
curved 279.7
convolutional 281.6
complex 798.4
inconstant 853.7
MC steward 574.4
theater man 704.23

master of ceremonies
743.20
broadcaster 1033.23
McCarthyism 389.3
MD 90.4
me 864.5
mea culpa
penitence 113.4
apology 658.2
meadow marsh 243.1
grassland 310.8
meager
insignificant 248.6
dwarf 258.13
narrow 270.14
lean 270.17
sparse 884.5
slight 991.10
meal repast 8.5
feed 10.4
cereal 10.33
powder 1049.5
meal ticket
support 449.3
financer 729.9
mealy colorless 36.7
powdery 1049.11
mealymouth 138.3
mealymouthed
obsequious 138.14
flattering 511.8
sanctimonious 693.5
insincere 354.31
mean
n median 246.1
middle course 467.3
middle 818.1
v augur 133.12
manifest 348.5
intend 380.4
indicate 517.17
signify 518.8
imply 519.4
evidence 956.8
adj irascible 110.20
humble 137.10
servile 138.13
malicious 144.20
cruel 144.26
envious 154.4
intervening 213.10
medium 246.3
insignificant 248.6
inadequate 250.7
niggardly 484.8
low 497.15
populational 606.8
ungenerous 651.6
base 661.12
middle 818.4
narrow-minded
979.10
meager 991.10
paltry 997.21
excellent 998.13
inferior 1004.9
difficult 1012.17
mean business 359.8
meander
n bend 279.3
convolution 281.1
complex 798.2

v stray 164.4
wander 177.23
convolve 281.4
go roundabout 913.4
meandering
n convolution 281.1
discursiveness 538.3
circuitousness 913.1
adj deviative 164.7
wandering 177.37
flowing 238.24
curved 279.7
convolutional 281.6
complex 798.4
circuitous 913.7
meanie 660.6
meaning
n ominousness 133.7
interpretation 341.1
intention 380.1
indication 517.3
significance 518.1
implication 519.2
lexicology 526.14
adj meaningful 518.10
meaningful
premonitory 133.16
indicative 517.23
meaning 518.10
expressive 544.10
meaningless
uncommunicative
344.8
useless 391.9
unmeaning 520.6
unordered 809.12
meanness
ill humor 110.3
humility 137.1
servility 138.1
malice 144.5
envy 154.1
insignificance 248.1
inadequacy 250.3
niggardliness 484.2
vulgarity 497.1
commonness 497.5
ungenerousness 651.2
baseness 661.3
narrow-mindedness
979.1
meagerness 991.2
paltriness 997.2
inferiority 1004.3
means mode 384
manner 384.1
way 384.2
supply 386.2
assets 471.7
funds 728.14
expedient 994.2
tool 1039.1
means to an end
means 384.2
expedient 994.2
meant
intentional 380.8
signified 518.11
implied 519.7
meantime
n meanwhile 825.2
adv meanwhile 825.5

meanwhile
n meantime 825.2
adv in the meantime
820.10
meantime 825.5
measly
anemic 85.60
base 661.12
insignificant 997.18
measurable
mensurable 300.14
calculable 1016.24
measure
n space 158.1
quantity 244.1
amount 244.2
degree 245.1
size 257.1
capacity 257.2
length 267.1
measurement 300.1
measuring instrument
300.2
act 328.3
portion 477.5
sign 517.1
harmony 533.2
law 673.3
air 708.4
passage 708.24
notation 709.12
rhythm 709.22
metrics 720.6
meter 720.7
poetry 720.9
process 888.2
expedient 994.2
v traverse 177.20
quantify 244.4
size 257.15
gauge 300.10
make agree 787.7
estimate 945.9
number 1016.16
calculate 1016.17
measured
quantitative 244.5
gauged 300.13
harmonious 533.8
temperate 668.9
rhythmic 709.28
metric 720.16
uniform 780.5
periodic 849.7
measure for measure
compensation 338.1
tit for tat 506.3
justice 649.1
interchange 862.1
measurement
quantity 244.1
size 257.1
quantification 300
measure 300.1
estimate 945.3
numeration 1016.9
measure out
measure off 300.11
parcel out 477.8
measure up to
equal 789.5
be comparable 942.7

measuring
n measurement 300.1
adj metric 300.12
meat
n meal 8.5
food 10.1
flesh 10.12
nut 10.37
sex object 75.4
copulation 75.7
essential content
196.5
support 449.3
summary 557.2
essence 766.2
major part 791.6
topic 936.1
salient point 996.6
v feed 8.18
meat-eater eater 8.16
strong man 15.7
violent person 671.10
meat-eating 8.31
meathead 923.4
meathooks 474.4
meaty
corpulent 257.18
meaningful 518.10
mechanic
aircraftsman 185.6
mender 396.10
worker 607.9
skilled worker 726.6
cheater 759.22
mechanician 1039.8
mechanical
uniform 780.5
involuntary 962.14
mechanistic 1038.7
machinelike 1039.10
mechanics art 413.7
the physics of force
and motion 1038
leverage 1038.1
mechanism
instrumentality 384.3
instrument 384.4
art 413.7
machinery 1039.3
works 1039.4
materialism 1050.6
mechanistic
mechanical 1038.7
materialist 1050.12
mechanize 1039.9
mechanized 1039.10
medal
military honor 646.6
insignia 647.1
relief 715.3
medalist 413.15
medallion
medal 646.6
relief 715.3
meddle
intermeddle 214.7
advise 422.5
pry 980.4
hinder 1011.10
meddler
intermeddler 214.4
adviser 422.3

meddlesome
meddling 214.9
prying 980.6
meddling
n intermeddling 214.2
adj meddlesome 214.9
media
communications
343.5
telecommunications
347.1
medial
intervening 213.10
medium 246.3
middle 818.4
median
n mean 246.1
middle 818.1
adj intervening 213.10
medium 246.3
middle 818.4
mediary 213.4
mediate
interpose 213.6
be instrumental 384.7
reconcile 465.8
intermediate 466.6
mediating
n mediation 466.1
adj modal 384.8
mediatory 466.8
mediation
instrumentality 384.3
pacification 465.1
intermediation 466
mediating 466.1
function of Christ
677.15
mediator
intermediary 213.4
instrument 384.4
intermediator 466.3
go-between 576.4
moderator 670.3
mediatory
mediatorial 466.8
divine 677.17
Medicaid
health care 83.5
welfarism 611.7
medical examiner
doctor 90.4
autopsy 307.18
medical practice
medicine 90.1
practice of medicine
90.13
Medicare
health care 83.5
welfarism 611.7
medicate 91.25
medication
medicine 86.4
therapy 91.1
treatment 91.14
medicinal
n medicine 86.4
adj remedial 86.39
medicine
n medicament 86.4
liquor 88.14
medical practice 90.1

v medicate 91.25
medicine man 690.7
medico 90.4
medieval 841.13
medievalist 841.5
mediocre
  medium 246.3
  inadequate 250.7
  unskillful 414.15
  middle 818.4
  usual 868.9
  imperfect 1002.4
  middling 1004.7
mediocrity mean 246.1
  inadequacy 250.3
  unskillfulness 414.1
  incompetent 414.7
  usualness 868.2
  a nobody 997.7
  imperfection 1002.1
  ordinariness 1004
  mediocreness 1004.1
  second-rater 1004.5
meditate
  contemplate 380.5
  consider 930.12
meditation
  inaction 329.1
  trance 691.3
  prayer 696.4
  consideration 930.2
  engrossment 982.3
meditative
  passive 329.6
  cognitive 930.21
  engrossed 982.17
  abstracted 984.11
medium
  n color 35.8
  essential content
    196.5
  natural environment
    209.4
  intermediary 213.4
  mean 246.1
  instrument 384.4
  mediator 466.3
  middle course 467.3
  volume 554.4
  go-between 576.4
  psychic 689.13
  lights 704.18
  art equipment 712.18
  doer 726.1
  substance 762.2
  immaterialist 1051.4
  adj done 11.7
  intervening 213.10
  mean 246.3
  middle 818.4
  mediocre 1004.7
medium of exchange
  728.1
medley
  n performance 708.33
  miscellany 769.13
  hodgepodge 796.6
  adj chromatic 35.15
  variegated 47.9
  mixed 796.14
Medusa 690.9
meed portion 477.5

  recompense 624.3
meek
  resigned 134.10
  humblehearted 137.11
  modest 139.9
  gentle 433.15
  unbelligerent 464.10
meerschaum 89.6
meet
  n contest 457.3
  game 743.9
  track meet 755.2
  assembly 769.2
  v converge 169.2
  confront 216.8
  encounter 223.11
  concur 332.9
  observe 434.2
  oppose 451.5
  compete 457.18
  brave 492.11
  come together 769.16
  convene 769.17
  join 799.11
  experience 830.8
  conform 866.3
  collide 901.13
  suffice 990.4
  adj decorous 496.10
  conventional 579.5
  just 649.8
  timely 842.9
  expedient 994.5
  approachable 167.5
meet halfway
  make up 465.10
  mediate 466.6
  compromise 468.2
meet head-on
  contrapose 215.4
  meet 223.11
  confront 451.5
  offer resistance 453.3
  brave 492.11
  counteract 899.6
meeting
  n convergence 169.1
  meeting up 223.4
  contest 457.3
  conference 541.6
  rendezvous 582.9
  divine service 696.8
  assembly 769.2
  joining 799.1
  impact 901.3
  adj converging 169.3
  in contact 223.17
  assembled 769.21
  joining 799.16
  concurrent 898.4
meetinghouse
  hall 197.4
  church 703.1
meeting of minds
  unanimity 332.5
  consensus 787.3
meet the eye show 31.4
  appear 33.8
  meet with attention
    982.11
mega 257.20
megacycles 1033.12

megaphone 48.8
melancholia
  mental disorder 92.14
  wretchedness 96.6
  melancholy 112.5
  depression 925.5
melancholic
  n personality type
    92.12
  sourpuss 112.13
  adj melancholy 112.23
  weary 118.11
melancholy
  n wretchedness 96.6
  melancholia 112.5
  weariness 118.3
  thoughtfulness 930.3
  adj sullen 110.24
  melancholic 112.23
  weary 118.11
  n sullenness 110.8
mélange 796.6
melanism 38.1
meld
  n compound 796.5
  combination 804.1
  v identify 777.5
  mix 796.10
  combine 804.3
melding
  identification 777.2
  combination 804.1
melee free-for-all 457.5
  commotion 809.4
meliorate
  improve 392.7
  make better 392.9
  be changed 851.6
  change 851.7
mellifluous sweet 66.4
  pleasant 97.6
  melodious 708.48
mellow
  v mature 303.9
  ripen 407.8
  evolve 860.5
  soften 1045.6
  adj soft-colored 35.21
  resonant 54.9
  intoxicated 88.31
  pleasant 97.6
  mature 303.13
  ripe 407.13
  melodious 708.48
  soft 1045.8
mellowing
  maturation 303.6
  softening 1045.5
melodics 709.1
melodist singer 710.13
  composer 710.20
melodrama 93.9
melodramatic
  emotionalistic 93.19
  sensational 105.32
  dramatic 704.33
melodramatics
  emotionalism 93.9
  dramatics 704.2
melody
  melodiousness 708.2
  air 708.4

melon
  political patronage
    609.36
  dividend 738.7
melt disappear 34.2
  affect 93.14
  have pity 145.4
  move 145.5
  flit 827.6
  melt down 1019.21
  liquefy 1062.5
meltable
  molten 1019.31
  liquefiable 1062.9
melt away
  disappear 34.2
  decrease 252.6
  cease to exist 761.6
meltdown
  outburst 671.6
  misfortune 1010.2
melt down
  extract 192.16
  explode 671.14
  melt 1019.21
  liquefy 1062.5
melted
  penitent 113.9
  molten 1019.31
  liquefied 1062.6
melting
  n disappearance 34.1
  fusion 1019.3
  liquefaction 1062.1
  adj vanishing 34.3
  loving 104.27
  pitying 145.7
  liquefying 1062.7
melting pot
  mixture 796.1
  mixer 796.9
  instrument of
    conversion 857.10
the melting pot 232.3
member appendage 2.7
  affiliate 617.11
  organ 792.4
membership
  association 582.6
  members 617.12
  inclusion 771.1
membrane
  membrana 2.6
  lamina 296.2
memento
  monument 549.12
  remembrance 988.7
memo 549.4
memoir
  memorandum 549.4
  treatise 556.1
  history 719.1
  remembering 988.4
memorabilia
  archives 549.2
  history 719.1
  memento 988.7
  matter of importance
    996.5
memorable
  rememberable 988.25
  notable 996.19

memorandum
memo 549.4
reminder 988.6
memorandum book
549.11
memorial
n record 549.1
memorandum 549.4
monument 549.12
history 719.1
memento 988.7
adj celebrative 487.3
commemorative
988.27
memorialize
petition 440.10
celebrate 487.2
memorize
get by rote 570.8
commit to memory
988.17
memory
engram 92.29
celebration 487.1
recording media
549.10
posthumous fame
662.7
retrospection 836.4
recollection 988
remembrance 988.1
storage 1041.7
men work force 18.9
mankind 76.3
staff 577.11
menace
n threat 514.1
danger 1005.1
v forebode 133.11
threaten 514.2
be imminent 839.2
work evil 999.6
menacing
ominous 133.17
threatening 514.3
imminent 839.3
ménage home 228.2
family 559.5
domestic
management 573.6
menagerie
zoo 228.19
collection 769.11
mend
n improvement
392.1
v get well 83.7
improve 392.7
make better 392.9
repair 396.14
mendacity
untruthfulness 354.8
lie 354.11
Mendel's law 560.6
mender 396.10
mendicancy
beggary 440.6
indigence 619.2
mendicant
n nonworker 331.11
beggar 440.8
ascetic 667.2

religious 699.15
adj supplicatory
440.16
indigent 619.8
ascetic 667.4
mending
n improvement 392.1
reparation 396.6
adj improving 392.15
menfolk 76.3
menial
n servant 577.2
worker 726.2
adj servile 138.13
serving 577.14
meniscus 279.5
menopause 303.7
menses 12.9
menstrual
bleeding 12.24
regular 849.8
menstrual discharge
12.9
menstruate 12.18
menstruation 12.9
mensuration
measurement 300.1
science of
measurement 300.8
menswear 5.1
mental
n psychotic 925.17
adj intellectual
918.7
crazy 925.27
cognitive 930.21
attitudinal 977.7
mental block 989.3
mental capacity 919.1
mental case 925.17
mental deficiency 925.1
mental disorder
emotional disorder
92.14
insanity 925.1
mental health
health 83.1
sanity 924.1
mental hospital 925.14
mental illness
mental disorder 92.14
insanity 925.1
mentality
intellect 918.1
intelligence 919.1
intelligent being 919.9
mentally retarded
921.22
mental picture
idea 931.1
visualization 985.6
mental telepathy 689.9
mention
n remark 524.4
information 551.1
citation 646.4
v remark 524.25
specify 864.11
call attention to
982.10
mentor preparer 405.5
adviser 422.3

teacher 571.1
wise man 920.1
Mentor 920.2
menu bill of fare 8.14
statement 870.5
schedule 964.3
meow 60.2
Mephistopheles 680.4
mercantile
business 730.12
commercial 731.21
mercantilism 731.12
mercantilistic 731.21
mercenary
n hireling 461.17
employee 577.3
adj greedy 100.27
employed 615.20
corruptible 645.23
merchandise
n provisions 385.2
goods 735
commodities 735.1
v deal in 731.15
sell 734.8
merchandising
n trade 731.2
selling 734.2
adj sales 734.13
merchant
n provider 385.6
businessperson 730
merchandiser 730.2
adj commercial
731.21
merchant marine
ships 180.10
branch 461.21
navy 461.27
merci! 150.6
merciful
kind 143.13
pitying 145.7
lenient 427.7
almighty 677.18
merciless
pitiless 146.3
savage 671.21
mercurial fast 174.15
active 330.17
irresolute 362.9
fickle 364.6
nonuniform 781.3
inconstant 853.7
flighty 984.17
brass 1056.17
mercury
swiftness 174.6
guide 574.7
changeableness 853.4
thermometer 1018.20
Mercury
messenger 353.1
planet 1070.9
mercy kindness 143.1
act of kindness 143.7
pity 145.1
leniency 427.1
mercy killing 308.1
mere
n lake 241.1
marsh 243.1

adj sheer 248.8
simple 797.6
mere caricature 786.1
mere child
simple soul 416.3
innocent 657.4
mere child's play
1013.3
mere existence 760.6
mere façade 500.1
mere farce 489.1
merely adequate 246.3
a mere nothing 997.6
mere show 500.1
mere skin and bones
270.17
mere subsistence 991.5
mere suggestion 551.4
mere technicality 997.6
meretricious
specious 354.26
coarse 497.11
gaudy 501.20
grandiloquent 545.8
prostitute 665.28
paltry 997.21
a mere trickle 991.9
merge
converge 169.2
submerge 367.7
cooperate 450.3
come together 769.16
identify 777.5
mix 796.10
put together 799.5
join 799.11
combine 804.3
merger
convergence 169.1
affiliation 450.2
identification 777.2
mixture 796.1
joining 799.1
combination 804.1
merging
converging 169.3
combining 804.7
meridian
n map 159.5
summit 198.2
zone 231.3
noon 314.5
orbit 1070.16
adj top 198.10
noon 314.7
meringue sweets 10.38
foam 320.2
merit
n importance 996.1
goodness 998.1
v deserve 639.5
merited
warranted 639.9
just 649.8
meritless 997.22
meritorious
praiseworthy 509.20
due 639.10
reputable 662.15
Merlin 690.6
mermaid
swimmer 182.12

mezzo-soprano
 n high voice 58.6
 voice 709.5
 adj high 58.13
miasma
 stench 71.1
 mephitis 1000.4
 vapor 1065.1
miasmic
 malodorous 71.5
 poisonous 82.7
 offensive 98.18
 vaporous 1065.9
Mick 232.7
Mickey Finn
 anesthetic 25.3
 chloral hydrate
  87.5
 drink 88.9
Mickey Mouse
 n finery 498.3
 trivia 997.4
 adj vulgar 497.10
 insignificant 997.18
 inferior 1004.9
 easy 1013.13
micro 258.12
microbe germ 85.41
 minute 258.7
 organism 305.2
microcosm 258.6
microdot 549.10
microfiche
 recording media
  549.10
 transcript 784.4
microfilm
 n recording media
  549.10
 film 714.10
 v photograph 714.14
 copy 784.8
microorganism
 germ 85.41
 minute 258.7
 organism 305.2
microphone mike 50.9
 radio transmitter
  1033.4
microscope 29.1
microscopic
 telescopic 29.10
 infinitesimal 258.14
 exact 972.17
microscopy optics 29.7
 littleness 258.18
microtome 801.7
microwave
 n radio wave 1033.11
 v cook 11.4
micturition 12.5
mid
 adj phonetic 524.31
 middle 818.4
 prep between 213.12
 among 796.17
Midas 618.8
midday
 n noon 314.5
 adj noon 314.7
midden dunghill 80.10
 derelict 370.4

trash pile 391.6
middle
 n center 208.2
 mean 246.1
 voice 530.14
 midpoint 818
 median 818.1
 v centralize 208.9
 seek the middle 818.3
 adj central 208.11
 intervening 213.10
 mediatory 466.8
 medial 818.4
middle age 303.4
middle-aged
 mid-life 303.14
 mature 304.7
Middle Ages 823.5
Middle America
 inland 207.3
 US region 231.7
 the people 606.1
 middle class 607.5
 mediocrity 1004.5
Middle American
 n conformist 866.2
 adj inland 207.7
middlebrow 929.8
middle class
 middle order 607.5
 mediocrity 1004.5
middle-class
 upper-class 607.10
 ordinary 1004.8
the middle class 606.1
Middle East 231.6
middle ground
 mean 246.1
 middle course 467.3
 mid-distance 818.2
middleman
 intermediary 213.4
 mediator 466.3
 go-between 576.4
 merchant 730.2
middlemost
 central 208.11
 middle 818.4
middle of the road
 middle course 467.3
 moderatism 611.2
 mid-distance 818.2
 mean 246.1
middle-of-the-road
 medium 246.3
 moderate 611.18
 middle 818.4
middle-of-the-roader
 centrist 611.10
 moderate 670.4
middle-of-the-roadism
 611.2
middle school 567.4
middleweight 297.3
the Middle West 231.7
middling
 medium 246.3
 middle 818.4
 mediocre 1004.7
middy 183.4
Mideast 231.6
midge dwarf 258.5

minute 258.7
midget
 n dwarf 258.5
 adj dwarf 258.13
midget hockey 749.1
midland
 n inland 207.3
 adj inland 207.7
 middle 818.4
Midland 523.7
midmost
 n middle 818.1
 adj central 208.11
 middle 818.4
midnight
 n dead of night
  315.6
 adj black 38.8
 nocturnal 315.9
midriff
 digestive system 2.16
 partition 213.5
 middle 818.1
midsection 213.5
midshipman
 navy man 183.4
 undergraduate 572.6
midst
 n middle 818.1
 prep between 213.12
 among 796.17
midterm 937.2
midtown
 n city district 230.6
 adj urban 230.11
mid-Victorian
 n prude 500.11
 back number 841.8
 adj prudish 500.19
 antiquated 841.13
midway
 n mid-distance 818.2
 adj neutral 467.7
 middle 818.4
 adv mediumly 246.4
 halfway 818.5
midwife
 health care
  professional 90.8
 instrument 384.4
mien looks 33.4
 exteriority 206.1
 behavior 321.1
miff
 n dudgeon 152.7
 v annoy 96.13
 provoke 152.24
miffed annoyed 96.21
 provoked 152.27
might strength 15.1
 power 18.1
 greatness 247.1
 authoritativeness
  417.2
might be 965.4
mighty
 adj strong 15.15
 powerful 18.12
 great 247.6
 huge 257.20
 authoritative 417.15
 eminent 662.18

adv very 247.18
migraine 26.5
migrant migrator 178.5
 bird 311.28
 worker 726.2
migrant worker
 migrant 178.5
 worker 726.2
 agriculturist 1067.5
migrate 177.22
migration
 transferal 176.1
 transmigration 177.4
 departure 188.1
mikado 575.9
mike 50.9
milady woman 77.5
 title 648.2
milch 1059.5
milcher 311.6
mild insipid 65.2
 bright 97.11
 good-natured 143.14
 lenient 427.7
 meek 433.15
 moderate 670.10
 warm 1018.24
 soft 1045.8
mildew
 n fetidness 71.2
 decay 393.6
 blight 1000.2
 v decay 393.22
mildewed
 malodorous 71.5
 blighted 393.42
 stale 841.14
mileage
 distance 261.1
 length 267.1
 benefit 387.4
 fee 624.5
 expedience 994.1
milepost post 273.4
 pointer 517.4
 marker 517.10
miles per hour 174.1
milestone
 marker 517.10
 salient point 996.6
milieu
 environment 209.1
 ambience 209.3
 region 231.1
 arena 463.1
 plot 722.4
militancy
 activity 330.1
 warlikeness 458.11
militant
 n man of action 330.8
 combatant 461.1
 believer 692.4
 adj active 330.17
 warlike 458.21
militarism
 warlikeness 458.11
 foreign policy 609.5
 government 612.4
militarist 461.5
militarization 458.10
militarize 458.20

military 458.21
military court 595.4
military operations
  war 458.1
  operation 458.5
military police 1007.17
military science 458.6
militate 888.7
militate against
  contend against 451.4
  counteract 899.6
militia 461.24
milk
  n humor 2.22
  whiteness 37.2
  fluid 1059.2
  v draw off 192.12
  exploit 387.16
  take from 480.21
  strip 480.24
  tend 1068.7
  adj milky 1059.5
milk and honey 1009.1
milk and water 16.7
milker 311.6
milking 192.3
milk run 184.11
milksop weakling 16.6
  effeminate male 77.10
  coward 491.5
  fool 923.1
milky
  wishy-washy 16.17
  white 37.7
  lacteal 1059.5
the Milky Way 1070.6
mill
  n money 728.7
  plant 739.3
  machinery 1039.3
  pulverizer 1049.7
  v notch 289.4
  come together 769.16
  process 891.9
  seethe 914.12
  tool 1039.9
  pulverize 1049.9
milled made 891.18
  powdery 1049.11
millenarian
  n optimist 124.6
  adj optimistic 124.12
millennial
  thousandth 881.30
  ideal 985.23
millennium
  moment 823.2
  thousand 881.10
  utopia 985.11
  good times 1009.4
milliner 5.36
millinery
  headdress 5.25
  garment making 5.31
milling
  production 891.2
  pulverization 1049.4
million
  n ten million 881.11
  adj numerous 883.6
millionaire 618.7
millions 618.2

millstone burden 297.7
  pulverizer 1049.7
millstone around one's
  neck affliction 96.8
  disadvantage 995.2
  impediment 1011.6
millstream 238.1
mill town 739.2
milord 648.2
milquetoast
  n manageability 433.4
  coward 491.5
  adj henpecked 326.5
  manageable 433.14
Milquetoast
  weakling 16.6
  vacillator 362.5
mime
  n imitator 336.4
  impersonation 349.4
  actor 707.2
  v mimic 336.6
  impersonate 349.12
  gesture 517.21
  act 704.29
mimeograph
  n printing 548.1
  v print 548.14
  copy 784.8
mimer imitator 336.4
  actor 707.2
mimetic
  imitative 336.9
  representational
    349.13
mimic
  n imitator 336.4
  actor 707.2
  v imitate 336.6
  impersonate 349.12
  resemble 783.7
  adj imitative 336.9
mimicry
  mockery 336.2
  impersonation 349.4
  acting 704.8
miming
  impersonation 349.4
  acting 704.8
minaret 272.6
minatory 514.3
mince
  n meat 10.12
  gait 177.12
  v walk 177.28
  be affected 500.14
  speak poorly 525.7
  extenuate 600.12
  shatter 801.13
mind
  n psyche 92.28
  desire 100.1
  will 323.1
  intention 380.1
  theosophy 689.18
  intellect 918.1
  intelligence 918.4
  opinion 952.6
  disposition 977.3
  mood 977.4
  attention 982.1
  memory 988.1

v take amiss 152.13
  refuse 325.3
  obey 326.2
  care 339.6
  beware 494.7
  heed 982.6
  remember 988.10
  care for 1007.19
Mind 677.6
mind-altering drug
  87.2
mind-blowing
  exciting 105.30
  hallucinatory 975.10
mind-boggler 522.8
mind-boggling
  deadening 25.9
  astonishing 122.12
  frightening 127.28
  unbelievable 954.10
minded willing 324.5
  moved 375.30
  disposed 977.8
mind-expanding
  psychochemical 86.46
  hallucinatory 975.10
mindful
  considerate 143.16
  careful 339.10
  observant 434.4
  cautious 494.8
  knowing 927.15
  attentive 982.15
  recollective 988.22
  remembering 988.24
mindless
  unconcerned 102.7
  inconsiderate 144.18
  cruel 144.26
  animal 311.38
  unrefined 497.12
  savage 671.21
  unintelligent 921.13
  unwise 922.10
  unaware 929.13
  purposeless 971.16
  incurious 981.3
mind one's own
  business
  not interfere 430.16
  take no interest in
    981.2
mind one's P's and Q's
  behave oneself 321.5
  be careful 339.7
  mind one's manners
    504.11
mind reader 689.15
mind reading 689.9
mind your own
  business 214.10
mine
  n pit 284.4
  trap 356.12
  source of supply 386.4
  entrenchment 460.5
  bomb 462.20
  rich source 618.4
  fountainhead 885.6
  quarry 1056.6
  v extract 192.10
  deepen 275.8

  excavate 284.15
  undermine 393.15
  blow up 395.18
  plant a mine 459.24
  fortify 460.9
  take from 480.21
  process 891.9
  quarry 1056.14
miner excavator 284.10
  mineworker 1056.9
mineral
  n inorganic substance
    1056.1
  ore 1056.2
  adj inorganic 1053.4
  inanimate 1056.15
mineral kingdom
  mineral 1056.1
  hierarchy 808.4
  inorganic matter
    1053.1
mineralogy 1056.10
mineral oil 1054.4
mineral spring 91.23
mineral water 1063.3
mineworker 1056.9
mingle 796.10
mingling 796.1
mingy niggardly 484.8
  ungenerous 651.6
mini
  n runt 258.4
  miniature 258.6
  adj miniature 258.12
miniature
  n mini 258.6
  image 349.5
  picture 712.11
  portrait 712.15
  adj insignificant 248.6
  diminutive 258.12
miniaturization 252.1
miniaturize 258.9
miniaturized
  reduced 252.10
  miniature 258.12
minim
  n modicum 248.2
  minute 258.7
  note 709.14
  rest 709.21
  adj least 250.8
minimal
  least 250.8
  miniature 258.12
  sufficient 990.6
minimization
  reduction 252.5
  underestimation
    949.1
minimize
  reduce 252.9
  disparage 512.8
  underestimate 949.2
  attach little
    importance to 997.12
minimum
  n modicum 248.2
  sufficiency 990.1
  adj least 250.8
  sufficient 990.6
minimum wage 624.4

mining
extraction 192.1
deepening 275.7
excavation 284.11
production 891.2
coal mining 1056.8
mining engineer
1056.12
minion favorite 104.16
sycophant 138.3
instrument 384.4
retainer 577.1
follower 616.8
minister
n public official
575.17
delegate 576.2
diplomat 576.6
clergyman 699.2
v officiate 701.15
ministerial
modal 384.8
helping 449.20
administrative 573.14
diplomatic 576.16
executive 612.19
ecclesiastic 698.13
ministering
modal 384.8
helping 449.20
serving 577.14
minister of state 575.17
minister to treat 91.24
be instrumental 384.7
aid 449.18
serve 577.13
care for 1007.19
ministration
aid 449.1
service 577.12
ministry aid 449.1
the authorities 575.15
service 577.12
bureau 594.4
cabinet 613.3
clergy 699.1
protectorship 1007.2
minor
n youngster 302.1
study 568.8
key 709.15
adj inferior 250.6
immature 301.10
insignificant 997.17
minority
n inability 19.2
inferiority 250.1
immaturity 301.3
race 312.2
least 884.3
adj least 884.7
minority group
party 617.4
minority 884.3
minority interests
609.31
minority leader 610.3
minority opinion 333.1
minor league 745.1
Minos
Pontius Pilate 596.5
justice 649.5

nether world deity
682.5
minstrel
n musical theater
708.34
singer 710.13
ballad singer 710.14
poet 720.11
v sing 708.38
minstrel show 708.34
mint
n lot 247.4
gain 472.3
wealth 618.3
plant 739.3
mold 785.6
v form 262.7
coin 728.28
innovate 840.5
originate 891.12
adj unused 390.12
new-made 840.9
undamaged 1001.8
mintage money 728.1
coining 728.24
production 891.1
product 892.1
mint condition
healthiness 83.2
newness 840.1
minted formative 262.9
invented 891.19
minus
n math terms 255.6
deduction 255.7
adj bereft 473.8
nonexistent 761.8
short of 910.5
positive 1031.34
prep off 255.14
without 991.17
minuscule
n type 548.6
adj miniature 258.12
literal 546.8
minute
n entry 628.5
period 823.1
moment 823.2
instant 829.3
time of day 831.2
the present 837.1
v record 549.15
keep accounts 628.8
adj tiny 258.11
meticulous 339.12
detailed 765.9
particular 864.12
insignificant 997.17
minutemen 461.24
minutes
memorandum 549.4
report 549.7
minutiae
modicum 248.2
detail 258.7
particular 765.3
trivia 997.4
minx woman 77.6
impudent person
142.5
brat 302.4

mischief-maker 322.3
miracle marvel 122.2
sign 869.8
miracle drug 86.29
miracle-worker 690.5
miraculous
wonderful 122.10
sorcerous 690.14
wondrous 869.16
mirage apparition 33.5
disappointment 132.1
deception 356.1
fata morgana 975.6
mire
n slime 80.8
receptacle of filth
80.12
marsh 243.1
mud 1060.8
v dirty 80.15
bemire 243.2
mirror
n glass 29.6
furniture 229.1
paragon 659.4
model 785.1
ideal 785.4
pattern of perfection
1001.4
v imitate 336.5
image 349.11
resemble 783.7
mirror image 778.2
mirroring
imitation 336.1
image 349.5
mirth merriment 109.5
amusement 743.1
miry dirty 80.22
marshy 243.3
slimy 1060.14
misadventure 1010.2
misalliance
marriage 563.1
misconnection 775.2
unfitness 788.3
misanthrope
hater 103.4
misanthropist 590.2
misanthropy
hate 103.1
people-hating 590
misanthropism 590.1
misapplication
misinterpretation
342.1
misuse 389.1
misconnection 775.2
sophistry 935.1
error 974.1
misapply
misinterpret 342.2
misuse 389.4
reason speciously
935.8
misdo 974.12
misapprehend
misinterpret 342.2
mistake 974.13
misapprehension
misinterpretation
342.1

mistake 974.3
misappropriate 389.4
misappropriation 389.1
misbegotten
deformed 265.12
illegitimate 674.7
freakish 869.13
unshapely 1014.8
misbehave
behave 321.4
misdemean 322.4
transgress 654.8
do wrong 655.4
misbehavior
good behavior 321.2
misconduct 322.1
wrongdoing 655.1
misbelief
heresy 688.2
unbelief 954.1
illusion 975.1
misbelieve err 688.8
disbelieve 954.5
misbeliever 688.5
miscalculate
misjudge 947.2
err 974.9
miscalculation
misjudgment 947.1
mistake 974.3
miscarriage
abortion 410.5
mistake 974.3
miscarriage of justice
650.4
miscarry
abort 410.15
miss 910.4
miscegenate
get married 563.15
hybridize 796.13
miscegenation
marriage 563.1
crossbreeding 796.4
miscellany
compilation 554.7
excerpts 557.4
assortment 769.13
hodgepodge 796.6
mischance 1010.2
mischief
mischievousness
322.2
mischief-maker 322.3
impairment 393.1
disaccord 456.1
disadvantage 995.2
evil 999.3
mischief-maker
mischief 322.3
instigator 375.11
troublemaker 593.2
mischievous
mischief-loving 322.6
impish 680.18
harmful 999.12
misconceive
misinterpret 342.2
mistake 974.13
misconception
misinterpretation
342.1

mistake 974.3
illusion 975.1
misconduct
  n misbehavior 322.1
misuse 389.1
mismanagement
  414.6
wrongdoing 655.1
  v mismanage 414.13
misdo 974.12
misconstruction
perversion 265.2
misinterpretation
  342.1
deliberate falsehood
  354.9
solecism 531.2
misjudgment 947.1
error 974.1
misconstrue
pervert 265.6
misinterpret 342.2
misjudge 947.2
miscue
  n bungle 414.5
slip 974.4
  v bungle 414.11
err 974.13
misdate
  n anachronism 832.1
  v mistime 832.2
misdated 832.3
misdating 832.1
misdeed 655.2
misdemeanor
misbehavior 322.1
misdeed 655.2
offense 674.4
misdirect pervert 265.6
mislead 356.16
mismanage 414.13
misteach 569.3
misdirected
botched 414.21
mistaught 569.5
misdirection
perversion 265.2
misleading 356.2
mismanagement
  414.6
misteaching 569.1
mise-en-scène
setting 209.2
production 704.13
stage setting 704.19
motion-picture studio
  706.3
miser niggard 484.4
collector 769.15
miserable
wretched 96.26
unhappy 112.21
base 661.12
paltry 997.21
adverse 1010.13
Miserere 696.3
miserly greedy 100.27
stingy 484.9
sparse 884.5
meager 991.10
misery pain 26.1
wretchedness 96.6

unhappiness 112.2
sorrow 112.10
misfeasance
misbehavior 322.1
misuse 389.1
mismanagement
  414.6
wrongdoing 655.1
misdeed 655.2
error 974.1
misfire
  n abortion 410.5
  v come to nothing
  410.13
miss 910.4
misfit
intruder 773.2
naysayer 788.4
nonconformist 867.3
misfortune 1010.2
misgiving
  n anxiety 126.1
apprehension 127.4
nervousness 128.1
foreboding 133.2
doubt 954.2
  adj anxious 126.7
apprehensive 127.24
misgovern 414.13
misguide
mislead 356.16
mismanage 414.13
misteach 569.3
misguided
botched 414.21
mistaught 569.5
unwise 922.10
mishandle
misuse 389.4
mistreat 389.5
mismanage 414.13
mishandling
misuse 389.1
mismanagement
  414.6
mishap 1010.2
mishmash
hodgepodge 796.6
jumble 809.3
misidentify 974.13
misinform
mislead 356.16
misteach 569.3
misinformation
misleading 356.2
misteaching 569.1
misinformed
mistaught 569.5
unlearned 929.14
misinterpret
pervert 265.6
misunderstand 342.2
misjudge 947.2
mistake 974.13
misinterpretation
perversion 265.2
misunderstanding
  342.1
misjudgment 947.1
error 974.1
misjudge
misinterpret 342.2

judge amiss 947.2
misjudgment
misinterpretation
  342.1
error in judgment 947
poor judgment 947.1
error 974.1
mistake 974.3
mislay misplace 160.7
lose 473.4
mislaying 160.3
mislead lie 354.18
misguide 356.16
misteach 569.3
betray 645.14
seduce 665.20
misleading
  n misguidance 356.2
misteaching 569.1
  adj deceptive 356.21
misteaching 569.6
illusory 975.8
mismanage
misuse 389.4
mishandle 414.13
misdo 974.12
mismanagement
misuse 389.1
mishandling 414.6
mismatch
  n misconnection 775.2
unfitness 788.3
  v disagree 788.5
mismatched
inappropriate 788.7
unequal 790.4
misname 527.12
misnomer
  n wrong name 527.9
  v misname 527.12
misogynist hater 103.4
celibate 565.2
misanthrope 590.2
misogyny hate 103.1
celibacy 565.1
misanthropy 590.1
misplace mislay 160.7
lose 473.4
misplaced
mislaid 160.11
inappropriate 788.7
disorderly 809.13
out of line 867.7
misplay
  n mistake 974.3
  v play 745.5
misdo 974.12
misprint
  n mistake 974.3
  v misdo 974.12
misprize disdain 157.3
underestimate 949.2
misprized disliked 99.9
underestimated 949.3
mispronounce 525.11
mispronunciation
misspeaking 525.5
grammatical error
  974.7
misquote
misinterpret 342.2
misrepresent 350.3

falsify 354.15
misdo 974.12
misquoted
falsified 265.11
unauthentic 974.19
misread
  v misinterpret 342.2
misjudge 947.2
misdo 974.12
  adj misinterpreted
  342.3
misreading
misinterpretation
  342.1
misjudgment 947.1
misremember 989.5
misrender
pervert 265.6
misinterpret 342.2
misrendering 342.1
misrepresent
pervert 265.6
belie 350.3
falsify 354.15
misrepresentation
perversion 265.2
distortion 350
misinterpretation
  350.1
deliberate falsehood
  354.9
misrepresented
  265.11
misrule
  n mismanagement
  414.6
anarchy 418.2
confusion 809.2
  v mismanage 414.13
miss
  n girl 302.6
near-miss 410.4
game 750.2
mistake 974.3
  v leave undone 340.7
miss the mark 410.14
lose 473.4
miscarry 910.4
be inattentive 983.2
want 991.7
fall short 1002.3
Miss 77.8
Miss America 1015.8
misshape
  n deformity 265.3
  v deform 263.3
distort 265.7
misshapen
deformed 265.12
unordered 809.12
freakish 869.13
unshapely 1014.8
missile
  n weapon 462.18
projectile 903.5
rocket 1072.3
  adj projectile 903.15
missilery
arms 462.1
ballistics 462.3
missile science 1072
rocketry 1072.1

missing
gone 34.4
absent 222.11
nonexistent 761.8
incomplete 794.4
wanting 991.13
missing link 841.7
mission
n Air Force mission
184.11
adventure 404.2
operation 458.5
delegation 576.13
commission 615.1
duty 641.1
church 703.1
task 724.2
vocation 724.6
v commission
615.10
missionary
evangelist 699.6
converter 857.9
missive 553.2
misspeak
mispronounce 525.11
blunder 974.14
misspell 974.12
misspent 486.9
misstate
misrepresent 350.3
falsify 354.15
misstatement
misrepresentation
350.1
deliberate falsehood
354.9
mistake 974.3
misstep misdeed 655.2
slip 974.4
miss the boat
miss an opportunity
843.5
be late 845.7
miss 910.4
miss the mark
err 410.14
miss 910.4
fall short 1002.3
mist
n rain 316.1
fog 319.2
obscurity 522.3
spirit 763.3
confusion 984.3
v blur 32.4
cloud 319.6
confuse 984.7
mistake
n miss 410.4
bungle 414.5
error 974.3
v misinterpret 342.2
make a mistake
974.13
err 974.13
mistaken
misinterpreted 342.3
in error 974.18
misteach
misrepresent 350.3
misinstruct 569.3

misteaching
n misrepresentation
350.1
misinstruction 569.1
adj misinstructive
569.6
Mister man 76.7
Sir 648.3
mistime misdate 832.2
ill-time 843.3
mistimed
anachronous 832.3
untimely 843.6
mistiming 832.1
mistral 318.9
mistreat
maltreat 389.5
work evil 999.6
mistreatment 389.2
mistress
ladylove 104.14
proprietor 470.2
teacher 571.2
governess 575.2
woman 665.17
wise woman 920.1
Mistress woman 77.8
madame 648.4
mistrial 598.5
mistrust
n suspiciousness 153.2
wariness 494.2
doubt 954.2
v suffer pangs of
jealousy 153.3
doubt 954.6
mistrustful wary 494.9
doubting 954.9
misty
inconspicuous 32.6
formless 263.4
thin 270.16
rainy 316.10
foggy 319.9
obscure 522.15
vague 970.19
muddled 984.13
misunderstand
misinterpret 342.2
mistake 974.13
misunderstanding
misinterpretation
342.1
disagreement 456.2
mistake 974.3
misunderstood
disliked 99.9
misinterpreted 342.3
misusage misuse 389.1
solecism 531.2
grammatical error
974.7
misuse
n perversion 265.2
use 387.1
misemployment 389
misusage 389.1
corruption 393.2
mistake 974.3
v pervert 265.6
exploit 387.16
misemploy 389.4

corrupt 393.12
misdo 974.12
mite
modicum 248.2
minute 258.7
child 302.3
insect 311.31
vermin 311.35
money 728.8
pittance 991.5
miter
n ecclesiastical
insignia 647.4
joint 799.4
v hook 799.8
mitigate
weaken 16.10
relieve 120.5
abate 252.8
extenuate 600.12
moderate 670.6
relax 670.9
be changed 851.6
change 851.7
qualify 958.3
mitigating
relieving 120.9
assuaging 670.14
qualifying 958.7
mitigation
weakening 16.5
relief 120.1
pity 145.1
decrease 252.1
extenuation 600.5
modulation 670.2
change 851.1
mitigator 670.3
mitosis 305.16
mitzvah
act of kindness 143.7
rule 419.2
mix
n motion-picture
editing 706.5
hodgepodge 796.6
predicament 1012.5
v make up 405.7
compose 795.3
admix 796.10
combine 804.3
confound 944.3
mixed
ambiguous 539.4
mingled 796.14
combined 804.5
imperfect 1002.4
mixed bag 796.6
mixed-blood 796.8
mixed marriage 563.1
mixed-up
complex 798.4
distracted 809.16
muddleheaded 921.18
confused 984.12
mixer
sociable person
582.16
dance 705.2
blender 796.9
control room 1033.7
radioman 1033.24

mixing mixture 796.1
radio broadcasting
1033.16
televising 1034.3
mixture
medicine 86.4
concoction 405.3
miscellany 769.13
difference 779.1
composition 795.1
blending 796
mixing 796.1
compound 796.5
combination 804.2
solution 1062.3
mix up mix 796.10
complicate 798.3
rearrange 810.3
confound 944.3
mistake 974.13
confuse 984.7
mix-up
rearrangement 809.2
confusion 984.3
mnemonic
n memory training
988.9
adj recollective 988.22
moan
n lament 115.3
v sigh 52.14
be discontented 108.6
lament 115.10
wail 115.13
complain 115.16
sough 318.21
moaning
n sigh 52.8
lamentation 115.1
adj lamenting 115.18
moat crack 224.2
trench 290.2
entrenchment 460.5
barrier 1011.5
mob association 617.1
clique 617.6
company 769.3
throng 769.4
multitude 883.3
the mob
the masses 606.2
the underworld
660.11
mobile
n work of art 712.10
sculpture 715.2
adj moving 172.7
upper-class 607.10
changeable 853.6
mobile home
trailer 179.19
abode 228.17
mobile unit 1034.7
mobility
motivity 172.3
class 607.1
changeableness 853.1
mobilization
motion 172.1
utilization 387.8
preparation 405.1
call to arms 458.8

militarization 458.10
enlistment 615.7
assemblage 769.1
mobilize
set in motion 172.6
prepare 405.6
call to arms 458.19
militarize 458.20
enlist 615.17
assemble 769.18
put together 799.5
Möbius strip 811.2
mob rule
anarchy 418.2
government 612.4
mobster bandit 483.4
evildoer 593.1
criminal 660.10
mock
n indignity 156.2
fake 354.13
gibe 508.2
v offend 156.5
impersonate 349.12
deceive 356.14
joke 489.13
scoff 508.9
adopt 621.4
adj imitation 336.8
spurious 354.25
similar 783.10
substitute 861.8
mocker 336.4
mockery
indignity 156.2
mimicry 336.2
insincerity 354.5
ridicule 508.1
burlesque 508.6
laughingstock 508.7
trifle 997.5
mock-heroic
comic 488.6
poetic 720.15
mocking
n adoption 621.2
adj ridiculing 508.12
mockingbird
imitator 336.4
songbird 710.23
mock-up
reproduction 336.3
artist's model 785.5
mod 840.13
modal
instrumental 384.8
conditional 764.6
modality
form 262.1
manner 384.1
instrumentality 384.3
state 764.1
mode
form 262.1
manner 384.1
mood 530.11
style 532.2
fashion 578.1
octave species 709.10
shape 764.1
manner 764.4
syllogism 934.6

model
n form 262.1
measure 300.2
reproduction 336.3
original 337.2
image 349.5
figure 349.6
paragon 659.4
celebrity 662.9
arrangement 709.11
essence 766.2
duplicate 784.3
thing copied 785
pattern 785.1
ideal 785.4
rule 868.4
philosophy 931.2
beauty 1015.8
v form 262.7
sculpture 715.5
adj praiseworthy
509.20
exemplary 785.8
normal 868.8
perfected 1001.9
modeled
formative 262.9
sculptured 715.7
modeler 716.6
modeling
forming 262.5
imitation 336.1
sculpture 715.1
moderate
n centrist 611.10
moderatist 670.4
v slow 175.9
limit 210.5
mediate 466.6
restrain 670.6
qualify 958.3
adj sedate 106.14
slow 175.10
medium 246.3
lenient 427.7
neutral 467.7
centrist 611.18
cheap 633.7
temperate 668.9
moderating 670.10
middle 818.4
tolerable 998.20
mediocre 1004.7
moderation
sedateness 106.4
limitation 210.2
middle course 467.3
temperance 668.1
restraint 670
moderateness 670.1
moderato 708.55
moderator
arbitrator 466.4
judge 596.1
mitigator 670.3
modern
n modern man 840.4
adj fashionable 578.11
present 837.2
contemporary 840.13
modernist
poet 720.11

modern 840.4
modernization 840.3
modernize 840.6
modest
humble 137.10
meek 139.9
inferior 250.6
demurring 325.7
reticent 344.10
cheap 633.7
decent 664.5
mediocre 1004.7
unselfish 652.5
modesty
humility 137.1
unpretentiousness 139
meekness 139.1
demur 325.2
reticence 344.3
unselfishness 652.1
decency 664.2
mediocrity 1004.1
modicum minim 248.2
portion 477.5
piece 792.3
modifiable
changeable 853.6
convertible 857.18
modification
speech sound 524.13
differentiation 779.4
change 851.1
qualification 958.1
modified
changed 851.10
qualified 958.10
modifier syntax 530.2
transformer 851.5
modify
differentiate 779.6
change 851.7
qualify 958.3
modish dressed up 5.45
stylish 578.12
modern 840.13
modiste 5.35
modular partial 792.7
component 795.5
modulate inflect 524.29
moderate 670.6
be changed 851.6
change 851.7
qualify 958.3
modulation
intonation 524.7
abatement 670.2
harmonization 709.2
change 851.1
amplitude
modulation 1033.14
modulator 670.3
module part 792.1
component 795.2
individual 871.4
spacecraft 1073.2
modus operandi 384.1
modus vivendi
behavior 321.1
truce 465.5
mogul skiing 753.1
personage 996.8
snow 1022.8

Mogul 575.10
moiety portion 477.5
community 617.2
piece 792.3
mid-distance 818.2
half 874.2
moil
n work 725.4
agitation 916.1
v drudge 725.14
seethe 914.12
moiré
n variegation 47.6
adj iridescent 47.10
moisten 1063.12
moistening
n wetting 1063.6
adj wetting 1063.18
moisture rain 316.1
liquidity 1059.1
dampness 1063
damp 1063.1
moisture-proof 1064.11
moisturizer 1063.3
molar 2.8
molasses
sweetening 66.2
adhesive 802.4
semiliquid 1060.5
mold
n germ 85.41
land 234.1
form 262.1
structure 266.1
plant 310.4
original 337.2
decay 393.6
nature 766.4
cast 784.6
die 785.6
kind 808.3
characteristic 864.4
disposition 977.3
blight 1000.2
v form 262.7
decay 393.22
sculpture 715.5
pot 742.6
conform 866.3
produce 891.8
imagine 985.14
moldable docile 433.13
teachable 570.18
pliant 1045.9
molded
formative 262.9
sculptured 715.7
made 891.18
molder
n sculptor 716.6
v quiet 173.8
decay 393.22
disintegrate 805.3
age 841.9
moldering
quiescent 173.12
blighted 393.42
disintegrative 805.5
stale 841.14
molding
forming 262.5
structure 266.1

sculpture 715.1
cast 784.6
production 891.2
moldy
malodorous 71.5
blighted 393.42
stale 841.14
mole the blind 30.4
growth 85.38
bulge 283.3
mark 517.5
buttress 900.4
blemish 1003.1
harbor 1008.6
barrier 1011.5
molecular 258.14
molecular weight
weight 297.5
chemistry 297.8
atomic weight 1058.5
molecule
modicum 248.2
atom 258.8
atomic cluster 1037.7
matter 1050.2
element 1058.2
molehill hill 237.4
pile 769.10
trifle 997.5
molest annoy 96.13
mistreat 389.5
work evil 999.6
mollify relieve 120.5
pacify 465.7
calm 670.7
soften 1045.6
mollifying
n softening 1045.5
adj pacificatory
465.12
tranquilizing 670.15
softening 1045.16
mollycoddle
n weakling 16.6
effeminate male 77.10
spoiled child 427.4
v indulge 427.6
molt shed 6.10
waste 473.5
molten melted 1019.31
liquefied 1062.6
mom 560.12
moment prestige 417.4
period 823.1
second 823.2
short time 827.3
instant 829.3
influence 893.1
impulse 901.1
importance 996.1
momentary
transient 827.7
instantaneous 829.4
momently 849.8
moment of truth
period 823.1
crucial moment 842.5
unreliability 970.6
urgency 996.4
momentous
authoritative 417.15
eventful 830.10

influential 893.13
important 996.17
momentum
motion 172.1
course 172.2
impulse 901.1
monad atom 258.8
something 762.3
one 871.3
matter 1050.2
monarch 575.8
monarchic
sovereign 417.17
governmental 612.17
monarchism
radicalism 611.4
government 612.8
monarchist 611.9
monarchy
government 612.4
absolutism 612.9
monasterial
monastic 698.14
claustral 703.16
monastery 703.6
monastic
n celibate 565.2
religious 699.15
adj celibate 565.6
monachal 698.14
claustral 703.16
monasticism
celibacy 565.1
asceticism 667.1
monachism 698.4
monaural system 50.11
monde 578.6
money wealth 618.1
currency 728.1
moneybags 618.7
money changer
banker 729.10
broker 730.9
money-hungry 100.27
money in hand 728.18
money in the bank
472.6
money-laundering
673.2
moneylender
lender 620.3
banker 729.10
money-mad 100.27
moneymaking
n acquisition 472.1
adj gainful 472.16
paying 624.21
occupied 724.15
moneyman 729.8
money market 728.16
money order 728.11
money-raising 621.1
money-saving 635.6
monger 730.2
mongolism 921.9
mongoloid 921.22
Mongoloid 312.2
mongoloid idiot 923.8
mongrel
n cur 311.19
beast 660.7
hybrid 796.8

adj hybrid 796.15
mongrelization 796.4
mongrelize 796.13
moniker 527.3
monition
dissuasion 379.1
warning 399.1
advice 422.1
tip 551.3
monitor
n warner 399.4
adviser 422.3
shackle 428.4
informant 551.5
teaching fellow 571.4
superintendent 574.2
examiner 937.17
radioman 1033.24
television technician
1034.13
output device 1041.9
v be taught 570.11
examine 937.23
check 1033.26
monitoring
vigilance 339.4
televising 1034.3
monitory
n advice 422.1
adj premonitory
133.16
dissuasive 379.5
warning 399.7
advisory 422.8
informative 551.18
monk
wild animal 311.23
celibate 565.2
religious 699.15
monkey
n temper 152.6
wild animal 311.23
imitator 336.4
dupe 358.1
laughingstock 508.7
cheater 759.22
v trifle 997.15
monkey business 356.5
monkeying 997.9
monkeyshines
buffoonery 489.5
prank 489.10
monkey with 214.7
monkhood 698.4
monkish
inornate 499.9
celibate 565.6
monastic 698.14
mono 50.11
monochrome
n color system 35.7
adj chromatic 35.15
pictorial 712.21
monocle 29.3
monocratic
authoritative 417.15
imperious 417.16
governmental
612.17
monody
dirge 115.6
harmony 708.3

monophony 708.21
monogamist 563.11
monogram
identification 517.11
signature 527.10
letter 546.1
monograph 556.1
monolith
monument 549.12
rock 1057.1
monolithic
uniform 780.5
simple 797.6
stony 1057.11
monologist 542.2
monologue
soliloquy 542.1
regularity 780.2
monomania
obsession 925.13
engrossment 982.3
monomaniac
n fanatic 925.18
adj obsessed 925.33
monopolist
n restrictionist 428.6
self-seeker 651.3
adj monopolistic
469.11
monopolize hog 469.6
appropriate 480.19
purchase 733.7
corner 737.26
engross 982.13
monopoly
restraint 428.1
monopolization 469.3
manipulation 737.20
monorail 179.14
monosyllable 526.1
monotheism 675.5
monotheist 675.16
monotheistic 675.25
monotone
n tone 50.2
regularity 780.2
series 811.2
repetitiousness 848.4
adj sounding 50.15
monotonous 848.15
monotonous
tedious 118.9
same 780.6
continuous 811.8
monotone 848.15
monotony tone 50.2
tedium 118.1
regularity 780.2
continuity 811.1
repetitiousness 848.4
monsieur 76.7
Monsignor 648.5
monsoon season 313.1
wet weather 316.4
monster
n frightener 127.9
beast 144.14
largeness 257.11
behemoth 257.14
fiend 593.6
violent person 671.9
monstrosity 869.6

building material
1052.2
v plaster 295.25
pull the trigger 459.22
mortar and pestle
1049.7
mortgage
n mortgage deed
438.4
v pledge 438.10
mortgage company
620.4
mortgaged 623.8
mortgagee
warrantee 438.7
lender 620.3
creditor 622.4
mortgaging 621.1
mortgagor
guarantor 438.6
debtor 623.4
mortician 309.8
mortification
gangrene 85.39
chagrin 96.4
embarrassment 98.6
humiliation 137.2
penance 658.3
asceticism 667.1
mortified
diseased 85.59
distressed 96.22
humiliated 137.14
decayed 393.40
mortify chagrin 96.15
embarrass 98.13
humiliate 137.4
decay 393.22
mortifying
embarrassing 98.21
humiliating 137.15
mortise interact 776.6
hook 799.8
mortuary
n morgue 309.9
adj deathly 307.29
funereal 309.22
mosaic
n check 47.4
picture 712.11
adj checked 47.14
Mosaic 683.10
mosey 175.6
Moslem
n Muslim 675.23
adj Muslim 675.31
Moslemism 675.13
mosque 703.2
mosquito 311.36
moss marsh 243.1
plant 310.4
mossback
back number 841.8
conservative 852.4
mossbacked 303.18
mossy 310.39
most
n supremacy 249.3
major part 791.6
majority 882.2
adj extreme 247.13
superlative 249.13

majority 882.9
adv extremely 247.22
the most 249.16
most likely 967.8
mot witticism 489.7
maxim 973.1
mote modicum 248.2
minute 258.7
lightness 298.2
stronghold 460.6
intruder 773.2
motel 228.16
moth-eaten trite 117.9
stricken in years
303.18
blighted 393.42
stale 841.14
mother
n parent 559.3
genetrix 560.11
bad person 660.6
author 885.4
producer 891.7
v procreate 78.8
foster 449.16
engender 817.14
care for 1007.19
adj native 226.5
Mother 648.5
Mother Earth 1070.10
mother figure 92.31
motherhood
blood relationship
559.1
maternity 560.3
mothering 449.3
mother-in-law 564.2
motherland 232.2
motherless
helpless 19.18
bereaved 307.35
forlorn 584.12
mother lode 618.4
Mother Nature 677.8
mother-of-pearl
n variegation 47.6
iridescence 1024.18
adj soft-colored 35.21
iridescent 47.10
mother superior
mistress 575.2
nun 699.17
mother tongue 523.3
motif edging 211.7
ornamental motif
498.7
passage 708.24
plot 722.4
topic 936.1
motile moving 172.7
changeable 853.6
motility
mobility 172.3
changeableness 853.1
motion
n exercise 84.2
movement 172.1
travel 177.1
activity 330.1
proposal 439.2
gesture 517.14
bill 613.9

baseball team 745.2
process 888.2
trend 895.2
mechanism 1039.4
v gesture 517.21
motionless
unmoving 173.13
passive 329.6
inactive 331.17
motion picture
cinematography 706.1
pictures 714.8
motion sickness 85.30
motivate
set in motion 172.6
move 375.12
induce 885.11
impel 901.11
motivated
moved 375.30
teachable 570.18
motivating force 17.6
motivation
motion 172.1
reason 375
moving 375.2
teachableness 570.5
motivational
moving 172.7
motivating 375.25
motive
n reason 375.1
intention 380.1
passage 708.24
topic 936.1
adj moving 172.7
motivating 375.25
impelling 901.21
propulsive 903.14
motive power
energizer 17.6
mobility 172.3
impulse 901.1
pushing 903.1
machinery 1039.3
motivity 172.3
motley
n costume 5.9
comedy 704.6
buffoon 707.10
v variegate 47.7
adj chromatic 35.15
variegated 47.9
mottled 47.12
different 779.7
mixed 796.14
nonuniform 781.3
motor
n automobile 179.9
instrument of
conversion 857.10
machinery 1039.3
v ride 177.33
adj moving 172.7
motorboat
n powerboat 180.4
v navigate 182.13
motorcade 811.3
motorcar 179.9
motorcycle
n cycle 179.8
v ride 177.33

motorcyclist 178.11
motor-driven 1039.10
motoring 177.6
motor inn 228.16
motorist 178.10
motorize 1039.9
motor launch 180.4
motorman 178.12
motor oil 1054.4
motor vehicle 179.9
mottle
n spottiness 47.3
mark 517.5
v variegate 47.7
mark 517.19
mottled 47.12
motto heraldry 647.2
caption 936.2
maxim 973.1
slogan 973.4
moue scowl 110.9
grimace 265.4
mound
n hill 237.4
monument 549.12
baseball 745.1
pile 769.10
barrier 1011.5
v pile 769.19
mount
n ascent 193.1
mountain 237.6
horse 311.10
hunter 311.13
jockey 757.2
frame 900.10
v copulate 75.21
move 172.5
go on horseback
177.34
soar 184.39
ascend 193.8
climb 193.11
get on 193.12
rise 200.8
increase 251.6
tower 272.10
grow 272.12
dramatize 704.28
give a lift 911.7
mountain mount 237.6
quantity 247.3
plateau 272.4
bulge 283.3
mountain climber
193.6
mountain dew 88.18
mountaineer
traveler 178.1
climber 193.6
wilderness settler
227.10
mountain lion 311.22
mountain man 227.10
mountainous
hilly 237.8
large 247.7
huge 257.20
high 272.18
mountain range
mountain 237.6
plateau 272.4

mountaintop
summit 198.2
mountain 237.6
mountebank
impostor 357.6
entertainer 707.1
mountebankery 354.7
mounted policeman
rider 178.8
policeman 1007.15
Mounties 1007.17
mounting
n course 172.2
ascent 193.1
increase 251.1
production 704.13
frame 900.10
adj flowing 172.8
ascending 193.14
high 272.14
Mount Olympus 681.9
mount up to
cost 630.13
total 791.8
mourn distress 98.14
grieve 112.17
lament 115.10
mourner
lamenter 115.8
griever 309.7
mournful
distressing 98.20
sorrowful 112.26
plaintive 115.19
funereal 309.22
mourning
n lamentation 115.1
weeds 115.7
adj lamenting 115.18
mouse woman 77.6
trauma 85.37
shrinking violet 139.6
runt 258.4
coward 491.5
input device 1041.4
mouse-colored 39.4
mouser 311.21
mousetrap trap 356.12
rocket launcher
1072.10
mousse sweets 10.38
foam 320.2
mousy gray 39.4
silent 51.10
fearful 127.23
shy 139.12
rodent 311.43
cowardly 491.10
mouth
n digestive system
2.16
eater 8.16
inlet 242.1
maw 292.4
v chew 8.27
lick 73.9
grimace 265.8
be hypocritical 354.22
speak 524.20
mumble 525.9
declaim 543.10
mouthful bite 8.2

high-sounding words
545.3
full measure 793.3
mouthing
hypocrisy 354.6
mumbling 525.4
lip service 693.2
mouth organ 711.10
mouthpiece
telephone 347.4
mediator 466.3
informant 551.5
spokesman 576.5
lawyer 597.3
wind instrument
711.6
boxing 754.1
mouthwash
cleanser 79.17
dentifrice 86.22
mouth-watering
n saliva 13.3
adj appetizing 63.10
desirable 100.30
alluring 377.8
mouthy 545.9
movable
transferable 176.18
changeable 853.6
influenceable 893.15
movable feast 20.4
movables
furniture 229.1
belongings 471.2
move
n act 328.3
attempt 403.2
stratagem 415.3
cheating 759.13
process 888.2
expedient 994.2
v affect 93.14
excite 105.12
touch 145.5
settle 159.17
progress 162.2
budge 172.5
set in motion 172.6
remove 176.11
travel 177.18
behave 321.4
act 328.4
motivate 375.12
admonish 422.6
propose 439.5
sell 734.8
influence 893.7
impel 901.11
push 903.9
move away
recede 168.2
depart 188.6
move back 163.6
moved
affected 93.23
excited 105.20
motivated 375.30
move in
settle 159.17
inhabit 225.7
take possession 472.10
gain influence 893.12

move into
inhabit 225.7
undertake 404.3
movement
defecation 12.2
feces 12.4
exercise 84.2
motion 172.1
moving 176.4
travel 177.1
behavior 321.1
act 328.3
activity 330.1
operation 458.5
gesture 517.14
front 609.33
passage 708.24
rhythm 709.22
style 712.8
meter 720.7
plot 722.4
company 769.3
cause 885.9
trend 895.2
mechanism 1039.4
move out 188.6
mover wanderer 178.2
prompter 375.10
doer 726.1
cheater 759.22
author 885.4
producer 891.7
movie
n motion pictures
706.1
adj motion-picture
706.8
moviegoer
playgoer 704.27
attender 221.5
movie star 707.4
moving
n motion 172.1
removal 176.4
travel 177.1
motivation 375.2
adj affecting 93.22
distressing 98.20
exciting 105.30
pitiful 145.8
progressive 162.6
stirring 172.7
traveling 177.36
motivating 375.25
lofty 544.14
impelling 901.23
moving spirit
inspiration 375.9
prompter 375.10
moving staircase 911.4
mow
n scowl 110.9
grimace 265.4
garner 386.7
pile 769.10
v grimace 265.8
shorten 268.6
smooth 287.5
harvest 1067.19
mow down raze 395.19
fell 912.5
moxie energy 17.3

power 18.1
liveliness 330.2
pluck 359.3
skill 413.1
fearlessness 492.4
MP legislator 610.3
policeman 1007.15
police 1007.17
Mr common man 606.5
man 76.7
Mr Universe 15.6
Mrs 77.8
Mrs Grundy
fussbudget 495.7
social convention
579.1
conventionalist 579.3
conformist 866.2
Ms 77.8
MS 547.10
much
n quantity 247.3
plenty 990.2
adj many 247.8
plentiful 990.7
adv greatly 247.15
**much ado about
nothing**
overreaction 355.2
triviality 997.3
mucilage
adhesive 802.4
lubricant 1054.2
semiliquid 1060.5
muck
n filth 80.7
slime 80.8
fertilizer 889.4
mud 1060.8
v dirty 80.15
muck around 997.15
mucked up
spoiled 393.29
complex 798.4
confused 809.16
muckrake 512.10
muckraker
disparager 512.6
critic 945.7
muckraking
defamation 512.2
smear campaign
609.14
muck up dirty 80.15
spoil 393.11
complicate 798.3
confuse 810.3
make a boner 974.15
mucky filthy 80.23
slimy 1060.14
mucous 1060.13
mucous membrane 2.6
mucus
digestive secretion
13.2
filth 80.7
lubricant 1054.2
semiliquid 1060.5
mud
dirt 80.6
marsh 243.1
muck 1060.8

slaughterous 308.23
savage 671.21
murderous insanity
  925.7
murk
  n gloom 112.7
  obscurity 522.3
  darkishness 1026.2
  v blacken 38.7
  darken 1026.9
  adj darkish 1026.15
murky dingy 38.11
  gloomy 112.24
  obscure 522.15
  vague 970.19
  stained 1003.10
  darkish 1026.15
murmur
  n murmuring 52.4
  lament 115.3
  v mutter 52.10
  complain 115.15
  sigh 318.21
  speak 524.26
  mumble 525.9
murmurer 108.3
murmuring
  n murmur 52.4
  complaint 115.4
  mumbling 525.4
  adj murmurous 52.18
  discontented 108.7
muscle
  n the muscles 2.3
  muscularity 15.2
  exertion 725.1
  v exert strength 15.12
  thrust 901.12
  adj skeleton 2.24
muscle-bound
  firm 425.7
  able-bodied 15.16
muscle in 214.5
muscle man
  strong man 15.6
  hulk 15.7
  ruffian 593.4
  violent person 671.10
muscular skeleton 2.24
  able-bodied 15.16
muscularity 15.2
musculature
  the muscles 2.3
  muscularity 15.2
muse
  n inspiration 375.9
  abstractedness 984.2
  creative thought 985.2
  v remark 524.25
  consider 930.12
  moon 984.9
Muse
  the Muses 720.10
  genius 919.8
museum gallery 386.9
  preserve 397.7
  collection 769.11
museum piece
  work of art 712.10
  oddity 869.5
mush
  n sentimentality 93.8

face 216.4
mouth 292.4
pulp 1061.2
v march 177.30
mushroom
  n drugs 87.18
  plant 310.4
  v grow 14.2
  expand 259.7
  grow round 282.7
mushy
  wishy-washy 16.17
  sentimental 93.21
  pulpy 1061.6
music
  harmonious sound
    708.1
  score 708.28
  harmonics 709.1
musical
  n musical theater
    708.34
  adj musically inclined
    708.47
  melodious 708.48
  rhyming 720.17
musical comedy 708.34
musicality
  melody 708.2
  musicianship 708.31
  harmonics 709.1
music box 711.15
music director 710.17
music festival 708.32
music hall hall 197.4
  theater 704.14
musician
  entertainer 707.1
  music maker 710
  musico 710.1
musicianship 708.31
music lover 710.21
music maker 710.1
musicologist 710.20
musicology 709.1
music roll score 708.28
  keyboard instrument
    711.12
music school 567.7
musing
  n consideration 930.2
  thoughtfulness 930.3
  abstractedness 984.2
  dreaminess 985.8
  adj cognitive 930.21
  abstracted 984.11
musk 70.2
musketeer
  infantryman 461.9
  shooter 903.8
musketry
  gunfire 459.8
  arms 462.1
  ballistics 462.3
  throwing 903.2
Muslim
  n Muhammadan
    675.23
  adj Islamic 675.31
Muslimism 675.13
Muslim rulers 608.7
muss 810.2

mussed up 809.14
mussy 809.15
must
  n fetidness 71.2
  wine 88.17
  duty 641.1
  requirement 962.2
  blight 1000.2
  v be necessary 962.10
  adj in heat 75.27
  mandatory 420.12
  obligatory 641.15
mustache 3.11
mustang 311.10
mustard plaster 86.33
muster
  n call to arms 458.8
  enlistment 615.7
  assemblage 769.1
  roll 870.6
  v avail oneself of
    387.14
  summon 420.11
  call to arms 458.19
  enlist 615.17
  come together 769.16
  assemble 769.18
mustering out 465.6
muster roll 870.6
muster up
  prompt 375.13
  summon 420.11
musty malodorous 71.5
  in heat 75.27
  trite 117.9
  blighted 393.42
  stale 841.14
mutability
  death rate 307.13
  nonuniformity 781.1
  transience 827.1
  changeableness 853.1
mutable mortal 307.34
  irresolute 362.9
  nonuniform 781.3
  transient 827.7
  changeable 853.6
mutant
  n violent person 671.9
  transformation 851.3
  adj savage 671.21
  changed 851.10
mutate diversify 781.2
  be changed 851.6
  change 851.7
mutation
  phonetics 524.14
  transformation 851.3
mute
  n dummy 51.3
  silencer 51.4
  mourner 309.7
  speech sound 524.13
  supporting actor
    707.7
  music 711.22
  v muffle 51.9
  adj mum 51.12
  taciturn 344.9
  stammering 525.13
  inanimate 1053.5
muted muffled 52.17

phonetic 524.31
mutilate excise 255.10
  deform 265.7
  injure 393.13
  tear apart 801.14
mutilated
  deformed 265.12
  impaired 393.27
  garbled 794.5
mutilation
  trauma 85.37
  excision 255.3
  deformity 265.3
  impairment 393.1
  severance 801.2
mutineer
  n rebel 327.5
  anarchist 418.3
  v revolt 327.7
mutinous
  unwilling 325.5
  rebellious 327.11
  lawless 418.5
mutiny
  n revolt 327.4
  lawlessness 418.1
  v revolt 327.7
mutter
  n murmur 52.4
  lament 115.3
  mumbling 525.4
  v murmur 52.10
  complain 115.15
  sigh 318.21
  speak 524.26
  mumble 525.9
mutterer 108.3
muttering
  n murmur 52.4
  mumbling 525.4
  adj murmuring 52.18
  discontented 108.7
mutton mouton 10.15
  sheep 311.7
muttonhead 923.4
muttonheaded 921.17
mutual
  cooperative 450.5
  communal 476.9
  accompanying 768.9
  correlative 776.11
  interchangeable 862.5
mutual attraction
  inclination 100.3
  relation 774.1
  attraction 906.1
mutual company
  1007.4
mutual fund 737.16
mutuality
  cooperation 450.1
  accord 455.1
  correlation 776.1
  interchange 862.1
mutual understanding
  unanimity 332.5
  understanding 787.2
muzzle
  n silencer 51.4
  nose 283.8
  mouth 292.4
  shackle 428.4

fabrication 722.3
narrative
  n story 719.3
  fiction 722.1
  narration 722.2
  fabrication 722.3
  adj narrational 719.8
  poetic 720.15
  fictional 722.8
narrator 722.5
narrow
  n inlet 242.1
  narrow place 270.3
  v limit 210.5
  contract 260.7
  constrict 270.11
  restrict 428.9
  simplify 797.4
  specialize 865.4
  qualify 958.3
  adj limited 210.7
  slender 270.14
  meticulous 339.12
  stingy 484.9
  prudish 500.19
  phonetic 524.31
  poor 619.7
  exclusive 772.9
  narrow-minded
    979.10
  meager 991.10
narrow down 159.11
narrow escape 369.2
narrow-gauge 270.14
narrowing
  n contraction 260.1
  tapering 270.2
  exclusion 772.1
  simplification 797.2
  adj restrictive 428.12
narrow margin 779.2
narrow-mindedness
  small-mindedness 979
  narrowness 979.1
narrows inlet 242.1
  narrow place 270.3
narrow the gap
  approach 167.3
  converge 169.2
nasal
  n speech sound 524.13
  adj respiratory 2.30
  phonetic 524.31
  inarticulate 525.12
nasalization 525.1
nasalize 525.10
nascency birth 1.1
  origin 817.4
nascent 817.15
nasty
  v defile 80.17
  adj unpleasant 64.7
  filthy 80.23
  offensive 98.18
  malicious 144.20
  ill-bred 505.6
  obscene 666.9
  terrible 999.9
nasty crack 489.7
nasty look 510.8
natal native 226.5
  beginning 817.15

nation
  population 227.1
  country 232.1
  humankind 312.1
  race 559.4
the nation 606.1
national
  n citizen 227.4
  adj public 312.16
  racial 559.7
  populational 606.8
  universal 863.14
national anthem
    458.12
national assembly
    613.1
national debt 623.1
national defense 460.2
national emergency
    458.10
National Guard 461.24
nationalism
  nationhood 232.6
  patriotism 591.2
  foreign policy 609.5
nationalist 591.3
nationality
  nativeness 226.1
  country 232.1
  nationhood 232.6
  humankind 312.1
  patriotism 591.2
nationalization
  naturalization 226.3
  communization 476.3
  attachment 480.5
  socialism 611.6
nationalize
  communize 476.7
  attach 480.20
  politicize 611.16
national park 397.7
native
  n dweller 227
  indigene 227.3
  adj indigenous 226.5
  undeveloped 406.13
  natural 416.6
  plain 499.7
  innate 766.8
native environment
    228.18
native land 232.2
native language 523.3
nativity birth 1.1
  nativeness 226.1
  origin 817.4
  astrology 1070.20
NATO 437.2
natter
  n chatter 540.3
  v speak 524.21
  chatter 540.5
natty chic 578.13
  tidy 806.8
natural
  n sure success 409.2
  talented person
    413.12
  note 709.14
  blackjack 759.11
  oddity 869.4

idiot 923.8
  adj typical 349.15
  native 406.13
  artless 416.6
  plain 499.7
  elegant 533.6
  plain-speaking 535.3
  related 559.6
  informal 581.3
  innate 766.8
  lifelike 783.16
  normal 868.8
  instinctive 933.6
  genuine 972.15
naturalism
  naturalness 416.2
  normality 868.1
  genuineness 972.7
  materialism 1050.6
naturalist
  n materialist 1050.7
  biologist 1066.2
  adj materialist
    1050.12
naturalistic
  descriptive 349.14
  typical 349.15
  normal 868.8
  genuine 972.15
  materialist 1050.12
naturalization
  naturalized
    citizenship 226.3
  habituation 373.8
  conversion 857.1
naturalize
  grant citizenship
    226.4
  accustom 373.10
  convert 857.11
naturalized
  adopted 226.6
  accustomed 373.16
  converted 857.19
naturalized citizen
    227.4
natural law 868.4
natural right 642.1
natural science
  science 927.10
  physics 1017.1
natural selection 860.3
natural state 406.3
natural world 1050.2
nature
  naturalness 406.3
  unaffectedness 416.2
  character 766.4
  kind 808.3
  characteristic 864.4
  disposition 977.3
  matter 1050.2
  universe 1070.1
Nature 677.8
naturist 6.3
naturistic naked 6.14
  normal 868.8
naught 761.2
naughty
  misbehaving 322.5
  disobedient 327.8
  wicked 654.16

nausea symptom 85.9
  nauseation 85.30
  unpleasure 96.1
  hostility 99.2
  vomiting 908.8
nauseant
  n nastiness 64.3
  cleanser 79.17
  emetic 86.18
  adj nasty 64.7
nauseate disgust 64.4
  offend 98.11
nauseated
  nauseous 85.56
  pleasureless 96.20
nauseating nasty 64.7
  filthy 80.23
  offensive 98.18
nauseous nasty 64.7
  nauseated 85.56
  pleasureless 96.20
nautical marine 182.57
  oceanic 240.8
naval 182.57
naval academy 567.6
naval cadet 183.4
naval officer
  ship's officer 183.7
  fleet admiral 575.20
naval vessel 180.6
navar navigation 184.6
  airborne radar 1035.2
nave center 208.2
  church 703.9
  axle 914.5
navel 208.2
navigate locate 159.11
  journey 177.21
  sail 182.13
  pilot 182.14
  fly 184.36
navigation
  guidance 159.3
  topography 159.8
  direction 161.1
  water travel 182.1
  aviation 184.6
  bearing 573.1
navigational
  locational 159.19
  nautical 182.57
navigator
  mariner 183.1
  hand 183.6
  ship's officer 183.7
  crew 185.4
  guide 574.7
navvy
  excavator 284.10
  worker 726.2
navy
  chewing tobacco 89.7
  ships 180.10
  branch 461.21
  naval forces 461.27
navy man 183.4
nay
  n negation 335.1
  vote 371.6
  refusal 442.1
  side 934.14
  inter no 335.8

nay-sayer
oppositionist 452.3
misfit 788.4
doubter 954.4
nay-saying
n negation 335.1
contrariety 778.1
adj negative 335.5
contrary 778.6
Nazarene 675.17
Nazism 612.8
NB 982.22
NCO 575.19
Neanderthal
n barbarian 497.7
adj unrefined 497.12
neap
n tide 238.13
low tide 274.2
adj low 274.7
near
v approach 167.3
come near 223.7
resemble 783.7
come 838.6
be imminent 839.2
adj approaching 167.4
left 220.4
close 223.14
narrow 270.14
stingy 484.9
familiar 587.19
approximate 774.8
approximating 783.14
imminent 839.3
adv nigh 223.20
nearly 223.22
prep at 159.27
nigh 223.24
nearby
adj handy 223.15
adv aside 218.10
near 223.20
Near East 231.6
nearer 223.18
nearest 223.19
nearing
n approach 167.1
adj approaching 167.4
near 223.14
future 838.8
imminent 839.3
near-miss
narrow escape 369.2
crash 184.20
meeting 223.4
miss 410.4
nearsighted
poor-sighted 28.11
undiscerning 921.14
narrow-minded
979.10
neat
n cattle 311.6
adj shipshape 180.20
shapely 264.5
skillful 413.22
elegant 533.6
plain-speaking 535.3
chic 578.13
unmixed 797.7
tidy 806.8

excellent 998.13
neaten 807.12
neat-fingered 413.23
neath 274.11
neb nose 283.8
point 285.3
nebbish weakling 16.6
thing of naught 763.2
a nobody 997.7
nebula light 1024.15
nebulosity 1070.7
nebulous cloudy 319.7
obscure 522.15
general 863.11
celestial 1070.25
necessaries 962.2
necessary
n latrine 12.10
adj obligatory 424.11
mandatory 641.15
required 962.12
requisite 962.13
inevitable 962.15
certain 969.13
necessitate
require 424.5
determine 885.12
oblige 962.8
destine 963.7
necessity
compulsion 424.1
indigence 619.2
prerequisite 962
necessariness 962.1
requirement 962.2
inevitability 962.7
predetermination
963.1
certainty 969.1
neck
n fowl part 10.22
contraction 260.1
narrow place 270.3
joint 799.4
supporter 900.2
v hang 604.18
neck-and-neck
equal 789.7
simultaneous 835.5
necking 562.2
necklace
circle 280.3
jewel 498.6
necrological
funereal 309.22
documentary 549.18
historical 719.7
necrology
obituary 307.14
monument 549.12
history 719.1
necromancer
psychic 689.13
sorcerer 690.5
necromancy
spiritualism 689.5
sorcery 690.1
necromantic
sorcerous 690.14
miraculous 869.16
necrophilia 75.11
necrophiliac 75.16

necrosis symptom 85.9
gangrene 85.39
nectar delicacy 10.8
sweetening 66.2
nectarous tasty 63.8
sweet 66.4
née 1.4
need
n desire 100.1
indigence 619.2
deficiency 794.2
requirement 962.2
want 991.4
v be poor 619.5
require 962.9
be necessary 962.10
want 991.7
adv necessarily 962.16
needing
desirous 100.21
incomplete 794.4
wanting 991.13
needle
n energizer 17.6
sound reproduction
system 50.11
mountain 237.6
point 285.3
thorn 285.5
leaf 310.17
pointer 517.4
compass 574.9
v annoy 96.13
perforate 292.15
goad 375.15
banter 490.6
sew 741.4
needless
unnecessary 391.10
superfluous 992.17
needlework 741.1
needleworker
garmentmaker 5.33
sewer 741.2
needling 375.5
need to 962.10
the needy 619.3
nefarious
wicked 654.16
base 661.12
terrible 999.9
negate abnegate 335.3
abolish 395.13
refuse 442.3
contradict 451.6
disagree 788.5
neutralize 899.7
disbelieve 954.5
disprove 957.4
negating
n negation 335.1
adj neutralizing
899.9
negation
disaffirmation 335
negating 335.1
extinction 395.6
refusal 442.1
opposition 451.1
nonexistence 761.1
disagreement 788.1
disproof 957.1

negative
n math terms 255.6
negation 335.1
refusal 442.1
veto 444.2
graphic arts 713.5
film 714.10
print 784.5
mold 785.6
v negate 335.3
abolish 395.13
refuse 442.3
veto 444.5
neutralize 899.7
disprove 957.4
adj pessimistic
125.16
negatory 335.5
unconsenting 442.6
oppositional 451.8
nonexistent 761.8
contrary 778.6
disagreeing 788.6
numeric 1016.22
electric 1031.34
inter no 335.8
negativism
defense mechanism
92.23
pessimism 125.6
negation 335.1
resistance 453.1
hindrance 1011.1
negativist
pessimist 125.7
oppositionist 452.3
hinderer 1011.8
neglect
n negligence 340
neglectfulness 340.1
nonaccomplishment
408.1
mismanagement
414.6
nonobservance 435.1
v slight 157.6
overlook 340.6
leave undone 408.2
disregard 435.3
neglected
unthanked 151.5
unattended to 340.14
needless 391.10
unaccomplished 408.3
neglecter 340.5
negligee 5.20
negligence
unconcern 102.2
neglect 340.1
thoughtlessness 365.3
improvidence 406.2
mismanagement
414.6
laxness 426.1
nonobservance 435.1
slovenliness 809.6
innaccuracy 974.2
inattention 983.1
negligent
n neglecter 340.5
adj unconcerned 102.7
neglectful 340.10

stay with it 360.4
stand fast 453.4
persist 855.5
nevertheless
notwithstanding
338.8
anyhow 384.10
nevus growth 85.38
bulge 283.3
mark 517.5
blemish 1003.1
new
adj additional 253.10
original 337.5
unaccustomed 374.4
unused 390.12
fashionable 578.11
present 837.2
young 840.7
adv newly 840.15
again 873.7
New Age 869.7
new arrival
newcomer 773.4
beginner 817.2
new birth revival 396.3
redemption 685.4
new start 857.2
newborn born 1.4
infant 301.12
new-made 840.9
newcomer
incomer 189.4
novice 572.9
new arrival 773.4
beginner 817.2
newel 273.4
newfangled 840.10
new-fashioned
fashionable 578.11
modern 840.13
New Left 611.4
new life 685.4
new look 840.2
newlywed 563.5
newlyweds 563.9
new moon 1070.11
news information 552
tidings 552.1
newspaper 555.2
newscast
n radiobroadcast
1033.18
television broadcast
1034.2
v broadcast 1033.25
newscaster 1033.23
new slant 931.5
newsletter 552.1
newsman 555.4
news media 552.1
newsmonger
informant 551.5
rumormonger 552.9
newspaper news 552.1
news medium 555.2
newspaperman
writer 547.15
newsmonger 552.9
journalist 555.4
author 718.4
news report 552.5

newsstand 736.3
newsworthy 552.13
newsy
v talkative 540.9
adj communicative
343.10
newsworthy 552.13
gossipy 552.14
New Testament 683.4
new to
unaccustomed 374.4
inexperienced 414.17
new twist 931.5
New World 231.6
next
adj adjacent 223.16
nearest 223.19
succeeding 814.4
adv subsequently
834.6
next life 834.1
next of kin 559.2
next to
v learn 551.14
prep at 159.27
the next world 838.2
nexus 811.2
Niagara 238.11
nib nose 283.8
point 285.3
extremity 819.2
nibble
n bite 8.2
v feed 8.18
pick 8.26
chew 8.27
kid oneself 953.6
trifle 997.14
nibbling 8.1
nice tasty 63.8
pleasant 97.6
kind 143.13
meticulous 339.12
dainty 495.11
elegant 496.9
right 637.3
conscientious 644.15
detailed 765.9
discriminating 943.7
exact 972.17
attentive 982.15
good 998.12
nice guy 659.2
nicety
meticulousness 339.3
niceness 495.3
taste 496.1
margin 779.2
discrimination 943.1
accuracy 972.5
niche
nook 197.3
recess 284.7
hiding place 346.4
nick
n notch 289.1
jail 429.9
mark 517.5
type 548.6
v notch 289.4
rob 482.16
mark 517.19

nickel
n money 728.7
precious metals
728.20
adj brass 1056.17
nickelodeon 50.11
nickname
n sobriquet 527.7
v name 527.11
nick of time 842.5
nicotine 89.9
nicotine addict 87.20
nicotine addiction
substance abuse 87.1
smoking 89.10
nicotinic 89.15
niece 559.3
nifty chic 578.13
excellent 998.13
niggard
n tightwad 484.4
adj niggardly 484.8
nigger 312.3
niggle
n criticism 510.4
v nag 510.16
trifle 997.14
niggling
n criticism 510.4
adj insignificant 248.6
critical 510.23
attentive 982.15
petty 997.20
nigh
v near 223.7
adj left 220.4
near 223.14
adv near 223.20
nearly 223.22
prep near 223.24
night
n blackness 38.4
close of day 315
nighttime 315.4
darkness 1026.1
adj nocturnal 315.9
night and day
n opposites 215.2
adv constantly 846.7
night blindness 30.2
nightcap
sleep-inducer 22.10
drink 88.9
night clothes 5.21
nightclub bar 88.20
theater 704.14
entertainment 743.13
night crawler 311.37
nightdress 5.21
nightfall 315.2
nightgown 5.21
nightie 5.21
nightingale 710.23
night letter 347.14
nightlong
adj nocturnal 315.9
continuing 826.12
adv nightly 315.11
nightmare
torment 96.7
frightener 127.9
dream 985.9

night prayer 696.8
nights 315.11
night spot
theater 704.14
entertainment 743.13
nighttime
n night 315.4
adj nocturnal 315.9
nightwalk
creep 177.26
noctambulate 177.32
lurk 346.9
nightwalking
n noctambulation
177.9
creeping 177.17
adj noctambulant
177.38
nihilism
pessimism 125.6
anarchy 418.2
radicalism 611.4
nihilist
n pessimist 125.7
destroyer 395.8
anarchist 418.3
savage 593.5
radical 611.12
adj destructive 395.26
nihilistic
pessimistic 125.16
destructive 395.26
anarchic 418.6
radical 611.20
unruly 671.19
nil 761.2
nimble fast 174.15
quick 330.18
alert 339.14
agile 413.23
smart 919.14
nimble-fingered 413.23
nimble-footed
agile 413.23
fast 174.15
nimble-witted
witty 489.15
smart 919.14
nimbus
illustriousness 662.6
halo 1024.14
Nimrod hunter 382.5
shooter 903.8
nincompoop 923.3
nine team 617.7
baseball team 745.2
card 758.2
ennead 881.5
nine days' wonder
marvel 122.2
great success 409.3
ephemeron 827.5
ninny 923.3
nip
n bite 8.2
drink 8.4
pang 26.2
zest 68.2
liquor 88.7
scrap 248.3
squeezing 260.2
hold 474.2

dose 792.5
cold 1022.1
v pain 26.7
bite 68.5
tipple 88.24
converge 169.2
speed 174.9
hasten off 188.10
excise 255.10
squeeze 260.8
shorten 268.6
put an end to 395.12
hold 474.6
seize 480.14
rob 482.16
freeze 1022.10
chill 1023.11
nip and tuck 789.7
nip in the bud
  kill 308.12
  put an end to 395.12
  stop 1011.13
nipped
  contracted 260.12
  shortened 268.9
nipper 302.3
nipple tube 239.6
  breast 283.6
nippy zestful 68.7
  cold 1022.14
nirvana
  unconsciousness 25.2
  undesirousness 102.3
  quiescence 173.1
  heaven 681.8
  thoughtlessness 932.1
  forgetfulness 989.1
nirvanic
  unconscious 25.8
  undesirous 102.8
  thoughtless 932.4
nit vermin 311.35
  criticism 510.4
NIT 747.1
nitpick
  find fault 510.15
  quibble 935.9
nitpicker
  perfectionist 495.6
  faultfinder 510.9
  quibbler 935.7
nit-picking
  n criticism 510.4
  quibbling 935.5
  adj quibbling 935.14
nitrate
  n fertilizer 889.4
  v chemicalize 1058.7
nitrogen 889.4
the nitty-gritty
  essential content
    196.5
  reality 760.2
  fact 760.3
  essence 766.3
nitwit 923.2
nitwitted 921.17
nival 1022.18
nix
  n negation 335.1
  refusal 442.1
  water god 678.10

nothing 761.3
inter nope 335.10
no
  n negation 335.1
  vote 371.6
  refusal 442.1
  side 934.14
  number 1016.3
  adv none 761.12
  inter nay 335.8
  phrs I refuse 442.7
no-account
  worthless 391.11
  uninfluential 894.3
nobby chic 578.13
  excellent 998.13
nobility
  proud bearing 136.2
  glory 247.2
  the best 249.5
  mastership 417.7
  grandeur 501.5
  loftiness 544.6
  upper class 607.2
  noble rank 608
  aristocracy 608.1
  nobleness 608.2
  probity 644.1
  magnanimity 652.2
  distinction 662.5
noble
  n nobleman 608.4
  adj dignified 136.12
  eminent 247.9
  grandiose 501.21
  lofty 544.14
  of rank 608.10
  honest 644.13
  magnanimous 652.6
  reputable 662.15
  unchangeable 854.17
  notable 996.19
  good 998.12
nobleman 608.4
noble-minded 652.6
noblesse oblige 504.2
noblewoman 608.6
nobody
  no one 222.6
  thing of naught 763.2
  mediocrity 1004.5
nobody's fool
  smart 919.14
  ungullible 955.5
no chance
  gambling odds 759.6
  impossibility 966.1
  not a prayer 971.10
no choice
  dilemma 371.3
  restriction 428.3
  choicelessness 962.6
noctambulation 177.9
nocturnal 315.9
nod
  n stupor 22.6
  obeisance 155.2
  affirmative 332.2
  summons 420.5
  consent 441.1
  permission 443.1
  approval 509.1

signal 517.15
hint 551.4
greeting 585.4
crouch 912.3
v bow 155.6
hang 202.6
assent 332.8
neglect 340.6
consent 441.2
signal 517.22
nodding
  n languor 331.6
  adj sleepy 22.21
  intoxicated 87.22
  drooping 202.10
  languid 331.20
  unalert 983.8
  abstracted 984.11
noddle head 198.6
  brain 918.6
node nodule 283.5
  wave 915.4
  dilemma 1012.7
  solid 1043.6
no-deposit 388.6
no doubt
  probably 967.8
  unquestionably
    969.25
nodular studded 283.17
  gnarled 288.8
nodule 283.5
nodus 1012.7
no end greatly 247.15
  chiefly 249.17
  numerously 883.12
  plentifully 990.9
no end to long 267.7
  infinite 822.3
  innumerable 883.10
noetic mental 918.7
  intelligent 919.12
  cognitive 930.21
noggin member 2.7
  head 198.6
  brain 918.6
no go 410.1
no-go useless 391.9
  impossible 125.14
no-good
  n wretch 660.2
  adj worthless 391.11
nohow
  adv noway 248.11
  anyhow 384.10
  inter by no means
    335.9
no ifs, ands, or buts
  really 760.16
  completely 793.14
no strings attached
  959.3
  certainly 969.23
noise
  n sound 50.1
  loud noise 53.3
  clash 61.2
  meaninglessness
    520.1
  Greek 522.7
  information theory
    551.7

pandemonium 809.5
radio reception
  1033.21
television reception
  1034.5
v sound 50.14
be noisy 53.9
noiseless 51.10
noisemaker 53.6
noiseproof 15.20
noisome nasty 64.7
  malodorous 71.5
  unhealthful 82.5
  offensive 98.18
  terrible 999.9
  harmful 999.12
noisy
  noiseful 53.13
  vociferous 59.10
  blustering 503.4
nomad
  n Bedouin 178.4
  adj wandering 177.37
nomadic 177.37
nomadism 177.3
no-man's-land
  prohibition 444.1
  battlefield 463.2
no matter 997.25
no matter what
  n whatever 863.6
  inter by no means
    335.9
nom de plume 527.8
nomen name 527.3
  term 527.6
nomenclature
  naming 527
  terminology 527.1
nominal
  n noun 530.5
  adj cognominal 527.15
  grammatical 530.17
  formal 580.7
  cheap 633.7
nominal charge 633.2
nominalism 864.1
nominate
  choose 371.19
  name 527.11
  support 609.41
  appoint 615.11
nomination
  designation 371.8
  caucus nomination
    609.11
  appointment 615.2
  holy orders 698.10
nominative
  n case 530.9
  adj nominal 527.15
  denominative 527.16
nominee 615.9
no more
  adj gone 34.4
  dead 307.30
  extinct 761.11
  past 836.7
  inter stop! 856.13
nonacceptance
  rejection 372.1
  refusal 442.1

nonaccomplishment
nonachievement
408.1
failure 410.1
nonadherent
nonobservant 435.5
incoherent 803.4
nonadmission 772.1
nonage 301.3
nonagenarian
old man 304.2
ninety 881.7
nonaggression 464.4
nonaggressive
indolent 331.19
unbelligerent 464.10
nonalcoholic 516.4
nonalcoholic beverage
10.47
nonaligned
independent 430.22
neutral 467.7
nonaligned nation
country 232.1
free agent 430.12
neutral 467.4
nonalignment
neutrality 467.1
moderatism 611.2
nonattendance 222.4
nonattendant 222.11
nonbeliever 695.11
nonbelieving 954.8
nonbelligerent 464.5
nonbreakable 1047.5
the nonce 837.1
nonce word 526.8
nonchalance
apathy 94.4
unconcern 102.2
casualness 106.5
nonchalant
apathetic 94.13
unconcerned 102.7
blasé 106.15
noncohering 801.20
noncohesion
nonadhesion 803
uncohesiveness 803.1
noncohesive
separate 801.20
incoherent 803.4
noncom 575.19
noncombatant
n nonbelligerent 464.5
adj unbelligerent
464.10
noncommissioned
officer
enlisted man 461.8
superintendent 574.2
noncommittal 494.8
noncommitted 467.7
noncommunicable
122.13
noncompetitive 450.5
noncompletion 408.1
noncompliance
disobedience 327.1
nonobservance 435.1
refusal 442.1
nonconformity 867.1

non compos mentis
925.26
nonconducting 1031.35
nonconductive 1031.35
nonconductor 1031.13
nonconforming
disobedient 327.8
dissenting 333.6
nonobservant 435.5
unconforming 867.5
nonconformist
n rebel 327.5
dissenter 333.3
heretic 688.5
misfit 788.4
unconformist 867.3
oddity 869.4
eccentric 926.3
adj nonuniform 781.3
individualistic 788.9
counteractive 899.8
nonconformity
obliquity 204.1
disobedience 327.1
dissent 333.1
nonobservance 435.1
unorthodoxy 688.1
extraneousness 773.1
difference 779.1
nonuniformity 781.1
inconsistency 788.2
particularity 864.1
nonconformance 867
unconformity 867.1
counteraction 899.1
eccentricity 926.1
noncontiguous 801.20
nonconvergent 203.6
noncooperation
disobedience 327.1
opposition 451.1
hostility 451.2
resistance 453.1
disaccord 456.1
noncooperative
insubordinate 327.9
oppositional 451.8
resistant 453.5
noncreative 890.5
nondenominational
nonsectarian 675.27
universal 863.14
nondescript
formless 263.4
simple 499.6
nondutiable 630.16
none
n divine service 696.8
not any 761.4
adv no 761.12
nonelastic 1044.12
nonemotional 94.9
nonentity
weakling 16.6
nonexistence 761.1
thing of naught 763.2
a nobody 997.7
mediocrity 1004.5
none of your business
214.10
nonessential
n inessential 767.2

adj needless 391.10
circumstantial 765.7
unessential 767.4
irrelevant 775.7
superfluous 992.17
insignificant 997.17
nonesuch
marvel 122.2
the best 998.8
nonetheless
anyhow 384.10
notwithstanding
338.8
nonexistence
absence 222.1
nonbeing 761
nonsubsistence 761.1
nonexistent gone 34.4
absent 222.11
unexistent 761.8
imaginary 985.19
nonexpectant 131.9
nonfactual 985.21
nonfeasance
disobedience 327.1
neglect 340.1
nonaccomplishment
408.1
mismanagement
414.6
nonobservance 435.1
misdeed 655.2
nonfertile 890.4
nonfiction 547.10
nonflammability
1021.1
nonflammable 1021.9
nonformal
n substandard
language 523.6
jargon 523.9
adj in dishabille 5.46
vernacular 523.18
nonuniform 781.3
slovenly 809.15
unconventional 867.6
nonfulfillment
nonaccomplishment
408.1
nonobservance 435.1
insufficiency 991.1
nonfunctional 391.14
nonhuman 869.15
nonimitation 337.1
nonintellectual 929.14
noninterference
neglect 340.1
nonintervention 430.9
policy 609.4
noninterruption 846.2
nonintervention
avoidance 368.1
noninterference 430.9
policy 609.4
noninvolvement
inaction 329.1
avoidance 368.1
neutrality 467.1
non-Jew 688.6
nonliving 1053.5
nonliving matter
1053.1

nonmalignant 998.21
nonmandatory 324.7
nonmedical therapist
90.9
nonmedical therapy
91.2
nonmetal 1056.3
nonmetallic 1056.16
nonmilitant 464.10
no-no prohibition 444.1
oath 513.4
nonobjective 979.12
nonobservance
nonadherence 435
inobservance 435.1
refusal 442.1
nonreligiousness
695.1
nonconformity 867.1
inattention 983.1
nonobservant
inobservant 435.5
nonreligious 695.15
nonconforming 867.5
nonoccupancy 222.2
nonoccurrence
absence 222.1
nonexistence 761.1
nonopposing 433.12
nonopposition 433.1
nonordained 700.3
nonpareil
marvel 122.2
superior 249.4
paragon 659.4
the best 998.8
nonparticipation 329.1
nonpartisan
n free agent 430.12
neutral 467.4
independent 609.28
adj autonomous
430.22
neutral 467.7
independent 609.45
nonpartisanism
neutrality 467.1
independence 609.26
nonpaying 625.10
nonpayment 625.1
nonperformance
neglect 340.1
nonaccomplishment
408.1
nonobservance 435.1
nonperishable 854.18
nonpermanent 827.7
nonphysical 1051.7
nonplus
n bewilderment 970.3
dilemma 1012.7
v refute 957.5
perplex 970.13
thwart 1011.15
nonplussed
in a dilemma 970.25
at an impasse 1012.24
nonpoetic 721.4
nonpoisonous 998.21
nonpolluted 79.25
nonporous 1043.12
nonproductive 890.4

nonprofessional
n amateur 726.5
adj avocational
724.17
nonprofit 617.16
nonrecognition
ingratitude 151.1
incognizance 929.3
nonreligious
unreligious 695.15
lay 700.3
nonrepresentationalism
350.1
nonresident 222.12
nonresistance
resignation 134.2
inaction 329.1
submission 433.1
foreign policy 609.5
nonresistive
submissive 433.12
soft 1045.8
nonrestrictive
negligent 340.10
unrestrictive 430.25
nonreturnable 854.17
nonsectarian
undenominational
675.27
universal 863.14
nonsense
stuff and nonsense
520.2
foolishness 922.1
absurdity 922.3
nonsense talk 540.3
nonsense verse 720.3
nonsensical
silly 520.7
absurd 922.11
non sequitur
discontinuity 812.1
specious argument
935.3
nonsked 184.10
nonsmoker 668.4
nonspecific
general 863.11
vague 970.19
nonspiritual
carnal 663.6
material 1050.10
nonstop
continuous 811.8
perpetual 828.7
nonsubjective 767.3
nontaxable 630.16
nontoxic 998.21
nonuniform
ununiform 781.3
dissimilar 786.4
unordered 809.12
discontinuous 812.4
irregular 850.3
changeable 853.6
nonuniformity
roughness 288.1
unevenness 781.1
multiformity 782.1
dissimilarity 786.1
inequality 790.1
disorder 809.1

discontinuity 812.1
irregularity 850.1
changeableness 853.1
nonunion 801.1
nonunion shop 727.3
nonuple 881.21
nonuse 390.1
nonviable 307.33
nonviolence
inaction 329.1
peaceableness 464.4
moderation 670.1
nonviolent
unbelligerent 464.10
moderate 670.10
nonvirulent 998.21
noodle
n member 2.7
head 198.6
brain 918.6
v think over 930.13
nook corner 197.3
angle 278.2
recess 284.7
hiding place 346.4
noon
n summit 198.2
noonday 314
midday 314.5
adj noonday 314.7
adv constantly 846.7
no one 222.6
noose
n circle 280.2
snare 356.13
execution 605.5
v trap 356.20
catch 480.17
hang 604.18
weave 740.6
noosphere
organic matter 305.1
biosphere 306.6
atmosphere 317.2
philosophy 931.2
nope 335.10
nor 335.7
nor'east 161.19
nor'easter 318.9
norm mean 246.1
measure 300.2
custom 373.5
precept 419.2
ethics 636.1
paragon 659.4
rule 868.4
normal
n vertical 200.2
mean 246.1
straight line 277.2
adj medium 246.3
right-angled 278.7
typical 349.15
customary 373.14
right 637.3
orderly 806.6
prevalent 863.12
natural 868.8
sane 924.4
ordinary 1004.8
normality
propriety 637.2

prevalence 863.2
typicality 868
normalness 868.1
sanity 924.1
ordinariness 1004.2
normalize
make uniform 780.4
order 806.4
organize 807.10
standardize 868.6
normative
customary 373.14
preceptive 419.4
right 637.3
model 785.8
normal 868.8
usual 868.9
north
n points of the
compass 161.3
adj northern 161.14
adv N 161.15
northeast
n points of the
compass 161.3
adj northern 161.14
adv nor'east 161.19
norther 318.9
northern 161.14
Northerner 227.11
northern lights 1024.16
North Pole
opposites 215.2
remote region 261.4
cold place 1022.4
north pole 1031.8
North Star
guiding star 574.8
stars 1070.4
northward
n points of the
compass 161.3
adv north 161.15
northwest
n points of the
compass 161.3
adj northern 161.14
adv nor'west 161.20
north wind 318.9
no say 894.1
nose
n olfactory organ 69.5
prow 216.3
nozzle 239.9
protuberance 283.8
person 312.5
v smell 69.8
stroke 73.8
meddle 214.7
trace 937.34
pry 980.4
nose around 937.30
nosebleed 12.8
nose count roll 870.6
summation 1016.11
nose dive
maneuvers 184.13
plunge 367.1
collapse 410.3
cheapening 633.4
nose-dive dive 184.41
plunge 367.6

cheapen 633.6
nosegay fragrance 70.1
bouquet 310.23
bundle 769.8
nose ring circle 280.3
jewel 498.6
nose-tickling 68.6
nosh
n light meal 8.7
v pick 8.26
no-show 222.5
nostalgia
sentimentality 93.8
wistfulness 100.4
yearning 100.5
melancholy 112.5
nostalgic
sentimental 93.21
wistful 100.23
melancholy 112.23
nostril 239.13
no strings attached
adj unrestricted
430.27
adv no ifs, ands, or
buts 959.3
nostrum 86.2
no sweat 1013.16
nosy
meddlesome 214.9
searching 937.37
prying 980.6
not 335.8
nota bene 982.22
notability glory 247.2
distinction 662.5
celebrity 662.9
noteworthiness 996.2
personage 996.8
not a bit
n none 761.4
adv noway 248.11
inter no 335.8
notable
n celebrity 662.9
personage 996.8
adj remarkable 247.10
conspicuous 348.12
distinguished 662.16
characteristic 864.13
memorable 988.25
noteworthy 996.19
not accept deny 335.4
not permit 444.4
refuse to believe 955.3
not admit deny 335.4
disbelieve 954.5
not allow 444.4
not all there
mentally deficient
921.22
crazy 925.27
notarize 332.12
notarized 332.14
notarized statement
deposition 334.3
certificate 549.6
notary endorser 332.7
recorder 550.1
not at all
adv noway 248.11
none 761.12

never 821.4
inter by no means 335.9
notate
represent 349.8
grammaticize 530.16
notation
comment 341.5
representation 349.1
memorandum 549.4
entry 628.5
score 708.28
character 709.12
addition 1016.2
number 1016.3
not bad
adj tolerable 998.20
inter bravo! 509.22
not believe 954.5
not budge
do nothing 329.2
balk 361.7
stand fast 854.11
not buy refuse 442.3
disbelieve 954.5
refuse to believe 955.3
not care
not mind 102.4
take no interest in 981.2
not care for
dislike 99.3
neglect 340.6
not care to 325.3
notch
n crack 224.2
ridge 237.5
degree 245.1
indentation 284.6
cleft 289
nick 289.1
mark 517.5
v indent 284.14
nick 289.4
mark 517.19
notched
indented 284.17
nicked 289.5
notching 289.2
not comparable
inadequate 250.7
uncomparable 786.6
not compare 250.4
not count 997.11
not counting 255.14
not cricket
wrong 638.3
unfair 650.10
unconventional 867.6
not done
underdone 11.8
wrong 638.3
unfair 650.10
unconventional 867.6
note
n observation 27.2
animal noise 60.1
milieu 209.3
added to writing 254.2
comment 341.5
sign 517.1

remark 524.4
memorandum 549.4
certificate 549.6
letter 553.2
treatise 556.1
entry 628.5
distinction 662.5
air 708.4
pitch 709.4
musical note 709.14
interval 709.20
paper money 728.5
negotiable instrument 728.11
cognizance 927.2
mood 977.4
attention 982.1
importance 996.1
v signify 517.17
remark 524.25
record 549.15
keep accounts 628.8
heed 982.6
not easy
adverse 1010.13
difficult 1012.17
notebook
record book 549.11
book 554.1
not enough 991.9
noteworthy
remarkable 247.10
particular 864.12
extraordinary 869.14
notable 996.19
not have a chance
be impossible 966.4
have no chance 971.14
not hesitate 359.10
nothing void 222.3
nil 761.2
thing of naught 763.2
nothing doing
inter nope 335.10
God forbid! 510.27
phrs I refuse 442.7
nothing like 786.5
nothingness
unconsciousness 25.2
space 158.1
void 222.3
nonexistence 761.1
nothing of the kind
n a different thing 779.3
adj nothing like 786.5
inter no 335.8
nothing special
n mediocrity 1004.5
adj ordinary 1004.8
not hold up 974.8
notice
n observation 27.2
announcement 352.2
press release 352.3
publicity 352.4
advertisement 352.6
warning 399.1
demand 421.1
information 551.1
commentary 556.2
cognizance 927.2

criticism 945.2
attention 982.1
v see 27.12
detect 940.5
heed 982.6
noticeable visible 31.6
remarkable 247.10
measurable 300.14
manifest 348.8
conspicuous 348.12
notification
informing 343.2
announcement 352.2
warning 399.1
information 551.1
notify herald 133.14
warn 399.5
inform 551.8
not in keeping with 788.10
not in the habit of 374.4
not in the mood 325.5
notion caprice 364.1
impulse 365.1
intention 380.1
plan 381.1
idea 931.1
suggestion 950.5
opinion 952.6
notional
capricious 364.5
ideational 931.9
theoretical 950.13
imaginative 985.18
imaginary 985.19
fanciful 985.20
notions 735.6
not know 929.11
not kosher
dishonest 645.16
unfair 650.10
unconventional 867.6
not likely 442.7
not listen
disobey 327.6
be inattentive 983.2
not make sense
be meaningless 520.4
be incomprehensible 522.10
not matter 997.11
not mind
not care 102.4
disobey 327.6
notoriety
conspicuousness 348.4
publicity 352.4
disreputability 661.2
repute 662.1
notorious
conspicuous 348.12
knavish 645.17
disreputable 661.10
distinguished 662.16
immodest 666.6
well-known 927.27
terrible 999.9
not permit 444.4
not remember 989.5

not right
mentally deficient 921.22
insane 925.26
crazy 925.27
erroneous 974.16
not stand for
not permit 444.4
discountenance 510.11
not surprised 130.11
not swallow
disbelieve 954.5
refuse to believe 955.3
not there 984.11
not to be believed 954.10
not to be had
inaccessible 966.9
scarce 991.11
not tolerate
not permit 444.4
discountenance 510.11
not to mention
adv additionally 253.11
prep with 253.12
not touch
avoid 368.6
not use 390.5
abstain 668.7
not true false 354.24
erroneous 974.16
not understand 522.11
not wash 974.8
not with it
unaware 929.13
oblivious 983.7
notwithstanding 338.8
not work
be impotent 19.7
fail 410.9
noun 530.5
nourish feed 7.15
nurture 8.19
encourage 375.21
foster 449.16
nourishing
n nutrition 7.1
adj nutritious 7.19
eating 8.31
nourishment
nutrition 7.1
nutriment 10.3
support 449.3
nous world spirit 677.7
intellect 918.1
smartness 919.2
nouveau riche
n vulgarian 497.6
upstart 606.7
modern 840.4
adj populational 606.8
nova 10.23
novel
n book 554.1
story 722.3
adj original 337.5
new 840.11
novelist writer 547.15
author 718.4

narrator 722.5
novelty
  nonimitation 337.1
  fad 578.5
  merchandise 735.6
  newness 840.1
  innovation 840.2
  alteration 851.4
novena
  divine service 696.8
  nine 881.5
novice novitiate 572.9
  nun 699.17
  beginner 817.2
  ignoramus 929.8
now
  n the present 837.1
  adj modern 840.13
  adv at once 829.8
  at present 837.3
  recently 840.16
  inter make haste!
    401.16
now and then
  discontinuously 812.5
  occasionally 847.5
noway
  adv noways 248.11
  inter by no means
    335.9
no way
  n despair 125.2
  inter nope 335.10
  God forbid! 510.27
  phrs I refuse 442.7
  no can do 966.11
nowhere
  n remote region 261.4
  adv in no place 222.17
nowise 248.11
now or never 842.12
noxious nasty 64.7
  malodorous 71.5
  unhealthful 82.5
  poisonous 82.7
  offensive 98.18
  malicious 144.20
  harmful 999.12
nozzle bib nozzle 239.9
  nose 283.8
  sprinkler 1063.8
nth degree 793.5
nuance degree 245.1
  implication 519.2
  margin 779.2
  distinction 943.3
nub
  essential content
    196.5
  center 208.2
  bulge 283.3
  texture 294.1
  essence 766.2
  salient point 996.6
nubbin runt 258.4
  bulge 283.3
nubby studded 283.17
  nappy 294.7
nubile grown 14.3
  adolescent 301.13
  adult 303.12
  marriageable 563.20

nuclear
  nucleate 208.12
  nucleal 305.21
  middle 818.4
  thermonuclear
    1037.19
nuclear energy
  energy 17.1
  atomic energy
    1037.15
nuclear fission 1037.8
nuclear fusion 1037.9
nuclear physicist
  1037.3
nuclear physics
  electronics 1032.1
  atomic science 1037
  particle physics
    1037.1
nuclear power
  atomic energy
    1037.15
  manpower 18.4
nuclear reactor 1037.13
nuclear weapons 462.1
nucleus center 208.2
  cell nucleus 305.7
  essence 766.2
  middle 818.1
  vital force 885.7
  elementary particle
    1037.6
nude
  n work of art 712.10
  adj naked 6.14
  unadorned 499.8
nudge
  n contact 223.5
  signal 517.15
  hint 551.4
  thrust 901.2
  v set in motion 172.6
  contact 223.10
  goad 375.15
  importune 440.12
  signal 517.22
  thrust 901.12
  remind 988.20
nudist
  n nudity 6.3
  adj naked 6.14
nudity nakedness 6.3
  unadornment 499.3
nudzh
  n tormentor 96.10
  v annoy 96.13
nugatory
  ineffective 19.15
  insignificant 248.6
  worthless 391.11
  trivial 997.19
nugget lump 257.10
  precious metals
    728.20
nuisance
  annoyance 96.2
  tormentor 96.10
  bore 118.4
nuisance value 1011.1
null vacant 222.14
  meaningless 520.6
  nonexistent 761.8

null and void
  vacant 222.14
  repealed 445.3
nullification
  denial 335.2
  extinction 395.6
  repeal 445.1
  policy 609.4
  neutralization 899.2
nullify deny 335.4
  abolish 395.13
  repeal 445.2
  declare a moratorium
    625.9
  neutralize 899.7
nullity
  meaninglessness
    520.1
  nonexistence 761.1
  thing of naught 763.2
  an insignificancy
    997.6
numb
  v deaden 25.4
  benumb 94.8
  relieve 120.5
  freeze 1022.10
  adj insensible 25.6
  apathetic 94.13
  unconcerned 102.7
  languid 331.20
number
  n amount 244.2
  deception 356.9
  singular 530.8
  edition 554.5
  act 704.7
  rhythm 709.22
  vocation 724.6
  part of writing 792.2
  numeral 1016.3
  sum 1016.6
  v quantify 244.4
  total 791.8
  itemize 800.7
  numerate 1016.16
number among 771.3
numbering
  n numeration 1016.9
  adj inclusive 771.6
numberless 883.10
number one
  n urine 12.5
  victor 411.2
  self 864.5
  v urinate 12.14
  adj governing 612.18
  paramount 996.24
numbers
  quantity 244.1
  rhythm 709.22
  metrics 720.6
  meter 720.7
  statistics 746.4
  multitude 883.3
  mathematics 1016.1
numbers runner 759.20
numbing
  n relief 120.1
  adj deadening 25.9
  anesthetic 86.47
  relieving 120.9

  cold 1022.14
numerable
  measurable 300.14
  calculable 1016.24
numeral
  n number 1016.3
  adj numeric 1016.22
numerate 1016.16
numeration 1016.9
numerative
  measuring 300.12
  numeric 1016.22
  enumerative 1016.23
numeric
  mathematical 1016.21
  numeral 1016.22
numerous
  much 247.8
  large 257.16
  plural 882.7
  many 883.6
  plentiful 990.7
numinous
  awesome 122.11
  unintelligible 522.13
  illustrious 662.19
  almighty 677.18
  sacred 685.7
  sorcerous 690.14
  supernatural 869.15
numismatic 728.30
numismatics 728.22
numskull 923.4
nun marker 517.10
  celibate 565.2
  sister 699.17
nuncio
  messenger 353.1
  diplomat 576.6
nunnery 703.6
nuptial
  v join in marriage
    563.14
  adj sexual 75.24
  matrimonial 563.18
nuptials 563.3
nurse
  n health care
    professional 90.8
  sister 90.10
  nursemaid 1007.8
  v nourish 8.19
  treat 91.24
  foster 449.16
  hold 474.7
  train 568.13
  care for 1007.19
nursemaid maid 577.8
  nurse 1007.8
nursery bedroom 197.7
  hospital room 197.25
  preschool 567.2
  birthplace 885.8
  conservatory 1067.11
nurseryman 1067.6
nursery school 567.2
nursing home 1008.4
nurture
  n nutrition 7.1
  nutriment 10.3
  support 449.3
  training 568.3

protectorship 1007.2
v nourish 7.15
feed 8.19
look after 339.9
encourage 375.21
make better 392.9
foster 449.16
hold 474.7
train 568.13
care for 1007.19
raise 1068.6
nut
n food 10.37
enthusiast 101.5
seed 310.29
specialist 865.3
oddity 869.4
lunatic 925.16
fanatic 925.18
freak 926.4
v harvest 1067.19
nuthouse 925.14
Nutrasweet 66.2
nutrient
n nutritive 7.3
adj nutritious 7.19
nutriment
nutrient 7.3
nourishment 10.3
nutrition
nourishment 7.1
eating 8.1
cooking 11.1
nutritionist 7.13
nutritious
nutritive 7.19
eating 8.31
nutritive value 7.1
nutriture 449.3
nuts
n genitals 2.11
bet 759.3
poker 759.10
adj crazy 925.27
nuts about
enthusiastic 101.11
crazy about 104.31
nutshell
n modicum 248.2
adj shortened 268.9
abridged 557.6
nutty flavorful 63.9
foolish 922.9
crazy 925.27
eccentric 926.6
nuzzle stroke 73.8
cuddle 562.17
nymph larva 302.12
embryo 305.14
insect 311.31
deity 678.9
nymphet
schoolgirl 302.8
strumpet 665.14
nymph 678.9
nymphomania
sexual desire 75.5
lasciviousness 665.5
nymphomaniac
sexual pervert 75.16
strumpet 665.14
oaf bungler 414.8

simple soul 416.3
lout 923.5
oafish bungling 414.20
stupid 921.15
oak
symbol of strength
15.8
hardness 1044.6
oak leaf 647.5
oar remi— 180.15
boatman 183.5
oarsman 183.5
oath vow 334.4
promise 436.1
profane oath 513.4
oats 10.4
obdurate
insensible 25.6
impenitent 114.5
heartless 144.25
tough 361.10
firm 425.7
hardened 654.17
hard 1044.10
obedience
resignation 134.2
compliance 326.1
submission 433.1
conformity 866.1
obedient
resigned 134.10
compliant 326.3
submissive 433.12
dutiful 641.13
conformable 866.5
obeisance
obsequiousness 138.2
reverence 155.2
submission 433.1
crouch 912.3
obeisant
obsequious 138.14
prostrate 155.10
deferential 433.16
obelisk tower 272.6
monument 549.12
Oberon 678.8
obese corpulent 257.18
oversize 257.23
obesity oversize 257.5
corpulence 257.8
obey accept 134.7
mind 326.2
submit 433.6
obfuscate deform 263.3
conceal 346.6
make unintelligible
522.12
misteach 569.3
darken 1026.9
obituary
n obit 307.14
monument 549.12
history 719.1
adj funereal 309.22
documentary 549.18
object
v protest 333.5
offer resistance
453.3
disapprove 510.10
disagree 788.5

object
n objective 380.2
intent 518.2
syntax 530.2
something 762.3
article 1050.4
objectify
externalize 206.5
visualize 985.15
objecting
protesting 333.7
resistant 453.5
objection demur 325.2
protest 333.2
resistance 453.1
disapproval 510.1
defense 600.2
obstacle 1011.4
objectionable
offensive 98.18
unacceptable 108.10
unpraiseworthy
510.24
objective
n will 323.1
object 380.2
adj unfeeling 94.9
impartial 649.10
real 760.15
extrinsic 767.3
true 972.13
unprejudiced 978.12
objectivity
unfeeling 94.1
extrinsicality 767.1
unprejudicedness 978.5
object lesson
warning 399.1
lesson 568.7
example 785.2
objector
dissenter 333.3
oppositionist 452.3
objet d'art 712.10
oblation gift 478.4
offering 696.7
obligate
v commit 436.5
oblige 641.12
adj obliged 641.16
obligated
promised 436.8
chargeable 623.9
obliged 641.16
obligation
act of kindness 143.7
gratitude 150.1
undertaking 404.1
compulsion 424.1
commitment 436.2
security 438.1
debt 623.1
duty 641.1
condition 958.2
necessity 962.1
obligative 530.11
obligatory
mandatory 420.12
compulsory 424.11
binding 641.15
necessary 962.12
oblige be kind 143.9

necessitate 424.5
indulge 427.6
accommodate 449.19
obligate 641.12
require 962.8
obliged grateful 150.5
obligated 641.16
obliging
n indulgence 427.3
adj considerate 143.16
indulgent 427.8
permissive 443.14
courteous 504.14
oblique
n diagonal 204.7
v deviate 204.9
adj transverse 170.9
devious 204.13
circumlocutory
538.14
circuitous 913.7
obliterate
expunge 395.16
declare a moratorium
625.9
efface from the
memory 989.6
obliteration
erasure 395.7
moratorium 625.2
forgetfulness 989.1
oblivion
unconsciousness 25.2
insensibility 94.2
carelessness 340.2
thoughtlessness 932.1
forgetfulness 989.1
oblivious asleep 22.22
unconscious 25.8
insensible 94.10
careless 340.11
thoughtless 932.4
inattentive 983.7
abstracted 984.11
forgetful 989.9
oblong
oblongated 267.9
quadrangular 278.9
obloquy criticism 510.4
vilification 513.2
infamy 661.4
obnoxious
offensive 98.18
base 661.12
terrible 999.9
oboist 710.4
obscene offensive 98.18
cursing 513.8
lascivious 665.29
lewd 666.9
coarse 497.11
obscenity filth 80.7
offensiveness 98.2
coarseness 497.2
cursing 513.3
oath 513.4
lasciviousness 665.5
dirtiness 666.4
obscure
n darkness 1026.1
v blind 30.7
deform 263.3

cover 295.19
cloud 319.6
conceal 346.6
make unintelligible
522.12
misteach 569.3
quibble 935.9
make uncertain
970.15
darken 1026.9
opaque 1030.2
adj inconspicuous
32.6
formless 263.4
concealed 346.11
hard to understand
522.14
vague 522.15
ambiguous 539.4
unrenowned 661.14
uncertain 970.19
dark 1026.13
opaque 1030.3
obscured blinded 30.10
covered 295.31
concealed 346.11
latent 519.5
hard to understand
522.14
dark 1026.13
obscurity
inconspicuousness
32.2
formlessness 263.1
obscuration 522.3
diffuseness 538.1
vagueness 970.4
darkness 1026.1
opaqueness 1030.1
obsequies 309.4
obsequious
servile 138.14
obeisant 155.10
deferential 433.16
flattering 511.8
observable visible 31.6
manifest 348.8
observance regard 27.2
obedience 326.1
vigilance 339.4
custom 373.1
adherence 434
observation 434.1
execution 437.4
celebration 487.1
ceremony 580.4
piety 692.1
rite 701.3
conformity 866.1
attention 982.1
observant
vigilant 339.13
respectful 434.4
dutiful 641.13
pious 692.8
belief 952.21
attentive 982.15
observation
regard 27.2
observance 434.1
remark 524.4
idea 931.1

surveillance 937.9
opinion 952.6
attention 982.1
observatory 1070.17
observatory
observation post 27.8
astronomical
observatory 1070.17
observe see 27.12
look 27.13
obey 326.2
keep 434.2
execute 437.9
celebrate 487.2
remark 524.25
formalize 580.5
perform a rite 701.14
conform 866.3
examine 937.23
heed 982.6
observer
military pilot 185.3
spectator 917.1
examiner 937.17
obsess oppress 98.16
demonize 680.16
bewitch 691.9
possess 925.25
engross 982.13
haunt 987.6
be remembered
988.14
obsessed affected 93.23
bewitched 691.13
possessed 925.33
engrossed 982.17
haunted 987.10
remembering 988.24
obsession
bewitchment 691.2
prepossession 925.13
engrossment 982.3
possession 987.5
obsessive
obsessional 925.34
engrossing 982.20
unforgettable 988.26
obsolesce
fall into disuse 390.9
age 841.9
obsolescence 390.1
obsolete
n archaism 526.12
adj out of action 19.17
disused 390.10
past 836.7
passé 841.15
obstacle
obstruction 293.3
hindrance 1011.4
obstetric 90.15
obstinacy
strength 15.1
refusal 325.1
defiance 327.2
resolution 359.1
perseverance 360.1
stubbornness 361
obstinateness 361.1
firmness 425.2
hostility 451.2
resistance 453.1

tenacity 802.3
uninfluenceability
894.2
obstinate strong 15.15
disobedient 327.8
resolute 359.11
persevering 360.8
stubborn 361.8
firm 425.7
oppositional 451.8
adhesive 802.12
uninfluenceable 894.4
obstreperous
noisy 53.13
vociferous 59.10
defiant 327.10
ungovernable 361.12
unruly 671.19
obstruct slow 175.9
stop 293.7
oppose 451.3
fend off 460.10
delay 845.8
get in the way 1011.12
obstructed
stopped 293.11
late 845.16
obstruction
slowing 175.4
clog 293.3
golf 751.1
delay 845.2
hindrance 1011.1
obstacle 1011.4
obstructionist
oppositionist 452.3
hinderer 1011.8
obstructive
n oppositionist 452.3
adj oppositional 451.8
resistant 453.5
dilatory 845.17
hindering 1011.17
obtain fetch 176.16
elicit 192.14
acquire 472.8
receive 479.6
exist 760.8
prevail 863.10
induce 885.11
obtainable
attainable 472.14
accessible 965.8
obtrude intrude 214.5
eject 908.13
obtrusive
conceited 140.11
insolent 142.9
intrusive 214.8
conspicuous 348.12
gaudy 501.20
obtuse insensible 25.6
unfeeling 94.9
blunt 286.3
negative 335.5
dull 921.16
obverse
n opposite side 215.3
front 216.1
likeness 783.3
adj contrapositive
215.5

contrary 778.6
obviate 1011.14
obvious distinct 31.7
manifest 348.8
patent 969.15
occasion
n pretext 376.1
circumstance 765.1
event 830.2
opportunity 842.2
cause 885.1
requirement 962.2
v be timely 842.6
cause 885.10
occasional
circumstantial 765.7
happening 830.9
incidental 842.11
casual 847.3
causal 885.13
occident 161.3
Occident 231.6
occidental 161.14
occipital 217.10
occlude close 293.6
obstruct 1011.12
occlusion seizure 85.6
closure 293.1
hindrance 1011.1
occlusive
n speech sound 524.13
adj phonetic 524.31
hindering 1011.17
occult
v cover 295.19
conceal 346.6
darken 1026.9
adj secret 345.11
concealed 346.11
latent 519.5
recondite 522.16
esoteric 689.23
supernatural 869.15
spectral 987.7
immaterial 1051.7
the occult secret 345.5
supernaturalism
869.7
immateriality 1051.1
occultation
disappearance 34.1
covering 295.1
concealment 346.1
eclipse 1026.8
occultism
supernaturalism 689
esoterics 689.1
immateriality 1051.1
occultist
esoteric 689.11
immaterialist 1051.4
occupancy
habitation 225.1
possession 469.1
occupant
inhabitant 227.2
tenant 470.4
occupation
habitation 225.1
action 328.1
possession 469.1
appropriation 480.4

work 724.1
vocation 724.6
operation 888.1
occupational hazard
85.32
occupied
inhabited 225.12
busy 330.21
engaged 724.15
absorbed in thought
930.22
engrossed 982.17
occupy pervade 221.7
inhabit 225.7
possess 469.4
appropriate 480.19
engage 724.10
include 771.3
occupy the mind
930.20
engross 982.13
occur be present 221.6
exist 760.8
happen 830.5
occur to 930.18
occurrence
appearance 33.1
presence 221.1
existence 760.1
circumstance 765.1
event 830.2
prevalence 863.2
ocean
vast body of water
240
sea 240.1
the deep 240.3
quantity 247.3
ocean depths
ocean 240.1
the deep sea 275.4
oceanic
nautical 182.57
marine 240.8
ocean liner 180.5
oceanographer
thalassographer 240.7
measurer 300.9
earth scientist 1069.2
oceanography
thalassography 240.6
sounding 275.5
earth science 1069.1
Oceanus
spirit of the sea 240.4
water god 678.10
ocelot
variegation 47.6
wild cat 311.22
ocherous orange 42.2
yellow 43.4
Ockham's razor 484.1
octagonal
pentagonal 278.10
eighth 881.20
octave harmonics 709.9
interval 709.20
poetry 720.9
eight 881.4
octet cooperation 450.1
part music 708.18
poetry 720.9

eight 881.4
electron 1032.3
octogenarian
old man 304.2
eighty 881.7
ocular visual 27.20
optic 29.9
oculist
ophthalmologist 29.8
doctor 90.4
OD
n mariner 183.1
ship's officer 183.7
commissioned officer
575.18
v take sick 85.46
commit suicide
308.21
odalisque subject 432.7
demimonde 665.15
odd remaining 256.7
dissimilar 786.4
occasional 847.3
queer 869.11
sole 871.9
insane 925.26
eccentric 926.5
numeric 1016.22
oddball
n intruder 773.2
misfit 788.4
oddity 869.4
freak 926.4
adj odd 869.11
eccentric 926.6
oddity queerness 869.3
character 869.4
curiosity 869.5
eccentricity 926.1
odd job 724.2
odds advantage 249.2
gambling odds 759.6
difference 779.1
inequality 790.1
probability 967.1
even chance 971.7
odds and ends
remainder 256.1
notions 735.6
miscellany 769.13
hodgepodge 796.6
Odin 458.13
odious filthy 80.23
offensive 98.18
unlikable 99.7
base 661.12
terrible 999.9
odium hate 103.1
infamy 661.4
odor smell 69.1
fragrance 70.1
characteristic 864.4
odorize scent 69.7
perfume 70.8
odorizer 70.6
odorless 72.5
odorous
odoriferous 69.9
fragrant 70.9
malodorous 71.5
odyssey 177.2
Oedipus complex 92.22

oeuvre
literature 547.12
complete works 718.1
of 774.13
of age adult 303.12
marriageable 563.20
of consequence 996.18
of course
adv consequently
886.7
certainly 969.23
inter yes 332.18
off
n horse race 757.3
v kill 308.13
put an end to 395.12
adj dissonant 61.4
right 219.4
idle 331.18
tainted 393.41
dissimilar 786.4
occasional 847.3
odd 869.11
insane 925.26
delirious 925.31
erroneous 974.16
imperfect 1002.4
below par 1004.10
adv hence 188.20
oceanward 240.11
at a distance 261.14
prep from 255.14
offal slough 80.9
refuse 391.4
off and on
adj occasional 847.3
adv infrequently 847.4
alternately 849.11
irregularly 850.3
changeably 853.8
to and fro 915.21
off-balance
confused 984.12
eccentric 160.12
unbalanced 790.5
off-base untimely 843.6
misbehaving 322.5
wrong 638.3
inaccurate 974.17
offbeat
n beat 709.26
adj dissimilar 786.4
unconventional 867.6
unusual 869.10
off-center
eccentric 160.12
distorted 265.10
off chance
possibility 965.1
small chance 971.9
off-color off-tone 35.20
ill 85.55
wrong 638.3
risqué 666.7
off duty
on vacation 20.12
idle 331.18
offend
give offense 98.11
provoke 152.21
affront 156.5
do wrong 655.4

offend the eye 1014.5
offender 660.9
offense umbrage 152.2
provocation 152.11
indignity 156.2
violation 435.2
attack 459.1
misdeed 655.2
wrong 674.4
basketball game 747.3
hockey 749.3
fight 754.3
offensive
n attack 459.1
adj nasty 64.7
malodorous 71.5
objectionable 98.18
insulting 156.8
warlike 458.21
combative 459.30
vulgar 497.10
ill-bred 505.6
obscene 666.9
terrible 999.9
hideous 1014.11
offer
n attempt 403.2
proffer 439
offering 439.1
giving 478.1
v put to choice 371.21
attempt 403.6
proffer 439.4
give 478.12
bid 733.9
play 745.5
answer 938.4
adduce 956.12
offered 324.7
offering offer 439.1
gift 478.4
donation 478.6
oblation 696.7
game 745.3
offertory
donation 478.6
paean 696.3
oblation 696.7
sacred music 708.17
off-guard
negligent 340.10
unalert 983.8
offhand
adj nonchalant 106.15
careless 340.11
unpremeditated
365.11
extemporaneous
365.12
informal 581.3
adv carelessly 340.18
extemporaneously
365.15
informally 581.4
office
n act of kindness
143.7
library 197.6
function 387.5
aid 449.1
ceremony 580.4
bureau 594.4

commission 615.1
divine service 696.8
rite 701.3
duty 724.3
position 724.5
shop 739.7
v direct 573.8
office boy
errand boy 353.4
attendant 577.5
officeholder
official 575.16
office-bearer 610.11
officer
n executive 574.3
official 575.16
commissioned officer
575.18
policeman 1007.15
v govern 612.12
official
n executive 574.3
officer 575.16
agent 576.3
football 746.3
basketball 747.3
tennis 748.2
golf 751.3
soccer 752.3
boxing 754.3
adj authoritative
417.15
preceptive 419.4
recorded 549.17
governmental 612.17
executive 612.19
occupational 724.16
correct 969.18
officialdom 575.15
officialese
jargon 523.10
political jargon
609.37
officiate
administer 573.11
minister 701.15
function 724.13
baseball 745.5
football 746.5
sit in judgment 945.12
officious
meddlesome 214.9
overactive 330.24
offing
the distance 261.3
the future 838.1
offish arrogant 141.12
reticent 344.10
aloof 583.6
off-key 61.4
off-limits
restricted 210.8
prohibited 444.7
offscourings offal 80.9
remainder 256.1
refuse 391.4
rabble 606.3
off-season
n season 313.1
adj seasonal 313.9
offset
n setoff 338.2

printing 548.1
print 548.3
offshoot 561.4
the opposite 778.2
counteractant 899.3
v set off 338.5
cushion 670.8
go contrary to 778.4
neutralize 899.7
adj neutralizing 899.9
offsetting
n compensation 338.1
neutralization 899.2
adj compensating
338.6
neutralizing 899.9
offshoot fork 171.4
adjunct 254.1
sprig 310.18
offset 561.4
party 617.4
branch 617.10
sect 675.3
member 792.4
effect 886.1
extract 892.3
offshore 240.11
offspring child 302.3
family 559.5
posterity 561.1
descendant 561.3
sequel 834.2
effect 886.1
product 892.1
off the beaten track
secluded 584.8
unusual 869.10
off the cuff
adj extemporaneous
365.12
adv extemporaneously
365.15
off the record
adj confidential
345.14
adv confidentially
345.20
off-the-wall
unexpected 131.10
odd 869.11
crazy 925.27
off year 843.2
often frequently 846.6
repeatedly 848.16
ogle
n gaze 27.5
flirtation 562.9
v scrutinize 27.14
gaze 27.15
flirt 562.20
spectate 917.5
ogre frightener 127.9
monster 593.6
oh O! 122.20
my! 122.21
ohm 1031.12
oil
n balm 86.11
flattery 511.1
painting 712.14
fuel 1020.1
illuminant 1024.20

oleum 1054.1
v medicate 91.25
smooth 287.5
provision 385.9
flatter 511.6
facilitate 1013.7
fuel 1020.7
grease 1054.8
oiling
facilitation 1013.5
lubrication 1054.6
oily
slippery 287.11
insincere 354.31
suave 504.18
flattering 511.8
greasy 1054.9
ointment
anesthetic 25.3
balm 86.11
unction 701.5
money 728.2
lubricant 1054.3
okay
n consent 441.1
permission 443.1
v consent 441.2
permit 443.9
adj acceptable 107.12
accurate 972.16
excellent 998.13
tolerable 998.20
inter yeah 332.19
old aged 303.16
disused 390.10
experienced 413.28
former 836.10
age-old 841.10
antiquated 841.13
old age age 303.5
oldness 841.1
the old country
world region 231.6
fatherland 232.2
old days 836.2
older
n senior 304.5
adj mature 304.7
previous 833.4
senior 841.19
oldest
n senior 304.5
adj older 841.19
Old Faithful 1018.10
old-fashioned
disused 390.10
gallant 504.15
old-fangled 841.16
conservative 852.8
old fogy
back number 841.8
conservative 852.4
dotard 923.9
old hand 413.16
old hat trite 117.9
old-fashioned 841.16
old lady
ladylove 104.15
old woman 304.3
wife 563.8
old-line
conservative 611.17

unchanged 852.8
established 854.13
old maid
fussbudget 495.7
prude 500.11
spinster 565.4
old man beau 104.13
elder 304.2
father 560.9
forefather 560.10
grandfather 560.13
husband 563.7
commissioned officer
575.18
back number 841.8
the Old Man
ship's officer 183.7
commissioned officer
575.18
old master
work of art 712.10
artist 716.1
old pro
veteran 413.16
professional 726.4
old salt mariner 183.3
veteran 413.16
old saw 973.3
old school 852.4
old story 973.3
Old Testament 683.3
old-timer
old man 304.2
veteran 413.16
back number 841.8
old times 836.2
old wives' tale 953.3
old woman
effeminate male 77.10
old lady 304.3
fussbudget 495.7
grandmother 560.16
wife 563.8
back number 841.8
Old World 231.6
old-world
gallant 504.15
antiquated 841.13
olfactories 69.5
olfactory 69.12
olio stew 10.11
hodgepodge 796.6
olive 44.4
olive branch 465.2
ology 927.10
Olympian
apathetic 94.13
arrogant 141.12
high 272.14
reticent 344.10
aloof 583.6
impartial 649.10
heavenly 681.12
Olympics 457.3
Olympus 681.9
ombudsman 466.3
omega 819.1
omelet 10.25
omen
n portent 133.3
warning sign 399.3
prediction 961.1

v foreshow 133.10

ominous
portentous 133.17
threatening 514.3
premonitory 961.12
harmful 999.12
unfortunate 1010.14

omission
deletion 255.5
neglect 340.1
nonaccomplishment
408.1
mismanagement
414.6
nonobservance 435.1
misdeed 655.2
exclusion 772.1
deficiency 794.2
slip 974.4
want 991.4

omit delete 255.12
leave undone 340.7
exclude 772.4

omitting 772.10

omnibus
n public vehicle
179.13
compilation 554.7
adj comprehensive
771.7
whole 791.9
thorough 793.10

omnifarious 782.3

omnipotence 18.3

omnipotent
powerful 18.13
almighty 677.18

omnipresence
all-presence 221.2
completeness 793.1

omnipresent
all-present 221.13
almighty 677.18
thorough 793.10

omniscience 927.6

omniscient
almighty 677.18
knowing 927.15

omnivorous
eating 8.31
greedy 100.27
gluttonous 672.6

on
adj addicted 87.24
happening 830.9
adv forward 162.8
on foot 177.43
under way 182.63
after which 834.7
across 900.25
prep at 159.27
toward 161.26
atop 198.16
against 223.25
upon 295.37
with relation to
774.13

on account 622.10

on account of
for 449.26
because of 887.9

on and off 853.8

on and on
increasingly 251.9
continuously 811.10
constantly 846.7

on a par 789.7

on approval
at choice 371.27
on trial 941.14

on behalf of for 449.26
instead of 861.12

on board here 159.23
on shipboard 182.62
present 221.12
joined 799.13

on call handy 387.20
on demand 421.12
cash 624.25

once
adj former 836.10
adv whenever 820.12
once upon a time
836.14
one time 847.6
singly 871.13

once in a while 847.5

once upon a time
836.14

oncoming
n approach 167.1
beginning 817.1
adj progressive 162.6
approaching 167.4

on condition 958.12

on demand
at demand 421.12
cash 624.25

on duty 330.21

one
n child 302.3
person 312.5
I 871.3
adj quantitative 244.5
married 563.21
almighty 677.18
identical 777.7
whole 791.9
combined 804.5
single 871.7

one and all
n entire 791.3
all 863.4
adj every 863.15
adv unanimously
332.17
completely 793.14

one and only
n one 871.3
adj sole 871.9

one-armed bandit
759.16

one at a time 871.13

one by one
separately 801.27
each 864.19
singly 871.13

on edge nervous 128.11
in suspense 130.12
impatient 135.6

one-horse
insignificant 248.6
inferior 250.6
little 258.10

unimportant 997.18

one-horse town 230.3

one mind 332.5

on end
vertically 200.13
continuously 811.10

oneness accord 455.1
sameness 777.1
agreement 787.1
whole 791.1
simplicity 797.1
particularity 864.1
singleness 871
unity 871.1

one-night stand
copulation 75.7
engagement 704.11

one-on-one
n basketball game
747.3
adj contrapositive
215.5
front 216.10
personal 312.15
in opposition 451.9
plain-speaking 535.3
familiar 587.19

one-piece 871.11

onerous
oppressive 98.24
heavy 297.17
laborious 725.18
hampering 1011.18
troublesome 1012.18

oneself 864.5
402.6

one-sided sided 218.7
distorted 265.10
partial 650.11
unipartite 871.11
discriminatory 979.12

onetime 836.10

one time
adj infrequent 847.2
adv once 847.6

one-track mind 925.13

one-upmanship
cunning 415.1
competition 457.2

one-way 161.12

ongoing
n progression 162.1
course 172.2
adj progressive 162.6
improving 392.15
happening 830.9
operating 888.11

on guard
vigilant 339.13
defensively 460.16
cautious 494.8

on hand
present 221.12
in store 386.16
handy 387.20
possessed 469.8

on high
high up 272.21
celestially 681.13

on hold
neglected 340.14
late 845.16

on ice
prearranged 964.8
assured 969.20

on loan 620.7

onlooker
neighbor 223.6
spectator 917.1

onlooking 917.7

only
adj sole 871.9
adv limited 248.10
simply 797.11
solely 871.14

onomatopoeic
imitative 336.9
representational
349.13
lexical 526.19

onomatopoeic word
526.16

on one's knees
humbled 137.13
humbly 137.16
obsequious 138.14
obsequiously 138.16
obeisant 155.10
deferential 433.16
supplicatory 440.16
worshipful 696.15

on one's last legs
burnt-out 21.10
stricken in years
303.18
dying 307.33
worn-out 393.36

on one's mind 930.24

on one's own
at will 323.5
independently 430.33
singly 871.13

on one's toes 339.14

on paper
adj written 547.22
adv theoretically
950.16

on purpose 380.10

on record 549.17

onrush course 172.2
flow 238.4

on schedule 130.14

onset attack 459.1
printing 548.1
beginning 817.1

onslaught attack 459.1
berating 510.7
unruliness 671.3
impact 901.3

onstage 704.36

on stream 405.22

on tap 387.20

on tenterhooks
anxious 126.7
in suspense 130.12
in a dilemma 970.25

on the ball alert 339.14
clear-witted 919.13
attentive 982.15

on the bare possibility
965.10

on the beam
laterally 218.8
straight 277.7

knowledgeable 927.17
on the blink
  unserviceable 391.14
  impaired 393.38
  disorderly 809.13
on the block 734.17
on the brink 211.15
on the cuff 622.10
on the double
  adj swiftly 174.17
  hurried 401.11
  inter make haste!
    401.16
on the fence
  neutral 467.7
  nonpartisan 609.45
on the fritz
  unserviceable 391.14
  impaired 393.38
  disorderly 809.13
on the go
  under way 172.9
  en route 177.42
  busy 330.21
on the house
  adj gratuitous 634.5
  adv as a gift 478.27
  gratuitously 634.6
on the job busy 330.21
  alert 339.14
  attentive 982.15
on the level 644.14
on the lookout 339.13
on the lookout for
  adj expectant 130.11
  searching 937.37
  prep after 382.12
on the loose
  escaped 369.11
  free 430.21
  festive 743.28
on the make
  aspiring 100.28
  out for 403.17
on the mend 392.15
on the move
  under way 172.9
  en route 177.42
  busy 330.21
on the nose
  directable 161.13
  accurate 972.16
on the other hand
  laterally 218.8
  aside 218.10
  notwithstanding
    338.8
  contrarily 778.9
  otherwise 779.11
  comparatively 942.10
  all things considered
    945.17
on the quiet 345.18
on the rocks
  aground 182.73
  insolvent 625.11
  stranded 1012.27
on the run
  adj busy 330.21
  adv under way 172.9
  on the move 177.42
  hastily 401.12

on the shelf
  neglected 340.14
  disused 390.10
on the side
  aside 218.10
  additionally 253.11
on the spot here 159.23
  hasty 401.9
  now 837.3
  promptly 844.15
  in danger 1005.13
  in trouble 1012.22
on the take 378.4
on the verge 211.15
on the wagon 668.10
on the way
  along the way 176.20
  in preparation 405.22
on the whole
  on the average 246.5
  in the long run 791.14
  generally 863.17
  all things considered
    945.17
on time
  on credit 622.10
  punctually 844.14
on to
  v learn 551.14
  adj cognizant of
    927.16
ontogeny 860.3
on top of atop 198.16
  additionally 253.11
  on 295.37
  restraining 428.11
  attentive 982.15
  protective 1007.23
on trial
  adv under
    examination 941.14
  phrs in litigation
    598.21
on trust
  on credit 622.10
  believingly 952.28
onus duty 641.1
  charge 643.3
  guilt 656.1
  stigma 661.6
  proof 956.3
  impediment 1011.6
onward
  v make one's way
    162.4
  adj progressive 162.6
  adv forward 162.8
  frontward 216.13
oodles 247.4
ooze
  n slime 80.8
  exuding 190.6
  mud 1060.8
  v exude 190.15
  be damp 1063.11
opacity
  obscurity 522.3
  stupidity 921.3
  opaqueness 1030.1
opalescence
  rainbow effect 47.2
  iridescence 1024.18

opalescent
  soft-colored 35.21
  rainbow-like 47.10
  iridescent 1024.37
opaque
  v darken 1030.2
  adj obscure 522.15
  stupid 921.15
  intransparent 1030.3
op cit 956.24
open
  v cleave 224.4
  spread 259.6
  ope 292.11
  disclose 351.4
  dramatize 704.28
  open up 817.12
  adj visible 31.6
  approachable 167.5
  receptive 187.16
  exterior 206.7
  available 222.15
  champaign 236.2
  spread 259.11
  unclosed 292.17
  communicative
    343.10
  overt 348.10
  published 352.17
  leisure 402.5
  artless 416.5
  free-acting 430.23
  unrestricted 430.27
  liberal 485.4
  phonetic 524.31
  plain-speaking 535.3
  hospitable 585.11
  candid 644.17
  incoherent 803.4
  influenceable 893.15
  liable 896.5
  accessible 965.8
  undecided 970.18
  open-minded 978.10
  exposed 1005.15
  adv without date
    821.5
the open 206.3
open-air outdoor 206.8
  airy 317.11
open and aboveboard
  644.14
open-and-shut
  manifest 348.8
  assured 969.20
open-and-shut case
  proof 956.3
  sure thing 969.2
open arms
  reception 187.1
  entree 187.3
  welcome 585.2
  greeting 585.4
open door entree 187.3
  hospitality 585.1
  foreign policy 609.5
opener
  can opener 292.10
  inauguration 817.5
open-eyed
  wondering 122.9
  vigilant 339.13

  curious 980.5
  attentive 982.15
open fire
  n fire 1018.13
  v pull the trigger
    459.22
  open 817.12
  inter attack! 459.32
open forum
  forum 423.3
  arena 463.1
  discussion 541.7
openhanded
  liberal 485.4
  magnanimous 652.6
openhearted
  artless 416.5
  liberal 485.4
  hospitable 585.11
  candid 644.17
opening
  appearance 33.1
  entree 187.3
  entrance 189.5
  outlet 190.9
  vacancy 222.2
  crack 224.2
  aperture 292.1
  display 348.2
  passageway 383.3
  position 724.5
  beginning 817.1
  opportunity 842.2
opening move 817.3
open market
  marketplace 736.2
  stock market 737.1
open mind 978.3
open-minded
  nonrestrictive 430.25
  influenceable 893.15
  open 978.10
openmouthed
  vociferous 59.10
  wondering 122.9
  gaping 292.18
  curious 980.5
  attentive 982.15
  surprised 131.12
openness
  approachability 167.2
  receptivity 187.9
  exteriority 206.1
  communicativeness
    343.3
  manifestness 348.3
  artlessness 416.1
  plain speech 535.1
  talkativeness 540.1
  candor 644.4
  inclusion 771.1
  influenceability 893.5
  susceptibility 896.2
  accessibility 965.3
  open-mindedness
    978.3
  exposure 1005.3
open question 970.8
the open road 177.3
open sesame
  n opener 292.10
  password 517.12

incantation 691.4
influence 893.6
inter open up! 292.23
open shop 727.3
open to liable to 896.6
accessible 965.8
open to question
970.17
open up
v spread 259.6
open 292.11
come out 348.6
disclose 351.4
confess 351.7
make public 352.11
let oneself go 430.19
propose 439.5
begin 817.12
facilitate 1013.7
inter open sesame!
292.23
open warfare 458.1
opera theater 704.14
score 708.28
musical theater
708.34
operable
usable 387.23
workable 888.10
practicable 965.7
practical 994.6
opera glasses 29.4
operagoer 710.21
opera house 704.14
operant
n doer 726.1
operator 888.4
adj operating 888.11
opera singer 710.13
operate
treat 91.24
pilot 182.14
act 328.4
plot 381.9
use 387.10
trade 737.23
function 888.5
be operative 888.7
operate on treat 91.24
act on 888.6
operatic
dramatic 704.33
vocal 708.50
operating
n motion 172.1
adj acting 328.10
operational 888.11
operating room 197.25
operation
surgery 90.2
surgical intervention
91.19
motion 172.1
action 328.1
act 328.3
function 387.5
utilization 387.8
undertaking 404.1
military operation
458.5
transaction 731.4
workings 888

functioning 888.1
performance 891.5
operational
acting 328.10
operative 888.9
operating 888.11
functional 888.12
operative
n secret agent 576.9
detective 576.10
doer 726.1
operator 888.4
adj powerful 18.12
acting 328.10
effectual 387.21
operational 888.9
operator surgeon 90.5
man of action 330.8
telephone operator
347.9
schemer 381.7
politics 610.6
doer 726.1
speculator 737.11
operative 888.4
liveware 1041.17
operetta 708.34
operose
painstaking 339.11
laborious 725.18
difficult 1012.17
ophthalmic eye 2.26
visual 27.20
optic 29.9
ophthalmologist 29.8
opiate
sleep-inducer 22.10
anesthetic 25.3
drug 87.2
opine remark 524.25
judge 945.8
suppose 950.10
think 952.11
opinion advice 422.1
idea 931.1
estimate 945.3
sentiment 952.6
attitude 977.1
opinionated
obstinate 361.8
dogmatic 969.22
opinion poll 937.14
opium 22.10
opossum 311.23
opponent
n adversary 452.1
adj oppositional 451.8
opportune apt 787.10
timely 842.9
expedient 994.5
opportunist
n timeserver 363.4
schemer 381.7
adj scheming 381.13
opportunity turn 824.2
probability 842.2
chance 971.1
oppose
contrapose 215.4
dissent 333.4
deny 335.4
counter 451.3

offer resistance 453.3
disapprove 510.10
go contrary to 778.4
counteract 899.6
compare 942.4
hinder 1011.10
oppose change 852.6
opposed
contrapositive 215.5
unwilling 325.5
oppositional 451.8
disapproving 510.21
contrary 778.6
adverse 1010.13
opposed to 451.10
opposed to change
852.8
opposer 452.3
opposing
n contraposition 215.1
opposition 451.1
resistance 453.1
comparison 942.1
adj contrapositive
215.5
dissenting 333.6
negative 335.5
oppositional 451.8
disapproving 510.21
contrary 778.6
opposing party 452.1
opposing side 452.1
opposite
n inverse 205.4
poles 215.2
contrary 778.2
adj contrapositive
215.5
fronting 216.11
oppositional 451.8
contrary 778.6
adverse 1010.13
adv poles apart 215.6
prep against 223.25
over against 778.10
opposite number
the opposite 778.2
equal 789.4
opposition
contraposition 215.1
refusal 325.1
dissent 333.1
opposing 451.1
resistance 453.1
disapproval 510.1
contrariety 778.1
difference 779.1
disagreement 788.1
counteraction 899.1
comparison 942.1
hindrance 1011.1
oppositional
opponent 451.8
contrary 778.6
counteractive 899.8
opposition party
609.24
oppress
burden 98.16
sadden 112.18
aggrieve 112.19
weight down 297.13

persecute 389.7
domineer 612.16
task 725.16
go hard with 1010.8
oppressed
sad 112.20
weighted 297.18
subjugated 432.14
downtrodden 432.16
oppression
affliction 96.8
dejection 112.3
stuffiness 173.6
burden 297.7
persecution 389.3
despotism 612.10
oppressive
burdensome 98.24
depressing 112.30
stuffy 173.16
onerous 297.17
imperious 417.16
laborious 725.18
hampering 1011.18
troublesome 1012.18
sultry 1018.28
oppressor 575.14
opprobrium
vilification 513.2
infamy 661.4
oppugn
contradict 451.6
quarrel 456.11
dispute 457.21
go contrary to 778.4
counteract 899.6
opt 371.13
optic
n eye 2.9
vision 27.9
adj eye 2.26
visual 27.20
optical 29.9
optical illusion 975.5
optical instrument 29.1
optician 29.8
optics
optical physics 29.7
light 1024.22
optimal 998.16
optimism
cheerfulness 109.1
optimisticalness 124.3
sanguine expectation
130.2
optimist 124.6
optimistic
cheerful 109.11
upbeat 124.12
expectant 130.11
optimum
n the best 998.8
adj best 998.16
option discretion 371.2
free will 430.6
first option 733.2
stock option 737.21
optional
voluntary 324.7
elective 371.22
optometrist
oculist 29.8

doctor 90.4
optometry 29.7
opulence wealth 618.1
plenty 990.2
opulent
wealthy 618.14
plentiful 990.7
opus writing 547.10
book 554.1
piece 708.5
product 892.1
or
n yellowness 43.1
heraldry 647.2
adj yellow 43.4
conj either . . . or
371.29
OR 197.25
oracle
n wise man 920.1
Delphic oracle 961.7
maxim 973.1
v dogmatize 969.10
oracular
predictive 961.11
dogmatic 969.22
oral
n examination 937.2
adj mouthlike 292.22
communicational
343.9
speech 524.30
traditional 841.12
orange
n orangeness 42.1
adj orangeish 42.2
orangery 1067.11
orate 543.10
oration 543.2
orator 543.6
oratorical 543.12
oratorio 708.17
oratory
public speaking 543.1
eloquence 544.1
chapel 703.3
orb
n eye 2.9
vision 27.9
region 231.2
sphere 282.2
royal insignia 647.3
occupation 724.4
stars 1070.4
adj spherical 282.9
orbit
n domain 231.2
rank 245.2
circle 280.2
sphere 282.2
route 383.1
occupation 724.4
sphere of influence
893.4
circuitousness 913.1
circuit 913.2
circle 1070.16
spacecraft 1073.2
v encircle 280.10
circle 913.5
orbiting 913.1
orchard 310.12

orchestra
audience 48.6
auditorium 704.15
stage 704.16
band 710.12
orchestrate 708.46
orchestration
piece 708.5
harmonization 709.2
orchestrator 710.20
ordain install 191.4
command 420.8
allot 477.9
legislate 613.10
appoint 615.11
legalize 673.8
frock 698.12
destine 963.7
ordained
in orders 698.17
destined 963.9
ordeal trial 96.9
occultism 690.3
test 941.2
order
n rank 245.2
manner 384.1
precept 419.1
command 420.1
demand 421.1
peacefulness 464.2
nomenclature 527.1
harmony 533.2
race 559.4
caste 607.1
community 617.2
fellowship 617.3
school 617.5
decoration 646.5
medal 646.6
sect 675.3
good condition 764.3
arrangement 806
taxonomy 806.1
arrangement 807.1
class 808.2
classifications 808.5
sequence 814.1
normality 868.1
verdict 945.5
biology 1066.1
v outfit 5.40
command 420.8
demand 421.5
request 440.9
direct 573.8
organize 806.4
arrange 807.8
classify 808.6
exercise influence
893.8
pass judgment 945.13
ordered
harmonious 533.8
uniform 780.5
orderly 806.6
arranged 807.14
regular 849.6
ordering
direction 573.1
class 607.1
arrangement 807.1

organization 807.2
orderless
formless 263.4
unordered 809.12
vague 970.19
orderly
n hospital staff 90.11
attendant 577.5
adj pacific 464.9
harmonious 533.8
punctilious 580.10
uniform 780.5
consistent 802.11
ordered 806.6
arranged 807.14
regular 849.6
normal 868.8
adv regularly 780.8
order of the day
affairs 830.4
schedule 964.3
ordinal
classificational 808.7
consecutive 811.9
numeric 1016.22
ordinance rule 419.2
decree 420.4
law 673.3
rite 701.3
ordinary
n food service 8.11
heraldry 647.2
the usual 868.3
adj medium 246.3
inferior 250.6
customary 373.14
common 497.14
simple 499.6
populational 606.8
prosaic 721.5
frequent 846.4
prevalent 863.12
usual 868.9
average 1004.8
ordinate
n coordinates 300.5
v appoint 615.11
ordination
admission 187.2
appointment 615.2
holy orders 698.10
organization 807.2
ordnance arms 462.1
artillery 462.11
ordure feces 12.4
filth 80.7
ore raw material 406.5
mineral 1056.2
or else 779.11
organ instrument 384.4
periodical 555.1
branch 617.10
keyboard wind
instrument 711.13
member 792.4
organ-grinder 710.9
organic
structural 266.6
organismic 305.17
innate 766.8
organic matter
living matter 305

animate matter 305.1
organism body 2.1
structure 266.1
organization 305.2
something 762.3
organist 710.8
organization
contour 262.2
structure 266.1
organism 305.2
plan 381.1
military unit 461.22
establishment 617.8
sect 675.3
workplace 739.1
composition 795.1
order 806.1
methodization 807.2
production 891.4
organizational
associational 617.17
formational 807.15
organize form 262.7
construct 266.5
plan 381.8
unionize 727.9
compose 795.3
league 804.4
order 806.4
methodize 807.10
establish 891.10
organized drunk 88.33
organic 305.17
planned 381.12
arranged 807.14
organized crime
the underworld
660.11
illicit business 732.1
organized labor 727.2
organizer
planner 381.6
unionist 727.4
arranger 807.5
producer 891.7
organ player 710.8
organ stop 711.19
orgasm
copulation 75.7
fury 105.8
spasm 916.6
orgasmic
lustful 75.26
frenzied 105.25
turbulent 671.18
convulsive 671.23
jerky 916.19
orgiastic
frenzied 105.25
carnal 663.6
incontinent 665.24
saturnalian 669.9
orgy spree 88.5
fury 105.8
dissipation 669.2
oriel 197.3
orient
n points of the
compass 161.3
v orientate 161.11
accustom 373.10
adj luminous 1024.30

Orient 231.6
oriental 161.14
Oriental 312.3
orientation
  navigation 159.3
  direction 161.1
  bearings 161.4
  habituation 373.8
orienter 422.3
orifice 292.1
origami 291.4
origin
  etymology 526.15
  beginning 817.1
  origination 817.4
  source 885.5
original
  n real thing 337.2
  writing 547.10
  model 785.1
  nonconformist 867.3
  oddity 869.4
  source 885.5
  adj basic 199.8
  native 226.5
  actual 337.5
  unused 390.12
  essential 766.9
  preceding 815.4
  beginning 817.15
  new 840.7
  novel 840.11
  unconventional 867.6
  primary 885.14
  genuine 972.15
  imaginative 985.18
originality
  nonimitation 337.1
  newness 840.1
  nonconformity 867.1
  unconventionality 867.2
  invention 985.3
original sin 655.3
originate
  invent 337.4
  initiate 817.10
  take origin 817.13
  cause 885.10
  result from 886.5
  produce 891.12
  imagine 985.14
origination
  beginning 817.1
  origin 817.4
  source 885.5
  production 891.1
  product 892.1
originative
  causal 885.13
  creative 891.16
  imaginative 985.18
originator
  author 885.4
  producer 891.7
oriole 710.23
orison 696.4
Ormazd 677.5
ornament
  n extra 254.4
  ornamentation 498.1
  figure of speech 536.1

ornateness 545.4
  honor 646.1
  decoration 646.5
  passage 708.24
  impromptu 708.27
  grace 709.18
  v add 253.4
  decorate 498.8
  make grandiloquent 545.7
ornamental
  decorative 498.10
  artistic 712.20
ornamentalist 716.11
ornamentation
  decoration 498
  ornament 498.1
  ornateness 545.4
  architectural element 717.2
  superfluity 992.4
ornamented
  adorned 498.11
  figurative 536.3
ornate elegant 498.12
  purple 545.11
ornery irascible 110.20
  malicious 144.20
  defiant 327.10
  negative 335.5
  perverse 361.11
  oppositional 451.8
  contrary 778.6
  disagreeing 788.6
  counteractive 899.8
orotund 545.8
orphan
  n survivor 256.3
  derelict 370.4
  v bereave 307.28
  adj bereaved 307.35
orphanage 1008.4
orthodontic 90.15
orthodox
  n true believer 687.4
  adj firm 425.7
  conventional 579.5
  orthodoxical 687.7
  conformist 866.6
Orthodox 675.30
orthodoxy
  firmness 425.2
  religion 675.1
  soundness of doctrine 687
  orthodoxness 687.1
  conformity 866.1
Orthodoxy 675.9
orthogonal
  perpendicular 200.12
  right-angled 278.7
  quadrangular 278.9
orthography 546.4
orthopedic 90.15
orts remainder 256.1
  refuse 391.4
Oscar 646.2
oscillate
  vacillate 362.8
  be frequent 846.3
  recur 849.5
  change 853.5

vibrate 915.10
oscillating
  vacillating 362.10
  constant 846.5
  oscillatory 915.15
oscillation
  vacillation 362.2
  constancy 846.2
  periodicity 849.2
  changing 853.3
  vibration 915.1
oscillator 915.9
oscillatory
  vacillating 362.10
  periodic 849.7
  oscillating 915.15
oscilloscope
  instrument 915.8
  radar 1035.1
osculate contact 223.10
  kiss 562.19
Osiris 682.5
osmose 187.13
osmosis
  transferal 176.1
  sorption 187.6
ossified skeleton 2.24
  hardened 1044.13
ossify callous 94.6
  harden 1044.7
ossuary
  mortuary 309.9
  urn 309.12
  tomb 309.16
ostensible
  apparent 33.11
  conspicuous 348.12
  specious 354.26
  pretexted 376.5
  illusory 975.8
ostentation
  display 348.2
  conspicuousness 348.4
  sham 354.3
  ornateness 498.2
  pretension 501
  ostentatiousness 501.1
  grandiloquence 545.1
ostentatious
  pretentious 501.18
  grandiloquent 545.8
  ornate 498.12
osteopath 90.4
ostracism
  disapproval 510.1
  ostracization 586.3
  elimination 772.2
  banishment 908.4
ostracize
  disapprove 510.10
  turn thumbs down 586.6
  exclude 772.4
  banish 908.17
other
  n a different thing 779.3
  adj additional 253.10
  unrelated 775.6
  another 779.8
  fresh 840.8
  substitute 861.8

other-directed
  extroverted 92.40
  moved 375.30
  conformable 866.5
other self
  friend 588.1
  self 864.5
other side 215.3
otherwise
  adj other 779.8
  adv contrarily 778.9
  in other ways 779.11
otherworldly
  heavenly 681.12
  supernatural 869.15
  visionary 985.24
  immaterial 1051.7
  extraterrestrial 1070.26
otic ear 2.26
  auditory 48.13
otiose idle 331.18
  fruitless 391.12
  unserviceable 391.14
  trivial 997.19
otology 48.9
ought to 641.3
oui 332.18
Ouija 689.6
ounce
  modicum 248.2
  weight 297.8
oust depose 447.4
  eject 908.13
  evict 908.15
ouster
  ejection 908.1
  eviction 908.2
  ejector 908.11
out
  n outlet 190.9
  excuse 600.4
  game 745.3
  v be revealed 351.8
  fight fire 1021.7
  adj asleep 22.22
  unconscious 25.8
  dead-drunk 88.32
  dislocated 160.9
  exterior 206.7
  disused 390.10
  dissimilar 786.4
  old-fashioned 841.16
  odd 869.11
  erroneous 974.16
  extinguished 1021.11
  adv to the point of exhaustion 21.14
  audibly 50.18
  hence 188.20
  forth 190.21
  externally 206.10
  at a loss 473.9
  prep from 188.21
  out of 190.22
outage 794.2
out-and-out
  downright 247.12
  thorough 793.10
  unqualified 959.2
outback
  n open space 158.4

hinterland 233.2
remote region 261.4
wasteland 890.2
adj hinterland 233.9
secluded 584.8
outbalance 297.14
outbrave 492.12
outbreak
emotional outburst
105.9
revolt 327.4
outburst 671.6
beginning 817.1
outbuilding 228.9
outburst
exclamation 59.2
emotional outburst
105.9
outburst of anger
152.9
ejection 190.3
outbreak 671.6
disgorgement 908.7
flare 1018.14
outcast
n recluse 584.5
social outcast 586.4
exclusiveness 772.3
alien 773.3
oddity 869.4
adj unplaced 160.10
forlorn 584.12
cast-off 586.10
outclass outdo 249.9
defeat 412.6
out cold asleep 22.22
unconscious 25.8
dead-drunk 88.32
outcome ending 190.9
event 830.1
effect 886.1
product 892.1
solution 939.1
outcrop
n visibility 31.1
v appear 33.8
outcry
n noise 53.3
vociferation 59.4
lament 115.3
auction 734.4
v vociferate 59.8
outdate 841.9
outdated
disused 390.10
old-fashioned 841.16
outdistance
distance 249.10
reach out 261.5
outdo outrival 249.9
defeat 412.6
excel 998.11
outdoor 206.8
outdoors
n outside 206.3
adv out of doors
206.11
outer 206.7
outermost 206.7
outer space
the universe 158.1
remote region 261.4

depths 275.3
space 1070.3
outface 492.12
outfield
playground 743.11
baseball 745.1
outfielder 745.2
outfit
n wardrobe 5.2
costume 5.9
equipment 385.4
military unit 461.22
impedimenta 471.3
clique 617.6
team 617.7
company 769.3
set 769.12
v costume 5.40
equip 385.8
outflank 415.11
outflow
n outflowing 190.4
flow 238.4
spendings 626.2
v run out 190.13
outflowing
n outflow 190.4
adj outgoing 190.19
out for after 382.12
out to 403.17
searching 937.37
outgoer 190.10
outgoing
n egress 190.2
adj outbound 190.19
communicative
343.10
extroverted 92.40
out-group
company 769.3
exclusiveness 772.3
outgrow develop 14.2
grow 259.7
outgrowth
bodily development
14.1
growth 85.38
expansion 259.3
effect 886.1
product 892.1
extract 892.3
outguess 415.11
outhouse latrine 12.10
hut 228.9
outing journey 177.5
disclosure 351.1
out in the open
openly 348.15
exposed 1005.15
outland
n outdoors 206.3
adj extraneous 773.5
outlander 773.3
outlandish
wonderful 122.10
extraterritorial 206.9
unrefined 497.12
inelegant 534.2
extraneous 773.5
unrelated 775.6
odd 869.11
fanciful 985.20

outlast outtalk 540.7
outstay 826.8
outlaw
n outcast 586.4
evildoer 593.1
criminal 660.10
exclusiveness 772.3
alien 773.3
oddity 869.4
v prohibit 444.3
ostracize 586.6
eliminate 772.5
banish 908.17
adj illegal 674.6
outlawed prohibited
444.7
outcast 586.10
illegal 674.6
outlawry
illegality 674.1
elimination 772.2
banishment 908.4
outlay
n spendings 626.2
v spend 626.5
outlet catharsis 92.25
egress 190.9
opening 292.1
escape 369.1
passageway 383.3
sale 734.1
outline
n exterior 206.2
boundary 211.2
contour 262.2
diagram 381.3
treatise 556.1
abridgment 557.1
reflection 784.7
structural outline
800.4
v contour 211.9
describe 349.9
line 381.11
abridge 557.5
itemize 800.7
outlive 826.8
outlook
n viewpoint 27.7
observation post 27.8
field of view 31.3
view 33.6
expectations 130.4
dueness 639.1
the future 838.1
probability 967.1
mental outlook 977.2
v outbrave 492.12
out loud 50.18
outlying exterior 206.7
extrinsic 767.3
outmaneuver
outdo 249.9
deceive 356.14
defeat 412.6
outwit 415.11
outmoded
disused 390.10
old-fashioned 841.16
outmost 206.7
outnumber 883.5
out of from 188.21

ex 190.22
escaped 369.11
bereft 473.8
wanting 991.13
out of bounds
n game 746.3
adj restricted 210.8
prohibited 444.7
overpriced 632.12
excessive 992.16
out of character 788.7
out of commission
out of action 19.17
motionless 173.13
impaired 393.38
out of condition 764.7
out of contact 94.9
out of control 430.24
out of danger 1006.6
out-of-date
anachronous 832.3
disused 390.10
old-fashioned 841.16
out-of-doors 206.8
out of favor
disliked 99.9
in disrepute 661.13
out of focus 32.6
out of hand
ungovernable 361.12
extemporaneously
365.15
unrestrained 430.24
out of harm's way
1006.6
out of humor
discontented 108.7
out of temper 110.17
unhappy 112.21
out of it
out of action 19.17
sleepy 22.21
unconscious 25.8
inadequate 250.7
foolish 922.9
unaware 929.13
oblivious 983.7
out of joint
dislocated 160.9
in disrepair 393.37
inappropriate 788.7
separated 801.21
disorderly 809.13
out of keeping
inappropriate
788.7
out of line 867.7
out of kilter
impaired 393.38
out of condition
764.7
disorderly 809.13
out of line
misbehaving 322.5
wrong 638.3
inappropriate 788.7
untimely 843.6
out of keeping 867.7
inaccurate 974.17
out of luck 1010.14
out of one's mind
925.26

out of order
unserviceable 391.14
in disrepair 393.37
out of condition 764.7
disorderly 809.13
out of line 867.7
inexpedient 995.5
misbehaving 322.5

out of phase
n wave 915.4
adj untimely 843.6

out of place
misplaced 160.11
inappropriate 788.7
disorderly 809.13
out of line 867.7
inexpedient 995.5

out-of-pocket
bereft 473.8
at a loss 473.9
poor 619.7
wanting 991.13

out of practice 414.18
out of print 991.11

out of proportion
inappropriate 788.7
inconsistent 788.8
unequal 790.4

out of reach
out-of-the-way 261.9
beyond reach 261.18
inaccessible 966.9

out of season
unseasonal 313.9
inappropriate 788.7
anachronous 832.3
old-fashioned 841.16
scarce 991.11

out of shape
deformed 265.12
out of practice
  414.18

out of sight
adj invisible 32.5
gone 34.4
blissful 97.9
absent 222.11
far 261.15
out of reach 261.18
overpriced 632.12
excessive 992.16
excellent 998.13
inter goody! 95.20

out of sorts
ill 85.55
out of humor 110.17
unhappy 112.21

out of step 867.7
out of style 841.16

out of the blue
unexpected 131.10
unexpectedly 131.14

out of the ordinary
unusual 869.10
notable 996.19

out of the question
adj hopeless 125.14
rejected 372.3
impossible 966.7
inter by no means
  335.9
phrs I refuse 442.7

out of the running
out of action 19.17
disappointing 132.6
inadequate 250.7

out-of-the-way
unexpected 131.10
deviative 164.7
godforsaken 261.9
out of reach 261.18
secluded 584.8
irrelevant 775.7
farfetched 775.8
occasional 847.3
unconventional 867.6
unusual 869.10
circuitous 913.7

out of this world
blissful 97.9
extreme 247.13
unusual 869.10
excessive 992.16
excellent 998.13
superb 998.15

out of touch 94.9

out of tune
dissonant 61.4
in disrepair 393.37
disaccordant 456.15
different 779.7
inappropriate 788.7
disorderly 809.13
out of line 867.7

out of whack
unserviceable 391.14
impaired 393.38
out of condition 764.7
disagreeing 788.6
disorderly 809.13

out of work 331.18

out on a limb
exposed 1005.15
in trouble 1012.22

outpatient 85.42
outperform 249.9

outpost
frontier 211.5
vanguard 216.2
hinterland 233.2
remote region 261.4
guard 1007.9

outpouring
n outflow 190.4
plenty 990.2
adj outgoing 190.19

output yield 472.5
receipts 627.1
production 892.2

outrage
n indignity 156.2
mistreatment 389.2
injustice 650.4
misdeed 655.2
evil 999.3
v offend 152.21
insult 156.5
mistreat 389.5
violate 435.4
work evil 999.6

outrageous
insulting 156.8
overpriced 632.12
undue 640.9

disgraceful 661.11
violent 671.16
absurd 922.11
excessive 992.16
terrible 999.9

outré 922.11

outreach
outdo 249.9
be long 267.5
deceive 356.14
outwit 415.11

outright
adj downright 247.12
thorough 793.10
unqualified 959.2
adv freely 430.32
free and clear 469.12
completely 793.14

outrun
n skiing 753.1
v overtake 174.13
outdo 249.9
defeat 412.6

outset
n beginning 817.1
v set out 188.8

outshine
outdo 249.9
defeat 412.6

outside
n appearance 33.2
exterior 206.2
outdoors 206.3
roulette 759.12
adj exterior 206.7
outdoor 206.8
extrinsic 767.3
extraneous 773.5
adv externally 206.10
outdoors 206.11

outside chance
possibility 965.1
small chance 971.9

outside of 772.10

outsider
exclusiveness 772.3
alien 773.3
oddity 869.4

outsize
n oversize 257.5
adj large 247.7
oversize 257.23

outskirts
environment 209.1
bounds 211.1
frontier 211.5
town 230.1
city district 230.6
remote region 261.4

outsmart
deceive 356.14
outwit 415.11

outspoken
communicative
  343.10
artless 416.5
free-acting 430.23
speaking 524.32
candid 644.17

outstanding
exterior 206.7
eminent 247.9

remarkable 247.10
superior 249.12
superlative 249.13
remaining 256.7
protruding 283.14
conspicuous 348.12
due 623.10
prominent 662.17
notable 996.19

outstare 492.12
outstretched 259.11
outstrip lead 165.2
overtake 174.13
loom 247.5
outdo 249.9

outtalk persuade
  375.23
outspeak 540.7
out to 403.17

outward
adj apparent 33.11
exterior 206.7
formal 580.7
extrinsic 767.3
adv forth 190.21

outwear 826.8
outweigh excel 249.6
overweigh 297.14
outwit outdo 249.9
deceive 356.14
outfox 415.11

outworn
disused 390.10
obsolete 841.15

oval
n ovule 280.6
playground 743.11
track 755.1
horse racing 757.1
adj ovate 280.12

ovarian genital 2.27
glandular 13.8
ovary 2.11

ovation
celebration 487.1
applause 509.2

oven kiln 742.5
hot place 1018.11

over
adj superior 249.12
remaining 256.7
higher 272.19
ended 819.8
past 836.7
surplus 992.18
adv inversely 205.8
additionally 253.11
on high 272.21
again 848.17
excessively 992.22
prep all over 159.28
through 161.27
beyond 261.21
on 295.37
during 820.14
in excess of 992.26

overabundance 992.2
overabundant 992.19

overact
affect 500.12
overdramatize 704.31
overdo 992.10

overacted
affected 500.15
dramatic 704.33
overdone 992.21
overactive 330.24
overactivity 330.9
overage excess 256.4
surplus 992.5
overall
adj cumulative 769.23
comprehensive 771.7
adv throughout
793.17
generally 863.17
overall length 267.1
overambitious 101.12
over and above
adj surplus 992.18
prep with 253.12
in excess of 992.26
over and over 848.16
over-anxious
overzealous 101.12
anxious 126.7
overassess 948.2
overawe
daunt 127.18
domineer 612.16
overbearing
n authoritativeness
417.3
adj arrogant 141.9
imperious 417.16
overblown
past one's prime
303.15
overfull 992.20
overboard 182.74
overburden
n onerousness 297.2
burden 297.7
overfullness 992.3
v burden 297.13
overload 992.15
go hard with 1010.8
overburdened
careworn 126.9
weighted 297.18
overfull 992.20
overcareful 494.11
overcast
n atmosphere 184.32
cloudiness 319.3
darkening 1026.6
v cloud 319.6
darken 1026.9
adj cloudy 319.7
gloomy 1026.14
overcautious 494.11
overcharge
n cathexis 92.34
surcharge 632.5
overfullness 992.3
v exaggerate 355.3
ornament 545.7
charge 630.12
overprice 632.7
overload 992.15
overclouded 319.7
overcoat 5.13
overcome
v unnerve 128.10

excel 249.6
defeat 411.5
surmount 412.7
overwrought 105.26
adj dead-drunk 88.32
crushed 112.29
unnerved 128.14
defeated 412.14
overcompensation
defense mechanism
92.23
inequality 790.1
overconfidence
rashness 493.1
confidence 969.5
overconfident
rash 493.7
confident 969.21
overconscientious
overfastidious 495.12
conscientious 644.15
overcooked 11.7
overcount 948.2
overcritical
overfastidious 495.12
critical 510.23
overcrossing 383.9
overcrowded
full 793.11
teeming 883.9
overfull 992.20
overdeveloped
grown 14.3
oversize 257.23
expanded 259.12
excessive 992.16
overdo
exaggerate 355.3
overindulge 669.5
go too far 992.10
overrun 909.4
overdone done 11.7
exaggerated 355.4
affected 500.15
grandiloquent 545.8
overwrought 992.21
overdose
n superabundance
992.2
cloyer 993.3
v take sick 85.46
commit suicide
308.21
oversupply 992.14
satiate 993.4
overdraft arrears 623.2
insolvency 625.3
overdraw
misrepresent 350.3
exaggerate 355.3
overspend 486.7
overextend 992.13
overdrawn
exaggerated 355.4
overdone 992.21
overdress 5.41
overdrive task 725.16
overdo 992.10
overdue
expected 130.13
anachronous 832.3
late 845.16

overeager
overzealous 101.12
reckless 493.8
overeat 672.5
overelaborate
v overdo 992.10
adj ornate 498.12
affected 533.9
grandiloquent 545.8
overemotional
emotionalistic 93.19
excitable 105.28
overemphasis
exaggeration 355.1
overdoing 992.6
overemphasize
overdo 992.10
emphasize 996.14
overenthusiastic
overzealous 101.12
reckless 493.8
fanatic 925.32
overestimate
n overestimation
948.1
v exaggerate 355.3
overpraise 511.7
overreckon 948.2
overestimated
exaggerated 355.4
overrated 948.3
overexcited 105.26
overexercise
n overdoing 992.6
v overdo 992.10
overexert strain 725.10
overdo 992.10
overexpand 992.13
overexpansion 992.7
overextend
strain 725.10
overdraw 992.13
overextension
overactivity 330.9
strain 725.2
overdrawing 992.7
overexuberant 992.19
overfed
oversize 257.23
overgorged 672.7
overfull 992.20
satiated 993.6
overfill fill 793.7
overload 992.15
satiate 993.4
overflow
n spillage 238.6
wordiness 538.2
plenty 990.2
overfullness 992.3
v flow over 238.17
teem with 883.5
run over 909.7
abound 990.5
superabound 992.8
overflowing
n overflow 238.6
overrunning 909.1
adj much 247.8
diffuse 538.11
teeming 883.9
plentiful 990.7

overfull 992.20
overfull full 793.11
overloaded 992.20
satiated 993.6
overgarment 5.12
overgrow grow 14.2
spread 259.6
expand 259.7
vegetate 310.31
overspread 909.5
superabound 992.8
overgrown grown 14.3
large 247.7
oversize 257.23
overdeveloped 259.12
luxuriant 310.40
overrun 909.10
excessive 992.16
overgrowth
bodily development
14.1
oversize 257.5
growth 259.3
overrunning 909.1
excess 992.1
overhang
n overhanging 202.3
v hang over 202.7
overlie 295.30
be imminent 839.2
overhanging
n overhang 202.3
adj overhung 202.11
imminent 839.3
overhaul
n reparation 396.6
examination 937.3
v overtake 174.13
repair 396.14
take account of 628.9
examine 937.23
check 1016.20
overhead
n roof 295.6
expenses 626.3
adv on high 272.21
overhear hear 48.11
know 551.15
overheated
hot 1018.25
heated 1019.29
overindulge
be intemperate 669.5
overeat 672.5
overdo 992.10
overindulgence
unstrictness 426.2
indulgence 427.3
intemperance 669.1
gluttony 672.1
excess 992.1
overindulgent
unstrict 426.5
indulgent 427.8
intemperate 669.7
overjoyed 95.16
overkill
exaggeration 355.1
attack 459.1
plenty 990.2
overdoing 992.6
overland 234.8

out of practice 414.18
overthrow
  n overturn 205.2
  fall 395.3
  defeat 412.1
  deposal 447.2
  change 851.2
  revolution 859.1
  downthrow 912.2
  refutation 957.2
  v turn over 205.6
  revolt 327.7
  destroy 395.20
  overcome 412.7
  depose 447.4
  change 851.7
  revolutionize 859.4
  overturn 912.6
  refute 957.5
overthrown
  ruined 395.28
  defeated 412.14
  disproved 957.7
overtime
  basketball game 747.3
  hockey 749.3
  shift 824.3
overtire 21.4
overtired 21.11
overtone tone 50.2
  milieu 209.3
  meaning 518.1
  implication 519.2
  harmonics 709.16
overture
  n offer 439.1
  prelude 708.26
  curtain-raiser 815.2
  v make advances 439.7
overturn
  n upset 205.2
  fall 395.3
  defeat 412.1
  revolution 859.1
  downthrow 912.2
  v capsize 182.44
  turn over 205.6
  destroy 395.20
  overcome 412.7
  revolutionize 859.4
  overthrow 912.6
  refute 957.5
overvalue 948.2
overview
  scrutiny 27.6
  abridgment 557.1
overweening
  n presumptuousness 141.2
  insolence 142.1
  confidence 969.5
  adj vain 140.8
  presumptuous 141.10
  insolent 142.9
  rash 493.7
  confident 969.21
  excessive 992.16
overweight
  n oversize 257.5
  weight 297.1
  overfullness 992.3

v burden 297.13
  outweigh 297.14
  overload 992.15
  adj corpulent 257.18
  oversize 257.23
  heavy 297.16
overwhelm
  be strong 15.9
  drown out 53.8
  aggrieve 112.19
  astonish 122.6
  pervade 221.7
  overflow 238.17
  submerge 367.7
  destroy 395.21
  whelm 412.8
  subdue 432.9
  raid 459.20
  teem with 883.5
  run over 909.7
  refute 957.5
  oversupply 992.14
overwhelmed
  overwrought 105.26
  overcome 112.29
  wondering 122.9
  flooded 238.25
  defeated 412.14
  overrun 909.10
overwhelming
  n permeation 221.3
  overflow 238.6
  overrunning 909.1
  adj impregnable 15.19
  exciting 105.30
  astonishing 122.12
  irresistible 412.18
  teeming 883.9
  evidential 956.16
overwork
  n overdoing 992.6
  v work hard 725.13
  task 725.16
  overdo 992.10
overworked
  ornate 498.12
  trite 863.16
overwrought
  overexcited 105.26
  exaggerated 355.4
  ornate 498.12
  grandiloquent 545.8
  overdone 992.21
overzealous
  ultrazealous 101.12
  obstinate 361.8
  reckless 493.8
  zealous 692.11
  fanatic 925.32
ovine 311.44
oviparous 305.23
ovoid
  n oval 280.6
  adj oval 280.12
  spherical 282.9
ovule
  oval 280.6
  ovum 305.12
  egg 305.15
ovum egg 305.12
  vital force 885.7
  copulation 75.7

owe be indebted 623.5
  be liable 896.3
owed payable 623.10
  due 639.7
owing payable 623.10
  due 639.7
  attributable 887.6
owing to
  conj resulting from 886.8
  prep because of 887.9
owl bird of ill omen 133.6
  bird 311.28
owlish 570.17
own
  v acknowledge 332.11
  confess 351.7
  have title to 469.5
  adj possessed 469.8
own accord 430.7
owner proprietor 470.2
  jockey 757.2
ownership 469.2
own free will 430.7
owning
  n confession 351.3
  possession 469.1
  adj possessing 469.9
ox
  symbol of strength 15.8
  beast of burden 176.8
  cattle 311.6
  bungler 414.8
oxcart 179.3
oxidation decay 393.6
  burning 1019.5
oxidize corrode 393.21
  burn 1019.24
  chemicalize 1058.7
oxygenate air 317.10
  vaporize 1065.8
oxymoron
  ambiguity 539.1
  self-contradiction 778.3
  inconsistency 788.2
  impossibility 966.1
  dilemma 1012.7
oyez! hark! 48.16
  attention! 982.22
oyster
  fowl part 10.22
  marine animal 311.30
ozone 317.1
pa 560.10
PA
  sound reproduction system 50.11
  hospital staff 90.11
  practice of medicine 90.13
pabulum 10.3
pace
  n velocity 172.4
  step 177.11
  gait 177.12
  v lead 165.2
  walk 177.27
  walk back and forth 177.28

go on horseback 177.34
  row 182.53
  measure 300.10
pacer race horse 311.14
  jockey 757.2
pacesetter leader 574.6
  jockey 757.2
pachyderm 311.4
pacific
  quiescent 173.12
  meek 433.15
  peaceful 464.9
  unbelligerent 464.10
  pacificatory 465.12
pacification
  peacemaking 465.1
  truce 465.5
  modulation 670.2
pacifier
  sedative 86.12
  peacemaker 466.5
  moderator 670.3
pacifism inaction 329.1
  peaceableness 464.4
  moderation 670.1
pacifist
  n pacificist 464.6
  adj unbelligerent 464.10
pacifistic 670.10
pacify quiet 173.8
  conciliate 465.7
  calm 670.7
  order 806.4
pacifying
  pacificatory 465.12
  tranquilizing 670.15
pack
  n freight 176.6
  parachute 181.13
  amount 244.2
  lot 247.4
  stopping 293.5
  film 714.10
  card 758.2
  company 769.3
  group of animals 769.5
  bundle 769.8
  multitude 883.3
  impediment 1011.6
  v load 159.15
  transport 176.12
  fill 196.7
  package 212.9
  stop 293.7
  wrap 295.20
  tamper with 354.16
  assemble 769.18
  bundle 769.20
  stuff 793.7
  teem with 883.5
  prearrange 964.5
  overload 992.15
  obstruct 1011.12
package
  n packaging 212.2
  bundle 769.8
  all 791.3
  combination 804.1
  v pack 212.9

wrap 295.20
bundle 769.20
packaged
  packed 212.12
  covered 295.31
  assembled 769.21
package deal
  transaction 731.4
  all 791.3
  combination 804.1
package tour
  vacation 20.3
  journey 177.5
packaging 212.2
pack animal 176.8
pack away load 159.15
  store 386.10
packed
  packaged 212.12
  stopped 293.11
  tampered with 354.29
  crowded 769.22
  full 793.11
  stuck 854.16
  teeming 883.9
  prearranged 964.8
  overfull 992.20
  dense 1043.12
packet dose 87.19
  ship 180.1
  wealth 618.3
  bundle 769.8
packet boat 353.6
pack in enter 189.7
  thrust in 191.7
  assemble 769.18
  densify 1043.9
packing
  placement 159.6
  transportation 176.3
  lining 196.3
  packaging 212.2
  stopping 293.5
packinghouse 739.3
pack off repulse 907.3
  dismiss 908.18
pack of troubles 96.8
pack rat 769.15
pact 437.1
pad
  n thud 52.3
  foot 199.5
  partition 213.5
  quarters 228.4
  race horse 311.14
  print 517.7
  record book 549.11
  bedding 900.20
  safeguard 1007.3
  v thud 52.15
  relieve 120.5
  creep 177.26
  walk 177.27
  fill 196.7
  protract 538.8
  complete 793.7
  iterate 848.8
padded cell 925.14
padding
  creeping 177.17
  lining 196.3
  extra 254.4

stopping 293.5
redundancy 848.3
superfluity 992.4
safeguard 1007.3
softening 1045.5
paddle
  n gait 177.12
  oar 180.15
  rod 605.2
  agitator 916.9
  v way of walking
    177.28
  row 182.53
  punish 604.15
  agitate 916.10
  moisten 1063.12
paddle wheel
  gambling wheel
    759.16
  propeller 903.6
paddling 604.5
paddy 1067.9
Paddy 232.7
paddy wagon 179.11
padlock
  n lock 428.5
  v close 293.6
padre clergyman 699.2
  priest 699.5
padrone 575.1
paean cheer 116.2
  thanks 150.2
  praise 509.5
  laud 696.3
  sacred music 708.17
paella 10.11
paesano
  fellow citizen 227.5
  friend 588.4
pagan
  n heathen 688.7
  unbeliever 695.11
  adj paganish 688.11
  unbelieving 695.19
  idolatrous 697.7
  unlearned 929.14
paganism
  heathenism 688.4
  idolatry 697.1
  unenlightenment
    929.4
page
  n makeup 554.12
  attendant 577.5
  part of writing 792.2
  paper 1052.5
  v summon 420.11
  number 1016.16
pageant spectacle 33.7
  display 501.4
pageantry
  spectacle 33.7
  display 501.4
paginate 1016.16
pagination 1016.9
pagoda tower 272.6
  temple 703.2
paid
  employed 615.20
  paid-up 624.22
pain
  n bread 10.27

physical suffering 26
suffering 26.1
symptom 85.9
annoyance 96.2
distress 96.5
tormentor 96.10
distressfulness 98.5
v give pain 26.7
grieve 96.17
distress 98.14
pained in pain 26.9
  grieved 96.23
painful hurtful 26.10
  distressing 98.20
  laborious 725.18
  troublesome 1012.18
pain in the neck
  annoyance 96.2
  tormentor 96.10
  tedious person 118.5
pain killer
  sedative 86.12
  anesthetic 25.3
painless 1013.13
pains
  painstakingness 339.2
  punishment 604.1
  exertion 725.1
painstaking
  n painstakingness
    339.2
  adj diligent 339.11
paint
  n color 35.8
  blanket 295.12
  horse 311.11
  art equipment 712.18
  card 758.2
  makeup 1015.12
  v color 35.13
  represent 349.8
  describe 349.9
  ornament 498.8
  figure 498.9
  portray 712.19
  beautify 1015.15
paintbrush 712.18
painter wild cat 311.22
  artist 716.4
painting
  paint-work 35.12
  coloring 712.4
  canvas 712.14
  graphic arts 713.1
paint the town red
  go on a spree 88.28
  make merry 743.24
pair
  n rig 179.5
  set 783.5
  two 872.2
  deuce 872.3
  v assemble 769.18
  put together 799.5
  league 804.4
  double 872.5
  adj numeric 1016.22
paired married 563.21
  accompanying 768.9
  joined 799.13
  leagued 804.6
  coupled 872.8

pairing joining 799.1
  doubleness 872.1
pair off average 246.2
  get married 563.15
  league 804.4
  double 872.5
paisano 227.5
pajamas 5.21
pal
  n friend 588.4
  v associate with
    582.18
palace 228.7
palace revolution 859.1
paladin defender 460.7
  brave person 492.8
palaestra 463.1
palatable edible 8.33
  tasty 63.8
  desirable 100.30
palate taste 62.1
  taste bud 62.5
  vocal organ 524.19
  discrimination 943.1
palatial
  residential 228.32
  grandiose 501.21
palaver
  n flattery 511.1
  nonsense 520.2
  speech 524.1
  chatter 540.3
  talk 541.3
  conference 541.6
  v flatter 511.5
  chatter 540.5
  confer 541.11
palazzo 228.7
pale
  n bounds 211.1
  enclosed place 212.3
  sphere 231.2
  plot 231.4
  leg 273.6
  heraldry 647.2
  v blur 32.4
  decolor 36.5
  lose color 36.6
  change color 105.19
  take fright 127.11
  fence 212.7
  adj inconspicuous
    32.6
  soft-colored 35.21
  colorless 36.7
  whitish 37.8
  unhealthy 85.53
  dull 117.6
  deathly 307.29
paleface 312.3
paleography
  exegetics 341.8
  linguistics 523.12
  writing system 546.3
  handwriting 547.3
paleolith 841.6
paleolithic 841.20
palette 712.18
palindrome
  grammar 205.3
  wordplay 489.8
palinode 363.3

palisade
  n precipice 200.3
  fence 212.4
  slope 237.2
  leg 273.6
  v fence 212.7
  fortify 460.9
pall
  n cover 295.2
  graveclothes 309.14
  veil of secrecy 345.3
  v be tedious 118.6
  satiate 993.4
palladium 1007.3
pallbearer 309.7
pallet 900.20
palliate relieve 120.5
  extenuate 600.12
  moderate 670.6
  qualify 958.3
palliative
  n alleviative 86.10
  extenuation 600.5
  moderator 670.3
  adj lenitive 86.40
  relieving 120.9
  justifying 600.13
  alleviative 670.16
  qualifying 958.7
pallid colorless 36.7
  dull 117.6
  terrified 127.26
pallor color 35.1
  paleness 36.2
  dullness 117.1
  deathliness 307.12
palm
  n clutches 474.4
  trophy 646.3
  v touch 73.6
  take 480.13
  steal 482.13
palmate 171.8
palmistry 961.2
palm off on 643.7
palm oil
  incentive 375.7
  gratuity 478.5
palmy 1009.13
palooka fighter 461.2
  boxer 754.2
  jockey 757.2
palp 73.4
palpable
  touchable 73.11
  weighable 297.19
  manifest 348.8
  substantial 762.6
palpate 73.6
palpitant staccato 55.7
  pulsative 915.18
palpitate drum 55.4
  be excited 105.18
  pulsate 915.12
  flutter 916.12
palpitating 915.18
palpitation
  staccato 55.1
  excitement 105.5
  trepidation 127.5
  pulsation 915.3
  flutter 916.4

palsied
  anemic 85.60
  stricken in years
    303.18
  shaking 916.17
palsy
  n paralysis 85.27
  shaking 916.2
  v deaden 25.4
  adj chummy 587.20
palsy-walsy
  n friend 588.4
  v befriend 587.11
  adj chummy 587.20
palter
  prevaricate 344.7
  quibble 935.9
paltry
  ungenerous 651.6
  base 661.12
  meager 991.10
  poor 997.21
  inferior 1004.9
paludal 243.3
pampas plain 236.1
  grassland 310.8
pamper
  indulge 427.6
  foster 449.16
pampering 427.3
pamphlet 554.11
pan
  n container 195.1
  face 216.4
  v cook 11.4
  criticize 510.14
  photograph 714.14
  mine 1056.14
Pan
  forest god 678.11
  fertility 889.5
panacea 86.3
panache feather 3.16
  showiness 501.3
pancake
  n griddlecake 10.43
  v land 184.43
panchromatic 714.17
pancreas viscera 2.14
  digestive organ 2.15
  digestion 7.8
pancreatic 13.8
pandect
  treatise 556.1
  abridgment 557.1
  code 673.5
pandemic
  n epidemic 85.5
  adj contagious 85.61
  prevalent 863.12
pandemonium
  noise 53.3
  turbulence 671.2
Pandemonium
  hell 682.1
  utopia 985.11
pander
  n procurer 665.18
  v vulgarize 497.9
  prostitute oneself
    665.21
pandering 665.8

pander to
  toady to 138.8
  aid 449.18
  serve 577.13
pandit 571.1
Pandora's box
  affliction 96.8
  trouble 1012.3
pandowdy 10.39
pane
  bread 10.27
  window 292.7
  lamina 296.2
  transparent substance
    1028.2
panegyric
  n praise 509.5
  adj approbatory
    509.16
panel
  n partition 213.5
  lamina 296.2
  forum 423.3
  discussion 541.7
  jury 596.6
  litigant 598.11
  assembly 769.2
  v select a jury 598.15
paneling 1052.3
panelist 543.4
panel show 1034.2
pang throe 26.2
  pain 96.5
  compunction 113.2
panhandle 440.15
panhandler
  nonworker 331.11
  beggar 440.8
panhandling 440.6
panic
  n fear 127.1
  nervousness 128.1
  joke 489.6
  bear panic 737.22
  v start 127.12
  put in fear 127.16
  overwhelm 412.8
panicked
  panicky 127.27
  defeated 412.14
panicky
  panic-prone 127.27
  nervous 128.11
  cowardly 491.10
panning
  n ridicule 508.1
  adj ridiculing 508.12
panoply armor 460.3
  throng 769.4
panorama view 33.6
  spectacle 33.7
  picture 712.11
panoramic 771.7
pan out 886.4
pan shot 714.8
pansy weakling 16.6
  homosexual 75.15
pant
  n breathing 2.19
  v burn out 21.5
  be excited 105.18
  speak 524.26

  be hot 1018.22
Pantaloon
  old man 304.2
  buffoon 707.10
pantheism
  religion 675.5
  philosophy 951.4
pantheistic 675.25
pantheon
  the gods 678.1
  temple 703.2
panther 311.22
panting
  n breathlessness 21.3
  trepidation 105.5
  adj respiratory 2.30
  breathless 21.12
  eager 101.8
  precipitate 401.10
pantomime
  n impersonation 349.4
  gesture 517.14
  actor 707.2
  v impersonate 349.12
  gesture 517.21
  act 704.29
pantry closet 197.15
  larder 386.8
pants 5.18
pantywaist
  weakling 16.6
  effeminate male 77.10
pap diet 7.11
  nutriment 10.3
  breast 283.6
  father 560.10
  semiliquid 1060.5
papa 560.10
papacy
  mastership 417.7
  papality 698.6
papal 698.15
Papal Court 595.3
papalism 675.8
paper
  n whiteness 37.2
  thinness 270.7
  writing 547.10
  document 549.5
  newspaper 555.2
  treatise 556.1
  complimentary ticket
    634.2
  negotiable instrument
    728.11
  paper stock 1052.5
  v face 295.23
paperback 554.3
paper profits 472.3
papers
  naturalization 226.3
  archives 549.2
paper tiger 500.7
paperweight 297.6
papery
  frail 16.14
  thin 270.16
  wasted 393.35
  fragile 763.7
papilla 283.6
papillary 283.19
papilloma 283.3

papist
n Catholic 675.19
adj Catholic 675.29
papal 698.15
papoose 302.9
pappose 3.25
pappy
n father 560.10
adj insipid 65.2
papyrus 547.11
par
n mean 246.1
price 738.9
round 751.3
equality 789.1
v golf 751.4
adj equal 789.7
parabola 279.2
parabolical
parabolic 279.13
fictional 722.7
parachute
n chute 181.13
life preserver 397.6
safeguard 1007.3
v bail out 184.47
descend 194.5
plunge 367.6
parachute jump
parachute 181.13
plunge 367.1
parachutist 185.8
parade
n spectacle 33.7
walk 177.10
path 383.2
display 501.4
procession 811.3
v go for a walk 177.29
march 177.30
manifest 348.5
flaunt 501.17
file 811.7
parade ground 463.1
paradiddle 55.1
paradigm
morphology 526.3
model 785.1
paradisal
blissful 97.9
heavenly 681.12
ideal 985.23
paradise
observation 27.8
happiness 95.2
preserve 397.7
auditorium 704.15
park 743.14
utopia 985.11
garden 1067.10
Paradise 838.2
paradisiac blissful 97.9
heavenly 681.12
paradox
self-contradiction
778.3
inconsistency 788.2
impossibility 966.1
dilemma 1012.7
paradoxical
self-contradictory
778.8

inconsistent 788.8
impossible 966.7
paradoxical sleep 22.5
paraffin 1024.20
paragon superior 249.4
ideal 659.4
model 785.4
the best 998.8
pattern of perfection
1001.4
beauty 1015.8
paragraph
n phrase 529.1
part 554.13
treatise 556.1
part of writing 792.2
v diction 532.4
parallel
n map 159.5
paralleler 203.2
zone 231.3
entrenchment 460.5
likeness 783.3
equal 789.4
v be parallel 203.4
relate 774.6
resemble 783.7
agree 787.6
equal 789.5
compare 942.4
be comparable 942.7
adj paralleling 203.6
side 218.6
accompanying 768.9
related 774.9
analogous 783.11
comparative 942.8
parallel bars 725.7
paralleling
parallel 203.6
analogous 783.11
parallelism
alignment 203
coextension 203.1
side 218.1
symmetry 264.1
accompaniment 768.1
similarity 783.1
agreement 787.1
equality 789.1
comparison 942.1
paralogism
syllogism 934.6
specious argument
935.3
paralysis
symptom 85.9
paralyzation 85.27
inaction 329.1
paralytic
n cripple 85.44
adj anemic 85.60
passive 329.6
paralyze disable 19.10
deaden 25.4
numb 94.8
astonish 122.6
terrify 127.17
paralyzed
disabled 19.16
drunk 88.33
terrified 127.26

passive 329.6
paramedic
hospital staff 90.11
parachutist 185.8
diver 367.4
parameter
measure 300.2
condition 958.2
paramount
n master 575.1
potentate 575.8
chief 996.10
adj top 198.10
chief 249.14
governing 612.18
principal 996.24
best 998.16
paramountcy
supremacy 249.3
importance 996.1
superexcellence 998.2
paramour lover 104.12
mistress 665.17
paranoia
mental disorder 92.14
dissociation 92.20
schizophrenia 925.4
paranoid
n psychotic 925.17
adj psychotic 925.28
paranymph
wedding party 563.4
deputy 576.1
assistant 616.6
parapet 1011.5
paraphernalia
equipment 385.4
belongings 471.2
paraphilia 75.11
paraphrase
n reproduction 336.3
translation 341.3
v imitate 336.5
rephrase 341.13
paraplegia 85.27
paraplegic 85.44
paraprofessional
teaching fellow 571.4
assistant 616.6
parapsychology 689.4
parasite
barnacle 138.5
follower 166.2
plant 310.4
vermin 311.35
bloodsucker 311.36
nonworker 331.11
attendance 768.6
parasitic
obsequious 138.14
indolent 331.19
rapacious 480.26
concurrent 898.4
parasitism
obsequiousness 138.2
concurrence 898.1
parasol
umbrella 295.7
shade 1027.1
paratrooper
parachutist 185.8
diver 367.4

paratroops
elite troops 461.15
army 461.23
parboiled 11.6
Parcae 963.3
parcel
n amount 244.2
real estate 471.6
bundle 769.8
part 792.1
a number 883.2
v package 212.9
quantify 244.4
apportion 477.6
portion out 477.8
bundle 769.20
separate 801.18
dispose 807.9
parceled packed 212.12
apportioned 477.12
parceling 477.1
parcel of land
plot 231.4
field 1067.9
parch shrink 260.9
be hot 1018.22
burn 1019.24
dry 1064.6
parched thirsty 100.26
shrunk 260.13
burned 1019.30
dried 1064.9
parchment
writing 547.10
manuscript 547.11
document 549.5
fragility 1048.2
dryness 1064.2
pardner friend 588.4
partner 616.2
pardon
n pity 145.1
excuse 148.2
acquittal 601.1
v have pity 145.4
forgive 148.3
acquit 601.4
pardonable 600.14
pare peel 6.8
reduce 252.7
excise 255.10
cheapen 633.6
sever 801.11
paregoric
n sedative 86.12
adj sedative 86.45
parent
n progenitor 560.8
author 885.4
v foster 449.16
adj ancestral 560.17
parentage 560.1
parental
loving 104.27
ancestral 560.17
protective 1007.23
parenthesis
grammar 205.3
interjection 213.2
discontinuity 812.1
parenthesize
bracket 212.8

grammaticize 530.16
parenthetical
  interjectional 213.9
  irrelevant 775.7
  incidental 842.11
paresis 85.27
par excellence 249.16
parfait 10.45
par for the course
  n rule 373.5
  predetermination
    963.1
  adj medium 246.3
  typical 349.15
  prevalent 863.12
parfum 70.2
parget
  color 35.13
  plaster 295.25
pariah
  recluse 584.5
  outcast 586.4
  oddity 869.4
parietal
  enclosing 212.11
  partitioned 213.11
parietes 213.5
pari-mutuel
  statistics 757.4
  betting system 759.4
  pari-mutuel machine
    759.17
paring flake 296.3
  piece 792.3
parish region 231.5
  diocese 698.8
  the laity 700.1
parishioner 700.2
parity price 738.9
  similarity 783.1
  equality 789.1
park
  n enclosed place 212.3
  green 310.7
  grassland 310.8
  woodland 310.11
  preserve 397.7
  armory 462.2
  public park 743.14
  baseball 745.1
  v place 159.12
  settle 159.17
parlance
  language 523.1
  diction 532.1
parlay
  n bet 759.3
  v increase 251.4
  bet 759.25
parley
  n advice 422.1
  peace offer 465.2
  conference 541.6
  v confer 541.11
parliament 613.1
parliamentarianism
  612.8
parliamentary
  n train 179.14
  adj governmental
    612.17
  legislative 613.11

parlor
  living room 197.5
  workplace 739.1
parlor car 197.10
parlous 1005.9
parochial
  local 231.9
  exclusive 772.9
  narrow-minded
    979.10
parochialism
  exclusiveness 772.3
  narrow-mindedness
    979.1
parochial school 567.8
parody
  n imitation 336.1
  reproduction 336.3
  bad likeness 350.2
  wit 489.1
  burlesque 508.6
  v imitate 336.5
  misrepresent 350.3
  burlesque 508.11
  lampoon 512.12
parol
  n utterance 524.3
  adj speech 524.30
parole
  n release 431.2
  promise 436.1
  language 523.1
  utterance 524.3
  v release 431.5
parolee 429.11
paroxysm pang 26.2
  seizure 85.6
  outburst 105.9
  fit 152.8
  upheaval 671.5
  spasm 916.6
  frenzy 925.7
parquet check 47.4
  ground covering 199.3
  auditorium 704.15
parrot
  n tedium 118.1
  imitator 336.4
  conformist 866.2
  v mimic 336.6
  repeat 848.7
  memorize 988.17
parrotlike
  tedious 118.9
  imitative 336.9
  diffuse 538.11
  repetitious 848.14
parrotry 336.2
parry prevaricate 344.7
  dodge 368.8
  fend off 460.10
  fight 754.4
  quibble 935.9
  refute 957.5
  prevent 1011.14
parrying
  prevarication 344.4
  fight 754.3
  quibbling 935.5
parse
  grammaticize 530.16
  itemize 800.7

parsimonious
  sparing 484.7
  economical 635.6
  meager 991.10
parsimony
  frugality 484
  parsimoniousness
    484.1
  thrift 635.1
  meagerness 991.2
parsing grammar 530.1
  itemization 800.2
parson 699.2
parsonage house 228.5
  pastorage 703.7
part
  n contents 196.1
  region 231.1
  amount 244.2
  a length 267.2
  function 387.5
  estate 471.4
  apportioning 477.5
  section 554.13
  role 704.10
  melody part 708.22
  passage 708.24
  score 708.28
  occupation 724.3
  mode 764.4
  particular 765.3
  portion 792.1
  component 795.2
  v interspace 224.3
  open 292.11
  die 307.19
  apportion 477.6
  divorce 566.5
  disband 770.8
  separate 801.8
  part company 801.19
  adj partial 792.7
  incomplete 794.4
  half 874.5
  adv limited 248.10
  partly 792.8
partake eat 8.20
  participate 476.5
  take 480.13
  be involved 897.3
partaking
  n participation 476.1
  association 582.6
  adj participating
    476.8
part and parcel 795.2
parterre 704.15
parthenogenesis 78.6
parthenogenetic 78.16
Parthian shot
  leave-taking 188.4
  gibe 508.2
  remark 524.4
  sequel 816.1
partial
  n tone 50.2
  adj partisan 617.19
  interested 650.11
  part 792.7
  incomplete 794.4
  half 874.5
  discriminatory 979.12

imperfect 1002.4
partiality
  inclination 100.3
  love 104.1
  preference 371.5
  partisanism 617.13
  one-sidedness 650.3
  prejudice 979.3
partial to
  desirous of 100.22
  fond of 104.30
partible 801.26
participant
  n participator 476.4
  adj participating
    476.8
participate
  take part 476.5
  be involved 897.3
participating 476.8
participation
  partaking 476.1
  association 582.6
  inclusion 771.1
participator 476.4
participial 530.17
participle 530.3
particle
  modicum 248.2
  minute 258.7
  part of speech 530.3
  piece 792.3
  powder 1049.5
parti-color
  n variegation 47.1
  v variegate 47.7
  adj variegated 47.9
particular
  n instance 765.3
  part 792.1
  event 830.2
  citation 956.5
  adj meticulous 339.12
  selective 371.23
  proportionate 477.13
  fastidious 495.9
  detailed 765.9
  classificational 808.7
  special 864.12
particularity
  meticulousness 339.3
  fastidiousness 495.1
  circumstantiality
    765.4
  uniqueness 864
  individuality 864.1
  characteristic 864.4
  oneness 871.1
particularization
  description 349.2
  circumstantiation
    765.5
  differentiation 779.4
  specialization 864.7
  reasoning 934.3
particularize
  amplify 538.7
  itemize 765.6
  differentiate 779.6
  specialize 864.9
  cite 956.13
  be accurate 972.11

parting
n departure 188.1
leave-taking 188.4
death 307.1
disbandment 770.3
separation 801.1
adj departing 188.18
separating 801.25

parting shot
leave-taking 188.4
gibe 508.2
sequel 816.1

partisan
n follower 166.2
irregular 461.16
friend 588.1
party member 609.27
supporter 616.9
adj polarizing 456.17
party 609.44
supporting 617.19
partial 650.11
discriminatory 979.12

partisanism
politics 609.1
partisanship 609.25
association 617.13
partiality 650.3
sectarianism 675.4

partisan politics 609.1

partition
n dividing wall 213.5
apportionment 477.1
separation 801.1
bisector 874.3
v set apart 213.8
apportion 477.6
diversify 781.2
separate 801.18

partitioned
walled 213.11
separate 801.20

part music 708.18

partner
n participator 476.4
spouse 563.6
companion 588.3
associate 616.2
bridge 758.3
accompanier 768.4
v cooperate 450.3
assemble 769.18
league 804.4

partner in crime 616.3

partnership
affiliation 450.2
participation 476.1
bar 597.4
association 617.1
company 768.2

part of speech 530.3

parts talent 413.4
substance 762.2
wits 918.2

part time 824.3

part-time 847.3

parturient
pregnant 78.18
beginning 817.15

parturition birth 1.1
origin 817.4

part with discard 390.7

relinquish 475.3
give away 478.21

party
n man 76.5
endorser 332.7
telephoner 347.11
participator 476.4
entertainment 582.11
litigant 598.11
accuser 599.5
political party 609.24
interest 617.4
sect 675.3
festival 743.4
revel 743.6
assembly 769.2
company 769.3
support 900.1
v enjoy oneself 95.13
have a party 582.21
dissipate 669.6
adj partisan 609.44
associating 617.19

party hack
partisan 609.27
politician 610.4

party line
line 347.17
policy 609.4

par value worth 630.2
price 738.9

parvenu
n vulgarian 497.6
upstart 606.7
rich man 618.7
modern 840.4
adj populational 606.8

pashadom
mastership 417.7
aristocracy 608.9

pass
n ridge 237.5
valley 237.7
narrow place 270.3
ravine 284.9
trick 356.6
passageway 383.3
proposal 439.2
passport 443.7
thrust 459.3
complimentary ticket 634.2
football 746.3
basketball game 747.3
hockey 749.3
hockey game 749.6
soccer 752.3
bridge 758.3
state 764.1
crisis 842.4
circuit 913.2
danger 1005.1
predicament 1012.4
v excrete 12.12
disappear 34.2
progress 162.2
overtake 174.13
transmit 176.10
travel 177.18
average 246.2
outdistance 249.10
die 307.19

ratify 332.12
communicate 343.7
adopt 371.15
spend 387.13
pass away 390.9
perish 395.23
succeed 409.7
promote 446.2
deliver 478.13
bequeath 478.18
not understand 522.11
legislate 613.10
transfer 629.4
change hands 629.4
football 746.5
basketball 747.4
hockey 749.7
soccer 752.4
bet 759.25
cease to exist 761.6
come to an end 819.6
elapse 820.5
flit 827.6
occur 830.5
be past 836.6
throw 903.10
go by 909.8
not know 929.11
stand the test 941.10
suffice 990.4
exceed 992.9
excel 998.11

passable
acceptable 107.12
tolerable 998.20
mediocre 1004.7

passage duct 2.21
progression 162.1
course 172.2
transferal 176.1
travel 177.1
migration 177.4
voyage 182.6
entrance 189.5
corridor 197.18
valley 237.7
channel 239.1
act 328.3
passageway 383.3
part 554.13
excerpt 557.3
legislation 613.5
phrase 708.24
ornament 709.18
part of writing 792.2
conversion 857.1

passageway
n entrance 189.5
corridor 197.18
channel 239.1
opening 292.1
pass 383.3
inter open up! 292.23

pass away 34.2

passbook 628.4

pass by slight 157.6
reject 372.2
be inattentive 983.2

passé past 836.7
obsolete 841.15

passed chosen 371.26
past 836.7

passenger 178.1

passerby traveler 178.1
transient 827.4
spectator 917.1
witness 956.6

pass for go for 349.10
impersonate 349.12
pose as 354.21

passim
here and there 159.25
scatteringly 770.12

passing
n disappearance 34.1
departure 188.1
death 307.1
promotion 446.1
legislation 613.5
basketball game 747.3
hockey 749.3
adj vanishing 34.3
flowing 172.8
traveling 177.36
medium 246.3
hasty 401.9
transient 827.7
happening 830.9
adv awesomely 122.15

passing by
n rejection 372.1
adj spectating 917.7
prep through 161.27

passing fancy
infatuation 104.4
caprice 364.1

passion
sexual desire 75.5
passionateness 93.2
pain 96.5
torment 96.7
desire 100.1
liking 100.2
zeal 101.2
love 104.1
fury 105.8
rage 152.10
will 323.1
vehemence 544.5
turbulence 671.2
sacred music 708.17
cause 885.9
mania 925.12
interest 982.2

passionate lustful 75.26
fervent 93.18
zealous 101.9
amorous 104.26
heated 105.22
fiery 105.29
hot-tempered 110.25
vehement 544.13
turbulent 671.22
interested 982.16

passionless
unfeeling 94.9
undesirous 102.8

passive
n voice 530.14
adj apathetic 94.13
resigned 134.10
inert 173.14
inactive 329.6
submissive 433.12

neutral 467.7
thoughtless 932.4
incurious 981.3
passive resistance
resignation 134.2
disobedience 327.1
inaction 329.1
resistance 453.1
passivity apathy 94.4
resignation 134.2
quiescence 173.1
inertness 173.4
inaction 329.1
languor 331.6
submission 433.1
thoughtlessness 932.1
incuriosity 981.1
passkey 292.10
pass muster
meet with approval
509.15
follow the rule 866.4
stand the test 941.10
suffice 990.4
pass out faint 25.5
disappear 34.2
be drunk 88.27
exit 190.12
die 307.20
issue 352.14
deliver 478.13
disperse 770.4
Passover 701.18
pass over
condone 148.4
consign 176.10
traverse 177.20
die 307.19
neglect 340.6
leave undone 340.7
slight 340.8
deliver 478.13
transfer 629.3
exclude 772.4
pass 909.8
examine 937.23
be inattentive 983.2
passport 443.7
pass the buck
transfer 176.10
outwit 415.11
impose on 643.7
be unfaithful 645.12
pass the hat 440.15
pass the time
waste time 331.13
occupy 724.10
vegetate 760.10
pass through
traverse 177.20
penetrate 189.8
experience 830.8
pass up slight 157.6
leave undone 340.7
reject 372.2
abstain 668.7
password 517.12
past
n tense 530.12
the past 836.1
adj gone 836.7
preterit 836.9

former 836.10
obsolete 841.15
prep beyond 261.21
unintelligible 522.26
after 834.8
in excess of 992.26
pasta 10.32
past due 832.3
paste
n noodles 10.32
fake 354.13
finery 498.3
jewelry 498.5
compound 796.5
adhesive 802.4
blow 901.5
semiliquid 1060.5
pulp 1061.2
v defeat 412.9
stick together 802.9
strike 901.15
pound 901.16
pastel
n softness 35.3
drawing 712.13
art equipment 712.18
adj soft-colored 35.21
pasteurization 79.3
pasteurize 79.24
pasteurized 79.27
pastiche
n imitation 336.1
reproduction 336.3
adoption 621.2
work of art 712.10
similarity 783.1
copy 784.1
hodgepodge 796.6
v imitate 336.5
pastille 70.4
pastime
avocation 724.7
amusement 743.1
past master
master 413.13
producer 891.7
pastor 699.2
pastoral
n scene 712.12
adj rustic 233.6
natural 416.6
pacific 464.9
ecclesiastic 698.13
poetic 720.15
pastoral staff
staff 273.2
ecclesiastical insignia
647.4
attire 702.3
pastorate
the ministry 698.1
parsonage 703.7
protectorship 1007.2
pastrami 10.13
pastry 10.39
pasturage feed 10.4
grassland 310.8
pasture
n eating 8.1
feed 10.4
grassland 310.8
farm 1067.8

v feed 8.18
pasty colorless 36.7
doughy 1045.12
viscous 1060.12
pulpy 1061.6
pat
n thud 52.3
lump 257.10
endearment 562.5
tap 901.7
v thud 52.15
caress 562.16
tap 901.18
adj apt 787.10
immovable 854.15
known 927.26
patch
n spottiness 47.3
plot 231.4
scrap 248.3
mark 517.5
military insignia
647.5
stain 1003.3
ray 1024.5
field 1067.9
v do carelessly 340.9
repair 396.14
patch test 91.15
patch up
do carelessly 340.9
remedy 396.13
repair 396.14
settle 466.7
patchwork check 47.4
hodgepodge 796.6
patchy spotted 47.13
shabby 393.32
incomplete 794.4
mixed 796.14
discontinuous 812.4
irregular 850.3
imperfect 1002.4
pate head 198.6
brain 918.6
pâté 10.20
patent
n copyright 210.3
exemption 430.8
permission 443.1
grant 443.5
privilege 642.2
church 703.10
safeguard 1007.3
v limit 210.5
preserve 397.8
authorize 443.11
protect 1007.18
adj distinct 31.7
manifest 348.8
obvious 969.15
patented limited 210.7
authorized 443.17
protected 1007.21
patent medicine
nostrum 86.2
medicine 86.4
pater father 560.9
ancestor 560.10
paterfamilias
father 560.9
master 575.1

paternal loving 104.27
ancestral 560.17
paternalism 612.9
paternity
blood relationship
559.1
fatherhood 560.2
Paternoster 696.4
path deviation 164.1
airway 184.33
way 383
route 383.1
trail 383.2
track 517.8
circuit 1031.4
pathetic affecting 93.22
distressing 98.20
pitiful 145.8
paltry 997.21
pathfinder
traveler 178.1
preparer 405.5
precursor 815.1
pathogen 85.41
pathogenic
unhealthful 82.5
disease-causing 85.52
pathological
unwholesome 85.54
diseased 85.59
pathology 85.1
pathos sympathy 93.5
distressfulness 98.5
sadness 112.1
pity 145.1
pathway 383.2
patience
inexcitability 106.1
forbearance 134
patientness 134.1
forgiveness 148.1
perseverance 360.1
leniency 427.1
tolerance 978.4
patient
n sick person 85.42
subject 941.7
adj inexcitable 106.10
armed with patience
134.9
forgiving 148.6
persevering 360.8
lenient 427.7
tolerant 978.11
patina verdigris 44.2
polish 287.2
lamina 296.2
patinate 44.3
patio 197.21
pâtisserie 10.39
pâtissier 11.2
patois dialect 523.7
jargon 523.9
pat on the back
n congratulation
149.1
encouragement 492.9
v comfort 121.6
motivate 375.21
encourage 492.16
compliment 509.14
patria 232.2

patriarch
old man 304.2
father 560.9
master 575.1
clergy 699.9
back number 841.8
patriarchal
aged 303.16
ancestral 560.17
governmental 612.17
primitive 841.11
patrician
n aristocrat 607.4
nobleman 608.4
adj upper-class 607.10
noble 608.10
patrilineage 559.1
patrilineal 559.6
patrimony 479.2
patriot 591.3
patriotic 591.4
patriotism 591.2
patrol
n protection 1007.1
watchman 1007.10
v traverse 177.20
watch 1007.20
patrol car 179.11
patrolman
watchman 1007.10
policeman 1007.15
patron
ship's officer 183.7
attender 221.5
provider 385.6
giver 478.11
master 575.1
benefactor 592.1
associate 616.9
supporter 704.26
financer 729.9
customer 733.4
protector 1007.5
patronage
fosterage 449.4
recommendation 509.4
political patronage 609.36
custom 731.6
market 733.3
protectorship 1007.2
patronize
condescend 137.8
give oneself airs 141.8
sponsor 449.15
finance 729.15
trade with 731.16
patronizing
n arrogance 141.1
adj arrogant 141.9
patroon 575.1
patsy dupe 358.2
cheater 759.22
scapegoat 861.3
trusting soul 953.4
patter
n thud 52.3
staccato 55.1
rain 316.1
jargon 523.9
acting 704.8

sales talk 734.5
v thud 52.15
drum 55.4
rain 316.9
speak 523.16
talk 524.20
chatter 540.5
act 704.29
pound 901.16
pattern gestalt 92.32
form 262.1
structure 266.1
measure 300.2
behavior 321.1
original 337.2
habit 373.4
diagram 381.3
motif 498.7
paragon 659.4
harmonics 709.11
essence 766.2
model 785.1
philosophy 931.2
paucity fewness 884.1
scarcity 991.3
Paul 684.2
paunch 2.16
paunchy 257.18
pauper 619.4
pauperism 619.2
pauperize 619.6
pauperized
indigent 619.8
ill-provided 991.12
pause
n respite 20.2
demur 325.2
juncture 524.10
hiatus 524.10
notation 709.12
rest 709.21
interruption 812.2
interim 825.1
delay 845.2
ceasing 856.3
grammar 856.4
v take a rest 20.8
demur 325.4
hesitate 362.7
intervene 825.3
cease 856.9
pave 295.22
paved 295.31
pavement
ground covering 199.3
rug 295.9
paving 383.6
foundation 900.6
building material 1052.2
pave the way
prepare the way 405.12
facilitate 1013.7
pavilion 228.9
paw
n member 2.7
foot 199.5
v touch 73.6
pawky
cunning 415.12
shrewd 919.15

pawn
n inferior 250.2
instrument 384.4
pledge 438.2
chessman 743.17
v pledge 438.10
borrow 621.3
pawnbroker
lender 620.3
lending institution 620.4
broker 730.9
pawnshop 620.4
paw print 517.7
pax
n peace 464.1
inter silence! 51.14
pax vobiscum
farewell! 188.22
peace! 464.11
pay
n punishment 604.1
payment 624.4
v do 328.6
avail 387.17
be profitable 472.13
requite 506.5
punish 604.11
render 624.10
spend 626.5
yield 627.4
overpay 632.8
experience 830.8
payable owed 623.10
due 639.7
pay as you go 624.17
pay a visit 582.19
pay back
compensate 338.4
make restitution 481.5
requite 506.5
repay 624.11
interchange 862.4
pay COD 624.17
pay damages 481.5
payday 624.4
pay dearly 632.8
pay dirt 1056.7
payee 479.3
payer 624.9
pay heed 982.8
pay homage to
show respect for 155.5
worship 696.10
pay in full 624.13
pay in kind 624.11
pay lip service 693.4
payload freight 176.6
load 196.2
charge 462.16
rocket 1072.3
paymaster
payer 624.9
treasurer 729.11
payment
incentive 375.7
punishment 604.1
defrayal 624
paying 624.1
pay 624.4
expenditure 626.1

pay no mind
not think 932.2
be inattentive 983.2
pay off
bring off the wind 182.23
drift off course 182.29
bribe 378.3
avail 387.17
be profitable 472.13
requite 506.5
pay in full 624.13
yield 627.4
payoff 766.3
payola 378.2
pay one's debt to society 429.18
pay one's dues
do one's duty 641.10
atone 658.4
pay one's respects 504.12
pay out
parcel out 477.8
punish 604.11
settle with 624.12
fork out 624.14
spend 626.5
pay phone 347.4
pay respect to 155.5
payroll 624.4
pay the bill
pay in full 624.13
pay for 624.18
treat 624.19
pay the penalty 658.4
pay the piper
take one's punishment 604.21
pay for 624.18
pay through the nose 632.8
pay tribute
praise 509.12
honor 646.8
pay TV 1034.1
pay up
contribute 478.14
pay in full 624.13
pay 624.16
PBX 347.8
PBX operator 347.9
PC 1041.2
PCP 87.17
PDQ
in short order 174.19
promptly 844.15
pea 310.4
peabrain 923.4
peace silence 51.1
drugs 87.17
comfortableness 121.2
quiescence 173.1
accord 455.1
peacefulness 464
pax 464.1
truce 465.5
agreement 787.1
order 806.1
peace and quiet 464.2
peace be with you!
farewell! 188.22

peace! 464.11
peaceful calm 106.12
 comfortable 121.11
 quiescent 173.12
 homelike 228.33
 in accord 455.3
 pacific 464.9
 moderate 670.10
peaceful coexistence
 peaceableness 464.4
 foreign policy 609.5
peace-keeping force
 465.1
peacemaker
 pacifist 464.6
 make-peace 466.5
 moderator 670.3
peace offering
 peace offer 465.2
 gift 478.4
 atonement 658.1
 oblation 696.7
peace officer 1007.15
peace of mind
 composure 106.2
 contentment 107.1
 peace of heart 464.3
peace pipe pipe 89.6
 peace offer 465.2
peach
 n first-rate 998.7
 beauty 1015.9
 v betray 351.6
 inform on 551.13
 adj orange 42.2
peaches-and-cream
 35.21
peach fuzz beard 3.8
 smoothness 294.3
peachy feathery 3.27
 excellent 998.13
peacock
 n variegation 47.6
 male animal 76.8
 bird 311.28
 strutter 501.10
 v pose 500.13
 strut 501.15
peak
 n summit 198.2
 highland 237.1
 mountain 237.6
 wave 238.14
 plateau 272.4
 projection 285.4
 speech sound 524.13
 business cycle 731.9
 limit 793.5
 acme of perfection
  1001.3
 v fail 85.47
 top 198.9
 billow 238.22
peaked
 unhealthy 85.53
 topped 198.12
 thin 270.20
peal
 n blare 53.5
 ringing 54.3
 boom 56.4
 v din 53.7

blare 53.10
 ring 54.8
 boom 56.9
peanut 258.4
peanut gallery
 observation post 27.8
 auditorium 704.15
peanuts
 petty cash 728.19
 trivia 997.4
pearl
 n whiteness 37.2
 drop 282.3
 good person 659.1
 good thing 998.5
 adj whitish 37.8
 gray 39.4
pearl diver 367.4
Pearl Harbor 459.2
pearly
 soft-colored 35.21
 whitish 37.8
 gray 39.4
 variegated 47.10
 iridescent 1024.37
pearly gates 87.9
pear-shaped 279.14
peasant
 vulgarian 497.6
 countryman 606.6
 agriculturist
  1067.5
peas in a pod 783.5
pea soup 319.2
peat bog 243.1
peat moss 889.4
pebble
 n modicum 248.2
 pebblestone 1057.4
 v floor 295.22
pebbled
 granular 1049.12
 stony 1057.11
peccadillo 655.2
peck
 n quantity 247.3
 lot 247.4
 tap 901.7
 v pick 8.26
 tap 901.18
pecking order 808.4
pectoral 283.19
peculiar
 personal 312.15
 indicative 517.23
 other 779.8
 differentiative 779.9
 classificational 808.7
 characteristic 864.13
 odd 869.11
 eccentric 926.5
peculiarity habit 373.4
 mannerism 500.2
 sign 517.1
 characteristic 864.4
 oddity 869.3
 eccentricity 926.1
pecuniary 728.30
pedagogical
 scholastic 568.19
 pedagogic 571.11
pedagogy 568.1

pedal
 n lever 905.4
 v ride 177.33
 push 903.9
 adj plantar 199.9
peddle 734.9
peddler 730.5
peddling 734.2
pedestal 900.8
pedestrian
 n walker 178.6
 adj dull 117.6
 traveling 177.36
 unskillful 414.15
 prosaic 721.5
pediatric 90.15
pedigree register 549.9
 genealogy 560.5
pee
 n urine 12.5
 v urinate 12.14
peek
 n glance 27.4
 v look 27.13
 pry 980.4
peekaboo 1028.4
peel
 n skin 295.3
 lamina 296.2
 stronghold 460.6
 v pare 6.8
 excise 255.10
 tear apart 801.14
peel off pilot 184.37
 come apart 801.9
peel out leave 222.10
 flee 368.11
peep
 n glance 27.4
 v look 27.13
 bird sound 60.5
 reconnoiter 937.27
 pry 980.4
peeper eye 2.9
 sight organ 27.9
peepers 29.3
peephole 27.8
peer
 n nobleman 608.4
 equal 789.4
 v look 27.13
 be curious 980.3
peer group
 company 769.3
 equal 789.4
peerless
 matchless 249.15
 best 998.16
 perfect 1001.6
peeve
 n hated thing 103.3
 complaint 115.4
 grudge 589.5
 v annoy 96.13
 provoke 152.24
peewee
 n runt 258.4
 adj tiny 258.11
peg
 n tooth 2.8
 drink 8.4
 liquor 88.7

degree 245.1
 leg 273.6
 bulge 283.3
 stopper 293.4
 throw 903.3
 v plod 175.7
 walk 177.27
 hustle 177.28
 drudge 725.14
 hook 799.8
 throw 903.10
Pegasus 311.15
pejorative 512.13
pellet
 n sphere 282.2
 shot 462.19
 v pelt 459.27
pell-mell
 agitation 105.4
 commotion 809.4
pelt
 n hair 3.2
 fur 4.2
 skin 295.3
 hit 901.4
 v rain 316.9
 stone 459.27
 pound 901.16
 throw 903.10
 shoot 903.12
pelvis 2.11
pen
 n enclosed place 212.3
 place of confinement
  429.7
 prison 429.8
 writing 547.1
 writer 547.13
 author 718.3
 farm 1067.8
 v enclose 212.5
 confine 429.12
 write 547.19
 compose 718.6
penal code 673.5
penal colony 429.8
penal institution 429.8
penalize
 bring in a verdict
  598.19
 condemn 602.3
 put a penalty on 603.4
 punish 604.10
penalty
 judgment 598.9
 penance 603
 penalization 603.1
 punishment 604.1
 football 746.3
 game 749.3
 sports event 749.6
 golf 751.3
 soccer 752.3
 impediment 1011.6
penalty box 749.1
penalty shot 749.6
penance
 regret 113.4
 penalty 603.1
 penitence 658.3
 seven sacraments
  701.4

pen-and-ink
writing 547.1
drawing 712.13
penchant
inclination 100.3
preference 371.5
tendency 895.1
pencil
n art equipment
712.18
ray 1024.5
v mark 517.19
write 547.19
portray 712.19
pendant hanger 202.4
adjunct 254.1
likeness 783.3
pending
adj pendent 202.9
overhanging 202.11
undecided 970.18
prep during 820.14
pendulous
pendent 202.9
oscillating 915.15
pendulum series 811.2
oscillator 915.9
penetrate bite 68.5
affect 93.14
interpenetrate 189.8
insert 191.3
pervade 221.7
perforate 292.15
get across 521.5
perceive 521.9
imbue 796.11
see through 940.8
be remembered
988.14
freeze 1022.10
penetrating
intense 15.22
acrimonious 17.14
shrill 58.14
pungent 68.6
strong 69.10
deep-felt 93.24
piercing 105.31
caustic 144.23
vigorous 544.11
sagacious 919.16
cold 1022.14
penile 2.27
peninsula
continent 235.1
point of land 283.9
penis 2.11
penitent
n confessor 113.5
adj repentant 113.9
penitentiary
n prison 429.8
priest 699.5
adj penitent 113.9
penmanship 547.3
pen name 527.8
pennant flag 647.6
baseball 745.1
penned enclosed 212.10
written 547.22
penniless bereft 473.8
destitute 619.9

Pennsylvania Dutch
523.7
penny money 728.7
cent 728.8
penny-ante
insignificant 248.6
inferior 250.6
worthless 391.11
penny pincher 484.4
**penny-wise and pound-
foolish**
parsimonious 484.7
prodigal 486.8
penologist 604.9
penology 604.1
pen pal 553.8
pension
n subsidy 478.8
v depose 447.4
subsidize 478.19
pensioner
dependent 432.6
beneficiary 479.4
student 572.7
employee 577.3
pension off scrap 390.8
depose 447.4
resign 448.2
subsidize 478.19
dismiss 908.19
pensive
melancholy 112.23
cognitive 930.21
abstracted 984.11
pentagon 881.1
pentagram 881.1
pentameter
meter 720.7
five 881.1
pentathlon
contest 755.2
track meet 755.8
five 881.1
penthouse house 228.5
apartment 228.13
roof 295.6
pent-up
enclosed 212.10
confined 429.19
peon sycophant 138.3
subject 432.7
retainer 577.1
peasant 606.6
people
n population 227.1
kinfolk 559.2
race 559.4
family 559.5
the laity 700.1
v settle 159.17
inhabit 225.9
people's republic 232.1
the people
human race 312.1
humankind 312.4
the population 606
the populace 606.1
pep energy 17.3
liveliness 330.2
spirit 544.4
pepper
n energy 17.3

v variegate 47.7
flavor 63.7
pull the trigger 459.22
mark 517.19
sprinkle 770.6
throw 903.10
shoot 903.12
pepper-and-salt 47.12
peppery zestful 68.7
hot-tempered 110.25
pep pills 87.3
peppy energetic 17.13
active 330.17
spirited 544.12
pep rally 375.4
pep talk 543.2
peptic 7.20
peptide 7.6
per by means of 384.13
for each 864.20
conformable to 866.9
per annum 864.19
per capita
proportionate 477.13
each 864.19
perceive sense 24.6
see 27.12
feel 93.10
understand 521.9
know 927.12
detect 940.5
percent 1016.7
percentage
incentive 375.7
benefit 387.4
estate 471.4
gain 472.3
portion 477.5
discount 631.1
part 792.1
expedience 994.1
ratio 1016.7
perceptible visible 31.6
measurable 300.14
manifest 348.8
knowable 927.25
perception
sensation 24.1
vision 27.1
sagacity 919.4
cognizance 927.2
idea 931.1
discernment 943.2
perceptive
sensible 24.11
sagacious 919.16
knowing 927.15
discerning 943.8
perch
n birdhouse 228.23
footing 900.5
v settle 159.17
sit 173.10
get down 194.7
inhabit 225.7
rest on 900.22
percolate refine 79.22
exude 190.15
trickle 238.18
be operative 888.7
liquefy 1062.5
be damp 1063.11

soak 1063.13
percolator 79.13
percussion noise 53.3
concussion 671.8
percussion
instrument 711.16
impact 901.3
percussionist 710.10
per diem 864.19
peregrine
n wanderer 178.2
adj traveling 177.36
perennial
n plant 310.3
adj ephemeral 310.41
continuous 811.8
durable 826.10
indeciduous 828.8
constant 846.5
perestroika
reproduction 78.1
reconstruction 396.5
rearrangement 807.7
change 851.1
perfect
n tense 530.12
v excel 249.6
touch up 392.11
accomplish 407.6
complete 819.7
develop 1001.5
adj downright 247.12
complete 407.12
unrestricted 430.27
thorough 793.10
unqualified 959.2
accurate 972.16
ideal 1001.6
perfect binding 554.14
perfected
improved 392.13
ended 819.8
finished 1001.9
perfection
development 392.2
accomplishment
407.2
completion 793.4
end 819.1
accuracy 972.5
flawlessness 1001
faultlessness 1001.1
acme of perfection
1001.3
perfectionist
n optimist 124.6
precision 495.6
conformist 866.2
adj optimistic 124.12
perforate
v pierce 292.15
adj apertured 292.19
perform
execute 328.9
manifest 348.5
impersonate 349.12
accomplish 407.4
practice 434.3
act 704.29
play 708.39
operate 888.5
be operative 888.7

do 891.11
performance
deed 328.2
act 328.3
display 348.2
impersonation 349.4
accomplishment
407.1
observance 434.1
ceremony 580.4
acting 704.8
theatrical
performance 704.12
execution 708.30
musical performance
708.33
operation 888.1
production 891.5
performer
phony 500.7
entertainer 707.1
musician 710.1
doer 726.1
perform one's duty
641.10
perfume
n fragrance 70.1
perfumery 70.2
v odorize 69.7
scent 70.8
vaporize 1065.8
perfunctory
indifferent 102.6
unwilling 325.5
reluctant 325.6
careless 340.11
perfuse
bleed 91.27
transfer 176.10
filter in 189.10
insert 191.3
pervade 221.7
perhaps
n guess 950.4
adv possibly 965.9
perigee
juxtaposition 223.3
orbit 1070.16
spacecraft 1073.2
peril
n unreliability 970.6
danger 1005.1
v endanger 1005.6
perimeter
environment 209.1
bounds 211.1
period
menstruation 12.9
degree 245.1
season 313.1
phrase 529.1
passage 708.24
meter 720.7
football 746.3
game 749.3
hockey 749.6
soccer 752.3
end 819.1
time 820.1
portion of time 823
point 823.1
grammar 856.4

wave 915.4
orbit 1070.16
periodic
continuous 811.8
recurrent 848.13
seasonal 849.7
oscillating 915.15
periodical
n publication 352.1
magazine 555
serial 555.1
adj journalistic 555.5
seasonal 849.7
periodic table 1058.2
peripatetic
n wanderer 178.2
pedestrian 178.6
adj traveling 177.36
discursive 538.13
peripheral
n circuitry 1041.3
adj exterior 206.7
environing 209.8
outlining 211.14
peripheral vision 27.1
periscope 367.5
perish
disappear 34.2
die 307.19
expire 395.23
cease to exist 761.6
age 841.9
perishable
mortal 307.34
transient 827.7
perish the thought!
510.27
perjury
deliberate falsehood
354.9
deceitfulness 645.3
perk
n gain 472.3
v be operative 888.7
adj conceited 140.11
perk up refresh 9.2
energize 17.10
cheer up 109.9
improve 392.7
recuperate 396.19
elevate 911.5
perky
lighthearted 109.12
conceited 140.11
active 330.17
permanent
n hairdo 3.15
adj persevering 360.8
almighty 677.18
durable 826.10
perpetual 828.7
changeless 852.7
unchangeable 854.17
permeable
exudative 190.20
pervious 292.21
permeate
pervade 221.7
imbue 796.11
soak 1063.13
permission
ratification 332.4

exemption 430.8
consent 441.1
okay 443
leave 443.1
permissive
n mood 530.11
adj negligent 340.10
lawless 418.5
unstrict 426.5
indulgent 427.8
nonrestrictive 430.25
consenting 441.4
admissive 443.14
permit
n license 443.6
v ratify 332.12
consent 441.2
allow 443.9
make possible 965.5
permutation
transformation 851.3
interchange 862.1
peroxide 36.5
perpendicular
n vertical 200.2
straight line 277.2
adj plumb 200.12
right-angled 278.7
perpetrate 328.6
perpetrator
evildoer 593.1
criminal 645.10
bad person 660.10
doer 726.1
perpetual
almighty 677.18
infinite 822.3
durable 826.10
everlasting 828.7
constant 846.5
permanent 852.7
perpetual motion 172.2
perpetuate
preserve 828.5
sustain 855.4
perplex
n complex 798.2
v astonish 122.6
be incomprehensible
522.10
complicate 798.3
be unbelievable 954.7
baffle 970.13
confuse 984.7
thwart 1011.15
trouble 1012.13
perquisite gain 472.3
gratuity 478.5
booty 482.11
bonus 624.6
per se
essentially 766.11
singly 871.13
persecute annoy 96.13
make anxious 126.5
oppress 389.7
work evil 999.6
persecution complex
92.22
persevere endure 134.5
persist 360.2
balk 361.7

carry on 780.3
continue 855.5
win through 409.13
persist
keep alive 306.10
persevere 360.2
insist 421.8
live on 760.9
prevail 780.3
cohere 802.6
endure 826.6
remain 852.5
continue 855.5
persistent
reverberating 54.11
resolute 359.11
persevering 360.8
habitual 373.15
demanding 421.9
uniform 780.5
adhesive 802.12
durable 826.10
permanent 852.7
continuing 855.7
unforgettable 988.26
person
human form 262.4
human 312.5
first person 530.7
role 704.10
someone 762.3
individual 871.4
body 1050.3
personable
influential 893.13
comely 1015.18
personal
n aspersion 512.4
adj individual 312.15
private 345.13
marked 517.24
particular 864.12
personal appearance
704.12
personal computer
1041.2
personal effects
equipment 385.4
belongings 471.2
personal initiative
430.7
personality
psyche 92.28
person 312.5
aspersion 512.4
something 762.3
particularity 864.1
influence 893.1
personage 996.8
personal matter 345.5
personal responsibility
430.7
persona non grata
outcast 586.4
bad person 660.1
exclusiveness 772.3
personify image 349.11
metaphorize 536.2
materialize 1050.9
personnel
work force 18.9
staff 577.11

baseball team 745.2
football team 746.2
basketball team 747.2
persons 606.1
person-to-person call
347.13
perspective
field of view 31.3
view 33.6
station 159.2
distance 261.1
treatment 712.9
outlook 977.2
perspiration
humor 2.22
sweat 12.7
perspire 12.16
persuade
prevail on 375.23
admonish 422.6
convert 857.16
influence 893.7
convince 952.18
seem true 972.9
persuasion
inducement 375.3
school 617.5
sect 675.3
company 769.3
kind 808.3
conversion 857.6
influence 893.1
conviction 952.5
persuasive
n incentive 375.7
adj suasive 375.29
influential 893.13
convincing 952.26
pert cheerful 109.13
conceited 140.11
impudent 142.10
active 330.17
defiant 454.7
immodest 666.6
pertain 774.5
pertinent relative 774.7
relevant 774.11
perturb distress 96.16
excite 105.14
disorder 809.9
discompose 810.4
agitate 916.10
bewilder 970.12
confuse 984.7
trouble 1012.13
peruke 3.14
peruse scrutinize 27.14
study 570.12
examine 937.23
pervade
permeate 221.7
imbue 796.11
pervasive
deep-felt 93.24
pervading 221.14
thorough 793.10
perverse
irascible 110.19
negative 335.5
obstinant 361.11
oppositional 451.8
contrary 778.6

nonconformist 788.9
counteractive 899.8
erroneous 974.16
unwieldy 1012.19
pervert
n sexual pervert 75.16
reprobate 660.5
v distort 265.6
misinterpret 342.2
misrepresent 350.3
falsify 354.15
misuse 389.4
corrupt 393.12
misteach 569.3
reason speciously
935.8
pervious
exudative 190.20
permeable 292.21
influenceable 893.15
accessible 965.8
pesky
annoying 98.22
importunate 440.18
pessimism
dejection 112.3
cynicism 125.6
suspense 130.3
pessimist
n killjoy 112.14
cynic 125.7
adj pessimistic 125.16
pest epidemic 85.5
annoyance 96.2
tormentor 96.10
bore 118.4
bane 1000.1
blight 1000.2
pester annoy 96.13
importune 440.12
nag 510.16
pesthole sty 80.11
epidemic 85.5
pesticide killer 308.10
poison 1000.3
pestilence
epidemic 85.5
bane 1000.1
pestle
n pulverizer 1049.7
v pulverize 1049.9
pet
n ladylove 104.15
favorite 104.16
dudgeon 152.7
endearment term
562.6
v stroke 73.8
indulge 427.6
caress 562.16
rub 1042.6
adj beloved 104.24
petal leaf 310.17
flower 310.26
peter out weaken 16.9
get tired 21.6
be disappointing
132.3
be consumed 388.4
come to nothing
410.13
cease to exist 761.6

be unproductive 890.3
fall through 910.3
pet food 10.4
petit 997.17
petite 258.10
petition
n request 440.1
prayer 696.4
v present a petition
440.10
pray 696.12
pet name 527.7
pet peeve
hated thing 103.3
complaint 115.4
grudge 589.5
petrified
terrified 127.26
antiquated 841.13
hardened 1044.13
mineral 1056.15
stone 1057.10
petroleum
illuminant 1024.20
rock oil 1054.4
petroleum jelly 1054.2
pet subject 865.1
petticoat 77.13
petting touching 73.2
indulgence 427.3
lovemaking 562.2
petty
insignificant 248.6
inadequate 250.7
ungenerous 651.6
base 661.12
quibbling 935.14
narrow-minded
979.10
puny 997.20
petty cash 728.19
petty larceny 482.2
petty officer first class
575.20
petulant
discontented 108.7
peevish 110.22
plaintive 115.19
capricious 364.5
pew
compartment 197.2
church 703.14
pewter 1056.17
pfc 461.8
PG 706.1
PGA 751.1
pH 1058.3
phalanx
military unit 461.22
company 769.3
phallic 2.27
phallic symbol 92.30
phantasm
deception 356.1
phantom 975.4
figment of the
imagination 985.5
specter 987.1
phantasmagoric 975.8
phantom
n apparition 33.5
whiteness 37.2

frightener 127.9
spirit 763.3
phantasm 975.4
figment of the
imagination 985.5
specter 987.1
adj illusory 975.8
spectral 987.7
immaterial 1051.7
pharaoh ruler 575.9
tyrant 575.14
pharmaceutical 86.50
pharmacist 86.35
pharmacy
pharmacology 86.34
drugstore 86.36
hospital room 197.25
pharynx
digestive system 2.16
vocal organ 524.19
phase 33.3
phase in 245.4
phase out
graduate 245.4
reduce 252.7
cease to use 390.4
end 819.5
turn off 856.12
phases of the moon
853.4
phenom
marvel 122.2
success 409.4
successful person
409.6
talented person
413.12
phenomenal
wonderful 122.10
eventful 830.10
extraordinary 869.14
phenomenology 977.2
phenomenon
apparition 33.5
marvel 122.2
event 830.2
phew! eeyuck! 98.31
oh! 122.20
philanderer
beau 104.13
lover 562.12
libertine 665.10
philanthropic
benevolent 143.15
eleemosynary 478.22
philanthropist
altruist 143.8
giver 478.11
philharmonic
n performance 708.33
adj musical 708.47
Philistine
n vulgarian 497.6
conformist 866.2
adj callous 94.12
common 497.14
secularist 695.16
unlearned 929.14
philosopher
wise man 920.1
scholar 928.3
reasoner 934.11

philosophizer 951.6
philosophical
  calm 106.12
  patient 134.9
  sensible 919.18
  philosophic 951.8
philosophize
  reason 934.15
  be philosophic 951.7
philosophy
  composure 106.2
  ideology 931.8
  reasoning 934.1
  school of thought 951
  physics 1017.1
phlebotomy
  bloodletting 91.20
  drawing 192.3
phlegm
  humor 2.22
  apathy 94.4
  languor 331.6
phlegmatic
  n personality type
   92.12
  adj apathetic 94.13
  inert 173.14
  languid 331.20
  incurious 981.3
phobia
  hated thing 103.3
  fear 127.1
phobic neurotic 92.38
  afraid 127.22
phoenix 659.5
phone
  n sound 50.1
  telephone 347.4
  speech sound 524.13
  v telephone 347.18
phone book
  telephone number
   347.12
  reference book 554.9
  directory 574.10
phoneme 524.13
phone number 347.12
phonetic
  n phonetic symbol
   546.2
  adj linguistic 523.17
  phonic 524.31
phonetic alphabet
  546.3
phonetics hearing 48.9
  articulatory phonetics
   524.14
  spelling 546.4
phonetic spelling 546.4
phonic auditory 48.13
  acoustic 50.17
  phonetic 524.31
phonograph 50.11
phonograph record
  record 50.12
  recording media
   549.10
phony
  n imitator 336.4
  fake 354.13
  impostor 357.6
  hypocrite 357.8

affecter 500.7
  copy 784.1
  substitute 861.2
  adj imitation 336.8
  spurious 354.25
  assumed 500.16
  similar 783.10
  substitute 861.8
phooey! 157.10
phosphate 889.4
phosphoresce 1024.26
photic 1024.41
photochemical 1058.8
photochemical process
  548.1
photocomposition
  548.2
photocopy 714.5
photoelectric
  electric 1031.29
  electronic 1032.15
photoengraving
  printing 548.1
  engraving 713.2
photo finish
  horse race 757.3
  the same 789.3
photogenic
  photographic 714.17
  luminescent 1024.38
photograph
  n description 349.2
  picture 712.11
  photo 714.3
  print 784.5
  v shoot 714.14
  n image 349.5
photograph album
  554.7
photographer
  journalist 555.4
  shutter-bug 714.2
  artist 716.5
photographic
  pictorial 712.21
  photo 714.17
photographic memory
  988.3
photographic
  reproduction 548.1
photography
  optics 29.7
  printing 548.1
  motion-picture
   photography 706.4
  visual arts 712.1
  graphic arts 713.1
  picture-taking 714.1
photometry 1024.22
photon
  energy unit 17.7
  ray 1024.5
  measurement of light
   1024.21
photo-offset 548.1
photo opportunity
  conference 541.6
  event 830.2
  interview 937.11
photoprint 714.5
photosensitive
  photographic 714.17

photophobic 1024.42
photosphere 1070.13
photostatic copy
  print 714.5
  copy 784.5
phrase
  n sign 518.6
  remark 524.4
  expression 529.1
  part 554.13
  passage 708.24
  part of writing 792.2
  maxim 973.1
  v say 524.23
  express 532.4
  adj phrasal 529.4
phraseology
  language 523.1
  jargon 523.9
  vocabulary 526.13
phrasing diction 529.2
  harmonics 709.2
phylogenesis 860.3
phylum
  nomenclature 527.1
  lineage 560.4
  kind 808.3
  classifications 808.5
  biology 1066.1
physic
  n medicine 86.4
  laxative 86.17
  health care 90.1
  physics 1017.1
  v treat 91.24
physical
  n checkup 937.6
  adj carnal 663.6
  innate 766.8
  aerophysical 1017.3
  material 1050.10
physical addiction 87.1
physical condition 83.1
physical development
  14.1
physical education
  physical culture 568.9
  exercise 725.6
physical examination
  diagnosis 91.12
  checkup 937.6
physical fitness
  health 83.1
  fitness 84.1
physical force 424.2
physical presence 221.1
physical therapist
  90.11
physician doctor 90.4
  health care
   professional 90.8
physicist
  aerophysicist 1017.2
  materialist 1050.7
physics
  physical science
   1017.1
physiological 305.17
physiotherapist 90.11
physique body 2.1
  the muscles 2.3
  muscularity 15.2

human form 262.4
  structure 266.1
  nature 766.4
  material body 1050.3
pi
  n type 548.6
  v compose 548.16
  confuse 810.3
PI 576.10
pianissimo
  n music 708.25
  adj faint 52.16
  music 708.53
  adv faintly 52.21
pianist 710.7
piano
  n music 708.25
  keyboard instrument
   711.12
  adj faint 52.16
  music 708.53
  adv faintly 52.21
piazza
  porch 197.21
  square 230.8
pica 548.6
picayune
  n unimportance 997.1
  trifle 997.5
  adj insignificant 248.6
  detailed 765.9
  quibbling 935.14
  petty 997.20
pick
  n choice 371.1
  plectrum 711.21
  warp 740.3
  basketball game 747.3
  tap 901.7
  the best 998.8
  v peck 8.26
  choose 371.13
  select 371.14
  collect 472.11
  strum 708.40
  play 747.4
  tap 901.18
  harvest 1067.19
pick a bone with
  456.13
pick and choose
  choose 371.13
  be hard to please
   495.8
  be discriminating
   943.5
pick at pick 8.26
  annoy 96.13
  goad 375.15
  deprecate 510.12
  nag 510.16
pick clean 480.24
picked chosen 371.26
  best 998.16
picker
  string musician 710.5
  agriculturist 1067.5
picket
  n leg 273.6
  striker 727.7
  guard 1007.9
  watchman 1007.10

picketer 1007.13
v fence 212.7
object 333.5
bind 428.10
torture 604.16
strike 727.10
picket line 1007.13
Pick Four 759.14
pickings gain 472.3
booty 482.11
pickle
n appetizer 10.9
sour 67.2
state 764.1
bewilderment 970.3
predicament 1012.5
v intoxicate 88.23
preserve 397.9
pickled sour 67.5
salty 68.9
drunk 88.33
picklepuss
malcontent 108.4
moaning Minnie
112.13
complainer 115.9
pick-me-up
refreshment 9.1
tonic 86.8
bracer 88.8
pickoff 745.3
pick off kill 308.13
shoot 903.12
pick on annoy 96.13
goad 375.15
deprecate 510.12
nag 510.16
pick one's brains
482.19
pick one's way 937.31
pick out see 27.12
extract 192.10
excise 255.10
select 371.14
designate 517.18
eliminate 772.5
segregate 772.6
specify 864.11
discriminate 943.4
call attention to
982.10
pickpocket 483.2
pick pockets 482.14
pickup
sound reproduction
system 50.11
bracer 88.8
acceleration 174.4
ride 177.7
intensification 251.2
improvement 392.1
friend 588.1
strumpet 665.14
outside pickup
1033.17
television camera
1034.10
pick up refresh 9.2
stimulate 105.13
cheer 109.7
fetch 176.16
improve 392.7

recuperate 396.19
arrest 429.15
acquire 472.9
collect 472.11
capture 480.18
take up 911.8
detect 940.5
receive 1035.17
pick up speed 174.10
pick-up sticks 743.16
pick up the check
support 449.12
subsidize 478.19
pay for 624.18
treat 624.19
picky fastidious 495.9
critical 510.23
detailed 765.9
picnic
n meal 8.6
victory 411.1
fun 743.2
festival 743.4
easy 1013.4
v dine 8.21
picnicker 8.16
pictograph 546.2
pictorial
n periodical 555.1
adj representational
349.13
pictural 712.21
picture
n description 349.2
representation 349.5
sign 517.1
motion pictures 706.1
image 712.11
photograph 714.3
copy 784.1
thought 931.1
visualization 985.6
thing of beauty 1015.7
television reception
1034.5
signal 1035.11
v represent 349.8
describe 349.9
portray 712.19
visualize 985.15
the picture plan 381.1
the facts 760.4
circumstances 765.2
picture frame 266.4
the picture of
the same 777.3
likeness 783.3
picture of health 83.2
picture postcard 553.3
picture show 706.1
picturesque
ornate 498.12
pictorial 712.21
picture-taking 714.1
picture tube 1034.11
piddling
n trifling 997.8
adj little 258.10
sparse 884.5
petty 997.20
pidgin English 523.11
pie pastry 10.39

easy 1013.4
piebald
n horse 311.11
adj mottled 47.12
piece
sex object 75.4
lump 257.10
distance 261.1
a length 267.2
schoolgirl 302.8
gun 462.10
gain 472.3
portion 477.5
writing 547.10
news item 552.3
treatise 556.1
stage show 704.4
role 704.10
opus 708.5
work of art 712.10
specie 728.4
money 728.8
chessman 743.17
sample 785.3
part 792.1
particle 792.3
piece by piece 792.9
pièce de résistance
dish 10.7
feature 996.7
the best 998.8
piecemeal
piece by piece 792.9
separately 801.27
piece of cake 1013.4
piece of one's mind
510.6
piece of the action
portion 477.5
part 792.1
piece out 793.6
piece together
compose 795.3
put together 799.5
produce 891.8
piecework 891.3
pie chart 381.3
piecrust crust 295.14
fragility 1048.2
pied
n foot 199.5
adj mottled 47.12
pied-à-terre 228.8
piedmont 237.1
Pied Piper of Hamelin
377.4
pie-eyed 88.33
pie in the sky
985.23
pier pillar 273.5
buttress 900.4
base 900.8
harbor 1008.6
pierce pain 26.7
affect 93.14
hurt 96.17
penetrate 189.8
perforate 292.15
injure 393.13
stab 459.25
perceive 521.9
freeze 1022.10

pierce the ears
din 53.7
grate on 58.11
piercing
n hole 292.3
stabbing 459.10
adj intense 15.22
acrimonious 17.14
painful 26.10
loud 53.11
shrill 58.14
pungent 68.6
deep-felt 93.24
penetrating 105.31
caustic 144.23
vigorous 544.11
violent 671.16
sagacious 919.16
cold 1022.14
piety religiousness 692
piousness 692.1
sanctimony 693.1
piffle
n bull 520.3
v talk nonsense 520.5
pig eater 8.16
pork 10.16
filthy person 80.13
cycle 179.8
heavyweight 257.12
swine 311.9
beast 660.7
glutton 672.3
jockey 757.2
slob 809.7
bigot 979.5
police 1007.16
cast 1056.5
pig's eye 758.2
pigeon
n bird 311.28
dupe 358.2
v deceive 356.14
cheat 356.18
pigeonhole
n small space 258.3
hiding place 346.4
class 808.2
v put away 390.6
legislate 613.10
classify 808.6
postpone 845.9
list 870.8
pigeonholed
neglected 340.14
classified 808.8
pigeonholes 870.3
pigeon loft 228.23
pigeon-toed 265.12
pig farm 1068.5
piggish
hoggish 80.24
greedy 100.27
ungulate 311.44
gluttonous 672.6
piggy 311.9
piggyback 900.25
piggy bank 729.12
pighead 361.6
pig in a poke
bargain 731.5
gamble 759.2

piglet
   fledgling 302.10
   swine 311.9
pigment
   n color 35.8
   paint 712.18
   v color 35.13
pigmentation 35.11
pig out stuff 8.25
   overeat 672.5
pigpen sty 80.11
   hovel 228.11
pigskin 746.2
pigsty sty 80.11
   hovel 228.11
pigtail braid 3.7
   chewing tobacco 89.7
   tail 217.6
   coil 281.2
piker vagabond 178.3
   gambler 759.21
pile
   n hair 3.2
   plant beard 3.9
   down 3.19
   lot 247.4
   structure 266.2
   leg 273.6
   texture 294.1
   leaf 310.17
   store 386.1
   gain 472.3
   wealth 618.3
   heap 769.10
   base 900.8
   reactor 1037.13
   v load 159.15
   pile on 769.19
piled on 643.8
piledriver
   strong man 15.6
   influence 893.6
pile in 193.12
pile into 459.15
pile it on
   exaggerate 355.3
   talk big 545.6
   lay it on 992.11
piles 85.36
pile up
   shipwreck 182.42
   store up 386.11
   pile 769.19
pilfer misuse 389.4
   steal 482.13
pilgrim
   n traveler 178.1
   religious 699.15
   v journey 177.21
pilgrimage
   n wandering 177.3
   journey 177.5
   adventure 404.2
   v journey 177.21
piling buttress 900.4
   base 900.8
piling on
   cruelty 144.11
   persecution 389.3
   overdoing 992.6
pill bolus 86.7
   tedious person 118.5

sphere 282.2
   bad person 660.6
the pill 86.23
pillage
   n plundering 482.6
   v seize 480.14
   plunder 482.17
   rage 671.11
pillar tower 272.6
   column 273.5
   cylinder 282.4
   monument 549.12
   base 900.8
   protector 1007.5
pillar of society
   bourgeois 607.6
   good citizen 659.3
   personage 996.8
pillar of strength 854.6
pillbox 460.6
pillory
   n shackle 428.4
   punishment 605.3
   v ridicule 508.8
   punish 604.10
   disgrace 661.8
   stigmatize 661.9
pillow
   n bedding 900.20
   softness 1045.4
   v support 900.21
pillowcase 295.10
pill popper 87.20
pilot
   n steersman 183.8
   aviator 185.1
   guide 574.7
   baseball team 745.2
   jockey 757.2
   safeguard 1007.3
   v steer 182.14
   control 184.37
   guide 573.9
   adj experimental
      941.11
piloting 161.1
pilot light 1019.10
pilot program 941.3
pimp
   n reprobate 660.5
   procurer 665.18
   v prostitute oneself
      665.21
pimple
   n sore 85.36
   swelling 283.4
   print 517.7
   blemish 1003.1
   v roughen 288.4
pin
   n member 2.7
   stopper 293.4
   jewel 498.6
   insignia 647.1
   bowling 750.1
   golf 751.1
   axle 914.5
   trifle 997.5
   v hook 799.8
   fell 912.5
PIN 517.11
pin a medal on 646.8

pinball machine 759.16
pince-nez 29.3
pincer movement 459.5
pincers
   extractor 192.9
   clutches 474.4
pinch
   n pang 26.2
   modicum 248.2
   small space 258.3
   squeezing 260.2
   urge 375.6
   arrest 429.6
   indigence 619.2
   crisis 842.4
   urgency 996.4
   danger 1005.1
   predicament 1012.4
   crux 1012.8
   v pain 26.7
   converge 169.2
   sail near the wind
      182.25
   squeeze 260.8
   arrest 429.16
   rob 482.16
   stint 484.5
   adj substitute 861.8
pinched limited 210.7
   contracted 260.12
   haggard 270.20
   poor 619.7
   straitened 1012.26
pinch-hit
   represent 576.14
   substitute for 861.5
pinch of snuff
   snuff 89.8
   trifle 997.5
pinch pennies 484.5
pin down locate 159.11
   bind 428.10
   stabilize 854.7
   specify 864.11
   fell 912.5
pine
   n basketball 747.1
   v weaken 16.9
   fail 85.47
   wish for 100.16
   grieve 112.17
   languish 393.18
pine barrens 310.11
pine cone cone 282.5
   plant 310.25
pine needle thorn 285.5
   leaf 310.17
ping 54.3
pinhead top part 198.4
   minute 258.7
   fool 923.4
pinion
   n feather 3.16
   member 792.4
   v bind 428.10
pink
   n pinkness 41.2
   radical 611.12
   acme of perfection
      1001.3
   v notch 289.4
   perforate 292.15

adj pinkish 41.8
   fresh 83.13
   radical 611.20
pink elephants 925.10
pink ladies 87.4
pinko 611.12
pink slip 908.5
pin money 728.19
pinnacle summit 198.2
   mountain 237.6
   tower 272.6
   limit 793.5
   acme of perfection
      1001.3
pin on blame 599.8
   attribute to 887.4
pin one's ears back
   510.18
pinpoint
   n location 159.1
   minute 258.7
   v locate 159.11
   attribute to 887.4
   receive 1035.17
   adj exact 972.17
pinprick
   shallowness 276.1
   trifle 997.5
pins 177.15
pins and needles
   insensibility 25.1
   tingle 74.1
   anxiety 126.1
pinstripe
   n stripe 47.5
   adj striped 47.15
pinstriper 574.3
pinto
   n horse 311.11
   adj mottled 47.12
pint-size
   insignificant 248.6
   dwarf 258.13
pinup
   photograph 714.3
   beauty 1015.9
pinwheel 743.16
pioneer
   n traveler 178.1
   vanguard 216.2
   settler 227.9
   engineer 461.14
   precursor 815.1
   v be in front 216.7
   go before 815.3
   initiate 817.10
   innovate 851.9
   adj original 337.5
pioneering
   front 216.10
   preceding 815.4
pious
   pietistic 692.8
   sanctimonious 693.5
   believing 952.21
pip disease 85.40
   seed 310.29
   military insignia
      647.5
   first-rate 998.7
pipe
   n screech 58.4

tobacco pipe 89.6
tube 239.6
cylinder 282.4
wind instrument
711.6
v blare 53.10
screech 58.8
bird sound 60.5
transport 176.14
channel 239.15
sigh 318.21
speak 524.26
sing 708.38
blow a horn 708.42
pipe cleaner 89.6
pipe down
v fall silent 51.7
inter silence! 51.14
pipe dream
airy hope 124.5
illusion 975.1
abstractedness 984.2
dream 985.9
pipe-dream muse 984.9
dream 985.17
pipeline
n tube 239.6
inside information
551.2
news channel 552.10
v transport 176.14
piper 710.4
pipes
ship's officer 183.7
bagpipe 711.9
pipette
n drawing off 192.9
tube 239.6
v draw off 192.12
pipe up
vociferate 59.8
blow 318.20
speak up 524.22
strike up 708.37
piping hot 1018.25
pippin 998.7
pips 1035.11
pip-squeak runt 258.4
a nobody 997.7
piquant
appetizing 63.10
pungent 68.6
exciting 105.30
provocative 375.27
alluring 377.8
spirited 544.12
interesting 982.19
pique
n offense 152.2
dudgeon 152.7
v annoy 96.13
stimulate 105.13
provoke 152.24
incite 375.17
rouse 375.19
interest 982.12
piracy
buccaneering 482.7
plagiarism 482.8
pirate
n mariner 183.1
corsair 483.7

plagiarist 483.9
v buccaneer 482.18
plagiarize 482.19
adopt 621.4
pirouette
n whirl 914.2
v rotate 914.9
piss
n humor 2.22
urine 12.5
v urinate 12.14
be discontented 108.6
complain 115.16
make angry 152.23
piss and vinegar
energy 17.3
gaiety 109.4
liveliness 330.2
piss away 486.5
pissed-off 152.30
piss-poor 999.8
pistol
n skillful person
413.14
first-rate 998.7
v strike dead
308.17
shoot 903.12
pistol-whip 604.13
piston 903.6
pit
n audience 48.6
deep 275.2
cavity 284.2
well 284.4
indentation 284.6
texture 294.1
tomb 309.16
seed 310.29
arena 463.1
sewer 654.7
auditorium 704.15
stage 704.16
stock exchange 737.7
race 756.3
blemish 1003.1
mine 1056.6
v indent 284.14
the pit 682.1
pit against 456.14
pit bull
sorehead 110.11
boxer 461.2
pitch
n blackness 38.4
tone 50.2
summit 198.2
inclination 204.2
incline 204.4
degree 245.1
plunge 367.1
intonation 524.7
speech 543.2
tuning 709.4
sales talk 734.5
baseball 745.3
field hockey 749.4
soccer 752.1
throw 903.3
flounder 916.8
v establish 159.16
toss 182.55

descend 194.5
tumble 194.8
erect 200.9
incline 204.10
camp 225.11
plunge 367.6
make advances 439.8
play 745.5
shuffle 758.4
throw 903.10
oscillate 915.10
flounder 916.15
adj phonetic 524.31
pitch-black black 38.8
dark 1026.13
pitched battle 457.4
pitcher
baseball team 745.2
thrower 903.7
pitcher's mound 745.1
pitchfork 903.10
pitch in eat 8.20
set to work 725.15
begin 817.7
pitchman
publicist 352.9
cheat 357.3
pitch pipe 711.22
piteous
distressing 98.20
pitiful 145.8
pitfall trap 356.12
hidden danger 1005.5
pith
essential content
196.5
center 208.2
pluck 359.3
fortitude 492.6
meaning 518.1
summary 557.2
essence 766.2
salient point 996.6
pulp 1061.2
pithy
meaningful 518.10
concise 537.6
aphoristic 973.6
spongy 1045.11
pulpy 1061.6
pitiless unpitying 146.3
savage 671.21
bright 1024.32
pit man 737.10
pit of one's stomach
93.3
the pits bottom 199.1
sewer 654.7
terribleness 999.2
pittance
modicum 248.2
donation 478.6
dole 991.5
pitted
indented 284.17
rough 288.6
nappy 294.7
pitter-patter
n thud 52.3
staccato 55.1
trepidation 105.5
rain 316.1

repetitiousness 848.4
pulsation 915.3
flutter 916.4
v drum 55.4
rain 316.9
flutter 916.12
pit viper 311.26
pity
n kindness 143.1
sympathy 145.1
leniency 427.1
abomination 638.2
v be sorry for 145.3
condole with 147.2
pivot
n center 208.2
basketball game
747.3
round 751.3
joint 799.4
fulcrum 905.3
axle 914.5
salient point 996.6
v turn round 163.9
rotate 914.9
pivotal
central 208.11
critical 842.10
causal 885.13
urgent 996.22
pivotal point 996.6
pixie
mischief-maker 322.3
fairy 678.8
imp 680.7
pixilated 925.29
pizzazz energy 17.3
power 18.1
liveliness 330.2
vigor 544.3
pizzeria 8.17
PJ's 5.21
placard
n poster 352.7
v publicize 352.15
placate 465.7
place
n serving 8.10
location 159.1
stead 159.4
abode 228.1
square 230.8
region 231.1
rank 245.2
arena 463.1
class 607.1
duty 641.1
function 724.3
position 724.5
state 764.1
continuity 806.2
turn 824.2
opportunity 842.2
outlook 977.2
v locate 159.11
put 159.12
install 615.12
impose 643.4
invest 729.16
race 757.5
dispose 807.9
classify 808.6

attribute 887.3
recognize 988.12
place against 942.4
place an order 421.5
place at one's disposal
  439.4
place a value on
  price 630.11
  estimate 945.9
place before 216.8
placebo 86.4
place confidence in
  believe in 952.15
  trust 952.17
placed
  located 159.18
  arranged 807.14
  classified 808.8
place emphasis on
  996.14
place horse 757.2
place in office
  establish 159.16
  elect 371.20
  install 615.12
a place in the sun 662.1
place itself 806.5
placekick 746.3
place kick 901.9
placement
  location 159.1
  positioning 159.6
  installation 615.3
  arrangement 807.1
  grouping 807.3
  classification 808.1
  attribution 887.1
placenta 816.3
place of residence
  228.1
place of worship 703.1
place side by side
  223.13
place the blame on
  blame 599.8
  attribute to 887.4
place trust in 952.17
place under arrest
  480.18
place under oath 334.7
place upon 887.4
placid
  calm 106.12
  quiescent 173.12
placing 159.6
plafond 295.6
plagiarize
  imitate 336.5
  pirate 482.19
  adopt 621.4
  repeat 848.7
plague
  n epidemic 85.5
  assemblage 769.6
  infestation 909.2
  bane 1000.1
  v annoy 96.13
  vex 98.15
  make anxious 126.5
  importune 440.12
  infest 909.6
  trouble 1012.13

plagued
  tormented 96.24
  worried 126.8
  remembering 988.24
  troubled 1012.20
plaid
  n check 47.4
  adj checked 47.14
plain
  n open space 158.4
  horizontal 201.3
  flat country 236
  prairie 236.1
  adj distinct 31.7
  audible 50.16
  dull 117.8
  humble 137.10
  horizontal 201.7
  homelike 228.33
  champaign 236.2
  mere 248.8
  manifest 348.8
  artless 416.5
  uncomplicated 499.6
  clear 521.11
  elegant 533.6
  plain-speaking 535.3
  informal 581.3
  populational 606.8
  candid 644.17
  prosaic 721.5
  thorough 793.10
  simple 797.6
  easy 1013.13
  ugly 1014.6
  adv absolutely 793.15
plain as day
  distinct 31.7
  manifest 348.8
plain as the nose on
  one's face
  distinct 31.7
  manifest 348.8
plainclothesman
  576.10
plain English
  clearness 521.2
  plain speech 535.1
plain folks 606.1
plains
  n the country 233.1
  plain 236.1
  adj rustic 233.6
plain sense 919.6
plaint
  lament 115.3
  accusation 599.1
plaintiff
  oppositionist 452.3
  litigant 598.11
  accuser 599.5
plaintive
  sorrowful 112.26
  plangent 115.19
the plain truth 972.3
plait
  n braid 3.7
  pleat 291.2
  lamina 296.2
  weave 740.2
  v fold 291.5
  weave 740.6

plan
  n structure 266.1
  representation 349.1
  intention 380.1
  scheme 381.1
  undertaking 404.1
  intent 518.2
  plot 722.4
  outline 800.4
  v intend 380.4
  plan on 380.6
  premeditate 380.7
  devise 381.8
  prepare 405.6
  organize 807.10
  come 838.6
  originate 891.12
  prearrange 964.4
plane
  n aircraft 181.1
  horizontal 201.3
  degree 245.1
  smoothness 287.3
  cutlery 1039.2
  v take off 193.10
  smooth 287.5
  adj horizontal 201.7
  smooth 287.9
plane crash 1010.2
planet 1070.9
planetarium 1070.17
planetary
  deviative 164.7
  circular 280.11
  universal 863.14
  celestial 1070.25
plangent
  loud 53.11
  resonant 54.9
  sorrowful 112.26
  plaintive 115.19
plank
  n strip 271.4
  lamina 296.2
  platform 609.7
  wood 1052.3
  v place violently
    159.13
  face 295.23
plankton 311.30
planned
  intentional 380.8
  devised 381.12
  prepared 405.16
  future 838.8
  prearranged 964.7
planned obsolescence
  390.1
planned parenthood
  890.1
plant
  n vegetable 310.3
  shill 357.5
  equipment 385.4
  factory 739.3
  v establish 159.16
  people 225.9
  secrete 346.7
  tamper with 354.16
  fix 854.9
  implant 1067.18
  adj biological 1066.3

plant and animal life
  305.1
plantation
  establishment 159.7
  peopling 225.2
  growth 310.2
  farm 1067.8
plant biology 1066.1
plant-eating 8.31
plant growth 14.1
plant oneself 159.17
plaque 549.12
plasma 2.23
plaster
  n dressing 86.33
  sculpture tool 715.4
  adhesive 802.4
  pulp 1061.2
  v intoxicate 88.23
  treat 91.24
  smooth 287.5
  coat 295.24
  cover 295.25
  adj on 295.43
plastic
  n credit instrument
    622.3
  thermoplastic 1052.6
  resin 1055.1
  adj formative 262.9
  plasmatic 262.10
  docile 433.13
  teachable 570.18
  changeable 853.6
  conformable 866.5
  conformist 866.6
  influenceable 893.15
  ordinary 1004.8
  pliant 1045.9
plastic wrap 295.18
plate
  n serving 8.10
  continent 235.1
  plating 295.13
  shell 295.15
  lamina 296.2
  label 517.13
  printing surface 548.8
  steel plate 713.6
  film 714.10
  v chromium-plate
    295.26
the plate 745.1
plateau
  plain 236.1
  highlands 237.1
  tableland 237.3
  degree 245.1
  mesa 272.4
  interim 825.1
plated
  chromium-plated
    295.33
  layered 296.6
platform
  n horizontal 201.3
  policy 381.4
  arena 463.1
  marker 517.10
  party platform 609.7
  stage 900.13
  v make a speech 543.9

platinum 37.7
platinum blond
  n hair color 35.9
  adj blond 37.9
platitude
  generalization 863.8
  cliché 973.3
Plato 920.2
Platonic
  continent 664.6
  Aristotelian 951.10
  idealist 1051.8
platoon
  military unit 461.22
  team 617.7
  company 769.3
platter
  recording media
    549.10
  baseball 745.1
plaudit 509.2
plausible
  specious 354.26
  logical 934.20
  sophistical 935.10
  believable 952.24
  possible 965.6
  colorable 967.7
play
  n room 158.3
  action 328.1
  latitude 430.4
  joke 489.6
  writing 547.10
  repute 662.1
  stage show 704.4
  fun 743.2
  frolic 743.5
  contest 743.9
  sport 744.1
  baseball 745.3
  football 746.3
  basketball game 747.3
  tennis 748.2
  game 749.3
  hockey 749.6
  round 751.3
  soccer 752.3
  bridge 758.3
  gambling 759.1
  bet 759.3
  flicker 1024.8
  v jet 238.20
  act 328.4
  impersonate 349.12
  sham 354.20
  use 387.10
  affect 500.12
  stage 704.29
  perform 708.39
  sport 743.23
  compete 744.2
  play baseball 745.5
  kick 746.5
  play basketball 747.4
  play tennis 748.3
  skate 749.7
  play golf 751.4
  play soccer 752.4
  gamble 759.23
  trifle 997.14
  flicker 1024.25

playa shore 234.2
  plain 236.1
playacting
  sham 354.3
  acting 704.8
play a joke on 489.14
play along
  be willing 324.3
  concur 332.9
  consent 441.2
play around flirt 562.20
  trifle 997.15
play around with
  consider 930.12
  experiment 941.8
play at cross-purposes
  oppose 451.3
  go contrary to 778.4
play a waiting game
  be patient 134.4
  do nothing 329.2
play back 50.14
play ball
  cooperate 450.3
  play baseball 745.5
  play basketball 747.4
playbill 964.3
playbook book 554.1
  script 704.21
**play both ends against
    the middle**
  play a double game
    354.23
  exploit 387.16
playboy
  sociable person
    582.16
  dissipater 669.3
  player 743.18
play by ear
  improvise 365.8
  be unprepared 406.6
  play 708.39
**play-by-play
    description**
  account 349.3
  circumstances 765.2
play by the rules 644.9
**play cat and mouse
    with** 389.7
play down
  minimize 252.9
  moderate 670.6
  attach little
    importance to 997.12
play dumb
  be silent 51.6
  keep secret 345.7
played out
  weakened 16.18
  tired 21.8
  worn-out 393.36
player
  competitor 452.2
  participator 476.4
  motion-picture studio
    706.3
  actor 707.2
  instrumentalist 710.3
  frolicker 743.18
  athlete 743.19
  golfer 751.2

  gambler 759.21
  component 795.2
  influence 893.6
player piano 711.12
play fair 649.7
**play fast and loose
    with** 156.4
play favorites 650.8
play for a sucker
  deceive 356.19
  exploit 387.16
  stultify 922.7
play for time 845.11
playful gay 109.14
  mischievous 322.6
  waggish 489.17
  sportive 743.29
play God 640.8
playground 743.11
play hard to get 562.20
play havoc with
  spoil 393.10
  bungle 414.11
  work evil 999.6
play hide and seek
    346.8
play hooky 222.9
playhouse
  small space 258.3
  theater 704.14
playing card 758.2
playing field arena
    463.1
  playground 743.11
playmaker
  basketball team 747.2
  hockey team 749.2
playmate companion
    588.3
  mistress 665.17
play musical chairs
    853.5
playoff baseball 745.1
  football 746.1
play off
  symmetrize 264.3
  offset 338.5
**play one's cards close
    to one's vest** 345.7
play one's cards right
    321.5
play one's trump card
    415.11
play on words
  n wordplay 489.8
  v joke 489.13
play opposite 704.30
play out 21.5
play politics 468.2
play possum 354.20
playroom
  recreation room
    197.12
  playground 743.11
play Russian roulette
    493.6
play safe
  take precautions
    494.6
  keep on the safe side
    1006.3
playschool 567.2

play second fiddle
  efface oneself 139.7
  retreat 163.6
  retract 168.3
  be inferior 250.4
  depend on 432.12
play the field 562.20
play the fool
  misbehave 322.4
  be foolish 922.6
play the game
  behave oneself 321.5
  conform 579.4
  play fair 649.7
  follow the rule 866.4
play the lead 704.29
play the market 737.23
play the ponies
  gamble 759.23
  bet 759.25
play the same old tune
    118.8
plaything dupe 358.1
  instrument 384.4
  toy 743.16
playtime 856.3
play tricks 489.14
play up 996.16
play upon 387.16
play up to
  curry favor 138.9
  flatter 511.6
  cultivate 587.12
play with fire
  not know what one is
    about 414.14
  court danger 493.6
  take chances 1005.7
playwright 704.22
plaza square 230.8
  marketplace 736.2
plea entreaty 440.2
  pleadings 598.6
  defense 600.2
  argument 934.5
plea-bargain sign 437.7
  compromise 468.2
plead entreat 440.11
  enter a plea 598.18
  argue 934.16
  adduce 956.12
plead guilty
  repent 113.7
  confess 351.7
plead ignorance 600.11
plead with 375.14
pleasant pleasing 97.6
  cheerful 109.11
  friendly 587.15
  melodious 708.48
  good 998.12
  rainless 1064.8
pleasantry
  pleasantness 97.1
  wit 489.1
  wittiness 489.2
  witticism 489.7
  banter 490.1
please
  v pleasure 95.5
  prefer 371.17
  indulge 427.6

inter prithee 440.20
pleasing to the eye
  1015.18
pleasure
  n enjoyment 95.1
  pleasantness 97.1
  desire 100.1
  will 323.1
  option 371.2
  command 420.1
  amusement 743.1
  v please 95.5
pleasure boat 180.3
pleasure principle
  psyche 92.28
  pleasure-loving 95.4
  desire 100.1
  sensuality 663.1
pleat
  n trench 290.2
  pleating 291.2
  v furrow 290.3
  fold 291.5
pleated furrowed 290.4
  folded 291.7
plebe 572.6
plebeian
  n common man 606.5
  adj common 497.14
  populational 606.8
plebiscite vote 371.6
  referendum 613.8
pledge
  n toast 88.10
  oath 334.4
  promise 436.1
  gage 438.2
  member 617.11
  debt 623.1
  v drink 8.29
  drink to 88.29
  promise 436.4
  give security 438.10
  contribute 478.14
  obligate 641.12
the pledge 668.2
Pleiades nymph 678.9
  star 1070.8
plenary great 247.6
  unrestricted 430.27
  full 793.11
plenary session 423.1
plenipotentiary
  omnipotent 18.13
  diplomatic 576.16
plenipotentiary power
  615.1
plenty
  n quantity 247.3
  store 386.1
  numerousness 883.1
  plenitude 990.2
  superabundance 992.2
  adj sufficient 990.6
  plentiful 990.7
  adv greatly 247.15
plenum
  omnipresence 221.2
  council 423.1
  assembly 769.2
  completeness 793.1
  series 811.2

matter 1050.2
  universe 1070.1
plethora fullness 793.2
  superabundance 992.2
  overfullness 992.3
plexus
  nervous system 2.12
  network 170.3
pliable folded 291.7
  weak-willed 362.12
  usable 387.23
  docile 433.13
  teachable 570.18
  influenceable 893.15
  handy 1013.15
  pliant 1045.9
pliers 192.9
plight
  n promise 436.1
  state 764.1
  bewilderment 970.3
  danger 1005.1
  adversity 1010.1
  predicament 1012.4
  v promise 436.4
plod
  n slow motion 175.2
  v plug 175.7
  way of walking 177.28
  keep doggedly at
    360.3
  drudge 725.14
plodder
  slowpoke 175.5
  drudge 726.3
plop
  v place violently
    159.13
  sink 194.6
  bubble 320.4
  plunge 367.6
  adv suddenly 829.9
plot
  n plot of ground 231.4
  diagram 381.3
  intrigue 381.5
  stratagem 415.3
  real estate 471.6
  fable 722.4
  field 1067.9
  v premeditate 380.7
  scheme 381.9
  map 381.10
  maneuver 415.10
  come 838.6
  prearrange 964.4
plot a course 182.27
plow maneuver 184.40
  furrow 290.3
  cultivate 1067.17
plow back into 729.16
plow into
  attack 459.15
  criticize 510.14
ploy trick 356.6
  stratagem 415.3
  revel 743.6
pluck
  n spunk 359.3
  courage 492.1
  jerk 904.3
  v divest 6.5

flunk 410.17
  collect 472.11
  strip 480.24
  strum 708.40
  cheat 759.26
  jerk 904.5
  harvest 1067.19
plucky
  spunky 359.14
  enterprising 404.8
  courageous 492.17
plug
  n hydrant 239.12
  stopper 293.4
  horse 311.12
  publicity 352.4
  snare 356.13
  commendation 509.3
  commercial 1033.20
  v plod 175.7
  stop 293.7
  top 295.21
  publicize 352.15
  keep doggedly at
    360.3
  commend 509.11
  drudge 725.14
  shoot 903.12
plug in 1031.25
plum
  desire 100.11
  political patronage
    609.36
  money 728.8
  dividend 738.7
  good thing 998.5
plumage 3.18
plumb
  n vertical 200.2
  instrument 200.6
  weight 297.6
  v plumb-line 200.10
  sound 275.9
  measure 300.10
  perceive 521.9
  investigate 937.22
  solve 939.2
  adj perpendicular
    200.12
  thorough 793.10
  adv perpendicularly
    200.14
  absolutely 793.15
  exactly 972.21
plumbing 385.4
plumb the depths
  lose heart 112.16
  sound 275.9
plume
  n feather 3.16
  v groom 79.20
  adorn 498.9
plume of smoke 1065.1
plump
  n thud 52.3
  v place violently
    159.13
  sink 194.6
  fatten 259.8
  plunge 367.6
  vote 371.18
  soften 1045.6

adj corpulent
    257.18
  adv suddenly 829.9
plunder
  n plundering 482.6
  booty 482.11
  v pillage 482.17
plunge
  n run 174.3
  tumble 194.3
  decline 252.2
  dive 367.1
  deterioration 393.3
  cheapening 633.4
  investment 729.3
  trading 737.19
  swimming pool
    743.12
  gamble 759.2
  flounder 916.8
  v move 172.5
  pitch 182.55
  descend 194.5
  decrease 252.6
  gravitate 297.15
  dive 367.6
  make haste 401.5
  rush into 401.7
  cheapen 633.6
  invest 729.16
  trade 737.23
  bet 759.25
  flounder 916.15
plunger
  diver 367.4
  speculator 737.11
  gambler 759.21
plunk
  n thud 52.3
  v thud 52.15
  place violently 159.13
  sink 194.6
  plunge 367.6
  strike 901.15
  adv suddenly 829.9
plural
  n number 530.8
  adj pluralized 882.7
pluralism
  government 612.8
  nonuniformity 781.1
  mixture 796.1
  plurality 882.1
  dualism 951.5
plurality
  major part 791.6
  more than one 882
  pluralness 882.1
  majority 882.2
plus
  n math terms 253.2
  surplus 992.5
  v add 253.4
  adj additional 253.10
  positive 1031.34
  adv additionally
    253.11
  prep with 253.12
plush
  n softness 1045.4
  adj grandiose 501.21
  velvety 1045.15

Pluto
nether world deity
682.5
planet 1070.9
plutocracy 618.6
ply
n fold 291.1
lamina 296.2
v touch 73.6
traverse 177.20
navigate 182.13
sail near the wind
182.25
change course 182.30
fold 291.5
use 387.10
urge upon 439.9
importune 440.12
exert 725.8
ply one's trade
work 724.12
trade 731.14
plywood lamina 296.2
wood 1052.3
PM afternoon 315.1
modulation 1033.14
PMS 92.14
pneumatic
bulging 283.15
airy 317.11
comely 1015.18
pneumatological
1038.10
vaporous 1065.9
poach cook 11.4
steal 482.13
poached eggs 10.25
pock
n sore 85.36
swelling 283.4
indentation 284.6
texture 294.1
blemish 1003.1
v indent 284.14
pocket
n atmosphere 184.32
bag 195.2
cavity 284.2
funds 728.14
purse 729.14
game 746.3
string 750.2
v patience 134.8
load 159.15
enclose 212.5
retain 474.5
take 480.13
legislate 613.10
receive 627.3
adj miniature 258.12
pocketbook
record book 549.11
purse 729.14
pocket veto
prohibition 444.2
veto 613.7
pockmarked
spotted 47.13
indented 284.17
pod
n marijuana 87.10
hull 295.16

seed vessel 310.28
group of animals
769.5
v husk 6.9
podiatrist 90.4
podium 900.13
poem writing 547.10
verse 720.4
thing of beauty 1015.7
poet composer 547.15
author 718.4
poetess 720.11
imaginer 985.12
poetic poetical 720.15
visionary 985.24
poetic justice
justice 649.1
poetics 720.2
poetic license 720.2
poetic prose 721.1
poet laureate 720.11
poetry fluency 544.2
verse 720
poesy 720.1
pogrom 308.4
poignant
acrimonious 17.14
sensitive 24.13
painful 26.10
pungent 68.6
deep-felt 93.24
distressing 98.20
vigorous 544.11
spirited 544.12
point
n acrimony 17.5
location 159.1
direction 161.1
leading 165.1
summit 198.2
vanguard 216.2
mountain 237.6
degree 245.1
modicum 248.2
minute 258.7
angle 278.2
point of land 283.9
tip 285.3
intention 380.1
benefit 387.4
joke 489.6
mark 517.5
meaning 518.1
punctuation 530.15
type 548.6
sculpture tool 715.4
tennis 748.2
hockey team 749.2
game 749.3
score 749.6
soccer 752.3
particular 765.3
precursor 815.1
extremity 819.2
period 823.1
grammar 856.4
individual 871.4
topic 936.1
watchman 1007.10
cutlery 1039.2
v direct 161.5
take direction 161.7

sharpen 285.7
gravitate 297.15
mark 517.19
grammaticize 530.16
tend 895.3
point-blank
plainly 535.4
exactly 972.21
pointer index 517.4
clue 551.3
guide 574.7
point guard 747.2
pointillism 47.3
point in question
topic 936.1
question 937.10
pointless dull 117.6
blunt 286.3
useless 391.9
point man
vanguard 216.2
hockey team 749.2
precursor 815.1
point of departure
188.5
point of interest 996.5
point of reference
159.2
point of view
viewpoint 27.7
narrator 722.5
opinion 952.6
outlook 977.2
point out
designate 517.18
specify 864.11
call attention to
982.10
points lending 620.1
interest 623.3
esteem 662.3
point the finger at
599.7
poise
n looks 33.4
equanimity 106.3
behavior 321.1
gesture 517.14
equality 789.1
confidence 969.5
v take off 193.10
equalize 789.6
poison
n poisonousness 82.3
liquor 88.14
killer 308.10
evil 999.3
venom 1000.3
v empoison 85.51
kill 308.12
corrupt 393.12
work evil 999.6
radioactivate 1036.9
poisonous nasty 64.7
toxic 82.7
harmful 999.12
poison pen 512.5
poke
n bag 195.2
signal 517.15
purse 729.14
bundle 769.8

thrust 901.2
hit 901.4
v go slow 175.6
dally 331.14
goad 375.15
signal 517.22
thrust 901.12
hit 901.14
search 937.30
poke at 459.16
poke full of holes 957.4
poke fun at joke 489.13
ridicule 508.8
poke one's nose in
meddle 214.7
pry 980.4
poker
draw poker 759.10
fire iron 1019.12
poker face
unfeeling 94.1
unastonishment 123.1
reticence 344.3
unexpressiveness
522.5
pokey 429.9
poky dull 117.6
slow 175.10
little 258.10
base 661.12
slovenly 809.15
insignificant 997.18
polar
contrapositive 215.5
final 819.11
magnetic 1031.30
polar coordinates 300.5
Polaris
guiding star 574.8
stars 1070.4
Polaroid glasses 29.3
the polar opposite
778.2
pole
n spar 180.13
oar 180.15
summit 198.2
remote region 261.4
tower 272.6
shaft 273.1
beam 273.3
race 756.3
extremity 819.2
base 900.8
axle 914.5
polarity 1031.8
wood 1052.3
v push 903.9
poleax
strike dead 308.17
do for 395.11
polecat
stinker 71.3
wild animal 311.23
beast 660.7
polemic
n quarrel 456.5
contention 457.1
argumentation 934.4
arguer 934.12
adj contentious 110.26
partisan 456.17

argumentative 934.19
pole position
advantage 249.2
race 756.3
precedence 813.1
poles apart
opposite 215.6
different 779.7
pole vault 366.1
police
n policeman 1007.15
police force 1007.17
v tidy 807.12
protect 1007.18
watch 1007.20
police car 179.11
police state 612.4
police station 230.5
policy plan 381.4
polity 609.4
judiciousness 919.7
insurance 1007.4
policyholder 438.7
policy maker 610.7
polio 85.27
polish
n gloss 287.2
smoother 287.4
cultivation 392.3
taste 496.1
good breeding 504.4
elegance 533.1
v shine 287.7
perfect 392.11
buff 1042.8
polish off kill 308.13
accomplish 407.4
end 819.5
polite 504.14
polite society 578.6
political
politic 609.43
governmental 612.17
**political action
committee**
pressure group 609.31
influence 893.6
political activist 330.8
political asylum 1008.1
political convention
609.8
political election 371.9
political influence
machination 415.4
wire-pulling 609.29
political machine
political party 609.24
association 617.1
political party
party 609.24
association 617.4
political prisoner
429.11
political science 609.2
politician
expert 413.11
Machiavellian 415.8
statesman 610
politico 610.1
politicize
politick 609.38
democratize 611.16

politics
Machiavellianism
415.2
statesmanship 609
polity 609.1
political science 609.2
polka dot
spottiness 47.3
mark 517.5
poll
n head 198.6
vote 371.6
balloting place 609.20
returns 609.21
roll 870.6
canvass 937.14
v shorten 268.6
vote 371.18
record 549.15
canvass 937.28
number 1016.16
pollen
n sperm 305.11
v fertilize 78.10
pollinate 78.10
polling booth 609.20
pollute defile 80.17
intoxicate 88.23
misuse 389.4
corrupt 393.12
blaspheme 694.5
adulterate 796.12
work evil 999.6
pollution
defilement 80.4
unhealthfulness 82.1
misuse 389.1
corruption 393.2
sacrilege 694.2
adulteration 796.3
evil 999.3
environmental
destruction 1071.2
Pollyanna 124.6
poltergeist imp 680.7
psychic phenomena
689.6
specter 987.1
polychrome
n variegation 47.1
v variegate 47.7
adj variegated 47.9
pictorial 712.21
polygraph 92.8
polyhedral sided 218.7
multilateral 278.11
polymer 1052.6
polymorphous 782.3
Polynesian race 312.2
polynomial 882.8
polyp 85.36
polysaccharide 7.5
polysyllabic 545.10
polyunsaturated fat
fat 7.7
oil 1054.1
pomade
n ointment 1054.3
v oil 1054.8
pommel
n saddle parts 900.18
v whip 604.13

pound 901.16
pomp spectacle 33.7
circumstance 501.6
formality 580.1
procession 811.3
pompadour 3.22
**pomp and
circumstance** 501.6
pom-pom 462.12
pompous stuffy 501.22
stiff 534.3
grandiloquent 545.8
ceremonious 580.8
confident 969.21
pond 241.1
ponder hesitate 362.7
consider 930.12
ponderous dull 117.6
bulky 257.19
heavy 297.16
bungling 414.20
stiff 534.3
unwieldy 1012.19
pone 10.28
pontificate
n mastership 417.7
papacy 698.6
v give oneself airs
501.14
talk big 545.6
criticize 945.14
dogmatize 969.10
Pontius Pilate 596.5
pontoon 180.11
pony
n runt 258.4
horse 311.10
translation 341.3
money 728.8
jockey 757.2
adj miniature 258.12
adv on foot 177.43
ponytail 3.5
pooch
n dog 311.17
v bulge 283.11
pooh-pooh
slight 157.6
scoff 508.9
disbelieve 954.5
pool
landlocked water 241
lake 241.1
company 617.9
funds 728.14
bear pool 737.17
swimming pool
743.12
pot 759.5
pool hall 743.11
poop
n energy 17.3
power 18.1
stern 217.7
v get tired 21.6
pooped weak 16.12
tired 21.8
languid 331.20
worn-out 393.36
poor weak 16.15
humble 137.10
haggard 270.20

unskillful 414.15
disapproving 510.21
ill off 619.7
base 661.12
sparse 884.5
unsound 935.12
meager 991.10
ill-provided 991.12
paltry 997.21
inferior 1004.9
poor judgment 947.1
poor man's roulette
759.8
**Poor Richard's
Almanac** 831.7
poor taste 497.1
poor timing 843.2
pop
n beverage 10.47
thud 52.3
detonation 56.3
vulgarity 497.1
father 560.10
grandfather 560.14
automobile racing
756.1
back number 841.8
v thud 52.15
blast 56.8
use 87.21
bulge 283.11
play 745.5
adj common 497.14
adv suddenly 829.9
pop in enter 189.7
insert 191.3
pop literature
writing 547.12
literature 718.1
pop music 708.7
pop pills 87.21
pop psychology 92.1
poppy 22.10
poppycock
bull 520.3
foolishness 922.1
pop quiz 937.2
pop the question
solicit 440.14
propose 562.22
populace 227.1
popular
desired 100.29
beloved 104.24
customary 373.14
communal 476.9
common 497.14
approved 509.19
fashionable 578.11
populational 606.8
distinguished 662.16
lay 700.3
prevalent 863.12
usual 868.9
popular belief
opinion 952.6
superstition 953.3
populate settle 159.17
people 225.9
population
n establishment 159.7
peopling 225.2

inhabitants 227.1
adj populational 606.8
population explosion 251.2
populous
 inhabited 225.12
 crowded 769.22
 teeming 883.9
pop up burst forth 33.9
 be unexpected 131.6
 arrive 186.6
 shoot up 193.9
 play 745.5
 turn up 830.6
 chance 971.11
porcelain
 n ceramic ware 742.2
 adj ceramic 742.7
porch
 propylaeum 189.6
 stoop 197.21
 church 703.9
porcine
 corpulent 257.18
 ungulate 311.44
porcupine 311.23
pore
 n duct 2.21
 outlet 190.9
 opening 292.1
 v scrutinize 27.14
pork food 10.16
 political patronage 609.36
pork barrel
 booty 482.11
 political patronage 609.36
 treasury 729.12
 trading 862.2
pork chop 10.18
porker
 heavyweight 257.12
 swine 311.9
porno film 666.4
pornography
 writing 547.12
 obscenity 666.4
 literature 718.1
porous
 exudative 190.20
 porose 292.20
porpoise
 n marine animal 311.30
 v maneuver 184.40
porridge
 semiliquid 1060.5
 pulp 1061.2
port
 n looks 33.4
 airport 184.22
 destination 186.5
 outlet 190.9
 left side 220.1
 behavior 321.1
 refuge 1008.1
 harbor 1008.6
 circuitry 1041.3
 adj left 220.4
 adv leftward 220.6
portable 176.18

portage
 transportation 176.3
 fee 630.6
portal entrance 189.5
 porch 189.6
 vestibule 197.19
portcullis 1011.5
portent omen 133.3
 ominousness 133.7
 forewarning 399.2
porter carrier 176.7
 trainman 178.13
 doorkeeper 1007.12
portfolio
 scepter 417.9
 bookholder 554.17
 stock 738.2
portico
 vestibule 197.19
 pillar 273.5
 passageway 383.3
port in a storm 1008.1
portion
 n serving 8.10
 remedy 86.6
 fix 87.19
 amount 244.2
 a length 267.2
 share 477.5
 endowment 478.9
 part 792.1
 dose 792.5
 fate 963.2
 v apportion 477.6
 divide 801.18
portly 257.18
port of call 1008.6
portrait
 description 349.2
 image 349.5
 portraiture 712.15
 photograph 714.3
 copy 784.1
portrait painter 716.4
portray represent 349.8
 describe 349.9
 enact 704.30
 picture 712.19
pose
 n behavior 321.1
 sham 354.3
 posing 500.3
 gesture 517.14
 v place 159.12
 propose 439.5
 posture 500.13
 postulate 950.12
pose a question 937.19
Poseidon
 mariner 183.1
 spirit of the sea 240.4
 water god 678.10
posh
 grandiose 501.21
 chic 578.13
 upper-class 607.10
 expensive 632.11
posing against
 contraposition 215.1
 symmetrization 264.2
position
 n location 159.1

navigation 159.3
 rank 245.2
 affirmation 334.1
 remark 524.4
 class 607.1
 policy 609.4
 prestige 662.4
 function 724.3
 job 724.5
 skiing 753.3
 race 756.3
 state 764.1
 classification 808.2
 premise 934.7
 opinion 952.6
 attitude 977.1
 outlook 977.2
 v locate 159.11
position paper
 affirmation 334.1
 announcement 352.2
 policy 381.4
 platform 609.7
 classification 800.3
 statement of belief 952.4
positive
 n photocopy 714.5
 print 784.5
 adj downright 247.12
 affirmative 334.8
 unpersuadable 361.13
 helpful 449.21
 real 760.15
 agreeing 787.9
 belief 952.21
 unqualified 959.2
 certain 969.13
 confident 969.16
 dogmatic 969.22
 emphatic 996.21
 numeric 1016.22
 plus 1031.34
positive reinforcement 92.26
posse
 military unit 461.22
 company 769.3
 search 937.15
 police 1007.17
possess
 have 469.4
 take 480.13
 demonize 680.16
 bewitch 691.9
 obsess 925.25
 know 927.12
 haunt 987.6
possessed
 overjoyed 95.16
 frenzied 105.25
 owned 469.8
 bewitched 691.13
 possessed with a demon 925.29
 obsessed 925.33
 haunted 987.10
possessive
 possessory 469.10
 selfish 651.5
possible
 latent 519.5

within the bounds of possibility 965.6
 numeric 1016.22
possum 311.23
post
 n station 159.2
 standard 273.4
 pillar 273.5
 messenger 353.1
 stronghold 460.6
 mail 553.4
 branch 617.10
 position 724.5
 market 736.1
 basketball game 747.3
 base 900.8
 wood 1052.3
 v place 159.12
 speed 174.8
 send 176.15
 publicize 352.15
 make haste 401.5
 pledge 438.10
 record 549.15
 wise up 551.9
 mail 553.12
 commission 615.10
 pay 624.16
 keep accounts 628.8
 list 870.8
 adj epistolary 553.14
 adv swiftly 174.17
 posthaste 401.13
postage 553.5
postage stamp 553.5
postal service 553.7
postcard 553.3
postdated 832.3
posted located 159.18
 pledged 438.12
 recorded 549.17
 informed 927.18
poster bill 352.7
 mail carrier 353.6
posterior
 n rear 217.1
 buttocks 217.4
 adj rear 217.9
 succeeding 814.4
 subsequent 834.4
posterity
 kinfolk 559.2
 progeny 561
 offspring 561.1
 successor 816.4
 sequel 834.2
postgraduate
 n graduate 572.8
 adj scholastic 568.19
 studentlike 572.12
posthaste
 swiftly 174.17
 in posthaste 401.13
posthumous
 postmortem 307.36
 after death 834.5
post-industrial 834.5
postman
 mailman 353.5
 postal service 553.7
postmark 553.5
postmaster 353.5

bar 597.4
rite 701.3
vocation 724.6
exercise 725.6
operation 888.1
tryout 941.3
notation 1016.2
v act 328.4
put into practice
328.8
use 384.5
employ 387.10
perform 434.3
train 568.13
study 570.12
rehearse 704.32
busy oneself with
724.11
exert 725.8
play 744.2
iterate 848.8
practiced
skilled 413.26
experienced 413.28
practice law 597.5
practice medicine
90.14
**practice what one
preaches**
observe 434.2
keep faith 644.9
practicing
n iteration 848.2
adj acting 328.10
observant 434.4
pious 692.8
Prado 386.9
pragmatic
sensible 919.18
realistic 986.6
practical 994.6
prairie
n open space 158.4
horizontal 201.3
plain 236.1
grassland 310.8
adj rustic 233.6
prairie dog 311.23
praise
n congratulation
149.1
thanks 150.2
approval 509.5
flattery 511.1
citation 646.4
glorification 696.2
v congratulate 149.2
give approval 509.12
flatter 511.5
honor 646.8
glorify 696.11
praise the Lord! 696.16
praiseworthy 509.20
pram 179.6
prance
n gait 177.12
caper 366.2
v way of walking
177.28
go on horseback
177.34
caper 366.6

strut 501.15
dance 705.5
prancer horse 311.10
race horse 311.14
prank
n trick 489.10
v dress up 5.41
ornament 498.8
pratfall tumble 194.3
collapse 410.3
goof 974.6
prattle
n nonsense 520.2
speech 524.1
chatter 540.3
v talk nonsense 520.5
chatter 540.5
chat 541.10
pray
v petition 440.10
entreat 440.11
supplicate 696.12
inter please 440.20
prayer entreaty 440.2
supplication 696.4
divine service 696.8
worshiper 696.9
prayer book 554.1
preach admonish 422.6
lecture 543.11
expound 568.16
preacher lecturer 543.5
informer 551.6
teacher 571.7
sermoner 699.3
preamble
n curtain-raiser 815.2
v prefix 813.3
prearrange plan 381.8
prepare 405.6
contract 437.5
precontrive 964.4
precarious
unreliable 970.20
ticklish 1005.12
precaution
n precautiousness
494.3
v forewarn 399.6
precede lead 165.2
rule 249.11
antecede 813.2
go before 815.3
initiate 817.10
be prior 833.3
precedent
n model 785.1
precursor 815.1
antecedent 833.2
verdict 945.5
adj leading 165.3
preceding 813.4
precept
rule 419
prescript 419.1
direction 420.3
a belief 952.2
maxim 973.1
precinct
enclosed place 212.3
nearness 223.1
sphere 231.2

region 231.5
arena 463.1
election district
609.16
precious
n endearment term
562.6
adj beloved 104.24
downright 247.12
overnice 500.18
affected 533.9
punctilious 580.10
dear 632.10
precious few 884.4
precious metals
gold 728.20
metal 1056.3
precious stone
jewel 498.6
gem 1057.6
precipice cliff 200.3
slope 237.2
precipitant
precipitate 401.10
reckless 493.8
sudden 829.5
precipitate
n dregs 256.2
effect 886.1
precipitation 1043.5
v descend 194.5
gravitate 297.15
rain 316.9
hasten 401.4
fell 912.5
deposit 1043.11
adj fast 174.15
impulsive 365.9
precipitant 401.10
unprepared 406.8
reckless 493.8
sudden 829.5
premature 844.8
precipitous
perpendicular 200.12
steep 204.18
precipitate 401.10
reckless 493.8
sudden 829.5
précis
n shortening 268.3
abridgment 557.1
iteration 848.2
v iterate 848.8
precise
v be accurate 972.11
adj meticulous 339.12
fastidious 495.9
punctilious 580.10
detailed 765.9
particular 864.12
discriminating 943.7
exact 972.17
precision
meticulousness 339.3
fastidiousness 495.1
elegance 533.1
accuracy 972.5
preclude
prohibit 444.3
exclude 772.4
prevent 1011.14

precocious 844.8
precognition
understanding 927.3
intuition 933.1
foreknowledge 960.3
preconceive 946.2
preconclusion 946.1
preconscious
n psyche 92.28
adj subconscious
92.41
preconsider 380.7
precursor
harbinger 133.5
leading 165.1
vanguard 216.2
settler 227.9
warning sign 399.3
precedence 813.1
forerunner 815.1
antecedent 833.2
early bird 844.4
transformer 851.5
producer 891.7
predate
date 831.13
be prior 833.3
predator 480.12
predecessor 815.1
predestine
predetermine 963.6
destine 963.7
predetermine
premeditate 380.7
prejudge 946.2
predecide 963.6
predicament
state 764.1
urgent need 962.4
bewilderment 970.3
danger 1005.1
adversity 1010.1
plight 1012.4
predicate
n affirmation 334.1
syntax 530.2
v affirm 334.5
postulate 950.12
predict
look forward to 130.6
foreshow 133.10
come 838.6
foresee 960.5
make a prediction
961.9
risk 971.12
predictable
stable 854.12
divinable 961.13
probable 967.6
reliable 969.17
predilection
inclination 100.3
love 104.1
preference 371.5
tendency 895.1
prejudgment 946.1
disposition 977.3
prejudice 979.3
predispose 893.7
predominant
chief 249.14

president principal
571.8
executive 574.3
head of state 575.7
presidential election
609.15
press
n extractor 192.9
squeezing 260.2
urge 375.6
presswork 548.9
printing office 548.11
publisher 554.2
enlistment 615.7
throng 769.4
thrust 901.2
urgency 996.4
v squeeze 260.8
hot-press 287.6
weigh on 297.11
urge 375.14
hasten 401.4
insist 421.8
bring pressure to bear
upon 424.6
urge upon 439.9
importune 440.12
attach 480.20
embrace 562.18
enlist 615.17
strain 725.10
thrust 901.12
densify 1043.9
the press
informant 551.5
news 552.1
journalism 555.3
press charges 599.7
press conference
conference 541.6
interview 937.11
press into service
387.14
pressman
printer 548.12
journalist 555.4
press one's luck
risk 971.12
take chances 1005.7
press release
release 352.3
message 552.4
pressroom 548.11
press the panic button
127.11
pressure
n touching 73.2
tension 128.3
squeezing 260.2
burden 297.7
urging 375.5
urge 375.6
prestige 417.4
insistence 421.4
coercion 424.3
importunity 440.3
influence 893.1
thrust 901.2
urgent need 962.4
urgency 996.4
adversity 1010.1
v urge 375.14

coerce 424.8
importune 440.12
pressure group
interest group 609.31
party 617.4
influence 893.6
pressure suit
blackout 184.21
space suit 1073.11
pressurize 260.8
presswork 548.9
prestidigitation
juggling 356.5
illusoriness 975.2
prestige
respect 155.1
superiority 249.1
authority 417.4
class 607.1
honor 662.4
influence 893.1
notability 996.2
presto
n music 708.25
tempo 709.24
adj music 708.55
instantaneous 829.4
presto chango 851.13
inter attention! 982.22
presume
hope 124.7
expect 130.5
have the audacity
142.7
imply 519.4
assume 640.6
entail 771.4
judge 945.8
prejudge 946.2
suppose 950.10
think 952.11
think likely 967.5
presume upon
exploit 387.16
impose on 640.7
inflict on 643.7
presumption
hope 124.1
presumptuousness
141.2
insolence 142.1
meddling 214.2
foolhardiness 493.3
implication 519.2
assumption 640.2
entailment 771.2
prejudgment 946.1
supposition 950.3
opinion 952.6
probability 967.1
presumptuous
arrogant 141.10
insolent 142.9
meddlesome 214.9
foolhardy 493.9
presuming 640.11
presuppose
imply 519.4
entail 771.4
prejudge 946.2
suppose 950.10
pre-teens 301.2

pretend sham 354.20
pretext 376.3
affect 500.12
presume 640.6
pretender
impostor 357.6
phony 500.7
usurper 640.4
pretentious
artificial 500.15
ostentatious 501.18
inflated 502.12
affected 533.9
grandiloquent 545.8
pretext
n sham 354.3
loophole 369.4
pretense 376.1
reason 885.2
v make a pretext of
376.3
pretreat 405.6
pretty
adj beautiful 1015.17
adv to a degree 245.7
very 247.18
tolerably 998.24
a pretty penny 632.3
pretzel 10.29
prevail excel 249.6
succeed 409.7
triumph 411.3
dominate 612.15
exist 760.8
persist 780.3
endure 826.6
predominate 863.10
prevailing sentiment
952.6
prevailing taste 578.1
prevailing wind 318.10
prevail upon 375.23
prevalent
customary 373.14
fashionable 578.11
governing 612.18
existent 760.13
happening 830.9
frequent 846.4
prevailing 863.12
plentiful 990.7
prevaricate
equivocate 344.7
lie 354.18
quibble 935.9
prevent prohibit 444.3
anticipate 844.6
hinder 1011.14
preventative
n prophylactic 86.20
counteractant 899.3
adj preventive 1011.19
prevention
avoidance 368.1
prohibition 444.1
stop 1011.2
preview
n look 27.3
motion pictures 706.1
foresight 960.1
v dramatize 704.28
previous prior 833.4

former 836.10
premature 844.8
earlier 844.10
prewar 833.5
prewarn 399.6
prey sufferer 96.11
desire 100.11
sweetheart 104.10
objective 380.2
quarry 382.7
price
n penalty 603.1
interest 623.3
recompense 624.3
charge 630
cost 630.1
quotation 738.9
gambling odds 759.6
v set a price 630.11
price-fixing 630.5
priceless
humorous 488.5
precious 632.10
price supports
policy 609.4
price controls 630.5
prick
n pang 26.2
point 285.3
goad 375.8
mark 517.5
bad person 660.6
v hurt 26.7
tingle 74.5
pain 96.17
come to a point 285.6
perforate 292.15
goad 375.15
mark 517.19
drive 1068.8
prickle
n tingle 74.1
point 285.3
thorn 285.5
adhesive 802.4
v tingle 74.5
prickly
sensitive 24.12
tingly 74.8
excitable 105.28
touchy 110.21
pricky 285.10
prick up the ears
listen 48.10
hearken to 982.7
pride self-esteem 136
proudness 136.1
vanity 140.2
arrogance 141.1
pomp 501.6
group of animals
769.5
confidence 969.5
good thing 998.5
priest celibate 565.2
holy orders 699.4
parish priest 699.5
teacher 699.9
clergy 699.10
priesthood
the ministry 698.1
clericalism 698.3

clergy 699.1
prig snob 141.7
prude 500.11
prim prudish 500.19
stiff 580.9
prima ballerina 707.6
primacy
supremacy 249.3
dominance 417.6
importance 996.1
superexcellence 998.2
prima donna
lead 707.6
singer 710.13
chief 996.10
prima facie
at sight 27.22
apparently 33.12
primal
n first 817.3
adj basic 199.8
chief 249.14
unimitated 337.6
natural 416.6
innate 766.8
essential 766.9
simple 797.6
beginning 817.15
original 885.14
primary
n color system 35.7
election 609.15
first 817.3
adj basic 199.8
front 216.10
chief 249.14
unimitated 337.6
essential 766.9
simple 797.6
beginning 817.15
original 885.14
paramount 996.24
primary election
609.15
primary school 567.3
primate
wild animal 311.23
ancient 841.7
prime
n maturity 303.2
spring 313.2
dawn 314.3
divine service 696.8
first 817.3
the best 998.8
v color 35.13
coat 295.24
load 405.9
tutor 568.11
shoot 903.12
adj front 216.10
chief 249.14
unimitated 337.6
simple 797.6
beginning 817.15
previous 833.4
primitive 841.11
paramount 996.24
best 998.16
numeric 1016.22
prime interest rate
623.3

prime meridian 231.3
prime minister 575.7
primer color 35.8
fuse 462.15
textbook 554.10
elementary education
568.5
basics 817.6
prime time 1034.2
primeval
beginning 817.15
former 836.10
primitive 841.11
original 885.14
primitive
n native 227.3
simple soul 416.3
root 526.2
ancient 841.7
adj basic 199.8
native 226.5
unimitated 337.6
natural 416.6
unrefined 497.12
essential 766.9
simple 797.6
beginning 817.15
former 836.10
primordial 841.11
original 885.14
primordial 841.11
primp dress up 5.41
ornament 498.8
primrose pink 41.8
yellow 43.4
prince potentate 575.8
nobleman 608.7
good person 659.1
Prince Charming
104.13
princess
sovereign queen
575.11
noblewoman 608.8
principal
n superior 249.4
headmaster 571.8
chief 575.3
lead 707.6
capital 728.15
most important
person 996.10
adj chief 249.14
first 817.17
paramount 996.24
principality
region 231.5
country 232.1
dominance 417.6
mastership 417.7
angel 679.1
principle motive 375.1
rule 419.2
essence 766.2
law 868.4
cause 885.1
commitment 885.9
foundation 900.6
a belief 952.2
axiom 973.2
print
n indentation 284.6

mark 517.7
imprint 548.3
type 548.6
picture 712.11
numbered print 713.5
photoprint 714.5
offprint 784.5
copy 784.5
impact 886.2
v represent 349.8
mark 517.19
imprint 548.14
engrave 713.9
process 714.15
fix 854.9
printed written 547.22
in print 548.19
engraved 713.11
printer typist 547.18
printworker 548.12
publisher 554.2
output device 1041.9
printing press 548.9
printmaking
printing 548.1
graphic arts 713.1
the print media 555.3
print run 554.5
print shop 548.11
prior
n religious 699.15
adj leading 165.3
preceding 813.4
previous 833.4
former 836.10
priority leading 165.1
front 216.1
superiority 249.1
prestige 417.4
precedence 813.1
sequence 814.1
previousness 833.1
importance 996.1
prism 29.2
prismatic
chromatic 35.15
variegated 47.9
multilateral 278.11
prison 429.8
prisoner captive 429.11
accused 599.6
prisoner of war 429.11
prissy effeminate 77.14
meticulous 339.12
fastidious 495.9
prudish 500.19
stiff 580.9
pristine
unimitated 337.6
unused 390.12
natural 406.13
unadorned 416.6
innocent 657.6
intact 791.10
simple 797.6
new 840.7
primitive 841.11
original 885.14
undamaged 1001.8
privacy
retirement 345.2
seclusion 584.1

aloneness 871.2
retreat 1008.5
private
n enlisted man 461.8
adj interior 207.6
closed 293.9
personal 312.15
privy 345.13
taking 480.25
privatistic 584.9
intrinsic 766.7
particular 864.12
alone 871.8
private detective
576.10
private enterprise
611.8
private sector
capitalism 611.8
economy 731.7
privation
loss 473.1
deprivation 480.6
indigence 619.2
privatization 584.1
privatize 611.16
privilege
n superiority 249.1
exemption 430.8
license 642.2
v authorize 443.11
privileged information
secret 345.5
inside information
551.2
privy
n latrine 12.10
hut 228.9
adj covert 345.12
private 345.13
privy council
council 423.1
cabinet 613.3
prize
n desire 100.11
booty 482.11
monument 549.12
award 646.2
leverage 905.1
lever 905.4
good thing 998.5
the best 998.8
v cherish 104.21
respect 155.4
measure 300.10
price 630.11
get a purchase 905.8
estimate 945.9
value 996.13
adj best 998.16
prized 104.24
prizefight 457.9
prizewinner 413.15
PR man 352.9
pro
n expert 413.11
professional 726.4
gambler 759.21
affirmative 934.14
adj approving 509.17
occupational 724.16
prep in favor of 509.21

proactive
energetic 17.13
enterprising 330.23
pro and con 934.19
probability
expectation 130.1
the future 838.1
tendency 895.1
liability 896.1
prediction 961.1
possibility 965.1
likelihood 967
chance 971.1
good chance 971.8
probable error
mathematical
probability 967.2
inaccuracy 974.2
probate
n bequest 478.10
v confirm 956.11
probation 941.2
probe
n nurse 90.10
investigation 937.4
search 937.15
feeler 941.4
test rocket 1072.6
artificial satellite
1073.6
v measure 300.10
investigate 937.22
sound out 941.9
philosophize 951.7
probity honesty 644
virtue 653.1
problem
annoyance 96.2
enigma 522.8
topic 936.1
question 937.10
bewilderment 970.3
fault 1002.2
trouble 1012.3
problematic
unbelievable 954.10
doubtful 970.17
bewildering 970.27
proboscis 283.8
procedure
behavior 321.1
rule 373.5
plan 381.1
policy 381.4
manner 384.1
process 888.2
proceed
progress 162.2
behave 321.4
act 328.4
take action 328.5
use 384.5
elapse 820.5
proceed from 886.5
proceedings
activity 330.1
report 549.7
lawsuit 598.1
affairs 830.4
proceeds gain 472.3
yield 472.5
receipts 627.1

production 892.2
process
n manner 384.1
procedure 888.2
v cut or dress the hair
3.22
prepare 405.6
develop 714.15
convert 891.9
gather materials
1052.7
processed
prepared 405.16
made 891.18
procession train 811.3
sequence 814.1
processor 1041.2
proclaim
herald 133.14
affirm 334.5
cry 352.13
command 420.8
state 524.24
be prior 833.3
dogmatize 969.10
proclamation
affirmation 334.1
announcement 352.2
decree 420.4
proclivity
inclination 100.3
preference 371.5
tendency 895.1
disposition 977.3
proconsul 575.13
procrastinate
let go 329.5
leave undone 340.7
not face up to 368.13
protract 826.9
be dilatory 845.11
procrastinator
slowpoke 175.5
neglecter 340.5
procreate grow 14.2
generate 78.8
develop 259.7
engender 817.14
originate 891.12
proctor
teaching fellow 571.4
superintendent 574.2
steward 574.4
lawyer 597.1
procure fetch 176.16
elicit 192.14
induce 375.22
acquire 472.8
prostitute oneself
665.21
purchase 733.7
cause 885.11
procurement
provision 385.1
acquisition 472.1
prod
n goad 375.8
thrust 901.2
v touch 73.6
goad 375.15
importune 440.12
thrust 901.12

prodigal
n wastrel 486.2
adj exaggerated 355.4
improvident 406.15
extravagant 486.8
diffuse 538.11
unvirtuous 654.12
intemperate 669.7
teeming 883.9
plentiful 990.7
superabundant 992.19
prodigal son
penitent 113.5
prodigal 486.2
returnee 858.3
prodigious
wonderful 122.10
large 247.7
huge 257.20
extraordinary 869.14
miraculous 869.16
produce
n vegetables 10.34
fruit 10.36
yield 472.5
receipts 627.1
groceries 735.7
production 892.2
v secrete 13.5
lengthen 267.6
do 328.6
manifest 348.5
accomplish 407.4
write 547.21
dramatize 704.28
pen 718.6
cause 885.10
be productive 889.7
create 891.8
bear 891.13
adduce 956.12
imagine 985.14
product yield 472.5
commodity 735.2
effect 886.1
end product 892
sum 1016.6
productivity
power 18.1
wordiness 538.2
productiveness 889.1
invention 985.3
product liability 641.2
profane
v misuse 389.4
desecrate 694.4
adj cursing 513.8
unsacred 686.3
impious 694.6
secularist 695.16
profanity cursing 513.3
unsanctity 686.1
sacrilege 694.2
profess affirm 334.5
sham 354.20
pretext 376.3
state 952.12
profession
acknowledgment
332.3
affirmation 334.1
claim 376.2

occupation 724.4
vocation 724.6
confession 952.7
testimony 956.2
professional
n expert 413.11
member of a learned
profession 726.4
adj skillful 413.22
skilled 413.26
scholastic 568.19
occupational 724.16
professional ethics
636.1
professor expert 413.11
teacher 571.1
academic rank 571.3
gambler 759.21
proffer
n offer 439.1
v offer 439.4
give 478.12
answer 938.4
adduce 956.12
proficient
n expert 413.11
adj fitted 405.17
skillful 413.22
perfected 1001.9
able 18.14
profile
n outline 211.2
side 218.1
contour 262.2
description 349.2
diagram 381.3
portrait 712.15
history 719.1
v outline 211.9
profit
n incentive 375.7
benefit 387.4
gain 472.3
expedience 994.1
good 998.4
v avail 387.17
make profit 472.12
expedite one's affair
994.3
do good 998.10
profitable useful 387.18
valuable 387.22
helpful 449.21
gainful 472.16
paying 624.21
expedient 994.5
good 998.12
profit sharing 476.2
profit-sharing 476.9
profligate
n reprobate 660.5
libertine 665.10
adj prodigal 486.8
corrupt 654.14
licentious 665.25
pro forma 580.11
profound
deep-felt 93.24
downright 247.12
huge 257.20
deep 275.10
recondite 522.16

protean
multiform 782.3
changeable 853.6
protect preserve 397.8
play safe 1006.3
guard 1007.18
aid 449.11
defend 460.8
protection
bribe 378.2
preservation 397.1
restraint 428.1
custody 429.5
pass 443.7
aid 449.1
defense 460.1
precaution 494.3
policy 609.4
safety 1006.1
safeguarding 1007
guard 1007.1
protectionist 428.6
protector
defender 460.7
regent 575.12
keeper 1007.5
protégé 432.6
protein 7.6
pro tem 827.9
proteolytic 805.6
protest
n complaint 115.4
demur 325.2
objection 333.2
affirmation 334.1
resistance 453.1
disapproval 510.1
nonpayment 625.1
nonconformity 867.1
v object 333.5
affirm 334.5
oppose 451.3
offer resistance 453.3
disapprove 510.10
not pay 625.6
not conform 867.4
Protestant
n non-Catholic 675.20
adj religious 675.28
protocol
treatment 91.14
rule 419.2
compact 437.1
etiquette 580.3
fact 760.3
knowledge 927.1
schedule 964.3
proton atom 258.8
elementary particle
1037.6
protoplasm 305.4
prototype form 262.1
original 337.2
model 785.1
philosophy 931.2
standard of perfection
1001.4
protozoan
microbic 258.15
invertebrate 311.49
protract lengthen 267.6
extend 538.8

prolong 826.9
postpone 845.9
sustain 855.4
protractor 278.4
protrude
emerge 190.11
protuberate 283.10
proud prideful 136.8
vain 140.9
arrogant 141.9
grandiose 501.21
confident 969.21
provable real 760.15
demonstrable 956.19
obvious 969.15
prove print 548.14
result 886.4
experiment 941.8
demonstrate 956.10
confirm 956.11
verify 969.12
check 1016.20
proven
trustworthy 644.19
proved 956.20
true 972.13
provender
n food 10.1
feed 10.4
provisions 10.5
supplies 385.2
v provision 385.9
proverb
n maxim 973.1
v aphorize 973.5
provide supply 385.7
prepare 405.6
furnish 478.15
provide against
prepare for 405.11
take precautions
494.6
provided
adj supplied 385.13
prepared 405.16
adv circumstantially
765.12
conj in the event that
830.13
provided that 958.12
provide for
provide 385.7
prepare for 405.11
furnish 478.15
take precautions
494.6
finance 729.15
allow for 958.5
care for 1007.19
providence
precaution 494.3
thrift 635.1
divine function 677.14
sagacity 919.4
judiciousness 919.7
foresight 960.1
Providence 963.3
provider 385.6
province sphere 231.2
region 231.5
country 232.1
the country 233.1

duty 641.1
diocese 698.8
function 724.3
occupation 724.4
science 927.10
provincial
n governor 575.13
peasant 606.6
adj local 231.9
rustic 233.6
idiomatic 523.20
narrow-minded
979.10
proving ground
laboratory 941.5
testing ground 1072.7
provision
n food 10.1
groceries 10.5
providing 385.1
supplies 385.2
store 386.1
preparation 405.1
stipulation 421.2
support 449.3
giving 478.1
precaution 494.3
substitution 861.1
condition 958.2
foresight 960.1
expedient 994.2
v feed 8.18
provender 385.9
provisional
government 612.4
proviso stipulation
421.2
bill 613.9
condition 958.2
provocateur 375.11
provocative appetizing
63.10
desirable 100.30
exciting 105.30
aggravating 119.5
provoking 375.27
alluring 377.8
hostile 589.10
interesting 982.19
provoke annoy 96.13
irritate 96.14
vex 98.15
stimulate 105.13
aggravate 119.2
be insolent 142.8
incense 152.24
prompt 375.13
incite 375.17
sow dissension 456.14
antagonize 589.7
induce 885.11
interest 982.12
provost principal 571.8
executive 574.3
prow 216.3
prowess skill 413.1
courage 492.1
prowl
n stealth 345.4
v wander 177.23
creep 177.26
lurk 346.9

prowler 483.1
proximate
n person 530.7
v approach 167.3
adj approaching 167.4
near 223.14
approximate 774.8
succeeding 814.4
proximity nearness
223.1
relation 774.1
proxy
n vote 371.6
deputy 576.1
ballot 609.19
voter 609.23
commission 615.1
substitute 861.2
adj substitute 861.8
prude 500.11
prudent vigilant 339.13
cautious 494.8
economical 635.6
moderate 670.10
judicious 919.19
foreseeing 960.7
prune excise 255.10
shorten 268.6
sever 801.11
cultivate 1067.17
prune-faced sour
110.23
aged 303.16
prurient lustful 75.26
craving 100.24
lascivious 665.29
curious 980.5
pruritus itch 74.3
symptom 85.9
twitching 916.5
pry
n meddler 214.4
leverage 905.1
lever 905.4
inquisitive person
980.2
v look 27.13
meddle 214.7
get a purchase 905.8
search 937.30
snoop 980.4
pry loose from 480.22
pry open 292.14
pry out extract 192.10
elicit 192.14
get a purchase 905.8
grill 937.21
search out 937.33
uncover 940.4
PS 816.1
psalm
n paean 696.3
sacred music 708.17
v sing 708.38
the Psalms 701.10
pseudo imitation 336.8
spurious 354.25
pseudonym 527.8
psst! 48.16
psyche psychic
apparatus 92.28
spirit 918.4

psychedelic
  n psychoactive drug
    86.13
  drug of abuse 87.2
  adj psychochemical
    86.46
  hallucinatory 975.10
psyched up 405.16
psychiatric
  psychological 92.36
  psychotherapeutic
    92.37
psychiatric hospital
  925.14
psychiatrist
  psychologist 92.10
  psychiatry 925.19
psychic
  n spiritualist 689.13
  predictor 961.4
  adj occult 689.24
  supernatural 869.15
  mental 918.7
  spectral 987.7
  immaterial 1051.7
psychic energy 92.28
psychic phenomena
  689.6
psychic research 1051.1
psycho
  n lunatic 925.16
  psychotic 925.17
  adj crazy 925.27
psychoactive drug
  hallucinogen 86.13
  drug of abuse 87.2
psychoanalysis 92.6
psychoanalyst 92.10
psychoanalyze 92.35
psychobabble
  psychology 92.1
  jargon 523.10
psychochemical
  n drug 87.2
  adj psychoactive 86.46
psychogenic 92.36
psychokinesis 689.6
psychological
  psychiatric 92.36
  mental 918.7
psychological
  dependence 87.1
psychological warfare
  127.6
psychologist 92.10
psychology science of
  the mind 92
  anthropology 312.10
  attitude 977.1
psychopathic
  psychological 92.36
  psychotic 925.28
psychopathological
  92.36
psychophysical 92.36
psychosexual 92.36
psychosis mental
  disorder 92.14
  psychopathy 925.3
psychosocial 92.36
psychosomatic 92.36
psychotherapeutic 92.37

psychotherapy therapy
  91.1
  science of the mind 92
  psychotherapeutics
    92.5
psychotic
  n insane 925.17
  adj psychological
    92.36
  psychopathic 925.28
psych out unnerve 128.10
  solve 939.2
ptomaine poisoning
  85.31
pub restaurant 8.17
  bar 88.20
puberty bodily
  development 14.1
  adolescence 301.6
pubescence hair 3.2
  bodily development
    14.1
  smoothness 294.3
  adolescence 301.6
pubic hair genitals 2.11
  hair 3.2
public
  n bar 88.20
  follower 166.2
  population 227.1
  market 733.3
  adj exterior 206.7
  general 312.16
  published 352.17
  communal 476.9
  common 497.14
  populational 606.8
  well-known 927.27
public acclaim 662.1
public address 543.2
public assistance
  subsidy 478.8
  welfarism 611.7
publication informing
  343.2
  manifestation 348.1
  dissemination 352
  publishing 352.1
  printing 548.1
  information 551.1
  book 554.1
  dispersion 770.1
public baths 79.10
public enemy enemy
  589.6
  evildoer 593.1
  criminal 660.10
public figure 662.9
publicist publicizer
  352.9
  journalist 555.4
  commentator 556.4
publicity publicness
  352.4
  information 551.1
  repute 662.1
public library 558.1
public nuisance
  annoyance 96.2
  tormentor 96.10
public official official
  575.16

  officeholder 610.11
public opinion political
  influence 609.29
  opinion 952.6
public-opinion poll
  937.14
public ownership
  communion 476.2
  socialism 611.6
public policy 609.4
public radio 1033.16
public records 549.2
public relations 352.4
public safety 1007.1
public school 567.4
public sector 731.7
public servant official
  575.16
  officeholder 610.11
public telephone 347.4
public welfare welfare
  143.5
  subsidy 478.8
publish divulge 351.5
  promulgate 352.10
  print 548.14
  codify 673.9
  disperse 770.4
publisher informant
  551.5
  book publisher 554.2
publishing house
  press 548.11
  publisher 554.2
puce 41.6
pucker
  n dither 105.6
  anxiety 126.1
  wrinkle 291.3
  confusion 984.3
  v contract 260.7
  wrinkle 291.6
pudding food 10.44
  softness 1045.4
  semiliquid 1060.5
  pulp 1061.2
puddle lake 241.1
  mud puddle 1060.9
pudgy corpulent 257.18
  stubby 268.10
puerile childish 301.11
  immature 406.11
  simple-minded 921.24
puff
  n breathing 2.19
  pastry 10.39
  smoking 89.10
  distension 259.2
  puff of air 318.4
  foam 320.2
  publicity 352.4
  commendation 509.3
  makeup 1015.12
  softness 1045.4
  v burn out 21.5
  use 87.21
  smoke 89.14
  enlarge 259.4
  blow 318.20
  publicize 352.15
  exaggerate 355.3
  boast 502.6

  commend 509.11
  praise 509.12
  let out 908.24
puffy corpulent 257.18
  distended 259.13
  windy 318.22
pug
  n foot 199.5
  fighter 461.2
  print 517.7
  boxer 754.2
  adj stubby 268.10
pugilist fighter 461.2
  boxer 754.2
pugnacious
  partisan 456.17
  warlike 458.21
puissant strong 15.15
  powerful 18.12
  authoritative 417.15
puke
  n vomiting 908.8
  v feel disgust 99.4
  vomit 908.27
pulchritude 1015.1
pule cry 60.2
  whine 115.14
Pulitzer Prize 646.2
pull
  n drink 8.4
  power 18.1
  swig 88.7
  proof 548.5
  strain 725.2
  favor 893.2
  pulling 904.1
  draw 904.2
  attraction 906.1
  v drink 8.29
  smoke 89.14
  deflect 164.5
  row 182.53
  extract 192.10
  lengthen 267.6
  restrain 428.7
  print 548.14
  strain 725.10
  play 751.4
  draw 904.4
  attract 906.4
pull a boner
  bungle 414.12
  make a boner 974.15
pull a fast one 415.11
pull ahead 249.10
pull a stunt
  deceive 356.19
  trick 489.14
pull away recede 168.2
  dodge 368.8
  separate 801.8
pull back regress 163.5
  withdraw 163.6
  retract 168.3
  demur 325.4
  hesitate 362.7
  dodge 368.8
  separate 801.8
  retreat 902.7
pull down raze 395.19
  acquire 472.9
  receive 479.6

be paid 624.20
depress 912.4
fell 912.5
pullet fledgling 302.10
poultry 311.29
pull for 403.9
pull in
  retract 168.3
  arrive 186.6
  restrain 428.7
  arrest 429.16
  stop 856.7
  reel in 905.9
pull it together
  order 806.4
  arrange 807.8
Pullman car 197.10
pull off do 328.6
  bring about 407.5
  achieve one's purpose
    409.8
  succeed with 409.11
pull one's leg
  fool 356.15
  trick 489.14
  ridicule 508.8
  flatter 511.6
pull one's punches
  limit 210.5
  allow for 958.5
pull one's weight 476.6
pull out retreat 163.6
  retract 168.3
  maneuver 184.40
  depart 188.6
  extract 192.10
  abandon 370.5
  defect 370.6
  separate 801.8
pull out all the stops
  430.19
pull rank 424.8
pull strings
  maneuver 415.10
  exercise influence
    893.9
pull the plug on 395.11
pull the trigger 459.22
pull the wool over
  one's eyes 356.17
pull through
  cure 396.15
  recover 396.20
pull together
  plan 381.8
  cooperate 450.3
pull up
  maneuver 184.40
  extract 192.10
  arraign 598.14
  stop 856.7
  put a stop to 856.11
pull up short 131.7
pull up stakes
  disappear 34.2
  depart 188.7
  decamp 188.14
  leave 222.10
  flee 368.10
pulmonary 2.30
pulp
  n semiliquid 1060.5

paste 1061.2
v soften 1045.6
pulpify 1061.5
pulpit rostrum 703.13
  platform 900.13
pulpy insipid 65.2
  spongy 1045.11
  semiliquid 1060.11
  pulpous 1061.6
pulsar 1070.8
pulsate drum 55.4
  recur 849.5
  pulse 915.12
pulse
  n plant 310.4
  beat 709.26
  round 849.3
  pulsation 915.3
  radio-frequency pulse
    1035.10
  v resonate 54.6
  recur 849.5
  pulsate 915.12
  flutter 916.12
pulverize
  demolish 395.17
  come apart 801.9
  shatter 801.13
  pound 901.16
  powder 1049.9
puma 311.22
pumice 287.8
pumice stone 79.17
pummel whip 604.13
  pound 901.16
pump
  n viscera 2.14
  extractor 192.9
  poker 759.10
  machinery 1039.3
  v draw off 192.12
  enlarge 259.4
  process 891.9
  alternate 915.14
  interrogate 937.20
pumped up
  energetic 17.13
  prepared 405.16
  overestimated 948.3
pumping iron 84.2
pumpkin 42.2
pun
  n wordplay 489.8
  ambiguity 539.2
  assonance 783.6
  v joke 489.13
  assonate 783.9
punch
  n energy 17.3
  power 18.1
  zest 68.2
  drink 88.9
  vigor 544.3
  engraving tool 713.8
  fight 754.3
  mold 785.6
  thrust 901.2
  hit 901.4
  boxing punch 901.6
  v indent 284.14
  perforate 292.15
  mark 517.19

fight 754.4
thrust 901.12
hit 901.14
Punch and Judy 707.10
punch bowl
  spirits 88.13
  cavity 284.2
punching bag 725.7
punch line 489.6
punch out
  check out 188.13
  ring in 831.12
  beat 901.17
punch the clock 831.12
punctual
  meticulous 339.12
  observant 434.4
  conscientious 644.15
  prompt 844.9
punctuate mark 517.19
  grammaticize 530.16
  emphasize 996.14
punctuation
  punctuation marks
    530.15
  written character
    547.9
puncture
  n trauma 85.37
  hole 292.3
  mark 517.5
  v collapse 260.10
  perforate 292.15
  injure 393.13
  mark 517.19
  disprove 957.4
puncture proof
  resistant 15.20
  impervious 293.13
pundit expert 413.11
  teacher 571.1
  clergy 699.12
  specialist 865.3
  intellectual 928.1
  scholar 928.3
pungent intense 15.22
  painful 26.10
  bitter 64.6
  sour 67.5
  piquant 68.6
  strong 69.10
  witty 489.15
  spirited 544.12
  aphoristic 973.6
punish
  torture 96.18
  penalize 603.4
  chastise 604.10
  get even with 506.7
punishment
  reprisal 506.2
  penalty 603.1
  disciplinary measure
    604
punk
  n homosexual 75.14
  brat 302.4
  a nobody 997.7
  tinder 1020.6
  adj insignificant
    997.18
  bad 999.8

inferior 1004.9
punt
  n game 746.3
  kick 901.9
  v row 182.53
  compromise 468.2
  play 746.5
  bet 759.25
puny frail 16.14
  little 258.10
  haggard 270.20
  meager 991.10
  petty 997.20
pupa 302.12
pupil eye 2.9
  sight organ 27.9
  student 572.1
puppet
  sycophant 138.3
  miniature 258.6
  figure 349.6
  instrument 384.4
  figurehead 575.5
  deputy 576.1
  agent 576.3
  follower 616.8
  toy 743.16
  thing of naught 763.2
puppet government
  country 232.1
  dependent 432.6
puppy
  member 2.7
  impudent person
    142.5
  boy 302.5
  fledgling 302.10
  dog 311.17
  dandy 500.9
puppy love 104.4
purchase
  n grasp 474.2
  buying 733.1
  influence 893.1
  footing 900.5
  hold 905.2
  tackle 905.6
  v bribe 378.3
  buy 733.7
purchasing agent 733.5
purchasing power
  pay 624.4
  purchase 733.1
pure clean 79.25
  essential 192.18
  tasteful 496.8
  elegant 533.6
  plain-speaking 535.3
  honest 644.13
  virtuous 653.7
  spotless 657.7
  chaste 664.4
  godly 692.9
  thorough 793.10
  simple 797.6
  genuine 972.15
  perfect 1001.6
purebred
  upper-class 607.10
  wellborn 608.11
purée 1060.5
pure white 37.7

purgatory
torment 96.7
place of confinement
429.7
penance 658.3
hell 682.1
purge
n defecation 12.2
cleansing 79.2
cleanser 79.17
laxative 86.17
release 120.2
homicide 308.2
extinction 395.6
deposal 447.2
elimination 772.2
v clean 79.18
treat 91.24
release 120.6
kill 308.12
murder 308.15
exterminate 395.14
depose 447.4
justify 600.9
acquit 601.4
eliminate 772.2
do away with 908.21
evacuate 908.22
purify clean 79.18
refine 79.22
subtract 255.9
make plain 499.5
sanctify 685.5
simplify 797.4
purist
n obstinate person
361.6
classicist 533.4
pedant 928.5
adj firm 425.7
strict 687.8
puritan
n prude 500.11
ascetic 667.2
adj firm 425.7
Puritan 859.3
purity
color quality 35.6
cleanness 79.1
plainness 499.1
elegance 533.1
probity 644.1
immaculacy 653.3
innocence 657.1
chastity 664.1
godliness 692.2
simplicity 797.1
oneness 871.1
perfection 1001.1
purl ripple 52.11
border 211.10
eddy 238.21
purlieu resort 228.27
arena 463.1
purloin 482.13
purple
n purpleness 46.1
royal insignia 647.3
v empurple 46.2
adj purpure 46.3
sovereign 417.17
ornate 545.11

purport
n meaning 518.1
v pretext 376.3
intend 380.4
purpose
n resolution 359.1
intention 380.1
function 387.5
intent 518.2
v resolve 359.7
intend 380.4
purr hum 52.13
be pleased 95.11
purse
n funds 728.14
wallet 729.14
v contract 260.7
wrinkle 291.6
purser hand 183.6
attendant 577.5
payer 624.9
treasurer 729.11
purse snatcher 483.2
purse strings 729.14
pursue follow 166.3
practice 328.8
prosecute 382.8
persecute 389.7
court 562.21
elaborate 860.6
specialize 865.4
seek 937.29
pursuer
enthusiast 101.4
lover 104.12
follower 166.2
pursuant 382.4
pursuit
following 166.1
intention 380.1
seeking 382
pursuing 382.1
vocation 724.6
specialty 865.1
purulent
puss-filled 2.31
festering 12.21
purvey 385.9
purview
vision 27.1
commission 615.1
pus humor 2.22
matter 12.6
filth 80.7
push
n energy 17.3
power 18.1
enterprise 330.7
urge 375.6
attack 459.1
poker 759.10
crisis 842.4
thrust 901.2
pushing 903.1
v use 87.21
make one's way 162.4
set in motion 172.6
hustle 330.13
urge 375.14
hasten 401.4
try hard 403.12
importune 440.12

launch an attack
459.17
deal illicitly 732.7
play 751.4
thrust 901.12
propel 903.9
dismiss 983.4
push around
torture 96.18
domineer 612.16
push aside reject 372.2
put away 390.6
postpone 845.9
push-button control
1040.4
push-button telephone
347.4
pushcart 736.6
pusher addict 87.20
propeller plane 181.2
writer 718.3
racketeer 732.4
push off
v get under way
182.19
depart 188.7
leave 222.10
repulse 907.3
inter go away! 908.32
push on hasten 401.4
make haste 401.5
push one's luck
risk 971.12
take chances 1005.7
pushover weakling 16.6
dupe 358.2
victory 411.1
trusting soul 953.4
easy thing 1013.4
push the panic button
127.11
push up daisies 307.20
pushy insolent 142.9
meddlesome 214.9
enterprising 330.23
strong-willed 359.15
pusillanimous 491.12
puss face 216.4
cat 311.21
pussy
n cat 311.21
adj oozing 2.31
festering 12.21
pussycat cat 311.21
good person 659.2
beauty 1015.9
pussyfoot
n quibbler 935.7
v creep 177.26
lurk 346.9
dodge 368.8
be cautious 494.5
quibble 935.9
adj in hiding 346.14
pustule sore 85.36
swelling 283.4
blemish 1003.1
put
n option 737.21
throw 903.3
v place 159.12
affirm 334.5

phrase 532.4
impose 643.4
invest 729.16
attribute 887.3
throw 903.10
adj phrased 532.5
**put a bee in one's
bonnet**
propose 439.5
hint 551.10
put about
turn round 163.9
change course 182.30
publish 352.10
put a crimp in 1011.16
put across do 328.6
deceive 356.14
make clear 521.6
impose on 643.7
put a curse on
curse 513.5
put a hex on 691.10
put a move on 439.8
put and call 737.21
put an end to
kill 308.12
make an end of 395.12
annihilate 761.7
end 819.5
put a stop to 856.11
halt 1011.13
put a question to
937.19
put aside
v remove 176.11
reserve 386.12
put away 390.6
save 635.4
segregate 772.6
postpone 845.9
dismiss 983.4
adj neglected 340.14
unused 390.12
put a spin on 350.3
put a stop to
call a halt to 856.11
stop 1011.13
put at
measure off 300.11
calculate 1016.17
putative
attributable 887.6
supposed 950.14
put away devour 8.22
ingest 187.11
kill 308.12
secrete 346.7
store 386.10
lay away 390.6
accomplish 407.4
divorce 566.5
put back
turn back 163.8
change course 182.30
impair 393.9
restore 396.11
fend off 460.10
return 481.4
repulse 907.3
put before
confront 216.8
propose 439.5

put by
 v store 386.10
 reserve 386.12
 put away 390.6
 adj reserved 386.15
 unused 390.12
put-down 137.2
put down
 v abase 137.5
 be disrespectful 156.6
 disdain 157.3
 deposit 159.14
 overshadow 249.8
 kill 308.12
 extinguish 395.15
 conquer 412.10
 suppress 428.8
 deprecate 510.12
 disparage 512.8
 record 549.15
 pay over 624.15
 impose 643.4
 underestimate 949.2
 adj conquered 412.17
 suppressed 428.14
put down roots 159.17
put faith in 952.10
put forth
 set out 188.8
 vegetate 310.31
 issue 352.14
 propose 439.5
 flaunt 501.17
 say 524.23
 exert 725.8
put in establish 159.16
 sail for 182.35
 land 186.8
 enter 189.7
 insert 191.3
 internalize 207.5
 interrupt 214.6
 spend 387.13
 install 615.12
 plant 1067.18
put in a call 347.18
put in a good word
 375.14
put in a hole 1012.15
put in an appearance
 appear 33.8
 arrive 186.6
 attend 221.8
put in a new light
 551.8
put in for 440.9
put in motion
 impel 901.11
 start 903.13
put in one's place 137.5
**put in one's two cents'
 worth**
 interrupt 214.6
 affirm 334.5
 speak up 524.22
 judge 945.8
put in order
 repair 396.14
 arrange 807.8
 classify 808.6
put in place 159.11
put in storage 159.15

put into effect 328.7
put into words
 say 524.23
 phrase 532.4
put in writing
 write 547.19
 record 549.15
put it all behind one
 465.10
put it away 8.24
put it on the line
 confront 216.8
 insist 421.8
put it to
 confront 216.8
 propose 439.5
put money in 729.16
put new life into
 refresh 9.2
 vivify 306.9
 revive 396.16
put off
 v take off 6.6
 offend 98.11
 get under way 182.19
 sail away from 182.36
 dodge 368.8
 not face up to 368.13
 disincline 379.4
 postpone 845.9
 adj averse 99.8
 late 845.16
put-off 376.1
put off mortality
 307.19
put on
 don 5.42
 accelerate 174.10
put on sail 182.20
put on
 intrude 214.5
 cover 295.19
 sham 354.20
 deceive 356.14
 fool 356.15
 trick 489.14
 banter 490.6
 affect 500.12
 give oneself airs
 501.14
 ridicule 508.8
 impose 643.4
 administer 643.6
 dramatize 704.28
 give a lift 911.7
 stultify 922.7
 call attention to
 982.10
put-on
 n fake 354.13
 affectation 500.1
 gibe 508.2
 adj spurious 354.25
 assumed 500.16
put on airs
 affect 500.12
 give oneself airs
 501.14
put on alert 399.5
put on an act 354.20
put on an even keel
 182.49

put on a pedestal
 respect 155.4
 praise 509.12
 overpraise 511.7
 exalt 911.6
 overestimate 948.2
put on a show
 cut a dash 501.13
 dramatize 704.28
put on blinders 979.6
**put one's cards on the
 table**
 confess 351.7
 shoot straight 644.10
put one's feet up
 rest 20.6
 be at ease 121.8
 be still 173.7
 do nothing 329.2
put one's finger on
 locate 159.11
 designate 517.18
 specify 864.11
 attention 982.1
 call attention to
 982.10
put one's foot down
 remain firm 359.9
 lay down the law
 420.10
 insist 421.8
 refuse 442.3
 stand fast 854.11
**put one's foot in one's
 mouth**
 bungle 414.12
 talk out of turn 843.4
 make a boner 974.15
 get into trouble
 1012.12
put one's hands on
 seize 480.14
 discover 940.2
**put one's house in
 order**
 prepare oneself 405.13
 order 806.4
 organize 807.10
**put one's life on the
 line** 492.11
**put one's money where
 one's mouth is**
 take action 328.5
 risk 971.12
**put one's nose out of
 joint**
 disappoint 132.2
 humiliate 137.6
 make angry 152.23
 make jealous 153.4
 overshadow 249.8
 thwart 1011.15
**put one's shoulder to
 the wheel**
 be determined 359.8
 undertake 404.3
 set to work 725.15
**put one's tail between
 one's legs**
 flinch 127.13
 lose one's nerve 491.8
put one's trust in 124.7

put oneself down for
 commit 436.5
 contribute 478.14
**put oneself in another's
 shoes** 336.7
**put one through the
 wringer** 604.11
put one wise
 disclose 351.4
 disillusion 976.2
 call attention to
 982.10
put on hold
 v put away 390.6
 postpone 845.9
 dismiss 983.4
 adj late 845.16
put on ice 845.9
put on notice 399.5
put on paper 549.15
put on parole 431.5
put on report 599.7
put on tape 549.15
put on the agenda
 v schedule 964.6
 adj listed 870.9
put on the air 1033.25
put on the alert 400.3
put on the back burner
 v put away 390.6
 postpone 845.9
 dismiss 983.4
 adj late 845.16
put on the block 734.11
put on the brakes
 slow 175.9
 put a stop to 856.11
 stop 1011.13
put on the feed bag
 8.20
**put on the finishing
 touches** 392.11
put on the map
 locate 159.11
 publicize 352.15
put on the market
 738.12
put on the right track
 161.6
put on the scales
 297.10
put on the shelf
 put away 390.6
 postpone 845.9
put on the spot 1005.6
put on the stand
 598.16
put on to 551.11
put on weight 259.8
put out
 chagrin 96.15
 dissatisfy 108.5
 dismay 127.19
 humiliate 137.4
 make public 352.11
 issue 352.14
 extinguish 395.15
 print 548.14
 spend 626.5
 exert 725.8
 eject 908.13
 evict 908.15

bewilder 970.12
confuse 984.7
inconvenience 995.4
trouble 1012.13
fight fire 1021.7
put-out
n game 745.3
adj distressed 96.22
provoked 152.27
bewildered 970.24
confused 984.12
put out feelers 941.9
put out of action 19.9
put out of business
625.8
put out of commission
19.9
put out of joint 160.5
put out of one's misery
145.4
put out of reach 966.6
put out of sight
conceal 346.6
secrete 346.7
put out the welcome
mat 585.7
put out to pasture
feed 8.18
scrap 390.8
depose 447.4
dismiss 908.19
put over
bring about 407.5
succeed with 409.11
manage 409.12
make clear 521.6
impose on 643.7
put pressure on 424.6
putrid
nasty 64.7
malodorous 71.5
filthy 80.23
decayed 393.40
bad 999.8
put right
direct to 161.6
remedy 396.13
put sanctions on 603.4
putsch 327.4
put six feet under
309.19
put straight
v straighten 277.5
make better 392.9
remedy 396.13
arrange 437.8
disillusion 976.2
adj disillusioned
976.5
putt 751.4
putter waste time
331.13
trifle 997.14
put the arm on 621.3
put the best face on
600.12
put the blame on
blame 599.8
attribute to 887.4
put the cart before the
horse
invert 205.5

misinterpret 342.2
not know what one is
about 414.14
put the fear of God
into 127.16
put the final touches on
819.7
put the finger on
inform on 551.13
accuse 599.7
attribute to 887.4
put the hammer down
756.4
put the heat on
coerce 424.8
threaten 514.2
put the icing on the
cake 407.6
put the kibosh on
disable 19.9
silence 51.8
do for 395.11
end 819.5
put the lid on
silence 51.8
close 293.6
top 295.21
cover up 345.8
complete 407.6
suppress 428.8
end 819.5
put the pedal to the
metal 174.9
put the pressure on
937.21
put the screws to
coerce 424.8
overprice 632.7
grill 937.21
put the shot 903.10
put the skids under
do for 395.11
end 819.5
put through
channel 239.15
do 328.6
carry out 328.7
bring about 407.5
succeed with 409.11
manage 409.12
execute 437.9
legislate 613.10
put through the third
degree 937.21
putting 159.6
putting green
green 310.7
playground 743.11
golf 751.1
put to 799.7
put to bed 548.14
put to death
kill 308.12
execute 604.17
put together
v make up 405.7
assemble 769.18
compose 795.3
join 799.5
combine 804.3
produce 891.8
adj made 891.18

put to good use
apply 387.11
avail oneself of 387.14
put to music 708.46
put to one side 176.11
put to rest
abolish 395.13
end 819.5
disprove 957.4
put to rights
remedy 396.13
arrange 807.8
put to sea
get under way 182.19
embark 188.15
put to shame
humiliate 137.4
overshadow 249.8
disgrace 661.8
put to sleep
lull to sleep 22.20
deaden 25.4
kill 308.12
put to the test 941.8
put to use apply 387.11
avail oneself of 387.14
put two and two
together
reason 934.15
conclude 945.10
putty softness 1045.4
semiliquid 1060.5
putty in one's hands
893.5
put under 22.20
put under arrest
arrest 429.15
capture 480.18
put under a spell 377.7
put under lock and key
429.14
put under oath 334.7
put under surveillance
937.27
put up
v establish 159.16
suspend 202.8
house 225.10
increase 251.4
sham 354.20
nominate 371.19
accommodate 385.10
store up 386.11
do up 397.11
pledge 438.10
offer 439.4
pay over 624.15
put up for sale 734.10
bet 759.25
produce 891.8
adj fabricated 354.28
pledged 438.12
prearranged 964.8
put up a fight
object 333.5
offer resistance
453.3
contend 457.13
put up a front
sham 354.20
pretext 376.3
affect 500.12

give oneself airs
501.14
defend 600.10
put up an argument
934.16
put up a roadblock
1011.12
put up as collateral
v pledge 438.10
adj pledged 438.12
put upon 214.5
put-upon 96.22
put up or shut up 328.5
put up to 375.17
put up with
endure 134.5
suffer 443.10
substitute 861.4
put words in one's
mouth 887.4
putz
stupid person 923.2
fool 923.4
puzzle
n enigma 522.8
the unknown 929.7
bewilderment 970.3
dilemma 1012.7
v think hard 930.9
perplex 970.13
trouble 1012.13
pygmy
n dwarf 258.5
human group 312.3
adj dwarf 258.13
pylon
flying and landing
guides marker
184.19
tower 272.6
pyramid
n structure 266.2
tower 272.6
tomb 309.16
monument 549.12
pile 769.10
hierarchy 808.4
v increase 251.4
trade 737.23
pile 769.19
pyre
mortuary 309.9
fire 1018.13
pyromaniac 1019.8
pyrotechnics
public speaking
543.1
fireworks 1018.17
heat 1018.21
pyrrhic 720.16
Pyrrhic victory 411.1
QED 956.25
quack
n impostor 357.6
v bird sound 60.5
adj quackish 354.27
quackery 354.7
quad
enclosed place 212.3
plot 231.4
space 548.7
four 878.1

quadrant
instrument 278.4
semicircle 280.8
part 792.1
quadratic 878.4
quadrennial 849.4
quadrilateral
n four 878.1
adj sided 218.7
quadrangular 278.9
four 878.4
quadriplegic 85.44
quadruped
n creature 311.3
adj four 878.4
quadruple
v quadruplicate 879.2
adj quadruplicate
879.3
quadruplet 878.1
quaff
n drink 8.4
v drink 8.29
tipple 88.24
quagmire
receptacle of filth
80.12
marsh 243.1
complex 798.2
predicament 1012.4
quail
flinch 127.13
demur 325.4
cower 491.9
pull back 902.7
quaint
humorous 488.4
odd 869.11
quake
n upheaval 671.5
shake 916.3
v be excited 105.18
tremble 127.14
shake 916.11
freeze 1022.9
qualification
ability 18.2
circumscription 210.2
minimization 252.5
eligibility 371.11
fitting 405.2
preparedness 405.4
talent 413.4
stipulation 421.2
restriction 428.3
extenuation 600.5
fitness 787.5
change 851.1
provision 958
limitation 958.1
qualifier 530.2
qualify
circumscribe 210.5
fit 405.8
measure up 405.15
succeed 409.7
stipulate 421.7
restrict 428.9
suit 787.8
change 851.7
limit 958.3
suffice 990.4

qualitative analysis
800.1
quality milieu 209.3
taste 496.1
aristocracy 607.3
nobility 608.2
nature 766.4
characteristic 864.4
goodness 998.1
quality control
examination 937.3
process control 1040.8
quality of life
contentment 107.1
courtesy 504.1
prosperity 1009.1
qualm nausea 85.30
compunction 113.2
apprehension 127.4
nervousness 128.1
demur 325.2
objection 333.2
conscientiousness
644.2
quandary
bewilderment 970.3
dilemma 1012.7
quantify
quantize 244.4
measure 300.10
number 1016.16
quantity
quantum 244.1
amount 244.2
numerousness 247.3
capacity 257.2
lump 257.10
measure 300.2
extent 300.3
vowel quantity 524.12
meter 720.7
sum 1016.6
quantum
energy unit 17.7
quantity 244.1
portion 477.5
measurement of light
1024.21
quantum leap
progression 162.1
improvement 392.1
innovation 851.4
revolution 859.1
quantum mechanics
mathematical
probability 967.2
nuclear physics
1037.1
quarantine
n enclosure 212.1
isolation 429.2
seclusion 584.1
exclusiveness 772.3
v enclose 212.5
isolate 429.13
segregate 772.6
quark 258.8
quarrel
n open quarrel 456.5
contention 457.1
fight 457.4
arrow 462.6

v dispute 456.11
contend 457.13
quarry
n desire 100.11
sweetheart 104.10
pit 284.4
objective 380.2
game 382.7
source of supply 386.4
fountainhead 885.6
mine 1056.6
v extract 192.10
excavate 284.15
mine 1056.14
quart 880.2
quarter
n pity 145.1
direction 161.1
side 218.1
region 231.1
heraldry 647.2
money 728.7
game 746.3
basketball game 747.3
soccer 752.3
part 792.1
moment 823.2
fourth 880.2
v house 225.10
divide by four 880.3
adj fourth 880.5
quarterback
n football team 746.2
v direct 573.8
quarter horse 757.2
quarterly
n periodical 555.1
adj momentary 849.8
quartermaster
ship's officer 183.7
steersman 183.8
provider 385.6
quarter note 709.14
quarter rest 709.21
quarters 228.4
quartet
cooperation 450.1
part music 708.18
four 878.1
quasar 1070.8
quash cover up 345.8
extinguish 395.15
suppress 428.8
quasi
adj imitation 336.8
spurious 354.25
nominal 527.15
approximating 783.14
adv imitatively 336.11
supposedly 950.17
quaternary
n four 878.1
adj four 878.4
quaver
n trepidation 105.5
speech defect 525.1
note 709.14
trill 709.19
shake 916.3
v be weak 16.8
be excited 105.18
tremble 127.14

speak poorly 525.7
sing 708.38
shake 916.11
queasy nauseated 85.56
overfastidious 495.12
queen
homosexual 75.15
ant 311.32
bee 311.33
sovereign queen
575.11
princess 608.8
chessman 743.17
card 758.2
the best 998.8
queen bee bee 311.33
chief 575.4
important person
996.9
Queensbury rules 754.1
queen size
n large size 257.4
adj large 257.16
queer
n homosexual 75.15
counterfeit 728.10
v disable 19.9
spoil 393.11
hinder 1011.16
adj homosexual 75.29
spurious 354.25
odd 869.11
insane 925.26
eccentric 926.5
quell extinguish 395.15
conquer 412.10
suppress 428.8
subdue 432.9
calm 670.7
quench gratify 95.7
disincline 379.4
extinguish 395.15
suppress 428.8
fight fire 1021.7
query
n question 937.10
v inquire 937.19
interrogate 937.20
doubt 954.6
be curious 980.3
que será será 963.11
quest
n intention 380.1
pursuit 382.1
adventure 404.2
search 937.15
v pursue 382.8
seek 937.29
question
n enigma 522.8
remark 524.4
bill 613.9
topic 936.1
query 937.10
doubt 954.2
gamble 970.8
v communicate with
343.8
inquire 937.19
interrogate 937.20
doubt 954.6
be uncertain 970.9

be curious 980.3
questionable
  deceptive 356.21
  dishonest 645.16
  unbelievable 954.10
  improbable 968.3
  doubtful 970.17
questioning
  n interrogation 937.12
  adj communicational
    343.9
  inquiring 937.35
  doubting 954.9
question mark
  enigma 522.8
  question 937.10
questionnaire
  n roll 870.6
  canvass 937.14
  v canvass 937.28
queue
  n braid 3.7
  tail 217.6
  series 811.2
  afterpart 816.2
  v line up 811.6
quibble
  n criticism 510.4
  quiddity 935.4
  v find fault 510.15
  argue 934.16
  cavil 935.9
quiche 10.39
quick
  adj eager 101.8
  hot-tempered 110.25
  fast 174.15
  living 306.11
  willing 324.5
  swift 330.18
  alert 339.14
  impulsive 365.9
  hasty 401.9
  skillful 413.22
  teachable 570.18
  brief 827.8
  sudden 829.5
  prompt 844.9
  smart 919.14
  adv swiftly 174.17
the quick
  sore spot 24.4
  provocation 152.11
  the living 306.4
  inner nature 766.5
quick and dirty
  extemporaneous
    365.12
  handy 387.20
  makeshift 994.7
quicken
  refresh 9.2
  energize 17.10
  sensitize 24.7
  stimulate 105.13
  accelerate 174.10
  come to life 306.8
  vivify 306.9
  hasten 401.4
  be useful 449.17
  facilitate 1013.7
quick fix 994.2

quick-freeze
  preserve 397.9
  freeze 1023.11
quick on the draw
  sensitive 24.12
  quick 330.18
  alert 339.14
  impulsive 365.9
  reactive 902.9
quicksand marsh 243.1
  danger 1005.1
  predicament 1012.4
quicksilver
  n swiftness 174.6
  changeableness 853.4
  adj active 330.17
  fickle 364.6
  brass 1056.17
quickstep march
  march 177.13
  military march 708.12
quid bite 8.2
  chewing tobacco 89.7
  money 728.8
quid pro quo
  offset 338.2
  tit for tat 506.3
  interaction 776.3
  substitution 861.1
  interchange 862.1
quiescent
  silent 51.10
  quiet 173.12
  passive 329.6
  inactive 331.17
  permanent 852.7
quiet
  n rest 20.1
  silence 51.1
  composure 106.2
  quiescence 173.1
  peacefulness 464.2
  order 806.1
  v fall silent 51.7
  silence 51.8
  quieten 173.8
  calm 670.7
  order 806.4
  adj vacational 20.10
  soft-colored 35.21
  silent 51.10
  calm 106.12
  reserved 139.11
  quiescent 173.12
  taciturn 344.9
  covert 345.12
  meek 433.15
  pacific 464.9
  tasteful 496.8
  inter silence! 51.14
quill
  n feather 3.16
  feather part 3.17
  thorn 285.5
  v fold 291.5
quilt 295.10
quintessential
  essential 192.18
  typical 349.15
  characteristic 864.13
  best 998.16
  perfected 1001.9

quintet
  cooperation 450.1
  part music 708.18
  five 881.1
quintuplets 881.1
quip
  n witticism 489.7
  gibe 508.2
  quirk 926.2
  quibble 935.4
  v joke 489.13
quirk distortion 265.1
  caprice 364.1
  mannerism 500.2
  characteristic 864.4
  twist 926.2
  quibble 935.4
quirky capricious 364.5
  eccentric 926.5
quit
  v vacate 188.9
  abandon 370.5
  cease to use 390.4
  resign 448.2
  requite 506.5
  repay 624.11
  cease 856.6
  adj clear 430.31
quite
  adv to a degree 245.7
  very 247.18
  positively 247.19
  absolutely 793.15
  inter yes 332.18
  right on! 972.25
quite the contrary
  adv contrarily 778.9
  inter no 335.8
  by no means 335.9
quitter 362.5
quiver
  n thrill 105.2
  trepidation 105.5
  trill 709.19
  bundle 769.8
  shake 916.3
  flutter 916.4
  flicker 1024.8
  v be weak 16.8
  be excited 105.18
  tremble 127.14
  shake 916.11
  freeze 1022.9
  flicker 1024.25
quixotic 985.24
quixotic ideal 124.5
quiz
  n examination 937.2
  questioning 937.12
  v interrogate 937.20
  be curious 980.3
quiz show 1034.2
quizzical
  humorous 488.4
  bantering 490.7
  ridiculing 508.12
  inquiring 937.35
  curious 980.5
Quonset hut 228.9
quorum 769.2
quota portion 477.5
  part 792.1

ratio 1016.7
quotation price 630.1
  stock price 738.9
  repetition 848.1
  citation 956.5
quote state 524.24
  repeat 848.7
  cite 956.13
quote out of context
  misinterpret 342.2
  distort 350.3
rabbi teacher 571.1
  master 575.1
  supporter 616.9
  clergy 699.10
  wise man 920.1
Rabbi 648.5
rabbinical 698.13
rabbit hare 311.24
  productiveness 889.6
rabbit's-foot 691.5
rabble
  rabblement 606.3
  throng 769.4
rabble-rouser
  instigator 375.11
  speaker 543.4
rabid
  frenzied 105.25
  infuriated 152.32
  maniac 925.30
  fanatic 925.32
rabies disease 85.40
  hydrophobia 925.6
raccoon 311.23
race
  n run 174.3
  stream 238.1
  flow 238.4
  watercourse 239.2
  humankind 312.1
  haste 401.1
  contest of speed
    457.12
  people 559.4
  lineage 560.4
  game 743.9
  skiing 753.1
  downhill race 753.3
  automobile racing
    756.1
  driving 756.3
  horse race 757.3
  class 808.2
  kind 808.3
  v speed 174.8
  accelerate 174.10
  make haste 401.5
  race with 457.19
  drive 756.4
  run 757.5
race against the clock
    1005.8
race against time
  n crisis 842.4
  v spend time 820.6
  be in danger 1005.8
race course 753.1
race hatred hate 103.1
  exclusiveness 772.3
  discrimination 979.4
race horse 311.14

racer speeder 174.5
  skier 753.2
  automobile racing
    756.1
racetrack 757.1
race walk 177.27
racial 559.7
racial segregation
  772.3
racing
  n track 457.11
  adj flowing 238.24
racing car 756.1
racing form 757.4
racism hate 103.1
  discrimination 979.4
racist
  n hater 103.4
  bigot 979.5
  adj discriminatory
    979.12
rack
  n agony 26.6
  torment 96.7
  slow motion 175.2
  gait 177.12
  storehouse 386.6
  destruction 395.1
  punishment 604.2
  torture 605.4
  strain 725.2
  gear 1039.5
  v pain 26.7
  torment 96.18
  way of walking 177.28
  torture 604.16
  strain 725.10
racked pained 26.9
  affected 93.23
  tortured 96.25
racket
  n noise 53.3
  rattle 55.3
  fraud 356.8
  stratagem 415.3
  turbulence 671.2
  vocation 724.6
  illicit business 732.1
  tennis 748.1
  cheating 759.13
  commotion 809.4
  pandemonium 809.5
  elastic 1046.3
  v be noisy 53.9
racketeer
  extortionist 480.12
  bandit 483.4
  evildoer 593.1
  criminal 660.10
  Mafioso 732.4
rack one's brains
  think hard 930.9
  try to recall 988.21
rack up 395.17
racy
  zestful 68.7
  spirited 544.12
  risqué 666.7
  interesting 982.19
radar
  radio navigation
    182.2

  electronic navigation
    184.6
  electronics 1032.1
  radio detection 1035
radar defenses 460.2
radar tracking station
  proving ground
    1072.7
  space station 1073.5
radial
  n divergence 171.1
  adj radiating 171.9
radiant
  n axle 914.5
  meteor 1070.15
  adj happy 95.15
  cheerful 109.11
  illustrious 662.19
  almighty 677.18
  gorgeous 1015.20
  luminous 1024.30
radiant energy
  light 1024.1
  radiation 1036.1
radiant heat 1018.1
radiate
  v exude cheerfulness
    109.6
  radiate out 171.6
  disperse 770.4
  shine 1024.23
  broadcast 1033.25
  transmit 1035.15
  adj radiating 171.9
radiation radius 171.2
  dispersion 770.1
  light 1024.1
  beam 1024.5
  radioactive
    emanation 1036
  radiant energy 1036.1
  ray 1036.3
  space hazard 1073.10
radiator 1036.5
radical
  n left side 220.1
  reformer 392.6
  morphology 526.3
  phonetic symbol 546.2
  extremist 611.12
  source 885.5
  foundation 900.6
  atomic cluster 1037.7
  adj basic 199.8
  left 220.4
  utmost 247.13
  emendatory 392.16
  extreme 611.20
  innate 766.8
  thorough 793.10
  revolutionary 859.5
  original 885.14
  numeric 1016.22
radical change
  upheaval 851.2
  revolution 859.1
radical group 1058.2
radical right 611.9
radicle 310.20
radio
  n radiotelephony
    347.3

  informant 551.5
  news 552.1
  electronics 1032.1
  radio communica-
    tions 1033
  wireless 1033.1
  radio receiver 1033.3
  v telegraph 347.19
  broadcast 1033.25
  adj communicational
    347.20
  wireless 1033.28
radioactive 1036.10
radioactive element
  1036.5
radioactive isotope
  1037.5
radioactive particle
  1036.4
radio broadcasting
  1033.16
radiocarbon dating
  1036.1
radio frequency
  1033.12
radio-frequency
  1033.28
radioisotope
  radiotherapy 91.8
  radioactive 1036.5
  isotope 1037.5
radiology
  radiography 91.7
  radiation physics
    1036.7
  nuclear physics
    1037.1
radioman 1033.24
radio signal 1033.10
radio station
  transmitting station
    1033.6
  space station 1073.5
radiotelephone 347.5
radio telescope
  radio 1033.3
  observatory 1070.17
radiotherapy
  radiation therapy 91.6
  radiation physics
    1036.7
radio transmitter
  1033.4
radium
  radiotherapy 91.8
  cauterant 1019.15
radius
  convergence 169.1
  radiation 171.2
  size 257.1
  diameter 269.3
  straight line 277.2
  circle 280.2
raffle 759.14
raft
  n float 180.11
  lot 247.4
  wealth 618.3
  v haul 176.13
rag
  n material 4.1
  garment 5.3

  sail 180.14
  newspaper 555.2
  rabble 606.3
  scenery 704.20
  dance music 708.8
  tempo 709.24
  v berate 510.19
  syncopate 708.43
  play 749.7
ragamuffin 178.3
rag doll 743.16
rage
  n fury 105.8
  fit 152.8
  passion 152.10
  fad 578.5
  violence 671.1
  turbulence 671.2
  frenzy 925.7
  mania 925.12
  v be excitable 105.16
  be angry 152.15
  blow 318.20
  bluster 503.3
  storm 671.11
  be insane 925.20
ragged
  raucous 58.15
  tormented 96.24
  rugged 288.7
  shabby 393.32
  nonuniform 781.3
  slovenly 809.15
ragging
  n bantering 490.3
  ridicule 508.1
  game 749.3
  adj ridiculing 508.12
raging
  n violence 671.1
  adj frenzied 105.25
  infuriated 152.32
  stormy 318.23
  blustering 503.4
  turbulent 671.18
  rabid 925.30
rags material 4.1
  clothing 5.1
  tatters 5.5
  remainder 256.1
  refuse 391.4
  poker 759.10
rags-to-riches 1009.12
ragtag 606.3
ragtime
  n dance music 708.8
  tempo 709.24
  adj syncopated 709.29
rah 116.2
raid
  n foray 459.4
  plundering 482.6
  manipulation 737.20
  v foray 459.20
  plunder 482.17
raider assailant 459.12
  plunderer 483.6
rail
  n fence 212.4
  thinness 270.7
  railway 383.7
  horse racing 757.1

luxuriant 310.40
tainted 393.41
wicked 654.16
base 661.12
vulgar 666.8
terrible 999.9
rank and file
army 461.23
the people 606.1
rankle fester 12.15
pain 26.7
provoke 152.24
decay 393.22
be remembered
988.14
rank-order 945.9
ransack
plunder 482.17
rummage 937.32
ransom
n rescue 398.1
recovery 481.3
v redeem 396.12
rescue 398.3
recover 481.6
rant
n bluster 503.1
nonsense 520.2
bombast 545.2
v be excitable 105.16
be angry 152.15
bluster 503.3
declaim 543.10
rage 671.11
overact 704.31
be insane 925.20
rap
n thud 52.3
report 56.1
criticism 510.4
discussion 541.7
condemnation 602.1
hit 901.4
tap 901.7
trifle 997.5
v thud 52.15
crack 56.6
criticize 510.14
discuss 541.12
pound 901.16
tap 901.18
rapacious
greedy 100.27
ravenous 480.26
gluttonous 672.6
rape
n sexual possession
480.3
plundering 482.6
seduction 665.6
unruliness 671.3
v possess sexually
480.15
seduce 665.20
rage 671.11
rapid
n rapids 238.10
adj fast 174.15
steep 204.18
constant 846.5
rapid deployment force
461.15

**rapid-eye-movement
sleep** 22.1
rapid fire 846.2
rapids rapid 238.10
outburst 671.6
rapist
sexual pervert 75.16
seducer 665.12
violent person 671.9
rap on the knuckles
n reproof 510.5
slap 604.3
v reprove 510.17
rapping
n speech 524.1
conversation 541.1
adj banging 56.11
rapport
pleasantness 97.1
accord 455.1
good terms 587.3
relation 774.1
rapt overjoyed 95.16
persevering 360.8
absorbed in thought
930.22
gripped 982.18
abstracted 984.11
rapture happiness 95.2
amorousness 104.3
fury 105.8
trance 691.3
rara avis 869.4
rare underdone 11.8
wonderful 122.10
superior 249.12
thin 270.16
rarefied 299.4
raw 406.10
other 779.8
infrequent 847.2
unusual 869.10
sparse 884.5
scarce 991.11
notable 996.19
rare-earth metals
1056.3
rarefaction 299.2
rarefied
diluted 16.19
dainty 248.7
thin 270.16
rare 299.4
tenuous 763.6
rarin' to go 135.6
rascal
mischief-maker 322.3
precious rascal 660.3
rash
n symptom 85.9
skin eruption 85.35
adj impulsive 365.9
precipitate 401.10
brash 493.7
rasp
n scratch 58.3
v pain 26.7
grate 58.10
irritate 96.14
abrade 1042.7
raspberry 508.3
rassle 457.13

rat
n false hair 3.13
traitor 357.10
informer 551.6
bad person 660.6
strikebreaker 727.8
v betray 351.6
inform on 551.13
break a strike 727.11
rat's nest
hodgepodge 796.6
complex 798.2
jumble 809.3
rat-a-tat staccato 55.1
pulsation 915.3
ratchet 285.4
rate
n velocity 172.4
rank 245.2
interest 623.3
price 630.1
worth 630.2
ratio 1016.7
v quantify 244.4
measure 300.10
reprove 510.17
berate 510.19
price 630.11
deserve 639.5
classify 808.6
precede 813.2
estimate 945.9
rank 945.15
rate of exchange 728.9
rate of interest 623.3
rate of pay 624.4
rather
v prefer 371.17
adv to a degree 245.7
notwithstanding
338.8
preferably 371.28
contrarily 778.9
instead 861.11
tolerably 998.24
inter yes 332.18
right on! 972.25
rathole sty 80.11
hovel 228.11
rathskeller 88.20
ratify endorse 332.12
adopt 371.15
consent 441.2
authorize 443.11
secure 854.8
confirm 956.11
rating rank 245.2
measurement 300.1
reproof 510.5
berating 510.7
credit 622.1
valuation 630.3
motion pictures 706.1
classification 808.1
class 808.2
estimate 945.3
ratings 1034.2
ratio
degree 245.1
intellect 918.1
comparability 942.3
rate 1016.7

ration
n amount 244.2
portion 477.5
v budget 477.10
rational mental 918.7
intelligent 919.12
sensible 919.18
sane 924.4
cognitive 930.21
reasoning 934.18
logical 934.20
open-minded 978.10
realistic 986.6
numeric 1016.22
rationale
explanation 341.4
announcement 352.2
reason 885.2
rationalize
explain 341.10
plan 381.8
justify 600.9
organize 807.10
classify 808.6
reason 934.15
reason speciously
935.8
rations board 10.6
store 386.1
rat race
futility 391.2
work 725.4
whirl 914.2
rattan rod 605.2
cane 1052.4
rattle
n noise 53.3
noisemaker 53.6
rattling 55.3
chatterer 540.4
throw 759.9
v weaken 16.10
ruckle 55.6
agitate 105.14
talk nonsense 520.5
chatter 540.5
thrust 901.12
confuse 984.7
rattle off repeat 848.7
memorize 988.17
ratty rodent 311.43
shabby 393.32
infested 909.11
raucous raucid 58.15
dissonant 61.4
raunchy coarse 497.11
obscene 666.9
bad 999.8
ravage
n destruction 395.1
plundering 482.6
seduction 665.6
infestation 909.2
v corrupt 393.12
destroy 395.10
plunder 482.17
seduce 665.20
infest 909.6
ravages of time
wear 393.5
disintegration 805.1
tract of time 820.3

rave
n party 582.12
v be enthusiastic
  101.7
be excitable 105.16
be angry 152.15
bluster 503.3
rage 671.11
be insane 925.20
raven
n blackness 38.4
bird of ill omen 133.6
v hunger 100.19
plunder 482.17
gluttonize 672.4
adj black 38.8
ravenous
hungry 100.25
greedy 100.27
rapacious 480.26
gluttonous 672.6
ravine valley 237.7
gulch 284.9
ravioli 10.32
ravish delight 95.9
corrupt 393.12
possess sexually
  480.15
plunder 482.17
seduce 665.20
raw
n sore spot 24.4
adj naked 6.14
sore 26.11
garish 35.19
callow 301.10
windblown 318.24
crude 406.10
immature 406.11
inexperienced 414.17
coarse 497.11
cursing 513.8
vulgar 666.8
new 840.7
ignorant 929.12
cold 1022.14
the raw 6.3
raw data 769.11
raw deal
injustice 650.4
bad luck 1010.5
rawhide
n fur 4.2
whip 605.1
v whip 604.13
raw material
unlicked cub 263.2
crude 406.5
materials 1052.1
raw nerve
sore spot 24.4
provocation 152.11
ray
n divergence 171.2
wave 915.4
light 1024.5
radiation 1036.3
v radiate 171.6
ray of sunshine
optimist 124.6
daylight 1024.10
raze level 201.6

obliterate 395.16
rase 395.19
fell 912.5
abrade 1042.7
razorback 311.9
razor-edged 285.8
razor-sharp 415.12
razz
n boo 508.3
v banter 490.6
razzledazzle 501.3
RBI 745.4
re 774.13
reach
n earshot 48.4
range 158.2
inlet 242.1
degree 245.1
size 257.1
distance 261.1
length 267.1
knowledge 927.1
v be heard 48.12
move 145.5
extend 158.8
travel 177.19
sail for 182.35
arrive 186.6
arrive at 186.7
extend to 261.6
communicate with
  343.8
bribe 378.3
deliver 478.13
equal 789.5
suffice 990.4
reachable 965.8
reach a compromise
  468.2
reach an agreement
  332.10
reach for the sky
  100.20
reach maturity 407.8
reach one's goal 409.8
reach orgasm 75.23
reach out
extend 158.8
stretch out 261.5
be long 267.5
**reach the breaking
  point** 992.13
react
be affected 93.11
respond 902.5
answer 938.4
reaction
mental disorder 92.14
feeling 93.1
regression 163.1
propulsion 184.25
resistance 453.1
conservatism 611.1
impact 886.2
counteraction 899.1
response 902
answer 938.4
opinion 952.6
reactionary
n malcontent 108.3
right side 219.1
conservative 611.9

back number 841.8
reactionist 902.4
adj regressive 163.11
right 219.4
conservative 611.17
reversionary 858.7
counteractive 899.8
reactive 902.9
reactivate
activate 17.12
restore 396.11
militarize 458.20
reactive 902.9
reactor 1037.13
read
interpret 341.9
understand 521.8
declaim 543.10
copyedit 548.17
study 570.12
sound out 941.9
read between the lines
interpret 341.9
explain 341.10
see through 940.8
reader
advertisement 352.6
lecturer 543.5
elocutionist 543.7
proofreader 548.13
textbook 554.10
journalist 555.4
academic rank 571.3
teacher 571.7
student 572.1
holy orders 699.4
input device 1041.4
reading
measure 300.2
interpretation 341.1
rendering 341.2
speech 543.2
elementary education
  568.5
study 570.3
scholarship 927.5
signal 1035.11
reading glasses 29.3
read into
interpret 341.9
explain 341.10
readjust 857.14
readmit 187.15
read my lips 535.5
read one's mind 689.22
read one loud and clear
  521.8
**read someone like a
  book**
perceive 521.9
see through 940.8
read tea leaves 961.9
read the riot act
lay down the law
  420.10
reprove 510.17
read up on
study 570.12
study up 570.14
search 937.30
ready
v repair 396.14

prepare 405.6
train 568.13
adj eager 101.8
expectant 130.11
willing 324.5
quick 330.18
alert 339.14
handy 387.20
prepared 405.16
skillful 413.22
cunning 415.12
consenting 441.4
teachable 570.18
prompt 844.9
foreseeing 960.7
ready-made
tailored 5.47
ready-formed 405.19
made 891.18
ready oneself 570.11
ready-to-wear
n ready-mades 5.4
adj tailored 5.47
ready-made 405.19
made 891.18
ready wit wit 489.1
smartness 919.2
reaffirm 848.8
real
adj land 471.9
actual 760.15
substantial 762.6
obvious 969.15
true 972.11
genuine 972.15
numeric 1016.22
adv very 247.18
real estate plot 231.4
land 234.1
realty 471.6
realign
parallelize 203.5
rearrange 807.13
change 851.7
realism
normality 868.1
genuineness 972.7
realisticness 986.2
materialism 1050.6
realistic
descriptive 349.14
typical 349.15
occupied 724.15
lifelike 783.16
normal 868.8
ungullible 955.5
genuine 972.15
realist 986.6
materialistic 1050.12
reality actuality 760.2
event 830.2
unquestionability
  969.3
truth 972.1
realize
externalize 206.5
do 328.6
image 349.11
accomplish 407.4
profit 472.12
understand 521.7
be sold 734.12

recess
  n respite 20.2
  nook 197.3
  interior 207.2
  recession 284.7
  hiding place 346.4
  seclusion 584.1
  interim 825.1
  pause 856.3
  retreat 1008.5
  v take a rest 20.8
  indent 284.14
  intervene 825.3
  postpone 845.9
  pause 856.9
recessed 284.16
recession
  regression 163.1
  motion from 168
  recedence 168.1
  recess 284.7
  surrender 433.2
  business cycle 731.9
  hard times 1010.6
recharge activate 17.12
  revive 396.16
recheck
  n re-examination
    937.7
  v re-examine 937.26
  verify 969.12
recidivism
  regression 163.1
  inversion 205.1
  ungovernability 361.4
  apostasy 363.2
  backsliding 394.2
  vice 654.1
  impiety 694.1
  reversion 858.1
recipe remedy 86.1
  formula 419.3
recipient
  n receiver 479.3
  adj receptive 187.16
  receiving 479.9
reciprocal
  n likeness 783.3
  adj cooperative 450.5
  communal 476.9
  retaliatory 506.8
  reciprocative 776.10
  periodic 849.7
  interchangeable 862.5
  alternate 915.19
  numeric 1016.22
reciprocate
  cooperate 450.3
  get along 455.2
  retaliate 506.4
  correspond 776.7
  interchange 862.4
  alternate 915.19
recital speech 543.2
  lesson 568.7
  performance 708.33
  fiction 722.1
  narration 722.2
  iteration 848.2
recite state 524.24
  declaim 543.10
  narrate 719.6

tell a story 722.6
  iterate 848.8
  memorize 988.17
  sum up 1016.18
reckless
  unconcerned 102.7
  fast 174.15
  careless 340.11
  impulsive 365.9
  devil-may-care 493.8
  unwise 922.10
reckon plan 380.6
  estimate 945.9
  suppose 950.10
  think 952.11
  calculate 1016.17
reckoning
  amount 244.2
  fee 624.5
  account 628.2
  statement 628.3
  estimate 945.3
  sum 1016.6
  calculation 1016.10
  summation 1016.11
reclaim
  redeem 396.12
  aid 449.11
  recover 481.6
  re-form 857.12
  rehabilitate 857.14
recline rest 20.6
  lie 201.5
  lie down 912.11
recluse
  n loner 584.5
  eccentric 926.3
  adj reclusive 584.10
recognition
  thanks 150.2
  acknowledgment
    332.3
  commendation 509.3
  due 639.2
  repute 662.1
  plot 722.4
  cognizance 927.2
  discovery 940.1
  identification 988.5
recognizance
  obligation 436.2
  pledge 438.2
recognize see 27.12
  thank 150.4
  acknowledge 332.11
  honor 646.8
  perceive 927.12
  detect 940.5
  know 988.12
recoil
  n demur 325.2
  retaliation 506.1
  impact 886.2
  counteraction 899.1
  rebound 902.2
  retreat 902.3
  v shudder at 99.5
  flinch 127.13
  demur 325.4
  dodge 368.8
  rebound 902.6
  pull back 902.7

recollect 988.10
recommend
  n recommendation
    509.4
  v urge 375.14
  advise 422.5
  propose 439.5
  commend 509.11
recommit
  commit 429.17
  restore 481.4
recompense
  n compensation 338.1
  reparation 396.6
  restitution 481.2
  reprisal 506.2
  remuneration 624.3
  atonement 658.1
  v compensate 338.4
  remedy 396.13
  make restitution
    481.5
  requite 506.5
  pay 624.10
  atone 658.4
recompose
  restore 396.11
  remake 396.18
reconcile
  bring to terms 465.8
  make agree 787.7
  conform 866.3
reconciliation
  contentment 107.1
  reconcilement 465.3
  adjustment 787.4
  conformity 866.1
recondition
  repair 396.14
  renovate 396.17
  rehabilitate 857.14
reconnaissance
  Air Force mission
    184.11
  reconnoitering
    937.8
reconnoiter
  n reconnaissance
    937.8
  v look 27.13
  traverse 177.20
  make a
    reconnaissance
    937.27
reconsider
  rethink 930.15
  re-examine 937.26
reconstitute
  reproduce 78.7
  restore 396.11
  remake 396.18
  rearrange 807.13
reconstruct
  reproduce 78.7
  remake 396.18
  change 851.7
Reconstruction Era
  823.5
record
  n phonograph record
    50.12
  supremacy 249.3

preparedness 405.4
  documentation 549
  recording 549.1
  report 549.7
  history 719.1
  chronicle 831.9
  data 1041.15
  v sound 50.14
  write 547.19
  put upon record
    549.15
  chronicle 719.5
  teleview 1034.15
record-breaker 249.4
recording
  n tape 50.12
  record 549.1
  registration 549.14
  history 719.1
  transcript 784.4
  adj recordative 549.16
record keeping
  registration 549.14
  automation 1040.7
record player 50.11
records 757.4
recount
  n returns 609.21
  summation 1016.11
  v narrate 719.6
  tell a story 722.6
  iterate 848.8
  sum up 1016.18
recoup
  n recovery 481.3
  reimbursement 624.2
  v redeem 396.12
  recover 481.6
  repay 624.11
recourse
  instrumentality 384.3
  resource 1008.2
recover
  get well 83.7
  recuperate 392.8
  redeem 396.12
  rally 396.20
  rescue 398.3
  regain 481.6
  rehabilitate 857.14
re-cover 295.29
recovery
  improvement 392.1
  reclamation 396.2
  rally 396.8
  rescue 398.1
  regaining 481.3
  business cycle 731.9
  rehabilitation 857.4
recovery room 197.25
re-create
  reproduce 78.7
  remake 396.18
  change 851.7
recreation
  refreshment 9.1
  amusement 743.1
rec room 197.12
recruit
  n rookie 461.18
  novice 572.9
  newcomer 773.4

beginner 817.2
v add to 253.5
provide 385.7
avail oneself of 387.14
restore 396.11
revive 396.16
recuperate 396.19
call to arms 458.19
employ 615.14
enlist 615.17
rectangular
oblong 267.9
right-angled 278.7
quadrangular 278.9
rectify refine 79.22
straighten 277.5
compensate 338.4
revise 392.12
remedy 396.13
make agree 787.7
conform 866.3
recto right side 219.1
makeup 554.12
rector principal 571.8
director 574.1
clergyman 699.2
rectory house 228.5
benefice 698.9
parsonage 703.7
rectum 2.16
recumbency
reclining 201.2
lowness 274.1
recuperate
get well 83.7
rally 392.8
recruit 396.19
recover 481.6
recur be frequent 846.3
repeat 848.11
reoccur 849.5
recur to the mind
988.15
recycle 396.12
red
n redness 41.1
radical 611.12
revolutionist 859.3
adj sore 26.11
reddish 41.6
blushing 139.13
raw 406.10
radical 611.20
Red
n Communist 611.13
revolutionist 859.3
adj Communist 611.21
red, white, and blue
647.6
red alert
warning sign 399.3
crisis 842.4
red-baiting 389.3
red-blooded
strong 15.15
resolute 492.18
redcap carrier 176.7
trainman 178.13
red carpet 580.1
red cent money 728.7
trifle 997.5
red corpuscle 2.23

redden make red 41.4
turn red 41.5
change color 105.19
blush 139.8
show resentment
152.14
reddish 41.6
redecorate 498.8
redeem reclaim 396.12
rescue 398.3
aid 449.11
recover 481.6
pay in full 624.13
pay for 624.18
atone 658.4
regenerate 685.6
re-form 857.12
substitute 861.4
redeeming feature
864.4
redemption
pardon 148.2
reclamation 396.2
rescue 398.1
recovery 481.3
atonement 658.1
function of Christ
677.15
redeemedness 685.4
new start 857.2
reversion 858.1
redesign
n reproduction 78.1
change 851.1
v reproduce 78.7
change 851.7
redevelop
reproduce 78.7
restore 396.11
red flag
warning sign 399.3
signal 517.15
red-handed
adj guilty 656.3
adv in the act 656.4
redhead 35.9
red herring fish 10.23
stratagem 415.3
red-hot fervent 93.18
zealous 101.9
heated 105.22
fiery 671.22
hot 1018.25
red ink 473.3
rediscover 940.2
redistribute 807.13
red-letter day
holiday 20.4
celebration 487.1
red light
warning sign 399.3
alarm 400.1
signal 517.15
traffic light 1025.4
red-light district
city district 230.6
brothel 665.9
redneck
n hater 103.4
wilderness settler
227.10
vulgarian 497.6

adj not urbane 233.8
boorish 497.13
redo reproduce 78.7
ornament 498.8
repeat 848.7
redolent odorous 69.9
fragrant 70.9
recollective 988.22
redouble
intensify 251.5
repeat 848.7
duplicate 873.3
redress
n compensation 338.1
reparation 396.6
restitution 481.2
recompense 624.3
atonement 658.1
v remedy 396.13
make restitution
481.5
requite 506.5
repay 624.11
atone 658.4
red tape routine 373.6
officialism 612.11
delay 845.2
reduce
n make small 258.9
v weaken 16.10
dilute 16.11
afflict 85.49
relieve 120.5
abase 137.5
quantify 244.4
decrease 252.7
subtract 255.9
contract 260.7
shorten 268.6
slenderize 270.13
conquer 412.10
subdue 432.9
demote 447.3
impoverish 619.6
discount 631.2
cheapen 633.6
moderate 670.6
simplify 797.4
analyze 800.6
depress 912.4
qualify 958.3
chemicalize 1058.7
reduce to 857.11
reduction in forces
deposal 447.2
economizing 635.2
redundancy 992.4
redundant
diffuse 538.11
repetitious 848.14
superfluous 992.17
reduplicate
reproduce 777.6
copy 784.8
repeat 848.7
duplicate 873.3
redux 396.24
red wine 88.17
reebok 311.5
reed tube 239.6
grass 310.5
stem 310.19

arrow 462.6
wind instrument 711.6
woodwind 711.8
reeducate teach 568.10
rehabilitate 857.14
reedy 58.14
reef
n island 235.2
shoal 276.2
point of land 283.9
v slow 175.9
reduce sail 182.50
reefer marijuana
cigarette 87.11
refrigerator truck
1023.4
reek
n stench 71.1
combustion product
1019.16
vapor 1065.1
v have an odor 69.6
stink 71.4
exude 190.15
let out 908.24
smoke 1018.23
vaporize 1065.8
reel
n windlass 905.7
whirl 914.2
swing 915.6
flounder 916.8
v be drunk 88.27
pitch 182.55
eddy 238.21
reel in 905.9
whirl 914.11
oscillate 915.10
flounder 916.15
reel in fish 382.10
wind in 905.9
reeling
n rotation 914.1
adj intoxicated 88.31
rotating 914.14
swinging 915.17
reel off chatter 540.5
repeat 848.7
memorize 988.17
reenactment 396.1
reenlist 824.5
reentry
regression 163.1
return 186.3
repetition 848.1
periodicity 849.2
spacecraft 1073.2
reestablish
reproduce 78.7
restore 396.11
resume 855.6
re-examine
reconsider 930.15
recheck 937.26
refashion
reproduce 78.7
remake 396.18
re-form 857.12
refer 887.3
referee
n arbitrator 466.4
judge 596.1

basketball game 747.3
hockey game 749.3
round 751.3
soccer game 752.3
fight 754.3
umpire 945.6
v mediate 466.6
sit in judgment 945.12
reference
n aspect 33.3
recommendation
509.4
meaning 518.1
punctuation 530.15
relevance 774.4
acknowledgment
887.2
citation 956.5
v refer to 956.14
reference book
book 554.1
work of reference
554.9
directory 574.10
referendum vote 371.6
election 609.15
constitutional
referendum 613.8
refer to
avail oneself of 387.14
designate 517.18
mean 518.8
remark 524.25
confer 541.11
relate to 774.5
attribute to 887.4
direct attention to
956.14
call attention to
982.10
refill restore 396.11
complete 793.6
refinance 729.15
refine sensitize 24.7
clarify 79.22
extract 192.16
subtract 255.9
spiritualize 763.4
simplify 797.4
process 891.9
melt 1019.21
refinery refiner 79.13
plant 739.3
refit renovate 396.17
change 851.7
reflect curve 279.6
imitate 336.5
image 349.11
remark 524.25
consider 930.12
remember 988.10
return 1035.16
reflectance 1024.9
reflection bend 279.3
image 349.5
criticism 510.4
aspersion 512.4
remark 524.25
stigma 661.6
reflex 784.7
reaction 902.1
judiciousness 919.7

consideration 930.2
idea 931.1
remembering 988.4
reflected light 1024.9
signal 1035.11
reflector mirror 29.6
observatory 1070.17
reflect upon 510.13
reflex
n conditioning 92.26
impulse 365.1
reflection 784.7
impact 886.2
reaction 902.1
instinct 933.2
v curve 279.6
adj backward 163.12
unpremeditated
365.11
reactive 902.9
involuntary 962.14
reflexive
n voice 530.14
adj unpremeditated
365.11
reactive 902.9
involuntary 962.14
refluence
regression 163.1
course 172.2
eddy 238.12
tide 238.13
reaction 902.1
reflux regression 163.1
course 172.2
eddy 238.12
tide 238.13
reaction 902.1
reforestation
woodland 310.11
forestry 1067.3
planting 1067.14
reform
n reformation 392.5
change 851.1
new start 857.2
v repent 113.7
make better 392.9
restore 396.11
redeem 685.6
change 851.7
re-form 857.12
Reform
n Protestantism
675.10
adj Jewish 675.30
Reformationist
n Protestant 675.20
adj Protestant 675.28
reformatory
n prison 429.8
reform school 567.9
adj emendatory
392.16
refracted 164.8
refractory
n ceramic ware 742.2
adj unwilling 325.5
defiant 327.10
ungovernable 361.12
oppositional 451.8
resistant 453.5

ceramic 742.7
nonconforming 867.5
refrain
n air 708.4
passage 708.24
poetry 720.9
sequel 816.1
repeat 848.5
v not do 329.3
not use 390.5
abstain 668.7
cease 856.6
refreeze 1023.11
refresh freshen 9.2
strengthen 15.13
air 317.10
revive 396.16
renovate 396.17
amuse 743.21
refrigerate 1023.10
refresher course 568.8
refreshment
meal 8.5
invigoration 9
refection 9.1
nutriment 10.3
strengthening 15.5
ventilation 317.8
revival 396.3
renovation 396.4
refrigerant
n coolant 1023.7
adj refrigerative
1023.12
refrigerate
preserve 397.9
freeze 1022.10
cool 1023.10
refrigerator 1023.4
refuel 1020.7
refuge reception 187.1
hiding place 346.4
pretext 376.1
preserve 397.7
protection 1007.1
sanctuary 1008.1
refugee goer 190.10
fugitive 368.5
alien 773.3
refund
n reparation 481.2
reimbursement 624.2
discount 631.1
v make restitution
481.5
repay 624.11
discount 631.2
refurbish
renovate 396.17
ornament 498.8
refusal
unwillingness 325.1
dissent 333.1
rejection 372.1
denial 442
prohibition 444.1
opposition 451.1
option 733.2
repulse 907.2
refuse
n offal 80.9
remainder 256.1

derelict 370.4
discard 390.3
waste 391.4
v be unwilling 325.3
reject 372.2
decline 442.3
prohibit 444.3
repulse 907.3
refuse comment 344.6
refusenik 327.5
refuse to admit
deny 335.4
disbelieve 954.5
refuse to believe 955.3
refuse to pay 625.6
refute deny 335.4
defend 600.10
rebut 938.5
confute 957.5
regain 481.6
regal dignified 136.12
sovereign 417.17
noble 608.10
good 998.12
regale
n refreshment 9.1
treat 95.3
v feed 8.18
feast 8.24
refresh 9.2
gratify 95.7
amuse 743.21
regalia
formal dress 5.11
insignia 647.1
royal insignia 647.3
regard
n observation 27.2
look 27.3
aspect 33.3
love 104.1
considerateness 143.3
respect 155.1
carefulness 339.1
good terms 587.3
esteem 662.3
particular 765.3
relevance 774.4
outlook 977.2
attention 982.1
v look 27.13
cherish 104.21
be considerate 143.10
respect 155.4
care 339.6
observe 434.2
relate to 774.5
think of 930.17
judge 945.8
consider 952.11
heed 982.6
regardless
adj unconcerned 102.7
careless 340.11
incurious 981.3
inattentive 983.6
adv anyhow 384.10
in spite of 338.9
regards
respects 155.3
compliments 504.8
greetings 585.3

regatta
race 457.12
tournament 743.10
regency
mastership 417.7
government 612.4
commission 615.1
regenerate
v reproduce 78.7
revive 396.16
redeem 685.6
re-form 857.12
adj redeemed 685.9
converted 692.10
regent 575.12
regimen diet 7.11
treatment 91.14
government 612.1
regiment
n military unit 461.22
company 769.3
v hold a tight hand upon 425.4
dispose 807.9
regimentation
strictness 425.1
arrangement 807.1
region
location 159.1
area 231.1
territory 231.5
land 234.1
plot 722.4
regional
locational 159.19
territorial 231.8
idiomatic 523.20
register
n range 158.2
record 549.1
memorandum 549.4
record book 549.11
registration 549.14
clerk 550.1
account book 628.4
pitch 709.4
scale 709.6
organ stop 711.19
chronicle 831.9
list 870.1
v be heard 48.12
limit 210.5
represent 349.8
preserve 397.8
get across 521.5
record 549.15
be taught 570.11
act 704.29
agree 787.6
list 870.8
protect 1007.18
register a complaint 115.15
registered trademark
patent 210.3
label 517.13
registered voter 609.23
registrar
recorder 549.13
clerk 550.1
accountant 628.7

registration
register 549.14
index 870.7
registry record 549.1
registry office 549.3
memorandum 549.4
registration 549.14
account book 628.4
chronicle 831.9
list 870.1
index 870.7
regress
n regression 163.1
reversion 858.1
v go backwards 163.5
move 172.5
be behind 217.8
deteriorate 393.16
relapse 394.4
revert 858.4
regret
n remorse 113
regrets 113.1
apology 658.2
v deplore 113.6
regrettable
distressing 98.20
much to be regretted 113.10
terrible 999.9
regroup 857.12
regular
n partisan 609.27
customer 733.4
baseball team 745.2
adj gradual 245.5
downright 247.12
symmetric 264.4
smooth 287.9
typical 349.15
customary 373.14
habitual 373.15
uniform 780.5
thorough 793.10
orderly 806.6
constant 846.5
systematic 849.6
usual 868.9
ordinary 1004.8
regularity
symmetry 264.1
smoothness 287.1
constancy 780.2
order 806.1
continualness 846.2
regularness 849.1
normality 868.1
regulate direct 573.8
govern 612.12
legalize 673.8
make uniform 780.4
make agree 787.7
order 806.4
organize 807.10
exercise influence 893.8
regulation
n rule 419.2
directive 420.3
direction 573.1
government 612.1
law 673.3

adjustment 787.4
organization 807.2
principle 868.4
adj customary 373.14
preceptive 419.4
usual 868.9
regulatory
directing 573.12
governing 612.18
regurgitate flow 238.16
repeat 848.7
vomit 908.26
pulp 1061.5
rehabilitate
restore 396.11
justify 600.9
re-form 857.12
recondition 857.14
rehash
n iteration 848.2
summation 1016.11
v paraphrase 341.13
iterate 848.8
sum up 1016.18
rehearse
report 552.11
train 568.13
practice 704.32
narrate 719.6
tell a story 722.6
iterate 848.8
sum up 1016.18
reheat 1019.17
reheated 1019.29
reign
n governance 417.5
government 612.1
influence 893.1
v rule 612.14
prevail 863.10
reigning
governing 612.18
prevalent 863.12
reign of terror
terrorization 127.7
despotism 612.10
reimburse
make restitution 481.5
repay 624.11
rein
n restraint 428.1
shackle 428.4
v restrain 428.7
reincarnate
repeat 848.7
materialize 1050.9
reindeer
beast of burden 176.8
hoofed animal 311.5
reinforce
n supporter 900.2
v strengthen 15.13
intensify 251.5
add to 253.5
bolster 449.12
support 900.21
confirm 956.11
stiffen 1044.9
reinforcements 449.8
rein in slow 175.9
restrain 428.7

reins 573.5
reinstate
restore 396.11
justify 600.9
reinstitute
reproduce 78.7
restore 396.11
reinvest restore 396.11
invest 729.16
reissue
n reproduction 78.1
print 548.3
iteration 848.2
v reproduce 78.7
print 548.14
monetize 728.26
iterate 848.8
reiterate
v iterate 848.8
persist 855.5
adj repeated 848.12
reject
n derelict 370.4
discard 390.3
v repudiate 372.2
discard 390.7
refuse 442.3
prohibit 444.3
contradict 451.6
disapprove 510.10
ostracize 586.6
exclude 772.4
eject 908.13
vomit 908.26
disbelieve 954.5
refuse to believe 955.3
rejoice cheer 109.7
jubilate 116.5
rejoice in 95.12
rejoinder answer 938.1
rebuttal 938.2
rejuvenate
make young 301.8
revive 396.16
rekindle revive 396.16
ignite 1019.22
relapse
n regression 163.1
apostasy 363.2
lapse 394
conversion 857.1
reversion 858.1
v regress 163.5
invert 205.5
deteriorate 393.16
lapse 394.4
go wrong 654.9
defect 857.13
revert 858.4
relate state 524.24
report 552.11
narrate 719.6
tell a story 722.6
associate 774.6
compare 942.4
sum up 1016.18
related kindred 559.6
connected 774.9
akin 774.10
relate to
communicate with 343.8

refer to 774.5
relation meaning 518.1
 blood relationship
  559.1
 fiction 722.1
 narration 722.2
 story 722.3
 connection 774
 relationship 774.1
 involvement 897.1
 comparison 942.1
relations
 copulation 75.7
 kinfolk 559.2
 relationship 774.1
 affairs 830.4
relationship
 blood relationship
  559.1
 relation 774.1
relative
 relational 774.7
 comparative 942.8
relative humidity
 1063.2
relatives 559.2
relativity
 fourth dimension
  158.6
 dependence 774.2
 correlation 776.1
 uncertainty 970.1
relativity theory 1017.1
relax
 v unlax 20.7
 compose oneself 106.7
 relieve 120.5
 release 120.6
 be at ease 121.8
 have pity 145.4
 slow 175.9
 not stand on
  ceremony 581.2
 unbend 670.9
 entertain 743.21
 amuse oneself 743.22
 loosen 803.3
 pause 856.9
 allow for 958.5
 soften 1045.6
 yield 1045.7
 inter cease! 856.13
relay
 n shift 824.3
 v transfer 176.10
relay station 1033.6
release
 n deliverance 120.2
 death 307.1
 press release 352.3
 escape 369.1
 rescue 398.1
 exemption 430.8
 freeing 431.2
 permission 443.1
 relinquishment 475.1
 information 551.1
 message 552.4
 acquittal 601.1
 acknowledgment
  627.2
 game 750.2

disbandment 770.3
 v free 120.6
 rescue 398.3
 exempt 430.14
 unhand 431.5
 extricate 431.7
 permit 443.9
 let go 475.4
 acquit 601.4
 disband 770.8
 detach 801.10
 dismiss 908.19
relegate commit 478.16
 exclude 772.4
 banish 908.17
relent have pity 145.4
 submit 433.6
 be moderate 670.5
 yield 1045.7
relentless pitiless 146.3
 industrious 330.22
 resolute 359.11
 persevering 360.8
 unyielding 361.9
 firm 425.7
 constant 846.5
 inevitable 962.15
relevant
 pertinent 774.11
 apt 787.10
reliability
 trustworthiness 644.6
 stability 854.1
 believability 952.8
 dependability 969.4
reliable
 trustworthy 644.19
 stable 854.12
 believable 952.24
 evidential 956.16
 dependable 969.17
 unhazardous 1006.5
relic remainder 256.1
 corpse 307.16
 record 549.1
 antiquity 841.6
 back number 841.8
 memento 988.7
relief remedy 86.1
 easement 120
 consolation 121.4
 welfare 143.5
 pity 145.1
 outline 211.2
 protuberance 283.2
 lightening 298.3
 aid 449.1
 reinforcements 449.8
 subsidy 478.8
 welfarism 611.7
 relievo 715.3
 turn 824.2
 interim 825.1
 substitute 861.2
relief pitcher 745.2
relieve give relief 120.5
 comfort 121.6
 lighten 298.6
 aid 449.11
 play 745.5
 take one's turn 824.5
 substitute for 861.5

disembarrass 1013.9
relieve of 480.21
relieve oneself
 excrete 12.12
 lighten 120.7
 speak up 524.22
relight revive 396.16
 ignite 1019.22
religion
 religious belief 675.1
 theology 676.1
 piety 692.1
 system of belief 952.3
religious
 n clergy 699.15
 adj meticulous 339.12
 conscientious 644.15
 theistic 675.25
 theological 676.4
 sacred 685.7
 pious 692.8
 exact 972.17
religious ceremony
 580.4
religious discourse
 543.3
religious faith 675.1
religious holiday 849.4
religious order 675.3
religious rites
 celebration 487.1
 ritualism 701
relinquish
 give up 370.7
 cease to use 390.4
 surrender 433.8
 resign 448.2
 yield 475.3
 discontinue 856.6
reliquary tomb 309.16
 monument 549.12
 shrine 703.4
 church vessels 703.11
relish
 n taste 62.1
 savor 63.2
 flavoring 63.3
 zest 68.2
 passion 93.2
 pleasure 95.1
 liking 100.2
 appetite 100.7
 v eat 8.20
 savor 63.5
 enjoy 95.12
relocate settle 159.17
 remove 176.11
reluctant slow 175.10
 renitent 325.6
 resistant 453.5
rely on hope 124.7
 rest on 900.22
 depend on 952.16
 trust 952.17
remain
 be still 173.7
 be present 221.6
 inhabit 225.7
 be left 256.5
 endure 826.6
 persist 852.5
 continue 855.3

remainder
 difference 255.8
 remains 256
 part 792.1
 subsequence 834.1
 surplus 992.5
remains
 remainder 256.1
 corpse 307.16
 record 549.1
 antiquity 841.6
remake reproduce 78.7
 reconstruct 396.18
 change 851.7
remand
 n commitment 429.4
 restitution 481.1
 v imprison 429.17
 commit 478.16
 restore 481.4
remark
 n interjection 213.2
 aspersion 512.4
 statement 524.4
 commentary 556.2
 attention 982.1
 v comment 524.25
 heed 982.6
remarkable
 wonderful 122.10
 outstanding 247.10
 extraordinary 869.14
 notable 996.19
remarry 563.15
remedial
 curative 86.39
 relieving 120.9
 tonic 396.22
 helpful 449.21
remedy
 n cure 86
 relief 120.1
 reparation 396.6
 therapy 396.7
 aid 449.1
 counteractant 899.3
 v cure 86.38
 treat 91.24
 rectify 396.13
 heal 396.15
 aid 449.11
remember
 recall 988.10
 remind 988.20
remembrance
 celebration 487.1
 monument 549.12
 posthumous fame
  662.7
 memory 836.4
 recollection 988.1
 remembering 988.4
 reminder 988.6
 memento 988.7
remind 988.20
reminder
 memorandum 549.4
 remembrance 988.6
reminisce 988.11
reminiscence
 memory 836.4
 remembering 988.4

remiss indolent 331.19
  negligent 340.10
  lax 426.4
  dilatory 845.17
remission relief 120.1
  pardon 148.2
  decline 252.2
  reduction 255.2
  restitution 481.1
  acquittal 601.1
  modulation 670.2
  pause 856.3
remit relieve 120.5
  have pity 145.4
  forgive 148.3
  send 176.15
  abate 252.8
  imprison 429.17
  exempt 430.14
  commit 478.16
  restore 481.4
  acquit 601.4
  pay 624.10
  be moderate 670.5
  relax 670.9
remittance
  subsidy 478.8
  payment 624.1
remnant
  n remainder 256.1
  adj remaining 256.7
remodel remake 396.18
  re-form 857.12
remonstrate
  object 333.5
  dissuade 379.3
  admonish 422.6
  offer resistance 453.3
remora adhesive 802.4
  curb 1011.7
remorse regret 113.1
  guilt 656.1
remorseless
  unregretful 114.4
  pitiless 146.3
remote aloof 141.12
  distant 261.8
  reticent 344.10
  standoffish 583.6
  secluded 584.8
  selfish 651.5
  farfetched 775.8
remote control 1040.4
remote past 836.3
remote possibility
  possibility 965.1
  small chance 971.9
remove
  n degree 245.1
  v divest 6.5
  take off 6.6
  release 120.6
  move 176.11
  quit 188.9
  extract 192.10
  subtract 255.9
  murder 308.15
  discard 390.7
  exterminate 395.14
  depose 447.4
  eliminate 772.5
  detach 801.10

eject 908.13
  dismiss 908.19
  evacuate 908.22
removed distant 261.8
  reticent 344.10
  aloof 583.6
  secluded 584.8
  unrelated 775.6
  separated 801.21
  alone 871.8
remove from office
  447.4
REM sleep
  sleepiness 22.1
  deep sleep 22.5
remunerate
  remedy 396.13
  make restitution
    481.5
  pay 624.10
renaissance 396.3
Renaissance man 413.3
renascent
  reproductive 78.14
  redivivus 396.24
rend pain 26.7
  injure 393.13
  demolish 395.17
  wrest 480.22
  sever 801.11
render
  extraction 192.16
  do 328.6
  translate 341.12
  communicate 343.7
  represent 349.8
  describe 349.9
  execute 437.9
  give 478.12
  deliver 478.13
  pay 624.10
  play 708.39
  convert 857.11
  melt 1019.21
render a service 143.12
render assistance
  449.11
rendering extract 192.7
  rendition 341.2
  representation 349.1
  description 349.2
  execution 708.30
rendezvous
  n tryst 582.9
  assembly 769.2
  v come together
    769.16
rendition
  extract 192.7
  rendering 341.2
  representation 349.1
  description 349.2
  restitution 481.1
  execution 708.30
renegade
  n apostate 363.5
  sacrilegist 694.3
  defector 857.8
  adj apostate 363.11
  impious 694.6
  traitorous 857.20
  nonobservant 435.5

renege
  n recant 363.8
  v abandon 370.5
  disregard 435.3
  repeal 445.2
  be unfaithful 645.12
  defect 857.13
renew refresh 9.2
  stimulate 105.13
  revive 396.16
  renovate 396.17
  innovate 840.5
  repeat 848.7
  change 851.7
  resume 855.6
  re-form 857.12
renewable
  remediable 396.25
  convertible 857.18
renitent
  reluctant 325.6
  resistant 453.5
  counteractive 899.8
  rigid 1044.11
renounce
  n recant 363.8
  v deny 335.4
  give up 370.7
  reject 372.2
  cease to use 390.4
  surrender 433.8
  relinquish 475.3
  swear off 668.8
  cease 856.6
renovate
  reproduce 78.7
  renew 396.17
  recover 481.6
  innovate 840.5
  perfect 392.1
renown glory 247.2
  repute 662.1
  notability 996.2
rent
  n trauma 85.37
  crack 224.2
  rental 615.6
  hire 630.8
  break 801.4
  v cleave 224.4
  inhabit 225.7
  open 292.11
  lease 615.15
  rent out 615.16
  adj cleft 224.7
  impaired 393.27
  severed 801.23
rental car 179.13
rent control 630.5
renter lodger 227.8
  tenant 470.4
reoccupy 481.6
reoccur repeat 848.11
  recur 849.5
reopen 855.6
reorder 807.13
reorganize
  reproduce 78.7
  rearrange 807.13
repair
  n reparation 396.6
  good condition 764.3

v perfect 392.11
  mend 396.14
  atone 658.4
repairman 396.10
repair shop 739.5
repair to 177.25
reparation
  compensation 338.1
  repair 396.6
  restitution 481.2
  recompense 624.3
  atonement 658.1
repartee
  witticism 489.7
  conversation 541.1
  answer 938.1
repast 8.5
repatriate restore 481.4
  rehabilitate 857.14
repave 295.22
repay
  compensate 338.4
  be profitable 472.13
  make restitution
    481.5
  requite 506.5
  pay back 624.11
repeal
  n revocation 445
  v abolish 395.13
  revoke 445.2
repeat
  n repetend 848.5
  encore 848.6
  duplication 873.2
  v reproduce 78.7
  imitate 336.5
  publish 352.10
  redo 848.7
  recur 848.11
  become cyclic 849.5
  duplicate 873.3
  memorize 988.17
repeatedly 846.6
repeat performance
  encore 848.6
  repeat 873.2
repeat word for word
  848.7
repel
  disgust 64.4
  offend 98.11
  cause dislike 99.6
  reject 372.2
  disincline 379.4
  rebuff 442.5
  resist 453.2
  fend off 460.10
  repulse 907.3
  prevent 1011.14
repellent
  offensive 98.18
  resistant 453.5
  repulsive 907.4
  hideous 1014.11
repent
  v think better of 113.7
  adj creeping 177.39
  reptile 311.46
repentant
  penitent 113.9
  atoning 658.7

repercussion
concussion 671.8
execution 708.30
impact 886.2
counteraction 899.1
recoil 902.2
repertoire store 386.1
repertory 704.9
repertory company
707.11
repetition
reproduction 78.1
triteness 117.3
tediousness 118.2
imitation 336.1
duplicate 784.3
constancy 846.2
redundancy 848.1
regularity 849.1
continuance 855.1
replication 873.1
repetitive
habitual 373.15
diffuse 538.11
same 780.6
continuous 811.8
repetitious 848.14
ceaseless 855.7
rephrase 341.13
replace
restore 396.11
depose 447.4
come after 834.3
substitute for 861.5
dismiss 908.19
replacement
restoration 396.1
deposal 447.2
successor 816.4
sequel 834.2
exchange 861.1
substitute 861.2
replant 91.24
replay 848.6
replenish provide 385.7
restore 396.11
complete 793.6
replete full 793.11
plentiful 990.7
overfull 992.20
satiated 993.6
replica
reproduction 336.3
the same 777.3
duplicate 784.3
replicate copy 784.8
double 872.5
duplicate 873.3
reply
n communication
343.1
retaliation 506.1
letter 553.2
defense 600.2
reaction 902.1
answer 938.1
v acknowledge 553.11
defend 600.10
react 902.5
answer 938.4
répondez s'il vous plaît
553.15

report
n crash 56.1
account 349.3
announcement 352.2
publicity 352.4
bulletin 549.7
information 551.1
rumor 552.6
commentary 556.2
repute 662.1
explosion 671.7
paean 696.3
note 709.14
criticism 945.2
v present oneself
221.11
communicate 343.7
announce 352.12
inform 551.8
give a report 552.11
accuse 599.7
narrate 719.6
tell a tale 722.6
pass judgment 945.13
reportage 552.1
reporter
informant 551.5
newsmonger 552.9
journalist 555.4
spokesman 576.5
repose
n rest 20.1
respite 20.2
sleep 22.2
quiescence 173.1
recumbency 201.2
leisure 402.1
moderation 670.1
v rest 20.6
be located 159.10
deposit 159.14
be still 173.7
lie 201.5
trust 952.17
repository
storehouse 386.6
friend 588.1
treasury 729.12
repossess 481.6
reprehensible
blameworthy 510.25
wicked 654.16
guilty 656.3
terrible 999.9
represent
be in front 216.7
manifest 348.5
delineate 349.8
describe 349.9
mediate 466.6
act for 576.14
enact 704.30
substitute for 861.5
visualize 985.15
representation
spectacle 33.7
reproduction 336.3
display 348.2
portrayal 349
delineation 349.1
description 349.2
representative 349.7

sham 354.3
vote 371.6
sign 517.1
bar 597.4
acting 704.8
picture 712.11
copy 784.1
duplicate 784.3
substitution 861.1
idea 931.1
representative
n representation 349.7
sign 517.1
deputy 576.1
legislator 610.3
example 785.2
substitute 861.2
adj representational
349.13
descriptive 349.14
indicative 517.23
deputy 576.15
model 785.8
repress inhibit 106.8
blunt 286.2
cover up 345.8
suppress 428.8
prohibit 444.3
retain 474.5
domineer 612.16
hinder 1011.10
reprieve
n release 120.2
pity 145.1
pardon 148.2
respite 601.3
delay 845.2
v release 120.6
have pity 145.4
respite 601.5
reprimand
n reproof 510.5
stigma 661.6
v reprove 510.17
stigmatize 661.9
reprint
n print 548.3
copy 784.5
iteration 848.2
v reproduce 78.7
print 548.14
iterate 848.8
reprisal requital 506.2
revenge 507.1
penalty 603.1
reprise 848.6
repro duplicate 784.3
print 784.5
duplication 873.1
reproach
n reproof 510.5
accusation 599.1
disgrace 661.5
stigma 661.6
v censure 510.13
accuse 599.7
disgrace 661.8
reprobate
n recreant 660.5
v censure 510.13
adj knavish 645.17
corrupt 654.14

wicked 654.16
unsacred 686.3
unregenerate 695.18
reproduce grow 14.2
remake 78.7
grow 259.9
copy 777.6
replicate 784.8
repeat 848.7
duplicate 873.3
produce 889.7
reproduction
bodily development
14.1
remaking 78
making 78.1
procreation 78.2
growth 259.3
replication 336.3
picture 712.11
duplication 784.2
double 784.3
repetition 848.1
imitation 873.1
proliferation 889.2
reproductive organs
2.11
reprove 510.17
reptile
n creature 311.3
reptilian 311.25
beast 660.7
adj creeping 177.39
reptilian 311.46
republic country 232.1
government 612.4
republican 612.17
repudiate
n recant 363.8
v deny 335.4
reject 372.2
refuse 442.3
not pay 625.6
exclude 772.4
repugnant
offensive 98.18
negative 335.5
oppositional 451.8
hostile 589.10
contrary 778.6
disagreeing 788.6
counteractive 899.8
hideous 1014.11
repulse
n snub 157.2
rejection 372.1
discomfiture 412.2
refuse 442.2
resistance 453.1
recoil 902.2
rebuff 907.2
v snub 157.5
reject 372.2
rebuff 442.5
resist 453.2
fend off 460.10
repel 907.3
repulsive
malodorous 71.5
filthy 80.23
offensive 98.18
repellent 907.4

terrible 999.9
hideous 1014.11
reputable
honest 644.13
highly reputed 662.15
influential 893.13
notable 996.19
reputation 996.2
repute
n reputation 662.1
custom 731.6
influence 893.1
notability 996.2
v suppose 950.10
request
n proposal 439.2
expressed desire 440
asking 440.1
v ask 440.9
requiem dirge 115.6
last offices 309.4
sacred music 708.17
requiescat in pace
309.24
require
prescribe 420.9
demand 421.5
oblige 424.5
charge 630.12
obligate 641.12
entail 771.4
determine 885.12
need 962.9
want 991.7
requirement
demand 421.1
study 568.8
requisite 962.2
requisite
n condition 958.2
requirement 962.2
adj needful 962.13
requisition
n summons 420.5
demand 421.1
request 440.1
appropriation 480.4
requirement 962.2
v summon 420.11
demand 421.5
request 440.9
appropriate 480.19
requite remedy 396.13
make restitution
481.5
quit 506.5
repay 624.11
interchange 862.4
rerun 1033.18
rescind delete 255.12
repeal 445.2
rescue
n escape 369.1
saving 398
deliverance 398.1
liberation 431.1
aid 449.1
v redeem 396.12
come to the rescue
398.3
liberate 431.4
aid 449.11

research
n investigation 937.4
v search 937.30
experiment 941.8
**research and
development** 941.1
researcher
seeker 937.18
experimenter 941.6
research paper 556.1
resection 801.2
resell 734.8
resemble be like 783.7
be comparable 942.7
resent
be resentful 152.12
envy 154.3
reservation
demur 325.2
objection 333.2
preserve 397.7
stipulation 421.2
engagement 615.4
doubt 954.2
qualification 958.1
prearrangement 964.1
reserve
n restraint 139.3
communicativeness
343.3
reticence 344.3
reserves 386.3
preserve 397.7
conciseness 537.1
v save 386.12
not use 390.5
allot 477.9
employ 615.14
postpone 845.9
prearrange 964.4
adj unused 390.12
substitute 861.8
reserve forces 449.8
reservoir
n lake 241.1
reserve 386.3
storehouse 386.6
v store 386.10
reset sharpen 285.7
plant 1067.18
reshape reproduce 78.7
change 851.7
re-form 857.12
reshuffle arrange 437.8
rearrange 807.13
reside
settle 159.17
inhabit 225.7
residence
habitation 225.1
abode 228.1
resident
n doctor 90.4
inhabitant 227.2
tenant 470.4
diplomat 576.6
benefice-holder 699.7
adj residentiary
225.13
intrinsic 766.7
residential 228.32
residual 256.8

residue
remainder 256.1
extract 892.3
resign give up 370.7
cease to use 390.4
submit 433.6
demit 448.2
relinquish 475.3
deliver 478.13
resign oneself to 134.7
resiliency
lightheartedness
109.3
pliancy 1045.2
elasticity 1046.1
resilient
lighthearted 109.12
recuperative 396.23
changeable 853.6
recoiling 902.10
pliant 1045.9
elastic 1046.7
resin
n gum 1055.1
v resinize 1055.2
resist oppose 451.3
contend against 451.4
withstand 453.2
counteract 899.6
hinder 1011.10
resistance
immunity 83.4
defense mechanism
92.23
suppression 92.24
drag 184.27
refusal 325.1
ungovernability 361.4
opposition 451.1
defiance 453
withstanding 453.1
defense 460.1
irregular 461.16
counteraction 899.1
hindrance 1011.1
ohm 1031.12
conductance 1032.9
friction 1042.1
hardness 1044.1
toughness 1047.1
resolute
zealous 101.9
resolved 359.11
persevering 360.8
trial 403.16
tough 492.18
resolution
distinctness 31.2
zeal 101.2
will 323.1
determination 359
resolve 359.1
perseverance 360.1
intention 380.1
decay 393.6
endeavor 403.1
proposal 439.2
adjustment 465.4
fortitude 492.6
legislation 613.5
passage 708.24
harmonization 709.2

analysis 800.1
itemization 800.2
dissection 801.5
disintegration 805.1
end 819.1
conversion 857.1
solution 939.1
judgment 945.1
verdict 945.5
resolve
n resolution 359.1
intention 380.1
v will 323.2
determine 359.7
intend 380.4
endeavor 403.5
reconcile 465.8
analyze 800.6
itemize 800.7
end 819.5
solve 939.2
decide 945.11
resolvent
n solvent 1062.4
adj disintegrative
805.5
solvent 1062.8
resonance
resoundingness 54
reaction 902.1
oscillation 915.1
wave 915.4
resonate vibrate 54.6
oscillate 915.10
resort haunt 228.27
instrumentality 384.3
entertainment 743.13
expedient 994.2
recourse 1008.2
resound
n reverberation 54.2
v sound 50.14
din 53.7
reverberate 54.7
repeat 848.11
resounding triumph
409.3
resource supply 386.2
reserve 386.3
source of supply 386.4
skill 413.1
expedient 994.2
recourse 1008.2
resourceful
skillful 413.22
versatile 413.25
cunning 415.12
respect
n observation 27.2
aspect 33.3
esteem 155
regard 155.1
observance 434.1
courtesy 504.1
approval 509.1
good terms 587.3
duty 641.1
honor 662.3
particular 765.3
relevance 774.4
outlook 977.2
attention 982.1

v be considerate
143.10
entertain respect for
155.4
observe 434.2
approve 509.9
relate to 774.5
respectable
honest 644.13
reputable 662.15
tolerable 998.20
mediocre 1004.7
respectful
regardful 155.8
observant 434.4
courteous 504.14
approbatory 509.16
dutiful 641.13
respective
proportionate 477.13
mutual 776.11
particular 864.12
respects regards 155.3
compliments 504.8
respiration 2.19
respirator 91.19
respiratory 2.30
respite
n recess 20.2
release 120.2
reprieve 601.3
interim 825.1
delay 845.2
pause 856.3
v reprieve 601.5
resplendent
illustrious 662.19
gorgeous 1015.20
bright 1024.32
respond sense 24.6
be affected 93.11
defend 600.10
interchange 862.4
react 902.5
answer 938.4
respondent
n accused 599.6
answerer 938.3
adj reactive 902.9
answering 938.6
response
sensation 24.1
feeling 93.1
sympathy 93.5
communication 343.1
meaning 518.1
defense 600.2
paean 696.3
responsory report
708.23
passage 708.24
impact 886.2
reaction 902.1
answer 938.1
responsibility
supervision 573.2
commission 615.1
incumbency 641.2
trustworthiness 644.6
attribution 887.1
operation 888.1
liability 896.1

responsible
chargeable 623.9
answerable 641.17
trustworthy 644.19
liable 896.5
responsive
sensitive 24.12
sympathetic 93.20
willing 324.5
communicational
343.9
influenceable 893.15
reactive 902.9
answering 938.6
pliant 1045.9
elastic 1046.7
rest
n respite 20
repose 20.1
silence 51.1
quiescence 173.1
step 193.5
remainder 256.1
death 307.1
leisure 402.1
musical pause 709.21
pause 856.3
supporter 900.2
fulcrum 905.3
v repose 20.6
be situated 159.10
deposit 159.14
be still 173.7
ride at anchor 182.16
remain 256.5
do nothing 329.2
plead 598.18
calm 670.7
pause 856.9
depend 958.6
rest assured
hope 124.7
be confident 952.14
be certain 969.9
restate
paraphrase 341.13
iterate 848.8
restaurant
eating place 8.17
dining room 197.11
workplace 739.1
rest easy
be content 107.5
persuade oneself
375.24
restful vacational 20.10
comfortable 121.11
quiescent 173.12
pacific 464.9
tranquilizing 670.15
restimulate 396.16
resting place
tomb 309.16
end 819.1
supporter 900.2
rest in peace 309.24
restitution
compensation 338.1
restoration 396.1
reparation 481
reimbursement 624.2
recompense 624.3

atonement 658.1
reversion 858.1
restive restless 105.27
discontented 108.7
impatient 135.6
reluctant 325.6
defiant 327.10
obstinate 361.8
ungovernable 361.12
restless wakeful 23.7
restive 105.27
discontented 108.7
impatient 135.6
bustling 330.20
inconstant 853.7
agitated 916.16
rest one's case 598.18
rest on one's laurels
be content 107.5
take it easy 331.15
restore vitaminize 7.18
reproduce 78.7
put back 396.11
return 481.4
justify 600.9
rehabilitate 857.14
recover 481.6
aid 449.11
restrain limit 210.5
compel 424.4
constrain 428.7
bind 428.10
confine 429.12
simplify 499.5
moderate 670.6
qualify 958.3
hinder 1011.10
restraint
suppression 92.24
equanimity 106.3
reserve 139.3
limitation 210.2
reticence 344.3
self-control 359.5
compulsion 424.1
constraint 428
shackle 428.4
confinement 429.1
subjection 432.1
restrainedness 496.4
elegance 533.1
temperance 668.1
moderation 670.1
hindrance 1011.1
restraint of trade
restraint 428.1
commerce 731.1
restrict bound 210.5
narrow 270.11
limit 428.9
confine 429.12
allot 477.9
specialize 865.4
qualify 958.3
restricted
bounded 210.7
out of bounds 210.8
narrow 270.14
secret 345.11
limited 428.15
confined 429.19
specialized 865.5

qualified 958.10
Restricted 706.1
rest room latrine 12.10
bathing place 79.10
bathroom 197.26
restructure
reproduce 78.7
rearrange 807.13
change 851.7
rest stop 856.2
result
n event 830.1
effect 886.1
product 892.1
solution 939.1
v turn out 830.7
follow after 834.3
ensue 886.4
resultant
n effect 886.1
adj happening 830.9
resulting 886.6
resume recover 481.6
iterate 848.8
repeat 848.11
recommence 855.6
résumé
summary 557.2
history 719.1
iteration 848.2
resupply 385.1
resurface floor 295.22
repeat 848.11
recur 849.5
recur to the mind
988.15
resurgent
reproductive 78.14
renascent 396.24
resurrect
reproduce 78.7
revive 396.16
resurrection
reproduction 78.1
revival 396.3
removal to heaven
681.11
resuscitate
stimulate 105.13
come to life 306.8
revive 396.16
aid 449.11
resume 855.6
retail
n sale 734.1
v publish 352.10
deal in 731.15
sell 734.8
disperse 770.4
iterate 848.8
adj commercial
731.21
sales 734.13
retailer provider 385.6
merchant 730.2
retail store 736.1
retain
reserve 386.12
keep 474.5
employ 615.14
stabilize 854.7
sustain 855.4

elimination 772.2
riddle
   n refinery 79.13
   network 170.3
   porousness 292.8
   conundrum 522.9
   arranger 807.5
   the unknown 929.7
   bewilderment 970.3
   v perforate 292.15
   strike dead 308.17
   mark 517.19
   be incomprehensible
      522.10
   segregate 772.6
   classify 807.11
   shoot 903.12
   solve 939.2
ride
   n drive 177.7
   merry-go-round
      743.15
   v annoy 96.13
   be disrespectful 156.6
   go for a ride 177.33
   go on horseback
      177.34
   ride at anchor 182.16
   weather the storm
      182.40
   float 182.54
   banter 490.6
   ridicule 508.8
   rest on 900.22
ride a broomstick
      690.10
ride and tie
   n race 457.12
   v alternate 915.13
   adv to and fro 915.21
ride down
   conquer 412.10
   run over 909.7
ride for a fall 493.6
ride full tilt against
      459.18
ride herd on
   wield authority
      417.13
   hold a tight hand
      upon 425.4
   supervise 573.10
   dominate 612.15
   care for 1007.19
   drive 1068.8
ride high 298.8
ride it out 854.11
**ride off in all
   directions at once**
      105.16
ride on a rail
   torture 604.16
   drive out 908.14
ride out
   race 757.5
   be safe 1006.2
rider
   equestrian 178.8
   added to writing
      254.2
   hunter 311.13
   bill 613.9

jockey 757.2
ride roughshod over
   conquer 412.10
   intimidate 424.7
   domineer 612.16
   run over 909.7
ride shotgun 1007.18
ride the gravy train
   take one's leisure
      402.4
   live well 1009.10
ride the high horse
      141.8
ride the pine 747.4
ride the sea 182.54
ridge
   n summit 198.2
   head 198.6
   back 217.3
   ridgeline 237.5
   plateau 272.4
   bulge 283.3
   wrinkle 291.3
   v emboss 283.12
   wrinkle 291.6
ridicule
   n impudence 142.2
   disrespect 156.1
   contempt 157.1
   banter 490.1
   derision 508.1
   deprecation 510.2
   v have the audacity
      142.7
   disrespect 156.4
   disdain 157.3
   joke 489.13
   deride 508.8
   deprecate 510.12
ridiculous
   humorous 488.4
   absurd 922.11
   unbelievable 954.10
   impossible 966.7
riding 231.5
riding horse 311.13
rid oneself of
   break the habit 374.3
   discard 390.7
   relinquish 475.3
   eliminate 772.5
rife reported 552.15
   prevalent 863.12
   teeming 883.9
   plentiful 990.7
riffraff offal 80.9
   rubbish 391.5
   rabble 606.3
rifle
   n military man 461.6
   infantryman 461.9
   gun 462.10
   v furrow 290.3
   plunder 482.17
   ransack 937.32
rift
   n crack 224.2
   valley 237.7
   falling-out 456.4
   break 801.4
   fault 1002.2
   blemish 1003.1

v open 292.11
   adj cleft 224.7
rig
   n wardrobe 5.2
   suit 5.6
   costume 5.9
   equipage 179.5
   truck 179.12
   rigging 180.12
   equipment 385.4
   ruler 575.9
   v outfit 5.40
   tamper with 354.16
   plot 381.9
   equip 385.8
   prearrange 964.5
rigamarole 520.2
rigger
   aircraftsman 185.6
   electrician 1031.21
rigging rig 180.12
   cordage 271.3
   intrigue 381.5
   equipment 385.4
   manipulation 737.20
   supporter 900.2
right
   n right side 219.1
   authority 417.1
   rights 430.2
   estate 471.4
   warrant 600.6
   conservative 611.9
   rightfulness 637.1
   due 639.2
   prerogative 642.1
   justice 649.1
   option 737.21
   accuracy 972.5
   v remedy 396.13
   make agree 787.7
   arrange 807.8
   adj right-hand 219.4
   straight 277.6
   decorous 496.10
   conventional 579.5
   rightful 637.3
   honest 644.13
   just 649.8
   orthodox 687.7
   apt 787.10
   sane 924.4
   accurate 972.16
   expedient 994.5
   adv directly 161.23
   rightward 219.7
   very 247.18
   rightly 637.4
   absolutely 793.15
   exactly 972.21
   right on! 972.24
   excellently 998.22
   inter yes 332.18
right-about-face
   n reverse 163.1
   change of mind 363.1
   turnabout 858.1
   v do an about-face
      163.10
right and left
   extensively 158.11
   all round 209.13

laterally 218.8
right-angle
   upright 200.2
   perpendicular 200.12
   right-angled 278.7
right as rain
   adj straight 644.14
   adv right! 972.24
right away at once 829.8
   promptly 844.15
righteous
   honest 644.13
   virtuous 653.6
   godly 692.9
   right 637.3
righteous indignation
      152.4
rightful right 637.3
   condign 639.8
   just 649.8
   legal 673.10
   genuine 972.15
right hand 616.7
right-hand
   starboard 219.4
   dexterous 219.5
right-handed 219.5
right-hand man
   subordinate 432.5
   employee 577.3
   right hand 616.7
**right of eminent
   domain** 480.5
right off the bat 829.6
right-of-way
   superiority 249.1
   road 383.5
right on
   adv you better believe
      it! 972.25
   inter congratulations
      149.5
   yeah 332.19
   phrs that's it 787.13
the Right Reverend
   n clergyman 699.2
   adj the Noble 648.8
right side 219
the right stuff 413.4
the right thing right
      637.1
   fairness 649.3
   virtue 653.1
right to vote vote 371.6
   suffrage 609.17
rightward clockwise
      161.24
   to the right 219.7
right wing
   right side 219.1
   conservative 611.9
right with 787.12
rigid firm 15.18
   meticulous 339.12
   unyielding 361.9
   strict 425.7
   formal 580.9
   permanent 852.7
   immovable 854.15
   exact 972.17
   stiff 1044.11
rigor acrimony 17.5

meticulousness 339.3
firmness 425.2
asceticism 667.1
violence 671.1
accuracy 972.5
adversity 1010.1
difficulty 1012.1
cold 1022.1
rigidity 1044.2
rigor mortis 307.1
rile annoy 96.13
provoke 152.24
agitate 916.10
rill 238.1
rim
n border 211.4
slope 237.2
felly 280.4
v border 211.10
rime 1022.7
rind exterior 206.2
shallowness 276.1
skin 295.3
lamina 296.2
ring
n ringing 54.3
circle 280.2
encircling thing 280.3
bulge 283.3
telephone call 347.13
fighting 457.9
arena 463.1
jewel 498.6
association 617.1
clique 617.6
insignia 647.1
ecclesiastical insignia
647.4
boxing 754.1
halo 1024.14
atomic cluster 1037.7
v din 53.7
tintinnabulate 54.8
check out 188.13
encircle 209.7
telephone 347.18
ring a bell 902.8
ringer impostor 357.6
substitute 861.2
ring in arrive 186.6
inaugurate 817.11
punch the clock 831.12
substitute 861.4
ringing in the ear 54.3
ringleader
instigator 375.11
leader 574.6
politics 610.7
ringlet lock 3.5
circlet 280.5
coil 281.2
ringmaster
theater man 704.23
circus artist 707.3
rings 725.7
ringside seat 27.8
ring true 972.9
rink playground 743.11
hockey 749.1
lawn bowling 750.3
rinse
n washing 79.5

cleanser 79.17
v wash 79.19
soak 1063.13
riot
n revolt 327.4
free-for-all 457.5
joke 489.6
unruliness 671.3
commotion 809.4
plenty 990.2
v vegetate 310.31
revolt 327.7
contend 457.13
rage 671.11
roister 809.10
riot police 1007.17
rip
n trauma 85.37
drinking spree 88.6
disrespect 156.3
tide 238.13
attempt 403.3
libertine 665.10
break 801.4
v torture 96.18
be disrespectful 156.6
speed 174.9
open 292.11
injure 393.13
wrest 480.22
RIP 309.24
rip cord 181.13
ripe
v ripen 407.8
adj mature 303.13
prepared 405.16
seasoned 407.13
experienced 413.28
marriageable 563.20
complete 793.9
timely 842.9
perfected 1001.9
ripen fester 12.15
grow 14.2
enlarge 259.7
mature 303.9
develop 392.10
bloom 407.8
evolve 860.5
perfect 1001.5
ripe old age 303.5
rip into
lift one's hand against
457.14
attack 459.15
criticize 510.14
rip off 482.16
rip-off fake 354.13
hoax 356.7
theft 482.4
ripped high 87.23
drunk 88.33
tortured 96.25
ripping
n extortion 192.6
severance 801.2
adj excellent 998.13
ripple
n splash 52.5
rapids 238.10
wave 238.14
roughness 288.2

wrinkle 291.3
attempt 403.3
v babble 52.11
wrinkle 291.6
agitate 916.10
ripple effect
divergence 171.1
transferal 176.1
permeation 221.3
expansion 259.1
dispersion 770.1
immediate cause
885.3
rip-roaring noisy 53.13
turbulent 671.18
riptide 238.13
rise
n appearance 33.1
ascent 193.1
rising 200.5
acclivity 204.6
slope 237.2
hill 237.4
wave 238.14
increase 251.1
height 272.2
improvement 392.1
promotion 446.1
evolution 860.1
source 885.5
reaction 902.1
v wake up 23.6
appear 33.8
din 53.7
move 172.5
ascend 193.8
arise 200.8
incline 204.10
billow 238.22
grow 251.6
tower 272.10
levitate 298.9
revolt 327.7
make good 409.10
originate 817.13
rise above accept 134.7
loom 247.5
tower above 272.11
defeat 411.5
rise again 306.8
rise and fall 238.22
rise from 886.5
rise in the world
make good 409.10
be prosperous 1009.9
riser 193.5
rise to mind 930.18
rise to the occasion
carry out 328.7
win through 409.13
rise to the surface
190.11
rise up ascend 193.8
rise 200.8
grow 272.12
revolt 327.7
rising
n appearance 33.1
sore 85.36
course 172.2
ascent 193.1
uprising 200.5

acclivity 204.6
swelling 283.4
revolt 327.4
adj flowing 172.8
ascending 193.14
sloping upward
204.17
increasing 251.8
risk
n investment 729.3
gamble 759.2
unreliability 970.6
chance 971.1
v invest 729.16
gamble 759.24
take a chance 971.12
endanger 1005.6
defy danger 1005.7
riskless 1006.5
risk-taking
defiance 454.1
daring 492.5
chance 971.1
risqué cursing 513.8
risky 666.7
rite celebration 487.1
amenity 504.7
ceremony 580.4
ritual 701.3
rite of confession 351.3
rite of passage 580.4
ritual
n custom 373.1
amenity 504.7
formality 580.1
ceremony 580.4
rite 701.3
adj ceremonious 580.8
ritualistic 701.18
ritual murder 308.1
ritual observance
celebration 487.1
rite 701.3
ritzy grandiose 501.21
chic 578.13
rival
n competitor 452.2
combatant 461.1
v contend against
451.4
compete 457.18
equal 789.5
be comparable 942.7
excel 998.11
adj oppositional 451.8
competitive 457.23
rivalry envy 154.1
hostility 451.2
competition 457.2
river stream 238.1
torrent 238.5
river bed 239.2
river gambler 759.21
riverside
n shore 234.2
adj coastal 234.7
rivet 799.8
riveted fixed 854.14
gripped 982.18
riveting alluring 377.8
engrossing 982.20
riviera 234.2

rivulet 238.1
RNA
  genetic material 305.9
  heredity 560.6
roach
  marijuana cigarette
    87.11
  remainder 256.1
  vermin 311.35
road seaway 182.10
  inlet 242.1
  route 383.1
  highway 383.5
  harbor 1008.6
ROAD 461.22
roadbed 383.7
roadblock 1011.5
road hog driver 178.10
  self-seeker 651.3
roadhouse inn 228.15
  entertainment 743.13
road map 574.10
road racing 744.1
road-test 941.8
the road to ruin 395.1
roadwork 84.2
roadworthy 1006.7
roam
  n wandering 177.3
  v wander 177.23
roan
  n horse 311.11
  adj reddish-brown
    40.4
roar
  n noise 53.3
  boom 56.4
  cry 59.1
  v be noisy 53.9
  boom 56.9
  cry 59.6
  animal sound 60.2
  laugh 116.8
  sigh 318.21
  speak 524.26
  rage 671.11
  overact 704.31
roaring
  thundering 56.12
  frenzied 105.25
roaring drunk 88.33
roaring fire 1018.13
roaring forties
  zone 231.3
  prevailing wind
    318.10
Roaring Twenties
  823.5
roast
  n dish 10.7
  meat 10.12
  celebration 487.1
  v cook 11.4
  be disrespectful 156.6
  banter 490.6
  ridicule 508.8
  criticize 510.20
  grill 937.21
  be hot 1018.22
  adj cooked 11.6
roast beef 10.13
roaster poultry 311.29

hot day 1018.8
rob
  n semiliquid 1060.5
  v commit robbery
    482.14
robbed of 473.8
robber thief 483.1
  holdup man 483.5
robber baron 730.1
robbery loss 473.1
  theft 482.3
robe
  n garment 5.3
  blanket 295.10
  frock 702.2
  v clothe 5.38
Robin Hood
  philanthropist 143.8
  thief 483.11
robot 1040.12
robot factory
  plant 739.3
  control system 1040.5
robotization
  automation 1040.1
  automatic control
    1040.3
robotlike 780.5
rob Peter to pay Paul
  861.4
robust strong 15.15
  energetic 17.13
  hale 83.12
rock
  n symbol of strength
    15.8
  dose 87.19
  missile 462.18
  rock-and-roll 708.10
  stability 854.6
  swing 915.6
  flounder 916.8
  protector 1007.5
  hardness 1044.6
  stone 1057.1
  v impress 93.15
  agitate 105.14
  pitch 182.55
  calm 670.7
  oscillate 915.10
  flounder 916.15
  adj instrumental
    708.51
  stone 1057.10
rock'n'roll 708.10
rock bottom
  bottom 199.1
  foundation 900.6
rockbound
  rugged 288.7
  firm 425.7
rockbound coast
  shore 234.2
  hidden danger 1005.5
rock climber 193.6
rocker refinery 79.13
  marvel 122.2
  engraving tool 713.8
  oscillator 915.9
rocket
  n swiftness 174.6
  rocket plane 181.4

ascent 193.7
  projectile 462.18
  signal 517.15
  rocketry 1072.1
  rocket engine 1072.2
  missile 1072.3
  spacecraft 1073.2
  v shoot up 193.9
  skyrocket 1072.12
rocket engine
  rocket 1072.2
  atomic power plant
    1073.4
rocket fuel 87.17
rocket launcher
  launcher 462.21
  projector 1072.10
rocket propulsion
  propulsion 184.25
  reaction propulsion
    1072.8
rocketry
  ballistics 462.3
  missile science 1072
  space travel 1073.1
rocket scientist
  talented person
    413.12
  intellectual 928.1
  rocketeer 1072.11
rock-fill dam 1011.5
rock-hard
  unyielding 361.9
  hard 1044.10
the Rockies 231.7
rockiness 85.1
rocking
  tranquilizing 670.15
  swinging 915.17
rocking chair 915.9
rocking horse 743.16
rocklike
  unyielding 361.9
  stable 854.12
  hard 1044.10
  stony 1057.11
rock music 708.10
Rock of Gibraltar
  854.6
rock pile 604.2
rocks genitals 2.11
  money 728.2
  hidden danger 1005.5
rock-steady 129.2
rock the boat 867.4
rock to sleep
  put to sleep 22.20
  calm 670.7
rocky
  unsteady 16.16
  tired 21.7
  ill 85.55
  rugged 288.7
  unsafe 1005.11
  hard 1044.10
  stony 1057.11
rococo
  n ornateness 498.2
  adj ornate 498.12
  freakish 869.13
  fanciful 985.20
rod shaft 273.1

scepter 417.9
  gun 462.10
  stick 605.2
  royal insignia 647.3
  nuclear reactor
    1037.13
rodent
  n creature 311.3
  adj rodential 311.43
rodeo 769.1
rodlike 1044.11
roe fish 10.23
  female animal 77.9
  egg 305.15
  hoofed animal 311.5
Roger 332.19
Roget's
  vocabulary 526.13
  reference book 554.9
  dictionary 870.4
rogue horse 311.12
  mischief-maker 322.3
  rascal 660.3
  jockey 757.2
rogues' gallery 714.3
roil
  n agitation 916.1
  opaqueness 1030.1
  v annoy 96.13
  provoke 152.24
  riot 809.10
  seethe 914.12
  agitate 916.10
role function 387.5
  part 704.10
  script 706.2
  occupation 724.3
  mode 764.4
role model
  paragon 659.4
  ideal 785.4
  standard of perfection
    1001.4
role-player 357.1
roll
  n bun 10.30
  staccato 55.1
  boom 56.4
  gait 177.12
  barrel roll 184.14
  wave 238.14
  a length 267.2
  coil 281.2
  cylinder 282.4
  record 549.1
  document 549.5
  film 714.10
  bankroll 728.17
  throw 759.9
  bundle 769.8
  roster 870.6
  rotation 914.1
  swing 915.6
  flounder 916.8
  v reverberate 54.7
  drum 55.4
  boom 56.9
  bird sound 60.5
  progress 162.2
  travel 177.18
  way of walking 177.28
  pitch 182.55

maneuver 184.40
level 201.6
billow 238.22
ball 282.7
smooth 287.5
press 287.6
rob 482.16
push 903.9
trundle 914.10
wallow 914.13
oscillate 915.10
flounder 916.15
go easily 1013.10
roll around 849.5
rollback
regression 163.1
curtailment 252.4
discount 631.1
economizing 635.2
roll back reduce 252.7
retrench 635.5
roll bar 756.1
roll call
legislative procedure
613.6
roll 870.6
rolled into one 871.10
roller dressing 86.33
billow 238.14
cylinder 282.4
smoother 287.4
game 745.3
rotator 914.4
wave 915.4
pulverizer 1049.7
roller coaster 743.15
roller-skate 177.35
roller skates 179.21
rollick
n frolic 743.5
v rejoice 116.5
bluster 503.3
play 743.23
roll in arrive 186.6
indulge 669.4
roll-in 749.6
rolling
n progression 162.1
maneuvers 184.13
throwing 903.2
rotation 914.1
television reception
1034.5
adj resonant 54.9
thundering 56.12
hilly 237.8
knobby 272.18
wavy 281.10
rotating 914.14
swinging 915.17
rolling pin 282.4
rolling stone
wanderer 178.2
changeableness 853.4
rotator 914.4
roll in the aisles 116.8
roll into one
put together 799.5
combine 804.3
roll it 817.7
roll of the dice 759.2
roll on march on 162.3

travel 177.18
elapse 820.5
roll out get up 23.6
manifest 348.5
roll out the red carpet
pay homage to 155.5
receive 187.10
welcome 585.9
honor 646.8
roll over 729.16
roll over and play dead
354.20
Rolls-Royce 249.4
roll up one's sleeves
prepare oneself 405.13
set to work 725.15
roll with the punches
keep cool 106.9
accept 134.7
Rolodex 870.7
roly-poly
n heavyweight 257.12
adj corpulent 257.18
roman 548.6
Roman calendar 831.8
Roman candle 517.15
Roman Catholic
n Catholic 675.19
adj Catholic 675.29
romance
n love affair 104.6
fabrication 354.10
figment of the
imagination 985.5
idealism 985.7
v narrate 722.6
idealize 985.16
Roman Christianity
675.7
Romanism 675.8
romanization 546.5
Roman numerals
1016.4
romantic
n visionary 985.13
adj sentimental
93.21
loving 104.27
fictional 722.7
visionary 985.24
Romeo 104.13
Romeo and Juliet
104.18
**Rome wasn't built in a
day** 134.13
romp
n mannish female
76.9
schoolgirl 302.8
victory 411.1
frolic 743.5
horse race 757.3
v exude cheerfulness
109.6
rejoice 116.5
caper 366.6
play 743.23
rompers 5.30
roof
n top 198.1
abode 228.1
home 228.2

house 228.5
roofing 295.6
v top 295.21
rook
n chessman 743.17
cheater 759.22
v deceive 356.19
cheat 759.26
rookery sty 80.11
birdhouse 228.23
birthplace 885.8
rookie recruit 461.18
novice 572.9
newcomer 773.4
beginner 817.2
room
n latitude 158.3
compartment 197
chamber 197.1
interval 224.1
quarters 228.4
capacity 257.2
latitude 430.4
opportunity 842.2
v inhabit 225.7
house 225.10
room and board 385.3
roomer lodger 227.8
tenant 470.4
rooming house 228.15
roommate 588.3
room temperature
1018.3
roomy
comfortable 121.11
spacious 158.10
broad 269.6
airy 317.11
roorback 552.6
roost
n birdhouse 228.23
v settle 159.17
sit 173.10
inhabit 225.7
rooster
male animal 76.8
poultry 311.29
root
n plant root 310.20
etymon 526.2
morphology 526.3
source 885.5
foundation 900.6
v vegetate 310.31
encourage 492.16
applaud 509.10
fix 854.9
lodge 854.10
search 937.30
root around 937.22
rooted
confirmed 373.19
innate 766.8
traditional 841.12
established 854.13
rooter enthusiast 101.5
commender 509.8
rooting out 395.5
root of all evil 728.1
root out dislodge 160.6
excise 255.10
exterminate 395.14

eliminate 772.5
search out 937.33
rope
n cigar 89.4
cord 271.2
latitude 430.4
hanging 604.7
execution 605.5
game 745.3
v restrain 428.10
catch 480.17
bind 799.9
roped off 429.20
**rope enough to hang
oneself** 430.4
rope in deceive 356.19
lure 377.5
rope ladder 193.4
rope off
circumscribe 210.4
quarantine 429.13
ropes 893.3
rosary 696.4
rose
n pinkness 41.2
nozzle 239.9
insignia 647.1
heraldry 647.2
adj pink 41.8
Rose Bowl 746.1
rose-colored glasses
optimism 124.3
idealism 985.7
rosé wine 88.17
rosin
n gum 1055.1
v resin 1055.2
roster record 549.1
baseball team 745.2
football team 746.2
basketball team 747.2
roll 870.6
schedule 964.3
rostrum prow 216.3
nose 283.8
pulpit 703.13
platform 900.13
rosy pink 41.8
red-complexioned
41.9
fresh 83.13
cheerful 109.11
optimistic 124.12
thriving 1009.13
rot
n filth 80.7
disease 85.40
rottenness 393.7
bull 520.3
blight 1000.2
v decay 393.22
rota 549.1
rotary flowing 172.8
periodic 849.7
circuitous 913.7
rotational 914.15
rotate move 172.5
take off 184.38
invert 205.5
recur 849.5
revolve 914.9
rote 988.4

rotgut 88.14
rotor propeller 903.6
  rotator 914.4
rotten unsound 16.15
  nasty 64.7
  malodorous 71.5
  filthy 80.23
  horrid 98.19
  decayed 393.40
  dishonest 645.16
  corrupt 654.14
rotten egg 71.3
rotten luck
  chance 971.1
  ill fortune 1010.5
rotund
  corpulent 257.18
  round 282.8
  convex 283.13
rouge
  n makeup 1015.12
  v make red 41.4
rough
  n roughness 288.2
  diagram 381.3
  combatant 461.1
  vulgarian 497.6
  ruffian 593.3
  golf 751.1
  v roughen 288.4
  mistreat 389.5
  adj acrimonious 17.14
  raucous 58.15
  bitter 64.6
  pungent 68.6
  harsh 144.24
  flowing 238.24
  unsmooth 288.6
  coarse 294.6
  undeveloped 406.12
  vulgar 497.11
  gruff 505.7
  violent 671.16
  boisterous 671.20
  nonuniform 781.3
  irregular 850.3
  jolting 916.20
  difficult 1012.17
  adv roughly 288.11
roughage 7.3
rough-and-ready
  unprepared 406.8
  unrefined 497.12
rough-and-tumble
  n commotion 809.4
  adj boisterous 671.20
roughhouse
  n misbehavior 322.1
  commotion 809.4
  v misbehave 322.4
  create disorder 809.11
rough idea 783.3
rough it 225.11
roughly speaking
  approximately 223.23
  generally 863.17
roughneck
  n vulgarian 497.6
  ruffian 593.4
  adj boorish 497.13
rough up
  roughen 288.4

mistreat 389.5
  injure 393.13
  punish 604.15
  beat 901.17
roulette 759.12
round
  n drink 88.7
  step 193.5
  sphere 231.2
  degree 245.1
  circle 280.2
  music 280.9
  routine 373.6
  route 383.1
  rondo 708.19
  occupation 724.4
  18 holes 751.3
  fight 754.3
  series 811.2
  turn 824.2
  revolution 849.3
  circuit 913.2
  whirl 914.2
  v turn round 163.9
  curve 279.6
  encircle 280.10
  round out 282.6
  circle 913.5
  turn 913.6
  rotate 914.9
  number 1016.16
  adj circular 280.11
  rotund 282.8
  elegant 533.6
  candid 644.17
  full 793.11
  circuitous 913.7
  adv about 209.12
  around 914.16
roundhouse
  garage 197.27
  repair shop 739.5
rounding out 407.2
round of applause
  509.2
round off
  complete 407.6
  number 1016.16
round robin 913.2
round table 423.3
round the clock
  adj uninterrupted 811.8
  adv continuously 811.10
round trip
  journey 177.5
  game 745.3
  circuit 913.2
roundup 769.1
rouse energize 17.10
  awake 23.4
  wake someone up 23.5
  excite 105.12
  elicit 192.14
  arouse 375.19
roustabout hand 183.6
  longshoreman 183.9
rout
  n retreat 163.2
  discomfiture 412.2
  rabble 606.3
  attendance 768.6
  throng 769.4

multitude 883.3
  agitation 916.1
  v overwhelm 412.8
route way 383
  path 383.1
routine
  n exercise 84.2
  run 373.6
  manner 384.1
  act 704.7
  order 806.1
  series 811.2
  software 1041.11
  adj medium 246.3
  habitual 373.15
  orderly 806.6
  frequent 846.4
  prevalent 863.12
rove
  n wandering 177.3
  v stray 164.4
  wander 177.23
row
  n series 811.2
  v navigate 182.13
  paddle 182.53
row
  n noise 53.4
  quarrel 456.6
  turbulence 671.2
  commotion 809.4
  agitation 916.1
  v be noisy 53.9
  quarrel 456.12
  push 903.9
  cause trouble 1012.14
rowdy
  n mischief-maker
    322.3
  combatant 461.1
  vulgarian 497.6
  ruffian 593.3
  adj noisy 53.13
  misbehaving 322.5
  boorish 497.13
  boisterous 671.20
royal
  n volume 554.4
  potentate 575.8
  adj dignified 136.12
  sovereign 417.17
  good 998.12
Royal Canadian
  Mounted Police
  1007.17
Royal Highness 648.2
royalist 611.9
royalty
  sovereignty 417.8
  potentate 575.8
  aristocracy 608.1
  nobility 608.2
  dividend 624.7
rpm velocity 174.1
  revolutions 914.3
RSVP 553.15
rub
  n touch 73.1
  contact 223.5
  disaccord 456.1
  bone of contention
    456.7

crisis 842.4
  crux 1012.8
  friction 1042.1
  v pain 26.7
  stroke 73.8
  treat 91.24
  contact 223.10
  polish 287.7
  represent 349.8
  banter 490.6
  frictionize 1042.6
  dry 1064.6
rubber
  n contraceptive 86.23
  eradicator 395.9
  bridge 758.3
  softness 1045.4
  elastic 1046.3
  v be curious 980.3
  elasticize 1046.6
  adj rubbery 1046.8
rubber band 1046.3
rubber check
  arrears 623.2
  counterfeit 728.10
rubberneck
  n traveler 178.1
  sightseer 917.3
  inquisitive person 980.2
  v journey 177.21
  be long 267.5
  sight-see 917.6
  be curious 980.3
  adj spectating 917.7
rubber stamp
  n ratification 332.4
  v ratify 332.12
rubbish
  n remainder 256.1
  derelict 370.4
  rubble 391.5
  nonsense 520.2
  rabble 606.3
  trivia 997.4
  v be disrespectful
    156.6
  censure 510.13
rubble rubbish 391.5
  rock 1057.1
rubdown 1042.3
rub down rub 1042.6
  tend 1068.7
rube
  n bungler 414.9
  simple soul 416.3
  peasant 606.6
  oaf 923.5
  adj not urbane 233.8
rub elbows with 582.17
rub it in 96.13
rub off wear 393.20
  abrade 1042.7
rub out delete 255.12
  kill 308.13
  obliterate 395.16
  abrade 1042.7
rub salt in the wound
  irritate 96.14
  aggravate 119.2
  impair 393.9
rub the wrong way
  288.5

ruby 41.6
ruckus noise 53.4
  quarrel 456.6
  turbulence 671.2
  commotion 809.4
rudder 573.5
ruddy red 41.6
  red-complexioned
    41.9
  fresh 83.13
  blushing 139.13
  curse 513.10
rude raucous 58.15
  hale 83.12
  impudent 142.10
  undeveloped 406.12
  coarse 497.11
  discourteous 505.4
  inelegant 534.2
  populational 606.8
  unlearned 929.14
rude awakening
  awakening 23.2
  disillusionment 976.1
rudiment
  embryo 305.14
  foundation 900.6
rudimentary
  basic 199.8
  dwarf 258.13
  undeveloped 406.12
  beginning 817.15
  original 885.14
rue
  n pity 145.1
  v regret 113.6
ruffian
  mischief-maker 322.3
  combatant 461.1
  vulgarian 497.6
  rough 593.3
ruffle
  n staccato 55.1
  agitation 105.4
  edging 211.7
  fold 291.1
  confusion 984.3
  v drum 55.4
  annoy 96.13
  perturb 105.14
  provoke 152.24
  wrinkle 288.5
  fold 291.5
  beat time 708.44
  disarrange 810.2
  agitate 916.10
  confuse 984.7
ruffles and flourishes
  708.27
rug wig 3.14
  carpet 295.9
  blanket 295.10
  bedding 900.20
rugged strong 15.15
  hale 83.12
  harsh 144.24
  ragged 288.7
  wrinkled 291.8
  strict 425.6
  sturdy 762.7
  difficult 1012.17
ruggedly 15.23

ruin
  n wreck 393.8
  destruction 395.1
  defeat 412.1
  loss 473.1
  antiquity 841.6
  v spoil 393.10
  destroy 395.10
  defeat 412.6
  bankrupt 625.8
  seduce 665.20
  rage 671.11
  thwart 1011.15
ruins remainder 256.1
  wreck 393.8
  antiquity 841.6
rule
  n mean 246.1
  supremacy 249.3
  straightedge 277.3
  measure 300.2
  norm 373.5
  governance 417.5
  law 419.2
  direction 420.3
  decree 420.4
  government 612.1
  ordinance 673.3
  game 752.3
  model 785.1
  the book 868.4
  influence 893.1
  syllogism 934.6
  axiom 973.2
  v oversee 249.11
  wield authority
    417.13
  command 420.8
  sway 612.14
  prevail 863.10
  exercise influence
    893.8
  pass judgment 945.13
rule against 444.3
rulebook 868.4
rulebook slowdown
  727.5
rule off 300.11
rule of law 612.8
rule of thumb 941.1
rule out
  excise 255.10
  close 293.6
  obliterate 395.16
  prohibit 444.3
  make impossible
    966.6
  prevent 1011.14
ruler superior 249.4
  straightedge 277.3
  governor 575.6
  potentate 575.8
  rod 605.2
rule the roost 612.15
rule with an iron fist
  612.16
ruling
  n decree 420.4
  law 673.3
  verdict 945.5
  adj powerful 18.12
  chief 249.14

  authoritative 417.15
  governing 612.18
  prevalent 863.12
  influential 893.14
ruling class
  the best 249.5
  mastership 417.7
  the authorities 575.15
  upper class 607.2
rum
  n spirits 88.13
  adj odd 869.11
  excellent 998.13
rumble
  n audio distortion
    50.13
  noise 53.4
  reverberation 54.2
  boom 56.4
  fight 457.4
  report 552.6
  v reverberate 54.7
  boom 56.9
  speak 524.26
rumble seat 217.1
ruminant 930.21
ruminate chew 8.27
  consider 930.12
rummage
  n search 937.15
  v ransack 937.32
rummage sale 734.3
rumor
  n report 552.6
  v publish 352.10
  report 552.11
rump buttocks 217.4
  remainder 256.1
rumple
  n wrinkle 291.3
  v ruffle 288.5
  wrinkle 291.6
  disarrange 810.2
  agitate 916.10
rumpus
  n noise 53.4
  quarrel 456.6
  turbulence 671.2
  commotion 809.4
  v be noisy 53.9
rumpus room 197.12
rumrunner 732.5
run
  n trauma 85.37
  direction 161.1
  course 172.2
  sprint 174.3
  migration 177.4
  journey 177.5
  voyage 182.6
  flight 184.9
  lair 228.26
  stream 238.1
  flow 238.4
  average 246.1
  a length 267.2
  routine 373.6
  route 383.1
  path 383.2
  freedom 430.1
  race 457.12
  engagement 704.11

  impromptu 708.27
  ornament 709.18
  home run 745.3
  round 751.3
  series 811.2
  continuance 855.1
  generality 863.3
  amount made 892.4
  trend 895.2
  v fester 12.15
  exercise 84.4
  extend 158.8
  move 172.5
  speed 174.8
  travel 177.18
  migrate 177.22
  navigate 182.13
  pilot 182.14
  sail before the wind
    182.22
  float 182.54
  meet 223.11
  flow 238.16
  flee 368.10
  nominate 371.19
  hunt 382.9
  injure 393.13
  make haste 401.5
  print 548.14
  direct 573.8
  guide 573.9
  run for office
    609.39
  go into politics
    610.13
  smuggle 732.8
  play 746.5
  ski 753.4
  race 757.5
  elapse 820.5
  endure 826.6
  operate 888.5
  be operative 888.7
  incur 896.4
  thrust 901.12
  corner 1012.16
  melt 1019.21
  computerize 1041.18
  liquefy 1062.5
  raise 1068.6
runabout 178.2
run across
  meet 223.11
  come across 940.3
run afoul of 457.15
run aground
  shipwreck 182.42
  come to grief 1010.10
run amok
  go berserk 671.15
  riot 809.10
  be insane 925.20
the runaround
  avoidance 368.1
  circumvention 415.5
run around like a
  chicken with its
  head cut off
  be excitable 105.16
  bustle 330.12
run a temperature
  take sick 85.46

get excited 105.17
run a tight ship 425.4
runaway
  n fugitive 368.5
  adj fugitive 368.16
  escaped 369.11
run away
  run along 188.12
  flee 368.10
run circles around
  outdo 249.9
  defeat 412.9
run counter to
  deny 335.4
  oppose 451.3
  go contrary to 778.4
  counteract 899.6
run down
  burn out 21.5
  fail 85.47
  quiet 173.8
  sail into 182.41
  decline 393.17
  arrest 429.15
  capture 480.18
  disparage 512.8
  run over 909.7
  trace 937.34
  discover 940.2
  underestimate 949.2
run-down tired 21.7
  unhealthy 85.53
  dilapidated 393.33
  worn-out 393.36
run dry 388.4
run for it 368.10
run for one's life
  run off 188.12
  flee 368.10
run for one's money
  457.2
run from 182.36
rung step 193.5
  degree 245.1
run in sail into 182.41
  thrust in 191.7
  interpose 213.6
  arrest 429.16
  capture 480.18
  visit 582.19
run-in
  n quarrel 456.6
  adj accustomed
  373.16
run in circles
  be impotent 19.7
  be useless 391.8
run in opposition to
  778.4
run in pursuit of 382.8
run interference for
  back 449.13
  facilitate 1013.7
run in the family 766.6
run into total 791.8
  sail into 182.41
  meet 223.11
  cost 630.13
  be converted into
  857.17
  collide 901.13
  come across 940.3

run into a brick wall
  856.7
run into debt
  borrow 621.3
  go in debt 623.6
run into the ground
  992.10
run it by again 848.7
run its course
  come to an end 819.6
  elapse 820.5
run it up the flagpole
  and see who salutes
  941.8
run neck and neck
  174.14
runner speeder 174.5
  sled 179.20
  channel 239.4
  branch 310.18
  messenger 353.1
  smuggler 732.5
  jockey 757.2
  member 792.4
runner-up 411.2
running
  n pus 12.6
  exercise 84.2
  motion 172.1
  direction 573.1
  supervision 573.2
  candidacy 609.10
  operation 888.1
  melting 1019.3
  liquefaction 1062.1
  adj flowing 172.8
  fast 174.15
  pouring 238.24
  cursive 547.22
  continuous 811.8
  present 837.2
  prevalent 863.12
  operating 888.11
  adv consecutively
  811.11
running away
  absence 222.4
  flight 368.4
running back 746.2
running commentary
  556.2
running head
  label 517.13
  caption 936.2
running mate 610.9
running sore 1000.1
running start
  advantage 249.2
  beginning 817.1
  earliness 844.1
running wild 925.30
runny exudative 190.20
  fluid 1059.4
runoff outflow 190.4
  election 609.15
run off
  run along 188.12
  flee 368.10
  print 548.14
  drive out 908.14
run off at the mouth
  talk nonsense 520.5

chatter 540.5
  persist 855.5
run off with
  steal 482.13
  abduct 482.20
run of luck
  chance 971.1
  stroke of luck 1009.3
run of the mill
  average 863.3
  mediocre 1004.8
run on march on 162.3
  chatter 540.5
  continue 811.4
  elapse 820.5
  endure 826.6
  continue 855.3
run out
  v burn out 21.5
  exit 190.12
  empty 190.13
  find vent 369.10
  be consumed 388.4
  perish 395.23
  protract 538.8
  come to an end 819.6
  elapse 820.5
  eject 908.13
  drive out 908.14
  adj past 836.7
  obsolete 841.15
run out of gas
  weaken 16.9
  stall 410.16
  flop 704.28
  fall short 910.2
run out on 370.5
run over
  overflow 238.17
  browse 570.13
  iterate 848.8
  overrun 909.7
  think over 930.13
  examine 937.23
  abound 990.5
  number 1016.16
run parallel to 898.3
run ragged 21.8
run rings around
  outdo 249.9
  defeat 412.9
run riot revolt 327.7
  dissipate 669.6
  run amok 671.15
  riot 809.10
  overspread 909.5
  superabound 992.8
run roughshod over
  412.10
runs 12.2
run scared 491.8
run short of 991.7
run smoothly 1013.10
runt shrimp 258.4
  a nobody 997.7
run the gauntlet 492.11
run the risk
  chance 759.24
  be liable 896.3
  take chances 1005.7
run through
  pervade 221.7

perforate 292.15
  stab 459.25
  squander 486.3
  browse 570.13
  spend 626.5
  rehearse 704.32
run-through
  summary 557.2
  production 704.13
  examination 937.3
run to extend to 261.6
  entreat 440.11
  cost 630.13
  equal 789.5
  total 791.8
run together 169.2
run to seed
  v waste 393.19
  go to ruin 395.24
  go to waste 473.6
  fall on evil days
  1010.11
  adj stricken in years
  303.18
  out of practice 414.18
  wasted 486.9
run true to form 780.3
run up grow 251.6
  improvise 365.8
  go before 815.3
  produce 891.8
run-up
  preparation 405.1
  precedence 813.1
  curtain-raiser 815.2
  forethought 960.2
run up against
  meet 223.11
  experience 830.8
  come across 940.3
run up a tab 623.6
runway taxiway 184.23
  path 383.2
runway lights 184.19
run with the pack
  332.9
rupture
  n trauma 85.37
  crack 224.2
  falling-out 456.4
  break 801.4
  v cleave 224.4
  breach 292.14
  injure 393.13
  be damaged 393.23
  break 801.12
rural rustic 233.6
  natural 416.6
  agricultural 1067.20
ruse trick 356.6
  stratagem 415.3
rush
  n substance abuse
  87.1
  thrill 105.2
  excitement 105.3
  course 172.2
  velocity 174.1
  run 174.3
  flow 238.4
  jet 238.9
  grass 310.5

sainthood
  sanctification 685.3
  godliness 692.2
Saint Nicholas 678.13
sake motive 375.1
  intention 380.1
salaam
  n obeisance 155.2
  crouch 912.3
  v make obeisance
    155.6
  bow 912.9
salad food 10.35
  hodgepodge 796.6
salad days 301.1
salamander
  amphibian 311.27
  spirit 678.6
  fire iron 1019.12
salaried worker
  bourgeois 607.6
  worker 726.2
salary
  n pay 624.4
  v pay 624.10
sale transfer 629.1
  selling 734
  wholesale 734.1
  closing-out sale 734.3
sales 734.13
salesmanship
  promotion 352.5
  inducement 375.3
  selling 734.2
salesperson 730.3
sales pitch 734.5
salient
  n region 231.1
  protuberance 283.2
  adj protruding 283.14
  conspicuous 348.12
  notable 996.19
saline 68.9
saliva
  digestive juice 2.15
  humor 2.22
  digestion 7.8
  spittle 13.3
salivary glands
  digestion 2.15
  digestive system 2.16
  ingestion 7.8
salivate 13.6
sallow
  v yellow 43.3
  adj colorless 36.7
  yellow 43.4
  yellow-faced 43.6
sally
  n journey 177.5
  attack 459.1
  witticism 489.7
  v set out 188.8
  emerge 190.11
sally forth set out 188.8
  emerge 190.11
salmon
  n marine animal
    311.30
  jumper 366.4
  adj pink 41.8
salon parlor 197.5

  museum 386.9
  society 578.6
  social gathering
    582.10
  market 736.1
  company 769.3
saloon bar 88.20
  parlor 197.5
  cabin 197.9
salsa 10.9
salt
  n saltiness 68.4
  mariner 183.1
  preservative 397.4
  veteran 413.16
  wit 489.1
  v flavor 63.7
  tamper with 354.16
  preserve 397.9
  falsify accounts
    628.10
  adj flavored 62.9
  salty 68.9
  witty 489.15
salt-and-pepper 39.4
salt away 386.10
salt flat plain 236.1
  wasteland 890.2
salt-free diet 7.11
saltine 10.29
salt in the wound 96.3
salt of the earth
  person of honor 644.8
  good citizen 659.3
  the best 998.8
salt water ocean 240.1
  water 1063.3
salud! 88.38
salute
  n obeisance 155.2
  celebration 487.1
  greeting 585.4
  v pay homage to 155.5
  greet another ship
    182.52
  praise 509.12
  signal 517.22
  address 524.27
  greet 585.10
  inter toast 88.38
salvage
  n reclamation 396.2
  preservation 397.1
  rescue 398.1
  recovery 481.3
  recompense 624.3
  fee 630.6
  v redeem 396.12
  rescue 398.3
salvageable
  remediable 396.25
  rescuable 398.4
salvager
  mender 396.10
  rescuer 398.2
salvation
  reclamation 396.2
  preservation 397.1
  rescue 398.1
  function of Christ
    677.15
  redemption 685.4

salve
  n balm 86.11
  gratuity 478.5
  moderator 670.3
  ointment 1054.3
  v medicate 91.25
  relieve 120.5
  redeem 396.12
  oil 1054.8
salvo detonation 56.3
  volley 459.9
  celebration 487.1
  shot 903.4
  qualification 958.1
Samaritan 592.1
same identical 777.7
  uniform 780.6
  former 813.5
same old story
  836.2
same old thing
  tedium 118.1
  regularity 780.2
sample
  n taste 62.4
  specimen 785.3
  part 792.1
  feeler 941.4
  subject 941.7
  v taste 62.7
  canvass 937.28
  experiment 941.8
  adj typical 349.15
sampler 937.16
Samson 15.6
samurai 608.3
sanctify
  glorify 662.13
  hallow 685.5
sanctimonious
  hypocritical 354.32
  prudish 500.19
  zealous 692.11
  self-righteous 693.5
sanction
  n ratification 332.4
  consent 441.1
  authorization 443.3
  approval 509.1
  legalization 673.2
  v ratify 332.12
  consent 441.2
  authorize 443.11
  approve 509.9
  legalize 673.8
sanctioned
  authorized 443.17
  legal 673.10
sanctity sacredness 685
  sanctitude 685.1
  godliness 692.2
sanctuary
  hiding place 346.4
  preserve 397.7
  holy of holies 703.5
  refuge 1008.1
sanctum
  sanctum sanctorum
    197.8
  retreat 584.6
  sanctuary 703.5
  refuge 1008.5

sand
  n grain 1049.6
  grain of sand 1057.2
  v grind 287.8
  buff 1042.8
sandalwood 70.4
sandbag
  n weight 297.6
  v weight 297.12
  defeat 412.9
  attack 459.15
  bet 759.25
  beat 901.17
  club 901.20
sandbagger 483.5
sandbar island 235.2
  shoal 276.2
  hidden danger 1005.5
  sand 1057.2
sandblast grind 287.8
  buff 1042.8
a sand castle 16.7
sand dune hill 237.4
  sand 1057.2
sandhog 284.10
sanding 1042.2
sandman 22.11
sandpaper
  n roughness 288.2
  v grind 287.8
  buff 1042.8
sands shore 234.2
  hidden danger 1005.5
sands of time 820.3
sandstone 1057.1
sandstorm 318.13
sand trap 751.1
sandwich
  n food 10.31
  v interpose 213.6
sandwich board 352.7
sandy yellow 43.4
  granular 1049.12
  stony 1057.11
  dry 1064.7
sane intelligent 919.12
  sensible 919.18
  sane-minded 924.4
  logical 934.20
  realistic 986.6
sanguine
  n personality type
    92.12
  adj sanguineous 41.7
  red-complexioned
    41.9
  cheerful 109.11
  hopeful 124.11
  expectant 130.11
sanitary hygienic 79.27
  healthful 81.5
sanitary landfill
  receptacle of filth
    80.12
  derelict 370.4
  trash pile 391.6
sanitation
  cleansing 79.3
  hygiene 81.2
sanity
  intelligence 919.1
  sensibleness 919.6

saneness 924.1

sans absent 222.19

without 991.17

sans serif 548.6

sans souci 107.7

Santa Claus

giver 478.11

cheerful giver 485.2

Santa 678.13

sap

n essential content 196.5

dupe 358.2

entrenchment 460.5

essence 766.2

fool 923.3

fluid 1059.2

v weaken 16.10

excavate 284.15

undermine 393.15

overthrow 395.20

spiritualize 763.4

sapling

youngster 302.1

sprout 302.11

tree 310.10

sapphire 45.3

sappy

sentimental 93.21

immature 301.10

foolish 922.9

fluid 1059.4

sarcasm wit 489.1

irony 508.5

sarcoma 85.38

sarcophagus 309.11

sardonic 508.13

sardonic grin

smile 116.3

scornful laugh 508.4

sartorial

clothing 5.44

tailored 5.47

sash waistband 5.19

frame 266.4

sashay travel 177.18

way of walking 177.28

sass

n back talk 142.4

v talk back 142.8

sassy 142.10

Satan demon 680.6

liar 357.9

the Devil 680.3

nether world deity 682.5

satanic cruel 144.26

diabolic 654.13

demoniac 680.17

execrable 999.10

Satanist 680.15

sate gratify 95.7

satiate 993.4

sated languid 331.20

satiated 993.6

satellite

hanger-on 138.6

follower 166.2

country 232.1

dependent 432.6

disciple 616.8

escort 768.5

moon 1070.11

artificial satellite 1073.6

satellite communication 347.1

satin

n smooth surface 287.3

fine texture 294.3

softness 1045.4

adj smooth 294.8

satire wit 489.1

sarcasm 508.5

burlesque 508.6

lampoon 512.5

satirist

humorist 489.1

lampooner 512.7

poet 720.11

satirize

burlesque 508.11

lampoon 512.12

satisfaction

pleasure 95.1

contentment 107.1

compensation 338.1

reparation 396.6

observance 434.1

duel 457.7

restitution 481.2

payment 624.1

recompense 624.3

atonement 658.1

sufficiency 990.1

satiety 993.1

satisfactory

satisfying 107.11

convincing 952.26

sufficient 990.6

tolerable 998.20

satisfy feed 8.18

gratify 95.7

content 107.4

indulge 427.6

observe 434.2

pay 624.10

pay in full 624.13

atone 658.4

convince 952.18

suffice 990.4

satiate 993.4

satisfying 97.6

saturate fill 793.7

imbue 796.11

overload 992.15

satiate 993.4

soak 1063.13

saturated fat 1054.1

saturation

colorfulness 35.4

color quality 35.6

fullness 793.2

imbuement 796.2

overfullness 992.3

satiety 993.1

soaking 1063.7

saturation point

fullness 793.2

satiety 993.1

radiation 1036.1

saturation raid 459.4

Saturn 1070.9

satyr

sexual pervert 75.16

lecher 665.11

forest god 678.11

sauce

n cooking 11.1

liquor 88.14

back talk 142.4

hodgepodge 796.6

admixture 796.7

pulp 1061.2

v flavor 63.7

talk back 142.8

saucer tableware 8.12

circle 280.2

saucer eyes

optic part 2.9

eye 27.9

defect 28.6

saucer-shaped

parabolic 279.13

concave 284.16

saucy impudent 142.10

defiant 454.7

sauna bath 79.8

bathing place 79.10

saunter

n slow motion 175.2

walk 177.10

gait 177.12

v go slowly 175.6

wander 177.23

way of walking 177.28

sausage 10.20

sausage meat 10.12

sauté brown 40.2

cook 11.4

savable 398.4

savage

n barbarian 497.7

brute 593.5

violent person 671.9

v torture 96.18

mistreat 389.5

injure 393.13

rage 671.11

work evil 999.6

adj cruel 144.26

pitiless 146.3

infuriated 152.32

deadly 308.22

warlike 458.21

unrefined 497.12

fierce 671.21

savagery cruelty 144.11

unrefinement 497.3

violence 671.1

unenlightenment 929.4

savanna

horizontal 201.3

the country 233.1

plain 236.1

grassland 310.8

savant expert 413.11

specialist 865.3

wise man 920.1

scientist 927.11

scholar 928.3

save

n soccer action 752.3

v store up 386.11

reserve 386.12

not use 390.5

preserve 397.8

rescue 398.3

aid 449.11

retain 474.5

economize 635.4

redeem 685.6

stop from scoring 752.4

be conservative 852.6

play safe 1006.3

prevent 1011.14

prep off 255.14

excluding 772.10

conj unless 958.16

save-all

n niggard 484.4

adj stingy 484.9

the saved 692.5

saved soul 679.1

save face 136.7

save for a rainy day

reserve 386.12

economize 635.4

save one's neck

rescue 398.3

benefit 592.3

be safe 1006.2

save the day 592.3

save your breath! 51.14

saving grace

extenuation 600.5

characteristic 864.4

savings reserve 386.3

funds 728.14

savings account

account 622.2

funds 728.14

savings institution

lending institution 620.4

bank 729.13

savior preserver 397.5

rescuer 398.2

redeemer 592.2

savoir-faire skill 413.1

mannerliness 504.3

savor

n taste 62.1

relish 63.2

odor 69.1

passion 93.2

characteristic 864.4

v eat 8.20

taste 62.7

relish 63.5

flavor 63.7

enjoy 95.12

savory

n food 10.8

adj edible 8.33

flavored 62.9

tasty 63.8

fragrant 70.9

delectable 97.10

savvy

n skill 413.1

smartness 919.2

understanding 927.3

discrimination 943.1

v understand 521.7
know 927.12

saw
  n notching 289.2
  maxim 973.1
  platitude 973.3
  cutlery 1039.2
  v fiddle 708.41
  sever 801.11
sawbones doctor 90.4
  surgeon 90.5
sawbuck money 728.7
  trestle 900.16
sawdust
  remainder 256.1
  powder 1049.5
sawed-off 258.13
sawhorse 900.16
sawmill 739.3
sawtooth
  n projection 285.4
  adj angular 278.6
  rugged 288.7
saw wood 22.13
saxophonist 710.4
say
  n supremacy 249.3
  affirmation 334.1
  vote 371.6
  authority 417.1
  free will 430.6
  remark 524.4
  speech 543.2
  turn 824.2
  influence 893.1
  v take leave 188.16
  affirm 334.5
  announce 352.12
  utter 524.23
  state 524.24
  answer 938.4
  suppose 950.10
  adv approximately
    223.23
say again 848.7
say a good word for
  509.11
say amen to 332.12
say a mouthful 972.10
say a word to the wise
  399.5
say aye 441.2
say goodbye to 370.5
say hello 585.10
say in a roundabout
  way
  prevaricate 344.7
  circumlocute 538.10
  go roundabout 913.4
say in defense 600.10
saying
  affirmation 334.1
  remark 524.4
  maxim 973.1
say in reply 938.4
say it all 1016.18
say loud and clear
  affirm 334.5
  speak up 524.22
say no refuse 442.3
  restrain oneself 668.6
say nothing 51.6

sayonara! 188.22
say one's prayers
  696.12
say out loud
  affirm 334.5
  speak up 524.22
say over and over
  848.10
say right to one's face
  454.3
say-so
  affirmation 334.1
  command 420.1
  free will 430.6
  administration 573.3
  influence 893.1
say the word
  command 420.8
  permit 443.9
say to oneself 542.3
say uncle flinch 127.13
  lose 412.12
  surrender 433.8
say under one's breath
  345.9
say what one thinks
  644.12
say yes 441.2
scab
  n sore 85.36
  crust 295.14
  strikebreaker 727.8
  blemish 1003.1
  v crust 295.27
  break a strike 727.11
  blemish 1003.4
scabies 85.40
scads lot 247.4
  plenty 990.2
scaffold
  execution 605.5
  scaffolding 900.12
scalawag horse 311.12
  rascal 660.3
scald
  n trauma 85.37
  burn 1019.6
  v injure 393.13
  be hot 1018.22
scalding 1018.25
scale
  n range 158.2
  map 159.5
  ladder 193.4
  step 193.5
  degree 245.1
  size 257.1
  blanket 295.12
  crust 295.14
  flake 296.3
  weighing 297.9
  measure 300.2
  gamut 709.6
  break 801.4
  series 811.2
  v flake 6.11
  climb 193.11
  layer 296.5
  raid 459.20
  break 801.12
scale down
  n make small 258.9

v reduce 252.7
scales of justice 649.1
scale up 259.4
scaling raid 459.4
  disruption 801.3
scallop
  n notching 289.2
  v cook 11.4
  convolve 281.4
  notch 289.4
scalloped cooked 11.6
  notched 289.5
scalp peel 6.8
  trade 737.23
scalper salesman 730.3
  speculator 737.11
scaly flaky 296.7
  powdery 1049.11
scam
  n deception 356.9
  cheating 759.13
  v deceive 356.14
  swindle 356.19
scamp
  n mischief-maker
    322.3
  rascal 660.3
  v slight 340.8
  stint 484.5
scamper
  n run 174.3
  haste 401.1
  v speed 174.8
  hasten off 188.10
  make haste 401.5
scan
  n field of view 31.3
  examination 937.3
  v browse 570.13
  rhyme 720.14
  itemize 800.7
  examine 937.23
  examine cursorily
    937.25
  receive 1035.17
scandal slander 512.3
  gossip 552.8
  abomination 638.2
  iniquity 654.3
  disgrace 661.5
  immodesty 666.2
scandalize 661.7
scandalmonger 552.9
scanner 1041.4
scanning
  n metrics 720.6
  televising 1034.3
  radar 1035.8
  adj metric 720.16
scant
  v limit 210.5
  stint 484.5
  adj narrow 270.14
  incomplete 794.4
  sparse 884.5
  meager 991.10
scantily clad 6.13
scanty narrow 270.14
  incomplete 794.4
  sparse 884.5
  meager 991.10
  scarce 991.11

scapegoat
  sacrifice 696.7
  whipping boy 861.3
  oddity 869.4
scar
  n precipice 200.3
  slope 237.2
  mark 517.5
  blemish 1003.1
  v mark 517.19
  blemish 1003.4
scarab 691.5
scarce infrequent 847.2
  in short supply 884.5
  sparse 991.11
scarcely any 884.4
scarcely to be expected
  968.3
scarcity
  infrequency 847.1
  fewness 884.1
  underproduction
    891.5
  scarceness 991.3
scare
  n fear 127.1
  v frighten 127.15
scarecrow figure 349.6
  eyesore 1014.4
scared to death
  afraid 127.22
  terrified 127.26
scare off 379.3
scare tactics
  terrorization 127.7
  coercion 424.3
  threat 514.1
scare up 472.9
scarf
  n food 10.2
  joint 799.4
  v hook 799.8
scarlet red 41.6
  prostitute 665.28
scarp precipice 200.3
  incline 204.4
  slope 237.2
scary fearful 127.23
  frightening 127.28
scat! 908.31
scathe
  n impairment 393.1
  v criticize 510.20
  work evil 999.6
scathing
  acrimonious 17.14
  caustic 144.23
scatter
  n deflection 164.2
  rarity 299.1
  dispersion 770.1
  v deflect 164.5
  radiate 171.6
  interspace 224.3
  rarefy 299.3
  overwhelm 412.8
  squander 486.3
  disperse 770.4
  disband 770.8
  shatter 801.13
  part company 801.19
  loosen 803.3

disarrange 810.2
scatterbrain
frivolous person 923.7
flightiness 984.5
scatter to the winds
squander 486.3
disperse 770.4
scavenge 79.18
scavenger
sweeper 79.16
creature 311.3
scenario project 381.2
playbook 704.21
script 706.2
effect 886.1
solution 939.1
scene look 27.3
view 33.6
outburst 152.9
setting 209.2
arena 463.1
act 704.7
scenery 704.20
landscape 712.12
scenery view 33.6
arena 463.1
decor 704.20
scent
n odor 69.1
sense of smell 69.4
fragrance 70.1
perfumery 70.2
track 517.8
clue 517.9
hint 551.4
v odorize 69.7
smell 69.8
perfume 70.8
catch the scent of
940.6
scepter rod 417.9
royal insignia 647.3
schedule
n plan 381.1
chronicle 831.9
list 870.1
program 964.3
v plan 381.8
allot 477.9
spend 626.5
list 870.8
line up 964.6
scheduled
planned 381.12
listed 870.9
slated 964.9
schematic
diagrammatic 381.14
analytical 800.9
scheme
n trick 356.6
plan 381.1
project 381.2
intrigue 381.5
stratagem 415.3
plot 722.4
outline 800.4
v premeditate 380.7
plot 381.9
maneuver 415.10
plot 838.6
prearrange 964.4

schism desertion 370.2
falling-out 456.4
sect 675.3
schizoid
n personality type
92.12
psychotic 925.17
adj crazy 925.27
psychotic 925.28
schizophrenia
mental disorder 92.14
dissociation 92.20
dementia praecox
925.4
schizophrenic
n psychotic 925.17
adj psychotic 925.28
schlock 1004.6
schmaltz 93.8
schnapps 88.13
schnoz 283.8
scholar
student 572.1
specialist 865.3
wise man 920.1
scientist 927.11
scholastic 928.3
scholarship
subsidy 478.8
studiousness 570.4
fellowship 646.7
erudition 927.5
scholastic
n theologian 676.3
scholar 928.3
adj institutional
567.13
academic 568.19
studious 570.17
learned 927.21
book-learned 927.22
school
n educational
institution 567.1
teaching 568.1
order 617.5
sect 675.3
style 712.8
group of animals
769.5
system of belief 952.3
v teach 568.10
adj scholastic 567.13
schoolbook
book 554.1
textbook 554.10
schoolboy boy 302.5
schoolchild 572.3
schoolbus 179.13
schooled 927.18
schoolgirl
schoolmaid 302.8
schoolchild 572.3
schoolhouse 567.10
schooling
teaching 568.1
learning 927.4
school library 558.1
school of thought 951.1
schoolroom 567.11
schoolteacher 571.1
sciatic 217.10

science art 413.7
ology 927.10
science fiction 1073.1
scientific
technical 927.28
exact 972.17
realistic 986.6
scientist 927.11
scintilla hint 248.4
spark 1018.15
glitter 1024.7
scintillate joke 489.13
be brilliant 919.11
glitter 1024.24
scintillating
witty 489.15
smart 919.14
burning 1018.27
glittering 1024.35
scion insert 191.2
sprout 302.11
branch 310.18
descendant 561.3
member 792.4
scissor 801.11
sclerosis symptom 85.9
hardening 1044.5
scoff
n food 10.2
indignity 156.2
gibe 508.2
v jeer 508.9
disbelieve 695.14
scofflaw 660.10
scold
n bitch 110.12
faultfinder 510.9
v bird sound 60.5
reprove 510.17
scoop
n cavity 284.2
information 551.1
news item 552.3
the facts 760.4
piece 792.3
v ladle 176.17
excavate 284.15
scoot 174.9
scope
n vision 27.1
telescope 29.4
field of view 31.3
range 158.2
degree 245.1
size 257.1
latitude 430.4
meaning 518.1
legality 673.1
opportunity 842.2
v look 27.13
scope out
look 27.13
examine 937.23
scorch
n trauma 85.37
burn 1019.6
v brown 40.2
speed 174.9
injure 393.13
criticize 510.20
stain 1003.6
be hot 1018.22

burn 1019.24
dry 1064.6
scorched earth 671.3
scorcher
speeder 174.5
game 745.3
hot day 1018.8
score
n crack 224.2
notch 289.1
furrow 290.1
representation 349.1
motive 375.1
hit 409.5
mark 517.5
line 517.6
debt 623.1
account 628.2
statement 628.3
price 630.1
playbook 704.21
piece 708.5
musical score 708.28
engraving 713.2
basketball game 747.3
tennis game 748.2
hockey game 749.3
string 750.2
round 751.3
soccer game 752.3
bridge 758.3
twenty 881.7
sum 1016.6
v use 87.21
notch 289.4
furrow 290.3
score a success 409.9
acquire 472.8
mark 517.19
compose 708.46
engrave 713.9
play football 746.5
play basketball 747.4
play tennis 748.3
play hockey 749.7
list 870.8
calculate 1016.17
the score
the facts 760.4
essence 766.3
score a bull's-eye
972.10
scorecard 549.10
scorekeeper 550.1
scoreless 412.16
scorer
recorder 550.1
composer 710.20
game 749.3
scorn
n hate 103.1
contempt 157.1
rejection 372.1
v hate 103.5
disdain 157.3
reject 372.2
flout 454.4
be hard to please
495.8
scorpion 311.31
scotch
n notch 289.1

mark 517.5
curb 1011.7
v notch 289.4
injure 393.13
mark 517.19
hinder 1011.10
thwart 1011.15
Scotch 635.6
scot-free
escaped 369.11
free 430.21
Scotland Yard 1007.17
scoundrel
criminal 645.10
rascal 660.3
scour
n abrasion 1042.2
v wash 79.19
speed 174.8
traverse 177.20
polish 287.7
ransack 937.32
abrade 1042.7
scourge
n epidemic 85.5
punishment 604.1
whip 605.1
bane 1000.1
v whip 604.13
scouring powder 79.17
scourings
remainder 256.1
refuse 391.4
scout
n vanguard 216.2
secret agent 576.9
baseball team 745.2
precursor 815.1
watchman 1007.10
v look 27.13
spurn 157.4
traverse 177.20
reject 372.2
flout 454.4
scoff 508.9
reconnoiter 937.27
scowl
n frown 110.9
offense 152.2
reproving look 510.8
v look sullen 110.15
show resentment
  152.14
scrabble
n creeping 177.17
scribbling 547.7
v creep 177.26
excavate 284.15
scribble 547.20
grope 937.31
scram
v depart 188.7
leave 222.10
flee 368.11
inter go away 908.32
scramble
n creeping 177.17
Air Force mission
  184.11
bustle 330.4
haste 401.1
fight 457.4

gibberish 522.7
hodgepodge 796.6
jumble 809.3
commotion 809.4
v speed 174.8
creep 177.26
hustle 330.13
make haste 401.5
contend 457.13
make unintelligible
  522.12
play football 746.5
mix 796.10
confuse 810.3
scrambled
meaningless 520.6
hard to understand
  522.14
mixed 796.14
scrambled eggs 10.25
scramble for 480.16
scrambler 347.4
scrap
n tatter 248.3
minute 258.7
rubbish 391.5
quarrel 456.6
piece 792.3
v junk 390.8
quarrel 456.12
end 819.5
scrapbook
record book 549.11
compilation 554.7
scrape
n rasp 58.3
trauma 85.37
obeisance 155.2
bewilderment 970.3
predicament 1012.5
abrasion 1042.2
v grate 58.10
touch lightly 73.7
bow 155.6
contact 223.10
excavate 284.15
grind 287.8
injure 393.13
economize 635.4
fiddle 708.41
engrave 713.9
abrade 1042.7
scrape by 990.4
**scrape the bottom of
  the barrel** 994.4
scrape together
collect 472.11
assemble 769.18
scrap heap
trash pile 391.6
derelict 370.4
scrap iron 391.4
scrapper
oppositionist 452.3
combatant 461.1
boxer 461.2
scrapple 10.12
scrappy
irascible 110.20
contentious 110.26
warlike 458.21
incomplete 794.4

discontinuous 812.4
irregular 850.3
scraps
remainder 256.1
refuse 391.4
scrap the plan 365.8
scratch
n feed 10.4
rasp 58.3
trauma 85.37
shallowness 276.1
furrow 290.1
bad likeness 350.2
mark 517.5
scribbling 547.7
engraving 713.2
money 728.2
blemish 1003.1
abrasion 1042.2
v grate 58.10
tingle 74.5
excavate 284.15
furrow 290.3
misdraw 350.4
injure 393.13
obliterate 395.16
mark 517.19
scribble 547.20
portray 712.19
engrave 713.9
work hard 725.13
end 819.5
cease 856.6
scratchboard 712.18
**scratch each other's
  back** 862.4
scratchiness 58.2
scratch pad 549.11
scratch player 751.2
scratch the surface
give a lick and a
  promise 206.6
touch upon 276.4
not know 929.11
scrawl
n illegibility 522.4
scribbling 547.7
v scribble 547.20
scrawny lean 270.17
meager 991.10
scream
n screech 58.4
cry 59.1
lament 115.3
joke 489.6
v screech 58.8
cry 59.6
animal cry 60.2
wail 115.13
wind sound 318.21
speak 524.26
scream bloody murder
cry 59.6
complain 115.16
screamer caption 936.2
goof 974.6
screaming garish 35.19
vociferous 59.10
gaudy 501.20
screaming halt 856.2
screech
n shriek 58.4

cry 59.1
v shriek 58.8
cry 59.6
animal sound 60.2
wind sound 318.21
speak 524.26
screen
n refinery 79.13
network 170.3
furniture 229.1
porousness 292.8
cover 295.2
veil 346.2
pretext 376.1
scenery 704.20
motion-picture
  theater 706.6
arranger 807.5
safeguard 1007.3
shade 1027.1
television picture
  tube 1034.11
v refine 79.22
cover 295.19
conceal 346.6
defend 460.8
project 714.16
shield 747.4
play 752.4
segregate 772.6
classify 807.11
discriminate 943.4
protect 1007.18
shade 1027.5
screening
n refinement 79.4
network 170.3
covering 295.1
concealment 346.1
basketball game 747.3
grouping 807.3
adj covering 295.35
defensive 460.11
protective 1007.23
shading 1027.6
screen pass 746.3
screenplay 706.2
screen test 706.4
screenwriter
dramatist 704.22
scriptwriter 706.3
screw
n distortion 265.1
coil 281.2
jailer 429.10
torture 605.4
propeller 903.6
v copulate 75.21
distort 265.5
convolve 281.4
deceive 356.19
mistreat 389.6
demand 421.5
wrest 480.22
stint 484.5
overprice 632.7
hook 799.8
rotate 914.9
screw around 997.15
screwball
n oddity 869.4
lunatic 925.16

freak 926.4
adj crazy 925.27
eccentric 926.6
screwed up
spoiled 393.29
botched 414.22
complex 798.4
confused 809.16
a screw loose 925.2
screwy foolish 922.9
crazy 925.27
eccentric 926.6
scribble
n bad likeness 350.2
illegibility 522.4
scribbling 547.7
v misdraw 350.4
scrabble 547.20
scribbler
hack writer 547.16
writer 718.3
literary hack 718.5
scribe
n writer 547.13
author 547.15
recorder 550.1
clergy 699.10
creative writer 718.4
v write 547.19
scrimmage fight 457.4
free-for-all 457.5
scrimmage line 746.3
scrimp stint 484.5
economize 635.4
scrip writing 547.10
document 549.5
money 728.1
paper money 728.5
token 728.12
script
representation 349.1
writing system 546.3
handwriting 547.3
writing 547.10
type 548.6
document 549.5
playbook 704.21
screenplay 706.2
scripture
sacred texts 683
scriptures 683.1
Scripture 683.2
scriptwriter
author 547.15
dramatist 704.22
screenwriter 706.3
creative writer 718.4
scroll
n coil 281.2
writing 547.10
manuscript 547.11
record 549.1
document 549.5
rare book 554.6
violin part 711.5
roll 870.6
v write 547.19
scrooge 484.4
scrotum 2.11
scrounge 440.15
scrounging
n beggary 440.6

theft 482.1
adj indolent 331.19
supplicatory 440.16
scrub
n washing 79.5
shrubbery 310.9
woodland 310.11
brush 310.14
a nobody 997.7
abrasion 1042.2
v wash 79.19
cease 856.6
abrade 1042.7
scrubby dwarf 258.13
arboreal 310.36
sylvan 310.37
vulgar 497.15
base 661.12
paltry 997.21
scrubland 310.11
scruffy dirty 80.22
shabby 393.32
base 661.12
paltry 997.21
scrumptious
tasty 63.8
excellent 998.13
scrunch
n rasp 58.3
v grate 58.10
pulverize 1049.9
scruple
n compunction 113.2
modicum 248.2
demur 325.2
objection 333.2
conscientiousness
644.2
doubt 954.2
v demur 325.4
object 333.5
hesitate 362.7
doubt 954.6
scrupulous
demurring 325.7
meticulous 339.12
observant 434.4
fastidious 495.9
punctilious 580.10
dutiful 641.13
conscientious 644.15
doubting 954.9
scrutinize survey 27.14
examine 937.23
make a close study of
937.24
pay attention 982.8
scrutiny overview 27.6
examination 937.3
close attention 982.4
scuba 367.5
scuba diver 367.4
scud
n run 174.3
rainstorm 316.2
gust 318.6
foam 320.2
v speed 174.8
float 182.54
scuff
n trauma 85.37
abrasion 1042.2

v way of walking
177.28
injure 393.13
abrade 1042.7
scuffle
n fight 457.4
struggle 725.3
v way of walking
177.28
contend 457.13
struggle 725.11
scull
n oar 180.15
v navigate 182.13
row 182.53
sculler 183.5
scullery 11.3
scullery maid
washer 79.15
maid 577.8
sculpt form 262.7
sculpture 715.5
sculptor
sculpture 715.1
artist 716.6
sculpture
n forming 262.5
figure 349.6
visual arts 712.1
statuary 715
sculpturing 715.1
carving 715.2
v form 262.7
engrave 713.9
sculpt 715.5
scum
n slime 80.8
offal 80.9
dregs 256.2
blanket 295.12
lamina 296.2
sperm 305.11
foam 320.2
refuse 391.4
rabble 606.3
v cover 295.19
foam 320.5
scum of the earth
offal 80.9
rabble 606.3
the wicked 660.12
scupper 239.5
scurrilous
caustic 144.23
insulting 156.8
disparaging 512.13
cursing 513.8
obscene 666.9
S-curve 279.3
scurvy vulgar 497.15
base 661.12
paltry 997.21
terrible 999.9
scurvy trick 356.6
scuttle
n run 174.3
gait 177.12
porch 189.6
haste 401.1
v speed 174.8
way of walking 177.28
capsize 182.44

sink 367.8
do for 395.11
make haste 401.5
lose one's nerve 491.8
bankrupt 625.8
scuttlebutt 552.6
scuzzy filthy 80.23
offensive 98.18
slovenly 809.15
paltry 997.21
scythe 279.5
sea wave 238.14
vast body of water
240
ocean 240.1
open water 240.3
quantity 247.3
sea anchor
safeguard 1007.3
curb 1011.7
seabed bed 199.4
ocean depths 275.4
Seabees 461.27
sea bird 311.28
Seabiscuit 311.15
seaboard 234.2
seaborne 182.57
sea breeze 318.5
seacoast 234.2
seafarer 183.1
seafood 10.23
seagoing 182.57
sea ice 1022.5
seal
n ratification 332.4
sign 517.1
print 517.7
label 517.13
signature 527.10
royal insignia 647.3
engraving tool 713.8
cast 784.6
mold 785.6
characteristic 864.4
v close 293.6
ratify 332.12
resolve 359.7
sign 437.7
mark 517.19
label 517.20
adj brown 40.3
sea lane seaway 182.10
route 383.1
sealed close 293.12
accepted 332.14
confidential 345.14
contracted 437.11
unknown 929.17
sea legs 182.3
sea level 201.3
seal of approval 509.1
seal off close 293.6
quarantine 429.13
seal one's lips 51.5
seam
n crack 224.2
layer 296.1
joint 799.4
deposit 1056.7
v mark 517.19
seamanship
shipmanship 182.3

sectary 675.26
sectarianism 617.13
section
n region 231.1
plot 231.4
military unit 461.22
part of book 554.13
passage 708.24
part 792.1
part of writing 792.2
severance 801.2
class 808.2
classifications 808.5
v apportion 801.18
sectional
regional 231.8
partisan 617.19
partial 792.7
sector semicircle 280.8
part 792.1
secular
n layman 700.2
adj unsacred 686.3
secularist 695.16
lay 700.3
momentary 849.6
hundredth 881.29
realistic 986.6
material 1050.10
secular humanist
695.13
secure
v fetch 176.16
elicit 192.14
close 293.6
bind 428.10
guarantee 438.9
defend 460.8
acquire 472.8
receive 479.6
fasten 799.7
make sure 854.8
stop work 856.8
protect 1007.18
adj fast 799.14
stable 854.12
belief 952.21
reliable 969.17
assured 969.20
confident 969.21
safe 1006.4
securities 738
security hope 124.1
veil of secrecy 345.3
guaranty 438
surety 438.1
stability 854.1
reliability 969.4
confidence 969.5
safety 1006.1
protection 1007.1
prosperity 1009.1
security blanket 900.1
Security Council 614.2
security risk 357.11
sedate
v put to sleep 22.20
relieve 120.5
moderate 670.6
adj staid 106.14
solemn 111.3
dignified 136.12

sedative
n sleep-inducer 22.10
anesthetic 25.3
sedative hypnotic
86.12
drug 87.2
moderator 670.3
adj sleep-inducing
22.23
calmative 86.45
palliative 670.16
sedentary inert 173.14
inactive 331.17
sedge 310.5
sediment
n deposit 176.9
dregs 256.2
v precipitate 1043.11
sedimentary rock
1057.1
sedition
rebelliousness 327.3
treason 645.7
seduce enamor 104.23
lure 377.5
betray 665.20
seductive
desirable 100.30
alluring 377.8
see
n diocese 698.8
v sense 24.6
behold 27.12
attend 221.8
perceive 521.9
visit 582.19
bet 759.25
spectate 917.5
know 927.12
think of 930.17
detect 940.5
heed 982.6
visualize 985.15
inter attention! 982.22
see about 930.14
see both sides 978.7
seed
n sperm 305.11
stone 310.29
lineage 560.4
offspring 561.1
card 758.2
vital force 885.7
v plant 1067.18
seedbed 1067.11
seed clouds 316.9
seedling sprout 302.11
plant 310.3
tree 310.10
see double
see badly 28.8
be drunk 88.27
seed pod 310.28
seedy tired 21.7
ill 85.55
shabby 393.32
slovenly 809.15
inferior 1004.9
see eye to eye
concur 332.9
agree 787.6
see fit 371.17

**see how the wind
blows** 494.6
seeing
n vision 27.1
distinctness 31.2
observatory 1070.17
adj visual 27.20
Seeing Eye dog
aid to the blind 30.6
dog 311.17
see in perspective 924.2
see in retrospect 988.10
see into perceive 521.9
investigate 937.22
see it through
prosecute to a
conclusion 360.5
be thorough 793.8
continue 855.3
persist 855.5
seek pursue 382.8
endeavor 403.5
solicit 440.14
hunt 937.29
be curious 980.3
seek refuge 1008.7
seem 33.10
seeming
n aspect 33.3
exteriority 206.1
sham 354.3
illusoriness 975.2
adj apparent 33.11
exterior 206.7
specious 354.26
illusory 975.8
seemly decorous 496.10
appropriate 533.7
conventional 579.5
right 637.3
decent 664.5
expedient 994.5
see off 188.16
see one's way clear to
441.3
seep
n exuding 190.6
v exude 190.15
trickle 238.18
be damp 1063.11
seepage
sorption 187.6
entrance 189.1
exuding 190.6
trickle 238.7
see red 152.18
seesaw
n playground
equipment 743.15
interaction 776.3
alternation 915.5
oscillator 915.9
v change 853.5
alternate 915.13
adj reciprocal 776.10
alternate 915.19
adv reciprocally
776.12
to and fro 915.21
seethe
n agitation 916.1
v be excitable 105.16

be angry 152.15
bubble 320.4
fume 671.12
come together 769.16
mill 914.12
flounder 916.15
be hot 1018.22
boil 1019.20
soak 1063.13
see the cloven hoof
940.8
see the difference 943.6
see the future 961.9
**see the handwriting on
the wall**
anticipate 844.6
foreknow 960.6
see the inside of 940.8
see the last of
not use 390.5
relinquish 475.3
eject 908.13
see the light
appear 33.8
come to life 306.8
be published 352.16
perceive 521.9
be converted 692.7
**see the light at the end
of the tunnel** 124.9
see the light of day
be born 1.2
appear 33.8
be published 352.16
originate 817.13
see to
prepare for 405.11
operate 888.5
seek 937.29
attend to 982.5
care for 1007.19
see what one can do
see what can be done
403.10
experiment 941.8
**see which way the
wind blows** 941.9
see you later! 188.22
segment
n straight line 277.2
portion 477.5
sect 675.3
part 792.1
part of writing 792.2
v analyze 800.6
apportion 801.18
segregate
quarantine 429.13
exclude 772.6
differentiate 779.6
separate 801.8
discriminate 943.4
seismic 671.23
seismic wave 915.4
seismograph 915.8
seismology 915.7
seize
take command 417.14
arrest 429.15
hold 474.6
take hold of 480.14
understand 521.7

usurp 640.8
secure 854.8
fix 854.10
stop 856.7
infest 909.6
know 927.12
seize on select 371.14
fasten upon 480.16
think of 930.16
pay attention 982.8
seize the day
make no provision
406.7
squander 486.3
seize the opportunity
use the occasion 842.7
improve the occasion
842.8
seize up be still 173.7
fix 854.10
stop 856.7
seizure pang 26.2
attack 85.6
symptom 85.9
outburst 105.9
authority 417.12
arrest 429.6
hold 474.2
seizing 480.2
take 480.10
usurpation 640.3
overrunning 909.1
spasm 916.6
frenzy 925.7
seldom
infrequently 847.4
unusually 869.17
select
n the best 998.8
v make a selection
371.14
designate 517.18
appoint 615.11
specify 864.11
discriminate 943.4
adj chosen 371.26
particular 495.13
exclusive 772.9
best 998.16
select a jury 598.15
select committee 423.2
selected works 554.7
selection
choice 371.1
indication 517.3
excerpt 557.3
appointment 615.2
grouping 807.3
specification 864.6
selective service
service 458.9
enlistment 615.7
selectman 575.17
self psyche 92.28
ego 864.5
soul 918.4
self-abasement
humiliation 137.2
unselfishness 652.1
crouch 912.3
self-absorbed
unfeeling 94.9

selfish 651.5
self-abuse 75.8
self-accusing 113.8
self-acting
voluntary 324.7
automated 1040.21
self-address 542.1
self-adhesive 802.12
self-adjusting 1040.21
self-admiring
vain 140.8
selfish 651.5
self-admission 351.3
self-adulation 502.3
self-advancement 651.1
self-advertisement
self-approbation 502.3
selfishness 651.1
self-analysis 113.3
self-appointed
presumptuous 141.10
meddlesome 214.9
self-approbation
complacency 107.2
vanity 140.1
self-praise 502.3
self-assertive 359.15
self-assured
composed 106.13
confident 969.21
self-avowal 351.3
self-centered
unfeeling 94.9
egotistic 140.10
selfish 651.5
self-complacent
complacent 107.10
vain 140.8
self-conceit 140.4
self-confessed
accepted 332.14
disclosive 351.10
self-confidence
equanimity 106.3
pride 136.1
confidence 969.5
self-congratulating
140.8
self-conscious 139.12
self-contained
independent 430.22
unsociable 583.5
selfish 651.5
separate 801.20
self-contained
    underwater breathing
    apparatus 367.5
self-content
n complacency 107.2
vanity 140.1
adj complacent 107.10
vain 140.8
self-contradiction
inconsistency 788.2
impossibility 966.1
error 974.1
self-control
n equanimity 106.3
patience 134.1
self-command 359.5
restraint 428.1
temperance 668.1

moderation 670.1
v self-govern 1040.20
self-deception
deception 356.1
illusion 975.1
self-defeating 922.10
self-defense
defense 460.1
justification 600.2
self-deluding 975.8
self-denial
self-control 359.5
unselfishness 652.1
asceticism 667.1
temperance 668.1
moderation 670.1
self-dependent 430.22
self-deprecating
self-abasing 137.12
self-effacing 139.10
self-destruct
blow up 395.18
be destroyed 395.22
self-destruction 308.5
self-destructive
murderous 308.23
destructive 395.26
self-determination
nationhood 232.6
voluntariness 324.2
independence 430.5
rallying device 458.12
automation 1040.1
self-discipline
self-control 359.5
temperance 668.1
self-discovery 940.1
self-doubt
self-effacement 139.2
doubt 954.2
self-dramatizing
n self-approbation
502.3
adj self-approving
502.11
self-driven 1040.22
self-educated 927.24
self-effacing
self-modest 139.10
unselfish 652.5
self-elected 141.10
self-employed person
726.2
self-esteem pride 136.1
vanity 140.1
selfishness 651.1
self-evident
manifest 348.8
real 760.15
obvious 969.15
self-examination 937.6
self-explanatory 348.8
self-expression 359.6
self-flagellation 113.3
self-fulfillment 92.27
self-glorification 502.3
self-governing 612.17
self-gratification 95.1
self-hatred 113.3
self-help 449.6
self-help group 449.2
self-humiliating 113.8

self-hypnosis 22.7
self-identity 864.1
self-immolation
suicide 308.5
unselfishness 652.1
oblation 696.7
burning 1019.5
self-importance
vanity 140.1
pompousness 501.7
confidence 969.5
importance 996.1
self-improvement
449.6
self-inflicted 643.8
self-interest
egotism 140.3
selfishness 651.1
selfish egotistic 140.10
self-seeking 651.5
self-isolation 651.1
selfless
impartial 649.10
unselfish 652.5
self-love vanity 140.1
selfishness 651.1
self-made 891.18
self-neglect 652.1
self-operating 1040.21
self-opinionated
conceited 140.11
dogmatic 969.22
self-pitiful 145.9
self-pity 145.1
self-possessed
composed 106.13
strong-willed 359.15
self-praise 502.3
self-preservation 460.1
self-priming 1040.21
self-proclaimed 141.10
self-promoting
n self-approbation
502.3
adj self-approving
502.11
selfish 651.5
self-propelled
jet-propelled 903.16
self-moved 1040.22
self-propulsion 1040.1
self-protection 460.1
self-punishment 113.3
self-regulating 1040.21
self-reliance
pride 136.1
independence 430.5
confidence 969.5
self-reproach 113.3
self-respect pride 136.1
vanity 140.1
self-restraint
equanimity 106.3
self-control 359.5
temperance 668.1
moderation 670.1
self-righteous 693.5
self-rule
communion 476.2
government 612.4
self-sacrifice
suicide 308.5

unselfishness 652.1
oblation 696.7
selfsame
n the same 777.3
adj identical 777.7
self-satisfied
complacent 107.10
vain 140.8
self-serving
n selfishness 651.1
adj selfish 651.5
self-starter 330.8
self-styled
spurious 354.25
nominal 527.15
self-sufficient
proud 136.8
vain 140.8
independent 430.22
unsociable 583.5
selfish 651.5
self-support 449.6
self-sustaining 449.23
self-taught
educated 570.16
self-educated 927.24
self-winding 1040.21
self-worship 140.1
self-worshiping 140.8
sell publicize 352.15
urge 375.14
persuade 375.23
provision 385.9
transfer 629.3
deal in 731.15
merchandise 734.8
be sold 734.12
convert 737.24
convince 952.18
sell at a loss
discount 631.2
sell 734.8
sell at auction 734.11
sell down the river
defect 370.6
betray 645.14
seller 730.3
seller's market
demand 421.1
insufficiency 991.1
roaring trade 1009.5
sell for cost 630.13
be sold 734.12
sell in futures 737.23
selling
n inducement 375.3
provision 385.1
merchandising 734.2
adj sales 734.13
sell off
discard 390.7
relinquish 475.3
transfer 629.3
sell 734.8
sell on credit 622.6
sell one a bill of goods
356.15
sell one on
persuade 375.23
convince 952.18
sell oneself
act the traitor 645.15

convince oneself
952.19
sell out defect 370.6
discard 390.7
inform on 551.13
betray 645.14
act the traitor 645.15
sell 734.8
sell stocks 737.24
sell short sell 734.8
sell stocks 737.24
underestimate 949.2
sell to the highest
bidder 734.11
sell under the counter
732.7
semantic
indicative 517.23
meaning 518.12
linguistic 523.17
semantics
meaning 518.7
lexicology 526.14
semaphore 517.15
semblance aspect 33.3
image 349.5
sham 354.3
pretext 376.1
similarity 783.1
copy 784.1
illusoriness 975.2
semen body fluid 13.2
sperm 305.11
semester 823.2
semi 179.12
semiannual 849.8
semi-automatic
1040.12
semicircle
crescent 279.5
half circle 280.8
half 874.2
semicolon 856.4
semiconductor 1031.13
semiconductor chip
1041.3
semiconductor circuit
1032.8
semiconscious 25.8
semifinalist 452.2
semigloss 35.21
seminal genital 2.27
secretory 13.7
reproductive 78.15
gametic 305.20
original 885.14
productive 889.9
fertilizing 889.11
imaginative 985.18
seminar
discussion 541.7
study 568.8
seminary school 567.1
secondary school
567.4
semiprecious stone
1057.6
semiretired 402.5
semiweekly 849.8
semiyearly 849.8
senary 881.18
senate 423.1

Senate committee
613.2
senator 610.3
send
n wave 238.14
v delight 95.10
remove 176.11
send off 176.15
billow 238.22
communicate 343.7
mail 553.12
start 903.13
broadcast 1033.25
transmit 1035.15
send abroad 190.17
send after 420.11
send a letter to 553.10
send a message
communicate 343.7
announce 352.12
state 524.24
send a statement
628.11
send away send 176.15
repulse 907.3
banish 908.17
send a wire 347.19
send back
reverberate 54.7
restore 481.4
send down 908.17
sender 347.2
send flying 412.7
send for 420.11
send forth send 176.15
issue 352.14
start 903.13
disgorge 908.25
send headlong 912.5
sending 343.2
send in one's papers
448.2
send off
send 176.15
begin 817.7
start 903.13
repulse 907.3
dismiss 908.18
send-off
leave-taking 188.4
beginning 817.1
send one's condolences
147.2
send one's regards
504.13
send out
commission 615.10
disgorge 908.25
vaporize 1065.8
send packing
reject 372.2
repulse 907.3
drive out 908.14
dismiss 908.18
send the wrong
message
pervert 265.6
misrepresent 350.3
send to Davy Jones's
locker 367.8
send to hell 682.6
send to jail 429.17

send to kingdom come
308.12
send to the gas
chamber 604.17
send up commit 429.17
lampoon 512.12
send-up 512.5
send up a trial balloon
941.9
send up the river
imprison 429.14
commit 429.17
send word
communicate 343.7
inform 551.8
senescence 303.6
senile
n dotard 923.9
adj stricken in years
303.18
old-fogyish 841.17
decrepit 921.23
senior
n superior 249.4
elder 304.5
undergraduate 572.6
chief 575.3
bridge 758.3
adj authoritative
417.15
previous 833.4
older 841.19
senior citizen 304.2
senior high school
567.4
seniority
superiority 249.1
eldership 303.3
prestige 417.4
oldness 841.1
señor 76.7
señora 77.8
señorita 77.8
sensation
physical sensibility 24
sense 24.1
feeling 93.1
thrill 105.2
marvel 122.2
success 409.4
brain 918.6
sensational
emotionalistic 93.19
lurid 105.32
wonderful 122.10
gaudy 501.20
vigorous 544.11
grandiloquent 545.8
superb 998.15
sense
n sensation 24.1
feeling 93.1
milieu 209.3
meaning 518.1
consensus 787.3
intelligence 919.1
sensibleness 919.6
cognizance 927.2
idea 931.1
hunch 933.3
logic 934.9
discrimination 943.1

suggestion 950.5
opinion 952.6
v perceive 24.6
feel 93.10
understand 521.7
intuit 933.4
detect 940.5
senseless
unconscious 25.8
cruel 144.26
meaningless 520.6
unordered 809.12
unintelligent 921.13
foolish 922.8
unwise 922.10
insane 925.26
illogical 935.11
inanimate 1053.5
sense of duty 641.2
sense of hearing 48.1
sense of humor 489.11
sense of relief 120.4
sense of rhythm 708.31
**sense of right and
    wrong** 636.5
sense of touch 73.1
sense of wonder 122.1
sense organ 24.5
senses five senses 24.5
wits 918.2
sanity 924.1
sensible sentient 24.11
sensitive 93.20
grateful 150.5
weighable 297.19
cheap 633.7
substantial 762.6
intelligent 919.12
reasonable 919.18
sane 924.4
knowing 927.15
logical 934.20
realistic 986.6
sensitive sensory 24.9
responsive 24.12
sore 26.11
sensible 93.20
excitable 105.28
touchy 110.21
confidential 345.14
fastidious 495.9
discriminating 943.7
tolerant 978.11
pliant 1045.9
sensitize 24.7
sensory
n brain 918.6
adj sensorial 24.9
sensual 663.5
sensual sexual 75.24
sensualist 663.5
lascivious 665.29
sensuous sensory 24.9
delightful 97.7
sensual 663.5
sentence
n remark 524.4
phrase 529.1
judgment 598.9
condemnation 602.1
part of writing 792.2
verdict 945.5

maxim 973.1
v condemn 602.3
pass judgment 945.13
sentence of death 307.1
sentient 24.11
sentiment feeling 93.1
sentimentality 93.8
love 104.1
idea 931.1
opinion 952.6
attitude 977.1
sentimental
maudlin 93.21
loving 104.27
foolish 922.8
sentry warner 399.4
watchman 1007.10
separable
different 779.7
severable 801.26
discriminable 943.9
separate
v refine 79.22
diverge 171.5
bound 211.8
partition 213.8
interspace 224.3
open 292.11
quarantine 429.13
fall out 456.10
sow dissension 456.14
divorce 566.5
disband 770.8
segregate 772.6
differentiate 779.6
apportion 792.6
analyze 800.6
divide 801.8
part company 801.19
classify 807.11
discriminate 943.4
adj secluded 584.8
different 779.7
distinct 801.20
alone 871.8
separate oneself
keep one's distance
    261.7
dissent 333.4
separate returns 630.9
**separate the wheat
    from the chaff**
select 371.14
discriminate 943.4
separatist
n dissenter 333.3
apostate 363.5
adj repudiative 363.12
separator
extractor 192.9
sieve 801.7
sepia 40.3
seppuku 308.5
septet
cooperation 450.1
part music 708.18
poetry 720.9
seven 881.5
septic unhealthful 82.5
diseased 85.59
putrefactive 393.39
septicemia 85.31

septic tank 80.12
septuagenarian
old man 304.2
seventy 881.7
septum 213.5
sepulcher 309.16
sequel following 166.1
continuation 816
consequence 816.1
follow-up 834.2
effect 886.1
sequence
following 166.1
consistency 802.2
continuity 806.2
series 811.2
progression 814
subsequence 834.1
effect 886.1
thoughts 930.4
sequester
reserve 386.12
attach 480.20
separate 801.8
sequester oneself
seclude oneself 584.7
stand alone 871.6
find refuge 1008.8
sequitur 816.1
seraglio 563.10
seraph 679.1
sere worn 393.31
wasted 393.35
unproductive 890.4
dried 1064.9
serenade
n courtship 562.7
v court 562.21
sing 708.38
serendipity
discovery 940.1
chance 971.1
serene calm 464.9
pacific 464.9
equable 670.13
light 1024.31
serf sycophant 138.3
subject 432.7
retainer 577.1
sergeant
Army
    noncommissioned
    officer 575.19
Navy officer 575.20
policeman 1007.15
sergeant-at-arms
ship's officer 183.7
policeman 1007.15
serial
n part 554.13
periodical 555.1
radiobroadcast
    1033.18
television broadcast
    1034.2
adj journalistic 555.5
consistent 802.11
consecutive 811.9
periodic 849.7
serial killer 308.10
serial number 517.11
series following 166.1

edition 554.5
hockey 749.1
set 769.12
classifications 808.5
succession 811.2
sequence 814.1
round 849.3
mathematical
    progression 1016.8
serif 548.6
serious zealous 101.9
sedate 106.14
solemn 111.3
great 247.6
resolute 359.11
lofty 544.14
cognitive 930.21
weighty 996.20
dangerous 1005.9
sermon
reproof 510.5
lecture 543.3
lesson 568.7
sermonize
lecture 543.11
expound 568.16
serpent snake 311.26
traitor 357.10
beast 660.7
serpentine
n variegation 47.6
v convolve 281.4
adj deviative 164.7
flowing 238.24
curved 279.7
convolutional 281.6
coiled 281.7
reptile 311.46
cunning 415.12
serrate
v notch 289.4
adj angular 278.6
rugged 288.7
notched 289.5
serum humor 2.22
blood 2.23
antitoxin 86.27
transfusion 91.18
servant
hanger-on 138.6
instrument 384.4
underling 432.5
subject 432.7
employee 577
servitor 577.2
assistant 616.6
believer 692.4
worker 726.2
serve
n game 748.2
v copulate 75.21
be inferior 250.4
act 328.4
be instrumental 384.7
avail 387.17
summon 420.11
lend oneself 449.18
do duty 458.18
give 478.12
work for 577.13
officiate 724.13
play tennis 748.3

shuffle 758.4
suit 787.8
tend 895.3
throw 903.10
suffice 990.4
expedite one's affair
994.3
do good 998.10
serve an
apprenticeship
570.11
serve-and-volley 748.2
serve as 349.10
serve notice 551.8
serve one right
requite 506.5
punish 604.10
get one's deserts 639.6
be just 649.6
serve out 477.8
serve time
be imprisoned 429.18
take one's turn 824.5
service
n serving 8.10
food service 8.11
act of kindness 143.7
rigging 180.12
obedience 326.1
instrumentality 384.3
benefit 387.4
subservience 432.2
aid 449.1
military service 458.9
military branch
461.21
servanthood 577.12
ceremony 580.4
divine service 696.8
rite 701.3
task 724.2
game 748.2
throw 903.3
v copulate 75.21
repair 396.14
serviceable
modal 384.8
useful 387.18
helpful 449.21
serviceable life 826.1
service academy 567.6
serviceman
mender 396.10
military man 461.6
service medal 646.6
servile slavish 138.13
inferior 250.6
subject 432.13
downtrodden 432.16
submissive 433.12
deferential 433.16
serving 577.14
serving
n service 8.10
rigging 180.12
adj acting 328.10
helping 449.20
servitorial 577.14
servitude
subjection 432.1
service 577.12
sesquicentennial 849.4

sesquipedality 545.3
session
ecclesiastical council
423.4
conference 541.6
assembly 769.2
moment 823.2
set
n navigation 159.3
direction 161.1
course 172.2
flow 238.4
form 262.1
sprout 302.11
edition 554.5
clique 617.6
setting 704.19
motion-picture studio
706.3
game 745.3
bridge 758.3
company 769.3
collection 769.12
group 783.5
all 791.3
cohesion 802.1
class 808.2
trend 895.2
disposition 977.3
radio 1033.3
v be pregnant 78.12
place 159.12
establish 159.16
direct 161.5
take direction 161.7
sit 173.10
sink 194.6
flow 238.16
form 262.7
sharpen 285.7
heal 396.21
prime 405.9
prescribe 420.9
allot 477.9
typeset 548.16
impose 643.4
put to music 708.46
make agree 787.7
fasten 799.7
cohere 802.6
fix 854.9
specify 864.11
tend 895.3
thicken 1043.10
solidify 1044.8
plant 1067.18
adj trite 117.9
located 159.18
circumscribed 210.6
sharp 285.8
firm 359.12
obstinate 361.8
customary 373.14
confirmed 373.19
planned 381.12
prepared 405.16
fast 799.14
cohesive 802.10
established 854.13
fixed 854.14
assured 969.20
hardened 1044.13

set about
undertake 404.3
begin 817.7
set above 371.17
set a course 817.8
set afire 375.18
set afloat cause 885.10
start 903.13
set against
v offset 338.5
sow dissension 456.14
antagonize 589.7
compare 942.4
adj oppositional 451.8
hostile 589.10
set against one another
215.4
set a limit 943.4
set an example 785.7
set apart
v partition 213.8
interspace 224.3
excise 255.10
reserve 386.12
allot 477.9
dedicate 477.11
sanctify 685.5
segregate 772.6
differentiate 779.6
separate 801.8
characterize 864.10
discriminate 943.4
adj sanctified 685.8
segregated 772.8
set a precedent 833.3
set a price 630.11
set aside
remove 176.11
excise 255.10
reserve 386.12
put away 390.6
repeal 445.2
segregate 772.6
separate 801.8
postpone 845.9
allow for 958.5
dismiss 983.4
set astir excite 105.12
rouse 375.19
set at undertake 404.3
set to work 725.15
set at each other's
throat 589.7
set at ease
content 107.4
lighten 120.7
comfort 121.6
set at intervals 224.3
set at large 431.4
set at odds
sow dissension 456.14
antagonize 589.7
set a trap for
ambush 346.10
trap 356.20
set at rest
v prove 956.10
make sure 969.11
adj accomplished
407.10
ended 819.8
set at variance 456.14

set a value on 945.9
setback
disappointment 132.1
regression 163.1
slowing 175.4
relapse 394.1
discomfiture 412.2
bridge 758.3
reverse 1010.3
hindrance 1011.1
set back
v daunt 127.18
slow 175.9
indent 284.14
impair 393.9
restrain 428.7
hinder 1011.10
adj retarded 175.12
set before
confront 216.8
prefer 371.17
put to choice 371.21
propose 439.5
set conditions
stipulate 421.7
qualify 958.3
set designer 704.23
set down
v abase 137.5
deposit 159.14
affirm 334.5
reprove 510.17
record 549.15
maintain 952.11
adj humbled 137.13
set down for hearing
598.12
set down to 887.4
set eyes on 27.12
set fire to excite 105.12
ignite 1019.22
set foot in go to 177.25
enter 189.7
attend 221.8
set foot on dry land
186.8
set for
prepared for 405.18
in preparation for
405.24
set forth set out 188.8
manifest 348.5
describe 349.9
propose 439.5
say 524.23
make a beginning
817.8
focus on 936.3
postulate 950.12
evidence 956.8
set free rescue 398.3
liberate 431.4
acquit 601.4
set in
insert 191.3
indent 284.14
blow 318.20
begin 817.7
fix 854.9
set in concrete
v prescribe 420.9
adj mandatory 420.12

set in motion
  move 172.6
  motivate 375.12
  execute 437.9
  impel 901.11
  start 903.13
set in one's ways
  obstinate 361.8
  confirmed 373.19
set in opposition 942.4
set in order 807.8
set in print 548.16
set limits
  differentiate 779.6
  qualify 958.3
set mind 361.1
set of conditions 765.2
set off border 211.10
  measure off 300.11
  offset 338.5
  kindle 375.18
  allot 477.9
  ornament 498.8
  explode 671.14
  go contrary to 778.4
  differentiate 779.6
  cause 885.10
  discriminate 943.4
  beautify 1015.15
set off against 942.4
set on
  v base on 199.6
  incite 375.17
  sow dissension 456.14
  attack 459.14
  adj desirous of 100.22
  determined upon
    359.16
set one's cap for
  desire 100.14
  court 562.21
set one's course for
  161.9
set one's heart on
  100.17
set one's house in order
  prepare for 405.11
  atone 658.4
set one's jaw 359.8
set one's mind at ease
  be composed 106.6
  content 107.4
  lighten 120.7
set one's sights on
  380.4
set one's teeth on edge
  grate on 58.11
  sour 67.4
  irritate 96.14
  get on one's nerves
    128.9
set one back 630.13
**set one back on his
  heels** 856.11
set on edge
  irritate 96.14
  ruffle 288.5
set oneself against
  refuse 442.3
  oppose 451.3
  disapprove 510.10
set on fire excite 105.12

  kindle 375.18
  ignite 1019.22
**set on the straight and
  narrow** 857.12
set out
  go forth 188.8
  plot 381.10
  ornament 498.8
  phrase 532.4
  dispose 807.9
  begin 817.7
  make a beginning
    817.8
set out for 161.9
set phrase 529.1
set point
  tennis score 748.2
  values 1040.10
set purpose 380.1
set right direct to 161.6
  compensate 338.4
  remedy 396.13
  teach 568.10
  atone 658.4
  make agree 787.7
  disillusion 976.2
set sail
  hoist sail 182.20
  set out 188.8
  begin 817.7
set side by side 223.13
set straight
  direct to 161.6
  straighten 277.5
  make better 392.9
  remedy 396.13
  arrange 437.8
  reprove 510.17
  re-form 857.12
set the ball rolling
  817.7
set the date 831.13
set the limit 210.4
set the mind to 982.5
set the pace lead 165.2
  set an example 785.7
  characterize 864.10
set the record straight
  420.10
set the stage 704.28
set the tone
  be fashionable 578.9
  characterize 864.10
setting
  n background 209.2
  nearness 223.1
  arena 463.1
  motif 498.7
  composition 548.2
  stage setting 704.19
  musical piece 708.5
  harmonization 709.2
  plot 722.4
  circumstances 765.2
  frame 900.10
  thickening 1043.4
  hardening 1044.5
  planting 1067.14
  adj descending 194.11
setting sun 315.2
settle
  settle down 159.17

  dive 184.41
  arrive 186.6
  sink 194.6
  get down 194.7
  people 225.9
  gravitate 297.15
  kill 308.13
  resolve 359.7
  do for 395.11
  defeat 412.9
  arrange 437.8
  pacify 465.7
  reconcile 465.8
  negotiate 466.7
  compromise 468.2
  punish 604.11
  pay in full 624.13
  transfer 629.3
  organize 807.10
  fix 854.9
  interchange 862.4
  conform 866.3
  decide 945.11
  prove 956.10
  refute 957.5
  make sure 969.11
settle accounts
  get even with 506.7
  punish 604.10
  pay in full 624.13
settle down
  settle 159.17
  land 184.43
  sink 194.6
  mature 303.9
  be moderate 670.5
settle for
  be content 107.5
  interchange 862.4
settle in arrive 186.6
  people 225.9
settlement
  establishment 159.7
  peopling 225.2
  country 232.1
  compact 437.1
  adjustment 465.4
  compromise 468.1
  estate 471.4
  endowment 478.9
  community 617.2
  payment 624.1
  transfer 629.1
  proof 956.3
settle one's differences
  465.10
settler incomer 189.4
  habitant 227.9
  giver 478.11
  newcomer 773.4
  finishing stroke 819.4
  conclusive argument
    957.3
settle the score
  get even with 506.7
  punish 604.11
settlings 256.2
set to undertake 404.3
  quarrel 456.11
  set to work 725.15
  fasten 799.7
  begin 817.7

  set-to 456.6
set to one side 176.11
set to rights
  remedy 396.13
  repair 396.14
  arrange 807.8
set toward 895.3
set to work 725.15
setup structure 266.1
  plan 381.1
  composition 795.1
  order 806.1
  prearrangement 964.2
  easy 1013.4
set up refresh 9.2
  provoke 152.24
  establish 159.16
  erect 200.9
  plan 381.8
  remedy 396.13
  aid 449.11
  trump up a charge
    599.12
  treat 624.19
  glorify 662.13
  finance 729.15
  order 806.4
  inaugurate 817.11
  cause 885.10
  produce 891.8
  found 891.10
  elevate 911.5
  prearrange 964.5
set up barriers 429.13
set up for 354.21
set up in business
  settle 159.17
  work 724.12
  finance 729.15
set upon 459.14
set up shop
  settle 159.17
  practice 328.8
  work 724.12
  set to work 725.15
  make a beginning
    817.8
seven
  playing card 758.2
  heptad 881.3
seven-card stud 759.10
sevenfold 881.19
the seven seas 240.1
Seven Sisters 1070.8
seventh
  n interval 709.20
  adj septimal 881.19
seventh heaven
  happiness 95.2
  summit 198.2
  heaven of heavens
    681.4
seventy 881.7
sever
  differentiate 779.6
  separate 801.11
  discriminate 943.4
several
  n plurality 882.1
  a number 883.2
  adj proportionate
    477.13

different 779.7
diversified 782.4
particular 864.12
plural 882.7
divers 883.7
severance
elimination 772.2
differentiation 779.4
disseverment 801.2
severance pay 624.4
severe
acrimonious 17.14
painful 26.10
pungent 68.6
harsh 144.24
imperious 417.16
strict 425.6
inornate 499.9
gruff 505.7
plain-speaking 535.3
violent 671.16
simple 797.6
exact 972.17
difficult 1012.17
cold 1022.14
severity acrimony 17.5
pungency 68.1
harshness 144.9
strictness 425.1
inornateness 499.4
gruffness 505.3
plain speech 535.1
violence 671.1
simplicity 797.1
accuracy 972.5
cold 1022.1
sew stitch 741.4
hook 799.8
sewage
feces 12.4
offal 80.9
refuse 391.4
sewed up
completed 407.11
prearranged 964.8
assured 969.20
sewer
needleworker 741.2
sewing machine 741.3
sewer
n receptacle of filth
80.12
drain 239.5
cave 284.5
gutter 654.7
adj cursing 513.8
sewing
bookbinding 554.14
needlework 741
sewing machine 741.3
sex
n gender 75.1
copulation 75.7
love 104.1
v sexualize 75.19
adj sexual 75.24
sexagenarian
old man 304.2
sixty 881.7
sex appeal
sexual attraction 75.3
attractiveness 377.2

sex chromosome
chromosome 305.8
heredity 560.6
sex discrimination
misanthropy 590.1
discrimination 979.4
sex drive 75.2
sex fiend 75.16
sex goddess
sex object 75.4
beauty 1015.8
sexism
sexual preference
75.10
misanthropy 590.1
discrimination 979.4
sexist
n misanthrope 590.2
bigot 979.5
adj misanthropic
590.3
discriminatory 979.12
sex kitten 1015.9
sexless 75.28
sex object
hot number 75.4
sweetheart 104.10
sexology 75.18
sex organs 2.11
sex shop 75.7
sex-starved 75.26
sextant
navigation 182.2
instrument 278.4
semicircle 280.8
sextet
cooperation 450.1
part music 708.18
poetry 720.9
six 881.2
sextuple
v sixfold 881.16
adj sixth 881.18
sextuplets 881.2
sexual
sex 75.24
gametic 305.20
lascivious 665.29
amorous 104.26
amatory 562.23
sexual abnormality
75.11
sexual abstinence
celibacy 565.1
abstinence 668.2
sexual abuse 75.11
sexual advance 439.2
sexual assault
sexual possession
480.3
seduction 665.6
sexual climax
copulation 75.7
spasm 916.6
sexual counselor 75.18
sexual customs 75.18
sexual desire
biological urge 75.5
desire 100.1
craving 100.6
will 323.1
heat metaphor 1018.2

sexual deviation 75.11
sexual excitement
105.7
sexual fantasy
masturbation 75.8
defense mechanism
92.23
sexual freedom 75.18
sexual intercourse
copulation 75.7
lovemaking 562.1
sexuality
sexual nature 75.2
lasciviousness 665.5
sexual love 104.1
sexually-transmitted
disease 85.18
sexual magnetism 75.3
sexual maturity 14.1
sexual morality 75.18
sexual mores 75.18
sexual orientation
75.10
sexual pathology
perversion 75.11
personality disorder
92.15
psychosis 925.3
sexual pleasure 95.1
sexual power 76.2
sexual practices 75.18
sexual preference 75.10
sexual relations 75.7
sexual revolution 75.18
sexual stereotyping
590.1
sexual surrogate 75.18
sexual union 75.7
sexy
sexual 75.24
lustful 75.26
delightful 97.7
amorous 97.8
desirable 100.30
alluring 377.8
lascivious 665.29
excellent 998.13
sh! 51.14
shabby
squalid 80.25
inadequate 250.7
worthless 391.11
shoddy 393.32
niggardly 484.8
cheap 633.7
base 661.12
slovenly 809.15
paltry 997.21
terrible 999.9
inferior 1004.9
shack 228.9
shackle
n restraint 428.4
curb 1011.7
v bind 428.10
confine 429.12
hamper 1011.11
shack up 75.21
shade
n color 35.1
degree 245.1
hint 248.4

admixture 796.7
psyche 918.4
phantom 975.4
specter 987.1
protection 1007.1
shadow 1026.3
screen 1027
v color 35.13
blacken 38.7
cloud 319.6
conceal 346.6
portray 712.19
darken 1026.9
screen 1027.5
shade of difference
margin 779.2
distinction 943.3
shades spectacles 29.3
eyeshade 1027.2
shade tree 310.10
shading
n blackening 38.5
gradation 245.3
treatment 712.9
darkening 1026.6
televising 1034.3
television reception
1034.5
adj screening 1027.6
shadow
n omen 133.3
hanger-on 138.6
follower 166.2
degree 245.1
hint 248.4
remainder 256.1
thinness 270.7
slim 270.8
image 349.5
treatment 712.9
spirit 763.3
reflection 784.7
psyche 918.4
phantom 975.4
specter 987.1
protection 1007.1
darkness 1026.3
shade 1027.1
v look 27.13
color 35.13
blacken 38.7
foreshow 133.10
follow 166.3
cloud 319.6
lurk 346.9
image 349.11
make unintelligible
522.12
trace 937.34
darken 1026.9
shade 1027.5
shadow-box 754.4
shadowing
n following 166.1
ambush 346.3
pursuit 382.1
surveillance 937.9
darkening 1026.6
adj shading 1027.6
shadow of death 307.1
shadow of doubt 954.2
shady dishonest 645.16

disreputable 661.10
shadowy 1026.16
shaded 1027.7
shady character 415.6
the shady side 303.5
shaft
  n feather part 3.17
  air passage 239.13
  tower 272.6
  pole 273.1
  hole 275.2
  pit 284.4
  arrow 462.6
  monument 549.12
  base 900.8
  mine 1056.6
  v mistreat 389.6
shag
  n hair 3.2
  head of hair 3.4
  tobacco 89.2
  texture 294.1
  v fetch 176.16
shaggy
  hairy 3.24
  rough 288.6
  nappy 294.7
  disheveled 809.14
shah 575.9
shake
  n beverage 10.47
  speech defect 525.1
  trill 709.19
  instant 829.3
  quake 916.3
  flutter 916.4
  search 937.15
  wood 1052.3
  v be weak 16.8
  weaken 16.10
  disturb 105.14
  be excited 105.18
  tremble 127.14
  frighten 127.15
  daunt 127.18
  unnerve 128.10
  startle 131.8
  face 295.23
  age 303.10
  evade 368.7
  break the habit 374.3
  sign 437.7
  speak poorly 525.7
  greet 585.10
  dance 705.5
  sing 708.38
  thrust 901.12
  oscillate 915.10
  wave 915.11
  alternate 915.14
  agitate 916.10
  quake 916.11
  ransack 937.32
  freeze 1022.9
shake a leg
  v be active 330.14
  inter make haste
    401.17
shakedown
  extortion 480.8
  search 937.15
  tryout 941.3

shakedown artist
  480.12
shakedown cruise
  voyage 182.6
  tryout 941.3
shake hands near 223.7
  sign 437.7
  make up 465.10
  greet 585.10
  strike a bargain
    731.18
shaken
  disturbed 105.23
  unnerved 128.14
  startled 131.13
  agitated 916.16
  confused 984.12
shake off evade 368.7
  free oneself from
    431.8
  do away with 908.21
shake one's fist at
  defy 454.3
  threaten 514.2
shake on it
  come to an agreement
    332.10
  strike a bargain
    731.18
shakeout
  elimination 772.2
  classification 800.3
  grouping 807.3
  distinction 943.3
shaker
  gambling wheel
    759.16
  agitator 916.9
Shaker
  n abstainer 668.4
  adj abstinent 668.10
the shakes
  shaking 916.2
  delirium tremens
    925.10
shake up
  weaken 16.10
  wake someone up 23.5
  disturb 105.14
  censure 510.13
  rearrange 807.13
  agitate 916.10
  soften 1045.6
shake-up
  rearrangement 807.7
  expedient 994.2
shaky unsteady 16.16
  fearful 127.23
  jittery 128.12
  stricken in years
    303.18
  unaccustomed 374.4
  inarticulate 525.12
  fragile 763.7
  loose 803.5
  shaking 916.17
  unreliable 970.20
  unsafe 1005.11
  feeling cold 1022.16
shaky ground 1005.2
shallow
  n shoal 276.2

v become less deep
  276.3
adj insignificant 248.6
  depthless 276.5
  superficial 921.20
  half-learned 929.15
  trivial 997.19
shallowness
  exteriority 206.1
  depthlessness 276.1
  superficiality 921.7
  slight knowledge
    929.6
  inattention 983.1
  triviality 997.3
shallows
  shoal 276.2
  hidden danger 1005.5
shalom!
  farewell! 188.22
  peace! 464.11
sham
  n fakery 354.3
  fake 354.13
  hoax 356.7
  impostor 357.6
  pretext 376.1
  affectation 500.1
  display 501.4
  v fake 354.20
  affect 500.12
  adj imitation 336.8
  spurious 354.25
  assumed 500.16
shaman
  n witch doctor 690.7
  adj sorcerous 690.14
shamble
  n slow motion 175.2
  gait 177.12
  v plod 175.7
  way of walking 177.28
shambles
  butchery 308.3
  place of killing 308.11
  destruction 395.1
  battlefield 463.2
shame
  n chagrin 96.4
  regret 113.1
  humiliation 137.2
  abomination 638.2
  iniquity 654.3
  disgrace 661.5
  decency 664.2
  v humiliate 137.4
  disgrace 661.8
  inter God forbid!
    510.27
shamed
  humiliated 137.14
  in disrepute 661.13
shamefaced
  regretful 113.8
  humiliated 137.14
  shy 139.12
shameful
  regretful 113.8
  wrong 638.3
  wicked 654.16
  disgraceful 661.11
  terrible 999.9

shameless
  unregretful 114.4
  brazen 142.11
  gaudy 501.20
  wrong 638.3
  dishonest 645.16
  hardened 654.17
  immodest 666.6
shampoo
  n washing 79.5
  cleanser 79.17
  v wash 79.19
shamrock
  insignia 647.1
  three 875.1
shamus 1007.16
shanghai coerce 424.7
  seize 480.14
  abduct 482.20
Shangri-la 985.11
shank member 2.7
  leg 177.14
  shaft 273.6
  type 548.6
shanty 228.9
shanty-town 230.6
shape
  n aspect 33.3
  appearance 33.5
  fitness 84.1
  form 262.1
  human form 262.4
  structure 266.1
  good condition 764.3
  mode 764.4
  kind 808.3
  characteristic 864.4
  illusion 975.4
  specter 987.1
  v form 262.7
  be formed 262.8
  plan 381.8
  pot 742.6
  compose 795.3
  conform 866.3
  produce 891.8
  imagine 985.14
shape a course
  pilot 182.14
  chart a course 182.27
  plan 381.8
shaped
  formative 262.9
  structural 266.6
  planned 381.12
  made 891.18
shapeless
  formless 263.4
  obscure 522.15
  unordered 809.12
  inconstant 853.7
  abnormal 869.9
  vague 970.19
  unshapely 1014.8
shapely
  well-shaped 264.5
  comely 1015.18
the shape of things
  764.2
shape up
  v be formed 262.8
  improve 392.7

be in a certain state
  764.5
compose 795.3
form 806.5
phrs don't rock the
  boat 866.10
shard
  n refuse 391.4
  piece 792.3
  v break 1048.3
  pulverize 1049.9
share
  n amount 244.2
  portion 477.5
  stockholding 738.3
  part 792.1
  v respond 93.11
  communicate 343.7
  share in 476.6
  apportion 477.6
  separate 792.6
share and share alike
  v share 476.6
  apportion 477.6
  bisect 874.4
  adj communal 476.9
  proportionately
    477.14
sharebroker 737.10
share certificate 622.3
sharecrop 1067.16
sharecropper 1067.5
shared 776.11
shareholder
  participator 476.4
  stockholder 737.14
share in 476.6
share one's sorrow
  147.2
share out
  apportion 477.6
  separate 792.6
shares 738.2
sharing
  n sympathy 93.5
  informing 343.2
  accord 455.1
  participation 476.1
  apportionment 477.1
  association 582.6
  adj participating
    476.8
  mutual 776.11
shark
  marine animal 311.30
  cheater 357.4
  expert 413.11
  extortionist 480.12
  savage 593.5
  gambler 759.21
sharp
  n cheat 357.3
  expert 413.11
  note 709.14
  gambler 759.21
  adj acrimonious 17.14
  sensitive 24.13
  painful 26.10
  shrill 58.14
  dissonant 61.4
  bitter 64.6
  pungent 68.6

strong 69.10
deep-felt 93.24
distressing 98.20
penetrating 105.31
caustic 144.23
steep 204.18
angular 278.6
keen 285.8
quick 330.18
alert 339.14
deceitful 356.22
cunning 415.12
witty 489.15
gruff 505.7
chic 578.13
violent 671.16
smart 919.14
cold 1022.14
adv suddenly 829.9
punctually 844.14
sharpen
  sensitize 24.7
  stimulate 105.13
  aggravate 119.2
  intensify 251.5
  edge 285.7
  tool 1039.9
sharpener 1039.2
sharpen the wits
  568.10
sharper cheat 357.3
  gambler 759.21
sharp eye
  keen eye 27.10
  vigilance 339.4
sharp pain 26.2
sharps and flats 709.15
sharpshooter
  infantryman 461.9
  shooter 903.8
sharp-witted 919.14
sharp words 456.5
sharpy
  expert 413.11
  person of fashion
    578.7
shatter
  demolish 395.17
  splinter 801.13
  madden 925.24
  break 1048.3
  pulverize 1049.9
shattered nerves 128.4
shatterproof
  resistant 15.20
  unbreakable 1047.5
shave
  contact 223.10
  excise 255.10
  shorten 268.6
  smooth 287.5
  deceive 356.19
  cheapen 633.6
  discount 728.27
shaven 6.17
shaver 302.3
shaving
  hairlessness 6.4
  remainder 256.1
  thinness 270.7
  flake 296.3
  refuse 391.4

piece 792.3
she female 77.4
  self 864.5
sheaf 769.8
shear divest 6.5
  excise 255.10
  shorten 268.6
  strip 480.24
sheath 295.17
sheathe clothe 5.38
  wrap 295.20
  face 295.23
shed
  n hangar 184.24
  hut 228.9
  v cast 6.10
  waste 473.5
shed blood bleed 12.17
  spill blood 308.14
  war 458.14
shed crocodile tears
  354.22
she-devil bitch 110.12
  witch 593.7
  demon 680.6
shed light upon
  explain 341.10
  illuminate 1024.28
shed tears 115.12
sheen 1024.2
sheep whiteness 37.2
  animal 311.7
  imitator 336.4
  the laity 700.1
  conformist 866.2
sheepdip dip 79.9
  liquor 88.14
  poison 1000.3
sheep dog dog 311.17
  watchdog 1007.11
sheep farm 1068.5
sheepherder 1068.3
sheepish penitent 113.9
  blushing 139.13
  ungulate 311.44
sheepskin 549.6
sheer
  n deviation 164.1
  bias 204.3
  v deviate 164.3
  change course 182.30
  oblique 204.9
  adj perpendicular
    200.12
  steep 204.18
  mere 248.8
  thorough 793.10
  unmixed 797.7
  transparent 1028.4
  adv perpendicularly
    200.14
  absolutely 793.15
sheer drop 200.3
sheer off
  avoid 164.6
  dodge 368.8
  pull back 902.7
sheet whiteness 37.2
  blanket 295.10
  lamina 296.2
  newspaper 555.2
  part of writing 792.2

paper 1052.5
sheet ice 1022.5
sheet lightning 1024.17
sheet metal 1056.5
sheet music 708.28
sheet of fire 1018.13
sheet of rain 316.1
sheik 104.13
sheikh ruler 575.9
  prince 608.7
  clergy 699.11
sheikhdom 417.7
shekels 728.2
shelf shoal 276.2
  layer 296.1
  storehouse 386.6
  ledge 900.14
shelf ice 1022.5
shelf life 826.1
shell
  n ear 2.10
  exterior 206.2
  frame 266.4
  cavity 284.2
  crust 295.14
  seashell 295.15
  hull 295.16
  armor 460.3
  cartridge 462.17
  shot 462.19
  stage 704.16
  electron 1032.3
  atom 1037.4
  v husk 6.9
  pull the trigger 459.22
shellac
  n liquor 88.14
  v color 35.13
  defeat 412.9
shellacked drunk 88.33
  sleek 287.10
  defeated 412.15
shellacking
  painting 35.12
  victory 411.1
  utter defeat 412.3
shellfish 10.24
shell game 356.10
shell out give 478.12
  pay out 624.14
  spend 626.5
shelter
  n quarters 228.4
  cover 295.2
  protection 1007.1
  refuge 1008.3
  v house 225.10
  protect 1007.18
sheltered
  quiescent 173.12
  protected 1007.21
shelve incline 204.10
  put away 390.6
  postpone 845.9
shenanigans
  buffoonery 489.5
  prank 489.10
shepherd
  n guide 574.7
  clergyman 699.2
  escort 768.5
  guardian 1007.6

herder 1068.3
v guide 573.9
escort 768.8
care for 1007.19
drive 1068.8
sherbet 10.45
sheriff 1007.15
Sherlock Holmes
576.10
Shetland pony 311.10
she-wolf bitch 110.12
witch 593.7
violent person 671.9
shibboleth
password 517.12
catchword 526.9
shield
n cover 295.2
shell 295.15
heraldry 647.2
safeguard 1007.3
v cover 295.19
defend 460.8
protect 1007.18
shield-bearer 176.7
shielded
covered 295.31
protected 1007.21
shift
n shirt 5.15
dislocation 160.1
deviation 164.1
moving 176.4
trick 356.6
stratagem 415.3
work shift 824.3
change 851.1
conversion 857.1
expedient 994.2
v deviate 164.3
move 172.5
remove 176.11
change course 182.30
vacillate 362.8
dodge 368.8
live by one's wits
415.9
be dishonest 645.11
be changed 851.6
change 853.5
convert 857.11
quibble 935.9
shift about 645.11
shifting
n deviation 164.1
changing 853.3
quibbling 935.5
adj deviative 164.7
wandering 177.37
inconstant 853.7
unreliable 970.20
shifting sands 853.4
shiftless
indolent 331.19
improvident 406.15
shift the blame
impose on 643.7
be unfaithful 645.12
shifty
covert 345.12
secretive 345.15
deceitful 356.22

evasive 368.15
cunning 415.12
dishonest 645.16
treacherous 645.21
inconstant 853.7
unreliable 970.20
Shiite
n Muslim 675.23
adj Muslim 675.31
shill
n decoy 357.5
by-bidder 733.6
v bid 733.9
shillelagh 273.2
shilling 728.8
shimmer
n glitter 1024.7
v glitter 1024.24
shimmy 705.5
shin
n part the body 2.7
leg 177.14
v climb 193.11
shindig party 582.12
dance 705.2
assembly 769.2
shine
n bootleg liquor 88.18
love 104.1
polish 287.2
glow 1024.2
daylight 1024.10
v polish 287.7
perfect 392.11
cut a dash 501.13
be eloquent 544.7
be somebody 662.10
look good 1015.16
give light 1024.23
buff 1042.8
shiner 85.37
shine through 31.4
shingle
n grain 1049.6
wood 1052.3
gravel 1057.3
v cut the hair 3.22
cover 295.23
overlap 295.30
shin guard
soccer equipment
752.1
safeguard 1007.3
shining
n abrasion 1042.2
adj illustrious
662.19
gorgeous 1015.20
luminous 1024.30
shiny 1024.33
shining example
paragon 659.4
ideal 785.4
shiny clean 79.25
sleek 287.10
luminous 1024.30
shining 1024.33
ship
n boat 180
aircraft 181.1
part of fleet 180.10
dirigible 181.11

v haul 176.13
send 176.15
ship's log 549.11
shipmaster 183.7
shipmate 588.3
shipment
transportation 176.3
freight 176.6
ship of war 180.6
shipshape trim 180.20
tidy 806.8
shipwreck
n debacle 395.4
misfortune 1010.2
v wreck 182.42
destroy 395.10
shipyard plant 739.3
harbor 1008.6
shirk
n shirker 368.3
v idle 331.12
leave undone 340.7
slack 368.9
shirt
n clothing 5.15
soccer 752.1
v cloak 5.39
shit
n defecation 12.2
feces 12.4
bullshit 520.3
bad person 660.6
nothing 761.3
v defecate 12.13
shitcan 391.7
shitfaced 88.33
shithead 660.6
shithouse 12.10
shit in one's pants
127.11
shit-kicker 606.6
shitkickers 5.27
shit list 870.1
shitload 883.3
shit or get off the pot
328.5
shitty
excremental 12.20
filthy 80.23
bad 999.8
shiv 1039.2
shiver
n thrill 105.2
trepidation 105.5
scrap 248.3
piece 792.3
shake 916.3
v be excited 105.18
tremble 127.14
shatter 801.13
shake 916.11
freeze 1022.9
shiver my timbers!
122.19
shoal
n shallow 276.2
group of animals
769.5
multitude 883.3
v become shallow
276.3
adj shallow 276.5

shock
n head of hair 3.4
stupor 22.6
symptom 85.9
trauma 85.26
pain 96.5
start 131.3
concussion 671.8
bunch 769.7
impact 901.3
shake 916.3
misfortune 1010.2
electric discharge
1031.6
v offend 98.11
agitate 105.14
terrify 127.17
startle 131.8
shake 916.11
electrify 1031.25
shock absorber 670.3
shocking horrid 98.19
frightening 127.30
surprising 131.11
downright 247.12
disgraceful 661.11
sudden 829.5
terrible 999.9
shock-resistant 1047.4
shock tactics 459.1
shock troops 461.15
shock wave
air speed 184.31
wave 915.4
shod 5.44
shoddy
n fake 354.13
rubbish 391.5
adj spurious 354.25
worthless 391.11
shabby 393.32
cheap 633.7
base 661.12
slovenly 809.15
paltry 997.21
terrible 999.9
shoe
n footwear 5.27
bowling 750.1
automobile racing
756.1
v cloak 5.39
the shoe is on the other
foot
what goes around
comes around 506.10
permanence 851.14
shoemaker 5.37
shogun 575.9
shoo
v do away with 908.21
inter go away! 908.31
begone 908.32
shoo-in
sure success 409.2
victor 411.2
horse race 757.3
sure thing 969.2
shook
startled 131.13
confused 984.12
shook up 128.12

shoot
 n pang 26.2
 journey 177.5
 rapids 238.10
 gutter 239.3
 sprout 302.11
 branch 310.18
 offshoot 561.4
 warp 740.3
 deposit 1056.7
 rocket launching
  1072.9
 v suffer 26.8
 inject 87.21
 immunize 91.28
 speed 174.8
 row 182.53
 float 182.54
 strike dead 308.17
 vegetate 310.31
 hunt 382.9
 pull the trigger 459.22
 execute 604.17
 explode 671.14
 film 706.7
 photograph 714.14
 play basketball 747.4
 play hockey 749.7
 play golf 751.4
 fire off 903.12
 shine 1024.23
 launch 1072.13
shoot ahead
 spurt 174.12
 outdistance 249.10
 hustle 330.13
shoot back 938.4
shoot craps 759.23
shoot down
 strike dead 308.17
 do for 395.11
 end 819.5
 shoot 903.12
shooter 903.8
shoot from the hip
 be impatient 135.4
 act on the spur of the
  moment 365.7
 prejudge 946.2
shoot full of holes
 957.4
shooting
 n pang 26.2
 killing 308.1
 hunting 382.2
 gunfire 459.8
 capital punishment
  604.7
 hockey game 749.3
 throwing 903.2
 adj painful 26.10
shooting gallery 87.19
shooting script
 playbook 704.21
 script 706.2
shooting star
 omen 133.6
 meteor 1070.15
shoot it out with
 457.17
shoot off one's mouth
 bluster 503.3

 talk nonsense 520.5
 speak 524.21
 chatter 540.5
shootout 752.3
shoot out 283.10
shoot straight with
 649.6
shoot the breeze
 speak 524.21
 converse 541.9
shoot the works
 be determined 359.8
 persevere 360.7
 do one's best 403.14
 do to perfection 407.7
 court danger 493.6
 risk 971.12
shoot up
 grow 14.2
 inject 87.21
 spring up 193.9
 increase 251.6
 expand 259.7
 grow higher 272.12
 protrude 283.10
 vegetate 310.31
shop
 n occupation 724.4
 market 736.1
 workplace 739.1
 office 739.7
 casino 759.19
 v inform on 551.13
 market 733.8
shop around
 choose 371.13
 shop 733.8
 be discriminating
  943.5
shop at 731.16
shopkeeper 730.2
shoplift 482.13
shoplifter 483.1
shopper 733.5
shopping-bag lady
 homeless person
  331.10
 poor person 619.4
shopping center
 metropolis 208.7
 city district 230.6
 marketplace 736.2
shopping list 870.1
shopping mall 739.1
shopping spree 733.1
shop steward 727.4
shoptalk 523.10
shopworn 393.31
shore
 n border 211.4
 side 218.1
 coast 234.2
 v buttress 449.12
 support 900.21
 adj aquatic 182.58
 coastal 234.7
shore bird 311.28
shore leave 20.3
shoreline
 n shore 234.2
 adj coastal 234.7
shore patrol 1007.17

shore up
 strengthen 15.13
 buttress 449.12
 support 900.21
 stiffen 1044.9
shorn 252.10
shorn of 473.8
short
 n car 179.10
 motion pictures 706.1
 bear account 737.12
 v electrify 1031.25
 adj insignificant 248.6
 little 258.10
 brief 268.8
 low 274.7
 taciturn 344.9
 gruff 505.7
 concise 537.6
 poor 619.7
 incomplete 794.4
 fleeting 827.8
 falling short of 910.5
 wanting 991.13
 imperfect 1002.4
 adv abruptly 268.13
shortage
 deficiency 794.2
 shortcoming 910.1
 want 991.4
 imperfection 1002.1
shortchange 356.18
short-circuit 1031.25
shortcoming
 inequality 790.1
 falling short 910.1
 want 991.4
 imperfection 1002.1
 fault 1002.2
shortcut cut 268.5
 straight line 277.2
 route 383.1
shorten
 n make small 258.9
 v reduce 252.7
 subtract 255.9
 contract 260.7
 abbreviate 268.6
 be brief 537.5
 abridge 557.5
shorten sail
 reduce sail 182.50
 take precautions
  494.6
shorter 252.10
shortfall
 deficiency 794.2
 shortcoming 910.1
 want 991.4
short fuse
 irascibility 110.2
 hot temper 110.4
shorthand
 n phonetic symbol
  546.2
 stenography 547.8
 adj written 547.22
 stenographic 547.27
shorthanded 991.12
short list 870.1
short-lived 827.7
short memory 989.1

short odds 759.6
short of breath 21.12
short-order cook 11.2
short range 223.2
short rations 515.2
shorts
 bear account 737.12
 soccer 752.1
short shrift
 pitilessness 146.1
 repulse 442.2
shortsighted
 poor-sighted 28.11
 undiscerning 921.14
 unwise 922.10
 narrow-minded
  979.10
shortstop 745.2
short story 722.3
short story writer
 author 547.15
 scribe 718.4
short subject 706.1
short supply 991.1
short temper
 irascibility 110.2
 hot temper 110.4
short-term 827.8
short-term memory
 988.1
short time
 shortness 268.1
 little while 827.3
shortwave
 n radio wave 1033.11
 v broadcast 1033.25
 adj radio 1033.28
shorty 258.4
shot
 n detonation 56.3
 dose 86.6
 fix 87.19
 drink 88.7
 inoculation 91.16
 disrespect 156.3
 swiftness 174.6
 attempt 403.3
 ball 462.19
 fee 630.6
 cinematography 706.4
 photograph 714.3
 motion picture
  segment 714.8
 baseball game 745.3
 basketball game 747.3
 tennis game 748.2
 hockey game 749.3
 golf stroke 751.3
 soccer game 752.3
 bet 759.3
 throw 759.9
 portion 792.5
 discharge 903.4
 shooter 903.8
 guess 950.4
 rocket launching
  1072.9
 adj variegated 47.9
 unnerved 128.14
 spoiled 393.29
 ruined 395.29
 ended 819.9

shotgun 308.17
shotgun wedding 563.3
shot in the arm 86.8
shot in the dark
  gamble 759.2
  guess 950.4
shot-put 903.3
shot through
  variegated 47.9
  permeated 221.15
  apertured 292.19
should
  ought to 641.3
  be necessary 962.10
shoulder
  n bulge 283.3
  type 548.6
  joint 799.4
  supporter 900.2
  buttress 900.4
  shelf 900.14
  v support 900.21
  thrust 901.12
shoulder patch 647.5
shoulder to shoulder
  adv cooperatively
    450.6
  hand in hand 768.10
  concurrently 898.5
  phrs side by side
    218.12
shout
  n cry 59.1
  cheer 116.2
  laughter 116.4
  v din 53.7
  cry 59.6
  cheer 116.6
  laugh 116.8
  be manifest 348.7
  proclaim 352.13
shout at the top of
  one's voice 59.9
shout down
  drown out 53.8
  run over 909.7
shout hallelujah 116.6
shout out 59.8
shove
  n thrust 901.2
  pushing 903.1
  v set in motion 172.6
  illicit goods 732.7
  thrust 901.12
  push 903.9
shove aside 164.6
shovel
  n cutlery 1039.2
  v ladle 176.17
  excavate 284.15
shove off
  v get under way
    182.19
  sail away from 182.36
  depart 188.7
  leave 222.10
  die 307.20
  inter go away 908.32
shoving match 457.4
show
  n appearance 33.2
  spectacle 33.7

externalization
  206.4
exhibition 348.2
sham 354.3
pretext 376.1
affectation 500.1
display 501.4
indication 517.3
stage show 704.4
theatrical
  performance 704.12
marketplace 736.2
illusoriness 975.2
v show up 31.4
appear 33.8
direct to 161.6
externalize 206.5
explain 341.10
manifest 348.5
disclose 351.4
signify 517.17
teach 568.10
project 714.16
finish third 757.5
evidence 956.8
prove 956.10
show a deficit 623.6
show a lack of respect
  for 156.4
show a percentage
  472.13
show aptitude for
  413.18
show a tendency
  tend 895.3
  be probable 967.4
showboat
  n show-off 501.11
  theater 704.14
  v exercise skill
    413.20
  show off 501.16
show business
  the entertainment
    industry 704
  theater 743.13
showcase
  n display 348.2
  theatrical
    performance 704.12
  counter 736.6
  transparent substance
    1028.2
  v manifest 348.5
show consideration
  670.8
show dog 311.17
showdown poker
  759.10
  contrariety 778.1
shower
  n bath 79.8
  showering apparatus
    79.12
  rain 316.1
  plenty 990.2
  sprinkle 1063.5
  sprinkler 1063.8
  v wash 79.19
  rain 316.9
  give 478.12
  abound 990.5

shower head
  showering apparatus
    79.12
  nozzle 239.9
  sprinkler 1063.8
show girl 707.1
show good faith 644.9
show horse 757.2
show how
  explain 341.10
  teach 568.10
showing
  n appearance 33.1
  externalization 206.4
  display 348.2
  indication 517.3
  adj divested 6.12
  visible 31.6
  manifesting 348.9
  disclosive 351.10
show its colors 351.8
show its face 351.8
show kindness 143.9
showman 704.23
showmanship 704.3
show no mercy 146.2
show off
  manifest 348.5
  grandstand 501.16
show-off 501.11
show of hands 371.6
show one's hand 351.7
show one's true colors
  come out 348.6
  confess 351.7
showpiece model 785.1
  standard of perfection
    1001.4
show pity 670.8
showplace 785.1
show preference 650.8
show promise 133.13
show respect for 155.5
showroom display
  room 197.24
  salesroom 736.5
show signs of
  appear to be 33.10
  augur 133.12
  evidence 956.8
showstopper 409.4
show the door 908.18
show the ropes 568.10
show the way
  direct to 161.6
  lead 165.2
  explain 341.10
  go before 815.3
show through
  show 31.4
  be transparent 1028.3
show up
  show 31.4
  appear 33.8
  arrive 186.6
  attend 221.8
  overshadow 249.8
  disclose 351.4
  turn up 830.6
  be discovered 940.9
  disprove 957.4
  disillusion 976.2

showy
  flaunting 501.19
  grandiloquent 545.8
shrapnel 462.19
shred
  n scrap 248.3
  piece 792.3
  v tear apart 801.14
  pulverize 1049.9
shredded
  severed 801.23
  powdery 1049.11
shredder 1049.7
shrew 110.12
shrewd cunning 415.12
  artful 919.15
  knowing 927.15
shrewish
  peevish 110.22
  ungovernable 361.12
  partisan 456.17
shriek
  n blare 53.5
  screech 58.4
  cry 59.1
  laughter 116.4
  v blare 53.10
  screech 58.8
  cry 59.6
  wail 115.13
  laugh 116.8
  sigh 318.21
  speak 524.26
shrift pardon 148.2
  confession 351.3
shrill
  n screech 58.4
  v squawk 58.8
  adj strident 58.14
  dissonant 61.4
shrimp
  n runt 258.4
  a nobody 997.7
  v fish 382.10
shrine
  n tomb 309.16
  monument 549.12
  holy place 703.4
  v enclose 212.5
shrink
  n psychologist 92.10
  v suffer 26.8
  flinch 127.13
  efface oneself 139.7
  recede 168.2
  retract 168.3
  decrease 252.6
  reduce 252.7
  shrivel 260.9
  demur 325.4
  dodge 368.8
  languish 393.18
  waste 473.5
  draw back 902.7
shrink from 99.5
shrinking violet 139.6
shrink-wrap
  package 212.9
  bind 799.9
shrivel
  shrink 260.9
  age 303.10

compromise 468.2
pull back 902.7
quibble 935.9
side street 383.4
sideswipe
  n impact 901.3
  v contact 223.10
  collide 901.13
side-to-side 218.8
sidetrack
  n digression 538.4
  v avoid 164.6
sidewalk 383.2
sideways
  adj flowing 172.8
  lateral 218.6
  adv crosswise 170.13
  obliquely 204.21
  laterally 218.8
sidewheeler 311.14
side with concur 332.9
  back 449.13
  take sides with 450.4
siding side 218.1
  building material
    1052.2
  wood 1052.3
sidle
  n gait 177.12
  v avoid 164.6
  creep 177.26
  way of walking 177.28
  incline 204.10
  go sideways 218.5
sidle up to 167.3
siege enclosure 212.1
  besiegement 459.5
sierra 237.6
Sierra Club 397.5
siesta 22.3
sieve
  n refinery 79.13
  network 170.3
  porousness 292.8
  separator 801.7
  arranger 807.5
  v refine 79.22
  segregate 772.6
  classify 807.11
  discriminate 943.4
sift refine 79.22
  select 371.14
  discuss 541.12
  segregate 772.6
  analyze 800.8
  classify 807.11
  investigate 937.22
  discriminate 943.4
sigh
  n breathing 2.19
  murmur 52.4
  sighing 52.8
  v murmur 52.10
  moan 52.14
  lament 115.10
  wind sound 318.21
  speak 524.26
sigh of relief 120.4
sight
  n sensation of seeing
    24.5
  vision 27.1

look 27.3
  optical device 29.5
  field of view 31.3
  view 33.6
  spectacle 33.7
  marvel 122.2
  lot 247.4
  opinion 952.6
  outlook 977.2
  eyesore 1014.4
  v see 27.12
sight for sore eyes
  1015.7
sighthole
  observation post 27.8
  optical device 29.5
sighting 940.1
sightly 1015.18
sight-see
  journey 177.21
  see the sights 917.6
sight-seeing tour
  journey 177.5
  sight-seeing 917.4
sight-unseen
  transaction 970.8
sigmoid
  crescent-shaped
    279.11
  convolutional 281.6
sign
  n prognosis 91.13
  omen 133.3
  poster 352.7
  telltale sign 517.1
  signal 517.15
  symbol 518.6
  letter 546.1
  hint 551.4
  musical notation
    709.12
  substitute 861.2
  miracle 869.8
  evidence 956.1
  number 1016.3
  v ratify 332.12
  shake hands 437.7
  secure 438.9
  signal 517.22
  inscribe 546.6
signal
  n sign 517.1
  beacon 517.15
  hint 551.4
  information theory
    551.7
  race 756.3
  radar signal 1035.11
  v make a signal
    182.52
  communicate 343.7
  flash 517.22
  adj remarkable 247.10
  communicational
    347.20
  notable 996.19
signal flag
  signal 517.15
  flag 647.6
signalman 399.4
signal of distress 400.1
sign a petition 440.10

signatory 332.7
signature
  ratification 332.4
  signing 437.3
  sign 517.1
  identification 517.11
  autograph 527.10
  book part 554.12
  bookbinding 554.14
  musical notation
    709.12
  part of writing 792.2
  acknowledgment
    887.2
  station identification
    1033.19
sign away 629.3
signed, sealed, and
  delivered 407.11
signed agreement 437.1
signer 332.7
signet
  ratification 332.4
  print 517.7
  label 517.13
  signature 527.10
  royal insignia 647.3
signet ring 498.6
significant
  n sign 518.6
  adj premonitory
    133.16
  indicative 517.23
  meaningful 518.10
  prominent 662.17
  evidential 956.16
  important 996.17
significant other
  lover 104.12
  friend 588.1
signify augur 133.12
  betoken 517.17
  mean 518.8
  specify 864.11
  evidence 956.8
  matter 996.12
sign in 186.6
sign language
  deaf-and-dumb
    alphabet 49.3
  gesture 517.14
sign off
  telegraph 347.19
  broadcast 1033.25
sign of the cross 696.5
sign of the times 133.3
sign on install 191.4
  telegraph 347.19
  participate 476.5
  employ 615.14
  broadcast 1033.25
sign one's death
  warrant
  condemn to death
    308.19
  condemn 602.3
signor 76.7
signora 77.8
sign out 188.13
sign over 629.3
signpost post 273.4
  pointer 517.4

sign up install 191.4
  employ 615.14
  enlist 615.17
  join 617.14
  take one's turn 824.5
Silas Marner 484.4
silence
  n noiselessness 51
  quiescence 173.1
  taciturnity 344.2
  v disable 19.10
  put to silence 51.8
  strike dead 308.17
  extinguish 395.15
  overcome 412.7
  suppress 428.8
  refute 957.5
  inter hush 51.14
silent
  n motion pictures
    706.1
  adj still 51.10
  taciturn 344.9
  unexpressed 519.9
silent majority
  middle class 607.5
  party 617.4
  mediocrity 1004.5
silent partner 616.2
silent treatment 908.4
silhouette
  n outline 211.2
  contour 262.2
  drawing 712.13
  portrait 712.15
  reflection 784.7
  shadow 1026.3
  v outline 211.9
silicon chip
  electronic circuit
    1032.8
  circuitry 1041.3
silicone 1054.2
silk material 4.1
  smoothness 287.3
  fine texture 294.3
  softness 1045.4
silk-screen printing
  printing 548.1
  stencil printing 713.4
silk-stocking
  n nobleman 608.4
  adj socially prominent
    578.16
silk-stocking district
  609.16
silkworm 271.5
silky threadlike 271.7
  smooth 287.9
  sleek 287.10
  fine-textured 294.8
  velvety 1045.15
silly
  n fool 923.6
  adj nonsensical 520.7
  foolish 922.8
  dazed 984.14
  trivial 997.19
silo granary 386.7
  rocket launcher
    1072.10
silt deposit 176.9

dregs 256.2
silver
n tableware 8.12
whiteness 37.1
alabaster 37.2
money 728.1
precious metals
728.20
v whiten 37.5
gray 39.3
adj white 37.7
gray 39.4
eloquent 544.8
brass 1056.17
Silver 311.15
silver dollar 728.7
silver lining 124.3
silver mine 1056.6
the silver screen 706.1
silver-tongued
eloquent 544.8
melodious 708.48
silverware
tableware 8.12
hard goods 735.4
silver wedding
anniversary 849.4
simian 311.23
similar
approximate 774.8
like 783.10
comparative 942.8
simile similarity 783.1
comparible 942.1
simmer
n boiling 1019.2
v cook 11.4
be angry 152.15
bubble 320.4
seethe 671.12
be hot 1018.22
boil 1019.20
simmer down 106.7
Simon Legree 575.14
simp 923.8
simpatico 587.15
simper
n smile 116.3
v smile 116.7
mince 500.14
simple
soft-colored 35.21
humble 137.10
homelike 228.33
mere 248.8
artless 416.5
tasteful 496.8
ordinary 499.6
elegant 533.6
plain-speaking 535.3
informal 581.3
real 760.15
essential 766.9
plain 797.6
one 871.7
mentally deficient
921.22
ignorant 929.12
gullible 953.9
genuine 972.15
easy 1013.13
simple existence 760.6

simple fact 760.3
simple matter 1013.3
simpleminded
artless 416.5
mentally deficient
921.22
simpleton 923.8
simplicity
prosaicness 117.2
rusticity 233.3
decrease 252.1
artlessness 416.1
restraint 496.4
ordinariness 499.1
clearness 521.2
elegance 533.1
plain speech 535.1
informality 581.1
simpleness 797
purity 797.1
oneness 871.1
mental deficiency
921.9
ignorance 929.1
gullibility 953.2
facility 1013.1
simulate imitate 336.5
fake 354.20
affect 500.12
adopt 621.4
resemble 783.7
simulation
imitation 336.1
sham 354.3
adoption 621.2
similarity 783.1
simultaneous 835.5
sin
n blackness 38.4
iniquity 654.3
wrongdoing 655.1
misdeed 655.2
error 974.1
v do wrong 654.8
transgress 655.4
since
adv subsequently
834.6
ago 836.15
ever since 836.17
conj because 887.10
sincere zealous 101.9
resolute 359.11
artless 416.5
candid 644.17
genuine 972.15
**the sincerest form of
flattery** 336.1
since time began
for a long time 826.14
since 836.17
sine qua non 196.5
sinew muscularity 15.2
power 18.1
vigor 544.3
sinewy
able-bodied 15.16
vigorous 544.11
tough 1047.4
sinful wrong 638.3
immoral 654.16
wicked 655.5

ungodly 695.17
bad 999.7
sing
n musical occasion
708.32
v bird sound 60.5
be pleased 95.11
exude cheerfulness
109.6
rejoice 116.5
wind sound 318.21
betray 351.6
speak 524.26
inform on 551.13
vocalize 708.38
poetize 720.13
sing a different tune
n change one's mind
363.6
v be changed 851.6
change 851.7
convert 857.11
singe
n burn 1019.6
v stain 1003.6
burn 1019.24
singer
entertainer 707.1
lead 707.6
vocalist 710.13
Singer 741.3
single
n celibate 565.2
baseball hit 745.3
individual 871.4
v hit a baseball 745.5
adj unmarried 565.7
simple 797.6
characteristic 864.13
one 871.7
single file 811.2
single-handed 871.8
single-minded
resolute 359.11
persevering 360.8
artless 416.5
engrossed 982.17
singleness of purpose
360.1
single out
select 371.14
specify 864.11
call attention to
982.10
single vote 371.6
sing out 59.8
singsong
n regularity 780.2
repetitiousness 848.4
adj tedious 118.9
monotonous 848.15
sing the blues
hang one's head
112.11
lament 115.10
sing the praises of
praise 509.12
glorify 696.11
sing 708.38
sing the same old song
harp on 118.8
dwell on 848.9

singular
n number 530.8
adj wonderful 122.10
particular 864.12
characteristic 864.13
odd 869.11
one 871.7
sole 871.9
eccentric 926.5
sinister
adj ominous 133.17
oblique 204.13
left 220.4
dishonest 645.16
bad 999.7
adverse 1010.13
adv leftward 220.6
sink
n washbasin 79.12
receptacle of filth
80.12
drain 239.5
cavity 284.2
den of iniquity 654.7
v weaken 16.9
burn out 21.5
disappear 34.2
languish 85.47
lose heart 112.16
sadden 112.18
recede 168.2
move 172.5
capsize 182.44
go down 194.6
decrease 252.6
deepen 275.8
be concave 284.12
excavate 284.15
gravitate 297.15
age 303.10
submerge 367.7
scuttle 367.8
spoil 393.11
decline 393.17
ruin 395.11
founder 410.11
bankrupt 625.8
invest 729.16
make a golf shot 751.4
flit 827.6
depress 912.4
come to grief 1010.10
fall on evil days
1010.11
sinkhole 284.3
sink in
impress 93.15
mire 243.2
get across 521.5
impress 930.19
be remembered
988.14
sinking fast 307.33
sinking heart 112.3
sink into despair
lose heart 112.16
despair 125.10
sink one's teeth into it
330.11
sink or swim
adv without fail
969.26

phrs come what may
359.20
sinner evildoer 593.1
wrongdoer 660.9
sinuous curved 279.7
convolutional 281.6
sinus 279.2
sip
n drink 8.4
taste 62.2
nip 88.7
hint 248.4
v drink 8.29
taste 62.7
tipple 88.24
siphon
n extractor 192.9
tube 239.6
v transport 176.14
channel 239.15
sir 76.7
Sir 648.3
sire
n senior 304.5
father 560.9
Sir 648.3
jockey 757.2
author 885.4
producer 891.7
v procreate 78.8
engender 817.14
cause 885.10
siren
n noisemaker 53.6
spirit of the sea 240.4
tempter 377.4
warning sign 399.3
alarm 400.1
witch 593.7
water god 678.10
bewitcher 690.9
adj alluring 377.8
Sir Galahad 608.5
sirocco
hot wind 318.7
dust storm 318.13
sissy
n weakling 16.6
effeminate male 77.10
spoiled child 427.4
coward 491.5
sister 559.3
adj effeminate 77.14
cowardly 491.10
sister woman 77.6
nurse 90.10
female sibling 559.3
member 617.11
nun 699.17
layman 700.2
likeness 783.3
Sister 648.5
sister-in-law 564.2
sit be pregnant 78.12
be seated 173.10
convene 769.17
sit around 331.12
sit at 221.8
sit at the feet of 570.11
sit back 329.2
sitcom 1034.2
sit-down meal 8.5

conference 541.6
strike 727.5
assembly 769.2
site
n location 159.1
arena 463.1
v locate 159.11
place 159.12
establish 159.16
sit idly by 329.3
sit-in
objection 333.2
assembly 769.2
sit in 333.5
sit in for 861.5
sit in judgment
administer justice
594.5
try 598.17
hold the scales 945.12
sit in on 48.10
sit it out 329.2
sit on cover up 345.8
suppress 428.8
participate 476.5
appropriate 480.19
disapprove 510.18
try 598.17
rest on 900.22
**sit on a barrel of
gunpowder**
court danger 493.6
take chances 1005.7
sit on the fence
n be a timeserver
363.9
v hesitate 362.7
dodge 368.8
remain neutral 467.5
sit on the sidelines
do nothing 329.2
remain neutral 467.5
sitter 1007.8
sit through 134.7
sit tight hide 346.8
stay with it 360.4
wait 845.12
sitting duck dupe 358.2
exposure 1005.3
easy thing 1013.3
sitting pretty
cheerful 109.11
successful 409.14
victorious 411.7
sitting room 197.5
situate
v locate 159.11
adj located 159.18
situation location 159.1
placement 159.6
environment 209.1
occupation 724.5
state 764.1
mental outlook 977.2
predicament 1012.4
sit up rise 200.8
wait 845.12
sit up and take notice
982.8
sitz bath 79.8
six playing card 758.2
number 881.2

six feet under
adj dead 307.30
adv buried 309.23
sixfold
v multiply by six
881.16
adj six times as much
881.18
**six of one and half a
dozen of the other**
n ambiguity 539.1
the same 789.3
choicelessness 962.6
adj coinciding 777.8
indistinguishable
944.6
sixteen 881.7
sixteenth note 709.14
sixteenth rest 709.21
sixth
n interval 709.20
adj ordinal number
881.18
n fraction 881.14
sixth sense senses 24.5
extrasensory
perception 689.8
intuition 933.1
sixtieth 881.27
sixty 881.7
**sixty-four dollar
question** 522.8
sixty-fourth note
709.14
sixty-fourth rest 709.21
sizable large 247.7
considerable 257.16
size
n dimension 257
largeness 257.1
extent 300.3
semiliquid 1060.5
v adjust 257.15
measure 300.10
classify 807.11
examine 937.23
size up scrutinize 27.14
measure 300.10
examine 937.23
estimate 945.9
sizzle
n energy 17.3
hissing 57.1
v hiss 57.2
drug use 87.21
be angry 152.15
speed 174.9
sizzler
speeder 174.5
hot day 1018.8
skate glide 177.35
play hockey 749.7
skateboard
n skates 179.21
v glide 177.35
skate on thin ice 1005.7
skating rink 743.11
skedaddle
n flight 368.4
v be frightened 127.12
speed 174.9
depart 188.7

leave 222.10
flee 368.11
lose one's nerve 491.8
inter go away! 908.32
skeet shooting
sport 744.1
trapshooting 903.2
skein cord 271.2
flock 769.6
skeleton
n base 199.2
outline 211.2
frame 266.4
thinness 270.7
thin person 270.8
corpse 307.16
diagram 381.3
wreck 393.8
abridgment 557.1
support 900.10
adj skeletal 2.24
skeleton crew 991.2
skeleton in the closet
secret 345.5
evil 999.3
skeleton key 292.10
skeptic
n agnostic 695.12
doubter 954.4
adj agnostic 695.20
sketch
n description 349.2
diagram 381.3
treatise 556.1
abridgment 557.1
act 704.7
drawing 712.13
likeness 783.3
v describe 349.9
plot 381.10
outline 381.11
abridge 557.5
act 704.29
portray 712.19
sketchbook
book 554.1
art equipment 712.18
sketchy
incomplete 794.4
imperfect 1002.4
skew
n deviation 164.1
bias 204.3
v squint 28.9
deflect 164.5
diverge 204.9
go sideways 218.5
unbalance 790.3
adj deflective 164.8
askew 204.14
unequal 790.4
skewer
perforate 292.15
stigmatize 661.9
hook 799.8
ski
n skate 179.21
v glide 177.35
sport 753.4
skid
n slide 194.4
v glide 177.35

maneuver 184.40
slide 194.9
go sideways 218.5
skid row 230.6
skier 753.2
skiing gliding 177.16
  sports 753.1
ski jump
  n leap 366.1
  v leap 366.5
ski lift
  cableway 383.8
  transport 753.1
skill superiority 249.1
  expertise 413
  skillfulness 413.1
  art 413.7
  production 891.2
  memory 988.1
skilled laborer 726.6
skillful expert 413.22
  good 998.12
skim
  n gliding 177.16
  v touch lightly 73.7
  speed 174.8
  glide 177.35
  float 182.54
  slide 194.9
  contact 223.10
  scratch the surface
   276.4
  slight 340.8
  cheat 356.18
  acquire 472.9
  take 480.13
  browse 570.13
  examine cursorily
   937.25
skimp
  v slight 340.8
  stint 484.5
  economize 635.4
  adj meager 991.10
skimpy sparse 884.5
  meager 991.10
skin
  n body covering 2.4
  fur 4.2
  contraceptive 86.23
  exterior 206.2
  shallowness 276.1
  skin 295.3
  blanket 295.12
  lamina 296.2
  money 728.6
  cash 728.7
  v peel 6.8
  best 249.7
  injure 393.13
  strip 480.24
  overprice 632.7
  cheat 759.26
  tear apart 801.14
  abrade 1042.7
skin alive best 249.7
  defeat 412.9
  criticize 510.20
skin and bones
  n shrinking 260.3
  leanness 270.5
  adj wasted 393.35

skin color 35.1
skin-deep
  cutaneous 2.25
  insignificant 248.6
  shallow 276.5
  epidermal 295.32
skin diver 367.4
skin flick 666.4
skinflint 484.4
skin game 356.10
skinny cutaneous 2.25
  lean 270.17
  skinlike 295.32
the skinny
  information 551.1
  the facts 760.4
  the truth 972.4
skinny-dip 182.56
skip
  n step 177.11
  leap 366.1
  wastepaper basket
   391.7
  lawn bowling 750.3
  v exude cheerfulness
   109.6
  rejoice 116.5
  way of walking 177.28
  depart 188.7
  leave undone 340.7
  leap 366.5
  caper 366.6
  flee 368.11
  escape 369.6
  dance 705.5
  play 743.23
skip it 997.25
skip over slight 340.8
  examine cursorily
   937.25
skipper
  n ship's officer 183.7
  v direct 573.8
skirl
  n screech 58.4
  v screech 58.8
skirmish
  n fight 457.4
  v contend 457.13
skirt
  n dress 5.16
  woman 77.6
  border 211.4
  girl 302.7
  v border 211.10
  flank 218.4
  contact 223.10
  evade 368.7
  circle 913.5
skirting
  n edging 211.7
  adj bordering 211.11
  flanking 218.6
ski slope 753.1
skit 704.7
skittish
  sensitive 24.12
  excitable 105.28
  frisky 109.14
  fearful 127.23
  jittery 128.12
  shy 139.12

  fickle 364.6
skoal! 88.38
skulduggery 356.4
skulk
  n shirker 368.3
  group of animals
   769.5
  v lurk 346.9
  shirk 368.9
  cower 491.9
skull cranium 198.7
  death 307.3
skull and crossbones
  death 307.3
  warning sign 399.3
  insignia 647.1
skunk
  n stinker 71.3
  wild animal 311.23
  bad person 660.7
  v defeat 412.9
sky
  n summit 198.2
  height 272.2
  the heavens 1070.2
  v hit golf ball 751.4
  elevate 911.5
skycap 176.7
sky dive
  parachute 181.13
  plunge 367.1
sky-high 272.15
skyjack 482.20
skyjacker 483.7
skylark
  n ascent 193.7
  v make merry 743.24
skylight roof 295.6
  shine 1024.2
skyline 201.4
skyrocket
  n ascent 193.7
  v shoot up 193.9
  improve 392.7
  rocket 1072.12
skyscraper
  structure 266.2
  tower 272.6
skyward up 193.16
  on high 272.21
skywriting 184.1
slab lamina 296.2
  wood 1052.3
slack
  n refuse 391.4
  coal dust 1020.2
  v relax 20.7
  leave undone 340.7
  shirk 368.9
  ease up 670.9
  loosen 803.3
  fight fire 1021.7
  adj weak 16.12
  apathetic 94.13
  inert 173.14
  slow 175.10
  indolent 331.19
  negligent 340.10
  lax 426.4
  wanton 665.26
  loose 803.5
  slovenly 809.15

  dilatory 845.17
slacker neglecter 340.5
  shirker 368.3
slack-jawed 292.18
slacks 5.18
slag dregs 256.2
  refuse 391.4
  combustion product
   1019.16
slake gratify 95.7
  relieve 120.5
  relax 670.9
  satiate 993.4
slalom 753.3
slam
  n explosive noise 56.1
  disrespect 156.3
  score 409.5
  jail 429.9
  criticism 510.4
  hit 901.4
  blow 901.5
  v make explosive
   noise 56.6
  be disrespectful 156.6
  close 293.6
  criticize 510.14
  strike 901.15
slammer 429.9
**slam the door in one's
face**
  snub 157.5
  avoid 368.6
  repulse 442.5
slander
  n monstrous lie
   354.12
  libel 512.3
  scandal 552.8
  v libel 512.11
slang
  n gibberish 522.7
  nonformal language
   523.5
  jargon 523.9
  barbarism 526.6
  v bluster 503.3
  adj jargonish 523.19
slant
  n glance 27.4
  aspect 33.3
  deviation 164.1
  inclination 204.2
  diagonal 204.7
  partiality 650.3
  plot 722.4
  tendency 895.1
  mental outlook 977.2
  disposition 977.3
  v incline 204.10
  go sideways 218.5
  pervert 265.6
  misrepresent 350.3
  falsify 354.15
  favor 650.8
  influence 893.7
  adj inclining
   204.15
  transverse 204.19
slap
  n explosive sound
   56.1

ceramics 742.3
error 974.4
harbor 1008.6
mud 1060.8
v glide 177.35
float 182.54
slide 194.9
decline 393.17
sink 410.11
miss 410.14
bungle 414.11
give 478.12
go wrong 654.9
elapse 820.5
err 974.9
fall on evil days
1010.11
slip by 836.6
slipcover 554.14
slip in enter 189.7
insert 191.3
interpose 213.6
intrude 214.5
slip off take off 6.6
absent oneself 222.8
slip of the tongue 974.4
slip on 5.42
slip one's mind 989.7
slip one a Mickey 25.4
slippery slick 287.11
deceitful 356.22
evasive 368.15
cunning 415.12
dishonest 645.16
treacherous 645.21
unreliable 970.20
precarious 1005.12
oily 1054.9
slipshod
careless 340.12
lax 426.4
ungrammatic 531.4
slovenly 809.15
slipstream 184.30
**slip through one's
fingers** 369.9
slit
n crack 224.2
furrow 290.1
break 801.4
v cleave 224.4
furrow 290.3
open 292.11
injure 393.13
sever 801.11
adj cleft 224.7
furrowed 290.4
impaired 393.27
severed 801.23
slither
n gait 177.12
gliding 177.16
slide 194.4
v way of walking
177.28
glide 177.35
slide 194.9
slit trench 460.5
sliver scrap 248.3
intruder 773.2
piece 792.3
slob bungler 414.9

slattern 809.7
ice 1022.5
mud 1060.8
slobber
n saliva 13.3
unction 511.2
v salivate 13.6
be stupid 921.12
be insane 925.20
moisten 1063.12
sloe
n blackness 38.4
adj black 38.8
slog
n walk 177.10
hit 901.4
v way of walking
177.28
keep doggedly at
360.3
drudge 725.14
strike 901.15
slogan
call to arms 458.8
catchword 526.9
motto 973.4
slop
n slime 80.8
offal 80.9
sentimentality 93.8
refuse 391.4
mud 1060.8
mud puddle 1060.9
v overflow 238.17
moisten 1063.12
slope
n inclination 204.2
incline 204.4
declivity 237.2
skiing 753.1
v incline 204.10
sloppy filthy 80.23
sentimental 93.21
slipshod 340.12
bungling 414.20
lax 426.4
loose 803.5
slovenly 809.15
slimy 1060.14
watery 1063.16
slosh
n lap 238.8
snow 1022.8
mud 1060.8
sprinkle 1063.5
v ripple 52.11
overflow 238.17
lap 238.19
moisten 1063.12
sloshed 88.33
slot
n crack 224.2
opening 292.1
syntax 530.2
gambling wheel
759.16
v cleave 224.4
sloth apathy 94.4
wretchedness 96.6
unconcern 102.2
dejection 112.3
despair 125.2

slowness 175.1
inaction 329.1
indolence 331.5
languor 331.6
group of animals
769.5
slot machine
vending machine
736.4
gambling wheel
759.16
slouch
n slow motion 175.2
gait 177.12
idler 331.8
bungler 414.8
v way of walking
177.28
sink 194.6
idle 331.12
slough
n shed skin 2.5
offal 80.9
gangrene 85.39
marsh 243.1
predicament 1012.4
mud puddle 1060.9
v shed 6.10
discard 390.7
slovenly dirty 80.22
slipshod 340.12
ungrammatic 531.4
slipshod 809.15
slow
v slow down 175.9
adj dull 117.6
not fast 175.10
reluctant 325.6
indolent 331.19
languid 331.20
leisurely 402.6
late 845.16
dilatory 845.17
infrequent 847.2
dull 921.16
adv slowly 175.13
late 845.19
tardily 845.20
slow burn 152.3
slowdown
slowing 175.4
decline 252.2
economizing 635.2
strike 727.5
delay 845.2
slow motion 175.2
slow on the draw
845.16
slowpoke 175.5
slow starter 845.6
slow time
march 177.13
time 831.3
slow-up 845.2
slow-witted 921.16
sludge slime 80.8
refuse 391.4
ice 1022.5
mud 1060.8
slug
n drink 8.4
slowpoke 175.5

idler 331.8
shot 462.19
line of type 548.2
type spacing 548.7
token 728.12
dose 792.5
blow 901.5
v fight 754.4
strike 901.15
slugger
baseball player 745.2
boxer 754.2
sluggish
apathetic 94.13
unconcerned 102.7
inert 173.14
slow 175.10
meandering 238.24
languid 331.20
dilatory 845.17
dull 921.16
sluice
n outlet 190.9
watercourse 239.2
drain 239.5
floodgate 239.11
v wash 79.19
flood 1063.14
slum sty 80.11
city district 230.6
slumber
n sleep 22.2
quiescence 173.1
v sleep 22.13
stagnate 173.9
slumlord 470.3
slump
n sinkage 194.2
decline 252.2
deterioration 393.3
cheapening 633.4
business cycle 731.9
declining market
737.5
shortcoming 910.1
hard times 1010.6
v sink 194.6
decline 393.17
cheapen 633.6
fall short 910.2
slur
n aspersion 512.4
stigma 661.6
musical execution
708.30
musical notation
709.12
v slight 340.8
defame 512.9
stigmatize 661.9
examine cursorily
937.25
stain 1003.6
slurp
n drink 8.4
ingestion 187.4
v lap up 8.30
draw in 187.12
slurry 796.6
slush slime 80.8
sentimentality 93.8
talkativeness 540.1

snootful 793.3
snooty snobbish 141.14
  contemptuous 157.8
snooze
  n nap 22.3
  v sleep 22.14
snore
  n breathing 2.19
  resonance 54.1
  sibilation 57.1
  rasp 58.3
  v sleep 22.13
  resonate 54.6
  sibilate 57.2
  sound harshly 58.9
snorkel tube 239.6
  diving equipment
    367.5
  extinguisher 1021.3
snort
  n drink 8.4
  sibilation 57.1
  drink 88.7
  laughter 116.4
  snub 157.2
  scornful laugh 508.4
  dose 792.5
  v sibilate 57.2
  grunt 60.3
  inhale a drug 87.21
  laugh 116.8
  speak 524.26
snot body fluid 2.22
  filth 80.7
snotty
  snobbish 141.14
  contemptuous 157.8
  mucous 1060.13
snout nozzle 239.9
  nose 283.8
snow
  n whiteness 37.2
  cocaine 87.6
  ice 1022.8
  television reception
    1034.5
  v deceive 356.14
  give 478.12
  hail 1022.11
snowball
  n accumulation 769.9
  snow 1022.8
  v grow 251.6
  enlarge 259.5
  ball 282.7
**a snowball's chance in
  hell** 966.1
snow-blind
  v blind 30.7
  adj dim-sighted 28.13
  blinded 30.10
snowdrift pile 769.10
  snow 1022.8
snowflake 1022.8
snow job
  deception 356.9
  inducement 375.3
snowman figure 349.6
  snow 1022.8
snowmobile 179.20
snowshoes 179.21
snowstorm storm 671.4

snow 1022.8
television reception
  1034.5
snub
  n rebuff 157.2
  repulse 907.2
  v rebuff 157.5
  shorten 268.6
  restrain 428.7
  refuse 442.5
  repulse 907.3
  banish 908.17
  hinder 1011.10
  adj shortened 268.9
snub-nosed
  deformed 265.12
  stubby 268.10
snuff
  n breathing 2.19
  sibilation 57.1
  tobacco 89.8
  drawing in 187.5
  v sibilate 57.2
  smell 69.8
  draw in 187.12
  kill 308.13
  fight fire 1021.7
snuffbox 89.8
snuff out
  extinguish 395.15
  fight fire 1021.7
snug
  v make comfortable
    121.9
  adj comfortable
    121.11
  seaworthy 180.18
  homelike 228.33
  close 293.12
  taciturn 344.9
  unsociable 583.5
  tidy 806.8
  cozy 1006.7
snuggery nook 197.3
  cottage 228.8
snuggle nestle 121.10
  cuddle 562.17
snug harbor 1008.1
so
  adj suchlike 783.12
  adv greatly 247.15
  very 247.18
  how 384.9
  thus 765.10
  similarly 783.18
  equally 789.11
  accurately 972.20
  conj for 380.11
  just so 958.15
soak
  n drunk 88.12
  soaking 1063.7
  v tipple 88.24
  extraction 192.16
  overprice 632.7
  strike 901.15
  overload 992.15
  liquefy 1062.5
  drench 1063.13
so-and-so 528.2
soap
  n cleanser 79.17

television broadcast
  1034.2
  v wash 79.19
  flatter 511.6
soapbox
  n platform 900.13
  v make a speech 543.9
soapbox racing 744.1
soap opera
  sentimentality 93.8
  radiobroadcast
    1033.18
  television broadcast
    1034.2
soapy foamy 320.7
  suave 504.18
  flattering 511.8
  oily 1054.9
soar move 172.5
  fly 184.36
  take off 193.10
  loom 247.5
  tower 272.10
soaring costs 632.3
sob
  n sexual pervert 75.16
  lament 115.3
  v sigh 52.14
  weep 115.12
  wind sound 318.21
  speak 524.26
  mumble 525.9
SOB 660.6
sober
  v moderate 670.6
  adj soft-colored 35.21
  dark 38.9
  gray 39.4
  sedate 106.14
  solemn 111.3
  dignified 136.12
  not intoxicated
    516.3
  plain-speaking 535.3
  temperate 668.9
  moderate 670.10
  real 760.15
  sensible 919.18
  cognitive 930.21
  weighty 996.20
sobering 996.20
sobriety
  darkness 38.2
  sedateness 106.4
  solemnity 111.1
  proud bearing 136.2
  unintoxicatedness 516
  temperance 668.1
  moderation 670.1
  sensibleness 919.6
  sanity 924.1
sobriquet 527.7
sob story 93.8
so-called
  spurious 354.25
  pretexted 376.5
  nominal 527.15
soccer 752
sociable
  n social gathering
    582.10
  v talkative 540.9

  adj communicative
    343.10
  informal 581.3
  social 582.22
  friendly 587.15
  associational 617.17
social
  n social gathering
    582.10
  adj public 312.16
  communal 476.9
  sociable 582.22
  associational 617.17
social behavior
  good behavior 321.2
  behaviorism 321.3
social class
  social circle 582.5
  class 607.1
  community 617.2
social climbing 100.10
social consciousness
  591.1
social democracy 612.4
social director 743.20
social disease 85.18
social drinker 88.11
social evolution 860.4
social gathering 582.10
social graces 580.3
social intercourse
  communication 343.1
  social life 582.4
socialism
  communion 476.2
  collective ownership
    611.6
  government 612.8
socialite
  n person of fashion
    578.7
  aristocrat 607.4
  adj upper-class 607.10
socialize
  make better 392.9
  communize 476.7
  attach 480.20
  politicize 611.16
social mobility
  class 607.1
  change 851.1
the social order 606.1
social outcast 586.4
social register 578.6
Social Register
  directory 549.9
  Bluebook 607.2
social security
  welfare 143.5
  subsidy 478.8
  welfarism 611.7
  insurance 1007.4
social services 449.3
social worker
  philanthropist 143.8
  professional 726.4
society
  n population 227.1
  humankind 312.1
  culture 373.3
  fashionable people
    578.6

so long! 188.22
so long as 958.15
solstice 313.7
soluble solvable 939.3
  liquefiable 1062.9
solution
  explanation 341.4
  harmonization 709.2
  answer to a problem
   939
  resolution 939.1
  expedient 994.2
  liquefaction 1062.1
  decoction 1062.3
solve explain 341.10
  resolve 939.2
  liquefy 1062.5
solvent
  n cleanser 79.17
  thinner 270.10
  dissolvent 1062.4
  adj unindebted 624.23
  sound 729.17
  disintegrative 805.5
  dissolvent 1062.8
soma body 2.1
  physical entity 1050.3
somber
  n gloom 1026.4
  v darken 1026.9
  adj soft-colored 35.21
  dark 38.9
  gray 39.4
  solemn 111.3
  grim 112.24
  ominous 133.17
  gloomy 1026.14
  lackluster 1026.17
some
  n quantity 244.3
  plurality 882.1
  adj quantitative 244.5
  skillful 413.22
  plural 882.7
  adv approximately
   244.6
somebody person 312.5
  celebrity 662.9
  personage 996.8
someday 838.12
somehow
  in some way 384.11
  by chance 971.19
someplace 159.26
somersault
  n overturn 205.2
  v capsize 182.44
something
  n some 244.3
  thing 762.3
  important person
   996.9
  object 1050.4
  prep about 223.26
something else
  n marvel 122.2
  a different thing 779.3
  first-rate 998.7
  adj nothing like 786.5
  excellent 998.13
something extra
  advantage 249.2

extra 254.4
  gratuity 478.5
  surplus 992.5
something like 783.10
something out of
  nothing 355.3
something special
  996.5
something terrible
  distressingly 247.21
  terribly 999.14
something to fall back
  on 386.3
something to spare
  992.5
something to write
  home about
  marvel 122.2
  matter of
   consequence 996.5
sometime
  adj former 836.10
  occasional 847.3
  adv someday 838.12
some time ago 836.16
somewhat
  n some 244.3
  adv to a degree 245.7
  limited 248.10
somewhere 159.26
somewhere else
  adj abstracted 984.11
  adv away 222.18
somnambulism
  sleep 22.2
  trance 92.19
  nightwalking 177.9
somnolent sleepy 22.21
  languid 331.20
so much for that
  inter that's that!
   407.15
  phrs that's all for
   819.14
son male child 559.3
  offspring 561.1
  descendant 561.3
sonar 182.2
song melody 708.4
  vocal music 708.13
  types 708.14
  poetry 720.1
song and dance
  deception 356.9
  act 704.7
songbird bird 311.28
  singer 710.13
  singing bird 710.23
sonic 50.17
sonic boom sonics 50.6
  noise 53.3
  air speed 184.31
son-in-law 564.2
son of a bitch 660.6
sonogram 91.9
sonorous
  sounding 50.15
  loud 53.11
  resonant 54.9
  grandiloquent 545.8
  melodious 708.48
soon in the future 838.9

presently 844.16
sooner than
  preferably 371.28
  instead of 861.12
soon to be 839.3
soot
  n blackness 38.4
  blacking 38.6
  dirt 80.6
  dregs 256.2
  combustion product
   1019.16
  powder 1049.5
  v blacken 38.7
  dirty 80.15
soothe
  relieve 120.5
  quiet 173.8
  pacify 465.7
  calm 670.7
soothing
  n palliative 86.10
  relief 120.1
  pacification 465.1
  modulation 670.2
  adj palliative 86.40
  sedative 86.45
  relieving 120.9
  pacificatory 465.12
  tranquilizing 670.15
  lubricant 1054.10
soothsayer 961.4
sooty dingy 38.11
  dirty 80.22
sop
  n weakling 16.6
  bribe 378.2
  fool 923.1
  v soak 1063.13
sophisticated
  experienced 413.28
  elegant 496.9
  chic 578.13
  ungullible 955.5
  disillusioned 976.5
sophistry
  insincerity 354.5
  cunning 415.1
  misteaching 569.1
  reasoning 934.1
  illogicalness 935.1
  specious argument
   935.3
  philosophy 951.1
sophomore
  undergraduate 572.6
  jockey 757.2
soporific
  n sleep-inducer 22.10
  adj sleepy 22.21
  sleep-inducing 22.23
  sedative 86.45
  apathetic 94.13
sopping wet 1063.17
soprano
  n high voice 58.6
  part 708.22
  voice 709.5
  adj high 58.13
  vocal 708.50
sorcerer
  Satanist 680.15

necromancer 690.5
  illusoriness 975.2
  diviner 689.16
sorceress 690.8
sordid squalid 80.25
  greedy 100.27
  niggardly 484.8
  disreputable 661.10
  slovenly 809.15
  terrible 999.9
sore
  n soreness 26.4
  symptom 85.9
  lesion 85.36
  pain 96.5
  adj raw 26.11
  distressing 98.20
  resentful 152.26
  angry 152.30
  hostile 589.10
  disastrous 1010.15
  straitened 1012.26
sorehead
  malcontent 108.4
  grouch 110.11
  complainer 115.9
sore point
  sore spot 24.4
  provocation 152.11
  bone of contention
   456.7
sorghum 66.2
sorority
  affiliation 450.2
  sisterhood 587.2
  club 617.3
sorrel
  n horse 311.11
  adj brown 40.3
sorrow
  n affliction 96.8
  grief 112.10
  regret 113.1
  lamentation 115.1
  v distress 98.14
  grieve 112.17
  aggrieve 112.19
  lament 115.10
sorry unhappy 112.21
  regretful 113.8
  low 497.15
  disgraceful 661.11
  paltry 997.21
sort
  n nature 766.4
  kind 808.3
  v size 257.15
  analyze 800.8
  arrange 807.11
  classify 808.6
  discriminate 943.4
sortie
  Air Force mission
   184.11
  attack 459.1
sort of
  to a degree 245.7
  so to speak 783.19
SOS 400.1
so-so
  adj medium 246.3
  mediocre 1004.7

v extend 158.8
overlie 295.30
measure 300.10
put together 799.5
double 872.5
spandex 1046.3
spangled spotted 47.13
ornamented 498.11
illuminated 1024.39
spaniel 138.3
Spanish fly 75.6
spank
n slap 901.8
v reprove 510.17
punish 604.13
pound 901.16
slap 901.19
spanking new 840.10
spar
n mast 180.13
beam 273.3
boxing 457.9
lever 905.4
v quarrel 456.11
contend 457.13
fight 754.4
argue 934.16
spare
n bowling 750.2
surplus 992.5
v have pity 145.4
forgive 148.3
refrain 329.3
not use 390.5
preserve 397.8
exempt 430.14
relinquish 475.3
give away 478.21
afford 626.7
abstain 668.7
adj additional
253.10
remaining 256.7
lean 270.17
reserved 386.15
unused 390.12
leisure 402.5
plain-speaking 535.3
economical 635.6
simple 797.6
occasional 847.3
substitute 861.8
meager 991.10
superfluous 992.17
surplus 992.18
spare no expense 485.3
spare part 386.3
spare room 158.3
spare the rod
be easy on 427.5
indulge 427.6
spare time 402.1
spare tire 2.17
spark
n hint 248.4
inspiration 375.9
prompter 375.10
dandy 500.9
immediate cause
885.3
fire 1018.15
glitter 1024.7

v motivate 375.12
kindle 375.18
court 562.21
cause 885.10
be hot 1018.22
glitter 1024.24
sparkle
n bubbling 320.3
spirit 544.4
spark 1018.15
glitter 1024.7
v exude cheerfulness
109.6
bubble 320.4
joke 489.13
be brilliant 919.11
glitter 1024.24
sparkling water 10.47
spark plug
energizer 17.6
prompter 375.10
sparring partner 754.2
sparse dispersed 770.9
infrequent 847.2
scant 884.5
scarce 991.11
Spartan
n stoic 134.3
man of few words
344.5
adj patient 134.9
strict 425.6
inornate 499.9
plain-speaking 535.3
concise 537.6
abstinent 668.10
meager 991.10
spasm pang 26.2
seizure 85.6
symptom 85.9
pain 96.5
outburst 105.9
bustle 330.4
upheaval 671.5
revolution 859.1
convulsion 916.6
frenzy 925.7
spastic
n sick person 85.42
idiot 923.8
adj convulsive 671.23
irregular 850.3
jerky 916.19
unintelligent 921.17
mentally deficient
921.22
foolish 922.8
spat
n quarrel 456.5
offspring 561.1
v quarrel 456.11
spate flow 238.4
torrent 238.5
quantity 247.3
lot 247.4
rainstorm 316.2
outburst 671.6
throng 769.4
plenty 990.2
superabundance 992.2
spatter
n staccato 55.1

stain 1003.3
sprinkle 1063.5
v splatter 80.18
rain 316.9
sprinkle 770.6
spot 1003.5
moisten 1063.12
spatula
art equipment 712.18
sculpture tool 715.4
spawn
n egg 305.15
offspring 561.1
v reproduce 78.9
originate 891.12
spay 255.11
spaying 255.4
speak sound 50.14
hail a ship 182.52
affirm 334.5
communicate 343.6
command 420.8
signal 517.22
use language 523.16
talk 524.20
remark 524.25
address 524.27
make a speech 543.9
speakeasy 88.20
speaker
loudspeaker 50.8
talker 524.18
speechmaker 543.4
chairman 574.5
spokesman 576.5
Speaker of the House
610.3
speak for
be in front 216.7
represent 576.14
defend 600.10
speak in tongues
talk nonsense 520.5
be incomprehensible
522.10
speak too soon 843.4
speak up affirm 334.5
come out 348.6
brave 492.11
speak out 524.22
spear
n leaf 310.17
branch 310.18
stem 310.19
weapon 462.8
v perforate 292.15
stab 459.25
catch 480.17
spearhead
n vanguard 216.2
v lead 165.2
special
n train 179.14
commodity 735.2
feature 865.2
adj student 572.12
detailed 765.9
other 779.8
classificational
808.7
particular 864.12
notable 996.19

special edition 555.2
special education
student 572.4
special effects 706.4
Special Forces 461.15
special interest
pressure group 609.31
interest 982.2
specialist
n doctor 90.4
dentist 90.6
stockbroker 737.10
specializer 865.3
adj specialized 865.5
specialize in
practice 328.8
study to be 570.15
go in for 865.4
special police 1007.17
special privilege 430.8
specialty study 568.8
occupation 724.4
vocation 724.6
component 795.2
particularity 864.2
characteristic 864.4
object of special
attention 865
speciality 865.1
science 927.10
specie money 728.1
hard money 728.4
species
nomenclature 527.1
race 559.4
kind 808.3
classifications 808.5
biology 1066.1
specific
n remedy 86.1
adj circumscribed
210.6
detailed 765.9
classificational 808.7
particular 864.12
specification
circumscription 210.1
description 349.2
indication 517.3
accusation 599.1
circumstantiation
765.5
differentiation 779.4
designation 864.6
qualification 958.1
condition 958.2
specific gravity
weight 297.5
density 1043.1
specify
circumscribe 210.4
designate 517.18
name 527.11
itemize 765.6
differentiate 779.6
specialize 864.11
focus on 936.3
call attention to
982.10
specimen sample 62.4
representative 349.7
model 785.3

specious
meretricious 354.26
pretexted 376.5
sophistical 935.10
illusory 975.8
speck
n spottiness 47.3
modicum 248.2
minute thing 258.7
mark 517.5
intruder 773.2
stain 1003.3
v variegate 47.7
mark 517.19
sprinkle 770.6
spot 1003.5
speckle
n spottiness 47.3
mark 517.5
stain 1003.3
v variegate 47.7
mark 517.19
sprinkle 770.6
spot 1003.5
spectacle sight 33.7
marvel 122.2
display 501.4
spectacles 29.3
spectacular
astonishing 122.12
gaudy 501.20
theatrical 501.24
dramatic 704.33
Spectacular Bid 311.15
spectator audience 48.6
attender 221.5
recipient 479.3
playgoer 704.27
gambler 759.21
observer 917.1
witness 956.6
specter apparition 33.5
frightener 127.9
spirit 678.5
phantom 975.4
ghost 987.1
spectrometer 29.1
spectroscope
optical instrument
29.1
astronomical
instrument 1070.17
spectrum
color system 35.7
variegation 47.6
range 158.2
series 811.2
optical illusion 975.5
frequency 1033.12
spectrum analysis
35.10
speculate invest 729.16
trade 737.23
gamble 759.23
consider 930.12
theorize 950.9
predict 961.9
speculator
stock investor 737.11
gambler 759.21
theorist 950.7
philosopher 951.6

speech
n communication
343.1
language 523.1
utterance 524
talk 524.1
diction 532.1
conversation 541.3
public speaking 543.2
story teller 722.4
adj communicational
343.9
language 524.30
speech impediment
525.1
speechless mute 51.12
taciturn 344.9
speechmaker 543.4
speech-writer 543.8
speed
n amphetamines 87.3
velocity 174.1
hastiness 401.2
v move 172.5
go fast 174.8
hasten 401.4
be useful 449.17
facilitate 1013.7
speedboat 180.4
speed bump
bulge 283.3
hindrance 1011.1
speed demon 174.5
speeder racer 174.5
driver 178.10
speed of light 174.2
speed of sound
sonics 50.6
sonic speed 174.2
air speed 184.31
speedometer 174.7
speed up
accelerate 174.10
hasten 401.4
speedway 756.1
speedwriting 547.8
speedy fast 174.15
quick 330.18
hasty 401.9
brief 827.8
sudden 829.5
prompt 844.9
spell
n sorcery 690.1
magic spell 691.1
period 823.1
term 823.3
period of duty 824
turn 824.2
round 849.3
superstition 953.3
bad influence 999.4
v augur 133.12
fascinate 377.7
mean 518.8
orthographize 546.7
cast a spell 691.7
take one's turn 824.5
substitute for 861.5
spellbound
wondering 122.9
enchanted 691.12

gripped 982.18
dreamy 985.25
speller 554.10
spelling bee 546.4
spell out
explain 341.10
simplify 499.5
make clear 521.6
spell 546.7
itemize 765.6
elaborate 860.6
particularize 864.9
spend
use up 387.13
consume 388.3
waste 486.4
expend 626.5
occupy 724.10
experience 830.8
spending money 728.19
spendthrift
n prodigal 486.2
adj prodigal 486.8
spend time 820.6
spent weakened 16.18
burnt-out 21.10
used up 388.5
worn-out 393.36
wasted 486.9
paid 624.22
sperm body fluid 13.2
copulation 75.7
spermatozoa 305.11
spermatozoa 305.11
spermicide 86.23
spew
n jet 238.9
outburst 671.6
vomiting 908.8
v salivate 13.6
run out 190.13
jet 238.20
erupt 671.13
disgorge 908.25
vomit 908.26
sphere
n space 158.1
domain 231.2
rank 245.2
ball 282.2
arena 463.1
occupation 724.4
science 927.10
stars 1070.4
v ball 282.7
spheres of influence
609.5
sphincter 280.2
spice
n flavoring 63.3
zest 68.2
fragrance 70.1
admixture 796.7
v flavor 63.7
spick and span 79.26
spicy zestful 68.7
fragrant 70.9
risqué 666.7
interesting 982.19
spider spinner 271.5
insect 311.31
spider's web 271.1

spiel
n sales talk 734.5
v publicize 352.15
speak 524.21
declaim 543.10
spiff up 5.41
spiffy chic 578.13
excellent 998.13
spigot valve 239.10
stopper 293.4
spike
n rig 179.5
thorn 285.5
stopper 293.4
plant part 310.25
ear of corn 310.27
card 758.2
v disable 19.9
perforate 292.15
stab 459.25
adulterate 796.12
thwart 1011.15
spill
n tumble 194.3
overturn 205.2
overflow 238.6
stopper 293.4
lighter 1020.4
v overflow 238.17
betray 351.6
confess 351.7
waste 486.4
spill over
overflow 238.17
superabound 992.8
spill the beans
disclose 351.4
betray 351.6
inform on 551.13
spillway 239.2
spin
n aspect 33.3
ride 177.7
air maneuver 184.15
perversion 265.2
misrepresentation
350.1
partiality 650.3
tennis play 748.2
tendency 895.1
rotation 914.1
whirl 914.2
v turn round 163.9
move 172.5
maneuver aircraft
184.40
eddy 238.21
make threads 271.6
rotate 914.9
whirl 914.11
adv at top speed 756.5
spin a long yarn 538.8
spindle 914.5
spindly
unsteady 16.16
lean 270.17
spine ridge 237.5
bulge 283.3
thorn 285.5
supporter 900.2
spineless weak 16.12
weak-willed 362.12

inconstant 853.7
spinning wheel 271.5
spin-off
  adjunct 254.1
  aftermath 816.3
  effect 886.1
  extract 892.3
spin one's wheels
  be impotent 19.7
  be useless 391.8
  miss 410.14
spin out
  v lengthen 267.6
  protract 538.8
  prolong 826.9
  postpone 845.9
  sustain 855.4
  adv at top speed 756.5
spinster woman 77.5
  spinner 271.5
  unmarried woman
    565.4
spiny pointed 285.9
  difficult 1012.17
spiracle
  outlet 190.9
  air passage 239.13
spiral
  n air maneuvers
    184.13
  coil 281.2
  circuitousness 913.1
  whirl 914.2
  galaxy 1070.6
  v maneuver aircraft
    184.40
  ascend 193.8
  circle 913.5
  rotate 914.9
  adj curled 281.8
  circuitous 913.7
  rotary 914.15
spiraling up 193.1
spiral notebook 549.11
spiral staircase 193.3
spire
  n summit 198.2
  tower 272.6
  projection 285.4
  leaf 310.17
  stem 310.19
  v ascend 193.8
  take off 193.10
  tower 272.10
spirit
  n animation 17.4
  passion 93.2
  heart 93.3
  eagerness 101.1
  zeal 101.2
  gaiety 109.4
  extract 192.8
  content 196.5
  milieu 209.3
  life force 306.3
  liveliness 330.2
  enterprise 330.7
  pluck 359.3
  fortitude 492.6
  meaning 518.1
  eloquence 544.4
  pagan diety 678.5

supernatural being
  678.12
spiritualism 689.5
theosophy 689.18
intangible thing 763.3
essence 766.2
nature 766.4
inner nature 766.5
psyche 918.4
genius 919.8
mood 977.4
specter 987.1
v inspire 375.20
Spirit 677.6
spirit away 482.20
spirited energetic 17.13
  eager 101.8
  zealous 101.9
  cheerful 109.14
  active 330.17
  resolute 492.18
  eloquent 544.12
the Spirit of God
  677.12
spirits liquor 88.13
  gaiety 109.4
  the gods 678.1
  mood 977.4
spiritual sacred 685.7
  psychic 689.24
  godly 692.9
  supernatural 869.15
  mental 918.7
  attitudinal 977.7
  spectral 987.7
  immaterial 1051.7
spiritual father 699.5
spiritual healer 90.9
spirochete 85.41
spit
  n body fluid 2.22
  saliva 13.3
  sibilation 57.1
  jet 238.9
  point of land 283.9
  fire iron 1019.12
  v salivate 13.6
  snapping noise 56.7
  sibilate 57.2
  growl 60.4
  show resentment
    152.14
  jet 238.20
  perforate 292.15
  rain 316.9
  stab 459.25
spit and polish
  meticulousness 339.3
  pretext 376.1
  strictness 425.1
  fastidiousness 495.1
spite hate 103.1
  spitefulness 144.6
  hostility 589.3
  grudge 589.5
spit it out 351.7
spitting 56.2
spitting image
  image 349.5
  the same 777.3
splash
  n spottiness 47.3

ripple 52.5
lap 238.8
display 501.4
mark 517.5
stain 1003.3
sprinkle 1063.5
v ripple 52.11
spatter 80.18
lap 238.19
cut a dash 501.13
sprinkle 770.6
dramatize 996.16
spot 1003.5
moisten 1063.12
splashdown 1073.2
splashy
  showy 501.19
  slimy 1060.14
  watery 1063.16
splat
  n explosive sound
    56.1
  wood 1052.3
  v make explosive
    sound 56.6
splatter
  n rain 316.1
  stain 1003.3
  sprinkle 1063.5
  v drum 55.4
  spatter 80.18
  sprinkle 770.6
  spot 1003.5
  moisten 1063.12
splay
  n expansion 259.1
  dispersion 770.1
  v diverge 171.5
  lie 201.5
  spread 259.6
  open 292.11
  disperse 770.4
  adj sprawled 201.8
  spread 259.11
spleen
  viscera 2.14
  unpleasure 96.1
  ill humor 110.1
  melancholy 112.5
  weariness 118.3
  bitterness 152.3
splendid
  grandiose 501.21
  illustrious 662.19
  good 998.12
  superb 998.15
  gorgeous 1015.20
  bright 1024.32
splendor
  grandeur 501.5
  illustriousness 662.6
  gorgeousness 1015.6
  brightness 1024.4
splice
  n joining 799.1
  fastening 799.3
  v join in marriage
    563.14
  weave 740.6
  put together 799.5
  bind 799.9
spline 271.4

splint
  n medical dressing
    86.33
  v treat 91.24
splinter
  n scrap 248.3
  thinness 270.7
  party 617.4
  intruder 773.2
  piece 792.3
  break 801.4
  v shatter 801.13
splinter group 617.4
split
  n crack 224.2
  opening 292.1
  falling-out 456.4
  stock 738.2
  bowling 750.2
  break 801.4
  blemish 1003.1
  v laugh 116.8
  depart 188.7
  leave 222.10
  cleave 224.4
  open 292.11
  flee 368.11
  be damaged 393.23
  demolish 395.17
  fall out 456.10
  apportion 477.6
  separate 801.8
  sever 801.11
  break off 801.12
  divide up 801.18
  disintegrate 805.3
  blemish 1003.4
  adj cleft 224.7
  impaired 393.27
  severed 801.23
  halved 874.6
  blemished 1003.8
split decision 754.3
split fifty fifty
  v double 872.5
  adj two 872.6
split hairs
  differentiate 779.6
  quibble 935.9
  discriminate 943.4
split-level 228.5
split off
  diverge 171.5
  interspace 224.3
  dissent 333.4
  separate 801.8
split personality 92.20
split second 829.3
split the atom 1037.17
split the difference
  average 246.2
  compromise 468.2
  share 476.6
split ticket 609.19
splotch
  n spottiness 47.3
  mark 517.5
  stain 1003.3
  v variegate 47.7
  spatter 80.18
  mark 517.19
  spot 1003.5

splurge
n display 501.4
v cut a dash 501.13
spend 626.5

spoil
n gain 472.3
booty 482.11
v mar 393.10
decay 393.22
bungle 414.11
indulge 427.6
plunder 482.17
thwart 1011.15
offend 1014.5

spoilage decay 393.6
rot 393.7

spoiled brat 302.4

spoiler
plunderer 483.6
automobile racing 756.1

spoil for 100.16

spoke radius 171.2
step 193.5
curb 1011.7

spoken
vernacular 523.18
speech 524.30

spoken for 421.10

spokesperson
mediator 466.3
informant 551.5
deputy 576.5

sponge medical 86.33

sponge
n washing 79.5
bath 79.8
drunk 88.12
parasite 138.5
absorption 187.6
porousness 292.8
lightness 298.2
marine animal 311.30
eradicator 395.9
pulp 1061.2
v wash 79.19
feed on 138.12
absorb 187.13
obliterate 395.16
freeload 634.4
moisten 1063.12
dry 1064.6

spongy
absorbent 187.17
porous 292.20
soft 1045.11
pulpy 1061.6

sponsor
n guarantor 438.6
supporter 616.9
financer 729.9
v secure 438.9
patronize 449.15
accept the
responsibility 641.9
finance 729.15

spontaneous
voluntary 324.7
unpremeditated 365.11
instinctive 933.6
automated 1040.21

spontaneous combustion 1019.5

spontaneous generation 78.6

spoof
n hoax 356.7
v fool 356.15

spook
n specter 987.1
v frighten 127.15
discompose 810.4
haunt 987.6

spoon ladle 176.17
make love 562.15

spoonerism
wordplay 489.8
word form 526.4
grammatical error 974.7

spoon-feed 449.16

spoor odor 69.1
track 517.8
clue 517.9
hint 551.4

sporadic
not highly contagious 85.61
dispersed 770.9
nonuniform 781.3
unordered 809.12
intermittent 850.3

spore germ 85.41
microspore 305.13

sport
n hunting 382.2
loser 412.5
joke 489.6
banter 490.1
dandy 500.9
fun 743.2
toy 743.16
athletics 744.1
gambler 759.21
misfit 788.4
transformation 851.3
v wear 5.43
hunt 382.9
flaunt 501.17
play 743.23
gamble 759.23

sporting
n hunting 382.2
gambling 759.1
adj fair-minded 649.9
sports 743.30

sporting goods
dry goods 735.3
hard goods 735.4

the sport of kings
racing 457.11
horse racing 757.1

sportscaster 1033.23

sportsman
hunter 382.5
athlete 743.19
gambler 759.21

sportsmanship
competition 457.2
fairness 649.3

sportswear
clothing 5.1
dry goods 735.3

sporty
casually dressed 5.46
showy 501.19

spot
n spottiness 47.3
soil 80.5
drink 88.7
location 159.1
modicum 248.2
advertisement 352.6
mark 517.5
stigma 661.6
lights 704.18
bowling 750.1
state 764.1
intruder 773.2
crisis 842.4
stain 1003.3
predicament 1012.5
commercial 1033.20
radar signal 1035.11
v see 27.12
variegate 47.7
soil 80.16
spatter 80.18
locate 159.11
mark 517.19
sprinkle 770.6
detect 940.5
recognize 988.12
bespot 1003.5
use radar 1035.17

spot check 937.6

spotless clean 79.25
honest 644.13
virtuous 653.7
innocent 657.7
chaste 664.4
perfect 1001.6

spotlight
n publicity 352.4
lights 704.18
v manifest 348.5
emphasize 996.14
illuminate 1024.28

spotter
secret agent 576.9
detective 576.11
watchman 1007.10

spotty
spotted 47.13
discontinuous 812.4
irregular 850.3
sparse 884.5
spotted 1003.9

spouse 563.6

spout
n outlet 190.9
ascent 193.1
jet 238.9
channel 239.8
rainstorm 316.2
disgorgement 908.7
v run out 190.13
jet 238.20
pledge 438.10
chatter 540.5
declaim 543.10
erupt 671.13
overact 704.31
disgorge 908.25

sprain 393.13

sprawl
n tumble 194.3
recumbency 201.2
oversize 257.5
v rest 20.6
tumble 194.8
lie 201.5
spread 259.6
be long 267.5

spray
n perfume 70.6
jet 238.9
branch 310.18
bouquet 310.23
foam 320.2
volley 459.9
member 792.4
shot 903.4
sprinkle 1063.5
sprinkler 1063.8
vaporizer 1065.6
v jet 238.20
moisten 1063.12
vaporize 1065.8

spray can 1063.8

spread
n meal 8.5
food 10.1
space 158.1
divergence 171.1
transferal 176.1
increase 251.1
size 257.1
expansion 259.1
breadth 269.1
blanket 295.10
publication 352.1
advertisement 352.6
stock option 737.21
dispersion 770.1
caption 936.2
v extend 158.8
diverge 171.5
radiate 171.6
transfer 176.10
grow 251.6
expand 259.6
broaden 269.4
open 292.11
publish 352.10
be published 352.16
report 552.11
disperse 770.4
generalize 863.9
adj recumbent 201.8
increased 251.7
spreading 259.11
published 352.17
dispersed 770.9

spread-eagle
tumble 194.8
fell 912.5

spread far and wide 352.10

spread it on thick
exaggerate 355.3
commend 509.11

spread like wildfire
spread 259.6
be published 352.16

spread oneself too thin
overindulge 669.5

strain 725.10
overdo 992.10
spreadsheet
arranger 807.5
list 870.1
systems program
1041.12
spree
n drinking bout 88.5
revel 743.6
v go on a spree
88.28
make merry 743.24
sprig youngster 302.1
sprout 302.11
branch 310.18
member 792.4
sprightly
cheerful 109.14
active 330.17
agile 413.23
witty 489.15
spring
n progression 162.1
ascent 193.1
resort 228.27
lake 241.1
springtime 313.2
leap 366.1
motive 375.1
source of supply 386.4
group of teal 769.6
fountainhead 885.6
bedding 900.20
recoil 902.2
resilience 1046.1
elastic object 1046.3
v speed 174.8
distort 265.5
leap 366.5
blow up 395.18
exempt 430.14
release 431.5
recoil 902.6
have resilience 1046.5
adj seasonal 313.9
spring a leak 393.23
springboard 1046.3
springbok 311.5
spring fever 331.5
spring for
subsidize 478.19
pay for 624.18
spring from 886.5
spring up grow 14.2
burst forth 33.9
shoot up 193.9
mature 259.7
originate 817.13
turn up 830.6
springy quick 330.18
recoiling 902.10
pliant 1045.9
elastic 1046.7
sprinkle
n rain 316.1
spray 1063.5
v variegate 47.7
rain 316.9
baptize 701.16
spatter 770.6
moisten 1063.12

sprinkler
extinguisher 1021.3
shower 1063.8
sprint
n run 174.3
v speed 174.8
sprinter 174.5
sprite fairy 678.8
imp 680.7
specter 987.1
spritz
n jet 238.9
v jet 238.20
rain 316.9
moisten 1063.12
sprocket 285.4
sprout
n seedling 302.11
branch 310.18
offshoot 561.4
upstart 606.7
v grow 14.2
enlarge 259.7
vegetate 310.31
spruce
v clean 79.18
perfect 392.11
tidy 807.12
adj dressed up 5.45
cleaned 79.26
shapely 264.5
chic 578.13
tidy 806.8
spry active 330.17
quick 330.18
agile 413.23
spud 10.34
spume
n lightness 298.2
foam 320.2
sprinkle 1063.5
v foam 320.5
spunk vim 17.2
sperm 305.11
enterprise 330.7
pluck 359.3
fearlessness 492.4
tinder 1020.6
spur
n mountain 237.6
point of land 283.9
projection 285.4
goad 375.8
offshoot 792.4
v sharpen 285.7
goad 375.15
hasten 401.4
drive 1068.8
spurious
ungenuine 354.25
assumed 500.16
illegitimate 674.7
unauthentic 974.19
spurn
n snub 157.2
v scorn 157.4
reject 372.2
be hard to please
495.8
have nothing to do
with 586.5
repulse 907.3

banish 908.17
spur-of-the-moment
extemporaneous
365.12
hasty 401.9
spurt
n run 174.3
ascent 193.1
jet 238.9
bustle 330.4
outburst 671.6
short time 827.3
disgorgement 908.7
v make a dash 174.12
run out 190.13
shoot up 193.9
jet 238.20
make haste 401.5
disgorge 908.25
sputnik 1073.6
sputter
n staccato 55.1
sibilation 57.1
bluster 503.1
flutter 916.4
v drum 55.4
sibilate 57.2
bluster 503.3
mumble 525.9
flutter 916.12
spy
n informer 551.6
secret agent 576.9
v see 27.12
reconnoiter 937.27
detect 940.5
pry 980.4
spy glass 29.4
squab 311.28
squabble
n quarrel 456.5
v quarrel 456.11
squad
military unit 461.22
team 617.7
baseball team 745.2
football team 746.2
basketball team 747.2
hockey team 749.2
soccer team 752.2
company 769.3
squad car 179.11
squadron
military unit 461.22
navy 461.27
air force 461.29
squalid sordid 80.25
base 661.12
slovenly 809.15
terrible 999.9
squall
n cry 59.1
windstorm 318.12
storm 671.4
v cry 59.6
animal sound 60.2
wail 115.13
blow 318.20
speak 524.26
squamous 296.7
squander
consume 388.3

waste 473.5
lavish 486.3
spend 626.5
square
n instrument 200.6
enclosed place 212.3
block 230.7
plaza 230.8
plot 231.4
straightedge 277.3
old-fashioned person
841.8
conformist 866.2
four 878.1
v plumb 200.10
offset 338.5
make restitution
481.5
pay in full 624.13
agree 787.6
equalize 789.6
quadrate 878.3
adj trite 117.9
corpulent 257.18
symmetric 264.4
quadrangular 278.9
straight 644.14
just 649.8
equal 789.7
old-fogyish 841.17
conformist 866.6
exact 972.17
adv perpendicularly
200.14
exactly 972.21
square circle 754.1
square dance
dance 705.2
four 878.1
Square Deal 609.6
square deal 649.3
squared off 778.6
square meal 8.8
square off
offer resistance 453.3
raise one's hand
against 457.14
disagree 788.5
square one
beginning 817.1
new start 857.2
revolution 859.1
**square peg in a round
hole** 867.3
square-rigged 180.17
squash
n sibilation 57.1
mud 1060.8
pulp 1061.2
v silence 51.8
sibilate 57.2
cover up 345.8
extinguish 395.15
suppress 428.8
shatter 801.13
refute 957.5
soften 1045.6
pulverize 1049.9
pulp 1061.5
squat
n nothing 761.3
crouch 912.3

standing ovation 509.2
standing room only
  adj full 793.11
  phrs all present and
    accounted for 221.19
stand in the way
  1011.12
standoff
  n contrariety 778.1
  the same 789.3
  stop 856.2
  even chance 971.7
  impasse 1012.6
  adj aloof 141.12
  reticent 344.10
  unsociable 583.6
stand on ceremony
  580.6
stand one's ground
  hold out 359.9
  offer resistance 453.3
  resist 453.4
  stand fast 854.11
stand one in good stead
  387.17
stand opposed 215.4
standout
  n superior 249.4
  paragon 659.4
  celebrity 662.9
  adj eminent 247.9
  notable 996.19
stand over
  supervise 573.10
  govern 612.12
  postpone 845.9
stand pat
  balk 361.7
  bet 759.25
  be conservative
    852.6
  stand fast 854.11
standpipe 272.6
standpoint
  viewpoint 27.7
  station 159.2
  outlook 977.2
stand ready 405.14
stand shoulder to
  shoulder 450.3
standstill
  quiescence 173.3
  stop 856.2
  impasse 1012.6
stand together
  cooperate 450.3
  agree 787.6
  league 804.4
stand to reason 934.17
stand up
  not weaken 15.10
  ascend 193.8
  stand 200.7
  rise 200.8
  stay with it 360.4
  resist 453.2
  stand the test 941.10
  be true 972.8
  suffice 990.4
stand-up comedian
  humorist 489.12
  comedian 707.9

stand up for
  secure 438.9
  defend 600.10
stand up to
  confront 216.8
  offer resistance 453.3
  brave 492.11
  meet an obligation
    641.11
Stanley Cup 749.1
stanza
  musical passage
    708.24
  poetry 720.9
  fight 754.3
staphylococcus 85.41
staple
  n source of supply
    386.4
  commodity 735.2
  marketplace 736.2
  materials 1052.1
  v fasten 799.8
  adj fixed 854.14
star
  n superior 249.4
  successful person
    409.6
  skillful person 413.14
  decoration 646.5
  military insignia
    647.5
  celebrity 662.9
  movie star 706.3
  lead 707.6
  chief 996.10
  first-rater 998.6
  heavenly body 1070.8
  v rule 249.11
  dramatize 704.28
  act 704.29
  matter 996.12
  emphasize 996.14
  feature 996.15
  adj chief 249.14
starboard
  n right side 219.1
  adj right 219.4
  adv rightward 219.7
starch
  n carbohydrate 7.5
  energy 17.3
  semiliquid 1060.5
  v stiffen 1044.9
  adj prim 580.9
stardom
  great success 409.3
  distinction 662.5
  notability 996.2
stare
  n gaze 27.5
  v gaze 27.15
  wonder 122.5
  be curious 980.3
stare down gaze 27.15
  defy 454.3
  outbrave 492.12
stargaze 984.9
stark
  adj downright 247.12
  mere 248.8
  inornate 499.9

plain-speaking 535.3
  simple 797.6
  adv absolutely 793.15
stark-naked 6.14
stark-raving mad
  925.30
starlet
  movie actress 706.3
  entertainer 707.4
starlight 1024.12
star of David 881.2
starring 704.10
starry-eyed
  happy 95.15
  visionary 985.24
Stars and Stripes 647.6
Star-Spangled Banner
  647.6
start
  n shock 131.3
  starting 188.2
  point of departure
    188.5
  boundary 211.3
  advantage 249.2
  auto race 756.3
  horse race 757.3
  beginning 817.1
  jerk 904.3
  v startle 127.12
  be startled 131.5
  set out 188.8
  leap 366.5
  hunt 382.9
  break 393.23
  propose 439.5
  drive 756.4
  race 757.5
  come apart 801.9
  begin 817.7
  set in motion 903.13
start all over 855.6
starter
  baseball team 745.2
  light source 1025.1
the starting gun 188.2
starting line
  point of departure
    188.5
  boundary 211.3
startle
  astonish 122.6
  start 127.12
  frighten 127.15
  be startled 131.5
  shock 131.8
  alarm 400.3
start the ball rolling
  begin 817.7
  inaugurate 817.11
  set in motion 903.13
start up
  burst forth 33.9
  shoot up 193.9
  protrude 283.10
  leap 366.5
  begin 817.7
  make a beginning
    817.8
  inaugurate 817.11
  set in motion 903.13
starvation diet 515.2

starvation wages 991.5
starve hunger 100.19
  die 307.24
  kill 308.12
  stint 484.5
  be poor 619.5
Star Wars 460.2
star worship 697.1
stash
  n hiding place 346.4
  v secrete 346.7
  store 386.10
stasis inertness 173.4
  inaction 329.1
  permanence 852.1
stat
  n print 784.5
  v copy 784.8
state
  n region 231.5
  country 232.1
  grandeur 501.5
  pomp 501.6
  mode 764.1
  v affirm 334.5
  announce 352.12
  declare 524.24
  phrase 532.4
  specify 864.11
  assert 952.12
  adj public 312.16
state assembly 613.1
stated
  circumscribed 210.6
  affirmed 334.9
  published 352.17
  fixed 854.14
  conditional 958.8
  assured 969.20
stately
  dignified 136.12
  grandiose 501.21
  lofty 544.14
  ceremonious 580.8
statement
  affirmation 334.1
  account 349.3
  announcement 352.2
  remark 524.4
  report 549.7
  information 551.1
  declaration 598.7
  bill 628.3
  passage 708.24
  list 870.5
  premise 934.7
  testimony 956.2
  summation 1016.11
state of affairs 830.4
state of emergency
  842.4
state of grace 685.3
state of mind 977.4
state-of-the-art 840.14
state one's case 956.9
state park 397.7
state police 1007.17
state prison 429.8
stateroom cabin 197.9
  room on train 197.10
states' rights 609.4
stateside 232.3

statesman
expert 413.11
politician 610.2
state-wide 863.14
static
n audio distortion
50.13
meaninglessness
520.1
pandemonium 809.5
reception 1033.21
adj motionless 173.13
inert 173.14
passive 329.6
inactive 331.17
permanent 852.7
electric 1031.29
biostatic 1038.8
station
n status 159.2
rank 245.2
class 607.1
prestige 662.4
position 724.5
state 764.1
category 808.2
farm 1068.5
v place 159.12
stationary
motionless 173.13
passive 329.6
inactive 331.17
permanent 852.7
immovable 854.15
stationed 159.18
stationery
handwriting style
547.4
paper 1052.5
statistical
probable 967.6
numerative 1016.23
statistician
calculator 1016.14
mathematician
1016.15
statistics
baseball 745.4
football 746.4
horse racing records
757.4
mathematical
probability 967.2
figures 1016.13
statuary
n sculptor 716.6
adj sculptural 715.6
statue figure 349.6
work of art 712.10
sculpture 715.2
statuesque
dignified 136.12
giant 272.16
sculptural 715.6
comely 1015.18
stature height 272.1
authority 417.4
prestige 662.4
status station 159.2
rank 245.2
class 607.1
prestige 662.4

state 764.1
category 808.2
status quo state 764.1
circumstances 765.2
statute
prohibition 444.1
law 673.3
statutory
preceptive 419.4
legal 673.10
staunch solid 15.18
close 293.12
firm 359.12
devoted 587.21
faithful 644.20
strict 687.8
reliable 969.17
stave step 193.5
staff 273.2
musical staff 708.29
poetry 720.9
supporter 900.2
wood 1052.3
stave in 292.14
stave off
fend off 460.10
prevent 1011.14
stay
n corset 5.23
respite 20.2
sojourn 225.5
exemption 601.2
delay 845.2
stop 856.2
pause 856.3
supporter 900.2
prevention 1011.2
curb 1011.7
v be still 173.7
slow 175.9
inhabit 225.7
sojourn 225.8
stop 293.7
cohere 802.6
endure 826.6
delay 845.8
postpone 845.9
wait 845.12
remain 852.5
continue 855.3
cease 856.6
put a stop to 856.11
support 900.21
prevent 1011.13
stay-at-home
n recluse 584.5
adj untraveled 173.15
recluse 584.10
staying
n habitation 225.1
prevention 1011.2
adj resident 225.13
durable 826.10
permanent 852.7
continuing 855.7
staying power
strength 15.1
perseverance 360.1
continuance 855.1
stay of execution 845.2
stay on endure 826.6
continue 855.3

stay over 225.8
stay put be still 173.7
cohere 802.6
stand fast 854.11
stay the course
stay with it 360.4
endure 826.6
stand fast 854.11
stay with it
hold on 360.4
continue 855.3
stead location 159.1
place 159.4
steadfast firm 359.12
persevering 360.8
devoted 587.21
faithful 644.20
uniform 780.5
durable 826.10
permanent 852.7
stable 854.12
reliable 969.17
steady
n lover 104.12
v calm 670.7
stabilize 854.7
adj inexcitable 106.10
unnervous 129.2
firm 359.12
persevering 360.8
faithful 644.20
sturdy 762.7
uniform 780.5
orderly 806.6
continuous 811.8
perpetual 828.7
constant 846.5
periodic 849.7
stable 854.12
continuing 855.7
reliable 969.17
unhazardous 1006.5
steady state
continuity 811.1
stability 854.1
automation 1040.9
steak 10.17
steal
n bargain 633.3
basketball game 747.3
v creep 177.26
lurk 346.9
thieve 482.13
adopt 621.4
play 747.4
take 480.13
steal away 368.12
steal one's thunder
1011.15
stealth secrecy 345.4
cunning 415.1
steal the show 704.29
stealthy covert 345.12
in hiding 346.14
cunning 415.12
steam
n energy 17.3
power 18.1
hot water 1018.10
water 1063.3
vapor 1065.1
v cook 11.4

be angry 152.15
make angry 152.23
navigate 182.13
let out 908.24
be hot 1018.22
heat 1019.17
vaporize 1065.8
steamboat
n steamer 180.2
v navigate 182.13
steam-clean 79.18
steamed up 105.20
steamer
steamboat 180.2
marine animal 311.30
steamroller
n force 424.2
pulverizer 1049.7
v level 201.6
raze 395.19
defeat 412.9
coerce 424.8
thrust 901.12
adj coercive 424.12
steamy
lustful 75.26
fervent 93.18
heated 105.22
vaporous 1065.9
steed 311.10
steel
n symbol of strength
15.8
sword 462.5
cutlery 1039.2
hardness 1044.6
v strengthen 15.13
make unfeeling 94.6
harden 1044.7
adj firm 425.7
metal 1056.17
steel mill 739.4
steel oneself
harden one's heart
114.3
be determined 359.8
get up nerve 492.13
steely strong 15.15
gray 39.4
callous 94.12
pitiless 146.3
firm 359.12
unyielding 361.9
strict 425.7
sturdy 762.7
hard 1044.10
like steel 1056.17
steep
n precipice 200.3
slope 237.2
v extract 192.16
imbue 796.11
liquefy 1062.5
soak 1063.13
adj perpendicular
200.12
precipitous 204.18
expensive 632.11
excessive 992.16
difficult 1012.17
steeple tower 272.6
projection 285.4

steeplechase
n leap 366.1
leaping 366.3
v leap 366.5
steer
n sexlessness 75.9
male animal 76.8
cattle 311.6
tip 551.3
v direct to 161.6
take direction 161.7
pilot 182.14
guide 573.9
steerage 182.4
steer clear of
snub 157.7
turn aside 164.6
keep one's distance 261.7
avoid 368.6
have nothing to do with 586.5
steering wheel 573.5
stellar chief 249.14
theatrical 704.33
celestial 1070.25
St Elmo's fire
fire 1018.13
luminescence 1024.13
stem
n fork 171.4
prow 216.3
tube 239.6
shaft 273.1
stalk 310.19
morphology 526.3
type 548.6
lineage 560.4
source 885.5
base 900.8
v progress 162.2
fork 171.7
confront 216.8
contend against 451.4
put a stop to 856.11
stemware 1028.2
stench
n odor 69.1
stink 71.1
v stop 293.7
stencil
n printing 548.1
picture 712.11
graphic art 713.4
v portray 712.19
stenographer
shorthand writer 547.17
recorder 550.1
stentorian
loud-voiced 53.12
vociferous 59.10
step
n velocity 172.4
pace 177.11
gait 177.12
stair 193.5
short distance 223.2
degree 245.1
layer 296.1
act 328.3
attempt 403.2

footprint 517.7
interval 709.20
process 888.2
expedient 994.2
v speed 174.9
walk 177.27
measure 300.10
step aside
turn aside 164.6
dodge 368.8
resign 448.2
separate 801.8
stepbrother
extended family 559.3
stepparent's son 564.3
step by step
by degrees 245.6
in order 806.10
consecutively 811.11
step down
reduce 252.7
reduce electric current 1031.25
step forward
progress 162.2
volunteer 439.10
step in enter 189.7
mediate 466.6
step into the breach
be willing 324.3
volunteer 439.10
mediate 466.6
stepladder 193.4
step lively speed 174.9
hustle 330.13
step off
measure off 300.11
die 307.20
step on it! 401.17
step on one's toes
cause resentment 152.21
offend 156.5
step out 743.24
step out of line
disobey 327.6
go wrong 654.9
misbelieve 688.8
steppe open space 158.4
horizontal 201.3
plain 236.1
grassland 310.8
stepped-up
aggravated 119.4
increased 251.7
step up
n promotion 446.1
v aggravate 119.2
approach 167.3
accelerate 174.10
intensify 251.5
make good 409.10
electrify 1031.25
stereophonic system 50.11
stereoscopic
optical 29.10
spatial 158.9
stereotype
n habit 373.4
printing surface 548.8

v autotype 548.15
make uniform 780.4
fix 854.9
generalize 863.9
sterile
ineffective 19.15
sanitary 79.27
dull 117.6
fruitless 391.12
unproductive 890.4
sterling
n money 728.1
adj honest 644.13
monetary 728.30
genuine 972.15
superb 998.15
stern
n rear 217.1
buttocks 217.5
heel 217.7
adj harsh 144.24
unyielding 361.9
strict 425.6
steroid 7.7
stet 854.19
stethoscope 48.8
stevedore
carrier 176.7
longshoreman 183.9
stew
n food 10.11
drunk 88.12
dither 105.6
anxiety 126.1
impatience 135.1
dudgeon 152.7
flight attendant 185.4
bustle 330.4
hostess 577.5
brothel 665.9
prostitute 665.16
hodgepodge 796.6
bewilderment 970.3
confusion 984.3
predicament 1012.5
v cook 11.4
intoxicate 88.23
feel anxious 126.6
be impatient 135.4
show resentment 152.14
be angry 152.15
seethe 671.12
be hot 1018.22
boil 1019.20
steward
n ship's crew 183.6
flight attendant 185.4
provider 385.6
bailiff 574.4
agent 576.3
attendant 577.5
major-domo 577.10
treasurer 729.11
jockey 757.2
guardian 1007.6
v treat 387.12
stewardess
ship's crew 183.6
flight attendant 185.4
attendant 577.5
stew over 930.9

stick
n marijuana cigarette 87.11
spar 180.13
slim 270.8
pole 273.1
staff 273.2
punishment 605.2
baton 711.22
field hockey 749.4
supporter 900.2
wood 1052.3
dryness 1064.2
v endure 134.6
place 159.12
be still 173.7
come to a point 285.6
perforate 292.15
deceive 356.19
remain firm 359.9
persevere 360.7
injure 393.13
stall 410.16
resist 453.4
stab 459.25
overprice 632.7
fasten 799.8
cohere 802.6
stabilize 854.7
fix 854.10
stop 856.7
stump 970.14
stick around 845.12
stick by 449.13
sticker thorn 285.5
label 517.13
enigma 522.8
price 630.1
adhesive 802.4
stick in
insert 191.3
interpose 213.6
stick in one's throat 98.11
stick-in-the-mud
n slowpoke 175.5
idler 331.8
conservative 852.4
adj untraveled 173.15
stick it out
endure 134.6
persevere 360.7
resist 453.4
keep up one's courage 492.15
stand fast 854.11
persist 855.5
stickler
obstinate person 361.6
perfectionist 495.6
tyrant 575.14
stick like glue 802.8
stick one's foot in it
bungle 414.12
make a boner 974.15
stick one's head in the sand 983.2
stick out like a sore thumb
show 31.4
be manifest 348.7

the sticks
the country 233.1
remote region 261.4
stick together
put together 799.5
cohere 802.6
cement 802.9
be true 972.8
stick to it
persevere 360.7
persist 855.5
stick to one's guns
remain firm 359.9
stay with it 360.4
balk 361.7
resist 453.4
keep up one's courage
492.15
stand fast 854.11
stick up rise 200.8
protrude 283.10
rob 482.16
elevate 911.5
stick up for
back 449.13
defend 600.10
stick with it
remain firm 359.9
persevere 360.7
be conservative 852.6
persist 855.5
sticky sweaty 12.22
sentimental 93.21
adhesive 802.12
difficult 1012.17
sultry 1018.28
viscous 1060.12
moist 1063.15
stiff
n vagabond 178.3
corpse 307.16
horse 311.12
bum 331.9
proletarian 607.9
wretch 660.2
laborer 726.2
blackjack 759.11
v mistreat 389.6
adj dull 117.6
seaworthy 180.18
stone-dead 307.31
unyielding 361.9
out of practice 414.18
bungling 414.20
strict 425.7
stilted 534.3
formal 580.9
expensive 632.11
excessive 992.16
rigid 1044.11
tough 1047.4
adv firmly 425.9
stifle silence 51.8
control feelings 106.8
strangle 308.18
cover up 345.8
extinguish 395.15
suppress 428.8
moderate 670.6
obstruct 1011.12
be hot 1018.22
fight fire 1021.7

stigma sore 85.36
flower 310.26
mark 517.5
disrepute 661.6
stain 1003.3
stigmatize
variegate 47.7
vilify 512.10
designate 517.18
mark 517.19
brand 661.9
stain 1003.6
stile stairs 193.3
post 273.4
stiletto 459.25
still
n silence 51.1
distillery 88.21
photograph 714.3
vaporizer 1065.6
v silence 51.8
calm 670.7
adj silent 51.10
quiescent 173.12
motionless 173.13
dead 307.30
adv quiescently
173.18
until now 837.4
notwithstanding
338.8
stillborn born 1.4
dead 307.30
unsuccessful 410.18
still life
work of art 712.10
picture 712.11
still photograph 714.3
stilt 270.8
stimulant
n energizer 17.6
tonic 86.9
drug 87.2
adj provocative 375.27
stimulate refresh 9.2
energize 17.10
sensitize 24.7
whet 105.13
elicit 192.14
motivate 375.12
interest 982.12
stimulus energizer 17.6
excitation 105.11
incentive 375.7
cause 885.1
sting
n acrimony 17.5
pain 26.3
tingle 74.1
point 285.3
deception 356.9
goad 375.8
cheating 759.13
stinger 1000.5
v pain 26.7
bite 68.5
tingle 74.5
affect 93.14
aggressive 96.17
offend 152.21
be sharp 285.6
deceive 356.19

goad 375.15
overprice 632.7
stingy illiberal 484.9
ungenerous 651.6
sparse 884.5
meager 991.10
stink
n odor 69.1
stench 71.1
v have an odor 69.6
smell 71.4
stinker stinkard 71.3
cigar 89.4
bad person 660.6
stint
n degree 245.1
restriction 428.3
task 724.2
shift 824.3
v limit 210.5
restrict 428.9
scrimp 484.5
stipend subsidy 478.8
fee 624.5
stipple
n spottiness 47.3
engraving 713.2
v color 35.13
variegate 47.7
engrave 713.9
stipulate fight for 421.7
contract 437.5
specify 864.11
suppose 950.10
make conditional
958.4
stir
n excitement 105.4
motion 172.1
activity 330.1
bustle 330.4
jail 429.9
commotion 809.4
agitation 916.1
v awake 23.4
sensitize 24.7
affect 93.14
excite 105.12
perturb 105.14
move 172.5
be active 330.11
bustle 330.12
rouse 375.19
seethe 671.12
be turbulent 914.12
agitate 916.10
stir-fry 11.4
stirrup ear 2.10
saddle parts 900.18
stir up excite 105.12
provoke 152.24
incite 375.17
rouse 375.19
mix 796.10
agitate 916.10
stir up a hornet's nest
1012.14
stitch
n pang 26.2
scrap 248.3
piece 792.3
joint 799.4

v sew 741.4
fasten 799.8
a stitch in time 844.1
stock
n stem 310.19
animal life 311.1
humankind 312.1
means 384.2
store 386.1
assets 471.7
portion 477.5
laughingstock 508.7
race 559.4
lineage 560.4
show business 704.1
repertoire 704.9
merchandise 735.1
shares 738.2
source 885.5
belief 952.1
materials 1052.1
paper 1052.5
mineral deposit
1056.7
v provide 385.7
gather materials
1052.7
adj trite 117.9
customary 373.14
usual 868.9
stockade 429.8
stockbroker
broker 730.9
sharebroker 737.10
stock dividend 738.7
stock exchange
exchange 737.7
workplace 739.1
stockholder 737.14
stockings 5.28
stock in trade
means 384.2
supply 386.2
stock market
the market 737.1
stock exchange
737.7
stockpile
n store 386.1
reserve 386.3
accumulation 769.9
v store up 386.11
stocks and bonds
securities 738.1
guarantee 438.1
stock up
store up 386.11
gather materials
1052.7
stocky
corpulent 257.18
stubby 268.10
stodgy dull 117.6
old-fogyish 841.17
viscous 1060.12
stogie 89.4
stoic
n Spartan 134.3
adj apathetic 94.13
inexcitable 106.10
patient 134.9
quiescent 173.12

stable 854.12
stoke ignite 1019.22
fuel 1020.7
stolen 482.23
stolid
inexcitable 106.10
quiescent 173.12
stable 854.12
incurious 981.3
unimaginative 986.5
stoma 292.1
stomach
n digestive system
2.16
taste 62.1
appetite 100.7
v endure 134.8
permit 443.10
stomachache 26.5
stomp
n stamp 901.10
v way of walking
177.28
stamp 901.22
stone
n fruit seed 310.29
pavement 383.6
missile 462.18
jewel 498.6
monument 549.12
lithographic plate
713.6
hardness 1044.6
building material
1052.2
rock 1057.1
v intoxicate 88.23
cover face 295.23
strike dead 308.17
pelt 459.27
execute 604.17
adj rock 1057.10
stone's throw 223.2
stone-cold
stone-dead 307.31
cold 1022.14
stoned
unconscious 25.8
high 87.23
drunk 88.33
stonewall be silent 51.6
outwit 415.11
delay 845.8
hinder 1011.10
stony callous 94.12
rugged 288.7
without money 619.10
hard 1044.10
rocky 1057.11
stooge
n flatterer 138.4
follower 166.2
dupe 358.1
instrument 384.4
loser 412.5
figurehead 575.5
retainer 577.1
flunky 616.8
actor 707.2
v act 704.29
stool
n defecation 12.2

feces 12.4
toilet 12.11
v defecate 12.13
betray 351.6
inform on 551.13
stool pigeon shill 357.5
informer 551.6
stoop
n descent 194.1
porch 197.21
plunge 367.1
crouch 912.3
v humble oneself
137.8
fawn 138.7
condescend 141.8
descend 194.5
plunge 367.6
bow down 433.10
incur disgrace 661.7
crouch 912.8
stop
n standstill 173.3
destination 186.5
sojourn 225.5
obstruction 293.3
stopper 293.4
speech sound 524.13
punctuation 530.15
delay 845.2
stoppage 856.2
prevention 1011.2
curb 1011.7
impasse 1012.6
v muffle 51.9
daunt 127.18
quiet 173.8
sojourn 225.8
stop up 293.7
be vigilant 339.8
disaccustom 374.2
break the habit 374.3
cease to use 390.4
fend off 460.10
swear off 668.8
end 819.5
delay 845.8
cease 856.6
come to a halt 856.7
put a stop to 856.11
stay 1011.13
stop at nothing 359.10
stopgap
n stopper 293.4
improvisation 365.5
expedient 994.2
adj extemporaneous
365.12
substitute 861.8
makeshift 994.7
stop in one's tracks
daunt 127.18
strike dead 308.17
stop 856.7
shoot 903.12
stop it! 856.13
stop light signal 517.15
traffic light 1025.4
stopoff 225.5
stop over sojourn 225.8
visit 582.19
stoppage seizure 85.6

obstruction 293.3
end 819.1
delay 845.2
cessation 856.2
prevention 1011.2
stopped
stopped up 293.11
phonetic 524.31
late 845.16
stopper
n plug 293.4
cover 295.5
baseball team 745.2
finishing stroke
819.4
v stop up 293.7
top 295.21
stop the clock 852.6
storage
placement 159.6
stowage 386.5
storehouse 386.6
fee 630.6
computer memory
1041.7
store
n provisions 10.5
supply 386
hoard 386.1
storehouse 386.6
preserve 397.7
gain 472.3
market 736.1
workplace 739.1
casino 759.19
belief 952.1
materials 1052.1
v load 159.15
provide 385.7
stow 386.10
put away 390.6
gather materials
1052.7
store-bought
tailored 5.47
bought 733.11
storekeeper
provider 385.6
merchant 730.2
the stork 1.1
storm
n frenzy 105.9
fit of anger 152.9
windstorm 318.12
attack 459.6
tempest 671.4
v be excitable 105.16
be angry 152.15
blow 318.20
raid 459.20
bluster 503.3
rage 671.11
cause trouble 1012.14
storm cellar
cellar 197.17
shelter 1008.3
storm clouds
bird of ill omen 133.6
danger 1005.1
storm troops
elite troops 461.15
army 461.23

stormy
passionate 105.29
tempestuous 318.23
cloudy 319.7
turbulent 671.18
gloomy 1026.14
story
n floor 197.23
layer 296.1
lie 354.11
joke 489.6
record 549.1
news item 552.3
gossip 552.7
history 719.1
tale 719.3
work of fiction 722.3
plot 722.4
v lie 354.18
storybook
n book 554.1
adj visionary 985.24
storyteller
liar 357.9
author 547.15
narrator 718.4
yarn spinner 722.5
stout strong 15.15
firm 15.18
hale 83.12
corpulent 257.18
courageous 492.17
sturdy 762.7
stouthearted 492.17
stove kiln 742.5
heater 1019.10
stove in 292.14
stovepipe 239.14
stow load 159.15
store 386.10
put away 390.6
stowaway 773.4
stow away
secrete 346.7
store 386.10
straddle
n stock option 737.21
v extend 158.8
way of walking 177.28
rest on 900.22
pass 909.8
adv on 900.25
straddle the fence
n be a timeserver
363.9
v hesitate 362.7
remain neutral 467.5
Stradivarius 711.5
strafe 459.22
straggle stray 164.4
lag 166.4
wander 177.23
way of walking 177.28
be behind 217.8
be long 267.5
straggler 178.2
straight
n heterosexual 75.13
straight line 277.2
adj directional 161.12
straight-lined 277.6
sober 516.3

stress
   n psychological stress
      92.17
   distress 96.5
   anxiety 126.1
   tension 128.3
   urge 375.6
   accent 524.11
   meter 720.7
   exertion 725.2
   thrust 901.2
   urgency 996.4
   adversity 1010.1
   v strain 725.10
   thrust 901.12
   emphasize 996.14
stress and strain
   tension 128.3
   strain 725.2
stress pattern 524.11
stretch
   n range 158.2
   walk 177.10
   distance 261.1
   length 267.1
   strain 725.2
   exercise 725.6
   racetrack 743.11
   period 823.1
   spell 824.1
   term 824.4
   overextension 992.7
   elasticity 1046.1
   extension 1046.2
   v exercise 84.4
   reach 158.8
   expand 259.4
   become larger 259.5
   be long 267.5
   lengthen 267.6
   exaggerate 355.3
   hang 604.18
   strain 725.10
   suffice 990.4
   overextend 992.13
   extend 1046.4
   adj elastic 1046.7
stretcher 900.19
stretcher-bearer 176.7
stretch limo 179.13
stretch of the
      imagination 985.5
stretch one's luck 493.6
stretch the legs 177.29
stretch the truth
   lie 354.18
   exaggerate 355.3
stretchy sleepy 22.21
   elastic 1046.7
strewn 770.9
striation stripe 47.5
   furrow 290.1
   line 517.6
stricken affected 93.23
   wretched 96.26
   overcome 112.29
   unnerved 128.14
strict
   meticulous 339.12
   imperious 417.16
   exacting 425.6
   fastidious 495.9

conscientious 644.15
   orthodox 687.8
   precise 972.17
strict interpretation
      687.5
strictly on the up-
      and-up 972.13
strictly speaking
   truly 972.18
   to be exact 972.22
stricture
   contraction 260.1
   narrowing 270.2
   censure 510.3
   criticism 510.4
   hindrance 1011.1
stride
   n velocity 172.4
   step 177.11
   gait 177.12
   distance 261.1
   jazz 708.9
   v walk 177.27
   way of walking 177.28
   straddle 900.22
strident
   acrimonious 17.14
   stridulant 58.12
   dissonant 61.4
strife quarrel 456.5
   contention 457.1
strike
   n revolt 327.4
   objection 333.2
   score 409.5
   attack 459.1
   walkout 727.5
   baseball 745.3
   bowling 750.2
   stop 856.2
   discovery 940.1
   v impress 93.15
   delete 255.12
   revolt 327.7
   object 333.5
   attack 459.14
   advance against
      459.17
   print 548.14
   slap 604.12
   go on strike 727.10
   stop work 856.8
   collide 901.13
   hit 901.14
   shoot 903.12
   occur to 930.18
   impress 930.19
   discover 940.2
strike a balance
   average 246.2
   weigh 297.10
   be neutral 467.6
   compromise 468.2
   pay in full 624.13
   keep accounts 628.8
   be moderate 670.5
   equalize 789.6
strike a bargain
   sign 437.7
   compromise 468.2
   make a deal 731.18
strike a blow 328.5

strike a pose 500.13
strike a sour note 61.3
strike back 506.4
strikebreaker
   apostate 363.5
   scab 727.8
strike dead
   astonish 122.6
   fell 308.17
strike down
   put an end to 395.12
   repeal 445.2
strike it rich
   grow rich 618.10
   be fortunate 1009.11
strike oil 1009.11
strike one's colors
      433.8
strike one's fancy
   please 95.5
   enamor 104.23
strike one as 33.10
strikeout 745.3
strike out set out 188.8
   delete 255.12
   obliterate 395.16
   fail 410.10
   baseball 745.5
   eliminate 772.5
   originate 891.12
strike out at
   lash out at 459.16
   criticize 510.14
strike out for 161.9
strike terror into
      127.17
strike the first blow
      457.14
strike up 708.37
strike up a
      conversation 541.9
strike up a tune 708.37
strike up the band
      708.37
strike while the iron is
      hot 842.8
striking
   n deletion 255.5
   coining 728.24
   adj powerful 18.12
   exciting 105.30
   wonderful 122.10
   remarkable 247.10
   conspicuous 348.12
   eloquent 544.11
   notable 996.19
striking resemblance
      783.4
string
   n swimwear 5.29
   step 193.5
   line 267.3
   cord 271.2
   utterance 524.3
   team 617.7
   violin family 711.5
   chord 711.20
   bowling 750.2
   company 769.3
   part of writing 792.2
   series 811.2
   procession 811.3

condition 958.2
   v tune 708.36
   continue 811.4
string along
   follow 166.3
   deceive 356.14
   flatter 511.6
stringent
   acrimonious 17.14
   harsh 144.24
   strict 425.6
stringer 555.4
string musician 710.5
string out
   lengthen 267.6
   protract 538.8
   align 811.5
   postpone 845.9
   sustain 855.4
strings
   proviso 421.3
   orchestra 710.12
   stringed instrument
      711.2
   backstairs influence
      893.3
string up 604.18
stringy
   threadlike 271.7
   tough 1047.4
   viscous 1060.12
strip
   n runway 184.23
   a length 267.2
   line 267.3
   strap 271.4
   stripe 517.6
   stock option 737.21
   horse racing 757.1
   v divest 6.5
   undress 6.7
   peel 6.8
   excise 255.10
   strip clean 480.24
   simplify 797.4
   tear apart 801.14
   dismiss 908.19
stripe
   n streak 47.5
   line 267.3
   slash 517.6
   corporal punishment
      604.4
   military insignia
      647.5
   nature 766.4
   kind 808.3
   slap 901.8
   disposition 977.3
   v variegate 47.7
   mark 517.19
   whip 604.13
striped streaked 47.15
   netlike 170.11
strip mining 1056.8
stripper nudity 6.3
   dancer 705.3
   entertainer 707.1
   separator 801.7
strive endeavor 403.5
   contend 457.13
   struggle 725.11

strobe light 1024.7
stroke
  n touch 73.1
  seizure 85.6
  paralysis 85.27
  pain 96.5
  act 328.3
  attempt 403.2
  stratagem 415.3
  compliment 509.6
  line 517.6
  upheaval 671.5
  work 725.4
  tennis 748.2
  hockey 749.6
  golf swing 751.3
  instant 829.3
  hit 901.4
  spasm 916.6
  expedient 994.2
  v pet 73.8
  delight 95.10
  encourage 375.21
  exploit 387.16
  flatter 511.6
  rub 1042.6
stroke of luck 1009.3
stroll
  n slow motion 175.2
  walk 177.10
  gait 177.12
  v go slowly 175.6
  wander 177.23
  way of walking 177.28
stroller wanderer 178.2
  baby carriage 179.6
  actor 707.2
strong forceful 15.15
  energetic 17.13
  powerful 18.12
  pungent 68.8
  strong-smelling 69.10
  malodorous 71.5
  hale 83.12
  alcoholic 88.37
  great 247.6
  tainted 393.41
  accented 524.31
  eloquent 544.11
  sturdy 762.7
  influential 893.13
  tough 1047.4
strong-arm
  v exert strength 15.12
  coerce 424.8
  adj coercive 424.12
strongbox
  storehouse 386.6
  treasury 729.12
stronghold
  fortification 460.6
  refuge 1008.1
strong language
  cursing 513.3
  vigor 544.3
strong-minded
  strong-willed 359.15
  intelligent 919.12
strong point
  talent 413.4
  stronghold 460.6
  specialty 865.1

good reasoning 934.10
strop
  n strip 271.4
  v sharpen 285.7
struck down 445.3
structural
  formal 266.6
  semantic 518.12
  linguistic 523.17
  grammatical 530.17
  organizational 807.15
  constructional 891.15
structure
  n house 228.5
  form 262.1
  arrangement 266
  construction 266.1
  building 266.2
  texture 294.1
  clearness 521.2
  syntax 530.2
  plot 722.4
  composition 795.1
  order 806.1
  v construct 266.5
  compose 795.3
  order 806.4
strudel 10.39
struggle
  n endeavor 403.1
  contention 457.1
  fight 457.4
  exertion 725.3
  v endeavor 403.5
  contend 457.13
  strive 725.11
  flounder 916.15
  have difficulty
    1012.11
strum 708.40
strut
  n gait 177.12
  swagger 501.8
  v way of walking
    177.28
  show defiance 454.5
  swagger 501.15
stub cigarette 89.5
  tail 217.6
  label 517.13
  extremity 819.2
stubble beard 3.8
  remainder 256.1
  bristle 288.3
  refuse 391.4
stubborn
  persevering 360.8
  obstinate 361.8
  strict 425.7
  tenacious 802.12
  inflexible 1044.12
  tough 1047.4
stubborn as a mule
    361.8
stubby 268.10
stub one's toe 414.12
stucco 295.25
stuck fastened 799.14
  cohesive 802.10
  caught 854.16
  baffled 970.26
  at an impasse 1012.24

stranded 1012.27
stuck-up
  conceited 140.11
  arrogant 141.9
  contemptuous 157.8
stuck with 643.8
stud
  n sex object 75.4
  man 76.5
  male animal 76.8
  beam 273.6
  knob 283.3
  horse 311.10
  print 517.7
  jockey 757.2
  poker 759.10
  v variegate 47.7
  roughen 288.4
  sprinkle 770.6
studded spotted 47.13
  knobbed 283.17
  gnarled 288.8
  bristly 288.9
  nappy 294.7
  ornamented 498.11
  sprinkled 770.10
  teeming 883.9
  illuminated 1024.39
student pupil 572.1
  scholar 928.3
stud farm 1068.5
studied
  intentional 380.8
  affected 533.9
  reasoned 934.21
studio library 197.6
  atelier 712.17
  workplace 739.1
  radio station 1033.6
study
  n diagnosis 91.12
  library 197.6
  intention 380.1
  discussion 541.7
  treatise 556.1
  branch of learning
    568.8
  studying 570.3
  work of art 712.10
  drawing 712.13
  office 739.7
  science 927.10
  consideration 930.2
  thoughtfulness 930.3
  examination 937.3
  engrossment 982.3
  abstractedness 984.2
  retreat 1008.5
  v endeavor 403.5
  discuss 541.12
  learn 570.12
  consider 930.12
  examine 937.23
  pay attention 982.8
  memorize 988.17
stuff
  n fabric 4.1
  essential content
    196.5
  equipment 385.4
  game 745.3
  substance 762.2

essence 766.2
  matter 1050.2
  materials 1052.1
  v nourish 8.19
  gorge 8.25
  cram 196.7
  clog 293.7
  embalm 397.10
  gluttonize 672.4
  fill 793.7
  overload 992.15
  satiate 993.4
stuffed clogged 293.11
  full 793.11
  overfull 992.20
  satiated 993.6
stuffed shirt 501.9
stuffing
  n food 10.26
  padding 196.3
  extra 254.4
  blockage 293.5
  embalming 397.3
  adj gluttonous 672.6
stuffy malodorous 71.5
  dull 117.6
  airless 173.16
  unyielding 361.9
  perverse 361.11
  prudish 500.19
  pompous 501.22
  old-fogyish 841.17
  conformist 866.6
  narrow-minded
    979.10
  unimaginative 986.5
  sultry 1018.28
stultify suppress 428.8
  neutralize 899.7
  make a fool of 922.7
stumble
  n tumble 194.3
  collapse 410.3
  bungle 414.5
  flounder 916.8
  slip 974.4
  v tumble 194.3
  not know one's own
    mind 362.6
  bungle 414.11
  stammer 525.8
  flounder 916.15
  err 974.9
stumblebum 414.9
stumble on
  arrive at 186.7
  come across 940.3
stumbling block 1011.4
stump
  n remainder 256.1
  public speaking 543.1
  art equipment 712.18
  piece 792.3
  extremity 819.2
  platform 900.13
  v plod 175.7
  way of walking 177.28
  make a speech 543.9
  electioneer 609.40
  go into politics 610.13
  boggle 970.14
  thwart 1011.15

stumper enigma 522.8
  campaigner 610.10
stumpy
  deformed 265.12
  stubby 268.10
  low 274.7
stun deaden 25.4
  deafen 49.5
  din 53.7
  numb 94.8
  astonish 122.6
  terrify 127.17
  startle 131.8
stung 96.23
stun gun 462.10
stunning
  deadening 25.9
  astonishing 122.12
  frightening 127.28
  terrifying 127.29
  surprising 131.11
  excellent 998.13
  beautiful 1015.21
stunt
  n act 328.3
  acting 704.8
  v air maneuver 184.40
  shorten 268.6
stunted dwarf 258.13
  undeveloped 406.12
  incomplete 794.4
  meager 991.10
stunt man 185.1
stupefy deaden 25.4
  numb 94.8
  astonish 122.6
  terrify 127.17
stupendous
  wonderful 122.10
  large 247.7
  huge 257.20
  extraordinary 869.14
stupid dumb 921.15
  foolish 922.8
stupidity
  stupidness 921.3
  foolishness 922.1
  folly 922.4
  blunder 974.5
stupor sleep 22.6
  unconsciousness 25.2
  trance 92.19
  apathy 94.4
  languor 331.6
sturdy strong 15.15
  firm 15.18
  hale 83.12
  stable 762.7
stutter
  n stammering 525.3
  v stammer 525.8
sty pigsty 80.11
  eye disease 85.36
  hovel 228.11
  blemish 1003.1
style
  n clothing 5.1
  aspect 33.3
  form 262.1
  flower part 310.26
  behavior 321.1
  preference 371.5

  manner 384.1
  skill 413.1
  motif 498.7
  name 527.3
  way of speaking 532.2
  fashion 578.1
  lines 712.8
  engraving tool 713.8
  race 753.3
  fight 754.3
  mode 764.4
  kind 808.3
  specialty 865.1
  v name 527.11
  phrase 532.4
stylish dressed up 5.45
  skillful 413.22
  modish 578.12
stylus 50.11
stymie
  n golf 751.3
  v stop 1011.13
styptic pencil 260.6
Styx
  river of death 307.4
  Hades 682.4
suave smooth 287.9
  glib 504.18
sub
  n submarine 180.9
  baseball 745.2
  football 746.2
  substitute 861.2
  adj inferior 250.6
subatomic particle
  minute particle 258.8
  elementary particle
    1037.6
subclass 808.5
subcommittee
  committee 423.2
  delegation 576.13
subconscious
  n psyche 92.28
  inmost mind 918.3
  adj unconscious 92.41
subconscious urge
  933.2
subcutaneous
  n injection 91.17
  adj cutaneous 2.25
subdivide
  analyze 800.6
  apportion 801.18
  classify 808.6
  bisect 874.4
  discriminate 943.4
subdue
  muffle 51.9
  relieve 120.5
  conquer 412.10
  suppress 428.8
  master 432.9
  moderate 670.6
  calm 670.7
  soften 1045.6
subhead
  n caption 936.2
  v focus on 936.3
subhuman
  cruel 144.26
  animal 311.38

subject
  n citizen 227.4
  vassal 432.7
  syntax 530.2
  discipline 568.8
  field of study 570.3
  passage 708.24
  plot 722.4
  doer 726.1
  topic 936.1
  examinee 937.18
  experimental subject
    941.7
  v subjugate 432.8
  adj inferior 250.6
  dependent 432.13
subjection
  inferiority 250.1
  subjugation 432.1
  submission 433.1
subjective
  introverted 92.39
  intrinsic 766.7
  mental 918.7
subjectivism 1051.3
subject oneself 652.3
subject to
  v impose 643.4
  adj liable to 896.6
  contingent 958.9
  conj provided 958.12
subjugate
  conquer 412.10
  subject 432.8
  appropriate 480.19
  domineer 612.16
sublet
  v rent 615.15
  rent out 615.16
  adj employed 615.20
sublimate
  n dregs 256.2
  v refine 79.22
  suppress 106.8
  vaporize 1065.8
sublime
  v refine 79.22
  vaporize 1065.8
  adj blissful 97.9
  distinguished 247.9
  lofty 272.14
  eloquent 544.14
  magnanimous 652.6
  eminent 662.18
  raised 911.9
  gorgeous 1015.20
subliminal
  n psyche 92.28
  adj subconscious
    92.41
  instinctive 933.6
submarine
  n sub 180.9
  diving equipment
    367.5
  adj underwater 275.13
submerge
  submarines 182.47
  sink 194.6
  overflow 238.17
  submerse 367.7
  flood 1063.14

submersible
  n submarine 180.9
  adj submergible 367.9
submission
  resignation 134.2
  obeisance 155.2
  obedience 326.1
  submittal 433.1
  offer 439.1
  consent 441.1
submissive
  resigned 134.10
  servile 138.13
  assenting 332.13
  compliant 433.12
  conformable 866.5
  pliant 1045.9
  obedient 326.3
  humblehearted 137.11
  obeisant 155.10
  downtrodden 432.16
  consenting 441.4
submit affirm 334.5
  nominate 371.19
  advise 422.5
  comply 433.6
  offer 439.4
  propose 439.5
  obey 326.2
  acquiesce 441.3
  yield 1045.7
subordinate
  n inferior 250.2
  junior 432.5
  retainer 577.1
  nonessential 767.2
  v subjugate 432.8
  arrange 807.11
  adj inferior 250.6
  subject 432.13
  unessential 767.4
suborn bribe 378.3
  induce 885.11
subpar 999.9
subplot 722.4
subpoena
  n summons 598.2
  v summon 420.11
  summons 598.13
sub rosa 345.17
subscribe abet 449.14
  contribute 478.14
  belong 617.15
subscription
  ratification 332.4
  giving 478.1
  donation 478.6
  signature 527.10
subsequent
  succeeding 814.4
  after 834.4
subservient
  servile 138.13
  inferior 250.6
  instrumental 384.8
  subject 432.13
  submissive 433.12
  deferential 433.16
  helping 449.20
subset 792.1
subside quiet 173.8
  sink 194.6

decrease 252.6
descend 297.15
decline 393.17
subsidiary
  n nonessential 767.2
  adj helping 449.20
  endowed 478.26
  unessential 767.4
subsidize
  provide 385.7
  support 449.12
  finance 478.19
  treat 624.19
  sponsor 729.15
  maintain 900.21
subsidy provision 385.1
  support 449.3
  grant 478.8
  treat 624.8
  financing 729.2
  upkeep 900.1
subsist remain 256.5
  live 306.7
  support oneself 385.12
  exist 760.8
  endure 826.6
  persist 852.5
subsistence
  n accommodations
    385.3
  support 449.3
  existence 760.1
  adj meager 991.10
subsisting 760.13
subspecies
  humankind 312.1
  part 792.1
  classifications 808.5
substance
  content 196.5
  quantity 244.1
  meaning 518.1
  summary 557.2
  warrant 600.6
  wealth 618.1
  funds 728.14
  substantiality 762.1
  stuff 762.2
  essence 766.2
  major part 791.6
  topic 936.1
  salient point 996.6
  matter 1050.2
substance abuse 87.1
substandard
  vernacular 523.18
  below par 1004.10
substantiate
  itemize 765.6
  test 941.8
  confirm 956.11
  materialize 1050.9
substantive
  n noun 530.5
  adj grammatical
    530.17
  substantial 762.6
  essential 766.9
  vital 996.23
substitute
  n surrogate 92.31
  deputy 576.1

supporting actor
  707.7
baseball team 745.2
football team 746.2
successor 816.4
replacement 861.2
  v exchange 861.4
  adj alternate 861.8
substitution
  defense mechanism
    92.23
  compensation 338.1
  switch 861
  substitute 861.2
subterfuge
  secrecy 345.1
  concealment 346.1
  deception 356.1
  trick 356.6
  pretext 376.1
  stratagem 415.3
  quibbling 935.5
subterranean 275.12
subtext 519.2
subtile dainty 248.7
  tenuous 763.6
  shrewd 919.15
  discriminating 943.7
subtitle
  n book 554.12
  caption 936.2
  v focus on 936.3
subtle
  soft-colored 35.21
  dainty 248.7
  thin 270.16
  rare 299.4
  meticulous 339.12
  cunning 415.12
  nice 495.11
  elegant 496.9
  tenuous 763.6
  complex 798.4
  shrewd 919.15
  discriminating 943.7
  exact 972.17
subtle distinction
  margin 779.2
  distinction 943.3
subtotal 253.2
subtract deduct 255.9
  separate 801.8
  calculate 1016.17
subtropics zone 231.3
  hot place 1018.11
suburb 230.1
suburban
  surrounding 209.8
  urban 230.11
  upper-class 607.10
  ordinary 1004.8
subversion
  overturn 205.2
  fall 395.3
  indoctrination 857.5
  revolution 859.1
  refutation 957.2
subversionary 395.26
subversive
  n rebel 327.5
  saboteur 357.11
  radical 611.12

revolutionist 859.3
  adj rebellious 327.11
  destructive 395.26
  radical 611.20
  changed 851.10
subway train 179.14
  underground area
    284.5
subzero 1022.14
succeed
  accomplish 407.4
  prevail 409.7
  triumph 411.3
  change hands 629.4
  be a hit 704.28
  be next 814.2
  follow 816.5
  come after 834.3
  substitute for 861.5
  prosper 1009.7
succession
  authority 417.12
  inheritance 479.2
  lineage 560.4
  offspring 561.1
  devolution 629.2
  series 811.2
  sequence 814.1
  subsequence 834.1
  constancy 846.2
  thoughts 930.4
successive
  consecutive 811.9
  succeeding 814.4
  subsequent 834.4
successor
  follower 166.2
  survivor 256.3
  heir 479.5
  replacement 816.4
  sequel 834.2
  substitute 861.2
successsion 861.1
success story 409.3
succinct short 268.8
  concise 537.6
  aphoristic 973.6
succor
  n remedy 86.1
  aid 449.1
  v aid 449.11
  benefit 592.3
succulent
  n plant 310.4
  adj edible 8.33
  tasty 63.8
  delectable 97.10
  interesting 982.19
  fluid 1059.4
  pulpy 1061.6
succumb burn out 21.5
  faint 25.5
  die 307.19
  perish 395.23
  lose 412.12
  submit 433.6
such 783.3
such as 783.12
suck
  n sip 8.4
  drink 88.7
  drawing in 187.5

  v sip 8.29
  perform oral sex 75.22
  draw in 187.12
  draw off 192.12
suck dry exploit 387.16
  consume 388.3
  strip 480.24
sucked into 897.5
sucker
  n sprout 302.11
  branch 310.18
  dupe 358.2
  customer 733.4
  cheater 759.22
  trusting soul 953.4
  v exploit 387.16
suck in drink 8.29
  draw in 187.12
  lure 377.5
suckle
  breast-feed 8.19
  drink 8.29
  draw in 187.12
  foster 449.16
suckling 302.9
suck up to
  curry favor 138.9
  cultivate 587.12
suction
  drawing in 187.5
  extraction 192.3
  favor 893.2
sudden
  adj unexpected 131.10
  impulsive 365.9
  precipitate 401.10
  abrupt 829.5
  adv suddenly 829.9
sudden death
  fatal disease 85.2
  early death 307.5
sudden death overtime
  749.3
sudden infant death
  syndrome 85.2
suddenly
  unexpectedly 131.14
  abruptly 268.13
suds
  n beer 88.16
  foam 320.2
  v foam 320.5
sue
  petition 440.10
  solicit 440.14
  court 562.21
  litigate 598.12
suet 10.13
suffer
  feel pain 26.8
  ail 85.45
  hurt 96.19
  endure 134.5
  submit 433.6
  countenance 443.10
  be punished 604.20
  experience 830.8
sufferer
  sick person 85.42
  victim 96.11
suffer the
  consequences 604.20

sufficient
satisfactory 107.11
valid 972.14
sufficing 990.6
tolerable 998.20
suffix
n addition 254.2
morphology 526.3
sequel 816.1
v add 253.4
place after 814.3
suffocate die 307.24
strangle 308.18
extinguish 395.15
suppress 428.8
obstruct 1011.12
be hot 1018.22
suffrage vote 371.6
participation 476.1
franchise 609.17
suffragette
suffrage 609.17
women's rightist
642.5
suffuse
pervade 221.7
imbue 796.11
suffused with light
1024.39
sugar
n carbohydrate 7.5
sweetening 66.2
LSD 87.9
loved one 104.11
endearment term
562.6
money 728.2
v sweeten 66.3
sugar daddy
beau 104.13
giver 478.11
suggest promise 133.13
advise 422.5
propose 439.5
signify 517.17
mean 518.8
imply 519.4
hint 551.10
resemble 783.7
evidence 956.8
remind 988.20
suggestion hint 248.4
advice 422.1
proposal 439.2
aspersion 512.4
indication 517.3
clue 517.9
implication 519.2
veiled reference 551.4
admixture 796.7
influence 893.1
supposition 950.5
suicidal
wretched 96.26
dejected 112.22
murderous 308.23
destructive 395.26
unwise 922.10
suicide 308.5
suit
n clothing 5.6
entreaty 440.2

solicitation 440.5
courtship 562.7
lawsuit 598.1
accusation 599.1
prayer 696.4
soccer 752.1
playing cards 758.2
bridge 758.3
set 769.12
important person
996.9
v outfit 5.40
please 95.5
be satisfactory 107.6
fit 405.8
agree 787.8
be timely 842.6
conform 866.3
suffice 990.4
suitable eligible 371.24
decorous 496.10
right 637.3
apt 787.10
timely 842.9
sufficient 990.6
expedient 994.5
suite apartment 228.13
furniture 229.1
attendance 768.6
set 769.12
suit oneself 430.20
suitor desirer 100.12
lover 104.12
petitioner 440.7
litigant 598.11
accuser 599.5
suit the occasion 994.3
suit up 5.42
sulfa drug 86.29
sulfate 1058.7
sulfuric 1056.15
sulk
n refusal 325.1
v mope 110.14
sulky
discontented 108.7
sullen 110.24
glum 112.25
unwilling 325.5
obstinate 361.8
perverse 361.11
sullen dark 38.9
sulky 110.24
glum 112.25
unwilling 325.5
obstinate 361.8
perverse 361.11
unsociable 583.5
sully soil 80.16
defile 80.17
vilify 512.10
corrupt 654.10
stigmatize 661.9
seduce 665.20
sultan 575.10
sultry
obscene 666.9
stifling 1018.28
sum
n quantity 244.1
amount 244.2
math terms 253.2

meaning 518.1
summary 557.2
amount of money
728.13
total 791.2
summation 1016.6
v compute 253.6
sum up 1016.18
summa cum laude
646.11
summarize
shorten 268.6
abridge 557.5
iterate 848.8
sum up 1016.18
summary
n shortening 268.3
résumé 557.2
iteration 848.2
summation 1016.11
adj short 268.8
concise 537.6
prompt 844.9
summary execution
604.7
summation
math terms 253.2
shortening 268.3
résumé 557.2
testimony 598.8
sum 1016.6
summary 1016.11
summer
n summertide 313.3
hot weather 1018.7
v vacation 313.8
spend time 820.6
adj seasonal 313.9
summer solstice 313.7
summery green 44.4
seasonal 313.9
warm 1018.24
summit top 198.2
mountain 237.6
supremacy 249.3
limit 793.5
acme of perfection
1001.3
summit conference
541.6
summon attract 377.6
call 420.11
invite 440.13
enlist 615.17
conjure 690.11
convene 769.17
summons
n bidding 420.5
invitation 440.4
call 517.16
subpoena 598.2
enlistment 615.7
v summon 420.11
issue a summons
598.13
sumo 457.10
sump
receptacle of filth
80.12
drain 239.5
lake 241.1
marsh 243.1

pit 284.4
sumptuous
grandiose 501.21
expensive 632.11
sum total 791.2
sum up
shorten 268.6
iterate 848.8
sum 1016.18
sun
n moment 823.2
light source 1025.1
orb of day 1070.13
v sunbathe 1019.19
dry 1064.6
the Sunbelt 231.7
sunblind 1027.1
sun-block 1054.3
sunburn
n burn 1019.6
v brown 40.2
sundae 10.45
Sunday
n day of rest 20.5
holy day 701.11
v vacation 20.9
Sunday school 567.8
sundown 315.2
sundry
diversified 782.4
several 883.7
sunglasses
spectacles 29.3
eyeshade 1027.2
sunk
concave 284.16
spoiled 393.29
depressed 912.12
sunless 1026.13
Sunni
n Muslim 675.23
adj Muslim 675.31
sunny
bright 97.11
cheerful 109.11
optimistic 124.12
warm 1018.24
luminous 1024.30
sunrise east 161.3
dawn 314.3
sunset
west 161.3
evening 315.2
sun worshiper 697.4
sup
n drink 8.4
sip 62.2
nip 88.7
hint 248.4
v dine 8.21
drink 8.29
taste 62.7
tipple 88.24
super
n volume 554.4
supporting actor or
actress 707.7
adj superior 249.12
excellent 998.13
magnificent 998.15
superb
eminent 247.9

good chance 971.8
adv surely 969.24
inter yeah 332.19
surety security 438.1
pledge 438.2
guarantor 438.6
belief 952.1
certainty 969.1
confidence 969.5
safety 1006.1
surf
n breaker 238.14
foam 320.2
wave 915.4
v navigate 182.13
surface
n space 158.1
top 198.1
exterior 206.2
shallowness 276.1
texture 294.1
tennis 748.1
v show 31.4
submarines 182.47
arrive 186.6
emerge 190.11
shoot up 193.9
cover 295.22
come out 348.6
be manifest 348.7
be revealed 351.8
adj apparent 33.11
spatial 158.9
exterior 206.7
shallow 276.5
formal 580.7
insufficient 991.9
surfboard 180.11
surfeit
n overfullness 992.3
satiety 993.1
v fill 793.7
overload 992.15
satiate 993.4
surge
n loudness 53.1
ascent 193.1
flow 238.4
billow 238.14
increase 251.1
whirl 914.2
wave 915.4
v din 53.7
run out 190.13
ascend 193.8
flow 238.16
jet 238.20
billow 238.22
come together 769.16
whirl 914.11
surgeon 90.5
surgery operation 90.2
surgical treatment
91.19
hospital room 197.25
severance 801.2
surgical strike 459.1
surly sullen 110.24
gruff 505.7
surmise
n supposition 950.3
guess 950.4

v suppose 950.10
think 952.11
surmount climb 193.11
top 198.9
rise above 272.11
defeat 411.5
overcome 412.7
surname 527.5
surpass excel 249.6
outdistance 249.10
exceed 992.9
do better 998.11
surplus
n difference 255.8
remainder 256.4
overrunning 909.1
excess 992.5
v dismiss 908.19
adj additional 253.10
remaining 256.7
excess 992.18
surprise
n wonder 122.1
astonishment 131.2
surprise attack 459.2
v astonish 122.6
take by surprise 131.7
attack 459.14
surreal odd 869.11
illusory 975.8
surrender
n abandonment 370.3
capitulation 433.2
compromise 468.1
relinquishment 475.1
giving 478.1
transfer 629.1
v weaken 16.9
yield 370.7
give up 433.8
compromise 468.2
relinquish 475.3
deliver 478.13
transfer 629.3
surreptitious
covert 345.12
in hiding 346.14
deceitful 356.22
surrogate
psychological
substitute 92.31
deputy 576.1
replacement 861.2
surround
n environment 209.1
setting 209.2
nearness 223.1
circumstances 765.2
frame 900.10
v devour 8.22
extend 158.8
internalize 207.5
envelop 209.6
circumscribe 210.4
bound 211.8
enclose 212.5
circle 280.10
wrap 295.20
besiege 459.19
go around 913.5
surveillance
vigilance 339.4

ambush 346.3
supervision 573.2
shadowing 937.9
survey
n scrutiny 27.6
field of view 31.3
measurement 300.1
treatise 556.1
abridgment 557.1
assemblage 769.1
examination 937.3
canvass 937.14
v scrutinize 27.14
measure 300.10
write upon 556.5
examine 937.23
canvass 937.28
surveyor
measurer 300.9
superintendent 574.2
survival of the fittest
860.4
survive remain 256.5
keep alive 306.10
support oneself 385.12
recover 396.20
endure 826.6
outlast 826.8
live on 838.7
sustain 855.4
persist 855.5
survivor 256.3
susceptible
sensible 24.11
sensitive 93.20
teachable 570.18
influenceable 893.15
liable 896.5
exposed 1005.15
pliant 1045.9
sushi 10.23
suspect
n accused 599.6
v be jealous 153.3
suppose 950.10
think 952.11
doubt 954.6
adj unbelievable
954.10
doubted 954.12
questionable 970.17
suspend release 120.6
hang 202.8
repeal 445.2
depose 447.4
postpone 845.9
interrupt 856.10
dismiss 908.19
suspenders 202.5
suspense anxiety 126.1
expectancy 130.3
inertness 173.4
pendency 202.1
uncertainty 970.1
suspension respite 20.2
release 120.2
pendency 202.1
inactivity 331.1
discontinuance 390.2
repeal 445.1
deposal 447.2
harmonization 709.2

elimination 772.2
interruption 812.2
delay 845.2
pause 856.3
dismissal 908.5
solution 1062.3
suspicion
suspiciousness 153.2
hint 248.4
small amount 258.7
wariness 494.2
leeriness 551.4
admixture 796.7
hunch 933.3
suggestion 950.5
doubt 954.2
incredulity 955.1
suspicious
jealous 153.5
wary 494.9
dishonest 645.16
doubting 954.9
unbelievable 954.10
incredulous 955.4
doubtful 970.17
sustain nourish 7.15
feed 8.18
strengthen 15.13
tolerate 134.5
buoy 298.8
preserve 397.8
maintain 449.12
foster 449.16
defend 600.10
endure 826.6
experience 830.8
protract 855.4
support 900.21
confirm 956.11
sustenance food 10.1
nutriment 10.3
maintenance 449.3
continuance 855.1
support 900.1
suttee suicide 308.5
oblation 696.7
burning 1019.5
suture filament 271.1
sewing 741.1
joint 799.4
svelte 270.16
Svengali hypnotist 22.9
influence 893.6
swab wash 79.19
dry 1064.6
swaddle
n children's wear 5.30
v clothe 5.38
wrap 295.20
bind 799.9
swag
n sinkage 194.2
hang 202.2
inclination 204.2
curve 279.2
booty 482.11
swing 915.6
v sink 194.6
hang 202.6
incline 204.10
curve 279.6
oscillate 915.10

adj drooping 202.10
swagger
  n gait 177.12
  strut 501.8
  boasting 502.1
  bluster 503.1
  v way of walking
    177.28
  strut 501.15
  boast 502.6
  bluster 503.3
swagger stick 273.2
swain
  n desirer 100.12
  beau 104.13
  escort 768.5
  v court 562.21
swale marsh 243.1
  lowland 274.3
  grassland 310.8
swallow
  n bite 8.2
  swiftness 174.6
  ingestion 187.4
  recant 363.8
  v devour 8.22
  endure 134.6
  disregard 134.8
  condone 148.4
  ingest 187.11
  consume 388.3
  believe 952.10
  kid oneself 953.6
swallow one's pride
  137.7
swamp
  n receptacle of filth
    80.12
  marsh 243.1
  predicament 1012.4
  v overflow 238.17
  overwhelm 395.21
  oversupply 992.14
  flood 1063.14
swan whiteness 37.2
  bird 311.28
swan dive 367.1
swanky
  grandiose 501.21
  chic 578.13
swan song
  leave-taking 188.4
  death song 307.10
  theatrical
    performance 704.12
  musical performance
    708.33
  sequel 816.1
  end 819.1
swap
  n explosive sound
    56.1
  bargain 731.5
  trading 862.2
  v make explosive
    sound 56.6
  trade 731.14
  interchange 862.4
swarm
  n migration 177.4
  assemblage 769.6
  multitude 883.3

infestation 909.2
  v migrate 177.22
  come together 769.16
  infest 909.6
  superabound 992.8
swarthy 38.9
swashbuckler
  combatant 461.1
  strutter 501.10
  blusterer 503.2
swastika cross 170.4
  insignia 647.1
  charm 691.5
swat
  n blow 901.5
  v strike 901.15
SWAT 1007.17
swatch 785.3
swath 811.2
sway
  n inclination 204.2
  supremacy 249.3
  authority 417.5
  dominance 417.6
  government 612.1
  influence 893.1
  swing 915.6
  flounder 916.8
  v pitch 182.55
  oblique 204.9
  incline 204.10
  induce 375.22
  persuade 375.23
  break down 393.24
  rule 612.14
  change 853.5
  influence 893.7
  oscillate 915.10
  flounder 916.15
  prejudice 979.9
sway-backed 265.12
swear affirm 334.6
  administer an oath
    334.7
  promise 436.4
  curse 513.6
  blaspheme 694.5
  state 952.12
  testify 956.9
swear by 952.16
swear in
  administer an oath
    334.7
  call to witness 598.16
swear off
  break the habit 374.3
  relinquish 475.3
  renounce 668.8
sweat
  n body fluid 2.22
  perspiration 12.7
  trepidation 127.5
  nervousness 128.2
  impatience 135.1
  bustle 330.4
  work 725.4
  confusion 984.3
  v perspire 12.16
  fear 127.10
  await 130.8
  be impatient 135.4
  trickle 238.18

endeavor 403.5
  work hard 725.13
  overwork 725.16
  be hot 1018.22
  be damp 1063.11
sweater shirt 5.15
  gambler 759.21
sweat it out
  be strong 15.11
  await 130.8
  be impatient 135.4
  wait impatiently
    845.13
Swedish bath 79.8
sweep
  n vision 27.1
  view 33.6
  sweeper 79.16
  range 158.2
  deviation 164.1
  gliding 177.16
  oar 180.15
  bend 279.3
  lottery 759.14
  v touch lightly 73.7
  clean 79.23
  extend 158.8
  speed 174.9
  traverse 177.20
  glide 177.35
  overflow 238.17
  curve 279.6
  plunder 482.17
  push 903.9
  go easily 1013.10
  receive 1035.17
sweeper 79.16
sweeping change 859.1
sweepings
  remainder 256.1
  refuse 391.4
sweep off one's feet
  enamor 104.23
  take one's breath
    away 122.7
  fascinate 377.7
  convince 857.16
sweepstakes
  award 646.2
  lottery 759.14
sweet
  n food 10.38
  sweetness 66.1
  endearment term
    562.6
  adj soft-colored 35.21
  flavored 62.9
  sweetish 66.4
  fragrant 70.9
  clean 79.25
  pleasant 97.6
  endearing 104.25
  good-natured 143.14
  harmonious 533.8
  melodious 708.48
sweetbread veal 10.14
  organ meat 10.19
sweetener 478.5
sweetheart
  n loved one 104.10
  endearment term
    562.6

good person 659.2
  first-rate 998.7
  v court 562.21
sweet nothings
  flattery 511.1
  endearment 562.5
sweets
  confectionery 10.38
  sweetening 66.2
  loved one 104.11
  endearment term
    562.6
the sweet science 754.1
sweet sixteen 301.14
swell
  n loudness 53.1
  hill 237.4
  wave 238.14
  distension 259.2
  dandy 500.9
  aristocrat 607.4
  nobleman 608.4
  notation 709.12
  keyboard 711.17
  v din 53.7
  be excited 105.18
  be vain 140.7
  billow 238.22
  grow 251.6
  enlarge 259.4
  increase 259.5
  bulge 283.11
  give oneself airs
    501.14
  overextend 992.13
  adj grandiose 501.21
  chic 578.13
  excellent 998.13
swelled head 140.4
swelter
  n sweat 12.7
  sultriness 1018.6
  v sweat 12.16
  be hot 1018.22
swept 238.25
swept-back 217.12
swept up 982.17
swerve
  n deviation 164.1
  bias 204.3
  angle 278.2
  v deviate 164.3
  change course 182.30
  oblique 204.9
  angle 278.5
  dodge 368.8
  be changed 851.6
  pull back 902.7
swift
  fast 174.15
  quick 330.18
  hasty 401.9
  brief 827.8
  sudden 829.5
  prompt 844.9
swig
  n drink 8.4
  snort 88.7
  v drink 8.29
  booze 88.25
swill
  n drink 8.4

feed 10.4
offal 80.9
snort 88.7
refuse 391.4
mud 1060.8
v drink 8.29
booze 88.25
ingest 187.11
swim
n aquatics 182.11
v bathe 182.56
conform 866.4
swim against the tide
dissent 333.4
not conform 867.4
counteract 899.6
swimming pool 743.12
swim suit 5.29
swindle
n fake 354.13
fraud 356.8
theft 482.1
v cheat 356.18
steal 482.13
overprice 632.7
swine
filthy person 80.13
pig 311.9
beast 660.7
sensualist 663.3
slob 809.7
swing
n room 158.3
gait 177.12
hang 202.2
latitude 430.4
thrust 459.3
supporting actor
  707.7
jazz 708.9
rhythm 709.22
meter 720.7
playground apparatus
  743.15
golf 751.3
trend 895.2
hit 901.4
swinging 915.6
oscillator 915.9
flounder 916.8
v turn round 163.9
way of walking 177.28
toss at sea 182.55
hang 202.6
do 328.6
accomplish 407.4
manage 409.12
be hanged 604.19
afford 626.7
be promiscuous
  665.19
syncopate 708.43
change 853.5
rotate 914.9
oscillate 915.10
wave 915.11
alternate 915.13
flounder 916.15
adj music 708.51
swinger
person of fashion
  578.7

libertine 665.10
swing into action
behave 321.4
take action 328.5
undertake 404.3
begin 817.7
swing shift 824.3
swing vote 609.28
swipe
n criticism 510.4
hit 901.4
v rob 482.16
hit 901.14
swirl
n excitement 105.4
eddy 238.12
coil 281.2
bustle 330.4
whirl 914.2
agitation 916.1
v eddy 238.21
convolve 281.4
whirl 914.11
agitate 916.10
swish
n sibilation 57.1
v ripple 52.11
rustle 52.12
sibilate 57.2
basketball 747.4
Swiss cheese 284.6
switch
n false hair 3.13
surprise 131.2
branch 310.18
apostatize 363.7
whip 605.2
plot 722.4
member 792.4
change 851.1
conversion 857.1
substitution 861.1
trading 862.2
v avoid 164.6
transfer 176.10
whip 604.13
trade 731.14
convert 857.11
substitute 861.4
interchange 862.4
switchback
zigzag 204.8
race 756.3
switchboard
telephone 347.8
stage 704.16
switch hitter 745.2
switch over
n apostatize 363.7
v convert 857.11
swivel
n axle 914.5
v turn round 163.9
rotate 914.9
swivet dither 105.6
confusion 984.3
swollen
diseased 85.59
puffed up 136.10
increased 251.7
corpulent 257.18
distended 259.13

bulged 283.16
pompous 501.22
boastful 502.12
bombastic 545.9
full 793.11
overfull 992.20
swoon
n stupor 22.6
unconsciousness 25.2
v faint 25.5
swoop
n descent 194.1
plunge 367.1
v descend 194.5
plunge 367.6
sword
n combatant 461.1
blade 462.5
cutlery 1039.2
v stab 459.25
sword of Damocles
threat 514.1
dangerousness 1005.2
sworn affirmed 334.9
, promised 436.8
sworn enemy 589.6
sworn statement
deposition 334.3
certificate 549.6
statement of
  principles 952.4
testimony 956.2
sycophant toady 138.3
flatterer 511.4
follower 616.8
syllabic
n letter 546.1
adj phonetic 524.31
syllable
n speech sound 524.13
word 526.1
poetry 720.9
v syllabify 546.7
syllabus 557.1
syllogism reasoning
  934.3
prosyllogism 934.6
sylvan hinterland 233.9
woodland 310.37
symbiotic
cooperative 450.5
agreeing 787.9
concurrent 898.4
symbol
n psychological
  symbol 92.30
representation 349.1
emblem 517.2
sign 518.6
letter 546.1
insignia 647.1
musical notation
  709.12
example 785.2
substitute 861.2
number 1016.3
v designate 517.18
symbolic indicative
  517.23
meaningful 518.10
semantic 518.12
figurative 519.10

symmetrical
balanced 264.4
harmonious 533.8
orderly 806.6
symmetry
balance 264
harmony 533.2
correlation 776.1
agreement 787.1
equality 789.1
order 806.1
sympathetic
sensitive 24.12
responsive 93.20
comforting 121.13
kind 143.13
pitying 145.7
condoling 147.3
in accord 455.3
related 774.9
attracting 906.5
tolerant 978.11
sympathy
sensitivity 24.3
fellow feeling 93.5
inclination 100.3
consolation 121.4
kindness 143.1
pity 145.1
condolence 147.1
patronage 449.4
accord 455.1
good terms 587.3
relation 774.1
attraction 906.1
tolerance 978.4
symphony accord 455.1
harmony 708.3
symposium
drinking 8.3
spree 88.5
forum 423.3
discussion 541.7
compilation 554.7
assembly 769.2
symptom
medical sign 91.13
warning sign 399.3
sign 517.1
hint 551.4
evidence 956.1
synagogue 703.2
synapse 2.12
sync
n agreement 787.1
v make agree 787.7
synchronized
harmonious 708.49
accompanying 768.9
agreeing 787.9
arranged 807.14
simultaneous 835.6
syncopation
dance music 708.8
tempo 709.24
syncope
unconsciousness 25.2
shortening 268.3
abbreviation 537.4
tempo 709.24
syndicate
n council 423.1

company 617.9
v combine 804.3
the syndicate
the underworld
660.11
illicit business 732.1
syndication 804.1
syndrome 85.1
synergy
cooperation 450.1
concurrence 898.1
synod council 423.1
ecclesiastical council
423.4
diocese 698.8
assembly 769.2
synonym word 526.1
the same 777.3
synopsis
shortening 268.3
abridgment 557.1
syntax
grammatical
structure 530.2
arrangement 807.1
synthesis
identification 777.2
composition 795.1
combination 804.1
reasoning 934.3
synthesize
identify 777.5
compose 795.3
combine 804.3
reason 934.15
synthesizer
musical instrument
711.1
reasoner 934.11
theorist 950.7
synthetic
n plastic 1052.6
adj imitation 336.8
spurious 354.25
similar 783.10
dialectic 934.22
synthetic fuels 1020.1
syringe
n sprinkler 1063.8
v wash 79.19
moisten 1063.12
syrup
sweetening 66.2
medicine 86.4
adhesive 802.4
semiliquid 1060.5
system
plan 381.1
manner 384.1
nature 766.4
order 806.1
orderliness 806.3
outlook 977.2
universe 1070.1
systematic
uniform 780.5
orderly 806.6
regular 849.6
systemic 1000.3
system of government
612.1
system of values 373.3

systems analysis
1040.2
syzygy
juxtaposition 223.3
meter 720.7
T 170.4
tab
n bulge 283.3
statement 628.3
price 630.1
scenery 704.20
afterpart 816.2
v label 517.20
appoint 615.11
tabby
n iridescence 47.2
cat 311.21
newsmonger 552.9
v variegate 47.7
adj striped 47.15
tabernacle 703.2
table
n meal 8.5
food 10.1
horizontal 201.3
furniture 229.1
plain 236.1
plateau 237.3
steppe 272.4
lamina 296.2
diagram 381.3
register 549.1
record book 549.11
outline 800.4
code 807.4
contents 870.2
board 900.15
summation 1016.11
v put away 390.6
legislate 613.10
postpone 845.9
tableau spectacle 33.7
picture 712.11
table manners 580.3
table of contents
book 554.12
outline 800.4
table 870.2
table setting 498.1
tablespoon 8.12
tablet pill 86.7
lamina 296.2
record book 549.11
monument 549.12
tabloid 555.2
taboo
n prohibition 444.1
exclusion 772.1
v prohibit 444.3
exclude 772.4
adj prohibited 444.7
jargonish 523.19
tabular
horizontal 201.7
classified 808.8
tabula rasa void 222.3
revolution 859.1
ignorance 929.1
thoughtlessness 932.1
tabulate record 549.15
classify 808.6
list 870.8

tachometer 174.7
tachycardia
symptom 85.9
pulsation 915.3
tacit
wordless 51.11
implicit 519.8
taciturn
untalkative 344.9
concise 537.6
tack
n direction 161.2
deviation 164.1
cordage 271.3
manner 384.1
harness 385.5
horse racing 757.1
inferiority 1004.3
v deviate 164.3
change course 182.30
fasten 799.8
be changed 851.6
tackle
n rigging 180.12
cordage 271.3
equipment 385.4
harness 385.5
impedimenta 471.3
linemen 746.2
football game 746.3
hockey game 749.6
soccer game 752.3
purchase 905.6
lifter 911.3
v practice 328.8
treat 387.12
attempt 403.7
undertake 404.3
set to work 725.15
football 746.5
hockey 749.7
soccer 752.4
reel in 905.9
tack on 253.4
tacky frail 16.14
unpleasant 98.17
shabby 393.32
vulgar 497.10
gaudy 501.20
base 661.12
adhesive 802.12
slovenly 809.15
inferior 1004.9
viscous 1060.12
moist 1063.15
tact sensitivity 24.3
considerateness 143.3
skill 413.1
courtesy 504.1
intuition 933.1
discrimination 943.1
tactic stratagem 415.3
expedient 994.2
tactical planned 381.12
cunning 415.12
tactician planner 381.6
strategist 415.7
tactile tactual 73.10
touchable 73.11
tad 302.3
tadpole
fledgling 302.10

amphibian 311.27
tag
n scrap 248.3
label 517.13
name 527.3
rabble 606.3
token 728.12
sequel 816.1
afterpart 816.2
extremity 819.2
v follow 166.3
add 253.4
allot 477.9
label 517.20
name 527.11
tag along 166.3
taiga 243.1
tail
n braid 3.7
follower 166.2
rear 217.1
buttocks 217.5
cauda 217.6
added to writing
254.2
book 554.12
appendage 792.4
afterpart 816.2
extremity 819.2
v look 27.13
follow 166.3
trace 937.34
adj rear 217.9
caudal 217.11
final 819.11
tailback 746.2
tail gunner 185.4
tail off weaken 16.9
recede 168.2
decrease 252.6
cease to exist 761.6
tailor
n garmentmaker 5.34
sewer 741.2
v outfit 5.40
form 262.7
sew 741.4
make agree 787.7
tailored
custom-made 5.47
formative 262.9
apt 787.10
tailpiece rear 217.1
tail 217.6
adjunct 254.1
coda 708.24
afterpart 816.2
tails
formal dress 5.11
opposite side 215.3
tailspin
air maneuver 184.15
collapse 410.3
tail wind
atmosphere 184.32
wind 318.1
nautical 318.11
taint
n infection 85.4
stigma 661.6
admixture 796.7
characteristic 864.4

fault 1002.2
stain 1003.3
v defile 80.17
infect 85.50
corrupt 393.12
stigmatize 661.9
blaspheme 694.5
work evil 999.6
stain 1003.6
take
n winnings 251.3
explanation 341.4
profit 472.3
catch 480.10
booty 482.11
receipts 627.1
shot 706.4
motion picture
714.8
change 851.1
production 892.2
answer 938.1
v eat 8.20
take sick 85.46
pocket 134.8
condone 148.4
transport 176.12
interpret 341.9
succeed 409.7
submit 433.6
acquire 472.8
receive 479.6
possess 480.13
possess sexually
480.15
catch 480.17
steal 482.13
understand 521.7
adopt 621.4
entail 771.4
combine 804.3
suppose 950.10
think 952.11
take aback
dismay 127.19
surprise 131.7
startle 131.8
take a back seat
efface oneself 139.7
retreat 163.6
retract 168.3
be inferior 250.4
depend on 432.12
take a break
take a rest 20.8
intervene 825.3
pause 856.9
interrupt 856.10
take a chance
venture 759.24
risk 971.12
take chances 1005.7
take action 328.5
take a cut 328.5
take a dim view of
shudder at 99.5
disapprove 510.10
take a dive 356.18
take advantage of
avail oneself of 387.15
exploit 387.16
impose on 643.7

improve the occasion
842.8
take a flier
trade 737.23
chance 759.24
take after
emulate 336.7
resemble 783.7
take a hard line 425.5
take a header
tumble 194.8
plunge 367.6
take a hike! 908.32
take aim at
intend 380.4
pull the trigger 459.22
take a liking to 104.22
take a load off 121.8
take a look at 27.13
take a nap
take a rest 20.8
sleep 22.13
take an interest in
love 104.19
be curious 980.3
attend to 982.5
take a nose dive
decrease 252.6
plunge 367.6
decline 393.17
take apart
demolish 395.17
tear apart 801.14
disassemble 801.15
take a peek 27.13
take a percentage 631.2
take a picture 714.14
take a powder
depart 188.7
flee 368.11
take a raincheck 329.2
take a reading 300.10
take a second look
repeat 848.7
re-examine 937.26
take a short cut 268.7
take a stab at 403.7
take a stand 348.6
take at one's word
believe 952.10
trust 952.11
**take a turn for the
better**
rally 392.8
recuperate 396.19
**take a turn for the
worse**
worsen 119.3
decline 393.17
take a walk
go for a walk 177.29
not interfere 430.17
take away
remove 176.11
subtract 255.9
take a whack at
attempt 403.7
enter 817.9
take back deny 335.4
recant 363.8
restore 481.4
recover 481.6

apologize 658.5
take by surprise 131.7
take by the hand
449.11
take care
be careful 339.7
beware 494.7
pay attention 982.8
take care of
kill 308.13
perform 328.9
look after 339.9
bribe 378.3
accomplish 407.4
supervise 573.10
serve 577.13
punish 604.11
operate 888.5
care for 1007.19
**take care of number
one** 651.4
take center stage
501.12
take charge
be able 18.11
take command 417.14
take comfort 121.7
take cover hide 346.8
take refuge 1008.7
take credit 622.7
take down devour 8.22
abase 137.5
raze 395.19
reprove 510.17
record 549.15
disassemble 801.15
depress 912.4
fell 912.5
take effect 888.7
take evasive action
368.8
take exception
dissent 333.4
find fault 510.15
take for
suppose 950.10
think 952.11
take for a ride
kill 308.13
deceive 356.19
take for granted
accept 123.2
expect 130.5
neglect 340.6
imply 519.4
suppose 950.10
believe 952.10
take heart
cheer up 109.9
be comforted 121.7
be hopeful 124.8
take courage 492.14
take heed
be careful 339.7
beware 494.7
pay attention 982.8
take hold of
seize 480.14
cohere 802.6
attend to 982.5
take-home pay
pay 624.4

standard of living
731.8
take in devour 8.22
see 27.12
hear 48.11
extend 158.8
let in 187.10
absorb 187.13
enter 189.7
attend 221.8
shorten 268.6
deceive 356.14
receive 479.6
capture 480.18
understand 521.7
learn 570.7
host 585.7
include 771.3
entail 771.4
put together 799.5
watch 917.5
take in stride
accept 123.2
patience 134.7
take in the sights 917.6
take into consideration
include 771.3
allow for 958.5
take cognizance of
982.9
take into custody
arrest 429.15
capture 480.18
take issue with
deny 335.4
oppose 451.3
dispute 457.21
take it be strong 15.11
endure 134.6
submit 433.6
suppose 950.10
think 952.11
suffice 990.4
take it easy rest 20.6
compose oneself 106.7
take things as they
come 331.15
be cautious 494.5
pause 856.9
swim with the stream
1013.12
take it lying down
take 134.8
submit 433.6
take it on the chin
be strong 15.11
endure 134.6
fail 410.10
take it or leave it
be indifferent 102.5
have no choice 962.11
take it out on 152.16
take it slow relax 20.7
go slowly 175.6
be cautious 494.5
take kindly to
assent 332.8
concur 332.9
consent 441.2
approve 509.9
take leave
vacation 20.9 .

depart 188.6
bid farewell 188.16
absent oneself 222.8
**take leave of one's
   senses**
be foolish 922.6
go mad 925.21
take legal action 673.8
take liberties
have the audacity
   142.7
presume on 640.7
take notice 982.6
taken up with 982.17
taken with
adj pleased 95.14
fond of 104.30
prep compared to
   942.11
take odds 759.25
takeoff flight 184.8
start 188.2
embarkation 188.3
point of departure
   188.5
ascent 193.1
imitation 336.1
burlesque 508.6
similarity 783.1
take off
remove 6.6
become airborne
   184.38
depart 188.7
leave the ground
   193.10
excise 255.10
kill 308.12
mimic 336.6
impersonate 349.12
improve 392.7
put an end to 395.12
gesture 517.21
discount 631.2
resemble 783.7
detach 801.10
begin 817.7
take offense 152.13
take off for 161.9
take office 615.13
take on
grieve 112.17
complain 115.16
feel anxious 126.6
be angry 152.15
practice 328.8
treat 387.12
attempt 403.7
undertake 404.3
contend against 451.4
engage 457.16
receive 479.6
employ 615.14
adopt 621.4
set to work 725.15
take one's leave
depart 188.6
separate 801.8
**take one's life in one's
   hands**
brave 492.11
risk one's neck 1005.7

take one's medicine
submit 433.6
take one's
   punishment 604.21
take one's own life
   308.21
take one's time
dawdle 175.8
idle 331.12
dally 331.14
take one's leisure
   402.4
wait 845.12
take one's word for
believe 952.10
rely on 952.16
take one step at a time
   494.5
take one up on
assent 332.8
acquiesce 441.3
take a dare 454.6
suppose 950.10
take orders obey 326.2
be ordained 698.11
takeout 8.6
take out extract 192.10
excise 255.10
kill 308.13
annihilate 761.7
escort 768.8
end 819.5
take out after
follow 166.3
pursue 382.8
censure 510.13
takeover
appropriation 480.4
stock trading 737.19
combination 804.1
take over
take command 417.14
take possession 472.10
receive 479.6
appropriate 480.19
adopt 621.4
usurp 640.8
combine 804.3
succeed 814.2
take pains
be careful 339.7
make a special effort
   403.11
take part 476.5
take pity on 145.4
take place 830.5
take pleasure in 95.12
take possession
appropriate 472.10
take 480.13
take precautions
take steps 494.6
play safe 1006.3
take precedence
rule 249.11
precede 813.2
take pride 136.5
take prisoner
arrest 429.15
capture 480.18
take refuge 1008.7
take refuge in 376.4

take revenge
get even with 506.7
avenge 507.4
take risks 492.10
take shape
be formed 262.8
form 806.5
take shelter 1008.7
take sides with
back 449.13
side with 450.4
take steps
take action 328.5
take precautions
   494.6
take stock
take account of 628.9
check 1016.20
take the bait
react 902.5
kid oneself 953.6
**take the bull by the
   horns**
be determined 359.8
attempt 403.6
undertake 404.3
brave 492.11
seize the opportunity
   842.7
take the cake
best 249.7
triumph 411.3
take the edge off
weaken 16.10
blunt 286.2
moderate 670.6
take the first step
   817.10
take the floor
speak up 524.22
make a speech 543.9
legislate 613.10
take the heat for
be responsible for
   641.6
accept the
   responsibility 641.9
**take the law into one's
   own hands**
have one's will 323.3
violate 435.4
break the law 674.5
take the lead
lead 165.2
be in front 216.7
take command 417.14
direct 573.8
dominate 612.15
initiate 817.10
take the next step
   816.5
take the offensive
   459.14
take the opportunity
   842.7
take the place of
follow after 834.3
substitute for 861.5
take the rap 604.21
take the stand
depose 334.6
call to witness 598.16

take the trouble 324.3
**take the wind out of
   one's sails**
disable 19.10
sadden 112.18
humiliate 137.6
becalm 173.11
disincline 379.4
refute 957.5
thwart 1011.15
**take the words out of
   one's mouth** 844.6
take the wraps off
   351.4
take the wrong way
   342.2
**take things as they
   come**
keep cool 106.9
accept 134.7
take it easy 331.15
take time
spend time 820.6
wait 845.12
take to desire 100.14
fall in love 104.22
practice 328.8
become used to
   373.12
avail oneself of 387.14
take to heart
respond 93.11
take amiss 152.13
internalize 207.5
believe 952.10
take to mean 341.9
take to task
reprove 510.17
accuse 599.7
punish 604.10
take to the cleaners
best 249.7
lose 473.4
strip 480.24
take turns 824.5
**take under
   consideration**
   930.14
take under one's wing
back 449.13
benefit 592.3
care for 1007.19
take up
absorb 187.13
practice 328.8
adopt 371.15
undertake 404.3
patronize 449.15
take possession 472.10
collect 472.11
appropriate 480.19
espouse 509.13
discuss 541.12
write upon 556.5
pay in full 624.13
busy oneself with
   724.11
assemble 769.18
include 771.3
enter 817.9
pick up 911.8
engross 982.13

stain 1003.3
  v decolor 36.5
  defile 80.17
  vilify 512.10
  stigmatize 661.9
  stain 1003.6
tarry
  v be still 173.7
  dawdle 175.8
  endure 826.6
  linger on 826.7
  wait 845.12
  continue 855.3
  adj black 38.8
tart
  n pastry 10.39
  strumpet 665.14
  adj acrimonious 17.14
  bitter 64.6
  sour 67.5
  caustic 144.23
tartan check 47.4
  insignia 647.1
Tartar 110.11
Tarzan 15.6
task
  n undertaking 404.1
  lesson 568.7
  commission 615.1
  charge 643.3
  job 724.2
  work 725.4
  v accuse 599.7
  impose 643.4
  work 725.16
task force
  military unit 461.22
  navy 461.27
taskmaster 574.2
taste
  n bite 8.2
  senses 24.5
  gust 62.1
  sample 62.4
  liking 100.2
  appetite 100.7
  hint 248.4
  preference 371.5
  fastidiousness 495.1
  tastefulness 496.1
  elegance 533.1
  specimen 785.3
  characteristic 864.4
  discrimination 943.1
  v eat 8.20
  sense 24.6
  taste of 62.7
  savor 63.5
  experience 830.8
  experiment 941.8
taste bud 62.5
tasteful
  in good taste 496.8
  elegant 533.6
  artistic 712.20
tasteless
  wishy-washy 16.17
  insipid 65.2
  dull 117.6
  vulgar 497.10
  inelegant 534.2
  base 661.12

tasty good 63.8
  delectable 97.10
tata 188.22
tater
  vegetables 10.34
  baseball 745.3
tatter
  n scrap 248.3
  piece 792.3
  v wear 393.20
tattle
  n gossip 552.7
  v betray 351.6
  inform on 551.12
  gossip 552.12
tattletale
  n informer 551.6
  newsmonger 552.9
  adj telltale 551.19
tattoo
  n fanfare 53.5
  staccato 55.1
  mark 517.5
  constancy 846.2
  hit 901.4
  shot 903.4
  v variegate 47.7
  rain 316.9
  mark 517.19
taught 927.18
taunt
  n indignity 156.2
  gibe 508.2
  v be insolent 142.7
  offend 156.5
  scoff 508.9
taupe gray 39.4
  brown 40.3
taut tense 128.13
  in suspense 130.12
  shipshape 180.20
  rigid 1044.11
tautology
  wordiness 538.2
  redundancy 848.3
  superfluity 992.4
tavern
  restaurant 8.17
  bar 88.20
  inn 228.15
  entertainment 743.13
tawdry gaudy 501.20
  paltry 997.21
tawny 40.3
tax
  n demand 421.1
  taxation 630.9
  charge 643.3
  overdoing 992.6
  v burden 297.13
  accuse 599.7
  charge 630.12
  impose 643.4
  strain 725.10
  task 725.16
taxable income
  pay 624.4
  tax 630.9
tax collector
  taxer 630.10
  collector 769.15
tax-deductible 630.16

tax evasion
  shirking 368.2
  tax 630.9
taxi
  n public vehicle
    179.13
  v ride 177.33
  take off 184.38
taxidermy 397.3
taxing
  n burden 297.7
  demand 421.1
  accusation 599.1
  imposition 643.1
  strain 725.2
  adj demanding 421.9
taxonomy
  biological
    classification 305.3
  nomenclature 527.1
  classification 800.3
  grouping 807.3
  arrangement 808.1
taxpayer payer 624.9
  good or respectable
    citizen 659.3
tax return 630.9
tea meal 8.6
  marijuana 87.10
  afternoon tea 582.13
teach 568.10
teacher preparer 405.5
  adviser 422.3
  tutor 568.1
  instructor 571.1
  master 575.1
  clergy 699.9
  professional 726.4
teacher's pet
  weakling 16.6
  favorite 104.16
teach one a lesson
    604.10
team
  n rig 179.5
  outfit 617.7
  baseball team 745.2
  football team 746.2
  basketball team 747.2
  hockey team 749.2
  attack 749.5
  lawn bowling 750.3
  golfer 751.2
  squad 752.2
  company 769.3
  two 872.2
  v double 872.5
teamed 804.6
teammate
  companion 588.3
  co-worker 616.5
teamster
  coachman 178.9
  driver 178.10
team up
  cooperate 450.3
  befriend 587.11
  double 872.5
tear
  n humor 2.22
  weeping 115.2
  v secrete 13.5

tear
  n trauma 85.37
  drinking spree 88.6
  break 801.4
  v pain 26.7
  speed 174.8
  hurry 174.9
  open 292.11
  injure 393.13
  make haste 401.5
  rage 671.11
  sever 801.11
tear apart
  demolish 395.17
  find fault 510.15
  pull apart 801.14
tear down
  blacken 38.7
  raze 395.19
  find fault 510.15
  defame 512.9
  disassemble 801.15
teardrop tear 2.22
  weeping 115.2
  drop 282.3
tearful
  sorrowful 112.26
  teary 115.21
tearing
  n severance 801.2
  adj welling 2.31
tearjerker 93.8
tear limb from limb
  torture 604.16
  rip apart 801.14
tearoom 8.17
tear open open 292.11
  breach 292.14
tears
  secretion 13.2
  weeping 115.2
tease
  n tormentor 96.10
  disappointment 132.1
  deceiver 357.1
  v annoy 96.13
  disappoint 132.2
  attract 377.6
  importune 440.12
  banter 490.5
teaspoon 8.12
teatime 8.6
teats 283.6
technical
  skilled 413.26
  occupational 724.16
  specialized 865.5
  scientific 927.28
  insignificant 997.17
technicality
  technical term 526.5
  complexity 798.1
  specialty 865.1
  an insignificancy
    997.6
technical knockout
    754.3
technician
  expert 413.11
  skilled worker 726.6
  engineer 726.7
  specialist 865.3

computer whiz
1041.17
technique
manner 384.1
skill 413.1
art 413.7
artistic treatment
712.9
skiing 753.3
knowledge 927.1
technology art 413.7
engineer 726.7
science 927.10
tectonics 266.1
teddy bear figure 349.6
toy 743.16
tedious dull 117.6
monotonous 118.9
same 780.6
repetitive 848.15
mediocre 1004.7
tee 751.1
teed off 152.30
teed up 405.16
teeming
n proliferation 889.2
infestation 909.2
adj pregnant 78.18
permeated 221.15
diffuse 538.11
crowded 769.22
swarming 883.9
productive 889.9
infested 909.11
imaginative 985.18
plentiful 990.7
superabundant 992.19
teen-aged 301.14
teenager 302.1
tee off on
attack 459.15
criticize 510.14
teeter
n alternation 915.5
oscillator 915.9
v be weak 16.8
vacillate 362.8
change 853.5
alternate 915.13
teeth
dentition 2.8
acrimony 17.5
clutches 474.4
speech organ 524.19
**sail in the teeth of the
wind** 182.24
teetotaler 668.4
Teflon-coated 1007.23
telecast
n television broadcast
1034.2
v publish 352.10
televise 1034.14
adj published 352.17
telecommunication
communications
343.5
signaling 347.1
radio 1033.1
teleconference
telephone call 347.13
conference 541.6

telegram
n telegraph 347.14
message 552.4
v telegraph 347.19
telegraph
n telegraph recorder
347.2
telegram 347.14
v send a message
347.19
telekinesis 689.6
telemarketing 347.13
telemetry
measurement 300.1
semiautomatic
control 1040.4
rocketry 1072.1
telepathic
communicational
343.9
psychic 689.24
telepathy
communication 343.1
mental telepathy
689.9
telephone
n communication
device 347.4
v phone 347.18
telephone book
reference book 554.9
directory 574.10
telephone number
347.12
telephone operator
347.9
telephoto 714.17
telescope
n optical instrument
29.4
observatory 1070.17
v shorten 268.6
televise publish 352.10
telecast 1034.14
television
communications
medium 347.3
informant 551.5
news 552.1
electronics 1032.1
TV 1034.1
television personality
1034.2
television repairman
1034.13
television studio 1034.6
telex
n telegraph 347.2
telegram 347.14
v telegraph 347.19
tell impress 93.15
communicate 343.7
divulge 351.5
say 524.23
inform 551.8
report 552.11
narrate 719.6
spin a yarn 722.6
have influence 893.10
evidence 956.8
recognize 988.12
matter 996.12

number 1016.16
teller
informant 551.5
banker 729.10
telling
n informing 343.2
fiction 722.1
narration 722.2
numeration 1016.9
adj powerful 18.12
exciting 105.30
vigorous 544.11
influential 893.13
evidential 956.16
notable 996.19
tell it like it is 644.12
tell off 510.18
tell on betray 351.6
inform on 551.13
telltale
n divulgence 351.2
clue 517.9
hint 551.4
informer 551.6
newsmonger 552.9
adj tattletale 551.19
tell the truth
confess 351.7
speak true 644.11
disillusion 976.2
temerity 493.1
temp worker 726.2
temperature 1018.3
temper
n firmness 15.3
hot temper 110.4
anger 152.6
nature 766.4
disposition 977.3
mood 977.4
tempering 1044.4
v strengthen 15.13
mature 303.9
moderate 670.6
imbue 796.11
qualify 958.3
harden 1044.7
toughen 1047.3
temperament
pitch 709.4
nature 766.4
disposition 977.3
temperance
sedateness 106.4
sobriety 516.1
cardinal virtues 653.4
temperateness 668.1
restraint 670.1
temperate
sedate 106.14
sober 516.3
moderate 668.9
mild 670.10
warm 1018.24
cool 1022.12
temperature 1018.3
temper tantrum 152.8
tempest outburst 105.9
windstorm 318.12
storm 671.4
tempest in a teacup
997.3

tempest in a teapot
355.2
template 785.6
temple side 218.1
religious building
703.2
tempo time 709.24
pulsation 915.3
temporal
unsacred 686.3
secularist 695.16
lay 700.3
chronological 820.7
transient 827.7
timekeeping 831.15
material 1050.10
temporary
n worker 726.2
adj interim 825.4
transient 827.7
substitute 861.8
conditional 958.8
unreliable 970.20
makeshift 994.7
temporize
n be a timeserver
363.9
v not face up to 368.13
protract 826.9
procrastinate 845.11
tempt seduce 104.23
induce 375.22
attract 377.6
temptress
tempter 377.4
seductress 665.15
tempus fugit 820.17
ten
n card 758.2
number 881.6
beauty 1015.9
v intervene 825.3
tenable
acceptable 107.12
defensible 460.15
believable 952.24
tenacious
resolute 359.11
persevering 360.8
obstinate 361.8
retentive 474.8
courageous 492.18
adhesive 802.12
tough 1047.4
viscous 1060.12
tenant
n inhabitant 227.2
lodger 227.8
occupant 470.4
v inhabit 225.7
Ten Commandments
ethics 636.1
ten 881.6
tend
take direction 161.7
gravitate 297.15
look after 339.9
serve 577.13
have a tendency 895.3
heed 982.6
care for 1007.19
groom 1068.7

tendency
  direction 161.1
  preference 371.5
  aptitude 413.5
  nature 766.4
  inclination 895.1
  probability 967.1
  disposition 977.3
tender
  n attendant 577.5
  v offer 439.4
  give 478.12
  pay 624.10
  adj sensitive 24.12
  sore 26.11
  soft-colored 35.21
  sympathetic 93.20
  loving 104.27
  kind 143.13
  pitying 145.7
  seaworthy 180.18
  light 298.12
  immature 301.10
  careful 339.10
  lenient 427.7
  unbalanced 790.5
  soft 1045.8
tenderfoot
  recruit 461.18
  novice 572.9
  jockey 757.2
  newcomer 773.4
  beginner 817.2
  ignoramus 929.8
tenderize 1045.6
tenderloin
  city district 230.6
  brothel 665.9
tendon 271.2
tendril filament 271.1
  coil 281.2
  branch 310.18
  part 792.4
tenement sty 80.11
  apartment 228.13
  high rise 228.14
tenet rule 419.2
  a belief 952.2
tennis 748
tennis ball
  tennis 748.1
  elastic 1046.3
tennis court
  smoothness 287.3
  playing area 743.11
  tennis 748.1
tenor
  n high voice 58.6
  direction 161.1
  meaning 518.1
  music part 708.22
  voice 709.5
  mode 764.4
  nature 766.4
  transcript 784.4
  trend 895.2
  adj high 58.13
  vocal 708.50
tenpins 750.1
tense
  n grammar 530.12
  time 820.1

v strain 725.10
  stiffen 1044.9
  adj restless 105.27
  anxious 126.7
  nervous 128.13
  in suspense 130.12
  phonetic 524.31
  unfriendly 589.9
  rigid 1044.11
tension
  n anxiety 126.1
  tenseness 128.3
  disaccord 456.1
  enmity 589.1
  strain 725.2
  overextension 992.7
  urgency 996.4
  voltage 1031.11
  rigidity 1044.2
  stretching 1046.2
  v stiffen 1044.9
tent
  n medical apparatus
    86.33
  canvas 295.8
  v camp 225.11
tentacles 474.4
tentative
  n attempt 403.2
  adj slow 175.10
  hesitant 362.11
  trial 403.16
  cautious 494.8
  interim 825.4
  substitute 861.8
  ignorant 929.12
  examining 937.36
  experimental 941.11
  unreliable 970.20
  makeshift 994.7
tenterhooks 126.1
tenth
  n fraction 881.14
  adj ordinal number
    881.22
ten to one 967.8
tenuous dainty 248.7
  infinitesimal 258.14
  thin 270.16
  rare 299.4
  ethereal 763.6
  incoherent 803.4
tenure possession 469.1
  position 724.5
  term 823.3
  period of duty 824.4
tepee 228.10
tepid indifferent 102.6
  warm 1018.24
term
  n boundary 211.3
  sign 518.6
  word 526.1
  phrase 529.1
  end 819.1
  time 820.1
  moment 823.2
  duration 823.3
  tenure 824.4
  v name 527.11
terminal
  n destination 186.5

railway 383.7
  speech component
    524.10
  end 819.1
  stop 856.2
  output device 1041.9
  adj unhealthy 85.53
  past hope 125.15
  limital 210.10
  bordering 211.11
  dying 307.33
  deadly 308.22
  completing 407.9
  final 819.11
  disastrous 1010.15
terminal illness 85.2
terminate
  complete 407.6
  end 819.5
  cease 856.6
  result 886.4
terminology
  nomenclature 527.1
  dictionary 870.4
termite 311.32
term paper 556.1
terra land 234.1
  Earth 1070.10
terrace
  balcony 197.22
  horizontal 201.3
  platform 900.13
terra cotta 715.2
terra-cotta 40.4
terra firma
  ground 199.3
  land 234.1
  foundation 900.6
terrain
  open space 158.4
  region 231.1
  land 234.1
  arena 463.1
terrapin 311.25
terrarium 228.24
terrestrial
  terrene 234.4
  secularist 695.16
  celestial 1070.25
terrible
  horrid 98.19
  frightening 127.30
  remarkable 247.11
  wrong 638.3
  dreadful 999.9
  hideous 1014.11
terrific
  frightening 127.30
  remarkable 247.11
  superb 998.15
terrified 127.26
territorial 231.8
territory
  open space 158.4
  region 231.1
  area 231.5
  country 232.1
  land 234.1
  sphere of influence
    893.4
terror
  n fear 127.1

frightener 127.9
  ruffian 593.4
  violent person 671.10
  adj terrifying 127.29
terrorism
  terrorization 127.7
  despotism 612.10
  violence 671.1
  revolutionism 859.2
terrorist
  n alarmist 127.8
  destroyer 395.8
  violent person 671.9
  revolutionist 859.3
  adj revolutionist 859.6
terrorize
  intimidate 127.20
  threaten 514.2
  rage 671.11
  domineer 612.16
terror-stricken
  terrified 127.26
  panicky 127.27
terse taciturn 344.9
  elegant 533.6
  concise 537.6
  aphoristic 973.6
tertiary
  n color system 35.7
  adj third 876.4
tessellation
  mosaic 47.4
  insertion 191.1
test
  n diagnosis 91.12
  shell 295.15
  measure 300.2
  contest 457.3
  examination 937.2
  trial 941.2
  v interrogate 937.20
  experiment 941.8
  verify 969.12
  adj experimental
    941.11
testament 478.10
Testament 683.2
test case 941.2
testes 2.11
test flight flight 184.9
  tryout 941.3
testicles 2.11
testify depose 334.6
  signify 517.17
  call to witness 598.16
  attest 956.9
testify against 551.12
testimonial
  n advertisement 352.6
  celebration 487.1
  recommendation
    509.4
  certificate 549.6
  monument 549.12
  testimony 956.2
  adj documentary
    549.18
testimony
  deposition 334.3
  evidence 598.8
  attestation 956.2
test pilot aviator 185.1

experimenter 941.6
test run 941.3
test the waters
try one's hand 403.10
sound out 941.9
test tube 857.10
testy
irascible 110.19
argumentative 934.19
tetanus 85.6
tête-à-tête
n chat 541.4
adj intimate 582.24
both 872.7
adv conversationally
541.14
tether
n shackle 428.4
v bind 428.10
yoke 799.10
secure 854.8
tetrad
n four 878.1
adj four 878.4
tetrahedral 278.9
Texas Leaguer 745.3
Texas tea 87.10
text
rendering 341.2
representation 349.1
sign 518.6
writing 547.10
literature 547.12
printed matter 548.10
textbook 554.10
book contents 554.12
playbook 704.21
musical score 708.28
book 718.1
part of writing 792.2
topic 936.1
maxim 973.1
textbook book 554.1
text 554.10
textile
n material 4.1
adj woven 740.7
texture material 4.1
network 170.3
structure 266.1
surface texture 294.1
weaving 740.1
than
adv otherwise 779.11
prep compared to
942.11
thank 150.4
thankful 150.5
thankless
unpleasant 98.17
disliked 99.9
ungrateful 151.4
thanksgiving
thanks 150.2
prayer 696.4
thank-you 150.2
that
adj this 864.14
conj lest 896.7
that's the ticket
inter bravo! 509.22
phrs that's it 787.13

thatch
n head of hair 3.4
v cover 295.23
thaw
n melting 1019.3
v have pity 145.4
melt 1019.21
liquefy 1062.5
theater hall 197.4
setting 209.2
enclosed place 212.3
arena 463.1
battlefield 463.2
schoolroom 567.11
the entertainment
industry 704
playhouse 704.14
theater of operations
war 458.1
battlefield 463.2
theater of the absurd
704.1
theatrical
n actor 707.2
adj emotionalistic
93.19
affected 500.15
stagy 501.24
dramatic 704.33
theatrics
emotionalism 93.9
display 501.4
dramatics 704.2
theft
taking 480.1
thievery 482.1
robbery 482.3
theism
monotheism 675.5
piety 692.1
them
the authorities 575.15
the others 864.5
thematic
recurrent 848.13
topical 936.4
theme
motif 498.7
identification
517.11
morphology 526.3
treatise 556.1
musical passage
708.24
plot 722.4
topic 936.1
theme park 743.14
theme song
identification 517.11
radio signature
1033.19
themselves 864.5
then
adj former 836.10
adv additionally
253.11
at that time 820.9
thereat 820.11
subsequently 834.6
formerly 836.13
hence 887.7
then and there 829.8

theocracy
government 612.4
hierarchy 698.7
theological
n theologian 676.3
adj religious 676.4
theologist 676.3
theology
religious doctrine
675.1
religion 676.1
theorem premise 934.7
axiom 973.2
theoretical
ideational 931.9
hypothetical 950.13
theorist 950.7
theory
harmonics 709.1
idea 931.1
hypothesis 950
theorization 950.1
explanation 950.2
opinion 952.6
theory of evolution
860.4
theory of relativity
158.6
therapeutic
remedial 86.39
helpful 449.21
therapist
health care
professional 90.8
psychologist 92.10
therapy
medicine 90.1
therapeutics 91.1
cure 396.7
aid 449.1
there
at that location
159.24
present 221.16
thereabouts
there 159.24
near 223.20
thereafter
subsequently 834.6
in future 838.10
thereby 384.12
therefore
accordingly 765.11
consequently 886.7
hence 887.7
all things considered
945.17
therein 207.10
thereof 188.20
thermal
n hot air 1018.9
adj warm 1018.24
thermal unit 1018.19
thermochemical
pyrological 1018.32
chemical 1058.8
thermodynamic
1018.32
thermometer 1018.20
thermonuclear 1037.19
thermonuclear power
nuclear energy 18.4

atomic energy
1037.15
thermonuclear
reaction
fission 1037.8
fusion 1037.9
thermonuclear
weapons 462.1
thermostat 1018.20
thesaurus
vocabulary 526.13
reference book 554.9
dictionary 870.4
these 864.14
thesis treatise 556.1
accent 709.25
meter 720.7
beat 849.3
premise 934.7
supposition 950.3
thespian
n actor 707.2
adj dramatic 704.33
thew 15.2
they
the authorities 575.15
exclusiveness 772.3
them 864.5
thick
n middle 818.1
v thicken 269.5
density 1043.10
adj raucous 58.15
three-dimensional
269.8
luxuriant 310.40
inarticulate 525.12
familiar 587.19
teeming 883.9
stupid 921.15
unbelievable 954.10
dense 1043.12
viscous 1060.12
adv densely 1043.15
thicken increase 251.4
grow thick 269.5
densify 1043.10
solidify 1044.8
emulsify 1060.10
thicket
dense plant growth
310.13
bunch 769.7
thick skin
insensibility 25.1
callousness 94.3
shell 295.15
armor 460.3
thief robber 483.1
evildoer 593.1
criminal 660.10
thigh body part 2.7
fowl part 10.22
leg 177.14
thimbleful 248.2
thin
v dilute 16.11
subtract 255.9
shrink 260.9
thin down 270.12
rarefy 299.3
dissipate 770.5

liquefy 1062.5
prune 1067.17
adj shrill 58.14
insipid 65.2
dainty 248.7
infinitesimal 258.14
shrunk 260.13
slender 270.16
shallow 276.5
rare 299.4
tenuous 763.6
sparse 884.5
unbelievable 954.10
meager 991.11
transparent 1028.4
adv thinly 270.23
thin air air 317.1
spirit 763.3
thing love affair 104.6
act 328.3
preference 371.5
occupation 724.1
something 762.3
mode 764.4
particular 765.3
affair 830.3
specialty 865.1
object 1050.4
things wardrobe 5.2
equipment 385.4
belongings 471.2
thingumajig 1050.5
thin ice 1005.1
think expect 130.5
care 339.6
intend 380.4
cogitate 930.8
suppose 950.10
opine 952.11
think ahead
anticipate 838.6
foresee 960.5
think back 988.10
think better of
repent 113.7
reconsider 930.15
thinker wise man 920.1
intellectual 928.1
reasoner 934.11
philosopher 951.6
think highly of
respect 155.4
value 996.13
think little of
disdain 157.3
not hesitate 359.10
disapprove 510.10
underestimate 949.2
be inattentive 983.2
attach little
importance to 997.12
think nothing of
disdain 157.3
not hesitate 359.10
underestimate 949.2
be inattentive 983.2
attach little
importance to 997.12
take it easy 1013.12
think out loud 542.3
think over 930.13
think tank 941.5

think the world of
104.21
think the worst of
125.9
think twice
be cautious 494.5
be unsure 970.10
thinner
paint 35.8
solvent 270.10
diluting agent 1062.4
thinning
n weakening 16.5
shrinking 260.3
rarefaction 299.2
dispersion 770.1
cultivation 1067.13
adj solvent 1062.8
thin-skinned
sensitive 24.12
touchy 110.21
third
n harmonic interval
709.20
baseball 745.1
fraction 877.2
mediocre 1004.6
v trisect 877.3
adj tertiary 876.4
the third-degree 937.13
third-degree burn
trauma 85.37
burn 1019.6
the third dimension
269.2
the third estate 606.1
third person 530.7
third-rate 1004.9
third string
n inferiority 250.1
team 617.7
substitute 861.2
adj inferior 250.6
third world
independents 430.12
neutral 467.4
the poor 619.3
thirst
n craving 100.6
appetite 100.7
tendency 895.1
dryness 1064.1
v hunger 100.19
drink up 1064.5
thirsty
craving 100.24
needing water 100.26
absorbent 187.17
dry 1064.7
thirteen 881.7
thirty-second note
709.14
thirty-two 881.7
this 864.14
this day
n the present 837.1
adv now 837.3
this instant 837.1
thistle thorn 285.5
insignia 647.1
thistledown
down 3.19

lightness 298.2
softness 1045.4
this way 765.10
thong
swimwear 5.29
strip 271.4
whip 605.1
Thor thunder 56.5
rain 316.6
lightning 1024.17
thorax 283.6
thorn
affliction 96.8
bramble 285.5
adhering thing 802.4
bane 1000.1
thorny
prickly 285.10
difficult 1012.17
thorough
downright 247.12
painstaking 339.11
meticulous 339.12
confirmed 373.19
complete 407.12
cautious 494.8
thoroughgoing 793.10
thoroughbred
n aristocrat 607.4
nobleman 608.4
horse 757.2
adj upper-class 607.10
wellborn 608.11
those 864.14
though 338.8
thought
n expectation 130.1
considerateness 143.3
swift thing 174.6
hint 248.4
advice 422.1
remark 524.4
admixture 796.7
intellect 918.1
act of thinking 930
idea 931.1
opinion 952.6
attention 982.1
adj cognitive 930.21
thoughtful
solemn 111.3
considerate 143.16
careful 339.10
courteous 504.14
judicious 919.19
cognitive 930.21
thoughtless
inconsiderate 144.18
careless 340.11
unthinking 365.10
improvident 406.15
unskillful 414.15
foolish 922.8
unwise 922.10
vacuous 932.4
inattentive 983.6
scatterbrained 984.16
thought-out 934.21
thought-provoking
982.19
thousand
n number 881.10

a myriad 883.4
adj numerous 883.6
thrash defeat 412.9
whip 604.13
separate 772.6
pound 901.16
thread
n symbol of weakness
16.7
filament 271.1
series 811.2
v continue 811.4
threadbare trite 117.9
worn 393.31
threads 5.1
threat warning 399.1
menace 514.1
danger 1005.1
threaten
intimidate 127.20
forebode 133.11
warn 399.5
menace 514.2
be in the future 838.6
be imminent 839.2
work evil 999.6
three
n playing card 758.2
trio 875.1
adj triple 875.3
three-alarm fire
1018.13
three cheers! 509.22
3-D
n photography 714.1
adj optical 29.10
spatial 158.9
photographic 714.17
three-dimensional
optical 29.10
spatial 158.9
thick 269.8
photographic 714.17
tripartite 877.4
threefold
v triplicate 876.2
adj triple 876.3
adv triply 876.5
three-in-one
almighty 677.18
three 875.3
three-legged race
457.12
The Three Musketeers
588.6
three-part harmony
708.3
**three sheets to the
wind** 88.33
three-sided sided 218.7
tripartite 877.4
threesome golfer 751.2
three 875.1
Three Wise Men 920.5
thresh separate 772.6
pound 901.16
threshold
n porch 189.6
vestibule 197.19
boundary 211.3
sill 900.9
adj bordering 211.11

thresh out 541.12

thrift
lending institution
620.4
economy 635.1
thrift institution 620.4
thrifty 635.6
thrill
n pang 26.2
tingle 74.1
excitement 105.2
v suffer 26.8
tingle 74.5
delight 95.9
tickle 105.15
be excited 105.18
thrive grow 14.2
have energy 17.11
enlarge 259.7
flourish 1009.8
throat
body passage 2.16
narrow place 270.3
throaty raucous 58.15
inarticulate 525.12
throb
n staccato 55.1
trepidation 105.5
beat 709.26
pulsation 915.3
flutter 916.4
v suffer 26.8
resonate 54.6
drum 55.4
be excited 105.18
pulsate 915.12
flutter 916.12
throes pang 26.2
seizure 85.6
distress 96.5
compunction 113.2
spasm 916.6
thrombosis 85.6
throne
n toilet 12.11
royal seat 417.11
v install 615.12
glorify 662.13
throng
n multitude 769.4
crowd 883.3
v come together
769.16
throttle disable 19.10
silence 51.8
strangle 308.18
suppress 428.8
seize 480.14
through
adj completed 407.11
ended 819.8
adv breadthwise 269.9
prep over 159.28
via 161.27
by means of 384.13
during 820.14
through and through
793.17
throughout
adv scatteringly
770.12
all over 793.17

prep over 159.28
during 820.14
through thick and thin
through fire and
water 360.10
throughout 793.17
through with 819.8
throw
n cast 759.9
toss 903.3
v give birth 1.3
place violently 159.13
make pottery 742.6
play baseball 745.5
discompose 810.4
fling 903.10
fell 912.5
prearrange 964.5
stump 970.14
throw a fit 152.15
throw a scare into
127.16
throw away
reject 372.2
consume 388.3
discard 390.7
squander 486.3
underact 704.31
eject 908.13
do away with 908.21
attach little
importance to 997.12
throwback
regression 163.1
relapse 394.1
atavism 858.2
reverse 1010.3
throw caution to the
wind brave 492.11
take chances 1005.7
throw down
raze 395.19
overthrow 395.20
fell 912.5
throw down the
gauntlet
confront 216.8
resist 453.2
defy 454.3
make war on 458.15
throw-in
basketball game
747.3
soccer game 752.3
throw in the towel
give up 370.7
lose 412.12
surrender 433.8
throw into chaos 984.7
throw into the street
908.15
throw in with
side with 450.4
league 804.4
throw light upon
explain 341.10
illuminate 1024.28
thrown for a loss
412.15
throw off take off 6.6
shed 6.10
dislodge 160.6

do carelessly 340.9
improvise 365.8
break the habit 374.3
free oneself from
431.8
say 524.23
separate 801.8
do away with 908.21
let out 908.24
throw off balance
790.3
throw off the scent
mislead 356.16
evade 368.7
distract 984.6
throw one's hat in the
ring 609.39
throw one's money
away 486.3
throw one's weight
around
urge 375.14
wield authority
417.13
exercise influence
893.9
throw one a curve
356.16
throw oneself at the
feet of fawn 138.7
beg for mercy 145.6
bow down 433.10
entreat 440.11
throw oneself on the
mercy of the court
repent 113.7
confess 351.7
plead 598.18
throw open 292.11
throw out
reject 372.2
discard 390.7
separate 801.8
eject 908.13
disgorge 908.25
throw out of joint
dislocate 160.5
disjoint 801.16
throw out the baby
with the bath water
486.4
throw overboard
discard 390.7
eliminate 772.5
eject 908.13
throw the book at
604.11
throw together
do carelessly 340.9
improvise 365.8
acquire 472.9
mix 796.10
throw to the wolves
abandon 370.5
discard 390.7
punish 604.11
throw up
give up 370.7
relinquish 475.3
vomit 908.26
elevate 911.5
thrush 710.23

thrust
n vim 17.2
power 18.4
acceleration 174.4
pass 459.3
major part 791.6
push 901.2
propulsion 903.1
rocketry 1072.8
v place violently
159.13
launch an attack
459.17
impel 901.11
push 901.12
propel 903.9
thrust and parry
457.13
thrust aside 983.4
thruster rocket 1072.2
spacecraft 1073.2
thrust upon
urge upon 439.9
force upon 478.20
thud
n dull sound 52.3
v make a dull sound
52.15
thug killer 308.10
combatant 461.1
bandit 483.4
ruffian 593.3
criminal 660.10
henchman 616.8
thumb
n finger 73.5
v touch 73.6
hitchhike 177.31
fight 754.4
thumbnail review
945.2
thumb one's nose at
disdain 157.3
flout 454.4
thumbprint 517.7
thumbscrew
contractor 260.6
torture 605.4
thumbs-down
refusal 442.1
veto 444.2
disapproval 510.1
banishment 908.4
thumbs-up
affirmative 332.2
permission 443.1
thumb through
browse 570.13
examine cursorily
937.25
thump
n dull sound 52.3
hit 901.4
v make a dull sound
52.15
drum 55.4
whip 604.13
beat time 708.44
hit 901.14
pound 901.16
thunder
n noise 53.3

reverberation 54.2
rumbling sound 56.5
v din 53.7
boom 56.9
proclaim 352.13
speak 524.26
thunderbolt
surprise 131.2
swiftness 174.6
lightning 1024.17
thunderclap noise 53.3
thunder 56.5
surprise 131.2
thunderhead
bird of ill omen 133.6
warning sign 399.3
thunderstorm
thunder 56.5
rain 316.3
storm 671.4
thunderstruck 122.9
thus how 384.9
thusly 765.10
similarly 783.18
hence 887.7
to illustrate 956.23
thus far so far 211.16
limited 248.10
until now 837.4
thwack
n explosive sound
56.1
hit 901.4
v make explosive
sound 56.6
hit 901.14
thwart
v disappoint 132.2
frustrate 412.11
neutralize 899.7
hinder 1011.15
adj across 170.9
transverse 204.19
adv crosswise 170.13
tiara jewel 498.6
royal insignia 647.3
ecclesiastical insignia
647.4
tic
nervousness 128.1
shake 916.3
obsession 925.13
tick
n faint sound 52.3
clicking 55.2
degree 245.1
insect 311.31
bloodsucker 311.36
mark 517.5
credit 622.1
instant 829.3
v make faint sound
52.15
click repeatedly 55.5
mark 517.19
be operative 888.7
pulsate 915.12
ticked off 152.30
ticker the heart 2.14
telegraph 347.2
stock exchange 737.7
timepiece 831.6

ticker tape
recording media
549.10
stock exchange 737.7
ticket
n permission 443.1
label 517.13
certificate 549.6
ballot 609.19
price 630.1
token 728.12
v label 517.20
tickle
n sensation 74.2
v titillate 74.6
delight 95.9
thrill 105.15
incite 375.17
attract 377.6
amuse 743.21
tap 901.18
interest 982.12
tickled pleased 95.14
amused 743.26
interested 982.16
tickler fisher 382.6
reminder 988.6
ticklish sensitive 24.12
tickling 74.9
touchy 110.21
unreliable 970.20
precarious 1005.12
difficult 1012.17
tick off
make angry 152.23
mark 517.19
tidal aquatic 182.58
coastal 234.7
flowing 238.24
tidal wave wave 238.14
election returns
609.21
upheaval 671.5
oscillation 915.4
tidbit delicacy 10.8
scandal 552.8
tide
n flow 238.4
tidal current 238.13
ocean 240.1
time 820.1
v conform 866.4
tide over 1006.2
tidewater
n shore 234.2
tide 238.13
adj gulfy 242.2
tidy
v clean 79.18
arrange 807.12
adj cleaned 79.26
large 257.16
trim 806.8
tolerable 998.20
tidy sum lot 247.4
large sum 618.2
multitude 883.3
tie
n intermediary 213.4
security 438.1
fidelity 644.7
insignia 647.1

musical notation
709.12
relation 774.1
the same 789.3
joining 799.1
dead heat 835.3
stop 856.2
v compel 424.4
bind 428.10
obligate 641.12
relate 774.6
equal 789.5
put together 799.5
fasten 799.9
secure 854.8
tiebreaker 748.2
tie clasp 498.6
tied up busy 330.21
bound 428.16
indebted 623.8
tie-dyed 35.16
tie hand and foot
disable 19.10
bind 428.10
tie-in affiliation 450.2
sale 734.1
relation 774.1
joining 799.1
tie into attack 459.15
criticize 510.14
tie in with
relate to 774.5
league 804.4
tie off 854.8
tie one on 88.26
tier layer 296.1
series 811.2
tie rod 799.4
Tierra del Fuego
remote region 261.4
cold place 1022.4
tie the knot
join in marriage
563.14
get married 563.15
put together 799.5
tie up anchor 182.15
land 186.8
bind 428.10
cooperate 450.3
monopolize 469.6
bundle 769.20
fasten 799.9
secure 854.8
tiff
n dudgeon 152.7
quarrel 456.5
v quarrel 456.11
tiger
wild cat 311.22
brave person 492.8
savage 593.5
violent person 671.9
tight
adj resistant 15.20
drunk 88.33
shipshape 180.20
narrow 270.14
close 293.12
stingy 484.9
concise 537.6
fastened 799.14

consistent 802.11
tidy 806.8
sparse 884.5
rigid 1044.11
adv securely 799.19
tight end 746.2
tighten one's belt
retrench 635.5
deny oneself 667.3
tighten the screws
119.2
tightfisted 484.9
tight grip 474.2
tight-knit joined 799.13
dense 1043.12
tight-lipped 344.9
tightrope walking
defiance 454.1
daring 492.5
foolhardiness 493.3
unreliability 970.6
tights 5.9
tight squeeze
narrowness 270.1
narrow escape 369.2
poverty 619.1
predicament 1012.5
tightwad 484.4
tigress
female animal 77.9
bitch 110.12
witch 593.7
violent person 671.9
tile
n pavement 383.6
ceramic ware 742.2
building material
1052.2
v cover 295.23
till
n booty 482.11
treasury 729.12
v cultivate 1067.17
prep until 820.15
till death do us part
828.13
tiller helm 573.5
agriculturist 1067.5
till hell freezes over
to the end 819.13
for a long time 826.14
forever 828.12
**till one is blue in the
face** 105.35
**till the cows come
home**
for a long time 826.14
forever 828.12
till the end of time
826.14
till then 825.5
till the soil 1067.17
tilt
n penchant 100.3
inclination 204.2
preference 371.5
contest 457.3
tendency 895.1
v tumble 194.8
incline 204.10
contend 457.13
tend 895.3

throw 903.10
tilt at windmills
be impotent 19.7
be useless 391.8
be foolish 922.6
timber spar 180.13
beam 273.3
tree 310.10
woodland 310.11
wood 1052.3
timber wolf 311.20
timbre tonality 50.3
manner of speaking
524.8
Timbuktu 261.4
time
n leisure 402.1
tempo 709.24
duration 820.1
period 823.1
term 823.3
age 823.4
turn 824.2
shift 824.3
tenure 824.4
time of day 831.2
date 831.4
opportunity 842.2
v fix the time 831.11
synchronize 835.4
time bomb 1005.1
time book 831.9
time frame
boundary 211.3
plan 381.1
time 820.1
period 823.1
time-honored
venerable 155.12
customary 373.14
traditional 841.12
timekeeper
recorder 550.1
hockey 749.6
boxing 754.3
timepiece 831.6
chronologist 831.10
timeless
almighty 677.18
dateless 821.3
perpetual 828.7
old 841.10
time limit 211.3
timely
well-timed 842.9
expedient 994.5
time off
n vacation 20.3
interim 825.1
pause 856.3
v take one's turn 824.5
time out
n respite 20.2
v punch the clock
831.12
timepiece 831.6
the times
affairs 830.4
the present 837.1
time scale 831.9
timetable plan 381.1
chronicle 831.9

time to spare
leisure 402.1
earliness 844.1
time warp
fourth dimension
158.6
time 820.1
timeworn trite 117.9
stricken in years
303.18
worn 393.31
stale 841.14
time zone 831.3
timid fearful 127.23
shy 139.12
hesitant 362.11
cowardly 491.10
timing
skill 413.1
tempo 709.24
agreement 787.1
chronology 831.1
timorous
fearful 127.23
shy 139.12
cowardly 491.10
tin
n money 728.2
v package 212.9
put up 397.11
adj spurious 354.25
metal 1056.17
tincture
n color 35.1
pigment 35.8
hint 248.4
heraldry 647.2
admixture 796.7
v color 35.13
imbue 796.11
tinder 1020.6
tin foil 295.18
tinge
n color 35.1
trace 62.3
hint 248.4
implication 519.2
admixture 796.7
v color 35.13
imbue 796.11
influence 893.7
tingle
n smart 26.3
ringing 54.3
tingling sensation
74.1
thrill 105.2
v have energy 17.11
suffer 26.8
ring 54.8
thrill 74.5
be excited 105.18
tinhorn
n gambler 759.21
mediocrity 1004.5
adj insignificant
997.18
tinker
n mender 396.10
v repair 396.14
rearrange 807.13
trifle 997.14

tinkle
n clinking sound 52.3
ringing 54.3
v clink 52.15
ring 54.8
tinny
lacking resonance
58.15
inferior 1004.9
metallic 1056.17
Tin Pan Alley 708.7
tinsel
n appearance 33.2
fake 354.13
finery 498.3
glitter 1024.7
v decorate 498.9
glitter 1024.24
adj spurious 354.25
specious 354.26
tint
n color 35.1
hue 35.6
engraving 713.2
admixture 796.7
v color 35.13
portray 712.19
tintinnabulation 54.3
tiny insignificant 248.6
little 258.11
tip
n summit 198.2
inclination 204.2
point 285.3
piece of advice 422.2
gratuity 478.5
part of tongue 524.19
clue 551.3
bonus 624.6
extremity 819.2
tap 901.7
surplus 992.5
v careen 182.43
crown 198.9
incline 204.10
top 295.21
warn 399.5
alert 551.11
tap 901.18
tip-off
warning 399.1
sign 517.1
clue 517.9
suggest 551.3
hint 551.4
tip of the iceberg
modicum 248.2
hint 248.4
sign 517.1
tipple drink 8.29
booze 88.24
tippytoe
n creeping 177.17
v creep 177.26
adj creeping 177.39
tip sheet 757.4
tipster informant 551.5
dopester 961.5
tipsy
intoxicated 88.31
inclining 204.15
tip the scales 297.10

tiptoe
n creeping 177.17
v creep 177.26
lurk 346.9
be cautious 494.5
adj creeping 177.39
adv on tiptoe 272.21
tip-top
n summit 198.2
adj top 198.10
superlative 249.13
first-rate 998.18
tirade
n lament 115.3
berating 510.7
wordiness 538.2
speech 543.2
v wail 115.13
tire
n rim 280.4
v clothe 5.38
fatigue 21.4
weary 21.5
oppress 98.16
be tedious 118.6
tired clothing 5.44
fatigued 21.7
weary 118.11
worn-out 393.36
aphoristic 973.6
tireless
industrious 330.22
persevering 360.8
tires 756.1
tiresome
fatiguing 21.13
annoying 98.22
boring 118.10
prosaic 721.5
tissue
n material 4.1
network 170.3
structure 266.1
organic matter 305.1
weaving 740.1
v weave 740.6
titan 257.13
titanic large 247.7
huge 257.20
tit for tat offset 338.2
retaliation 506.3
reciprosity 776.3
substitution 861.1
interchange 862.1
tit-for-tat 776.10
tithe
n donation 478.6
tax 630.9
tenth part 881.14
v charge 630.12
adj tenth 881.22
titillate tickle 74.6
delight 95.9
thrill 105.15
attract 377.6
amuse 743.21
interest 982.12
title
n possession 469.1
ownership 469.2
estate 471.4
name 527.3

book 554.1
book part 554.12
prerogative 642.1
honorific 648.1
golf 751.1
class 808.2
caption 936.2
v name 527.11
focus on 936.3
titled named 527.14
noble 608.10
titleholder 470.2
title page label 517.13
book part 554.12
caption 936.2
titrate 800.6
tits
n bosom 283.7
adj excellent 998.13
tizzy dither 105.6
confusion 984.3
TKO 754.2
TLC carefulness 339.1
support 449.3
to at 159.27
toward 161.26
into 189.14
as far as 261.20
for the purpose of
380.11
until 820.15
toad sycophant 138.3
amphibian 311.27
to a degree
to some extent 245.7
limited 248.10
relatively 774.12
toad-stool 310.4
to advantage
usefully 387.26
helpfully 449.24
profitably 472.17
expediently 994.8
toady
n sycophant 138.3
assenter 332.6
v fawn 138.7
to a fault 992.23
to a great extent 247.15
to all appearances
apparently 33.12
externally 206.10
to a man 332.17
to and fro
reciprocally 776.12
alternately 849.11
changeably 853.8
back and forth 915.21
toast
n pledge 88.10
celebration 487.1
fine lady 500.10
v drink 8.29
cook 11.4
drink to 88.29
be hot 1018.22
adj brown 40.3
delightful 97.8
to a T
to completion 407.14
exactly 972.21
to a nicety 972.23

to perfection 1001.11
to a turn
carefully 339.15
to completion 407.14
to a nicety 972.23
to perfection 1001.11
tobacco
n tabac 89.1
adj tobaccoey 89.15
to beat the band
swiftly 174.18
utterly 793.16
to perfection 1001.11
to be brief 537.8
to be desired
desirable 100.30
expedient 994.5
to be exact 972.22
to be expected
adj as expected 130.14
adv imminently 839.4
normally 868.10
to be fair 649.12
to be reckoned with
893.13
to be seen
visible 31.6
manifest 348.8
to be specific 864.15
to be sure
adv surely 969.24
inter yes 332.18
toboggan 177.35
to boot 253.11
to come
approaching 167.4
future 838.8
imminent 839.3
scheduled 964.9
to completion 407.14
tocsin
warning sign 399.3
alarm 400.1
to date 837.4
today
n the present 837.1
adv now 837.3
toddler 302.9
to-do
excitement 105.4
bustle 330.4
commotion 809.4
agitation 916.1
toe base 199.2
foot 199.5
toehold hold 474.2
wrestling 474.3
footing 900.5
purchase 905.2
toe the mark
obey 326.2
follow the rule 866.4
toe-to-toe 778.6
to extremes
intemperately 669.10
in or to excess 992.23
tofu 10.46
together
v assemble 769.18
adj composed 106.13
in accord 455.3
sane 924.4

adv unanimously
332.17
cooperatively 450.6
collectively 768.11
jointly 799.18
continuously 811.10
simultaneously 835.7
concurrently 898.5
togetherness
accord 455.1
accompaniment 768.1
toggle 799.8
to good use 387.26
togs clothing 5.1
garment 5.3
toil
n work 725.4
v work 724.12
drudge 725.14
hamper 1011.11
toilet
n latrine 12.10
stool 12.11
bathroom 197.26
casino 759.19
adj cursing 513.8
toiletries 735.6
to infinity 822.4
token
n omen 133.3
symbol 517.2
password 517.12
label 517.13
sign 518.6
record 549.1
counter 728.12
substitute 861.2
characteristic 864.4
evidence 956.1
memento 988.7
v augur 133.12
manifest 348.5
adj cheap 633.7
substitute 861.8
token gesture 354.6
to leeward
leeward 182.68
windward 218.9
tolerable
bearable 107.13
satisfactory 998.20
mediocre 1004.7
tolerance
resistance 87.1
patience 134.1
forgiveness 148.1
leniency 427.1
latitude 430.4
liberalism 430.10
sufferance 443.2
inclusion 771.1
inaccuracy 974.2
broad-mindedness
978.4
tolerate endure 134.5
be easy on 427.5
suffer 443.10
keep an open mind
978.7
toll
n ringing 54.3
fee 630.6

tax 630.9
v ring 54.8
tollbooth 228.9
tomahawk 745.5
**to make a long story
short** 537.8
tomato
vegetables 10.34
woman 77.6
girl 302.7
tomb
n sepulcher 309.16
monument 549.12
v inter 309.19
tomboy mannish
female 76.9
schoolgirl 302.8
tomcat
male animal 76.8
cat 311.21
tome book 554.1
volume 554.4
tomorrow
n the future 838.1
adv in the future 838.9
tom-tom 55.1
ton quantity 247.3
fashion 578.1
popularity 578.2
tonal sounding 50.15
phonetic 524.31
harmonics 709.27
tone
n muscularity 15.2
color 35.1
hue 35.6
audio frequency 50.2
fitness 84.1
feeling 93.1
milieu 209.3
behavior 321.1
manner 384.1
intonation 524.7
voice 524.8
melody 708.2
tonality 709.3
pitch 709.4
note 709.14
interval 709.20
artistic treatment
712.9
plot 722.4
nature 766.4
trend 895.2
mood 977.4
elasticity 1046.1
v color 35.13
influence 893.7
tone-deaf 49.6
tone down decolor 36.5
muffle 51.9
moderate 670.6
tune 708.36
dull 1026.10
soften 1045.6
toneless colorless 36.7
monotone 50.15
tongs 1019.12
tongue
n food 10.19
bell 54.4
taste 62.1

grandiloquent 545.8
torture
  n agony 26.6
  torment 96.7
  harshness 98.4
  deflection 164.2
  punishment 604.2
  v pain 26.7
  torment 96.18
  agonize 98.12
  bear malice 144.15
  deflect 164.5
  pervert 265.6
  deform 265.7
  misinterpret 342.2
  put to the question
    604.16
  work evil 999.6
Tory 611.9
to spare
  remaining 256.7
  unused 390.12
  superfluous 992.17
toss
  n gamble 759.2
  throw 903.3
  flounder 916.8
  search 937.15
  even chance 971.7
  v be excited 105.18
  place violently 159.13
  pitch 182.55
  billow 238.22
  gamble 759.23
  throw 903.10
  oscillate 915.10
  flounder 916.15
  ransack 937.32
toss and turn
  keep awake 23.3
  be excited 105.18
  flounder 916.15
toss-up election 609.15
  uncertainty 759.2
  stop 856.2
  gamble 970.8
  even chance 971.7
total
  n amount 244.2
  math terms 253.2
  whole 791.2
  sum 1016.6
  v compute 253.6
  spoil 393.11
  demolish 395.17
  amount to 791.8
  sum up 1016.18
  adj great 247.6
  downright 247.12
  unmitigated 671.17
  cumulative 769.23
  comprehensive 771.7
  whole 791.9
  complete 793.9
  thorough 793.10
  universal 863.14
  unqualified 959.2
  sound 1001.7
total assets
  assets 471.7
  funds 728.14
total darkness 1026.1

total eclipse
  darkness 1026.8
  sun 1070.13
totaled high 87.23
  spoiled 393.29
  disintegrative 805.5
  ended 819.9
totalitarian
  authoritative 417.15
  governmental 612.17
totality whole 791.1
  wholeness 791.5
  completeness 793.1
  all 863.4
  universe 1070.1
total lack 222.1
total loss
  wreck 393.8
  debacle 395.4
  failure 410.2
  loss 473.1
total recall 988.3
total victory 411.1
total war
  death struggle 457.6
  war 458.1
tote board 759.17
to tell the truth
  truthfully 644.22
  truly 972.18
totem symbol 517.2
  race 559.4
  familiar spirit 678.12
  idol 697.3
totem pole
  shaft 273.1
  symbol 517.2
tote up compute 253.6
  sum up 1016.18
to the contrary
  adv contrarily 778.9
  inter no 335.8
  by no means 335.9
to the death
  deathly 307.37
  throughout 793.17
to the end to
  completion 407.14
  throughout 793.17
  to the bitter end
    819.13
to the extreme 992.23
to the four winds
  from everywhere
    158.13
  in every direction
    161.25
to the good
  helpfully 449.24
  profitably 472.17
  to one's account
    622.9
to the heart of 207.13
to the hilt
  completely 793.14
  throughout 793.17
to the letter 972.21
to the limit
  to completion 407.14
  utterly 793.16
to the max
  utterly 793.16

in excess 992.23
to the nth degree
  793.16
to the point
  adj concise 537.6
  relevant 774.11
  apt 787.10
  adv plainly 535.4
to the second 844.14
to the side
  adj side 218.6
  adv aside 218.10
to the tune of
  adv at a price 630.17
  prep to the amount of
    244.7
tots 302.2
totter
  n gait 177.12
  flounder 916.8
  v be weak 16.8
  way of walking 177.28
  tumble 194.8
  age 303.10
  vacillate 362.8
  break down 393.24
  change 853.5
  flounder 916.15
touch
  n senses 24.5
  sense of touch 73.1
  contact 223.5
  hint 248.4
  communication 343.1
  skill 413.1
  knack 413.6
  motif 498.7
  signal 517.15
  implication 519.2
  execution 708.30
  admixture 796.7
  tap 901.7
  v sense 24.6
  feel 73.6
  affect 93.14
  move 145.5
  contact 223.10
  beg 440.15
  signal 517.22
  borrow 621.3
  relate to 774.5
  equal 789.5
  tap 901.18
touch and go
  gamble 759.2
  uncertainty 970.8
  even chance 971.7
touch a nerve 24.8
touchdown
  landing 184.18
  score 409.5
  game 746.3
touché
  adv right! 972.24
  phrs that's it 787.13
touched affected 93.23
  penitent 113.9
  insane 925.26
touch off
  kindle 375.18
  explode 671.14
  ignite 1019.22

touch on
  remark 524.25
  evidence 956.8
  call attention to
    982.10
touch up 392.11
touchy sensitive 24.12
  excitable 105.28
  tetchy 110.21
  partisan 456.17
  precarious 1005.12
tough
  n strong man 15.7
  combatant 461.1
  ruffian 593.4
  violent person 671.10
  adj firm 15.18
  obdurate 361.10
  strict 425.6
  resolute 492.18
  hard to understand
    522.14
  violent 671.16
  laborious 725.18
  sturdy 762.7
  adhesive 802.12
  durable 826.10
  excellent 998.13
  difficult 1012.17
  hard 1044.10
  resistant 1047.4
  viscous 1060.12
tough act to follow
  expert 413.11
  first-rater 998.6
tough as nails 1047.4
tough break 1010.5
tough guy
  strong man 15.7
  violent person 671.10
tough it out
  be strong 15.11
  endure 134.6
  confront 216.8
  persevere 360.7
  offer resistance 453.3
  stand fast 854.11
tough luck
  chance 971.1
  bad luck 1010.5
toupee 3.14
tour
  n journey 177.5
  tower 272.6
  route 383.1
  engagement 704.11
  bowling 750.1
  golf 751.1
  shift 824.3
  term 824.4
  circuit 913.2
  sight-seeing 917.4
  v journey 177.21
tour de force
  act 328.3
  masterpiece 413.10
tourist
  traveler 178.1
  sightseer 917.3
tournament
  contest 457.3
  tourney 743.10

trajectory course 172.2
route 383.1
orbit 1070.16
rocket launching 1072.9
tram 179.17
tramp
n walk 177.10
vagabond 178.3
bum 331.9
beggar 440.8
wretch 660.2
transient 827.4
oddity 869.4
v plod 175.7
wander 177.23
march 177.30
trample stamp 901.22
run over 909.7
trampoline
exerciser 725.7
elastic 1046.3
trance
n stupor 22.6
hypnosis 22.7
daze 92.19
ecstasy 691.3
abstractedness 984.2
v put to sleep 22.20
cast a spell 691.7
tranquil calm 106.12
quiescent 173.12
pacific 464.9
equable 670.13
thoughtless 932.4
tranquilizer
anesthetic 25.3
sedative 86.12
moderator 670.3
transact perform 328.9
execute 437.9
transaction
performance 328.2
act 328.3
compact 437.1
execution 437.4
business transaction 731.4
affair 830.3
transatlantic 261.11
transcend
loom 247.5
excel 249.6
exceed 992.9
transcendental
n immaterialism 1051.3
adj superior 249.12
recondite 522.16
heavenly 681.12
supernatural 869.15
visionary 985.24
numeric 1016.22
extraterrestrial 1070.26
transcontinental 261.11
transcribe
translate 341.12
letter 546.6
write 547.19
compose 708.46

copy 784.8
transducer 857.10
transect 874.4
transept
crosspiece 170.5
church 703.9
transfer
n transferal 176.1
informing 343.2
transference 629.1
transcript 784.4
v transmit 176.10
communicate 343.7
deliver 478.13
commission 615.10
convey 629.3
transfigure
make better 392.9
transform 851.8
transfix
perforate 292.15
stab 459.25
stabilize 854.7
transform
make better 392.9
transfigure 851.8
convert 857.11
transfusion
blood transfusion 91.18
transferal 176.1
permeation 221.3
transgress
disobey 327.6
violate 435.4
do wrong 655.4
break the law 674.5
overstep 909.9
transiency 827.1
transient
n traveler 178.1
lodger 227.8
guest 827.4
adj vanishing 34.3
wandering 177.37
emerging 190.18
short 268.8
mortal 307.34
transitory 827.7
changeable 853.6
transistor 1032.12
transit
n crossing 170.1
transferal 176.1
travel 177.1
instrument 278.4
conversion 857.1
v traverse 177.20
transition
transferal 176.1
motion-picture editing 706.5
change 851.1
conversion 857.1
transitive
n verb 530.4
adj grammatical 530.17
transient 827.7
translate
transfer 176.10
render 341.12

transform 851.8
translation
transferal 176.1
transcription 341.3
removal to heaven 681.11
transformation 851.3
translucent
clear 521.11
light 1024.31
lucent 1029.5
transmigration
transferal 176.1
migration 177.4
transformation 851.3
materialization 1050.8
transmission
transferal 176.1
informing 343.2
information 551.1
conveyance 629.1
radio broadcasting 1033.16
gear 1039.5
transmit
change over 176.10
send 176.15
communicate 343.7
bequeath 478.18
transfer 629.3
broadcast 1033.25
send 1035.15
transmitter
telegraph 347.2
telephone 347.4
radio transmitter 1033.4
televisor 1034.8
transmogrification 851.3
transoceanic 261.11
transom
crosspiece 170.5
stern 217.7
air passage 239.13
transparency
clearness 521.2
photograph 714.3
print 714.5
nonopacity 1028
transparence 1028.1
transparent
clear 521.11
candid 644.17
light 1024.31
transpicuous 1028.4
transpire
exude 190.15
be revealed 351.8
occur 830.5
transplant
n insertion 191.1
plant 739.3
v treat 91.24
transfer 176.10
implant 191.8
set 1067.18
transport
n happiness 95.2
fury 105.8

transportation 176.3
trance 691.3
v delight 95.9
convey 176.12
fascinate 377.7
banish 908.17
transportation
transplacement 176
conveyance 176.3
banishment 908.4
transpose
transfer 176.10
invert 205.5
compose 708.46
reverse 778.5
interchange 862.4
transsexual 75.17
transverse
n crosspiece 170.5
diagonal 204.7
v cross 170.6
adj transversal 170.9
crosswise 204.19
adv crossways 170.13
transvestite
n sexual pervert 75.16
adj homosexual 75.29
trap
n mouth 292.4
ambush 346.3
gin 356.12
lure 377.3
basketball game 747.3
soccer 752.3
hidden danger 1005.5
v entrap 356.20
catch 480.17
play 752.4
trapeze 725.7
trapezoid 278.9
trapper 382.5
trappings
wardrobe 5.2
harness 385.5
belongings 471.2
finery 498.3
Trappist
n religious person 667.2
adj ascetic 667.4
trap shooting 744.1
trash
n derelict 370.4
rubbish 391.5
nonsense 520.2
rabble 606.3
poker 759.10
trivia 997.4
v be disrespectful 156.6
censure 510.13
trashy worthless 391.11
nonsensical 520.7
paltry 997.21
trauma shock 85.26
wound 85.37
psychological stress 92.17
traumatic 393.27
travail
n birth 1.1

work 725.4
v give birth 1.3
drudge 725.14
travel
  n progression 162.1
  course 172.2
  transportation 176.3
  journeying 177
  traveling 177.1
  v progress 162.2
  move 172.5
  go 177.18
  journey 177.21
travel agency 177.5
travels 177.2
traverse
  n crosspiece 170.5
  v cross 170.6
  travel 177.20
  navigate 182.13
  oppose 451.3
  contradict 451.6
  ski 753.4
  adj transverse 170.9
  adv crosswise 170.13
travesty
  n reproduction 336.3
  bad likeness 350.2
  exaggeration 355.1
  wit 489.1
  burlesque 508.6
  v misrepresent 350.3
  exaggerate 355.3
  burlesque 508.11
trawler 382.6
treacherous
  falsehearted 354.30
  deceitful 356.22
  perfidious 645.21
  unreliable 970.20
  unsafe 1005.11
treachery
  falseheartedness 354.4
  treacherousness 645.6
  unreliability 970.6
treacle sweetening 66.2
  semiliquid 1060.5
tread
  n velocity 172.4
  travel 177.11
  gait 177.12
  step 193.5
  degree 245.1
  v walk 177.27
  stamp 901.22
treading water 182.11
treadmill
  n routine 373.6
  punishment 605.3
  work 725.4
  adj tedious 118.9
tread underfoot
  conquer 412.10
  subdue 432.9
  domineer 612.16
treason apostasy 363.2
  petty crime 645.7
  conversion 857.3
treasure
  n store 386.1
  wealth 618.1
  funds 728.14

collection 769.11
good thing 998.5
v cherish 104.21
store up 386.11
hold 474.7
keep in memory
  988.13
value 996.13
treasurer
  executive 574.3
  payer 624.9
  financial officer
  729.11
treasury store 386.1
  bank 386.6
  funds 728.14
  cash 728.18
  treasure-house 729.12
  collection 769.11
treasury bill 728.11
treat
  n meal 8.5
  delicacy 10.8
  regalement 95.3
  payment 624.8
  v remedy 86.38
  practice medicine
  90.14
  doctor 91.24
  use 321.6
  handle 387.12
  prepare 405.6
  discuss 541.12
  write upon 556.5
  pay for 624.19
  operate on 888.6
treatise tract 556
  piece 556.1
treatment
  medicine 90.1
  therapy 91.1
  medical attention
  91.14
  usage 387.2
  preparation 405.1
  discussion 541.7
  treatise 556.1
  script 706.2
  technique 712.9
treaty 437.2
treble
  n stridency 58.6
  air 708.4
  part 708.22
  voice 709.5
  v triplicate 876.2
  adj high 58.13
  vocal 708.50
  triple 876.3
tree
  n cross 170.4
  spar 180.13
  timber 310.10
  genealogy 560.5
  execution 605.5
  v corner 1012.16
tree line 237.2
trek
  n migration 177.4
  journey 177.5
  v journey 177.21
  migrate 177.22

trellis
  n network 170.3
  v net 170.7
tremble
  n trepidation 105.5
  trill 709.19
  agitate 916.3
  v be weak 16.8
  be excited 105.18
  shake 127.14
  fidget 128.6
  quiver 916.11
  freeze 1022.9
tremendous
  terrible 127.30
  large 247.7
  huge 257.20
  superb 998.15
tremor thrill 105.2
  trepidation 105.5
  speech defect 525.1
  trill 709.19
  shake 916.3
tremulous
  fearful 127.23
  jittery 128.6
  inarticulate 525.12
  shaking 916.17
trench
  n crack 224.2
  channel 239.1
  ocean depths 275.4
  valley 284.9
  trough 290.2
  entrenchment 460.5
  shelter 1008.3
  v intrude 214.5
  cleave 224.4
  channel 239.15
  excavate 284.15
  furrow 290.3
trenchant
  energetic 17.13
  acrimonious 17.14
  pungent 68.6
  caustic 144.23
  vigorous 544.11
  sagacious 919.16
trencherman eater 8.16
  glutton 672.3
trend
  n direction 161.1
  course 172.2
  flow 238.4
  fashion 578.1
  drift 895.2
  v take direction 161.7
  deviate 164.3
  flow 238.16
  tend 895.3
trendsetter 578.7
trendy
  fashionable 578.11
  faddish 578.15
  knowledgeable 927.17
trepidation
  trepidity 105.5
  fear 127.5
  nervousness 128.1
  agitation 916.1
très bien 332.18
très bon 998.12

trespass
  n intrusion 214.1
  violation 435.2
  usurpation 640.3
  misdeed 655.2
  lawbreaking 674.3
  overstepping 909.3
  v intrude 214.5
  violate 435.4
  usurp 640.8
  do wrong 655.4
  break the law 674.5
  overstep 909.9
tresses 3.4
trestle
  railway 383.7
  horse 900.16
trey card 758.2
  three 875.1
trial
  n annoyance 96.2
  tribulation 96.9
  attempt 403.2
  preparation 405.1
  contest 457.3
  number 530.8
  legal action 598.5
  experiment 941.1
  test 941.2
  adversity 1010.1
  adj tentative 403.16
  three 875.3
  experimental 941.11
trial and error
  attempt 403.2
  experiment 941.1
trial balloon
  question 937.10
  feeler 941.4
trial by jury 598.5
trials and tribulations
  96.9
triangle bell 54.4
  love affair 104.6
  straightedge 277.3
  punishment 605.3
  three 875.1
triangulate
  v locate 159.11
  measure 300.10
  adj tripartite 877.4
triathlon sport 744.1
  track meet 755.2
tribe race 559.4
  company 769.3
  kind 808.3
  classifications 808.5
tribunal
  n council 423.1
  court 595
  forum 595.1
  platform 900.13
  adj judicial 595.7
tributary
  n feeder 238.3
  adj subject 432.13
tribute demand 421.1
  gift 478.4
  celebration 487.1
  praise 509.5
  fee 624.5
  tax 630.9

citation 646.4
acknowledgment
  887.2
trick
  n act 328.3
  artifice 356.6
  habit 373.4
  pretext 376.1
  intrigue 381.5
  knack 413.6
  stratagem 415.3
  prank 489.10
  mannerism 500.2
  style 532.2
  bridge 758.3
  shift 824.3
  characteristic 864.4
  quirk 926.2
  goof 974.6
  illusion 975.1
  expedient 994.2
  v deceive 356.14
  fool 356.15
  live by one's wits
    415.9
  play a practical joke
    489.14
trickle
  n leakage 190.5
  tricklet 238.7
  a few 884.2
  v leak 190.14
  dribble 238.18
tricks of the trade
  356.6
tricky deceptive 356.21
  deceitful 356.22
  cunning 415.12
  waggish 489.17
  dishonest 645.16
  improper 645.18
  treacherous 645.21
  difficult 1012.17
tricycle 179.8
trident
  n fork 171.4
  three 875.1
  adj tripartite 877.4
tried and true
  experienced 413.28
  devoted 587.21
  trustworthy 644.19
  traditional 841.12
  proven 941.12
trifle
  n hardly anything
    248.5
  thing of naught 763.2
  particular 765.3
  triviality 997.5
  v waste time 331.13
  leave undone 340.7
  make love 562.14
  be foolish 922.6
  dally 997.14
trifle with
  disrespect 156.4
  do carelessly 340.9
trigger
  n immediate cause
    885.3
  v kindle 375.18

explode 671.14
cause 885.10
receive 1035.17
trigger-happy
  jittery 128.12
  warlike 458.21
trigger man
  killer 308.10
  ruffian 593.4
triglyceride 7.7
trigonal
  triangular 278.8
  tripartite 877.4
trigonometry 278.3
trihedral sided 218.7
  tripartite 877.4
trilateral sided 218.7
  triangular 278.8
  tripartite 877.4
trill
  n trillo 709.19
  v ripple 52.11
  bird sound 60.5
  leak 190.14
  sing 708.38
trilogy 875.1
trim
  n ornamentation
    498.1
  good condition 764.3
  v cut the hair 3.22
  trim ship 182.49
  border 211.10
  shorten 268.6
  prepare 405.6
  defeat 412.9
  remain neutral 467.5
  ornament 498.8
  disapprove 510.18
  punish 604.15
  cheapen 633.6
  fasten 799.7
  sever 801.11
  tidy 807.12
  reel in 905.9
  adj in trim 180.19
  shipshape 180.20
  shapely 264.5
  elegant 533.6
  chic 578.13
  tidy 806.8
trimester
  moment 823.2
  three 875.1
trim sail 182.20
trim size volume 554.4
  makeup 554.12
trinity three 875.1
  threeness 875.2
  Godhead 677.9
trinket gewgaw 498.4
  toy 743.16
  trifle 997.5
Trinkgeld 478.5
trinomial
  n three 875.1
  adj terminological
    527.17
trio
  cooperation 450.1
  part music 708.18
  three 875.1

trip
  n journey 177.5
  flight 184.9
  tumble 194.3
  bungle 414.5
  misdeed 655.2
  group of animals
    769.5
  slip 974.4
  illusion 975.1
  figment of the
    imagination 985.5
  v use 87.21
  speed 174.8
  way of walking 177.28
  tumble 194.8
  trap 356.20
  caper 366.6
  overcome 412.7
  bungle 414.11
  go wrong 654.9
  explode 671.14
  dance 705.5
  play 743.23
  fell 912.5
  err 974.9
  dream 985.17
tripartite 877.4
tripe food 10.19
  bull 520.3
triple
  n game 745.3
  v intensify 251.5
  play 745.5
  triplicate 876.2
  adj three 875.3
  triplicate 876.3
triple crown
  ecclesiastical insignia
    647.4
  horse racing 757.1
  three 875.1
triple play 745.3
triplet note 709.14
  tempo 709.24
  poetry 720.9
  three 875.1
triplicate
  n reproduce 784.3
  triplication 876.1
  v copy 784.8
  triple 876.2
  adj triple 876.3
tripod three 875.1
  fire iron 1019.12
tripping
  n hallucination 975.7
  adj high 87.23
  harmonious 533.8
  fluent 544.9
trip up
  abase 137.5
  trap 356.20
  overcome 412.7
  discompose 810.4
  fell 912.5
  make a boner 974.15
  distract 984.6
tripwire 1005.5
trisect 877.3
trite corny 117.9
  habitual 373.15

commonplace 863.16
well-known 927.27
aphoristic 973.6
trivial 997.19
tritium 1037.5
Triton
  spirit of the sea 240.4
  water god 678.10
triumph
  n rejoicing 116.1
  great success 409.3
  victory 411.1
  celebration 487.1
  crowing 502.4
  v best 249.7
  win through 409.13
  prevail 411.3
  exult 502.9
triumphant
  successful 409.14
  victorious 411.7
  crowing 502.13
triumvirate
  cooperation 450.1
  government 612.4
  three 875.1
trivet
  three 875.1
  fire iron 1019.12
trivial
  insignificant 248.6
  inadequate 250.7
  shallow 276.5
  worthless 391.11
  quibbling 935.14
  trifling 997.19
troglodyte
  barbarian 497.7
  ancient 841.7
troika
  cooperation 450.1
  three 875.1
Trojan horse
  subversive 357.11
  language 1041.13
troll
  n round 708.19
  v fish 382.10
  sing 708.38
  push 903.9
  pull 904.4
  roll 914.10
trolley handcar 179.16
  streetcar 179.17
trollop reprobate 660.5
  strumpet 665.14
  slob 809.7
trombonist 710.4
troop
  military unit 461.22
  company 769.3
  group of animals
    769.5
trooper
  cavalryman 461.12
  war-horse 461.30
  policeman 1007.15
trophy
  desire 100.11
  victory 411.1
  monument 549.12
  laurel 646.3

tennis 748.1
memento 988.7
good thing 998.5
tropical 1018.24
Tropic of Cancer 231.3
Tropic of Capricorn
231.3
tropics zone 231.3
hot place 1018.11
trot
n run 174.3
gait 177.12
old woman 304.3
translation 341.3
repetitiousness 848.4
v speed 174.8
go on horseback
177.34
depart 188.7
trot out 348.5
trotter foot 199.5
race horse 311.14
jockey 757.2
troubadour
wanderer 178.2
minstrel 710.14
poet 720.11
trouble
n annoyance 96.2
affliction 96.8
anxiety 126.1
imposition 643.1
exertion 725.1
commotion 809.4
inconvenience 995.3
adversity 1010.1
impediment 1011.6
the matter 1012.3
v distress 96.16
vex 98.15
excite 105.14
concern 126.4
presume upon 640.7
discompose 810.4
agitate 916.10
inconvenience 995.4
beset 1012.13
trouble-free
perfect 1001.6
unhazardous 1006.5
troublemaker
rebel 327.5
instigator 375.11
mischief-maker 593.2
troubleshooter 396.10
trouble spot 458.1
trough
n atmosphere 184.32
wave 238.14
channel 239.1
gutter 239.3
cavity 284.2
valley 284.9
trench 290.2
oscillation 915.4
v excavate 284.15
furrow 290.3
trounce
best 249.7
defeat 412.9
criticize 510.20
whip 604.13

troupe
n cast 707.11
company 769.3
v act 704.29
trousers 5.18
trousseau 5.2
trove find 472.6
discovery 940.1
trowel 1039.2
truant
n absentee 222.5
shirker 368.3
wretch 660.2
adj absent without
leave 222.13
truce armistice 465.5
pause 856.3
truck
n lorry 179.12
communication 343.1
rubbish 391.5
impedimenta 471.3
commerce 731.1
groceries 735.7
relation 774.1
v haul 176.13
trade 731.14
truculent
cruel 144.26
warlike 458.21
gruff 505.7
trudge
n slow motion 175.2
walk 177.10
v plod 175.7
way of walking 177.28
true
v make agree 787.7
adj straight 277.6
firm 359.12
observant 434.4
devoted 587.21
honest 644.16
trustworthy 644.19
faithful 644.20
orthodox 687.7
real 760.15
certain 969.13
truthful 972.13
true believer
orthodox Christian
687.4
believer 952.9
true blue fidelity 644.7
person of honor 644.8
true course
direction 161.2
course 184.34
true meaning 518.1
true to form
typical 349.15
characteristic 864.13
true to life
descriptive 349.14
lifelike 783.16
genuine 972.15
truism
generalization 863.8
axiom 973.2
truly
adv really 760.16
certainly 969.23

inter yes 332.18
trump
n good person 659.2
bridge 758.3
expedient 994.2
v excel 249.6
trump card
opportunity 842.2
influence 893.1
trumped-up 354.28
trumpet
n blare 53.5
v blare 53.10
proclaim 352.13
flaunt 501.17
praise 509.12
speak 524.26
blow a horn 708.42
truncate excise 255.10
deform 265.7
shorten 268.6
truncheon
n scepter 417.9
v whip 604.13
trundle push 903.9
roll 914.10
trunk
cylinder 282.4
nose 283.8
stem 310.19
line 347.17
base 900.8
body 1050.3
trunk line 347.17
trunks 5.29
truss
n bundle 769.8
v bundle 769.20
bind 799.9
trust
n hope 124.1
estate 471.4
commission 615.1
association 617.9
credit 622.1
investment company
737.16
belief 952.1
confidence 969.5
v hope 124.7
commit 478.16
give credit 622.6
believe 952.10
confide in 952.17
trustee
fiduciary 470.5
recipient 479.3
treasurer 729.11
trust fund 737.16
trustworthy
trusty 644.19
believable 952.24
reliable 969.17
unhazardous 1006.5
trusty
n prisoner 429.11
person of honor 644.8
adj trustworthy
644.19
dependable 952.22
believable 952.24
reliable 969.17

truth
honesty 644.3
reality 760.2
certainty 969.1
trueness 972.1
axiom 973.2
**the truth, the whole
truth, and nothing
but the truth** 972.3
the truth of the matter
fact 760.3
existence 760.4
the real story 972.3
try
n attempt 403.3
test 941.2
v refine 79.22
attempt 403.6
try a case 598.17
experiment 941.8
sit in judgment 945.12
trying
n experiment 941.1
adj weakening 16.20
fatiguing 21.13
oppressive 98.24
examining 937.36
experimental 941.11
adverse 1010.13
troublesome 1012.18
tryout
audition 48.2
preparation 405.1
theatrical
performance 704.12
workout 941.3
tryst 582.9
T square
instrument 200.6
straightedge 277.3
tsunami wave 238.14
upheaval 671.5
wave 915.4
tub
n bath 79.8
washbasin 79.12
car 179.10
ship 180.1
heavyweight 257.12
v wash 79.19
tubby corpulent 257.18
stubby 268.10
tube
n train 179.14
pipe 239.6
cylinder 282.4
wave 915.4
electronics 1032.10
v transport 176.14
tuber 310.20
tuberculosis
epidemic 85.5
white plague 85.17
tubing 239.6
tub-thumper 543.4
tubular tubate 239.16
cylindric 282.11
tuck
n food 10.2
fold 291.1
game 746.3
race 753.3

v fold 291.5
tuckered out 21.8
tuff 1057.1
tuft flock 3.6
 beard 3.8
 feather 3.16
 growth 310.2
 bunch 769.7
tug
 n strain 725.2
 pull 904.2
 attraction 906.1
 v strain 725.10
 pull 904.4
 attract 906.4
tug-of-war fight 457.4
 pulling 904.1
tuition 568.1
tumble
 n fall 194.3
 collapse 410.3
 jumble 809.3
 flounder 916.8
 v be excited 105.18
 pitch 182.55
 fall 194.8
 be destroyed 395.22
 lose 412.12
 confuse 810.3
 fell 912.5
 wallow 914.13
 flounder 916.15
 confound 944.3
tummy goozle 2.17
 middle 818.1
tummyache 26.5
tumor symptom 85.9
 growth 85.38
 swelling 283.4
tumult noise 53.3
 excitement 105.4
 bustle 330.4
 turbulence 671.2
 commotion 809.4
 agitation 916.1
tundra plain 236.1
 cold place 1022.4
tune
 n melody 708.2
 harmony 708.3
 air 708.4
 pitch 709.4
 v fit 405.8
 harmonize 708.35
 tune up 708.36
 make agree 787.7
 organize 807.10
 rearrange 807.13
tune in
 listen in 1033.27
 receive 1035.17
tune out exclude 772.4
 be inattentive 983.2
 listen in 1033.27
tune up tune 708.36
 organize 807.10
 rearrange 807.13
 listen in 1033.27
tuning fork 711.22
tunnel
 n lair 228.26
 channel 239.1

cave 284.5
 passageway 383.3
 entrenchment 460.5
 v deepen 275.8
 excavate 284.15
tunnel vision
 faulty eyesight 28.1
 narrow-mindedness
  979.1
turbid
 disorderly 809.13
 opaque 1030.3
 fluid 1059.4
 slimy 1060.14
turbine 903.6
turbocharger 756.1
turbojet 181.3
turbulent
 noisy 53.13
 tumultuous 105.24
 stormy 318.23
 rebellious 327.11
 bustling 330.20
 violent 671.18
 disorderly 809.13
 agitated 916.16
turd feces 12.4
 bad person 660.6
turf abode 228.1
 sod 310.6
 arena 463.1
 occupation 724.4
 horse racing 757.1
 sphere of influence
  893.4
turgid
 distended 259.13
 bulged 283.16
 pompous 501.22
 stiff 534.3
 bombastic 545.9
turkey
 poultry 311.29
 failure 410.2
 loser 410.8
 stage show 704.4
 game 750.2
Turkish bath 79.8
turmoil
 excitement 105.4
 anarchy 418.2
 turbulence 671.2
 jumble 809.3
 commotion 809.4
 agitation 916.1
turn
 n looks 33.4
 inclination 100.3
 start 131.3
 act of kindness 143.7
 deviation 164.1
 journey 177.5
 walk 177.10
 bias 204.3
 form 262.1
 distortion 265.1
 bend 279.3
 act 328.3
 aptitude 413.5
 show business 704.7
 ornament 709.18
 transaction 731.4

trading 737.19
 ski move 753.3
 race 756.3
 bout 824.2
 shift 824.3
 crisis 842.4
 round 849.3
 change 851.1
 reversion 858.1
 tendency 895.1
 circuitousness 913.1
 circuit 913.2
 whirl 914.2
 disposition 977.3
 v direct 161.5
 take direction 161.7
 turn round 163.9
 deviate 164.3
 change course 182.30
 oblique 204.9
 distort 265.5
 curve 279.6
 convolve 281.4
 blunt 286.2
 ski 753.4
 recur 849.5
 be changed 851.6
 change 853.5
 turn back 858.5
 tend 895.3
 go around 913.6
 rotate 914.9
turn a blind eye
 take 134.8
 exclude 772.4
 be inattentive 983.2
turnabout
 n regression 163.3
 reverse 363.1
 apostate 363.5
 change 851.1
 reversion 858.1
 v turn 163.9
turn a deaf ear
 be deaf 49.4
 show no mercy 146.2
 exclude 772.4
turn against
 act the traitor 645.15
 defect 857.13
turnaround
 n regression 163.3
 reverse 363.1
 v turn 163.9
turn aside
 deviate 164.3
 avoid 164.6
 disincline 379.4
 fend off 460.10
 digress 538.9
 be changed 851.6
 pull back 902.7
 prevent 1011.14
turn away avoid 164.6
 reject 372.2
 disincline 379.4
turn back
 put back 163.8
 avoid 164.6
 change course 182.30
 repeat 848.11
 convert 857.11

change back 858.5
 repulse 907.3
turn back the clock
 make young 301.8
 be conservative 852.6
turncoat
 n traitor 357.10
 apostate 363.5
 convert 857.8
 adj traitorous 645.22
turn down invert 205.5
 refuse 442.3
turn down the volume
 670.6
turned 393.41
turn in go to bed 22.18
 invert 205.5
 betray 645.14
turn informer 551.12
turning point
 crisis 842.4
 crucial moment 842.5
 urgency 996.4
 salient point 996.6
turn in one's badge
 448.2
turn inside out
 invert 205.5
 ransack 937.32
turn into
 translate 341.12
 become 760.12
 be changed 851.6
 convert 857.11
 be converted into
  857.17
turnip 831.6
turn loose 431.5
turn of events 830.2
turn off offend 98.11
 disincline 379.4
 shut off 856.12
 dismiss 908.18
 stop 908.19
 electrify 1031.25
turn of phrase 529.1
turn of the screw 251.2
turn on excite 105.12
 rouse 375.19
 inaugurate 817.11
 result from 886.5
 depend 958.6
 electrify 1031.25
turn on a dime 163.9
turn one's back on
 quit 188.9
 slight 340.8
 defect 370.6
 reject 372.2
 refuse 442.3
turn one's stomach
 64.4
turnout
 wardrobe 5.2
 rig 179.5
 attendance 221.4
 assembly 769.2
turn out outfit 5.40
 get up 23.6
 invert 205.5
 reject 372.2
 equip 385.8

two 872.6
twofold 873.5
two of a kind 783.5
two-party system
609.24
two-sided sided 218.7
ambiguous 539.4
two 872.6
two-timer cheat 357.3
criminal 660.10
two-way 776.11
tycoon ruler 575.9
businessman 730.1
personage 996.8
type
n omen 133.3
form 262.1
measure 300.2
representative 349.7
preference 371.5
symbol 517.2
sign 518.6
print 548.6
nature 766.4
model 785.1
example 785.2
kind 808.3
specialty 865.1
oddity 869.4
disposition 977.3
v write 547.19
classify 808.6
type A 2.23
type AB 2.23
Type A behavior 321.1
type B 2.23
Type B behavior 321.1
typeface 548.6
type O 2.23
typeset 548.19
typesetter 548.12
type size 548.6
typewritten 547.22
typhoon
windstorm 318.12
whirlwind 318.14
storm 671.4
typical typic 349.15
indicative 517.23
model 785.8
classificational 808.7
normal 868.8
typify augur 133.12
designate 517.18
typographer 548.12
typographical error
974.3
tyranny
force 424.2
subjection 432.1
government 612.4
absolutism 612.9
despotism 612.10
tyrant 575.14
ubiquitous
omnipresent 221.13
almighty 677.18
thorough 793.10
recurrent 848.13
U-boat 180.9
udder 283.6
UFO 1073.3

ugly
unpleasant 98.17
irascible 110.20
dangerous 1005.9
unsightly 1014.6
ugly duckling
nonconformist 867.3
eyesore 1014.4
UHF 1033.12
UK 232.4
ulcer 85.36
ulterior
additional 253.10
thither 261.10
secret 345.11
extraneous 773.5
ultimate
n acme of perfection
1001.3
adj top 198.10
farthest 261.12
completing 407.9
mandatory 420.12
ending 819.10
final 819.11
eventual 830.11
future 838.8
ultimatum
warning 399.1
demand 421.1
last word 439.3
condition 958.2
ultra
n radical 611.12
adj extreme 247.13
ultraconservative
n political principles
611.9
conservative 852.4
adj conservative
611.17
radical 611.20
political 852.8
ultrahigh frequency
1033.12
ultramodern 840.13
ultrasonic
acoustic 50.17
supersonic 174.16
ultrasound sound 50.1
diagnosis 91.9
ultraviolet light 1024.1
ultra-violet radiation
1036.1
Ulysses 178.2
umber 40.3
umbilical 208.11
umbrage offense 152.2
foliage 310.16
shadow 1026.3
umbrella
parachute 181.13
Air Force mission
184.11
gamp 295.7
safeguard 1007.3
shade 1027.1
umlaut 524.14
umpire
n arbitrator 466.4
judge 596.1
game 745.3

referee 747.3
mediator 748.2
linesman 749.6
ruler 945.6
v mediate 466.6
play 745.5
sit in judgment 945.12
UN 614.1
unabashed
brazen 142.11
undaunted 492.21
immodest 666.6
unabated
unweakened 15.21
undiminished 247.14
unmitigated 671.17
unable incapable 19.14
incompetent 414.19
unabridged 791.12
unacceptable
inadmissible 108.10
unpraiseworthy
510.24
unwelcome 586.9
unaccompanied
separate 801.20
alone 871.8
unaccountable
lawless 418.5
exempt 430.30
inexplicable 522.18
inconstant 853.7
fantastic 869.12
uncertain 970.16
purposeless 971.16
unaccustomed 374.4
unadorned mere 248.8
natural 416.6
undecorated 499.8
elegant 533.6
plain-speaking 535.3
simple 797.6
unadulterated
clean 79.25
unadorned 499.8
unmixed 797.7
unqualified 959.2
genuine 972.15
perfect 1001.6
unaffected
unmoved 94.11
unyielding 361.9
natural 416.6
tasteful 496.8
plain 499.7
elegant 533.6
plain-speaking 535.3
informal 581.3
undeceptive 644.18
uninfluenced 894.5
genuine 972.15
unaffectionate
unfeeling 94.9
unkind 144.16
unafraid
unfearing 492.20
confident 969.21
unaided
adj alone 871.8
adv singly 871.13
unalterable
unyielding 361.9

unchangeable 854.17
inflexible 1044.12
unamazed 123.3
unambiguous
clear 521.11
certain 969.13
unambitious
undesirous 102.8
modest 139.9
unanimous
solid 332.15
agreeing 787.9
unannounced 131.10
unanswerable
exempt 430.30
obvious 969.15
unanticipated
unexpected 131.10
sudden 829.5
unappealing 98.17
unappeased 100.27
unappetizing
unsavory 64.5
unpleasant 98.17
unappreciated 99.9
unapprehended 929.17
unapproachable
peerless 249.15
out-of-the-way 261.9
reticent 344.10
aloof 583.6
inaccessible 966.9
unarguable 969.15
unarmed
unfitted 406.9
unprotected 1005.14
unaroused 173.14
unashamed
unregretful 114.4
immodest 666.6
unaspiring
undesirous 102.8
modest 139.9
unimaginative 986.5
unassailable 15.19
unassisted 871.8
unassuming
modest 139.9
natural 416.6
plain 499.7
informal 581.3
undeceptive 644.18
genuine 972.15
unattached
free 430.21
separate 801.20
unattainable
impracticable 966.8
inaccessible 966.9
unattended
separate 801.20
alone 871.8
unprotected 1005.14
unattracted 102.8
unauthorized
prohibited 444.7
illegal 674.6
unavailable 966.9
unavailing
ineffective 19.15
useless 391.9
unavoidable 962.15

unconnected
  unintelligible 522.13
  unrelated 775.6
  separate 801.20
  incoherent 803.4
  discontinuous 812.4
  illogical 935.11
unconquered
  undefeated 411.8
  unsubject 430.29
unconscionable
  downright 247.12
  overpriced 632.12
  dishonest 645.16
  unjustifiable 650.12
  violent 671.16
  excessive 992.16
unconscious
  n psyche 92.28
  adj asleep 22.22
  senseless 25.8
  subconscious 92.41
  insensible 94.10
  unpremeditated
    365.11
  unaware 929.13
  instinctive 933.6
  involuntary 962.14
  unintentional 971.17
  oblivious 983.7
  abstracted 984.11
  inanimate 1053.5
unconsidered
  neglected 340.14
  unheeded 340.15
  unexamined 340.16
  unpremeditated
    365.11
  unwise 922.10
  unthought-of 932.5
unconstitutional
  674.6
unconstrained
  communicative
    343.10
  unrestrained 430.24
  informal 581.3
  candid 644.17
  intemperate 669.7
unconsumed
  remaining 256.7
  unused 390.12
uncontaminated
  natural 416.6
  perfect 1001.6
uncontested
  unanimous 332.15
  believed 952.23
  undoubted 969.16
uncontrollable
  frenzied 105.25
  ungovernable 361.12
  rabid 925.30
  inevitable 962.15
unconventional
  informal 581.3
  unorthodox 867.6
  eccentric 926.5
unconvinced
  unbelieving 954.8
  uncertain 970.16
uncooked 406.10

uncooperative
  inconsiderate 144.18
  insubordinate 327.9
  obstinate 361.8
  unconsenting 442.6
  oppositional 451.8
  resistant 453.5
uncoordinated 414.20
uncork 292.12
uncorroborated
  unproved 957.8
  unauthoritative
    970.21
uncounted
  innumerable 883.10
  undecided 970.18
uncouple 801.8
uncouth
  countrified 233.7
  bungling 414.20
  unrefined 497.12
  inelegant 534.2
  vulgar 666.8
uncover divest 6.5
  disinter 192.11
  unclose 292.12
  disclose 351.4
  greet 585.10
  unearth 940.4
uncritical
  obedient 326.3
  unmeticulous 340.13
  uncriticizing 509.18
  undiscriminating
    944.5
  credulous 953.8
unction balm 86.11
  flattery 511.2
  function of Holy
    Ghost 677.16
  sanctimony 693.1
  sacred unction 701.5
  ointment 1054.3
  lubrication 1054.6
uncultivated
  countrified 233.7
  undeveloped 406.12
  fallow 406.14
  unrefined 497.12
  unproductive 890.4
  unlearned 929.14
uncultured
  countrified 233.7
  undeveloped 406.12
  unrefined 497.12
  unlearned 929.14
uncurl 277.5
uncut unformed 263.5
  undeveloped 406.12
  undivided 791.11
  complete 793.9
undamaged
  preserved 397.13
  intact 791.10
  unharmed 1001.8
  safe 1006.4
undaunted
  persevering 360.8
  undismayed 492.21
undecided
  irresolute 362.9
  undetermined 970.18

undecided issue 970.8
undeclared 519.9
undefeated 411.8
undefended 1005.14
undefined
  inconspicuous 32.6
  formless 263.4
  anonymous 528.3
  almighty 677.18
  vague 970.19
undeflected 277.6
undeformed 1001.8
undemanding
  unstrict 426.5
  undiscriminating
    944.5
undeniable
  downright 247.12
  real 760.15
  obvious 969.15
undependable
  fickle 364.6
  untrustworthy 645.19
  inconstant 853.7
  unreliable 970.20
  unsafe 1005.11
under
  adj lower 274.8
  adv below 274.10
  prep below 274.11
  beneath 432.17
underachiever 572.4
under a cloud
  accused 599.15
  in disrepute 661.13
  unreliable 954.11
  doubted 954.12
under advisement
  937.38
underage
  n deficiency 794.2
  shortcoming 910.1
  adj immature 301.10
under arrest 429.22
under a spell 691.12
under attack
  adj accused 599.15
  adv under fire 459.31
underbelly
  digestive system 2.16
  bottom 199.1
underbrush 310.15
undercarriage 900.6
the underclass
  the underprivileged
    607.8
  the poor 619.3
  unfortunate 1010.7
underclothes 5.22
undercoating
  color 35.8
  painting 35.12
under consideration
  937.38
under construction
  in preparation 405.22
  in production 891.21
under control
  adj restrained 428.13
  adv in hand 612.20
undercooked
  underdone 11.8

raw 406.10
under cost 631.3
undercover
  adj covert 345.12
  adv secretly 345.17
undercurrent
  feeling 93.1
  flow 238.4
  wind 318.1
  opposition 451.1
  implication 519.2
  counterforce 899.4
  hidden danger 1005.5
undercut
  sell 734.8
  disprove 957.4
underdeveloped
  undeveloped 406.12
  incomplete 794.4
underdog 412.5
underdone
  undercooked 11.8
  raw 406.10
under duress 514.4
underestimate
  n underestimation
    949.1
  v misestimate 949.2
under fire
  adj accused 599.15
  adv under attack
    459.31
underfoot 274.10
under full steam
  174.20
undergarments 5.22
undergo afford 626.7
  experience 830.8
undergraduate
  n undergrad 572.6
  adj studentlike 572.12
underground
  n train 179.14
  dissent 333.1
  secret passage 346.5
  subversive 357.11
  irregular 461.16
  adj subterranean
    275.12
  dissenting 333.6
  covert 345.12
  concealed 346.11
  adv beneath the sod
    309.23
  secretly 345.17
undergrowth 310.15
underhanded
  covert 345.12
  deceitful 356.22
  dishonest 645.16
under handicap
  1011.21
under house arrest
  concealed 346.11
  under arrest 429.22
under investigation
  937.38
underlayer
  bottom 199.1
  layer 296.1
underlie base on 199.6
  lie low 274.5

be latent 519.3
support 900.21
underline
  n line 517.6
  v mark 517.19
    emphasize 996.14
underling
  inferior 250.2
  subordinate 432.5
  retainer 577.1
under lock and key
  jailed 429.21
  in safety 1006.6
underlying
  basic 199.8
  latent 519.5
  essential 766.9
undermine
  weaken 16.10
  sap 393.15
  overthrow 395.20
  refute 957.5
underneath
  n bottom 199.1
  prep below 274.11
  under 432.17
**under no
  circumstances**
  adv no way 248.11
  inter by no means
    335.9
undernourish 270.12
under oath
  adj promissory 436.7
  adv affirmatively
    334.10
under one's nose
  before 216.12
  near 223.20
  openly 348.15
under one's thumb
  subjugated 432.14
  influenceable 893.15
underpaid 625.12
underpass 383.3
underpinning 900.6
under power 182.63
under pressure 325.8
underprice 633.6
underprivileged
  inferior 250.6
  indigent 619.8
  unfortunate 1010.14
under protest
  adj protesting 333.7
  adv reluctantly 325.9
underrated 949.3
under restraint
  restrained 428.13
  confined 429.19
under sail
  under way 172.9
  traveling 182.63
underscore
  n line 517.6
  v mark 517.19
  emphasize 996.14
undersecretary 575.17
undersell 734.8
underside 199.1
under siege 459.31
the undersigned 332.7

undersized
  dwarf 258.13
  lean 270.17
understaffed 991.9
understand
  interpret 341.9
  comprehend 521.7
  know 927.12
  suppose 950.10
understanding
  n unanimity 332.5
  obligation 436.2
  compact 437.1
  accord 455.1
  compromise 468.1
  entente 787.2
  intellect 918.1
  intelligence 919.1
  comprehension 927.3
  adj patient 134.9
  pitying 145.7
  in accord 455.3
  intelligent 919.12
  sagacious 919.16
  knowing 927.15
understated 496.8
understructure
  understruction 266.3
  foundation 900.6
understudy
  n deputy 576.1
  supporting actor
    707.7
  substitute 861.2
  v represent 576.14
under surveillance
  937.38
under suspicion
  adj doubted 954.12
  adv on trial 941.14
undertake
  practice 328.8
  attempt 403.6
  assume 404.3
  commit 436.5
  contract 437.5
  set to work 725.15
undertaker 309.8
**under the
  circumstances**
  765.11
under-the-counter
  covert 345.12
  illegal 674.6
under the gun
  obligatorily 424.15
  under duress 514.4
under the impression
  952.21
under the influence
  intoxicated 87.22
  inebriated 88.31
under the sun
  adj existent 760.13
  adv everywhere
    158.12
  on earth 234.9
under the surface
  adj latent 519.5
  adv internally 207.9
under the table
  adj dead-drunk 88.32

  adv surreptitiously
    345.18
under the weather
  85.55
under the wire 845.19
undertone
  murmur 52.4
  milieu 209.3
  meaning 518.1
  implication 519.2
undertow flow 238.4
  opposition 451.1
  hidden danger 1005.5
undervalue 949.2
underwater 275.13
under way
  adj undertaken 404.7
  in preparation 405.22
  happening 830.9
  adv under sail 172.9
  making way 182.63
underwear 5.22
underweight
  n leanness 270.5
  weight 297.1
  adj lean 270.17
  lightweight 298.13
underworld 682.1
under wraps
  secret 345.11
  concealed 346.11
underwrite
  ratify 332.12
  promise 436.4
  secure 438.9
  protect 1007.18
underwriter
  endorser 332.7
  guarantor 438.6
  insurance 1007.4
undeserved
  undue 640.9
  unjust 650.9
undesirable
  n outcast 586.4
  bad person 660.1
  adj unpleasant 98.17
  unacceptable 108.10
  unwelcome 586.9
  inexpedient 995.5
undetached
  partial 650.11
  discriminatory 979.12
undetectable 32.5
undetermined
  irresolute 362.9
  unproved 957.8
  undecided 970.18
  vague 970.19
  chance 971.15
undeveloped
  immature 301.10
  unfinished 406.12
  inexperienced 414.17
  incomplete 794.4
  new 840.7
  imperfect 1002.4
undeviating
  directional 161.12
  straight 277.6
  uniform 780.5
  unchangeable 854.17

exact 972.17
undifferentiated
  identical 777.7
  uniform 780.5
  simple 797.6
  continuous 811.8
  general 863.11
  indistinguishable
    944.6
undigested 406.11
undignified
  vulgar 497.10
  inelegant 534.2
undiluted 797.7
undiminished
  unweakened 15.21
  unabated 247.14
  undivided 791.11
  complete 793.9
undiscernible 32.5
undisciplined
  disobedient 327.8
  lawless 418.5
  intemperate 669.7
  inconstant 853.7
undisclosed
  invisible 32.5
  secret 345.11
  unrevealed 346.12
  unknown 929.17
undiscovered
  unrevealed 346.12
  unknown 929.17
undisguised
  visible 31.6
  unhidden 348.11
  undeceptive 644.18
  genuine 972.15
undismayed 492.21
undisputed
  believed 952.23
  undoubted 969.16
undistorted
  straight 277.6
  genuine 972.15
undisturbed
  unexcited 106.11
  untroubled 107.8
  quiescent 173.12
undivided uncut 791.11
  joined 799.13
  one 871.7
undo take off 6.6
  unnerve 128.10
  unclose 292.12
  do for 395.11
  abolish 395.13
  demolish 395.17
  defeat 412.6
  detach 801.10
  neutralize 899.7
  solve 939.2
undoing
  destruction 395.1
  defeat 412.1
  disassembly 801.6
  neutralization 899.2
undoubted
  believed 952.23
  not to be doubted
    969.16
  true 972.13

undress
  n dishabille 5.20
  unadornment 499.3
  v unclothe 6.7
undue
  overpriced 632.12
  wrong 638.3
  unowed 640.9
  unjust 650.9
  excessive 992.16
undulate
  v maneuver 184.40
  billow 238.22
  recur 849.5
  wave 915.11
  adj wavy 281.10
unduplicated 337.6
undying
  immortal 828.9
  indestructible 854.18
  continuing 855.7
uneager 102.8
unearned 640.9
unearth extract 192.10
  uncover 940.4
unearthly
  deathly 307.29
  heavenly 681.12
  godly 692.9
  extraneous 773.5
  odd 869.11
  supernatural 869.15
  unbelievable 954.10
  weird 987.9
  immaterial 1051.7
unease
  unpleasure 96.1
  discontent 108.1
  anxiety 126.1
  agitation 916.1
uneasy
  pleasureless 96.20
  distressed 96.22
  restless 105.27
  discontented 108.7
  anxious 126.7
  nervous 128.11
  impatient 135.6
  agitated 916.16
uneconomical 406.15
uneducated
  vernacular 523.18
  unlearned 929.14
unembellished
  natural 416.6
  unadorned 499.8
  prosaic 721.5
unemotional 94.9
unemployed
  motionless 173.13
  idle 331.18
  unused 390.12
unencumbered
  lightened 298.11
  unhampered 430.26
unending
  continuous 811.8
  perpetual 828.7
  continuing 855.7
unendurable 98.25
unenjoyable
  unpleasant 98.17

uninteresting 117.7
unenlightened
  blind 30.9
  ignorant 929.12
unenvied 156.9
unequaled 249.15
unequipped
  unfitted 406.9
  incompetent 414.19
unequivocal
  downright 247.12
  unrestricted 430.27
  clear 521.11
  candid 644.17
  unqualified 959.2
  certain 969.13
unerring
  uncorrupt 653.8
  infallible 969.19
  exact 972.17
unescorted 871.8
unessential
  n nonessential 767.2
  adj needless 391.10
  circumstantial
    765.7
  extrinsic 767.4
  irrelevant 775.7
  superfluous 992.17
  insignificant 997.17
unestablished
  unplaced 160.10
  unproved 957.8
  undecided 970.18
unethical
  dishonest 645.16
  vice-prone 654.11
uneven
  rough 288.6
  unjust 650.9
  nonuniform 781.3
  unequal 790.4
  irregular 850.3
  imperfect 1002.4
uneventful
  uninteresting 117.7
  tedious 118.9
unexamined 340.16
unexceptional
  normal 868.8
  ordinary 1004.8
unexhausted
  unwearied 9.5
  unweakened 15.21
unexpected
  unanticipated 131.10
  sudden 829.5
  unusual 869.10
  fantastic 869.12
  improbable 968.3
  chance 971.15
unexplained
  unrevealed 346.12
  unknown 929.17
unexplored
  unexamined 340.16
  unrevealed 346.12
  unknown 929.17
unexposed
  unrevealed 346.12
  unknown 929.17
unfabricated 972.15

unfaded
  unweakened 15.21
  undamaged 1001.8
unfailing
  persevering 360.8
  faithful 644.20
  permanent 852.7
  reliable 969.17
unfair 650.10
unfaithful
  nonobservant 435.5
  faithless 645.20
unfamiliar
  novel 840.11
  unusual 869.10
  ignorant 929.12
  unknown 929.17
unfashionable
  old-fashioned 841.16
  unconventional 867.6
unfastened 801.22
unfathomable
  abysmal 275.11
  unintelligible 522.13
  infinite 822.3
unfavorable
  ominous 133.17
  oppositional 451.8
  disapproving 510.21
  untimely 843.6
  disadvantageous
    995.6
  bad 999.7
  adverse 1010.13
unfed fasting 515.5
  ill-provided 991.12
unfeeling
  n insensibility 25.1
  unfeelingness 94.1
  heartlessness 144.10
  adj insensible 25.6
  unemotional 94.9
  heartless 144.25
  pitiless 146.3
  inanimate 1053.5
unfelt 25.6
unfertile 890.4
unfettered
  unbound 430.28
  unfastened 801.22
unfilled hungry 100.25
  available 222.15
unfinished
  undeveloped 406.12
  unaccomplished 408.3
  unskilled 414.16
  incomplete 794.4
  imperfect 1002.4
unfit
  v disable 19.9
  adj unable 19.14
  unserviceable 391.14
  unfitted 406.9
  incompetent 414.19
  wrong 638.3
  inappropriate 788.7
  untimely 843.6
  inexpedient 995.5
unflagging
  unweakened 15.21
  industrious 330.22
  persevering 360.8

unflappable
  inexcitable 106.10
  firm 359.12
  stable 854.12
unflattering
  undeceptive 644.18
  genuine 972.15
unflavored 65.2
unflinching
  unnervous 129.2
  unhesitating 359.13
  persevering 360.8
  undaunted 492.21
  stable 854.12
unfold spread 259.6
  unclose 292.12
  explain 341.10
  manifest 348.5
  disclose 351.4
  amplify 538.7
  unroll 860.7
  result 886.4
unforced
  adj voluntary 324.7
  unrestrained 430.24
  adv at will 323.5
unforeseen
  unexpected 131.10
  sudden 829.5
  chance 971.15
unforgettable
  never to be forgotten
    988.26
  notable 996.19
unforgivable
  unjustifiable 650.12
  wicked 654.16
unforgotten 988.23
unfortified
  unmixed 797.7
  unprotected 1005.14
unfortunate
  n unlucky person
    1010.7
  adj ominous 133.17
  unsuccessful 410.18
  untimely 843.6
  inexpedient 995.5
  unlucky 1010.14
unfounded
  false 354.24
  unsubstantial 763.8
  baseless 935.13
  unproved 957.8
  unauthentic 974.19
  illusory 975.8
unfreeze 1019.21
unfriendly
  unpleasant 98.17
  averse 99.8
  oppositional 451.8
  warlike 458.21
  unsociable 583.5
  inhospitable 586.7
  inimical 589.9
unfrozen 1018.24
unfulfilled
  pleasureless 96.20
  discontented 108.7
  unaccomplished 408.3
unfurl disclose 351.4
  unfold 860.7

UNIX 1041.12
unjust 650.9
unkempt rough 288.6
  unrefined 497.12
  slovenly 809.15
unkind
  nasty 144.16
  bad 999.7
unknowing
  n ignorance 929.1
  adj ignorant 929.12
  unaware 929.13
unknown
  concealed 346.11
  anonymous 528.3
  unrenowned 661.14
  unbeknown 929.17
unlaced 801.22
unlatch unclose 292.12
  loose 431.6
unlawful
  prohibited 444.7
  wrong 638.3
  unjust 650.9
  illegal 674.6
unleash liberate 431.6
  detach 801.10
  loosen 803.3
unleavened 797.7
unless 958.16
unlicensed 444.7
unlighted 1026.13
unlike different 779.7
  dissimilar 786.4
  incomparable 942.9
unlikely 968.3
unlimber 1044.12
unlimited
  omnipotent 18.13
  unrestricted 430.27
  intemperate 669.7
  almighty 677.18
  infinite 822.3
  unqualified 959.2
unlisted number
  347.12
unlit 1026.13
unlivable 586.8
unload
  relieve 120.7
  lighten 298.6
  deal 734.8
  sell 737.24
  off-load 908.23
  disembarrass 1013.9
unlock
  unclose 292.12
  explain 341.10
  loose 431.6
  solve 939.2
unloved 99.10
unlucky
  ominous 133.17
  speculative 759.27
  untimely 843.6
  unfortunate 1010.14
unmade
  unprepared 406.8
  uncreated 761.10
unmanageable
  ungovernable 361.12
  unwieldy 1012.19

unmaneuverable
  1012.19
unmanned
  impotent 19.19
  terrified 127.26
  unnerved 128.14
  available 222.15
  downtrodden 432.16
  cowardly 491.10
unmarked
  unheeded 340.15
  undamaged 1001.8
unmarried
  n celibate 565.2
  adj unwedded 565.7
unmask 351.4
unmatched
  peerless 249.15
  dissimilar 786.4
  best 998.16
  first-rate 998.17
unmentionable
  indescribable 122.13
  base 661.12
unmerciful
  heartless 144.25
  pitiless 146.3
unmet 256.7
unmindful
  unconcerned 102.7
  inconsiderate 144.18
  ungrateful 151.4
  careless 340.11
  unaware 929.13
  incurious 981.3
  inattentive 983.6
  forgetful 989.9
unmistakable
  distinct 31.7
  manifest 348.8
  clear 521.11
  unqualified 959.2
  certain 969.13
unmitigated
  downright 247.12
  undiminished 247.14
  unsoftened 671.17
  thorough 793.10
  changed 851.10
  unqualified 959.2
unmixed
  unmitigated 671.17
  unmingled 797.7
  perfect 1001.6
unmolested 1006.4
unmotivated 971.16
unmoved
  unaffected 94.11
  unastonished 123.3
  quiescent 173.12
  motionless 173.13
  unyielding 361.9
  uninfluenced 894.5
unnamed 528.3
unnatural
  heartless 144.25
  spurious 354.25
  affected 500.15
  elegant 533.9
  abnormal 869.9
  eccentric 926.5
unnavigable 276.6

unnecessary
  needless 391.10
  unessential 767.4
  superfluous 992.17
unneighborly 586.7
unnerving
  weakening 16.20
  frightening 127.28
  nerve-racking 128.15
unnoticed
  invisible 32.5
  unheeded 340.15
  unrenowned 661.14
unnumbered
  infinite 822.3
  innumerable 883.10
unobjectionable
  desirable 100.30
  acceptable 107.12
  justifiable 600.14
  inculpable 657.8
  tolerable 998.20
unobliging 144.18
unobscured
  unhidden 348.11
  light 1024.31
unobserved
  invisible 32.5
  unheeded 340.15
unobstructed
  open 292.17
  unhampered 430.26
unobtainable 966.9
unobtrusive
  modest 139.9
  covert 345.12
  tasteful 496.8
unoccupied
  available 222.15
  idle 331.18
  leisure 402.5
  thoughtless 932.4
unofficial
  informal 581.3
  illegal 674.6
  unauthoritative
    970.21
unopen 293.9
unopposed 332.15
unordered
  formless 263.4
  orderless 809.12
unordinary 869.10
unorganized
  formless 263.4
  unprepared 406.8
  unordered 809.12
  inorganic 1053.4
unorthodox
  nonorthodox 688.9
  nonuniform 781.3
  nonconformist 788.9
  unconventional 867.6
  erroneous 974.16
unpack disclose 351.4
  unload 908.23
unpaid due 623.10
  unremunerated
    625.12
unpalatable
  unsavory 64.5
  unpleasant 98.17

unparalleled
  peerless 249.15
  extraordinary 869.14
  best 998.16
unpardonable
  unjustifiable 650.12
  wicked 654.16
unpayable
  irredeemable 625.13
  expensive 632.11
unperceptive
  insensible 25.6
  undiscerning 921.14
unperformed 408.3
unperturbed
  unexcited 106.11
  untroubled 107.8
  quiescent 173.12
unplanned
  unprepared 406.8
  unintentional 971.17
unpleasant
  unsavory 64.5
  unpleasing 98.17
  unlikable 99.7
  bad 999.7
unplug 292.12
unpolished
  countrified 233.7
  rough 288.6
  undeveloped 406.12
  unskilled 414.16
  unrefined 497.12
  inelegant 534.2
unpolluted 79.25
unpopular
  disliked 99.9
  unrenowned 661.14
unpopulated 222.15
unpracticed
  unaccustomed 374.4
  inexperienced 414.17
unprecedented
  wonderful 122.10
  original 337.5
  unimitated 337.6
  extraordinary 869.14
unprecise
  unmeticulous 340.13
  inaccurate 974.17
unpredictable
  unexpected 131.10
  fickle 364.6
  unessential 767.4
  inconstant 853.7
  improbable 968.3
  uncertain 970.16
  chance 971.15
  unsafe 1005.11
unprejudiced 978.12
unpremeditated
  unmeditated 365.11
  unprepared 406.8
  premature 844.8
  unintentional 971.17
unprepared
  inexpectant 131.9
  careless 340.11
  unready 406.8
  unskilled 414.16
  premature 844.8
  unalert 983.8

unprepossessing 1014.7
unpretentious
  humble 137.10
  modest 139.9
  natural 416.6
  plain 499.7
  unselfish 652.5
unprincipled 645.16
unprintable 666.9
unprocessed 406.12
unproductive
  fruitless 391.12
  nonproductive 890.4
unprofessional 414.16
unprofitable
  fruitless 391.12
  inexpedient 995.5
  disadvantageous
    995.6
unpronounced
  silent 51.10
  unexpressed 519.9
unprotected
  helpless 19.18
  unshielded 1005.14
unprovable
  controvertible 957.9
  uncertain 970.16
unproved
  unsound 935.12
  not proved 957.8
  unauthoritative
    970.21
  erroneous 974.16
unprovoked 640.9
unpublished 519.9
unqualified
  unable 19.14
  downright 247.12
  unfitted 406.9
  incompetent 414.19
  unrestricted 430.27
  inappropriate 788.7
  thorough 793.10
  unconditional 959.2
  genuine 972.15
  insufficient 991.9
  sound 1001.7
unquenchable
  greedy 100.27
  indestructible 854.18
unquestionable
  downright 247.12
  intrinsic 766.7
  believable 952.24
  obvious 969.15
  true 972.13
unravel extract 192.10
  explain 341.10
  extricate 431.7
  disinvolve 797.5
  come apart 801.9
  loosen 803.3
  solve 939.2
unreachable 966.9
unread 929.14
unreadable 522.19
unready
  inexpectant 131.9
  careless 340.11
  unprepared 406.8
  untimely 843.6

late 845.16
  unalert 983.8
unreal
  spurious 354.25
  unrealistic 761.9
  thin 763.6
  illusory 975.8
  imaginary 985.19
unrealistic
  unreal 761.9
  imaginary 985.19
  visionary 985.24
unrealized
  invisible 32.5
  unaccomplished 408.3
unreasonable
  capricious 364.5
  overpriced 632.12
  unjustifiable 650.12
  unwise 922.10
  fanatic 925.32
  illogical 935.11
  excessive 992.16
unreceptive
  inhospitable 586.7
  uninfluenceable 894.4
unrecognizable 32.6
unreconstructed
  impenitent 114.5
  ungovernable 361.12
  unsubject 430.29
  conservative 611.17
  permanent 852.8
unrecorded 519.9
unredeemable 654.18
unreduced
  undiminished 247.14
  undivided 791.11
unrefined
  countrified 233.7
  rough 288.6
  coarse 294.6
  undeveloped 406.12
  unpolished 497.12
  ill-bred 505.6
  inelegant 534.2
  unlearned 929.14
unregenerate
  obstinate 361.8
  irreclaimable 654.18
  unsacred 686.3
  unredeemed 695.18
unregretful 114.4
unregulated
  permitted 443.16
  illegal 674.6
unrehearsed 365.12
unrelated 775.6
unrelaxed tense 128.13
  rigid 1044.11
unrelenting
  persevering 360.8
  unyielding 361.9
  firm 425.7
  wordy 538.12
  constant 846.5
unreliable fickle 364.6
  untrustworthy 645.19
  inconstant 853.7
  under a cloud 954.11
  undependable 970.20
  inauthentic 974.19

unsafe 1005.11
unrelieved
  vacant 222.14
  downright 247.12
  same 780.6
  continuous 811.8
unreligious 695.15
unremarkable 1004.8
unremitting
  industrious 330.22
  persevering 360.8
  continuous 811.8
  perpetual 828.7
  constant 846.5
  unchangeable 854.17
  continuing 855.7
unremorseful
  unregretful 114.4
  pitiless 146.3
unrepentant 114.5
unrequited
  unthanked 151.5
  unpaid 625.12
unreserved
  communicative
    343.10
  artless 416.5
  unrestrained 430.24
  candid 644.17
  thorough 793.10
  unqualified 959.2
unresisting
  resigned 134.10
  submissive 433.12
unresolved
  remaining 256.7
  irresolute 362.9
unresponsive
  unfeeling 94.9
  heartless 144.25
  uninfluenceable 894.4
unrest
  trepidation 105.5
  motion 172.1
  agitation 916.1
unrestored 21.7
unrestrained
  fervent 93.18
  communicative
    343.10
  capricious 364.5
  lawless 418.5
  lax 426.4
  unconstrained 430.24
  candid 644.17
  incontinent 665.24
  intemperate 669.7
  inconstant 853.7
  excessive 992.16
unrestricted
  undiminished 247.14
  open 292.17
  communicative
    343.10
  unconfined 430.27
  thorough 793.10
  unqualified 959.2
unrevealing 346.15
unrewarded
  unthanked 151.5
  unpaid 625.12
unripe sour 67.5

immature 301.10
  unprepared 406.11
  inexperienced 414.17
  untimely 843.6
  premature 844.8
  ignorant 929.12
unrivaled 249.15
unrobed 6.13
unroll unclose 292.12
  disclose 351.4
  unfold 860.7
unruffled
  unaffected 94.11
  unexcited 106.11
  quiescent 173.12
  smooth 287.9
  uniform 780.5
unruly
  defiant 327.10
  ungovernable 361.12
  anarchic 418.6
  unrestrained 430.24
  disorderly 671.19
unsafe 1005.11
unsaid tacit 51.11
  unexpressed 519.9
unsalvageable 125.15
unsanctioned 444.7
unsanitary 82.5
unsatisfactory
  dissatisfactory 108.9
  disappointing 132.6
  insufficient 991.9
unsaturated fat 1054.1
unsavory
  unpalatable 64.5
  insipid 65.2
  unpleasant 98.17
  dishonest 645.16
  disreputable 661.10
unscathed
  undamaged 1001.8
  safe 1006.4
unscented 72.5
unschooled
  unskilled 414.16
  unlearned 929.14
unscientific 935.11
unscramble
  disinvolve 797.5
  solve 939.2
  disembarrass 1013.9
unscratched 1001.8
unscrew 801.10
unscrubbed 80.20
unscrupulous
  unmeticulous 340.13
  dishonest 645.16
unseal 292.12
unsearched 340.16
unseasonable
  inappropriate 788.7
  anachronous 832.3
  untimely 843.6
  inexpedient 995.5
unseat
  dislodge 160.6
  depose 447.4
  disjoint 801.16
unseeing blind 30.9
  unwise 922.10
  unaware 929.13

unseemly
  vulgar 497.10
  inelegant 534.2
  wrong 638.3
  indecent 666.5
  inappropriate 788.7
  inexpedient 995.5
unseen invisible 32.5
  unheeded 340.15
  unrevealed 346.12
unselfish
  liberal 485.4
  impartial 649.10
  selfless 652.5
unserviceable 391.14
unsettle excite 105.14
  disorder 809.9
  discompose 810.4
  agitate 916.10
  confuse 984.7
unshaded 348.11
unshakeable 326.3
unshaken
  unweakened 15.21
  unnervous 129.2
  firm 359.12
unshaven 3.25
unsheathed 6.12
unshielded 1005.14
unsightly
  slovenly 809.15
  ugly 1014.6
unsimulated 972.15
unskilled 414.16
unskilled laborer 726.2
unsmiling
  solemn 111.3
  unhappy 112.21
unsnap 801.10
unsnarl
  straighten 277.5
  extricate 431.7
  disinvolve 797.5
  arrange 807.8
  disembarrass 1013.9
unsociable
  uncommunicative
    344.8
  insociable 583.5
  unfriendly 589.9
  misanthropic 590.3
unsoiled clean 79.25
  spotless 657.7
  chaste 664.4
unsold 734.15
unsolicited
  voluntary 324.7
  neglected 340.14
unsolid unsound 16.15
  unsubstantial 763.5
  unreliable 970.20
unsolved 346.12
unsophisticated
  artless 416.5
  unadorned 499.8
  unmixed 797.7
  gullible 953.9
unsound infirm 16.15
  unhealthy 85.53
  unwholesome 85.54
  unorthodox 688.9
  insolvent 729.18

fragile 763.7
  unwise 922.10
  insane 925.26
  unsubstantial 935.12
  unreliable 970.20
  imperfect 1002.4
  unsafe 1005.11
unsparing harsh 144.24
  industrious 330.22
  strict 425.6
  liberal 485.4
unspeakable
  horrid 98.19
  indescribable 122.13
  insulting 156.8
  wicked 654.16
  base 661.12
  sacred 685.7
  extraordinary 869.14
unspecified
  anonymous 528.3
  general 863.11
  vague 970.19
unspectacular 1004.8
unspoiled
  downright 247.12
  preserved 397.13
  natural 416.6
  intact 791.10
  unmixed 797.7
  undamaged 1001.8
unspoken tacit 51.11
  secret 345.11
  unexpressed 519.9
unsportsmanlike
  650.10
unspotted clean 79.25
  honest 644.13
  spotless 657.7
  chaste 664.4
  perfect 1001.6
unstable
  unsound 16.15
  nonuniform 781.3
  unbalanced 790.5
  transient 827.7
  inconstant 853.7
  unreliable 970.20
  unsafe 1005.11
unstained clean 79.25
  honest 644.13
  chaste 664.4
unsteady shaky 16.16
  nonuniform 781.3
  unbalanced 790.5
  irregular 850.3
  inconstant 853.7
  fluttering 916.18
  unreliable 970.20
  unsafe 1005.11
unstick detach 801.10
  loosen 803.3
unstoppable 962.15
unstrap loose 431.6
  detach 801.10
unstructured
  unformed 263.5
  diffuse 538.11
unstuck 801.22
unsturdy 16.15
unsubstantial
  frail 16.14

weak 16.15
  rare 299.4
  unreal 761.9
  insubstantial 763.5
  unsound 935.12
  unreliable 970.20
  illusory 975.8
  immaterial 1051.7
unsubstantiated 957.8
unsuccessful 410.18
unsuitable
  unacceptable 108.10
  unserviceable 391.14
  vulgar 497.10
  wrong 638.3
  inappropriate 788.7
  untimely 843.6
  inexpedient 995.5
unsuited
  unfitted 406.9
  inappropriate 788.7
unsullied clean 79.25
  natural 406.13
  honest 644.13
  spotless 657.7
  chaste 664.4
unsung
  disliked 99.9
  unexpressed 519.9
  unrenowned 661.14
unsupportable
  baseless 935.13
  unprovable 957.9
unsuppressed
  communicative
    343.10
  unrestrained 430.24
unsure
  untrustworthy 645.19
  ignorant 929.12
  uncertain 970.16
  unreliable 970.20
  unconfident 970.23
  unsafe 1005.11
unsurpassed
  peerless 249.15
  best 998.16
unsuspecting
  inexpectant 131.9
  unaware 929.13
  trusting 952.22
  credulous 953.8
  unprotected 1005.14
unsustained
  unsound 935.12
  baseless 935.13
  unproved 957.8
unswayed
  impartial 649.10
  uninfluenced 894.5
  unprejudiced 978.12
unsweetened 67.5
unswept 80.20
unswerving
  directional 161.12
  straight 277.6
  firm 359.12
  persevering 360.8
  faithful 644.20
unsymmetrical
  distorted 265.10
  unordered 809.12

unsympathetic
  insensible 25.6
  unfeeling 94.9
  unkind 144.16
  pitiless 146.3
unsynchronized 456.15
untactful
  careless 340.11
  undiscriminating
    944.5
untainted clean 79.25
  preserved 397.13
  natural 416.6
  spotless 657.7
  chaste 664.4
  perfect 1001.6
untalented
  unable 19.14
  unskilled 414.16
  unintelligent 921.13
untamed
  defiant 327.10
  unsubject 430.29
  unrefined 497.12
  savage 671.21
untangle
  extricate 431.7
  disinvolve 797.5
  solve 939.2
untapped 390.12
untarnished
  clean 79.25
  honest 644.13
  chaste 664.4
untaxed 634.5
unteachable 921.15
untenable
  helpless 19.18
  unacceptable 108.10
  baseless 935.13
untended
  available 222.15
  neglected 340.14
untested 957.8
unthawed 1022.13
unthinkable
  unbelievable 954.10
  impossible 966.7
unthinking
  inconsiderate 144.18
  careless 340.11
  unreasoning 365.10
  unintelligent 921.13
  unwise 922.10
  thoughtless 932.4
  credulous 953.8
  involuntary 962.14
  unintentional 971.17
unthoughtful
  inconsiderate 144.18
  unthinking 365.10
  unwise 922.10
untidy dirty 80.22
  slipshod 340.12
  slovenly 809.15
untied adrift 182.61
  unbound 430.28
  liberated 431.10
  unfastened 801.22
until 820.15
until we meet again!
  188.22

untimely
inappropriate 788.7
unseasonable 843.6
premature 844.8
late 845.16
inexpedient 995.5
unto 820.15
untogether 809.12
untold
secret 345.11
unexpressed 519.9
infinite 822.3
innumerable 883.10
undecided 970.18
untouchable
n outcast 586.4
adj unfeeling 94.9
disliked 99.9
out-of-the-way 261.9
prohibited 444.7
sacred 685.7
untouched
unaffected 94.11
impenitent 114.5
unused 390.12
natural 406.13
intact 791.10
unmixed 797.7
new 840.7
unknown 929.17
undamaged 1001.8
safe 1006.4
untoward
ominous 133.17
untimely 843.6
bad 999.7
adverse 1010.13
untracked 346.12
untrained
unaccustomed 374.4
unskilled 414.16
untrammeled
lawless 418.5
lax 426.4
unhampered 430.26
profligate 665.25
untreated 406.12
untried
inexperienced 414.17
new 840.7
unproved 957.8
untrimmed
unadorned 499.8
undeceptive 644.18
untroubled
unexcited 106.11
unbothered 107.8
quiescent 173.12
pacific 464.9
untrue
adj false 354.24
nonobservant 435.5
unfaithful 645.20
erroneous 974.16
adv erroneously
974.20
untruthfulness 354.8
untwist
disinvolve 797.5
solve 939.2
untying 431.2
unusable 391.14

unused
remaining 256.7
unaccustomed 374.4
unutilized 390.12
new 840.7
surplus 992.18
unusual novel 840.11
infrequent 847.2
nonconforming 867.5
unordinary 869.10
unutterable
indescribable 122.13
secret 345.11
sacred 685.7
unvarnished
natural 416.6
unadorned 499.8
plain-speaking 535.3
undeceptive 644.18
genuine 972.15
unvarying
tedious 118.9
uniform 780.5
constant 846.5
permanent 852.7
unchangeable 854.17
unveil divest 6.5
unclose 292.12
disclose 351.4
unventilated
stuffy 173.16
closed 293.9
unverified
unproved 957.8
unauthoritative
970.21
unwanted
unwished 99.11
unwelcome 586.9
unwarranted
overpriced 632.12
undue 640.9
illegal 674.6
baseless 935.13
unauthoritative
970.21
unwary
negligent 340.10
artless 416.5
rash 493.7
unalert 983.8
unwashed 80.20
unwatched
neglected 340.14
unprotected 1005.14
unwavering
unnervous 129.2
persevering 360.8
stable 854.12
confident 969.21
unwed 565.7
unwelcome
unpleasant 98.17
unwanted 99.11
inhospitable 586.9
unwieldy bulky 257.19
onerous 297.17
bungling 414.20
stiff 534.3
inconvenient 995.7
unmanageable
1012.19

unwilling
disinclined 325.5
unconsenting 442.6
involuntary 962.14
unwind relax 20.7
compose oneself 106.7
disinvolve 797.5
unfold 860.7
unwise
unintelligent 921.13
injudicious 922.10
inexpedient 995.5
unwitting
unaware 929.13
involuntary 962.14
unintentional 971.17
unworkable
unserviceable 391.14
impracticable 966.8
inexpedient 995.5
unworldly
heavenly 681.12
godly 692.9
supernatural 869.15
immaterial 1051.7
unworn
unweakened 15.21
undamaged 1001.8
unworthy
n bad person 660.1
adj undue 640.9
wicked 654.16
worthless 997.22
unwrap
take off 6.6
unclose 292.12
disclose 351.4
unwritten
unexpressed 519.9
speech 524.30
traditional 841.12
unyielding
impregnable 15.19
pitiless 146.3
resolute 359.12
unbending 361.9
firm 425.7
resistant 453.5
sturdy 762.7
immovable 854.15
uninfluenceable 894.4
inevitable 962.15
inflexible 1044.12
unzipped 801.22
up
n increase 251.1
v ascend 193.8
increase 251.4
enlarge 259.4
promote 446.2
elevate 911.5
adj awake 23.8
adv upward 193.16
vertically 200.13
on high 272.21
prep toward 161.26
up against
adj contrapositive
215.5
resistant 453.5
prep near 223.25
up and about 83.10

up and at 'em! 459.32
up and down
perpendicularly
200.14
alternately 849.11
to and fro 915.21
up-and-up 644.14
up a tree
unfortunate 1010.14
in trouble 1012.22
cornered 1012.25
upbeat
n improvement 392.1
beat 709.26
round 849.3
adj optimistic 124.12
upbraid 510.17
upcoming
n ascent 193.1
adj approaching 167.4
ascending 193.14
imminent 839.3
update date 831.13
modernize 840.6
updraft
ascent 193.1
wind 318.1
upended 200.11
up for grabs 970.18
up for sale 734.16
up front 817.18
upgrade
n ascent 193.1
acclivity 204.6
improvement 392.1
v make better 392.9
promote 446.2
adj ascending 193.14
sloping upward
204.17
adv slantingly 204.23
upheaval
outburst 105.9
fall 395.3
convulsion 671.5
revolution 851.2
elevation 911.1
upheld 900.24
uphill
n ascent 193.1
acclivity 204.6
adj ascending 193.14
sloping upward
204.17
laborious 725.18
difficult 1012.17
adv up 193.16
slantingly 204.23
uphold buoy 298.8
preserve 397.8
aid 449.12
approve 509.9
defend 600.10
support 900.21
elevate 911.5
confirm 956.11
upholstered 295.34
UPI 555.3
up in arms
adj prepared 405.16
resistant 453.5
at odds 456.16

adv in opposition
451.9
at war 458.24
up in the air 970.18
upkeep
  n preservation 397.1
  aid 449.3
  support 900.1
  v aid 449.12
  support 900.21
upland area 237.1
uplift
  n ascent 193.1
  acclivity 204.6
  improvement 392.1
  elevation 911.1
  v elate 109.8
  erect 200.9
  buoy 298.8
  make better 392.9
  glorify 662.13
  elevate 911.5
upon
  adv after which 834.7
  prep toward 161.26
  atop 198.16
  against 223.25
  on 295.37
  relation to 774.13
up on skilled in 413.27
  informed 927.18
  versed in 927.19
up one's sleeve 345.17
upper
  n excitement 105.3
  adj superior 249.12
  higher 272.19
upper case 548.6
upper class
  the best 249.5
  social status 607.2
  aristocracy 608.1
upperclassman 572.6
upper crust
  the best 249.5
  society 578.6
  upper class 607.2
  aristocracy 608.1
upper hand
  advantage 249.2
  dominance 417.6
  influence 893.1
upper middle class
  607.5
uppermost top 198.10
  superlative 249.13
  higher 272.19
  paramount 996.24
uppers 87.3
uppity arrogant 141.9
  insolent 142.9
upraised
  vertical 200.11
  raised 911.9
upright
  n vertical 200.2
  post 273.4
  base 900.8
  v erect 200.9
  adj vertical 200.11
  straight 277.6
  honest 644.13

virtuous 653.6
raised 911.9
  adv vertically 200.13
uprising
  n ascent 193.1
  rising 200.5
  acclivity 204.6
  revolt 327.4
  adj ascending 193.14
  sloping upward
  204.17
uproar
  noise 53.3
  outcry 59.4
  agitation 105.4
  turbulence 671.2
  commotion 809.4
uproot
  dislodge 160.6
  extract 192.10
  exterminate 395.14
upscale
  upper-class 607.10
  wealthy 618.15
  expensive 632.11
  prosperous 1009.12
upset
  n anxiety 126.1
  dislodgment 160.2
  overturn 205.2
  fall 395.3
  turbulence 671.2
  disorder 809.1
  revolution 859.1
  agitation 916.1
  refutation 957.2
  bewilderment 970.3
  confusion 984.3
  frustration 1011.3
  v chagrin 96.15
  distress 96.16
  excite 105.14
  concern 126.4
  make anxious 126.5
  unnerve 128.10
  capsize 182.44
  overturn 205.6
  overthrow 395.20
  overcome 412.7
  unbalance 790.3
  disorder 809.9
  discompose 810.4
  revolutionize 859.4
  agitate 916.10
  refute 957.5
  bewilder 970.12
  confuse 984.7
  thwart 1011.15
  adj distressed 96.22
  excited 105.23
  overwrought 105.26
  unnerved 128.14
  defeated 412.14
  disorderly 809.13
  agitated 916.16
  disproved 957.7
  bewildered 970.24
  confused 984.12
upshoot
  n ascent 193.1
  v grow 14.2
  shoot up 193.9

expand 259.7
upside-down
  inverted 205.7
  confused 809.16
upstage
  n stage 704.16
  v snub 157.5
  act 704.29
  adj arrogant 141.9
  adv on the stage
  704.36
upstairs up 193.16
  on high 272.21
upstanding
  vertical 200.11
  honest 644.13
upstart
  n impudent person
  142.5
  vulgarian 497.6
  parvenu 606.7
  modern 840.4
  v shoot up 193.9
  adj populational 606.8
upstream
  v ascend 193.8
  adv up 193.16
upsurge
  n ascent 193.1
  increase 251.1
  v ascend 193.8
upswing ascent 193.1
  increase 251.1
  improvement 392.1
uptake 938.1
up the creek
  unfortunate 1010.14
  in trouble 1012.22
uptight
  tense 128.13
  conformist 866.6
up to
  v be able 18.11
  adj able 18.14
  prepared for 405.18
  competent 413.24
  sufficient 990.6
  prep until 820.15
up-to-date
  fashionable 578.11
  present 837.2
  modern 840.13
  informed 927.18
up to no good
  dishonest 645.16
  wicked 654.16
up to snuff
  competent 413.24
  in order 806.7
  up to par 998.19
up-to-the-minute
  fashionable 578.11
  present 837.2
  modern 840.13
  state-of-the-art 840.14
uptown
  n city district 230.6
  adj urban 230.11
  adv up 193.16
upturn
  n uptrend 193.2
  overturn 205.2

increase 251.1
business cycle 731.9
  v turn up 193.13
  overturn 205.6
upward mobility
  improvement 392.1
  class 607.1
  change 851.1
  prosperity 1009.1
upwind
  land 184.43
  ascend 193.8
upwind
  leeward 182.68
  windward 218.9
uranium 1037.5
Uranus 1070.9
urban 230.11
urbane decorous 496.10
  courteous 504.14
  sociable 582.22
urban renewal 396.4
urchin vagabond 178.3
  brat 302.4
urea 12.5
urethra 2.21
urge
  n desire 100.1
  impulse 365.1
  urgency 375.6
  v press 375.14
  insist 421.8
  admonish 422.6
  importune 440.12
  hasten 401.4
urgent
  motivating 375.25
  hasty 401.9
  demanding 421.9
  importunate 440.18
  vehement 544.13
  necessary 962.12
  imperative 996.22
urinal latrine 12.10
  toilet 12.11
urinate 12.14
urine humor 2.22
  water 12.5
urn
  cinerary urn 309.12
  ceramic ware 742.2
USA 232.3
usable 387.23
USAF 461.29
usage custom 373.1
  habit 373.4
  use 387.1
  treatment 387.2
  acceptation 518.4
  language 523.1
  word 526.1
  phrase 529.1
  diction 532.1
US Air Force 461.29
US Cabinet 423.1
use
  n custom 373.1
  habit 373.4
  employment 387.1
  utility 387.3
  benefit 387.4
  function 387.5

wear 393.5
estate 471.4
expenditure 626.1
v be on 87.21
treat 321.6
practice 328.8
handle 384.5
utilize 387.10
treat 387.12
exploit 387.16
spend 626.5
exert 725.8
used
employed 387.24
lost 473.7
wasted 486.9
secondhand 841.18
used to
accustomed 373.16
familiar with 373.17
habituated 373.18
use force 15.12
useful modal 384.8
employable 387.18
helpful 449.21
expedient 994.5
good 998.12
useless
ineffective 19.15
of no use 391.9
unsuccessful 410.18
disadvantageous
995.6
use one's head
have all one's wits
about one 919.10
think 930.8
user addict 87.20
use 387.7
employer 387.9
user-friendly 1013.15
use some elbow grease
endeavor 403.5
exert oneself 725.9
use up fatigue 21.4
spend 387.13
consume 388.3
waste 486.4
usher
n wedding party 563.4
attendant 577.5
theater man 704.23
escort 768.5
doorkeeper 1007.12
v escort 768.8
usual medium 246.3
typical 349.15
customary 373.14
same 780.6
orderly 806.6
frequent 846.4
prevalent 863.12
regular 868.9
ordinary 1004.8
usurp
take command 417.14
appropriate 480.19
arrogate 640.8
overstep 909.9
usury lending 620.1
interest 623.3
illicit business 732.1

utensil container 195.1
tool 1039.1
uterus genitals 2.11
vital force 885.7
utilitarian
useful 387.18
occupied 724.15
utility
n usefulness 387.3
helpfulness 449.10
machinery 1039.3
adj substitute 861.8
utility man
deputy 576.1
actor 707.2
utility player
baseball team 745.2
substitute 861.2
utility pole 273.1
utilize manage 384.5
use 387.10
gather materials
1052.7
utmost
n limit 793.5
adj extreme 247.13
superlative 249.13
trial 403.16
Utopia 985.11
utopian
n optimist 124.6
reformer 392.6
visionary 985.13
adj optimistic 124.12
emendatory 392.16
ideal 985.23
utter
v divulge 351.5
say 524.23
monetize 728.26
coin 728.28
disperse 770.4
adj downright 247.12
thorough 793.10
unqualified 959.2
sound 1001.7
U-turn reverse 163.3
bend 279.3
change of mind 363.1
V fork 171.4
five 881.1
vacancy vacuity 222.2
absence 222.2
position 724.5
nonexistence 761.1
empty-headedness
921.6
thoughtlessness 932.1
vacate quit 188.9
abandon 370.5
repeal 445.2
resign 448.2
relinquish 475.3
vacation
n holiday 20.3
absence 222.4
repeal 445.1
interim 825.1
pause 856.3
v get away from it all
20.9
absent oneself 222.8

vacational 20.10
vaccine
vaccination 86.28
inoculation 91.16
vacillate waver 362.8
blow hot and cold
364.4
change 853.5
oscillate 915.10
hang in doubt 970.10
vacuous vacant 222.14
nonexistent 761.8
empty-headed 921.19
ignorant 929.12
thoughtless 932.4
trivial 997.19
vacuum
n void 222.3
nonexistence 761.1
deficiency 794.2
empty-headedness
921.6
v sweep 79.23
vacuum-packed 212.12
vacuum tube 1032.10
vagabond
n displaced person
160.4
vagrant 178.3
wretch 660.2
transient 827.4
v wander 177.23
adj wandering 177.37
vagary obliquity 204.1
caprice 364.1
vagina genitals 2.11
duct 2.21
vagrancy
wandering 177.3
indolence 331.5
vagrant
n vagabond 178.3
bum 331.9
wretch 660.2
adj deviative 164.7
wandering 177.37
capricious 364.5
inconstant 853.7
vague
inconspicuous 32.6
formless 263.4
thin 270.16
obscure 522.15
unordered 809.12
general 863.11
indefinite 970.19
inaccurate 974.17
vain ineffective 19.15
conceited 136.9
vainglorious 140.8
futile 391.13
boastful 502.10
baseless 935.13
trivial 997.19
valedictorian 543.4
valedictory
n leave-taking 188.4
speech 543.2
adj departing 188.18
valence electrons
1032.3
valentine 562.13

valet
n man 577.4
v serve 577.13
valiant
n brave person 492.8
adj courageous 492.17
valid powerful 18.12
legal 673.10
evidential 956.16
sound 972.14
good 998.12
validate ratify 332.12
authorize 443.11
legalize 673.8
experiment 941.8
confirm 956.11
verify 969.12
valley crack 224.2
vale 237.7
pit 275.2
concavity 284.9
valor 492.1
valuable
of value 387.22
precious 632.10
value
n color quality 35.6
measure 300.2
benefit 387.4
meaning 518.1
worth 630.2
preciousness 632.2
importance 996.1
goodness 998.1
v respect 155.4
measure 300.10
price 630.11
estimate 945.9
esteem 996.13
value judgment 945.3
valve gate 239.10
stopper 293.4
wind instrument
711.6
electron tube 1032.10
cutlery 1039.2
vamp
n lover 104.12
tempter 377.4
flirt 562.11
demimonde 665.15
overture 708.26
impromptu 708.27
fire fighter 1021.4
v enamor 104.23
improvise 365.8
fascinate 377.7
perfect 392.11
vampire lover 104.12
frightener 127.9
tempter 377.4
extortionist 480.12
monster 593.6
demimonde 665.15
demon 680.6
bewitcher 690.9
van leading 165.1
wagon 179.2
vanguard 216.2
guard 1007.9
vandal destroyer 395.8
savage 593.5

vandalism
cruelty 144.11
misbehavior 322.1
destruction 395.1
violence 671.1
vane 318.17
vanguard leading 165.1
border 211.4
van 216.2
precursor 815.1
novelty 840.2
guard 1007.9
vanilla
unadorned 499.8
elegant 533.6
simple 797.6
vanish disappear 34.2
quit 188.9
perish 395.23
cease to exist 761.6
flit 827.6
vanishing cream
1015.12
vanishing point
disappearance 34.1
convergence 169.1
minute 258.7
the distance 261.3
vanity pride 136.1
self-admiration 140
vainness 140.1
futility 391.2
boasting 502.1
triviality 997.3
vanity press 554.2
vanquish 412.10
vantage viewpoint 27.7
advantage 249.2
vantage point 272.2
vapid
wishy-washy 16.17
insipid 65.2
dull 117.6
prosaic 721.5
empty-headed 921.19
trivial 997.19
mediocre 1004.7
vapor
n fog 319.2
spirit 763.3
illusion 975.1
figment of the
imagination 985.5
hot water 1018.10
volatile 1065
steam 1065.1
v boast 502.6
bluster 503.3
talk nonsense 520.5
talk big 545.6
let out 908.24
vaporize
strike dead 308.17
destroy 395.10
evaporate 1065.8
vaquero rider 178.8
herder 1068.3
variable
n process variable
1040.9
adj relative 774.7
nonuniform 781.3

multiform 782.3
irregular 850.3
changeable 853.6
inconstant 853.7
uncertain 970.16
variable-rate mortgage
438.4
variance dissent 333.1
permission 443.1
disaccord 456.2
relativity 774.2
difference 779.1
disagreement 788.1
variation
deviation 164.1
passage 708.24
difference 779.1
differentiation 779.4
nonuniformity 781.1
multiformity 782.1
change 851.1
inconstancy 853.2
changing 853.3
varicose vein 2.21
varied different 779.7
diversified 782.4
mixed 796.14
variegated
chromatic 35.15
many-colored 47.9
different 779.7
nonuniform 781.3
variety sect 675.3
show business 704.1
miscellany 769.13
difference 779.1
nonuniformity 781.1
multiformity 782.1
kind 808.3
classifications 808.5
change 851.1
inconstancy 853.2
plurality 882.1
various different 779.7
nonuniform 781.3
diversified 782.4
plural 882.7
several 883.7
varnish
n blanket 295.12
sham 354.3
pretext 376.1
extenuation 600.5
art equipment 712.18
v color 35.13
pervert 265.6
polish 287.7
conceal 346.6
falsify 354.15
ornament 545.7
extenuate 600.12
varsity 617.7
vary deviate 164.3
vacillate 362.8
differ 779.5
differentiate 779.6
diversify 781.2
multiform 782.2
disguise 786.3
disagree 788.5
intermit 850.2
shift 851.6

alternate 851.7
change 853.5
vas 2.21
vascular 2.31
vase 742.2
Vaseline 1054.2
vassal
n subject 432.7
retainer 577.1
adj subject 432.13
vast spacious 158.10
large 247.7
huge 257.20
vat 386.6
the Vatican 698.6
Vatican Library 558.1
vaudeville 704.1
vault
n ascent 193.1
compartment 197.2
arch 279.4
tomb 309.16
leap 366.1
storehouse 386.6
treasury 729.12
the heavens 1070.2
v curve 279.6
leap 366.5
vaulter 366.4
vaunt
n display 501.4
boasting 502.1
v flaunt 501.17
boast 502.6
VCR record 50.12
television receiver
1034.11
VD 85.18
veal 10.14
vector infection 85.4
carrier 85.43
direction 161.2
course 184.34
straight line 277.2
the Vedas 683.7
veep 574.3
veer
n deviation 164.1
bias 204.3
angle 278.2
v turn round 163.9
deviate 164.3
change course 182.30
oblique 204.9
go sideways 218.5
angle 278.5
be changed 851.6
vegetable
n plant 310.3
adj vegetal 310.33
passive 329.6
languid 331.20
permanent 852.7
vegetarian
n eater 8.16
abstainer 668.4
adj eating 8.31
vegetable 310.33
abstinent 668.10
vegetate develop 14.2
stagnate 173.9
grow 259.7

sprout 310.31
do nothing 329.2
merely exist 760.10
vegetation
physical development
14.1
inertness 173.4
growth 259.3
plants 310.1
life 310.30
inaction 329.1
mere existence 760.6
vehement
acrimonious 17.14
zealous 101.9
passionate 105.29
industrious 330.22
emphatic 544.13
violent 671.16
vehicle color 35.8
means of travel 179
conveyance 179.1
instrument 384.4
stage show 704.4
film 714.10
veil
n clothing 5.26
cover 295.2
veil of secrecy 345.3
curtain 346.2
pretext 376.1
shade 1027.1
v cover 295.19
keep secret 345.7
conceal 346.6
shade 1027.5
veiled covered 295.31
latent 519.5
vague 970.19
shaded 1027.7
vein
n duct 2.21
thinness 270.7
source of supply 386.4
style 532.2
mode 764.4
nature 766.4
disposition 977.3
mood 977.4
deposit 1056.7
v variegate 47.7
veld the country 233.1
plain 236.1
grassland 310.8
velocity rate 172.4
speed 174.1
gait 177.12
velvet comfort 121.1
smoothness 287.3
texture 294.3
prosperity 1009.1
easy 1013.4
softness 1045.4
vena cava 2.21
venal greedy 100.27
bribable 378.4
corruptible 645.23
vendetta quarrel 456.5
revenge 507.1
animosity 589.4
vending machine 736.4
vendor peddler 730.5

vending machine
736.4

veneer
n shallowness 276.1
blanket 295.12
lamina 296.2
v face 295.23

venerable
dignified 136.12
reverend 155.12
aged 303.16
reputable 662.15
sacred 685.7
old 841.10
traditional 841.12

venerate
respect 155.4
worship 696.10

venereal disease 85.18

vengeance
revenge 507.1
deserts 639.3

venial 600.14

venison 10.12

venom
poisonousness 82.3
rancor 144.7
animosity 589.4
violence 671.1
evil 999.3
bane 1000.3

vent
n parachute 181.13
emergence 190.1
outlet 190.9
air passage 239.13
escape 369.1
v divulge 351.5
evacuate 908.22

ventilate
deodorize 72.4
air 317.10
disclose 351.4
divulge 351.5
make public 352.11
discuss 541.12
refrigerate 1023.10

ventral 2.29

ventricular 2.29

ventriloquist 524.16

venture
n undertaking 404.1
investment 729.3
trading 737.19
gamble 759.2
v attempt 403.6
dare 492.10
presume 640.6
invest 729.16
trade 737.23
chance 759.24

venture capital
supply 386.2
capital 728.15
trading 737.19

venue 159.2

Venus Love 104.8
beauty 1015.10
stars 1070.4
planet 1070.9

Venus's flytrap 356.12

Venus de Milo 1015.10

veracity honesty 644.3
truth 972.1

veranda 197.21

verb 530.4

verbal
n verb 530.4
adj communicational
343.9
semantic 518.12
speech 524.30
vocabular 526.18
grammatical 530.17
genuine 972.15

verbalize 524.23

verbatim
adj genuine 972.15
adv exactly 972.21

verbiage diction 532.1
wordiness 538.2

verboten 444.7

verdant green 44.4
verdurous 310.39

verdict judgment 598.9
solution 939.1
decision 945.5

verge
n border 211.4
insignia 647.1
v take direction 161.7
border 211.10
tend 895.3

verify
experiment 941.8
collate 942.5
confirm 956.11
certify 969.12
check 1016.20

verisimilitude
probability 967.1
genuineness 972.7

veritable
straight 644.14
real 760.15
thorough 793.10
true 972.13

vérité 706.1

vermicelli 10.32

vermicide
vermifuge 86.24
poison 1000.3

vermiform coiled 281.7
wormlike 311.51

vermilion
v make red 41.4
adj red 41.6

vermin
creature 311.3
parasite 311.35
rabble 606.3
beast 660.7

vernacular
n dead language 523.2
mother tongue 523.3
nonformal speech
523.5
substandard language
523.6
jargon 523.9
plain speech 535.1
adj local 231.9
common 497.14
colloquial 523.18

usual 868.9

vernal green 44.4
immature 301.10
seasonal 313.9
new 840.7

vernal equinox
season 313.7
orbit 1070.16

versatile fickle 364.6
handy 387.20
ambidextrous 413.25
multiform 782.3

verse
n part 554.13
passage 708.24
poetry 720.1
poem 720.4
part of writing 792.2
curtain-raiser 815.2
maxim 973.1
v inform 551.8
poetize 720.13

versed in
skilled in 413.27
informed in 927.19

version
reproduction 336.3
rendering 341.2
writing 547.10
sect 675.3
score 708.28
story 722.3

verso left side 220.1
makeup 554.12

versus toward 161.26
against 215.7
opposed to 451.10

vertebrate
n creature 311.3
adj chordate 311.39

vertex summit 198.2
angle 278.2

vertical
n upright 200.2
adj top 198.10
upright 200.11
steep 204.18
straight 277.6

vertigo symptom 85.9
ear disease 85.15
dizziness 984.4

verve vim 17.2
passion 93.2
eagerness 101.1
gaiety 109.4
liveliness 330.2
spirit 544.4
lively imagination
985.4

very to a degree 245.7
exceedingly 247.18

vesicle bulge 283.3
bubble 320.1
blemish 1003.1

vespers 696.8

vessel duct 2.21
ship 180.1
container 195.1

vest
n waistcoat 5.14
v establish 159.16
endow 478.17

commission 615.10

vestal virgin 565.4

vested clothing 5.44
established 854.13

vested interest
estate 471.4
pressure group 609.31
prerogative 642.1

vestibule ear 2.10
entrance 189.5
portal 197.19

vestige
remainder 256.1
print 517.7
clue 517.9
record 549.1
admixture 796.7
antiquity 841.6

vestment
clothing 5.1
garment 5.3
cover 295.2

vest-pocket
insignificant 248.6
miniature 258.12
shortened 268.9
concise 537.6

vestry
ecclesiastical council
423.4
church 703.9

veteran
n old man 304.2
vet 413.16
combat participant
461.19
adj experienced
413.28

veterinarian 90.7

veto
n negative 444.2
executive privilege
613.7
v put one's veto upon
444.5
oppose 451.3
disapprove 510.10
legislate 613.10

vex annoy 96.13
irk 98.15
make anxious 126.5
provoke 152.24
trouble 1012.13

V formation 184.12

VHF 1033.12

via 161.27

viable energizing 17.15
acceptable 107.12
living 306.11
workable 888.10
practicable 965.7
of importance 996.18

viaduct crossing 170.2
bridge 383.9

vibrant energetic 17.13
resonant 54.9

vibrate resonate 54.6
be frequent 846.3
oscillate 915.10
shake 916.11

vibrato
n screech 58.4

trill 709.19
adj shrill 58.14
vicar deputy 576.1
substitute 861.2
vicarious 861.8
vice
n misbehavior 322.1
deputy 576.1
moral badness 654
viciousness 654.1
weakness 654.2
wrongdoing 655.1
substitute 861.2
prep instead of 861.12
vice-president
executive 574.3
vice-chairman 576.8
substitute 861.2
viceroy
governor 575.13
vice-president 576.8
vice versa
inversely 205.8
reciprocally 776.12
contrarily 778.9
vicinity
environment 209.1
nearness 223.1
region 231.1
vicious cruel 144.26
vice-prone 654.11
wicked 654.16
savage 671.21
bad 999.7
harmful 999.12
vicious circle
circle 280.2
futility 391.2
sophistry 935.1
vicissitudes 971.5
vicious cycle 391.2
vicissitude
changing 853.3
adversity 1010.1
victim
sick person 85.42
sufferer 96.11
dupe 358.1
quarry 382.7
loser 412.5
laughingstock 508.7
cheater 759.22
unfortunate 1010.7
victimize cheat 356.18
persecute 389.7
outwit 415.11
overprice 632.7
victor
successful person
409.6
winner 411.2
Victorian
n prude 500.11
adj prudish 500.19
antiquated 841.13
victorious 411.7
victory
success 409.1
triumph 411
win 411.1
victuals food 10.2
groceries 735.7

video
n television 1034.1
adj televisional
1034.16
video-cassette recorder
record 50.12
television receiver
1034.11
videotape
n recording media
549.10
v record 549.15
vie compete 457.18
be comparable 942.7
excel 998.11
Vietcong
n irregular 461.16
revolutionist 859.3
adj revolutionist 859.6
view
n look 27.3
field of view 31.3
aspect 33.3
appearance 33.6
intention 380.1
scene 712.12
estimate 945.3
opinion 952.6
outlook 977.2
v see 27.12
look 27.13
think of 930.17
take the attitude
977.6
heed 982.6
viewer
optical instrument
29.1
recipient 479.3
spectator 917.1
televiewer 1034.12
viewpoint
standpoint 27.7
field of view 31.3
aspect 33.3
station 159.2
outlook 977.2
vigil wakefulness 23.1
vigilance 339.4
vigilant wakeful 23.7
wary 339.13
prepared 405.16
protective 1007.23
vignette
description 349.2
drawing 712.13
print 713.5
vigor strength 15.1
energy 17.1
power 18.1
haleness 83.3
gaiety 109.4
force 544.3
vigorish 792.1
viking mariner 183.1
pirate 483.7
vile nasty 64.7
malodorous 71.5
filthy 80.23
offensive 98.18
low 497.15
cursing 513.8

knavish 645.17
wicked 654.16
base 661.12
obscene 666.9
paltry 997.21
terrible 999.9
vilify berate 510.19
revile 512.10
abuse 513.7
stigmatize 661.9
blaspheme 694.5
villa 228.7
village
n hamlet 230.2
region 231.5
adj urban 230.11
villain evildoer 593.1
rascal 660.3
role 704.10
actor 707.2
vim verve 17.2
power 18.1
gaiety 109.4
liveliness 330.2
vinaigrette 70.6
vindicate justify 600.9
acquit 601.4
vindictive 507.7
vine 310.4
vinegar sour 67.2
preservative 397.4
vineyard 1067.10
vintage 472.5
violate disobey 327.6
misuse 389.4
corrupt 393.12
break 435.4
possess sexually
480.15
seduce 665.20
rage 671.11
break the law 674.5
work evil 999.6
violence acrimony 17.5
excitability 105.10
cruelty 144.11
rage 152.10
mistreatment 389.2
coercion 424.3
vehement action 671
agitation 671.1
violet
n purpleness 46.1
adj purple 46.3
violinist 710.5
VIP celebrity 662.9
influence 893.6
important person
996.9
viper serpent 311.26
beast 660.7
virgin
n schoolgirl 302.8
single woman 565.4
adj hinterland 233.9
natural 406.13
unmarried 565.7
continent 664.6
intact 791.10
unmixed 797.7
new 840.7
unproductive 890.4

unknown 929.17
undamaged 1001.8
virgule diagonal 204.7
line 517.6
virile potent 76.12
courageous 492.17
virtual 519.5
virtue power 18.1
courage 492.1
morality 636.3
probity 644.1
moral goodness 653
virtuousness 653.1
chastity 664.1
goodness 998.1
virtuoso
n superior 249.4
master 413.13
connoisseur 496.7
musician 710.1
first-rater 998.6
adj skillful 413.22
musical 708.47
virtuous honest 644.13
good 653.6
chaste 664.4
pure 998.12
virulent
acrimonious 17.14
poisonous 82.7
rancorous 144.22
resentful 152.26
deadly 308.22
hostile 589.10
violent 671.16
harmful 999.12
virus infection 85.4
germ 85.41
organism 305.2
poison 1000.3
visa
n ratification 332.4
pass 443.7
signature 527.10
certificate 549.6
v ratify 332.12
visage looks 33.4
face 216.4
vis à vis 789.4
viscera vitals 2.14
heart 93.3
insides 207.4
viscount 608.4
viscous thick 269.8
dense 1043.12
viscid 1060.12
vise 260.6
visible visual 27.20
clear 31.6
apparent 33.11
manifest 348.8
vision
n sight 27
optics 27.1
apparition 33.5
deception 356.1
phantom 975.4
figment of the
imagination 985.5
visualization 985.6
dream 985.9
specter 987.1

thing of beauty 1015.7
v visualize 985.15
visit
n chat 541.4
social call 582.7
v go to 177.25
enter 189.7
attend 221.8
chat 541.10
pay a visit 582.19
visitor traveler 178.1
incomer 189.4
attender 221.5
superintendent 574.2
guest 585.6
examiner 937.17
visor cover 356.11
eyeshade 1027.2
vista field of view 31.3
view 33.6
visual eye 2.26
ocular 27.20
visible 31.6
visualize
think of 930.17
vision 985.15
vital
powerful 18.12
hale 83.12
eager 101.8
gay 109.14
organic 305.17
living 306.11
vigorous 544.11
durable 826.10
requisite 962.13
all-important 996.23
vitality
strength 15.1
energy 17.1
power 18.1
haleness 83.3
eagerness 101.1
gaiety 109.4
life 306.1
vigor 544.3
toughness 1047.1
vital statistics 1016.13
vitamin 7.4
vitamin complex 7.4
vitamin deficiency
991.6
vitiate impair 393.12
corrupt 654.10
neutralize 899.7
vitreous 1028.5
vitriolic
acrimonious 17.14
pungent 68.6
rancorous 144.22
hostile 589.10
vituperate
berate 510.19
vilify 513.7
viva! 509.23
vivacious
energetic 17.13
eager 101.8
gay 109.14
active 330.17
spirited 544.12
vive! 509.23

vivid energetic 17.13
sensitive 24.13
colorful 35.18
eager 101.8
representational
349.13
descriptive 349.14
expressive 544.10
remembered 988.23
bright 1024.32
vivisection 801.5
vixen
female animal 77.9
bitch 110.12
witch 593.7
violent person 671.9
viz
by interpretation
341.18
namely 864.18
vocabulary
n jargon 523.9
lexis 526.13
reference book 554.9
dictionary 870.4
adj verbal 526.18
vocal speech 524.30
singing 708.50
vocal cords 524.19
vocalist 710.13
vocalize say 524.23
sing 708.38
vocation motive 375.1
the ministry 698.1
occupation 724.6
specialty 865.1
vociferous noisy 53.13
vociferant 59.10
vogue
n fashion 578.1
repute 662.1
adj stylish 578.12
voice
n vote 371.6
approval 509.1
utterance 524.3
manner of speaking
524.8
speech sound 524.13
active voice 530.14
spokesman 576.5
part 708.22
voce 709.5
singer 710.13
v publish 352.10
say 524.23
tune 708.36
voiceless mute 51.12
phonetic 524.31
voicemail 347.13
void
n space 158.1
vacuum 222.3
crack 224.2
nonexistence 761.1
v defecate 12.13
delete 255.12
abolish 395.13
repeal 445.2
neutralize 899.7
evacuate 908.22
adj vacant 222.14

repealed 445.3
nonexistent 761.8
voilà
so much for that!
407.15
attention! 982.22
volatile
n vapor 1065.1
adj light 298.10
fickle 364.6
transient 827.7
inconstant 853.7
superficial 921.20
flighty 984.17
vaporable 1065.10
volcanic fervent 93.18
excitable 105.28
passionate 105.29
hot-tempered 110.25
explosive 671.24
volcano
mountain 237.6
outburst 671.6
volition will 323.1
choice 371.1
volley
n detonation 56.3
salvo 459.9
arrow 462.6
shot 903.4
v play tennis 748.3
volt 1031.11
voltage 1031.11
voluble 540.9
volume loudness 53.1
space 158.1
quantity 247.3
size 257.1
capacity 257.2
book 554.1
tome 554.4
edition 554.5
part 554.13
voluminous
spacious 158.10
large 247.7
capacious 257.17
voluntary
n overture 708.26
curtain-raiser 815.2
adj volitional 323.4
volunteer 324.7
elective 371.22
intentional 380.8
volunteer
n voluntariness 324.2
v do voluntarily 324.4
step forward 439.10
adj voluntary 324.7
voluptuous
sexual 75.24
delightful 97.7
sensual 663.5
vomit
n emetic 86.18
vomiting 908.8
v feel disgust 99.4
jet 238.20
erupt 671.13
spew 908.26
voodoo
n animism 675.6

sorcery 690.1
shaman 690.7
charm 691.5
bad influence 999.4
v bewitch 691.9
adj sorcerous 690.14
voracious
hungry 100.25
greedy 100.27
gluttonous 672.6
vortex agitation 105.4
wash 184.30
eddy 238.12
coil 281.2
bustle 330.4
whirl 914.2
vote
n choice 371.6
approval 509.1
voting 609.18
legislative procedure
613.6
v cast one's vote
371.18
participate 476.5
voter selector 371.7
elector 609.23
vouch
n affirmation 334.1
v depose 334.6
promise 436.4
testify 956.9
voucher
recommendation
509.4
certificate 549.6
acknowledgment
627.2
negotiable paper
728.11
witness 956.6
vouchsafe
condescend 137.8
give oneself airs 141.8
permit 443.9
give 478.12
vow
n oath 334.4
promise 436.1
v depose 334.6
promise 436.4
state 952.12
vowel
n speech sound 524.13
adj phonetic 524.31
vox populi
unanimity 332.5
opinion 952.6
voyage
n journey 177.5
ocean trip 182.6
v traverse 177.20
journey 177.21
navigate 182.13
voyager 178.1
voyeur
sexual pervert 75.16
inquisitive person
980.2
vs 451.10
V-shaped forked 171.10
angular 278.6

Vulcan 726.8
vulcanize burn 1019.24
  elasticize 1046.6
vulgar inferior 250.6
  disreputable 497.10
  gaudy 501.20
  ill-bred 505.6
  vernacular 523.18
  inelegant 534.2
  populational 606.8
  base 661.12
  uncouth 666.8
vulgarity
  inadequacy 250.3
  commonness 497
  vulgarness 497.1
  discourtesy 505.1
  inelegance 534.1
  baseness 661.3
  uncouthness 666.3
vulnerable
  helpless 19.18
  influenceable 893.15
  liable 896.5
  pregnable 1005.16
  brittle 1048.4
vulture 480.12
vulva 2.11
vying
  n hostility 451.2
  contention 457.1
  competition 457.2
  adj competitive
    457.23
wacky foolish 922.9
  crazy 925.27
  eccentric 926.6
wad
  n lot 247.4
  lump 257.10
  wealth 618.3
  bankroll 728.17
  accumulation 769.9
  v fill 196.7
  stuff 793.7
wadding
  lining 196.3
  stopping 293.5
waddle
  n slow motion 175.2
  gait 177.12
  v go slow 175.6
  way of walking 177.28
wade 182.56
wade into
  confront 216.8
  attack 459.15
  set to work 725.15
wading bird 311.28
wafer biscuit 10.29
  thinness 270.7
  lamina 296.2
  Eucharist 701.7
waffle
  n pancake 10.43
  bull 520.3
  v slight 340.8
  prevaricate 344.7
  vacillate 362.8
  remain neutral 467.5
  talk nonsense 520.5
  change 853.5

waft
  n transportation 176.3
  puff 318.4
  v transport 176.12
  buoy 298.8
  blow 318.20
wag
  n mischief-maker
    322.3
  humorist 489.12
  swing 915.6
  wiggle 916.7
  v oscillate 915.10
  wave 915.11
  wiggle 916.14
wage
  n pay 624.4
  v practice 328.8
wager
  n bet 759.3
  gamble 970.8
  v chance 759.24
  bet 759.25
wagon vehicle 179.2
  police car 179.11
waif vagabond 178.3
  derelict 370.4
wail
  n screech 58.4
  lament 115.3
  v screech 58.8
  cry 60.2
  ululate 115.13
  sigh 318.21
  speak 524.26
wainscot
  n lining 196.3
  base 199.2
  v fill 196.7
waist shirt 5.15
  middle 818.1
waistband 5.19
waistcoat 5.14
waistline 818.1
wait
  n minstrel 710.14
  delay 845.2
  v await 130.8
  be patient 134.4
  serve 577.13
  delay 845.12
waiter 577.7
waiting list 870.1
wait on await 130.8
  toady to 138.8
  extend courtesy
    504.12
  serve 577.13
  accompany 768.7
  escort 768.8
waitress 577.7
wait up 845.12
waive
  give up 370.7
  reject 372.2
  cease to use 390.4
  not use 390.5
  permit 443.9
  repeal 445.2
  relinquish 475.3
  postpone 845.9
  allow for 958.5

waiver
  relinquishment 370.3
  discontinuance 390.2
  permission 443.1
  repeal 445.1
  quitclaim 475.2
  qualification 958.1
wake
  n wakefulness 23.1
  track 182.7
  wash 184.30
  last offices 309.4
  sign 517.8
  social gathering
    582.10
  afterpart 816.2
  aftereffect 886.3
  v awake 23.4
  get up 23.5
  excite 105.12
wale sore 85.36
  bulge 283.3
  texture 294.1
  blemish 1003.1
walk
  n slow motion 175.2
  ramble 177.10
  gait 177.12
  sphere 231.2
  route 383.1
  path 383.2
  race 457.12
  arena 463.1
  occupation 724.4
  vocation 724.6
  game 745.3
  circuit 913.2
  v exercise 84.4
  go slow 175.6
  ambulate 177.27
  get off 369.7
  win hands down 411.4
  be free 430.18
  liberate 431.9
  strike 727.10
  play 745.5
walk all over 612.16
walk a tightrope
    1012.11
walk away quit 188.9
  outdistance 249.10
  abandon 370.5
  dismiss 983.4
walker
  pedestrian 178.6
  baby carriage 179.6
walking papers 908.5
walk-on role 704.10
  supporting actor
    707.7
walk out exit 190.12
  strike 727.10
  stop work 856.8
walkover 411.1
walk-through 704.13
walkup 228.13
walkway 383.2
wall
  n precipice 200.3
  fence 212.4
  partition 213.5
  slope 237.2

  barrier 1011.5
  v fence 212.7
  fortify 460.9
walled-in
  enclosed 212.10
  covered 295.31
wallet 729.14
wall off partition 213.8
  quarantine 429.13
wallop
  n blow 901.5
  v punish 604.15
  strike 901.15
  beat 901.17
  flounder 916.15
wallow
  n marsh 243.1
  flounder 916.8
  v pitch 182.55
  be promiscuous
    665.19
  bow 912.9
  welter 914.13
  flounder 916.15
wallpaper 295.23
Wall Street
  stock market 737.1
  stock exchange 737.7
  financial district
    737.8
wall-to-wall
  adj comprehensive
    771.7
  same 780.6
  thorough 793.10
  continuous 811.8
  adv continuously
    811.10
wall-to-wall carpet
    295.9
walnut 40.3
waltz
  n easy 1013.4
  v win hands down
    411.4
  dance 705.5
wampum jewel 498.6
  money 728.2
  names for 728.3
wan
  v lose color 36.6
  adj tired-looking 21.9
  colorless 36.7
  deathly 307.29
  languid 331.20
  lackluster 1026.17
wand fitness 84.1
  scepter 417.9
  insignia 647.1
  wish-bringer 691.6
  dowsing 961.3
wander deviate 164.4
  roam 177.23
  digress 538.9
  misbelieve 688.8
  be insane 925.20
  err 974.9
  stray 983.3
  muse 984.9
wanderer rover 178.2
  alien 773.3
  transient 827.4

wash one's hands of
give up 370.7
refuse 442.3
relinquish 475.3
disapprove 510.10
washout washing 79.5
airmanship 184.3
overflow 238.6
debacle 395.4
scrub 410.2
abortion 410.5
failure 410.8
wash over 238.17
wasp
sorehead 110.11
bee 311.33
waste
n excrement 12.3
offal 80.9
decrement 252.3
remainder 256.1
derelict 370.4
consumption 388.1
refuse 391.4
wastage 393.4
destruction 395.1
loss 473.2
prodigality 486.1
disintegration 805.1
wasteland 890.2
extract 892.3
v disappear 34.2
fail 85.47
decrease 252.6
shrink 260.9
kill 308.13
be consumed 388.4
impair 393.19
destroy 395.10
put an end to 395.12
deplete 473.5
consume 486.4
annihilate 761.7
end 819.5
adj hinterland 233.9
unproductive 890.4
wastebasket 391.7
waste disposal 390.3
wasteful
destructive 395.26
prodigal 486.8
wasteland
hinterland 233.2
waste 890.2
wastrel
vagabond 178.3
bum 331.9
derelict 370.4
prodigal 486.2
wretch 660.2
watch
n observation 27.2
hand 183.6
vigilance 339.4
assemblage 769.6
shift 824.3
timepiece 831.6
watchman 1007.10
v look 27.13
await 130.8
attend 221.8
be vigilant 339.8

spectate 917.5
reconnoiter 937.27
be curious 980.3
heed 982.6
care for 1007.19
protect 1007.20
watchdog dog 311.17
guard dog 1007.11
watchful
wakeful 23.7
vigilant 339.13
attentive 982.15
protective 1007.23
watchtower
observation post 27.8
marker 517.10
watchword
call to arms 458.8
password 517.12
motto 973.4
watch your step!
494.14
water
n urine 12.5
sweat 12.7
symbol of weakness
16.7
sounding 275.5
painting 712.14
changeableness 853.4
extinguisher 1021.3
fluid 1059.2
aqua 1063.3
v secrete 13.5
dilute 16.11
abate 252.8
thin 270.12
rarefy 299.3
corrupt 393.12
dissipate 770.5
adulterate 796.12
moisten 1063.12
tend 1068.7
watercolor 712.14
waterfall
descent 194.1
cataract 238.11
waterfowl 311.28
waterfront 234.2
watering
n weakening 16.5
rarefaction 299.2
dispersion 770.1
adulteration 796.3
wetting 1063.6
adj secretory 13.7
wetting 1063.18
watering hole
bar 88.20
lake 241.1
waterlogged 1063.17
Waterloo 412.1
watermark
waterline 300.6
mark 517.5
water pollution
unhealthfulness 82.1
environmental
destruction 1071.2
waterproof
v proof 15.14
adj seaworthy 180.18

close 293.12
watertight 1064.11
water sport 744.1
waterspout spout 239.8
rainstorm 316.2
whirlwind 318.14
watertight
resistant 15.20
seaworthy 180.18
close 293.12
waterproof 1064.11
water under the bridge
836.1
waterway
seaway 182.10
stream 238.1
watercourse 239.2
waterworks
channel 239.2
water 1063.3
watery secretory 13.7
wishy-washy 16.17
insipid 65.2
thin 270.16
meager 991.10
fluid 1059.4
moist 1063.16
WATS line 347.17
watts 1031.17
wave
n hairdo 3.15
billow 238.14
convolution 281.1
greeting 585.4
waving 915.2
oscillation 915.4
swing 915.6
v cut the hair 3.22
billow 238.22
manifest 348.5
flaunt 501.17
signal 517.22
oscillate 915.10
undulate 915.11
flutter 916.12
wavelength
oscillation 915.4
radio wave 1033.11
wavelet 238.14
wave off 772.4
waver
n swing 915.6
flutter 916.4
v demur 325.4
vacillate 362.8
diversify 781.2
change 853.5
oscillate 915.10
flutter 916.12
flicker 1024.25
wave the white flag
surrender 433.8
make peace 465.9
wavy curved 279.7
undulant 281.10
inconstant 853.7
wax
n whiteness 37.2
record 50.12
fit 152.8
softness 1045.4
lubricant 1054.2

v grow 14.2
increase 251.6
expand 259.7
polish 287.7
evolve 860.5
oil 1054.8
wax and wane
change 853.5
alternate 915.13
waxen 36.7
way room 158.3
direction 161.1
progression 162.1
progress 182.9
entrance 189.5
channel 239.1
behavior 321.1
custom 373.1
habit 373.4
plan 381.1
route 383.1
manner 384.1
knack 413.6
latitude 430.4
style 532.2
mode 764.4
nature 766.4
continuance 855.1
specialty 865.1
wayfarer 178.1
waylay 346.10
way of life
behavior 321.1
preference 371.5
custom 373.1
mode 764.4
specialty 865.1
the way of the world
764.2
way out
n outlet 190.9
loophole 369.4
excuse 600.4
adj extreme 247.13
nothing like 786.5
modern 840.13
unconventional 867.6
ways and means 384.2
**the way the ball
bounces** 971.1
wayward
disobedient 327.8
perverse 361.11
capricious 364.5
unvirtuous 654.12
wanton 665.26
inconstant 853.7
weak weakly 16.12
impotent 19.13
tired 21.7
inconspicuous 32.6
colorless 36.7
faint 52.16
insipid 65.2
thin 270.16
stricken in years
303.18
human 312.13
weak-willed 362.12
lax 426.4
cowardly 491.10
phonetic 524.31

assent 332.1
liberality 485.1
hospitality 585.2
v receive 187.10
assent 332.8
be hospitable 585.9
incur 896.4
adj pleasant 97.6
hospitable 585.12
weld
n joint 799.4
v sculpture 715.5
relate 774.6
put together 799.5
stick together 802.9
burn 1019.24
welder
blowtorch 1019.14
machinery 1039.3
welfare
n kindness 143.5
subsidy 478.8
welfarism 611.7
good 998.4
prosperity 1009.1
adj benevolent 143.15
welfare state
welfare 143.5
relief 611.7
government 612.4
welfare worker 143.8
well
n lake 241.1
depth 275.2
pit 284.4
source of supply 386.4
fountainhead 885.6
v run out 190.13
jet 238.20
adj unailing 83.10
adv ably 18.16
kindly 143.18
successfully 409.15
skillfully 413.31
excellently 998.22
well-advised 919.19
well-balanced
composed 106.13
symmetric 264.4
stable 854.12
sensible 919.18
well-being health 83.1
pleasure 95.1
contentment 107.1
comfort 121.1
good 998.4
prosperity 1009.1
well-bred
highbred 504.17
upper-class 607.10
wellborn 608.11
well-built
able-bodied 15.16
sturdy 762.7
made 891.18
comely 1015.18
well-defined
distinct 31.7
clear 521.11
well-deserving 509.20
well-developed
grown 14.3

expanded 259.12
mature 303.13
well-disposed
well-meaning 143.17
willing 324.5
favorable 449.22
approving 509.17
friendly 587.15
well-educated 927.20
well-established
sturdy 762.7
established 854.13
obvious 969.15
well-fed 257.18
well-known trite 117.9
distinguished 662.16
real 760.15
well-kenned 927.27
well-made
shapely 264.5
sturdy 762.7
made 891.18
comely 1015.18
well-mannered
mannerly 504.16
ceremonious 580.8
well-meaning
well-meant 143.17
favorable 449.22
friendly 587.15
harmless 998.21
well-nigh 223.22
well-off 618.14
well-prepared 405.16
well-preserved
young 301.9
preserved 397.13
well-proportioned
shapely 264.5
comely 1015.18
well-put 533.7
well-rounded 413.25
well-suited
fitted 405.17
competent 413.24
well-thought-of
respected 155.11
approved 509.19
reputable 662.15
well-to-do 618.14
well-traveled 177.40
well-versed
skilled in 413.27
knowledgeable 927.18
well-informed 927.20
welsh
n recant 363.8
v shirk 368.9
repeal 445.2
not pay 625.6
welt
n sore 85.36
edging 211.7
bulge 283.3
blemish 1003.1
v punish 604.15
welterweight 297.3
wench
woman 77.6
girl 302.6
maid 577.8
strumpet 665.14

werewolf
frightener 127.9
monster 593.6
evil spirit 680.12
west
n points of the
compass 161.3
adj directional 161.14
adv W 161.18
Western Hemisphere
231.6
wet
n drink 88.7
rain 316.1
weather 316.4
liberal 611.11
moisture 1063.1
v urinate 12.14
moisten 1063.12
adj left 220.4
liberal 611.19
foolish 922.8
fluid 1059.4
moist 1063.15
wetback migrant 178.5
derogatory names
232.7
fugitive 368.5
wet behind the ears
untried 301.10
immature 406.11
inexperienced 414.17
wet blanket
killjoy 112.14
bore 118.4
deterrent 379.2
spoilsport 1011.9
extinguisher 1021.3
wetlands shore 234.2
shoal 276.2
wet-nurse nourish 8.19
foster 449.16
whack
n report 56.1
attempt 403.3
slap 604.3
turn 824.2
hit 901.4
v crack 56.6
slap 604.12
hit 901.14
whale
n largeness 257.11
heavyweight 257.12
behemoth 257.14
marine animal 311.30
v fish 382.10
whip 604.13
punish 604.15
wham
n report 56.1
v crack 56.6
strike 901.15
whammy
n gaze 27.5
malevolence 144.4
curse 513.1
spell 691.1
charm 691.5
bad influence 999.4
v bring bad luck
1010.12

wharf 1008.6
what 863.6
whatever
n no matter what
863.6
adv any kind 808.9
**what goes around
comes around** 886.9
**what goes up must
come down** 886.9
wheat 10.4
wheedle urge 375.14
importune 440.12
flatter 511.5
wheel
n cycle 179.8
circle 280.2
change one's mind
363.6
helm 573.5
torture 605.4
potter's wheel 742.4
automobile racing
756.1
roulette 759.12
round 849.3
propeller 903.6
whirl 914.2
rotator 914.4
important person
996.9
v turn about 163.9
ride 177.33
recur 849.5
circle 913.5
rotate 914.9
whirl 914.11
wheel chair 179.7
wheeler-dealer
man of action 330.8
politics 610.6
influence 893.6
wheel of fortune
gambling wheel
759.16
changeableness 853.4
fate 963.2
Chance 971.2
wheeze
n breathing 2.19
sibilation 57.1
joke 489.6
v burn out 21.5
sibilate 57.2
whelp
n boy 302.5
fledgling 302.10
dog 311.17
beast 660.7
v give birth 1.3
whenever
when 820.8
time 820.12
when hell freezes over
821.2
when least expected
unexpectedly 131.14
suddenly 829.9
where 159.21
whereabouts
n location 159.1
adv where 159.21

whereas
n condition 958.2
prep when 820.16
conj because 887.10
whereby 384.12
wherein 207.10
where it's at fact 760.3
state of affairs 764.2
essence 766.3
novelty 840.2
what's what 972.4
salient point 996.6
wherever 159.22
wherewithal
n means 384.2
funds 728.14
adv herewith 384.12
whet
n appetizer 10.9
incentive 375.7
v sensitize 24.7
stimulate 105.13
intensify 251.5
sharpen 285.7
incite 375.17
whew! 122.20
whey 1059.2
whichever
n whatever 863.6
adj every 863.15
while
n time 820.1
period 823.1
meantime 825.2
v spend 387.13
prep when 820.16
while away
spend 387.13
fritter away 486.5
whim caprice 364.1
quirk 926.2
figment of the
imagination 985.5
whimper
n lament 115.3
v sigh 52.14
weep 115.12
whine 115.14
whimsical
capricious 364.5
humorous 488.4
witty 489.15
inconstant 853.7
eccentric 926.5
uncertain 970.16
fanciful 985.20
whine
n screech 58.4
lament 115.3
v sigh 52.14
screech 58.8
cry 60.2
whimper 115.14
speak 524.26
nasalize 525.10
whinny 60.2
whiny
discontented 108.7
plaintive 115.19
whip
n driver 178.9
goad 375.8

lash 605.1
legislator 610.3
merry-go-round
743.15
slap 901.8
v best 249.7
foam 320.5
goad 375.15
hasten 401.4
defeat 412.9
give a beating 604.13
pound 901.16
slap 901.19
agitate 916.10
emulsify 1060.10
drive 1068.8
whip into shape
complete 407.6
arrange 807.8
perfect 1001.5
whiplash trauma 85.37
goad 375.8
whip 605.1
whipped cream 10.38
whippersnapper
impudent person
142.5
brat 302.4
a nobody 997.7
whipping boy 861.3
whip up
excite 105.12
improvise 365.8
incite 375.17
seize 480.14
agitate 916.10
whir
n rotation 914.1
v hum 52.13
whirl
n agitation 105.4
ride 177.7
eddy 238.12
coil 281.2
bustle 330.4
round of pleasure
743.7
wheel 914.2
v turn around 163.9
move 172.5
eddy 238.21
convolve 281.4
whirligig 914.11
Whirlaway 311.15
whirlpool
n eddy 238.12
whirl 914.2
v rotation 914.11
whirlwind
outburst 105.9
wind 318.14
whirl 914.2
whirlybird 181.5
whisk
n tap 901.7
agitator 916.9
v sweep 79.23
speed 174.9
transport 176.12
foam 320.5
tap 901.18
agitate 916.10

whisker
n bristle 288.3
v grow hair 3.20
whiskey 88.13
whisper
n murmur 52.4
touch 73.1
mumbling 525.4
tip-off 551.3
hint 551.4
report 552.6
v murmur 52.10
sigh 318.21
tell confidentially
345.9
publish 352.10
say 524.23
speak 524.26
mumble 525.9
tip 551.11
adj murmuring 52.18
whistle
n blare 53.5
noisemaker 53.6
sibilation 57.1
screech 58.4
alarm 400.1
call 517.16
v blare 53.10
sibilate 57.2
screech 58.8
bird sound 60.5
exude cheerfulness
109.6
rejoice 116.5
sigh 318.21
sing 708.38
blow a horn 708.42
whistle-stop campaign
609.13
whit 248.2
white
n whiteness 37.1
cocaine 87.6
egg 305.15
v whiten 37.5
whitewash 37.6
adj pure 37.7
clean 79.25
vacant 222.14
aged 303.16
spotless 657.7
chaste 664.4
white-bearded 303.16
whitecap
body of water 238.14
wave 915.4
white-collar crime
655.2
white-collar worker
bourgeois 607.6
worker 726.2
white corpuscle 2.23
white elephant 1011.6
white flag
peace offer 465.2
signal 517.15
race 756.3
white-hot zealous 101.9
fiery 671.22
hot 1018.25
White House 228.5

white lie 354.11
white lightning
liquor 88.14
bootleg 88.18
white meat 10.22
white out 35.13
white supremacist
103.4
whitewash
n appearance 33.2
whitening agent 37.4
pretext 376.1
utter defeat 412.3
extenuation 600.5
v color 35.13
whiten 37.5
hide 37.6
scratch the surface
206.6
conceal 346.6
falsify 354.15
acquit 601.4
white water
rapids 238.10
foam 320.2
whittle
n cutlery 1039.2
v form 262.7
sever 801.11
whiz
n sibilation 57.1
skillful person 413.14
first-rate 998.7
v hum 52.13
sibilate 57.2
speed 174.9
whiz kid 413.12
Who's Who 549.9
whoa! 856.13
whoever 863.7
who knows? 929.19
whole
n contents 196.1
quantity 244.1
inclusion 771.1
totality 791.1
all 863.4
sum 1016.6
adj healthy 83.11
comprehensive 771.7
total 791.9
complete 793.9
one 871.7
unqualified 959.2
sound 1001.7
wholehearted 359.11
whole kit and caboodle
791.4
whole nine yards 791.4
whole note 709.14
whole rest 709.21
wholesale
n sale 734.1
v deal in 731.15
sell 734.8
adj commercial
731.21
sales 734.13
thorough 793.10
extensive 863.13
undiscriminating
944.5

plentiful 990.7
adv cheaply 633.10
wholesome
healthful 81.5
sound 83.11
sane 924.4
whomever 863.7
whomp
n report 56.1
slap 604.3
impact 901.3
v crack 56.6
defeat 412.9
slap 604.12
collide 901.13
whoop
n cry 59.1
v cry 59.6
whoop it up
be noisy 53.9
have a party 582.21
make merry 743.24
create disorder
809.11
whoops! 974.22
whoosh
n sibilation 57.1
v sibilate 57.2
whopper
largeness 257.11
monstrous lie 354.12
whore
n flirt 562.11
reprobate 660.5
strumpet 665.14
prostitute 665.16
card 758.2
v be promiscuous
665.19
whorehouse
disapproved place
228.28
brothel 665.9
whorl
n coil 281.2
v convolve 281.4
why
n enigma 522.8
adv whyever 887.8
wick
village 230.2
taper 1025.7
wicked
malicious 144.20
wrong 638.3
evil 654.16
wrongdoing 655.5
ungodly 695.17
bad 999.7
difficult 1012.17
wicker 170.3
wide
adj spacious 158.10
voluminous 257.17
broad 269.6
phonetic 524.31
extensive 863.13
erroneous 974.16
broad-minded 978.8
adv far and wide
261.16
clear 261.19

wide-awake
awake 23.8
alert 339.14
clear-witted 919.13
wide berth 430.4
widen grow 251.6
enlarge 259.4
expand 259.5
spread 259.6
broaden 269.4
generalize 863.9
wide of the mark
adj irrelevant 775.7
erroneous 974.16
adv wide 261.19
wide open 174.20
wide-ranging
spacious 158.10
broad 269.6
extensive 863.13
broad-minded 978.8
wide receiver 746.2
widespread
spacious 158.10
spread 259.11
broad 269.6
customary 373.14
dispersed 770.9
extensive 863.13
widget 1050.5
widow
n survivor 256.3
widow woman 566.4
v bereave 307.28
leave behind 566.6
widow's peak 3.6
widower survivor 256.3
widow 566.4
width size 257.1
breadth 269.1
wield touch 73.6
use 387.10
wave 915.11
wieldy 1013.15
wiener roast 8.6
Wiener Schnitzel 10.18
wife woman 77.5
married woman 563.8
wig 3.14
wiggle
n wriggle 916.7
v be excited 105.18
way of walking 177.28
wriggle 916.14
wig out use 87.21
get excited 105.17
lose self-control 128.8
fly into a rage 152.20
go mad 925.22
wigwam 228.10
wild
n wasteland 890.2
adj overzealous 101.12
frenzied 105.25
passionate 105.29
infuriated 152.32
hinterland 233.9
animal 311.38
defiant 327.10
ungovernable 361.12
unrestrained 430.24
reckless 493.8

foolhardy 493.9
unrefined 497.12
profligate 665.25
turbulent 671.18
unruly 671.19
boisterous 671.20
savage 671.21
absurd 922.11
rabid 925.30
distracted 984.10
fanciful 985.20
wild about 101.11
wild animals 311.1
wildcat strike 727.5
wildebeest 311.5
wilderness
n open space 158.4
hinterland 233.2
complex 798.2
wasteland 890.2
adj hinterland 233.9
wild-eyed
frenzied 105.25
turbulent 671.18
fanatic 925.32
wildfire 1018.13
wildflower 310.22
wild-goose chase
lost cause 125.8
labor in vain 391.3
abortion 410.5
wild guess 950.4
wildlife 311.1
wildlife preserve 397.7
wild man
daredevil 493.4
savage 593.5
wild West 233.2
wiles 415.1
will
n desire 100.1
volition 323
resolution 359.1
will power 359.4
choice 371.1
intention 380.1
command 420.1
bequest 478.10
v see fit 323.2
resolve 359.7
bequeath 478.18
willful
disobedient 327.8
obstinate 361.8
intentional 380.8
lawless 418.5
willies 128.2
willing volitional 323.4
willinghearted 324.5
obedient 326.3
trial 403.16
consenting 441.4
teachable 570.18
will-o'-the-wisp
deception 356.1
illusion 975.1
mirage 975.6
fire 1018.13
luminescence 1024.13
willowy thin 270.16
folded 291.7
pliant 1045.9

will power will 323.1
resolution 359.4
wilt sweat 12.16
weaken 16.9
fatigue 21.4
burn out 21.5
fail 85.47
languish 393.18
wily deceitful 356.22
cunning 415.12
shrewd 919.15
wimp weakling 16.6
impotent 19.6
vacillator 362.5
coward 491.5
wimpy weak 16.12
impotent 19.13
irresolute 362.12
cowardly 491.10
uninfluential 894.3
win
n victory 411.1
fight 754.3
v best 249.7
persuade 375.23
triumph 411.3
acquire 472.8
race 757.5
win back 396.12
win by a nose 411.3
wince
n retreat 902.3
v suffer 26.8
flinch 127.13
retract 168.3
demur 325.4
pull back 902.7
winch
n windlass 905.7
v reel in 905.9
wind
stray 164.4
change course 182.30
curve 279.6
convolve 281.4
trap 356.20
prime 405.9
rotate 914.9
wind
n breathing 2.19
swiftness 174.6
current 318.1
bull 520.3
wind instrument
711.6
belch 908.9
fart 908.10
v fatigue 21.4
blare 53.10
air 317.10
blow a horn 708.42
windbag
braggart 502.5
chatterer 540.4
windblown 318.24
wind chill 318.8
wind down
decrease 252.6
cease to exist 761.6
turn off 856.12
windfall find 472.6
good thing 998.5

winding
deviative 164.7
convolutional 281.6
wind instrument 711.6
windjammer
sailboat 180.3
mariner 183.1
braggart 502.5
chatterer 540.4
windmill
rotor plane 181.5
automobile racing 756.1
window
casement 292.7
radar 1035.13
window dressing
appearance 33.2
front 216.1
sham 354.3
ornamentation 498.1
window frame
structure 266.4
opening 292.7
windowpane
window 292.7
transparent substance
1028.2
window-shop 733.8
windpipe 2.20
windshield 1007.3
wind sock
flying and landing
guides marker
184.19
weather vane 318.17
windstorm
high wind 318.12
storm 671.4
windsurfing 182.11
wind tunnel 239.13
windup
completion 407.2
game 745.3
end 819.1
wind up prime 405.9
complete 407.6
end 819.5
turn off 856.12
result 886.4
windward
n windward side
218.3
adj side 218.6
adv clockwise 161.24
leeward 182.68
side 218.9
windy
n braggart 502.5
v talkative 540.9
adj distended 259.13
rare 299.4
blowy 318.22
inflated 502.12
wordy 538.12
bombastic 545.9
thin 763.6
trivial 997.19
wine
n kinds of 88.17
adj red 41.6
wine cellar
room 197.17

storehouse 386.6
wine cooler 1023.3
win friends and
influence people
893.7
wing
n fowl part 10.22
adjunct 254.3
air force 461.29
party 617.4
branch 617.10
scenery 704.20
company 769.3
member 792.4
protectorship 1007.2
v disable 19.9
transport 176.12
fly 184.36
cripple 393.14
make good 409.10
wing it improvise 365.8
do easily 1013.8
wingspan 257.1
win hands down
1013.11
wink
n nap 22.3
glance 27.4
signal 517.15
hint 551.4
instant 829.3
v blink 28.10
signal 517.22
the wink of an eye 827.3
wink of sleep 22.3
winner superior 249.4
man of action 330.8
sure success 409.2
successful person
409.6
victor 411.2
jockey 757.2
good thing 998.5
winning
n victory 411.1
acquisition 472.1
adj delightful 97.7
desirable 100.30
endearing 104.25
alluring 377.8
victorious 411.7
in the money 757.6
speculative 759.27
influential 893.13
winnings
increase 251.3
gain 472.3
winnow
n refinery 79.13
v refine 79.22
air 317.10
select 371.14
segregate 772.6
classify 800.8
discriminate 943.4
wino 88.12
win one's wings
succeed 409.7
triumph 411.3
win over
persuade 375.23
convert 857.16

convince 952.18
seem true 972.9
winsome
delightful 97.7
endearing 104.25
cheerful 109.11
alluring 377.8
Winston Churchill
543.6
winter
n wintertide 313.6
cold weather 1022.3
v summer 313.8
spend time 820.6
adj seasonal 313.9
winter solstice 313.7
wintry seasonal 313.9
cold 1022.14
wipe
n disappearance 34.1
v clean 79.18
dry 1064.6
wipe off the map
395.16
wipeout 34.1
wipe out clean 79.18
excise 255.10
kill 308.13
exterminate 395.14
obliterate 395.16
bankrupt 625.8
declare a moratorium
625.9
annihilate 761.7
end 819.5
wipe up the floor with
604.11
wire
n cord 271.2
telegram 347.14
automobile racing
756.1
end 819.1
electrical device
1031.20
v telegraph 347.19
bind 799.9
electrify 1031.25
wired high 87.23
assured 969.20
wireless
n communications
347.3
radiophone 347.5
radio 1033.1
radio receiver 1033.3
v broadcast 1033.25
adj communicational
347.20
radio 1033.28
wire-puller
schemer 381.7
strategist 415.7
politician 609.30
politics 610.6
influence 893.6
wire service
telegraph 347.2
news 552.1
the press 555.3
wiretap
n surveillance 937.9

v listen 48.10
wiry able-bodied 15.16
threadlike 271.7
tough 1047.4
wisdom
mental grasp 919
ripe wisdom 919.5
understanding 927.3
maxim 973.1
expedience 994.1
wisdom tooth 2.8
wise
n aspect 33.3
manner 384.1
adj sage 919.17
learned 927.21
ungullible 955.5
wisecrack
n witticism 489.7
v joke 489.13
wise guy
impudent person
142.6
wiseacre 920.6
wise man
intelligence 919.9
wise woman 920.1
intellectual 928.1
wise to 927.16
wise up 551.9
wish
n desire 100.1
will 323.1
request 440.1
v desire 100.14
request 440.9
wishbone
fowl part 10.22
fork 171.4
wish-bringer 691.6
wishful 100.23
wishful thinking
defense mechanism
92.23
wistfulness 100.4
deception 356.1
credulity 953.1
idealism 985.7
wishing well 691.6
wishy-washy
tasteless 16.17
insipid 65.2
inconstant 853.7
mediocre 1004.7
wisp runt 258.4
bunch 769.7
luminescence 1024.13
wispy
frail 16.14
thin 270.16
wistful
wishful 100.23
melancholy 112.23
regretful 113.8
cognitive 930.21
wit
skill 413.1
cunning 415.1
pleasantry 489
humor 489.1
humorist 489.12
intelligence 919.1

witch
n bitch 110.12
frightener 127.9
old woman 304.3
hag 593.7
violent person 671.9
sorceress 690.8
eyesore 1014.4
v fascinate 377.7
bewitch 691.9
adj sorcerous 690.14
witchcraft 690.1
witch-hunt
persecution 389.3
investigation 937.4
the witching hour
315.6
with
adv in spite of 338.9
prep at 159.27
plus 253.12
by means of 384.13
in cooperation with
450.8
in company with
768.12
in agreement with
787.12
among 796.17
with abandon 430.32
with a grain of salt
unbelievingly 954.13
conditionally 958.11
with all haste
swiftly 174.17
hastily 401.12
with a straight face
unfeelingly 94.14
solemnly 111.4
with authority 417.18
with a vengeance
powerfully 18.15
extremely 247.22
violently 671.25
utterly 793.16
with bated breath
adj in suspense 130.12
adv in an undertone
52.22
fearfully 127.32
expectantly 130.15
humbly 137.16
secretly 345.17
with care
carefully 339.15
cautiously 494.12
with child 78.18
with difficulty
disadvantageously
995.9
difficultly 1012.28
with dignity
solemnly 111.4
dignifiedly 136.14
with dispatch
quickly 330.26
hastily 401.12
withdraw
n recant 363.8
v use 87.21
retreat 163.6
recede 168.2

retract 168.3
quit 188.9
extract 192.10
subtract 255.9
dissent 333.4
hesitate 362.7
abandon 370.5
repeal 445.2
separate 801.8
stand alone 871.6
withdrawal
substance abuse 87.1
defense mechanism
92.23
unfeeling 94.1
retreat 163.2
recession 168.1
departure 188.1
extraction 192.1
dissent 333.1
reticence 344.3
recantation 363.3
abandonment 370.1
repeal 445.1
resignation 448.1
seclusion 584.1
elimination 772.2
separation 801.1
aloneness 871.2
incuriosity 981.1
with ease 121.14
wither
fail 85.47
decrease 252.6
shrink 260.9
age 303.10
languish 393.18
dry 1064.6
with feeling 93.25
with finesse
skillfully 413.31
discriminatingly
943.9
with flying colors
501.25
with gusto
eagerly 101.13
gaily 109.18
actively 330.25
with haste 401.12
withhold
keep secret 345.7
reserve 386.12
restrain 428.7
deny 442.4
hold back 484.6
abstain 668.7
withholding 442.1
within
adv in 207.10
prep in 207.13
within easy reach 633.7
within range 223.20
within reach
adj present 221.12
cheap 633.7
accessible 965.8
adv near 223.20
within reason
moderately 670.17
reasonably 934.24
with intent 380.10

with interest 982.21
**within the realm of
possibility** 965.6
with it
adj knowledgeable
927.17
adv in step 787.11
with love 104.32
**with malice
aforethought**
malevolently 144.30
intentionally 380.10
with might and main
powerfully 18.15
by force 18.17
laboriously 725.19
**with no strings
attached**
extremely 247.22
completely 793.14
with no time to spare
844.12
**with one foot in the
grave**
stricken in years
303.18
dying 307.33
**with one hand tied
behind one's back**
1013.16
with one voice
adj unanimous 332.15
adv unanimously
332.17
cooperatively 450.6
in step 787.11
simultaneously 835.7
concurrently 898.5
with open arms
eagerly 101.13
willingly 324.8
hospitably 585.13
amicably 587.22
without
adv externally 206.10
prep absent 222.19
off 255.14
excluding 772.10
minus 991.17
conj unless 958.16
without a break 811.10
without a clue 970.24
without a stitch 6.14
without charge
adj costless 634.5
adv gratuitously 634.6
without contradiction
332.17
without delay
at once 829.8
promptly 844.15
without difficulty
1013.16
without distinction
adj identical 777.7
indistinguishable
944.6
adv justly 649.11
equally 789.11
without doubt
positively 247.19
believingly 952.28

unquestionably
969.25
without end
adj long 267.7
infinite 822.3
perpetual 828.7
innumerable 883.10
adv infinitely 822.4
perpetually 828.10
without equal 249.15
without exception
adj comprehensive
771.7
unqualified 959.2
adv regularly 780.8
always 828.11
universally 863.18
without fail 969.26
without foundation
unsubstantiated 763.8
baseless 935.13
without further ado
suddenly 829.9
promptly 844.15
without hesitation
324.9
without mercy 146.3
without merit 598.20
without question
willingly 324.8
believingly 952.28
unquestionably
969.25
truly 972.18
**without rhyme or
reason**
adj meaningless 520.6
illogical 935.11
adv capriciously
364.7
without shame 645.16
without warning
adj unexpected 131.10
adv unexpectedly
131.14
suddenly 829.9
with permission 443.19
with pleasure 95.18
with pride 136.13
with purpose 380.10
with regard to 774.13
with relish
eagerly 101.13
willingly 324.8
with respect 443.20
with respect to 774.13
withstand oppose 451.3
resist 453.2
defend 453.3
with taste 496.11
with the exception of
prep off 255.14
excluding 772.10
with the understanding
958.12
with tongue in cheek
489.19
witless
unintelligent 921.13
foolish 922.8
unwise 922.10
insane 925.26

unaware 929.13
scatterbrained 984.16
witness
  n certificate 549.6
  informant 551.5
  litigant 598.11
  function of Holy
    Ghost 677.16
  spectator 917.1
  examinee 937.18
  testimony 956.2
  eyewitness 956.6
  v see 27.12
  attend 221.8
  depose 334.6
  be pious 692.6
  spectate 917.5
  testify 956.9
witness stand 595.6
wits 918.2
witticism
  pleasantry 489.7
  maxim 973.1
witty humorous 488.4
  amusing 489.15
wizard
  n master 413.13
  sorcerer 690.5
  adj excellent 998.13
wizened dwarf 258.13
  shrunk 260.13
  haggard 270.20
  stricken in years
    303.18
  wasted 393.35
  dried 1064.9
wobble
  n irregularity 850.1
  shake 916.3
  v way of walking
    177.28
  vacillate 362.8
  change 853.5
  oscillate 915.10
  shake 916.11
woe wretchedness 96.6
  affliction 96.8
  distressfulness 98.5
  sorrow 112.10
  evil 999.3
  bane 1000.1
wolf
  n discord 61.1
  fox 311.20
  philanderer 562.12
  libertine 665.10
  violent person 671.9
  v gobble 8.23
  gluttonize 672.4
wolf at the door 619.2
wolverine 311.23
woman
  womankind 77.3
  Eve 77.5
  adult 304.1
  person 312.5
  wife 563.8
  mistress 665.17
womanizer 665.10
woman of means 618.7
woman of substance
  618.7

woman of the world
  578.7
womb genitals 2.11
  vital force 885.7
women's liberation
  liberation 431.1
  women's rights 642.4
wonder
  n awe 122
  wonderment 122.1
  marvel 122.2
  miracle 869.8
  first-rater 998.6
  v marvel 122.5
  not know 929.11
  be uncertain 970.9
wonderful
  wondrous 122.10
  remarkable 247.10
  extraordinary 869.14
  superb 998.15
wondrous
  adj wonderful 122.10
  miraculous 869.16
  adv intensely 247.20
wont
  n custom 373.1
  habit 373.4
  v accustom 373.10
  be used to 373.12
  adj accustomed
    373.16
won ton 10.32
woo lure 377.5
  solicit 440.14
  court 562.21
wood woodland 310.11
  gambler 759.21
  firewood 1020.3
  lumber 1052.3
wood carving 349.6
woodchuck 311.23
woodcut
  scenery 704.20
  print 713.5
wooded 310.37
wooden dumb 117.6
  inexpressive 522.20
  dull 921.16
woodenheaded 921.17
woodland
  n the country 233.1
  land 234.1
  wood 310.11
  adj hinterland 233.9
  sylvan 310.37
woods hinterland 233.2
  woodland 310.11
  woodwind 711.8
woodwind
  orchestra 710.12
  wood instrument
    711.8
woodwork 712.3
wool hair 3.2
  whiteness 37.2
  softness 1045.4
woolens 5.22
woolly
  hairy 3.24
  fluffy 1045.14
woozy 984.14

word
  n affirmation 334.1
  oath 334.4
  account 349.3
  command 420.1
  promise 436.1
  sign 518.6
  utterance 524.3
  remark 524.4
  term 526
  free form 526.1
  information 551.1
  news 552.1
  message 552.4
  testimony 956.2
  maxim 973.1
  v say 524.23
  phrase 532.4
worded 532.5
word for word 972.21
wordless tacit 51.11
  mute 51.12
  taciturn 344.9
  unexpressed 519.9
word of advice 422.2
the Word of God 683.2
word of honor 436.1
word of mouth 524.3
word origin 526.15
word processor 1041.12
words quarrel 456.5
  contention 457.1
  speech 524.1
  vocabulary 526.13
  diction 532.1
wordsmith
  writer 547.15
  author 718.4
word to the wise
  warning 399.1
  piece of advice 422.2
  tip-off 551.3
wordy 538.12
work
  n action 328.1
  act 328.3
  function 387.5
  undertaking 404.1
  fortification 460.4
  writing 547.10
  literature 547.12
  book 554.1
  stage show 704.4
  piece 708.5
  work of art 712.10
  literature 718.1
  occupation 724.1
  task 724.2
  vocation 724.6
  labor 725.4
  operation 888.1
  product 892.1
  barrier 1011.5
  v bubble 320.4
  act 328.4
  be busy 330.10
  use 387.10
  accomplish 407.4
  toil 724.12
  labor 725.12
  task 725.16
  mix 796.10

  cause 885.10
  operate 888.5
  be operative 888.7
  perform 891.11
  influence 893.7
  solve 939.2
  suffice 990.4
  expedite one's affair
    994.3
  chemicalize 1058.7
  cultivate 1067.17
workable
  operable 888.10
  solvable 939.3
  possible 965.7
  practical 994.6
workaday
  habitual 373.15
  simple 499.6
  occupied 724.15
work against 899.6
workaholic 330.8
workbench
  workplace 739.1
  table 900.15
workbook
  record book 549.11
  textbook 554.10
**work both sides of the
    street** 354.23
worked up
  affected 93.23
  excited 105.20
  angry 152.28
worker ant 311.32
  bee 311.33
  employee 577.3
  workman 607.9
  agent 726
  doer 726.1
  laborer 726.2
  cheater 759.22
work for assist 449.18
  serve 577.13
  aid 724.12
workhorse
  hunter 311.13
  drudge 726.3
working class
  n lower class 607.7
  adj upper-class 607.10
working girl
  worker 607.9
  employee 726.2
working plan 381.1
workings pit 284.4
  action 328.1
  operation 888.1
  mechanism 1039.4
  mine 1056.6
workings of the mind
  930.1
working stiff
  worker 607.9
  laborer 726.2
working together 450.1
working toward 895.5
work like a dog 725.13
workload 725.4
workmanlike
  skillful 413.22
  tolerable 998.20

workmanship
  skill 413.1
  production 891.2
**workmen's
  compensation**
  welfarism 611.7
  recompense 624.3
work of art 712.10
work on urge 375.14
  exploit 387.16
  importune 440.12
  impose on 643.7
  operate on 888.6
  exert influence 893.9
workout
  exercise 725.6
  tryout 941.3
work over
  revise 392.12
  punish 604.15
  beat 901.17
workplace
  library 197.6
  worksite 739.1
workroom
  library 197.6
  workplace 739.1
works viscera 2.14
  benevolences 143.6
  insides 207.4
  act 328.3
  writing 547.12
  literature 718.1
  plant 739.3
  mechanism 1039.4
the works 791.4
workshop 739.1
work stoppage
  strike 727.5
  stop 856.2
work up excite 105.12
  provoke 152.24
  incite 375.17
  plan 381.8
  agitate 916.10
work well
  succeed 409.7
  go easily 1013.10
world
  n quantity 247.3
  plot 722.4
  outlook 977.2
  universe 1070.1
  v meet one's Maker
    307.21
the world
  affairs 830.4
  Earth 1070.10
World Almanac 831.7
World Bank 729.13
world champion 413.15
world-class
  chief 249.14
  distinguished 662.16
  paramount 996.24
  superior 998.14
worldly
  experienced 413.28
  unsacred 686.3
  secularist 695.16
  realistic 986.6
  material 1050.10

world politics 609.5
world power
  country 232.1
  supremacy 249.3
World Series 745.1
world-traveler 178.1
worm
  n earthworm 311.37
  beast 660.7
  blight 1000.2
  v go slow 175.6
  creep 177.26
  convolve 281.4
worm's-eye view
  viewpoint 27.7
  appearance 33.6
worn weakened 16.18
  tired 21.7
  fatigued 21.9
  trite 117.9
  reduced 252.10
  impaired 393.31
  disintegrative 805.5
  stale 841.14
  secondhand 841.18
worn away
  used up 388.5
  lost 473.7
worry
  n annoyance 96.2
  worriment 126.2
  trouble 1012.3
  v annoy 96.13
  distress 96.16
  vex 98.15
  make anxious 126.5
  feel anxious 126.6
  trouble 1012.13
worrywart
  pessimist 125.7
  worrier 126.3
worse aggravated 119.4
  impaired 393.27
  changed 851.10
the worse for wear
  stricken in years
    303.18
  worn 393.31
  dilapidated 393.33
worsen irritate 96.14
  aggravate 119.2
  get worse 119.3
  impair 393.9
  deteriorate 393.16
  be changed 851.6
  change 851.7
worship
  n love 104.1
  respect 155.1
  piety 692.1
  reverence 696
  worshiping 696.1
  v cherish 104.21
  respect 155.4
  adore 696.10
Worship 648.2
worst
  v best 249.7
  defeat 412.6
  adj terrible 999.9
worst-case
  depressing 112.30

  hopeless 125.12
worth
  n benefit 387.4
  assets 471.7
  value 630.2
  preciousness 632.2
  funds 728.14
  importance 996.1
  goodness 998.1
  adj possessing 469.9
  priced 630.14
worthless
  valueless 391.11
  disadvantageous
    995.6
  paltry 997.21
  unworthy 997.22
  terrible 999.9
worthwhile
  valuable 387.22
  gainful 472.16
  expedient 994.5
worthy
  n good person 659.1
  celebrity 662.9
  personage 996.8
  adj dignified 136.12
  eligible 371.24
  competent 413.24
  praiseworthy 509.20
  precious 632.10
  warranted 639.9
  honest 644.13
  reputable 662.15
would-be
  presumptuous 141.10
  nominal 527.15
wound
  n trauma 85.37
  displease 96.5
  v pain 26.7
  hurt 96.17
  offend 152.21
  injure 393.13
  work evil 999.6
wound up
  completed 407.11
  ended 819.8
  past 836.7
woven webbed 170.12
  loomed 740.7
wow
  n audio distortion
    50.13
  success 409.4
  joke 489.6
  first-rate 998.7
  v delight 95.10
  amuse 743.21
wracked 93.23
wraith phantom 975.4
  specter 987.1
  double 987.3
wrangle
  n quarrel 456.5
  v quarrel 456.11
  argue 934.16
  drive 1068.8
wrangler
  oppositionist 452.3
  combatant 461.1
  student 572.7

  arguer 934.12
  herder 1068.3
wrap
  n dishabille 5.20
  wrapper 295.18
  v clothe 5.38
  surround 209.6
  enclose 212.5
  package 212.9
  fold 291.5
  enwrap 295.20
  bundle 769.20
  bind 799.9
  end 819.5
wrapped up
  completed 407.11
  assembled 769.21
wrapped up in
  fond of 104.30
  involved in 897.5
  engrossed 982.17
wrapper
  dishabille 5.20
  wrapping 295.18
  bookbinding 554.14
wrath anger 152.5
  revenge 507.1
wrath of God
  revenge 507.1
  deserts 639.3
wreak havoc
  destroy 395.10
  rage 671.11
wreath circle 280.2
  bouquet 310.23
  trophy 646.3
  heraldry 647.2
  braid 740.2
wreck
  n nervousness 128.5
  car 179.10
  ruins 393.8
  destruction 395.1
  debacle 395.4
  misfortune 1010.2
  v disable 19.9
  shipwreck 182.42
  spoil 393.10
  destroy 395.10
  demolish 395.17
  rage 671.11
wreckage 395.5
wrench
  n pang 26.2
  trauma 85.37
  pain 96.5
  extortion 192.6
  distortion 265.1
  jerk 904.3
  tool 1039.1
  v pain 26.7
  distort 265.5
  misinterpret 342.2
  misrepresent 350.3
  injure 393.13
  wrest 480.22
  jerk 904.5
wrest
  n extortion 192.6
  distortion 265.1
  v extort 192.15
  distort 265.5

follower 616.8
conformist 866.2
yesterday
　n the past 836.1
　adv formerly 836.13
yet
　additionally 253.11
　notwithstanding
　　338.8
　previously 833.6
　until now 837.4
yield
　n output 472.5
　receipts 627.1
　dividend 738.7
　production 892.2
　v weaken 16.9
　acknowledge 332.11
　hesitate 362.7
　give up 370.7
　provide 385.7
　cede 433.7
　compromise 468.2
　relinquish 475.3
　allow 478.12
　bring in 627.4
　conform 866.3
　bear 891.13
　soften 1045.7
　stretch 1046.5
yield the floor 613.10
yo! hark! 48.16
　greeting 585.16
　hey! 982.23
yodel
　n vocal music 708.13
　v sing 708.38
yodeler 710.13
yoga occultism 689.1
　exercise 725.6
yogi ascetic 667.2
　occultist 689.11
　clergy 699.12
yogurt 67.2
yoke
　n shackle 428.4
　two 872.2
　v put together 799.5
　hitch up 799.10
　combine 804.3
　league 804.4
　double 872.5
　tend 1068.7

yokel
　n bungler 414.8
　simple soul 416.3
　vulgarian 497.6
　peasant 606.6
　oaf 923.5
　adj not urbane 233.8
yolk 305.15
Yom Kippur
　fast day 515.3
　penance 658.3
yonder
　adj thither 261.10
　adv yon 261.13
yore 836.2
you 864.5
young
　n young people 302.2
　adj youngling 301.9
　new 840.7
youngster
　young person 302
　adolescent 302.1
yourself 864.5
yours truly 864.5
youth early years 301
　youthhead 301.1
　youngster 302.1
　young people 302.2
　boy 302.5
　origin 817.4
　memory 836.4
yowl
　n cry 59.1
　lament 115.3
　v cry 59.6
　yelp 60.2
　wail 115.13
yo-yo 923.3
Y-shaped forked 171.10
　angular 278.6
yucca 285.5
yuck 116.4
the Yukon 1022.4
yummy tasty 63.8
　delightful 97.8
yuppie 866.2
zany humorist 489.12
　buffoon 707.10
　fool 923.1
zap kill 308.13
　do for 395.11
　annihilate 761.7

end 819.5
zeal vim 17.2
　passion 93.2
　ardor 101.2
　anxiety 126.1
　willingness 324.1
　turbulence 671.2
　zealousness 692.3
　cause 885.9
　interest 982.2
zealot
　enthusiast 101.4
　believer 692.4
　oddity 869.4
　fanatic 925.18
zebra variegation 47.6
　crossing 170.2
　game 746.3
zenith summit 198.2
　supremacy 249.3
　height 272.2
zephyr breeze 318.5
　softness 1045.4
zeppelin 181.11
zero
　roulette 759.12
　nothing 761.2
　thing of naught 763.2
　temperature 1018.3
zero hour
　time of attack 459.13
　crucial moment 842.5
zero in 797.4
zero option
　dilemma 371.3
　restriction 428.3
　choicelessness 962.6
zero-sum
　compensating 338.6
　equal 789.7
　neutralizing 899.9
zest
　animation 17.4
　savor 63.2
　zestfulness 68.2
　pleasure 95.1
　eagerness 101.1
　gaiety 109.4
Zeus 316.6
zigzag
　n deviation 164.1
　zig 204.8
　angle 278.2

avoidance 368.1
　v deflect 164.5
　zig 204.12
　angle 278.5
　alternate 915.13
　adj deviative 164.7
　crooked 204.20
　angular 278.6
zilch 761.3
zip
　n energy 17.3
　sibilation 57.1
　zest 68.2
　gaiety 109.4
　address 553.9
　nothing 761.3
　v sibilate 57.2
　speed 174.9
zip code 553.9
zipper
　close 293.6
　hook 799.8
ziti 10.32
zodiac
　circle 280.3
　orbit 1070.16
　astrology
　　1070.20
zombie 987.1
zone
　n region 231.1
　climate 231.3
　circle 280.3
　layer 296.1
　address 553.9
　middle 818.1
　orbit 1070.16
　v encircle 209.7
　apportion 801.18
zoning law 444.1
zoo
　menagerie 228.19
　collection 769.11
zoological
　animal 311.38
　biological 1066.3
zoologist 1066.2
zoom
　n maneuvers
　　184.13
　v speed 174.8
　ascend 184.39
　take off 193.10